COSMOPOLITAN

WORLD ATLAS

RAND McNALLY

Contents

Cosmopolitan World Atlas

Cartography
Michael W. Dobson, V. Patrick Healy, Winifred V. Farbman, Susan K. Hudson, Robert K. Argersinger, Jim Purvis, Charlene Smith, Patty Porter.

Editorial and Design
Jon M. Leverenz, Brett R. Gover, John C. Nelson, Donna M. McGrath, Vito M. DePinto.

The Real World was developed by Rand McNally with Dr. Marvin W. Mikesell, Department of Geography, University of Chicago. Artimus Keiffer, Geography Department, Kent State University, contributed the section on communication using data from *Telegeography 1993*, Telegeography, Inc., Washington, D.C. Satellite image on pages viii-A·1: Mendoza, Argentina. Processed by Earth Information Systems Corporation, Austin, TX; Laser film writing by Cirrus Technology, Inc., Nashua, N.H.

Library of Congress Cataloging-in-Publication Data

Rand McNally and Company.
    Cosmopolitan world atlas.
        p. cm.
    Rev. ed. of: The new cosmopolitan world atlas. 1993.
    Includes index.
    ISBN 0-528-83674-9
    1. Atlases. I. Rand McNally and Company. New cosmopolitan world atlas. II. Title.
G1021.R35 1994 <G&M>   94-15785
                                                                                    CIP
                                                                                    MAP

MAPS AND ATLASES

Satellite images of the world (figure 1) constantly give us views of the shape and size of the earth. It is hard, therefore, to imagine how difficult it once was to ascertain the look of our planet. Yet from early history we have evidence of humans trying to work out what the world actually looked like.

Twenty-five hundred years ago, on a tiny clay tablet the size of a hand, the Babylonians inscribed the earth as a flat disk (figure 2) with Babylon at the center. The section of the Cantino map of 1502 (figure 3) is an example of a *portolan* chart used by mariners to chart the newly discovered Americas. Handsome and useful maps have been produced by many cultures. The Mexican map drawn in 1583 marks hills with wavy lines and roads with footprints between parallel lines (figure 4). The methods and materials used to create these maps were dependent upon the technology available, and their accuracy suffered considerably. A modern topographic map (figure 5), as well as those in this atlas, shows the detail and accuracy that cartographers are now able to achieve. They benefit from our ever-increasing technology, including satellite imagery and computer assisted cartography.

In 1589 Gerardus Mercator used the word *atlas* to describe a collection of maps. Atlases now bring together not only a variety of maps, but an assortment of tables and other reference material as well. They have become a unique and indispensable reference for graphically defining the world and answering the question, *where?*. Only on a map can the countries, cities, roads, rivers, and lakes covering a vast area be simultaneously viewed in their relative locations. Routes between places can be traced, trips planned, boundaries of neighboring states and countries examined, distances between places measured, the meandering of rivers and streams and the sizes of lakes visualized—and remote places imagined.

FIGURE 1

FIGURE 4

FIGURE 2

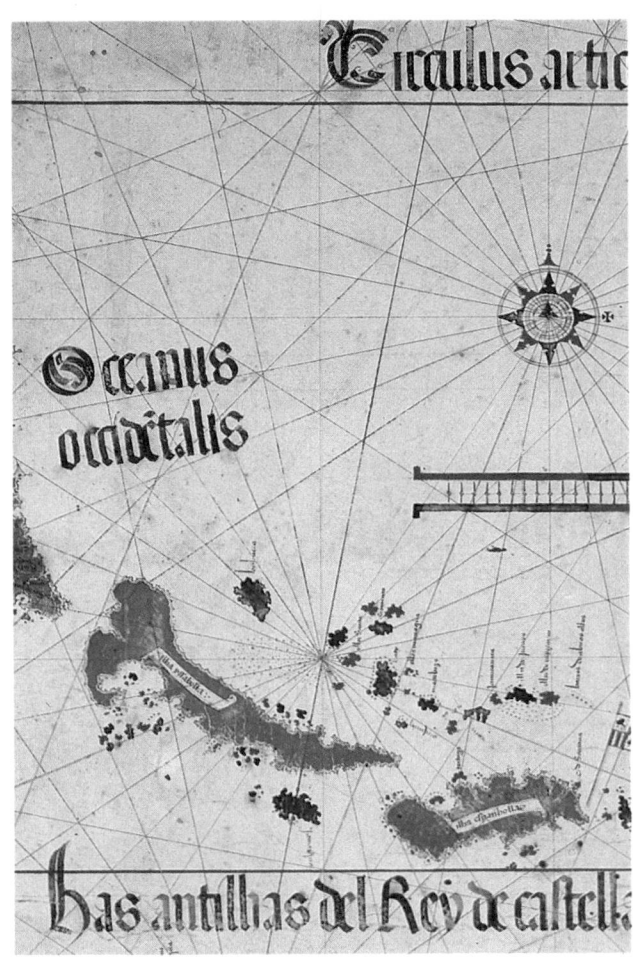

FIGURE 3

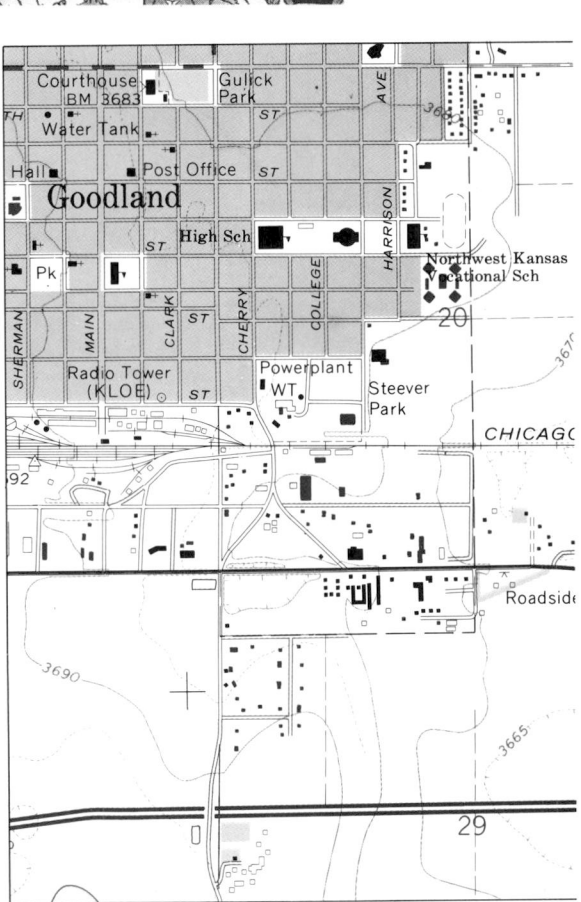

FIGURE 5

SEQUENCE OF THE MAPS

The world is made up of seven major landmasses: the continents of Europe, Asia, Africa, Antarctica, Australia, South America, and North America (figure 6). The maps in this atlas follow this continental sequence. To allow for the inclusion of detail, each continent is broken down into a series of maps, and this grouping is arranged so that as consecutive pages are turned, a continuous successive part of the continent is shown. Larger-scale maps are used for regions of greater detail (having many cities, for example) or for areas of global significance.

GETTING THE INFORMATION

An atlas can be used for many purposes, from planning a trip to finding hot spots in the news and supplementing world knowledge. To realize the potential of an atlas the user must be able to:

1. Find places on the maps
2. Measure distances
3. Determine directions
4. Understand map symbols

FIGURE 6

Yangguanpu, China	C4	34
Yangjia, China	I7	32
Yangjiang, China	G9	30
Yangkoushi, China	G7	34
Yangliuqing, China	D5	32
Yanglousi, China	F2	34
Yangon (Rangoon), Mya.	B2	38
Yangp'yŏng, S. Kor.	F15	32
Yangquan, China	F1	32
Yangsan, S. Kor.	H17	32
Yangshuling, China	B6	32
Yangtze see Chang, stm., China	E10	30
Yangxiaodian, China	D5	34
Yangyang, S. Kor.	E16	32
Yangzhou, China	C8	34
Yanheying, China	C7	32
Yanji, China	A17	32
Yankdŏk, N. Kor.	D14	32

FIGURE 7

FINDING PLACES

One of the most common and important tasks facilitated by an atlas is finding the location of a place in the world. A river's name in a book, a city mentioned in the news, or a vacation spot may prompt your need to know where the place is located. The illustrations and text below explain how to find Yangon (Rangoon), Myanmar.

1. Look up the place-name in the index at the back of the atlas. Yangon, Myanmar can be found on the map on page 38, and it can be located on the map by the letter-number key *B2* (figure 7).

2. Turn to the map of Southeastern Asia found on page 38. Note that the letters *A* through *H* and the numbers *1* through *11* appear in the margins of the map.

3. To find Yangon, on the map, place your left index finger on *B* and your right index finger on *2*. Move your left finger across the map and your right finger down the map. Your fingers will meet in the area in which Yangon is located (figure 8).

MEASURING DISTANCES

In planning trips, determining the distance between two places is essential, and an atlas can help in travel preparation. For instance, to determine the approximate distance between Paris and Rouen, France, follow these three steps:

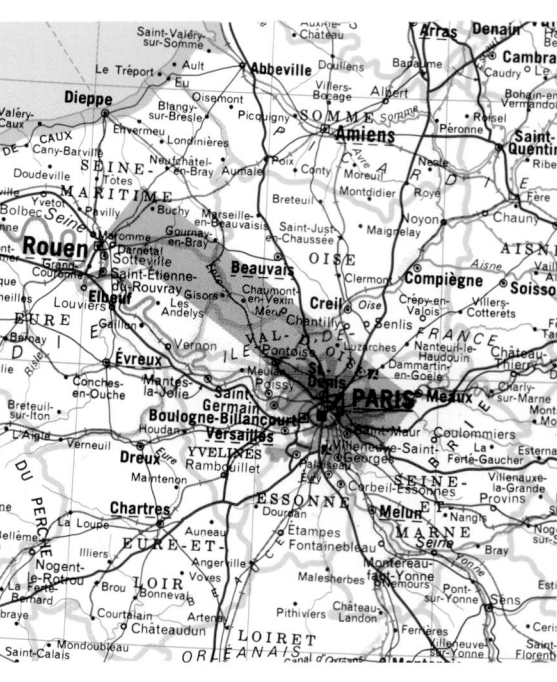

FIGURE 9

1. Lay a slip of paper on the map on page 14 so that its edge touches the two cities. Adjust the paper so one corner touches Rouen. Mark the paper directly at the spot where Paris is located (figure 9).

2. Place the paper along the scale of miles beneath the map. Position the corner at 0 and line up the edge of the paper along the scale. The pencil mark on the paper indicates Rouen is between 50 and 100 miles from Paris (figure 10).

3. To find the exact distance, move the paper to the right so that the pencil mark is at 100 on the scale. The corner of the paper stands on the fourth 5-mile unit on the scale. This means that the two towns are 50 plus 20, or 70 miles apart (figure 11).

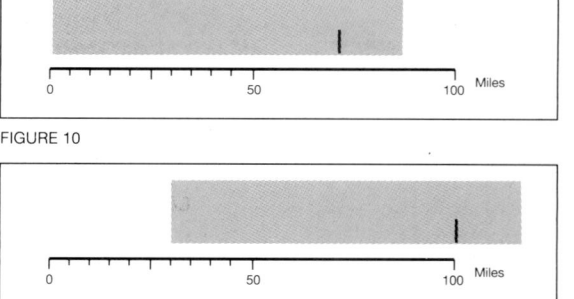

FIGURE 10

FIGURE 11

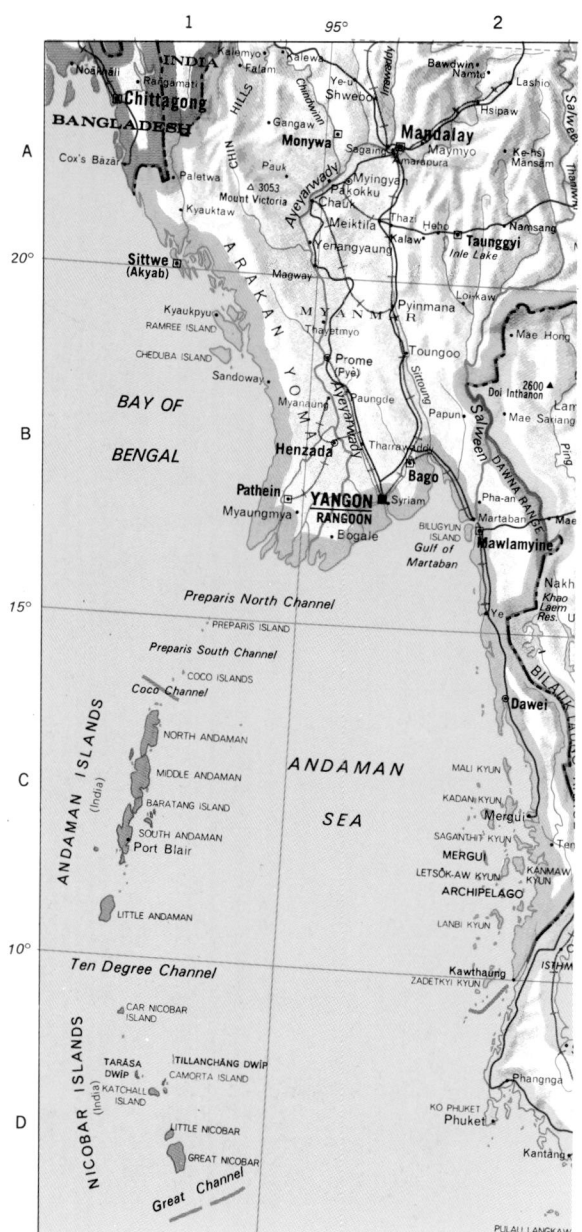

FIGURE 8

DETERMINING DIRECTIONS

Most of the maps in the atlas are drawn so that when oriented for normal reading, north is at the top of the map, south is at the bottom, west is at the left, and east is at the right. Most maps have a series of lines drawn across them—the lines of *latitude* and *longitude*. Lines of latitude, or *parallels* of latitude, are drawn east and west. Lines of longitude, or *meridians* of longitude, are drawn north and south (figure 9).

Parallels and meridians appear as either curved or straight lines. For example, in the section of the map of Europe (figure 10) the parallels of latitude appear as curved lines. The meridians of longitude are straight lines that come together toward the top of the map. Latitude and longitude lines help locate places on maps. Parallels of latitude are numbered in degrees north and south of the *Equator*. Meridians of longitude are numbered in degrees east and west of a line called the *Prime Meridian*, running through Greenwich, England, near London. Any place on earth can be located by the latitude and longitude lines running through it.

To determine directions or locations on the map, you must use the parallels and meridians. For example, suppose you want to know which is farther north, Bergen, Norway, or Norrköping, Sweden. The map (figure 10) shows that Norrköping is south of the 60° parallel of latitude and Bergen is north of it. Bergen is farther north than Norrköping. By looking at the meridians of longitude, you can determine which

city is farther east. Bergen is approximately 5° east of the 0° meridian (Prime Meridian), and Norrköping is more than 15° east of it. Norrköping is farther east than Bergen.

UNDERSTANDING MAP SYMBOLS

In a very real sense, the whole map is a symbol, representing the world or a part of it. It is a reduced representation of the earth; each of the world's features—cities, rivers, etc.—is represented on the map by a symbol. Map symbols may take the form of points, such as dots or squares (often used for cities, capital cities, or points of interest), or lines (roads, railroads, rivers). Symbols may also occupy an area, showing extent of coverage (terrain, forests, deserts). They seldom look like the feature they represent and therefore must be identified and interpreted. For instance, the maps in this atlas define political units by a colored line depicting their boundaries. Neither the colors nor the boundary lines are actually found on the surface of the earth, but because countries and states are such important political components of the world, strong symbols are used to represent them. The Map Symbols page in this atlas identifies the symbols used on the maps.

FIGURE 12

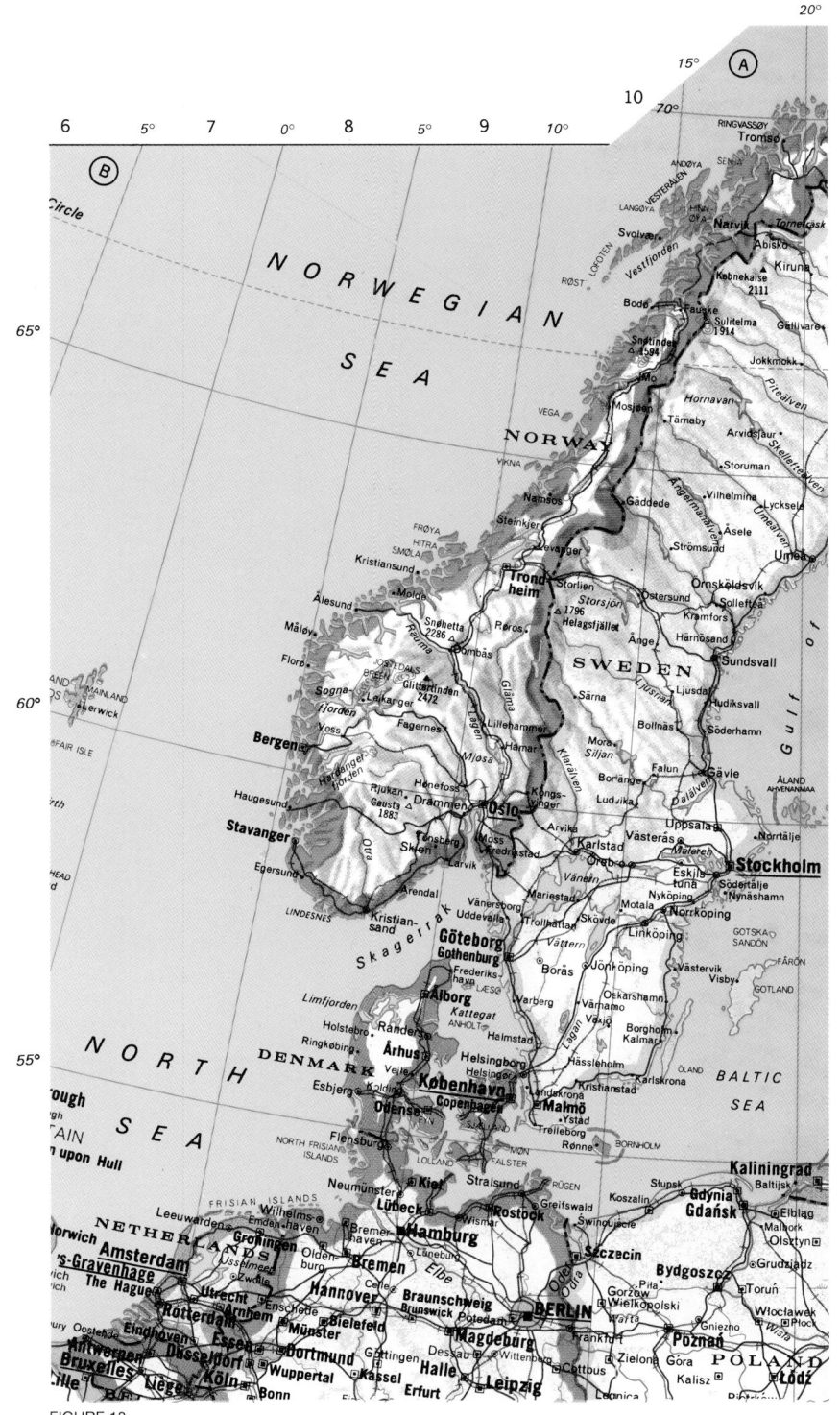

FIGURE 13

The Real World

Marvin W. Mikesell
Professor of Geography, University of Chicago

VIEWED FROM SPACE, THE EARTH APPEARS AS A MAJESTIC SPHERE, BLUE-GRAY AND WHITE, OUTLINED AGAINST THE STARRY BLACKNESS OF THE UNIVERSE. SWIRLING CLOUD FORMATIONS STREAK THE ATMOSPHERE, GIVING THE SPHERE'S SURFACE THE LOOK OF POLISHED MARBLE.

As we draw closer to the planet, the solid blue-gray separates into the great oceans and land masses of this world. Reaching the outer atmosphere, we can begin to make out the complex shades of blue, green, and brown that speak of the Earth's astonishing diversity of terrain, vegetation and climatic zones.

At this distance, mountain ranges appear as little more than wrinkles in the planet's surface, rivers as fine, branching lines tracing across the continents, and lakes as still, blue puddles. Moving closer toward the surface, we discern the shapes of ancient craters, volcanoes, fissures and canyons, great stretches of desert, and long, fertile valleys surrounded by arid lands.

But only when we descend to the lower atmosphere do the telltale signs of human existence become visible. Cities line the coastal fringes of the continents and dot the inner regions, glowing at night like constellations. Highways and railroads criss-cross the settled areas of the Earth, often paralleling coastlines or river courses. Patchworks of farmlands, quarries, mines, and logging operations mark our economic activities around the globe.

Scholars generally believe that there is a fundamental order and logic in the distribution of humanity and our activities over the Earth—a kind of "human geography" ruled by natural and cultural forces. The following sequence of special maps explores this order and logic, portraying the major geographic distributions affecting human existence. By understanding more about human geography, we may learn how to deal with the problems we face and to preserve the diversity and beauty of the planet we have affected so profoundly.

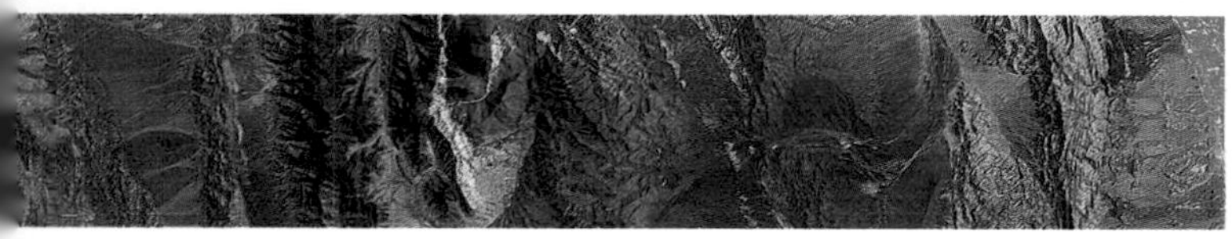

THE SURFACE OF OUR PLANET EXISTS IN A CONSTANT STATE OF CHANGE: CONTINENTS DRIFT TO NEW POSITIONS; OCEANS SHRINK AND DISAPPEAR WHILE NEW ONES ARE BEING

born; mountain ranges rise and gradually vanish. But on a human time scale, geologic processes are so gradual as to be almost unnoticeable. Only in the sudden, violent moments of an earthquake, a volcanic eruption, or a major storm do we glimpse the powerful forces that shape the face of our planet.

The greatest shaping force is the movement of the brittle crustal pieces that make up the Earth's surface. These pieces, called "tectonic plates," float on a dense fluid portion of the upper mantle. Convection currents rising from the lower mantle keep them in constant motion—colliding, moving apart, sliding over or under one another. The result is the tremendously varied terrain depicted on the relief map on these pages.

Asia's massive Himalayan mountains were born when the Indo-Australian Plate collided with the Eurasian Plate, crumpling the crustal material at the plate edges and slowly thrusting it upward to heights of five and a half miles above sea level. The Red Sea and Africa's great Rift Valley were created through a different kind of tectonic process: the African plate is literally splitting apart. Eventually, the land east of the rift will be torn from the continent to form an enormous offshore island.

In the vast Pacific Ocean, volcanic activity is creating a long chain of islands as the Pacific Plate slides over a "hot spot" in the mantle. The Hawaiian Islands are the newest additions to this chain, which stretches northwest all the way to Russia's Kamchatka Peninsula.

Besides plate movement, wind and water are the most powerful forces shaping the Earth's surface. Wind and rain carry away soil and sediment, while rivers sculpt valleys and gorges, such as the Grand Canyon, and create fertile flood plains and deltas. The advance and retreat of glaciers during the great ice ages vastly altered terrain in the northern latitudes. Norway's fjords and North America's Great Lakes are among the glaciers' legacies.

Over the last few centuries, humans have had an increasingly significant impact on the face of the Earth. We have turned arid regions into farmlands, and have made forests and grasslands into deserts. We have reclaimed land from the sea and dammed rivers to create new lakes. Our mining and quarrying operations have left huge scars on the landscape.

Today, as population soars and technology leaps forward, our potential for changing the face of the earth, and our responsibility to change it for the better, is greater than ever.

Equatorial Scale
© Rand McNally
X-510000-792-1E-1E-1E-3B

CONTINENTAL DRIFT
Geologic evidence indicates that the Earth's landmasses have migrated to their present positions over millions of years. These maps illustrate the positions of the continents in the past and where they are at present.

225 million years ago.
All of the world's land masses were joined together, forming a single supercontinent which we call Pangaea. Panthalassa is the name given to the single ancestral ocean. The Tethys Sea, predecessor of the Mediterranean Sea, separated Eurasia and Africa.

180 million years ago.
Pangaea split up. The northern block of continents, Laurasia, drifted northward, and the southern block, Gondwanaland, broke up into South America/Africa, India, and Australia/Antarctica.

65 million years ago.
Madagascar moved away from Africa, and the Tethys Sea all but disappeared as the Mediterranean Sea began to form. The ocean basins took shape as South America moved from Africa and India headed toward a collision with Asia. Australia was still joined with Antarctica.

The present day.
India has completed its northward migration and collided with Asia to form the Himalayas. Australia and Antarctica have separated, and North America has split from Eurasia, leaving Greenland as an island between them. During the past 65 million years, nearly one-half of the world's ocean floor has been created.

COSMOPOLITAN

WORLD ATLAS

RAND McNALLY

COSMOPOLITAN

WORLD ATLAS

RAND McNALLY

Contents

Cosmopolitan World Atlas

Cartography
Michael W. Dobson, V. Patrick Healy, Winifred V. Farbman, Susan K. Hudson, Robert K. Argersinger, Jim Purvis, Charlene Smith, Patty Porter.

Editorial and Design
Jon M. Leverenz, Brett R. Gover, John C. Nelson, Donna M. McGrath, Vito M. DePinto.

The Real World was developed by Rand McNally with Dr. Marvin W. Mikesell, Department of Geography, University of Chicago. Artimus Keiffer, Geography Department, Kent State University, contributed the section on communication using data from *Telegeography 1993*, Telegeography, Inc., Washington, D.C. Satellite image on pages viii-A•1: Mendoza, Argentina. Processed by Earth Information Systems Corporation, Austin, TX; Laser film writing by Cirrus Technology, Inc., Nashua, N.H.

Printed in the United States of America.

Library of Congress Cataloging-in-Publication Data

Rand McNally and Company.
    Cosmopolitan world atlas.
        p. cm.
    Rev. ed. of: The new cosmopolitan world atlas. 1993.
    Includes index.
    ISBN 0-528-83674-9
    1. Atlases. I. Rand McNally and Company. New cosmopolitan world atlas. II. Title.
G1021.R35 1994 <G&M>

94-15785
CIP
MAP

MAPS AND ATLASES

Satellite images of the world (figure 1) constantly give us views of the shape and size of the earth. It is hard, therefore, to imagine how difficult it once was to ascertain the look of our planet. Yet from early history we have evidence of humans trying to work out what the world actually looked like.

Twenty-five hundred years ago, on a tiny clay tablet the size of a hand, the Babylonians inscribed the earth as a flat disk (figure 2) with Babylon at the center. The section of the Cantino map of 1502 (figure 3) is an example of a *portolan* chart used by mariners to chart the newly discovered Americas. Handsome and useful maps have been produced by many cultures. The Mexican map drawn in 1583 marks hills with wavy lines and roads with footprints between parallel lines (figure 4). The methods and materials used to create these maps were dependent upon the technology available, and their accuracy suffered considerably. A modern topographic map (figure 5), as well as those in this atlas, shows the detail and accuracy that cartographers are now able to achieve. They benefit from our ever-increasing technology, including satellite imagery and computer assisted cartography.

In 1589 Gerardus Mercator used the word *atlas* to describe a collection of maps. Atlases now bring together not only a variety of maps, but an assortment of tables and other reference material as well. They have become a unique and indispensable reference for graphically defining the world and answering the question, *where?*. Only on a map can the countries, cities, roads, rivers, and lakes covering a vast area be simultaneously viewed in their relative locations. Routes between places can be traced, trips planned, boundaries of neighboring states and countries examined, distances between places measured, the meandering of rivers and streams and the sizes of lakes visualized—and remote places imagined.

FIGURE 1

FIGURE 4

FIGURE 2

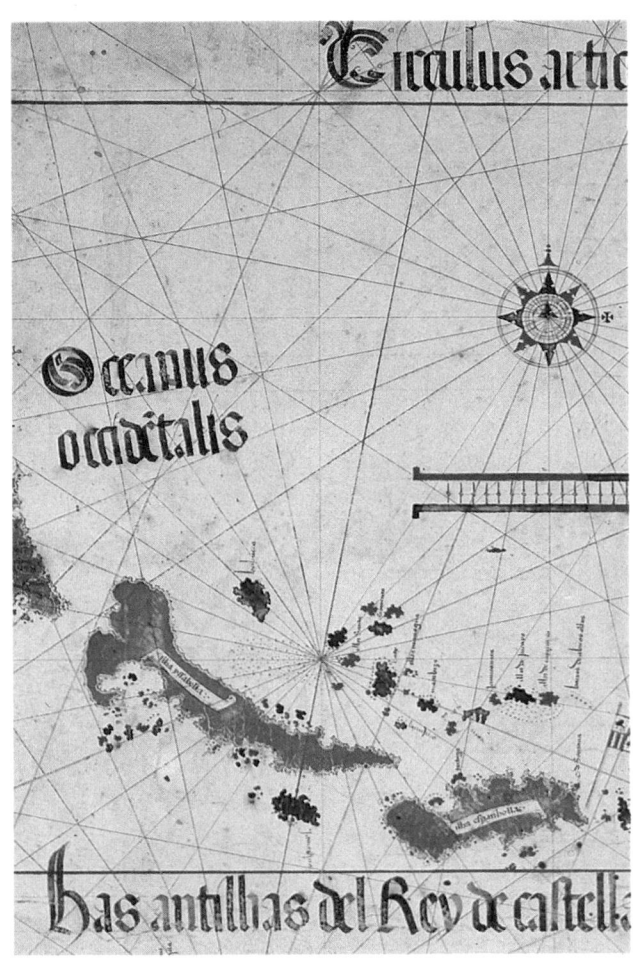

FIGURE 3

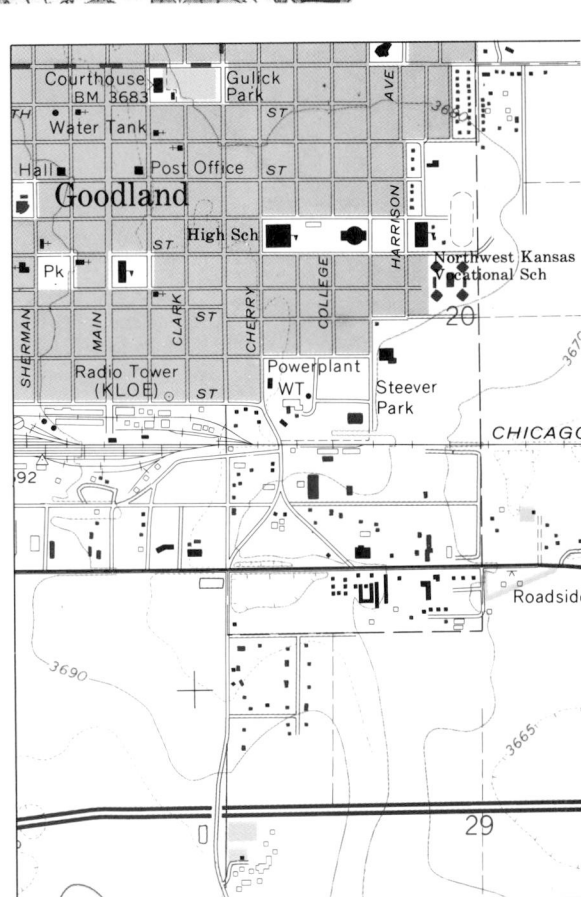

FIGURE 5

SEQUENCE OF THE MAPS

The world is made up of seven major landmasses: the continents of Europe, Asia, Africa, Antarctica, Australia, South America, and North America (figure 6). The maps in this atlas follow this continental sequence. To allow for the inclusion of detail, each continent is broken down into a series of maps, and this grouping is arranged so that as consecutive pages are turned, a continuous successive part of the continent is shown. Larger-scale maps are used for regions of greater detail (having many cities, for example) or for areas of global significance.

GETTING THE INFORMATION

An atlas can be used for many purposes, from planning a trip to finding hot spots in the news and supplementing world knowledge. To realize the potential of an atlas the user must be able to:

1. Find places on the maps
2. Measure distances
3. Determine directions
4. Understand map symbols

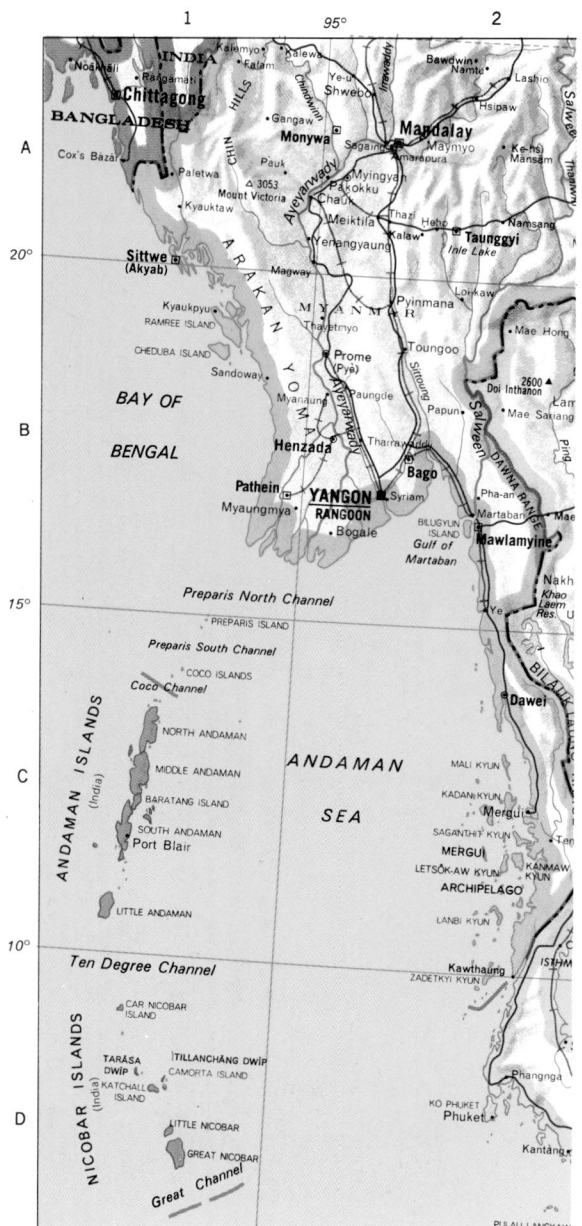

FIGURE 6

FIGURE 7

Yangguanpu, China	C4	34
Yangjia, China	I7	32
Yangjiang, China	G9	30
Yangkoushi, China	G7	34
Yangliuqing, China	D5	32
Yanglousi, China	F2	34
Yangon (Rangoon), Mya.	B2	38
Yangp'yŏng, S. Kor.	F15	32
Yangquan, China	F1	32
Yangsan, S. Kor.	H17	32
Yangshuling, China	B6	32
Yangtze see Chang, stm., China	E10	30
Yangxiaodian, China	D5	34
Yangyang, S. Kor.	E16	32
Yangzhou, China	C8	34
Yanheying, China	C7	32
Yanji, China	A17	32
Yankdŏk, N. Kor.	D14	32

FINDING PLACES

One of the most common and important tasks facilitated by an atlas is finding the location of a place in the world. A river's name in a book, a city mentioned in the news, or a vacation spot may prompt your need to know where the place is located. The illustrations and text below explain how to find Yangon (Rangoon), Myanmar.

1. Look up the place-name in the index at the back of the atlas. Yangon, Myanmar can be found on the map on page 38, and it can be located on the map by the letter-number key *B2* (figure 7).

2. Turn to the map of Southeastern Asia found on page 38. Note that the letters *A* through *H* and the numbers *1* through *11* appear in the margins of the map.

3. To find Yangon, on the map, place your left index finger on *B* and your right index finger on *2*. Move your left finger across the map and your right finger down the map. Your fingers will meet in the area in which Yangon is located (figure 8).

MEASURING DISTANCES

In planning trips, determining the distance between two places is essential, and an atlas can help in travel preparation. For instance, to determine the approximate distance between Paris and Rouen, France, follow these three steps:

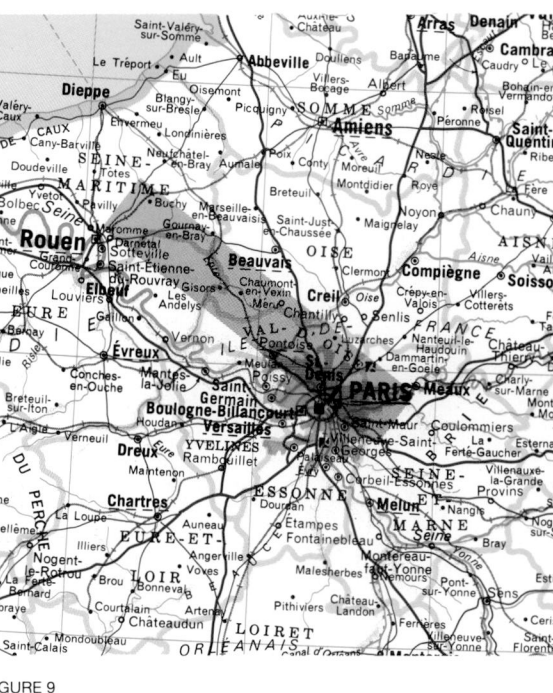

FIGURE 9

1. Lay a slip of paper on the map on page 14 so that its edge touches the two cities. Adjust the paper so one corner touches Rouen. Mark the paper directly at the spot where Paris is located (figure 9).

2. Place the paper along the scale of miles beneath the map. Position the corner at 0 and line up the edge of the paper along the scale. The pencil mark on the paper indicates Rouen is between 50 and 100 miles from Paris (figure 10).

3. To find the exact distance, move the paper to the right so that the pencil mark is at 100 on the scale. The corner of the paper stands on the fourth 5-mile unit on the scale. This means that the two towns are 50 plus 20, or 70 miles apart (figure 11).

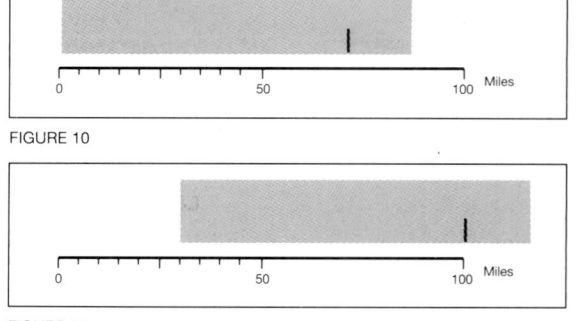

FIGURE 10

FIGURE 11

FIGURE 8

DETERMINING DIRECTIONS

Most of the maps in the atlas are drawn so that when oriented for normal reading, north is at the top of the map, south is at the bottom, west is at the left, and east is at the right. Most maps have a series of lines drawn across them—the lines of *latitude* and *longitude*. Lines of latitude, or *parallels* of latitude, are drawn east and west. Lines of longitude, or *meridians* of longitude, are drawn north and south (figure 9).

Parallels and meridians appear as either curved or straight lines. For example, in the section of the map of Europe (figure 10) the parallels of latitude appear as curved lines. The meridians of longitude are straight lines that come together toward the top of the map. Latitude and longitude lines help locate places on maps. Parallels of latitude are numbered in degrees north and south of the *Equator*. Meridians of longitude are numbered in degrees east and west of a line called the *Prime Meridian*, running through Greenwich, England, near London. Any place on earth can be located by the latitude and longitude lines running through it.

To determine directions or locations on the map, you must use the parallels and meridians. For example, suppose you want to know which is farther north, Bergen, Norway, or Norrköping, Sweden. The map (figure 10) shows that Norrköping is south of the 60° parallel of latitude and Bergen is north of it. Bergen is farther north than Norrköping. By looking at the meridians of longitude, you can determine which city is farther east. Bergen is approximately 5° east of the 0° meridian (Prime Meridian), and Norrköping is more than 15° east of it. Norrköping is farther east than Bergen.

UNDERSTANDING MAP SYMBOLS

In a very real sense, the whole map is a symbol, representing the world or a part of it. It is a reduced representation of the earth; each of the world's features—cities, rivers, etc.—is represented on the map by a symbol. Map symbols may take the form of points, such as dots or squares (often used for cities, capital cities, or points of interest), or lines (roads, railroads, rivers). Symbols may also occupy an area, showing extent of coverage (terrain, forests, deserts). They seldom look like the feature they represent and therefore must be identified and interpreted. For instance, the maps in this atlas define political units by a colored line depicting their boundaries. Neither the colors nor the boundary lines are actually found on the surface of the earth, but because countries and states are such important political components of the world, strong symbols are used to represent them. The Map Symbols page in this atlas identifies the symbols used on the maps.

FIGURE 12

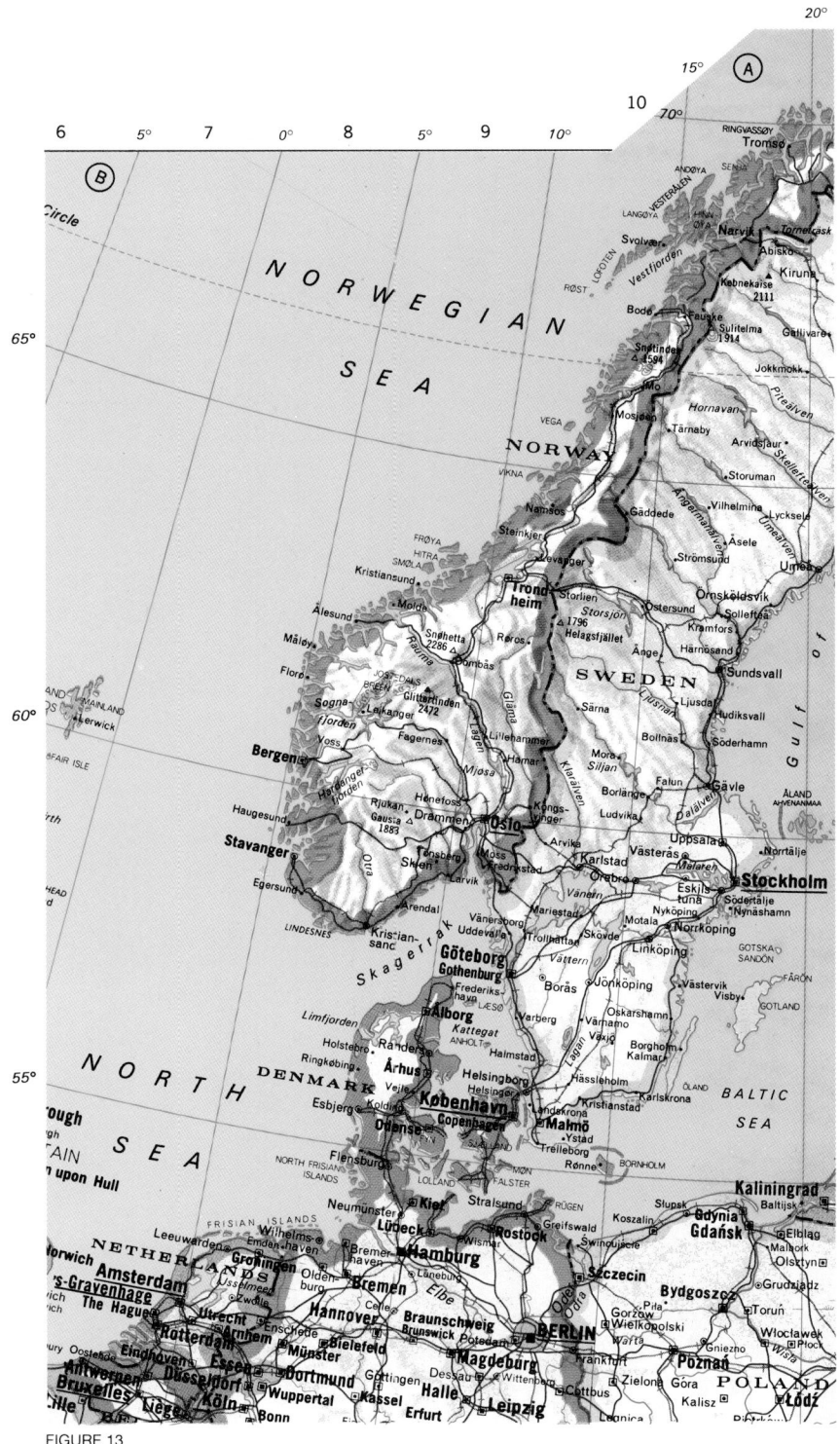

FIGURE 13

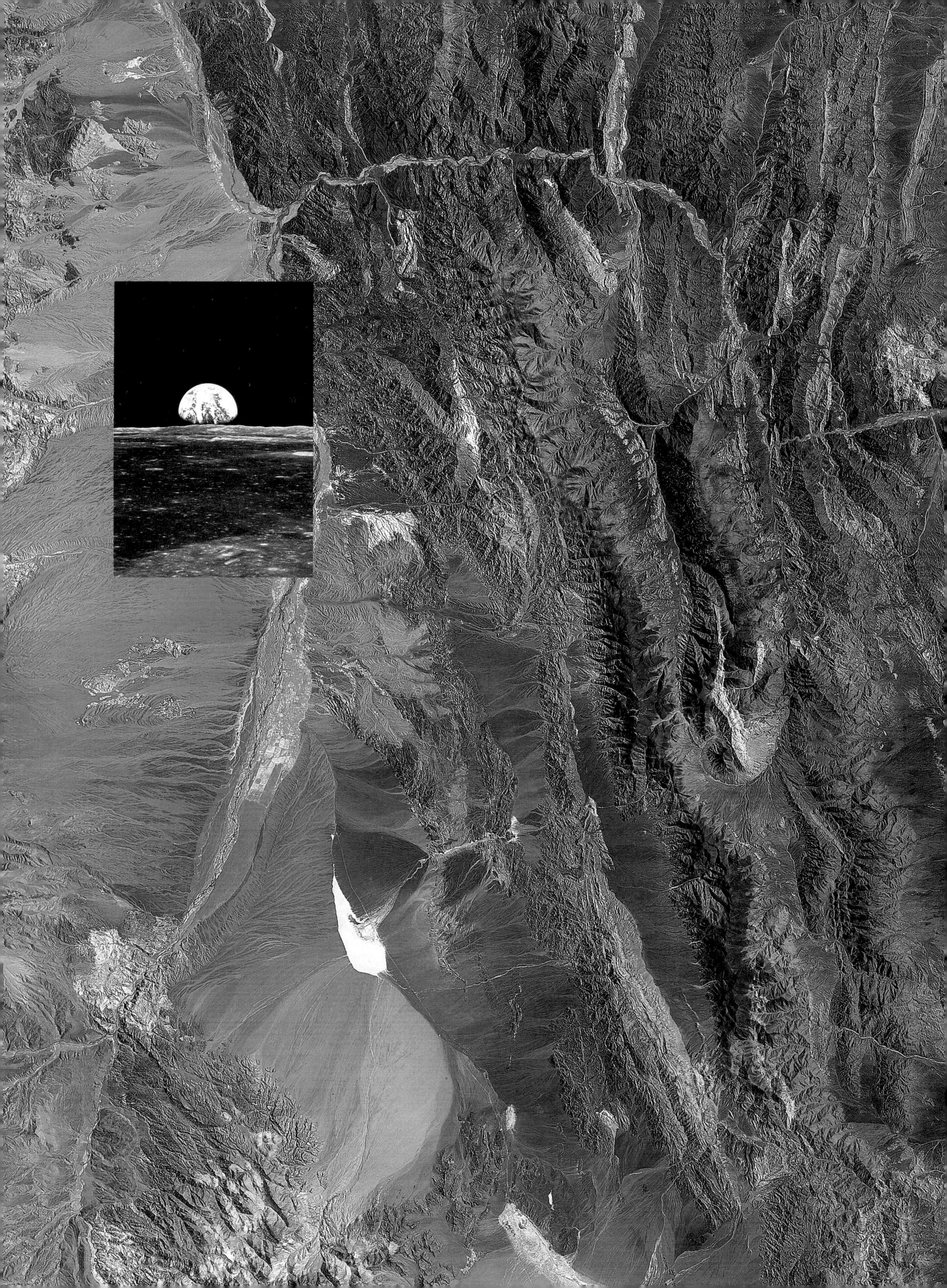

The Real World

Marvin W. Mikesell
Professor of Geography, University of Chicago

**VIEWED FROM SPACE, THE EARTH APPEARS AS
A MAJESTIC SPHERE, BLUE-GRAY AND WHITE,
OUTLINED AGAINST THE STARRY BLACKNESS OF
THE UNIVERSE. SWIRLING CLOUD FORMATIONS
STREAK THE ATMOSPHERE, GIVING THE SPHERE'S
SURFACE THE LOOK OF POLISHED MARBLE.**

As we draw closer to the planet, the solid blue-gray separates
into the great oceans and land masses of this world. Reaching
the outer atmosphere, we can begin to make out the complex
shades of blue, green, and brown that speak of the Earth's
astonishing diversity of terrain, vegetation and climatic zones.

At this distance, mountain ranges appear as little more than
wrinkles in the planet's surface, rivers as fine, branching lines
tracing across the continents, and lakes as still, blue puddles.
Moving closer toward the surface, we discern the shapes of
ancient craters, volcanoes, fissures and canyons, great stretches
of desert, and long, fertile valleys surrounded by arid lands.

But only when we descend to the lower atmosphere do the
telltale signs of human existence become visible. Cities line
the coastal fringes of the continents and dot the inner regions,
glowing at night like constellations. Highways and railroads
criss-cross the settled areas of the Earth, often paralleling
coastlines or river courses. Patchworks of farmlands, quarries,
mines, and logging operations mark our economic activities
around the globe.

Scholars generally believe that there is a fundamental order
and logic in the distribution of humanity and our activities
over the Earth—a kind of "human geography" ruled by
natural and cultural forces. The following sequence of special
maps explores this order and logic, portraying the major
geographic distributions affecting human existence. By
understanding more about human geography, we may learn
how to deal with the problems we face and to preserve the
diversity and beauty of the planet we have affected so profoundly.

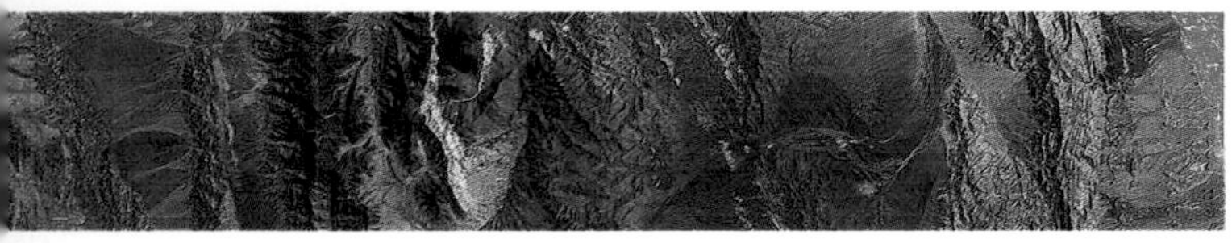

THE SURFACE OF OUR PLANET EXISTS IN
A CONSTANT STATE OF CHANGE: CONTINENTS
DRIFT TO NEW POSITIONS; OCEANS SHRINK
AND DISAPPEAR WHILE NEW ONES ARE BEING

born; mountain ranges rise and gradually vanish. But
on a human time scale, geologic processes are so gradual
as to be almost unnoticeable. Only in the sudden, violent
moments of an earthquake, a volcanic eruption, or a
major storm do we glimpse the powerful forces that
shape the face of our planet.

The greatest shaping force is the movement of the brittle
crustal pieces that make up the Earth's surface. These
pieces, called "tectonic plates," float on a dense fluid
portion of the upper mantle. Convection currents
rising from the lower mantle keep them in constant
motion—colliding, moving apart, sliding over or under
one another. The result is the tremendously varied
terrain depicted on the relief map on these pages.

Asia's massive Himalayan mountains were born when
the Indo-Australian Plate collided with the Eurasian
Plate, crumpling the crustal material at the plate edges
and slowly thrusting it upward to heights of five and a
half miles above sea level. The Red Sea and Africa's
great Rift Valley were created through a different kind
of tectonic process: the African plate is literally splitting
apart. Eventually, the land east of the rift will be torn
from the continent to form an enormous offshore island.

In the vast Pacific Ocean, volcanic activity is creating
a long chain of islands as the Pacific Plate slides over a
"hot spot" in the mantle. The Hawaiian Islands are the
newest additions to this chain, which stretches northwest
all the way to Russia's Kamchatka Peninsula.

Besides plate movement, wind and water are the most
powerful forces shaping the Earth's surface. Wind and
rain carry away soil and sediment, while rivers sculpt
valleys and gorges, such as the Grand Canyon, and create
fertile flood plains and deltas. The advance and retreat
of glaciers during the great ice ages vastly altered terrain
in the northern latitudes. Norway's fjords and North
America's Great Lakes are among the glaciers' legacies.

Over the last few centuries, humans have had an
increasingly significant impact on the face of the Earth.
We have turned arid regions into farmlands, and have
made forests and grasslands into deserts. We have
reclaimed land from the sea and dammed rivers to
create new lakes. Our mining and quarrying operations
have left huge scars on the landscape.

Today, as population soars and technology leaps forward,
our potential for changing the face of the earth, and
our responsibility to change it for the better, is greater
than ever.

0	1000	2000	3000 Km.
0	1000	2000	3000 Mi.

Equatorial Scale
© Rand McNally
X-510000-792-1E-1E-1E-3B

CONTINENTAL DRIFT
*Geologic evidence indicates that the Earth's landmasses have migrated to their present positions over millions of years. These maps illustrate
the positions of the continents in the past and where they are at present.*

225 million years ago.
*All of the world's land masses
were joined together, forming a
single supercontinent which we
call Pangaea. Panthalassa is the
name given to the single ancestral
ocean. The Tethys Sea, predecessor of the Mediterranean Sea,
separated Eurasia and Africa.*

180 million years ago.
*Pangaea split up. The northern
block of continents, Laurasia,
drifted northward, and the
southern block, Gondwanaland,
broke up into South America/
Africa, India, and Australia/
Antarctica.*

65 million years ago.
*Madagascar moved away from
Africa, and the Tethys Sea all but
disappeared as the Mediterranean
Sea began to form. The ocean
basins took shape as South
America moved from Africa and
India headed toward a collision
with Asia. Australia was still
joined with Antarctica.*

The present day.
*India has completed its northward
migration and collided with Asia
to form the Himalayas. Australia
and Antarctica have separated,
and North America has split from
Eurasia, leaving Greenland as
an island between them. During
the past 65 million years, nearly
one-half of the world's ocean
floor has been created.*

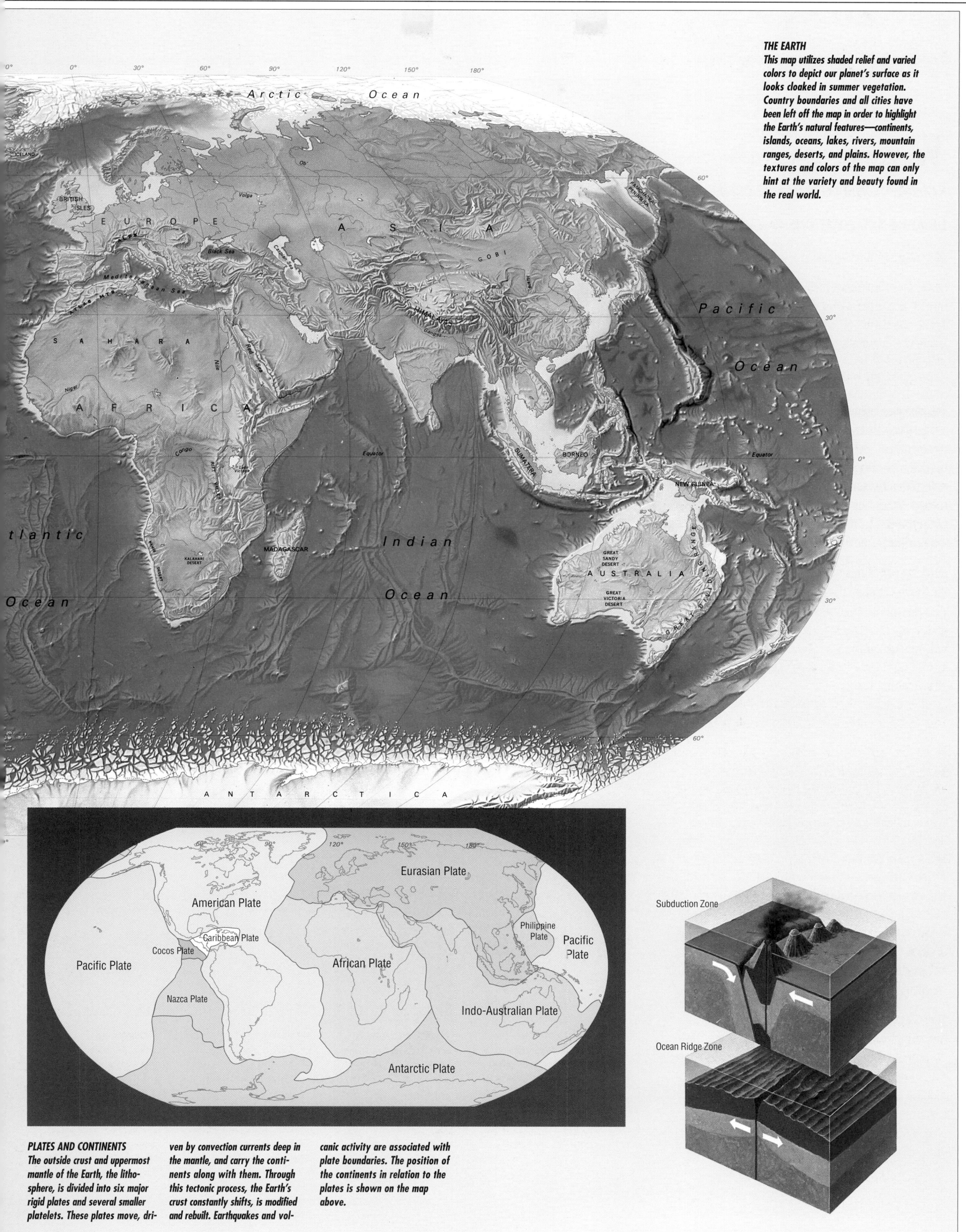

THE EARTH
This map utilizes shaded relief and varied colors to depict our planet's surface as it looks cloaked in summer vegetation. Country boundaries and all cities have been left off the map in order to highlight the Earth's natural features—continents, islands, oceans, lakes, rivers, mountain ranges, deserts, and plains. However, the textures and colors of the map can only hint at the variety and beauty found in the real world.

Arctic Ocean

ICELAND

BRITISH ISLES

EUROPE

ASIA

Ob'

Volga

Black Sea

Caspian Sea

GOBI

Mediterranean Sea

Atlas Mtns.

SAHARA

Nile

Red Sea

HIMALAYAS

Pacific

AFRICA

Niger

Ganges

Ocean

Congo

Rift Valley

Lake Victoria

SUMATRA

BORNEO

Equator

Equator

NEW GUINEA

Atlantic

Indian

GREAT SANDY DESERT

KALAHARI DESERT

MADAGASCAR

Ocean

AUSTRALIA

GREAT DIVIDING RANGE

Ocean

GREAT VICTORIA DESERT

ANTARCTICA

Subduction Zone

Eurasian Plate

American Plate

Philippine Plate

Pacific Plate

Caribbean Plate

Cocos Plate

African Plate

Pacific Plate

Nazca Plate

Indo-Australian Plate

Ocean Ridge Zone

Antarctic Plate

PLATES AND CONTINENTS
The outside crust and uppermost mantle of the Earth, the lithosphere, is divided into six major rigid plates and several smaller platelets. These plates move, driven by convection currents deep in the mantle, and carry the continents along with them. Through this tectonic process, the Earth's crust constantly shifts, is modified and rebuilt. Earthquakes and volcanic activity are associated with plate boundaries. The position of the continents in relation to the plates is shown on the map above.

WHILE CALM, CLEAR SKIES PREVAIL OVER NORTH AMERICA'S GREAT PLAINS, A VIOLENT HURRICANE BATTERS A CHAIN OF CARIBBEAN ISLANDS. IN EASTERN AFRICA, RAINSTORMS break a two-year drought, but northern European farmers watch their crops dry up in a heat wave. Mild spring winds arrive over Argentina, and in southeast Asia monsoon winds bring lightning and torrential rains.

The infinite variety of our planet's weather is created by the complex relationship of air, water, and land. Air masses ebb and flow around the globe, as moist tropical air moves toward the poles and drier polar air descends toward the equator. The spinning of the Earth helps to direct the air masses. Ocean currents circulate "rivers" of warmer and cooler waters around the globe. Great mountain ranges trap air masses and disrupt the world-wide flow. The 23½° inclination of our planet as it revolves around the sun creates the yearly cycle of seasons.

Over time, this constant interaction of natural forces establishes consistent weather patterns which, in turn, define the major climatic regions of the world, which are depicted on the adjacent map. Within each region, char-acteristic soils and related plant and animal life evolve.

Generally predictable patterns of weather within these regions have permitted humanity to develop an array of economic and cultural systems, each closely related to the area's normal climatic conditions.

It is the abnormal climatic occurrence—sometimes called a "climatic anomaly"—that causes the most human turmoil, as well as shock to the natural order. For example, a combination of cold Pacific currents and dry air masses makes the northern coast of Chile one of the driest places on Earth. The lifestyle of the region is based upon this prevailing climate. When the phenomenon known as *El Niño* occurs, the usual northerly flow of cold air and water reverses itself, and warm equatorial air and water flow south onto the coast of Chile. These unexpected conditions dramatically increase rainfall, leading to disastrous flooding, and completely disrupting the cultural and natural order.

Today there is growing awareness and concern about humanity's increasing impact on climate. In many large urban areas, the heat-absorbing artificial terrain, combined with air pollution from automobiles and industry, has created "micro-climates" characterized by higher temperatures and excessive smog. A far greater potential problem is global warming resulting from the so-called "greenhouse effect." The burning of fossil fuels adds carbon dioxide to the atmosphere, which causes the atmosphere to trap heat that would normally radiate out into space. If global temperatures rise even a few degrees, the consequences could be disastrous.

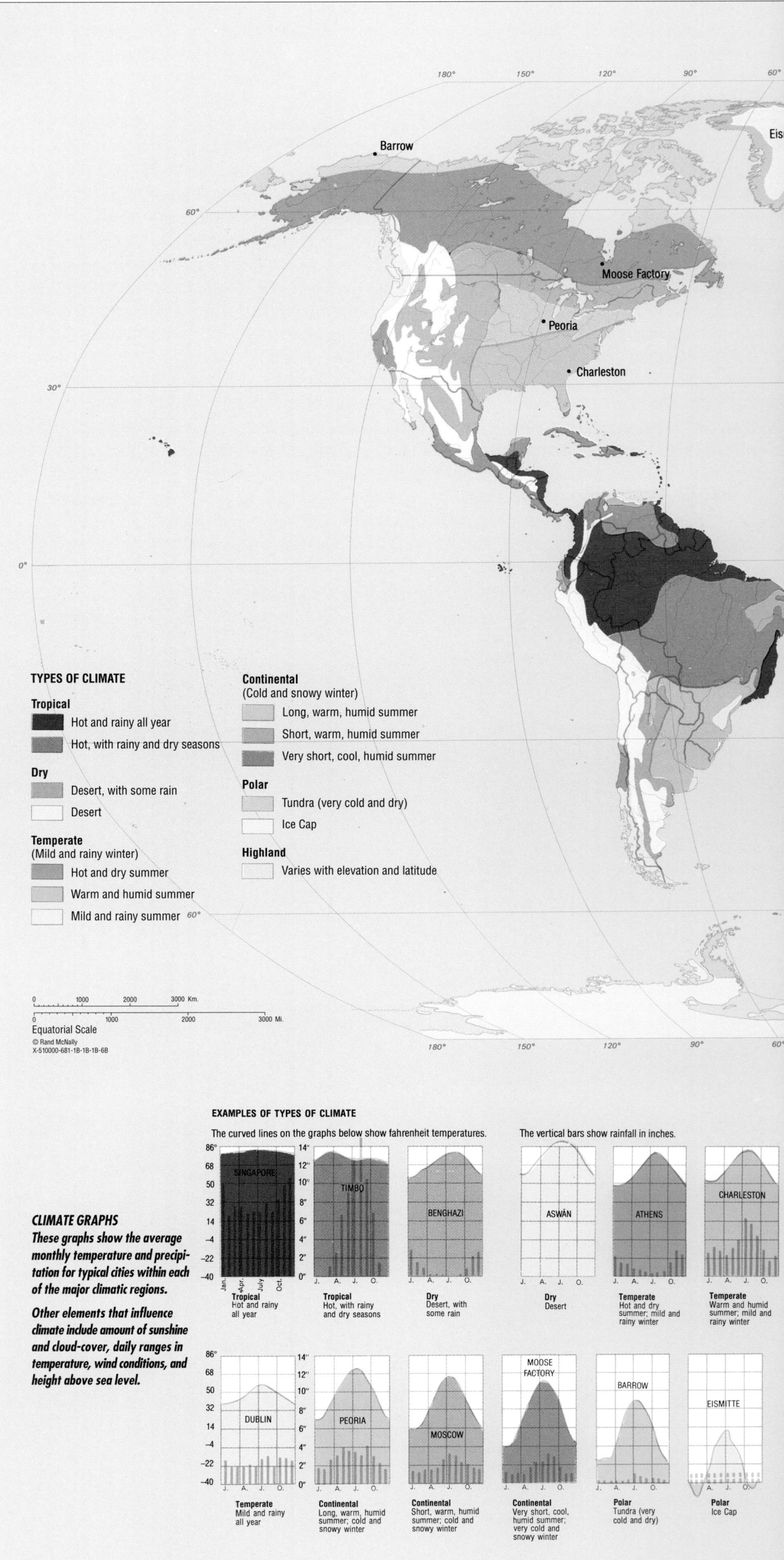

TYPES OF CLIMATE

Tropical
- Hot and rainy all year
- Hot, with rainy and dry seasons

Dry
- Desert, with some rain
- Desert

Temperate
(Mild and rainy winter)
- Hot and dry summer
- Warm and humid summer
- Mild and rainy summer

Continental
(Cold and snowy winter)
- Long, warm, humid summer
- Short, warm, humid summer
- Very short, cool, humid summer

Polar
- Tundra (very cold and dry)
- Ice Cap

Highland
- Varies with elevation and latitude

Equatorial Scale
© Rand McNally
X-510000-681-1B-1B-1B-6B

EXAMPLES OF TYPES OF CLIMATE

The curved lines on the graphs below show fahrenheit temperatures.   The vertical bars show rainfall in inches.

CLIMATE GRAPHS
These graphs show the average monthly temperature and precipi-tation for typical cities within each of the major climatic regions.

Other elements that influence climate include amount of sunshine and cloud-cover, daily ranges in temperature, wind conditions, and height above sea level.

SINGAPORE
Tropical
Hot and rainy all year

TIMBO
Tropical
Hot, with rainy and dry seasons

BENGHAZI
Dry
Desert, with some rain

ASWAN
Dry
Desert

ATHENS
Temperate
Hot and dry summer; mild and rainy winter

CHARLESTON
Temperate
Warm and humid summer; mild and rainy winter

DUBLIN
Temperate
Mild and rainy all year

PEORIA
Continental
Long, warm, humid summer; cold and snowy winter

MOSCOW
Continental
Short, warm, humid summer; cold and snowy winter

MOOSE FACTORY
Continental
Very short, cool, humid summer; very cold and snowy winter

BARROW
Polar
Tundra (very cold and dry)

EISMITTE
Polar
Ice Cap

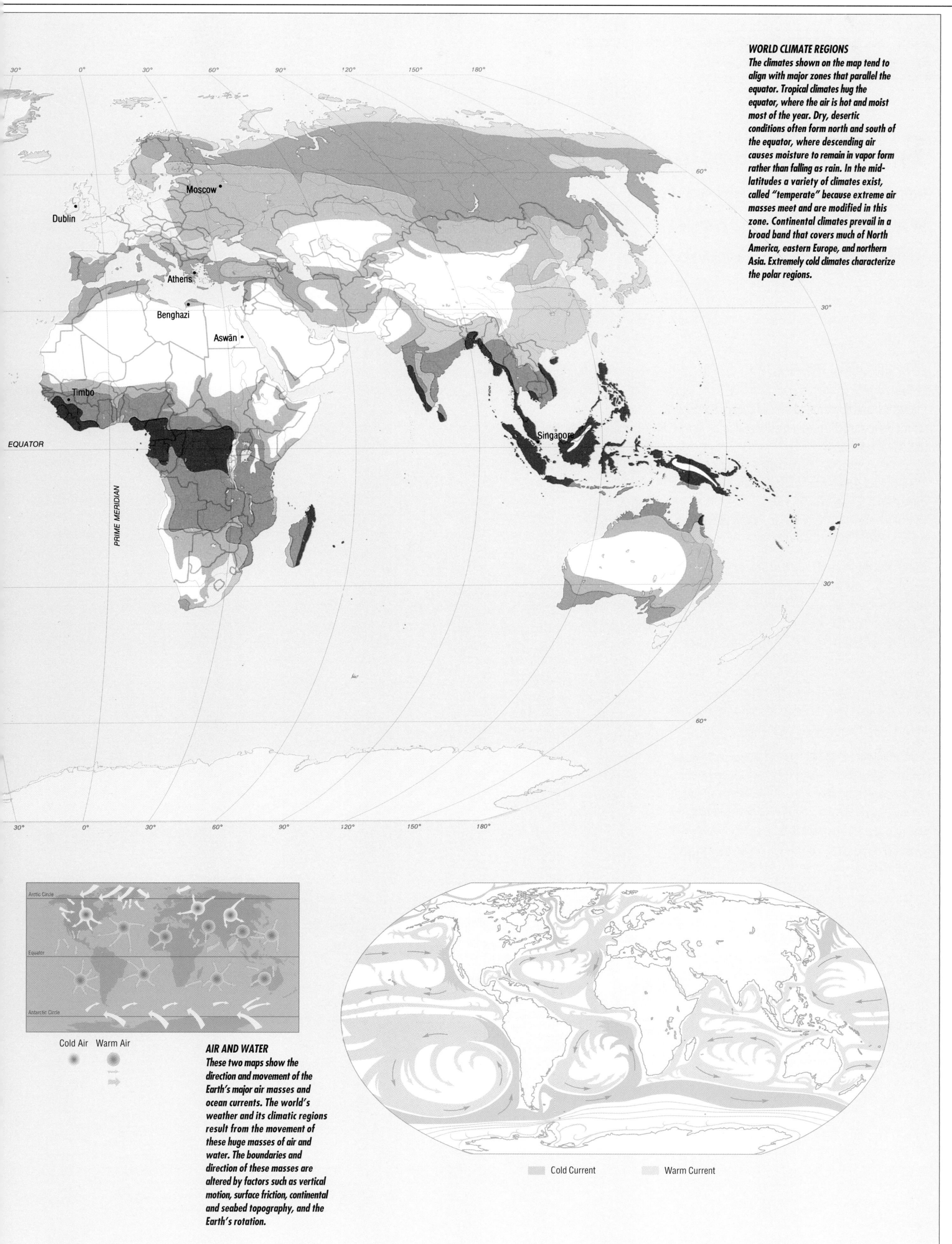

WORLD CLIMATE REGIONS
The climates shown on the map tend to align with major zones that parallel the equator. Tropical climates hug the equator, where the air is hot and moist most of the year. Dry, desertic conditions often form north and south of the equator, where descending air causes moisture to remain in vapor form rather than falling as rain. In the mid-latitudes a variety of climates exist, called "temperate" because extreme air masses meet and are modified in this zone. Continental climates prevail in a broad band that covers much of North America, eastern Europe, and northern Asia. Extremely cold climates characterize the polar regions.

Cold Air   Warm Air

AIR AND WATER
These two maps show the direction and movement of the Earth's major air masses and ocean currents. The world's weather and its climatic regions result from the movement of these huge masses of air and water. The boundaries and direction of these masses are altered by factors such as vertical motion, surface friction, continental and seabed topography, and the Earth's rotation.

Cold Current   Warm Current

SETTLEMENT

THE HISTORY OF HUMAN SETTLEMENT IS THE STORY OF A SEARCH FOR FERTILE LAND, ABUNDANT SOURCES OF WATER, SUITABLE TERRAIN, AND CLIMATES WITH ADEQUATE

growing seasons. Wherever nature supplies all of these elements, human settlements flourish. When they are scarce or disappear, communities are few and may eventually be abandoned.

Since humans began practicing agriculture about 10,000 years ago, the greatest limitation on settlement has been the length of the growing season. Areas with fewer than 90 days free of frost per year are not suitable for most forms of agriculture. Without an abundant food supply, settlements cannot grow beyond a limited size. Outside the regions where agriculture is viable, people must depend on imported food or live by hunting, fishing, and trapping—activities that can support only small communities.

Human settlement is also restricted by the amount of precipitation an area receives. Farming is not practical where annual rainfall is less than 10 inches (24.5 cm) in temperate areas and less than 20 inches (51 cm) in hotter regions. At various times, people have developed large-scale irrigation systems to pipe water into once-arid lands. In this way, human patterns of settlement have appeared in desert areas of the American Southwest, the Middle East, and parts of Africa. However, the process is costly and usually draws heavily on underground reservoirs.

Finally, terrain and soil also limit human settlement. Much of the world is simply too mountainous or the soil too poor for people to settle. At high elevations, the growing season is often too short for cultivation. Taiga forests and equatorial rainforests generally create a thin, acidic soil that is often too infertile to sustain permanent agricultural communities.

Human settlement patterns have shifted dramatically from rural to urban in the last two centuries. Advances in agricultural technology and methods have produced growing food supplies able to support larger and larger urban populations. The industrial and technological revolution has created job opportunities that are nearly always in urban areas. In 1925, approximately 20% of the world's population was urban. Today the figure is approaching 50%. It is estimated that by 2025, five out of eight people will live in cities.

Until the early part of this century, this trend was largely confined to the developed countries, but it has since spread to much of the rest of the world. Today the strongest urbanization trends are in the developing countries of South America and Africa, where the problems indigenous to urban living—overcrowding, pollution, inadequate sanitation, disease—are often magnified by inadequate economic resources.

LIMITS OF THE HABITABLE WORLD

- Annual rainfall under 10 inches
- Annual growing season under 90 days
- Rough, mountainous land

One dot represents 100,000 people

1000   2000   3000 Km.
1000   2000   3000 Mi.

Equatorial Scale
© Rand McNally
X-510000-6L50-1B-1B-1B-1B

URBANIZATION

Percentage of population living in urban areas

World Average ►
43 %

- Over 60 %
- 45 to 60 %
- 30 to 45 %
- 15 to 30 %
- Under 15 %
- Uninhabited or sparsely populated

● Metropolitan areas over 5,000,000 population
○ Metropolitan areas 2,000,000 to 5,000,000 population

WORLD URBAN AND RURAL POPULATION
Though urban populations dominate extensive areas of the Earth, southern and eastern Asia, with one-half of the world's people and more than 30 of its largest urban centers, are still characterized by a very dense rural population. Africa is another part of the world where rural populations predominate. Future growth in urban areas is expected to take place in African countries, as well as in other developing regions where city populations are already large.

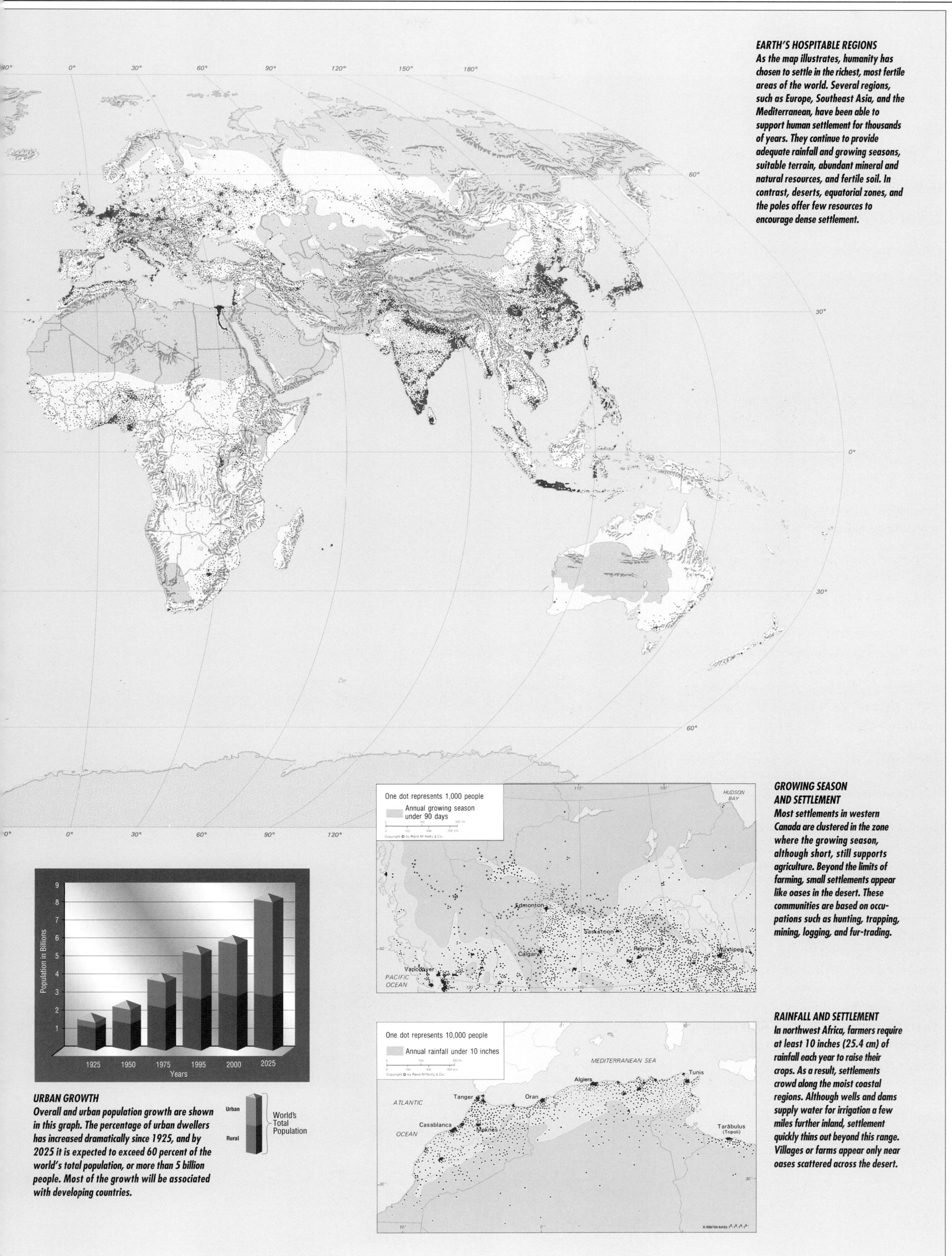

EARTH'S HOSPITABLE REGIONS
As the map illustrates, humanity has chosen to settle in the richest, most fertile areas of the world. Several regions, such as Europe, Southeast Asia, and the Mediterranean, have been able to support human settlement for thousands of years. They continue to provide adequate rainfall and growing seasons, suitable terrain, abundant mineral and natural resources, and fertile soil. In contrast, deserts, equatorial zones, and the poles offer few resources to encourage dense settlement.

GROWING SEASON AND SETTLEMENT
Most settlements in western Canada are clustered in the zone where the growing season, although short, still supports agriculture. Beyond the limits of farming, small settlements appear like oases in the desert. These communities are based on occupations such as hunting, trapping, mining, logging, and fur-trading.

One dot represents 1,000 people
Annual growing season under 90 days
Copyright © by Rand McNally & Co.

HUDSON BAY

Edmonton
Saskatoon
Calgary
Regina
Winnipeg
Vancouver
PACIFIC OCEAN

URBAN GROWTH
Overall and urban population growth are shown in this graph. The percentage of urban dwellers has increased dramatically since 1925, and by 2025 it is expected to exceed 60 percent of the world's total population, or more than 5 billion people. Most of the growth will be associated with developing countries.

Population in Billions

9 8 7 6 5 4 3 2 1

1925 1950 1975 1995 2000 2025
Years

Urban
Rural
World's Total Population

RAINFALL AND SETTLEMENT
In northwest Africa, farmers require at least 10 inches (25.4 cm) of rainfall each year to raise their crops. As a result, settlements crowd along the moist coastal regions. Although wells and dams supply water for irrigation a few miles further inland, settlement quickly thins out beyond this range. Villages or farms appear only near oases scattered across the desert.

One dot represents 10,000 people
Annual rainfall under 10 inches
Copyright © by Rand McNally & Co.

MEDITERRANEAN SEA
ATLANTIC OCEAN
Tanger
Oran
Algiers
Tunis
Casablanca
Meknes
Tarābulus (Tripoli)

X-589700-6ASO-P⁴P⁴P⁵

POPULATION

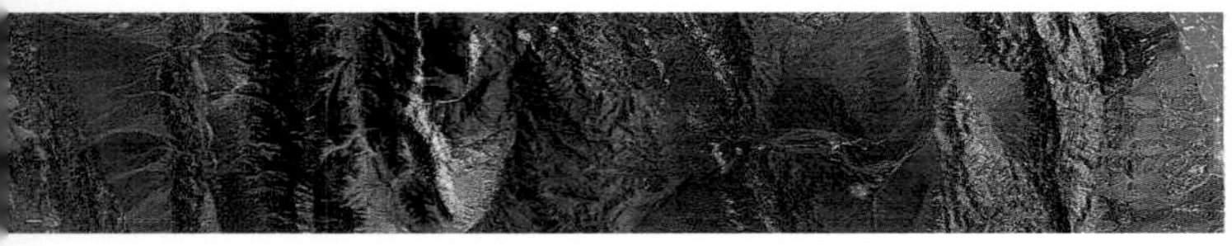

NEARLY 1.6 MILLION YEARS AGO, OUR
HUMAN ANCESTORS STRUGGLED TO SURVIVE
IN THE FORESTS AND FERTILE PLAINS
OF EASTERN AFRICA. TODAY, HUMANITY

inhabits every continent on earth. World population is
approaching 6 billion, with 80 million new lives added
every year. More people are alive now than have existed
since the dawn of human history.

This explosive growth is fueled not only by a rising birth
rate but by longer average life spans and by a sharp
reduction in the number of children who die young.
With births far outstripping deaths, predictions are that
world population will not stablize until the year 2010,
when over 10 billion people will share the planet.

The most densely settled parts of the Earth appear in
the industrial areas of Europe, North America, and
Japan, and the predominantly rural areas of India,
China, and Southeast Asia. In developed areas, modern
technology has encouraged the growth of large urban
districts. The heavily populated rural areas of Asian
countries reflect nearly 4,000 years of agricultural
civilization.

Even with the surge in population, however, substantial
areas of the Earth remain underpopulated or virtually
empty. Some regions offer striking contrasts between
crowded and open spaces. In Russia, a narrow band of
population stretches along the Trans-Siberian Railway.
The eastern shore of the Mediterranean Sea, with its
crowded coastal fringe of Israel, Lebanon, and Syria,
stands out sharply against the barren, uninhabited
land beyond.

Several natural and cultural factors help explain the
uneven distribution of humanity. Nature imposes
limits on agricultural development: many areas are too
dry or mountainous or have growing seasons too short
to support a large population. The harsher climate and
terrain of the polar regions and great deserts of the
world show only widely scattered human settlements.

Cultural factors also influence where populations are
likely to concentrate. Nearly 2.5 billion people now
live in urban centers, half of them in cities that number
500,000 or more. By the year 2000, the urban
population in less-developed countries will double, as
the rural poor seek greater opportunities in the already-
crowded cities. Religion and cultural values also
influence a nation's ability to control its birth rate.
Until curbing population becomes a worldwide goal,
our growing numbers will continue to exert increasing
pressure on the Earth's resources.

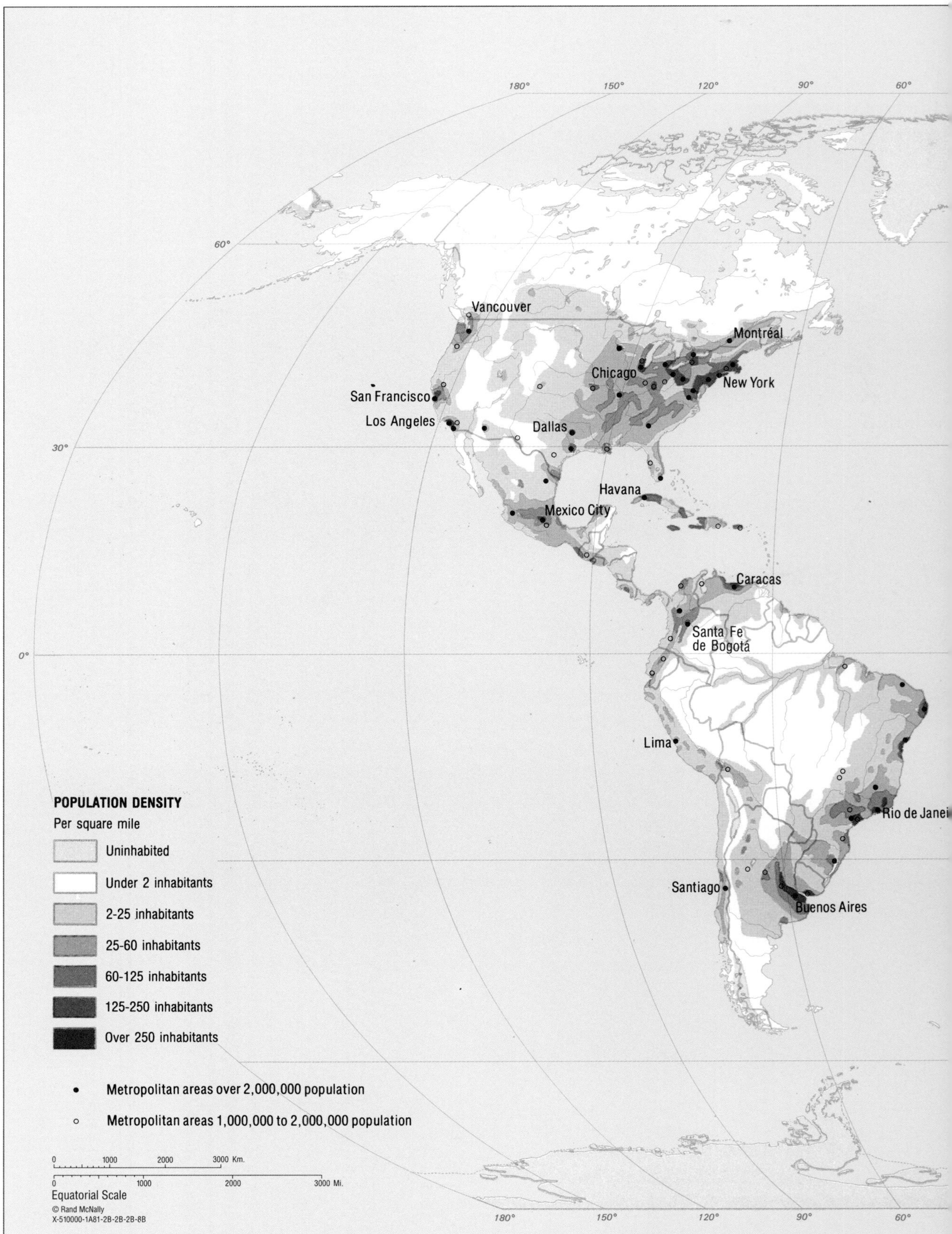

POPULATION DENSITY
Per square mile

- Uninhabited
- Under 2 inhabitants
- 2-25 inhabitants
- 25-60 inhabitants
- 60-125 inhabitants
- 125-250 inhabitants
- Over 250 inhabitants

● Metropolitan areas over 2,000,000 population

○ Metropolitan areas 1,000,000 to 2,000,000 population

```
0    1000    2000    3000 Km.
0         1000        2000         3000 Mi.
```
Equatorial Scale
© Rand McNally
X-510000-1A81-2B-2B-2B-8B

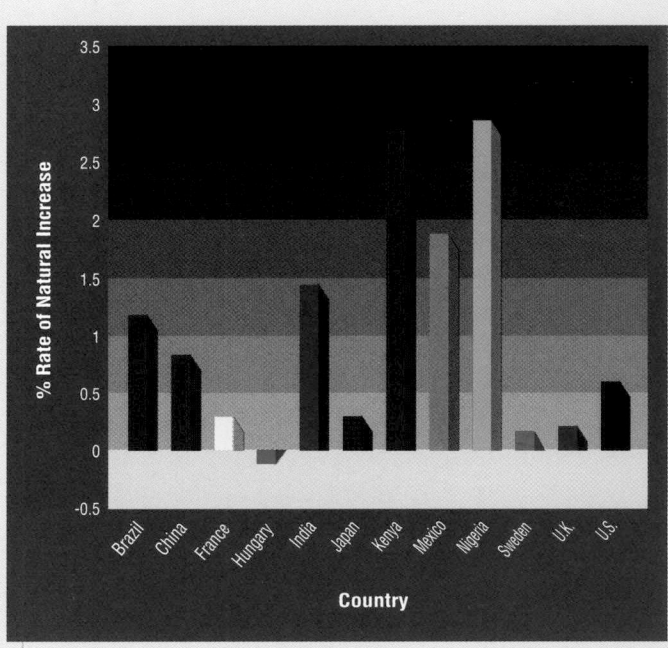

POPULATION GROWTH
*In densely populated countries,
extremely high growth rates can
cripple efforts to develop viable
economies. Through state-
encouraged family planning,
China has managed to decrease
its growth rate and thus improve
the economic well-being of its
people. Low rates of growth in
industrialized countries have
resulted in economies which are
able to support relatively high
standards of living.*

*(Rate of natural growth per year = birth rate
minus death rate. Immigration and emigration
are not included in this formulation.)*

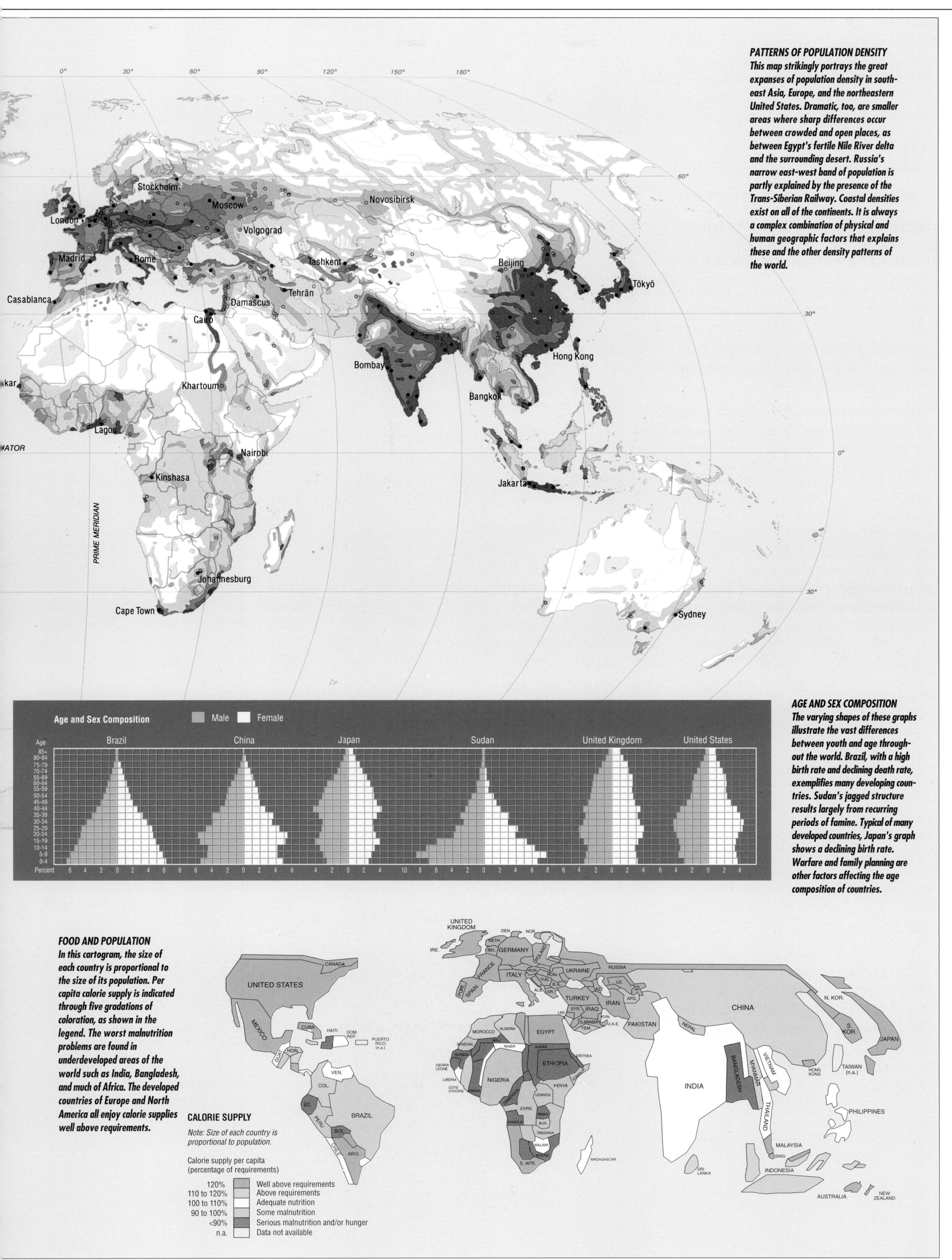

PATTERNS OF POPULATION DENSITY
This map strikingly portrays the great expanses of population density in south-east Asia, Europe, and the northeastern United States. Dramatic, too, are smaller areas where sharp differences occur between crowded and open places, as between Egypt's fertile Nile River delta and the surrounding desert. Russia's narrow east-west band of population is partly explained by the presence of the Trans-Siberian Railway. Coastal densities exist on all of the continents. It is always a complex combination of physical and human geographic factors that explains these and the other density patterns of the world.

Stockholm
Moscow
London
Novosibirsk
Volgograd
Madrid
Rome
Tashkent
Beijing
Casablanca
Tōkyō
Damascus
Tehrān
Cairo
Hong Kong
Bombay
kar
Khartoum
Bangkok
Lagos
Nairobi
Jakarta
Kinshasa
ATOR
PRIME MERIDIAN
Johannesburg
Sydney
Cape Town

AGE AND SEX COMPOSITION
The varying shapes of these graphs illustrate the vast differences between youth and age throughout the world. Brazil, with a high birth rate and declining death rate, exemplifies many developing countries. Sudan's jagged structure results largely from recurring periods of famine. Typical of many developed countries, Japan's graph shows a declining birth rate. Warfare and family planning are other factors affecting the age composition of countries.

Age and Sex Composition   Male   Female

| Age | Brazil | China | Japan | Sudan | United Kingdom | United States |

Age: 85+ 80-84 75-79 70-74 65-69 60-64 55-59 50-49 45-49 40-44 35-39 30-34 25-29 20-24 15-19 10-14 5-9 0-4

Percent

FOOD AND POPULATION
In this cartogram, the size of each country is proportional to the size of its population. Per capita calorie supply is indicated through five gradations of coloration, as shown in the legend. The worst malnutrition problems are found in underdeveloped areas of the world such as India, Bangladesh, and much of Africa. The developed countries of Europe and North America all enjoy calorie supplies well above requirements.

UNITED STATES
CANADA
MEXICO
CUBA
HAITI
DOM. REP.
PUERTO RICO (n.a.)
GUAT.
HON.
VEN.
COL.
EC.
PERU
BOL.
BRAZIL
CHILE
ARG.

UNITED KINGDOM
DEN.
NOR.
IRE.
NETH.
BEL.
GERMANY
POLAND
SPAIN
FRANCE
ITALY
HUN.
UKRAINE
RUSSIA
PORT.
ALB.
GR.
TURKEY
UZ.
AFG.
IRAN
MOROCCO
ALGERIA
EGYPT
PAKISTAN
NEPAL
CHINA
N. KOR.
S. KOR.
JAPAN
SENEGAL
MALI
NIGER
SUDAN
ETHIOPIA
ERITREA
BANGLADESH
VIETNAM
HONG KONG
TAIWAN (n.a.)
SIERRA LEONE
GUINEA
NIGERIA
KENYA
INDIA
MYANMAR
THAILAND
PHILIPPINES
LIBERIA
COTE D'IVOIRE
GHANA
UGANDA
ZAIRE
RWANDA
BUR.
TANZANIA
MALAYSIA
SING.
ANGOLA
INDONESIA
MALAWI
S. AFR.
MADAGASCAR
SRI LANKA
AUSTRALIA
NEW ZEALAND

CALORIE SUPPLY
Note: Size of each country is proportional to population.

Calorie supply per capita (percentage of requirements)

120%	Well above requirements
110 to 120%	Above requirements
100 to 110%	Adequate nutrition
90 to 100%	Some malnutrition
<90%	Serious malnutrition and/or hunger
n.a.	Data not available

RESOURCES ALONE DO NOT ACCOUNT FOR THE DISTRIBUTION OF INDUSTRIAL DEVELOPMENT AROUND THE WORLD. THE LARGEST OIL AND NATURAL GAS DEPOSITS

are in the Sahara and the Persian Gulf region, yet most Middle Eastern countries have little industry beyond refineries. The location and development of industries depend upon several factors—energy, skilled labor, capital and technology, transportation, markets, government planning, and trade alliances.

In North America, industrial sites, large urban markets, and concentrations of resources coincide. These regions are also blessed with abundant skilled labor and large capital markets to fund development. In South America, industrial districts are confined primarily to the main urban centers. Some countries, such as Venezuela and Chile, have adequate natural resources but lack the skilled labor or national markets to sustain industrial development.

Europe, the former Soviet Union, and Japan have developed in widely different ways. In the industrial districts of England, Belgium, northern France, and Germany, large deposits of coal and iron ore have fueled the growth of heavy industries. But in countries where raw materials are scarce, such as Italy, development is due mainly to individual initiative. The pattern of development in the former Soviet Union is tied directly to this region's enormous stores of coal, oil, iron ore, and other natural resources. In contrast, nearly all of Japan's raw materials are imported. Ample capital and skilled labor have made this country a leader in such areas as electronics and automobiles.

Industrial development in other regions of the world reflects a mixture of natural resources and cultural influences. India has only one major industrial district, the product of government initiatives and local supplies of coal and oil. China is taking advantage of rich deposits of coal and iron ore and an abundant labor supply to move rapidly toward modernization. Africa, from an industrial point of view, remains the least developed continent. It has significant hydroelectric potential and mineral resources, but lacks skilled labor and capital.

The trend in industrial development is toward light industries such as electronics and food processing. Concentrations of this type of industry can be found near large urban centers in many countries, including Taiwan, the Philippines, Mexico, and Korea.

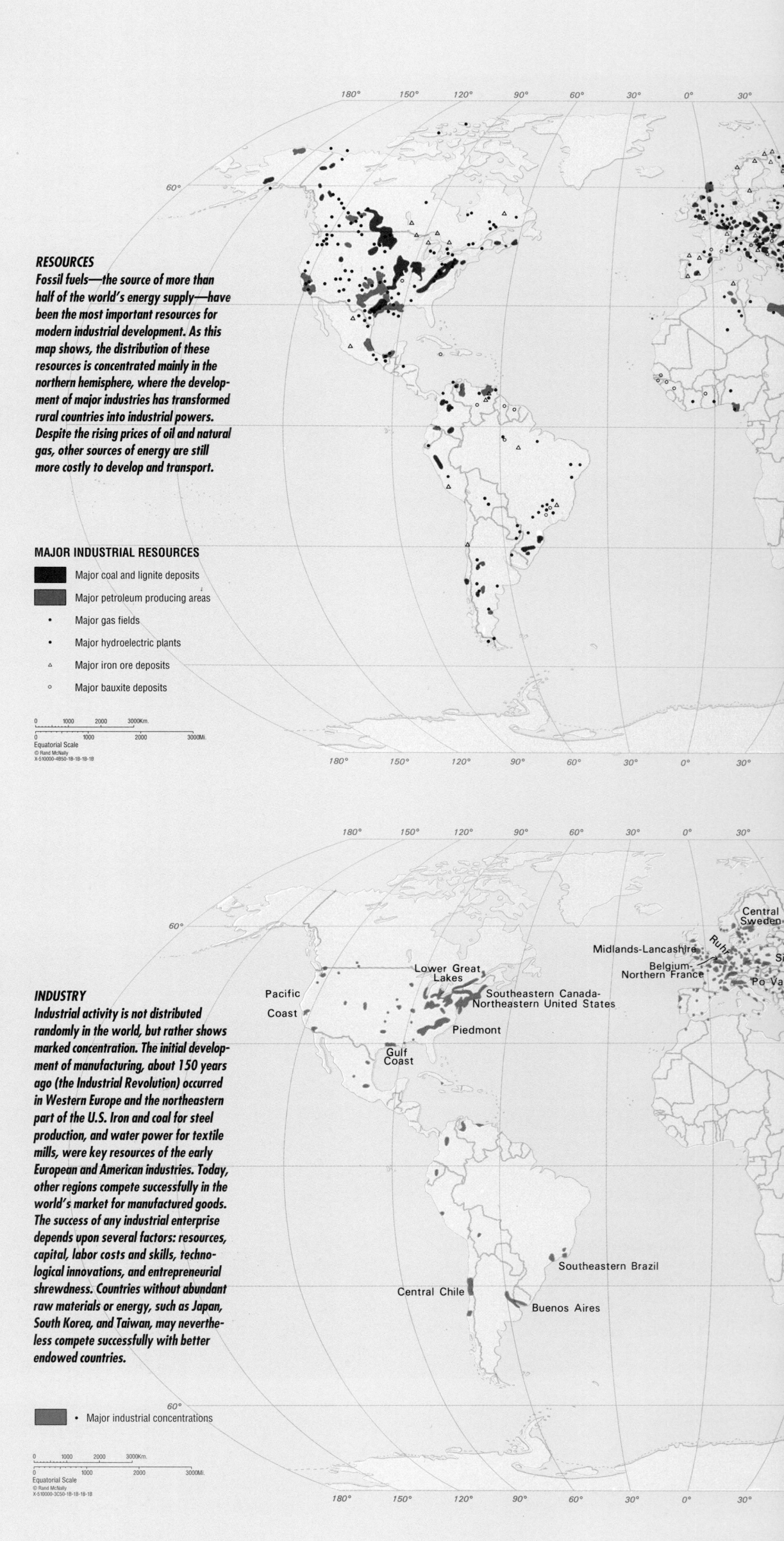

RESOURCES
Fossil fuels—the source of more than half of the world's energy supply—have been the most important resources for modern industrial development. As this map shows, the distribution of these resources is concentrated mainly in the northern hemisphere, where the development of major industries has transformed rural countries into industrial powers. Despite the rising prices of oil and natural gas, other sources of energy are still more costly to develop and transport.

MAJOR INDUSTRIAL RESOURCES

- ■ Major coal and lignite deposits
- ■ Major petroleum producing areas
- • Major gas fields
- • Major hydroelectric plants
- △ Major iron ore deposits
- ○ Major bauxite deposits

0   1000   2000   3000Km.
0   1000   2000   3000Mi.
Equatorial Scale
© Rand McNally
X-510000-4850-18-18-18-18

INDUSTRY
Industrial activity is not distributed randomly in the world, but rather shows marked concentration. The initial development of manufacturing, about 150 years ago (the Industrial Revolution) occurred in Western Europe and the northeastern part of the U.S. Iron and coal for steel production, and water power for textile mills, were key resources of the early European and American industries. Today, other regions compete successfully in the world's market for manufactured goods. The success of any industrial enterprise depends upon several factors: resources, capital, labor costs and skills, technological innovations, and entrepreneurial shrewdness. Countries without abundant raw materials or energy, such as Japan, South Korea, and Taiwan, may nevertheless compete successfully with better endowed countries.

- ■ • Major industrial concentrations

0   1000   2000   3000Km.
0   1000   2000   3000Mi.
Equatorial Scale
© Rand McNally
X-510000-3C50-18-18-18-18

ENERGY PRODUCTION AND CONSUMPTION

A large percentage of the world's energy is used for manufacturing. This fact helps explain the enormous variance—by country and by continent—in the production and consumption of energy. The United States, with only 5% of the world's population, consumes 25% of the world's energy, and nearly five times as much as Africa and South America combined.

However, the United States produces 80% of the energy it consumes, and is therefore less dependent on foreign sources than several other industrialized countries. Germany, for example, produces only 54% of the energy it consumes, and Japan only 7%.

Major energy exporting countries include oil-rich Saudi Arabia, Iran, and Venezuela.

Total World Production: 11,411,215,000 metric tons of coal equivalent
Total World Consumption: 11,037,655,000 metric tons of coal equivalent

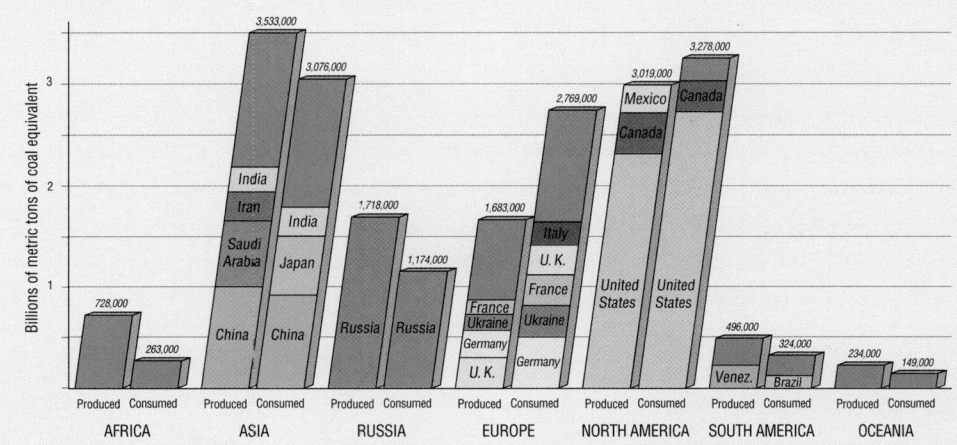

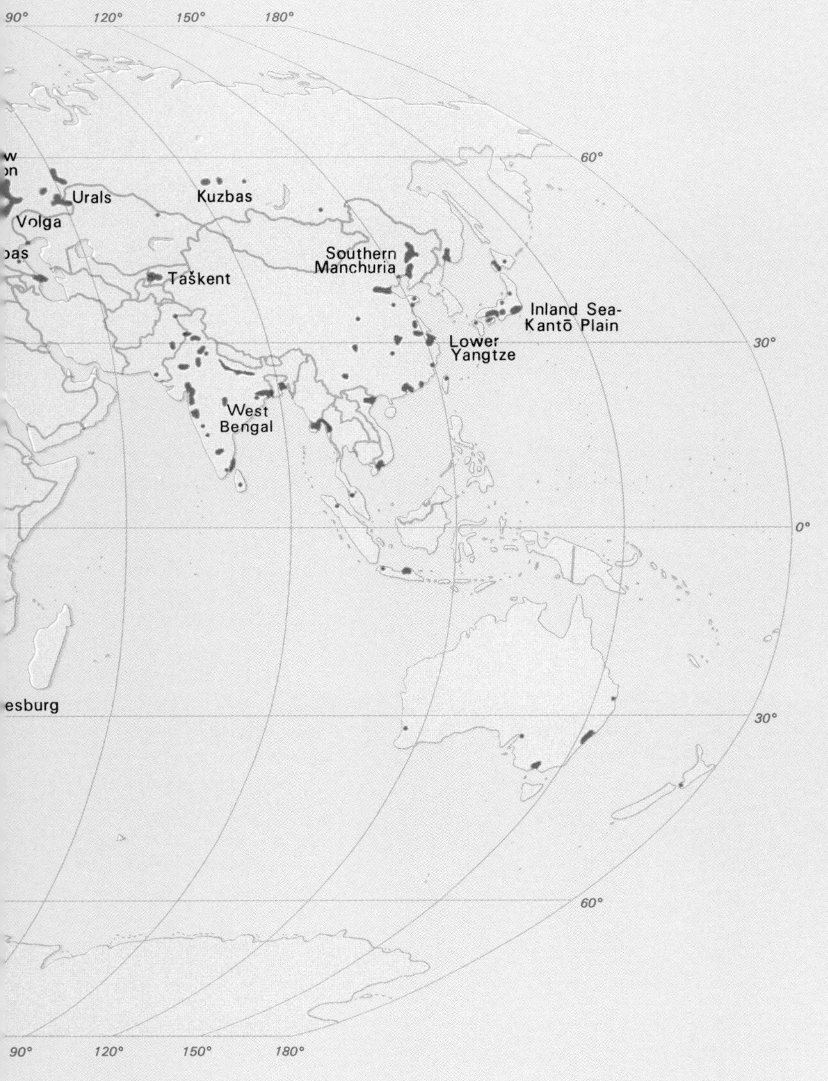

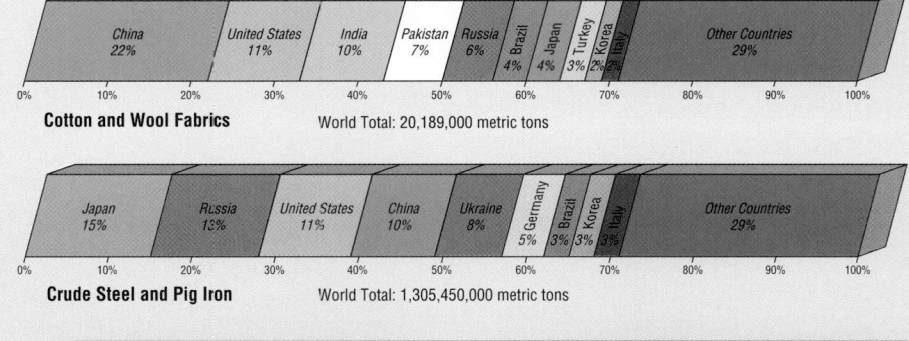

Cotton and Wool Fabrics World Total: 20,189,000 metric tons

Crude Steel and Pig Iron World Total: 1,305,450,000 metric tons

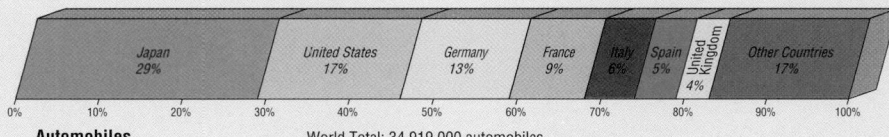

Automobiles World Total: 34,919,000 automobiles

MANUFACTURING

These graphs deal with three very different types of manufacturing activities.

Textile manufacturing is a relatively basic industry—it does not require a great deal of technology, capital, or energy. Textiles are basic goods that are needed in every country, regardless of economic status. (It is not surprising that China, with 1.1 billion people, should lead this category.)

Crude steel and pig iron manufacturing provide a raw material that is used in many products, including automobiles, machinery, and building materials.

Automobile production is a rather sophisticated manufacturing activity, requiring significant amounts of energy and capital, and involving sophisticated technology and the complex logistics of assembling many different parts and materials.

More than anything else, the graphs show the industrial dominance of Japan, the U.S., China, and Europe (including Russia), which together produce 48% of the world's cotton and wool fabrics, 65% of the crude steel and pig iron, and 83% of the automobiles.

SINCE HUMANS FIRST BEGAN USING TOOLS, CULTIVATING THE SOIL, AND FASHIONING ARTICLES TO TRADE, THEY HAVE MADE USE OF THE EARTH'S RESOURCES TO EARN A

living. Economic activities generally fall into two basic categories: herding and farming, and industrial production and commerce.

Nomadic herding and farming are perhaps the oldest economic activities practiced by humans. Today, only a smattering of people in Asia and Africa still follow the nomadic way of life. Farming, however, thrives in nearly every country, ranging from small family or tribal plots to the commercial farms of industrialized countries. Particularly in the United States, small, family-owned farms have given way to huge commercial agribusiness firms. With advanced methods of fertilization and mechanized harvesting, these agricultural businesses can raise enough food to feed the population of the country and still export surpluses around the world.

In contrast, subsistence farming, which produces little or no surplus for sale, is the mainstay of rural populations in Asia, Africa, and parts of South America. The large areas devoted to this type of farming represent essentially closed economic systems. It is in these areas that the challenge of economic development is greatest, for this type of farming is often the struggle on an impoverished people to wrest a living from tiny plots of land. Per capita income may be only a few hundred dollars per year. Release from such grinding poverty and toil is possible only where industries provide an alternative to rural life, and where systems of transportation and storage permit farming on a large scale.

Although subsistence agriculture still occupies large tracts of land in the world, developing countries are seeking to change this state of affairs in the near future. They wish to improve their agricultural output, increase industrialization, and raise their countries' standards of living.

Only a small portion of the Earth's surface is devoted to manufacturing and commerce—the foundations of national wealth and power. These areas generally coincide with the major urban centers of the world. In the United States alone, slightly over one percent of the land provides employment and residence for nearly 70 percent of the population. Urban centers in Europe are somewhat smaller but also account for a disproportionate amount of economic activity. As a result, per capita income in industrialized countries is high.

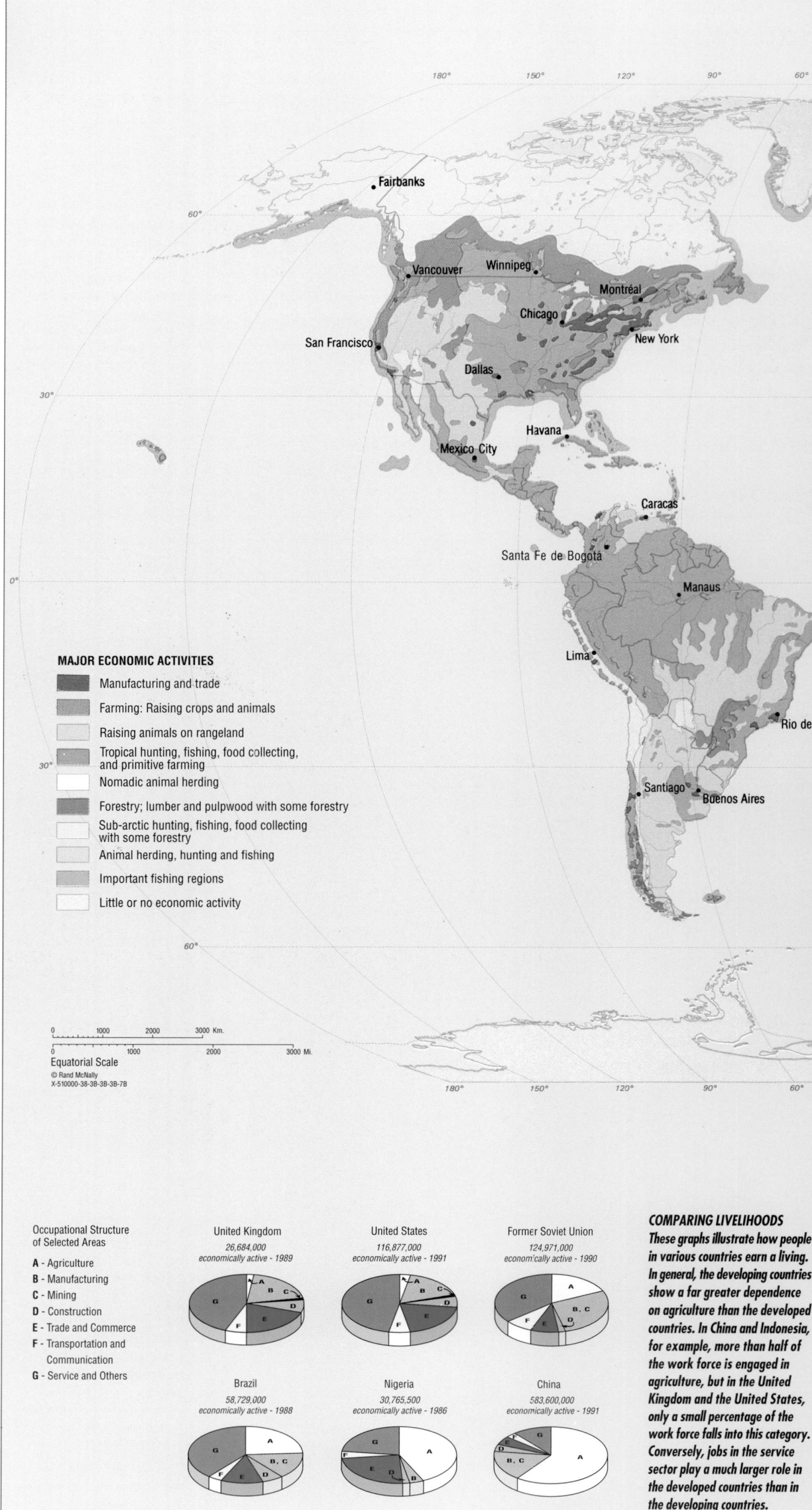

MAJOR ECONOMIC ACTIVITIES

- Manufacturing and trade
- Farming: Raising crops and animals
- Raising animals on rangeland
- Tropical hunting, fishing, food collecting, and primitive farming
- Nomadic animal herding
- Forestry; lumber and pulpwood with some forestry
- Sub-arctic hunting, fishing, food collecting with some forestry
- Animal herding, hunting and fishing
- Important fishing regions
- Little or no economic activity

0   1000   2000   3000 Km.
0   1000   2000   3000 Mi.
Equatorial Scale
© Rand McNally
X-510000-38-38-38-38-7B

Occupational Structure of Selected Areas

- A - Agriculture
- B - Manufacturing
- C - Mining
- D - Construction
- E - Trade and Commerce
- F - Transportation and Communication
- G - Service and Others

United Kingdom
26,684,000
economically active - 1989

United States
116,877,000
economically active - 1991

Former Soviet Union
124,971,000
economically active - 1990

Brazil
58,729,000
economically active - 1988

Nigeria
30,765,500
economically active - 1986

China
583,600,000
economically active - 1991

COMPARING LIVELIHOODS
These graphs illustrate how people in various countries earn a living. In general, the developing countries show a far greater dependence on agriculture than the developed countries. In China and Indonesia, for example, more than half of the work force is engaged in agriculture, but in the United Kingdom and the United States, only a small percentage of the work force falls into this category. Conversely, jobs in the service sector play a much larger role in the developed countries than in the developing countries.

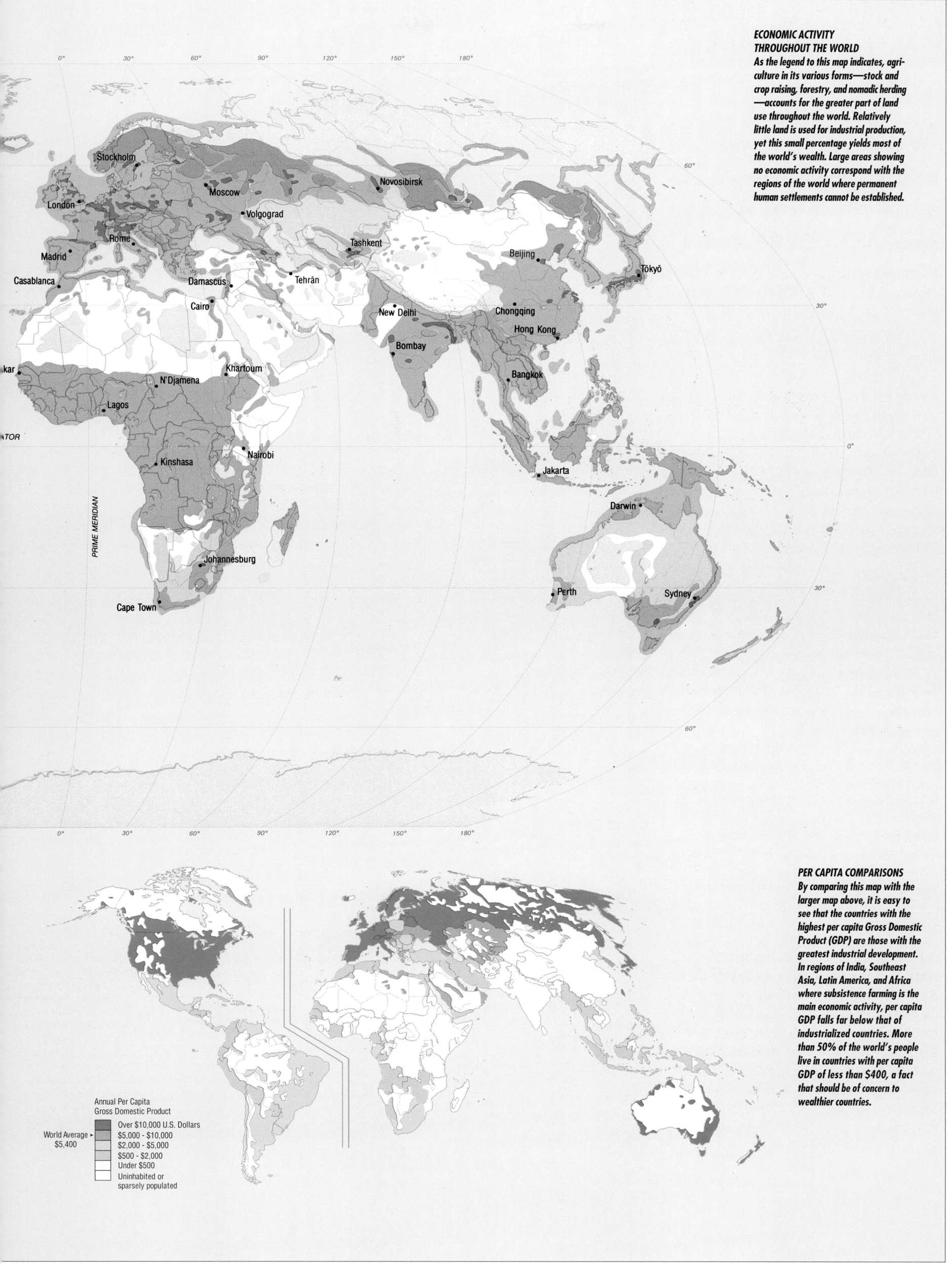

**ECONOMIC ACTIVITY
THROUGHOUT THE WORLD**
As the legend to this map indicates, agriculture in its various forms—stock and
crop raising, forestry, and nomadic herding
—accounts for the greater part of land
use throughout the world. Relatively
little land is used for industrial production,
yet this small percentage yields most of
the world's wealth. Large areas showing
no economic activity correspond with the
regions of the world where permanent
human settlements cannot be established.

PER CAPITA COMPARISONS
By comparing this map with the
larger map above, it is easy to
see that the countries with the
highest per capita Gross Domestic
Product (GDP) are those with the
greatest industrial development.
In regions of India, Southeast
Asia, Latin America, and Africa
where subsistence farming is the
main economic activity, per capita
GDP falls far below that of
industrialized countries. More
than 50% of the world's people
live in countries with per capita
GDP of less than $400, a fact
that should be of concern to
wealthier countries.

Annual Per Capita
Gross Domestic Product

- Over $10,000 U.S. Dollars
- $5,000 - $10,000
- World Average ► $5,400
- $2,000 - $5,000
- $500 - $2,000
- Under $500
- Uninhabited or
  sparsely populated

WE HUMANS, UNLIKE ANY OTHER SPECIES ON EARTH, HAVE RADICALLY RESHAPED THE ENVIRONMENT TO SUIT OUR OWN NEEDS. OVER COUNTLESS CENTURIES, WE HAVE cleared vast tracts of forest, dotted the landscape with cities—some covering hundreds of square miles—and altered the natural landscape to such a degree that we can almost speak of a "human-engineered" environment. But this reshaping carries a high price: mass extinctions of plant and animal life, damage to the atmosphere, and pollution on a worldwide scale. In the future, we must learn how to live in the world without destroying it.

The most obvious sign of our efforts to modify the environment has been the clearing of much of the world's forestland. At one time, the mid-latitude zones of both the Old and New Worlds were virtually covered with deciduous and evergreen trees. Over several hundred years, human settlers cleared the forests so vigorously that by the 17th century, wood was in short supply. These latitudes are now the most heavily populated on Earth, with new "forests" of glass, steel, and concrete.

The destruction of the world's forests and the overcultivation and overgrazing of exposed land has damaged the soil and accelerated the erosion process in many areas. The loss of productive land is especially serious today when a rapid increase in population raises the spectre of widespread famine.

Modern technology has enabled us to create artificial environments to live more comfortably in different climates. Central heating and cooling systems keep our buildings at a uniform temperature year-round. Some future planners envision entire dome-covered cities, with climate and temperature controlled by computer.

Pollution of air, water, and soil is perhaps the most pressing problem brought on by human activity. The Earth's atmosphere and hydrosphere are closed circulating systems. Industrial and household wastes are being dumped into these systems at a rate that far exceeds nature's ability to absorb them. Conservation and recycling programs seek to restore the environment and prevent further degradation. But much remains to be done, particularly in developing countries. The future quality of our environment will rest on our ability to cooperate as a world community.

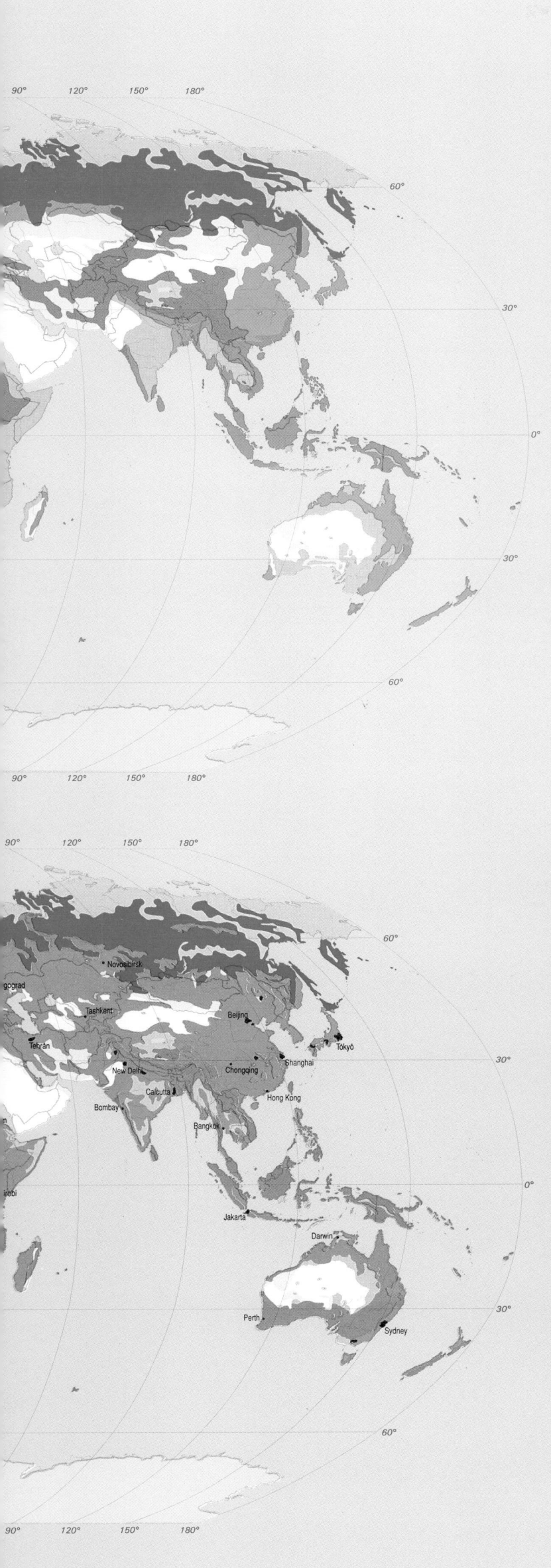

THE NATURAL WORLD

This map shows the world's "natural" vegetation—that is, the vegetation patterns that are thought to have existed before humans began to have a significant impact on the world environment. Tropical and subtropical forests, which harbor a majority of the world's plant species, are clustered near the equator. Savanna and desert regions are found to the north and south of these forests, where hot and dry climates prevail. Mediterranean vegetation, temperate grasslands, and temperate forests appear mainly in the temperate zones of the northern hemisphere, where rainfall is abundant and growing seasons are long. North of these zones are great stretches of the northern coniferous forests called "taiga." The extreme northern and southern latitudes are characterized by tundra and polar ice cap. The world's mountainous regions, though shown here in a uniform color, actually support an incredible diversity of vegetation.

TODAY'S WORLD

The extent to which humans have impacted and reshaped the natural world is evident on this map. The Mediterranean area and most of Europe, once heavily forested, are now cropland, grassland, or near-desert environments. The same is true of south and east Asia. In North America, only pockets remain of the temperate forests and grasslands that once covered much of the central part of the continent. Vast urban areas have sprung up throughout the world, replacing the original environments.

Today, the eyes of the world are on South America, where the vast rain forest of the Amazon basin is being destroyed at a rapid pace to create new cropland and grazing land. This rain forest is thought to play an important role in the Earth's weather systems as well as in the purification of air through the absorption of carbon dioxide and the production of oxygen. Its destruction could be disastrous to the entire world ecosystem.

VEGETATION

This legend applies to both maps

Tropical and sub-tropical forests

Savanna

Desert

Mediterranean

Temperate grassland

Temperate forest

Taiga (northern forests)

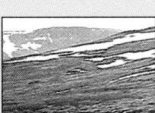
Tundra (lichen and moss)

Mountain

Polar and high mountain

HUMAN ENVIRONMENTS

This legend applies to the bottom map only

Cropland

Cropland and woodland

Cropland and grazing land

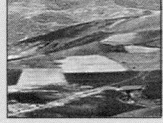
Grassland, grazing land

Urban

EVERY GREAT CIVILIZATION IN HUMAN HISTORY HAS CREATED A COMPLEX, OFTEN FAR-FLUNG TRANSPORTATION NETWORK LINKING IT TO THE OUTSIDE WORLD. CITIES

and industry in any era depend on supply lines and trade routes to survive. As the adjacent map shows, these land and sea routes underscore the world's uneven distribution of human settlement.

The greatest systems of surface transportation are found in North America and Europe, where nearly every inhabited locale can be reached by car, train, bus, or airline. This dense network thins out only in the western United States and in western and northern Canada. The more open network of the former Soviet Union traces the well-populated area west of the Ural Mountains and a narrow corridor between central Asia and Siberia. South America's transportation network is a study in contrasts between densely settled metropolitan areas and the more inaccessible interior regions. Until recently, much of the vast Amazon basin was accessible only via waterways, but development of the rain forest has spurred the construction of new highways and roads. The Pan American Highway, stretching from Mexico to Chile, is a major link among South American countries.

Africa, the Middle East, and Asia are more complex. In Africa, only South Africa, northern Morocco, Algeria, and Tunisia have well-developed transportation systems. The Middle East boasts some of humanity's oldest routes along the sea coast, but further inland the desert has few roads. Only in the oil-producing regions are transportation lines in abundant supply. Vast areas of the Asian continent are sparsely populated, and transportation facilities here are poor or nonexistent. India and Pakistan have roads and rail systems built on a European model, but only Japan's transportation network rivals those of the United States and Europe. In Australia, the transportation lines clearly mark where human settlements end and the "outback" regions begin. A single rail line cuts through the desert, connecting rural settlements with the major cities along the coast.

Transportation patterns also reveal something about the culture and economic development of a country or region. The complex network in Europe, for example, means that every factory, farm, and home is connected into a national and continental system of communication. In contrast, people in more remote areas may not be exposed to new ideas and methods as easily. Whether a country is connected into a vital network of communication or is relatively isolated has a significant impact on its rate of development and progress.

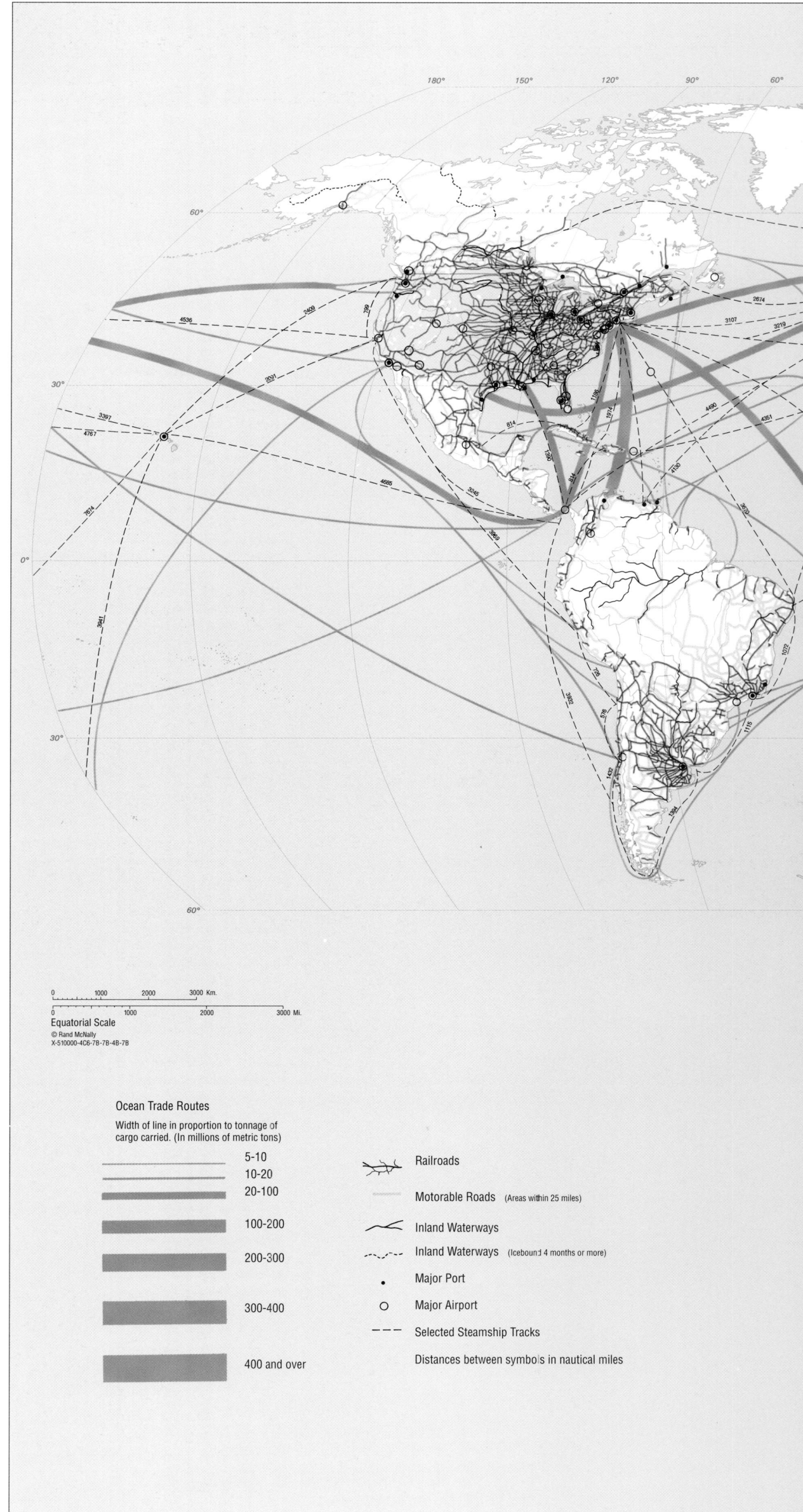

Equatorial Scale
© Rand McNally
X-510000-4C6-7B-7B-4B-7B

Ocean Trade Routes

Width of line in proportion to tonnage of cargo carried. (In millions of metric tons)

	5-10
	10-20
	20-100
	100-200
	200-300
	300-400
	400 and over

Railroads

Motorable Roads (Areas within 25 miles)

Inland Waterways

Inland Waterways (Icebound 4 months or more)

• Major Port

○ Major Airport

--- Selected Steamship Tracks

Distances between symbols in nautical miles

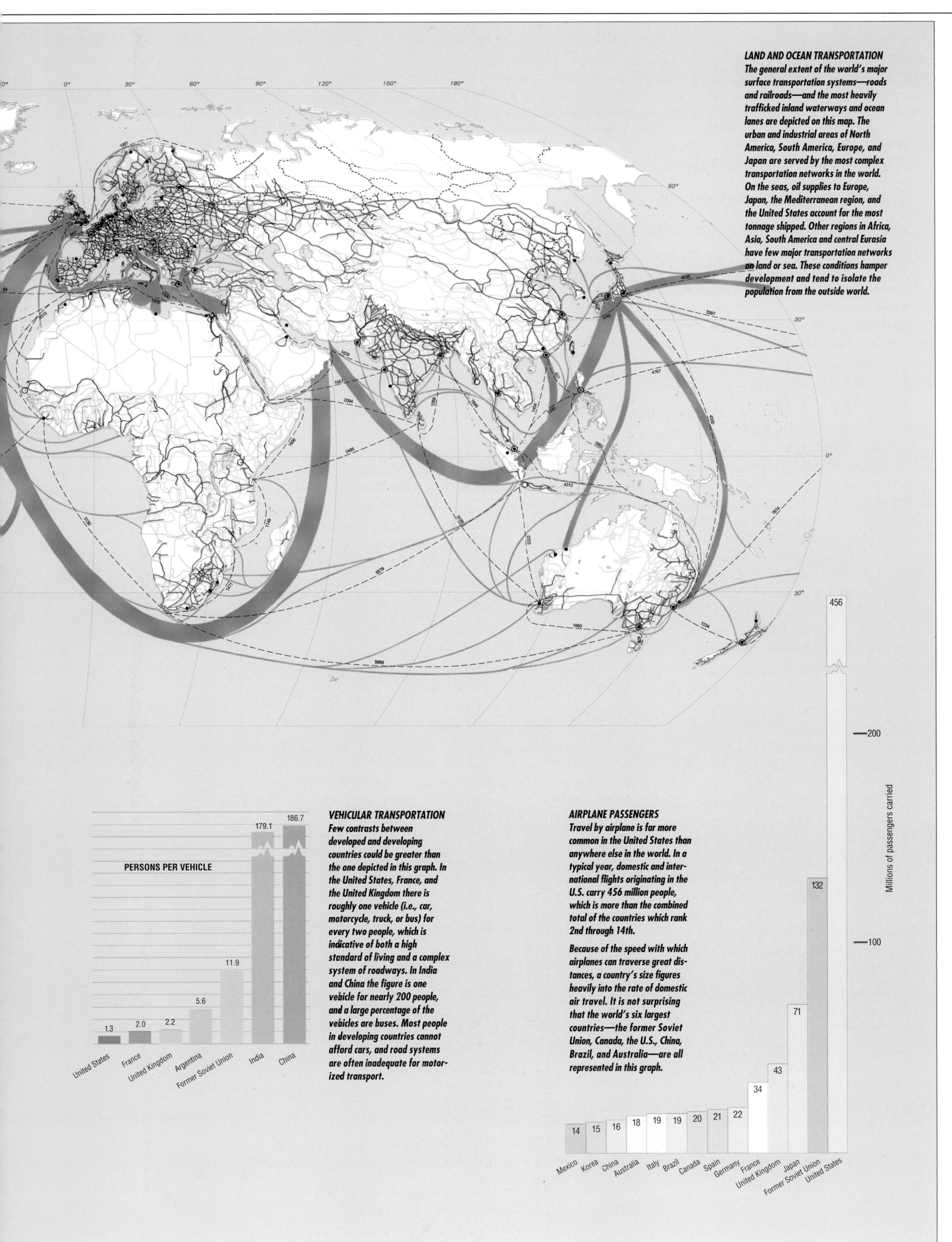

LAND AND OCEAN TRANSPORTATION
The general extent of the world's major surface transportation systems—roads and railroads—and the most heavily trafficked inland waterways and ocean lanes are depicted on this map. The urban and industrial areas of North America, South America, Europe, and Japan are served by the most complex transportation networks in the world. On the seas, oil supplies to Europe, Japan, the Mediterranean region, and the United States account for the most tonnage shipped. Other regions in Africa, Asia, South America and central Eurasia have few major transportation networks on land or sea. These conditions hamper development and tend to isolate the population from the outside world.

VEHICULAR TRANSPORTATION
Few contrasts between developed and developing countries could be greater than the one depicted in this graph. In the United States, France, and the United Kingdom there is roughly one vehicle (i.e., car, motorcycle, truck, or bus) for every two people, which is indicative of both a high standard of living and a complex system of roadways. In India and China the figure is one vehicle for nearly 200 people, and a large percentage of the vehicles are buses. Most people in developing countries cannot afford cars, and road systems are often inadequate for motorized transport.

PERSONS PER VEHICLE

United States	France	United Kingdom	Argentina	Former Soviet Union	India	China
1.3	2.0	2.2	5.6	11.9	179.1	186.7

AIRPLANE PASSENGERS
Travel by airplane is far more common in the United States than anywhere else in the world. In a typical year, domestic and international flights originating in the U.S. carry 456 million people, which is more than the combined total of the countries which rank 2nd through 14th.

Because of the speed with which airplanes can traverse great distances, a country's size figures heavily into the rate of domestic air travel. It is not surprising that the world's six largest countries—the former Soviet Union, Canada, the U.S., China, Brazil, and Australia—are all represented in this graph.

Millions of passengers carried

— 200
— 100

Mexico	Korea	China	Australia	Italy	Brazil	Canada	Spain	Germany	France	United Kingdom	Japan	Former Soviet Union	United States
14	15	16	18	19	19	20	21	22	34	43	71	132	456

FEW ACTIVITIES HAVE HAD AS PROFOUND AN IMPACT ON HUMAN DEVELOPMENT AS COMMUNICATION. YET UNLIKE AGRICULTURE OR TRANSPORTATION, COMMUNICATION

networks leave little imprint on the landscape. In modern times, this dynamic, invisible network has linked countries around the world, effectively conquering the barriers of time and distance. Today's telecommunications equipment can transmit and receive messages in milliseconds over distances that once took days, even months, to cross.

Throughout history, however, whether a country or region was included in a communications network or relatively isolated greatly affected its rate of cultural evolution. The invention of moveable type and printing in Europe in the 1400s, for example, had a tremendous cultural impact on the Western world. Information could now be disseminated to a wide audience, aiding in the exchange of ideas and new discoveries among the countries of Europe, North Africa, and the Far East. From that time on, the cultural development of these countries began to accelerate. Regions outside this network, such as sub-Saharan Africa and parts of Asia, slowly began to fall behind in technology and economic growth.

In the 1800s, advances in the understanding of electricity led to the invention of the telegraph, telephone, and radio. By 1866, the first transatlantic telegraph cable linked North America and Europe, laying the foundation for the modern era of electronic information exchange. Since the turn of the twentieth century, the explosive growth in communication devices and networks has ushered in the so-called "Information Age," the hallmark of which is the virtual elimination of geographic barriers to communication. Satellites, television and video, computer and data networks, modems, fax machines, electronic and voice mail, and cellular telephones have created a type of global information highway, along which information and communications flow with astonishing speed.

Although its full potential has not yet been realized, this new and vital highway is already beginning to transform the way we live, work, and view the world. For example, computer networking and fax machines allow many people in the service sector to work out of their homes instead of commuting to an office. Global positioning systems make it possible to track ocean-going vessels, trucks and individual parcels. Satellite geographic information systems aid in resource management by revealing global rates of deforestation, flood damage, and suburban sprawl.

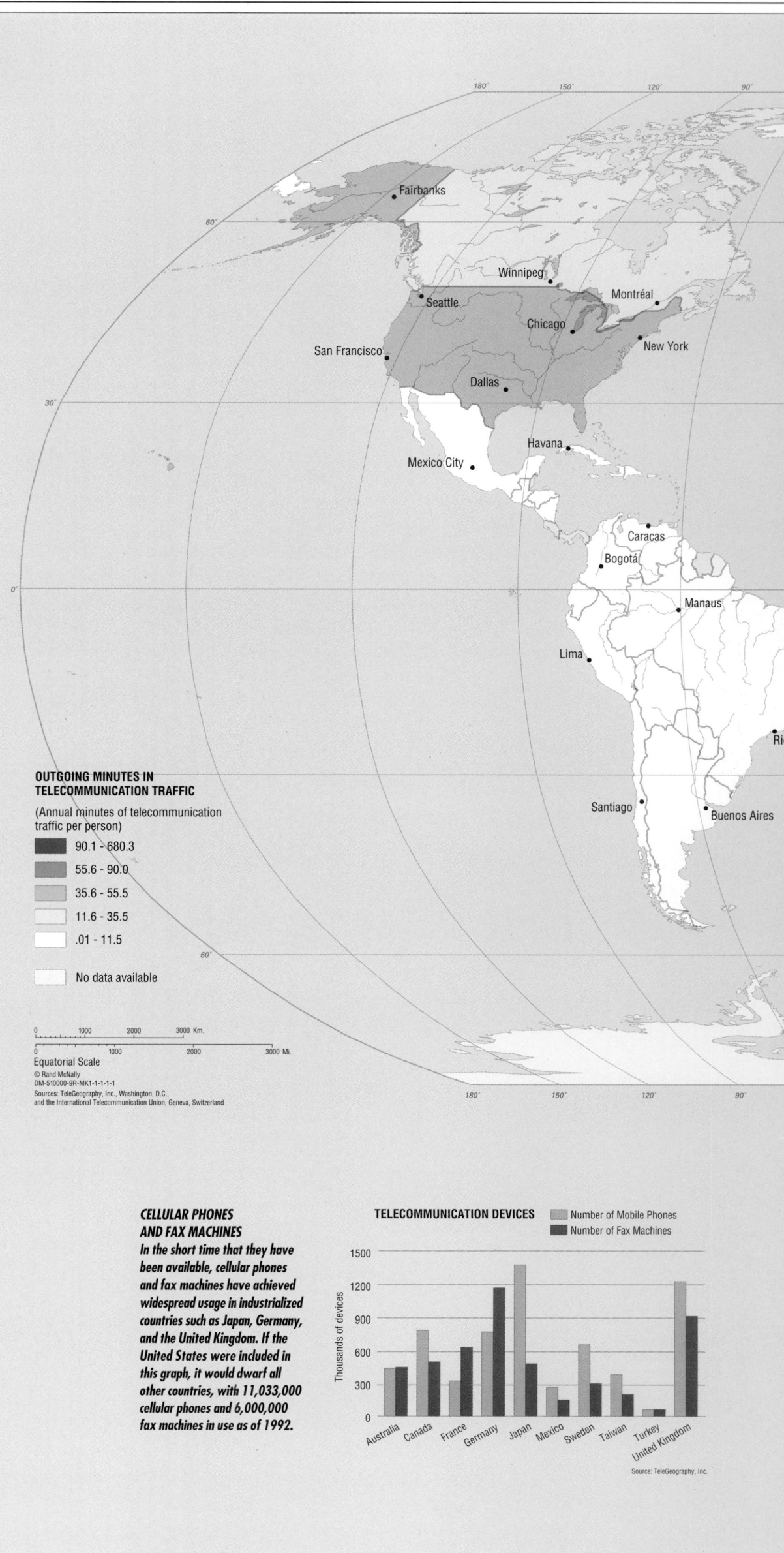

OUTGOING MINUTES IN TELECOMMUNICATION TRAFFIC

(Annual minutes of telecommunication traffic per person)

- 90.1 - 680.3
- 55.6 - 90.0
- 35.6 - 55.5
- 11.6 - 35.5
- .01 - 11.5

- No data available

Equatorial Scale
© Rand McNally
DM-510000-9R-MK1-1-1-1-1
Sources: TeleGeography, Inc., Washington, D.C.,
and the International Telecommunication Union, Geneva, Switzerland

CELLULAR PHONES AND FAX MACHINES
In the short time that they have been available, cellular phones and fax machines have achieved widespread usage in industrialized countries such as Japan, Germany, and the United Kingdom. If the United States were included in this graph, it would dwarf all other countries, with 11,033,000 cellular phones and 6,000,000 fax machines in use as of 1992.

TELECOMMUNICATION DEVICES
- Number of Mobile Phones
- Number of Fax Machines

Thousands of devices

Australia, Canada, France, Germany, Japan, Mexico, Sweden, Taiwan, Turkey, United Kingdom

Source: TeleGeography, Inc.

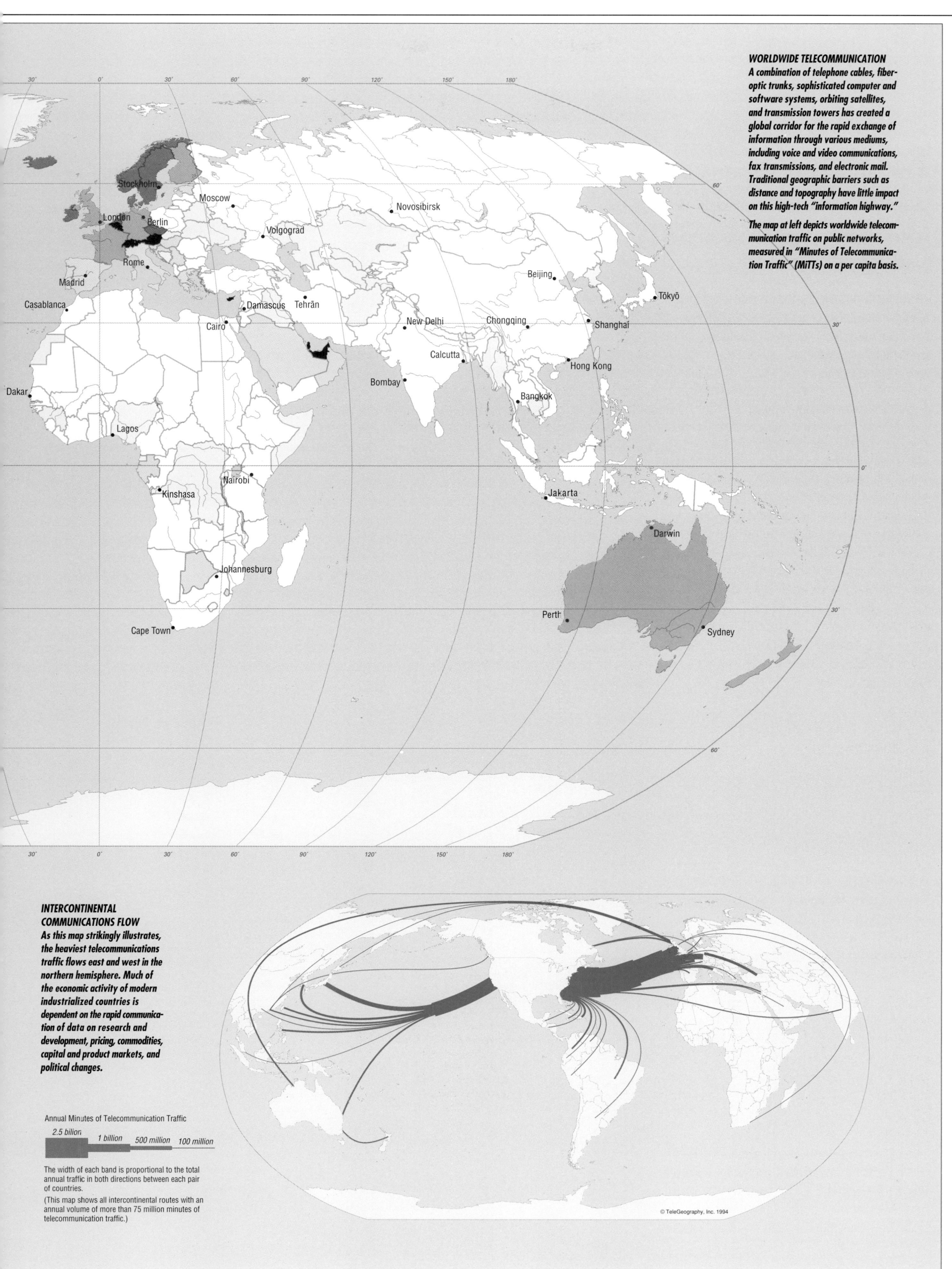

WORLDWIDE TELECOMMUNICATION
A combination of telephone cables, fiber-optic trunks, sophisticated computer and software systems, orbiting satellites, and transmission towers has created a global corridor for the rapid exchange of information through various mediums, including voice and video communications, fax transmissions, and electronic mail. Traditional geographic barriers such as distance and topography have little impact on this high-tech "information highway."

The map at left depicts worldwide telecommunication traffic on public networks, measured in "Minutes of Telecommunication Traffic" (MiTTs) on a per capita basis.

INTERCONTINENTAL COMMUNICATIONS FLOW
As this map strikingly illustrates, the heaviest telecommunications traffic flows east and west in the northern hemisphere. Much of the economic activity of modern industrialized countries is dependent on the rapid communication of data on research and development, pricing, commodities, capital and product markets, and political changes.

Annual Minutes of Telecommunication Traffic

2.5 billion   1 billion   500 million   100 million

The width of each band is proportional to the total annual traffic in both directions between each pair of countries.

(This map shows all intercontinental routes with an annual volume of more than 75 million minutes of telecommunication traffic.)

© TeleGeography, Inc. 1994

LANGUAGE, RELIGION, AND ETHNIC IDENTITY—THESE HELP TO DEFINE HUMAN COMMUNITIES IN A WAY THAT TRANSCENDS POLITICAL BOUNDARIES. LANGUAGE, OF course, is the most effective means of communication among members of a group. It serves as a cohesive force for the members and helps to distinguish one community from another.

The map to the right shows only the major language groups, such as the Germanic branch of the Indo-European family. A map that displayed all known languages would require thousands of colors and labels. The Chinese branch of the Sino-Tibetan family ranks first in the number of speakers. English ranks second, but is the world's most important medium for scientific and commercial communication.

English enjoys absolute predominance in only four countries: the United Kingdom, the U.S., Australia, and New Zealand. However, it is spoken by a majority of people in Ireland and Canada and is the preferred second language in many other countries. French, Spanish, and Russian are also widely used as second languages. The importance of two other languages is suggested by the number of countries in which they have official status: Arabic (18 countries) and Spanish (20 countries).

Religion, like language, is a means of communication and a mechanism that promotes social cohesion. The map here shows the most important universalizing religions (Christianity, Islam, and Buddhism) that are held to be appropriate for all of humankind and so are propagated by missionary activities. Religions associated with particular peoples, such as Judaism and Hinduism, seldom entail missionary activity.

Countries cannot always be neatly divided into religious groups, however. In China, for example, Buddhism, Confucianism, and Taoism are so entwined that one has to speak of a Chinese religious system rather than a Chinese religion. Elsewhere in the world, and especially in Africa, a wide array of tribal religions can be identified, and many of these have incorporated some of the practices and beliefs of one of the universalizing religions. Over time, most religions tend to split into factions or denominations. The division of Christianity into Catholic, Orthodox, and Protestant branches is striking evidence of this tendency, as is the split of the Islamic religion into Sunni and Shi'ite factions after the death of Muhammad in A.D. 632.

The country boundaries that appear as lines under the patterns of religions and languages remind us of an important fact about our world: very few of the 184 member states of the United Nations are nations in the strict or singular sense of the word. Most are a collection

Continued on page A·22

WORLD LANGUAGES

INDO-EUROPEAN
- 1 Germanic
- 2 Romance
- 3 Indo-Aryan
- 4 Greek
- 5 Celtic
- 6 Iranian
- 7 Slavic
- 8 Baltic
- 9 Armenian
- 10 Albanian

URALIC
- 11 Samoyed
- 12 Finnic
- 13 Ugrian

CAUCASIC
- 14 Kartvelian, Adyo-Abkaz, Nakh, Dagestan
- Basque

ALTAIC
- 16 Turkic
- 17 Mongolic
- 18 Tungus-Manchu
- 19 Korean
- Japanese

SINO-TIBETAN
- 21 Tibetan-Burmese
- 22 Chinese (Sinitic)
- 23 Thai-Chuang
- 24 Vietnamese
- Miao-Yao
- 25 Mon-Khmer
- 27 Dravidian
- 28 Mundar
- 29 Andaman

AUSTRONESIAN
- 30 Indonesian
- 31 Melanesian
- 32 Polynesian
- 33 Micronesian
- Papuan
- 35 Australian Aboriginie
- 36 Paleoasiatic
- Eskimo-Aleut
- 38 Native American

AFRO-ASIATIC
- 39 Arabic
- 40 Hebrew
- 41 Cushitic
- Berber

- 43 Bantu
- 44 Central and East Sudan
- 45 Mande
- 46 Guinean
- Songai
- Hausa
- 49 Koisan
- 50 Kanuri
- 51 Nilot

- Uninhabited

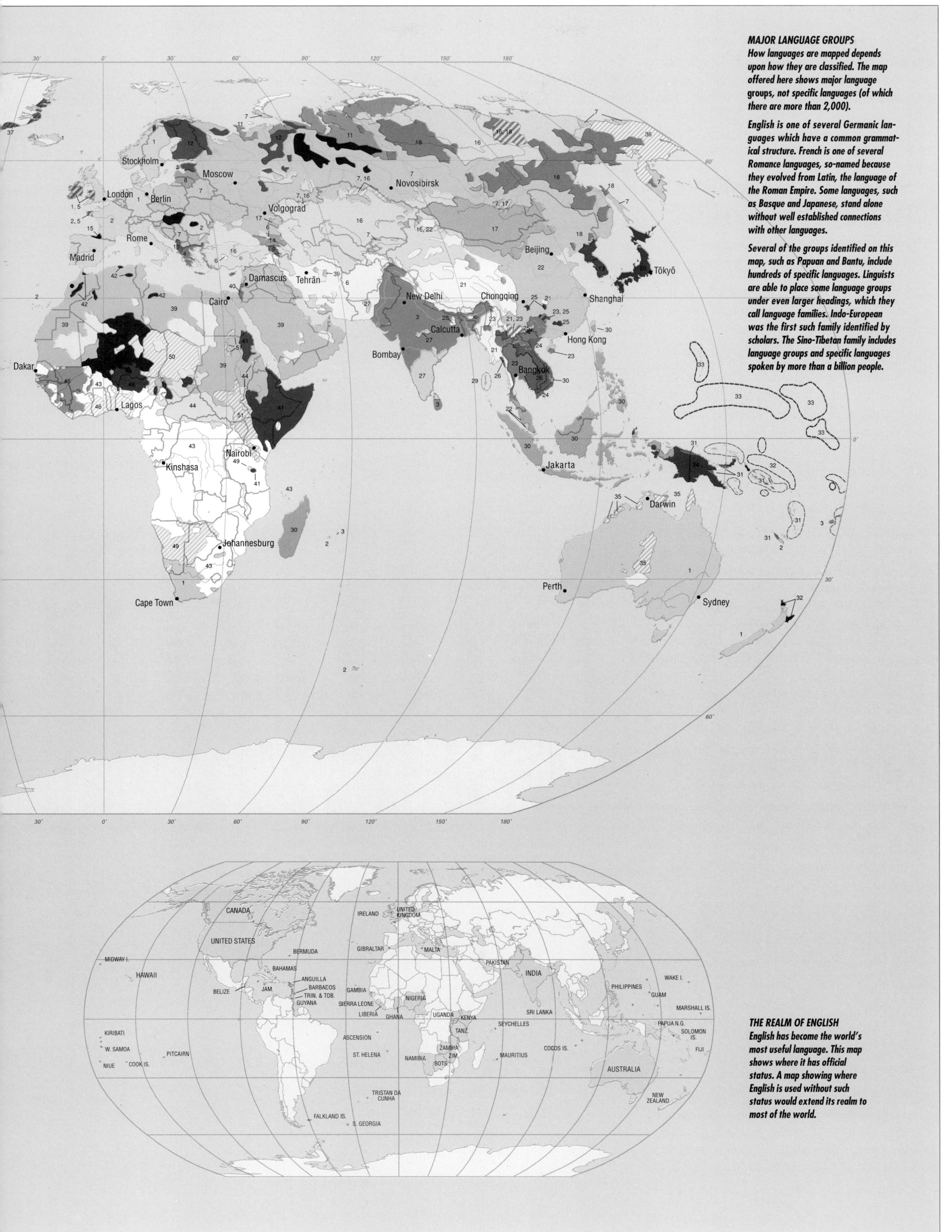

MAJOR LANGUAGE GROUPS
How languages are mapped depends upon how they are classified. The map offered here shows major language groups, not specific languages (of which there are more than 2,000).

English is one of several Germanic languages which have a common grammatical structure. French is one of several Romance languages, so-named because they evolved from Latin, the language of the Roman Empire. Some languages, such as Basque and Japanese, stand alone without well established connections with other languages.

Several of the groups identified on this map, such as Papuan and Bantu, include hundreds of specific languages. Linguists are able to place some language groups under even larger headings, which they call language families. Indo-European was the first such family identified by scholars. The Sino-Tibetan family includes language groups and specific languages spoken by more than a billion people.

THE REALM OF ENGLISH
English has become the world's most useful language. This map shows where it has official status. A map showing where English is used without such status would extend its realm to most of the world.

PEOPLES AND COUNTRIES

Continued from page A·20

of different groups speaking a variety of languages and maintaining diverse religious and cultural beliefs. In Western Europe, only Denmark and Portugal are homogeneous countries where everyone speaks the same language and belongs to the same church. In Africa, only Tunisia shares this distinction.

It is hard to find a comparable example in the Middle East, even among countries predominantly Islamic in faith and Arabic in speech. Saudi Arabia, if its large foreign labor population is ignored, is the only example of a true nation state in this region. Elsewhere in Asia, Japan and the two Korean states are rare exceptions to the more common pattern of cultural complexity. In Latin America, Spanish or Portuguese speech and Roman Catholicism are cultural common denominators, but Native American languages are still spoken in most countries. In contrast, Argentina and Brazil are cultural melting pots like the United States. Costa Rica and Uruguay may be the only New World states without significant minorities.

The fact that cultural uniformity is so rare, and only one perfect example can be cited (Iceland), means that the familiar political map not only differs from the less familiar maps of language and religion, but may actually conflict with them. Some countries have laws and institutions that permit citizens of different faiths and languages to live in peace and prosperity. For example, the Swiss live in harmony in spite of speaking four languages (German, French, Italian, and Romansch) and having Catholic and Protestant affiliations. Unfortunately, such happy examples of cultural accommodation are offset by numerous instances of tension and conflict. The ethnic warfare within recent decades in Sri Lanka, Bosnia, Sudan, Lebanon, and Rwanda are conspicuous examples of the potential for violence that often exists in states that are not true nation states or have borders that do not coincide with ethnic realities. The collapse of the Soviet Union exposed many problems of this nature.

Since the world is never likely to have only one language or one religion, comparison of maps showing cultural patterns with those indicating political jurisdiction reveals an important truth about our troubled world. In order to understand why ethnic conflict occurs so frequently we need an appropriate vocabulary. We need to be able to distinguish among the following cultural-political categories: *nation states* (homogeneous countries, such as Iceland and Denmark); *multinational states* (countries made up of diverse ethnic and linguistic groups, such as India); *multi-state nations* (multiple countries that share language and religion, such as the Arabic-Islamic realm); *non-nation states* (Vatican City is the only example); and, finally, *non-state nations* (regions where people share language and religion but have no political state, such as Kurdistan and Palestine).

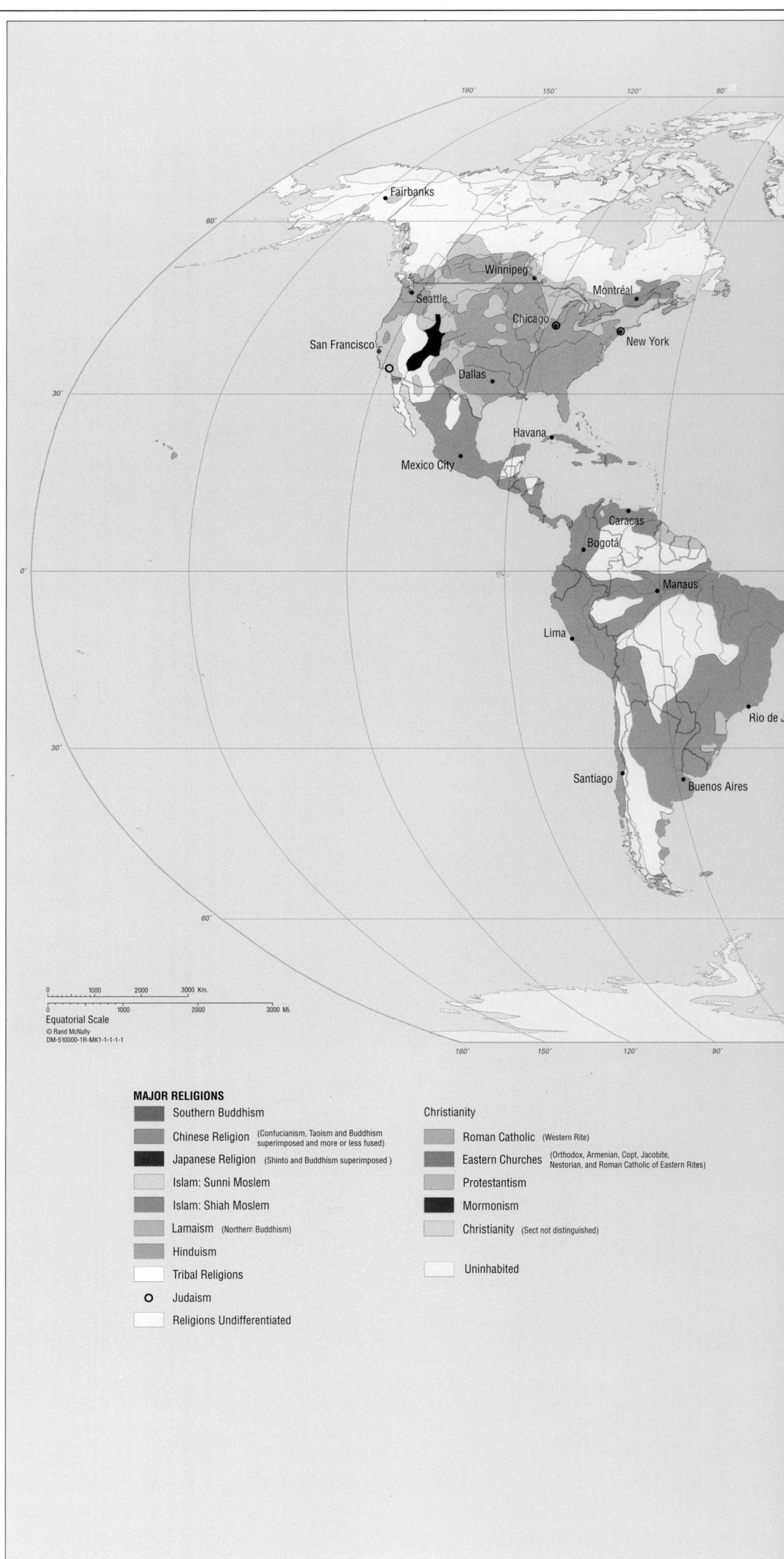

MAJOR RELIGIONS

- Southern Buddhism
- Chinese Religion (Confucianism, Taoism and Buddhism superimposed and more or less fused)
- Japanese Religion (Shinto and Buddhism superimposed)
- Islam: Sunni Moslem
- Islam: Shiah Moslem
- Lamaism (Northern Buddhism)
- Hinduism
- Tribal Religions
- ○ Judaism
- Religions Undifferentiated

Christianity

- Roman Catholic (Western Rite)
- Eastern Churches (Orthodox, Armenian, Copt, Jacobite, Nestorian, and Roman Catholic of Eastern Rites)
- Protestantism
- Mormonism
- Christianity (Sect not distinguished)
- Uninhabited

0   1000   2000   3000 Km.
0   1000   2000   3000 Mi.
Equatorial Scale
© Rand McNally
DM-510000-1R-MK1-1-1-1-1

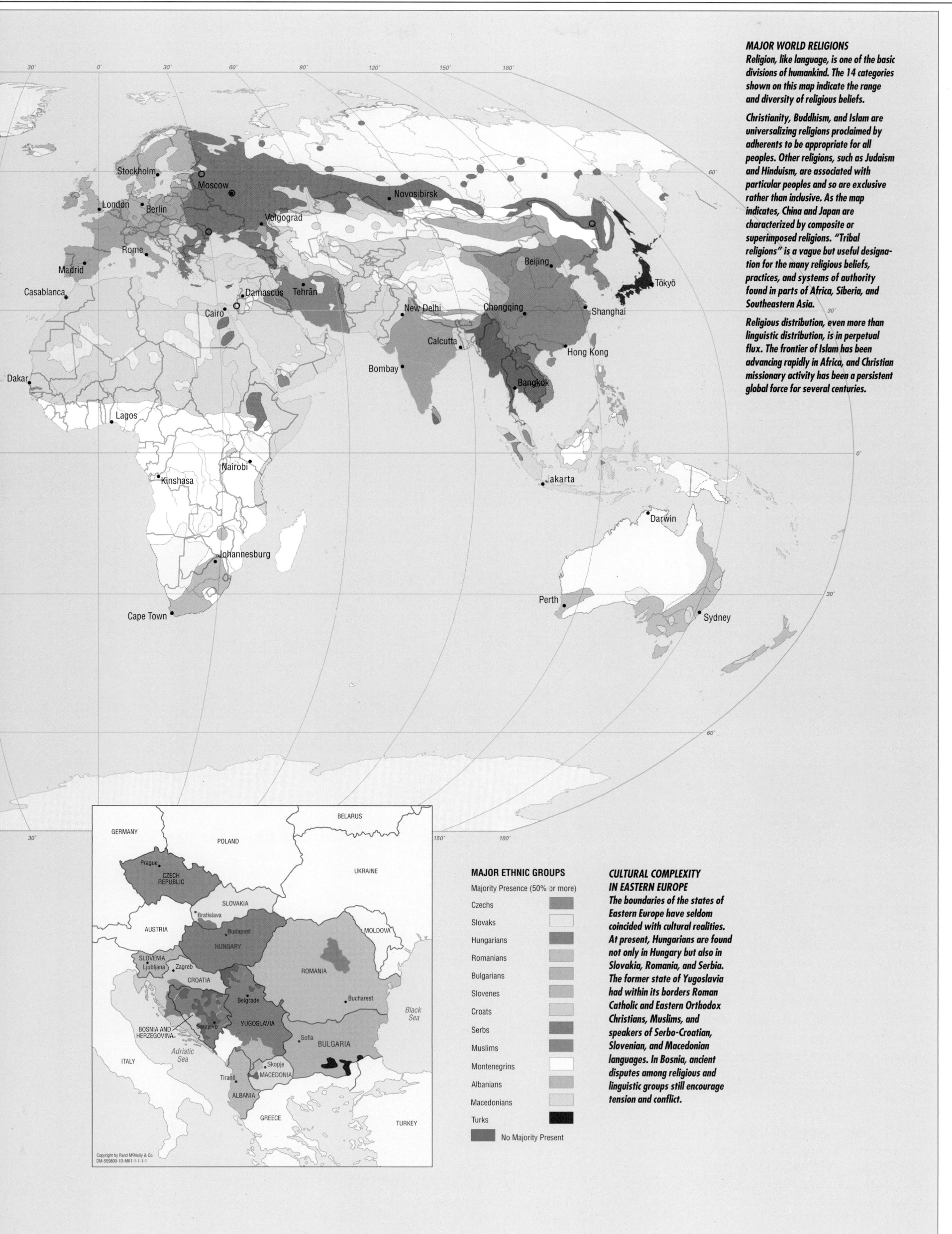

MAJOR WORLD RELIGIONS

Religion, like language, is one of the basic divisions of humankind. The 14 categories shown on this map indicate the range and diversity of religious beliefs.

Christianity, Buddhism, and Islam are universalizing religions proclaimed by adherents to be appropriate for all peoples. Other religions, such as Judaism and Hinduism, are associated with particular peoples and so are exclusive rather than inclusive. As the map indicates, China and Japan are characterized by composite or superimposed religions. "Tribal religions" is a vague but useful designation for the many religious beliefs, practices, and systems of authority found in parts of Africa, Siberia, and Southeastern Asia.

Religious distribution, even more than linguistic distribution, is in perpetual flux. The frontier of Islam has been advancing rapidly in Africa, and Christian missionary activity has been a persistent global force for several centuries.

MAJOR ETHNIC GROUPS

Majority Presence (50% or more)

- Czechs
- Slovaks
- Hungarians
- Romanians
- Bulgarians
- Slovenes
- Croats
- Serbs
- Muslims
- Montenegrins
- Albanians
- Macedonians
- Turks

No Majority Present

CULTURAL COMPLEXITY IN EASTERN EUROPE

The boundaries of the states of Eastern Europe have seldom coincided with cultural realities. At present, Hungarians are found not only in Hungary but also in Slovakia, Romania, and Serbia. The former state of Yugoslavia had within its borders Roman Catholic and Eastern Orthodox Christians, Muslims, and speakers of Serbo-Croatian, Slovenian, and Macedonian languages. In Bosnia, ancient disputes among religious and linguistic groups still encourage tension and conflict.

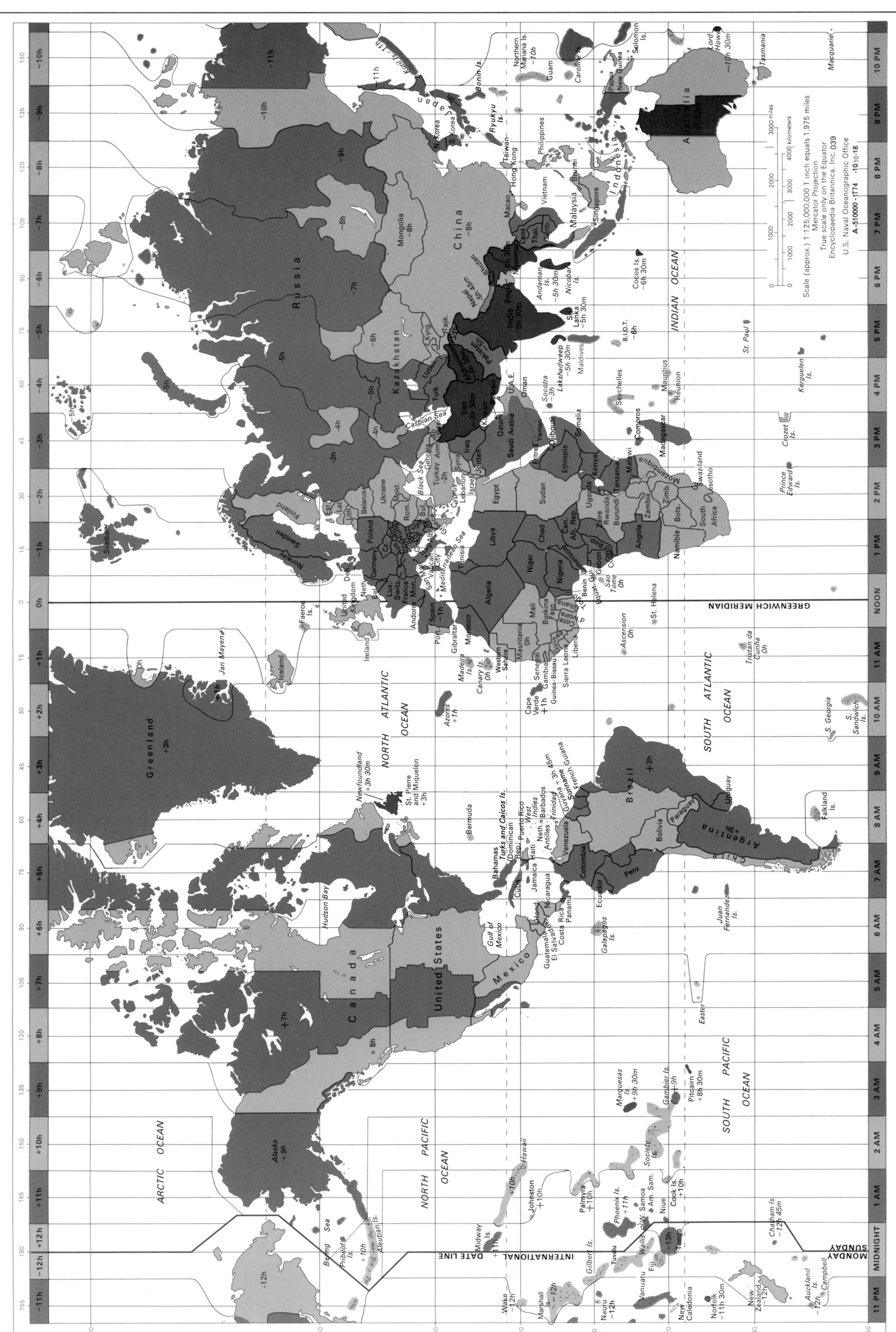

The standard time zone system, fixed by international agreement and by law in each country, is based on a theoretical division of the globe into 24 zones of 15° longitude each. The mid-meridian of each zone fixes the hour for the entire zone. The zero time zone extends 7½° east and 7½° west of the Greenwich meridian, 0° longitude. Since the earth rotates toward the east, time zones to the west of Greenwich are earlier, to the east, later.

Plus and minus hours at the top of the map are added to or subtracted from local time to find Greenwich time. Local standard time can be determined for any area in the world by adding one hour for each time zone counted in an easterly direction from one's own, or by subtracting one hour for each zone counted in a westerly direction. To separate one day from the next, the 180th meridian has been designated as the international date line. On both sides of the line the time of day is the same, but west of the line it is one day later than it is to the east.

Countries that adhere to the international zone system adopt the zone applicable to their location. Some countries, however, establish time zones based on political boundaries, or adopt the time zone of a neighboring unit. For all or part of the year some countries also advance their time by one hour, thereby utilizing more daylight hours each day.

Time Zones

■ Standard time zone of even-numbered hours from Greenwich time

■ Standard time zone of odd-numbered hours from Greenwich time

■ Time varies from the standard time zone by half an hour

■ Time varies from the standard time zone by other than half an hour

| h | m | hours, minutes

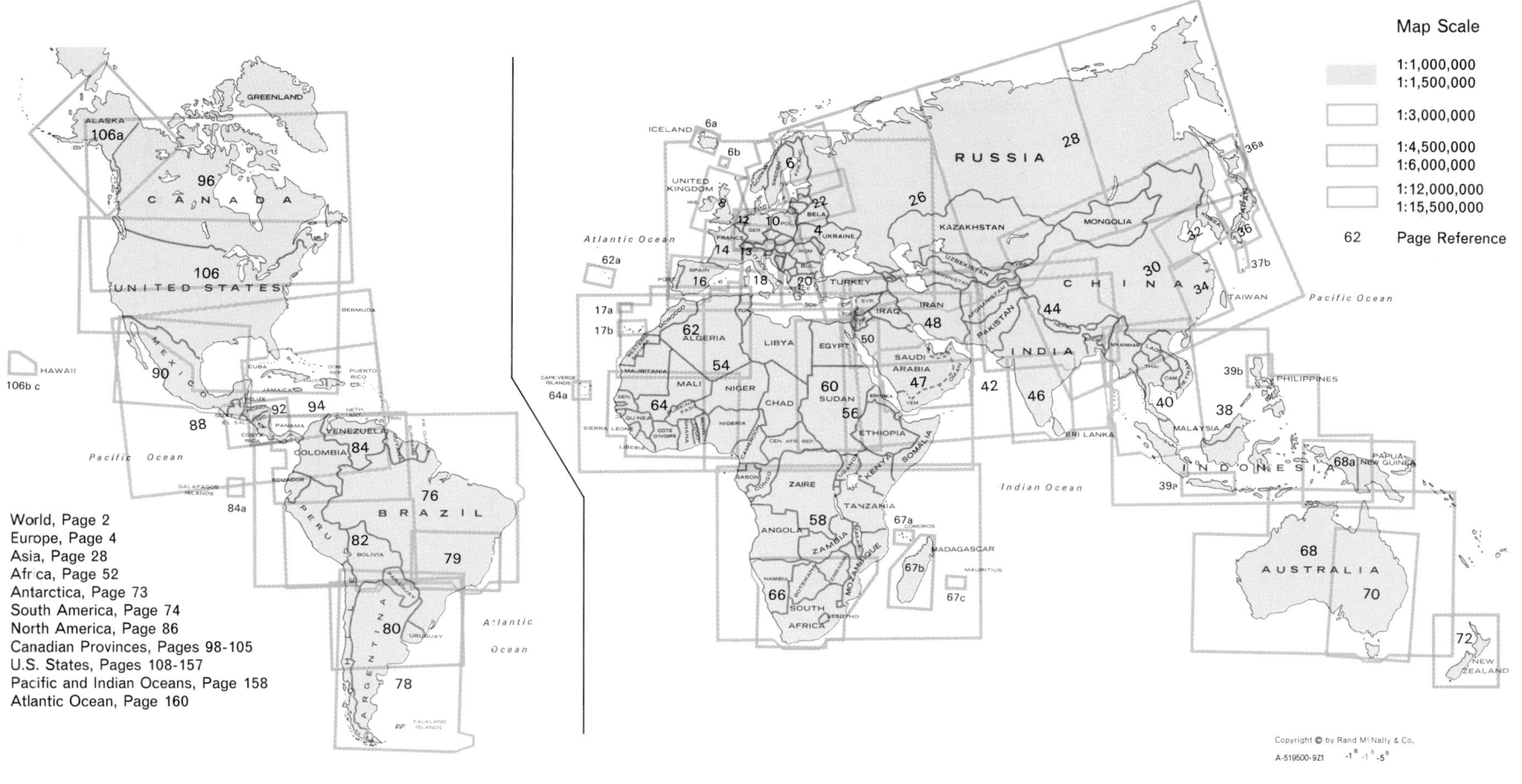

Map Scale

	1:1,000,000 1:1,500,000
	1:3,000,000
	1:4,500,000 1:6,000,000
	1:12,000,000 1:15,500,000

62   Page Reference

World Maps Symbols

Inhabited Localities

The size of type indicates the relative economic and political importance of the locality

Écommoy	Lisieux	**Rouen**
Trouville	**Orléans**	**PARIS**
Bîr Safâjah °	Oasis	

The symbol represents the population of the locality

1:1,000,000- 1:6,000,000	1:12,000,000- 1:15,500,000	1:24,000,000- 1:48,000,000
• 0—10,000	• 0—50,000	• 0—100,000
○ 10,000—25,000	⊙ 50,000—100,000	⊙ 100,000—1,500,000
⊙ 25,000—100,000	⊙ 100,000—250,000	■ >1,500,000
▣ 100,000—250,000	▣ 250,000—1,000,000	
▣ 250,000—1,000,000	■ >1,000,000	
■ >1,000,000		

English or second official language names are shown in reduced size lettering. Historical or other alternate names in the local language are shown in parentheses.

Urban Area (Area of continuous industrial, commercial, and residential development)

Capitals of Political Units

BUDAPEST   Independent Nation

Cayenne   Dependency (Colony, protectorate, etc.)

Recife   State, Province, County, Oblast, etc.

State, Province Maps Symbols

✪	Capital	
○	County Seat	
▲	Military Installation	
△	Point of Interest	
+	Mountain Peak	

·············	International Boundary
·············	State, Province Boundary
·············	County Boundary
————	Railroad
————	Road
	Urban Area

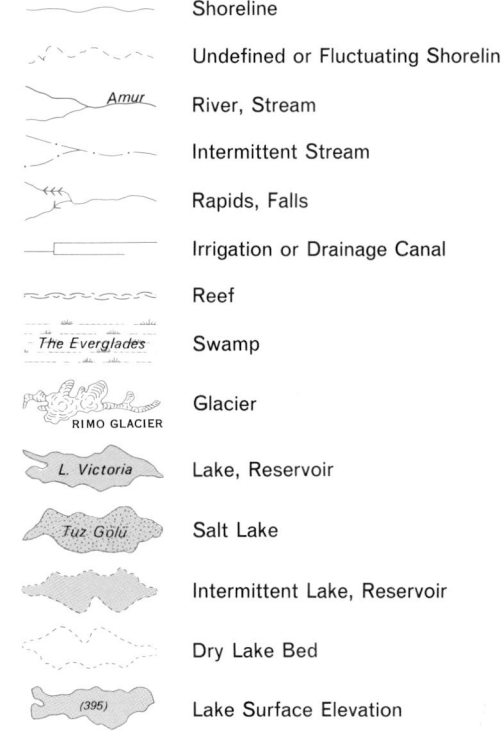

Political Boundaries

International (First-order political unit)

	Demarcated and Undemarcated
— · — · —	Disputed de jure
	Indefinite or Undefined
—————	Demarcation Line

Internal

	State, Province, etc. (Second-order political unit)
MURCIA	Historical Region (No boundaries indicated)
GALAPAGOS (Ecuador)	Administering Country

Transportation

————	Primary Road
————	Secondary Road
----------	Minor Road, Trail
—+—+—	Railway
Canal du Midi	Navigable Canal
	Bridge
—)---(—	Tunnel
TO MALMÖ	Ferry

Hydrographic Features

	Shoreline
	Undefined or Fluctuating Shoreline
Amur	River, Stream
	Intermittent Stream
◄◄◄	Rapids, Falls
	Irrigation or Drainage Canal
	Reef
The Everglades	Swamp
RIMO GLACIER	Glacier
L. Victoria	Lake, Reservoir
Tuz Gölü	Salt Lake
	Intermittent Lake, Reservoir
	Dry Lake Bed
(395)	Lake Surface Elevation

Topographic Features

Matterhorn △ 4478	Elevation Above Sea Level
76 ▽	Elevation Below Sea Level
Mount Cook ▲ 3764	Highest Elevation in Country
133 ▼	Lowest Elevation in Country
Khyber Pass ═ 1067	Mountain Pass

Elevations are given in meters.
The highest and lowest elevations in a continent are underlined

	Sand Area
	Lava
	Salt Flat

1

ARCTIC OCEAN
Beaufort Sea
GREENLAND
(Den.)
Greenland Sea
Baffin Bay
Thule
Godhavn
Godthåb
Angmagssalik
Denmark Strait
Reykjavík
ICELAND
FAEROE ISLANDS
(Den.)
Davis Strait
BAFFIN ISLAND
VICTORIA ISLAND
RUSSIA
Bering Strait
Nome
UNITED STATES
Arctic Circle
Yukon
Fairbanks
Inuvik
Mackenzie
Mount McKinley
6194
Anchorage
Yellowknife
Bering Sea
Gulf of Alaska
ALEUTIAN ISLANDS
Juneau
Hudson Bay
Churchill
CANADA
ROCKY MOUNTAINS
Edmonton
Calgary
Vancouver
Seattle
Portland
Winnipeg
Lake Superior
Lake Huron
NEWFOUNDLAND
St. John's
Québec
Ottawa
Montréal
Minneapolis
Lake Ontario
Toronto
Halifax
NORTH AMERICA
CHICAGO
DETROIT
Lake Michigan
L. Erie
Boston
NEW YORK
PHILADELPHIA
WASHINGTON
APPALACHIAN MOUNTAINS
SAN FRANCISCO
Salt Lake City
Denver
UNITED STATES
St. Louis
LOS ANGELES
San Diego
Phoenix
El Paso
Dallas
Atlanta
Mississippi
Rio Grande
Houston
New Orleans
BERMUDA
(U.K.)
ATLANTIC OCEAN
PACIFIC OCEAN
MIDWAY ISLANDS
(U.S.)
HAWAIIAN ISLANDS
(U.S.)
Honolulu
Tropic of Cancer
Gulf of Mexico
Monterrey
Miami
BAHAMAS
CABO SAN LUCAS
MEXICO
Guadalajara
CIUDAD DE MÉXICO
MEXICO CITY
LA HABANA
CUBA
HAITI
DOMINICAN REPUBLIC
Port-au-Prince
SANTO DOMINGO
PUERTO RICO (U.S.)
SAN JUAN
JAMAICA
Kingston
GUADELOUPE (Fr.)
MARTINIQUE (Fr.)
BARBADOS
TRINIDAD AND TOBAGO
Port of Spain
GUATEMALA
BELIZE
HONDURAS
Tegucigalpa
San Salvador
EL SALVADOR
NICARAGUA
Managua
Caribbean Sea
SAN JOSÉ
COSTA RICA
Panamá
PANAMA
JOHNSTON ATOLL
(U.S.)
ÎLE CLIPPERTON
(Fr.)
POLYNESIA
CARACAS
VENEZUELA
GUYANA
Georgetown
Paramaribo
SURINAME
FRENCH GUIANA
Medellín
SANTA FE DE BOGOTÁ
Cali
COLOMBIA
Equator
QUITO
ECUADOR
Guayaquil
ARCHIPIÉLAGO DE COLÓN
GALÁPAGOS ISLANDS
(Ec.)
Iquitos
Manaus
Amazon
Belém
Fortaleza
Natal
Recife
KIRIBATI
PHOENIX ISLANDS
TOKELAU
(N.Z.)
ÎLES MARQUISES
WALLIS AND FUTUNA
(Fr.)
W. SAMOA
Apia
AM. SAMOA
FIJI
TONGA
NIUE
(N.Z.)
COOK ISLANDS
(N.Z.)
ÎLES TUAMOTU
FRENCH POLYNESIA
Trujillo
ANDES
PERU
LIMA
BRAZIL
Madeira
SOUTH AMERICA
Salvador
Arequipa
LA PAZ
BOLIVIA
Sucre
Goiânia
BRASÍLIA
Belo Horizonte
PARAGUAY
SÃO PAULO
RIO DE JANEIRO
Santos
Curitiba
Asunción
Antofagasta
Tropic of Capricorn
PITCAIRN
(U.K.)
ISLA DE PASCUA
EASTER ISLAND
(Chile)
ISLA SAN AMBROSIO
(Chile)
CHILE
Co. Aconcagua
6959
Córdoba
Paraná
Porto Alegre
Valparaíso
SANTIAGO
Rosario
URUGUAY
BUENOS AIRES
MONTEVIDEO
ARCHIPIÉLAGO JUAN FERNÁNDEZ
(Chile)
ARGENTINA
Concepción
Mar del Plata
Bahía Blanca
International Date Line
CHATHAM ISLANDS
(N.Z.)
FALKLAND ISLANDS
(U.K.)
Punta Arenas
CABO DE HORNOS
CAPE HORN
SOUTH GEORGIA
(U.K.)
Drake Passage
SOUTH ORKNEY ISLANDS
(U.K.)
Antarctic Circle
ANTARCTIC PENINSULA
Bellingshausen Sea
Weddell Sea
Ross Sea
MARIE BYRD LAND
ROSS ICE SHELF
Vinson Massif
4897
ANTAR
Norw
IRELAND
DUBLIN
Glasgow
Porto
PORTUGAL
LISBOA
AÇORES AZORES
(Port.)
GIBRALTAR
(U.K.)
RABAT
Casablanca
MOROCCO
ARQUIPÉLAGO DA MADEIRA
(Port.)
ISLAS CANARIAS
CANARY ISLANDS
(Sp.)
WESTERN SAHARA
MAURITANIA
Nouakchott
CAPE VERDE
SENEGAL
DAKAR
GAMBIA
Banjul
Bamako
GUINEA-BISSAU
GUINEA
Conakry
SIERRA LEONE
Freetown
Monrovia
LIBERIA
ABIDJAN
SAINT HELENA
(U.K.)
180° 1 165° 2 150° 3 135° 4 120° 5 105° 6 90° 7 75° 8 60° 9 45° 10 30° 11 15° 12 0°
A B C D E F G H I J K L
90° 75° 60° 45° 30° 15° 0° 15° 30° 45° 60° 75° 90°

14 30° 15 45° 16 60° 17 75° 18 90° 19 105° 20 120° 21 135° 22 150° 23 165° 24 180° 90°

ARCTIC OCEAN

A

75°

Barents
Sea
ZEML'A FRANCA-IOSIFA
NOVOSIBIRSKIJE
OSTROVA

SALBARD
(Nor.)
Hammerfest
NOVAJA
ZEML'A
Karskoje
more
Dikson
Chatanga
Tiksi
Arctic Circle
B

Narvik
WAY
Murmansk
Noril'sk
Verchojansk
Anadyr

SWEDEN
FINLAND
Vorkuta
Jenisej
Igarsa
Jakutsk

HELSINKI
Ladozskoje
ozero
Archangel'sk
Ob
Lensk
60°

STOCKHOLM
SANKT-PETERBURG
ST. PETERSBURG
Salechard
Lena
Magadan
Ochotsk
Bering Sea
C

LITH.
BELARUS
Niznij Novgorod
Perm'
RUSSIA
Irkutsk
Cita
Nikolajevsk
OSTROV
SACHALIN
PETROPAVLOVSK-
Kamcatskij
ALEUTIAN IS.
(U.S.)

BERLIN
POLAND
MOSKVA
Jekaterinburg
Čel'abinsk
Omsk
Novosibirsk
ozero
Bajkal
Ulaanbaatar
Chabarovsk
45°

GERMANY
WARSZAWA
UKRAINE
KYYIV
Volgograd
Samara
KAZAKHSTAN
Karaganda
MONGOLIA
GOBI
Harbin
Vladivostok
Sapporo
JAPAN
D

Bonn
BUDAPEST
Dnepr
Volga
ALTAJ
SHAN
Hohhot
BEIJING
PEKING
Shenyang
N. KOREA
Sea of
Japan
Sendai

30°

ROM.
BUCUREŞTI
Aral
More
ALMA-ATA
ÜRÜMQI
Tianjin
Dalian
PYONGYANG
SEOUL
S. KOREA
Pusan
OSAKA
TŌKYŌ
HONSHŪ

Black Sea
Caspian
BAKU
TAŠKENT
TIAN
CHINA
Lanzhou
Xi'an
Qingdao
Yellow
Sea
Fukuoka

TURKEY
ANKARA
UZBEKISTAN
TURKMENISTAN
TADŽ.
KYRG.
Shache
HIMALAYAS
Lhasa
Chengdu
Nanjing
Wuhan
SHANGHAI
OGASAWARA-GUNTŌ
(Japan)
PACIFIC

SYRIA
TEHRĀN
Esfahan
KĀBOL
AFGHANISTAN
Islāmābād
Rawalpindi
Chongqing
Changsha
NANSEI-
SHOTŌ

IRAQ
BAGHDĀD
IRAN
Lahore
Mount
Everest
8848
DELHI
Kunming
Guangzhou
HONG
KONG
(U.K.)
T'AIPEI
OCEAN
E

Ābādān
PAKISTAN
New Delhi
NEPAL
Kāthmāndu
DHAKA
Tropic of Cancer
MYANMAR
HA NOI
TAIWAN
Philippine
WAKE
ISLAND
(U.S.)

KUWAIT
QATAR
UNITED
ARAB
EMIRATES
Karāchi
Ahmadābād
CALCUTTA
YANGON
Sea

AR-RIYĀD
SAUDI
ARABIA
Masqat
INDIA
Hyderābād
Bay of
Bengal
ANDAMAN
ISLANDS
(India)
South
China
VIETNAM
MANILA
NORTHERN
MARIANA
ISLANDS
(U.S.)
MARSHALL
ISLANDS

OMAN
BOMBAY
Madras
KRUNG THEP
BANGKOK
THAILAND
Sea
GUAM (U.S.)
PHILIPPINES
M

ABA
Bangalore
Phnum Penh
Thanh Pho
Ho Chi Minh
PALAU
(T.T.P.I.)
I

NIGER
CHAD
AL-KHARTŪM
SUDAN
Sana
VIENTEN
CAMB.
Cochin
SRI LANKA
NICOBAR
ISLANDS
(India)
Davao
FEDERATED STATES
OF MICRONESIA
C

Kano
N'Djamena
ERITREA
ṢAN'Ā'
COLOMBO
Medan
BRUNEI
R

ETHIOPIA
ADIS ABEBA
Djibouti
MALDIVES
MALAYSIA
KUALA LUMPUR
SINGAPORE
BORNEO
SULAWESI
O

NIGERIA
Abuja
DJIBOUTI
SOMALIA
Equator
SUMATRA
PAPUA
NEW GUINEA
NAURU
KIRIBATI
TUVALU
N

CEN.
AFR. REP.
GEES GWARDAFUY
Equator
E

Yaoundé
UGANDA
KAMPALA
KENYA
NAIROBI
SEYCHELLES
BRITISH
INDIAN OCEAN
TERRITORY
Palembang
Banjarmasin
Ljungpandang
INDONESIA
Mount Wilhelm
4509
NEW
GUINEA
S

ATORIAL
GUINEA
Libreville
ZAIRE
RWANDA
BURUNDI
Lake
Victoria
Kilimanjaro 5895
Mombasa
JAKARTA
JAWA
Surabaya
TIMOR
Port Moresby
SOLOMON
ISLANDS
I

GABON
Brazzaville
KINSHASA
CONGO
Lake
Tanganyika
Dodoma
Zanzibar
TANZANIA
DAR ES SALAAM
CHRISTMAS ISLAND
(Aust.)
CAPE YORK
Darwin
Gulf of
Carpentaria
A

LUANDA
Lubumbashi
Lake
Nyasa
INDIAN
COCOS
ISLANDS
(Aust.)
VANUATU
SUVA

Lobito
ANGOLA
ZAMBIA
Lilongwe
MALAWI
Zambezi
OCEAN
Coral
Sea
NEW
CALEDONIA
(Fr.)
Nouméa
FIJI

Lusaka
HARARE
Alice Springs
Rockhampton

Windhoek
BOTSWANA
ZIMBABWE
Mozambique Channel
MADAGASCAR
MAURITIUS
REUNION
(Fr.)
Tropic of Capricorn
Cairns
NORFOLK
ISLAND
(Aust.)
H

Walvis Bay
NAMIBIA
Gaborone
PRETORIA
MAPUTO
ANTANANARIVO
AUSTRALIA
Darling
Brisbane
30°

Johannesburg
SWAZILAND
LESOTHO
Perth
Sydney

SOUTH
AFRICA
Durban
ÎLES KERGUÉLEN
(Fr.)
Adelaide
Canberra
Mount Kosciusko
2228
Melbourne
Tasman Sea
Auckland
NORTH ISLAND
45°
I

CAPE TOWN
Port Elizabeth
CAPE AGULHAS
NEW
ZEALAND
Wellington

TASMANIA
Hobart
SOUTH
ISLAND
Christchurch

SOUTHERN
60°

OCEAN
J

75°
K

Antarctic Circle

ENDERBY LAND
WILKES
LAND
Copyright © by Rand McNally & Co.
Map prepared by Rand McNally & Co.
A-510000-264   -30°-20°-40°
L

CTICA

14 30° 15 45° 16 60° 17 75° 18 90° 19 105° 20 120° 21 135° 22 150° 23 165° 24 180° 90°

Kilometers   0   1000   2000   3000   Km.
Statute Miles   0   1000   2000   3000   Mi.

One centimeter represents 750 kilometers.
One inch represents approximately 1200 miles.
Robinson Projection
Scale 1:75,000,000

3

ATLANTIC OCEAN
NORWEGIAN SEA
NORTH SEA
BALTIC SEA
MEDITERRANEAN SEA
Tyrrhenian Sea
Ionian Sea
Adriatic Sea
Bay of Biscay
English Channel
CELTIC SEA
Irish Sea
Skagerrak
Kattegat
Arctic Circle
ICELAND
Reykjavík
FAEROE ISLANDS (Den.)
SHETLAND ISLANDS
ORKNEY ISLANDS
HEBRIDES
IRELAND
DUBLIN
Cork
UNITED KINGDOM
GREAT BRITAIN
SCOTLAND
WALES
ENGLAND
LONDON
Birmingham
Manchester
Liverpool
Leeds
Glasgow
Edinburgh
Aberdeen
Belfast
Cardiff
Bristol
NORWAY
Oslo
Bergen
Stavanger
Trondheim
SWEDEN
STOCKHOLM
Göteborg
Malmö
DENMARK
KØBENHAVN
COPENHAGEN
NETHERLANDS
AMSTERDAM
's-Gravenhage
The Hague
Rotterdam
BRUXELLES
BELGIUM
LUXEMBOURG
GERMANY
BERLIN
Hamburg
Bremen
Hannover
Köln
Düsseldorf
Frankfurt
Stuttgart
München
Leipzig
Dresden
Nürnberg
POLAND
Gdańsk
Poznań
Wrocław
CZECH REP.
PRAHA
PRAGUE
AUSTRIA
WIEN
VIENNA
SWITZERLAND
Bern
Zürich
Genève
FRANCE
PARIS
Lyon
Marseille
Bordeaux
Toulouse
Nantes
Brest
Le Havre
Strasbourg
Nice
MONACO
ANDORRA
SPAIN
MADRID
Barcelona
Valencia
Sevilla
Zaragoza
Bilbao
Málaga
PORTUGAL
LISBOA
LISBON
Porto
ITALY
ROMA
Milano
Torino
Genova
Venezia
Firenze
Bologna
Napoli
Palermo
SICILY
SARDEGNA
SARDINIA
CORSE
CORSICA
MALTA
Valletta
SLOVENIA
Ljubljana
CROATIA
Zagreb
BOSNIA AND HERZEGOVINA
Sarajevo
HUNGARY
BUDAPEST
SLOVAKIA
Bratislava
ALBANIA
MOROCCO
RABAT
Casablanca
ALGERIA
EL DJAZAÏR
ALGIERS
TUNISIA
TUNIS
Gibraltar (U.K.)
ILLES BALEARS
BALEARIC ISLANDS
MALLORCA
ATLAS MOUNTAINS
Copyright © by Rand McNally & Co.
Map prepared by Esselte Map Service AB, Stockholm.

One centimeter represents 120 kilometers.
One inch represents approximately 190 miles.

Scale 1:12,000,000

Miller Oblated Stereographic Projection

5

a
GREENLAND SEA
Denmark Strait
Arctic Circle
ICELAND
ÍSLAND
Reykjavík
Akureyri
Húnaflói
Faxaflói
VATNAJÖKULL
HOFSJÖKULL
LANGJÖKULL
MÝRDALSJÖKULL
DRANGAJÖKULL
ATLANTIC
OCEAN
Vestmannaeyjar
© R.MᶜN.
b
FAEROE ISLANDS
FØROYAR
(Denmark)
NORWEGIAN SEA
Tórshavn
ATLANTIC
OCEAN
© R.MᶜN.
NORWEGIAN
SEA
NORTH
SEA
Skagerrak
Kattegat
BALTIC
SEA
Arctic Circle
NORWAY
SWEDEN
FINLAND
DENMARK
GERMANY
Oslo
Bergen
Trondheim
Stavanger
Haugesund
Kristiansand
Ålesund
Bodø
Skien
Drammen
Fredrikstad
Östersund
Sundsvall
Falun
Uppsala
Västerås
Örebro
Karlstad
Eskilstuna
STOCKHOLM
Norrköping
Linköping
Jönköping
Göteborg
Gothenburg
Borås
Halmstad
Helsingborg
Malmö
Lund
Kristianstad
Karlskrona
Växjö
Kalmar
Västervik
GOTLAND
ÖLAND
Ålborg
Århus
Randers
Esbjerg
Odense
KØBENHAVN
COPENHAGEN
Flensburg
Schleswig
Kiel
Rendsburg
Neumünster
Vänern
Vättern
TO LERWICK
TO NEWCASTLE
TO HARWICH
Copyright © by Rand McNally & Co.

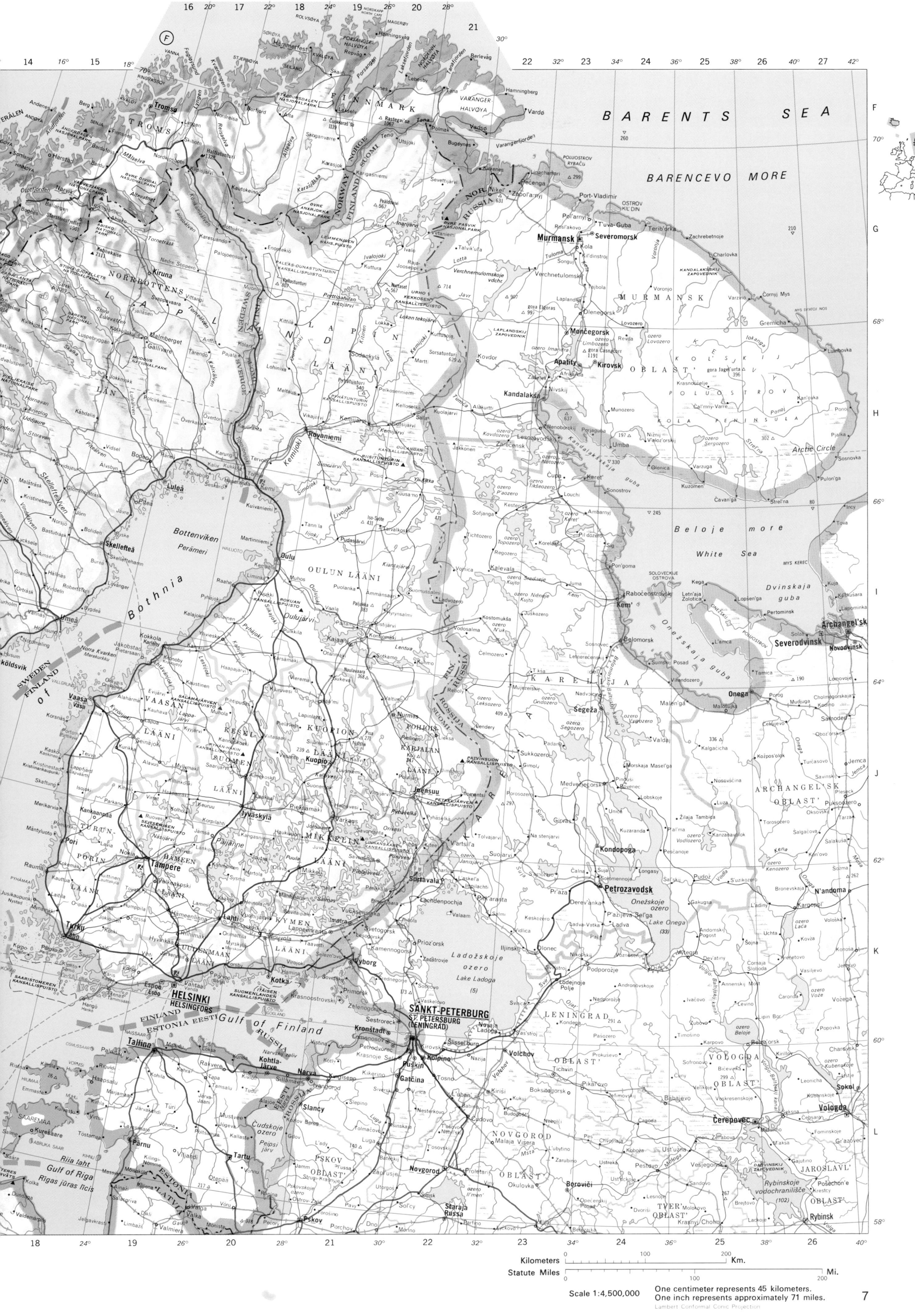

Kilometers 0 ... 100 ... 200 Km.

Statute Miles 0 ... 100 ... 200 Mi.

Scale 1:4,500,000

One centimeter represents 45 kilometers.
One inch represents approximately 71 miles.

Lambert Conformal Conic Projection

British Isles

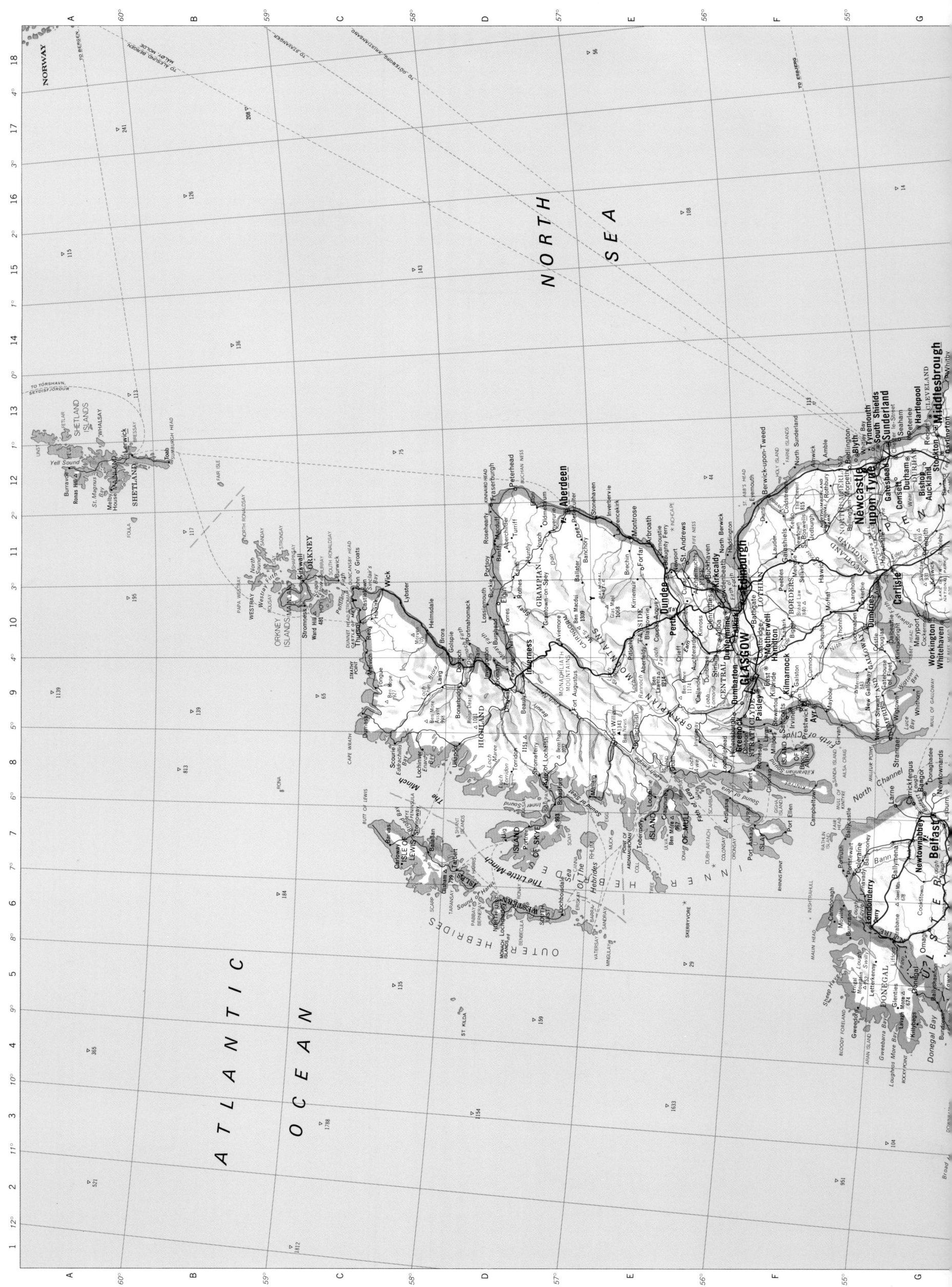

NORWAY
NORTH SEA
ATLANTIC OCEAN
SHETLAND ISLANDS
SHETLAND
Lerwick
ORKNEY ISLANDS
ORKNEY
Kirkwall
Wick
Inverness
Aberdeen
Dundee
Perth
Edinburgh
GLASGOW
Paisley
Kilmarnock
Ayr
Carlisle
Newcastle upon Tyne
Sunderland
Middlesbrough
Belfast
Londonderry
OUTER HEBRIDES
ISLE OF SKYE
The Minch
North Channel
GRAMPIAN MOUNTAINS
HIGHLAND
ST KILDA

Kilometers
Statute Miles

Scale 1:3,000,000

One centimeter represents 30 kilometers.
One inch represents approximately 47 miles.
Conic Projection, Two Standard Parallels

Central Europe

NORTH SEA

10

Scale 1:3,000,000

Kilometers
Statute Miles

One centimeter represents 30 kilometers.
One inch represents approximately 47 miles.
Conic Projection, Two Standard Parallels.

BALTIC SEA
Gulf of Gdansk
Pomeranian Bay
RÜGEN
Kaliningrad
(Königsberg)
RUSSIA
POLAND
POLSKA
LITHUANIA
BELARUS
Gdańsk
(Danzig)
Gdynia
Szczecin
(Stettin)
Koszalin
Słupsk
Elbląg
Olsztyn
Toruń
Bydgoszcz
Białystok
Poznań
WARSZAWA WARSAW
Łódź
Lublin
Radom
Kielce
Częstochowa
Wrocław
(Breslau)
Opole
Katowice
Kraków
Rzeszów
Przemyśl
BERLIN
Frankfurt an der Oder
Dresden
Cottbus
Görlitz
Chemnitz
PRAHA
PRAGUE
Plzeň
Liberec
Hradec Králové
Pardubice
Ostrava
Olomouc
Brno
Zlín
Jihlava
České Budějovice
Znojmo
WIEN
VIENNA
Linz
Graz
Klagenfurt
Villach
Sankt Pölten
Bratislava
Trnava
Nitra
Žilina
Martin
Banská Bystrica
Poprad
Košice
Prešov
Uzhhorod
Mukacheve
BUDAPEST
Győr
Miskolc
Debrecen
Nyíregyháza
Szeged
Pécs
Kecskemét
Székesfehérvár
Veszprém
Szombathely
Sopron
Eger
Oradea
Arad
Subotica
Maribor
Balaton
Danube
Dunaj
CARPATHIAN MOUNTAINS
WIELKOPOLSKA
MAZURY
KUJAWY
CZECH REPUBLIC
AUSTRIA
ÖSTERREICH
HUNGARY
MAGYARORSZÁG
ROMANIA
SLOVENSKO
SERBIA
SRBIJA
CROATIA
HRVATSKA
UKRAINE
GERMANY

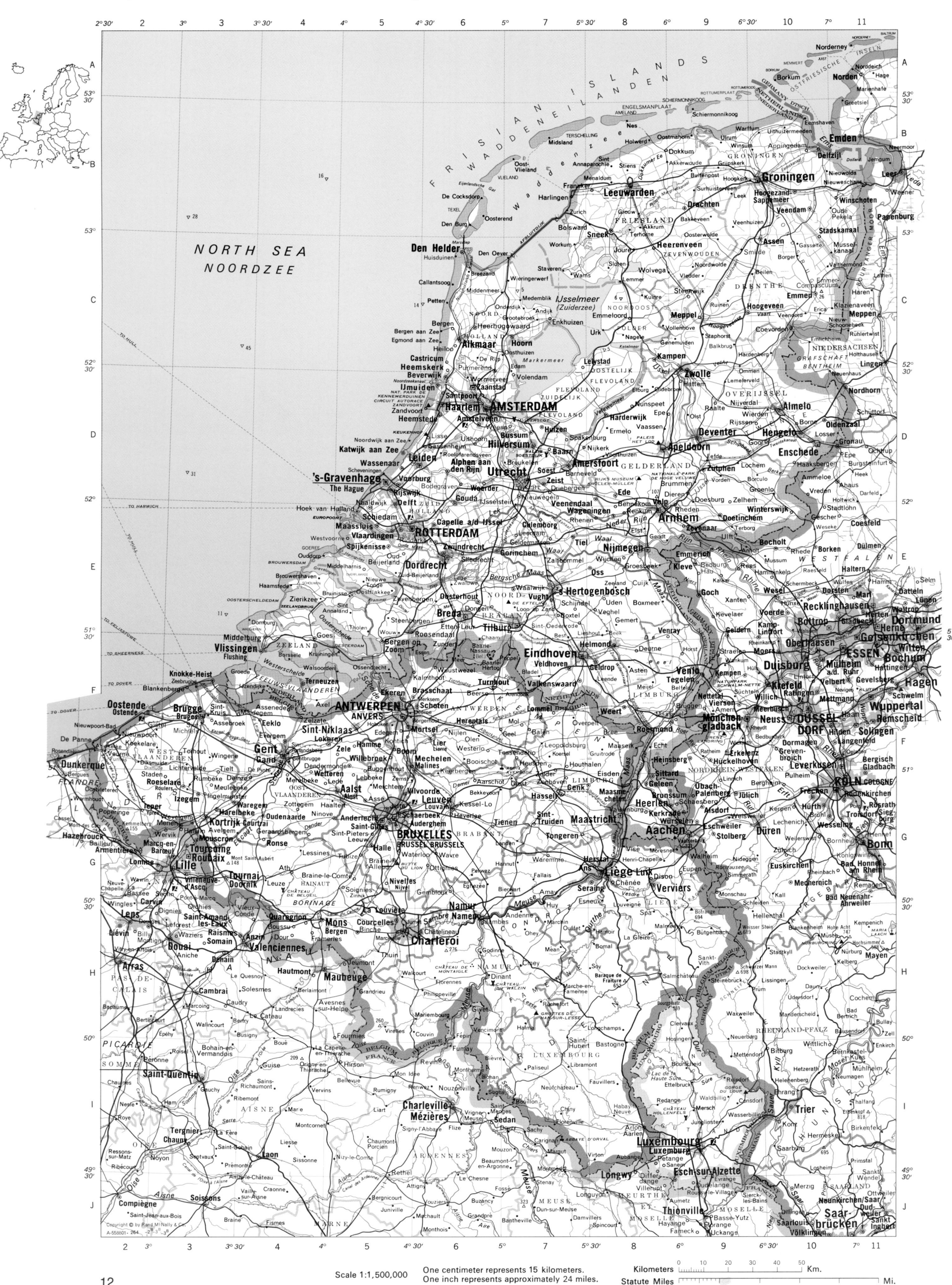

Scale 1:1,500,000

One centimeter represents 15 kilometers.
One inch represents approximately 24 miles.

Lambert Conformal Conic Projection

Kilometers
Statute Miles

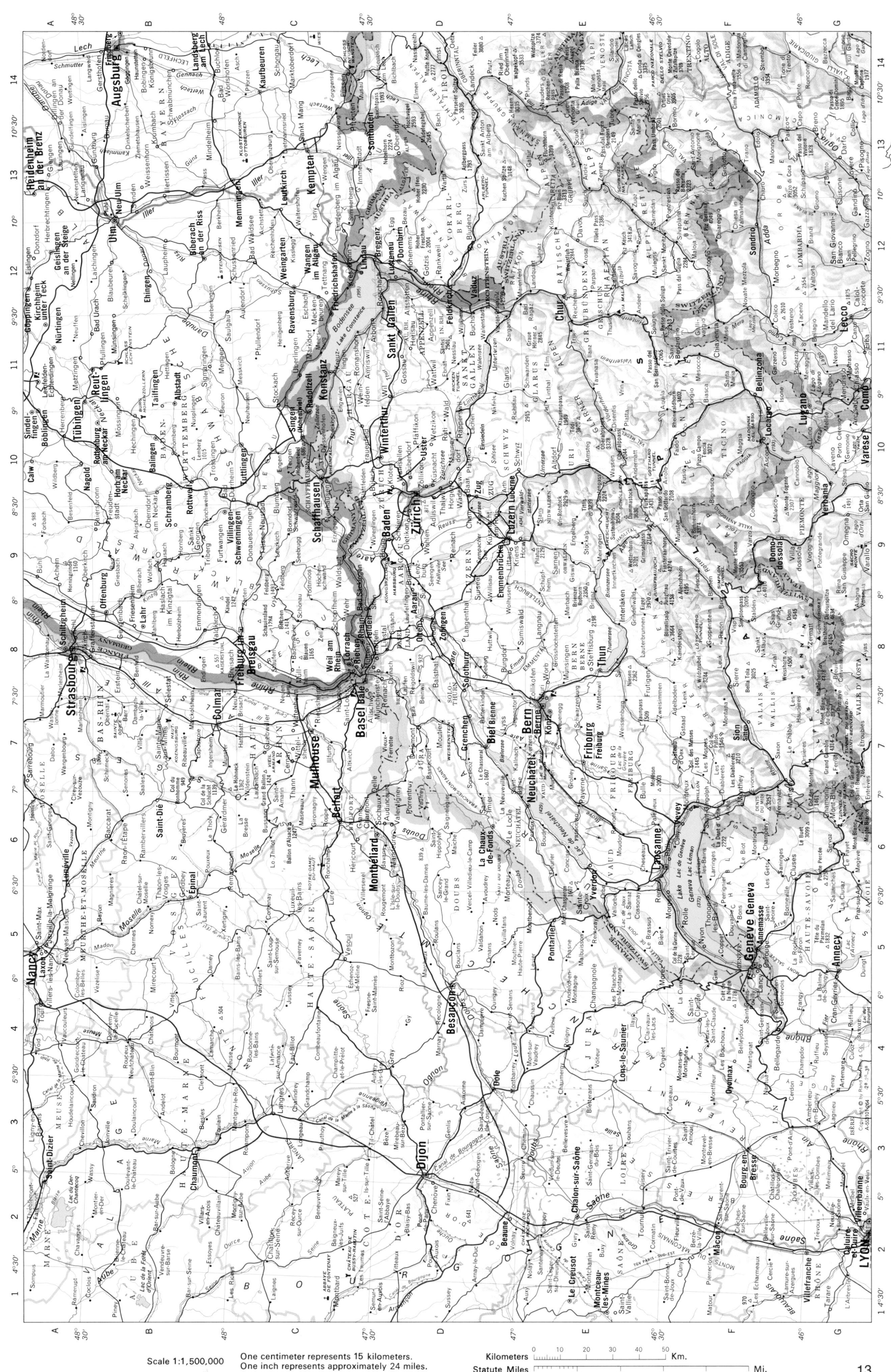

Scale 1:1,500,000

One centimeter represents 15 kilometers.
One inch represents approximately 24 miles.
Lambert Conformal Conic Projection

Kilometers 0 10 20 30 40 50 Km.

Statute Miles 0 10 20 30 40 50 Mi.

English Channel
La Manche
ATLANTIC
OCEAN
Bay of Biscay
Golfe de Saint-Malo
Baie de la Seine
CHANNEL ISLANDS
GUERNSEY (U.K.)
St. Peter Port
JERSEY (U.K.)
St. Helier
UNITED KINGDOM
FRANCE
Strait of Dover
Pas de Calais
PARIS
BRUXELLES
Southampton
Portsmouth
Bournemouth
Brighton
Plymouth
Torquay
Exeter
Dover
Folkestone
Dunkerque
Calais
Lille
Roubaix
Amiens
Rouen
Le Havre
Caen
Cherbourg
Brest
Quimper
Lorient
Vannes
Rennes
Saint-Brieuc
Saint-Malo
Nantes
Saint-Nazaire
Angers
Le Mans
Tours
Orléans
Chartres
Versailles
Troyes
Reims
Poitiers
Limoges
La Rochelle
Rochefort
Niort
Angoulême
Bordeaux
Périgueux
Clermont-Ferrand
Saint-Étienne
Toulouse
Montpellier
Nîmes
Narbonne
Carcassonne
Perpignan
Béziers
Bayonne
Biarritz
Pau
Tarbes
Agen
Montauban
Albi
Rodez
Le Puy
Vichy
Moulins
Nevers
Bourges
Châteauroux
Vierzon
Blois
Laval
Alençon
Évreux
Dieppe
Abbeville
Beauvais
Compiègne
Soissons
Laon
Saint-Quentin
Cambrai
Valenciennes
Arras
Lens
Douai
Béthune
Boulogne-sur-Mer
Santander
Bilbao
Donostia
San Sebastián
Vitoria Gasteiz
Pamplona
Logroño
Burgos
Andorra
ANDORRA
SPAIN
PYRÉNÉES
MASSIF CENTRAL
BRETAGNE
NORMANDIE
LOIRE
DORDOGNE
GIRONDE
LANDES
GASCOGNE
ATLANTIC
CANTABRIA
NAVARRA
CATALUNYA
ARAGÓN
LA RIOJA
CASTILLA-LEÓN
EUSKAL HERRIKO

Kilometers
Statute Miles

One centimeter represents 30 kilometers.
One inch represents approximately 47 miles.

Scale 1:3,000,000

15

Lambert Conformal Conic Projection

Copyright by Rand McNally & Co.
Map prepared by Rand McNally GmbH. Stuttgart.
A-559495-764

MEDITERRANEAN SEA
Golfe du Lion
ILLES BALEARS
BALEARIC ISLANDS
MALLORCA
MAJORCA
MENORCA
MINORCA
EIVISSA
IBIZA
FORMENTERA
Palma
Maó
Ciutadella
BARCELONA
L'Hospitalet de Llobregat
València
Alacant
Murcia
Cartagena
Zaragoza
Tarragona
Castelló de la Plana
Lleida
Girona
Perpignan
Marseille
Toulon
Nice
Montpellier
Toulouse
Nîmes
Narbonne
Carcassonne
ANDORRA
FRANCE
SPAIN
ESPAÑA
CATALUNYA
PYRÉNÉES
DELTA DE L'EBRE
Golf de València
a
ARQUIPÉLAGO DA MADEIRA
MADEIRA ISLANDS
(Portugal)
MADEIRA
Funchal
Porto Santo
ILHAS DESERTAS
ATLANTIC OCEAN
b
ISLAS CANARIAS
CANARY ISLANDS
(Spain)
LA PALMA
TENERIFE
Santa Cruz de Tenerife
GOMERA
HIERRO
GRAN CANARIA
Las Palmas de Gran Canaria
FUERTEVENTURA
LANZAROTE
Arrecife
ATLANTIC OCEAN
WESTERN SAHARA
ALGERIA
ALGÉRIE
Wahran
Oran
Kilometers
Km.
Statute Miles
Mi.
Scale 1:3,000,000
One centimeter represents 30 kilometers.
One inch represents approximately 47 miles.
Conic Projection, Two Standard Parallels
© R. McN.

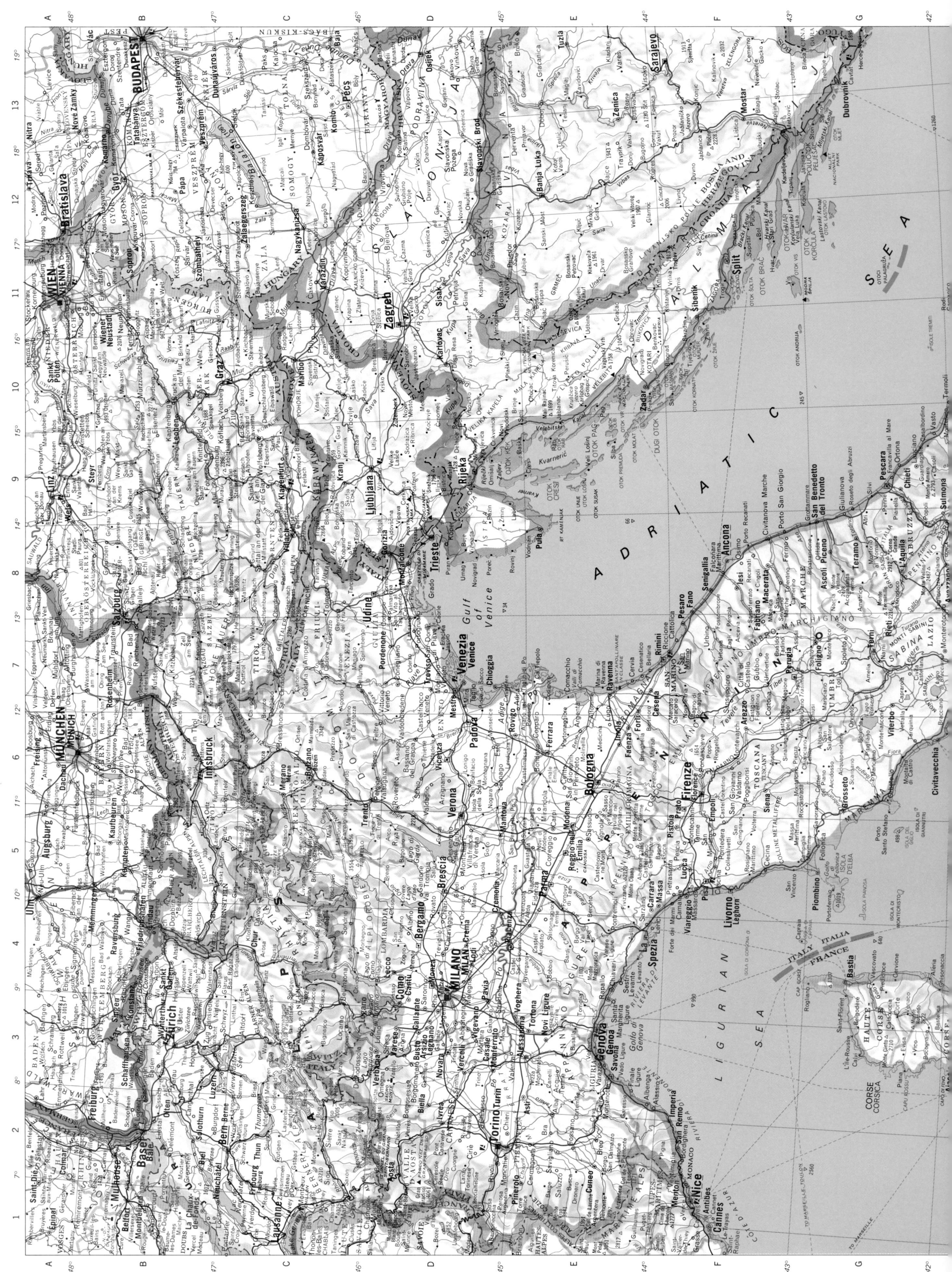
ADRIATIC SEA
LIGURIAN SEA
Gulf of Venice
MILANO
Venezia
Venice
Zagreb
WIEN
VIENNA
BUDAPEST
MÜNCHEN
MUNICH
Bologna
Firenze
Genova
Torino
Ljubljana
Trieste
Rijeka
Innsbruck
Salzburg
Bratislava
Zürich
Basel
Bern
Sarajevo
Split
Ancona
Pescara
Livorno
Nice
ITALY
FRANCE
CORSE
CORSICA

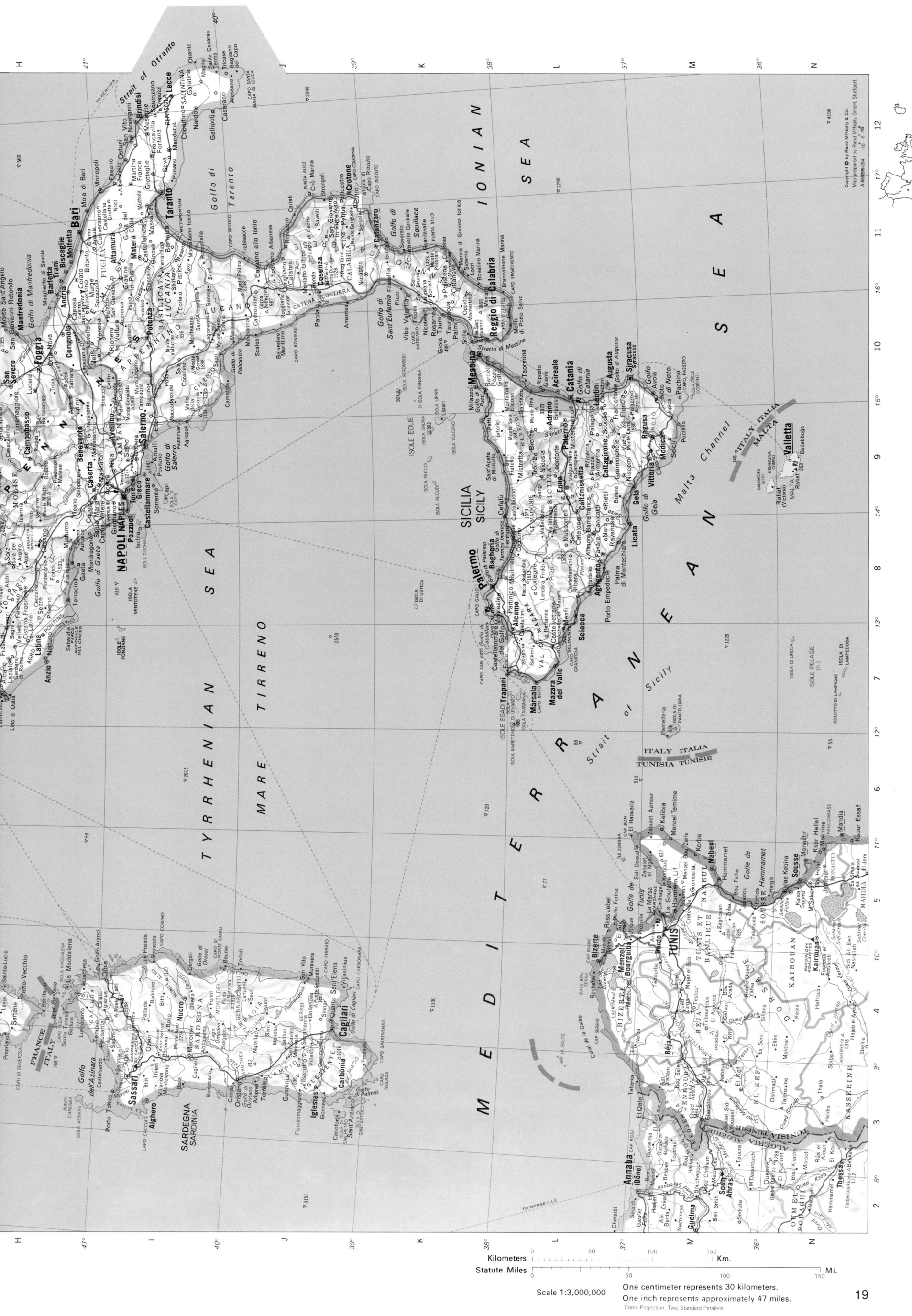

Kilometers

Statute Miles

Scale 1:3,000,000

One centimeter represents 30 kilometers.
One inch represents approximately 47 miles.

Conic Projection, Two Standard Parallels

BLACK SEA
Mouths of the Danube
CARPATHIAN MOUNTAINS
TRANSYLVANIAN ALPS
BUDAPEST
BUCUREŞTI
BEOGRAD
SOFIJA
Chişinău
Constanţa

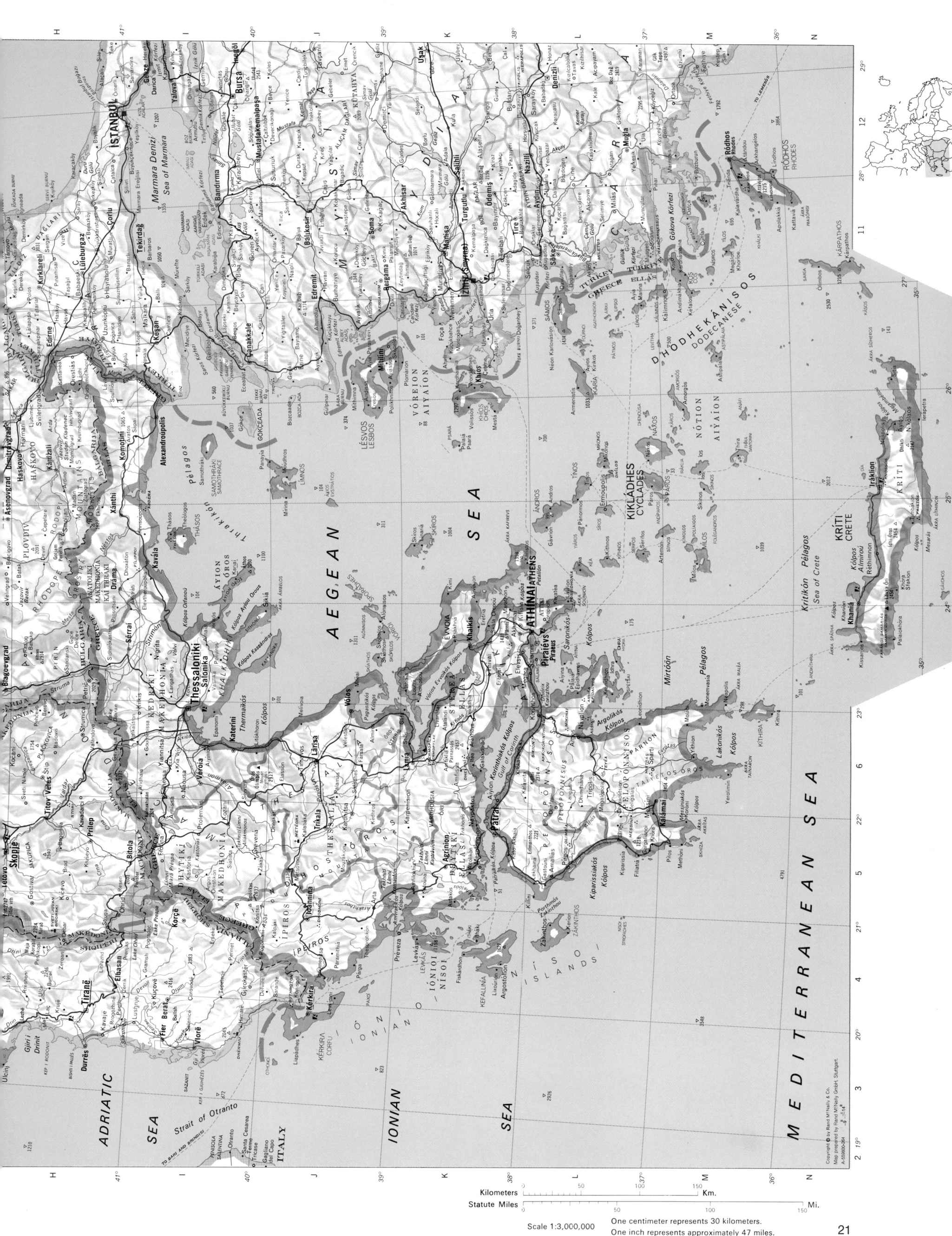

Kilometers 0 50 100 150 Km.

Statute Miles 0 50 100 150 Mi.

Scale 1:3,000,000

One centimeter represents 30 kilometers.
One inch represents approximately 47 miles.
Conic Projection, Two Standard Parallels

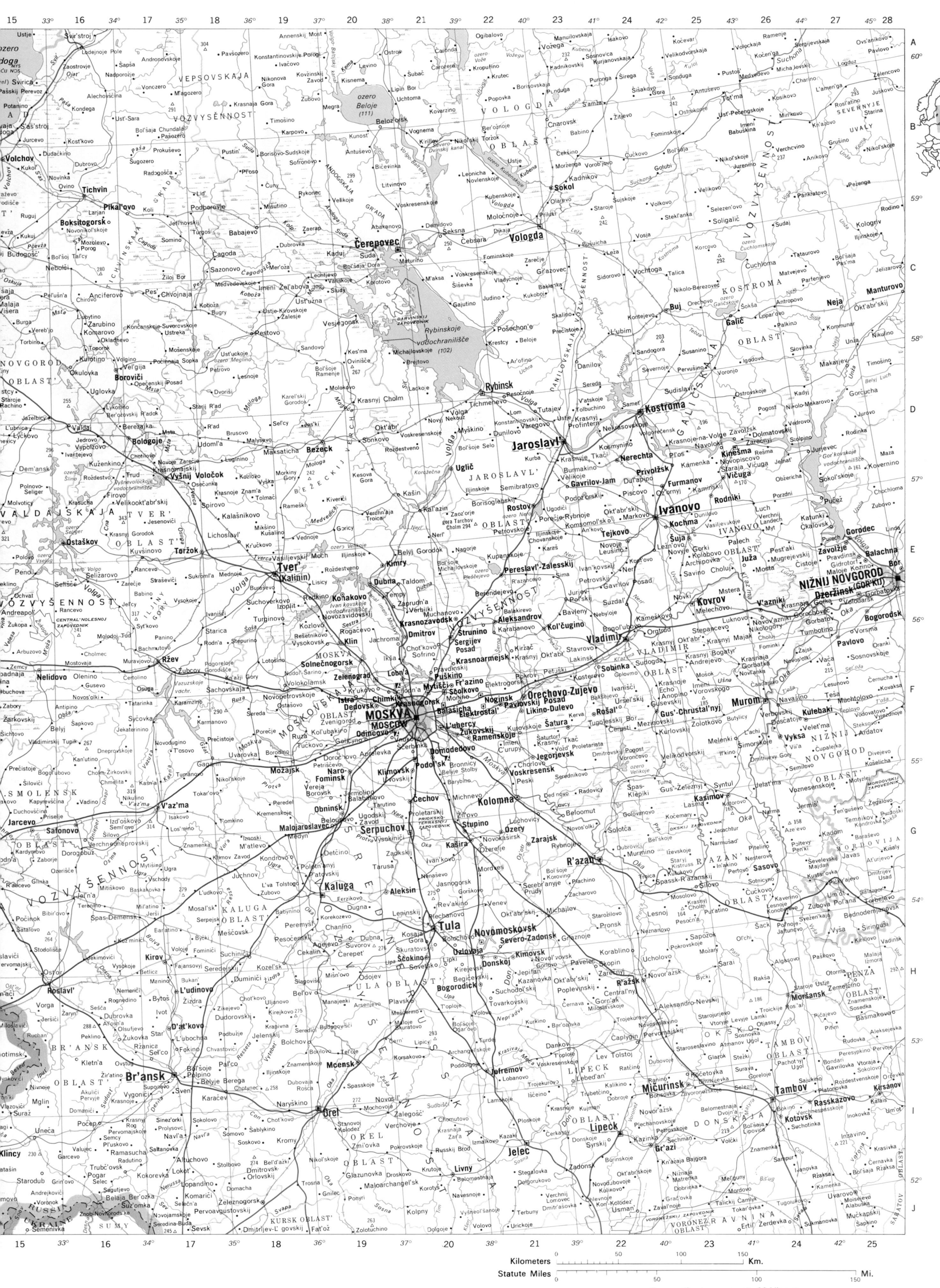

Kilometers 0 50 100 150 Km.

Statute Miles 0 50 100 150 Mi.

Scale 1:3,000,000

One centimeter represents 30 kilometers.

One inch represents approximately 47 miles.

Lambert Conformal Conic Projection

ARCTIC OCEAN
North Pole
ATLANTIC OCEAN
GREENLAND (Den.)
ICELAND
Reykjavík
Greenland Sea
Norwegian Sea
Barents Sea
Kara Sea
Laptev Sea
East Siberian Sea
Chukchi Sea
Bering Sea
Sea of Okhotsk
Sea of Japan
Yellow Sea
EAST CHINA SEA
North Sea
Baltic Sea
Black Sea
Caspian Sea
Aral Sea
Arctic Circle
SVALBARD
FRANZ JOSEF LAND
SEVERNAJA ZEML'A
NOVOSIBIRSKIJE OSTROVA
OSTROV VRANGEL'A
ALEUTIAN ISLANDS
KURIL ISLANDS
UNITED STATES
Bering Strait
UNITED KINGDOM
IRELAND
NORWAY
SWEDEN
FINLAND
DENMARK
NETHERLANDS
BELGIUM
GERMANY
POLAND
BELARUS
UKRAINE
ROMANIA
BULGARIA
HUNGARY
AUSTRIA
TURKEY
ASIA MINOR
SYRIA
IRAQ
IRAN
SAUDI ARABIA
AFGHANISTAN
KAZAKHSTAN
UZBEKISTAN
TURKMENISTAN
KYRGYZSTAN
MONGOLIA
NORTH KOREA
SOUTH KOREA
RUSSIA
EUROPE
ASIA
CHINA
CAUCASUS
URAL'SKIJE GORY
URAL MOUNTAINS
ZAPADNO-SIBIRSKAJA RAVNINA
SREDNESIBIRSKOJE PLOSKOGORJE
SIBERIA
SIBIR'
CHREBET ČERSKOGO
TIEN SHAN
KUNLUN SHAN
TARIM PENDI
GOBI
ALTAI
HINDU KUSH
PAMIR
DA HINGGAN LING
SICHOTE-ALIN
LONDON
DUBLIN
AMSTERDAM
BRUXELLES
BERLIN
KØBENHAVN
OSLO
STOCKHOLM
HELSINKI
Tallinn
RIGA
Vilnius
MINSK
WARSZAWA
PRAHA
WIEN
BUDAPEST
BEOGRAD
BUCUREȘTI
SOFIJA
KYYIV
MOSKVA
SANKT-PETERBURG
ISTANBUL
ANKARA
TBILISI
JEREVAN
BAKI
TEHRĀN
BAGHDĀD
DIMASHQ
AMMAN
TAŠKENT
ALMA-ATA
Biškek
Dušanbe
KABOL
ULAANBAATAR
BEIJING
P'YONGYANG
SOUL
TOKYO
Lena
Ob'
Jenisej
Amur
Volga
Irtyš
Angara
Tunguska
ozero Bajkal
Lake Baikal
Ozero Balchaš
Lake Balkhash
Murmansk
Archangel'sk
Vorkuta
Noril'sk
Jakutsk
Magadan
Petropavlovsk-Kamčatskij
Vladivostok
Chabarovsk
Irkutsk
Krasnojarsk
Novosibirsk
Omsk
Jekaterinburg
Perm'
Kazan'
Samara
Saratov
Volgograd
Harbin
SHANGHAI

INDIAN OCEAN
ARABIAN SEA
Bay of Bengal
Andaman Sea
SOUTH CHINA SEA
Philippine Sea
Sulu Sea
Celebes Sea
Java Sea
Lakshadweep Sea
Gulf of Aden
Gulf of Oman
Red Sea
Gulf of Thailand
Gulf of Tonkin
INDIA
PAKISTAN
NEPAL
BHUTAN
BANGLADESH
MYANMAR (BURMA)
THAILAND
LAOS
CAMBODIA
VIETNAM
MALAYSIA
SINGAPORE
BRUNEI
INDONESIA
PHILIPPINES
SRI LANKA
MALDIVES
OMAN
YEMEN
SOMALIA
ETHIOPIA
DJIBOUTI
SEYCHELLES
MAURITIUS
MADAGASCAR
AUSTRALIA
ARABIAN PENINSULA
AR-RUB' AL-KHĀLĪ
SUMATERA
BORNEO
JAWA
SULAWESI
GREATER SUNDA ISLANDS
DELHI
New Delhi
CALCUTTA
BOMBAY
MADRAS
BANGALORE
Hyderābād
KARĀCHI
AHMADĀBĀD
COLOMBO
DHAKA
YANGON (RANGOON)
KRUNG THEP (BANGKOK)
HA NOI
THANH PHO HO CHI MINH (SAIGON)
KUALA LUMPUR
JAKARTA
SURABAYA
MANILA
HONG KONG
ANTANANARIVO
Muqdisho
Perth
Tropic of Cancer
Tropic of Capricorn
Equator
CARLSBERG RIDGE
MID-INDIAN RIDGE
NINETYEAST RIDGE
BROKEN RIDGE
WHARTON BASIN
JAVA TRENCH
MASCARENE PLATEAU
SOMALI BASIN
MADAGASCAR BASIN
Kilometers
Statute Miles
Scale 1:24,000,000
One centimeter represents 240 kilometers.
One inch represents approximately 380 miles.
Lambert Azimuthal Equal-Area Projection
Copyright © by Rand McNally & Co.
Map prepared by Rand McNally & Co.

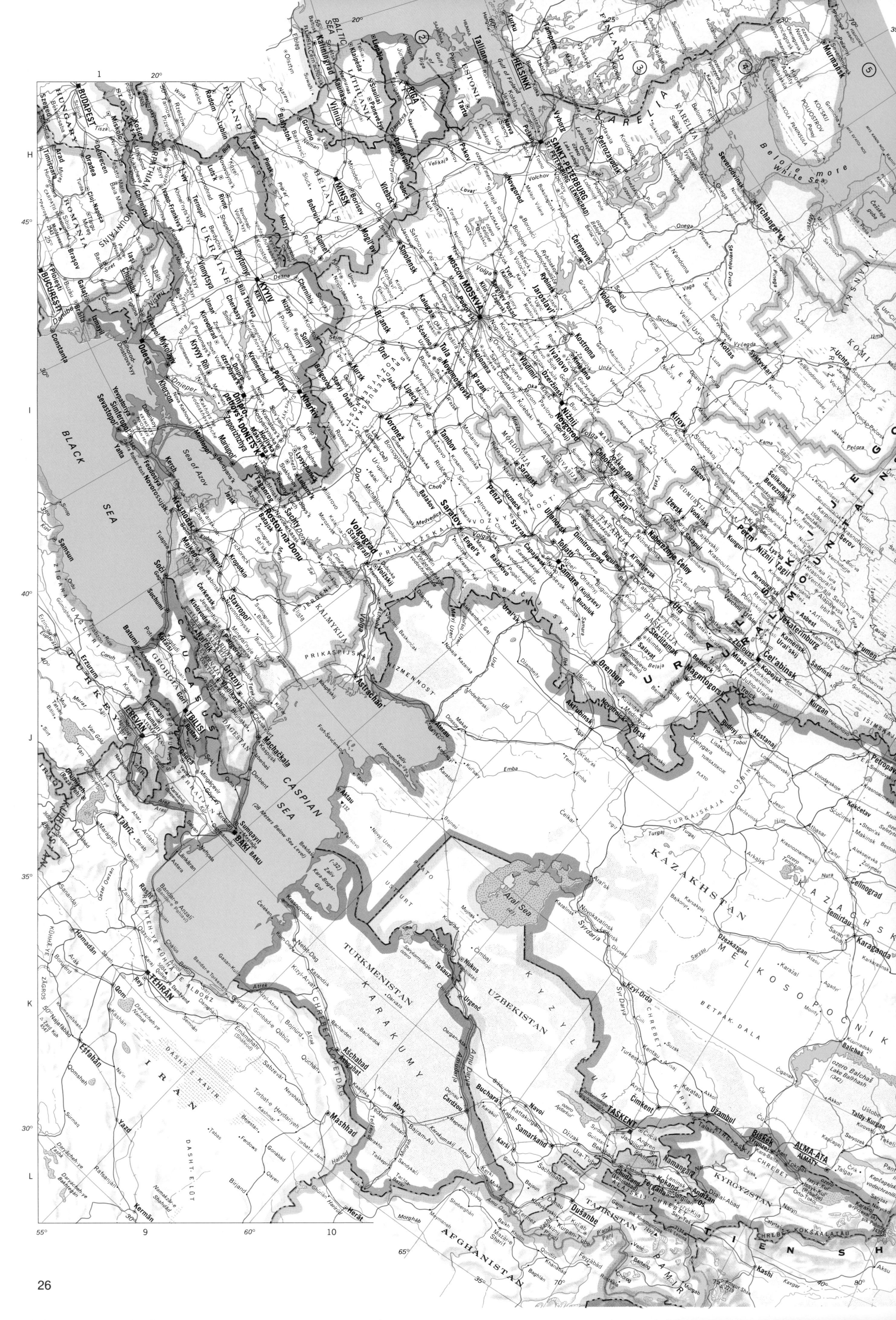

BALTIC SEA
FINLAND
ESTONIA
LATVIA
LITHUANIA
POLAND
BELARUS
UKRAINE
HUNGARY
ROMANIA
KARELIA
KOMI
Beloje more
White Sea
HELSINKI
TALLINN
RIGA
VILNIUS
MINSK
SANKT-PETERBURG (LENINGRAD)
MOSCOW MOSKVA
KYYIV (KIEV)
BUDAPEST
BUCUREŞTI
Sea of Azov
BLACK SEA
CASPIAN SEA
(28 Meters Below Sea Level)
Aral Sea
GEORGIA
CAUCASUS
TBILISI
JEREVAN
BAKU
TURKEY
IRAN
TEHRĀN
TURKMENISTAN
KARAKUMY
UZBEKISTAN
KAZAKHSTAN
KYRGYZSTAN
TAJIKISTAN
AFGHANISTAN
TAŠKENT
ALMA-ATA
DUŠANBE
AŠCHABAD
Lake Balkhash

Kilometers

Statute Miles

Scale 1:12,000,000

One centimeter represents 120 kilometers.
One inch represents approximately 190 miles.
Lambert Conformal Conic Projection

Kilometers
Statute Miles

Scale 1:12,000,000
One centimeter represents 120 kilometers.
One inch represents approximately 190 miles.
Lambert Conformal Conic Projection

ALASKA
UNITED STATES
Chukchi Sea
Bering Strait
Arctic Circle
ČUKOTSKIJ POLUOSTROV
SAINT LAWRENCE ISLAND
NUNIVAK ISLAND
SAINT MATTHEW ISLAND
OSTROV VRANGEL'A
proliv Longa
VOSTOČNO-SIBIRSKOJE MORE
EAST SIBERIAN SEA
OSTROV KOTEL'NYJ
proliv Sannikova
proliv Dmitrija Lapteva
OSTROV NOVAJA SIBIR'
Anadyrskij zaliv
zaliv Kresta
Provideniya
Anadyr'
ANADYRSKOJE PLOSKOGORJE
ANJUJSKIJ CHREBET
Malyj Anjuj
Bol'šoj Anjuj
KOR'AKSKOJE NAGORJE
Bering Sea
Kolyma
Indigirka
Omolon
KOLYMSKAJA NIZMENNOST'
JUKAGIRSKOJE PLOSKOGORJE
MOMSKIJ CHREBET
CHREBET ČERSKOGO
Janskij zaliv
Jana
Verchojansk
VERCHOJANSKIJ CHREBET
JAKUTIJA
SIBERIA
CHREBET SUNTAR-CHAJATA
CHREBET SETTE-DABAN
Lena
Aldan
Jakutsk
Magadan
Tauijskaja guba
Penžinskaja guba
Gižiginskaja guba
zaliv Šelichova
Ochotsk
POLUOSTROV KAMČATKA
KAMCHATKA
SREDINNYJ CHREBET
Petropavlovsk-Kamčatskij
KOMANDORSKIJE OSTROVA
SEA OF OKHOTSK
OCHOTSKOJE MORE
ALDANSKOJE NAGORJE
STANOVOJ CHREBET
CHREBET DŽUGDŽUR
Zejskoje vodochranilišče
Zeja
Amur
Heilong
Svobodnyj
Blagoveščensk
Komsomol'sk-na-Amure
Chabarovsk
SICHOTE-ALIN'
OSTROV SACHALIN
SAKHALIN
Južno-Sachalinsk
Tatarskij proliv
La Perouse Strait
KURIL'SKIJE OSTROVA
KURIL ISLANDS
Habomai, Shikotan, Kunashiri, and Etorofu, occupied since 1945, are claimed by Japan pending a final peace treaty.
HOKKAIDO
Sapporo
Asahikawa
Kushiro
Obihiro
Hakodate
HONSHU
JAPAN
SEA OF JAPAN
PACIFIC OCEAN
Vladivostok
Nachodka
Ussurijsk
Harbin
MANCHURIA
CHINA
HEILONGJIANG
NEI MONGGOL ZIZHIQU
DA HINGGAN LING
XIAO HINGGAN LING
Qiqihar Tsitsihar
Jiamusi
Mudanjiang
Yichun
Aomori
Akita
Morioka

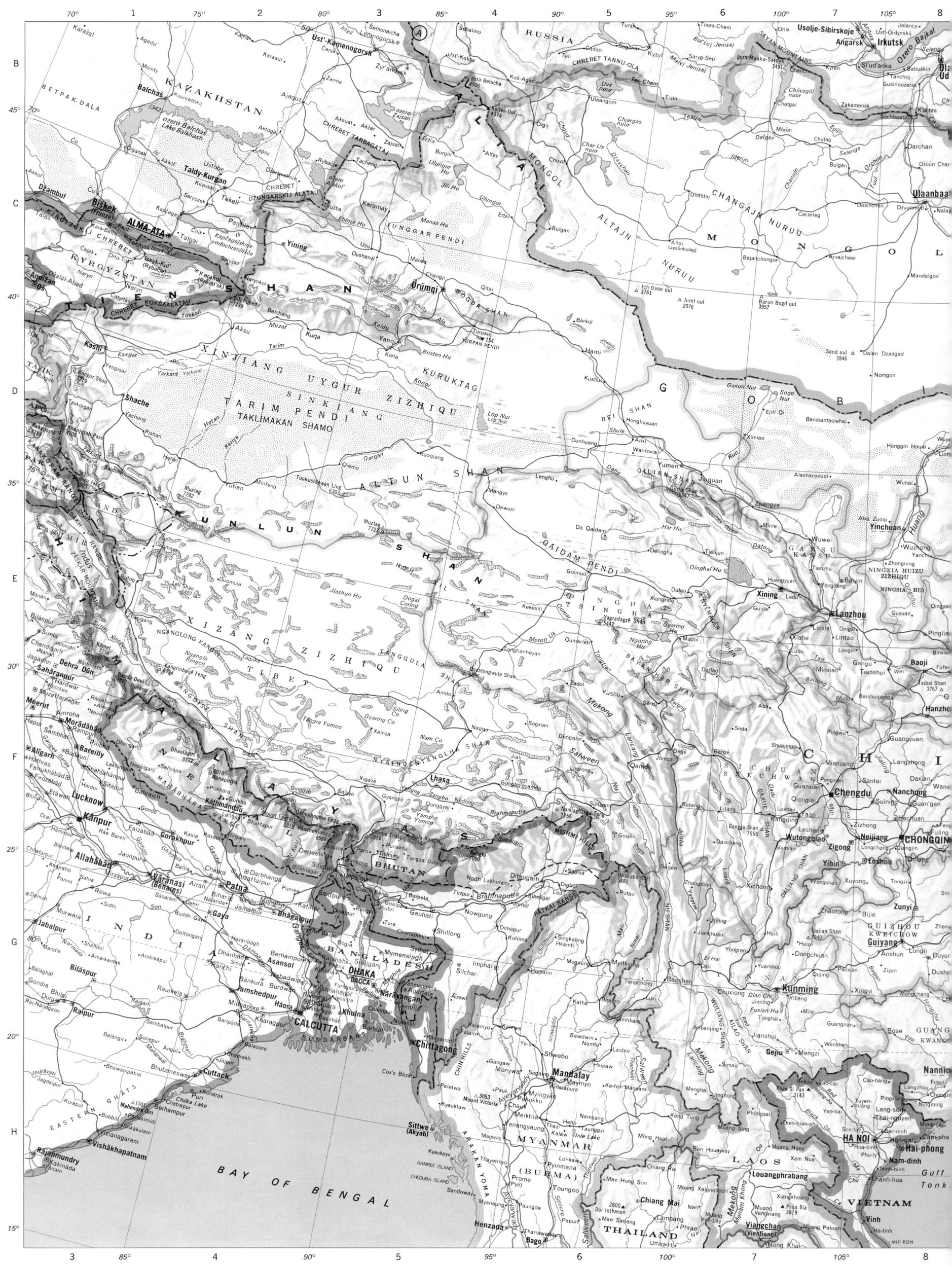
RUSSIA
KAZAKHSTAN
BETPAK-DALA
Balchaš
ozero Balchaš
Lake Balkhash
Ust'-Kamenogorsk
Semipalatinsk
Taldy-Kurgan
Džambul
Biškek (Frunze)
ALMA-ATA
KYRGYZSTAN
TIEN SHAN
Yining
Ürümqi
Karamay
JUNGGAR PENDI
ALTAI
MONGOL ALTAJN NURUU
CHANGAJN NURUU
Irkutsk
Angarsk
Ulaanbaatar
MONGOLIA
GOBI
Kashi
Aksu
Kuqa
Turpan
TURPAN PENDI
Hami
XINJIANG UYGUR ZIZHIQU
SINKIANG
TARIM PENDI
TAKLIMAKAN SHAMO
KURUKTAG
Lop Nur
Shache
Hotan
ALTUN SHAN
KUNLUN SHAN
QAIDAM PENDI
QINGHAI
TSINGHAI
Xining
Lanzhou
Yinchuan
XIZANG ZIZHIQU
TIBET
Lhasa
NYAINQENTANGLHA SHAN
TANGGULA SHAN
Mekong
Salween
Brahmaputra
NEPAL
Kathmandu
HIMALAYA
BHUTAN
Thimphu
Chengdu
CHONGQING
Kunming
Guiyang
SICHUAN
SZECHWAN
YUNNAN
INDIA
Delhi
Lucknow
Kanpur
Allahabad
Varanasi (Benares)
Patna
Gaya
Bhagalpur
Jabalpur
Jamshedpur
Asansol
CALCUTTA
BANGLADESH
DHAKA (DACCA)
Chittagong
Khulna
Nārāyanganj
Cuttack
Vishākhapatnam
Rajahmundry
EASTERN GHATS
BAY OF BENGAL
MYANMAR (BURMA)
Mandalay
Sittwe (Akyab)
Bago
Henzada
THAILAND
Chiang Mai
LAOS
Louangphrabang
Viangchan (Vientiane)
VIETNAM
HA NOI
Hai-phong
Nam-dinh
Vinh
Gulf of Tonkin

Scale 1:12,000,000

One centimeter represents 120 kilometers.
One inch represents approximately 190 miles.
Lambert Conformal Conic Projection

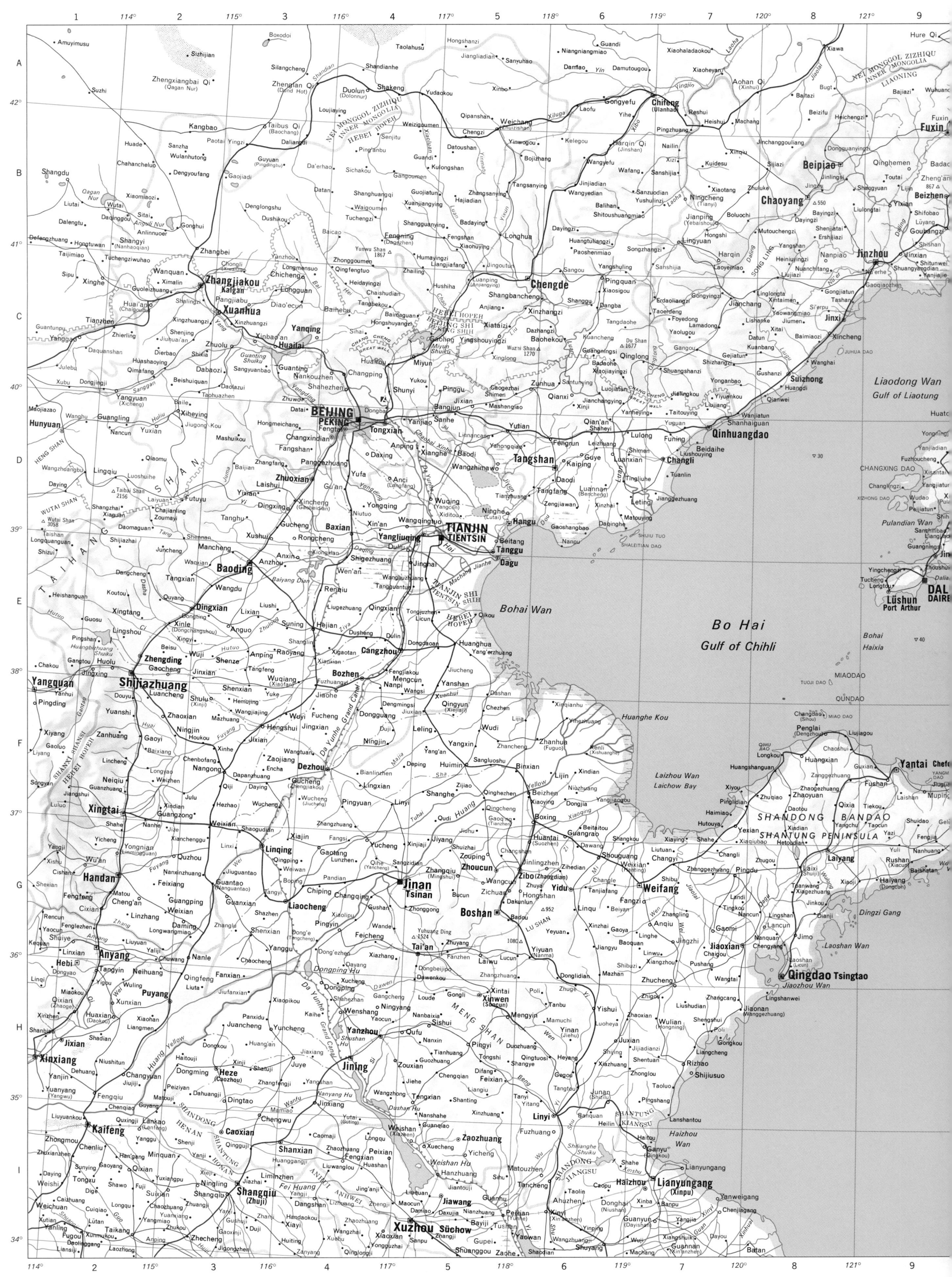

MANCHURIA
SEA OF JAPAN
Korea Bay
YELLOW SEA
Western Channel
Korea Strait
Tsushima-kaikyō
Eastern Channel
SOUTH KOREA
JAPAN
NIHON
CHINA
RUSSIA
NORTH KOREA
CHINA
ZHONGGUO
HAMGYŎNG PUKDO
HAMGYŎNG NAMDO
YANGGANG DO
CHAGANG DO
P'YŎNGAN PUKDO
P'YŎNGAN NAMDO
HWANGHAE PUKDO
HWANGHAE NAMDO
KANGWŎN DO
KYŎNGGI DO
CH'UNGCH'ŎNG PUKDO
CH'UNGCH'ŎNG NAMDO
KYŎNGSANG PUKDO
KYŎNGSANG NAMDO
CHŎLLA PUKDO
CHŎLLA NAMDO
CHANGBAI SHAN
HAMGYŎNG-SANMAEK
KANGNAM-SANMAEK
NANGNIM-SANMAEK
T'AEBAEK-SANMAEK
SOBAEK-SANMAEK
LIAODONG BANDAO
LIAOTUNG PENINSULA
P'yŏngyang
SŎUL
SEOUL
Inch'ŏn
Pusan
Taegu
Kwangju
Taejŏn
Ch'ŏngjin
Hamhŭng
Hŭngnam
Wŏnsan
Kaesŏng
Namp'o
Sinŭiju
Kimch'aek
Tanch'ŏn
Kanggye
Hyesan
Haeju
Sariwŏn
Chŏnju
Kunsan
Mokp'o
Yŏsu
Masan
Ulsan
P'ohang
Kangnŭng
Ch'unch'ŏn
Wŏnju
Ch'ŏngju
Suwŏn
Anyang
Sŏngnam-si
Chinju
Tsushima
Dandong
FUSHUN
SHENYANG
MUKDEN
Anshan
Liaoyang
Benxi
Dalian
Tonghua
Weihai
Sea of Japan
Tongjosŏn-man
Sŏjosŏn-man
Kyŏnggi-man
Copyright © by Rand McNally & Co.
Map compiled by Cartographia, Budapest
Map produced by Rand McNally & Co.
A-564400-264
Kilometers
Km.
Statute Miles
Mi.
Scale 1:3,000,000
One centimeter represents 30 kilometers.
One inch represents approximately 47 miles.
Lambert Conformal Conic Projection

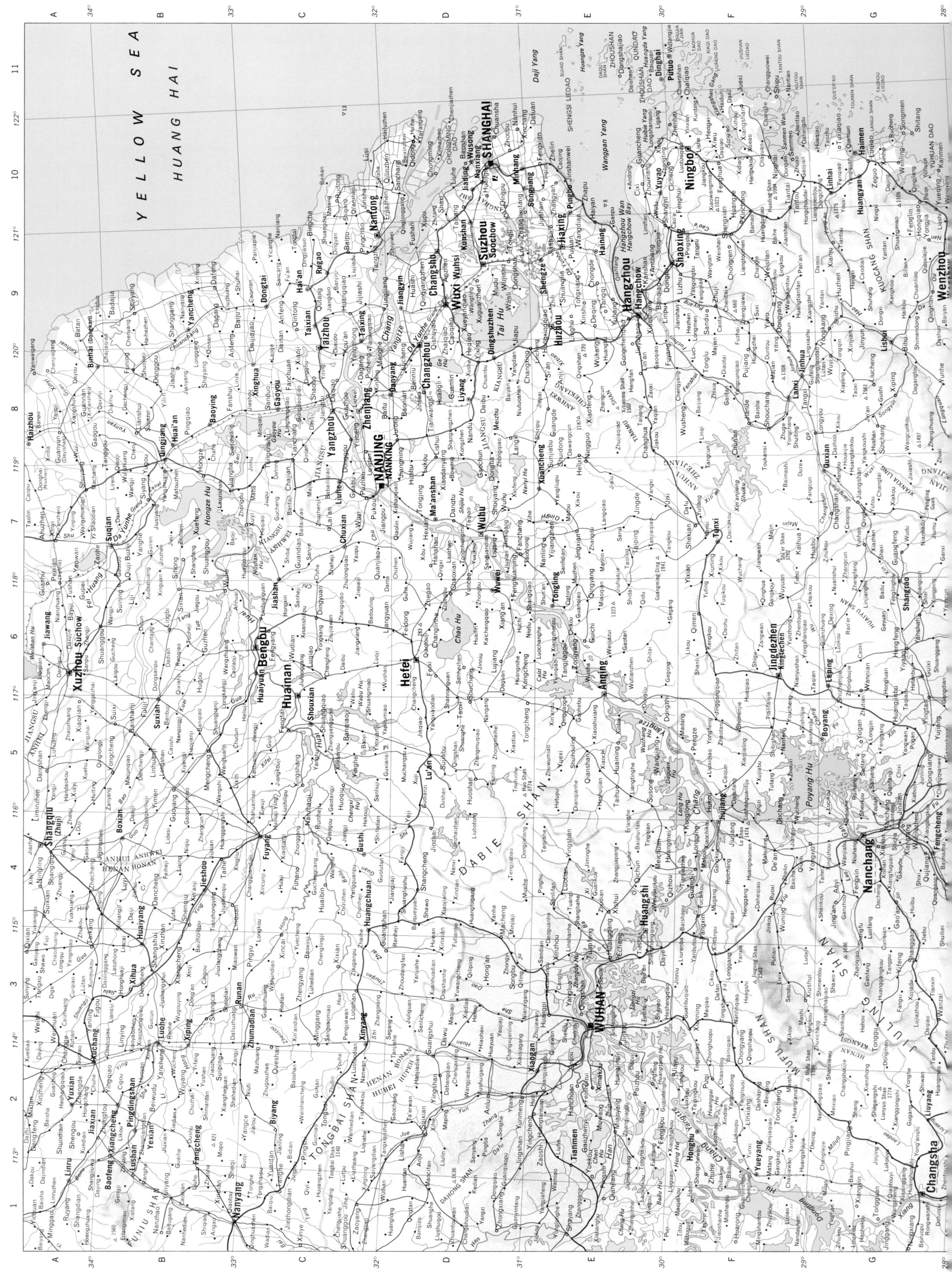

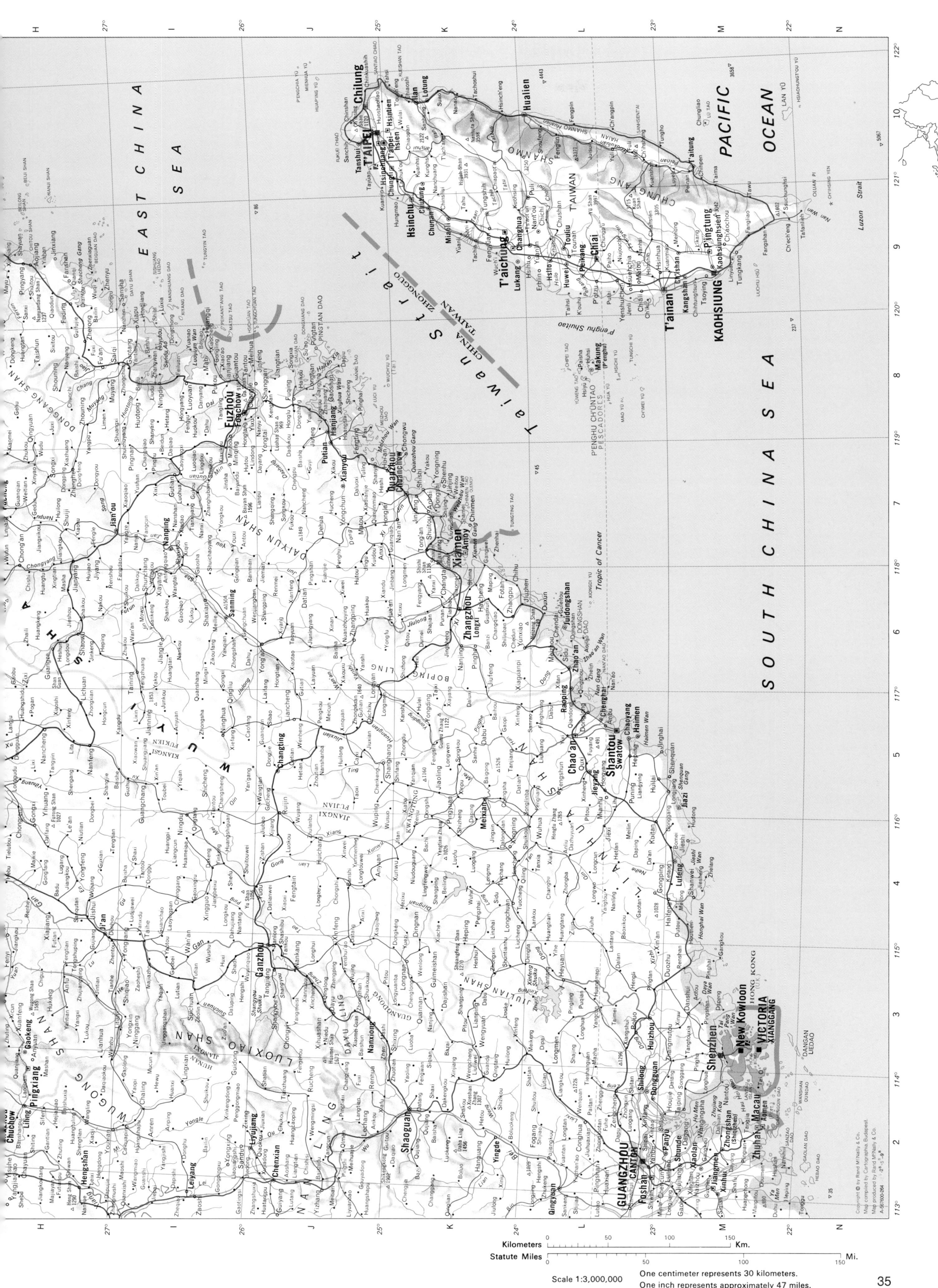

Kilometers

Statute Miles

Scale 1:3,000,000

One centimeter represents 30 kilometers.
One inch represents approximately 47 miles.
Lambert Conformal Conic Projection

35

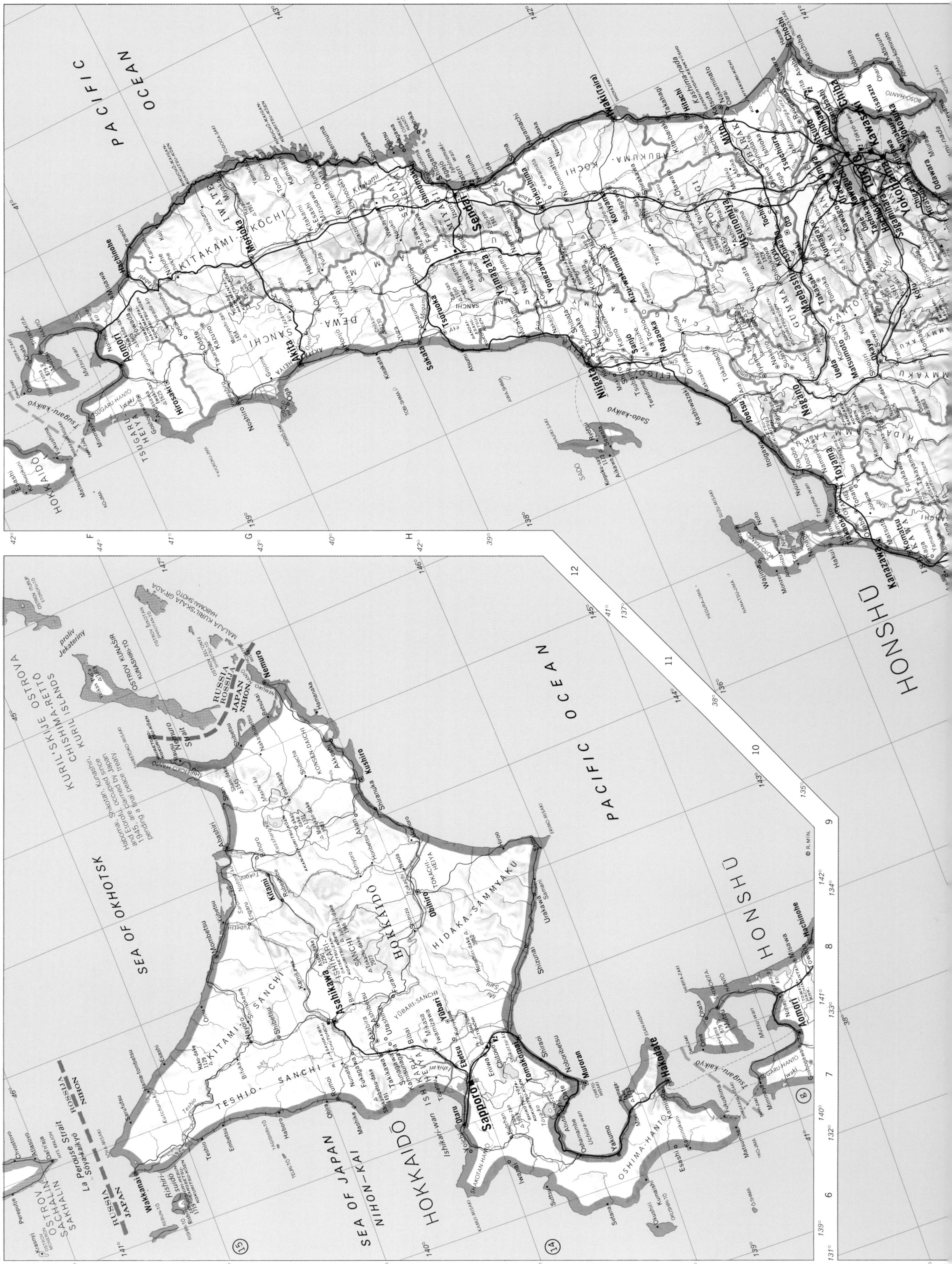

PACIFIC OCEAN

SEA OF OKHOTSK

SEA OF JAPAN
NIHON-KAI

HOKKAIDO

HONSHŪ

KITAKAMI KOCHI
IWATE
DEWA SANCHI
ABUKUMA KOCHI
KANTO
ECHIGO
HIDA

Morioka
Hachinohe
Aomori
Hirosaki
Akita
Sakata
Niigata
Sendai
Fukushima
Yonezawa
Yamagata
Tsuruoka
Nagano
Maebashi
Takasaki
Toyama
Kanazawa
Komatsu
Chiba
Yokohama
Ueda
Matsumoto
Nagaoka
Sado
Sado-kaikyo
Tsugaru-kaikyo
TSUGARU HEIYA
OGA
BOSO-HANTO
NOTO-HANTO

KURIL'SKIJE OSTROVA
KURIL'SKIE RETTO
CHISHIMA-RETTO
KURIL ISLANDS
proliv Jekateriny
OSTROV KUNASIR
KUNASHIR-TO
MALAJA KURIL'SKAJA GR. ADA
HABOMAI-SHOTO
RUSSIA / JAPAN NIHON
Nemuro
Nemuro strait
Hanasaka

KITAMI SANCHI
TESHIO SANCHI
ISHIKARI SANCHI
YUBARI-SANCHI
HIDAKA-SAMMYAKU
KONSEN-DAICHI
TOKACHI-HEIYA

Wakkanai
Rishiri
Asahikawa
Kitami
Kushiro
Obihiro
Sapporo
Otaru
Muroran
Tomakomai
Hakodate
Aomori
Hachinohe

OSHIMA-HANTO
SHAKOTAN-HANTO
ISHIKARI-WAN
UCHIURA-WAN

La Pérouse Strait
RUSSIA / JAPAN
OSTROV SAKHALIN
SAKHALIN

SEA OF JAPAN
NIHON-KAI

PACIFIC OCEAN

HONSHŪ
Tsugaru-kaikyo
TSUGARU-HANTO

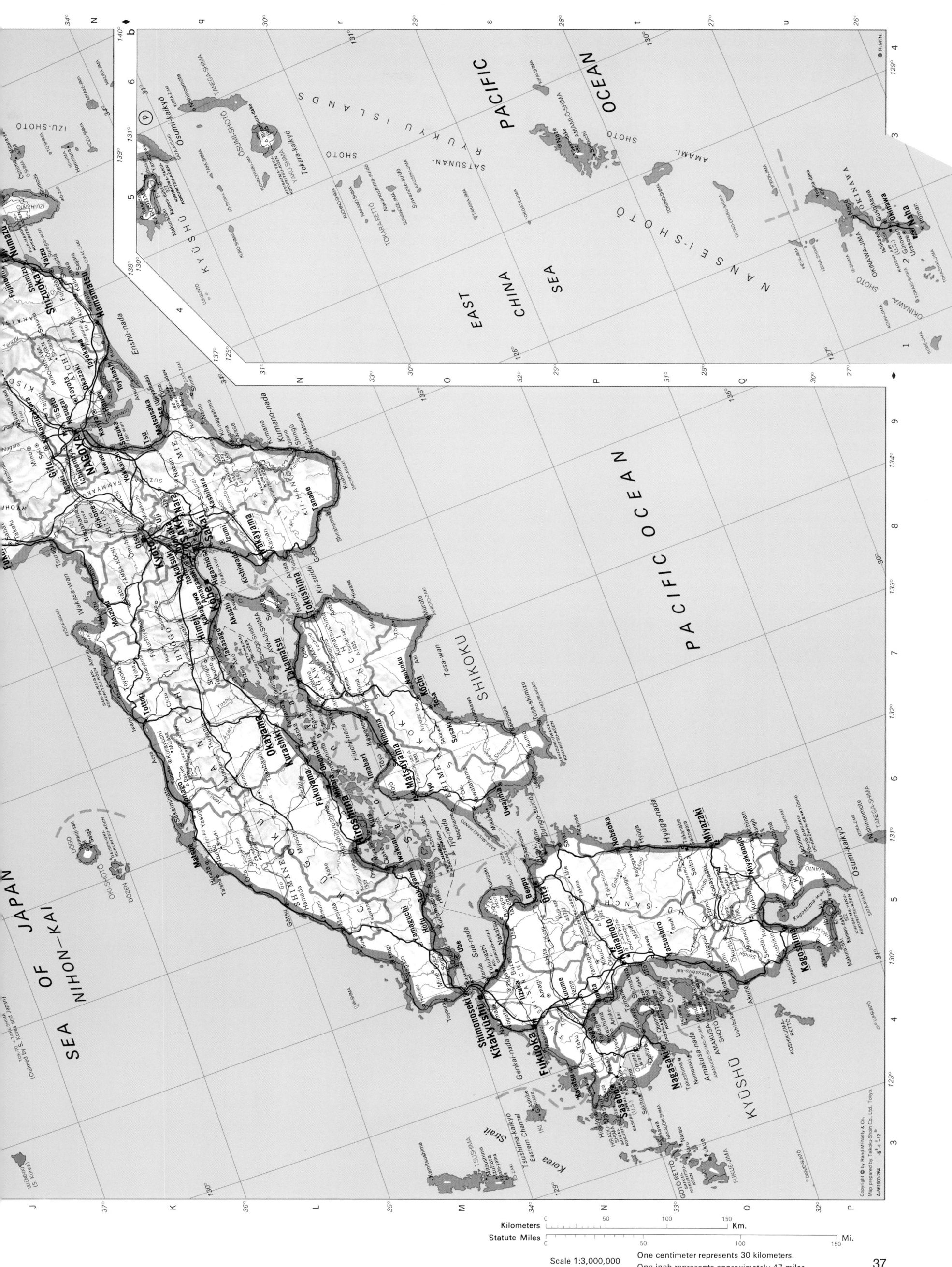

SEA OF JAPAN

NIHON-KAI

(Claimed by S. Korea and Japan)

PACIFIC OCEAN

EAST CHINA SEA

PACIFIC OCEAN

RYUKYU ISLANDS

NANSEI-SHOTO

KYŪSHŪ

SHIKOKU

NAGOYA

ŌSAKA

KYŌTO

Hiroshima

Fukuoka

Kitakyūshū

Shimonoseki

Nagasaki

Sasebo

Kumamoto

Kagoshima

Miyazaki

Matsuyama

Kōchi

Takamatsu

Tokushima

Okayama

Kurashiki

Fukuyama

Himeji

Sakai

Wakayama

Tanabe

Tsu

Matsusaka

Shizuoka

Hamamatsu

Naha

Okinawa

Kilometers   0   50   100   150   Km.

Statute Miles   0   50   100   150   Mi.

Scale 1:3,000,000

One centimeter represents 30 kilometers.
One inch represents approximately 47 miles.
Lambert Conformal Conic Projection

37

Copyright © by Rand McNally & Co.
Map prepared by Teikoku-Shoin Co., Ltd., Tokyo.
A-661900-264   -5-4-12

CHINA
YUNNAN
GUANGXI
Nanning
ZHUANGZU
GUANGDONG
GUANGZHOU
CANTON
Shantou
Swatow
New Kowloon Xinjiulong
VICTORIA XIANGGANG
HONG KONG
(U.K.)
Macau
Zhanjiang
Haikou
HAINAN
HAINAN DAO
Gulf of
Tonkin
HA NOI
Hai Phong
Nam Dinh
LAOS
Louangphrabang
Viangchan
(Vientiane)
MYANMAR
(BURMA)
Mandalay
Monywa
Taunggyi
Sittwe
(Akyab)
Henzada
Pathein
YANGON
RANGOON
Bago
Mawlamyine
BANGLADESH
Chittagong
INDIA
BAY OF
BENGAL
THAILAND
Chiang
Mai
Nakhon
Ratchasima
Khon Kaen
KRUNG THEP
BANGKOK
INDOCHINA
VIETNAM
Vinh
Hue
Da Nang
Qui Nhon
Nha Trang
CAMBODIA
Phnum Penh
THANH PHO HO CHI MINH
(SAIGON)
Can Tho
Bien Hoa
Gulf of
Thailand
ANDAMAN
SEA
ANDAMAN ISLANDS
(India)
Port Blair
NICOBAR ISLANDS
(India)
Ten Degree Channel
SOUTH CHINA
SEA
XISHA QUNDAO
PARACEL ISLANDS
(claimed by China, Taiwan and Vietnam)
SPRATLY
ISLANDS
Songkhla
Hat Yai
George Town
(Pinang)
Kota Baharu
Ipoh
Kuala Terengganu
MALAYSIA
SEMENANJUNG
MALAYSIA
KUALA LUMPUR
Seremban
Melaka
Johor Baharu
SINGAPORE
Banda Aceh
Medan
Pematangsiantar
Pekanbaru
SUMATERA
SUMATRA
Padang
Jambi
Palembang
Bengkulu
Tanjungkarang-
Telukbetung
Pangkalpinang
PULAU BANGKA
KEPULAUAN
NATUNA BESAR
KEPULAUAN LINGGA
KEPULAUAN RIAU
BRUNEI
SABAH
Kota Kinabalu
(Jesselton)
SARAWAK
Kuching
Pontianak
BORNEO
KALIMANTAN
Samarinda
Balikpapan
Banjarmasin
GREATER SUNDA ISLANDS
INDONESIA
LAUT JAWA
JAVA SEA
JAKARTA
BANDUNG
Cirebon
Semarang
SURABAYA
Yogyakarta
Surakarta
Malang
JAWA
JAVA
MADURA
Denpasar
INDIAN OCEAN
CHRISTMAS ISLAND
(Austl.)
Equator

TAIWAN
T'AIWAN
Tropic of Cancer
Bashi Channel
Luzon Strait
BATAN ISLANDS
BABUYAN ISLANDS
LUZON
MANILA
PHILIPPINES
MINDORO
PANAY
NEGROS
SAMAR
LEYTE
Cebu
Iloilo
Bacolod
MINDANAO
Davao
Zamboanga
Moro Gulf
SULU SEA
SULU ARCHIPELAGO
PACIFIC
OCEAN
PALAU
BELAU
(T.T.P.I.)
CELEBES
SEA
LAUT JAWA
JAVA SEA
JAKARTA
BANDUNG
Semarang
SURABAYA
Surakarta
Yogyakarta
MADURA
JAWA
JAVA
INDIAN OCEAN
SUMATERA
SUMATRA
Scale 1:6,000,000
Km.
Mi.
Babuyan Channel
PHILIPPINE
SEA
Quezon City
Scale 1:6,000,000
Manado
HALMAHERA
LAUT MALUKU
MOLUCCA SEA
Teluk Tomini
SULAWESI
CELEBES
LAUT SERAM
CERAM SEA
BURU
Ambon
Ujungpandang
LAUT BANDA
BANDA SEA
MOLUCCAS
KEPULAUAN ARU
KEPULAUAN TANIMBAR
FLORES
Flores Sea
SUMBA
Laut Sawu
Savu Sea
TIMOR
TIMOR SEA
Kupang
Dili
ARAFURA SEA
AUSTRALIA
Equator
Teluk Cenderawasih
Jayapura (Sukarnapura)
PAPUA NEW GUINEA
NEW GUINEA
Puncak Jaya
Gulf of Papua
Torres Strait
Kilometers
Statute Miles
Km.
Mi.
Scale 1:12,000,000
One centimeter represents 120 kilometers.
One inch represents approximately 190 miles.
Lambert Conformal Conic Projection

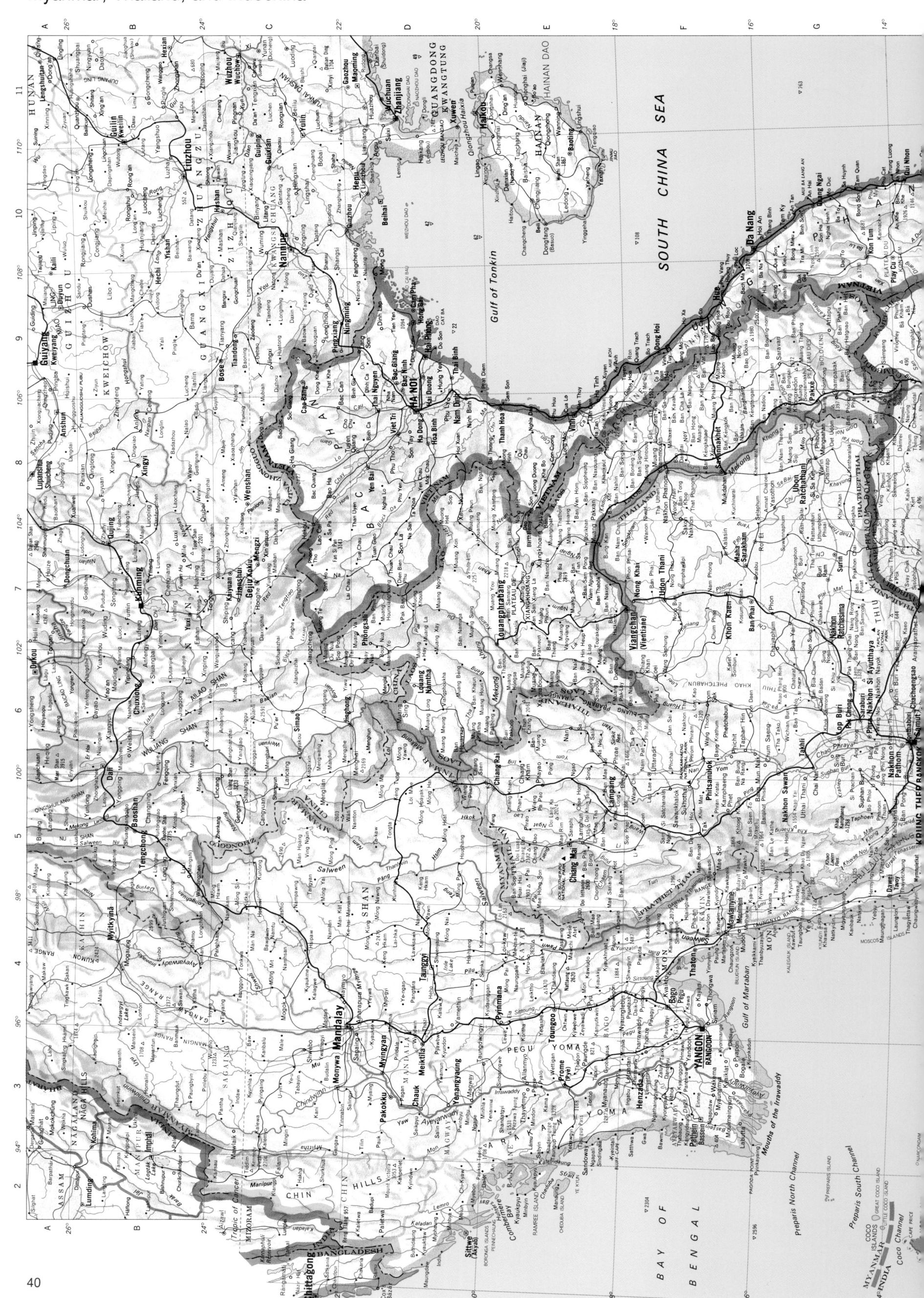
SOUTH CHINA SEA
Gulf of Tonkin
HAINAN DAO
BAY OF BENGAL
Gulf of Martaban
Mouths of the Irrawaddy
Preparis North Channel
Preparis South Channel
Coco Channel
COCO ISLANDS
HA NOI
YANGON
RANGOON
Mandalay
Viangchan
(Vientiane)
Kunming
Nanning
Guiyang
Da Nang
Hue
Chiang Mai
Myitkyinā
Chittagong
Haikou
Zhanjiang
Guilin
Liuzhou
BANGLADESH
MYANMAR
INDIA
SHAN
CHIN HILLS
NAGA HILLS
Tropic of Cancer

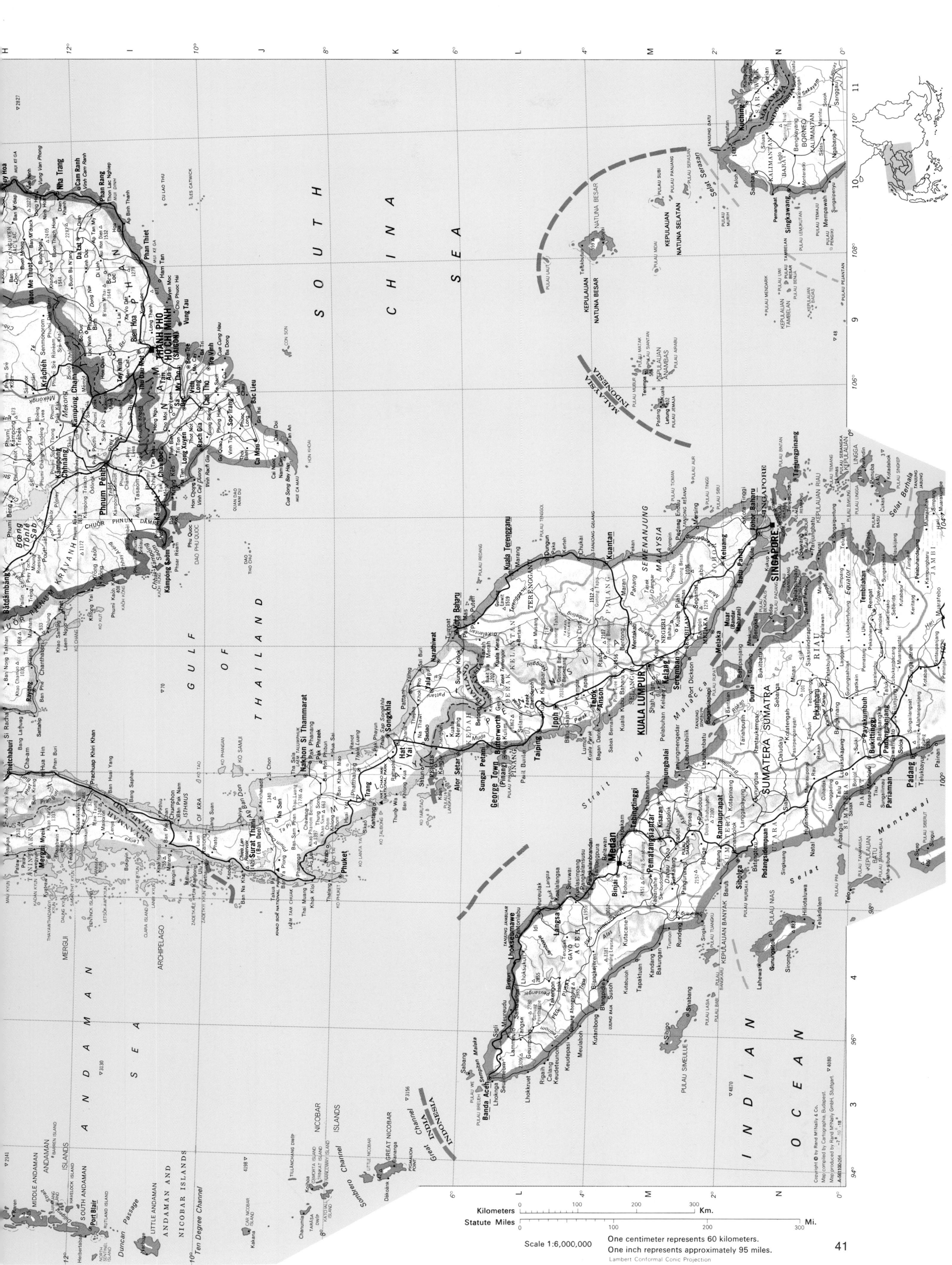

Kilometers 0   100   200   300 Km.

Statute Miles 0   100   200   300 Mi.

Scale 1:6,000,000

One centimeter represents 60 kilometers.
One inch represents approximately 95 miles.
Lambert Conformal Conic Projection

Copyright © by Rand McNally & Co.
Map compiled by Cartographia, Budapest.
Map produced by Rand McNally GmbH, Stuttgart.
A-580100-264

Kilometers
Statute Miles

Scale 1:12,000,000

One centimeter represents 120 kilometers.
One inch represents approximately 190 miles.
Lambert Conformal Conic Projection

KAZAKHSTAN
KYRGYZSTAN
TAJIKISTAN
TIEN SHAN
PAMIR
XINJIANG UYGUR ZIZHIQU
SINKIANG
TARIM PENDI
TAKLIMAKAN SHAMO
ALTUN SHAN
QAIDAM PENDI
QINGHAI
GANSU
KUNLUN SHAN
CHINA
XIZANG ZIZHIQU
TIBET
HINDU KUSH
KARAKORAM RANGE
JAMMU AND KASHMIR
LADAKH RANGE
PIR PANJAL RANGE
HIMACHAL PRADESH
PUNJAB
HARYANA
UTTAR PRADESH
NEPAL
BHUTAN
SIKKIM
ASSAM
ARUNACHAL PRADESH
MEGHALAYA
NAGALAND
MANIPUR
MIZORAM
TRIPURA
BANGLADESH
MYANMAR (BURMA)
AFGHANISTAN
PAKISTAN
KIRTHAR RANGE
SULAIMAN RANGE
TOBA KAKAR RANGE
THAR DESERT
GREAT INDIAN DESERT
RAJASTHAN
ARAVALLI RANGE
RANN OF KUTCH
GUJARAT
KATHIAWAR PENINSULA
MADHYA PRADESH
VINDHYA RANGE
SATPURA RANGE
AJANTA RANGE
MAHARASHTRA
BIHAR
WEST BENGAL
ORISSA
EASTERN GHATS
WESTERN GHATS
DECCAN
ANDHRA PRADESH
KARNATAKA
TAMIL NADU
KERALA
MALABAR COAST
COROMANDEL COAST
SRI LANKA
Lakshadweep Sea
LAKSHADWEEP (India)
Nine Degree Channel
Gulf of Mannar
Palk Strait
BAY OF BENGAL
ARABIAN SEA
INDIAN OCEAN
ANDAMAN ISLANDS (India)
NORTH ANDAMAN
MIDDLE ANDAMAN
SOUTH ANDAMAN
LITTLE ANDAMAN
Port Blair
COCO ISLANDS (Myanmar)
Coco Channel
Taškent
Samarkand
Dušanbe
Kabol
Peshāwar
Islāmābād
Rāwalpindi
Lahore
Faisalabad
Multān
Quetta
Sukkur
Hyderābād
Karāchi
Srīnagar
Amritsar
Ludhiāna
Chandīgarh
Delhi
New Delhi
Jaipur
Jodhpur
Agra
Lucknow
Kānpur
Vārānasi (Benares)
Patna
Kāthmāndau
Lhasa
Calcutta
Dhaka
Chittagong
Ahmadābād
Vadodara
Sūrat
Bhopāl
Indore
Jabalpur
Nāgpur
Raipur
Cuttack
Bombay
Pune (Poona)
Hyderābād
Vishākhapatnam
Vijayawāda
Madras
Bangalore
Mysore
Coimbatore
Madurai
Cochin
Trivandrum
Jaffna
Colombo
Sri Jayawardenepura (Kotte)
Copyright © by Rand McNally & Co.
Map prepared by Esselte Map Service AB, Stockholm.
A-569400-264
The boundary between India and Pakistan through the disputed state of Jammu and Kashmir follows the "line of control" agreed upon by both countries in 1972.

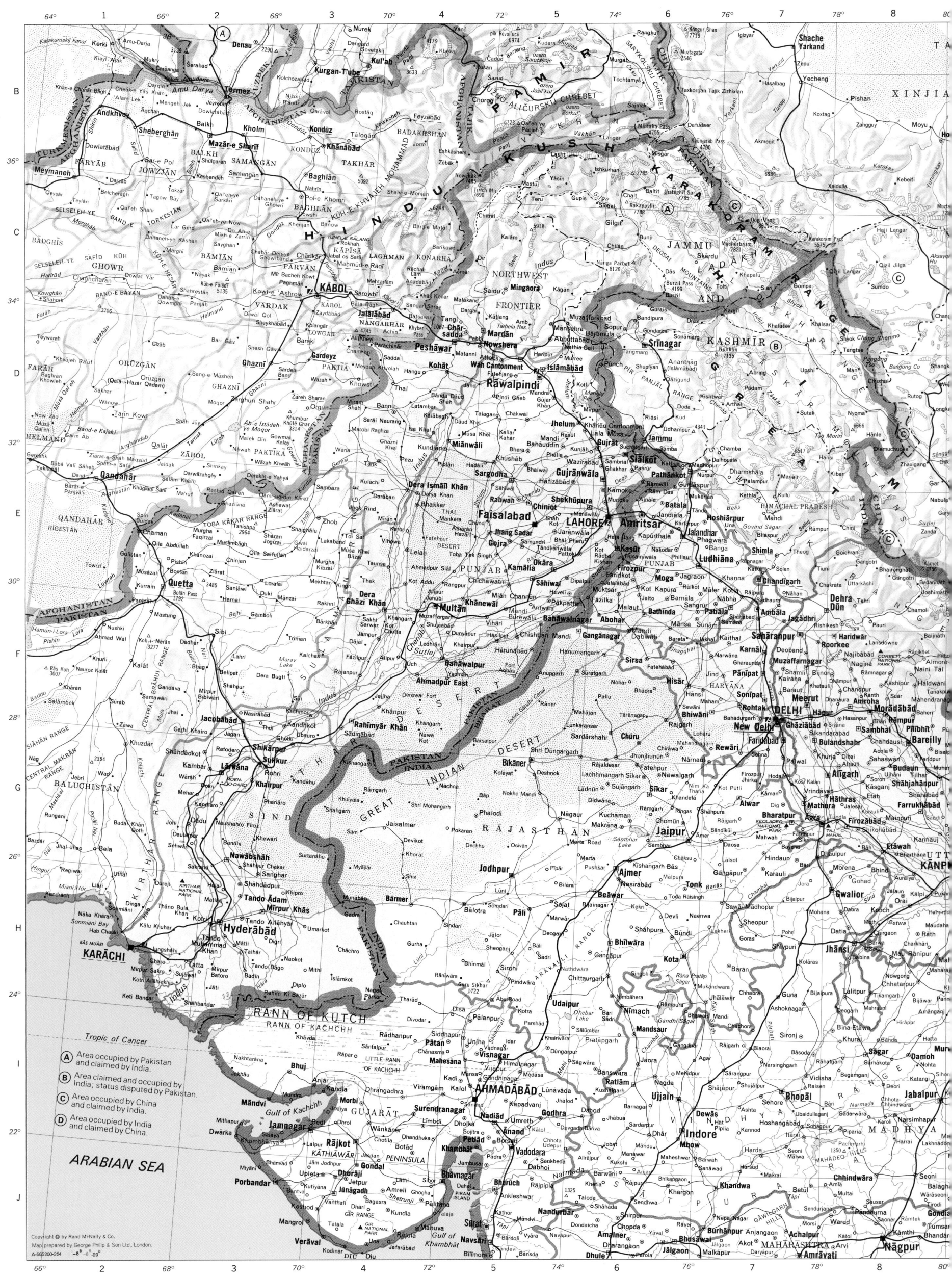

Area occupied by Pakistan
and claimed by India.

Area claimed and occupied by
India; status disputed by Pakistan.

Area occupied by China
and claimed by India.

Area occupied by India
and claimed by China.

Tropic of Cancer

ARABIAN SEA

Copyright © Rand McNally & Co.
Map prepared by George Philip & Son Ltd., London.
A-562,200-264

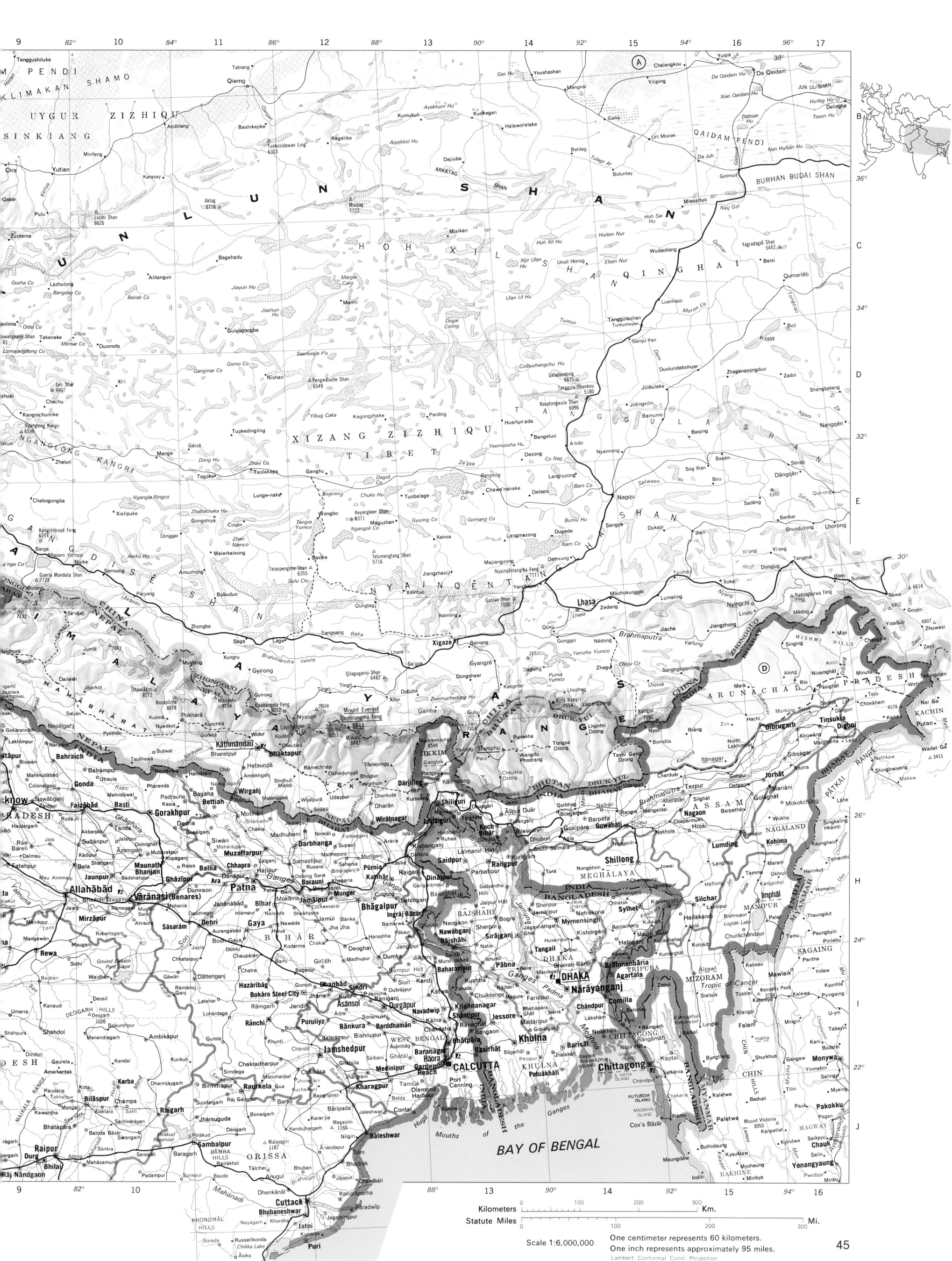

9
82°
10
84°
11
86°
12
88°
13
90°
14
92°
15
94°
16
96°
17
UYGUR ZIZHIQU
SINKIANG
QAIDAM PENDI
BURHAN BUDAI SHAN
KUNLUN SHAN
HOH XIL SHAN
QINGHAI
TANGGULA SHAN
XIZANG ZIZHIQU
TIBET
GANGDISE SHAN
NYAINQÊNTANGLHA SHAN
HIMALAYA RANGE
Mount Everest
Qomolangma Feng
8848
Lhasa
Xigazê
Nagqu
Golmud
ARUNACHAL PRADESH
ASSAM
NAGALAND
MANIPUR
MEGHALAYA
MIZORAM
TRIPURA
SIKKIM
BHUTAN
DRUK-YUL
NEPAL
BANGLADESH
INDIA
CHINA
ZHONGGUO
MYANMAR
BIHAR
WEST BENGAL
ORISSA
Kathmandu
Thimphu
DHAKA
CALCUTTA
Patna
Vārānasi (Benares)
Allahābād
Gorakhpur
Shillong
Guwāhāti
Dibrugarh
Imphāl
Chittagong
Khulna
Jamshedpur
Cuttack
Bhubaneshwar
Puri
Tropic of Cancer
Mouths of the Ganges
BAY OF BENGAL
Brahmaputra
Ganges
Yarlung
PĀTKAI RANGE
CHIN HILLS
SAGAING
MAGWAY
RAKHINE
Kilometers 0 100 200 300 Km.
Statute Miles 0 100 200 300 Mi.
Scale 1:6,000,000
One centimeter represents 60 kilometers.
One inch represents approximately 95 miles.
Lambert Conformal Conic Projection

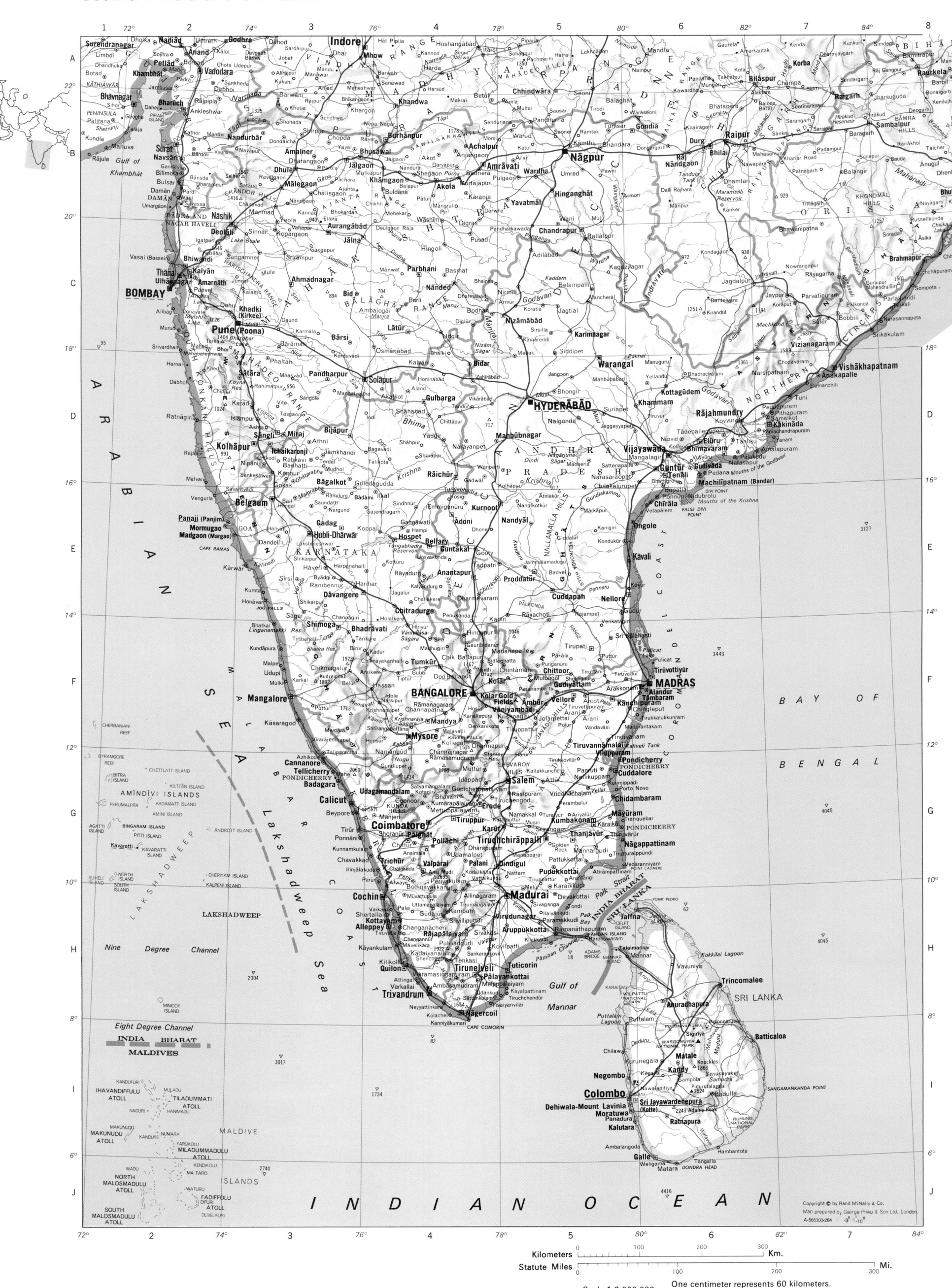

Kilometers 0   100   200   300
Statute Miles 0   100   200   300

Scale 1:6,000,000

One centimeter represents 60 kilometers.
One inch represents approximately 95 miles.
Lambert Conformal Conic Projection

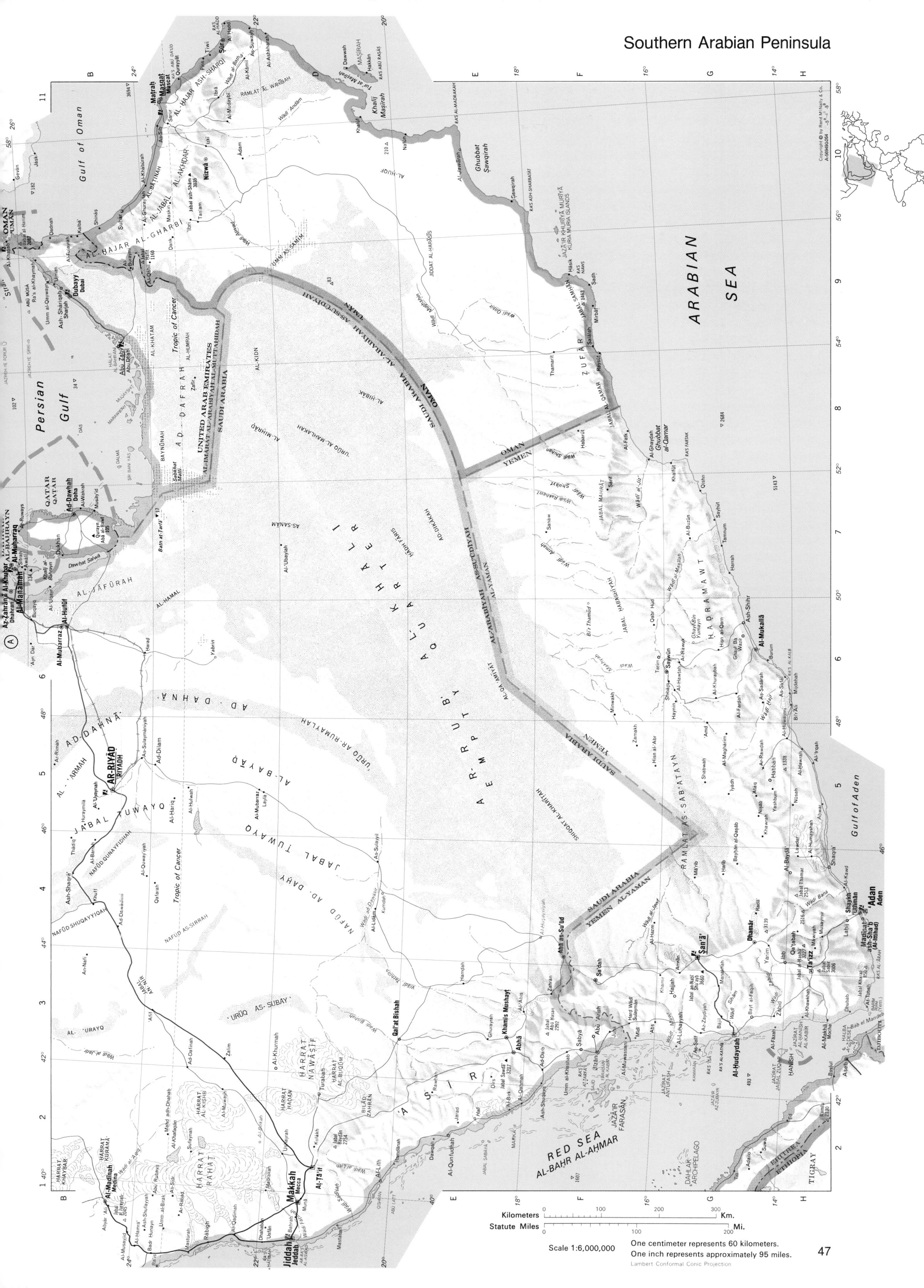

Kilometers 0   100   200   300 Km.

Statute Miles 0   100   200 Mi.

Scale 1:6,000,000   One centimeter represents 60 kilometers.
One inch represents approximately 95 miles.

Lambert Conformal Conic Projection

47

The Middle East

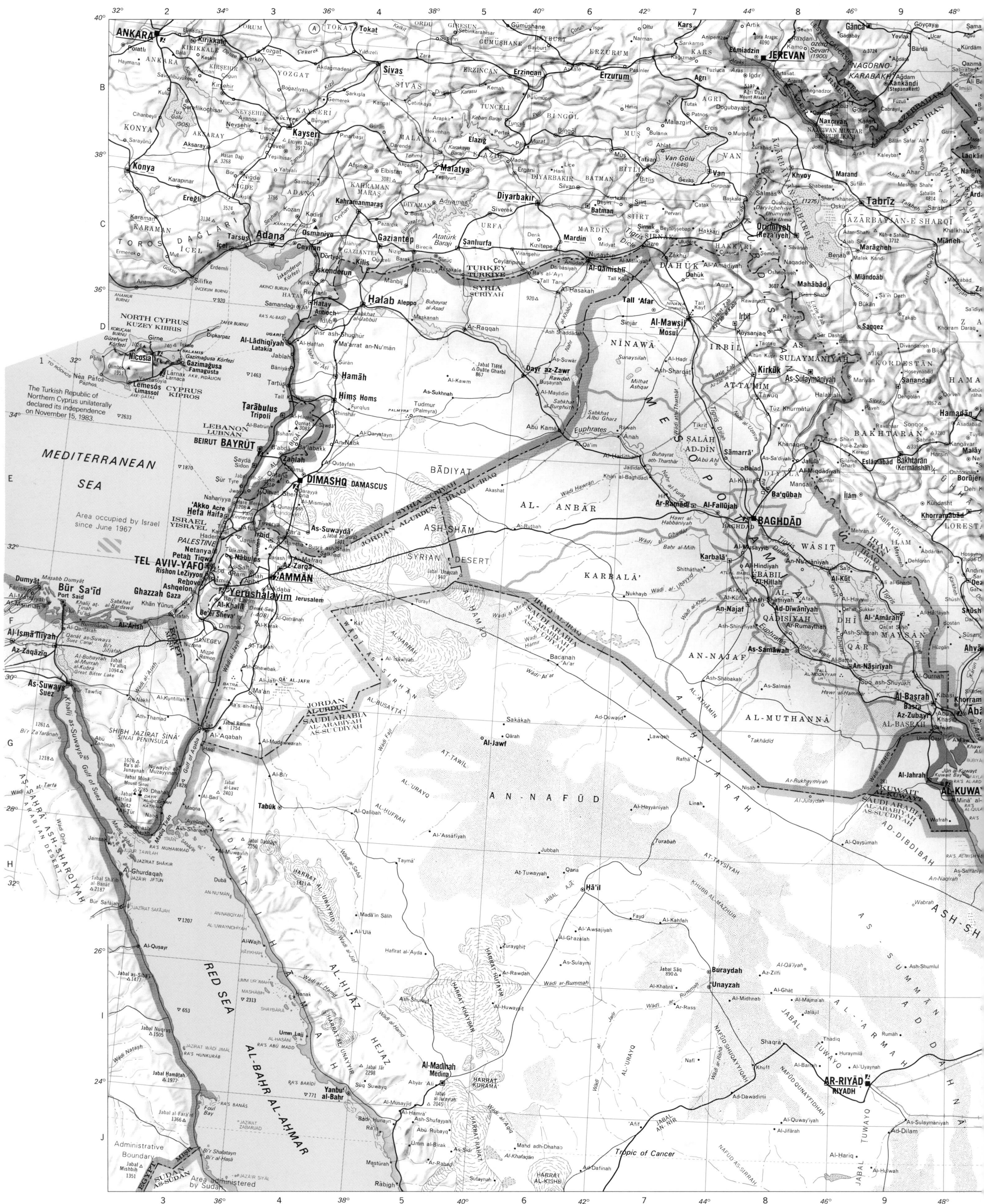

Kilometers

Statute Miles

Scale 1:6,000,000

One centimeter represents 60 kilometers.
One inch represents approximately 95 miles.

Lambert Conformal Conic Projection

49

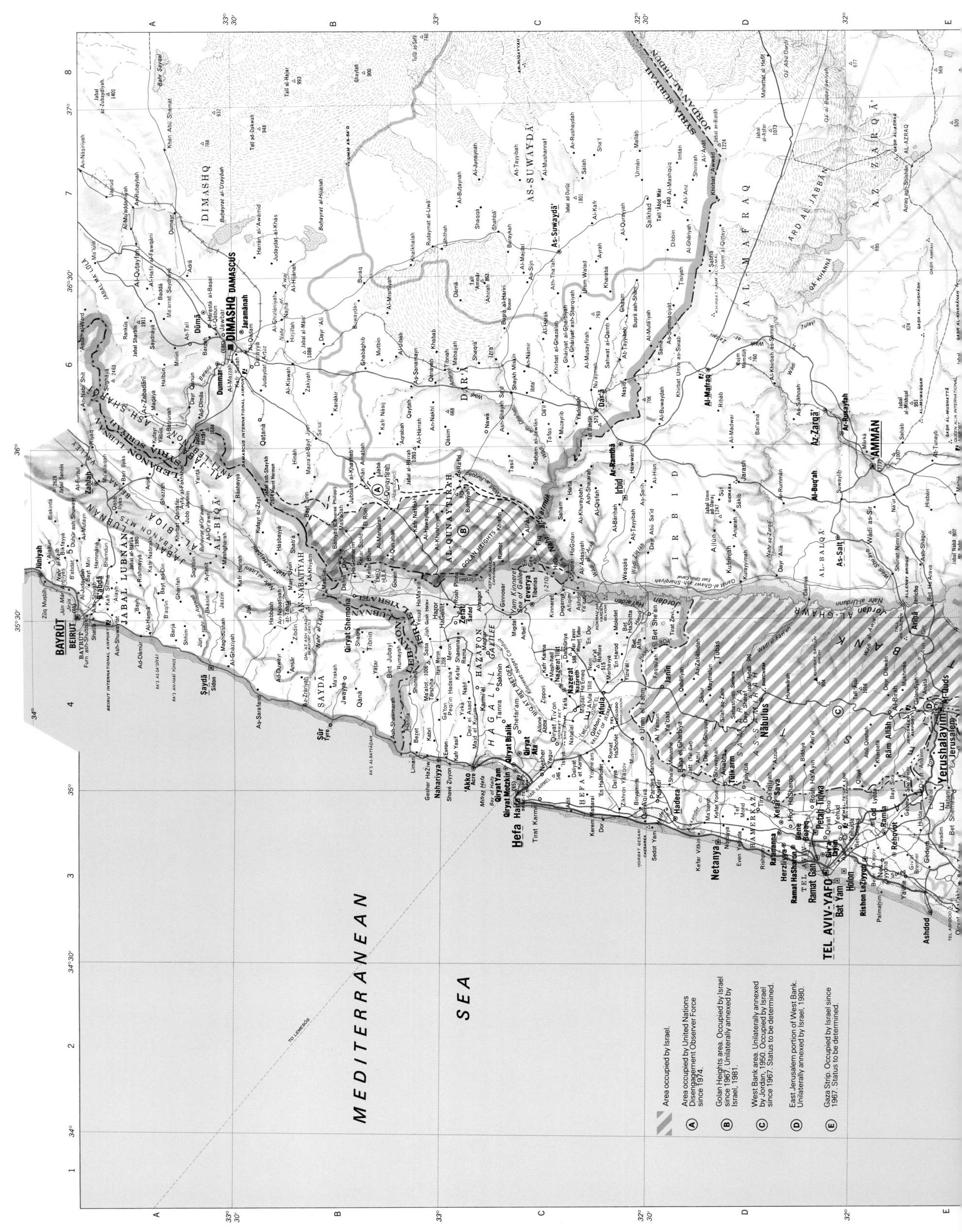

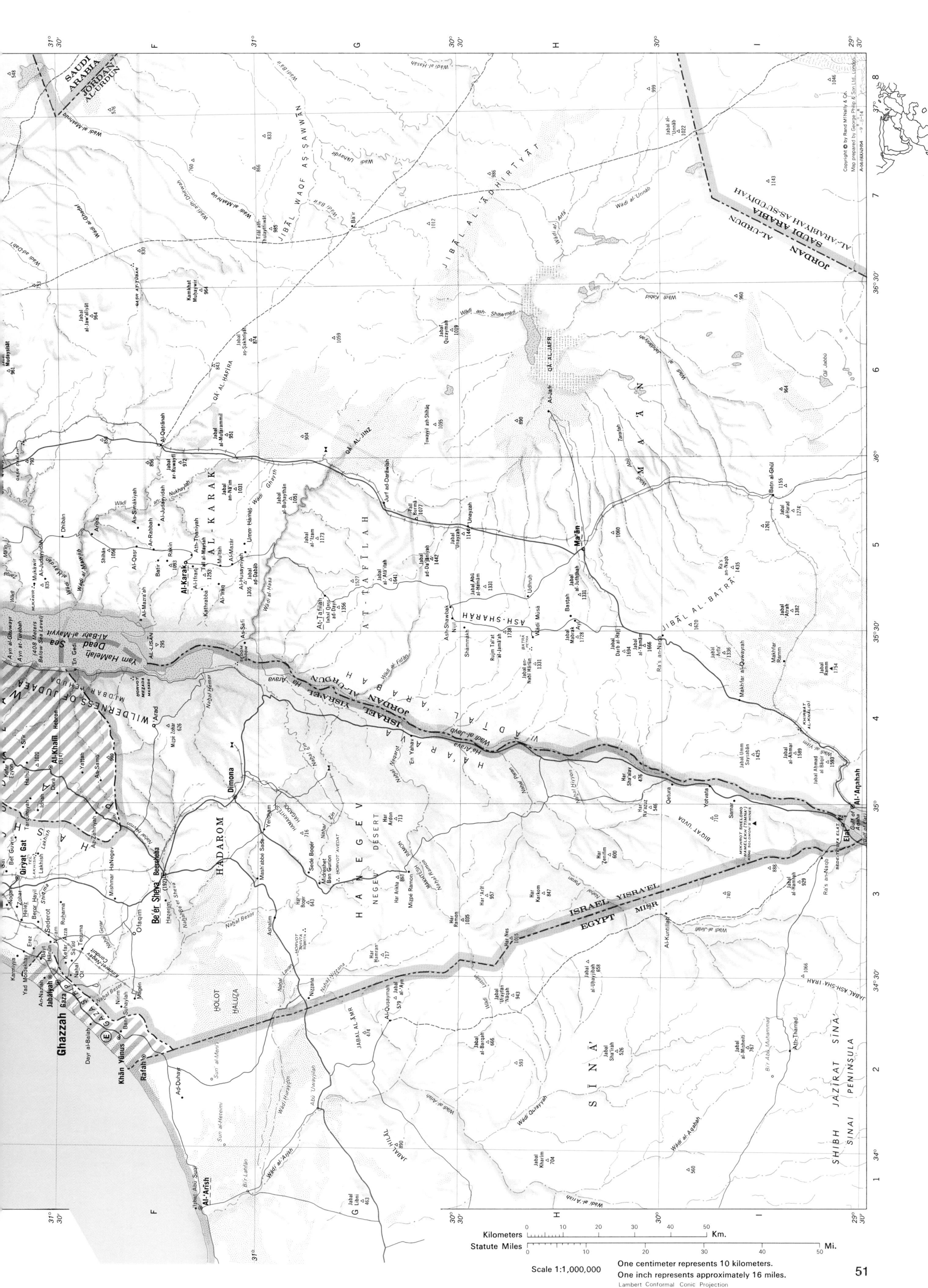

Kilometers ⊢——————————————————⊣ Km.
0 10 20 30 40 50

Statute Miles ⊢——————————————————⊣ Mi.
0 10 20 30 40 50

Scale 1:1,000,000

One centimeter represents 10 kilometers.
One inch represents approximately 16 miles.

Lambert Conformal Conic Projection

51

ATLANTIC
MID-ATLANTIC RIDGE
OCEAN
WEST EUROPEAN BASIN
AZORES-GIBRALTAR RIDGE
CANARY BASIN
LABRADOR BASIN
Labrador Sea
NORWEGIAN BASIN
Norwegian Sea
Barents Sea
Mediterranean Sea
Black Sea
Caspian Sea
EUROPE
ASIA
RUSSIA
KAZAKHSTAN
UZBEKISTAN
TURKMENISTAN
IRAN
IRAQ
SYRIA
TURKEY
SAUDI ARABIA
EGYPT
LIBYA
ALGERIA
MOROCCO
TUNISIA
MAURITANIA
MALI
NIGER
SAHARA
WESTERN SAHARA
ICELAND
GREENLAND
IRELAND
UNITED KINGDOM
FRANCE
SPAIN
PORTUGAL
GERMANY
POLAND
UKRAINE
BELARUS
FINLAND
NORWAY
SWEDEN
ITALY
ROMANIA
BULGARIA
GREECE
HUNGARY
AUSTRIA
CZECH REP.
DENMARK
URAL'SKIJE GORY
URAL MOUNTAINS
CAUCASUS
ALPS
ATLAS MOUNTAINS
ZAPADNO-SIBIRSKAJA RAVNINA

Scale 1:24,000,000
One centimeter represents 240 kilometers.
One inch represents approximately 380 miles.
Lambert Azimuthal Equal-Area Projection

Kilometers
Km.
0 200 400 600 800

Statute Miles
Mi.
0 200 400 600 800

Copyright © by Rand McNally & Co.
Map prepared by Rand McNally & Co.
A-519394-264

ARQUIPÉLAGO DA MADEIRA
MADEIRA ISLANDS
(Portugal)
Funchal
ISLAS CANARIAS
CANARY ISLANDS
(Spain)
Santa Cruz de Tenerife
Las Palmas de Gran Canaria
Western Sahara has been occupied by Morocco
Tropic of Cancer
ATLANTIC
OCEAN
CAPE VERDE
Mindelo
Praia
MOROCCO
Casablanca
RABAT
Marrakech
Agadir
Tanger
Fès
Meknès
Oujda
Béchar
El Aaiún
WESTERN SAHARA
MAURITANIA
Nouakchott
Nouâdhibou
Saint-Louis
DAKAR
SENEGAL
Banjul
GAMBIA
GUINEA-BISSAU
Bissau
GUINEA
Conakry
SIERRA LEONE
Freetown
LIBERIA
Monrovia
COTE D'IVOIRE
(IVORY COAST)
ABIDJAN
MALI
Bamako
Tombouctou
BURKINA FASO
Ouagadougou
GHANA
Kumasi
ACCRA
TOGO
Lomé
SAHARA
SUDAN
Equator
Copyright © by Rand McNally & Co.
Map prepared by Esselte Map Service AB, Stockholm.

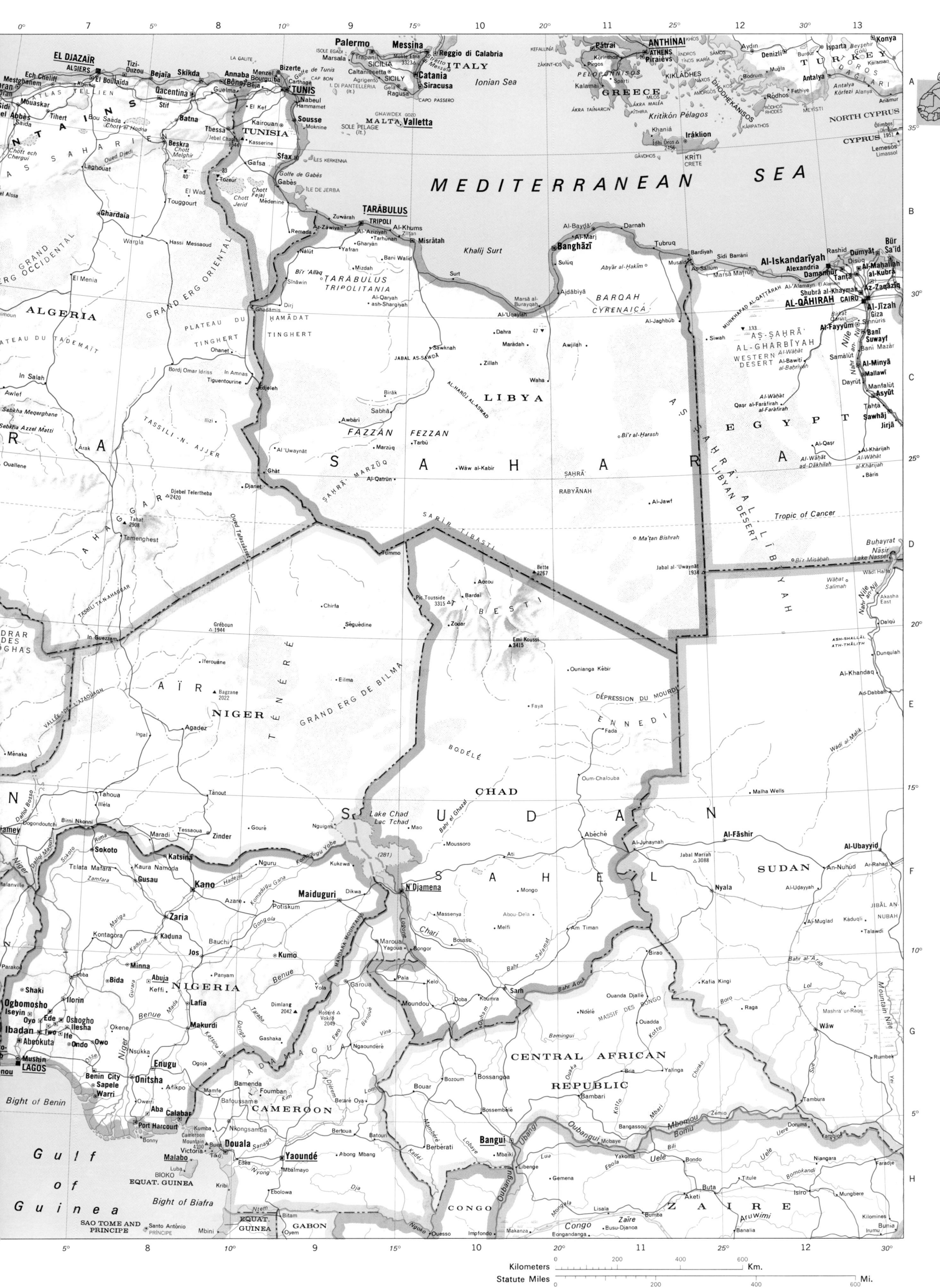

Kilometers 0 200 400 600 Km.

Statute Miles 0 200 400 600 Mi.

Scale 1:12,000,000

One centimeter represents 120 kilometers.

One inch represents approximately 190 miles.

Miller Oblated Stereographic Projection

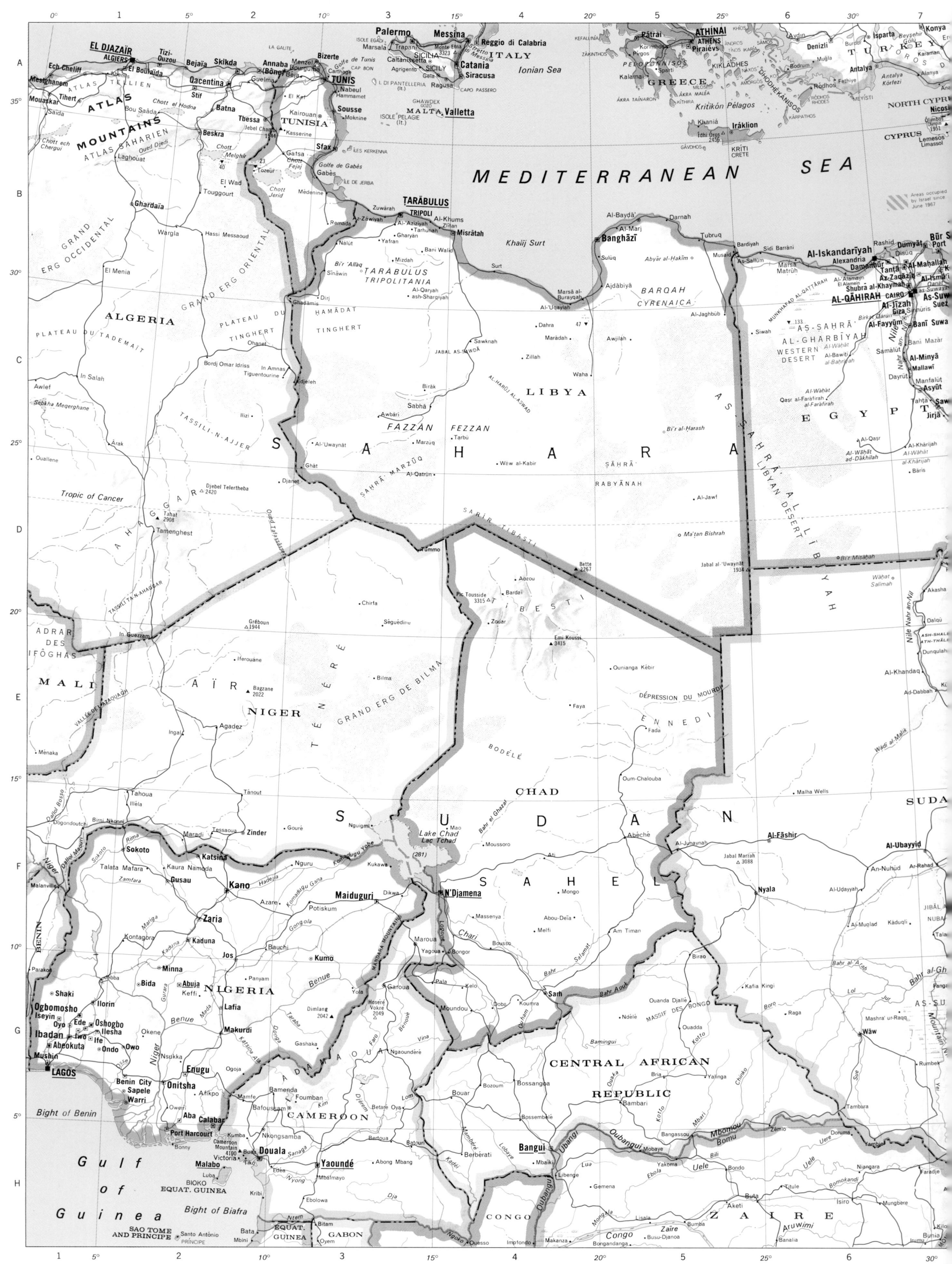

Kilometers 0 200 400 600 Km.

Statute Miles 0 200 400 600 Mi.

Scale 1:12,000,000

One centimeter represents 120 kilometers.
One inch represents approximately 190 miles.

Miller Oblated Stereographic Projection

Southern Africa

INDIAN OCEAN

Equator

SOMALIA

KENYA

NAIROBI

Mombasa

TANZANIA

MASAI STEPPE

Tanga

Zanzibar

DAR ES SALAAM

SEYCHELLES

PRASLIN ISLAND   LA DIGUE
SILHOUETTE   Victoria
MAHÉ ISLAND

AMIRANTE ISLANDS
(Sey.)   ÎLE DESROCHES
(Sey.)   PLATTE ISLAND (Sey.)

ALPHONSE ISLAND (Sey.)   COETIVY ISLAND
(Sey.)

PROVIDENCE ISLAND
(Sey.)

ALDABRA ISLAND
(Sey.)   COSMOLEDO I.
(Sey.)   SAINT PIERRE ISLAND
(Sey.)   CERF ISLAND
(Sey.)

ASSUMPTION ISLAND
(Sey.)   ASTOVE ISLAND
(Sey.)   FARQUHAR GROUP
(Sey.)

AGALEGA ISLANDS
(Mauritius)

COMOROS

Moroni

ARCHIPEL DES COMORES

MAYOTTE
(Fr.)

ÎLES GLORIEUSES
(Fr.)   CAP D'AMBRE

CAP SAINT-SÉBASTIEN   Antsiranana

NOSY MITSIO

MASSIF DU TSARATANANA

MALAWI

Lake Nyasa

Lake Malawi

Blantyre

Nacala

Moçambique

Nampula

MOZAMBIQUE

Quelimane

Chimoio

Beira

MADAGASCAR

Mahajanga

ANTANANARIVO

Antsirabe

Toamasina

Fianarantsoa

Toliara

Faradofay

CAP SAINTE-MARIE

Tropic of Capricorn

Port Louis
Curepipe   Mahébourg
MAURITIUS

Le Port   Saint-Denis
Saint-Paul   RÉUNION
Saint-Pierre   (Fr.)

MASCARENE ISLANDS

ÎLE TROMELIN
(Fr.)

INDIAN OCEAN

Copyright © by Rand McNally & Co.
Map prepared by Esselte Map Service AB, Stockholm.
A-589200-264

Kilometers   0   200   400   600   Km.

Statute Miles   0   200   400   600   Mi.

Scale 1:12,000,000

One centimeter represents 120 kilometers.
One inch represents approximately 190 miles.

Miller Oblated Stereographic Projection

59

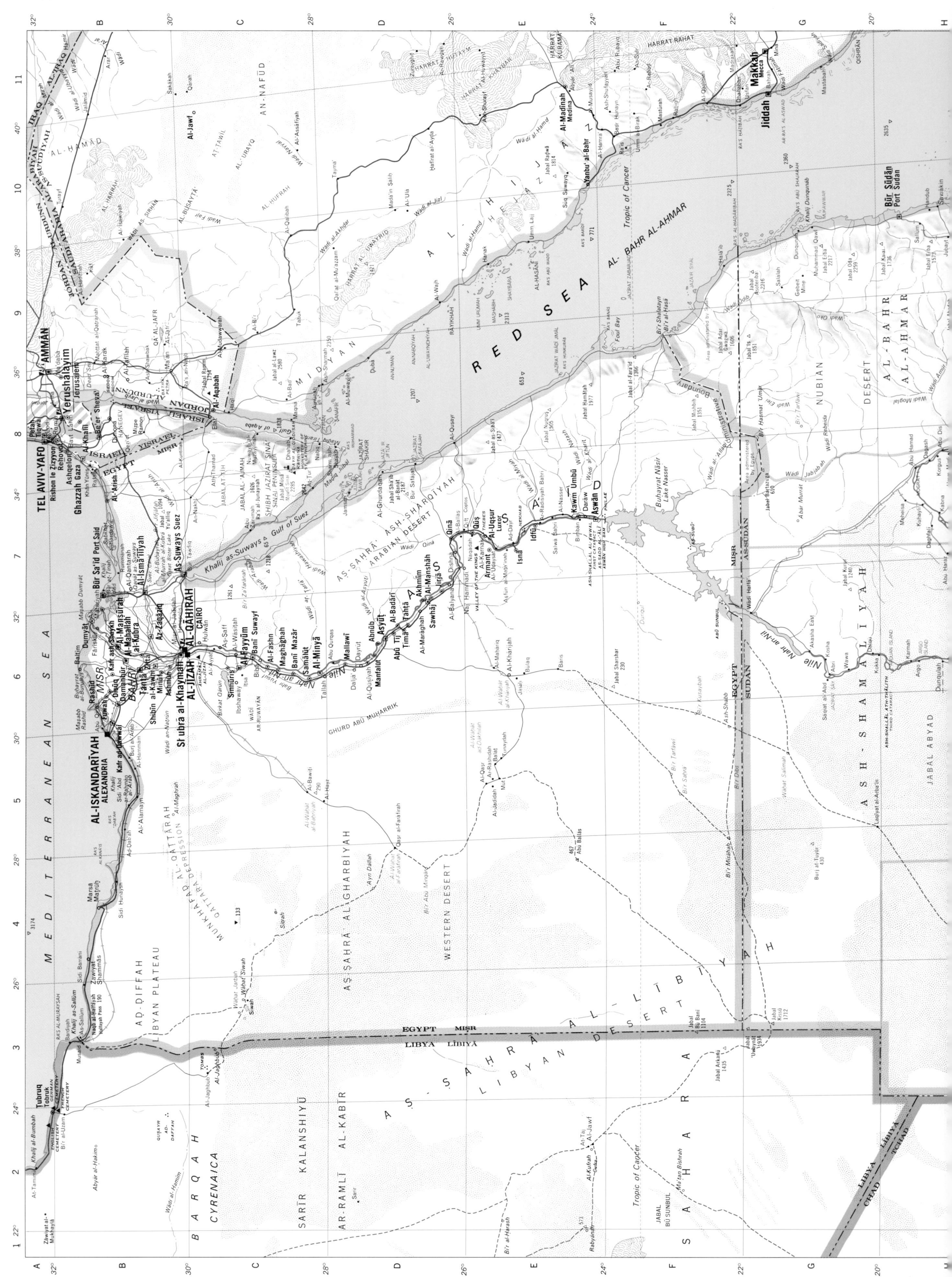
MEDITERRANEAN SEA
RED SEA
AL-BAHR AL-AHMAR
AL-ISKANDARĪYAH
ALEXANDRIA
AL-QĀHIRAH
CAIRO
AL-JĪZAH
Būr Sa'īd Port Said
As-Suways Suez
Gulf of Suez
Gulf of Aqaba
TEL AVIV-YAFO
Yerushalayim
Jerusalem
'AMMĀN
Jiddah
Makkah
Mecca
Al-Madīnah
Medina
Būr Sūdān
Port Sudan
Aswān
Al-Uqṣur
Luxor
Qinā
Asyūṭ
Al-Minyā
Al-Fayyūm
Banī Suwayf
Tropic of Cancer
ARABIAN DESERT
WESTERN DESERT
LIBYAN DESERT
NUBIAN
DESERT
LIBYAN PLATEAU
CYRENAICA
SINAI PENINSULA
Buhayrat Nāsir
Lake Nasser
EGYPT
MIṢR
LIBYA
LĪBIYĀ
SUDAN
AS-SŪDĀN
CHAD
TCHAD
ISRAEL
YISRA'EL
JORDAN
AL-URDUNN
SAUDI ARABIA
AS-SU'ŪDĪYAH
IRAQ
AL-'IRĀQ
Nile
Nahr an-Nīl

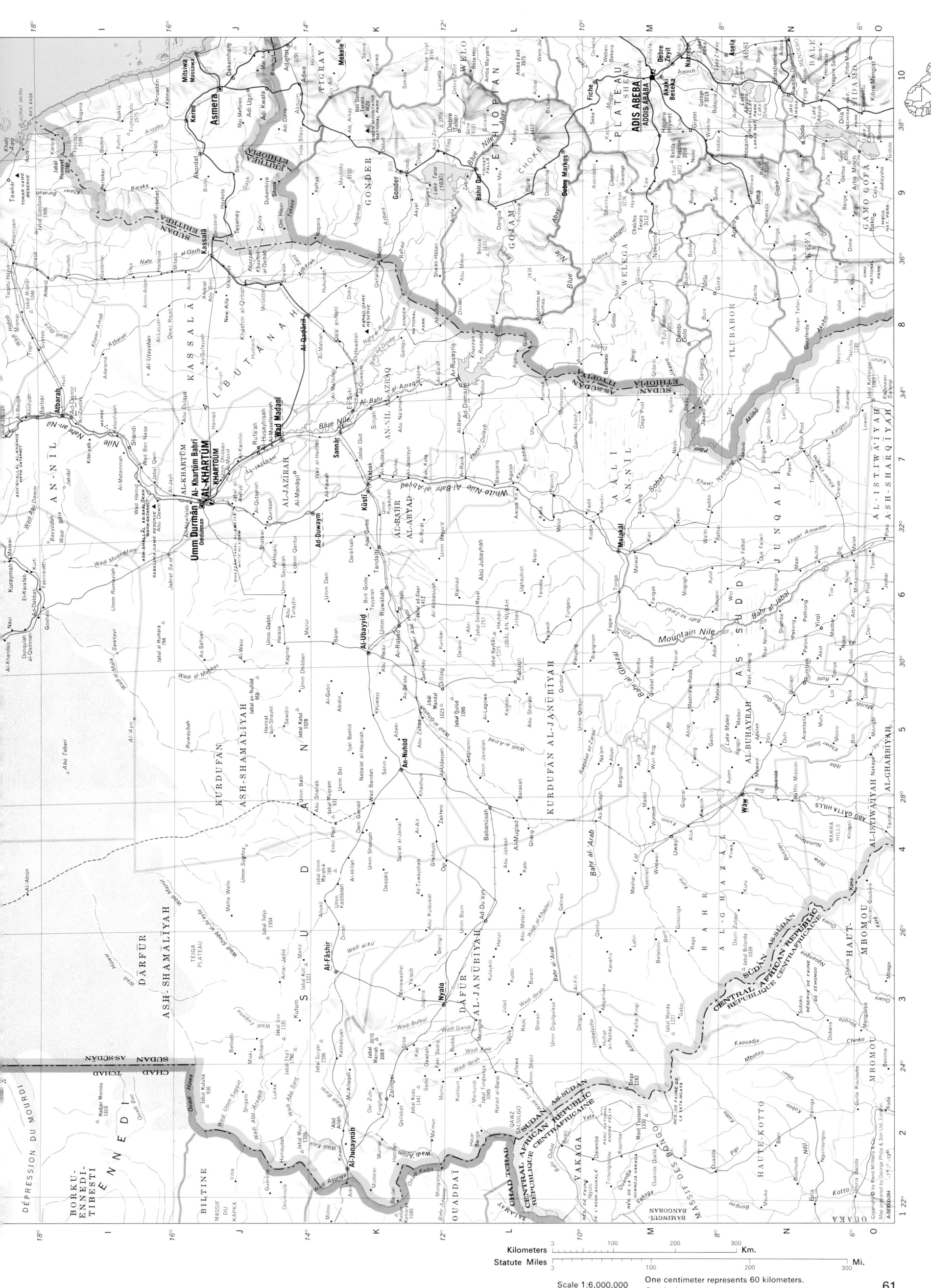

Kilometers 100 200 300 Km.

Statute Miles 100 200 300 Mi.

Scale 1:6,000,000   One centimeter represents 60 kilometers.
One inch represents approximately 95 miles.
Lambert Azimuthal Equal-Area Projection

61

Western Sahara has been
occupied by Morocco.

MEDITERRANEAN SEA
EL DJAZAÏR
ALGIERS
Annaba (Bône)
Skikda (Philippeville)
Qacentina (Constantine)
Bejaïa (Bougie)
Tizi-Ouzou
Sétif
Batna
Biskra
Wahran (Oran)
Mestghanem
Ech Cheliff (Orléansville)
Tihert
Sidi bel Abbès
Tilimsen
Oujda
Melilla (Sp.)
Tunis
Bizerte
Sousse
Sfax
Gafsa
Gabès
Golfe de Gabès
Golfe de Hammamet
Almería
Granada
Murcia
Cartagena
HAUTS PLATEAUX
ATLAS SAHARIEN
Chott Melrhir
Chott Jerid
Laghouat
Ghardaïa
Wargla
Touggourt
El Menia
Béchar
Hassi Messaoud
GRAND ERG OCCIDENTAL
GRAND ERG ORIENTAL
PLATEAU DU TINGHERT
HAMĀDAT TINGHERT
PLATEAU DU TADEMAÏT
SAHARA
TIDIKELT
In Salah
Adrar
Reggâne
TANEZROUFT
TASSILI
AHAGGAR
Tamenghest
Tahat 2908
Djebel Serkout
Ghadamis
Ghāt
ERG D'ADMER
Tropic of Cancer
TUNISIA / ALGERIA
ALGERIA / LIBYA
ALGERIA / MALI
ALGERIA / NIGER
TÉNÉRÉ DU TAFASSÂSSET
AGADEZ
GAO
Kilometers
Statute Miles
Km.
Mi.
Scale 1:6,000,000
One centimeter represents 60 kilometers.
One inch represents approximately 95 miles.
Lambert Azimuthal Equal-Area Projection

DAKHLET NOUADHIBOU
INCHIRI
ADRAR
PARC NATIONAL DU BANC D'ARGUIN
Nouâmghâr
ADÂFER EL ABIOD
TAGANT
HODH ECH CHARGUI
Nouakchott
TRARZA
BRAKNA
MALI
MAURITANIA
MAURITANIE
AOUÂNA
TOMBO
Boûmdeïd
Tidjikja
Aleg
Kiffa
EL 'AÇÂBA
HODH EL GHARBI
Néma
Oualâta
Sénégal
Saint-Louis
Louga
Thiès
DAKAR
Rufisque
Diourbel
DIOURBEL
LOUGA
FERLO
SAINT-LOUIS
GORGOL
GUIDIMAKA
KAOLACK
Kaolack
FATICK
Fatick
Mbour
TAMBACOUNDA
Tambacounda
Banjul (Bathurst)
CAPE SAINT MARY
GAMBIA
Gambia
KOLDA
Kolda
SENEGAL
SÉNÉGAL
Ziguinchor
GUINEA-BISSAU
GUINÉ-BISSAU
Bissau
ARQUIPÉLAGO DOS BIJAGÓS
Kayes
KAYES
KOULIKORO
Koulikoro
Bamako
Ségou
SÉGOU
Mopti
SIKASSO
Sikasso
Niger
Bani
Kita
MASSIF DU TAMGUÉ
FOUTA DJALON
Labé
Siguiri
Kankan
GUINEA
GUINÉE
Conakry
Kindia
Fria
Boké
SIERRA LEONE
Freetown
WESTERN AREA
NORTHERN
EASTERN
SOUTHERN
Makeni
Bo
Kenema
Koidu
LIBERIA
Monrovia
Buchanan
Greenville
Harper
CÔTE D'IVOIRE
Man
Daloa
Bouaké
Korhogo
Yamoussoukro
ABIDJAN
San Pédro
Gagnoa
Divo
ATLANTIC OCEAN
GRAIN COAST
IVORY COAST
BURKINA
Bobo Dioulasso
CAPE VERDE
CABO VERDE
SANTO ANTÃO
SÃO VICENTE
Mindelo
SÃO NICOLAU
SAL
BOA VISTA
MAIO
SANTIAGO
FOGO
BRAVA
Praia
ATLANTIC
OCEAN
Copyright © by Rand McNally & Co.
Map prepared by George Philip & Son Ltd., London.

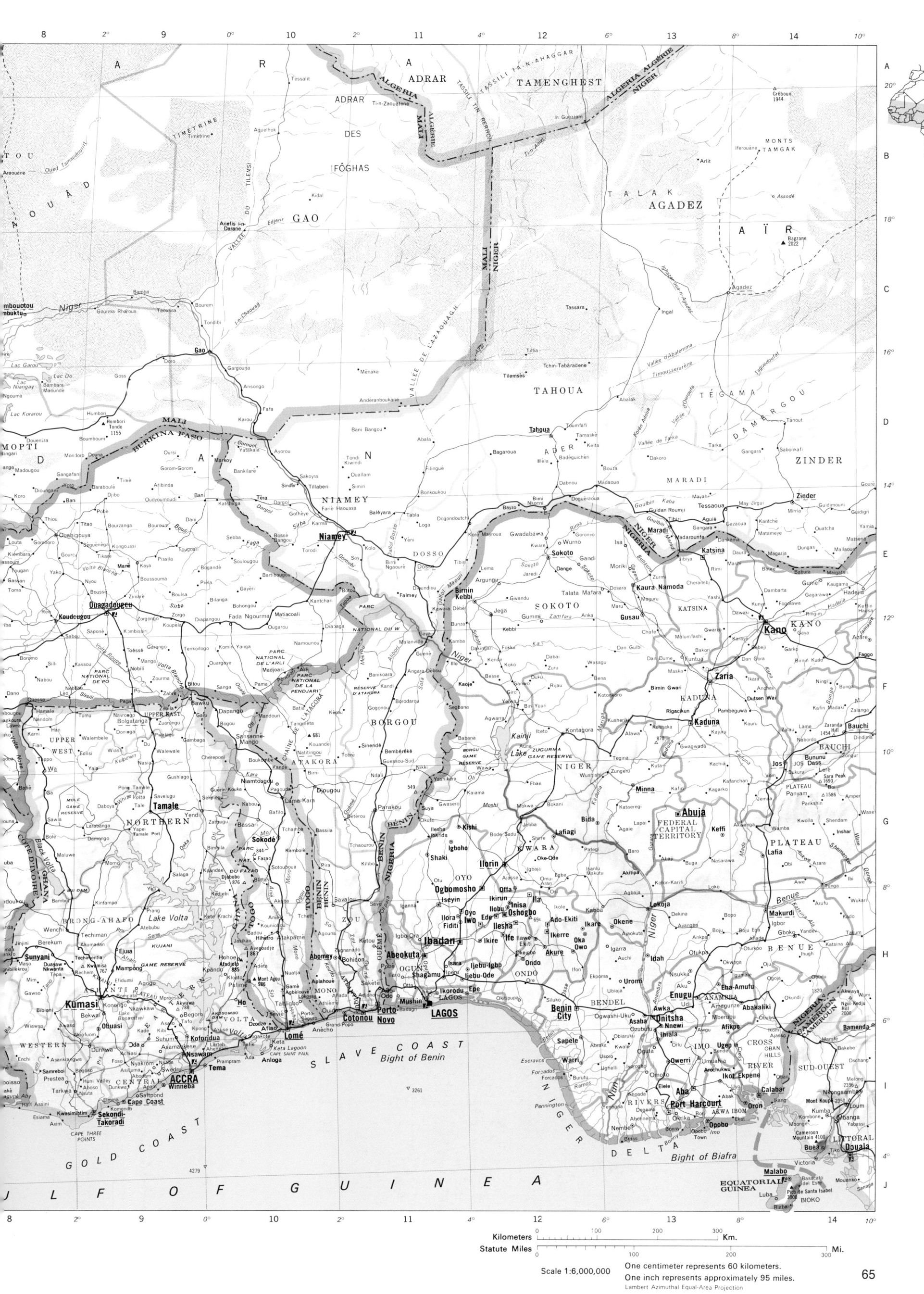

Kilometers

Statute Miles

Scale 1:6,000,000

One centimeter represents 60 kilometers.
One inch represents approximately 95 miles.

Lambert Azimuthal Equal-Area Projection

65

Southern Africa and Madagascar

Copyright © by Rand McNally & Co.
Map prepared by George Philip & Son Ltd., London.
A-589292-264

Kilometers
0   100   200   300   Km.

Statute Miles
0   100   200   300   Mi.

Scale 1:6,000,000
One centimeter represents 60 kilometers.
One inch represents approximately 95 miles.
Lambert Azimuthal Equal-Area Projection

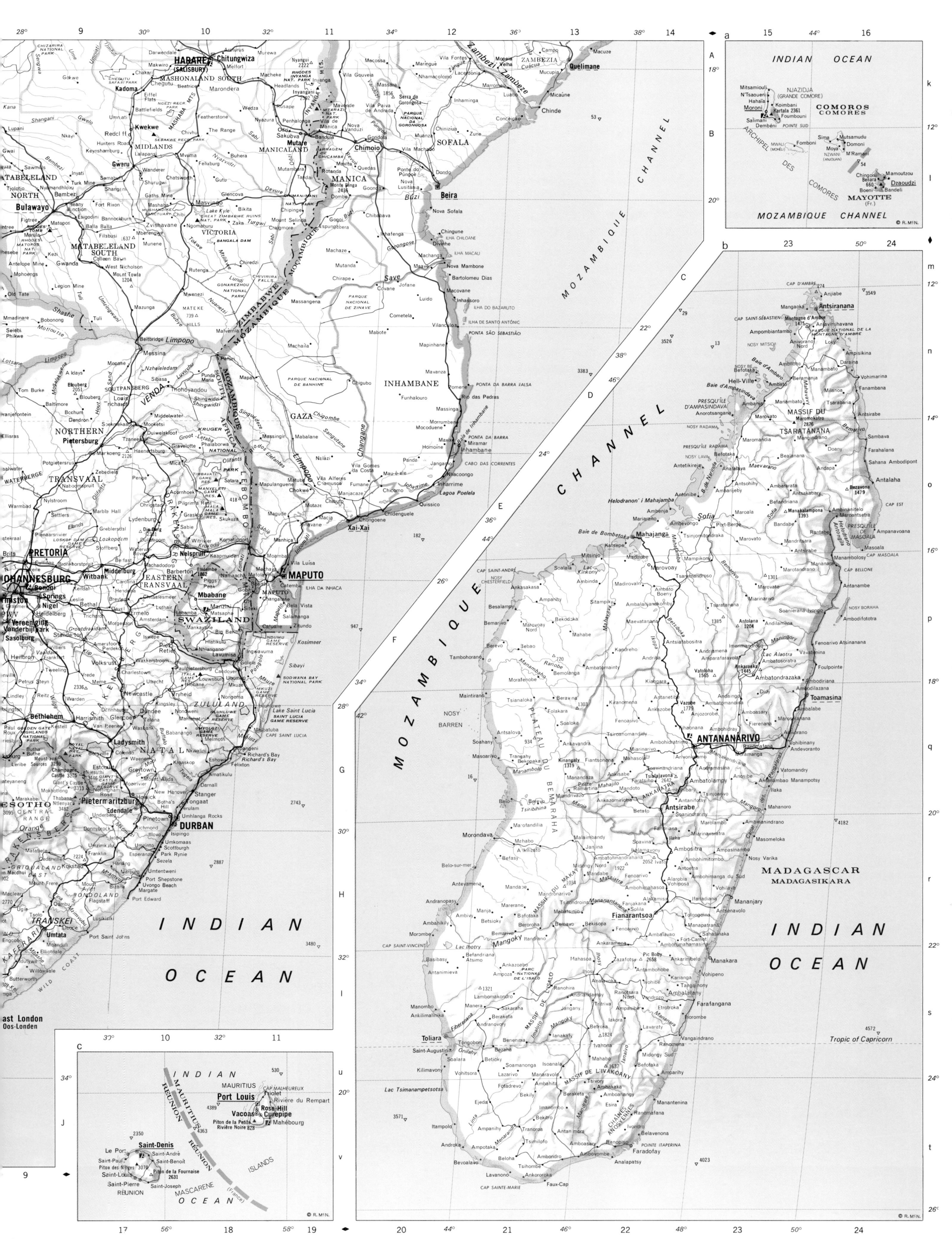

INDIAN OCEAN
MOZAMBIQUE CHANNEL
NJAZIDJA (GRANDE COMORE)
Moroni
COMOROS
COMORES
ARCHIPEL DES COMORES
MAYOTTE (Fr.)
Dzaoudzi
HARARE (SALISBURY)
Chitungwiza
MASHONALAND SOUTH
Kadoma
Kwekwe
MIDLANDS
Gweru
MATABELELAND NORTH
Bulawayo
MATABELELAND SOUTH
VICTORIA
Masvingo
MANICALAND
Mutare
ZAMBEZIA
Quelimane
SOFALA
Beira
Chimoio
MANICA
ZIMBABWE
MOZAMBIQUE
INHAMBANE
GAZA
Limpopo
Xai-Xai
MAPUTO
NORTHERN
Pietersburg
TRANSVAAL
PRETORIA
JOHANNESBURG
EASTERN TRANSVAAL
Mbabane
SWAZILAND
Nelspruit
ZULULAND
NATAL
Ladysmith
Pietermaritzburg
DURBAN
LESOTHO
TRANSKEI
Umtata
East London
Oos-Londen
Bethlehem
MADAGASCAR
MADAGASIKARA
Antsiranana
Mahajanga
Toamasina
ANTANANARIVO
Antsirabe
Fianarantsoa
Toliara
Tropic of Capricorn
MAURITIUS
Port Louis
Curepipe
Saint-Denis
RÉUNION
MASCARENE ISLANDS

PACIFIC OCEAN
Equator
PULAU WAIGEO
KEPULAUAN SCHOUTEN
Selat Dampier
Sorong
Manokwari
BIAK
SALAWATI
PULAU MISOOL
Teluk Berau
Teluk Cenderawasih
Jayapura (Sukarnapura)
SERAM
Fakfak
Bula
PEGUNUNGAN MAOKE
Puncak Jaya 5030m
Puncak Trikora 4750m
INDONESIA
PULAU ADI
KEPULAUAN KAI
KAI KECIL
Dobo
PULAU WOKAM
KEPULAUAN ARU
PULAU KOBROOR
PULAU YAMDENA
PULAU TRANGAN
KEPULAUAN TANIMBAR
PULAU SELARU
Arafura Sea
NEW GUINEA
PAPUA NEW GUINEA
Mt. Giluwe 4368m
Mt. Wilhelm 4509m
Aitape
Wewak
Sepik
Madang
Lae
Huon Gulf
Morobe
Gulf of Papua
Merauke
Digul
Fly
Strickland
Torres Strait
Port Moresby
Popondetta
OWEN STANLEY RANGE
Samarai
NINIGO GROUP
HERMIT ISLANDS
ADMIRALTY ISLANDS
MANUS ISLAND
MUSSAU ISLAND
EMIRAU ISLAND
NEW HANOVER
Kavieng
NEW IRELAND
BISMARCK ARCHIPELAGO
Namatanai
Rabaul
Kokopo
KARKAR ISLAND
WITU ISLANDS
UMBOI ISLAND
Talasea
NEW BRITAIN
KIRIWINA ISLANDS
WOODLARK ISLAND
D'ENTRECASTEAUX ISLANDS
Coral Sea
Gulf of Carpentaria
MELVILLE ISLAND
CROKER ISLAND
WESSEL ISLANDS
BATHURST ISLAND
Van Diemen Gulf
Darwin
AUSTRALIA
MOA ISLAND
CAPE YORK PEN.
GREAT BARRIER REEF
0 100 200 300 Km.
0 100 200 Mi.
A-592200-264-1-1-1-2
©1979 R.MSN.
Laut Sawu
Savu Sea
TIMOR
Kupang
Soe
PULAU ROTI
Timor Sea
HIBERNIA REEF
ASHMORE ISLANDS
CARTIER ISLANDS (Austl.)
BROWSE ISLAND
CAPE LONDONDERRY
Admiralty Gulf
Joseph Bonaparte Gulf
BONAPARTE ARCHIPELAGO
York Sound
Queens Channel
MELVILLE ISLAND
BATHURST ISLAND
CAPE CROKER
CROKER ISLAND
COBOURG PENINSULA
Van Diemen Gulf
Beagle Gulf
Clarence Strait
Darwin
Humpty Doo
Jabiru
POINT BLAZE
Rum Jungle
ARNHEM LAND
Pine Creek
Daly
Katherine
Victoria
Victoria River Downs
Daly Waters
Newcastle Waters
Lake Woods
Wave Hill
Wyndham
Ord
Kununurra
Lake Argyle
Drysdale
KIMBERLEY PLATEAU
DURACK RANGES
KING LEOPOLD RANGES
Mount Ord 937
ADÈLE ISLAND
BEAGLE REEF
BUCCANEER ARCHIPELAGO
Collier Bay
CAPE LEVEQUE
King Sound
Derby
Fitzroy
Fitzroy Crossing
Halls Creek
ROWLEY SHOALS
Broome
CAPE LATOUCHE TREVILLE
La Grange
EIGHTY MILE BEACH
NORTHERN TERRITORY
TANAMI DESERT
Lake Gregory
Lake White
Barrow Creek
INDIAN OCEAN
MONTE BELLO ISLANDS
DAMPIER ARCHIPELAGO
Port Hedland
Goldsworthy
Shay Gap
De Grey
Dampier
Karratha
Roebourne
Marble Bar
GREAT SANDY DESERT
Lake Wills
Lake Mackay
BARROW ISLAND
Nullagine
Lake Dora
Lake Auld
MUIRON ISLANDS
NORTH WEST CAPE
Exmouth
Exmouth Gulf
Onslow
Pannawonica
Fortescue
HAMERSLEY RANGE
Wittenoom
Mount Brockman 1132
Mount Bruce 1235
Tom Price
Mount Meharry 1251
Paraburdoo
Ashburton
Newman
Savory Cr.
Lake Disappointment
Mount Leisler 897
Mount Liebig 1524
Mount Zeil 1511
Alice Springs
MACDONNELL RANGES
Lake Macdonald
POINT CLOATES
WESTERN AUSTRALIA
GIBSON DESERT
Lake Neale
Lake Amadeus
Mount Olga 1069
Ayers Rock 867
Mount Cockburn 1138
CAPE CUVIER
Lake Macleod
Lyons
1105
Mount Augustus
906 Mount Essendon
Tropic of Capricorn
Geographe Channel
Carnarvon
BERNIER ISLAND
DORRE ISLAND
Shark Bay
Naturaliste Channel
DIRK HARTOG ISLAND
STEEP POINT
Denham
Gascoyne
Wooramel
ROBINSON RANGE
Peak Hill
Lake Carnegie
Lake Gillen
Mount Aloysius 1085
Mount Woodroffe 1440
Meekatharra
Wiluna
Lake Wells
Murchison
Nannine
Cue
Lake Austin
Sandstone
Kalbarri
Agnew
Mount Redcliffe 562
Yeo Lake
GREAT VICTORIA DESERT
Laverton
Leonora
Malcolm
Lake Carey
Lake Ballard
Lake Raeside
Lake Minigwal
Lake Maurice
Mount Magnet
Northampton
Mullewa
Yalgoo
Pindar
HOUTMAN ABROLHOS
Geraldton
Mongers Lake
Lake Barlee
Menzies
Maralinga
Ooldea
Dongara
Three Springs
Lake Moore
Forrest
Deakin
GREEN HEAD
Dalwallinu
Bonnie Rock
Kalgoorlie
Boulder
Zanthus
Rawlinna
Haig
NULLARBOR PLAIN
Moora
Bencubbin
Bullfinch
Lake Lefroy
Eucla
DARLING RANGE
Northam
Merredin
Kellerberrin
Southern Cross
Lake Cowan
CAPE ADIEU
SAINT PETER ISLAND
Streaky
Wanneroo
Perth
Fremantle
York
Beverley
Brookton
Hyden
Lake Johnston
Norseman
Lake Dundas
Eyre
Pinjarra
POINT CULVER
Narrogin
Newdegate
Wagin
Nyabing
Katanning
Gnowangerup
Ravensthorpe
Esperance
CAPE ARID
Great Australian Bight
INVESTIGATOR
Geographe Bay
CAPE NATURALISTE
Bunbury
Collie
Busselton
Bridgetown
Manjimup
Bluff Knoll 1096
Hopetoun
HOOD POINT
Esperance Bay
ARCHIPELAGO OF THE RECHERCHE
CAPE LEEUWIN
Augusta
Pemberton
Mount Barker
Albany
Denmark
CAPE VANCOUVER
POINT D'ENTRECASTEAUX
WEST CAPE HOWE
King George Sound
SOUTHERN OCEAN
Copyright © by Rand McNally & Co.
Map prepared by Esselte Map Service AB, Stockholm.
A-590200-264

Scale 1:12,000,000

One centimeter represents 120 kilometers.
One inch represents approximately 190 miles.

Lambert Conformal Conic Projection

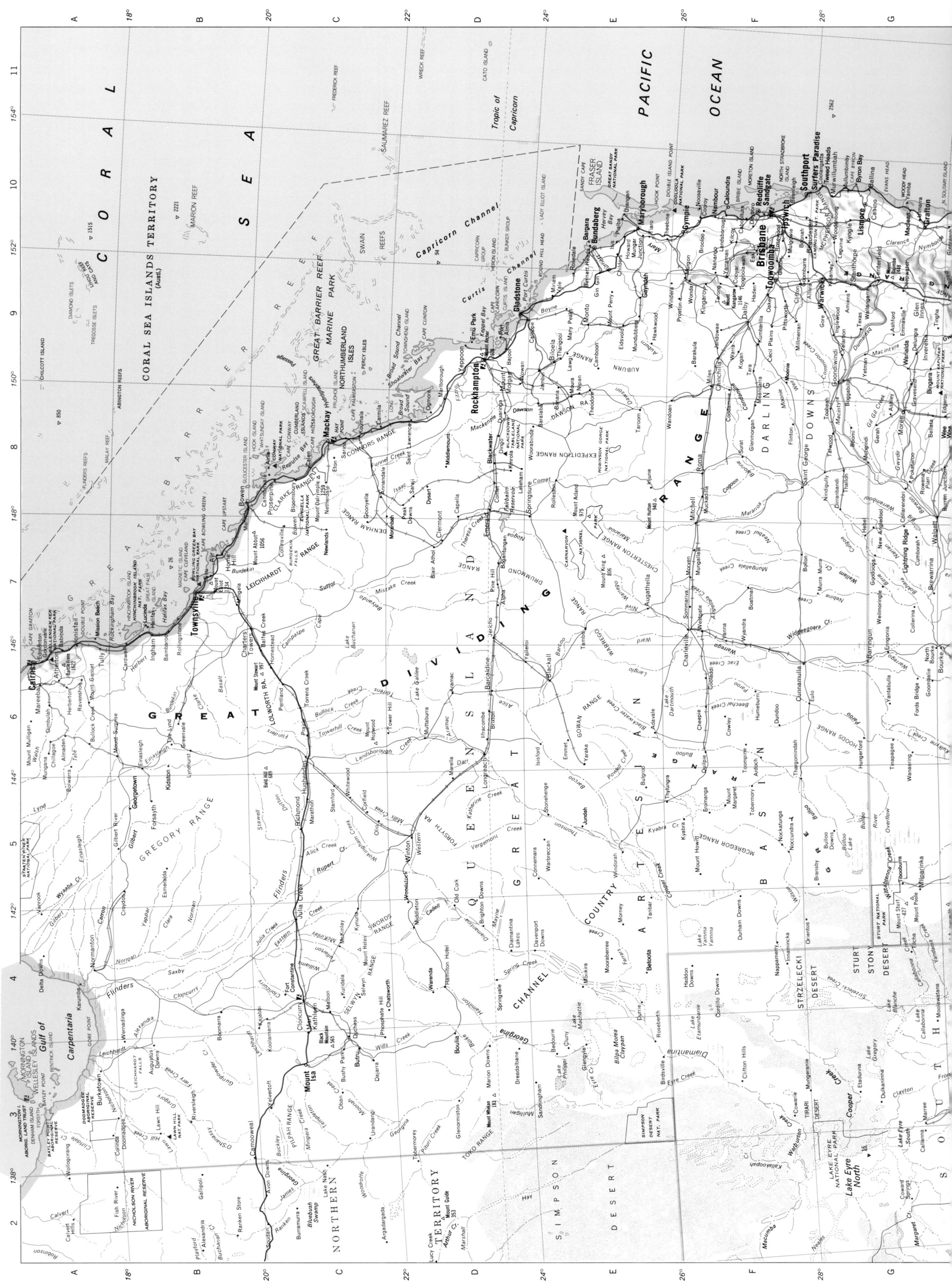
CORAL SEA
CORAL SEA ISLANDS TERRITORY (Austl.)
PACIFIC OCEAN
Tropic of Capricorn
Capricorn Channel
GREAT BARRIER REEF
GREAT BARRIER REEF MARINE PARK
Gulf of Carpentaria
QUEENSLAND
GREAT DIVIDING RANGE
GREAT ARTESIAN BASIN
NORTHERN TERRITORY
SIMPSON DESERT
STURT STONY DESERT
STRZELECKI DESERT
DARLING DOWNS
CHANNEL COUNTRY
GREGORY RANGE
Cairns
Townsville
Mackay
Rockhampton
Gladstone
Bundaberg
Maryborough
Brisbane
Toowoomba
Ipswich
Southport
Mount Isa
Cloncurry
Longreach
Charleville
Roma
Emerald
Winton
Camooweal

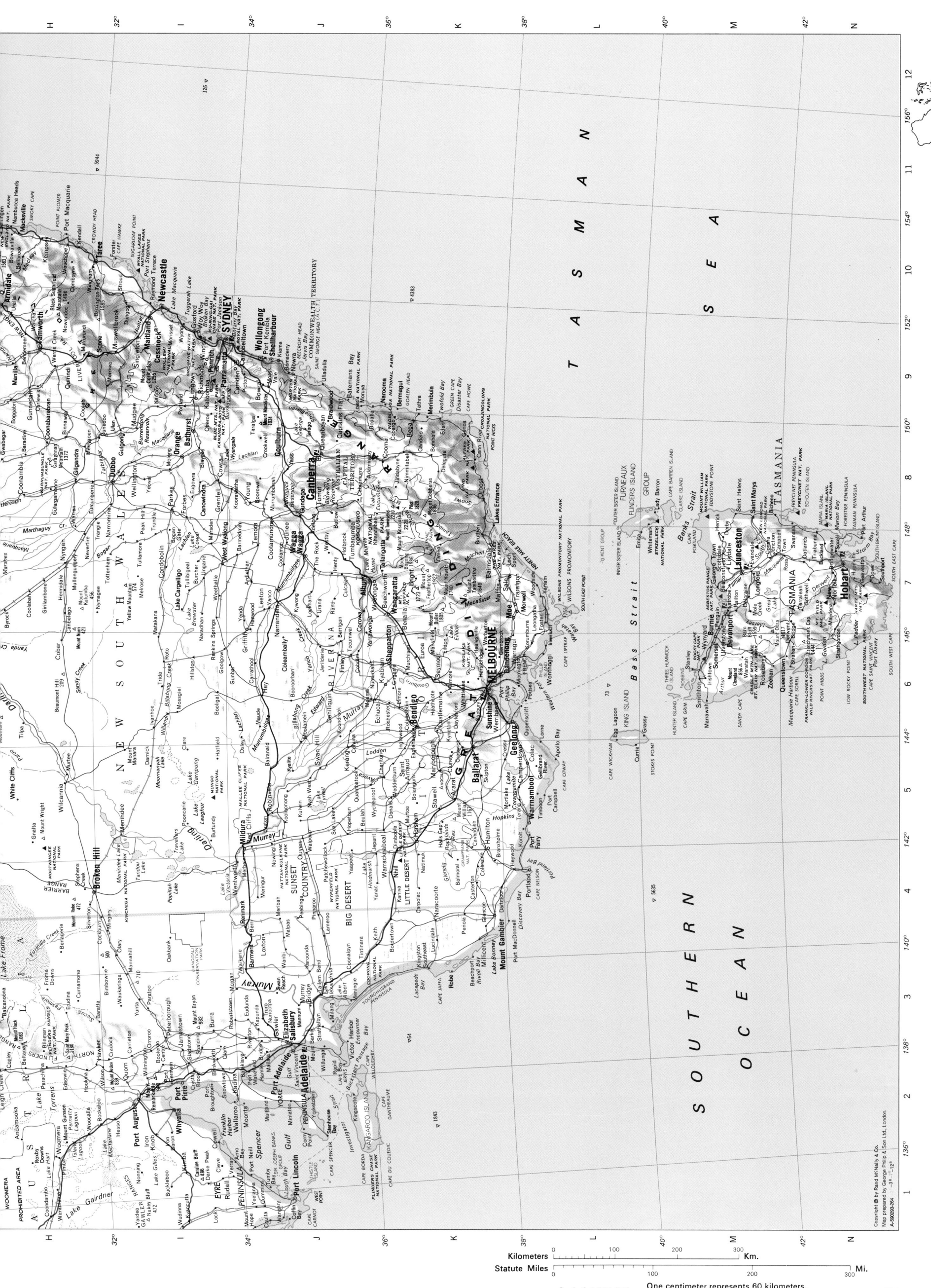

Kilometers
Statute Miles

Scale 1:6,000,000

One centimeter represents 60 kilometers.
One inch represents approximately 95 miles.

Lambert Conformal Conic Projection

71

New Zealand

Scale 1:6,000,000

One centimeter represents 60 kilometers.
One inch represents approximately 95 miles.
Lambert Conformal Conic Projection

Kilometers
Statute Miles

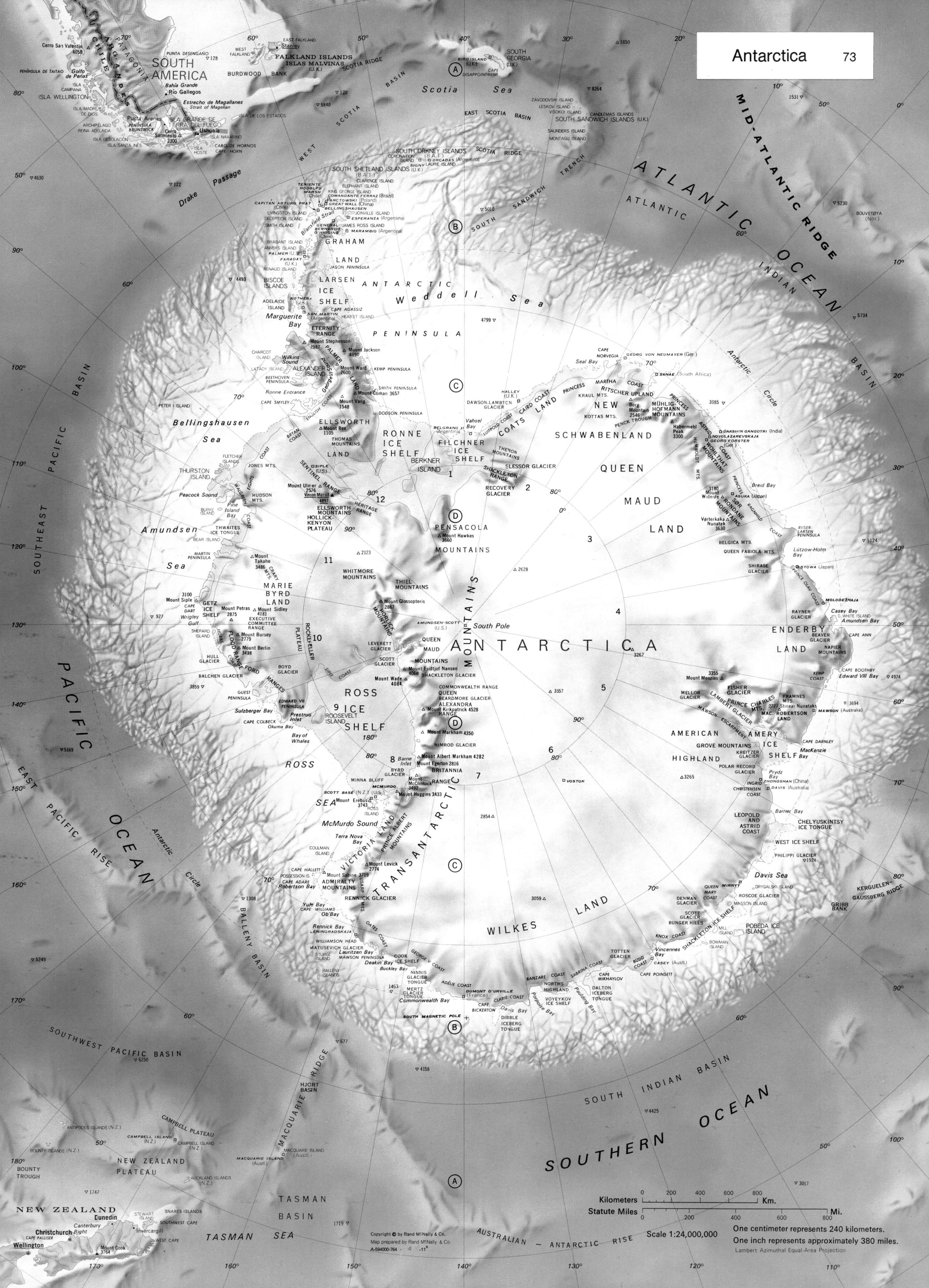

Scale 1:24,000,000

One centimeter represents 240 kilometers.
One inch represents approximately 380 miles.

Lambert Azimuthal Equal-Area Projection

Copyright by Rand McNally & Co.
Map prepared by Rand McNally & Co.
A-694000-764   -11"

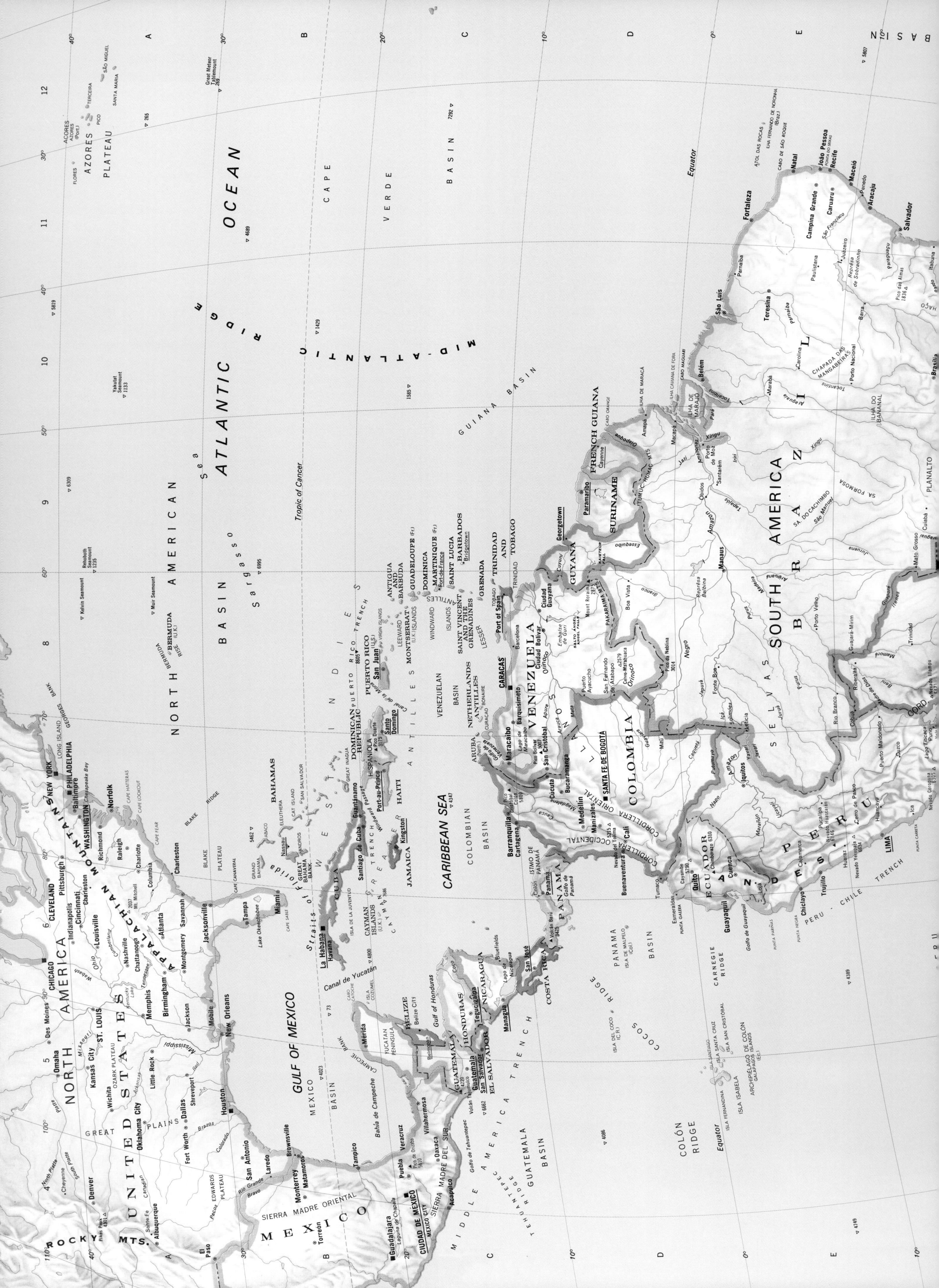

NORTH AMERICA
UNITED STATES
ROCKY MTS.
APPALACHIAN MOUNTAINS
GREAT PLAINS
MEXICO
SIERRA MADRE ORIENTAL
SIERRA MADRE DEL SUR
GULF OF MEXICO
CARIBBEAN SEA
ATLANTIC OCEAN
NORTH AMERICAN BASIN
Sargasso Sea
MID-ATLANTIC RIDGE
Tropic of Cancer
Equator
BAHAMAS
CUBA
JAMAICA
HAITI
DOMINICAN REPUBLIC
PUERTO RICO
WEST INDIES
GREATER ANTILLES
LESSER ANTILLES
BELIZE
GUATEMALA
HONDURAS
EL SALVADOR
NICARAGUA
COSTA RICA
PANAMA
VENEZUELA
COLOMBIA
ECUADOR
PERU
GUYANA
SURINAME
FRENCH GUIANA
SOUTH AMERICA
BRAZIL
ANDES
CHICAGO
NEW YORK
PHILADELPHIA
WASHINGTON
CIUDAD DE MÉXICO
LA HABANA
CARACAS
SANTA FE DE BOGOTÁ
LIMA
Quito
AZORES PLATEAU
CAPE VERDE BASIN
GUIANA BASIN
COLOMBIAN BASIN
VENEZUELAN BASIN
GUATEMALA BASIN
PANAMA BASIN
MIDDLE AMERICA TRENCH
PERU-CHILE TRENCH
COCOS RIDGE
CARNEGIE RIDGE
COLÓN RIDGE
ARCHIPIÉLAGO DE COLÓN

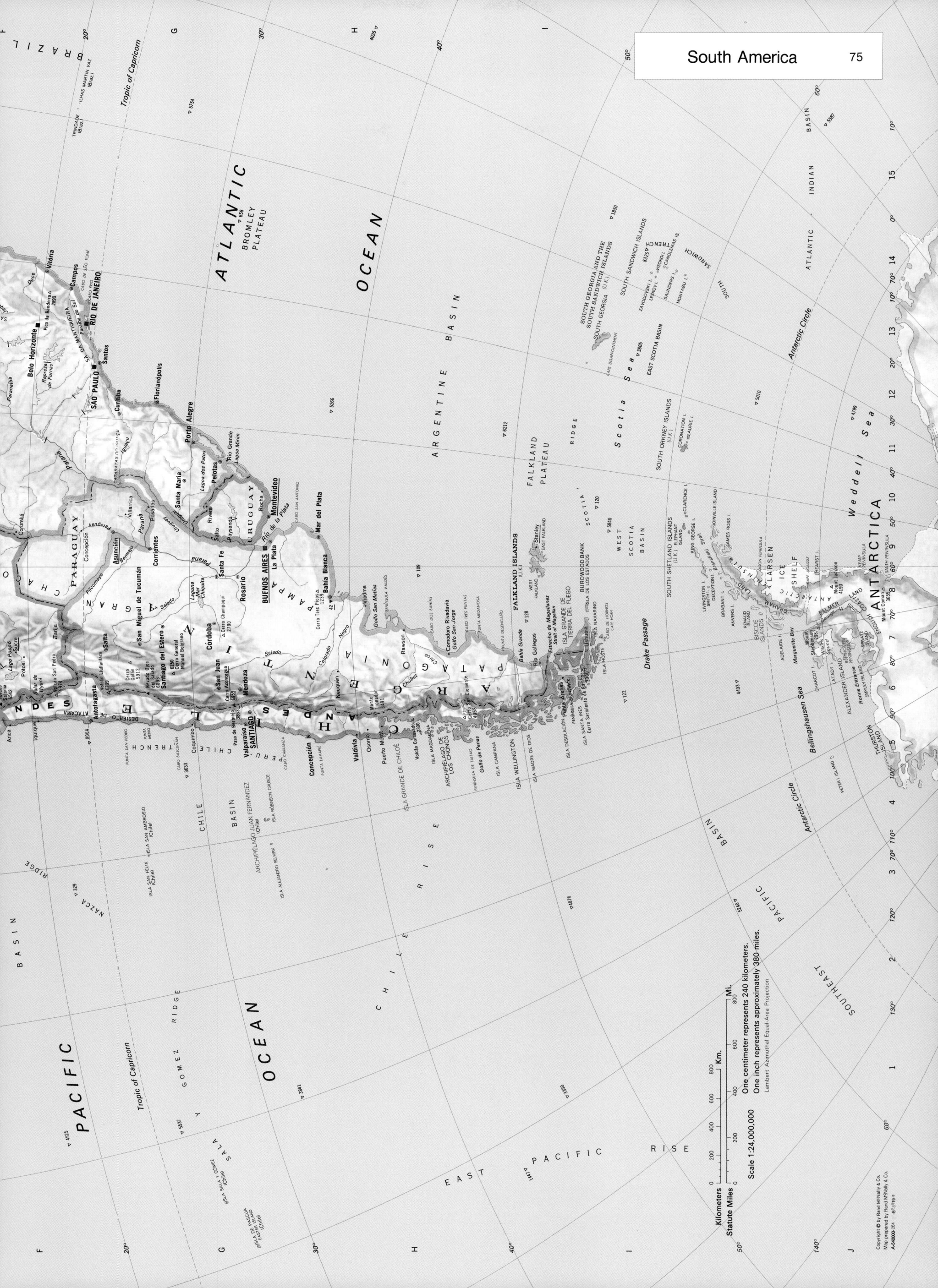
PACIFIC
OCEAN
ATLANTIC
OCEAN
BROMLEY PLATEAU
ARGENTINE BASIN
FALKLAND PLATEAU
FALKLAND ISLANDS (U.K.)
SOUTH GEORGIA AND THE SOUTH SANDWICH ISLANDS
SOUTH GEORGIA (U.K.)
SOUTH SANDWICH ISLANDS
SOUTH SANDWICH TRENCH
EAST SCOTIA BASIN
Scotia Sea
WEST SCOTIA BASIN
SOUTH ORKNEY ISLANDS (U.K.)
SOUTH SHETLAND ISLANDS (U.K.)
Drake Passage
BURDWOOD BANK
ISLA GRANDE DE TIERRA DEL FUEGO
Estrecho de Magallanes
Strait of Magellan
Weddell Sea
ANTARCTICA
LARSEN ICE SHELF
Bellingshausen Sea
ALEXANDER ISLAND
THURSTON ISLAND
PETER I ISLAND
Antarctic Circle
ATLANTIC - INDIAN BASIN
SOUTHEAST PACIFIC BASIN
CHILE BASIN
CHILE RISE
EAST PACIFIC RISE
NAZCA RIDGE
SALA Y GOMEZ RIDGE
Tropic of Capricorn
BRAZIL
PARAGUAY
URUGUAY
CHACO
PAMPAS
PATAGONIA
ANDES
Belo Horizonte
Vitória
Campos
RIO DE JANEIRO
SÃO PAULO
Santos
Curitiba
Florianópolis
Porto Alegre
Pelotas
Montevideo
BUENOS AIRES
La Plata
Mar del Plata
Bahía Blanca
Rosario
Santa Fe
Córdoba
Corrientes
Asunción
San Miguel de Tucumán
Santiago del Estero
Salta
Mendoza
San Juan
SANTIAGO
Valparaíso
Concepción
Valdivia
Puerto Montt
Comodoro Rivadavia
Río Gallegos
Ushuaia
Stanley
Antofagasta
Arica
Iquique
ARCHIPIÉLAGO JUAN FERNÁNDEZ (Chile)
ISLA DE PASCUA (EASTER ISLAND) (Chile)
Kilometers 0 200 400 600 800 Km.
Statute Miles 0 200 400 600 800 Mi.
Scale 1:24,000,000
One centimeter represents 240 kilometers.
One inch represents approximately 380 miles.
Lambert Azimuthal Equal-Area Projection
Copyright © by Rand McNally & Co.
Map prepared by Rand McNally & Co.

Copyright © by Rand McNally & Co.
Map prepared by Esselte Map Service AB, Stockholm.
A-549100-264

Kilometers
Statute Miles

Scale 1:12,000,000

One centimeter represents 120 kilometers.
One inch represents approximately 190 miles.
Oblique Conic Conformal Projection

ATLANTIC OCEAN
Equator
Tropic of Capricorn
BRAZIL
SURINAME
FRENCH GUIANA
GUYANA
AMAPÁ
PARÁ
MARANHÃO
PIAUÍ
CEARÁ
RIO GRANDE DO NORTE
PARAÍBA
PERNAMBUCO
ALAGOAS
SERGIPE
BAHIA
TOCANTINS
GOIÁS
MATO GROSSO
MATO GROSSO DO SUL
MINAS GERAIS
ESPÍRITO SANTO
RIO DE JANEIRO
SÃO PAULO
D.F.
PLANALTO CENTRAL
PLANALTO DO MATO GROSSO
TUMUC-HUMAC MTS.
ACARAÍ MTS.
SERRA DOS CARAJÁS
SERRA DO CACHIMBO
SERRA DO RONCADOR
SERRA DO ESPINHAÇO
SERRA DA MANTIQUEIRA
SERRA DO CAIAPÓ
CHAPADA DAS MANGABEIRAS
ILHA DE MARAJÓ
ILHA DO BANANAL
ILHA FERNANDO DE NORONHA (Brazil)
ATOL DAS ROCAS
CABO ORANGE
CABO MAGUARI
CABO DE SÃO ROQUE
PONTA DO SEIXAS
CABO DE SÃO TOMÉ
CABO FRIO
Amazon
Amazonas
Tocantins
Araguaia
Xingu
Tapajós
São Francisco
Represa de Tucuruí
Represa de Sobradinho
Represa Boa Esperança
Represa de Três Marias
Paramaribo
Cayenne
Georgetown
Macapá
Belém
São Luís
Fortaleza
Teresina
Natal
João Pessoa
Recife
Maceió
Aracaju
Salvador
Palmas
BRASÍLIA
Goiânia
Anápolis
Cuiabá
Campo Grande
Belo Horizonte
Vitória
RIO DE JANEIRO
SÃO PAULO
Santarém
Marabá
Imperatriz
Juazeiro
Petrolina
Campina Grande
Feira de Santana
Ilhéus
Vitória da Conquista
Montes Claros
Uberlândia
Uberaba
Ribeirão Preto
Campinas
Santos
Juiz de Fora
Niterói
Corumbá
Rondonópolis
Presidente Prudente
△ Pico das Almas 1836
▲ Juliana Top 1230

Southern South America

Kilometers

Statute Miles

Scale 1:12,000,000

One centimeter represents 120 kilometers.
One inch represents approximately 190 miles.
Oblique Conic Conformal Projection

Copyright © by Rand McNally & Co.
Map prepared by Esselte Map Service AB, Stockholm.
A-549200-264

ATLANTIC

OCEAN

Kilometers
Statute Miles

Scale 1:6,000,000

One centimeter represents 60 kilometers.
One inch represents approximately 95 miles.

Oblique Conic Conformal Projection

79

PACIFIC
OCEAN
Tropic of Capricorn
Antofagasta
Calama
Chuquicamata
Tocopilla
Copiapó
La Serena
Coquimbo
Ovalle
Viña del Mar
Valparaíso
SANTIAGO
Rancagua
Curicó
Talca
Linares
Chillán
Concepción
Talcahuano
Los Angeles
Temuco
San Miguel de Tucumán
Salta
San Salvador de Jujuy
Santiago del Estero
La Rioja
San Juan
Mendoza
San Luis
Córdoba
Río Cuarto
Villa María
Santa Rosa
Bahía Blanca
Neuquén
Cipolletti
General Roca
Rosario
Punta Alta
A N D E S
PUNA DE ATACAMA
DESIERTO DE ATACAMA
LA PAMPA
GRAN CHACO
JUJUY
SALTA
TUCUMÁN
CATAMARCA
LA RIOJA
SAN JUAN
MENDOZA
SAN LUIS
CÓRDOBA
SANTA FE
BUENOS
NEUQUÉN
RÍO NEGRO
POTOSÍ
TARIJA
BOQUERÓN
BOLIVIA
CHILE
ARGENTINA
Copyright © by Rand McNally & Co.
Map prepared by Rand McNally & Co.
A-540191-264

Kilometers

Statute Miles

Scale 1:6,000,000

One centimeter represents 60 kilometers.
One inch represents approximately 95 miles.
Oblique Conic Conformal Projection

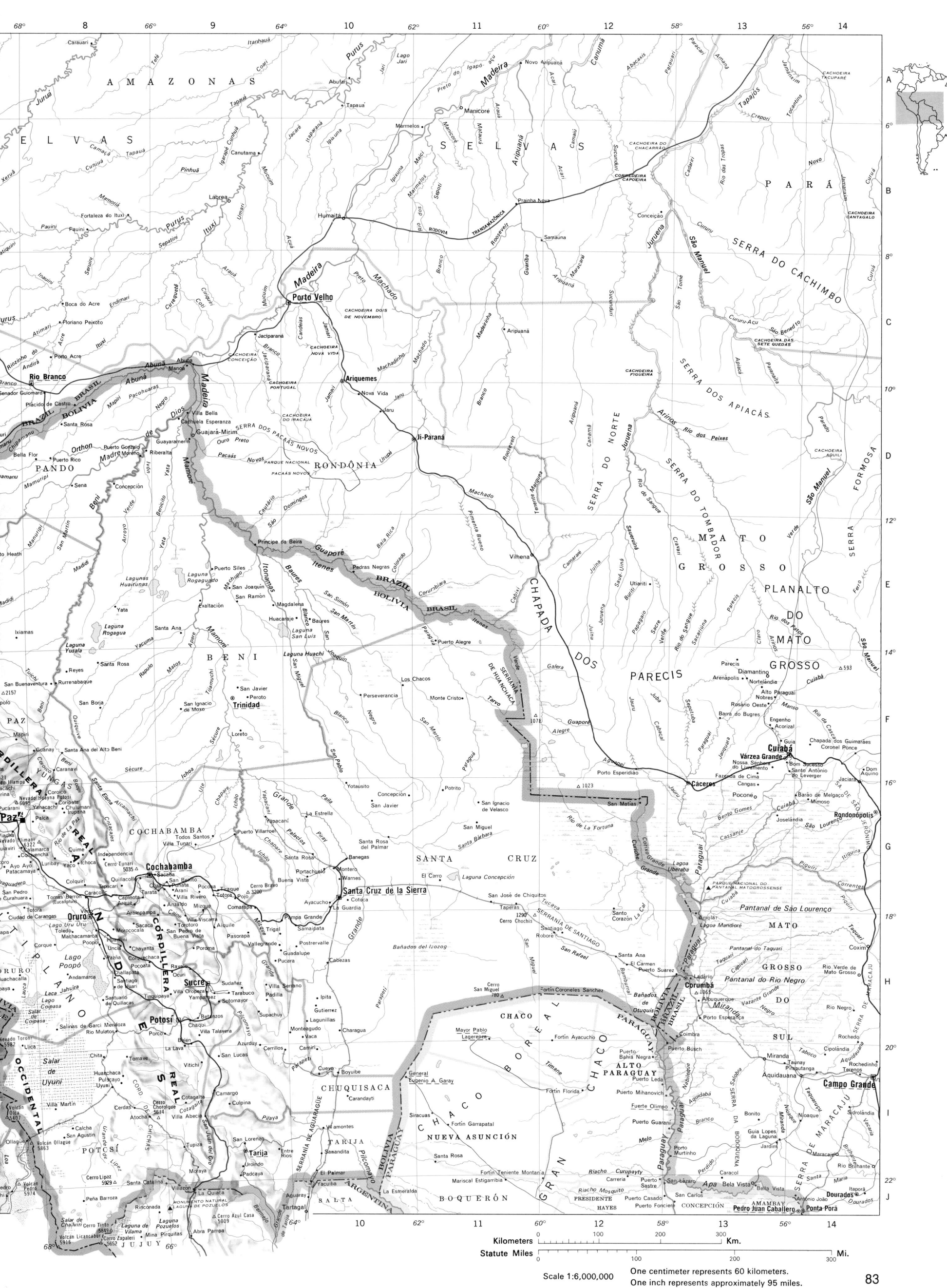

Kilometers

Statute Miles

Scale 1:6,000,000

One centimeter represents 60 kilometers.
One inch represents approximately 95 miles.
Oblique Conic Conformal Projection

CARIBBEAN SEA
PACIFIC OCEAN
NICARAGUA
ARUBA (Neth.)
Oranjestad
SAN ANDRÉS Y PROVIDENCIA (Col.)
Puerto Limón
Colón
Panamá
ISTMO DE PANAMÁ
Golfo de los Mosquitos
Golfo de Chiriquí
Golfo de Panamá
David
Santiago
Chitré
ISLA DE COIBA
PENÍNSULA DE AZUERO
ARCH. DE LAS PERLAS
Golfo de Urabá
Riohacha
Santa Marta
Barranquilla
Ciénaga
Cartagena
Valledupar
Maracaibo
Lago de Maracaibo
Cabimas
Ciudad Ojeda
Carora
Golfo de Venezuela
PENÍNSULA DE LA GUAJIRA
LA GUAJIRA
ZULIA
Sincelejo
Montería
Magangué
CÓRDOBA
SUCRE
BOLÍVAR
MAGDALENA
CESAR
ATLÁNTICO
Mérida
Barinas
BARINAS
San Cristóbal
Cúcuta
Pamplona
Ocaña
NORTE DE SANTANDER
SANTANDER
Bucaramanga
Floridablanca
Barrancabermeja
ANTIOQUIA
Medellín
Quibdó
CHOCÓ
ARAUCA
CASANARE
BOYACÁ
Tunja
Sogamoso
Duitama
CUNDINAMARCA
SANTA FE DE BOGOTÁ
Manizales
Pereira
Armenia
Ibagué
Girardot
Villavicencio
META
Buenaventura
VALLE DEL CAUCA
Cali
Palmira
Tuluá
Buga
TOLIMA
CAUCA
Popayán
Neiva
HUILA
Florencia
CAQUETÁ
GUAVIARE
VAUPÉS
Pasto
NARIÑO
Tumaco
Ipiales
PUTUMAYO
AMAZONAS
Leticia
Esmeraldas
ESMERALDAS
CARCHI
IMBABURA
Ibarra
Quito
PICHINCHA
SUCUMBÍOS
NAPO
MANABÍ
Manta
Portoviejo
Santo Domingo de los Colorados
Quevedo
Latacunga
Ambato
Riobamba
Babahoyo
GUAYAS
Guayaquil
Milagro
Golfo de Guayaquil
ISLA PUNÁ
Cuenca
AZUAY
CAÑAR
MORONA-SANTIAGO
PASTAZA
Machala
EL ORO
Loja
LOJA
ZAMORA-CHINCHIPE
Tumbes
Talara
Sullana
PIURA
LORETO
Iquitos
COLOMBIA
ECUADOR
PERU
BRAZIL
Amazon
Putumayo
Caquetá
Napo
Marañón
Magdalena
Cauca
Meta
Equator
PACIFIC OCEAN
ARCHIPIÉLAGO DE COLÓN
GALAPAGOS ISLANDS
ISLA ISABELA
ISLA FERNANDINA
ISLA SANTIAGO
ISLA SANTA CRUZ
ISLA SAN CRISTÓBAL
GALÁPAGOS (Ec.)
Puerto Ayora
Puerto Baquerizo Moreno
ISLA SANTA MARÍA
ISLA ESPAÑOLA
ISLA MARCHENA
ISLA GENOVESA
ISLA PINTA
ISLA DARWIN
ISLA WOLF

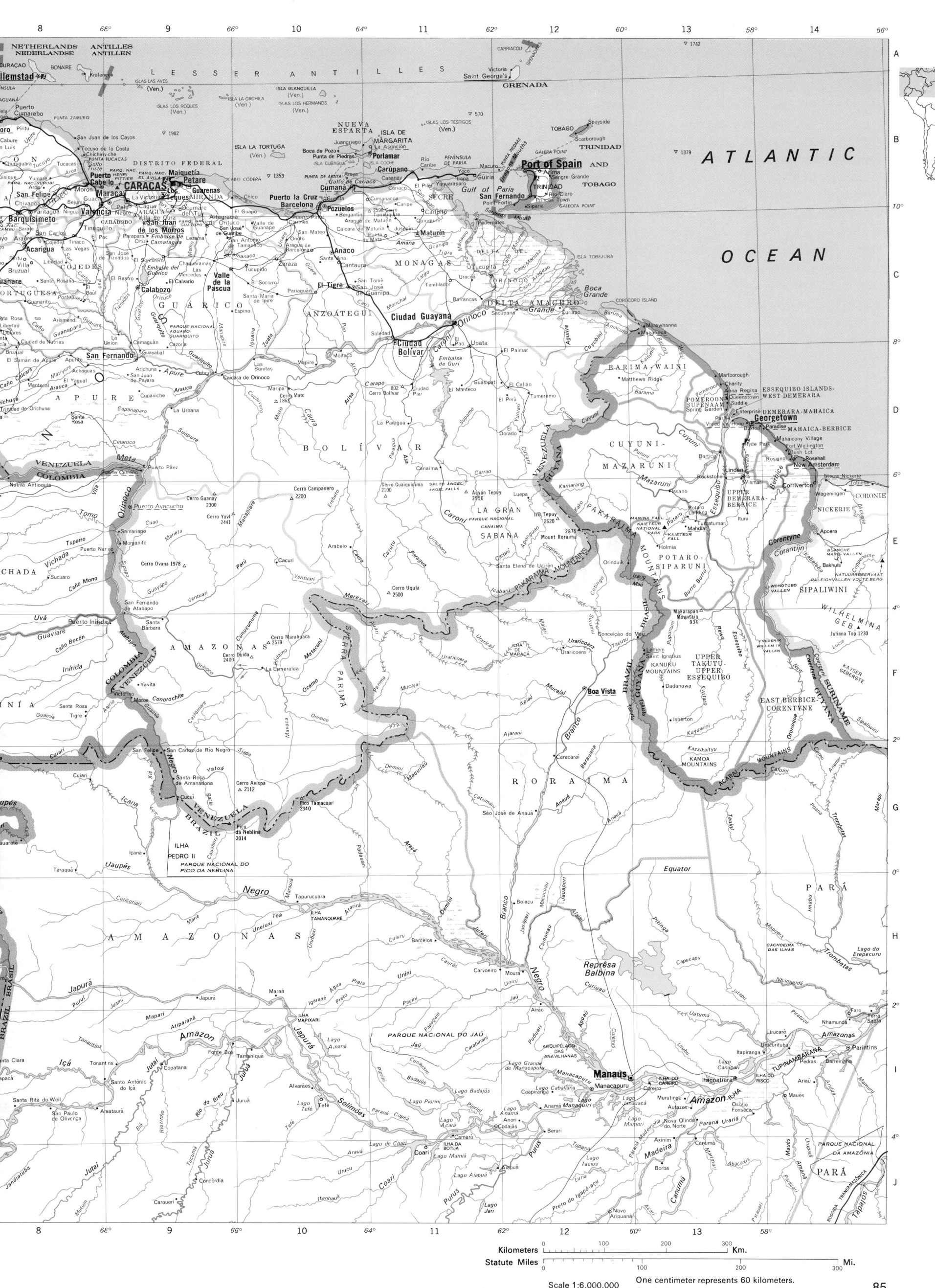

Kilometers 0 100 200 300 Km.
Statute Miles 0 100 200 300 Mi.

Scale 1:6,000,000
One centimeter represents 60 kilometers.
One inch represents approximately 95 miles.
Oblique Conic Conformal Projection

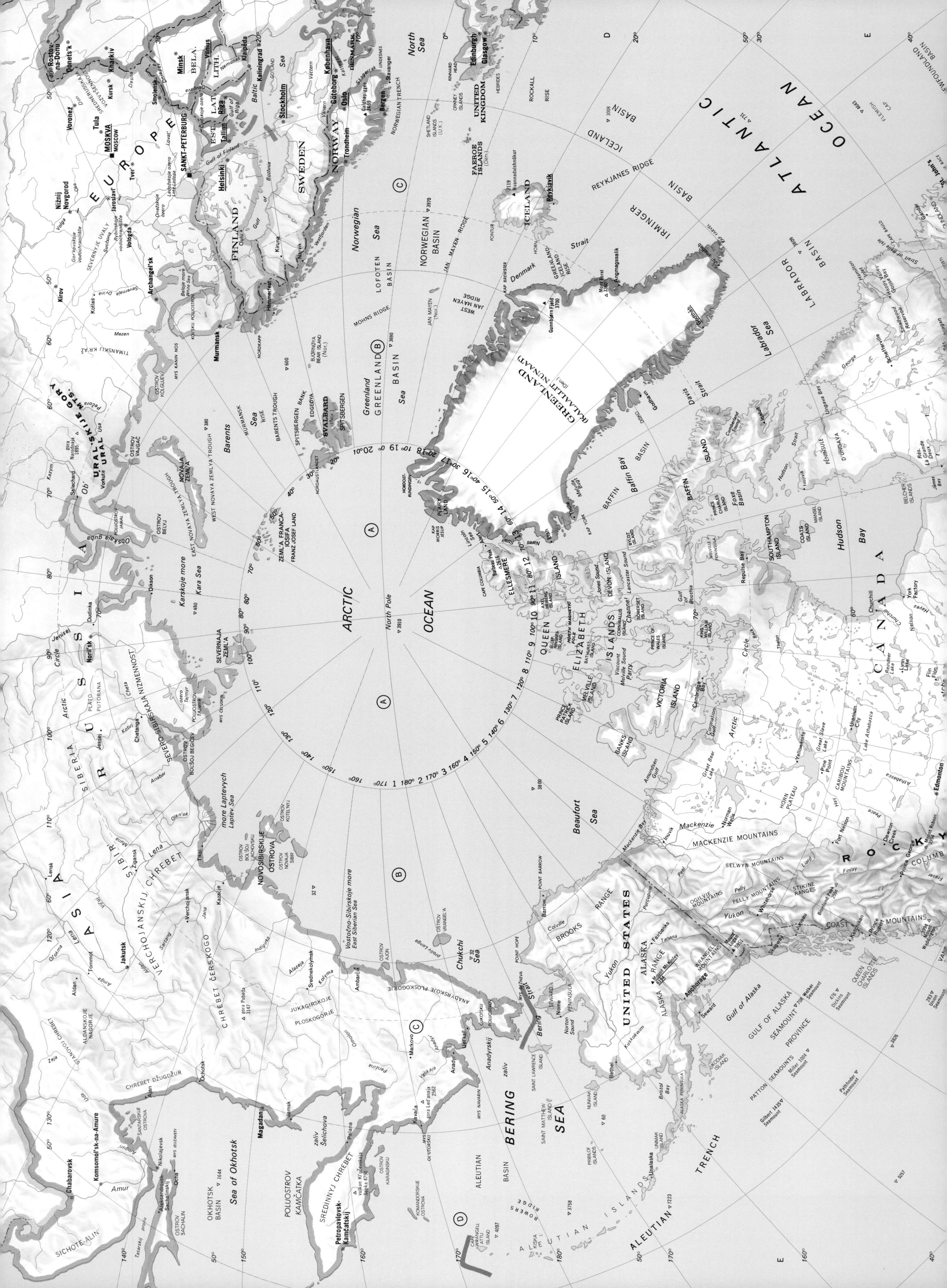

ARCTIC
OCEAN
North Pole
ATLANTIC
OCEAN
EUROPE
ASIA
RUSSIA
CANADA
UNITED STATES
GREENLAND
(KALAALLIT NUNAAT)
ICELAND
NORWAY
SWEDEN
FINLAND
UNITED KINGDOM
Norwegian Sea
Greenland Sea
Barents Sea
Karskoje more
Kara Sea
more Laptevych
Laptev Sea
Vostočno-Sibirskoje more
East Siberian Sea
Chukchi Sea
Beaufort Sea
BERING SEA
Sea of Okhotsk
Gulf of Alaska
Hudson Bay
Baffin Bay
Labrador Sea
Davis Strait
Denmark Strait
North Sea
ALEUTIAN ISLANDS
ALEUTIAN TRENCH
SVALBARD
SPITSBERGEN
ZEML'A FRANCA-IOSIFA
FRANZ JOSEF LAND
NOVAJA ZEML'A
SEVERNAJA ZEML'A
NOVOSIBIRSKIJE OSTROVA
ELLESMERE ISLAND
QUEEN ELIZABETH ISLANDS
VICTORIA ISLAND
BANKS ISLAND
BAFFIN ISLAND
SOUTHAMPTON ISLAND
MACKENZIE MOUNTAINS
BROOKS RANGE
ALASKA RANGE
ROCKY
URAL'SKIJE GORY
URAL MTS.
SIBIR'
SIBERIA
MOSKVA
MOSCOW
SANKT-PETERBURG
Murmansk
Archangel'sk
Noril'sk
Jakutsk
Magadan
Petropavlovsk-Kamčatskij
Anchorage
Fairbanks
Reykjavík
Helsinki
Stockholm
Oslo
København
Edmonton
Churchill

Scale 1:24,000,000

One centimeter represents 240 kilometers.
One inch represents approximately 380 miles.

Lambert Azimuthal Equal-Area Projection

Copyright © by Rand McNally & Co.

UNITED STATES
MEXICO
GULF OF MEXICO
PACIFIC OCEAN
SIERRA MADRE OCCIDENTAL
SIERRA MADRE ORIENTAL
SIERRA MADRE DEL SUR
Golfo de California
BAJA CALIFORNIA
Tropic of Cancer
Bahía de Campeche
Golfo de Tehuantepec
YUCATAN PENINSULA
BELIZE
GUATEMALA
EL SALVADOR
ISLAS REVILLAGIGEDO
ÎLE CLIPPERTON (Fr.)
CIUDAD DE MÉXICO
MEXICO CITY
Guadalajara
Monterrey
Puebla
León
San Luis Potosí
Aguascalientes
Chihuahua
Hermosillo
Culiacán
Mazatlán
Torreón
Durango
Tampico
Veracruz
Acapulco
Oaxaca
Mérida
Campeche
Tijuana
Mexicali
Ciudad Juárez
El Paso
San Diego
Phoenix
Tucson
Albuquerque
Amarillo
Lubbock
Oklahoma City
Tulsa
Dallas
Fort Worth
Houston
San Antonio
Austin
Corpus Christi
Brownsville
New Orleans
Baton Rouge
Memphis
Little Rock
Jackson
Shreveport
Belize City
Guatemala
San Salvador
Tegucigalpa
Copyright © by Rand McNally & Co.
Map prepared by Esselte Map Service AB, Stockholm.

Kilometers |0 200 400 600 Km.

Statute Miles |0 200 400 600 Mi.

Scale 1:12,000,000
One centimeter represents 120 kilometers.
One inch represents approximately 190 miles.
Oblique Conic Conformal Projection

89

Mexico

PACIFIC

OCEAN

Kilometers

Statute Miles

Scale 1:6,000,000

One centimeter represents 60 kilometers.
One inch represents approximately 95 miles.

Lambert Conformal Conic Projection

GULF
OF
MEXICO
Bahía de Campeche
Golfo de Tehuantepec
Gulf of Honduras
Tropic of Cancer
TEXAS
LOUISIANA
MISSISSIPPI
ALABAMA
EDWARDS PLATEAU
UNITED STATES
MEXICO
GUATEMALA
BELIZE
HONDURAS
YUCATAN PENINSULA
YUCATÁN
CAMPECHE
QUINTANA ROO
TABASCO
CHIAPAS
OAXACA
VERACRUZ
PUEBLA
TAMAULIPAS
NUEVO LEÓN
SAN LUIS POTOSÍ
QUERÉTARO
HIDALGO
MÉXICO
MORELOS
GUERRERO
MICHOACÁN
GUANAJUATO
SIERRA MADRE ORIENTAL
SIERRA MADRE DEL SUR
SIERRA MADRE DE CHIAPAS
ISTMO DE TEHUANTEPEC
MAYA MOUNTAINS
Fort Worth
Dallas
Arlington
Abilene
Longview
Shreveport
Jackson
Meridian
Monroe
Tyler
Waco
San Angelo
Killeen
Temple
Bryan
College Station
Austin
Houston
Galveston
Beaumont
Port Arthur
Lake Charles
Lafayette
Baton Rouge
New Orleans
Mobile
Hattiesburg
Gulfport
Biloxi
Alexandria
San Antonio
Corpus Christi
Laredo
Nuevo Laredo
Brownsville
Matamoros
Reynosa
McAllen
Harlingen
Monterrey
Saltillo
Ciudad Victoria
Tampico
Ciudad Madero
San Luis Potosí
León
Querétaro
Pachuca
CIUDAD DE MÉXICO
MEXICO CITY
Puebla
Cuernavaca
Toluca
Morelia
Acapulco
Oaxaca
Veracruz
Xalapa
Orizaba
Córdoba
Tuxpan
Coatzacoalcos
Minatitlán
Villahermosa
Tuxtla Gutiérrez
Tapachula
Ciudad del Carmen
Campeche
Mérida
Progreso
Cancún
Cozumel
Chetumal
Belmopan
Belize City
San Pedro Sula
GUATEMALA
Ciudad Acuña
Del Rio
Piedras Negras
Eagle Pass
Nueva Rosita
Monclova
Victoria
Laguna Madre
PADRE ISLAND

Central America

PACIFIC
OCEAN
Gulf of Honduras
Golfo de Fonseca
MEXICO
MÉXICO
GUATEMALA
BELIZE
HONDURAS
EL SALVADOR
ISLAS DE LA BAHÍA
CHIAPAS
SIERRA MADRE DE CHIAPAS
PETÉN
ALTA VERAPAZ
BAJA VERAPAZ
QUICHÉ
HUEHUETENANGO
SAN MARCOS
TOTONICAPÁN
QUETZALTENANGO
SOLOLÁ
CHIMALTENANGO
SUCHITEPÉQUEZ
RETALHULEU
ESCUINTLA
SANTA ROSA
JUTIAPA
JALAPA
CHIQUIMULA
ZACAPA
EL PROGRESO
IZABAL
SIERRA DE LAS MINAS
SIERRA DE SANTA CRUZ
CORTÉS
ATLÁNTIDA
YORO
SANTA BÁRBARA
COPÁN
OCOTEPEQUE
LEMPIRA
INTIBUCÁ
COMAYAGUA
LA PAZ
FRANCISCO MORAZÁN
EL PARAÍSO
VALLE
CHOLUTECA
CHINANDEGA
LEÓN
MANAGUA
MASAYA
CARAZO
ESTELÍ
NUEVA SEGOVIA
MADRIZ
Tapachula
Guatemala
Escuintla
Quetzaltenango
Mazatenango
Retalhuleu
Huehuetenango
Cobán
Puerto Barrios
Puerto Cortés
San Pedro Sula
El Progreso
Tela
La Ceiba
Tegucigalpa
Comayagua
Siguatepeque
Santa Ana
San Salvador
Nueva San Salvador
Sonsonate
San Miguel
La Unión
Usulután
Zacatecoluca
San Vicente
Cojutepeque
Chalchuapa
Choluteca
Chinandega
León
Managua
Masaya
Tipitapa
Estelí
Comitán de Domínguez
Puerto San José
La Libertad
Acajutla
Copyright © by Rand McNally & Co.
Map prepared by Rand McNally & Co.
A-533600-264

Kilometers
Statute Miles

Scale 1:3,000,000
One centimeter represents 30 kilometers.
One inch represents approximately 47 miles.
Lambert Conformal Conic Projection

93

Caribbean Region

Kilometers |C|_____|100|_____|200|_____|300| Km.

Statute Miles |C|_____|100|_____|200|_____|300| Mi.

Scale 1:6,000,000

One centimeter represents 60 kilometers.
One inch represents approximately 95 miles.

Lambert Conformal Conic Projection

95

Beaufort Sea
PACIFIC OCEAN
Gulf of Alaska
ALASKA
UNITED STATES
CANADA
Yukon
ALASKA RANGE
Fairbanks
Anchorage
Cook Inlet
OGILVIE MTS.
RICHARDSON MTS.
MACKENZIE MTS.
SELWYN MTS.
PELLY MOUNTAINS
COAST MOUNTAINS
ROCKY MOUNTAINS
COLUMBIA MOUNTAINS
N O R T H W E S T
BANKS ISLAND
VICTORIA ISLAND
Amundsen Gulf
Great Bear Lake
Great Slave Lake
Lake Athabasca
Mackenzie
Whitehorse
Dawson
Inuvik
Yellowknife
QUEEN CHARLOTTE ISLANDS
VANCOUVER ISLAND
Prince Rupert
Prince George
Vancouver
Victoria
Seattle
Tacoma
Spokane
Portland
Salem
Eugene
A L B E R T A
Edmonton
Calgary
Lethbridge
S A S K A T C H E W A N
Saskatoon
Regina
Moose Jaw
Prince Albert
M A N I T O B A
Winnipeg
Lake Winnipeg
Churchill
O R E G O N
I D A H O
Boise
M O N T A N A
Great Falls
Missoula
Helena
Butte
Billings
W Y O M I N G
NORTH DAKOTA
Bismarck
Grand Forks
Fargo
SOUTH DAKOTA
Rapid City
Sioux Falls
MINNESOTA
Minneapolis
NEBRASKA
IOWA
N E V A D A
Reno
Salt Lake City
Ogden
Provo
UTAH
COLORADO
CALIFORNIA
SAN FRANCISCO
Sacramento
Oakland
San Jose
Stockton
Modesto
Fresno
CASCADE RANGE
SIERRA NEVADA
GREAT BASIN

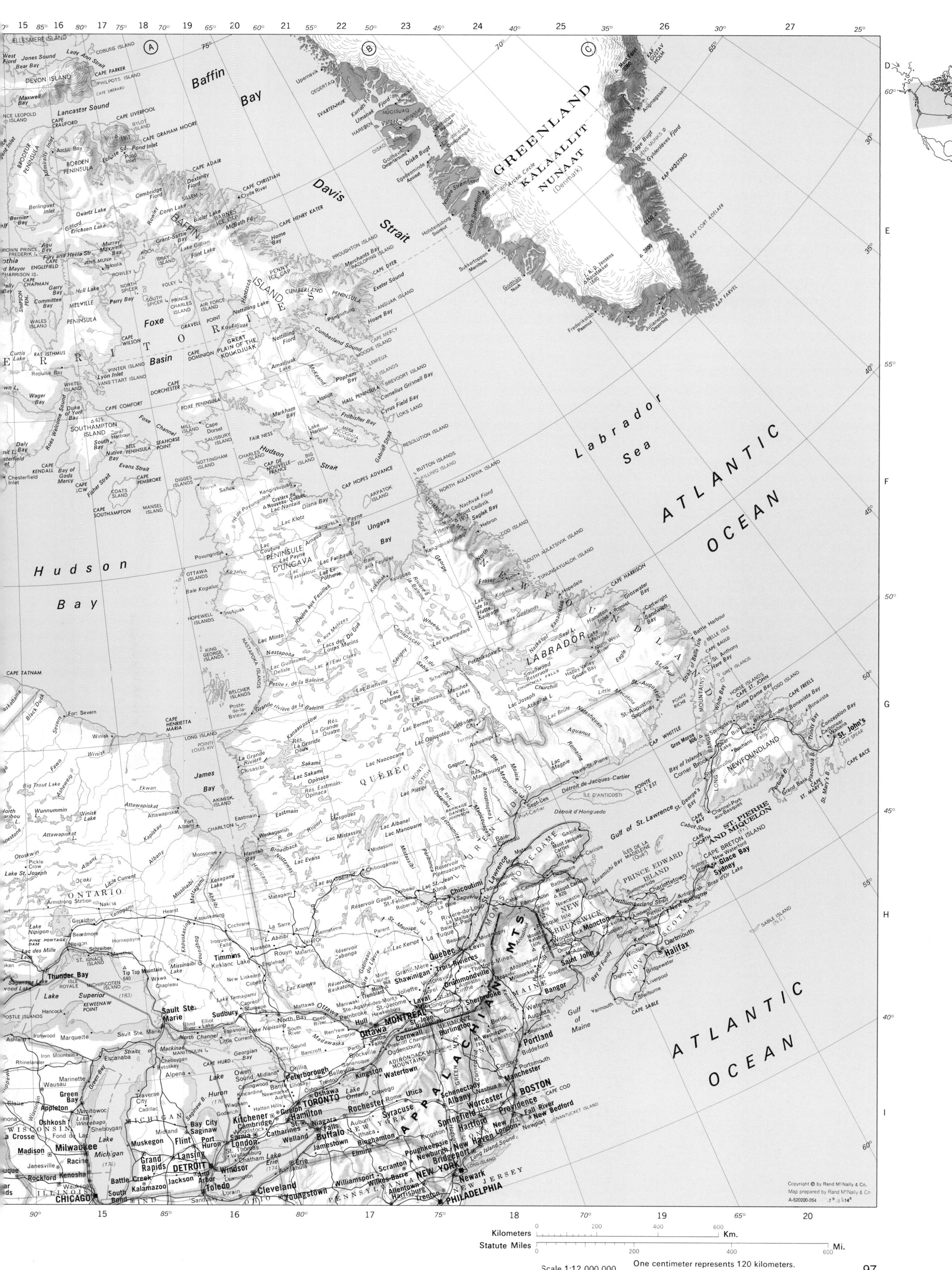

Copyright © by Rand McNally & Co.
Map prepared by Rand McNally & Co.
A-520200-264

Kilometers

Statute Miles

Scale 1:12,000,000

One centimeter represents 120 kilometers.
One inch represents approximately 190 miles.
Lambert Conformal Conic Projection

97

Alberta

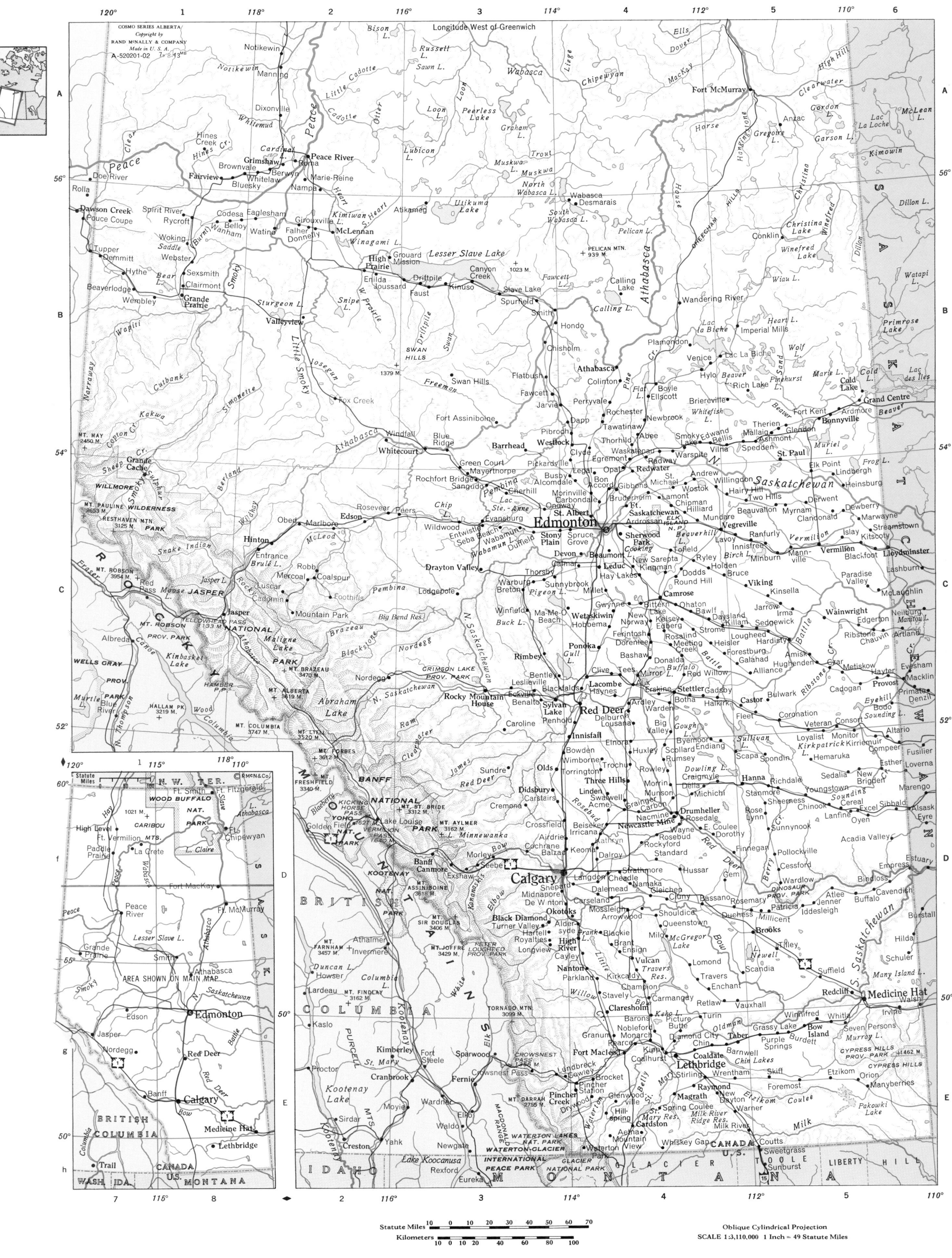

Statute Miles 10 0 10 20 30 40 50 60 70

Kilometers 10 0 10 20 40 60 80 100

Oblique Cylindrical Projection

SCALE 1:3,110,000 1 Inch = 49 Statute Miles

Oblique Cylindrical Projection
SCALE 1:4,255,000 1 Inch = 67 Statute Miles

Statute Miles
Kilometers

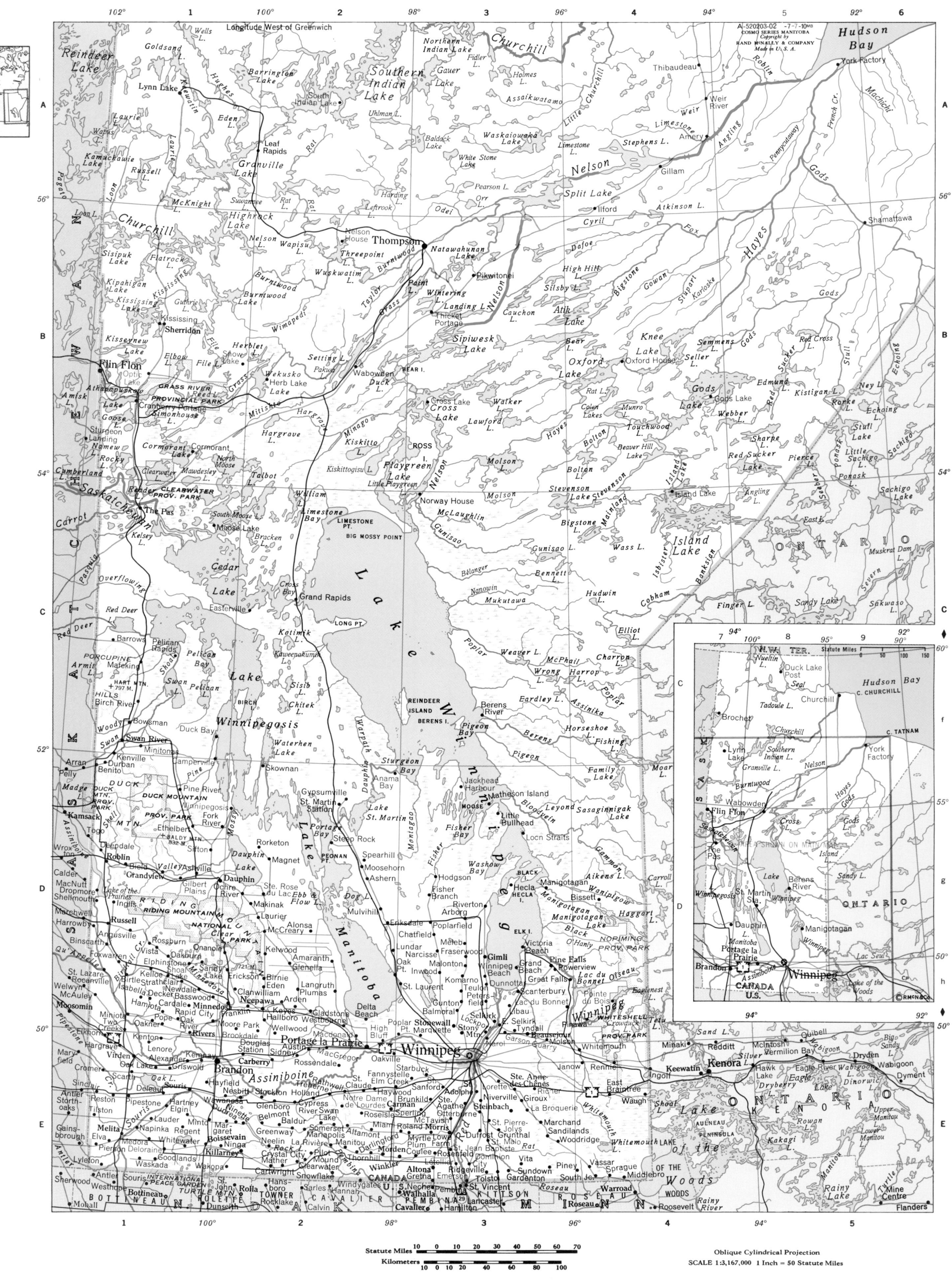
Longitude West of Greenwich
A-520203-02 -7-7-10MB
COSMO SERIES MANITOBA
Copyright by
RAND McNALLY & COMPANY
Made in U. S. A.
Hudson Bay
Reindeer Lake
Southern Indian Lake
Churchill
Nelson
Lynn Lake
Leaf Rapids
Granville Lake
Thompson
Split Lake
Gillam
York Factory
Shamattawa
Flin Flon
Sherridon
The Pas
Cedar Lake
Grand Rapids
Oxford Lake
Gods Lake
Island Lake
Cross Lake
Norway House
Playgreen Lake
Lake Winnipeg
Lake Winnipegosis
Lake Manitoba
Swan River
Dauphin
Russell
Minnedosa
Neepawa
Brandon
Virden
Portage la Prairie
Winnipeg
Selkirk
Steinbach
Morden
Winkler
Altona
Carman
Souris
Melita
Boissevain
Killarney
Gimli
Berens River
Pine Falls
Kenora
Keewatin
Lake of the Woods
ONTARIO
SASKATCHEWAN
NORTH DAKOTA
MINNESOTA
CANADA
U.S.
GRASS RIVER PROVINCIAL PARK
CLEARWATER PROV. PARK
DUCK MOUNTAIN PROV. PARK
RIDING MOUNTAIN NATIONAL PARK
WHITESHELL PROV. PARK
NOPIMING PROV. PARK
INTERNATIONAL PEACE GARDEN
Statute Miles 10 0 10 20 30 40 50 60 70
Kilometers 10 0 10 20 40 60 80 100
Oblique Cylindrical Projection
SCALE 1:3,167,000 1 Inch = 50 Statute Miles
N.W. TER.
Duck Lake Post
Churchill
C. CHURCHILL
C. TATNAM
Brochet
AREA SHOWN ON MAIN MAP

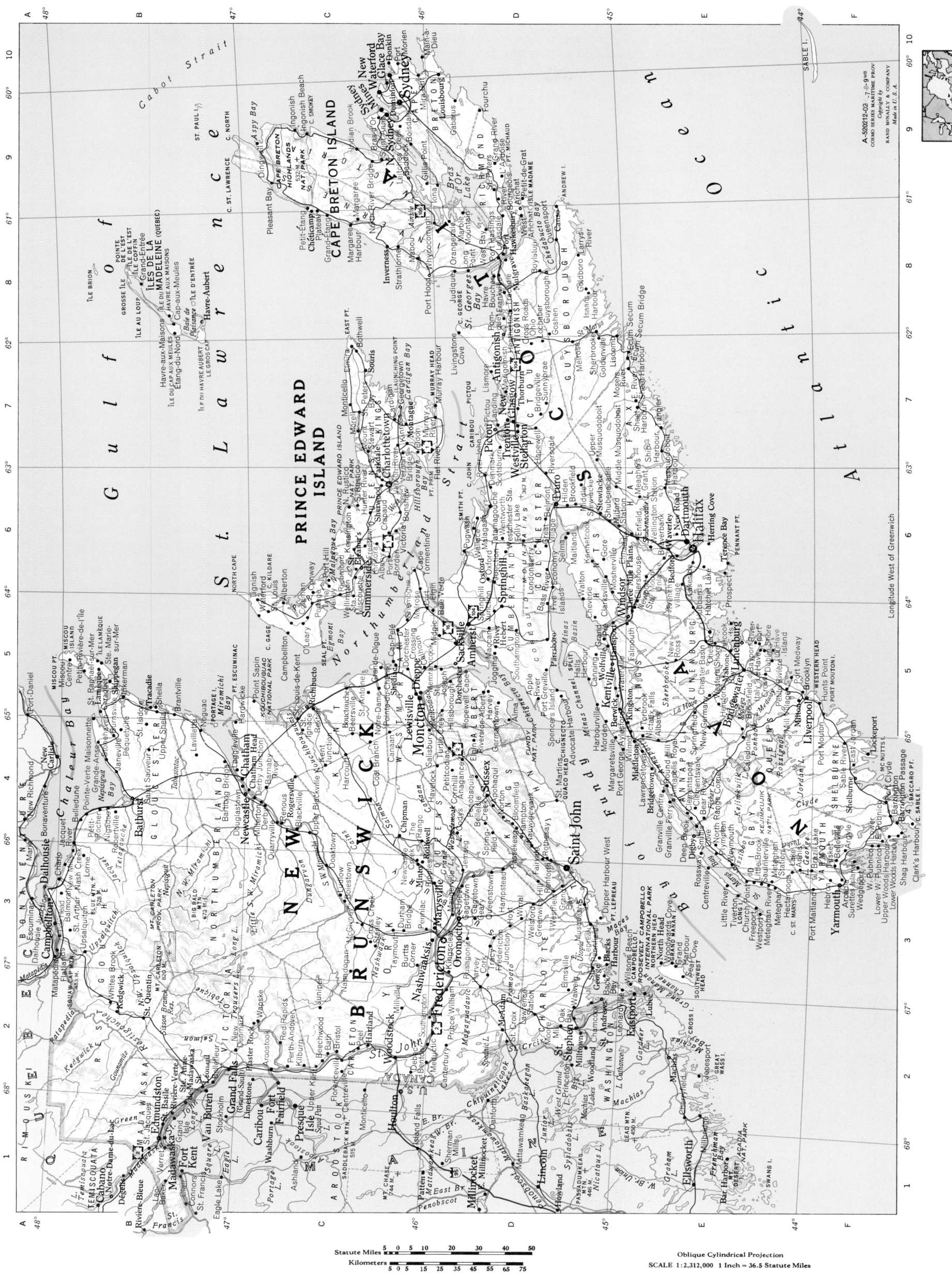

Oblique Cylindrical Projection
SCALE 1:2,312,000 1 Inch = 36.5 Statute Miles

Newfoundland

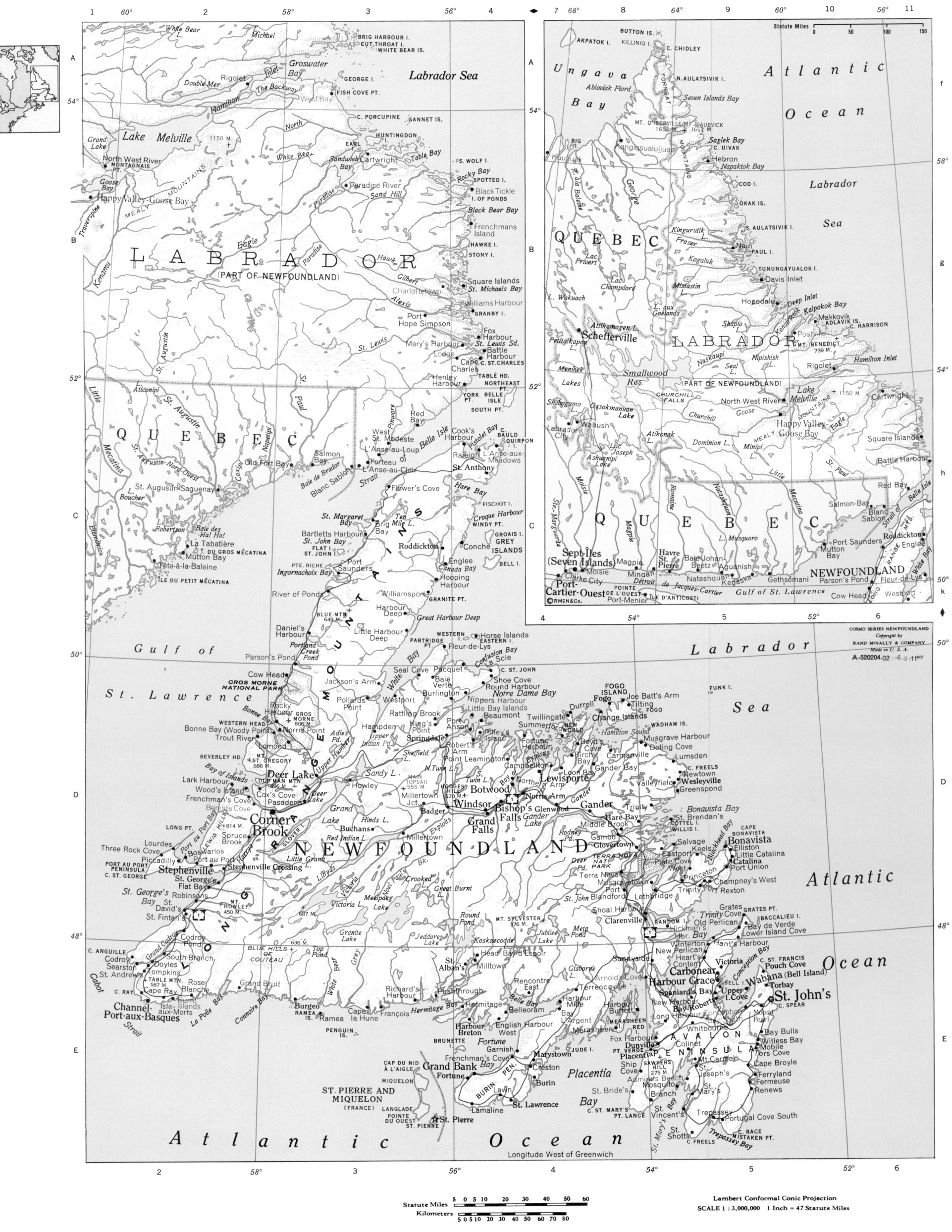

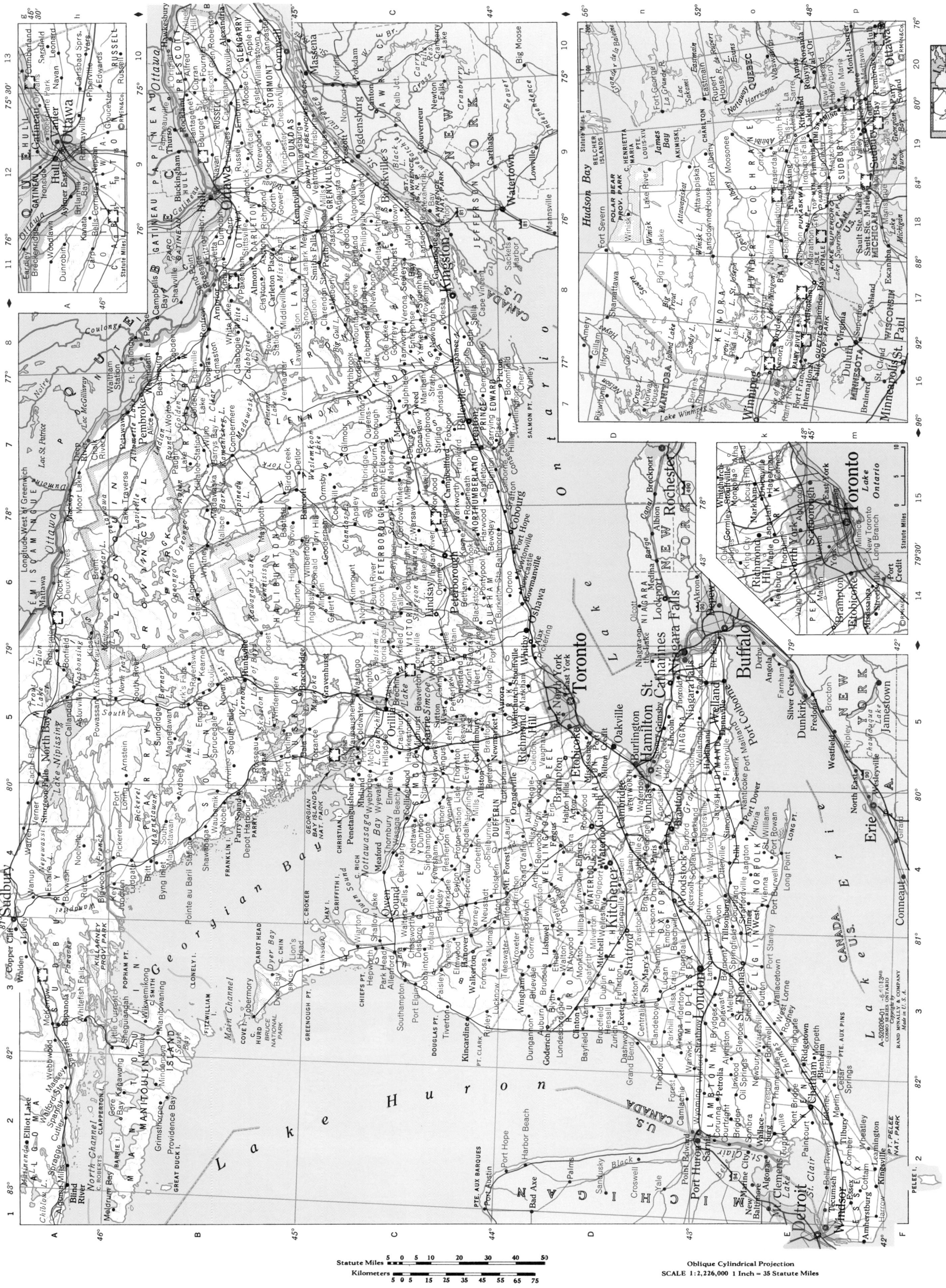

Oblique Cylindrical Projection
SCALE 1:2,226,000 1 Inch = 35 Statute Miles

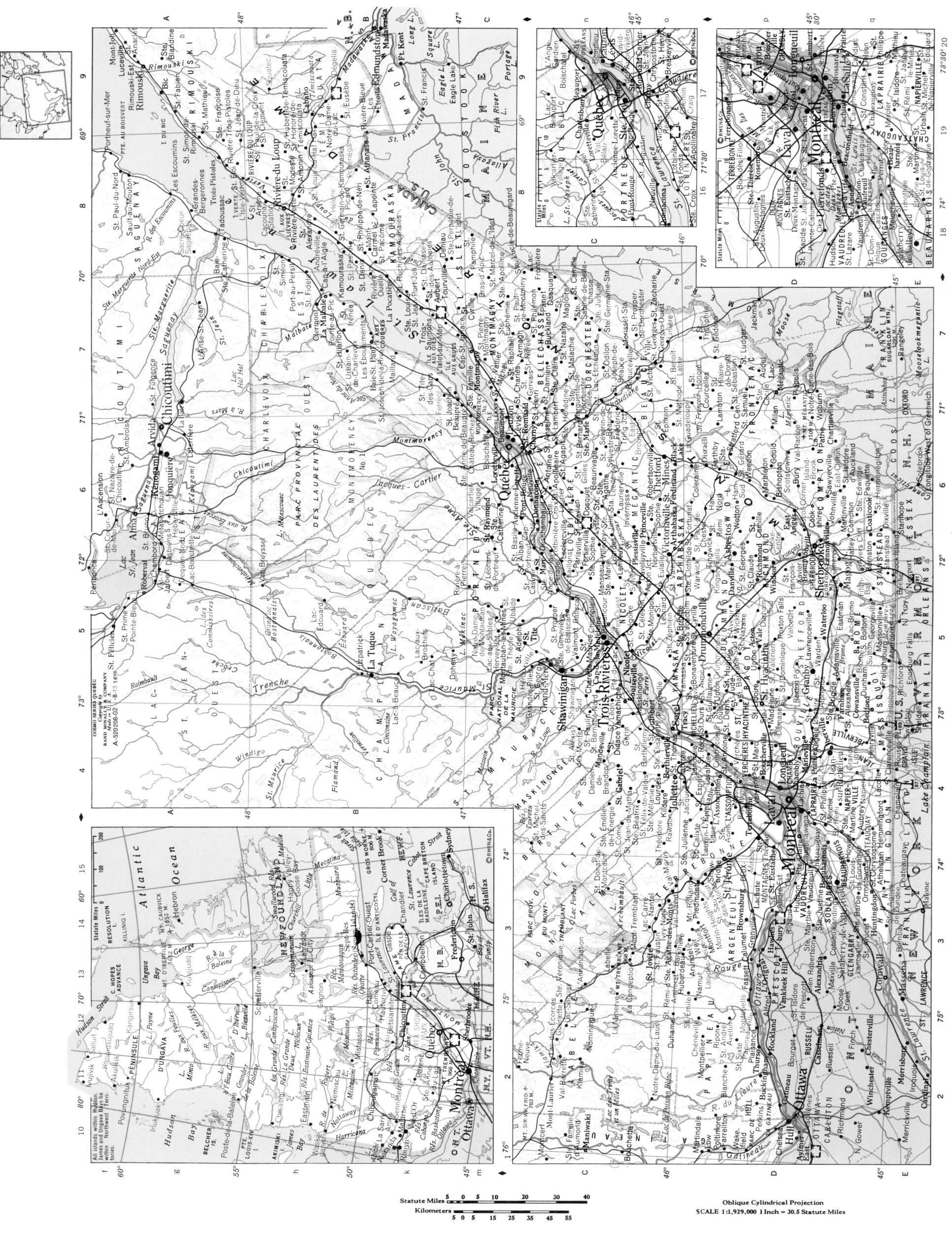

Statute Miles

Kilometers

Oblique Cylindrical Projection
SCALE 1:1,929,000 1 Inch = 30.5 Statute Miles

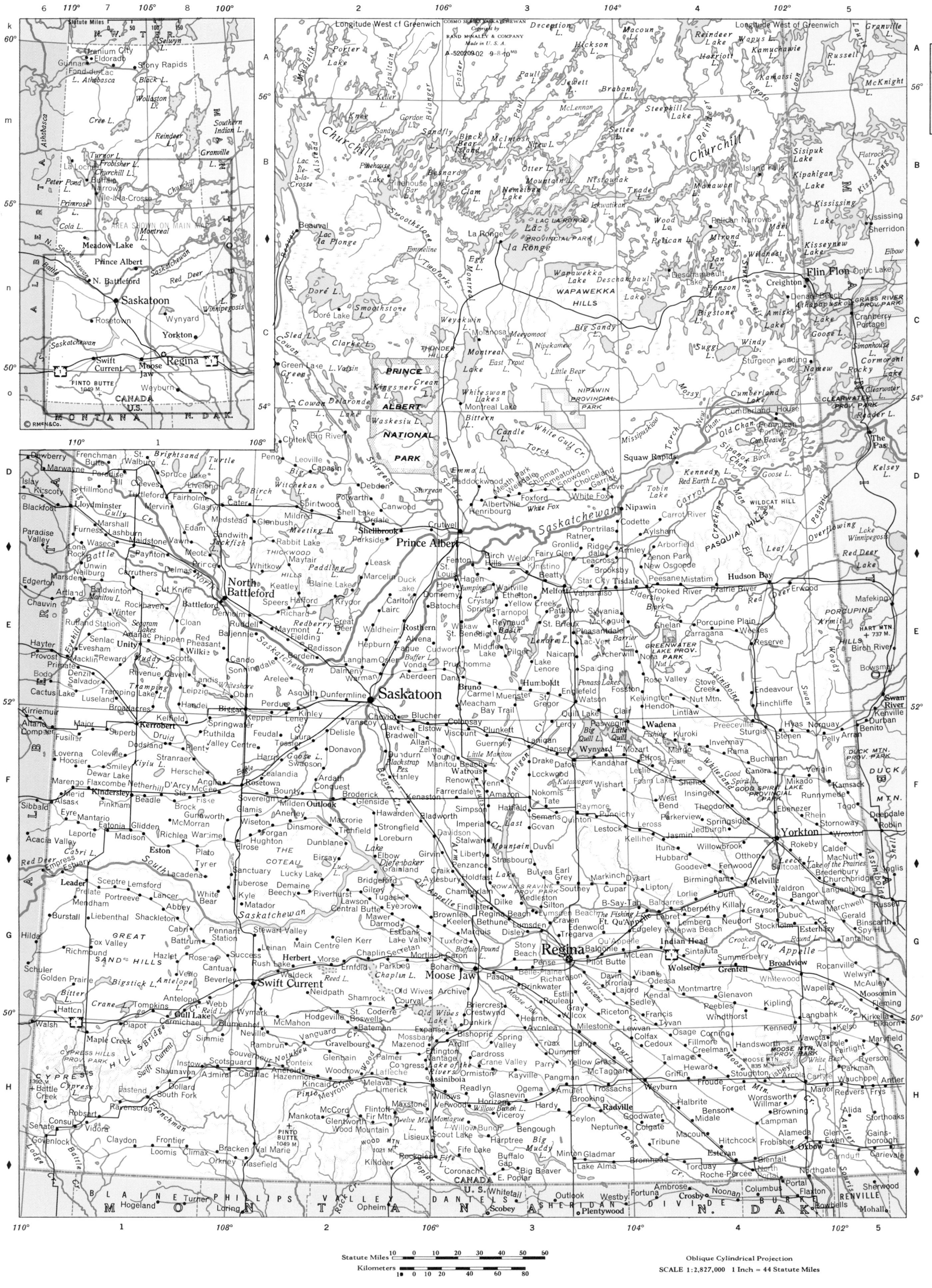
Longitude West of Greenwich
COSMO SERIES SASKATCHEWAN
Copyright by RAND McNALLY & COMPANY
Made in U. S. A.
AREA SHOWN ON MAIN MAP
N. W. TERR.
ALBERTA
MONTANA
N. DAK.
CANADA
U.S.
FINTO BUTTE 1049 M.
© RMcN&Co.
Uranium City
Eldorado
Stony Rapids
L. Athabasca
Cree L.
Wollaston L.
Reindeer L.
Southern Indian L.
La Loche
Buffalo Narrows
Ile-à-la-Crosse
Meadow Lake
Prince Albert
N. Battleford
Saskatoon
Rosetown
Wynyard
Yorkton
Swift Current
Moose Jaw
Regina
Weyburn
Churchill
La Ronge
Lac la Ronge
LAC LA RONGE PROVINCIAL PARK
WAPAWEKKA HILLS
Flin Flon
Creighton
PRINCE ALBERT NATIONAL PARK
Waskesiu L.
NIPAWIN PROVINCIAL PARK
Cumberland House
The Pas
Saskatchewan
Nipawin
Tisdale
Melfort
Hudson Bay
PASQUIA HILLS
North Battleford
Battleford
Lloydminster
Unity
Humboldt
Wadena
Kindersley
Rosetown
Outlook
Lake Diefenbaker
Yorkton
Melville
Indian Head
Moose Jaw
Swift Current
Gull Lake
Maple Creek
CYPRESS HILLS PROV. PARK
GREAT SAND HILLS
Assiniboia
Weyburn
Estevan
Oxbow
MOOSE MTN. PROV. PARK
DUCK MTN. PROV. PARK
GOOD SPIRIT LAKE PROVINCIAL PARK
GREENWATER LAKE PROV. PARK
PINTO BUTTE 1049 M.
WOOD MTN 1021 M.
Statute Miles
Kilometers
Oblique Cylindrical Projection
SCALE 1:2,827,000 1 Inch = 44 Statute Miles

PACIFIC
OCEAN
CANADA
UNITED STATES
MEXICO
BRITISH COLUMBIA
ALBERTA
SASKATCHEWAN
MANITOBA
WASHINGTON
OREGON
IDAHO
MONTANA
WYOMING
NORTH DAKOTA
SOUTH DAKOTA
NEBRASKA
KANSAS
OKLAHOMA
TEXAS
NEW MEXICO
COLORADO
UTAH
NEVADA
ARIZONA
CALIFORNIA
ROCKY MOUNTAINS
GREAT BASIN
SIERRA NEVADA
CASCADE RANGE
COAST RANGES
VANCOUVER ISLAND
Vancouver
Victoria
Seattle
Tacoma
Spokane
Portland
Salem
Eugene
Boise
Salt Lake City
Ogden
Provo
Reno
Sacramento
SAN FRANCISCO
Oakland
San Jose
Fresno
Bakersfield
LOS ANGELES
Long Beach
San Diego
Tijuana
Las Vegas
Phoenix
Tucson
Albuquerque
Santa Fe
El Paso
Ciudad Juárez
Denver
Colorado Springs
Pueblo
Cheyenne
Billings
Great Falls
Helena
Butte
Calgary
Edmonton
Regina
Saskatoon
Winnipeg
Bismarck
Fargo
Rapid City
Amarillo
Lubbock
Oklahoma City
Wichita
Fort Worth
San Antonio
Austin
ALASKA
ARCTIC OCEAN
Beaufort Sea
Chukchi Sea
BERING SEA
Bering Strait
Gulf of Alaska
BROOKS RANGE
ALASKA RANGE
Mount McKinley 6194
Anchorage
Fairbanks
Juneau
ALEUTIAN ISLANDS
Arctic Circle
RUSSIA
OAHU
Honolulu
MOLOKAI
LANAI
MAUI
HAWAII
Hilo
KAUAI
NIHAU
Kilometers
Miles
Copyright © by Rand McNally & Co.

Kilometers
Statute Miles

Scale 1:12,000,000   One centimeter represents 120 kilometers.
One inch represents approximately 190 miles.
Albers Conical Equal-Area Projection

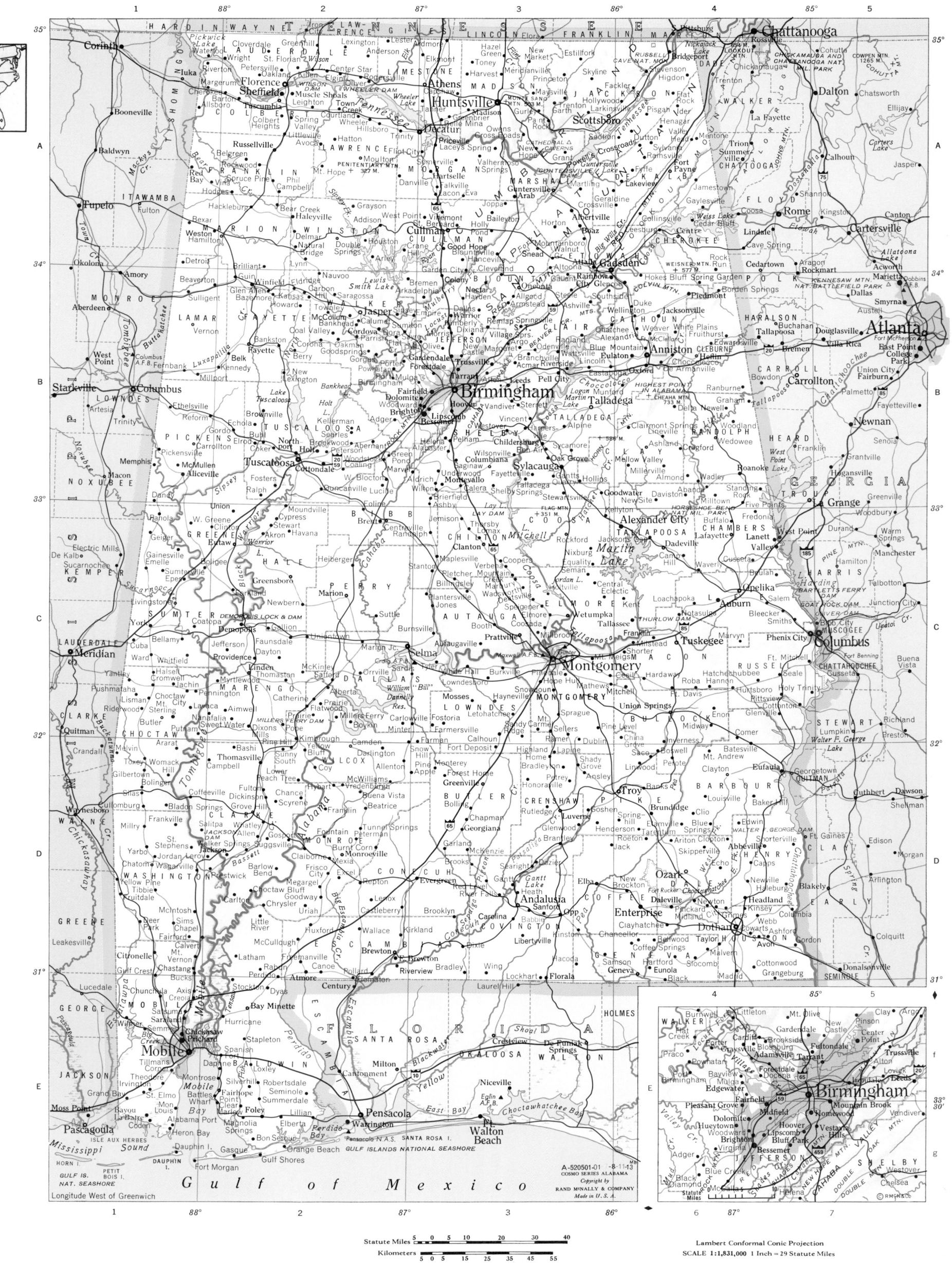
Gulf of Mexico
Longitude West of Greenwich
A-520501-01 -8-11-13
COSMO SERIES ALABAMA
Copyright by
RAND McNALLY & COMPANY
Made in U. S. A.
Statute Miles 5 0 5 10 20 30 40
Kilometers 5 0 5 15 25 35 45 55
Lambert Conformal Conic Projection
SCALE 1:1,831,000 1 Inch = 29 Statute Miles
Birmingham
Montgomery
Mobile
Huntsville
Tuscaloosa
Atlanta
Chattanooga
Columbus
Meridian
Pensacola
TENNESSEE
GEORGIA
FLORIDA

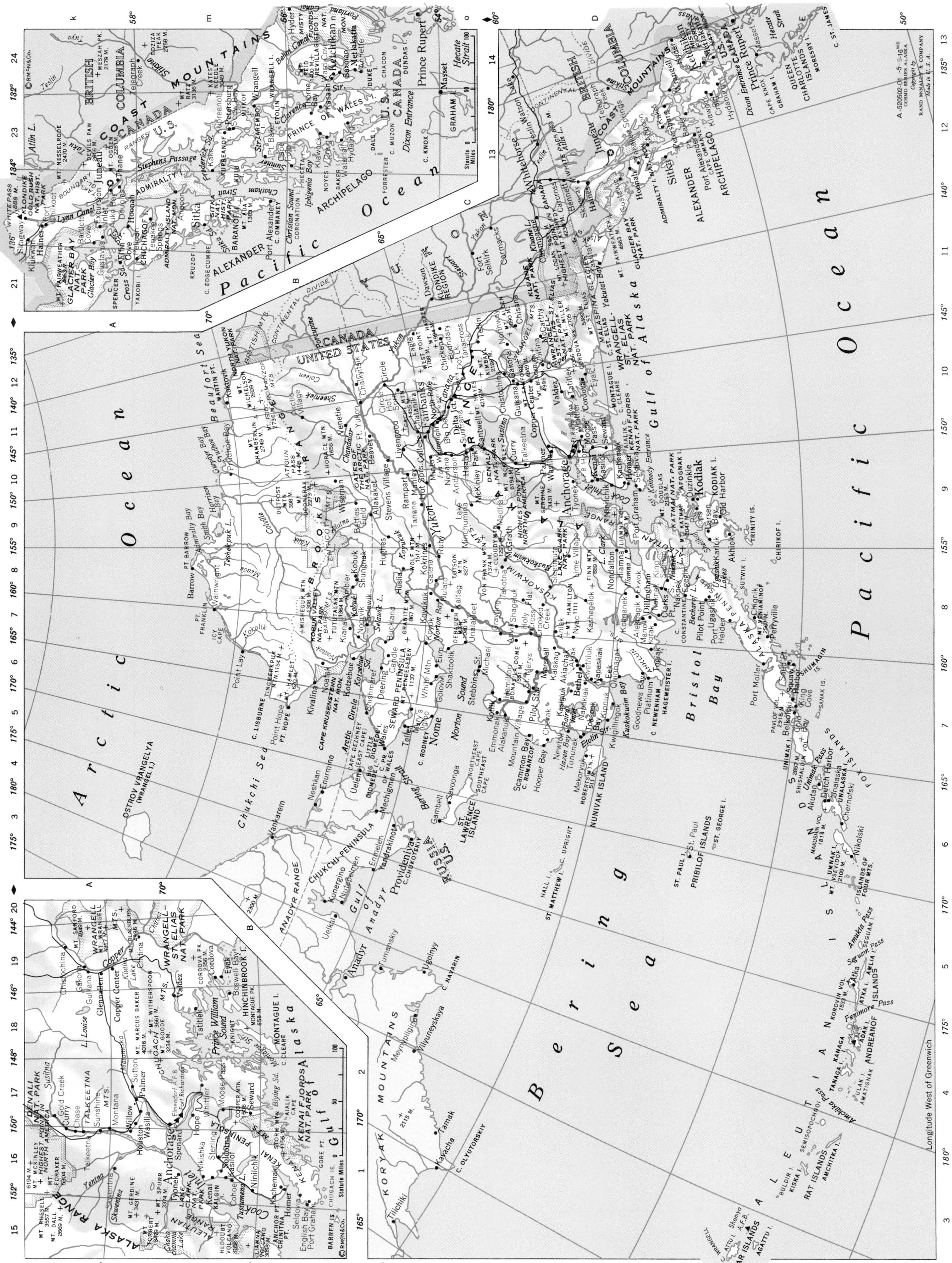

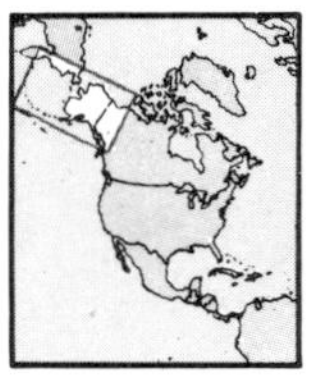

Arctic Ocean

Pacific Ocean

Bering Sea

Beaufort Sea

Chukchi Sea

Gulf of Alaska

Bristol Bay

CANADA
UNITED STATES

BRITISH COLUMBIA

COAST MOUNTAINS

U.S.

BROOKS RANGE

ALASKA RANGE

ALEUTIAN ISLANDS

Anchorage
Fairbanks
Juneau
Sitka
Nome
Kodiak
Bethel
Valdez
Seward
Homer
Kotzebue
Barrow
Prince Rupert
Ketchikan
Wrangell
Skagway
Haines

DENALI NAT. PARK
MT. McKINLEY
KATMAI NAT. PARK
GLACIER BAY NAT. PARK
WRANGELL-ST. ELIAS NAT. PARK
KENAI FJORDS NAT. PARK
LAKE CLARK NAT. PARK
GATES OF THE ARCTIC NAT. PARK
KLONDIKE GOLD RUSH NAT. HIST. PARK

ALEXANDER ARCHIPELAGO

ADMIRALTY ISLAND
BARANOF ISLAND
PRINCE OF WALES I.
NUNIVAK ISLAND
ST. LAWRENCE ISLAND
PRIBILOF ISLANDS
KODIAK I.
UNIMAK I.

St. Paul
St. George

OSTROV VRANGELYA (WRANGEL I.)

RUSSIA
CHUKCHI PENINSULA
ANADYR RANGE
KORYAK MOUNTAINS

Norton Sound

SEWARD PENINSULA
KENAI PENINSULA
Cook Inlet
Prince William Sound

Yukon

KOYUKUK

Statute Miles 50 25 0 50 100 150 200 250
Kilometers 50 0 100 200 300

Polyconic Projection
SCALE 1:12,000,000 1 Inch = 189 Statute Miles

Longitude West of Greenwich

Arizona

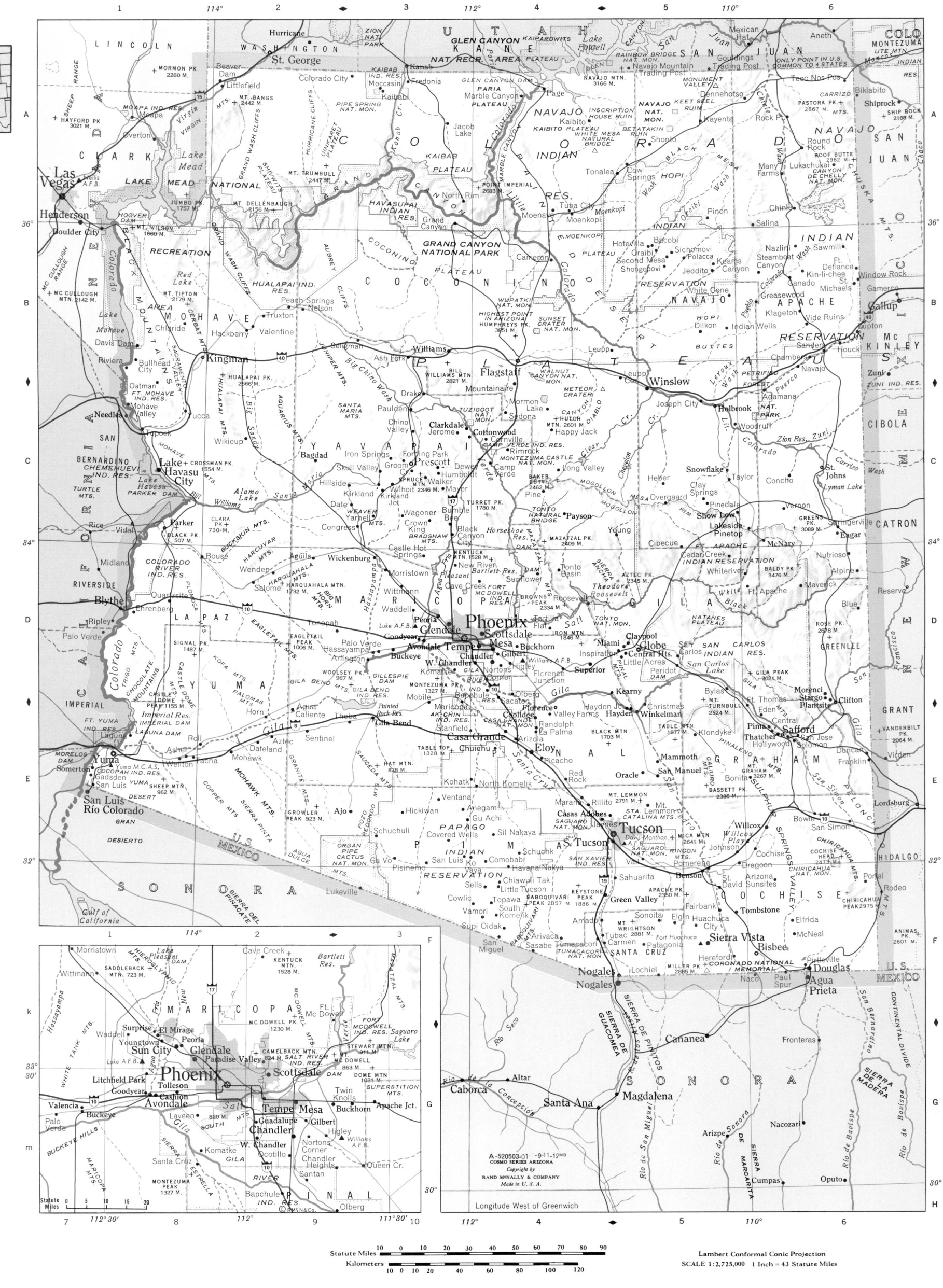

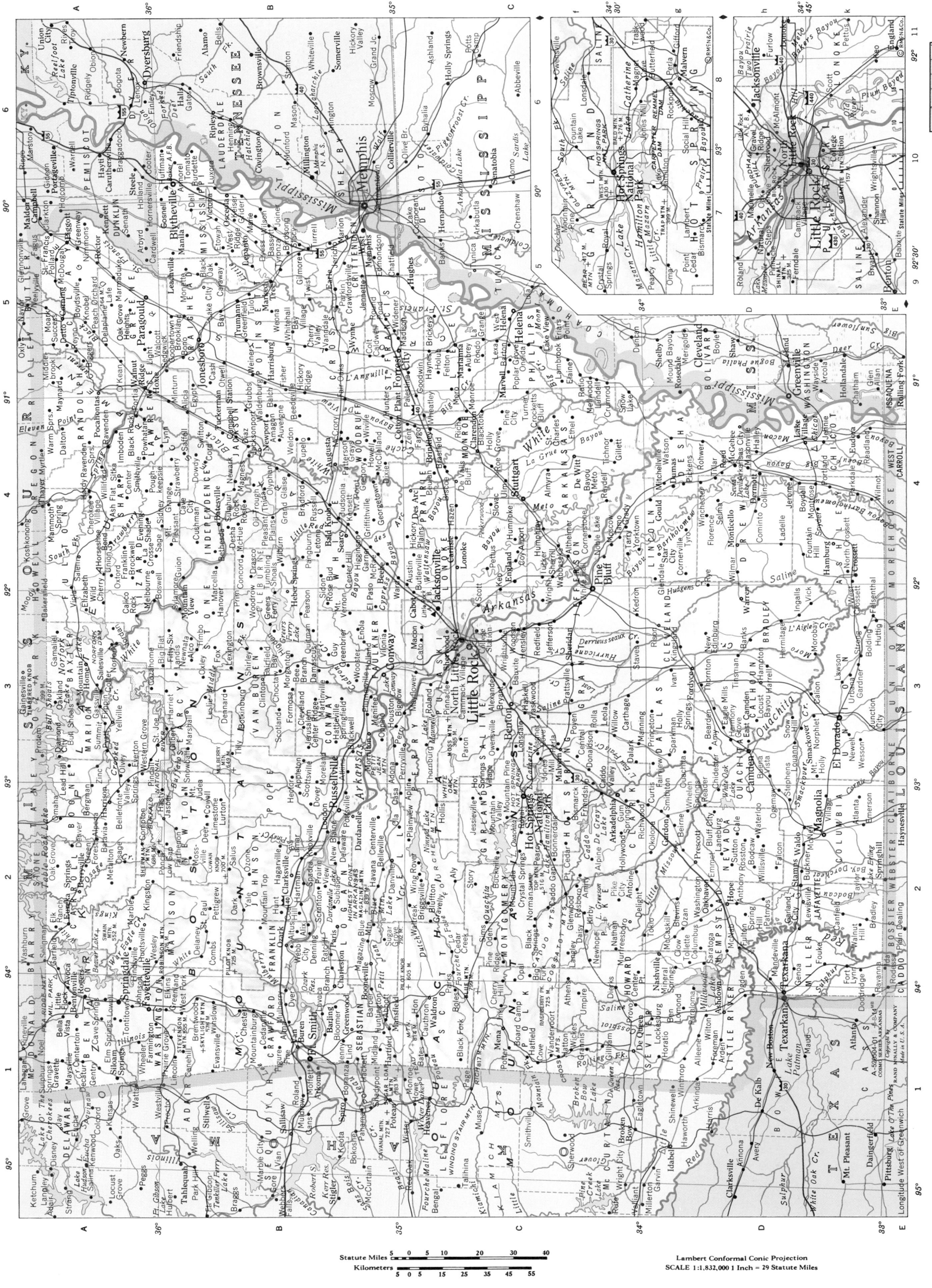

Statute Miles 5 0 5 10 20 30 40
Kilometers 5 0 5 15 25 35 45 55

Lambert Conformal Conic Projection
SCALE 1:1,832,000 1 Inch = 29 Statute Miles

California

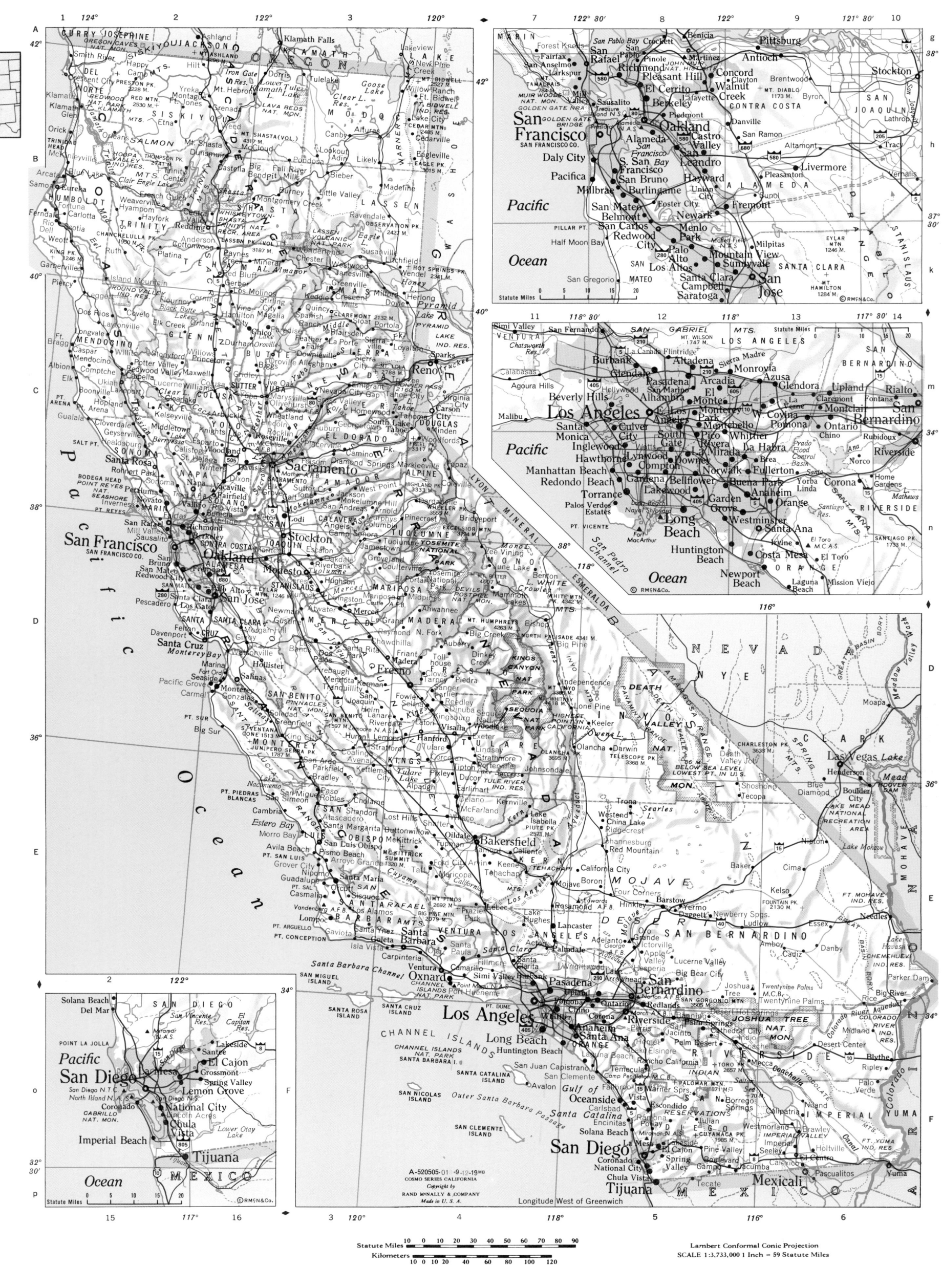

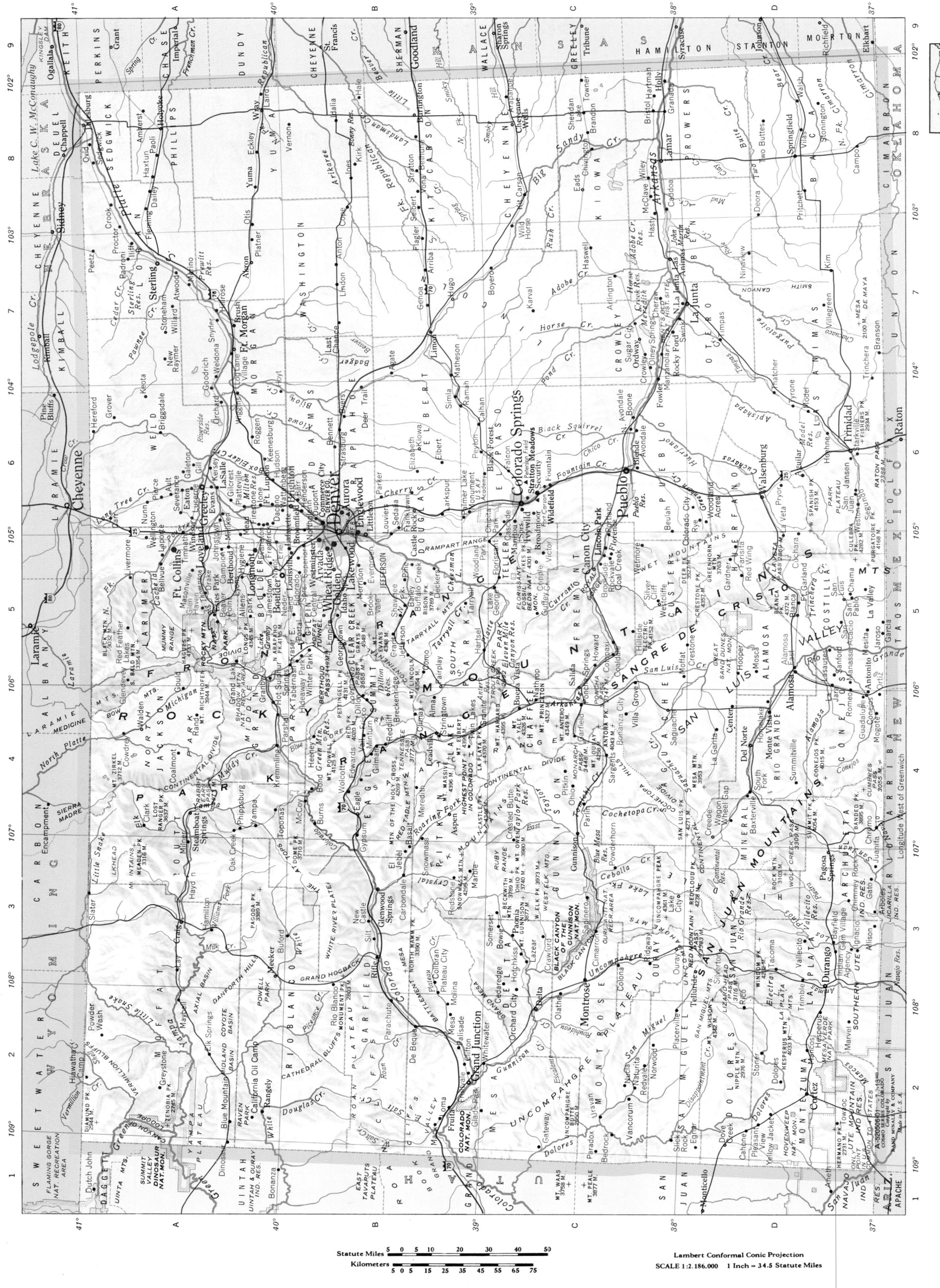

Statute Miles 5 0 5 10   20   30   40   50
Kilometers 5 0 5 15 25 35 45 55 65 75

Lambert Conformal Conic Projection
SCALE 1:2,186,000   1 Inch = 34.5 Statute Miles

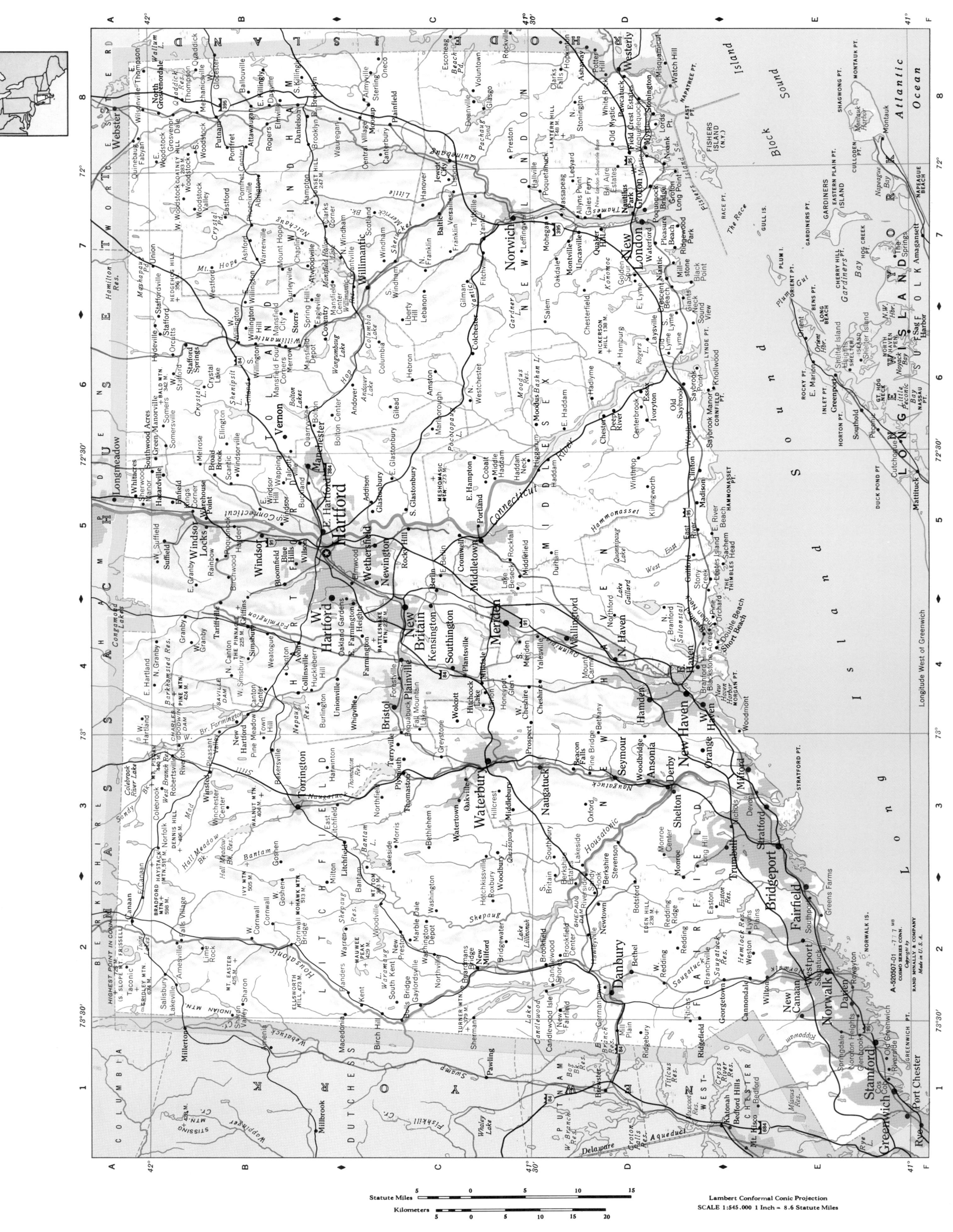
Statute Miles
5 0 5 10 15
Kilometers
5 0 5 10 15 20
Lambert Conformal Conic Projection
SCALE 1:545,000 1 Inch = 8.6 Statute Miles

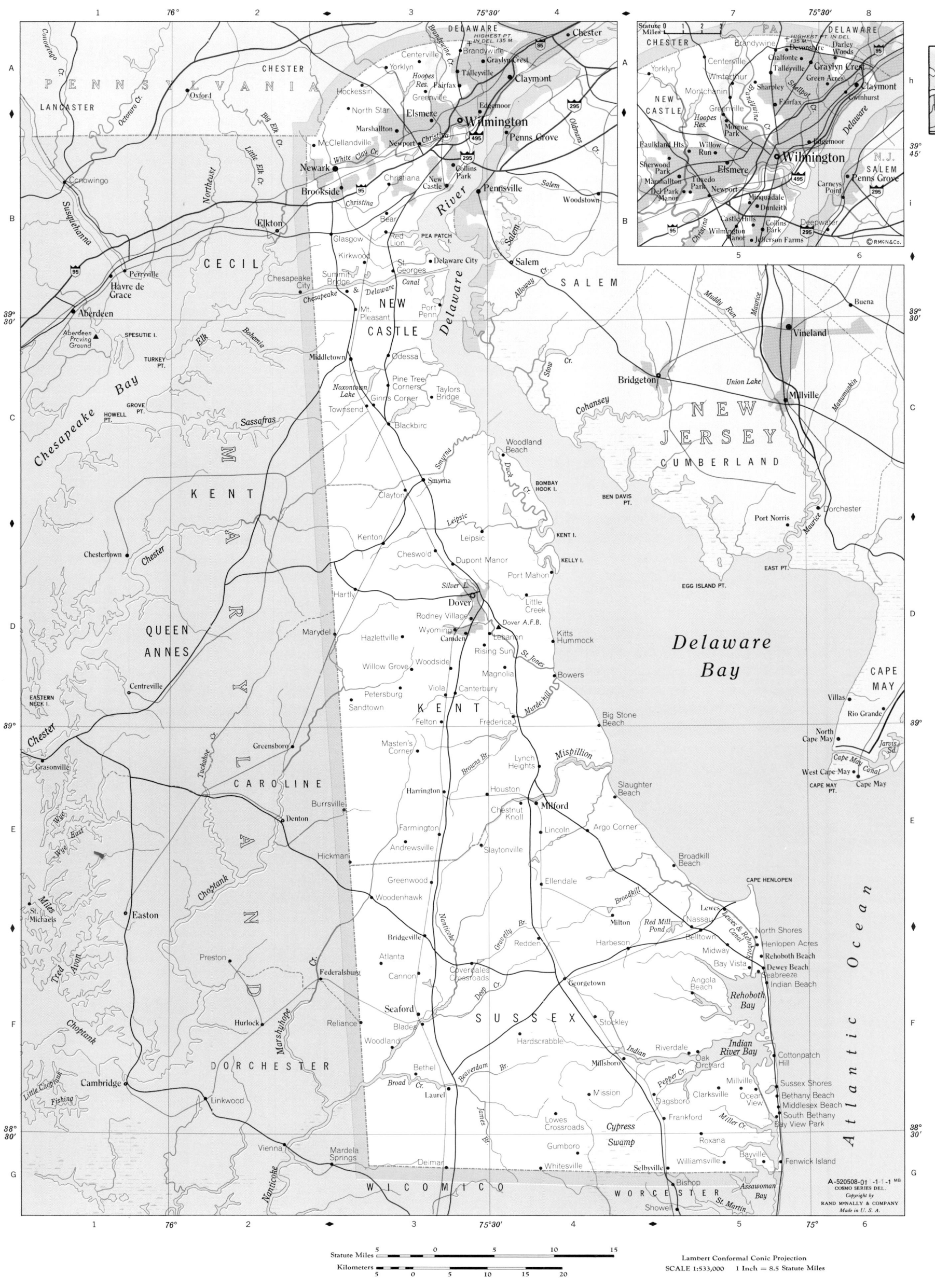

Statute Miles 5 0 5 10 15

Kilometers 5 0 5 10 15 20

Lambert Conformal Conic Projection

SCALE 1:533,000 1 Inch = 8.5 Statute Miles

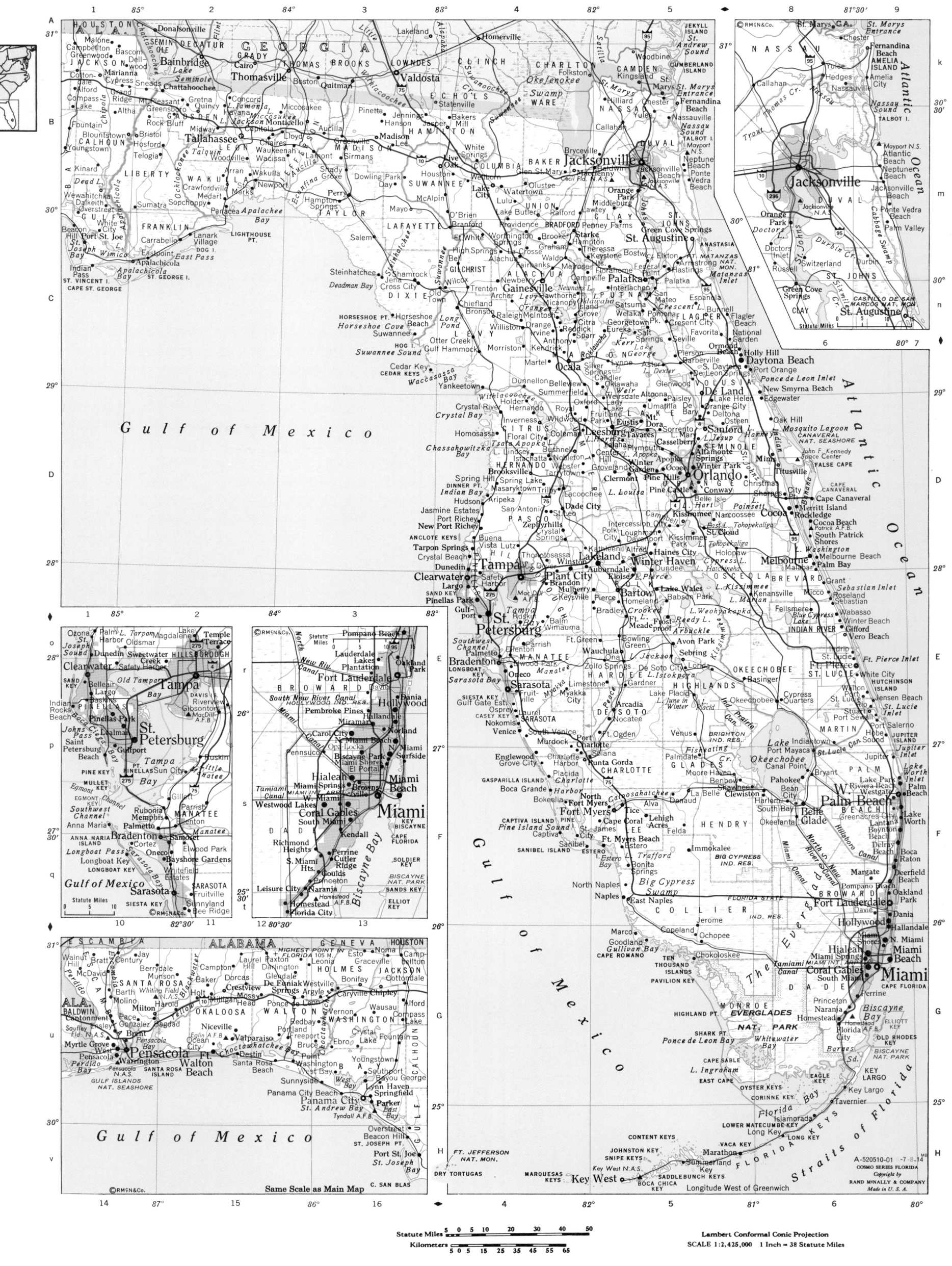
Gulf of Mexico
Atlantic Ocean
Straits of Florida
Florida Bay
Biscayne Bay
GEORGIA
ALABAMA
ALA.
Jacksonville
Tallahassee
Pensacola
Gainesville
Ocala
Orlando
Daytona Beach
Tampa
St. Petersburg
Clearwater
Sarasota
Bradenton
Lakeland
Fort Myers
W. Palm Beach
Fort Lauderdale
Hollywood
Miami
Miami Beach
Coral Gables
Hialeah
Key West
Panama City
St. Augustine
Melbourne
Lake Okeechobee
The Everglades
EVERGLADES NAT. PARK
Big Cypress Swamp
Okefenokee Swamp
Same Scale as Main Map
A-520510-01 -7-8-14
COSMO SERIES FLORIDA
Copyright by RAND McNALLY & COMPANY
Made in U. S. A.
Longitude West of Greenwich
Statute Miles 5 0 5 10 20 30 40 50
Kilometers 5 0 5 15 25 35 45 55 65
Lambert Conformal Conic Projection
SCALE 1:2,425,000 1 Inch = 38 Statute Miles

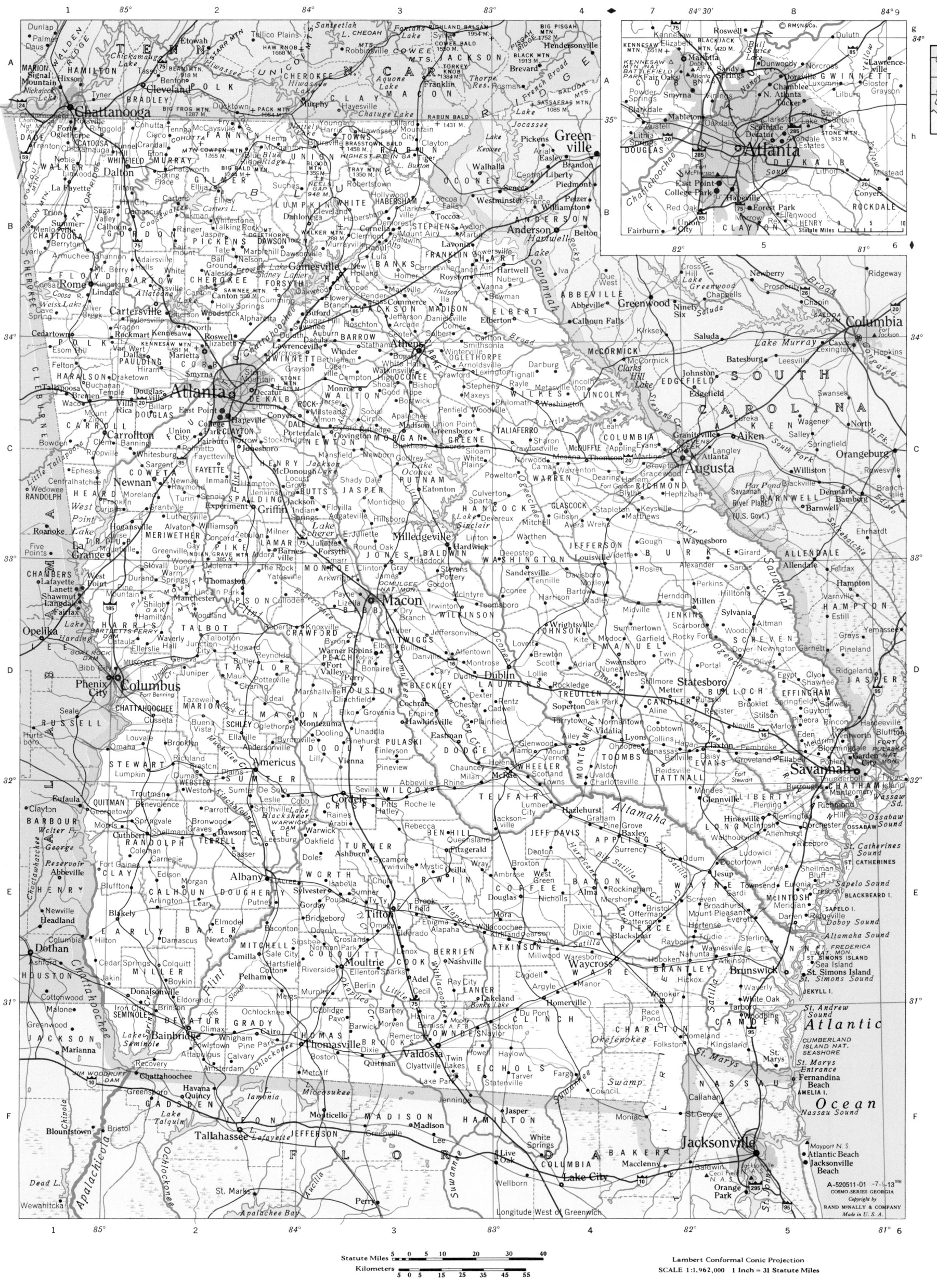

Statute Miles 5 0 5 10 20 30 40
Kilometers 5 0 5 15 25 35 45 55

Lambert Conformal Conic Projection
SCALE 1:1,962,000   1 Inch = 31 Statute Miles

Hawaii

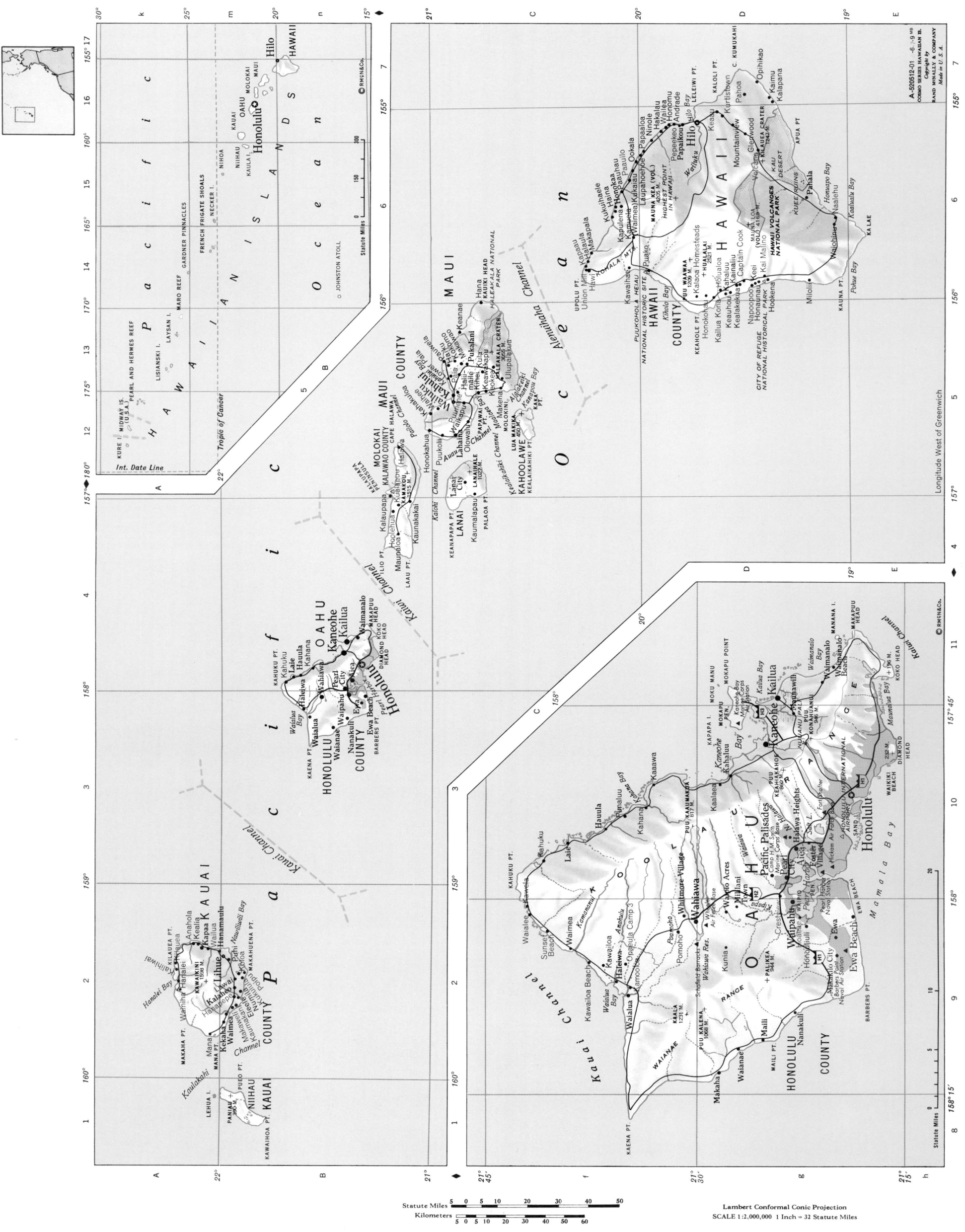

Statute Miles 5 0 10 20 30 40 50
Kilometers 5 0 5 10 20 30 40 50 60

Lambert Conformal Conic Projection
SCALE 1:2,000,000 1 Inch = 32 Statute Miles

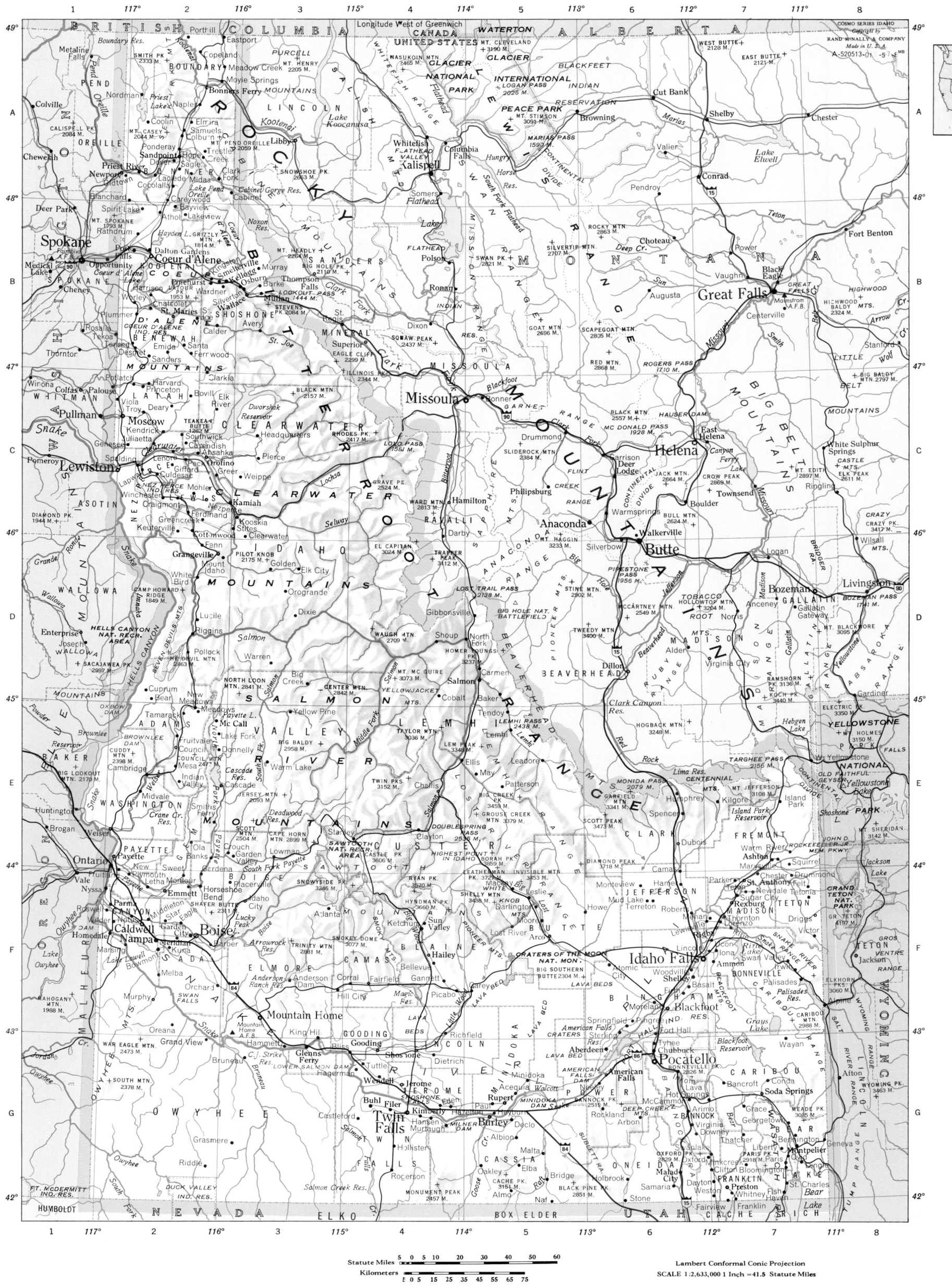

Statute Miles

Kilometers

Lambert Conformal Conic Projection
SCALE 1:2,633,000 1 Inch = 41.5 Statute Miles

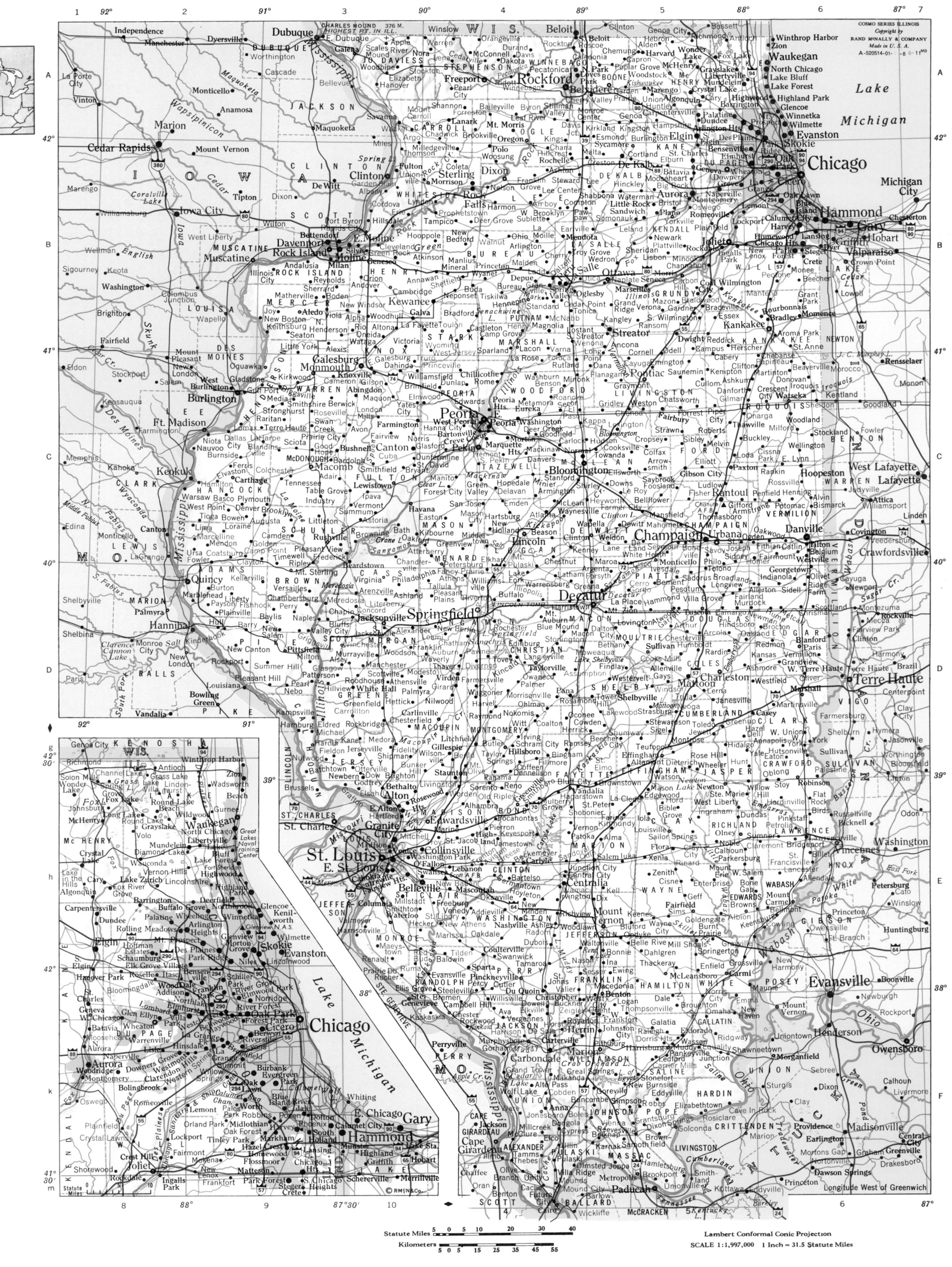
COSMO SERIES ILLINOIS
Copyright by
RAND McNALLY & COMPANY
Made in U. S. A.
Lake Michigan
Chicago
Rockford
Peoria
Springfield
Champaign
Decatur
St. Louis
Statute Miles
Kilometers
Lambert Conformal Conic Projection
SCALE 1:1,997,000 1 Inch = 31.5 Statute Miles
Longitude West of Greenwich

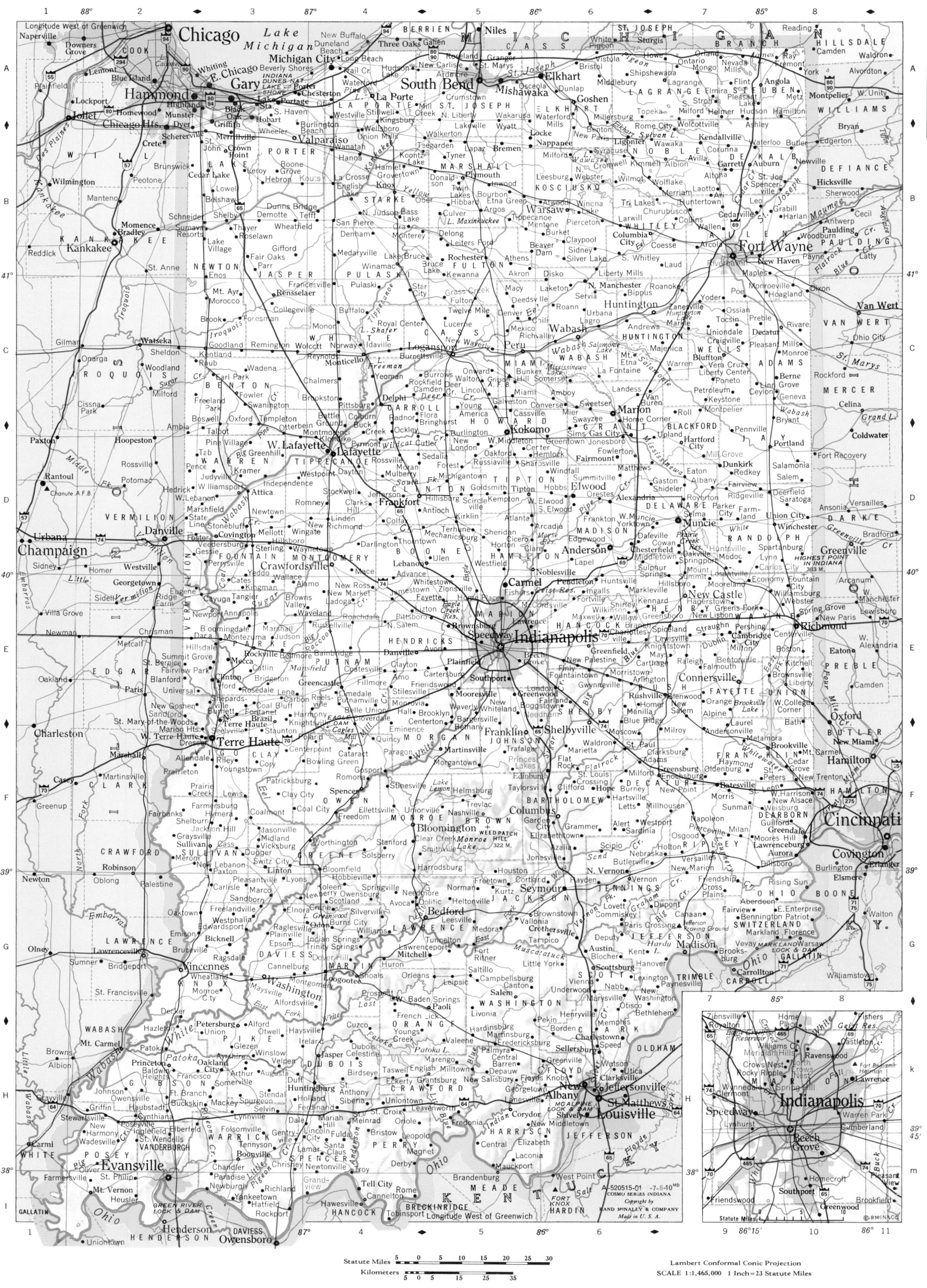

Statute Miles 5 0 5 10 15 20 25 30
Kilometers 5 0 5 10 15 25 35

Lambert Conformal Conic Projection
SCALE 1:1,465,000   1 Inch=23 Statute Miles

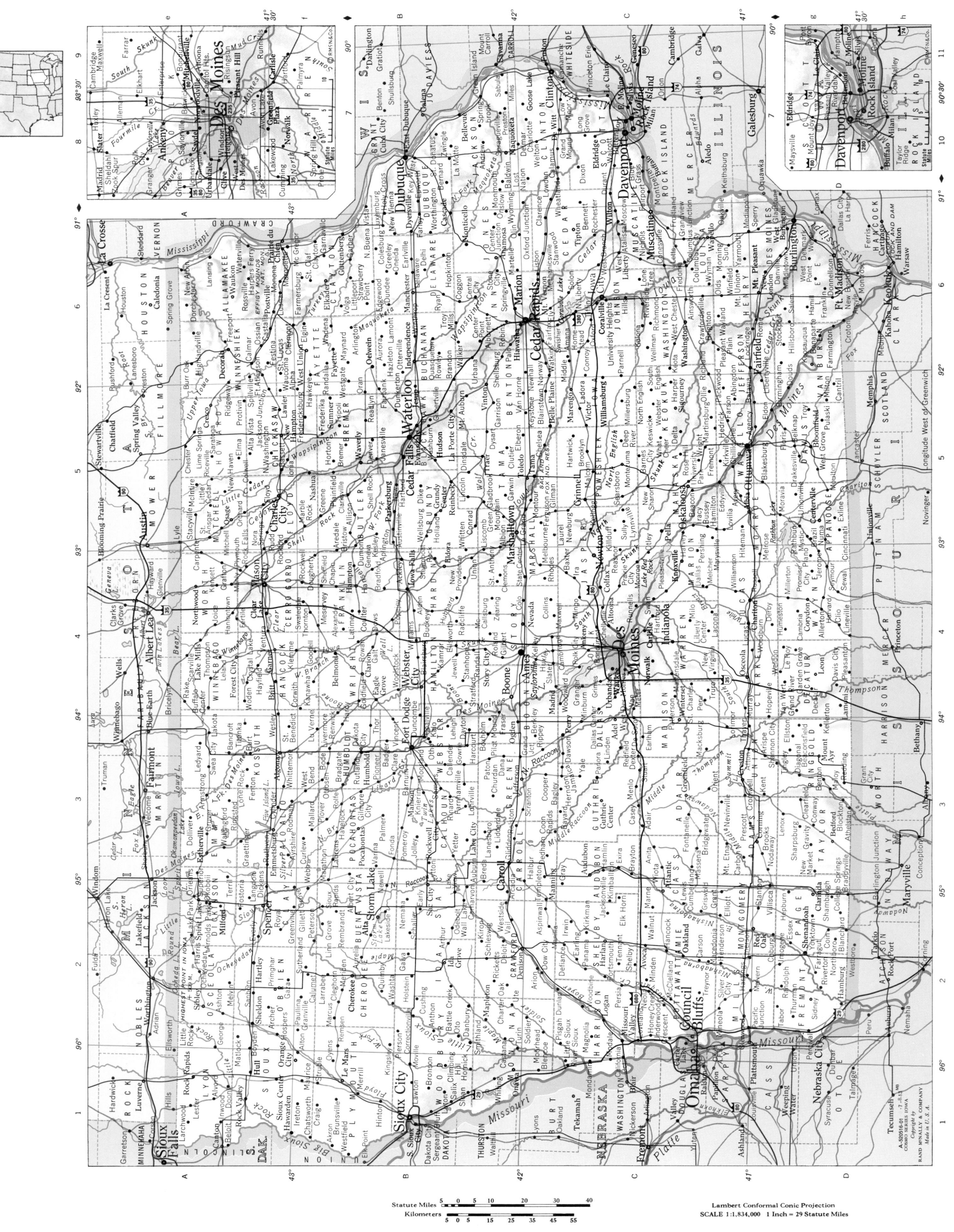
Statute Miles 5 0 5 10 20 30 40
Kilometers 5 0 5 15 25 35 45 55
Lambert Conformal Conic Projection
SCALE 1:1,834,000 1 Inch = 29 Statute Miles

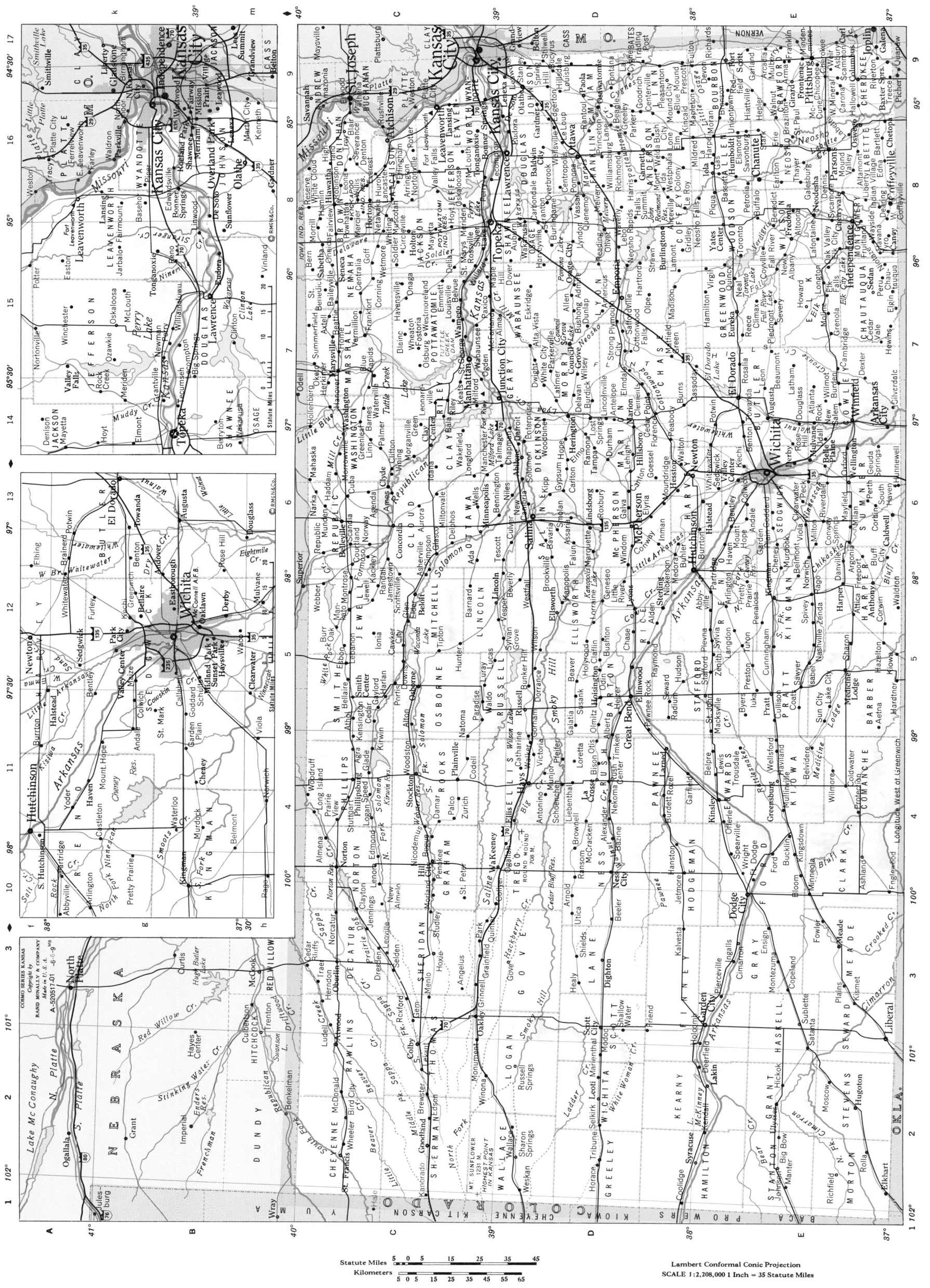

Statute Miles

Kilometers

Lambert Conformal Conic Projection
SCALE 1:2,208,000 1 Inch = 35 Statute Miles

Kentucky

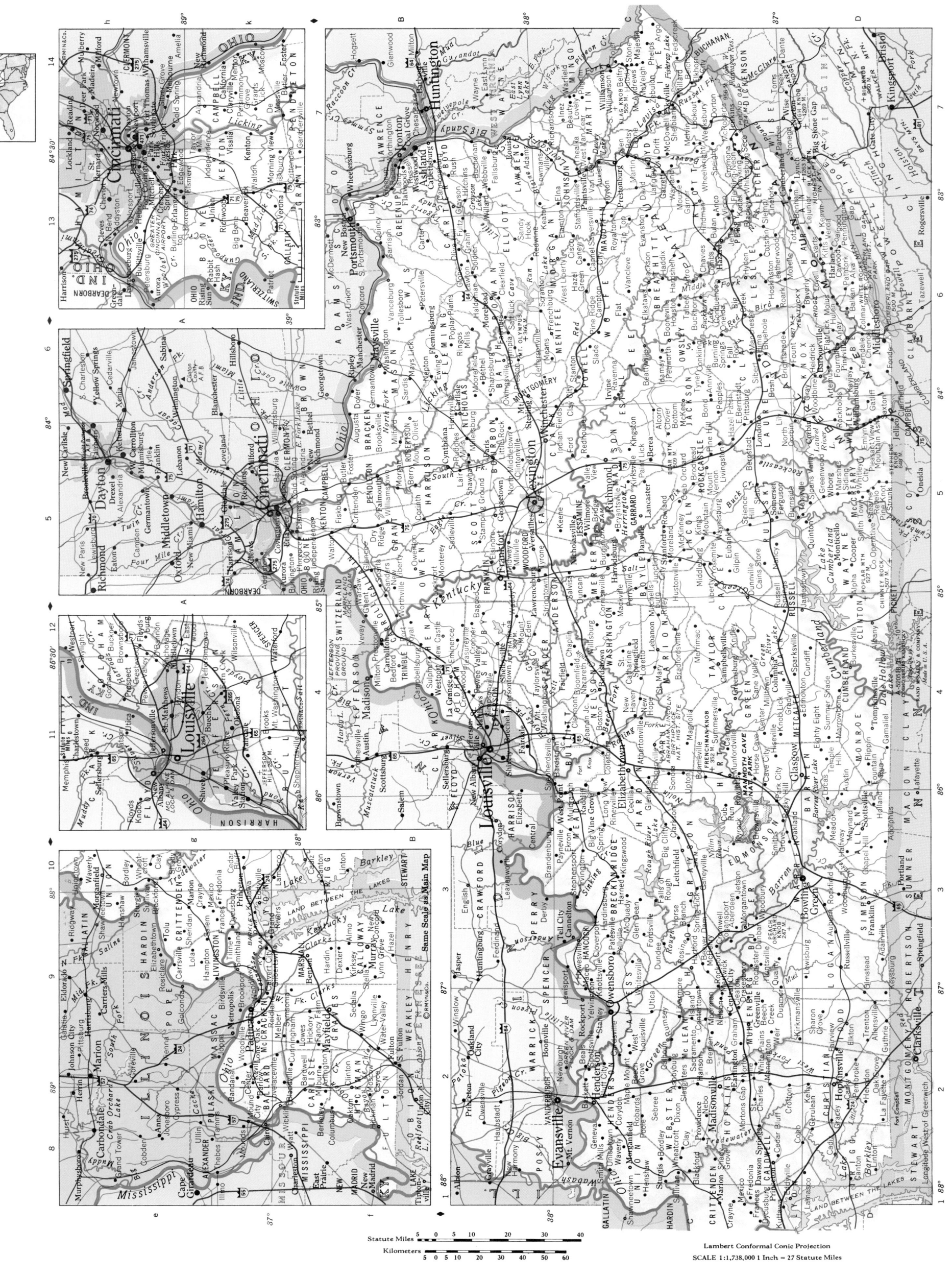

Statute Miles

5   0   5   10   20   30   40

Kilometers

5 0 5 10   20   30   40   50   60

Lambert Conformal Conic Projection
SCALE 1:1,738,000 1 Inch = 27 Statute Miles

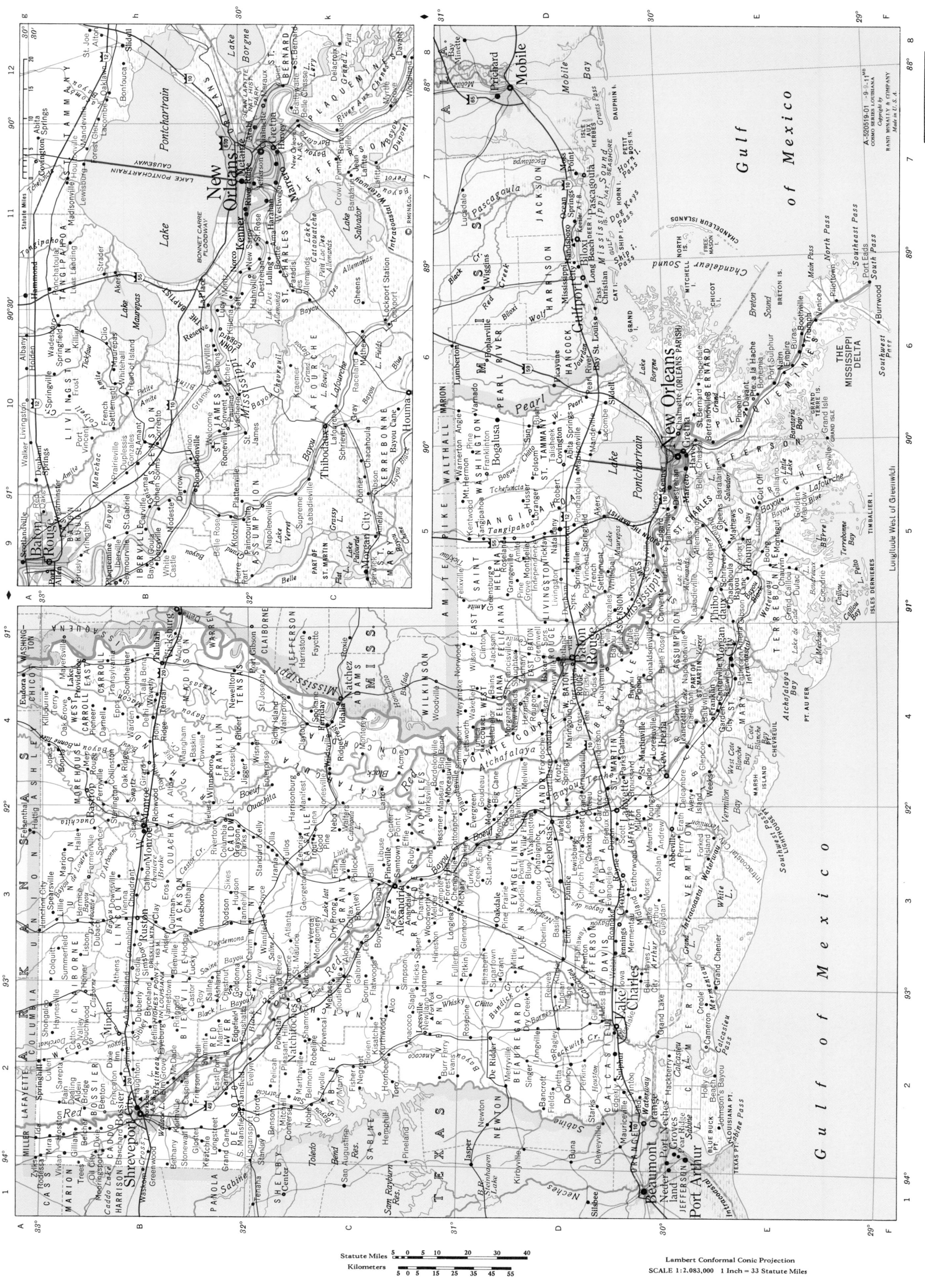

Statute Miles
Kilometers

Lambert Conformal Conic Projection
SCALE 1:2,083,000   1 Inch = 33 Statute Miles

Maine

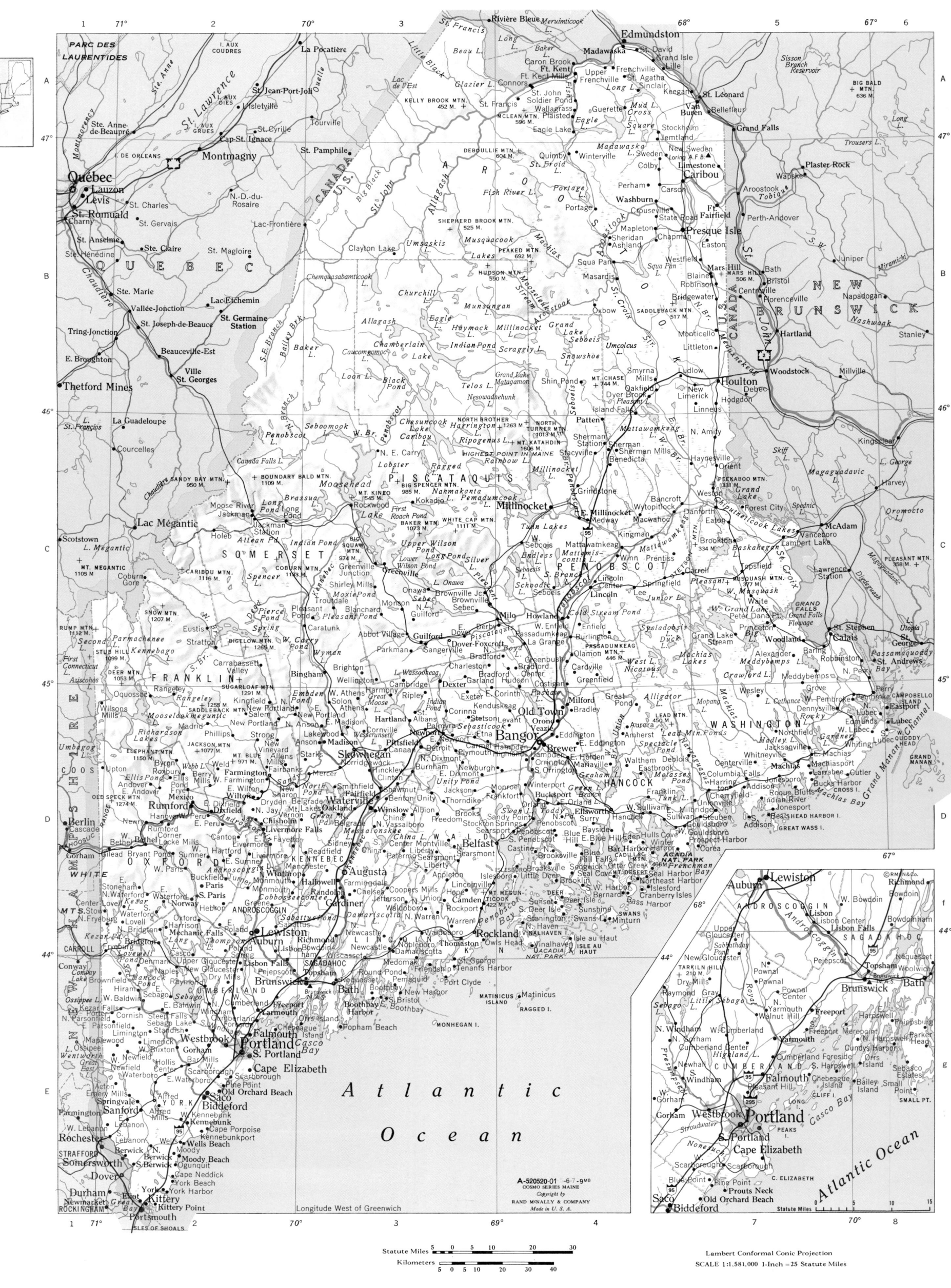

Q U E B E C
N E W B R U N S W I C K
Atlantic Ocean
Edmundston
Québec
Lac Mégantic
Thetford Mines
Caribou
Presque Isle
Houlton
Millinocket
Bangor
Augusta
Lewiston
Auburn
Portland
S. Portland
Cape Elizabeth
Saco
Biddeford
Brunswick
Bath
Rockland
Belfast
Old Town
Calais
Eastport
Berlin
Rochester
Dover
Portsmouth
Kittery
Somersworth
A R O O S T O O K
P I S C A T A Q U I S
S O M E R S E T
F R A N K L I N
P E N O B S C O T
W A S H I N G T O N
H A N C O C K
W A L D O
K E N N E B E C
O X F O R D
A N D R O S C O G G I N
S A G A D A H O C
L I N C O L N
C U M B E R L A N D
Y O R K
MT. KATAHDIN 1606 M.
HIGHEST POINT IN MAINE
Moosehead Lake
A-520520-01 -6-7-9MB
COSMO SERIES MAINE
Copyright by RAND McNALLY & COMPANY
Made in U. S. A.
Longitude West of Greenwich
Statute Miles 5 0 5 10 20 30
Kilometers 5 0 5 10 20 30 40
Lambert Conformal Conic Projection
SCALE 1:1,581,000 1 Inch = 25 Statute Miles

Statute Miles
Kilometers

Lambert Conformal Conic Projection
SCALE 1:985,000 1 Inch = 15.5 Statute Miles

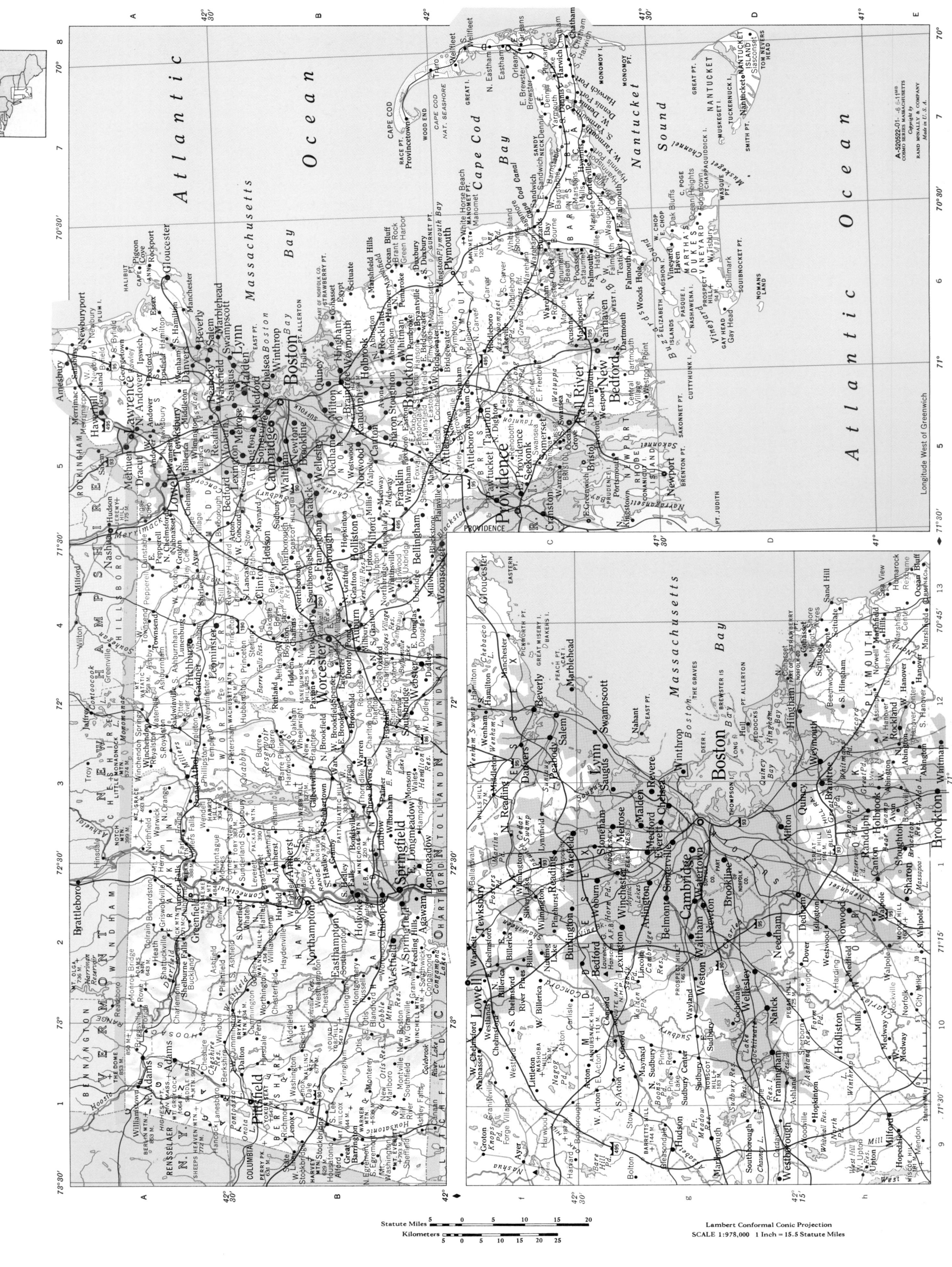

Statute Miles

Kilometers

Lambert Conformal Conic Projection
SCALE 1:978,000   1 Inch = 15.5 Statute Miles

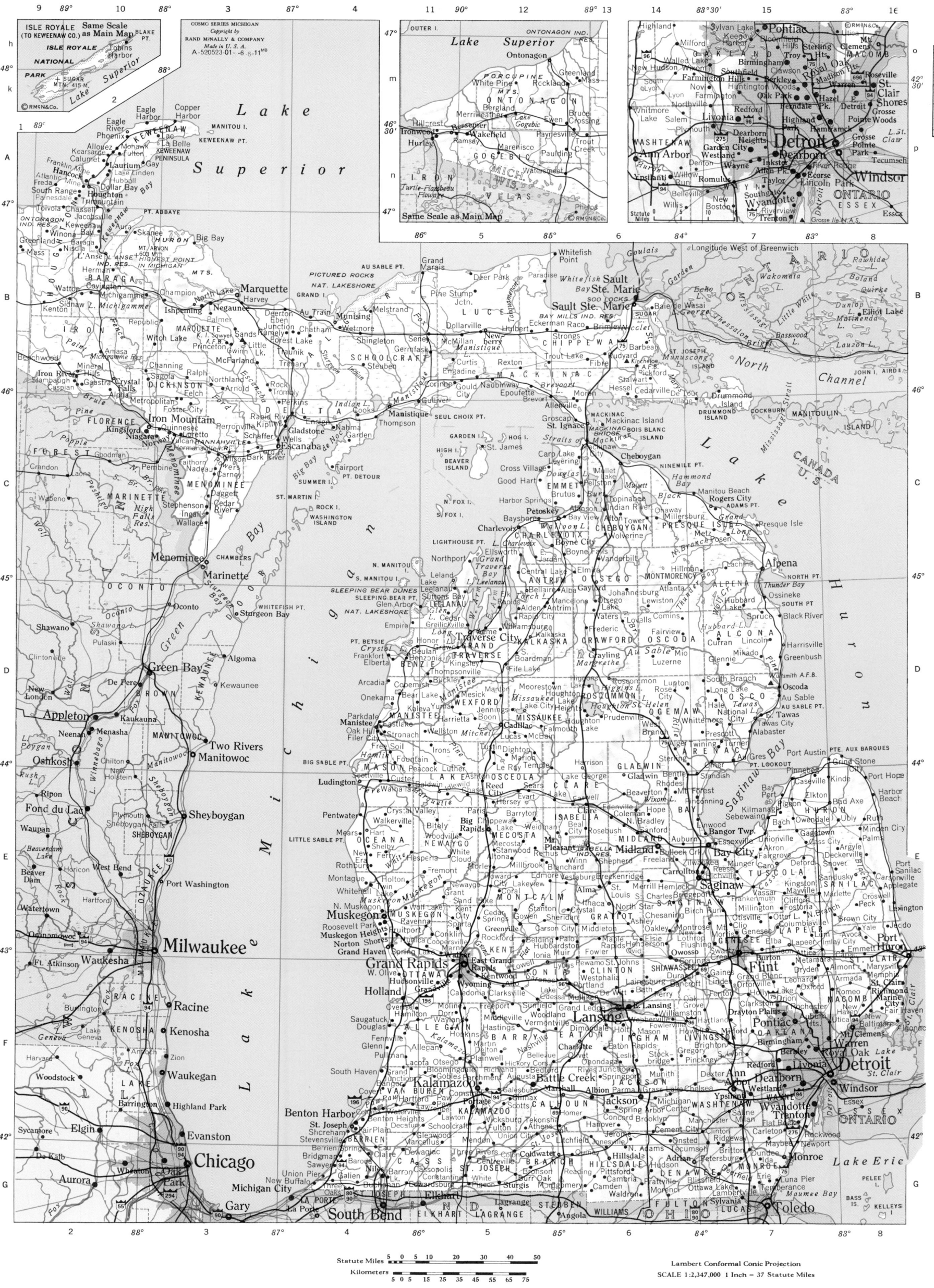

Statute Miles
5 0 5 10   20   30   40   50

Kilometers
5 0 5 15 25 35 45 55 65 75

Lambert Conformal Conic Projection
SCALE 1:2,347,000 1 Inch = 37 Statute Miles

Minnesota

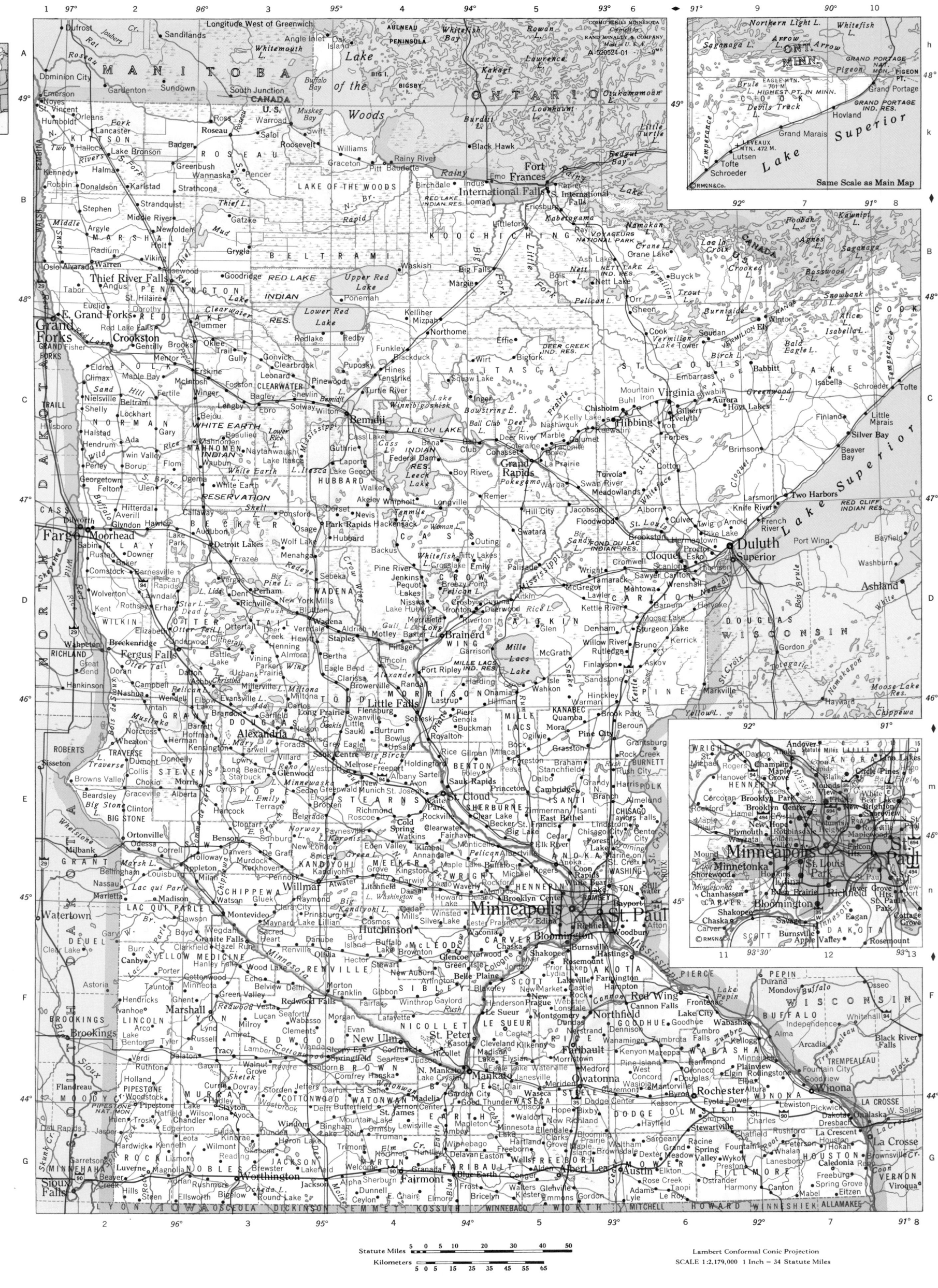

Longitude West of Greenwich
MANITOBA
ONTARIO
CANADA
U.S.
Lake of the Woods
Rainy Lake
Lake Superior
Upper Red Lake
Lower Red Lake
Mille Lacs Lake
Leech Lake
NORTH DAKOTA
SOUTH DAKOTA
IOWA
WISCONSIN
Grand Forks
Fargo
Moorhead
Thief River Falls
Crookston
International Falls
Fort Frances
Bemidji
Grand Rapids
Hibbing
Virginia
Duluth
Superior
Brainerd
Fergus Falls
Alexandria
Little Falls
St. Cloud
Willmar
Minneapolis
St. Paul
Bloomington
Hutchinson
Marshall
New Ulm
Mankato
Red Wing
Northfield
Faribault
Owatonna
Rochester
Winona
La Crosse
Albert Lea
Austin
Worthington
Fairmont
Sioux Falls
Brookings
Watertown
Same Scale as Main Map
Statute Miles 5 0 5 10 20 30 40 50
Kilometers 5 0 5 15 25 35 45 55 65
Lambert Conformal Conic Projection
SCALE 1:2,179,000 1 Inch = 34 Statute Miles

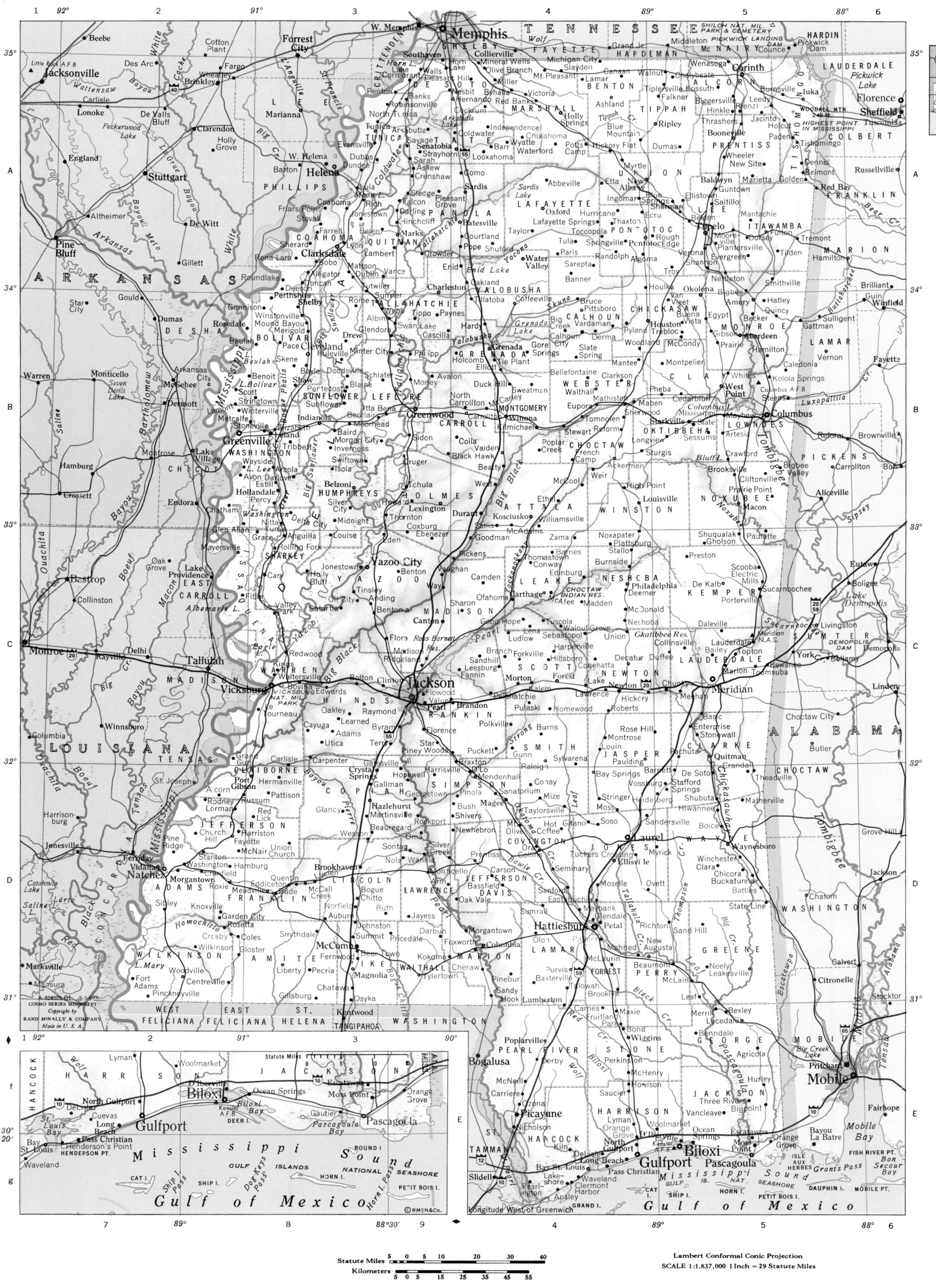

Statute Miles 5 0 5 10 20 30 40
Kilometers 5 0 5 15 25 35 45 55

Lambert Conformal Conic Projection
SCALE 1:1,837,000 1 Inch = 29 Statute Miles

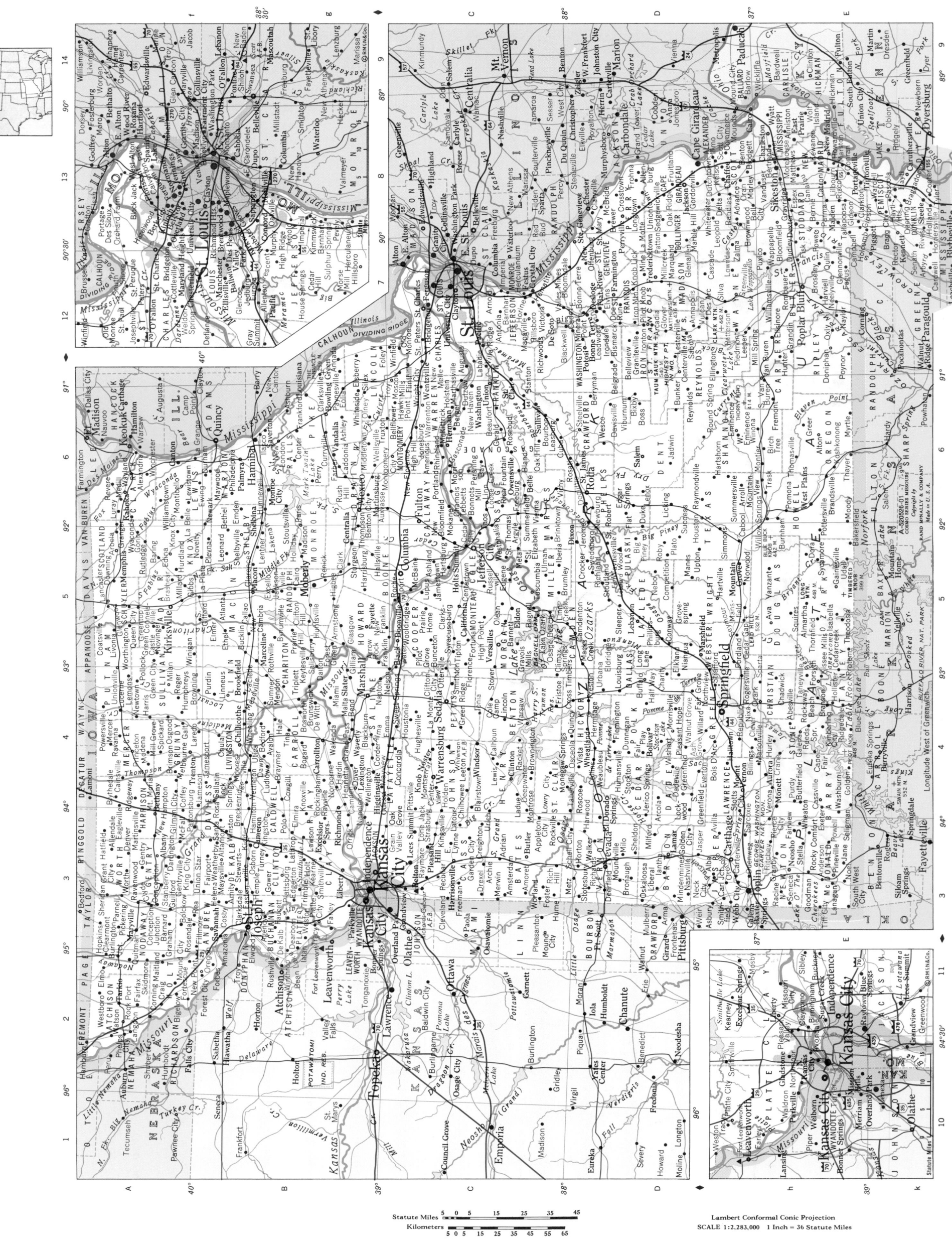

Statute Miles 5 0 5 15 25 35 45
Kilometers 5 0 5 15 25 35 45 55 65

Lambert Conformal Conic Projection
SCALE 1:2,283,000   1 Inch = 36 Statute Miles

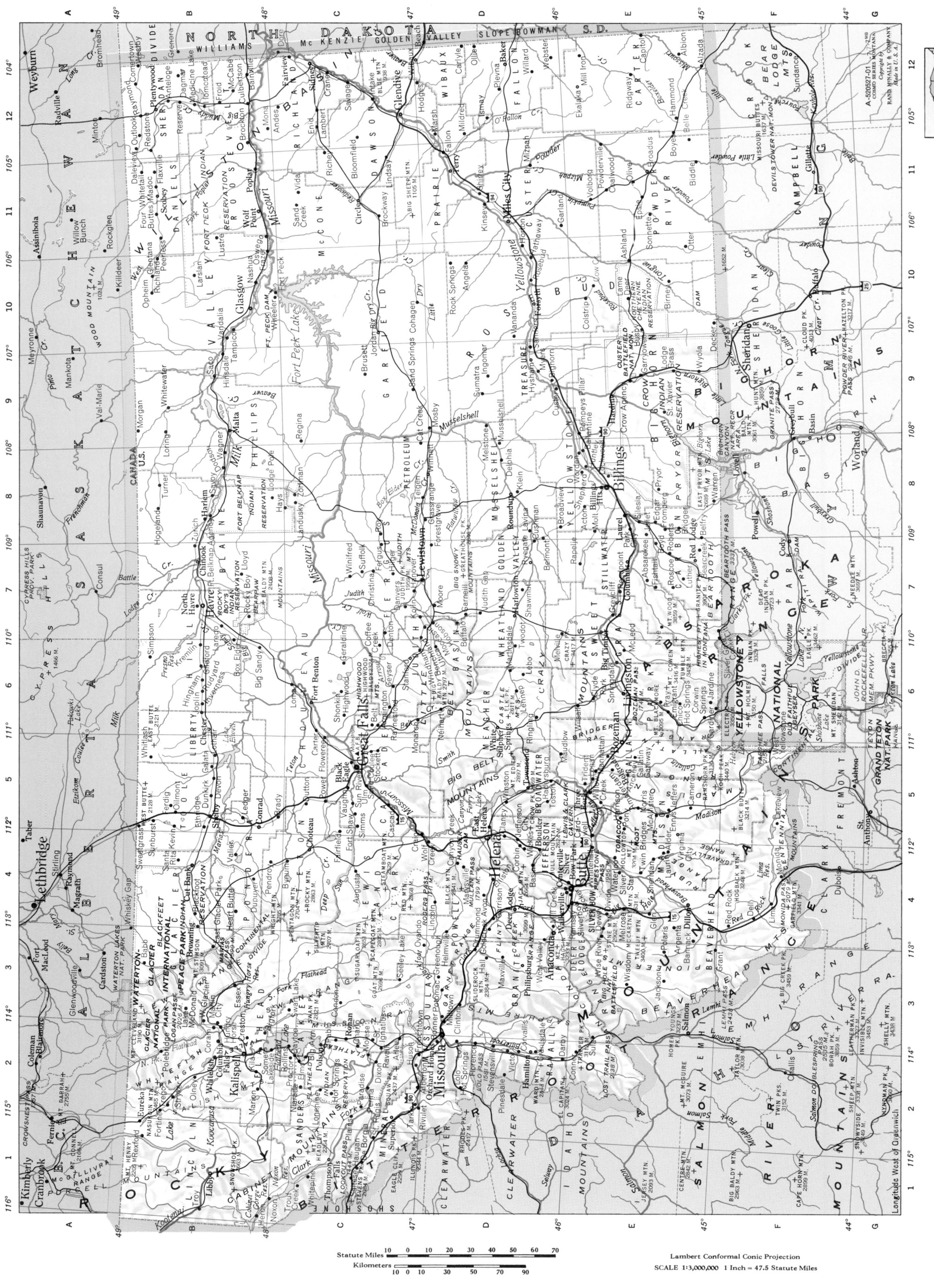

Statute Miles 10 0 10 20 30 40 50 60 70
Kilometers 10 0 10 30 50 70 90

Lambert Conformal Conic Projection
SCALE 1:3,000,000 1 Inch = 47.5 Statute Miles

Nebraska

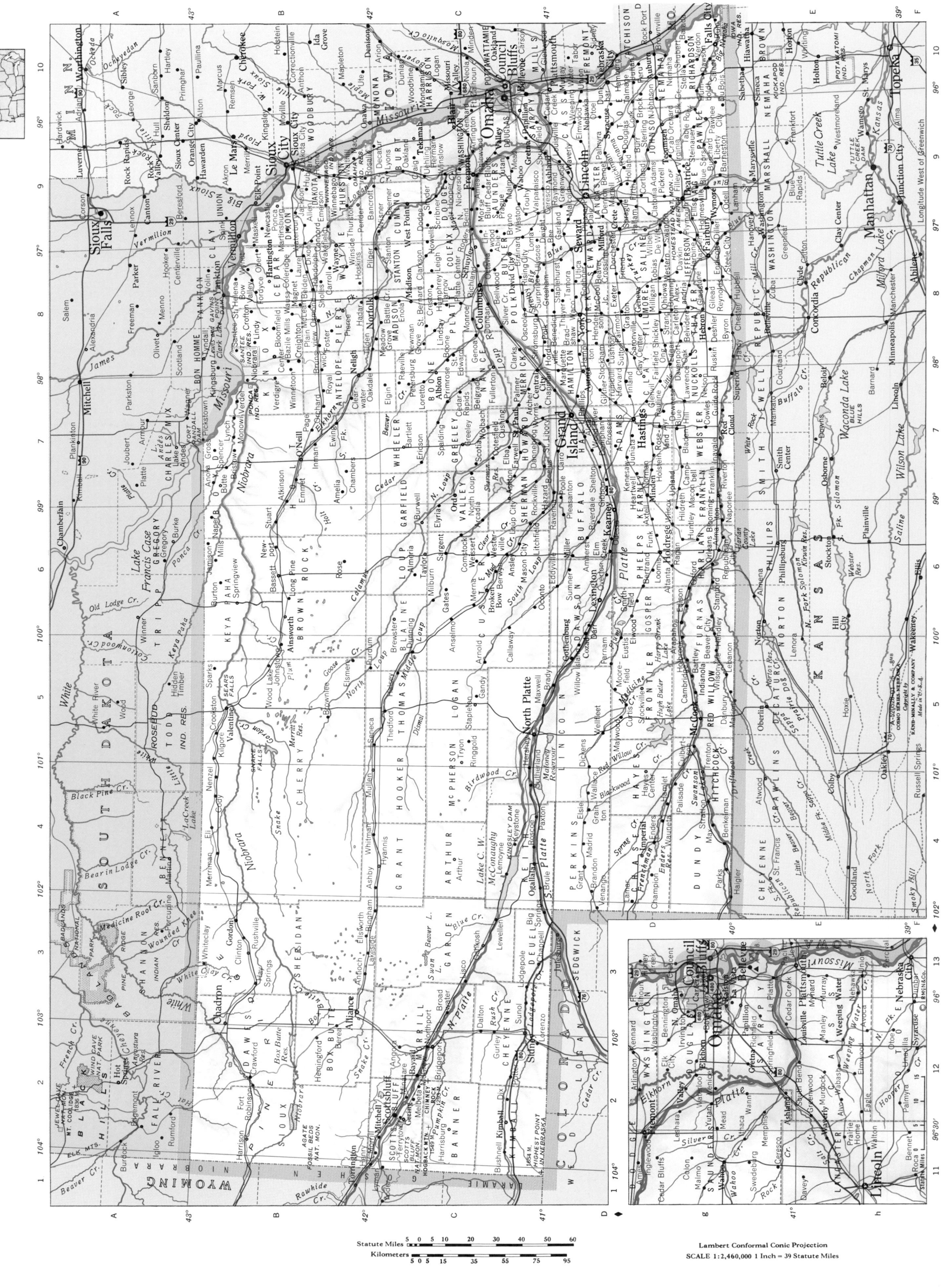

Statute Miles 5 0 5 10 20 30 40 50 60
Kilometers 5 0 5 15 35 55 75 95

Lambert Conformal Conic Projection
SCALE 1:2,460,000 1 Inch = 39 Statute Miles

134

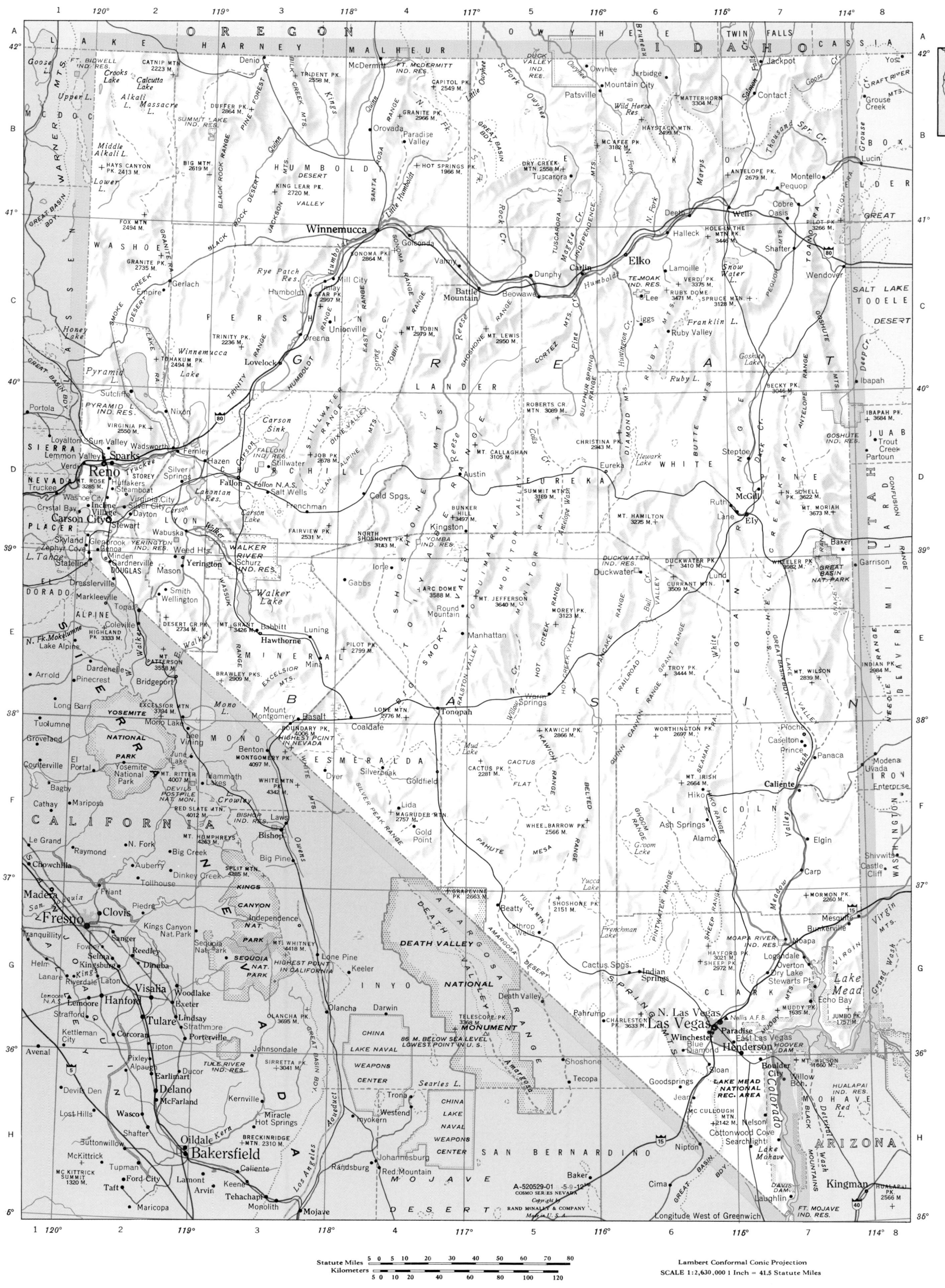

Lambert Conformal Conic Projection
SCALE 1:2,630,000 1 Inch = 41.5 Statute Miles

Statute Miles
Kilometers

A-520529-01 5-9-12
COSMO SERIES NEVADA
Copyright by
RAND M⁽ᴺᴬˡˡʸ & COMPANY
Made in U.S.A.

Longitude West of Greenwich

New Hampshire

Same Scale as Main Map

Statute Miles 5 0 5 10 20

Kilometers 5 0 5 10 15 20 25

Lambert Conformal Conic Projection

SCALE 1:792,000 1 Inch = 12.75 Statute Miles

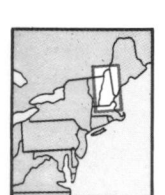

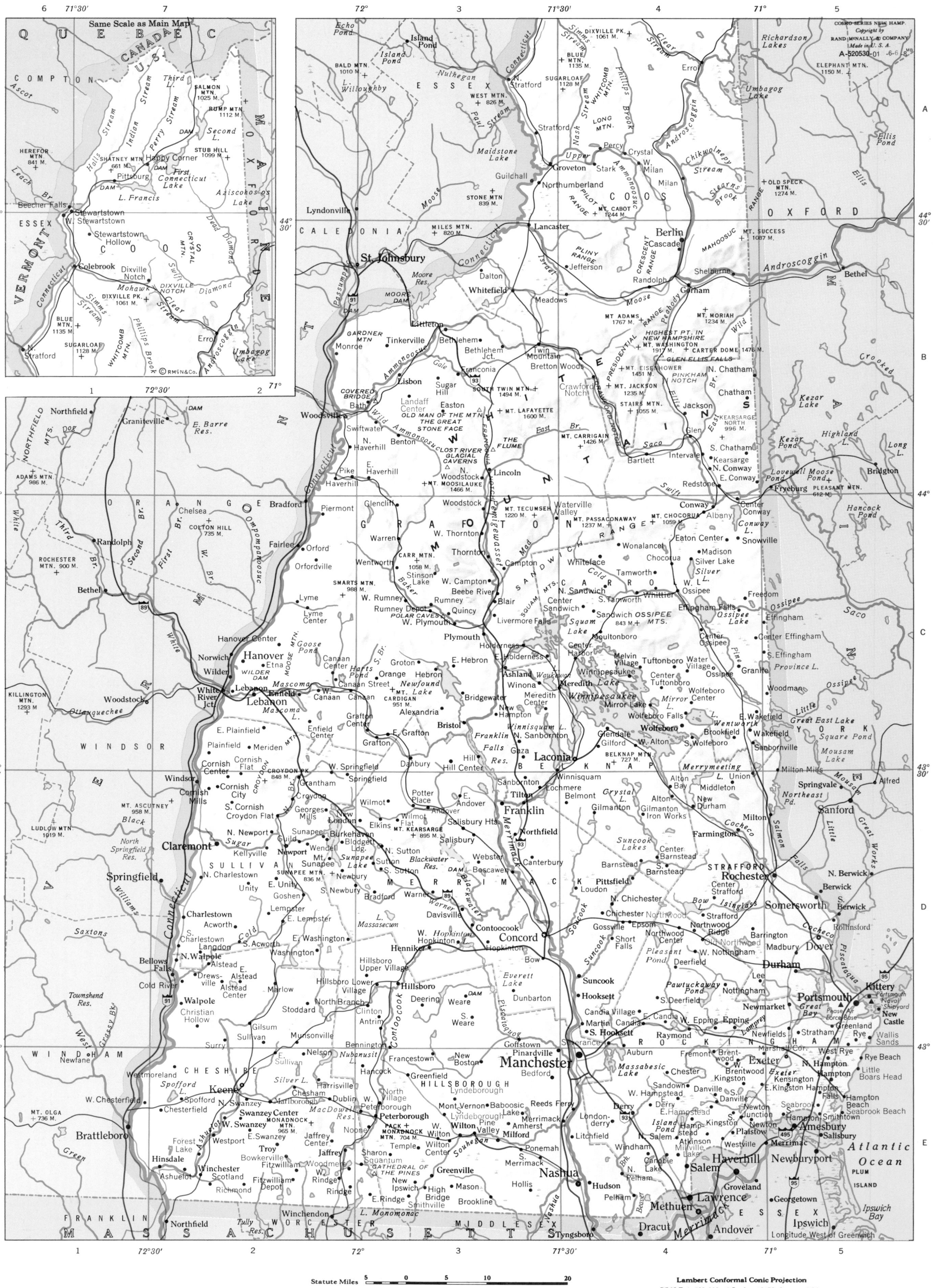

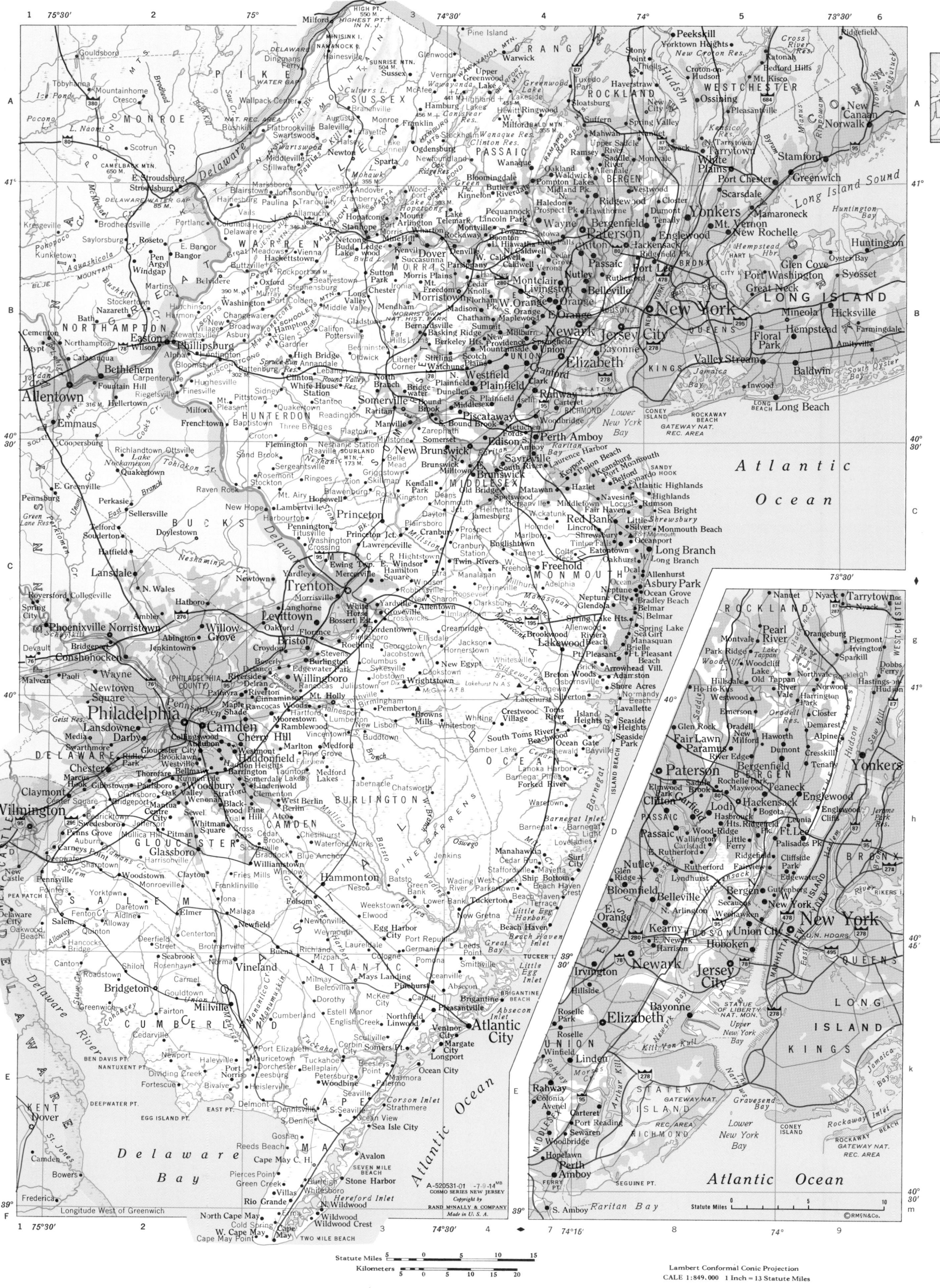

New Mexico

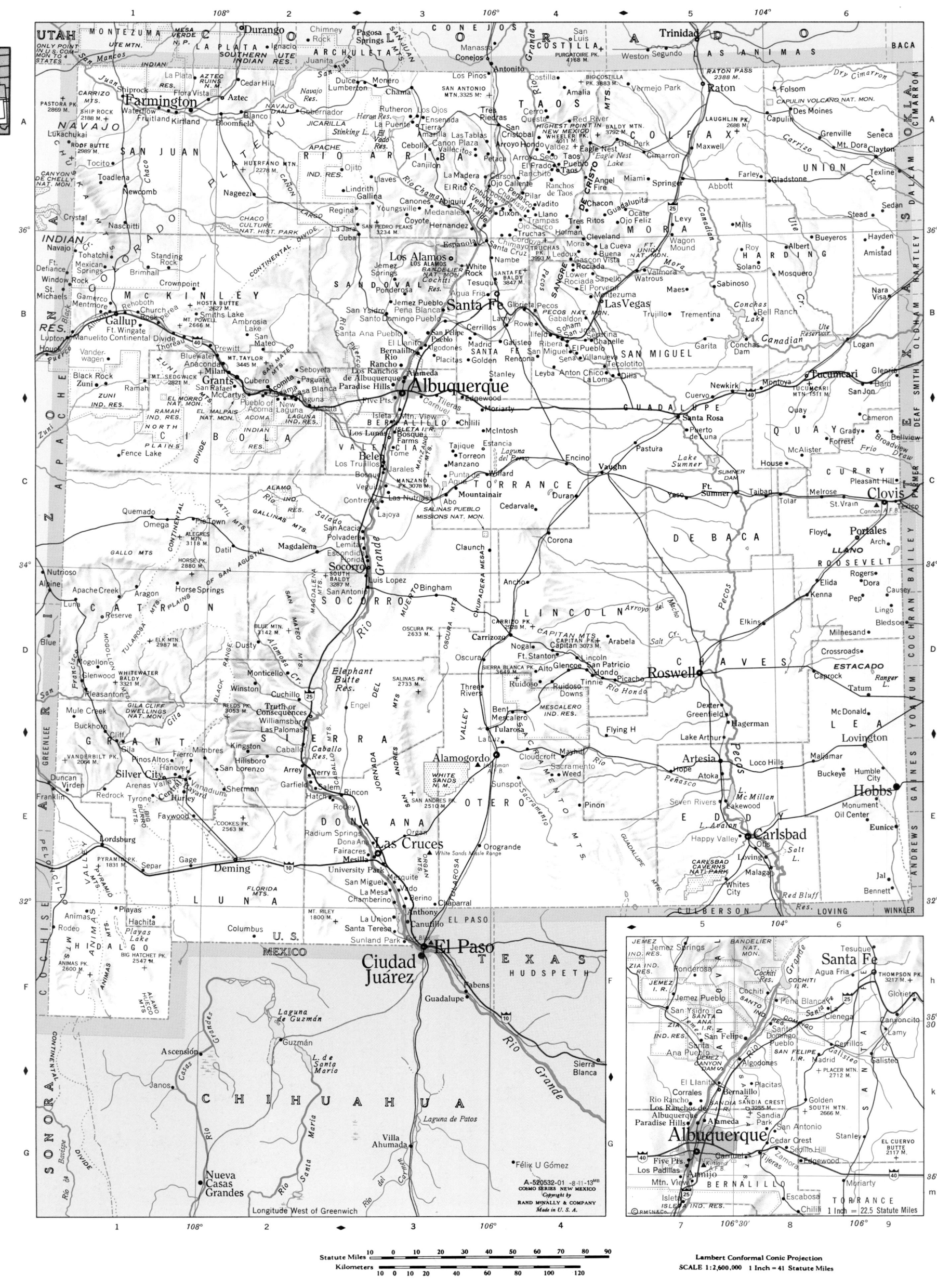
UTAH
COLORADO
ARIZONA
TEXAS
OKLA.
MEXICO
CHIHUAHUA
SONORA
SAN JUAN
RIO ARRIBA
TAOS
COLFAX
UNION
MORA
HARDING
McKINLEY
SANDOVAL
SANTA FE
SAN MIGUEL
GUADALUPE
QUAY
CURRY
CIBOLA
VALENCIA
BERNALILLO
TORRANCE
DE BACA
ROOSEVELT
CATRON
SOCORRO
LINCOLN
CHAVES
GRANT
SIERRA
OTERO
LEA
EDDY
DONA ANA
LUNA
HIDALGO
Farmington
Gallup
Grants
Albuquerque
Santa Fe
Los Alamos
Las Vegas
Raton
Tucumcari
Clovis
Portales
Socorro
Roswell
Alamogordo
Las Cruces
Deming
Silver City
Lordsburg
Artesia
Carlsbad
Hobbs
Lovington
Ruidoso
Santa Rosa
Belen
Truth or Consequences
El Paso
Ciudad Juárez
Rio Grande
Pecos
Canadian
Lambert Conformal Conic Projection
SCALE 1:2,600,000 1 Inch = 41 Statute Miles
Statute Miles
Kilometers
Longitude West of Greenwich
A-520532-01 -8-11-13MB
COSMO SERIES NEW MEXICO
Copyright by RAND McNALLY & COMPANY
Made in U. S. A.
1 Inch = 22.5 Statute Miles

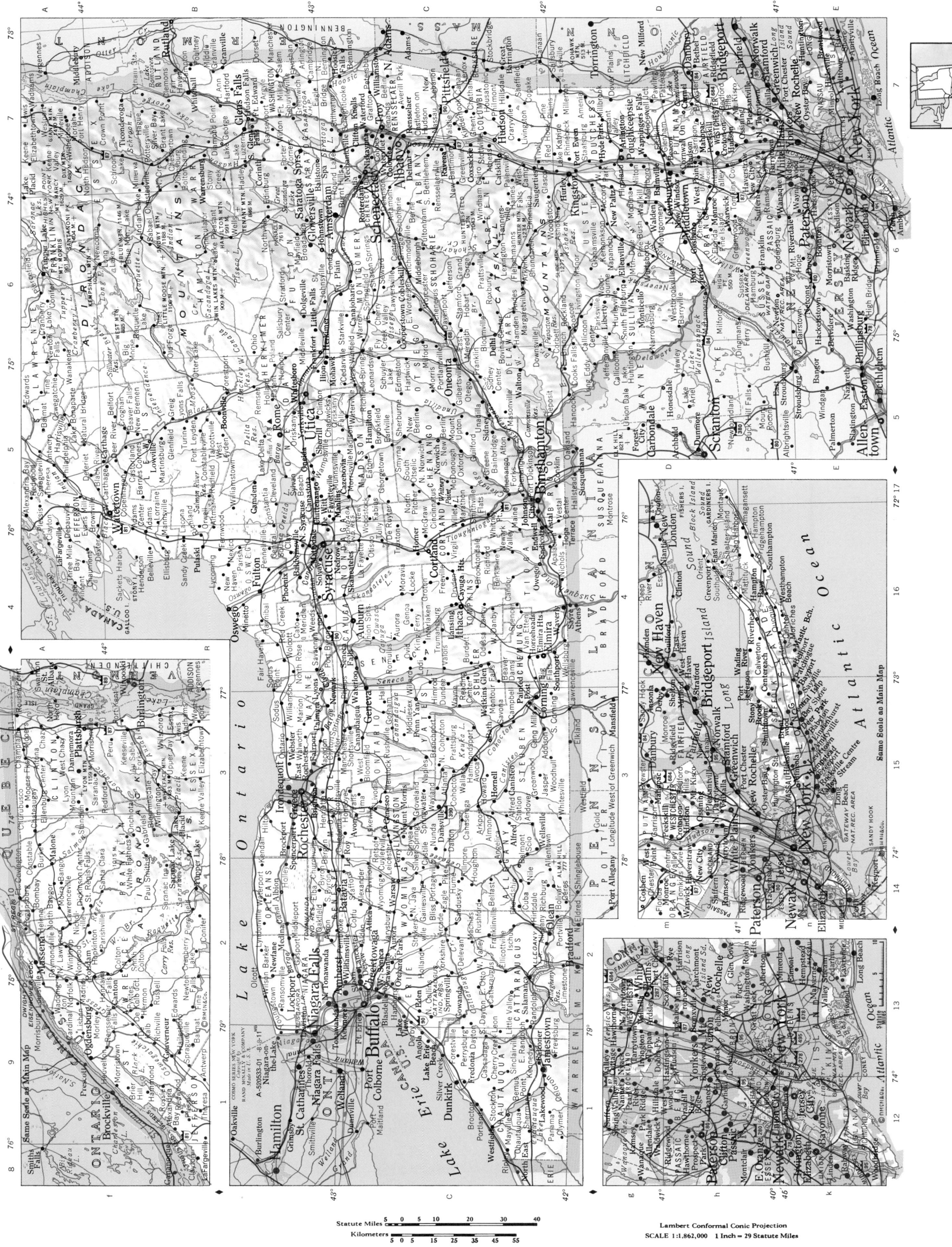

Statute Miles
Kilometers

Lambert Conformal Conic Projection
SCALE 1:1,862,000   1 Inch = 29 Statute Miles

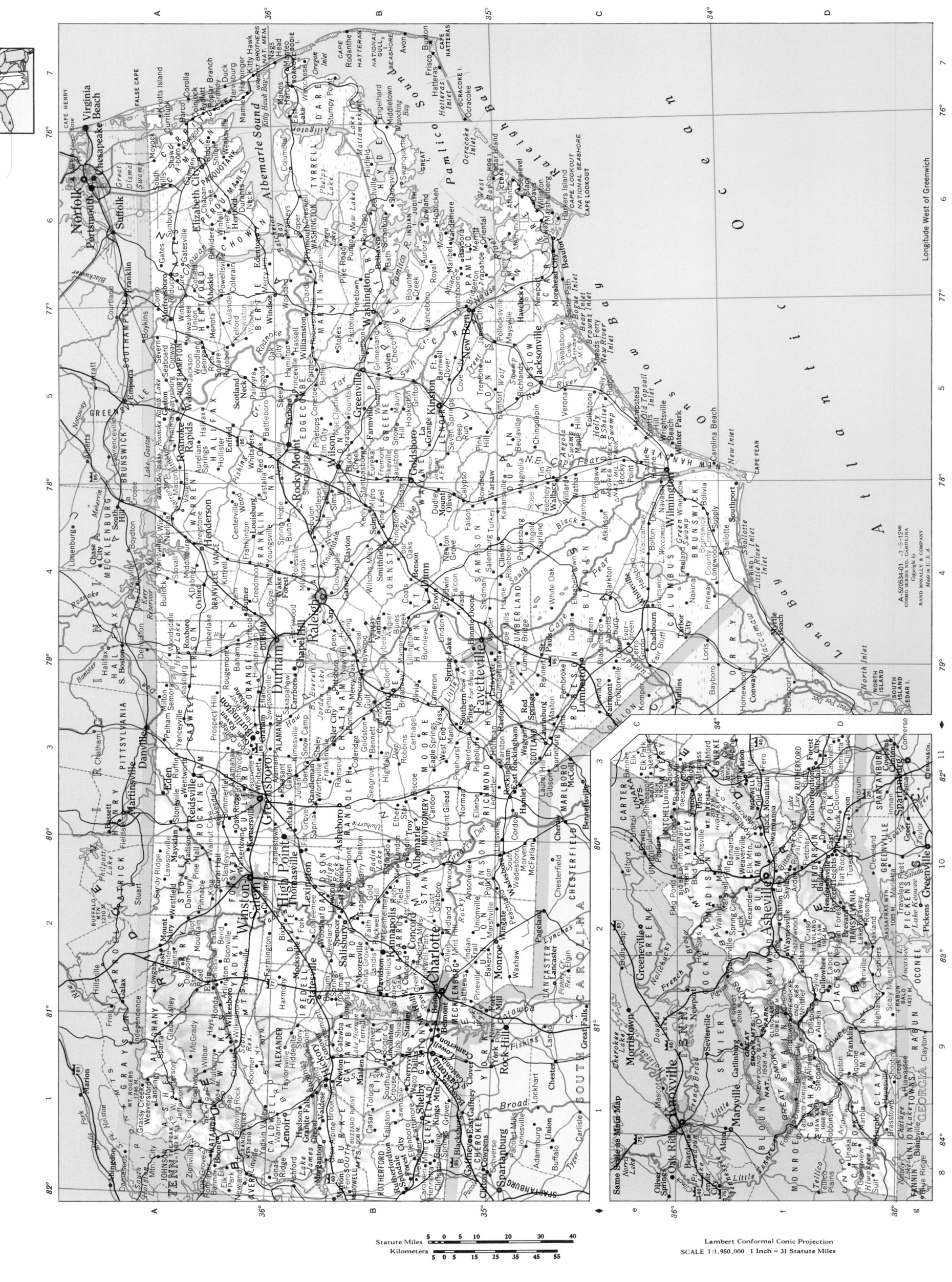

Statute Miles
Kilometers

Lambert Conformal Conic Projection
SCALE 1:1,950,000   1 Inch = 31 Statute Miles

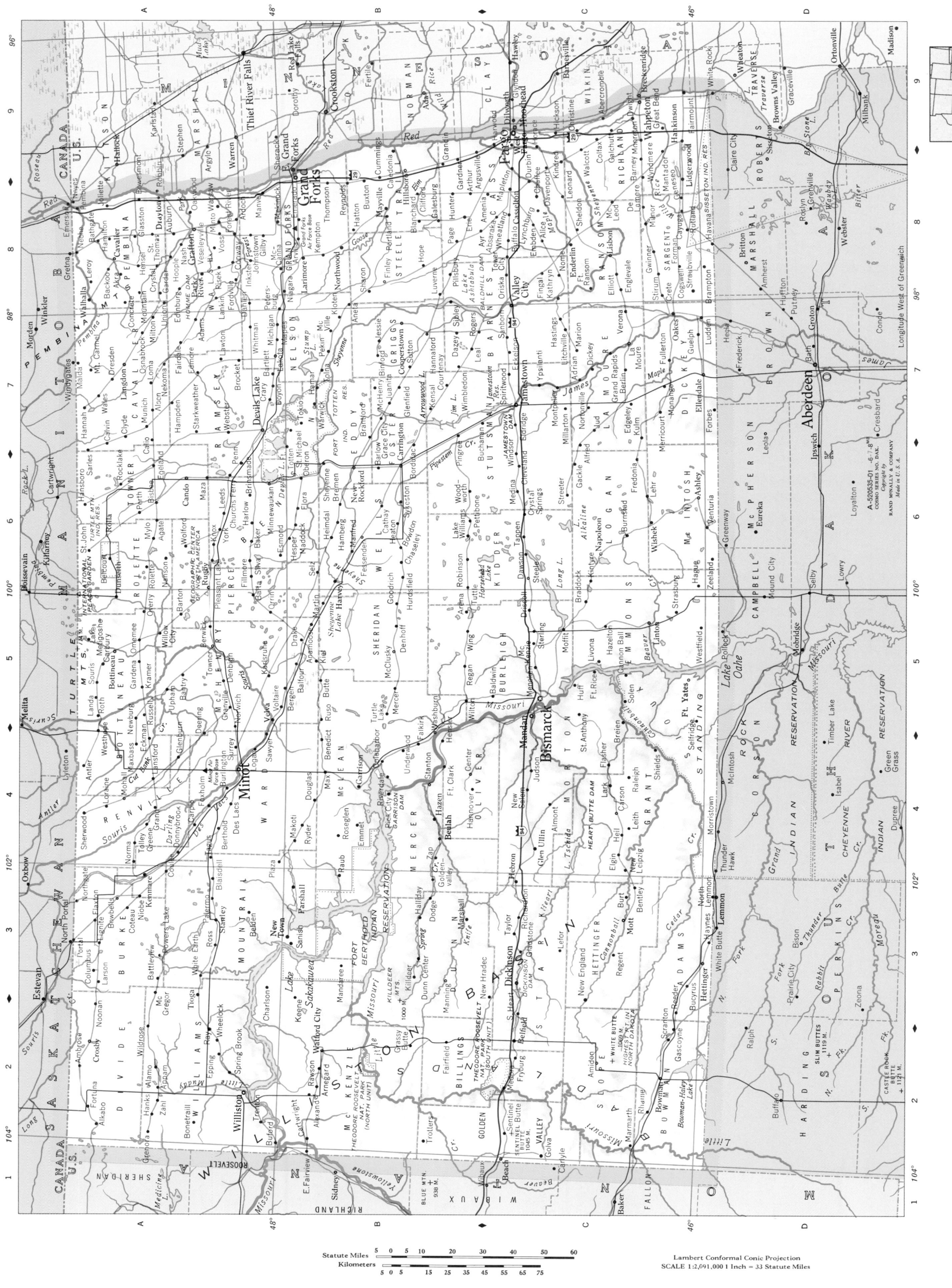

Statute Miles
Kilometers

Lambert Conformal Conic Projection
SCALE 1:2,091,000 1 Inch = 33 Statute Miles

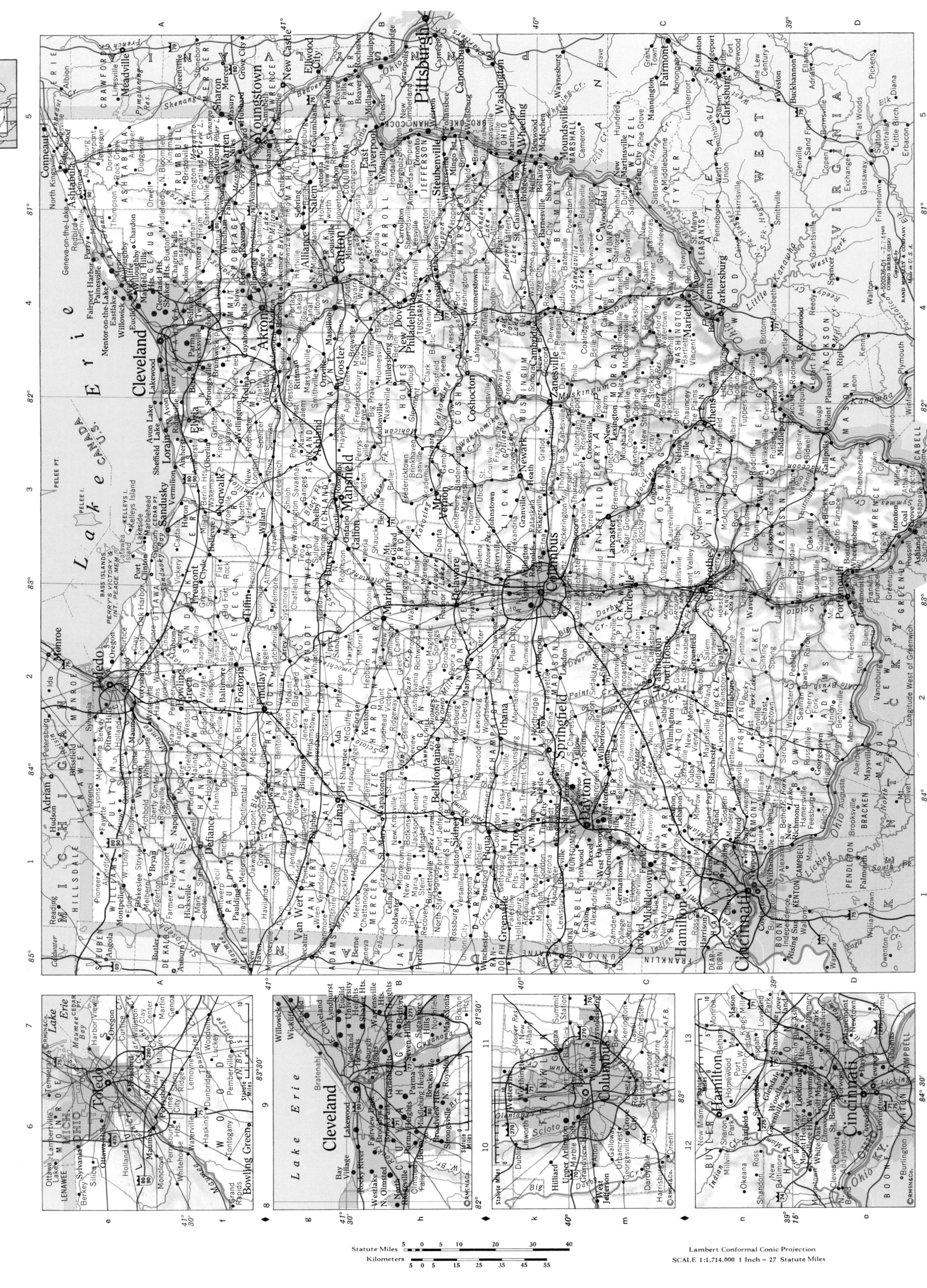
Lake Erie
CANADA
U.S.
MICHIGAN
INDIANA
KENTUCKY
WEST VIRGINIA
PENNSYLVANIA
Cleveland
Toledo
Columbus
Cincinnati
Dayton
Akron
Youngstown
Canton
Pittsburgh
Springfield
Mansfield
Hamilton
Longitude West of Greenwich
A-520536-D1 -7-7-11
COSMO SERIES OHIO
Copyright by RAND McNALLY & COMPANY
Made in U.S.A.
Statute Miles 5 0 5 10 20 30 40
Kilometers 5 0 5 15 25 35 45 55
Lambert Conformal Conic Projection
SCALE 1:1,714,000 1 Inch = 27 Statute Miles

Oklahoma

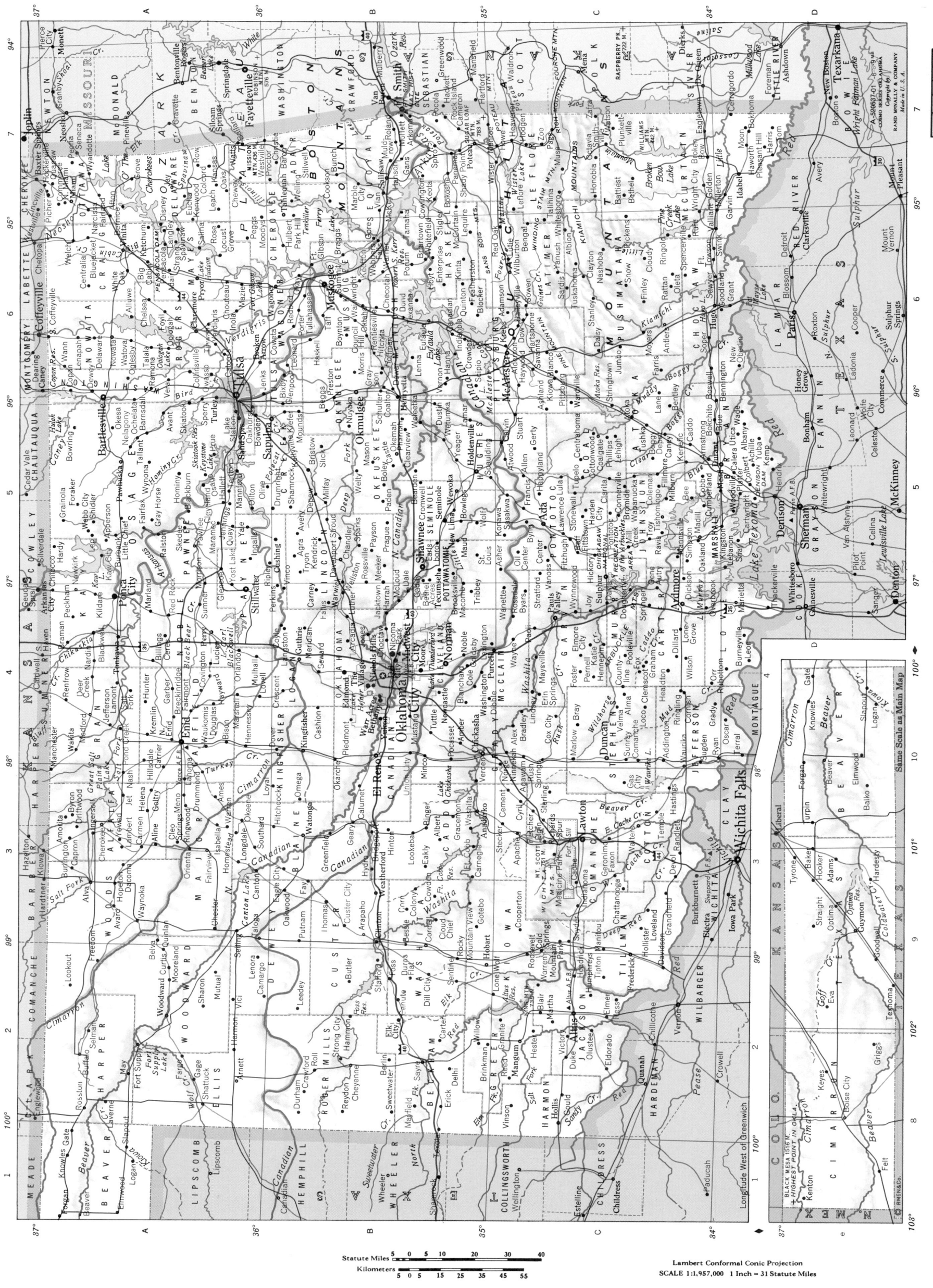

Statute Miles

Kilometers

Lambert Conformal Conic Projection
SCALE 1:1,957,000 1 Inch = 31 Statute Miles

Same Scale as Main Map

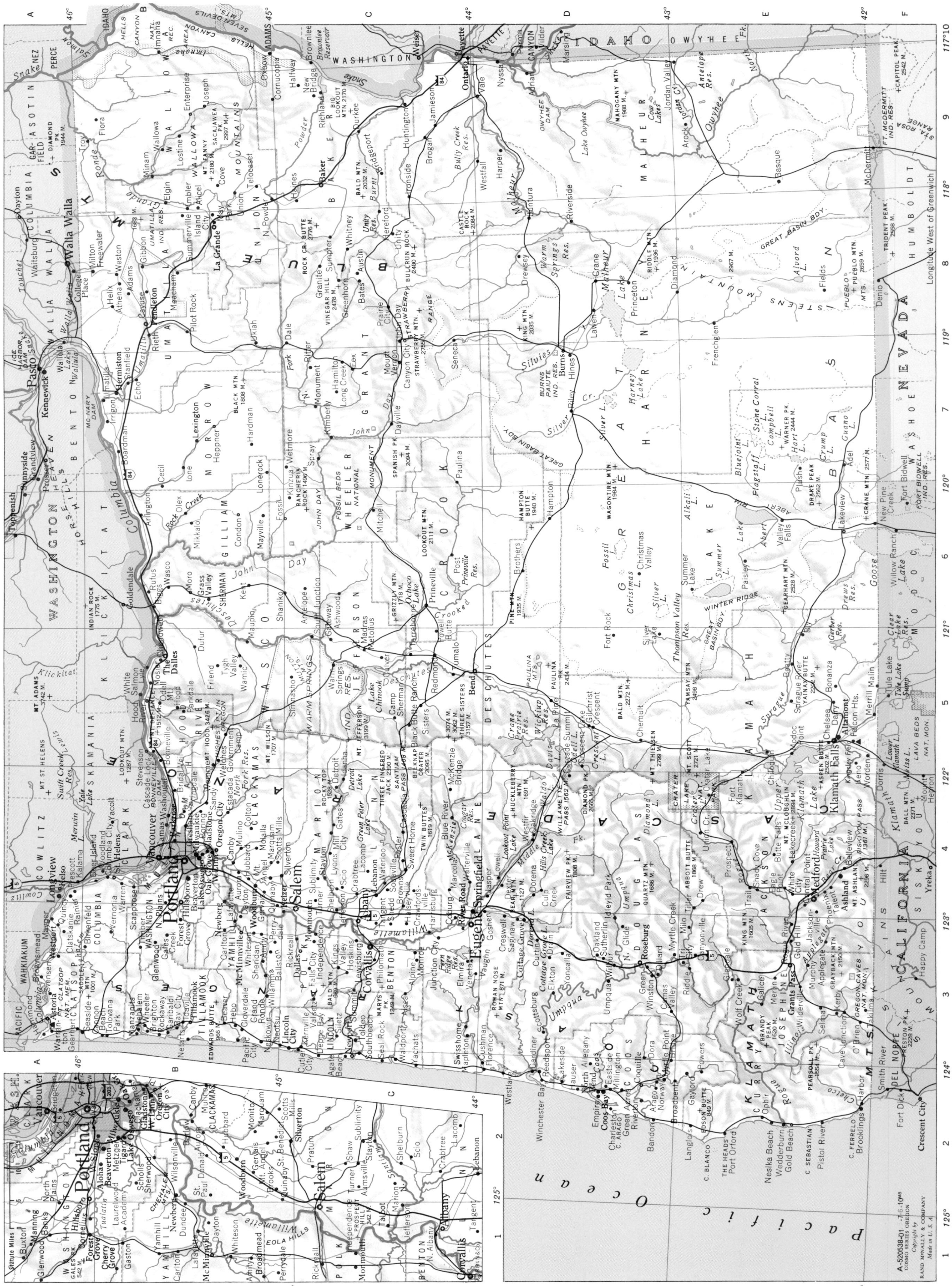

Lambert Conformal Conic Projection
SCALE 1:2,329,000 1 Inch = 37 Statute Miles

Statute Miles 5 0 5 10 20 30 40 50
Kilometers 5 0 5 15 25 35 45 55 65 75

A-520538-O1   7-6-70³³
COSMO SERIES OREGON
Copyright by
RAND M°NALLY & COMPANY
Made in U.S.A.

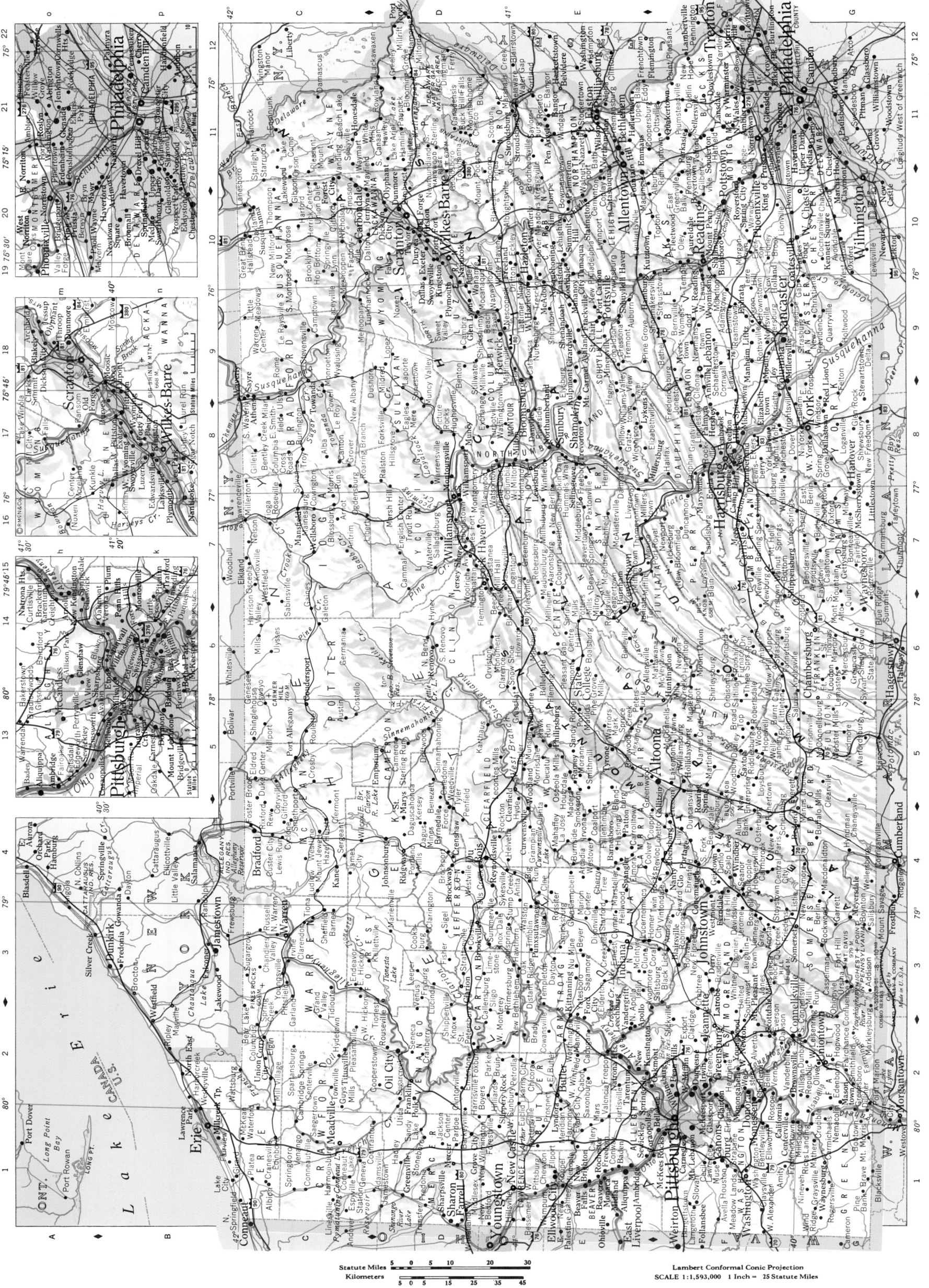

Statute Miles
Kilometers

Lambert Conformal Conic Projection
SCALE 1:1,593,000   1 Inch = 25 Statute Miles

Rhode Island

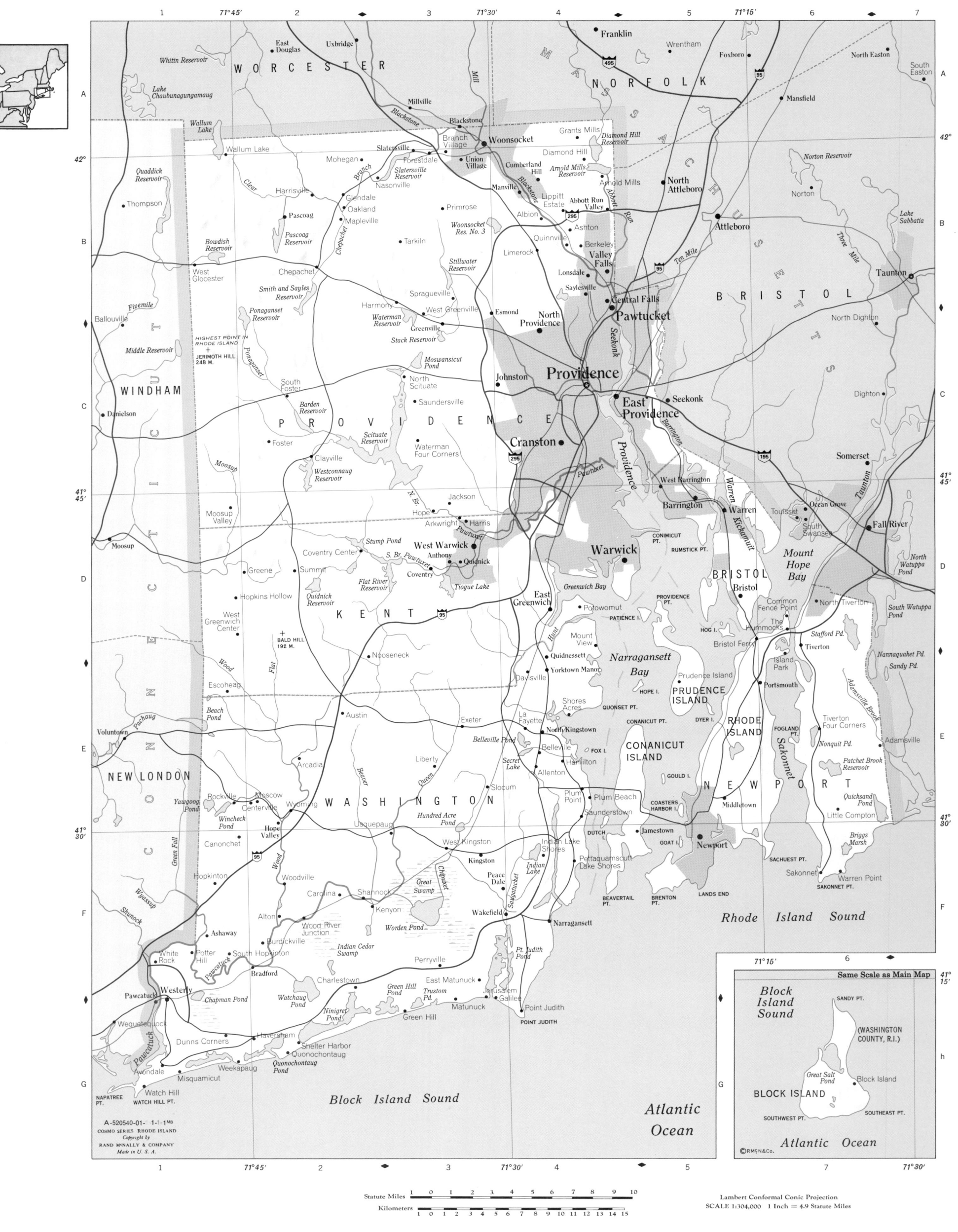

Statute Miles 1 0 1 2 3 4 5 6 7 8 9 10

Kilometers 1 0 1 2 3 4 5 6 7 8 9 10 11 12 13 14 15

Lambert Conformal Conic Projection
SCALE 1:304,000   1 Inch = 4.9 Statute Miles

A-520540-01- 1-1-1 MB
COSMO SERIES RHODE ISLAND
Copyright by
RAND MCNALLY & COMPANY
Made in U.S.A.

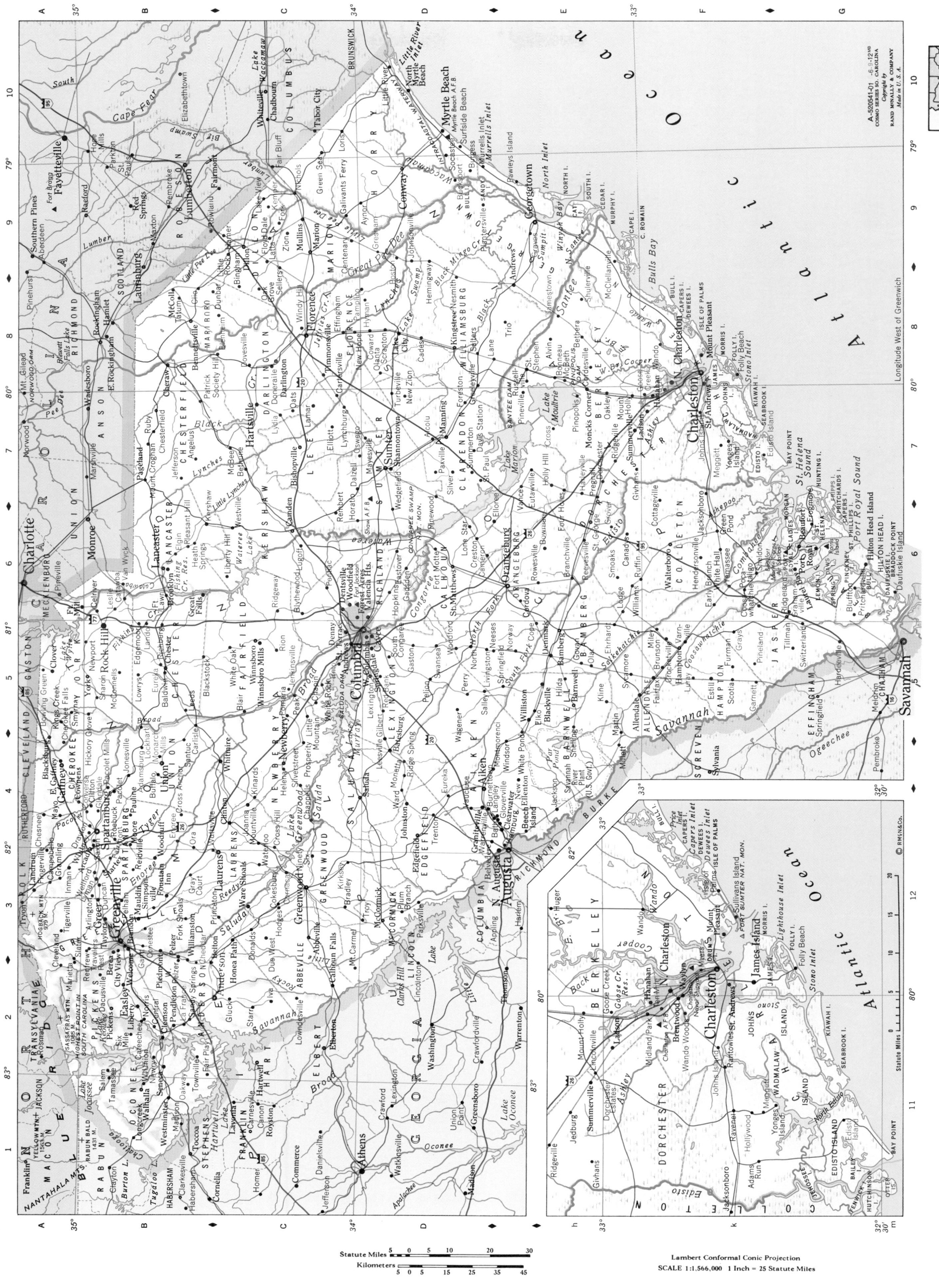

Lambert Conformal Conic Projection
SCALE 1:1,566,000   1 Inch = 25 Statute Miles

Statute Miles
Kilometers

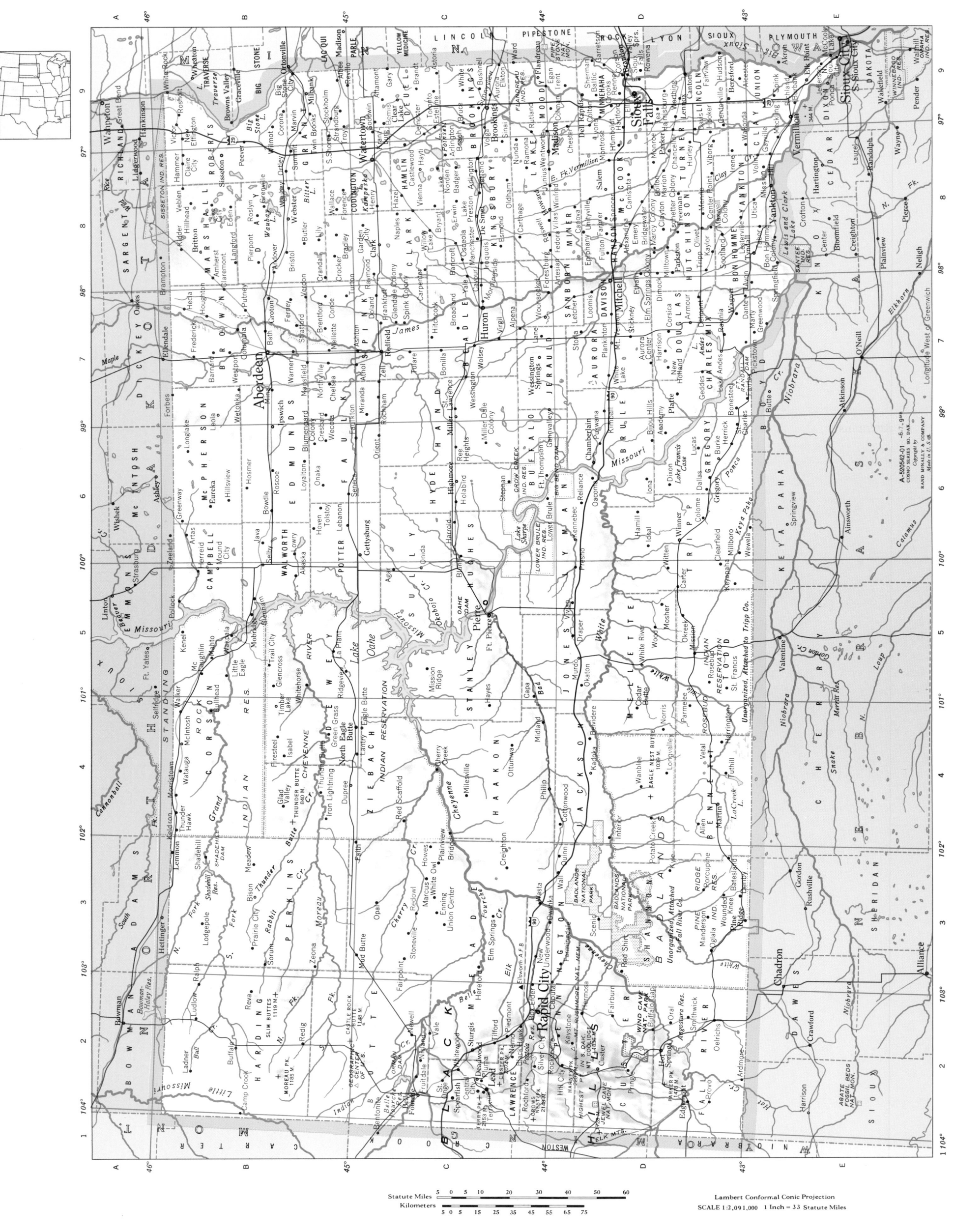

Statute Miles 5 0 5 10 20 30 40 50 60
Kilometers 5 0 5 15 25 35 45 55 65 75

Lambert Conformal Conic Projection
SCALE 1:2,091,000   1 Inch = 33 Statute Miles

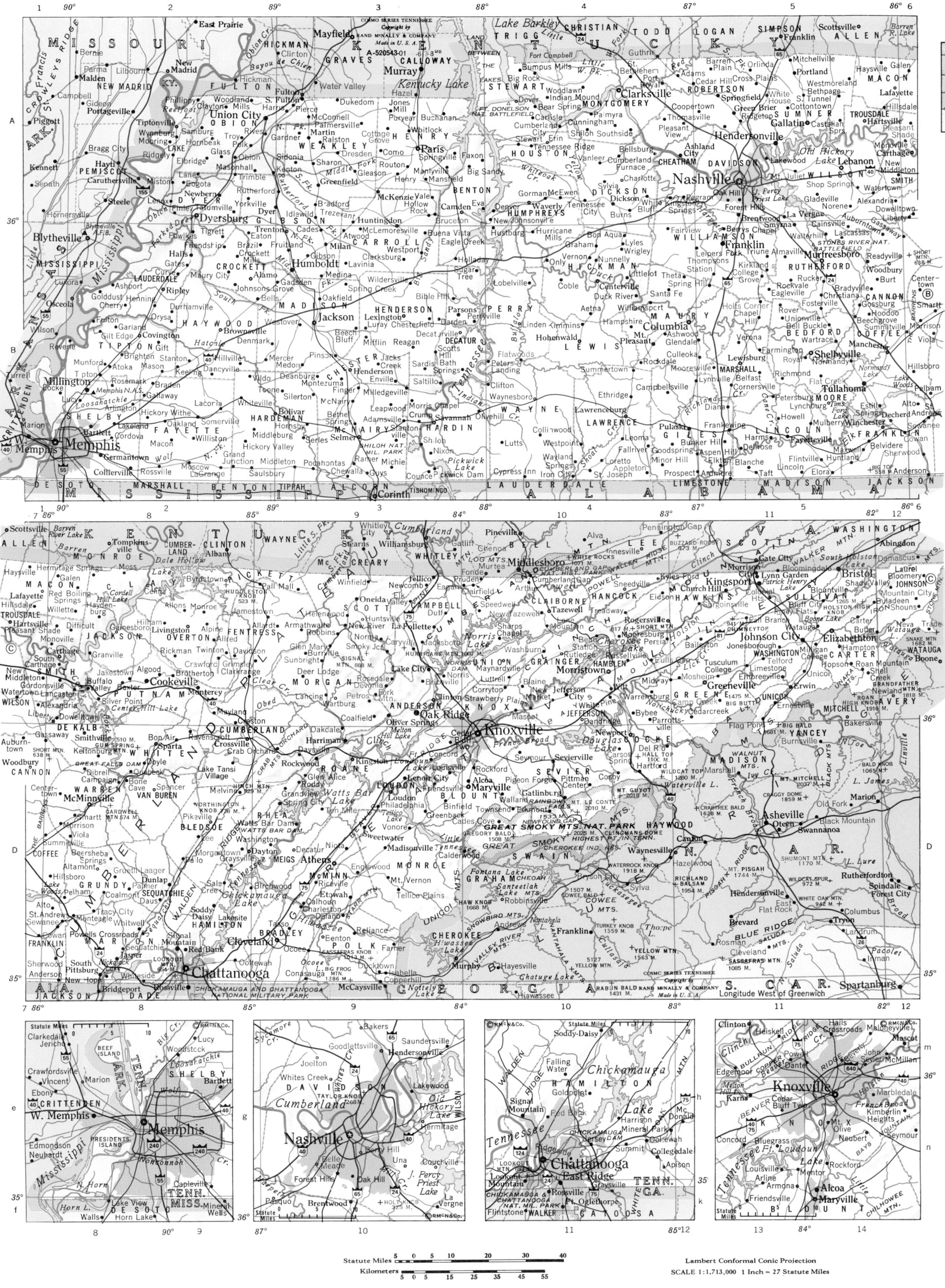

Lambert Conformal Conic Projection
SCALE 1:1,713,000 1 Inch = 27 Statute Miles

Texas

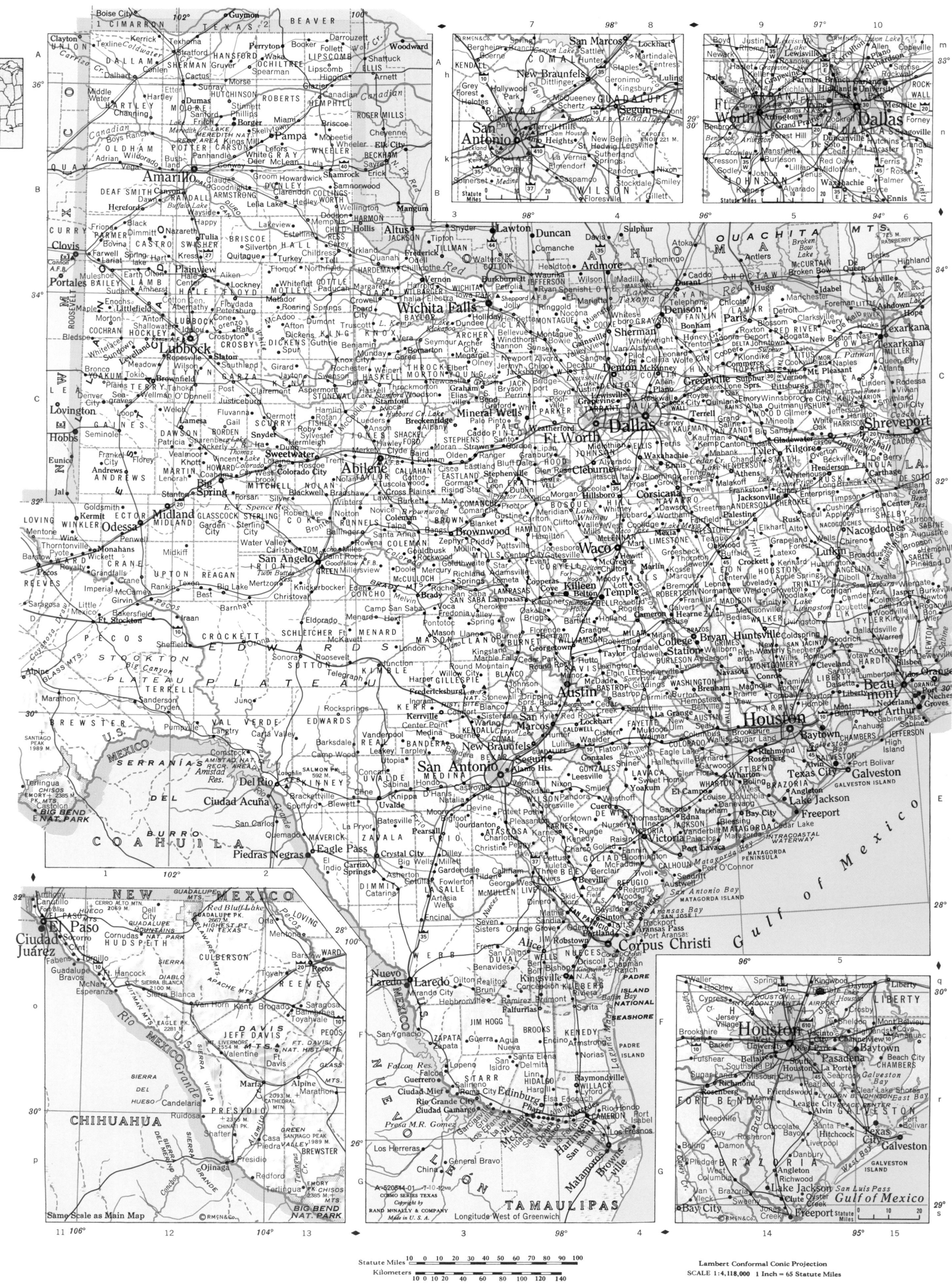

Statute Miles 10 0 10 20 30 40 50 60 70 80 90 100
Kilometers 10 0 10 20 40 60 80 100 120 140

Lambert Conformal Conic Projection
SCALE 1:4,118,000 1 Inch = 65 Statute Miles

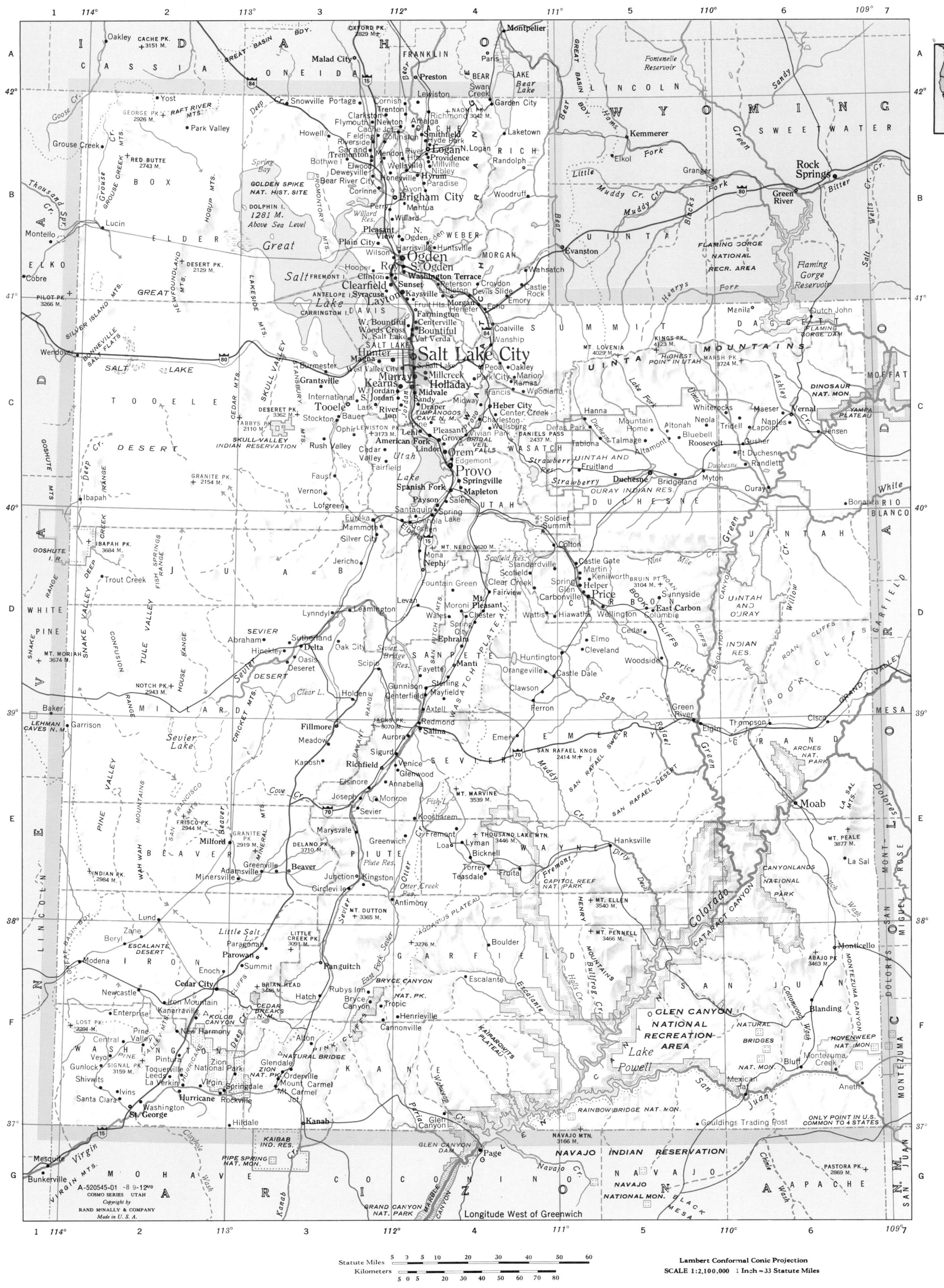

Statute Miles
Kilometers

Lambert Conformal Conic Projection
SCALE 1:2,100,000   1 Inch = 33 Statute Miles

Longitude West of Greenwich

A-520545-01 -8 9-12 MB
COSMO SERIES UTAH
Copyright by
RAND McNALLY & COMPANY
Made in U.S.A.

Vermont

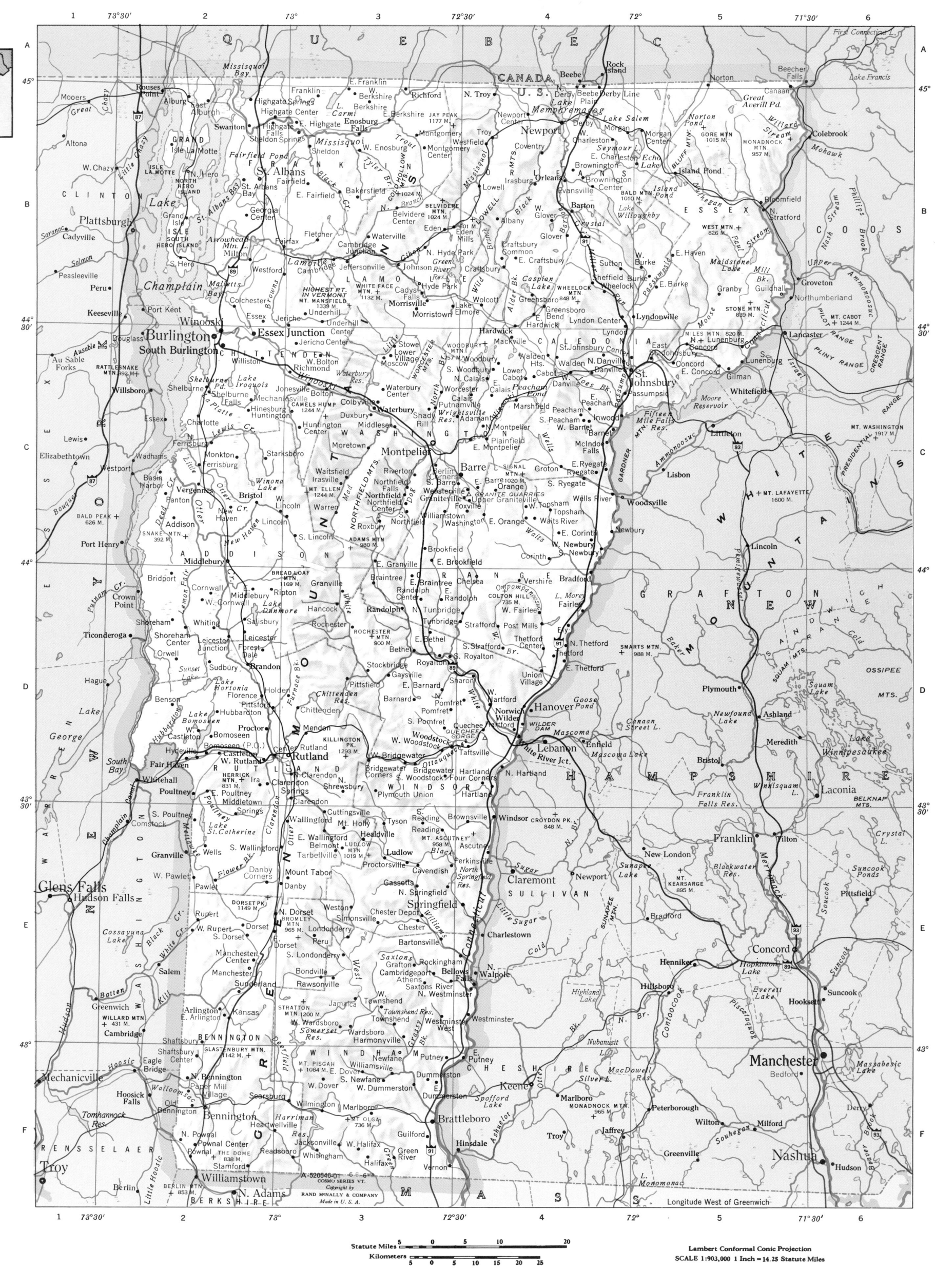

Q U E B E C
CANADA
U. S.
CLINTON
ESSEX
GRAND ISLE
FRANKLIN
LAMOILLE
ORLEANS
ESSEX
COOS
CALEDONIA
CHITTENDEN
WASHINGTON
ADDISON
ORANGE
GRAFTON
RUTLAND
WINDSOR
SULLIVAN
BENNINGTON
WINDHAM
CHESHIRE
RENSSELAER
BERKSHIRE
M A S S.
NEW YORK
WASHINGTON
WARREN
NEW HAMPSHIRE
GREEN MOUNTAINS
WHITE MOUNTAINS
Lake Champlain
Lake Memphremagog
Lake George
Connecticut
Burlington
South Burlington
Montpelier
Barre
Rutland
St. Albans
St. Johnsbury
Newport
Bennington
Brattleboro
Springfield
Plattsburgh
Glens Falls
Hudson Falls
Troy
Manchester
Concord
Nashua
Laconia
Keene
Claremont
Hanover
Lebanon
White River Jct.
North Adams
Williamstown
Essex Junction
Winooski
HIGHEST PT. IN VERMONT MT. MANSFIELD 1339 M.
A-520546-01 COSMO SERIES VT.
Copyright by RAND McNALLY & COMPANY Made in U. S. A.
Longitude West of Greenwich
Statute Miles 5 0 5 10 20
Kilometers 5 0 5 10 15 20 25
Lambert Conformal Conic Projection
SCALE 1:903,000 1 Inch = 14.25 Statute Miles

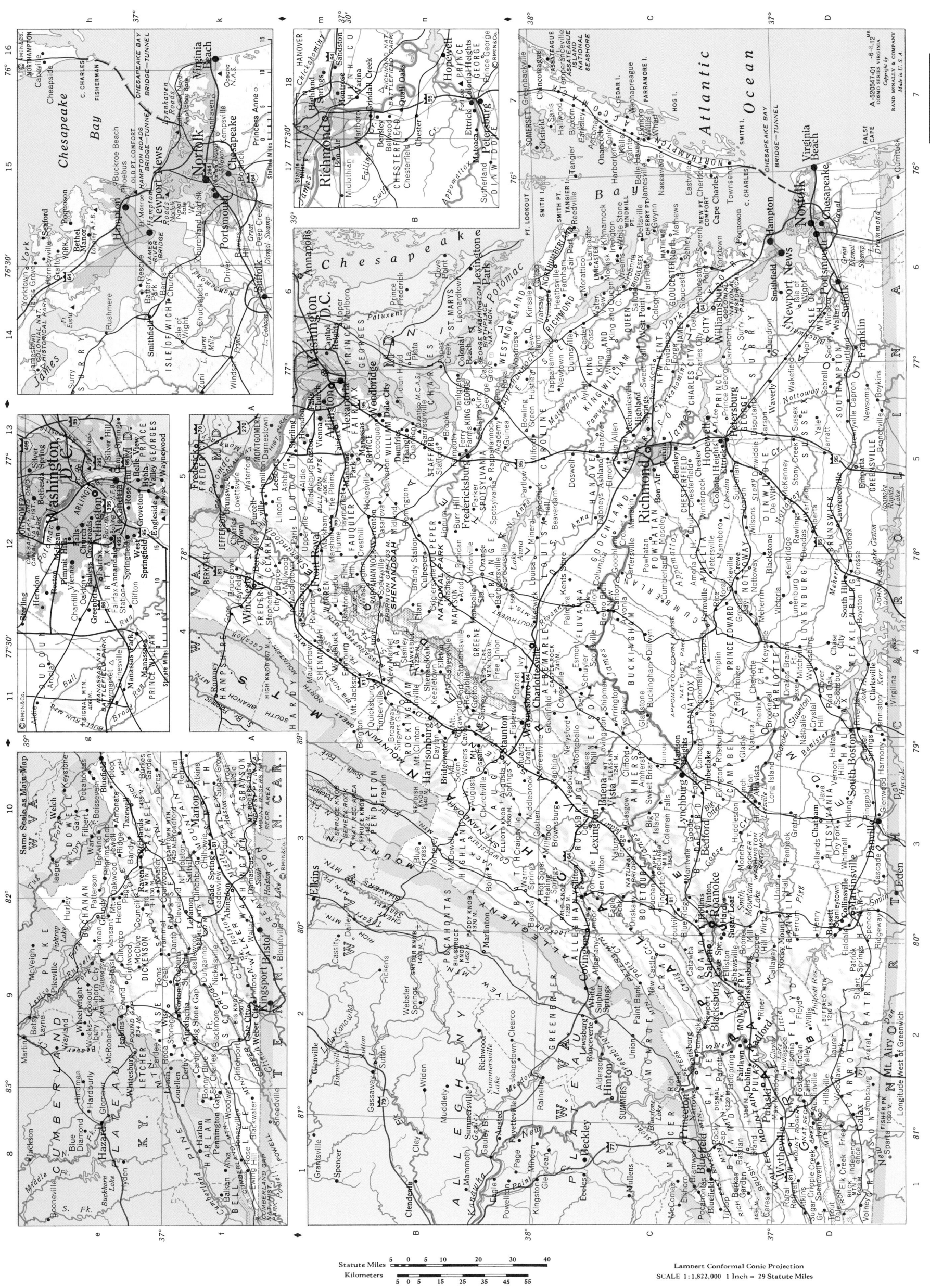

Lambert Conformal Conic Projection
SCALE 1:1,822,000 1 Inch = 29 Statute Miles

Statute Miles
Kilometers

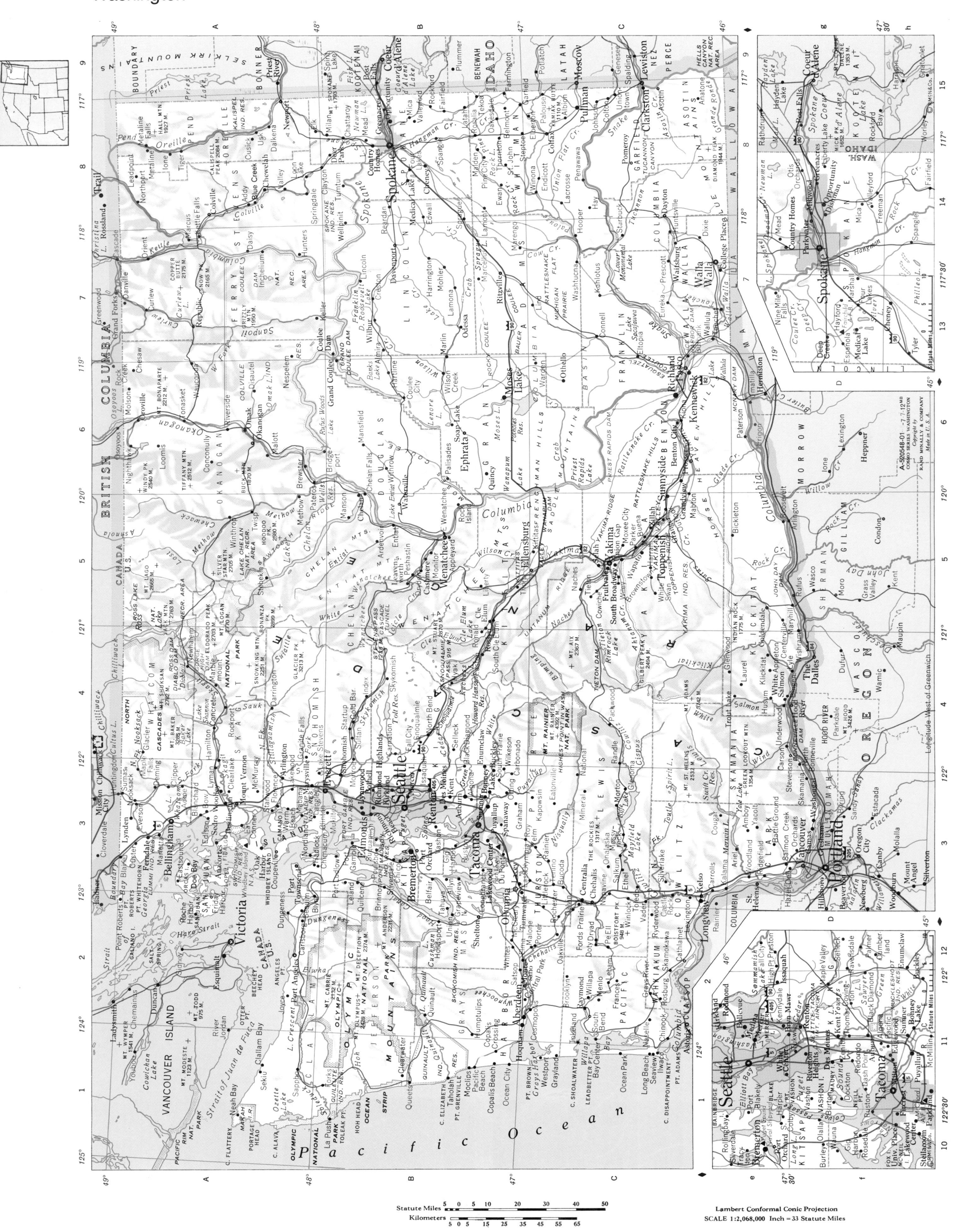
Pacific Ocean
BRITISH COLUMBIA
CANADA
IDAHO
OREGON
Statute Miles 5 0 5 10 20 30 40 50
Kilometers 5 0 5 15 25 35 45 55 65
Lambert Conformal Conic Projection
SCALE 1:2,068,000 Inch = 33 Statute Miles

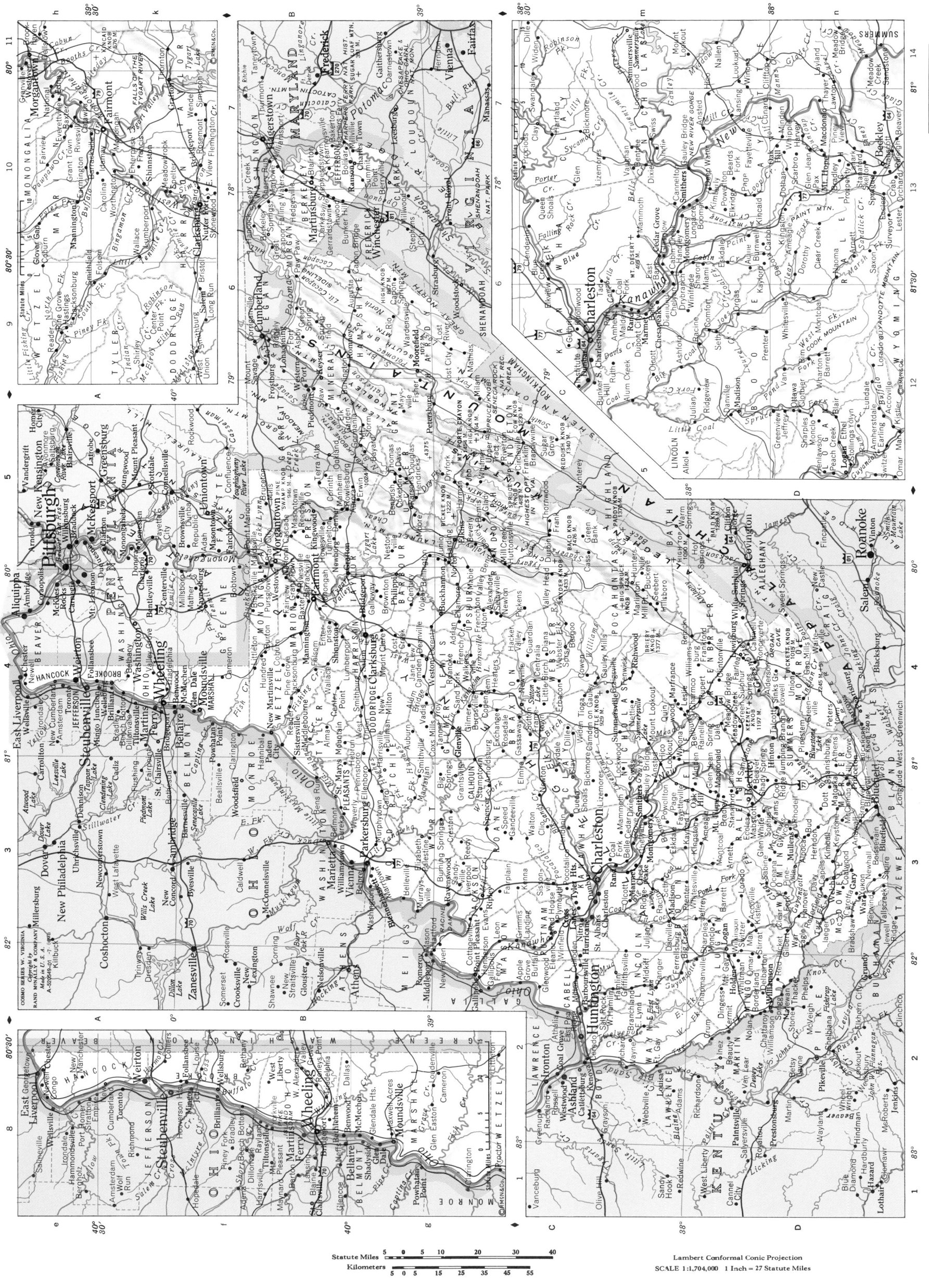

Lambert Conformal Conic Projection
SCALE 1:1,704,000 1 Inch = 27 Statute Miles

Statute Miles
Kilometers

Wisconsin

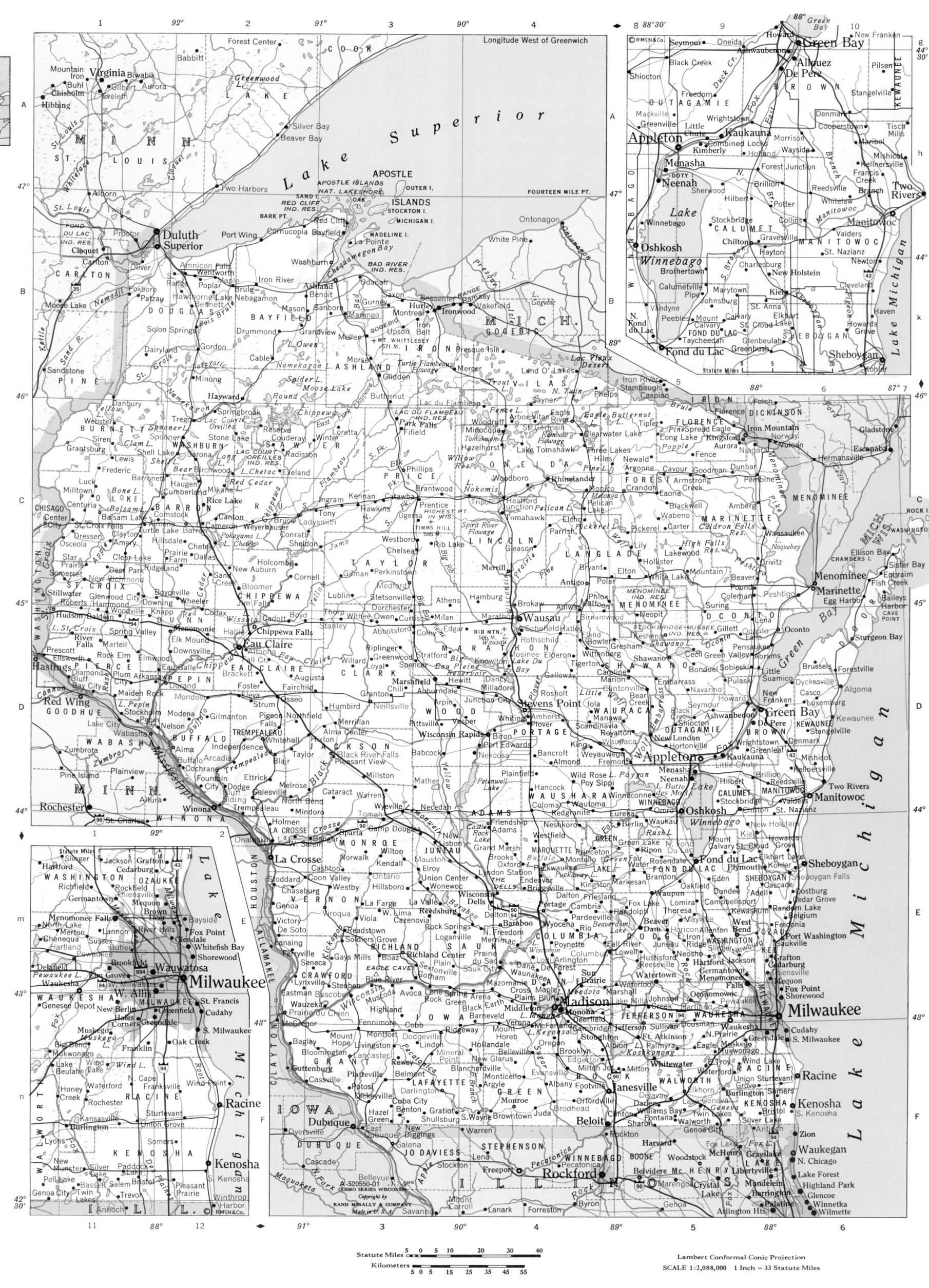
Longitude West of Greenwich
Lake Superior
Lake Michigan
Green Bay
MINN.
MICH.
IOWA
ILLINOIS
Milwaukee
Madison
Green Bay
Appleton
Oshkosh
La Crosse
Eau Claire
Wausau
Duluth
Superior
Racine
Kenosha
Sheboygan
Manitowoc
Janesville
Beloit
Rockford
Dubuque
Stevens Point
Fond du Lac
Statute Miles 5 0 5 10 20 30 40
Kilometers 5 0 5 15 25 35 45 55
Lambert Conformal Conic Projection
SCALE 1:2,088,000 1 Inch = 33 Statute Miles
A-520550-01
COSMO SERIES WISCONSIN
Copyright by RAND McNALLY & COMPANY
Made in U. S. A.
© RM&Co.

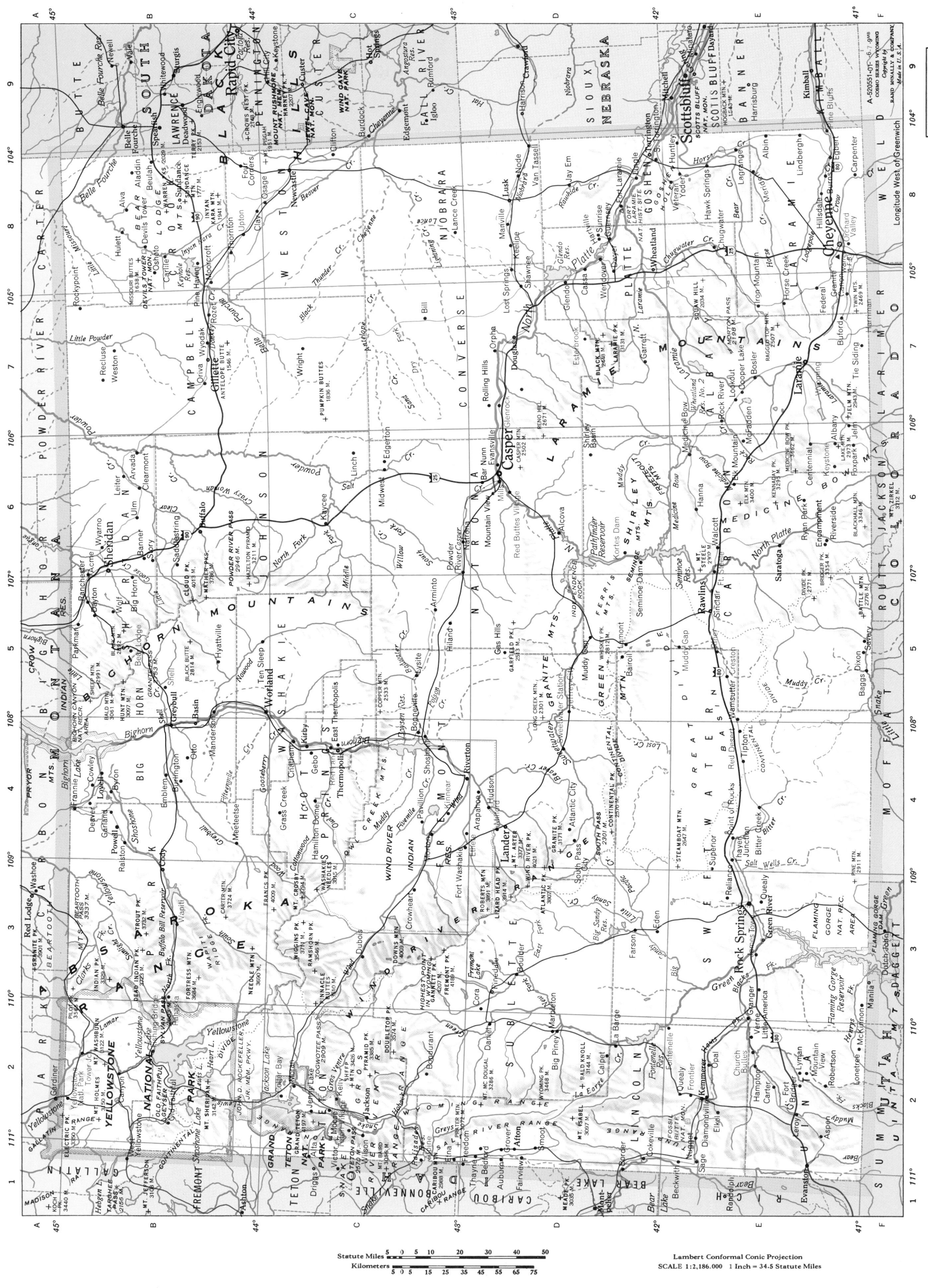

Statute Miles 5 0 5 10 20 30 40 50
Kilometers 5 0 5 15 25 35 45 55 65 75

Lambert Conformal Conic Projection
SCALE 1:2,186,000   1 Inch = 34.5 Statute Miles

GREENLAND
Greenland Sea
Barents Sea
Norwegian Sea
Arctic Circle
ICELAND
Reykjavik
FAEROE IS.
NORWAY
SWEDEN
FINLAND
HELSINKI
SANKT-PETERBURG
Baltic Sea
North Sea
UNITED KINGDOM
IRELAND
DUBLIN
LONDON
DENMARK
KØBENHAVN
BERLIN
POLAND
WARSZAWA
MOSKVA
FRANCE
PARIS
AUSTRIA
HUNGARY
BUDAPEST
ROMANIA
BUCURESTI
BULGARIA
SOFIJA
UKRAINE
KYYIV
Black Sea
İSTANBUL
ANKARA
TURKEY
ASIA MINOR
MEDITERRANEAN SEA
TUNISIA
LIBYA
EGYPT
AL-QAHIRAH
SAHARA
Tropic of Cancer
SUDAN
AL-KHARTŪM
AFRICA
ETHIOPIA
ADIS ABEBA
SOMALIA
KENYA
NAIROBI
TANZANIA
DAR ES SALAAM
ZAMBIA
ZIMBABWE
HARARE
MOZAMBIQUE
MAPUTO
BOTSWANA
PRETORIA
SOUTH AFRICA
CAPE TOWN
MADAGASCAR
ANTANANARIVO
URAL'SKIJE GORY
URAL MOUNTAINS
ZAPADNO-SIBIRSKAJA RAVNINA
SREDNESIBIRSKOJE PLOSKOGORJE
RUSSIA
SIBERIA
KAZAKHSTAN
Caspian Sea
Aral Sea
UZBEK.
TURK.
TIEN SHAN
MONGOLIA
GOBI
CHINA
BEIJING
SHANGHAI
Yellow Sea
East China Sea
Sea of Japan
JAPAN
TŌKYŌ
Sea of Okhotsk
SYRIA
IRAQ
BAGHDĀD
JORDAN
SAUDI ARABIA
AR-RIYĀD
YEMEN
OMAN
IRAN
TEHRĀN
AFGHANISTAN
KABOL
PAKISTAN
HIMALAYAS
Mount Everest
NEPAL
INDIA
DELHI
ARABIAN SEA
Bay of Bengal
SRI LANKA
COLOMBO
MYANMAR
THAILAND
KRUNG THEP
VIET-NAM
South China Sea
PHILIPPINES
MANILA
Philippine Sea
MALAYSIA
KUALA LUMPUR
SINGAPORE
INDONESIA
JAKARTA
GREATER SUNDA ISLANDS
PAPUA NEW GUINEA
Coral Sea
Timor Sea
Arafura Sea
Gulf of Carpentaria
AUSTRALIA
GREAT SANDY DESERT
GREAT VICTORIA DESERT
GREAT DIVIDING RANGE
Great Australian Bight
Perth
Adelaide
Melbourne
Sydney
Canberra
Brisbane
TASMANIA
Hobart
INDIAN OCEAN
Equator
Tropic of Capricorn
MID-INDIAN RIDGE
NINETY EAST RIDGE
SOUTHWEST INDIAN RIDGE
SOUTHEAST INDIAN RIDGE
ATLANTIC-INDIAN RIDGE
JAVA TRENCH
SOUTH AUSTRALIAN BASIN
SOUTH INDIAN BASIN
ATLANTIC-INDIAN BASIN
SOUTHERN OCEAN
Antarctic Circle
ENDERBY LAND
AMERY ICE SHELF
AMERICAN HIGHLAND
WILKES LAND
ANTARCTICA

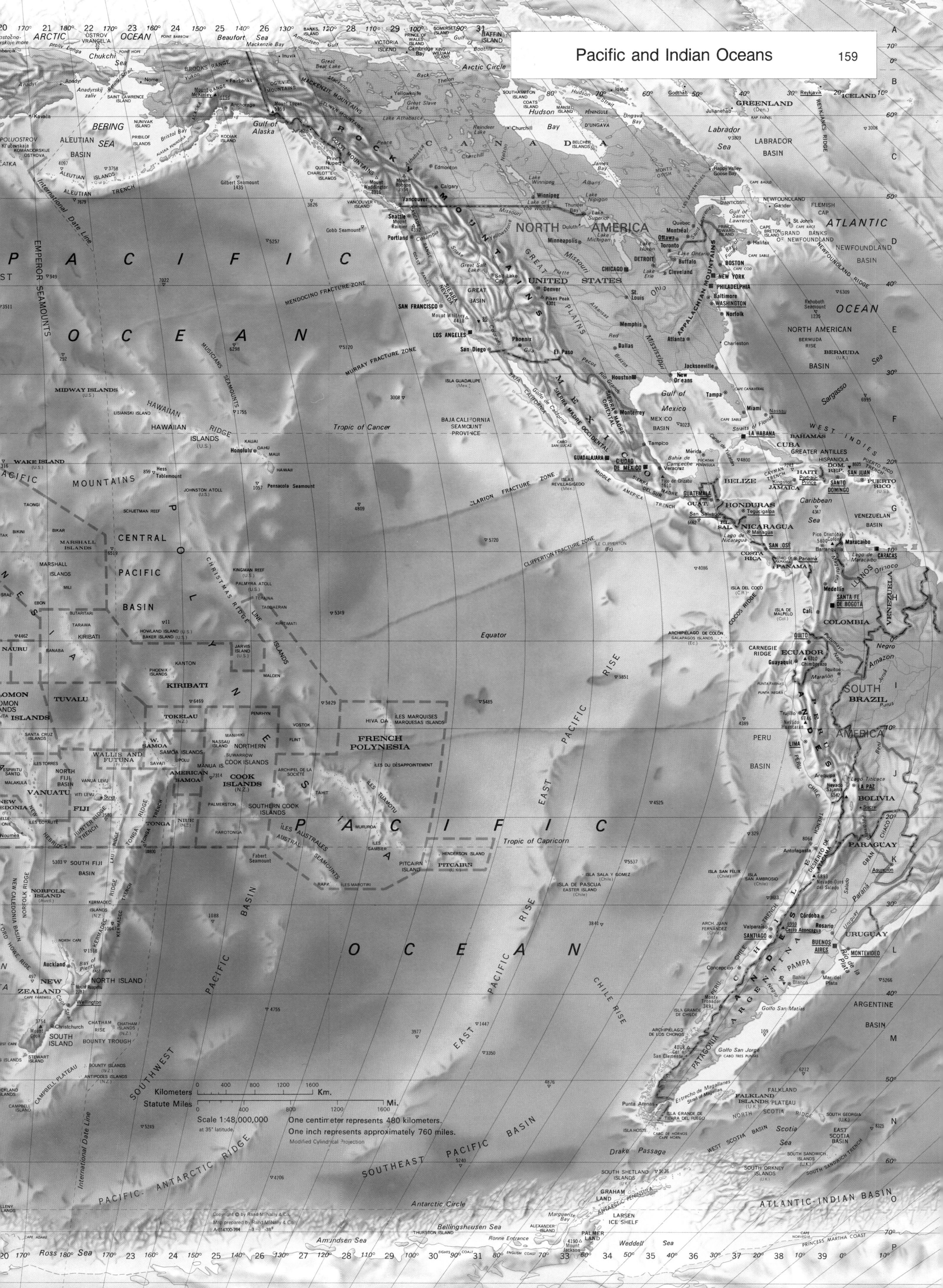
ARCTIC
OCEAN
Beaufort Sea
Chukchi Sea
BERING SEA
ALEUTIAN BASIN
ALEUTIAN ISLANDS
ALEUTIAN TRENCH
Gulf of Alaska
BROOKS RANGE
MACKENZIE MOUNTAINS
ROCKY MOUNTAINS
COAST MOUNTAINS
Hudson Bay
Labrador Sea
LABRADOR BASIN
GREENLAND
ICELAND
REYKJANES RIDGE
C A N A D A
NORTH AMERICA
UNITED STATES
GREAT PLAINS
GREAT BASIN
SIERRA NEVADA
APPALACHIAN MOUNTAINS
ATLANTIC
OCEAN
NEWFOUNDLAND BASIN
NORTH AMERICAN BASIN
Sargasso Sea
Gulf of Mexico
MEXICO BASIN
SIERRA MADRE OCCIDENTAL
SIERRA MADRE ORIENTAL
MIDDLE AMERICA TRENCH
WEST INDIES
GREATER ANTILLES
Caribbean Sea
VENEZUELAN BASIN
CUBA
BAHAMAS
HAITI
DOM. REP.
JAMAICA
PUERTO RICO
BELIZE
GUATEMALA
HONDURAS
NICARAGUA
COSTA RICA
PANAMA
International Date Line
EMPEROR SEAMOUNTS
MUSICIANS SEAMOUNTS
MENDOCINO FRACTURE ZONE
MURRAY FRACTURE ZONE
CLARION FRACTURE ZONE
CLIPPERTON FRACTURE ZONE
P A C I F I C
O C E A N
MIDWAY ISLANDS (U.S.)
HAWAIIAN RIDGE
HAWAIIAN ISLANDS (U.S.)
Honolulu
Tropic of Cancer
BAJA CALIFORNIA SEAMOUNT PROVINCE
WAKE ISLAND (U.S.)
PACIFIC MOUNTAINS
JOHNSTON ATOLL (U.S.)
MARSHALL ISLANDS
CENTRAL PACIFIC BASIN
CHRISTMAS RIDGE
LINE ISLANDS
KIRIBATI
NAURU
TUVALU
SOLOMON ISLANDS
TOKELAU (N.Z.)
W. SAMOA
AMERICAN SAMOA
WALLIS AND FUTUNA
FIJI
VANUATU
TONGA
NIUE (N.Z.)
COOK ISLANDS (N.Z.)
FRENCH POLYNESIA
ÎLES MARQUISES
ÎLES TUAMOTU
ÎLES AUSTRALES
PITCAIRN
Tropic of Capricorn
Equator
COCOS RIDGE
CARNEGIE RIDGE
ARCHIPIÉLAGO DE COLÓN (GALAPAGOS ISLANDS) (Ec.)
EAST PACIFIC RISE
CHILE RISE
PERU BASIN
PERU-CHILE TRENCH
NEW ZEALAND
NORTH ISLAND
SOUTH ISLAND
Wellington
Auckland
KERMADEC TRENCH
SOUTH FIJI BASIN
SOUTHWEST PACIFIC BASIN
PACIFIC-ANTARCTIC RIDGE
SOUTHEAST PACIFIC BASIN
Antarctic Circle
Bellingshausen Sea
Amundsen Sea
Ross Sea
Weddell Sea
Drake Passage
SCOTIA RIDGE
Scotia Sea
ATLANTIC-INDIAN BASIN
ARGENTINE BASIN
FALKLAND ISLANDS (U.K.)
SOUTH AMERICA
COLOMBIA
VENEZUELA
ECUADOR
PERU
BOLIVIA
BRAZIL
PARAGUAY
URUGUAY
ARGENTINA
CHILE
ANDES
PATAGONIA
Kilometers 0 400 800 1200 1600 Km.
Statute Miles 0 400 800 1200 1600 Mi.
Scale 1:48,000,000 at 35° latitude.
One centimeter represents 480 kilometers.
One inch represents approximately 760 miles.
Modified Cylindrical Projection

GREENLAND
ICELAND
Norwegian Sea
Barents Sea
Labrador Sea
LABRADOR BASIN
Hudson Bay
NORTH AMERICA
CANADA
UNITED STATES
MEXICO
Gulf of Mexico
Caribbean Sea
ATLANTIC OCEAN
NORTH AMERICAN BASIN
WEST EUROPEAN BASIN
MID-ATLANTIC RIDGE
Sargasso Sea
Tropic of Cancer
CAPE VERDE BASIN
GUIANA BASIN
Equator
SOUTH AMERICA
BRAZIL
BRAZIL BASIN
ANGOLA BASIN
Tropic of Capricorn
ARGENTINE BASIN
CAPE BASIN
AGULHAS BASIN
PACIFIC OCEAN
INDIAN OCEAN
Scotia Sea
Drake Passage
Weddell Sea
Antarctic Circle
ANTARCTICA
EUROPE
AFRICA
Mediterranean Sea
Black Sea
Caspian Sea
Kilometers
Statute Miles
Scale 1:48,000,000
One centimeter represents 480 kilometers.
One inch represents approximately 760 miles.
Modified Cylindrical Projection
Copyright © by Rand McNally & Co.
Map prepared by Rand McNally & Co.

Index to World Reference Maps

Introduction to the Index

This universal index includes in a single alphabetical list approximately 69,000 names of features that appear on the reference maps. Each name is followed by the name of the country or continent in which it is located, a map-reference key and a page reference.

Names The names of cities appear in the index in regular type. The names of all other features appear in *italics*, followed by descriptive terms (hill, mtn., state) to indicate their nature.

Names that appear in shortened versions on the maps due to space limitations are spelled out in full in the index. The portions of these names omitted from the maps are enclosed in brackets — for example, Acapulco [de Juárez].

Abbreviations of names on the maps have been standardized as much as possible. Names that are abbreviated on the maps are generally spelled out in full in the index.

Country names and names of features that extend beyond the boundaries of one country are followed by the name of the continent in which each is located. Country designations follow the names of all other places in the index. The locations of places in the United States, Canada, and the United Kingdom are further defined by abbreviations that indicate the state, province, or political division in which each is located.

All abbreviations used in the index are defined in the List of Abbreviations below.
Alphabetization Names are alphabetized in the order of the letters of the English alphabet. Spanish *ll* and *ch*, for example, are not treated as distinct letters. Furthermore, diacritical marks are disregarded in alphabetization — German or Scandinavian *ä* or *ö* are treated as *a* or *o*.

The names of physical features may appear inverted, since they are always alphabetized under the proper, not the generic, part of the name, thus: 'Gibraltar, Strait of'. Otherwise every entry, whether consisting of one word or more, is alphabetized as a single continuous entity. 'Lakeland', for example, appears after 'La Crosse' and before 'La Salle'. Names beginning with articles (Le Havre, Den Helder, Al Mansūrah) are not inverted. Names beginning 'St.', 'Ste.' and 'Sainte' are alphabetized as though spelled 'Saint'.

In the case of identical names, towns are listed first, then political divisions, then physical features. Entries that are completely identical are listed alphabetically by country name.
Map-Reference Keys and Page References The map-reference keys and page references are found in the last two columns of each entry.

Each map-reference key consists of a letter and number. The letters appear along the sides of the maps. Lowercase letters indicate reference to inset maps. Numbers appear across the tops and bottoms of the maps.

Map reference keys for point features, such as cities and mountain peaks, indicate the locations of the symbols. For extensive areal features, such as countries or mountain ranges, locations are given for the approximate centers of the features. Those for linear features, such as canals and rivers, are given for the locations of the names.

The page number generally refers to the main map for the country in which the feature is located. Page references to two-page maps always refer to the left-hand page.

List of Abbreviations

Afg.	Afghanistan	C.V.	Cape Verde	Jam.	Jamaica	N. Ire., U.K.	Northern Ireland, U.K.	Sri L.	Sri Lanka
Afr.	Africa	Cyp.	Cyprus	Jord.	Jordan			*state*	state, republic, canton
Ak., U.S.	Alaska, U.S.	Czech Rep.	Czech Republic	Kaz.	Kazakhstan	N.J., U.S.	New Jersey, U.S.		
Al., U.S.	Alabama, U.S.	D.C., U.S.	District of Columbia, U.S.	Kir.	Kiribati	N. Kor.	North Korea	St. Hel.	St. Helena
Alb.	Albania			Ks., U.S.	Kansas, U.S.	N.M., U.S.	New Mexico, U.S.	St. K./N	St. Kitts and Nevis
Alg.	Algeria	De., U.S.	Delaware, U.S.	Kuw.	Kuwait	N. Mar. Is.	Northern Mariana Islands	St. Luc.	St. Lucia
Alta., Can.	Alberta, Can.	Den.	Denmark	Ky., U.S.	Kentucky, U.S.			*stm.*	stream (river, creek)
Am. Sam.	American Samoa	*dep.*	dependency, colony	Kyrg.	Kyrgyzstan	Nmb.	Namibia	S. Tom./P.	Sao Tome and Principe
anch.	anchorage	*depr.*	depression	*l.*	lake, pond	Nor.	Norway		
And.	Andorra	*dept.*	department, district	La., U.S.	Louisiana, U.S.	Norf. I.	Norfolk Island	St. P./M.	St. Pierre and Miquelon
Ang.	Angola	*des.*	desert	Lat.	Latvia	N.S., Can.	Nova Scotia, Can.		
Ant.	Antarctica	Dji.	Djibouti	Leb.	Lebanon	Nv., U.S.	Nevada, U.S.	*strt.*	strait, channel, sound
Antig.	Antigua and Barbuda	Dom.	Dominica	Leso.	Lesotho	N.W. Ter., Can.	Northwest Territories, Can.		
		Dom. Rep.	Dominican Republic	Lib.	Liberia			St. Vin.	St. Vincent and the Grenadines
Ar., U.S.	Arkansas, U.S.	Ec.	Ecuador	Liech.	Liechtenstein	N.Y., U.S.	New York, U.S.		
Arg.	Argentina	El Sal.	El Salvador	Lith.	Lithuania	N.Z.	New Zealand	Sud.	Sudan
Arm.	Armenia	Eng., U.K.	England, U.K.	Lux.	Luxembourg	Oc.	Oceania	Sur.	Suriname
Aus.	Austria	Eq. Gui.	Equatorial Guinea	Ma., U.S.	Massachusetts, U.S.	Oh., U.S.	Ohio, U.S.	*sw.*	swamp, marsh
Austl.	Australia	Erit.	Eritrea			Ok., U.S.	Oklahoma, U.S.	Swaz.	Swaziland
Az., U.S.	Arizona, U.S.	*est.*	estuary	Mac.	Macedonia	Ont., Can.	Ontario, Can.	Swe.	Sweden
Azer.	Azerbaijan	Est.	Estonia	Madag.	Madagascar	Or., U.S.	Oregon, U.S.	Switz.	Switzerland
b.	bay, gulf, inlet, lagoon	Eth.	Ethiopia	Malay.	Malaysia	Pa., U.S.	Pennsylvania, U.S.	Tai.	Taiwan
		Eur.	Europe	Mald.	Maldives	Pak.	Pakistan	Taj.	Tajikistan
Bah.	Bahamas	Faer. Is.	Faeroe Islands	Man., Can.	Manitoba, Can.	Pan.	Panama	Tan.	Tanzania
Bahr.	Bahrain	Falk. Is.	Falkland Islands	Marsh. Is.	Marshall Islands	Pap. N. Gui.	Papua New Guinea	T./C. Is.	Turks and Caicos Islands
Barb.	Barbados	Fin.	Finland	Mart.	Martinique	Para.	Paraguay		
B.A.T.	British Antarctic Territory	Fl., U.S.	Florida, U.S.	Maur.	Mauritania	P.E.I., Can.	Prince Edward Island, Can.	*ter.*	territory
		for.	forest, moor	May.	Mayotte			Thai.	Thailand
B.C., Can.	British Columbia, Can.	Fr.	France	Md., U.S.	Maryland, U.S.	*pen.*	peninsula	Tn., U.S.	Tennessee, U.S.
Bdi.	Burundi	Fr. Gu.	French Guiana	Me., U.S.	Maine, U.S.	Phil.	Philippines	Tok.	Tokelau
Bel.	Belgium	Fr. Poly.	French Polynesia	Mex.	Mexico	Pit.	Pitcairn	Trin.	Trinidad and Tobago
Bela.	Belarus	F.S.A.T.	French Southern and Antarctic Territory	Mi., U.S.	Michigan, U.S.	*pl.*	plain, flat		
Ber.	Bermuda			Micron.	Federated States of Micronesia	*plat.*	plateau, highland	Tun.	Tunisia
Bhu.	Bhutan	Ga., U.S.	Georgia, U.S.			Pol.	Poland	Tur.	Turkey
B.I.O.T.	British Indian Ocean Territory	Gam.	Gambia	Mid. Is.	Midway Islands	Port.	Portugal	Turk.	Turkmenistan
		Gaza	Gaza Strip	*mil.*	military installation	P.R.	Puerto Rico	Tx., U.S.	Texas, U.S.
Bngl.	Bangladesh	Geor.	Georgia	Mn., U.S.	Minnesota, U.S.	*prov.*	province, region	U.A.E.	United Arab Emirates
Bol.	Bolivia	Ger.	Germany	Mo., U.S.	Missouri, U.S.	Que., Can.	Quebec, Can.		
Boph.	Bophuthatswana	Gib.	Gibraltar	Mol.	Moldova	*reg.*	physical region	Ug.	Uganda
Bos.	Bosnia and Herzegovina	Golan	Golan Heights	Mon.	Monaco	*res.*	reservoir	U.K.	United Kingdom
		Grc.	Greece	Mong.	Mongolia	Reu.	Reunion	Ukr.	Ukraine
Bots.	Botswana	Gren.	Grenada	Monts.	Montserrat	*rf.*	reef, shoal	Ur.	Uruguay
Braz.	Brazil	Grnld.	Greenland	Mor.	Morocco	R.I., U.S.	Rhode Island, U.S.	U.S.	United States
Bru.	Brunei	Guad.	Guadeloupe	Moz.	Mozambique	Rom.	Romania	Ut., U.S.	Utah, U.S.
Br. Vir. Is.	British Virgin Islands	Guat.	Guatemala	Mrts.	Mauritius	Rw.	Rwanda	Uzb.	Uzbekistan
Bul.	Bulgaria	Gui.	Guinea	Ms., U.S.	Mississippi, U.S.	S.A.	South America	Va., U.S.	Virginia, U.S.
Burkina	Burkina Faso	Gui.-B.	Guinea-Bissau	Mt., U.S.	Montana, U.S.	S. Afr.	South Africa	*val.*	valley, watercourse
c.	cape, point	Guy.	Guyana	*mth.*	river mouth or channel	Sask., Can.	Saskatchewan, Can.	Vat.	Vatican City
Ca., U.S.	California, U.S.	Hi., U.S.	Hawaii, U.S.					Ven.	Venezuela
Cam.	Cameroon	*hist.*	historic site, ruins	*mtn.*	mountain	Sau. Ar.	Saudi Arabia	Viet.	Vietnam
Camb.	Cambodia	*hist. reg.*	historic region	*mts.*	mountains	S.C., U.S.	South Carolina, U.S.	V.I.U.S.	Virgin Islands (U.S.)
Can.	Canada	H.K.	Hong Kong	Mwi.	Malawi	*sci.*	scientific station	*vol.*	volcano
Cay. Is.	Cayman Islands	Hond.	Honduras	Mya.	Myanmar	Scot., U.K.	Scotland, U.K.	Vt., U.S.	Vermont, U.S.
Cen. Afr. Rep.	Central African Republic	Hung.	Hungary	N.A.	North America	S.D., U.S.	South Dakota, U.S.	Wa., U.S.	Washington, U.S.
		i.	island	N.B., Can.	New Brunswick, Can.	Sen.	Senegal	Wal./F.	Wallis and Futuna
Christ. I.	Christmas Island	Ia., U.S.	Iowa, U.S.			Sey.	Seychelles	Wi., U.S.	Wisconsin, U.S.
C. Iv.	Cote d'Ivoire	Ice.	Iceland	N.C., U.S.	North Carolina, U.S.	Sing.	Singapore	W. Sah.	Western Sahara
clf.	cliff, escarpment	*ice*	ice feature, glacier	N. Cal.	New Caledonia	S. Geor.	South Georgia	W. Sam.	Western Samoa
co.	county, parish	Id., U.S.	Idaho, U.S.	N. Cyp.	North Cyprus	S. Kor.	South Korea	*wtfl.*	waterfall
Co., U.S.	Colorado, U.S.	Il., U.S.	Illinois, U.S.	N.D., U.S.	North Dakota, U.S.	S.L.	Sierra Leone	W.V., U.S.	West Virginia, U.S.
Col.	Colombia	In., U.S.	Indiana, U.S.	Ne., U.S.	Nebraska, U.S.	Slvk.	Slovakia	Wy., U.S.	Wyoming, U.S.
Com.	Comoros	Indon.	Indonesia	Neth.	Netherlands	Slvn.	Slovenia	Yugo.	Yugoslavia
cont.	continent	I. of Man	Isle of Man	Neth. Ant.	Netherlands Antilles	S. Mar.	San Marino	Yukon, Can.	Yukon Territory, Can.
C.R.	Costa Rica	Ire.	Ireland	Newf., Can.	Newfoundland, Can.	Sol. Is.	Solomon Islands		
crat.	crater	*is.*	islands	N.H., U.S.	New Hampshire, U.S.	Som.	Somalia	Zam.	Zambia
Cro.	Croatia	Isr.	Israel			Sp. N. Afr.	Spanish North Africa	Zimb.	Zimbabwe
Ct., U.S.	Connecticut, U.S.	Isr. Occ.	Israeli Occupied Territories	Nic.	Nicaragua				
ctry.	country			Nig.	Nigeria				

Index

A

Name	Map Ref.	Page

Name — Map Ref. — Page

Al-Qāhirah (Cairo), Egypt B6 60
Al-Qaḥmah, Sau. Ar. E2 47
Al-Qalībah, Sau. Ar. G4 48
Al-Qāmishlī, Syria C6 48
Al-Qanṭarah, Egypt B7 60
Al-Qaryah ash-Sharqīyah, Libya B3 56
Al-Qaṣr, Egypt E5 60
Al-Qaṣr, Jord. F5 50
Al-Qaṭīf, Sau. Ar. A7 47
Al-Qaṭrānah, Jord. F6 50
Al-Qaṭrūn, Libya D3 56
Al-Qayṣūmah, Sau. Ar. G9 48
Al-Qiṣfah, Jord. C5 50
Al-Quds see Yerushalayim, Isr. E4 50
Al-Qunayṭirah, Syria B5 50
Al-Qunfudhah, Sau. Ar. E2 47
Al-Qurnah, Iraq F9 48
Al-Quṣaymah, Egypt G2 50
Al-Quṣayr, Egypt D8 60
Al-Qūṣīyah, Egypt D6 60
Al-Quṭayfah, Syria A7 50
Al-Quṭaynah, Sud. J7 60
Al-Quway'īyah, Sau. Ar. B4 47
Al-Quwaysī, Sud. K8 60
Alsace, hist. reg., Fr. D14 14
Alsask, Sask., Can. F1 105
Alsea, Or., U.S. C3 144
Alsen, N.D., U.S. A7 141
Alsey, Il., U.S. D3 120
Alsfeld, Ger. E9 10
Alsina, Arg. G9 80
Alstead, N.H., U.S. D2 136
Alstead, stm., Sask., Can. B2 105
Alstead Center, N.H., U.S. D2 136
Alston, Ga., U.S. D4 117
Alsunga, Lat. E4 22
Alta, Ia., U.S. B2 122
Alta, Wy., U.S. C1 157
Altadena, Ca., U.S. m12 112
Alta Gracia, Arg. F6 80
Altagracia, Nic. F9 92
Altagracia, Ven. B7 84
Altagracia de Orituco, Ven. C9 84
Altai, mts., Asia H16 26
Altaj (Jesönbulag), Mong. B6 30
Altaj, state, Russia G15 26
Altamaha, stm., Ga., U.S. E4 117
Altamaha Sound, strt., Ga., U.S. E5 117
Altamira, Braz. D8 76
Altamira, Chile C4 80
Altamira, C.R. G10 92
Altamont, Man., Can. E2 100
Altamont, Il., U.S. D5 120
Altamont, Ks., U.S. E8 123
Altamont, Mo., U.S. B3 132
Altamont, N.Y., U.S. C6 139
Altamont, Or., U.S. E5 144
Altamont, Tn., U.S. D8 149
Altamonte Springs, Fl., U.S. D5 116
Altamura, Italy I11 18
Altamura, Isla, i., Mex. E5 90
Altar, Mex. B4 90
Altar, stm., Mex. B4 90
Altar, Desierto de, des., Mex. B3 90
Altar de Los Sacrificios, hist., Guat. I14 90
Altario, Alta., Can. D5 98
Altata, Mex. E6 90
Alta Verapaz, dept., Guat. B4 92
Alta Vista, Ia., U.S. A5 122
Alta Vista, Ks., U.S. D7 123
Altavista, Va., U.S. C3 153
Altay, China B4 30
Altay see Altaj, state, Russia G15 26
Altdorf, Switz. E10 13
Altenburg, Ger. E12 10
Altenburg, Mo., U.S. D8 132
Altha, Fl., U.S. B1 116
Altheimer, Ar., U.S. C4 111
Althofen, Aus. I14 10
Altinópolis, Braz. F5 79
Altiplano, plat., S.A. H7 82
Altkirch, Fr. E14 14
Altmark, reg., Ger. C11 10
Altmühl, stm., Ger. F10 10
Alto, Ga., U.S. B3 117
Alto, N.M., U.S. D4 138
Alto, Tx., U.S. D5 150
Alto Araguaia, Braz. D2 79
Alto Cedro, Cuba D7 94
Alto Coité, Braz. C1 79
Alto del Carmen, Chile E3 80
Alto do Rio Doce, Braz. F7 79
Alto Garças, Braz. D2 79
Altomünster, Ger. G11 10
Alton, Al., U.S. B3 108
Alton, Il., U.S. E3 120
Alton, Ia., U.S. B2 122
Alton, Ks., U.S. C5 123
Alton, La., U.S. h12 125
Alton, Mo., U.S. E6 132
Alton, N.H., U.S. D4 136
Altona, Man., Can. E3 100
Altona, Il., U.S. B3 120
Altona, In., U.S. B7 121
Alton Bay, N.H., U.S. D4 136
Altoona, Al., U.S. A3 108
Altoona, Fl., U.S. D5 116
Altoona, Ia., U.S. C4 122
Altoona, Ks., U.S. E8 123
Altoona, Pa., U.S. E5 145
Altoona, Wi., U.S. D2 156
Alto Paraguai, Braz. F13 82
Alto Paraguay, dept., Para. I12 82
Alto Paraíso de Goiás, Braz. C5 79
Alto Paraná, dept., Para. C11 80
Alto Parnaíba, Braz. E9 76
Alto Pass, Il., U.S. F4 120
Alto Purús, stm., Peru D6 82
Alto Río Senguer, Arg. F2 78
Alto Sucuriú, Braz. E2 79
Altötting, Ger. G12 10
Alto Yurua, stm., Peru C5 82
Altro, Ky., U.S. C6 124
Altstätten, Switz D12 13
Altuchovo, Russia I17 22
Altunoluk, Tur. J10 20
Altun Shan, mts., China D4 30
Altura, Mn., U.S. F7 130
Alturas, Ca., U.S. B3 112
Altus, Ar., U.S. B2 111
Altus, Ok., U.S. C2 143
Altus Air Force Base, mil., Ok., U.S. C2 143
Altus Reservoir, res., Ok., U.S. C2 143
Al-'Ubaylah, Sau. Ar. D7 47
Al-Ubayyiḍ, Sud. K6 60
Al-'Udaysāt, Egypt E7 60
Al-Uḍayyah, Sud. K5 60
Aluk, Sud. M4 60
Alūksne, Lat. D10 22
Al-'Ulā, Sau. Ar. H4 48
Alum Bank, Pa., U.S. F4 145
Alum Creek, W.V., U.S. m12 155
Alum Creek, stm., Oh., U.S. k11 142
Aluminé, Lago, l., Arg. J3 80
Al-'Uqaylah, Libya B4 56
Al-'Uqayr, Sau. Ar. B7 47
Al-Uqṣur (Luxor), Egypt E7 60
Al-'Uwaynāt, Libya C3 56
Al-'Uyaynah, Sau. Ar. B5 47
Alva, Fl., U.S. F5 116
Alva, Ok., U.S. A3 143
Alva, Wy., U.S. B8 157
Alvarado, Mex. H12 90
Alvarado, Mn., U.S. B2 130
Alvarado, Tx., U.S. C4 150
Alvarães, Braz. I10 84
Álvaro Obregón, Presa, res., Mex. D5 90
Alvdal, Nor. J12 6
Alvear, Arg. E10 80
Alvena, Sask., Can. E2 105
Alvernia, Mount, hill, Bah. B7 94
Alvesta, Swe. M14 6
Alvin, Il., U.S. C6 120
Alvin, Tx., U.S. E5 150
Alvinópolis, Braz. F7 79
Alvinston, Ont., Can. E3 103
Alvito, Port. G4 16
Älvkarleby, Swe. K15 6
Alvo, Ne., U.S. h12 134
Alvord, Ia., U.S. A1 122
Alvord, Tx., U.S. C4 150
Alvord Lake, l., Or., U.S. E8 144
Älvros, Swe. J14 6
Älvsborgs Län, co., Swe. L13 6
Al-Wajh, Sau. Ar. H4 48
Al-Wakrah, Qatar I11 48
Alwar, India G7 44
Al-Wāsiṭah, Egypt C6 60
Al-Wazz, Sud. J6 60
Alxa Zuoqi, China D8 30
Alytus, Lith. G7 22
Alzamaj, Russia F11 28
Alzira (Alcira), Spain F11 16
Ama, La., U.S. k11 125
Amacuro, stm., S.A. C12 84
Amadeus, Lake, l., Austl. D6 68
Amadjuak Lake, l., N.W. Ter., Can. C18 96
Amador, co., Ca., U.S. C3 112
Amagansett, N.Y., U.S. n16 139
Amagasaki, Japan M10 36
Amagi, Japan N5 36
Amagon, Ar., U.S. B4 111
Amagunze, Nig. H13 64
Amahai, Indon. F8 38
Amaichá del Valle, Arg. D6 80
Amajac, stm., Mex. G10 90
Amaka, stm., Nic. C9 92
Amakusa-shotō, is., Japan O5 36
Amakuso-Shimo-shima, i., Japan O5 36
Åmål, Swe. L13 6
Amalfi, Col. D5 84
Amalfi, Italy I9 18
Amalga, Ut., U.S. B4 151
Amalia, N.M., U.S. A4 138
Amaliás, Grc. L5 20
Amambaí, Braz. G1 79
Amambaí, stm., Braz. G1 79
Amambay, dept., Para. B10 80
Amami-Ō-shima, i., Japan s4 37b
Amami-shotō, is., Japan F12 30
Amami-shotō, is., Japan t3 37b
Amana, Ia., U.S. C6 122
Amanã, stm., Braz. J14 84
Amana, stm., Ven. J13 94
Amaná, Lago, l., Braz. I10 84
Amanda, Oh., U.S. C3 142
Amapá, Braz. D9 74
Amapá, Braz. C8 76
Amapala, Hond. D7 92
Amapala, Punta de, c., El Sal. D7 92
Amarante, Braz. E10 76
Amaranth, Man., Can. D2 100
Amarapura, Mya. D4 40
'Amārat Abū Sinn, Sud. J8 60
Amares, Port. D3 16
Amargosa, Braz. B9 79
Amargosa, stm., U.S. D5 112
Amargosa Desert, des., U.S. G5 135
Amargosa Range, mts., U.S. G5 135
Amarillo, Tx., U.S. B2 150
'Amar Jadīd, Sud. J3 60
Amarkantak, India G3 30
Amarnāth, India C2 46
Amasa, Mi., U.S. B2 129
Amasya, Tur. G15 4
Amataurá, Braz. I8 84
Amatignak Island, i., Ak., U.S. E4 109
Amatikulu, S. Afr. G10 66
Amatique, Bahía de, b., N.A. B6 92
Amatitlán, Guat. C4 92
Amatitlán, Lago de, l., Guat. C4 92
Amazon (Solimões) (Amazonas), stm., S.A. D7 76
Amazonas, state, Braz. H10 84
Amazonas, dept., Col. H7 84
Amazonas, dept., Peru A2 82
Amazonas, ter., Ven. F9 84
Amazonia, Mo., U.S. B3 132
Ambakaka, Madag. t22 67b
Ambāla, India E7 44
Ambalanjanakomby, Madag. p22 67b
Ambalavao, Madag. r22 67b
Amba Maryam, Eth. L10 60
Ambanja, Madag. n23 67b
Ambar, Peru D3 82
Ambararata, Madag. o23 67b
Ambarčik, Russia D24 28
Ambargasta, Salinas de, pl., Arg. E6 80
Ambarnyj, Russia I23 6
Ambato, Ec. H3 84
Ambatofinandrahana, Madag. r22 67b
Ambatolampy, Madag. q22 67b
Ambatondrazaka, Madag. p23 67b
Ámbelos, Ákra, c., Grc. J7 20
Ambenja, Madag. o22 67b
Amber, Ok., U.S. B4 143
Amberg, Ger. F11 10
Amberg, Wi., U.S. C6 156
Ambergris Cay, i., Belize H16 90
Ambérieu-en-Bugey, Fr. G12 14
Ambert, Fr. G10 14
Ambevongo, Madag. o22 67b
Ambia, In., U.S. D2 121
Ambikāpur, India I10 44
Ambilobe, Madag. n23 67b
Ambinanindrano, Madag. r23 67b
Ambivy, Madag. r21 67b
Ambler, Ak., U.S. B8 109
Ambler, Pa., U.S. F11 145
Ambo, Peru D3 82
Amboahangy, Madag. t22 67b
Ambodifototra, Madag. p23 67b
Ambodiriana, Madag. p23 67b
Ambohidray, Madag. q23 67b
Ambohimahamasina, Madag. r22 67b
Amboise, Fr. E7 14
Ambon, Indon. F8 38
Ambondro, Madag. t21 67b
Ambositra, Madag. r22 67b
Ambovombe, Madag. t22 67b
Amboy, Il., U.S. B4 120
Amboy, In., U.S. C6 121
Amboy, Mn., U.S. G4 130
Amboy, Wa., U.S. D3 154
Ambre, Cap d', c., Madag. m23 67b
Ambridge, Pa., U.S. E1 145
Ambrières, Fr. D6 14
Ambriz, Ang. C2 58
Ambrose, Ga., U.S. E4 117
Ambunti, Pap. N. Gui. F11 38
Amchitka Island, i., Ak., U.S. E3 109
Amchitka Pass, strt., Ak., U.S. E4 109
'Amd, Yemen G6 47
Amderma, Russia D10 26
Amdo, China E5 30
Ameagle, W.V., U.S. D3 155
Ameca, Mex. G7 90
Ameca, stm., Mex. G7 90
Amecameca [de Juárez], Mex. H10 90
Ameghino, Arg. H7 80
Ameland, i., Neth. B8 12
Amelia, Italy G7 18
Amelia, La., U.S. E4 125
Amelia, Oh., U.S. C1 142
Amelia, co., Va., U.S. C4 153
Amelia Court House, Va., U.S. C5 153
Amelia Island, i., Fl., U.S. k9 116
Amenia, N.Y., U.S. D7 139
Amenia, N.D., U.S. B8 141
Āmer, India G6 44
American, stm., Ca., U.S. C3 112
American, South Fork, stm., Ca., U.S. C3 112
Americana, Braz. G5 79
American Falls, Id., U.S. G6 119
American Falls Dam, Id., U.S. G6 119
American Falls Reservoir, res., Id., U.S. F5 119
American Fork, Ut., U.S. C4 151
American Highland, plat., Ant. C5 73
American Samoa, dep., Oc. G1 2
Americus, Ga., U.S. D2 117
Americus, Ks., U.S. D7 123
Amersfoort, Neth. D7 12
Amersfoort, S. Afr. F9 66
Amery, Wi., U.S. C1 156
Amery Ice Shelf, Ant. B5 73
Ames, Ia., U.S. B4 122
Ames, Ok., U.S. A3 143
Amesbury, Ma., U.S. A6 128
Ámfissa, Grc. K6 20
Amga, Russia E18 28
Amga, stm., Russia E18 28
Amguema, stm., Russia D27 28
Amguid, Alg. G13 62
Amgun', stm., Russia G19 28
Amherst, N.S., Can. D5 101
Amherst, Ma., U.S. B2 128
Amherst, Ne., U.S. D6 134
Amherst, N.H., U.S. E3 136
Amherst, N.Y., U.S. C2 139
Amherst, Oh., U.S. A3 142
Amherst, S.D., U.S. B8 148
Amherst, Tx., U.S. B1 150
Amherst, Va., U.S. C3 153
Amherst, Wi., U.S. D4 156
Amherst, co., Va., U.S. C3 153
Amherstburg, Ont., Can. E1 103
Amherstdale, W.V., U.S. n12 155
Amiens, Fr. C9 14
Amili, China F16 44
Amīndīvi Islands, is., India G2 46
Aminga, Arg. E5 80
Aminuis, Nmb. D4 66
Amirante Islands, is., Sey. C10 58
Amisk, Alta., Can. C5 98
Amisk Lake, l., Sask., Can. C4 105
Amistad, Parque Internacional de la, C.R. H11 92
Amistad National Recreation Area, Tx., U.S. E2 150
Amite, La., U.S. D5 125
Amite, co., Ms., U.S. D3 131
Amite, stm., La., U.S. D5 125
Amity, Ar., U.S. C2 111
Amity, Or., U.S. B3 144
Amityville, N.Y., U.S. E7 139
Amizmiz, Mor. E6 62
Amlia Island, i., Ak., U.S. E5 109
'Amm-Adām, Sud. I9 60
'Ammān, Jord. E5 50
Ammarnäs, Swe. I15 6
Ammon, Id., U.S. F7 119
Ammonoosuc, stm., N.H., U.S. B3 136
Amne Machin Shan see A'nyêmaqên Shan, mts., China D6 30
Amnok-kang (Yalu), stm., Asia C13 32
Amo, In., U.S. E4 121
Amo, stm., Asia G13 44
Āmol, Iran C12 48
Amolar, Braz. H13 82
Amonate, Va., U.S. e10 153
Amoret, Mo., U.S. C3 132
Amorgós, i., Grc. M9 20
Amorinópolis, Braz. D3 79
Amory, Ms., U.S. B5 131
Amos, Que., Can. k11 104
Amoy see Xiamen, China K7 34
Ampanihy, Madag. t21 67b
Amparihy, Madag. s22 67b
Amparo, Braz. G5 79
Ampato, Nevado, mtn., Peru F6 82
Amper, Nig. G14 64
Ampombiantambo, Madag. n23 67b
Amposta, Spain E12 16
Ampotaka, Madag. t21 67b
'Amrān, Yemen G3 47
Amrāvati, India J7 44
Amreli, India J4 44
Amritsar, India E6 44
Amroha, India F8 44
Amsel, Alg. I13 62
Åmsele, Swe. I16 6
Amsteg, Switz. E10 13
Amsterdam, Neth. D6 12
Amsterdam, S. Afr. F10 66
Amsterdam, Ga., U.S. F2 117
Amsterdam, Mo., U.S. C3 132
Amsterdam, Mt., U.S. E5 133
Amsterdam, N.Y., U.S. C6 139
Amsterdam, Oh., U.S. B5 142
Amsterdam, Île, i., F.S.A.T. L11 158
Amsterdam-Rijnkanaal, Neth. E7 12
Amstetten, Aus. G14 10
Amston, Ct., U.S. C6 114
Am Timan, Chad F5 56
Amubri, C.R. H12 92
Amu-Darja, Turk. C18 48
Amu Darya (Amudarja), stm., Asia B2 44
Amukta Pass, strt., Ak., U.S. E5 109
Amundsen Gulf, b., N.W. Ter., Can. B8 96
Amundsen-Scott, sci., Ant. D10 73
Amundsen Sea, Ant. C11 73
Amuntai, Indon. F6 38
Amur (Heilong), stm., Asia B14 30
Amurrio, Spain I3 14
Amuzhong, China E11 44
Amvrakikós Kólpos, b., Grc. K4 20
Amy, Ar., U.S. D3 111
Anabar, stm., Russia C14 28
Anaco, Ven. C10 84
Anacoco, La., U.S. C2 125
Anacoco, Bayou, stm., La., U.S. D2 125
Anaconda, Mt., U.S. D4 133
Anaconda, N.M., U.S. B2 138
Anaconda Range, mts., Mt., U.S. E3 133
Anacortes, Wa., U.S. A3 154
Anacostia, stm., U.S. C4 127
Anacostia, Northwest Branch, stm., Md., U.S. B3 127
Anadarko, Ok., U.S. B3 143
Anadyr', Russia E27 28
Anadyr', stm., Russia E26 28
Anadyrskij zaliv, b., Russia E28 28
Anadyrskoje ploskogorje, plat., Russia D26 28
Anagance, N.B., Can. D4 101
Anagni, Italy H8 18
'Ānah, Iraq D6 48
Anaheim, Ca., U.S. F5 112
Anahim Lake, B.C., Can. C5 99
Anahola, Hi., U.S. A2 118
Anáhuac, Mex. C6 90
Anáhuac, Mex. D9 90
Anahuac, Tx., U.S. E5 150
Anahulu, stm., Hi., U.S. f9 118
Ānai Mudi, mtn., India G4 46
Analalava, Madag. o22 67b
Analapatsy, Madag. t22 67b
Anamã, Braz. I12 84
Anamã, Lago, l., Braz. I12 84
Anama Bay, Man., Can. D2 100
Ana María, Golfo de, b., Cuba D5 94
Anambas, Kepulauan, is., Indon. M9 40
Anamoose, N.D., U.S. B5 141
Anamosa, Ia., U.S. B6 122
Anamu, stm., Braz. G14 84
Anamur, Tur. C2 48
Ānand, India I5 44
Anandale, La., U.S. C3 125
Ananea, Peru F7 82
Anantapur, India E4 46
Anantnāg (Islāmābād), India D6 44
Anan'yiv, Ukr. B13 20
Anápolis, Braz. D4 79
Anār, Iran F13 48
Anārak, Iran E12 48
Anār Darreh, Afg. E16 48
Anastácio, Braz. F1 79
Anastasia Island, i., Fl., U.S. C5 116
'Anātā, W.B. E4 50
Anatolikí Makedhonía kaí Thráki, prov., Grc. H9 20
Añatuya, Arg. E7 80
Anauá, stm., Braz. G12 84
Anaurilândia, Braz. G2 79
Anavilhanas, Arquipélago das, is., Braz. I12 84
Anawalt, W.V., U.S. D3 155
Anbanjing, China C6 40
Anbu, China L5 34
Anbyŏn, N. Kor. D15 32
Ancash, dept., Peru C3 82
Ancaster, Ont., Can. D4 103
Ancasti, Arg. E6 80
Ancasti, Sierra de, mts., Arg. E6 80
Ancha, Sierra, mts., Az., U.S. D4 110
Anchang, China E9 34
Anchorage, Ak., U.S. C10 109
Anchorage, Ky., U.S. g11 124
Anchorena, Arg. H6 80
Anchor Point, Ak., U.S. D9 109
Anchor Point, c., Ak., U.S. h15 109
Anci (Langfang), China D4 32
Ancien Goubéré, Cen. Afr. Rep. O4 60
Ancienne-Lorette, Que., Can. C6 104
Anciferovo, Russia C17 22
Anclote Keys, is., Fl., U.S. D4 116
Anco, Ky., U.S. C6 124
Ancón, Peru D3 82
Ancona, Italy F8 18
Ancón de Sardinas, Bahía de, b., S.A. G3 84
Ancoraimes, Bol. F7 82
Ancud, Chile E2 78
Ancud, Golfo de, b., Chile E2 78
Anda, China B12 30
Andacollo, Arg. I3 80
Andacollo, Chile F3 80
Andahuaylas, Peru E5 82
Andale, Ks., U.S. E6 123
Andalgalá, Arg. D5 80
Åndalsnes, Nor. J10 6
Andalucía, prov., Spain H7 16
Andalucía, hist. reg., Spain H7 16
Andalusia, Al., U.S. D3 108
Andalusia, Il., U.S. B3 120
Andaman Islands, is., India H2 40
Andaman Sea, Asia I3 40
Andamarca, Bol. H8 82
Andamarca, Peru D4 82
Andamooka, Austl. H2 70
Andapa, Madag. o23 67b
Andaraí, Braz. B8 79
Andaray, Peru F5 82
Andeer, Switz. E11 13
Andelot, Fr. D12 14
Andenes, Nor. G15 6
Andéranboukane, Mali D11 64
Andermatt, Switz. E10 13
Andernach, Ger. E7 10
Anderson, Al., U.S. A2 108
Anderson, Ak., U.S. C10 109
Anderson, Ca., U.S. B2 112
Anderson, In., U.S. D6 121
Anderson, Mo., U.S. E3 132
Anderson, S.C., U.S. B2 147
Anderson, Tn., U.S. D8 149
Anderson, Tx., U.S. D4 150
Anderson, co., Ks., U.S. D8 123
Anderson, co., Ky., U.S. C4 124
Anderson, co., S.C., U.S. B2 147
Anderson, co., Tn., U.S. C9 149
Anderson, co., Tx., U.S. D5 150
Anderson, stm., N.W. Ter., Can. C7 96
Anderson, stm., In., U.S. H4 121
Anderson, Mount, mtn., Wa., U.S. B2 154
Anderson Ranch Reservoir, res., Id., U.S. F3 119
Andersonville, Ga., U.S. D2 117
Andersonville, In., U.S. F7 121
Andes, Col. E5 84
Andes, mts., S.A. G8 74
Andes, Lake, l., S.D., U.S. D7 148
Andevoranto, Madag. q23 67b
Andhra Pradesh, state, India D5 46
Andikíthira, i., Grc. N7 20
Andimákhia, Grc. M11 20
Andīmeshk, Iran E10 48
Andirá, stm., Braz. I14 84
Andirá, Riozinho do, stm., Braz. C8 82
Andirlang, China B10 44
Ándissa, Grc. J9 20
Andižan, Uzb. I12 26
Andkhvoy, Afg. B1 44
Andoas, Peru I4 84
Andong, S. Kor. G16 32
Andorra, And. C13 16
Andorra, ctry., Eur. G8 4
Andover, Ct., U.S. C6 114
Andover, Il., U.S. B3 120
Andover, Ks., U.S. g12 123
Andover, Me., U.S. D2 126
Andover, Ma., U.S. A5 128
Andover, Mn., U.S. m12 130
Andover, N.H., U.S. D3 136
Andover, N.Y., U.S. C3 139
Andover, Oh., U.S. A5 142
Andover, S.D., U.S. B8 148
Andover Lake, res., Ct., U.S. C6 114
Andøya, i., Nor. G14 6
Andrade, Hi., U.S. D6 118
Andradina, Braz. F3 79
Andranopasy, Madag. r20 67b
Andranovory, Madag. s21 67b
Andreanof Islands, is., Ak., U.S. E4 109
Andreapol', Russia E15 22
Andrejevo, Russia F24 22
Andréville, Que., Can. B8 104
Andrew, Alta., Can. C4 98
Andrew, Ia., U.S. B7 122
Andrew, co., Mo., U.S. B3 132
Andrew Island, i., N.S., Can. D9 101
Andrews, In., U.S. C6 121
Andrews, N.C., U.S. f9 140
Andrews, S.C., U.S. E8 147
Andrews, Tx., U.S. C1 150
Andrews, co., Tx., U.S. C1 150
Andrews Air Force Base, mil., Md., U.S. C4 127
Andria, Italy H11 18
Andriamena, Madag. p22 67b
Andriandampy, Madag. s21 67b
Andrijevica, Yugo. G3 20
Androka, Madag. t21 67b
Ándros, Grc. L8 20
Andros, i., Bah. B6 94
Ándros, i., Grc. L8 20
Androscoggin, co., Me., U.S. D2 126
Androscoggin, stm., Me., U.S. D2 126
Androscoggin Lake, l., Me., U.S. D2 126
Andros Town, Bah. B6 94
Āndrott Island, i., India G2 46
Andrychów, Pol. F19 10
Andújar, Spain G7 16
Anécho, Togo H10 64
Anegada, i., Br. Vir. Is. E12 94
Anegada Passage, strt., N.A. E13 94
Añelo, Arg. J4 80
Aneroid, Sask., Can. H2 105
Aneta, N.D., U.S. B8 141
Aneth, Ut., U.S. F6 151
Aneto, Pico de, mtn., Spain C12 16
Anfeng, China B9 34
Anfeng, China C9 34
Anfengqiao, China I7 34
Anfu, China H3 34
Angamos, Punta, c., Chile B3 80
Ang'angxi, China B11 30
Angao, China B1 34
Angara, stm., Russia F17 26
Angara-Débou, Benin F11 64
Angarbaka, Sud. M3 60
Angarsk, Russia G12 28
Angastaco, Arg. C5 80
Angatuba, Braz. G4 79
Ángel, Salto (Angel Falls), wtfl, Ven. E11 84
Ángel de la Guarda, Isla, i., Mex. C3 90
Angeles, Phil. n19 39b
Angeles Point, c., Wa., U.S. A2 154
Angel Falls see Ángel, Salto, wtfl, Ven. E11 84
Angelica, N.Y., U.S. C2 139
Angelina, co., Tx., U.S. D5 150
Angels Camp, Ca., U.S. C3 112
Angereb, stm., Afr. K9 60
Angermünde, Ger. B14 10
Angers, Fr. E6 14
Angerville, Fr. D9 14
Angical, Braz. B6 79
Angicos, Braz. E11 76
Angier, N.C., U.S. B4 140
Angkor Wat, hist., Camb. H7 40
Ângk Tasaôm, Camb. I8 40
Angle Inlet, Mn., U.S. A3 130
Anglesey, i., Wales, U.K. H9 8
Angleton, Tx., U.S. E5 150
Angling Lake, l., Man., Can. C5 100
Angmagssalik, Grnld. C16 86
Angoche, Moz. E7 58
Angoche, Ilha, i., Moz. E7 58
Angol, Chile I2 80
Angola, In., U.S. A8 121
Angola, N.Y., U.S. C1 139
Angola, ctry., Afr. D3 58
Angola Swamp, sw., N.C., U.S. C5 140
Angoon, Ak., U.S. D13 109
Angora see Ankara, Tur. B2 48
Angoram, Pap. N. Gui. F11 38
Angostura, Mex. E5 90
Angostura, Presa de la, res., Mex. I13 90
Angostura Reservoir, res., S.D., U.S. D2 148
Angoulême, Fr. G7 14
Angoumois, hist. reg., Fr. G6 14
Angra dos Reis, Braz. G6 79
Angren, Uzb. I12 26
Angualasto, Arg. F4 80
Anguciana, Cerro, mtn., C.R. I11 92
Anguilla, Ms., U.S. C3 131
Anguilla, dep., N.A. E13 94
Anguilla Cays, is., Bah. C5 94
Anguille, Cape, c., Newf., Can. E2 102
Anguo, China E3 32
Angusville, Man., Can. D1 100
Anhai, China K7 34
Anhui (Anhwei), prov., China E10 30
Aniak, Ak., U.S. C8 109
Aniche, Fr. H3 12
Anicuns, Braz. D4 79
Anié, Togo H10 64
Animas, N.M., U.S. F1 138
Animas, stm., U.S. D3 113
Animas Mountains, mts., N.M., U.S. F1 138
Animas Peak, mtn., N.M., U.S. F2 138
Animas Valley, val., N.M., U.S. F1 138
Anina, Rom. D5 20
Anita, Ia., U.S. C3 122
Anita, Pa., U.S. D4 145
Aniva, zaliv, b., Russia H20 28
Anivorano, Madag. q23 67b
Anjangaon, India B4 46
Anjār, India I4 44
'Anjar, Leb. A5 50
Anji, China E8 34
Anjiabe, Madag. n23 67b
Anjiang, China C5 32
Anjou, Que., Can. p19 104
Anjou, hist. reg., Fr. E6 14
Anju, N. Kor. D13 32
Ankang, China E8 30
Ankara, Tur. B2 48
Ankaratra, mts., Madag. q22 67b
Ankarimbelo, Madag. s22 67b
Ankasakasa, Madag. p21 67b
Ankavandra, Madag. q21 67b
Ankazoabo, Madag. s21 67b
Ankazobe, Madag. q22 67b
Ankazomiriotra, Madag. q22 67b
Ankeny, Ia., U.S. C4 122
Ankilimalinika, Madag. s20 67b
Ankisabe, Madag. q22 67b
Ankleshwar, India B2 46
Ankober, Eth. G8 56
Ankou, China J2 34
An'kovo, Russia E22 22
Ankpa, Nig. H13 64
Anliu, China L4 34
Anlu, China D2 34
Ann, Cape, c., Ant. B4 73
Ann, Cape, c., Ma., U.S. A6 128
Anna, Il., U.S. F4 120
Anna, Oh., U.S. B1 142
Anna, Lake, res., Va., U.S. B5 153
Annaba (Bône), Alg. B14 62
Annabella, Ut., U.S. E3 151
Annaberg-Buchholz, Ger. E13 10
An-Nabk, Syria D4 48
An-Nafī, Sau. Ar. B3 47
An-Nafūd, des., Sau. Ar. G6 48

Name — Map Ref. — Page

An-Najaf, Iraq F8 48
An-Nakhl, Egypt C7 60
Anna Maria, Fl., U.S. p10 116
Anna Maria Island, i., Fl., U.S. q10 116
Annamitique, Chaîne, mts., Asia F9 40
Annandale, Austl. C8 70
Annandale, Mn., U.S. E4 130
Annandale, N.J., U.S. B3 137
Annandale, Va., U.S. g12 153
Annapolis, In., U.S. E3 121
Annapolis, Md., U.S. C5 127
Annapolis, Mo., U.S. D7 132
Annapolis, stm., N.S., Can. E4 101
Annapolis Junction, Md., U.S. B4 127
Annapolis Royal, N.S., Can. E4 101
Annapūrna, mtn., Nepal F10 44
Ann Arbor, Mi., U.S. F7 129
Anna Regina, Guy. D13 84
An-Nāṣirīyah, Iraq F9 48
An-Nāṣirīyah, Syria A7 50
Annawan, Il., U.S. B4 120
An-Nawfalāb, Sud. J7 60
Anne Arundel, co., Md., U.S. B4 127
Annecy, Fr. G13 14
Annemasse, Fr. F13 14
Annenskij Most, Russia A20 22
An Nhon, Viet. H10 40
Anniston, Al., U.S. B4 108
Anniston, Mo., U.S. E8 132
Annobón, i., Eq. Gui. B1 58
Annonay, Fr. G11 14
An-Nuhūd, Sud. K5 60
An-Nu'mānīyah, Iraq E8 48
Annursnack Hill, hill, Ma., U.S. g10 128
Annville, Ky., U.S. C6 124
Annville, Pa., U.S. F8 145
Anoka, Mn., U.S. E5 130
Anoka, co., Mn., U.S. E5 130
Anopino, Russia F23 22
Anori, Braz. I12 84
Anorí, Col. D5 84
Anping, China D4 32
Anpu, China D11 40
Anqing, China E6 34
Anqiu, China G7 32
Ansbach, Ger. F10 10
Anse-d'Hainault, Haiti E7 94
Anselmo, Ne., U.S. C6 134
Anserma, Col. E5 84
Anshan, China B10 32
Anshun, China A8 40
Ansina, Ur. F11 80
Ansley, Ms., U.S. E4 131
Ansley, Ne., U.S. C6 134
Anson, Me., U.S. D3 126
Anson, Tx., U.S. C3 150
Anson, co., N.C., U.S. B2 140
Ansŏng, S. Kor. F15 32
Ansongo, Mali D10 64
Ansonia, Ct., U.S. D3 114
Ansonia, Oh., U.S. B1 142
Ansonville, N.C., U.S. B2 140
Ansted, W.V., U.S. C3 155
Anta, Peru E5 82
Antabamba, Peru F5 82
Antalaha, Madag. o24 67b
Antalivtsi, Ukr. G22 10
Antalya, Tur. H14 4
Antalya Körfezi, b., Tur. H14 4
Antambohobe, Madag. s22 67b
Antanambao Manampotsy, Madag. q23 67b
Antananarivo, Madag. q22 67b
Antanetibe, Madag. q22 67b
Antanifotsy, Madag. q22 67b
Antarctica D5 73
Antarctic Peninsula, pen., Ant. B12 73
Antas, Rio das, stm., Braz. E13 80
Antelope, Mt., U.S. B12 133
Antelope, co., Ne., U.S. B7 134
Antelope Butte, mtn., Wy., U.S. B7 157
Antelope Creek, stm., Wy., U.S. C7 157
Antelope Island, i., Ut., U.S. B3 151
Antelope Mine, Zimb. C9 66
Antelope Peak, mtn., Nv., U.S. B7 135
Antelope Range, mts., Nv., U.S. D7 135
Antelope Reservoir, res., Or., U.S. E9 144
Antelope Wash, val., Nv., U.S. D5 135
Antequera, Para. C10 80
Antequera, Spain H7 16
Antero, Mount, mtn., Co., U.S. C4 113
Antero Reservoir, res., Co., U.S. C5 113
Antevamena, Madag. r21 67b
Anthon, Ia., U.S. B2 122
Anthony, Fl., U.S. C4 116
Anthony, Ks., U.S. E5 123
Anthony, N.M., U.S. F3 138
Anthony, R.I., U.S. D3 146
Anthony, Tx., U.S. o11 150
Anthony Creek, stm., W.V., U.S. D4 155
Anti-Atlas, mts., Mor. E6 62
Antibes, Fr. I14 14
Anticosti, Île d', i., Que., Can. k14 104
Antietam Creek, stm., Md., U.S. B2 127
Antietam National Battlefield, hist., Md., U.S. B2 127
Antigo, Wi., U.S. C4 156
Antigonish, N.S., Can. D8 101
Antigua, i., Antig. F14 94
Antigua and Barbuda, ctry., N.A. F14 94
Antigua Guatemala, Guat. C4 92
Antiguo Morelos, Mex. F10 90
Anti-Lebanon see Sharqī, Al-Jabal ash-, mts., Asia A6 50
Antilla, Arg. D6 80
Antilla, Cuba D7 94
Antioch see Hatay, Tur. C4 48
Antioch, Ca., U.S. h9 112
Antioch, Il., U.S. A5 120
Antioquia, Col. D5 84
Antioquia, dept., Col. D5 84
Antipodes Islands, is., N.Z. M21 158
Antizana, vol., Ec. H3 84
Antlers, Ok., U.S. C6 143
Antofagasta, Chile B3 80
Antofagasta, prov., Chile B4 80
Antofagasta de la Sierra, Arg. D5 80
Antofalla, Salar de, pl., Arg. C5 80
Antofalla, Volcán, vol., Arg. C5 80
Antoine, Ar., U.S. C2 111
Antón, Pan. C2 84
Anton, Tx., U.S. C1 150
Anton Chico, N.M., U.S. B4 138
Antongila, Helodrano, b., Madag. o23 67b
Antonia, Mo., U.S. C7 132
Antonina, Braz. C14 80
Antonio Amaro, Mex. E7 90
Antônio Prado, Braz. E13 80
Antonito, Co., U.S. D5 113
Antón Lizardo, Punta, c., Mex. H12 90
Antopol', Bela. I7 22
Antora Peak, mtn., Co., U.S. C4 113
Antou, China I7 34
Antrain, Fr. D5 14
Antrim, N. Ire., U.K. G7 8
Antrim, N.H., U.S. D3 136
Antrim, co., Mi., U.S. C5 129
Antrodoco, Italy G8 18
Antropovo, Russia C26 22
Antsalova, Madag. q21 67b
Antsenavolo, Madag. r23 67b
Antsiafabositra, Madag. p22 67b
Antsirabe, Madag. o23 67b
Antsirabe, Madag. q22 67b
Antsiranana, Madag. n23 67b
Antsla, Est. D9 22
Antsohihy, Madag. o22 67b
Antuševo, Russia B20 22
Antwerp see Antwerpen, Bel. F5 12
Antwerp, Oh., U.S. A1 142
Antwerpen (Anvers), Bel. F5 12
Antwerpen, prov., Bel. F6 12
Anugul, India B8 46
Anuradhapura, Sri L. H6 46
Anvers (Antwerpen), Bel. F5 12
Anvers Island, i., Ant. B12 73
Anxi, China C6 30
Anxi, China J7 34
Anxin, China E3 32
Anyama, C. Iv. I7 64
Anyang, China G2 32
A'nyêmaqên Shan, mts., China D6 30
Anyi, China G4 34
Anykščiai, Lith. F8 22
Anyuan, China H2 34
Anzac, Alta., Can. A5 98
Anzaldo, Bol. G9 82
Anžero-Sudženskij, Russia F15 26
Anzhen, China D9 34
Anzhou, China E3 32
Anzin, Fr. B10 14
Anzio, Italy H7 18
Anzoátegui, state, Ven. C10 84
Anžu, ostrova, is., Russia B20 28
Aoga-shima, i., Japan E14 30
Aohan Qi (Xinhui), China A7 32
Aoji, N. Kor. A18 32
Aojiang, China H9 34
Aojiao, China L6 34
Aomori, Japan G15 36
Aóös (Vijosë), stm., Eur. J4 20
Aôral, Phnum, mtn., Camb. H8 40
Aosta, Italy D2 18
Aotou, China M3 34
Aouderas, Niger C14 64
Aouk, Bahr, stm., Afr. G5 56
Aoukâr, reg., Maur. B5 64
Aourou, Mali D4 64
Aozou, Chad D4 56
Apa, stm., S.A. B10 80
Apache, Ok., U.S. C3 143
Apache, co., Az., U.S. B6 110
Apache Junction, Az., U.S. m9 110
Apache Peak, mtn., Az., U.S. F5 110
Apalachee, Ga., U.S. C3 117
Apalachee Bay, b., Fl., U.S. B2 116
Apalachicola, Fl., U.S. C2 116
Apalachicola, stm., Fl., U.S. B1 116
Apalachicola Bay, b., Fl., U.S. C2 116
Apalachin, N.Y., U.S. C4 139
Apanas, Laguna de, res., Nic. D9 92
Apaporis, stm., S.A. H7 84
Aparados da Serra, Parque Nacional de, Braz. E13 80
Aparri, Phil. I19 39b
Apaseo El Grande, Mex. G9 90
Apatin, Yugo. D2 20
Apatity, Russia D4 26
Apatzingán de la Constitución, Mex. H8 90
Apaxtla de Castrejón, Mex. H10 90
Apayacu, stm., Peru I6 84
Ape, Lat. D9 22
Apeldoorn, Neth. D8 12
Apennines see Appennino, mts., Italy F7 18
Apex, N.C., U.S. B4 140
Api, mtn., Nepal F9 44
Apía, Col. E5 84
Apia, W. Sam. G1 2
Apiacá, stm., Braz. C13 82
Apiacás, Serra dos, plat., Braz. D13 82
Apiaí, Braz. C14 80
Apiaú, stm., Braz. F12 84
Apishapa, stm., Co., U.S. D6 113
Apison, Tn., U.S. h11 149
Apizaco, Mex. H10 90
Apizolaya, Mex. E8 90
Aplahoué, Benin H10 64
Aplao, Peru G5 82
Aplin, Ar., U.S. C3 111
Aplington, Ia., U.S. B5 122
Apo, Mount, mtn., Phil. D8 38
Apohaqui, N.B., Can. D4 101
Apolakkiá, Grc. M11 20
Apolda, Ger. D11 10
Apolinario Saravia, Arg. C6 80
Apollo, Pa., U.S. E2 145
Apolo, Bol. F7 82
Apón, stm., Ven. B6 84
Aponguao, stm., Ven. E12 84
Apopa, El Sal. D5 92
Apopka, Fl., U.S. D5 116
Apopka, Lake, l., Fl., U.S. D5 116
Aporé, Braz. E2 79
Aporé, stm., Braz. E3 79
Apostle Islands, is., Wi., U.S. A3 156
Apostle Islands National Lakeshore, Wi., U.S. A3 156
Apóstoles, Arg. D11 80
Apostolove, Ukr. H4 26
Appalachia, Va., U.S. f9 153
Appalachian Mountains, mts., N.A. C11 106
Appanoose, co., Ia., U.S. D5 122
Appennino (Apennines), mts., Italy F7 18
Appenzell, Switz. D11 13
Appenzell-Ausserrhoden, state, Switz. D11 13
Apple, stm., Wi., U.S. C1 156
Apple Creek, Oh., U.S. B4 142
Applegate, Or., U.S. E3 144
Applegate, stm., Or., U.S. E3 144
Apple Grove, W.V., U.S. C2 155
Apple Hill, Ont., Can. B10 103
Apple Orchard Mountain, mtn., Va., U.S. C3 153
Apple River, N.S., Can. D5 101
Apple River, Il., U.S. A3 120
Appleton, Ar., U.S. B3 111
Appleton, Mn., U.S. E2 130
Appleton, Wi., U.S. D5 156
Appleton City, Mo., U.S. C3 132
Apple Valley, Ca., U.S. E5 112
Apple Valley, Mn., U.S. n12 130
Applewood, Co., U.S. *B5 113
Appleyard, Wa., U.S. B5 154
Appling, Ga., U.S. C4 117
Appling, co., Ga., U.S. E4 117
Appomattox, Va., U.S. C4 153
Appomattox, co., Va., U.S. C4 153
Appomattox, stm., Va., U.S. C4 153
Appomattox Court House National Historical Park, Va., U.S. C4 153
Aprelevka, Russia F20 22
Apsley, Ont., Can. C6 103
Apt, Fr. I12 14
Apua Point, c., Hi., U.S. D6 118
Apuaú, stm., Braz. I12 84
Apucarana, Braz. G3 79
Apure, state, Ven. D8 84
Apure, stm., Ven. D9 84
Apurímac, dept., Peru E5 82
Apurímac, stm., Peru E5 82
Apurito, Ven. D8 84
Aqaba, Gulf of, b. C8 60
'Aqiq, Sud. H10 60
Aquarius Mountains, mts., Az., U.S. C2 110
Aquarius Plateau, plat., Ut., U.S. E4 151
Aquidabã, stm., Braz. I13 82
Aquidabán, stm., Para. B10 80
Aquidauana, Braz. I14 82
Aquidauana, stm., Braz. I14 82
Aquila, Mex. H8 90
Aquila, Switz. E10 13
Aquiles Serdán, Mex. E11 90
Aquiles Serdán, Mex. C7 90
Aquin, Haiti E8 94
Aquio, stm., Col. F9 84
Ara, India H11 44
Arab, Al., U.S. A3 108
'Arab, Baḥr al-, stm., Sud. M4 60
'Arab, Shaṭṭ al-, stm., Asia G10 48
'Arab, Wādī al-, val., Jord. C5 50
'Arabah, Wādī al- (Ha'Arava), val., Asia G4 50
Arabako, prov., Spain C9 16
Arabelo, Ven. E10 84
Arabi, Ga., U.S. E3 117
Arabi, La., U.S. k11 125
Arabian Desert see Sharqīyah, Aṣ-Ṣaḥrā' ash-, des., Egypt D7 60
Arabian Gulf see Persian Gulf, b., Asia H11 48
Arabian Peninsula, pen., Asia G5 24
Arabian Sea H7 24
Araçá, stm., Braz. G11 84
Aracaju, Braz. F11 76
Aracataca, Col. B5 84
Aracati, Braz. D11 76
Araçatuba, Braz. F3 79
Aracena, Spain H5 16
Aracruz, Braz. E8 79
Araçuaí, Braz. D7 79
Araçuaí, stm., Braz. D7 79
Arad, Rom. C5 20
Arad, co., Rom. C5 20
Arada, Hond. C6 92
Arafura Sea I17 158
Aragarças, Braz. C2 79
Arago, Cape, c., Or., U.S. D2 144
Aragon, Ga., U.S. B1 117
Aragon, N.M., U.S. D1 138
Aragón, prov., Spain D10 16
Aragón, stm., Spain C10 16
Aragua, state, Ven. B9 84
Araguacema, Braz. E9 76
Araguaçu, Braz. B4 79
Aragua de Barcelona, Ven. C10 84
Aragua de Maturín, Ven. C11 84
Araguaia, stm., Braz. E9 76
Araguaia, Braço Menor, stm., Braz. B3 79
Araguainha, Braz. D2 79
Araguao, Caño, mth., Ven. C12 84
Araguari, Braz. E4 79
Araguari, stm., Braz. C8 76
Araguari, stm., Braz. E4 79
Araguatins, Braz. E9 76
Arak, Alg. H12 62
Arāk, Iran D10 48
Arakan Yoma, mts., Mya. E3 40
Arákhthos, stm., Grc. J4 20
Aral Sea, Asia H10 26
Aral'sk, Kaz. H10 26
Aramac, Austl. D6 70
Aramac, stm., Austl. D6 70
Aramari, Braz. B9 79
Aramberri, Mex. E10 90
Arampampa, Bol. G8 82
Aramtalla, Sud. N5 60
Ārān, Iran D11 48
Aranda de Duero, Spain D8 16
Arandas, Mex. G8 90
Arandelovac, Yugo. E4 20
Arandis, Nmb. D2 66
Arani, Bol. G9 82
Aran Islands, is., Ire. H4 8
Aranjuez, Spain E8 16
Aransas, co., Tx., U.S. E4 150
Aransas Bay, b., Tx., U.S. E4 150
Aransas Pass, Tx., U.S. F4 150
Aranyaprathet, Thai. H7 40
Arao, Japan O5 36
Araouane, Mali E6 54
Arapa, Laguna, l., Peru F6 82
Arapaho, Ok., U.S. B3 143
Arapahoe, Co., U.S. C8 113
Arapahoe, Ne., U.S. D6 134
Arapahoe, N.C., U.S. B6 140
Arapahoe, co., Co., U.S. B6 113
Arapey, Ur. F10 80
Arapey Chico, stm., Ur. F10 80
Arapey Grande, stm., Ur. F10 80
Arapiraca, Braz. E11 76
Arapkir, Tur. B5 48
Arapongas, Braz. G3 79
Arapoti, Braz. H4 79
'Ar'ar, Sau. Ar. F6 48
'Ar'ar, Wādī, val., Asia B11 60
Araranguá, Braz. E14 80
Araraquara, Braz. F4 79
Araras, Braz. G5 79
Ararat, Arm. B8 48
Ararat, Austl. K5 70
Ararat, Mount see Ağrı Dağı, mtn., Tur. B8 48
Ararirá, stm., Braz. H10 84
Araruama, Lagoa de, b., Braz. G7 79
Aras (Araz), stm., Asia B10 48
Aratos, Grc. H9 20
Aratuípe, Braz. B9 79
Arauá, stm., Braz. A11 82
Arauá, stm., Braz. C9 82
Arauá, stm., Braz. J10 84
Arauca, Col. D7 84
Arauca, dept., Col. D7 84
Arauca, stm., S.A. D9 84
Araucária, Braz. C14 80
Arauco, Chile I2 80
Arauco, Golfo de, b., Chile I2 80
Araújos, Braz. E6 79
Arauquita, Col. D7 84
Araure, Ven. C8 84
Arāvalli Range, mts., India H5 44
Araxá, Braz. E5 79
Araya, Ven. B10 84
Araya, Punta de, c., Ven. B10 84
Araz (Aras), stm., Asia B10 48
Arba Minch, Eth. N9 60
Arboga, Swe. L14 6
Arbois, Fr. F12 14
Arboledas, Arg. I8 80
Arboletes, Col. C4 84
Arbon, Switz. C11 13
Arborfield, Sask., Can. D4 105
Arborg, Man., Can. D3 100
Arbroath, Scot., U.K. E11 8
Arbuckle, Ca., U.S. C2 112
Arbuckle, Lake, l., Fl., U.S. E5 116
Arbuckle Mountains, mts., Ok., U.S. C4 143
Arbuckles, Lake of the, res., Ok., U.S. C5 143
Arbyrd, Mo., U.S. E7 132
Arc, Bayou des, stm., Ar., U.S. B4 111
Arcachon, Fr. H5 14
Arcade, Ca., U.S. *C3 112
Arcade, Ga., U.S. B3 117
Arcade, N.Y., U.S. C2 139
Arcadia, N.S., Can. F3 101
Arcadia, Ca., U.S. m12 112
Arcadia, Fl., U.S. E5 116
Arcadia, In., U.S. D5 121
Arcadia, Ia., U.S. B2 122
Arcadia, Ks., U.S. E9 123
Arcadia, La., U.S. B3 125
Arcadia, Mi., U.S. D4 129
Arcadia, Mo., U.S. D7 132
Arcadia, Ne., U.S. C6 134
Arcadia, Oh., U.S. A2 142
Arcadia, Ok., U.S. B4 143
Arcadia, S.C., U.S. B4 147
Arcadia, Wi., U.S. D2 156
Arcanum, Oh., U.S. C1 142
Arcas, Cayos, is., Mex. G14 90
Arcata, Ca., U.S. B1 112
Arcatao, El Sal. C6 92
Arc Dome, mtn., Nv., U.S. E4 135
Arcelia, Mex. H9 90
Archambault, Lac, l., Que., Can. C3 104
Archangel'sk, Russia E6 26
Archbald, Pa., U.S. m18 145
Archbold, Oh., U.S. A1 142
Archdale, N.C., U.S. B3 140
Archer, Fl., U.S. C4 116
Archer, co., Tx., U.S. C3 150
Archer City, Tx., U.S. C3 150
Archerwill, Sask., Can. E4 105
Arches National Park, Ut., U.S. E6 151
Archidona, Spain H7 16
Archie, Mo., U.S. C3 132
Archipovka, Russia E24 22
Archuleta, co., Co., U.S. D3 113
Arco, Id., U.S. F5 119
Arcola, Sask., Can. H4 105
Arcola, Il., U.S. D5 120
Arcola, Ms., U.S. B3 131
Arcola, Va., U.S. g11 153
Arcos, Braz. F6 79
Arcos de la Frontera, Spain I6 16
Arcot, India F5 46
Arcoverde, Braz. E11 76
Arctic Bay, N.W. Ter., Can. B15 96
Arctic Ocean A1 86
Arctic Red, stm., N.W. Ter., Can. C6 96
Arctowski, sci., Ant. B1 73
Arcturus, Zimb. A10 66
Arda, stm., Eur. H9 20
Ardabīl, Iran B10 48
Ardahan, Tur. G16 4
Ardakān, Iran E12 48
Ardakān, Iran F12 48
Ardalstangen, Nor. K10 6
Ardatov, Russia F26 22
Ardèche, dept., Fr. H11 14
Arden, Man., Can. D2 100
Arden, Ont., Can. C8 103
Arden, Ar., U.S. D1 111
Arden, Mount, mtn., Austl. I2 70
Ardennes, dept., Fr. C11 14
Ardennes, reg., Eur. E5 10
Ardestān, Iran E12 48
Ardila, stm., Eur. G4 16
Ardino, Bul. H9 20
Ardlethan, Austl. J7 70
Ardmore, Alta., Can. B5 98
Ardmore, Al., U.S. A3 108
Ardmore, In., U.S. A5 121
Ardmore, Ok., U.S. C4 143
Ardmore, Pa., U.S. F11 145
Ardmore, Tn., U.S. B5 149
Ardoch, Austl. F6 70
Ardrossan, Alta., Can. C4 98
Ardsley, N.Y., U.S. g13 139
Åre, Swe. J13 6
Areado, Braz. F5 79
Arecibo, P.R. E11 94
Areguá, Para. C10 80
Areia, Ribeirão da, stm., Braz. C6 79
Areia Branca, Braz. D11 76
Arena, Wi., U.S. E4 156
Arena, Point, c., Ca., U.S. C2 112
Arena, Punta, c., Mex. F5 90
Arenac, co., Mi., U.S. D7 129
Arena de la Ventana, Punta, c., Mex. E5 90
Arenal, C.R. G10 92
Arenal, Laguna de, l., C.R. G10 92
Arenal, Volcán, vol., C.R. G10 92
Arenápolis, Braz. F13 82
Arenas, Cayo, i., Mex. F14 90
Arenas Valley, N.M., U.S. E1 138
Arendal, Nor. L11 6
Arendtsville, Pa., U.S. G7 145
Arenillas, Ec. I2 84
Arenys de Mar, Spain D14 16
Arenzville, Il., U.S. D3 120
Arequipa, Peru G6 82
Arequipa, dept., Peru F5 82
Arequito, Arg. G8 80
Arès, Fr. H5 14
Arezzo, Italy F6 18
Argadargada, Austl. C2 70
Arganda, Spain E8 16
Arga-Sala, stm., Russia D13 28
Argelès-Gazost, Fr. I7 14
Argelès-sur-Mer, Fr. J10 14
Argenta, Italy E6 18
Argenta, Il., U.S. D5 120
Argentan, Fr. D6 14
Argentat, Fr. G8 14
Argentera, mtn., Italy E2 18
Argentina, ctry., S.A. C4 78
Argentino, Lago, l., Arg. G2 78
Argenton-Château, Fr. F6 14
Argenton-sur-Creuse, Fr. F8 14
Argentré, Fr. D6 14
Argeș, co., Rom. E8 20
Argeș, stm., Rom. E9 20
Arghandāb, stm., Afg. D2 44
Argo, Sud. H6 60
Argo, Al., U.S. B3 108
Argo, Ky., U.S. C7 124
Argo Corner, De., U.S. E4 115
Argolikós Kólpos, b., Grc. L6 20
Argonia, Ks., U.S. E6 123
Argonne, Wi., U.S. C5 156
Argonne, reg., Fr. C12 14
Árgos, Grc. L6 20
Argos, In., U.S. B5 121
Argostólion, Grc. K4 20
Argun' (Ergun), stm., Asia G16 28
Argusville, N.D., U.S. B9 141
Argyle, N.S., Can. F4 101
Argyle, Ga., U.S. E4 117
Argyle, Mn., U.S. B2 130
Argyle, Mo., U.S. C5 132
Argyle, Wi., U.S. F4 156
Argyle, Lake, res., Austl. C5 68
Århus, Den. M12 6
Ariana, Tun. M5 18
Ariano Irpino, Italy H10 18
Ariari, stm., Col. F6 84
Arias, Arg. G7 80
Ariaú, Braz. I14 84
Aribinda, Burkina D9 64
Arica, Chile H6 82
Arica, Col. I7 84
Arichat, N.S., Can. D8 101
Arichuna, Ven. D9 84
Arid, Cape, c., Austl. F4 68
Ariège, dept., Fr. J8 14
Ariguaní, stm., Col. C6 84
Arīḥā, Jord. F5 50
Arīḥā (Jericho), W.B. E4 50
Arikaree, stm., U.S. B8 113
Arima, Trin. I14 94
Arimo, Id., U.S. G6 119
Arinos, stm., Braz. D12 82
Ario de Rosales, Mex. H9 90
Ariogala, Lith. F6 22
Ariporo, stm., Col. D7 84
Aripuanã, Braz. C11 82
Aripuanã, stm., Braz. B11 82
Ariquemes, Braz. C10 82
Arisa, stm., Ven. D10 84
'Arīsh, Wādī al-, val., Egypt B7 60
Arismendi, Ven. C8 84
Aristazabal Island, i., B.C., Can. C3 99
Ariton, Al., U.S. D4 108
Arivaca, Az., U.S. F4 110
Arivonimamo, Madag. q22 67b
Arízaro, Salar de, pl., Arg. C5 80
Arizgoiti, Spain B9 16
Arizona, Arg. H6 80
Arizona, state, U.S. C4 110
Arizona Sunsites, Az., U.S. F6 110
Arizpe, Mex. B4 90
Arjay, Ky., U.S. D6 124
Arjeplog, Swe. H15 6
Arjona, Col. B5 84
Arkabutla, Ms., U.S. A3 131
Arkabutla Lake, res., Ms., U.S. A4 131
Arkadelphia, Ar., U.S. C2 111
Arkalyk, Kaz. G11 26
Arkansas, co., Ar., U.S. C4 111
Arkansas, state, U.S. C3 111
Arkansas, stm., U.S. D8 106
Arkansas, Salt Fork, stm., U.S. A3 143
Arkansas City, Ar., U.S. D4 111
Arkansas City, Ks., U.S. E6 123
Arkhangelsk see Archangel'sk, Russia E6 26
Arklow, Ire. I7 8
Arkoma, Ok., U.S. B7 143
Arkona, Ont., Can. D3 103
Arkona, Kap, c., Ger. A13 10
Arktičeskij, mys, c., Russia A11 28
Arktičeskogo Instituta, ostrova, is., Russia B14 26
Arkwright, Ga., U.S. D3 117
Arlbergpass, Aus. D13 13
Arlberg-Tunnel, Aus. D13 13
Arlee, Mt., U.S. C2 133
Arles, Fr. I11 14
Arley, Al., U.S. A2 108
Arli, Burkina F10 64
Arlington, Az., U.S. D3 110
Arlington, Ga., U.S. E2 117
Arlington, Il., U.S. B4 120
Arlington, In., U.S. E6 121
Arlington, Ia., U.S. B6 122
Arlington, Ks., U.S. E5 123
Arlington, Ky., U.S. f9 124
Arlington, La., U.S. h9 125
Arlington, Ma., U.S. B5 128
Arlington, Mn., U.S. F4 130
Arlington, Ne., U.S. C9 134
Arlington, N.Y., U.S. D7 139
Arlington, N.C., U.S. A2 140
Arlington, Oh., U.S. B2 142
Arlington, Or., U.S. B6 144
Arlington, S.C., U.S. B3 147
Arlington, S.D., U.S. C8 148
Arlington, Tn., U.S. B2 149
Arlington, Tx., U.S. n9 150
Arlington, Vt., U.S. E2 152
Arlington, Va., U.S. B5 153
Arlington, Wa., U.S. A3 154
Arlington, Wi., U.S. E4 156
Arlington, co., Va., U.S. g12 153
Arlington, Lake, res., Tx., U.S. n9 150
Arlington Heights, Il., U.S. A5 120
Arlit, Niger B13 64
Arm, stm., Sask., Can. F3 105
Arma, Ks., U.S. E9 123
Armada, Mi., U.S. F8 129
Armageddon see Tel Megiddo, hist., Isr. C4 50
Armagh, Que., Can. C7 104
Armagh, N. Ire., U.K. G7 8
Armagnac, hist. reg., Fr. I7 14
Armant, Egypt E7 60
Armavir, Russia H6 26
Armazém, Braz. E14 80
Armenia, Col. E5 84
Armenia, ctry., Asia I6 26
Armeniya see Armenia, ctry., Asia I6 26
Armentières, Fr. B9 14
Armería, Mex. H8 90
Armero, Col. E5 84
Armidale, Austl. H9 70
Armijo, N.M., U.S. k7 138
Armington, Il., U.S. C4 120
Armington, Mt., U.S. C6 133
Armorel, Ar., U.S. B6 111
Armour, S.D., U.S. D7 148
Armstrong, Arg. G8 80
Armstrong, B.C., Can. D8 99
Armstrong, Il., U.S. C6 120
Armstrong, Ia., U.S. A3 122
Armstrong, Mo., U.S. B5 132
Armstrong, co., Pa., U.S. E2 145
Armstrong, co., Tx., U.S. B2 150
Armstrong Creek, stm., W.V., U.S. m13 155
Armuchee, Ga., U.S. B1 117
Arnaudville, La., U.S. D4 125
Arnay-le-Duc, Fr. E11 14
Arnedo, Spain C9 16
Arnegard, N.D., U.S. B2 141
Årnes, Nor. K12 6
Arnett, Ok., U.S. A2 143
Arnett, W.V., U.S. D3 155
Arnhem, Neth. E8 12
Arnhem, Cape, c., Austl. B7 68
Arnhem Land, reg., Austl. B6 68
Árnissa, Grc. I5 20
Arno, stm., Italy F5 18
Arno Bay, Austl. I2 70
Arnold, Ca., U.S. C3 112
Arnold, Md., U.S. B5 127
Arnold, Mn., U.S. D6 130
Arnold, Mo., U.S. C7 132
Arnold, Ne., U.S. C5 134
Arnold, Pa., U.S. h14 145
Arnold Mills, R.I., U.S. B4 146
Arnold Mills Reservoir, res., R.I., U.S. B4 146
Arnold's Cove, Newf., Can. E4 102
Arnolds Park, Ia., U.S. A2 122
Arnoldsville, Ga., U.S. C3 117
Arnprior, Ont., Can. B8 103
Arnsberg, Ger. D8 10
Arnstadt, Ger. E10 10
Arnstein, Ont., Can. B5 103
Aro, stm., Ven. D10 84
Aroa, Ven. B8 84
Aroa, stm., Ven. B8 84
Aroab, Nmb. F4 66
Aroma, Sud. J9 60
Aroma Park, Il., U.S. B6 120
Arona, Italy D3 18
Aroostook, N.B., Can. C2 101
Aroostook, co., Me., U.S. B4 126
Aros, stm., Mex. C5 90
Arosa, Switz. E12 13
Arpin, Wi., U.S. D3 156
Arque, Bol. G8 82
Ar-Rabad, Sau. Ar. K8 47
Ar-Radīsīyah Baḥrī, Egypt E7 60
Arraga, Arg. E6 80
Ar-Rahad, Sud. K6 60

Name	Map Ref.	Page
Arraial do Cabo, Braz.	G7	79
Arraias, Braz.	B5	79
Arraias, stm., Braz.	A1	79
Arraias, stm., Braz.	B5	79
Ar-Ramādī, Iraq	E7	48
Ar-Ramthā, Jord.	C6	50
Arran, Sask., Can.	F5	105
Arran, Island of, i., Scot., U.K.	F8	8
Ar-Rank, Sud.	L7	60
Ar-Raqqah, Syria	D5	48
Arras, Fr.	B9	14
Ar-Rāshidah, Egypt	E5	60
Ar-Rass, Sau. Ar.	I7	48
Ar-Rawḍah, Sau. Ar.	H6	48
Ar-Rāwuk, Yemen	G6	47
Ar-Rayyān, Qatar	I11	48
Arrecife, Spain	o27	17b
Arrecifes, Arg.	H8	80
Arrey, N.M., U.S.	E2	138
Arriaga, Mex.	I13	90
Arriba, Co., U.S.	B7	113
Ar-Rimāh, Sau. Ar.	B5	47
Arrington, Va., U.S.	C4	153
Ar-Riyāḍ (Riyadh), Sau. Ar.	B5	47
Arroio Grande, Braz.	G12	80
Arrojado, stm., Braz.	B6	79
Arronches, Port.	F4	16
Arrow Creek, stm., Mt., U.S.	C6	133
Arrowhead Mountain Lake, res., Vt., U.S.	B2	152
Arrowrock Reservoir, res., Id., U.S.	F3	119
Arrowsmith, Il., U.S.	C5	120
Arrowsmith, Mount, mtn., Austl.	H4	70
Arrowwood, Alta., Can.	D4	98
Arrowwood Lake, res., N.D., U.S.	B7	141
Arroyito, Arg.	F7	80
Arroyo de la Luz, Spain	F5	16
Arroyo Grande, Ca., U.S.	E3	112
Arroyo Hondo, N.M., U.S.	A4	138
Arroyo Seco, Arg.	G8	80
Arroyo Seco, N.M., U.S.	A4	138
Arroyos y Esteros, Para.	C10	80
Ar-Ruʿat, Sud.	K7	60
Ar-Rubʿ al-Khālī (Empty Quarter), des., Asia	D7	47
Ar-Rukhaymīyah, well, Asia	G8	48
Ar-Rumaythah, Iraq	F8	48
Ar-Rummān, Jord.	D5	50
Ar-Ruṣayfah, Jord.	D6	50
Ar-Ruṣayriṣ, Sud.	L8	60
Ar-Ruṭbah, Iraq	E6	48
Ar-Ruways, Qatar	H11	48
Arsenjev, Russia	I18	28
Arsenjevo, Russia	H19	22
Árta, Grc.	J4	20
Artašat, Arm.	B8	48
Arteaga, Mex.	H8	90
Artemisa, Cuba	C3	94
Artémou, Maur.	D3	64
Artemus, Ky., U.S.	D6	124
Artenay, Fr.	D8	14
Arter, Mount, mtn., Wy., U.S.	D4	157
Artesia, Ms., U.S.	B5	131
Artesia, N.M., U.S.	E5	138
Artesian, S.D., U.S.	C8	148
Arth, Switz.	D10	13
Arthabaska, Que., Can.	C6	104
Arthur, Ont., Can.	D4	103
Arthur, Il., U.S.	D5	120
Arthur, Ia., U.S.	B2	122
Arthur, Ne., U.S.	C4	134
Arthur, N.D., U.S.	B8	141
Arthur, Tn., U.S.	C10	149
Arthur, co., Ne., U.S.	C4	134
Arthur, Lake, l., La., U.S.	D3	125
Arthur, Lake, res., Pa., U.S.	E1	145
Arthur Kill, stm., N.J., U.S.	k8	137
Arthur's Town, Bah.	B7	94
Artibonite, stm., Haiti	E8	94
Artigas, Ur.	F10	80
Artik, Arm.	A7	48
Artois, hist. reg., Fr.	B9	14
Art'om, Russia	I18	28
Art'omovsk, Russia	G10	28
Art'omovskij, Russia	F10	26
Artsyz, Ukr.	C13	20
Artvin, Tur.	G16	4
Artyk, Russia	E21	28
Artyom, Azer.	A11	48
Aru, Kepulauan, is., Indon.	G9	38
Aruaddin, Erit.	I10	60
Aruanã, Braz.	C3	79
Aruba, dep., N.A.	H9	94
Arunāchal Pradesh, state, India	F16	44
Arundel, Que., Can.	D3	104
Aruppukkottai, India	H5	46
Arusha, Tan.	B7	58
Aruwimi, stm., Zaire	H6	56
Arvada, Co., U.S.	B5	113
Arvada, Wy., U.S.	B6	157
Arvajcheer, Mong.	B7	30
Arvi, India	B5	46
Arvidsjaur, Swe.	I16	6
Arvika, Swe.	L13	6
Arvilla, N.D., U.S.	B8	141
Arvin, Ca., U.S.	E4	112
Arvon, Mount, mtn., Mi., U.S.	B2	129
Arvonia, Va., U.S.	C4	153
Arvorezinha, Braz.	E12	80
Arxan, China	H15	28
Arys', Kaz.	I11	26
Arzachena, Italy	H4	18
Arzamas, Russia	F6	26
Arziw, Alg.	C10	62
Aš, Czech Rep.	E12	10
Aša, Russia	F9	26
Asa, stm., Ven.	D11	84
Asab, Nmb.	E3	66
Asad, Buḥayrat al-, res., Syria	C5	48
Asahikawa, Japan	d17	36a
Asamankese, Ghana	I9	64
Asansol, India	I12	44
Asbest, Russia	F10	26
Asbestos, Que., Can.	D6	104
Asbury, Mo., U.S.	D3	132
Asbury Park, N.J., U.S.	C4	137
Ascensión, Mex.	B6	90
Ascension, co., La., U.S.	D5	125
Ascension, i., St. Hel.	I5	52
Aščhabad (Ashgabat), Turk.	J9	26
Aschach an der Donau, Aus.	A9	18
Aschaffenburg, Ger.	F9	10
Aschersleben, Ger.	D11	10
Ascoli Piceno, Italy	G8	18
Ascona, Switz.	F10	13
Ascope, Peru	B2	82
Ascotán, Chile	A4	80
Ascutney, Vt., U.S.	E4	152
Ascutney, Mount, mtn., Vt., U.S.	E4	152
Aseb, Erit.	H3	47
Åseda, Swe.	M14	6
Asela, Eth.	N10	60
Åsele, Swe.	I15	6
Asendabo, Eth.	M9	60
Asenovgrad, Bul.	G8	20
Aṣfūn al-Maṭāʿinah, Egypt	E7	60
Ashaway, R.I., U.S.	F1	146
Ashburn, Ga., U.S.	E3	117
Ashburn, Va., U.S.	A5	153
Ashburnham, Ma., U.S.	A4	128
Ashburton, N.Z.	E3	72
Ashburton, stm., Austl.	D3	68
Ashby, Al., U.S.	B3	108
Ashby, Mn., U.S.	D3	130
Ashby, Ne., U.S.	B4	134
Ashcroft, B.C., Can.	D7	99
Ashdod, Isr.	E3	50
Ashdot Yaʿaqov, Isr.	C5	50
Ashdown, Ar., U.S.	D1	111
Ashe, co., N.C., U.S.	A1	140
Asheboro, N.C., U.S.	B3	140
Ashepoo, stm., S.C., U.S.	F6	147
Asher, Ok., U.S.	C5	143
Ashern, Man., Can.	D2	100
Asherton, Tx., U.S.	E3	150
Asheville, N.C., U.S.	f10	140
Ashfield, Ma., U.S.	A2	128
Ash Flat, Ar., U.S.	A4	111
Ashford, Austl.	G9	70
Ashford, Al., U.S.	D4	108
Ashford, W.V., U.S.	m12	155
Ash Fork, Az., U.S.	B3	110
Ash Grove, Mo., U.S.	D4	132
Ashibetsu, Japan	d17	36a
Ashikaga, Japan	K14	36
Ashkhabad see Aščhabad, Turk.	J9	26
Ashkum, Il., U.S.	C6	120
Ashland, Al., U.S.	B4	108
Ashland, Il., U.S.	D3	120
Ashland, Ks., U.S.	E4	123
Ashland, Ky., U.S.	B7	124
Ashland, La., U.S.	B2	125
Ashland, Me., U.S.	B4	126
Ashland, Ma., U.S.	g10	128
Ashland, Ms., U.S.	A4	131
Ashland, Mo., U.S.	C5	132
Ashland, Mt., U.S.	E10	133
Ashland, Ne., U.S.	C9	134
Ashland, N.H., U.S.	C3	136
Ashland, Oh., U.S.	B3	142
Ashland, Or., U.S.	E4	144
Ashland, Pa., U.S.	E9	145
Ashland, Va., U.S.	C5	153
Ashland, Wi., U.S.	B3	156
Ashland, co., Oh., U.S.	B3	142
Ashland, co., Wi., U.S.	B3	156
Ashland, Mount, mtn., Or., U.S.	E4	144
Ashland City, Tn., U.S.	A4	149
Ashland Reservoir, res., Ma., U.S.	h10	128
Ashley, Il., U.S.	E4	120
Ashley, In., U.S.	A7	121
Ashley, Mi., U.S.	E6	129
Ashley, N.D., U.S.	C6	141
Ashley, Oh., U.S.	B3	142
Ashley, Pa., U.S.	n17	145
Ashley, co., Ar., U.S.	D4	111
Ashley, stm., S.C., U.S.	F7	147
Ashley Creek, stm., Ut., U.S.	C6	151
Ashmont, Alta., Can.	B5	98
Ashmore, Il., U.S.	D5	120
Ashmore Islands, is., Austl.	B4	68
Ashmūn, Egypt	B6	60
Ashokan Reservoir, res., N.Y., U.S.	D6	139
Ashport, Tn., U.S.	B2	149
Ashqelon, Isr.	E3	50
Ash-Shajarah, Jord.	C5	50
Ash-Shaqrā', Sau. Ar.	B4	47
Ash-Shāriqah (Sharjah), U.A.E.	B9	47
Ash-Sharmah, Sau. Ar.	G3	48
Ash-Shaṭrah, Iraq	F9	48
Ash-Shawbak, Jord.	G5	50
Ash-Shawmarah, Leb.	B4	50
Ash-Shiḥr, Yemen	G6	47
Ash-Shufayyah, Sau. Ar.	C1	47
Ash-Shumlul, Sau. Ar.	H9	48
Ash-Shuqayq, Sau. Ar.	F3	47
Ash-Shurayf, Sau. Ar.	I5	48
Ash-Shurayk, Sud.	H7	60
Ashtabula, Oh., U.S.	A5	142
Ashtabula, co., Oh., U.S.	A5	142
Ashtabula, Lake, res., N.D., U.S.	B8	141
Ashton, Ont., Can.	B8	103
Ashton, S. Afr.	I5	66
Ashton, Id., U.S.	E7	119
Ashton, Il., U.S.	B4	120
Ashton, Ia., U.S.	A2	122
Ashton, Md., U.S.	B3	127
Ashton, Ne., U.S.	C7	134
Ashton, R.I., U.S.	B4	146
Ashton, S.D., U.S.	C7	148
Ashuanipi Lake, l., Newf., Can.	h8	102
Ashuelot, N.H., U.S.	E2	136
Ashuelot, stm., N.H., U.S.	E2	136
Ashville, Man., Can.	D1	100
Ashville, Al., U.S.	B3	108
Ashville, Oh., U.S.	C3	142
Ashwaubenon, Wi., U.S.	D5	156
Ashwood, Tn., U.S.	B4	149
Asi (Nahr al-ʿĀṣī), stm., Asia	C3	48
Asia	D11	24
Asia, Kepulauan, is., Indon.	E9	38
Asia Minor, hist. reg., Tur.	H14	4
Asilah, Mor.	C7	62
Asino, Russia	F9	28
ʿAsīr, reg., Sau. Ar.	E2	47
Aşkale, Tur.	B6	48
Askew, Ms., U.S.	A3	131
Askham, S. Afr.	F5	66
Askov, Mn., U.S.	D6	130
Asmār, Afg.	C4	44
Asmara see Asmera, Erit.	J10	60
Asmera, Erit.	J10	60
Asnebumskit Hill, hill, Ma., U.S.	B4	128
Asola, Italy	D5	18
Asosa, Eth.	F7	56
Asotin, Wa., U.S.	C8	154
Asotin, co., Wa., U.S.	C8	154
Asotin Creek, stm., Wa., U.S.	C8	154
Asp, Spain	G11	16
Aspang Markt, Aus.	H16	10
Aspen, Co., U.S.	B4	113
Aspen Butte, mtn., Or., U.S.	E4	144
Aspen Hill, Md., U.S.	B3	127
Aspermont, Tx., U.S.	C2	150
Aspinwall, Pa., U.S.	k14	145
Aspres-sur-Buëch, Fr.	H12	14
Aspy Bay, b., N.S., Can.	C9	101
Asquith, Sask., Can.	E2	105
As-Saʿata, Sud.	K5	60
Assabet, stm., Ma., U.S.	g9	128
Aṣ-Ṣaff, Egypt	C6	60
As-Saffānīyah, Sau. Ar.	H10	48
Aṣ-Ṣāfī, Jord.	F4	50
Aṣ-Ṣāfiyah, Sud.	J6	60
Assaí, Braz.	G3	79
ʿAssāl al-Ward, Syria	A6	50
As-Sallūm, Egypt	B3	60
As-Salṭ, Jord.	D5	50
Assam, state, India	G15	44
As-Samāwah, Iraq	F8	48
Assaria, Ks., U.S.	D6	123
Aṣ-Ṣarīḥ, Jord.	C5	50
Assateague Island, i., U.S.	D7	127
Assateague Island National Seashore, U.S.	D7	127
Assawoman Bay, b., Md., U.S.	D7	127
Assawompset Pond, l., Ma., U.S.	C6	128
Assekaifaf, Alg.	G15	62
Assenede, Bel.	F4	12
As-Sidr, Sau. Ar.	C1	47
Assiniboia, Sask., Can.	H2	105
Assiniboine, stm., Can.	E2	100
Assiniboine, Mount, mtn., Can.	D3	98
Assinippi, Ma., U.S.	h12	128
Assis, Braz.	G3	79
Assisi, Italy	F7	18
Assomada, C.V.	m17	64a
Assonet, Ma., U.S.	C5	128
As-Sudd, reg., Sud.	N6	60
Aṣ-Ṣufayyah, Sud.	J8	60
As-Sulaymānīyah, Iraq	D8	48
As-Sulaymānīyah, Sau. Ar.	B5	47
As-Sulaymī, Sau. Ar.	H6	48
As-Sulayyil, Sau. Ar.	D4	47
As-Sumayḥ, Sud.	M4	60
Assumption, Il., U.S.	D4	120
Assumption, co., La., U.S.	E4	125
Assumption Island, i., Sey.	C9	58
As-Suwaydā', Syria	C7	50
As-Suways (Suez), Egypt	C7	60
Astaffort, Fr.	H7	14
Āstāneh, Iran	C10	48
Āstāneh, Iran	E10	48
Astara, Azer.	J7	26
Āstārā, Iran	B10	48
Asti, Italy	E3	18
Astica, Arg.	F5	80
Astillero, Spain	B8	16
Astipálaia, Grc.	M10	20
Astipálaia, i., Grc.	M10	20
Aston Jonction, Que., Can.	C5	104
Astor, Fl., U.S.	C5	116
Astorga, Braz.	G3	79
Astorga, Spain	C5	16
Astoria, Il., U.S.	C3	120
Astoria, Or., U.S.	A3	144
Astoria, S.D., U.S.	C9	148
Astrachan', Russia	F17	4
Asturias, prov., Spain	B5	16
Asuka, sci., Ant.	C3	73
Asunción, Para.	C10	80
Asunción, Bahía, b., Mex.	D2	90
Asunción Mita, Guat.	C5	92
Asunción Nochixtlán, Mex.	I11	90
Asunga, Wādī, val., Afr.	K2	60
Aswān, Egypt	E7	60
Aswān High Dam see ʿĀli, As-Sadd al-, Egypt	D7	60
Asyūṭ, Egypt	D6	60
Aszód, Hung.	H19	10
Atabapo, stm., S.A.	F9	84
Atacama, prov., Chile	D3	80
Atacama, Desierto de, des., Chile	G8	74
Atacama, Puna de, plat., S.A.	C5	80
Atacama, Salar de, pl., Chile	B4	80
Ataco, Col.	F5	84
Atacuari, stm., Peru	I7	84
Atakpamé, Togo	H10	64
Atalándi, Grc.	K7	20
Atalaya, Pan.	I14	92
Atalaya, Peru	D5	82
Atalaya, Cerro, mtn., Peru	E6	82
Atalissa, Ia., U.S.	C6	122
Atami, Japan	L14	36
Atâr, Maur.	A3	64
Atascadero, Ca., U.S.	E3	112
Atascosa, co., Tx., U.S.	E3	150
Atasu, Kaz.	H12	26
Atauro, Pulau, i., Indon.	G8	38
Atbara (ʿAṭbarah), stm., Afr.	I8	60
ʿAṭbarah, Sud.	I7	60
ʿAṭbarah (Atbara), stm., Afr.	E7	56
Atbasar, Kaz.	G11	26
Atchafalaya, stm., La., U.S.	D4	125
Atchafalaya Bay, b., La., U.S.	E4	125
Atchison, Ks., U.S.	C8	123
Atchison, co., Ks., U.S.	C8	123
Atchison, co., Mo., U.S.	A2	132
Atco, N.J., U.S.	D3	137
Atebubu, Ghana	H9	64
Ateca, Spain	D10	16
Atelchu, stm., Braz.	B1	79
Atenguillo, Mex.	G7	90
Aterau, Kaz.	H8	26
Aterno, stm., Italy	G8	18
Ath (Aat), Bel.	G4	12
Athabasca, Alta., Can.	B4	98
Athabasca, stm., Alta., Can.	f8	98
Athabasca, Lake, l., Can.	m7	105
Athārān Hazāri, Pak.	E5	44
Athena, Or., U.S.	B8	144
Athens, Ont., Can.	C9	103
Athens see Athínai, Grc.	L7	20
Athens, Al., U.S.	A3	108
Athens, Ar., U.S.	C2	111
Athens, Ga., U.S.	C3	117
Athens, Il., U.S.	D4	120
Athens, In., U.S.	B5	121
Athens, La., U.S.	B2	125
Athens, Me., U.S.	D3	126
Athens, Mi., U.S.	F5	129
Athens, N.Y., U.S.	C7	139
Athens, Oh., U.S.	C3	142
Athens, Pa., U.S.	C8	145
Athens, Tn., U.S.	D9	149
Athens, Tx., U.S.	C5	150
Athens, W.V., U.S.	D3	155
Athens, Wi., U.S.	C3	156
Athens, co., Oh., U.S.	C3	142
Atherley, Ont., Can.	C5	103
Atherton, Austl.	A6	70
Athiémé, Benin	H10	64
Athínai (Athens), Grc.	L7	20
Athlone, Ire.	H6	8
Athok, Mya.	F3	40
Athol, Id., U.S.	B2	119
Athol, Ma., U.S.	A3	128
Athol, S.D., U.S.	C7	148
Áthos, mtn., Grc.	I8	20
Ath-Thamad, Egypt	C8	60
Ati, Chad	F4	56
Atico, Peru	G5	82
Aticonipi, Lac, l., Que., Can.	C2	102
Atik Lake, l., Man., Can.	B4	100
Atikonak Lake, l., Newf., Can.	h8	102
Atimari, stm., Braz.	C8	82
Atiparaná, mth., Braz.	I9	84
Atiquizaya, El Sal.	D5	92
Atitlán, Lago de, l., Guat.	C3	92
Atitlán, Volcán, vol., Guat.	C3	92
Atka, Russia	E22	28
Atka Island, i., Ak., U.S.	E5	109
Atkarsk, Russia	G7	26
Atkins, Ar., U.S.	B3	111
Atkins, Va., U.S.	D1	153
Atkinson, Ga., U.S.	E5	117
Atkinson, Il., U.S.	B3	120
Atkinson, Ne., U.S.	B7	134
Atkinson, N.H., U.S.	E4	136
Atkinson, co., Ga., U.S.	E4	117
Atlanta, Ar., U.S.	D2	111
Atlanta, Ga., U.S.	C2	117
Atlanta, Il., U.S.	C4	120
Atlanta, In., U.S.	D5	121
Atlanta, Ks., U.S.	E7	123
Atlanta, Mi., U.S.	C6	129
Atlanta, Mo., U.S.	B5	132
Atlanta, Ne., U.S.	D6	134
Atlanta, Tx., U.S.	C5	150
Atlantic, Ia., U.S.	C2	122
Atlantic, N.C., U.S.	C6	140
Atlantic, co., N.J., U.S.	E3	137
Atlantic Beach, Fl., U.S.	m9	116
Atlantic City, N.J., U.S.	E4	137
Atlantic Highlands, N.J., U.S.	C4	137
Atlantic-Indian Ridge	N5	158
Atlantic Mine, Mi., U.S.	A2	129
Atlántico, dept., Col.	B5	84
Atlantic Ocean	I11	160
Atlantic Peak, mtn., Wy., U.S.	D3	157
Atlántida, Ur.	H11	80
Atlántida, dept., Hond.	B7	92
Atlas Mountains, mts., Afr.	B6	54
Atlas Saharien, mts., Alg.	D11	62
Atlas Tellien, mts., Alg.	C11	62
Atlin, B.C., Can.	m16	99
Atlin Lake, l., Can.	E6	96
ʿAtlit, Isr.	C3	50
Atmore, Al., U.S.	D2	108
Atna Peak, mtn., B.C., Can.	C3	99
Atocha, Bol.	I8	82
Atoka, Ok., U.S.	C5	143
Atoka, Tn., U.S.	B2	149
Atoka, co., Ok., U.S.	C5	143
Atoka Reservoir, res., Ok., U.S.	C5	143
Atotonilco, Mex.	E8	90
Atoui, Khatt (Khaṭṭ Atoui), val., Afr.	J3	62
Atoyac, stm., Mex.	H10	90
Atoyac de Álvarez, Mex.	I9	90
Atoyaquillo, stm., Mex.	I11	90
Atrak (Atrek), l., Asia	C12	48
Atrato, stm., Col.	D4	84
Atrek (Atrak), stm., Asia	C12	48
Atri, Italy	G8	18
Aṭ-Ṭafīlah, Jord.	G5	50
Aṭ-Ṭā'if, Sau. Ar.	D2	47
At-Tāj, Libya	E2	60
Attala, co., Ms., U.S.	B4	131
At-Tall, Syria	A6	50
Attalla, Al., U.S.	A3	108
Attapu, Laos	G9	40
Attapulgus, Ga., U.S.	F2	117
Attawapiskat, stm., Ont., Can.	n18	103
Attawaugan, Ct., U.S.	B8	114
Attean Pond, l., Me., U.S.	C2	126
Attica, In., U.S.	D3	121
Attica, Ks., U.S.	E5	123
Attica, Mi., U.S.	E7	129
Attica, N.Y., U.S.	C2	139
Attica, Oh., U.S.	A3	142
Attica see Attikí, hist. reg., Grc.	K7	20
Attigny, Fr.	C11	14
Attikí, prov., Grc.	K7	20
Attikí, hist. reg., Grc.	K7	20
Attir, Sud.	N6	60
Attleboro, Ma., U.S.	C5	128
Attock, Pak.	D5	44
Attu Island, i., Ak., U.S.	E2	109
Aṭ-Ṭunayb, Jord.	E5	50
Aṭ-Ṭūr, Egypt	C7	60
Āttūr, India	G5	46
Aṭ-Ṭuwayshah, Sud.	K4	60
Aṭ-Ṭuwayyah, Sau. Ar.	H6	48
Atucatiquini, stm., Braz.	B7	82
Atucha, Arg.	G9	80
Atuel, stm., Arg.	H5	80
Atuel, Bañados del, sw., Arg.	I5	80
Atuntaqui, Ec.	G3	84
Atwater, Sask., Can.	G4	105
Atwater, Ca., U.S.	D3	112
Atwater, Mn., U.S.	E4	130
Atwood, Ont., Can.	D3	103
Atwood, Co., U.S.	A7	113
Atwood, Il., U.S.	D5	120
Atwood, In., U.S.	B6	121
Atwood, Ks., U.S.	C2	123
Atwood, Ok., U.S.	C5	143
Atwood, Tn., U.S.	B3	149
Atwood Lake, res., Oh., U.S.	B4	142
Auari, stm., Braz.	F11	84
Auau Channel, strt., Hi., U.S.	C5	118
Aubagne, Fr.	I12	14
Aube, dept., Fr.	D11	14
Aube, stm., Fr.	D11	14
Auberry, Ca., U.S.	D4	112
Aubigny-sur-Nère, Fr.	E9	14
Aubin, Fr.	H9	14
Aubrey, Ar., U.S.	C5	111
Aubrey Cliffs, clf, Az., U.S.	B2	110
Auburn, Ont., Can.	D3	103
Auburn, Al., U.S.	C4	108
Auburn, Ca., U.S.	C3	112
Auburn, Ga., U.S.	B3	117
Auburn, Il., U.S.	D4	120
Auburn, In., U.S.	B7	121
Auburn, Ia., U.S.	B3	122
Auburn, Ks., U.S.	D8	123
Auburn, Ky., U.S.	D3	124
Auburn, Me., U.S.	D2	126
Auburn, Ma., U.S.	B4	128
Auburn, Mi., U.S.	E6	129
Auburn, Ne., U.S.	D10	134
Auburn, N.H., U.S.	D4	136
Auburn, N.Y., U.S.	C4	139
Auburn, Pa., U.S.	E9	145
Auburn, Wa., U.S.	B3	154
Auburn, Wy., U.S.	D1	157
Auburn, stm., Austl.	E9	70
Auburndale, Fl., U.S.	D5	116
Auburndale, Wi., U.S.	D3	156
Auburn Heights, Mi., U.S.	F7	129
Auburn Range, mts., Austl.	E9	70
Auburntown, Tn., U.S.	B5	149
Aubusson, Fr.	G9	14
Auca Mahuida, Arg.	I4	80
Auca Mahuida, Cerro, mtn., Arg.	I4	80
Aucará, Peru	F4	82
Auce, Lat.	E5	22
Auch, Fr.	I7	14
Aucilla, stm., Fl., U.S.	B3	116
Auckland, N.Z.	B5	72
Auckland Islands, is., N.Z.	N20	158
Aude, dept., Fr.	I9	14
Aude, stm., Fr.	I10	14
Audierne, Fr.	D2	14
Audincourt, Fr.	E13	14
Audrain, co., Mo., U.S.	B6	132
Audubon, Ia., U.S.	C3	122
Audubon, Mn., U.S.	D3	130
Audubon, N.J., U.S.	D2	137
Audubon, co., Ia., U.S.	C2	122
Aue, Ger.	E12	10
Augathella, Austl.	E7	70
Auglaize, co., Oh., U.S.	B1	142
Auglaize, stm., Oh., U.S.	A1	142
Au Gres, Mi., U.S.	D7	129
Augsburg, Ger.	G10	10
Augšlīgatne, Lat.	D8	22
Augusta, Austl.	F3	68
Augusta, Italy	L10	18
Augusta, Ar., U.S.	B4	111
Augusta, Ga., U.S.	C5	117
Augusta, Il., U.S.	C3	120
Augusta, Ks., U.S.	E7	123
Augusta, Ky., U.S.	B6	124
Augusta, Me., U.S.	D3	126
Augusta, Mi., U.S.	F5	129
Augusta, Mo., U.S.	C7	132
Augusta, Mt., U.S.	C4	133
Augusta, Wi., U.S.	D2	156
Augusta, co., Va., U.S.	B3	153
Augusta Springs, Va., U.S.	B3	153
Augustów, Pol.	B22	10
Auila, Ribeirão, stm., Braz.	B2	79
Aulander, N.C., U.S.	A5	140
Aulnay, Fr.	F6	14
Aulneau Peninsula, pen., Ont., Can.	E4	100
Ault, Fr.	B8	14
Ault, Co., U.S.	A6	113
Aumale, Fr.	C8	14
Aumsville, Or., U.S.	k12	144
Auna, Nig.	F12	64
Auneau, Fr.	D8	14
Auob, stm., Afr.	F5	66
Aurangābād, India	C3	46
Auray, Fr.	E4	14
Aurelia, Ia., U.S.	B2	122
Aurès, Massif de l', mts., Alg.	C14	62
Aurich, Ger.	B7	10
Auriflama, Braz.	F3	79
Aurilândia, Braz.	D3	79
Aurillac, Fr.	H9	14
Aurora, Ont., Can.	C5	103
Aurora, Co., U.S.	B6	113
Aurora, Il., U.S.	B5	120
Aurora, In., U.S.	F8	121
Aurora, Ks., U.S.	C6	123
Aurora, Mn., U.S.	C6	130
Aurora, Mo., U.S.	E4	132
Aurora, Ne., U.S.	D7	134
Aurora, N.C., U.S.	B6	140
Aurora, Oh., U.S.	A4	142
Aurora, Or., U.S.	B4	144
Aurora, S.D., U.S.	C9	148
Aurora, Ut., U.S.	E4	151
Aurora, W.V., U.S.	B5	155
Aurora, Wi., U.S.	C5	156
Aurora, co., S.D., U.S.	D7	148
Aurora do Norte, Braz.	B5	79
Aurukun, Austl.	B8	68
Aus, Nmb.	F3	66
Au Sable, Mi., U.S.	D7	129
Au Sable, stm., Mi., U.S.	D6	129
Ausable, stm., N.Y., U.S.	f11	139
Au Sable, North Branch, stm., Mi., U.S.	D6	129
Au Sable Forks, N.Y., U.S.	f11	139
Au Sable Point, c., Mi., U.S.	D7	129
Au Sable Point, c., Mi., U.S.	B4	129
Auschwitz see Oświęcim, Pol.	E19	10
Aust-Agder, co., Nor.	L10	6
Austell, Ga., U.S.	h7	117
Austin, Man., Can.	E2	100
Austin, Ar., U.S.	C4	111
Austin, In., U.S.	G6	121
Austin, Mn., U.S.	G6	130
Austin, Nv., U.S.	D4	135
Austin, Tx., U.S.	D4	150
Austin, co., Tx., U.S.	E4	150
Austinburg, Oh., U.S.	A5	142
Austin Channel, strt., N.W. Ter., Can.	A12	96
Austintown, Oh., U.S.	A5	142
Austinville, Va., U.S.	D2	153
Australes, Îles, is., Fr. Poly.	K24	158
Australia, ctry., Oc.	D7	68
Australian Capital Territory, ter., Austl.	G9	68
Austria (Österreich), ctry., Eur.	F10	4
Autauga, co., Al., U.S.	C3	108
Autaugaville, Al., U.S.	C3	108
Autazes, Braz.	I13	84
Autlán de Navarro, Mex.	H7	90
Au Train, Mi., U.S.	B4	129
Autun, Fr.	F11	14
Auvergne, Ar., U.S.	B4	111
Auvergne, hist. reg., Fr.	G9	14
Auxerre, Fr.	E10	14
Auxier, Ky., U.S.	C7	124
Auxi-le-Château, Fr.	B9	14
Auxonne, Fr.	E12	14
Auxvasse, Mo., U.S.	B6	132
Auyán Tepuy, mtn., Ven.	E11	84
Auzances, Fr.	F9	14
Auzangate, Nevado, mtn., Peru	E6	82
Ava, Il., U.S.	F4	120
Ava, Mo., U.S.	E5	132
Avaí, Braz.	G4	79
Avallon, Fr.	E10	14
Avalon, Ca., U.S.	F4	112
Avalon, Ga., U.S.	B3	117
Avalon, Ms., U.S.	B3	131
Avalon, N.J., U.S.	E3	137
Avalon, Pa., U.S.	h13	145
Avalon, Lake, res., N.M., U.S.	E5	138
Avalon Peninsula, pen., Newf., Can.	E5	102
Ávalos, Mex.	C6	90
Avanos, Tur.	B3	48
Avant, Ok., U.S.	A5	143
Avaré, Braz.	G4	79
Avegbadje, mtn., Afr.	H10	64
Aveiro, Port.	E3	16
Avelgem, Bel.	G3	12
Avella, Pa., U.S.	F1	145
Avellaneda, Arg.	E9	80
Avellaneda, Arg.	H9	80
Avellino, Italy	I9	18
Avenal, Ca., U.S.	E3	112
Avenel, N.J., U.S.	k7	137
Avening, Ont., Can.	C4	103
Avera, Ga., U.S.	C4	117
Averill Park, N.Y., U.S.	C7	139
Aversa, Italy	I9	18
Avery, Id., U.S.	B3	119
Avery, Ia., U.S.	C5	122
Avery, co., N.C., U.S.	e11	140
Avery Island, La., U.S.	E4	125
Aveyron, dept., Fr.	H9	14
Avezzano, Italy	G8	18
Aviemore, Scot., U.K.	D10	8
Avigliano, Italy	I10	18
Avignon, Fr.	I11	14
Ávila, Spain	E7	16
Ávila, prov., Spain	E7	16
Avila Beach, Ca., U.S.	E3	112
Avilés, Spain	B6	16
Avilla, In., U.S.	B7	121
Avis, Pa., U.S.	D7	145
Avispa, Cerro, mtn., Ven.	G10	84
Aviston, Il., U.S.	E4	120
Aviz, Port.	F4	16
Avoca, Ar., U.S.	A1	111
Avoca, In., U.S.	G4	121
Avoca, Ia., U.S.	C2	122
Avoca, Mn., U.S.	G3	130
Avoca, Ne., U.S.	h12	134
Avoca, N.Y., U.S.	C3	139
Avoca, Pa., U.S.	m18	145
Avoca, Wi., U.S.	E3	156
Avola, B.C., Can.	D8	99
Avola, Italy	M10	18
Avon, Ont., Can.	E4	103
Avon, Ct., U.S.	B4	114
Avon, Il., U.S.	C3	120
Avon, In., U.S.	E5	121
Avon, Ma., U.S.	B5	128
Avon, Mn., U.S.	E4	130
Avon, Ms., U.S.	B2	131
Avon, Mt., U.S.	D4	133
Avon, N.Y., U.S.	C3	139
Avon, N.C., U.S.	B7	140
Avon, Oh., U.S.	A3	142
Avon, S.D., U.S.	E7	148
Avon, co., Eng., U.K.	J11	8
Avon, stm., Eng., U.K.	I12	8
Avondale, Az., U.S.	D3	110
Avondale, Co., U.S.	C6	113
Avondale, Mo., U.S.	h10	132
Avondale, Pa., U.S.	G10	145
Avondale Estates, Ga., U.S.	h8	117
Avon Downs, Austl.	C2	70
Avon Lake, Ia., U.S.	e8	122
Avon Lake, Oh., U.S.	A3	142
Avonlea, Sask., Can.	G3	105
Avonmore, Pa., U.S.	E3	145
Avon Park, Fl., U.S.	E5	116
Avontuur, S. Afr.	I6	66
Avoyelles, co., La., U.S.	C3	125
Avranches, Fr.	D5	14
Aʿwaj, Nahr al-, stm., Syria	B6	50
Awaji-shima, i., Japan	M9	36
ʿAwālī, Bahr.	H11	48
Awasa, Eth.	N10	60
Awash, Eth.	G9	56
Awash, stm., Eth.	M10	60

Name	Map Ref.	Page
Awaso, Ghana	H8	64
Awbārī, Libya	C3	56
Awe, Nig.	G14	64
Awegyun, Mya.	H5	40
Awjilah, Libya	C5	56
Awled Djellal, Alg.	C13	62
Awlef, Alg.	G11	62
Aworo Kit, Sud.	L7	60
Axel Heiberg Island, i., N.W. Ter., Can.	B10	86
Axial Basin, Co., U.S.	A2	113
Axim, Ghana	I8	64
Axinim, Braz.	J13	84
Axiós (Vardar), stm., Eur.	I6	20
Axis, Al., U.S.	E1	108
Ax-les-Thermes, Fr.	J8	14
Axson, Ga., U.S.	E4	117
Axtell, Ks., U.S.	C7	123
Axtell, Ne., U.S.	D6	134
Ayabaca, Peru	J3	84
Ayabe, Japan	L10	36
Ayacucho, Arg.	I9	80
Ayacucho, Bol.	G10	82
Ayacucho, Peru	E4	82
Ayacucho, dept., Peru	E4	82
Ayamonte, Spain	H4	16
Ayangba, Nig.	H13	64
Ayapel, Col.	C5	84
Ayarza, Laguna de, l., Guat.	C4	92
Ayaviri, Peru	F6	82
Ayaviri, stm., Peru	F6	82
Ayden, N.C., U.S.	B5	140
Aydın, Tur.	L11	20
Ayer, Ma., U.S.	A4	128
Ayers Cliff, Que., Can.	D5	104
Ayers Rock, mtn., Austl.	E6	68
Ayeyarwady (Irrawaddy), stm., Mya.	F3	40
Ayía Paraskeví, Grc.	J10	20
Ayiássos, Grc.	J10	20
Áyion Óros, pen., Grc.	I8	20
Áyios Kírikos, Grc.	L10	20
Áyios Nikólaos, Grc.	N9	20
Ayíou Órous, Kólpos, b., Grc.	I8	20
Ayl, Jord.	H5	50
Aylen Lake, l., Ont., Can.	B7	103
Aylesbury, Sask., Can.	G3	105
Aylesbury, Eng., U.K.	J13	8
Aylesford, N.S., Can.	D5	101
Aylmer, Mount, mtn., Alta., Can.	D3	98
Aylmer East, Que., Can.	D2	104
Aylmer Lake, l., N.W. Ter., Can.	D11	96
Aylmer West, Ont., Can.	E4	103
Aylsham, Sask., Can.	D4	105
ʻAyn Dār, Sau. Ar.	B6	47
Aynor, S.C., U.S.	D9	147
ʻAynūnah, Sau. Ar.	G3	48
Ayo, Peru	F5	82
Ayo Ayo, Bol.	G7	82
Ayod, Sud.	M6	60
Ayom, Sud.	N5	60
'Ayoûn el 'Atroûs, Maur.	C5	64
Ayr, Austl.	B7	70
Ayr, Scot., U.K.	F9	8
Ayr, Ne., U.S.	D7	134
ʻAytā al-Fakhkhār, Leb.	A5	50
Ayton, Ont., Can.	C4	103
Ayu, Kepulauan, is., Indon.	E9	38
Ayutla, Mex.	G7	90
Ayutla de los Libres, Mex.	I10	90
Ayvacık, Tur.	J10	20
Ayvalık, Tur.	J10	20
Azacualpa, Hond.	B6	92
Azacualpa, Hond.	C8	92
Azalia, In., U.S.	F6	121
Azambuja, Port.	F3	16
Āzamgarh, India	G10	44
Azángaro, Peru	F6	82
Azángaro, stm., Peru	F6	82
Azaouagh, Vallée de l', val., Afr.	D11	64
Azapa, Quebrada de, stm., Chile	H6	82
Azar, val., Afr.	C12	64
Azare, Nig.	F15	64
Āzar Shahr, Iran	C8	48
Azazga, Alg.	B13	62
Azeffâl, dunes, Afr.	J4	62
Azeffoun, Alg.	B13	62
Azemmour, Mor.	D6	62
Azerbaijan (Azạrbaycan), ctry., Asia	I7	26
Azerbaydzan see Azerbaijan, ctry., Asia	I7	26
Azezo, Eth.	K9	60
Aziscohos Lake, l., Me., U.S.	C1	126
Azle, Tx., U.S.	n9	150
Azogues, Ec.	I3	84
Azores see Açores, is., Port.	k19	62a
Azoum, Bahr (Wādī ʻAẓūm), val., Afr.	K2	60
Azov, Russia	H5	26
Azov, Sea of, Eur.	H5	26
Azpeitia, Spain	B9	16
Azraq, Al-Baḥr al- see Blue Nile, stm., Afr.	K8	60
Azrou, Mor.	D8	62
Aztec, N.M., U.S.	A2	138
Aztec Peak, mtn., Az., U.S.	D5	110
Aztec Ruins National Monument, N.M., U.S.	A1	138
Azua, Dom. Rep.	E9	94
Azuaga, Spain	G6	16
Azuay, prov., Ec.	I3	84
Azucena, Arg.	I9	80
Azuero, Península de, pen., Pan.	D2	84
Azul, Arg.	I9	80
Azul, Cerro, mtn., C.R.	H9	92
Azul, Cerro, mtn., Hond.	C6	92
Azur, Côte d', Fr.	I14	14
Azurduy, Bol.	H9	82
Azusa, Ca., U.S.	m13	112
Az-Zabadānī, Syria	A6	50
Az-Ẓahrān (Dhahran), Sau. Ar.	A7	47
Az-Zaqāzīq, Egypt	B6	60
Az-Zarqā', Jord.	D6	50
Az-Zāwiyah, Libya	B3	56
Az-Zaydīyah, Yemen	G3	47
Azzel Matti, Sebkha, pl., Alg.	H11	62
Az-Zilfī, Sau. Ar.	H8	48
Az-Zubayr, Iraq	F9	48

B

Name	Map Ref.	Page
Ba, stm., Viet.	H10	40
Baalbek see Baʻlabakk, Leb.	D4	48
Baar, Switz.	D10	13
Baardheere, Som.	H9	56
Baarle-Hertog (Baerle-Duc), Bel.	F6	12
Baarle-Nassau, Bel.	F6	12
Baba, Ec.	H3	84
Babadağ, Tur.	L12	20
Babahoyo, Ec.	H3	84
Babailiqiao, China	C7	34
Babajevo, Russia	B18	22
Babana, Nig.	F11	64
Babanango, S. Afr.	G10	66
Babanūsah, Sud.	L4	60
Babar, Kepulauan, is., Indon.	G8	38
Babar, Pulau, i., Indon.	G8	38
Babb Creek, stm., Pa., U.S.	C7	145
Babbie, Al., U.S.	D3	108
Babbitt, Mn., U.S.	C7	130
Babbitt, Nv., U.S.	E3	135
Bab el Mandeb see Mandeb, Bab el, strt.	H3	47
Babimost, Pol.	C15	10
Babina Greda, Cro.	D2	20
Babinda, Austl.	A6	70
Babine, stm., B.C., Can.	B4	99
Babine Lake, l., B.C., Can.	B5	99
Babine Range, mts., B.C., Can.	B4	99
Babino, Russia	B14	22
Babino, Russia	B23	22
Babo, Indon.	F9	38
Bābol, Iran	C12	48
Bābol Sar, Iran	C12	48
Baboosic Lake, N.H., U.S.	E3	136
Baboquivari Mountains, mts., Az., U.S.	F4	110
Baboquivari Peak, mtn., Az., U.S.	F4	110
Babson Park, Fl., U.S.	E5	116
Babuškin, Russia	G13	28
Babuyan Islands, is., Phil.	B7	38
Babylon, N.Y., U.S.	n15	139
Babynino, Russia	G18	22
Baca, co., Co., U.S.	D8	113
Bacabal, Braz.	D10	76
Bacadéhuachi, Mex.	C5	90
Bacan, Pulau, i., Indon.	F8	38
Bacău, Rom.	C10	20
Bacău, co., Rom.	C10	20
Bac Can, Viet.	C8	40
Baccarat, Fr.	D13	14
Baccaro Point, c., N.S., Can.	F4	101
Bacerac, Mex.	B5	90
Bac Giang, Viet.	D9	40
Bachaquero, Ven.	C7	84
Bacharden, Turk.	J9	26
Bachi, China	K4	34
Bachiniva, Mex.	C6	90
Bachmutovo, Russia	E17	22
Bachu, China	D2	30
Bachuma, Eth.	N8	60
Back, stm., N.W. Ter., Can.	C13	96
Back, stm., S.C., U.S.	h12	147
Bačka Palanka, Yugo.	D3	20
Bačka Topola, Yugo.	D3	20
Back Bay, N.B., Can.	D3	101
Backbone Mountain, mtn., U.S.	m12	127
Backnang, Ger.	G9	10
Backstairs Passage, strt., Austl.	J2	70
Bac Lieu, Viet.	J8	40
Bac Ninh, Viet.	D9	40
Bacoachi, Mex.	B5	90
Bacobi, Az., U.S.	B5	110
Bacolod, Phil.	C7	38
Bacon, co., Ga., U.S.	E4	117
Baconton, Ga., U.S.	E2	117
Bacoor, Phil.	n19	39b
Bács-Kiskun, co., Hung.	I19	10
Bácum, Mex.	D4	90
Bad, stm., S.D., U.S.	C5	148
Bad, stm., Wi., U.S.	B3	156
Badagara, India	G3	46
Badajia, China	B9	34
Badajós, stm., Braz.	I11	84
Badajós, Lago, l., Braz.	I11	84
Badajoz, Spain	G5	16
Badalona, Spain	D14	16
Bādāmi, India	E3	46
Badanah, Sau. Ar.	F6	48
Badaohao, China	B9	32
Badaohe, China	C10	32
Bad Aussee, Aus.	H13	10
Bad Axe, Mi., U.S.	E8	129
Bad Brückenau, Ger.	E9	10
Baddeck, N.S., Can.	C9	101
Bad Doberan, Ger.	A11	10
Bad Dürkheim, Ger.	F8	10
Bad Dürrenberg, Ger.	D12	10
Badeggi, Nig.	G13	64
Badéguichéri, Niger	D12	64
Bad Ems, Ger.	E7	10
Baden, Ont., Can.	D4	103
Baden, Erit.	I9	60
Baden, Switz.	D9	13
Baden, Pa., U.S.	E1	145
Baden-Baden, Ger.	G8	10
Badenweiler, Ger.	H7	10
Baden-Württemberg, state, Ger.	G8	10
Badgastein, Aus.	H13	10
Badger, Newf., Can.	D3	102
Badger, Ia., U.S.	B3	122
Badger, Mn., U.S.	B2	130
Badger, S.D., U.S.	C8	148
Badger Creek, stm., Co., U.S.	B7	113
Bad Hall, Aus.	G14	10
Bad Harzburg, Ger.	D10	10
Bad Hersfeld, Ger.	E9	10
Bad Homburg [vor der Höhe], Ger.	E8	10
Badin, N.C., U.S.	B2	140
Badin Lake, res., N.C., U.S.	B2	140
Badiraguato, Mex.	E6	90
Bad Kissingen, Ger.	E10	10
Bad Kreuznach, Ger.	F7	10
Badlands, hills, S.D., U.S.	D3	148
Badlands, reg., U.S.	C2	141
Badlands National Park, S.D., U.S.	D3	148
Bad Langensalza, Ger.	D10	10
Bad Lauterberg, Ger.	D10	10
Bad Leonfelden, Aus.	G14	10
Bad Mergentheim, Ger.	F9	10
Bad Muskau, Ger.	D14	10
Bad Nauheim, Ger.	E8	10
Bad Neustadt an der Saale, Ger.	E10	10
Bad Oeynhausen, Ger.	C8	10
Badogo, Mali	F5	64
Bad Oldesloe, Ger.	B10	10
Badou, China	G5	32
Badou, Togo	H10	64
Badoumbé, Mali	E4	64
Bad Pyrmont, Ger.	D9	10
Bad Ragaz, Switz.	D12	13
Bad Reichenhall, Ger.	H12	10
Badr Ḥunayn, Sau. Ar.	C1	47
Bad River Indian Reservation, Wi., U.S.	B3	156
Bad Salzuflen, Ger.	C8	10
Bad Salzungen, Ger.	E10	10
Bad Sankt Leonhard im Lavanttal, Aus.	I14	10
Bad Schwalbach, Ger.	E8	10
Bad Schwartau, Ger.	B10	10
Bad Segeberg, Ger.	B10	10
Bad Tölz, Ger.	H11	10
Badu, China	I8	34
Badulla, Sri L.	I6	46
Badupi, Mya.	D2	40
Bad Vöslau, Aus.	H16	10
Bad Waldsee, Ger.	H9	10
Badwater Creek, stm., Wy., U.S.	C5	157
Bad Wildungen, Ger.	D9	10
Baediam, Maur.	D4	64
Baena, Spain	H7	16
Baependi, Braz.	F6	79
Baeza, Ec.	H4	84
Bafatá, Gui.-B.	E2	64
Baffin Bay, b., N.A.	B13	86
Baffin Bay, b., Tx., U.S.	E4	150
Baffin Island, i., N.W. Ter., Can.	C18	96
Bafing, stm., Afr.	F4	54
Bafoulabé, Mali	E4	64
Bafoussam, Cam.	G9	54
Bāfq, Iran	F13	48
Bāft, Iran	G14	48
Bafwasende, Zaire	A5	58
Bagaces, C.R.	G9	92
Bagagem, stm., Braz.	C4	79
Bāgalkot, India	D3	46
Bagansiapiapi, Indon.	M6	40
Bağarası, Tur.	L11	20
Bagawi, Sud.	K8	60
Bagdad see Baghdād, Iraq	E8	48
Bagdad, Az., U.S.	C2	110
Bagdad, Fl., U.S.	u14	116
Bagdad, Ky., U.S.	B4	124
Bagdarin, Russia	G14	28
Bagé, Braz.	F11	80
Baggs, Wy., U.S.	E5	157
Baghdād, Iraq	E8	48
Bagheria, Italy	K8	18
Baghlān, Afg.	B3	44
Bagley, Ia., U.S.	C3	122
Bagley, Mn., U.S.	C3	130
Bagley, Wi., U.S.	F2	156
Bagnell Dam, Mo., U.S.	C5	132
Bagnères-de-Bigorre, Fr.	I7	14
Bagnères-de-Luchon, Fr.	J7	14
Bagnols-sur-Cèze, Fr.	H11	14
Bago (Pegu), Mya.	F4	40
Bagoé, stm., Afr.	F6	64
Bagrationovsk, Russia	G3	22
Baguio, Phil.	m19	39b
Bagzane, mtn., Niger	C14	64
Bahama, N.C., U.S.	A4	140
Bahamas, ctry., N.A.	D9	88
Bahār, Iran	D10	48
Baharampur, India	H13	44
Bahāwalnagar, Pak.	F5	44
Bahāwalpur, Pak.	F4	44
Bahechuan, China	C12	32
Bahia, state, Braz.	B7	79
Bahía, Islas de la, is., Hond.	A8	92
Bahía Azul, Pan.	H13	92
Bahía Blanca, Arg.	J7	80
Bahía Kino, Mex.	C4	90
Bahir Dar, Eth.	L9	60
Baḥrah, Sau. Ar.	D1	47
Bahraich, India	G9	44
Bahrain (Al-Baḥrayn), ctry., Asia	D5	42
Baḥrayn, Khalīj al-, b., Asia	B7	47
Bāhū Kalāt, Iran	I16	48
Baï, Mali	E8	64
Baia Mare, Rom.	B7	20
Baía Rica, stm., Braz.	E10	82
Baia Sprie, Rom.	B7	20
Baicao, China	B4	32
Baicheng, China	C3	30
Baicheng, China	B11	30
Baie-Comeau, Que., Can.	k13	104
Baie-d'Urfé, Que., Can.	q19	104
Baie-Saint-Paul, Que., Can.	B7	104
Baie Verte, N.B., Can.	C5	101
Baie Verte, Newf., Can.	D3	102
Baigong, China	K5	34
Baihebu, China	C4	32
Baijian, China	D3	32
Baiju, China	B9	34
Baikal, Lake see Bajkal, ozero, l., Russia	G13	28
Bailadores, Ven.	C7	84
Baile, China	D2	32
Baile Átha Cliath see Dublin, Ire.	H7	8
Băile Govora, Rom.	D8	20
Bailén, Spain	G8	16
Băileşti, Rom.	E7	20
Bailey, Co., U.S.	B5	113
Bailey, N.C., U.S.	B4	140
Bailey, co., Tx., U.S.	B1	150
Bailey Brook, stm., Me., U.S.	B2	126
Bailey Island, Me., U.S.	g8	126
Bailey Island, i., S.C., U.S.	k11	147
Baileys Crossroads, Va., U.S.	g12	153
Baileys Harbor, Wi., U.S.	C6	156
Baileyton, Al., U.S.	A3	108
Baileyton, Tn., U.S.	C11	149
Baileyville, Il., U.S.	A4	120
Baileyville, Ks., U.S.	C7	123
Bailin, China	H9	34
Bailique, Ilha, i., Braz.	C9	76
Bailong, stm., China	E7	30
Bailundo, Ang.	D3	58
Baimaguan, China	C4	32
Baimashi, China	F7	34
Baimiaozi, China	C8	32
Bainbridge, Ga., U.S.	F2	117
Bainbridge, In., U.S.	E4	121
Bainbridge, N.Y., U.S.	C5	139
Bainbridge, Oh., U.S.	C2	142
Bainbridge Island, i., Wa., U.S.	e10	154
Bain-de-Bretagne, Fr.	E5	14
Bainiqiao, China	F3	34
Bains-les-Bains, Fr.	D13	14
Bainville, Mt., U.S.	B12	133
Baipu, China	C9	34
Baiquan, China	E11	34
Baird, Tx., U.S.	C3	150
Bairdford, Pa., U.S.	h14	145
Baird Inlet, b., Ak., U.S.	C7	109
Baird Mountains, mts., Ak., U.S.	B7	109
Bairin Zuoqi, China	C10	30
Bairnsdale, Austl.	K7	70
Bairoil, Wy., U.S.	D5	157
Bairuopu, China	G1	34
Baisha, China	E10	40
Baishanji, China	B5	34
Baishatan, China	G9	32
Baishuifan, China	E4	34
Baishuijiang, China	E8	30
Baisogala, Lith.	F6	22
Baitazi, China	A8	32
Baitu, China	D8	34
Baixa Grande, Braz.	A8	79
Baixiang, China	F2	32
Baiyin, China	D7	30
Baizhongpu, China	B3	34
Baja, Hung.	I18	10
Baja, Punta, c., Mex.	C2	90
Baja California, state, Mex.	C2	90
Baja California, pen., Mex.	C3	90
Baja California Sur, state, Mex.	E4	90
Bajada del Agrio, Arg.	J3	80
Bajanaul, Kaz.	G13	26
Bajanchongor, Mong.	B7	30
Bajánsenye, Hung.	I16	10
Baja Verapaz, dept., Guat.	B4	92
Bajdarackaja guba, b., Russia	D11	26
Bajestān, Iran	D15	48
Bajiazi, China	B11	32
Bajimba, Mount, mtn., Austl.	G10	70
Bajkal, ozero (Lake Baikal), l., Russia	G13	28
Bajkal'skoje, Russia	F13	28
Bajmak, Russia	G9	26
Bajo Baudó, Col.	E4	84
Bajo Boquete, Pan.	C1	84
Bajos de Haina, Dom. Rep.	E9	94
Bajram-Ali, Turk.	J10	26
Bakebe, Cam.	I14	64
Bakel, Sen.	D3	64
Baker, Ca., U.S.	E5	112
Baker, Fl., U.S.	u15	116
Baker, La., U.S.	D4	125
Baker, Mt., U.S.	D12	133
Baker, Nv., U.S.	D7	135
Baker, Or., U.S.	C9	144
Baker, co., Fl., U.S.	B4	116
Baker, co., Ga., U.S.	E2	117
Baker, co., Or., U.S.	C9	144
Baker, stm., N.H., U.S.	C3	136
Baker, Mount, mtn., Wa., U.S.	A4	154
Baker Air Force Base, mil., Ar., U.S.	B6	111
Baker Butte, mtn., Az., U.S.	C4	110
Baker Hill, Al., U.S.	D4	108
Baker Island, i., Oc.	H22	158
Baker Island, i., Ak., U.S.	n22	109
Baker Lake, N.W. Ter., Can.	D13	96
Baker Lake, l., N.W. Ter., Can.	D13	96
Baker Lake, l., Me., U.S.	B3	126
Baker Lake, res., Wa., U.S.	A4	154
Baker Mountain, mtn., Me., U.S.	C3	126
Bakers, N.C., U.S.	B2	140
Bakers Bayou, stm., Ar., U.S.	k11	111
Bakersfield, Ca., U.S.	E4	112
Bakersfield, Mo., U.S.	E5	132
Bakersfield, Vt., U.S.	B3	152
Bakers Island, i., Ma., U.S.	f12	128
Bakerstown, Pa., U.S.	h14	145
Bakersville, Ct., U.S.	B3	114
Bakersville, N.C., U.S.	e10	140
Bakerton, W.V., U.S.	B7	155
Bākhtarān (Kermānshāh), Iran	D9	48
Bakhtegān, Daryācheh-ye, l., Iran	G13	48
Bakı (Baku), Azer.	I7	26
Bakkagerði, Ice.	B7	6a
Baklanka, Russia	C23	22
Bako, Eth.	O9	60
Bakony, mts., Hung.	H17	10
Bakoy, stm., Afr.	F5	54
Baku see Bakı, Azer.	I7	26
Bakun, China	D9	44
Bala, Ont., Can.	B5	103
Bala, Sen.	D3	64
Balâ, Tur.	B2	48
Balabac Strait, strt., Asia	D6	38
Baʻlabakk, Leb.	D4	48
Balabanovo, Russia	F19	22
Balachna, Russia	E26	22
Balad, Iraq	D8	48
Bālāghāt, India	J9	44
Balaguer, Spain	D12	16
Balakirevo, Russia	E21	22
Balaklava, Austl.	J3	70
Balakovo, Russia	G7	26
Balallan, Scot., U.K.	C7	8
Bālā Morghāb, Afg.	D17	48
Balāngīr, India	B7	46
Balašicha, Russia	F20	22
Balašov, Russia	G6	26
Balassagyarmat, Hung.	G19	10
Balāṭ, Egypt	E5	60
Balatina, Mol.	B11	20
Balaton, Mn., U.S.	F3	130
Balaton, l., Hung.	I17	10
Balayan, Phil.	o19	39b
Balbieriškis, Lith.	G6	22
Balbina, Reprêsa, res., Braz.	H13	84
Balbirini, Austl.	C7	68
Balboa, Pan.	I15	92
Balbriggan, Ire.	H7	8
Balcanoona, Austl.	H3	70
Balcarce, Arg.	I9	80
Balcarres, Sask., Can.	G4	105
Balchaš, Kaz.	H12	26
Balchaš, ozero (Lake Balkhash), l., Kaz.	H12	26
Balde, Arg.	G5	80
Bald Eagle Lake, l., Mn., U.S.	C7	130
Bald Eagle Lake, l., Mn., U.S.	m12	130
Bald Hill, hill, R.I., U.S.	D2	146
Baldhill Dam, N.D., U.S.	B7	141
Baldim, Braz.	E7	79
Bald Knob, Ar., U.S.	B4	111
Bald Knob, mtn., Va., U.S.	c3	153
Bald Knob, mtn., W.V., U.S.	C5	155
Bald Knoll, mtn., Wy., U.S.	D2	157
Bald Mountain, mtn., Ct., U.S.	B6	114
Bald Mountain, mtn., N.J., U.S.	A4	137
Bald Mountain, mtn., Or., U.S.	C9	144
Bald Mountain, mtn., Or., U.S.	D5	144
Bald Mountain, mtn., Vt., U.S.	B5	152
Bald Mountain, mtn., Wy., U.S.	B5	157
Bald Mountains, mts., N.C., U.S.	f10	140
Baldone, Lat.	E7	22
Baldur, Man., Can.	E2	100
Baldwin, Fl., U.S.	B5	116
Baldwin, Ga., U.S.	B3	117
Baldwin, Il., U.S.	E4	120
Baldwin, La., U.S.	E4	125
Baldwin, Mi., U.S.	E5	129
Baldwin, Pa., U.S.	k14	145
Baldwin, S.C., U.S.	B5	147
Baldwin, Wi., U.S.	D1	156
Baldwin, co., Al., U.S.	E2	108
Baldwin, co., Ga., U.S.	C3	117
Baldwin City, Ks., U.S.	D8	123
Baldwinsville, N.Y., U.S.	B4	139
Baldwinville, Ma., U.S.	A3	128
Baldwyn, Ms., U.S.	A5	131
Baldy Mountain, mtn., B.C., Can.	D7	99
Baldy Mountain, mtn., Man., Can.	D1	100
Baldy Mountain, mtn., Mt., U.S.	B7	133
Baldy Mountain, mtn., N.M., U.S.	A4	138
Baldy Peak, mtn., Az., U.S.	D6	110
Balearic Islands see Balears, Illes, is., Spain	F15	16
Balears, prov., Spain	F15	16
Balears, Illes (Balearic Islands), is., Spain	F15	16
Baleia, Ponta da, c., Braz.	D9	79
Baleine, Rivière à la, stm., Que., Can.	g13	104
Balej, Russia	G15	28
Baler, Phil.	n19	39b
Bāleshwar, India	J12	44
Baléyara, Niger	E11	64
Balfate, Hond.	B8	92
Balfes Creek, Austl.	C6	70
Balfour, N.C., U.S.	f10	140
Balgonie, Sask., Can.	G3	105
Bali, Laut (Bali Sea), Indon.	G6	38
Bali, Selat, strt., Indon.	G5	38
Balihan, China	B6	32
Balıkesir, Tur.	J11	20
Balikpapan, Indon.	F6	38
Balimo, Pap. N. Gui.	G11	38
Balin, China	B11	30
Balingen, Ger.	G8	10
Balintang Channel, strt., Phil.	B7	38
Baliza, Braz.	D2	79
Balkan Mountains see Stara Planina, mts., Eur.	G8	20
Balkan Peninsula, pen., Eur.	D9	52
Balkaria see Kabardino-Balkarija, state, Russia	I6	26
Balkbrug, Neth.	C9	12
Balkh, Afg.	B2	44
Balkh, stm., Afg.	B2	44
Balkhash, Lake see Balchaš, ozero, l., Kaz.	H12	26
Ball, La., U.S.	C3	125
Ballachulish, Scot., U.K.	E8	8
Ballangen, Nor.	G15	6
Ballantine, Mt., U.S.	E8	133
Ballarat, Austl.	K5	70
Ballard, co., Ky., U.S.	e8	124
Ballardvale, Ma., U.S.	f11	128
Ball Club Lake, l., Mn., U.S.	C5	130
Ballé, Mali	D5	64
Ballenas, Bahía de, b., Mex.	D3	90
Balleny Islands, is., Ant.	B8	73
Balleroy, Fr.	C6	14
Ballesteros, Arg.	G7	80
Balleza, Mex.	D6	90
Balleza, stm., Mex.	D6	90
Ball Ground, Ga., U.S.	B2	117
Ballia, India	H11	44
Ballina, Austl.	G10	70
Ballina, Ire.	G4	8
Ballinger, Tx., U.S.	D3	150
Ball Mountain Lake, res., Vt., U.S.	E3	152
Ballon, Fr.	M14	8
Ballouville, Ct., U.S.	B8	114
Balls Pyramid, i., Austl.	F11	68
Ballston Spa, N.Y., U.S.	B7	139
Ballwin, Mo., U.S.	f12	132
Bally, Pa., U.S.	F10	145
Balm, Fl., U.S.	E4	116
Balmaceda, Chile	F2	78
Balmoral, Man., Can.	D3	100
Balmoral, N.B., Can.	B3	101
Balmorhea, Tx., U.S.	o13	150
Balmville, N.Y., U.S.	D6	139
Balnearia, Arg.	F7	80
Balonne, stm., Austl.	F8	70
Bālotra, India	H5	44
Balovale, Zam.	D4	58
Baloži, Lat.	E7	22
Balrāmpur, India	G10	44
Balranald, Austl.	J5	70
Balsam, N.C., U.S.	f9	140
Balsam Lake, Wi., U.S.	C1	156
Balsam Lake, l., Ont., Can.	C6	103
Balsam Lake, l., Wi., U.S.	C1	156
Bálsamo, Braz.	F2	79
Balsas, Braz.	E9	76
Balsas, stm., Mex.	H8	90
Balsas, Rio das, stm., Braz.	E9	76
Balsas Sur, Mex.	I10	90
Balsthal, Switz.	D8	13
Balta, Ukr.	H3	26
Balta, N.D., U.S.	A5	141
Baltasar Brum, Ur.	F10	80
Bălţi, Mol.	H3	26
Baltic, Ct., U.S.	C7	114
Baltic, Oh., U.S.	B4	142
Baltic, S.D., U.S.	D9	148
Baltic Sea, Eur.	M16	6
Baltijsk, Russia	G2	22
Baltijskaja kosa, spit, Eur.	A19	10
Balṭīm, Egypt	B6	60
Baltimore, Ont., Can.	C6	103
Baltimore, Ire.	J4	8
Baltimore, S. Afr.	D9	66
Baltimore, Md., U.S.	B4	127
Baltimore, Oh., U.S.	C3	142
Baltimore, co., Md., U.S.	B4	127
Baltimore Highlands, Md., U.S.	h11	127
Baluarte, stm., Mex.	F7	90
Balvi, Lat.	D10	22
Balya, Tur.	J11	20
Balykši, Kaz.	H8	26
Balzar, Ec.	H3	84
Bam, Iran	G15	48
Bama, China	B9	40
Bamaga, Austl.	B8	68
Bamako, Mali	E5	64
Bamba, Mali	C9	64
Bambamarca, Peru	B2	82
Bambana, stm., Nic.	D11	92
Bambara Maoundé, Mali	D8	64
Bambari, Cen. Afr. Rep.	G5	56
Bambaroo, Austl.	B7	70
Bamberg, Ger.	F10	10
Bamberg, S.C., U.S.	E5	147
Bamberg, co., S.C., U.S.	E5	147
Bambesi, Eth.	M8	60
Bambezi, Zimb.	C9	66
Bambuí, Braz.	F6	79
Bamburral, stm., S.A.	H12	82
Bam Co, l., China	E14	44
Bamenda, Cam.	I15	64
Bami, Turk.	B14	48
Bamingui, stm., Cen. Afr. Rep.	G4	56
Bampūr, Iran	H16	48
Bamumo, China	D15	44
Ba Na, Viet.	G9	40
Banaba, i., Kir.	I20	158
Banalia, Zaire	A5	58
Banana, Zaire	C2	58
Bananal, Ilha do, i., Braz.	F8	76
Banana River, b., Fl., U.S.	D6	116
Banarlı, Tur.	H11	20
Banās, Ra's, c., Egypt	F8	60
Banat, hist. reg., Eur.	D4	20
Banbuji, China	B5	34
Banco, Punta, c., C.R.	I11	92
Bancroft, Ont., Can.	B7	103
Bancroft, Id., U.S.	G7	119
Bancroft, Ia., U.S.	A3	122
Bancroft, Mi., U.S.	F6	129
Bancroft, Ne., U.S.	B9	134
Bānda, India	H9	44
Banda, Kepulauan, is., Indon.	F8	38
Banda, Laut (Banda Sea), Indon.	G8	38
Banda Aceh, Indon.	L3	40
Bānda Dāūd Shāh, Pak.	D4	44
Banda del Río Salí, Arg.	D6	80
Bandama, stm., C. Iv.	H7	64
Bandama Blanc, stm., C. Iv.	G7	64
Bandama Rouge, stm., C. Iv.	G6	64
Bandana, Ky., U.S.	e9	124
Bandar see Machilīpatnam, India	D6	46
Bandar Beheshtī, Iran	I16	48
Bandar-e ʻAbbās, Iran	H14	48
Bandar-e Anzalī (Bandar-e Pahlavī), Iran	C10	48
Bandar-e Būshehr, Iran	G11	48
Bandar-e Deylam, Iran	F11	48
Bandar-e Khomeynī (Bandar-e Shāhpūr), Iran	F10	48
Bandar-e Lengeh, Iran	H13	48
Bandar-e Māh Shahr, Iran	F10	48
Bandar-e Rīg, Iran	G11	48
Bandar-e Torkeman, Iran	C13	48
Bandar Seri Begawan, Bru.	E5	38
Banded Peak, mtn., Co., U.S.	D4	113
Bandeira, Pico da, mtn., Braz.	F8	79
Bandeirantes, Braz.	B3	79
Bandeirantes, Braz.	E1	79
Bandeirantes, Braz.	G3	79
Bandelier National Monument, N.M., U.S.	B3	138
Bandera, Arg.	E7	80
Bandera, Tx., U.S.	E3	150
Bandera, co., Tx., U.S.	E3	150
Bandera, Alto, mtn., Dom. Rep.	E9	94
Banderas, Bahía de, b., Mex.	G7	90
Bandiagara, Mali	D8	64
Bandiantaolehai, China	C7	30
Bandırma, Tur.	I11	20
Bandon, Ire.	J5	8
Bandon, Or., U.S.	D2	144

Name — Map Ref. — Page

Ban Don, Ao, b., Thai. J5 40
Bandula, Moz. B11 66
Bandundu, Zaire B3 58
Bandung, Indon. j13 39a
Bāneh, Iran D8 48
Banes, Cuba D7 94
Banff, Scot., U.K. D11 8
Banff National Park, Alta., Can. D2 98
Banfora, Burkina F7 64
Bangalore, India F4 46
Bangaon, India I13 44
Bangassou, Cen. Afr. Rep. H5 56
Banggai, Indon. F7 38
Banggai, Kepulauan, is., Indon. F7 38
Banghāzī, Libya B5 56
Bangil, Indon. j16 39a
Bangjang, Sud. L7 60
Bangjun, China D5 32
Bangka, Pulau, i., Indon. F4 38
Bangkalan, Indon. j16 39a
Bangkok see Krung Thep, Thai. H6 40
Bangladesh, ctry., Asia E13 42
Bang Mun Nak, Thai. F6 40
Bangolo, C. Iv. H6 64
Bangor, Sask., Can. G4 105
Bangor, N. Ire., U.K. G8 8
Bangor, Wales, U.K. H9 8
Bangor, Me., U.S. D4 126
Bangor, Mi., U.S. F4 129
Bangor, Pa., U.S. E11 145
Bangor, Wi., U.S. E3 156
Bangor Township, Mi., U.S. E7 129
Bangs, Tx., U.S. D3 150
Bangs, Mount, mtn., Az., U.S. A2 110
Bang Saphan, Thai. I5 40
Bangshi, China C10 32
Bangued, Phil. m19 39b
Bangui, Cen. Afr. Rep. H4 56
Bangweulu, Lake, l., Zam. D5 58
Ban Hin Heup, Laos E7 40
Ban Houayxay, Laos D6 40
Bani, Burkina D9 64
Baní, Dom. Rep. E9 94
Bani, stm., Mali E7 64
Baniachang, Bngl. H14 44
Banikoara, Benin F11 64
Banī Mazār, Egypt C6 60
Banister, stm., Va., U.S. D4 153
Banī Suwayf, Egypt C6 60
Banī Walīd, Libya B3 56
Bāniyās, Golan B5 50
Banja Luka, Bos. E12 18
Banjarmasin, Indon. F5 38
Banjin, China C9 34
Banjul (Bathurst), Gam. E1 64
Bankas, Mali D8 64
Bankhead Lake, res., Al., U.S. B2 108
Bankilaré, Niger D10 64
Banks, Al., U.S. D4 108
Banks, Or., U.S. g11 144
Banks, co., Ga., U.S. B3 117
Banks Island, i., B.C., Can. C2 99
Banks Island, i., N.W. Ter., Can. B8 96
Banks Lake, res., Ga., U.S. E3 117
Banks Lake, res., Wa., U.S. B6 154
Banks Peninsula, pen., N.Z. E4 72
Banks Strait, strt., Austl. M8 70
Bankston, Al., U.S. B2 108
Bānkura, India I12 44
Ban Mit, Laos E6 40
Bann, stm., N. Ire., U.K. G7 8
Ban Nahin, Laos E8 40
Ban Namnga, Laos D7 40
Banner, co., Ne., U.S. C2 134
Banner Elk, N.C., U.S. A1 140
Ban Ngam, Laos D8 40
Banning, Ca., U.S. F5 112
Banning, Ga., U.S. C2 117
Bannock, co., Id., U.S. G6 119
Bannockburn, Ont., Can. C7 103
Bannock Peak, mtn., Id., U.S. F6 119
Bannock Range, mts., Id., U.S. G6 119
Bannu, Pak. D4 44
Banon, Fr. H12 14
Baños, Ec. H3 84
Baños, Peru D3 82
Ban Pakneun, Laos E6 40
Ban Pong, Thai. H5 40
Banpu, China A8 34
Banqiao, China E9 34
Banqiaoji, China C5 34
Banquan, China H6 32
Banshi, China J4 34
Banská Bystrica, Slvk. G19 10
Banská Štiavnica, Slvk. G18 10
Ban Songkhon, Laos F8 40
Bānswāra, India I6 44
Bantam, Ct., U.S. C3 114
Bantam, stm., Ct., U.S. B3 114
Bantam Lake, l., Ct., U.S. C3 114
Ban Thanoun, Laos E6 40
Bantry, Ire. J4 8
Ban Xènkhalôk, Laos E6 40
Banyak, Kepulauan, is., Indon. M4 40
Banyoles, Spain C14 16
Banzare Coast, Ant. B7 73
Banzhi, China K6 34
Baode, China D9 30
Baoding, China E3 32
Baofeng, China B2 34
Bao Ha, Viet. C8 40
Baohekou, China C6 32
Baoji, China E8 30
Bao Lac, Viet. I9 40
Baonian, China D8 34
Baoquan, China G7 32
Baoshan, China D10 34
Baoshan, China B5 40
Baoting, China H8 30
Baotou, China C8 30
Baowei, China C9 40
Baoxinji, China C4 34
Baoying, China B8 34
Bāpatla, India E6 46
Bapaume, Fr. B9 14
Bapchule, Az., U.S. D4 110
Baptiste, Ont., Can. B6 103
Bāqa el Gharbīya, Isr. D4 50
Baqên, China E16 44
B'aqlīn, Leb. A5 50
Ba'qūbah, Iraq E8 48
Baquedano, Chile B4 80
Bar, Yugo. G3 20
Baraawe, Som. H9 56
Barabinsk, Russia F7 28
Barabinskaja step', pl., Russia F7 28
Baraboo, Wi., U.S. E4 156
Baraboo, stm., Wi., U.S. E3 156
Baraboulé, Burkina D9 64
Baracaju, stm., Braz. B3 79
Baracaldo, Spain B9 16
Barachit, Erit. J10 60
Baracoa, Cuba D7 94
Baracoa, Hond. B7 92
Baradero, Arg. G9 80
Baradine, Austl. H8 70
Baraga, Mi., U.S. B2 129
Baraga, co., Mi., U.S. B2 129
Baragarh, India B7 46
Bārah, Sud. K6 60
Barahona, Dom. Rep. E9 94
Barak, Tur. C4 48
Baraka, val., Afr. E8 56
Baralaba, Austl. E8 70
Baram, stm., Malay. E5 38
Barama, stm., Guy. D13 84
Baran', Bela. G13 22
Baranagar, India I13 44
Baranoa, Col. B5 84
Baranof Island, i., Ak., U.S. m22 109
Baranoviči, Bela. H9 22
Baranya, co., Hung. J18 10
Barão de Melgaço, Braz. G14 82
Baratang Island, i., India H2 40
Barataria, La., U.S. E5 125
Barataria, Bayou, stm., La., U.S. k11 125
Barataria Bay, b., La., U.S. E6 125
Barat Daya, Kepulauan, is., Indon. G8 38
Bar'atino, Russia G17 22
Barauana, stm., Braz. G12 84
Barauni, India H11 44
Baraut, India F7 44
Baraya, Col. F5 84
Barbacena, Braz. F7 79
Barbacoas, Col. G3 84
Barbados, ctry., N.A. H15 94
Barbar, Sud. H7 60
Barbareta, Isla, i., Hond. A8 92
Barbas, Cap, c., W. Sah. I2 62
Barbastro, Spain C12 16
Barbate de Franco, Spain I6 16
Barbeau Peak, mtn., N.W. Ter., Can. A12 86
Barber, co., Ks., U.S. E5 123
Barberena, Guat. C4 92
Barbers Point, c., Hi., U.S. B3 118
Barbers Point Naval Air Station, mil., Hi., U.S. g9 118
Barberton, S. Afr. E10 66
Barberton, Oh., U.S. A4 142
Barbezieux, Fr. G6 14
Barbil, India I11 44
Barbosa, Col. E6 84
Barbosa, Col. D5 84
Barbour, co., Al., U.S. D4 108
Barbour, co., W.V., U.S. B4 155
Barboursville, W.V., U.S. C2 155
Barbourville, Ky., U.S. D6 124
Barbuda, i., Antig. F14 94
Barby, Ger. D11 10
Barcaldine, Austl. D6 70
Barcău (Berettyó), stm., Eur. B6 20
Barce see Al-Marj, Libya B5 56
Barcellona Pozzo di Gotto, Italy K10 18
Barcelona, Mex. D8 90
Barcelona, Spain D14 16
Barcelona, Ven. B10 84
Barcelos, Braz. H11 84
Barcin, Pol. C17 10
Barco, N.C., U.S. A7 140
Barcoo, stm., Austl. E5 70
Barcroft, Lake, res., Va., U.S. g12 153
Barcs, Hung. J17 10
Barczewo, Pol. B20 10
Bärdä, Azer. A9 48
Barda del Medio, Arg. J4 80
Bardaï, Chad D4 56
Bardai, Sud. K1 60
Bardawīl, Sabkhat al-, sw., Egypt F2 48
Barddhamān, India I12 44
Bardejov, Slvk. F21 10
Barden Reservoir, res., R.I., U.S. C2 146
Bardi, Italy E4 18
Bardīyah, Libya B3 60
Bardo, Tun. M5 18
Bardolph, Il., U.S. C3 120
Bardonecchia, Italy D1 18
Bardstown, Ky., U.S. C4 124
Bardu, Nor. G16 6
Bardufoss, Nor. G16 6
Bardwell, Ky., U.S. f9 124
Bardwell Lake, res., Tx., U.S. C4 150
Bare Hill Pond, l., Ma., U.S. g9 128
Bareilly, India F8 44
Barents Sea, Eur. B24 24
Barentu, Erit. J9 60
Barfleur, Fr. C5 14
Barge, Eth. N9 60
Bargersville, In., U.S. E5 121
Bargnop, Sud. M5 60
Barguzin, stm., Russia G14 28
Bar Harbor, Me., U.S. D4 126
Bari, Italy H11 18
Baria, stm., Ven. G9 84
Barichara, Col. D6 84
Barillas, Guat. B3 92
Barīm (Perim), i., Yemen H3 47
Barima, stm., S.A. C12 84
Barima-Waini, prov., Guy. D13 84
Barinas, Ven. C7 84
Barinas, state, Ven. C8 84
Baring, Me., U.S. C5 126
Baring, Mo., U.S. A5 132
Baring, Cape, c., N.W. Ter., Can. B9 96
Barinitas, Ven. C7 84
Bāripada, India J12 44
Bariri, Braz. G4 79
Bārīs, Egypt E6 60
Barisāl, Bngl. I14 44
Barisan, Pegunungan, mts., Indon. F3 38
Barito, stm., Indon. F5 38
Barium Springs, N.C., U.S. B2 140
Barjols, Fr. I13 14
Barkal, Bngl. I15 44
Barker Heights, N.C., U.S. f10 140
Barkhamsted Reservoir, res., Ct., U.S. B3 114
Bark Lake, l., Ont., Can. B7 103
Barkley, Lake, res., U.S. f10 124
Barkley Dam, Ky., U.S. e9 124
Barkley Sound, strt., B.C., Can. E5 99
Barkly East, S. Afr. H8 66
Barkly Tableland, plat., Austl. C7 68
Barkly West, S. Afr. G7 66
Barkmere, Que., Can. C3 104
Barkol, China C5 30
Bark Point, c., Wi., U.S. B2 156
Bark River, Mi., U.S. C3 129
Barksdale Air Force Base, mil., La., U.S. B2 125
Bârlad, Rom. C11 20
Bar-le-Duc, Fr. D12 14
Barlee, Lake, l., Austl. E3 68
Barletta, Italy H11 18
Barling, Ar., U.S. B1 111
Barlow, Ky., U.S. e8 124
Bārmer, India H4 44
Bar Mills, Me., U.S. E2 126
Barnaby River, N.B., Can. C4 101
Barnard, Ks., U.S. C5 123
Barnard, Mo., U.S. A3 132
Barnard, Vt., U.S. D3 152
Barnard Castle, Eng., U.K. G15 8
Barnardsville, N.C., U.S. f10 140
Barnaul, Russia G14 26
Barn Bluff, mtn., Austl. M6 70
Barnegat, N.J., U.S. D4 137
Barnegat Bay, b., N.J., U.S. D4 137
Barnegat Inlet, b., N.J., U.S. D4 137
Barnes, Ks., U.S. C7 123
Barnes, co., N.D., U.S. B7 141
Barnesboro, Pa., U.S. E4 145
Barnes City, Ia., U.S. C5 122
Barnes Creek, stm., La., U.S. D2 125
Barnes Ice Cap, N.W. Ter., Can. B18 96
Barnes Sound, strt., Fl., U.S. G6 116
Barneston, Ne., U.S. D9 134
Barnesville, Ga., U.S. C2 117
Barnesville, Mn., U.S. D2 130
Barnesville, Oh., U.S. C4 142
Barnet, Vt., U.S. C4 152
Barnett, Mo., U.S. C5 132
Barneveld, Wi., U.S. E4 156
Barney, Ga., U.S. F3 117
Barney, N.D., U.S. C8 141
Barnhart, Mo., U.S. C7 132
Barnsdall, Ok., U.S. A5 143
Barnstable, Ma., U.S. C7 128
Barnstable, co., Ma., U.S. C7 128
Barnstaple, Eng., U.K. J9 8
Barnstead, N.H., U.S. D4 136
Barnum, Mn., U.S. D6 130
Bar Nunn, Wy., U.S. D6 157
Barnwell, Alta., Can. E4 98
Barnwell, S.C., U.S. E5 147
Barnwell, co., S.C., U.S. E5 147
Baro, stm., Afr. G8 56
Baroda, Mi., U.S. G4 129
Barons, Alta., Can. E4 98
Barpeta, India G14 44
Barqa, China E9 44
Barqah (Cyrenaica), hist. reg., Libya C2 60
Barque Canada Reef, rf., Asia D5 38
Barques, Pointe aux, c., Mi., U.S. D8 129
Barquisimeto, Ven. B8 84
Barr, Co., U.S. B6 113
Barra, Braz. F10 76
Barra, Ponta da, c., Moz. D12 66
Barraba, Austl. H9 70
Barrackville, W.V., U.S. B4 155
Barra da Estiva, Braz. B8 79
Barra do Bugres, Braz. F13 82
Barra do Corda, Braz. E9 76
Barra do Cuanza, Ang. C2 58
Barra do Garças, Braz. C2 79
Barra do Mendes, Braz. A7 79
Barra do Piraí, Braz. G7 79
Barra do Ribeiro, Braz. F13 80
Barra Falsa, Ponta da, c., Moz. D12 66
Barrafranca, Italy L9 18
Barra Mansa, Braz. G6 79
Barranca, Peru A3 82
Barranca, Peru D3 82
Barrancabermeja, Col. D6 84
Barrancas, Col. B6 84
Barrancas, Ven. C11 84
Barrancas, Ven. C7 84
Barrancas, stm., Arg. I3 80
Barranqueras, Arg. D9 80
Barranquilla, Col. B5 84
Barras, Braz. D10 76
Barre, Ma., U.S. B3 128
Barre, Vt., U.S. C4 152
Barre, Lake, l., La., U.S. E5 125
Barreal, Arg. F4 80
Barre Falls Reservoir, res., Ma., U.S. B4 128
Barreiras, Braz. B6 79
Barreirinha, Braz. I14 84
Barreiro, Port. G2 16
Barreiro, stm., Braz. C2 79
Barreiros, Braz. E11 76
Barren, co., Ky., U.S. D4 124
Barren, stm., Ky., U.S. D3 124
Barren, Nosy, is., Madag. q20 67b
Barren Island, i., Md., U.S. D5 127
Barren Islands, is., Ak., U.S. h15 109
Barren River Lake, res., Ky., U.S. D3 124
Barretos, Braz. F4 79
Barrett, Mn., U.S. E3 130
Barrett, W.V., U.S. D3 155
Barretts Hill, hill, Ma., U.S. g9 128
Barrhead, Alta., Can. B3 98
Barrie, Ont., Can. C5 103
Barrie Island, i., Ont., Can. B2 103
Barrière, B.C., Can. D7 99
Barrier Range, mts., Austl. H4 70
Barrington, N.S., Can. F4 101
Barrington, Il., U.S. A5 120
Barrington, N.H., U.S. D4 136
Barrington, N.J., U.S. D2 137
Barrington, R.I., U.S. D5 146
Barrington, stm., R.I., U.S. C5 146
Barrington Lake, l., Man., Can. A1 100
Barrington Passage, N.S., Can. F4 101
Barringun, Austl. G6 70
Barrita Vieja, Guat. D4 92
Barro Alto, Braz. C4 79
Barron, Wi., U.S. C2 156
Barron, co., Wi., U.S. C2 156
Barron Lake, Mi., U.S. G4 129
Barrow, Arg. J8 80
Barrow, Ak., U.S. A8 109
Barrow, co., Ga., U.S. B3 117
Barrow, Point, c., Ak., U.S. A8 109
Barrow Creek, Austl. D6 68
Barrow-in-Furness, Eng., U.K. G10 8
Barrow Island, i., Austl. D3 68
Barrows, Man., Can. C1 100
Barrow Strait, strt., N.W. Ter., Can. B13 96
Barry, Il., U.S. D2 120
Barry, co., Mi., U.S. F5 129
Barry, co., Mo., U.S. E4 132
Barrys Bay, Ont., Can. B7 103
Barryton, Mi., U.S. E5 129
Bārsi, India C3 46
Barsinghausen, Ger. C9 10
Barstow, Ca., U.S. E5 112
Barstow, Tx., U.S. D1 150
Bar-sur-Aube, Fr. D11 14
Bar-sur-Seine, Fr. D11 14
Bartang, stm., Taj. A5 44
Bartelso, Il., U.S. E4 120
Barthélemy, Deo, Viet. E8 40
Bartholomew, co., In., U.S. F6 121
Bartholomew, Bayou, stm., U.S. D4 111
Bartibog Bridge, N.B., Can. B4 101
Bartica, Guy. D13 84
Bartle Frere, mtn., Austl. A6 70
Bartlesville, Ok., U.S. A6 143
Bartlett, Ks., U.S. E8 123
Bartlett, Ne., U.S. C7 134
Bartlett, N.H., U.S. B4 136
Bartlett, Tn., U.S. B2 149
Bartlett, Tx., U.S. D4 150
Bartlett Reservoir, res., Az., U.S. D4 110
Bartletts Ferry Dam, U.S. C4 108
Bartletts Harbour, Newf., Can. C3 102
Bartley, Ne., U.S. D5 134
Bartolomé de las Casas, Arg. C9 80
Bartolomeu Dias, Moz. C12 66
Barton, Al., U.S. A2 108
Barton, Ar., U.S. C5 111
Barton, Md., U.S. k12 127
Barton, Oh., U.S. B5 142
Barton, Vt., U.S. B4 152
Barton, co., Ks., U.S. D5 123
Barton, co., Mo., U.S. D3 132
Barton, stm., Vt., U.S. B4 152
Bartonsville, Vt., U.S. E3 152
Barton-upon-Humber, Eng., U.K. H13 8
Bartonville, Il., U.S. C4 120
Bartoszyce, Pol. A20 10
Bartow, Fl., U.S. E5 116
Bartow, Ga., U.S. D4 117
Bartow, co., Ga., U.S. B2 117
Barú, Volcán, vol., Pan. I12 92
Baruun-Urt, Mong. B9 30
Barva, Volcán, vol., C.R. G10 92
Barwāni, India I6 44
Barwick, Ga., U.S. F3 117
Barwon, stm., Austl. G8 70
Barybino, Russia F20 22
Baryš, Russia G7 26
Basacato del Este, Eq. Gui. J14 64
Basail, Arg. D9 80
Basalt, Co., U.S. B3 113
Basalt, Id., U.S. F6 119
Basankusu, Zaire A3 58
Basarabeasca, Mol. C12 20
Basarabi, Rom. E12 20
Basatongwula Shan, mtn., China D14 44
Basavilbaso, Arg. G9 80
Basco, Phil. A7 38
Bascom, Oh., U.S. A2 142
Bascuñán, Cabo, c., Chile G7 74
Basehor, Ks., U.S. k16 123
Basel (Bâle), Switz. C8 13
Basey, Phil. C8 38
Bashan Lake, l., Ct., U.S. D6 114
Bashaw, Alta., Can. C4 98
Bashi, Al., U.S. D2 108
Bashi Channel, strt., Asia G11 30
Bashkortostan see Baškirija, state, Russia G9 26
Basile, La., U.S. D3 125
Basilicata, prov., Italy I11 18
Basin, Mt., U.S. D4 133
Basin, Wy., U.S. B4 157
Basīrhāt, India I13 44
Baskahegan Lake, l., Me., U.S. C5 126
Baskakovka, Russia G17 22
Baskatong, Réservoir, res., Que., Can. k11 104
Baskett, Ky., U.S. C2 124
Baskin, Fl., U.S. p10 116
Basking Ridge, N.J., U.S. B3 137
Baškirija, state, Russia G9 26
Bašmakovo, Russia H26 22
Basoko, Zaire A4 58
Basque Lands see Euskal Herriko, prov., Spain B9 16
Basra see Al-Başrah, Iraq F9 48
Bas-Rhin, dept., Fr. D14 14
Bassano, Alta., Can. D4 98
Bassano del Grappa, Italy D6 18
Bassari, Togo G10 64
Bassas da India, rf., Afr. F7 58
Bassecourt, Switz. D7 13
Bassein see Pathein, Mya. F3 40
Bassein, mth., Mya. F3 40
Basse-Terre, Guad. F14 94
Basseterre, St. K./N. F13 94
Basse-Terre, i., Guad. F14 94
Bassett, Ar., U.S. B5 111
Bassett, Ne., U.S. B6 134
Bassett, Va., U.S. D3 153
Bassett, Wi., U.S. n11 156
Bassett Creek, stm., Al., U.S. D2 108
Bassett Peak, mtn., Az., U.S. E5 110
Basse-Yutz, Fr. J9 12
Bassfield, Ms., U.S. D4 131
Bass Harbor, Me., U.S. D4 126
Bassikounou, Maur. D7 64
Bassila, Benin G10 64
Bass Islands, is., Oh., U.S. A3 142
Bass Lake, In., U.S. B4 121
Bass River, N.S., Can. D6 101
Bass Strait, strt., Austl. L6 70
Basswood, Man., Can. D1 100
Basswood Lake, l., Mn., U.S. B7 130
Baştah, Jord. H5 50
Bastak, Iran H13 48
Bastelica, Fr. I24 15a
Basti, India G10 44
Bastia, Fr. J16 14
Bastian, Va., U.S. C1 153
Bastimentos, Pan. H12 92
Bastimentos, Isla, i., Pan. H12 92
Bastogne (Bastenaken), Bel. H8 12
Bastrop, La., U.S. B4 125
Bastrop, Tx., U.S. D4 150
Bastrop, co., Tx., U.S. D4 150
Basuträsk, Swe. I17 6
Basutoland see Lesotho, ctry., Afr. G5 58
Bata, Eq. Gui. A1 58
Bataan Peninsula, pen., Phil. n19 39b
Batabanó, Golfo de, b., Cuba C3 94
Bataguassu, Braz. F2 79
Bataiporã, Braz. G2 79
Batajsk, Russia H5 26
Batala, India E6 44
Batan, China A9 34
Batang, China E6 30
Batangas, Phil. o19 39b
Batan Islands, is., Phil. A7 38
Bátaszék, Hung. I18 10
Batatais, Braz. F5 79
Batavia, Arg. H6 80
Batavia, Il., U.S. B5 120
Batavia, Ia., U.S. D5 122
Batavia, N.Y., U.S. C2 139
Batavia, Oh., U.S. C1 142
Batchelor Bay, b., N.C., U.S. B6 140
Batchtown, Il., U.S. D3 120
Bătdâmbâng, Camb. H7 40
Bateckij, Russia C13 22
Batemans Bay, Austl. J9 70
Bates, Ar., U.S. C1 111
Bates, co., Mo., U.S. C3 132
Batesburg, S.C., U.S. D4 147
Batesland, S.D., U.S. D3 148
Batesville, Ar., U.S. B4 111
Batesville, In., U.S. F7 121
Batesville, Ms., U.S. A4 131
Batesville, Tx., U.S. E3 150
Bath, N.B., Can. C2 101
Bath, Ont., Can. C8 103
Bath, Eng., U.K. J11 8
Bath, Il., U.S. C3 120
Bath, Me., U.S. E3 126
Bath, Mi., U.S. F6 129
Bath, N.H., U.S. B3 136
Bath, N.Y., U.S. C3 139
Bath, Pa., U.S. E11 145
Bath, S.C., U.S. D4 147
Bath, S.D., U.S. B7 148
Bath, co., Ky., U.S. B6 124
Bath, co., Va., U.S. B3 153
Bathinda, India E6 44
Bathsheba, Barb. H15 94
Bathurst, Austl. I8 70
Bathurst, N.B., Can. B4 101
Bathurst see Banjul, Gam. E1 64
Bathurst, S. Afr. I8 66
Bathurst, Cape, c., N.W. Ter., Can. B7 96
Bathurst Inlet, b., N.W. Ter., Can. C11 96
Bathurst Island, i., Austl. B6 68
Bathurst Island, i., N.W. Ter., Can. A12 96
Batia, Benin F10 64
Batié, Burkina G8 64
Bāţin, Wādī al-, val., Asia G9 48
Batiscan, stm., Que., Can. B5 104
Batkanu, S.L. G3 64
Batlow, Austl. J8 70
Batman, Tur. C6 48
Batna, Alg. C14 62
Baţn al-Ghūl, Jord. I5 50
Baton Rouge, La., U.S. D4 125
Batouri, Cam. H9 54
Batovi, Braz. C2 79
Batrā (Petra), hist., Jord. H4 50
Batsto, stm., N.J., U.S. D3 137
Batten Kill, stm., U.S. E2 152
Battery Park, Va., U.S. k14 153
Batticaloa, Sri L. I6 46
Battiest, Ok., U.S. C7 143
Battle, stm., Can. F10 96
Battle, stm., Can. A4 106
Battleboro, N.C., U.S. A5 140
Battle Creek, Ia., U.S. B2 122
Battle Creek, Mi., U.S. F5 129
Battle Creek, Ne., U.S. C8 134
Battleford, Sask., Can. E1 105
Battle Ground, In., U.S. C4 121
Battle Ground, Wa., U.S. D3 154
Battle Lake, Mn., U.S. D3 130
Battlement Mesa, mtn., Co., U.S. B2 113
Battle Mountain, Nv., U.S. C5 135
Battle Mountain, mtn., Wy., U.S. E5 157
Battles, Ms., U.S. D5 131
Battles Wharf, Al., U.S. E2 108
Battonya, Hung. I21 10
Batu, mtn., Eth. G8 56
Batu, Kepulauan, is., Indon. O5 40
Batumi, Geor. I6 26
Batu Pahat, Malay. N7 40
Baturité, Braz. D11 76
Bat Yam, Isr. D3 50
Baubau, Indon. G7 38
Bauchi, Nig. F14 64
Baud, Fr. E3 14
Baudette, Mn., U.S. B4 130
Baudó, stm., Col. E4 84
Bauer Coulee, val., Wa., U.S. B7 154
Bauld, Cape, c., Newf., Can. C4 102
Baume-les-Dames, Fr. E13 14
Baures, Bol. E10 82
Baures, stm., Bol. E10 82
Bauru, Braz. G4 79
Baús, Braz. E2 79
Bauska, Lat. E7 22
Bautzen, Ger. D14 10
Bauxite, Ar., U.S. C3 111
Bavaria, Ks., U.S. D6 123
Bavaria see Bayern, state, Ger. F11 10
Bavispe, Mex. B5 90
Bavispe, stm., Mex. C5 90
Bavleny, Russia E22 22
Bawdwin, Mya. C4 40
Bawku, Ghana F9 64
Bawlf, Alta., Can. C4 98
Baxian, China D4 32
Baxley, Ga., U.S. E4 117
Baxter, Ia., U.S. C4 122
Baxter, Mn., U.S. D4 130
Baxter, Tn., U.S. C8 149
Baxter, W.V., U.S. B4 155
Baxter, co., Ar., U.S. A3 111
Baxter Springs, Ks., U.S. E9 123
Baxterville, Ms., U.S. D4 131
Bay, Ar., U.S. B5 111
Bay, co., Fl., U.S. u16 116
Bay, co., Mi., U.S. E6 129
Bayamo, Cuba D6 94
Bayamón, P.R. E11 94
Bayan Har Shan, mts., China E6 30
Bayano, Lago, res., Pan. C3 84
Bayan Obo, China C9 30
Bayard, Ia., U.S. C3 122
Bayard, Ne., U.S. C2 134
Bayard, N.M., U.S. E1 138
Bayard, W.V., U.S. B5 155
Bayberry, N.Y., U.S. *B4 139
Bayboro, N.C., U.S. B6 140
Bay Bulls, Newf., Can. E5 102
Bayburt, Tur. A6 48
Bay Center, Wa., U.S. C2 154
Bay City, Mi., U.S. E7 129
Bay City, Or., U.S. B3 144
Bay City, Tx., U.S. E5 150
Bay City, Wi., U.S. D1 156
Bay de Verde, Newf., Can. D5 102
Baydhabo, Som. H9 56
Bayerische Alpen, mts., Eur. H11 10
Bayern, state, Ger. F11 10
Bayeux, Fr. C6 14
Bayfield, Ont., Can. D3 103
Bayfield, Co., U.S. D3 113
Bayfield, Wi., U.S. B3 156
Bayfield, co., Wi., U.S. B2 156
Bayiji, China A6 34
Bayingzi, China B8 32
Bay L'Argent, Newf., Can. E4 102
Baylis, Il., U.S. D3 120
Baylor, co., Tx., U.S. C3 150
Bay Mills Indian Reservation, Mi., U.S. B6 129
Bay Minette, Al., U.S. E2 108
Bayombong, Phil. m19 39b
Bayon, Fr. D13 14
Bayonne, Fr. I5 14
Bayonne, N.J., U.S. B4 137
Bayou Bodcau Reservoir, res., La., U.S. B2 125
Bayou Cane, La., U.S. E5 125
Bayou D'Arbonne Lake, res., La., U.S. B3 125
Bayou George, Fl., U.S. u16 116
Bayou Goula, La., U.S. D4 125
Bayou La Batre, Al., U.S. E1 108
Bayou Pigeon, La., U.S. D4 125
Bayovar, Peru A1 82
Bay Point, c., S.C., U.S. G7 147
Bayport, N.S., Can. E5 101
Bay Port, Mi., U.S. E7 129
Bayport, Mn., U.S. E6 130
Bayport, N.Y., U.S. n15 139
Bayreuth, Ger. F11 10
Bay Ridge, Md., U.S. C5 127
Bayrischzell, Ger. H12 10
Bay Roberts, Newf., Can. E5 102
Bayrūt (Beirut), Leb. A5 50
Bays, Lake of, l., Ont., Can. B5 103
Bay Saint Louis, Ms., U.S. E4 131
Bay Shore, N.Y., U.S. E7 139
Bayshore Gardens, Fl., U.S. q10 116
Bayside, Wi., U.S. m12 156
Bays Mountain, mtn., Tn., U.S. C10 149
Bay Springs, Ms., U.S. D4 131
Bayt al-Faqīh, Yemen G3 47
Bayt Jinn, Syria B5 50
Bayt Lahm (Bethlehem), W.B. E4 50
Bayt Mirī, Leb. A5 50
Baytown, Tx., U.S. E5 150
Bayview, Al., U.S. f7 108
Bayview, Id., U.S. B2 119
Bay View Park, De., U.S. F5 115
Bay Village, Oh., U.S. h9 142
Bayville, De., U.S. G5 115
Bayville, N.J., U.S. D4 137
Bayzo, Niger E12 64
Baza, Spain H9 16
Bazaruto, Ilha do, i., Moz. C12 66
Bazas, Fr. H6 14
Bazdār, Pak. G1 44
Bazi, China K2 34
Bazine, Ks., U.S. D4 123
Be, Nosy, i., Madag. n23 67b
Beach, Il., U.S. h9 120
Beach, N.D., U.S. C1 141
Beachburg, Ont., Can. B8 103

Name — Map Ref. — Page

Berchtesgaden, Ger. H13 10
Berdigest'ach, Russia E17 28
Berdsk, Russia G8 28
Berdyans'k, Ukr. H5 26
Berdychiv, Ukr. H3 26
Berea, Ky., U.S. C5 124
Berea, Oh., U.S. A4 142
Berea, S.C., U.S. B3 147
Berehomet, Ukr. A9 20
Berehove, Ukr. G22 10
Berekua, Dom. G14 94
Berendejevo, Russia E22 22
Berens, stm., Can. C3 100
Berens River, Man., Can. C3 100
Beresford, S.D., U.S. D9 148
Berettyó (Barcău), stm., Eur. B5 20
Berevo, Madag. q21 67b
Berezajka, Russia D16 22
Berezino, Bela. G11 22
Berezino, Bela. H11 22
Berezniki, Russia F9 26
Berezyne, Ukr. C13 20
Berg, Nor. G15 6
Berga, Spain C13 16
Bergama, Tur. J11 20
Bergamo, Italy D4 18
Bergantín, Ven. B10 84
Bergara, Spain B9 16
Bergby, Swe. K15 6
Bergen (Mons), Bel. H4 12
Bergen, Ger. C10 10
Bergen, Neth. C6 12
Bergen, Nor. K9 6
Bergen, N.Y., U.S. B3 139
Bergen, co., N.J., U.S. A4 137
Bergen aan Zee, Neth. C6 12
Bergen [auf Rügen], Ger. A13 10
Bergenfield, N.J., U.S. B4 137
Bergen op Zoom, Neth. E5 12
Berger, Mo., U.S. C6 132
Bergerac, Fr. H7 14
Bergholz, Oh., U.S. B5 142
Bergisch Gladbach, Ger. E7 10
Bergland, Mi., U.S. m12 129
Bergman, Ar., U.S. A2 111
Bergoo, W.V., U.S. C4 155
Bergsche Maas, stm., Neth. E6 12
Bergsjö, Swe. K15 6
Bergstrom Air Force Base, mil., Tx., U.S. D4 150
Berguent, Mor. C9 62
Bergues, Fr. B9 14
Berhala, Selat, strt., Indon. O8 40
Beringa, ostrov, i., Russia F25 28
Bering Sea C2 86
Bering Strait, strt. m18 106a
Berino, N.M., U.S. E3 138
Berja, Spain I9 16
Berkane, Mor. C9 62
Berkeley, Ont., Can. C4 103
Berkeley, Ca., U.S. D2 112
Berkeley, Mo., U.S. f13 132
Berkeley, R.I., U.S. B4 146
Berkeley, co., S.C., U.S. E8 147
Berkeley, co., W.V., U.S. B6 155
Berkeley Heights, N.J., U.S. B4 137
Berkeley Springs, W.V., U.S. B6 155
Berkley, Mi., U.S. F7 129
Berkner Island, i., Ant. C1 73
Berks, co., Pa., U.S. F9 145
Berkshire, Vt., U.S. B3 152
Berkshire, co., Eng., U.K. J12 8
Berkshire, co., Ma., U.S. B1 128
Berkshire Hills, hills, Ma., U.S. B1 128
Berlaimont, Fr. B10 14
Berland, stm., Alta., Can. C1 98
Berlin, Ger. C13 10
Berlin, S. Afr. I8 66
Berlin, Ct., U.S. C5 114
Berlin, Ga., U.S. E3 117
Berlin, Md., U.S. D7 127
Berlin, N.H., U.S. B4 136
Berlin, N.J., U.S. D3 137
Berlin, N.Y., U.S. C7 139
Berlin, Oh., U.S. B4 142
Berlin, Pa., U.S. G4 145
Berlin, Wi., U.S. E5 156
Berlin, Mount, mtn., Ant. C10 73
Berlin Corners, Vt., U.S. C3 152
Berlin Heights, Oh., U.S. A3 142
Berlin Lake, res., Oh., U.S. A4 142
Berlin Mountain, mtn., U.S. A1 128
Bermejillo, Mex. E8 90
Bermejo, Arg. F5 80
Bermejo, stm., Arg. F5 80
Bermejo, stm., S.A. C9 80
Bermejo, Paso del, S.A. G3 80
Bermeo, Spain B9 16
Bermuda, dep., N.A. B12 88
Bern (Berne), Switz. E7 13
Bern, Ks., U.S. C8 123
Bern (Berne), state, Switz. E8 13
Bernalda, Italy I11 18
Bernalillo, N.M., U.S. B3 138
Bernalillo, co., N.M., U.S. C3 138
Bernard, Me., U.S. D4 126
Bernardsville, N.J., U.S. B3 137
Bernasconi, Arg. I7 80
Bernau bei Berlin, Ger. C13 10
Bernay, Fr. C7 14
Bernburg, Ger. D11 10
Berne, In., U.S. C8 121
Berner Alpen, mts., Switz. F7 13
Bernice, La., U.S. B3 125
Bernice, Ok., U.S. A7 143
Bernie, Mo., U.S. E8 132
Bernier Bay, b., N.W. Ter., Can. B15 96
Bernina, mts., Eur. F12 13
Bernina, Passo del, Switz. F13 13
Bernina, Piz, mtn., Eur. F16 14
Bernville, Pa., U.S. F9 145
Beromünster, Switz. H8 10
Berón de Astrada, Arg. D10 80
Beroroha, Madag. r21 67b
Ber'ostovica, Bela. H6 22
Beroun, Czech Rep. F14 10
Berounka, stm., Czech Rep. F13 10
Berovo, Mac. H6 20
Ber'oza, Bela. I7 22
Ber'ozovo, Russia E11 26
Berrechid, Mor. D7 62
Berri, Austl. J4 70
Berrien, co., Ga., U.S. E3 117
Berrien, co., Mi., U.S. F4 129
Berrien Springs, Mi., U.S. G4 129
Berrigan, Austl. J6 70
Berriyyane, Alg. D12 62
Berry, Al., U.S. B2 108
Berry, Ky., U.S. B5 124
Berry, hist. reg., Fr. E9 14
Berry Creek, stm., Alta., Can. D5 98
Berryessa, Lake, res., Ca., U.S. C2 112
Berry Hill, Tn., U.S. g10 149
Berry Islands, is., Bah. B6 94
Berrys Chapel, Tn., U.S. B5 149
Berryton, Ga., U.S. B1 117
Berryville, Ar., U.S. A2 111
Berryville, Va., U.S. A5 153
Berseba, Nmb. F3 66
Bersenbrück, Ger. C7 10
Bershad', Ukr. A13 20
Bertha, Mn., U.S. D3 130
Berthierville, Que., Can. C4 104
Berthold, N.D., U.S. A4 141
Berthoud, Co., U.S. A5 113
Berthoud Pass, Co., U.S. B5 113
Bertie, co., N.C., U.S. A5 140
Bertoua, Cam. H9 54
Bertram, Tx., U.S. D4 150
Bertrand, Mo., U.S. E8 132
Bertrand, Ne., U.S. D6 134
Beruri, Braz. I12 84
Berwick, N.S., Can. D5 101
Berwick, Il., U.S. C3 120
Berwick, Ia., U.S. e8 122
Berwick, La., U.S. E4 125
Berwick, Me., U.S. E2 126
Berwick, Pa., U.S. D9 145
Berwick-upon-Tweed, Eng., U.K. F11 8
Berwind, W.V., U.S. D3 155
Berwyn, Alta., Can. A2 98
Berwyn, Il., U.S. k9 120
Berwyn, Ne., U.S. C6 134
Berwyn, Pa., U.S. o20 145
Besalampy, Madag. p21 67b
Besançon, Fr. E13 14
Besbes, Alg. M2 18
Bešenkoviči, Bela. F12 22
Beskid Mountains, mts., Eur. F20 10
Beskra, Alg. C13 62
Besni, Tur. C4 48
Besor, Naḥal, val., Asia F2 50
Bessarabia, hist. reg., Mol. C12 20
Besse, Nig. F12 64
Bessemer, Al., U.S. B3 108
Bessemer, Mi., U.S. n11 129
Bessemer, Pa., U.S. E1 145
Bessemer City, N.C., U.S. B1 140
Bessie, Ok., U.S. B3 143
Best'ach, Russia E17 28
Bestobe, Kaz. G12 26
Betafo, Madag. q22 67b
Betanzos, Bol. H9 82
Betanzos, Spain B3 16
Betaré Oya, Cam. G9 54
Betatakin Ruin, hist., Az., U.S. A5 110
Betbetti, Sud. J3 60
Bete Hor, Eth. L10 60
Bétera, Spain F11 16
Bétérou, Benin G11 64
Bet Guvrin, Isr. E3 50
Bet Ha'arava, W.B. E5 50
Bethal, S. Afr. F9 66
Bethalto, Il., U.S. E3 120
Bethanien, Nmb. F3 66
Bethany, Ont., Can. C6 103
Bethany, Ct., U.S. D4 114
Bethany, Il., U.S. D5 120
Bethany, Mo., U.S. A3 132
Bethany, Ok., U.S. B4 143
Bethany, W.V., U.S. A4 155
Bethany Beach, De., U.S. F5 115
Bethel, Ak., U.S. C7 109
Bethel, Ct., U.S. D2 114
Bethel, De., U.S. F3 115
Bethel, Ky., U.S. B6 124
Bethel, Me., U.S. D2 126
Bethel, N.C., U.S. B5 140
Bethel, Oh., U.S. D1 142
Bethel, Ok., U.S. C7 143
Bethel, Pa., U.S. F9 145
Bethel, Vt., U.S. D3 152
Bethel Acres, Ok., U.S. B5 143
Bethel Park, Pa., U.S. k14 145
Bethel Springs, Tn., U.S. B3 149
Bethesda, Ar., U.S. B4 111
Bethesda, Md., U.S. C3 127
Bethesda, Oh., U.S. B4 142
Bethlehem, S. Afr. G9 66
Bethlehem, Ct., U.S. C3 114
Bethlehem, Ga., U.S. C3 117
Bethlehem, N.H., U.S. B3 136
Bethlehem, Pa., U.S. E11 145
Bethlehem see Bayt Laḥm, W.B. E4 50
Bethpage, Tn., U.S. A5 149
Bethune, Sask., Can. G3 105
Béthune, Fr. B9 14
Bethune, Co., U.S. B8 113
Bethune, S.C., U.S. C7 147
Beticos, Sistemas, mts., Spain H8 16
Betijoque, Ven. C7 84
Betioky, Madag. s21 67b
Betlica, Russia G16 22
Betong, Thai. L6 40
Betoota, Austl. E4 70
Betpak-Dala, des., Kaz. H12 26
Betroka, Madag. s22 67b
Bet Sh'ean, Isr. C5 50
Bet Shemesh, Isr. E4 50
Betsiboka, stm., Madag. p22 67b
Betsie, Point, c., Mi., U.S. D4 129
Betsioky, Madag. r21 67b
Betsy Layne, Ky., U.S. C7 124
Bette, mtn., Libya D4 56
Bettendorf, Ia., U.S. C7 122
Bettsville, Oh., U.S. A2 142
Betūl, India J7 44
Betzdorf, Ger. E7 10
Beulah, Al., U.S. C4 108
Beulah, Co., U.S. C6 113
Beulah, Mi., U.S. D4 129
Beulah, Ms., U.S. B3 131
Beulah, N.D., U.S. B4 141
Beulah, Wy., U.S. B8 157
Beulah, Lake, l., Ms., U.S. B3 131
Beulaville, N.C., U.S. C5 140
Bevensen, Ger. B10 10
B. Everett Jordan Lake, res., N.C., U.S. B3 140
Beverley, Austl. F3 68
Beverley, Eng., U.K. H13 8
Beverley Head, c., Newf., Can. D2 102
Beverly, Ks., U.S. C6 123
Beverly, Ma., U.S. A6 128
Beverly, N.J., U.S. C3 137
Beverly, Oh., U.S. C4 142
Beverly, Tn., U.S. m14 149
Beverly, W.V., U.S. C5 155
Beverly Hills, Ca., U.S. m12 112
Beverly Shores, In., U.S. A4 121
Beverwijk, Neth. D6 12
Bewdley, Ont., Can. C6 103
Bexar, co., Tx., U.S. E3 150
Bexley, Oh., U.S. m11 142
Beyçayırı, Tur. I10 20
Beylul, Erit. H3 47
Beypazarı, Tur. G14 4
Beyşehir Gölü, l., Tur. H14 4
Bezaha, Madag. s21 67b
Bežanicy, Russia E12 22
Bezau, Aus. H9 10
Bežeck, Russia D19 22
Bezerra, stm., Braz. B5 79
Béziers, Fr. I10 14
Bezmein, Turk. B15 48
Bhadrak, India J12 44
Bhadrāvati, India F3 46
Bhāg, Pak. F2 44
Bhāgalpur, India H12 44
Bhakkar, Pak. E4 44
Bhakkar, Pak. E4 44
Bhaktapur, Nepal G11 44
Bhamo, Mya. B4 40
Bhandāra, India J8 44
Bharatpur, India G7 44
Bharatpur, Nepal G11 44
Bharūch, India J5 44
Bhātāpāra, India B6 46
Bhātpāra, India I13 44
Bhāvnagar, India J5 44
Bhawānipatna, India C7 46
Bhera, Pak. D5 44
Bhilai, India J9 44
Bhīlwāra, India H6 44
Bhind, India G8 44
Bhiwandi, India C2 46
Bhiwāni, India F7 44
Bhongīr, India D5 46
Bhopāl, India I7 44
Bhubaneshwar, India J11 44
Bhuj, India I3 44
Bhusāwal, India J6 44
Bhutan (Druk-Yul), ctry., Asia D13 42
Bia, stm., Afr. H8 64
Biá, stm., Braz. I9 84
Bia, Phou, mtn., Laos E7 40
Biabo, stm., Peru B3 82
Biafra, Bight of, Afr. H8 54
Biak, i., Indon. F10 38
Biała, Pol. E17 10
Biała Podlaska, Pol. C23 10
Biała Rawska, Pol. D20 10
Białogard, Pol. A16 10
Białystok, Pol. B23 10
Bianco, Monte (Mont Blanc), mtn., Eur. G13 14
Biarritz, Fr. I5 14
Biasca, Switz. F10 13
Bibā, Egypt C6 60
Bibai, Japan d16 36a
Bibala, Ang. D2 58
Bibb, co., Al., U.S. C2 108
Bibb, co., Ga., U.S. D3 117
Bibb City, Ga., U.S. D2 117
Biberach an der Riss, Ger. G9 10
Bibiani, Ghana H8 64
Biblián, Ec. I3 84
Bic, Que., Can. A9 104
Bic, Île du, i., Que., Can. A9 104
Bicas, Braz. F7 79
Bicaz, Rom. C10 20
Bičevinka, Russia B20 22
Biche, Lac la, l., Alta., Can. B4 98
Bichena, Eth. L10 60
Bickett Knob, mtn., W.V., U.S. D4 155
Bickle Knob, mtn., W.V., U.S. C5 155
Bicknell, In., U.S. G3 121
Bicknell, Ut., U.S. E4 151
Bicol Peninsula, pen., Phil. C7 38
Bicske, Hung. H18 10
Bicudo, stm., Braz. E6 79
Bīd, India C3 46
Bida, Nig. G13 64
Bīdar, India D4 46
Biddeford, Me., U.S. E2 126
Bidian, China C2 34
Bidwell, Mount, mtn., Ca., U.S. B3 112
Bieber, Ca., U.S. B3 112
Biecz, Pol. F21 10
Biedenkopf, Ger. E8 10
Biel (Bienne), Switz. D7 13
Bielawa, Pol. E16 10
Bielefeld, Ger. C8 10
Bielersee, l., Switz. D7 13
Biella, Italy D3 18
Bielsko-Biała, Pol. F19 10
Bielsk Podlaski, Pol. C23 10
Bienfait, Sask., Can. H4 105
Bien Hoa, Viet. I9 40
Bienville, La., U.S. B3 125
Bienville, co., La., U.S. B2 125
Bienville, Lac, l., Que., Can. g12 104
Big, stm., Mo., U.S. c7 132
Biga, Tur. I11 20
Big A Mountain, mtn., Va., U.S. e9 153
Big Arm, Mt., U.S. C2 133
Big Bald, mtn., U.S. f10 140
Big Bald, mtn., Ga., U.S. B2 117
Big Bald Mountain, mtn., N.B., Can. B3 101
Big Baldy, mtn., Id., U.S. E3 119
Big Baldy Mountain, mtn., Mt., U.S. D6 133
Big Bay, Mi., U.S. B3 129
Big Bay De Noc, b., Mi., U.S. C4 129
Big Bayou, stm., Ar., U.S. D4 111
Big Bear City, Ca., U.S. E5 112
Big Beaver, Sask., Can. H3 105
Big Belt Mountains, mts., Mt., U.S. D5 133
Big Bend, Swaz. F10 66
Big Bend, Wi., U.S. n11 156
Big Bend Dam, S.D., U.S. C6 148
Big Bend National Park, Tx., U.S. E1 150
Big Birch Lake, l., Mn., U.S. E4 130
Big Black, stm., Me., U.S. B3 126
Big Black, stm., Ms., U.S. C3 131
Big Blue, stm., In., U.S. E6 121
Big Burro Mountains, mts., N.M., U.S. E1 138
Big Butt, mtn., Tn., U.S. C11 149
Big Cabin, Ok., U.S. A6 143
Big Cabin Creek, stm., Ok., U.S. A6 143
Big Canyon, val., Tx., U.S. D1 150
Big Chino Wash, val., Az., U.S. B3 110
Big Clifty, Ky., U.S. C3 124
Big Coal, stm., W.V., U.S. C3 155
Big Costilla Peak, mtn., N.M., U.S. A4 138
Big Creek, B.C., Can. D6 99
Big Creek, Ca., U.S. D4 112
Big Creek, Ky., U.S. C6 124
Big Creek, W.V., U.S. C2 155
Big Creek, stm., Ar., U.S. C5 111
Big Creek, stm., In., U.S. H2 121
Big Creek, stm., In., U.S. G7 121
Big Creek, stm., Ks., U.S. D4 123
Big Creek, stm., La., U.S. B4 125
Big Creek, stm., Ms., U.S. D5 131
Big Creek, stm., Mo., U.S. C3 132
Big Creek, stm., Tn., U.S. e8 149
Big Creek Lake, res., Al., U.S. E1 108
Big Creek Peak, mtn., Id., U.S. E5 119
Big Cypress Indian Reservation, Fl., U.S. F5 116
Big Cypress Swamp, sw., Fl., U.S. F5 116
Big Darby Creek, stm., Oh., U.S. C2 142
Big Delta, Ak., U.S. C10 109
Big Desert, des., Austl. J4 70
Big Dry Creek, stm., Mt., U.S. C10 133
Big Duke Dam, N.C., U.S. B2 140
Big Eau Pleine, stm., Wi., U.S. D3 156
Big Eau Pleine Reservoir, res., Wi., U.S. D4 156
Big Elk Creek, stm., Md., U.S. A6 127
Bigelow, Ar., U.S. B3 111
Bigelow, Mount, mtn., Me., U.S. C2 126
Big Escambia Creek, stm., U.S. D2 108
Big Falls, Mn., U.S. B5 130
Big Flat Mountain, mtn., Va., U.S. B4 153
Big Flats, N.Y., U.S. C4 139
Bigfork, Mn., U.S. C5 130
Bigfork, Mt., U.S. B2 133
Big Fork, stm., Mn., U.S. B5 130
Big Frog Mountain, mtn., Tn., U.S. D9 149
Biggar, Sask., Can. E1 105
Biggar, Scot., U.K. F10 8
Biggers, Ar., U.S. A5 111
Biggersville, Ms., U.S. A5 131
Biggs, Ca., U.S. C3 112
Biggsville, Il., U.S. C3 120
Big Hatchet Peak, mtn., N.M., U.S. F1 138
Big Hole, stm., Mt., U.S. E4 133
Big Hole National Battlefield, hist., Mt., U.S. E3 133
Big Horn, Wy., U.S. B5 157
Big Horn, co., Mt., U.S. E9 133
Big Horn, co., Wy., U.S. B4 157
Bighorn, stm., U.S. B5 106
Bighorn Canyon National Recreation Area, U.S. F8 133
Bighorn Lake, res., U.S. E8 133
Bighorn Mountains, mts., U.S. B5 157
Big Horn Mountains, mts., Az., U.S. D2 110
Big Island, Va., U.S. C3 153
Big Island, i., N.W. Ter., Can. D18 96
Big Island, i., N.W. Ter., Can. f8 102
Big Kandiyohi Lake, l., Mn., U.S. F4 130
Big Knob, mtn., Pa., U.S. F6 145
Big Knob, mtn., Va., U.S. f9 153
Big Lake, Mn., U.S. E5 130
Big Lake, Tx., U.S. D2 150
Big Lake, l., Me., U.S. C5 126
Biglerville, Pa., U.S. G7 145
Big Lookout Mountain, mtn., Or., U.S. C9 144
Big Lost, stm., Id., U.S. F5 119
Big Mossy Point, c., Man., Can. C2 100
Big Mountain, mtn., Nv., U.S. B2 135
Big Muddy, stm., Il., U.S. F4 120
Big Muddy Creek, stm., Mt., U.S. B12 133
Bignasco, Switz. F10 13
Big Nemaha, stm., Ne., U.S. D10 134
Bignona, Sen. E1 64
Big North Mountain, mts., Va., U.S. B4 153
Big Otter, stm., Va., U.S. C3 153
Big Pine, Ca., U.S. D4 112
Big Pine Creek, stm., In., U.S. D3 121
Big Pine Lake, l., Mn., U.S. D3 130
Big Pine Mountain, mtn., Ca., U.S. E4 112
Big Piney, Wy., U.S. D2 157
Big Piney, stm., Mo., U.S. D5 132
Big Piney Creek, stm., Ar., U.S. B2 111
Big Pipe Creek, stm., Md., U.S. A3 127
Bigpoint, Ms., U.S. E5 131
Big Raccoon Creek, stm., In., U.S. E4 121
Big Rapids, Mi., U.S. E5 129
Big Rib, stm., Wi., U.S. C3 156
Big River, Sask., Can. D2 105
Big River, Ca., U.S. E6 112
Big Rock, Il., U.S. B5 120
Big Rock, Tn., U.S. A4 149
Big Rock Mountain, mtn., Ar., U.S. h10 111
Big Run, Pa., U.S. E4 145
Big Sable Point, c., Mi., U.S. D4 129
Big Sandy, Mt., U.S. B6 133
Big Sandy, Tn., U.S. A3 149
Big Sandy, Tx., U.S. C5 150
Big Sandy, stm., U.S. C2 155
Big Sandy, stm., Az., U.S. C2 110
Big Sandy, stm., Tn., U.S. B3 149
Big Sandy, stm., Wy., U.S. D3 157
Big Sandy Creek, stm., Co., U.S. C8 113
Big Sandy Creek, stm., Mt., U.S. B6 133
Big Sandy Creek, stm., W.V., U.S. C3 155
Big Sandy Lake, l., Mn., U.S. D5 130
Big Sandy Reservoir, res., Wy., U.S. D3 157
Big Satilla Creek, stm., Ga., U.S. E4 117
Big Savage Mountain, mtn., U.S. k12 127
Big Sheep Mountain, mtn., Mt., U.S. C11 133
Big Shiney Mountian, mtn., Pa., U.S. n18 145
Big Sioux, stm., U.S. E9 148
Big Slough, stm., Ga., U.S. F2 117
Big Smoky Valley, val., Nv., U.S. E4 135
Big Snowy Mountains, mts., Mt., U.S. D7 133
Big Southern Butte, mtn., Id., U.S. F5 119
Big South Fork, stm., Ky., U.S. k13 124
Big Spencer Mountain, mtn., Me., U.S. C3 126
Big Spring, Tx., U.S. C2 150
Big Springs, Ne., U.S. C3 134
Big Spruce Knob, mtn., W.V., U.S. C4 155
Big Squaw Mountain, mtn., Me., U.S. C3 126
Big Stone, co., Mn., U.S. E2 130
Bigstone, stm., Man., Can. B4 100
Big Stone City, S.D., U.S. B9 148
Big Stone Gap, Va., U.S. f9 153
Big Stone Lake, l., U.S. E2 130
Big Sunflower, stm., Ms., U.S. B3 131
Big Sur, Ca., U.S. D3 112
Big Thompson, stm., Co., U.S. A5 113
Big Timber, Mt., U.S. E7 133
Big Top, mtn., Tn., U.S. B5 149
Big Trout Lake, l., Ont., Can. n17 103
Biguaçu, Braz. D14 80
Big Valley, Alta., Can. C4 98
Big Walnut Creek, stm., Oh., U.S. m11 142
Big Warrambool, stm., Austl. G8 70
Big Water, Ut., U.S. F4 151
Big Wells, Tx., U.S. E3 150
Big Wills Creek, stm., Al., U.S. A3 108
Bigwood, Ont., Can. A4 103
Big Wood, stm., Id., U.S. F4 119
Bihać, Bos. E10 18
Bihār, India H11 44
Bihār, state, India H11 44
Bihor, co., Rom. B6 20
Bija, stm., Russia G15 26
Bijagós, Arquipélago dos, is., Gui.-B. F1 64
Bījār, Iran D9 48
Bijeljina, Bos. E3 20
Bijelo Polje, Yugo. F3 20
Bijie, China F8 30
Bijou Creek, stm., Co., U.S. B6 113
Bijsk, Russia G9 28
Bīkāner, India F5 44
Bikeqi, China C9 30
Bikin, Russia H18 28
Bikin, stm., Russia H19 28
Bikini, atoll, Marsh. Is. G20 158
Bikoro, Zaire B3 58
Bilac, Braz. F3 79
Bilāspur, India I10 44
Bila Tserkva, Ukr. H4 26
Bilauktaung Range, mts., Asia H5 40
Bilbao, Spain B9 16
Bilhorod-Dnistrovs'kyy, Ukr. H4 26
Bilian, China G9 34
Bīlimora, India B2 46
Bilin, Mya. F4 40
Bílina, Czech Rep. E13 10
Bilk Creek Mountains, mts., Nv., U.S. B3 135
Billabong Creek, stm., Austl. J6 70
Billerica, Ma., U.S. A5 128
Billings, Mo., U.S. D4 132
Billings, Mt., U.S. E8 133
Billings, Ok., U.S. A4 143
Billings, co., N.D., U.S. B2 141
Billings Heights, Mt., U.S. E8 133
Billingsley, Al., U.S. C3 108
Billom, Fr. G10 14
Bill Williams, stm., Az., U.S. C1 110
Bill Williams Mountain, mtn., Az., U.S. B3 110
Bilma, Niger E9 54
Biloela, Austl. E9 70
Biloxi, Ms., U.S. E5 131
Biloxi, stm., Ms., U.S. E4 131
Biloxi Bay, b., Ms., U.S. f8 131
Biltmore Forest, N.C., U.S. f10 140
Bilugyun Island, i., Mya. F4 40
Bilwaskarma, Nic. C11 92
Bilyayivka, Ukr. C14 20
Bim, W.V., U.S. n12 155
Bimbān, Egypt E7 60
Bimbila, Ghana G10 64
Bimini Islands, is., Bah. B5 94
Binche, Bel. H5 12
Bindura, Zimb. E6 58
Binéfar, Spain D12 16
Binford, N.D., U.S. B7 141
Binga, Monte, mtn., Afr. B11 66
Bingamon Creek, stm., W.V., U.S. k10 155
Bingara, Austl. G9 70
Bingen, Ger. F7 10
Bingen, Wa., U.S. D4 154
Binger, Ok., U.S. B3 143
Bingham, Me., U.S. C3 126
Bingham, co., Id., U.S. F6 119
Bingham Lake, Mn., U.S. G3 130
Binghamton, N.Y., U.S. C5 139
Bingöl, Tur. B6 48
Binhai (Dongkan), China A8 34
Binjai, Indon. M5 40
Binscarth, Man., Can. D1 100
Bintan, Pulau, i., Indon. N8 40
Bintang, Gam. E1 64
Bintimani, mtn., S.L. G4 64
Bint Jubayl, Leb. B4 50
Bintulu, Malay. E5 38
Binxian, China D8 30
Binyamina, Isr. C3 50
Binyang, China C10 40
Bin Yauri, Nig. F12 64
Bíobío, prov., Chile I3 80
Bíobío, stm., Chile F3 80
Biobío, stm., Chile I2 80
Bioko, i., Eq. Gui. J14 64
Bippus, In., U.S. C6 121
Birāk, Libya C3 56
Bi'r al-Uzam, Libya B2 60
Birao, Cen. Afr. Rep. L2 60
Birātnagar, Nepal F4 30
Birch, stm., W.V., U.S. C4 155
Birch Hills, Sask., Can. E3 105
Birch Island, B.C., Can. D8 99
Birch Island, i., Man., Can. C2 100
Birch Lake, l., Mn., U.S. C7 130
Birch River, Man., Can. C1 100
Birch Rock Hill, mtn., Pa., U.S. F3 145
Birch Run, Mi., U.S. E7 129
Birch Tree, Mo., U.S. E6 132
Birchwood, Ct., U.S. B5 114
Birchwood, Tn., U.S. D9 149
Birchwood, Wi., U.S. C2 156
Birchwood City, Md., U.S. *f9 127
Birchy Bay, Newf., Can. D4 102
Bird City, Ks., U.S. C2 123
Bird Creek, stm., Ok., U.S. A6 143
Bird Island, Mn., U.S. F4 130
Bird Island, i., N.C., U.S. D4 140
Bird Island, sci., S. Geor. A1 73
Bird Islet, i., Austl. D11 68
Birdsboro, Pa., U.S. F10 145
Birds Creek, Ont., Can. B7 103
Birdseye, In., U.S. H4 121
Birdsong, Ar., U.S. B5 111
Birdsville, Austl. E3 70
Birdtown, N.C., U.S. f9 140
Birdum, Austl. C6 68
Birdwood Creek, stm., Ne., U.S. C4 134
Birecik, Tur. C4 48
Bir el Ater, Alg. C15 62
Bir Enzaran, W. Sah. I3 62
Birigui, Braz. F3 79
Biril'ussy, Russia F16 26
Bīrjand, Iran E15 48
Birkenhead, Eng., U.K. H10 8
Birkfeld, Aus. H15 10
Birmingham, Eng., U.K. I12 8
Birmingham, Al., U.S. B3 108
Birmingham, Ia., U.S. D6 122
Birmingham, Mi., U.S. F7 129
Birmingham, Mo., U.S. h11 132
Birmitrapur, India I11 44
Bîr Mogreïn (Fort-Trinquet), Maur. H5 62
Birnamwood, Wi., U.S. D4 156
Birni, Benin F10 64
Birnie, Man., Can. D2 100
Birni Ngaouré, Niger E11 64
Birnin Gwari, Nig. F13 64
Birni Nkonni, Niger E12 64
Birnin Kudu, Nig. F14 64
Birobidžan, Russia H18 28
Birobijan see Jevrej, state, Russia H18 28
Biron, Wi., U.S. D4 156
Birrie, stm., Austl. G7 70
Birsay, Sask., Can. F2 105
Birsk, Russia F9 26
Birtle, Man., Can. D1 100
Bir'usa, stm., Russia F17 26
Biržai, Lith. E7 22
Bîrzava, stm., Eur. D5 20
Bisbee, Az., U.S. F6 110
Bisbee, N.D., U.S. A6 141
Biscarrosse, Fr. H5 14
Biscay, Bay of, b., Eur. H3 14
Biscayne, Key, i., Fl., U.S. s13 116
Biscayne Bay, b., Fl., U.S. G6 116
Biscayne National Monument, Fl., U.S. G6 116
Biscayne Park, Fl., U.S. s13 116
Bisceglie, Italy H11 18
Bischofswerda, Ger. D14 10
Biscoe, Ar., U.S. C4 111
Biscoe, N.C., U.S. B3 140
Biscoe Islands, is., Ant. B12 73
Biscucuy, Ven. C8 84
Bisha, Erit. J9 60
Bishkek see Biškek, Kyrg. I12 26
Bisho, S. Afr. I8 66
Bishop, Ca., U.S. D4 112
Bishop, Ga., U.S. C3 117
Bishop, Tx., U.S. F4 150
Bishop Auckland, Eng., U.K. G12 8
Bishop's Falls, Newf., Can. D4 102
Bishops Mills, Ont., Can. C9 103
Bishopton, Que., Can. D6 104
Bishopville, S.C., U.S. C7 147
Bishrah, Ma'ṭan, well, Libya F2 60
Biškek (Frunze), Kyrg. I12 26
Bislig, Phil. D8 38
Bismarck, Ar., U.S. C2 111

Name | Map Ref. | Page

Bismarck, Il., U.S. C6 120
Bismarck, Mo., U.S. D7 132
Bismarck, N.D., U.S. C5 141
Bismarck Archipelago, is., Pap. N. Gui. k16 68a
Bismarck Range, mts., Pap. N. Gui. m15 68a
Bismarck Sea, Pap. N. Gui. I18 158
Bismuna, Laguna, b., Nic. C11 92
Bison, Ks., U.S. D4 123
Bison, S.D., U.S. B3 148
Bison Peak, mtn., Co., U.S. B5 113
Bissau, Gui.-B. F3 54
Bissett, Man., Can. D4 100
Bissikrima, Gui. F4 64
Bissorã, Gui.-B. E2 64
Bistineau, Lake, res., La., U.S. B2 125
Bistrița, Rom. B8 20
Bistrița, stm., Rom. C10 20
Bistrița-Năsăud, co., Rom. B8 20
Bisztynek, Pol. A20 10
Bitam, Gabon A2 58
Bitburg, Ger. F6 10
Bitche, Fr. C14 14
Bitlis, Tur. B7 48
Bitola, Mac. H5 20
Bitonto, Italy H11 18
Bitter Creek, stm., Wy., U.S. E4 157
Bitterfeld, Ger. D12 10
Bitterfontein, S. Afr. H4 66
Bitter Lake, l., S.D., U.S. B8 148
Bittern Lake, Alta., Can. C4 98
Bitterroot, stm., Mt., U.S. D2 133
Bitterroot Range, mts., U.S. B3 119
Bitti, Italy I4 18
Bitung, Indon. E8 38
Bituruna, Braz. D13 80
Biwabik, Mn., U.S. C6 130
Biwa-ko, l., Japan L11 36
Bixby, Ok., U.S. B6 143
Biyang, China C2 34
Bizana, S. Afr. H9 66
Bizerte, Tun. L4 18
Bizkaiko, prov., Spain B9 16
Bjala Slatina, Bul. F7 20
Bjelovar, Cro. D11 18
Bjork Lake, l., Sask., Can. E4 105
Björna, Swe. J16 6
Bjørnøya (Bear Island), i., Sval. B2 24
Bla, Mali E7 64
Black, Al., U.S. D4 108
Black (Lixian) (Da), stm., Asia D8 40
Black, stm., Man., Can. D4 100
Black, stm., Az., U.S. D5 110
Black, stm., Ar., U.S. B4 111
Black, stm., La., U.S. C4 125
Black, stm., Mi., U.S. E8 129
Black, stm., N.Y., U.S. B4 139
Black, stm., N.C., U.S. C4 140
Black, stm., S.C., U.S. D8 147
Black, stm., Vt., U.S. B4 152
Black, stm., Vt., U.S. E3 152
Black, stm., Wi., U.S. D3 156
Black, Bayou, stm., La., U.S. E5 125
Blackall, Austl. E6 70
Black Bear Creek, stm., Ok., U.S. A4 143
Blackbeard Island, i., Ga., U.S. E5 117
Black Bear Island Lake, l., Sask., Can. B3 105
Blackbird, De., U.S. C3 115
Blackburn, Mo., U.S. B4 132
Blackburn, Mount, mtn., Ak., U.S. C11 109
Black Butte, mtn., Mt., U.S. F5 133
Black Butte, mtn., Wy., U.S. B5 157
Black Butte Lake, res., Ca., U.S. C2 112
Black Canyon, val., Co., U.S. C3 113
Black Canyon City, Az., U.S. C3 110
Black Canyon of the Gunnison National Monument, Co., U.S. C3 113
Black Creek, B.C., Can. E5 99
Black Creek, N.C., U.S. B5 140
Black Creek, Wi., U.S. D5 156
Black Creek, stm., U.S. B1 138
Black Creek, stm., Ms., U.S. D4 131
Black Creek, stm., S.C., U.S. B7 147
Black Diamond, Alta., Can. D3 98
Black Diamond, Al., U.S. g6 108
Black Diamond, Wa., U.S. B4 154
Blackduck, Mn., U.S. C4 130
Black Duck, stm., Can. E15 96
Black Eagle, Mt., U.S. C5 133
Black Earth, Wi., U.S. E4 156
Blackey, Ky., U.S. C7 124
Blackfalds, Alta., Can. C4 98
Blackfeet Indian Reservation, Mt., U.S. B4 133
Blackfoot, Alta., Can. C5 98
Blackfoot, Id., U.S. F6 119
Blackfoot, Mt., U.S. B4 133
Blackfoot, stm., Mt., U.S. C3 133
Blackfoot Mountains, mts., Id., U.S. F7 119
Blackfoot Reservoir, res., Id., U.S. G7 119
Blackford, co., In., U.S. D7 121
Black Forest, Co., U.S. C6 113
Black Forest see Schwarzwald, mts., Ger. G8 10
Blackhall Mountain, mtn., Wy., U.S. E6 157
Black Hawk, S.D., U.S. C2 148
Black Hawk, co., Ia., U.S. B5 122
Black Hills, mts., U.S. C2 148
Blackie, Alta., Can. D4 98
Blackjack Mountain, mtn., Ga., U.S. h8 117
Black Lake, Que., Can. C6 104
Black Lake, l., Sask., Can. m7 105
Black Lake, l., Mi., U.S. C6 129
Black Lake, l., N.Y., U.S. f9 139
Black Lake Bayou, stm., La., U.S. B2 125
Black Lick, Pa., U.S. F3 145
Blacklick Estates, Oh., U.S. *m11 142
Black Mesa, mtn., Az., U.S. A5 110
Black Mesa, mtn., Ok., U.S. e8 143
Black Mingo Creek, stm., S.C., U.S. D9 147
Blackmore, Mount, mtn., Mt., U.S. E6 133
Black Mountain, N.C., U.S. f10 140
Black Mountain, mtn., U.S. D7 124
Black Mountain, mtn., Az., U.S. E4 110
Black Mountain, mtn., Co., U.S. A5 113
Black Mountain, mtn., Id., U.S. C3 119
Black Mountain, mtn., Mt., U.S. D4 133
Black Mountain, mtn., Or., U.S. B7 144
Black Mountain, mtn., Wy., U.S. B5 157
Black Mountain, mtn., Wy., U.S. D7 157
Black Mountains, mts., Az., U.S. B1 110
Black Oak, Ar., U.S. B5 111
Black Peak, mtn., Az., U.S. C1 110
Black Pine Peak, mtn., Id., U.S. G5 119
Black Pond, l., Me., U.S. B3 126
Blackpool, Eng., U.K. H10 8
Black Range, mts., N.M., U.S. D2 138
Black River, N.Y., U.S. A5 139
Black River Falls, Wi., U.S. D3 156
Black Rock, Ar., U.S. A4 111
Black Rock, N.M., U.S. B1 138
Black Rock, S. Geor. G8 78
Black Rock Desert, des., Nv., U.S. B3 135
Black Rock Range, mts., Nv., U.S. B3 135
Blacksburg, S.C., U.S. A4 147
Blacksburg, Va., U.S. C2 153
Black Sea G15 4
Blacks Fork, stm., U.S. E3 157
Blacks Harbour, N.B., Can. D3 101
Blackshear, Ga., U.S. E4 117
Blackshear, Lake, res., Ga., U.S. E2 117
Black Squirrel Creek, stm., Co., U.S. C6 113
Blackstock, Ont., Can. C6 103
Blackstone, Ma., U.S. B4 128
Blackstone, Va., U.S. C5 153
Blackstone, stm., R.I., U.S. B4 146
Black Thunder Creek, stm., Wy., U.S. C8 157
Black Tickle, Newf., Can. B4 102
Blackville, N.B., Can. C4 101
Blackville, S.C., U.S. E5 147
Black Volta (Volta Noire), stm., Afr. G6 54
Blackwalnut Point, c., Md., U.S. C5 127
Black Warrior, stm., Al., U.S. C2 108
Blackwater, Mo., U.S. C5 132
Blackwater, stm., Ire. I5 8
Blackwater, stm., Fl., U.S. u15 116
Blackwater, stm., Md., U.S. D5 127
Blackwater, stm., N.H., U.S. D3 136
Blackwater, stm., Va., U.S. D6 153
Blackwater Reservoir, res., N.H., U.S. D3 136
Blackwell, Ar., U.S. B3 111
Blackwell, Ok., U.S. A4 143
Blackwood, N.J., U.S. D2 137
Blackwood Creek, stm., Ne., U.S. D4 134
Bladel, Neth. F7 12
Bladen, Ne., U.S. D7 134
Bladen, co., N.C., U.S. C4 140
Bladenboro, N.C., U.S. C4 140
Bladensburg, Md., U.S. f9 127
Blades, De., U.S. F3 115
Bladgrond, S. Afr. G4 66
Bladon Springs, Al., U.S. D1 108
Bladworth, Sask., Can. F2 105
Blaeberry, stm., B.C., Can. D2 98
Blagodarnyj, Russia H6 26
Blagoevgrad, Bul. G7 20
Blagoveščensk, Russia G17 28
Blain, Fr. E5 14
Blaine, Me., U.S. B5 126
Blaine, Mn., U.S. m12 130
Blaine, Tn., U.S. C10 149
Blaine, Wa., U.S. A3 154
Blaine, co., Id., U.S. F4 119
Blaine, co., Mt., U.S. B7 133
Blaine, co., Ne., U.S. C6 134
Blaine, co., Ok., U.S. B3 143
Blaine Creek, stm., Ky., U.S. B7 124
Blaine Lake, Sask., Can. E2 105
Blair, Ne., U.S. C9 134
Blair, Ok., U.S. C2 143
Blair, W.V., U.S. n12 155
Blair, Wi., U.S. D2 156
Blair, co., Pa., U.S. E5 145
Blair Athol, Austl. D7 70
Blairsburg, Ia., U.S. B4 122
Blairstown, Ia., U.S. C5 122
Blairstown, Mo., U.S. C4 132
Blairsville, Ga., U.S. B3 117
Blairsville, Pa., U.S. F3 145
Blake Island, i., Wa., U.S. e11 154
Blakely, Ga., U.S. E2 117
Blakely, Pa., U.S. m18 145
Blake Point, c., Mi., U.S. h10 129
Blakesburg, Ia., U.S. D5 122
Blanc, Mont (Monte Bianco), mtn., Eur. G13 14
Blanca, Co., U.S. D5 113
Blanca, Bahía, b., Arg. J7 80
Blanca, Isla, i., Peru C2 82
Blanca, Punta, c., Chile C3 80
Blanca, Sierra, mtn., Tx., U.S. o12 150
Blanca Peak, mtn., Co., U.S. D5 113
Blancas, Peñas, mts., Nic. D9 92
Blanchard, Id., U.S. A2 119
Blanchard, La., U.S. B2 125
Blanchard, Mi., U.S. E5 129
Blanchard, Ok., U.S. B4 143
Blanchard, Pa., U.S. D6 145
Blanchard, stm., Oh., U.S. A1 142
Blanchardville, Wi., U.S. F4 156
Blanche, Lake, l., Austl. G3 70
Blanchester, Oh., U.S. C2 142
Blanco, N.M., U.S. A2 138
Blanco, Tx., U.S. D3 150
Blanco, co., Tx., U.S. D3 150
Blanco, stm., Arg. E4 80
Blanco, stm., Bol. E10 82
Blanco, stm., Ec. G3 84
Blanco, Cabo, c., C.R. H9 92
Blanco, Cape, c., Or., U.S. E2 144
Bland, Mo., U.S. C6 132
Bland, Va., U.S. C1 153
Bland, co., Va., U.S. C1 153
Blandburg, Pa., U.S. E5 145
Blandford, Ma., U.S. B2 128
Blanding, Ut., U.S. F6 151
Blandinsville, Il., U.S. C3 120
Blanes, Spain D14 16
Blanford, In., U.S. E2 121
Blangy-sur-Bresle, Fr. C8 14
Blankenberge, Bel. F3 12
Blankenburg, Ger. D10 10
Blanquilla, Isla, i., Ven. B10 84
Blantyre, Mwi. E7 58
Blarney Castle, hist., Ire. J5 8
Blasdell, N.Y., U.S. C2 139
Blatná, Czech Rep. F13 10
Blaufelden, Ger. F9 10
Blawnox, Pa., U.S. k14 145
Blaye-et-Sainte-Luce, Fr. G6 14
Blayney, Austl. I8 70
Bleckley, co., Ga., U.S. D3 117
Bledsoe, co., Tn., U.S. D8 149
Bleiburg, Aus. I14 10
Blekinge Län, co., Swe. M14 6
Blencoe, Ia., U.S. C1 122
Blende, Co., U.S. C6 113
Blenheim, Ont., Can. E3 103
Blenheim, N.Z. D4 72
Blennerhassett, W.V., U.S. B3 155
Blessing, Tx., U.S. E4 150
Bletterans, Fr. F12 14
Blevins, Ar., U.S. D2 111
Blind, stm., La., U.S. h10 125
Blind River, Ont., Can. A2 103
Bliss, Id., U.S. G4 119
Blissfield, Mi., U.S. G7 129
Blitar, Indon. k16 39a
Blocher, In., U.S. G6 121
Blocker, Ok., U.S. B6 143
Block Island, R.I., U.S. h7 146
Block Island, i., R.I., U.S. h7 146
Block Island Sound, strt., U.S. G2 146
Blockton, Ia., U.S. D3 122
Blodgett, Mo., U.S. D8 132
Bloemfontein, S. Afr. G8 66
Bloemhof, S. Afr. F7 66
Blois, Fr. E8 14
Blönduós, Ice. B3 6a
Blood Mountain, mtn., Ga., U.S. B3 117
Bloodsworth Island, i., Md., U.S. D5 127
Bloodvein, stm., Can. D3 100
Bloomdale, Oh., U.S. A2 142
Bloomer, Ar., U.S. B1 111
Bloomer, Wi., U.S. C2 156
Bloomfield, N.B., Can. D4 101
Bloomfield, Ont., Can. D7 103
Bloomfield, Ct., U.S. B5 114
Bloomfield, In., U.S. F4 121
Bloomfield, Ia., U.S. D5 122
Bloomfield, Ky., U.S. C4 124
Bloomfield, Mo., U.S. E8 132
Bloomfield, Ne., U.S. B8 134
Bloomfield, N.J., U.S. h8 137
Bloomfield, N.M., U.S. A2 138
Bloomfield Hills, Mi., U.S. o15 129
Bloomingburg, Oh., U.S. C2 142
Bloomingdale, Ga., U.S. D5 117
Bloomingdale, Il., U.S. k8 120
Bloomingdale, In., U.S. E3 121
Bloomingdale, Mi., U.S. F5 129
Bloomingdale, N.J., U.S. A4 137
Bloomingdale, Tn., U.S. C11 149
Blooming Grove, Tx., U.S. C4 150
Blooming Prairie, Mn. U.S. G5 130
Bloomington, Id., U.S. G7 119
Bloomington, Il., U.S. C4 120
Bloomington, In., U.S. F4 121
Bloomington, Mn., U.S. F5 130
Bloomington, Ne., U.S. D6 134
Bloomington, Tx., U.S. E4 150
Bloomington, Wi., U.S. F3 156
Bloomington, Lake, res., Il., U.S. C5 120
Bloomsburg, Pa., U.S. E9 145
Bloomsdale, Mo., U.S. C7 132
Bloomville, Oh., U.S. A2 142
Blora, Indon. j15 39a
Blossburg, Al., U.S. f7 108
Blossburg, Pa., U.S. C7 145
Blossom, Tx., U.S. C5 150
Bloumet, Alg. I14 62
Blount, co., Al., U.S. B3 108
Blount, co., Tn., U.S. D10 149
Blountstown, Fl., U.S. B1 116
Blountsville, Al., U.S. A3 108
Blountville, Tn., U.S. C11 149
Blovice, Czech Rep. F13 10
Blowering Reservoir, res., Austl. J8 70
Blowing Rock, N.C., U.S. A1 140
Bloxom, Va., U.S. C7 153
Bludenz, Aus. H9 10
Blue, Ok., U.S. C5 143
Blue, stm., Co., U.S. B4 113
Blue, stm., In., U.S. H5 121
Blue, stm., Mo., U.S. k10 132
Blue, stm., Ok., U.S. C5 143
Blue, Bayou, stm., La., U.S. E5 125
Blue, Mount, mtn., Me., U.S. D2 126
Blue Ash, Oh., U.S. o13 142
Blueberry, stm., B.C., Can. A7 99
Blue Buck Knob, hill, Mo., U.S. E5 132
Blue Buck Point, c., La., U.S. D2 125
Blue Creek, Al., U.S. g6 108
Blue Creek, W.V., U.S. m13 155
Blue Creek, stm., Ne., U.S. C3 134
Blue Creek, stm., W.V., U.S. m13 155
Blue Cypress Lake, l., Fl., U.S. E6 116
Blue Diamond, Nv., U.S. G6 135
Blue Earth, Mn., U.S. G4 130
Blue Earth, co., Mn., U.S. G4 130
Blue Earth, stm., Mn., U.S. G4 130
Bluefield, Va., U.S. C1 153
Bluefield, W.V., U.S. D3 155
Bluefields, Nic. E11 92
Bluefields, Bahía de, b., Nic. F11 92
Blue Grass, Ia., U.S. C7 122
Blue Hill, Me., U.S. D4 126
Blue Hill, Ne., U.S. D7 134
Blue Hill Range, hills, Ma., U.S. h11 128
Blue Hills, Ct., U.S. B5 114
Bluehole, Ky., U.S. C6 124
Blue Island, Il., U.S. B6 120
Bluejoint Lake, l., Or., U.S. E7 144
Blue Knob, mtn., Pa., U.S. F4 145
Blue Lake, Ca., U.S. B2 112
Blue Mesa Reservoir, res., Co., U.S. C3 113
Blue Mound, Il., U.S. D4 120
Blue Mound, Ks., U.S. D8 123
Blue Mountain, Al., U.S. B4 108
Blue Mountain, Ar., U.S. B2 111
Blue Mountain, Ms., U.S. A4 131
Blue Mountain, mtn., Newf., Can. C3 102
Blue Mountain, mtn., Ar., U.S. C1 111
Blue Mountain, mtn., Mt., U.S. C12 133
Blue Mountain, mtn., N.H., U.S. A4 136
Blue Mountain, mtn., N.M., U.S. D2 138
Blue Mountain, mtn., N.Y., U.S. B6 139
Blue Mountain, mtn., Pa., U.S. F6 145
Blue Mountain Lake, res., Ar., U.S. B2 111
Blue Mountain Peak, mtn., Jam. E6 94
Blue Mountains, mts., U.S. B3 106
Blue Nile (Al-Bahr al-Azraq) (Abay), stm., Afr. F7 56
Blue Point, Me., U.S. g7 126
Blue Rapids, Ks., U.S. C7 123
Blue Ridge, Alta., Can. B3 98
Blue Ridge, In., U.S. E6 121
Blue Ridge, Va., U.S. C3 153
Blue Ridge, mts., U.S. D10 106
Blue Ridge Lake, res., Ga., U.S. B2 117
Blue Ridge Summit, Pa., U.S. G7 145
Blue River, B.C., Can. C8 99
Blue River, Or., U.S. C4 144
Blue River, Wi., U.S. E3 156
Bluesky, Alta., Can. A1 98
Blue Springs, Al., U.S. D4 108
Blue Springs, Mo., U.S. h11 132
Blue Springs, Ne., U.S. D9 134
Bluestone, stm., W.V., U.S. D3 155
Bluestone Lake, res., U.S. D4 155
Bluevale, Ont., Can. D3 103
Bluewater, N.M., U.S. B2 138
Bluewell, W.V., U.S. D3 155
Bluff, N.Z. G2 72
Bluff, Ut., U.S. F6 151
Bluff City, Ar., U.S. D2 111
Bluff City, Il., U.S. E4 120
Bluff City, Tn., U.S. C11 149
Bluff Creek, stm., Ks., U.S. E4 123
Bluff Creek, stm., Ok., U.S. A4 143
Bluff Lake, res., Ms., U.S. B5 131
Bluff Mountain, mtn., Vt., U.S. B5 152
Bluff Park, Al., U.S. g7 108
Bluffs, Il., U.S. D3 120
Bluffton, Ga., U.S. E2 117
Bluffton, In., U.S. C7 121
Bluffton, Mn., U.S. D3 130
Bluffton, Oh., U.S. B2 142
Bluffton, S.C., U.S. G6 147
Bluford, Il., U.S. E5 120
Blumberg, Ger. H8 10
Blumenau, Braz. D14 80
Blunt, S.D., U.S. C6 148
Bly, Or., U.S. E5 144
Blying Sound, strt., Ak., U.S. h17 109
Blyth, Ont., Can. D3 103
Blythe, Ca., U.S. F6 112
Blythe, Ga., U.S. C4 117
Blytheville, Ar., U.S. B6 111
Bø, Nor. L11 6
Bø, Nor. G14 6
Bo, S.L. H4 64
Boaco, Nic. E9 92
Boaco, dept., Nic. E9 92
Boa Esperança, Braz. F6 79
Boa Esperança, Represa, res., Braz. E10 76
Boalsburg, Pa., U.S. E6 145
Boa Nova, Braz. C8 79
Boardman, Oh., U.S. A5 142
Boardman, Or., U.S. B7 144
Boatman, Austl. F7 70
Boa Vista, Braz. F12 84
Boa Vista, i., C.V. m17 64a
Boavita, Col. D6 84
Boaz, Al., U.S. A3 108
Bobai, China C10 40
Bobbili, India C7 46
Bobbio, Italy E4 18
Bobcaygeon, Ont., Can. C6 103
Böblingen, Ger. G9 10
Bobo Dioulasso, Burkina F7 64
Bobolice, Pol. B16 10
Bobonaza, stm., Ec. I4 84
Bobonong, Bots. C9 66
Bobr, Bela. G12 22
Bobrujsk, Bela. H12 22
Bobtown, Pa., U.S. G2 145
Bobures, Ven. C7 84
Boby, Pic, mtn., Madag. s22 67b
Boca Brava, Isla, i., Pan. I12 92
Boca Chica Key, i., Fl., U.S. H5 116
Boca Ciega Bay, b., Fl., U.S. p10 116
Boca del Monte, Pan. I12 92
Boca de Pozo, Ven. B10 84
Boca do Acre, Braz. C8 82
Boca Grande, Fl., U.S. F4 116
Bocaiúva, Braz. D7 79
Bocanda, C. Iv. H7 64
Boca Raton, Fl., U.S. F6 116
Bocas del Toro, Pan. C1 84
Bocas del Toro, prov., Pan. I12 92
Bocas del Toro, Archipiélago de, is., Pan. H12 92
Bocay, Nic. C9 92
Bocay, stm., Nic. C9 92
Bochnia, Pol. F20 10
Bocholt, Ger. D6 10
Bochum, Ger. D7 10
Bochum, S. Afr. D9 66
Bocón, Caño, stm., Col. F8 84
Boconó, Ven. C7 84
Bodajbo, Russia F14 28
Bodcau Creek, stm., Ar., U.S. D2 111
Bodcaw, Ar., U.S. D2 111
Bode, Ia., U.S. B3 122
Bodega Head, c., Ca., U.S. C2 112
Bodegraven, Neth. D6 12
Bodélé, reg., Chad E4 56
Boden, Swe. I17 6
Bodensee (Lake Constance), l., Eur. E16 14
Bodh Gaya, India E11 42
Bodie Island, i., N.C., U.S. B7 140
Bodinayakkanūr, India G4 46
Bodkin Point, c., Md., U.S. B5 127
Bodo, Alta., Can. C5 98
Bodø, Nor. H14 6
Bodoquena, Serra da, plat., Braz. I13 82
Bodrog, stm., Eur. A5 20
Bodrum, Tur. L11 20
Boelus, Ne., U.S. C7 134
Boende, Zaire B4 58
Boeo, Capo, c., Italy L7 18
Boerne, Tx., U.S. E3 150
Boeuf, stm., La., U.S. C4 125
Boeuf, Bayou, stm., La., U.S. D3 125
Boeuf, Lake, l., La., U.S. k10 125
Bogale, Mya. F3 40
Bogalusa, La., U.S. D6 125
Bogan, stm., Austl. H7 70
Bogandé, Burkina E9 64
Bogard, Mo., U.S. B4 132
Bogart, Ga., U.S. C3 117
Bogata, Tx., U.S. C5 150
Boğazlıyan, Tur. B3 48
Bogda Shan, mts., China C4 30
Boger City, N.C., U.S. B1 140
Boggabri, Austl. H9 70
Boggstown, In., U.S. E6 121
Bogo, Phil. C7 38
Bogol'ubovo, Russia E23 22
Bogong, Mount, mtn., Austl. K7 70
Bogor, Indon. j13 39a
Bogorodick, Russia H21 22
Bogorodsk, Russia E26 22
Bogotá see Santa Fe de Bogotá, Col. E5 84
Bogota, N.J., U.S. h8 137
Bogota, Tn., U.S. A2 149
Bogotol, Russia F9 28
Bogou, Togo F10 64
Bogra, Bngl. H13 44
Bogué, Maur. C2 64
Bogue, Ks., U.S. C4 123
Bogue Chitto, Ms., U.S. D3 131
Bogue Chitto, stm., U.S. D5 125
Bogue Inlet, b., N.C., U.S. C5 140
Bogue Phalia, stm., Ms., U.S. B3 131
Boguševsk, Bela. G13 22
Bo Hai (Gulf of Chihli), b., China E8 32
Bohai Haixia, strt., China E9 32
Bohain-en-Vermandois, Fr. C10 14
Bohan, Bel. I6 12
Bohemia see Čechy, hist. reg., Czech Rep. F14 10
Bohemian Forest, mts., Eur. F12 10
Bohicon, Benin H11 64
Bohol, i., Phil. D7 38
Bohol Sea, Phil. D7 38
Boiaçu, Braz. H12 84
Boiestown, N.B., Can. C3 101
Boigu Island, i., Austl. A8 68
Boiling Springs, N.C., U.S. B1 140
Boiling Springs, Pa., U.S. F7 145
Boipeba, Ilha de, i., Braz. B9 79
Bois, Rio dos, stm., Braz. E3 79
Bois Blanc Island, i., Mi., U.S. C6 129
Bois Brule, stm., Wi., U.S. B2 156
Boischâtel, Que., Can. C6 104
Boisdale, N.S., Can. C9 101
Bois D'Arc, Mo., U.S. D4 132
Bois-des-Filion, Que., Can. p19 104
Bois de Sioux, stm., Mn., U.S. E2 130
Boise, Id., U.S. F2 119
Boise, co., Id., U.S. F3 119
Boise City, Ok., U.S. e8 143
Bois Fort, Mn., U.S. B5 130
Boissevain, Man., Can. E1 100
Boissevain, Va., U.S. e10 153
Boistfort Peak, mtn., Wa., U.S. C2 154
Boisvert, Pointe au, c., Que., Can. A8 104
Bojayá, stm., Col. D4 84
Bojeador, Cape, c., Phil. I19 39b
Bojnūrd, Iran C14 48
Bojonegoro, Indon. j15 39a
Boju, Nig. H13 64
Bojuru, Braz. F13 80
Bokani, Nig. G12 64
Bokchito, Ok., U.S. C5 143
Boké, Gui. F2 64
Bokeelia, Fl., U.S. F4 116
Bokhara, stm., Austl. G7 70
Bokino, Russia I24 22
Bokolako, Sen. E3 64
Bokoshe, Ok., U.S. B7 143
Boksitogorsk, Russia B16 22
Bokungu, Zaire B4 58
Bol, Cro. F11 18
Bolama, Gui.-B. F2 64
Bolaños, stm., Mex. F8 90
Bolaños de Calatrava, Spain G8 16
Bolbec, Fr. C7 14
Bolchov, Russia H19 22
Bolckow, Mo., U.S. A3 132
Boles, Ar., U.S. C1 111
Bolesławiec, Pol. D15 10
Boleszkowice, Pol. C14 10
Boley, Ok., U.S. B5 143
Bolgatanga, Ghana F9 64
Bolhrad, Ukr. D12 20
Boli, China B13 30
Boli, Sud. N5 60
Boligee, Al., U.S. C1 108
Boling, Tx., U.S. E5 150
Bolingbrook, Il., U.S. k8 120
Bolinger, Al., U.S. D1 108
Bolívar, Col. E4 84
Bolívar, Col. G4 84
Bolívar, Col. E4 84
Bolívar, Peru B3 82
Bolivar, Mo., U.S. D4 132
Bolivar, N.Y., U.S. C2 139
Bolivar, Oh., U.S. B4 142
Bolivar, Tn., U.S. B3 149
Bolivar, W.V., U.S. B7 155
Bolívar, state, Ven. D11 84
Bolívar, prov., Ec. H3 84
Bolívar, dept., Col. C5 84
Bolivar, co., Ms., U.S. B3 131
Bolívar, Cerro, mtn., Ven. D11 84
Bolivar, Lake, l., Ms., U.S. B3 131
Bolívar, Pico, mtn., Ven. C7 84
Bolivia, ctry., S.A. F8 74
Bollène, Fr. H11 14
Bollinger, co., Mo., U.S. D7 132
Bollnäs, Swe. K15 6
Bollon, Austl. G7 70
Bollullos par del Condado, Spain H5 16
Bolobo, Zaire B3 58
Bolochovo, Russia G20 22
Bologna, Italy E6 18
Bolognesi, Peru B5 82
Bologoje, Russia D17 22
Bolomba, Zaire A3 58
Bolonchén de Rejón, Mex. G15 90
Bolotnoje, Russia F14 26
Bolovens, Plateau des, plat., Laos G9 40
Bol'šaja Balachn'a, stm., Russia C12 28
Bol'šaja Čheta, stm., Russia D14 26
Bol'šaja Čuja, stm., Russia F14 28
Bol'šaja Ižora, Russia B12 22
Bol'šaja Kuonamka, stm., Russia D13 28
Bol'šaja Lipovica, Russia I24 22
Bol'šaja Murta, Russia F16 26
Bol'šaja Višera, Russia C15 22
Bol'šakovo, Russia G4 22
Bolsena, Italy G6 18
Bolsena, Lago di, l., Italy G6 18
Bol'šereck, Russia G23 28
Bol'ševik, Bela. I13 22
Bol'ševik, Russia E21 28
Bol'ševik, ostrov, i., Russia B12 28
Bol'šezemel'skaja Tundra, reg., Russia D9 26
Bol'šoj An'uj, stm., Russia D24 28
Bol'šoj Begičev, ostrov, i., Russia C14 28
Bol'šoje Michajlovskoje, Russia E21 22
Bol'šoje Polpino, Russia H17 22
Bol'šoj Jenisej, stm., Russia G11 28
Bol'šoj L'achovskij, ostrov, i., Russia C20 28
Bol'šoj Tal'cy, Russia B16 22
Bol'šoj T'uters, ostrov, i., Russia B10 22
Bol'šoj Uzen', stm., Eur. H7 26
Bolton, Ms., U.S. C3 131
Bolton, N.C., U.S. C4 140
Bolton Lakes, l., Ct., U.S. B6 114
Bolton Landing, N.Y., U.S. B7 139
Bolu, Tur. G14 4
Boluntay, China B15 44
Boluochi, China B7 32
Bóly, Hung. J18 10
Bolzano (Bozen), Italy C6 18
Boma, Zaire C2 58
Bomaderry, Austl. J9 70
Bombala, Austl. K8 70
Bombarral, Port. F2 16
Bombay, India C2 46
Bombay Hook Island, i., De., U.S. C4 115
Bomberai, Semenanjung, pen., Indon. F9 38
Bom Despacho, Braz. E6 79
Bomei, China M4 34
Bom Jardim de Goiás, Braz. D2 79
Bom Jesus da Lapa, Braz. B7 79
Bom Jesus de Goiás, Braz. E4 79
Bomoseen, Vt., U.S. D2 152
Bomoseen, Lake, l., Vt., U.S. D2 152
Bom Retiro, Braz. D14 80
Bom Sucesso, Braz. G3 79
Bom Sucesso, Braz. F13 82
Bomu (Mbomou), stm., Afr. H5 56
Bon, Cap, c., Tun. L6 18
Bon Accord, Alta., Can. C4 98
Bon Air, Tn., U.S. D8 149
Bon Air, Va., U.S. C5 153
Bonaire, Ga., U.S. D3 117
Bonaire, i., Neth. Ant. H10 94
Bonampak, hist., Mex. I14 90
Bonanza, Nic. C10 92
Bonanza, Ar., U.S. B1 111
Bonanza, Or., U.S. E5 144
Bonanza Peak, mtn., Wa., U.S. A5 154
Bonao, Dom. Rep. E9 94
Bonaparte, Ia., U.S. D6 122
Bonaparte, Mount, mtn., Wa., U.S. A6 154
Bonaparte Archipelago, is., Austl. B5 68
Bonaparte Lake, l., B.C., Can. D7 99
Bon Aqua, Tn., U.S. B4 149
Bonarbridge, Scot., U.K. D9 8
Bonarcado, Italy I3 18
Bonasila Dome, mtn., Ak., U.S. C7 109
Bonaventure, Que., Can. A4 101
Bonavista, Newf., Can. D5 102
Bonavista, Cape, c., Newf., Can. D5 102

Name	Map Ref.	Page
Breukelen, Neth.	D7	12
Brevard, N.C., U.S.	f10	140
Brevard, co., Fl., U.S.	E6	116
Breves, Braz.	D8	76
Brevoort Lake, l., Mi., U.S.	B6	129
Brewarrina, Austl.	G7	70
Brewer, Me., U.S.	D4	126
Brewster, Ks., U.S.	C2	123
Brewster, Ma., U.S.	C7	128
Brewster, Mn., U.S.	G3	130
Brewster, N.Y., U.S.	D7	139
Brewster, Oh., U.S.	B4	142
Brewster, Wa., U.S.	A6	154
Brewster, co., Tx., U.S.	E1	150
Brewster, Kap, c., Grnld.	B17	86
Brewster, Lake, l., Austl.	I7	70
Brewster Islands, is., Ma., U.S.	g12	128
Brewton, Al., U.S.	D2	108
Brewton, Ga., U.S.	D4	117
Brežice, Slvn.	D10	18
Brézina, Alg.	D11	62
Breznik, Bul.	G6	20
Bria, Cen. Afr. Rep.	N1	60
Brian Boru Peak, mtn., B.C., Can.	B4	99
Briançon, Fr.	H13	14
Brian Head, mtn., Ut., U.S.	F3	151
Briare, Fr.	E9	14
Bricelyn, Mn., U.S.	G5	130
Briceni, Mol.	A11	20
Briceville, Tn., U.S.	C9	149
Brick [Township], N.J., U.S.	C4	137
Bricquebec, Fr.	C5	14
Bridal Veil Falls, wtfl, Ut., U.S.	C4	151
Bridesville, B.C., Can.	E8	99
Bridgeboro, Ga., U.S.	E3	117
Bridgehampton, N.Y., U.S.	n16	139
Bridgeport, Al., U.S.	A4	108
Bridgeport, Ca., U.S.	C4	112
Bridgeport, Ct., U.S.	E3	114
Bridgeport, Il., U.S.	E6	120
Bridgeport, Mi., U.S.	E7	129
Bridgeport, Ne., U.S.	C2	134
Bridgeport, Oh., U.S.	B5	142
Bridgeport, Pa., U.S.	o20	145
Bridgeport, Tx., U.S.	C4	150
Bridgeport, Wa., U.S.	B6	154
Bridgeport, W.V., U.S.	B4	155
Bridger, Mt., U.S.	E8	133
Bridger Peak, mtn., Wy., U.S.	E5	157
Bridger Range, mts., Mt., U.S.	E6	133
Bridgeton, In., U.S.	E3	121
Bridgeton, Mo., U.S.	C7	132
Bridgeton, N.J., U.S.	E2	137
Bridgeton, N.C., U.S.	B5	140
Bridgetown, Austl.	F3	68
Bridgetown, Barb.	H15	94
Bridgetown, N.S., Can.	E4	101
Bridgeville, De., U.S.	F3	115
Bridgeville, Pa., U.S.	k13	145
Bridgewater, Austl.	N7	70
Bridgewater, N.S., Can.	E5	101
Bridgewater, Ct., U.S.	C2	114
Bridgewater, Ia., U.S.	C3	122
Bridgewater, Me., U.S.	B5	126
Bridgewater, Ma., U.S.	C6	128
Bridgewater, N.J., U.S.	B3	137
Bridgewater, S.D., U.S.	D8	148
Bridgewater, Vt., U.S.	D3	152
Bridgewater, Va., U.S.	B4	153
Bridgman, Mi., U.S.	G4	129
Bridgton, Me., U.S.	D2	126
Bridgwater, Eng., U.K.	J10	8
Bridport, Vt., U.S.	D2	152
Brie, reg., Fr.	D10	14
Briec, Fr.	D2	14
Brielle, N.J., U.S.	C4	137
Brienne-le-Château, Fr.	D11	14
Brienz, Switz.	E9	13
Brienzersee, l., Switz.	E9	13
Brier Creek, stm., Ga., U.S.	C5	117
Briercrest, Sask., Can.	G3	105
Brierfield, Al., U.S.	B3	108
Briery Knob, mtn., W.V., U.S.	C4	155
Briey, Fr.	C12	14
Brig, Switz.	F9	13
Brigantine, N.J., U.S.	E4	137
Brigantine Beach, N.J., U.S.	E4	137
Brig Bay, Newf., Can.	C3	102
Brigden, Ont., Can.	E2	103
Briggs Marsh, sw., R.I., U.S.	F6	146
Briggsville, Wi., U.S.	E4	156
Brigham City, Ut., U.S.	B3	151
Brig Harbour Island, i., Newf., Can.	A3	102
Bright, Austl.	K7	70
Bright, Ont., Can.	D4	103
Brighton, Ont., Can.	C7	103
Brighton, Eng., U.K.	K13	8
Brighton, Al., U.S.	B3	108
Brighton, Co., U.S.	B6	113
Brighton, Il., U.S.	D3	120
Brighton, Ia., U.S.	C6	122
Brighton, Mi., U.S.	F7	129
Brighton, N.Y., U.S.	B3	139
Brighton, Tn., U.S.	B2	149
Brighton Downs, Austl.	D4	70
Brighton Indian Reservation, Fl., U.S.	E5	116
Brignoles, Fr.	I13	14
Brikama, Gam.	E1	64
Brilhante, stm., Braz.	F1	79
Brilliant, B.C., Can.	E9	99
Brilliant, Al., U.S.	A2	108
Brilliant, Oh., U.S.	B5	142
Brillion, Wi., U.S.	D5	156
Brilon, Ger.	D8	10
Brimfield, Il., U.S.	C4	120
Brimhall, N.M., U.S.	B1	138
Brimley, Mi., U.S.	B6	129
Brindisi, Italy	I12	18
Bringhurst, In., U.S.	C5	121
Brinje, Cro.	D10	18
Brinkley, Ar., U.S.	C4	111
Brinnon, Wa., U.S.	B3	154
Brinson, Ga., U.S.	F2	117
Brion, Île, i., Que., Can.	B8	101
Brioude, Fr.	G10	14
Briouze, Fr.	D6	14
Brisbane, Austl.	F10	70
Briscoe, co., Tx., U.S.	B2	150
Bristol, N.B., Can.	C2	101
Bristol, Eng., U.K.	J11	8
Bristol, Co., U.S.	C8	113
Bristol, Ct., U.S.	C4	114
Bristol, Fl., U.S.	B2	116
Bristol, Ga., U.S.	E4	117
Bristol, Il., U.S.	B5	120
Bristol, In., U.S.	A6	121
Bristol, Me., U.S.	D4	126
Bristol, N.H., U.S.	C3	136
Bristol, R.I., U.S.	D5	146
Bristol, S.D., U.S.	B8	148
Bristol, Tn., U.S.	C11	149
Bristol, Vt., U.S.	C2	152
Bristol, Va., U.S.	f9	153
Bristol, co., Ma., U.S.	C5	128
Bristol, co., R.I., U.S.	D5	146
Bristol [Township], Pa., U.S.	F12	145
Bristolville, Oh., U.S.	A5	142
Bristow, Ne., U.S.	B7	134
Bristow, Ok., U.S.	B5	143
Britânia, Braz.	C3	79
Britannia Beach, B.C., Can.	E6	99
British Antarctic Territory, dep., S.A.	B1	73
British Columbia, prov., Can.	C6	99
British Honduras see Belize, ctry., N.A.	I15	90
British Indian Ocean Territory, dep., Afr.	J8	24
British Virgin Islands, dep., N.A.	E12	94
Brits, S. Afr.	E8	66
Britstown, S. Afr.	H6	66
Britt, Ia., U.S.	A4	122
Brittany see Bretagne, hist. reg., Fr.	D3	14
Britton, Mi., U.S.	G7	129
Britton, S.D., U.S.	B8	148
Brive-la-Gaillarde, Fr.	G8	14
Brixton, Austl.	D6	70
Brno, Czech Rep.	F16	10
Broa, Ensenada de la, b., Cuba	C3	94
Broad, stm., Ga., U.S.	B4	117
Broad, stm., S.C., U.S.	C5	147
Broadalbin, N.Y., U.S.	B6	139
Broadbent, Or., U.S.	E2	144
Broad Brook, Ct., U.S.	B5	114
Broad Creek, stm., De., U.S.	F3	115
Broadford, Scot., U.K.	D8	8
Broadford, Va., U.S.	f10	153
Broadkill, stm., De., U.S.	E4	115
Broadkill Beach, De., U.S.	E5	115
Broadlands, Il., U.S.	C6	120
Broad Run, stm., Va., U.S.	g11	153
Broad Sound, strt., Austl.	D8	70
Broad Sound Channel, strt., Austl.	D9	70
Broadus, Mt., U.S.	E11	133
Broadview, Sask., Can.	G4	105
Broadview, Mt., U.S.	D8	133
Broadview Heights, Oh., U.S.	h9	142
Broadwater, Ne., U.S.	C3	134
Broadwater, co., Mt., U.S.	D5	133
Broadway, N.C., U.S.	B3	140
Broadway, Va., U.S.	B4	153
Brocēni, Lat.	E5	22
Brochet, Man., Can.	f7	100
Brock, Sask., Can.	F1	105
Brock, Ne., U.S.	D10	134
Brocket, N.D., U.S.	A7	141
Brockport, N.Y., U.S.	B3	139
Brockton, Ma., U.S.	B5	128
Brockton, Mt., U.S.	B12	133
Brockton Reservoir, res., Ma., U.S.	h11	128
Brockville, Ont., Can.	C9	103
Brockway, Pa., U.S.	D4	145
Brocton, Il., U.S.	D6	120
Brocton, N.Y., U.S.	C1	139
Broderick, Sask., Can.	F2	105
Brodeur Peninsula, pen., N.W. Ter., Can.	B15	96
Brodhead, Ky., U.S.	C5	124
Brodhead, Wi., U.S.	F4	156
Brodheadsville, Pa., U.S.	E11	145
Brodnax, Va., U.S.	D4	153
Brodnica, Pol.	B19	10
Broken Arrow, Ok., U.S.	A6	143
Broken Bay, b., Austl.	I9	70
Broken Bow, Ne., U.S.	C6	134
Broken Bow, Ok., U.S.	C7	143
Broken Bow Lake, res., Ok., U.S.	C7	143
Broken Hill, Austl.	H4	70
Brokopondo, Sur.	B8	76
Brokopondo Stuwmeer, res., Sur.	C7	76
Brome, Que., Can.	D5	104
Brome, Lac, l., Que., Can.	D5	104
Bromley Mountain, mtn., Vt., U.S.	E3	152
Bromptonville, Que., Can.	D6	104
Bronaugh, Mo., U.S.	D3	132
Bronnicy, Russia	F21	22
Bronnoje, Bela.	I13	22
Bronson, Fl., U.S.	C4	116
Bronson, Ia., U.S.	B1	122
Bronson, Ks., U.S.	E8	123
Bronson, Mi., U.S.	G5	129
Bronte, Italy	L9	18
Bronte, Tx., U.S.	D2	150
Bronwood, Ga., U.S.	E2	117
Bronx, co., N.Y., U.S.	E7	139
Bronxville, N.Y., U.S.	h13	139
Brook, In., U.S.	C3	121
Brookdale, Man., Can.	D2	100
Brooke, co., W.V., U.S.	A4	155
Brookfield, N.S., Can.	D6	101
Brookfield, Ct., U.S.	D2	114
Brookfield, Il., U.S.	k9	120
Brookfield, Ma., U.S.	B3	128
Brookfield, Mo., U.S.	B4	132
Brookfield, Va., U.S.	*B5	153
Brookfield, Wi., U.S.	m11	156
Brookfield Center, Vt., U.S.	D2	152
Brookford, N.C., U.S.	B1	140
Brookhaven, Ms., U.S.	D3	131
Brookhaven, W.V., U.S.	h11	155
Brookings, Or., U.S.	E2	144
Brookings, S.D., U.S.	C9	148
Brookings, co., S.D., U.S.	C9	148
Brookland, Ar., U.S.	B5	111
Brooklandville, Md., U.S.	g10	127
Brooklawn, N.J., U.S.	D2	137
Brooklet, Ga., U.S.	D5	117
Brooklin, Me., U.S.	D4	126
Brookline, Ma., U.S.	B5	128
Brookline, N.H., U.S.	E3	136
Brooklyn, N.S., Can.	E5	101
Brooklyn, Al., U.S.	D3	108
Brooklyn, Ct., U.S.	B8	114
Brooklyn, In., U.S.	E5	121
Brooklyn, Ia., U.S.	C5	122
Brooklyn, Mi., U.S.	F6	129
Brooklyn, Ms., U.S.	D4	131
Brooklyn, Oh., U.S.	h9	142
Brooklyn, S.C., U.S.	B6	147
Brooklyn, Wi., U.S.	F4	156
Brooklyn Center, Mn., U.S.	E5	130
Brooklyn Park, Md., U.S.	h11	127
Brooklyn Park, Mn., U.S.	m12	130
Brookneal, Va., U.S.	C4	153
Brook Park, Oh., U.S.	h9	142
Brookport, Il., U.S.	F5	120
Brooks, Alta., Can.	D5	98
Brooks, Ky., U.S.	g11	124
Brooks, Me., U.S.	D3	126
Brooks, Mn., U.S.	C2	130
Brooks, Or., U.S.	h12	144
Brooks, co., Ga., U.S.	F3	117
Brooks, co., Tx., U.S.	F3	150
Brooks Air Force Base, mil., Tx., U.S.	k7	150
Brookshire, Tx., U.S.	E5	150
Brookside, Al., U.S.	f7	108
Brookside, Co., U.S.	C5	113
Brookside, De., U.S.	B3	115
Brookston, In., U.S.	C4	121
Brookston, Mn., U.S.	C6	130
Brooksville, Fl., U.S.	D4	116
Brooksville, Ky., U.S.	B5	124
Brooksville, Ms., U.S.	B5	131
Brookton, Austl.	F3	68
Brookvale, Co., U.S.	B5	113
Brookville, In., U.S.	F8	121
Brookville, Oh., U.S.	C1	142
Brookville, Pa., U.S.	D3	145
Brookville Lake, res., In., U.S.	E7	121
Brookwood, Al., U.S.	B2	108
Brookwood, N.J., U.S.	C4	137
Broomall, Pa., U.S.	p20	145
Broome, Austl.	C4	68
Broome, co., N.Y., U.S.	C5	139
Broomes Island, Md., U.S.	C4	127
Broomfield, Co., U.S.	B5	113
Broons, Fr.	D4	14
Brooten, Mn., U.S.	E3	130
Brora, Scot., U.K.	C10	8
Brossard, Que., Can.	q20	104
Brotas de Macaúbas, Braz.	B7	79
Brou, Fr.	D8	14
Broughton, Il., U.S.	F5	120
Broughty Ferry, Scot., U.K.	E11	8
Broussard, La., U.S.	D4	125
Brouwersdam, Neth.	E4	12
Brouwershaven, Neth.	E4	12
Broward, co., Fl., U.S.	F6	116
Browerville, Mn., U.S.	D4	130
Brown, co., Il., U.S.	D3	120
Brown, co., In., U.S.	F5	121
Brown, co., Ks., U.S.	C8	123
Brown, co., Mn., U.S.	F4	130
Brown, co., Ne., U.S.	B6	134
Brown, co., Oh., U.S.	D2	142
Brown, co., S.D., U.S.	B7	148
Brown, co., Tx., U.S.	D3	150
Brown, co., Wi., U.S.	D6	156
Brown, Point, c., Wa., U.S.	C1	154
Brown City, Mi., U.S.	E8	129
Brown Deer, Wi., U.S.	m12	156
Brownfield, Tx., U.S.	C1	150
Browning, Mo., U.S.	A4	132
Browning, Mt., U.S.	B3	133
Brownlee, Sask., Can.	G2	105
Brownlee Reservoir, res., U.S.	C10	144
Browns, Il., U.S.	E6	120
Browns, stm., Vt., U.S.	B2	152
Brownsboro, Ky., U.S.	g11	124
Browns Branch, stm., De., U.S.	E3	115
Brownsburg, Que., Can.	D3	104
Brownsburg, In., U.S.	E5	121
Brownsdale, Mn., U.S.	G6	130
Browns Inlet, b., N.C., U.S.	C5	140
Browns Mills, N.J., U.S.	D3	137
Browns Peak, mtn., Az., U.S.	D4	110
Brownstown, Il., U.S.	E5	120
Brownstown, In., U.S.	G5	121
Brownstown, Pa., U.S.	F9	145
Browns Valley, Mn., U.S.	E2	130
Brownsville, Fl., U.S.	s13	116
Brownsville, In., U.S.	E7	121
Brownsville, Ky., U.S.	C3	124
Brownsville, Mn., U.S.	G7	130
Brownsville, Or., U.S.	C4	144
Brownsville, Pa., U.S.	F2	145
Brownsville, Tn., U.S.	B2	149
Brownsville, Tx., U.S.	G4	150
Brownton, Mn., U.S.	F4	130
Brownton, W.V., U.S.	B4	155
Brownvale, Alta., Can.	A2	98
Brownville, Me., U.S.	C3	126
Brownville, N.Y., U.S.	A5	139
Brownville Junction, Me., U.S.	C3	126
Brownwood, Mo., U.S.	D5	132
Brownwood, Tx., U.S.	D3	150
Brownwood, Lake, res., Tx., U.S.	D3	150
Browse Island, i., Austl.	B4	68
Broxton, Ga., U.S.	E4	117
Broža, Bela.	I12	22
Bruay-en-Artois, Fr.	B9	14
Bruce, Alta., Can.	C4	98
Bruce, Ms., U.S.	B4	131
Bruce, S.D., U.S.	C9	148
Bruce, Wi., U.S.	C2	156
Bruce, Mount, mtn., Austl.	D3	68
Bruce Crossing, Mi., U.S.	m12	129
Brucefield, Ont., Can.	D3	103
Bruce National Park, Ont., Can.	B3	103
Bruce Peninsula, pen., Ont., Can.	B3	103
Bruceton, Tn., U.S.	A3	149
Bruceville, In., U.S.	G3	121
Bruchsal, Ger.	F8	10
Bruck an der Mur, Aus.	H15	10
Bruderheim, Alta., Can.	C4	98
Bruges (Brugge), Bel.	F3	12
Brugg, Switz.	D9	13
Brugge (Bruges), Bel.	F3	12
Brugge-Gent, Kanaal, Bel.	F3	12
Brühl, Ger.	E6	10
Bruinisse, Neth.	E5	12
Bruin Point, mtn., Ut., U.S.	D5	151
Bruja, Cerro, mtn., Pan.	H15	92
Brule, Ne., U.S.	C4	134
Brule, stm., U.S.	C5	156
Brûlé, Lac, l., Can.	F20	96
Brule Lake, l., Mn., U.S.	k9	130
Brumadinho, Braz.	F6	79
Brumado, Braz.	C8	79
Brumath, Fr.	D14	14
Brumley Mountain, mtn., Va., U.S.	f9	153
Brundidge, Al., U.S.	D4	108
Bruneau, Id., U.S.	G3	119
Bruneau, stm., U.S.	G3	119
Brunei, ctry., Asia	E5	38
Brunette Island, i., Newf., Can.	E4	102
Bruning, Ne., U.S.	D8	134
Brunkild, Man., Can.	E3	100
Bruno, Sask., Can.	E3	105
Bruno, Ne., U.S.	C9	134
Brunson, S.C., U.S.	F5	147
Brunswick see Braunschweig, Ger.	C10	10
Brunswick, Ga., U.S.	E5	117
Brunswick, In., U.S.	B2	121
Brunswick, Me., U.S.	E3	126
Brunswick, Md., U.S.	B2	127
Brunswick, Mo., U.S.	B4	132
Brunswick, Ne., U.S.	B8	134
Brunswick, N.C., U.S.	C4	140
Brunswick, Oh., U.S.	A4	142
Brunswick, co., N.C., U.S.	C4	140
Brunswick, co., Va., U.S.	D5	153
Brunswick, Península, pen., Chile	G2	78
Brunswick Naval Air Station, mil., Me., U.S.	E3	126
Bruntál, Czech Rep.	F17	10
Brus, Laguna de, b., Hond.	B10	92
Brush, Co., U.S.	A7	113
Brushy Mountain, mtn., Va., U.S.	C1	153
Brushy Mountains, mts., N.C., U.S.	B1	140
Brusly, La., U.S.	D4	125
Brusovo, Russia	D18	22
Brusque, Braz.	D14	80
Brussels see Bruxelles, Bel.	G5	12
Brussels, Ont., Can.	D3	103
Bruthen, Austl.	K7	70
Bruxelles (Brussel) (Brussels), Bel.	G5	12
Bruyères, Fr.	D13	14
Bruzual, Ven.	C8	84
Bryan, Oh., U.S.	A1	142
Bryan, Tx., U.S.	D4	150
Bryan, co., Ga., U.S.	D5	117
Bryan, co., Ok., U.S.	D5	143
Bryansk see Br'ansk, Russia	H17	22
Bryans Road, Md., U.S.	C3	127
Bryant, Ar., U.S.	C3	111
Bryant, Fl., U.S.	F6	116
Bryant, Il., U.S.	C4	120
Bryant, S.D., U.S.	C8	148
Bryant Creek, stm., Mo., U.S.	E5	132
Bryant Mountain, mtn., Ma., U.S.	B2	128
Bryantown, Md., U.S.	C4	127
Bryant Pond, Me., U.S.	D2	126
Bryantville, Ma., U.S.	B6	128
Bryce Canyon National Park, Ut., U.S.	F3	151
Bryn Mawr, Pa., U.S.	o20	145
Bryson, Tx., U.S.	C3	150
Bryson City, N.C., U.S.	f9	140
Brzeg, Pol.	E17	10
Brzesko, Pol.	F20	10
Brzeziny, Pol.	D19	10
B-Say-Tah, Sask., Can.	G4	105
Bsharrī, Leb.	D4	48
Bua Yai, Thai.	G7	40
Buba, Gui.-B.	F2	64
Bū Bānī, Jabal, mtn., Afr.	F3	60
Būbīyān, i., Kuw.	G10	48
Bucaramanga, Col.	D6	84
Buccaneer Archipelago, is., Austl.	C4	68
Buccino, Italy	I10	18
Buchanan, Sask., Can.	F4	105
Buchanan, Lib.	I4	64
Buchanan, Ga., U.S.	C1	117
Buchanan, Mi., U.S.	G4	129
Buchanan, N.D., U.S.	B7	141
Buchanan, Tn., U.S.	A3	149
Buchanan, Va., U.S.	C3	153
Buchanan, co., Ia., U.S.	B6	122
Buchanan, co., Mo., U.S.	B3	132
Buchanan, co., Va., U.S.	e9	153
Buchanan, Lake, l., Austl.	C6	70
Buchanan, Lake, l., Tx., U.S.	D3	150
Buchans, Newf., Can.	D3	102
Bucharest see București, Rom.	E10	20
Buchholz, Ger.	B9	10
Buchloe, Ger.	G10	10
Buchs, Switz.	D11	13
Buchtel, Oh., U.S.	C3	142
Buchy, Fr.	C8	14
Buckatunna, Ms., U.S.	D5	131
Buck Creek, In., U.S.	D4	121
Buck Creek, stm., Ga., U.S.	D2	117
Buck Creek, stm., In., U.S.	m11	121
Buck Creek, stm., Ky., U.S.	C5	124
Buckeye, Az., U.S.	D3	110
Buckeye, W.V., U.S.	C4	155
Buckeye Hills, hills, Az., U.S.	m7	110
Buckeye Lake, Oh., U.S.	C3	142
Buckfield, Me., U.S.	D2	126
Buckhannon, W.V., U.S.	C4	155
Buckhaven, Scot., U.K.	E10	8
Buckhead, Ga., U.S.	C3	117
Buck Hill Falls, Pa., U.S.	D11	145
Buckhorn, Ky., U.S.	C6	124
Buckhorn Knob, mtn., W.V., U.S.	D4	155
Buckhorn Lake, res., Ky., U.S.	C6	124
Buckie, Scot., U.K.	D11	8
Buckingham, Que., Can.	D2	104
Buckingham, co., Va., U.S.	C4	153
Buckingham Bay, b., Austl.	B7	68
Buckinghamshire, co., Eng., U.K.	J13	8
Buckland, Que., Can.	C7	104
Buckland, Ak., U.S.	B7	109
Bucklands, S. Afr.	G6	66
Buckley, Il., U.S.	C5	120
Buckley, Mi., U.S.	D5	129
Buckley, Wa., U.S.	B3	154
Bucklin, Ks., U.S.	E4	123
Bucklin, Mo., U.S.	B5	132
Buck Mountain, mtn., Austl.	C3	70
Buck Mountain, mtn., Va., U.S.	D1	153
Buck Mountain, mtn., Wa., U.S.	A6	154
Buckner, Ar., U.S.	D2	111
Buckner, Il., U.S.	F4	120
Buckner, Ky., U.S.	g12	124
Buckner, Mo., U.S.	h11	132
Buckow, Ger.	C14	10
Bucks, Al., U.S.	D1	108
Bucks, co., Pa., U.S.	F11	145
Buckskin, In., U.S.	H3	121
Buckskin Mountains, mts., Az., U.S.	C2	110
Bucksport, Me., U.S.	D4	126
Bucksport, S.C., U.S.	D9	147
Bucoda, Wa., U.S.	C3	154
Bucovăț, Mol.	B12	20
Bucun, China	C10	30
București (Bucharest), Rom.	E10	20
București, co., Rom.	E10	20
Bucyrus, Ks., U.S.	D9	123
Bucyrus, Oh., U.S.	B3	142
Bud, W.V., U.S.	D3	155
Buda, Il., U.S.	B4	120
Buda, Tx., U.S.	D4	150
Budapest, Hung.	H19	10
Budardalur, Ice.	B3	6a
Budaun, India	F8	44
Budd Lake, l., N.J., U.S.	B3	137
Buddu, Sud.	L3	60
Bude, Ms., U.S.	D3	131
Büdingen, Ger.	E9	10
Budogošč', Russia	B15	22
Budonnovsk, Russia	I6	26
Budweis see České Budějovice, Czech Rep.	G14	10
Buea, Cam.	I14	64
Buena, N.J., U.S.	D3	137
Buena, Wa., U.S.	C5	154
Buena Esperanza, Arg.	H6	80
Buena Park, Ca., U.S.	n12	112
Buenaventura, Col.	F4	84
Buenaventura, Mex.	C6	90
Buena Vista, Bol.	G10	82
Buena Vista, Para.	D10	80
Buena Vista, Co., U.S.	C4	113
Buena Vista, Fl., U.S.	D5	116
Buena Vista, Ga., U.S.	D2	117
Buena Vista, N.M., U.S.	B4	138
Buena Vista, Va., U.S.	C3	153
Buena Vista, co., Ia., U.S.	B2	122
Buena Vista, Lago (Lago General Carrera), l., S.A.	F2	78
Buendía, Embalse de, res., Spain	E9	16
Buenópolis, Braz.	D6	79
Buenos Aires, Arg.	H9	80
Buenos Aires, Col.	F4	84
Buenos Aires, C.R.	H11	92
Buenos Aires, prov., Arg.	I8	80
Buenos Aires, Lago (Lago General Carrera), l., S.A.	F2	78
Buerarema, Braz.	C9	79
Buesaco, Col.	G4	84
Buffalo, Il., U.S.	D4	120
Buffalo, Ia., U.S.	C7	122
Buffalo, Ks., U.S.	E8	123
Buffalo, Ky., U.S.	C4	124
Buffalo, Mn., U.S.	E5	130
Buffalo, Mo., U.S.	D4	132
Buffalo, N.Y., U.S.	C2	139
Buffalo, N.D., U.S.	C8	141
Buffalo, Oh., U.S.	C4	142
Buffalo, S.C., U.S.	B4	147
Buffalo, S.D., U.S.	B2	148
Buffalo, Tn., U.S.	B4	149
Buffalo, Tx., U.S.	D5	150
Buffalo, W.V., U.S.	C3	155
Buffalo, Wy., U.S.	B6	157
Buffalo, co., Ne., U.S.	D6	134
Buffalo, co., S.D., U.S.	C6	148
Buffalo, co., Wi., U.S.	D2	156
Buffalo, stm., U.S.	E10	96
Buffalo, stm., Ar., U.S.	B3	111
Buffalo Bill Reservoir, res., Wy., U.S.	B3	157
Buffalo Center, Ia., U.S.	A4	122
Buffalo Creek, Co., U.S.	B5	113
Buffalo Creek, stm., W.V., U.S.	h10	155
Buffalo Creek, stm., W.V., U.S.	n12	155
Buffalo Gap, S.D., U.S.	D2	148
Buffalo Grove, Il., U.S.	h9	120
Buffalo Lake, l., Alta., Can.	C4	98
Buffalo Lake, res., Tx., U.S.	B1	150
Buffalo Lake, res., Wi., U.S.	E4	156
Buffalo Mountain, mtn., Va., U.S.	D2	153
Buffumville Lake, res., Ma., U.S.	B4	128
Buford, Ga., U.S.	B2	117
Bug, stm., Eur.	E12	4
Buga, Col.	F4	84
Buga, Nig.	G13	64
Bugalagrande, Col.	E4	84
Bugeat, Fr.	G8	14
Bugg, Russia	C18	22
Bugt, China	B11	30
Bugt, China	A8	32
Bugul'ma, Russia	G8	26
Buguruslan, Russia	G8	26
Buhera, Zimb.	B10	66
Buhl, Al., U.S.	B2	108
Buhl, Id., U.S.	G4	119
Buhl, Mn., U.S.	C6	130
Buhler, Ks., U.S.	D6	123
Buhuşi, Rom.	C10	20
Buies Creek, N.C., U.S.	B4	140
Builth Wells, Wales, U.K.	I10	8
Buin, Chile	G3	80
Buin, Piz, mtn., Eur.	E13	13
Buir Nuur, l., Asia	B10	30
Buj, Russia	C24	22
Bujalance, Spain	H7	16
Bujnaksk, Russia	I7	26
Bujumbura, Bdi.	B5	58
Bukačača, Russia	G15	28
Bukama, Zaire	C5	58
Būkān, Iran	C9	48
Bukavu, Zaire	B5	58
Bukittinggi, Indon.	O6	40
Bukovina, hist. reg., Eur.	B9	20
Bülach, Switz.	C10	13
Bulan, Phil.	o20	39b
Bulan, Ky., U.S.	o6	124
Bulandshahr, India	F7	44
Būlāq, Egypt	E6	60
Bulawayo, Zimb.	C9	66
Buldir Island, i., Ak., U.S.	E13	109
Bulgan, Mong.	B7	30
Bulgan, Mong.	B5	30
Bulgaria (Bălgarija), ctry., Eur.	G13	4
Bulki, Eth.	N9	60
Bulkley, stm., B.C., Can.	B4	99
Bulkley Ranges, mts., B.C., Can.	B4	99
Bullard, Ga., U.S.	D3	117
Bullas, Spain	G10	16
Bull Creek, stm., Nv., U.S.	E6	135
Buller, Mount, mtn., Austl.	K7	70
Buller, stm., N.Z.	F3	63
Bullfrog Creek, stm., Ut., U.S.	F5	151
Bullhead, S.D., U.S.	B4	148
Bullhead City, Az., U.S.	B1	110
Bull Island, i., S.C., U.S.	D9	147
Bull Island, i., S.C., U.S.	F8	147
Bull Island, i., S.C., U.S.	G6	147
Bullitt, co., Ky., U.S.	C4	124
Bullittsville, Ky., U.S.	h13	124
Bull Mountain, mtn., Mt., U.S.	D4	133
Bulloch, co., Ga., U.S.	D5	117
Bullock, N.C., U.S.	A6	140
Bullock, co., Al., U.S.	C4	108
Bullock Creek, Austl.	A6	70
Bulloo, stm., Austl.	G5	70
Bull Run Mountains, mts., Va., U.S.	B5	153
Bullrun Ridge, mtn., Tn., U.S.	m13	149
Bullrun Rock, mtn., Or., U.S.	C8	144
Bulls Bay, b., S.C., U.S.	F8	147
Bull Shoals, Ar., U.S.	A3	111
Bull Shoals Lake, res., U.S.	A3	111
Bull Sluice Lake, res., Ga., U.S.	h8	117
Bully Creek Reservoir, res., Or., U.S.	C9	144
Bulnes, Chile	I2	80
Bultfontein, S. Afr.	G6	66
Bulukumba, Indon.	G7	38
Bulyea, Sask., Can.	G3	105
Bumba, Zaire	A4	58
Bumping, stm., Wa., U.S.	C4	154
Bumpus Mills, Tn., U.S.	A4	149
Buna, Tx., U.S.	D6	150
Bunbury, Austl.	F3	68
Buncombe, Il., U.S.	F5	120
Buncombe, co., N.C., U.S.	f10	140
Bundaberg, Austl.	E10	70
Bünde, Ger.	C8	10
Bundi, India	H6	44
Bundick Creek, stm., La., U.S.	D2	125
Bungo-suidō, strt., Japan	N7	36
Bunia, Zaire	A6	58
Bunker, Mo., U.S.	D6	132
Bunker Group, is., Austl.	D10	70
Bunker Hill, Il., U.S.	D4	120
Bunker Hill, In., U.S.	C5	121
Bunker Hill, Ks., U.S.	D5	123
Bunker Hill, W.V., U.S.	B6	155
Bunker Hill, mtn., Nv., U.S.	D4	135
Bunkerville, Nv., U.S.	G7	135
Bunn, N.C., U.S.	B4	140
Bunnell, Fl., U.S.	C5	116
Bunnlevel, N.C., U.S.	B4	140
Bünyan, Tur.	B3	48
Bunyolo, Spain	F11	16
Bunza, Nig.	E11	64
Buon Me Thuot, Viet.	H10	40
Buor-Chaja, guba, b., Russia	C18	28
Buor-Chaja, mys, c., Russia	C18	28
Buqayq, Saur. Ar.	B7	47
Bura, Kenya	B7	58
Buram, Sud.	L3	60

Name	Map Ref.	Page
Burang, China	E3	30
Buranhém, stm., Braz.	D9	79
Buras, La., U.S.	E6	125
Buraydah, Sau. Ar.	H7	48
Burbank, Ca., U.S.	E4	112
Burbank, Il., U.S.	k9	120
Burbank, S.D., U.S.	E9	148
Burbank, Wa., U.S.	C7	154
Burchard, Ne., U.S.	D9	134
Burcher, Austl.	I7	70
Burco, Som.	G10	56
Burdekin, stm., Austl.	B7	70
Burden, Ks., U.S.	E7	123
Burdett, Alta., Can.	E5	98
Burdett, Ks., U.S.	D4	123
Burdette, Ar., U.S.	B6	111
Burdickville, R.I., U.S.	F2	146
Burdur, Tur.	H14	4
Bure, Eth.	M8	60
Bure, Eth.	L9	60
Bureau, Il., U.S.	B4	120
Bureau, co., Il., U.S.	B4	120
Bureinskij chrebet, mts., Russia	G18	28
Bureja, stm., Russia	G18	28
Büren, Ger.	D8	10
Būr Fu'ād, Egypt	F2	48
Burgas, Bul.	G11	20
Burg [auf Fehmarn], Ger.	A11	10
Burgaw, N.C., U.S.	C5	140
Burg [bei Magdeburg], Ger.	C11	10
Burgdorf, Switz.	D8	13
Burgenland, state, Aus.	H16	10
Burgeo, Newf., Can.	E3	102
Burgersdorp, S. Afr.	H8	66
Burgettstown, Pa., U.S.	F1	145
Burgin, China	B4	30
Burgin, Ky., U.S.	C5	124
Burglengenfeld, Ger.	F12	10
Burgos, Mex.	E10	90
Burgos, Spain	C8	16
Burgos, prov., Spain	C8	16
Burgstädt, Ger.	E12	10
Burgundy see Bourgogne, hist. reg., Fr.	E11	14
Burhaniye, Tur.	J10	20
Burhānpur, India	J7	44
Buri, Braz.	G4	79
Burica, Punta, c., N.A.	I12	92
Burila Mare, Rom.	E6	20
Burin, Newf., Can.	E4	102
Burin Peninsula, pen., Newf., Can.	E4	102
Buri Ram, Thai.	G7	40
Buritama, Braz.	F3	79
Buriti, Braz.	D2	79
Buriti, stm., Braz.	E12	82
Buriti Alegre, Braz.	E4	79
Buritizeiro, Braz.	D6	79
Burj al-'Arab, Egypt	B5	60
Burjassot, Spain	F11	16
Burjatija, state, Russia	G20	26
Burkburnett, Tx., U.S.	B3	150
Burke, S.D., U.S.	D6	148
Burke, co., Ga., U.S.	C4	117
Burke, co., N.C., U.S.	B1	140
Burke, co., N.D., U.S.	A3	141
Burke, stm., Austl.	D3	70
Burke Channel, strt., B.C., Can.	C4	99
Burkesville, Ky., U.S.	D4	124
Burket, In., U.S.	B6	121
Burketown, Austl.	A3	70
Burkeville, Tx., U.S.	D6	150
Burkeville, Va., U.S.	C4	153
Burkina Faso, ctry., Afr.	F6	54
Burkley, Ky., U.S.	f8	124
Burk's Falls, Ont., Can.	B5	103
Burkville, Al., U.S.	C3	108
Burleigh, co., N.D., U.S.	C5	141
Burleson, Tx., U.S.	n9	150
Burleson, co., Tx., U.S.	D4	150
Burley, Id., U.S.	G5	119
Burley, Wa., U.S.	f10	154
Burlingame, Ca., U.S.	h8	112
Burlingame, Ks., U.S.	D8	123
Burlington, Newf., Can.	D3	102
Burlington, Ont., Can.	D5	103
Burlington, Co., U.S.	B8	113
Burlington, Il., U.S.	A5	120
Burlington, In., U.S.	D5	121
Burlington, Ia., U.S.	D6	122
Burlington, Ks., U.S.	D8	123
Burlington, Ky., U.S.	A5	124
Burlington, Me., U.S.	C4	126
Burlington, Ma., U.S.	f11	128
Burlington, N.J., U.S.	C3	137
Burlington, N.C., U.S.	A3	140
Burlington, N.D., U.S.	A4	141
Burlington, Vt., U.S.	C2	152
Burlington, Wa., U.S.	A3	154
Burlington, Wi., U.S.	F5	156
Burlington, Wy., U.S.	B4	157
Burlington, co., N.J., U.S.	D3	137
Burlington Beach, In., U.S.	B3	121
Burlington Junction, Mo., U.S.	A2	132
Burma see Myanmar, ctry., Asia	A2	38
Burmā, Tall, mtn., Jord.	G5	50
Burmakino, Russia	D23	22
Burnaby, B.C., Can.	E6	99
Burnaby Island, i., B.C., Can.	C2	99
Burnet, Tx., U.S.	D3	150
Burnet, co., Tx., U.S.	D3	150
Burnett, In., U.S.	E3	121
Burnett, co., Wi., U.S.	C1	156
Burnett, stm., Austl.	E10	70
Burnettown, S.C., U.S.	D4	147
Burnettsville, In., U.S.	C4	121
Burney, Ca., U.S.	B3	112
Burney, In., U.S.	F6	121
Burnham, Me., U.S.	D3	126
Burnham, Pa., U.S.	E6	145
Burnie, Austl.	M6	70
Burning Springs, Ky., U.S.	C6	124
Burnley, Eng., U.K.	H11	8
Burns, Ks., U.S.	D7	123
Burns, Or., U.S.	D7	144
Burns, Tn., U.S.	A4	149
Burns, Wy., U.S.	E8	157
Burns Flat, Ok., U.S.	B2	143
Burnside, Ky., U.S.	D5	124
Burnside, stm., N.W. Ter., Can.	C11	96
Burns Lake, B.C., Can.	B5	99
Burns Paiute Indian Reservation, Or., U.S.	D7	144
Burnsville, N.B., Can.	B4	101
Burnsville, Al., U.S.	C3	108
Burnsville, Mn., U.S.	F5	130
Burnsville, Ms., U.S.	A5	131
Burnsville, N.C., U.S.	f10	140
Burnsville, W.V., U.S.	C4	155
Burnsville Lake, res., W.V., U.S.	C4	155
Burnt Corn, Al., U.S.	D2	108
Burnt Hills, N.Y., U.S.	C7	139
Burnt Islands, Newf., Can.	E2	102
Burnt Mills, Lake, l., Va., U.S.	k14	153
Burnt River, Ont., Can.	C6	103
Burntside Lake, l., Mn., U.S.	C6	130
Burntwood, stm., Man., Can.	B2	100
Burntwood Lake, l., Man., Can.	B1	100
Burnwell, Al., U.S.	f6	108
Burra, Austl.	I3	70
Burragorang, Lake, res., Austl.	I9	70
Burramurra, Austl.	C2	70
Burrendong Reservoir, res., Austl.	I8	70
Burrinjuck Reservoir, res., Austl.	J8	70
Burr Oak, Ks., U.S.	C5	123
Burr Oak, Mi., U.S.	G5	129
Burr Oak Reservoir, res., Oh., U.S.	C3	142
Burro Burro, stm., Guy.	E13	84
Burroughs, Ga., U.S.	E5	117
Burrows, In., U.S.	C5	121
Burrton, Ks., U.S.	D6	123
Burruyacú, Arg.	D6	80
Bursa, Tur.	I13	20
Būr Safājah, Egypt	D7	60
Būr Sa'īd (Port Said), Egypt	B7	60
Burstall, Sask., Can.	G1	105
Būr Sūdān (Port Sudan), Sud.	H9	60
Burt, Ia., U.S.	A3	122
Burt, co., Ne., U.S.	C9	134
Būr Tawfīq, Egypt	G2	48
Burt Lake, l., Mi., U.S.	C6	129
Burton, B.C., Can.	D9	99
Burton, Mi., U.S.	F7	129
Burton, Oh., U.S.	A4	142
Burton, Wa., U.S.	f11	154
Burton, W.V., U.S.	B4	155
Burton, Lake, res., Ga., U.S.	B3	117
Burtrum, Mn., U.S.	E4	130
Burtts Corner, N.B., Can.	C3	101
Burtundy, Austl.	I5	70
Buru, i., Indon.	F8	38
Burūm, Yemen	G6	47
Burundi, ctry., Afr.	B6	58
Burun-Šibertuj, gora, mtn., Russia	H13	28
Burwell, Ne., U.S.	C6	134
Burwick, Scot., U.K.	C11	8
Bury, Que., Can.	D6	104
Buryatia see Burjatija, state, Russia	G20	26
Bury Saint Edmunds, Eng., U.K.	I14	8
Busby, Alta., Can.	C4	98
Busby, Mt., U.S.	E10	133
Busca, Italy	E2	18
Bushkill, Pa., U.S.	D11	145
Bush Lot, Guy.	D14	84
Bushnell, Fl., U.S.	D4	116
Bushnell, Il., U.S.	C3	120
Bushnell, Ne., U.S.	C2	134
Bush River, b., Md., U.S.	B5	127
Bushton, Ks., U.S.	D5	123
Bushtyna, Ukr.	A7	20
Buskerud, co., Nor.	K11	6
Busko Zdrój, Pol.	E20	10
Buṣrá al-Ḥarīrī (Bosor), Syria	C6	50
Buṣrá ash-Shām, Syria	C6	50
Busselton, Austl.	F3	68
Bussey, Ia., U.S.	C5	122
Bussum, Neth.	D7	12
Bustamante, Mex.	D9	90
Busteni, Rom.	D9	20
Busto Arsizio, Italy	D3	18
Busu-Djanoa, Zaire	A4	58
Bušuicha, Russia	B23	22
Buta, Zaire	H5	56
Butajira, Eth.	M10	60
Buta Ranquil, Arg.	I4	80
Butare, Rw.	B5	58
Bute Inlet, b., B.C., Can.	D5	99
Butera, Italy	L9	18
Butere, Kenya	A6	58
Butha Qi, China	B11	30
Butiá, Braz.	F13	80
Butler, Al., U.S.	C1	108
Butler, Ga., U.S.	D2	117
Butler, In., U.S.	B8	121
Butler, Ky., U.S.	B5	124
Butler, Mo., U.S.	C3	132
Butler, N.J., U.S.	B4	137
Butler, Oh., U.S.	B3	142
Butler, Ok., U.S.	B2	143
Butler, Pa., U.S.	E2	145
Butler, Tn., U.S.	C11	149
Butler, Wi., U.S.	m11	156
Butler, co., Al., U.S.	D3	108
Butler, co., Ia., U.S.	B5	122
Butler, co., Ks., U.S.	E7	123
Butler, co., Ky., U.S.	C3	124
Butler, co., Mo., U.S.	E7	132
Butler, co., Ne., U.S.	C8	134
Butler, co., Oh., U.S.	C1	142
Butler, co., Pa., U.S.	E2	145
Butlerville, In., U.S.	F6	121
Butner, N.C., U.S.	A4	140
Buton, Pulau, i., Indon.	G7	38
Butru, Austl.	C3	70
Buttahatchee, stm., U.S.	B5	131
Butte, Mt., U.S.	E4	133
Butte, Ne., U.S.	B7	134
Butte, N.D., U.S.	B5	141
Butte, co., Ca., U.S.	C3	112
Butte, co., Id., U.S.	F5	119
Butte, co., S.D., U.S.	C2	148
Butte des Morts, Lake, l., Wi., U.S.	D5	156
Butte du Lion, hist., Bel.	G5	12
Butte Falls, Or., U.S.	E4	144
Butte Mountains, mts., Nv., U.S.	D6	135
Butterfield, Ar., U.S.	g8	111
Butterfield, Mn., U.S.	G4	130
Butterfield, Mo., U.S.	E4	132
Butternut, Wi., U.S.	B3	156
Butternut Lake, l., Wi., U.S.	C5	156
Butters, N.C., U.S.	C4	140
Butterworth, Malay.	L6	40
Butterworth, S. Afr.	I9	66
Button Islands, is., N.W. Ter., Can.	f8	102
Buttonwillow, Ca., U.S.	E4	112
Butts, co., Ga., U.S.	C3	117
Butuan, Phil.	D8	38
Butylicy, Russia	F24	22
Butzbach, Ger.	E8	10
Bützow, Ger.	B11	10
Buurgplaatz, mtn., Lux.	H9	12
Buxtehude, Ger.	B9	10
Buxton, Guy.	D13	84
Buxton, S. Afr.	F7	66
Buxton, N.C., U.S.	B7	140
Buxton, N.D., U.S.	B8	141
Buxy, Fr.	F11	14
Buyo, C. Iv.	H6	64
Buzançais, Fr.	F8	14
Buzău, Rom.	D10	20
Buzău, co., Rom.	D10	20
Buzău, stm., Rom.	D11	20
Buzen, Japan	N6	36
Búzi, stm., Moz.	B12	66
Búzios, Ponta dos, c., Braz.	G8	79
Buzuluk, Russia	G8	26
Buzzard Roost, mtn., N.C., U.S.	B1	140
Buzzards Bay, Ma., U.S.	C6	128
Buzzards Bay, b., Ma., U.S.	C6	128
Byam Martin Channel, strt., N.W. Ter., Can.	A12	96
Byam Martin Island, i., N.W. Ter., Can.	A12	96
Byars, Ok., U.S.	C4	143
Bybee, Tn., U.S.	C10	149
Bychov, Bela.	H13	22
Bydgoszcz, Pol.	B18	10
Byelorussia see Belarus, ctry., Eur.	E13	4
Byemoor, Alta., Can.	D4	98
Byers, Co., U.S.	B6	113
Byesville, Oh., U.S.	C4	142
Byfield, Ma., U.S.	A6	128
Bygdin, Nor.	K11	6
Byhalia, Ms., U.S.	A4	131
Bykle, Nor.	L10	6
Bylas, Az., U.S.	D5	110
Bylot Island, i., N.W. Ter., Can.	B17	96
Byng, Ok., U.S.	C5	143
Byng Inlet, Ont., Can.	B4	103
Bynum, N.C., U.S.	B3	140
Byram, Ms., U.S.	C3	131
Byrdstown, Tn., U.S.	C8	149
Byromville, Ga., U.S.	D3	117
Byron, Ca., U.S.	h9	112
Byron, Ga., U.S.	D3	117
Byron, Il., U.S.	A4	120
Byron, Mn., U.S.	F6	130
Byron, Ne., U.S.	D8	134
Byron, Wy., U.S.	B4	157
Byron, Cape, c., Austl.	G10	70
Byron Bay, Austl.	G10	70
Byrranga, gory, mts., Russia	B12	28
Bystřice, Czech Rep.	F14	10
Bystrzyca Kłodzka, Pol.	E16	10
Bytantaj, stm., Russia	D18	28
Bytkiv, Ukr.	A8	20
Bytom (Beuthen), Pol.	E18	10
Bytoš', Russia	H17	22
Bytów, Pol.	A17	10

C

Name	Map Ref.	Page
Ca, stm., Asia	E8	40
Caacupé, Para.	C10	80
Caaguazú, Para.	C10	80
Caaguazú, dept., Para.	C11	80
Caála, Ang.	D3	58
Caapiranga, Braz.	I12	84
Caapucú, Para.	D10	80
Caarapó, Braz.	G1	79
Caazapá, Para.	D10	80
Caazapá, dept., Para.	D10	80
Cabaçal, stm., Braz.	F12	82
Cabaiguán, Cuba	C5	94
Caballana, Lago, l., Braz.	I12	84
Caballo, N.M., U.S.	E2	138
Caballo Mountains, mts., N.M., U.S.	E2	138
Caballo Reservoir, res., N.M., U.S.	E2	138
Cabana, Peru	C2	82
Cabanaconde, Peru	F6	82
Cabanatuan, Phil.	n19	39b
Cabano, Que., Can.	B9	104
Cabarrus, co., N.C., U.S.	B2	140
Cabbage Swamp, sw., Fl., U.S.	m9	116
Cabeceiras, Braz.	C5	79
Cabedelo, Braz.	E12	76
Cabell, co., W.V., U.S.	C2	155
Cabery, Il., U.S.	C5	120
Cabeza del Buey, Spain	G6	16
Cabezas, Bol.	H10	82
Cabildo, Arg.	J8	80
Cabildo, Chile	G3	80
Cabimas, Ven.	B7	84
Cabin Creek, W.V., U.S.	m13	155
Cabin Creek, stm., W.V., U.S.	m13	155
Cabinda, Ang.	C2	58
Cabinda, dept., Ang.	C2	58
Cabinet Gorge Reservoir, res., U.S.	B1	133
Cabinet Mountains, mts., Mt., U.S.	B1	133
Cabin John, Md., U.S.	C3	127
Cabixi, stm., Braz.	E11	82
Cable, Wi., U.S.	B2	156
Cabo, Braz.	E11	76
Cabo Frio, Braz.	G7	79
Cabo Gracias a Dios, Nic.	C11	92
Cabonga, Réservoir, res., Que., Can.	k11	104
Cabool, Mo., U.S.	D5	132
Caboolture, Austl.	F10	70
Cabora Bassa Dam, Moz.	E6	58
Caborca, Mex.	B3	90
Cabot, Ar., U.S.	C3	111
Cabot, Vt., U.S.	C4	152
Cabot, Mount, mtn., N.H., U.S.	A4	136
Cabot Head, c., Ont., Can.	B3	103
Cabot Strait, strt., Can.	G20	96
Cabra, Spain	H7	16
Cabramurra, Austl.	J8	70
Cabrera, stm., Col.	F5	84
Cabrera, Illa de, i., Spain	F14	16
Cabri, Sask., Can.	G1	105
Cabrillo National Monument, Ca., U.S.	o15	112
Cabruta, Ven.	D9	84
Cabure, Ven.	B8	84
Cabuya, C.R.	H9	92
Cabuyal, C.R.	G9	92
Cabuyaro, Col.	E6	84
Caçador, Braz.	D13	80
Čačak, Yugo.	F4	20
Cacaohatán, Mex.	C2	92
Caçapava, Braz.	G6	79
Caçapava do Sul, Braz.	F12	80
Cacapon, stm., W.V., U.S.	B6	155
Caccamo, Italy	L8	18
Cacequi, Braz.	E11	80
Cáceres, Braz.	G13	82
Cáceres, Col.	D5	84
Cáceres, Spain	F5	16
Cacharí, Arg.	I9	80
Cache, Ok., U.S.	C3	143
Cache, co., Ut., U.S.	B4	151
Cache, stm., Ar., U.S.	C4	111
Cache, stm., Il., U.S.	F4	120
Cache Bay, Ont., Can.	A5	103
Cache Creek, B.C., Can.	D7	99
Cache Creek, stm., Ca., U.S.	C2	112
Cache la Poudre, stm., Co., U.S.	A5	113
Cache la Poudre, North Fork, stm., Co., U.S.	A5	113
Cache Mountain, mtn., Ak., U.S.	B10	109
Cache Peak, mtn., Id., U.S.	G5	119
Cacheu, Gui.-B.	E1	64
Cachí, Arg.	C5	80
Cachimbo, Serra do, mts., Braz.	C13	82
Cachoeira Alta, Braz.	E3	79
Cachoeira de Goiás, Braz.	D3	79
Cachoeira do Sul, Braz.	F12	80
Cachoeiras de Macacu, Braz.	G7	79
Cachoeiro de Itapemirim, Braz.	F8	79
Cachuela Esperanza, Bol.	D9	82
Cacine, Gui.-B.	F2	64
Cacólo, Ang.	D3	58
Caconda, Ang.	D3	58
Cacra, Peru	E4	82
Cactus, Tx., U.S.	A2	150
Cactus Flat, pl., Nv., U.S.	F5	135
Cactus Peak, mtn., Nv., U.S.	F5	135
Caçu, Braz.	E3	79
Caculé, Braz.	C7	79
Čadan, Russia	G16	26
Cadariri, stm., Braz.	B13	82
Caddo, Ok., U.S.	C5	143
Caddo, co., La., U.S.	B2	125
Caddo, co., Ok., U.S.	B3	143
Caddo, stm., Ar., U.S.	C2	111
Caddo Creek, stm., Ok., U.S.	C4	143
Caddo Gap, Ar., U.S.	C2	111
Caddo Lake, res., U.S.	B2	125
Caddo Mountains, mtn., Ar., U.S.	C2	111
Caddo Valley, Ar., U.S.	C2	111
Cade, La., U.S.	D4	125
Cadereyta de Jiménez, Mex.	E9	90
Cades, S.C., U.S.	D8	147
Cadet, Mo., U.S.	C7	132
Cadillac, Sask., Can.	H2	105
Cadillac, Mi., U.S.	D5	129
Cadillac Mountain, mtn., Me., U.S.	D4	126
Cádiz, Spain	I5	16
Cadiz, Ky., U.S.	D2	124
Cadiz, Oh., U.S.	B4	142
Cádiz, Golfo de, b., Eur.	I4	16
Čadobec, stm., Russia	F11	28
Cadogan, Alta., Can.	C5	98
Cadomin, Alta., Can.	C2	98
Cadott, Wi., U.S.	D2	156
Cadron Creek, stm., Ar., U.S.	B3	111
Cadwell, Ga., U.S.	D3	117
Cadys Falls, Vt., U.S.	B3	152
Caen, Fr.	C6	14
Caernarfon, Wales, U.K.	H9	8
Caesar Creek Lake, res., Oh., U.S.	C2	142
Cæsarea see Qesari, Ḥorbat, hist., Isr.	C3	50
Caetanópolis, Braz.	E6	79
Caeté, Braz.	E7	79
Caeté, stm., Braz.	C7	82
Caetité, Braz.	C7	79
Cafayate, Arg.	D6	80
Cafelândia do Leste, Braz.	D2	79
Cafuini, stm., Braz.	G14	84
Cagayan, stm., Phil.	I19	39b
Cagayan de Oro, Phil.	D7	38
Çağış, Tur.	J12	20
Cagles Mill Lake, res., In., U.S.	F4	121
Cagli, Italy	F7	18
Cagliari, Italy	J4	18
Cagliari, Golfo di, b., Italy	J4	18
Cagnes, Fr.	I14	14
Čagoda, Russia	B18	22
Cagua, Ven.	B9	84
Caguán, stm., Col.	G5	84
Caguas, P.R.	E11	94
Cahaba, stm., Al., U.S.	C2	108
Cahaba Valley, val., Al., U.S.	B3	108
Cahabón, Guat.	B5	92
Cahabón, stm., Guat.	B5	92
Cahokia, Il., U.S.	E3	120
Cahors, Fr.	H8	14
Cahuinari, stm., Col.	H7	84
Cahuita, Punta, c., C.R.	H12	92
Cahul, Mol.	H3	26
Caí, stm., Braz.	E13	80
Caia, stm., Eur.	F4	16
Caiapó, stm., Braz.	D3	79
Caiapó, Serra do, mts., Braz.	D2	79
Caiapônia, Braz.	D3	79
Caibarién, Cuba	C5	94
Cai Bau, Dao, i., Viet.	D9	40
Caiçara, Braz.	C3	79
Caicara, Caño, stm., Ven.	D8	84
Caicara de Maturín, Ven.	C11	84
Caicara de Orinoco, Ven.	D9	84
Caicara de Orinoco, Ven.	G11	88
Caicedonia, Col.	E5	84
Caicó, Braz.	E11	76
Caicos Islands, is., T./C. Is.	D9	94
Caicos Passage, strt., N.A.	C8	94
Caigou, China	B3	34
Cailloma, Peru	F6	82
Caillou Bay, b., La., U.S.	E5	125
Caillou Lake, l., La., U.S.	E5	125
Caimanera, Cuba	E7	94
Caine, stm., Bol.	G9	82
Cainsville, Mo., U.S.	A4	132
Caird Coast, Ant.	C2	73
Cairnbrook, Pa., U.S.	F4	145
Cairns, Austl.	A6	70
Cairo see Al-Qāhirah, Egypt	B6	60
Cairo, Ga., U.S.	F2	117
Cairo, Il., U.S.	F4	120
Cairo, Mo., U.S.	B5	132
Cairo, Ne., U.S.	D7	134
Cairo, N.Y., U.S.	C6	139
Cairo, W.V., U.S.	B3	155
Cairo Montenotte, Italy	E3	18
Cairu, Braz.	B9	79
Caiundo, Ang.	E3	58
Caixi, China	J5	34
Cajabamba, Ec.	H3	84
Cajabamba, Peru	B2	82
Cajacay, Peru	D3	82
Cajamarca, Peru	B2	82
Cajamarca, dept., Peru	B2	82
Cajatambo, Peru	D3	82
Cajàzeiras, Braz.	E11	76
Čajek, Kyrg.	I12	26
Čajkovskij, Russia	F8	26
Cajones, Cayos, rf., Hond.	A11	92
Cajuru, Braz.	F5	79
Čakeni, Ang.	A4	66
Čakovec, Cro.	C11	18
Cala, S. Afr.	H8	66
Calabar, Nig.	I14	64
Calabasas, Ca., U.S.	m11	112
Calabozo, Ven.	C9	84
Calabozo, Ensenada de, b., Ven.	B7	84
Calabria, prov., Italy	J11	18
Calahorra, Spain	C10	16
Calais, Fr.	B8	14
Calais, Me., U.S.	C5	126
Calais, Pas de (Strait of Dover), strt., Eur.	J15	8
Calalaste, Sierra de, mts., Arg.	C5	80
Calama, Chile	B4	80
Calamar, Col.	B5	84
Calamar, Col.	G6	84
Calamarca, Bol.	G7	82
Calamus, Ia., U.S.	C7	122
Calamus, stm., Ne., U.S.	B6	134
Calapan, Phil.	o19	39b
Călărași, Mol.	B12	20
Călărași, Rom.	E11	20
Calarcá, Col.	E5	84
Calatayud, Spain	D10	16
Calau, Ger.	D13	10
Calaveras, co., Ca., U.S.	C3	112
Calbayog, Phil.	C7	38
Calca, Peru	E6	82
Calcasieu, co., La., U.S.	D2	125
Calcasieu, stm., La., U.S.	D2	125
Calcasieu Lake, l., La., U.S.	E2	125
Calcasieu Pass, strt., La., U.S.	E2	125
Calceta, Ec.	H2	84
Calcha, Bol.	I8	82
Calchaquí, Arg.	E8	80
Calchaquí, stm., Arg.	C5	80
Calçoene, Braz.	C8	76
Calcutta, India	I13	44
Calcutta, Oh., U.S.	B5	142
Calcutta Lake, l., Nv., U.S.	B2	135
Caldas, Braz.	F5	79
Caldas, Col.	D5	84
Caldas, dept., Col.	E5	84
Caldas Novas, Braz.	D4	79
Calder, Sask., Can.	F5	105
Calder, Id., U.S.	B2	119
Caldera, Chile	D3	80
Calderwood, Tn., U.S.	D10	149
Caldron Falls Reservoir, res., Wi., U.S.	C5	156
Caldwell, Ar., U.S.	B5	111
Caldwell, Id., U.S.	F2	119
Caldwell, Ks., U.S.	E6	123
Caldwell, N.J., U.S.	B4	137
Caldwell, Oh., U.S.	C4	142
Caldwell, Tx., U.S.	D4	150
Caldwell, W.V., U.S.	D4	155
Caldwell, co., Ky., U.S.	C2	124
Caldwell, co., La., U.S.	B3	125
Caldwell, co., Mo., U.S.	B3	132
Caldwell, co., N.C., U.S.	B1	140
Caldwell, co., Tx., U.S.	E4	150
Caledon, Ont., Can.	D5	103
Caledon, stm., Afr.	H8	66
Caledonia, Belize	H15	90
Caledonia, N.S., Can.	E4	101
Caledonia, Il., U.S.	A5	120
Caledonia, Mi., U.S.	F5	129
Caledonia, Mn., U.S.	G7	130
Caledonia, Ms., U.S.	B5	131
Caledonia, N.Y., U.S.	C3	139
Caledonia, N.D., U.S.	B9	141
Caledonia, Oh., U.S.	B3	142
Caledonia, co., Vt., U.S.	C4	152
Calella, Spain	D14	16
Calera, Spain	o23	17b
Calera, Al., U.S.	B3	108
Calera, Ok., U.S.	D5	143
Caleta del Sebo, Spain	n27	17b
Caleufú, Arg.	H6	80
Calexico, Ca., U.S.	F6	112
Calgary, Alta., Can.	D3	98
Calhan, Co., U.S.	B6	113
Calhoun, N.B., Can.	C5	101
Calhoun, Al., U.S.	C3	108
Calhoun, Ga., U.S.	B2	117
Calhoun, Ky., U.S.	C2	124
Calhoun, La., U.S.	B3	125
Calhoun, Mo., U.S.	C4	132
Calhoun, Tn., U.S.	D9	149
Calhoun, co., Al., U.S.	B4	108
Calhoun, co., Ar., U.S.	D3	111
Calhoun, co., Fl., U.S.	B1	116
Calhoun, co., Ga., U.S.	E2	117
Calhoun, co., Il., U.S.	D3	120
Calhoun, co., Ia., U.S.	B3	122
Calhoun, co., Mi., U.S.	F5	129
Calhoun, co., Ms., U.S.	B4	131
Calhoun, co., S.C., U.S.	D6	147
Calhoun, co., Tx., U.S.	E4	150
Calhoun, co., W.V., U.S.	C3	155
Calhoun City, Ms., U.S.	B4	131
Calhoun Falls, S.C., U.S.	C2	147
Cali, Col.	F4	84
Calico Rock, Ar., U.S.	A3	111
Calicut, India	G3	46
Caliente, Nv., U.S.	F7	135
Califon, N.J., U.S.	B3	137
California, Md., U.S.	D4	127
California, Mo., U.S.	C5	132
California, Pa., U.S.	F2	145
California, state, U.S.	D4	112
California, Golfo de, b., Mex.	D4	90
California Aqueduct, Ca., U.S.	E4	112
California City, Ca., U.S.	E5	112
Călilabad, Azer.	B10	48
Calilegua, Arg.	B6	80
Calimere, Point, c., India	G5	46
Calindó, stm., Braz.	C6	79
Calingasta, Arg.	F4	80
Calion, Ar., U.S.	D3	111
Calipatria, Ca., U.S.	F6	112
Calispell Peak, mtn., Wa., U.S.	A8	154
Calistoga, Ca., U.S.	C2	112
Calitri, Italy	I10	18
Callabonna, Lake, l., Austl.	G4	70
Callac, Fr.	D3	14
Callaghan, Mount, mtn., Nv., U.S.	D5	135
Callahan, Fl., U.S.	B5	116
Callahan, co., Tx., U.S.	C3	150
Callanmarca, Peru	E4	82
Callanna, Austl.	G2	70
Callao, Peru	E3	82
Callao, Mo., U.S.	B5	132
Callao, Va., U.S.	C6	153
Callaway, Md., U.S.	D4	127
Callaway, Ne., U.S.	C6	134
Callaway, co., Mo., U.S.	C6	132
Callender, Ia., U.S.	B3	122
Calling Lake, l., Alta., Can.	B4	98
Callosa d'En Sarrià, Spain	G11	16
Callosa de Segura, Spain	G11	16
Calloway, co., Ky., U.S.	f9	124
Calmar, Alta., Can.	C4	98
Calmar, Ia., U.S.	A6	122
Calobre, Pan.	I14	92
Caloosahatchee, stm., Fl., U.S.	F5	116
Caloundra, Austl.	F10	70
Calp, Spain	G12	16
Caltagirone, Italy	L9	18
Caltanissetta, Italy	L9	18
Calumet, Que., Can.	D3	104
Calumet, Mi., U.S.	A2	129
Calumet, Mn., U.S.	C5	130
Calumet, Ok., U.S.	B3	143
Calumet, co., Wi., U.S.	D5	156
Calumet, Lake, l., Il., U.S.	k9	120
Calumet City, Il., U.S.	B6	120
Calumet Sag Channel, Il., U.S.	k9	120
Calunda, Ang.	D4	58
Caluula, Som.	F11	56
Calvados, dept., Fr.	C6	14
Calvary, Ga., U.S.	F2	117
Calvert, Al., U.S.	D1	108
Calvert, Tx., U.S.	D4	150
Calvert, co., Md., U.S.	C4	127
Calvert City, Ky., U.S.	e9	124
Calvert Island, i., B.C., Can.	D3	99
Calverton, Md., U.S.	*B4	127
Calverton, N.Y., U.S.	n16	139
Calverton Park, Mo., U.S.	f13	132
Calvi, Fr.	I23	15a
Calvia, Spain	F14	16
Calvillo, Mex.	G8	90
Calvin, Ok., U.S.	C5	143
Calvinia, S. Afr.	H4	66
Calw, Ger.	G8	10
Calypso, N.C., U.S.	B4	140
Calzada, Peru	B3	82
Camabatela, Ang.	C3	58
Camaçã, stm., Braz.	B8	82
Camaçari, Braz.	B9	79
Camacupa, Ang.	D3	58
Camaguán, Ven.	C9	84
Camagüey, Cuba	D6	94
Camaiore, Italy	F5	18
Camaiú, stm., Braz.	B12	82
Camajuaní, Cuba	C5	94
Camak, Ga., U.S.	C4	117
Camamu, Braz.	B9	79
Camaná, Peru	G5	82
Camaná, stm., Peru	G5	82
Camanaú, stm., Braz.	H12	84
Camanche, Ia., U.S.	C7	122
Camano Island, i., Wa., U.S.	A3	154
Camapuã, Braz.	E1	79
Camaquã, Braz.	F13	80
Camaquã, stm., Braz.	F12	80
Camará, Braz.	I11	84
Camararé, stm., Braz.	E12	82
Camarès, Fr.	I9	14
Camargo, Bol.	I9	82
Camargo, Mex.	D7	90
Camargo, Il., U.S.	D5	120
Camargo, Ok., U.S.	B2	143
Camargue, reg., Fr.	I11	14
Camarillo, Ca., U.S.	E4	112
Camarón, Cabo, c., Hond.	A9	92
Camarones, Arg.	E3	78
Camas, Spain	H5	16

Name	Map Ref.	Page
Camas, Wa., U.S.	D3	154
Camas, co., Id., U.S.	F4	119
Camas Valley, Or., U.S.	D3	144
Ca Mau, Viet.	J8	40
Ca Mau, Mui, c., Viet.	J8	40
Cambados, Spain	C3	16
Cambará, Braz.	G3	79
Cambodia (Kâmpŭchéa), ctry., Asia	C4	38
Camboon, Austl.	E9	70
Camboriú, Braz.	D14	80
Cambrai, Fr.	B10	14
Cambria, Ca., U.S.	E3	112
Cambria, Wi., U.S.	E4	156
Cambria, co., Pa., U.S.	E4	145
Cambrian Mountains, mts., Wales, U.K.	I10	8
Cambridge, Ont., Can.	D4	103
Cambridge, N.Z.	B5	72
Cambridge, Eng., U.K.	I14	8
Cambridge, Id., U.S.	E2	119
Cambridge, Il., U.S.	B3	120
Cambridge, Ia., U.S.	C4	122
Cambridge, Md., U.S.	C5	127
Cambridge, Ma., U.S.	B5	128
Cambridge, Mn., U.S.	E5	130
Cambridge, Ne., U.S.	D5	134
Cambridge, N.Y., U.S.	B7	139
Cambridge, Oh., U.S.	B4	142
Cambridge, Vt., U.S.	B3	152
Cambridge, Wi., U.S.	F4	156
Cambridge Bay, N.W. Ter., Can.	C11	96
Cambridge City, In., U.S.	E7	121
Cambridge Reservoir, res., Ma., U.S.	g10	128
Cambridgeshire, co., Eng., U.K.	I13	8
Cambridge Springs, Pa., U.S.	C1	145
Cambriú, Ponta de, c., Braz.	C15	80
Cambuí, Braz.	G5	79
Cambundi-Catembo, Ang.	D3	58
Camden, Austl.	J9	70
Camden, Al., U.S.	D2	108
Camden, Ar., U.S.	D3	111
Camden, De., U.S.	D3	115
Camden, In., U.S.	C4	121
Camden, Me., U.S.	D3	126
Camden, Mi., U.S.	G6	129
Camden, Ms., U.S.	C4	131
Camden, Mo., U.S.	B3	132
Camden, N.J., U.S.	D2	137
Camden, N.Y., U.S.	B5	139
Camden, N.C., U.S.	A6	140
Camden, Oh., U.S.	C1	142
Camden, S.C., U.S.	C6	147
Camden, Tn., U.S.	A3	149
Camden, co., Ga., U.S.	F5	117
Camden, co., Mo., U.S.	C5	132
Camden, co., N.J., U.S.	D3	137
Camden, co., N.C., U.S.	A6	140
Camdenton, Mo., U.S.	D5	132
Camelback Mountain, mtn., Az., U.S.	k9	110
Camels Hump, mtn., Vt., U.S.	C3	152
Camenca, Mol.	A12	20
Cameron, Az., U.S.	B4	110
Cameron, La., U.S.	E2	125
Cameron, Mo., U.S.	B3	132
Cameron, Ok., U.S.	B7	143
Cameron, S.C., U.S.	D6	147
Cameron, Tx., U.S.	D4	150
Cameron, W.V., U.S.	B4	155
Cameron, Wi., U.S.	C2	156
Cameron, co., La., U.S.	E2	125
Cameron, co., Pa., U.S.	D5	145
Cameron, co., Tx., U.S.	F4	150
Cameron Hills, hills, Can.	E9	96
Cameroon (Cameroun), ctry., Afr.	G9	54
Cameroon Mountain, mtn., Cam.	I14	64
Cametá, Braz.	D9	76
Camiling, Phil.	n19	39b
Camilla, Ga., U.S.	E2	117
Camiña, Chile	H7	82
Camino, Ca., U.S.	C3	112
Camiranga, Braz.	D9	76
Camiri, Bol.	I10	82
Camisea, stm., Peru	D5	82
Camissombo, Ang.	C4	58
Camlachie, Ont., Can.	D2	103
Cammack Village, Ar., U.S.	C3	111
Camoapa, Nic.	E9	92
Camocim, Braz.	D10	76
Camooweal, Austl.	B3	70
Camorta Island, i., India	J2	40
Camp, co., Tx., U.S.	C5	150
Campaign, Tn., U.S.	D8	149
Campamento, Hond.	C8	92
Campana, Arg.	H9	80
Campana, Isla, i., Chile	I7	74
Campanario, Spain	G6	16
Campanario, Cerro de, mtn., Peru	A3	82
Campanero, Cerro, mtn., Ven.	E10	84
Campania, prov., Italy	I9	18
Campania Island, i., B.C., Can.	C3	99
Campbell, Ca., U.S.	k8	112
Campbell, Fl., U.S.	D5	116
Campbell, Mo., U.S.	E7	132
Campbell, Ne., U.S.	D7	134
Campbell, Oh., U.S.	A5	142
Campbell, co., Ky., U.S.	B5	124
Campbell, co., S.D., U.S.	B5	148
Campbell, co., Tn., U.S.	C9	149
Campbell, co., Va., U.S.	C3	153
Campbell, co., Wy., U.S.	B7	157
Campbell, Cape, c., N.Z.	D5	72
Campbellford, Ont., Can.	C7	103
Campbell Hill, Il., U.S.	F4	120
Campbell Hill, hill, Oh., U.S.	B2	142
Campbell Island, i., N.Z.	N20	158
Campbell Lake, l., Or., U.S.	E7	144
Campbellsburg, In., U.S.	G5	121
Campbellsburg, Ky., U.S.	B4	124
Campbells Creek, stm., W.V., U.S.	m13	155
Campbellsport, Wi., U.S.	E5	156
Campbell Station, Ar., U.S.	B4	111
Campbellsville, Ky., U.S.	C4	124
Campbellton, N.B., Can.	A3	101
Campbellton, Newf., Can.	D4	102
Campbellton, P.E.I., Can.	C5	101
Campbelltown, Austl.	J9	70
Campbell Town, Austl.	M7	70
Camp Crook, S.D., U.S.	B2	148
Camp Douglas, Wi., U.S.	E3	156
Campeche, Mex.	H14	90
Campeche, state, Mex.	H14	90
Campeche, Bahía de, b., Mex.	H12	90
Campechuela, Cuba	D6	94
Camperdown, Austl.	L5	70
Camperville, Man., Can.	D1	100
Cam Pha, Viet.	D9	40
Camp Hill, Al., U.S.	C4	108
Camp Hill, Pa., U.S.	F8	145
Camp H. M. Smith Marine Corps Base, mil., Hi., U.S.	g10	118
Camp Howard Ridge, mtn., Id., U.S.	D2	119
Campillos, Spain	H7	16
Câmpina, Rom.	D9	20
Campina Grande, Braz.	E11	74
Campina Grande, Braz.	E11	76
Campinas, Braz.	G5	79
Campina Verde, Braz.	E4	79
Campion, Co., U.S.	A5	113
Camp Lejeune Marine Corps Base, mil., N.C., U.S.	C5	140
Campo, Co., U.S.	D8	113
Campoalegre, Col.	F5	84
Campo Alegre de Goiás, Braz.	D5	79
Campobasso, Italy	H9	18
Campobello, S.C., U.S.	A3	147
Campobello Island, i., N.B., Can.	E3	101
Campo Belo, Braz.	F6	79
Campo de Criptana, Spain	F8	16
Campo de la Cruz, Col.	B5	84
Campo Erê, Braz.	D12	80
Campo Florido, Braz.	E4	79
Campo Gallo, Arg.	D7	80
Campo Grande, Arg.	D11	80
Campo Grande, Braz.	F1	79
Campo Largo, Arg.	D8	80
Campo Largo, Braz.	C14	80
Campo Maior, Braz.	D10	76
Campo Mourão, Braz.	H2	79
Campo Novo, Braz.	D12	80
Campo Quijano, Arg.	C6	80
Camporredondo, Peru	B2	82
Campos, Braz.	F8	79
Campos Altos, Braz.	E5	79
Campo Santo, Arg.	C6	80
Campos Belos, Braz.	B5	79
Campos do Jordão, Braz.	G6	79
Campos Gerais, Braz.	F6	79
Campos Novos, Braz.	D13	80
Camp Pendleton Marine Corps Base, mil., Ca., U.S.	F5	112
Camp Point, Il., U.S.	C2	120
Camp Springs, Md., U.S.	f9	127
Campti, La., U.S.	C2	125
Campton, Ga., U.S.	C3	117
Campton, Ky., U.S.	C6	124
Campton, N.H., U.S.	C3	136
Câmpulung, Rom.	D9	20
Câmpulung Moldovenesc, Rom.	B9	20
Campuya, stm., Peru	H5	84
Camp Verde, Az., U.S.	C4	110
Camp Verde Indian Reservation, Az., U.S.	C4	110
Camp Wood, Tx., U.S.	E2	150
Cam Ranh, Viet.	I10	40
Cam Ranh, Vinh, b., Viet.	I10	40
Camrose, Alta., Can.	C4	98
Camu, stm., Braz.	G14	84
Canaan, N.B., Can.	C4	101
Canaan, Ct., U.S.	A2	114
Canaan, Me., U.S.	D3	126
Canaan, N.H., U.S.	C2	136
Canaan, Vt., U.S.	A5	152
Canaan, stm., N.B., Can.	C4	101
Canaan Center, N.H., U.S.	C2	136
Canaan Street, N.H., U.S.	C2	136
Cana-brava, stm., Braz.	B4	79
Cana-brava, stm., Braz.	B4	79
Canaçari, Lago, l., Braz.	I13	84
Canada, ctry., N.A.	D13	96
Canada Bay, b., Newf., Can.	C3	102
Cañada de Gómez, Arg.	G8	80
Canada Falls Lake, res., Me., U.S.	C2	126
Cañada Honda, Arg.	F4	80
Canadensis, Pa., U.S.	D11	145
Canadian, Ok., U.S.	B6	143
Canadian, Tx., U.S.	B2	150
Canadian, co., Ok., U.S.	B3	143
Canadian, stm., U.S.	D6	106
Canaguá, stm., Ven.	C7	84
Canaima, Ven.	D11	84
Canaima, Parque Nacional, Ven.	E11	84
Canajoharie, N.Y., U.S.	C6	139
Çanakkale, Tur.	I10	20
Çanakkale Boğazı (Dardanelles), strt., Tur.	I10	20
Canal Flats, B.C., Can.	D10	99
Canal Fulton, Oh., U.S.	B4	142
Canalou, Mo., U.S.	E8	132
Canal Point, Fl., U.S.	F6	116
Canals, Arg.	G7	80
Canal Winchester, Oh., U.S.	C3	142
Canamã, stm., Braz.	D12	82
Canandaigua, N.Y., U.S.	C3	139
Canandaigua Lake, l., N.Y., U.S.	C3	139
Cananea, Mex.	B4	90
Cananéia, Braz.	C15	80
Canápolis, Braz.	E4	79
Cañar, Ec.	I3	84
Cañar, prov., Ec.	I3	84
Canarias, Islas (Canary Islands), is., Spain	o25	17b
Canarreos, Archipiélago de los, is., Cuba	D4	94
Canary Islands see Canarias, Islas, is., Spain	C3	54
Cañas, C.R.	G9	92
Cañasgordas, Col.	D4	84
Canastota, N.Y., U.S.	B5	139
Canatlán, Mex.	E7	90
Canaveral, Cape, c., Fl., U.S.	D6	116
Canaveral National Seashore, Fl., U.S.	D6	116
Canavieiras, Braz.	C9	79
Cañazas, Pan.	C2	84
Canberra, Austl.	J8	70
Canby, Ca., U.S.	B3	112
Canby, Mn., U.S.	F2	130
Canby, Or., U.S.	B4	144
Cancale, Fr.	D5	14
Canchaque, Peru	A2	82
Cancún, Mex.	G16	90
Cancún, Punta, c., Mex.	D1	94
Candarave, Peru	G6	82
Candás, Spain	B6	16
Candé, Fr.	E5	14
Candeias, Braz.	B9	79
Candeias, Braz.	F6	79
Candeias, stm., Braz.	C10	82
Candela, Mex.	D9	90
Candela, stm., Mex.	D9	90
Candelaria, Arg.	D11	80
Candelaria, Arg.	G6	80
Candelária, Braz.	E12	80
Candelaria, Col.	F4	84
Candelaria, Cuba	C3	94
Candelaria, stm., Mex.	H14	90
Candeleda, Spain	E6	16
Candia see Iráklion, Grc.	N9	20
Candia, N.H., U.S.	D4	136
Candiac, Que., Can.	q19	104
Candia Village, N.H., U.S.	D4	136
Cándido Aguilar, Mex.	E10	90
Cândido de Abreu, Braz.	C13	80
Candle Lake, l., Sask., Can.	D3	105
Candlemas Islands, is., S. Geor.	A2	73
Candlemas Islands, is., S. Geor.	J12	74
Candler, Fl., U.S.	C5	116
Candler, co., Ga., U.S.	D4	117
Candlewood, Lake, l., Ct., U.S.	D1	114
Candlewood Isle, Ct., U.S.	D2	114
Candlewood Shores, Ct., U.S.	D2	114
Cando, Sask., Can.	E1	105
Cando, N.D., U.S.	A6	141
Candor, N.Y., U.S.	C4	139
Candor, N.C., U.S.	B3	140
Cane, stm., La., U.S.	C2	125
Canea see Khaniá, Grc.	N8	20
Canehill, Ar., U.S.	B1	111
Canela, Braz.	E13	80
Canelas, Mex.	E6	90
Canelli, Italy	E3	18
Canelones, Ur.	H10	80
Cañete, Chile	I2	80
Cañete, Spain	E10	16
Cane Valley, Ky., U.S.	C4	124
Caney, Ks., U.S.	E8	123
Caney, Ky., U.S.	C6	124
Caney, stm., Ok., U.S.	A5	143
Caney Creek, stm., Tx., U.S.	r14	150
Caney Fork, stm., Tn., U.S.	C8	149
Caneyville, Ky., U.S.	C3	124
Canfield, Oh., U.S.	A5	142
Cangallo, Peru	E4	82
Cangas, Braz.	G13	82
Cangkuang, Tanjung, c., Indon.	j12	39a
Cangombe, Ang.	D3	58
Canguçu, Braz.	F12	80
Cangzhou, China	E4	32
Caniapiscau, stm., Que., Can.	g13	104
Canicattì, Italy	L8	18
Canim Lake, l., B.C., Can.	D7	99
Canindeyú, dept., Para.	C11	80
Canistear Reservoir, res., N.J., U.S.	A4	137
Canisteo, N.Y., U.S.	C3	139
Canisteo, stm., N.Y., U.S.	C3	139
Canistota, S.D., U.S.	D8	148
Cañitas de Felipe Pescador, Mex.	F8	90
Canjilon, N.M., U.S.	A3	138
Cankton, La., U.S.	D3	125
Canmer, Ky., U.S.	C4	124
Canmore, Alta., Can.	D3	98
Cannanore, India	G3	46
Cannel City, Ky., U.S.	C6	124
Cannelton, In., U.S.	I4	121
Cannelton, W.V., U.S.	m13	155
Cannes, Fr.	I14	14
Cannes, Bayou des, stm., La., U.S.	D3	125
Canning, N.S., Can.	D5	101
Cannon, De., U.S.	F3	115
Cannon, co., Tn., U.S.	B5	149
Cannon, stm., Mn., U.S.	F5	130
Cannon Air Force Base, mil., N.M., U.S.	C6	138
Cannon Ball, N.D., U.S.	C5	141
Cannonball, stm., N.D., U.S.	C5	141
Cannon Beach, Or., U.S.	B3	144
Cannondale, Ct., U.S.	E2	114
Cannon Falls, Mn., U.S.	F6	130
Cannonsburg, Ky., U.S.	B7	124
Cannonsville Reservoir, res., N.Y., U.S.	C5	139
Cann River, Austl.	K8	70
Caño, Isla del, i., C.R.	I11	92
Canoas, Braz.	E13	80
Canoas, stm., Braz.	D13	80
Canoe, Al., U.S.	D2	108
Canoinhas, Braz.	D13	80
Canon, Ga., U.S.	B3	117
Canon City, Co., U.S.	C5	113
Caño Negro, C.R.	G10	92
Canonsburg, Pa., U.S.	F1	145
Canoochee, stm., Ga., U.S.	D5	117
Canora, Sask., Can.	F4	105
Canosa [di Puglia], Italy	H11	18
Canossa, hist., Italy	E5	18
Canouan, i., St. Vin.	H14	94
Canova, S.D., U.S.	D8	148
Canowindra, Austl.	I8	70
Cansado, Maur.	J2	62
Canso, N.S., Can.	D8	101
Canta, Peru	D3	82
Cantabria, prov., Spain	B7	16
Cantábrica, Cordillera, mts., Spain	B6	16
Cantagalo, Braz.	F7	79
Cantal, dept., Fr.	G9	14
Cantanhede, Port.	E3	16
Cantaura, Ven.	C10	84
Canterbury, N.B., Can.	D2	101
Canterbury, Eng., U.K.	J15	8
Canterbury, De., U.S.	D3	115
Canterbury, N.H., U.S.	D3	136
Canterbury Bight, N.Z.	F4	72
Can Tho, Viet.	I8	40
Canton see Guangzhou, China	L2	34
Canton, Ct., U.S.	B4	114
Canton, Ga., U.S.	B2	117
Canton, Il., U.S.	C3	120
Canton, In., U.S.	G5	121
Canton, Ks., U.S.	D6	123
Canton, Me., U.S.	D2	126
Canton, Ma., U.S.	B5	128
Canton, Mn., U.S.	G7	130
Canton, Ms., U.S.	C3	131
Canton, Mo., U.S.	A6	132
Canton, N.Y., U.S.	f9	139
Canton, N.C., U.S.	f10	140
Canton, Oh., U.S.	B4	142
Canton, Ok., U.S.	A3	143
Canton, Pa., U.S.	C8	145
Canton, S.D., U.S.	D9	148
Canton, Tx., U.S.	C5	150
Canton Center, Ct., U.S.	B4	114
Canton Lake, res., Ok., U.S.	A3	143
Cantonment, Fl., U.S.	u14	116
Cantril, Ia., U.S.	D5	122
Cantù, Italy	D4	18
Cantu, stm., Braz.	C12	80
Cantwell, Ak., U.S.	C10	109
Cañuelas, Arg.	H9	80
Canumã, Braz.	J13	84
Canumã, stm., Braz.	J13	84
Canutama, Braz.	B9	82
Canute, Ok., U.S.	B2	143
Canutillo, Tx., U.S.	o11	150
Canwood, Sask., Can.	D2	105
Čany, ozero, l., Russia	G13	26
Cany-Barville, Fr.	C7	14
Canyon, Tx., U.S.	B2	150
Canyon, co., Id., U.S.	F2	119
Canyon City, Or., U.S.	C8	144
Canyon Creek, Alta., Can.	B3	98
Canyon de Chelly National Monument, Az., U.S.	A6	110
Canyon Ferry Lake, res., Mt., U.S.	D5	133
Canyon Lake, Tx., U.S.	E3	150
Canyon Lake, res., Tx., U.S.	E3	150
Canyonlands National Park, Ut., U.S.	E6	151
Canyonville, Or., U.S.	E3	144
Cao Bang, Viet.	C9	40
Caojun, China	F5	34
Caomaji, China	I4	32
Caoping, China	G7	34
Caoqiao, China	D8	34
Caota, China	F9	34
Caoxian, China	I3	32
Caoyangxi, China	I7	34
Cap, Pointe du, c., St. Luc.	G14	94
Capac, Mi., U.S.	F8	129
Čapajevsk, Russia	G7	26
Cap-à-l'Aigle, Que., Can.	B7	104
Capanaparo, stm., S.A.	D9	84
Capanema, Braz.	C12	80
Capão Bonito, Braz.	H4	79
Capão Doce, Morro do, mtn., Braz.	D13	80
Caparaó, Parque Nacional do, Braz.	F8	79
Caparo Viejo, stm., Ven.	D7	84
Capatárida, Ven.	B7	84
Cap-aux-Meules, Que., Can.	B8	101
Cap aux Meules, Île du, i., Que., Can.	B8	101
Cap-de-la-Madeleine, Que., Can.	C5	104
Cape, stm., Austl.	C7	70
Cape Arid National Park, Austl.	F4	68
Cape Barren Island, i., Austl.	M8	70
Cape Breton Highlands National Park, N.S., Can.	C9	101
Cape Breton Island, i., N.S., Can.	C9	101
Cape Broyle, Newf., Can.	E5	102
Cape Canaveral, Fl., U.S.	D6	116
Cape Charles, Va., U.S.	C6	153
Cape Coast, Ghana	I9	64
Cape Cod Bay, b., Ma., U.S.	C7	128
Cape Cod Canal, Ma., U.S.	C6	128
Cape Cod National Seashore, Ma., U.S.	C7	128
Cape Coral, Fl., U.S.	F5	116
Cape Dorset, N.W. Ter., Can.	D17	96
Cape Elizabeth, Me., U.S.	E2	126
Cape Fair, Mo., U.S.	E4	132
Cape Fear, stm., N.C., U.S.	C4	140
Cape Girardeau, Mo., U.S.	D8	132
Cape Girardeau, co., Mo., U.S.	D8	132
Cape Hatteras National Seashore, N.C., U.S.	B7	140
Cape Horn Mountain, mtn., Id., U.S.	E3	119
Cape Island, i., S.C., U.S.	E9	147
Capelinha, Braz.	D7	79
Capel'ka, Russia	C11	22
Capelle [aan den IJssel], Neth.	E6	12
Capelongo, Ang.	D3	58
Cape Lookout National Seashore, N.C., U.S.	C6	140
Capels, W.V., U.S.	D3	155
Cape May, N.J., U.S.	F3	137
Cape May, co., N.J., U.S.	E3	137
Cape May Court House, N.J., U.S.	E3	137
Cape Neddick, Me., U.S.	E2	126
Cape Porpoise, Me., U.S.	E2	126
Cape Ray, Newf., Can.	E2	102
Capernaum see Kefar Naḥum, hist., Isr.	C5	50
Capers Inlet, b., S.C., U.S.	k12	147
Capers Island, i., S.C., U.S.	F8	147
Capers Island, i., S.C., U.S.	G6	147
Cape Sable Island, i., N.S., Can.	F4	101
Cape Tormentine, N.B., Can.	C6	101
Cape Town (Kaapstad), S. Afr.	I4	66
Cape Verde (Cabo Verde), ctry., Afr.	E2	54
Cape York Peninsula, pen., Austl.	B8	68
Cap-Haïtien, Haiti	E8	94
Capilla de Farruco, Ur.	G11	80
Capilla del Monte, Arg.	F6	80
Capim, stm., Braz.	D9	76
Capinópolis, Braz.	E4	79
Capinota, Bol.	G8	82
Capinzal, Braz.	D13	80
Capira, Pan.	C3	84
Capitan, N.M., U.S.	D4	138
Capitán Arturo Prat, sci., Ant.	B1	73
Capitán Bado, Para.	B11	80
Capitán Bermúdez, Arg.	G8	80
Capitán Meza, Para.	D11	80
Capitan Mountains, mts., N.M., U.S.	D4	138
Capitan Peak, mtn., N.M., U.S.	D4	138
Capitán Sarmiento, Arg.	H9	80
Capitol Heights, Ia., U.S.	e8	122
Capitol Heights, Md., U.S.	C4	127
Capitol Peak, mtn., Nv., U.S.	B4	135
Capitol Reef National Park, Ut., U.S.	E4	151
Capivari, Braz.	G5	79
Capivari, stm., Braz.	B8	79
Capivari, stm., Braz.	H13	82
Capleville, Tn., U.S.	e9	149
Caplina, stm., Peru	G6	82
Čaplygin, Russia	H22	22
Capon Springs, W.V., U.S.	B6	155
Capote Knob, mtn., Tx., U.S.	k8	150
Cap-Pelé, N.B., Can.	C5	101
Capreol, Ont., Can.	p19	103
Capri, Isola di, i., Italy	I9	18
Capricorn, Cape, c., Austl.	D9	70
Capricorn Channel, strt., Austl.	D10	70
Capricorn Group, is., Austl.	D10	70
Caprivi Zipfel (Caprivi Strip), hist. reg., Nmb.	A6	66
Capron, Il., U.S.	A5	120
Cap-Rouge, Que., Can.	n17	104
Cap-Saint-Ignace, Que., Can.	B7	104
Capshaw, Al., U.S.	A3	108
Captain Cook, Hi., U.S.	D6	118
Captains Flat, Austl.	J8	70
Captiva, Fl., U.S.	F4	116
Captiva Island, i., Fl., U.S.	F4	116
Capua, Italy	H9	18
Capuça I, Ang.	A5	66
Capucapu, stm., Braz.	H13	84
Capulin Volcano National Monument, N.M., U.S.	A6	138
Caquetá, ter., Col.	G5	84
Caquetá (Japurá), stm., S.A.	H7	84
Caquiaviri, Bol.	G7	82
Çara, Eth.	O9	60
Čara, stm., Russia	E16	28
Carabaya, stm., Peru	F7	82
Carabaya, Cordillera de, mts., Peru	E6	82
Carabinani, stm., Braz.	I11	84
Carabobo, state, Ven.	J10	94
Caracal, Rom.	E8	20
Caracaraí, Braz.	G12	84
Caracas, Ven.	B9	84
Carache, Ven.	C7	84
Caracol, Braz.	B10	80
Caracollo, Bol.	G8	82
Caraguatatuba, Braz.	G6	79
Caraguatay, Para.	C10	80
Caraí, Braz.	D8	79
Caraibamba, Peru	F5	82
Caraigres, Cerro, mtn., C.R.	H10	92
Caraíva, stm., Braz.	D9	79
Carajás, Braz.	E8	76
Carajás, Serra dos, mts., Braz.	E8	76
Caranavi, Bol.	F8	82
Carandaí, Braz.	F7	79
Carandayti, Bol.	I10	82
Carangola, Braz.	F7	79
Caransebeş, Rom.	D6	20
Carapá, stm., Para.	C11	80
Cara-Paraná, stm., Col.	H6	84
Carapeguá, Para.	C10	80
Carapo, stm., Ven.	D11	84
Caraquet, N.B., Can.	B5	101
Caráquez, Ec.	H2	84
Carare, stm., Col.	D5	84
Caraş-Severin, co., Rom.	D5	20
Caratasca, Laguna de, b., Hond.	B11	92
Caratinga, Braz.	E7	79
Carauari, Braz.	J9	84
Caravaca, Spain	G10	16
Caravaggio, Italy	D4	18
Caravelas, Braz.	D9	79
Caravelí, Peru	F5	82
Caraway, Ar., U.S.	B5	111
Carayaó, Para.	C10	80
Caraz, Peru	C3	82
Carazinho, Braz.	E12	80
Carazo, dept., Nic.	F8	92
Carballiño, Spain	C3	16
Carballo, Spain	B3	16
Carberry, Man., Can.	E2	100
Carbo, Mex.	C4	90
Carbon, Alta., Can.	D4	98
Carbon, In., U.S.	E3	121
Carbon, W.V., U.S.	m13	155
Carbon, co., Mt., U.S.	E7	133
Carbon, co., Pa., U.S.	E10	145
Carbon, co., Ut., U.S.	D5	151
Carbon, co., Wy., U.S.	E5	157
Carbonado, Wa., U.S.	B3	154
Carbondale, Alta., Can.	C4	98
Carbondale, Co., U.S.	B3	113
Carbondale, Il., U.S.	F4	120
Carbondale, Ks., U.S.	D8	123
Carbondale, Pa., U.S.	C10	145
Carbonear, Newf., Can.	E5	102
Carbon Hill, Al., U.S.	B2	108
Carbon Hill, Il., U.S.	B5	120
Carbonia, Italy	J3	18
Carbonville, Ut., U.S.	D5	151
Carcaixent, Spain	F11	16
Carcarañá, Arg.	G8	80
Carcarañá, stm., Arg.	G8	80
Carcassonne, Fr.	I9	14
Carchi, prov., Ec.	G3	84
Carcross, Yukon, Can.	D6	96
Cardale, Man., Can.	D1	100
Čardarinskoje vodochranilišče, res., Asia	I11	26
Cárdenas, Cuba	C4	94
Cárdenas, Mex.	I13	90
Cárdenas, Mex.	F10	90
Cárdenas, Nic.	F9	92
Cárdenas, Bahía de, b., Cuba	C4	94
Çardi, Tur.	J13	20
Cardiel, Lago, l., Arg.	F2	78
Cardiff, Wales, U.K.	J10	8
Cardiff, Md., U.S.	A5	127
Cardigan, P.E.I., Can.	C7	101
Cardigan, Mount, mtn., N.H., U.S.	C3	136
Cardigan Bay, b., P.E.I., Can.	C7	101
Cardigan Bay, b., Wales, U.K.	I9	8
Cardinal, Ont., Can.	C9	103
Cardington, Oh., U.S.	B3	142
Cardona, Ur.	G10	80
Cardonal, Punta, c., Mex.	C4	90
Cardoso, Braz.	F4	79
Cardozo, Ur.	G10	80
Cardston, Alta., Can.	E4	98
Cardwell, Austl.	B7	70
Cardwell, Mo., U.S.	E7	132
Cardwell Mountain, mtn., Tn., U.S.	D8	149
Čardžou, Turk.	J10	26
Carei, Rom.	B6	20
Careiro, Braz.	I13	84
Careiro, Ilha do, i., Braz.	I13	84
Carén, Chile	F3	80
Carencro, La., U.S.	D3	125
Carentan, Fr.	C5	14
Cares, stm., Spain	B7	16
Caretta, W.V., U.S.	D3	155
Carey, Id., U.S.	F5	119
Carey, Oh., U.S.	B2	142
Carey, Lake, l., Austl.	E4	68
Careysburg, Lib.	H4	64
Carhaix-Plouguer, Fr.	D3	14
Carhuamayo, Peru	D3	82
Carhuanca, Peru	E5	82
Carhuaz, Peru	C3	82
Carhué, Arg.	I7	80
Cariacica, Braz.	F8	79
Cariaco, Ven.	B11	84
Cariaco, Golfo de, b., Ven.	B10	84
Cariamanga, Ec.	J3	84
Caribana, Punta, c., Col.	C4	84
Caribbean Sea	G8	94
Cariboo Mountains, mts., B.C., Can.	C7	99
Caribou, Me., U.S.	B5	126
Caribou, co., Id., U.S.	G7	119
Caribou Island, i., N.S., Can.	D7	101
Caribou Lake, l., Me., U.S.	C3	126
Caribou Mountain, mtn., Id., U.S.	F7	119
Caribou Mountain, mtn., Me., U.S.	C2	126
Caribou Mountains, mts., Alta., Can.	f7	98
Caribou Range, mts., Id., U.S.	F7	119
Carichic, Mex.	D6	90
Carievale, Sask., Can.	H5	105
Carignan, Fr.	C12	14
Carinhanha, Braz.	C7	79
Carinhanha, stm., Braz.	C6	79
Carini, Italy	K8	18
Caripe, Ven.	B11	84
Caripito, Ven.	B11	84
Carl Blackwell, Lake, res., Ok., U.S.	A4	143
Carleton, Mi., U.S.	F7	129
Carleton, Ne., U.S.	D8	134
Carleton, Mount, mtn., N.B., Can.	B3	101
Carleton Place, Ont., Can.	B8	103
Carlin, Nv., U.S.	C5	135
Carlinville, Il., U.S.	D4	120
Carlisle, Eng., U.K.	G11	8
Carlisle, Ar., U.S.	C4	111
Carlisle, In., U.S.	G3	121
Carlisle, Ia., U.S.	C4	122
Carlisle, Ky., U.S.	B5	124
Carlisle, Oh., U.S.	C1	142
Carlisle, Pa., U.S.	F7	145
Carlisle, S.C., U.S.	B5	147
Carlisle, co., Ky., U.S.	f8	124
Carl Junction, Mo., U.S.	D3	132
Carlock, Il., U.S.	C4	120
Carlópolis, Braz.	G4	79
Carlos, Mn., U.S.	E3	130
Carlos Barbosa, Braz.	E13	80
Carlos Casares, Arg.	H8	80
Carlos Chagas, Braz.	D8	79
Carlos Forseca Amador, Nic.	F8	92
Carlos Pellegrini, Arg.	G8	80
Carlos Reyles, Ur.	G10	80
Carlos Tejedor, Arg.	H7	80
Carlotta, Ca., U.S.	B1	112
Carlow, Ire.	I7	8
Carlow, co., Ire.	I7	8
Carlowville, Al., U.S.	C2	108
Carlsbad see Karlovy Vary, Czech Rep.	E12	10
Carlsbad, Ca., U.S.	F5	112
Carlsbad, N.M., U.S.	E5	138
Carlsbad, Tx., U.S.	D2	150
Carlsbad Caverns National Park, N.M., U.S.	E5	138
Carlsbad Springs, Ont., Can.	h13	103
Carlsborg, Wa., U.S.	A2	154
Carlstadt, N.J., U.S.	h8	137
Carlton, Sask., Can.	E2	105
Carlton, Ga., U.S.	B3	117
Carlton, Mn., U.S.	D6	130

Name	Map Ref.	Page

Name	Map Ref.	Page

Name	Map Ref.	Page

Name — Map Ref. — Page

Name — Map Ref. — Page

Derdepoort, S. Afr. E8 66
Derecske, Hung. H21 10
Derev'anka, Russia K24 6
De Ridder, La., U.S. D2 125
Derik, Tur. C6 48
Derma, Ms., U.S. B4 131
Dermott, Ar., U.S. D4 111
Dernieres, Isles, is., La., U.S. E5 125
Déroute, Passage de la, strt., Eur. L11 8
Derrieusseaux Creek, stm., Ar., U.S. C3 111
Derry see Londonderry, N. Ire., U.K. F6 8
Derry, N.H., U.S. E4 136
Derry, N.M., U.S. E2 138
Derry, Pa., U.S. F3 145
Derudeb, Sud. I9 60
De Rust, S. Afr. I6 66
Derval, Fr. E5 14
Derventa, Bos. E1 20
Derwent, Alta., Can. C5 98
Derwent, stm., Austl. N7 70
Derwood, Md., U.S. B3 127
Deržavinsk, Kaz. G11 26
Desaguadero, stm., Arg. G5 80
Desaguadero, stm., Bol. G7 82
Des Allemands, La., U.S. E5 125
Des Arc, Ar., U.S. C4 111
Des Arc, Mo., U.S. D7 132
Desbiens, Que., Can. A6 104
Desboro, Ont., Can. C3 103
Descabezado Grande, Volcán, vol., Chile H3 80
Descanso, Braz. D12 80
Descartes, Fr. F7 14
Deschaillons [-sur-Saint-Laurent], Que., Can. C5 104
Deschambault, Que., Can. C6 104
Deschambault Lake, Sask., Can. C4 105
Deschambault Lake, l., Sask., Can. C4 105
Deschutes, co., Or., U.S. D5 144
Deschutes, stm., Or., U.S. B6 144
Desdunes, Haiti E8 94
Dese, Eth. F8 56
Deseado, stm., Arg. F3 78
Desengaño, Punta, c., Arg. F3 78
Desenzano del Garda, Italy D5 18
Deseret, Ut., U.S. D3 151
Deseret Peak, mtn., Ut., U.S. C3 151
Deseronto, Ont., Can. C7 103
Desert, Mount, mtn., W.V., U.S. m13 155
Desertas, Ilhas, is., Port. m21 17a
Desert Creek Peak, mtn., Nv., U.S. E2 135
Desert Hot Springs, Ca., U.S. F5 112
Desert Peak, mtn., Ut., U.S. B2 151
Desert Valley, val., Nv., U.S. B3 135
Desha, Ar., U.S. B4 111
Desha, co., Ar., U.S. D4 111
Desheng, China B10 40
Deshler, Ne., U.S. D8 134
Deshler, Oh., U.S. A2 142
Desiderio Tello, Arg. F5 80
Des Lacs, N.D., U.S. A4 141
Des Lacs, stm., N.D., U.S. A4 141
Desloge, Mo., U.S. D7 132
Desmarais, Alta., Can. B4 98
Desmet, Id., U.S. B2 119
De Smet, S.D., U.S. C8 148
Des Moines, Ia., U.S. C4 122
Des Moines, N.M., U.S. A6 138
Des Moines, Wa., U.S. B3 154
Des Moines, co., Ia., U.S. D6 122
Des Moines, stm., U.S. D5 122
Des Moines, East Fork, stm., U.S. A3 122
Desna, stm., Eur. G4 26
Desolación, Isla, i., Chile J7 74
Desolation Canyon, val., Ut., U.S. D5 151
De Soto, Ga., U.S. E2 117
De Soto, Il., U.S. F4 120
De Soto, Ia., U.S. C3 122
De Soto, Ks., U.S. D9 123
De Soto, Mo., U.S. C7 132
De Soto, Tx., U.S. n10 150
De Soto, Wi., U.S. E2 156
De Soto, co., Fl., U.S. E5 116
De Soto, co., La., U.S. B2 125
De Soto, co., Ms., U.S. A3 131
De Soto City, Fl., U.S. E5 116
Despard, W.V., U.S. k10 155
Des Peres, Mo., U.S. f13 132
Des Plaines, Il., U.S. A6 120
Des Plaines, stm., U.S. k8 120
Desroches, Île, i., Sey. C10 58
Dessau, Ger. D12 10
Destin, Fl., U.S. u15 116
Destrehan, La., U.S. E5 125
Desvres, Fr. B8 14
Deta, Rom. D5 20
Detčino, Russia G19 22
Dete, Zimb. B8 66
Detlor, Ont., Can. B7 103
Detmold, Ger. D8 10
Detour, Point, c., Mi., U.S. C4 129
De Tour Village, Mi., U.S. C7 129
Detroit, Al., U.S. A1 108
Detroit, Ks., U.S. D6 123
Detroit, Me., U.S. D3 126
Detroit, Mi., U.S. F7 129
Detroit, Or., U.S. C4 144
Detroit, Tx., U.S. C5 150
Detroit Lake, res., Or., U.S. C4 144
Detroit Lakes, Mn., U.S. D3 130
Deuel, co., Ne., U.S. C3 134
Deuel, co., S.D., U.S. C9 148
Deurne, Bel. F5 12
Deurne, Neth. F8 12
Deutsche Bucht, b., Ger. A7 10
Deux-Montagnes, Que., Can. p19 104
Deux Montagnes, Lac des, l., Que., Can. q19 104
Deux-Sèvres, dept., Fr. F6 14
Deva, Rom. D6 20
Devakottai, India H5 46
De Valls Bluff, Ar., U.S. C4 111
Dev'atiny, Russia K25 6
Dévaványa, Hung. H20 10
Devecser, Hung. H17 10
Deventer, Neth. D9 12
Devereux, Ga., U.S. C3 117
DeView, Bayou, stm., Ar., U.S. B4 111
Devils Island see Diable, Île du, i., Fr. Gu. B8 76
Devils Lake, N.D., U.S. A7 141
Devils Lake, l., N.D., U.S. A6 141
Devils Paw, mtn., Ak., U.S. k23 109
Devils Postpile National Monument, Ca., U.S. D4 112
Devils Tower, Wy., U.S. B8 157
Devils Tower National Monument, Wy., U.S. B8 157
Devil Track Lake, l., Mn., U.S. k9 130
Devine, Tx., U.S. E3 150
DeVola, Oh., U.S. C4 142
Devon, Alta., Can. C4 98
Devon, Ks., U.S. E9 123
Devon, co., Eng., U.K. K10 8
Devon Island, i., N.W. Ter., Can. B11 86
Devonport, Austl. M7 70
Devonport, N.Z. B5 72
Devonshire, De., U.S. h7 115
Devoto, Arg. F7 80
Dewar, Ok., U.S. B6 143
Dewās, India I7 44
Dewberry, Alta., Can. C5 98
Dewees Inlet, b., S.C., U.S. k12 147
Dewees Island, i., S.C., U.S. F8 147
Dewetsdorp, S. Afr. G8 66
Dewey, Az., U.S. C3 110
Dewey, Ok., U.S. A6 143
Dewey, co., Ok., U.S. B2 143
Dewey, co., S.D., U.S. B4 148
Dewey Beach, De., U.S. F5 115
Dewey Lake, res., Ky., U.S. C7 124
Deweyville, Tx., U.S. D6 150
Deweyville, Ut., U.S. B3 151
De Winton, Alta., Can. D3 98
De Witt, Ar., U.S. C4 111
De Witt, Ia., U.S. C7 122
De Witt, Mi., U.S. F6 129
De Witt, Ne., U.S. D9 134
De Witt, N.Y., U.S. B4 139
De Witt, co., Il., U.S. C4 120
De Witt, co., Tx., U.S. E4 150
Dexter, Ga., U.S. D3 117
Dexter, Ia., U.S. C3 122
Dexter, Ks., U.S. E7 123
Dexter, Ky., U.S. f9 124
Dexter, Me., U.S. C3 126
Dexter, Mi., U.S. F7 129
Dexter, Mn., U.S. G6 130
Dexter, Mo., U.S. E8 132
Dexter, N.M., U.S. D5 138
Dexter, N.Y., U.S. A4 139
Dexter, Or., U.S. D4 144
Dexter, Lake, l., Fl., U.S. C5 116
Deyhūk, Iran E14 48
Deyyer, Iran H11 48
Dezfūl, Iran E10 48
Dezhou, China F4 32
Dežneva, mys, c., Russia D30 28
Dháfni, Grc. L6 20
Dhahab, Egypt C8 60
Dhahabān, Sau. Ar. D1 47
Dhahran see Az-Zahrān, Sau. Ar. A7 47
Dhaka, Bngl. I14 44
Dhamār, Yemen G4 47
Dhamtari, India B6 46
Dhanbād, India I12 44
Dhangadhī, Nepal F9 44
D'Hanis, Tx., U.S. E3 150
Dhār, India I6 44
Dharangaon, India B3 46
Dhārāpuram, India G4 46
Dharmavaram, India E4 46
Dharmshāla, India D7 44
Dhaulpur, India G7 44
Dhawlāgiri, mtn., Nepal F10 44
Dhelfoí, hist., Grc. K6 20
Dhenoúsa, i., Grc. L9 20
Dhībān, Jord. E5 50
Dhodhekánisos (Dodecanese), is., Grc. M10 20
Dholka, India I5 44
Dhorāji, India J4 44
Dhuburi, India G13 44
Dhule, India J6 44
Dhytikí Ellás, prov., Grc. K5 20
Dhytikí Makedhonía, prov., Grc. I5 20
Diable, Île du, i., Fr. Gu. B8 76
Diablo, Canyon, val., Az., U.S. C4 110
Diablo, Mount, mtn., Ca., U.S. h9 112
Diablo, Pico del, mtn., Mex. B2 90
Diablo Dam, Wa., U.S. A4 154
Diablo Lake, res., Wa., U.S. A4 154
Diablo Range, mts., Ca., U.S. D3 112
Diablotins, Morne, mtn., Dom. G14 94
Diagonal, Ia., U.S. D3 122
Diaka, mth., Mali D4 64
Dialakoto, Sen. E3 64
Diamante, Arg. G8 80
Diamante, stm., Arg. H5 80
Diamantina, Braz. E7 79
Diamantina, stm., Austl. F3 70
Diamantino, Braz. F13 82
Diamantino, stm., Braz. D2 79
Diamond, W.V., U.S. m12 155
Diamond City, Alta., Can. E4 98
Diamond City, Ar., U.S. A3 111
Diamond Harbour, India I13 44
Diamond Head, crat., Hi., U.S. B4 118
Diamond Hill, R.I., U.S. B4 146
Diamond Hill Reservoir, res., R.I., U.S. A4 146
Diamond Islets, is., Austl. A9 70
Diamond Lake, Il., U.S. h9 120
Diamond Lake, l., Or., U.S. D4 144
Diamond Mountains, mts., Nv., U.S. D6 135
Diamond Peak, mtn., Co., U.S. A2 113
Diamond Peak, mtn., Id., U.S. E5 119
Diamond Peak, mtn., Or., U.S. D4 144
Diamond Peak, mtn., Wa., U.S. C8 154
Diamond Springs, Ca., U.S. C3 112
Diamondville, Wy., U.S. E2 157
Diana, W.V., U.S. C4 155
Diana Bay, b., Can. D19 96
Dian Chi, l., China B7 40
Diangounté Kamara, Mali D5 64
Dianhu, China B8 34
Dianópolis, Braz. F9 76
Diapaga, Burkina E10 64
Diaz, Ar., U.S. B4 111
Dibaya, Zaire C4 58
Dibeng, S. Afr. F6 66
D'Iberville, Ms., U.S. E5 131
Dibete, Bots. D8 66
Diboll, Tx., U.S. D5 150
Dibrell, Tn., U.S. D8 149
Dibrugarh, India G16 44
Dickens, co., Tx., U.S. C2 150
Dickenson, co., Va., U.S. e9 153
Dickerson, Md., U.S. B3 127
Dickey, co., N.D., U.S. C7 141
Dickeyville, Wi., U.S. F3 156
Dickinson, Al., U.S. D2 108
Dickinson, N.D., U.S. C3 141
Dickinson, co., Ia., U.S. A2 122
Dickinson, co., Ks., U.S. D6 123
Dickinson, co., Mi., U.S. B3 129
Dickinson Dam, N.D., U.S. C3 141
Dickson, Ok., U.S. C5 143
Dickson, Tn., U.S. A4 149
Dickson, co., Tn., U.S. A4 149
Dickson City, Pa., U.S. D10 145
Didimbo, Ang. A5 66
Didsbury, Alta., Can. D3 98
Die, Fr. H12 14
Diébougou, Burkina F8 64
Dieciocho de Julio, Ur. G12 80
Diefenbaker, Lake, res., Sask., Can. F2 105
Diego de Almagro, Chile D3 80
Diego de Ocampo, Pico, mtn., Dom. Rep. E9 94
Diego Garcia, i., B.I.O.T. J8 24
Diego Ramírez, Islas, is., Chile H3 78
Diembéring, Sen. E1 64
Dien Bien Phu, Viet. D7 40
Dieppe, N.B., Can. C5 101
Dieppe, Fr. L15 8
Dieren, Neth. D9 12
Dierks, Ar., U.S. C1 111
Diessenhofen, Switz. C10 13
Dieterich, Il., U.S. D5 120
Dietikon, Switz. D9 13
Dietrich, Id., U.S. G4 119
Dieulefit, Fr. H12 14
Dieuze, Fr. D13 14
Diez de Octubre, Mex. E7 90
Dif, Kenya A8 58
Difang, China H5 32
Differdange, Lux. I8 12
Difficult, Tn., U.S. C8 149
Digboi, India G16 44
Digby, N.S., Can. E4 101
Digges Islands, is., N.W. Ter., Can. D17 96
Dighton, Ks., U.S. D3 123
Dighton, Ma., U.S. C5 128
Digne, Fr. H13 14
Digoin, Fr. F10 14
Digras, India B4 46
Digri, Pak. H3 44
Digul, stm., Indon. G11 38
Dijon, Fr. E12 14
Dikaja, Russia B22 22
Dike, Ia., U.S. B5 122
Dikhil, Dji. F9 56
Dikili, Tur. J10 20
Dikodougou, C. Iv. G7 64
Diksmuide (Dixmude), Bel. F2 12
Dikson, Russia C8 28
Dikwa, Nig. F9 54
Dila, Eth. N10 60
Dili, Indon. G8 38
Dilke, Sask., Can. G3 105
Dilkon, Az., U.S. B5 110
Dillard, Ga., U.S. B3 117
Dillard, Or., U.S. D3 144
Dill City, Ok., U.S. B2 143
Dille, W.V., U.S. C4 155
Diller, Ne., U.S. D9 134
Dilley, Tx., U.S. E3 150
Dilling, Sud. K5 60
Dillingen [an der Donau], Ger. G10 10
Dillingham, Ak., U.S. D8 109
Dillon, Co., U.S. B4 113
Dillon, Mt., U.S. E4 133
Dillon, S.C., U.S. C9 147
Dillon, co., S.C., U.S. C9 147
Dillon Lake, res., Oh., U.S. B3 142
Dillon Reservoir, res., Co., U.S. B4 113
Dillonvale, Oh., U.S. B5 142
Dillsboro, In., U.S. F7 121
Dillsburg, Pa., U.S. F7 145
Dillwyn, Va., U.S. C4 153
Dilly, Mali D6 64
Dilolo, Zaire E4 58
Dilworth, Mn., U.S. D2 130
Dimāpur, India H15 44
Dimashq (Damascus), Syria A6 50
Dimboola, Austl. K5 70
Dime, Eth. N9 60
Dimitrovgrad, Bul. G9 20
Dimitrovgrad, Russia G7 26
Dimlang, mtn., Nig. G9 54
Dimmit, co., Tx., U.S. E3 150
Dimmitt, Tx., U.S. B1 150
Dimock, S.D., U.S. D8 148
Dimona, Isr. F4 50
Dimondale, Mi., U.S. F6 129
Dinājpur, Bngl. H13 44
Dinan, Fr. D4 14
Dinant, Bel. H6 12
Dinara (Dinaric Alps), mts., Eur. F11 18
Dinara Planina, mts., Eur. F3 20
Dinard, Fr. D4 14
Dinaric Alps see Dinara, mts., Eur. F11 18
Dindar, Nahr ad- (Dinder), stm., Afr. K8 60
Dindigul, India G4 46
Dindima, Nig. F15 64
Dingalan Bay, b., Phil. n19 39b
Dingess, W.V., U.S. D2 155
Dinggyê, China F4 30
Dinghai, China E11 34
Dingle, Id., U.S. G7 119
Dingle Bay, b., Ire. I3 8
Dingmans Ferry, Pa., U.S. D12 145
Dingnan, China K3 34
Dingolfing, Ger. G12 10
Dingshuzhen, China D8 34
Dinguiraye, Gui. F4 64
Dingwall, N.S., Can. C9 101
Dingxi, China D7 30
Dingxian, China E2 32
Dingyuan, China C6 34
Dinh Lap, Viet. D9 40
Dinkelsbühl, Ger. F10 10
Dinner Point, c., Fl., U.S. D4 116
Dinokwe, Bots. D8 66
Dinosaur, Co., U.S. A1 113
Dinosaur National Monument, U.S. C6 151
Dinsmore, Sask., Can. F2 105
Dinuba, Ca., U.S. D4 112
Dinwiddie, co., Va., U.S. C5 153
Dioila, Mali E6 64
Dionísio, Braz. E7 79
Dionísio Cerqueira, Braz. D12 80
Diorama, Braz. D3 79
Diouloulou, Sen. E1 64
Dioundiou, Niger E11 64
Dioura, Mali D7 64
Diourbel, Sen. D1 64
Dipkarpaz, N. Cyp. D3 48
Dipolog, Phil. D7 38
Dipper Harbour West, N.B., Can. D3 101
Dippoldiswalde, Ger. E13 10
Dīr, Pak. C4 44
Dire Dawa, Eth. G9 56
Diriamba, Nic. F8 92
Dirico, Ang. A5 66
Diriomo, Nic. F8 92
Dirj, Libya E16 62
Dirk Hartog Island, i., Austl. E2 68
Dirrah, Sud. K4 60
Dirranbandi, Austl. G8 70
Dirs, Sau. Ar. E3 47
Dirty Devil, stm., Ut., U.S. E5 151
Disappointment, Cape, c., S. Geor. J11 74
Disappointment, Cape, c., Wa., U.S. C1 154
Disappointment, Lake, l., Austl. D4 68
Disappointment Creek, stm., Co., U.S. D2 113
Disaster Bay, b., Austl. K9 70
Discovery Bay, b., Austl. L4 70
Disentis, Switz. E10 13
Dishman, Wa., U.S. g14 154
Dishnā, Egypt D7 60
Disko, i., Grnld. C14 86
Disley, Sask., Can. G3 105
Dismal, stm., Ne., U.S. C5 134
Dismal Peak, mtn., Va., U.S. C2 153
Disna, Bela. F11 22
Disney, Ok., U.S. A6 143
Disputanta, Va., U.S. C5 153
Disraëli, Que., Can. D6 104
Distant, Pa., U.S. E3 145
District of Columbia, dept., U.S. f8 127
Distrito Federal, dept., Braz. C5 79
Distrito Federal, dept., Ven. B9 84
Disūq, Egypt B6 60
Diu, India J4 44
Divalá, Pan. I12 92
Divenskaja, Russia B13 22
Divernon, Il., U.S. D4 120
Divide, co., N.D., U.S. A2 141
Divide Peak, mtn., Wy., U.S. E5 157
Dividing Creek, stm., Md., U.S. D6 127
Divin, Bela. J7 22
Divinhe, Moz. C12 66
Divino, Braz. F7 79
Divinópolis, Braz. F6 79
Divisor, Serra do (Cordillera Ultraoriental), plat., S.A. C5 82
Divnoje, Russia H6 26
Divriği, Tur. B5 48
Dix, Il., U.S. E5 120
Dix, Ne., U.S. C2 134
Dix, stm., Ky., U.S. C5 124
Dix Dam, Ky., U.S. C5 124
Dixfield, Me., U.S. D2 126
Dixiana, Al., U.S. B3 108
Dixie, Ga., U.S. F3 117
Dixie, Wa., U.S. C7 154
Dixie, W.V., U.S. C3 155
Dixie, co., Fl., U.S. C3 116
Dixie Inn, La., U.S. B2 125
Dixie Union, Ga., U.S. E4 117
Dixie Valley, val., Nv., U.S. D4 135
Dix Mountain, mtn., N.Y., U.S. A7 139
Dixmude (Diksmuide), Bel. F2 12
Dixon, Ca., U.S. C3 112
Dixon, Il., U.S. B4 120
Dixon, Ia., U.S. C7 122
Dixon, Ky., U.S. C2 124
Dixon, Mo., U.S. D5 132
Dixon, Mt., U.S. C2 133
Dixon, N.M., U.S. A4 138
Dixon, Wy., U.S. E5 157
Dixon, co., Ne., U.S. B9 134
Dixons Mills, Al., U.S. C2 108
Dixonville, Alta., Can. A2 98
Dixonville, Pa., U.S. E3 145
Dixville, Que., Can. D6 104
Dixville Notch, N.H., U.S. g7 136
Dixville Notch, N.H., U.S. g7 136
Dixville Peak, mtn., N.H., U.S. g7 136
Diyālā (Sīrvān), stm., Asia E8 48
Diyarbakır, Tur. C6 48
Dizhou, China C9 40
Dja, stm., Afr. H9 54
Djakarta see Jakarta, Indon. j13 39a
Djamâa, Alg. D13 62
Djambala, Congo B2 58
Djanet, Alg. H15 62
Djedi, Oued, val., Alg. C13 62
Djema, Cen. Afr. Rep. N3 60
Djemila, hist., Alg. B13 62
Djénné, Mali E7 64
Djérem, stm., Cam. G9 54
Djibo, Burkina D9 64
Djibouti, Dji. F9 56
Djibouti, ctry., Afr. F9 56
Djokupunda, Zaire C4 58
Djougou, Benin G10 64
Djúpivogur, Ice. B6 6a
Djurås, Swe. K14 6
D'Lo, Ms., U.S. D4 131
Dmitrija Lapteva, proliv, strt., Russia C20 28
Dmitrijevka, Russia I23 22
Dmitrijev-L'govskij, Russia I18 22
Dmitrov, Russia E20 22
Dmitrovskij Pogost, Russia F22 22
Dmitrovsk-Orlovskij, Russia I18 22
Dnepropetrovsk see Dnipropetrovs'k, Ukr. H4 26
Dneprovsko-Bugskij kanal, Bela. I7 22
Dnieper, stm., Eur. H4 26
Dniester see Dnister, stm., Eur. H3 26
Dniprodzerzhyns'k, Ukr. H4 26
Dnipropetrovs'k, Ukr. H4 26
Dnister (Nistru), stm., Eur. H3 26
Dnistrovs'kyy lyman, l., Ukr. C14 20
Dno, Russia D12 22
Doaktown, N.B., Can. C3 101
Doany, Madag. o23 67b
Doba, Chad E4 56
Dobane, Cen. Afr. Rep. N3 60
Dobbiaco, Italy C7 18
Dobbins Air Force Base, mil., Ga., U.S. h7 117
Dobbs Ferry, N.Y., U.S. g13 139
Dobczyce, Pol. F20 10
Dobele, Lat. E6 22
Döbeln, Ger. D13 10
Doberai, Jazirah, pen., Indon. F9 38
Doboj, Bos. E2 20
Doboy Sound, b., Ga., U.S. E5 117
Dobr'anka, Russia F9 26
Dobrič, Bul. F11 20
Dobrinka, Russia I23 22
Dobříš, Czech Rep. F14 10
Dobromyl', Ukr. F22 10
Dobrudžansko plato, plat., Bul. F11 20
Dobruja, hist. reg., Eur. E12 20
Dobruš, Bela. I14 22
Dobson, N.C., U.S. A2 140
Doce, stm., Braz. E3 79
Doce, stm., Braz. E8 79
Docena, Al., U.S. f7 108
Dock Junction, Ga., U.S. *E5 117
Dockton, Wa., U.S. f11 154
Doctor Arroyo, Mex. F9 90
Doctor Cecilio Báez, Para. C10 80
Doctor Pedro P. Peña, Para. B7 80
Doctors Inlet, Fl., U.S. m8 116
Doctors Lake, l., Fl., U.S. m8 116
Dod Ballāpur, India F4 46
Doddridge, Ar., U.S. D2 111
Doddridge, co., W.V., U.S. B4 155
Dodecanese see Dhodhekánisos, is., Grc. M10 20
Dodge, Ne., U.S. C9 134
Dodge, N.D., U.S. B3 141
Dodge, co., Ga., U.S. D3 117
Dodge, co., Mn., U.S. G6 130
Dodge, co., Ne., U.S. C9 134
Dodge, co., Wi., U.S. E5 156
Dodge Center, Mn., U.S. F6 130
Dodge City, Ks., U.S. E3 123
Dodgeville, Wi., U.S. F3 156
Dodola, Eth. N10 60
Dodoma, Tan. C7 58
Dodsland, Sask., Can. F1 105
Dodson, La., U.S. B3 125
Dodson, Mt., U.S. B8 133
Doerun, Ga., U.S. E3 117
Doe Run, Mo., U.S. D7 132
Doetinchem, Neth. E9 12
Dog, stm., Vt., U.S. C3 152
Dogai Coring, l., China C13 44
Dog Island, i., Anguilla E13 94
Dog Island, i., Fl., U.S. C2 116
Dog Keys Pass, strt., Ms., U.S. g8 131
Dog Lake, l., Man., Can. D2 100
Dōgo, i., Japan K8 36
Do Gonbadān, Iran F11 48
Dogondoutchi, Niger E12 64
Doğubayazıt, Tur. B8 48
Doha see Ad-Dawḥah, Qatar B7 47
Doiran, Lake, l., Eur. H6 20
Dois de Novembro, Cachoeira, wtfl, Braz. C10 82
Dokka, Nor. K12 6
Dokšicy, Bela. G10 22
Doksy, Czech Rep. E14 10
Doland, S.D., U.S. C7 148
Dolbeau, Que., Can. k12 104
Dol-de-Bretagne, Fr. D5 14
Dole, Fr. E12 14
Dolega, Pan. C1 84
Doles, Ga., U.S. E3 117
Dolgeville, N.Y., U.S. B6 139
Dolgoje, Russia I20 22
Dolgorukovo, Russia I21 22
Dolinsk, Russia H20 28
Dolisie, Congo B2 58
Dolj, co., Rom. E7 20
Dollar Bay, Mi., U.S. A2 129
Dollard, Sask., Can. H1 105
Dollard, b., Eur. B11 12
Dolmatovskij, Russia D25 22
Dolomite, Al., U.S. B3 108
Dolomites see Dolomiti, mts., Italy C6 18
Dolomiti, mts., Italy C6 18
Dolores, Arg. I10 80
Dolores, Col. F5 84
Dolores, Guat. I15 90
Dolores, Co., U.S. D2 113
Dolores, Ur. G9 80
Dolores, Ven. C8 84
Dolores, co., Co., U.S. D2 113
Dolores, stm., U.S. E7 151
Dolores Hidalgo, Mex. G9 90
Dolphin and Union Strait, strt., N.W. Ter., Can. C9 96
Dolphin Island, i., Ut., U.S. B3 151
Dolton, Il., U.S. k9 120
Dolzhak, Ukr. A10 20
Dom Aquino, Braz. C1 79
Domažlice, Czech Rep. F12 10
Dombarovskij, Russia G9 26
Dombås, Nor. J11 6
Dombrád, Hung. G21 10
Dom Cavati, Braz. E7 79
Dome Mountain, mtn., Az., U.S. k9 110
Dome Peak, mtn., Co., U.S. B3 113
Domeyko, Chile E3 80
Domeyko, Cordillera, mts., Chile B4 80
Domfront, Fr. D6 14
Domiciano Ribeiro, Braz. B5 79
Domingo M. Irala, Para. C11 80
Domingos Martins, Braz. F8 79
Dominica, ctry., N.A. G14 94
Dominical, C.R. H11 92
Dominican Republic (República Dominicana), ctry., N.A. E9 94
Dominica Passage, strt., N.A. G14 94
Dominion, N.S., Can. C9 101
Dominion, Cape, c., N.W. Ter., Can. C18 96
Dominion City, Man., Can. E3 100
Dom Joaquim, Braz. E7 79
Domo, Eth. G10 56
Domodedovo, Russia F20 22
Domodossola, Italy C3 18
Domoni, Com. I16 67a
Dom Pedrito, Braz. F11 80
Domremy, Sask., Can. E3 105
Dom Silvério, Braz. F7 79
Domuyo, Volcán, vol., Arg. I3 80
Don, stm., Russia H6 26
Don, stm., Scot., U.K. D11 8
Dona Ana, N.M., U.S. E3 138
Dona Ana, co., N.M., U.S. E2 138
Donadeu, Arg. D7 80
Donald, Austl. K5 70
Donald, Or., U.S. h12 144
Donalda, Alta., Can. C4 98
Donalds, S.C., U.S. C3 147
Donaldson, Ar., U.S. C3 111
Donaldsonville, La., U.S. D4 125
Donalsonville, Ga., U.S. E2 117
Doñana, Parque Nacional de, Spain H5 16
Donaueschingen, Ger. H8 10
Donauwörth, Ger. G10 10
Don Benito, Spain G6 16
Doncaster, Eng., U.K. H12 8
Dondo, Ang. C2 58
Dondo, Moz. B12 66
Dondra Head, c., Sri L. J6 46
Dondușeni, Mol. A11 20
Donegal, Ire. G5 8
Donegal, co., Ire. G5 8
Donegal Bay, b., Ire. G5 8
Doneraile, S.C., U.S. C8 147
Donets'k, Ukr. H5 26
Dong, stm., China L6 34
Donga, stm., Nig. G15 64
Dong'an, China B3 34
Dongara, Austl. E2 68
Dongba, China D8 34
Dongchuan, China A7 40
Dongdaoan, China E5 32
Dong'ezhen, China G4 32
Dongfeng (Basuo), China E10 40
Dongfeng, China A13 32
Donggu, China I4 34
Dongguan, China L2 34
Dongguanyingzi, China B8 32
Donghai Dao, i., China D11 40
Dong Hoi, Viet. F9 40
Dongmen, China G3 34
Dong Nai, stm., Viet. I9 40
Dongola, Il., U.S. F4 120
Dongshi, China K7 34
Dongtai, China C9 34
Dongting Hu, l., China G1 34
Dongyang, China F9 34
Dongzhi, China E5 34
Doniphan, Mo., U.S. E7 132
Doniphan, Ne., U.S. D7 134
Doniphan, co., Ks., U.S. C8 123
Donji Vakuf, Bos. E12 18
Donkey Creek, stm., Wy., U.S. B7 157
Donkin, N.S., Can. C10 101
Donley, co., Tx., U.S. B2 150
Don Matías, Col. D5 84
Donna, Tx., U.S. F3 150
Donnacona, Que., Can. C6 104
Donnellson, Ia., U.S. D6 122
Donnelly, Alta., Can. B2 98
Donnelly, Id., U.S. E2 119
Donner Pass, Ca., U.S. C3 112
Donnybrook, N.D., U.S. A4 141
Donora, Pa., U.S. F2 145
Donostia (San Sebastián), Spain B10 16
Donovan, Il., U.S. C6 120
Don Peninsula, pen., B.C., Can. C3 99
Donskoj, Russia H21 22
Donskoje, Russia I22 22
Doolittle, Mo., U.S. D6 132
Doolow, Som. H9 56
Dooly, co., Ga., U.S. D3 117
Doomadgee, Austl. A3 70
Doon, Ia., U.S. A1 122
Doonerak, Mount, mtn., Ak., U.S. B9 109
Door, co., Wi., U.S. D6 156
Doornik (Tournai), Bel. G3 12
Dora, Al., U.S. B2 108
Dora, N.M., U.S. D6 138
Doraville, Ga., U.S. h8 117
Dorcheat, Bayou, stm., U.S. B2 125
Dorchester, N.B., Can. D5 101
Dorchester, Eng., U.K. K11 8
Dorchester, Ga., U.S. E5 117
Dorchester, Ne., U.S. D8 134
Dorchester, S.C., U.S. E7 147
Dorchester, Wi., U.S. C3 156

Name | Map Ref. | Page

E

Eagl-Elgi

Name — Map Ref. — Page

Eagletown, Ok., U.S. C7 143
Eagleville, Mo., U.S. A4 132
Eagleville, Tn., U.S. B5 149
Eakly, Ok., U.S. B3 143
Earle, Ar., U.S. B5 111
Earl Grey, Sask., Can. G3 105
Earlham, Ia., U.S. C3 122
Earlimart, Ca., U.S. E4 112
Earling, Ia., U.S. C2 122
Earling, W.V., U.S. n12 155
Earlington, Ky., U.S. C2 124
Earl Park, In., U.S. C3 121
Earlsboro, Ok., U.S. B5 143
Earlville, Il., U.S. B5 120
Earlville, Ia., U.S. B6 122
Earlville, N.Y., U.S. C5 139
Early, Ia., U.S. B2 122
Early, co., Ga., U.S. E2 117
Earth, Tx., U.S. B1 150
Easley, S.C., U.S. B2 147
East, stm., Ct., U.S. D5 114
East, stm., N.Y., U.S. k13 139
East, stm., Wi., U.S. h9 156
Eastaboga, Al., U.S. B3 108
Eastabuchie, Ms., U.S. D4 131
East Acton, Ma., U.S. g10 128
East Alstead, N.H., U.S. D2 136
East Alton, Il., U.S. E3 120
East Andover, N.H., U.S. D3 136
East Angus, Que., Can. D6 104
East Arlington, Vt., U.S. E2 152
East Aurora, N.Y., U.S. C2 139
East Baldwin, Me., U.S. E2 126
East Bangor, Pa., U.S. E11 145
East Bank, W.V., U.S. m13 155
East Barre, Vt., U.S. C4 152
East Baton Rouge, co., La., U.S. D4 125
East Bay, b., Fl., U.S. u16 116
East Bay, b., Tx., U.S. R15 150
East Beckwith Mountain, mtn., Co., U.S. C3 113
East Bend, N.C., U.S. A2 140
East Berbice-Corentyne, prov., Guy. E13 84
East Berlin, Ct., U.S. C5 114
East Berlin, Pa., U.S. G8 145
East Bernard, Tx., U.S. E4 150
East Bernstadt, Ky., U.S. C5 124
East Bethel, Mn., U.S. E5 130
East Bethel, Vt., U.S. D3 152
East Billerica, Ma., U.S. f11 128
East Blue Hill, Me., U.S. D4 126
East Bonne Terre, Mo., U.S. D7 132
East Boothbay, Me., U.S. E3 126
Eastborough, Ks., U.S. g12 123
East Brady, Pa., U.S. E2 145
East Branch Clarion River Lake, res., Pa., U.S. C4 145
East Brewton, Al., U.S. D2 108
East Bridgewater, Ma., U.S. B6 128
East Brimfield Lake, res., Ma., U.S. B3 128
East Brookfield, Ma., U.S. B3 128
East Brooklyn, Ct., U.S. B8 114
East Broughton, Que., Can. C6 104
East Brunswick, N.J., U.S. C4 137
East Burke, Vt., U.S. B5 152
East Butler, Pa., U.S. E2 145
East Butte, mtn., Mt., U.S. B5 133
East Cache Creek, stm., Ok., U.S. C3 143
East Caicos, i., T./C. Is. D9 94
East Calais, Vt., U.S. C4 152
East Camden, Ar., U.S. D3 111
East Canaan, Ct., U.S. A2 114
East Candia, N.H., U.S. D4 136
East Cape, c., N.Z. B7 72
East Cape, c., Fl., U.S. G5 116
East Carbon, Ut., U.S. D5 151
East Carroll, co., La., U.S. B4 125
East Chain, Mn., U.S. G3 130
East Chicago, In., U.S. A3 121
East China Sea, Asia r3 37b
East Chop, c., Ma., U.S. D6 128
East Cleveland, Oh., U.S. g9 142
East Concord, Vt., U.S. C5 152
East Corinth, Me., U.S. D3 126
East Cote Blanche Bay, b., La., U.S. E4 125
East Coulee, Alta., Can. D4 98
East Dennis, Ma., U.S. C7 128
East Derry, N.H., U.S. E4 136
East Detroit, Mi., U.S. p16 129
East Dorset, Vt., U.S. E2 152
East Douglas, Ma., U.S. B4 128
East Dover, Vt., U.S. F3 152
East Dubuque, Il., U.S. A3 120
East Dummerston, Vt., U.S. F3 152
East Eddington, Me., U.S. D4 126
East Ellijay, Ga., U.S. B2 117
Eastend, Sask., Can. H1 105
Easter, Mount, mtn., Ct., U.S. B2 114
Easter Island see Pascua, Isla de, i., Chile G4 74
Eastern Bay, b., Md., U.S. C5 127
Eastern Cape, prov., S. Afr. I8 66
Eastern Ghāts, mts., India F5 46
Eastern Neck Island, i., Md., U.S. B5 127
Eastern Point, c., Ma., U.S. f13 128
Eastern Transvaal, prov., S. Afr. E10 66
Easterville, Man., Can. C2 100
East Fairfield, Vt., U.S. B3 152
East Fairview, N.D., U.S. B1 141
East Falkland, i., Falk. Is. G5 78
East Falmouth, Ma., U.S. C6 128
East Farmington Heights, Ct., U.S. C4 114
East Feliciana, co., La., U.S. D4 125
East Flat Rock, N.C., U.S. f10 140
Eastford, Ct., U.S. B7 114
East Fork, stm., Wy., U.S. D3 157
East Fork Lake, res., Oh., U.S. C1 142
East Foxboro, Ma., U.S. B5 128
East Frisian Islands see Ostfriesische Inseln, is., Ger. B7 10
East Fultonham, Oh., U.S. C3 142
East Gaffney, S.C., U.S. A4 147
East Galesburg, Il., U.S. C3 120
East Glacier Park, Mt., U.S. B3 133
East Glastonbury, Ct., U.S. C5 114
East Granby, Ct., U.S. B5 114
East Grand Forks, Mn., U.S. C2 130
East Grand Rapids, Mi., U.S. F5 129
East Greenville, Pa., U.S. F10 145
East Greenwich, R.I., U.S. D4 146
East Gwillimbury, Ont., Can. C5 103
East Haddam, Ct., U.S. D6 114
Eastham, Ma., U.S. C8 128
East Hampstead, N.H., U.S. E4 136
East Hampton, Ct., U.S. C5 114
Easthampton, Ma., U.S. B2 128
East Hampton, N.Y., U.S. n16 139
East Hanover, N.J., U.S. *B4 137
East Hardwick, Vt., U.S. B4 152
East Hartford, Ct., U.S. B5 114
East Hartland, Ct., U.S. B4 114
East Haven, Ct., U.S. D4 114
East Haverhill, N.H., U.S. B3 136
East Helena, Mt. U.S. D5 133
East Holden, Me., U.S. D4 126
East Jordan, N.S., Can. F4 101
East Jordan, Mi., U.S. C5 129
East Juliette, Ga., U.S. C3 117
East Kilbride, Scot., U.K. F9 8
East Killingly, Ct., U.S. B8 114
East Kingston, N.H., U.S. E4 136
Eastlake, Mi., U.S. D4 129
Eastlake, Oh., U.S. A4 142
East Lake, l., Ont., Can. C5 100
East Lake Tohopekaliga, l., Fl., U.S. D5 116
Eastland, Tx., U.S. C3 150
Eastland, co., Tx., U.S. C3 150
East Lansing, Mi., U.S. F6 129
East Las Vegas, Nv., U.S. G6 135
East Laurinburg, N.C., U.S. C3 140
East Lempster, N.H., U.S. D2 136
East Liverpool, Oh., U.S. B5 142
East London (Oos-Londen), S. Afr. I8 66
East Longmeadow, Ma., U.S. B2 128
East Los Angeles, Ca., U.S. m12 112
East Lyme, Ct., U.S. D7 114
East Lynn, Il., U.S. C6 120
East Lynn, W.V., U.S. C2 155
East Lynne, Mo., U.S. C3 132
East Lynn Lake, res., W.V., U.S. C2 155
East Machias, Me., U.S. D5 126
East Madison, Me., U.S. D3 126
Eastmain-Opinaca, Réservoir, res., Que., Can. h11 104
Eastman, Que., Can. D5 104
Eastman, Ga., U.S. D3 117
Eastman, Wi., U.S. E2 156
East Marion, N.Y., U.S. m16 139
East Matunuck, R.I., U.S. F3 146
East Middlebury, Vt., U.S. D2 152
East Millbury, Ma., U.S. B4 128
East Millinocket, Me., U.S. C4 126
East Moline, Il., U.S. B3 120
East Montpelier, Vt., U.S. C4 152
East Naples, Fl., U.S. F5 116
East Newark, N.J., U.S. k8 137
East Newnan, Ga., U.S. C2 117
East Nishnabotna, stm., Ia., U.S. C2 122
East Norriton, Pa., U.S. o20 145
East Olympia, Wa., U.S. C3 154
Easton, Il., U.S. C4 120
Easton, Ks., U.S. k15 123
Easton, Me., U.S. B5 126
Easton, Md., U.S. C5 127
Easton, Mo., U.S. B3 132
Easton, Pa., U.S. E11 145
Easton, Wa., U.S. B4 154
Easton Reservoir, res., Ct., U.S. E2 114
East Orange, N.J., U.S. B4 137
East Orleans, Ma., U.S. C8 128
Eastover, S.C., U.S. D6 147
East Palatka, Fl., U.S. C5 116
East Palestine, Oh., U.S. B5 142
East Parsonfield, Me., U.S. E2 126
East Pass, strt., Fl., U.S. C2 116
East Pea Ridge, W.V., U.S. C2 155
East Peoria, Il., U.S. C4 120
East Pepperell, Ma., U.S. A4 128
East Petersburg, Pa., U.S. F9 145
East Pittsburgh, Pa., U.S. k14 145
Eastpoint, Fl., U.S. C2 116
East Point, Ga., U.S. C2 117
East Point, c., P.E.I., Can. C8 101
East Point, c., Ma., U.S. B6 128
East Point, c., N.J., U.S. E2 137
Eastport, Newf., Can. D5 102
Eastport, Me., U.S. D6 126
Eastport, N.Y., U.S. n16 139
East Poultney, Vt., U.S. D2 152
East Prairie, Mo., U.S. E8 132
East Providence, R.I., U.S. C4 146
East Pryor Mountain, mtn., Mt., U.S. E8 133
East Quogue, N.Y., U.S. n16 139
East Range, mts., Nv., U.S. C4 135
East Ridge, Tn., U.S. h11 149
East Rindge, N.H., U.S. E3 136
East River, Ct., U.S. D5 114
East River Mountain, mts., U.S. C1 153
East Rochester, N.Y., U.S. B3 139
East Rockingham, N.C., U.S. C3 140
East Rutherford, N.J., U.S. h8 137
East Saint Johnsbury, Vt., U.S. C5 152
East Saint Louis, Il., U.S. E3 120
East Salt Creek, stm., Co., U.S. B2 113
East Sandwich, Ma., U.S. C7 128
East Sebago, Me., U.S. E2 126
East Selkirk, Man., Can. D3 100
East Siberian Sea see Vostočno-Sibirskoje more, Russia C23 28
East Sioux Falls, S.D., U.S. D9 148
Eastsound, Wa., U.S. A3 154
East Sparta, Oh., U.S. B4 142
East Spencer, N.C., U.S. B2 140
East Stroudsburg, Pa., U.S. D11 145
East Sullivan, Me., U.S. D4 126
East Sullivan, N.H., U.S. E2 136
East Swanzey, N.H., U.S. E2 136
East Tawas, Mi., U.S. D7 129
East Templeton, Ma., U.S. A3 128
East Thermopolis, Wy., U.S. C4 157
East Thompson, Ct., U.S. A8 114
East Troy, Wi., U.S. F5 156
East Vestal, N.Y., U.S. C4 139
East View, W.V., U.S. k10 155
East Walker, stm., U.S. E2 135
East Wallingford, Vt., U.S. E3 152
East Walpole, Ma., U.S. h11 128
East Wareham, Ma., U.S. C6 128
East Washington, Pa., U.S. F1 145
East Waterboro, Me., U.S. E2 126
East Wenatchee, Wa., U.S. B5 154
East Wilton, Me., U.S. D6 126
East Windsor, N.J., U.S. C3 137
Eastwood, Ky., U.S. g12 124
East York, Ont., Can. D5 103
Eaton, Co., U.S. A6 113
Eaton, In., U.S. D7 121
Eaton, Oh., U.S. C1 142
Eaton, co., Mi., U.S. F6 129
Eatonia, Sask., Can. F1 105
Eaton Rapids, Mi., U.S. F6 129
Eatonton, Ga., U.S. C3 117
Eatontown, N.J., U.S. C4 137
Eatonville, Wa., U.S. C3 154
Eau Claire, Mi., U.S. G4 129
Eau Claire, Wi., U.S. D2 156
Eau Claire, co., Wi., U.S. D2 156
Eau Claire, stm., Wi., U.S. D2 156
Eau Claire, Lac à l', l., Que., Can. g11 104
Eauze, Fr. I7 14
Eban, Nig. G12 64
Ebano, Mex. F10 90
Ebb and Flow Lake, l., Man., Can. D2 100
Ebbw Vale, Wales, U.K. J10 8
Ebenezer, Sask., Can. F4 105
Eben Junction, Mi., U.S. B4 129
Ebensburg, Pa., U.S. F4 145
Ebensee, Aus. H13 10
Eberbach, Ger. F8 10
Ebermannstadt, Ger. F11 10
Eberndorf, Aus. I14 10
Ebersbach, Ger. D14 10
Ebersberg, Ger. G11 10
Eberstein, Aus. I14 10
Eberswalde, Ger. C13 10
Ebetsu, Japan d16 36a
Ebinur Hu, l., China C3 30
Ebnat, Switz. D11 13
Eboli, Italy I10 18
Ebolowa, Cam. H9 54
Ebony, Nmb. D2 66
Ebro (Ebre), stm., Spain E12 16
Ebro, Embalse del, res., Spain B8 16
Eccles, W.V., U.S. n13 155
Echaporã, Braz. G3 79
Ech Cheliff (Orléansville), Alg. B11 62
Echeconnee Creek, stm., Ga., U.S. D3 117
Echo, Al., U.S. D4 108
Echo, La., U.S. C3 125
Echo, Mn., U.S. F3 130
Echo, Or., U.S. B7 144
Echo Bay, Nv., U.S. G7 135
Echoing Lake, l., Ont., Can. B5 100
Echo Lake, l., Me., U.S. D3 126
Echo Lake, l., Vt., U.S. B5 152
Echols, co., Ga., U.S. F4 117
Echt, Neth. F8 12
Echuca, Austl. K6 70
Écija, Spain H6 16
Eckernförde, Ger. A9 10
Eckerty, In., U.S. H4 121
Eckhart Mines, Md., U.S. k13 127
Eckley, Co., U.S. A8 113
Eckville, Alta., Can. C3 98
Eclectic, Al., U.S. C3 108
Eclipse Sound, strt., N.W. Ter., Can. B17 96
Ečmiadzin, Arm. I6 26
Econfina, stm., Fl., U.S. B3 116
Economy, N.S., Can. D6 101
Economy, In., U.S. E7 121
Economy, Pa., U.S. *h13 145
Écorces, Rivière aux, stm., Que., Can. A6 104
Ecorse, Mi., U.S. p15 129
Écrins, Barre des, mtn., Fr. H13 14
Ecru, Ms., U.S. A4 131
Ector, co., Tx., U.S. D1 150
Ecuador, ctry., S.A. D3 76
Ecum Secum, N.S., Can. E7 101
Ecum Secum Bridge, N.S., Can. E7 101
Ed, Erit. H2 47
Edam, Sask., Can. D1 105
Edam, Neth. C7 12
Edberg, Alta., Can. C4 98
Edcouch, Tx., U.S. F4 150
Eddiceton, Ms., U.S. D3 131
Eddy, co., N.M., U.S. E5 138
Eddy, co., N.D., U.S. B7 141
Eddystone, Pa., U.S. p20 145
Eddystone Point, c., Austl. M8 70
Eddyville, Ia., U.S. C5 122
Eddyville, Ky., U.S. e9 124
Eddyville, Ne., U.S. C6 134
Ede, Nig. H12 64
Edéa, Cam. H9 54
Edéia, Braz. D4 79
Edelény, Hung. G20 10
Eden, Austl. K8 70
Eden, Man., Can. D2 100
Eden, Az., U.S. E6 110
Eden, Ga., U.S. D5 117
Eden, Id., U.S. G4 119
Eden, Md., U.S. D6 127
Eden, N.Y., U.S. C2 139
Eden, N.C., U.S. A3 140
Eden, S.D., U.S. B8 148
Eden, Tx., U.S. D3 150
Eden, Ut., U.S. B4 151
Eden, Wi., U.S. E5 156
Eden, Wy., U.S. D3 157
Edenburg, S. Afr. G7 66
Eden Hill, hill, Ct., U.S. D2 114
Eden Prairie, Mn., U.S. n12 130
Edenton, N.C., U.S. A6 140
Eden Valley, Mn., U.S. E4 130
Edenville, S. Afr. F8 66
Edenville, Mi., U.S. E6 129
Edenwold, Sask., Can. G3 105
Edeowie, Austl. H3 70
Eder, stm., Ger. D8 10
Edfu see Idfū, Egypt E7 60
Edgar, Ne., U.S. D8 134
Edgar, Wi., U.S. D4 156
Edgar, co., Il., U.S. D6 120
Edgard, La., U.S. D5 125
Edgar Springs, Mo., U.S. D6 132
Edgartown, Ma., U.S. D6 128
Edgecombe, co., N.C., U.S. B5 140
Edgecumbe, Cape, c., Ak., U.S. m21 109
Edgefield, S.C., U.S. D4 147
Edgefield, co., S.C., U.S. D4 147
Edgeley, N.D., U.S. C7 141
Edgemere, Md., U.S. B5 127
Edgemont, S.D., U.S. D2 148
Edgemoor, De., U.S. A3 115
Edgemoor, S.C., U.S. B5 147
Edgemoor, Tn., U.S. m13 149
Edgeøya, i., Sval. B3 24
Edgerly, La., U.S. D2 125
Edgerton, Alta., Can. C5 98
Edgerton, Ks., U.S. D8 123
Edgerton, Mn., U.S. G2 130
Edgerton, Mo., U.S. B3 132
Edgerton, Oh., U.S. A1 142
Edgerton, Wi., U.S. F4 156
Edgerton, Wy., U.S. C6 157
Edgewater, Al., U.S. f7 108
Edgewater, Fl., U.S. D6 116
Edgewater, Md., U.S. C4 127
Edgewater, N.J., U.S. h9 137
Edgewater Park, N.J., U.S. C3 137
Edgewood, B.C., Can. E8 99
Edgewood, Il., U.S. E5 120
Edgewood, In., U.S. D6 121
Edgewood, Ia., U.S. B6 122
Edgewood, Ky., U.S. h13 124
Edgewood, Md., U.S. B5 127
Edgewood, N.M., U.S. B3 138
Edgewood, Oh., U.S. A5 142
Edgewood, Pa., U.S. k14 145
Edgewood, Wa., U.S. f11 154
Edgeworth, Pa., U.S. h13 145
Édhessa, Grc. I6 20
Edina, Mn., U.S. F5 130
Edina, Mo., U.S. A5 132
Edinboro, Pa., U.S. C1 145
Edinburg, Il., U.S. D4 120
Edinburg, N.D., U.S. A8 141
Edinburg, Tx., U.S. F3 150
Edinburg, Va., U.S. B4 153
Edinburgh, Scot., U.K. F10 8
Edinburgh, In., U.S. F6 121
Edinburgh, Arrecife, rf., Nic. C12 92
Edinburgh Channel, strt., Nic. C12 92
Edincik, Tur. I11 20
Edirne, Tur. H10 20
Edison, Ga., U.S. E2 117
Edison, Ne., U.S. D6 134
Edison, N.J., U.S. B4 137
Edison, Wa., U.S. A3 154
Edisto, stm., S.C., U.S. E6 147
Edisto, North Fork, stm., S.C., U.S. D5 147
Edisto, South Fork, stm., S.C., U.S. E5 147
Edisto Island, i., S.C., U.S. F7 147
Edith, Mount, mtn., Mt., U.S. D5 133
Edjeleh, Alg. G15 62
Edmond, Ok., U.S. B4 143
Edmonds, Wa., U.S. B3 154
Edmondson, Ar., U.S. B5 111
Edmondson Heights, Md., U.S. *g10 127
Edmonson, co., Ky., U.S. C3 124
Edmonton, Austl. A6 70
Edmonton, Alta., Can. C4 98
Edmonton, Ky., U.S. D4 124
Edmore, Mi., U.S. E5 129
Edmore, N.D., U.S. A7 141
Edmunds, co., S.D., U.S. B6 148
Edmundston, N.B., Can. B1 101
Edna, Ks., U.S. E8 123
Edna, Tx., U.S. E4 150
Edolo, Italy C5 18
Edon, Oh., U.S. A1 142
Édouard, Lac, l., Que., Can. B5 104
Edremit, Tur. J11 20
Edsbro, Swe. L16 6
Edsbyn, Swe. K14 6
Edson, Alta., Can. C2 98
Edson Butte, mtn., Or., U.S. E2 144
Eduardo Castex, Arg. H6 80
Edward, Lake, l., Afr. B5 58
Edwards, Co., U.S. B4 113
Edwards, Il., U.S. C4 120
Edwards, Ms., U.S. C3 131
Edwards, co., Il., U.S. E5 120
Edwards, co., Ks., U.S. E4 123
Edwards, co., Tx., U.S. E2 150
Edwards Air Force Base, mil., Ca., U.S. E5 112
Edwardsburg, Mi., U.S. G4 129
Edwards Butte, mtn., Or., U.S. B3 144
Edwards Plateau, plat., Tx., U.S. D2 150
Edwardsport, In., U.S. G3 121
Edwardsville, Al., U.S. B4 108
Edwardsville, Il., U.S. E4 120
Edwardsville, Ks., U.S. k16 123
Edwardsville, Pa., U.S. n17 145
Edward VII Peninsula, pen., Ant. C9 73
Edwin, Al., U.S. D4 108
Eek, Ak., U.S. C7 109
Eeklo, Bel. F4 12
Eel, stm., Ca., U.S. B2 112
Eel, stm., In., U.S. C6 121
Eel, stm., In., U.S. F3 121
Effigy Mounds National Monument, Ia., U.S. A6 122
Effingham, Il., U.S. D5 120
Effingham, Ks., U.S. C8 123
Effingham, co., Ga., U.S. D5 117
Effingham, co., Il., U.S. D5 120
Efland, N.C., U.S. A3 140
Ega, stm., Spain C9 16
Egadi, Isole, is., Italy L7 18
Egan, S.D., U.S. D9 148
Egaña, Arg. I9 80
Egan Range, mts., Nv., U.S. E7 135
Eganville, Ont., Can. B7 103
Egegik, Ak., U.S. D8 109
Egeland, N.D., U.S. A6 141
Eger see Cheb, Czech Rep. E12 10
Eger, Hung. H20 10
Egersund, Nor. L10 6
Eggenburg, Aus. G15 10
Egg Harbor City, N.J., U.S. D3 137
Egg Island Point, c., N.J., U.S. E2 137
Egilsstadir, Ice. B6 6a
Eglin Air Force Base, mil., Fl., U.S. u15 116
Egmont, Mount, mtn., N.Z. C4 72
Egmont Bay, b., P.E.I., Can. C5 101
Egmont Channel, strt., Fl., U.S. p10 116
Egmont Key, i., Fl., U.S. p10 116
Egremont, Alta., Can. B4 98
Éguas, Rio das, stm., Braz. D6 79
Egypt, Ar., U.S. B5 111
Egypt, Ga., U.S. D5 117
Egypt, Ma., U.S. B6 128
Egypt (Miṣr), ctry., Afr. C7 56
Egypt, Lake of, res., Il., U.S. F5 120
Ehrenberg, Az., U.S. D1 110
Ehrhardt, S.C., U.S. E5 147
Eibar, Spain B9 16
Eichstätt, Ger. G11 10
Eidsvåg, Nor. J11 6
Eidsvold, Austl. E9 70
Eielson Air Force Base, mil., Ak., U.S. C10 109
Eifel, mts., Ger. E6 10
Eiger, mtn., Switz. E9 13
Eight Degree Channel, strt., Asia I2 46
Eightmile Creek, stm., Ks., U.S. h12 123
Eights Coast, Ant. C11 73
Eighty Eight, Ky., U.S. D4 124
Eighty Mile Beach, Austl. C4 68
Eildon, Austl. K6 70
Eildon, Lake, res., Austl. K6 70
Eilenburg, Ger. D12 10
Einasleigh, Austl. B6 70
Einasleigh, stm., Austl. A5 70
Einbeck, Ger. D9 10
Eindhoven, Neth. F7 12
Einsiedeln, Switz. D10 13
Eiru, stm., Braz. B6 82
Eirunepé, Braz. B7 82
Eisden, Bel. G8 12
Eisenach, Ger. E10 10
Eisenberg, Ger. E11 10
Eisenerz, Aus. H14 10
Eisenhower, Mount, mtn., N.H., U.S. B4 136
Eisenhüttenstadt, Ger. C14 10
Eisenkappel, Aus. I14 10
Eisenstadt, Aus. H16 10
Eišiškės, Lith. G8 22
Eisleben, Ger. D11 10
Eitorf, Ger. E7 10
Eivissa, Spain G13 16
Eivissa (Ibiza), i., Spain G13 16
Ejea de los Caballeros, Spain C10 16
Ejeda, Madag. t21 67b
Ejido, Ven. C7 84
Ejido Jaboncillos, Mex. C8 90
Ejin Qi, China C7 30
Ejutla de Crespo, Mex. I11 90
Ekalaka, Mt., U.S. E12 133
Eket, Nig. I13 64
Ekibastuz, Kaz. G7 28
Ekpoma, Nig. H13 64
Eksjö, Swe. M14 6
Ela, Mya. E4 40
El Aaiún (La'youn), W. Sah. G4 62
El Abiadh Sidi Cheikh, Alg. D11 62
El Adeb Larache, Alg. G15 62
El Adelanto, Guat. C5 92
El Agreb, Alg. E13 62
El Aguilar, Arg. B6 80
Elaine, Ar., U.S. C5 111
El Alamein see Al-'Alamayn, Egypt B5 60
El Alia, Tun. L5 18
El Alto, Arg. E6 80
El Alto, Peru J2 84
El Amparo de Apure, Ven. D7 84
Elamville, Al., U.S. D4 108
Elandsvlei, S. Afr. I4 66
El Angel, Ec. G4 84
El Aouinet, Alg. N2 18
El Arahal, Spain H6 16
El Arco, Mex. C3 90
El Aricha, Alg. C10 62
El Aroussa, Tun. M4 18
Elat, Isr. I3 50
El Ávila, Parque Nacional, Ven. B9 84
Elazığ, Tur. B5 48
Elba, Al., U.S. D3 108
Elba, Ne., U.S. C7 134
Elba, Isola d', i., Italy G5 18
El Banco, Col. C6 84
El Barco de Valdeorras, Spain C5 16
Elbasan, Alb. H4 20
El Baúl, Ven. C8 84
El Baúl, Cerro, mtn., Mex. I12 90
El Baúl, Cerro, mtn., Mex. I9 90
Elbe (Labe), stm., Eur. B9 10
Elberfeld, In., U.S. H3 121
Elberon, Ia., U.S. B5 122
Elbert, Co., U.S. B6 113
Elbert, co., Co., U.S. B6 113
Elbert, co., Ga., U.S. B4 117
Elbert, Mount, mtn., Co., U.S. B4 113
Elberta, Al., U.S. E2 108
Elberta, Ga., U.S. D3 117
Elberta, Mi., U.S. D4 129
Elberton, Ga., U.S. B4 117
Elbeuf, Fr. C8 14
El Beyyadh, Alg. D11 62
Elbing, Ks., U.S. f12 123
Elbistan, Tur. B4 48
Elbląg (Elbing), Pol. A19 10
El Bluff, Nic. F11 92
El-Borouj, Mor. D7 62
El Boulaïda, Alg. B12 62
Elbow, Sask., Can. F2 105
Elbow, stm., Alta., Can. D3 98
Elbow Cay, i., Bah. C4 94
Elbow Lake, Mn., U.S. E3 130
El'brus, gora, mtn., Russia I6 26
Elbrus, Mount see El'brus, gora, mtn., Russia I6 26
Elburn, Il., U.S. B5 120
El Cabezo, Arrecife, rf., Mex. H12 90
El Caburé, Arg. D7 80
El Caimanero, Laguna, b., Mex. F6 90
El Cajon, Ca., U.S. F5 112
El Cajón, Embalse, res., Hond. B7 92
El Calafate, Arg. G2 78
El Callao, Ven. D12 84
El Calvario, Col. E6 84
El Calvario, Ven. C9 84
El Campo, Tx., U.S. E4 150
El Capitan, mtn., Mt., U.S. D2 133
El Capitan Reservoir, res., Ca., U.S. o16 112
El Carmen, Arg. C6 80
El Cármen, Bol. H12 82
El Carmen, Col. C6 84
El Carmen, Peru E3 82
El Carmen, stm., Mex. B6 90
El Carmen de Bolívar, Col. C5 84
El Carricito, Mex. C8 90
El Carril, Arg. C6 80
El Castillo de La Concepción, Nic. F10 92
El Cedral, Guat. A4 92
El Cedrito, Mex. C9 90
El Centro, Ca., U.S. F6 112
El Cerrito, Col. F4 84
El Cerrito, Ca., U.S. h8 112
El Cerro, Bol. G11 82
El Chile, Montaña, mtn., Hond. C8 92
Elcho, Wi., U.S. C4 156
El Chorrillo, Arg. G5 80
El Cocuy, Col. D6 84
El Colorado, Arg. D9 80
El Cóndor, Cerro, mtn., Arg. D4 80
El Congo, El Sal. D5 92
El Corazón, Ec. H3 84
El Corpus, Hond. D7 92
El Coyote, stm., Mex. B3 90
El Cozón, Mex. B3 90
El Cuco, El Sal. D6 92
El Cuervo, Laguna, l., Mex. C7 90
El Cuervo Butte, mtn., N.M., U.S. k9 138
Elda, Spain G11 16
El Dátil, Mex. B3 90
Eldersburg, Md., U.S. B4 127
Eldersley, Sask., Can. E4 105
El Desemboque, Mex. C3 90
El Desemboque, Mex. B3 90
El'dikan, Russia E19 28
El Diviso, Col. G3 84
El Djazaïr (Algiers), Alg. B12 62
El Djelfa, Alg. C12 62
Eldon, P.E.I., Can. C7 101
Eldon, Ia., U.S. D5 122
Eldon, Mo., U.S. C5 132
Eldora, Ia., U.S. B4 122
Eldorado, Arg. D11 80
Eldorado, Braz. C14 80
Eldorado, Ont., Can. C7 103
El Dorado, Mex. E6 90
El Dorado, Ar., U.S. D3 111
Eldorado, Ga., U.S. E3 117
Eldorado, Il., U.S. F5 120
El Dorado, Ks., U.S. E7 123
Eldorado, Oh., U.S. C1 142
Eldorado, Ok., U.S. C2 143
Eldorado, Tx., U.S. D2 150
El Dorado, Ven. D12 84
El Dorado, co., Ca., U.S. C3 112
Eldorado Peak, mtn., Wa., U.S. A4 154
Eldorado Springs, Co., U.S. B5 113
El Dorado Springs, Mo., U.S. D3 132
Eldorendo, Ga., U.S. E2 117
Eldoret, Kenya A7 58
Eldred, Il., U.S. D3 120
Eldred, Pa., U.S. C5 145
Eldridge, Al., U.S. B2 108
Eldridge, Ia., U.S. C7 122
Eleanor, W.V., U.S. C3 155
Electra, Tx., U.S. C3 150
Electra Lake, res., Co., U.S. D3 113
Electric Peak, mtn., Co., U.S. C5 113
Electric Peak, mtn., Mt., U.S. E6 133
Elefante, Isla del see Elephant Island, i., Ant. B1 73
Elefantes, Rio dos (Olifants), stm., Afr. E11 66
Elei, Wādī, val., Afr. G8 60
Eleja, Lat. E6 22
Elektrogorsk, Russia F21 22
Elektrostal', Russia F21 22
El Encanto, Col. H6 84
El Encanto, Guat. I15 90
Elephant Butte Reservoir, res., N.M., U.S. D2 138
Elephant Island, i., Ant. K9 74
Elephant Mountain, mtn., Me., U.S. D2 126
El Estor, Guat. B5 92
El Eulma, Alg. B13 62
Eleuthera, i., Bah. B6 94
Eleuthera Point, c., Bah. B6 94
Eleva, Wi., U.S. D2 156
Eleven Mile Canyon Reservoir, res., Co., U.S. C5 113
Eleven Point, stm., U.S. A4 111
Elevsis, Grc. K7 20
El Fahs, Tun. M4 18
El Ferrol del Caudillo, Spain B3 16
Elfrida, Az., U.S. F6 110
Elfros, Sask., Can. F4 105
El Fuerte, Mex. D5 90
El Galpón, Arg. C6 80
El Ghazawet, Alg. C10 62
Elgin, Man., Can. E1 100
Elgin, N.B., Can. D4 101
Elgin, Scot., U.K. D10 8
Elgin, Al., U.S. A2 108
Elgin, Il., U.S. A5 120

Name	Map Ref.	Page

Name | Map Ref. | Page

Fear, Cape, c., N.C., U.S. D5 140
Feather, stm., Ca., U.S. C3 112
Feather, Middle Fork, stm., Ca., U.S. C3 112
Featherston, Ok., U.S. B6 143
Feathertop, Mount, mtn., Austl. K7 70
Fécamp, Fr. C7 14
Federación, Arg. F10 80
Federal, Arg. F9 80
Federalsburg, Md., U.S. C6 127
Fedora, S.D., U.S. C8 148
Fedscreek, Ky., U.S. C7 124
Feeding Hills, Ma., U.S. B2 128
Fehérgyarmat, Hung. H22 10
Fehmarn, i., Ger. A11 10
Fehmarn Belt, strt., Eur. A11 10
Feia, Lagoa, b., Braz. G8 79
Feijó, Braz. C6 82
Feira, Zam. E6 58
Feira de Santana, Braz. B9 79
Feixiang, China G2 32
Fejaj, Chott, sw., Tun. D15 62
Fejér, co., Hung. H18 10
Felanitx, Spain F15 16
Feldbach, Aus. I15 10
Feldkirch, Aus. H9 10
Felhit, Erit. I10 60
Feliciano, Arroyo, stm., Arg. F9 80
Felicity, Oh., U.S. D1 142
Felix, Cape, c., N.W. Ter., Can. C13 96
Felixlândia, Braz. E6 79
Felixstowe, Eng., U.K. J15 8
Felixton, S. Afr. G10 66
Félix U. Gómez, Mex. C4 90
Fellbach, Ger. G9 10
Felletin, Fr. G9 14
Fellsmere, Fl., U.S. E6 116
Felton, Ca., U.S. D2 112
Felton, De., U.S. D3 115
Felton, Ga., U.S. C1 117
Feltre, Italy C6 18
Femund, l., Nor. J12 6
Femundsenden, Nor. K12 6
Fen, stm., China D9 30
Fence, stm., Mi., U.S. B2 129
Fence Lake, l., Wi., U.S. C4 156
Fenelon Falls, Ont., Can. C6 103
Fengcheng, China C12 32
Fengcheng, China G4 34
Fengdu, China F8 30
Fengfeng, China G2 32
Fenghuanjing, China D6 34
Fengjia, China F9 32
Fenglin, Tai. L10 34
Fengxin, China G4 34
Fengyang, China E10 30
Fengyüan, Tai. K9 34
Fengzhen, China C9 30
Feni, Bngl. I14 44
Fenimore Pass, strt., Ak., U.S. E4 109
Fennimore, Wi., U.S. F3 156
Fennville, Mi., U.S. F4 129
Fenoarivo Atsinanana, Madag. p23 67b
Fenshui'ao, China J3 34
Fenton, Ia., U.S. A3 122
Fenton, La., U.S. D3 125
Fenton, Mi., U.S. F7 129
Fentress, co., Tn., U.S. C9 149
Fenwick, W.V., U.S. C4 155
Fenwick Island, De., U.S. G5 115
Fenwick Island, i., S.C., U.S. k11 147
Fenwood, Sask., Can. G4 105
Fenyang, China D9 30
Feodosiya, Ukr. H5 26
Fer, Point au, c., La., U.S. E4 125
Ferdinand, Id., U.S. C2 119
Ferdinand, In., U.S. H4 121
Ferdows, Iran D15 48
Fergana, Uzb. I12 26
Fergus, Ont., Can. D4 103
Fergus, co., Mt., U.S. C7 133
Fergus Falls, Mn., U.S. D2 130
Ferguson, Ky., U.S. C5 124
Ferguson, Mo., U.S. C7 132
Fériana, Tun. C15 62
Ferintosh, Alta., Can. C4 98
Ferkéssédougou, C. Iv. G7 64
Ferlo, Vallée du, val., Sen. D2 64
Ferme-Neuve, Que., Can. C2 104
Fermeuse, Newf., Can. E5 102
Fermo, Italy F8 18
Fermont, Que., Can. h13 104
Fernández, Arg. D7 80
Fernandina, Isla, i., Ec. j13 84a
Fernandina Beach, Fl., U.S. B5 116
Fernando de la Mora, Para. C10 80
Fernando de Noronha, Ilha, i., Braz. D12 76
Fernandópolis, Braz. F3 79
Fernando Póo see Bioko, i., Eq. Gui. J14 64
Fernán-Núñez, Spain H7 16
Fern Creek, Ky., U.S. g11 124
Fern Creek, stm., Ky., U.S. g11 124
Ferndale, Ar., U.S. h9 111
Ferndale, Ca., U.S. B1 112
Ferndale, Ky., U.S. D6 124
Ferndale, Md., U.S. B4 127
Ferndale, Mi., U.S. P15 129
Ferndale, Pa., U.S. F4 145
Ferndale, Wa., U.S. A3 154
Fernie, B.C., Can. E10 99
Fernley, Nv., U.S. D2 135
Fern Ridge Lake, res., Or., U.S. C3 144
Fernwood, Id., U.S. B2 119
Fernwood, Ms., U.S. D3 131
Ferrara, Italy E6 18
Ferrellsburg, W.V., U.S. C2 155
Ferrelo, Cape, c., Or., U.S. E2 144
Ferreñafe, Peru B2 82
Ferreyra, Arg. F6 80
Ferriday, La., U.S. C4 125
Ferrières, Fr. D9 14
Ferris, Tx., U.S. C4 150
Ferrisburg, Vt., U.S. C2 152
Ferris Mountains, mts., Wy., U.S. D5 157
Ferro, stm., Braz. B1 79
Ferrol, Península de, pen., Peru C2 82
Ferron, Ut., U.S. D4 151
Ferros, Braz. E7 79
Ferrum, Va., U.S. D2 153
Ferry, co., Wa., U.S. A7 154
Ferry Farms, Va., U.S. B5 153
Ferryland, Newf., Can. E5 102
Ferry Point, c., N.J., U.S. k7 137
Fertile, Ia., U.S. A4 122
Fertile, Mn., U.S. C2 130
Fès, Mor. C8 62
Feshi, Zaire C3 58
Fessenden, N.D., U.S. B6 141
Festus, Mo., U.S. C7 132
Fété Bowé, Sen. D3 64
Fetești, Rom. E11 20
Fethiye, Tur. M13 20
Feuchtwangen, Ger. F10 10
Feuet, Libya H16 62
Feuilles, Rivière aux, stm., Que., Can. g12 104
Feversham, Ont., Can. C4 103
Feyzābād, Afg. B4 44
Fez see Fès, Mor. C8 62
Fiambalá, Arg. D5 80
Fianarantsoa, Madag. r22 67b
Fiantsonana, Madag. q22 67b
Fiche, Eth. M10 60
Fichtelberg, mtn., Ger. E12 10
Fichtelgebirge, mts., Eur. E11 10
Ficksburg, S. Afr. G8 66
Fidalgo Island, i., Wa., U.S. A3 154
Fidenza, Italy E5 18
Fidler Lake, l., Man., Can. A3 100
Field, B.C., Can. D9 99
Fieldale, Va., U.S. D3 153
Fielding, Ut., U.S. B3 151
Fieldon, Il., U.S. D3 120
Fields, Lake, l., Fl., U.S. B3 116
Fields, Lake, l., La., U.S. k10 125
Fier, Alb. I3 20
Fiesch, Switz. F9 13
Fife, prov., Scot., U.K. E10 8
Fife Lake, Sask., Can. H3 105
Fife Lake, Mi., U.S. D5 129
Fife Lake, l., Sask., Can. H3 105
Fifield, Wi., U.S. C3 156
Fifteenmile Creek, stm., Wy., U.S. B4 157
Fifteen Mile Falls Reservoir, res., U.S. C5 152
Fifty Lakes, Mn., U.S. D4 130
Fifty-Six, Ar., U.S. B3 111
Figueira da Foz, Port. E3 16
Figueres, Spain C14 16
Figuig, Mor. D10 62
Fiji, ctry., Oc. H24 2
Filabusi, Zimb. C9 66
Filadelfia, C.R. G9 92
Filchner Ice Shelf, Ant. C1 73
File Lake, l., Man., Can. B1 100
Filer, Id., U.S. G4 119
Filer City, Mi., U.S. D4 129
Filingué, Niger D11 64
Filley, Ne., U.S. D9 134
Fillmore, Sask., Can. H4 105
Fillmore, Ca., U.S. E4 112
Fillmore, Il., U.S. D4 120
Fillmore, In., U.S. E4 121
Fillmore, Mo., U.S. A3 132
Fillmore, Ut., U.S. E3 151
Fillmore, co., Mn., U.S. G6 130
Fillmore, co., Ne., U.S. D8 134
Finale Ligure, Italy E3 18
Finarwa, Eth. K10 60
Fincastle, Va., U.S. C3 153
Finch, Ont., Can. B9 103
Findlater, Sask., Can. G3 105
Findlay, Il., U.S. D5 120
Findlay, Oh., U.S. A2 142
Fingal, N.D., U.S. C8 141
Finger, Tn., U.S. B3 149
Finger Lake, l., Ont., Can. C5 100
Fingerville, S.C., U.S. A3 147
Fingoè, Moz. E6 58
Finistère, dept., Fr. D2 14
Finisterre, Cabo de, c., Spain C2 16
Finke, Austl. E6 68
Finke, stm., Austl. E7 68
Finksburg, Md., U.S. B4 127
Finland, Mn., U.S. C7 130
Finland (Suomi), ctry., Eur. C13 4
Finland, Gulf of, b., Eur. L20 6
Finley, Austl. J6 70
Finley, N.D., U.S. B8 141
Finley, Tn., U.S. A2 149
Finleyson, Ga., U.S. D3 117
Finly, In., U.S. E6 121
Finn, stm., Eur. G6 8
Finney, co., Ks., U.S. D3 123
Finnmark, co., Nor. F19 6
Finn Mountain, mtn., Ak., U.S. C8 109
Fins, Oman C11 47
Finsteraarhorn, mtn., Switz. E9 13
Finsterwalde, Ger. D13 10
Fiora, stm., Italy G6 18
Fiq, Golan C5 50
Firavitoba, Col. E6 84
Fircrest, Wa., U.S. f10 154
Firebaugh, Ca., U.S. D3 112
Firenze (Florence), Italy F6 18
Firestone, Co., U.S. A6 113
Firmat, Arg. G8 80
Firminópolis, Braz. D3 79
Firminy, Fr. G11 14
Firovo, Russia D16 22
Fīrozābād, India G8 44
Fīrozpur, India E6 44
First Connecticut Lake, l., N.H., U.S. f7 136
First Roach Pond, l., Me., U.S. C3 126
Firth, Id., U.S. F6 119
Firth, Ne., U.S. D9 134
Firth, stm., N.A. C4 96
Fīrūzābād, Iran G12 48
Fīrūz Kūh, Iran D12 48
Fish (Vis), stm., Nmb. F3 66
Fish, stm., Al., U.S. E2 108
Fish, stm., Me., U.S. A4 126
Fish Creek, stm., W.V., U.S. g8 155
Fisheating Creek, stm., Fl., U.S. F5 116
Fisher, Ar., U.S. B5 111
Fisher, Il., U.S. C5 120
Fisher, La., U.S. C2 125
Fisher, Mn., U.S. C2 130
Fisher, co., Tx., U.S. C2 150
Fisher Bay, b., Man., Can. D3 100
Fisher Branch, Man., Can. D3 100
Fisher Lake, l., N.S., Can. E4 101
Fishermans Island, i., Va., U.S. h15 153
Fishers, In., U.S. E5 121
Fishers Island, i., N.Y., U.S. m16 139
Fishers Peak, mtn., Co., U.S. D6 113
Fisher Strait, strt., N.W. Ter., Can. D16 96
Fishersville, Va., U.S. B4 153
Fishertown, Pa., U.S. F4 145
Fish Haven, Id., U.S. G7 119
Fishing Bay, b., Md., U.S. D5 127
Fishing Creek, Md., U.S. D5 127
Fishing Creek, stm., N.C., U.S. A5 140
Fishing Creek, stm., S.C., U.S. B5 147
Fishing Creek, stm., W.V., U.S. B4 155
Fishing Creek, North Fork, stm., W.V., U.S. h9 155
Fishing Creek, South Fork, stm., W.V., U.S. h9 155
Fishing Creek Reservoir, res., S.C., U.S. B6 147
Fishkill, N.Y., U.S. D7 139
Fish Lake, l., Ut., U.S. E4 151
Fish River Lake, l., Me., U.S. B4 126
Fish Springs Range, mts., Ut., U.S. D2 151
Fishtail, Mt., U.S. E7 133
Fishtrap Lake, res., Ky., U.S. C7 124
Fisk, Mo., U.S. E7 132
Fiskdale, Ma., U.S. B3 128
Fiske, Sask., Can. F1 105
Fismes, Fr. C10 14
Fitchburg, Ma., U.S. A4 128
Fitchville, Ct., U.S. C7 114
Fithian, Il., U.S. C6 120
Fittstown, Ok., U.S. C5 143
Fitzgerald, Ga., U.S. E3 117
Fitzgerald River National Park, Austl. F3 68
Fitzroy, stm., Austl. C4 68
Fitzroy, stm., Austl. D9 70
Fitzroy, Monte (Cerro Chaltel), mtn., S.A. F2 78
Fitzroy Crossing, Austl. C5 68
Fitzwilliam, N.H., U.S. E2 136
Fitzwilliam Depot, N.H., U.S. E2 136
Fitzwilliam Island, i., Ont., Can. B3 103
Fiume see Rijeka, Cro. D9 18
Fiumicino, Italy H7 18
Five Island Lake, l., Ia., U.S. A3 122
Five Islands, N.S., Can. D5 101
Fivemile Creek, stm., Wy., U.S. C4 157
Five Points, Al., U.S. B4 108
Five Points, N.M., U.S. B3 138
Fizi, Zaire B5 58
Fjällåsen, Swe. H17 6
Fkih-Ben-Salah, Mor. D7 62
Flag Knob, mtn., Ky., U.S. C7 124
Flagler, Co., U.S. B7 113
Flagler, co., Fl., U.S. C5 116
Flagler Beach, Fl., U.S. C5 116
Flag Mountain, hill, Al., U.S. C3 108
Flagstaff, Az., U.S. B4 110
Flagstaff Lake, l., Or., U.S. E7 144
Flambeau, stm., Wi., U.S. C3 156
Flambeau, South Fork, stm., Wi., U.S. C3 156
Fläming, reg., Ger. D12 10
Flaming Gorge Dam, Ut., U.S. C6 151
Flaming Gorge National Recreation Area, U.S. E3 157
Flaming Gorge Reservoir, res., U.S. E3 157
Flanagan, Il., U.S. C5 120
Flanders (Flandre), hist. reg., Eur. G2 12
Flandes, Col. E5 84
Flandreau, S.D., U.S. C9 148
Flandreau Indian Reservation, S.D., U.S. C9 148
Flasher, N.D., U.S. C4 141
Flat, stm., Mi., U.S. E5 129
Flat, stm., N.C., U.S. A4 140
Flat, stm., R.I., U.S. E2 146
Flat Bay, Newf., Can. D2 102
Flat Brook, stm., N.J., U.S. A3 137
Flatbush, Alta., Can. B3 98
Flat Creek, Tn., U.S. B5 149
Flatey, Ice. B2 6a
Flateyri, Ice. B2 6a
Flathead, co., Mt., U.S. B2 133
Flathead, South Fork, stm., Mt., U.S. C3 133
Flathead Indian Reservation, Mt., U.S. C2 133
Flathead Lake, l., Mt., U.S. C2 133
Flathead Valley, val., Mt., U.S. C2 133
Flat Lake, l., Alta., Can. B4 98
Flat Lake, l., La., U.S. k9 125
Flatlands, N.B., Can. B3 101
Flat Lick, Ky., U.S. D6 124
Flatonia, Tx., U.S. E4 150
Flat River, P.E.I., Can. C7 101
Flat River, Mo., U.S. D7 132
Flat River Reservoir, res., R.I., U.S. D3 146
Flat Rock, Al., U.S. A4 108
Flat Rock, Il., U.S. E6 120
Flat Rock, In., U.S. F6 121
Flat Rock, Mi., U.S. F7 129
Flat Rock, N.C., U.S. f10 140
Flatrock, stm., In., U.S. F6 121
Flattery, Cape, c., Wa., U.S. A1 154
Flatwoods, Ky., U.S. B7 124
Flatwoods, Tn., U.S. B4 149
Flaxcombe, Sask., Can. F1 105
Flaxton, N.D., U.S. A3 141
Flaxville, Mt., U.S. B11 133
Fleet, Alta., Can. C5 98
Fleetwood, Pa., U.S. F10 145
Fleming, Sask., Can. G5 105
Fleming, Co., U.S. A8 113
Fleming, Ga., U.S. E5 117
Fleming, co., Ky., U.S. B6 124
Fleming-Neon, Ky., U.S. C7 124
Flemingsburg, Ky., U.S. B6 124
Flemington, Ga., U.S. E5 117
Flemington, N.J., U.S. B3 137
Flemington, Pa., U.S. D7 145
Flemington, W.V., U.S. k10 155
Flensburg, Ger. A9 10
Flesherton, Ont., Can. C4 103
Fletcher, Ont., Can. E2 103
Fletcher, N.C., U.S. f10 140
Fletcher, Oh., U.S. B1 142
Fletcher, Ok., U.S. C3 143
Fleurance, Fr. I7 14
Fleur-de-Lys, Newf., Can. C3 102
Fleurier, Switz. E6 13
Flevoland, prov., Neth. D7 12
Flinders, stm., Austl. A4 70
Flinders Island, i., Austl. M8 70
Flinders Reefs, rf., Austl. A8 70
Flin Flon, Man., Can. B1 100
Flint, Mi., U.S. E7 129
Flint, stm., Ga., U.S. E2 117
Flint City, Al., U.S. A3 108
Flint Creek, stm., Al., U.S. A3 108
Flint Creek Range, mts., Mt., U.S. D3 133
Flinthill, Mo., U.S. C7 132
Flint Hill, Va., U.S. B4 153
Flint Hills, hills, Ks., U.S. D7 123
Flinton, Ont., Can. C7 103
Flint Run, stm., W.V., U.S. k9 155
Flintstone, Md., U.S. k13 127
Flintville, Tn., U.S. B5 149
Flippin, Ar., U.S. A3 111
Flisa, Nor. K13 6
Flize, Fr. C11 14
Flomaton, Al., U.S. D2 108
Floodwood, Mn., U.S. D6 130
Flora, Il., U.S. E5 120
Flora, In., U.S. C4 121
Flora, Ms., U.S. C3 131
Florac, Fr. H10 14
Florahome, Fl., U.S. C5 116
Florala, Al., U.S. D3 108
Floral City, Fl., U.S. D4 116
Flora Vista, N.M., U.S. A1 138
Florence see Firenze, Italy F6 18
Florence, Al., U.S. A2 108
Florence, Az., U.S. D4 110
Florence, Co., U.S. C5 113
Florence, In., U.S. G8 121
Florence, Ks., U.S. D7 123
Florence, Ky., U.S. A5 124
Florence, Ms., U.S. C3 131
Florence, Mt., U.S. D2 133
Florence, N.J., U.S. C3 137
Florence, Or., U.S. D2 144
Florence, S.C., U.S. C8 147
Florence, S.D., U.S. B8 148
Florence, Tx., U.S. D4 150
Florence, Wi., U.S. C5 156
Florence, co., S.C., U.S. C8 147
Florence, co., Wi., U.S. C5 156
Florenceville, N.B., Can. C2 101
Florencia, Col. G5 84
Florencio Sánchez, Ur. G10 80
Flores, Braz. E11 76
Flores, i., Indon. G7 38
Flores, i., Port. k18 62a
Flores, Laut (Flores Sea), Indon. G7 38
Flores da Cunha, Braz. E13 80
Flores de Goiás, Braz. C5 79
Floresta Azul, Braz. C9 79
Florești, Mol. B12 20
Floresville, Tx., U.S. E3 150
Florham Park, N.J., U.S. B4 137
Floriano, Braz. E10 76
Floriano Peixoto, Braz. C8 82
Florianópolis, Braz. D14 80
Florida, Col. F4 84
Florida, Cuba D5 94
Florida, Hond. B6 92
Florida, Peru A3 82
Florida, N.M., U.S. C3 138
Florida, N.Y., U.S. D6 139
Florida, Ur. H10 80
Florida, state, U.S. E5 116
Florida, Cape, c., Fl., U.S. G6 116
Florida, Straits of, strt., N.A. B4 94
Florida Bay, b., Fl., U.S. H6 116
Floridablanca, Col. D6 84
Florida City, Fl., U.S. G6 116
Florida Keys, is., Fl., U.S. H6 116
Florida Mountains, mts., N.M., U.S. E2 138
Florida State Indian Reservation, Fl., U.S. F5 116
Floridia, Italy L10 18
Florido, stm., Mex. D7 90
Florien, La., U.S. C2 125
Florina, Grc. I5 20
Florissant, Co., U.S. C5 113
Florissant, Mo., U.S. f13 132
Florissant Fossil Beds National Monument, Co., U.S. C5 113
Florø, Nor. K9 6
Flossmoor, Il., U.S. k9 120
Flourtown, Pa., U.S. o21 145
Flovilla, Ga., U.S. C3 117
Flower Brook, stm., Vt., U.S. E2 152
Flower's Cove, Newf., Can. C3 102
Flower Station, Ont., Can. B8 103
Flowery Branch, Ga., U.S. B3 117
Flowood, Ms., U.S. C3 131
Floyd, Ia., U.S. A5 122
Floyd, N.M., U.S. C6 138
Floyd, Va., U.S. D2 153
Floyd, co., Ga., U.S. B1 117
Floyd, co., In., U.S. H6 121
Floyd, co., Ia., U.S. A5 122
Floyd, co., Ky., U.S. C7 124
Floyd, co., Tx., U.S. B2 150
Floyd, co., Va., U.S. D2 153
Floyd, stm., Ia., U.S. B1 122
Floydada, Tx., U.S. C2 150
Floydsburg, Ky., U.S. g12 124
Floyds Fork, stm., Ky., U.S. B4 124
Floyds Knobs, In., U.S. H6 121
Fluchthorn, mtn., Eur. E13 13
Flushing, Mi., U.S. E7 129
Flushing, Oh., U.S. B4 142
Fluvanna, co., Va., U.S. C4 153
Fly, stm. m15 68a
Foam Lake, Sask., Can. F4 105
Foard, co., Tx., U.S. B3 150
Foča, Bos. F2 20
Foça, Tur. K10 20
Focșani, Rom. D11 20
Fodé, Cen. Afr. Rep. O2 60
Fodécontea, Gui. F2 64
Foggaret el Arab, Alg. G12 62
Foggaret ez Zoua, Alg. G12 62
Foggia, Italy H10 18
Fogland Point, c., R.I., U.S. E6 146
Fogo, Newf., Can. D4 102
Fogo, i., C.V. m16 64a
Fogo, Cape, c., Newf., Can. D5 102
Fogo Island, i., Newf., Can. D4 102
Fogolawa, Nig. E14 64
Fohnsdorf, Aus. H14 10
Foix, Fr. J8 14
Foix, hist. reg., Fr. J8 14
Fokino, Russia H17 22
Folakara, Madag. q21 67b
Folégandros, i., Grc. M8 20
Foley, Al., U.S. E2 108
Foley, Mn., U.S. E5 130
Foley, Mo., U.S. B7 132
Foligno, Italy G7 18
Folkestone, Eng., U.K. J15 8
Folkston, Ga., U.S. F4 117
Follansbee, W.V., U.S. A4 155
Follonica, Italy G5 18
Follonica, Golfo di, b., Italy G5 18
Folly Beach, S.C., U.S. F8 147
Folly Island, i., S.C., U.S. F8 147
Folly Lake, N.S., Can. D6 101
Folsom, Ca., U.S. C3 112
Folsom, La., U.S. D5 125
Folsom, N.J., U.S. D3 137
Folsom, W.V., U.S. B4 155
Fomboni, Com. I15 67a
Fonda, Ia., U.S. B3 122
Fonda, N.Y., U.S. C6 139
Fond du Lac, Wi., U.S. E5 156
Fond du Lac, co., Wi., U.S. E5 156
Fond du Lac Indian Reservation, Mn., U.S. D6 130
Fondi, Italy H8 18
Fondouk el Aouareb, Tun. N4 18
Fonni, Italy I4 18
Fonseca, Col. B6 84
Fonseca, Golfo de, b., N.A. D7 92
Fontainebleau, Fr. D9 14
Fontana, Arg. D9 80
Fontana, Ca., U.S. m14 112
Fontana, Ks., U.S. D9 123
Fontana, Wi., U.S. F5 156
Fontana Lake, res., N.C., U.S. f9 140
Fontanelle, Ia., U.S. C3 122
Fontanet, In., U.S. E3 121
Fontas, stm., Can. E8 96
Fonte Boa, Braz. I9 84
Fontenelle Reservoir, res., Wy., U.S. D2 157
Fontur, c., Ice. A6 6a
Fonyód, Hung. I17 10
Foochow see Fuzhou, China I8 34
Footville, Wi., U.S. F4 156
Forada, Mn., U.S. E3 130
Foraker, Mount, mtn., Ak., U.S. f16 109
Forbach, Fr. C13 14
Forbes, Austl. I8 70
Forbes, Mount, mtn., Alta., Can. D2 98
Force, Pa., U.S. D4 145
Forchheim, Ger. F11 10
Ford, Ks., U.S. E4 123
Ford, Ky., U.S. C5 124
Ford, co., Il., U.S. C5 120
Ford, co., Ks., U.S. E4 123
Ford, stm., Mi., U.S. C3 129
Ford City, Ca., U.S. E4 112
Ford City, Pa., U.S. E2 145
Fordland, Mo., U.S. D5 132
Fordoche, La., U.S. D4 125
Ford Ranges, mts., Ant. C10 73
Fords, N.J., U.S. B4 137
Fords Prairie, Wa., U.S. C2 154
Fordsville, Ky., U.S. C3 124
Fordville, N.D., U.S. A8 141
Fordwich, Ont., Can. D3 103
Fordyce, Ar., U.S. D3 111
Fordyce, Ne., U.S. B8 134
Forel, Mont, mtn., Grnld. C16 86
Foreman, Ar., U.S. D1 111
Foremost, Alta., Can. E5 98
Forest, Ont., Can. D2 103
Forest, In., U.S. D5 121
Forest, Ms., U.S. C4 131
Forest, Oh., U.S. B2 142
Forest, Va., U.S. C3 153
Forest, co., Pa., U.S. C3 145
Forest, co., Wi., U.S. C5 156
Forest, stm., N.D., U.S. A8 141
Forest Acres, S.C., U.S. C6 147
Forestburg, Alta., Can. C4 98
Forestburg, S.D., U.S. C7 148
Forest City, Il., U.S. C4 120
Forest City, Ia., U.S. A4 122
Forest City, Mo., U.S. B2 132
Forest City, N.C., U.S. B1 140
Forest City, Pa., U.S. C11 145
Forestdale, Al., U.S. B3 108
Forestdale, R.I., U.S. B3 146
Forest Dale, Vt., U.S. D2 152
Forest Glen, La., U.S. h12 125
Forest Grove, Or., U.S. B3 144
Forest Hill, La., U.S. C3 125
Forest Hill, Md., U.S. A5 127
Forest Hill, Tx., U.S. n9 150
Forest Hills, Pa., U.S. k14 145
Forest Hills, Tn., U.S. A5 149
Forest Home, Al., U.S. D3 108
Forest Knolls, Ca., U.S. g7 112
Forest Lake, Mn., U.S. E6 130
Forestón, Mn., U.S. E5 130
Forest Park, Ga., U.S. h8 117
Forest Park, Il., U.S. k9 120
Forest Park, La., U.S. *B3 125
Forest Park, Oh., U.S. *n12 142
Forestport, N.Y., U.S. B5 139
Forest River, N.D., U.S. A8 141
Forestville, Wi., U.S. D6 156
Forfar, Scot., U.K. E11 8
Forgan, Ok., U.S. A1 143
Forget, Sask., Can. H4 105
Forillon, Parc National de, Que., Can. k14 104
Fork Creek, stm., W.V., U.S. m12 155
Forked Deer, stm., Tn., U.S. B2 149
Forked Deer, Middle Fork, stm., Tn., U.S. D3 149
Forked Deer, North Fork, stm., Tn., U.S. B3 149
Forked Deer, South Fork, stm., Tn., U.S. B2 149
Forked Island, La., U.S. E3 125
Forked River, N.J., U.S. D4 137
Forkland, Al., U.S. C2 108
Fork River, Man., Can. D1 100
Forks, Wa., U.S. B1 154
Fork Union, Va., U.S. C4 153
Forkville, Ms., U.S. C4 131
Forlì, Italy E7 18
Forman, N.D., U.S. C8 141
Formentera, i., Spain G13 16
Formia, Italy H8 18
Formiga, Braz. F6 79
Formosa, Arg. D9 80
Formosa, Braz. C5 79
Formosa, Ont., Can. C3 103
Formosa, Ar., U.S. B3 111
Formosa, prov., Arg. C9 80
Formosa see Taiwan, ctry., Asia L9 34
Formosa, Serra, plat., Braz. D14 82
Formoso, Ks., U.S. C6 123
Formoso, stm., Braz. E2 79
Formoso, stm., Braz. B6 79
Forney, Tx., U.S. C4 150
Fornosovo, Russia B13 22
Forres, Arg. D7 80
Forrest, Austl. F5 68
Forrest, Il., U.S. C5 120
Forrest, co., Ms., U.S. D4 131
Forrest City, Ar., U.S. B5 111
Forrester Island, i., Ak., U.S. n23 109
Forreston, Il., U.S. A4 120
Forsayth, Austl. B5 70
Forst, Ger. D14 10
Forster, Austl. I10 70
Forsyth, Ga., U.S. C3 117
Forsyth, Il., U.S. D5 120
Forsyth, Mo., U.S. E4 132
Forsyth, Mt., U.S. D10 133
Forsyth, co., Ga., U.S. B2 117
Forsyth, co., N.C., U.S. A2 140
Forsyth Range, mts., Austl. D5 70
Fort Adams, Ms., U.S. D2 131
Fortaleza, Braz. D11 76
Fortaleza, stm., Peru D3 82
Fortaleza de Santa Teresa, hist., Ur. G12 80
Fortaleza do Ituxi, Braz. B8 82
Fort Apache, Az., U.S. D6 110
Fort Apache Indian Reservation, Az., U.S. D5 110
Fort Ashby, W.V., U.S. B6 155
Fort Assiniboine, Alta., Can. B3 98
Fort Atkinson, Ia., U.S. A6 122
Fort Atkinson, Wi., U.S. F5 156
Fort Barnwell, N.C., U.S. B5 140
Fort Beaufort, S. Afr. I8 66
Fort Belknap Agency, Mt., U.S. B8 133
Fort Belknap Indian Reservation, Mt., U.S. B8 133
Fort Belvoir, mil., Va., U.S. g12 153
Fort Bend, co., Tx., U.S. E5 150
Fort Benjamin Harrison, mil., In., U.S. k10 121
Fort Benning, mil., Ga., U.S. D2 117
Fort Benton, Mt., U.S. C6 133
Fort Berthold Indian Reservation, N.D., U.S. B3 141
Fort Bidwell Indian Reservation, Ca., U.S. B3 112
Fort Blackmore, Va., U.S. f9 153
Fort Bliss, mil., Tx., U.S. o11 150
Fort Bragg, Ca., U.S. C2 112
Fort Bragg, mil., N.C., U.S. B3 140
Fort Branch, In., U.S. H2 121
Fort Bridger, Wy., U.S. E2 157
Fort Calhoun, Ne., U.S. C9 134
Fort Campbell, mil., U.S. A4 149
Fort-Carnot, Madag. r22 67b
Fort Carson, mil., Co., U.S. C6 113
Fort Chipewyan, Alta., Can. f8 98
Fort Clatsop National Memorial, hist., Or., U.S. A3 144
Fort Cobb, Ok., U.S. B3 143
Fort Cobb Reservoir, res., Ok., U.S. B3 143
Fort Collins, Co., U.S. A5 113
Fort Coulonge, Que., Can. B8 103
Fort Covington, N.Y., U.S. f10 139
Fort Davis, Al., U.S. C4 108
Fort Davis, Tx., U.S. o13 150
Fort Davis National Historic Site, hist., Tx., U.S. o13 150
Fort Defiance, Az., U.S. B6 110
Fort-de-France, Mart. G14 94
Fort Deposit, Al., U.S. D3 108
Fort Detrick, mil., Md., U.S. B3 127
Fort Devens, mil., Ma., U.S. f9 128
Fort Dix, mil., N.J., U.S. C3 137
Fort Dodge, Ia., U.S. B3 122
Fort Dodge, Ks., U.S. D4 123
Fort Donelson National Battlefield, Tn., U.S. A4 149
Fort Duchesne, Ut., U.S. C6 151
Forteau, Newf., Can. C3 102
Fort Edward, N.Y., U.S. B7 139
Fort Erie, Ont., Can. E6 103
Fortescue, stm., Austl. D3 68
Fort Eustis, mil., Va., U.S. h14 153
Fortezza, Italy C6 18
Fort Fairfield, Me., U.S. B5 126
Fort Frances, Ont., Can. o16 103
Fort Franklin, N.W. Ter., Can. C8 96
Fort Fraser, B.C., Can. B5 99
Fort Frederica National Monument, Ga., U.S. E5 117
Fort Gaines, Ga., U.S. E1 117
Fort Garland, Co., U.S. D5 113
Fort Gay, W.V., U.S. C2 155
Fort Gibson, Ok., U.S. B6 143

Name — Map Ref. — Page

Fort Gibson Lake, res., Ok., U.S. A6 143
Fort Good Hope, N.W. Ter., Can. C7 96
Fort Gordon, mil., Ga., U.S. C4 117
Fort Greely, mil., Ak., U.S. C10 109
Forth, Firth of, b., Scot., U.K. E11 8
Fort Hall, Id., U.S. F6 119
Fort Hall Indian Reservation, Id., U.S. F6 119
Fort Hancock, Tx., U.S. o12 150
Fort Hood, mil., Tx., U.S. D4 150
Fort Howard, Md., U.S. B5 127
Fort Huachuca, mil., Az., U.S. F5 110
Fortierville, Que., Can. C5 104
Fortín Ayacucho, Para. H12 82
Fortín Coroneles Sanchez, Para. H12 82
Fortine, Mt., U.S. B2 133
Fortín Florida, Para. I12 82
Fortín Garrapatal, Para. I11 82
Fortín Teniente Montanía, Para. B9 80
Fortín Uno, Arg. J6 80
Fort Jackson, mil., S.C., U.S. C6 147
Fort Jefferson National Monument, Fl., U.S. H4 116
Fort Jones, Ca., U.S. B2 112
Fort Kent, Alta., Can. B5 98
Fort Kent, Me., U.S. A4 126
Fort Kent Mills, Me., U.S. A4 126
Fort Knox, mil., Ky., U.S. B4 124
Fort-Lamy see N'Djamena, Chad F4 56
Fort Laramie, Wy., U.S. D8 157
Fort Laramie National Historic Site, hist., Wy., U.S. D8 157
Fort Lauderdale, Fl., U.S. F6 116
Fort Lawn, S.C., U.S. B6 147
Fort Leavenworth, mil., Ks., U.S. C9 123
Fort Lee, N.J., U.S. B5 137
Fort Lee, mil., Va., U.S. C5 153
Fort Leonard Wood, mil., Mo., U.S. D5 132
Fort Lewis, mil., Wa., U.S. B3 154
Fort Liard, N.W. Ter., Can. D8 96
Fort-Liberté, Haiti E9 94
Fort Loramie, Oh., U.S. B1 142
Fort Loudon, Pa., U.S. G6 145
Fort Loudoun Lake, res., Tn., U.S. D9 149
Fort Lupton, Co., U.S. A6 113
Fort MacArthur, mil., Ca., U.S. n12 112
Fort MacKay, Alta., Can. f8 98
Fort Macleod, Alta., Can. E4 98
Fort Madison, Ia., U.S. D6 122
Fort Matanzas National Monument, Fl., U.S. C5 116
Fort McClellan, mil., Al., U.S. B4 108
Fort McDermitt Indian Reservation, U.S. B4 135
Fort McDowell, Az., U.S. k9 110
Fort McDowell Indian Reservation, Az., U.S. D4 110
Fort McHenry National Monument And Historic Shrine, Md., U.S. g11 127
Fort McMurray, Alta., Can. A5 98
Fort McPherson, N.W. Ter., Can. C6 96
Fort Meade, Fl., U.S. E5 116
Fort Meade, mil., Md., U.S. B4 127
Fort Meadow Reservoir, res., Ma., U.S. g9 128
Fort Mill, S.C., U.S. A6 147
Fort Mitchell, Al., U.S. C4 108
Fort Mitchell, Ky., U.S. h13 124
Fort Mojave Indian Reservation, U.S. C1 110
Fort Monmouth, mil., N.J., U.S. C4 137
Fort Monroe, mil., Va., U.S. h15 153
Fort Morgan, Co., U.S. A7 113
Fort Myer, mil., Va., U.S. g12 153
Fort Myers, Fl., U.S. F5 116
Fort Myers Beach, Fl., U.S. F5 116
Fort Nelson, B.C., Can. m18 99
Fort Norman, N.W. Ter., Can. D7 96
Fort Ogden, Fl., U.S. E5 116
Fort Oglethorpe, Ga., U.S. B1 117
Fort Ord, mil., Ca., U.S. D3 112
Fort Payne, Al., U.S. A4 108
Fort Peck, Mt., U.S. B10 133
Fort Peck Dam, Mt., U.S. B10 133
Fort Peck Indian Reservation, Mt., U.S. B11 133
Fort Peck Lake, res., Mt., U.S. C9 133
Fort Pierce, Fl., U.S. E6 116
Fort Pierce Inlet, b., Fl., U.S. E6 116
Fort Pierre, S.D., U.S. C5 148
Fort Plain, N.Y., U.S. C6 139
Fort Polk, mil., La., U.S. C2 125
Fort Portal, Ug. A6 58
Fort Providence, N.W. Ter., Can. D9 96
Fort Qu'Appelle, Sask., Can. G4 105
Fort Randall Dam, S.D., U.S. D7 148
Fort Ransom, N.D., U.S. C8 141
Fort Recovery, Oh., U.S. B1 142
Fort Resolution, N.W. Ter., Can. D10 96
Fortress Mountain, mtn., Wy., U.S. B3 157
Fort Richardson, mil., Ak., U.S. C10 109
Fort Riley, mil., Ks., U.S. C7 123
Fort Ritchie, mil., Md., U.S. A3 127
Fort Rucker, mil., Al., U.S. D4 108
Fort Saint James, B.C., Can. B5 99
Fort Saint John, B.C., Can. A7 99
Fort Sam Houston, mil., Tx., U.S. k7 150
Fort Saskatchewan, Alta., Can. C4 98
Fort Scott, Ks., U.S. E9 123
Fort-Ševčenko, Kaz. I8 26
Fort Severn, Ont., Can. n18 103
Fort Shafter, mil., Hi., U.S. g10 118
Fort Shaw, Mt., U.S. C5 133
Fort Shawnee, Oh., U.S. B1 142
Fort Sheridan, mil., Il., U.S. h9 120
Fort Sill, mil., Ok., U.S. C3 143
Fort Simpson, N.W. Ter., Can. D8 96
Fort Smith, N.W. Ter., Can. D10 96
Fort Smith, Ar., U.S. B1 111
Fort Stanton, N.M., U.S. D4 138
Fort Steele, B.C., Can. E10 99
Fort Stewart, mil., Ga., U.S. D5 117
Fort Stockton, Tx., U.S. D1 150
Fort Sumner, N.M., U.S. C5 138
Fort Sumter National Monument, S.C., U.S. k12 147
Fort Supply, Ok., U.S. A2 143
Fort Supply Lake, res., Ok., U.S. A2 143
Fort Thomas, Az., U.S. D6 110
Fort Thomas, Ky., U.S. h14 124
Fort Thompson, S.D., U.S. C6 148
Fort Totten, N.D., U.S. B7 141
Fort Totten Indian Reservation, N.D., U.S. B7 141
Fort Towson, Ok., U.S. C6 143
Fortuna, Arg. H6 80
Fortuna, C.R. G10 92
Fortuna, Ca., U.S. B1 112
Fortuna, Mo., U.S. C5 132
Fortuna, Río de la, stm., Bol. G12 82
Fortune, Newf., Can. E4 102
Fortune Bay, b., Newf., Can. E4 102
Fortune Harbour, Newf., Can. D4 102
Fort Union National Monument, N.M., U.S. B5 138
Fort Valley, Ga., U.S. D3 117
Fort Vermilion, Alta., Can. f7 98
Fortville, In., U.S. E6 121
Fort Wainwright, mil., Ak., U.S. C10 109
Fort Walton Beach, Fl., U.S. u15 116
Fort Washakie, Wy., U.S. C4 157
Fort Washington, Pa., U.S. o21 145
Fort Washington Forest, Md., U.S. C4 127
Fort Wayne, In., U.S. B7 121
Fort Wellington, Guy. D14 84
Fort William, Scot., U.K. E8 8
Fort Wingate, N.M., U.S. B1 138
Fort Worth, Tx., U.S. C4 150
Fort Wright, Ky., U.S. h13 124
Fort Yates, N.D., U.S. C5 141
Forty Fort, Pa., U.S. D10 145
Fort Yukon, Ak., U.S. B10 109
Fort Yuma Indian Reservation, Ca., U.S. F6 112
Foshan, China L2 34
Fossano, Italy E2 18
Fossil, Or., U.S. B6 144
Fossil Butte National Monument, Wy., U.S. E2 157
Fossil Lake, l., Or., U.S. D6 144
Foss Reservoir, res., Ok., U.S. B2 143
Fosston, Sask., Can. E4 105
Fosston, Mn., U.S. C3 130
Foster, Austl. L7 70
Foster, Mo., U.S. C3 132
Foster, Or., U.S. C4 144
Foster, co., N.D., U.S. B6 141
Foster Brook, Pa., U.S. C4 145
Foster City, Ca., U.S. h8 112
Foster City, Mi., U.S. C3 129
Fosters, Al., U.S. B2 108
Fosters Pond, l., Ma., U.S. f11 128
Foster Village, Hi., U.S. g10 118
Fosterville, Tn., U.S. B5 149
Fostoria, Al., U.S. C3 108
Fostoria, Ia., U.S. A2 122
Fostoria, Mi., U.S. E7 129
Fostoria, Oh., U.S. A2 142
Fouesnant, Fr. E2 14
Fougamou, Gabon B2 58
Fougères, Fr. D5 14
Fouke, Ar., U.S. D2 111
Foul Bay, b., Egypt J3 48
Foulpointe, Madag. p23 67b
Foulwind, Cape, c., N.Z. D3 72
Foumban, Cam. G9 54
Foumbouni, Com. k15 67a
Foum-el-Hisn, Mor. F6 62
Foum-Zguid, Mor. E7 62
Foundiougne, Sen. D1 64
Fountain, Al., U.S. D2 108
Fountain, Co., U.S. C6 113
Fountain, Fl., U.S. B1 116
Fountain, Mn., U.S. G6 130
Fountain, N.C., U.S. B5 140
Fountain, co., In., U.S. D3 121
Fountain City, In., U.S. E8 121
Fountain City, Wi., U.S. D2 156
Fountain Creek, stm., Co., U.S. C6 113
Fountain Green, Ut., U.S. D4 151
Fountain Hill, Ar., U.S. D4 111
Fountain Hill, Pa., U.S. E11 145
Fountain Inn, S.C., U.S. B3 147
Fountain Lake, Ar., U.S. f8 111
Fountain Peak, mtn., Ca., U.S. E6 112
Fountain Place, La., U.S. *D4 125
Fountain Run, Ky., U.S. D4 124
Fountaintown, In., U.S. E6 121
Fourche Creek, stm., Ar., U.S. k10 111
Fourche LaFave, stm., Ar., U.S. C2 111
Fourche Maline, stm., Ok., U.S. C6 143
Fourche Mountain, mtn., Ar., U.S. C2 111
Fouriesburg, S. Afr. G9 66
Four Lakes, Wa., U.S. B8 154
Fourmies, Fr. B11 14
Fourmile, Ky., U.S. D6 124
Fourmile Creek, stm., Ia., U.S. e8 122
Four Mountains, Islands of, is., Ak., U.S. E6 109
Fournier, Ont., Can. B10 103
Four Oaks, N.C., U.S. B4 140
Fouta Djalon, reg., Gui. F3 64
Foux, Cap à, c., Haiti E8 94
Foveaux Strait, strt., N.Z. G1 72
Fowler, Ca., U.S. D4 112
Fowler, Co., U.S. C6 113
Fowler, Il., U.S. C2 120
Fowler, In., U.S. C3 121
Fowler, Ks., U.S. E3 123
Fowler, Mi., U.S. E6 129
Fowlerton, In., U.S. D6 121
Fowlerville, Mi., U.S. F6 129
Fowlkes, Tn., U.S. B2 149
Fowlstown, Ga., U.S. F2 117
Fowman, Iran C10 48
Fox, Ar., U.S. B3 111
Fox, Ok., U.S. C4 143
Fox, stm., Man., Can. B4 100
Fox, stm., U.S. B5 120
Fox, stm., U.S. A6 132
Fox, stm., Mi., U.S. B4 129
Fox, stm., Wi., U.S. D5 156
Foxboro, Ont., Can. C7 103
Foxboro, Ma., U.S. B5 128
Fox Creek, Alta., Can. B2 98
Foxe Basin, b., N.W. Ter., Can. C17 96
Foxe Channel, strt., N.W. Ter., Can. D16 96
Foxe Peninsula, pen., N.W. Ter., Can. D17 96
Fox Harbour, Newf., Can. E5 102
Fox Island, i., R.I., U.S. E4 146
Fox Island, i., Wa., U.S. f10 154
Fox Islands, is., Ak., U.S. E6 109
Fox Lake, Il., U.S. A5 120
Fox Lake, Wi., U.S. E5 156
Fox Lake, l., Il., U.S. h8 120
Fox Mountain, mtn., Nv., U.S. B2 135
Foxpark, Wy., U.S. E6 157
Fox Point, Wi., U.S. E6 156
Fox River Grove, Il., U.S. h8 120
Fox Valley, Sask., Can. G1 105
Foxville, Vt., U.S. C4 152
Foxwarren, Man., Can. D1 100
Foxworth, Ms., U.S. D4 131
Foyle, Lough, b., Eur. F6 8
Foz do Cunene, Ang. E2 58
Foz do Iguaçu, Braz. C11 80
Foz do Jordão, Braz. C6 82
Foz Giraldo, Port. E4 16
Foziling, China D5 34
Frackville, Pa., U.S. E9 145
Fraga, Arg. G6 80
Fraile Muerto, Ur. G11 80
Framingham, Ma., U.S. B5 128
Frampol, Pol. E22 10
Franca, Braz. F5 79
Franca-Iosifa, Zemľa (Franz Josef Land), is., Russia A6 24
Francavilla Fontana, Italy I12 18
France, ctry., Eur. F8 4
Francestown, N.H., U.S. E3 136
Francés Viejo, Cabo, c., Dom. Rep. E10 94
Francesville, In., U.S. C4 121
Franceville, Gabon B2 58
Franche-Comté, hist. reg., Fr. F12 14
Francia, Ur. G10 80
Francis, Sask., Can. G4 105
Francis, Ok., U.S. C5 143
Francis, Ut., U.S. C4 151
Francis, Lake, l., N.H., U.S. f7 136
Francis Case, Lake, res., S.D., U.S. D6 148
Francisco, In., U.S. H3 121
Francisco Beltrão, Braz. D12 80
Francisco I. Madero, Mex. E7 90
Francisco I. Madero, Mex. E8 90
Francisco Morazán, dept., Hond. C7 92
Francisco Murguía, Mex. E8 90
Francisco Sá, Braz. D7 79
Francis Creek, Wi., U.S. h10 156
Francistown, Bots. C8 66
Francofonte, Italy L9 18
François, Newf., Can. E3 102
Franconia, N.H., U.S. B3 136
Franconia Notch, N.H., U.S. B3 136
Francs Peak, mtn., Wy., U.S. C3 157
Frangy, Fr. F12 14
Frankenmuth, Mi., U.S. E7 129
Frankford, Ont., Can. C7 103
Frankford, De., U.S. F5 115
Frankford, Mo., U.S. B6 132
Frankford, W.V., U.S. D4 155
Frankfort, S. Afr. I8 66
Frankfort, S. Afr. F9 66
Frankfort, Il., U.S. m9 120
Frankfort, In., U.S. D4 121
Frankfort, Ks., U.S. C7 123
Frankfort, Ky., U.S. B5 124
Frankfort, Me., U.S. D4 126
Frankfort, Mi., U.S. D4 129
Frankfort, N.Y., U.S. B5 139
Frankfort, Oh., U.S. C2 142
Frankfort, S.D., U.S. C7 148
Frankfurt am Main, Ger. E8 10
Frankfurt an der Oder, Ger. C14 10
Franklin, Man., Can. D2 100
Franklin, Al., U.S. D2 108
Franklin, Az., U.S. E6 110
Franklin, Ar., U.S. A4 111
Franklin, Ga., U.S. C1 117
Franklin, Id., U.S. G7 119
Franklin, Il., U.S. D3 120
Franklin, In., U.S. F5 121
Franklin, Ks., U.S. E9 123
Franklin, Ky., U.S. D3 124
Franklin, La., U.S. E4 125
Franklin, Me., U.S. D4 126
Franklin, Ma., U.S. B5 128
Franklin, Mn., U.S. F4 130
Franklin, Mo., U.S. B5 132
Franklin, Ne., U.S. D7 134
Franklin, N.H., U.S. D3 136
Franklin, N.J., U.S. A3 137
Franklin, N.C., U.S. f9 140
Franklin, Oh., U.S. C1 142
Franklin, Pa., U.S. D2 145
Franklin, Tn., U.S. B5 149
Franklin, Tx., U.S. D4 150
Franklin, Va., U.S. D6 153
Franklin, W.V., U.S. C5 155
Franklin, Wi., U.S. n11 156
Franklin, co., Al., U.S. A2 108
Franklin, co., Ar., U.S. B2 111
Franklin, co., Fl., U.S. C2 116
Franklin, co., Ga., U.S. B3 117
Franklin, co., Id., U.S. G7 119
Franklin, co., Il., U.S. E4 120
Franklin, co., In., U.S. F7 121
Franklin, co., Ia., U.S. B4 122
Franklin, co., Ks., U.S. D8 123
Franklin, co., Ky., U.S. B5 124
Franklin, co., La., U.S. B4 125
Franklin, co., Me., U.S. C2 126
Franklin, co., Ma., U.S. A2 128
Franklin, co., Ms., U.S. D3 131
Franklin, co., Mo., U.S. C6 132
Franklin, co., Ne., U.S. D7 134
Franklin, co., N.Y., U.S. f10 139
Franklin, co., N.C., U.S. A4 140
Franklin, co., Oh., U.S. B2 142
Franklin, co., Pa., U.S. G6 145
Franklin, co., Tn., U.S. B5 149
Franklin, co., Tx., U.S. C5 150
Franklin, co., Vt., U.S. B2 152
Franklin, co., Va., U.S. D3 153
Franklin, co., Wa., U.S. C6 154
Franklin, Point, c., Ak., U.S. A8 109
Franklin Bay, b., N.W. Ter., Can. C7 96
Franklin D. Roosevelt Lake, res., Wa., U.S. B7 154
Franklin Falls Reservoir, res., N.H., U.S. C3 136
Franklin Grove, Il., U.S. B4 120
Franklin Harbor, b., Austl. I2 70
Franklin Island, i., Ont., Can. B4 103
Franklin Lake, l., Nv., U.S. C6 135
Franklin Mine, Mi., U.S. A2 129
Franklin Mountains, mts., N.W. Ter., Can. D8 96
Franklin Park, Il., U.S. k9 120
Franklin Park, Pa., U.S. *h13 145
Franklin Strait, strt., N.W. Ter., Can. B13 96
Franklinton, La., U.S. D5 125
Franklinton, N.C., U.S. A4 140
Franklinville, N.J., U.S. D2 137
Franklinville, N.Y., U.S. C2 139
Franklinville, N.C., U.S. B3 140
Frankston, Tx., U.S. C5 150
Franksville, Wi., U.S. n12 156
Frankton, In., U.S. D6 121
Frankville, N.S., Can. D8 101
Frankville, Al., U.S. D1 108
Frannie, Wy., U.S. B4 157
Franz Josef Land see Franca Iosifa, Zemľa, is., Russia A6 24
Frascati, Italy H7 18
Fraser, Co., U.S. B5 113
Fraser, stm., B.C., Can. E7 99
Fraser, stm., Newf., Can. g9 102
Fraser, Mount, mtn., Can. C8 99
Fraserburg, S. Afr. H5 66
Fraser Island, i., Austl. E10 70
Fraser Lake, B.C., Can. B5 99
Fraser Plateau, plat., B.C., Can. D6 99
Fraserwood, Man., Can. D3 100
Frauenfeld, Switz. C10 13
Fray Bentos, Ur. G9 80
Fray Luis Beltrán, Arg. J6 80
Fray Marcos, Ur. H11 80
Frazee, Mn., U.S. D3 130
Frazer, Mt., U.S. B10 133
Frazeysburg, Oh., U.S. B3 142
Frazier Park, Ca., U.S. E4 112
Fr'azino, Russia F21 22
Frederic, Mi., U.S. D6 129
Frederic, Wi., U.S. C1 156
Frederica, De., U.S. D4 115
Fredericia, Den. N11 6
Frederick, Co., U.S. A6 113
Frederick, Md., U.S. B3 127
Frederick, Ok., U.S. C2 143
Frederick, S.D., U.S. B7 148
Frederick, co., Md., U.S. B3 127
Frederick, co., Va., U.S. A4 153
Frederick Reef, rf., Austl. C11 70
Fredericksburg, In., U.S. H5 121
Fredericksburg, Ia., U.S. B5 122
Fredericksburg, Oh., U.S. B4 142
Fredericksburg, Pa., U.S. F9 145
Fredericksburg, Tx., U.S. D3 150
Fredericksburg, Va., U.S. B5 153
Frederick Sound, strt., Ak., U.S. m23 109
Fredericktown, Mo., U.S. D7 132
Fredericktown, Oh., U.S. B3 142
Fredericktown, Pa., U.S. F1 145
Frederico Westphalen, Braz. D12 80
Fredericton, N.B., Can. D3 101
Fredericton Junction, N.B., Can. D3 101
Frederikshavn, Den. M12 6
Frederiksted, V.I.U.S. F12 94
Frederik Willem IV Vallen, wtfl, Sur. F14 84
Fredonia, Col. E5 84
Fredonia, Az., U.S. A3 110
Fredonia, Ia., U.S. C6 122
Fredonia, Ks., U.S. E8 123
Fredonia, Ky., U.S. C1 124
Fredonia, N.Y., U.S. C1 139
Fredonia, Pa., U.S. D1 145
Fredonia, Wi., U.S. E6 156
Fredrikstad, Nor. L12 6
Freeborn, Mn., U.S. G5 130
Freeborn, co., Mn., U.S. G5 130
Freeburg, Il., U.S. E4 120
Freeburg, Mo., U.S. C6 132
Freeburg, Pa., U.S. E8 145
Freedom, In., U.S. F4 121
Freedom, N.H., U.S. C4 136
Freedom, Ok., U.S. A2 143
Freedom, Pa., U.S. E1 145
Freedom, Wi., U.S. h9 156
Freedom, Wy., U.S. D2 157
Freehold, N.J., U.S. C4 137
Freeland, Mi., U.S. E6 129
Freeland, Pa., U.S. D10 145
Freelandville, In., U.S. G3 121
Freel Peak, mtn., Ca., U.S. C4 112
Freels, Cape, c., Newf., Can. D5 102
Freels, Cape, c., Newf., Can. E5 102
Freeman, Mo., U.S. C3 132
Freeman, S.D., U.S. D8 148
Freeman, Lake, l., In., U.S. C4 121
Freemansburg, Pa., U.S. E11 145
Freemanville, Al., U.S. D2 108
Freemason Island, i., La., U.S. E7 125
Freeport, Bah. A5 94
Freeport, N.S., Can. E3 101
Freeport, Fl., U.S. u15 116
Freeport, Il., U.S. A4 120
Freeport, Me., U.S. E2 126
Freeport, Mi., U.S. F5 129
Freeport, Mn., U.S. E4 130
Freeport, N.Y., U.S. n15 139
Freeport, Pa., U.S. E2 145
Freeport, Tx., U.S. E5 150
Freer, Tx., U.S. F3 150
Freestone, co., Tx., U.S. D4 150
Freetown, P.E.I., Can. C6 101
Freetown, S.L. G3 64
Freetown, In., U.S. G5 121
Freezeout Mountains, mts., Wy., U.S. D6 157
Fregenal de la Sierra, Spain G5 16
Freiberg, Ger. E13 10
Freiburg [im Breisgau], Ger. H7 10
Freirina, Chile E3 80
Freising, Ger. G11 10
Freistadt, Aus. G14 10
Freital, Ger. D13 10
Fréjus, Fr. I13 14
Fremantle, Austl. F3 68
Fremont, Ca., U.S. D2 112
Fremont, In., U.S. A8 121
Fremont, Ia., U.S. C5 122
Fremont, Mi., U.S. E5 129
Fremont, Mo., U.S. E6 132
Fremont, Ne., U.S. C9 134
Fremont, N.H., U.S. E4 136
Fremont, N.C., U.S. B5 140
Fremont, Oh., U.S. A2 142
Fremont, Ut., U.S. E4 151
Fremont, Wi., U.S. D5 156
Fremont, co., Co., U.S. C5 113
Fremont, co., Id., U.S. E7 119
Fremont, co., Ia., U.S. D2 122
Fremont, co., Wy., U.S. C4 157
Fremont, stm., Ut., U.S. E4 151
Fremont Island, i., Ut., U.S. B3 151
Fremont Lake, l., Wy., U.S. D3 157
Fremont Peak, mtn., Wy., U.S. C3 157
French Broad, stm., U.S. D10 149
Frenchburg, Ky., U.S. C6 124
French Camp, Ms., U.S. B4 131
French Creek, stm., Pa., U.S. C2 145
French Frigate Shoals, rf., Hi., U.S. m14 118
French Guiana (Guyane française), dep., S.A. C8 76
French Gulch, Ca., U.S. B2 112
French Island, i., Austl. L6 70
French Lick, In., U.S. G4 121
Frenchman Bay, b., Me., U.S. D4 126
Frenchman Butte, Sask., Can. D1 105
Frenchman Creek, stm., U.S. D4 134
Frenchman Hills, hills, Wa., U.S. C6 154
Frenchman Knob, mtn., Ky., U.S. C4 124
Frenchman Lake, l., Nv., U.S. G6 135
Frenchmans Cap, mtn., Austl. N6 70
Frenchman's Cove, Newf., Can. D2 102
Frenchman's Cove, Newf., Can. E4 102
French Polynesia, dep., Oc. H3 2
French River, Mn., U.S. D7 130
French Settlement, La., U.S. D5 125
French Southern and Antarctic Territories, dep., Afr. M10 158
Frenchtown, Mt., U.S. C2 133
Frenchtown, N.J., U.S. B2 137
French Village, N.S., Can. E6 101
Frenchville, Me., U.S. A4 126
Frenda, Alg. C11 62
Fresco, stm., Braz. E8 76
Freshfield, Mount, mtn., Can. D2 98
Fresne-Saint-Mamès, Fr. E12 14
Fresnes-en-Woëvre, Fr. C12 14
Fresnillo, Mex. F8 90
Fresno, Col. E5 84
Fresno, Ca., U.S. D4 112
Fresno, co., Ca., U.S. D4 112
Fresno Reservoir, res., Mt., U.S. B6 133
Frewsburg, N.Y., U.S. C1 139
Freycinet Peninsula, pen., Austl. N8 70
Freyre, Arg. F7 80
Fria, Cape, c., Nmb. E2 58
Friant, Ca., U.S. D4 112
Friars Point, Ms., U.S. A3 131
Frías, Arg. E6 80
Frías, Peru A2 82
Fribourg (Freiburg), Switz. E7 13
Fribourg (Freiburg), state, Switz. E7 13
Friday Harbor, Wa., U.S. A2 154
Fridley, Mn., U.S. m12 130
Fridtjof Nansen, Mount, mtn., Ant. D9 73
Friedberg, Aus. H16 10
Friedberg, Ger. E8 10
Friedberg, Ger. G10 10
Friedland, Ger. B13 10
Friedrichshafen, Ger. H9 10
Friedrichsort, Ger. A10 10
Friedrichstadt, Ger. A9 10
Friend, Ne., U.S. D8 134
Friendship, Ar., U.S. C3 111
Friendship, Me., U.S. E3 126
Friendship, N.Y., U.S. C2 139
Friendship, Oh., U.S. D2 142
Friendship, Tn., U.S. B2 149
Friendship, Wi., U.S. E4 156
Friendsville, Md., U.S. k12 127
Friendsville, Tn., U.S. D9 149
Friendswood, Tx., U.S. r14 150
Fries, Va., U.S. D2 153
Friesach, Aus. I14 10
Friesland, prov., Neth. B8 12
Friguia, Gui. E4 64
Frio, co., Tx., U.S. E3 150
Frío, stm., N.A. G10 92
Frio, stm., Tx., U.S. E3 150
Frio, Cabo, c., Braz. G7 79
Frio Draw, val., U.S. C6 138
Friona, Tx., U.S. B1 150
Fripps Island, i., S.C., U.S. G7 147
Frisco, Co., U.S. B4 113
Frisco, N.C., U.S. B7 140
Frisco City, Al., U.S. D2 108
Frisco Peak, mtn., Ut., U.S. E2 151
Frisian Islands, is., Eur. E9 4
Frissell, Mount, mtn., U.S. A2 114
Fritch, Tx., U.S. B2 150
Friuli-Venezia-Giulia, prov., Italy C7 18
Friza, proliv, strt., Russia H21 28
Frobisher, Sask., Can. H4 105
Frobisher Bay, b., N.W. Ter., Can. D19 96
Frobisher Lake, l., Sask., Can. m7 105
Frohna, Mo., U.S. D8 132
Frohnleiten, Aus. H15 10
Froid, Mt., U.S. B12 133
Frolovo, Russia H6 26
Fromberg, Mt., U.S. E8 133
Frombork, Pol. A19 10
Frome, stm., Austl. G3 70
Frome, Lake, l., Austl. H3 70
Frontenac, Ks., U.S. E9 123
Frontenac, Mn., U.S. F6 130
Frontera, Mex. H13 90
Frontera, Mex. D9 90
Frontier, Sask., Can. H1 105
Frontier, Wy., U.S. E2 157
Frontier, co., Ne., U.S. D5 134
Frontino, Col. D4 84
Frontino, Páramo, mtn., Col. D4 84
Front Range, mts., Co., U.S. A5 113
Front Royal, Va., U.S. B4 153
Frosinone, Italy H8 18
Frost, Tx., U.S. C4 150
Frostburg, Md., U.S. k13 127
Frostproof, Fl., U.S. E5 116
Frøya, i., Nor. J11 6
Fruges, Fr. B9 14
Fruita, Co., U.S. B2 113
Fruitdale, Al., U.S. D1 108
Fruit Heights, Ut., U.S. B4 151
Fruithurst, Al., U.S. B4 108
Fruitland, Id., U.S. F2 119
Fruitland, Ia., U.S. C6 122
Fruitland, Md., U.S. D6 127
Fruitland, N.M., U.S. A1 138
Fruitland, Tn., U.S. B3 149
Fruitland Park, Fl., U.S. D5 116
Fruitport, Mi., U.S. E4 129
Fruitvale, B.C., Can. E9 99
Fruitvale, Co., U.S. B2 113
Fruitvale, Id., U.S. E2 119
Fruitvale, Wa., U.S. C5 154
Fruitville, Fl., U.S. E4 116
Frunze see Biškek, Kyrg. I12 26
Frunzivka, Ukr. B13 20
Frutal, Braz. F4 79
Frutigen, Switz. E8 13
Frýdek-Místek, Czech Rep. F18 10
Fryeburg, Me., U.S. D2 126
Fuchang, China E2 34
Fuchū, Japan M8 36
Fuchun, stm., China F8 34
Fuding, China H9 34
Fuego, Volcán de, vol., Guat. C4 92
Fuencaliente de la Palma, Spain o23 17b
Fuensalida, Spain E7 16
Fuente de Cantos, Spain G5 16
Fuente de Oro, Col. F6 84
Fuentesaúco, Spain D6 16
Fuerte, stm., Mex. D5 90
Fuerte Olimpo, Para. I13 82
Fuerteventura, i., Spain o26 17b
Fufeng, China E8 30
Fuhe, China L2 34
Fuhu, China F7 34
Fuji, Japan L13 36
Fujian (Fukien), prov., China F10 30
Fujieda, Japan M13 36
Fujin, China B13 30
Fujinomiya, Japan L13 36
Fuji-san (Fujiyama), vol., Japan L13 36
Fujisawa, Japan L14 36
Fujiyama see Fuji-san, vol., Japan L13 36
Fuji-yoshida, Japan L13 36
Fukagawa, Japan d17 36a
Fukou, China I6 34
Fukuchiyama, Japan L10 36
Fukue-jima, i., Japan O3 36
Fukui, Japan K11 36
Fukuoka, Japan N5 36
Fukushima, Japan J15 36
Fukuyama, Japan M8 36
Fulacunda, Gui.-B. F2 64
Fūlādī, Kūh-e, mtn., Afg. C2 44
Fulda, Ger. E9 10
Fulda, In., U.S. H4 121
Fulda, Mn., U.S. G3 130
Fulda, stm., Ger. D9 10
Fulechang, China B8 40
Fuling, China F8 30
Fullarton, Ont., Can. D3 103
Fullerton, Ca., U.S. n13 112
Fullerton, Ne., U.S. C8 134
Fullerton, N.D., U.S. C7 141
Fulpmes, Aus. H11 10
Fulshear, Tx., U.S. r14 150
Fulton, Al., U.S. D2 108
Fulton, Ar., U.S. D2 111
Fulton, Il., U.S. B3 120
Fulton, In., U.S. C5 121
Fulton, Ks., U.S. D9 123
Fulton, Ky., U.S. f9 124
Fulton, Md., U.S. B4 127
Fulton, Mi., U.S. A2 129

Name	Map Ref.	Page

Name | Map Ref. | Page

Gorgona, Isola di, i., Italy F4 18
Gorgor, Peru D3 82
Gorgora, Eth. K9 60
Gorham, Il., U.S. F4 120
Gorham, Ks., U.S. D4 123
Gorham, Me., U.S. E2 126
Gorham, N.H., U.S. B4 136
Gorham, N.Y., U.S. C3 139
Gori, Geor. I6 26
Goricy, Russia D19 22
Gorinchem, Neth. E7 12
Goris, Arm. B9 48
Gorizia, Italy D8 18
Gorj, co., Rom. E7 20
Gorkhā, Nepal F11 44
Gorki, Bela. G13 22
Gor'kovskoje vodochranilišče, res., Russia D26 22
Gorky see Nižnij Novgorod, Russia E27 22
Gorlice, Pol. F21 10
Görlitz, Ger. D14 10
Gorlovka see Horlivka, Ukr. H5 26
Gorlovo, Russia H22 22
Gorman, Tx., U.S. C3 150
Gormania, W.V., U.S. B5 155
Gorn'ackij, Russia D10 26
Gorn'ak, Russia H22 22
Gornji Milenovac, Yugo. E4 20
Gorno-Altajsk, Russia G9 28
Gorno-Altay see Altaj, state, Russia G15 26
Gornozavodsk, Russia H20 28
Gorochovec, Russia E25 22
Gorodec, Russia C12 22
Gorodec, Russia E26 22
Gorodeja, Bela. H9 22
Gorodišče, Bela. H9 22
Gorodišče, Bela. H12 22
Gorodok, Bela. F12 22
Goroka, Pap. N. Gui. G12 38
Gorontalo, Indon. E7 38
Gorouol, stm., Afr. D10 64
Gorrie, Ont., Can. D3 103
Gorutuba, stm., Braz. C7 79
Gorzów Wielkopolski (Landsberg an der Warthe), Pol. C15 10
Gosford, Austl. I9 70
Goshabi, Sud. I6 60
Goshen, N.S., Can. D8 101
Goshen, Al., U.S. D3 108
Goshen, Ct., U.S. B3 114
Goshen, In., U.S. A6 121
Goshen, Ky., U.S. g11 124
Goshen, N.H., U.S. D2 136
Goshen, N.Y., U.S. D6 139
Goshen, Oh., U.S. C1 142
Goshen, Ut., U.S. D4 151
Goshen, Va., U.S. C3 153
Goshen, co., Wy., U.S. D8 157
Goshen Hole, Wy., U.S. D8 157
Goshute Indian Reservation, U.S. D7 135
Goshute Lake, l., Nv., U.S. C7 135
Goshute Mountains, mts., Nv., U.S. C7 135
Goslar, Ger. D10 10
Gosnell, Ar., U.S. B6 111
Gosper, co., Ne., U.S. D6 134
Gosport, In., U.S. F4 121
Gossas, Sen. D1 64
Gossi, Mali D9 64
Gossville, N.H., U.S. D4 136
Gostivar, Mac. H4 20
Gostyń, Pol. D17 10
Gostynin, Pol. C19 10
Göta älv, stm., Swe. M13 6
Gotebo, Ok., U.S. B3 143
Göteborg (Gothenburg), Swe. M12 6
Göteborgs och Bohus län, co., Swe. L12 6
Gotemba, Japan L13 36
Gotești, Mol. C12 20
Gotha, Ger. E10 10
Gotham, Wi., U.S. E3 156
Gothenburg see Göteborg, Swe. M12 6
Gothenburg, Ne., U.S. D5 134
Gothèye, Niger E10 64
Gotland, i., Swe. M16 6
Gotlands Län, co., Swe. M16 6
Gotō-rettō, is., Japan O3 36
Göttingen, Ger. D9 10
Gouarec, Fr. D3 14
Gouda, Neth. D6 12
Goudge, Arg. H4 80
Goudiry, Sen. D3 64
Gough, Ga., U.S. C4 117
Gough Island, i., St. Hel. M6 52
Gouin, Réservoir, res., Que., Can. k12 104
Goulburn, Austl. J8 70
Goulburn Islands, is., Austl. B6 68
Gould, Ar., U.S. D4 111
Gould, Ok., U.S. C2 143
Goulding, Fl., U.S. u14 116
Gould Island, i., R.I., U.S. E5 146
Goulds, Fl., U.S. s13 116
Gouldsboro, Me., U.S. D4 126
Goulimime, Mor. F5 62
Gounamitz, stm., N.B., Can. B2 101
Goundam, Mali C8 64
Gourdon, Fr. H8 14
Gouré, Niger E15 64
Gourin, Fr. D3 14
Gourma Rharous, Mali C9 64
Gournay-en-Bray, Fr. C8 14
Gouveia, Braz. E7 79
Gouverneur, N.Y., U.S. f9 139
Gouyadong, China J1 34
Govan, Sask., Can. F3 105
Gove, Ks., U.S. D3 123
Gove, co., Ks., U.S. D3 123
Govena, mys, c., Russia F25 28
Governador Valadares, Braz. E8 79
Government Camp, Or., U.S. B5 144
Governor's Harbour, Bah. B6 94
Govind Ballabh Pant Sāgar, res., India H10 44
Govind Sāgar, res., India E7 44
Gowanda, N.Y., U.S. C2 139
Gowan Range, mts., Austl. E6 70
Gowen, Mi., U.S. E5 129
Gowen, Ok., U.S. C6 143
Gower, Mo., U.S. B3 132
Gowmal (Gumal), stm., Asia D3 44
Gowrie, Ia., U.S. B3 122
Goya, Arg. E9 80
Göyçay, Azer. I7 26
Göytäpä, Azer. B10 48
Gozo see Għawdex, i., Malta M9 18
Graaff-Reinet, S. Afr. I7 66
Grabill, In., U.S. B8 121
Grabo, C. Iv. I6 64
Grabowiec, Pol. E23 10
Gračanica, Bos. E2 20
Grace, Id., U.S. G7 119
Grace, Ms., U.S. C3 131
Grace, Mount, mtn., Ma., U.S. A3 128
Grace City, N.D., U.S. B7 141
Gracemont, Ok., U.S. B3 143
Graceville, Fl., U.S. u16 116
Graceville, Mn., U.S. E2 130
Gracewood, Ga., U.S. C4 117
Gracey, Ky., U.S. D2 124
Gracias, Hond. C6 92
Gracias a Dios, dept., Hond. B10 92
Gracias a Dios, Cabo, c., N.A. B11 92
Gradačac, Bos. E2 20
Gradaús, Braz. E8 76
Grado, Italy D8 18
Grady, Ar., U.S. C4 111
Grady, N.M., U.S. C6 138
Grady, co., Ga., U.S. F2 117
Grady, co., Ok., U.S. C4 143
Graettinger, Ia., U.S. A3 122
Grafenau, Ger. G13 10
Gräfenhainichen, Ger. D12 10
Grafing [bei München], Ger. G11 10
Graford, Tx., U.S. C3 150
Grafton, Austl. G10 70
Grafton, Ont., Can. D6 103
Grafton, Il., U.S. E3 120
Grafton, Ia., U.S. A4 122
Grafton, Ma., U.S. B4 128
Grafton, Ne., U.S. D8 134
Grafton, N.H., U.S. C3 136
Grafton, N.D., U.S. A8 141
Grafton, Oh., U.S. A3 142
Grafton, Vt., U.S. E3 152
Grafton, Va., U.S. h15 153
Grafton, W.V., U.S. B4 155
Grafton, Wi., U.S. E6 156
Grafton, co., N.H., U.S. C3 136
Grafton, Cape, c., Austl. A6 70
Graham, Ky., U.S. C2 124
Graham, Mo., U.S. A2 132
Graham, N.C., U.S. A3 140
Graham, Ok., U.S. C4 143
Graham, Tx., U.S. C3 150
Graham, co., Az., U.S. E5 110
Graham, co., Ks., U.S. C4 123
Graham, co., N.C., U.S. f9 140
Graham, Lake, res., Tx., U.S. C3 150
Graham, Mount, mtn., Az., U.S. E6 110
Graham Creek, stm., In., U.S. G6 121
Graham Island, i., B.C., Can. C1 99
Graham Lake, l., Me., U.S. D4 126
Graham Land, reg., Ant. B12 73
Graham Moore, Cape, c., N.W. Ter., Can. B17 96
Graham Moore Bay, b., N.W. Ter., Can. A12 96
Grahamstown, S. Afr. I8 66
Grahamsville, N.Y., U.S. D6 139
Grahn, Ky., U.S. B6 124
Grain Coast, Lib. I5 64
Grainfield, Ks., U.S. C3 123
Grainger, co., Tn., U.S. C10 149
Grain Valley, Mo., U.S. B3 132
Grajaú, Braz. E9 76
Grajaú, stm., Braz. D9 76
Grajewo, Pol. B22 10
Gramada, Bul. F6 20
Gramado, Braz. E13 80
Gramalote, Col. D6 84
Grambling, La., U.S. B3 125
Gramercy, La., U.S. h10 125
Gramilla, Arg. D6 80
Gramling, S.C., U.S. A3 147
Grammer, In., U.S. F6 121
Grammichele, Italy L9 18
Grampian, prov., Scot., U.K. D11 8
Grampian Mountains, mts., Scot., U.K. E9 8
Grampians National Park, Austl. K5 70
Granada, Col. F6 84
Granada, Nic. F9 92
Granada, Spain H8 16
Granada, Co., U.S. C8 113
Granada, Mn., U.S. G4 130
Granada, dept., Nic. F8 92
Granadilla de Abona, Spain o24 17b
Granbury, Tx., U.S. C4 150
Granby, Que., Can. D5 104
Granby, Co., U.S. A5 113
Granby, Ct., U.S. B4 114
Granby, Ma., U.S. B2 128
Granby, Mo., U.S. E3 132
Granby, Lake, res., Co., U.S. A5 113
Gran Canaria, i., Spain o25 17b
Gran Chaco, pl., S.A. C8 80
Grand, co., Co., U.S. A4 113
Grand, co., Ut., U.S. E6 151
Grand, stm., Ont., Can. D4 103
Grand, stm., Mi., U.S. E5 129
Grand, stm., Mo., U.S. A3 132
Grand, stm., Oh., U.S. A4 142
Grand, stm., S.D., U.S. B4 148
Grand, North Fork, stm., U.S. B2 148
Grand, South Fork, stm., S.D., U.S. B3 148
Grand Bahama, i., Bah. A5 94
Grand Bank, Newf., Can. E4 102
Grand Banks of Newfoundland E14 86
Grand-Bassam, C. Iv. I8 64
Grand Bay, N.B., Can. D3 101
Grand Bay, Al., U.S. E1 108
Grand Bayou, stm., La., U.S. k10 125
Grand Bayou, stm., La., U.S. h9 125
Grand Bend, Ont., Can. D3 103
Grand Blanc, Mi., U.S. F7 129
Grand Bruit, Newf., Can. E2 102
Grand Caillou, La., U.S. E5 125
Grand Canal see Da Yunhe, China E10 30
Grand Canal, Ire. H6 8
Grand Canyon, Az., U.S. A3 110
Grand Canyon, val., Az., U.S. A3 110
Grand Canyon National Park, Az., U.S. B3 110
Grand Cayman, i., Cay. Is. E4 94
Grand Centre, Alta., Can. B5 98
Grand Cess, Lib. I5 64
Grand Chenier, La., U.S. E3 125
Grand Codroy, stm., Newf., Can. E2 102
Grand Combin, mtn., Switz. G7 13
Grand Coteau, La., U.S. D3 125
Grand Coulee, Wa., U.S. B6 154
Grand Coulee Dam, Wa., U.S. B6 154
Grand-Couronne, Fr. C8 14
Grande, stm., Arg. C6 80
Grande, stm., Arg. I4 80
Grande, stm., Bol. G9 82
Grande, stm., Braz. F10 76
Grande, stm., Braz. E3 79
Grande, stm., Chile F3 80
Grande, stm., Nic. E8 92
Grande, stm., Pan. I14 92
Grande, stm., Peru F4 82
Grande, Arroyo, stm., Ur. G10 80
Grande, Bahia, Arg. G3 78
Grande, Boca, mth., Ven. C12 84
Grande, Cerro, mtn., Mex. C6 90
Grande, Cerro, mtn., Mex. G8 90
Grande, Corixa, stm., S.A. G7 76
Grande, Corixa (Curiche Grande), sw., S.A. G12 82
Grande, Cuchilla, mtn., Ur. G11 80
Grande, Ilha, i., Braz. G6 79
Grande, Ilha, i., Braz. B11 80
Grande, Ponta, c., Braz. D9 79
Grande, Punta, c., Chile A3 80
Grande, Rio (Bravo del Norte), stm., N.A. F7 106
Grande-Anse, N.B., Can. B4 101
Grande Cache, Alta., Can. C1 98
Grande Cayemite, i., Haiti E8 94
Grand Ecore, La., U.S. C2 125
Grande de Lipez, stm., Bol. I8 82
Grande de Manacapuru, Lago, l., Braz. I12 84
Grande de Matagalpa, stm., Nic. D11 92
Grande de Santiago, stm., Mex. G7 90
Grande de Tarija, stm., S.A. J9 82
Grande de Térraba, stm., C.R. I11 92
Grande-Digue, N.B., Can. C5 101
Grande do Gurupá, Ilha, i., Braz. D8 76
Grand-Entrée, Que., Can. B8 101
Grande Prairie, Alta., Can. B1 98
Grand Erg de Bilma, des., Niger E9 54
Grand Erg Occidental, des., Alg. E11 62
Grand Erg Oriental, des., Alg. E14 62
Grande rivière de la Baleine, stm., Que., Can. g11 104
Grande Ronde, stm., U.S. C8 154
Grandes, Salinas, pl., Arg. B6 80
Grandes, Salinas, pl., Arg. F6 80
Grandes-Bergeronnes, Que., Can. A8 104
Grand-Étang, N.S., Can. C8 101
Grande-Terre, i., Guad. F14 94
Grand Falls (Grand-Sault), N.B., Can. B2 101
Grandfalls, Tx., U.S. D1 150
Grand Falls, wtfl, Me., U.S. C5 126
Grand Falls [-Windsor], Newf., Can. D4 102
Grandfather Mountain, mtn., N.C., U.S. A1 140
Grandfield, Ok., U.S. C3 143
Grand Forks, B.C., Can. E8 99
Grand Forks, N.D., U.S. B8 141
Grand Forks, co., N.D., U.S. B8 141
Grand Forks Air Force Base, mil., N.D., U.S. B8 141
Grand Gorge, N.Y., U.S. C6 139
Grand Harbour, N.B., Can. E3 101
Grand Haven, Mi., U.S. E4 129
Grand Hers, stm., Fr. I8 14
Grand Hogback, mtn., Co., U.S. B3 113
Grandiči, Bela. H6 22
Grandin, Mo., U.S. E7 132
Grandin, N.D., U.S. B9 141
Grand Island, Ne., U.S. D7 134
Grand Island, i., La., U.S. D6 125
Grand Island, i., Mi., U.S. B4 129
Grand Isle, La., U.S. E6 125
Grand Isle, Me., U.S. A4 126
Grand Isle, Vt., U.S. B2 152
Grand Isle, co., Vt., U.S. B2 152
Grand Isle, i., La., U.S. E6 125
Grand Junction, Co., U.S. B2 113
Grand Junction, Ia., U.S. B3 122
Grand Junction, Tn., U.S. B2 149
Grand lac Bostonnais, l., Que., Can. B5 104
Grand-Lahou, C. Iv. I7 64
Grand Lake, Co., U.S. A5 113
Grand Lake, l., N.B., Can. D3 101
Grand Lake, l., Newf., Can. B1 102
Grand Lake, l., Newf., Can. D3 102
Grand Lake, l., La., U.S. E3 125
Grand Lake, l., La., U.S. E6 125
Grand Lake, l., Mi., U.S. C7 129
Grand Lake, l., Oh., U.S. B1 142
Grand Lake Matagamon, l., Me., U.S. B4 126
Grand Lake Seboeis, l., Me., U.S. B4 126
Grand Lake Stream, Me., U.S. C5 126
Grand Ledge, Mi., U.S. F6 129
Grand Manan Island, i., N.B., Can. E3 101
Grand Marais, Mi., U.S. B5 129
Grand Marais, Mn., U.S. k9 130
Grand Marsh, Wi., U.S. E4 156
Grand Meadow, Mn., U.S. G6 130
Grand-Mère, Que., Can. C5 104
Grand Mesa, mtn., Co., U.S. C2 113
Grand Mound, Ia., U.S. C7 122
Grand-Popo, Benin H10 64
Grand Portage, Mn., U.S. k10 130
Grand Portage Indian Reservation, Mn., U.S. k10 130
Grand Portage National Monument, Mn., U.S. h10 130
Grand Prairie, Tx., U.S. n10 150
Grand Pré, N.S., Can. D5 101
Grand Rapids, Mi., U.S. F5 129
Grand Rapids, Mn., U.S. C5 130
Grand Rapids, Oh., U.S. f6 142
Grand Ridge, Fl., U.S. B1 116
Grand Ridge, Il., U.S. B5 120
Grandrieu, Bel. H5 12
Grand River, N.S., Can. D9 101
Grand Rivers, Ky., U.S. f9 124
Grand Ronde, Or., U.S. B3 144
Grand-Saint-Bernard, Col du, Eur. G7 13
Grand-Saint-Bernard, Tunnel du, Eur. G14 14
Grand Saline, Tx., U.S. C5 150
Grand Terre Islands, is., La., U.S. E6 125
Grand Teton, mtn., Wy., U.S. C2 157
Grand Teton National Park, Wy., U.S. C2 157
Grand Tower, Il., U.S. F4 120
Grand Traverse, co., Mi., U.S. D5 129
Grand Traverse Bay, b., Mi., U.S. C5 129
Grand Traverse Bay, East Arm, b., Mi., U.S. D5 129
Grand Traverse Bay, West Arm, b., Mi., U.S. D5 129
Grand Turk, T./C. Is. D9 94
Grand Valley, Ont., Can. D4 103
Grand Valley, val., U.S. B2 113
Grandview, Man., Can. D1 100
Grand View, Id., U.S. G2 119
Grandview, In., U.S. I4 121
Grandview, Ia., U.S. C6 122
Grandview, Mo., U.S. C3 132
Grandview, Tn., U.S. D9 149
Grandview, Wa., U.S. C6 154
Grandview Heights, Oh., U.S. m10 142
Grandville, Mi., U.S. F5 129
Grand Wash Cliffs, clf, Az., U.S. B2 110
Grandy, Mn., U.S. E5 130
Grandy, N.C., U.S. A7 140
Graneros, Chile H3 80
Granger, In., U.S. A5 121
Granger, Ia., U.S. C4 122
Granger, Tx., U.S. D4 150
Granger, Wa., U.S. C5 154
Granger, Wy., U.S. E3 157
Grangeville, Id., U.S. D2 119
Gran Guardia, Arg. C9 80
Granisle, B.C., Can. B4 99
Granite, Ok., U.S. C2 143
Granite, co., Mt., U.S. D3 133
Granite Canon, Wy., U.S. E7 157
Granite City, Il., U.S. E3 120
Granite Falls, Mn., U.S. F3 130
Granite Falls, N.C., U.S. B1 140
Granite Falls, Wa., U.S. A4 154
Granite Lake, res., Newf., Can. D3 102
Granite Mountain, mtn., Ak., U.S. B7 109
Granite Mountains, mts., Az., U.S. E2 110
Granite Mountains, mts., Wy., U.S. D5 157
Granite Pass, Wy., U.S. B5 157
Granite Peak, mtn., Mt., U.S. E7 133
Granite Peak, mtn., Nv., U.S. C2 135
Granite Peak, mtn., Nv., U.S. B4 135
Granite Peak, mtn., Ut., U.S. E3 151
Granite Peak, mtn., Ut., U.S. C2 151
Granite Peak, mtn., Wy., U.S. D4 157
Granite Quarry, N.C., U.S. B2 140
Granite Range, mts., Nv., U.S. C2 135
Graniteville, Ma. U.S. f10 128
Graniteville, S.C., U.S. D4 147
Graniteville, Vt., U.S. C4 152
Grannis, Ar., U.S. C1 111
Granollers, Spain D14 16
Gran Pajonal, mts., Peru D4 82
Gran Paradiso, mtn., Italy D2 18
Gran Sasso d'Italia, mts., Italy G8 18
Grant, Al., U.S. A3 108
Grant, Fl., U.S. E6 116
Grant, Mi., U.S. E5 129
Grant, Ne., U.S. D4 134
Grant, Ok., U.S. D6 143
Grant, co., Ar., U.S. C3 111
Grant, co., In., U.S. D6 121
Grant, co., Ks., U.S. E2 123
Grant, co., Ky., U.S. B5 124
Grant, co., La., U.S. C3 125
Grant, co., Mn., U.S. E2 130
Grant, co., Ne., U.S. C4 134
Grant, co., N.M., U.S. E1 138
Grant, co., N.D., U.S. C4 141
Grant, co., Ok., U.S. A4 143
Grant, co., Or., U.S. C7 144
Grant, co., S.D., U.S. B8 148
Grant, co., Wa., U.S. B6 154
Grant, co., W.V., U.S. B5 155
Grant, co., Wi., U.S. F3 156
Grant, Mount, mtn., Nv., U.S. E3 135
Gran Tarajal, Spain o26 17b
Grant City, Mo., U.S. A3 132
Grantham, N.H., U.S. D2 136
Granton, Ont., Can. D3 103
Granton, Wi., U.S. D3 156
Grant Park, Il., U.S. B6 120
Grant Range, mts., Nv., U.S. E6 135
Grants, N.M., U.S. B2 138
Grantsboro, N.C., U.S. B6 140
Grantsburg, In., U.S. H5 121
Grantsburg, Wi., U.S. C1 156
Grantsdale, Mt., U.S. D2 133
Grants Pass, Or., U.S. E3 144
Grantsville, Md., U.S. k12 127
Grantsville, Ut., U.S. C3 151
Grantsville, W.V., U.S. C3 155
Grant Town, W.V., U.S. B4 155
Grantville, Ga., U.S. C2 117
Grantville, Ks., U.S. k14 123
Granum, Alta., Can. E4 98
Granville, Fr. D5 14
Granville, Il., U.S. B4 120
Granville, Ia., U.S. B2 122
Granville, N.Y., U.S. B7 139
Granville, N.D., U.S. A5 141
Granville, Oh., U.S. B3 142
Granville, Vt., U.S. D3 152
Granville, W.V., U.S. h11 155
Granville, co., N.C., U.S. A4 140
Granville Centre, N.S., Can. E4 101
Granville Ferry, N.S., Can. E4 101
Granville Lake, l., Man., Can. A1 100
Granvin, Nor. K10 6
Grão Mogol, Braz. D7 79
Grapeland, Tx., U.S. D5 150
Grapeview, Wa., U.S. B3 154
Grapevine, Tx., U.S. C4 150
Grapevine Lake, res., Tx., U.S. n9 150
Grapevine Peak, mtn., Nv., U.S. G4 135
Grasmere, S. Afr. F8 66
Grasonville, Md., U.S. C5 127
Grass, stm., Man., Can. B2 100
Grass, stm., N.Y., U.S. f9 139
Grass Creek, In., U.S. C5 121
Grasse, Fr. I13 14
Grassflat, Pa., U.S. D5 145
Grass Lake, Il., U.S. h8 120
Grass Lake, Mi., U.S. F6 129
Grass Lake, l., Il., U.S. h8 120
Grassrange, Mt., U.S. C8 133
Grass Valley, Ca., U.S. C3 112
Grassy, Austl. M6 70
Grassy Brook, stm., Vt., U.S. E3 152
Grassy Lake, Alta., Can. E5 98
Grassy Lake, l., La., U.S. k9 125
Grates Cove, Newf., Can. D5 102
Grates Point, c., Newf., Can. D5 102
Gratiot, co., Mi., U.S. E6 129
Gratis, Oh., U.S. C1 142
Gratz, Pa., U.S. E8 145
Graubünden (Grischun), state, Switz. E11 13
Gravatá, Braz. E11 76
Gravatá, stm., Braz. D7 79
Grave Creek, stm., W.V., U.S. g8 155
Gravelines, Fr. B9 14
Gravell Point, c., N.W. Ter., Can. C17 96
Gravelly, Ar., U.S. C2 111
Gravelly Branch, stm., De., U.S. F4 115
Gravelly Range, mts., Mt., U.S. E4 133
Gravel Ridge, Ar., U.S. h10 111
Gravenhurst, Ont., Can. C5 103
Grave Peak, mtn., Id., U.S. C4 119
Graves, co., Ky., U.S. f9 124
Gravette, Ar., U.S. A1 111
Gravina in Puglia, Italy I11 18
Gravity, Ia., U.S. D3 122
Gray, Sask., Can. G3 105
Gray, Fr. E12 14
Gray, Ga., U.S. C3 117
Gray, Ky., U.S. D5 124
Gray, La., U.S. k10 125
Gray, Me., U.S. g7 126
Gray, co., Ks., U.S. E3 123
Gray, co., Tx., U.S. B2 150
Grayback Mountain, mtn., Or., U.S. E3 144
Gray Court, S.C., U.S. B3 147
Grayland, Wa., U.S. C1 154
Grayling, Ak., U.S. C7 109
Grayling, Mi., U.S. D6 129
Graylyn Crest, De., U.S. A3 115
Grays Harbor, co., Wa., U.S. B2 154
Grays Harbor, b., Wa., U.S. C1 154
Grayslake, Il., U.S. A5 120
Grays Lake, sw., Id., U.S. F7 119
Grayson, Sask., Can. G4 105
Grayson, Al., U.S. A2 108
Grayson, Ga., U.S. C3 117
Grayson, Ky., U.S. B7 124
Grayson, La., U.S. B3 125
Grayson, co., Ky., U.S. C3 124
Grayson, co., Tx., U.S. C4 150
Grayson, co., Va., U.S. D1 153
Grayson Lake, res., Ky., U.S. B7 124
Grays Peak, mtn., Co., U.S. B5 113
Grays River, Wa., U.S. C2 154
Gray Summit, Mo., U.S. g12 132
Graysville, Al., U.S. f7 108
Graysville, Tn., U.S. D8 149
Grayville, Il., U.S. E5 120
Graz, Aus. H15 10
Grazalema, Spain I6 16
Gr'azi, Russia I22 22
Gr'aznoje, Russia G22 22
Gr'azovec, Russia C23 22
Greasewood, Az., U.S. B6 110
Great Artesian Basin, Austl. E5 70
Great Australian Bight, Austl. F5 68
Great Averill Pond, l., Vt., U.S. B5 152
Great Barrier Island, i., N.Z. B5 72
Great Barrier Reef, rf., Austl. C9 68
Great Barrier Reef Marine Park, Austl. C9 68
Great Barrington, Ma., U.S. B1 128
Great Basin, U.S. C3 106
Great Basin National Park, Nv., U.S. E7 135
Great Bay, b., N.H., U.S. D5 136
Great Bay, b., N.J., U.S. D4 137
Great Bear Lake, l., N.W. Ter., Can. C8 96
Great Bend, Ks., U.S. D5 123
Great Bend, N.D., U.S. C9 141
Great Bend, Pa., U.S. C10 145
Great Blue Hill, hill, Ma., U.S. B5 128
Great Britain, i., U.K. E7 4
Great Burnt Lake, l., Newf., Can. D3 102
Great Cacapon, W.V., U.S. B6 155
Great Captain Island, i., Ct., U.S. F1 114
Great Channel, strt., Asia K3 40
Great Dismal Swamp, sw., U.S. D6 153
Great Divide Basin, Wy., U.S. E4 157
Great Dividing Range, mts., Austl. E9 68
Great Duck Island, i., Ont., Can. B2 103
Great East Lake, l., U.S. C5 136
Great Egg Harbor, stm., N.J., U.S. D3 137
Greater Antilles, is., N.A. D7 94
Greater Cincinnati Airport, Ky., U.S. h13 124
Greater Khingan Range see Da Hinggan Ling, mts., China B11 30
Greater Sunda Islands, is., Asia F5 38
Great Exuma, i., Bah. C7 94
Great Falls, Man., Can. D3 100
Great Falls, Mt., U.S. C5 133
Great Falls, S.C., U.S. B6 147
Great Falls, wtfl, Md., U.S. B3 127
Great Falls Dam, Tn., U.S. D6 149
Great Guana Cay, i., Bah. B6 94
Greathouse Peak, mtn., Mt., U.S. D7 133
Great Inagua, i., Bah. D8 94
Great Indian Desert (Thar Desert), des., Asia G4 44
Great Island, spit, Ma., U.S. C7 128
Great Island, i., N.C., U.S. B6 140
Great Karroo, plat., S. Afr. I6 66
Great Lake, l., Austl. M7 70
Great Lakes Naval Training Center, mil., Il., U.S. h9 120
Great Miami, stm., U.S. C1 142
Great Misery Island, i., Ma., U.S. f12 128
Great Moose Lake, l., Me., U.S. D3 126
Great Namaqualand, hist. reg., Nmb. E3 66
Great Neck, N.Y., U.S. h13 139
Great Nicobar, i., India K2 40
Great North Mountain, mtn., U.S. C6 155
Great Palm Island, i., Austl. B7 70
Great Pee Dee, stm., U.S. D9 147
Great Plain of the Koukdjuak, pl., N.W. Ter., Can. C18 96
Great Plains, pl., N.A. E9 86
Great Point, c., Ma., U.S. D7 128
Great Pond, l., Me., U.S. D3 126
Great Pond, l., Ma., U.S. h12 128
Great Pond, l., Ma., U.S. h11 128
Great Quittacas Pond, l., Ma., U.S. C6 128
Great Ruaha, stm., Tan. C7 58
Great Sacandaga Lake, l., N.Y., U.S. C6 139
Great Saint Bernard Pass see Grand-Saint-Bernard, Col du, Eur. G7 13
Great Salt Lake, l., Ut., U.S. B3 151
Great Salt Lake Desert, des., Ut., U.S. C2 151
Great Salt Plains Lake, res., Ok., U.S. A3 143
Great Salt Pond, b., R.I., U.S. h7 146
Great Sand Dunes National Monument, Co., U.S. D5 113
Great Sand Hills, hills, Sask., Can. G1 105
Great Sandy Desert, des., Austl. D4 68
Great Scarcies (Kolenté), stm., Afr. G3 64
Great Seneca Creek, stm., Md., U.S. B3 127
Great Slave Lake, l., N.W. Ter., Can. D10 96
Great Smoky Mountains, mts., U.S. B8 149
Great Smoky Mountains National Park, U.S. B8 149
Great Swamp, sw., R.I., U.S. F3 146
Great Valley, val., U.S. C2 153
Great Victoria Desert, des., Austl. E5 68
Great Village, N.S., Can. D6 101
Great Wall, sci., Ant. B1 73
Great Wall see Chang Cheng, hist., China C4 32
Great Wass Island, i., Me., U.S. D5 126
Great Yarmouth, Eng., U.K. I15 8
Great Zab (Büyükzap) (Az-Zāb al-Kabīr), stm., Asia C7 48
Gréboun, mtn., Niger A14 64
Grecia, C.R. G10 92
Greco, Ur. G10 80
Greece, N.Y., U.S. B3 139
Greece (Ellás), ctry., Eur. H12 4
Greeley, Co., U.S. A6 113
Greeley, Ia., U.S. B6 122
Greeley, Ks., U.S. D8 123
Greeley, Ne., U.S. C7 134
Greeley, Pa., U.S. D12 145

Name — Map Ref. — Page

Greeley, co., Ks., U.S. D2 123
Greeley, co., Ne., U.S. C7 134
Greeleyville, S.C., U.S. D8 147
Green, Ks., U.S. C6 123
Green, Or., U.S. D3 144
Green, co., Ky., U.S. C4 124
Green, co., Wi., U.S. F4 156
Green, stm., N.B., Can. B1 101
Green, stm., U.S. D5 106
Green, stm., U.S. A1 113
Green, stm., U.S. F3 152
Green, stm., Il., U.S. B4 120
Green, stm., Ky., U.S. C2 124
Green, stm., Wa., U.S. B3 154
Green Acres, De., U.S. h8 115
Greenacres, Wa., U.S. B8 154
Greenacres City, Fl., U.S. F6 116
Greenback, Tn., U.S. D9 149
Greenbackville, Va., U.S. C7 153
Green Bank, W.V., U.S. C5 155
Green Bay, Wi., U.S. D6 156
Green Bay, b., U.S. D3 129
Greenbelt, Md., U.S. C4 127
Greenbriar, Va., U.S. g12 153
Greenbrier, Al., U.S. A3 108
Greenbrier, Ar., U.S. B3 111
Green Brier, Tn., U.S. A5 149
Greenbrier, co., W.V., U.S. D4 155
Greenbrier, stm., W.V., U.S. D4 155
Greenbush, Me., U.S. C4 126
Greenbush, Mn., U.S. B2 130
Greencastle, In., U.S. E4 121
Green Castle, Mo., U.S. A5 132
Greencastle, Pa., U.S. G6 145
Green City, Mo., U.S. A5 132
Green Court, Alta., Can. B3 98
Green Cove Springs, Fl., U.S. C5 116
Green Creek, N.J., U.S. E3 137
Greendale, In., U.S. F8 121
Greendale, Wi., U.S. F6 156
Greene, Ia., U.S. B5 122
Greene, Me., U.S. D2 126
Greene, N.Y., U.S. C5 139
Greene, co., Al., U.S. C1 108
Greene, co., Ar., U.S. A5 111
Greene, co., Ga., U.S. C3 117
Greene, co., Il., U.S. D3 120
Greene, co., In., U.S. F4 121
Greene, co., Ia., U.S. B3 122
Greene, co., Ms., U.S. D5 131
Greene, co., Mo., U.S. D4 132
Greene, co., N.Y., U.S. C6 139
Greene, co., N.C., U.S. B5 140
Greene, co., Oh., U.S. C2 142
Greene, co., Pa., U.S. G1 145
Greene, co., Tn., U.S. C11 149
Greene, co., Va., U.S. B4 153
Greeneville, Tn., U.S. C11 149
Green Fall, stm., U.S. F1 146
Greenfield, Ar., U.S. B5 111
Greenfield, Ca., U.S. D3 112
Greenfield, Il., U.S. D3 120
Greenfield, In., U.S. E6 121
Greenfield, Ia., U.S. C3 122
Greenfield, Ma., U.S. A2 128
Greenfield, Mo., U.S. D4 132
Greenfield, N.H., U.S. E3 136
Greenfield, N.M., U.S. D5 138
Greenfield, Oh., U.S. C2 142
Greenfield, Ok., U.S. B3 143
Greenfield, Tn., U.S. A3 149
Greenfield, Wi., U.S. n12 156
Greenfield Plaza, Ia., U.S. e8 122
Green Forest, Ar., U.S. A2 111
Green Harbor, Ma., U.S. B6 128
Green Head, c., Austl. F2 68
Greenhill, Al., U.S. A2 108
Green Hill Pond, I., R.I., U.S. G3 146
Greenhills, Oh., U.S. n12 142
Greenhorn Creek, stm., Co., U.S. D6 113
Green Lake, Sask., Can. C2 105
Green Lake, Wi., U.S. E5 156
Green Lake, co., Wi., U.S. E4 156
Green Lake, I., Me., U.S. D4 126
Green Lake, I., Wi., U.S. E5 156
Greenland, Ar., U.S. B1 111
Greenland, Mi., U.S. B1 129
Greenland, N.H., U.S. D5 136
Greenland (Kalaallit Nunaat), dep., N.A. B15 86
Greenland Sea B20 86
Greenleaf, Ks., U.S. C7 123
Greenleaf, Wi., U.S. D5 156
Greenlee, co., Az., U.S. D6 110
Green Lookout Mountain, mtn., Wa., U.S. D3 154
Greenmount, Md., U.S. A4 127
Green Mountain, Ia., U.S. B5 122
Green Mountain, mtn., Wy., U.S. D5 157
Green Mountain Reservoir, res., Co., U.S. B4 113
Green Mountains, mts., Vt., U.S. F2 152
Greenock, Pa., U.S. F2 145
Green Peter Lake, res., Or., U.S. C4 144
Green Pond, Al., U.S. B2 108
Green Pond, I., N.J., U.S. A4 137
Green Pond Mountain, mtn., N.J., U.S. B3 137
Greenport, N.Y., U.S. m16 139
Green Ridge, Mo., U.S. C4 132
Green River, Ut., U.S. E5 151
Green River, Wy., U.S. E3 157
Green River Lake, res., Ky., U.S. C4 124
Green River Lock and Dam, U.S. I2 121
Green River Reservoir, res., Vt., U.S. B3 152
Green Rock, Il., U.S. B3 120
Greensboro, Al., U.S. C2 108
Greensboro, Fl., U.S. B2 116
Greensboro, Ga., U.S. C3 117
Greensboro, In., U.S. E7 121
Greensboro, Md., U.S. C6 127
Greensboro, N.C., U.S. A3 140
Greensboro, Vt., U.S. B4 152
Greensboro Bend, Vt., U.S. B4 152
Greensburg, In., U.S. F7 121
Greensburg, Ks., U.S. E4 123
Greensburg, Ky., U.S. C4 124
Greensburg, La., U.S. D5 125
Greensburg, Pa., U.S. F2 145
Greens Fork, In., U.S. E7 121
Greens Peak, mtn., Az., U.S. C6 110
Greenspond, Newf., Can. D5 102
Green Spring, W.V., U.S. B6 155
Green Springs, Oh., U.S. A2 142
Greensville, co., Va., U.S. D5 153
Green Swamp, sw., N.C., U.S. C4 140
Greentop, Mo., U.S. A5 132
Greentown, In., U.S. D6 121
Greenup, Il., U.S. D5 120
Greenup, Ky., U.S. B7 124
Greenup, co., Ky., U.S. B7 124
Greenvale, Austl. B6 70
Green Valley, Az., U.S. F5 110
Green Valley, Il., U.S. C4 120
Green Valley, val., Tx., U.S. p13 150
Greenview, Il., U.S. C4 120
Greenview, W.V., U.S. n12 155
Greenville, Lib. I5 64
Greenville, Al., U.S. D3 108
Greenville, Ca., U.S. B3 112
Greenville, De., U.S. A3 115
Greenville, Fl., U.S. B3 116
Greenville, Ga., U.S. C2 117
Greenville, Il., U.S. E4 120
Greenville, In., U.S. H6 121
Greenville, Ky., U.S. C2 124
Greenville, Me., U.S. C3 126
Greenville, Mi., U.S. E5 129
Greenville, Ms., U.S. B2 131
Greenville, Mo., U.S. D7 132
Greenville, N.H., U.S. E3 136
Greenville, N.C., U.S. B5 140
Greenville, Oh., U.S. B1 142
Greenville, Pa., U.S. D1 145
Greenville, R.I., U.S. C3 146
Greenville, S.C., U.S. B3 147
Greenville, Tx., U.S. C4 150
Greenville, Va., U.S. B3 153
Greenville, co., S.C., U.S. B3 147
Greenville Creek, stm., Oh., U.S. B1 142
Greenville Junction, Me., U.S. C3 126
Greenway, Ar., U.S. A5 111
Greenwich, Ct., U.S. E1 114
Greenwich, N.Y., U.S. B7 139
Greenwich, Oh., U.S. A3 142
Greenwich Bay, b., R.I., U.S. D4 146
Greenwich Hill, N.B., Can. D3 101
Greenwich Point, c., Ct., U.S. E1 114
Greenwood, B.C., Can. E8 99
Greenwood, Ar., U.S. B1 111
Greenwood, De., U.S. E3 115
Greenwood, Fl., U.S. B1 116
Greenwood, In., U.S. E5 121
Greenwood, La., U.S. B2 125
Greenwood, Ms., U.S. B3 131
Greenwood, Mo., U.S. k11 132
Greenwood, Ne., U.S. D9 134
Greenwood, Pa., U.S. E5 145
Greenwood, S.C., U.S. C3 147
Greenwood, S.D., U.S. E7 148
Greenwood, Wi., U.S. D3 156
Greenwood, co., Ks., U.S. E7 123
Greenwood, co., S.C., U.S. C3 147
Greenwood, Lake, res., In., U.S. G4 121
Greenwood, Lake, res., S.C., U.S. C4 147
Greenwood Lake, N.Y., U.S. D6 139
Greenwood Lake, I., U.S. A4 137
Greenwood Lake, I., Mn., U.S. C7 130
Greer, S.C., U.S. B3 147
Greer, co., Ok., U.S. C2 143
Greers Ferry, Ar., U.S. B3 111
Greers Ferry Lake, res., Ar., U.S. B3 111
Greeson, Lake, res., Ar., U.S. C2 111
Gregg, co., Tx., U.S. C5 150
Gregoire Lake, I., Alta., Can. A5 98
Gregório, stm., Braz. B6 82
Gregory, Ar., U.S. B4 111
Gregory, Mi., U.S. F6 129
Gregory, S.D., U.S. D6 148
Gregory, co., S.D., U.S. D6 148
Gregory, stm., Austl. B3 70
Gregory, Lake, I., Austl. G3 70
Gregory Bald, mtn., U.S. D10 149
Gregory Range, mts., Austl. B5 70
Greifswald, Ger. A13 10
Greilickville, Mi., U.S. D5 129
Greiz, Ger. E12 10
Grem'ačinsk, Russia F9 26
Grenada, Ca., U.S. B2 112
Grenada, Ms., U.S. B4 131
Grenada, co., Ms., U.S. B4 131
Grenada, ctry., N.A. H14 94
Grenada Lake, res., Ms., U.S. B4 131
Grenadines, is., N.A. H14 94
Grenchen, Switz. D7 13
Grenfell, Austl. I8 70
Grenfell, Sask., Can. G4 105
Grenoble, Fr. G12 14
Grenola, Ks., U.S. E7 123
Grenora, N.D., U.S. A2 141
Grenville, Que., Can. D3 104
Grenville, Cape, c., Austl. B8 68
Grenville, Point, c., Wa., U.S. B1 154
Gréoux-les-Bains, Fr. I12 14
Gresham, Ne., U.S. C8 134
Gresham, Or., U.S. B4 144
Gresham, Wi., U.S. D5 156
Gresik, Indon. j16 39a
Gresten, Aus. G15 10
Gretna, Man., Can. E3 100
Gretna, Fl., U.S. B2 116
Gretna, La., U.S. E5 125
Gretna, Ne., U.S. C9 134
Gretna, Va., U.S. D3 153
Greven, Ger. C7 10
Grevená, Grc. I5 20
Grevenbroich, Ger. D6 10
Grey, stm., Newf., Can. E3 102
Greybull, Wy., U.S. B4 157
Greybull, stm., Wy., U.S. B4 157
Grey Eagle, Mn., U.S. E4 130
Greylock, Mount, mtn., Ma., U.S. A1 128
Greymouth, N.Z. E3 72
Grey Range, mts., Austl. G5 70
Greys, stm., Wy., U.S. C2 157
Greytown, S. Afr. G10 66
Gribanovskij, Russia G6 26
Gridley, Ca., U.S. C3 112
Gridley, Il., U.S. C5 120
Gridley, Ks., U.S. D8 123
Gridley Mountain, mtn., Ct., U.S. A2 114
Griesbach, Ger. G13 10
Griesheim, Ger. F8 10
Griffin, Sask., Can. H4 105
Griffin, Ga., U.S. C2 117
Griffin, In., U.S. H2 121
Griffiss Air Force Base, mil., N.Y., U.S. B5 139
Griffith, Austl. J7 70
Griffith, In., U.S. A3 121
Griffith Island, i., Ont., Can. C4 103
Griffithsville, W.V., U.S. C3 155
Griffithville, Ar., U.S. B4 111
Grifton, N.C., U.S. B5 140
Griggs, co., N.D., U.S. B7 141
Griggsville, Il., U.S. D3 120
Grignan, Fr. H11 14
Grigoriopol, Mol. B13 20
Grijalva, stm., Mex. I13 90
Grijalva (Cuilco), stm., N.A. B3 92
Grijpskerk, Neth. B9 12
Grim, Cape, c., Austl. M6 70
Grimes, Al., U.S. D4 108
Grimes, Ia., U.S. C4 122
Grimes, co., Tx., U.S. D4 150
Grimesland, N.C., U.S. B5 140
Grimma, Ger. D12 10
Grimsby, Ont., Can. D5 103
Grimsby, Eng., U.K. H13 8
Grimselpass, Switz. E9 13
Grimshaw, Alta., Can. A2 98
Grimsley, Tn., U.S. C9 149
Grímsstaðir, Ice. B5 6a
Grimstad, Nor. L11 6
Grímsvötn, mtn., Ice. B5 6a
Grindall Creek, Va., U.S. n18 153
Grindelwald, Switz. E9 13
Grinnell, Ia., U.S. C5 122
Grinnell, Ks., U.S. C3 123
Grinnell Peninsula, pen., N.W. Ter., Can. A13 96
Gris-Nez, Cap, c., Fr. B8 14
Grissom Air Force Base, mil., In., U.S. C5 121
Griswold, Man., Can. E1 100
Griswold, Ia., U.S. C2 122
Grizzly Bear Mountain, mtn., N.W. Ter., Can. C8 96
Grizzly Mountain, mtn., Id., U.S. B2 119
Grizzly Mountain, mtn., Or., U.S. C6 144
Grizzly Mountain, mtn., Wa., U.S. A7 154
Groais Island, i., Newf., Can. C4 102
Grobiņa, Lat. E4 22
Groblersdal, S. Afr. E9 66
Groblershoop, S. Afr. G5 66
Grodków, Pol. E17 10
Grodno, Bela. H6 22
Grodzisk Mazowiecki, Pol. C20 10
Groede, Neth. F4 12
Groenlo, Neth. D10 12
Groesbeck, Tx., U.S. D4 150
Groesbeek, Neth. E8 12
Groix, Fr. E3 14
Grójec, Pol. D20 10
Grombalia, Tun. M5 18
Gronau, Ger. C7 10
Groningen, Neth. B10 12
Groningen, prov., Neth. B10 12
Gronlid, Sask., Can. D3 105
Groom, Tx., U.S. B2 150
Groom Lake, I., Nv., U.S. F6 135
Groom Range, mts., Nv., U.S. F6 135
Groot-Brakrivier, S. Afr. J5 66
Groote Eylandt, i., Austl. B7 68
Grootfontein, Nmb. B4 66
Groot Karasberge, mts., Nmb. F4 66
Groot-Kei, stm., S. Afr. I9 66
Groot Laagte, stm., Afr. C5 66
Groot-Marico, S. Afr. E8 66
Groot-Vis, stm., S. Afr. I8 66
Gros-Mécatina, Île du, i., Que., Can. C2 102
Gros Morne, mtn., Newf., Can. D3 102
Gros Morne National Park, Newf., Can. D3 102
Grosse Île, i., Que., Can. B8 101
Grosse Isle Naval Air Station, mil., Mi., U.S. p15 129
Grossenhain, Ger. D13 10
Grosse Pointe, Mi., U.S. *p16 129
Grosse Pointe Park, Mi., U.S. p16 129
Grosse Pointe Woods, Mi., U.S. p16 129
Grosse Tete, La., U.S. D4 125
Grosseto, Italy G6 18
Gross-Gerau, Ger. F8 10
Grossglockner, mtn., Aus. H12 10
Grosshöchstetten, Switz. E8 13
Grossmont, Ca., U.S. o16 112
Grossräschen, Ger. D14 10
Grosvenor Dale, Ct., U.S. B8 114
Gros Ventre, stm., Wy., U.S. C2 157
Gros Ventre Range, mts., Wy., U.S. C2 157
Groton, Ct., U.S. D7 114
Groton, Ma., U.S. A4 128
Groton, N.H., U.S. C3 136
Groton, N.Y., U.S. C4 139
Groton, S.D., U.S. B7 148
Groton, Vt., U.S. C4 152
Groton Long Point, Ct., U.S. D7 114
Grottaglie, Italy I12 18
Grottoes, Va., U.S. B4 153
Grouard Mission, Alta., Can. B2 98
Grouse Creek, stm., Ks., U.S. E7 123
Grouse Creek, stm., Ut., U.S. B2 151
Grouse Creek Mountain, mtn., Id., U.S. E5 119
Grouse Creek Mountains, mts., Ut., U.S. B2 151
Grovania, Ga., U.S. D3 117
Grove, Ok., U.S. A7 143
Grove City, Fl., U.S. F4 116
Grove City, Mn., U.S. E4 130
Grove City, Oh., U.S. C2 142
Grove City, Pa., U.S. D1 145
Grove Hill, Al., U.S. D2 108
Groveland, Fl., U.S. D5 116
Groveland, Ga., U.S. D5 117
Groveland, Ma., U.S. A5 128
Grove Point, c., Md., U.S. B5 127
Groveport, Oh., U.S. C3 142
Grover, Co., U.S. A6 113
Grover, N.C., U.S. B1 140
Grover, Wy., U.S. D2 157
Grover City, Ca., U.S. E3 112
Grover Hill, Oh., U.S. A1 142
Groves, Tx., U.S. E6 150
Grovespring, Mo., U.S. D5 132
Groveton, N.H., U.S. A3 136
Groveton, Tx., U.S. D5 150
Groveton, Va., U.S. g12 153
Groveton Gardens, Va., U.S. *B5 153
Grovetown, Ga., U.S. C4 117
Groveville, N.J., U.S. C3 137
Growler Peak, mtn., Az., U.S. E2 110
Groznyj, Russia I7 26
Grubbs, Ar., U.S. B4 111
Grudziądz, Pol. B18 10
Gruetli-Laager, Tn., U.S. D8 149
Gruitrode, Bel. F8 12
Grulla, Tx., U.S. F3 150
Grünau, Nmb. F4 66
Grünau [im Almtal], Aus. H13 10
Grundy, Va., U.S. e9 153
Grundy, co., Il., U.S. B5 120
Grundy, co., Ia., U.S. B5 122
Grundy, co., Mo., U.S. A4 132
Grundy, co., Tn., U.S. D8 149
Grundy Center, Ia., U.S. B5 122
Grunthal, Man., Can. E3 100
Gruver, Tx., U.S. A2 150
Gruziya see Georgia, ctry., Asia I6 26
Grybów, Pol. F20 10
Gryfice, Pol. B15 10
Gstaad, Switz. F7 13
Guabito, Pan. H12 92
Guacanayabo, Golfo de, b., Cuba D6 94
Guacara, Ven. B9 84
Guacarí, Col. F4 84
Gu Achi, Az., U.S. E3 110
Guachiría, stm., Col. E7 84
Guachochi, Mex. D6 90
Guaçuí, Braz. F8 79
Guadalajara, Mex. G8 90
Guadalajara, Spain E8 16
Guadalcanal, i., Sol.Is. I20 158
Guadalén, stm., Spain G8 16
Guadalén, Embalse de, res., Spain G8 16
Guadalmena, stm., Spain G9 16
Guadalquivir, stm., Spain H6 16
Guadalupe, Bol. H9 82
Guadalupe, Col. F5 84
Guadalupe, C.R. H10 92
Guadalupe, Mex. E9 90
Guadalupe, Mex. F8 90
Guadalupe, Peru B2 82
Guadalupe, Az., U.S. m9 110
Guadalupe, Ca., U.S. E3 112
Guadalupe, Co., U.S. D4 113
Guadalupe, co., N.M., U.S. C5 138
Guadalupe, co., Tx., U.S. E4 150
Guadalupe [Bravos], Mex. B6 90
Guadalupe Mountains, mts., U.S. E5 138
Guadalupe Mountains National Park, Tx., U.S. o12 150
Guadalupe Peak, mtn., Tx., U.S. o12 150
Guadalupe Victoria, Mex. E7 90
Guadalupita, N.M., U.S. A4 138
Guadarrama, Sierra de, mts., Spain E7 16
Guadeloupe, dep., N.A. F14 94
Guadeloupe Passage, strt., N.A. F14 94
Guadiana, stm., Eur. H4 16
Guadix, Spain H8 16
Guaíba, Braz. F13 80
Guaíba, est., Braz. F13 80
Guaihe, China B1 34
Guaimaca, Hond. C8 92
Guaimoreto, Laguna de, b., Hond. B9 92
Guainía, dept., Col. F8 84
Guainía, stm., S.A. F9 84
Guaiquinima, Cerro, mtn., Ven. E11 84
Guaíra, Braz. F4 79
Guaíra, Braz. C11 80
Guairá, dept., Para. C10 80
Guáitara, stm., Col. G4 84
Guajaba, Cayo, i., Cuba D6 94
Guajará-Mirim, Braz. D9 82
Gualaca, Pan. C1 84
Gualaceo, Ec. I3 84
Gualala, Ca., U.S. C2 112
Gualán, Guat. B5 92
Gualaquiza, Ec. I3 84
Gualdo Tadino, Italy F7 18
Gualeguay, Arg. G9 80
Gualeguay, stm., Arg. G9 80
Gualeguaychú, Arg. G9 80
Gualicho, Salina del, pl., Arg. E3 78
Guam, dep., Oc. F22 2
Guamal, Col. C5 84
Guamal, Col. F6 84
Guaminí, Arg. I7 80
Guamo, Col. E5 84
Guamote, Ec. H3 84
Guamúchil, Mex. E5 90
Guamués, stm., Col. G4 84
Guanacaste, prov., C.R. G9 92
Guanacaste, Cordillera de, mts., C.R. G9 92
Guanacaste, Parque Nacional, C.R. G9 92
Guanacaure, Cerro, mtn., Hond. D7 92
Guanaceví, Mex. E7 90
Guanache, stm., Peru B4 82
Guanahacabibes, Golfo de, b., Cuba C2 94
Guanaja, Hond. A9 92
Guanaja, Isla de, i., Hond. A9 92
Guanajay, Cuba C3 94
Guanajuato, Mex. G9 90
Guanajuato, state, Mex. G9 90
Guanambi, Braz. C7 79
Guanaparo, Caño, stm., Ven. C8 84
Guañape, Islas, is., Peru C2 82
Guanare, Ven. C8 84
Guanare, stm., Ven. C8 84
Guanarito, Ven. C8 84
Guanay, Bol. F8 82
Guanay, Cerro, mtn., Ven. E9 84
Guanbuqiao, China F3 34
Guandacol, Arg. E4 80
Guandanghu, China E2 34
Guandian, China C7 34
Guane, Cuba C2 94
Guang'an, China E8 30
Guangde, China E8 34
Guangdong (Kwangtung), prov., China G9 30
Guanghua, China E9 30
Guangnan, China G8 30
Guangrao, China F6 32
Guangxi Zhuangzu Zizhiqu (Kwangsi Chuang), prov., China G8 30
Guangyuan, China E8 30
Guangzhou (Canton), China L2 34
Guanhães, Braz. E7 79
Guanipa, stm., Ven. C11 84
Guankou, China E4 34
Guano, Ec. H3 84
Guano Lake, I., Or., U.S. E7 144
Guanqian, China E6 34
Guanqiaopu, China D1 34
Guanta, Ven. B10 84
Guantánamo, Cuba D7 94
Guantao (Nanguantao), China G3 32
Guantou, China G9 34
Guanxian, China E7 30
Guanyintang, China D1 34
Guanzhuang, China F2 32
Guanzhuang, China C3 34
Guapí, Col. F4 84
Guapiara, Braz. H4 79
Guápiles, C.R. G11 92
Guaporé, Braz. E13 80
Guaporé (Itenes), stm., S.A. E10 82
Guaqui, Bol. G7 82
Guará, stm., Braz. B6 79
Guarabira, Braz. E11 76
Guaraçaí, Braz. F3 79
Guaraci, Braz. F4 79
Guaraciaba, Braz. D7 79
Guaramirim, Braz. D14 80
Guaranda, Ec. H3 84
Guaraniaçu, Braz. C12 80
Guarani das Missões, Braz. E11 80
Guarani de Goiás, Braz. B5 79
Guarapari, Braz. F8 79
Guarapuava, Braz. C13 80
Guaraqueçaba, Braz. C14 80
Guararé, Pan. D2 84
Guaratinguetá, Braz. G6 79
Guaratuba, Braz. C14 80
Guarda, Port. E4 16
Guardafui, Cape see Caseyr, c., Som. F11 56
Guardavalle, Italy K11 18
Guardia Escolta, Arg. E7 80
Guardiagrele, Italy G9 18
Guardo, Spain C7 16
Guareña, Spain G5 16
Guarenas, Ven. B9 84
Guariba, stm., Braz. C11 82
Guarico, Ven. C8 84
Guárico, state, Ven. C9 84
Guárico, stm., Ven. C9 84
Guárico, Embalse del, res., Ven. C9 84
Guariquito, stm., Ven. D9 84
Guarizama, Hond. C8 92
Guarulhos, Braz. G5 79
Guasare, stm., Ven. B6 84
Guasave, Mex. E5 90
Guasdualito, Ven. D7 84
Guasipati, Ven. D12 84
Guastalla, Italy E5 18
Guastatoya, Guat. C4 92
Guatajiagua, El Sal. D6 92
Guatemala, Guat. C4 92
Guatemala, dept., Guat. C4 92
Guatemala, ctry., N.A. E6 88
Guateque, Col. E6 84
Guatimozín, Arg. G7 80
Guatopo, Parque Nacional, Ven. C9 84
Guatraché, Arg. I7 80
Guaviare, ter., Col. F6 84
Guaviare, stm., Col. F8 84
Guaxupé, Braz. F5 79
Guayabal, Cuba D6 94
Guayabal, Ven. C9 84
Guayabero, stm., Col. F6 84
Guayacán, Chile E3 80
Guayama, P.R. F11 94
Guayambre, stm., Hond. C8 92
Guayape, Hond. C8 92
Guayape, stm., Hond. C9 92
Guayapo, stm., Ven. E9 84
Guayaquil, Ec. I3 84
Guayaquil, Golfo de, b., S.A. I2 84
Guayaramerín, Bol. D9 82
Guayas, prov., Ec. H2 84
Guayas, stm., Col. G5 84
Guayas, stm., Ec. I3 84
Guayatayoc, Laguna de, I., Arg. B6 80
Guaycora, Mex. C5 90
Guaymas, Mex. D4 90
Guayquiraró, stm., Arg. F9 80
Guayuriba, stm., Col. F6 84
Guazacapán, Guat. C4 92
Guazapares, Mex. D5 90
Guazárachi, Mex. D6 90
Guba, Eth. L8 60
Gubacha, Russia F9 26
Gubbio, Italy F7 18
Guben, Ger. D14 10
Gubin, Pol. D14 10
Gubkin, Russia G5 26
Gucheng, China C7 34
Güdalür, India H4 46
Gudermes, Russia I7 26
Gudianzi, China D5 34
Gudiyāttam, India F5 46
Güdür, India E5 46
Guebwiller, Fr. E14 14
Güéjar, stm., Col. F6 84
Guelma, Alg. B14 62
Guelph, Ont., Can. D4 103
Guéméné-sur-Scorff, Fr. D3 14
Guené, Benin F11 64
Guérande, Fr. E4 14
Guercif, Mor. C9 62
Güere, stm., Ven. C10 84
Guéréda, Chad J2 60
Guéret, Fr. F8 14
Guernsey, Sask., Can. F3 105
Guernsey, Wy., U.S. D8 157
Guernsey, co., Oh., U.S. B4 142
Guernsey, dep., Eur. F7 4
Guerrero, Mex. C6 90
Guerrero, state, Mex. I9 90
Guerzim, Alg. F10 62
Guessou-Sud, Benin F11 64
Gueydan, La., U.S. D3 125
Gugang, China G2 34
Guge, mtn., Eth. N9 60
Guia, Braz. F13 82
Guía de Isora, Spain o24 17b
Guia Lopes da Laguna, Braz. I13 82
Guibes, Nmb. F3 66
Güicán, Col. D6 84
Guichen, Fr. E5 14
Guichón, Ur. G10 80
Guidan Roumji, Niger E13 64
Guide, China D7 30
Guide Rock, Ne., U.S. D7 134
Guidigri, Niger E14 64
Guidimouni, Niger E14 64
Guiding, China A9 40
Guifujie, China H9 34
Guiglo, C. Iv. H6 64
Güija, Lago de, I., N.A. C5 92
Guild, N.H., U.S. D2 136
Guildford, Eng., U.K. J13 8
Guilford, Ct., U.S. D5 114
Guilford, Me., U.S. C3 126
Guilford, Vt., U.S. F3 152
Guilford, co., N.C., U.S. A3 140
Guilin (Kweilin), China B11 40
Guillaumes, Fr. H13 14
Güimar, Spain o24 17b
Guimarães, Port. D3 16
Guin, Al., U.S. B2 108
Guinea (Guinée), ctry., Afr. F4 54
Guinea, Gulf of, b., Afr. H7 52
Guinea-Bissau (Guiné-Bissau), ctry., Afr. F3 54
Güines, Cuba C3 94
Guînes, Fr. B8 14
Guingamp, Fr. D3 14
Güinope, Hond. D8 92
Guiones, Punta, c., C.R. H9 92
Guiping, China C11 40
Guir, Hammada du, des., Afr. E9 62
Guir, Oued, val., Afr. E9 62
Güira de Melena, Cuba C3 94
Guiraí, stm., Braz. G2 79
Guiratinga, Braz. D2 79
Güiria, Ven. B11 84
Guiricema, Braz. F7 79
Güisisil, mtn., Nic. E8 92
Guist Creek, stm., Ky., U.S. B4 124
Guita Koulouba, Cen. Afr. Rep. O2 60
Guitou, China K2 34
Guîtres, Fr. G6 14
Guiuan, Phil. C8 38
Guixi, China G6 34
Guixian, China C10 40
Guiyang (Kweiyang), China A9 40
Güiza, stm., Col. G3 84
Guizhou (Kweichow), prov., China F8 30
Gujarāt, state, India I4 44
Gujrānwāla, Pak. D6 44
Gujrāt, Pak. D6 44
Gulbarga, India D4 46
Gulbene, Lat. D9 22
Guledagudda, India D3 46
Guleitou, China L6 34
Gulf, co., Fl., U.S. C1 116
Gulf Gate Estates, Fl., U.S. E4 116
Gulf Hammock, Fl., U.S. C4 116
Gulf Islands National Seashore, U.S. E5 131
Gulfport, Fl., U.S. E4 116
Gulf Port, Il., U.S. C2 120
Gulfport, Ms., U.S. E4 131
Gulf Shores, Al., U.S. E2 108
Gulgong, Austl. I8 70
Gulistān, Pak. E2 44
Gulistan, Uzb. I11 26
Gulkana, Ak., U.S. C10 109
Gull Island, i., N.C., U.S. B7 140
Gullivan Bay, b., Fl., U.S. G5 116
Gull Lake, Sask., Can. G1 105
Gull Lake, I., Alta., Can. C4 98
Gull Lake, I., Mn., U.S. D4 130
Güllük, Tur. L11 20
Gulnam, Sud. N5 60
Gülpınar, Tur. J10 20
Guluy, Erit. J9 60
Gumal (Gowmal), stm., Asia D3 44
Gumare, Bots. B6 66
Gumboro, De., U.S. G4 115
Gumiao, China C2 34
Gummersbach, Ger. D7 10
Gummi, Nig. E12 64
Gum Spring Mountain, mtn., Tn., U.S. D8 149
Gum Springs, Ar., U.S. C2 111
Gum Swamp Creek, stm., Ga., U.S. D3 117
Gümüşhane, Tur. A5 48

Name | Map Ref. | Page

Guna, India H7 44
Gundagai, Austl. J8 70
Gungu, Zaire C3 58
Gunisao, stm., Man., Can. C3 100
Gunisao Lake, l., Man., Can. C3 100
Gunnbjørn Fjeld, mtn., Grnld. C17 86
Gunnedah, Austl. H9 70
Gunnison, Co., U.S. C4 113
Gunnison, Ms., U.S. B3 131
Gunnison, Ut., U.S. D4 151
Gunnison, co., Co., U.S. C3 113
Gunnison, stm., Co., U.S. C2 113
Gunnison, Mount, mtn., Co., U.S. C3 113
Gunpowder Creek, stm., Ky., U.S. k13 124
Gunpowder Neck, c., Md., U.S. B5 127
Gunpowder River, b., Md., U.S. B5 127
Guntakal, India E4 46
Gunter Air Force Base, mil., Al., U.S. C3 108
Guntersville, Al., U.S. A3 108
Guntersville Dam, Al., U.S. A3 108
Guntersville Lake, res., Al., U.S. A3 108
Gunton, Man., Can. D3 100
Guntown, Ms., U.S. A5 131
Guntūr, India D6 46
Gunungsitoli, Indon. N4 40
Gunzenhausen, Ger. F10 10
Guolutan, China C4 34
Guozhuang, China H5 32
Gupei, China I5 32
Guraferda, Eth. N8 60
Gura Galbehei, Mol. C12 20
Gurara, stm., Nig. G13 64
Gurdāspur, India D6 44
Gurdon, Ar., U.S. D2 111
Güre, Tur. K13 20
Gurgueia, stm., Braz. E10 76
Guri, Embalse de, res., Ven. D11 84
Gurjevsk, Russia G3 22
Gurjevsk, Russia G15 26
Gurley, Al., U.S. A3 108
Gurley, Ne., U.S. C3 134
Gurnee, Il., U.S. h9 120
Gurnet Point, c., Ma., U.S. B6 128
Gurupá, Braz. D8 76
Gurupi, Braz. F9 76
Gurupi, stm., Braz. D9 76
Gusau, Nig. E13 64
Gus'-Chrustal'nyj, Russia F23 22
Gusev, Russia G5 22
Gusevskij, Russia F23 22
Gushanzi, China C8 32
Gushi, China C4 34
Gushikawa, Japan u2 37b
Gusino, Russia G14 22
Gusinoozersk, Russia G13 28
Guspini, Italy J3 18
Gustavus, Ak., U.S. D12 109
Gustine, Ca., U.S. D3 112
Güstrow, Ger. B12 10
Gus'-Železnyj, Russia F24 22
Gütersloh, Ger. D8 10
Guthrie, Ky., U.S. D2 124
Guthrie, Ok., U.S. B4 143
Guthrie, W.V., U.S. m12 155
Guthrie, co., Ia., U.S. C3 122
Guthrie Center, Ia., U.S. C3 122
Gutian, China I7 34
Gutierrez, Bol. H10 82
Gutiérrez Zamora, Mex. G11 90
Guttenberg, Ia., U.S. B6 122
Guttenberg, N.J., U.S. h8 137
Gutu, Zimb B10 66
Gu Vo, Az., U.S. E3 110
Guwāhāti, India G14 44
Guxian, China F9 32
Guxiansi, China C5 34
Guy, Ar., U.S. B3 111
Guyana, ctry., S.A. B7 76
Guyandotte, stm., W.V., U.S. C2 155
Guyandotte Mountain, mtn., W.V., U.S. n12 155
Guyi, China J7 34
Guymon, Ok., U.S. e9 143
Guyot, Mount, mtn., U.S. D10 149
Guyra, Austl. H9 70
Guys, Tn., U.S. B3 149
Guysborough, N.S., Can. D8 101
Guyton, Ga., U.S. D5 117
Guyuan, China D8 30
Guzar, Uzb. J11 26
Guzhu, China I5 34
Guzmán, Mex. B6 90
Guzmán, Laguna, l., Mex. B6 90
Gvardejsk, Russia G4 22
Gwa, Mya. F3 40
Gwadabawa, Nig. E12 64
Gwādar, Pak. I17 48
Gwai, Zimb B8 66
Gwāl Haidarzai, Pak. E3 44
Gwalior, India G8 44
Gwanda, Zimb. C9 66
Gwandu, Nig. E12 64
Gwardafuy, Gees, c., Som. F11 56
Gwātar Bay, b., Asia I16 48
Gwent, co., Wales, U.K. J11 8
Gweru, Zimb. B9 66
Gweta, Bots. C7 66
Gwinhurst, De., U.S. h8 115
Gwinn, Mi., U.S. B3 129
Gwinner, N.D., U.S. C8 141
Gwinnett, co., Ga., U.S. C2 117
Gwydyr Bay, b., Ak., U.S. A10 109
Gwynedd, co., Wales, U.K. H9 8
Gwynn, Va., U.S. C6 153
Gwynne, Alta., Can. C4 98
Gwynneville, In., U.S. E6 121
Gwynns Falls, stm., Md., U.S. g10 127
Gy, Fr. E12 14
Gyangzê, China F4 30
Gyaring Co, l., China E13 44
Gyaring Hu, l., China E6 30
Gydanskaja guba, b., Russia C13 26
Gydanskij poluostrov, pen., Russia C13 26
Gyirong, China F11 44
Gympie, Austl. F10 70
Gyobingauk, Mya. E3 40
Gyoma, Hung. I20 10
Gyöngyös, Hung. H19 10
Győr, Hung. H17 10
Győr-Moson-Sopron, co., Hung. H17 10
Gypsum, Co., U.S. B4 113
Gypsum, Ks., U.S. D6 123
Gypsum Point, c., N.W. Ter., Can. D10 96
Gypsumville, Man., Can. D2 100
Gyula, Hung. I21 10

H

Haag in Oberbayern, Ger. G12 10
Haakon, co., S.D., U.S. C4 148
Haalenberg, Nmb. F2 66
Haaltert, Bel. G5 12
Haapajärvi, Fin. J19 6
Haapamäki, Fin. J19 6
Haapsalu, Est. C6 22
Ha'Arava (Wādī al-Jayb), val., Asia H4 50
Ha'Arava (Wādī al-'Arabah), val., Asia G4 50
Haarlem, Neth. D6 12
Ḥabarūt, Yemen F8 47
Ḥabbān, Yemen G5 47
Ḥabbūsh, Leb. B4 50
Habermehl Peak, mtn., Ant. C3 73
Habersham, co., Ga., U.S. B3 117
Habiganj, Bngl. H14 44
Habomai-shotō see Malaja Kuril'skaja Gr'ada, is., Russia d21 36a
Hachijō-jima, i., Japan E14 30
Hachinohe, Japan G16 36
Hachiōji, Japan L14 36
Hacienda Miravalles, C.R. G9 92
Hacienda Murciélago, C.R. G9 92
Hackberry, La., U.S. E2 125
Hackberry Creek, stm., Ks., U.S. D3 123
Hackensack, N.J., U.S. B4 137
Hackensack, stm., N.J., U.S. h8 137
Hacker Valley, W.V., U.S. C4 155
Hackett, Ar., U.S. B1 111
Hackettstown, N.J., U.S. B3 137
Hackleburg, Al., U.S. A2 108
Hack Point, Md., U.S. B6 127
Hadalīya, Sud. I9 60
Hadar, Ne., U.S. B8 134
Hadd, Ra's al-, c., Oman C11 47
Haddam, Ct., U.S. D5 114
Haddam, Ks., U.S. C6 123
Haddington, Scot., U.K. F11 8
Haddix, Ky., U.S. C6 124
Haddock, Ga., U.S. C3 117
Haddonfield, N.J., U.S. D2 137
Haddon Heights, N.J., U.S. D2 137
Hadejia, Nig. E14 64
Hadejia, stm., Nig. E14 64
Ḥadera, Isr. D3 50
Ḥadera, stm., Asia D3 50
Hadley, Ma., U.S. B2 128
Hadley, N.Y., U.S. B7 139
Hadley Bay, b., N.W. Ter., Can. B11 96
Hadley Lake, l., Me., U.S. D5 126
Hadlock, Wa., U.S. A3 154
Hadlyme, Ct., U.S. D6 114
Ha Dong, Viet. B8 40
Ḥaḍramawt, reg., Yemen G6 47
Haeju, N. Kor. E13 32
Haenam, S. Kor. I14 32
Hafford, Sask., Can. E2 105
Haffouz, Tun. N4 18
Hafīrat al-'Ayda, Sau. Ar. H5 48
Hafnarfjörður, Ice. B3 6a
Haft Gel, Iran F10 48
Hafun, Ras, c., Som. F11 56
Hagan, Ga., U.S. D5 117
Hagarville, Ar., U.S. B2 111
Hagemeister Island, i., Ak., U.S. D7 109
Hagen, Ger. D7 10
Hagensborg, B.C., Can. C4 99
Hagere Hiywet, Eth. M9 60
Hagere Selam, Eth. N10 60
Hagerman, Id., U.S. G4 119
Hagerman, N.M., U.S. D5 138
Hagerstown, In., U.S. E7 121
Hagerstown, Md., U.S. A2 127
Hagetmau, Fr. I6 14
Haggin, Mount, mtn., Mt., U.S. D3 133
Ha Giang, Viet. C8 40
Hagondange, Fr. C13 14
Hague, Sask., Can. E2 105
Hague, N.D., U.S. C6 141
Hague, Cap de la, c., Fr. C5 14
Haguenau, Fr. D14 14
Hagues Peak, mtn., Co., U.S. A5 113
Ha! Ha!, Baie des, b., Que., Can. C2 102
Hahaīa, Com. k15 67a
Hahira, Ga., U.S. F3 117
Hahnville, La., U.S. E5 125
Haian Shanmo, mts., Tai. L10 34
Haicheng, China D10 32
Haīdra, Tun. N3 18
Hai Duong, Viet. D9 40
Haifa see Hefa, Isr. C4 50
Haifeng, China M4 34
Haig, Austl. F5 68
Haigler, Ne., U.S. D4 134
Haikang (Leizhou), China D11 40
Haikou, China D11 40
Haiku, Hi., U.S. C5 118
Hā'il, Sau. Ar. H6 48
Hailākāndi, India H15 44
Hailar, China B10 30
Hailar, stm., China B11 30
Hailey, Id., U.S. F4 119
Haileybury, Ont., Can. p20 103
Haileyville, Ok., U.S. C6 143
Hailong (Meihekou), China A13 32
Hailun, China B12 30
Haimen, China G10 34
Haimen, China L5 34
Hainan, prov., China H8 30
Hainan Dao, i., China E11 40
Hainaut, prov., Bel. G4 12
Hainaut, hist. reg., Eur. H4 12
Haines, Ak., U.S. D12 109
Haines, Or., U.S. C9 144
Haines City, Fl., U.S. D5 116
Haines Falls, N.Y., U.S. C6 139
Haines Junction, Yukon, Can. D5 96
Hainesport, N.J., U.S. D3 137
Hainfeld, Aus. G15 10
Hai Phong, Viet. D9 40
Hairy Hill, Alta., Can. C5 98
Haiti (Haïti), ctry., N.A. E8 94
Haitou, China I7 32
Haiyaopu, China A6 40
Haizhou, China A8 34
Hajdú-Bihar, co., Hung. H21 10
Hajdúböszörmény, Hung. H21 10
Hajdúnánás, Hung. H21 10
Hajeb el Ayoun, Tun. N4 18
Haji Langar, China C8 44
Hājīpur, India H11 44
Ḥajjah, Yemen G3 47
Hajnówka, Pol. C23 10
Hakalau, Hi., U.S. D6 118
Ḥakīm, Abyār al-, well, Libya B2 60
Hakkâri, Tur. C7 48
Hakodate, Japan f15 36a
Hakui, Japan K11 36
Ḥalab (Aleppo), Syria C4 48
Ḥalabjah, Iraq D8 48
Halachó, Mex. G14 90
Halā'ib, Egypt F9 60
Halaula, Hi., U.S. C6 118
Halawa, Cape, c., Hi., U.S. B5 118
Halawa Heights, Hi., U.S. g10 118
Halawotelake, China B14 44
Halberstadt, Ger. D11 10
Halbrite, Sask., Can. H4 105
Halbur, Ia., U.S. C3 122
Haldeman, Ky., U.S. B6 124
Haldimand, Ont., Can. E5 103
Haldwāni, India F8 44
Hale, Mi., U.S. D7 129
Hale, Mo., U.S. B4 132
Hale, co., Al., U.S. C2 108
Hale, co., Tx., U.S. B2 150
Haleakala Crater, crat., Hi., U.S. C5 118
Haleakala National Park, Hi., U.S. C6 118
Hale Center, Tx., U.S. B2 150
Haleiwa, Hi., U.S. B3 118
Hales Corners, Wi., U.S. n11 156
Halethorpe, Md., U.S. B4 127
Haleyville, Al., U.S. A2 108
Half Moon Bay, Ca., U.S. k8 112
Halfway, Md., U.S. A2 127
Half Way, Mo., U.S. D4 132
Halfway, Or., U.S. C9 144
Haliburton, Ont., Can. B6 103
Halibut Point, c., Ma., U.S. A6 128
Halifax, Austl. B7 70
Halifax, N.S., Can. E6 101
Halifax, Ma., U.S. C6 128
Halifax, N.C., U.S. A5 140
Halifax, Pa., U.S. F8 145
Halifax, Va., U.S. D4 153
Halifax, co., N.C., U.S. A5 140
Halifax, co., Va., U.S. D4 153
Halifax Bay, b., Austl. B7 70
Haliimaile, Hi., U.S. C5 118
Halkirk, Alta., Can. C4 98
Hall, Mt., U.S. D3 133
Hall, co., Ga., U.S. B3 117
Hall, co., Ne., U.S. D7 134
Hall, co., Tx., U.S. B2 150
Hallam, Ne., U.S. D9 134
Hallam Peak, mtn., B.C., Can. C8 99
Hallandale, Fl., U.S. G6 116
Hallands Län, co., Swe. M13 6
Halla-san, mtn., S. Kor. E12 30
Halle (Hal), Bel. G5 12
Halle, Ger. D11 10
Hallein, Aus. H13 10
Hallettsville, Tx., U.S. E4 150
Halley, Ar., U.S. D4 111
Halliday, N.D., U.S. B3 141
Hallie, Wi., U.S. D2 156
Hall in Tirol, Aus. H11 10
Hall Island, i., Ak., U.S. C5 109
Hall Meadow Brook, stm., Ct., U.S. B3 114
Hall Meadow Brook Reservoir, res., Ct., U.S. B3 114
Hall Mountain, mtn., Wa., U.S. A8 154
Hällnäs, Swe. I16 6
Hallock, Mn., U.S. B2 130
Hallowell, Ks., U.S. E9 123
Hallowell, Me., U.S. D3 126
Hall Peninsula, pen., N.W. Ter., Can. D19 96
Halls, Tn., U.S. B2 149
Hallsberg, Swe. L14 6
Hallsboro, N.C., U.S. C4 140
Halls Creek, Austl. C5 68
Halls Creek, stm., Ut., U.S. F5 151
Halls Crossroads, Tn., U.S. m14 149
Halls Harbour, N.S., Can. D5 101
Halls Stream, stm., N.H., U.S. f7 136
Hallstavik, Swe. K16 6
Hallstead, Pa., U.S. C10 145
Hallsville, Mo., U.S. B5 132
Hallsville, Tx., U.S. C5 150
Hall Top, mtn., Tn., U.S. D10 149
Halltown, Mo., U.S. D4 132
Hallwood, Va., U.S. C7 153
Halma, Bel. H7 12
Halmahera, i., Indon. E8 38
Halmahera, Laut (Halmahera Sea), Indon. F8 38
Halmstad, Swe. M13 6
Halsell, Al., U.S. C1 108
Halsey, Ne., U.S. C5 134
Halsey, Or., U.S. C3 144
Hälsingborg see Helsingborg, Swe. M13 6
Halstad, Mn., U.S. C2 130
Halstead, Ks., U.S. E6 123
Haltern, Ger. D7 10
Haltiatunturi, mtn., Eur. G17 6
Halton Hills, Ont., Can. D5 103
Hamad, Sud. J7 60
Hamada, Japan M7 36
Hamadān, Iran D10 48
Ḥamāh, Syria D4 48
Hamale, Ghana F8 64
Hamamatsu, Japan M12 36
Hamar, Nor. K12 6
Ḥamātah, Jabal, mtn., Egypt I3 48
Hamblen, co., Tn., U.S. C10 149
Hamburg, Ger. B9 10
Hamburg, Ar., U.S. D4 111
Hamburg, Ia., U.S. D2 122
Hamburg, N.J., U.S. A3 137
Hamburg, N.Y., U.S. C2 139
Hamburg, Pa., U.S. E10 145
Hamburg Mountains, mts., N.J., U.S. A3 137
Ḥamdānah, Sau. Ar. E2 47
Hamden, Ct., U.S. D4 114
Hamden, Oh., U.S. C3 142
Hämeen lääni, prov., Fin. K19 6
Hämeenlinna, Fin. K19 6
Hamel, Mn., U.S. m11 130
Hameln, Ger. C9 10
Hamer, S.C., U.S. C9 147
Hamersley Range, mts., Austl. D3 68
Hamersley Range National Park, Austl. D3 68
Hamersville, Oh., U.S. D2 142
Hamhŭng, N. Kor. D15 32
Hami, China C5 30
Hamill, S.D., U.S. D6 148
Hamilton, Austl. K5 70
Hamilton, Ber. B12 88
Hamilton, Ont., Can. D5 103
Hamilton, N.Z. B5 72
Hamilton, Scot., U.K. F9 8
Hamilton, Al., U.S. A2 108
Hamilton, Ga., U.S. D2 117
Hamilton, Il., U.S. C2 120
Hamilton, In., U.S. A8 121
Hamilton, Ks., U.S. E7 123
Hamilton, Ma., U.S. A6 128
Hamilton, Mi., U.S. F4 129
Hamilton, Ms., U.S. B5 131
Hamilton, Mo., U.S. B3 132
Hamilton, Mt., U.S. D2 133
Hamilton, N.Y., U.S. C5 139
Hamilton, N.C., U.S. B5 140
Hamilton, Oh., U.S. C1 142
Hamilton, Tx., U.S. D3 150
Hamilton, Va., U.S. A5 153
Hamilton, Wa., U.S. A4 154
Hamilton, co., Fl., U.S. B3 116
Hamilton, co., Il., U.S. E5 120
Hamilton, co., In., U.S. D5 121
Hamilton, co., Ia., U.S. B4 122
Hamilton, co., Ks., U.S. E2 123
Hamilton, co., Ne., U.S. D7 134
Hamilton, co., N.Y., U.S. B6 139
Hamilton, co., Oh., U.S. C1 142
Hamilton, co., Tn., U.S. D8 149
Hamilton, co., Tx., U.S. D3 150
Hamilton, stm., Austl. D4 70
Hamilton, Lake, res., Ar., U.S. C2 111
Hamilton, Mount, mtn., Ak., U.S. C8 109
Hamilton, Mount, mtn., Ca., U.S. k9 112
Hamilton, Mount, mtn., Nv., U.S. D6 135
Hamilton City, Ca., U.S. C2 112
Hamilton Dome, Wy., U.S. C4 157
Hamilton Hotel, Austl. D4 70
Hamilton Inlet, b., Newf., Can. A2 102
Hamilton Mountain, mtn., N.Y., U.S. B6 139
Hamilton Reservoir, res., Ma., U.S. B3 128
Hamilton Sound, strt., Newf., Can. D4 102
Hamilton Square, N.J., U.S. C3 137
Hamina, Fin. K20 6
Hamiota, Man., Can. D1 100
Ḥāmir, Wādī, val., Asia F7 48
Hamīrpur, India H9 44
Hamler, Oh., U.S. A1 142
Hamlet, In., U.S. B4 121
Hamlet, N.C., U.S. C3 140
Hamlet, Mount, mtn., Ak., U.S. B6 109
Hamlin, Pa., U.S. D11 145
Hamlin, Tx., U.S. C2 150
Hamlin, W.V., U.S. C2 155
Hamlin, co., S.D., U.S. C8 148
Hamlin Lake, l., Mi., U.S. D4 129
Hamm, Ger. D7 10
Hammamet, Alg N2 18
Hammamet, Tun. M5 18
Hammamet, Golfe de, b., Tun. M5 18
Hamman Lif, Tun. M5 18
Ḥammār, Hawr al-, l., Iraq F9 48
Hamme, Bel. F5 12
Hammerdal, Swe. J14 6
Hammerfest, Nor. F18 6
Hammett, Id., U.S. G3 119
Hammon, Ok., U.S. B2 143
Hammonasset, stm., Ct., U.S. D5 114
Hammonasset Point, c., Ct., U.S. E5 114
Hammond, Il., U.S. D5 120
Hammond, In., U.S. A2 121
Hammond, La., U.S. D5 125
Hammond, Or., U.S. A3 144
Hammond, Wi., U.S. D1 156
Hammond Bay, b., Mi., U.S. C6 129
Hammondsport, N.Y., U.S. C3 139
Hammonton, N.J., U.S. D3 137
Ham-Nord, Que., Can. D6 104
Hamoyet, Jabal, mtn., Afr. I10 60
Hampden, Newf., Can. D3 102
Hampden, Me., U.S. D4 126
Hampden, Ma., U.S. B3 128
Hampden, N.D., U.S. A7 141
Hampden, co., Ma., U.S. B2 128
Hampden Highlands, Me., U.S. D4 126
Hampshire, Il., U.S. A5 120
Hampshire, Tn., U.S. B4 149
Hampshire, co., Eng., U.K. J12 8
Hampshire, co., Ma., U.S. B2 128
Hampshire, co., W.V., U.S. B6 155
Hampstead, N.B., Can. D3 101
Hampstead, Md., U.S. A4 127
Hampstead, N.H., U.S. E4 136
Hampstead, N.C., U.S. C5 140
Hampton, N.B., Can. D4 101
Hampton, Ar., U.S. D3 111
Hampton, Ct., U.S. B7 114
Hampton, Ga., U.S. C2 117
Hampton, Ia., U.S. B4 122
Hampton, Mn., U.S. F5 130
Hampton, Ne., U.S. D8 134
Hampton, N.H., U.S. E5 136
Hampton, N.J., U.S. B3 137
Hampton, S.C., U.S. F5 147
Hampton, Tn., U.S. C11 149
Hampton, Va., U.S. C6 153
Hampton, co., S.C., U.S. F5 147
Hampton Bays, N.Y., U.S. n16 139
Hampton Beach, N.H., U.S. E5 136
Hampton Butte, mtn., Or., U.S. D6 144
Hampton Falls, N.H., U.S. E5 136
Hampton Roads, Va., U.S. k15 153
Hampton Roads Bridge-Tunnel, Va., U.S. k15 153
Hamra, As Saquia al, val., W. Sah. G4 62
Hams Fork, stm., Wy., U.S. E2 157
Hamtramck, Mi., U.S. p15 129
Hamyang, S. Kor. H15 32
Han, stm., China E9 30
Hana, Hi., U.S. C6 118
Hanahan, S.C., U.S. F7 147
Hanalei, Hi., U.S. A2 118
Hanalei Bay, b., Hi., U.S. A2 118
Hanamaki, Japan H16 36
Hanamaulu, Hi., U.S. B2 118
Hanapepe, Hi., U.S. B2 118
Hanau, Ger. E8 10
Hanbury, stm., N.W. Ter., Can. D11 96
Hâncești, Mol. C12 20
Hanceville, B.C., Can. D6 99
Hanceville, Al., U.S. A3 108
Hancheng, China D9 30
Hancock, Ia., U.S. C2 122
Hancock, Me., U.S. D4 126
Hancock, Md., U.S. A1 127
Hancock, Mi., U.S. A2 129
Hancock, Mn., U.S. E3 130
Hancock, N.H., U.S. E3 136
Hancock, N.Y., U.S. D5 139
Hancock, Vt., U.S. D3 152
Hancock, Wi., U.S. D4 156
Hancock, co., Ga., U.S. C3 117
Hancock, co., Il., U.S. C2 120
Hancock, co., In., U.S. E6 121
Hancock, co., Ia., U.S. A4 122
Hancock, co., Ky., U.S. C3 124
Hancock, co., Me., U.S. D4 126
Hancock, co., Ms., U.S. E4 131
Hancock, co., Oh., U.S. A2 142
Hancock, co., Tn., U.S. C10 149
Hancock, co., W.V., U.S. A4 155
Hancock Pond, l., Me., U.S. E2 126
Hancocks Bridge, N.J., U.S. D2 137
Hand, co., S.D., U.S. C6 148
Handa, Japan M11 36
Handa, Som. F11 56
Handan, China G2 32
Handley, W.V., U.S. m13 155
Handub, Sud. H9 60
HaNegev (Negev Desert), reg., Isr. G3 50
Hanford, Ca., U.S. D4 112
Han'gang, China I2 32
Han-gang, stm., Asia F14 32
Hangchow see Hangzhou, China E9 34
Hanggin Houqi, China C8 30
Hanggin Qi, China D8 30
Hangman Creek, stm., Wa., U.S. B8 154
Hangö (Hanko), Fin. L18 6
Hangu, China D5 32
Hangu, Pak. D4 44
Hangzhou (Hangchow), China E9 34
Hangzhou Wan (Hangchow Bay), b., China E10 34
Hani, Tur. B6 48
Ḥanīsh, is., Yemen H3 47
Ḥanita, Isr. B4 50
Hanjiang, China J8 34
Hankey, S. Afr. I7 66
Hankinson, N.D., U.S. C9 141
Hankö see Hangö, Fin. D12 4
Hankow see Wuhan, China E3 34
Hanksville, Ut., U.S. E5 151
Hanley, Sask., Can. F2 105
Hanna, Alta., Can. D5 98
Hanna, In., U.S. B4 121
Hanna, Wy., U.S. E6 157
Hanna City, Il., U.S. C4 120
Hannaford, N.D., U.S. B7 141
Hannahville Indian Reservation, Mi., U.S. C3 129
Hannibal, Mo., U.S. B6 132
Hannibal, Oh., U.S. C5 142
Hannover, Ger. C9 10
Ha Noi, Viet. D8 40
Hanover, Ont., Can. C3 103
Hanover see Hannover, Ger. C9 10
Hanover, Ct., U.S. C7 114
Hanover, Il., U.S. A3 120
Hanover, In., U.S. G7 121
Hanover, Ks., U.S. C7 123
Hanover, Me., U.S. D2 126
Hanover, Ma., U.S. B6 128
Hanover, Mi., U.S. F6 129
Hanover, Mn., U.S. m11 130
Hanover, N.H., U.S. C2 136
Hanover, N.M., U.S. E1 138
Hanover, Oh., U.S. B3 142
Hanover, Pa., U.S. G8 145
Hanover, Va., U.S. C5 153
Hanover, co., Va., U.S. C5 153
Hanover Center, Ma., U.S. h12 128
Hanover Park, Il., U.S. k8 120
Hansen, Id., U.S. G4 119
Hansford, co., Tx., U.S. A2 150
Hānsi, India F6 44
Hanska, Mn., U.S. F4 130
Hanson, Ky., U.S. C2 124
Hanson, Ma., U.S. B6 128
Hanson, co., S.D., U.S. D8 148
Hanston, Ks., U.S. D4 123
Hant's Harbour, Newf., Can. D5 102
Hantsport, N.S., Can. D5 101
Hanumangarh, India F6 44
Hanušovice, Czech Rep. E16 10
Hanwood, Austl. J7 70
Hanzhong, China E8 30
Hanzhuang, China I5 32
Haohekou, China G1 34
Hāora, India I13 44
Hapeville, Ga., U.S. C2 117
Happy, Tx., U.S. B2 150
Happy Jack, Az., U.S. C4 110
Happy Valley, N.M., U.S. E5 138
Happy Valley-Goose Bay, Newf., Can. B1 102
Hāpur, India F7 44
Haquira, Peru F5 82
Ḥarad, Sau. Ar. B6 47
Ḥarad, Jabal al-, mtn., Jord. I5 50
Harahan, La., U.S. k11 125
Haralson, co., Ga., U.S. C1 117
Harare (Salisbury), Zimb. A10 66
Harash, Bi'r al-, well, Libya E2 60
Harbeson, De., U.S. F4 115
Harbin, China B12 30
Harbinger, N.C., U.S. A7 140
Harbor, Or., U.S. E2 144
Harbor Beach, Mi., U.S. E8 129
Harborcreek, Pa., U.S. B2 145
Harbor Springs, Mi., U.S. C6 129
Harborton, Va., U.S. C7 153
Harbour Breton, Newf., Can. E4 102
Harbour Grace, Newf., Can. E5 102
Harbour Mille, Newf., Can. E4 102
Harbourville, N.S., Can. D5 101
Harcourt, N.B., Can. C4 101
Harcourt, Ia., U.S. B3 122
Harcuvar Mountains, mts., Az., U.S. D2 110
Harda, India I7 44
Hardangerfjorden, Nor. K10 6
Hardaway, Al., U.S. C4 108
Hardee, co., Fl., U.S. E5 116
Hardeeville, S.C., U.S. G5 147
Hardeman, co., Tn., U.S. B2 149
Hardeman, co., Tx., U.S. B3 150
Harderwijk, Neth. D8 12
Hardesty, Ok., U.S. e9 143
Hardin, Il., U.S. D3 120
Hardin, Ky., U.S. f9 124
Hardin, Mo., U.S. B4 132
Hardin, Mt., U.S. E9 133
Hardin, co., Il., U.S. F5 120
Hardin, co., Ia., U.S. B4 122
Hardin, co., Ky., U.S. C4 124
Hardin, co., Oh., U.S. B2 142
Hardin, co., Tn., U.S. B3 149
Hardin, co., Tx., U.S. D5 150
Harding, S. Afr. H9 66
Harding, co., N.M., U.S. B5 138
Harding, co., S.D., U.S. B2 148
Harding, Lake, res., U.S. C4 108
Hardinsburg, In., U.S. H5 121
Hardinsburg, Ky., U.S. C3 124
Hardisty, Alta., Can. C5 98
Hardoi, India G9 44
Hardshell, Ky., U.S. C6 124
Hardtner, Ks., U.S. E5 123
Hardwick, Ga., U.S. C3 117
Hardwick, Vt., U.S. B4 152
Hardwicke, N.B., Can. B5 101
Hardwood Ridge, mtn., Pa., U.S. D11 145
Hardy, Ar., U.S. A4 111
Hardy, Ne., U.S. D8 134
Hardy, co., W.V., U.S. B6 155
Hardy Lake, res., In., U.S. G6 121
Hare Bay, Newf., Can. D4 102
Hare Bay, b., Newf., Can. C4 102
Harer, Eth. G9 56
Hareto, Eth. M9 60
Harford, co., Md., U.S. A5 127
Hargeysa, Som. G9 56
Harghita, co., Rom. C9 20
Hargill, Tx., U.S. F3 150
Har Hu, l., China D6 30
Hari, stm., Indon. F3 38
Haría, Spain n27 17b
Haridwār, India F8 44
Harihar, India E3 46
Haringvliet, strt., Neth. E5 12
Harīrūd (Tedžen), stm., Asia C16 48
Harkers Island, N.C., U.S. C6 140
Harlan, In., U.S. B8 121
Harlan, Ia., U.S. C2 122
Harlan, Ky., U.S. D6 124
Harlan, co., Ky., U.S. D6 124
Harlan, co., Ne., U.S. D6 134
Harlan County Lake, res., Ne., U.S. E6 134
Harlem, Fl., U.S. F6 116
Harlem, Ga., U.S. C4 117
Harlem, Mt., U.S. B8 133
Harleyville, S.C., U.S. E7 147
Harlingen, Neth. B7 12
Harlingen, Tx., U.S. F4 150
Harlowton, Mt., U.S. D7 133
Harman, Va., U.S. e9 153
Harmanli, Bul. H9 20
Harmon, co., Ok., U.S. C2 143
Harmon Creek, stm., W.V., U.S. f8 155
Harmony, In., U.S. E3 121
Harmony, Me., U.S. D3 126
Harmony, Mn., U.S. G6 130
Harmony, Pa., U.S. E1 145
Harmony, R.I., U.S. B3 146
Harmony Grove, Ar., U.S. D3 111
Harned, Ky., U.S. C3 124
Harnett, co., N.C., U.S. B4 140
Harney, co., Or., U.S. D7 144
Harney, Lake, l., Fl., U.S. D5 116
Harney Lake, l., Or., U.S. D7 144
Harney Peak, mtn., S.D., U.S. D2 148
Härnösand, Swe. J15 6
Haro, Spain C9 16
Haro, Cabo, c., Mex. D4 90
Haro Strait, strt., Wa., U.S. A2 154
Harper, Lib. I6 64
Harper, Ks., U.S. E5 123
Harper, Wa., U.S. e10 154
Harper, co., Ks., U.S. E5 123
Harper, co., Ok., U.S. A2 143

Name — Map Ref. — Page

Herring Cove, N.S., Can. E6 101
Herring Run, stm., Md., U.S. g11 127
Herrington Lake, res., Ky., U.S. C5 124
Herschel, Sask., Can. F1 105
Herschel Island, i., Yukon, Can. C5 96
Herscher, Il., U.S. B5 120
Hersey, Mi., U.S. E5 129
Hershey, Ne., U.S. C5 134
Hershey, Pa., U.S. F8 145
Herstal, Bel. G8 12
Hertford, N.C., U.S. A6 140
Hertford, co., N.C., U.S. A5 140
Hertfordshire, co., Eng., U.K. J13 8
Hervey Bay, b., Austl. E10 70
Herzberg, Ger. D13 10
Herzberg [am Harz], Ger. D10 10
Herzliyya, Isr. D3 50
Hesdin, Fr. B9 14
Heshangqiao, China A2 34
Heshi, China J7 34
Heshuijian, China E5 34
Hesperia, Ca., U.S. E5 112
Hesperia, Mi., U.S. E4 129
Hesperus, Co., U.S. D2 113
Hesperus Mountain, mtn., Co., U.S. D2 113
Hessen, state, Ger. E9 10
Hessisch Lichtenau, Ger. D9 10
Hessmer, La., U.S. C3 125
Hesston, Ks., U.S. D6 123
Hetang, China I8 34
Hetou, China K2 34
Hettick, Il., U.S. D3 120
Hettinger, N.D., U.S. D3 141
Hettinger, co., N.D., U.S. C3 141
Hettstedt, Ger. D11 10
Hetupu, China E5 34
Heves, Hung. H20 10
Heves, co., Hung. H20 10
Ḥevron, Naḥal, val., Asia F3 50
Hewitt, Mn., U.S. D3 130
Hewitt, Tx., U.S. D4 150
Hewitt, Wi., U.S. D3 156
Hexi, China K6 34
Hexian, China G9 30
Heyang, China H6 32
Heyburn, Id., U.S. G5 119
Heywood, Austl. L4 70
Heyworth, Il., U.S. C5 120
Heze (Caozhou), China H3 32
Hezhen, China F9 34
Hialeah, Fl., U.S. G6 116
Hiattville, Ks., U.S. E9 123
Hiawassee, Ga., U.S. B3 117
Hiawatha, Ia., U.S. B6 122
Hiawatha, Ks., U.S. C8 123
Hibbing, Mn., U.S. C6 130
Hibbs, Point, c., Austl. N6 70
Hibernia Reef, rf., Austl. B4 68
Hickam Air Force Base, mil., Hi., U.S. g10 118
Hickman, De., U.S. E3 115
Hickman, Ky., U.S. f8 124
Hickman, Ne., U.S. D9 134
Hickman, co., Ky., U.S. f8 124
Hickman, co., Tn., U.S. B4 149
Hickman's Harbour, Newf., Can. D5 102
Hickory, Ky., U.S. f9 124
Hickory, Ms., U.S. C4 131
Hickory, N.C., U.S. B1 140
Hickory, co., Mo., U.S. D4 132
Hickory Flat, Ms., U.S. A4 131
Hickory Plains, Ar., U.S. C4 111
Hickory Ridge, Ar., U.S. B5 111
Hickory Valley, Tn., U.S. B2 149
Hicks, Point, c., Austl. K8 70
Hickson, Ont., Can. D4 103
Hicksville, N.Y., U.S. E7 139
Hicksville, Oh., U.S. A1 142
Hico, Tx., U.S. D3 150
Hico, W.V., U.S. C3 155
Hidalgo, Mex. E10 90
Hidalgo, Mex. E9 90
Hidalgo, Mex. D10 90
Hidalgo, Mex. F8 90
Hidalgo, Tx., U.S. F3 150
Hidalgo, state, Mex. G10 90
Hidalgo, co., N.M., U.S. F1 138
Hidalgo, co., Tx., U.S. F3 150
Hidalgo del Parral, Mex. D7 90
Hida-sammyaku, mts., Japan K12 36
Hiddenite, N.C., U.S. B1 140
Hidrolândia, Braz. D4 79
Hidrolina, Braz. C4 79
Hieflau, Aus. H14 10
Hieroglyphic Mountains, mts., Az., U.S. k8 110
Hierro (Ferro), i., Spain p22 17b
Higashine, Japan I15 36
Higashiōsaka, Japan M10 36
Higbee, Mo., U.S. B5 132
Higdon, Al., U.S. A4 108
Higganum, Ct., U.S. D5 114
Higgins Lake, Mi., U.S. D6 129
Higgins Lake, l., Mi., U.S. D6 129
Higgins Millpond, res., Md., U.S. C6 127
Higginson, Ar., U.S. B4 111
Higginsville, Mo., U.S. B4 132
High Bluff, Man., Can. D2 100
High Bridge, N.J., U.S. B3 137
High Falls Reservoir, res., Wi., U.S. C5 156
Highfield, Md., U.S. A3 127
Highgate, Ont., Can. E3 103
Highgate Falls, Vt., U.S. B2 152
High Hill, Mo., U.S. C6 132
High Island, Tx., U.S. E5 150
High Island, i., Mi., U.S. C5 129
High Knob, mtn., U.S. A4 153
High Knob, mtn., W.V., U.S. C5 155
Highland, Il., U.S. E4 120
Highland, In., U.S. A3 121
Highland, Ks., U.S. C8 123
Highland, Mi., U.S. o14 129
Highland, N.Y., U.S. D7 139
Highland, Wi., U.S. E3 156
Highland, prov., Scot., U.K. D8 8
Highland, co., Oh., U.S. C2 142
Highland, co., Va., U.S. B3 153
Highland Grove, Ont., Can. B6 103
Highland Home, Al., U.S. D3 108
Highland Lake, l., Me., U.S. g7 126
Highland Lakes, N.J., U.S. A4 137
Highland Park, Il., U.S. A6 120
Highland Park, Mi., U.S. p15 129
Highland Park, Tx., U.S. n10 150
Highland Peak, mtn., Ca., U.S. C4 112
Highland Point, c., Fl., U.S. G5 116
Highlands, N.J., U.S. C5 137
Highlands, N.C., U.S. f9 140
Highlands, Tx., U.S. r14 150
Highlands, co., Fl., U.S. E5 116
Highland Springs, Va., U.S. C5 153
High Level, Alta., Can. F7 98
Highmore, S.D., U.S. C6 148
High Point, N.C., U.S. B2 140
High Point, Wa., U.S. e12 154
High Prairie, Alta., Can. B2 98
High Ridge, Mo., U.S. g12 132
High River, Alta., Can. D4 98
High Rock, mtn., Md., U.S. k12 127
Highrock Lake, l., Man., Can. B1 100
High Rock Lake, res., N.C., U.S. B2 140
High Shoals, Ga., U.S. C3 117
High Shoals, N.C., U.S. B1 140
High Spire, Pa., U.S. F8 145
High Springs, Fl., U.S. C4 116
High Top, mtn., W.V., U.S. C5 155
Hightstown, N.J., U.S. C3 137
Highwood, Il., U.S. A6 120
Highwood, Mt., U.S. C6 133
Highwood Baldy, mtn., Mt., U.S. C6 133
Highwood Mountains, mts., Mt., U.S. C6 133
High Wycombe, Eng., U.K. J13 8
Higley, Az., U.S. D4 110
Higuera de Abuya, Mex. E6 90
Higuera de Zaragoza, Mex. E5 90
Higüero, Punta, c., P.R. E11 94
Higüey, Dom. Rep. E10 94
Higuito, stm., Hond. C6 92
Hiiumaa, i., Est. C5 22
Hiko, Nv., U.S. F6 135
Hikone, Japan L11 36
Hiko Range, mts., Nv., U.S. F6 135
Hilbert, Wi., U.S. D5 156
Hilda, Alta., Can. D5 98
Hilda, S.C., U.S. E5 147
Hildale, Ut., U.S. F3 151
Hildburghausen, Ger. E10 10
Hilden, N.S., Can. D6 101
Hildesheim, Ger. C9 10
Hildreth, Ne., U.S. D6 134
Hill, N.H., U.S. C3 136
Hill, co., Mt., U.S. B6 133
Hill, co., Tx., U.S. D4 150
Hillaby, Mount, mtn., Barb. H15 94
Hill Bank, Belize I15 90
Hill City, Ga., U.S. B2 117
Hill City, Ks., U.S. C4 123
Hill City, Mn., U.S. D5 130
Hill City, S.D., U.S. D2 148
Hillcrest, Il., U.S. B4 120
Hillcrest, Mi., U.S. n11 129
Hillcrest Heights, Md., U.S. C4 127
Hilli, Bngl. H13 44
Hilliard, Alta., Can. C4 98
Hilliard, Fl., U.S. B5 116
Hilliard, Oh., U.S. k10 142
Hillier, Ont., Can. D7 103
Hillsburg, In., U.S. D5 121
Hill Lake, l., Ar., U.S. h10 111
Hillman, Mi., U.S. C7 129
Hillrose, Co., U.S. A7 113
Hills, Ia., U.S. C6 122
Hills, Mn., U.S. G2 130
Hillsboro, Al., U.S. A2 108
Hillsboro, Ga., U.S. C3 117
Hillsboro, Il., U.S. D4 120
Hillsboro, In., U.S. D3 121
Hillsboro, Ks., U.S. D6 123
Hillsboro, Ms., U.S. C4 131
Hillsboro, Mo., U.S. C7 132
Hillsboro, N.H., U.S. D3 136
Hillsboro, N.M., U.S. E2 138
Hillsboro, N.D., U.S. B8 141
Hillsboro, Oh., U.S. C2 142
Hillsboro, Or., U.S. B4 144
Hillsboro, Tn., U.S. D8 149
Hillsboro, Tx., U.S. C4 150
Hillsboro, Wi., U.S. E3 156
Hillsboro Canal, Fl., U.S. F6 116
Hillsborough, N.B., Can. D5 101
Hillsborough, N.C., U.S. A3 140
Hillsborough, co., Fl., U.S. E4 116
Hillsborough, co., N.H., U.S. E3 136
Hillsborough, Cape, c., Austl. C8 70
Hillsborough Bay, b., P.E.I., Can. C6 101
Hillsborough Lower Village, N.H., U.S. D3 136
Hillsborough Upper Village, N.H., U.S. D3 136
Hillsburgh, Ont., Can. D4 103
Hills Creek Lake, res., Or., U.S. D4 144
Hillsdale, Ont., Can. C5 103
Hillsdale, Il., U.S. B3 120
Hillsdale, In., U.S. E3 121
Hillsdale, Ks., U.S. D9 123
Hillsdale, Mi., U.S. G6 129
Hillsdale, N.J., U.S. g8 137
Hillsdale, Wy., U.S. E8 157
Hillsdale, co., Mi., U.S. G6 129
Hillside, N.J., U.S. k8 137
Hillspring, Alta., Can. E4 98
Hillston, Austl. I6 70
Hillsville, Pa., U.S. D1 145
Hillsville, Va., U.S. D2 153
Hilltonia, Ga., U.S. D5 117
Hillview, Il., U.S. D3 120
Hilo, Hi., U.S. D6 118
Hilo Bay, b., Hi., U.S. D6 118
Hilton, N.Y., U.S. B3 139
Hilton Head Island, S.C., U.S. G6 147
Hilton Head Island, i., S.C., U.S. G6 147
Hilversum, Neth. D7 12
Hima, Ky., U.S. C6 124
Himāchal Pradesh, state, India E7 44
Himalayas, mts., Asia F11 44
Himeji, Japan M9 36
Himi, Japan K11 36
Ḥimṣ (Homs), Syria D4 48
Hinche, Haiti E8 94
Hinchinbrook Island, i., Austl. B7 70
Hinchinbrook Island, i., Ak., U.S. g18 109
Hinch Mountain, mtn., Tn., U.S. D9 149
Hinckley, Il., U.S. B5 120
Hinckley, Me., U.S. D3 126
Hinckley, Mn., U.S. D6 130
Hinckley, Oh., U.S. A4 142
Hinckley, Ut., U.S. D3 151
Hinckley Reservoir, res., N.Y., U.S. B5 139
Hindaun, India G7 44
Hindman, Ky., U.S. C7 124
Hindmarsh, Lake, l., Austl. K4 70
Hinds, co., Ms., U.S. C3 131
Hindsboro, Il., U.S. D5 120
Hinds Lake, l., Newf., Can. D3 102
Hindu Kush, mts., Asia B4 44
Hindupur, India F4 46
Hines, Or., U.S. D7 144
Hinesburg, Vt., U.S. C2 152
Hines Creek, Alta., Can. A1 98
Hineston, La., U.S. C3 125
Hinesville, Ga., U.S. E5 117
Hinganghāt, India B5 46
Hingham, Ma., U.S. B6 128
Hingham, Mt., U.S. B6 133
Hingham Bay, b., Ma., U.S. g12 128
Hingol, stm., Pak. H1 44
Hingoli, India C4 46
Hınıs, Tur. B6 48
Hinkle, Ms., U.S. A5 131
Hinkley, Ca., U.S. E5 112
Hinnøya, i., Nor. G14 6
Hinojosa del Duque, Spain G6 16
Hinsdale, Il., U.S. k9 120
Hinsdale, Ma., U.S. B1 128
Hinsdale, Mt., U.S. B9 133
Hinsdale, N.H., U.S. E2 136
Hinsdale, N.Y., U.S. C2 139
Hinsdale, co., Co., U.S. D3 113
Hinterrhein, stm., Switz. E11 13
Hinton, Alta., Can. C2 98
Hinton, Ia., U.S. B1 122
Hinton, Ok., U.S. B3 143
Hinton, W.V., U.S. D4 155
Hipólito, Mex. E9 90
Hipólito Yrigoyen, Arg. G5 80
Hirado, Japan N4 36
Hīrākud Reservoir, res., India B7 46
Hiram, Ga., U.S. C2 117
Hiram, Me., U.S. E2 126
Hiram, Oh., U.S. A4 142
Hirata, Japan L7 36
Hiratsuka, Japan L14 36
Hirhafok, Alg. I13 62
Hirjillah, Syria B6 50
Hirosaki, Japan G15 36
Hiroshima, Japan M7 36
Hirson, Fr. C11 14
Hisār, India F6 44
Hisbān, Jord. E5 50
Hiseville, Ky., U.S. C4 124
Ḥiṣn al-Qarn, Yemen G6 47
Hispaniola, i., N.A. E9 94
Hita, Japan N5 36
Hitachi, Japan K15 36
Hitchcock, Sask., Can. H4 105
Hitchcock, S.D., U.S. C7 148
Hitchcock, Tx., U.S. r14 150
Hitchcock, co., Ne., U.S. D4 134
Hitchcock Lake, Ct., U.S. C4 114
Hitchins, Ky., U.S. B7 124
Hitoyoshi, Japan O5 36
Hitra, i., Nor. J11 6
Hiva Oa, i., Fr. Poly. I26 158
Hiwannee, Ms., U.S. D5 131
Hiwassee, stm., Tn., U.S. D9 149
Hiwassee Lake, res., N.C., U.S. f8 140
Hixon, B.C., Can. C6 99
Hixton, Wi., U.S. D3 156
Hkakabo Razi, mtn., Mya. F6 30
Hkok (Kok), stm., Asia D5 40
Hlatikulu, Swaz. F10 66
Hlegu, Mya. F4 40
Hlinsko, Czech Rep. F15 10
Hlobane, S. Afr. F10 66
Hlohovec, Slvk. G17 10
Hluboká nad Vltavou, Czech Rep. F14 10
Hlučín, Czech Rep. F18 10
Hlyboka, Ukr. A9 20
Hmawbi, Mya. F4 40
Ho, Ghana H10 64
Hoa Binh, Viet. D8 40
Hoagland, In., U.S. C8 121
Hoback, stm., Wy., U.S. C2 157
Hobart, Austl. N7 70
Hobart, In., U.S. A3 121
Hobart, Ok., U.S. B2 143
Hobbema, Alta., Can. C4 98
Hobbs, In., U.S. D6 121
Hobbs, N.M., U.S. E6 138
Hobe Sound, Fl., U.S. E6 116
Hobgood, N.C., U.S. A5 140
Hobo, Col. F5 84
Hoboken, Bel. F5 12
Hoboken, Ga., U.S. E4 117
Hoboken, N.J., U.S. k8 137
Hobson, Mt., U.S. D7 133
Hobucken, N.C., U.S. B6 140
Hobyo, Som. G10 56
Hochalmspitze, mtn., Aus. H13 10
Ho Chi Minh City see Thanh Pho Ho Chi Minh, Viet. C4 38
Hochkönig, mtn., Aus. H13 10
Höchstadt an der Aisch, Ger. F10 10
Hockenheim, Ger. F8 10
Hockessin, De., U.S. A3 115
Hocking, co., Oh., U.S. C3 142
Hocking, stm., Oh., U.S. C3 142
Hockley, Tx., U.S. q14 150
Hockley, co., Tx., U.S. C1 150
Hodeida see Al-Hudaydah, Yemen G3 47
Hodgdon, Me., U.S. B5 126
Hodge, La., U.S. B3 125
Hodgeman, co., Ks., U.S. D4 123
Hodgen, Ok., U.S. C7 143
Hodgenville, Ky., U.S. C4 124
Hodges, Al., U.S. A2 108
Hodges Village Reservoir, res., Ma., U.S. B4 128
Hodgeville, Sask., Can. G2 105
Hodgson, Man., Can. D3 100
Hódmezővásárhely, Hung. I20 10
Hodna, Chott el, l., Alg. C13 62
Hodonín, Czech Rep. G17 10
Hoehne, Co., U.S. D6 113
Hoek van Holland, Neth. E5 12
Hoeryŏng, N. Kor. A17 32
Hoey, Sask., Can. E3 105
Hoeyang, N. Kor. E15 32
Hof, Ger. E11 10
Hof, Ice. B6 6a
Hoffman, Mn., U.S. E3 130
Hoffman, N.C., U.S. B3 140
Hoffman Estates, Il., U.S. h8 120
Hofheim, Ger. E8 10
Hofmeyr, S. Afr. H7 66
Höfn, Ice. B6 6a
Hofors, Swe. K15 6
Hōfu, Japan M6 36
Hofuf see Al-Hufūf, Sau. Ar. I10 48
Hogansville, Ga., U.S. C2 117
Hogback Mountain, mtn., Mt., U.S. F4 133
Hogback Mountain, mtn., Ne., U.S. C2 134
Hogback Mountain, mtn., S.C., U.S. A3 147
Hoggar see Ahaggar, mts., Alg. I13 62
Hog Island, i., Fl., U.S. C3 116
Hog Island, i., Mi., U.S. C5 129
Hog Island, i., N.C., U.S. B6 140
Hog Island, i., R.I., U.S. D5 146
Hog Island, i., Va., U.S. C7 153
Högsby, Swe. M15 6
Hogup Mountains, mts., Ut., U.S. B2 151
Hoh, stm., Wa., U.S. B1 154
Hohenau, Para. D11 80
Hohenau an der March, Aus. G16 10
Hohenthurn, Aus. I13 10
Hohenwald, Tn., U.S. B4 149
Hoher Dachstein, mtn., Aus. H13 10
Hohe Tauern, mts., Aus. H12 10
Hoh Head, c., Wa., U.S. B1 154
Hohhot, China C9 30
Hohoe, Ghana H10 64
Ho-Ho-Kus, N.J., U.S. h8 137
Hoh Xil Shan, mts., China C13 44
Hoi An, Viet. G10 40
Hoisington, Ks., U.S. D5 123
Hojāi, India G15 44
Hokah, Mn., U.S. G7 130
Hoke, co., N.C., U.S. B3 140
Hokes Bluff, Al., U.S. B4 108
Hokitika, N.Z. E3 72
Hokkaidō, i., Japan d17 36a
Holbrook, Austl. J7 70
Holbrook, Az., U.S. C5 110
Holbrook, Id., U.S. G6 119
Holbrook, Ma., U.S. B5 128
Holbrook, Ne., U.S. D5 134
Holcomb, Ks., U.S. E3 123
Holcomb, Ms., U.S. B4 131
Holcomb, Mo., U.S. E7 132
Holcombe, Wi., U.S. C2 156
Holden, Alta., Can. C4 98
Holden, La., U.S. g10 125
Holden, Ma., U.S. B4 128
Holden, Mo., U.S. C4 132
Holden, Ut., U.S. D3 151
Holden, W.V., U.S. D2 155
Holdenville, Ok., U.S. B5 143
Holder, Fl., U.S. D4 116
Holderness, N.H., U.S. C3 136
Holdfast, Sask., Can. G3 105
Holdingford, Mn., U.S. E4 130
Holdrege, Ne., U.S. D6 134
Hole in the Mountain Peak, mtn., Nv., U.S. C6 135
Holgate, Oh., U.S. A1 142
Holguín, Cuba D6 94
Holič, Slvk. G17 10
Hollabrunn, Aus. G16 10
Holladay, Ut., U.S. C4 151
Holland, Man., Can. E2 100
Holland, In., U.S. H3 121
Holland, Ia., U.S. B5 122
Holland, Ky., U.S. D3 124
Holland, Mi., U.S. F4 129
Holland, Mo., U.S. E8 132
Holland, Ne., U.S. D9 134
Holland, N.Y., U.S. C2 139
Holland, Oh., U.S. A2 142
Holland, Tx., U.S. D4 150
Holland see Netherlands, ctry., Eur. E9 4
Hollandale, Ms., U.S. B3 131
Holland Centre, Ont., Can. C4 103
Holland Island, i., Md., U.S. D5 127
Holland Point, c., Md., U.S. C4 127
Hollandsbird Island, i., S. Afr. E2 66
Hollandsch Diep, strt., Neth. E5 12
Holland Straits, strt., Md., U.S. D5 127
Holley, N.Y., U.S. B2 139
Holliday, Tx., U.S. C3 150
Hollidaysburg, Pa., U.S. F5 145
Hollins, Al., U.S. B3 108
Hollins, Va., U.S. C3 153
Hollis, N.H., U.S. E3 136
Hollis, Ok., U.S. C2 143
Hollis Center, Me., U.S. E2 126
Hollister, Ca., U.S. D3 112
Hollister, Id., U.S. G4 119
Hollister, Mo., U.S. E4 132
Hollister, N.C., U.S. A5 140
Holliston, Ma., U.S. B5 128
Holloman Air Force Base, mil., N.M., U.S. E3 138
Hollow Rock, Tn., U.S. A3 149
Hollowtop Mountain, mtn., Mt., U.S. E4 133
Hollsopple, Pa., U.S. F4 145
Holly, Co., U.S. C8 113
Holly, Mi., U.S. F7 129
Holly Bluff, Ms., U.S. C3 131
Holly Grove, Ar., U.S. C4 111
Holly Hill, Fl., U.S. C5 116
Holly Hill, S.C., U.S. E7 147
Holly Pond, Al., U.S. A3 108
Holly Ridge, N.C., U.S. C5 140
Holly Shelter Swamp, sw., N.C., U.S. C5 140
Holly Springs, Ga., U.S. B2 117
Holly Springs, Ms., U.S. A4 131
Holly Springs, N.C., U.S. B4 140
Hollywood, Al., U.S. A4 108
Hollywood, Az., U.S. E6 110
Hollywood (part of Los Angeles), Ca., U.S. m12 112
Hollywood, Fl., U.S. F6 116
Hollywood, Ga., U.S. B3 117
Hollywood, Md., U.S. D4 127
Hollywood, S.C., U.S. k11 147
Hollywood Indian Reservation, Fl., U.S. r3 116
Hollywood Park, Tx., U.S. h7 150
Holman, N.W. Ter., Can. B9 96
Holman, N.M., U.S. A4 138
Holmen, Wi., U.S. E2 156
Holmes, co., Fl., U.S. u16 116
Holmes, co., Ms., U.S. B3 131
Holmes, co., Oh., U.S. B4 142
Holmes, Mount, mtn., Wy., U.S. B2 157
Holmestrand, Nor. L12 6
Holmesville, Ne., U.S. D9 134
Holmia, Guy. E13 84
Holod, Rom. C6 20
Holoit, Punta, c., Mex. G15 90
Ḥolon, Isr. D3 50
Holoog, Nmb. F3 66
Holovanivs'k, Ukr. A14 20
Holstebro, Den. M11 6
Holstein, Ont., Can. C4 103
Holstein, Ia., U.S. B2 122
Holstein, Ne., U.S. D7 134
Holston, stm., Tn., U.S. C11 149
Holston, Middle Fork, stm., Va., U.S. f10 153
Holston High Knob, mtn., Tn., U.S. C11 149
Holt, Al., U.S. B2 108
Holt, Fl., U.S. u15 116
Holt, Mi., U.S. F6 129
Holt, Mo., U.S. B3 132
Holt, co., Mo., U.S. A2 132
Holt, co., Ne., U.S. B7 134
Holt Creek, stm., Ne., U.S. B6 134
Holt Knob, mtn., Tn., U.S. g10 149
Holt Lake, res., Al., U.S. B2 108
Holton, In., U.S. F7 121
Holton, Ks., U.S. C8 123
Holton, Mi., U.S. E4 129
Holtville, Al., U.S. C3 108
Holtville, Ca., U.S. F6 112
Holualoa, Hi., U.S. D6 118
Holy Cross, Ak., U.S. C8 109
Holy Cross, Ia., U.S. B7 122
Holy Cross, Mountain of the, mtn., Co., U.S. B4 113
Holyoke, Co., U.S. A8 113
Holyoke, Ma., U.S. B2 128
Holyoke Range, hills, Ma., U.S. B2 128
Holyrood, Ks., U.S. D5 123
Holy Trinity, Al., U.S. C4 108
Holzkirchen, Ger. H11 10
Holzminden, Ger. D9 10
Homalin, Mya. B3 40
Homathko, stm., B.C., Can. D5 99
Homberg, Ger. D9 10
Hombori Tondo, mtn., Mali D9 64
Hombre Muerto, Salar del, pl., Arg. C5 80
Homburg see Bad Homburg vor der Höhe, Ger. E8 10
Homburg, Ger. F7 10
Home, Ks., U.S. C7 123
Home Corner, In., U.S. C6 121
Homecroft, In., U.S. m10 121
Homedale, Id., U.S. F2 119
Home Gardens, Ca., U.S. n14 112
Home Hill, Austl. B7 70
Homelake, Co., U.S. D4 113
Homeland, Fl., U.S. E5 116
Homeland, Ga., U.S. F4 117
Home Place, In., U.S. E5 121
Homer, Ak., U.S. D9 109
Homer, Ga., U.S. B3 117
Homer, Il., U.S. C6 120
Homer, In., U.S. E6 121
Homer, La., U.S. B2 125
Homer, Mi., U.S. F6 129
Homer, Ne., U.S. B9 134
Homer, N.Y., U.S. C4 139
Homer City, Pa., U.S. E3 145
Homerville, Ga., U.S. E4 117
Homer Youngs Peak, mtn., Mt., U.S. E3 133
Homestead, Fl., U.S. G6 116
Homestead, Ia., U.S. C6 122
Homestead, Pa., U.S. k14 145
Homestead Air Force Base, mil., Fl., U.S. G6 116
Homestead National Monument of America, Ne., U.S. D9 134
Homewood, Al., U.S. g7 108
Homewood, Ca., U.S. C3 112
Homewood, Il., U.S. B6 120
Homewood, Oh., U.S. C1 142
Hominy, Ok., U.S. A5 143
Hominy Creek, stm., Ok., U.S. A5 143
Homme Dam, N.D., U.S. A8 141
Homochitto, stm., Ms., U.S. D2 131
Homosassa, Fl., U.S. D4 116
Homs see Al-Khums, Libya B3 56
Homs see Ḥimṣ, Syria D4 48
Honaker, Va., U.S. e10 153
Honan see Henan, prov., China E9 30
Honaunau, Hi., U.S. D6 118
Honaz, Tur. L13 20
Honda, Col. E5 84
Honda, Bahía, b., Col. A7 84
Hondeklipbaai, S. Afr. H3 66
Hondo, N.M., U.S. D4 138
Hondo, Tx., U.S. E3 150
Hondo, stm., N.A. H15 90
Hondo, Río, stm., N.M., U.S. D4 138
Hondsrug, hills, Neth. C10 12
Honduras, ctry., N.A. B8 92
Honduras, Cabo de, c., Hond. A8 92
Honduras, Gulf of, b., N.A. E7 88
Honduras, Port, b., Belize A6 92
Honea Path, S.C., U.S. C3 147
Hønefoss, Nor. K12 6
Honeoye Falls, N.Y., U.S. C3 139
Honesdale, Pa., U.S. C11 145
Honey Brook, Pa., U.S. F10 145
Honey Creek, Wi., U.S. n11 156
Honey Grove, Tx., U.S. C5 150
Honey Lake, l., Ca., U.S. B3 112
Honeymoon Bay, B.C., Can. E5 99
Honeypot Glen, Ct., U.S. C4 114
Honeyville, Ut., U.S. B3 151
Honfleur, Fr. C7 14
Hong see Red, stm., Asia C8 40
Hon Gai, Viet. D9 40
Hong'an, China D3 34
Honga River, b., Md., U.S. D5 127
Hongch'ŏn, S. Kor. F15 32
Hongcun, China H5 34
Honghu, China F2 34
Hongjiang, China F8 30
Hong Kong, dep., Asia G9 30
Honglai, China J7 34
Hongliuyuan, China C6 30
Honglu, China J8 34
Hongmendu, China A7 40
Hong Ngu, Viet. I8 40
Hongshi, China B7 32
Hongshui, stm., China C10 40
Hongshuyangzi, China C4 32
Hongsŏng, S. Kor. G14 32
Hongtong, China D9 30
Hongwŏn, N. Kor. C15 32
Hongxingqiao, China E8 34
Hongyang, China L5 34
Hongze Hu, l., China B7 34
Honiara, Sol.Is. I19 158
Honobia, Ok., U.S. C7 143
Honokaa, Hi., U.S. C6 118
Honokahua, Hi., U.S. B5 118
Honokohau, Hi., U.S. D6 118
Honolulu, Hi., U.S. B4 118
Honolulu, co., Hi., U.S. B3 118
Honolulu International Airport, Hi., U.S. g10 118
Honomu, Hi., U.S. D6 118
Honouliuli, Hi., U.S. g9 118
Hon Quan, Viet. I9 40
Honshū, i., Japan K13 36
Honuapo Bay, b., Hi., U.S. D6 118
Hood, co., Tx., U.S. C4 150
Hood, Mount, mtn., Or., U.S. B5 144
Hood Canal, b., Wa., U.S. B2 154
Hoodoo Peak, mtn., Wa., U.S. A5 154
Hood Point, c., Austl. F3 68
Hood River, Or., U.S. B5 144
Hood River, co., Or., U.S. B5 144
Hoodsport, Wa., U.S. B2 154
Hoods Range, mts., Austl. G6 70
Hooker, Ok., U.S. e9 143
Hooker, co., Ne., U.S. C4 134
Hookerton, N.C., U.S. B5 140
Hookina, Austl. H3 70
Hook Island, i., Austl. C8 70
Hooks, Tx., U.S. C5 150
Hooksett, N.H., U.S. D4 136
Hoolehua, Hi., U.S. B4 118
Hoonah, Ak., U.S. D12 109
Hoopa Valley Indian Reservation, Ca., U.S. B2 112
Hooper, Co., U.S. D5 113
Hooper, Ne., U.S. C9 134
Hooper, Ut., U.S. B3 151
Hooper Bay, Ak., U.S. C6 109
Hooper Creek, stm., Ne., U.S. h12 134
Hooper Islands, is., Md., U.S. D5 127
Hooper Strait, strt., Md., U.S. D5 127
Hoopes Reservoir, res., De., U.S. A3 115
Hoopeston, Il., U.S. C6 120
Hoople, N.D., U.S. A8 141
Hoosac Range, mts., U.S. A1 128
Hoosic, stm., U.S. C7 139
Hoosick Falls, N.Y., U.S. C7 139
Hoosuc Range, mts., U.S. D1 126
Hoover, Al., U.S. B3 108
Hoover Dam, U.S. G7 135
Hoover Reservoir, res., Oh., U.S. B3 142
Hooverson Heights, W.V., U.S. f8 155
Hooversville, Pa., U.S. F4 145
Hopatcong, N.J., U.S. B3 137
Hopatcong, Lake, l., N.J., U.S. A3 137
Hope, B.C., Can. E7 99
Hope, Ak., U.S. C10 109
Hope, Ar., U.S. D2 111
Hope, In., U.S. F6 121
Hope, Ks., U.S. D6 123
Hope, Mn., U.S. G5 130
Hope, N.M., U.S. E5 138
Hope, N.D., U.S. B8 141
Hope, R.I., U.S. D3 146
Hope, Point, c., Ak., U.S. B6 109
Hopedale, Newf., Can. g9 102
Hopedale, Il., U.S. C4 120
Hopedale, La., U.S. E6 125
Hopedale, Ma., U.S. B4 128
Hopedale, Oh., U.S. B5 142
Hopefield, S. Afr. I4 66
Hope Hull, Al., U.S. C3 108
Hope Island, i., R.I., U.S. E5 146
Hopelchén, Mex. H15 90
Hope Mills, N.C., U.S. C4 140
Hopes Advance, Cap, c., Que., Can. f13 104
Hopetoun, Austl. F4 68
Hopetoun, Austl. J5 70
Hopetown, S. Afr. G7 66
Hope Valley, R.I., U.S. E2 146
Hopewell, N.S., Can. D7 101
Hopewell, N.J., U.S. C3 137
Hopewell, Oh., U.S. C3 142
Hopewell, Va., U.S. C5 153
Hopewell Cape, N.B., Can. D5 101
Hopewell Junction, N.Y., U.S. D7 139

Name — Map Ref. — Page

Hyères, Fr. I13 14
Hyères, Îles d', is., Fr. B18 16
Hyesan, N. Kor. B16 32
Hygiene, Co., U.S. A5 113
Hyland, stm., Can. D7 96
Hylo, Alta., Can. B4 98
Hymaya, stm., Mex. E6 90
Hymera, In., U.S. F3 121
Hyndman, Pa., U.S. G4 145
Hyndman Peak, mtn., Id., U.S. F4 119
Hyŏpch'ŏn, S. Kor. H16 32
Hyrra Banda, Cen. Afr. Rep. O2 60
Hyrum, Ut., U.S. B4 151
Hysham, Mt., U.S. D9 133
Hythe, Alta., Can. B1 98

I

Iacanga, Braz. F4 79
Iaciara, Braz. C5 79
Iaco (Yaco), stm., S.A. C7 82
Iaçu, Braz. B8 79
Iaeger, W.V., U.S. D3 155
Ialomița, co., Rom. E11 20
Ialomița, stm., Rom. E11 20
Iamonia, Lake, l., Fl., U.S. B2 116
Ianakafy, Madag. s21 67b
Iantha, Mo., U.S. D3 132
Iapó, stm., Braz. C13 80
Iapu, Braz. E7 79
Iargara, Mol. C12 20
Iași, Rom. B11 20
Iași, co., Rom. B11 20
Iatt, Lake, res., La., U.S. C3 125
Iauaretê, Braz. G8 84
Ibadan, Nig. H11 64
Ibagué, Col. E5 84
Ibaiti, Braz. G3 79
Ibans, Laguna de, b., Hond. B10 92
Ibapah Peak, mtn., Ut., U.S. D2 151
Ibarra, Ec. G3 84
Ibarreta, Arg. C9 80
Ibb, Yemen G4 47
Ibbenbüren, Ger. C7 10
Iberia, Mo., U.S. C5 132
Iberia, co., La., U.S. E4 125
Ibérica, Península, pen., Eur. E6 52
Ibérico, Sistema, mts., Spain D9 16
Iberville, Que., Can. D4 104
Iberville, La., U.S. D4 125
Iberville, co., La., U.S. D4 125
Iberville, Mont d' (Mount Caubvick), mtn., Can. g14 104
Ibeto, Nig. F12 64
Ibiá, Braz. E5 79
Ibicaraí, Braz. C9 79
Ibicuí, Braz. C9 79
Ibicuí, stm., Braz. E10 80
Ibicuy, Arg. G9 80
Ibiquera, Braz. B8 79
Ibiraci, Braz. F5 79
Ibiraçu, Braz. E8 79
Ibirama, Braz. D14 80
Ibirapuã, Braz. D8 79
Ibirapuitã, stm., Braz. F11 80
Ibirataia, Braz. C9 79
Ibirubá, Braz. E12 80
Ibitiara, Braz. B7 79
Ibitinga, Braz. F4 79
Ibo, Moz. D8 58
Ibotirama, Braz. B7 79
'Ibrī, Oman C10 47
Ibshawāy, Egypt C6 60
Ibusuki, Japan P5 36
Ica, Peru F4 82
Ica, dept., Peru F4 82
Ica, stm., Peru F4 82
Içá (Putumayo), stm., S.A. I8 84
Icabarú, stm., Ven. E11 84
Icamaquã, stm., Braz. E11 80
Içana, Braz. G9 84
Içana (Isana), stm., S.A. G9 84
Icaño, Arg. E7 80
Icaño, Arg. E6 80
Ice Harbor Dam, Wa., U.S. C7 154
İçel, Tur. C3 48
Iceland (Ísland), ctry., Eur. B4 4
Icém, Braz. F4 79
Ichaikaronji, India D3 46
Ichikawa, Japan L14 36
Ichilo, stm., Bol. G9 82
Ichinomiya, Japan L11 36
Ichinoseki, Japan I16 36
Ichkeul, Lac, l., Tun. L4 18
Ichoa, stm., Bol. F9 82
Ichoca, Bol. G8 82
Ich'on, N. Kor. E14 32
Ich'ŏn, S. Kor. F15 32
Icicle Creek, stm., Wa., U.S. B5 154
Ičinskaja Sopka, vulkan, vol., Russia F23 28
Icó, Braz. E11 76
Iconha, Braz. F8 79
Icy Cape, c., Ak., U.S. A7 109
Icy Strait, strt., Ak., U.S. k22 109
Ida, La., U.S. A2 125
Ida, Mi., U.S. G7 129
Ida, co., Ia., U.S. B2 122
Ida, Lake, l., Mn., U.S. D3 130
Idabel, Ok., U.S. D7 143
Ida Grove, Ia., U.S. B2 122
Idah, Nig. H13 64
Idaho, co., Id., U.S. D3 119
Idaho, state, U.S. E3 119
Idaho City, Id., U.S. F3 119
Idaho Falls, Id., U.S. F6 119
Idaho Springs, Co., U.S. B5 113
Idalia, Co., U.S. B8 113
Idalou, Tx., U.S. C2 150
Idamay, W.V., U.S. k10 155
Idana, Ks., U.S. C6 123
Idanha, Or., U.S. C4 144
Idanre, Nig. H12 64
Idāppādi, India G4 46
Idar-Oberstein, Ger. F7 10
Idaville, In., U.S. C4 121
Ideal, Ga., U.S. D2 117
Idelès, Alg. I13 62
Ider, Al., U.S. A4 108
Idfū, Egypt E7 60
Ídhi Óros, mtn., Grc. N8 20
Ídhra (Hydra), i., Grc. L7 20
Idi, Indon. L4 40
Idiofa, Zaire C3 58
Idlewild, Tn., U.S. A3 149
Idleyld Park, Or., U.S. D3 144
Idlib, Syria D4 48
Idre, Swe. K13 6
Idrica, Russia E11 22
Idrija, Slvn. C9 18
Idutywa, S. Afr. I9 66
Iecava, Lat. E7 22
Iepê, Braz. G3 79
Ieper (Ypres), Bel. G2 12
Ierisós, Grc. I7 20
Ife, Nig. H12 64
Iferouâne, Niger B14 64
Ifni, hist. reg., Mor. F5 62
Ifôghas, Adrar des, mts., Afr. E7 54
Ifon-Oshogbo, Nig. H12 64
Igal, Hung. I17 10
Iganna, Nig. H11 64
Igaporã, Braz. B7 79
Igara Paraná, stm., Col. H6 84
Igarka, Russia D9 28
Igbasa-Odo, Nig. H11 64
Iğdır, Tur. B8 48
Igharghar, Oued, val., Afr. J14 62
Igizyar, China A7 44
Iglesia, Arg. F4 80
Iglesias, Italy J3 18
Igli, Alg. E9 62
Igloolik, N.W. Ter., Can. C16 96
Ignacio, Co., U.S. D3 113
Ignacio Zaragoza, Mex. C6 90
Ignalina, Lith. F9 22
Ignatei, Mol. B12 20
İğneada, Tur. H11 20
Iguaçu, stm., S.A. C12 80
Iguaçu, Cataratas do (Iguassu Falls), wtfl, S.A. C11 80
Iguaí, Braz. C8 79
Iguala, Mex. H10 90
Igualada, Spain D13 16
Iguana, stm., Ven. C10 84
Iguape, Braz. C15 80
Iguassu Falls see Iguaçu, Cataratas do, wtfl, S.A. C11 80
Iguatemi, Braz. G1 79
Iguatemi, stm., Braz. G1 79
Iguatu, Braz. E11 76
Iguazú, Parque Nacional, S.A. C11 80
Iguéla, Gabon B1 58
Iguîdi, 'Erg, dunes, Afr. C5 54
Igžej, Russia G12 28
Iheya-shima, i., Japan t2 37b
Ihiala, Nig. I13 64
Ihosy, Madag. s22 67b
Ihtiman, Bul. G7 20
Iida, Japan L12 36
Iisaku, Est. B10 22
Ii-shima, i., Japan F12 30
Iiyama, Japan K13 36
Iizuka, Japan N5 36
Ijâfene, des., Afr. D5 54
Ijaji, Eth. M9 60
Ijebu-Igbo, Nig. H12 64
IJmuiden, Neth. D6 12
IJssel, stm., Neth. C8 12
IJsselmeer (Zuiderzee), Neth. C7 12
IJsselstein, Neth. D7 12
Ijuí, Braz. E12 80
Ijuí, stm., Braz. E11 80
Ikalamavony, Madag. r22 67b
Ikang, Nig. I14 64
Ikaría, i., Grc. L10 20
Ikeja, Nig. H11 64
Ikela, Zaire B4 58
Ikirun, Nig. H12 64
Ikot Ekpene, Nig. I13 64
Ikša, Russia E20 22
Ila, Ga., U.S. B3 117
Ilabaya, Peru G6 82
Ilagan, Phil. m19 39b
Ilaka, Madag. q23 67b
Īlām, Iran E9 48
Ilām, Nepal G12 44
Ilan, Tai. K10 34
Ilanskij, Russia F17 26
Ilanz, Switz. E11 13
Ilaro, Nig. H11 64
Iława, Pol. B19 10
Ilbenge, Russia E16 28
Ilchester, Md., U.S. B4 127
Ilderton, Ont., Can. D3 103
Île-à-la-Crosse, Sask., Can. m7 105
Île-à-la-Crosse, Lac, l., Sask., Can. B2 105
Ilebo, Zaire B4 58
Île-de-France, hist. reg., Fr. C9 14
Ilek, stm., Asia G8 26
Île-Perrot, Que., Can. q19 104
Ilesha, Nig. H12 64
Ilesha Ibarida, Nig. G11 64
Ilford, Man., Can. A4 100
Ilfracombe, Austl. D6 70
Ilhabela, Braz. G6 79
Ilha Grande, Baía da, b., Braz. G6 79
Ilha Solteira, Represa de, res., Braz. F3 79
Ilhéus, Braz. C9 79
Ili, stm., Asia H12 26
Iliamna Lake, l., Ak., U.S. D8 109
Iliamna Volcano, vol., Ak., U.S. C9 109
Ilicínia, Braz. F6 79
Iliff, Co., U.S. A7 113
Iligan, Phil. D7 38
Ilimsk, Russia F12 28
Ilinza, mtn., Ec. H3 84
Ilion, N.Y., U.S. B5 139
Ilio Point, c., Hi., U.S. B4 118
Ilizi, Alg. G15 62
Iljinskij, Russia K23 6
Iljinskij, Russia H20 28
Iljinskoje, Russia D21 22
Iljinskoje, Russia E20 22
Iljinskoje-Chovanskoje, Russia E22 22
Ilkal, India E4 46
Il'kino, Russia F24 22
Illampu, Nevado, mtn., Bol. F7 82
Illapel, Chile F3 80
Ille-et-Vilaine, dept., Fr. D5 14
Illéla, Niger D12 64
Iller, stm., Ger. H10 10
Illescas, Mex. F8 90
Illescas, Spain E8 16
Illiers, Fr. D8 14
Illimani, Nevado, mtn., Bol. G8 82
Illimo, Peru B2 82
Illinois, state, U.S. C4 120
Illinois, stm., U.S. A7 143
Illinois, stm., Il., U.S. B5 120
Illinois, stm., Or., U.S. E3 144
Illinois City, Il., U.S. B3 120
Illinois Peak, mtn., Id., U.S. B3 119
Illiopolis, Il., U.S. D4 120
Illmo, Mo., U.S. D8 132
Il'men', ozero, l., Russia C14 22
Ilo, Peru G6 82
Ilobasco, El Sal. D6 92
Iloilo, Phil. C7 38
Ilopango, Lago de, l., El Sal. D5 92
Ilora, Nig. H11 64
Ilorin, Nig. G12 64
Ilūkste, Lat. F9 22
Ilwaco, Wa., U.S. C1 154
Ilwaki, Indon. G8 38
Imabari, Japan M8 36
Imabu, stm., Braz. H14 84
Imandra, ozero, l., Russia H23 6
Imari, Japan N4 36
Imaruí, Braz. E14 80
Imaruí, Lagoa do, b., Braz. E14 80
Imatra, Fin. K21 6
Imbabura, prov., Ec. G3 84
Imbituba, Braz. E14 80
Imbituva, Braz. C13 80
Imbler, Or., U.S. B9 144
Imboden, Ar., U.S. A4 111
Imeni Babuškina, Russia B26 22
Imeni C'urupy, Russia F21 22
Imeni Vorovskogo, Russia F24 22
Imeni Žel'abova, Russia C19 22
Imerimandroso, Madag. p23 67b
Imi, Eth. G9 56
Imías, Cuba D7 94
Imilac, Chile C4 80
Imi-n'Tanout, Mor. E6 62
İmişli, Azer. B10 48
Imjin-gang, stm., Asia F14 32
Imlay, Nv., U.S. C3 135
Imlay City, Mi., U.S. E7 129
Immingham Dock, Eng., U.K. H13 8
Immokalee, Fl., U.S. F5 116
Imnaha, stm., Or., U.S. B10 144
Imola, Italy E6 18
Imotski, Cro. F12 18
Imperatriz, Braz. E9 76
Imperia, Italy F3 18
Imperial, Sask., Can. F3 105
Imperial, Peru E3 82
Imperial, Ca., U.S. F6 112
Imperial, Mo., U.S. C7 132
Imperial, Ne., U.S. D4 134
Imperial, Pa., U.S. k13 145
Imperial, Tx., U.S. D1 150
Imperial, co., Ca., U.S. F6 112
Imperial, stm., Chile J2 80
Imperial Beach, Ca., U.S. o15 112
Imperial Dam, U.S. E1 110
Imperial Mills, Alta., Can. B5 98
Imperial Reservoir, res., U.S. E1 110
Imperial Valley, val., Ca., U.S. F6 112
Impfondo, Congo A3 58
Imphāl, India H15 44
Impilachti, Russia K22 6
Imsil, S. Kor. H15 32
Imuris, Mex. B4 90
Ina, Japan L12 36
Ina, Il., U.S. E5 120
Inambari, stm., Peru E7 82
In Amguel, Alg. I13 62
In Amnas, Alg. F15 62
Iñapari, Peru D7 82
In'aptuk, gora, mtn., Russia F14 28
Inari, Fin. G20 6
Inarijärvi, l., Fin. G20 6
Inauini, stm., Braz. C8 82
Inavale, Ne., U.S. D7 134
Inawashiro-ko, l., Japan J15 36
In Belbel, Alg. G11 62
Inca, Spain F14 16
Inca de Oro, Chile D4 80
Incaguasi, Chile E3 80
İncesu, Tur. B3 48
Inchelium, Wa., U.S. A7 154
Inch'ŏn, S. Kor. F14 32
Incline Village, Nv., U.S. D2 135
Incomáti (Komati), stm., Afr. E11 66
Indaiá, stm., Braz. E6 79
Inda Silase, Eth. J10 60
Indaw, Mya. C3 40
Indé, Mex. E7 90
Independence, Ca., U.S. D4 112
Independence, In., U.S. D3 121
Independence, Ia., U.S. B6 122
Independence, Ks., U.S. E8 123
Independence, Ky., U.S. B5 124
Independence, La., U.S. D5 125
Independence, Ms., U.S. A4 131
Independence, Mo., U.S. B3 132
Independence, Or., U.S. C3 144
Independence, Va., U.S. D1 153
Independence, Wi., U.S. D2 156
Independence, co., Ar., U.S. B4 111
Independence, stm., N.Y., U.S. B5 139
Independence Mountains, mts., Nv., U.S. C5 135
Independence National Historical Park, Pa., U.S. p21 145
Independence Rock, mtn., Wy., U.S. D5 157
Independencia, Bol. G8 82
Independencia, Isla, i., Peru F3 82
India (Bhārat), ctry., Asia E10 42
Indiahoma, Ok., U.S. C3 143
Indian, stm., Ont., Can. B7 103
Indian, stm., De., U.S. F4 115
Indian, stm., Mi., U.S. B4 129
Indian, stm., N.Y., U.S. A5 139
Indiana, Pa., U.S. E3 145
Indiana, co., Pa., U.S. E3 145
Indiana, state, U.S. E5 121
Indiana Dunes National Lakeshore, In., U.S. A3 121
Indianapolis, In., U.S. E5 121
Indian Bay, b., Fl., U.S. D4 116
Indian Brook, N.S., Can. C9 101
Indian Cedar Swamp, sw., R.I., U.S. F2 146
Indian Church, Belize I15 90
Indian Creek, stm., In., U.S. H5 121
Indian Creek, stm., Md., U.S. C4 127
Indian Creek, stm., Oh., U.S. C1 142
Indian Creek, stm., S.D., U.S. B2 148
Indian Creek, stm., Tn., U.S. B3 149
Indian Creek, stm., W.V., U.S. D4 155
Indian Creek, stm., W.V., U.S. k9 155
Indian Grave Mountain, hill, Ga., U.S. C2 117
Indian Head, Sask., Can. G4 105
Indian Head, Md., U.S. C3 127
Indian Island, i., N.C., U.S. B6 140
Indian Lake, l., Mi., U.S. C4 129
Indian Lake, l., N.Y., U.S. B6 139
Indian Lake, l., Oh., U.S. B2 142
Indian Lake, l., R.I., U.S. F4 146
Indian Mound, Tn., U.S. A4 149
Indian Mound Beach, Ma., U.S. *C6 128
Indian Mountain, mtn., Ct., U.S. B2 114
Indian Neck, Ct., U.S. D4 114
Indian Ocean J11 158
Indianola, Il., U.S. D6 120
Indianola, Ia., U.S. C4 122
Indianola, Ms., U.S. B3 131
Indianola, Ne., U.S. D5 134
Indianópolis, Braz. E5 79
Indian Peak, mtn., Ut., U.S. E2 151
Indian Peak, mtn., Wy., U.S. B3 157
Indian Pond, l., Me., U.S. D3 126
Indian Pond, l., Me., U.S. C3 126
Indian Pond, l., Me., U.S. B3 126
Indian Prairie Canal, Fl., U.S. E5 116
Indian River, Ont., Can. C6 103
Indian River, Mi., U.S. C6 129
Indian River, co., Fl., U.S. E6 116
Indian River, b., Fl., U.S. D6 116
Indian River Bay, b., De., U.S. F5 115
Indian Rock, mtn., Wa., U.S. D5 154
Indian Rocks Beach, Fl., U.S. p10 116
Indian Springs, Ga., U.S. C3 117
Indian Springs, Nv., U.S. G6 135
Indian Stream, stm., N.H., U.S. f7 136
Indiantown, Fl., U.S. E6 116
Indian Trail, N.C., U.S. B2 140
Indian Village, Ks., U.S. E8 123
Indian Village, La., U.S. D3 125
Indiaporã, Braz. E3 79
Indibir, Eth. M9 60
Indigirka, stm., Russia D21 28
Indio, Ca., U.S. F5 112
Indio, stm., Nic. F10 92
Indio, stm., Pan. H14 92
Indira Gandhi Canal, India F5 44
Indispensable Reefs, rf., Sol.Is. B12 68
Indochina, reg., Asia H11 24
Indonesia, ctry., Asia G7 38
Indore, India I6 44
Indragiri, stm., Indon. O7 40
Indrāvati, stm., India C6 46
Indre, dept., Fr. F8 14
Indre-et-Loire, dept., Fr. E7 14
Indrio, Fl., U.S. E6 116
Indura, Bela. H6 22
Indus, stm., Asia H2 44
Industry, Il., U.S. C3 120
Indwe, S. Afr. H8 66
İnece, Tur. H11 20
In Ecker, Alg. H13 62
İnegöl, Tur. I13 20
Inez, Ky., U.S. C7 124
Inez, Tx., U.S. E4 150
Inferior, Laguna, b., Mex. I12 90
Infiernillo, Presa del, res., Mex. H9 90
Ingal, Niger C13 64
Ingalls, In., U.S. E6 121
Ingalls, Ks., U.S. E3 123
Ingalls Park, Il., U.S. B5 120
Ingelheim, Ger. F8 10
Ingelmunster, Bel. G3 12
Ingende, Zaire B3 58
Ingeniero Luiggi, Arg. H6 80
Ingeniero Luis A. Huergo, Arg. J5 80
Ingeniero White, Arg. J7 80
Ingenio La Esperanza, Arg. C6 80
Ingenio Santa Ana, Arg. D6 80
Ingersoll, Ont., Can. D4 103
Ingham, Austl. B7 70
Ingham, co., Mi., U.S. F6 129
Ingleside, Tx., U.S. F4 150
Inglewood, Austl. G9 70
Inglewood, Ca., U.S. n12 112
Inglewood, Ne., U.S. C9 134
Inglis, Man., Can. D1 100
Ingoda, stm., Russia G14 28
Ingoldsby, Ont., Can. C6 103
Ingolstadt, Ger. G11 10
Ingomar, Ms., U.S. A4 131
Ingonish, N.S., Can. C9 101
Ingonish Beach, N.S., Can. C9 101
Ingraham, Lake, l., Fl., U.S. G5 116
Ingrāj Bāzār, India H13 44
Ingram, Pa., U.S. k13 145
Ingram, Tx., U.S. D3 150
In Guezzam, Alg. B12 64
Ingwiller, Fr. D14 14
Inhaca, Ilha da, i., Moz. F11 66
Inhafenga, Moz. C11 66
Inhambane, Moz. D12 66
Inhambupe, Braz. A9 79
Inhaminga, Moz. B12 66
Inhanduí, stm., Braz. F1 79
Inhapim, Braz. E7 79
Inharrime, Moz. E12 66
Inhaúma, Braz. E6 79
Inhumas, Braz. D4 79
Inimutaba, Braz. E6 79
Inírida, stm., Col. F8 84
Inisa, Nig. H12 64
Inishmore, i., Ire. H4 8
Injibara, Eth. L9 60
Injune, Austl. E8 70
Inkerman, N.B., Can. B5 101
Inkom, Id., U.S. G6 119
Inkster, Mi., U.S. p15 129
Inkster, N.D., U.S. A8 141
Inland Sea see Seto-naikai, Japan M7 36
Inle Lake, l., Mya. D4 40
Inman, Ga., U.S. C2 117
Inman, Ks., U.S. D6 123
Inman, Ne., U.S. B7 134
Inman, S.C., U.S. A3 147
Inn (En), stm., Eur. D20 14
Innamincka, Austl. F4 70
Inner Channel, strt., Belize I15 90
Inner Hebrides, is., Scot., U.K. E7 8
Inner Mongolia see Nei Monggol Zizhiqu, prov., China C10 30
Innertkirchen, Switz. E9 13
Innisfail, Austl. A7 70
Innisfail, Alta., Can. C4 98
Innisfree, Alta., Can. C5 98
Innsbruck, Aus. H11 10
Innviertel, reg., Aus. G13 10
Inocência, Braz. E3 79
Inola, Ok., U.S. A6 143
Inongo, Zaire B3 58
Inowrocław, Pol. C18 10
In Rhar, Alg. G11 62
In Salah, Alg. G12 62
Inscription House Ruin, hist., Az., U.S. A5 110
Ińsko, Pol. B15 10
Institute, W.V., U.S. m12 155
Inta, Russia D10 26
Intendente Alvear, Arg. H7 80
İntepe, Tur. I10 20
Intercession City, Fl., U.S. D5 116
Interlachen, Fl., U.S. C5 116
Interlaken, Switz. E8 13
Interlândia, Braz. D4 79
International Falls, Mn., U.S. B5 130
Intervale, N.H., U.S. B4 136
Inthanon, Doi, mtn., Thai. E5 40
Intibucá, Hond. C6 92
Intibucá, dept., Hond. C6 92
Intipucá, El Sal. D6 92
Intiyaco, Arg. E8 80
Intracoastal Waterway, U.S. E4 125
Intuto, Peru I5 84
Inukjuak, Que., Can. g11 104
Inuvik, N.W. Ter., Can. C6 96
Inuya, stm., Peru D5 82
Invercargill, N.Z. G2 72
Inverell, Austl. G9 70
Invergordon, Scot., U.K. D9 8
Inver Grove Heights, Mn., U.S. n12 130
Invermay, Sask., Can. F4 105
Invermere, B.C., Can. D9 99
Inverness, Que., Can. C6 104
Inverness, Scot., U.K. D9 8
Inverness, Ca., U.S. C2 112
Inverness, Fl., U.S. D4 116
Inverness, Ms., U.S. B3 131
Inverness, Mt., U.S. B6 133
Investigator Group, is., Austl. F6 68
Investigator Strait, strt., Austl. J2 70
Invisible Mountain, mtn., Id., U.S. F5 119
Inwood, Man., Can. D3 100
Inwood, Ont., Can. E3 103
Inwood, In., U.S. B5 121
Inwood, Ia., U.S. A1 122
Inwood, N.Y., U.S. k13 139
Inwood, W.V., U.S. B6 155
Inyangani, mtn., Zimb. B11 66
Inyan Kara Creek, stm., Wy., U.S. B8 157
Inyan Kara Mountain, mtn., Wy., U.S. B8 157
Inyantue, Zimb. B8 66
Inyati, Zimb. B9 66
Inyo, co., Ca., U.S. D5 112
Inyo, Mount, mtn., Ca., U.S. D5 112
Inyo Mountains, mts., Ca., U.S. D4 112
Inywa, Mya. C4 40
Inza, Russia G7 26
Inzana Lake, l., B.C., Can. B5 99
Inžavino, Russia I25 22
Ioánnina, Grc. J4 20
Iō-jima (Iwo Jima), i., Japan F18 158
Iola, Ks., U.S. E8 123
Iola, Wi., U.S. D4 156
Iolotan', Turk. J10 26
Iona, N.S., Can. D9 101
Iona, Id., U.S. F7 119
Iona, Mn., U.S. G3 130
Ione, Ca., U.S. C3 112
Ione, Or., U.S. B7 144
Ione, Wa., U.S. A8 154
Ionia, Ia., U.S. A5 122
Ionia, Mi., U.S. F5 129
Ionia, co., Mi., U.S. F5 129
Ionian Islands see Iónioi Nísoi, is., Grc. K4 20
Ionian Sea, Eur. H11 4
Iónioi Nísoi, prov., Grc. K4 20
Iónioi Nísoi, is., Grc. K4 20
Íos, i., Grc. M9 20
Iosco, co., Mi., U.S. D7 129
Iosegun, stm., Alta., Can. B2 98
Iota, La., U.S. D3 125
Iowa, La., U.S. D2 125
Iowa, co., Ia., U.S. C5 122
Iowa, co., Wi., U.S. E3 156
Iowa, state, U.S. C4 122
Iowa, stm., Ia., U.S. C6 122
Iowa, West Branch, stm., Ia., U.S. B4 122
Iowa City, Ia., U.S. C6 122
Iowa Falls, Ia., U.S. B4 122
Iowa Indian Reservation, U.S. C8 123
Iowa Lake, l., U.S. A3 122
Iowa Park, Tx., U.S. C3 150
Ipameri, Braz. D4 79
Ipatinga, Braz. E7 79
Ipava, Il., U.S. C3 120
Ípeiros, hist. reg., Grc. J4 20
Ipel' (Ipoly), stm., Eur. G19 10
Iphigenia Bay, b., Ak., U.S. n22 109
Ipiales, Col. G4 84
Ipiaú, Braz. C9 79
Ipirá, Braz. B9 79
Ipiranga, Braz. C13 80
Ípiros, prov., Grc. J4 20
Ipita, Bol. H10 82
Ipixuna, stm., Braz. B5 82
Ipixuna, stm., Braz. B10 82
Ipixuna, stm., Braz. B10 82
Ipoh, Malay. L6 40
Ipoly (Ipel'), stm., Eur. G18 10
Iporã, Braz. G2 79
Iporá, Braz. D3 79
Ipoti-Ekiti, Nig. H12 64
Ipswich, Austl. F10 70
Ipswich, Eng., U.K. I15 8
Ipswich, Ma., U.S. A6 128
Ipswich, S.D., U.S. B6 148
Ipswich, stm., Ma., U.S. A5 128
Ipu, Braz. D10 76
Ipupiara, Braz. A7 79
Iqaluit, N.W. Ter., Can. D19 96
Iquique, Chile G7 74
Iquique, Chile I6 82
Iquitos, Peru I6 84
Iraan, Tx., U.S. D2 150
Iracajá, Cachoeira do, wtfl, Braz. D9 82
Iraí, Braz. D12 80
Iráklia, i., Grc. M9 20
Iráklion, Grc. N9 20
Iran (Īrān), ctry., Asia C5 42
Iran, Pegunungan, mts., Asia E5 38
Īrānshahr, Iran H16 48
Irapa, Ven. B11 84
Irapuato, Mex. G9 90
Iraq (Al-'Irāq), ctry., Asia C3 42
Irará, Braz. B9 79
Irasburg, Vt., U.S. B4 152
Irati, Braz. C13 80
Irazú, Volcán, vol., C.R. H11 92
Irbeni väin (Irbes jūras šaurums), strt., Eur. D5 22
Irbes jūras šaurums (Irbeni väin), strt., Eur. D5 22
Irbid, Jord. C5 50
Irbīl, Iraq C8 48
Irbit, Russia F10 26
Iredell, co., N.C., U.S. B2 140
Ireland, In., U.S. H3 121
Ireland (Éire), ctry., Eur. E6 4
Irene, S. Afr. E9 66
Irene, S.D., U.S. D8 148
Ireng (Maú), stm., S.A. E13 84
Ireton, Ia., U.S. B1 122
Irgiz, Kaz. H10 26
Iri, S. Kor. H14 32
Iriba, Chad J2 60
Irîgui, reg., Afr. C7 64
Iringa, Tan. C7 58
Irion, co., Tx., U.S. D2 150
Iriona, Hond. B9 92
Iriri, stm., Braz. D8 76
Irish, Mount, mtn., Nv., U.S. F6 135
Irish Sea, Eur. H8 8
Irkutsk, Russia G12 28
Irma, Alta., Can. C5 98
Irmo, S.C., U.S. C5 147
Iron, co., Mi., U.S. B2 129
Iron, co., Mo., U.S. D7 132
Iron, co., Ut., U.S. F2 151
Iron, co., Wi., U.S. B3 156
Iron Belt, Wi., U.S. B3 156
Iron City, Ga., U.S. E2 117
Iron City, Tn., U.S. B4 149
Irondale, Al., U.S. f7 108
Irondale, Mo., U.S. D7 132
Irondequoit, N.Y., U.S. B3 139
Iron Gate, Va., U.S. C3 153
Iron Gate, val., Eur. E6 20
Iron Gate Reservoir, res., Eur. E6 20
Iron Gate Reservoir, res., Ca., U.S. B2 112
Ironia, N.J., U.S. B3 137
Iron Knob, Austl. I2 70
Iron Mountain, Mi., U.S. C2 129
Iron Mountain, Mo., U.S. D7 132
Iron Mountain, mtn., Az., U.S. D4 110
Iron Mountains, mts., U.S. D1 153
Iron Range, Austl. B8 68
Iron Ridge, Wi., U.S. E5 156
Iron River, Mi., U.S. B2 129
Iron River, Wi., U.S. B2 156
Ironton, Mn., U.S. D5 130
Ironton, Mo., U.S. D7 132
Ironton, Oh., U.S. D3 142
Ironwood, Mi., U.S. n11 129
Iroquois, Ont., Can. C9 103
Iroquois, S.D., U.S. C8 148
Iroquois, co., Il., U.S. C6 120
Iroquois, stm., U.S. C6 120
Iroquois, Lake, l., Vt., U.S. B2 152
Iroquois Falls, Ont., Can. o19 103
Irrawaddy see Ayeyarwady, stm., Mya. F3 40
Irricana, Alta., Can. D4 98
Irrigon, Or., U.S. B7 144
Irshava, Ukr. A7 20
Irtyš (Ertix), stm., Asia E11 26
Irtyš (Ertix), stm., Asia A3 30
Irtyšsk, Kaz. G13 26
Irumu, Zaire A5 58
Irún, Spain B10 16
Irupana, Bol. G8 82
Irurzun, Spain C10 16
Irú Tepuy, mtn., Ven. E12 84
Irvine, Alta., Can. E5 98
Irvine, Scot., U.K. F9 8
Irvine, Ca., U.S. n13 112
Irvine, Ky., U.S. C6 124
Irving, Il., U.S. D4 120
Irving, Tx., U.S. n10 150
Irvington, Al., U.S. E1 108
Irvington, Il., U.S. E4 120
Irvington, Ky., U.S. C3 124
Irvington, Ne., U.S. g12 134
Irvington, N.J., U.S. k8 137
Irvington, N.Y., U.S. g13 139
Irvington, Va., U.S. C6 153
Irvona, Pa., U.S. E4 145

Name — Map Ref. — Page

Irwin, Id., U.S. F7 119
Irwin, Ia., U.S. C2 122
Irwin, Pa., U.S. F2 145
Irwin, co., Ga., U.S. E3 117
Irwinton, Ga., U.S. D3 117
Irwinville, Ga., U.S. E3 117
Isaac, stm., Austl. D8 70
Isaac Lake, l., B.C., Can. C7 99
Isabel, Ks., U.S. E5 123
Isabel, S.D., U.S. B4 148
Isabel, Mount, mtn., Wy., U.S. D2 157
Isabela, Phil. D7 38
Isabela, Cabo, c., Dom. Rep. E9 94
Isabela, Isla, i., Ec. j13 84a
Isabela, Isla, i., Mex. G7 90
Isabelia, Cordillera, mts., Nic. D9 92
Isabella, Ga., U.S. E3 117
Isabella, Mo., U.S. E5 132
Isabella, Tn., U.S. D9 149
Isabella, co., Mi., U.S. E6 129
Isabella Indian Reservation, Mi., U.S. E6 129
Isabella Lake, l., Mn., U.S. C7 130
Isaccea, Rom. D12 20
Ísafjörður, Ice. A2 6a
Isahaya, Japan O5 36
Īsa Khel, Pak. D4 44
Işalniţa, Rom. E7 20
Isana (Içana), stm., S.A. G8 84
Isanti, Mn., U.S. E5 130
Isanti, co., Mn., U.S. E5 130
Isar, stm., Eur. G11 10
Isara, Nig. H11 64
Ischia, Italy I8 18
Ischia, Isola d', i., Italy I8 18
Iscuandé, stm., Col. F4 84
Ise (Uji-yamada), Japan M11 36
Iselin, N.J., U.S. B4 137
Iseo, Lago d', l., Italy D5 18
Isère, dept., Fr. G12 14
Isère, stm., Fr. G12 14
Iserlohn, Ger. D7 10
Isernia, Italy H9 18
Isesaki, Japan K14 36
Iset', stm., Russia F11 26
Iseyin, Nig. H11 64
Isherton, Guy. F13 84
Ishinomaki, Japan I16 36
Ishioka, Japan K15 36
Ishpeming, Mi., U.S. B3 129
Isigny, Fr. C5 14
Isil'kul', Russia G12 26
Išim, Russia F11 26
Išim, stm., Asia F12 26
Išimbaj, Russia G9 26
Isinglass, stm., N.H., U.S. D4 136
Isiolo, Kenya A7 58
Isipingo, S. Afr. G10 66
Isiro, Zaire H6 56
Isisford, Austl. E6 70
Iskăr, stm., Bul. F8 20
Iskăr, Jazovir, res., Bul. G7 20
İskele, N. Cyp. D2 48
İskenderun, Tur. C4 48
İskenderun Körfezi, b., Tur. H15 4
Iskitim, Russia G8 28
Isla, Mex. H12 90
Isla, Salar de la, pl., Chile C4 80
Isla Cristina, Spain H4 16
Isla de Maipo, Chile G3 80
Islāmābād, Pak. D5 44
Islāmkot, Pak. H4 44
Islamorada, Fl., U.S. H6 116
Islāmpur, India D3 46
Isla Mujeres, Mex. G16 90
Island, Ky., U.S. C2 124
Island, co., Wa., U.S. A3 154
Island Beach, N.J., U.S. D4 137
Island City, Or., U.S. B8 144
Island Falls, Me., U.S. B4 126
Island Heights, N.J., U.S. D4 137
Island Lagoon, l., Austl. H2 70
Island Lake, l., Man., Can. C4 100
Island Lake, stm., Man., Can. B4 100
Island Park, Id., U.S. E7 119
Island Park, R.I., U.S. E6 146
Island Park Reservoir, res., Id., U.S. E7 119
Island Pond, Vt., U.S. B5 152
Island Pond, l., N.H., U.S. E4 136
Islands, Bay of, b., Newf., Can. D2 102
Isla Patrulla, Ur. G11 80
Islas de la Bahía, dept., Hond. A8 92
Isla Verde, Arg. G7 80
Isla Vista, Ca., U.S. E4 112
Islay, Alta., Can. C5 98
Islay, i., Scot., U.K. F7 8
Islay, Punta, c., Peru G5 82
Isle, Mn., U.S. D5 130
Isle-aux-Morts, Newf., Can. E2 102
Isle of Man, dep., Eur. E7 4
Isle of Palms, S.C., U.S. k12 147
Isle of Wight, co., Eng., U.K. K12 8
Isle of Wight, co., Va., U.S. D6 153
Isle of Wight Bay, b., Md., U.S. D7 127
Isle Royale National Park, Mi., U.S. h9 129
Islesboro Island, i., Me., U.S. D4 126
Isleta, N.M., U.S. C3 138
Isleta Indian Reservation, N.M., U.S. C3 138
Isleton, Ca., U.S. C3 112
Islington, Ma., U.S. h11 128
Islón, Chile E3 80
Ismael Cortinas, Ur. G10 80
Ismailia see Al-Ismā'īlīyah, Egypt B7 60
Ismailli, Tur. K11 20
Isnā, Egypt E7 60
Isojoki, Fin. J17 6
Isola, Ms., U.S. B3 131
Isone, Switz. F10 13
Isparta, Tur. H14 4
İspir, Tur. A6 48
Israel (Yisra'el), ctry., Asia C2 42
Israel, stm., N.H., U.S. B3 136
Issano, Guy. E13 84
Issaquah, Wa., U.S. B3 154
Issaquena, co., Ms., U.S. C2 131
Issoire, Fr. G10 14
Issoudun, Fr. F9 14
Is-sur-Tille, Fr. E12 14
Issyk-Kul' (Rybačje), Kyrg. I13 26
Issyk-Kul', ozero, l., Kyrg. I13 26
İstanbul, Tur. H12 20
İstanbul Boğazı (Bosporus), strt., Tur. H13 20
Istmina, Col. E4 84
Isto, Mount, mtn., Ak., U.S. B11 109
Istokpoga, Lake, l., Fl., U.S. E5 116
Istra, Russia F19 22
Istra, pen., Eur. D8 18
Istria see Istra, pen., Eur. D8 18
Itá, Para. C10 80
Itabaiana, Braz. F11 76
Itabaiana, Braz. E11 76
Itabapoana, Braz. F8 79
Itaberá, Braz. G4 79
Itaberaba, Braz. B8 79
Itaberaí, Braz. D4 79
Itabira, Braz. E7 79
Itabuna, Braz. C9 79
Itacambiruçu, stm., Braz. D7 79
Itacaré, Braz. C9 79
Itacoatiara, Braz. I13 84
Itacurubí del Rosario, Para. C10 80
Itaeté, Braz. B8 79
Itagi, Braz. C8 79
Itaguaçu, Braz. E8 79
Itaguajé, Braz. G3 79
Itaguara, Braz. F6 79
Itaguari, stm., Braz. C6 79
Itaguaru, Braz. C4 79
Itagüí, Col. D5 84
Itaí, Braz. G4 79
Itá-Ibaté, Arg. D10 80
Itaiópolis, Braz. D14 80
Itaipu, Represa de, res., S.A. C11 80
Itaituba, Braz. D7 76
Itajá, Braz. E3 79
Itajaí, Braz. D14 80
Itajaí do Sul, stm., Braz. D14 80
Itajubá, Braz. G6 79
Itaju do Colônia, Braz. C9 79
Itajuípe, Braz. C9 79
Italy, Tx., U.S. C4 150
Italy (Italia), ctry., Eur. G10 4
Italy Cross, N.S., Can. E5 101
Itamaraju, Braz. D9 79
Itamarandiba, Braz. D7 79
Itamarandiba, stm., Braz. D7 79
Itamari, Braz. B9 79
Itambacuri, Braz. E8 79
Itambé, Braz. C8 79
Itami, Japan M10 36
Itanhaém, Braz. H5 79
Itanhauã, stm., Braz. A9 82
Itanhém, Braz. D8 79
Itanhomi, Braz. E8 79
Itaobim, Braz. D8 79
Itapaci, Braz. C4 79
Itapagipe, Braz. E4 79
Itaparanã, stm., Braz. B10 82
Itaparica, Ilha de, i., Braz. B9 79
Itapaya, Bol. G8 82
Itapé, Braz. C9 79
Itapebi, Braz. C9 79
Itapecerica, Braz. F6 79
Itapecuru-Mirim, Braz. D10 76
Itapemirim, Braz. F8 79
Itaperuna, Braz. F8 79
Itapetinga, Braz. C8 79
Itapetininga, Braz. G4 79
Itapetininga, stm., Braz. G5 79
Itapeva, Braz. G4 79
Itapicuru, stm., Braz. F11 76
Itapicuru, stm., Braz. D10 76
Itapira, Braz. G5 79
Itapiranga, Braz. D12 80
Itapiranga, Braz. I13 84
Itapirapuã, Braz. C3 79
Itapitanga, Braz. C9 79
Itápolis, Braz. F4 79
Itaporã, Braz. G1 79
Itaporanga, Braz. G4 79
Itapúa, dept., Para. D11 80
Itapuranga, Braz. C4 79
Itaquaí, stm., Braz. J7 84
Itaquara, Braz. B9 79
Itaquari, Braz. F8 79
Itaqui, Braz. E10 80
Itaquyry, Para. C11 80
Itarantim, Braz. C8 79
Itararé, Braz. H4 79
Itārsi, India I7 44
Itarumã, Braz. E3 79
Itasca, Il., U.S. k8 120
Itasca, Tx., U.S. C4 150
Itasca, co., Mn., U.S. C5 130
Itasca, Lake, l., Mn., U.S. C3 130
Itata, stm., Chile I2 80
Itatí, Arg. D9 80
Itatiaia, Parque Nacional do, Braz. G6 79
Itatinga, Braz. G4 79
Itaúna, Braz. F6 79
Itawamba, co., Ms., U.S. A5 131
Itenes (Guaporé), stm., S.A. E10 82
Ithaca, Mi., U.S. E6 129
Ithaca, Ne., U.S. g11 134
Ithaca, N.Y., U.S. C4 139
Itháki, Grc. K4 20
Itháki, i., Grc. K4 20
Itinga, Braz. D8 79
Itinga, stm., Braz. D8 79
Itiquira, Braz. D1 79
Itirapina, Braz. G5 79
Itiruçu, Braz. B8 79
Itō, Japan M14 36
Itoigawa, Japan J12 36
Itonamas, stm., Bol. E9 82
Itororó, Braz. C8 79
Itsā, Egypt C6 60
Itta Bena, Ms., U.S. B3 131
Itú, Braz. G5 79
Itu, stm., Braz. E11 80
Ituaçu, Braz. B8 79
Ituango, Col. D5 84
Ituberá, Braz. B9 79
Itucumã, stm., Braz. B7 82
Itueta, Braz. E8 79
Ituí, stm., Braz. J7 84
Ituim, stm., Braz. E13 80
Ituiutaba, Braz. E4 79
Itumbiara, Braz. E4 79
Ituna, Sask., Can. F4 105
Ituni, Guy. E13 84
Ituporanga, Braz. D14 80
Iturama, Braz. E3 79
Iturbe, Para. D10 80
Iturbide, Mex. H15 90
Iturup, ostrov (Etorofu-tō), i., Russia c22 36a
Ituverava, Braz. F5 79
Ituxi, stm., Braz. B9 82
Ituzaingó, Arg. D10 80
Itzehoe, Ger. B9 10
Iuka, Il., U.S. E5 120
Iuka, Ks., U.S. E5 123
Iuka, Ms., U.S. A5 131
Iúna, Braz. F8 79
Iva, S.C., U.S. C2 147
Ivacevičì, Bela. I8 22
Ivahona, Madag. s22 67b
Ivaí, stm., Braz. G2 79
Ivaiporã, Braz. C13 80
Ivane-Puste, Ukr. A10 20
Ivangorod, Russia B11 22
Ivangrad, Yugo. G3 20
Ivanhoe, Austl. I6 70
Ivanhoe, Mn., U.S. F2 130
Ivanhoe, Va., U.S. D2 153
Ivan'kovo, Russia G20 22
Ivan'kovskij, Russia E23 22
Ivan'kovskoje vodochranilišče, res., Russia E19 22
Ivano-Frankivs'k, Ukr. H2 26
Ivanovo, Bela. I8 22
Ivanovo, Russia D23 22
Ivato, Madag. r22 67b
Ivatuba, Braz. G2 79
Ivdel', Russia E10 26
Ivenec, Bela. H9 22
Ivesdale, Il., U.S. D5 120
Ivinheima, stm., Braz. G2 79
Ivins, Ut., U.S. F2 151
Ivje, Bela. H8 22
Ivón, stm., Bol. D8 82
Ivor, Va., U.S. D6 153
Ivorogbo, Nig. I13 64
Ivory Coast see Cote d'Ivoire, ctry., Afr. G5 54
Ivory Coast, C. Iv. I7 64
Ivoryton, Ct., U.S. D6 114
Ivrea, Italy D2 18
İvrindi, Tur. J11 20
Ivujivik, Que., Can. f11 104
Ivy, Va., U.S. B4 153
Ivydale, W.V., U.S. C3 155
Ivy Mountain, mtn., Ct., U.S. B3 114
Iwaki (Taira), Japan J15 36
Iwakuni, Japan M7 36
Iwamizawa, Japan d16 36a
Iwanai, Japan e15 36a
Iwo, Nig. H12 64
Iwo Jima see Iō-jima, i., Japan F18 158
Iwŏn, N. Kor. C16 32
Ixcán, stm., N.A. B3 92
Ixchiguán, Guat. B3 92
Ixiamas, Bol. E7 82
Iximché, hist., Guat. C4 92
Ixmiquilpan, Mex. G10 90
Ixopo, S. Afr. H10 66
Ixtahuacán, Guat. B3 92
Ixtapa, Mex. I9 90
Ixtepec, Mex. I12 90
Ixtlán de Juárez, Mex. I11 90
Ixtlán del Río, Mex. G7 90
'Iyāl Bakhīt, Sud. K5 60
Iyo-mishima, Japan N8 36
Izabal, Guat. B5 92
Izabal, dept., Guat. B5 92
Izabal, Lago de, l., Guat. B5 92
Īzad Khvāst, Iran F12 48
Izalco, El Sal. D5 92
Izamal, Mex. G15 90
Izapa, hist., Mex. J13 90
Izard, co., Ar., U.S. A4 111
'Izbat Abū Suql, Egypt F1 50
Izberbaš, Russia I7 26
Izbica, Pol. A17 10
Izd'oškovo, Russia F16 22
Izegem, Bel. G3 12
Īzeh, Iran F10 48
Iževsk, Russia F8 26
Izkī, Oman C10 47
Ižma, stm., Russia E8 26
Izmalkovo, Russia I20 22
Izmayil, Ukr. H3 26
İzmir (Smyrna), Tur. K11 20
İzmit, Tur. G13 4
Iznajar, Embalse de, res., Spain H7 16
Izoplit, Russia E19 22
Izopo, Punta, c., Hond. B7 92
Izozog, Bañados del, sw., Bol. H10 82
Izra', Syria C6 50
Izsák, Hung. I19 10
Iztaccíhuatl, Volcán, vol., Mex. H10 90
Iztaccíhuatl y Popocatépetl, Parques Nacionales, Mex. H10 90
Iztapa, Guat. D4 92
Izucar de Matamoros, Mex. H10 90
Izuhara, Japan M4 36
Izumi, Japan O5 36
Izumi, Japan M10 36
Izumi, Japan I15 36
Izumo, Japan L7 36
Izu-shotō, is., Japan E15 30
Izvestij CIK, ostrova, is., Russia B14 26
Izyum, Ukr. H5 26

J

Jaba, Eth. N8 60
Jabal al-Awliyā', Sud. J7 60
Jabalpur, India I8 44
Jabālyah, Gaza E2 50
Jabiru, Austl. B6 68
Jabjabah, Wādī, val., Afr. G7 60
Jablah, Syria D3 48
Jablonec nad Nisou, Czech Rep. E15 10
Jabłonka, Pol. F19 10
Jablonovyj chrebet, mts., Russia G14 28
Jaboatão, Braz. E11 76
Jaborandi, Braz. F4 79
Jaboticabal, Braz. F4 79
Jabung, Tanjung, c., Indon. O8 40
Jaca, Spain C11 16
Jacala, Mex. G10 90
Jacaleapa, Hond. C8 92
Jacaltenango, Guat. B3 92
Jacaraci, Braz. C7 79
Jacaré, stm., Braz. B8 79
Jacaré, stm., Braz. B10 82
Jacareí, Braz. G6 79
Jacarezinho, Braz. G4 79
Jaceel, val., Som. F11 56
Jáchal, stm., Arg. F4 80
Jachin, Al., U.S. C1 108
Jachroma, Russia E20 22
Jaciara, Braz. C1 79
Jacinto, Braz. D8 79
Jacinto, Ms., U.S. A5 131
Jacinto Aráuz, Arg. J7 80
Jacinto City, Tx., U.S. r14 150
Jacinto Machado, Braz. E14 80
Jaciparaná, Braz. C9 82
Jaciparaná, stm., Braz. D9 82
Jack, co., Tx., U.S. C3 150
Jackfish Lake, l., Sask., Can. D1 105
Jackman, Me., U.S. C2 126
Jackman Station, Me., U.S. C2 126
Jack Mountain, mtn., Mt., U.S. D4 133
Jack Mountain, mtn., Va., U.S. B3 153
Jack Mountain, mtn., Wa., U.S. A5 154
Jackpot, Nv., U.S. B7 135
Jacksboro, Tn., U.S. C9 149
Jacksboro, Tx., U.S. C3 150
Jacks Creek, Tn., U.S. B3 149
Jacks Mountain, mtn., Pa., U.S. E6 145
Jackson, Al., U.S. D2 108
Jackson, Ca., U.S. C3 112
Jackson, Ga., U.S. C3 117
Jackson, Ky., U.S. C6 124
Jackson, La., U.S. D4 125
Jackson, Mi., U.S. F6 129
Jackson, Mn., U.S. G4 130
Jackson, Ms., U.S. C3 131
Jackson, Mo., U.S. D8 132
Jackson, Mt., U.S. E3 133
Jackson, Ne., U.S. B9 134
Jackson, N.H., U.S. B4 136
Jackson, N.C., U.S. A5 140
Jackson, Oh., U.S. C3 142
Jackson, S.C., U.S. E4 147
Jackson, Tn., U.S. B3 149
Jackson, Wi., U.S. E5 156
Jackson, Wy., U.S. C2 157
Jackson, co., Al., U.S. A3 108
Jackson, co., Ar., U.S. B4 111
Jackson, co., Co., U.S. A4 113
Jackson, co., Fl., U.S. B1 116
Jackson, co., Ga., U.S. B3 117
Jackson, co., Il., U.S. F4 120
Jackson, co., In., U.S. G5 121
Jackson, co., Ia., U.S. B7 122
Jackson, co., Ks., U.S. C8 123
Jackson, co., Ky., U.S. C5 124
Jackson, co., La., U.S. B3 125
Jackson, co., Mi., U.S. F6 129
Jackson, co., Mn., U.S. G3 130
Jackson, co., Ms., U.S. E5 131
Jackson, co., Mo., U.S. B3 132
Jackson, co., N.C., U.S. f9 140
Jackson, co., Oh., U.S. C3 142
Jackson, co., Ok., U.S. C2 143
Jackson, co., Or., U.S. E4 144
Jackson, co., S.D., U.S. D4 148
Jackson, co., Tn., U.S. C8 149
Jackson, co., Tx., U.S. E4 150
Jackson, co., W.V., U.S. C3 155
Jackson, co., Wi., U.S. D3 156
Jackson, stm., Va., U.S. C3 153
Jackson, Lake, l., Fl., U.S. E5 116
Jackson, Lake, l., Fl., U.S. B2 116
Jackson, Mount, mtn., Ant. C12 73
Jackson, Mount, mtn., N.H., U.S. B4 136
Jacksonboro, S.C., U.S. F7 147
Jacksonburg, W.V., U.S. B4 155
Jackson Center, Oh., U.S. B1 142
Jackson Dam, Al., U.S. D2 108
Jackson Lake, res., Ga., U.S. C3 117
Jackson Lake, res., Wy., U.S. C2 157
Jackson Mountain, mtn., Me., U.S. D2 126
Jackson Mountains, mts., Nv., U.S. B3 135
Jacksonport, Ar., U.S. B4 111
Jackson's Arm, Newf., Can. D3 102
Jacksons Gap, Al., U.S. C4 108
Jacksonville, Al., U.S. B4 108
Jacksonville, Ar., U.S. C3 111
Jacksonville, Fl., U.S. B5 116
Jacksonville, Ga., U.S. E4 117
Jacksonville, Il., U.S. D3 120
Jacksonville, Me., U.S. D5 126
Jacksonville, N.C., U.S. C5 140
Jacksonville, Oh., U.S. C3 142
Jacksonville, Or., U.S. E4 144
Jacksonville, Tx., U.S. D5 150
Jacksonville, Vt., U.S. F3 152
Jacksonville Beach, Fl., U.S. B5 116
Jacksonville Naval Air Station, mil., Fl., U.S. B5 116
Jacks Peak, mtn., Ut., U.S. E3 151
Jacmel, Haiti E8 94
Jaco, Mex. D7 90
Jacobābād, Pak. F3 44
Jacobina, Braz. F10 76
Jacobsdal, S. Afr. G7 66
Jacques-Cartier, stm., Que., Can. B6 104
Jacques-Cartier, Détroit de, strt., Que., Can. h8 102
Jacquet, stm., N.B., Can. B3 101
Jacquet River, N.B., Can. B4 101
Jacqueville, C. Iv. I7 64
Jacuba, stm., Braz. E2 79
Jacuí, stm., Braz. F12 80
Jacuipe, stm., Braz. B9 79
Jacumba, Ca., U.S. F5 112
Jacupiranga, Braz. C14 80
Jaén, Peru A2 82
Jaén, Spain H8 16
Jāfarābād, India B1 46
Jaffa, Cape, c., Austl. K3 70
Jaffa, Tel Aviv- see Tel Aviv-Yafo, Isr. D3 50
Jaffna, Sri L. H6 46
Jaffrey, N.H., U.S. E2 136
Jaffrey Center, N.H., U.S. E2 136
Jafr, Qā' al-, depr., Jord. H6 50
Jagādhri, India E7 44
Jagdalpur, India C7 46
Jagersfontein, S. Afr. G7 66
Jagodnoje, Russia E21 28
Jagraon, India E6 44
Jagtiāl, India C5 46
Jaguaquara, Braz. B9 79
Jaguarão, Braz. G12 80
Jaguarão (Yaguarón), stm., S.A. G12 80
Jaguari, Braz. E11 80
Jaguariaíva, Braz. C14 80
Jaguaribe, stm., Braz. E11 76
Jaguaripe, Braz. B9 79
Jaguaruna, Braz. E14 80
Jagüé, Arg. E4 80
Jagüey Grande, Cuba C4 94
Jahānābād, India H11 44
Jahrom, Iran G12 48
Jailolo, Indon. E8 38
Jaipur, India G6 44
Jaisalmer, India G4 44
Jaja, Russia F15 26
Jājapur, India J12 44
Jajce, Bos. E12 18
Jakarta, Indon. j13 39a
Jakestown, Tn., U.S. C8 149
Jakin, Ga., U.S. E2 117
Jakobstad (Pietarsaari), Fin. J18 6
Jakša, Russia E9 26
Jakutija, state, Russia D18 28
Jakutsk, Russia E17 28
Jal, N.M., U.S. E6 138
Jalālābād, Afg. C4 44
Jalāmīd, Sau. Ar. B10 60
Jalán, stm., Hond. C8 92
Jalandhar, India E6 44
Jalapa, Guat. C5 92
Jalapa, Nic. D8 92
Jalapa, dept., Guat. C5 92
Jālgaon, India J6 44
Jalisco, state, Mex. G7 90
Jālna, India C3 46
Jālor, India H5 44
Jalostotitlán, Mex. G8 90
Jalpa, Mex. G8 90
Jalpāiguri, India G13 44
Jalpan, Mex. G10 90
Jaltepec, stm., Mex. I12 90
Jalūlā', Iraq D8 48
Jalutorovsk, Russia F11 26
Jamaame, Som. A8 58
Jamaica, Ia., U.S. C3 122
Jamaica, Vt., U.S. E3 152
Jamaica, ctry., N.A. E6 94
Jamaica Bay, b., N.Y., U.S. k13 139
Jamaica Channel, strt., N.A. E7 94
Jamal, poluostrov, pen., Russia C12 26
Jamalo-Neneckij, state, Russia D12 26
Jamālpur, Bngl. H13 44
Jamālpur, India H12 44
Jamantau, gora, mtn., Russia G9 26
Jamanxim, stm., Braz. A13 82
Jamari, stm., Braz. C10 82
Jamarovka, Russia G14 28
Jambelí, Canal de, strt., Ec. I2 84
Jambi, Indon. F3 38
Jambol, Bul. G10 20
James, Ga., U.S. D3 117
James, stm., Alta., Can. D3 98
James, stm., U.S. C7 106
James, stm., Mo., U.S. E4 132
James, stm., Va., U.S. C5 153
James, Lake, l., In., U.S. A7 121
James, Lake, res., N.C., U.S. B1 140
James Bay, b., Can. F16 96
James Bay, b., Can. A10 106
James Branch, stm., De., U.S. F3 115
Jamesburg, N.J., U.S. C4 137
James City, N.C., U.S. B5 140
James City, co., Va., U.S. C6 153
James Craik, Arg. G7 80
James Island, S.C., U.S. k12 147
James Island, i., Md., U.S. C5 127
James Island, i., S.C., U.S. F8 147
Jamesport, Mo., U.S. B4 132
James River Bridge, Va., U.S. k15 153
James Ross, Cape, c., N.W. Ter., Can. B10 96
James Ross Strait, strt., N.W. Ter., Can. C13 96
Jamestown, Austl. I3 70
Jamestown, S. Afr. H8 66
Jamestown, Ca., U.S. D3 112
Jamestown, Co., U.S. A5 113
Jamestown, In., U.S. E4 121
Jamestown, Ks., U.S. C6 123
Jamestown, Ky., U.S. D4 124
Jamestown, Mo., U.S. C5 132
Jamestown, N.Y., U.S. C1 139
Jamestown, N.C., U.S. B3 140
Jamestown, N.D., U.S. C7 141
Jamestown, Oh., U.S. C2 142
Jamestown, Pa., U.S. D1 145
Jamestown, R.I., U.S. F5 146
Jamestown, Tn., U.S. C9 149
James Town, Wy., U.S. E3 157
Jamestown Dam, N.D., U.S. C7 141
Jamestown Reservoir, res., N.D., U.S. C7 141
Jamesville, N.C., U.S. B6 140
Jaminauá, stm., Braz. C6 82
Jamkhandi, India D3 46
Jamm, Russia C11 22
Jammu, India D6 44
Jammu and Kashmīr, dep., Asia C10 42
Jamnagar, India I4 44
Jamsah, Egypt D7 60
Jamshedpur, India I12 44
Jamsk, Russia F22 28
Jämtlands Län, co., Swe. J13 6
Jamūi, India H12 44
Jamuna, stm., Bngl. H13 44
Jamundí, Col. F4 84
Jana, stm., Russia C19 28
Janauacá, Lago, l., Braz. I12 84
Janaúba, Braz. C7 79
Janaucu, Ilha, i., Braz. C8 76
Jand, Pak. D5 44
Jandaia, Braz. D3 79
Jandaia do Sul, Braz. G3 79
Jandaq, Iran D13 48
Jandiāla, India E6 44
Jandiatuba, stm., Braz. J8 84
Janeiro, Rio de, stm., Braz. A6 79
Jane Lew, W.V., U.S. B4 155
Janesville, Ca., U.S. B3 112
Janesville, Ia., U.S. B5 122
Janesville, Mn., U.S. F5 130
Janesville, Wi., U.S. F4 156
Janeville, N.B., Can. B4 101
Jangijul', Uzb. I11 26
Jangīpur, India H13 44
Janīn, W.B. D4 50
Janjina, Madag. r21 67b
Jan Kempdorp (Andalusia), S. Afr. F7 66
Jan Mayen, i., Sval. A6 52
Janos, Mex. B5 90
Jánoshalma, Hung. I19 10
Jánosháza, Hung. H17 10
Janoviči, Bela. F13 22
Jansen, Sask., Can. F3 105
Jansen, Co., U.S. D6 113
Jansen, Ne., U.S. D8 134
Janskij zaliv, b., Russia C19 28
Jantarnyj, Russia G2 22
Januária, Braz. C6 79
Janzé, Fr. E5 14
Jaora, India I6 44
Japan (Nihon), ctry., Asia D14 30
Japan, Sea of (Nihon-kai), Asia K7 36
Japim, Braz. B5 82
Japurá, Braz. H9 84
Japurá (Caquetá), stm., S.A. H8 84
Jaqué, Pan. D3 84
Jaquí, Peru F4 82
Jarābulus, Syria C5 48
Jarad, Sau. Ar. E2 47
Jaraguá, Braz. C4 79
Jaraguá do Sul, Braz. D14 80
Jaraiz de la Vera, Spain E6 16
Jarales, N.M., U.S. C3 138
Jarama, stm., Spain E8 16
Jaramānah, Syria B6 50
Jaransk, Russia F7 26
Jarash, Jord. D5 50
Jarbalo, Ks., U.S. k15 123
Jarcevo, Russia F15 22
Jardim, Braz. I13 82
Jardín América, Arg. D11 80
Jardine River National Park, Austl. B8 68
Jardines de la Reina, Archipiélago de los, is., Cuba D5 94
Jardinópolis, Braz. F5 79
Jaredi, Nig. E12 64
Jarensk, Russia E7 26
Jargeau, Fr. E9 14
Jari, stm., Braz. A10 82
Jari, Lago, l., Braz. J11 84
Jaridih, India I12 44
Jarnac, Fr. G6 14
Jarocin, Pol. D17 10
Jaroměř, Czech Rep. E15 10
Jaroslavl', Russia D22 22
Jarosław, Pol. E22 10
Jarratt, Va., U.S. D5 153
Jarrettsville, Md., U.S. A5 127
Jaru, Braz. D10 82
Jaru, stm., Braz. D10 82
Järva-Jaani, Est. B8 22
Järvenpää, Fin. K19 6
Jarvie, Alta., Can. B4 98
Jarvis Island, i., Oc. I23 158
Jaša Tomić, Yugo. D4 20
Jasikan, Ghana H10 64
Jāsk, Iran I14 48
Jasło, Pol. F21 10
Jasmine Estates, Fl., U.S. D4 116
Jasnogorsk, Russia G20 22
Jason Islands, is., Falk. Is. G4 78
Jasonville, In., U.S. F3 121
Jasper, Ont., Can. C9 103
Jasper, Al., U.S. B2 108
Jasper, Ar., U.S. B2 111
Jasper, Fl., U.S. B4 116
Jasper, Ga., U.S. B2 117
Jasper, In., U.S. H4 121
Jasper, Mn., U.S. G2 130
Jasper, Mo., U.S. D3 132
Jasper, Tn., U.S. D8 149
Jasper, Tx., U.S. D6 150
Jasper, co., Ga., U.S. C3 117
Jasper, co., Il., U.S. D5 120
Jasper, co., In., U.S. B3 121
Jasper, co., Ia., U.S. C4 122
Jasper, co., Ms., U.S. C4 131
Jasper, co., Mo., U.S. D3 132
Jasper, co., S.C., U.S. G5 147
Jasper, co., Tx., U.S. D5 150
Jasper Lake, l., Alta., Can. C1 98
Jasper National Park, Alta., Can. C1 98
Jászapáti, Hung. H20 10
Jászberény, Hung. H19 10
Jász-Nagykun-Szolnok, co., Hung. H20 10
Jataí, Braz. D3 79
Jatapu, stm., Braz. H13 84
Jatatè, stm., Mex. I14 90
Jatni, India J11 44
Jatobá, stm., Braz. B1 79
Jaú, Braz. G4 79
Jaú, stm., Braz. H12 84
Jaú, Parque Nacional do, Braz. I11 84
Jauaperi, stm., Braz. H12 84
Jauja, Peru D4 82
Jaungulbene, Lat. D9 22
Jaunjelgava, Lat. E8 22
Jaunpiebalga, Lat. D9 22

Name	Map Ref.	Page
Jaunpur, India	H10	44
Jaupaci, Braz.	D3	79
Jauquara, stm., Braz.	F13	82
Jauru, stm., Braz.	E1	79
Jauru, stm., Braz.	G13	82
Java, S.D., U.S.	B6	148
Java see Jawa, i., Indon.	j15	39a
Javari (Yavarí), stm., S.A.	D4	76
Javas, Russia	G25	22
Java Sea see Jawa, Laut, Indon.	G5	38
Java Trench	J11	24
Jawa (Java), i., Indon.	j15	39a
Jawa, Laut (Java Sea), Indon.	G5	38
Jawbar, Syria	A6	50
Jawor, Pol.	D16	10
Jaworzno, Pol.	E19	10
Jay, Fl., U.S.	u14	116
Jay, Me., U.S.	D2	126
Jay, Ok., U.S.	A7	143
Jay, co., In., U.S.	D7	121
Jaya, Puncak, mtn., Indon.	F10	38
Jayanca, Peru	B2	82
Jayapura (Sukarnapura), Indon.	F11	38
Jayb, Wādī al- (Ha'Arava), val., Asia	H4	50
Jay Peak, mtn., Vt., U.S.	B3	152
Jaypur, India	C7	46
Jayton, Tx., U.S.	C2	150
Jaželbicy, Russia	C15	22
J. B. Thomas, Lake, res., Tx., U.S.	C2	150
Jean, Nv., U.S.	H6	135
Jeanerette, La., U.S.	E4	125
Jean Lafitte, La., U.S.	k11	125
Jean Lafitte National Historical Park, La., U.S.	k12	125
Jeannette, Pa., U.S.	F2	145
Jebba, Nig.	G12	64
Jebeniana, Tun.	C16	62
Jeberos, Peru	A3	82
Jechegnadzor, Arm.	B8	48
Jedburg, Mo., U.S.	f12	132
Jeddore Lake, res., Newf., Can.	D3	102
Jędrzejów, Pol.	E20	10
Jefawa, Sud.	L2	60
Jeff, Ky., U.S.	C6	124
Jeffara (Al-Jifārah), pl., Afr.	D16	62
Jeff Davis, co., Ga., U.S.	E4	117
Jeff Davis, co., Tx., U.S.	o12	150
Jeffers, Mn., U.S.	F3	130
Jeffers, Mt., U.S.	E5	133
Jefferson, Al., U.S.	C2	108
Jefferson, Ar., U.S.	C3	111
Jefferson, Co., U.S.	B5	113
Jefferson, Ga., U.S.	B3	117
Jefferson, In., U.S.	D4	121
Jefferson, Ia., U.S.	B3	122
Jefferson, La., U.S.	k11	125
Jefferson, Me., U.S.	D3	126
Jefferson, Ma., U.S.	B4	128
Jefferson, N.H., U.S.	B4	136
Jefferson, N.C., U.S.	A1	140
Jefferson, Oh., U.S.	A5	142
Jefferson, Or., U.S.	C3	144
Jefferson, S.C., U.S.	B7	147
Jefferson, S.D., U.S.	E9	148
Jefferson, Tx., U.S.	C5	150
Jefferson, Wi., U.S.	E5	156
Jefferson, co., Al., U.S.	B3	108
Jefferson, co., Ar., U.S.	C3	111
Jefferson, co., Co., U.S.	B5	113
Jefferson, co., Fl., U.S.	B3	116
Jefferson, co., Ga., U.S.	C4	117
Jefferson, co., Id., U.S.	F6	119
Jefferson, co., Il., U.S.	E5	120
Jefferson, co., In., U.S.	G6	121
Jefferson, co., Ia., U.S.	C5	122
Jefferson, co., Ks., U.S.	C8	123
Jefferson, co., Ky., U.S.	B4	124
Jefferson, co., La., U.S.	E5	125
Jefferson, co., Ms., U.S.	D2	131
Jefferson, co., Mo., U.S.	C7	132
Jefferson, co., Mt., U.S.	D4	133
Jefferson, co., Ne., U.S.	D8	134
Jefferson, co., N.Y., U.S.	A5	139
Jefferson, co., Oh., U.S.	B5	142
Jefferson, co., Ok., U.S.	C4	143
Jefferson, co., Or., U.S.	C5	144
Jefferson, co., Pa., U.S.	D3	145
Jefferson, co., Tn., U.S.	C10	149
Jefferson, co., Tx., U.S.	E5	150
Jefferson, co., Wa., U.S.	B1	154
Jefferson, co., W.V., U.S.	B7	155
Jefferson, co., Wi., U.S.	E5	156
Jefferson, stm., Mt., U.S.	E5	133
Jefferson, Mount, mtn., Id., U.S.	E7	119
Jefferson, Mount, mtn., Nv., U.S.	E5	135
Jefferson, Mount, mtn., Or., U.S.	C5	144
Jefferson City, Mo., U.S.	C5	132
Jefferson City, Mt., U.S.	D5	133
Jefferson City, Tn., U.S.	C10	149
Jefferson Davis, co., La., U.S.	D3	125
Jefferson Davis, co., Ms., U.S.	D4	131
Jefferson Farms, De., U.S.	i7	115
Jefferson Heights, Md., U.S.	B2	127
Jefferson Hill, hill, Ky., U.S.	g11	124
Jefferson Proving Ground, mil., In., U.S.	G7	121
Jeffersontown, Ky., U.S.	B4	124
Jeffersonville, Ga., U.S.	D3	117
Jeffersonville, In., U.S.	H6	121
Jeffersonville, Ky., U.S.	C6	124
Jeffersonville, Oh., U.S.	C2	142
Jeffersonville, Vt., U.S.	B3	152
Jeffrey, W.V., U.S.	D3	155
Jeffrey City, Wy., U.S.	D5	157
Jeffries Creek, stm., S.C., U.S.	C8	147
Jefimovskij, Russia	L24	6
Jefremov, Russia	G5	26
Jega, Nig.	E12	64
Jegenstorf, Switz.	D8	13
Jegorjevsk, Russia	F22	22
Jehossee Island, i., S.C., U.S.	k11	147
Jejsk, Russia	H5	26
Jēkabpils, Lat.	E8	22
Jekaterinburg, Russia	F10	26
Jekateriny, proliv, strt., Russia	I21	28
Jekimoviči, Russia	G16	22
Jekyll Island, i., Ga., U.S.	E5	117
Jelabuga, Russia	F8	26
Jelancy, Russia	G13	28
Jel'cy, Russia	E16	22
Jelec, Russia	I21	22
Jelenia Góra (Hirschberg), Pol.	E15	10
Jelenskij, Russia	H18	22
Jelgava, Lat.	E6	22
Jelizarovo, Russia	C27	22
Jelizavety, mys, c., Russia	G20	28
Jelizovo, Bela.	H12	22
Jellico, Tn., U.S.	C9	149
Jelm Mountain, mtn., Wy., U.S.	E7	157
Jel'n'a, Russia	G16	22
Jelnat', Russia	D25	22
Jeloguj, stm., Russia	E15	26
Jelšava, Slvk.	G20	10
Jemanželinsk, Russia	G10	26
Jember, Indon.	G5	38
Jemca, Russia	J27	6
Jemez, stm., N.M., U.S.	k7	138
Jemez Canyon Dam, N.M., U.S.	k7	138
Jemez Indian Reservation, N.M., U.S.	h7	138
Jemez Pueblo, N.M., U.S.	B3	138
Jemez Springs, N.M., U.S.	B3	138
Jemison, Al., U.S.	C3	108
Jemmal, Tun.	N5	18
Jemseg, N.B., Can.	D3	101
Jena, Ger.	E11	10
Jena, La., U.S.	C3	125
Jenašimskij Polkan, gora, mtn., Russia	F16	26
Jenbach, Aus.	H11	10
Jendouba (Souk el Arba), Tun.	M3	18
Jenisej (Yenisey), stm., Russia	D15	26
Jenisejsk, Russia	F10	28
Jenisejskij kr'až, mts., Russia	F16	26
Jenisejskij zaliv, b., Russia	C8	28
Jenkins, Ky., U.S.	C7	124
Jenkins, Mn., U.S.	D4	130
Jenkins, co., Ga., U.S.	D5	117
Jenkinsburg, Ga., U.S.	C2	117
Jenkintown, Pa., U.S.	o21	145
Jenks, Ok., U.S.	A6	143
Jenner, Alta., Can.	D5	98
Jenners, Pa., U.S.	F3	145
Jennersdorf, Aus.	I16	10
Jennette, Ar., U.S.	B5	111
Jennie, Ar., U.S.	D4	111
Jennings, Fl., U.S.	B3	116
Jennings, Ks., U.S.	C3	123
Jennings, La., U.S.	D3	125
Jennings, Mo., U.S.	f13	132
Jennings, Ok., U.S.	A5	143
Jennings, co., In., U.S.	G6	121
Jenny Jump Mountain, mtn., N.J., U.S.	B3	137
Jenny Lind, Ar., U.S.	B1	111
Jensen, Ut., U.S.	C6	151
Jensen Beach, Fl., U.S.	E6	116
Jeparit, Austl.	K4	70
Jepelacio, Peru	B3	82
Jepifan', Russia	H21	22
Jeptha Knob, hill, Ky., U.S.	B4	124
Jequeri, Braz.	F7	79
Jequetepeque, stm., Peru	B2	82
Jequié, Braz.	B8	79
Jequitaí, Braz.	D6	79
Jequitinhonha, Braz.	D8	79
Jequitinhonha, stm., Braz.	D9	79
Jerada, Mor.	C9	62
Jeradou, Tun.	M5	18
Jerauld, co., S.D., U.S.	C7	148
Jerba, Île de, i., Tun.	D16	62
Jerécuaro, Mex.	G9	90
Jérémie, Haiti	E7	94
Jeremoabo, Braz.	F11	76
Jerevan, Arm.	I6	26
Jerez de García Salinas, Mex.	F8	90
Jerez de la Frontera, Spain	I5	16
Jerez de los Caballeros, Spain	G5	16
Jergeni, hills, Russia	H6	26
Jericho, Ar., U.S.	B5	111
Jericho, Vt., U.S.	B3	152
Jericho see Arīḥā, W.B.	E4	50
Jericó, Col.	E5	84
Jerico Springs, Mo., U.S.	D4	132
Jerid, Chott, sw., Tun.	D15	62
Jerilderie, Austl.	J6	70
Jerimoth Hill, hill, R.I., U.S.	C1	146
Jermiš', Russia	G25	22
Jermolajevo, Russia	E19	4
Jermolino, Russia	F19	22
Jermyn, Pa., U.S.	C10	145
Jeroaquara, Braz.	C3	79
Jerofej Pavlovič, Russia	G16	28
Jerome, Az., U.S.	C3	110
Jerome, Fl., U.S.	F5	116
Jerome, Id., U.S.	G4	119
Jerome, Mo., U.S.	D6	132
Jerome, Pa., U.S.	F4	145
Jerome, co., Id., U.S.	G4	119
Jeromesville, Oh., U.S.	B3	142
Jersey, Ga., U.S.	C3	117
Jersey, co., Il., U.S.	D3	120
Jersey, dep., Eur.	F7	4
Jersey City, N.J., U.S.	B4	137
Jersey Mountain, mtn., Id., U.S.	E3	119
Jersey Shore, Pa., U.S.	D7	145
Jersey Village, Tx., U.S.	r14	150
Jerseyville, Il., U.S.	D3	120
Jeršov, Russia	G7	26
Jerusalem see Yerushalayim, Isr.	E4	50
Jerusalem, Ar., U.S.	B3	111
Jervis, Cape, c., Austl.	J3	70
Jervis Bay, b., Austl.	J9	70
Jervis Inlet, b., B.C., Can.	D6	99
Jesenice, Czech Rep.	E13	10
Jesi, Italy	F8	18
Jesil', Kaz.	G11	26
Jessamine, co., Ky., U.S.	C5	124
Jessentuki, Russia	I6	26
Jessieville, Ar., U.S.	C2	111
Jessore, Bngl.	I13	44
Jessup, Md., U.S.	B4	127
Jessup, Pa., U.S.	m18	145
Jesup, Ga., U.S.	E5	117
Jesup, Ia., U.S.	B5	122
Jesup, Lake, l., Fl., U.S.	D5	116
Jesús, Para.	D11	80
Jésus, Île, i., Que., Can.	p19	104
Jesús Carranza, Mex.	I12	90
Jesús de Otoro, Hond.	C7	92
Jesús María, Arg.	F6	80
Jesús María, Mex.	E6	90
Jesús María, stm., Mex.	F7	90
Jesús Menéndez, Cuba	D6	94
Jet, Ok., U.S.	A3	143
Jetmore, Ks., U.S.	D4	123
Jetpur, India	J4	44
Jette, Bel.	G5	12
Jeumont, Fr.	B11	14
Jever, Ger.	B7	10
Jevrej, state, Russia	H18	28
Jewel Cave National Monument, S.D., U.S.	D2	148
Jewell, Ia., U.S.	B4	122
Jewell, Ks., U.S.	C5	123
Jewell, co., Ks., U.S.	C5	123
Jewell Ridge, Va., U.S.	e10	153
Jewett, Oh., U.S.	B4	142
Jewett, Tx., U.S.	D4	150
Jewett City, Ct., U.S.	C8	114
Jewett Lake, l., Sask., Can.	A3	105
Jezerce, mtn., Alb.	G3	20
Jezerišće, Bela.	F12	22
Jeziorany, Pol.	B20	10
Jhābua, India	I6	44
Jhālāwār, India	H7	44
Jhal Jhao, Pak.	G1	44
Jhang Sadar, Pak.	E5	44
Jhānsi, India	H8	44
Jharia, India	I12	44
Jhārsuguda, India	B8	46
Jhelum, Pak.	D5	44
Jhelum, stm., Asia	E5	44
Jhok Rind, Pak.	E4	44
Jhunjhunūn, India	F6	44
Jiaban, China	B9	40
Jiāganj, India	H13	44
Jiakou, China	E8	34
Jiali, China	E5	30
Jialing, stm., China	E8	30
Jialou, China	C2	34
Jiamusi, China	B13	30
Ji'an, China	H3	34
Jianchang, China	B12	32
Jianchuan, China	A5	40
Jiangbeixu, China	I4	34
Jiangbianzhai, China	C6	40
Jiangcun, China	G6	34
Jiangdihe, China	B6	40
Jiangduo, China	C9	34
Jianggezhuang, China	D7	32
Jiangji, China	C4	34
Jiangjin, China	F8	30
Jiangkou, China	G9	30
Jiangkou, China	H7	34
Jiangkouji, China	C5	34
Jiangliadian, China	A5	32
Jiangmen, China	M2	34
Jiangsu (Kiangsu), prov., China	E10	30
Jiangtun, China	B10	32
Jiangxi (Kiangsi), prov., China	F10	30
Jiangxiang, China	C6	34
Jiangyin, China	D9	34
Jiangzhasiji, China	E13	44
Jianli, China	F1	34
Jianning, China	I5	34
Jian'ou, China	H7	34
Jianshan, China	F9	34
Jianshui, China	C7	40
Jiantouji, China	I5	34
Jiaohe, China	C12	30
Jiaomei, China	K6	34
Jiaoshanhe, China	F1	34
Jiaoxian, China	G7	32
Jiaozuo, China	D9	30
Jiashan, China	C7	34
Jiashun Hu, l., China	C12	44
Jiawang, China	A6	34
Jiaxian, China	B2	34
Jiaxing, China	E9	34
Jiayu, China	F2	34
Jiazi, China	M5	34
Jibiya, Nig.	E13	64
Jiboa, stm., El Sal.	D5	92
Jicarilla Apache Indian Reservation, N.M., U.S.	A2	138
Jicarón, Isla, i., Pan.	D2	84
Jicatuyo, stm., Hond.	C6	92
Jiddah (Jeddah), Sau. Ar.	D1	47
Jidingxilin, China	D15	44
Jiedong, China	I2	34
Jiehe, China	H5	32
Jieji, China	B7	34
Jiepai, China	E8	34
Jiesheng, China	M4	34
Jieshou, China	B8	34
Jieshou, China	B4	34
Jieyang, China	L5	34
Jieznas, Lith.	G7	22
Jigongzhen, China	A4	34
Jiguaní, Cuba	D6	94
Jiguanshan, China	A12	32
Jigüey, Bahía de, b., Cuba	C5	94
Jihlava, Czech Rep.	F15	10
Jijel, Alg.	B13	62
Jijiadianzi, China	H6	32
Jikawo, Eth.	M7	60
Jikawo, stm., Afr.	M8	60
Jilib, Som.	A8	58
Jili Hu, l., China	B4	30
Jilin, China	C12	30
Jilin (Kirin), prov., China	C12	30
Jill, Kediet ej, mtn., Maur.	I4	62
Jima, Eth.	N9	60
Jimbolia, Rom.	D4	20
Jiménez, Mex.	D7	90
Jiménez, Mex.	C9	90
Jiménez del Téul, Mex.	F7	90
Jim Hogg, co., Tx., U.S.	F3	150
Jim Lake, res., N.D., U.S.	B7	141
Jimo, China	G8	32
Jim Thorpe, Pa., U.S.	E10	145
Jim Wells, co., Tx., U.S.	F3	150
Jin (Gam), stm., Asia	C8	40
Jināh, Egypt	E6	60
Jinan (Tsinan), China	G4	32
Jinbang, China	J7	34
Jincheng, China	D9	30
Jīnd, India	F7	44
Jindřichův Hradec, Czech Rep.	F15	10
Jingangtou, China	H2	34
Jingcheng, China	K6	34
Jingdezhen (Kingtechen), China	F6	34
Jinggang, China	G1	34
Jinggangshan (Ciping), China	I3	34
Jinghai, China	E4	32
Jinghaiwei, China	G10	32
Jinghong, China	C6	40
Jingning, China	H8	34
Jingoutun, China	B5	32
Jingxi, China	C9	40
Jingxian, China	F4	32
Jingyu, China	A14	32
Jingzhi, China	G7	32
Jinhua, China	F8	34
Jining, China	C9	30
Jining, China	H4	32
Jinja, Ug.	A6	58
Jinjiang, China	A6	40
Jinjing, China	G2	34
Jinkeng, China	H6	34
Jinkou, China	G8	32
Jinlingzhen, China	G6	32
Jinmu Jiao, c., China	H8	30
Jinning, China	B7	40
Jinotega, Nic.	D8	92
Jinotega, dept., Nic.	D9	92
Jinotepe, Nic.	F8	92
Jinping, China	A10	40
Jinrui, China	H3	34
Jinsha, stm., China	F6	30
Jinshan, China	E10	34
Jinshi, China	F9	30
Jintian, China	H3	34
Jinxi, China	C8	32
Jinxian, China	D9	32
Jinyun, China	G9	34
Jinzhaizhen, China	D4	34
Jinzhou (Chinchou), China	B9	32
Ji-Paraná, Braz.	D11	82
Jipijapa, Ec.	H2	84
Jiquilisco, El Sal.	D6	92
Jiquilisco, Bahía de, b., El Sal.	D6	92
Jiquiriçá, stm., Braz.	B8	79
Jirāfī, Wādī al- (Naḥal Paran), val.	I3	50
Jirbān, Sud.	L6	60
Jirjā, Egypt	D6	60
Jirkov, Czech Rep.	E13	10
Jīroft, Iran	G14	48
Jisr ash-Shughūr, Syria	D4	48
Jitan, China	K4	34
Jitaúna, Braz.	C9	79
Jiu, stm., Rom.	F7	20
Jiubao, China	J4	34
Jiucheng, China	E5	32
Jiuguan, China	E9	32
Jiuhu, China	F5	32
Jiuhuaxian, China	L2	34
Jiujiang, China	F4	34
Jiukou, China	E1	34
Jiulian Shan, mts., China	K3	34
Jiuling Shan, mts., China	G3	34
Jiulong, China	K1	34
Jiumianyang, China	E2	34
Jiuningyang, China	J6	34
Jiuquan, China	D6	30
Jiushangshui, China	H3	34
Jiutai, China	C12	30
Jiuxian, China	B2	34
Jiuxiangcheng, China	B3	34
Jixi, China	B13	30
Jixian, China	H2	32
Jixian, China	C5	32
Jixingji, China	C5	34
Jiyang, China	G5	32
Jīzān, Sau. Ar.	F3	47
Joaçaba, Braz.	D13	80
Joaíma, Braz.	D8	79
Joanna, S.C., U.S.	C4	147
João Neiva, Braz.	E8	79
João Pessoa, Braz.	E12	76
João Pinheiro, Braz.	D5	79
Joaquim Távora, Braz.	G4	79
Joaquín V. González, Arg.	C6	80
Job Peak, mtn., Nv., U.S.	D3	135
Jocassee, Lake, res., U.S.	B1	147
Jocolí, Arg.	G4	80
Jocón, Hond.	B8	92
Jocoro, El Sal.	D6	92
Jocotán, Guat.	C5	92
Jódar, Spain	H8	16
Jo Daviess, co., Il., U.S.	A3	120
Jodhpur, India	G5	44
Jodie, W.V., U.S.	m13	155
Joe Batt's Arm [-Barr'd Islands-Shoal Bay], Newf., Can.	D4	102
Joensuu, Fin.	J21	6
Joes Brook, stm., Vt., U.S.	C4	152
Joes Creek, stm., W.V., U.S.	m12	155
Joetsu, Japan	J13	36
Joffre, Mount, mtn., Can.	D3	98
Jõgeva, Est.	C9	22
Jog Falls, wtfl, India	E3	46
Joggins, N.S., Can.	D5	101
Jogui, stm., Braz.	G1	79
Johannesburg, S. Afr.	F9	66
John, Cape, c., N.S., Can.	D6	101
John Day, Or., U.S.	C8	144
John Day, stm., Or., U.S.	B6	144
John Day, North Fork, stm., Or., U.S.	C7	144
John Day Dam, U.S.	D5	154
John Day Fossil Beds National Monument, Or., U.S.	C6	144
John F. Kennedy Space Center, sci., Fl., U.S.	D6	116
John H. Kerr Dam, Va., U.S.	D4	153
John H. Kerr Reservoir, res., U.S.	D4	153
John Martin Reservoir, res., Co., U.S.	C7	113
John Muir National Historical Site, hist., Ca., U.S.	h8	112
John o' Groats, Scot., U.K.	C10	8
John Redmond Reservoir, res., Ks., U.S.	D8	123
Johnsburg, Il., U.S.	h8	120
John Sevier, Tn., U.S.	m14	149
Johns Island, S.C., U.S.	F7	147
Johns Island, i., S.C., U.S.	F7	147
Johnson, Ar., U.S.	A1	111
Johnson, Ks., U.S.	E2	123
Johnson, Ne., U.S.	D10	134
Johnson, Vt., U.S.	B3	152
Johnson, co., Ar., U.S.	B2	111
Johnson, co., Ga., U.S.	D4	117
Johnson, co., Il., U.S.	F5	120
Johnson, co., In., U.S.	F5	121
Johnson, co., Ia., U.S.	C6	122
Johnson, co., Ks., U.S.	D9	123
Johnson, co., Ky., U.S.	C7	124
Johnson, co., Mo., U.S.	C4	132
Johnson, co., Ne., U.S.	D9	134
Johnson, co., Tn., U.S.	C12	149
Johnson, co., Tx., U.S.	C4	150
Johnson, co., Wy., U.S.	B6	157
Johnsonburg, Pa., U.S.	D4	145
Johnson City, N.Y., U.S.	C5	139
Johnson City, Tn., U.S.	C11	149
Johnson City, Tx., U.S.	D3	150
Johnson Creek, Wi., U.S.	E5	156
Johnsonville, S.C., U.S.	D9	147
Johns Pass, strt., Fl., U.S.	p10	116
Johnston, Ia., U.S.	e8	122
Johnston, R.I., U.S.	C4	146
Johnston, S.C., U.S.	D4	147
Johnston, co., N.C., U.S.	B4	140
Johnston, co., Ok., U.S.	C5	143
Johnston Atoll, atoll, Oc.	G23	158
Johnston City, Il., U.S.	F5	120
Johnstone Strait, strt., B.C., Can.	D4	99
Johnston Key, i., Fl., U.S.	H5	116
Johnstown, Co., U.S.	A6	113
Johnstown, N.Y., U.S.	B6	139
Johnstown, Oh., U.S.	B3	142
Johnstown, Pa., U.S.	F4	145
Johnsville, Md., U.S.	A3	127
John W. Flannagan Reservoir, res., Va., U.S.	e9	153
Johor Baharu, Malay.	N7	40
Joice, Ia., U.S.	A4	122
Joigny, Fr.	E10	14
Joiner, Ar., U.S.	B5	111
Joinville, Braz.	D14	80
Joinville, Fr.	D12	14
Joinville Island, i., Ant.	B1	73
Jokkmokk, Swe.	H16	6
Jolārpettai, India	F5	46
Jolfā, Iran	B8	48
Joliet, Il., U.S.	B5	120
Joliet, Mt., U.S.	E8	133
Joliette, Que., Can.	C4	104
Jolo, Phil.	D7	38
Jomda, China	E6	30
Jonava, Lith.	F7	22
Jones, Al., U.S.	C3	108
Jones, Ok., U.S.	B4	143
Jones, co., Ga., U.S.	C3	117
Jones, co., Ia., U.S.	B6	122
Jones, co., Ms., U.S.	D4	131
Jones, co., N.C., U.S.	B5	140
Jones, co., S.D., U.S.	D5	148
Jones, co., Tx., U.S.	C3	150
Jonesboro, Ar., U.S.	B5	111
Jonesboro, Ga., U.S.	C2	117
Jonesboro, Il., U.S.	F4	120
Jonesboro, In., U.S.	D6	121
Jonesboro, La., U.S.	B3	125
Jonesboro, Me., U.S.	D5	126
Jonesborough, Tn., U.S.	C11	149
Jonesburg, Mo., U.S.	C6	132
Jones Creek, Tx., U.S.	s14	150
Jones Mill, Ar., U.S.	C3	111
Jonesport, Me., U.S.	D5	126
Jones Sound, strt., N.W. Ter., Can.	A15	96
Jonestown, Ms., U.S.	C3	131
Jonestown, Ms., U.S.	A3	131
Jonestown, Pa., U.S.	F9	145
Jonesville, In., U.S.	F6	121
Jonesville, La., U.S.	C4	125
Jonesville, Mi., U.S.	G6	129
Jonesville, N.C., U.S.	A2	140
Jonesville, S.C., U.S.	B4	147
Jonesville, Vt., U.S.	C3	152
Jonesville, Va., U.S.	f8	153
Joniškėlis, Lith.	E7	22
Joniškis, Lith.	E6	22
Jönköping, Swe.	M14	6
Jonquière, Que., Can.	A6	104
Jonuta, Mex.	H13	90
Joplin, Mo., U.S.	D3	132
Joplin, Mt., U.S.	B6	133
Joppa, Al., U.S.	A3	108
Joppa, Il., U.S.	F5	120
Joppatowne, Md., U.S.	B5	127
Jordan, Al., U.S.	D1	108
Jordan, Mn., U.S.	F5	130
Jordan, Mt., U.S.	C10	133
Jordan, N.Y., U.S.	B4	139
Jordan (Al-Urdunn), ctry., Asia	C2	42
Jordan (Nahr al-Urdunn) (HaYarden), stm., Asia	E5	50
Jordan, stm., Ut., U.S.	C4	151
Jordan Creek, stm., U.S.	E9	144
Jordânia, Braz.	C8	79
Jordan Lake, l., N.S., Can.	E4	101
Jordan Lake, res., Al., U.S.	C3	108
Jordanów, Pol.	F19	10
Jordan Valley, Or., U.S.	D9	144
Jordão, stm., Braz.	C13	80
Jordet, Nor.	K13	6
Jorhāt, India	G16	44
Jornado del Muerto, des., N.M., U.S.	D3	138
Jos, Nig.	G14	64
José Batlle y Ordóñez, Ur.	G11	80
José Bonifácio, Braz.	F4	79
José Francisco Vergara, Chile	B4	80
Joselândia, Braz.	G13	82
José Pedro Varela, Ur.	G11	80
Joseph, Or., U.S.	B9	144
Joseph, Lac, l., Newf., Can.	h8	102
Joseph Bonaparte Gulf, b., Austl.	B5	68
Joseph City, Az., U.S.	C5	110
Josephine, co., Or., U.S.	E3	144
Josephville, Mo., U.S.	f12	132
Joshua, Tx., U.S.	n9	150
Joshua Tree, Ca., U.S.	E5	112
Joshua Tree National Monument, Ca., U.S.	F6	112
Joškar-Ola, Russia	F7	26
Josselin, Fr.	E4	14
Joubertina, S. Afr.	I6	66
Jourdanton, Tx., U.S.	E3	150
Joussard, Alta., Can.	B3	98
Jovellanos, Cuba	C4	94
Joviânia, Braz.	D4	79
Jowhar, Som.	H10	56
Joy, Il., U.S.	B3	120
Joyce, La., U.S.	C3	125
Józefów, Pol.	C21	10
J. Percy Priest Lake, res., Tn., U.S.	A5	149
Juab, co., Ut., U.S.	D2	151
Juami, stm., Braz.	H9	84
Juan Aldama, Mex.	E8	90
Juan B. Arruabarrena, Arg.	F9	80
Juan Bautista Alberdi, Arg.	D6	80
Juan de Fuca, Strait of, strt., N.A.	A1	154
Juan de Mena, Para.	C10	80
Juan de Nova, Île, i., Afr.	E8	58
Juan E. Barra, Arg.	I8	80
Juan Eugenio, Mex.	E8	90
Juan Fernández, Archipiélago, is., Chile	C1	78
Juangriego, Ven.	B11	84
Juan Guerra, Peru	B3	82
Juan Jorba, Arg.	G6	80
Juan José Castelli, Arg.	C8	80
Juán José Perez, Bol.	F7	82
Juanjuí, Peru	B3	82
Juan L. Lacaze, Ur.	H10	80
Juan N. Fernández, Arg.	J9	80
Juan Viñas, C.R.	H11	92
Juárez, Mex.	D9	90
Juárez, Mex.	B5	90
Juárez see Ciudad Juárez, Mex.	B6	90
Juárez, Sierra de, mts., Mex.	B2	90
Juatinga, Ponta de, c., Braz.	G6	79
Juàzeiro, Braz.	E10	76
Juazeiro do Norte, Braz.	E11	76
Jūbā, Sud.	H7	56
Juba, stm., Braz.	F12	82
Jūbāl, Madīq, strt., Egypt	D7	60
Jubal, Strait of see Jūbāl, Madīq, strt., Egypt	D7	60
Jubaysho, Eth.	O9	60
Jubayt, Sud.	H9	60
Jubba (Genale), stm., Afr.	H9	56
Jubbah, Sau. Ar.	G6	48
Jubones, stm., Ec.	I3	84
Juby, Cap, c., Mor.	G4	62
Júcar (Xúquer), stm., Spain	F10	16
Juçara, Braz.	C3	79
Júcaro, Cuba	D5	94
Juchipila, Mex.	G8	90
Juchitán de Zaragoza, Mex.	I12	90
Juchnov, Russia	G18	22
Juchoviči, Bela.	E11	22
Jucuapa, El Sal.	D6	92
Jucurucu, stm., Braz.	D9	79
Jud, N.D., U.S.	C7	141
Juda, Wi., U.S.	F4	156
Judaea, hist. reg., Asia	E4	50
Judas, Punta, c., C.R.	H10	92
Judenburg, Aus.	H14	10
Judique, N.S., Can.	D8	101
Judith, stm., Mt., U.S.	C7	133
Judith, Point, c., R.I., U.S.	G4	115
Judith Basin, co., Mt., U.S.	C6	133
Judith Gap, Mt., U.S.	D7	133
Judith Island, i., N.C., U.S.	B6	140
Judith Mountains, mts., Mt., U.S.	C7	133
Judith Peak, mtn., Mt., U.S.	C7	133
Judson, Mn., U.S.	F4	130
Judson, N.D., U.S.	C4	141
Judsonia, Ar., U.S.	B4	111
Juexi, China	F10	34
Jufari, stm., Braz.	H11	84
Jugon, Fr.	D4	14
Juḥā, Sau. Ar.	F3	47
Juidongshan, China	L6	34
Juigalpa, Nic.	E9	92
Juína, stm., Braz.	E12	82
Juiz de Fora, Braz.	F7	79
Jujuy, prov., Arg.	B5	80
Jukagirskoje ploskogorje, plat., Russia	D23	28
Julesburg, Co., U.S.	A8	113
Juli, Peru	G7	82
Juliaca, Peru	F6	82
Julia Creek, Austl.	C4	70
Juliaetta, Id., U.S.	C2	119
Julian, Ca., U.S.	F5	112
Julian, W.V., U.S.	C3	155
Julianakanaal, Neth.	F8	12
Julian Alps, mts., Eur.	C8	13
Juliana Top, mtn., Sur.	F14	84
Julianehåb, Grnld.	C15	86
Jülich, Ger.	E6	10
Juliette, Ga., U.S.	C3	117
Julimes, Mex.	C7	90
Júlio de Castilhos, Braz.	E12	80
Julu, China	F3	32
Juma, Russia	I23	6
Jumay, Volcán, vol., Guat.	C5	92
Jumbilla, Peru	A3	82
Jumboo, Som.	B8	58
Jumbo Peak, mtn., Nv., U.S.	G7	135
Jumentos Cays, is., Bah.	C7	94
Jumet, Bel.	H5	12
Jumilla, Spain	G10	16
Jump, stm., Wi., U.S.	C3	156
Jump, North Fork, stm., Wi., U.S.	C3	156
Jump, South Fork, stm., Wi., U.S.	C3	156
Jumping Branch, W.V., U.S.	D4	155
Jumping Lake, l., Sask., Can.	E3	105
Jūnāgadh, India	J4	44

Name — Map Ref. — Page

Junaynah, Ra's al-, mtn., Egypt G2 48
Junction, Il., U.S. F5 120
Junction, Tx., U.S. D3 150
Junction City, Ar., U.S. D3 111
Junction City, Ga., U.S. D2 117
Junction City, Il., U.S. E4 120
Junction City, Ks., U.S. C7 123
Junction City, Ky., U.S. C5 124
Junction City, La., U.S. A3 125
Junction City, Oh., U.S. C3 142
Junction City, Or., U.S. C3 144
Junction City, Wi., U.S. D4 156
Jundiaí, Braz. G5 79
Jundiaí do Sul, Braz. G3 79
Juneau, Ak., U.S. D13 109
Juneau, Wi., U.S. E5 156
Juneau, co., Wi., U.S. E3 156
Junee, Austl. J7 70
June in Winter, Lake, l., Fl., U.S. E5 116
June Lake, Ca., U.S. D4 112
Jungar Qi, China D9 30
Jungfrau, mtn., Switz. E8 13
Junggar Pendi, China B4 30
Jungshāhi, Pak. H2 44
Juniata, Ne., U.S. D7 134
Juniata, co., Pa., U.S. F7 145
Juniata, stm., Pa., U.S. F7 145
Juniata, Raystown Branch, stm., Pa., U.S. F5 145
Junín, Arg. H8 80
Junín, Ec. H2 84
Junín, Peru D3 82
Junín, dept., Peru D4 82
Junín, Lago de, l., Peru D3 82
Junior, W.V., U.S. C5 155
Junior Lake, l., Me., U.S. C4 126
Juniper, N.B., Can. C2 101
Juniper Mountains, mts., Az., U.S. B2 110
Junipero Serra Peak, mtn., Ca., U.S. D3 112
Juniville, Fr. C11 14
Junqueirópolis, Braz. F3 79
Juntas, C.R. G9 92
Junxian, China E9 30
Juozapinės kalnas, hill, Lith. G8 22
Juparanã, Lagoa, l., Braz. E8 79
Jupilingo, stm., Guat. C5 92
Jupiter, Fl., U.S. F6 116
Jupiter Inlet, b., Fl., U.S. F6 116
Jupiter Island, i., Fl., U.S. E6 116
Juquiá, Braz. C15 80
Juquiá, Ponta do, c., Braz. C15 80
Jur, stm., Sud. M5 60
Jura, state, Switz. D7 13
Jura, dept., Fr. F12 14
Jura, mts., Eur. F13 14
Jura, i., Scot., U.K. E8 8
Juramento, Braz. D7 79
Juratiški, Bela. G8 22
Jurbarkas, Lith. F5 22
Jurf ad-Darāwīsh, Jord. G5 50
Jurga, Russia F8 28
Jurjevec, Russia D26 22
Jurjev-Pol'skij, Russia E22 22
Jūrmala, Lat. E6 22
Jurty, Russia F17 26
Juruá, Braz. I9 84
Juruá, stm., S.A. D5 76
Juruá-mirim, stm., Braz. C5 82
Juruena, stm., Braz. B12 82
Jurupari, stm., Braz. C7 82
Jur'uzan', Russia G9 26
Juscelândia, Braz. C3 79
Jusepín, Ven. C11 84
Juskatla, B.C., Can. C1 99
Jussey, Fr. E12 14
Justin, Tx., U.S. C4 150
Justiniano Posse, Arg. G7 80
Justo Daract, Arg. G6 80
Jutaí, Braz. A7 82
Jutaí, stm., Braz. D5 76
Jüterbog, Ger. D13 10
Juti, Braz. G1 79
Jutiapa, Guat. C5 92
Jutiapa, dept., Guat. C5 92
Juticalpa, Hond. C8 92
Jutiquile, Hond. C8 92
Jutland see Jylland, pen., Den. M11 6
Juva, Fin. K20 6
Juventud, Isla de la (Isla de Pinos), i., Cuba D3 94
Juxi, China H8 34
Juža, Russia E25 22
Južno-Sachalinsk, Russia H20 28
Južno-Ural'sk, Russia G10 26
Južnyj, mys, c., Russia F23 28
Jwayyā, Leb. B4 50
Jylland, reg., Den. M11 6
Jyväskylä, Fin. J19 6

K

K2 (Qogir Feng), mtn., Asia C7 44
Kaaawa, Hi., U.S. f10 118
Kaachka, Turk. J9 26
Kaachka, Turk. C15 48
Kaala, mtn., Hi., U.S. f9 118
Kaalualu Bay, b., Hi., U.S. E6 118
Kaapstad see Cape Town, S. Afr. I4 66
Kaaumakua, Puu, mtn., Hi., U.S. f10 118
Kabah, hist., Mex. G15 90
Kabale, Ug. B5 58
Kabalega Falls, wtfl, Ug. H7 56
Kabalo, Zaire C5 58
Kabambare, Zaire B5 58
Kabardino-Balkarija, state, Russia I6 26
Kabba, Nig. H13 64
Kabetogama Lake, l., Mn., U.S. B5 130
Kabinda, Zaire C4 58
Kabīr Kūh, mts., Iran E9 48
Kabkābīyah, Sud. K3 60
Kabna, Sud. H7 60
Kābol, Afg. C3 44
Kābol, stm., Asia C4 44
Kabompo, stm., Zam. D4 58
Kabongo, Zaire C5 58
Kabot, Gui. F2 64
Kabou, Togo G10 64
Kabr, Sud. L4 60
Kābul see Kābol, Afg. C3 44
Kaburuang, Pulau, i., Indon. E8 38
Kabwe (Broken Hill), Zam. D5 58
Kačanik, Yugo. G5 20
Kačerginė, Lith. G6 22
Kachchh, Gulf of, b., India I3 44
Kachemak, Ak., U.S. D9 109
Kachess Lake, res., Wa., U.S. B4 154
Kachisi, Eth. M9 60
K'achta, Russia G13 28
Kačug, Russia G13 28
Kadaiyanallūr, India H4 46
Kadanai (Kadaney), stm., Asia E2 44
Kadaney (Kadanai), stm., Asia E2 44
Kadan Kyun, i., Mya. H5 40
Kade, Ghana H9 64
Kadéï, stm., Afr. H4 56
Kadi, India I5 44
Kadiana, Mali F6 64
Kadina, Austl. I2 70
Kadiri, India E5 46
Kadirli, Tur. C4 48
Kadja, Ouadi (Wādī Kaja), val., Afr. L3 60
Kadnikov, Russia B23 22
Kadnikovskij, Russia A23 22
Kado, Nig. H14 64
Kadodo, Sud. L5 60
Kadoka, S.D., U.S. D4 148
Kadom, Russia G25 22
Kadoma, Zimb. B9 66
Kaduj, Russia B20 22
Kaduna, Nig. F13 64
Kaduna, stm., Nig. G12 64
Kāduqlī, Sud. L5 60
Kadyj, Russia D26 22
Kadykčan, Russia E21 28
Kadžerom, Russia E9 26
Kaech'ŏn, N. Kor. D13 32
Kaédi, Maur. C3 64
Kaena Point, c., Hi., U.S. B3 118
Kaesŏng, N. Kor. F14 32
Kāf, Sau. Ar. F4 48
Kafan, Arm. B9 48
Kafanchan, Nig. G14 64
Kaffraria, hist. reg., S. Afr. H9 66
Kaffrine, Sen. D2 64
Kafia Kingi, Sud. M3 60
Kafin Madaki, Nig. F14 64
Kafirévs, Ákra, c., Grc. K8 20
Kafr ad-Dawwār, Egypt B6 60
Kafr ash-Shaykh, Egypt B6 60
Kafue, stm., Zam. E5 58
Kagan, Uzb. J10 26
Kagawong, Ont., Can. B2 103
Kagaznagar, India C5 46
Kagelike, China B12 44
Kagera, stm., Afr. B6 58
Kağızman, Tur. A7 48
Kagmar, Sud. J6 60
Kagoshima, Japan P5 36
Kagoshima-wan, b., Japan P5 36
Kahakuloa, Hi., U.S. B5 118
Kahaluu, Hi., U.S. D6 118
Kahaluu, Hi., U.S. g10 118
Kahana, Hi., U.S. B4 118
Kahana Bay, b., Hi., U.S. f10 118
Kahayan, stm., Indon. F5 38
Kahemba, Zaire C3 58
Kahnūj, Iran H14 48
Kahoka, Mo., U.S. A6 132
Kahoolawe, i., Hi., U.S. C5 118
Kahramanmaraş, Tur. C4 48
Kahuku, Hi., U.S. B4 118
Kahuku Point, c., Hi., U.S. B4 118
Kahului, Hi., U.S. C5 118
Kahului Bay, b., Hi., U.S. C5 118
Kai, Kepulauan, is., Indon. G9 38
Kaiama, Nig. G11 64
Kaiapoi, N.Z. E4 72
Kaibab Indian Reservation, Az., U.S. A3 110
Kaibab Plateau, plat., Az., U.S. A3 110
Kaibito, Az., U.S. A4 110
Kaibito Plateau, plat., Az., U.S. A4 110
Kaidu, stm., China C4 30
Kaieteur Fall, wtfl, Guy. E13 84
Kaifeng, China I2 32
Kaikoura, N.Z. E4 72
Kailahun, S.L. G4 64
Kaili, China A9 40
Kailu, China C11 30
Kailua, Hi., U.S. B4 118
Kailua Bay, b., Hi., U.S. g11 118
Kailua Kona, Hi., U.S. D6 118
Kai Malino, Hi., U.S. D6 118
Kaimanawa Mountains, mts., N.Z. C5 72
Kainaliu, Hi., U.S. D6 118
Kainan, Japan M10 36
Kaipara Harbour, b., N.Z. B5 72
Kaiparowits Plateau, plat., Ut., U.S. F4 151
Kaiping, China G9 30
Kaipokok Bay, b., Newf., Can. g10 102
Kairāna, India F7 44
Kairouan, Tun. N5 18
Kaiserslautern, Ger. F7 10
Kaishantun, China A17 32
Kaišiadorys, Lith. G7 22
Kaitangata, N.Z. G2 72
Kaithal, India F7 44
Kaituma, stm., Guy. D13 84
Kaiwi Channel, strt., Hi., U.S. B4 118
Kaiyuan, China A12 32
Kaja, Wādī (Ouadi Kadja), val., Afr. L3 60
Kajaani, Fin. I20 6
Kajang, Malay. M6 40
Kajnar, Kaz. H13 26
Kaka, Cen. Afr. Rep. N4 60
Kākā, Sud. L7 60
Kakadu National Park, Austl. B6 68
Kakamas, S. Afr. G5 66
Kaka Point, c., Hi., U.S. C5 118
Kake, Ak., U.S. D13 109
Kakegawa, Japan M13 36
Kakhovs'ke vodoskhovyshche, res., Ukr. H4 26
Kākināda, India D7 46
Kako, stm., Guy. E12 84
Kakoaka, Bots. B7 66
Kakogawa, Japan M9 36
Kaktovik, Ak., U.S. A11 109
Kalaa Kebira, Tun. N5 18
Kalaallit Nunaat see Greenland, dep., N.A. B15 86
Kalaa Sghira, Tun. N5 18
Kālābagh, Pak. D4 44
Kalabo, Zam. D4 58
Kalač, Russia G6 26
Kalačinsk, Russia F12 26
Kalač-na-Donu, Russia H6 26
Kaladan, stm., Asia D2 40
Kaladar, Ont., Can. C7 103
Ka Lae, c., Hi., U.S. E6 118
Kalagwe, Mya. C4 40
Kalahari Desert, des., Afr. E5 66
Kalaheo, Hi., U.S. B2 118
Kalai-Chumb, Taj. A4 44
Kalai-Mor, Turk. D17 48
Kalajoki, Fin. I18 6
Kalakamate, Bots. C8 66
Kalām, Pak. C5 44
Kalama, Wa., U.S. C3 154
Kalámai, Grc. L6 20
Kalamazoo, Mi., U.S. F5 129
Kalamazoo, co., Mi., U.S. F5 129
Kalamazoo, stm., Mi., U.S. F5 129
Kalaoa Homesteads, Hi., U.S. D6 118
Kalasin, Thai. F7 40
Kalašnikovo, Russia D18 22
Kalāt, Pak. F2 44
Kalaupapa, Hi., U.S. B5 118
Kalaupapa Peninsula, pen., Hi., U.S. B5 118
Kalaw, Mya. D4 40
Kalawao, co., Hi., U.S. B5 118
Kal'azin, Russia D20 22
Kalb, Ra's al-, c., Yemen G6 47
Kalbā', U.A.E. B10 47
Kalbarri, Austl. E2 68
Kale, Tur. L12 20
Kaleden, B.C., Can. E8 99
Kalemie (Albertville), Zaire C5 58
Kalemyo, Mya. C3 40
Kalena, Puu, mtn., Hi., U.S. g9 118
Kaletwa, Mya. D2 40
Kaleva, Mi., U.S. D4 129
Kalevala, Russia D4 26
Kalewa, Mya. C3 40
Kálfafell, Ice. C5 6a
Kalgan see Zhangjiakou, China C2 32
Kalgin Island, i., Ak., U.S. g16 109
Kalgoorlie-Boulder, Austl. F4 68
Kali, Mali E4 64
Kaliakra, nos, c., Bul. F12 20
Kalibo, Phil. C7 38
Kalima, Zaire B5 58
Kalimantan see Borneo, i., Asia E5 38
Kálimnos, Grc. M10 20
Kālimpang, India G13 44
Kalinin see Tver', Russia E18 22
Kaliningrad (Königsberg), Russia G3 22
Kalinkoviči, Bela. I12 22
Kalinovik, Bos. F2 20
Kalispel Indian Reservation, Wa., U.S. A8 154
Kalispell, Mt., U.S. B2 133
Kalisz, Pol. D18 10
Kalkaska, Mi., U.S. D5 129
Kalkaska, co., Mi., U.S. D5 129
Kalkfontein, Bots. D5 66
Kallaste, Est. C10 22
Kallavesi, l., Fin. J20 6
Kallnach, Switz. D7 13
Kalmar, Swe. M15 6
Kalmykia see Kalmykija, state, Russia H7 26
Kalmykija, state, Russia H7 26
Kālna, India I13 44
Kalnciems, Lat. E6 22
Kalocsa, Hung. C13 18
Kalohi Channel, strt., Hi., U.S. C4 118
Kālol, India I5 44
Kaloli Point, c., Hi., U.S. D7 118
Kalomo, Zam. E5 58
Kalona, Ia., U.S. C6 122
Kalone Peak, mtn., B.C., Can. C4 99
Kalpeni Island, i., India G2 46
Kalskag, Ak., U.S. C7 109
Kaltag, Ak., U.S. C8 109
Kaltan, Russia G15 26
Kaluga, Russia G19 22
Kalundborg, Den. N12 6
Kałuszyn, Pol. C21 10
Kalutara, Sri L. I5 46
Kalvarija, Lith. G6 22
Kalyān, India C2 46
Kama, stm., Russia F8 26
Kamaishi, Japan H16 36
Kamakou, mtn., Hi., U.S. B5 118
Kamakura, Japan L14 36
Kamamaung, Mya. F4 40
Kamananui Stream, stm., Hi., U.S. f9 118
Kamanjab, Nmb. B2 66
Kamarān, i., Yemen G3 47
Kamarang, stm., S.A. E12 84
Kamas, Ut., U.S. C4 151
Kamatsi Lake, l., Sask., Can. A4 105
Kamba, Nig. F11 64
Kambam, India H4 46
Kambar, Pak. G3 44
Kambarka, Russia F8 26
Kambia, S.L. G3 64
Kamčatka, poluostrov (Kamchatka), pen., Russia F24 28
Kamčatskij zaliv, b., Russia F24 28
Kamchatka see Kamčatka, poluostrov, pen., Russia F24 28
Kâmchay Méa, Camb. I8 40
Kamčija, stm., Bul. F11 20
Kamen', Bela. F11 22
Kamen', gora, mtn., Russia D16 26
Kamenec, Bela. I6 22
Kamenjak, Rt, c., Cro. E8 18
Kamenka, Russia G6 26
Kamen'-na-Obi, Russia G8 28
Kamennogorsk, Russia K21 6
Kamensk-Ural'skij, Russia F10 26
Kameškovo, Russia E24 22
Kāmet, mtn., Asia E8 44
Kamiah, Id., U.S. C2 119
Kamiak Butte, mtn., Wa., U.S. C8 154
Kamienna Góra, Pol. E16 10
Kamieńsk, Pol. D19 10
Kamina, Zaire C5 58
Kaminaljuyú, hist., Guat. J14 90
Kaminaljuyú, hist., Guat. C4 92
Kaminoyama, Japan I15 36
Kaminskij, Russia D24 22
Kamisunagawa, Japan d17 36a
Kamloops, B.C., Can. D7 99
Kamo, Arm. A8 48
Kamoa Mountains, mts., Guy. G13 84
Kamooloa, Hi., U.S. f9 118
Kamouraska, Que., Can. B8 104
Kampala, Ug. A6 58
Kampar, Malay. L6 40
Kampar, stm., Indon. N7 40
Kampen, Neth. C8 12
Kampeska, Lake, l., S.D., U.S. C8 148
Kamphaeng Phet, Thai. F5 40
Kamp'o, S. Kor. H17 32
Kâmpóng Cham, Camb. H8 40
Kâmpóng Chhnăng, Camb. H8 40
Kâmpóng Saôm, Camb. I7 40
Kâmpóng Saôm, Chhâk, b., Camb. I7 40
Kâmpóng Thum, Camb. H8 40
Kâmpôt, Camb. I8 40
Kampsville, Il., U.S. D3 120
Kâmpŭchéa see Cambodia, ctry., Asia C4 38
Kamrar, Ia., U.S. B4 122
Kamsack, Sask., Can. F5 105
Kamskoje vodochranilišče, res., Russia F9 26
Kāmthi, India B5 46
Kamuela (Waimea), Hi., U.S. C6 118
Kámuk, Cerro, mtn., C.R. H11 92
Kam'yanets'-Podil's'kyy, Ukr. H3 26
Kamyšin, Russia G7 26
Kamyšlov, Russia F10 26
Kanab, Ut., U.S. F3 151
Kanab Creek, stm., U.S. A3 110
Kanabec, co., Mn., U.S. E5 130
Kanafis, Sud. M3 60
Kanaga Island, i., Ak., U.S. E4 109
Kanairiktok, stm., Newf., Can. g9 102
Kananga (Luluabourg), Zaire C4 58
Kanapou Bay, b., Hi., U.S. C5 118
Kanarraville, Ut., U.S. F2 151
Kanaš, Russia F7 26
Kanata, Ont., Can. B9 103
Kanauga, Oh., U.S. D3 142
Kanawha, Ia., U.S. B4 122
Kanawha, co., W.V., U.S. C3 155
Kanawha, stm., W.V., U.S. C3 155
Kanazawa, Japan K11 36
Kanchanaburi, Thai. G5 40
Kānchenjunga, mtn., Asia G13 44
Kānchipuram, India F5 46
Kandalakša, Russia D4 26
Kandalakšskaja guba, b., Russia H23 6
Kandangan, Indon. F6 38
Kandava, Lat. D5 22
Kandersteg, Switz. E8 13
Kandi, Benin F11 64
Kandi, India I13 44
Kandiāro, Pak. G3 44
Kandiyohi, Mn., U.S. E4 130
Kandiyohi, co., Mn., U.S. E3 130
Kandos, Austl. I8 70
Kandrāch, Pak. H1 44
Kandy, Sri L. I6 46
Kane, Il., U.S. D3 120
Kane, Pa., U.S. C4 145
Kane, co., Il., U.S. B5 120
Kane, co., Ut., U.S. F3 151
Kaneohe, Hi., U.S. B4 118
Kaneohe Bay, b., Hi., U.S. g10 118
Kaneohe Bay Marine Corps Air Station, mil., Hi., U.S. g10 118
Kang, Bots. D6 66
Kangal, Tur. B4 48
Kangalassy, Russia E17 28
Kangar, Malay. K6 40
Kangaroo Island, i., Austl. J2 70
Kangāvar, Iran D9 48
Kangding, China E7 30
Kangdong, N. Kor. D14 32
Kangean, Kepulauan, is., Indon. G6 38
Kanggye, N. Kor. C14 32
Kanghwa, S. Kor. F14 32
Kanghwa-man, b., S. Kor. F14 32
Kangiqsualujjuaq, Que., Can. f8 102
Kangiqsujuaq, Que., Can. f12 104
Kangirsuk, Que., Can. f12 104
Kangjin, S. Kor. I14 32
Kangley, Il., U.S. B5 120
Kangnichumike, China D9 44
Kangnŭng, S. Kor. F16 32
Kango, Gabon A2 58
Kangping, China A11 32
Kangrinboqê Feng, mtn., China E9 44
Kangshan, Tai. M9 34
Kangsŏ, N. Kor. E13 32
Kangto, mtn., Asia G15 44
Kangyidaung, Mya. F3 40
Kani, Mya. C3 40
Kaniama, Zaire C4 58
Kanin, poluostrov, pen., Russia D7 26
Kanin Nos, mys, c., Russia D6 26
Kaniva, Austl. K4 70
Kanjiža, Yugo. C4 20
Kankakee, Il., U.S. B6 120
Kankakee, co., Il., U.S. B6 120
Kankakee, stm., U.S. B5 120
Kankan, Gui. F5 64
Kankéla, Mali F6 64
Kankossa, Maur. D4 64
Kanmaw Kyun, i., Mya. I5 40
Kannapolis, N.C., U.S. B2 140
Kannauj, India G8 44
Kano, Nig. E14 64
Kanonji, Japan M8 36
Kanopolis, Ks., U.S. D5 123
Kanopolis Lake, res., Ks., U.S. D5 123
Kanorado, Ks., U.S. C1 123
Kanosh, Ut., U.S. E3 151
Kanoya, Japan P5 36
Kānpur, India G9 44
Kansas, Al., U.S. B2 108
Kansas, Il., U.S. D6 120
Kansas, Ok., U.S. A7 143
Kansas, state, U.S. D5 123
Kansas, stm., Ks., U.S. C7 123
Kansas City, Ks., U.S. C9 123
Kansas City, Mo., U.S. B3 132
Kansau, Mya. C2 40
Kanshan, China E9 34
Kansk, Russia F11 28
Kansu see Gansu, prov., China D7 30
Kant, Kyrg. I12 26
Kantang, Thai. K5 40
Kantché, Niger E14 64
Kantō-sanchi, mts., Japan K13 36
Kantunilkin, Mex. G16 90
Kanuku Mountains, mts., Guy. F13 84
Kanuma, Japan K14 36
Kanus, Nmb. F4 66
Kan'utino, Russia F16 22
Kanye, Bots. E7 66
Kanyu, Bots. C7 66
Kaohsiung, Tai. M9 34
Kaohsiunghsien, Tai. M9 34
Kaokoland, dept., Nmb. A1 66
Kaoko Veld, plat., Nmb. B1 66
Kaolack, Sen. D1 64
Kaoma, Zam. D4 58
Kaoshanpu, China E3 34
Kapaa, Hi., U.S. A2 118
Kapaau, Hi., U.S. C6 118
Kapadvanj, India I5 44
Kapanga, Zaire C4 58
Kapapa Island, i., Hi., U.S. g10 118
Kapčagaj, Kaz. I13 26
Kapčagajskoje vodochranilišče, res., Kaz. I13 26
Kapfenberg, Aus. H15 10
Kaplan, La., U.S. D3 125
Kapoe, Thai. J5 40
Kapos, stm., Hung. C13 18
Kaposvár, Hung. I17 10
Kapowsin, Wa., U.S. C3 154
Kappeln, Ger. A9 10
Kapps, Nmb. D3 66
Kaprun, Aus. H12 10
Kapsan, N. Kor. B16 32
Kapuas, stm., Indon. F4 38
Kapuas Hulu, Pegunungan, mts., Asia E5 38
Kapulena, Hi., U.S. C6 118
Kapunda, Austl. J3 70
Kapūrthala, India E6 44
Kapuskasing, Ont., Can. o19 103
Kapuvár, Hung. H17 10
Kara, stm., Afr. G10 64
Kara-Balta, Kyrg. I12 26
Karabanovo, Russia E21 22
Karabaš, Russia F10 26
Karabekaul, Turk. B18 48
Kara-Bogaz-Gol, zaliv, b., Turk. I8 26
Karabük, Tur. G14 4
Karacabey, Tur. I12 20
Karacadağ, Tur. H11 20
Karačev, Russia H18 22
Karāchi, Pak. H2 44
Karād, India D3 46
Karaganda, Kaz. H12 26
Karaginskij, ostrov, i., Russia F24 28
Karaginskij zaliv, b., Russia F24 28
Karagoš, gora, mtn., Russia G15 26
Kāraikāl, India G5 46
Kāraikkudi, India G5 46
Karaj, Iran D11 48
Karakax, stm., China B8 44
Karakelong, Pulau, i., Indon. E8 38
Karakol (Prževal'sk), Kyrg. I13 26
Karakoram Pass, Asia C7 44
Karakoram Range, mts., Asia C7 44
Karakoro, stm., Afr. D4 64
Karakumskij kanal, Turk. C16 48
Karakumy, des., Turk. J9 26
Karaman, Tur. L13 20
Karaman, Tur. C2 48
Karamay, China B3 30
Karamea Bight, N.Z. D3 72
Karamürsel, Tur. I13 20
Karamyševo, Russia D11 22
Kāranja, India B4 46
Karapınar, Tur. C2 48
Karasburg, Nmb. G4 66
Karasburg, dept., Nmb. G4 66
Kara Sea see Karskoje more, Russia C11 26
Karasjok, Nor. G19 6
Karasu, stm., Tur. B5 48
Karasuk, Russia G7 28
Karatau, Kaz. I12 26
Karatau, chrebet, mts., Kaz. I12 26
Karaton, Kaz. H8 26
Karatsu, Japan N4 36
Karauli, India G7 44
Karawang, Indon. j13 39a
Karawang, Tanjung, c., Indon. i13 39a
Karawanken, mts., Eur. C9 18
Karaye, Nig. F14 64
Karažal, Kaz. H12 26
Karbalā', Iraq E8 48
Karcag, Hung. H20 10
Kardhítsa, Grc. J5 20
Kärdla, Est. B5 22
Kardymovo, Russia G15 22
Kărdžali, Bul. H9 20
Karelia see Karelija, state, Russia E4 26
Karelia, hist. reg., Eur. J22 6
Karelija, state, Russia E4 26
Karesuando, Swe. G18 6
Kargopol', Russia E5 26
Karia-ba-Mohammed, Mor. C8 62
Kariba, Zimb. E5 58
Kariba, Lake, res., Afr. E5 58
Karibib, Nmb. C2 66
Karigasniemi, Fin. G19 6
Karimata, Kepulauan, is., Indon. F4 38
Karimata, Selat (Karimata Strait), strt., Indon. F4 38
Karīmnagar, India C5 46
Karimunjawa, Kepulauan, is., Indon. G5 38
Karin, Som. F10 56
Karis (Karjaa), Fin. K18 6
Karisimbi, Volcan, vol., Afr. B5 58
Kariya, Japan M11 36
Kārīz, Iran D16 48
Karkaralinsk, Kaz. H13 26
Karl-Marx-Stadt see Chemnitz, Ger. E12 10
Karloske, stm., Man., Can. B4 100
Karlovac, Cro. D10 18
Karlovo, Bul. G8 20
Karlovy Vary, Czech Rep. E12 10
Karlsborg, Swe. I18 6
Karlskoga, Swe. L14 6
Karlskrona, Swe. M14 6
Karlsruhe, Ger. F8 10
Karlsruhe, N.D., U.S. A5 141
Karlstad, Mn., U.S. B2 130
Karlstadt, Ger. F9 10
Karma, Niger E10 64
Karmah, Sud. H6 60
Karmel, Har (Mount Carmel), mtn., Isr. C4 50
Karmiyya, Isr. E3 50
Karnak see Al-Karnak, Egypt E7 60
Karnak, Il., U.S. F5 120
Karnāl, India F7 44
Karṇālī, stm., Asia F9 44
Karnātaka, state, India E3 46
Karnes, co., Tx., U.S. E4 150
Karnes City, Tx., U.S. E4 150
Karnobat, Bul. G10 20
Karns, Tn., U.S. n13 149
Kärnten, state, Aus. I13 10
Karonga, Mwi. C6 58
Karora, Sud. I10 60
Káros, i., Grc. M9 20
Kárpathos, i., Grc. N11 20
Karpenísion, Grc. K5 20
Karpinsk, Russia F10 26
Karpogory, Russia E6 26
Karratha, Austl. D3 68
Kars, Tur. A7 48
Karsakpaj, Kaz. H11 26
Kärsämäki, Fin. J19 6
Kārsava, Lat. E10 22
Karši, Uzb. J11 26
Karsin, Pol. B17 10
Karskije Vorota, proliv, strt., Russia C9 26
Karskoje more (Kara Sea), Russia C11 26
Kartaly, Russia G10 26
Kartuzy, Pol. A18 10
Karukuwisa, Nmb. B4 66
Karūr, India G5 46
Karval, Co., U.S. C7 113
Karviná, Czech Rep. F18 10
Kārwār, India E3 46
Karymskoje, Russia G14 28
Kas, Sud. K3 60
Kasai (Cassai), stm., Afr. B3 58
Kasaji, Zaire D4 58
Kasama, Zam. D6 58
Kasan, Uzb. B18 48
Kasane, Bots. A7 66
Kasanga, Tan. C6 58
Kasaoka, Japan M8 36
Kāsaragod, India F3 46
Kasba Lake, l., N.W. Ter., Can. D12 96
Kasba-Tadla, Mor. D7 62
Kaseda, Japan P5 36
Kasempa, Zam. D5 58
Kasenga, Zaire D5 58
Kasese, Zaire B5 58
Kāsganj, India G8 44
Kāshān, Iran K8 26
Kashgar see Kashi, China D2 30
Kashi, China F8 24
Kashi, China D2 30
Kashihara, Japan M10 36
Kashima, Japan N5 36
Kāshīpur, India F8 44
Kashiwazaki, Japan J13 36
Kāshmar, Iran D15 48
Kashmir see Jammu and Kashmīr, dep., Asia C10 42
Kashmor, Pak. F3 44
Kasigluk, Ak., U.S. C7 109
Kasilof, Ak., U.S. C9 109
Kasimov, Russia G24 22
Kašin, Russia D20 22
Kasinka, Bots. B7 66
Kašira, Russia G21 22
Kasiruta, Pulau, i., Indon. F8 38
Kaskaskia, Il., U.S. F4 120
Kaskaskia, stm., Il., U.S. D5 120
Kaskö (Kaskinen), Fin. J17 6
Kasli, Russia F10 26
Kaslo, B.C., Can. E9 99
Kasn'a, Russia F17 22
Kasongo, Zaire B5 58
Kasongo-Lunda, Zaire C3 58
Kásos, i., Grc. N10 20
Kasota, Mn., U.S. F5 130
Kaspijsk, Russia I7 26
Kaspijskij, Russia H7 26
Kasr, Ra's, c., Afr. H10 60
Kassalā, Sud. J9 60
Kassándra, pen., Grc. I7 20
Kassándras, Kólpos, b., Grc. I7 20
Kassel, Ger. D9 10
Kasserine, Tun. C15 62
Kassikaityu, stm., Guy. G13 84
Kassinger, Sud. H6 60
Kasson, Mn., U.S. F6 130
Kastamonu, Tur. G14 4
Kastoría, Grc. I5 20
Kastrávion, Tekhnití Límni, res., Grc. K5 20
Kasūr, Pak. E6 44
Kataeregi, Nig. G13 64

Name	Map Ref.	Page
Katahdin, Mount, mtn., Me., U.S.	C4	126
Katanga, hist. reg., Zaire	D5	58
Katanga, stm., Russia	F12	28
Katanning, Austl.	F3	68
Katchall Island, i., India	K2	40
Katélé, Mali	F7	64
Katepwa Beach, Sask., Can.	G4	105
Kateríni, Grc.	I6	20
Kates Needle, mtn., Ak., U.S.	m24	109
Katha, Mya.	B4	40
Katherine, Austl.	B6	68
Kāthiāwār Peninsula, pen., India	I4	44
Kathleen, Fl., U.S.	D4	116
Kāṭhmāṇḍau, Nepal	G11	44
Kathmandu see Kāṭhmāṇḍau, Nepal	G11	44
Kathrabbā, Jord.	F5	50
Katihār, India	F4	30
Katiola, C. Iv.	G7	64
Katmai, Mount, mtn., Ak., U.S.	D9	109
Katmai National Park, Ak., U.S.	D9	109
Kātmāndu see Kāṭhmāṇḍau, Nepal	G11	44
Katoomba, Austl.	I9	70
Katoúna, Grc.	K5	20
Katowice, Pol.	E19	10
Kātrīnā, Jabal, mtn., Egypt	C7	60
Katsepe, Madag.	o22	67b
Katsina, Nig.	E13	64
Katsina Ala, Nig.	H14	64
Katsina Ala, stm., Afr.	G8	54
Katsuta, Japan	K15	36
Katsuura, Japan	L15	36
Katsuyama, Japan	K11	36
Kattakurgan, Uzb.	J11	26
Kattaviá, Grc.	N11	20
Kattegat, strt., Eur.	M12	6
Katun', stm., Russia	G9	28
Katunki, Russia	E26	22
Kātwa, India	I13	44
Katwijk aan Zee, Neth.	D5	12
Katy, Tx., U.S.	r14	150
Katyn, Russia	G14	22
Kauai, co., Hi., U.S.	B1	118
Kauai, i., Hi., U.S.	A2	118
Kauai Channel, strt., Hi., U.S.	B3	118
Kau Desert, des., Hi., U.S.	D6	118
Kaufbeuren, Ger.	H10	10
Kaufman, Tx., U.S.	C4	150
Kaufman, co., Tx., U.S.	C4	150
Kauiki Head, c., Hi., U.S.	C6	118
Kaukauna, Wi., U.S.	D5	156
Kaukau Veld, plat., Afr.	B5	66
Kaula Island, i., Hi., U.S.	m15	118
Kaulakahi Channel, strt., Hi., U.S.	A2	118
Kauliranta, Fin.	H18	6
Kaumakani, Hi., U.S.	B2	118
Kaumalapau, Hi., U.S.	C5	118
Kaunakakai, Hi., U.S.	B4	118
Kauna Point, c., Hi., U.S.	D6	118
Kaunas, Lith.	G6	22
Kaura Namoda, Nig.	E13	64
Kauru, Nig.	F14	64
Kaustinen, Fin.	J18	6
Kautokeino, Nor.	G18	6
Kavacık, Tur.	J12	20
Kavajë, Alb.	H3	20
Kavála, Grc.	I8	20
Kavalerovo, Russia	I19	28
Kāvali, India	E5	46
Kavaratti Island, i., India	G2	46
Kāveri, stm., India	G5	46
Kāveri Falls, wtfl, India	F4	46
Kaverino, Russia	G24	22
Kavieng, Pap. N. Gui.	k17	68a
Kavimba, Bots.	B7	66
Kavīr, Dasht-e, des., Iran	D13	48
Kawagoe, Japan	L14	36
Kawaguchi, Japan	L14	36
Kawaihae, Hi., U.S.	C6	118
Kawaihoa Point, c., Hi., U.S.	B1	118
Kawaikini, mtn., Hi., U.S.	A2	118
Kawailoa, Hi., U.S.	f9	118
Kawailoa Beach, Hi., U.S.	f9	118
Kawambwa, Zam.	C5	58
Kawara Débé, Niger	E11	64
Kawasaki, Japan	L14	36
Kaw City, Ok., U.S.	A5	143
Kawdut, Mya.	G4	40
Kaweenakumik Lake, l., Man., Can.	C2	100
Kawela, Hi., U.S.	f9	118
Kawich Peak, mtn., Nv., U.S.	F5	135
Kawich Range, mts., Nv., U.S.	F5	135
Kaw Lake, res., Ok., U.S.	A5	143
Kawludo, Mya.	E4	40
Kawm Umbū, Egypt	E7	60
Kawthaung, Mya.	J5	40
Kaxgar, stm., China	D2	30
Kay, co., Ok., U.S.	A4	143
Kaya, Burkina	E9	64
Kayan, Mya.	F4	40
Kayan, stm., Indon.	E6	38
Kāyankulam, India	H4	46
Kaycee, Wy., U.S.	C6	157
Kayenta, Az., U.S.	A5	110
Kayes, Congo	B2	58
Kayes, Mali	D4	64
Kayford, W.V., U.S.	C3	155
Kayjay, Ky., U.S.	D6	124
Kaylor, S.D., U.S.	D8	148
Kayser Gebergte, mts., Sur.	F14	84
Kayseri, Tur.	B3	48
Kaysville, Ut., U.S.	B4	151
Kayville, Sask., Can.	H3	105
Kazachskij melkosopočnik, hills, Kaz.	H12	26
Kazachstan see Kazakhstan, ctry., Asia	H11	26
Kazačinskoje, Russia	F16	26
Kazakhstan, ctry., Asia	H11	26
Kazaki, Russia	I21	22
Kazakstan see Kazakhstan, ctry., Asia	H11	26
Kazalinsk, Kaz.	H10	26
Kazan', Russia	F7	26
Kazan, stm., N.W. Ter., Can.	D13	96
Kazandžik, Turk.	J9	26
Kazanlăk, Bul.	G9	20
Kazanovka, Russia	H21	22
Kazbek, gora, mtn.	I6	26
Kāzerūn, Iran	G11	48
Kazimierza Wielka, Pol.	E20	10
Kazincbarcika, Hung.	G20	10
Kazinka, Russia	I22	22
Kazlų Rūda, Lith.	G6	22
Kazungula, Zam.	A7	66
Kazym, stm., Russia	E5	28
Kazyr, stm., Russia	G17	26
Kcynia, Pol.	B17	10
Kdyně, Czech Rep.	F13	10
Kéa, i., Grc.	L8	20
Keaau, Hi., U.S.	D6	118
Keahiakahoe, Puu, mtn., Hi., U.S.	g10	118
Keahole Point, c., Hi., U.S.	D5	118
Kealaikahiki Channel, strt., Hi., U.S.	C5	118
Kealaikahiki Point, c., Hi., U.S.	C5	118
Kealakekua, Hi., U.S.	D6	118
Kealia, Hi., U.S.	A2	118
Keams Canyon, Az., U.S.	B5	110
Keanae, Hi., U.S.	C5	118
Keanapapa Point, c., Hi., U.S.	C4	118
Keansburg, N.J., U.S.	C4	137
Kearney, Ont., Can.	B5	103
Kearney, Mo., U.S.	B3	132
Kearney, Ne., U.S.	D6	134
Kearney, co., Ne., U.S.	D7	134
Kearneysville, W.V., U.S.	B7	155
Kearns, Ut., U.S.	C4	151
Kearny, Az., U.S.	D5	110
Kearny, N.J., U.S.	h8	137
Kearny, co., Ks., U.S.	D2	123
Kearsarge, N.H., U.S.	B4	136
Kearsarge, Mount, mtn., N.H., U.S.	D3	136
Kearsarge North, mtn., N.H., U.S.	B4	136
Keatchie, La., U.S.	B2	125
Keaton, Ky., U.S.	C7	124
Keats, Ks., U.S.	C7	123
Keauhou, Hi., U.S.	D6	118
Kebeiti, China	B8	44
Kébémer, Sen.	D1	64
Kebili, Tun.	D15	62
Kebnekaise, mtn., Swe.	H16	6
Kebri Dehar, Eth.	G9	56
Kecel, Hung.	I19	10
Kech, stm., Pak.	H17	48
Kecskemét, Hung.	I19	10
Kėdainiai, Lith.	F7	22
Kedges Straits, strt., Md., U.S.	D5	127
Kedgwick, N.B., Can.	B2	101
Kediri, Indon.	j16	39a
Kédougou, Sen.	E3	64
Kedrikí Makedhonía, prov., Grc.	I6	20
Kędzierzyn Kozle, Pol.	E18	10
Keedysville, Md., U.S.	B2	127
Keegan, Me., U.S.	A5	126
Keego Harbor, Mi., U.S.	o15	129
Keei, Hi., U.S.	D6	118
Keele Peak, mtn., Yukon, Can.	D6	96
Keeling Islands see Cocos Islands, dep., Oc.	K10	24
Keels, Newf., Can.	D5	102
Keene, Ont., Can.	C6	103
Keene, Ky., U.S.	C5	124
Keene, N.H., U.S.	E2	136
Keene, Tx., U.S.	n9	150
Keenesburg, Co., U.S.	A6	113
Keeney Knob, mtn., W.V., U.S.	D4	155
Keensburg, Il., U.S.	E6	120
Keerbergen, Bel.	F6	12
Keeseville, N.Y., U.S.	f11	139
Keesler Air Force Base, mil., Ms., U.S.	E5	131
Keetmanshoop, Nmb.	F4	66
Keet Seel Ruin, hist., Az., U.S.	A5	110
Keewatin, Ont., Can.	E4	100
Keewatin, Mn., U.S.	C5	130
Keewatin, stm., Man., Can.	A1	100
Keezletown, Va., U.S.	B4	153
Kefallinía, i., Grc.	K4	20
Kefar Blum, Isr.	B5	50
Kefar 'Eẓyon, W.B.	E4	50
Kefar Naḥum (Capernaum), hist., Isr.	C5	50
Kefar Sava, Isr.	D3	50
Keffi, Nig.	G13	64
Keffin Hausa, Nig.	E14	64
Keflavík, Ice.	B2	6a
Keftya, Eth.	K9	60
Ke Ga, Mui, c., Viet.	H10	40
Kegonsa, Lake, l., Wi., U.S.	F4	156
Kegums, Lat.	E7	22
Kehra, Est.	B8	22
Ke-hsi Mānsām, Mya.	D4	40
Keila, Est.	B7	22
Keimoes, S. Afr.	G5	66
Keiser, Ar., U.S.	B5	111
Keith, Scot., U.K.	D11	8
Keith, co., Ne., U.S.	C4	134
Keith Arm, b., N.W. Ter., Can.	C8	96
Keithsburg, Il., U.S.	B3	120
Keizer, Or., U.S.	C3	144
Kejimkujik National Park, N.S., Can.	E4	101
Kekaha, Hi., U.S.	B2	118
Kékes, mtn., Hung.	H20	10
Kekexili, China	D5	30
Kelafo, Eth.	G9	56
Kelang, Malay.	M6	40
Kelantan, stm., Malay.	L7	40
Kelegou, China	B6	32
Kelibia, Tun.	M6	18
Kell, Il., U.S.	E5	120
Keller, Tx., U.S.	n9	150
Keller, Va., U.S.	C7	153
Keller, Wa., U.S.	A7	154
Kellerberrin, Austl.	F3	68
Kellerman, Al., U.S.	B2	108
Kellerton, Ia., U.S.	D3	122
Kellett, Cape, c., N.W. Ter., Can.	B7	96
Kelley, Ia., U.S.	C4	122
Kelleys Island, i., Oh., U.S.	A3	142
Kelliher, Sask., Can.	F4	105
Kelliher, Mn., U.S.	C4	130
Kellnersville, Wi., U.S.	D6	156
Kellogg, Id., U.S.	B2	119
Kellogg, Ia., U.S.	C5	122
Kellogg, Mn., U.S.	F6	130
Kelly, Wy., U.S.	C2	157
Kelly Air Force Base, mil., Tx., U.S.	k7	150
Kelly Brook Mountain, mtn., Me., U.S.	A3	126
Kelly Island, i., De., U.S.	D4	115
Kelly Lake, B.C., Can.	B7	99
Kellyton, Al., U.S.	C3	108
Kellyville, N.H., U.S.	D2	136
Kellyville, Ok., U.S.	B5	143
Kelmė, Lith.	F5	22
Kel'mentsi, Ukr.	A10	20
Kelmet, Erit.	I10	60
Kelo, Chad	G4	56
Kelolokan, Indon.	E6	38
Kelowna, B.C., Can.	E8	99
Kelsey Lake, l., Man., Can.	C1	100
Kelseyville, Ca., U.S.	C2	112
Kelso, Mo., U.S.	D8	132
Kelso, Wa., U.S.	C3	154
Keluang, Malay.	M7	40
Kelvington, Sask., Can.	E4	105
Kelwood, Man., Can.	D2	100
Kem', Russia	E4	26
Kemalpaşa, Tur.	K11	20
Kemano, B.C., Can.	C4	99
Kemer Barajı, res., Tur.	L12	20
Kemerovo, Russia	F9	28
Kemi, Fin.	I19	6
Kemijärvi, Fin.	H20	6
Kemijoki, stm., Fin.	H19	6
Kemmerer, Wy., U.S.	E2	157
Kemnath, Ger.	F11	10
Kemnay, Man., Can.	E1	100
Kemp, Tx., U.S.	C4	150
Kemp, Lake, res., Tx., U.S.	C3	150
Kemparana, Mali	E7	64
Kempele, Fin.	I19	6
Kemper, co., Ms., U.S.	C5	131
Kemps Bay, Bah.	B6	94
Kempsey, Austl.	H10	70
Kempshall Mountain, mtn., N.Y., U.S.	A6	139
Kempten [Allgäu], Ger.	H10	10
Kempton, Il., U.S.	C5	120
Kempton, In., U.S.	D5	121
Kemptville, Ont., Can.	B9	103
Kenai, Ak., U.S.	C9	109
Kenai Fjords National Park, Ak., U.S.	D10	109
Kenai Mountains, mts., Ak., U.S.	h16	109
Kenai Peninsula, pen., Ak., U.S.	h16	109
Kenansville, Fl., U.S.	E6	116
Kenansville, N.C., U.S.	C5	140
Kenaston, Sask., Can.	F2	105
Kenbridge, Va., U.S.	D4	153
Kendal, Sask., Can.	G4	105
Kendal, S. Afr.	F9	66
Kendall, Fl., U.S.	s13	116
Kendall, Ks., U.S.	E2	123
Kendall, Wi., U.S.	E3	156
Kendall, co., Il., U.S.	B5	120
Kendall, co., Tx., U.S.	E3	150
Kendall, Cape, c., N.W. Ter., Can.	D15	96
Kendall Park, N.J., U.S.	C3	137
Kendallville, In., U.S.	B7	121
Kendari, Indon.	F7	38
Kendrāparha, India	J12	44
Kendrick, Id., U.S.	C2	119
Kenduskeag, Me., U.S.	D4	126
Kenedy, Tx., U.S.	E4	150
Kenedy, co., Tx., U.S.	F4	150
Kenel, S.D., U.S.	B5	148
Kenema, S.L.	H4	64
Kenesaw, Ne., U.S.	D7	134
Kenge, Zaire	B3	58
Kengtian, China	J8	34
Kēng Tung, Mya.	D5	40
Kenhardt, S. Afr.	G5	66
Kenilworth, Il., U.S.	h9	120
Kenilworth, Ut., U.S.	D5	151
Kenitra, Mor.	C7	62
Kenly, N.C., U.S.	B4	140
Kenmare, N.D., U.S.	A3	141
Kenmore, N.Y., U.S.	C2	139
Kenna, W.V., U.S.	C3	155
Kennaday Peak, mtn., Wy., U.S.	E6	157
Kennard, In., U.S.	E6	121
Kennard, Ne., U.S.	C9	134
Kennebago Lake, l., Me., U.S.	C2	126
Kennebec, S.D., U.S.	D5	148
Kennebec, co., Me., U.S.	D3	126
Kennebec, stm., Me., U.S.	D3	126
Kennebunk, Me., U.S.	E2	126
Kennebunkport, Me., U.S.	E2	126
Kennedy, Sask., Can.	G4	105
Kennedy, Al., U.S.	B2	108
Kennedy, Mn., U.S.	B2	130
Kennedy, Zimb.	B8	66
Kennedy, Mount, mtn., Yukon, Can.	D5	96
Kennedy Entrance, strt., Ak., U.S.	D9	109
Kenner, La., U.S.	E5	125
Kennesaw, Ga., U.S.	B2	117
Kennesaw Mountain, mtn., Ga., U.S.	C2	117
Kennesaw Mountain National Battlefield Park, Ga., U.S.	h7	117
Kennetcook, N.S., Can.	D6	101
Kennett, Mo., U.S.	E7	132
Kennett Square, Pa., U.S.	G10	145
Kennewick, Wa., U.S.	C6	154
Kenney, Il., U.S.	C4	120
Kenn Reef, rf., Austl.	D11	68
Kennydale, Wa., U.S.	e11	154
Keno, Or., U.S.	E5	144
Kénogami, Lac, l., Que., Can.	A6	104
Kenora, Ont., Can.	o16	103
Kenosha, Wi., U.S.	F6	156
Kenosha, co., Wi., U.S.	F5	156
Kenova, W.V., U.S.	C2	155
Kensal, N.D., U.S.	B7	141
Kensett, Ar., U.S.	B4	111
Kensett, Ia., U.S.	A4	122
Kensico Reservoir, res., N.Y., U.S.	g13	139
Kensington, P.E.I., Can.	C6	101
Kensington, Ct., U.S.	C4	114
Kensington, Ks., U.S.	C4	123
Kensington, Md., U.S.	B3	127
Kensington, Mn., U.S.	E3	130
Kensington, N.H., U.S.	E5	136
Kent, S.L.	G3	64
Kent, Al., U.S.	C4	108
Kent, Ct., U.S.	C2	114
Kent, Oh., U.S.	A4	142
Kent, Wa., U.S.	B3	154
Kent, co., Eng., U.K.	J14	8
Kent, co., De., U.S.	D3	115
Kent, co., Md., U.S.	B5	127
Kent, co., Mi., U.S.	E5	129
Kent, co., R.I., U.S.	D2	146
Kent, co., Tx., U.S.	C2	150
Kentau, Kaz.	I11	26
Kent Bridge, Ont., Can.	E2	103
Kent City, Mi., U.S.	E5	129
Kent Group, is., Austl.	L7	70
Kent Island, i., De., U.S.	D4	115
Kent Island, i., Md., U.S.	C5	127
Kent Junction, N.B., Can.	C4	101
Kentland, In., U.S.	C3	121
Kenton, Man., Can.	E1	100
Kenton, De., U.S.	D3	115
Kenton, Ky., U.S.	k14	124
Kenton, Oh., U.S.	B2	142
Kenton, Tn., U.S.	A2	149
Kenton, co., Ky., U.S.	B5	124
Kent Peninsula, pen., N.W. Ter., Can.	C11	96
Kent Point, c., Md., U.S.	C5	127
Kentucky, state, U.S.	C4	124
Kentucky, stm., Ky., U.S.	B5	124
Kentucky, Middle Fork, stm., Ky., U.S.	C6	124
Kentucky, North Fork, stm., Ky., U.S.	C6	124
Kentucky, South Fork, stm., Ky., U.S.	C6	124
Kentucky Dam, Ky., U.S.	e9	124
Kentucky Lake, res., U.S.	D9	106
Kentucky Ridge, mtn., Ky., U.S.	D6	124
Kentville, N.S., Can.	D5	101
Kentwood, La., U.S.	D5	125
Kentwood, Mi., U.S.	F5	129
Kenvil, N.J., U.S.	B3	137
Kenville, Man., Can.	D1	100
Kenvir, Ky., U.S.	D6	124
Kenya, ctry., Afr.	B7	58
Kenya, Mount see Kirinyaga, mtn., Kenya	B7	58
Kenyon, Mn., U.S.	F6	130
Kenyon, R.I., U.S.	F2	146
Keo, Ar., U.S.	C3	111
Keokea, Hi., U.S.	C5	118
Keokuk, Ia., U.S.	D6	122
Keokuk, co., Ia., U.S.	C5	122
Keokuk Lock and Dam, U.S.	D6	122
Keoma, Alta., Can.	D4	98
Keo Neua, Col de, Asia	E8	40
Keosauqua, Ia., U.S.	D6	122
Keota, Ia., U.S.	C6	122
Keota, Ok., U.S.	B7	143
Keowee, Lake, res., S.C., U.S.	B2	147
Kępice, Pol.	A16	10
Kępno, Pol.	D17	10
Keppel Bay, b., Austl.	D9	70
Kequan, China	G2	32
Kerala, state, India	G4	46
Kerang, Austl.	J5	70
Kerby, Or., U.S.	E3	144
Kerch, Ukr.	H5	26
Keremeos, B.C., Can.	E8	99
Keren, Erit.	J10	60
Kerend, Iran	D9	48
Kerens, Tx., U.S.	C4	150
Keret', ozero, l., Russia	I23	6
Kerewan, Gam.	E1	64
Kerguélen, Îles, is., F.S.A.T.	M10	158
Kerhonkson, N.Y., U.S.	D6	139
Kericho, Kenya	B7	58
Keri Kera, Sud.	K7	60
Kerinci, Gunung, mtn., Indon.	F3	38
Keriya, stm., China	B9	44
Kerkebet, Erit.	I9	60
Kerkenna, Îles, is., Tun.	C16	62
Kerkhoven, Mn., U.S.	E3	130
Kerki, Turk.	J11	26
Kérkira (Corfu), Grc.	J3	20
Kérkira (Corfu), i., Grc.	J3	20
Kerkrade, Neth.	G9	12
Kermadec Islands, is., N.Z.	K22	158
Kermān, Iran	F14	48
Kerman, Ca., U.S.	D3	112
Kermit, Tx., U.S.	D1	150
Kermit, W.V., U.S.	D2	155
Kermode, Mount, mtn., B.C., Can.	C2	99
Kern, co., Ca., U.S.	E4	112
Kern, stm., Ca., U.S.	E4	112
Kernersville, N.C., U.S.	A2	140
Kernville, Ca., U.S.	E4	112
Kérou, Benin	F11	64
Kerr, co., Tx., U.S.	D3	150
Kerr, Lake, l., Fl., U.S.	C5	116
Kerrobert, Sask., Can.	F1	105
Kerrville, Tx., U.S.	D3	150
Kerry, co., Ire.	I4	8
Kersey, Co., U.S.	A6	113
Kersey, Pa., U.S.	D4	145
Kershaw, S.C., U.S.	B6	147
Kershaw, co., S.C., U.S.	C6	147
Kersley, B.C., Can.	C6	99
Kerulen (Cherlen) (Herlen), stm., Asia	B10	30
Kerzaz, Alg.	F10	62
Kerzers, Switz.	E7	13
Keşan, Tur.	I10	20
Kesennuma, Japan	I16	36
Keshena, Wi., U.S.	D5	156
Keshendeh, Afg.	B2	44
Keshod, India	J4	44
Keskin, Tur.	B2	48
Keski-Suomen lääni, prov., Fin.	J19	6
Keskozero, Russia	K23	6
Kes'ma, Russia	C20	22
Kesova Gora, Russia	D20	22
Kesra, Tun.	N4	18
Kesten'ga, Russia	I22	6
Keswick, Ia., U.S.	C5	122
Keszthely, Hung.	I17	10
Ket', stm., Russia	F8	28
Keta, Ghana	I10	64
Keta, ozero, l., Russia	D10	28
Ketama, Mor.	K7	16
Ketang, China	M4	34
Ketchikan, Ak., U.S.	D13	109
Ketchum, Id., U.S.	F4	119
Ketchum, Ok., U.S.	A6	143
Kete Krachi, Ghana	H9	64
Kétou, Benin	H11	64
Kętrzyn (Rastenburg), Pol.	A21	10
Kettering, Eng., U.K.	I13	8
Kettering, Oh., U.S.	C1	142
Kettle, stm., Mn., U.S.	D6	130
Kettle Creek, stm., Pa., U.S.	D6	145
Kettle Creek Lake, res., Pa., U.S.	D6	145
Kettle Falls, Wa., U.S.	A7	154
Kettleman City, Ca., U.S.	E4	112
Kettle River, Mn., U.S.	D6	130
Keuka Lake, l., N.Y., U.S.	C3	139
Kevil, Ky., U.S.	e9	124
Kevin, Mt., U.S.	B5	133
Kew, T./C. Is.	D8	94
Kewanee, Il., U.S.	B4	120
Kewanee, Mo., U.S.	E8	132
Kewanna, In., U.S.	B5	121
Kewaskum, Wi., U.S.	E5	156
Kewaunee, Wi., U.S.	D6	156
Kewaunee, co., Wi., U.S.	D6	156
Keweenaw, co., Mi., U.S.	A2	129
Keweenaw Bay, b., Mi., U.S.	B2	129
Keweenaw Peninsula, pen., Mi., U.S.	A3	129
Keweenaw Point, c., Mi., U.S.	A3	129
Keya Paha, co., Ne., U.S.	B6	134
Keya Paha, stm., U.S.	A5	134
Keyes, Ok., U.S.	e8	143
Keyesport, Il., U.S.	E4	120
Keyhole Reservoir, res., Wy., U.S.	B8	157
Key Largo, Fl., U.S.	G6	116
Keymar, Md., U.S.	A3	127
Keyport, N.J., U.S.	C4	137
Keyser, W.V., U.S.	B6	155
Keystone, In., U.S.	C7	121
Keystone, Ia., U.S.	C5	122
Keystone, S.D., U.S.	D2	148
Keystone, W.V., U.S.	D3	155
Keystone Heights, Fl., U.S.	C4	116
Keystone Lake, res., Ok., U.S.	A5	143
Keystone Peak, mtn., Az., U.S.	F4	110
Keysville, Ga., U.S.	C4	117
Keysville, Va., U.S.	C4	153
Keytesville, Mo., U.S.	B5	132
Key West, Fl., U.S.	H5	116
Key West, Ia., U.S.	B7	122
Key West Naval Air Station, mil., Fl., U.S.	H5	116
Kezar Falls, Me., U.S.	E2	126
Kezar Lake, l., Me., U.S.	D2	126
Kezar Pond, l., Me., U.S.	D2	126
Kežmarok, Slvk.	F20	10
Kgalagadi, dept., Bots.	E5	66
Kgatleng, dept., Bots.	E8	66
Khābūr, Nahr al-, stm., Asia	D6	48
Khadki (Kirkee), India	C2	46
Khairpur, Pak.	G3	44
Khajrāho, India	H8	44
Khakassia see Chakasija, state, Russia	G15	26
Khakhea, Bots.	E6	66
Khalkhalah, Syria	B7	50
Khálki, i., Grc.	M11	20
Khalkidhikí, hist. reg., Grc.	I7	20
Khalkís, Grc.	K7	20
Khalūf, Oman	D11	47
Khambhāliya, India	I3	44
Khambhāt, India	I5	44
Khambhāt, Gulf of, b., India	J5	44
Khāmgaon, India	B4	46
Khamir, Yemen	F3	47
Khamīs Mushayṭ, Sau. Ar.	E3	47
Khamkeut, Laos	E8	40
Khammam, India	D6	46
Khānābād, Afg.	B3	44
Khān al-Baghdādī, Iraq	E7	48
Khānaqīn, Iraq	D8	48
Khancoban, Austl.	K8	70
Khandwa, India	J7	44
Khānewāl, Pak.	E4	44
Khāngarh, Pak.	F4	44
Khaniá, Grc.	N8	20
Khānpur, Pak.	F4	44
Khān Yūnus, Gaza	F2	50
Kharagpur, India	I12	44
Kharānoq, Iran	E13	48
Kharg Island see Khārk, Jazīreh-ye, i., Iran	G11	48
Khargon, India	J6	44
Khāriān Cantonment, Pak.	D5	44
Khārk, Jazīreh-ye, i., Iran	G11	48
Kharkiv, Ukr.	G5	26
Kharkov see Kharkiv, Ukr.	G5	26
Khartoum see Al-Kharṭūm, Sud.	J7	60
Khartoum North see Al-Kharṭūm Baḥrī, Sud.	J7	60
Khartum see Al-Kharṭūm, Sud.	J7	60
Khasebake, Bots.	C7	66
Khāsh, Afg.	F17	48
Khāsh, Iran	G16	48
Khashm al-Qirbah, Sud.	J8	60
Khatt, Oued al, val., W. Sah.	G4	62
Khawsa, Mya.	G4	40
Khemis, Alg.	B12	62
Khemmarat, Thai.	F8	40
Khenchla, Alg.	C14	62
Khenifra, Mor.	D8	62
Kherrata, Alg.	B13	62
Kherson, Ukr.	H4	26
Khíos, Grc.	K10	20
Khíos (Chios), i., Grc.	K10	20
Khirbat 'Awwād, Syria	D7	50
Khlong Thom, Thai.	K5	40
Khmel'nyts'kyy, Ukr.	H3	26
Kholm, Afg.	B2	44
Khomeyn, Iran	E11	48
Khomeynīshahr, Iran	E11	48
Khomodimo, Bots.	D6	66
Khon Kaen, Thai.	F7	40
Khóra, Grc.	L5	20
Khorramābād, Iran	E10	48
Khorramshahr, Iran	F10	48
Khossanto, Sen.	E4	64
Khotyn, Ukr.	A10	20
Khouribga, Mor.	D7	62
Khowst, Afg.	D3	44
Khuff, Sau. Ar.	B4	47
Khugaung, Mya.	A5	40
Khuis, Bots.	F5	66
Khu Khan, Thai.	G8	40
Khulna, Bngl.	I13	44
Khūnjerāb Pass, Asia	B6	44
Khurai, India	H8	44
Khurīyā Murīyā, Jazā'ir, is., Oman	F10	47
Khurja, India	F7	44
Khust, Ukr.	H2	26
Khuzdār, Pak.	G2	44
Khvāf, Iran	D16	48
Khvor, Iran	E13	48
Khvormūj, Iran	G11	48
Khvoy, Iran	B8	48
Khwae Noi, stm., Thai.	G5	40
Khyber Pass, Asia	C4	44
Khyriv, Ukr.	F22	10
Kiama, Austl.	J9	70
Kiamichi, stm., Ok., U.S.	C6	143
Kiamika, stm., Que., Can.	C2	104
Kiana, Ak., U.S.	B7	109
Kiangarow, Mount, mtn., Austl.	F9	70
Kiangsi see Jiangxi, prov., China	F10	30
Kiangsu see Jiangsu, prov., China	E10	30
Kiawah Island, i., S.C., U.S.	F7	147
Kibangou, Congo	B2	58
Kibombo, Zaire	B5	58
Kibre Mengist, Eth.	O10	60
Kičevo, Mac.	H4	20
Kickamuit, stm., R.I., U.S.	D5	146
Kickapoo, stm., Wi., U.S.	E3	156
Kickapoo, Lake, res., Tx., U.S.	C3	150
Kickapoo Creek, stm., Il., U.S.	C4	120
Kickapoo Indian Reservation, Ks., U.S.	C8	123
Kicking Horse Pass, Can.	D2	99
Kidal, Mali	B10	64
Kidder, Mo., U.S.	B3	132
Kidder, S.D., U.S.	B8	143
Kidder, co., N.D., U.S.	C6	141
Kidira, Sen.	D3	64
Kiefer, Ok., U.S.	B5	143
Kiel, Ger.	A10	10
Kiel, Wi., U.S.	E5	156
Kiel Canal see Nord-Ostsee-Kanal, Ger.	A9	10
Kielce, Pol.	E20	10
Kieler Bucht, b., Ger.	A10	10
Kiester, Mn., U.S.	G5	130
Kiev see Kyyiv, Ukr.	G4	26
Kiffa, Maur.	C4	64
Kifisiá, Grc.	K7	20
Kifrī, Iraq	D8	48
Kigali, Rw.	B6	58
Kigille, Sud.	M8	60
Kigoma, Tan.	B5	58
Kihei, Hi., U.S.	C5	118
Kihniö, Fin.	J18	6
Kihnu, i., Est.	C7	22
Kiholo Bay, b., Hi., U.S.	D5	118
Kii-suidō, strt., Japan	N9	36
Kikerino, Russia	B12	22
Kikinda, Yugo.	D4	20
Kikládhes (Cyclades), is., Grc.	L9	20
Kikori, Pap. N. Gui.	G11	38
Kikwit, Zaire	C3	58
Kila, Mt., U.S.	B2	133
Kilambé, Cerro, mtn., Nic.	D9	92
Kilauea, Hi., U.S.	A2	118
Kilauea Crater, crat., Hi., U.S.	D6	118
Kilauea Point, c., Hi., U.S.	A2	118
Kilbourne, Il., U.S.	C4	120
Kilbourne, La., U.S.	B4	125
Kilburn, N.B., Can.	C2	101
Kilchu, N. Kor.	C17	32
Kilcoy, Austl.	F10	70
Kildare, Ire.	H7	8
Kildare, co., Ire.	H7	8
Kil'din, ostrov, i., Russia	G24	6
Kil'dinstroj, Russia	G23	6
Kilgore, Tx., U.S.	C5	150
Kilibo, Benin	G11	64
Kilikollūr, India	H4	46
Kilimanjaro, mtn., Tan.	B7	58
Kilimavony, Madag.	s20	67b
Kilingi-Nõmme, Est.	C7	22
Kilis, Tur.	C4	48
Kiliya, Ukr.	D13	20
Kilkenny, Ire.	I6	8
Kilkenny, Mn., U.S.	F5	130
Kilkenny, co., Ire.	I6	8
Kilkís, Grc.	H6	20
Killaloe, Ire.	I5	8
Killaloe Station, Ont., Can.	B7	103
Killaly, Sask., Can.	G4	105
Killam, Alta., Can.	C5	98
Killarney, Man., Can.	E2	100
Killarney, Ire.	I4	8
Killarney Provincial Park, Ont., Can.	A3	103
Killbuck, Oh., U.S.	B4	142
Killdeer, N.D., U.S.	B3	141
Killdeer Mountains, mts., N.D., U.S.	B3	141
Killeen, Tx., U.S.	D4	150
Killen, Al., U.S.	A2	108
Killian, La., U.S.	h10	125
Killik, stm., Ak., U.S.	B9	109
Killington Peak, mtn., Vt., U.S.	D3	152
Killinkoski, Fin.	J18	6

Name	Map Ref.	Page
Killona, La., U.S.	h11	125
Kilmarnock, Scot., U.K.	F9	8
Kilmarnock, Va., U.S.	C6	153
Kilmichael, Ms., U.S.	B4	131
Kiln, Ms., U.S.	E4	131
Kilomines, Zaire	A6	58
Kilosa, Tan.	C7	58
Kilpisjärvi, Fin.	G17	6
Kilrush, Ire.	I4	8
Kilttān Island, i., India	G2	46
Kilwa, Zaire	C5	58
Kim, stm., Cam.	G9	54
Kimba, Austl.	I2	70
Kimball, Mn., U.S.	E4	130
Kimball, Ne., U.S.	C2	134
Kimball, S.D., U.S.	D7	148
Kimball, W.V., U.S.	D3	155
Kimball, co., Ne., U.S.	C2	134
Kimball, Mount, mtn., Ak., U.S.	C11	109
Kimballton, Ia., U.S.	C2	122
Kimberley, B.C., Can.	E9	99
Kimberley, S. Afr.	G7	66
Kimberley Plateau, plat., Austl.	C5	68
Kimberling City, Mo., U.S.	E4	132
Kimberlin Heights, Tn., U.S.	n14	149
Kimberly, Al., U.S.	B3	108
Kimberly, Id., U.S.	G4	119
Kimberly, W.V., U.S.	m13	155
Kimberly, Wi., U.S.	h9	156
Kimble, co., Tx., U.S.	D3	150
Kimbrough, Al., U.S.	C2	108
Kimch'aek (Sŏngjin), N. Kor.	C17	32
Kimch'ŏn, S. Kor.	G16	32
Kimito (Kemiö), Fin.	K18	6
Kimiwan Lake, l., Alta., Can.	B2	98
Kimje, S. Kor.	H14	32
Kimmell, In., U.S.	B6	121
Kimovsk, Russia	H21	22
Kimry, Russia	E20	22
Kinabalu, Gunong, mtn., Malay.	D6	38
Kinbasket Lake, res., B.C., Can.	D8	99
Kinburn, Ont., Can.	B8	103
Kincaid, Sask., Can.	H2	105
Kincaid, Il., U.S.	D4	120
Kincaid, Ks., U.S.	D8	123
Kincaid, W.V., U.S.	m13	155
Kincaid, Lake, res., Il., U.S.	D4	120
Kincaid Knob, mtn., W.V., U.S.	k11	155
Kincardine, Ont., Can.	C3	103
Kinchafoonee Creek, stm., Ga., U.S.	E2	117
Kincheloe Air Force Base, mil., Mi., U.S.	B6	129
Kindberg, Aus.	H15	10
Kinde, Mi., U.S.	E8	129
Kinder, La., U.S.	D3	125
Kinderhook, Il., U.S.	D2	120
Kinderhook, N.Y., U.S.	C7	139
Kindersley, Sask., Can.	F1	105
Kindia, Gui.	F3	64
Kindred, N.D., U.S.	C9	141
Kindu, Zaire	B5	58
Kinel', Russia	G8	26
Kineo, Mount, mtn., Me., U.S.	C3	126
Kinešma, Russia	D25	22
King, N.C., U.S.	A2	140
King, Wi., U.S.	D4	156
King, co., Tx., U.S.	C2	150
King, co., Wa., U.S.	B3	154
King and Queen, co., Va., U.S.	C6	153
Kingaroy, Austl.	F9	70
King City, Ca., U.S.	D3	112
King City, Mo., U.S.	A3	132
King Cove, Ak., U.S.	E7	109
Kingfield, Me., U.S.	D2	126
Kingfisher, Ok., U.S.	B4	143
Kingfisher, co., Ok., U.S.	B3	143
King George, Va., U.S.	B5	153
King George, co., Va., U.S.	B5	153
King George Island, i., Ant.	B1	73
King George Islands, is., N.W. Ter., Can.	E17	96
King Hill, Id., U.S.	F3	119
Kingisepp, Russia	B11	22
King Island, i., Austl.	L6	70
King Island, i., B.C., Can.	C4	99
King Lear Peak, mtn., Nv., U.S.	B3	135
King Leopold Ranges, mts., Austl.	C5	68
Kingman, Alta., Can.	C4	98
Kingman, Az., U.S.	B1	110
Kingman, In., U.S.	E3	121
Kingman, Ks., U.S.	E5	123
Kingman, Me., U.S.	C4	126
Kingman, co., Ks., U.S.	E5	123
Kingman Reef, rf., Oc.	H23	158
King Mountain, mtn., Ok., U.S.	C2	143
King Mountain, mtn., Or., U.S.	D8	144
King Mountain, mtn., Or., U.S.	E3	144
King of Prussia, Pa., U.S.	F11	145
King Peak, mtn., Ca., U.S.	B1	112
Kings, Il., U.S.	A4	120
Kings, Ms., U.S.	C3	131
Kings, co., Ca., U.S.	D4	112
Kings, co., N.Y., U.S.	E7	139
Kings, stm., Ar., U.S.	A2	111
Kings, stm., Ca., U.S.	D4	112
Kings, stm., Nv., U.S.	B3	135
King Salmon, Ak., U.S.	D8	109
Kingsburg, Ca., U.S.	D4	112
Kingsbury, In., U.S.	A4	121
Kingsbury, co., S.D., U.S.	C8	148
Kings Canyon National Park, Ca., U.S.	D4	112
Kingsclear, N.B., Can.	D3	101
Kingscote, Austl.	J2	70
Kingsdown, Ks., U.S.	E4	123
Kingsey-Falls, Que., Can.	D5	104
Kingsford, Mi., U.S.	C2	129
Kingsgate, B.C., Can.	E9	99
Kingsland, Ar., U.S.	D3	111
Kingsland, Ga., U.S.	F5	117
Kingsland, Tx., U.S.	D3	150
Kingsley, Ia., U.S.	B2	122
Kingsley, Mi., U.S.	D5	129
Kingsley Dam, Ne., U.S.	C4	134
King's Lynn, Eng., U.K.	I14	8
Kings Mills, Oh., U.S.	C1	142
Kings Mountain, N.C., U.S.	B1	140
King Solomon's Mines see Mikhrot Shelomo Hamelekh, hist., Isr.	I3	50
King Sound, strt., Austl.	C4	68
Kings Park West, Va., U.S.	*B5	153
Kings Peak, mtn., Ut., U.S.	C5	151
King's Point, Newf., Can.	D3	102
Kingsport, Tn., U.S.	C11	149
Kingston, Ont., Can.	C8	103
Kingston, Jam.	E6	94
Kingston, N.Z.	F2	72
Kingston, Ar., U.S.	A2	111
Kingston, Ga., U.S.	B2	117
Kingston, Id., U.S.	B2	119
Kingston, Il., U.S.	A5	120
Kingston, Ky., U.S.	C5	124
Kingston, Ma., U.S.	C6	128
Kingston, Mi., U.S.	E7	129
Kingston, Mo., U.S.	B3	132
Kingston, N.H., U.S.	E4	136
Kingston, N.J., U.S.	C3	137
Kingston, N.Y., U.S.	D6	139
Kingston, Oh., U.S.	C3	142
Kingston, Ok., U.S.	D5	143
Kingston, Pa., U.S.	D10	145
Kingston, R.I., U.S.	F3	146
Kingston, Tn., U.S.	D9	149
Kingston, Wi., U.S.	E4	156
Kingston Southeast, Austl.	K3	70
Kingston Springs, Tn., U.S.	A4	149
Kingston upon Hull, Eng., U.K.	H13	8
Kingstown, St. Vin.	H14	94
Kingstown, Md., U.S.	B5	127
Kingstree, S.C., U.S.	D8	147
Kingsville, Ont., Can.	E2	103
Kingsville, Md., U.S.	B5	127
Kingsville, Mo., U.S.	C3	132
Kingsville (North Kingsville), Oh., U.S.	A5	142
Kingsville, Tx., U.S.	F4	150
Kingsville Naval Air Station, mil., Tx., U.S.	F4	150
Kingswood, Ky., U.S.	C3	124
King William, co., Va., U.S.	C5	153
King William Island, i., N.W. Ter., Can.	C13	96
King William's Town, S. Afr.	I8	66
Kingwood, Tx., U.S.	q14	150
Kingwood, W.V., U.S.	B5	155
Kinistino, Sask., Can.	E3	105
Kinkaid Lake, res., Il., U.S.	F4	120
Kinkony, Lac, l., Madag.	p21	67b
Kinkora, P.E.I., Can.	C6	101
Kinley, Sask., Can.	E2	105
Kin-li-chee, Az., U.S.	B6	110
Kinloch, Mo., U.S.	f13	132
Kinmount, Ont., Can.	C6	103
Kinmundy, Il., U.S.	E5	120
Kinnaird Head, c., Scot., U.K.	D11	8
Kinnear, Wy., U.S.	C4	157
Kinnelon, N.J., U.S.	B4	137
Kinneret, Yam (Sea of Galilee), l., Isr.	C5	50
Kinney, co., Tx., U.S.	E2	150
Kinross, P.E.I., Can.	C7	101
Kinsale, Va., U.S.	B6	153
Kinsale, Old Head of, c., Ire.	J5	8
Kinsella, Alta., Can.	C5	98
Kinsey, Al., U.S.	D4	108
Kinshasa (Léopoldville), Zaire	B3	58
Kinsley, Ks., U.S.	E4	123
Kinsman, Oh., U.S.	A5	142
Kinston, Al., U.S.	D3	108
Kinston, N.C., U.S.	B5	140
Kinta, Ok., U.S.	B6	143
Kintampo, Ghana	G9	64
Kintyre, pen., Scot., U.K.	F8	8
Kintyre, Mull of, c., Scot., U.K.	F8	8
Kinuso, Alta., Can.	B3	98
Kinyeti, mtn., Sud.	H7	56
Kinzua, Or., U.S.	C6	144
Kiosk, Ont., Can.	A6	103
Kiowa, Co., U.S.	B6	113
Kiowa, Ks., U.S.	E5	123
Kiowa, Ok., U.S.	C6	143
Kiowa, co., Co., U.S.	C8	113
Kiowa, co., Ks., U.S.	E4	123
Kiowa, co., Ok., U.S.	C2	143
Kiowa Creek, stm., Co., U.S.	B6	113
Kiowa Creek, stm., Ok., U.S.	A1	143
Kipapa Stream, stm., Hi., U.S.	g9	118
Kipengere Range, mts., Tan.	C6	58
Kipling, Sask., Can.	G4	105
Kipling, Mi., U.S.	C3	129
Kipnuk, Ak., U.S.	C7	109
Kipp, Ks., U.S.	D6	123
Kipushi, Zaire	D5	58
Kirane, Mali	D4	64
Kirazlı, Tur.	I10	20
Kirby, Ar., U.S.	C2	111
Kirby, Wy., U.S.	C4	157
Kirbyville, Tx., U.S.	D6	150
Kirchberg, Ger.	F9	10
Kirchheim, Ger.	G9	10
Kirchheimbolanden, Ger.	F8	10
Kirchmöser, Ger.	C12	10
Kirchschlag in der Buckligen Welt, Aus.	H16	10
Kirejevsk, Russia	H20	22
Kirenga, stm., Russia	F13	28
Kirensk, Russia	F13	28
Kirghizia see Kyrgyzstan, ctry., Asia	I13	26
Kirgizskij chrebet, mts., Asia	I12	26
Kiri, Zaire	B3	58
Kiribati, ctry., Oc.	F24	2
Kırıkhan, Tur.	C4	48
Kırıkkale, Tur.	B2	48
Kirillov, Russia	B21	22
Kirillovskoje, Russia	A12	22
Kirin see Jilin, China	C12	30
Kirin see Jilin, prov., China	C12	30
Kirinyaga, mtn., Kenya	B7	58
Kiriši, Russia	B15	22
Kiriwina Islands, is., Pap. N. Gui.	A10	68
Kirk, Co., U.S.	B8	113
Kırkağaç, Tur.	J11	20
Kirkcaldy, Scot., U.K.	E10	8
Kirkcudbright, Scot., U.K.	G9	8
Kirkenes, Nor.	G22	6
Kirkersville, Oh., U.S.	C3	142
Kirkfield, Ont., Can.	C5	103
Kirkjubæjarklaustur, Ice.	C4	6a
Kirkland, Al., U.S.	D2	108
Kirkland, Il., U.S.	A5	120
Kirkland, Wa., U.S.	B3	154
Kirkland Lake, Ont., Can.	o19	103
Kırklareli, Tur.	H11	20
Kirklin, In., U.S.	D5	121
Kirkpatrick, Mount, mtn., Ant.	D8	73
Kirksey, Ky., U.S.	f9	124
Kirksville, Ky., U.S.	C5	124
Kirksville, Mo., U.S.	A5	132
Kirkton, Ont., Can.	D3	103
Kirkūk, Iraq	D8	48
Kirkwall, Scot., U.K.	C11	8
Kirkwood, S. Afr.	I7	66
Kirkwood, De., U.S.	B3	115
Kirkwood, Il., U.S.	C3	120
Kirkwood, Mo., U.S.	f13	132
Kiron, Ia., U.S.	B2	122
Kirov, Russia	G17	22
Kirov, Russia	F7	26
Kirovakan, Arm.	I6	26
Kirovgrad, Russia	F10	26
Kirovohrad, Ukr.	H4	26
Kirovsk, Bela.	H12	22
Kirovsk, Russia	B14	22
Kirovsk, Russia	D4	26
Kirovskij, Kaz.	I13	26
Kirs, Russia	F8	26
Kirsanov, Russia	I25	22
Kırşehir, Tur.	B3	48
Kīrthar Range, mts., Pak.	G2	44
Kirtland, N.M., U.S.	A1	138
Kirtland Air Force Base, mil., N.M., U.S.	k7	138
Kiruna, Swe.	H17	6
Kirwin, Ks., U.S.	C4	123
Kirwin Reservoir, res., Ks., U.S.	C4	123
Kiryū, Japan	K14	36
Kiržač, Russia	E21	22
Kisa, Swe.	M14	6
Kisangani (Stanleyville), Zaire	A5	58
Kisarazu, Japan	L14	36
K.I. Sawyer Air Force Base, mil., Mi., U.S.	B3	129
Kisbey, Sask., Can.	H4	105
Kisel'ovsk, Russia	G9	28
Kishanganj, India	G12	44
Kishangarh Bās, India	G6	44
Kishi, Nig.	G11	64
Kishinev see Chişinău, Mol.	B12	20
Kishiwada, Japan	M10	36
Kishorganj, Bngl.	H14	44
Kishwaukee, stm., Il., U.S.	A5	120
Kisii, Kenya	B6	58
Kisiwa Creek, stm., Ks., U.S.	g11	123
Kiska Island, i., Ak., U.S.	E3	109
Kiskittogisu Lake, l., Man., Can.	B2	100
Kiskunfélegyháza, Hung.	I19	10
Kiskunhalas, Hung.	I19	10
Kiskunmajsa, Hung.	I19	10
Kislovodsk, Russia	I6	26
Kismaayo, Som.	B8	58
Kismet, Ks., U.S.	E3	123
Kiso-sammyaku, mts., Japan	L12	36
Kissee Mills, Mo., U.S.	E4	132
Kissidougou, Gui.	G4	64
Kissimmee, Fl., U.S.	D5	116
Kissimmee, stm., Fl., U.S.	E5	116
Kissimmee, Lake, l., Fl., U.S.	E5	116
Kissimmee Park, Fl., U.S.	D5	116
Kississing Lake, l., Man., Can.	B1	100
Kistler, W.V., U.S.	D3	155
Kisújszállás, Hung.	H20	10
Kisumu, Kenya	B6	58
Kisvárda, Hung.	G22	10
Kita, Mali	E5	64
Kita-Daitō-jima, i., Japan	F13	30
Kitaibaraki, Japan	K15	36
Kitakata, Japan	J14	36
Kitakyūshū, Japan	N5	36
Kitale, Kenya	A7	58
Kitami, Japan	d18	36a
Kitami-sanchi, mts., Japan	c17	36a
Kit Carson, Co., U.S.	C8	113
Kit Carson, co., Co., U.S.	B8	113
Kitchener, Ont., Can.	D4	103
Kite, Ga., U.S.	D4	117
Kiteiyab, Sud.	I7	60
Kíthira, Grc.	M7	20
Kíthira, i., Grc.	M6	20
Kíthnos, i., Grc.	L8	20
Kitimat, B.C., Can.	B3	99
Kitsap, co., Wa., U.S.	B3	154
Kitscoty, Alta., Can.	C5	98
Kitsman', Ukr.	A9	20
Kittanning, Pa., U.S.	E2	145
Kittatinny Mountain, mtn., U.S.	B2	137
Kittery, Me., U.S.	E2	126
Kittery Point, Me., U.S.	E2	126
Kittilä, Fin.	H19	6
Kittitas, Wa., U.S.	C5	154
Kittitas, co., Wa., U.S.	B4	154
Kittitas Valley, val., Wa., U.S.	B5	154
Kitts, Ky., U.S.	D6	124
Kitts Hummock, De., U.S.	D4	115
Kittson, co., Mn., U.S.	B2	130
Kitty Hawk, N.C., U.S.	A7	140
Kitty Hawk Bay, b., N.C., U.S.	A7	140
Kitui, Kenya	B7	58
Kitwanga, B.C., Can.	B3	99
Kitwe, Zam.	D5	58
Kitwitwi, Nmb.	A4	66
Kitzbühel, Aus.	H12	10
Kitzingen, Ger.	F10	10
Kiukiang see Jiujiang, China	F4	34
Kivalina, Ak., U.S.	B7	109
Kiviõli, Est.	B9	22
Kivu, Lac, l., Afr.	B5	58
Kıyıköy, Tur.	H12	20
Kizel, Russia	F9	26
Kızıl, stm., Tur.	A2	48
Kızıltepe, Tur.	C6	48
Kizl'ar, Russia	I7	26
Kizyl-Arvat, Turk.	J9	26
Kizyl-Atrek, Turk.	J8	26
Kizyl-Su, Turk.	B12	48
Kjustendil, Bul.	G6	20
Kladanj, Bos.	E2	20
Kladno, Czech Rep.	E14	10
Klagenfurt, Aus.	I14	10
Klagetoh, Az., U.S.	B6	110
Klaipėda (Memel), Lith.	F4	22
Klaksvík, Faer. Is.	D8	6b
Klamath, Ca., U.S.	B1	112
Klamath, co., Or., U.S.	E5	144
Klamath, stm., U.S.	B2	112
Klamath Falls, Or., U.S.	E5	144
Klamath Glen, Ca., U.S.	B2	112
Klamath Mountains, mts., U.S.	E2	144
Klangpi, Mya.	C2	40
Klarälven, stm., Eur.	K13	6
Kl'asticy, Bela.	F11	22
Klatovy, Czech Rep.	F13	10
Klawer, S. Afr.	H4	66
Klawock, Ak., U.S.	D13	109
Kl'az'ma, stm., Russia	E25	22
Kleberg, co., Tx., U.S.	F4	150
Kleck, Bela.	H9	22
Kleena Kleene, B.C., Can.	D5	99
Klemme, Ia., U.S.	A4	122
Klerksdorp, S. Afr.	F8	66
Klet', mtn., Czech Rep.	G14	10
Kletn'a, Russia	H16	22
Kleve, Ger.	D6	10
Kličev, Bela.	H12	22
Klickitat, Wa., U.S.	D4	154
Klickitat, co., Wa., U.S.	D4	154
Klickitat, stm., Wa., U.S.	C4	154
Klimoviči, Bela.	H14	22
Klimovo, Russia	I15	22
Klimovsk, Russia	F20	22
Klin, Russia	E19	22
Klincy, Russia	I15	22
Klipplaat, S. Afr.	I7	66
Klishkivtsi, Ukr.	A10	20
Kłobuck, Pol.	E18	10
Kłodzko, Pol.	E16	10
Klondike, hist. reg., Yukon, Can.	D5	96
Klondike Gold Rush National Historical Park, Ak., U.S.	k22	109
Klosterneuburg, Aus.	G16	10
Klosters, Switz.	E12	13
Kloten, Switz.	D10	13
Klötze, Ger.	C11	10
Klotzville, La., U.S.	h9	125
Klouto, Togo	H10	64
Kluane Lake, l., Yukon, Can.	D5	96
Kl'učevskaja Sopka, vulkan, vol., Russia	F24	28
Kl'uči, Russia	F24	28
Kluczbork, Pol.	E18	10
Klukwan, Ak., U.S.	k22	109
Klutina Lake, l., Ak., U.S.	g19	109
Knapp, Wi., U.S.	D1	156
Knapp Creek, stm., W.V., U.S.	C5	155
Knäred, Swe.	M13	6
Kn'ažji Gory, Russia	E18	22
Knee Lake, l., Man., Can.	B4	100
Knevicy, Russia	D15	22
Kneža, Bul.	F8	20
Knič, Yugo.	F4	20
Knife, stm., N.D., U.S.	B3	141
Knife River, Mn., U.S.	D7	130
Knifley, Ky., U.S.	C4	124
Knightdale, N.C., U.S.	B4	140
Knight Inlet, b., B.C., Can.	D5	99
Knight Island, i., Ak., U.S.	g18	109
Knights Landing, Ca., U.S.	C3	112
Knightstown, In., U.S.	E6	121
Knightsville, In., U.S.	E3	121
Knightville Reservoir, res., Ma., U.S.	B2	128
Knin, Cro.	E11	18
Knittelfeld, Aus.	H14	10
Knob Creek, stm., Ky., U.S.	g11	124
Knobel, Ar., U.S.	A5	111
Knobly Mountain, mtn., W.V., U.S.	B5	155
Knob Noster, Mo., U.S.	C4	132
Knokke-Heist, Bel.	F3	12
Knollwood, Ct., U.S.	D6	114
Knollwood, W.V., U.S.	m12	155
Knops Pond, l., Ma., U.S.	f9	128
Knott, co., Ky., U.S.	C6	124
Knotts Island, N.C., U.S.	A7	140
Knottsville, Ky., U.S.	C3	124
Knox, In., U.S.	B4	121
Knox, Pa., U.S.	D2	145
Knox, co., Il., U.S.	B3	120
Knox, co., In., U.S.	G3	121
Knox, co., Ky., U.S.	D6	124
Knox, co., Me., U.S.	D4	126
Knox, co., Mo., U.S.	A5	132
Knox, co., Ne., U.S.	B8	134
Knox, co., Oh., U.S.	B3	142
Knox, co., Tn., U.S.	C10	149
Knox, co., Tx., U.S.	C3	150
Knox, Cape, c., B.C., Can.	B1	99
Knox City, Mo., U.S.	A5	132
Knox City, Tx., U.S.	C3	150
Knox Coast, Ant.	B6	73
Knoxville, Ar., U.S.	B2	111
Knoxville, Ga., U.S.	D3	117
Knoxville, Il., U.S.	C3	120
Knoxville, Ia., U.S.	C4	122
Knoxville, Tn., U.S.	D10	149
Knysna, S. Afr.	J6	66
Knyszyn, Pol.	B22	10
Kobar Sink, depr., Eth.	F9	56
Kobayashi, Japan	P5	36
Kōbe, Japan	M10	36
København (Copenhagen), Den.	N13	6
Koblenz, Ger.	E7	10
Koboža, Russia	C18	22
Kobrin, Bela.	I7	22
Kobrinskoje, Russia	B13	22
Kobuk, stm., Ak., U.S.	B8	109
Kobuk Valley National Park, Ak., U.S.	B8	109
Kobylin, Pol.	D17	10
Kočani, Mac.	H6	20
Kočečum, stm., Russia	D12	28
Kočetovka, Russia	I23	22
Kočevje, Slvn.	D9	13
Kŏch'ang, S. Kor.	H14	32
Kochanovo, Bela.	G13	22
Koch Bihār, India	G13	44
Kōchi, Japan	N8	36
Kochma, Russia	E24	22
Koch Peak, mtn., Mt., U.S.	E5	133
Kodaikānal, India	G4	46
Kodak, Ky., U.S.	C6	124
Kodāri, Nepal	G11	44
Kodiak, Ak., U.S.	D9	109
Kodiak Island, i., Ak., U.S.	D9	109
Kodino, Russia	J26	6
Kodok, Sud.	M7	60
Kodyma, Ukr.	A13	20
Koekelare, Bel.	F2	12
Koersel, Bel.	F7	12
Koes, Nmb.	E4	66
Kofa Mountains, mts., Az., U.S.	D2	110
Köflach, Aus.	H15	10
Koforidua, Ghana	H9	64
Kōfu, Japan	L13	36
Koga, Japan	K14	36
Kogaluk, stm., Newf., Can.	g9	102
Kogan, Austl.	F9	70
Køge, Den.	N13	6
Kogoni, Mali	D6	64
Kohala Mountains, mts., Hi., U.S.	C6	118
Kohāt, Pak.	D4	44
Kohila, Est.	B7	22
Kohīma, India	H16	44
Kohler, Wi., U.S.	E6	156
Kohtla-Järve, Est.	B10	22
Kohŭng, S. Kor.	I15	32
Kohunlich, hist., Mex.	H15	90
Koidu, S.L.	G4	64
Koigi, Est.	C8	22
Koimbani, Com.	k15	67a
Kojgorodok, Russia	E8	26
Kojŏ, N. Kor.	E15	32
Kok (Hkok), stm., Asia	D5	40
Kokand, Uzb.	I12	26
Kokanee Glacier Provincial Park, B.C., Can.	E9	99
Kokčetav, Kaz.	G11	26
Koki, Sen.	D2	64
Kokka, Sud.	G6	60
Kokkola (Karleby), Fin.	J18	6
Koknese, Lat.	E8	22
Koko, Nig.	F12	64
Kokoda, Pap. N. Gui.	A9	68
Koko Head, c., Hi., U.S.	B4	118
Kokolik, stm., Ak., U.S.	B7	109
Kokomo, Hi., U.S.	C5	118
Kokomo, In., U.S.	D5	121
Kokomo, Ms., U.S.	D3	131
Kokong, Bots.	E6	66
Koko Nor see Qinghai Hu, l., China	D7	30
Kokopo, Pap. N. Gui.	k17	68a
Kokorevka, Russia	I17	22
Kokosing, stm., Oh., U.S.	B3	142
Kokšaalatau, chrebet, mts., Asia	I13	26
Koksan, N. Kor.	E14	32
Koksilah, B.C., Can.	g12	99
Koksŏng, S. Kor.	H15	32
Kokstad, S. Afr.	H9	66
Kola, Russia	G23	6
Kolahun, Lib.	G4	64
Kola Peninsula see Kol'skij poluostrov, pen., Russia	D5	26
Kolār, India	F5	46
Kolār Gold Fields, India	F5	46
Kolárovo, Slvk.	H18	10
Kolbio, Kenya	B8	58
Kolchozabad, Taj.	B3	44
Kol'čugino, Russia	E22	22
Kolda, Sen.	E2	64
Kolenté (Great Scarcies), stm., Afr.	G3	64
Kolgujev, ostrov, i., Russia	D7	26
Kolhāpur, India	D3	46
Kolia, C. Iv.	G6	64
Koliba (Corubal), stm., Afr.	E3	64
Koliganek, Ak., U.S.	D8	109
Kolimbine, stm., Afr.	D4	64
Kolín, Czech Rep.	E15	10
Kolisne, Ukr.	C13	20
Kolka, Lat.	D5	22
Kolkasrags, c., Lat.	D5	22
Kollegāl, India	F4	46
Köln (Cologne), Ger.	E6	10
Kolno, Pol.	B21	10
Kolo, Niger	E11	64
Koło, Pol.	C18	10
Koloa, Hi., U.S.	B2	118
Kolob Canyon, val., Ut., U.S.	F2	151
Kolobovo, Russia	E24	22
Kołobrzeg, Pol.	A15	10
Kolodn'a, Russia	G15	22
Kologriv, Russia	C27	22
Koloko, Burkina	F7	64
Kolola Springs, Ms., U.S.	B5	131
Kolomna, Russia	F21	22
Kolomyya, Ukr.	H3	26
Kolpaševo, Russia	F8	28
Kolpino, Russia	B13	22
Kolpny, Russia	I20	22
Kol'skij poluostrov (Kola Peninsula), pen., Russia	D5	26
Kol'ubakino, Russia	F19	22
Kolwezi, Zaire	D5	58
Kolyma, stm., Russia	D23	28
Kolymskaja nizmennost', pl., Russia	D22	28
Koma, Eth.	M9	60
Komadugu Gana, stm., Nig.	F9	54
Komadugu Yobe, stm., Afr.	F9	54
Komandorskije ostrova, is., Russia	F25	28
Komariči, Russia	I17	22
Komarno, Man., Can.	D3	100
Komárno, Slvk.	H18	10
Komarnyky, Ukr.	F23	10
Komárom, Hung.	H18	10
Komárom-Esztergom, co., Hung.	H18	10
Komarovo, Russia	C16	22
Komati (Incomáti), stm., Afr.	E10	66
Komatipoort, S. Afr.	E10	66
Komatke, Az., U.S.	D3	110
Komatsu, Japan	K11	36
Komatsushima, Japan	M9	36
Kombone, Cam.	I14	64
Komi, state, Russia	E8	26
Komin Yanga, Burkina	F10	64
Komló, Hung.	I18	10
Kommunizma, pik, mtn., Taj.	J12	26
Komodo, Pulau, i., Indon.	G6	38
Komoé, stm., Afr.	G6	54
Komotiní, Grc.	H9	20
Komsomolec, Kaz.	G10	26
Komsomolec, ostrov, i., Russia	A17	26
Komsomolec, zaliv, b., Kaz.	H8	26
Komsomol'sk, Russia	D23	22
Komsomol'sk, Turk.	B17	48
Komsomol'sk-na-Amure, Russia	G19	28
Komsomol'skoj Pravdy, ostrova, is., Russia	B13	28
Kona, Mali	D8	64
Konahuanui, Puu, mtn., Hi., U.S.	g10	118
Konakovo, Russia	E19	22
Konakpınar, Tur.	J11	20
Konar, stm., Asia	C4	44
Konārak, India	K12	44
Konawa, Ok., U.S.	C5	143
Konch, India	H8	44
Konda, stm., Russia	E5	28
Kondoa, Tan.	B7	58
Kondopoga, Russia	E4	26
Kondratjevo, Russia	A11	22
Kondrovo, Russia	G18	22
Kondūz, Afg.	B3	44
Konfara, Gui.	F5	64
Kŏng, stm., Asia	H9	40
Kongcheng, China	D6	34
Kongfang, China	H5	34
Kongju, S. Kor.	G15	32
Konglong, China	F4	34
Kongolo, Zaire	C5	58
Kongor, Sud.	N6	60
Kongsvinger, Nor.	K13	6
Kongur Shan, mtn., China	D2	30
Kongzhen, China	D8	34
Konice, Czech Rep.	F16	10
Königswinter, Ger.	E7	10
Konin, Pol.	C18	10
Köniz, Switz.	E7	13
Konjic, Bos.	F1	20
Könkämäälven, stm., Eur.	G17	6
Kon'-Kolodez', Russia	I22	22
Konkouré, stm., Gui.	F3	64
Konnur, India	D3	46
Konomoc, Lake, res., Ct., U.S.	D7	114
Konoša, Russia	E6	26
Konotop, Ukr.	G4	26
Kon'ovo, Russia	J26	6
Konqi, stm., China	C4	30
Końskie, Pol.	D20	10
Konstantinovskij, Russia	D22	22
Konstanz, Ger.	H9	10
Kontagora, Nig.	F12	64
Kontejevo, Russia	C24	22
Kontich, Bel.	F5	12
Kontiomäki, Fin.	I21	6
Kontseba, Ukr.	A13	20
Kon Tum, Viet.	G10	40
Kontum, Plateau du, plat., Viet.	H10	40
Konya, Tur.	C2	48
Konza, Kenya	B7	58
Konžakovskij Kamen', gora, mtn., Russia	F9	26
Koochiching, co., Mn., U.S.	B4	130
Koolamarra, Austl.	C4	70
Koolau Range, mts., Hi., U.S.	f10	118
Kooloonong, Austl.	J5	70
Koondrook, Austl.	J6	70
Koontz Lake, In., U.S.	B5	121
Koosharem, Ut., U.S.	E4	151
Kooskia, Id., U.S.	C3	119
Koossa, Gui.	G5	64
Kootenai, co., Id., U.S.	B2	119
Kootenay Lake, l., B.C., Can.	E9	99
Kootenay National Park, B.C., Can.	D9	99
Kootjieskolk, S. Afr.	H5	66
Kopargaon, India	C3	46
Kópasker, Ice.	A5	6a
Kopceviči, Bela.	I11	22
Kopejsk, Russia	F10	26
Koper, Slvn.	D8	18
Kopetdag, chrebet, mts., Asia	C15	48
Koppal, India	E4	46
Kopparbergs Län, co., Swe.	K14	6
Koppel, Pa., U.S.	E1	145
Koprivnica, Cro.	C11	18
Kopt'ovo, Russia	E23	22
Kopyl', Bela.	H10	22
Kopys', Bela.	G13	22
Korab (Maja e Korabit), mtn., Eur.	H4	20
Korabit, Maja e (Korab), mtn., Eur.	H4	20
Korablino, Russia	H23	22
Kor'akskaja Sopka, vulkan, vol., Russia	G23	28
Korāput, India	C7	46
Korba, Tun.	M5	18
Korbach, Ger.	D8	10
Korbous, Tun.	M5	18
Korçë, Alb.	I4	20
Korčula, Otok, i., Cro.	G11	18
Kord Kūy, Iran	C13	48
Korea, North, ctry., Asia	C12	30
Korea, South, ctry., Asia	D12	30
Korea Bay, b., Asia	E11	32
Korea Strait, strt., Asia	I16	32
Korekozevo, Russia	G19	22
Koreliči, Bela.	H9	22
Korfovskij, Russia	H19	28
Korgus, Sud.	H7	60
Korhogo, C. Iv.	G7	64
Korinthiakós Kólpos (Gulf of Corinth), b., Grc.	K6	20
Kórinthos (Corinth), Grc.	L6	20

Name — Map Ref. — Page

Korínthou, Dhiórix, Grc. L6 20
Kōriyama, Japan J15 36
Korkino, Russia G10 26
Korla, China C4 30
Korneuburg, Aus. G16 10
Koro, Mali D8 64
Korogwe, Tan. C7 58
Koroit, Austl. L5 70
Koroleve, Ukr. A7 20
Koróni, Grc. M5 20
Koronis, Lake, l., Mn., U.S. E4 130
Koronowo, Pol. B17 10
Körös, stm., Hung. I21 10
Korosten', Ukr. G3 26
Korotovo, Russia C20 22
Korovin Volcano, vol., Ak., U.S. E5 109
Korpilahti, Fin. J19 6
Korpo (Korppoo), Fin. K17 6
Korsakov, Russia H20 28
Korsør, Den. N12 6
Korsze, Pol. A21 10
Kortrijk (Courtrai), Bel. G3 12
Koruçam Burnu, c., N. Cyp. D2 48
Korumburra, Austl. L6 70
Koryŏng, S. Kor. H16 32
Kos, Grc. M11 20
Kos (Cos), i., Grc. M11 20
Kosa, Eth. N9 60
Kosa, Russia F8 26
Koš-Agač, Russia G15 26
Kosaja Gora, Russia G20 22
Kosčagyl, Kaz. H8 26
Kościan, Pol. C16 10
Kościerzyna, Pol. A18 10
Kosciusko, Ms., U.S. B4 131
Kosciusko, co., In., U.S. B6 121
Kosciusko, Mount, mtn., Austl. K8 70
Kosciusko National Park, Austl. K8 70
Koshikijima-rettō, is., Japan P4 36
Koshkonong, Mo., U.S. E6 132
Koshkonong, Lake, l., Wi., U.S. F5 156
Košice, Slvk. G21 10
Kosiv, Ukr. A9 20
Köşk, Tur. L12 20
Koski, Fin. K18 6
Koslan, Russia E7 26
Kosmynino, Russia D23 22
Kosŏng, N. Kor. E16 32
Kosovo-Metohija, prov., Yugo. G5 20
Kosovska Mitrovica, Yugo. G4 20
Kosse, Tx., U.S. D4 150
Kossuth, Ms., U.S. A5 131
Kossuth, co., Ia., U.S. A3 122
Koster, S. Afr. E8 66
Kosterevo, Russia F22 22
Kostroma, Russia D23 22
Kostroma, stm., Russia C23 22
Kostryzhivka, Ukr. A9 20
Kostrzyn, Pol. C14 10
Kost'ukoviči, Bela. H15 22
Kost'ukovka, Bela. I13 22
Kostyantynivka, Ukr. H5 26
Koszalin (Köslin), Pol. A16 10
Kőszeg, Hung. H16 10
Kota, India H6 44
Kota Baharu, Malay. K7 40
Kotabaru, Indon. F6 38
Kotabumi, Indon. F3 38
Kotadabok, Indon. O8 40
Kotel'nič, Russia F7 26
Kotel'nikovo, Russia H6 26
Kotel'nyj, ostrov, i., Russia B19 28
Köthen, Ger. D11 10
Kotka, Fin. K20 6
Kot Kapūra, India E6 44
Kotlas, Russia E7 26
Kotli, Pak. D5 44
Kotlik, Ak., U.S. C7 109
Kotlin, ostrov, i., Russia A12 22
Kotly, Russia B11 22
Koton-Karifi, Nig. G13 64
Kotonkoro, Nig. F12 64
Kotor, Yugo. G2 20
Kotoriba, Cro. C11 18
Kotorovo, Russia G24 22
Kotouba, C. Iv. G8 64
Kotovsk, Russia I24 22
Kotovs'k, Ukr. H3 26
Kottagūdem, India D6 46
Kottayam, India H4 46
Kotto, stm., Cen. Afr. Rep. G5 56
Kotuj, stm., Russia C12 28
Kotzebue, Ak., U.S. B7 109
Kotzebue Sound, strt., Ak., U.S. B7 109
Kötzting, Ger. F12 10
Kou'an, China C8 34
Kouandé, Benin F10 64
Kouchibouguac National Park, N.B., Can. C5 101
Koudougou, Burkina E8 64
Kouéré, Burkina F8 64
Koukdjuak, stm., N.W. Ter., Can. C18 96
Koulamoutou, Gabon B2 58
Koulikoro, Mali E6 64
Koulouguidi, Mali E4 64
Koulountou, stm., Afr. E3 64
Koumbakara, Sen. E3 64
Koumbal, Cen. Afr. Rep. M2 60
Koumpentoum, Sen. E2 64
Koumra, Chad G4 56
Koundara, Gui. E3 64
Koungheul, Sen. E2 64
Kounradskij, Kaz. H13 26
Kountze, Tx., U.S. D5 150
Koupéla, Burkina E9 64
Kouroukoto, Mali E4 64
Kouroussa, Gui. F5 54
Koussanar, Sen. E2 64
Koussané, Mali D4 64
Koussane, Sen. D3 64
Koussi, Emi, mtn., Chad E4 56
Koussili, Mali E4 64
Koutia Ba, Sen. D2 64
Koutiala, Mali E7 64
Kouto, C. Iv. G6 64
Koutou, China E2 32
Kouts, In., U.S. B3 121
Kovarskas, Lith. F7 22
Kovdor, Russia H22 6
Kovel', Ukr. G2 26
Kovernino, Russia D26 22
Kovilpatti, India H4 46
Kovrov, Russia F6 26
Kovvur, India D6 46
Kowalewo Pomorskie, Pol. B18 10
Kowŏn, N. Kor. D15 32
Koyna Reservoir, res., India D2 46
Koyuk, Ak., U.S. C7 109
Koyukuk, Ak., U.S. C8 109
Koyukuk, stm., Ak., U.S. B8 109
Kozan, Tur. C3 48
Kozáni, Grc. I5 20
Kozel'sk, Russia G18 22
Kozlov Bereg, Russia C10 22
Kozlovo, Russia E19 22
Kozlovščina, Bela. H8 22
Kpandae, Ghana G9 64
Kpandu, Ghana H10 64
Kra, Isthmus of, Asia I5 40
Krabi, Thai. J5 40
Krâchéh, Camb. H9 40
Kraemer, La., U.S. k10 125
Kragerø, Nor. L11 6
Kragujevac, Yugo. E4 20
Krajenka, Pol. B17 10
Krakatoa see Rakata, Pulau, i., Indon. j12 39a
Krâkôr, Camb. H8 40
Kraków, Pol. E19 10
Kralendijk, Neth. Ant. H10 94
Kraljevo, Yugo. F4 20
Kralovice, Czech Rep. F13 10
Kramators'k, Ukr. H5 26
Kranj, Slvn. C9 18
Kranzberg, Nmb. C2 66
Kranzburg, S.D., U.S. C9 148
Kraskino, Russia A18 32
Krāslava, Lat. F10 22
Krasnaja Gorbatka, Russia F24 22
Krasnaja Gorka, Russia E26 22
Krasnaja Zar'a, Russia I20 22
Kraśnik, Pol. E22 10
Krasni Okny, Ukr. B13 20
Krasnoarmejsk, Russia E21 22
Krasnodar, Russia H5 26
Krasnofarfornyj, Russia B14 22
Krasnogorsk, Russia F20 22
Krasnogorsk, Russia H20 28
Krasnoil's'k, Ukr. A9 20
Krasnojarsk, Russia F10 28
Krasnojarskoje vodochranilišče, res., Russia F16 26
Krasnoje, Bela. G10 22
Krasnoje Echo, Russia F23 22
Krasnoje-na-Volge, Russia D24 22
Krasnoje Selo, Russia B13 22
Krasnoje Znam'a, Turk. C17 48
Krasnokamsk, Russia F9 26
Krasnolesje, Russia G5 22
Krasnoslobodsk, Russia H6 26
Krasnoturjinsk, Russia F10 26
Krasnoufimsk, Russia D19 4
Krasnoural'sk, Russia F10 26
Krasnovišersk, Russia E9 26
Krasnovodsk, Turk. I8 26
Krasnovodskij poluostrov, pen., Turk. A12 48
Krasnovodskij zaliv, b., Turk. B12 48
Krasnozavodsk, Russia E21 22
Krasnoznamenskij, Kaz. G11 26
Krasnoz'orskoje, Russia G13 26
Krasnyj Bogatyr', Russia E24 22
Krasnyj Cholm, Russia C20 22
Krasnyje Tkači, Russia D22 22
Krasnyj Kut, Russia G7 26
Krasnyj Luč, Russia D13 22
Krasnyj Okt'abr', Russia E21 22
Krasnyj Profintern, Russia D23 22
Krasnyj Rog, Russia I16 22
Krasnyj Tkač, Russia F22 22
Krasnystaw, Pol. E23 10
Krasnyy Luch, Ukr. H5 26
Kraszna (Crasna), stm., Eur. A6 20
Krebs, Ok., U.S. C6 143
Krečetovo, Russia K26 6
Krečevicy, Russia C14 22
Krefeld, Ger. D6 10
Kremastón, Tekhnití Límni, res., Grc. K5 20
Kremenchuk, Ukr. H4 26
Kremenchuts'ke vodoskhovyshche, res., Ukr. H4 26
Kremlin, Mt., U.S. B6 133
Kremlin, Ok., U.S. A4 143
Kremmling, Co., U.S. A4 113
Krems an der Donau, Aus. G15 10
Kress, Tx., U.S. B2 150
Kresta, zaliv, b., Russia D28 28
Krestcy, Russia C15 22
Kretinga, Lith. F4 22
Kribi, Cam. H8 54
Kričov, Bela. H14 22
Kriens, Switz. D9 13
Kriljon, mys, c., Russia b17 36a
Křimice, Czech Rep. F13 10
Krishna, stm., India D5 46
Krishnagiri, India F5 46
Krishnanagar, India I13 44
Krishnarāja Sāgara, res., India F4 46
Kristdala, Swe. M15 6
Kristiansand, Nor. L11 6
Kristianstad, Swe. M14 6
Kristiansund, Nor. J10 6
Kristineberg, Swe. I16 6
Kríti, prov., Grc. N8 20
Kríti (Crete), i., Grc. N8 20
Kritikón Pélagos (Sea of Crete), Grc. N8 20
Kriva Palanka, Mac. G6 20
Kriviči, Bela. G10 22
Krivodol, Bul. F7 20
Križevci, Cro. C11 18
Krk, Otok, i., Cro. D9 18
Krnov, Czech Rep. E17 10
Krobia, Pol. D16 10
Krokek, Swe. L15 6
Kroken, Nor. I14 6
Krokowa, Pol. A18 10
Krombi Pits, Bots. B7 66
Kroměříž, Czech Rep. F17 10
Kromy, Russia I18 22
Kronau, Sask., Can. G3 105
Krŏng Kaôh Kŏng, Camb. I7 40
Krŏng Kêb, Camb. I8 40
Kronobergs Län, co., Swe. M14 6
Kronoby (Kruunupyy), Fin. J18 6
Kronockaja Sopka, vulkan, vol., Russia G24 28
Kronockij zaliv, b., Russia G24 28
Kronštadt, Russia B12 22
Kroonstad, S. Afr. F8 66
Kropotkin, Russia H6 26
Krosno, Pol. F21 10
Krotoszyn, Pol. D17 10
Krotz Springs, La., U.S. D4 125
Kr'učkovo, Russia D18 22
Krugersdorp, S. Afr. F8 66
Kruidfontein, S. Afr. I5 66
Kruisfontein, S. Afr. J7 66
Krukira, Laguna de, b., Nic. D11 92
Kr'ukovo, Russia F20 22
Krulevščina, Bela. F10 22
Krumbach [Schwaben], Ger. G10 10
Krung Thep (Bangkok), Thai. H6 40
Krupka, Czech Rep. E13 10
Krupki, Bela. G12 22
Kruševac, Yugo. F5 20
Kruševo, Mac. H5 20
Krušné hory (Erzgebirge), mts., Eur. B19 14
Kruszwica, Pol. C18 10
Krutoje, Russia I20 22
Kruzenšterna, proliv, strt., Russia H22 28
Kruzof Island, i., Ak., U.S. m21 109
Krydor, Sask., Can. E2 105
Kryms'kyy pivostriv (Crimean Peninsula), pen., Ukr. H4 26
Krynica, Pol. F20 10
Krynychne, Ukr. D12 20
Kryve Ozero, Ukr. B14 20
Kryvyy Rih, Ukr. H4 26
Kryzhopil', Ukr. A12 20
Ksar Chellala, Alg. C12 62
Ksar el Barka, Maur. B3 64
Ksar-el-Kebir, Mor. J6 16
Ksar-el-Seghir, Mor. J6 16
Ksar Hellal, Tun. N5 18
Ksenjevka, Russia G15 28
Ksour, Monts des, mts., Alg. D10 62
Ksour Essaf, Tun. N6 18
Kuala Kangsar, Malay. L6 40
Kualakapuas, Indon. F5 38
Kuala Lipis, Malay. L7 40
Kuala Lumpur, Malay. M6 40
Kuala Pilah, Malay. M7 40
Kualapuu, Hi., U.S. B4 118
Kuala Terengganu, Malay. L7 40
Kuancheng, China C6 32
Kuantan, Malay. M7 40
Kuban', stm., Russia H5 26
Kubbum, Sud. L2 60
Kubenskoje, Russia B22 22
Kubenskoje, ozero, l., Russia B22 22
Kučevo, Yugo. E5 20
Kuchāman, India G6 44
Kuching, Malay. N11 40
Kuçovë, Alb. I3 20
Kudirkos Naumiestis, Lith. G5 22
Kudus, Indon. j15 39a
Kudymkar, Russia F8 26
Kuee Ruins, hist., Hi., U.S. D6 118
Kufstein, Aus. H12 10
Kūhdasht, Iran E9 48
Kūhpāyeh, Iran E12 48
Kuidesu, China B7 32
Kuidou, China J7 34
Kuiseb, stm., S. Afr. D2 66
Kuito, Ang. D3 58
Kuiu Island, i., Ak., U.S. m23 109
Kujang, N. Kor. D14 32
Kujbyšev, Russia F13 26
Kujbyšev see Samara, Russia G8 26
Kujbyševskij, Uzb. J11 26
Kujbyševskoje vodochranilišče, res., Russia G7 26
Kujman', Russia I22 22
Kukalaya, stm., Nic. D11 92
Kukawa, Nig. F9 54
Kukawa, Nig. F3 56
Kukkola, Fin. I19 6
Kukuihaele, Hi., U.S. C6 118
Kukuiula, Hi., U.S. B2 118
Kula, Hi., U.S. C5 118
Kula, Yugo. D3 20
Kul'ab, Taj. J11 26
Kula Kangri, mtn., Bhu. F14 44
Kulākh, Sau. Ar. D2 47
Kulautuva, Lith. G6 22
Kulaykilī, Sud. L3 60
Kuldīga, Lat. E4 22
Kule, Bots. D5 66
Kulebaki, Russia F25 22
Kulikovo, Russia I22 22
Kulim, Malay. L6 40
Kulm, N.D., U.S. C7 141
Kulmbach, Ger. E11 10
Kuloj, Russia E6 26
Kulongshan, China B4 32
Kulotino, Russia C16 22
Kulpmont, Pa., U.S. E9 145
Kul'sary, Kaz. H8 26
Kulti, India I12 44
Kulumadau, Pap. N. Gui. A10 68
Kulundinskaja step', pl., Asia G7 28
Kuma, stm., Russia I7 26
Kumagaya, Japan K14 36
Kumajri, Arm. I6 26
Kumamoto, Japan O5 36
Kumanovo, Mac. G5 20
Kumārapālaiyam, India G4 46
Kumasi, Ghana H9 64
Kumba, Cam. I14 64
Kumbakonam, India G5 46
Kumba Pits, Bots. B7 66
Kŭmch'ŏn, N. Kor. E14 32
Kum-Dag, Turk. J8 26
Kume-jima, i., Japan u31 37b
Kŭmhwa, S. Kor. E15 32
Kumla, Swe. L14 6
Kumo, Nig. F9 54
Kumukahi, Cape, c., Hi., U.S. D7 118
Kumukuli, China B13 44
Kumzār, Oman A10 47
Kuna, Id., U.S. F2 119
Kunašir, ostrov (Kunashiri-tō), i., Russia c21 36a
Kunchhā, Nepal F11 44
Kunda, Est. B9 22
Kundar, stm., Asia E3 44
Kunene (Cunene), stm., Afr. E2 58
Kunghit Island, i., B.C., Can. C2 99
Kungrad, Uzb. I9 26
Kungsbacka, Swe. M13 6
Kungur, Russia F9 26
Kunhegyes, Hung. H20 10
Kunia, Hi., U.S. g9 118
Kunja, Russia E13 22
Kunjāh, Pak. D5 44
Kunlong, Mya. C5 40
Kunlun Shan, mts., China B12 44
Kunming, China B7 40
Kunsan, S. Kor. H14 32
Kunshan, China D9 34
Kunszentmárton, Hung. I20 10
Kuntair, Gam. E1 64
Kuntaur, Gam. E2 64
Kunting, China F10 34
Kununurra, Austl. C5 68
Kunwi, S. Kor. G16 32
Kuokegan, China B13 44
Kuopio, Fin. J20 6
Kuopion lääni, prov., Fin J20 6
Kupang, Indon. H7 38
Kupanskoje, Russia E21 22
Kupino, Russia G7 28
Kupiškis, Lith. F7 22
Küplü, Tur. H10 20
Kupreanof Island, i., Ak., U.S. m23 109
Kup'yans'k, Ukr. H5 26
Kuqa, China C3 30
Kür, stm., Asia B10 48
Kurashiki, Japan M8 36
Kuraymah, Sud. H6 60
Kurayyimah, Jord. D5 50
Kurba, Russia D22 22
Kürdämir, Azer. A10 48
Kür dili, spit, Azer. B10 48
Kurdistan, hist. reg., Asia B4 42
Kure, Japan M7 36
Kure Island, i., Hi., U.S. k12 118
Kurejka, stm., Russia D9 28
Kuressaare, Est. C5 22
Kurgan, Russia F11 26
Kurgan-T'ube, Taj. J11 26
Kuria Muria Islands see Khurīyā Murīyā, is., Oman F10 47
Kuridala, Austl. C4 70
Kurīgrām, Bngl. H13 44
Kuril Islands see Kuril'skije ostrova, is., Russia H22 28
Kuril'skije ostrova (Kuril Islands), is., Russia H22 28
Kuril Strait see Pervyj Kuril'skij proliv, strt., Russia G23 28
Kuril Trench D19 158
Kurinwás, stm., Nic. E11 92
Kurkino, Russia H21 22
Kurlovskij, Russia F23 22
Kurmuk, Sud. L8 60
Kurnool, India E5 46
Kuroki, Sask., Can. F4 105
Kurovskoje, Russia F21 22
Kurow, N.Z. F3 72
Kuršėnai, Lith. E5 22
Kursk, Russia G5 26
Kurskaja kosa, spit, Eur. F4 22
Kurskij zaliv, b., Eur. F3 22
Kürtī, Sud. H6 60
Kurtistown, Hi., U.S. D6 118
Kuru, Sud. N4 60
Kuruman, S. Afr. F6 66
Kuruman, stm., S. Afr. F5 66
Kurumanheuwels, hills, S. Afr. F6 66
Kurume, Japan N5 36
Kurumkan, Russia G14 28
Kurun, stm., Afr. O8 60
Kurunegala, Sri L. I6 46
Kurzeme, hist. reg., Lat. E5 22
Kusa, Russia F9 26
Kušalino, Russia D19 22
Kusel, Ger. F7 10
Kushaka, Nig. F13 64
Kushiro, Japan e19 36a
Kushnytsya, Ukr. A7 20
Kushtia, Bngl. I13 44
Kushui, China C5 30
Kuška, Turk. J10 26
Kuška, stm., Asia C17 48
Kuskokwim, stm., Ak., U.S. C8 109
Kuskokwim Bay, b., Ak., U.S. D7 109
Kuskokwim Mountains, mts., Ak., U.S. C8 109
Kušmurun, Kaz. G10 26
Küsnacht, Switz. D10 13
Kusŏng, N. Kor. D13 32
Kussharo-ko, l., Japan d19 36a
Küssnacht am Rigi, Switz. D9 13
Kustanaj, Kaz. G10 26
Kustar'ovka, Russia G25 22
Kūstī, Sud. K7 60
Kušva, Russia F9 26
Kut, Ko, i., Thai. I7 40
Kuta, Nig. G13 64
Kütahya, Tur. H13 4
Kutaisi, Geor. I6 26
Kutch, Rann of (Rann of Kachchh), reg., Asia H4 44
Kutina, Cro. D11 18
Kutná Hora, Czech Rep. F15 10
Kutno, Pol. C19 10
Kutse Game Reserve, Bots. D6 66
Kuttawa, Ky., U.S. e9 124
Kuttura, Fin. G20 6
Kuttusoja, Fin. H21 6
Kutu, Zaire B3 58
Kutum, Sud. J3 60
Kuty, Ukr. A9 20
Kutztown, Pa., U.S. E10 145
Kuujjuaq, Que., Can. g13 104
Kuusamo, Fin. I21 6
Kuusankoski, Fin K20 6
Kuvandyk, Russia G9 26
Kuvango, Ang. D3 58
Kuvšinovo, Russia D17 22
Kuwait see Al-Kuwayt, Kuw. G9 48
Kuwait (Al-Kuwayt), ctry., Asia D4 42
Kuwana, Japan L11 36
Kuwayt, Jūn al- (Kuwait Bay), b., Kuw. G10 48
Kuybyshev see Samara, Russia G8 26
Kūysanjaq, Iraq C8 48
Kuyuwini, stm., Guy. F13 84
Kuženkino, Russia D16 22
Kuzneck, Russia G7 26
Kuzneckij Alatau, mts., Russia G9 28
Kvaløy, i., Nor. G16 6
Kwai see Khwae Noi, stm., Thai. G5 40
Kwajok, Sud. M4 60
Kwakoegron, Sur. B7 76
Kwando (Cuando), stm., Afr. E4 58
Kwangchow see Guangzhou, China L2 34
Kwangju, S. Kor. H14 32
Kwango (Cuango), stm., Afr. B3 58
Kwangtung see Guangdong, prov., China G9 30
Kwangyang, S. Kor. I15 32
Kwazulu see Natal, prov., S. Afr. G10 66
Kweisui see Hohhot, China C9 30
Kwekwe, Zimb. B9 66
Kweneng, dept., Bots. E7 66
Kwenge, stm., Afr. C3 58
Kwethluk, Ak., U.S. C7 109
Kwidzyn, Pol. B18 10
Kwigillingok, Ak., U.S. D7 109
Kwilu (Cuilo), stm., Afr. B3 58
Kwitaro, stm., Guy. F13 84
Kwolla, Nig. G14 64
Kyabra, Austl. F5 70
Kyabram, Austl. K6 70
Kyaiklat, Mya. F3 40
Kyaikto, Mya. F4 40
Kyaukhnyat, Mya. F4 40
Kyaukpyu, Mya. E2 40
Kyaukse, Mya. D4 40
Kyauktaw, Mya. D2 40
Kyaunggon, Mya. F3 40
Kybartai, Lith. G5 22
Kyeikdon, Mya. F5 40
Kyindwe, Mya. D2 40
Kyle, Sask., Can. G1 105
Kyle, S.D., U.S. D3 148
Kyle, Tx., U.S. E4 150
Kyle of Lochalsh, Scot., U.K. D8 8
Kymen lääni, prov., Fin. K20 6
Kyneton, Austl. K6 70
Kyoga, Lake, l., Ug. A6 58
Kyogle, Austl. G10 70
Kyŏnggi-man, b., Asia F13 32
Kyŏngju, S. Kor. H17 32
Kyŏngsan, S. Kor. H16 32
Kyŏngsŏng, N. Kor. B17 32
Kyŏngwŏn, N. Kor. A18 32
Kyōto, Japan L10 36
Kyren, Russia G12 28
Kyrgyzstan, ctry., Asia I13 26
Kyritz, Ger. C12 10
Kyštovka, Russia F13 26
Kyštym, Russia F10 26
Kyunhla, Mya. C3 40
Kyuquot, B.C., Can. D4 99
Kyuquot Sound, strt., B.C., Can. E4 99
Kyūshū, i., Japan O5 36
Kywebwe, Mya. E4 40
Kywong, Austl. J7 70
Kyyiv (Kiev), Ukr. G4 26
Kyyivs'ke vodoskhovyshche, res., Ukr. G4 26
Kyyjärvi, Fin. J19 6
Kyzyl, Russia G10 28
Kyzyl-Kija, Kyrg. I12 26
Kyzylkum, des., Asia I10 26
Kzyl-Orda, Kaz. I11 26
Kzyltu, Kaz. G12 26

L

Laa an der Thaya, Aus. G16 10
La Aguja, Cabo de, c., Col. B5 84
La Alcarria, reg., Spain E9 16
La Algaba, Spain H5 16
La Antigua, Salina, pl., Arg. E5 80
La Araucanía, prov., Chile J2 80
La Arena, Pan. J14 92
Laas Caanood, Som. G10 56
La Ascensión, Mex. E10 90
La Asunción, Ven. B11 84
La Atravesada, Loma, hill, Mex. C3 90
Laau Point, c., Hi., U.S. B4 118
La Babia, Mex. C8 90
Labadie, Mo., U.S. C7 132
Labadieville, La., U.S. E5 125
La Banda, Arg. D6 80
La Bandera, Cerro, mtn., Mex. E7 90
La Bañeza, Spain C6 16
La Barca, Mex. G8 90
La Barge, Wy., U.S. D2 157
La Barge Creek, stm., Wy., U.S. D2 157
La Barra, Nic. E11 92
La Barrita, Guat. C3 92
La Baule-Escoublac, Fr. E4 14
Labé, Gui. F3 64
Labe (Elbe), stm., Eur. B9 10
La Belle, Fl., U.S. F5 116
La Belle, Mo., U.S. A6 132
Labette, co., Ks., U.S. E8 123
Labette Creek, stm., Ks., U.S. E8 123
Labin, Cro. D9 18
Labinsk, Russia I6 26
La Bisbal, Spain D15 16
La Blanca Grande, Laguna, l., Arg. J7 80
Labná, hist., Mex. G15 90
Laboe, Ger. A10 10
Laborde, Arg. G7 80
Labouheyre, Fr. H6 14
Laboulaye, Arg. H7 80
Labrador, reg., Newf., Can. g9 102
Labrador City, Newf., Can. h8 102
Labrador Sea, N.A. E22 96
Lábrea, Braz. E6 76
Lábrea, Braz. B9 82
Labrit, Fr. H6 14
La Broquerie, Man., Can. E3 100
Labutta, Mya. F3 40
Labytnangi, Russia D11 26
Lača, ozero, l., Russia K26 6
Laca Jahuira, stm., Bol. H8 82
La Cal, stm., Bol. G12 82
La Calera, Chile G3 80
La Campana, Spain H6 16
La Canada Flintridge, Ca., U.S. m12 112
La Candelaria, Arg. D6 80
Lacantún, stm., Mex. I14 90
La Capelle [-en-Thierache], Fr. C10 14
Lacapelle-Marival, Fr. H8 14
La Carlota, Arg. G7 80
La Carolina, Spain G8 16
Lacaune, Fr. I9 14
Lac-Baker, N.B., Can. B1 101
Lac-Bouchette, Que., Can. A5 104
Lac-Brome, Que., Can. D5 104
Laccadive Islands see Lakshadweep, is., India G2 46
Lac-Carré, Que., Can. C3 104
Lac Courte Oreilles Indian Reservation, Wi., U.S. C2 156
Lac du Bonnet, Man., Can. D3 100
Lac du Flambeau, Wi., U.S. B4 156
Lac du Flambeau Indian Reservation, Wi., U.S. C3 156
La Ceiba, Hond. B8 92
La Ceiba, Ven. C7 84
La Center, Ky., U.S. e9 124
Lac-Etchemin, Que., Can. C7 104
Lacey, Wa., U.S. B3 154
Laceys Spring, Al., U.S. A3 108
La Chambre, Fr. G13 14
La Chapelle-d'Angillon, Fr. E9 14
La Chartre-sur-le-Loir, Fr. E7 14
La Châtaigneraie, Fr. F6 14
La Chaux-de-Fonds, Switz. D6 13
Lachay, Punta, c., Peru D3 82
Lachdenpochja, Russia K22 6
Lachen, Switz. D10 13
Lachhmangarh Sīkar, India G6 44
Lachine, Que., Can. D4 104
Lachlan, stm., Austl. J6 70
La Chorrera, Col. H6 84
La Chorrera, Pan. C3 84
L'achoviči, Bela. H9 22
L'achovskije ostrova, is., Russia C20 28
Lachute, Que., Can. D3 104
Lachva, Bela. I10 22
La Ciénaga, Arg. D5 80
La Cienega, N.M., U.S. h8 138
La Ciotat, Fr. I12 14
La Citadelle, hist., Haiti E8 94
La Ciudad, Mex. F7 90
Lackawanna, N.Y., U.S. C2 139
Lackawanna, co., Pa., U.S. D10 145
Lackawaxen, Pa., U.S. D12 145
Lackland Air Force Base, mil., Tx., U.S. k7 150
Lac La Biche, Alta., Can. B5 98
Lac la Hache, B.C., Can. D7 99
Laclede, Id., U.S. A2 119
Laclede, Mo., U.S. B4 132
Laclede, co., Mo., U.S. D5 132
La Clotilde, Arg. D8 80
Lac-Mégantic, Que., Can. D7 104
La Cocha, Arg. D6 80
Lacolle, Que., Can. D4 104
La Colorada, Mex. C4 90
La Coma, Mex. E10 90
Lacombe, Alta., Can. C4 98
Lacombe, La., U.S. D6 125
Lacombe Bayou, stm., La., U.S. h12 125
Lacon, Il., U.S. B4 120
Lacona, Ia., U.S. C4 122
La Concepción, Pan. C1 84
La Concepción, Ven. B7 84
Laconia, N.H., U.S. C4 136
La Conner, Wa., U.S. A3 154
La Consulta, Arg. G4 80
Lacoochee, Fl., U.S. D4 116
La Coruña, Spain B3 16
Lac qui Parle, co., Mn., U.S. F2 130
Lac qui Parle, stm., Mn., U.S. F2 130
Lac qui Parle, West Branch, stm., Mn., U.S. F2 130
La Creek Lake, l., S.D., U.S. D4 148
La Crescent, Mn., U.S. G7 130
La Crete, Alta., Can. f7 98
La Crosse, In., U.S. B4 121
La Crosse, Ks., U.S. D4 123
La Crosse, Va., U.S. D4 153
Lacrosse, Wa., U.S. C8 154
La Crosse, Wi., U.S. E2 156
La Crosse, co., Wi., U.S. E2 156
La Crosse, stm., Wi., U.S. E3 156
La Cruz, Arg. E10 80
La Cruz, Col. G4 84
La Cruz, C.R. F9 92
La Cruz, Ur. G10 80
La Cruz, Cerro, mtn., Mex. I9 90
La Cruz de Río Grande, Nic. D10 92
Lac-Saguay, Que., Can. C2 104
La Cuesta, C.R. I12 92
La Cumbre, Arg. F6 80
Lac-Vert, Sask., Can. E3 105
La Cygne, Ks., U.S. D9 123
Ladainha, Braz. D8 79
Ladākh Range, mts., Asia C7 44
Ladário, Braz. H13 82
Ladd, Il., U.S. B4 120
Ladder Creek, stm., Ks., U.S. D2 123
Laddonia, Mo., U.S. B6 132
La Désirade, i., Guad. F14 94
Ladies Island, i., S.C., U.S. G6 147
La Digue, i., Sey. B11 58
Ladismith, S. Afr. I5 66
Lādīz, Iran G16 48

Name	Map Ref.	Page
Lādnūn, India	G6	44
Ladoga, In., U.S.	E4	121
Ladoga, Lake see Ladožskoje ozero, l., Russia	E4	26
Ladonia, Tx., U.S.	C5	150
Ladora, Ia., U.S.	C5	122
La Dorada, Col.	E5	84
La Dormida, Arg.	G5	80
Ladožskoje Ozero, Russia	A14	22
Ladožskoje ozero (Lake Ladoga), l., Russia	E4	26
Ladson, S.C., U.S.	F7	147
Laduškin, Russia	G3	22
Ladva-Vetka, Russia	K24	6
L'ady, Russia	C11	22
Lady Ann Strait, strt., N.W. Ter., Can.	A16	96
Ladybrand, S. Afr.	G8	66
Lady Elliot Island, i., Austl.	E10	70
Lady Lake, Fl., U.S.	D5	116
Lady Laurier, Mount, mtn., B.C., Can.	A6	99
Ladysmith, B.C., Can.	E6	99
Ladysmith, S. Afr.	G9	66
Ladysmith, Wi., U.S.	C2	156
Lae, Pap. N. Gui.	m16	68a
La Encantada, Mex.	E9	90
La Esmeralda, Mex.	D8	90
La Esmeralda, Para.	B7	80
La Esmeralda, Ven.	F10	84
La Esperanza, Cuba	C3	94
La Esperanza, Hond.	C6	92
La Estrella, Bol.	G10	82
La Falda, Arg.	F6	80
La Farge, Wi., U.S.	E3	156
Lafayette, Al., U.S.	C4	108
Lafayette, Ca., U.S.	h8	112
Lafayette, Co., U.S.	B5	113
Lafayette, Ga., U.S.	B1	117
La Fayette, Il., U.S.	B4	120
Lafayette, In., U.S.	D4	121
Lafayette, La., U.S.	D3	125
Lafayette, Mn., U.S.	F4	130
Lafayette, N.C., U.S.	B3	140
Lafayette, Or., U.S.	B3	144
La Fayette, R.I., U.S.	E4	146
Lafayette, Tn., U.S.	A5	149
Lafayette, co., Ar., U.S.	D2	111
Lafayette, co., Fl., U.S.	C3	116
Lafayette, co., La., U.S.	D3	125
Lafayette, co., Ms., U.S.	A4	131
Lafayette, co., Mo., U.S.	B4	132
Lafayette, co., Wi., U.S.	F3	156
Lafayette, Mount, mtn., N.H., U.S.	B3	136
La Fé, Cuba	D3	94
Lafe, Ar., U.S.	A5	111
La Fère, Fr.	C10	14
La Feria, Tx., U.S.	F4	150
La Ferté-Bernard, Fr.	D7	14
La Ferté-Gaucher, Fr.	D10	14
La Ferté-Macé, Fr.	D6	14
La Ferté-Saint-Aubin, Fr.	E8	14
Lafferty, Oh., U.S.	B4	142
Lafia, Nig.	G14	64
Lafitte, La., U.S.	k11	125
Laflèche, Sask. Can.	H2	105
La Flèche, Fr.	E6	14
La Florida, Guat.	I14	90
Lafnitz, stm., Eur.	H16	10
La Follette, Tn., U.S.	C9	149
La Fontaine, In., U.S.	C6	121
Lafontaine, Ks., U.S.	E8	123
Lafourche, La., U.S.	E5	125
Lafourche, co., La., U.S.	E5	125
Lafourche, Bayou, stm., La., U.S.	E5	125
La Fragua, Arg.	D6	80
La France, S.C., U.S.	B2	147
La Francia, Arg.	F7	80
La Fría, Ven.	C6	84
La Galite, i., Tun.	L3	18
La Gallareta, Arg.	E8	80
Lagangzong, China	F14	44
Lagarto, C.R.	G10	92
Lagawe, Phil.	m19	39b
Lage, China	F11	44
Lågen, stm., Nor.	K12	6
Lågen, stm., Nor.	K11	6
Lages, Braz.	D13	80
Lage Zwaluwe, Neth.	E6	12
Laghouat, Alg.	D12	62
La Gleize, Bel.	H8	12
La Gloria, Col.	C6	84
Lago, Mount, mtn., Wa., U.S.	A5	154
Lagoa da Prata, Braz.	F6	79
Lagoa Formosa, Braz.	E5	79
Lagoa Santa, Braz.	E7	79
Lagoa Vermelha, Braz.	E13	80
Lagolândia, Braz.	C4	79
Lagos, Nig.	H11	64
Lagos, Port.	H3	16
Lagos de Moreno, Mex.	G9	90
La Gouèra, W. Sah.	J2	62
La Goulette, Tun.	M5	18
La Grand'Combe, Fr.	H11	14
La Grande, Or., U.S.	B8	144
La Grande, stm., Que., Can.	h11	104
La Grande Deux, Réservoir, res., Que., Can.	h11	104
La Grange, Austl.	C4	68
La Grange, Ar., U.S.	C5	111
La Grange, Ga., U.S.	C1	117
La Grange, Il., U.S.	B6	120
Lagrange, In., U.S.	A7	121
La Grange, Ky., U.S.	B4	124
La Grange, Mo., U.S.	A6	132
La Grange, N.C., U.S.	B5	140
Lagrange, Oh., U.S.	A3	142
La Grange, Tn., U.S.	B2	149
La Grange, Tx., U.S.	E4	150
Lagrange, Wy., U.S.	E8	157
Lagrange, co., In., U.S.	A7	121
La Grange Park, Il., U.S.	k9	120
La Gran Sabana, pl., Ven.	E12	84
La Grita, Ven.	C7	84
Lagro, In., U.S.	C6	121
La Grue Bayou, stm., Ar., U.S.	C4	111
Lagu, China	A6	40
La Guadeloupe (Saint-Evariste), Que., Can.	D7	104
La Guajira, dept., Col.	B6	84
La Guajira, Península de, pen., S.A.	A7	84
La Guardia, Arg.	E6	80
La Guardia, Bol.	G10	82
La Guardia, Spain	D3	16
La Guerche-de-Bretagne, Fr.	E5	14
La Guerche-sur-l'Aubois, Fr.	F9	14
Laguna, Braz.	E14	80
Laguna, N.M., U.S.	B2	138
Laguna, Ilha da, i., Braz.	D8	76
Laguna Beach, Ca., U.S.	F5	112
Laguna Dam, U.S.	E1	110
Laguna Indian Reservation, N.M., U.S.	C2	138
Laguna Larga, Arg.	F7	80
Laguna Limpia, Arg.	D9	80
Laguna Paiva, Arg.	F8	80
Lagunas, Peru	A4	82
Lagunas de Chacagua, Parque Nacional, Mex.	I11	90
Lagunas de Montebello, Parque Nacional, Mex.	A3	92
Lagunillas, Bol.	H10	82
Lagunillas, Ven.	C7	84
Lagunillás, Laguna, l., Peru	F6	82
Laguntara, b., Hond.	B10	92
La Habana (Havana), Cuba	C3	94
La Habra, Ca., U.S.	n13	112
Lahaina, Hi., U.S.	C5	118
La Harpe, Il., U.S.	C3	120
La Harpe, Ks., U.S.	E8	123
Lahat, Indon.	F3	38
La Have, stm., N.S., Can.	E5	101
La Have Island, N.S., Can.	E5	101
La Haye-du-Puits, Fr.	C5	14
La Higuera, Chile	E3	80
Laḥij, Yemen	H4	47
Lāhījān, Iran	C11	48
Lahnstein, Ger.	E7	10
Lahoma, Ok., U.S.	A3	143
Lahontan Reservoir, res., Nv., U.S.	D2	135
Lahore, Pak.	E6	44
La Horqueta, Col.	F6	84
Lahr, Ger.	G7	10
Lahri, Pak.	F3	44
Lahti, Fin.	K19	6
La Huaca, Peru	A1	82
La Huacana, Mex.	H9	90
Laibin, China	C10	40
Lai Chau, Viet.	C7	40
Laie, Hi., U.S.	B4	118
Laifang, China	J5	34
L'Aigle, Fr.	D7	14
L'Aigle Creek, stm., Ar., U.S.	D3	111
Laignes, Fr.	E11	14
La Independencia, Bahía de, b., Peru	F3	82
Laingsburg, S. Afr.	I5	66
Laingsburg, Mi., U.S.	F6	129
La Inmaculada, Mex.	C4	90
Laird, Sask., Can.	E2	105
Laird, Co., U.S.	A8	113
Laishan, China	F9	32
Laishui, China	D3	32
Laiwu, China	G5	32
Laiyang, China	G8	32
Laizhou Wan (Laichow Bay), b., China	F7	32
Laja, stm., Chile	I3	80
Laja, Laguna de la, l., Chile	I3	80
Laja, Salto del, wtfl, Chile	I3	80
La Jalca, Peru	B3	82
La Jara, Co., U.S.	D5	113
Lajas, Cuba	C4	94
Laje, Braz.	B9	79
Lajeado, Braz.	E13	80
Lajes, Braz.	E11	76
Lajinha, Braz.	F8	79
La Jolla, Point, c., Ca., U.S.	o15	112
Lajosmizse, Hung.	H19	10
La Joya, Peru	G6	82
Lajoya, N.M., U.S.	C3	138
La Joya, Tx., U.S.	F3	150
La Junta, Co., U.S.	D7	113
Lakamané, Mali	D5	64
Lake, Mi., U.S.	E5	129
Lake, Ms., U.S.	C4	131
Lake, co., Ca., U.S.	C2	112
Lake, co., Co., U.S.	B4	113
Lake, co., Fl., U.S.	D5	116
Lake, co., Il., U.S.	A6	120
Lake, co., In., U.S.	B3	121
Lake, co., Mi., U.S.	E5	129
Lake, co., Mn., U.S.	C7	130
Lake, co., Mt., U.S.	C2	133
Lake, co., Oh., U.S.	A4	142
Lake, co., Or., U.S.	E6	144
Lake, co., S.D., U.S.	C8	148
Lake, co., Tn., U.S.	A2	149
Lake Alfred, Fl., U.S.	D5	116
Lake Alma, Sask., Can.	H3	105
Lake Andes, S.D., U.S.	D7	148
Lake Ariel, Pa., U.S.	D11	145
Lake Arrowhead, Ca., U.S.	E5	112
Lake Arthur, La., U.S.	D3	125
Lake Arthur, N.M., U.S.	D5	138
Lake Barcroft, Va., U.S.	*B5	153
Lake Benton, Mn., U.S.	F2	130
Lake Beseck, Ct., U.S.	C5	114
Lake Beulah, Wi., U.S.	n11	156
Lake Bluff, Il., U.S.	A6	120
Lake Bronson, Mn., U.S.	B2	130
Lake Butler, Fl., U.S.	B4	116
Lake Cargelligo, Austl.	I7	70
Lake Charles, La., U.S.	D2	125
Lake Chelan National Recreation Area, Wa., U.S.	A5	154
Lake City, Ar., U.S.	B5	111
Lake City, Co., U.S.	C3	113
Lake City, Fl., U.S.	B4	116
Lake City, Ia., U.S.	B3	122
Lake City, Mi., U.S.	D5	129
Lake City, Mn., U.S.	F6	130
Lake City, Pa., U.S.	B1	145
Lake City, S.C., U.S.	D8	147
Lake City, Tn., U.S.	C9	149
Lake Clark National Park, Ak., U.S.	C9	109
Lake Cormorant, Ms., U.S.	A3	131
Lake Cowichan, B.C., Can.	g11	99
Lake Creek, stm., Wa., U.S.	B7	154
Lake Crystal, Mn., U.S.	F4	130
Lake Delta, N.Y., U.S.	B5	139
Lake Delton, Wi., U.S.	E4	156
Lake Elsinore, Ca., U.S.	F5	112
Lake Erie Beach, N.Y., U.S.	C1	139
Lakefield, Ont., Can.	C6	103
Lakefield, Mn., U.S.	G3	130
Lakefield National Park, Austl.	C8	68
Lake Forest, Il., U.S.	A6	120
Lake Fork, stm., Co., U.S.	C3	113
Lake Fork, stm., Ut., U.S.	C5	151
Lake Geneva, Wi., U.S.	F5	156
Lake George, Co., U.S.	C5	113
Lake George, Mi., U.S.	E6	129
Lake George, N.Y., U.S.	B7	139
Lake Hamilton, Ar., U.S.	g7	111
Lake Harbour, N.W. Ter., Can.	D19	96
Lake Havasu City, Az., U.S.	C1	110
Lake Helen, Fl., U.S.	D5	116
Lake Hubert, Mn., U.S.	D4	130
Lake Hughes, Ca., U.S.	E4	112
Lakehurst, N.J., U.S.	C4	137
Lakehurst Naval Air Station, mil., N.J., U.S.	C4	137
Lake in the Hills, Il., U.S.	h8	120
Lake Isabella, Ca., U.S.	E4	112
Lake Itasca, Mn., U.S.	C3	130
Lake Jackson, Tx., U.S.	r14	150
Lake Katrine, N.Y., U.S.	D7	139
Lakeland, Fl., U.S.	D5	116
Lakeland, Ga., U.S.	E3	117
Lakeland, Tn., U.S.	B2	149
Lake Leelanau, Mi., U.S.	D5	129
Lake Lenore, Sask., Can.	E3	105
Lake Linden, Mi., U.S.	A2	129
Lake Louise, Alta., Can.	D2	98
Lake Luzerne, N.Y., U.S.	B7	139
Lake Magdalene, Fl., U.S.	o11	116
Lake Mary, Fl., U.S.	D5	116
Lake Mead National Recreation Area, U.S.	H7	135
Lake Meredith National Recreation Area, Tx., U.S.	B2	150
Lake Metigoshe, N.D., U.S.	A5	141
Lake Mills, Ia., U.S.	A4	122
Lake Mills, Wi., U.S.	E5	156
Lakemore, Oh., U.S.	A4	142
Lake Mountain, mtn., Wy., U.S.	E6	157
Lakenan, Mo., U.S.	B5	132
Lake Nash, Austl.	C2	70
Lake Nebagamon, Wi., U.S.	B2	156
Lake Norden, S.D., U.S.	C8	148
Lake Odessa, Mi., U.S.	F5	129
Lake of the Woods, co., Mn., U.S.	B4	130
Lake Orion, Mi., U.S.	F7	129
Lake Oswego, Or., U.S.	B4	144
Lake Ozark, Mo., U.S.	C5	132
Lake Park, Fl., U.S.	F6	116
Lake Park, Ga., U.S.	F3	117
Lake Park, Ia., U.S.	A2	122
Lake Park, Mn., U.S.	D2	130
Lake Placid, Fl., U.S.	E5	116
Lake Placid, N.Y., U.S.	A7	139
Lake Pontchartrain Causeway, La., U.S.	h11	125
Lakeport, Ca., U.S.	C2	112
Lake Preston, S.D., U.S.	C8	148
Lake Providence, La., U.S.	B4	125
Lake Range, mts., Nv., U.S.	C2	135
Lake Ridge, Va., U.S.	*B5	153
Lake Shore, Md., U.S.	B5	127
Lakeshore, Ms., U.S.	E4	131
Lakeside, N.S., Can.	E6	101
Lakeside, Az., U.S.	C6	110
Lakeside, Ca., U.S.	F5	112
Lakeside, Ct., U.S.	D3	114
Lakeside, Ct., U.S.	C3	114
Lakeside, Ia., U.S.	B2	122
Lakeside, Mt., U.S.	B2	133
Lakeside, Oh., U.S.	A3	142
Lakeside, Or., U.S.	D2	144
Lakeside Mountains, mts., Ut., U.S.	B3	151
Lakeside Park, Ky., U.S.	h13	124
Lakesite, Tn., U.S.	D8	149
Lake Station, In., U.S.	A3	121
Lake Station, Ok., U.S.	A5	143
Lake Stevens, Wa., U.S.	A3	154
Lake Superior Provincial Park, Ont., Can.	p18	103
Lake Swamp, stm., S.C., U.S.	D8	147
Lake Tansi Village, Tn., U.S.	D8	149
Lake Telemark, N.J., U.S.	B4	137
Lake Tomahawk, Wi., U.S.	C4	156
Laketon, In., U.S.	C6	121
Laketown, Ut., U.S.	B4	151
Lake Valley, Sask., Can.	G2	105
Lake Valley, val., Nv., U.S.	E7	135
Lake View, Ar., U.S.	C5	111
Lake View, Ia., U.S.	B2	122
Lakeview, Mi., U.S.	E5	129
Lake View, N.Y., U.S.	C2	139
Lakeview, Oh., U.S.	B2	142
Lakeview, Or., U.S.	E6	144
Lake View, S.C., U.S.	C9	147
Lake Villa, Il., U.S.	h8	120
Lake Village, Ar., U.S.	D4	111
Lake Village, In., U.S.	B3	121
Lakeville, Ct., U.S.	B2	114
Lakeville, In., U.S.	A5	121
Lakeville, Ma., U.S.	C6	128
Lakeville, Mn., U.S.	F5	130
Lakeville, N.Y., U.S.	C3	139
Lake Waccamaw, N.C., U.S.	C4	140
Lake Wales, Fl., U.S.	E5	116
Lake Wilson, Mn., U.S.	G3	130
Lakewood, Ca., U.S.	n12	112
Lakewood, Co., U.S.	B5	113
Lakewood, Il., U.S.	D5	120
Lakewood, Ia., U.S.	f8	122
Lakewood, N.J., U.S.	C4	137
Lakewood, N.Y., U.S.	C1	139
Lakewood, Oh., U.S.	A4	142
Lakewood, Tn., U.S.	A5	149
Lakewood, Wa., U.S.	A3	154
Lakewood Center, Wa., U.S.	B3	154
Lake Worth, Fl., U.S.	F6	116
Lake Worth Inlet, b., Fl., U.S.	F7	116
Lake Zurich, Il., U.S.	h8	120
Lakhīmpur, India	G9	44
Lakhish, val., Asia	E3	50
Lakin, Ks., U.S.	E2	123
Lakinsk, Russia	E22	22
Lakonikós Kólpos, b., Grc.	M6	20
Lakota, Ia., U.S.	A3	122
Lakota, N.D., U.S.	A7	141
Lakshadweep, ter., India	H2	46
Lakshadweep, is., India	G2	46
Lakshadweep Sea, Asia	H3	46
La Lajilla, Mex.	D10	90
L'Albufera, l., Spain	F11	16
La Leonesa, Arg.	D9	80
Lalibela, Eth.	K10	60
La Libertad, El Sal.	D5	92
La Libertad, Guat.	I14	90
La Libertad, Hond.	C7	92
La Libertad, Nic.	E9	92
La Libertad, dept., Peru	B2	82
La Ligua, Chile	G3	80
La Lima, Hond.	B7	92
La Línea, Spain	I6	16
Lalitpur, India	H8	44
Lālmanir Hāt, Bngl.	H13	44
La Loche, Sask., Can.	m7	105
La Loupe, Fr.	D8	14
Lalupon, Nig.	H12	64
La Luz, Mex.	E11	90
La Luz, Nic.	D10	92
La Luz, N.M., U.S.	E4	138
Lama, ozero, l., Russia	D16	26
La Macarena, Serranía de, mts., Col.	F6	84
La Maddalena, Italy	H4	18
La Madera, N.M., U.S.	A3	138
Lamadong, China	C7	32
La Madrid, Arg.	D6	80
La Malbaie, Que., Can.	B7	104
Lamaline, Newf., Can.	E4	102
La Mancha, reg., Spain	G8	16
Lamar, Ar., U.S.	B2	111
Lamar, Co., U.S.	C8	113
Lamar, Mo., U.S.	D3	132
Lamar, Pa., U.S.	D7	145
Lamar, S.C., U.S.	C7	147
Lamar, co., Al., U.S.	B1	108
Lamar, co., Ga., U.S.	C2	117
Lamar, co., Ms., U.S.	D4	131
Lamar, co., Tx., U.S.	C5	150
Lamar, stm., Wy., U.S.	B2	157
Lamarche, Fr.	D12	14
La Mariscala, Ur.	H11	80
Lamarque, Arg.	J6	80
La Marsa, Tun.	M5	18
Lamas, Peru	B3	82
Lamasco, Ky., U.S.	f10	124
La Masica, Hond.	B7	92
Lamastre, Fr.	H11	14
La Mauricie, Parc National de, Que., Can.	C5	104
Lamb, co., Tx., U.S.	B1	150
Lamballe, Fr.	D4	14
Lambaréné, Gabon	B2	58
Lambari, stm., Braz.	F6	79
Lambayeque, Peru	B2	82
Lambayeque, dept., Peru	B1	82
Lambayeque, stm., Peru	B2	82
Lambert, Ms., U.S.	A3	131
Lambert, Mt., U.S.	C12	133
Lambert Glacier, Ant.	C5	73
Lamberton, Mn., U.S.	F3	130
Lambert's Bay, S. Afr.	I4	66
Lambertville, Mi., U.S.	G7	129
Lambertville, N.J., U.S.	C3	137
Lambomakondro, Madag.	s21	67b
Lambrama, Peru	E5	82
Lambrook, Ar., U.S.	C5	111
Lambton, Cape, c., N.W. Ter., Can.	B8	96
Lame Deer, Mt., U.S.	E10	133
La Media Luna, Arrecifes de, rf., Hond.	B12	92
La Mendieta, Arg.	C6	80
Lamèque, N.B., Can.	B5	101
Lamèque, Île, i., N.B., Can.	B5	101
La Merced, Arg.	E6	80
La Merced, Arg.	C6	80
La Merced, Peru	D4	82
La Mesa, Pan.	I13	92
La Mesa, Ca., U.S.	F5	112
La Mesa, N.M., U.S.	E3	138
Lamesa, Tx., U.S.	C2	150
Lamía, Grc.	K6	20
L'amin, stm., Russia	E12	26
La Minerve, Que., Can.	C3	104
La Moille, Il., U.S.	B4	120
Lamoille, Nv., U.S.	C6	135
Lamoille, co., Vt., U.S.	B3	152
Lamoille, stm., Vt., U.S.	B3	152
Lamoille, North Branch, stm., Vt., U.S.	B3	152
La Moine, stm., Il., U.S.	C3	120
Lamon Bay, b., Phil.	n19	39b
Lamoni, Ia., U.S.	D4	122
Lamont, Alta., Can.	C4	98
Lamont, Ca., U.S.	E4	112
Lamont, Ia., U.S.	B6	122
Lamont, Ok., U.S.	A4	143
La Monte, Mo., U.S.	C4	132
La Mosquitia, hist. reg., Hond.	B11	92
La Mothe-Achard, Fr.	F5	14
La Motte, Ia., U.S.	B7	122
La Motte, Isle, i., Vt., U.S.	B2	152
Lamotte-Beuvron, Fr.	E9	14
La Moure, N.D., U.S.	C7	141
La Moure, co., N.D., U.S.	C7	141
Lampa, Peru	F6	82
Lampang, Thai.	E5	40
Lampasas, Tx., U.S.	D3	150
Lampasas, co., Tx., U.S.	D3	150
Lampazos de Naranjo, Mex.	D9	90
Lampedusa, Isola di, i., Italy	N7	18
Lamphun, Thai.	E5	40
Lampman, Sask., Can.	H4	105
Lamprey, stm., N.H., U.S.	D4	136
Lamud, Peru	B3	82
La Muerte, Cerro, mtn., C.R.	H11	92
Lana, Italy	C6	18
Lanagan, Mo., U.S.	E3	132
Lanai, i., Hi., U.S.	C4	118
Lanai City, Hi., U.S.	C5	118
Lanaihale, mtn., Hi., U.S.	C5	118
Lanalhue, Lago, l., Chile	I2	80
Lanare, Ca., U.S.	D4	112
Lanark, Ont., Can.	C8	103
Lanark, Il., U.S.	A4	120
Lanark, W.V., U.S.	D3	155
Lanark Village, Fl., U.S.	C2	116
Lanbi Kyun, i., Mya.	I5	40
Lancashire, co., Eng., U.K.	H11	8
Lancaster, Ont., Can.	B10	103
Lancaster, Eng., U.K.	G11	8
Lancaster, Ca., U.S.	E4	112
Lancaster, Ks., U.S.	C8	123
Lancaster, Ky., U.S.	C5	124
Lancaster, Ma., U.S.	B4	128
Lancaster, Mn., U.S.	B2	130
Lancaster, Mo., U.S.	A5	132
Lancaster, N.H., U.S.	B3	136
Lancaster, N.Y., U.S.	C2	139
Lancaster, Oh., U.S.	C3	142
Lancaster, Pa., U.S.	F9	145
Lancaster, S.C., U.S.	B6	147
Lancaster, Tn., U.S.	C8	149
Lancaster, Tx., U.S.	n10	150
Lancaster, Wi., U.S.	F3	156
Lancaster, co., Ne., U.S.	D9	134
Lancaster, co., Pa., U.S.	G9	145
Lancaster, co., S.C., U.S.	B6	147
Lancaster, co., Va., U.S.	C6	153
Lancaster Sound, strt., N.W. Ter., Can.	B16	96
Lance, Point, c., Newf., Can.	E4	102
Lance Creek, Wy., U.S.	C8	157
Lance Creek, stm., Wy., U.S.	C8	157
Lancer, Sask., Can.	G1	105
Lanchyn, Ukr.	A8	20
Lanciano, Italy	G9	18
Lancing, Tn., U.S.	C8	149
Lancones, Peru	J2	84
Lancun, China	G8	32
Łańcut, Pol.	E22	10
Lancy, Switz.	F5	13
Landau, Ger.	F8	10
Landau an der Isar, Ger.	G12	10
Land Between the Lakes, U.S.	f9	124
Landeck, Aus.	H10	10
Landen, Bel.	G7	12
Lander, Wy., U.S.	D4	157
Lander, co., Nv., U.S.	C4	135
Landerneau, Fr.	D2	14
Landes, dept., Fr.	H6	14
Landess, In., U.S.	C6	121
Landete, Spain	F10	16
Landing Lake, l., Man., Can.	B3	100
Landis, Sask., Can.	E1	105
Landis, N.C., U.S.	B2	140
Landivisiau, Fr.	D2	14
Lando, S.C., U.S.	B5	147
Land O' Lakes, Wi., U.S.	B4	156
Landquart, Switz.	E12	13
Landrum, S.C., U.S.	A3	147
Landsberg [am Lech], Ger.	G10	10
Land's End, c., Eng., U.K.	K8	8
Lands End, c., R.I., U.S.	F5	146
Landshut, Ger.	G12	10
Landskrona, Swe.	N13	6
Landsman Creek, stm., Co., U.S.	B8	113
Lane, Ks., U.S.	D8	123
Lane, Ok., U.S.	C6	143
Lane, S.C., U.S.	D8	147
Lane, co., Ks., U.S.	D3	123
Lane, co., Or., U.S.	C4	144
Laneburg, Ar., U.S.	D2	111
La Negra, Chile	B3	80
Lanesboro, Ma., U.S.	A1	128
Lanesboro, Mn., U.S.	G7	130
Lanesboro, Pa., U.S.	C10	145
Lanesville, In., U.S.	H6	121
Lanett, Al., U.S.	C4	108
Lang, Sask., Can.	H3	105
Langano, Lake, l., Eth.	N10	60
Langarūd, Iran	C11	48
Lang Bay, B.C., Can.	E5	99
Langdon, Alta., Can.	D4	98
Langdon, N.H., U.S.	D2	136
Langdon, N.D., U.S.	A7	141
Langeac, Fr.	G10	14
Langeais, Fr.	E7	14
Langeloth, Pa., U.S.	F1	145
Langenburg, Sask., Can.	G5	105
Langenhagen, Ger.	C9	10
Langenthal, Switz.	D8	13
Langford, S.D., U.S.	B8	148
Langham, Sask., Can.	E2	105
Langholm, Scot., U.K.	F10	8
Langhorne, Pa., U.S.	F12	145
Langlade, co., Wi., U.S.	C4	156
Langley, B.C., Can.	f13	99
Langley, Ky., U.S.	C7	124
Langley, Ok., U.S.	A6	143
Langley, S.C., U.S.	E4	147
Langley, Wa., U.S.	A3	154
Langley Air Force Base, mil., Va., U.S.	h15	153
Langley Park, Md., U.S.	f9	127
Langleyville, Il., U.S.	D4	120
Langlo, stm., Austl.	E6	70
Langnau, Switz.	E8	13
Langogne, Fr.	H10	14
Langon, Fr.	H6	14
Langøya, i., Nor.	G14	6
Langqiao, China	E7	34
Langres, Fr.	E12	14
Langruth, Man., Can.	D2	100
Langsa, Indon.	L4	40
Lang Son, Viet.	D9	40
Langston, Ok., U.S.	B4	143
Langtian, China	J2	34
Langton, Ont., Can.	E4	103
Langue, Hond.	D7	92
Languedoc, hist. reg., Fr.	I9	14
Langui Layo, Laguna de, l., Peru	F6	82
L'Anguille, stm., Ar., U.S.	B5	111
Langxi, China	D8	34
Langzhong, China	E8	30
Lanham, Md., U.S.	C4	127
Lanier, co., Ga., U.S.	E3	117
Lanigan, Sask., Can.	F3	105
Länkäran, Azer.	J7	26
Lankin, N.D., U.S.	A8	141
Lankou, China	L4	34
Lannemezan, Fr.	I7	14
Lannilis, Fr.	D2	14
Lannion, Fr.	D3	14
Lannon, Wi., U.S.	m11	156
L'Annonciation, Que., Can.	C3	104
Lanoka Harbor, N.J., U.S.	D4	137
Lanquín, Guat.	B5	92
Lansdale, Pa., U.S.	F11	145
Lansdowne, Ont., Can.	C8	103
Lansdowne, Md., U.S.	B4	127
L'Anse, Mi., U.S.	B2	129
L'Anse-au-Clair, Newf., Can.	C3	102
L'Anse-au-Loup, Newf., Can.	C3	102
L'Anse-aux-Meadows, Newf., Can.	C4	102
L'Anse Indian Reservation, Mi., U.S.	B2	129
Lansford, N.D., U.S.	A4	141
Lansford, Pa., U.S.	E10	145
Lansing, Il., U.S.	B6	120
Lansing, Ia., U.S.	A6	122
Lansing, Ks., U.S.	C9	123
Lansing, Mi., U.S.	F6	129
Lansing, N.Y., U.S.	C4	139
Lansing, W.V., U.S.	m13	155
Lanslebourg, Fr.	G13	14
Lantana, Fl., U.S.	F6	116
Lantang, China	L3	34
Lantau Island, i., H.K.	M2	34
Lantern Hill, hill, Ct., U.S.	D8	114
Lantsch, Switz.	E12	13
Lanusei, Italy	J4	18
Lanxi, China	F8	34
Lanzarote, i., Spain	n27	17b
Lanzhou, China	D7	30
Laoag, Phil.	I19	39b
Lao Cai, Viet.	C7	40
Laochang, China	B8	40
Laoge, China	C8	34
Laoha, stm., China	A7	32
Laois, co., Ire.	I6	8
Laojie, China	B5	40
La Oliva, Spain	o27	17b
Laon, Fr.	C10	14
Laona, Wi., U.S.	C5	156
La Orchila, Isla, i., Ven.	B10	84
La Orchila, Isla, i., Ven.	I11	94
La Orotava, Spain	o24	17b
La Oroya, Peru	D4	82
Laos (Lao), ctry., Asia	B3	38
Laotto, In., U.S.	B7	121
Laoxinkou, China	E1	34
Laoyingpan, China	I4	34
Laozishan, China	B7	34
Lapa, Braz.	C14	80
Lapalisse, Fr.	F10	14
La Palma, Col.	E5	84
La Palma, El Sal.	C5	92
La Palma, Pan.	C3	84
La Palma, Pan.	D2	84
La Palma, Az., U.S.	E4	110
La Palma, i., Spain	o23	17b
La Palma del Condado, Spain	H5	16
La Paloma, Ur.	H11	80
La Pampa, prov., Arg.	I5	80
La Paragua, Ven.	D11	84
La Pasión, Río de, stm., Guat.	I14	90
La Passe, Ont., Can.	B8	103
La Patrie, Que., Can.	D6	104
La Paz, Arg.	G5	80
La Paz, Arg.	F9	80
La Paz, Bol.	G7	82
La Paz, Col.	B6	84
La Paz, Hond.	C7	92
La Paz, Mex.	E4	90
La Paz, Mex.	F9	90
Lapaz, In., U.S.	B5	121
La Paz, Ur.	H10	80
La Paz, dept., Bol.	F7	82
La Paz, dept., Hond.	C7	92
La Paz, co., Az., U.S.	D2	110
La Paz, Bahía, b., Mex.	E4	90
La Paz, Río de, stm., Bol.	G8	82
La Paz Centro, Nic.	E8	92
La Pedrera, Col.	H8	84
Lapeer, Mi., U.S.	E7	129
Lapeer, co., Mi., U.S.	E7	129
Lapel, In., U.S.	D6	121
La Perla, Mex.	C7	90
La Perouse Strait (Sōya-kaikyō), strt., Asia	b17	36a
La Pesca, Mex.	F11	90
La Piedad de Cabadas, Mex.	G8	90
Lapine, Al., U.S.	D3	108
La Pine, Or., U.S.	D5	144
Lapin lääni, prov., Fin.	H20	6
Lapinlahti, Fin.	J20	6
La Pintada, Pan.	I14	92
La Place, Il., U.S.	D5	120
La Place, La., U.S.	h11	125
Lapland, hist. reg., Eur.	H18	6
La Plata, Arg.	H10	80
La Plata, Col.	F5	84
La Plata, Md., U.S.	C4	127
La Plata, Mo., U.S.	A5	132
La Plata, co., Co., U.S.	D3	113
La Plata Mountains, mts., Co., U.S.	D3	113
La Plata Peak, mtn., Co., U.S.	B4	113
La Platte, Ne., U.S.	g13	134
La Platte, stm., Vt., U.S.	C2	152
La Pobla de Segur, Spain	C12	16
La Pocatière, Que., Can.	B7	104
La Poile Bay, b., Newf., Can.	E2	102
Lapoint, Ut., U.S.	C6	151
Laporte, Co., U.S.	A5	113
La Porte, In., U.S.	A4	121
La Porte, Tx., U.S.	r14	150
La Porte, co., In., U.S.	A4	121
La Porte City, Ia., U.S.	B5	122
La Poza Grande, Mex.	E3	90
Lappeenranta, Fin.	K21	6
Lappfjärd (Lapväärtti), Fin.	J17	6
La Prairie, Que., Can.	D4	104
La Prairie, Mn., U.S.	C5	130
La Presa, stm., Mex.	E4	90
Laprida, Arg.	I8	80
Laprida, Arg.	E6	80
La Pryor, Tx., U.S.	E3	150
Lâpseki, Tur.	I10	20
Laptev Sea see Laptevych, more, Russia	B17	28
Laptevych, more (Laptev Sea), Russia	B17	28
La Puebla de Cazalla, Spain	H6	16

Name	Map Ref.	Page
La Puebla de Montalbán, Spain	F7	16
La Puerta, Arg.	E6	80
La Purísima, Mex.	D3	90
Lăpuș, Rom.	B8	20
La Push, Wa., U.S.	B1	154
Lapwai, Id., U.S.	C2	119
La Quiaca, Arg.	B6	80
La Quiaca, Arg.	J9	82
L'Aquila, Italy	G8	18
Lār, Iran	H13	48
Lara, state, Ven.	B8	84
Larache, Mor.	J5	16
Laragne-Montéglin, Fr.	H12	14
Laramate, Peru	F4	82
Laramie, Wy., U.S.	E7	157
Laramie, co., Wy., U.S.	E8	157
Laramie, stm., U.S.	E7	157
Laramie Mountains, mts., Wy., U.S.	D7	157
Laramie Peak, mtn., Wy., U.S.	D7	157
Laranjaí, stm., Braz.	G1	79
Laranjal, Braz.	F7	79
Laranjeiras do Sul, Braz.	C12	80
Laraos, Peru	E4	82
Larap, Phil.	n20	39b
La Raya, Abra, Peru	F6	82
L'Arbresle, Fr.	G11	14
Larche, Col de, Eur.	H13	14
Larchmont, N.Y., U.S.	h13	139
Larchwood, Ia., U.S.	A1	122
Lardeau, B.C., Can.	D9	99
L'Ardoise, N.S., Can.	D9	101
Laredo, Spain	B8	16
Laredo, Mo., U.S.	A4	132
Laredo, Tx., U.S.	F3	150
La Reforma, Mex.	E5	90
La Réole, Fr.	H6	14
Lares, Peru	E5	82
La Restinga, Spain	p23	17b
Largo, Fl., U.S.	E4	116
Largo, Cañon, val., N.M., U.S.	A2	138
Largo, Cayo, i., Cuba	D4	94
Largo, Key, i., Fl., U.S.	G6	116
Largs, Scot., U.K.	F9	8
Lari, Peru	F6	82
Larimer, co., Co., U.S.	A5	113
Larimore, N.D., U.S.	B8	141
Larino, Italy	H9	18
La Rioja, Arg.	E5	80
La Rioja, prov., Arg.	E5	80
La Rioja, prov., Spain	C9	16
Lárisa, Grc.	J6	20
La Rivière, Man., Can.	E2	100
Lark, Ut., U.S.	C3	151
Lārkāna, Pak.	G3	44
Lark Harbour, Newf., Can.	D2	102
Larkinsville, Al., U.S.	A3	108
Larkspur, Ca., U.S.	h7	112
Larkspur, Co., U.S.	B6	113
Larksville, Pa., U.S.	n17	145
Lárnax (Larnaca), Cyp.	D2	48
Larned, Ks., U.S.	D4	123
La Rochefoucauld, Fr.	G7	14
La Rochelle, Fr.	F5	14
La Roche-sur-Yon, Fr.	F5	14
La Roda, Spain	F9	16
La Romana, Dom. Rep.	E10	94
La Ronge, Sask., Can.	B3	105
Larose, La., U.S.	E5	125
La Rosita, Nic.	D10	92
Larreynaga, Nic.	E8	92
Larroque, Arg.	G9	80
Larrys River, N.S., Can.	D8	101
Larsen Bay, Ak., U.S.	D9	109
Larsen Ice Shelf, Ant.	B12	73
Larteh Aheneasi, Ghana	I10	64
La Rubia, Arg.	F8	80
La Rue, Oh., U.S.	B2	142
Larue, co., Ky., U.S.	C4	124
Laruns, Fr.	J6	14
Larvik, Nor.	L12	6
Larwill, In., U.S.	B6	121
La Sabana, Arg.	D9	80
La Sal, Ut., U.S.	E6	151
LaSalle, Que., Can.	q19	104
La Salle, Co., U.S.	A6	113
La Salle, Il., U.S.	B4	120
La Salle, co., Il., U.S.	B4	120
La Salle, co., La., U.S.	C3	125
La Salle, co., Tx., U.S.	E3	150
Las Almejas, Bahía, b., Mex.	E4	90
La Sal Mountains, mts., Ut., U.S.	E6	151
Las Animas, Co., U.S.	C7	113
Las Animas, co., Co., U.S.	D6	113
La Sarraz, Switz.	E6	13
La Sarre, Que., Can.	k11	104
Las Arrias, Arg.	F7	80
Las Aves, Islas, is., Ven.	A9	84
Las Ballenas, Canal de, strt., Mex.	C3	90
Las Bonitas, Ven.	D10	84
Las Breñas, Arg.	D8	80
Las Cabezas de San Juan, Spain	I6	16
Las Cabras, Chile	H3	80
Lascano, Ur.	G11	80
Lascar, Volcán, vol., Chile	B5	80
Las Catitas, Arg.	G4	80
Lascaux, Grotte de, Fr.	G8	14
Las Cejas, Arg.	D6	80
Las Choapas, Mex.	I12	90
La Scie, Newf., Can.	D4	102
Las Cruces, N.M., U.S.	E3	138
Las Cuevas, Mex.	C9	90
Las Delicias, Mex.	J14	90
La Selle, Morne, mtn., Haiti	E9	94
La Serena, Chile	E3	80
La Seyne, Fr.	I12	14
Las Flores, Arg.	I9	80
Las Flores, Arg.	F4	80
Las Flores, Arroyo, stm., Arg.	H9	80
Las Flores, Cerro, mtn., Mex.	I12	90
Las Garcitas, Arg.	D9	80
Las Guayabas, Mex.	E11	90
Lashburn, Sask., Can.	D1	105
Lāsh-e Joveyn, Afg.	F16	48
Las Heras, Arg.	G4	80
Lashio, Mya.	C4	40
Las Hormigas, Mex.	E10	90
La Sierra, Montaña, mts., Hond.	C7	92
Las Iglesias, Cerro, mtn., Mex.	D6	90
Łasin, Pol.	B19	10
Łask, Pol.	D19	10
L'askel'a, Russia	K22	6
Las Lajas, Arg.	J3	80
Las Lajas, Pan.	C2	84
Las Lajitas, Arg.	C6	80
Las Lomas, Peru	J2	84
Las Lomitas, Arg.	C8	80
Lašma, Russia	G24	22
Las Malvinas, Arg.	H4	80
Las Margaritas, Mex.	I14	90
Las Marianas, Arg.	H9	80
Las Mercedes, Ven.	C9	84
Las Minas, Cerro, mtn., Hond.	C6	92
Las Nieves, Mex.	D7	90
Las Nopaleras, Cerro, mtn., Mex.	E8	90
La Solana, Spain	G8	16
La Soledad, Cerro, mtn., Mex.	D6	90
Las Ovejas, Arg.	I3	80
Las Palmas, Arg.	D9	80
Las Palmas, Pan.	C2	84
Las Palmas, prov., Spain	o26	17b
Las Palmas de Gran Canaria, Spain	o25	17b
La Spezia, Italy	E4	18
Las Piedras, Ur.	H10	80
Las Piedras, Río de, stm., Peru	E7	82
Las Plumas, Arg.	E3	78
Las Rosas, Arg.	G8	80
Las Rosas, Mex.	I13	90
Lassance, Braz.	D6	79
Lassay, Fr.	D6	14
Lassen, co., Ca., U.S.	B3	112
Lassen Peak, vol., Ca., U.S.	B3	112
Lassen Volcanic National Park, Ca., U.S.	B3	112
L'Assomption, Que., Can.	D4	104
Las Tablas, Pan.	D2	84
Las Tinajas, Arg.	D7	80
Last Mountain Lake, l., Sask., Can.	F3	105
Las Toscas, Arg.	E9	80
Lastoursville, Gabon	B2	58
Las Tunas, Cuba	D6	94
Las Tunas Grandes, Laguna, l., Arg.	I7	80
La Suze, Fr.	E7	14
Las Varas, Mex.	C5	90
Las Varas, Mex.	G7	90
Las Varillas, Arg.	F7	80
Las Vegas, Nv., U.S.	G6	135
Las Vegas, N.M., U.S.	B4	138
Las Vegas, Ven.	C8	84
Latacunga, Ec.	H3	84
Latady Island, i., Ant.	C12	73
La Tagua, Col.	H5	84
Latah, co., Id., U.S.	C2	119
Latakia see Al-Lādhiqīyah, Syria	D3	48
La Teste-de-Buch, Fr.	H5	14
La Tetilla, Cerro, mtn., Mex.	G7	90
Latham, Il., U.S.	D4	120
Latham, Ks., U.S.	E7	123
Lathrop, Ca., U.S.	h10	112
Lathrop, Mo., U.S.	B3	132
Lathrop Wells, Nv., U.S.	G5	135
Latimer, Ia., U.S.	B4	122
Latimer, co., Ok., U.S.	C6	143
Latina, Italy	H7	18
Latisana, Italy	D8	18
La Toma, Arg.	G6	80
Laton, Ca., U.S.	D4	112
La Tortuga, Isla, i., Ven.	B10	84
Latorytsya, stm., Eur.	G22	10
Latouche Treville, Cape, c., Austl.	C4	68
La Tour-du-Pin, Fr.	G12	14
Latour Peak, mtn., Id., U.S.	B2	119
Latowicz, Pol.	C21	10
La Tremblade, Fr.	G5	14
La Trimouille, Fr.	F8	14
La Trinidad, Arg.	D6	80
La Trinidad, Nic.	E8	92
La Trinidad de Orichuna, Ven.	D8	84
La Trinitaria, Mex.	I13	90
La Trinité, Mart.	G14	94
Latrobe, Austl.	M7	70
Latrobe, Pa., U.S.	F3	145
Latta, S.C., U.S.	C9	147
Lattimer Mines, Pa., U.S.	E10	145
La Tuque, Que., Can.	B5	104
Lātūr, India	C4	46
Latvia (Latvija), ctry., Eur.	D8	22
Lauca, stm., Bol.	H7	82
Lauchhammer, Ger.	D13	10
Lauder, Man., Can.	E1	100
Lauder, Scot., U.K.	F11	8
Lauderdale, Ms., U.S.	C5	131
Lauderdale, co., Al., U.S.	A2	108
Lauderdale, co., Ms., U.S.	C5	131
Lauderdale, co., Tn., U.S.	B2	149
Lauderdale Lakes, Fl., U.S.	r13	116
Lauf an der Pegnitz, Ger.	F11	10
Läufelfingen, Switz.	D8	13
Laufen, Switz.	D8	13
Laughery Creek, stm., In., U.S.	F7	121
Laughlin, Nv., U.S.	H7	135
Laughlin Air Force Base, mil., Tx., U.S.	E2	150
Laughlin Peak, mtn., N.M., U.S.	A5	138
Laughlintown, Pa., U.S.	F3	145
Laukuva, Lith.	F5	22
Launceston, Austl.	M7	70
Launceston, Eng., U.K.	K9	8
Launching Point, c., P.E.I., Can.	C7	101
La Unión, Chile	E2	78
La Unión, Col.	G4	84
La Unión, El Sal.	D7	92
La Unión, Mex.	I9	90
La Unión, Peru	A1	82
La Unión, Peru	C3	82
La Unión, Spain	H11	16
La Union, N.M., U.S.	F3	138
La Unión, Ven.	C9	84
Laupahoehoe, Hi., U.S.	D6	118
Laura, Austl.	C8	68
La Urbana, Ven.	D9	84
Laurel, Ont., Can.	D4	103
Laurel, De., U.S.	F3	115
Laurel, Fl., U.S.	E4	116
Laurel, In., U.S.	F7	121
Laurel, Ia., U.S.	C5	122
Laurel, Md., U.S.	B4	127
Laurel, Ms., U.S.	D4	131
Laurel, Mt., U.S.	E8	133
Laurel, Ne., U.S.	B8	134
Laurel, Va., U.S.	C5	153
Laurel, co., Ky., U.S.	C5	124
Laurel, stm., Ky., U.S.	D5	124
Laurel Bay, S.C., U.S.	G6	147
Laurel Bloomery, Tn., U.S.	C12	149
Laurel Creek, stm., W.V., U.S.	n14	155
Laurel Creek, stm., W.V., U.S.	m12	155
Laureldale, Pa., U.S.	F10	145
Laureles, Ur.	F11	80
Laurel Fork, stm., W.V., U.S.	C5	155
Laurel Hill, Fl., U.S.	u15	116
Laurel Hill, N.C., U.S.	C3	140
Laurel Mountain, mtn., W.V., U.S.	B5	155
Laurel River Lake, res., Ky., U.S.	D5	124
Laurel Run, Pa., U.S.	n17	145
Laurelville, Oh., U.S.	C3	142
Laurence G. Hanscom Air Force Base, mil., Ma., U.S.	g10	128
Laurence Harbor, N.J., U.S.	C4	137
Laurens, Ia., U.S.	B3	122
Laurens, S.C., U.S.	C3	147
Laurens, co., Ga., U.S.	D4	117
Laurens, co., S.C., U.S.	C4	147
Laurentides, Que., Can.	D4	104
Laurentides, Parc Provincial des, Que., Can.	B6	104
Lauria, Italy	I10	18
Laurie Island, i., Ant.	B1	73
Laurie Island, i., Ant.	K10	74
Laurier, Man., Can.	D2	100
Laurier, Que., Can.	C6	104
Laurière, Fr.	F8	14
Laurierville, Que., Can.	C6	104
Laurinburg, N.C., U.S.	C3	140
Laurium, Mi., U.S.	A2	129
Lausanne, Switz.	E6	13
Laut, Pulau, i., Indon.	F6	38
Lauta, Ger.	D14	10
Lautaro, Chile	J2	80
Lauterbach, Ger.	E9	10
Lauterbrunnen, Switz.	E8	13
Lauter [Sachsen], Ger.	E12	10
Laut Kecil, Kepulauan, is., Indon.	F6	38
Lauzon (part of Lévis-Lauzon), Que., Can.	C6	104
Lava (Łyna), stm., Eur.	G4	22
Lava, Nosy, i., Madag.	o22	67b
Lava Beds National Monument, Ca., U.S.	B3	112
Lavaca, Al., U.S.	C1	108
Lavaca, Ar., U.S.	B1	111
Lavaca, co., Tx., U.S.	E4	150
Lava Hot Springs, Id., U.S.	G6	119
Lavaisse, Arg.	G6	80
Laval, Que., Can.	D4	104
Laval, Fr.	D6	14
La Vale, Md., U.S.	k13	127
La Vall d'Uixo, Spain	F11	16
Lavalle, Arg.	E6	80
Lavalle, Arg.	E9	80
La Valle, Wi., U.S.	E3	156
Lavallette, N.J., U.S.	D4	137
La Valley, Co., U.S.	D5	113
Lavaltrie, Que., Can.	D4	104
Lavapié, Punta, c., Chile	I2	80
Lávara, Grc.	H10	20
Lavardac, Fr.	H7	14
Lava-Tudo, stm., Braz.	E13	80
Laveen, Az., U.S.	m8	110
La Vega, Dom. Rep.	E9	94
La Vela, Cabo de, c., Col.	A6	84
La Vela de Coro, Ven.	B8	84
Lavelanet, Fr.	J8	14
Lavello, Italy	H10	18
L'Avenir, Que., Can.	D5	104
La Venta, hist., Mex.	H12	90
La Ventura, Mex.	E9	90
La Verde, Arg.	D9	80
La Vergne, Tn., U.S.	A5	149
La Verkin, Ut., U.S.	F2	151
La Verne, Ca., U.S.	m13	112
Laverne, Ok., U.S.	A2	143
La Vernia, Tx., U.S.	E3	150
Laverton, Austl.	E4	68
La Veta, Co., U.S.	D5	113
La Victoria, Ven.	B9	84
La Vila Joiosa, Spain	G11	16
La Villa, stm., Pan.	J14	92
Lavillette, N.B., Can.	B4	101
La Viña, Arg.	C6	80
Lavina, Mt., U.S.	D8	133
La Virginia, Col.	E5	84
La Vista, Ga., U.S.	*h8	117
La Vista, Ne., U.S.	g12	134
Lavonia, Ga., U.S.	B3	117
Lavon Lake, res., Tx., U.S.	m10	150
La Voulte-sur-Rhône, Fr.	H11	14
Lavoy, Alta., Can.	C5	98
Lavras, Braz.	F6	79
Lavras do Sul, Braz.	F12	80
Lavumisa, Swaz.	F10	66
Lawai, Hi., U.S.	B2	118
Lawdar, Yemen	H4	47
Lawford Lake, l., Man., Can.	B3	100
Lawksawk, Mya.	D4	40
Lawler, Ia., U.S.	A5	122
Lawn, Newf., Can.	E4	102
Lawndale, N.C., U.S.	B1	140
Lawn Hill, Austl.	B3	70
Lawrence, In., U.S.	E5	121
Lawrence, Ks., U.S.	D8	123
Lawrence, Ma., U.S.	A5	128
Lawrence, Mi., U.S.	F4	129
Lawrence, Ms., U.S.	C4	131
Lawrence, Ne., U.S.	D7	134
Lawrence, N.Y., U.S.	k13	139
Lawrence, Pa., U.S.	F1	145
Lawrence, co., Al., U.S.	A2	108
Lawrence, co., Ar., U.S.	A4	111
Lawrence, co., Il., U.S.	E6	120
Lawrence, co., In., U.S.	G4	121
Lawrence, co., Ky., U.S.	B7	124
Lawrence, co., Ms., U.S.	D3	131
Lawrence, co., Mo., U.S.	D4	132
Lawrence, co., Oh., U.S.	D3	142
Lawrence, co., Pa., U.S.	E1	145
Lawrence, co., Tn., U.S.	B4	149
Lawrenceburg, In., U.S.	F8	121
Lawrenceburg, Ky., U.S.	B5	124
Lawrenceburg, Tn., U.S.	B4	149
Lawrence Park, Pa., U.S.	B1	145
Lawrence Station, N.B., Can.	D2	101
Lawrencetown, N.S., Can.	E4	101
Lawrenceville, Que., Can.	D5	104
Lawrenceville, Ga., U.S.	C3	117
Lawrenceville, Il., U.S.	E6	120
Lawrenceville, N.J., U.S.	C3	137
Lawrenceville, Va., U.S.	D5	153
Lawson, Ar., U.S.	D3	111
Lawson, Mo., U.S.	B3	132
Lawsonia, Md., U.S.	E6	127
Lawtell, La., U.S.	D3	125
Lawtey, Fl., U.S.	B4	116
Lawton, Ia., U.S.	B1	122
Lawton, Mi., U.S.	F5	129
Lawton, Ok., U.S.	C3	143
Lawz, Jabal al-, mtn., Sau. Ar.	G3	48
Laxå, Swe.	L14	6
Lay Dam, Al., U.S.	C3	108
Laylā, Sau. Ar.	C5	47
Lay Lake, res., Al., U.S.	B3	108
Layland, W.V., U.S.	n14	155
Laysan Island, i., Hi., U.S.	k13	118
Laysville, Ct., U.S.	D6	114
Layton, Ut., U.S.	B4	151
Laytonville, Ca., U.S.	C2	112
La Zarca, Mex.	E7	90
Lázaro Cárdenas, Mex.	I8	90
Lázaro Cárdenas, Mex.	B2	90
Lázaro Cárdenas, Presa, res., Mex.	E7	90
Lazdijai, Lith.	G6	22
Lazhulong, China	C9	44
Lazio, prov., Italy	G7	18
Lea, co., N.M., U.S.	D6	138
Léach, Camb.	H7	40
Leachville, Ar., U.S.	B5	111
Lead, S.D., U.S.	C2	148
Leadbetter Point, c., Wa., U.S.	C1	154
Leader, Sask., Can.	G1	105
Lead Hill, Ar., U.S.	A3	111
Lead Hill, hill, Mo., U.S.	D5	132
Lead Mountain, mtn., Me., U.S.	D4	126
Lead Mountain Ponds, l., Me., U.S.	D4	126
Leadville, Co., U.S.	B4	113
Leadwood, Mo., U.S.	D7	132
Leaf, stm., Ms., U.S.	D5	131
Leaf Rapids, Man., Can.	A1	100
Leaf River, Il., U.S.	A4	120
League City, Tx., U.S.	r14	150
Leake, co., Ms., U.S.	C4	131
Leakesville, Ms., U.S.	D5	131
Lealman, Fl., U.S.	p10	116
Leamington, Ont., Can.	E2	103
Leamington, Ut., U.S.	D3	151
Leán, stm., Hond.	B7	92
Leandro N. Alem, Arg.	D11	80
Leary, Ga., U.S.	E2	117
Leasburg, Mo., U.S.	C6	132
Leask, Sask., Can.	E2	105
Leatherman Peak, mtn., Id., U.S.	E5	119
Leatherwood, Ky., U.S.	C6	124
L'Eau Frais Creek, stm., Ar., U.S.	C3	111
Leavenworth, In., U.S.	H5	121
Leavenworth, Ks., U.S.	C9	123
Leavenworth, Wa., U.S.	B5	154
Leavenworth, co., Ks., U.S.	C8	123
Leavittsburg, Oh., U.S.	A5	142
Leawood, Ks., U.S.	D9	123
Lebak, Phil.	D7	38
Lebam, Wa., U.S.	C2	154
Lebanon, Ct., U.S.	C7	114
Lebanon, De., U.S.	D4	115
Lebanon, Il., U.S.	E4	120
Lebanon, In., U.S.	D5	121
Lebanon, Ks., U.S.	C5	123
Lebanon, Ky., U.S.	C4	124
Lebanon, Mo., U.S.	D5	132
Lebanon, N.H., U.S.	C2	136
Lebanon, N.J., U.S.	B3	137
Lebanon, Oh., U.S.	C1	142
Lebanon, Ok., U.S.	D5	143
Lebanon, Or., U.S.	C4	144
Lebanon, Pa., U.S.	F9	145
Lebanon, S.D., U.S.	B6	148
Lebanon, Tn., U.S.	A5	149
Lebanon, Va., U.S.	f9	153
Lebanon, co., Pa., U.S.	F8	145
Lebanon (Lubnān), ctry., Asia	C2	42
Lebanon Junction, Ky., U.S.	C4	124
Leb'ažje, Kaz.	G13	26
Lebec, Ca., U.S.	E4	112
Lebed'an', Russia	H22	22
Le Blanc, Fr.	F8	14
Lebo, Ks., U.S.	D8	123
Lebombo Mountains, hills, Afr.	E10	66
Lębork, Pol.	A17	10
Lebret, Sask., Can.	G4	105
Lebrija, Spain	I5	16
Lebrija, stm., Col.	D6	84
Lebu, Chile	I2	80
Le Cannet, Fr.	I14	14
Le Cateau, Fr.	B10	14
Lecce, Italy	I13	18
Lecco, Italy	D4	18
Le Center, Mn., U.S.	F5	130
Lech, stm., Eur.	G10	10
Le Châble, Switz.	F7	13
Le Chesne, Fr.	C11	14
Le Cheylard, Fr.	H11	14
Lechiguanas, Islas de las, is., Arg.	G9	80
Lechtaler Alpen, mts., Aus.	H10	10
Lechuguilla, Cerro, mtn., Mex.	F7	90
Le Claire, Ia., U.S.	C7	122
Leclercville, Que., Can.	C6	104
Lecompte, La., U.S.	C3	125
Lecompton, Ks., U.S.	C8	123
Leconte, Mount, mtn., Tn., U.S.	D10	149
Le Creusot, Fr.	F11	14
Łęczyca, Pol.	C19	10
Led'anaja, gora, mtn., Russia	E26	28
Lede, Bel.	G4	12
Ledford, Il., U.S.	F5	120
Ledgewood, N.J., U.S.	B3	137
Ledo, India	D14	42
Ledong, China	E10	40
Ledoux, N.M., U.S.	B4	138
Ledu, China	D7	30
Leduc, Alta., Can.	C4	98
Lee, Il., U.S.	B5	120
Lee, Me., U.S.	C4	126
Lee, Ma., U.S.	B1	128
Lee, co., Al., U.S.	C4	108
Lee, co., Ar., U.S.	C5	111
Lee, co., Fl., U.S.	F5	116
Lee, co., Ga., U.S.	E2	117
Lee, co., Il., U.S.	B4	120
Lee, co., Ia., U.S.	D6	122
Lee, co., Ky., U.S.	C6	124
Lee, co., Ms., U.S.	A5	131
Lee, co., N.C., U.S.	B3	140
Lee, co., S.C., U.S.	C7	147
Lee, co., Tx., U.S.	D4	150
Lee, co., Va., U.S.	f8	153
Lee, Lake, l., Ms., U.S.	B3	131
Lee Center, Il., U.S.	B4	120
Leechburg, Pa., U.S.	E2	145
Leech Lake, l., Mn., U.S.	C4	130
Leech Lake Indian Reservation, Mn., U.S.	C4	130
Lee Creek, stm., U.S.	B1	111
Leedey, Ok., U.S.	B2	143
Leeds, Eng., U.K.	H12	8
Leeds, Al., U.S.	B3	108
Leeds, N.D., U.S.	A6	141
Leeds, Ut., U.S.	F2	151
Leek, Neth.	B9	12
Leelanau, co., Mi., U.S.	D5	129
Leelanau, Lake, l., Mi., U.S.	C5	129
Leende, Neth.	F8	12
Lee Park, Pa., U.S.	n17	145
Leeper, Mo., U.S.	D7	132
Leer, Ger.	B7	10
Leesburg, Al., U.S.	A4	108
Leesburg, Fl., U.S.	D5	116
Leesburg, Ga., U.S.	E2	117
Leesburg, In., U.S.	B6	121
Leesburg, Oh., U.S.	C2	142
Leesburg, Va., U.S.	A5	153
Lees Summit, Mo., U.S.	C3	132
Leesville, La., U.S.	C2	125
Leesville, S.C., U.S.	D4	147
Leesville Lake, res., Va., U.S.	C3	153
Leeton, Austl.	J7	70
Leeton, Mo., U.S.	C4	132
Leetonia, Oh., U.S.	B5	142
Leetsdale, Pa., U.S.	h13	145
Leeuwarden, Neth.	B8	12
Leeuwin, Cape, c., Austl.	F3	68
Lee Vining, Ca., U.S.	D4	112
Leeward Islands, is., N.A.	F13	94
Leffingwell, Ct., U.S.	C7	114
Leflore, co., Ms., U.S.	B3	131
Le Flore, co., Ok., U.S.	C7	143
Lefor, N.D., U.S.	C3	141
Lefors, Tx., U.S.	B2	150
Leftrook Lake, l., Man., Can.	A2	100
Legal, Alta., Can.	C4	98
Leganés, Spain	E8	16
Legaspi, Phil.	o20	39b
Leggett, Ca., U.S.	C2	112
Leghorn see Livorno, Italy	F5	18
Legion Mine, Zimb.	C9	66
Legionowo, Pol.	C20	10
Legnago, Italy	D6	18
Legnano, Italy	D3	18
Legnica (Liegnitz), Pol.	D16	10
Le Grand, Ca., U.S.	D3	112
Le Grand, Ia., U.S.	B5	122
Le Grand-Lucé, Fr.	E7	14
Le Grau-du-Roi, Fr.	I11	14
Leh, India	C7	44
Le Havre, Fr.	C7	14
Lehi, Ut., U.S.	C4	151
Lehigh, Ia., U.S.	B3	122
Lehigh, Ks., U.S.	D6	123
Lehigh, Ok., U.S.	C5	143
Lehigh, co., Pa., U.S.	E10	145
Lehigh, stm., Pa., U.S.	E10	145
Lehigh Acres, Fl., U.S.	F5	116
Lehighton, Pa., U.S.	E10	145
Leho, Sud.	N7	60
Lehr, N.D., U.S.	C6	141
Lehrte, Ger.	C9	10
Lehtse, Est.	B8	22
Lehua Island, i., Hi., U.S.	A1	118
Lehututu, Bots.	D5	66
Leiah, Pak.	E4	44
Leibnitz, Aus.	I15	10
Leicester, Eng., U.K.	I12	8
Leicester, Ma., U.S.	B4	128
Leicestershire, co., Eng., U.K.	I12	8
Leichhardt, stm., Austl.	A3	70
Leichhardt Range, mts., Austl.	C7	70
Leiden, Neth.	D6	12
Leie (Lys), stm., Eur.	B10	14
Leigh, Ne., U.S.	C8	134
Leigh Creek, Austl.	H3	70
Leighton, Al., U.S.	A2	108
Leikanger, Nor.	K10	6
Leine, stm., Ger.	C9	10
Leinster, hist. reg., Ire.	H6	8
Leipers Fork, Tn., U.S.	B5	149
Leipsic, De., U.S.	D3	115
Leipsic, Oh., U.S.	A2	142
Leipsic, stm., De., U.S.	C3	115
Leipzig, Ger.	D12	10
Leisure City, Fl., U.S.	s13	116
Leitches Creek, N.S., Can.	C9	101
Leitchfield, Ky., U.S.	C3	124
Leitersburg, Md., U.S.	A2	127
Leiters Ford, In., U.S.	B5	121
Leitha, stm., Eur.	H16	10
Leitrim, co., Ire.	H6	8
Leiyang, China	I1	34
Leizhou Bandao, pen., China	D11	40
Leizhuang, China	D6	32
Lejunior, Ky., U.S.	D6	124
Lek, stm., Neth.	E6	12
Le Kreïder, Alg.	C11	62
Leksand, Swe.	K14	6
Leksozero, ozero, l., Russia	J22	6
Le Lamentin, Mart.	G14	94
Leland, Il., U.S.	B5	120
Leland, Ia., U.S.	A4	122
Leland, Mi., U.S.	C5	129
Leland, Ms., U.S.	B3	131
Leleiwi Point, c., Hi., U.S.	D7	118
Leleque, Arg.	E2	78
Le Limbé, Haiti	E8	94
Leli Shan, mtn., China	D9	44
Le Locle, Switz.	D6	13
Leloup, Ks., U.S.	D8	123
Le Lude, Fr.	E7	14
Lelystad, Neth.	C7	12
Lema, Nig.	E12	64
Le Maire, Estrecho de, strt., Arg.	G4	73
Le Mans, Fr.	D7	14
Le Mars, Ia., U.S.	B1	122
Lemberg, Sask., Can.	G4	105
Lemdiyya, Alg.	B12	62
Leme, Braz.	G5	79
Lemesós (Limassol), Cyp.	D2	48
Lemgo, Ger.	C8	10
Lemhi, co., Id., U.S.	E4	119
Lemhi, stm., Id., U.S.	E5	119
Lemhi Pass, Id., U.S.	E5	119
Lemhi Range, mts., Id., U.S.	E5	119
Lemieux Islands, is., N.W. Ter., Can.	D20	96
Lemin, China	D10	40
Lemitar, N.M., U.S.	C3	138
Lemmon, S.D., U.S.	B3	148
Lemmon, Mount, mtn., Az., U.S.	E5	110
Lemmon Valley, Nv., U.S.	D2	135
Lemnos see Límnos, i., Grc.	J9	20
Lemon, Lake, l., In., U.S.	F5	121
Lemon Fair, stm., Vt., U.S.	C2	152
Lemon Grove, Ca., U.S.	o15	112
Lemon Island, i., S.C., U.S.	G6	147
Lemont, Il., U.S.	B5	120
Lemont, Pa., U.S.	E6	145
Le Mont-Saint-Michel, Fr.	D5	14
Lemonweir, stm., Wi., U.S.	D3	156
Lemoore, Ca., U.S.	D4	112
Lemoore Naval Air Station, mil., Ca., U.S.	D4	112
Le Moule, Guad.	F14	94
Lemoyne, Ne., U.S.	C4	134
Lempa, stm., N.A.	D6	92
Lem Peak, mtn., Id., U.S.	E5	119
Lempira, dept., Hond.	C6	92
Lempster, N.H., U.S.	D2	136
Lemsid, W. Sah.	G4	62
Lena, Il., U.S.	A4	120
Lena, La., U.S.	C3	125
Lena, Ms., U.S.	C4	131
Lena, Wi., U.S.	D5	156
Lena, stm., Russia	C17	28
Lenapah, Ok., U.S.	A6	143
Lenawee, co., Mi., U.S.	G6	129
Lençóis, Braz.	B8	79
Lendery, Russia	J22	6
Lenexa, Ks., U.S.	D9	123
Lenghu, China	D5	30
Lenhovda, Swe.	M14	6
Lenina, pik, mtn., Asia	J12	26
Leningrad see Sankt-Peterburg, Russia	B13	22
Leningradskaja, sci., Ant.	B8	73
Leninogorsk, Kaz.	G8	28
Leninogorsk, Russia	G8	26
Leninsk, Kaz.	H10	26
Leninsk, Uzb.	I12	26
Leninsk-Kuzneckij, Russia	G9	28
Lenk, Switz.	F7	13
Lennox, S.D., U.S.	D9	148
Lennox, Isla, i., Chile	H3	78
Lennoxville, Que., Can.	D6	104
Lenoir, N.C., U.S.	B1	140
Lenoir, co., N.C., U.S.	B5	140
Lenoir City, Tn., U.S.	D9	149
Lenora, Ks., U.S.	C4	123
Lenore, Man., Can.	E1	100
Lenore, Id., U.S.	C2	119
Lenore Lake, l., Sask., Can.	E3	105
Lenore Lake, l., Wa., U.S.	B6	154
Lenox, Ga., U.S.	E3	117
Lenox, Ia., U.S.	D3	122
Lenox, Ma., U.S.	B1	128
Lenox, Tn., U.S.	A2	149
Lens, Fr.	B9	14
Lensk, Russia	E14	28
Lenti, Hung.	I16	10
Lentini, Italy	L10	18
Lentner, Mo., U.S.	B5	132
Lentvaris, Lith.	G8	22
Lenzburg, Switz.	D9	13
Léo, Burkina	F8	64
Leo, In., U.S.	B7	121
Leoben, Aus.	H15	10
Léogâne, Haiti	E8	94
Leola, Ar., U.S.	C3	111
Leola, S.D., U.S.	B7	148
Leoma, Tn., U.S.	B4	149
Leominster, Ma., U.S.	A4	128
Léon, Fr.	I5	14
León, Nic.	E8	92
León, Spain	C6	16
Leon, Ia., U.S.	D4	122
Leon, Ks., U.S.	E7	123
León, dept., Nic.	E8	92
Leon, co., Fl., U.S.	B2	116
Leon, co., Tx., U.S.	D4	150
León, hist. reg., Spain	D6	16
Leona, Punta, c., C.R.	H10	92
Leonard, Ont., Can.	h13	103
Leonard, Mi., U.S.	F7	129
Leonard, N.D., U.S.	C8	141
Leonard, Ok., U.S.	B6	143
Leonard, Tx., U.S.	C4	150
Leonardo, N.J., U.S.	C4	137
Leonardtown, Md., U.S.	D4	127
Leonardville, N.B., Can.	E3	101
Leonardville, Ks., U.S.	C7	123
León [de los Aldamas], Mex.	G9	90
Leones, Arg.	G7	80

Name	Map Ref.	Page
Mackinaw, Il., U.S.	C4	120
Mackinaw, stm., Il., U.S.	C4	120
Mackinaw City, Mi., U.S.	C6	129
Mackinnon Road, Kenya	B7	58
Macklin, Sask., Can.	E1	105
Macks Creek, Mo., U.S.	D5	132
Macksville, Austl.	H10	70
Macksville, Ks., U.S.	E5	123
Mackville, Ky., U.S.	C4	124
Maclean, Austl.	G10	70
Macleod, Lake, l., Austl.	D2	58
Maclovia Herrera, Mex.	C7	90
Macmillan, stm., Yukon, Can.	D6	96
MacNutt, Sask., Can.	F5	105
Macomb, Il., U.S.	C3	120
Macomb, co., Mi., U.S.	F8	129
Macomer, Italy	I3	18
Mâcon, Fr.	F11	14
Macon, Ar., U.S.	C3	111
Macon, Ga., U.S.	D3	117
Macon, Il., U.S.	D5	120
Macon, Ms., U.S.	B5	131
Macon, Mo., U.S.	B5	132
Macon, Tn., U.S.	B2	149
Macon, co., Al., U.S.	C4	108
Macon, co., Ga., U.S.	D2	117
Macon, co., Il., U.S.	D4	120
Macon, co., Mo., U.S.	B5	132
Macon, co., N.C., U.S.	f9	140
Macon, co., Tn., U.S.	A5	149
Macon, Bayou, stm., U.S.	B4	125
Macorís, Cabo, c., Dom. Rep.	E9	94
Macoun, Sask., Can.	H4	105
Macoupin, co., Il., U.S.	D4	120
Macoupin Creek, stm., Il., U.S.	D3	120
Macquarie, stm., Austl.	H7	70
Macquarie, stm., Austl.	M7	70
Macquarie Harbour, b., Austl.	N6	70
Macquarie Island, i., Austl.	A8	73
Mac. Robertson Land, reg., Ant.	B5	73
Macroom, Ire.	J5	8
Macrorie, Sask., Can.	F2	105
MacTier, Ont., Can.	B5	103
Macucuau, stm., Braz.	H12	84
Macuelizo, Hond.	B6	92
Macujer, Col.	G6	84
Macungie, Pa., U.S.	E10	145
Macunqiao, China	B5	34
Macuro, Ven.	B12	84
Macusani, Peru	F6	82
Macuspana, Mex.	I13	90
Macusse, Ang.	A5	56
Macy, In., U.S.	C5	121
Macy, Ne., U.S.	B9	134
Mad, stm., Ca., U.S.	B2	112
Mad, stm., Ct., U.S.	B3	114
Mad, stm., N.H., U.S.	C3	136
Mad, stm., Oh., U.S.	C2	142
Mad, stm., Vt., U.S.	C3	152
Ma'dabā, Jord.	E5	50
Madagascar (Madagasikara), ctry., Afr.	E9	58
Madā'in Ṣāliḥ, Sau. Ar.	H4	48
Madame, Isle, i., N.S., Can.	D9	101
Madanapalle, India	F5	46
Madang, Pap. N. Gui.	m16	68a
Mādārīpur, Bngl.	I14	44
Madawaska, Ont., Can.	B7	103
Madawaska, Me., U.S.	A4	126
Madawaska, stm., Can.	B9	104
Madawaska, stm., Ont., Can.	B7	103
Madawaska Lake, l., Me., U.S.	A4	126
Maddaloni, Italy	H9	18
Madden, Ms., U.S.	C4	131
Maddock, N.D., U.S.	B6	141
Madeira, Oh., U.S.	o13	142
Madeira, i., Port.	m21	17a
Madeira, stm., S.A.	E6	76
Madeira, Arquipélago da, is., Port.	m21	17a
Madeirinha, stm., Braz.	C11	82
Madeirinha, Paraná, mth., Braz.	I13	84
M'adel', Bela.	G9	22
Mädelegabel, mtn., Eur.	E17	14
Madeleine, Îles de la, is., Que., Can.	B8	101
Madelia, Mn., U.S.	F4	130
Madeline Island, i., Wi., U.S.	B3	156
Maden, Tur.	B5	48
Madera, Mex.	C5	90
Madera, Ca., U.S.	D3	112
Madera, Pa., U.S.	E5	145
Madera, co., Ca., U.S.	D4	112
Maderas, Volcán, vol., Nic.	F9	92
Madhubani, India	G12	44
Madhya Pradesh, state, India	I8	44
Madibogo, S. Afr.	F7	66
Madidi, stm., Bol.	E8	82
Madill, Ok., U.S.	C5	143
Madimba, Zaire	B3	58
Madina do Boé, Gui.-B.	F2	64
Madinani, C. Iv.	G6	64
Madīnat ash-Sha'b (Al-Ittihad), Yemen	H4	47
Madingou, Congo	B2	58
Madirobe, Madag.	p22	67b
Madison, Al., U.S.	A3	108
Madison, Ar., U.S.	B5	111
Madison, Ct., U.S.	D5	114
Madison, Fl., U.S.	B3	116
Madison, Ga., U.S.	C3	117
Madison, Il., U.S.	E3	120
Madison, In., U.S.	G7	121
Madison, Ks., U.S.	D7	123
Madison, Me., U.S.	D3	126
Madison, Mn., U.S.	E2	130
Madison, Ms., U.S.	C3	131
Madison, Mo., U.S.	B5	132
Madison, Ne., U.S.	C8	134
Madison, N.H., U.S.	C4	136
Madison, N.J., U.S.	B4	137
Madison, N.C., U.S.	A3	140
Madison, Oh., U.S.	A4	142
Madison, S.D., U.S.	D8	148
Madison, Va., U.S.	B4	153
Madison, W.V., U.S.	C3	155
Madison, Wi., U.S.	E4	156
Madison, co., Al., U.S.	A3	108
Madison, co., Ar., U.S.	B2	111
Madison, co., Fl., U.S.	B3	116
Madison, co., Ga., U.S.	B3	117
Madison, co., Id., U.S.	F7	119
Madison, co., Il., U.S.	E4	120
Madison, co., In., U.S.	D6	121
Madison, co., Ia., U.S.	C3	122
Madison, co., Ky., U.S.	C5	124
Madison, co., La., U.S.	B4	125
Madison, co., Ms., U.S.	C4	131
Madison, co., Mo., U.S.	D7	132
Madison, co., Mt., U.S.	E5	133
Madison, co., Ne., U.S.	C8	134
Madison, co., N.Y., U.S.	C5	139
Madison, co., N.C., U.S.	f10	140
Madison, co., Oh., U.S.	C2	142
Madison, co., Tn., U.S.	B3	149
Madison, co., Tx., U.S.	D5	150
Madison, co., Va., U.S.	B4	153
Madison, stm., Mt., U.S.	E5	133
Madison Heights, Mi., U.S.	o15	129
Madison Heights, Va., U.S.	C3	153
Madison Lake, Mn., U.S.	F5	130
Madison Range, mts., Mt., U.S.	E5	133
Madisonville, Ky., U.S.	C2	124
Madisonville, La., U.S.	D5	125
Madisonville, Tn., U.S.	D9	149
Madisonville, Tx., U.S.	D5	150
Madiun, Indon.	j15	39a
Madoc, Ont., Can.	C7	103
Madoi, China	E6	30
Madol, Sud.	M4	60
Madona, Lat.	E9	22
Madougou, Mali	D8	64
Madrakah, Sau. Ar.	D1	47
Madrakah, Ra's al-, c., Oman	E10	47
Madras, India	G11	42
Madras, Or., U.S.	C5	144
Madras see Tamil Nādu, state, India	G5	46
Madre, Laguna, b., Mex.	E11	90
Madre, Laguna, b., Tx., U.S.	F4	150
Madre, Sierra, mts., Phil.	m20	39b
Madre de Chiapas, Sierra, mts., N.A.	B2	92
Madre de Dios, dept., Peru	D6	82
Madre de Dios, stm., S.A.	D8	82
Madre de Dios, Isla, i., Chile	A12	73
Madre de Dios, Isla, i., Chile	J7	74
Madre del Sur, Sierra, mts., Mex.	I10	90
Madre Occidental, Sierra, mts., Mex.	E6	90
Madre Oriental, Sierra, mts., Mex.	F9	90
Madre Vieja, stm., Guat.	C3	92
Madrid, Col.	E5	84
Madrid, Spain	E8	16
Madrid, Al., U.S.	D4	108
Madrid, Ia., U.S.	C4	122
Madrid, Ne., U.S.	D4	134
Madrid, N.Y., U.S.	f9	139
Madrid, prov., Spain	E8	16
Madridejos, Spain	F8	16
Madriz, dept., Nic.	D8	92
Madura, i., Indon.	j16	39a
Madurai, India	H5	46
Maebashi, Japan	K14	36
Mae Hong Son, Thai.	E4	40
Mae Klong, stm., Thai.	G5	40
Maengsan, N. Kor.	D14	32
Mae Sariang, Thai.	E4	40
Maeser, Ut., U.S.	C6	151
Mae Sot, Thai.	F5	40
Maestra, Sierra, mts., Cuba	D6	94
Maevatanana, Madag.	p22	67b
Mafeking, Man., Can.	C1	100
Mafeteng, Leso.	G8	66
Maffra, Austl.	K7	70
Mafia Island, i., Tan.	C7	58
Mafikeng, S. Afr.	G5	58
Mafikeng, S. Afr.	E7	66
Mafra, Braz.	D14	80
Magadan, Russia	F22	28
Magadi, Kenya	B7	58
Magalia, Ca., U.S.	C3	112
Magallanes, Phil.	o20	39b
Magallanes, Estrecho de (Strait of Magellan), strt., S.A.	G3	78
Magangué, Col.	C5	84
Magazine, Ar., U.S.	B2	111
Magazine Mountain, mtn., Ar., U.S.	B2	111
Magburaka, S.L.	G4	64
Magdagači, Russia	G17	28
Magdalena, Arg.	H10	80
Magdalena, Bol.	E9	82
Magdalena, Mex.	G8	90
Magdalena, Peru	B3	82
Magdalena, N.M., U.S.	C2	138
Magdalena, dept., Col.	B5	84
Magdalena, stm., Col.	C5	84
Magdalena, stm., Mex.	B4	90
Magdalena, Bahía, b., Mex.	E3	90
Magdalena, isla, i., Chile	E2	78
Magdalena, isla, i., Mex.	E3	90
Magdalena, Punta, c., Col.	F4	84
Magdalena de Kino, Mex.	B4	90
Magdalena Mountains, mts., N.M., U.S.	D2	138
Magdeburg, Ger.	C11	10
Magee, Ms., U.S.	D4	131
Magelang, Indon.	j15	39a
Magellan, Strait of see Magallanes, Estrecho de, strt., S.A.	G3	78
Magenta, Italy	D3	18
Maggia, Switz.	F10	13
Maggie Creek, stm., Nv., U.S.	C5	135
Maggiore, Lago, l., Eur.	C3	18
Maghāghah, Egypt	C6	60
Maghama, Maur.	D3	64
Maghniyya, Alg.	C10	62
Magic Reservoir, res., Id., U.S.	F4	119
Magione, Italy	F7	18
Maglaj, Bos.	E2	20
Magna, Ut., U.S.	C3	151
Magness, Ar., U.S.	B4	111
Magnetawan, Ont., Can.	B5	103
Magnetawan, stm., Ont., Can.	B4	103
Magnet Cove, Ar., U.S.	C3	111
Magnitogorsk, Russia	G9	26
Magnolia, Ar., U.S.	D2	111
Magnolia, De., U.S.	D4	115
Magnolia, Il., U.S.	B4	120
Magnolia, Ia., U.S.	C2	122
Magnolia, Ky., U.S.	C4	124
Magnolia, Mn., U.S.	G2	130
Magnolia, Ms., U.S.	D3	131
Magnolia, N.C., U.S.	C4	140
Magnolia, Oh., U.S.	B4	142
Magnolia, Tx., U.S.	D5	150
Magnolia Springs, Al., U.S.	E2	108
Magoffin, co., Ky., U.S.	C6	124
Magog, Que., Can.	D5	104
Magothy River, b., Md., U.S.	B4	127
Magozal, Mex.	G11	90
Magpie, stm., Que., Can.	h8	102
Magrath, Alta., Can.	E4	98
Magruder Mountain, mtn., Nv., U.S.	F4	135
Maguari, Cabo, c., Braz.	D9	76
Maguzhan, China	E13	44
Magway, Mya.	D3	40
Mahābād, Iran	C8	48
Mahābaleshwar, India	F9	42
Mahābhārat Lek, mts., Nepal	F10	44
Mahabo, Madag.	s22	67b
Mahabo, Madag.	r21	67b
Mahaica-Berbice, prov., Guy.	D14	84
Mahaicony Village, Guy.	D14	84
Mahajamba, Helodranon' i, b., Madag.	o22	67b
Mahajanga, Madag.	o22	67b
Mahākālī (Sārda), stm., Asia	F9	44
Mahakam, stm., Indon.	E6	38
Mahalatswe, Bots.	D8	66
Mahallāt, Iran	E11	48
Mahanoro, Madag.	q23	67b
Mahanoy City, Pa., U.S.	E9	145
Mahārāshtra, state, India	C3	46
Maha Sarakham, Thai.	F7	40
Mahaska, co., Ia., U.S.	C5	122
Mahasoa, Madag.	s22	67b
Mahasolo, Madag.	q22	67b
Mahates, Col.	B5	84
Mahatsinjo, Madag.	r21	67b
Mahaṭṭat al-Hafīf, Jord.	D8	50
Mahbūbnagar, India	D4	46
Mahd adh-Dhahab, Sau. Ar.	C2	47
Mahdia, Tun.	N6	18
Mahe, India	G3	46
Mahébourg, Mrts.	v18	67c
Mahé Island, i., Sey.	B11	58
Mahendra Giri, mtn., India	C8	46
Mahesāna, India	I5	44
Mahia Peninsula, pen., N.Z.	C7	72
Mahned, Ms., U.S.	D4	131
Mahnomen, Mn., U.S.	C3	130
Mahnomen, co., Mn., U.S.	C3	130
Mahoba, India	H8	44
Mahogany Mountain, mtn., Or., U.S.	D9	144
Mahomet, Il., U.S.	C5	120
Mahone Bay, N.S., Can.	E5	101
Mahoning, co., Oh., U.S.	B5	142
Mahoning, stm., U.S.	A5	142
Mahoosuc Range, mts., N.H., U.S.	B4	136
Mahopac, N.Y., U.S.	D7	139
Mahres, Tun.	C16	62
Mahtowa, Mn., U.S.	D6	130
Mahuva, India	B1	46
Mahwah, N.J., U.S.	A4	137
Mai Aini, Erit.	J10	60
Maicao, Col.	B6	84
Maîche, Fr.	E13	14
Maici, stm., Braz.	B11	82
Maicuru, stm., Braz.	D8	76
Maiden, N.C., U.S.	B1	140
Maidenhead, Eng., U.K.	J13	8
Maidstone, Sask., Can.	D1	105
Maidstone, Eng., U.K.	J14	8
Maidstone Lake, l., Vt., U.S.	B5	152
Maidsville, W.V., U.S.	B5	155
Maiduguri, Nig.	F9	54
Maienfeld, Switz.	D12	13
Maigatari, Nig.	E14	64
Maignelay, Fr.	C9	14
Maili, Hi., U.S.	g9	118
Maili Point, c., Hi., U.S.	g9	118
Maillezais, Fr.	F6	14
Mai Mefales, Erit.	J10	60
Main, stm., Ger.	F9	10
Main-à-Dieu, N.S., Can.	C10	101
Main Channel, strt., Ont., Can.	B3	103
Mai-Ndombe, Lac, l., Zaire	B3	58
Maine, N.Y., U.S.	C4	139
Maine, hist. reg., Fr.	D6	14
Maine, state, U.S.	C3	126
Maine, Gulf of, b., N.A.	C13	106
Maine-et-Loire, dept., Fr.	E6	14
Mainhardt, Ger.	F9	10
Mainland, i., Scot., U.K.	A12	8
Mainland, i., Scot., U.K.	B10	8
Main Pass, strt., La., U.S.	E6	125
Mainpuri, India	G8	44
Maintenon, Fr.	D8	14
Maintirano, Madag.	q21	67b
Main Topsail, mtn., Newf., Can.	D3	102
Mainz, Ger.	E8	10
Maio, i., C.V.	m17	64a
Maipo, stm., Chile	G3	80
Maipo, Volcán, vol., S.A.	H4	80
Maipú, Arg.	I10	80
Maipú, Arg.	G4	80
Maipú, Chile	G3	80
Maiquetía, Ven.	B9	84
Mairipotaba, Braz.	D4	79
Maisonnette, N.B., Can.	B4	101
Maitengwe, Bots.	C8	66
Maitengwe, stm., Afr.	C8	66
Maitland, Austl.	J2	70
Maitland, Austl.	I9	70
Maitland, N.S., Can.	D6	101
Maitland, Ont., Can.	C9	103
Maitland, Mo., U.S.	A2	132
Maíz, stm., Nic.	F10	92
Maíz, Islas del, is., Nic.	E11	92
Maize, Ks., U.S.	g12	123
Maizuru, Japan	L10	36
Maja, stm., Russia	F18	28
Majagual, Col.	C5	84
Majari, stm., Braz.	F12	84
Majé, Braz.	G7	79
Majestic, Ky., U.S.	C7	124
Maji, Eth.	N8	60
Majia, China	C7	34
Majie, China	B7	40
Majja, Russia	E18	28
Majkain, Kaz.	G13	26
Majkop, Russia	I6	26
Major, Sask., Can.	F1	105
Major, co., Ok., U.S.	A3	143
Majorca see Mallorca, i., Spain	F15	16
Maka, Sen.	E2	64
Makabana, Congo	B2	58
Makaha, Hi., U.S.	g9	118
Makaha Point, c., Hi., U.S.	A2	118
Makah Indian Reservation, Wa., U.S.	A1	154
Makahuena Point, c., Hi., U.S.	B2	118
Makakilo City, Hi., U.S.	g9	118
Makalamabedi, Bots.	C6	66
Makallé, Arg.	D9	80
Makālu, mtn., Asia	G12	44
Makanda, Il., U.S.	F4	120
Makanza, Zaire	A3	58
Makapala, Hi., U.S.	C6	118
Makapuu Head, c., Hi., U.S.	B4	118
Makarjev, Russia	D26	22
Makarov, Russia	H20	28
Makarska, Cro.	F12	18
Makasar, Selat (Makassar Strait), strt., Indon.	F6	38
Makassar Strait see Makasar, Selat, strt., Indon.	F6	38
Makat, Kaz.	H8	26
Makawao, Hi., U.S.	C5	118
Makaweli, Hi., U.S.	B2	118
Makedonija see Macedonia, ctry., Eur.	H5	20
Makeni, S.L.	G3	64
Makeyevka see Makiyivka, Ukr.	H5	26
Makgadikgadi, pl., Bots.	C7	66
Makgadikgadi Pans Game Reserve, Bots.	C7	66
Makhfar al-Quwayrah, Jord.	I4	50
Makhfar Ramn, Jord.	I4	50
Makhrūq, Wādī al-, val., Asia	F7	50
Makindu, Kenya	B7	58
Makinsk, Kaz.	G12	26
M'akiševo, Russia	E11	22
M'akit, Russia	E22	28
Makiyivka, Ukr.	H5	26
Makkah (Mecca), Sau. Ar.	D1	47
Makkovik, Newf., Can.	g10	102
Makó, Hung.	I20	10
Makokou, Gabon	A2	58
Makoti, N.D., U.S.	B4	141
Makoua, Congo	A3	58
Makrāna, India	G6	44
Makran Coast, Asia	I16	48
M'aksa, Russia	C21	22
Maksatícha, Russia	D18	22
Makthar, Tun.	N4	18
Mākū, Iran	B8	48
Makumbi, Zaire	C4	58
Makung (P'enghu), Tai.	L8	34
Makurdi, Nig.	H14	64
Makushin Volcano, vol., Ak., U.S.	E6	109
Makwassie, S. Afr.	F8	66
Mal, Maur.	C3	64
Mala, Peru	E3	82
Mala, stm., Peru	E3	82
Mala, Punta, c., Pan.	D3	84
Malabang, Phil.	D7	38
Malabar, Fl., U.S.	D6	116
Malabar Coast, India	F3	46
Malabo, Eq. Gui.	J14	64
Malacacheta, Braz.	D7	79
Malacca, Strait of, strt., Asia	M6	40
Malacky, Slvk.	G17	10
Malad City, Id., U.S.	G6	119
Málaga, Col.	D6	84
Málaga, Spain	I7	16
Malaga, N.J., U.S.	D2	137
Malaga, N.M., U.S.	E5	138
Malagash, N.S., Can.	D6	101
Malagasy Republic see Madagascar, ctry., Afr.	E9	58
Malagón, Spain	F8	16
Malaimbandy, Madag.	r21	67b
Malaja Kuril'skaja Gr'ada (Habomai-Shotō), is., Russia	d21	36a
Malaja Višera, Russia	C15	22
Malakāl, Sud.	M6	60
Malakoff, Tx., U.S.	C4	150
Malambo, Col.	B5	84
Malān, Mya.	B4	40
Malang, Indon.	j16	39a
Malanggwā, Nepal	G11	44
Malanje, Ang.	C3	58
Malanville, Benin	F11	64
Malanzán, Arg.	F5	80
Mälaren, l., Swe.	L15	6
Malargüe, Arg.	H4	80
Malartic, Que., Can.	k11	104
Malaspina Glacier, Ak., U.S.	D11	109
Malatya, Tur.	B5	48
Malaut, India	E6	44
Malawi, ctry., Afr.	D6	58
Malawi, Lake see Nyasa, Lake, l., Afr.	D6	58
Malaybalay, Phil.	D8	38
Malāyer, Iran	D10	48
Malay Peninsula, pen., Asia	K6	40
Malay Reef, rf., Austl.	A8	70
Malaysia, ctry., Asia	E3	38
Malazgirt, Tur.	B7	48
Malbaie, stm., Que., Can.	B7	104
Malbork, Pol.	A19	10
Malbrán, Arg.	E7	80
Malcolm, Austl.	E4	68
Malcolm, Ne., U.S.	D9	134
Malcom, Ia., U.S.	C5	122
Maldegem, Bel.	F3	12
Malden, Il., U.S.	B4	120
Malden, Ma., U.S.	B5	128
Malden, Mo., U.S.	E8	132
Malden, W.V., U.S.	m12	155
Maldive Islands, is., Mald.	I2	46
Maldives, ctry., Asia	I8	24
Maldonado, Ur.	H11	80
Malé, Italy	C5	18
Male', Mald.	I8	24
Maléa, Ákra, c., Grc.	M7	20
Mālegaon, India	B3	46
Malek, Sud.	N6	60
Malek Sīāh, Kūh-e, mtn., Asia	G16	48
Malema, Moz.	D7	58
Malen'ga, Russia	J25	6
Māler Kotla, India	E6	44
Malesherbes, Fr.	D9	14
Malestroit, Fr.	E4	14
Malha Wells, Sud.	J4	60
Malheur, co., Or., U.S.	D9	144
Malheur, stm., Or., U.S.	D9	144
Malheur Lake, l., Or., U.S.	D8	144
Mali, ctry., Afr.	E6	54
Mali, stm., Mya.	A4	40
Malibu, Ca., U.S.	m11	112
Malik, Wādī al-, val., Sud.	I6	60
Mali Kyun, i., Mya.	H5	40
Malin, Or., U.S.	E5	144
Malinalco, hist., Mex.	H10	90
Malinaltepec, Mex.	I10	90
Malines (Mechelen), Bel.	F5	12
Malin Head, c., Ire.	F6	8
Maliwun, Mya.	I5	40
Maljamar, N.M., U.S.	E6	138
Malka, Russia	G23	28
Malkāpur, India	B4	46
Malkara, Tur.	I10	20
Mallāh, Syria	C7	50
Mallaig, Alta., Can.	B5	98
Mallaig, Scot., U.K.	D8	8
Mallala, Austl.	J3	70
Mallaoua, Niger	E14	64
Mallard, Ia., U.S.	B3	122
Mallawī, Egypt	D6	60
Mallet, Braz.	C13	80
Malletts Bay, b., Vt., U.S.	B2	152
Malligasta, Arg.	E5	80
Mallnitz, Aus.	I13	10
Mallorca, i., Spain	F15	16
Mallow, Ire.	I5	8
Malmédy, Bel.	H9	12
Malmesbury, S. Afr.	I4	66
Malmö, Swe.	N13	6
Malmo, Ne., U.S.	C9	134
Malmöhus Län, co., Swe.	N13	6
Malmstrom Air Force Base, mil., Mt., U.S.	C5	133
Maloarchangel'sk, Russia	I19	22
Maloja, Switz.	F12	13
Malojaroslavec, Russia	F19	22
Maloje Kozino, Russia	E26	22
Maloje Skuratovo, Russia	H20	22
Malolos, Phil.	n19	39b
Malone, Fl., U.S.	B1	116
Malone, N.Y., U.S.	f10	139
Malone, Wa., U.S.	C2	154
Maloney Reservoir, res., Ne., U.S.	C5	134
Malonga, Zaire	D4	58
Małopolska, reg., Pol.	E21	10
Malošujka, Russia	E5	26
Malott, Wa., U.S.	A6	154
Måløy, Nor.	K9	6
Malpaisillo, Nic.	E8	92
Malpas, Austl.	J4	70
Malpelo, Isla de, i., Col.	C2	76
Malpeque Bay, b., P.E.I., Can.	C6	101
Malta, Lat.	E10	22
Malta, Id., U.S.	G5	119
Malta, Il., U.S.	B5	120
Malta, Mt., U.S.	B9	133
Malta, Oh., U.S.	C4	142
Malta, ctry., Eur.	H10	4
Malta, i., Malta	N9	18
Malta Bend, Mo., U.S.	B4	132
Malta Channel, strt., Eur.	M9	18
Maltahöhe, Nmb.	E3	66
Maltepe, Tur.	I11	20
Maluku (Moluccas), is., Indon.	F8	38
Maluku, Laut (Molucca Sea), Indon.	F7	38
Malumfashi, Nig.	F13	64
Malvern, Al., U.S.	D4	108
Malvern, Ar., U.S.	C3	111
Malvern, Ia., U.S.	D2	122
Malvern, Oh., U.S.	B4	142
Malvern, Pa., U.S.	o19	145
Malverne, N.Y., U.S.	k13	139
Malvinas, Arg.	E9	80
Malwal, Sud.	M6	60
Malý Dunaj, stm., Slvk.	H17	10
Malyj, ostrov, i., Russia	A11	22
Malyj An'uj, stm., Russia	D24	28
Malyj Jenisej, stm., Russia	G11	28
Malyj Tajmyr, ostrov, i., Russia	B13	28
Malyj T'uters, ostrov, i., Russia	B9	22
Malyj Uzen', stm., Eur.	H7	26
Malyševo, Russia	D18	22
Mamala Bay, b., Hi., U.S.	g10	118
Mamara, Peru	F5	82
Mamaroneck, N.Y., U.S.	h13	139
Mambaí, Braz.	C5	79
Mamberamo, stm., Indon.	F10	38
Mambéré, stm., Cen. Afr. Rep.	H4	56
Ma-Me-O Beach, Alta., Can.	C4	98
Mamers, Fr.	D7	14
Mamfe, Cam.	G8	54
Mamiá, Lago, l., Braz.	J11	84
Mamiña, Chile	I7	82
Mammoth, Az., U.S.	E5	110
Mammoth, W.V., U.S.	C3	155
Mammoth Cave National Park, Ky., U.S.	C4	124
Mammoth Lakes, Ca., U.S.	D4	112
Mammoth Spring, Ar., U.S.	A4	111
Mamonovo, Russia	G2	22
Mamoré, stm., S.A.	D9	82
Mamori, Lago, l., Braz.	I12	84
Mamoriá, stm., Braz.	B8	82
Mamou, Gui.	F3	64
Mamou, La., U.S.	D3	125
Mamoutzou, May.	I16	67a
Mampikony, Madag.	p22	67b
Mamry, Jezioro, l., Pol.	A21	10
Mamuchi, China	H6	32
Ma'mūn, Sud.	K2	60
Mamuno, Bots.	D5	66
Mamuru, stm., Braz.	I14	84
Man, C. Iv.	H6	64
Man, W.V., U.S.	D3	155
Mana, stm., Fr. Gu.	B8	76
Manabí, prov., Ec.	H2	84
Manacacías, stm., Col.	F6	84
Manacapuru, Braz.	I12	84
Manacor, Spain	F15	16
Manado, Indon.	E7	38
Managua, Nic.	E8	92
Managua, dept., Nic.	E8	92
Managua, Lago de, l., Nic.	E8	92
Manahawkin, N.J., U.S.	D4	137
Manakara, Madag.	s23	67b
Manakin, Va., U.S.	C5	153
Manāli, India	C10	42
Manama see Al-Manāmah, Bahr.	H11	48
Manambato, Madag.	n23	67b
Manambolosy, Madag.	p23	67b
Mánamo, Caño, mth., Ven.	C11	84
Manana Island, i., Hi., U.S.	g11	118
Mananara, Madag.	p23	67b
Mananjary, Madag.	r23	67b
Manantenina, Madag.	t22	67b
Manantico Creek, stm., N.J., U.S.	E3	137
Manapiare, stm., Ven.	E9	84
Manapire, stm., Ven.	C9	84
Mana Point, c., Hi., U.S.	A2	118
Manaquiri, Lago, l., Braz.	I12	84
Manaravolo, Madag.	s21	67b
Manas, China	C4	30
Manās, stm., Asia	G14	44
Manas Hu, l., China	B4	30
Manāslu, mtn., Nepal	F11	44
Manasquan, N.J., U.S.	C4	137
Manasquan, stm., N.J., U.S.	C4	137
Manassa, Co., U.S.	D5	113
Manassas, Ga., U.S.	D4	117
Manassas, Va., U.S.	B5	153
Manassas National Battlefield Park, Va., U.S.	g11	153
Manassas Park, Va., U.S.	B5	153
Manatee, co., Fl., U.S.	E4	116
Manatee, stm., Fl., U.S.	E4	116
Manatí, Col.	B5	84
Manatí, P.R.	E11	94
Manaung, Mya.	E2	40
Manaus, Braz.	I12	84
Manawa, Wi., U.S.	D5	156
Manbij, Syria	C4	48
Mancelona, Mi., U.S.	D5	129
Manchac, Bayou, stm., La., U.S.	h10	125
Mancha Real, Spain	H8	16
Manchaug, Ma., U.S.	B4	128
Manche, dept., Fr.	C5	14
Manchester, Eng., U.K.	H11	8
Manchester, Ct., U.S.	B5	114
Manchester, Ga., U.S.	D2	117
Manchester, Il., U.S.	D3	120
Manchester, Ia., U.S.	B6	122
Manchester, Ky., U.S.	C6	124
Manchester, Me., U.S.	D3	126
Manchester, Md., U.S.	A4	127
Manchester, Ma., U.S.	A6	128
Manchester, Mi., U.S.	F6	129
Manchester, Mo., U.S.	f12	132
Manchester, N.H., U.S.	E4	136
Manchester, N.Y., U.S.	C3	139
Manchester, Oh., U.S.	D2	142
Manchester, Pa., U.S.	F8	145
Manchester, Tn., U.S.	B5	149
Manchester, Vt., U.S.	E2	152
Manchester Center, Vt., U.S.	E2	152
Manchón, Guat.	C2	92
Manchuria, hist. reg., China	B12	30
Máncora, Peru	J2	84
Mancos, Co., U.S.	D2	113
Mancos, stm., U.S.	D2	113
Mandabe, Madag.	r21	67b
Mandaguari, Braz.	G3	79
Mandal, Nor.	L10	6
Mandala, Puncak, mtn., Indon.	F11	38
Mandalay, Mya.	C4	40
Mandalgov', Mong.	B8	30
Mandalī, Iraq	E8	48
Mandan, N.D., U.S.	C5	141
Mandara Mountains, mts., Afr.	F9	54
Mandaree, N.D., U.S.	B3	141
Mandas, Italy	J4	18
Mandeb, Bab el, strt.	H3	47
Mandel, Afg.	E16	48
Manderson, S.D., U.S.	D3	148
Manderson, Wy., U.S.	B5	157
Mandeville, Jam.	E6	94
Mandeville, Ar., U.S.	D2	111
Mandeville, La., U.S.	D5	125
Mandi, India	E7	44
Mandiana, Gui.	F5	64
Mandimba, Moz.	D7	58
Mandioli, Pulau, i., Indon.	F8	38
Mandioré, Lagoa, l., S.A.	H13	82
Mandla, India	A6	46
Mandoto, Madag.	q22	67b
Mandouri, Togo	F10	64
Mandra, Pak.	D5	44
Mandritsara, Madag.	o23	67b
Mandronarivo, Madag.	r21	67b
Mandsaur, India	H6	44
Manduria, Italy	I12	18
Māndvi, India	I3	44
Mandya, India	F4	46
Manfalūt, Egypt	D6	60
Manfredonia, Italy	H10	18
Manfredonia, Golfo di, b., Italy	H11	18
Manga, Braz.	C7	79
Manga, Burkina	F9	64
Mangabeiras, Chapada das, hills, Braz.	F9	76
Mangalagiri, India	D6	46
Mangalore, India	F3	46
Mangaoka, Madag.	n23	67b
Mangchang, China	F8	30
Mange, China	D10	44
Mange, S.L.	G4	64
Mangham, La., U.S.	B4	125
Manglares, Cabo, c., Col.	G3	84
Mangochi, Mwi.	D7	58

Name	Map Ref.	Page
Mangoky, stm., Madag.	r21	67b
Mangole, Pulau, i., Indon.	F8	38
Mangoupa, Cen. Afr. Rep.	O3	60
Mangrol, India	J4	44
Mangrove Cay, i., Bah.	B6	94
Mangueira, Lagoa, b., Braz.	G12	80
Mangueirinha, Braz.	C12	80
Mangulile, Hond.	B8	92
Mangum, Ok., U.S.	C2	143
Mangya, China	D5	30
Manhattan, Ks., U.S.	C7	123
Manhattan, Mt., U.S.	E5	133
Manhattan Beach, Ca., U.S.	n12	112
Manhattan Island, i., N.Y., U.S.	h13	139
Manheim, Pa., U.S.	F9	145
Manhuaçu, Braz.	F7	79
Manhuaçu, stm., Braz.	E8	79
Manhumirim, Braz.	F8	79
Maniago, Italy	C7	18
Maniamba, Moz.	D7	58
Manicoré, Braz.	A11	82
Manicoré, stm., Braz.	B11	82
Manicouagan, Réservoir, res., Que., Can.	h13	104
Manignan, C. Iv.	F6	64
Manigotagan, Man., Can.	D3	100
Manila, Phil.	n19	39b
Manila, Ar., U.S.	B5	111
Manila, Ut., U.S.	C6	151
Manila Bay, b., Phil.	n19	39b
Manilla, Austl.	H9	70
Manilla, In., U.S.	E6	121
Manilla, Ia., U.S.	C2	122
Manily, Russia	E25	28
Manimpé, Mali	D7	64
Manino, Russia	H17	22
Manipur, state, India	H15	44
Manipur, stm., Asia	C2	40
Manisa, Tur.	K11	20
Manissauá-Miçu, stm., Braz.	A1	79
Manistee, Mi., U.S.	D4	129
Manistee, co., Mi., U.S.	D4	129
Manistee, stm., Mi., U.S.	D5	129
Manistique, Mi., U.S.	C4	129
Manistique, stm., Mi., U.S.	B4	129
Manistique Lake, l., Mi., U.S.	B5	129
Manito, Il., U.S.	C4	120
Manitoba, prov., Can.	C3	100
Manitoba, Lake, l., Man., Can.	D2	100
Manitou, Man., Can.	E2	100
Manitou, Ok., U.S.	C3	143
Manitou, stm., Ont., Can.	E5	100
Manitou, Lake, l., Ont., Can.	B3	103
Manitou Beach, Sask., Can.	F3	105
Manitou Island, i., Mi., U.S.	A3	129
Manitou Lake, l., Ont., Can.	A6	103
Manitou Lake, l., Sask., Can.	E1	105
Manitoulin Island, i., Ont., Can.	B2	103
Manitou Springs, Co., U.S.	C6	113
Manitowaning, Ont., Can.	B3	103
Manitowoc, Wi., U.S.	D6	156
Manitowoc, co., Wi., U.S.	D6	156
Manitowoc, stm., Wi., U.S.	h10	156
Manitowoc, North Branch, stm., Wi., U.S.	h9	156
Manitowoc, South Branch, stm., Wi., U.S.	k9	156
Maniwaki, Que., Can.	C2	104
Manizales, Col.	E5	84
Manja, Madag.	r21	67b
Manjacaze, Moz.	E11	66
Manjakandriana, Madag.	q22	67b
Manjimup, Austl.	F3	68
Mankato, Ks., U.S.	C5	123
Mankato, Mn., U.S.	F5	130
Mankayane, Swaz.	F10	66
Mankota, Sask., Can.	H2	105
Manley, Ne., U.S.	h12	134
Manlius, Il., U.S.	B4	120
Manlius, N.Y., U.S.	C5	139
Manlleu, Spain	C14	16
Manly, Ia., U.S.	A4	122
Manmād, India	B3	46
Mannahill, Austl.	I3	70
Mannar, Gulf of, b., Asia	H5	46
Mannārgudi, India	G5	46
Männedorf, Switz.	D10	13
Mannford, Ok., U.S.	A5	143
Mannheim, Ger.	F8	10
Manni, China	C12	44
Manning, Alta., Can.	A2	98
Manning, Ia., U.S.	C2	122
Manning, S.C., U.S.	D7	147
Mannington, Ky., U.S.	C2	124
Mannington, W.V., U.S.	B4	155
Manns Creek, stm., W.V., U.S.	n14	155
Manns Harbor, N.C., U.S.	B7	140
Mannsville, Ok., U.S.	C5	143
Mannum, Austl.	J3	70
Mannville, Alta., Can.	C5	98
Mano, stm., Afr.	H4	64
Manoa, Bol.	C9	82
Manoel Ribas, Braz.	C13	80
Manokin, stm., Md., U.S.	D6	127
Manokotak, Ak., U.S.	D8	109
Manombo, Madag.	s20	67b
Manomet, Ma., U.S.	C6	128
Manomet Hill, hill, Ma., U.S.	C6	128
Manomet Point, c., Ma., U.S.	C6	128
Manono, Zaire	C5	58
Manor, Sask., Can.	H4	105
Manor, Ga., U.S.	E4	117
Manor, Tx., U.S.	D4	150
Manosque, Fr.	I12	14
Manouane, Lac, l., Que., Can.	h12	104
Manp'o, N. Kor.	B14	32
Manresa, Spain	D13	16
Mānsa, India	F6	44
Mansa, Zam.	D5	58
Manseau, Que., Can.	C5	104
Mansel Island, i., N.W. Ter., Can.	D17	96
Mansfield, Austl.	K7	70
Mansfield, Ar., U.S.	B1	111
Mansfield, Ga., U.S.	C3	117
Mansfield, Il., U.S.	C5	120
Mansfield, La., U.S.	B2	125
Mansfield, Ma., U.S.	B5	128
Mansfield, Mo., U.S.	D5	132
Mansfield, Oh., U.S.	B3	142
Mansfield, Pa., U.S.	C7	145
Mansfield, S.D., U.S.	B7	148
Mansfield, Tn., U.S.	A3	149
Mansfield, Tx., U.S.	n9	150
Mansfield, Wa., U.S.	B6	154
Mansfield, Mount, mtn., Vt., U.S.	B3	152
Mansfield Center, Ct., U.S.	B7	114
Mansfield Depot, Ct., U.S.	B6	114
Mansfield Hollow Lake, res., Ct., U.S.	B7	114
Mansión, C.R.	G9	92
Mansle, Fr.	G7	14
Manso, stm., Braz.	F13	82
Manson, Ia., U.S.	B3	122
Manson, Wa., U.S.	B5	154
Manson Creek, B.C., Can.	B5	99
Mansonville, Que., Can.	D5	104
Mansura see Al-Manṣūrah, Egypt	B6	60
Mansura, La., U.S.	C3	125
Manta, Ec.	H2	84
Manta, Bahía de, b., Ec.	H2	84
Mantachie, Ms., U.S.	A5	131
Mantador, N.D., U.S.	C9	141
Mantaro, stm., Peru	E4	82
Manteca, Ca., U.S.	D3	112
Mantecal, Ven.	D8	84
Manteno, Il., U.S.	B6	120
Manteo, N.C., U.S.	B7	140
Manter, Ks., U.S.	E2	123
Mantes-la-Jolie, Fr.	D8	14
Manti, Ut., U.S.	D4	151
Mantiqueira, Serra da, mts., Braz.	G6	79
Manton, Mi., U.S.	D5	129
Mantorville, Mn., U.S.	F6	130
Mantos Blancos, Chile	B3	80
Mantova, Italy	D5	18
Mantua, Cuba	C2	94
Mantua see Mantova, Italy	D5	18
Mantua, N.J., U.S.	D2	137
Mantua, Oh., U.S.	A4	142
Mantua, Ut., U.S.	B4	151
Manturovo, Russia	C27	22
Mäntyharju, Fin.	K20	6
Manu, Peru	E6	82
Manú, stm., Peru	E6	82
Manu, Parque Nacional del, Peru	E6	82
Manua Islands, is., Am. Sam.	J23	158
Manuel, Mex.	F10	90
Manuel Antonio, Parque Nacional, C.R.	H10	92
Manuel Benavides, Mex.	C8	90
Manuel Derqui, Arg.	D9	80
Manuel Urbano, Braz.	C7	82
Manumuskin, stm., N.J., U.S.	E3	137
Manuripe (Mamuripi), stm., S.A.	D8	82
Manuripi, stm., Bol.	E8	82
Manus Island, i., Pap. N. Gui.	k16	68a
Manvel, N.D., U.S.	A8	141
Manvel, Tx., U.S.	r14	150
Manville, N.J., U.S.	B3	137
Manville, R.I., U.S.	B4	146
Manville, Wy., U.S.	D8	157
Many, La., U.S.	C2	125
Manyana, Bots.	D5	66
Manyara, Lake, l., Tan.	B7	58
Manyberries, Alta., Can.	E5	98
Manyč, stm., Russia	H6	26
Many Farms, Az., U.S.	A6	110
Manzanares, Spain	F8	16
Manzanillo, Cuba	D6	94
Manzanillo, Mex.	H7	90
Manzanillo, Punta, c., Pan.	H15	92
Manzanillo Bay, b., N.A.	E9	94
Manzanita, Or., U.S.	B3	144
Manzanola, Co., U.S.	C7	113
Manzano Mountains, mts., N.M., U.S.	C3	138
Manzano Peak, mtn., N.M., U.S.	C3	138
Manzhouli, China	B10	30
Manzini, Swaz.	F10	66
Mao, Chad	F4	56
Mao, Dom. Rep.	E9	94
Maó, Spain	F16	16
Maoke, Pegunungan, mts., Indon.	F10	38
Maoming, China	G9	30
Maouri, Dallol, val., Niger	E11	64
Mapari, stm., Braz.	I9	84
Mapastepec, Mex.	J13	90
Mapaville, Mo., U.S.	C7	132
Mapia, Kepulauan, is., Indon.	E9	38
Mapimí, Mex.	E8	90
Mapimí, Bolsón de, des., Mex.	D8	90
Maping, China	D2	34
Mapinhane, Moz.	D12	66
Mapire, Ven.	D10	84
Mapiri, Bol.	F7	82
Mapiri, stm., Bol.	D8	82
Mapixari, Ilha, i., Braz.	I10	84
Maple, stm., U.S.	A7	148
Maple, stm., Ia., U.S.	B2	122
Maple, stm., N.D., U.S.	C8	141
Maple Bluff, Wi., U.S.	E4	156
Maple Creek, Sask., Can.	H1	105
Maple Creek, stm., Ne., U.S.	C9	134
Maple Falls, Wa., U.S.	A3	154
Maple Grove, Mn., U.S.	m12	130
Maple Heights, Oh., U.S.	h9	142
Maple Hill, Ks., U.S.	C7	123
Maple Island, Mn., U.S.	G5	130
Maple Lake, Mn., U.S.	E5	130
Maple Mount, Ky., U.S.	C2	124
Maple Plain, Mn., U.S.	m11	130
Maple Rapids, Mi., U.S.	E6	129
Maple Shade, N.J., U.S.	D2	137
Maplesville, Al., U.S.	C3	108
Mapleton, Ia., U.S.	B2	122
Mapleton, Me., U.S.	B4	126
Mapleton, Mn., U.S.	G5	130
Mapleton, N.D., U.S.	C8	141
Mapleton, Or., U.S.	C3	144
Mapleton, Ut., U.S.	C4	151
Maple Valley, Wa., U.S.	f11	154
Mapleville, R.I., U.S.	B2	146
Maplewood, Mn., U.S.	n12	130
Maplewood, Mo., U.S.	f13	132
Maplewood, N.J., U.S.	B4	137
Mapuera, stm., Braz.	H14	84
Mapulanguene, Moz.	E11	66
Maputo, Moz.	E11	66
Maputo, stm., Afr.	F11	66
Maqna, Sau. Ar.	G3	48
Maquela do Zombo, Ang.	C3	58
Maquiläu, stm., Braz.	G11	84
Maquinchao, Arg.	E3	78
Maquoketa, Ia., U.S.	B7	122
Maquoketa, stm., Ia., U.S.	B6	122
Maquoketa, North Fork, stm., Ia., U.S.	B7	122
Maquon, Il., U.S.	C3	120
Mar, Serra do, clf, Braz.	C14	80
Mara, Peru	F5	82
Mara, stm., Afr.	B6	58
Maraã, Braz.	H10	84
Marabá, Braz.	E9	76
Maracá, Ilha de, i., Braz.	F12	84
Maracaí, Braz.	G3	79
Maracaibo, Ven.	B7	84
Maracaibo, Lago de, l., Ven.	C7	84
Maracaju, Braz.	F1	79
Maracaju, Serra de, hills, S.A.	F1	79
Maracanã, stm., Braz.	C12	82
Maracás, Braz.	B8	79
Maracay, Ven.	B9	84
Marādah, Libya	C4	56
Maradi, Niger	E13	64
Maradi, Goulbin, stm., Afr.	E13	64
Marāgheh, Iran	C9	48
Maragogipe, Braz.	F11	76
Maragogipe, Braz.	B9	79
Marahuaca, Cerro, mtn., Ven.	F10	84
Marais des Cygnes, stm., U.S.	D8	123
Marajó, Baía de, b., Braz.	D9	76
Marajó, Ilha de, i., Braz.	D9	76
Marakabei, Leso.	G9	66
Maralal, Kenya	A7	58
Maralaleng, Bots.	E6	66
Marampa, S.L.	G3	64
Maramureș, co., Rom.	B8	20
Maran, Malay.	M7	40
Marana, Az., U.S.	E4	110
Marand, Iran	B8	48
Marangani, Peru	F6	82
Maranguape, Braz.	D11	76
Maranhão, stm., Braz.	C4	79
Maranoa, stm., Austl.	E9	68
Marañón, stm., Peru	D3	76
Marapanim, Braz.	D9	76
Marapi, stm., Braz.	G14	84
Maras, Peru	E5	82
Marathon, Austl.	C5	70
Marathón, Grc.	K7	20
Marathon, Fl., U.S.	H5	116
Marathon, Ia., U.S.	B3	122
Marathon, N.Y., U.S.	C4	139
Marathon, Tx., U.S.	D1	150
Marathon, Wi., U.S.	D4	156
Marathon, co., Wi., U.S.	D4	156
Maraú, Braz.	C9	79
Marau, Braz.	E12	80
Marauiá, stm., Braz.	H10	84
Maravilha, Braz.	D12	80
Maravillas, Mex.	D7	90
Marawī, Sud.	H6	60
Marayes, Arg.	F5	80
Marbach, Switz.	E8	13
Marbella, Spain	I7	16
Marble, Ar., U.S.	A2	111
Marble, Mn., U.S.	C5	130
Marble, N.C., U.S.	f9	140
Marble Bar, Austl.	D3	68
Marble Canyon, Az., U.S.	A4	110
Marble Canyon, val., Az., U.S.	A4	110
Marble City, Ok., U.S.	B7	143
Marble Cliff, Oh., U.S.	m10	142
Marbledale, Tn., U.S.	n14	149
Marble Falls, Tx., U.S.	D3	150
Marble Hall, S. Afr.	E9	66
Marblehead, Ma., U.S.	B6	128
Marblehead, Oh., U.S.	A3	142
Marblehill, Ga., U.S.	B2	117
Marble Hill, Mo., U.S.	D8	132
Marblemount, Wa., U.S.	A4	154
Marble Mountain, N.S., Can.	D8	101
Marble Rock, Ia., U.S.	B5	122
Marbleton, Que., Can.	D6	104
Marbleton, Wy., U.S.	D2	157
Marburg, Ger.	E8	10
Marbury, Al., U.S.	C3	108
Marbury, Md., U.S.	C3	127
Marcala, Hond.	C6	92
Marcali, Hung.	I17	10
Marcaria, Italy	D5	18
Marcelin, Sask., Can.	E2	105
Marceline, Mo., U.S.	B5	132
Marcelino Ramos, Braz.	D13	80
Marcellus, Mi., U.S.	F5	129
March (Morava), stm., Eur.	G16	10
Marcha, stm., Russia	E15	28
March Air Force Base, mil., Ca., U.S.	F5	112
Marchand, Man., Can.	E3	100
Marche, prov., Italy	F8	18
Marche, hist. reg., Fr.	F8	14
Marche-en-Famenne, Bel.	H7	12
Marchegg, Aus.	G16	10
Marchena, Spain	H6	16
Mar Chiquita, Laguna, b., Arg.	I10	80
Mar Chiquita, Laguna, l., Arg.	F7	80
Marchwell, Sask., Can.	G5	105
Marcigny, Fr.	F11	14
Marco, Fl., U.S.	G5	116
Marcola, Or., U.S.	C4	144
Marcona, Peru	F4	82
Marcos Juárez, Arg.	G7	80
Marcos Paz, Arg.	H9	80
Marcus, Ia., U.S.	B2	122
Marcus Baker, Mount, mtn., Ak., U.S.	g18	109
Marcus Hook, Pa., U.S.	G11	145
Marcy, Mount, mtn., N.Y., U.S.	A7	139
Mardān, Pak.	C5	44
Mardarivka, Ukr.	B13	20
Mar del Plata, Arg.	J10	80
Mardin, Tur.	C6	48
Marea de Portillo, Cuba	E6	94
Marechal Cândido Rondon, Braz.	C11	80
Marechal Taumaturgo, Braz.	C5	82
Mareeba, Austl.	A6	70
Marengo, Sask., Can.	F1	105
Marengo, Il., U.S.	A5	120
Marengo, In., U.S.	H5	121
Marengo, Ia., U.S.	C5	122
Marengo, co., Al., U.S.	C2	108
Marenisco, Mi., U.S.	n12	129
Marfa, Tx., U.S.	o12	150
Margaree, N.S., Can.	C8	101
Margaree Harbour, N.S., Can.	C8	101
Margaret, Al., U.S.	B3	108
Margaretsville, N.S., Can.	D4	101
Margarita, Isla, i., Col.	C5	84
Margarita, Isla de, i., Ven.	B10	84
Margarita Belén, Arg.	D9	80
Margate, S. Afr.	H10	66
Margate, Eng., U.K.	J15	8
Margate, Fl., U.S.	F6	116
Margate City, N.J., U.S.	E3	137
Margecany, Slvk.	G21	10
Margherita Peak, mtn., Afr.	A5	58
Marghī, Afg.	C2	44
Margilan, Uzb.	I12	26
Margo, Sask., Can.	F4	105
Margos, Peru	D3	82
Mārgow, Dasht-e, des., Afg.	F17	48
Margrethe, Lake, l., Mi., U.S.	D6	129
Marguerite Bay, b., Ant.	B12	73
Marhanets', Ukr.	H4	26
María Cleofas, Isla, i., Mex.	G6	90
María Elena, Chile	B4	80
Maria Gail, Aus.	I13	10
Mariah Hill, In., U.S.	H4	121
María Ignacia (Vela), Arg.	I9	80
Maria Island, i., Austl.	N8	70
María la Baja, Col.	C5	84
María Madre, Isla, i., Mex.	G6	90
María Magdalena, Isla, i., Mex.	G6	90
Marian, Lake, l., Fl., U.S.	E5	116
Mariana, Braz.	F7	79
Mariana Islands, is., Oc.	G18	158
Mariana Trench	G18	158
Mariāni, India	G16	44
Marianna, Ar., U.S.	C5	111
Marianna, Fl., U.S.	B1	116
Mariano I. Loza, Arg.	E9	80
Mariano Moreno, Arg.	J3	80
Mariánské Lázně, Czech Rep.	F12	10
Mariapolis, Man., Can.	E2	100
Marias, stm., Mt., U.S.	B4	133
Marías, Islas, is., Mex.	G6	90
Marias Pass, Mt., U.S.	B3	133
María Teresa, Arg.	H8	80
Mariato, Punta, c., Pan.	D2	84
Mā'rib, Yemen	G4	47
Maribel, Wi., U.S.	h10	156
Maribor, Slvn.	C10	18
Marica (Évros) (Meriç), stm., Eur.	H10	20
Marico, stm., Afr.	E8	66
Maricopa, Az., U.S.	E3	110
Maricopa, Ca., U.S.	E4	112
Maricopa, co., Az., U.S.	D3	110
Maricopa Mountains, mts., Az., U.S.	m7	110
Maricunga, Salar de, pl., Chile	D4	80
Marie, Ar., U.S.	B5	111
Marié, stm., Braz.	H9	84
Marie Byrd Land, reg., Ant.	C10	73
Marie-Galante, i., Guad.	G14	94
Mariehamn, Fin.	K16	6
Mari El see Marij El, state, Russia	F7	26
Mariemont, Oh., U.S.	o13	142
Marienbad see Mariánské Lázně, Czech Rep.	F12	10
Marienburg see Malbork, Pol.	A19	10
Mariental, Nmb.	E3	66
Marienthal, Ks., U.S.	D2	123
Marienville, Pa., U.S.	D3	145
Marie-Reine, Alta., Can.	A2	98
Maries, co., Mo., U.S.	C6	132
Mariestad, Swe.	L13	6
Marieta, stm., Ven.	E9	84
Marietta, Ga., U.S.	C2	117
Marietta, In., U.S.	F6	121
Marietta, Ms., U.S.	A5	131
Marietta, Oh., U.S.	C4	142
Marietta, Ok., U.S.	D4	143
Marietta, S.C., U.S.	A2	147
Marietta, Wa., U.S.	A3	154
Marieville, Que., Can.	D4	104
Mariga, stm., Nig.	F13	64
Marignane, Fr.	I12	14
Marigot, Dom.	G14	94
Marigot, Guad.	E13	94
Mariinsk, Russia	F9	28
Marijampole, Lith.	G6	22
Marij El, state, Russia	F7	26
Marikana, S. Afr.	E8	66
Mari Lake, l., Sask., Can.	B4	105
Marília, Braz.	G4	79
Marimari, stm., Braz.	J13	84
Marimba, Ang.	C3	58
Marín, Spain	C3	16
Marin, co., Ca., U.S.	C2	112
Marina, Ca., U.S.	D3	112
Marina di Ravenna, Italy	E7	18
Marina Fall, wtfl, Guy.	E13	84
Marine, Il., U.S.	E4	120
Marine City, Mi., U.S.	F8	129
Marine On St. Croix, Mn., U.S.	E6	130
Marinette, Wi., U.S.	C6	156
Marinette, co., Wi., U.S.	C5	156
Maringá, Braz.	G3	79
Maringouin, La., U.S.	D4	125
Maringuè, Moz.	A12	66
Marion, Al., U.S.	C2	108
Marion, Ar., U.S.	B5	111
Marion, Ct., U.S.	C4	114
Marion, Il., U.S.	F5	120
Marion, In., U.S.	C6	121
Marion, Ia., U.S.	B6	122
Marion, Ks., U.S.	D6	123
Marion, Ky., U.S.	e9	124
Marion, La., U.S.	B3	125
Marion, Ma., U.S.	C6	128
Marion, Mi., U.S.	D5	129
Marion, Ms., U.S.	C5	131
Marion, Mt., U.S.	B2	133
Marion, Ne., U.S.	D5	134
Marion, N.Y., U.S.	B3	139
Marion, N.C., U.S.	B1	140
Marion, N.D., U.S.	C7	141
Marion, Oh., U.S.	B2	142
Marion, Pa., U.S.	G6	145
Marion, S.C., U.S.	C9	147
Marion, S.D., U.S.	D8	148
Marion, Va., U.S.	f10	153
Marion, Wi., U.S.	D5	156
Marion, co., Al., U.S.	A2	108
Marion, co., Ar., U.S.	A3	111
Marion, co., Fl., U.S.	C4	116
Marion, co., Ga., U.S.	D2	117
Marion, co., Il., U.S.	E4	120
Marion, co., In., U.S.	E5	121
Marion, co., Ia., U.S.	C4	122
Marion, co., Ks., U.S.	D6	123
Marion, co., Ky., U.S.	C4	124
Marion, co., Ms., U.S.	D4	131
Marion, co., Mo., U.S.	B6	132
Marion, co., Oh., U.S.	B2	142
Marion, co., Or., U.S.	C4	144
Marion, co., S.C., U.S.	C9	147
Marion, co., Tn., U.S.	D8	149
Marion, co., Tx., U.S.	C5	150
Marion, co., W.V., U.S.	B4	155
Marion, Lake, res., S.C., U.S.	E7	147
Marion Heights, In., U.S.	F3	121
Marion Junction, Al., U.S.	C2	108
Marion Reef, rf., Austl.	B10	70
Marion Station, Md., U.S.	D6	127
Marionville, Mo., U.S.	D4	132
Mariópolis, Braz.	D12	80
Maripa, Ven.	D10	84
Mariposa, Ca., U.S.	D4	112
Mariposa, co., Ca., U.S.	D3	112
Mariquita, Col.	E5	84
Mariscal Estigarribia, Para.	B8	80
Marissa, Il., U.S.	E4	120
Maritime Alps, mts., Eur.	H14	14
Maritime Atlas see Atlas Tellien, mts., Alg.	C11	62
Mariupol' (Ždanov), Ukr.	H5	26
Mariusa, Caño, mth., Ven.	C12	84
Marīvān, Iran	D9	48
Märjamaa, Est.	C7	22
Marjina Gorka, Bela.	H11	22
Marjinsko, Russia	C11	22
Mark, Il., U.S.	B4	120
Marka, Som.	H9	56
Markala, Mali	E6	64
Markdale, Ont., Can.	C4	103
Marked Tree, Ar., U.S.	B5	111
Markesan, Wi., U.S.	E5	156
Markham, Ont., Can.	D5	103
Markham, Il., U.S.	k9	120
Markham, Tx., U.S.	E4	150
Markham, Mount, mtn., Ant.	D8	73
Markinch, Sask., Can.	G3	105
Markland Lock and Dam, U.S.	B5	124
Markle, In., U.S.	C7	121
Markleville, In., U.S.	E6	121
Markovo, Russia	D23	22
Markovo, Russia	E26	28
Marks, Russia	G7	26
Marks, Ms., U.S.	A3	131
Marksville, La., U.S.	C3	125
Marktheidenfeld, Ger.	F9	10
Marktoberdorf, Ger.	H10	10
Marktredwitz, Ger.	E12	10
Mark Twain Lake, res., Mo., U.S.	B6	132
Markundi, Sud.	L2	60
Marland, Ok., U.S.	A4	143
Marlbank, Ont., Can.	C7	103
Marlboro, Alta., Can.	C2	98
Marlboro, N.Y., U.S.	D6	139
Marlboro, Vt., U.S.	F3	152
Marlboro, Va., U.S.	n17	153
Marlboro, co., S.C., U.S.	B8	147
Marlborough, Austl.	D8	70
Marlborough, Guy.	D13	84
Marlborough, Eng., U.K.	J12	8
Marlborough, Ct., U.S.	C6	114
Marlborough, Ma., U.S.	B4	128
Marlborough, N.H., U.S.	E2	136
Marle, Fr.	C10	14
Marlette, Mi., U.S.	E7	129
Marley, Md., U.S.	B4	127
Marlin, Tx., U.S.	D4	150
Marlinton, W.V., U.S.	C4	155
Marlow, Al., U.S.	E2	108
Marlow, Ga., U.S.	D5	117
Marlow, N.H., U.S.	D2	136
Marlow, Ok., U.S.	C4	143
Marlowe, W.V., U.S.	B7	155
Marlton, N.J., U.S.	D3	137
Marmaduke, Ar., U.S.	A5	111
Marmande, Fr.	H7	14
Marmara Denizi (Sea of Marmara), Tur.	I12	20
Marmara Ereğlisi, Tur.	I11	20
Marmaris, Tur.	M12	20
Marmarth, N.D., U.S.	C2	141
Marmelos, Braz.	B11	82
Marmelos, Rio dos, stm., Braz.	B11	82
Marmet, W.V., U.S.	C3	155
Marmora, Ont., Can.	C7	103
Mar Muerto, Laguna, b., Mex.	I12	90
Marnay, Fr.	E12	14
Marne, Mi., U.S.	E5	129
Marne, dept., Fr.	D11	14
Marne, stm., Fr.	C10	14
Marne au Rhin, Canal de la, Fr.	D13	14
Maroa, Il., U.S.	C5	120
Maroa, Ven.	F9	84
Maroala, Madag.	o22	67b
Maroantsetra, Madag.	o23	67b
Maroelaboom, Nmb.	B4	66
Marolambo, Madag.	r23	67b
Maromme, Fr.	C8	14
Maromokotro, mtn., Madag.	o23	67b
Marondera, Zimb.	B10	66
Maroni, stm., S.A.	C8	76
Maro Reef, rf., Hi., U.S.	k13	118
Maros (Mureș), stm., Eur.	C4	20
Maroseranana, Madag.	q23	67b
Maroua, Cam.	F9	54
Marovato, Madag.	o23	67b
Marovoay, Madag.	p22	67b
Marquand, Mo., U.S.	D7	132
Marquesas Islands see Marquises, Îles, is., Fr. Poly.	I26	158
Marquesas Keys, is., Fl., U.S.	H4	116
Marquette, Man., Can.	D3	100
Marquette, Ia., U.S.	A6	122
Marquette, Ks., U.S.	D6	123
Marquette, Mi., U.S.	B3	129
Marquette, Ne., U.S.	D8	134
Marquette, co., Mi., U.S.	B3	129
Marquette, co., Wi., U.S.	E4	156
Marquette Heights, Il., U.S.	C4	120
Marquis, Sask., Can.	G3	105
Marquise, Fr.	B8	14
Marquises, Îles (Marquesas Islands), is., Fr. Poly.	I26	158
Marrah, Jabal, mtn., Sud.	K3	60
Marrakech, Mor.	E6	62
Marrawah, Austl.	M6	70
Marree, Austl.	G3	70
Marrero, La., U.S.	E5	125
Marromeu, Moz.	B12	66
Mars, Pa., U.S.	E1	145
Marsā al-Burayqah, Libya	B4	56
Marsabit, Kenya	H8	56
Marsala, Italy	L7	18
Marsā Maṭrūḥ, Egypt	B4	60
Marsden, Austl.	I7	70
Marsden, Sask., Can.	E1	105
Marseille, Fr.	I12	14
Marseille-en-Beauvaisis, Fr.	C8	14
Marseilles, Il., U.S.	B5	120
Marshall, Sask., Can.	D1	105
Marshall, Lib.	G4	54
Marshall, Lib.	H4	64
Marshall, Ak., U.S.	C7	109
Marshall, Ar., U.S.	B3	111
Marshall, Il., U.S.	D6	120
Marshall, In., U.S.	E3	121
Marshall, Mi., U.S.	F6	129
Marshall, Mn., U.S.	F3	130
Marshall, Mo., U.S.	B4	132
Marshall, N.C., U.S.	f10	140
Marshall, Ok., U.S.	A4	143
Marshall, Tx., U.S.	C5	150
Marshall, Va., U.S.	B5	153
Marshall, Wi., U.S.	E4	156
Marshall, co., Al., U.S.	A3	108
Marshall, co., Il., U.S.	B4	120
Marshall, co., In., U.S.	B5	121
Marshall, co., Ia., U.S.	C4	122
Marshall, co., Ks., U.S.	C7	123
Marshall, co., Ky., U.S.	f9	124
Marshall, co., Mn., U.S.	B2	130
Marshall, co., Ms., U.S.	A4	131
Marshall, co., Ok., U.S.	C5	143
Marshall, co., S.D., U.S.	B8	148
Marshall, co., Tn., U.S.	B5	149
Marshall, co., W.V., U.S.	B4	155
Marshallberg, N.C., U.S.	C6	140
Marshall Islands, ctry., Oc.	H20	158
Marshall Islands, is., Oc.	H20	158
Marshallton, De., U.S.	B3	115
Marshalltown, Ia., U.S.	B5	122
Marshallville, Ga., U.S.	D3	117
Marshallville, Oh., U.S.	B4	142
Marshes Siding, Ky., U.S.	D5	124
Marshfield, Ma., U.S.	B6	128
Marshfield, Mo., U.S.	D5	132
Marshfield, Vt., U.S.	C4	152
Marshfield, Wi., U.S.	D3	156
Marshfield Hills, Ma., U.S.	B6	128
Marsh Fork, stm., W.V., U.S.	n13	155
Marsh Harbour, Bah.	A6	94
Mars Hill, Me., U.S.	B5	126
Mars Hill, N.C., U.S.	f10	140
Mars Hill, mtn., Me., U.S.	B5	126
Marsh Island, i., La., U.S.	E4	125
Marsh Lake, res., Mn., U.S.	E2	130
Marsh Peak, mtn., Ut., U.S.	C6	151
Marshville, N.C., U.S.	C2	140
Marshyhope Creek, stm., Md., U.S.	C6	127
Marsing, Id., U.S.	F2	119
Marston, Mo., U.S.	E8	132
Marstons Mills, Ma., U.S.	C7	128
Mart, Tx., U.S.	D4	150
Martaban, Mya.	F4	40
Martaban, Gulf of, b., Mya.	F4	40
Martapura, Indon.	F5	38
Martell, Ne., U.S.	D9	134
Martelle, Ia., U.S.	B6	122
Martensdale, Ia., U.S.	C4	122
Marte R. Gómez, Presa, res., Mex.	D10	90
Martha, Ok., U.S.	C2	143
Marthasville, Mo., U.S.	C6	132
Martha's Vineyard, i., Ma., U.S.	D6	128
Marthaville, La., U.S.	C2	125
Martí, Cuba	D6	94
Martigny, Switz.	F7	13
Martigues, Fr.	I12	14
Martil, Mor.	J6	16
Martin, Slvk.	F18	10
Martin, Ga., U.S.	B3	117
Martin, Ky., U.S.	C7	124
Martin, La., U.S.	B2	125
Martin, Mi., U.S.	F5	129
Martin, N.D., U.S.	B5	141
Martin, S.D., U.S.	D4	148
Martin, Tn., U.S.	A3	149
Martin, Ut., U.S.	D5	151
Martin, co., Fl., U.S.	E6	116
Martin, co., In., U.S.	G4	121
Martin, co., Ky., U.S.	C7	124
Martin, co., Mn., U.S.	G4	130
Martin, co., N.C., U.S.	B5	140
Martin, co., Tx., U.S.	C2	150
Martina Franca, Italy	I12	18
Martin City, Mt., U.S.	B3	133
Martindale, Tx., U.S.	h8	150
Martinez, Ca., U.S.	C2	112
Martinez, Ga., U.S.	C4	117
Martínez de la Torre, Mex.	G11	90
Martinho Campos, Braz.	E6	79
Martinique, dep., N.A.	G14	94

Name	Map Ref.	Page
Martinique Passage, strt., N.A.	G14	94
Martin Lake, res., Al., U.S.	C4	108
Martinniemi, Fin.	I19	6
Martin Point, c., Ak., U.S.	A11	109
Martinsberg, Aus.	G15	10
Martinsburg, In., U.S.	H5	121
Martinsburg, Mo., U.S.	B6	132
Martinsburg, Pa., U.S.	F5	145
Martinsburg, W.V., U.S.	B7	155
Martins Ferry, Oh., U.S.	B5	142
Martins Pond, l., Ma., U.S.	f11	128
Martinsville, Il., U.S.	D6	120
Martinsville, In., U.S.	F5	121
Martinsville, Ms., U.S.	D3	131
Martinsville, Va., U.S.	D3	153
Martinton, Il., U.S.	C5	120
Martin Vaz, Ilhas, is., Braz.	G12	74
Martisovo, Russia	E14	22
Martos, Spain	H8	16
Martre, Lac la, l., N.W. Ter., Can.	D9	96
Martti, Fin.	H21	6
Marty, S.D., U.S.	E7	148
Maru, Nig.	E13	64
Marugame, Japan	M8	36
Marula, Zimb.	C9	66
Marumsco Creek, stm., Md., U.S.	D6	127
Marunga, Ang.	A5	66
Marungu, mts., Zaire	C5	58
Ma'rūt, Afg.	E2	44
Marv Dasht, Iran	G12	48
Marvejols, Fr.	H10	14
Marvel, Al., U.S.	B2	108
Marvel, Co., U.S.	D2	113
Marvell, Ar., U.S.	C5	111
Marvine, Mount, mtn., Ut., U.S.	E4	151
Marwayne, Alta., Can.	C5	98
Mary, Turk.	J10	26
Mary, Lake, l., Mn., U.S.	E3	130
Mary, Lake, l., Ms., U.S.	D2	131
Maryborough, Austl.	E10	70
Maryborough, Austl.	K5	70
Marydale, S. Afr.	G6	66
Marydel, De., U.S.	D3	115
Maryfield, Sask., Can.	H5	105
Mary Kathleen, Austl.	C3	70
Maryland, state, U.S.	B4	127
Maryland City, Md., U.S.	B4	127
Maryland Heights, Mo., U.S.	f13	132
Maryland Point, c., Md., U.S.	D3	127
Marys, stm., Nv., U.S.	B6	135
Mary's Harbour, Newf., Can.	B4	102
Mary's Igloo, Ak., U.S.	B6	109
Marys Peak, mtn., Or., U.S.	C3	144
Marystown, Newf., Can.	E4	102
Marysvale, Ut., U.S.	E3	151
Marysville, Ca., U.S.	C3	112
Marysville, Id., U.S.	F7	119
Marysville, Ks., U.S.	C7	123
Marysville, Mi., U.S.	F8	129
Marysville, Oh., U.S.	B2	142
Marysville, Pa., U.S.	F8	145
Marysville, Wa., U.S.	A3	154
Maryville, Mo., U.S.	A3	132
Maryville, Tn., U.S.	D10	149
Marzagão, Braz.	D4	79
Marzo, Punta, c., Col.	D4	84
Marzūq, Libya	C3	56
Marzūq, Ṣaḥrā', des., Libya	D3	56
Masachapa, Nic.	F8	92
Masada see Meẓada, Ḥorvot, hist., Isr.	F4	50
Masagua, Guat.	C4	92
Masai Steppe, plat., Tan.	B7	58
Masaka, Ug.	B6	58
Masallı, Azer.	B10	48
Masan, S. Kor.	H16	32
Masaryktown, Fl., U.S.	D4	116
Masasi, Tan.	D7	58
Masatepe, Nic.	F8	92
Masaya, Nic.	F8	92
Masaya, dept., Nic.	E8	92
Masbate, Phil.	C7	38
Mascarene Islands, is., Afr.	F11	58
Mascasín, Arg.	F5	80
Mascoma, stm., N.H., U.S.	C2	136
Mascoma Lake, l., N.H., U.S.	C2	136
Mascot, Tn., U.S.	C10	149
Mascota, Mex.	G7	90
Mascouche, Que., Can.	D4	104
Mascoutah, Il., U.S.	E4	120
Maseru, Leso.	G8	66
Mashaba Mountains, mts., Zimb.	B10	66
Mashābih, i., Sau. Ar.	I4	48
Mashapaug Pond, l., Ct., U.S.	A7	114
Mashar, Sud.	M4	60
Mashhad, Iran	C15	48
Mashīz, Iran	G14	48
Māshkel, Hāmūn-i-, l., Pak.	G17	48
Māshkel, Rūd-i- (Māshkīd), stm., Asia	G17	48
Mashra'ur-Raqq, Sud.	M5	60
Masi Manimba, Zaire	B3	58
Maṣīrah, Khalīj, b., Oman	E11	47
Masisea, Peru	C4	82
Masjed-e Soleymān, Iran	F10	48
Mask, Lough, l., Ire.	H4	8
Maska, Nig.	F13	64
Maskanah, Syria	C5	48
Maskin, Oman	C10	47
Maskinongé, Que., Can.	C4	104
Masoala, Madag.	o24	67b
Masoala, Cap, c., Madag.	o24	67b
Masoala, Presqu'île de, pen., Madag.	o24	67b
Masoarivo, Madag.	q21	67b
Masomeloka, Madag.	r23	67b
Mason, Il., U.S.	E5	120
Mason, Mi., U.S.	F6	129
Mason, Nv., U.S.	E2	135
Mason, N.H., U.S.	E3	136
Mason, Oh., U.S.	C1	142
Mason, Tn., U.S.	B2	149
Mason, Tx., U.S.	D3	150
Mason, W.V., U.S.	B2	155
Mason, co., Il., U.S.	C4	120
Mason, co., Ky., U.S.	B6	124
Mason, co., Mi., U.S.	D4	129
Mason, co., Tx., U.S.	D3	150
Mason, co., Wa., U.S.	B2	154
Mason, co., W.V., U.S.	C3	155
Mason City, Il., U.S.	C4	120
Mason City, Ia., U.S.	A4	122
Mason City, Ne., U.S.	C6	134
Masonhall, Tn., U.S.	A2	149
Masontown, Pa., U.S.	G2	145
Masontown, W.V., U.S.	B5	155
Masonville, Co., U.S.	A5	113
Masqaṭ (Muscat), Oman	C11	47
Massa, Italy	E5	18
Massabesic Lake, l., N.H., U.S.	E4	136
Massac, co., Il., U.S.	F5	120
Massachusetts, state, U.S.	B4	128
Massachusetts Bay, b., Ma., U.S.	B6	128
Massacre Lake, l., Nv., U.S.	B2	135
Massaemett Mountain, mtn., Ma., U.S.	A2	128
Massafra, Italy	I12	18
Massa Marittima, Italy	F5	18
Massangena, Moz.	C11	66
Massanutten Mountain, mts., Va., U.S.	B4	153
Massapoag Lake, l., Ma., U.S.	h11	128
Massarosa, Italy	F5	18
Massasecum, Lake, l., N.H., U.S.	D3	136
Massena, Ia., U.S.	C3	122
Massena, N.Y., U.S.	f10	139
Massenya, Chad	F4	56
Masset, B.C., Can.	C1	99
Masseube, Fr.	I7	14
Massey, Ont., Can.	A2	103
Massillon, Oh., U.S.	B4	142
Massina, reg., Mali	D7	64
Massinga, Moz.	D12	66
Massive, Mount, mtn., Co., U.S.	B4	113
Mastābah, Sau. Ar.	D1	47
Maştağa, Azer.	I8	26
Masterton, N.Z.	D5	72
Mastic Beach, N.Y., U.S.	n16	139
Mastung, Pak.	F2	44
Mastūrah, Sau. Ar.	C1	47
Masuda, Japan	M6	36
Masury, Oh., U.S.	A5	142
Masvingo, Zimb.	C10	66
Matachewan, Ont., Can.	p19	103
Matacuni, stm., Ven.	F10	84
Mata de São João, Braz.	B9	79
Matadi, Zaire	C2	58
Matador, Tx., U.S.	B2	150
Matagalpa, Nic.	E9	92
Matagalpa, dept., Nic.	E9	92
Matagorda, Tx., U.S.	E5	150
Matagorda, co., Tx., U.S.	E5	150
Matagorda Bay, b., Tx., U.S.	E4	150
Matagorda Island, i., Tx., U.S.	E4	150
Matagorda Peninsula, pen., Tx., U.S.	E5	150
Matale, Sri L.	I6	46
Matam, Sen.	D3	64
Matamá, Cerro, mtn., C.R.	H11	92
Matamoras, Pa., U.S.	D12	145
Matamoros, Mex.	E8	90
Matamoros, Mex.	E11	90
Matane, Que., Can.	k13	104
Matanuska, stm., Ak., U.S.	g18	109
Matanzas, Cuba	C4	94
Matanzas, Mex.	G9	90
Matanzas Inlet, b., Fl., U.S.	C5	116
Matapalo, Cabo, c., C.R.	I11	92
Matape, stm., Mex.	C4	90
Mataquito, stm., Chile	H3	80
Matará, Peru	B2	82
Matara, Sri L.	J6	46
Mataram, Indon.	G6	38
Matarani, Peru	G5	82
Mataró, Spain	D14	16
Matatiele, S. Afr.	H9	66
Mataurá, stm., Braz.	B11	82
Matawan, N.J., U.S.	C4	137
Mateare, Nic.	E8	92
Matehuala, Mex.	F9	90
Matera, Italy	I11	18
Mátészalka, Hung.	H22	10
Mateur, Tun.	L4	18
Matewan, W.V., U.S.	D2	155
Mather, Man., Can.	E2	100
Mather, Pa., U.S.	G1	145
Mather Air Force Base, mil., Ca., U.S.	C3	112
Mather Peaks, mts., Wy., U.S.	B5	157
Matherville, Il., U.S.	B3	120
Matheson, Co., U.S.	B7	113
Matheson Island, Man., Can.	D3	100
Mathews, Al., U.S.	C3	108
Mathews, La., U.S.	E5	125
Mathews, Va., U.S.	C6	153
Mathews, co., Va., U.S.	C6	153
Mathews, Lake, l., Ca., U.S.	n14	112
Mathias, W.V., U.S.	C6	155
Mathis, Tx., U.S.	E4	150
Mathiston, Ms., U.S.	B4	131
Mathura, India	G7	44
Matiacoali, Burkina	E10	64
Matias Barbosa, Braz.	F7	79
Matías Romero, Mex.	I12	90
Matícora, stm., Ven.	B7	84
Matignon, Fr.	D4	14
Matiguás, Nic.	E9	92
Matinenda Lake, l., Ont., Can.	A2	103
Matinicus Island, i., Me., U.S.	E3	126
Matipó, Braz.	F7	79
Matiyure, stm., Ven.	D8	84
Matlamanyane, Bots.	B7	66
M'atlevo, Russia	G18	22
Matmata, Tun.	D15	62
Mato, stm., Ven.	D10	84
Mato, Cerro, mtn., Ven.	D10	84
Matoaca, Va., U.S.	n18	153
Matoaka, W.V., U.S.	D3	155
Matočkin Šar, proliv, strt., Russia	C8	26
Mato Grosso, state, Braz.	D13	82
Mato Grosso, Planalto do, plat., Braz.	G7	76
Mato Grosso do Sul, state, Braz.	G8	76
Matopo Hills, hills, Zimb.	C9	66
Matos, stm., Bol.	F9	82
Matosinhos, Port.	D3	16
Matou, Tai.	L9	34
Matoury, Fr. Gu.	C8	76
Matouying, China	D6	32
Mato Verde, Braz.	C7	79
Matozinhos, Braz.	E6	79
Matraḥ, Oman	C11	47
Matrei in Osttirol, Aus.	H12	10
Matru, S.L.	H3	64
Matsapha, Swaz.	F10	66
Matsqui, B.C., Can.	f13	99
Matsudo, Japan	L14	36
Matsue, Japan	L8	36
Matsumae, Japan	F15	36
Matsumoto, Japan	K12	36
Matsu Tao, i., Tai.	I8	34
Matsuyama, Japan	N7	36
Mattamiscontis Lake, l., Me., U.S.	C4	126
Mattamuskeet, Lake, l., N.C., U.S.	B6	140
Mattapoisett, Ma., U.S.	C6	128
Mattaponi, stm., Va., U.S.	C5	153
Mattawa, Ont., Can.	A6	103
Mattawamkeag, Me., U.S.	C4	126
Mattawamkeag, stm., Me., U.S.	C4	126
Mattawamkeag, East Branch, stm., Me., U.S.	C4	126
Mattawamkeag, West Branch, stm., Me., U.S.	C4	126
Mattawamkeag Lake, l., Me., U.S.	C4	126
Mattawoman Creek, stm., Md., U.S.	C3	127
Matterhorn, mtn., Eur.	G14	14
Matterhorn, mtn., Nv., U.S.	B6	135
Mattersburg, Aus.	H16	10
Matteson, Il., U.S.	k9	120
Matthews, Ga., U.S.	C4	117
Matthews, In., U.S.	D7	121
Matthews, Mo., U.S.	E8	132
Matthews, N.C., U.S.	B2	140
Matthews Mountain, mtn., Mo., U.S.	D6	132
Matthews Ridge, Guy.	D12	84
Matthew Town, Bah.	D8	94
Mattī, Sabkhat, l., Asia	J2	48
Mattighofen, Aus.	G13	10
Mattituck, N.Y., U.S.	n16	139
Mattoon, Il., U.S.	D5	120
Mattoon, Wi., U.S.	C4	156
Mattoon, Lake, res., Il., U.S.	D5	120
Mattydale, N.Y., U.S.	B4	139
Matuba, Moz.	E11	66
Matucana, Peru	D3	82
Matunuck, R.I., U.S.	G3	146
Maturín, Ven.	C11	84
Maturino, Russia	B20	22
Matutina, Braz.	E6	79
Maú (Ireng), stm., S.A.	E13	84
Maúa, Moz.	D7	58
Maubeuge, Fr.	B10	14
Maud, Oh., U.S.	n13	142
Maud, Ok., U.S.	B5	143
Maude, Austl.	J6	70
Maués, Braz.	I14	84
Maués, stm., Braz.	I14	84
Maugansville, Md., U.S.	A2	127
Maugerville, N.B., Can.	D3	101
Maui, co., Hi., U.S.	B5	118
Maui, i., Hi., U.S.	C6	118
Mauk, Ga., U.S.	D2	117
Mauldin, S.C., U.S.	B3	147
Maule, prov., Chile	H2	80
Maule, stm., Chile	H2	80
Maule, Laguna del, l., Chile	I3	80
Mauléon, Fr.	F6	14
Maumee, Oh., U.S.	A2	142
Maumee, stm., U.S.	A2	142
Maumee Bay, b., U.S.	G7	129
Maumelle, Ar., U.S.	h10	111
Maumelle, Lake, res., Ar., U.S.	C3	111
Maun, Bots.	C6	66
Mauna Kea, vol., Hi., U.S.	D6	118
Maunaloa, Hi., U.S.	B4	118
Mauna Loa, vol., Hi., U.S.	D6	118
Maunalua Bay, b., Hi., U.S.	g10	118
Maunath Bhanjan, India	H10	44
Maunatlala, Bots.	D8	66
Maunawili, Hi., U.S.	g10	118
Maungdaw, Mya.	D2	40
Maupin, Or., U.S.	B5	144
Mau Rānīpur, India	H8	44
Maure-de-Bretagne, Fr.	E5	14
Maurepas, Lake, l., La., U.S.	D5	125
Maurertown, Va., U.S.	B4	153
Mauri, stm., Bol.	G7	82
Mauriac, Fr.	G9	14
Maurice, Ia., U.S.	B1	122
Maurice, La., U.S.	D3	125
Maurice, stm., N.J., U.S.	E2	137
Mauritania (Mauritanie), ctry., Afr.	D4	54
Mauritius, ctry., Afr.	F11	58
Mauritius, i., Mrts.	v18	67c
Mauron, Fr.	D4	14
Maury, N.C., U.S.	B5	140
Maury, co., Tn., U.S.	B4	149
Maury City, Tn., U.S.	B2	149
Maury Island, i., Wa., U.S.	f11	154
Mauston, Wi., U.S.	E3	156
Mauterndorf, Aus.	H13	10
Mauthausen, Aus.	G14	10
Mauvezin, Fr.	I7	14
Mauwee Peak, mtn., Ct., U.S.	C2	114
Mavaca, stm., Ven.	F10	84
Maverick, co., Tx., U.S.	E2	150
Mavinga, Ang.	E4	58
Mawchi, Mya.	E4	40
Maw-daung Pass, Asia	I5	40
Mawkhi, Mya.	F5	40
Mawlaik, Mya.	C3	40
Mawlamyine (Moulmein), Mya.	F4	40
Maw Taung, mtn., Asia	I5	40
Max, Ne., U.S.	D4	134
Max, N.D., U.S.	B4	141
Maxbass, N.D., U.S.	A4	141
Maxcanú, Mex.	G15	90
Maxeys, Ga., U.S.	C3	117
Maxinkuckee, Lake, l., In., U.S.	B5	121
Maxixe, Moz.	D12	66
Max Meadows, Va., U.S.	D2	153
Maxton, N.C., U.S.	C3	140
Maxville, Ont., Can.	B10	103
Maxwell, Ca., U.S.	C2	112
Maxwell, In., U.S.	E6	121
Maxwell, Ia., U.S.	C4	122
Maxwell, Ne., U.S.	C5	134
Maxwell, N.M., U.S.	A5	138
Maxwell, Tn., U.S.	B5	149
Maxwell Acres, W.V., U.S.	g8	155
Maxwell Air Force Base, mil., Al., U.S.	C3	108
May, Id., U.S.	E5	119
Maya, Mesa de, mtn., Co., U.S.	D7	113
Mayaguana, i., Bah.	C8	94
Mayaguana Passage, strt., Bah.	C8	94
Mayagüez, P.R.	E11	94
Mayaky, Ukr.	C14	20
Mayales, Punta, c., Nic.	F9	92
Maya Mountains, mts., N.A.	I15	90
Mayapan, hist., Mex.	G15	90
Mayarí, Cuba	D7	94
Maybee, Mi., U.S.	F7	129
Maybell, Co., U.S.	A2	113
Maybole, Scot., U.K.	F9	8
Mayenne, Fr.	M13	8
Mayenne, dept., Fr.	D6	14
Mayer, Az., U.S.	C3	110
Mayersville, Ms., U.S.	C2	131
Mayerthorpe, Alta., Can.	C3	98
Mayes, co., Ok., U.S.	A6	143
Mayesville, S.C., U.S.	D7	147
Mayetta, Ks., U.S.	C8	123
Mayfair, Sask., Can.	E2	105
Mayfield, Ks., U.S.	E6	123
Mayfield, Ky., U.S.	f9	124
Mayfield, N.Y., U.S.	B4	139
Mayfield, Pa., U.S.	C10	145
Mayfield, Ut., U.S.	D4	151
Mayfield Heights, Oh., U.S.	A4	142
Mayfield Lake, res., Wa., U.S.	C3	154
Mayflower, Ar., U.S.	C3	111
Mayhill, N.M., U.S.	E4	138
May Jirgui, Niger	E14	64
Mayking, Ky., U.S.	C7	124
Mayland, Tn., U.S.	C8	149
Maymont, Sask., Can.	E2	105
Maymyo, Mya.	C4	40
Maynard, Ar., U.S.	A5	111
Maynard, Ia., U.S.	B6	122
Maynard, Ma., U.S.	B5	128
Maynard, Mn., U.S.	F3	130
Maynardville, Tn., U.S.	C10	149
Mayne, B.C., Can.	g12	99
Mayne, stm., Austl.	D4	70
Mayne Island, i., B.C., Can.	g12	99
Maynooth, Ont., Can.	B7	103
Mayo, Yukon, Can.	D5	96
Mayo, Fl., U.S.	B3	116
Mayo, Md., U.S.	C4	127
Mayo, S.C., U.S.	A4	147
Mayo, co., Ire.	H4	8
Mayo, stm., Col.	G4	84
Mayo, stm., Mex.	D5	90
Mayo, stm., Peru	B3	82
Mayodan, N.C., U.S.	A3	140
Mayon Volcano, vol., Phil.	o20	39b
Mayor Buratovich, Arg.	J7	80
Mayor Pablo Lagerenza, Para.	H11	82
Mayotte, dep., Afr.	D9	58
May Park, Or., U.S.	B8	144
May Pen, Jam.	F6	94
Mayport Naval Station, mil., Fl., U.S.	B5	116
Mayrhofen, Aus.	H11	10
Mays, In., U.S.	E7	121
Mays Landing, N.J., U.S.	E3	137
Mays Lick, Ky., U.S.	B6	124
Maysville, Al., U.S.	A3	108
Maysville, Ar., U.S.	A1	111
Maysville, Ga., U.S.	B3	117
Maysville, Ky., U.S.	B6	124
Maysville, Mo., U.S.	B3	132
Maysville, N.C., U.S.	C5	140
Maysville, Ok., U.S.	C4	143
Mayumba, Gabon	B2	58
Māyūram, India	G5	46
Mayview, Mo., U.S.	B4	132
Mayville, Mi., U.S.	E7	129
Mayville, N.Y., U.S.	C1	139
Mayville, N.D., U.S.	B8	141
Mayville, Wi., U.S.	E5	156
Maywood, Il., U.S.	k9	120
Maywood, Mo., U.S.	B6	132
Maywood, Ne., U.S.	D5	134
Maywood, N.J., U.S.	h8	137
Maywood Park, Or., U.S.	*B4	144
Maza, Arg.	I7	80
Mazabuka, Zam.	E5	58
Mazagan see El-Jadida, Mor.	D6	62
Mazagão, Braz.	D8	76
Mazamet, Fr.	I9	14
Mazán, stm., Peru	I6	84
Mazār, Jabal, mtn., Asia	A6	50
Mazara del Vallo, Italy	L7	18
Mazār-e Sharīf, Afg.	B2	44
Mazarn Creek, stm., Ar., U.S.	g7	111
Mazaruni, stm., Guy.	E13	84
Mazatenango, Guat.	C3	92
Mazatlán, Mex.	F6	90
Mazatzal Mountains, mts., Az., U.S.	C4	110
Mazatzal Peak, mtn., Az., U.S.	C4	110
Mažeikiai, Lith.	E5	22
Mazeppa, Mn., U.S.	F6	130
Mazhuang, China	C3	34
Mazirbe, Lat.	D5	22
Mazoe, stm., Afr.	E6	58
Mazomanie, Wi., U.S.	E4	156
Mazon, Il., U.S.	B5	120
Mazsalaca, Lat.	D8	22
Mazunga, Zimb.	C9	66
Mazury, reg., Pol.	B20	10
Mbabane, Swaz.	F10	66
Mbacké, Sen.	D2	64
Mbage, Cen. Afr. Rep.	O3	60
Mbaïki, Cen. Afr. Rep.	H4	56
Mbala, Zam.	C6	58
Mbale, Ug.	A6	58
Mbalmayo, Cam.	H9	54
Mbamba Bay, Tan.	D6	58
Mbandaka (Coquilhatville), Zaire	A3	58
Mbanga, Cam.	I14	64
M'banza Congo, Ang.	C2	58
Mbanza-Ngungu, Zaire	C2	58
Mbarara, Ug.	B6	58
Mbari, stm., Cen. Afr. Rep.	G5	56
Mbashe, stm., S. Afr.	I9	66
M'bengué, C. Iv.	F7	64
Mbeya, Tan.	C6	58
Mbinda, Congo	B2	58
Mbini, Eq. Gui.	H8	54
Mbomou (Bomu), stm., Afr.	H5	56
Mbonge, Cam.	I14	64
Mboro, Sud.	N5	60
Mbour, Sen.	D1	64
Mbout, Maur.	C3	64
Mbuji-Mayi (Bakwanga), Zaire	C4	58
Mburucuyá, Arg.	E9	80
McAdam, N.B., Can.	D2	101
McAdams, Ms., U.S.	B4	131
McAdoo, Pa., U.S.	E9	145
McAfee Peak, mtn., Nv., U.S.	B6	135
McAlester, Ok., U.S.	C6	143
McAlester, Lake, res., Ok., U.S.	B6	143
McAlisterville, Pa., U.S.	E7	145
McAllen, Tx., U.S.	F3	150
McAlmont, Ar., U.S.	h10	111
McAlpine, Md., U.S.	B4	127
McAlpine Lock and Dam, U.S.	H6	121
McAndrews, Ky., U.S.	C7	124
McArthur, Oh., U.S.	C3	142
McAuley, Man., Can.	D1	100
McBain, Mi., U.S.	D5	129
McBee, S.C., U.S.	C7	147
McBride, B.C., Can.	C7	99
McCall, Id., U.S.	E2	119
McCalla, Al., U.S.	g6	108
McCallsburg, Ia., U.S.	B4	122
McCamey, Tx., U.S.	D1	150
McCammon, Id., U.S.	G6	119
McCandless, Pa., U.S.	h13	145
McCartney Mountain, mtn., Mt., U.S.	E4	133
McCartys, N.M., U.S.	B2	138
McCauley Island, i., B.C., Can.	C2	99
McCaysville, Ga., U.S.	B2	117
McChord Air Force Base, mil., Wa., U.S.	f11	154
McClain, co., Ok., U.S.	C4	143
McClave, Co., U.S.	C8	113
McCleary, Wa., U.S.	B2	154
McClellan Air Force Base, mil., Ca., U.S.	C3	112
McClellandville, De., U.S.	B2	115
McClellanville, S.C., U.S.	E9	147
McClintock, Mount, mtn., Ant.	D8	73
McCloud, Ca., U.S.	B2	112
McClure, Il., U.S.	F4	120
McClure, Oh., U.S.	A2	142
McClure, Pa., U.S.	E7	145
McClure, Va., U.S.	e9	153
McClusky, N.D., U.S.	B5	141
McColl, S.C., U.S.	B8	147
McCollum, Al., U.S.	B2	108
McComas, W.V., U.S.	D3	155
McComb, Ms., U.S.	D3	131
McComb, Oh., U.S.	A2	142
McCone, co., Mt., U.S.	C11	133
McConnell, Il., U.S.	A4	120
McConnell Air Force Base, mil., Ks., U.S.	g12	123
McConnellsburg, Pa., U.S.	G6	145
McConnellstown, Pa., U.S.	F5	145
McConnelsville, Oh., U.S.	C4	142
McCook, Ne., U.S.	D5	134
McCook, co., S.D., U.S.	D8	148
McCook Lake, S.D., U.S.	E9	148
McCool, Ms., U.S.	B4	131
McCool Junction, Ne., U.S.	D8	134
McCordsville, In., U.S.	E6	121
McCormick, S.C., U.S.	D3	147
McCormick, co., S.C., U.S.	D3	147
McCracken, Ks., U.S.	D4	123
McCracken, co., Ky., U.S.	e9	124
McCreary, Man., Can.	D2	100
McCreary, co., Ky., U.S.	D5	124
McCrory, Ar., U.S.	B4	111
McCulloch, co., Tx., U.S.	D3	150
McCullough, Al., U.S.	D2	108
McCullough Mountain, mtn., Nv., U.S.	H6	135
McCune, Ks., U.S.	E8	123
McCurtain, Ok., U.S.	B7	143
McCurtain, co., Ok., U.S.	C7	143
McDermitt, Nv., U.S.	B4	135
McDermott, Oh., U.S.	D2	142
McDonald, Ks., U.S.	C2	123
McDonald, Tn., U.S.	h12	149
McDonald, co., Mo., U.S.	E3	132
McDonald Creek, stm., Mt., U.S.	C8	133
McDonough, Ga., U.S.	C2	117
McDonough, co., Il., U.S.	C3	120
McDougal, Ar., U.S.	A5	111
McDougall, Mount, mtn., Wy., U.S.	D2	157
McDowell, Ky., U.S.	C7	124
McDowell, co., N.C., U.S.	f10	140
McDowell, co., W.V., U.S.	D3	155
McDowell Mountains, mts., Az., U.S.	k9	110
McDowell Peak, mtn., Az., U.S.	k9	110
McDuffie, co., Ga., U.S.	C4	117
McElroy Creek, stm., W.V., U.S.	k9	155
Mcensk, Russia	H19	22
McEwen, Tn., U.S.	A4	149
McFadden, Wy., U.S.	E6	157
McFarland, Ca., U.S.	E4	112
McFarland, Ks., U.S.	C7	123
McFarland, Wi., U.S.	E4	156
McGaheysville, Va., U.S.	B4	153
McGehee, Ar., U.S.	D4	111
McGill, Nv., U.S.	D7	135
McGivney, N.B., Can.	C3	101
McGrath, Ak., U.S.	C8	109
McGraw, N.Y., U.S.	C4	139
McGraws, W.V., U.S.	D3	155
McGregor, Ia., U.S.	A6	122
McGregor, Mn., U.S.	D5	130
McGregor, N.D., U.S.	A3	141
McGregor, Tx., U.S.	D4	150
McGregor, stm., B.C., Can.	B7	99
McGregor Lake, l., Alta., Can.	D4	98
McGregor Range, mts., Austl.	F5	70
McGuffey, Oh., U.S.	B2	142
McGuire, Mount, mtn., Id., U.S.	D4	119
McGuire Air Force Base, mil., N.J., U.S.	C3	137
McHenry, Il., U.S.	A5	120
McHenry, Ky., U.S.	C3	124
McHenry, Md., U.S.	k12	127
McHenry, Ms., U.S.	E4	131
McHenry, N.D., U.S.	B7	141
McHenry, co., Il., U.S.	A5	120
McHenry, co., N.D., U.S.	A5	141
Mchinji, Mwi.	D6	58
McIndoe Falls, Vt., U.S.	C4	152
McIntosh, Al., U.S.	D1	108
McIntosh, Fl., U.S.	C4	116
McIntosh, Ga., U.S.	E5	117
McIntosh, Mn., U.S.	C3	130
McIntosh, S.D., U.S.	B4	148
McIntosh, co., Ga., U.S.	E5	117
McIntosh, co., N.D., U.S.	C6	141
McIntosh, co., Ok., U.S.	B6	143
McIntosh Lake, l., Sask., Can.	B3	105
McIntosh Run, stm., Md., U.S.	D4	127
McIntyre, Ga., U.S.	D3	117
McKean, co., Pa., U.S.	C4	145
McKee, Ky., U.S.	C6	124
McKee City, N.J., U.S.	E3	137
McKeesport, Pa., U.S.	F2	145
McKees Rocks, Pa., U.S.	F1	145
McKenney, Va., U.S.	D5	153
McKenzie, Al., U.S.	D3	108
McKenzie, Tn., U.S.	A3	149
McKenzie, co., N.D., U.S.	B2	141
McKenzie, stm., Or., U.S.	C4	144
McKerrow, Ont., Can.	A3	103
McKinley, co., N.M., U.S.	B1	138
McKinley, Mount, mtn., Ak., U.S.	C9	109
McKinley Park, Ak., U.S.	C10	109
McKinleyville, Ca., U.S.	B1	112
McKinney, Ky., U.S.	C5	124
McKinney, Tx., U.S.	C4	150
McKinney, Lake, l., Ks., U.S.	E2	123
McKittrick Summit, mtn., Ca., U.S.	E4	112
McLain, Ms., U.S.	D5	131
McLaughlin, Alta., Can.	C5	98
McLaughlin, S.D., U.S.	B5	148
McLaurin, Ms., U.S.	D4	131
McLean, Sask., Can.	G3	105
McLean, Il., U.S.	C4	120
McLean, Tx., U.S.	B2	150
McLean, Va., U.S.	g12	153
McLean, co., Il., U.S.	C4	120
McLean, co., Ky., U.S.	C2	124
McLean, co., N.D., U.S.	B4	141
McLean Lake, l., Sask., Can.	A6	98
McLean Mountain, mtn., Me., U.S.	A4	126
McLeansboro, Il., U.S.	E5	120
McLemoresville, Tn., U.S.	B3	149
McLennan, Alta., Can.	B2	98
McLennan, co., Tx., U.S.	D4	150
McLeod, N.D., U.S.	C8	141
McLeod, co., Mn., U.S.	F4	130
McLeod, stm., Alta., Can.	C2	98
McLeod Bay, b., N.W. Ter., Can.	D10	96
McLeod Lake, B.C., Can.	B6	99
M'Clintock Channel, strt., N.W. Ter., Can.	B12	96
McLoud, Ok., U.S.	B4	143
McLoughlin, Mount, mtn., Or., U.S.	D4	144
McLouth, Ks., U.S.	C8	123
M'Clure Strait, strt., N.W. Ter., Can.	B9	96
McMechen, W.V., U.S.	B4	155
McMillan, Lake, res., N.M., U.S.	E5	138
McMillin, Wa., U.S.	f11	154
McMinn, co., Tn., U.S.	D9	149
McMinnville, Or., U.S.	B3	144
McMinnville, Tn., U.S.	D8	149
McMullen, co., Tx., U.S.	E3	150
McMurdo, sci., Ant.	C8	73
McMurdo Sound, strt., Ant.	C8	73
McNabb, Il., U.S.	B4	120
McNairy, co., Tn., U.S.	B3	149
McNary, Az., U.S.	C6	110
McNary Dam, U.S.	B7	144
McNeil, Ar., U.S.	D2	111
McNeil, Mount, mtn., B.C., Can.	B2	99
McNeil Island, i., Wa., U.S.	f10	154
McNeill, Ms., U.S.	E4	131
McPherson, Ks., U.S.	D6	123
McPherson, co., Ks., U.S.	D6	123
McPherson, co., Ne., U.S.	C4	134
McPherson, co., S.D., U.S.	B6	148
McPherson Range, mts., Austl.	G10	70
McQueeney, Tx., U.S.	h7	150
McRae, Ar., U.S.	B4	111
McRae, Ga., U.S.	D4	117
McRoberts, Ky., U.S.	C7	124
McSherrystown, Pa., U.S.	G7	145
McTaggart, Sask., Can.	H3	105
McTavish, Man., Can.	E3	100
McVeigh, Ky., U.S.	C7	124
McVille, N.D., U.S.	B7	141
McWilliams, Al., U.S.	D2	108
M'Daourouch, Alg.	M2	18
Meacham, Sask., Can.	E3	105
Mead, Co., U.S.	A6	113
Mead, Ne., U.S.	C9	134
Mead, Wa., U.S.	B8	154
Mead, Lake, res., U.S.	A1	110
Meade, Ks., U.S.	E3	123

Name — Map Ref. — Page

Meade, co., Ks., U.S. E3 123
Meade, co., Ky., U.S. C3 124
Meade, co., S.D., U.S. C3 148
Meade, stm., Ak., U.S. B8 109
Meaden Peak, mtn., Co., U.S. A3 113
Meade Peak, mtn., Id., U.S. G7 119
Meadow, Tx., U.S. C1 150
Meadow, Ut., U.S. E3 151
Meadow, stm., W.V., U.S. C4 155
Meadow Bridge, W.V., U.S. D4 155
Meadowbrook, W.V., U.S. k10 155
Meadow Creek, W.V., U.S. D4 155
Meadow Creek, stm., W.V., U.S. n14 155
Meadow Grove, Ne., U.S. B8 134
Meadow Lake, Sask., Can. n7 105
Meadow Lands, Pa., U.S. F1 145
Meadow Mountain, mtn., U.S. k12 127
Meadows, Id., U.S. E2 119
Meadow Valley Wash, val., Nv., U.S. F7 135
Meadowview, Va., U.S. f10 153
Meadville, Ms., U.S. D3 131
Meadville, Mo., U.S. B4 132
Meadville, Pa., U.S. C1 145
Meaford, Ont., Can. C4 103
Meagher, co., Mt., U.S. D6 133
Meaghers Grant, N.S., Can. E6 101
Mealy Mountains, mts., Newf., Can. h9 102
Méan, Bel. H7 12
Meana, Turk. C16 48
Meandarra, Austl. F8 70
Meander Creek Reservoir, res., Oh., U.S. A5 142
Means, Ky., U.S. C6 124
Mears, Mi., U.S. E4 129
Meath, co., Ire. H7 8
Meath, hist. reg., Ire. H6 8
Meath Park, Sask., Can. D3 105
Meaux, Fr. D9 14
Mebane, N.C., U.S. A3 140
Mecaya, stm., Col. G5 84
Mecca see Makkah, Sau. Ar. D1 47
Mecca, Ca., U.S. F5 112
Mecca, In., U.S. E3 121
Mechanic Falls, Me., U.S. D2 126
Mechanicsburg, In., U.S. D5 121
Mechanicsburg, Oh., U.S. B2 142
Mechanicsburg, Pa., U.S. F7 145
Mechanicsville, Ia., U.S. C6 122
Mechanicsville, Md., U.S. D4 127
Mechanicsville, Va., U.S. C5 153
Mechanicville, N.Y., U.S. C7 139
Mechant, Lake, l., La., U.S. E4 125
Mechelen (Malines), Bel. F5 12
Mechita, Arg. H8 80
Mechra Safsaf, Mor. K9 16
Mechriyya, Alg. D10 62
Mechroha, Alg. M2 18
Mecklenburg, co., N.C., U.S. B2 140
Mecklenburg, co., Va., U.S. D4 153
Mecklenburg, hist. reg., Ger. B12 10
Mecklenburger Bucht, b., Ger. A11 10
Mecklenburg-Vorpommern, state, Ger. B12 10
Meckling, S.D., U.S. E8 148
Mecosta, Mi., U.S. E5 129
Mecosta, co., Mi., U.S. E5 129
Meda, Port. E4 16
Medan, Indon. M5 40
Medanales, N.M., U.S. A3 138
Médanos, Arg. J7 80
Medanosa, Punta, c., Arg. F3 78
Medaryville, In., U.S. B4 121
Meddybumps Lake, l., Me., U.S. C5 126
Mede, Italy D3 18
Medeiros Neto, Braz. D8 79
Medellín, Col. D5 84
Médenine, Tun. D16 62
Mederdra, Maur. C2 64
Medfield, Ma., U.S. h10 128
Medford, Ma., U.S. B5 128
Medford, Mn., U.S. F5 130
Medford, N.J., U.S. D3 137
Medford, Ok., U.S. A4 143
Medford, Or., U.S. E4 144
Medford, Wi., U.S. C3 156
Medford Lakes, N.J., U.S. D3 137
Medgidia, Rom. E12 20
Media, Pa., U.S. G11 145
Mediapolis, Ia., U.S. C6 122
Mediaș, Rom. C8 20
Medical Lake, Wa., U.S. B8 154
Medicina, Italy E6 18
Medicine Bow, Wy., U.S. E6 157
Medicine Bow, stm., Wy., U.S. E6 157
Medicine Bow Mountains, mts., U.S. E6 157
Medicine Bow Peak, mtn., Wy., U.S. E6 157
Medicine Creek, stm., Mo., U.S. B4 132
Medicine Creek, stm., Ne., U.S. D5 134
Medicine Hat, Alta., Can. D5 98
Medicine Lake, Mt., U.S. B12 133
Medicine Lodge, Ks., U.S. E5 123
Medicine Lodge, stm., U.S. E4 123
Medicine Park, Ok., U.S. C3 143
Medina, Braz. D8 79
Medina see Al-Madīnah, Sau. Ar. B1 47
Medina, N.Y., U.S. B2 139
Medina, N.D., U.S. C6 141
Medina, Oh., U.S. A4 142
Medina, Tn., U.S. B3 149
Medina, Wa., U.S. e11 154
Medina, co., Oh., U.S. A4 142
Medina, co., Tx., U.S. E3 150
Medina, stm., Tx., U.S. k7 150
Medina del Campo, Spain D7 16
Medininkai, Lith. G8 22
Medinīpur, India I12 44
Medio, Punta, c., Chile D3 80
Mediterranean Sea E9 52
Medjerda, Monts de la, mts., Afr. M3 18
Mednogorsk, Russia G9 26
Mednoje, Russia E18 22
Mednyj, ostrov, i., Russia G25 28
Médoc, reg., Fr. G6 14
Medora, Man., Can. E1 100
Medora, Il., U.S. D3 120
Medora, In., U.S. G5 121
Medora, N.D., U.S. C2 141
Médouneu, Gabon A2 58
Medstead, Sask., Can. D1 105
Meductic, N.B., Can. D2 101
Medveđa, Yugo. G5 20
Medvedevskoje, Russia C18 22
Medvedica, stm., Russia G6 26
Medvežjegorsk, Russia E4 26
Medvežji ostrova, is., Russia C24 28
Medway, Me., U.S. C4 126
Medway, Ma., U.S. B5 128
Medway, stm., N.S., Can. E5 101
Medyn', Russia G18 22
Meekatharra, Austl. E3 68
Meeker, Co., U.S. A3 113
Meeker, Ok., U.S. B5 143
Meeker, co., Mn., U.S. E4 130
Meelpaeg Lake, res., Newf., Can. D3 102
Meer, Bel. F6 12
Meerane, Ger. E12 10
Meerut, India F7 44
Meeteetse, Wy., U.S. B4 157
Meeting Creek, Alta., Can. C4 98
Mega, Eth. H8 56
Mégantic, Lac, l., Que., Can. D7 104
Mégantic, Mont, mtn., Que., Can. D6 104
Mégara, Grc. K7 20
Megargel, Al., U.S. D2 108
Meggett, S.C., U.S. F7 147
Meghālaya, state, India H14 44
Meghna, stm., Bngl. H14 44
Megunticook, Mount, mtn., Me., U.S. D3 126
Mehadia, Rom. E6 20
Mehar, Pak. G2 44
Mehdia, Alg. C11 62
Mehedinți, co., Rom. E6 20
Meherrin, stm., U.S. A4 140
Mehlville, Mo., U.S. f13 132
Mehrān, Iran E9 48
Meia Ponte, Rio da, stm., Braz. D4 79
Meigs, Ga., U.S. E2 117
Meigs, co., Oh., U.S. C3 142
Meigs, co., Tn., U.S. D9 149
Meiktila, Mya. D3 40
Meilie, China I6 34
Meiningen, Ger. E10 10
Meiringen, Switz. E9 13
Meissen, Ger. D13 10
Meixian, China K5 34
Meiyino, Sud. N8 60
Meizhai, China B10 40
Mejerda, Oued (Oued Medjerda), stm., Afr. M4 18
Mejez el Bab, Tun. M4 18
Mejicanos, El Sal. D5 92
Mejillones, Chile B3 80
Mejillones, Península, pen., Chile B3 80
Mejillones del Sur, Bahía de, b., Chile B3 80
Mékambo, Gabon A2 58
Mekele, Eth. K10 60
Mekinock, N.D., U.S. A8 141
Meknès, Mor. D8 62
Mekong, stm., Asia H8 40
Mekoryuk, Ak., U.S. C6 109
Mékrou, stm., Afr. F7 54
Melado, stm., Chile H3 80
Melaka, Malay. M7 40
Melanesia, is., Oc. I19 158
Melba, Id., U.S. F2 119
Melber, Ky., U.S. f9 124
Melbeta, Ne., U.S. C2 134
Melbourne, Austl. K6 70
Melbourne, Ont., Can. E3 103
Melbourne, Ar., U.S. A4 111
Melbourne, Fl., U.S. D6 116
Melbourne, Ia., U.S. C4 122
Melbourne, Ky., U.S. h14 124
Melbourne Beach, Fl., U.S. D6 116
Melby House, Scot., U.K. A12 8
Melcher, Ia., U.S. C4 122
Melchor Múzquiz, Mex. D9 90
Meldorf, Ger. A9 10
Meldrim, Ga., U.S. D5 117
Melechovo, Russia E24 22
Melegnano, Italy D4 18
Melenki, Russia F24 22
Meleuz, Russia G9 26
Mélèzes, Rivière aux, stm., Que., Can. g12 104
Melfi, Chad F4 56
Melfi, Italy H10 18
Melfort, Sask., Can. E3 105
Melgaço, Port. C3 16
Melghir, Chott, l., Alg. C14 62
Melhus, Nor. J12 6
Meli, stm., Afr. G4 64
Meliane, Oued, stm., Tun. M5 18
Melide, Switz. G10 13
Melilla, Sp. N. Afr. C9 62
Melincué, Arg. G8 80
Melipilla, Chile G3 80
Melita, Man., Can. E1 100
Melitopol', Ukr. F15 4
Mellègue, Oued, stm., Afr. M3 18
Mellen, Wi., U.S. B3 156
Mellette, S.D., U.S. B7 148
Mellette, co., S.D., U.S. D5 148
Mellott, In., U.S. D3 121
Mellwood, Ar., U.S. C5 111
Mělník, Czech Rep. E14 10
Mel'nytsya-Podil's'ka, Ukr. A10 20
Melo, Ur. G11 80
Melo, stm., Para. I12 82
Melocheville, Que., Can. q19 104
Melong, Cam. I14 64
Melos see Mílos, i., Grc. M8 20
Melrose, N.B., Can. C6 101
Melrose, N.S., Can. D7 101
Melrose, Ct., U.S. B5 114
Melrose, Fl., U.S. C4 116
Melrose, Ma., U.S. B5 128
Melrose, Mn., U.S. E4 130
Melrose, N.M., U.S. C6 138
Melrose, Wi., U.S. D2 156
Melstone, Mt., U.S. D9 133
Melton Hill Lake, res., Tn., U.S. D9 149
Melton Mowbray, Eng., U.K. I13 8
Melúa, Col. F6 84
Melun, Fr. D9 14
Melun, Mya. D2 40
Melvern, Ks., U.S. D8 123
Melvern Lake, res., Ks., U.S. D8 123
Melville, Sask., Can. G4 105
Melville, La., U.S. D4 125
Melville, Lake, l., Newf., Can. B2 102
Melville Bugt, b., Grnld. B13 86
Melville Island, i., Austl. B6 68
Melville Island, i., N.W. Ter., Can. B8 86
Melville Peninsula, pen., N.W. Ter., Can. C16 96
Melville Sound, strt., N.W. Ter., Can. C11 96
Melvin, Al., U.S. D1 108
Melvin, Il., U.S. C5 120
Melvin, Ia., U.S. A2 122
Melvin, Ky., U.S. C7 124
Melvin, Lough, l., Eur. G5 8
Melvin Village, N.H., U.S. C4 136
Melyana, Alg. B12 62
Melzo, Italy D4 18
Memel, S. Afr. F9 66
Memel see Nemunas, stm., Eur. F6 22
Memmingen, Ger. H10 10
Memo, stm., Ven. C9 84
Mémót, Camb. I9 40
Mempawah, Indon. N10 40
Memphis, Fl., U.S. p10 116
Memphis, In., U.S. H6 121
Memphis, Mi., U.S. F8 129
Memphis, Mo., U.S. A5 132
Memphis, Ne., U.S. g12 134
Memphis, Tn., U.S. B1 149
Memphis, Tx., U.S. B2 150
Memphis Naval Air Station, mil., Tn., U.S. B2 149
Memramcook, N.B., Can. C5 101
Mena, Ar., U.S. C1 111
Menahga, Mn., U.S. D3 130
Ménaka, Mali D11 64
Menaldum, Neth. B8 12
Menan, Id., U.S. F7 119
Menands, N.Y., U.S. C7 139
Menard, Tx., U.S. D3 150
Menard, co., Il., U.S. C4 120
Menard, co., Tx., U.S. D3 150
Menasha, Wi., U.S. D5 156
Menawashei, Sud. K3 60
Mendawai, stm., Indon. F5 38
Mende, Fr. H10 14
Mendenhall, Ms., U.S. D4 131
Mendes, Ga., U.S. E5 117
Méndez, Mex. E10 90
Mendham, Sask., Can. G1 105
Mendham, N.J., U.S. B3 137
Mendi, Eth. M8 60
Mendi, Pap. N. Gui. G11 38
Mendocino, Ca., U.S. C2 112
Mendocino, co., Ca., U.S. C2 112
Mendon, Il., U.S. C2 120
Mendon, Ma., U.S. h9 128
Mendon, Mi., U.S. F5 129
Mendon, Mo., U.S. B4 132
Mendon, Oh., U.S. B1 142
Mendon, Ut., U.S. B4 151
Mendota, Ca., U.S. D3 112
Mendota, Il., U.S. B4 120
Mendota, Lake, l., Wi., U.S. E4 156
Mendoza, Arg. G4 80
Mendoza, Peru B3 82
Mendoza, prov., Arg. H4 80
Mendoza, stm., Arg. G4 80
Ménéac, Fr. D4 14
Mene de Mauroa, Ven. B7 84
Mene Grande, Ven. C7 84
Menemen, Tur. K11 20
Menen (Menin), Bel. G3 12
Menfi, Italy L7 18
Mengcheng, China E10 30
Menggala, Indon. F4 38
Menggu, China A7 40
Menghai, China C6 40
Mengla, China D6 40
Mengzhi, China B5 40
Mengzi, China C7 40
Menifee, Ar., U.S. B3 111
Menifee, co., Ky., U.S. C6 124
Menindee, Austl. I5 70
Menindee Lake, l., Austl. I5 70
Menlo, Ga., U.S. B1 117
Menlo, Ia., U.S. C3 122
Menlo, Wa., U.S. C2 154
Menlo Park, Ca., U.S. k8 112
Menno, S.D., U.S. D8 148
Menominee, Mi., U.S. C3 129
Menominee, co., Mi., U.S. C3 129
Menominee, co., Wi., U.S. C5 156
Menominee, stm., U.S. C6 156
Menominee Indian Reservation, Wi., U.S. C5 156
Menomonee, stm., Wi., U.S. m11 156
Menomonee Falls, Wi., U.S. E5 156
Menomonie, Wi., U.S. D2 156
Menongue, Ang. D3 58
Menorca, i., Spain F16 16
Mens, Fr. H12 14
Mentawai, Kepulauan, is., Indon. F2 38
Mentawai, Selat, strt., Indon. F3 38
Mentmore, N.M., U.S. B1 138
Menton, Fr. I14 14
Mentone, Al., U.S. A4 108
Mentone, In., U.S. B5 121
Mentor, Ky., U.S. k14 124
Mentor, Oh., U.S. A4 142
Mentor, Tn., U.S. n13 149
Mentor-on-the-Lake, Oh., U.S. A4 142
Menzel Bourguiba, Tun. L4 18
Menzel Bou Zelfa, Tun. M5 18
Menzel Djemil, Tun. L4 18
Menzel Temime, Tun. M5 18
Menzies, Austl. E4 68
Menzies, Mount, mtn., Ant. C5 73
Meoqui, Mex. C7 90
Meota, Sask., Can. D1 105
Meppel, Neth. C9 12
Meppen, Ger. C7 10
Meqerghane, Sebkha, pl., Alg. G11 62
Mequon, Wi., U.S. E6 156
Mer, Fr. E8 14
Meramec, stm., Mo., U.S. C7 132
Merano (Meran), Italy C6 18
Merasheen Island, i., Newf., Can. E4 102
Merate, Italy D4 18
Merauke, Indon. G11 38
Meraux, La., U.S. k12 125
Mercaderes, Col. G4 84
Mercāra, India F3 46
Merced, Ca., U.S. D3 112
Merced, co., Ca., U.S. D3 112
Merced, stm., Ca., U.S. D3 112
Mercedario, Cerro, mtn., Arg. F3 80
Mercedes, Arg. G6 80
Mercedes, Arg. E9 80
Mercedes, Arg. H9 80
Mercedes, Tx., U.S. F4 150
Mercedes, Ur. G9 80
Mercer, Mo., U.S. A4 132
Mercer, N.D., U.S. B5 141
Mercer, Pa., U.S. D1 145
Mercer, Tn., U.S. B2 149
Mercer, Wi., U.S. B3 156
Mercer, co., Il., U.S. B3 120
Mercer, co., Ky., U.S. C5 124
Mercer, co., Mo., U.S. A4 132
Mercer, co., N.J., U.S. C3 137
Mercer, co., N.D., U.S. B4 141
Mercer, co., Oh., U.S. B1 142
Mercer, co., Pa., U.S. D1 145
Mercer, co., W.V., U.S. D3 155
Mercer Island, Wa., U.S. B3 154
Mercer Island, i., Wa., U.S. e11 154
Mercersburg, Pa., U.S. G6 145
Mercerville, N.J., U.S. C3 137
Merchtem, Bel. G5 12
Mercier, Que., Can. D4 104
Mercy, Cape, c., N.W. Ter., Can. D20 96
Meredith, N.H., U.S. C3 136
Meredith, Lake, l., Co., U.S. C7 113
Meredith, Lake, res., Tx., U.S. B2 150
Meredith Center, N.H., U.S. C3 136
Meredosia, Il., U.S. D3 120
Meredosia Lake, l., Il., U.S. D3 120
Mereeg, Som. H10 56
Merenkurkku (Norra Kvarken), strt., Eur. J17 6
Merevari, stm., Ven. E10 84
Merewa, Eth. N9 60
Mergui (Myeik), Mya. H5 40
Mergui Archipelago, is., Mya. H5 40
Meriç (Marica) (Évros), stm., Eur. H10 20
Mérida, Mex. G15 90
Mérida, Spain G5 16
Mérida, Ven. C7 84
Mérida, state, Ven. C7 84
Mérida, Cordillera de, mts., Ven. C7 84
Meriden, Ct., U.S. C4 114
Meriden, Ks., U.S. C8 123
Meriden, N.H., U.S. C2 136
Meriden, Wy., U.S. E8 157
Meridian, Ga., U.S. E5 117
Meridian, Id., U.S. F2 119
Meridian, Ms., U.S. C5 131
Meridian, Pa., U.S. E2 145
Meridian, Tx., U.S. D4 150
Meridian Hills, In., U.S. k10 121
Meridian Naval Air Station, mil., Ms., U.S. C5 131
Meridianville, Al., U.S. A3 108
Mérignac, Fr. H6 14
Merigold, Ms., U.S. B3 131
Merigomish, N.S., Can. D7 101
Merimbula, Austl. K8 70
Merín, Laguna (Lagoa Mirim), b., S.A. G12 80
Merino, Co., U.S. A7 113
Merinos, Ur. G10 80
Meriwether, co., Ga., U.S. C2 117
Merkel, Tx., U.S. C2 150
Merkendorf, Ger. F10 10
Merkinė, Lith. G7 22
Merkuloviči, Bela. I13 22
Merlin, Ont., Can. E2 103
Merlin, Or., U.S. E3 144
Merlo, Arg. G6 80
Mermentau, La., U.S. D3 125
Mermentau, stm., La., U.S. E3 125
Merna, Ne., U.S. C6 134
Mernye, Hung. I17 10
Merom, In., U.S. F2 121
Meron, Hare, mtn., Isr. C4 50
Merredin, Austl. F3 68
Merriam, Ks., U.S. k16 123
Merrick, co., Ne., U.S. C7 134
Merrick Brook, stm., Ct., U.S. C7 114
Merrickville, Ont., Can. C9 103
Merrifield, Mn., U.S. D4 130
Merrill, Ia., U.S. B1 122
Merrill, Mi., U.S. E6 129
Merrill, Or., U.S. E5 144
Merrill, Wi., U.S. C4 156
Merrillan, Wi., U.S. D3 156
Merrillville, In., U.S. B3 121
Merrimac, Ma., U.S. A5 128
Merrimac, Wi., U.S. E4 156
Merrimack, N.H., U.S. E4 136
Merrimack, co., N.H., U.S. D3 136
Merrimack, stm., U.S. A5 128
Merriman, Ne., U.S. B4 134
Merritt, B.C., Can. D7 99
Merritt Island, Fl., U.S. D6 116
Merritt Reservoir, res., Ne., U.S. B5 134
Merriwa, Austl. I9 70
Mer Rouge, La., U.S. B4 125
Merrymeeting Lake, l., N.H., U.S. D4 136
Merryville, La., U.S. D2 125
Mersch, Lux. I9 12
Merseburg, Ger. D11 10
Mersey, stm., Austl. M7 70
Mershon, Ga., U.S. E4 117
Mersing, Malay. M7 40
Mērsrags, Lat. D6 22
Merthyr Tydfil, Wales, U.K. J10 8
Mértola, Port. H4 16
Merton, Wi., U.S. m11 156
Mertzon, Tx., U.S. D2 150
Méru, Fr. C9 14
Meru, Kenya A7 58
Meru, Mount, mtn., Tan. B7 58
Mervin, Sask., Can. D1 105
Merwin Lake, res., Wa., U.S. C3 154
Méry, Fr. D10 14
Merzig, Ger. F6 10
Mesa, Az., U.S. D4 110
Mesa, Co., U.S. B2 113
Mesa, co., Co., U.S. C2 113
Mesa, stm., Spain D10 16
Mesabi Range, hills, Mn., U.S. C6 130
Mesagne, Italy I12 18
Mesa Mountain, mtn., Co., U.S. D4 113
Mesa Verde National Park, Co., U.S. D2 113
Mescalero, N.M., U.S. D4 138
Mescalero Indian Reservation, N.M., U.S. D4 138
Meschede, Ger. D8 10
Meščovsk, Russia G18 22
Mesena, Ga., U.S. C4 117
Meservey, Ia., U.S. B4 122
Mesfinto, Eth. K9 60
Meshgīn Shahr, Iran B9 48
Meshomasic Mountain, mtn., Ct., U.S. C5 114
Mesick, Mi., U.S. D5 129
Mesilla, N.M., U.S. E3 138
Mesita, N.M., U.S. C2 138
Meskiana, Alg. C14 62
Meslay-du-Maine, Fr. E6 14
Mesocco, Switz. F11 13
Mesolóngion, Grc. K5 20
Mesopotamia, hist. reg., Asia D8 48
Mesquita, Braz. E7 79
Mesquite, Nv., U.S. G7 135
Mesquite, N.M., U.S. E3 138
Mesquite, Tx., U.S. n10 150
Messalo, stm., Moz. D7 58
Messalonskee Lake, l., Me., U.S. D3 126
Messina, Italy K10 18
Messina, S. Afr. D10 66
Messina, Stretto di, strt., Italy K10 18
Messini, Grc. L6 20
Messiniakós Kólpos, b., Grc. M6 20
Messojacha, stm., Russia D13 26
Mestá, Grc. K9 20
Mesta (Néstos), stm., Eur. H7 20
Mestasa, Mor. C8 62
Mestghanem, Alg. C11 62
Mestre, Italy D7 18
Meta, Mo., U.S. C5 132
Meta, dept., Col. F6 84
Meta, stm., S.A. D9 84
Métabetchouan, Que., Can. A6 104
Métabetchouane, stm., Que., Can. A5 104
Meta Incognita Peninsula, pen., N.W. Ter., Can. D19 96
Metairie, La., U.S. k11 125
Metaline, Wa., U.S. A8 154
Metaline Falls, Wa., U.S. A8 154
Metamora, Il., U.S. C4 120
Metamora, In., U.S. F7 121
Metamora, Mi., U.S. F7 129
Metamora, Oh., U.S. A2 142
Metán, Arg. C6 80
Metapán, El Sal. C5 92
Meta Pond, l., Newf., Can. D4 102
Metcalf, Ga., U.S. F3 117
Metcalf, Il., U.S. D6 120
Metcalfe, Ont., Can. B9 103
Metcalfe, Ms., U.S. B2 131
Metcalfe, co., Ky., U.S. C4 124
Metedeconk, North Branch, stm., N.J., U.S. C4 137
Metedeconk, South Branch, stm., N.J., U.S. C3 137
Meteghan, N.S., Can. E3 101
Meteghan River, N.S., Can. E3 101
Meteghan Station, N.S., Can. E3 101
Metema, Eth. K9 60
Meteor Crater, crat., Az., U.S. C4 110
Methóni, Grc. M5 20
Methow, stm., Wa., U.S. A5 154
Methuen, Ma., U.S. A5 128
Metiskow, Alta., Can. C5 98
Metković, Cro. F12 18
Metlakatla, Ak., U.S. D13 109
Metlaoui, Tun. C15 62
Metlatonoc, Mex. I10 90
Meto, Bayou, stm., Ar., U.S. C4 111
Metolius, Or., U.S. C5 144
Metonga, Lake, l., Wi., U.S. C5 156
Metropolis, Il., U.S. F5 120
Metsematluku, Bots. E7 66
Mettawee, stm., U.S. E2 152
Metter, Ga., U.S. D4 117
Mettuppālaiyam, India G4 46
Mettūr, India G4 46
Metu, Eth. M8 60
Metuchen, N.J., U.S. B4 137
Metulla, Isr. B5 50
Metz, Fr. C13 14
Metzger, Or., U.S. h12 144
Meulan, Fr. C8 14
Meureudu, Indon. L4 40
Meurthe, stm., Fr. D13 14
Meurthe-et-Moselle, dept., Fr. D13 14
Meuse, dept., Fr. D12 14
Meuse (Maas), stm., Eur. E5 10
Meuselwitz, Ger. D12 10
Mexia, Al., U.S. D2 108
Mexia, Tx., U.S. D4 150
Mexia, Lake, res., Tx., U.S. D4 150
Mexiana, Ilha, i., Braz. D9 76
Mexicali, Mex. A2 90
Mexican Springs, N.M., U.S. B1 138
Mexico, In., U.S. C5 121
Mexico, Me., U.S. D2 126
Mexico, Mo., U.S. B6 132
Mexico, N.Y., U.S. B4 139
México, state, Mex. H10 90
Mexico (México), ctry., N.A. F9 90
Mexico, Gulf of, b., N.A. C6 88
Mexico City see Ciudad de México, Mex. H10 90
Meximieux, Fr. G12 14
Meycauayan, Phil. n19 39b
Meyersdale, Pa., U.S. G3 145
Meyísti, i., Grc. H13 4
Meymac, Fr. G9 14
Meymaneh, Afg. C1 44
Meymeh, stm., Asia E9 48
Meyrargues, Fr. I12 14
Mezada, Horvot (Masada), hist., Isr. F4 50
Mezapa, Hond. B7 92
Mezcala, Mex. I10 90
Mezcalapa, stm., Mex. I13 90
Meždurečensk, Russia G9 28
Mèze, Fr. I10 14
Mezen', Russia D6 26
Mezen', stm., Russia D6 26
Mézin, Fr. H7 14
Mezinovskij, Russia F23 22
Mezőberény, Hung. I21 10
Mezőcsát, Hung. H20 10
Mezőkovácsháza, Hung. I20 10
Mezőkövesd, Hung. H20 10
Mezőtúr, Hung. H20 10
Mezquital, Mex. F7 90
Mezquital, stm., Mex. F7 90
Mglin, Russia H15 22
M'goun, Irhil, mtn., Mor. E7 62
Mhow, India I6 44
Miahuatlán de Porfirio Díaz, Mex. I11 90
Miajadas, Spain F6 16
Miami, Man., Can. E2 100
Miami, Az., U.S. D5 110
Miami, Fl., U.S. G6 116
Miami, In., U.S. C5 121
Miami, N.M., U.S. A5 138
Miami, Ok., U.S. A7 143
Miami, Tx., U.S. B2 150
Miami, W.V., U.S. m13 155
Miami, co., In., U.S. C5 121
Miami, co., Ks., U.S. D9 123
Miami, co., Oh., U.S. B1 142
Miami Beach, Fl., U.S. G6 116
Miami Canal, Fl., U.S. F6 116
Miami International Airport, Fl., U.S. G6 116
Miamisburg, Oh., U.S. C1 142
Miami Shores, Fl., U.S. G6 116
Miami Springs, Fl., U.S. G6 116
Miamitown, Oh., U.S. o12 142
Mīāndoāb, Iran C9 48
Miandrivazo, Madag. q21 67b
Mīāneh, Iran C9 48
Miangas, Pulau, i., Indon. D8 38
Mianhu, China L5 34
Mianus Reservoir, res., U.S. E1 114
Miānwāli, Pak. D4 44
Mianyang, China E7 30
Mianyang, China E2 34
Miaoli, Tai. K9 34
Miarinavaratra, Madag. r22 67b
Miass, Russia G10 26
Miastko, Pol. A17 10
Mica Creek, B.C., Can. C8 99
Mica Mountain, mtn., Az., U.S. E5 110
Micanopy, Fl., U.S. C4 116
Micaúne, Moz. B13 66
Micco, Fl., U.S. E6 116
Miccosukee, Lake, res., Fl., U.S. B2 116
Michajlov, Russia G22 22
Michajlovka, Russia G6 26
Michanoviči, Bela. H10 22
Michaud, Point, c., N.S., Can. D9 101
Michelson, Mount, mtn., Ak., U.S. B11 109
Miches, Dom. Rep. E10 94
Michichi, Alta., Can. D4 98
Michie, Tn., U.S. B3 149
Michigamme, Mi., U.S. B2 129
Michigamme, Lake, l., Mi., U.S. B2 129
Michigamme Reservoir, res., Mi., U.S. B2 129
Michigan, N.D., U.S. A7 141
Michigan, state, U.S. E6 129
Michigan, stm., Co., U.S. A4 113
Michigan, Lake, l., U.S. C9 106
Michigan Center, Mi., U.S. F6 129
Michigan City, In., U.S. A4 121
Michigan City, Ms., U.S. A4 131
Michigan Island, i., Wi., U.S. B3 156
Michigan Prairie, reg., Wa., U.S. C7 154
Michigantown, In., U.S. D5 121
Michnevo, Russia F20 22
Michoacán, state, Mex. H9 90
Mico, stm., Nic. E10 92
Mico, Montañas del, mts., Guat. B6 92
Micro, N.C., U.S. B4 140
Micronesia, is., Oc. G19 158
Micronesia, Federated States of, ctry., Oc. H19 158
Mičurinsk, Russia I23 22
Midale, Sask., Can. H4 105
Midar, Mor. C9 62
Mid-Atlantic Ridge F9 160
Middelburg, Neth. E4 12
Middelburg, S. Afr. E9 66
Middelburg, S. Afr. H7 66
Middelfart, Den. N11 6
Middelharnis, Neth. E5 12
Middelpos, S. Afr. H5 66
Middelwater, S. Afr. D10 66
Middenmeer, Neth. C7 12
Middle, Ia., U.S. C6 122
Middle, stm., Ia., U.S. C3 122
Middle, stm., Mn., U.S. B2 130
Middle America Trench H10 86
Middle Andaman, i., India H2 40
Middleboro (Middleborough Center), Ma., U.S. C6 128
Middlebourne, W.V., U.S. B4 155
Middlebranch, Oh., U.S. B4 142

Name — Map Ref. — Page

Middlebro, Man., Can. E4 100
Middlebrook, Va., U.S. B3 153
Middleburg, Fl., U.S. B5 116
Middleburg, Ky., U.S. C5 124
Middleburg, Pa., U.S. E7 145
Middleburg, Va., U.S. B5 153
Middleburgh, N.Y., U.S. C6 139
Middleburg Heights, Oh., U.S. h9 142
Middlebury, Ct., U.S. C3 114
Middlebury, In., U.S. A6 121
Middlebury, Vt., U.S. C2 152
Middle Caicos, i., T./C. Is. D9 94
Middlefield, Ct., U.S. C5 114
Middlefield, Oh., U.S. A4 142
Middle Haddam, Ct., U.S. C5 114
Middle Island Creek, stm., W.V., U.S. B3 155
Middle Lake, Sask., Can. E3 105
Middle Loup, stm., Ne., U.S. C5 134
Middle Musquodoboit, N.S., Can. D6 101
Middle Nodaway, stm., Ia., U.S. C3 122
Middle Park, val., Co., U.S. A4 113
Middle Patuxent, stm., Md., U.S. B4 127
Middle Point, Oh., U.S. B1 142
Middleport, N.Y., U.S. B2 139
Middleport, Oh., U.S. C3 142
Middle Raccoon, stm., Ia., U.S. C3 122
Middle River, Md., U.S. B5 127
Middle River, Mn., U.S. B2 130
Middlesboro, Ky., U.S. D6 124
Middlesbrough, Eng., U.K. G12 8
Middlesex, Belize I15 90
Middlesex, N.J., U.S. B4 137
Middlesex, N.C., U.S. B4 140
Middlesex, Vt., U.S. C3 152
Middlesex, co., Ct., U.S. D5 114
Middlesex, co., Ma., U.S. A5 128
Middlesex, co., N.J., U.S. C4 137
Middlesex, co., Va., U.S. C6 153
Middlesex Fells Reservation, Ma., U.S. g11 128
Middle Stewiacke, N.S., Can. D6 101
Middleton, N.S., Can. E4 101
Middleton, Id., U.S. F2 119
Middleton, Ma., U.S. A5 128
Middleton, Mi., U.S. E6 129
Middleton, N.H., U.S. D4 136
Middleton, Tn., U.S. B3 149
Middleton, Wi., U.S. E4 156
Middletown, Ca., U.S. C2 112
Middletown, Ct., U.S. C5 114
Middletown, De., U.S. C3 115
Middletown, Il., U.S. C4 120
Middletown, In., U.S. D6 121
Middletown, Ia., U.S. D6 122
Middletown, Ky., U.S. g11 124
Middletown, Md., U.S. B2 127
Middletown, Mo., U.S. B6 132
Middletown, N.J., U.S. C4 137
Middletown, N.Y., U.S. D6 139
Middletown, Oh., U.S. C1 142
Middletown, Pa., U.S. F8 145
Middletown, R.I., U.S. E5 146
Middletown, Va., U.S. A4 153
Middletown Springs, Vt., U.S. E2 152
Middleville, Mi., U.S. F5 129
Midelt, Mor. D8 62
Midfield, Al., U.S. g7 108
Midgic, N.B., Can. D5 101
Mid Glamorgan, co., Wales, U.K. J10 8
Midhurst, Ont., Can. C5 103
Midi, Canal du, Fr. I9 14
Midi de Bigorre, Pic du, mtn., Fr. J7 14
Midkiff, W.V., U.S. C2 155
Midland, Ont., Can. C5 103
Midland, Ar., U.S. B1 111
Midland, In., U.S. F3 121
Midland, La., U.S. D3 125
Midland, Md., U.S. k13 127
Midland, Mi., U.S. E6 129
Midland, N.C., U.S. B2 140
Midland, Pa., U.S. E1 145
Midland, S.D., U.S. C4 148
Midland, Tx., U.S. D1 150
Midland, co., Mi., U.S. E6 129
Midland, co., Tx., U.S. D1 150
Midland Basin, Co., U.S. A2 113
Midland City, Al., U.S. D4 108
Midland Park, Ks., U.S. g12 123
Midland Park, N.J., U.S. B4 137
Midland Park, S.C., U.S. k11 147
Midlothian, Il., U.S. k9 120
Midlothian, Md., U.S. k13 127
Midlothian, Tx., U.S. C4 150
Midlothian, Va., U.S. m17 153
Midnight, Ms., U.S. B3 131
Midongy Sud, Madag. s22 67b
Miduzhen, China B6 40
Midvale, Id., U.S. E2 119
Midvale, Oh., U.S. B4 142
Midvale, Ut., U.S. C4 151
Midville, Ga., U.S. D4 117
Midway, B.C., Can. E8 99
Midway, Al., U.S. C4 108
Midway, De., U.S. F5 115
Midway, Fl., U.S. B2 116
Midway, Ky., U.S. B5 124
Midway, Pa., U.S. G7 145
Midway, Tn., U.S. C11 149
Midway, Ut., U.S. C4 151
Midway Islands, dep., Oc. E1 2
Midway Range, mts., B.C., Can. E8 99
Midwest, Wy., U.S. C6 157
Midwest City, Ok., U.S. B4 143
Midyat, Tur. C6 48
Midžor (Midžur), mtn., Eur. F6 20
Miechów, Pol. E20 10
Międzychód, Pol. C15 10
Międzyrzec Podlaski, Pol. C22 10
Międzyrzecz, Pol. C15 10
Miélan, Fr. I7 14
Mielec, Pol. E21 10
Mier, Mex. D10 90
Mier, In., U.S. C6 121
Miercurea-Ciuc, Rom. C9 20
Mieres, Spain B6 16
Mier y Noriega, Mex. F9 90
Miesbach, Ger. H11 10
Mifflin, Pa., U.S. E7 145
Mifflin, co., Pa., U.S. E6 145
Mifflinburg, Pa., U.S. E7 145
Mifflintown, Pa., U.S. E7 145
Mifflinville, Pa., U.S. D9 145
Migdal, Isr. C5 50
Miguel Alemán, Presa, res., Mex. H11 90
Miguel Auza, Mex. E8 90
Miguel de la Borda, Pan. H14 92
Miguel Hidalgo, Presa, res., Mex. D5 90
Miguelópolis, Braz. F4 79
Miguel Riglos, Arg. I7 80
Mihajlovgrad, prov., Bul. F7 20
Mihara, Japan M8 36
Mijdahah, Yemen G6 47
Mikado, Sask., Can. F4 105
Mikana, Wi., U.S. C2 156
Mikaševiči, Bela. I10 22
Mikhrot Shelomo Hamelekh (Timna') (King Solomon's Mines), hist., Isr. I3 50
Mikkeli, Fin. K20 6
Mikkelin lääni, prov., Fin. J20 6
Mikołajki, Pol. B21 10
Mikołów, Pol. E18 10
Mikonos, Grc. L9 20
Mikun', Russia E8 26
Milaca, Mn., U.S. E5 130
Milagro, Ec. I3 84
Milam, co., Tx., U.S. D4 150
Milan see Milano, Italy D4 18
Milan, Ga., U.S. D3 117
Milan, Il., U.S. B3 120
Milan, In., U.S. F7 121
Milan, Ks., U.S. E6 123
Milan, Mi., U.S. F7 129
Milan, Mn., U.S. E3 130
Milan, Mo., U.S. A4 132
Milan, N.H., U.S. A4 136
Milan, N.M., U.S. B2 138
Milan, Oh., U.S. A3 142
Milan, Tn., U.S. B3 149
Milano (Milan), Italy D4 18
Milanoa, Madag. n23 67b
Milazzo, Italy K10 18
Milbank, S.D., U.S. B9 148
Milbridge, Me., U.S. D5 126
Milburn, Ky., U.S. f9 124
Milburn, Ok., U.S. C5 143
Milden, Sask., Can. F2 105
Mildmay, Ont., Can. C3 103
Mildred, Pa., U.S. D9 145
Mildura, Austl. J5 70
Mile, China B7 40
Miles, Austl. F9 70
Miles, Ia., U.S. B7 122
Miles, Tx., U.S. D2 150
Milesburg, Pa., U.S. E6 145
Miles City, Mt., U.S. D11 133
Miles Mountain, mtn., Vt., U.S. C5 152
Milestone, Sask., Can. G3 105
Milevsko, Czech Rep. F14 10
Milford, Ct., U.S. E3 114
Milford, De., U.S. E4 115
Milford, Il., U.S. C6 120
Milford, In., U.S. B6 121
Milford, Ia., U.S. A2 122
Milford, Ks., U.S. C7 123
Milford, Me., U.S. D4 126
Milford, Ma., U.S. B4 128
Milford, Mi., U.S. F7 129
Milford, Ne., U.S. D8 134
Milford, N.H., U.S. E3 136
Milford, N.J., U.S. B2 137
Milford, Oh., U.S. C1 142
Milford, Pa., U.S. D12 145
Milford, Ut., U.S. E2 151
Milford, Va., U.S. B5 153
Milford Center, Oh., U.S. B2 142
Milford Haven, Wales, U.K. J8 8
Milford Lake, res., Ks., U.S. C6 123
Milford Station, N.S., Can. D6 101
Milh, Bahr al-, l., Iraq E7 48
Milicz, Pol. D17 10
Mililani Town, Hi., U.S. g9 118
Milk Creek, stm., Co., U.S. A3 113
Mil'kovo, Russia G23 28
Milk River, Alta., Can. E4 98
Mill, stm., Ma., U.S. h9 128
Milladore, Wi., U.S. D4 156
Millard, co., Ut., U.S. D2 151
Millau, Fr. H10 14
Millbank, Ont., Can. D4 103
Millboro, Va., U.S. C3 153
Millbrae, Ca., U.S. h8 112
Millbrook, Ont., Can. C6 103
Millbrook, Al., U.S. C3 108
Millbrook, N.Y., U.S. D7 139
Mill Brook, stm., Vt., U.S. B5 152
Millburn, N.J., U.S. B4 137
Millbury, Ma., U.S. B4 128
Millbury, Oh., U.S. e7 142
Mill City, Or., U.S. C4 144
Mill Creek, In., U.S. A4 121
Mill Creek, Ok., U.S. C5 143
Millcreek, Ut., U.S. C4 151
Mill Creek, W.V., U.S. C5 155
Mill Creek, stm., In., U.S. F4 121
Mill Creek, stm., Ks., U.S. C6 123
Mill Creek, stm., Ks., U.S. C7 123
Mill Creek, stm., N.J., U.S. D4 137
Mill Creek, stm., Oh., U.S. B2 142
Mill Creek, stm., Tn., U.S. g10 149
Mill Creek, stm., W.V., U.S. m13 155
Mill Creek, stm., W.V., U.S. C3 155
Millcreek Township, Pa., U.S. B1 145
Milldale, Ct., U.S. C4 114
Milledgeville, Ga., U.S. C3 117
Milledgeville, Il., U.S. B4 120
Milledgeville, Tn., U.S. B3 149
Mille Îles, Rivière des, stm., Que., Can. p19 104
Mille Lacs, co., Mn., U.S. E5 130
Mille Lacs Indian Reservation, Mn., U.S. D5 130
Mille Lacs Lake, l., Mn., U.S. D5 130
Millen, Ga., U.S. D5 117
Miller, Ne., U.S. D6 134
Miller, S.D., U.S. C7 148
Miller, co., Ar., U.S. D2 111
Miller, co., Ga., U.S. E2 117
Miller, co., Mo., U.S. C5 132
Miller, Mount, mtn., Ak., U.S. C11 109
Miller Creek, stm., De., U.S. F5 115
Millerovo, Russia H6 26
Miller Peak, mtn., Az., U.S. F5 110
Miller Run, stm., Vt., U.S. B4 152
Millers, stm., Ma., U.S. A3 128
Millersburg, In., U.S. A6 121
Millersburg, Ky., U.S. B5 124
Millersburg, Oh., U.S. B4 142
Millersburg, Pa., U.S. E8 145
Millers Falls, Ma., U.S. A3 128
Millers Ferry, Al., U.S. C2 108
Millers Ferry Dam, Al., U.S. C2 108
Millersport, Oh., U.S. C3 142
Millerstown, Pa., U.S. E7 145
Millersville, Pa., U.S. F9 145
Millerton, N.B., Can. C4 101
Millerton, N.Y., U.S. D7 139
Millerton, Ok., U.S. D6 143
Millertown, Newf., Can. D3 102
Millerville, Al., U.S. B4 108
Millet, Alta., Can. C4 98
Millevaches, Plateau de, plat., Fr. G9 14
Mill Grove, In., U.S. D7 121
Mill Hall, Pa., U.S. D7 145
Millheim, Pa., U.S. E7 145
Millhousen, In., U.S. F7 121
Millicent, Austl. K4 70
Milligan, Fl., U.S. u15 116
Milligan, Ne., U.S. D8 134
Milliken, Co., U.S. A6 113
Millington, Mi., U.S. E7 129
Millington, Or., U.S. D2 144
Millington, Tn., U.S. B2 149
Millinocket, Me., U.S. C4 126
Millinocket Lake, l., Me., U.S. C4 126
Millinocket Lake, l., Me., U.S. B4 126
Millis, Ma., U.S. B5 128
Millmerran, Austl. F9 70
Millport, Al., U.S. B1 108
Mill Run, Pa., U.S. G3 145
Millry, Al., U.S. D1 108
Mills, Wy., U.S. D6 157
Mills, co., Ia., U.S. C2 122
Mills, co., Tx., U.S. D3 150
Millsboro, De., U.S. F4 115
Millsboro, Pa., U.S. G1 145
Mill Shoals, Il., U.S. E5 120
Mill Spring, Mo., U.S. D7 132
Millstadt, Il., U.S. E3 120
Millstatt, Aus. I13 10
Millstone, stm., N.J., U.S. C4 137
Millstream Chichester National Park, Austl. D3 68
Milltown, In., U.S. H5 121
Milltown, Ky., U.S. C4 124
Milltown, Mt., U.S. D3 133
Milltown, N.J., U.S. C4 137
Milltown, Wi., U.S. C1 156
Milltown [-Head of Bay d'Espoir], Newf., Can. E4 102
Millvale, Pa., U.S. k14 145
Mill Valley, Ca., U.S. D2 112
Mill Village, N.S., Can. E5 101
Millville, N.B., Can. C2 101
Millville, De., U.S. F5 115
Millville, Ky., U.S. B5 124
Millville, Ma., U.S. B4 128
Millville, N.J., U.S. E2 137
Millville, Oh., U.S. n12 142
Millville, Pa., U.S. D9 145
Millville, Ut., U.S. B4 151
Millville, W.V., U.S. B7 155
Millville Lake, N.H., U.S. E4 136
Millwood, Ga., U.S. E4 117
Millwood, Va., U.S. A4 153
Millwood, Wa., U.S. g14 154
Millwood Lake, res., Ar., U.S. D1 111
Milne Bay, b., Pap. N. Gui. B10 68
Milner, Co., U.S. A3 113
Milner, Ga., U.S. C2 117
Milner Dam, Id., U.S. G5 119
Milnor, N.D., U.S. C8 141
Milo, Alta., Can. D4 98
Milo, Ia., U.S. C4 122
Milo, Me., U.S. C4 126
Milo, Or., U.S. E3 144
Mílos, Grc. M8 20
Mílos, i., Grc. M8 20
Miloslavskoje, Russia H22 22
Milparinka, Austl. G4 70
Milpitas, Ca., U.S. k9 112
Milroy, In., U.S. F7 121
Milroy, Mn., U.S. F3 130
Milroy, Pa., U.S. E6 145
Milstead, Al., U.S. C4 108
Milstead, Ga., U.S. C3 117
Miltenberg, Ger. F9 10
Milton, Ont., Can. D5 103
Milton, N.Z. G2 72
Milton, De., U.S. E4 115
Milton, Fl., U.S. u14 116
Milton, Il., U.S. D3 120
Milton, In., U.S. E7 121
Milton, Ia., U.S. D5 122
Milton, Ky., U.S. B4 124
Milton, La., U.S. D3 125
Milton, Ma., U.S. B5 128
Milton, N.H., U.S. D5 136
Milton, N.Y., U.S. D7 139
Milton, N.D., U.S. A7 141
Milton, Pa., U.S. D8 145
Milton, Vt., U.S. B2 152
Milton, Wa., U.S. f11 154
Milton, W.V., U.S. C2 155
Milton, Wi., U.S. F5 156
Milton, Lake, l., Oh., U.S. A4 142
Miltona, Mn., U.S. D3 130
Miltona, Lake, l., Mn., U.S. D3 130
Milton-Freewater, Or., U.S. B8 144
Milton Mills, N.H., U.S. C5 136
Milton Reservoir, res., Co., U.S. A6 113
Miltonvale, Ks., U.S. C6 123
Milverton, Ont., Can. D4 103
Milwaukee, Wi., U.S. E6 156
Milwaukee, co., Wi., U.S. E6 156
Milwaukee, stm., Wi., U.S. m12 156
Milwaukie, Or., U.S. B4 144
Mim, Ghana H8 64
Mimoso, Braz. C4 79
Mimoso, Braz. G14 82
Mimoso do Sul, Braz. F8 79
Mims, Fl., U.S. D6 116
Min, stm., China E7 30
Min, stm., China I7 34
Mina, Nv., U.S E3 135
Mīnāb, Iran H14 48
Mina El Limón, Nic. E8 92
Minahasa, pen., Indon. E7 38
Minamata, Japan O5 36
Minami-Daitō-jima, i., Japan F13 30
Mina Pirquitas, Arg. B5 80
Minas, Cuba D6 94
Minas, Ur. H11 80
Minas, Sierra de las, mts., Guat. B5 92
Minas Basin, b., N.S., Can. D5 101
Minas Channel, strt., N.S., Can. D5 101
Minas de Barroterán, Mex. D9 90
Minas de Corrales, Ur. F11 80
Minas de Matahambre, Cuba C3 94
Minas de Oro, Hond. C7 92
Minas Gerais, state, Braz. E6 79
Minas Novas, Braz. D7 79
Minatare, Ne., U.S. C2 134
Minatitlán, Mex. I12 90
Minbu, Mya. D3 40
Minburn, Alta., Can. C5 98
Minburn, Ia., U.S. C3 122
Minco, Ok., U.S. B4 143
Mindanao, i., Phil. D8 38
Mindelo, C.V. k16 64a
Mindemoya, Ont., Can. B2 103
Minden, Ont., Can. C6 103
Minden, Ger. C8 10
Minden, Ia., U.S. C2 122
Minden, La., U.S. B2 125
Minden, Ne., U.S. D7 134
Minden, Nv., U.S. E2 135
Minden, W.V., U.S. D3 155
Mindenmines, Mo., U.S. D3 132
Mindon, Mya. E3 40
Mindoro, i., Phil. C7 38
Mindoro Strait, strt., Phil. C7 38
Mine Centre, Ont., Can. E5 100
Minechoag Mountain, hill, Ma., U.S. B3 128
Mine Hill, N.J., U.S. B3 137
Mineiros, Braz. D2 79
Mineola, N.Y., U.S. E7 139
Mineola, Tx., U.S. C5 150
Miner, Mo., U.S. E8 132
Miner, co., S.D., U.S. D8 148
Mineral, Il., U.S. B4 120
Mineral, Va., U.S. B5 153
Mineral, Wa., U.S. C3 154
Mineral, co., Co., U.S. D4 113
Mineral, co., Mt., U.S. C1 133
Mineral, co., Nv., U.S. E3 135
Mineral, co., W.V., U.S. B6 155
Mineral City, Oh., U.S. B4 142
Mineral de Cucharas, Mex. F7 90
Mineral Mountains, mts., Ut., U.S. E3 151
Mineral'nyje Vody, Russia I6 26
Mineral Point, Mo., U.S. D7 132
Mineral Point, Wi., U.S. F3 156
Mineral Springs, Ar., U.S. D2 111
Mineral Wells, Ms., U.S. A4 131
Mineral Wells, Tx., U.S. C3 150
Minersville, Pa., U.S. E9 145
Minersville, Ut., U.S. E3 151
Minerva, Oh., U.S. B4 142
Minervino Murge, Italy H11 18
Minetto, N.Y., U.S. B4 139
Mineville, N.Y., U.S. A7 139
Minfeng, China D3 30
Mingäçevir, Azer. I7 26
Mingela, Austl. B7 70
Minggang, China C3 34
Mingo, Ia., U.S. C4 122
Mingo, co., W.V., U.S. D2 155
Mingo Junction, Oh., U.S. B5 142
Minhang, China D10 34
Minhla, Mya. F3 40
Minho, hist. reg., Port. D3 16
Minho (Miño), stm., Eur. D3 16
Minhou, China I8 34
Minicoy Island, i., India H2 46
Minidoka, co., Id., U.S. G5 119
Minidoka Dam, Id., U.S. G5 119
Minier, Il., U.S. C4 120
Minīn, Syria A6 50
Miniota, Man., Can. D1 100
Minipi Lake, l., Newf., Can. h9 102
Minisink Island, i., N.J., U.S. A3 137
Minitonas, Man., Can. C1 100
Minjar, Russia F9 26
Min'kovo, Russia B26 22
Minlaton, Austl. J2 70
Minle, China D7 30
Minna, Nig. G13 64
Minneapolis, Ks., U.S. C6 123
Minneapolis, Mn., U.S. F5 130
Minnedosa, Man., Can. D2 100
Minnedosa, stm., Man., Can. D1 100
Minnehaha, co. S.D., U.S. D9 148
Minneola, Ks., U.S. E3 123
Minneota, Mn., U.S. F3 130
Minnesota, state, U.S. E4 130
Minnesota, stm., Mn., U.S. F2 130
Minnesota Lake, Mn., U.S. G5 130
Minnetonka, Mn., U.S. n12 130
Minnetonka, Lake, l., Mn., U.S. n11 130
Minnewaska, Lake, l., Mn., U.S. E3 130
Minnewaukan, N.D., U.S. A6 141
Miño (Minho), stm., Eur. D3 16
Minocqua, Wi., U.S. C4 156
Minonk, Il., U.S. C4 120
Minooka, Il., U.S. B5 120
Minor Hill, Tn., U.S. B4 149
Minot, Ma., U.S. h12 128
Minot, N.D., U.S. A4 141
Minot Air Force Base, mil., N.D., U.S. A4 141
Minquadale, De., U.S. i7 115
Minsk, Bela. H10 22
Mińsk Mazowiecki, Pol. C21 10
Minster, Oh., U.S. B1 142
Mintaka Pass, Asia B6 44
Minter City, Ms., U.S. B3 131
Mint Hill, N.C., U.S. B2 140
Minto, Man., Can. E1 100
Minto, N.B., Can. C3 101
Minto, Ak., U.S. C10 109
Minto, N.D., U.S. A8 141
Minto, Mount, mtn., Ant. C8 73
Minto Inlet, b., N.W. Ter., Can. B9 96
Minton, Sask., Can. H3 105
Minturn, Ar., U.S. B4 111
Minturn, Co., U.S. B4 113
Minturno, Italy H8 18
Minusinsk, Russia G10 28
Minute Man National Historical Park, Ma., U.S. g10 128
Minxian, China E7 30
Minya see Al-Minyā, Egypt C6 60
Minya Konka see Gongga Shan, mtn., China F7 30
Mio, Mi., U.S. D6 129
Miory, Bela. F10 22
Mir, Bela. H9 22
Mira, Port. E3 16
Mira, stm., Col. G3 84
Mirabel, Que., Can. D3 104
Miracema do Tocantins, Braz. E9 76
Mirador, Braz. E10 76
Miradouro, Braz. F7 79
Miraflores, Arg. E6 80
Miraflores, Col. G6 84
Miraflores, Col. E6 84
Miraflores, Esclusas de, Pan. I15 92
Mira Gut, N.S., Can. C10 101
Mīrah, Wādī al-, val., Asia B11 60
Miraj, India D3 46
Miramar, Arg. J10 80
Miramar, Arg. F7 80
Miramar, C.R. G10 92
Miramar, Fl., U.S. s13 116
Miramar Naval Air Station, mil., Ca., U.S. F5 112
Miramas, Fr. I12 14
Miramichi Bay, b., N.B., Can. B5 101
Miranda, Braz. I13 82
Miranda, Col. F4 84
Miranda, state, Ven. B9 84
Miranda, stm., Braz. H13 82
Miranda de Ebro, Spain C9 16
Miranda do Douro, Port. D5 16
Mirande, Fr. I7 14
Mirandela, Port. D4 16
Mirandola, Italy E6 18
Mirante do Paranapanema, Braz. G3 79
Mirapuxi, stm., Braz. B3 79
Mira Taglio, Italy D7 18
Miravalles, Volcán, vol., C.R. G9 92
Mirbāṭ, Oman F9 47
Mirebeau-sur-Bèze, Fr. E12 14
Mirecourt, Fr. D13 14
Miri, Malay. E5 38
Miriam Vale, Austl. E9 70
Mirim, Lagoa, b., S.A. H9 74
Mirim, Lagoa (Laguna Merín), b., S.A. G12 80
Miriñay, stm., Arg. E10 80
Miritiparaná, stm., Col. H7 84
Mīrjāveh, Iran G16 48
Mirnyj, Russia E14 28
Mirnyy, sci., Ant. B6 73
Mirow, Ger. B12 10
Mīrpur, Pak. D5 44
Mīrpur Khās, Pak. H3 44
Mirria, Niger E14 64
Mirror, Alta., Can. C4 98
Mirror Lake, N.H., U.S. C4 136
Mirror Lake, l., N.H., U.S. C4 136
Mirzāpur, India H10 44
Misāḥah, Bi'r, well, Egypt F4 60
Misantla, Mex. H11 90
Miscoe Hill, hill, Ma., U.S. h9 128
Miscou Centre, N.B., Can. B5 101
Miscouche, P.E.I., Can. C6 101
Miscou Island, i., N.B., Can. B5 101
Miscou Point, c., N.B., Can. A5 101
Misenheimer, N.C., U.S. B2 140
Mishagua, stm., Peru D5 82
Mishan, China B13 30
Mishawaka, In., U.S. A5 121
Mishbiḥ, Jabal, mtn., Egypt J3 48
Misheguk Mountain, mtn., Ak., U.S. B7 109
Mishicot, Wi., U.S. D6 156
Misikan, China C13 44
Misilmeri, Italy K8 18
Misiones, prov., Arg. D11 80
Misiones, dept., Para. D10 80
Misión San Francisco de Laishí, Arg. D9 80
Misión San Vicente, Mex. B1 90
Miskī, Sud. J3 60
Miskito Channel, strt., Nic. C11 92
Miskitos, Cayos, is., Nic. C12 92
Miskitos Reef, rf., Nic. C12 92
Miskolc, Hung. G20 10
Mislata, Spain A10 62
Misool, Pulau, i., Indon. F9 38
Mispillion, stm., De., U.S. E4 115
Misrātah, Libya B4 56
Missaukee, co., Mi., U.S. D5 129
Missaukee, Lake, l., Mi., U.S. D5 129
Mission, Ks., U.S. m16 123
Mission, S.D., U.S. D5 148
Mission, Tx., U.S. F3 150
Mission Hill, S.D., U.S. E8 148
Mission Mountain, mtn., Ok., U.S. A7 145
Mission Range, mts., Mt., U.S. C3 133
Mission Viejo, Ca., U.S. n13 112
Missisquoi, stm., Vt., U.S. B3 152
Missisquoi Bay, b., Vt., U.S. A2 152
Mississauga, Ont., Can. D5 103
Mississinewa, stm., U.S. D7 121
Mississinewa Lake, res., In., U.S. C6 121
Mississippi, co., Ar., U.S. B5 111
Mississippi, co., Mo., U.S. E8 132
Mississippi, state, U.S. C4 131
Mississippi, stm., U.S. E8 106
Mississippi Delta, La., U.S. E6 125
Mississippi Lake, l., Ont., Can. B8 103
Mississippi Sound, strt., U.S. E5 131
Mississippi State, Ms., U.S. B5 131
Missoula, Mt., U.S. D2 133
Missoula, co., Mt., U.S. D2 133
Missouri, state, U.S. C5 132
Missouri, stm., U.S. C7 106
Missouri Buttes, mtn., Wy., U.S. B8 157
Missouri City, Mo., U.S. h11 132
Missouri City, Tx., U.S. r14 150
Missouri Valley, Ia., U.S. C2 122
Mistaken Point, c., Newf., Can. E5 102
Mistassini, Que., Can. h12 104
Mistassini, Lac, l., Que., Can. h12 104
Mistastin Lake, l., Newf., Can. g9 102
Mistatim, Sask., Can. E4 105
Mistelbach, Aus. G16 10
Misterbianco, Italy L10 18
Misterei, Sud. K2 60
Misti, Volcán, vol., Peru G6 82
Mistretta, Italy L9 18
Mita, Punta, c., Mex. G7 90
Mitchell, Austl. F7 70
Mitchell, Ont., Can. D3 103
Mitchell, Ga., U.S. C4 117
Mitchell, Il., U.S. E3 120
Mitchell, In., U.S. G5 121
Mitchell, Ne., U.S. C2 134
Mitchell, S.D., U.S. D7 148
Mitchell, co., Ga., U.S. E2 117
Mitchell, co., Ia., U.S. A5 122
Mitchell, co., Ks., U.S. C5 123
Mitchell, co., N.C., U.S. e10 140
Mitchell, co., Tx., U.S. C2 150
Mitchell, stm., Austl. K7 70
Mitchell, Lake, l., Mi., U.S. D5 129
Mitchell, Lake, res., Al., U.S. C3 108
Mitchell, Mount, mtn., N.C., U.S. f10 140
Mitchell Island, i., La., U.S. E6 125
Mitchellsburg, Ky., U.S. C5 124
Mitchellville, Ar., U.S. D4 111
Mitchellville, Ia., U.S. C4 122
Mitchellville, Tn., U.S. A5 149
Mitilíni, Grc. J10 20
Mitkof Island, i., Ak., U.S. m23 109
Mitla, hist., Mex. I11 90
Mito, Japan k15 36
Mitsamiouli, Com. k15 67a
Mitsinjo, Madag. p21 67b
Mitsio, Nosy, i., Madag. n23 67b
Mitsiwa (Massawa), Erit. J10 60
Mittellandkanal, Ger. C9 10
Mittenwald, Ger. H11 10
Mittersill, Aus. H12 10
Mitú, Col. G7 84
Mitumba, Monts, mts., Zaire B5 58
Mitwaba, Zaire C5 58
Mitzic, Gabon A2 58
Miura, Japan L14 36
Mixco Viejo, hist., Guat. C4 92
Miyake-jima, i., Japan M14 36
Miyako, Japan H16 36
Miyakonojō, Japan P6 36
Miyazaki, Japan P6 36
Miyazu, Japan L10 36
Miyun, China C4 32
Mizan Teferi, Eth. N8 60
Mizdah, Libya B3 56
Mize, Ms., U.S. D4 131
Mizen Head, c., Ire. J4 8
Mizhhir'ya, Ukr. A7 20
Mizoram, state, India I15 44
Mizpah, N.J., U.S. E3 137
Mizpah Creek, stm., Mt., U.S. E11 133
Miẕpé Ramon, Isr. G3 50
Mizque, Bol. G9 82
Mizque, stm., Bol. H9 82
Mjøsa, l., Nor. K12 6
Mladá Boleslav, Czech Rep. E14 10
Mladenovac, Yugo. E4 20
Mlanje Peak see Sapitwa, mtn., Mwi. E7 58
Mława, Pol. B20 10
Mmabatho, S. Afr. E7 66
Mmadinare, Bots. C8 66
Mo, Nor. H14 6
Mo, stm., Afr. G10 64
Moa, stm., Afr. G4 54
Moa, stm., Braz. B5 82
Moab, Ut., U.S. E6 151
Moaco, stm., Braz. C7 82
Moa Island, i., Austl. B8 68
Moama, Austl. K6 70
Moanda, Gabon B2 58
Moapa, Nv., U.S. G7 135
Moapa River Indian Reservation, Nv., U.S. G7 135
Moark, Ar., U.S. A5 111
Mobara, Japan L15 36
Mobaye, Cen. Afr. Rep. H5 56
Moberly, Mo., U.S. B5 132
Moberly Lake, B.C., Can. B7 99
Mobile, Newf., Can. E5 102
Mobile, Al., U.S. E1 108
Mobile, co., Al., U.S. E1 108
Mobile, stm., Al., U.S. E1 108
Mobile Bay, b., Al., U.S. E1 113
Mobridge, S.D., U.S. B5 148
Moca, Dom. Rep. E9 94
Mocal, stm., N.A. C6 92
Moçambique, Moz. E8 58
Mocanal, Spain p23 17b
Mocanaqua, Pa., U.S. D9 145
Moccasin, Az., U.S. A3 110
Moccasin, Mt., U.S. C7 133
Mocha see Al-Makhā', Yemen H3 47
Mocha, Isla, i., Chile J2 80
Moche, stm., Peru C2 82
Moche, hist., Peru C2 82
Mochudi, Bots. E8 66
Mocímboa da Praia, Moz. D8 58
Mocksville, N.C., U.S. B2 140
Moclips, Wa., U.S. B1 154
Môco, Serra do, mtn., Ang. D3 58
Mocoa, Col. G4 84
Mococa, Braz. F5 79
Mocoduene, Moz. D12 66

Name — Map Ref. — Page

Mocoretá, Arg. F10 80
Mocorito, Mex. E6 90
Moctezuma, Mex. C5 90
Moctezuma, stm., Mex. G10 90
Moctezuma, stm., Mex. C5 90
Mocuba, Moz. E7 58
Modale, Ia., U.S. C2 122
Modane, Fr. G13 14
Modderrivier, S. Afr. G7 66
Model Reservoir, res., Co., U.S. D6 113
Modena, Italy E5 18
Modena, N.Y., U.S. D6 139
Modesto, Ca., U.S. D3 112
Modesto, Il., U.S. D4 120
Modica, Italy M9 18
Mödling, Aus. G16 10
Modoc, In., U.S. D7 121
Modoc, co., Ca., U.S. B3 112
Moe, Austl. L7 70
Moeda, Braz. F6 79
Moema, Braz. E6 79
Moengo, Sur. B8 76
Moenkopi, Az., U.S. A4 110
Moenkopi Plateau, plat., Az., U.S. B4 110
Moenkopi Wash, val., Az., U.S. A5 110
Moffat, co., Co., U.S. A2 113
Moffat Tunnel, Co., U.S. B5 113
Moffett, Ok., U.S. B7 143
Moffett Field Naval Air Station, mil., Ca., U.S. k8 112
Moffit, N.D., U.S. C5 141
Moga, India E6 44
Mogadiscio see Muqdisho, Som. H10 56
Mogadishu see Muqdisho, Som. H10 56
Mogadore, Oh., U.S. A4 142
Mogán, Spain p25 17b
Mogapinyana, Bots. D8 66
Mogaung, Mya. B4 40
Mogil'ov, Bela. H13 22
Mogincual, Moz. E8 58
Mogliano Veneto, Italy D7 18
Mogoča, Russia G15 28
Mogogh, Sud. M6 60
Mogok, Mya. C4 40
Mogollon Mesa, mtn., Az., U.S. C4 110
Mogollon Mountains, mts., N.M., U.S. D1 138
Mogollon Rim, clf, Az., U.S. C5 110
Mogote, Co., U.S. D4 113
Mogotes, Col. D6 84
Mogotón, mtn., N.A. D8 92
Moguer, Spain H5 16
Mogzon, Russia G14 28
Mohács, Hung. J18 10
Mohall, N.D., U.S. A4 141
Mohammedia (Fedala), Mor. D7 62
Mohave, co., Az., U.S. B1 110
Mohave, Lake, res., U.S. H7 135
Mohave Mountains, mts., Az., U.S. C1 110
Mohave Valley, Az., U.S. C1 110
Mohawk, Mi., U.S. A2 129
Mohawk, N.Y., U.S. C5 139
Mohawk, stm., N.H., U.S. g7 136
Mohawk, stm., N.Y., U.S. C6 139
Mohawk Lake, l., N.J., U.S. A3 137
Mohawk Mountain, mtn., Ct., U.S. B2 114
Mohawk Mountains, mts., Az., U.S. E2 110
Mohe, China A11 30
Mohican, stm., Oh., U.S. B3 142
Mohican, Black Fork, stm., Oh., U.S. B3 142
Mohican, Clear Fork, stm., Oh., U.S. B3 142
Mohnton, Pa., U.S. F10 145
Moho, stm., Belize A6 92
Mohyliv-Podil's'kyy, Ukr. H3 26
Moinești, Rom. C10 20
Mointy, Kaz. H12 26
Moiporá, Braz. D3 79
Mõisaküla, Est. C8 22
Moisés Ville, Arg. F8 80
Moisie, Que., Can. h8 102
Moissac, Fr. H8 14
Moitaco, Ven. C10 84
Mojana, Brazo, mth., Col. C5 84
Mojave, Ca., U.S. E4 112
Mojave, stm., Ca., U.S. E5 112
Mojave Desert, des., Ca., U.S. E5 112
Mojicuaçu, stm., Braz. F5 79
Mojimirim, Braz. G5 79
Mojjero, stm., Russia D12 28
Mojo, Eth. M10 60
Mokāma, India H11 44
Mokane, Mo., U.S. C6 132
Mokapu Peninsula, pen., Hi., U.S. g10 118
Mokapu Point, c., Hi., U.S. g11 118
Mokelumne, stm., Ca., U.S. C3 112
Mokelumne Hill, Ca., U.S. C3 112
Mokena, Il., U.S. k9 120
Moknine, Tun. N5 18
Mokp'o, S. Kor. I14 32
Mokrisset, Mor. K6 16
Mokša, stm., Russia G24 22
Moku Manu, i., Hi., U.S. g11 118
Mokwa, Nig. G12 64
Mol, Bel. F7 12
Mola di Bari, Italy H12 18
Molalla, Or., U.S. B4 144
Molasses Pond, l., Me., U.S. D4 126
Moldau see Vltava, stm., Czech Rep. F14 10
Moldavia see Moldova, ctry., Eur. F13 4
Moldavia, hist. reg., Rom. B11 20
Molde, Nor. J10 6
Moldova, ctry., Eur. F13 4
Moldoveanu, Vârful, mtn., Rom. D8 20
Môle, Cap du, c., Haiti E8 94
Molena, Ga., U.S. C2 117
Molepolole, Bots. E7 66
Molėtai, Lith. F8 22
Molfetta, Italy H11 18
Molina, Chile H3 80
Molina de Segura, Spain G10 16
Moline, Il., U.S. B3 120
Moline, Ks., U.S. E7 123
Moline, Mi., U.S. F5 129
Molino, Fl., U.S. u14 116
Molinos, Arg. C5 80
Molins de Rei, Spain D14 16
Molise, prov., Italy H9 18
Mollendo, Peru G5 82
Mollepata, Peru E5 82
Mölln, Ger. B10 10
Mölndal, Swe. M13 6
Moločnoje, Russia B22 22
Molodečno, Bela. G9 22
Mologa, stm., Russia C19 22
Molokai, i., Hi., U.S. B5 118
Molokini, i., Hi., U.S. C5 118
Molong, Austl. I8 70
Molopo, stm., Afr. F5 66
Molotov see Perm', Russia F9 26
Molou, Chad K1 60
Molsheim, Fr. D14 14
Molson, stm., Man., Can. C3 100
Molson Lake, l., Man., Can. B3 100
Molteno, S. Afr. H8 66
Moluccas see Maluku, is., Indon. F8 38
Molucca Sea see Maluku, Laut, Indon. F7 38
Molus, Ky., U.S. D6 124
Moma, Moz. E7 58
Moma, stm., Russia D20 28
Momanga, Nmb. B5 66
Mombachito, Cerro, mtn., Nic. E9 92
Mombacho, Volcán, vol., Nic. F9 92
Mombasa, Kenya B7 58
Mombetsu, Japan c18 36a
Momence, Il., U.S. B6 120
Momotombo, Volcán, vol., Nic. E8 92
Mompós, Col. C5 84
Mona, Ut., U.S. D4 151
Mona, Canal de la, strt., N.A. E11 94
Mona, Isla de, i., P.R. E11 94
Mona, Punta, c., C.R. H12 92
Monaca, Pa., U.S. E1 145
Monaco, ctry., Eur. G9 4
Monadnock, Mount, mtn., N.H., U.S. E2 136
Monadnock Mountain, mtn., Vt., U.S. B5 152
Monagas, state, Ven. C11 84
Monaghan, co., Ire. G6 8
Monagrillo, Pan. D2 84
Monahans, Tx., U.S. D1 150
Monarch, Alta., Can. E4 98
Monarch, Mt., U.S. C6 133
Monarch Mills, S.C., U.S. B4 147
Monarch Pass, Co., U.S. C4 113
Monashee Mountains, mts., B.C., Can. D8 99
Monastir see Bitola, Mac. H5 20
Monastir, Tun. N5 18
Monastyrščina, Russia G14 22
Moncalieri, Italy D2 18
Monção, Braz. D9 76
Mončegorsk, Russia D4 26
Mönchengladbach, Ger. D6 10
Moncks Corner, S.C., U.S. E7 147
Monclo, W.V., U.S. D3 155
Monclova, Mex. D9 90
Moncontour, Fr. D4 14
Moncoutant, Fr. F6 14
Moncton, N.B., Can. C5 101
Moncure, N.C., U.S. B3 140
Mondaí, Braz. D12 80
Mondamin, Ia., U.S. C1 122
Monday, stm., Para. C11 80
Mondoro, Mali D9 64
Mondoubleau, Fr. E7 14
Mondovi, Wi., U.S. D2 156
Mondragone, Italy H8 18
Monee, Il., U.S. B6 120
Moneron, ostrov, i., Russia a16 36a
Monessen, Pa., U.S. F2 145
Monesterio, Spain G5 16
Monett, Mo., U.S. E4 132
Monette, Ar., U.S. B5 111
Monfalcone, Italy D8 18
Monflanquin, Fr. H7 14
Monforte, Port. F4 16
Monforte de Lemos, Spain C4 16
Monfort Heights, Oh., U.S. *o12 142
Monguaguá, Braz. H5 79
Mongalla, Sud. G7 56
Mong Cai, Viet. D9 40
Mongers Lake, l., Austl. E3 68
Monghyr, India H12 44
Mŏng Hsat, Mya. D5 40
Mŏng Mit, Mya. C4 40
Mongo, Chad F4 56
Mongo, In., U.S. A7 121
Mongo, stm., Afr. G4 64
Mongol Altajn nuruu, mts., Asia H16 26
Mongolia (Mongol Ard Uls), ctry., Asia B8 30
Mongororo, Chad K2 60
Mong Pai, Mya. E4 40
Mongu, Zam. E4 58
Mŏng Yawng, Mya. D6 40
Monhegan Island, i., Me., U.S. E3 126
Monheim, Ger. G10 10
Monida Pass, U.S. E6 119
Monino, Russia F21 22
Moniquirá, Col. E6 84
Monistrol-sur-Loire, Fr. G11 14
Moniteau, co., Mo., U.S. C5 132
Monitor, Alta., Can. D5 98
Monitor Range, mts., Nv., U.S. E5 135
Monitor Valley, val., Nv., U.S. D5 135
Monkey River, Belize A6 92
Mońki, Pol. B22 10
Monkira, Austl. E4 70
Monkton, Ont., Can. D3 103
Monkton, Vt., U.S. C2 152
Mon Louis, Al., U.S. E1 108
Monmouth, Il., U.S. C3 120
Monmouth, Me., U.S. D2 126
Monmouth, Or., U.S. C3 144
Monmouth, co., N.J., U.S. C4 137
Monmouth Beach, N.J., U.S. C5 137
Monmouth Junction, N.J., U.S. C3 137
Monmouth Mountain, mtn., B.C., Can. D6 99
Mono, co., Ca., U.S. D4 112
Mono, stm., Afr. G7 54
Mono, Caño, stm., Col. E8 84
Mono, Punta, c., Nic. F11 92
Monocacy, stm., Md., U.S. B3 127
Mono Lake, l., Ca., U.S. D4 112
Monomonac, Lake, l., U.S. E3 136
Monomoy Island, i., Ma., U.S. C7 128
Monomoy Point, c., Ma., U.S. C7 128
Monon, In., U.S. C4 121
Monona, Ia., U.S. A6 122
Monona, Wi., U.S. E4 156
Monona, co., Ia., U.S. B1 122
Monona, Lake, l., Wi., U.S. E4 156
Monongah, W.V., U.S. B4 155
Monongahela, Pa., U.S. F2 145
Monongahela, stm., U.S. G2 145
Monongalia, co., W.V., U.S. B4 155
Monopoli, Italy I12 18
Monóver, Spain G11 16
Monreale, Italy K8 18
Monroe, Ar., U.S. C4 111
Monroe, Ct., U.S. D3 114
Monroe, Ga., U.S. C3 117
Monroe, In., U.S. C8 121
Monroe, Ia., U.S. C4 122
Monroe, La., U.S. B3 125
Monroe, Mi., U.S. G7 129
Monroe, Ne., U.S. C8 134
Monroe, N.H., U.S. B2 136
Monroe, N.Y., U.S. D6 139
Monroe, N.C., U.S. C2 140
Monroe, Oh., U.S. C1 142
Monroe, Ok., U.S. C7 143
Monroe, Or., U.S. C3 144
Monroe, S.D., U.S. D8 148
Monroe, Ut., U.S. E3 151
Monroe, Va., U.S. C3 153
Monroe, Wa., U.S. B4 154
Monroe, Wi., U.S. F4 156
Monroe, co., Al., U.S. D2 108
Monroe, co., Ar., U.S. C4 111
Monroe, co., Fl., U.S. G5 116
Monroe, co., Ga., U.S. D3 117
Monroe, co., Il., U.S. E3 120
Monroe, co., In., U.S. F4 121
Monroe, co., Ia., U.S. D5 122
Monroe, co., Ky., U.S. D4 124
Monroe, co., Mi., U.S. G7 129
Monroe, co., Ms., U.S. B5 131
Monroe, co., Mo., U.S. B5 132
Monroe, co., N.Y., U.S. B3 139
Monroe, co., Oh., U.S. C4 142
Monroe, co., Pa., U.S. D11 145
Monroe, co., Tn., U.S. D9 149
Monroe, co., W.V., U.S. D4 155
Monroe, co., Wi., U.S. E3 156
Monroe Center, Ct., U.S. D3 114
Monroe Center, Il., U.S. A5 120
Monroe City, In., U.S. G3 121
Monroe City, Mo., U.S. B6 132
Monroe Lake, res., In., U.S. F5 121
Monroe Park, De., U.S. h7 115
Monroeville, Al., U.S. D2 108
Monroeville, In., U.S. C8 121
Monroeville, Oh., U.S. A3 142
Monroeville, Pa., U.S. k14 145
Monrovia, Lib. H4 64
Monrovia, Ca., U.S. m13 112
Monrovia, In., U.S. E5 121
Mons (Bergen), Bel. H4 12
Monsefú, Peru B2 82
Monselice, Italy D6 18
Monson, Me., U.S. C3 126
Monson, Ma., U.S. B3 128
Montabaur, Ger. E7 10
Montagnana, Italy D6 18
Montagu, S. Afr. I5 66
Montague, P.E.I., Can. C7 101
Montague, Ca., U.S. B2 112
Montague, Mi., U.S. E4 129
Montague, co., Tx., U.S. C4 150
Montague, Isla, i., Mex. B2 90
Montague Island, i., Ak., U.S. D10 109
Montague Peak, mtn., Ak., U.S. g18 109
Montague Strait, strt., Ak., U.S. h18 109
Montagu Island, i., S. Geor. A2 73
Montaigu, Fr. F5 14
Montalcino, Italy F6 18
Montalegre, Port. D4 16
Mont Alto, Pa., U.S. G6 145
Montana, Bul. F7 20
Montana, Switz. F7 13
Montana, state, U.S. D7 133
Montandon, Pa., U.S. E8 145
Montargis, Fr. D9 14
Montauban, Fr. H8 14
Montbard, Fr. E11 14
Montbarrey, Fr. E12 14
Montbéliard, Fr. E13 14
Mont Belvieu, Tx., U.S. E5 150
Mont Blanc, Tunnel du, Eur. G6 13
Montbrison, Fr. G11 14
Montbron, Fr. G7 14
Montcalm, co., Mi., U.S. E5 129
Montceau [-les-Mines], Fr. F11 14
Montchanin, Fr. F11 14
Montchanin, De., U.S. h7 115
Montclair, Ca., U.S. m13 112
Montclair, N.J., U.S. B4 137
Mont Clare, Pa., U.S. o19 145
Montcoal, W.V., U.S. D3 155
Mont-de-Marsan, Fr. I6 14
Montdidier, Fr. C9 14
Monte, Laguna del, l., Arg. I7 80
Monteagle, Tn., U.S. D8 149
Monteagudo, Bol. H10 82
Monte Albán, hist., Mex. I11 90
Monte Alegre, Braz. D8 76
Monte Alegre de Goiás, Braz. B5 79
Monte Alegre de Minas, Braz. E4 79
Monte Azul, Braz. C7 79
Monte Azul Paulista, Braz. F4 79
Montebello, Que., Can. D3 104
Montebello, Ca., U.S. m12 112
Monte Bello Islands, is., Austl. D3 68
Monte Buey, Arg. G7 80
Montecarlo, Arg. D11 80
Monte Caseros, Arg. F10 80
Montecassino, Abbazia di, Italy H8 18
Montecatini-Terme, Italy F5 18
Montecillos, Cordillera de, mts., Hond. C7 92
Monte Comán, Arg. H5 80
Monte Cristi, Dom. Rep. E9 94
Montecristi, Ec. H2 84
Monte Cristo, Bol. F11 82
Monte Escobedo, Mex. F8 90
Montego Bay, Jam. E6 94
Monte Grande, Chile F3 80
Montegut, La., U.S. E5 125
Montelíbano, Col. C5 84
Montélimar, Fr. H11 14
Montelindo, stm., Para. B9 80
Montellano, Spain H6 16
Montello, Nv., U.S. B7 135
Montello, Wi., U.S. E4 156
Monte Maíz, Arg. G7 80
Montemorelos, Mex. E10 90
Montemor-o-Novo, Port. G3 16
Montemor-o-Velho, Port. E3 16
Montendre, Fr. G6 14
Montenegro, Braz. E13 80
Montenegro see Crna Gora, state, Yugo. G2 20
Monte Pascoal, Parque Nacional de, Braz. D9 79
Monte Patria, Chile F3 80
Montepuez, Moz. D7 58
Montepulciano, Italy F6 18
Monte Quemado, Arg. C7 80
Montereau-Faut-Yonne, Fr. D9 14
Monterey, Ca., U.S. D3 112
Monterey, In., U.S. B4 121
Monterey, Ky., U.S. B5 124
Monterey, Tn., U.S. C8 149
Monterey, Va., U.S. B3 153
Monterey, co., Ca., U.S. D3 112
Monterey Bay, b., Ca., U.S. D2 112
Monterey Park, Ca., U.S. m12 112
Montería, Col. C5 84
Montero, Bol. G10 82
Monteros, Arg. D6 80
Monterotondo, Italy G7 18
Monterrey, Mex. E9 90
Montesano, Italy I10 18
Montesano, Wa., U.S. C2 154
Monte Sano Mountain, mtn., Al., U.S. A3 108
Monte Sant'Angelo, Italy H10 18
Montesarchio, Italy H9 18
Montes Claros, Braz. F10 74
Montes Claros, Braz. D7 79
Montevallo, Al., U.S. B3 108
Montevarchi, Italy F6 18
Montevideo, Mn., U.S. F3 130
Montevideo, Ur. H10 80
Monte Vista, Co., U.S. D4 113
Montezuma, Ga., U.S. D2 117
Montezuma, In., U.S. E3 121
Montezuma, Ia., U.S. C5 122
Montezuma, Ks., U.S. E3 123
Montezuma, N.M., U.S. B4 138
Montezuma, co., Co., U.S. D2 113
Montezuma Canyon, val., Ut., U.S. F6 151
Montezuma Castle National Monument, Az., U.S. C4 110
Montezuma Creek, Ut., U.S. F6 151
Montezuma Peak, mtn., Az., U.S. D3 110
Montfort, Fr. D5 14
Montfort, Wi., U.S. F3 156
Montgomery, Al., U.S. C3 108
Montgomery, Ga., U.S. E5 117
Montgomery, Il., U.S. B5 120
Montgomery, In., U.S. G3 121
Montgomery, La., U.S. C3 125
Montgomery, Mi., U.S. G6 129
Montgomery, Mn., U.S. F5 130
Montgomery, N.Y., U.S. D6 139
Montgomery, Oh., U.S. o13 142
Montgomery, Pa., U.S. D8 145
Montgomery, Vt., U.S. B3 152
Montgomery, W.V., U.S. C3 155
Montgomery, co., Al., U.S. C3 108
Montgomery, co., Ar., U.S. C2 111
Montgomery, co., Ga., U.S. D4 117
Montgomery, co., Il., U.S. D4 120
Montgomery, co., In., U.S. D4 121
Montgomery, co., Ia., U.S. C2 122
Montgomery, co., Ks., U.S. E8 123
Montgomery, co., Ky., U.S. B6 124
Montgomery, co., Md., U.S. B3 127
Montgomery, co., Ms., U.S. B4 131
Montgomery, co., Mo., U.S. C6 132
Montgomery, co., N.Y., U.S. C6 139
Montgomery, co., N.C., U.S. B3 140
Montgomery, co., Oh., U.S. C1 142
Montgomery, co., Pa., U.S. F11 145
Montgomery, co., Tn., U.S. A4 149
Montgomery, co., Tx., U.S. D5 150
Montgomery, co., Va., U.S. C2 153
Montgomery Center, Vt., U.S. B3 152
Montgomery City, Mo., U.S. C6 132
Montgomery Creek, Ca., U.S. B3 112
Monthermé, Fr. C11 14
Monthey, Switz. F6 13
Monthois, Fr. C11 14
Monticello, P.E.I., Can. C7 101
Monticello, Ar., U.S. D4 111
Monticello, Fl., U.S. B3 116
Monticello, Ga., U.S. C3 117
Monticello, Il., U.S. C5 120
Monticello, In., U.S. C4 121
Monticello, Ia., U.S. B6 122
Monticello, Ky., U.S. D5 124
Monticello, Me., U.S. B5 126
Monticello, Mn., U.S. E5 130
Monticello, Ms., U.S. D3 131
Monticello, N.Y., U.S. D6 139
Monticello, Ut., U.S. F6 151
Monticello, Wi., U.S. F4 156
Montichiari, Italy D5 18
Montier, Mo., U.S. D6 132
Montignac, Fr. G8 14
Montigny-le-Roi, Fr. D12 14
Montigny-sur-Aube, Fr. E11 14
Montijo, Pan. D2 84
Montijo, Port. G3 16
Montijo, Spain G5 16
Montijo, Golfo de, b., Pan. D2 84
Montilla, Spain H7 16
Montividiu, Braz. D3 79
Montivilliers, Fr. C7 14
Mont-Joli, Que., Can. A9 104
Mont-Laurier, Que., Can. C2 104
Mont-Louis, Fr. J9 14
Montluçon, Fr. F9 14
Montluel, Fr. G12 14
Montmagny, Que., Can. C7 104
Montmartre, Sask., Can. G4 105
Montmédy, Fr. C12 14
Montmirail, Fr. D10 14
Montmorenci, In., U.S. D3 121
Montmorenci, S.C., U.S. D4 147
Montmorency, co., Mi., U.S. C6 129
Montmorillon, Fr. F7 14
Monto, Austl. E9 70
Montoro, Spain G7 16
Montour, Ia., U.S. C5 122
Montour, co., Pa., U.S. D8 145
Montour Falls, N.Y., U.S. C4 139
Montoursville, Pa., U.S. D8 145
Montpelier, Id., U.S. G7 119
Montpelier, In., U.S. C7 121
Montpelier, Ia., U.S. C7 122
Montpelier, Oh., U.S. A1 142
Montpelier, Vt., U.S. C3 152
Montpellier, Que., Can. D2 104
Montpellier, Fr. I10 14
Montpon-Ménesterol, Fr. G7 14
Montréal, Que., Can. D4 104
Montreal, Wi., U.S. B3 156
Montréal, Île de, i., Que., Can. q19 104
Montreal Lake, l., Sask., Can. C3 105
Montréal-Nord, Que., Can. p19 104
Montreat, N.C., U.S. f10 140
Montreuil, Fr. B8 14
Montreux, Switz. F6 13
Montrevel [-en-Bresse], Fr. F12 14
Mont-Rolland, Que., Can. D3 104
Montrose, B.C., Can. E9 99
Montrose, Scot., U.K. E11 8
Montrose, Al., U.S. E2 108
Montrose, Ar., U.S. D4 111
Montrose, Co., U.S. C3 113
Montrose, Ga., U.S. D3 117
Montrose, Il., U.S. D5 120
Montrose, Ia., U.S. D6 122
Montrose, Mi., U.S. E7 129
Montrose, Mo., U.S. C4 132
Montrose, Pa., U.S. C10 145
Montrose, S.D., U.S. D8 148
Montrose, Va., U.S. m18 153
Montrose, co., Co., U.S. C2 113
Montross, Va., U.S. B6 153
Mont-Royal, Que., Can. p19 104
Mont-Saint-Michel see Le Mont-Saint-Michel, Fr. D5 14
Montserrat, Mo., U.S. C4 132
Montserrat, dep., N.A. F13 94
Mont-Tremblant, Parc Provincial du, Que., Can. C3 104
Montvale, N.J., U.S. A4 137
Montvale, Va., U.S. C3 153
Mont Vernon, N.H., U.S. E3 136
Montville, Ct., U.S. D7 114
Montville, N.J., U.S. B4 137
Montz, La., U.S. h11 125
Monument, Co., U.S. B6 113
Monument, N.M., U.S. E6 138
Monument Beach, Ma., U.S. C6 128
Monument Peak, mtn., Co., U.S. B3 113
Monument Peak, mtn., Id., U.S. G4 119
Monument Valley, val., Az., U.S. A5 110
Monywa, Mya. C3 40
Monza, Italy D4 18
Monzón, Peru C3 82
Monzón, Spain D12 16
Moodus, Ct., U.S. D6 114
Moodus Reservoir, res., Ct., U.S. C6 114
Moody, Me., U.S. E2 126
Moody, Tx., U.S. D4 150
Moody, co., S.D., U.S. C9 148
Moody Air Force Base, mil., Ga., U.S. F3 117
Mooirivier, S. Afr. G9 66
Mookane, Bots. E7 66
Moolawatana, Austl. G3 70
Moonie, stm., Austl. F8 70
Moon Lake, l., Ms., U.S. A3 131
Moon Run, Pa., U.S. k13 145
Moonta, Austl. J2 70
Moora, Austl. F3 68
Moorcroft, Wy., U.S. B8 157
Moore, Id., U.S. F5 119
Moore, Mt., U.S. D7 133
Moore, Ok., U.S. B4 143
Moore, co., N.C., U.S. B3 140
Moore, co., Tn., U.S. B5 149
Moore, co., Tx., U.S. B2 150
Moore, Lake, l., Austl. E3 68
Moore Dam, U.S. B3 136
Moorefield, Ont., Can. D4 103
Moorefield, Ky., U.S. B6 124
Moorefield, W.V., U.S. B6 155
Moore Haven, Fl., U.S. F5 116
Mooreland, In., U.S. E7 121
Mooreland, Ok., U.S. A2 143
Moore Mill, N.B., Can. D2 101
Moore Reservoir, res., U.S. B3 136
Mooresburg, Tn., U.S. C10 149
Moores Creek National Military Park, N.C., U.S. C4 140
Moores Hill, In., U.S. F7 121
Moorestown, N.J., U.S. D3 137
Mooresville, In., U.S. E5 121
Mooresville, N.C., U.S. B2 140
Mooreton, N.D., U.S. C9 141
Mooreville, Ms., U.S. A5 131
Moorhead, Ia., U.S. C2 122
Moorhead, Mn., U.S. D2 130
Moorhead, Ms., U.S. B3 131
Mooringsport, La., U.S. B2 125
Moorland, Ia., U.S. B3 122
Moorman, Ky., U.S. C2 124
Moornanyah Lake, l., Austl. I5 70
Moorreesburg, S. Afr. I4 66
Moosburg, Ger. G11 10
Moose, Wy., U.S. C2 157
Moose, stm., N.H., U.S. B4 136
Moose, stm., N.Y., U.S. B5 139
Moose, stm., Vt., U.S. B5 152
Moose Creek, Ont., Can. B10 103
Moosehead Lake, l., Me., U.S. C3 126
Mooseheart, Il., U.S. B5 120
Moose Hill, hill, Ma., U.S. h11 128
Moosehorn, Man., Can. D2 100
Moose Jaw, Sask., Can. G3 105
Moose Jaw, stm., Sask., Can. G3 105
Moose Lake, Man., Can. C1 100
Moose Lake, Mn., U.S. D6 130
Moose Lake, l., B.C., Can. C1 98
Moose Lake, l., Wi., U.S. B2 156
Mooseleuk Stream, stm., Me., U.S. B4 126
Mooselookmeguntic Lake, l., Me., U.S. D2 126
Moose Mountain, mtn., Sask., Can. H4 105
Moose Mountain, mtn., N.H., U.S. C2 136
Moose Mountain Creek, stm., Sask., Can. H4 105
Moose Mountain Provincial Park, Sask., Can. H4 105
Moose River, Me., U.S. C2 126
Moosic, Pa., U.S. m18 145
Moosilauke, Mount, mtn., N.H., U.S. B3 136
Moosomin, Sask., Can. G5 105
Moosonee, Ont., Can. o19 103
Moosup, Ct., U.S. C8 114
Moosup, stm., U.S. C1 146
Mopane, S. Afr. D9 66
Mopang Lake, l., Me., U.S. D5 126
Mopipi, Bots. C7 66
Mopti, Mali D7 64
Moquegua, Peru G6 82
Moquegua, dept., Peru G6 82
Mór, Hung. H18 10
Mora, Spain F8 16
Mora, Swe. K14 6
Mora, Mn., U.S. E5 130
Mora, N.M., U.S. B4 138
Mora, co., N.M., U.S. A5 138
Mora, stm., N.M., U.S. B5 138
Morādābād, India F8 44
Morada Nova de Minas, Braz. E6 79
Moradel, Montaña de, mtn., Hond. B8 92
Mora de Rubielos, Spain E11 16
Morafenobe, Madag. p21 67b
Mórahalom, Hung. I19 10
Mor'akovskij Zaton, Russia F14 26
Moraleda, Canal, strt., Chile E2 78
Morales, Guat. B6 92
Morales, Peru B3 82
Morales, Laguna, b., Mex. F11 90
Moran, Ks., U.S. E8 123
Morant Bay, Jam. F6 94
Morant Cays, is., Jam. F7 94
Morant Point, c., Jam. F6 94
Moratalla, Spain G10 16
Moratico, Va., U.S. C6 153
Moratuwa, Sri L. I5 46
Morava, hist. reg., Czech Rep. F17 10
Morava (March), stm., Eur. G16 10
Moravia, C.R. H11 92
Moravia, Ia., U.S. D5 122
Moravia, N.Y., U.S. C4 139
Moravia see Morava, hist. reg., Czech Rep. F17 10
Morawhanna, Guy. C13 84
Moraya, Bol. I9 82
Moray Firth, est., Scot., U.K. D10 8
Morazán, Guat. C4 92
Morazán, Hond. B7 92
Morbegno, Italy C4 18
Morbi, India I4 44
Morbihan, dept., Fr. E4 14
Morcenx, Fr. H6 14
Morden, Man., Can. E2 100
Morden, N.S., Can. D5 101
Mordovija, state, Russia G6 26
Mordovo, Russia I23 22
Mordves, Russia G21 22
Mordvinia see Mordovija, state, Russia G6 26
Moreau, stm., S.D., U.S. B3 148
Moreau, North Fork, stm., S.D., U.S. B2 148
Moreau, South Fork, stm., S.D., U.S. B2 148
Moreau Peak, mtn., S.D., U.S. B2 148
Moreauville, La., U.S. C4 125
Moree, Austl. G8 70
Morée, Fr. E8 14
Morehead, Ky., U.S. B6 124
Morehead City, N.C., U.S. C6 140
Morehouse, Mo., U.S. E8 132
Morehouse, co., La., U.S. B4 125
Moreland, Ar., U.S. B3 111
Moreland, Ga., U.S. C2 117
Moreland, Id., U.S. F6 119
Morelia, Mex. H9 90
Morell, P.E.I., Can. C7 101
Morelos, Mex. D6 90
Morelos, state, Mex. H10 90
Moremi Wildlife Reserve, Bots. B6 66
Morena, India G8 44
Morena, Sierra, mts., Spain G6 16
Morenci, Az., U.S. D6 110
Morenci, Mi., U.S. G6 129
Moreno, Bahía, b., Chile B3 80
Møre og Romsdal, co., Nor. J10 6
Moresby Island, i., B.C., Can. C2 99
Mores Island, i., Bah. A6 94
Moresnet, Bel. G8 12
Moreton Island, i., Austl. F10 70
Moretown, Vt., U.S. C3 152
Moreuil, Fr. C9 14
Morewood, Ont., Can. B9 103
Morey, Lake, l., Vt., U.S. D4 152
Morey Peak, mtn., Nv., U.S. E5 135
Morez, Fr. F13 14

Name	Map Ref.	Page
Morgan, Ga., U.S.	E2	117
Morgan, Mn., U.S.	F4	130
Morgan, Ut., U.S.	B4	151
Morgan, co., Al., U.S.	A3	108
Morgan, co., Co., U.S.	A7	113
Morgan, co., Ga., U.S.	C3	117
Morgan, co., Il., U.S.	D3	120
Morgan, co., In., U.S.	F5	121
Morgan, co., Ky., U.S.	C6	124
Morgan, co., Mo., U.S.	C5	132
Morgan, co., Oh., U.S.	C4	142
Morgan, co., Tn., U.S.	C9	149
Morgan, co., Ut., U.S.	B4	151
Morgan, co., W.V., U.S.	B6	155
Morgan Center, Vt., U.S.	B5	152
Morgan City, La., U.S.	E4	125
Morganfield, Ky., U.S.	C2	124
Morgan Hill, Ca., U.S.	D3	112
Morgan Island, i., S.C., U.S.	G6	147
Morganito, Ven.	E9	84
Morgan Point, c., Ct., U.S.	E4	114
Morganton, Ga., U.S.	B2	117
Morganton, N.C., U.S.	B1	140
Morgantown, In., U.S.	F5	121
Morgantown, Ky., U.S.	C3	124
Morgantown, Ms., U.S.	D2	131
Morgantown, Ms., U.S.	D4	131
Morgantown, Pa., U.S.	F10	145
Morgantown, Tn., U.S.	D8	149
Morgantown, W.V., U.S.	B5	155
Morganville, Ks., U.S.	C6	123
Morganville, N.J., U.S.	C4	137
Morganza, La., U.S.	D4	125
Morgenzon, S. Afr.	F9	66
Morghāb (Murgab), stm., Asia	B16	48
Moriah, Mount, mtn., Nv., U.S.	D7	135
Moriah, Mount, mtn., N.H., U.S.	B4	136
Moriarty, N.M., U.S.	C3	138
Moribaya, Gui.	G5	64
Morice Lake, l., B.C., Can.	B4	99
Morichal Largo, stm., Ven.	C11	84
Moriki, Nig.	E13	64
Moringen, Ger.	D9	10
Morino, Russia	D13	22
Morinville, Alta., Can.	C4	98
Morioka, Japan	H16	36
Morisset, Austl.	I9	70
Morkiny Gory, Russia	D19	22
Morkoka, stm., Russia	D14	28
Morlaix, Fr.	D3	14
Morland, Ks., U.S.	C3	123
Morley, Mi., U.S.	E5	129
Morley, Mo., U.S.	D8	132
Mormal', Bela.	I12	22
Mormon Lake, Az., U.S.	C4	110
Mormon Peak, mtn., Nv., U.S.	G7	135
Morney, Austl.	E4	70
Morningdale, Ma., U.S.	B4	128
Morningside, S.D., U.S.	C7	148
Morning Sun, Ia., U.S.	C6	122
Mornington, Austl.	L6	70
Mornington, Isla, i., Chile	F1	78
Mornington Island, i., Austl.	A3	70
Morning View, Ky., U.S.	k14	124
Moro, Ar., U.S.	C5	111
Moro, Or., U.S.	B6	144
Moro, stm., Afr.	H4	64
Morobe, Pap. N. Gui.	m16	68a
Morocco, In., U.S.	C3	121
Morocco (Al-Magreb), ctry., Afr.	B5	54
Morococala, Bol.	H8	82
Morococha, Peru	D3	82
Moro Creek, stm., Ar., U.S.	D3	111
Morogoro, Tan.	C7	58
Moro Gulf, b., Phil.	D7	38
Moroleón, Mex.	G9	90
Morombe, Madag.	r20	67b
Morón, Arg.	H9	80
Morón, Cuba	C5	94
Mörön, Mong.	B7	30
Morón, Ven.	B8	84
Morona, stm., Peru	I4	84
Morona-Santiago, prov., Ec.	I3	84
Morondava, Madag.	r21	67b
Morón de la Frontera, Spain	H6	16
Moroni, Com.	k15	67a
Moroni, Ut., U.S.	D4	151
Morotai, i., Indon.	E8	38
Morozovsk, Russia	H6	26
Morpeth, Ont., Can.	E3	103
Morrill, Ks., U.S.	C8	123
Morrill, Ne., U.S.	C2	134
Morrill, co., Ne., U.S.	C2	134
Morrilton, Ar., U.S.	B3	111
Morrin, Alta., Can.	D4	98
Morrinhos, Braz.	D4	79
Morrinsville, N.Z.	B5	72
Morris, Man., Can.	E3	100
Morris, Al., U.S.	B3	108
Morris, Ga., U.S.	E2	117
Morris, Il., U.S.	B5	120
Morris, In., U.S.	F7	121
Morris, Mn., U.S.	E3	130
Morris, Ok., U.S.	B6	143
Morris, co., Ks., U.S.	D7	123
Morris, co., N.J., U.S.	B3	137
Morris, co., Tx., U.S.	C5	150
Morris, Mount, mtn., N.Y., U.S.	A6	139
Morrisburg, Ont., Can.	C9	103
Morrisdale, Pa., U.S.	E5	145
Morris Island, i., S.C., U.S.	F8	147
Morris Jesup, Kap, c., Grnld.	A16	86
Morrison, Arg.	G7	80
Morrison, Co., U.S.	B5	113
Morrison, Il., U.S.	B4	120
Morrison, Mo., U.S.	C6	132
Morrison, Ok., U.S.	A4	143
Morrison, Tn., U.S.	D8	149
Morrison, co., Mn., U.S.	D4	130
Morrison City, Tn., U.S.	C11	149
Morrisonville, Il., U.S.	D4	120
Morrisonville, N.Y., U.S.	f11	139
Morris Plains, N.J., U.S.	B4	137
Morristown, Az., U.S.	D3	110
Morristown, In., U.S.	E6	121
Morristown, Mn., U.S.	F5	130
Morristown, N.J., U.S.	B4	137
Morristown, Tn., U.S.	C10	149
Morristown National Historical Park, N.J., U.S.	B3	137
Morrisville, Mo., U.S.	D4	132
Morrisville, N.Y., U.S.	C5	139
Morrisville, Pa., U.S.	F12	145
Morrisville, Vt., U.S.	B3	152
Morrito, Nic.	F9	92
Morro, Ec.	I2	84
Morro, Punta, c., Mex.	H14	90
Morro Bay, Ca., U.S.	E3	112
Morro del Jable, Spain	o26	17b
Morro do Chapéu, Braz.	F10	76
Morropón, Peru	A1	82
Morrosquillo, Golfo de, b., Col.	C5	84
Morrow, Ga., U.S.	C2	117
Morrow, La., U.S.	D3	125
Morrow, Oh., U.S.	C1	142
Morrow, co., Oh., U.S.	B3	142
Morrow, co., Or., U.S.	B7	144
Morrowville, Ks., U.S.	C6	123
Morrumbene, Moz.	D12	66
Moršansk, Russia	H24	22
Morse, Sask., Can.	G2	105
Morse, La., U.S.	D3	125
Morse Bluff, Ne., U.S.	C9	134
Morse Mill, Mo., U.S.	g12	132
Morse Reservoir, res., In., U.S.	D5	121
Morses Creek, stm., N.J., U.S.	k8	137
Mortagne, Fr.	D7	14
Mortagne-sur-Sèvre, Fr.	E6	14
Mortain, Fr.	D6	14
Mortara, Italy	D3	18
Morteau, Fr.	E13	14
Morteros, Arg.	F7	80
Mortes, Rio das, stm., Braz.	B3	79
Mortesoro, Sud.	L8	60
Mortlach, Sask., Can.	G2	105
Mortlake, Austl.	L5	70
Morton, Il., U.S.	C4	120
Morton, Mn., U.S.	F4	130
Morton, Ms., U.S.	C4	131
Morton, Tx., U.S.	C1	150
Morton, Wa., U.S.	C3	154
Morton, co., Ks., U.S.	E2	123
Morton, co., N.D., U.S.	C4	141
Morton Grove, Il., U.S.	h9	120
Morton Pass, Wy., U.S.	E7	157
Mortons Gap, Ky., U.S.	C2	124
Moruya, Austl.	J9	70
Morven, Austl.	F7	70
Morven, Ga., U.S.	F3	117
Morven, N.C., U.S.	C2	140
Morwell, Austl.	L7	70
Morženga, Russia	B23	22
Mosal'sk, Russia	G17	22
Mosby, Mo., U.S.	h11	132
Moščnyj, ostrov, i., Russia	A10	22
Moscow see Moskva, Russia	F20	22
Moscow, Ar., U.S.	C4	111
Moscow, Id., U.S.	C2	119
Moscow, Ia., U.S.	C6	122
Moscow, Ks., U.S.	E2	123
Moscow, Pa., U.S.	m18	145
Moscow, Tn., U.S.	B2	149
Moscow, Vt., U.S.	C3	152
Moscow Mills, Mo., U.S.	C7	132
Mosel (Moselle), stm., Eur.	C13	14
Moselle, Ms., U.S.	D4	131
Moselle, dept., Fr.	D13	14
Moselle (Mosel), stm., Eur.	D13	14
Mosers River, N.S., Can.	E7	101
Moses Coulee, val., Wa., U.S.	B6	154
Moses Lake, Wa., U.S.	B6	154
Moses Lake, l., Wa., U.S.	B6	154
Mosetse, Bots.	C8	66
Moshanpu, China	F1	34
Moshaweng, stm., S. Afr.	F6	66
Mosheim, Tn., U.S.	C11	149
Mosherville, N.S., Can.	D6	101
Moshi, Tan.	B7	58
Mosina, Pol.	C16	10
Mosinee, Wi., U.S.	D4	156
Mosjøen, Nor.	I13	6
Moskva (Moscow), Russia	F20	22
Moskva, stm., Russia	F21	22
Moskvy, kanal imeni, Russia	E20	22
Mošok, Russia	F24	22
Mosolovo, Russia	G23	22
Mosomane, Bots.	E8	66
Mosonmagyaróvár, Hung.	H17	10
Mosopa, Bots.	E7	66
Mosquera, Col.	F3	84
Mosquero, N.M., U.S.	B6	138
Mosquito, Punta, c., Pan.	C4	84
Mosquito, Riacho, stm., Para.	B9	80
Mosquito Creek, stm., Ia., U.S.	C2	122
Mosquito Creek Lake, res., Oh., U.S.	A5	142
Mosquito Lagoon, b., Fl., U.S.	D6	116
Mosquitos, Costa de, hist. reg., Nic.	D11	92
Mosquitos, Golfo de los, b., Pan.	H13	92
Moss, Nor.	L12	6
Moss, Ms., U.S.	D4	131
Moss, Tn., U.S.	C8	149
Mossaka, Congo	B3	58
Mossâmedes, Braz.	D3	79
Mossbank, Sask., Can.	H3	105
Moss Bluff, La., U.S.	D2	125
Mosselbaai, S. Afr.	J6	66
Mossendjo, Congo	B2	58
Mossleigh, Alta., Can.	D4	98
Moss Mountain, mtn., Ar., U.S.	C3	111
Mossoró, Braz.	E11	76
Moss Point, Ms., U.S.	E5	131
Moss Vale, Austl.	J9	70
Mossyrock, Wa., U.S.	C3	154
Most, Czech Rep.	E13	10
Mosta, Russia	E25	22
Mostar, Bos.	F12	18
Mostardas, Braz.	F13	80
Mostok, Bela.	H13	22
Mosty, Bela.	H7	22
Mostys'ka, Ukr.	F23	10
Mosul see Al-Mawṣil, Iraq	C7	48
Moswansicut Pond, l., R.I., U.S.	C3	146
Mota, Eth.	L9	60
Motagua, stm., N.A.	B6	92
Motala, Swe.	L14	6
Motatán, Ven.	C7	84
Motherwell, Scot., U.K.	F9	8
Motihāri, India	G11	44
Motley, Mn., U.S.	D4	130
Motley, co., Tx., U.S.	B2	150
Motloutse, Bots.	C8	66
Motozintla de Mendoza, Mex.	J13	90
Motril, Spain	I8	16
Motru, Rom.	E7	20
Mott, N.D., U.S.	C3	141
Mottola, Italy	I12	18
Motueka, N.Z.	D4	72
Motul [de Felipe Carrillo Puerto], Mex.	G15	90
Motupe, Peru	B2	82
Mouaskar, Alg.	C11	62
Mouchoir Passage, strt., N.A.	D9	94
Moudjéria, Maur.	C3	64
Moudon, Switz.	E6	13
Mouila, Gabon	B2	58
Mouit, Maur.	C3	64
Mouka, Cen. Afr. Rep.	N1	60
Moulamein, Austl.	J6	70
Moulay-Idriss, Mor.	C8	62
Moulins, Fr.	F10	14
Moulins-la-Marche, Fr.	D7	14
Moulmein see Mawlamyine, Mya.	F4	40
Moulmeingyun, Mya.	F3	40
Moulouya, Oued, stm., Mor.	C9	62
Moulton, Al., U.S.	A2	108
Moulton, Ia., U.S.	D5	122
Moultonboro, N.H., U.S.	C4	136
Moultrie, Ga., U.S.	E3	117
Moultrie, co., Il., U.S.	D5	120
Moultrie, Lake, res., S.C., U.S.	E7	147
Mound, Mn., U.S.	n11	130
Mound Bayou, Ms., U.S.	B3	131
Mound City, Il., U.S.	F4	120
Mound City, Ks., U.S.	D9	123
Mound City, Mo., U.S.	A2	132
Mound City, S.D., U.S.	B5	148
Mound City Group National Monument, Oh., U.S.	C2	142
Moundou, Chad	G4	56
Moundridge, Ks., U.S.	D6	123
Mounds, Il., U.S.	F4	120
Mounds, Ok., U.S.	B5	143
Mounds View, Mn., U.S.	m12	130
Moundsville, W.V., U.S.	B4	155
Mound Valley, Ks., U.S.	E8	123
Moundville, Al., U.S.	C2	108
Mounlapamôk, Laos	G8	40
Mountain, N.D., U.S.	A8	141
Mountainair, N.M., U.S.	C3	138
Mountainaire, Az., U.S.	B4	110
Mountainboro, Al., U.S.	A3	108
Mountain Brook, Al., U.S.	g7	108
Mountainburg, Ar., U.S.	B1	111
Mountain City, Ga., U.S.	B3	117
Mountain City, Nv., U.S.	B6	135
Mountain City, Tn., U.S.	C12	149
Mountain Fork, stm., U.S.	C7	143
Mountain Grove, Ont., Can.	C8	103
Mountain Grove, Mo., U.S.	D5	132
Mountain Home, Ar., U.S.	A3	111
Mountain Home, Id., U.S.	F3	119
Mountainhome, Pa., U.S.	D11	145
Mountain Home Air Force Base, mil., Id., U.S.	F3	119
Mountain Iron, Mn., U.S.	C6	130
Mountain Lake, Mn., U.S.	G4	130
Mountain Lake Park, Md., U.S.	m12	127
Mountain Nile (Baḥr al-Jabal), stm., Sud.	M6	60
Mountain Park, Ok., U.S.	C3	143
Mountain Pine, Ar., U.S.	C2	111
Mountainside, N.J., U.S.	B4	137
Mountain Valley, Ar., U.S.	C2	111
Mountain View, Alta., Can.	E4	98
Mountain View, Ar., U.S.	B3	111
Mountain View, Ca., U.S.	k8	112
Mountainview, Hi., U.S.	D6	118
Mountain View, Mo., U.S.	D6	132
Mountain View, N.M., U.S.	C3	138
Mountain View, Ok., U.S.	B3	143
Mountain View, Wy., U.S.	E2	157
Mountain View, Wy., U.S.	D6	157
Mountain Village, Ak., U.S.	C7	109
Mount Airy, Ga., U.S.	B3	117
Mount Airy, Md., U.S.	B3	127
Mount Airy, N.C., U.S.	A2	140
Mount Albert, Ont., Can.	C5	103
Mount Alida, S. Afr.	G10	66
Mount Angel, Or., U.S.	B4	144
Mount Arlington, N.J., U.S.	B3	137
Mount Auburn, Il., U.S.	D4	120
Mount Ayr, In., U.S.	C3	121
Mount Ayr, Ia., U.S.	D3	122
Mount Barker, Austl.	F3	68
Mount Barker, Austl.	J3	70
Mount Berry, Ga., U.S.	B1	117
Mount Calvary, Wi., U.S.	E5	156
Mount Carmel, Al., U.S.	C3	108
Mount Carmel, Il., U.S.	E6	120
Mount Carmel, Oh., U.S.	o13	142
Mount Carmel, Pa., U.S.	E9	145
Mount Carmel [-Mitchell's Brook-Saint Catherine's], Newf., Can.	E5	102
Mount Carroll, Il., U.S.	A4	120
Mount Clare, W.V., U.S.	B4	155
Mount Clemens, Mi., U.S.	F8	129
Mount Crawford, Va., U.S.	B4	153
Mount Desert Island, i., Me., U.S.	D4	126
Mount Dora, Fl., U.S.	D5	116
Mount Eden, Ky., U.S.	B4	124
Mount Elgin, Ont., Can.	E4	103
Mount Enterprise, Tx., U.S.	D5	150
Mount Forest, Ont., Can.	D4	103
Mount Freedom, N.J., U.S.	B3	137
Mount Gambier, Austl.	K4	70
Mount Garnet, Austl.	A6	70
Mount Gay, W.V., U.S.	D2	155
Mount Gilead, N.C., U.S.	B3	140
Mount Gilead, Oh., U.S.	B3	142
Mount Hagen, Pap. N. Gui.	G11	38
Mount Healthy, Oh., U.S.	o12	142
Mount Holly, Ar., U.S.	D3	111
Mount Holly, N.J., U.S.	D3	137
Mount Holly, N.C., U.S.	B1	140
Mount Holly, Vt., U.S.	E3	152
Mount Holly Springs, Pa., U.S.	F7	145
Mount Hope, Austl.	J1	70
Mount Hope, Al., U.S.	A2	108
Mount Hope, Ks., U.S.	E6	123
Mount Hope, W.V., U.S.	D3	155
Mount Hope, stm., Ct., U.S.	B7	114
Mount Hope Bay, b., U.S.	D6	146
Mount Horeb, Wi., U.S.	E4	156
Mount Ida, Ar., U.S.	C2	111
Mount Isa, Austl.	C3	70
Mount Jackson, Va., U.S.	B4	153
Mount Jewett, Pa., U.S.	C4	145
Mount Joy, Ia., U.S.	h10	122
Mount Joy, Pa., U.S.	F9	145
Mount Juliet, Tn., U.S.	A5	149
Mount Kisco, N.Y., U.S.	D7	139
Mount Lebanon, Pa., U.S.	F1	145
Mount Lemmon, Az., U.S.	E5	110
Mount Lookout, W.V., U.S.	C4	155
Mount Magnet, Austl.	E3	68
Mount Manara, Austl.	I5	70
Mount Meigs, Al., U.S.	C3	108
Mount Morgan, Austl.	D9	70
Mount Morris, Il., U.S.	A4	120
Mount Morris, Mi., U.S.	E7	129
Mount Morris, N.Y., U.S.	C3	139
Mount Morris, Pa., U.S.	G1	145
Mount Mulligan, Austl.	A6	70
Mount Olive, Al., U.S.	B3	108
Mount Olive, Il., U.S.	D4	120
Mount Olive, Ms., U.S.	D4	131
Mount Olive, N.C., U.S.	B4	140
Mount Olive, Tn., U.S.	n14	149
Mount Olivet, Ky., U.S.	B5	124
Mount Orab, Oh., U.S.	C2	142
Mount Pearl, Newf., Can.	E5	102
Mount Penn, Pa., U.S.	F10	145
Mount Perry, Austl.	E9	70
Mount Pleasant, Ar., U.S.	B4	111
Mount Pleasant, Ia., U.S.	D6	122
Mount Pleasant, Mi., U.S.	E6	129
Mount Pleasant, Ms., U.S.	A4	131
Mount Pleasant, N.C., U.S.	B2	140
Mount Pleasant, Pa., U.S.	F2	145
Mount Pleasant, S.C., U.S.	F8	147
Mount Pleasant, Tn., U.S.	B4	149
Mount Pleasant, Tx., U.S.	C5	150
Mount Pleasant, Ut., U.S.	D4	151
Mount Pocono, Pa., U.S.	D11	145
Mount Prospect, Il., U.S.	A6	120
Mount Pulaski, Il., U.S.	C4	120
Mountrail, co., N.D., U.S.	A3	141
Mount Rainier, Md., U.S.	f9	127
Mount Rainier National Park, Wa., U.S.	C4	154
Mount Revelstoke National Park, B.C., Can.	D8	99
Mount Rogers National Recreation Area, Va., U.S.	D1	153
Mount Rushmore National Memorial, hist., S.D., U.S.	D2	148
Mount Savage, Md., U.S.	k13	127
Mount Shasta, Ca., U.S.	B2	112
Mount Sidney, Va., U.S.	B4	153
Mount Sterling, Il., U.S.	D3	120
Mount Sterling, Ky., U.S.	B6	124
Mount Sterling, Oh., U.S.	C2	142
Mount Stewart, P.E.I., Can.	C7	101
Mount Stewart, S. Afr.	I7	66
Mount Storm, W.V., U.S.	B5	155
Mount Summit, In., U.S.	D7	121
Mount Sunapee, N.H., U.S.	D2	136
Mount Surprise, Austl.	B6	70
Mount Uniacke, N.S., Can.	E6	101
Mount Union, Pa., U.S.	F6	145
Mount Vernon, Al., U.S.	D1	108
Mount Vernon, Ar., U.S.	B3	111
Mount Vernon, Ga., U.S.	D4	117
Mount Vernon, Il., U.S.	E5	120
Mount Vernon, In., U.S.	I2	121
Mount Vernon, Ia., U.S.	C6	122
Mount Vernon, Ky., U.S.	C5	124
Mount Vernon, Me., U.S.	D3	126
Mount Vernon, Mo., U.S.	D4	132
Mount Vernon, N.Y., U.S.	h13	139
Mount Vernon, Oh., U.S.	B3	142
Mount Vernon, Or., U.S.	C7	144
Mount Vernon, S.D., U.S.	D7	148
Mount Vernon, Tn., U.S.	D9	149
Mount Vernon, Tx., U.S.	C5	150
Mount Vernon, Wa., U.S.	A3	154
Mount Victory, Oh., U.S.	B2	142
Mount View, R.I., U.S.	D4	146
Mountville, Ga., U.S.	C2	117
Mount Washington, Ky., U.S.	B4	124
Mount Wolf, Pa., U.S.	F8	145
Mount Zion, Ga., U.S.	C1	117
Mount Zion, Il., U.S.	D5	120
Moura, Austl.	E8	70
Moura, Braz.	H12	84
Moura, Port.	G4	16
Mourdi, Dépression du, depr., Chad	E5	56
Mourdiah, Mali	D6	64
Mourne Mountains, mts., N. Ire., U.K.	G7	8
Mousie, Ky., U.S.	C7	124
Moussoro, Chad	F4	56
Moutier, Switz.	D7	13
Moûtiers, Fr.	G13	14
Mouzon, Fr.	C12	14
Moville, Ire.	F6	8
Moville, Ia., U.S.	B1	122
Moweaqua, Il., U.S.	D4	120
Mower, co., Mn., U.S.	G6	130
Moxee City, Wa., U.S.	C5	154
Moxie Pond, l., Me., U.S.	C3	126
Moya, Com.	I16	67a
Moya, Peru	E4	82
Moyahua, Mex.	G8	90
Moyamba, S.L.	G3	64
Moyen Atlas, mts., Mor.	D8	62
Moyeuvre-Grande, Fr.	C13	14
Moyie, B.C., Can.	E10	99
Moyie Springs, Id., U.S.	A2	119
Moyobamba, Peru	B3	82
Moyock, N.C., U.S.	A6	140
Moyogalpa, Nic.	F9	92
Moyuta, Volcán, vol., Guat.	C4	92
Možajsk, Russia	F19	22
Mozambique (Moçambique), ctry., Afr.	E7	58
Mozambique Channel, strt., Afr.	E8	58
Mozarlândia, Braz.	C3	79
Mozart, Sask., Can.	F3	105
Mozdok, Russia	I6	26
Mozelle, Ky., U.S.	D6	124
Možga, Russia	F8	26
Mozyr', Bela.	G3	26
Mphoengs, Zimb.	C8	66
Mpika, Zam.	D6	58
Mpraeso, Ghana	H9	64
Mpwapwa, Tan.	C7	58
Mqanduli, S. Afr.	H9	66
Mrągowo, Pol.	B21	10
M'Ramani, Com.	I16	67a
Mrkopalj, Cro.	D9	18
M'Saken, Tun.	N5	18
M'Sila, Alg.	C13	62
Mšinskaja, Russia	B12	22
Msta, Russia	D17	22
Msta, stm., Russia	C14	22
Mstera, Russia	E24	22
Mstislavl', Bela.	G14	22
Mszczonów, Pol.	D20	10
Mtamvuna, stm., S. Afr.	H9	66
Mtwara, Tan.	D8	58
Mu, Cerro, mtn., S.A.	C6	84
Muanda, Zaire	C2	58
Muang Hôngsa, Laos	E6	40
Muang Huang, Laos	E7	40
Muang Khammouan, Laos	F8	40
Muang Khi, Laos	E6	40
Muang Không, Laos	G8	40
Muang Khôngxédôn, Laos	G8	40
Muang Long, Laos	D6	40
Muang Ngoy, Laos	D7	40
Muang Ou Nua, Laos	C6	40
Muang Ou Tai, Laos	C6	40
Muang Pak-Lay, Laos	E6	40
Muang Pakxan, Laos	E7	40
Muang Phiang, Laos	E6	40
Muang Phoun, Laos	E7	40
Muang Sing, Laos	D6	40
Muang Souy, Laos	E7	40
Muang Thadua, Laos	E6	40
Muang Vangviang, Laos	E7	40
Muang Vapi, Laos	G8	40
Muang Xaignabouri, Laos	E6	40
Muang Xay, Laos	D6	40
Muang Xépôn, Laos	F9	40
Muang Xon, Laos	D7	40
Muang You, Laos	E7	40
Muar (Bandar Maharani), Malay.	M7	40
Muarasiberut, Indon.	F2	38
Mucajaí, stm., Braz.	F12	84
Muchanovo, Russia	E21	22
Muchinga Mountains, mts., Zam.	D6	58
Muchtolovo, Russia	F26	22
Muckadilla, Austl.	F8	70
Muckalee Creek, stm., Ga., U.S.	D2	117
Mučkapskij, Russia	J25	22
Muckleshoot Indian Reservation, Wa., U.S.	f11	154
Muconda, Ang.	D4	58
Mucuchíes, Ven.	C7	84
Mucugê, Braz.	B8	79
Mucuim, stm., Braz.	B9	82
Muçum, Braz.	E13	80
Mucupia, Moz.	B13	66
Mucupina, Monte, mtn., Hond.	B8	92
Mucur, Tur.	B3	48
Mucuri, Braz.	E9	79
Mucuri, stm., Braz.	E9	79
Mucusso, Ang.	B5	66
Mud, stm., Ky., U.S.	C3	124
Mud, stm., Mn., U.S.	B3	130
Mud, stm., W.V., U.S.	C2	155
Mudan, stm., China	B12	30
Mudanjiang, China	C12	30
Mud Creek, stm., Al., U.S.	g6	108
Mud Creek, stm., Co., U.S.	D8	113
Mud Creek, stm., Ia., U.S.	e9	122
Mud Creek, stm., Ne., U.S.	C6	134
Mud Creek, stm., Ok., U.S.	C4	143
Muddy Boggy Creek, stm., Ok., U.S.	C6	143
Muddy Creek, stm., Co., U.S.	A4	113
Muddy Creek, stm., Ks., U.S.	k14	123
Muddy Creek, stm., Ut., U.S.	E4	151
Muddy Creek, stm., Wy., U.S.	C4	157
Muddy Creek, stm., Wy., U.S.	E5	157
Muddy Creek, stm., Wy., U.S.	E2	157
Muddy Creek, stm., Wy., U.S.	D6	157
Muddy Mountains, mts., Nv., U.S.	G7	135
Muddy Peak, mtn., Nv., U.S.	G7	135
Mudgee, Austl.	I8	70
Mudjuga, Russia	J26	6
Mud Lake, Id., U.S.	F6	119
Mud Lake, l., Me., U.S.	A4	126
Mud Lake, l., Nv., U.S.	F4	135
Mud Lick Creek, stm., Ky., U.S.	k13	124
Mudon, Mya.	F4	40
Mudu, China	D9	34
Muelle de los Bueyes, Nic.	E10	92
Muenster, Sask., Can.	E3	105
Muenster, Tx., U.S.	C4	150
Muerto, stm., Arg.	B7	80
Mufulira, Zam.	D5	58
Mu Gia, Deo, Asia	F8	40
Muğla, Tur.	L12	20
Mugron, Fr.	I6	14
Muḥammad, Ra's, c., Egypt	D8	60
Muḥammad Qawl, Sud.	G9	60
Mühlacker, Ger.	G8	10
Mühldorf, Ger.	G12	10
Muhlenberg, co., Ky., U.S.	C2	124
Mühlhausen, Ger.	D10	10
Mühlig-Hofmann Mountains, mts., Ant.	C3	73
Muhu, i., Est.	C6	22
Muhu väin, strt., Est.	C6	22
Muir, Mi., U.S.	E6	129
Muirkirk, Md., U.S.	B4	127
Muiron Islands, is., Austl.	D2	68
Muir Woods National Monument, Ca., U.S.	h7	112
Muisne, Ec.	G2	84
Mujang-ni, S. Kor.	H14	32
Mujezerskij, Russia	J22	6
Mujnak, Uzb.	I9	26
Muju, S. Kor.	G15	32
Mukacheve, Ukr.	H2	26
Mukah, Malay.	E5	38
Mukdahan, Thai.	F8	40
Mukden see Shenyang, China	B11	32
Mukilteo, Wa., U.S.	B3	154
Mukry, Turk.	J11	26
Muktsar, India	E6	44
Mukwonago, Wi., U.S.	F5	156
Mula, Spain	G10	16
Mulanje, Mwi.	E7	58
Mulas, Punta de, c., Cuba	D7	94
Mulatos, Mex.	C5	90
Mulberry, Ar., U.S.	B1	111
Mulberry, Fl., U.S.	E4	116
Mulberry, In., U.S.	D4	121
Mulberry, Ks., U.S.	E9	123
Mulberry, N.C., U.S.	A1	140
Mulberry, Oh., U.S.	C1	142
Mulberry, Tn., U.S.	B5	149
Mulberry, stm., Ar., U.S.	B1	111
Mulberry Fork, stm., Al., U.S.	B3	108
Mulberry Grove, Il., U.S.	E4	120
Mulberry Mountain, mtn., Ar., U.S.	B3	111
Mulchén, Chile	I2	80
Mulde, stm., Ger.	D12	10
Muldraugh, Ky., U.S.	C4	124
Muldrow, Ok., U.S.	B7	143
Mulegé, Mex.	D3	90
Mulegns, Switz.	E12	13
Muleshoe, Tx., U.S.	B1	150
Mulga, Al., U.S.	B3	108
Mulgowie, Austl.	F10	70
Mulgrave, N.S., Can.	D8	101
Mulhacén, mtn., Spain	H8	16
Mulhouse, Fr.	E14	14
Mulino, Or., U.S.	B4	144
Mull, Island of, i., Scot., U.K.	E7	8
Mullan, Id., U.S.	B3	119
Mullan Pass, Mt., U.S.	D4	133
Mullen, Ne., U.S.	B4	134
Mullengudgery, Austl.	H7	70
Mullens, W.V., U.S.	D3	155
Muller, Pegunungan, mts., Indon.	E5	38
Mullet Key, i., Fl., U.S.	p10	116
Mullett Lake, l., Mi., U.S.	C6	129
Mullewa, Austl.	E3	68
Mullica, stm., N.J., U.S.	D3	137
Mullica Hill, N.J., U.S.	D2	137
Mulligan, stm., Austl.	D3	70
Mulliken, Mi., U.S.	F6	129
Mullingar, Ire.	H6	8
Mullins, S.C., U.S.	C9	147
Mullinville, Ks., U.S.	E4	123
Mullumbimby, Austl.	G10	70
Multān, Pak.	E4	44
Multnomah, co., Or., U.S.	B4	144
Mulvane, Ks., U.S.	E6	123
Mulvihill, Man., Can.	D2	100
Mulyah Mountain, mtn., Austl.	H6	70
Mumbwa, Zam.	D5	58
Mummy Range, mts., Co., U.S.	A5	113
Mumu, Sud.	K2	60
Mumungwe, Bots.	C8	66
Mun, stm., Thai.	G8	40
Muna, Mex.	G15	90
Munā, Sau. Ar.	D1	47
Muna, stm., Russia	D15	28
Münchberg, Ger.	E11	10
München (Munich), Ger.	G11	10
München-Gladbach see Mönchengladbach, Ger.	D6	10
Münchenstein, Switz.	C8	13
Munchique, Cerro, mtn., Col.	F4	84
Munch'ŏn, N. Kor.	D15	32
Muncie, In., U.S.	D7	121
Muncy, Pa., U.S.	D8	145
Mundare, Alta., Can.	C4	98
Munday, Tx., U.S.	C3	150
Mundelein, Il., U.S.	A5	120
Münden, Ger.	D9	10
Munden, Ks., U.S.	C6	123
Mundo Novo, Braz.	A8	79
Mundubbera, Austl.	E9	70
Munene, Zimb.	C10	66
Munford, Al., U.S.	B4	108
Munford, Tn., U.S.	B2	149
Munfordville, Ky., U.S.	C4	124
Mungallala, Austl.	F7	70
Mungbere, Zaire	H6	56
Munger, India	H12	44
Mungindi, Austl.	G8	70
Munhall, Pa., U.S.	k14	145
Munhango, Ang.	D3	58
Munich see München, Ger.	G11	10
Munich, N.D., U.S.	A7	141
Munising, Mi., U.S.	B4	129
Munith, Mi., U.S.	F6	129
Muniz Freire, Braz.	F8	79
Munjor, Ks., U.S.	D4	123
Munku-Sardyk, gora, mtn., Asia	G12	28
Munsan, S. Kor.	F14	32
Münsingen, Switz.	E8	13
Munson, Alta., Can.	D4	98
Munsonville, N.H., U.S.	D2	136
Munster, Fr.	D14	14
Munster, Ger.	C10	10
Münster, Ger.	D7	10
Munster, In., U.S.	A2	121
Munster, hist. reg., Ire.	I5	8
Munsungan Lake, l., Me., U.S.	B3	126
Munuscong Lake, l., Mi., U.S.	B6	129
Muong Saiapoun, Laos	E6	40
Muonio, Fin.	H18	6
Muqayshiṭ, i., U.A.E.	B8	47
Muqdisho (Mogadishu), Som.	H10	56
Muqi, China	B12	32
Muqui, Braz.	F8	79

Name	Map Ref.	Page

Name	Map Ref.	Page
Oriximiná, Braz.	D7	76
Orizaba, Mex.	H11	90
Orizaba, Pico de (Volcán Citlaltépetl), vol., Mex.	H11	90
Orizona, Braz.	D4	79
Orkney, S. Afr.	F8	66
Orkney, prov., Scot., U.K.	B10	8
Orkney Islands, is., Scot., U.K.	B10	8
Orland, Ca., U.S.	C2	112
Orland, In., U.S.	A7	121
Orland, Me., U.S.	D4	126
Orlândia, Braz.	F5	79
Orlando, Fl., U.S.	D5	116
Orland Park, Il., U.S.	k9	120
Orléanais, hist. reg., Fr.	E8	14
Orléans, Fr.	E8	14
Orleans, Ca., U.S.	B2	112
Orleans, In., U.S.	G5	121
Orleans, Ia., U.S.	A2	122
Orleans, Ma., U.S.	C7	128
Orleans, Ne., U.S.	D6	134
Orleans, Vt., U.S.	B4	152
Orleans, co., La., U.S.	E6	125
Orleans, co., N.Y., U.S.	B2	139
Orleans, co., Vt., U.S.	B4	152
Orléans, Île d', i., Que., Can.	C6	104
Orlinda, Tn., U.S.	A5	149
Orlová, Czech Rep.	F18	10
Orman Dam, S.D., U.S.	C2	148
Ormāra, Pak.	I18	48
Ormiston, Sask., Can.	H3	105
Ormoc, Phil.	C7	38
Ormond Beach, Fl., U.S.	C5	116
Ormsby, Mn., U.S.	G4	130
Ormstown, Que., Can.	D3	104
Ornans, Fr.	E13	14
Orne, dept., Fr.	D7	14
Orne, stm., Fr.	D6	14
Örnsköldsvik, Swe.	J16	6
Oro, N. Kor.	C15	32
Orocué, Col.	E7	84
Orocuina, Hond.	D7	92
Orodara, Burkina	F7	64
Orofino, Id., U.S.	C2	119
Oro Grande, Ca., U.S.	E5	112
Oromocto, N.B., Can.	D3	101
Oromocto Lake, l., N.B., Can.	D2	101
Oron, Nig.	I14	64
Orono, Me., U.S.	D4	126
Oronoco, Mn., U.S.	F6	130
Oronogo, Mo., U.S.	D3	132
Oronoque, stm., Guy.	F14	84
Orosháza, Hung.	I20	10
Orosí, Volcán, vol., C.R.	G9	92
Oroszlány, Hung.	B13	18
Oroville, Ca., U.S.	C3	112
Oroville, Wa., U.S.	A6	154
Oroville, Lake, res., Ca., U.S.	C3	112
Orr, Mn., U.S.	B6	130
Orrick, Mo., U.S.	B3	132
Orrington, Me., U.S.	D4	126
Orroroo, Austl.	I3	70
Orrs Island, Me., U.S.	E3	126
Orrville, Ont., Can.	B5	103
Orrville, Al., U.S.	C2	108
Orrville, Oh., U.S.	B4	142
Orša, Bela.	G13	22
Orsières, Switz.	F7	13
Orsk, Russia	G9	26
Orta Nova, Italy	H10	18
Ortega, Col.	F5	84
Ortegal, Cabo, c., Spain	B4	16
Orteguaza, stm., Col.	G5	84
Orthez, Fr.	I6	14
Orthon, stm., Bol.	D8	82
Orting, Wa., U.S.	B3	154
Ortisei, Italy	C6	18
Ortiz, Mex.	C4	90
Ortiz, Co., U.S.	D4	113
Ortiz, Ven.	C9	84
Ortles (Ortler), mtn., Italy	E14	13
Ortona, Italy	G9	18
Ortonville, Mi., U.S.	F7	129
Ortonville, Mn., U.S.	E2	130
Orūmīyeh (Rezā'īyeh), Iran	C8	48
Orūmīyeh, Daryācheh-ye (Lago Urmia), l., Iran	C8	48
Oruro, Bol.	G8	82
Oruro, dept., Bol.	H8	82
Orvieto, Italy	G7	18
Orwell, Oh., U.S.	A5	142
Orwell, Vt., U.S.	D2	152
Orwigsburg, Pa., U.S.	E9	145
Orxon, stm., China	B10	30
Or Yehuda, Isr.	D3	50
Orzinuovi, Italy	D4	18
Orzola, Spain	n27	17b
Orzysz, Pol.	B21	10
Oš, Kyrg.	I12	26
Osa, Península de, pen., C.R.	I11	92
Osage, Ia., U.S.	A5	122
Osage, Mn., U.S.	D3	130
Osage, Wy., U.S.	C8	157
Osage, co., Ks., U.S.	D8	123
Osage, co., Mo., U.S.	C6	132
Osage, co., Ok., U.S.	A5	143
Osage, stm., Mo., U.S.	C3	132
Osage Beach, Mo., U.S.	C5	132
Osage City, Ks., U.S.	D8	123
Osage Creek, stm., Ar., U.S.	A2	111
Ōsaka, Japan	M10	36
Ōsaka-wan, b., Japan	M10	36
Osakis, Mn., U.S.	E3	130
Osakis, Lake, l., Mn., U.S.	E3	130
Osan, S. Kor.	F15	32
Osawatomie, Ks., U.S.	D9	123
Osborn, Mo., U.S.	B3	132
Osborne, Ks., U.S.	C5	123
Osborne, co., Ks., U.S.	C5	123
Osburn, Id., U.S.	B3	119
Osceola, Ar., U.S.	B6	111
Osceola, In., U.S.	A5	121
Osceola, Ia., U.S.	C4	122
Osceola, Mo., U.S.	C4	132
Osceola, Ne., U.S.	C8	134
Osceola, Wi., U.S.	C1	156
Osceola, co., Fl., U.S.	E5	116
Osceola, co., Ia., U.S.	A2	122
Osceola, co., Mi., U.S.	E5	129
Osceola Mills, Pa., U.S.	E5	145
Oschatz, Ger.	D13	10
Oschersleben, Ger.	C11	10
Oscoda, Mi., U.S.	D7	129
Oscoda, co., Mi., U.S.	D6	129
Oscura Mountains, mts., N.M., U.S.	D3	138
Osgood, In., U.S.	F7	121
O'Shanassy, stm., Austl.	B3	70
Oshawa, Ont., Can.	D6	103
Oshigambo, Nmb.	A3	66
Ō-shima, i., Japan	M14	36
Ō-shima, i., Japan	f14	36a
Oshkosh, Ne., U.S.	C3	134
Oshkosh, Wi., U.S.	D5	156
Oshnovīyeh, Iran	C8	48
Oshogbo, Nig.	H12	64
Oshwe, Zaire	B3	58
Osi, Nig.	G12	64
Osich'ŏn-ni, N. Kor.	B16	32
Osijek, Cro.	D2	20
Osimo, Italy	F8	18
Osinniki, Russia	G9	28
Osipoviči, Bela.	H11	22
Osire, Nmb.	C3	66
Oskaloosa, Ia., U.S.	C5	122
Oskaloosa, Ks., U.S.	C8	123
Oskarshamn, Swe.	M15	6
Oskū, Iran	C9	48
Osler, Sask., Can.	E2	105
Oslo, Nor.	L12	6
Oslo, Mn., U.S.	B1	130
Osmānābād, India	C4	46
Osmaniye, Tur.	C4	48
Osm'any, Bela.	G8	22
Osmond, Ne., U.S.	B8	134
Osmore, stm., Peru	G6	82
Osnabrock, N.D., U.S.	A7	141
Osnabrück, Ger.	C8	10
Osório Fonseca, Braz.	I13	84
Osorno, Chile	E2	78
Osoyoos, B.C., Can.	E8	99
Osoyoos Lake, l., Wa., U.S.	A6	154
Ospino, Ven.	C8	84
Osprey, Fl., U.S.	E4	116
Ossa, Mount, mtn., Austl.	M7	70
Ossabaw Island, i., Ga., U.S.	E5	117
Ossabaw Sound, strt., Ga., U.S.	E6	117
Osse, stm., Nig.	H12	64
Osseo, Mn., U.S.	m12	130
Osseo, Wi., U.S.	D2	156
Ossian, In., U.S.	C7	121
Ossian, Ia., U.S.	A6	122
Ossining, N.Y., U.S.	D7	139
Ossipee, N.H., U.S.	C4	136
Ossipee, stm., U.S.	C5	136
Ossipee Lake, l., N.H., U.S.	C4	136
Ossipee Mountains, mts., N.H., U.S.	C4	136
Ossora, Russia	F24	28
Ošta, Russia	K24	6
Ostaškov, Russia	D16	22
Osteen, Fl., U.S.	D5	116
Ostende (Oostende), Bel.	F2	12
Osterburg, Ger.	C11	10
Östergötlands Län, co., Swe.	L14	6
Osterholz-Scharmbeck, Ger.	B8	10
Osterode, Ger.	D10	10
Östersund, Swe.	J14	6
Osterville, Ma., U.S.	C7	128
Osterwieck, Ger.	D10	10
Østfold, co., Nor.	L12	6
Ostfriesische Inseln, is., Ger.	B7	10
Ostfriesland, hist. reg., Ger.	B7	10
Ost'or, Russia	G15	22
Ostrander, Mn., U.S.	G6	130
Ostrava, Czech Rep.	F18	10
Ostróda, Pol.	B19	10
Ostrogožsk, Russia	G5	26
Ostrołęka, Pol.	B21	10
Ostrošickij Gorodok, Bela.	G10	22
Ostrov, Czech Rep.	E12	10
Ostrov, Russia	D11	22
Ostrov, i., Slvk.	H17	10
Ostrovno, Bela.	F12	22
Ostrovskoje, Russia	D25	22
Ostrowiec Świętokrzyski, Pol.	E21	10
Ostrów Mazowiecka, Pol.	C21	10
Ostrów Wielkopolski, Pol.	D17	10
Ostrzeszów, Pol.	D17	10
Ostúa, stm., N.A.	C5	92
Ostuni, Italy	I12	18
Ōsumi-kaikyō, strt., Japan	Q5	36
Ōsumi-shotō, is., Japan	q5	37b
Osuna, Spain	H6	16
Osvaldo Cruz, Braz.	F3	79
Osveja, Bela.	E11	22
Oswegatchie, stm., N.Y., U.S.	f9	139
Oswego, Il., U.S.	B5	120
Oswego, Ks., U.S.	E8	123
Oswego, N.Y., U.S.	B4	139
Oswego, co., N.Y., U.S.	B4	139
Oswego, stm., N.J., U.S.	D4	137
Oswego, stm., N.Y., U.S.	B4	139
Oświęcim, Pol.	E19	10
Osyka, Ms., U.S.	D3	131
Otaci, Mol.	A11	20
Otaki, N.Z.	D5	72
Otanmäki, Fin.	I20	6
Otaru, Japan	d16	36a
Otava, Fin.	K20	6
Otava, stm., Czech Rep.	F13	10
Otavalo, Ec.	G3	84
Otavi, Nmb.	B3	66
Oteen, N.C., U.S.	f10	140
Otego, N.Y., U.S.	C5	139
Otepää, Est.	C9	22
Otero, co., Co., U.S.	D7	113
Otero, co., N.M., U.S.	E3	138
Oteros, stm., Mex.	D5	90
Othello, Wa., U.S.	C6	154
Óthiris, Óros, mts., Grc.	J6	20
Otho, Ia., U.S.	B3	122
Oti, stm., Afr.	G7	54
Otinapa, Mex.	E7	90
Otis, Co., U.S.	A8	113
Otis, In., U.S.	A4	121
Otis, Ks., U.S.	D4	123
Otisco, In., U.S.	G6	121
Otis Orchards, Wa., U.S.	g14	154
Otis Reservoir, res., Ma., U.S.	B1	128
Otisville, Mi., U.S.	E7	129
Otjimbingue, Nmb.	D3	66
Otjiwarongo, Nmb.	C3	66
Otley, Ia., U.S.	C4	122
Otočac, Cro.	E10	18
Otoe, Ne., U.S.	D9	134
Otoe, co., Ne., U.S.	D9	134
Otoque, Isla, i., Pan.	I15	92
Otoro, stm., Hond.	C6	92
Otra, stm., Nor.	L10	6
Otradnyj, Russia	G8	26
Otranto, Italy	I13	18
Otranto, Strait of, strt., Eur.	I2	20
Otsego, Mi., U.S.	F5	129
Otsego, co., Mi., U.S.	C6	129
Otsego, co., N.Y., U.S.	C5	139
Otsego Lake, l., N.Y., U.S.	C6	139
Ōtsu, Japan	L10	36
Otta, Nor.	K11	6
Ottauquechee, stm., Vt., U.S.	D4	152
Ottawa, Ont., Can.	B9	103
Ottawa, Il., U.S.	B5	120
Ottawa, Ks., U.S.	D8	123
Ottawa, Oh., U.S.	A1	142
Ottawa, W.V., U.S.	n12	155
Ottawa, co., Ks., U.S.	C6	123
Ottawa, co., Mi., U.S.	F4	129
Ottawa, co., Oh., U.S.	A2	142
Ottawa, co., Ok., U.S.	A7	143
Ottawa, stm., Can.	G17	96
Ottawa, stm., Can.	B11	106
Ottawa, stm., Oh., U.S.	e6	142
Ottawa Hills, Oh., U.S.	e6	142
Ottawa Islands, is., N.W. Ter., Can.	E16	96
Otter, stm., Alta., Can.	A2	98
Otterbein, In., U.S.	D3	121
Otter Brook, stm., N.H., U.S.	E2	136
Otter Brook Lake, res., N.H., U.S.	E2	136
Otterburne, Man., Can.	E3	100
Otter Creek, Me., U.S.	D4	126
Otter Creek, stm., Ut., U.S.	E4	151
Otter Creek, stm., Vt., U.S.	C2	152
Otter Creek Reservoir, res., Ut., U.S.	E4	151
Otter Islands, is., S.C., U.S.	m11	147
Otter Lake, Mi., U.S.	E7	129
Ottertail, Mn., U.S.	D3	130
Otter Tail, co., Mn., U.S.	D3	130
Otter Tail, stm., Mn., U.S.	D2	130
Otter Tail Lake, l., Mn., U.S.	D3	130
Otterville, Ont., Can.	E4	103
Otterville, Mo., U.S.	C4	132
Otthon, Sask., Can.	F4	105
Otto, Wy., U.S.	B4	157
Ottoville, Oh., U.S.	B1	142
Ottumwa, Ia., U.S.	C5	122
Ottweiler, Ger.	F7	10
Otu, Nig.	G11	64
Otumpa, Arg.	D7	80
Otuquis, Bañados de, sw., Bol.	H12	82
Oturkpo, Nig.	H14	64
Otway, Cape, c., Austl.	L5	70
Otwell, Ar., U.S.	B5	111
Otwell, In., U.S.	H3	121
Otwock, Pol.	C21	10
Otyniya, Ukr.	A8	20
Ötztaler Alpen, mts., Eur.	C5	18
Ou, stm., China	J2	34
Ou, stm., Laos	D7	40
Ouachita, co., Ar., U.S.	D3	111
Ouachita, co., La., U.S.	B3	125
Ouachita, Lake, res., Ar., U.S.	C2	111
Ouachita Mountains, mts., U.S.	E8	106
Ouadâne, Maur.	J5	62
Ouadda, Cen. Afr. Rep.	M2	60
Ouagadougou, Burkina	E9	64
Ouahigouya, Burkina	F6	54
Ouahigouya, Burkina	E8	64
Ouaka, stm., Cen. Afr. Rep.	G5	56
Oualâta, Maur.	C6	64
Oualé, stm., Afr.	F10	64
Oualidia, Mor.	D6	62
Ouallam, Niger	D11	64
Ouallene, Alg.	H11	62
Ouanda Djallé, Cen. Afr. Rep.	M2	60
Ouaninou, C. Iv.	G6	64
Ouan Taredert, Alg.	G15	62
Ouarâne, reg., Maur.	A4	64
Ouarkziz, Jbel, mts., Afr.	F6	62
Ouarzazate, Mor.	E7	62
Ouassoulou, stm., Afr.	F5	64
Ouatcha, Niger	E14	64
Oubangui (Ubangi), stm., Afr.	H8	52
Oud-Beijerland, Neth.	E5	12
Ouddorp, Neth.	F4	12
Oudenaarde (Audenarde), Bel.	G4	12
Oude Pekela, Neth.	B10	12
Oudtshoorn, S. Afr.	I6	66
Oudyoumoudi, Burkina	D9	64
Oued Cheham, Alg.	M2	18
Oued Meliz, Tun.	M3	18
Oued Tlelat, Alg.	J11	16
Oued Zarga, Tun.	M4	18
Oued-Zem, Mor.	D7	62
Ouémé, stm., Benin	H11	64
Ouenza, Alg.	N3	18
Ouessant, Île d' (Ushant), i., Fr.	D1	14
Ouesso, Congo	A3	58
Ouezzane, Mor.	C8	62
Ouham, stm., Afr.	G4	56
Ouidah, Benin	H11	64
Ouistreham, Fr.	C6	14
Oujda, Mor.	C10	62
Oulainen, Fin.	I19	6
Oulu, Fin.	I19	6
Oulujärvi, l., Fin.	I20	6
Oulujoki, stm., Fin.	I20	6
Oulun lääni, prov., Fin.	I20	6
Oum-Chalouba, Chad	E5	56
Oum El Bouagui, Alg.	C14	62
Oum er Rbia, Oued, stm., Mor.	D7	62
Ounara, Mor.	E6	62
Ounianga Kébir, Chad	E5	56
Ouray, Co., U.S.	C3	113
Ouray, co., Co., U.S.	C3	113
Ouray, Mount, mtn., Co., U.S.	C4	113
Ourinhos, Braz.	G4	79
Ouro, Paraná do, stm., Braz.	C6	82
Ouro Fino, Braz.	G5	79
Ouro Preto, Braz.	F7	79
Ouro Preto, stm., Braz.	D9	82
Oursi, Burkina	D9	64
Ourthe, stm., Bel.	H8	12
Ōu-sammyaku, mts., Japan	I15	36
Ouse, stm., Eng., U.K.	H12	8
Outagamie, co., Wi., U.S.	D5	156
Outardes Quatre, Réservoir, res., Que., Can.	h13	104
Outer Hebrides, is., Scot., U.K.	D6	8
Outer Island, i., Wi., U.S.	A3	156
Outer Santa Barbara Passage, strt., Ca., U.S.	F4	112
Outjo, Nmb.	C3	66
Outlook, Sask., Can.	F2	105
Outlook, Mt., U.S.	B12	133
Outlook, Wa., U.S.	C5	154
Outpost Mountain, mtn., Ak., U.S.	B9	109
Outremont, Que., Can.	p19	104
Ouvidor, Braz.	E5	79
Ouyen, Austl.	J5	70
Ouzinkie, Ak., U.S.	D9	109
Ouzouer-le-Marché, Fr.	E8	14
Ouzzal, Oued i-n-, val., Alg.	J12	62
Ovalle, Chile	F3	80
Ovamboland, hist. reg., Nmb.	A3	66
Ovana, Cerro, mtn., Ven.	E9	84
Ovando, Mt., U.S.	C3	133
Ovejas, Col.	C5	84
Overbrook, Ks., U.S.	D8	123
Overflakkee, i., Neth.	E5	12
Overgaard, Az., U.S.	C5	110
Overhalla, Nor.	I12	6
Overijssel, prov., Neth.	D9	12
Overland, Mo., U.S.	f13	132
Overland Park, Ks., U.S.	m16	123
Overlea, Md., U.S.	B4	127
Overpelt, Bel.	F7	12
Overton, Ne., U.S.	D6	134
Overton, Nv., U.S.	G7	135
Overton, Tx., U.S.	C5	150
Overton, co., Tn., U.S.	C8	149
Övertorneå, Swe.	H18	6
Ovett, Ms., U.S.	D4	131
Ovid, Co., U.S.	A8	113
Ovid, Id., U.S.	G7	119
Ovid, Mi., U.S.	E6	129
Oviedo, Spain	B6	16
Ovino, Russia	B16	22
Ovstug, Russia	H16	22
Owando, Congo	B3	58
Owaneco, Il., U.S.	D4	120
Owasco Lake, l., N.Y., U.S.	C4	139
Owasso, Ok., U.S.	A6	143
Owatonna, Mn., U.S.	F5	130
Owbeh, Afg.	D17	48
Owego, N.Y., U.S.	C4	139
Owen, Wi., U.S.	D3	156
Owen, co., In., U.S.	F4	121
Owen, co., Ky., U.S.	B5	124
Owen, Lake, l., Wi., U.S.	B2	156
Owen, Mount, mtn., Co., U.S.	C3	113
Owens, stm., Ca., U.S.	D4	112
Owensboro, Ky., U.S.	C2	124
Owensburg, In., U.S.	G4	121
Owens Creek, stm., Md., U.S.	A3	127
Owens Cross Roads, Al., U.S.	A3	108
Owens Lake, l., Ca., U.S.	D5	112
Owen Sound, Ont., Can.	C4	103
Owen Sound, b., Ont., Can.	C4	103
Owen Stanley Range, mts., Pap. N. Gui.	m16	68a
Owensville, Ar., U.S.	C3	111
Owensville, In., U.S.	H2	121
Owensville, Mo., U.S.	C6	132
Owensville, Oh., U.S.	C1	142
Owenton, Ky., U.S.	B5	124
Owerri, Nig.	I13	64
Owings, Md., U.S.	C4	127
Owings Mills, Md., U.S.	B4	127
Owingsville, Ky., U.S.	B6	124
Owl Creek, stm., Wy., U.S.	C4	157
Owl Creek Mountains, mts., Wy., U.S.	C4	157
Owls Head, Me., U.S.	D3	126
Owo, Nig.	H12	64
Owosso, Mi., U.S.	E6	129
Owsley, co., Ky., U.S.	C6	124
Owyhee, Nv., U.S.	B5	135
Owyhee, co., Id., U.S.	G2	119
Owyhee, stm., U.S.	E9	144
Owyhee, Lake, res., Or., U.S.	D9	144
Owyhee, North Fork, stm., U.S.	E9	144
Owyhee, South Fork, stm., U.S.	G2	119
Owyhee Dam, Or., U.S.	D9	144
Owyhee Mountains, mts., U.S.	G2	119
Oxapampa, Peru	D4	82
Oxbow, Sask., Can.	H4	105
Oxbow Dam, U.S.	E2	119
Oxford, N.S., Can.	D6	101
Oxford, Eng., U.K.	J12	8
Oxford, Al., U.S.	B4	108
Oxford, Ar., U.S.	A4	111
Oxford, Ct., U.S.	D3	114
Oxford, Fl., U.S.	D4	116
Oxford, Ga., U.S.	C3	117
Oxford, In., U.S.	C3	121
Oxford, Ia., U.S.	C6	122
Oxford, Ks., U.S.	E6	123
Oxford, Me., U.S.	D2	126
Oxford, Md., U.S.	C5	127
Oxford, Ma., U.S.	B4	128
Oxford, Mi., U.S.	F7	129
Oxford, Ms., U.S.	A4	131
Oxford, Ne., U.S.	D6	134
Oxford, N.J., U.S.	B3	137
Oxford, N.Y., U.S.	C5	139
Oxford, N.C., U.S.	A4	140
Oxford, Oh., U.S.	C1	142
Oxford, Pa., U.S.	G10	145
Oxford, Wi., U.S.	E4	156
Oxford, co., Me., U.S.	D2	126
Oxford Junction, N.S., Can.	D6	101
Oxford Junction, Ia., U.S.	C7	122
Oxford Lake, l., Man., Can.	B4	100
Oxford Peak, mtn., Id., U.S.	G6	119
Oxfordshire, co., Eng., U.K.	J12	8
Oxkutzcab, Mex.	G15	90
Oxley, Austl.	J6	70
Oxly, Mo., U.S.	E7	132
Oxnard, Ca., U.S.	E4	112
Oxon Hill, Md., U.S.	f9	127
Oyama, B.C., Can.	D8	99
Oyama, Japan	K14	36
Oyem, Gabon	A2	58
Oyen, Alta., Can.	D5	98
Oyo, Nig.	H11	64
Oyón, Peru	D3	82
Oyonnax, Fr.	F12	14
Oyotún, Peru	B2	82
Oyster Bay, N.Y., U.S.	E7	139
Oyster Creek, Tx., U.S.	r14	150
Oyster Keys, is., Fl., U.S.	G6	116
Ozamiz, Phil.	D7	38
Ozariči, Bela.	I12	22
Ozark, Al., U.S.	D4	108
Ozark, Ar., U.S.	B2	111
Ozark, Mo., U.S.	D4	132
Ozark, co., Mo., U.S.	E5	132
Ozark Escarpment, clf, U.S.	B4	111
Ozark Plateau, plat., U.S.	D8	106
Ozark Reservoir, res., Ar., U.S.	B1	111
Ozarks, Lake of the, res., Mo., U.S.	C5	132
Ozaukee, co., Wi., U.S.	E6	156
Ozawkie, Ks., U.S.	k15	123
Ózd, Hung.	G20	10
Ožerelje, Russia	G21	22
Ozernovskij, Russia	G23	28
Ozery, Russia	G21	22
Ozette Lake, l., Wa., U.S.	A1	154
Ozieri, Italy	I4	18
Ozimek, Pol.	E18	10
Ozona, Fl., U.S.	o10	116
Ozona, Ms., U.S.	E4	131
Ozona, Tx., U.S.	D2	150
Ozone, Ar., U.S.	B2	111
Ozorków, Pol.	D19	10
Oz'ornyj, Russia	D23	22
Oz'ory, Bela.	H7	22
Ozubulu, Nig.	I13	64
Ozuluama, Mex.	G11	90

P

Name	Map Ref.	Page
Paarl, S. Afr.	I4	66
Paauhau, Hi., U.S.	C6	118
Paauilo, Hi., U.S.	C6	118
Pabellones, Ensenada, b., Mex.	E6	90
Pabianice, Pol.	D19	10
Pablo, Mt., U.S.	C2	133
Pābna, Bngl.	H13	44
Pabradė, Lith.	G8	22
Pacaás Novas, Parque Nacional, Braz.	D10	82
Pacaás Novos, stm., Braz.	D9	82
Pacaás Novos, Serra dos, mts., Braz.	D10	82
Pacaembu, Braz.	F3	79
Pacaltsdorp, S. Afr.	J6	66
Pacarán, Peru	E3	82
Pacaraos, Peru	D3	82
Pacasmayo, Peru	B2	82
Pace, Fl., U.S.	u14	116
Pace, Ms., U.S.	B3	131
Pachacamac, hist., Peru	E3	82
Pachaug Pond, l., Ct., U.S.	C8	114
Pachino, Italy	M10	18
Pachitea, stm., Peru	C4	82
Pachiza, Peru	B3	82
Pachmarhi, India	I8	44
Pacho, Col.	E5	84
Pachuca [de Soto], Mex.	G10	90
Pachuta, Ms., U.S.	C5	131
Pacific, Mo., U.S.	C7	132
Pacific, Wa., U.S.	f11	154
Pacific, co., Wa., U.S.	C2	154
Pacifica, Ca., U.S.	h8	112
Pacific Beach, Wa., U.S.	B1	154
Pacific City, Or., U.S.	B3	144
Pacific Creek, stm., Wy., U.S.	D3	157
Pacific Grove, Ca., U.S.	D3	112
Pacific Junction, Ia., U.S.	C2	122
Pacific Ocean	J24	158
Pacific Palisades, Hi., U.S.	g10	118
Pacific Ranges, mts., B.C., Can.	D4	99
Pacific Rim National Park, B.C., Can.	E5	99
Peckard Mountain, hill, Ma., U.S.	B3	128
Pack Monadnock Mountain, mtn., N.H., U.S.	E3	136
Packwaukee, Wi., U.S.	E4	156
Packwood, Ia., U.S.	C5	122
Packwood, Wa., U.S.	C4	154
Pacllón, Peru	D3	82
Pacohuaras, stm., Bol.	D8	82
Pacolet, S.C., U.S.	B4	147
Pacolet, stm., S.C., U.S.	A4	147
Pacolet Mills, S.C., U.S.	B4	147
Pacora, Pan.	C3	84
Pacquet, Newf., Can.	D4	102
Pactola Reservoir, res., S.D., U.S.	C2	148
Pacuare, stm., C.R.	G11	92
Pacuí, stm., Braz.	D6	79
Pacuneiro, stm., Braz.	B2	79
Padamo, stm., Ven.	F10	84
Padang, Indon.	O6	40
Padang Endau, Malay.	M7	40
Padangpanjang, Indon.	O6	40
Padangsidempuan, Indon.	N5	40
Padauari, stm., Braz.	G10	84
Padcaya, Bol.	I9	82
Paddle Prairie, Alta., Can.	f7	98
Paddock Lake, Wi., U.S.	n11	156
Paddockwood, Sask., Can.	D3	105
Paddy Knob, mtn., U.S.	C5	155
Paden, Ok., U.S.	B5	143
Paden City, W.V., U.S.	B4	155
Paderborn, Ger.	D8	10
Padilla, Bol.	H9	82
Padova, Italy	D6	18
Padre Bernardo, Braz.	C4	79
Padre Island, i., Tx., U.S.	F4	150
Padre Island National Seashore, Tx., U.S.	F4	150
Padre Paraíso, Braz.	D8	79
Padroni, Co., U.S.	A7	113
Padua see Padova, Italy	D6	18
Paducah, Ky., U.S.	e9	124
Paducah, Tx., U.S.	B2	150
Paektu-san, mtn., Asia	A16	32
Páez, stm., Col.	F4	84
Pafúri, Moz.	D10	66
Pag, Cro.	E10	18
Pag, Otok, i., Cro.	E10	18
Pagadian, Phil.	D7	38
Pagai Selatan, Pulau, i., Indon.	F3	38
Pagai Utara, Pulau, i., Indon.	F3	38
Pagan, Mya.	D3	40
Pagancillo, Arg.	E4	80
Pagasitikós Kólpos, b., Grc.	J6	20
Page, Az., U.S.	A4	110
Page, Ne., U.S.	B7	134
Page, N.D., U.S.	B8	141
Page, W.V., U.S.	C3	155
Page, co., Ia., U.S.	D2	122
Page, co., Va., U.S.	B4	153
Pagėgiai, Lith.	F4	22
Pageland, S.C., U.S.	B7	147
Pagoda Peak, mtn., Co., U.S.	A3	113
Pagoda Point, c., Mya.	G3	40
Pagon, Bukit, mtn., Asia	E6	38
Pagosa Springs, Co., U.S.	D3	113
Pagouda, Togo	G10	64
Paguate, N.M., U.S.	B2	138
Pahala, Hi., U.S.	D6	118
Pahang, stm., Malay.	M7	40
Páhara, Laguna, b., Nic.	C11	92
Pahoa, Hi., U.S.	D7	118
Pahokee, Fl., U.S.	F6	116
Pahrump, Nv., U.S.	G6	135
Pahute Mesa, mtn., Nv., U.S.	F5	135
Pai, stm., Asia	E5	40
Paia, Hi., U.S.	C5	118
Paico, Peru	F5	82
Paide, Est.	C8	22
Paignton, Eng., U.K.	K10	8
Paiguano, Chile	F3	80
Paiján, Peru	B2	82
Päijänne, l., Fin.	K19	6
Paila, stm., Bol.	G10	82
Pailin, Camb.	H7	40
Pailitas, Col.	C6	84
Pailolo Channel, strt., Hi., U.S.	B5	118
Paimpol, Fr.	D3	14
Paincourt, Ont., Can.	E2	103
Paincourtville, La., U.S.	k9	125
Painesdale, Mi., U.S.	A2	129
Painesville, Oh., U.S.	A4	142
Paint, stm., Mi., U.S.	B2	129
Paint Creek, stm., Oh., U.S.	C2	142
Paint Creek, stm., W.V., U.S.	m13	155
Paint Creek, North Fork, stm., Oh., U.S.	C2	142
Paint Creek Lake, res., Oh., U.S.	C2	142
Painted Desert, des., Az., U.S.	B4	110
Painted Post, N.Y., U.S.	C3	139
Painted Rock Reservoir, res., Az., U.S.	D3	110
Painter, Va., U.S.	C7	153
Paint Lick, Ky., U.S.	C5	124
Paint Mountain, mtn., W.V., U.S.	n13	155
Paint Rock, Al., U.S.	A3	108
Paintsville, Ky., U.S.	C7	124
Paisley, Ont., Can.	C3	103
Paisley, Scot., U.K.	F9	8
Paisley, Fl., U.S.	D5	116
Paisley, Or., U.S.	E6	144
Paita, Peru	A1	82
Paita, Bahía de, b., Peru	A1	82
Paizhou, China	E2	34
Pajala, Swe.	H18	6
Pajan, Ec.	H2	84
Pájara, Spain	o26	17b
Pajjer, gora, mtn., Russia	D10	26
Pakaraima Mountains, mts., S.A.	D8	74
Pakaraima Mountains, mts., S.A.	E12	84
Pak Ban, Laos	D7	40
Pakch'ŏn, N. Kor.	D13	32
Pakeng, Sud.	N6	60
Pakenham, Ont., Can.	B8	103
Pakhoi see Beihai, China	G8	30
Pakistan (Pākistān), ctry., Asia	C9	42
Pakokku, Mya.	D3	40
Pakouabo, C. Iv.	H7	64
Pakowki Lake, l., Alta., Can.	E5	98
Pākpattan, Pak.	E5	44
Pak Phanang, Thai.	J6	40
Pak Phraek, Thai.	J6	40
Pakrac, Cro.	D12	18
Pakruojis, Lith.	F6	22
Paks, Hung.	I18	10
P'akupur, stm., Russia	E7	28
Pakxé, Laos	G8	40
Pala, Chad	G3	56
Palacca Point, c., Bah.	D8	94
Palacios, Tx., U.S.	E4	150
Palacios, stm., Bol.	G10	82
Palagonia, Italy	L9	18
Palagruža, Otoci, is., Cro.	G11	18
Pālakodu, India	D5	46
Palamós, Spain	D15	16
Palana, Russia	F23	28

Name — Map Ref. — Page

Pátzcuaro, Mex. H9 90
Patzicía, Guat. C4 92
Patzún, Guat. C3 92
Pau, Fr. I6 14
Pau Brasil, Braz. C9 79
Paucarbamba, Peru E4 82
Paucarpata, Peru G6 82
Paucartambo, Peru E6 82
Pauini, Braz. B8 82
Pauini, stm., Braz. B8 82
Pauini, stm., Braz. H11 84
Pauk, Mya. D3 40
Paul, Id., U.S. G5 119
Paulaya, stm., Hond. B9 92
Paulding, Ms., U.S. C4 131
Paulding, Oh., U.S. A1 142
Paulding, co., Ga., U.S. C2 117
Paulding, co., Oh., U.S. A1 142
Paulhan, Fr. I10 14
Paulicéia, Braz. F3 79
Paulina, La., U.S. h10 125
Paulina Mountains, mts., Or., U.S. D5 144
Paulina Peak, mtn., Or., U.S. E5 144
Pauline, S.C., U.S. B4 147
Paulins Kill, stm., N.J., U.S. A3 137
Paul Island, i., Newf., Can. g9 102
Paulistana, Braz. E10 76
Paulistas, Braz. E7 79
Paullina, Ia., U.S. B2 122
Paulo Afonso, Braz. E11 76
Paulo de Faria, Braz. F4 79
Paulpietersburg, S. Afr. F10 66
Paulsboro, N.J., U.S. D2 137
Paul Stream, stm., Vt., U.S. B5 152
Pauls Valley, Ok., U.S. C4 143
Paungbyin, Mya. B3 40
Paungde, Mya. E3 40
Paupack, Pa., U.S. D11 145
Pausa, Peru F5 82
Paute, Ec. I3 84
Paute, stm., Ec. I3 84
Pauto, stm., Col. E7 84
Pauwela, Hi., U.S. C5 118
Pavant Range, mts., Ut., U.S. E3 151
Pāveh, Iran D9 48
Pavelec, Russia H22 22
Pavia, Italy D4 18
Pavilion Key, i., Fl., U.S. G5 116
Pavillion, Wy., U.S. C4 157
Pavilly, Fr. C7 14
Pāvilosta, Lat. E4 22
Pavlikeni, Bul. F9 20
Pavlodar, Kaz. G7 28
Pavlof Volcano, vol., Ak., U.S. D7 109
Pavlovo, Russia F26 22
Pavlovsk, Russia B13 22
Pavlovskij Posad, Russia F21 22
Pavo, Ga., U.S. F3 117
Pavón, Col. F6 84
Pawcatuck, Ct., U.S. D8 114
Pawcatuck, stm., R.I., U.S. G1 146
Paw Creek, N.C., U.S. B2 140
Pawhuska, Ok., U.S. A5 143
Pawlet, Vt., U.S. E2 152
Pawling, N.Y., U.S. D7 139
Pawnee, Il., U.S. D4 120
Pawnee, Ok., U.S. A5 143
Pawnee, co., Ks., U.S. D4 123
Pawnee, co., Ne., U.S. D9 134
Pawnee, co., Ok., U.S. A5 143
Pawnee, stm., Ks., U.S. D3 123
Pawnee City, Ne., U.S. D9 134
Pawnee Creek, stm., Co., U.S. A7 113
Pawnee Rock, Ks., U.S. D5 123
Pawpaw, Il., U.S. B5 120
Paw Paw, Mi., U.S. F5 129
Paw Paw, W.V., U.S. B6 155
Paw Paw, stm., Mi., U.S. F4 129
Pawpaw Creek, stm., W.V., U.S. h10 155
Pawtuckaway Pond, l., N.H., U.S. D4 136
Pawtucket, R.I., U.S. C4 146
Pawtuxet, stm., R.I., U.S. C4 146
Pawtuxet, North Branch, stm., R.I., U.S. D3 146
Pawtuxet, South Branch, stm., R.I., U.S. D3 146
Paxico, Ks., U.S. C7 123
Paxton, Fl., U.S. u15 116
Paxton, Il., U.S. C5 120
Paxton, In., U.S. F3 121
Paxton, Ma., U.S. B4 128
Paxton, Ne., U.S. C4 134
Paya, Hond. B9 92
Payakumbuh, Indon. O6 40
Payas, Cerro, mtn., Hond. B9 92
Payerne, Switz. E6 13
Payette, Id., U.S. E2 119
Payette, co., Id., U.S. E2 119
Payette, North Fork, stm., Id., U.S. E2 119
Payette, South Fork, stm., Id., U.S. E3 119
Payette Lake, res., Id., U.S. E3 119
Payne, Ga., U.S. D3 117
Payne, Oh., U.S. A1 142
Payne, co., Ok., U.S. A4 143
Payne, Lac, l., Que., Can. g12 104
Payne Bay, b., Can. D19 96
Paynesville, Mn., U.S. E4 130
Payneville, Ky., U.S. C3 124
Paynton, Sask., Can. D1 105
Paysandú, Ur. H9 74
Paysandú, Ur. G9 80
Payson, Az., U.S. C4 110
Payson, Il., U.S. D2 120
Payson, Ut., U.S. C4 151
Payún, Cerro, mtn., Arg. I4 80
Paz, stm., N.A. D4 92
Pazardžik, Bul. G8 20
Pazarköy, Tur. J11 20
Paz de Ariporo, Col. E7 84
Paz de Río, Col. E6 84
P'ažijeva Sel'ga, Russia K24 6
Pazin, Cro. D8 18
Pazña, Bol. H8 82
Pea, stm., Al., U.S. D3 108
Peabody, Ks., U.S. D6 123
Peabody, Ma., U.S. A6 128
Peabody, stm., N.H., U.S. B4 136
Peace, stm., Can. E10 96
Peace, stm., Fl., U.S. E5 116
Peace Dale, R.I., U.S. F3 146
Peace River, Alta., Can. A2 98
Peach, co., Ga., U.S. D3 117
Peacham, Vt., U.S. C4 152
Peacham Pond, res., Vt., U.S. C4 152
Peach Creek, W.V., U.S. D5 155
Peach Orchard, Ar., U.S. A5 111
Peach Orchard Knob, mtn., Ky., U.S. C3 124
Peach Point, c., Ma., U.S. f12 128
Peach Springs, Az., U.S. B2 110
Peaked Mountain, mtn., Me., U.S. B4 126
Peak Hill, Austl. E3 68
Peak Hill, Austl. I8 70
Peaks Island, i., Me., U.S. g7 126
Peale, Mount, mtn., Ut., U.S. E6 151
Pea Patch Island, i., De., U.S. B3 115
Pearcy, Ar., U.S. C2 111
Pea Ridge, Ar., U.S. A1 111
Pea Ridge National Military Park, Ar., U.S. A1 111
Pearisburg, Va., U.S. C2 153
Pearl, Ms., U.S. C3 131
Pearl, stm., U.S. D3 131
Pearland, Tx., U.S. r14 150
Pearl and Hermes Reef, rf., Hi., U.S. k12 118
Pearl City, Hi., U.S. B4 118
Pearl City, Il., U.S. A4 120
Pearl Harbor, b., Hi., U.S. B3 118
Pearl Harbor Naval Station, mil., Hi., U.S. g10 118
Pearlington, Ms., U.S. E4 131
Pearl River, La., U.S. D6 125
Pearl River, N.Y., U.S. g12 139
Pearl River, co., Ms., U.S. E4 131
Pearsall, Tx., U.S. E3 150
Pearsoll Peak, mtn., Or., U.S. E3 144
Pearson, Ga., U.S. E4 117
Pearston, S. Afr. I7 66
Peary Land, reg., Grnld. A16 86
Pease, Mn., U.S. E5 130
Pease, stm., Tx., U.S. B3 150
Pease Air Force Base, mil., N.H., U.S. D5 136
Pebane, Moz. E7 58
Pebas, Peru I7 84
Peć, Yugo. G4 20
Peçanha, Braz. E7 79
Peças, Ilha das, i., Braz. C14 80
Pecatonica, Il., U.S. A4 120
Pecatonica, stm., U.S. A4 120
Pecatonica, East Branch, stm., Wi., U.S. F4 156
Pečenga, Russia D4 26
Pechenizhyn, Ukr. A8 20
Pechora see Pečora, stm., Russia D8 26
Pecica, Rom. C5 20
Peck, Id., U.S. C2 119
Peck, Ks., U.S. E6 123
Peck, Mi., U.S. E8 129
Peckerwood Lake, res., Ar., U.S. C4 111
Pečora, Russia D9 26
Pečora, stm., Russia D8 26
Pečorskaja guba, b., Russia D8 26
Pečorskoje more, Russia D8 26
Pečory, Russia D10 22
Pecos, N.M., U.S. B4 138
Pecos, Tx., U.S. D1 150
Pecos, co., Tx., U.S. D1 150
Pecos, stm., U.S. E6 106
Pecos National Monument, N.M., U.S. B4 138
Pécs, Hung. I18 10
Peculiar, Mo., U.S. C3 132
Pedasí, Pan. D2 84
Peddāpuram, India D7 46
Pedder, Lake, res., Austl. N7 70
Peddocks Island, i., Ma., U.S. g12 128
Pedernales, Arg. H9 80
Pedernales, Dom. Rep. E9 94
Pedernales, Ven. C11 84
Pedernales, Salar de, pl., Chile D4 80
Pedra Azul, Braz. D8 79
Pedra Grande, Recifes da, rf., Braz. D9 79
Pedra Lume, C.V. k17 64a
Pedras, Braz. I14 84
Pedras Negras, Braz. E10 82
Pedraza, Col. B5 84
Pedregal, Pan. C1 84
Pedregal, Ven. B7 84
Pedregulho, Braz. F5 79
Pedreiras, Braz. D10 76
Pedriceña, Mex. E8 90
Pedricktown, N.J., U.S. D2 137
Pedro Afonso, Braz. E9 76
Pedro Cays, is., Jam. F6 94
Pedrógão Grande, Port. F3 16
Pedro Gomes, Braz. E1 79
Pedro II, Braz. D10 76
Pedro II, Ilha, i., S.A. G9 84
Pedro Juan Caballero, Para. B11 80
Pedro Leopoldo, Braz. E6 79
Pedro Luro, Arg. J7 80
Pedro Muñoz, Spain F9 16
Pedro Osório, Braz. F12 80
Pedro R. Fernández, Arg. E9 80
Peebinga, Austl. J4 70
Peebles, Oh., U.S. D2 142
Peekaboo Mountain, hill, Me., U.S. C5 126
Peekskill, N.Y., U.S. D7 139
Peel, N.B., Can. C2 101
Peel, I. of Man G9 8
Peel, stm., Can. C5 96
Pe Ell, Wa., U.S. C2 154
Peel Point, c., N.W. Ter., Can. B10 96
Peel Sound, strt., N.W. Ter., Can. B13 96
Peene, stm., Ger. B13 10
Peerless, Mt., U.S. B11 133
Peers, Alta., Can. C3 98
Peetz, Co., U.S. A7 113
Peever, S.D., U.S. B9 148
Pegan Hill, hill, Ma., U.S. g10 128
Pegasus Bay, b., N.Z. E4 72
Pegnitz, Ger. F11 10
Pegnitz, stm., Ger. F11 10
Pego, Spain G11 16
Pegram, Tn., U.S. A4 149
Pegu see Bago, Mya. F4 40
Pegu Yoma, mts., Mya. E3 40
Pehčevo, Mac. H6 20
Pehuajó, Arg. H8 80
Peikang, Tai. L9 34
Peine, Ger. C10 10
Peipus, Lake see Čudskoje ozero, l., Eur. C10 22
Peissenberg, Ger. H11 10
Peixe, Braz. B4 79
Peixe, Rio do, stm., Braz. G3 79
Peixe, Rio do, stm., Braz. C3 79
Peixian, China E10 30
Peiziyan, China H3 32
Pejepscot, Me., U.S. E2 126
Pekalongan, Indon. j14 39a
Pekanbaru, Indon. N6 40
Pekin, Il., U.S. C4 120
Pekin, In., U.S. G5 121
Pekin, N.D., U.S. B7 141
Peking see Beijing, China D4 32
Peklino, Russia H16 22
Pelabuhan Kelang, Malay. M6 40
Pelagie, Isole, is., Italy N7 18
Pelahatchie, Ms., U.S. C4 131
Pełczyce, Pol. B15 10
Pelechuco, Bol. F7 82
Pelée, Montagne, mtn., Mart. G14 94
Pelee Island, i., Ont., Can. F2 103
Pelega, Vârful, mtn., Rom. D6 20
Pelham, Ont., Can. D5 103
Pelham, Al., U.S. B3 108
Pelham, Ga., U.S. E2 117
Pelham, N.H., U.S. E4 136
Pelham, S.C., U.S. B3 147
Pelham, Tn., U.S. D8 149
Pelham Manor, N.Y., U.S. h13 139
Pelhřimov, Czech Rep. F15 10
Pelican, Ak., U.S. m21 109
Pelican Bay, b., Man., Can. C1 100
Pelican Lake, l., Man., Can. C1 100
Pelican Lake, l., Mn., U.S. E5 130
Pelican Lake, l., Mn., U.S. B6 130
Pelican Lake, l., Mn., U.S. D3 130
Pelican Lake, l., Mn., U.S. D4 130
Pelican Lake, l., Wi., U.S. C4 156
Pelican Mountain, mtn., Alta., Can. B4 98
Pelican Narrows, Sask., Can. B4 105
Pelican Rapids, Man., Can. C1 100
Pelican Rapids, Mn., U.S. D2 130
Pelileo, Ec. H3 84
Pelion, S.C., U.S. D5 147
Pelister, mtn., Mac. H5 20
Pelkosenniemi, Fin. H20 6
Pella, Ia., U.S. C5 122
Pell City, Al., U.S. B3 108
Pellegrini, Arg. I7 80
Pellegrini, Lago, l., Arg. J4 80
Pell Lake, Wi., U.S. n11 156
Pello, Fin. H19 6
Pellston, Mi., U.S. C6 129
Pelly, Sask., Can. F5 105
Pelly, stm., Yukon, Can. D6 96
Pelly Bay, b., N.W. Ter., Can. C14 96
Pelly Crossing, Yukon, Can. D5 96
Pelly Mountains, mts., Yukon, Can. D6 96
Pelón, Cerro, mtn., Mex. G10 90
Peloncillo Mountains, mts., U.S. E1 138
Peloponnesos see Pelopónnisos, pen., Grc. L6 20
Pelopónnisos (Peloponnesus), pen., Grc. L6 20
Pelotas, Braz. F12 80
Pelotas, stm., Braz. D13 80
Pelton, Lake, l., La., U.S. E5 125
Pel'ušn'a, Russia C15 22
Pemadumcook Lake, l., Me., U.S. C3 126
Pemalang, Indon. j14 39a
Pematangsiantar, Indon. M5 40
Pemba, Moz. D8 58
Pemba, i., Tan. C7 58
Pemberton, Austl. F3 68
Pemberton, B.C., Can. D6 99
Pemberton, N.J., U.S. D3 137
Pemberville, Oh., U.S. A2 142
Pembina, N.D., U.S. A8 141
Pembina, co., N.D., U.S. A8 141
Pembina, stm., Alta., Can. C3 98
Pembine, Wi., U.S. C6 156
Pembroke, Ont., Can. B7 103
Pembroke, Wales, U.K. J9 8
Pembroke, Ga., U.S. D5 117
Pembroke, Ky., U.S. D2 124
Pembroke, Me., U.S. D5 126
Pembroke, Ma., U.S. B6 128
Pembroke, N.C., U.S. C3 140
Pembroke, Va., U.S. C2 153
Pembroke, Cape, c., N.W. Ter., Can. D16 96
Pembroke Pines, Fl., U.S. r13 116
Pemigewasset, stm., N.H., U.S. C3 136
Pemigewasset, East Branch, stm., N.H., U.S. B3 136
Pemiscot, co., Mo., U.S. E8 132
Pemmican Portage, Sask., Can. D4 105
Pemuco, Chile I2 80
Peña Barroza, Bol. J8 82
Peña Blanca, Pan. I13 92
Pena Blanca, N.M., U.S. B3 138
Penafiel, Port. D3 16
Peña Gorda, Cerro, mtn., Mex. G7 90
Penápolis, Braz. F3 79
Peñaranda de Bracamonte, Spain E6 16
Pen Argyl, Pa., U.S. E11 145
Peñarroya-Pueblonuevo, Spain G6 16
Penas, Golfo de, b., Chile F2 78
Penasco, N.M., U.S. A4 138
Peñasco, Rio, stm., N.M., U.S. E4 138
Penbrook, Pa., U.S. F8 145
Pencahue, Chile H3 80
Pendembu, S.L. G3 64
Pender, Ne., U.S. B9 134
Pender, co., N.C., U.S. C4 140
Pendergrass, Ga., U.S. B3 117
Pendjari, stm., Afr. F7 54
Pendleton, In., U.S. E6 121
Pendleton, Or., U.S. B8 144
Pendleton, S.C., U.S. B2 147
Pendleton, co., Ky., U.S. B5 124
Pendleton, co., W.V., U.S. C5 155
Pendley Hills, Ga., U.S. *h8 117
Pend Oreille, co., Wa., U.S. A8 154
Pend Oreille, Lake, l., Id., U.S. A2 119
Pend Oreille, Mount, mtn., Id., U.S. A2 119
Penedo, Braz. F11 76
Penedono, Port. E4 16
Penetanguishene, Ont., Can. C5 103
Penfield, Ga., U.S. C3 117
Penfield, Il., U.S. C6 120
Penfield, Pa., U.S. D4 145
Penganga, stm., India C5 46
Penge, S. Afr. E10 66
P'enghu Ch'üntao (Pescadores), is., Tai. L8 34
P'enghu Shuitao, strt., Tai. L8 34
Pengkou, China J5 34
Penglai (Dengzhou), China F8 32
Pengshui, China F8 30
Penguin, Austl. M7 70
Pengxian, China E7 30
Penha, Braz. D14 80
Penhold, Alta., Can. C4 98
Peniche, Port. F2 16
Peninsula, Oh., U.S. A4 142
Penitentiary Mountain, hill, Al., U.S. A2 108
Penjamillo [de Degollado], Mex. G9 90
Pennant Point, c., N.S., Can. E6 101
Pennant Station, Sask., Can. G1 105
Pennask Mountain, mtn., B.C., Can. E7 99
Penne, Italy G8 18
Pennell, Mount, mtn., Ut., U.S. F5 151
Penney Farms, Fl., U.S. C5 116
Pennfield, N.B., Can. D3 101
Penn Hills, Pa., U.S. k14 145
Penniac, N.B., Can. C3 101
Pennines, mts., Eng., U.K. G11 8
Pennines, Alpes, mts., Eur. C2 18
Pennington, Al., U.S. C1 108
Pennington, N.J., U.S. C3 137
Pennington, co., Mn., U.S. B2 130
Pennington, co., S.D., U.S. D2 148
Pennington Gap, Va., U.S. f8 153
Pennock, Mn., U.S. E3 130
Pennsauken, N.J., U.S. D2 137
Pennsboro, W.V., U.S. B4 155
Pennsburg, Pa., U.S. F11 145
Penns Grove, N.J., U.S. D2 137
Pennsville, N.J., U.S. D1 137
Pennsylvania, state, U.S. E7 145
Pennville, In., U.S. D7 121
Penny, B.C., Can. C7 99
Penn Yan, N.Y., U.S. C3 139
Pennycutaway, stm., Man., Can. A5 100
Penny Ice Cap, N.W. Ter., Can. C19 96
Penny Strait, strt., N.W. Ter., Can. A13 96
Peno, Russia E15 22
Penobscot, co., Me., U.S. C4 126
Penobscot, stm., Me., U.S. C4 126
Penobscot, East Branch, stm., Me., U.S. C4 126
Penobscot, North Branch, stm., Me., U.S. B2 126
Penobscot, West Branch, stm., Me., U.S. C3 126
Penobscot Bay, b., Me., U.S. D3 126
Penobscot Lake, l., Me., U.S. C2 126
Penokee, Ks., U.S. C4 123
Penola, Austl. K4 70
Peñón Blanco, Mex. E7 90
Penong, Austl. F6 68
Penonomé, Pan. C2 84
Penrith, Austl. I9 70
Pensacola, Fl., U.S. u14 116
Pensacola Bay, b., Fl., U.S. u14 116
Pensacola Dam, Ok., U.S. A6 143
Pensacola Mountains, mts., Ant. D1 73
Pensacola Naval Air Station, mil., Fl., U.S. u14 116
Pense, Sask., Can. G3 105
Pensilvania, Col. E5 84
Pentagon Mountain, mtn., Mt., U.S. C3 133
Penticton, B.C., Can. E8 99
Pentland, Austl. C6 70
Pentland Firth, strt., Scot., U.K. C10 8
Pentwater, Mi., U.S. E4 129
Pènwègon, Mya. E4 40
Penza, Russia G7 26
Penzance, Sask., Can. F3 105
Penzance, Eng., U.K. K8 8
Penzberg, Ger. H11 10
Penžina, stm., Russia E25 28
Penžinskaja guba, b., Russia E24 28
Peonan Point, c., Man., Can. D2 100
Peoria, Az., U.S. D3 110
Peoria, Il., U.S. C4 120
Peoria, co., Il., U.S. C4 120
Peoria Heights, Il., U.S. C4 120
Peotone, Il., U.S. B6 120
Pepacton Reservoir, res., N.Y., U.S. C6 139
Pepeekeo, Hi., U.S. D6 118
Pepel, S.L. G3 64
Peper, Sud. N7 60
Pepin, Wi., U.S. D1 156
Pepin, co., Wi., U.S. D2 156
Pepin, Lake, l., U.S. D1 156
Pepper Creek, stm., De., U.S. F5 115
Pepperell, Ma., U.S. A4 128
Pequannock, N.J., U.S. B4 137
Pequest, stm., N.J., U.S. B2 137
Pequop Mountains, mts., Nv., U.S. C7 135
Pequot Lakes, Mn., U.S. D4 130
Perabumulih, Indon. F3 38
Perak, stm., Malay. L6 40
Peralillo, Chile H3 80
Perämeri (Bottenviken), b., Eur. I18 6
Perchtoldsdorf, Aus. G16 10
Percy, Il., U.S. E4 120
Percy Isles, is., Austl. C9 70
Perdeberg, S. Afr. G7 66
Perdido, Al., U.S. D2 108
Perdido, stm., Braz. I13 82
Perdido, stm., U.S. E2 108
Perdido, Monte, mtn., Spain C12 16
Perdido Bay, b., Al., U.S. E2 108
Perdizes, Braz. E5 79
Perdue, Sask., Can. E2 105
Perechyn, Ukr. G22 10
Perehonivka, Ukr. A14 20
Pereira, Col. E5 84
Pereira Barreto, Braz. F3 79
Pere Marquette, stm., Mi., U.S. E4 129
Peremyšl', Russia G19 22
Perené, stm., Peru D4 82
Pereslavl'-Zalesskij, Russia E21 22
Peresypkino Pervoje, Russia I25 22
Pérez, Arg. G8 80
Perg, Aus. G14 10
Pergamino, Arg. G8 80
Pergine Valsugana, Italy C6 18
Pergola, Italy F7 18
Perham, Mn., U.S. D3 130
Perico, Arg. C6 80
Pericos, Mex. E6 90
Peridot, Az., U.S. D5 110
Périers, Fr. C5 14
Périgord, hist. reg., Fr. G7 14
Périgueux, Fr. G7 14
Perijá, Serranía De, mts., S.A. B6 84
Periyakulam, India G4 46
Perkasie, Pa., U.S. F11 145
Perkins, Que., Can. D2 104
Perkins, Ga., U.S. D5 117
Perkins, Mi., U.S. C3 129
Perkins, Ok., U.S. B4 143
Perkins, co., Ne., U.S. D4 134
Perkins, co., S.D., U.S. B3 148
Perkinston, Ms., U.S. E4 131
Perla, Ar., U.S. C3 111
Perlas, Archipiélago de las, is., Pan. C3 84
Perlas, Laguna de, b., Nic. E11 92
Perlas, Punta de, c., Nic. E11 92
Perleberg, Ger. B11 10
Perm', Russia F9 26
Pernatty Lagoon, l., Austl. H2 70
Pernell, Ok., U.S. C4 143
Pernik, Bul. G7 20
Péronne, Fr. C9 14
Perot, Bayou, stm., La., U.S. k11 125
Perote, Mex. H11 90
Peroto, Bol. F9 82
Perpignan, Fr. J9 14
Perquimans, co., N.C., U.S. A6 140
Perrine, Fl., U.S. G6 116
Perris, Ca., U.S. F5 112
Perro, Laguna del, l., N.M., U.S. C4 138
Perros, Bahía de, b., Cuba C5 94
Perrot, Île, i., Que., Can. q19 104
Perry, Ar., U.S. B3 111
Perry, Fl., U.S. B3 116
Perry, Ga., U.S. D3 117
Perry, Il., U.S. D3 120
Perry, Ia., U.S. C3 122
Perry, Ks., U.S. C8 123
Perry, Mi., U.S. F6 129
Perry, Mo., U.S. B6 132
Perry, N.Y., U.S. C2 139
Perry, Oh., U.S. A4 142
Perry, Ok., U.S. A4 143
Perry, Ut., U.S. B3 151
Perry, co., Al., U.S. C2 108
Perry, co., Ar., U.S. C3 111
Perry, co., Il., U.S. E4 120
Perry, co., In., U.S. H4 121
Perry, co., Ky., U.S. C6 124
Perry, co., Ms., U.S. D4 131
Perry, co., Mo., U.S. D8 132
Perry, co., Oh., U.S. C3 142
Perry, co., Pa., U.S. F7 145
Perry, co., Tn., U.S. B4 149
Perry Hall, Md., U.S. B5 127
Perry Lake, res., Ks., U.S. C8 123
Perryman, Md., U.S. B5 127
Perry Peak, mtn., Ma., U.S. B1 128
Perry Point, Md., U.S. A5 127
Perrysburg, Oh., U.S. A2 142
Perrysburg Heights, Oh., U.S. e6 142
Perry Stream, stm., N.H., U.S. f7 136
Perry's Victory and International Peace Memorial, hist., Oh., U.S. A2 142
Perrysville, In., U.S. D3 121
Perrysville, Oh., U.S. B3 142
Perryton, Tx., U.S. A2 150
Perryville, Ak., U.S. D8 109
Perryville, Ar., U.S. B3 111
Perryville, Ky., U.S. C5 124
Perryville, Md., U.S. A5 127
Perryville, Mo., U.S. D8 132
Perryville, Tn., U.S. B3 149
Peršaj, Bela. G9 22
Perseverancia, Bol. F10 82
Pershing, In., U.S. E7 121
Pershing, Ia., U.S. C4 122
Pershing, co., Nv., U.S. C3 135
Persia, Ia., U.S. C2 122
Persia see Iran, ctry., Asia C5 42
Persian Gulf (Arabian Gulf), b., Asia H11 48
Persimmon Grove, Ky., U.S. k14 124
Person, co., N.C., U.S. A3 140
Pertek, Tur. B5 48
Perth, Austl. F3 68
Perth, Ont., Can. C8 103
Perth, Scot., U.K. E10 8
Perth Amboy, N.J., U.S. B4 137
Perth-Andover, N.B., Can. D10 101
Pertokar, Erit. I9 60
Peru, Il., U.S. B4 120
Peru, In., U.S. C5 121
Peru, Ks., U.S. E7 123
Peru, Ne., U.S. D10 134
Peru, N.Y., U.S. f11 139
Peru, Vt., U.S. E3 152
Peru (Perú), ctry., S.A. E3 76
Peruaçu, stm., Braz. C6 79
Peru-Chile Trench G7 74
Perugia, Italy F7 18
Perugorría, Arg. E9 80
Peruíbe, Braz. C15 80
Peruípe, stm., Braz. D9 79
Pervoavgustovskij, Russia I18 22
Pervomajskij, Bela. H8 22
Pervomajskij, Russia H23 22
Pervomays'k, Ukr. H4 26
Pervoural'sk, Russia F9 26
Pervyj Kuril'skij proliv, strt., Russia G23 28
Pes', Russia C17 22
Pesaro, Italy F7 18
Pesca, Col. E6 84
Pescadero, Ca., U.S. D2 112
Pescadores see P'enghu Ch'üntao, is., Tai. L8 34
Pescadores, Punta, c., Mex. F5 90
Pescadores, Punta, c., Peru G5 82
Peščanoje, Russia J24 6
Pescara, Italy G9 18
Pescia, Italy F5 18
Pesé, Pan. D2 84
Peseux, Switz. E6 13
Peshastin, Wa., U.S. B5 154
Peshāwar, Pak. C4 44
Peshtigo, Wi., U.S. C6 156
Peshtigo, stm., Wi., U.S. C5 156
Peski, Russia F21 22
Pesmes, Fr. E12 14
Pesočenskij, Russia G19 22
Pesočnoje, Russia C22 22
Pesočnyj, Russia A13 22
Peso da Régua, Port. D4 16
Pesotum, Il., U.S. D5 120
Pespire, Hond. D7 92
Pesqueira, Braz. E11 76
Pessac, Fr. H6 14
Pest, co., Hung. H19 10
Pest'aki, Russia E25 22
Peštera, Bul. G8 20
Pestovo, Russia C18 22
Petacalco, Bahía, b., Mex. I8 90
Petah Tiqwa, Isr. D3 50
Petal, Ms., U.S. D4 131
Petalcingo, Mex. I13 90
Petalión, Kólpos, b., Grc. L8 20
Petaluma, Ca., U.S. C2 112
Pétange, Lux. I8 12
Petare, Ven. B9 84
Petatlán, Mex. I9 90
Petawawa, Ont., Can. B7 103
Petawawa, stm., Ont., Can. A6 103
Petén, dept., Guat. A5 92
Petén Itzá, Lago, l., Guat. I15 90
Petenwell Lake, res., Wi., U.S. D4 156
Peterborough, Austl. I3 70
Peterborough, Ont., Can. C6 103
Peterborough, Eng., U.K. I13 8
Peterborough, N.H., U.S. E3 136
Peterculter, Scot., U.K. D11 8
Peter Dana Point, Me., U.S. C5 126
Peterhead, Scot., U.K. D12 8
Peter I Island, i., Ant. B11 73
Peterman, Al., U.S. D2 108
Peter Pond Lake, l., Sask., Can. m7 105
Petersburg, Ak., U.S. D13 109
Petersburg, De., U.S. D3 115
Petersburg, Il., U.S. C4 120
Petersburg, In., U.S. H3 121
Petersburg, Ky., U.S. h13 124
Petersburg, Mi., U.S. G7 129
Petersburg, Ne., U.S. C7 134
Petersburg, N.D., U.S. A8 141
Petersburg, Oh., U.S. B5 142
Petersburg, Tn., U.S. B5 149
Petersburg, Tx., U.S. C2 150
Petersburg, Va., U.S. C5 153
Petersburg, W.V., U.S. B5 155
Peters Creek, stm., W.V., U.S. m14 155
Petersfield, Man., Can. D3 100
Peters Mountain, mtn., U.S. D4 155
Peterson, Al., U.S. B2 108
Peterson, Ia., U.S. B2 122
Peterson, Mn., U.S. G7 130
Peterson Field, mil., Co., U.S. C6 113
Peterstown, W.V., U.S. D4 155
Petersville, Al., U.S. A2 108
Pétervására, Hung. G20 10
Petilia Policastro, Italy J11 18
Pétionville, Haiti E8 94
Petit Bois Island, i., Ms., U.S. E5 131
Petitcodiac, N.B., Can. D4 101
Petitcodiac, stm., N.B., Can. C5 101
Petit-de-Grat, N.S., Can. D9 101
Petite Amite, stm., La., U.S. h10 125
Petite Rivière, N.S., Can. E5 101
Petite-Rivière-de-l'Île, N.B., Can. B5 101
Petite Rivière Noire, Piton de la, mtn., Mrts. v18 67c
Petit-Étang, N.S., Can. C9 101
Petit-Goâve, Haiti E8 94
Petit Jean, stm., Ar., U.S. B2 111

Port-Prud

Name | Map Ref. | Page

Port Elizabeth, S. Afr. I7 66
Port Elizabeth, N.J., U.S. E3 137
Port-en-Bessin, Fr. C6 14
Porter, Al., U.S. B2 108
Porter, In., U.S. A3 121
Porter, Me., U.S. E2 126
Porter, Ok., U.S. B6 143
Porter, Tx., U.S. D5 150
Porter, co., In., U.S. B3 121
Porter Creek, stm., W.V., U.S. m13 155
Porterdale, Ga., U.S. C3 117
Porterville, Ca., U.S. D4 112
Portete, Bahía, b., Col. A6 84
Port Ewen, N.Y., U.S. D7 139
Port Fairy, Austl. L5 70
Port Gamble, Wa., U.S. B3 154
Port Gamble Indian Reservation, Wa., U.S. B3 154
Port Gentil, Gabon B1 58
Port George, N.S., Can. D4 101
Port Germein, Austl. I3 70
Port Gibson, Ms., U.S. D3 131
Port Graham, Ak., U.S. D9 109
Port Greville, N.S., Can. D5 101
Port Harcourt, Nig. I13 64
Port Hastings, N.S., Can. D8 101
Port Hawkesbury, N.S., Can. D8 101
Port Hedland, Austl. D3 68
Port Heiden, Ak., U.S. D8 109
Port Henry, N.Y., U.S. A7 139
Port Hill, P.E.I., Can. C6 101
Port Hood, N.S., Can. C8 101
Port Hope, Ont., Can. D6 103
Port Hope, Mi., U.S. E8 129
Port Hope Simpson, Newf., Can. B3 102
Port Howe, Bah. B7 94
Port Hueneme, Ca., U.S. E4 112
Port Huron, Mi., U.S. F8 129
Portia, Ar., U.S. A4 111
Port-İliç, Azer. B10 48
Portimão, Port. H3 16
Portis, Ks., U.S. C5 123
Port Isabel, Tx., U.S. F4 150
Port Jefferson, N.Y., U.S. n15 139
Port Jervis, N.Y., U.S. D6 139
Port Kembla, Austl. J9 70
Portland, Austl. L4 70
Portland, Austl. I9 70
Portland, Ont., Can. C8 103
Portland, Ar., U.S. D4 111
Portland, Ct., U.S. C5 114
Portland, In., U.S. D8 121
Portland, Me., U.S. E2 126
Portland, Mi., U.S. F6 129
Portland, Mo., U.S. C6 132
Portland, N.Y., U.S. C1 139
Portland, N.D., U.S. B8 141
Portland, Or., U.S. B4 144
Portland, Tn., U.S. A5 149
Portland, Tx., U.S. F4 150
Portland, Bill of, c., Eng., U.K. K11 8
Portland, Cape, c., Austl. M7 70
Portland Bay, b., Austl. L4 70
Portland Bight, Jam. F6 94
Portland Creek Pond, l., Newf., Can. C3 102
Portland Inlet, b., B.C., Can. B2 99
Portland Point, c., Jam. F6 94
Port Laoise, Ire. H6 8
Port Lavaca, Tx., U.S. E4 150
Port Lincoln, Austl. J1 70
Port Lions, Ak., U.S. D9 109
Port Loko, S.L. G3 64
Port Loring, Ont., Can. B4 103
Port-Louis, Fr. E3 14
Port Louis, Mrts. v18 67c
Port Ludlow, Wa., U.S. B3 154
Port Macquarie, Austl. H10 70
Port Madison Indian Reservation, Wa., U.S. B3 154
Port Maitland, N.S., Can. F3 101
Port Maria, Jam. E6 94
Port Matilda, Pa., U.S. E5 145
Port McNeil, B.C., Can. D4 99
Port McNicoll, Ont., Can. C5 103
Port Medway, N.S., Can. E5 101
Port Monmouth, N.J., U.S. C4 137
Port Moresby, Pap. N. Gui. m16 68a
Port Morien, N.S., Can. C10 101
Port Mouton, N.S., Can. F5 101
Port Neches, Tx., U.S. E6 150
Portneuf, Que., Can. C6 104
Port Nolloth, S. Afr. G3 66
Port Norris, N.J., U.S. E2 137
Porto, Port. D3 16
Porto Acre, Braz. C8 82
Porto Alegre, Braz. F13 80
Porto Amboim, Ang. D2 58
Porto Belo, Braz. D14 80
Portobelo, Pan. C3 84
Port O'Connor, Tx., U.S. E4 150
Porto de Moz, Braz. D8 76
Porto de Pedras, Braz. E11 76
Porto Empedocle, Italy L8 18
Porto Esperança, Braz. H13 82
Porto Esperidião, Braz. F12 82
Porto Farina, Tun. L5 18
Porto Feliz, Braz. G5 79
Porto Ferreira, Braz. F5 79
Port of Spain, Trin. I14 94
Portogruaro, Italy D7 18
Porto Inglês, C.V. m17 64a
Portola, Ca., U.S. C3 112
Porto Lucena, Braz. D11 80
Pörtom (Pirttikylä), Fin. J17 6
Porto Mendes, Braz. C11 80
Porto Murtinho, Braz. I13 82
Porto Nacional, Braz. F9 76
Porto-Novo, Benin H11 64
Port Orange, Fl., U.S. C6 116
Port Orchard, Wa., U.S. B3 154
Porto Recanati, Italy F8 18
Port Orford, Or., U.S. E2 144
Porto San Giorgio, Italy F8 18
Porto Santo, i., Port. I21 17a
Porto São José, Braz. G2 79
Porto Seguro, Braz. D9 79
Porto-Séguro, Togo H10 64
Porto Torres, Italy I3 18
Porto União, Braz. D13 80
Porto Válter, Braz. C5 82
Porto-Vecchio, Fr. m24 15a
Porto Velho, Braz. C10 82
Portoviejo, Ec. H2 84
Port Penn, De., U.S. B3 115
Port Phillip Bay, b., Austl. L6 70
Port Pirie, Austl. I3 70
Port Reading, N.J., U.S. k8 137
Port Renfrew, B.C., Can. E5 99
Port Republic, N.J., U.S. D4 137
Port Rexton, Newf., Can. D5 102
Port Richey, Fl., U.S. D4 116
Port Rowan, Ont., Can. E4 103
Port Royal, Ky., U.S. B4 124
Port Royal, Pa., U.S. E7 145
Port Royal, S.C., U.S. G6 147
Port Royal, Va., U.S. B5 153
Port Royal Island, i., S.C., U.S. G6 147
Port Royal Sound, strt., S.C., U.S. G6 147
Port Said see Būr Sa'īd, Egypt B7 60
Port Saint Joe, Fl., U.S. C1 116
Port Saint Johns, S. Afr. H9 66
Port Saint Lucie, Fl., U.S. E6 116
Port Salerno, Fl., U.S. E6 116
Port Sanilac, Mi., U.S. E8 129
Port Saunders, Newf., Can. C3 102
Portsea, Austl. L6 70
Port Sewall, Fl., U.S. E6 116
Port Shepstone, S. Afr. H10 66
Portsmouth, Eng., U.K. K12 8
Portsmouth, N.H., U.S. D5 136
Portsmouth, Oh., U.S. D3 142
Portsmouth, R.I., U.S. E6 146
Portsmouth, Va., U.S. D6 153
Portsmouth Naval Shipyard, mil., Me., U.S. D5 136
Portsoy, Scot., U.K. D11 8
Port Stanley, Ont., Can. E3 103
Port Sudan see Būr Sūdān, Sud. H9 60
Port Sulphur, La., U.S. E6 125
Port Talbot, Wales, U.K. J10 8
Port Taufiq see Būr Tawfīq, Egypt G2 48
Porttipahdan tekojärvi, res., Fin. G20 6
Port Townsend, Wa., U.S. A3 154
Portugal, ctry., Eur. H6 4
Portugal, Cachoeira, wtfl, Braz. C9 82
Portugal Cove South, Newf., Can. E5 102
Portugalete, Spain B8 16
Portuguesa, state, Ven. C8 84
Portuguesa, stm., Ven. C9 84
Portuguese Guinea see Guinea-Bissau, ctry., Afr. F3 54
Port Union, Newf., Can. D5 102
Port-Vendres, Fr. J10 14
Portville, N.Y., U.S. C2 139
Port Vincent, La., U.S. D5 125
Port Wakefield, Austl. J3 70
Port Washington, N.Y., U.S. h13 139
Port Washington, Oh., U.S. B4 142
Port Washington, Wi., U.S. E6 156
Port Wentworth, Ga., U.S. D5 117
Porum, Ok., U.S. B6 143
Porvenir, Chile G2 78
Porvenir, Mex. B7 90
Porzuna, Spain F7 16
Posada, Italy I4 18
Posadas, Arg. D11 80
Posadas, Spain H6 16
Poschiavo, Switz. F13 13
Pošechon'e, Russia C22 22
Posen see Poznań, Pol. C16 10
Posen, Il., U.S. k9 120
Posey, co., In., U.S. H2 121
Poseyville, In., U.S. H2 121
Positano, Italy I9 18
Posjet, Russia I18 28
Posse, Braz. C5 79
Possession Islands, is., Ant. C8 73
Pössneck, Ger. E11 10
Post, Tx., U.S. C2 150
Postavy, Bela. F9 22
Poste Ramartina, Madag. q21 67b
Post Falls, Id., U.S. B2 119
Post Mills, Vt., U.S. D4 152
Postojna, Slvn. D9 18
P'ostraja Dresva, Russia E23 28
Postrevalle, Bol. H10 82
Postville, Newf., Can. g10 102
Postville, Ia., U.S. A6 122
Pótam, Mex. D4 90
Potaro, stm., Guy. E13 84
Potaro Landing, Guy. E13 84
Potaro-Siparuni, prov., Guy. E13 84
Potawatomi Indian Reservation, Ks., U.S. C8 123
Poté, Braz. D8 79
Poteau, Ok., U.S. B7 143
Poteau, stm., U.S. B7 143
Poteau Mountain, mtn., U.S. C1 111
Poteet, Tx., U.S. E3 150
Potenza, Italy I10 18
Potes, Spain B7 16
Potgietersrus, S. Afr. E9 66
Poth, Tx., U.S. E3 150
Potholes Reservoir, res., Wa., U.S. B6 154
Poti, Geor. I6 26
Poti, stm., Braz. E10 76
Potiraguá, Braz. C9 79
Potirendaba, Braz. F4 79
Potiskum, Nig. F9 54
Potlatch, Id., U.S. C2 119
Potomac, Il., U.S. C6 120
Potomac, Md., U.S. B3 127
Potomac, stm., U.S. D4 127
Potomac, North Branch, stm., U.S. m12 127
Potomac, South Branch, stm., U.S. B6 155
Potomac, South Branch, North Fork, stm., W.V., U.S. C5 155
Potomac, South Branch, South Fork, stm., U.S. B6 155
Potomac Heights, Md., U.S. C3 127
Potomac Park, Md., U.S. k13 127
Potosí, Bol. F8 74
Potosí, Bol. H9 82
Potosi, Mo., U.S. D7 132
Potosi, Wi., U.S. F3 156
Potosí, dept., Bol. I8 82
Potrerillos, Chile D4 80
Potrerillos, Hond. B7 92
Potrerillos Arriba, Pan. I12 92
Potrero, C.R. G9 92
Potrero Grande, C.R. H11 92
Potro, Cerro del, mtn., S.A. E4 80
Potsdam, Ger. C13 10
Potsdam, N.Y., U.S. f10 139
Pottawatomie, co., Ks., U.S. C7 123
Pottawatomie, co., Ok., U.S. B4 143
Pottawatomie Creek, stm., Ks., U.S. D8 123
Pottawattamie, co., Ia., U.S. C2 122
Potter, Ks., U.S. C8 123
Potter, Ne., U.S. C2 134
Potter, co., Pa., U.S. C6 145
Potter, co., S.D., U.S. B6 148
Potter, co., Tx., U.S. B2 150
Potter Place, N.H., U.S. D3 136
Potter Valley, Ca., U.S. C2 112
Potterville, Ga., U.S. D2 117
Potts Camp, Ms., U.S. A4 131
Potts Creek, stm., U.S. C2 153
Pottstown, Pa., U.S. F10 145
Pottsville, Ar., U.S. B2 111
Pottsville, Pa., U.S. E9 145
Potwin, Ks., U.S. E6 123
P'otzu, Tai. L9 34
Pouancé, Fr. E5 14
Pouce Coupe, B.C., Can. B7 99
Pouch Cove, Newf., Can. E5 102
Poughkeepsie, N.Y., U.S. D7 139
Poulan, Ga., U.S. E3 117
Poulsbo, Wa., U.S. B3 154
Poultney, Vt., U.S. D2 152
Poultney, stm., Vt., U.S. D2 152
Poŭn, S. Kor. G15 32
Pound, Va., U.S. e9 153
Pound, Wi., U.S. C5 156
Pound Gap, U.S. C7 124
Pouso Alegre, Braz. G6 79
Pouso Redondo, Braz. D14 80
Poŭthisăt, Camb. H7 40
Považská Bystrica, Slvk. F18 10
Povenec, Russia J24 6
Póvoa de Varzim, Port. D3 16
Povorino, Russia G6 26
Povungnituk, Que., Can. f11 104
Powassan, Ont., Can. A5 103
Poway, Ca., U.S. F5 112
Powder, stm., U.S. B5 106
Powder, stm., Or., U.S. C9 144
Powder, Middle Fork, stm., Wy., U.S. C6 157
Powder, North Fork, stm., Wy., U.S. C6 157
Powder, South Fork, stm., Wy., U.S. C6 157
Powder River, Wy., U.S. C6 157
Powder River, co., Mt., U.S. E11 133
Powder River Pass, Wy., U.S. B5 157
Powder Springs, Ga., U.S. h8 117
Powell, Oh., U.S. B2 142
Powell, Tn., U.S. m13 149
Powell, Wy., U.S. B4 157
Powell, co., Ky., U.S. C6 124
Powell, co., Mt., U.S. D4 133
Powell, stm., U.S. C10 149
Powell, Lake, res., U.S. F5 151
Powell, Mount, mtn., Co., U.S. B4 113
Powell, Mount, mtn., N.M., U.S. B1 138
Powell Butte, Or., U.S. C5 144
Powell Mountain, mtn., U.S. C10 149
Powell Park, reg., Co., U.S. A2 113
Powell River, B.C., Can. E5 99
Powell's Crossroads, Al., U.S. A4 108
Powells Crossroads, Tn., U.S. D8 149
Powellton, W.V., U.S. C3 155
Power, Mt., U.S. C5 133
Power, co., Id., U.S. G5 119
Powers, Or., U.S. E2 144
Powers Lake, N.D., U.S. A3 141
Powerview, Man., Can. D3 100
Poweshiek, co., Ia., U.S. C5 122
Powhatan, Va., U.S. C5 153
Powhatan, co., Va., U.S. C5 153
Powhatan Point, Oh., U.S. C5 142
Powhattan, Ks., U.S. C8 123
Pownal, Vt., U.S. F2 152
Pownal Center, Vt., U.S. F2 152
Powys, co., Wales, U.K. I10 8
Poxoréo, Braz. C1 79
Poyang Hu, l., China F5 34
Poyen, Ar., U.S. C3 111
Poygan, Lake, l., Wi., U.S. D5 156
Poynette, Wi., U.S. E4 156
Poynor, Mo., U.S. E7 132
Poy Sippi, Wi., U.S. D4 156
Požarevac, Yugo. E5 20
Poza Rica, Mex. G11 90
Poznań, Pol. C16 10
Pozo Almonte, Chile I7 82
Pozoblanco, Spain G7 16
Pozo Colorado, Para. B9 80
Pozo del Molle, Arg. G7 80
Pozo del Tigre, Arg. C8 80
Pozo Hondo, Arg. D6 80
Pozo Negro, Spain o27 17b
Pozo Redondo Mountains, mts., Az., U.S. E3 110
Pozuelo de Alarcón, Spain E8 16
Pozuelos, Ven. B10 84
Pozuelos, Laguna, l., Arg. B6 80
Pozuzo, Peru D4 82
Pozuzo, stm., Peru C4 82
Pozzallo, Italy M9 18
Pozzuoli, Italy I9 18
Prachin Buri, Thai. G6 40
Prachuap Khiri Khan, Thai. I5 40
Praco, Al., U.S. f6 108
Pradera, Col. F4 84
Prades, Fr. J9 14
Prado, Braz. D9 79
Prado Flood Control Basin, Ca., U.S. n13 112
Prados, Braz. F6 79
Prague see Praha, Czech Rep. E14 10
Prague, Ne., U.S. C9 134
Prague, Ok., U.S. B5 143
Praha (Prague), Czech Rep. E14 10
Prahova, co., Rom. D10 20
Praia, C.V. m17 64a
Praia Grande, Braz. E14 80
Prainha Nova, Braz. B11 82
Prairie, Ms., U.S. B5 131
Prairie, co., Ar., U.S. C4 111
Prairie, co., Mt., U.S. D11 133
Prairie, stm., Mn., U.S. C5 130
Prairie, stm., Wi., U.S. C4 156
Prairie Bayou, stm., Ar., U.S. g7 111
Prairie City, Il., U.S. C3 120
Prairie City, Ia., U.S. C4 122
Prairie City, Or., U.S. C8 144
Prairie Creek, In., U.S. F3 121
Prairie Creek Reservoir, res., In., U.S. D7 121
Prairie Dog Creek, stm., U.S. C3 123
Prairie du Chien, Wi., U.S. E2 156
Prairie Du Rocher, Il., U.S. E3 120
Prairie du Sac, Wi., U.S. E4 156
Prairie Farm, Wi., U.S. C2 156
Prairie Grove, Ar., U.S. B1 111
Prairie Home, Mo., U.S. C5 132
Prairie River, Sask., Can. E4 105
Prairies, Rivière des, stm., Que., Can. p19 104
Prairieton, In., U.S. F3 121
Prairie View, Ar., U.S. B2 111
Prairie View, Ks., U.S. C4 123
Prairie View, Tx., U.S. D5 150
Prairie Village, Ks., U.S. m16 123
Prairieville, La., U.S. h10 125
Prampram, Ghana I10 64
Pran Buri, Thai. H5 40
Praslin Island, i., Sey. B11 58
Prata, Braz. E4 79
Prata, Rio da, stm., Braz. D5 79
Prata, Rio da, stm., Braz. E4 79
Pratāpgarh, India H6 44
Pratápolis, Braz. F5 79
Pratas Island see Tungsha Tao, i., Tai. G10 30
Prater Mountain, mtn., Wy., U.S. C2 157
Pratinha, Braz. E5 79
Prato, Italy F6 18
Pratt, Ks., U.S. E5 123
Pratt, co., Ks., U.S. E5 123
Prattsburg, N.Y., U.S. C3 139
Prattsville, Ar., U.S. C3 111
Prattville, Al., U.S. C3 108
Pratudão, stm., Braz. B6 79
Pravdinsk, Russia G4 22
Pravdinsk, Russia E26 22
Pravdinskij, Russia E20 22
Praya, Indon. G6 38
Pr'aža, Russia K23 6
Preble, In., U.S. C7 121
Preble, co., Oh., U.S. C1 142
Prečistoje, Russia C23 22
Prečistoje, Russia F15 22
Preda, Switz. E12 13
Predazzo, Italy C6 18
Predeal, Rom. D9 20
Predeşti, Rom. E7 20
Predlitz [-Turrach], Aus. H13 10
Preeceville, Sask., Can. F4 105
Pré-en-Pail, Fr. D6 14
Preetz, Ger. A10 10
Pregarten, Aus. G14 10
Pregol'a, stm., Russia G4 22
Pregonero, Ven. C7 84
Preila, Lith. F4 22
Preiļi, Lat. E9 22
Prelate, Sask., Can. G1 105
Premnitz, Ger. C12 10
Premont, Tx., U.S. F3 150
Prenter, W.V., U.S. C3 155
Prentice, Wi., U.S. C3 156
Prentiss, Ms., U.S. D4 131
Prentiss, co., Ms., U.S. A5 131
Prenzlau, Ger. B13 10
Preparis Island, i., Mya. G2 40
Preparis North Channel, strt., Mya. G3 40
Preparis South Channel, strt., Mya. G3 40
Přerov, Czech Rep. F17 10
Prescott, Ont., Can. C9 103
Prescott, Az., U.S. C3 110
Prescott, Ar., U.S. D2 111
Prescott, Ia., U.S. C3 122
Prescott, Ks., U.S. D9 123
Prescott, Mi., U.S. D7 129
Prescott, Wa., U.S. C7 154
Prescott, Wi., U.S. D1 156
Preševo, Yugo. G5 20
Presho, S.D., U.S. D5 148
Presidencia de la Plaza, Arg. D9 80
Presidencia Roca, Arg. D9 80
Presidencia Roque Sáenz Peña, Arg. D8 80
Presidente Epitácio, Braz. F2 79
Presidente Getúlio, Braz. D14 80
Presidente Hayes, dept., Para. C9 80
Presidente Olegário, Braz. E5 79
Presidente Prudente, Braz. G3 79
Presidente Venceslau, Braz. F3 79
Presidential Range, mts., N.H., U.S. B4 136
Presidents Island, i., Tn., U.S. e8 149
Presidio, Tx., U.S. p12 150
Presidio, co., Tx., U.S. o12 150
Presidio, stm., Mex. F7 90
Presidio of San Francisco, mil., Ca., U.S. h8 112
Prešov, Slvk. F21 10
Prespa, Lake, l., Eur. I5 20
Presque Isle, Me., U.S. B5 126
Presque Isle, co., Mi., U.S. C6 129
Preston, Eng., U.K. H11 8
Preston, Ga., U.S. D2 117
Preston, Id., U.S. G7 119
Preston, Ia., U.S. B7 122
Preston, Ks., U.S. E5 123
Preston, Ky., U.S. B6 124
Preston, Md., U.S. C6 127
Preston, Mn., U.S. G6 130
Preston, Ok., U.S. B6 143
Preston, Wa., U.S. e12 154
Preston, co., W.V., U.S. B5 155
Preston Peak, mtn., Ca., U.S. B2 112
Prestonsburg, Ky., U.S. C7 124
Prestonville, Ky., U.S. B4 124
Prestwick, Scot., U.K. F9 8
Presumpscot, stm., Me., U.S. g7 126
Preto, stm., Braz. F4 79
Preto, stm., Braz. E3 79
Preto, stm., Braz. D5 79
Preto, stm., Braz. B4 79
Preto, stm., Braz. C10 82
Preto, stm., Braz. H10 84
Preto do Igapó-açu, stm., Braz. J12 84
Pretoria, S. Afr. E9 66
Pretoria-Witwatersrand-Vereeniging (P.W.V.), prov., S. Afr. F9 66
Prettyboy Reservoir, res., Md., U.S. A4 127
Pretty Prairie, Ks., U.S. E5 123
Préveza, Grc. K4 20
Prewitt, N.M., U.S. B1 138
Prewitt Reservoir, res., Co., U.S. A7 113
Prey Vêng, Camb. I8 40
Pribilof Islands, is., Ak., U.S. D5 109
Priboj, Yugo. F3 20
Příbram, Czech Rep. F14 10
Price, Tx., U.S. C5 150
Price, Ut., U.S. D5 151
Price, co., Wi., U.S. C3 156
Price, stm., Ut., U.S. D5 151
Price Inlet, b., S.C., U.S. k12 147
Priceville, Ont., Can. C4 103
Priceville, Al., U.S. A3 108
Prichard, Al., U.S. E1 108
Prichard, W.V., U.S. C2 155
Priego de Córdoba, Spain H7 16
Priekule, Lat. E4 22
Priekule, Lith. F4 22
Prienai, Lith. G6 22
Prieska, S. Afr. G6 66
Priest Lake, l., Id., U.S. A2 119
Priest Rapids Dam, Wa., U.S. C6 154
Priest Rapids Lake, res., Wa., U.S. C6 154
Priest River, Id., U.S. A2 119
Prievidza, Slvk. G18 10
Prijedor, Bos. E11 18
Prijutovo, Russia G8 26
Prikaspijskaja nizmennost', pl. H7 26
Prilep, Mac. H5 20
Priluki, Ukr. G4 26
Prim, Point, c., P.E.I., Can. C6 101
Primate, Sask., Can. E1 105
Primeiro de Maio, Braz. G3 79
Primero, stm., Arg. F7 80
Primghar, Ia., U.S. A2 122
Primorje [Warnicken], Russia G3 22
Primorsk, Russia G3 22
Primorsk, Russia A11 22
Primrose, R.I., U.S. B3 146
Prince, Sask., Can. E1 105
Prince, Lake, res., Va., U.S. k14 153
Prince Albert, Sask., Can. D3 105
Prince Albert, S. Afr. I6 66
Prince Albert Mountains, mts., Ant. C8 73
Prince Albert National Park, Sask., Can. C2 105
Prince Albert Sound, strt., N.W. Ter., Can. B9 96
Prince Charles Island, i., N.W. Ter., Can. C17 96
Prince Charles Mountains, mts., Ant. C5 73
Prince Edward, co., Va., U.S. C4 153
Prince Edward Island, prov., Can. C6 101
Prince Edward Island National Park, P.E.I., Can. C6 101
Prince Edward Islands, is., S. Afr. M7 158
Prince Frederick, Md., U.S. C4 127
Prince George, B.C., Can. C6 99
Prince George, co., Va., U.S. C5 153
Prince Georges, co., Md., U.S. C4 127
Prince of Wales, Cape, c., Ak., U.S. B6 109
Prince of Wales Island, i., Austl. B8 68
Prince of Wales Island, i., N.W. Ter., Can. B13 96
Prince of Wales Island, i., Ak., U.S. n23 109
Prince of Wales Strait, strt., N.W. Ter., Can. B9 96
Prince Olav Coast, Ant. B4 73
Prince Patrick Island, i., N.W. Ter., Can. B8 86
Prince Regent Inlet, b., N.W. Ter., Can. B14 96
Prince Rupert, B.C., Can. B2 99
Princes Lakes, In., U.S. F5 121
Princess Anne, Md., U.S. D6 127
Princess Astrid Coast, Ant. C3 73
Princess Martha Coast, Ant. C2 73
Princess Ragnhild Coast, Ant. C3 73
Princess Royal Channel, strt., B.C., Can. C3 99
Princess Royal Island, i., B.C., Can. C3 99
Princes Town, Trin. I14 94
Princeton, B.C., Can. E7 99
Princeton, Newf., Can. D5 102
Princeton, Ont., Can. D4 103
Princeton, Al., U.S. A3 108
Princeton, Ca., U.S. C2 112
Princeton, Fl., U.S. G6 116
Princeton, Id., U.S. C2 119
Princeton, Il., U.S. B4 120
Princeton, In., U.S. H2 121
Princeton, Ia., U.S. C7 122
Princeton, Ks., U.S. D8 123
Princeton, Ky., U.S. C2 124
Princeton, Me., U.S. C5 126
Princeton, Ma., U.S. B4 128
Princeton, Mn., U.S. E5 130
Princeton, Mo., U.S. A4 132
Princeton, N.J., U.S. C3 137
Princeton, N.C., U.S. B4 140
Princeton, W.V., U.S. D3 155
Princeton, Wi., U.S. E4 156
Princeton, Mount, mtn., Co., U.S. C4 113
Princeton Junction, N.J., U.S. C3 137
Princeville, Que., Can. C6 104
Princeville, Il., U.S. C4 120
Princeville, N.C., U.S. B5 140
Prince William, co., Va., U.S. B5 153
Prince William Sound, strt., Ak., U.S. g18 109
Príncipe, i., S. Tom./P. A1 58
Principe Channel, strt., B.C., Can. C3 99
Príncipe da Beira, Braz. E9 82
Prineville, Or., U.S. C6 144
Prineville Reservoir, res., Or., U.S. C6 144
Pringle, S.D., U.S. D2 148
Prinsburg, Mn., U.S. F3 130
Prinzapolka, Nic. D11 92
Prinzapolka, stm., Nic. D11 92
Prior, Cabo, c., Spain B3 16
Prior Lake, Mn., U.S. F5 130
Prioz'orsk, Russia K22 6
Prip'at', stm., Eur. G3 26
Pripet Marshes see Polesje, reg., Eur. G3 26
Priština, Yugo. G5 20
Pritchards Island, i., S.C., U.S. G6 147
Pritchett, Co., U.S. D8 113
Pritzwalk, Ger. B12 10
Privas, Fr. H11 14
Priverno, Italy H8 18
Privolžsk, Russia D24 22
Privolžskaja vozvyšennost', plat., Russia G7 26
Privolžskij, Russia G7 26
Prizren, Yugo. G4 20
Prizzi, Italy L8 18
Prnjavor, Bos. E12 18
Probolinggo, Indon. j16 39a
Probstzella, Ger. E11 10
Procter, B.C., Can. E9 99
Proctor, Mn., U.S. D6 130
Proctor, Vt., U.S. D2 152
Proctor Lake, res., Tx., U.S. C3 150
Proctorsville, Vt., U.S. E3 152
Proctorville, Oh., U.S. D3 142
Proddatūr, India E5 46
Progreso, Mex. G15 90
Progreso, Ur. H10 80
Prokopjevsk, Russia G9 28
Prokuplje, Yugo. F5 20
Proletarij, Russia C14 22
Proletarskij, Russia F20 22
Prome (Pyè), Mya. E3 40
Promissão, Braz. F4 79
Promontogno, Switz. F12 13
Promontory Mountains, mts., Ut., U.S. B3 151
Pronsk, Russia G22 22
Prophetstown, Il., U.S. B4 120
Propriá, Braz. F11 76
Propriano, Fr. m23 15a
Proserpine, Austl. C8 70
Prospect, N.S., Can. E6 101
Prospect, Ct., U.S. C4 114
Prospect, In., U.S. G4 121
Prospect, Ky., U.S. g11 124
Prospect, Oh., U.S. B2 142
Prospect, Or., U.S. E4 144
Prospect, Pa., U.S. E1 145
Prospect, Tn., U.S. B4 149
Prospect, Va., U.S. C4 153
Prospect Harbor, Me., U.S. D4 126
Prospect Hill, mtn., Or., U.S. k11 144
Prospect Hill, hill, Ma., U.S. D6 128
Prospect Hill, hill, Ma., U.S. g10 128
Prospect Park, N.J., U.S. B4 137
Prospect Park, Pa., U.S. p20 145
Prosperity, S.C., U.S. C4 147
Prosperity, W.V., U.S. n13 155
Prosser, Wa., U.S. C6 154
Prostějov, Czech Rep. F17 10
Proston, Austl. F9 70
Protection, Ks., U.S. E4 123
Protem, S. Afr. J5 66
Protivin, Ia., U.S. A5 122
Proton Station, Ont., Can. C4 103
Protville, Tun. M5 18
Provadija, Bul. F11 20
Provencal, La., U.S. C2 125
Provence, hist. reg., Fr. I13 14
Providence, Ky., U.S. C2 124
Providence, R.I., U.S. C4 146
Providence, Ut., U.S. B4 151
Providence, co., R.I., U.S. C2 146
Providence, stm., R.I., U.S. C5 146
Providence, Cape, c., N.Z. F1 72
Providence Bay, Ont., Can. B2 103
Providence Forge, Va., U.S. C5 153
Providence Island, i., Sey. C10 58
Providence Point, c., R.I., U.S. D5 146
Providencia, Isla de, i., Col. H4 94
Providenciales, i., T./C. Is. D8 94
Providenija, Russia E29 28
Province Lake, l., N.H., U.S. C5 136
Provincetown, Ma., U.S. B7 128
Provins, Fr. D10 14
Provo, S.D., U.S. D2 148
Provo, Ut., U.S. C4 151
Provo, stm., Ut., U.S. C4 151
Provost, Alta., Can. C5 98
Prowers, co., Co., U.S. D8 113
Pruden, Tn., U.S. C10 149

Name — Map Ref. — Page

Prudence Island, i., R.I., U.S. E5 146
Prudentópolis, Braz. C13 30
Prudenville, Mi., U.S. D6 129
Prudhoe Bay, b., Ak., U.S. A10 139
Prudhoe Island, i., Austl. C8 70
Prud'homme, Sask., Can. E3 105
Prudnik, Pol. E17 10
Prudy, Bela. H9 22
Prue, Ok., U.S. A5 143
Prüm, Ger. E6 10
Pruszków, Pol. C20 10
Prut, stm., Eur. D12 20
Prutz, Aus. H10 10
Pružany, Bela. I7 22
Prydz Bay, b., Ant. B5 73
Pryor, Mt., U.S. E8 133
Pryor, Ok., U.S. A6 143
Pryor Mountains, mts., Mt., U.S. E8 133
Przasnysz, Pol. B20 10
Przedbórz, Pol. D19 10
Przemyśl, Pol. F22 10
Przeworsk, Pol. E22 10
Pskov, Russia D11 22
Pskovskoje ozero, l., Eur. C11 22
Pszczyna, Pol. F18 10
Ptarmigan, Cape, c., N.W. Ter., Can. B9 96
Ptolemaís, Grc. I5 20
Ptuj, Slvn. C10 18
Puán, Arg. I7 80
Puan, S. Kor. H14 32
Pucallpa, Peru C4 82
Pucara, Bol. H9 82
Pucarani, Bol. G7 82
Puccha, stm., Peru C3 82
Pučež, Russia E26 22
Pucheng, China H7 34
Pucheta, Arg. E10 80
Puchoviči, Bela. H11 22
Puck, Pol. A18 10
Puckaway Lake, l., Wi., U.S. E4 156
Puckett, Ms., U.S. C4 131
Pudož, Russia E5 26
Puduari, stm., Braz. I12 84
Puduhe, China B7 40
Pudukkottai, India G5 46
Puebla, state, Mex. H10 90
Puebla [de Zaragoza], Mex. H10 90
Pueblo, Co., U.S. C6 113
Pueblo, co., Co., U.S. C6 113
Pueblo Colorado Wash, val., Az., U.S. B6 110
Pueblo Libertador, Arg. F9 80
Pueblo Mountain, mtn., Or., U.S. E8 144
Pueblo Mountains, mts., Or., U.S. E8 144
Pueblo Nuevo, Col. C5 84
Pueblo Nuevo, Nic. D8 92
Pueblo Nuevo, Ven. B8 84
Pueblo Nuevo Tiquisate, Guat. C3 92
Pueblo of Acoma, N.M., U.S. C2 138
Pueblo Reservoir, res., Co., U.S. C6 113
Puebloviejo, Ec. H3 84
Pueblo Viejo, Laguna, b., Mex. F11 90
Pueblo Yaqui, Mex. D4 90
Puelches, Arg. J6 80
Puente Alto, Chile G3 80
Puente-Genil, Spain H7 16
Pueo Point, c., Hi., U.S. B1 118
Puerco, stm., U.S. C6 110
Puerco, Rio, stm., N.M., U.S. B2 138
Puerto Acosta, Bol. F7 82
Puerto Adela, Para. C11 80
Puerto Aisén, Chile F2 78
Puerto Alegre, Bol. E11 82
Puerto Ángel, Mex. J11 90
Puerto Arista, Mex. J13 90
Puerto Armuelles, Pan. C1 84
Puerto Asís, Col. G4 84
Puerto Ayacucho, Ven. E9 84
Puerto Bahía Negra, Para. I12 82
Puerto Baquerizo Moreno, Ec. m16 84a
Puerto Barrios, Guat. B6 92
Puerto Bermejo, Arg. D9 80
Puerto Bermúdez, Peru D4 82
Puerto Berrío, Col. D5 84
Puerto Bolívar, Ec. I3 84
Puerto Boyacá, Col. E5 84
Puerto Busch, Bol. I13 82
Puerto Cabello, Ven. B8 84
Puerto Cabezas, Nic. C11 92
Puerto Carreño, Col. D9 84
Puerto Casado, Para. B10 80
Puerto Castilla, Hond. A8 92
Puerto Chicama, Peru B2 82
Puerto Colombia, Col. B5 84
Puerto Cortés, Hond. B7 92
Puerto Cumarebo, Ven. B8 84
Puerto de Eten, Peru B2 82
Puerto de la Cruz, Spain o24 17b
Puerto Delicia, Arg. D11 80
Puerto de Lomas, Peru F4 82
Puerto Delón, Hond. C9 92
Puerto del Rosario, Spain o27 17b
Puerto de Luna, N.M., U.S. C5 138
Puerto El Triunfo, El Sal. D6 92
Puerto Escondido, Mex. J11 90
Puerto Esperanza, Arg. D11 80
Puerto Fonciere, Para. B10 80
Puerto Francisco de Orellana, Ec. H4 84
Puerto Guaraní, Para. I13 82
Puerto Heath, Bol. E7 82
Puerto Iguazú, Arg. C11 80
Puerto Inírida, Col. F9 84
Puerto Jiménez, C.R. I11 92
Puerto Juárez, Mex. G16 90
Puerto la Cruz, Ven. B10 84
Puerto Leda, Para. I12 82
Puerto Leguízamo, Col. H5 84
Puerto Lempira, Hond. B11 92
Puerto Libertad, Arg. C11 80
Puerto Libertad, Mex. C3 90
Puerto Limón, Col. F6 84
Puerto Limon, C.R. A2 76
Puerto Limón, C.R. G11 92
Puertollano, Spain G7 16
Puerto López, Col. E6 84
Puerto Madero, Mex. C2 92
Puerto Maldonado, Peru E7 82
Puerto Manatí, Cuba D6 94
Puerto Mihanovich, Para. I13 82
Puerto Montt, Chile E2 78
Puerto Morazán, Nic. E7 92
Puerto Morelos, Mex. G16 90
Puerto Nariño, Col. E9 84
Puerto Natales, Chile G2 78
Puerto Padre, Cuba D6 94
Puerto Páez, Ven. D9 84
Puerto Peñasco, Mex. B3 90
Puerto Pilón, Pan. H15 92
Puerto Pinasco, Para. B10 80
Puerto Piray, Arg. D11 80
Puerto Píritu, Ven. B10 84
Puerto Plata, Dom. Rep. E9 94
Puerto Portillo, Peru C5 82
Puerto Princesa, Phil. D6 38
Puerto Real, Spain I5 16
Puerto Rico, Arg. D11 80
Puerto Rico, Bol. D8 82
Puerto Rico, Col. G5 84
Puerto Rico, dep., N.A. E11 94
Puerto Rico Trench G13 86
Puerto Rondón, Col. D7 84
Puerto Saavedra, Chile J2 80
Puerto Salgar, Col. E5 84
Puerto Sandino, Nic. E8 92
Puerto San José, Guat. D4 92
Puerto San Julián, Arg. F3 78
Puerto Santa Cruz, Arg. G3 78
Puerto Sastre, Para. B10 80
Puerto Siles, Bol. E9 82
Puerto Suarez, Bol. H13 82
Puerto Supe, Peru D3 82
Puerto Tejada, Col. F4 84
Puerto Tolosa, Col. H5 84
Puerto Umbría, Col. G4 84
Puerto Vallarta, Mex. G7 90
Puerto Varas, Chile E2 78
Puerto Victoria, Arg. D11 80
Puerto Victoria, Peru C4 82
Puerto Viejo, C.R. G11 92
Puerto Viejo, C.R. H12 92
Puerto Villamil, Ec. j13 84a
Puerto Villamizar, Col. C6 84
Puerto Villarroel, Bol. G9 82
Puerto Wilches, Col. D6 84
Puerto Ybapobó, Para. B10 80
Pueyrredón, Lago (Lago Cochrane), l., S.A. F2 78
Pugačov, Russia G7 26
Puget Sound, strt., Wa., U.S. B3 154
Puget Sound Naval Shipyard, mil., Wa., U.S. e10 154
Puget-Théniers, Fr. I13 14
Puglia, prov., Italy I11 18
Pugwash, N.S., Can. D6 101
Puhi, Hi., U.S. B2 118
Puica, Peru F5 82
Puigcerdà, Spain C13 16
Puigmal, mtn., Eur. C14 16
Puinahua, Canal de, mth., Peru A4 82
Pujehun, S.L. H4 64
Pujiang, China F8 34
Pujilí, Ec. H3 84
Pukalani, Hi., U.S. C5 118
Pukaskwa National Park, Ont., Can. o18 103
Pukch'ang, N. Kor. D14 32
Pukch'ŏng, N. Kor. C16 32
Pukeashun Mountain, mtn., B.C., Can. D8 99
Pukekohe, N.Z. B5 72
Pukhan-gang, stm., Asia F15 32
Pukou, China C7 34
Puksoozero, Russia J27 6
Pukwana, S.D., U.S. D6 148
Pula, Cro. E8 18
Pulacayo, Bol. I8 82
Púlar, Cerro, mtn., Chile C4 80
Pulaski, Ga., U.S. D5 117
Pulaski, Il., U.S. F4 120
Pulaski, In., U.S. C4 121
Pulaski, Ia., U.S. D5 122
Pulaski, N.Y., U.S. B4 139
Pulaski, Tn., U.S. B4 149
Pulaski, Va., U.S. C2 153
Pulaski, Wi., U.S. D5 156
Pulaski, co., Ar., U.S. C3 111
Pulaski, co., Ga., U.S. D3 117
Pulaski, co., Il., U.S. F4 120
Pulaski, co., In., U.S. B4 121
Pulaski, co., Ky., U.S. C5 124
Pulaski, co., Mo., U.S. D5 132
Pulaski, co., Va., U.S. C2 153
Puławy, Pol. D21 10
Pulgaon, India B5 46
Puli, Tai. L9 34
Puliyangudi, India H4 46
Pullman, Mi., U.S. F4 129
Pullman, Wa., U.S. C8 154
Púllo, Peru F5 82
Pully, Switz. E6 13
Pulog, Mount, mtn., Phil. m19 39b
Pulsano, Italy I12 18
Pultusk, Pol. C21 10
Pumphrey, Md., U.S. h11 127
Pumpkin Buttes, mtn., Wy., U.S. C7 157
Pumpkin Creek, stm., Mt., U.S. E11 133
Pumpkin Creek, stm., Ne., U.S. C2 134
Puná, Isla, i., Ec. I2 84
Punakha, Bhu. G13 44
Punata, Bol. G9 82
Pūnch, India D6 44
Punduga, Russia A23 22
Pune (Poona), India C2 46
Púngoè, stm., Afr. B11 66
Pungo Lake, l., N.C., U.S. B6 140
P'ungsan, N. Kor. C16 32
Punia, Zaire B5 58
Punilla, Sierra de la, mts., Arg. E4 80
Puning, China L5 34
Punitaqui, Chile C2 78
Punitaqui, Chile F3 80
Punjab, state, India E6 44
Punnichy, Sask., Can. F3 105
Puno, Peru F6 82
Puno, dept., Peru F6 82
Punta, Cerro de, mtn., P.R. E11 94
Punta Alta, Arg. J7 80
Punta Arenas, Chile G2 78
Punta Banda, Cabo, c., Mex. B1 90
Punta Cardón, Ven. B7 84
Punta Colnett, Mex. B1 90
Punta de Bombón, Peru G6 82
Punta de Díaz, Chile E3 80
Punta del Cobre, Chile D3 80
Punta del Este, Ur. H11 80
Punta de los Llanos, Arg. F5 80
Punta de Mata, Ven. C11 84
Punta de Piedras, Ven. B10 84
Punta Gorda, Belize I15 90
Punta Gorda, Nic. F11 92
Punta Gorda, Fl., U.S. F4 116
Punta Gorda, stm., Nic. F11 92
Punta Gorda, Bahía de, b., Nic. F11 92
Punta Negra, Salar de, pl., Chile C4 80
Punta Prieta, Mex. C2 90
Puntarenas, C.R. H10 92
Puntarenas, prov., C.R. I11 92
Puntas del Sauce, Ur. G10 80
Punto Fijo, Ven. B7 84
Punxsutawney, Pa., U.S. E4 145
Puolanka, Fin. I20 6
Puqi, China F9 30
Puquio, Peru F4 82
Pur, stm., Russia D7 28
Puracé, Volcán, vol., Col. F4 84
Purcell, Mo., U.S. D3 132
Purcell, Ok., U.S. B4 143
Purcellville, Va., U.S. A5 153
Purdham Hill, mtn., Ar., U.S. h10 111
Purdin, Mo., U.S. B4 132
Purdy, Mo., U.S. E4 132
Purgatoire, stm., Co., U.S. D7 113
Purgatoire Peak, mtn., Co., U.S. D5 113
Puri, India K11 44
Purificación, Col. F5 84
Purificación, Mex. H7 90
Purificación, stm., Mex. E10 90
Purikari neem, c., Est. B8 22
Purmerend, Neth. C6 12
Pūrnia, India H12 44
Purple Springs, Alta., Can. E5 98
Purros, Nmb. B1 66
Pursglove, W.V., U.S. B4 155
Puruí, stm., Braz. H8 84
Puruliya, India I12 44
Puruni, stm., Guy. D13 84
Purus (Purús), stm., S.A. D6 76
Purvis, Ms., U.S. D4 131
Purwakarta, Indon. j13 39a
Purwokerto, Indon. j13 39a
Puryear, Tn., U.S. A3 149
Pusan, S. Kor. H17 32
Pushaw Lake, l., Me., U.S. D4 126
Pushkar, India G6 44
Pushmataha, Al., U.S. C1 108
Pushmataha, co., Ok., U.S. C6 143
Puškin, Russia B13 22
Puškino, Russia E20 22
Puškinskije Gory, Russia D11 22
Püspökladány, Hung. H21 10
Püssi, Est. B10 22
Pustoška, Russia E12 22
Putaendo, Chile G3 80
Putao, Mya. G17 44
Put'atino, Russia G24 22
Putian, China J8 34
Putina, Peru F7 82
Puting, Tanjung, c., Indon. F5 38
Putnam, Al., U.S. C1 108
Putnam, Ct., U.S. B8 114
Putnam, co., Fl., U.S. C5 116
Putnam, co., Ga., U.S. C3 117
Putnam, co., Il., U.S. B4 120
Putnam, co., In., U.S. E4 121
Putnam, co., Mo., U.S. A4 132
Putnam, co., N.Y., U.S. D7 139
Putnam, co., Oh., U.S. B1 142
Putnam, co., Tn., U.S. C8 149
Putnam, co., W.V., U.S. C3 155
Putnamville, In., U.S. E4 121
Putney, Ga., U.S. E2 117
Putney, Vt., U.S. F3 152
Putorana, plato, plat., Russia D17 26
Putre, Chile H7 82
Puttalam, Sri L. H5 46
Puttgarden, Ger. A11 10
Putú, Chile H2 80
Putumayo, ter., Col. G4 84
Putumayo (Içá), stm., S.A. I7 84
Putuo, China F11 34
Putyla, Ukr. A9 20
Puukohola Heiau National Historic Site, hist., Hi., U.S. D6 118
Puukolii, Hi., U.S. C5 118
Puula, l., Fin. K20 6
Puumala, Fin. K21 6
Puunene, Hi., U.S. C5 118
Puurmani, Est. C9 22
Puxi, China J8 34
Puxico, Mo., U.S. E7 132
Puyallup, Wa., U.S. B3 154
Puyallup, stm., Wa., U.S. C3 154
Puyang, China H2 32
Puyango (Tumbes), stm., S.A. I3 84
Puy-de-Dôme, dept., Fr. G10 14
Puylaurens, Fr. I9 14
Puyo, Ec. H4 84
Puyŏ, S. Kor. G14 32
Pweto, Zaire C5 58
P.W.V. see Pretoria-Witwatersrand-Vereeniging, prov., S. Afr. F9 66
Pyapon, Mya. F3 40
Pyatt, Ar., U.S. A3 111
Pyaye, Mya. E3 40
Pyhäjoki, Fin. I19 6
Pyhäselkä, l., Fin. J21 6
Pyinmana, Mya. E4 40
Pyles Fork, stm., W.V., U.S. h10 155
Pymatuning Reservoir, res., U.S. C1 145
Pyŏktong, N. Kor. C13 32
Pyŏlch'ang-ni, N. Kor. D14 32
P'yŏngch'ang, S. Kor. F16 32
P'yŏngsan, N. Kor. E14 32
P'yŏngt'aek, S. Kor. F15 32
P'yŏngyang, N. Kor. D13 32
Pyramid Lake, l., Nv., U.S. C2 135
Pyramid Lake Indian Reservation, Nv., U.S. D2 135
Pyramid Mountains, mts., N.M., U.S. E1 138
Pyramid Peak, mtn., N.M., U.S. E1 138
Pyramid Peak, mtn., Wy., U.S. C2 157
Pyrenees, mts., Eur. C13 16
Pyrénées-Atlantiques, dept., Fr. I6 14
Pyrénées-Orientales, dept., Fr. J9 14
Pyrmont, In., U.S. D4 121
Pyrzyce, Pol. B14 10
Pytalovo, Russia D10 22
Pyu, Mya. E4 40
Pyuntaza, Mya. F4 40

Q

Qacentina (Constantine), Alg. B14 62
Qā'emshahr, Iran C12 48
Qā'en, Iran E15 48
Qaidam Pendi, China B16 44
Qalāt, Afg. D2 44
Qal'at ash-Shaqīf (Beaufort Castle), hist., Leb. B5 50
Qal'at Bīshah, Sau. Ar. D3 47
Qal'at Şāliḩ, Iraq F9 48
Qal'at Sukkar, Iraq F9 48
Qal'eh-ye Now, Afg. C2 44
Qallābāt, Sud. K9 60
Qalqīlya, W.B. D3 50
Qamar, Ghubbat al-, b., Yemen F8 47
Qamdo, China E6 30
Qānā, Leb. B4 50
Qanā, Sau. Ar. H6 48
Qandahār, Afg. E1 44
Qandala, Som. F10 56
Qantur, Sud. M3 60
Qārah, Sau. Ar. G6 48
Qardho, Som. G10 56
Qarqan, stm., China D4 30
Qārūn, Birkat, l., Egypt C6 60
Qāsh, Nahr al- (Gash), stm., Afr. E8 56
Qaşr al-Farāfirah, Egypt D4 60
Qasr el-Boukhari, Alg. C12 62
Qaşr-e Shīrīn, Iraq D8 48
Qa'ṭabah, Yemen H4 47
Qaṭanā, Syria B6 50
Qatar (Qaṭar), ctry., Asia D5 42
Qattara Depression see Qaṭṭārah, Munkhafaḑ al-, depr., Egypt B4 60
Qaṭṭārah, Munkhafaḑ al- (Qattara Depression), depr., Egypt B4 60
Qazımämmäd, Azer. I7 26
Qazvīn, Iran C11 48
Qesari, Horbat (Cæsarea), hist., Isr. C3 50
Qeshm, Iran H14 48
Qeshm, Jazīreh-ye, i., Iran H13 48
Qetura, Isr. I4 50
Qezel Owzan, stm., Iran C10 48
Qianfang, China G5 34
Qianqi, China H9 34
Qianyang, China F9 30
Qiaogou, China C4 34
Qiddīsah Kātrīnā, Dayr al- (Monastery of Saint Catherine), Egypt G3 48
Qidong, China D10 34
Qidu, China E6 34
Qiemo, China A11 44
Qift (Coptos), Egypt D7 60
Qijiang, China F8 30
Qijiawan, China E3 34
Qila Lādgasht, Pak. H17 48
Qilian Shan, mtn., China D6 30
Qilian Shan, mts., China D6 30
Qimen, China J2 34
Qinā, Egypt D7 60
Qinā, Wādī, val., Egypt H2 48
Qingchengzi, China C11 32
Qingdao (Tsingtao), China G8 32
Qinghai (Tsinghai), prov., China D6 30
Qinghai Hu, l., China D7 30
Qinghezhen, China F5 32
Qingjiang, China G4 34
Qingjiang, China B8 34
Qinglian, China K1 34
Qinglong, China B8 40
Qingpu, China D10 34
Qingshan, China E3 34
Qingshui, stm., China D8 30
Qingshui, stm., China F8 30
Qingtang, China K2 34
Qingyang, China D8 30
Qingyangzhen, China D9 34
Qingyuan, China G8 30
Qingyuan, China L2 34
Qingzhou, China L5 34
Qinhuangdao (Chinwangtao), China D7 32
Qin Ling, mts., China E8 30
Qinzhou, China D10 40
Qionglai, China E7 30
Qiongzhong, China E10 40
Qiongzhou Haixia, strt., China D11 40
Qipanshan, China A5 32
Qiqian, China A11 30
Qiqihar (Tsitsihar), China B11 30
Qiryat Ata, Isr. C4 50
Qiryat Bialik, Isr. C4 50
Qiryat Gat, Isr. E3 50
Qiryat Mal'akhi, Isr. E3 50
Qiryat Motzkin, Isr. C4 50
Qiryat Ono, Isr. D3 50
Qiryat Shemona, Isr. B5 50
Qiryat Yam, Isr. C4 50
Qishn, Yemen G7 47
Qishon, stm., Asia C4 50
Qishuyan, China D9 34
Qitai, China C4 30
Qiyang, China A11 40
Qnadsa, Alg. E9 62
Qogir Feng (K2), mtn., Asia C7 44
Qom, Iran D11 48
Qomsheh, Iran E11 48
Qondūz, Afg. J11 26
Qondūz, stm., Afg. B3 44
Qonggyai, China F5 30
Qorveh, Iran D9 48
Quabbin Reservoir, res., Ma., U.S. B3 128
Quaco Head, c., N.B., Can. D4 101
Quaddick, Ct., U.S. B8 114
Quaddick Reservoir, res., Ct., U.S. B8 114
Quadros, Lagoa dos, b., Braz. E13 80
Quail Oaks, Va., U.S. n18 153
Quakenbrück, Ger. C7 10
Quaker City, Oh., U.S. C4 142
Quaker Hill, Ct., U.S. D7 114
Quakertown, Pa., U.S. F11 145
Qualicum Beach, B.C., Can. E5 99
Quanah, Tx., U.S. B3 150
Quangang, China G4 34
Quang Ngai, Viet. G10 40
Quang Trach, Viet. F9 40
Quannapowitt, Lake, l., Ma., U.S. f11 128
Quantico, Va., U.S. B5 153
Quantico Marine Corps Air Station, mil., Va., U.S. B5 153
Quanzhou (Chuanchou), China K7 34
Quapaw, Ok., U.S. A7 143
Qu'Appelle, Sask., Can. G4 105
Qu'Appelle, stm., Can. G4 105
Quaraí, Braz. F10 80
Quaraí, stm., S.A. F10 80
Quarryville, N.B., Can. C4 101
Quarryville, Ct., U.S. B6 114
Quarryville, Pa., U.S. G9 145
Quartu Sant'Elena, Italy J4 18
Quartz Mountain, mtn., Or., U.S. D4 144
Quartzsite, Az., U.S. D1 110
Quasqueton, Ia., U.S. B6 122
Quassapaug, Lake, l., Ct., U.S. C3 114
Quatsino Sound, strt., B.C., Can. D3 99
Quay, co., N.M., U.S. C6 138
Quba, Azer. I7 26
Qūchān, Iran C15 48
Queanbeyan, Austl. J8 70
Québec, Que., Can. C6 104
Quebec, prov., Can. C5 104
Quebra-Anzol, stm., Braz. E5 79
Quebracho, Ur. F10 80
Quechee, Vt., U.S. D4 152
Quechee Gorge, val., Vt., U.S. D4 152
Quedas, Moz. B11 66
Quedlinburg, Ger. D11 10
Queen, stm., R.I., U.S. E3 146
Queen Alexandra Range, mts., Ant. D8 73
Queen Annes, co., Md., U.S. B5 127
Queen Bess, Mount, mtn., B.C., Can. D5 99
Queen Charlotte, B.C., Can. C1 99
Queen Charlotte Islands, is., B.C., Can. C1 99
Queen Charlotte Mountains, mts., B.C., Can. C1 99
Queen Charlotte Sound, strt., B.C., Can. n17 99
Queen Charlotte Strait, strt., B.C., Can. D4 99
Queen City, Mo., U.S. A5 132
Queen City, Tx., U.S. C5 150
Queen Creek, Az., U.S. m9 110
Queen Elizabeth Islands, is., N.W. Ter., Can. B9 86
Queen Mary Coast, Ant. B6 73
Queen Maud Gulf, b., N.W. Ter., Can. C12 96
Queen Maud Land, reg., Ant. C3 73
Queen Maud Mountains, mts., Ant. D9 73
Queens, co., N.Y., U.S. E7 139
Queensborough, Ont., Can. C7 103
Queenscliff, Austl. L6 70
Queensland, Ga., U.S. E3 117
Queensland, state, Austl. D9 68
Queenstown, Austl. N6 70
Queenstown, N.B., Can. D3 101
Queenstown, Guy. D13 84
Queenstown, N.Z. F2 72
Queenstown, S. Afr. H8 66
Queenstown, Md., U.S. C5 127
Queets, Wa., U.S. B1 154
Queguay Grande, stm., Ur. G10 80
Queimados, Braz. G7 79
Quelimane, Moz. A13 66
Quemado, N.M., U.S. C1 138
Quemado, Tx., U.S. E2 150
Quemado, Punta de, c., Cuba D7 94
Quemado de Güines, Cuba C4 94
Quemoy see Chinmen Tao, i., Tai. K7 34
Quemú Quemú, Arg. I7 80
Quenemo, Ks., U.S. D8 123
Quepos, C.R. H10 92
Quequén, Arg. J9 80
Querary, stm., Col. G7 84
Quercy, hist. reg., Fr. H8 14
Querecotillo, Peru A1 82
Querétaro, Mex. G9 90
Querétaro, state, Mex. G10 90
Querobabi, Mex. B4 90
Quesada, C.R. G10 92
Quesada, Spain H8 16
Queshan, China C3 34
Quesnel, B.C., Can. C6 99
Quesnel, stm., B.C., Can. C6 99
Quesnel Lake, l., B.C., Can. C7 99
Questa, N.M., U.S. A4 138
Quetico Provincial Park, Ont., Can. o17 103
Quetta, Pak. E2 44
Quettehou, Fr. C5 14
Quetzaltenango, Guat. C3 92
Quetzaltenango, dept., Guat. C3 92
Quevedo, Ec. H3 84
Quezaltepeque, El Sal. D5 92
Quezaltepeque, Guat. C5 92
Quezon City, Phil. n19 39b
Qufu, China H5 32
Quibdó, Col. E4 84
Quiberon, Fr. E3 14
Quíbor, Ven. C8 84
Quiches, Peru C3 82
Quicksand Pond, l., R.I., U.S. E6 146
Quidnessett, R.I., U.S. E4 146
Quidnick, R.I., U.S. D3 146
Quidnick Reservoir, res., R.I., U.S. D2 146
Quiindy, Para. C10 80
Quila, Mex. E6 90
Quilalí, Nic. D8 92
Quilcene, Wa., U.S. B3 154
Quileute Indian Reservation, Wa., U.S. B1 154
Quilimarí, Chile G3 80
Quilino, Arg. F6 80
Quillabamba, Peru E5 82
Quillacollo, Bol. G8 82
Quillagua, Chile I7 82
Quillan, Fr. J9 14
Quill Lake, Sask., Can. E3 105
Quillota, Chile G3 80
Quilon, India H4 46
Quilpie, Austl. F6 70
Quilpué, Chile G3 80
Quimarí, Alto de, mtn., Col. C4 84
Quimbaya, Col. E5 84
Quimby, Ia., U.S. B2 122
Quime, Bol. G8 82
Quimilí, Arg. D7 80
Quimper, Fr. D2 14
Quimperlé, Fr. E3 14
Quinault, Wa., U.S. B2 154
Quinault, stm., Wa., U.S. B1 154
Quinault, Lake, l., Wa., U.S. B2 154
Quinault Indian Reservation, Wa., U.S. B1 154
Quince Mil, Peru E6 82
Quinches, Peru E3 82
Quincy, Ca., U.S. C3 112
Quincy, Fl., U.S. B2 116
Quincy, Il., U.S. D2 120
Quincy, In., U.S. F4 121
Quincy, Ky., U.S. B6 124
Quincy, Ma., U.S. B5 128
Quincy, Mi., U.S. G6 129
Quincy, Ms., U.S. B5 131
Quincy, Oh., U.S. B2 142
Quincy, Wa., U.S. B6 154
Quincy Bay, b., Ma., U.S. g12 128
Quindío, dept., Col. E5 84
Quinebaug, Ct., U.S. A8 114
Quinebaug, stm., Ct., U.S. C8 114
Quines, Arg. G6 80
Quinga, Moz. E8 58
Quinhagak, Ak., U.S. D7 109
Qui Nhon, Viet. H10 40
Quinlan, Tx., U.S. C4 150
Quinn, stm., Nv., U.S. B3 135
Quinn Canyon Range, mts., Nv., U.S. F6 135
Quinnesec, Mi., U.S. C3 129
Quinnipiac, stm., Ct., U.S. D4 114
Quintanar de la Orden, Spain F8 16
Quintana Roo, state, Mex. H15 90
Quinter, Ks., U.S. C3 123
Quintero, Chile G3 80
Quintin, Fr. D4 14
Quinto, stm., Arg. H6 80
Quinto de Noviembre, Presa, El Sal. D6 92
Quinton, Sask., Can. F3 105
Quinton, Ok., U.S. B6 143
Quinwood, W.V., U.S. C4 155
Quirauk Mountain, mtn., Md., U.S. A2 127
Quiriguá, hist., Guat. B5 92
Quirihue, Chile I2 80
Quirindi, Austl. H9 70
Quirinópolis, Braz. E3 79
Quiriquire, Ven. C11 84
Quiroga, Mex. H9 90
Quiroga, Spain C4 16
Quirós, Arg. E6 80
Quissanga, Moz. D8 58
Quitaque, Tx., U.S. B2 150
Quitilipi, Arg. D8 80
Quitman, Ar., U.S. B3 111
Quitman, Ga., U.S. F3 117
Quitman, Ms., U.S. C5 131
Quitman, Tx., U.S. C5 150
Quitman, co., Ga., U.S. E1 117
Quitman, co., Ms., U.S. A3 131
Quitman Mountains, mts., Tx., U.S. o12 150
Quito, Ec. H3 84
Quivilla, Peru C3 82
Quixadá, Braz. D11 76
Quixito, stm., Braz. J7 84
Qujiang, China K2 34
Qujing, China B7 40
Qulin, Mo., U.S. E7 132
Qumar, stm., China D5 30
Qumarlêb, China E6 30
Quonnipaug Lake, l., Ct., U.S. D5 114
Quonochontaug, R.I., U.S. G2 146
Quonochontaug Pond, l., R.I., U.S. G2 146
Quonset Point, c., R.I., U.S. E4 146
Qurayyāt, Oman C11 47
Qurdūd, Sud. L5 60
Qūş, Egypt E7 60
Quthing, Leso. H8 66
Quxi, China L5 34
Quxian, China G7 34
Quyquyó, Para. D10 80

Name — Map Ref. — Page

Quzhou, China G2 32

R

Raab (Rába), stm., Eur. H15 10
Raahe, Fin. I19 6
Raalte, Neth. D9 12
Ra'anana, Isr. D3 50
Raasiku, Est. B8 22
Raba, Indon. G6 38
Rába (Raab), stm., Eur. H17 10
Rabak, Sud. K7 60
Rabat (Victoria), Malta M9 18
Rabat, Mor. C7 62
Rabaul, Pap. N. Gui. k17 68a
Rabbit Creek, stm., S.D., U.S. B3 148
Rabbit Ears Pass, Co., U.S. A4 113
Rabbit Lake, Sask., Can. D2 105
Rābigh, Sau. Ar. C1 47
Rābigh, Sau. Ar. J5 48
Rabinal, Guat. B4 92
Rabka, Pol. F19 10
Rabkavi Banhatti, India D3 46
Râbnița (Rybnica), Mol. B13 20
Raboćeostrovsk, Russia I24 6
Rabun, Al., U.S. D2 108
Rabun, co., Ga., U.S. B3 117
Rabun Bald, mtn., Ga., U.S. B3 117
Rabyānah, Ṣaḥrā', des., Libya D5 56
Raccoon Creek, stm., Oh., U.S. D3 142
Raccourci Island, i., La., U.S. D4 125
Race, Cape, c., Newf., Can. E5 102
Raceland, Ky., U.S. B7 124
Raceland, La., U.S. E5 125
Race Point, c., Ma., U.S. B7 128
Race Pond, Ga., U.S. F4 117
Rach'a, Russia A13 22
Rach Gia, Viet. I8 40
Racibórz (Ratibor), Pol. E18 10
Racine, Mn., U.S. G6 130
Racine, Mo., U.S. E3 132
Racine, Oh., U.S. D4 142
Racine, W.V., U.S. C3 155
Racine, Wi., U.S. F6 156
Racine, co., Wi., U.S. F5 156
Racine Dam, U.S. C3 155
Ráckeve, Hung. H18 10
Rădăuți, Rom. B9 20
Radcliff, Ky., U.S. C4 124
Radcliffe, Ia., U.S. B4 122
Radeberg, Ger. D13 10
Radebeul, Ger. D13 10
Rades, Tun. B16 62
Radford, Va., U.S. C2 153
Rādhanpur, India I4 44
Radisson, Sask., Can. E2 105
Radium Hot Springs, B.C., Can. D9 99
Radium Springs, N.M., U.S. E3 138
Radofinnikovo, Russia B13 22
Radolfzell, Ger. H8 10
Radom, Pol. D21 10
Radomsko, Pol. D19 10
Radoškoviči, Bela. G10 22
Radoviš, Mac. H6 20
Radun', Bela. G8 22
Radviliškis, Lith. F6 22
Radville, Sask., Can. H3 105
Raḍwá, Jabal, mtn., Sau. Ar. E10 60
Radway, Alta., Can. B4 98
Rae, N.W. Ter., Can. D9 96
Rāe Bareli, India G9 44
Raeford, N.C., U.S. C3 140
Rae Isthmus, N.W. Ter., Can. C15 96
Rae Strait, strt., N.W. Ter., Can. C13 96
Raetihi, N.Z. C5 72
Rafaela, Arg. F8 80
Rafah, Gaza F2 50
Raffadali, Italy L8 18
Rafḥā', Sau. Ar. G7 48
Rafsanjān, Iran F14 48
Raft, stm., Id., U.S. G5 119
Raft River Mountains, mts., Ut., U.S. B2 151
Rafz, Switz. C10 13
Raga, Sud. M3 60
Ragged Island, i., Bah. C7 94
Ragged Island, i., Me., U.S. E4 126
Ragged Island Range, is., Bah. C7 94
Ragged Lake, l., Me., U.S. C3 126
Ragged Top Mountain, mtn., Wy., U.S. E7 157
Ragland, Al., U.S. B3 108
Ragusa, Italy M9 18
Raguva, Lith. F7 22
Rahad, Nahr ar-, stm., Afr. F8 56
Rahad al-Bardī, Sud. L2 60
Rahīmyār Khān, Pak. F4 44
Rahway, N.J., U.S. B4 137
Rahway, stm., N.J., U.S. k7 137
Rāichūr, India D4 46
Raiganj, India H13 44
Raigarh, India J10 44
Railroad Valley, val., Nv., U.S. E6 135
Railton, Austl. M7 70
Rainbow Bridge National Monument, Ut., U.S. F5 151
Rainbow City, Al., U.S. *A3 108
Rainbow Falls, wtfl, Tn., U.S. D10 149
Rainbow Flowage, res., Wi., U.S. C4 156
Rainbow Lake, l., Me., U.S. C3 126
Rainelle, W.V., U.S. D4 155
Rainier, Or., U.S. A4 144
Rainier, Wa., U.S. C3 154
Rainier, Mount, mtn., Wa., U.S. C4 154
Rains, co., Tx., U.S. C5 150
Rainsville, Al., U.S. A4 108
Rainy Lake, l., Mn., U.S. B5 130
Rainy River, Ont., Can. o16 103
Raipur, India J9 44
Ra'īs, Sau. Ar. C1 47
Raití, Nic. C9 92
Rājahmundry, India D6 46
Rajāj, Sud. L3 60
Rajang, stm., Malay. E5 38
Rājapālaiyam, India H4 46
Rājasthān, state, India G5 44
Rajčichinsk, Russia H17 28
Rajka, Hung. G17 10
Rājkot, India I4 44
Rāj Nāndgaon, India J9 44
Rājpīpla, India B2 46
Rājshāhi, Bngl. H13 44
Rakamaz, Hung. G21 10
Rakaposhi, mtn., Pak. B6 44
Rakata, Pulau, i., Indon. j12 39a
Rake, Ia., U.S. A4 122
Rakhiv, Ukr. A8 20
Rakops, Bots. C7 66
Rakovník, Czech Rep. E13 10
Rakvere, Est. B9 22
Raleigh, Newf., Can. C4 102
Raleigh, Il., U.S. F5 120
Raleigh, Ms., U.S. C4 131
Raleigh, N.C., U.S. B4 140
Raleigh, W.V., U.S. n13 155
Raleigh, co., W.V., U.S. D3 155
Raleigh Bay, b., N.C., U.S. C6 140
Ralls, Tx., U.S. C2 150
Ralls, co., Mo., U.S. B6 132
Ralph, Al., U.S. B2 108
Ralston, Ne., U.S. g12 134
Ralston, Ok., U.S. A5 143
Ralston, Wy., U.S. B4 157
Ralston Valley, val., Nv., U.S. E4 135
Rama, Sask., Can. F4 105
Rama, Isr. C4 50
Rama, Nic. E10 92
Rama, stm., Nic. F10 92
Ramacca, Italy L9 18
Ramah, N.M., U.S. B1 138
Ramah Indian Reservation, N.M., U.S. C1 138
Rām Allāh, W.B. E4 50
Rāmanāthapuram, India H5 46
Ramapo, stm., N.J., U.S. A4 137
Ramapo Mountains, mts., N.J., U.S. A4 137
Ramasucha, Russia I16 22
Ramat Gan, Isr. D3 50
Ramat HaSharon, Isr. D3 50
Ramathlabama, Bots. E7 66
Rambervillers, Fr. D13 14
Ramblewood, N.J., U.S. D3 137
Rambouillet, Fr. D8 14
Ramea, Newf., Can. E3 102
Ramenskoje, Russia F21 22
Ramer, Al., U.S. C3 108
Ramer, Tn., U.S. B3 149
Rameški, Russia D19 22
Rāmeswaram, India H10 42
Rāmhormoz, Iran F10 48
Ramingstein, Aus. H13 10
Ramiriquí, Col. E6 84
Ramla, Isr. E3 50
Ramlu, mtn., Afr. F9 56
Ramm, Jabal, mtn., Jord. I4 50
Râmnicu Sărat, Rom. D11 20
Râmnicu Vâlcea, Rom. D8 20
Ramona, Ca., U.S. F5 112
Ramona, Ks., U.S. D6 123
Ramona, Ok., U.S. A6 143
Ramona, S.D., U.S. C8 148
Ramos, Mex. F9 90
Ramos, stm., Mex. E7 90
Ramot, Golan C5 50
Ramotswa, Bots. E7 66
Rampart Range, mts., Co., U.S. B5 113
Rāmpur, India F8 44
Rāmpur Hāt, India H12 44
Ramree Island, i., Mya. E2 40
Ramsay, Mi., U.S. n12 129
Ramseur, N.C., U.S. B3 140
Ramsey, I. of Man G9 8
Ramsey, Il., U.S. D4 120
Ramsey, Mn., U.S. *E5 130
Ramsey, N.J., U.S. A4 137
Ramsey, co., Mn., U.S. E5 130
Ramsey, co., N.D., U.S. A7 141
Rāmshīr, Iran F10 48
Ramshorn Peak, mtn., Mt., U.S. E5 133
Ramshorn Peak, mtn., Wy., U.S. C3 157
Ramu, stm., Pap. N. Gui. m16 68a
Ramygala, Lith. F7 22
Rānāghāt, India I13 44
Ranburne, Al., U.S. B4 108
Rancagua, Chile H3 80
Rance, stm., Fr. D4 14
Rancevo, Russia E17 22
Rancharia, Braz. G3 79
Ranchería, stm., Col. B6 84
Rancheria Rock, mtn., Or., U.S. C6 144
Ranchester, Wy., U.S. B5 157
Rānchi, India I11 44
Ranchillos, Arg. D6 80
Ranchito, N.M., U.S. A4 138
Rancho California, Ca., U.S. F5 112
Rancho Palos Verdes, Ca., U.S. *n12 112
Ranchos de Taos, N.M., U.S. A4 138
Rancocas Creek, stm., N.J., U.S. C3 137
Rancocas Creek, South Branch, stm., N.J., U.S. D3 137
Rancocas Woods, N.J., U.S. D3 137
Rancul, Arg. H6 80
Rand, W.V., U.S. C3 155
Randall, Mn., U.S. D4 130
Randall, co., Tx., U.S. B2 150
Randallstown, Md., U.S. B4 127
Randers, Den. M12 6
Randle, Wa., U.S. C4 154
Randleman, N.C., U.S. B3 140
Randlett, Ok., U.S. C3 143
Randolph, Al., U.S. C3 108
Randolph, Az., U.S. E4 110
Randolph, Ia., U.S. D2 122
Randolph, Me., U.S. D3 126
Randolph, Ma., U.S. B5 128
Randolph, Ms., U.S. A4 131
Randolph, Ne., U.S. B8 134
Randolph, N.H., U.S. B4 136
Randolph, N.Y., U.S. C2 139
Randolph, Oh., U.S. A4 142
Randolph, Ut., U.S. B4 151
Randolph, Vt., U.S. D3 152
Randolph, Wi., U.S. E5 156
Randolph, co., Al., U.S. B4 108
Randolph, co., Ar., U.S. A4 111
Randolph, co., Ga., U.S. E2 117
Randolph, co., Il., U.S. E4 120
Randolph, co., In., U.S. D7 121
Randolph, co., Mo., U.S. B5 132
Randolph, co., N.C., U.S. B3 140
Randolph, co., W.V., U.S. C5 155
Randolph Air Force Base, mil., Tx., U.S. h7 150
Randolph Center, Vt., U.S. D3 152
Randolph Hills, Md., U.S. B3 127
Random Island, i., Newf., Can. D5 102
Random Lake, Wi., U.S. E6 156
Råneå, Swe. I18 6
Ranfurly, Alta., Can. C5 98
Rāngāmāti, Bngl. I15 44
Rangeley, Me., U.S. D2 126
Rangeley Lake, l., Me., U.S. D2 126
Rangely, Co., U.S. A2 113
Ranger, Ga., U.S. B2 117
Ranger, Tx., U.S. C3 150
Ranger, W.V., U.S. C2 155
Ranger Lake, l., N.M., U.S. D6 138
Rangoon see Yangon, Mya. B2 38
Rangpur, Bngl. H13 44
Ranguana Cay, i., Belize A6 92
Ranguana Entrance, strt., Belize A6 92
Rānībennur, India E3 46
Ranier, Mn., U.S. B5 130
Rānīganj, India I12 44
Rānikhet, India F8 44
Ranken, stm., Austl. C2 70
Ranken Store, Austl. B2 70
Rankin, Il., U.S. C6 120
Rankin, Pa., U.S. k14 145
Rankin, Tx., U.S. D2 150
Rankin, co., Ms., U.S. C4 131
Rankin Inlet, N.W. Ter., Can. D14 96
Ranohira, Madag. s21 67b
Ranomafana, Madag. t22 67b
Ranong, Thai. J5 40
Ranopiso, Madag. t22 67b
Ranotsara Nord, Madag. s22 67b
Ransom, Il., U.S. B5 120
Ransom, Ks., U.S. D4 123
Ransom, co., N.D., U.S. C8 141
Ransomville, N.Y., U.S. B2 139
Ranson, W.V., U.S. B7 155
Rantauprapat, Indon. M5 40
Rantekombola, Bulu, mtn., Indon. F7 38
Rantoul, Il., U.S. C5 120
Rantoul, Ks., U.S. D8 123
Rantowles, S.C., U.S. k11 147
Ranua, Fin. I20 6
Ranwanalenaus, Bots. B6 66
Raoping, China L6 34
Raoul, Ga., U.S. B3 117
Rapa, Ponta do, c., Braz. D14 80
Rapallo, Italy E4 18
Rapel, stm., Chile G3 80
Rapelje, Mt., U.S. E7 133
Rapelli, Arg. D6 80
Raphine, Va., U.S. C3 153
Rapid, stm., Mn., U.S. B4 130
Rapid, North Branch, stm., Mn., U.S. B4 130
Rapid City, Man., Can. D1 100
Rapid City, Mi., U.S. D5 129
Rapid City, S.D., U.S. C2 148
Rapides, co., La., U.S. C3 125
Rapid River, Mi., U.S. C4 129
Rapids City, Il., U.S. B3 120
Räpina, Est. C10 22
Rapla, Est. B7 22
Rappahannock, co., Va., U.S. B4 153
Rappahannock, stm., Va., U.S. B5 153
Rapperswil, Switz. D10 13
Rāpti, stm., Asia G10 44
Rapulo, stm., Bol. F8 82
Raquette, stm., N.Y., U.S. f10 139
Raquette Lake, l., N.Y., U.S. B6 139
Raritan, N.J., U.S. B3 137
Raritan, stm., N.J., U.S. C4 137
Raritan, South Branch, stm., N.J., U.S. B3 137
Raritan Bay, b., N.J., U.S. C4 137
Raron, Switz. F8 13
Rasa, Punta, c., Arg. I10 80
Ra's al-'Ayn, Syria C6 48
Ra's al-Khaymah, U.A.E. B9 47
Ra's an-Naqb, Egypt I3 50
Ra's an-Naqb, Jord. H4 50
Râșcani, Mol. B11 20
Rașcov, Mol. B12 20
Ras Dashen Terara, mtn., Eth. K10 60
Raseiniai, Lith. F6 22
Râs el Aïoun, Alg. N3 18
Ras el Ma, Alg. C10 62
Rashād, Sud. L6 60
Rashīd, Egypt B6 60
Rasht, Iran C10 48
Rāsipuram, India G5 46
Raška, Yugo. F4 20
Raspberry Peak, mtn., Ar., U.S. C1 111
Rass Jebel, Tun. L5 18
Rasskazovo, Russia I24 22
Rasšua, ostrov, i., Russia H22 28
Ra's Tannūrah, Sau. Ar. H11 48
Rastatt, Ger. G8 10
Rastede, Ger. B8 10
Rasūl, Pak. D5 44
Ratangarh, India F6 44
Rätansbyn, Swe. J14 6
Ratcliff, Ar., U.S. B2 111
Rāth, India H8 44
Rathbun Lake, res., Ia., U.S. D5 122
Rathdrum, Id., U.S. B2 119
Rathenow, Ger. C12 10
Rathwell, Man., Can. E2 100
Rat Islands, is., Ak., U.S. E3 109
Rat Lake, l., Man., Can. B4 100
Ratlām, India I6 44
Ratnāgiri, India D2 46
Ratnapura, Sri L. I6 46
Ratomka, Bela. H10 22
Raton, N.M., U.S. A5 138
Raton Pass, N.M., U.S. A5 138
Rattan, Ok., U.S. C6 143
Rattlesnake Creek, stm., Ks., U.S. E4 123
Rattlesnake Creek, stm., Oh., U.S. C2 142
Rattlesnake Creek, stm., Wa., U.S. C6 154
Rattlesnake Flat, pl., Wa., U.S. C7 154
Rattlesnake Hills, hills, Wa., U.S. C6 154
Rattlesnake Mountain, mtn., Ct., U.S. C4 114
Rattling Brook, Newf., Can. D3 102
Ratzeburg, Ger. B10 10
Raub, Malay. M6 40
Rauch, Arg. I9 80
Raul Soares, Braz. F7 79
Rauma, Fin. K17 6
Raurkela, India I11 44
Ravalli, Mt., U.S. C2 133
Ravalli, co., Mt., U.S. D2 133
Ravanusa, Italy L8 18
Rāvar, Iran F14 48
Ravelo, Bol. H9 82
Raven, Va., U.S. e10 153
Ravena, N.Y., U.S. C7 139
Ravenden, Ar., U.S. A4 111
Ravenden Springs, Ar., U.S. A4 111
Ravenel, S.C., U.S. k11 147
Ravenna, Italy E7 18
Ravenna, Ky., U.S. C6 124
Ravenna, Mi., U.S. E5 129
Ravenna, Ne., U.S. C7 134
Ravenna, Oh., U.S. A4 142
Raven Park, reg., Co., U.S. A2 113
Ravensburg, Ger. H9 10
Ravenscroft, Tn., U.S. D8 149
Ravensdale, Wa., U.S. f12 154
Ravenshoe, Austl. A6 70
Ravensthorpe, Austl. F4 68
Ravenswood, In., U.S. k10 121
Ravenswood, W.V., U.S. C3 155
Ravenwood, Mo., U.S. A3 132
Rāvi, stm., Asia E5 44
Ravia, Ok., U.S. C5 143
Ravinia, S.D., U.S. D7 148
Ravnina, Turk. C17 48
Rāwalpindi, Pak. D5 44
Rawa Mazowiecka, Pol. D20 10
Rawāndūz, Iraq C8 48
Rawdon, Que., Can. C4 104
Rawhide Creek, stm., Wy., U.S. D8 157
Rawicz, Pol. D16 10
Rawlings, Md., U.S. k13 127
Rawlinna, Austl. F5 68
Rawlins, Wy., U.S. E5 157
Rawlins, co., Ks., U.S. C2 123
Rawson, Arg. E3 78
Rawson, Arg. H8 80
Raxāul, India D11 42
Ray, In., U.S. A8 121
Ray, N.D., U.S. A2 141
Ray, co., Mo., U.S. B3 132
Ray, Cape, c., Newf., Can. E2 102
Raya, Bukit, mtn., Indon. F5 38
Rāyadurg, India E4 46
Ray City, Ga., U.S. E3 117
Rayle, Ga., U.S. C4 117
Raymond, Alta., Can. E4 98
Raymond, Ca., U.S. D4 112
Raymond, Ga., U.S. C2 117
Raymond, Il., U.S. D4 120
Raymond, Ks., U.S. D5 123
Raymond, Me., U.S. E2 126
Raymond, Mn., U.S. E3 130
Raymond, Ms., U.S. C3 131
Raymond, Ne., U.S. D9 134
Raymond, N.H., U.S. D4 136
Raymond, S.D., U.S. C8 148
Raymond, Wa., U.S. C2 154
Raymond Terrace, Austl. I9 70
Raymondville, Mo., U.S. D6 132
Raymondville, Tx., U.S. F4 150
Raymore, Sask., Can. F3 105
Raymore, Mo., U.S. C3 132
Rayne, La., U.S. D3 125
Raynham, Ma., U.S. C5 128
Raynham Center, Ma., U.S. C5 128
Rayón, Mex. C4 90
Rayones, Mex. E9 90
Rayong, Thai. H6 40
Raytown, Mo., U.S. h11 132
Rayville, La., U.S. B4 125
Rayville, Mo., U.S. B3 132
Razan, Iran D10 48
R'azan', Russia G22 22
R'azancevo, Russia E22 22
Ražanj, Yugo. F5 20
Razdan, Arm. A8 48
Razdil'na, Ukr. C14 20
Răzeni, Mol. C12 20
Razgrad, Bul. F10 20
Razgrad, prov., Bul. F10 20
R'ažsk, Russia H23 22
Ré, Île de, i., Fr. F5 14
Reader, W.V., U.S. B4 155
Reader Lake, l., Man., Can. C1 100
Readfield, Me., U.S. D3 126
Reading, Eng., U.K. J13 8
Reading, Ks., U.S. D8 123
Reading, Ma., U.S. A5 128
Reading, Mi., U.S. G6 129
Reading, Oh., U.S. C1 142
Reading, Pa., U.S. F10 145
Reading, Vt., U.S. E3 152
Readland, Ar., U.S. D4 111
Readlyn, Ia., U.S. B5 122
Readsboro, Vt., U.S. F3 152
Readstown, Wi., U.S. E3 156
Readyville, Tn., U.S. B5 149
Reagan, Tn., U.S. B3 149
Reagan, co., Tx., U.S. D2 150
Real, co., Tx., U.S. E3 150
Real, Cordillera, mts., S.A. H9 82
Real, Estero, stm., Nic. E7 92
Real del Padre, Arg. H5 80
Realicó, Arg. H6 80
Reamstown, Pa., U.S. F9 145
Reardan, Wa., U.S. B8 154
Reata, Mex. D9 90
Reay, Scot., U.K. C10 8
Rebecca, Ga., U.S. E3 117
Rebersburg, Pa., U.S. E7 145
Reboly, Russia J22 6
Rebouças, Braz. C13 80
Rebun-tō, i., Japan b16 36a
Recalde, Arg. I8 80
Recanati, Italy F8 18
Rečane, Russia E14 22
Recherche, Archipelago of the, is., Austl. F4 68
Rečica, Bela. I13 22
Recife, Braz. E12 76
Recinto, Chile I3 80
Recklinghausen, Ger. D7 10
Reconquista, Arg. E9 80
Recreio, Braz. F7 79
Recreo, Arg. E6 80
Rector, Ar., U.S. A5 111
Recuay, Peru C3 82
Red (Hong) (Yuan), stm., Asia C8 40
Red, stm., N.A. B7 106
Red, stm., U.S. E8 106
Red, stm., Ky., U.S. C6 124
Red, stm., Tn., U.S. A4 149
Red, Elm Fork, stm., U.S. B2 143
Red, North Fork, stm., U.S. B1 143
Red, Salt Fork, stm., U.S. C2 143
Red, South Fork, stm., U.S. A5 149
Red, West Fork, stm., U.S. A4 149
Redange, Lux. I8 12
Red Bank, N.J., U.S. C4 137
Red Bank, S.C., U.S. D5 147
Red Bank, Tn., U.S. D8 149
Red Banks, Ms., U.S. A4 131
Red Bay, Newf., Can. C3 102
Red Bay, Al., U.S. A1 108
Redberry Lake, l., Sask., Can. E2 105
Redbird, Oh., U.S. A4 142
Red Bird, stm., Ky., U.S. C6 124
Red Bluff, Ca., U.S. B2 112
Red Bluff Lake, res., U.S. o12 150
Red Bluff Reservoir, res., U.S. B8 90
Red Boiling Springs, Tn., U.S. C8 149
Red Bud, Il., U.S. E4 120
Red Butte, mtn., Ut., U.S. B2 151
Red Buttes Village, Wy., U.S. D6 157
Redby, Mn., U.S. C4 130
Red Cedar, stm., Wi., U.S. C2 156
Red Cedar Lake, l., Wi., U.S. C2 156
Redcliff, Alta., Can. D5 98
Redcliff, Co., U.S. B4 113
Redcliff, Zimb. B9 66
Redcliffe, Austl. F10 70
Red Cliff Indian Reservation, Wi., U.S. B2 156
Red Cliffs, Austl. J5 70
Red Cloud, Ne., U.S. D7 134
Redcloud Peak, mtn., Co., U.S. D3 113
Red Creek, stm., Ms., U.S. E4 131
Red Cross Lake, l., Man., Can. B5 100
Red Deer, Alta., Can. C4 98
Red Deer, stm., Can. D4 98
Red Deer, stm., Can. E4 105
Reddell, La., U.S. D3 125
Reddick, Fl., U.S. C4 116
Reddick, Il., U.S. B5 120
Redding, Ca., U.S. B2 112
Redding, Ct., U.S. D2 114
Redding Ridge, Ct., U.S. D2 114
Reddish Knob, mtn., U.S. C5 155
Redeye, stm., Mn., U.S. D3 130
Red Feather Lakes, Co., U.S. A5 113
Redfield, Ar., U.S. C3 111
Redfield, Ia., U.S. C3 122
Redfield, Ks., U.S. E9 123
Redfield, S.D., U.S. C7 148
Redford, Mi., U.S. F7 129
Redgranite, Wi., U.S. D4 156
Red Hook, N.Y., U.S. C7 139
Red House, W.V., U.S. C3 155
Red Indian Lake, l., Newf., Can. D3 102
Red Jacket, W.V., U.S. D2 155
Redkey, In., U.S. D7 121
Redkino, Russia E19 22
Redlake, Mn., U.S. C3 130
Red Lake, co., Mn., U.S. C2 130
Red Lake, l., Az., U.S. B1 110
Red Lake, stm., Mn., U.S. C2 130
Red Lake Falls, Mn., U.S. C2 130
Red Lake Indian Reservation, Mn., U.S. B3 130
Redlands, S. Afr. G6 66
Redlands, Ca., U.S. E5 112
Red Level, Al., U.S. D3 108
Red Lick, Ms., U.S. D3 131
Red Lion, Pa., U.S. G8 145
Red Lodge, Mt., U.S. E7 133
Red Mill Pond, l., De., U.S. E5 115
Redmon, Il., U.S. D6 120
Redmond, Or., U.S. C5 144
Redmond, Ut., U.S. E4 151
Redmond, Wa., U.S. e11 154
Red Mountain, mtn., Al., U.S. B3 108
Red Mountain, mtn., Ca., U.S. B2 112
Red Mountain, mtn., Mt., U.S. C4 133
Red Mountain Pass, Co., U.S. D3 113
Red Oak, Ga., U.S. h7 117
Red Oak, Ia., U.S. D2 122
Red Oak, Ok., U.S. C6 143
Red Oak, Tx., U.S. n10 150
Red Oaks, La., U.S. h9 125
Redon, Fr. E4 14
Redonda, i., Antig. F13 94
Redondo, Port. G4 16
Redondo, Wa., U.S. f11 154
Redondo Beach, Ca., U.S. n12 112
Redoubt Volcano, vol., Ak., U.S. g15 109
Red Peak, mtn., Co., U.S. B4 113
Red Rapids, N.B., Can. C2 101
Red River, N.M., U.S. A4 138
Red River, co., La., U.S. B2 125
Red River, co., Tx., U.S. C5 150
Red Rock, B.C., Can. C6 99
Red Rock, Az., U.S. E4 110
Red Rock, Ok., U.S. A4 143
Red Rock, stm., Mt., U.S. F4 133
Red Rock, Lake, res., Ia., U.S. C4 122
Red Scaffold, S.D., U.S. C4 148
Red Sea D8 56
Red Springs, N.C., U.S. C3 140
Redstone, Co., U.S. B3 113
Redstone, N.H., U.S. B4 136
Red Sucker, stm., Man., Can. B5 100
Red Table Mountain, mts., Co., U.S. B4 113
Redvale, Co., U.S. C2 113
Redvers, Sask., Can. H5 105
Redwater, Alta., Can. C4 98
Redwater, stm., Mt., U.S. C11 133
Red Willow, Alta., Can. C4 98
Red Willow, co., Ne., U.S. D5 134
Redwillow, stm., Can. B7 99
Red Willow Creek, stm., Ne., U.S. D5 134
Red Wing, Mn., U.S. F6 130
Redwood, Ms., U.S. C3 131
Redwood, co., Mn., U.S. F3 130
Redwood, stm., Mn., U.S. F3 130
Redwood City, Ca., U.S. D2 112
Redwood Falls, Mn., U.S. F3 130
Redwood National Park, Ca., U.S. B2 112
Redwood Valley, Ca., U.S. C2 112
Ree, Lough, l., Ire. H5 8
Reed, Ar., U.S. D4 111
Reed City, Mi., U.S. E5 129
Reeder, N.D., U.S. C3 141
Reed Lake, l., Man., Can. B1 100
Reedley, Ca., U.S. D4 112
Reedpoint, Mt., U.S. E7 133
Reedsburg, Wi., U.S. E3 156
Reeds Peak, mtn., N.M., U.S. D2 138
Reedsport, Or., U.S. D2 144
Reeds Spring, Mo., U.S. E4 132
Reedsville, Pa., U.S. E6 145
Reedsville, W.V., U.S. B5 155
Reedsville, Wi., U.S. D6 156
Reedville, Va., U.S. C6 153
Reedy, W.V., U.S. C3 155
Reedy, stm., S.C., U.S. C3 147
Reedy Lake, l., Fl., U.S. E5 116
Reefton, N.Z. E3 72
Ree Heights, S.D., U.S. C6 148
Reelfoot Lake, l., Tn., U.S. A2 149
Reelsville, In., U.S. E4 121
Reese, Mi., U.S. E7 129
Reese, stm., Nv., U.S. C4 135
Reese Air Force Base, mil., Tx., U.S. C1 150
Reese Station, Oh., U.S. m11 142
Reeseville, Wi., U.S. E5 156
Reeves, co., Tx., U.S. o13 150
Reform, Al., U.S. B1 108
Refugio, Tx., U.S. E4 150
Refugio, co., Tx., U.S. E4 150
Regaïa, Mor. J6 16
Regência, Braz. E9 79
Regensburg, Ger. F12 10
Regent, N.D., U.S. C3 141
Reggâne, Alg. G11 62
Reggello, Italy F6 18
Reggio di Calabria, Italy K10 18
Reggio nell'Emilia, Italy E5 18
Reghin, Rom. C8 20
Regina, Sask., Can. G3 105
Régina, Fr. Gu. C8 76
Regina Beach, Sask., Can. G3 105
Región Metropolitana, prov., Chile G3 80
Register, Ga., U.S. D5 117
Registro, Braz. C15 80
Registro do Araguaia, Braz. C3 79
Regnéville, Fr. C5 14
Reguengos de Monsaraz, Port. G4 16
Rehau, Ger. E12 10
Rehoboth, Nmb. D3 66
Rehoboth, N.M., U.S. B1 138
Rehoboth Bay, b., De., U.S. F5 115
Rehoboth Beach, De., U.S. F5 115
Reḥovot, Isr. E3 50
Reichenau, Switz. E11 13
Reichenbach, Ger. E12 10
Reid, Mount, mtn., Ak., U.S. n24 109
Reidland, Ky., U.S. e9 124
Reidsville, Ga., U.S. D4 117
Reidsville, N.C., U.S. A3 140
Reidville, S.C., U.S. B3 147
Reigate, Eng., U.K. J13 8
Reigoldswil, Switz. D8 13
Reims, Fr. C11 14
Reinach, Switz. C8 13
Reinach, Switz. D9 13
Reinbeck, Ia., U.S. B5 122
Reindeer Island, i., Man., Can. C3 100
Reindeer Lake, l., Can. m8 105
Reinga, Cape, c., N.Z. A4 72
Reinosa, Spain B7 16
Reisdorf, Lux. I9 12
Reisterstown, Md., U.S. B4 127
Reitz, S. Afr. F9 66
Reliance, De., U.S. F3 115
Reliance, S.D., U.S. D6 148
Reliance, Tn., U.S. D9 149
Reliance, Wy., U.S. E3 157
Remada, Tun. D16 62
Remagen, Ger. E7 10
Remagen, Ger. B14 14
Remanso, Braz. E10 76
Rembang, Indon. j15 39a
Rembert, S.C., U.S. C6 147
Rembrandt, Ia., U.S. B2 122

Reme-Robi

Name — Map Ref. — Page

Remecó, Arg. I7 80
Remedios, Col. D5 84
Remedios, Pan. C2 84
Remedios, Punta, c., El Sal. D5 92
Remer, Mn., U.S. C5 130
Remerton, Ga., U.S. F3 117
Remeshk, Iran H15 48
Remington, In., U.S. C3 121
Remington, Va., U.S. B5 153
Remiremont, Fr. D13 14
Remlap, Al., U.S. B3 108
Remmel Dam, Ar., U.S. g8 111
Remoulins, Fr. I11 14
Remscheid, Ger. D7 10
Remsen, Ia., U.S. B2 122
Remus, Mi., U.S. E5 129
Renaix (Ronse), Bel. G4 12
Rena Lara, Ms., U.S. A3 131
Renault, Il., U.S. E3 120
Renčeni, Lat. D8 22
Rencontre East, Newf., Can. E4 102
Rende, Italy J11 18
Rend Lake, res., Il., U.S. E5 120
Rendsburg, Ger. A9 10
Renens, Switz. E6 13
Renews [-Cappahayden], Newf., Can. E5 102
Renforth, N.B., Can. D4 101
Renfrew, Ont., Can. B8 103
Rengat, Indon. O7 40
Rengo, Chile H3 80
Reng Tlāng, mtn., Asia J15 44
Renhua, China J2 34
Reni, Ukr. D12 20
Renick, Mo., U.S. B5 132
Renmark, Austl. J4 70
Rennell, i., Sol.Is. B12 68
Renner, S.D., U.S. D9 148
Rennes, Fr. D5 14
Rennick Glacier, Ant. C8 73
Rennie, Man., Can. E4 100
Reno, Nv., U.S. D2 135
Reno, Oh., U.S. C4 142
Reno, co., Ks., U.S. E5 123
Reno, stm., Italy E6 18
Reno, Lake, l., Mn., U.S. E3 130
Reno Hill, mtn., Wy., U.S. D6 157
Renous, N.B., Can. C4 101
Renovo, Pa., U.S. D6 145
Renshou, China H6 34
Rensselaer, In., U.S. C3 121
Rensselaer, N.Y., U.S. C7 139
Rensselaer, co., N.Y., U.S. C7 139
Rentería, Spain B10 16
Renton, Wa., U.S. B3 154
Rentz, Ga., U.S. D4 117
Renville, Mn., U.S. F3 130
Renville, co., Mn., U.S. F4 130
Renville, co., N.D., U.S. A4 141
Renwick, Ia., U.S. B4 122
Répce, stm., Eur. H16 10
Repentigny, Que., Can. D4 104
Repetek, Turk. J10 26
Repino, Russia A12 22
Repton, Al., U.S. D2 108
Republic, Ks., U.S. C6 123
Republic, Mi., U.S. B3 129
Republic, Mo., U.S. D4 132
Republic, Oh., U.S. A2 142
Republic, Pa., U.S. G2 145
Republic, Wa., U.S. A7 154
Republic, co., Ks., U.S. C6 123
Republican, stm., U.S. C6 123
Republican, North Fork, stm., U.S. A8 113
Republican, South Fork, stm., U.S. E4 134
Republican City, Ne., U.S. D6 134
Repulse Bay, N.W. Ter., Can. C15 96
Repulse Bay, b., Austl. C8 70
Requena, Peru A5 82
Requena, Spain F10 16
Réquista, Fr. H9 14
Reschenpass, Eur. F17 14
Rescue, Va., U.S. k14 153
Resen, Mac. H5 20
Reserva, Braz. C13 80
Reserve, Ks., U.S. C8 123
Reserve, La., U.S. h10 125
Reserve, Mt., U.S. B12 133
Reserve, N.M., U.S. D1 138
Reservoir Pond, l., Ma., U.S. h11 128
Rešetnikovo, Russia E19 22
Resistencia, Arg. D9 80
Reşiţa, Rom. D5 20
Rešma, Russia D25 22
Resolute, N.W. Ter., Can. B14 96
Resolution Island, i., N.W. Ter., Can. D20 96
Resolution Island, i., N.Z. F1 72
Resplendor, Braz. E8 79
Restín, Punta, c., Peru J2 84
Restinga, Mor. J6 16
Restinga Seca, Braz. E12 80
Reston, Man., Can. E1 100
Reston, Va., U.S. B5 153
Restrepo, Col. F4 84
Restrepo, Col. E6 84
Retalhuleu, Guat. C3 92
Retalhuleu, dept., Guat. C3 92
Retamosa, Ur. G11 80
Rethel, Fr. C11 14
Réthimnon, Grc. N8 20
Reunion (Réunion), dep., Afr. F11 58
Reus, Spain D13 16
Reuss, stm., Switz. D9 13
Reuterstadt Stavenhagen, Ger. B12 10
Reutlingen, Ger. G9 10
Rev'akino, Russia G20 22
Revda, Russia F9 26
Revelo, Ky., U.S. D5 124
Revelstoke, B.C., Can. D8 99
Revelstoke, Lake, res., B.C., Can. D8 99
Reventazón, Peru B1 82
Reventazón, stm., C.R. G11 92
Revere, Ma., U.S. g11 128
Revigny-sur-Ornain, Fr. D11 14
Revillagigedo, Islas, is., Mex. H4 90
Revillagigedo Island, i., Ak., U.S. n24 109
Revillo, S.D., U.S. B9 148
Revin, Fr. C11 14
Revloc, Pa., U.S. F4 145
Revol'ucii, pik, mtn., Taj. A5 44
Revolución Mexicana, Mex. A1 92
Revuè, stm., Afr. B11 66
Rewa, India H9 44
Rewa, stm., Guy. F13 84
Rewāri, India F7 44
Rex, Ga., U.S. h8 117
Rexburg, Id., U.S. F7 119
Rexford, Ks., U.S. C3 123
Rexford, Mt., U.S. B1 133
Rexton, N.B., Can. C5 101
Rey, Isla del, i., Pan. C3 84
Rey, Laguna del, l., Mex. D8 90
Reydon, Ok., U.S. B2 143
Reyes, Bol. F8 82
Reyes, Point, c., Ca., U.S. C2 112
Reyhanlı, Tur. C4 48
Reykjanes, pen., Ice. C2 6a
Reykjavík, Ice. B3 6a
Reyno, Ar., U.S. A5 111
Reynolds, Ga., U.S. D2 117
Reynolds, Il., U.S. B3 120
Reynolds, In., U.S. C4 121
Reynolds, Mo., U.S. D6 132
Reynolds, Ne., U.S. D8 134
Reynolds, N.D., U.S. B8 141
Reynolds, co., Mo., U.S. D6 132
Reynoldsburg, Oh., U.S. C3 142
Reynoldsville, Pa., U.S. D4 145
Reynosa, Mex. D10 90
Rež, Russia F10 26
Reza, gora (Kūh-e Rīzeh), mtn., Asia C15 48
Rezé, Fr. E5 14
Rēzekne, Lat. E10 22
Rezina, Mol. B12 20
Rezovska (Mutlu), stm., Eur. G11 20
Rhaetian Alps, mts., Eur. F16 14
Rhame, N.D., U.S. C2 141
Rhea, co., Tn., U.S. D9 149
Rheda-Wiedenbrück, Ger. D8 10
Rheims see Reims, Fr. C11 14
Rhein, Sask., Can. F4 105
Rhein see Rhine, stm., Eur. D6 10
Rheine, Ger. C7 10
Rheinland-Pfalz, state, Ger. E6 10
Rhine, Ga., U.S. E3 117
Rhine (Rhein) (Rhin), stm., Eur. D6 10
Rhinebeck, N.Y., U.S. D7 139
Rhineland, Mo., U.S. C6 132
Rhinelander, Wi., U.S. C4 156
Rhir, Cap, c., Mor. E6 62
Rho, Italy D4 18
Rhode Island, state, U.S. D3 146
Rhode Island, i., R.I., U.S. E5 146
Rhode Island Sound, strt., U.S. F5 146
Rhodell, W.V., U.S. D3 155
Rhodes see Ródhos, Grc. M12 20
Rhodes see Ródhos, i., Grc. M12 20
Rhodesia see Zimbabwe, ctry., Afr. E5 58
Rhodes Peak, mtn., Id., U.S. C4 119
Rhodhiss, N.C., U.S. B1 140
Rhodope Mountains (Rodopi) (Orosirá Rodhópis), mts., Eur. H8 20
Rhome, Tx., U.S. m9 150
Rhön, mts., Ger. E9 10
Rhône, dept., Fr. G11 14
Rhône, stm., Eur. H11 14
Rhône au Rhin, Canal du, Fr. H7 10
Rhourde-el-Baguel, Alg. E14 62
Riaba, Eq. Gui. J14 64
Riachão, Braz. E9 76
Riacho de Santana, Braz. B7 79
Rialma, Braz. C4 79
Rialto, Ca., U.S. m14 112
Rianápolis, Braz. C4 79
Riangnom, Sud. M6 60
Riaño, Spain C6 16
Riau, Kepulauan, is., Indon. N8 40
Ribas do Rio Pardo, Braz. F2 79
Ribeauvillé, Fr. D14 14
Ribeira, Braz. C14 80
Ribeira do Iguape, stm., Braz. C14 80
Ribeira Grande, C.V. k16 64a
Ribeirão do Pinhal, Braz. G3 79
Ribeirão Preto, Braz. F5 79
Ribeirão Vermelho, Braz. F6 79
Ribeirãozinho, Braz. D2 79
Ribemont, Fr. C10 14
Ribera, Italy L8 18
Ribera, N.M., U.S. B4 138
Riberalta, Bol. D8 82
Rib Lake, Wi., U.S. C3 156
Rib Mountain, mtn., Wi., U.S. D4 156
Ribnica, Slvn. D9 18
Ribnitz-Damgarten, Ger. A12 10
Ribstone, Alta., Can. C5 98
Ricardo Flores Magón, Mex. C6 90
Ricaurte, Col. G4 84
Riccia, Italy H9 18
Riccione, Italy F7 18
Rice, Mn., U.S. E4 130
Rice, Va., U.S. C4 153
Rice, co., Ks., U.S. D5 123
Rice, co., Mn., U.S. F5 130
Riceboro, Ga., U.S. E5 117
Rice Creek, stm., Mn., U.S. m12 130
Rice Lake, Wi., U.S. C2 156
Rice Lake, l., Ont., Can. C6 103
Rice Lake, l., Mn., U.S. D5 130
Riceton, Sask., Can. G3 105
Riceville, Ia., U.S. A5 122
Riceville, Tn., U.S. D9 149
Rich, co., Ut., U.S. B4 151
Rich, Cape, c., Ont., Can. C4 103
Richard Collinson Inlet, b., N.W. Ter., Can. B10 96
Richard's Bay, S. Afr. G11 66
Richard's Bay, b., S. Afr. G11 66
Richards-Gebaur Air Force Base, mil., Mo., U.S. C3 132
Richards Island, i., N.W. Ter., Can. C6 96
Richardson, Tx., U.S. n10 150
Richardson, co., Ne., U.S. D10 134
Richardson, stm., Can. E10 96
Richardson Lakes, l., Me., U.S. D2 126
Richardson Mountains, mts., Can. C5 96
Richardton, N.D., U.S. C3 141
Richburg, S.C., U.S. B5 147
Rich Creek, Va., U.S. C2 153
Riche, Pointe, c., Newf., Can. C3 102
Richelieu, Fr. E7 14
Richer, Man., Can. E3 100
Richey, Mt., U.S. C11 133
Richfield, Id., U.S. F4 119
Richfield, Mn., U.S. F5 130
Richfield, N.C., U.S. B2 140
Richfield, Pa., U.S. E7 145
Richfield, Ut., U.S. E3 151
Richfield, Wi., U.S. m11 156
Richfield Springs, N.Y., U.S. C5 139
Richford, Vt., U.S. B3 152
Rich Fountain, Mo., U.S. C6 132
Rich Hill, Mo., U.S. C3 132
Richibucto, N.B., Can. C5 101
Richisau, Switz. D10 13
Richland, Ga., U.S. D2 117
Richland, In., U.S. I3 121
Richland, Ia., U.S. C6 122
Richland, Mi., U.S. F5 129
Richland, Mo., U.S. D5 132
Richland, N.J., U.S. D3 137
Richland, Wa., U.S. C6 154
Richland, co., Il., U.S. E5 120
Richland, co., La., U.S. B4 125
Richland, co., Mt., U.S. C12 133
Richland, co., N.D., U.S. C8 141
Richland, co., Oh., U.S. B3 142
Richland, co., S.C., U.S. D6 147
Richland, co., Wi., U.S. E3 156
Richland Balsam, mtn., N.C., U.S. f10 140
Richland Center, Wi., U.S. E3 156
Richland Creek, stm., Tn., U.S. B5 149
Richlands, N.C., U.S. C5 140
Richlands, Va., U.S. e10 153
Richlandtown, Pa., U.S. F11 145
Richmond, Austl. C5 70
Richmond, Austl. I9 70
Richmond, B.C., Can. E6 99
Richmond, P.E.I., Can. C6 101
Richmond, Que., Can. D5 104
Richmond, N.Z. D4 72
Richmond, S. Afr. G10 66
Richmond, S. Afr. H6 66
Richmond, Ca., U.S. D2 112
Richmond, Il., U.S. A5 120
Richmond, In., U.S. E8 121
Richmond, Ks., U.S. D8 123
Richmond, Ky., U.S. C5 124
Richmond, Me., U.S. D3 126
Richmond, Mi., U.S. F8 129
Richmond, Mn., U.S. E4 130
Richmond, Mo., U.S. B4 132
Richmond, Tx., U.S. E5 150
Richmond, Ut., U.S. B4 151
Richmond, Vt., U.S. C3 152
Richmond, Va., U.S. C5 153
Richmond, co., Ga., U.S. C4 117
Richmond, co., N.Y., U.S. E6 139
Richmond, co., N.C., U.S. B3 140
Richmond, co., Va., U.S. C6 153
Richmond Beach, Wa., U.S. B3 154
Richmond Dale, Oh., U.S. C3 142
Richmond Heights, Fl., U.S. s13 116
Richmond Heights, Mo., U.S. f13 132
Richmond Highlands, Wa., U.S. B3 154
Richmond Hill, Ont., Can. D5 103
Richmond Hill, Ga., U.S. E5 117
Richmond National Battlefield Park, Va., U.S. n18 153
Richmondville, N.Y., U.S. C6 139
Richmound, Sask., Can. G1 105
Rich Mountain, mtn., U.S. C1 111
Rich Mountain, mtn., Va., U.S. C1 153
Rich Mountain, mtn., W.V., U.S. C5 155
Rich Square, N.C., U.S. A5 140
Richthofen, Mount, mtn., Co., U.S. A5 113
Richton, Ms., U.S. D5 131
Richview, Il., U.S. E4 120
Richville, Mi., U.S. E7 129
Richwood, La., U.S. B3 125
Richwood, Oh., U.S. B2 142
Richwood, Tx., U.S. r14 150
Richwood, W.V., U.S. C4 155
Richwoods, Mo., U.S. C7 132
Rickenbacker Air Force Base, mil., Oh., U.S. m11 142
Rickman, Tn., U.S. C8 149
Riddle, Or., U.S. E3 144
Riddle Mountain, mtn., Or., U.S. D8 144
Rideau, stm., Ont., Can. B9 103
Riderwood, Al., U.S. C1 108
Ridgecrest, Ca., U.S. E5 112
Ridgecrest, La., U.S. C4 125
Ridgecrest, N.C., U.S. f10 140
Ridgedale, Sask., Can. D3 105
Ridgedale, Mo., U.S. E4 132
Ridge Farm, Il., U.S. D6 120
Ridgefield, Ct., U.S. D2 114
Ridgefield, N.J., U.S. h8 137
Ridgefield, Wa., U.S. D3 154
Ridgefield Park, N.J., U.S. B4 137
Ridgeland, Ms., U.S. C3 131
Ridgeland, S.C., U.S. G6 147
Ridgeley, W.V., U.S. B6 155
Ridgely, Md., U.S. C6 127
Ridgely, Tn., U.S. A2 149
Ridgeside, Tn., U.S. h11 149
Ridge Spring, S.C., U.S. D4 147
Ridgetop, Tn., U.S. A5 149
Ridgetown, Ont., Can. E3 103
Ridgeview, W.V., U.S. C3 155
Ridgeville, Man., Can. E3 100
Ridgeville, Ga., U.S. E5 117
Ridgeville, In., U.S. D7 121
Ridgeville, S.C., U.S. E7 147
Ridgeville Corners, Oh., U.S. A1 142
Ridgeway, Ia., U.S. A6 122
Ridgeway, Mo., U.S. A4 132
Ridgeway, S.C., U.S. C6 147
Ridgeway, Va., U.S. D3 153
Ridgeway, Wi., U.S. E4 156
Ridgewood, N.J., U.S. B4 137
Ridgewood Park, Ct., U.S. D7 114
Ridgway, Co., U.S. C3 113
Ridgway, Il., U.S. F5 120
Ridgway, Pa., U.S. D4 145
Riding Mountain, hills, Man., Can. D1 100
Riding Mountain National Park, Man., Can. D1 100
Ridley Park, Pa., U.S. p20 145
Ried im Innkreis, Aus. G13 10
Rienzi, Ms., U.S. A5 131
Riesa, Ger. D13 10
Riesco, Isla, i., Chile G2 78
Riesi, Italy L9 18
Rietavas, Lith. F4 22
Rietfontein, Nmb. C5 66
Rieti, Italy G7 18
Rif, mts., Mor. C8 62
Riffe Lake, res., Wa., U.S. C3 154
Rifle, Co., U.S. B3 113
Rifle, stm., Mi., U.S. D6 129
Rift Valley, val., Afr. I9 52
Rīga, Lat. E7 22
Riga, Gulf of (Rīgas jūras līcis) (Riia laht), b., Eur. D6 22
Rigacikun, Nig. F13 64
Rīgān, Iran G15 48
Rigaud, Que., Can. D3 104
Rigby, Id., U.S. F7 119
Rīgestān, reg., Afg. E1 44
Riggins, Id., U.S. D2 119
Rigi, mtn., Switz. D10 13
Rigo, Pap. N. Gui. A9 68
Rigolet, Newf., Can. A2 102
Riiser-Larsen Peninsula, pen., Ant. B4 73
Rijeka, Cro. D9 18
Rijswijk, Neth. D5 12
Riley, In., U.S. F3 121
Riley, Ks., U.S. C7 123
Riley, co., Ks., U.S. C7 123
Riley, Mount, mtn., N.M., U.S. F2 138
Rillito, Az., U.S. E4 110
Rima, stm., Nig. E12 64
Rímac, stm., Peru D3 82
Rimachi, Laguna, l., Peru J4 84
Rimavská Sobota, Slvk. G20 10
Rimbey, Alta., Can. C3 98
Rimersburg, Pa., U.S. D3 145
Rimi, Nig. E13 64
Rimini, Italy E7 18
Rimouski, Que., Can. A9 104
Rimouski, stm., Que., Can. A9 104
Rimouski-Est, Que., Can. A9 104
Rimrock, Az., U.S. C4 110
Rimrock Lake, res., Wa., U.S. C4 154
Rincón, C.R. I11 92
Rincon, Ga., U.S. D5 117
Rincon, N.M., U.S. E2 138
Rinconada, Arg. B5 80
Rincón de la Vieja, Parque Nacional, C.R. G9 92
Rincón del Bonete, Lago Artificial de, res., Ur. G11 80
Rincón del Ocote, Cerro, mtn., Hond. D7 92
Rincón de Romos, Mex. F8 90
Rincon Mountains, mts., Az., U.S. E5 110
Rindal, Nor. J11 6
Rindge, N.H., U.S. E2 136
Riner, Va., U.S. C2 153
Rineyville, Ky., U.S. C4 124
Ringebu, Nor. K12 6
Ringgold, Ga., U.S. B1 117
Ringgold, La., U.S. B2 125
Ringgold, Va., U.S. D3 153
Ringgold, co., Ia., U.S. D3 122
Ringim, Nig. E14 64
Ringling, Ok., U.S. C4 143
Ringoes, N.J., U.S. C3 137
Ringsted, Ia., U.S. A3 122
Ringwood, N.J., U.S. A4 137
Ringwood, Ok., U.S. A3 143
Rinjani, Gunung, mtn., Indon. G6 38
Rinteln, Ger. C9 10
Rio, Fl., U.S. E6 116
Rio, Il., U.S. B3 120
Rio, Wi., U.S. E4 156
Rio Arriba, co., N.M., U.S. A2 138
Rio Azul, Braz. C13 80
Riobamba, Ec. H3 84
Río Blanco, Chile G3 80
Rio Blanco, co., Co., U.S. B2 113
Rio Branco, Braz. C8 82
Río Branco, Ur. G12 80
Río Bravo, Mex. E10 90
Rio Brilhante, Braz. F1 79
Río Caribe, Ven. B11 84
Rio Casca, Braz. F7 79
Río Ceballos, Arg. F6 80
Río Chico, Ven. B10 84
Rio Claro, Braz. G5 79
Rio Claro, Trin. I14 94
Río Colorado, Arg. J6 80
Río Cuarto, Arg. G6 80
Rio de Contas, Braz. B8 79
Rio de Janeiro, Braz. G7 79
Rio de Janeiro, state, Braz. G7 79
Río de Jesús, Pan. J13 92
Rio Dell, Ca., U.S. B1 112
Río de Oro, Col. C6 84
Rio do Prado, Braz. D8 79
Rio do Sul, Braz. D14 80
Rio Espera, Braz. F7 79
Río Gallegos, Arg. G3 78
Rio Grande, Braz. G12 80
Río Grande, Mex. F8 90
Río Grande, Nic. E8 92
Rio Grande, N.J., U.S. E3 137
Rio Grande, Oh., U.S. D3 142
Rio Grande, co., Co., U.S. D4 113
Rio Grande see Grande, Rio, stm., N.A. F7 106
Rio Grande City, Tx., U.S. F3 150
Rio Grande do Sul, state, Braz. E11 80
Rio Grande Reservoir, res., Co., U.S. D3 113
Ríohacha, Col. B6 84
Río Hato, Pan. C2 84
Rio Hondo, Tx., U.S. F4 150
Rioja, Peru B3 82
Rio Lagartos, Mex. G15 90
Riolândia, Braz. E4 79
Rio Largo, Braz. E11 76
Riom, Fr. G10 14
Río Mulatos, Bol. H8 82
Riondel, B.C., Can. E9 99
Rio Negro, Braz. E1 79
Rio Negro, Braz. D14 80
Rionegro, Col. D5 84
Rionegro, Col. D6 84
Río Negro, prov., Arg. J6 80
Rio Negro, Pantanal do, sw., Braz. H13 82
Rionero in Vulture, Italy I10 18
Rio Novo do Sul, Braz. F8 79
Rio Pardo, Braz. E12 80
Rio Pardo de Minas, Braz. C7 79
Río Piedras, Arg. C6 80
Río Pilcomayo, Parque Nacional, Arg. C9 80
Rio Piracicaba, Braz. E7 79
Rio Pomba, Braz. F7 79
Rio Preto, Braz. G7 79
Rio Rancho, N.M., U.S. B3 138
Río San Juan, dept., Nic. F10 92
Río Segundo, Arg. F7 80
Riosucio, Col. E5 84
Riosucio, Col. D4 84
Río Tercero, Arg. G6 80
Rio Tinto, Braz. E11 76
Rio Verde, Braz. D3 79
Rioverde, Mex. G10 90
Rio Verde de Mato Grosso, Braz. E1 79
Rio Vermelho, Braz. E7 79
Rio Vista, Ca., U.S. C3 112
Rioz, Fr. E13 14
Riozinho, stm., Braz. I9 84
Ripley, Ont., Can. C3 103
Ripley, Ca., U.S. F6 112
Ripley, Ms., U.S. A5 131
Ripley, N.Y., U.S. C1 139
Ripley, Oh., U.S. D2 142
Ripley, Ok., U.S. A5 143
Ripley, Tn., U.S. B2 149
Ripley, W.V., U.S. C3 155
Ripley, co., In., U.S. F7 121
Ripley, co., Mo., U.S. E7 132
Ripogenus Pond, l., Me., U.S. C3 126
Ripoll, Spain C14 16
Ripon, Que., Can. D2 104
Ripon, Eng., U.K. G12 8
Ripon, Wi., U.S. E5 156
Riposto, Italy L10 18
Rippey, Ia., U.S. C3 122
Ripples, N.B., Can. D3 101
Rippowam, stm., Ct., U.S. E1 114
Ririe, Id., U.S. F7 119
Ririe Lake, res., Id., U.S. F7 119
Risaralda, dept., Col. E4 84
Riscle, Fr. I6 14
Risco, Mo., U.S. E8 132
Risco, Ilha do, i., Braz. I13 84
Rishiri-tō, i., Japan b16 36a
Rishmayyā, Leb. A5 50
Rishon LeẔiyyon, Isr. E3 50
Rising City, Ne., U.S. C8 134
Rising Star, Tx., U.S. C3 150
Rising Sun, De., U.S. D3 115
Rising Sun, In., U.S. G8 121
Rising Sun, Md., U.S. A5 127
Risingsun, Oh., U.S. A2 142
Rison, Ar., U.S. D3 111
Rison, Md., U.S. C3 127
Risør, Nor. L11 6
Rissani, Mor. E8 62
Risti, Est. C7 22
Ritchie, co., W.V., U.S. B3 155
Ritter, Mount, mtn., Ca., U.S. D4 112
Rittman, Oh., U.S. B4 142
Ritzville, Wa., U.S. B7 154
Riva, Italy D5 18
Rivadavia, Arg. H7 80
Rivadavia, Arg. C7 80
Rivadavia, Arg. G4 80
Rivadavia, Arg. F4 80
Rivadavia, Chile E3 80
Rivanna, stm., Va., U.S. C4 153
Rivas, Nic. F9 92
Rivas, dept., Nic. F8 92
Rive-de-Gier, Fr. G11 14
Rivera, Arg. I7 80
Rivera, Col. F5 84
Rivera, Ur. F11 80
Riverbank, Ca., U.S. D3 112
River Bourgeois, N.S., Can. D9 101
River Cess, Lib. I5 64
Riverdale, Ca., U.S. D4 112
Riverdale, Il., U.S. k9 120
Riverdale, Ia., U.S. g11 122
Riverdale, Md., U.S. C4 127
Riverdale, Ne., U.S. D6 134
Riverdale, N.J., U.S. B4 137
Riverdale, N.D., U.S. B4 141
Riverdale, Va., U.S. D4 153
River Edge, N.J., U.S. h8 137
River Falls, Al., U.S. D3 108
River Falls, Wi., U.S. D1 156
River Forest, Il., U.S. k9 120
Rivergaro, Italy E4 18
River Grove, Il., U.S. k9 120
Riverhaven, In., U.S. B7 121
Riverhead, N.Y., U.S. n16 139
River Hebert, N.S., Can. D5 101
River Heights, Ut., U.S. B4 151
River Hills, Wi., U.S. m12 156
Riverhurst, Sask., Can. G2 105
Riverina, reg., Austl. J6 70
River John, N.S., Can. D6 101
River Jordan, B.C., Can. h11 99
River of Ponds, Newf., Can. C3 102
River Pines, Ma., U.S. f10 128
Riverport, N.S., Can. E5 101
River Ridge, La., U.S. k11 125
River Road, Or., U.S. C3 144
River Rouge, Mi., U.S. p15 129
Rivers, Man., Can. D1 100
Riversdale, S. Afr. J5 66
Riverside, Al., U.S. B3 108
Riverside, Ca., U.S. F5 112
Riverside, Il., U.S. k9 120
Riverside, Ia., U.S. C6 122
Riverside, N.J., U.S. C3 137
Riverside, Pa., U.S. E8 145
Riverside, Ut., U.S. B3 151
Riverside, Wa., U.S. A6 154
Riverside, Wy., U.S. E6 157
Riverside, co., Ca., U.S. F5 112
Riverside-Albert, N.B., Can. D5 101
Riverside Reservoir, res., Co., U.S. A6 113
Riverton, Man., Can. D3 100
Riverton, N.Z. G2 72
Riverton, Ct., U.S. B3 114
Riverton, Il., U.S. D4 120
Riverton, Ia., U.S. D2 122
Riverton, Ks., U.S. E9 123
Riverton, Ne., U.S. D7 134
Riverton, N.J., U.S. C3 137
Riverton, Ut., U.S. C4 151
Riverton, Vt., U.S. C3 152
Riverton, Va., U.S. B4 153
Riverton, Wy., U.S. C4 157
Riverton Heights, Wa., U.S. f11 154
River Vale, N.J., U.S. h8 137
Riverview, Fl., U.S. p11 116
Riverview, Mi., U.S. p15 129
Rives, Tn., U.S. A2 149
Rivesaltes, Fr. J9 14
Rives Junction, Mi., U.S. F6 129
Rivesville, W.V., U.S. B4 155
Riviera, Tx., U.S. F4 150
Riviera Beach, Fl., U.S. F6 116
Riviera Beach, Md., U.S. B4 127
Rivière-à-Pierre, Que., Can. B5 104
Rivière-du-Loup, Que., Can. B8 104
Rivière-Trois-Pistoles, Que., Can. A8 104
Rivière-Verte, N.B., Can. B1 101
Riviersonderend, S. Afr. J4 66
Rivne, Ukr. G3 26
Rivoli, Italy D2 18
Riyadh see Ar-Riyāḍ, Sau. Ar. B5 47
Rize, Tur. G16 4
Rizhao, China H7 32
Roa, Nor. K12 6
Roachdale, In., U.S. E4 121
Road Town, Br. Vir. Is. E12 94
Roan Cliffs, clf, U.S. B1 113
Roan Creek, stm., Co., U.S. B2 113
Roane, co., Tn., U.S. D9 149
Roane, co., W.V., U.S. C3 155
Roan High Knob, mtn., U.S. C11 149
Roan Mountain, Tn., U.S. C11 149
Roann, In., U.S. C6 121
Roanne, Fr. F11 14
Roanoke, Al., U.S. B4 108
Roanoke, Il., U.S. C4 120
Roanoke, In., U.S. C7 121
Roanoke, La., U.S. D3 125
Roanoke, Tx., U.S. m9 150
Roanoke, Va., U.S. C3 153
Roanoke, co., Va., U.S. C2 153
Roanoke, stm., U.S. A5 140
Roanoke Island, i., N.C., U.S. B7 140
Roanoke Rapids, N.C., U.S. A5 140
Roanoke Rapids Lake, res., U.S. A5 140
Roan Plateau, plat., U.S. B2 113
Roaring Fork, stm., Co., U.S. C4 113
Roaring Spring, Pa., U.S. F5 145
Roark, Ky., U.S. C6 124
Roatán, Hond. A8 92
Roatán, Isla de, i., Hond. A8 92
Robâa Oued Yahia, Tun. M4 18
Robāṭ Karīm, Iran D11 48
Robb, Alta., Can. C2 98
Robbins, Il., U.S. k9 120
Robbins, N.C., U.S. B3 140
Robbins, Tn., U.S. C9 149
Robbinsdale, Mn., U.S. m12 130
Robbins Island, i., Austl. M6 70
Robbinston, Me., U.S. C5 126
Robbinsville, N.C., U.S. f9 140
Röbel, Ger. B12 10
Robersonville, N.C., U.S. B5 140
Roberta, Ga., U.S. D2 117
Robert Lee, Tx., U.S. D2 150
Roberts, Id., U.S. F6 119
Roberts, Il., U.S. C5 120
Roberts, Mt., U.S. E7 133
Roberts, Wi., U.S. C1 156
Roberts, co., S.D., U.S. B8 148
Roberts, co., Tx., U.S. B2 150
Roberts, Point, c., Wa., U.S. A2 154
Robert's Arm, Newf., Can. D4 102
Roberts Creek Mountain, mtn., Nv., U.S. D5 135
Robertsdale, Al., U.S. E2 108
Robertsdale, Pa., U.S. F5 145
Robertsfield, Lib. H4 64
Robert S. Kerr Reservoir, res., Ok., U.S. B6 143
Roberts Mountain, mtn., Ak., U.S. C6 109
Roberts Mountain, mtn., Wy., U.S. D3 157
Robertson, S. Afr. I4 66
Robertson, co., Ky., U.S. B5 124
Robertson, co., Tn., U.S. A5 149
Robertson, co., Tx., U.S. D4 150
Robertsonville, Que., Can. C6 104
Robertsport, Lib. H4 64
Robertstown, Ga., U.S. B3 117
Robertville, N.B., Can. B4 101
Roberval, Que., Can. A5 104
Robeson, co., N.C., U.S. C3 140
Robins, Ia., U.S. B6 122
Robins Air Force Base, mil., Ga., U.S. D3 117

Name | Map Ref. | Page

Robinson, Il., U.S. D6 120
Robinson, Ks., U.S. C8 123
Robinson, Me., U.S. B5 126
Robinson, N.D., U.S. B6 141
Robinson, Pa., U.S. F3 145
Róbinson Crusoe, Isla, i., Chile H7 74
Robinson Fork, stm., W.V., U.S. k9 155
Robinson Fork, stm., W.V., U.S. m14 155
Robinson Mountain, mtn., Ar., U.S. A1 111
Robinson Range, mts., Austl. E3 68
Robinsons, Newf., Can. D2 102
Robinsonville, Ms., U.S. A3 131
Robinvale, Austl. J5 70
Roblin, Man., Can. D1 100
Roboré, Bol. H12 82
Robson, Mount, mtn., B.C., Can. C8 99
Robstown, Tx., U.S. F4 150
Roby, Tx., U.S. C2 150
Roca, Cabo da, c., Port. G2 16
Rocafuerte, Ec. H2 84
Rocanville, Sask., Can. G5 105
Roca Partida, Isla, i., Mex. H3 90
Roca Partida, Punta, c., Mex. H12 90
Rocas, Atol das, atoll, Braz. D12 76
Roccastrada, Italy F6 18
Rocciamelone, mtn., Italy D2 18
Rocha, Ur. H9 74
Rocha, Ur. H11 80
Rochdale, Ma., U.S. B4 128
Rochedinho, Braz. F1 79
Rochedinho, Braz. I14 82
Rochedo, Braz. E1 79
Rochefort, Bel. H7 12
Rochefort, Fr. G6 14
Roche Harbor, Wa., U.S. A2 154
Rochelle, Ga., U.S. E3 117
Rochelle, Il., U.S. B4 120
Rochelle Park, N.J., U.S. h8 137
Roche-Percée, Sask., Can. H4 105
Rocheport, Mo., U.S. C5 132
Rochester, Austl. K6 70
Rochester, Alta., Can. B4 98
Rochester, Il., U.S. D4 120
Rochester, In., U.S. B5 121
Rochester, Ky., U.S. C3 124
Rochester, Mi., U.S. F7 129
Rochester, Mn., U.S. F6 130
Rochester, N.H., U.S. D5 136
Rochester, N.Y., U.S. B3 139
Rochester, Pa., U.S. E1 145
Rochester, Vt., U.S. D3 152
Rochester, Wa., U.S. C2 154
Rochester, Wi., U.S. n11 156
Rochester Mountain, mtn., Vt., U.S. D3 152
Rochfort Bridge, Alta., Can. C3 98
Rochlitz, Ger. D12 10
Rock, Mi., U.S. B3 129
Rock, co., Mn., U.S. G2 130
Rock, co., Ne., U.S. B6 134
Rock, co., Wi., U.S. F4 156
Rock, stm., U.S. B3 120
Rock, stm., U.S. A1 122
Rockall, i., Scot., U.K. D5 4
Rockaway, N.J., U.S. B3 137
Rockaway, Or., U.S. B3 144
Rockaway Beach, Mo., U.S. E4 132
Rockbridge, Il., U.S. D3 120
Rockbridge, co., Va., U.S. C3 153
Rockcastle, co., Ky., U.S. C5 124
Rockcastle, stm., Ky., U.S. C5 124
Rockcliffe Park, Ont., Can. h12 103
Rock Creek, B.C., Can. E8 99
Rock Creek, Mn., U.S. E6 130
Rock Creek, Oh., U.S. A5 142
Rock Creek, stm., U.S. B3 127
Rock Creek, stm., U.S. h14 154
Rock Creek, stm., Il., U.S. B4 120
Rock Creek, stm., Ks., U.S. g10 123
Rock Creek, stm., Ne., U.S. g11 134
Rock Creek, stm., Nv., U.S. C5 135
Rock Creek, stm., Or., U.S. B6 144
Rock Creek, stm., Wa., U.S. D5 154
Rock Creek, stm., Wa., U.S. B8 154
Rock Creek, stm., Wy., U.S. E6 157
Rock Creek Butte, mtn., Or., U.S. C8 144
Rockdale, Il., U.S. B5 120
Rockdale, Md., U.S. B4 127
Rockdale, Tx., U.S. D4 150
Rockdale, co., Ga., U.S. C3 117
Rockefeller Plateau, plat., Ant. D10 73
Rockenhausen, Ger. F7 10
Rockfall, Ct., U.S. C5 114
Rock Falls, Il., U.S. B4 120
Rockfield, In., U.S. C4 121
Rockfield, Ky., U.S. D3 124
Rockford, Al., U.S. C3 108
Rockford, Il., U.S. A4 120
Rockford, Ia., U.S. A5 122
Rockford, Mi., U.S. E5 129
Rockford, Mn., U.S. E5 130
Rockford, Oh., U.S. B1 142
Rockford, Tn., U.S. D10 149
Rockford, Wa., U.S. B8 154
Rockglen, Sask., Can. H3 105
Rock Hall, Md., U.S. B5 127
Rockhampton, Austl. D9 70
Rock Hill, S.C., U.S. B5 147
Rockholds, Ky., U.S. D5 124
Rockingham, N.C., U.S. C3 140
Rockingham, co., N.H., U.S. D4 136
Rockingham, co., N.C., U.S. A3 140
Rockingham, co., Va., U.S. B4 153
Rockingham Bay, b., Austl. B7 70
Rock Island, Que., Can. D5 104
Rock Island, Il., U.S. B3 120
Rock Island, Ok., U.S. B7 143
Rock Island, Wa., U.S. B5 154
Rock Island, co., Il., U.S. B3 120
Rock Island, i., Fl., U.S. C3 116
Rock Island, i., Wi., U.S. C7 156
Rocklake, N.D., U.S. A6 141
Rock Lake, l., Man., Can. E2 100
Rock Lake, l., Wa., U.S. B8 154
Rockland, Ont., Can. B9 103
Rockland, Id., U.S. G6 119
Rockland, Me., U.S. D3 126
Rockland, Ma., U.S. B6 128
Rockland, Mi., U.S. m12 129
Rockland, co., N.Y., U.S. D6 139
Rocklands Reservoir, res., Austl. K5 70
Rockledge, Fl., U.S. D6 116
Rockledge, Ga., U.S. D4 117
Rockledge, Pa., U.S. o20 145
Rocklin, Ca., U.S. C3 112
Rockmart, Ga., U.S. B1 117
Rock Mountain, mtn., Al., U.S. B2 108
Rock Mountain, mtn., Co., U.S. D3 113
Rock Point, Az., U.S. A6 110
Rockport, Ar., U.S. g8 111
Rockport, Il., U.S. D2 120
Rockport, In., U.S. I3 121
Rockport, Ky., U.S. C3 124
Rockport, Me., U.S. D3 126
Rockport, Ma., U.S. A6 128
Rock Port, Mo., U.S. A2 132
Rockport, Tx., U.S. F4 150
Rockport, Wa., U.S. A4 154
Rock Rapids, Ia., U.S. A1 122
Rock River, Wy., U.S. E7 157
Rock Run, Al., U.S. A4 108
Rock Sound, Bah. B6 94
Rocksprings, Tx., U.S. D2 150
Rock Springs, Wi., U.S. E4 156
Rock Springs, Wy., U.S. E3 157
Rockstone, Guy. E13 84
Rockton, Il., U.S. A4 120
Rockvale, Co., U.S. C5 113
Rockvale, Tn., U.S. B5 149
Rock Valley, Ia., U.S. A1 122
Rockville, In., U.S. E3 121
Rockville, Md., U.S. B3 127
Rockville, Mn., U.S. E4 130
Rockville, Mo., U.S. C3 132
Rockville Centre, N.Y., U.S. n15 139
Rockwall, Tx., U.S. C4 150
Rockwall, co., Tx., U.S. C4 150
Rockwell, Ia., U.S. B4 122
Rockwell, N.C., U.S. B2 140
Rockwell City, Ia., U.S. B3 122
Rockwell Park, N.C., U.S. B2 140
Rockwood, Me., U.S. C3 126
Rockwood, Mi., U.S. F7 129
Rockwood, Pa., U.S. G3 145
Rockwood, Tn., U.S. D9 149
Rocky, stm., N.C., U.S. B2 140
Rocky, stm., S.C., U.S. C2 147
Rocky, East Branch, stm., Oh., U.S. h9 142
Rocky, West Branch, stm., Oh., U.S. h9 142
Rocky Boy, Mt., U.S. B7 133
Rocky Boys Indian Reservation, Mt., U.S. B7 133
Rocky Comfort, Mo., U.S. E3 132
Rocky Coulee, val., Wa., U.S. B6 154
Rockyford, Alta., Can. D4 98
Rocky Ford, Co., U.S. C7 113
Rocky Ford, Ga., U.S. D5 117
Rocky Fork Lake, l., Oh., U.S. C2 142
Rocky Gap, Va., U.S. C1 153
Rocky Harbour, Newf., Can. D3 102
Rocky Hill, Ct., U.S. C5 114
Rocky Hill, Ky., U.S. C3 124
Rocky Lake, l., Man., Can. B1 100
Rocky Lake, l., Me., U.S. D5 126
Rocky Mount, N.C., U.S. B5 140
Rocky Mount, Va., U.S. D3 153
Rocky Mountain, mtn., Mt., U.S. C4 133
Rocky Mountain House, Alta., Can. C3 98
Rocky Mountain National Park, Co., U.S. A5 113
Rocky Mountains, mts., N.A. E8 86
Rocky Point, N.C., U.S. C5 140
Rocky Ripple, In., U.S. k10 121
Rocky River, Oh., U.S. A4 142
Rocky Top, mtn., Or., U.S. C4 144
Roda, Va., U.S. f9 153
Rodalben, Ger. F7 10
Rødbyhavn, Den. N12 6
Roddickton, Newf., Can. C3 102
Roddy, Tn., U.S. D9 149
Rodeo, Arg. F4 80
Rodeo, Mex. E7 90
Rodeo, N.M., U.S. F1 138
Roderfield, W.V., U.S. D3 155
Roderick Island, i., B.C., Can. C3 99
Rodessa, La., U.S. B2 125
Rodewisch, Ger. E12 10
Rodey, N.M., U.S. E2 138
Rodez, Fr. H9 14
Ródhos (Rhodes), Grc. M12 20
Ródhos (Rhodes), i., Grc. M12 20
Rodi Garganico, Italy H10 18
Roding, Ger. F12 10
Rodney, Ont., Can. E3 103
Rodney, Cape, c., Ak., U.S. C6 109
Rodney Pond, l., Newf., Can. D4 102
Rodney Village, De., U.S. D3 115
Rodniki, Russia D24 22
Rodrigues, i., Mrts. K7 24
Roe, Ar., U.S. C4 111
Roebling, N.J., U.S. C3 137
Roebourne, Austl. D3 68
Roebuck, S.C., U.S. B4 147
Roeland Park, Ks., U.S. k16 123
Roelofarendsveen, Neth. D6 12
Roer (Rur), stm., Eur. F9 12
Roermond, Neth. F9 12
Roes Welcome Sound, strt., N.W. Ter., Can. D15 96
Roff, Ok., U.S. C5 143
Rogačevo, Russia E20 22
Rogačov, Bela. H13 22
Rogagua, Laguna, l., Bol. E8 82
Rogaguado, Laguna, l., Bol. E9 82
Rogaland, co., Nor. L10 6
Rogatica, Bos. F3 20
Roger Mills, co., Ok., U.S. B2 143
Rogers, Ar., U.S. A1 111
Rogers, Ct., U.S. B8 114
Rogers, Mn., U.S. E5 130
Rogers, Tx., U.S. D4 150
Rogers, co., Ok., U.S. A6 143
Rogers, Mount, mtn., Va., U.S. f10 153
Rogers City, Mi., U.S. C7 129
Rogers Lake, res., Ct., U.S. D6 114
Rogers Pass, Mt., U.S. C4 133
Rogersville, N.B., Can. C4 101
Rogersville, Al., U.S. A2 108
Rogersville, Mo., U.S. D4 132
Rogersville, Tn., U.S. C10 149
Roggen, Co., U.S. A6 113
Rogliano, Fr. J16 14
Rogoźno, Pol. C17 10
Rogue, stm., Or., U.S. E2 144
Rogue River, Or., U.S. E3 144
Rohnert Park, Ca., U.S. C2 112
Rohtak, India F7 44
Rohunta, Laguna, b., Hond. B11 92
Roi Et, Thai. F7 40
Roisel, Fr. C10 14
Roja, Lat. D5 22
Rojas, Arg. H8 80
Rojo, Cabo, c., Mex. G11 90
Rojo, Cabo, c., P.R. F11 94
Rokeby National Park, Austl. B8 68
Rokiškis, Lith. F8 22
Rokycany, Czech Rep. F13 10
Roland, Man., Can. E3 100
Roland, Ar., U.S. C3 111
Roland, Ia., U.S. B4 122
Roland, Ok., U.S. B7 143
Roland, Lake, res., Md., U.S. g11 127
Rolândia, Braz. G3 79
Røldal, Nor. L10 6
Roldán, Arg. G8 80
Roldanillo, Col. E4 84
Rolesville, N.C., U.S. B4 140
Rolette, N.D., U.S. A6 141
Rolette, co., N.D., U.S. A6 141
Rolfe, Ia., U.S. B3 122
Roll, Az., U.S. E2 110
Rolla, B.C., Can. B7 99
Rolla, Ks., U.S. E2 123
Rolla, Mo., U.S. D6 132
Rolla, N.D., U.S. A6 141
Rolle, Switz. F5 13
Rolleston, Austl. E8 70
Rollingbay, Wa., U.S. e10 154
Rolling Fork, Ms., U.S. C3 131
Rolling Fork, stm., Ar., U.S. C1 111
Rolling Fork, stm., Ky., U.S. C4 124
Rolling Hills, Wy., U.S. D7 157
Rolling Meadows, Il., U.S. h8 120
Rollingstone, Austl. B7 70
Rollingstone, Mn., U.S. F7 130
Rollins, Mt., U.S. C2 133
Rollinsford, N.H., U.S. D5 136
Roma, Austl. F8 70
Roma (Rome), Italy H7 18
Roma, Tx., U.S. F3 150
Romagna, hist. reg., Italy H18 14
Romain, Cape, c., S.C., U.S. F9 147
Romaine, stm., Can. A14 106
Roman, Rom. C10 20
Romania (România), ctry., Eur. F13 4
Romankivtsi, Ukr. A11 20
Roman-Kosh, hora, mtn., Ukr. I4 26
Roman Nose Mountain, mtn., Md., U.S. m12 127
Roman Nose Mountain, mtn., Or., U.S. D3 144
Romano, Cape, c., Fl., U.S. G5 116
Romano, Cayo, i., Cuba C6 94
Romanshorn, Switz. C11 13
Romans [-sur-Isère], Fr. G12 14
Romanzof, Cape, c., Ak., U.S. C6 109
Romanzof Mountains, mts., Ak., U.S. B11 109
Romayor, Tx., U.S. D5 150
Rombauer, Mo., U.S. E7 132
Rome see Roma, Italy H7 18
Rome, Ga., U.S. B1 117
Rome, Il., U.S. C4 120
Rome, Ms., U.S. B3 131
Rome, N.Y., U.S. B5 139
Rome, Oh., U.S. D3 142
Rome City, In., U.S. B7 121
Romeo, Co., U.S. D4 113
Romeo, Mi., U.S. F7 129
Romeoville, Il., U.S. k8 120
Rometan, Uzb. B18 48
Romilly-sur-Seine, Fr. D10 14
Rommani, Mor. C7 62
Romney, In., U.S. D4 121
Romney, W.V., U.S. B6 155
Romny, Ukr. G4 26
Romont, Switz. E6 13
Romorantin-Lanthenay, Fr. E8 14
Romulus, Mi., U.S. p15 129
Ron, Mui, c., Viet. E9 40
Ronald, Wa., U.S. B4 154
Ronan, Mt., U.S. C2 133
Roncador, Serra do, plat., Braz. F8 76
Ronceverte, W.V., U.S. D4 155
Ronchamp, Fr. E13 14
Ronda, Spain I6 16
Rønde, Den. M12 6
Rondo, Ar., U.S. C5 111
Rondon, Braz. G2 79
Rondônia, state, Braz. D10 82
Rondonópolis, Braz. D1 79
Ronge, Lac la, l., Sask., Can. B3 105
Rongshui, China B10 40
Rõngu, Est. C9 22
Rønne, Den. N14 6
Ronneby, Swe. M14 6
Ronne Entrance, b., Ant. C12 73
Ronne Ice Shelf, Ant. C12 73
Ronse (Renaix), Bel. G4 12
Ronuro, stm., Braz. B1 79
Roodhouse, Il., U.S. D3 120
Roof Butte, mtn., Az., U.S. A6 110
Rooiboklaagte, stm., Nmb. C5 66
Rooks, co., Ks., U.S. C4 123
Roopville, Ga., U.S. C1 117
Roorkee, India F7 44
Roosendaal, Neth. E5 12
Roosevelt, Az., U.S. D4 110
Roosevelt, Mn., U.S. B3 130
Roosevelt, Ok., U.S. C2 143
Roosevelt, Ut., U.S. C5 151
Roosevelt, co., Mt., U.S. B11 133
Roosevelt, co., N.M., U.S. C6 138
Roosevelt, stm., Braz. B11 82
Roosevelt Island, i., Ant. C9 73
Roosevelt Park, Mi., U.S. E4 129
Root, stm., Mn., U.S. G7 130
Root, stm., Wi., U.S. n12 156
Rootstown, Oh., U.S. A4 142
Roper, N.C., U.S. B6 140
Roper, stm., Austl. B6 68
Roquefort, Fr. H6 14
Roque Pérez, Arg. H9 80
Roraima, state, Braz. G12 84
Roraima, Mount, mtn., S.A. E12 84
Rorketon, Man., Can. D2 100
Røros, Nor. J12 6
Rorschach, Switz. D12 13
Rørvik, Nor. I12 6
Rosa, Lake, l., Bah. D8 94
Rosa, Monte, mtn., Eur. G8 13
Rošal', Russia F22 22
Rosales, Mex. C7 90
Rosalia, Ks., U.S. E7 123
Rosalia, Wa., U.S. B8 154
Rosalie, Ne., U.S. B9 134
Rosalind, Alta., Can. C4 98
Rosamond, Ca., U.S. E4 112
Rosamond, Il., U.S. D4 120
Rosamorada, Mex. F7 90
Rosana, Braz. B12 80
Rosario, Arg. G8 80
Rosário, Braz. D10 76
Rosario, Mex. D5 90
Rosario, Mex. F7 90
Rosario, Para. C10 80
Rosario, Ur. H10 80
Rosario, Ven. B6 84
Rosario, stm., Arg. C6 80
Rosario, Bahía, b., Mex. C2 90
Rosario, Islas del, is., Col. B5 84
Rosario de Arriba, Mex. B2 90
Rosario de la Frontera, Arg. C6 80
Rosario de Lerma, Arg. C6 80
Rosario del Tala, Arg. G9 80
Rosário do Sul, Braz. F11 80
Rosário Oeste, Braz. F13 82
Rosarito, Mex. D4 90
Rosarno, Italy K10 18
Roščino, Russia A12 22
Roscoe, Il., U.S. A5 120
Roscoe, N.Y., U.S. D6 139
Roscoe, Pa., U.S. F2 145
Roscoe, S.D., U.S. B6 148
Roscoe, Tx., U.S. C2 150
Roscommon, Ire. H5 8
Roscommon, Mi., U.S. D6 129
Roscommon, co., Ire. H5 8
Roscommon, co., Mi., U.S. D6 129
Roscrea, Ire. I6 8
Rose, Mount, mtn., Nv., U.S. D2 135
Roseau, Dom. G14 94
Roseau, Mn., U.S. B3 130
Roseau, co., Mn., U.S. B3 130
Roseau, South Fork, stm., Mn., U.S. B3 130
Rosebery, Austl. M6 70
Rose-Blanche [-Harbour le Cou], Newf., Can. E2 102
Roseboro, N.C., U.S. C4 140
Rosebud, Alta., Can. D4 98
Rose Bud, Ar., U.S. B3 111
Rosebud, Mo., U.S. C6 132
Rosebud, Mt., U.S. D10 133
Rosebud, S.D., U.S. D5 148
Rosebud, Tx., U.S. D4 150
Rosebud, co., Mt., U.S. D10 133
Rosebud, stm., Alta., Can. D4 98
Rosebud Creek, stm., Mt., U.S. E10 133
Rosebud Indian Reservation, S.D., U.S. D5 148
Roseburg, Or., U.S. D3 144
Rosebush, Mi., U.S. E6 129
Rose City, Mi., U.S. D6 129
Rose Creek, Mn., U.S. G6 130
Rosedale, Austl. E9 70
Rosedale, Alta., Can. D4 98
Rosedale, In., U.S. E3 121
Rosedale, Md., U.S. g11 127
Rosedale, Ms., U.S. B2 131
Rosedale, Wa., U.S. f10 154
Rosehall, Guy. D14 84
Rosehearty, Scot., U.K. D11 8
Rose-Hill, Mrts. v18 67c
Rose Hill, Ks., U.S. E6 123
Rose Hill, Ms., U.S. C4 131
Rose Hill, N.C., U.S. C4 140
Rose Hill, Va., U.S. f8 153
Roseisle, Man., Can. E2 100
Roseland, Fl., U.S. E6 116
Roseland, In., U.S. A5 121
Roseland, La., U.S. D5 125
Roseland, Ne., U.S. D7 134
Roseland, Oh., U.S. B3 142
Roselawn, In., U.S. B3 121
Roselle, Il., U.S. k8 120
Roselle, N.J., U.S. k7 137
Roselle Park, N.J., U.S. k7 137
Rosemary, Alta., Can. D4 98
Rosemère, Que., Can. p19 104
Rosemont, W.V., U.S. k10 155
Rosemount, Mn., U.S. F5 130
Rosenberg, Tx., U.S. E5 150
Rosendal, Nor. L10 6
Rosendale, Mo., U.S. A3 132
Rosendale, Wi., U.S. E5 156
Roseneath, Ont., Can. C6 103
Rosenfeld, Man., Can. E3 100
Rosenheim, Ger. H12 10
Rose Peak, mtn., Az., U.S. D6 110
Rosepine, La., U.S. D2 125
Rose Point, c., B.C., Can. B2 99
Roseto, Pa., U.S. E11 145
Rosetown, Sask., Can. F1 105
Rosetta see Rashīd, Egypt B6 60
Rose Valley, Sask., Can. E4 105
Roseville, Ca., U.S. C3 112
Roseville, Il., U.S. C3 120
Roseville, Mi., U.S. o16 129
Roseville, Mn., U.S. m12 130
Roseville, Oh., U.S. C3 142
Rosewood, Austl. F10 70
Rosewood Heights, Il., U.S. E3 120
Rosharon, Tx., U.S. r14 150
Rosh Ha'Ayin, Isr. D3 50
Rosholt, S.D., U.S. B9 148
Rosholt, Wi., U.S. D4 156
Rosh Pinna, Isr. C5 50
Rosiclare, Il., U.S. F5 120
Rosignano Marittimo, Italy F5 18
Rosignol, Guy. D14 84
Roşiori de Vede, Rom. E9 20
Roskilde, Den. N13 6
Rosl'akovo, Russia G23 6
Rosl'atino, Russia B27 22
Roslavl', Russia H15 22
Roslyn, S.D., U.S. B8 148
Roslyn, Wa., U.S. B4 154
Roslyn Heights, N.Y., U.S. h13 139
Rosporden, Fr. E3 14
Ross, Austl. N7 70
Ross, N.Z. E3 72
Ross, Oh., U.S. C1 142
Ross, co., Oh., U.S. C2 142
Rossano, Italy J11 18
Ross Barnett Reservoir, res., Ms., U.S. C3 131
Rossburn, Man., Can. D1 100
Ross Dam, Wa., U.S. A4 154
Rosseau, Ont., Can. B5 103
Rossell y Rius, Ur. G11 80
Rossendale, Man., Can. E2 100
Rossford, Oh., U.S. A2 142
Ross Ice Shelf, Ant. D9 73
Rossignol, Lake, l., N.S., Can. E4 101
Ross Island, i., Ant. C8 73
Ross Island, i., Man., Can. B3 100
Rossiter, Pa., U.S. E4 145
Rossiya see Russia, ctry., Eur. E14 26
Ross Lake National Recreation Area, Wa., U.S. A5 154
Rossland, B.C., Can. E9 99
Rosslare, Ire. I7 8
Rosslau, Ger. D12 10
Rosso, Maur. C2 64
Ross-on-Wye, Eng., U.K. J11 8
Rossony, Bela. F11 22
Rossoš', Russia G5 26
Ross River, Yukon, Can. D6 96
Ross Sea, Ant. C9 73
Rosston, Ar., U.S. D2 111
Rossville, Ga., U.S. B1 117
Rossville, Il., U.S. C6 120
Rossville, In., U.S. D4 121
Rossville, Ks., U.S. C8 123
Rossville, Tn., U.S. B2 149
Rossway, N.S., Can. E4 101
Rosthern, Sask., Can. E2 105
Rostock, Ger. A12 10
Rostov, Russia D22 22
Rostov-na-Donu, Russia H5 26
Roswell, Ga., U.S. B2 117
Roswell, Id., U.S. F2 119
Roswell, N.M., U.S. D5 138
Rota, Spain I5 16
Rotan, Tx., U.S. C2 150
Rotenburg, Ger. B9 10
Rotenburg, Ger. D9 10
Roth, Ger. F11 10
Rothaargebirge, mts., Ger. D8 10
Rothbury, Mi., U.S. E4 129
Rothenburg ob der Tauber, Ger. F10 10
Rothesay, N.B., Can. D4 101
Rothsay, Mn., U.S. D2 130
Rothschild, Wi., U.S. D4 156
Rothsville, Pa., U.S. F9 145
Roti, Pulau, i., Indon. H7 38
Roto, Austl. I6 70
Rotondella, Italy I11 18
Rotorua, N.Z. C6 72
Rott am Inn, Ger. H12 10
Rottenburg, Ger. G8 10
Rottenmann, Aus. H14 10
Rotterdam, Neth. E5 12
Rotterdam, N.Y., U.S. C6 139
Rottweil, Ger. G8 10
Roubaix, Fr. B10 14
Roubideau Creek, stm., Co., U.S. C2 113
Roudnice, Czech Rep. E14 10
Rouen, Fr. C8 14
Rougé, Fr. E5 14
Rouge, stm., Que., Can. D3 104
Rougemont, Fr. E13 14
Rougemont, N.C., U.S. A4 140
Rough, stm., Ky., U.S. C3 124
Rough River Lake, res., Ky., U.S. C3 124
Rougon, La., U.S. D4 125
Rouillac, Fr. G6 14
Rouleau, Sask., Can. G3 105
Roulette, Pa., U.S. C5 145
Round Harbour, Newf., Can. D4 102
Round Hill, Alta., Can. C4 98
Round Hill, N.S., Can. E4 101
Round Hill, Va., U.S. A5 153
Round Hill Head, c., Austl. E9 70
Round Island, i., Ms., U.S. g8 131
Round Lake, Il., U.S. h8 120
Round Lake, Mn., U.S. G3 130
Round Lake, l., Ont., Can. B7 103
Round Lake, l., Sask., Can. G4 105
Round Lake Beach, Il., U.S. h8 120
Round Mound, hill, Ks., U.S. D4 123
Round Mountain, Nv., U.S. E4 135
Round Mountain, mtn., Austl. H10 70
Round Oak, Ga., U.S. C3 117
Round Pond, Ar., U.S. B5 111
Round Pond, Me., U.S. E3 126
Round Rock, Az., U.S. A6 110
Round Rock, Tx., U.S. D4 150
Round Top Hill, mtn., Ma., U.S. B2 128
Roundup, Mt., U.S. D8 133
Round Valley Indian Reservation, Ca., U.S. C2 112
Round Valley Reservoir, res., N.J., U.S. B3 137
Rouses Point, N.Y., U.S. f11 139
Roussillon, hist. reg., Fr. J9 14
Routt, co., Co., U.S. A3 113
Rouxville, S. Afr. H8 66
Rouyn [-Noranda], Que., Can. k11 104
Rouzerville, Pa., U.S. G6 145
Rovaniemi, Fin. H19 6
Rovato, Italy D5 18
Rover, Ar., U.S. C2 111
Rover, Tn., U.S. B5 149
Rovereto, Italy D6 18
Roversi, Arg. D8 80
Rovigo, Italy D6 18
Rovira, Col. E5 84
Rovuma (Ruvuma), stm., Afr. D7 58
Rowan, co., Ky., U.S. B6 124
Rowan, co., N.C., U.S. B2 140
Rowan Lake, l., Ont., Can. E5 100
Rowe, N.M., U.S. B4 138
Rowland, N.C., U.S. C3 140
Rowlesburg, W.V., U.S. B5 155
Rowletts, Ky., U.S. C4 124
Rowley, Ia., U.S. B6 122
Rowley, Ma., U.S. A6 128
Rowley Island, i., N.W. Ter., Can. C17 96
Rowley Shoals, rf., Austl. C3 68
Roxana, De., U.S. G5 115
Roxas, Phil. C7 38
Roxboro, N.C., U.S. A4 140
Roxburgh, N.Z. F2 72
Roxbury, Ks., U.S. D6 123
Roxbury, Vt., U.S. C3 152
Roxie, Ms., U.S. D2 131
Roxo, Cap, c., Afr. E1 64
Roxton, Tx., U.S. C5 150
Roxton Falls, Que., Can. D5 104
Roxton Pond, Que., Can. D5 104
Roy, Mt., U.S. C8 133
Roy, N.M., U.S. B5 138
Roy, Ut., U.S. B3 151
Roy, Wa., U.S. C3 154
Royal, Ar., U.S. C2 111
Royal, Ia., U.S. A2 122
Royal, Tn., U.S. B5 149
Royal, stm., Me., U.S. g7 126
Royal Canal, Ire. H6 8
Royal Center, In., U.S. C4 121
Royale, Isle, i., Mi., U.S. h9 129
Royal Gorge, val., Co., U.S. C5 113
Royal Leamington Spa, Eng., U.K. I12 8
Royal Oak, Md., U.S. C5 127
Royal Oak, Mi., U.S. F7 129
Royal Pines, N.C., U.S. f10 140
Royalton, Il., U.S. F4 120
Royalton, Ky., U.S. C6 124
Royalton, Mn., U.S. E4 130
Royal Tunbridge Wells, Eng., U.K. J14 8
Royan, Fr. G5 14
Roye, Fr. C9 14
Royersford, Pa., U.S. F10 145
Royerton, In., U.S. D7 121
Roylyanka, Ukr. C13 20
Royse City, Tx., U.S. C4 150
Royston, B.C., Can. E5 99
Royston, Ga., U.S. B3 117
Rožaj, Yugo. G4 20
Roždestvo, Russia D16 22
Rozel, Ks., U.S. D4 123
Rozet, Wy., U.S. B7 157
Rožňava, Slvk. G20 10
Roznov, Rom. C10 20
Roztocze, hills, Eur. E22 10
Rtiščevo, Russia G6 26
Ruacaná, Nmb. A2 66
Ruacana Falls, wtfl, Afr. A2 66
Ruapehu, mtn., N.Z. C5 72
Ruapehu, Mount, mtn., N.Z. L21 158
Rub' al Khali see Ar-Rub' al-Khālī, des., Asia D7 47
Rubcovsk, Russia G8 28
Rubiataba, Braz. C4 79
Rubidoux, Ca., U.S. n14 112
Rubim, Braz. D8 79
Rubino, C. Iv. H7 64
Rubio, Ven. D6 84
Rubizhne, Ukr. H5 26
Ruboani, Sud. M6 60
Rubonia, Fl., U.S. p10 116
Ruby, Ak., U.S. C8 109
Ruby, S.C., U.S. B7 147
Ruby Dome, mtn., Nv., U.S. C6 135
Ruby Lake, l., Nv., U.S. C6 135
Ruby Mountains, mts., Nv., U.S. C6 135
Ruby Range, mts., Co., U.S. C3 113
Ruby Range, mts., Mt., U.S. E4 133
Rucava, Lat. E4 22
Rudall, Austl. I2 70
Rudall River National Park, Austl. D4 68
Ruda Śląska, Pol. E18 10
Rūdbār, Afg. F17 48
Rudd, Ia., U.S. A5 122
Ruddels Mills, Ky., U.S. B5 124
Rudensk, Bela. H10 22
Rüdersdorf, Ger. C13 10
Rūdiškės, Lith. G7 22
Rudn'a, Russia G14 22
Rudnyj, Kaz. G10 26
Rudnytsya, Ukr. A12 20
Rudo, Bos. F3 20
Rudolf, Lake (Lake Turkana), l., Afr. H8 56
Rudolph, Oh., U.S. A2 142
Rudolstadt, Ger. E11 10
Rudong, China C10 34
Rūdsar, Iran C11 48
Rudyard, Mi., U.S. B6 129
Rudyard, Mt., U.S. B6 133
Rue, Fr. B8 14
Ruen, mtn., Eur. G6 20
Rufā'ah, Sud. J7 60
Ruffieux, Fr. G12 14

Name	Map Ref.	Page
Ruffin, S.C., U.S.	E6	147
Rufino, Arg.	H7	80
Rufisque, Sen.	D1	64
Rufus, Or., U.S.	B6	144
Rufus Woods Lake, res., Wa., U.S.	A6	154
Rugao, China	C9	34
Rugby, Eng., U.K.	I12	8
Rugby, N.D., U.S.	A6	141
Rügen, i., Ger.	A13	10
Ruhr, stm., Ger.	F10	12
Rui'an, China	H9	34
Ruidoso, N.M., U.S.	D4	138
Ruidoso Downs, N.M., U.S.	D4	138
Ruijin, China	J5	34
Ruivo, Pico, mtn., Port.	m21	17a
Ruiz, Mex.	G7	90
Ruiz, Nevado del, vol., Col.	A5	84
Ruiz de Montoya, Arg.	D11	80
Rūjiena, Lat.	D8	22
Rukwa, Lake, l., Tan.	C6	58
Rule, Tx., U.S.	C3	150
Rule Creek, stm., Co., U.S.	D7	113
Ruleville, Ms., U.S.	B3	131
Rulo, Ne., U.S.	D10	134
Rum, stm., Mn., U.S.	D5	130
Ruma, Il., U.S.	E3	120
Ruma, Yugo.	D3	20
Rumbek, Sud.	N5	60
Rumbeke, Bel.	G3	12
Rum Cay, i., Bah.	C7	94
Rum Creek, stm., W.V., U.S.	n12	155
Rumford, Me., U.S.	D2	126
Rumia, Pol.	A18	10
Rumigny, Fr.	C11	14
Rum Jungle, Austl.	B6	68
Rummānah, Egypt	B7	60
Rumney, N.H., U.S.	C3	136
Rumney Depot, N.H., U.S.	C3	136
Rumoi, Japan	d16	36a
Rump Mountain, mtn., Me., U.S.	C1	126
Rumsey, Alta., Can.	D4	98
Rumsey, Ky., U.S.	C2	124
Rumson, N.J., U.S.	C4	137
Rumstick Point, c., R.I., U.S.	D5	146
Runan, China	B3	34
Runanga, N.Z.	E3	72
Rundu, Nmb.	A4	66
Runge, Tx., U.S.	E4	150
Rungwa, Tan.	C6	58
Rungwa, stm., Tan.	C6	58
Runnells, Ia., U.S.	C4	122
Runnels, co., Tx., U.S.	D3	150
Runnemede, N.J., U.S.	D2	137
Ruo, stm., China	C6	30
Ruoqiang, China	D4	30
Ruoxi, China	F4	34
Rupea, Rom.	C9	20
Rupert, Id., U.S.	G5	119
Rupert, W.V., U.S.	D4	155
Rupert, Rivière de, stm., Que., Can.	h11	104
Rupununi, stm., Guy.	F13	84
Ruqqād, Wādī ar-, val., Asia	C5	50
Rur (Roer), stm., Eur.	F9	12
Rural Hall, N.C., U.S.	A2	140
Rural Retreat, Va., U.S.	D1	153
Rurrenabaque, Bol.	F8	82
Rurstausee, res., Ger.	G9	12
Rusagonis, N.B., Can.	D3	101
Rušan, Taj.	B4	44
Rusape, Zimb.	B11	66
Ruṣayriṣ, Khazzān ar-, res., Afr.	L8	60
Ruse, Bul.	F9	20
Rush, Ky., U.S.	B7	124
Rush, co., In., U.S.	E6	121
Rush, co., Ks., U.S.	D4	123
Rush, stm., Mn., U.S.	F4	130
Rush, stm., Wi., U.S.	D1	156
Rush Center, Ks., U.S.	D4	123
Rush City, Mn., U.S.	E6	130
Rush Creek, stm., Co., U.S.	C7	113
Rush Creek, stm., Ne., U.S.	C3	134
Rush Creek, stm., Oh., U.S.	B2	142
Rush Creek, stm., Ok., U.S.	C4	143
Rushford, Mn., U.S.	G7	130
Rush Lake, Sask., Can.	G2	105
Rush Lake, l., Mn., U.S.	D3	130
Rush Lake, l., Mn., U.S.	E5	130
Rush Lake, l., Wi., U.S.	E5	156
Rushmere, Va., U.S.	h14	153
Rushmore, Mn., U.S.	G3	130
Rush Springs, Ok., U.S.	C4	143
Rushsylvania, Oh., U.S.	B2	142
Rush Valley, Ut., U.S.	C3	151
Rushville, Il., U.S.	C3	120
Rushville, In., U.S.	E7	121
Rushville, Mo., U.S.	B2	132
Rushville, Ne., U.S.	B3	134
Rusk, Tx., U.S.	D5	150
Rusk, co., Tx., U.S.	C5	150
Rusk, co., Wi., U.S.	C2	156
Ruskin, Fl., U.S.	E4	116
Ruskin, Ne., U.S.	D8	134
Russas, Braz.	D11	76
Russell, Man., Can.	D1	100
Russell, Ont., Can.	B9	103
Russell, Ar., U.S.	B4	111
Russell, Ia., U.S.	D4	122
Russell, Ks., U.S.	D5	123
Russell, Ky., U.S.	B7	124
Russell, Ma., U.S.	B2	128
Russell, Mn., U.S.	F3	130
Russell, Pa., U.S.	C3	145
Russell, co., Al., U.S.	C4	108
Russell, co., Ks., U.S.	D5	123
Russell, co., Ky., U.S.	D4	124
Russell, co., Va., U.S.	f9	153
Russell, Cape, c., N.W. Ter., Can.	A9	96
Russell, Mount, mtn., Ak., U.S.	f16	109
Russell Cave National Monument, Al., U.S.	A4	108
Russell Fork, stm., U.S.	C7	124
Russell Island, i., N.W. Ter., Can.	B13	96
Russell Lake, l., Alta., Can.	A3	98
Russell Springs, Ky., U.S.	C4	124
Russellville, Al., U.S.	A2	108
Russellville, Ar., U.S.	B2	111
Russellville, In., U.S.	E4	121
Russellville, Ky., U.S.	D3	124
Russellville, Mo., U.S.	C5	132
Russellville, Tn., U.S.	C10	149
Rüsselsheim, Ger.	E8	10
Russia, ctry., Eur.	E14	26
Russian, stm., Ca., U.S.	C2	112
Russiaville, In., U.S.	D5	121
Russkij, ostrov, i., Russia	B17	26
Rust, Aus.	H16	10
Rustavi, Geor.	I7	26
Rustburg, Va., U.S.	C3	153
Rustenburg, S. Afr.	E8	66
Ruston, La., U.S.	B3	125
Ruston, Wa., U.S.	B3	154
Rute, Spain	H7	16
Ruteng, Indon.	G7	38
Rutenga, Zimb.	C10	66
Ruth, Ms., U.S.	D3	131
Ruth, Nv., U.S.	D6	135
Ruth, W.V., U.S.	m12	155
Rutherford, N.J., U.S.	B4	137
Rutherford, Tn., U.S.	A3	149
Rutherford, co., N.C., U.S.	B1	140
Rutherford, co., Tn., U.S.	B5	149
Rutherfordton, N.C., U.S.	B1	140
Rutherglen, Ont., Can.	A5	103
Rutheron, N.M., U.S.	A3	138
Ruthton, Mn., U.S.	F2	130
Ruthven, Ia., U.S.	A3	122
Rüti, Switz.	D10	13
Rutland, Il., U.S.	C4	120
Rutland, Ma., U.S.	B4	128
Rutland, N.D., U.S.	C8	141
Rutland, S.D., U.S.	C9	148
Rutland, Vt., U.S.	D3	152
Rutland, co., Vt., U.S.	D2	152
Rutledge, Al., U.S.	D3	108
Rutledge, Ga., U.S.	C3	117
Rutledge, Mn., U.S.	D6	130
Rutledge, Tn., U.S.	C10	149
Rutog, China	D8	44
Rutshuru, Zaire	B5	58
Ruvuma (Rovuma), stm., Afr.	D7	58
Ruy Barbosa, Braz.	B8	79
Ruza, Russia	F19	22
Ruzajevka, Russia	G6	26
Ružany, Bela.	I7	22
Ružomberok, Slvk.	F19	10
Rwanda, ctry., Afr.	B6	58
Ryan, Ia., U.S.	B6	122
Ryan, Ok., U.S.	C4	143
Ryan Creek, stm., Al., U.S.	A3	108
Ryan Peak, mtn., Id., U.S.	F4	119
Rybačij, poluostrov, pen., Russia	G23	6
Rybačje, Kaz.	H8	28
Rybinsk, Russia	C21	22
Rybinskoje vodochranilišče, res., Russia	C21	22
Rybnik, Pol.	E18	10
Rybnoje, Russia	G22	22
Rycroft, Alta., Can.	B1	98
Ryd, Swe.	M14	6
Ryde, Eng., U.K.	K12	8
Ryder, N.D., U.S.	B4	141
Ryderwood, Wa., U.S.	C2	154
Rye, Co., U.S.	D6	113
Rye, N.H., U.S.	D5	136
Rye, N.Y., U.S.	h13	139
Rye Beach, N.H., U.S.	E5	136
Ryegate, Mt., U.S.	D7	133
Rye Patch Dam, Nv., U.S.	C3	135
Rye Patch Reservoir, res., Nv., U.S.	C3	135
Ryes, Fr.	C6	14
Ryley, Alta., Can.	C4	98
Rymanów, Pol.	F21	10
Rypin, Pol.	B19	10
Rysy, mtn., Eur.	F20	10
Ryukyu Islands see Nansei-shotō, is., Japan	F12	30
Ryukyu Trench	F16	158
Ržaksa, Russia	I25	22
Ržanica, Russia	H16	22
Rzeszów, Pol.	E22	10
Ržev, Russia	E17	22

S

Name	Map Ref.	Page
Saale, stm., Ger.	D11	10
Saales, Fr.	D14	14
Saalfeld, Ger.	E11	10
Saar see Saarland, state, Ger.	F6	10
Saar, stm., Eur.	J10	12
Saarbrücken, Ger.	F6	10
Saarburg, Ger.	F6	10
Sääre, Est.	D5	22
Saaremaa, i., Est.	C5	22
Saarland, state, Ger.	F6	10
Saarlouis, Ger.	F6	10
Saas Grund, Switz.	F8	13
Saatlı, Azer.	B10	48
Saavedra, Arg.	I7	80
Saba, i., Neth. Ant.	F13	94
Šabac, Yugo.	E3	20
Sabadell, Spain	D14	16
Sabae, Japan	L11	36
Sabah, hist. reg., Malay.	D6	38
Sabana, Archipiélago de, is., Cuba	C4	94
Sabana de La Mar, Dom. Rep.	E10	94
Sabana de Mendoza, Ven.	C7	84
Sabanagrande, Hond.	D7	92
Sabanalarga, Col.	B5	84
Sabancuy, Mex.	H14	90
Sabaneta, Dom. Rep.	E9	94
Sabaneta, Ven.	C8	84
Sabang, Indon.	E6	38
Sabang, Indon.	L3	40
Sabanillas, Mex.	E9	90
Sabará, Braz.	E7	79
Sabastīyah (Samaria), W.B.	D4	50
Sabattus, Me., U.S.	D2	126
Sabattus Pond, l., Me., U.S.	D2	126
Sabaudia, Italy	H8	18
Sabaya, Bol.	H7	82
Şabāyā, Jabal, i., Sau. Ar.	E2	47
Sabbathday Pond, l., Me., U.S.	g7	126
Ṣāberī, Hāmūn-e, l., Asia	F16	48
Sabetha, Ks., U.S.	C8	123
Sabhā, Libya	C3	56
Sabi (Save), stm., Afr.	C11	66
Sābiē, stm., Afr.	E11	66
Sabile, Lat.	D5	22
Sabillasville, Md., U.S.	A3	127
Sabin, Mn., U.S.	D2	130
Sabina, Oh., U.S.	C2	142
Sabinal, Tx., U.S.	E3	150
Sabinal, Cayo, i., Cuba	D6	94
Sabiñánigo, Spain	C11	16
Sabinas, Mex.	D9	90
Sabinas, stm., Mex.	D9	90
Sabinas, stm., Mex.	D10	90
Sabinas Hidalgo, Mex.	D9	90
Sabine, W.V., U.S.	D3	155
Sabine, co., La., U.S.	C2	125
Sabine, co., Tx., U.S.	D6	150
Sabine, stm., U.S.	D6	150
Sabine Bay, b., N.W. Ter., Can.	A11	96
Sabine Lake, l., U.S.	E2	125
Sabine Pass, Tx., U.S.	E6	150
Sabine Pass, strt., U.S.	E2	125
Sabine Peninsula, pen., N.W. Ter., Can.	A11	96
Sabinópolis, Braz.	E7	79
Sabinosa, Spain	p22	17b
Sabirabad, Azer.	A10	48
Sable, Cape, c., Fl., U.S.	G5	116
Sable, Île de, i., N. Cal.	C11	68
Sable Island, i., N.S., Can.	F10	101
Sable River, N.S., Can.	F4	101
Sablé-sur-Sarthe, Fr.	E6	14
Sabogal, stm., C.R.	G10	92
Sabonkafi, Niger	D14	64
Sabou, Burkina	E8	64
Sabres, Fr.	H6	14
Sabrina Coast, Ant.	B7	73
Sabula, Ia., U.S.	B7	122
Şabyā, Sau. Ar.	F3	47
Sabzevār, Iran	C14	48
Sac, co., Ia., U.S.	B2	122
Sac, stm., Mo., U.S.	D4	132
Sacaba, Bol.	G8	82
Sacaca, Bol.	H8	82
Sacajawea, Lake, res., Wa., U.S.	C7	154
Sacajawea Peak, mtn., Or., U.S.	B9	144
Sacanche, Peru	B3	82
Sacandaga Lake, l., N.Y., U.S.	B6	139
Sac and Fox Indian Reservation, Ia., U.S.	C5	122
Sacariúna, stm., Braz.	E13	82
Sacaton, Az., U.S.	D4	110
Sac City, Ia., U.S.	B2	122
Săcele, Rom.	D9	20
Sachalin, ostrov (Sakhalin), i., Russia	G20	28
Sachalinskij zaliv, b., Russia	G20	28
Sachayoj, Arg.	D8	80
Sachem Head, Ct., U.S.	E5	114
Sachigo Lake, l., Ont., Can.	C5	100
Šachovskaja, Russia	E18	22
Šachrisabz, Uzb.	J11	26
Sachse, Tx., U.S.	n10	150
Sachsen, state, Ger.	D13	10
Sachsen-Anhalt, state, Ger.	C11	10
Sachs Harbour, N.W. Ter., Can.	B7	96
Šachty, Russia	H6	26
Sachuest Point, c., R.I., U.S.	F6	146
Šachunja, Russia	F7	26
Šack, Russia	G24	22
Sackets Harbor, N.Y., U.S.	B4	139
Sackville, N.B., Can.	D5	101
Saco, Me., U.S.	E2	126
Saco, Mt., U.S.	B9	133
Saco, stm., U.S.	E2	126
Saco, East Branch, stm., N.H., U.S.	B4	136
Sacramento, Braz.	E5	79
Sacramento, Ca., U.S.	C3	112
Sacramento, Ky., U.S.	C2	124
Sacramento, N.M., U.S.	E4	138
Sacramento, co., Ca., U.S.	C3	112
Sacramento, stm., Ca., U.S.	C3	112
Sacramento, stm., N.M., U.S.	E4	138
Sacramento, Pampa del, pl., Peru	C4	82
Sacramento Mountains, mts., N.M., U.S.	E4	138
Sacramento Valley, val., Az., U.S.	B1	110
Sacramento Valley, val., Ca., U.S.	C2	112
Sacre, stm., Braz.	E12	82
Sacré-Coeur-Saguenay, Que., Can.	A8	104
Sacred Heart, Mn., U.S.	F3	130
Sacupana, Ven.	C12	84
Sada, Spain	B3	16
Sa'dah, Yemen	F3	47
Saddle (Burnt), stm., Alta., Can.	B1	98
Saddle, stm., N.J., U.S.	h8	137
Saddleback Mountain, mtn., Az., U.S.	k8	110
Saddleback Mountain, mtn., Me., U.S.	D2	126
Saddleback Mountain, mtn., Me., U.S.	B4	126
Saddle Ball Mountain, mtn., Ma., U.S.	A1	128
Saddle Brook, N.J., U.S.	h8	137
Saddlebunch Keys, is., Fl., U.S.	H5	116
Saddle Mountain, mtn., Or., U.S.	B3	144
Saddle Mountains, mts., Wa., U.S.	C5	154
Saddle River, N.J., U.S.	A4	137
Sa Dec, Viet.	I8	40
Sadêng, China	E16	44
Sadieville, Ky., U.S.	B5	124
Sadiola, Mali	E4	64
Sadiya, India	D14	42
Sado, i., Japan	I13	36
Sadorus, Il., U.S.	D5	120
Šadrinsk, Russia	F10	26
Sädvaluspen, Swe.	H15	6
Saegertown, Pa., U.S.	C1	145
Safad see Ẕefat, Isr.	C5	50
Safājah, Jazīrat, i., Egypt	H2	48
Safety Harbor, Fl., U.S.	E4	116
Saffell, Ar., U.S.	B4	111
Safford, Al., U.S.	C2	108
Safford, Az., U.S.	E6	110
Safi, Mor.	D6	62
Safonovo, Russia	F4	26
Saga, China	F4	30
Saga, Japan	N5	36
Sagadahoc, co., Me., U.S.	E3	126
Sagaing, Mya.	D3	40
Sagamihara, Japan	L14	36
Sagami-nada, b., Japan	L14	36
Sagamore, Ma., U.S.	C6	128
Sagamore, Pa., U.S.	E3	145
Sagamore Hills, Oh., U.S.	h9	142
Saganaga Lake, l., Mn., U.S.	B7	130
Saganthit Kyun, i., Mya.	I5	40
Sāgar, India	I8	44
Sag Harbor, N.Y., U.S.	m16	139
Saginaw, Al., U.S.	B3	108
Saginaw, Mi., U.S.	E7	129
Saginaw, Tx., U.S.	n9	150
Saginaw, co., Mi., U.S.	E6	129
Saginaw Bay, b., Mi., U.S.	E7	129
Sagle, Id., U.S.	A2	119
Sagleipie, Lib.	H5	64
Saglek Bay, b., Newf., Can.	f9	102
Šagonar, Russia	G16	26
Saguache, Co., U.S.	C4	113
Saguache, co., Co., U.S.	C4	113
Saguache Creek, stm., Co., U.S.	C4	113
Sagua de Tánamo, Cuba	D7	94
Sagua la Grande, Cuba	C4	94
Saguaro Lake, res., Az., U.S.	k10	110
Saguaro National Monument, Az., U.S.	E5	110
Saguaro National Monument (Tucson Mountain Section), Az., U.S.	E4	110
Saguenay, stm., Que., Can.	A7	104
Sagunt, Spain	F11	16
Sa'gya, China	F13	44
Sahāb, Jord.	E6	50
Sahaba, Sud.	H6	60
Sahagún, Col.	C5	84
Sahara, des., Afr.	F7	52
Sahāranpur, India	F7	44
Sahaswān, India	F8	44
Şahbuz, Azer.	B8	48
Sahel see Sudan, reg., Afr.	F11	54
Sāhibganj, India	H12	44
Şahin, Tur.	H10	20
Sāhīwal, Pak.	E5	44
Sahuaripa, Mex.	C5	90
Sahuarita, Az., U.S.	F5	110
Sahuayo de José María Morelos, Mex.	G8	90
Sai Buri, Thai.	K6	40
Saïda, Alg.	C11	62
Saïdia, Mor.	C9	62
Saidpur, Bngl.	H13	44
Saidu, Pak.	C5	44
Saignelégier, Switz.	D7	13
Saigon see Thanh Pho Ho Chi Minh, Viet.	I9	40
Saijō, Japan	N8	36
Saiki, Japan	O6	36
Saimaa, l., Fin.	K20	6
Saín Alto, Mex.	F8	90
Saint Adolphe, Man., Can.	E3	100
Saint-Affrique, Fr.	I9	14
Saint Agatha, Me., U.S.	A4	126
Sainte Agathe, Man., Can.	E3	100
Sainte-Agathe, Que., Can.	C6	104
Sainte-Agathe-des-Monts, Que., Can.	C3	104
Saint-Aimé (Massueville), Que., Can.	D5	104
Saint-Alban, Que., Can.	C5	104
Saint Alban's, Newf., Can.	E4	102
Saint Albans, Eng., U.K.	J13	8
Saint Albans, Me., U.S.	D3	126
Saint Albans, Vt., U.S.	B2	152
Saint Albans, W.V., U.S.	C3	155
Saint Albans Bay, Vt., U.S.	B2	152
Saint Albans Bay, b., Vt., U.S.	B2	152
Saint Albert, Alta., Can.	C4	98
Saint-Alexandre, Que., Can.	D4	104
Saint-Amand-Montrond, Fr.	F9	14
Saint Amant, La., U.S.	h10	125
Saint-Ambroise, Que., Can.	A6	104
Saint-Amour, Fr.	F12	14
Saint-Anaclet, Que., Can.	A9	104
Saint-André, Reu.	v17	67c
Saint-André, Cap, c., Madag.	p21	67b
Saint-André-Avellin, Que., Can.	D2	104
Saint-André-Est, Que., Can.	D3	104
Saint Andrew Bay, b., Fl., U.S.	u16	116
Saint Andrews, N.B., Can.	D2	101
Saint Andrew's, Newf., Can.	E2	102
Saint Andrews, Scot., U.K.	E11	8
Saint Andrews, S.C., U.S.	C5	147
Saint Andrews, S.C., U.S.	F7	147
Saint Andrews, Tn., U.S.	D8	149
Saint Andrew Sound, strt., Ga., U.S.	F5	117
Saint Anne, Il., U.S.	B6	120
Sainte-Anne, stm., Que., Can.	B6	104
Sainte-Anne, Lac, l., Alta., Can.	C3	98
Sainte-Anne-de-Beaupré, Que., Can.	B7	104
Sainte-Anne [-de-Bellevue], Que., Can.	q19	104
Sainte Anne-de-Madawaska, N.B., Can.	B1	101
Sainte Anne-des-Chênes, Man., Can.	E3	100
Sainte-Anne-du-Lac, Que., Can.	k11	104
Sainte-Anne du Nord, stm., Que., Can.	B7	104
Saint Anne's, Eng., U.K.	H10	8
Saint Anns, N.S., Can.	C9	101
Saint Ann's Bay, Jam.	E6	94
Saint-Anselme, Que., Can.	C7	104
Saint Ansgar, Ia., U.S.	A5	122
Saint Anthony, Newf., Can.	C4	102
Saint Anthony, Id., U.S.	F7	119
Saint Anthony, In., U.S.	H4	121
Saint Anthony, N.D., U.S.	C5	141
Saint Antoine, N.B., Can.	C5	101
Saint-Antoine [-sur-Richelieu], Que., Can.	D4	104
Saint-Apollinaire, Que., Can.	C6	104
Saint Arnaud, Austl.	K5	70
Saint-Arsène, Que., Can.	B8	104
Saint Arthur, N.B., Can.	B3	101
Saint-Athanase, Que., Can.	B8	104
Saint-Aubert, Que., Can.	B7	104
Saint Augustin, stm., Can.	C2	102
Saint Augustine, Fl., U.S.	C5	116
Saint-Augustin-Nord-Ouest, stm., Que., Can.	C2	102
Saint-Avold, Fr.	C13	14
Saint-Barthélemy, i., Guad.	F13	94
Saint Basile, N.B., Can.	B1	101
Saint-Basile [-Sud], Que., Can.	C6	104
Saint-Béat, Fr.	J7	14
Saint Bees Head, c., Eng., U.K.	F10	8
Saint Benedict, Sask., Can.	E3	105
Saint-Benoît-Labre, Que., Can.	C7	104
Saint-Bernard, Que., Can.	C6	104
Saint Bernard, Al., U.S.	A3	108
Saint Bernard, La., U.S.	E6	125
Saint Bernard, Oh., U.S.	o13	142
Saint Bernard, co., La., U.S.	E6	125
Saint Bernice, In., U.S.	E2	121
Saint Bethlehem, Tn., U.S.	A4	149
Saint-Blaise, Switz.	D6	13
Saint-Bonaventure, Que., Can.	D5	104
Saint-Bonnet, Fr.	H13	14
Saint-Bonnet-de-Joux, Fr.	F11	14
Saint Brendan's, Newf., Can.	D5	102
Saint Bride, Mount, mtn., Alta., Can.	D3	98
Saint Bride's, Newf., Can.	E4	102
Saint-Brieuc, Fr.	D4	14
Saint Brieux, Sask., Can.	E3	105
Saint-Bruno, Que., Can.	A6	104
Saint-Calais, Fr.	E7	14
Saint-Camille [-de-Bellechasse], Que., Can.	C7	104
Saint-Casimir, Que., Can.	C5	104
Saint Catharine, Ky., U.S.	C4	124
Saint Catharines, Ont., Can.	D5	103
Saint Catherine, Lake, l., Vt., U.S.	E2	152
Saint Catherines Island, i., Ga., U.S.	E5	117
Saint Catherines Sound, strt., Ga., U.S.	E5	117
Saint-Célestin (Annaville), Que., Can.	C5	104
Saint-Cergue, Switz.	F5	13
Saint-Césaire, Que., Can.	D4	104
Saint-Chamond, Fr.	G11	14
Saint-Charles, Que., Can.	C7	104
Saint Charles, Ar., U.S.	C4	111
Saint Charles, Id., U.S.	G7	119
Saint Charles, Il., U.S.	B5	120
Saint Charles, Ia., U.S.	C4	122
Saint Charles, Ky., U.S.	C2	124
Saint Charles, Md., U.S.	C4	127
Saint Charles, Mi., U.S.	E6	129
Saint Charles, Mn., U.S.	G6	130
Saint Charles, Mo., U.S.	C7	132
Saint Charles, Va., U.S.	f8	153
Saint Charles, co., La., U.S.	E5	125
Saint Charles, co., Mo., U.S.	C7	132
Saint Christopher (Saint Kitts), i., St. K./N.	F13	94
Saint Christopher-Nevis see Saint Kitts and Nevis, ctry., N.A.	F13	94
Saint-Chrysostome, Que., Can.	D4	104
Saint Clair, Mi., U.S.	F8	129
Saint Clair, Mn., U.S.	F5	130
Saint Clair, Mo., U.S.	C6	132
Saint Clair, Pa., U.S.	E9	145
Saint Clair, co., Al., U.S.	B3	108
Saint Clair, co., Il., U.S.	E3	120
Saint Clair, co., Mi., U.S.	F8	129
Saint Clair, co., Mo., U.S.	C4	132
Saint Clair Shores, Mi., U.S.	p16	129
Saint Clairsville, Oh., U.S.	B5	142
Saint Claude, Man., Can.	E2	100
Saint-Claude, Fr.	F12	14
Saint Clements Creek, stm., Md., U.S.	D4	127
Sainte-Clothilde, Que., Can.	D5	104
Saint Cloud, Fl., U.S.	D5	116
Saint Cloud, Mn., U.S.	E4	130
Saint Cloud, Wi., U.S.	E5	156
Saint-Coeur-de-Marie, Que., Can.	A6	104
Saint-Constant, Que., Can.	q19	104
Saint Croix, N.B., Can.	D2	101
Sainte-Croix, Que., Can.	C6	104
Sainte-Croix, Switz.	E6	13
Saint Croix, co., Wi., U.S.	C1	156
Saint Croix, i., V.I.U.S.	F12	94
Saint Croix, stm., U.S.	C1	156
Saint Croix, Lake, l., U.S.	D1	156
Saint Croix Falls, Wi., U.S.	C1	156
Saint Croix Stream, stm., Me., U.S.	B4	126
Saint-Damase, Que., Can.	D4	104
Saint-Damase-des-Aulnaies, Que., Can.	B7	104
Saint David, Az., U.S.	F5	110
Saint David, Il., U.S.	C3	120
Saint-David-de-l'Auberivière, Que., Can.	n17	104
Saint David's, Newf., Can.	D2	102
Saint David's Head, c., Wales, U.K.	J8	8
Saint-Denis, Que., Can.	D4	104
Saint-Denis, Fr.	D9	14
Saint-Denis, Reu.	v17	67c
Saint-Denis [-de-la-Bouteillerie], Que., Can.	B8	104
Saint-Dié, Fr.	D13	14
Saint-Dizier, Fr.	D11	14
Saint-Dominique, Que., Can.	D5	104
Saint Edward, Ne., U.S.	C8	134
Saint Eleanor's, P.E.I., Can.	C6	101
Saint Elias, Cape, c., Ak., U.S.	D11	109
Saint Elias, Mount, mtn., N.A.	D4	96
Saint-Élie, Fr. Gu.	C8	76
Saint Elizabeth, Mo., U.S.	C5	132
Saint Elmo, Al., U.S.	E1	108
Saint Elmo, Il., U.S.	D5	120
Saint-Éloi, Que., Can.	A8	104
Saint-Émile [-de-Suffolk], Que., Can.	D3	104
Saint-Éphrem [-de-Tring], Que., Can.	C7	104
Saint-Étienne, Fr.	G11	14
Saint-Eusèbe, Que., Can.	B9	104
Saint-Eustache, Que., Can.	D4	104
Saint-Félicien, Que., Can.	A5	104
Saint-Félix-de-Valois, Que., Can.	C4	104
Saint-Ferdinand (Bernierville), Que., Can.	C6	104
Saint-Ferréol [-les-Neiges], Que., Can.	B7	104
Saint Fintan's, Newf., Can.	D2	102
Saint-Flavien, Que., Can.	C6	104
Saint-Florent, Fr.	I24	15a
Saint Florian, Al., U.S.	A2	108
Saint-Flour, Fr.	G10	14
Sainte-Foy, Que., Can.	n17	104
Sainte-Foy-la-Grande, Fr.	H7	14
Saint Francis, Ks., U.S.	C2	123
Saint Francis, Me., U.S.	A4	126
Saint Francis, Mn., U.S.	E5	130
Saint Francis, S.D., U.S.	D5	148
Saint Francis, Wi., U.S.	n12	156
Saint Francis, co., Ar., U.S.	B5	111
Saint Francis, stm., U.S.	A5	111
Saint Francis, Cape, c., Newf., Can.	E5	102
Saint Francisville, Il., U.S.	E6	120
Saint Francisville, La., U.S.	D4	125
Saint Francois, co., Mo., U.S.	D7	132
Saint-François, stm., Que., Can.	D5	104
Saint-François, Lac, l., Que., Can.	D6	104
Saint Francois Mountains, hills, Mo., U.S.	D7	132
Saint-Frédéric, Que., Can.	C7	104
Saint Froid Lake, l., Me., U.S.	B4	126
Saint-Fulgence, Que., Can.	A7	104
Saint-Gabriel, Que., Can.	C4	104
Saint Gabriel, La., U.S.	h9	125
Saint-Gaudens, Fr.	I7	14
Saint-Gédéon, Que., Can.	D7	104
Sainte Genevieve, Mo., U.S.	D7	132
Sainte Genevieve, co., Mo., U.S.	D7	132
Saint George, Austl.	G8	70
Saint George, N.B., Can.	D3	101
Saint George, Ont., Can.	D4	103
Saint George, Ga., U.S.	F4	117
Saint George, Ks., U.S.	C7	123
Saint George, Me., U.S.	D3	126
Saint George, S.C., U.S.	E6	147
Saint George, Ut., U.S.	F2	151
Saint George, Cape, c., Newf., Can.	D2	102
Saint George, Cape, c., Fl., U.S.	C1	116
Saint George Island, i., Ak., U.S.	D6	109
Saint George Island, i., Fl., U.S.	C2	116
Saint George's, Newf., Can.	D2	102
Saint-Georges, Que., Can.	C5	104
Saint-Georges, Fr. Gu.	C8	76
Saint George's, Gren.	H14	94
Saint Georges, De., U.S.	B3	115
Saint George's Bay, b., Newf., Can.	D2	102
Saint Georges Bay, b., N.S., Can.	D8	101
Saint George's Channel, strt., Eur.	J7	8
Saint-Georges [-de-Windsor], Que., Can.	D6	104
Saint Georges Head, c., Austl.	J9	70
Saint-Georges-Ouest (part of Ville-Saint-Georges), Que., Can.	C7	104
Saint-Gérard, Que., Can.	D6	104
Saint-Germain, Fr.	D9	14
Saint Germain, Wi., U.S.	C4	156
Saint-Germain-du-Bois, Fr.	F12	14
Saint-Gervais, Que., Can.	C7	104
Saint-Géry, Fr.	H8	14
Saint-Gilles (Sint-Gillis), Bel.	G5	12
Saint-Gilles, Que., Can.	C6	104
Saint-Gingolph, Switz.	F6	13
Saint-Girons, Fr.	J8	14
Saint-Grégoire (Larochelle), Que., Can.	C5	104
Saint Gregor, Sask., Can.	E3	105
Saint Gregory, Mount, mtn., Newf., Can.	D2	102
Saint-Guénolé, Fr.	E2	14
Saint-Guillaume-d'Upton, Que., Can.	D5	104
Saint Hedwig, Tx., U.S.	k7	150
Saint Helen, Lake, l., Mi., U.S.	D6	129
Saint Helena, Ca., U.S.	C2	112
Saint Helena, co., La., U.S.	D5	125
Saint Helena, dep., Afr.	J6	52
Saint Helena Island, i., S.C., U.S.	G6	147
Saint Helena Sound, strt., S.C., U.S.	G7	147
Sainte-Hélène [-de-Kamouraska], Que., Can.	B8	104
Saint Helens, Austl.	M8	70
Saint Helens, Or., U.S.	B4	144
Saint Helens, Mount, vol., Wa., U.S.	C3	154

Sama-Sanm

Name	Map Ref.	Page
Samā, Jord.	D6	50
Sama, stm., Peru	G6	82
Samacá, Col.	E6	84
Sama [de Langreo], Spain	B6	16
Samaipata, Bol.	H10	82
Samalá, stm., Guat.	C3	92
Sāmalkot, India	D7	46
Samālūt, Egypt	C6	60
Samambaia, stm., Braz.	G2	79
Samaná, Dom. Rep.	E10	94
Samaná, Bahía de, b., Dom. Rep.	E10	94
Samaná, Cabo, c., Dom. Rep.	E10	94
Samana Cay, i., Bah.	C8	94
Samandağı, Tur.	C3	48
Samaniego, Col.	G4	84
Samar, Isr.	I4	50
Samara (Kujbyšev), Russia	G8	26
Samara, stm., Russia	G8	26
Samarai, Pap. N. Gui.	n17	68a
Samaria, Id., U.S.	G6	119
Samariapo, Ven.	E9	84
Samarinda, Indon.	F6	38
Samarkand, Uzb.	J11	26
Sāmarrā', Iraq	D7	48
Samastīpur, India	H11	44
Samaúna, Braz.	B11	82
Şamaxı, Azer.	A10	48
Sambalpur, India	J10	44
Sambas, Indon.	N10	40
Sambava, Madag.	o24	67b
Sambawizi, Zimb.	B8	66
Sambhal, India	F8	44
Sāmbhar, India	G6	44
Sambir, Ukr.	F23	10
Sâmbor, Camb.	H8	40
Samborombón, stm., Arg.	H10	80
Samborombón, Bahía, b., Arg.	I10	80
Samborondón, Ec.	H3	84
Sambre, stm., Eur.	B11	14
Sambú, stm., Pan.	C3	84
Samburg, Tn., U.S.	A2	149
Sambusu, Nmb.	A4	66
Samch'ŏk, S. Kor.	F17	32
Samch'ŏnp'o, S. Kor.	I16	32
Samedan, Switz.	E12	13
Samho, N. Kor.	D15	32
Samiria, stm., Peru	J5	84
Sammamish Lake, l., Wa., U.S.	e11	154
Samnaungruppe, mts., Eur.	D13	13
Samnye, S. Kor.	H15	32
Samoa, Ca., U.S.	B1	112
Samoa Islands, is., Oc.	J22	158
Samo Alto, Chile	F3	80
Samoded, Russia	E6	26
Sámos, Grc.	L11	20
Sámos, i., Grc.	L10	20
Samoset, Fl., U.S.	q10	116
Samosir, Pulau, i., Indon.	M5	40
Samothrace see Samothráki, i., Grc.	I9	20
Samothráki (Samothrace), i., Grc.	I9	20
S'amozero, Russia	K23	6
Sampacho, Arg.	G6	80
Sampit, Indon.	F5	38
Sampit, stm., S.C., U.S.	E9	147
Sampson, co., N.C., U.S.	B4	140
Sampués, Col.	C5	84
Sampur, Russia	I24	22
Sam Rayburn Reservoir, res., Tx., U.S.	D5	150
Samre, Eth.	K10	60
Samreboi, Ghana	I8	64
Samson, Al., U.S.	D3	108
Samsun, Tur.	G15	4
Samtown, La., U.S.	C3	125
Samuels, Id., U.S.	A2	119
Samuhú, Arg.	D8	80
Samui, Ko, i., Thai.	J6	40
Samut Prakan, Thai.	H6	40
Samut Sakhon, Thai.	H6	40
Samut Songkhram, Thai.	H6	40
S'amža, Russia	A24	22
San, Mali	E7	64
San (Xan), stm., Asia	H9	40
San, stm., Eur.	E22	10
Saña, Peru	B2	82
Şan'ā', Yemen	G4	47
Sanaba, stm., Afr.	D4	64
San Acacia, N.M., U.S.	C3	138
Sanaga, stm., Cam.	J14	64
San Agustín, Arg.	J9	80
San Agustín, Arg.	F6	80
San Agustín, Col.	G4	84
San Agustin, Plains of, pl., N.M., U.S.	C2	138
San Agustín de Valle Fértil, Arg.	F5	80
Sanak Islands, is., Ak., U.S.	E7	109
San Alejo, El Sal.	D7	92
Sanalona, Presa, res., Mex.	E6	90
San Ambrosio, Isla, i., Chile	B1	78
Sanana, Pulau, i., Indon.	F8	38
Sanandaj, Iran	D9	48
Sanandita, Bol.	I10	82
San Andreas, Ca., U.S.	C3	112
San Andrés, Col.	H4	94
San Andrés, Mex.	D2	90
San Andrés, Pan.	I12	92
San Andrés, Isla de, i., Col.	H4	94
San Andrés de Giles, Arg.	H9	80
San Andres Mountains, mts., N.M., U.S.	E3	138
San Andres Peak, mtn., N.M., U.S.	E3	138
San Andrés Sajcabajá, Guat.	B4	92
San Andrés Tuxtla, Mex.	H12	90
San Andrés y Providencia, ter., Col.	H4	94
Sananduva, Braz.	D13	80
San Angelo, Tx., U.S.	D2	150
San Anselmo, Ca., U.S.	h7	112
San Antero, Col.	C5	84
San Antonio, Arg.	C6	80
San Antonio, Arg.	E6	80
San Antonio, Belize	A5	92
San Antonio, Chile	D3	80
San Antonio, Chile	G3	80
San Antonio, Col.	F5	84
San Antonio, C.R.	G9	92
San Antonio, Peru	B3	82
San Antonio, Fl., U.S.	D4	116
San Antonio, N.M., U.S.	D3	138
San Antonio, Tx., U.S.	E3	150
San Antonio, Ur.	F10	80
San Antonio, stm., Mex.	B2	90
San Antonio, Cabo, c., Arg.	I10	80
San Antonio, Cabo de, c., Cuba	D2	94
San Antonio, Punta, c., Mex.	D4	90
San Antonio, Punta, c., Mex.	C2	90
San Antonio Bay, b., Tx., U.S.	E4	150
San Antonio de Areco, Arg.	H9	80
San Antonio de los Baños, Cuba	C3	94
San Antonio de los Cobres, Arg.	C5	80
San Antonio del Táchira, Ven.	D6	84
San Antonio de Tamanaco, Ven.	C9	84
San Antonio El Bravo, Mex.	B7	90
San Antonio Mountain, mtn., N.M., U.S.	A3	138
San Antonio Suchitepéquez, Guat.	C3	92
San Ardo, Ca., U.S.	D3	112
Sanatorium, Ms., U.S.	D4	131
San Augustine, Tx., U.S.	D5	150
San Augustine, co., Tx., U.S.	D5	150
San Bartolomé, Spain	n27	17b
San Benedetto del Tronto, Italy	G8	18
San Benedicto, Isla, i., Mex.	H4	90
San Benito, Bol.	G9	82
San Benito, Guat.	I15	90
San Benito, Peru	B2	82
San Benito, Tx., U.S.	F4	150
San Benito, co., Ca., U.S.	D3	112
San Benito Mountain, mtn., Ca., U.S.	D3	112
San Bernardino, Switz.	F11	13
San Bernardino, Ca., U.S.	E5	112
San Bernardino, co., Ca., U.S.	E5	112
San Bernardo, Arg.	D8	80
San Bernardo, Chile	G3	80
San Bernardo, Mex.	E7	90
San Bernardo, Isla, i., Nic.	F9	92
San Bernardo, Islas de, is., Col.	C4	84
San Bernardo del Viento, Col.	C5	84
San Blas, Mex.	G7	90
San Blas, Mex.	D5	90
San Blas, Cape, c., Fl., U.S.	v16	116
San Blas, Golfo de, b., Pan.	C3	84
San Blas, Serranía De, mts., Pan.	C3	84
San Blas de los Sauces, Arg.	E5	80
San Borja, Bol.	F8	82
Sanborn, Ia., U.S.	A2	122
Sanborn, Mn., U.S.	F3	130
Sanborn, N.D., U.S.	C7	141
Sanborn, co., S.D., U.S.	D7	148
Sanbornton, N.H., U.S.	D3	136
Sanbornville, N.H., U.S.	C4	136
San Bruno, Ca., U.S.	D2	112
San Buenaventura, Bol.	F8	82
San Buenaventura, Mex.	D9	90
Sancang, China	C9	34
San Carlos, Arg.	D11	80
San Carlos, Arg.	G4	80
San Carlos, Arg.	C6	80
San Carlos, Chile	I3	80
San Carlos, Mex.	C9	90
San Carlos, Mex.	E10	90
San Carlos, Nic.	F10	92
San Carlos, Pan.	C3	84
San Carlos, Para.	B10	80
San Carlos, Phil.	C7	38
San Carlos, Phil.	n19	39b
San Carlos, Az., U.S.	D5	110
San Carlos, Ca., U.S.	k8	112
San Carlos, Ur.	H11	80
San Carlos, Ven.	C8	84
San Carlos, stm., C.R.	G10	92
San Carlos, stm., Ven.	C8	84
San Carlos, Riacho, stm., Para.	B9	80
San Carlos Centro, Arg.	F8	80
San Carlos de Bariloche, Arg.	E2	78
San Carlos de Bolívar, Arg.	I8	80
San Carlos de Guaroa, Col.	F6	84
San Carlos del Zulia, Ven.	C7	84
San Carlos de Río Negro, Ven.	G9	84
San Carlos Indian Reservation, Az., U.S.	D5	110
San Carlos Lake, res., Az., U.S.	D5	110
San Cataldo, Italy	L8	18
San Cayetano, Arg.	J9	80
Sancerre, Fr.	E9	14
Sánchez, Dom. Rep.	E10	94
Sanch'ŏng, S. Kor.	H15	32
San Ciro de Acosta, Mex.	G10	90
San Clemente, Spain	F9	16
San Clemente, Ca., U.S.	F5	112
San Clemente, Cerro, mtn., Chile	F2	78
San Clemente Island, i., Ca., U.S.	F4	112
San Cosme, Arg.	D9	80
San Cristóbal, Arg.	F8	80
San Cristóbal, Dom. Rep.	E9	94
San Cristóbal, N.M., U.S.	A4	138
San Cristóbal, Ven.	D6	84
San Cristóbal, Bahía, b., Mex.	D2	90
San Cristóbal, Isla, i., Ec.	j14	84a
San Cristóbal, Volcán, vol., Nic.	E7	92
San Cristóbal de la Laguna, Spain	o24	17b
San Cristóbal de las Casas, Mex.	I13	90
San Cristóbal Totonicapán, Guat.	C3	92
San Cristóbal Verapaz, Guat.	B4	92
Sancti Spíritus, Cuba	D5	94
Sancy, Puy de, mtn., Fr.	G9	14
Sand, stm., Alta., Can.	B5	98
San Damián, Peru	E3	82
Sandaré, Mali	D4	64
Sandborn, In., U.S.	G3	121
Sand Coulee, Mt., U.S.	C5	133
Sand Creek, stm., In., U.S.	F6	121
Sand Creek, stm., Ks., U.S.	g12	123
Sand Creek, stm., Wy., U.S.	C7	157
Sanders, Az., U.S.	B6	110
Sanders, Ky., U.S.	B5	124
Sanders, co., Mt., U.S.	C1	133
Sanderson, Tx., U.S.	D1	150
Sandersville, Ga., U.S.	D4	117
Sandersville, Ms., U.S.	D4	131
Sandfly Lake, l., Sask., Can.	B2	105
Sandford, In., U.S.	E2	121
Sandgate, Austl.	F10	70
Sand Hill, Ma., U.S.	h13	128
Sandhill, Ms., U.S.	C4	131
Sand Hill, Ms., U.S.	D5	131
Sand Hill, stm., Newf., Can.	B3	102
Sand Hill, stm., Mn., U.S.	C2	130
Sandia, Peru	F7	82
Sandia Crest, mtn., N.M., U.S.	k8	138
Sandia Indian Reservation, N.M., U.S.	k7	138
Sandia Mountains, mts., N.M., U.S.	k8	138
Sandia Park, N.M., U.S.	k8	138
San Diego, Ca., U.S.	F5	112
San Diego, Tx., U.S.	F3	150
San Diego, co., Ca., U.S.	F5	112
San Diego, stm., Ca., U.S.	o15	112
San Diego, Cabo, c., Arg.	G3	78
San Diego de la Unión, Mex.	G9	90
San Diego Naval Station, mil., Ca., U.S.	o15	112
San Diego Naval Training Center, mil., Ca., U.S.	o15	112
Sandilands, Man., Can.	E3	100
San Dionisio, Nic.	E9	92
Sand Island, i., Hi., U.S.	g10	118
Sand Island, i., Wi., U.S.	B3	156
Sand Key, i., Fl., U.S.	E4	116
Sand Lake, Mi., U.S.	E5	129
Sandlick Creek, stm., W.V., U.S.	n13	155
Sand Mountain, mtn., U.S.	A3	108
Sandoa, Zaire	C4	58
Sandomierz, Pol.	E21	10
Sandoná, Col.	G4	84
San Donà di Piave, Italy	D7	18
Sandoval, Il., U.S.	E4	120
Sandoval, co., N.M., U.S.	B2	138
Sandovalina, Braz.	G3	79
Sandovo, Russia	C19	22
Sandoway, Mya.	E3	40
Sandown, N.H., U.S.	E4	136
Sand Point, Ont., Can.	B8	103
Sand Point, Ak., U.S.	D7	109
Sandpoint, Id., U.S.	A2	119
Sandringham, Eng., U.K.	I13	8
Sands Key, i., Fl., U.S.	s3	116
Sandspit, B.C., Can.	C2	99
Sand Springs, Ok., U.S.	A5	143
Sandston, Va., U.S.	m18	153
Sandstone, Austl.	E3	68
Sandstone, Mn., U.S.	D6	130
Sandstone, W.V., U.S.	D4	155
Sandtown, De., U.S.	D3	115
Sandu Ao, b., China	I8	34
Sandusky, Mi., U.S.	E8	129
Sandusky, Oh., U.S.	A3	142
Sandusky, co., Oh., U.S.	A2	142
Sandusky, stm., Oh., U.S.	B2	142
Sandusky Bay, b., Oh., U.S.	A3	142
Sandvika, Nor.	L12	6
Sandviken, Swe.	K15	6
Sandwich, Il., U.S.	B5	120
Sandwich, Ma., U.S.	C7	128
Sandwich Bay, b., Newf., Can.	B3	102
Sandwich Range, mts., N.H., U.S.	C3	136
Sandwīp Island, i., Bngl.	I14	44
Sandy, Or., U.S.	B4	144
Sandy, Ut., U.S.	C4	151
Sandy, stm., Me., U.S.	D2	126
Sandy Bay, b., Nic.	C11	92
Sandy Bay Mountain, mtn., Me., U.S.	C2	126
Sandy Brook, stm., Ct., U.S.	A3	114
Sandy Cape, c., Austl.	E10	70
Sandy Creek, stm., Oh., U.S.	B4	142
Sandy Creek, stm., Ok., U.S.	C2	143
Sandy Hook, Ct., U.S.	D2	114
Sandy Hook, Ky., U.S.	B6	124
Sandy Hook, spit, N.J., U.S.	C5	137
Sandy Island, i., S.C., U.S.	D9	147
Sandykači, Turk.	J10	26
Sandy Lake, Man., Can.	D1	100
Sandy Lake, l., Newf., Can.	D3	102
Sandy Lake, l., Ont., Can.	n16	103
Sandy Lake, l., Sask., Can.	B2	105
Sandy Neck, pen., Ma., U.S.	C7	128
Sandy Point, c., R.I., U.S.	h7	146
Sandy Point Town, St. K./N.	F13	94
Sandy Pond, l., Ma., U.S.	g10	128
Sandy Ridge, Al., U.S.	C3	108
Sandy Ridge, mtn., Va., U.S.	e9	153
Sandy Springs, Ga., U.S.	h8	117
Sandy Springs, S.C., U.S.	B2	147
Sandyville, Md., U.S.	A4	127
Sandyville, W.V., U.S.	C3	155
San Enrique, Arg.	H8	80
San Estanislao, Para.	C10	80
San Esteban, Hond.	B9	92
San Esteban, Isla, i., Mex.	C3	90
San Felipe, Chile	G3	80
San Felipe, Col.	G9	84
San Felipe, Mex.	B2	90
San Felipe, Mex.	G9	90
San Felipe, Phil.	n19	39b
San Felipe, Ven.	B8	84
San Felipe, Castillo de, hist., Guat.	B5	92
San Felipe, Cayos de, is., Cuba	D3	94
San Felipe de Vichayal, Peru	A1	82
San Felipe Indian Reservation, N.M., U.S.	k8	138
San Felipe Nuevo Mercurio, Mex.	E8	90
San Felipe Pueblo, N.M., U.S.	B3	138
San Félix, stm., Pan.	I13	92
San Félix, Isla, i., Chile	K31	158
San Fernando, Chile	H3	80
San Fernando, Mex.	E10	90
San Fernando, Phil.	m19	39b
San Fernando, Phil.	n19	39b
San Fernando, Spain	I5	16
San Fernando, Trin.	I14	94
San Fernando, Ca., U.S.	m12	112
San Fernando, Ven.	D9	84
San Fernando de Atabapo, Ven.	E9	84
San Fernando del Valle de Catamarca, Arg.	E6	80
Sanford, Co., U.S.	D5	113
Sanford, Fl., U.S.	D5	116
Sanford, Me., U.S.	E2	126
Sanford, Mi., U.S.	E6	129
Sanford, N.C., U.S.	B3	140
Sanford, Mount, mtn., Ak., U.S.	C11	109
San Francisco, Arg.	F7	80
San Francisco, Col.	G4	84
San Francisco, C.R.	H9	92
San Francisco, El Sal.	D6	92
San Francisco, Pan.	I14	92
San Francisco, Ca., U.S.	D2	112
San Francisco, co., Ca., U.S.	D2	112
San Francisco, stm., Arg.	B6	80
San Francisco, stm., U.S.	D6	110
San Francisco, Paso de, S.A.	D4	80
San Francisco Bay, b., Ca., U.S.	h8	112
San Francisco de Borja, Mex.	D6	90
San Francisco de la Paz, Hond.	C8	92
San Francisco del Chañar, Arg.	E7	80
San Francisco del Monte de Oro, Arg.	G5	80
San Francisco del Oro, Mex.	D7	90
San Francisco del Rincón, Mex.	G9	90
San Francisco de Macoris, Dom. Rep.	E9	94
San Francisco de Mostazal, Chile	G3	80
San Francisco Libre, Nic.	E8	92
San Francisco Mountains, mts., Ut., U.S.	E2	151
San Franco, Cerro, mtn., Hond.	B7	92
San Gabriel, Ec.	G4	84
San Gabriel, Ca., U.S.	*m12	112
San Gabriel Chilac, Mex.	H11	90
San Gabriel Mountains, mts., Ca., U.S.	m12	112
Sangamner, India	C3	46
Sangamon, co., Il., U.S.	D4	120
Sangamon, stm., Il., U.S.	C3	120
Sanga Puitã, Braz.	G1	79
Sangay, vol., Ec.	H3	84
Sangayán, Isla, i., Peru	E3	82
Sangchungshih, Tai.	J10	34
Sang-e Māsheh, Afg.	D2	44
Sanger, Ca., U.S.	D4	112
Sanger, Tx., U.S.	C4	150
Sângera, Mol.	B12	20
Sangerhausen, Ger.	D11	10
San Germán, Cuba	D6	94
San Germán, P.R.	E11	94
Sangerville, Me., U.S.	C3	126
Sanggan, stm., China	C9	30
Sangha, stm., Afr.	A3	58
Sangihe, Kepulauan, is., Indon.	E8	38
Sangihe, Pulau, i., Indon.	E8	38
San Gil, Col.	D6	84
San Gimignano, Italy	F6	18
San Giovanni in Fiore, Italy	J11	18
San Giovanni in Persiceto, Italy	E6	18
San Giovanni Rotondo, Italy	H10	18
San Giovanni Valdarno, Italy	F6	18
Sangju, S. Kor.	G16	32
Sāngli, India	D3	46
Sangolquí, Ec.	H3	84
San Gorgonio Mountain, mtn., Ca., U.S.	E5	112
San Gottardo, Passo del, Switz.	E10	13
San Gregorio, Arg.	H7	80
San Gregorio, Ur.	G11	80
Sangre Grande, Trin.	I14	94
Sangrūr, India	E6	44
Sanguandian, China	D7	34
Sangudo, Alta., Can.	C3	98
Sangue, Rio do, stm., Braz.	D12	82
Sanhecun, China	A17	32
San Hipólito, Punta, c., Mex.	D3	90
Sanibel, Fl., U.S.	F4	116
Sanibel Island, i., Fl., U.S.	F4	116
San Ignacio, Arg.	D11	80
San Ignacio, C.R.	H10	92
San Ignacio, Hond.	C7	92
San Ignacio, Mex.	F9	90
San Ignacio, Mex.	D3	90
San Ignacio, Para.	D10	80
San Ignacio, Isla, i., Mex.	E5	90
San Ignacio, Laguna, l., Mex.	D3	90
San Ignacio de Moxo, Bol.	F9	82
San Ignacio de Velasco, Bol.	G11	82
Sanilac, co., Mi., U.S.	E8	129
San Ildefonso, Cerro, mtn., Hond.	B6	92
San Isidro, Arg.	H9	80
San Isidro, Arg.	E6	80
San Isidro, C.R.	H11	92
San Isidro, Nic.	E8	92
San Isidro, Tx., U.S.	F3	150
San Jacinto, Col.	C5	84
San Jacinto, Ca., U.S.	F5	112
San Jacinto, co., Tx., U.S.	D5	150
San Jacinto, stm., Tx., U.S.	r14	150
San Javier, Arg.	D11	80
San Javier, Arg.	F9	80
San Javier, Bol.	F9	82
San Javier, Bol.	G10	82
San Javier, Ur.	G9	80
San Javier, stm., Arg.	E9	80
San Javier de Loncomilla, Chile	H3	80
Sanjāwi, Pak.	E3	44
San Jerónimo, Guat.	B4	92
San Jerónimo Norte, Arg.	F8	80
Sanjō, Japan	J13	36
San Joaquín, Bol.	E9	82
San Joaquín, Para.	C10	80
San Joaquin, Ca., U.S.	D3	112
San Joaquin, co., Ca., U.S.	D3	112
San Joaquín, stm., Bol.	E10	82
San Joaquin, stm., Ca., U.S.	D3	112
San Joaquin Valley, val., Ca., U.S.	D3	112
San Jon, N.M., U.S.	B6	138
San Jorge, Arg.	F8	80
San Jorge, El Sal.	D6	92
San Jorge, Nic.	F9	92
San Jorge, stm., Col.	C5	84
San Jorge, Bahía, b., Mex.	B3	90
San Jorge, Golfo, b., Arg.	F3	78
San José, Arg.	D11	80
San José, C.R.	H10	92
San José, Para.	C10	80
San Jose, Phil.	n19	39b
San Jose, Az., U.S.	E6	110
San Jose, Ca., U.S.	D3	112
San Jose, Il., U.S.	C4	120
San Jose, N.M., U.S.	B4	138
San José, prov., C.R.	H11	92
San José, Isla, i., Mex.	E4	90
San José, Isla, i., Pan.	C3	84
San José Batuc, Mex.	C5	90
San José Buena Vista, Guat.	D4	92
San José de Bácum, Mex.	D4	90
San José de Chiquitos, Bol.	G11	82
San José de Copán, Hond.	C6	92
San José de Feliciano, Arg.	F9	80
San José de Guanipa, Ven.	C10	84
San José de Guaribe, Ven.	C10	84
San José de Jáchal, Arg.	F4	80
San José de la Esquina, Arg.	G8	80
San José de las Lajas, Cuba	C3	94
San José de las Raíces, Mex.	E9	90
San José del Cabo, Mex.	F5	90
San José del Guaviare, Col.	F6	84
San José de los Molinos, Peru	E4	82
San José de Mayo, Ur.	H10	80
San José de Ocuné, Col.	E7	84
San José de Sisa, Peru	B3	82
San José de Tiznados, Ven.	C9	84
San Jose Island, i., Tx., U.S.	E4	150
San Juan, Arg.	F4	80
San Juan, Guat.	B6	92
San Juan, Peru	F4	82
San Juan, P.R.	E11	94
San Juan, Tx., U.S.	F3	150
San Juan, prov., Arg.	F4	80
San Juan, co., Co., U.S.	D3	113
San Juan, co., N.M., U.S.	A1	138
San Juan, co., Ut., U.S.	F5	151
San Juan, co., Wa., U.S.	A2	154
San Juan, stm., Arg.	G5	80
San Juan, stm., Col.	E4	84
San Juan, stm., Mex.	E10	90
San Juan, stm., N.A.	G10	92
San Juan, stm., Peru	E4	82
San Juan, stm., S.A.	G3	84
San Juan, stm., U.S.	D5	106
San Juan, stm., Ven.	B11	84
San Juan, Pico, mtn., Cuba	D4	94
San Juan Bautista, Para.	D10	80
San Juan Capistrano, Ca., U.S.	F5	112
San Juan Cotzal, Guat.	B3	92
San Juan de Abajo, Mex.	G7	90
San Juan de Colón, Ven.	C6	84
San Juan de Guadalupe, Mex.	E8	90
San Juan [de la Maguana], Dom. Rep.	E9	94
San Juan del César, Col.	B6	84
San Juan del Norte, Nic.	G11	92
San Juan del Oro, stm., Bol.	I9	82
San Juan de los Cayos, Ven.	B8	84
San Juan de los Morros, Ven.	C9	84
San Juan del Río, Mex.	E7	90
San Juan del Río, Mex.	G9	90
San Juan del Sur, Nic.	F9	92
San Juan de Micay, stm., Col.	F4	84
San Juan de Payara, Ven.	D9	84
San Juan Evangelista, Mex.	I12	90
San Juanico, Mex.	D3	90
San Juanillo, C.R.	G9	92
San Juan Island, i., Wa., U.S.	A2	154
San Juanito, Isla, i., Mex.	G6	90
San Juan Mountains, mts., Co., U.S.	D3	113
San Juan Nepomuceno, Col.	C5	84
San Juan Nepomuceno, Para.	D11	80
San Juan Sacatepéquez, Guat.	C4	92
San Juan Teotihuacán, Mex.	H10	90
San Justo, Arg.	F8	80
Sankarani, stm., Afr.	F5	64
Sankosh, stm., Asia	G14	44
Sankt Aegyd am Neuwalde, Aus.	H15	10
Sankt Anton [am Arlberg], Aus.	H10	10
Sankt Gallen, Aus.	H14	10
Sankt Gallen, Switz.	D11	13
Sankt Gallen, state, Switz.	D11	13
Sankt Gilgen, Aus.	H13	10
Sankt Goar, Ger.	E7	10
Sankt Goarshausen, Ger.	E7	10
Sankt Ingbert, Ger.	F7	10
Sankt Johann im Pongau, Aus.	H13	10
Sankt Johann in Tirol, Aus.	H12	10
Sankt Moritz, Switz.	E12	13
Sankt Niklaus, Switz.	F8	13
Sankt Paul [im Lavanttal], Aus.	I14	10
Sankt Peter, Ger.	A8	10
Sankt-Peterburg (Saint Petersburg), Russia	B13	22
Sankt Pölten, Aus.	G15	10
Sankt Valentin, Aus.	G14	10
Sankt Veit an der Glan, Aus.	I14	10
Sankt Vith (Saint-Vith), Bel.	H9	12
Sankt Wendel, Ger.	F7	10
San Lázaro, Para.	B10	80
San Lázaro, Cabo, c., Mex.	E3	90
San Leandro, Ca., U.S.	h8	112
Sanlicheng, China	D3	34
Şanlıurfa, Tur.	C5	48
San Lope, Col.	D7	84
San Lorenzo, Arg.	E9	80
San Lorenzo, Arg.	G8	80
San Lorenzo, Bol.	I9	82
San Lorenzo, Ec.	G3	84
San Lorenzo, Hond.	D7	92
San Lorenzo, Mex.	E8	90
San Lorenzo, Nic.	E9	92
San Lorenzo, N.M., U.S.	E2	138
San Lorenzo, Ven.	C7	84
San Lorenzo, stm., Mex.	E6	90
San Lorenzo, Bahía de, b., Hond.	D7	92
San Lorenzo, Cabo, c., Ec.	H2	84
San Lorenzo, Isla, i., Mex.	C3	90
San Lorenzo, Isla, i., Peru	E3	82
San Lorenzo de El Escorial, Spain	E7	16
Sanlúcar de Barrameda, Spain	I5	16
Sanlúcar la Mayor, Spain	H5	16
San Lucas, Bol.	I9	82
San Lucas, Ec.	I3	84
San Lucas, Mex.	F5	90
San Lucas, Cabo, c., Mex.	F5	90
San Luis, Arg.	G5	80
San Luis, Cuba	D7	94
San Luis, Guat.	A5	92
San Luis, Az., U.S.	E1	110
San Luis, Co., U.S.	D5	113
San Luis, Ven.	B8	84
San Luis, prov., Arg.	H5	80
San Luís, Laguna, l., Bol.	E9	82
San Luis, Point, c., Ca., U.S.	E3	112
San Luis, Sierra de, mts., Arg.	G6	80
San Luis Creek, stm., Co., U.S.	C5	113
San Luis de la Paz, Mex.	G9	90
San Luis del Cordero, Mex.	E7	90
San Luis del Palmar, Arg.	D9	80
San Luis Gonzaga, Mex.	E4	90
San Luis Gonzaga, Bahía, b., Mex.	C2	90
San Luis Jilotepeque, Guat.	C5	92
San Luis Obispo, Ca., U.S.	E3	112
San Luis Obispo, co., Ca., U.S.	E3	112
San Luis Pass, strt., Tx., U.S.	r14	150
San Luis Peak, mtn., Co., U.S.	D4	113
San Luis Potosí, Mex.	F9	90
San Luis Potosí, state, Mex.	F9	90
San Luis Río Colorado, Mex.	A2	90
San Luis Valley, val., Co., U.S.	D4	113
Sanluri, Italy	J3	18
San Manuel, Arg.	I9	80
San Manuel, Az., U.S.	E5	110
San Marcial, stm., Mex.	C4	90
San Marcos, Chile	F3	80
San Marcos, Col.	C5	84
San Marcos, C.R.	H10	92
San Marcos, El Sal.	D5	92
San Marcos, Guat.	C3	92
San Marcos, Hond.	C6	92
San Marcos, Hond.	B6	92
San Marcos, Mex.	I10	90
San Marcos, Tx., U.S.	E4	150
San Marcos, dept., Guat.	B3	92
San Marcos, stm., Tx., U.S.	h8	150
San Marcos, Isla, i., Mex.	D3	90
San Marcos de Colón, Hond.	D8	92
San Marino, S. Mar.	F7	18
San Marino, Ca., U.S.	m12	112
San Marino, ctry., Eur.	G10	4
San Martín, Arg.	E6	80
San Martín, Arg.	G4	80
San Martín, Col.	F6	84
San Martín, dept., Peru	B8	82
San Martín, stm., Bol.	F10	82
San Martín, stm., Bol.	E10	82
San Martín, Lago (Lago O'Higgins), l., S.A.	F2	78
San Martín de los Andes, Arg.	E2	78
San Martín Texmelucan, Mex.	H10	90
San Mateo, Ca., U.S.	D2	112
San Mateo, Fl., U.S.	C5	116
San Mateo, N.M., U.S.	B2	138
San Mateo, Ven.	C10	84
San Mateo, co., Ca., U.S.	D2	112
San Mateo Ixtatán, Guat.	B3	92

Name	Map Ref.	Page
São Tomé, S. Tom./P.	A1	58
São Tomé, i., S. Tom./P.	A1	58
São Tomé, stm., Braz.	C13	82
São Tomé, Cabo de, c., Braz.	F8	79
Sao Tomé and Principe (São Tomé e Principe), ctry., Afr.	A1	58
Saoura, Oued, val., Alg.	F10	62
São Vicente, Braz.	G5	79
São Vicente, i., C.V.	k16	64a
São Vicente, Cabo de (Cape Saint Vincent), c., Port.	H2	16
São Vicente de Minas, Braz.	F6	79
Sapé, Braz.	E11	76
Sapele, Nig.	I12	64
Sapello, N.M., U.S.	B4	138
Sapelo Island, i., Ga., U.S.	E5	117
Sapelo Sound, strt., Ga., U.S.	E5	117
Şaphane, Tur.	J13	20
Šapitwa, mtn., Mwi.	E7	58
Šapki, Russia	B14	22
Sa Pobla, Spain	F15	16
Sapodilla Cays, i., Belize	A6	92
Saponé, Burkina	E9	64
Saposoa, Peru	B3	82
Sapožok, Russia	H23	22
Sappa Creek, stm., U.S.	E5	134
Sappa Creek, Middle Fork, stm., Ks., U.S.	C2	123
Sappa Creek, South Fork, stm., Ks., U.S.	C3	123
Sapphire Mountains, mts., Mt., U.S.	D3	133
Sapporo, Japan	d16	36a
Sapri, Italy	I10	18
Saptakośī, stm., Nepal	G12	44
Sapulpa, Ok., U.S.	B5	143
Sāqiat al-'Abd, Sud.	G6	60
Saqqez, Iran	C9	48
Saquena, Peru	A5	82
Saquisilí, Ec.	H3	84
Sarāb, Iran	C9	48
Saraburi, Thai.	G6	40
Saracura, stm., Braz.	B8	79
Saragossa see Zaragoza, Spain	D11	16
Saragossa, Al., U.S.	B2	108
Saraguro, Ec.	I3	84
Sarah, Ms., U.S.	A3	131
Sarai, Russia	H24	22
Sarajevo, Bos.	F2	20
Sarakhs, Iran	C16	48
Saraland, Al., U.S.	E1	108
Saran', Kaz.	H12	26
Saranac, Mi., U.S.	F5	129
Saranac, stm., N.Y., U.S.	F11	139
Saranac Lake, N.Y., U.S.	f10	139
Saranac Lakes, I., N.Y., U.S.	f10	139
Sarandi, Braz.	D12	80
Sarandí del Yi, Ur.	G11	80
Sarandí Grande, Ur.	G10	80
Saransk, Russia	G7	26
Sarapiquí, stm., C.R.	G11	92
Sarapul, Russia	F8	26
Sarare, Ven.	C8	84
Sara Sara, Nevado, mtn., Peru	F5	82
Sarasota, Fl., U.S.	E4	116
Sarasota, co., Fl., U.S.	E4	116
Sarasota Bay, b., Fl., U.S.	E4	116
Sarata, Ukr.	C13	20
Saratoga, Ar., U.S.	D2	111
Saratoga, Ca., U.S.	k8	112
Saratoga, In., U.S.	D8	121
Saratoga, Tx., U.S.	D5	150
Saratoga, Wy., U.S.	E6	157
Saratoga, co., N.Y., U.S.	B7	139
Saratoga Lake, I., N.Y., U.S.	C7	139
Saratoga National Historical Park, N.Y., U.S.	B7	139
Saratoga Springs, N.Y., U.S.	B7	139
Saratov, Russia	G7	26
Saratovskoje vodochranilišče, res., Russia	G7	26
Saraurcu, mtn., Ec.	H4	84
Saravan, Laos	G9	40
Sarawak, hist. reg., Malay.	E5	38
Saraya, Gui.	F4	64
Sarayköy, Tur.	L12	20
Sarbāz, Iran	H16	48
Sárbogárd, Hung.	I18	10
Sarcoxie, Mo., U.S.	D3	132
Sārda (Mahākālī), stm., Asia	F9	44
Sardārshahr, India	F6	44
Sardegna, prov., Italy	I4	18
Sardegna (Sardinia), i., Italy	I4	18
Sardinal, C.R.	G9	92
Sardinata, Col.	C6	84
Sardinia, In., U.S.	F6	121
Sardinia, Oh., U.S.	C2	142
Sardinia see Sardegna, i., Italy	I4	18
Sardis, Al., U.S.	C2	108
Sardis, Ga., U.S.	D5	117
Sardis, Ky., U.S.	B6	124
Sardis, Ms., U.S.	A4	131
Sardis, Oh., U.S.	C5	142
Sardis, Ok., U.S.	C6	143
Sardis, Tn., U.S.	B3	149
Sardis Lake, res., Ms., U.S.	A4	131
Sar-e Pol, Afg.	B1	44
Sarepta, La., U.S.	B2	125
Sargans, Switz.	D11	13
Sargasso Sea	B8	74
Sargasso Sea	F8	160
Sargent, Ga., U.S.	C2	117
Sargent, Ne., U.S.	C6	134
Sargent, co., N.D., U.S.	C8	141
Sargodha, Pak.	D5	44
Sarh, Chad	G4	56
Sārī, Iran	C12	48
Saric, Mex.	B4	90
Şarīf, Yemen	F7	47
Sarıkamış, Tur.	A7	48
Sarina, Austl.	C8	70
Sariñena, Spain	D11	16
Sarīr, Libya	D2	60
Sariwŏn, N. Kor.	E13	32
Šarja, Russia	F7	26
Sark, i., Guernsey	L11	8
Sarkad, Hung.	I21	10
Şarkışla, Tur.	B4	48
Šarkovščina, Bela.	F10	22
Şarköy, Tur.	I11	20
Šarlauk, Turk.	B13	48
Sarles, N.D., U.S.	A6	141
Sármellék, Hung.	I17	10
Sarmiento de Gamboa, Cerro, mtn., Chile	G2	78
Särna, Swe.	K13	6
Sarnen, Switz.	E9	13
Sarnia, Ont., Can.	E2	103
Sarno, Italy	I9	18
Saron, S. Afr.	I4	66
Saronikós Kólpos, b., Grc.	L7	20
Saronno, Italy	D4	18
Sárospatak, Hung.	G21	10
Sarpsborg, Nor.	L12	6
Sarpy, co., Ne., U.S.	C9	134
Sarralbe, Fr.	C14	14
Sarrebourg, Fr.	D14	14
Sarreguemines, Fr.	C14	14
Sarre-Union, Fr.	D14	14
Sarro, Mali	E7	64
Sarsfield, Ont., Can.	h13	103
Sarstoon (Sarstún), stm., N.A.	B5	92
Sarstún (Sarstoon), stm., N.A.	B5	92
Sartang, stm., Russia	D18	28
Sartell, Mn., U.S.	E4	130
Sartène, Fr.	m23	15a
Sarthe, dept., Fr.	D7	14
Sartilly, Fr.	D5	14
Saruhanlı, Tur.	K11	20
Sarūr, Oman	C11	47
Sárvár, Hung.	H16	10
Sarvestān, Iran	G12	48
Saryg-Sep, Russia	G17	26
Sarykamskoje ozero, I., Asia	I9	26
Sarykol'skij chrebet, mts., Asia	A6	44
Saryozek, Kaz.	I13	26
Sarysu, stm., Kaz.	H11	26
Sary-Taš, Kyrg.	J12	26
Sarzana, Italy	E4	18
Sāsarām, India	H11	44
Sásd, Hung.	I18	10
Sasebo, Japan	N4	36
Saskatchewan, prov., Can.	E3	105
Saskatchewan, stm., Can.	F12	96
Saskatoon, Sask., Can.	E2	105
Saslaya, Cerro, mtn., Nic.	H2	94
Sasolburg, S. Afr.	F8	66
Sasovo, Russia	G24	22
Sassafras, stm., Md., U.S.	B5	127
Sassafras Mountain, mtn., U.S.	A2	147
Sassandra, C. Iv.	I6	64
Sassandra, stm., C. Iv.	I6	64
Sassari, Italy	I3	18
Sasser, Ga., U.S.	E2	117
Sassoferrato, Italy	F7	18
Sasso Marconi, Italy	E6	18
S'as'stroj, Russia	A15	22
Sassuolo, Italy	E5	18
Sastown, Lib.	I5	64
Sastre, Arg.	F8	80
Sasyk, ozero, I., Ukr.	D13	20
Satah Mountain, mtn., B.C., Can.	C5	99
Šatalovo, Russia	G15	22
Sata-misaki, c., Japan	Q5	36
Satanta, Ks., U.S.	E3	123
Sātāra, India	D2	46
Satara, S. Afr.	E10	66
Satélite, Mex.	B6	90
Satilla, stm., Ga., U.S.	E5	117
Satipo, Peru	D4	82
Satīt (Tekeze), stm., Afr.	J9	60
Satka, Russia	F9	26
Satna, India	H9	44
Sátoraljaújhely, Hung.	G21	10
Sātpura Range, mts., India	J7	44
Satsop, Wa., U.S.	B2	154
Satsuma, Al., U.S.	E1	108
Satsuma, Fl., U.S.	C5	116
Satsunan-shotō, is., Japan	r4	37b
Sattahip, Thai.	H6	40
Satthwa, Mya.	F3	40
Satu Mare, Rom.	B6	20
Satu Mare, co., Rom.	B6	20
Satun, Thai.	K6	40
Šatura, Russia	F22	22
Saturna Island, i., B.C., Can.	E6	99
Saturnino M. Laspiur, Arg.	F7	80
Šaturtorf, Russia	F22	22
Satus Creek, stm., Wa., U.S.	C5	154
Sauce, Arg.	F9	80
Sauce, Peru	B3	82
Sauce, Ur.	H10	80
Sauce Corto, Arroyo, stm., Arg.	I8	80
Sauceda Mountains, mts., Az., U.S.	E3	110
Saucier, Ms., U.S.	E4	131
Saucillo, Mex.	C7	90
Sauda, Nor.	L10	6
Saudi Arabia (Al-'Arabīyah as-Su'ūdīyah), ctry., Asia	D4	42
Sauer (Sûre), stm., Eur.	I10	12
Saueruiná, stm., Braz.	E12	82
Sauê-Uiná, stm., Braz.	E12	82
Saufley Field Naval Air Station, mil., Fl., U.S.	u14	116
Saugatuck, Mi., U.S.	F4	129
Saugatuck, stm., Ct., U.S.	D2	114
Saugatucket, stm., R.I., U.S.	F4	146
Saugatuck Reservoir, res., Ct., U.S.	D2	114
Saugerties, N.Y., U.S.	C7	139
Saugus, Ma., U.S.	B5	128
Saugus, stm., Ma., U.S.	g11	128
Saujil, Arg.	E5	80
Sauk, co., Wi., U.S.	E4	156
Sauk, stm., Mn., U.S.	E4	130
Sauk, stm., Wa., U.S.	A4	154
Sauk Centre, Mn., U.S.	E4	130
Sauk City, Wi., U.S.	E4	156
Sauk Rapids, Mn., U.S.	E4	130
Saukville, Wi., U.S.	E6	156
Saül, Fr. Gu.	C8	76
Saulgau, Ger.	G9	10
Saulieu, Fr.	E11	14
Saulkrasti, Lat.	D7	22
Saulnierville, N.S., Can.	E3	101
Sault-au-Mouton, Que., Can.	A8	104
Sault Sainte Marie, Ont., Can.	p18	103
Sault Sainte Marie, Mi., U.S.	B6	129
Saumarez Reef, rf., Austl.	C10	70
Saumur, Fr.	E6	14
Saunders, co., Ne., U.S.	C9	134
Saunders Island, i., S. Geor.	A2	73
Saunders Island, i., S. Geor.	J12	74
Saunderstown, R.I., U.S.	E4	146
Saunemin, Il., U.S.	C5	120
Saurimo, Ang.	C4	58
Sausalito, Ca., U.S.	D2	112
Sauveterre-de-Béarn, Fr.	I6	14
Sauvo, Fin.	K18	6
Sava, Italy	I12	18
Sava, stm., Eur.	F11	4
Savage, Md., U.S.	B4	127
Savage, Ms., U.S.	A3	131
Savage, Mt., U.S.	C12	133
Savage, stm., Md., U.S.	k12	127
Savage River Reservoir, res., Md., U.S.	k12	127
Savai'i, i., W. Sam.	J22	158
Savalou, Benin	H10	64
Savanna, Il., U.S.	A3	120
Savanna, Ok., U.S.	C6	143
Savannah, Ga., U.S.	D5	117
Savannah, Mo., U.S.	B3	132
Savannah, Tn., U.S.	B3	149
Savannah, stm., U.S.	F5	147
Savannah River Plant, sci., S.C., U.S.	E4	147
Savannakhét, Laos	F8	40
Savanna Lake, I., Md., U.S.	D6	127
Savanna-la-Mar, Jam.	E5	94
Savé, Benin	G11	64
Save (Sabi), stm., Afr.	C12	66
Sāveh, Iran	D11	48
Savelli, Italy	J11	18
Saverdun, Fr.	I8	14
Saverne, Fr.	D14	14
Savigliano, Italy	E2	18
Saville Dam, Ct., U.S.	B4	114
Savino, Russia	E24	22
Savinskij, Russia	J27	6
Šavnik, Yugo.	G3	20
Savognin, Switz.	E12	13
Savoie, dept., Fr.	G13	14
Savona, B.C., Can.	D7	99
Savona, Italy	E3	18
Savona, N.Y., U.S.	C3	139
Savoonga, Ak., U.S.	C5	109
Savoy, Il., U.S.	C5	120
Savran', Ukr.	A14	20
Savu Sea see Sawu, Laut, Indon.	G7	38
Sawahlunto, Indon.	O6	40
Sawāi Mādhopur, India	H7	44
Sawākin, Sud.	H9	60
Sawankhalok, Thai.	F5	40
Sawatch Range, mts., Co., U.S.	B4	113
Sawdā', Jabal, mtn., Sau. Ar.	E3	47
Sawdā', Jabal as-, hills, Libya	C4	56
Sawdā', Qurnat as-, mtn., Leb.	D4	48
Sawdirī, Sud.	J5	60
Sawhāj, Egypt	D6	60
Sawknah, Libya	C4	56
Sawmill, Az., U.S.	B6	110
Sawnee Mountain, mtn., Ga., U.S.	B2	117
Şawqirah, Ghubbat, b., Oman	E10	47
Sawtooth Mountains, mts., Id., U.S.	F4	119
Sawtooth National Recreation Area, Id., U.S.	E3	119
Sawtooth Ridge, mtn., Wa., U.S.	A5	154
Sawu, Laut (Savu Sea), Indon.	G7	38
Sawu, Pulau, i., Indon.	H7	38
Sawyer, Ks., U.S.	E5	123
Sawyer, Mi., U.S.	G4	129
Sawyer, Mn., U.S.	D6	130
Sawyer, N.D., U.S.	A4	141
Sawyer, co., Wi., U.S.	C2	156
Sawyerville, Que., Can.	D6	104
Saxapahaw, N.C., U.S.	B3	140
Saxby, stm., Austl.	C8	70
Saxis, Va., U.S.	C7	153
Saxman, Ak., U.S.	n24	109
Saxon, Switz.	F7	13
Saxonburg, Pa., U.S.	E2	145
Saxony see Sachsen, state, Ger.	C9	10
Saxton, Pa., U.S.	F5	145
Saxtons, stm., Vt., U.S.	E3	152
Saxtons River, Vt., U.S.	E3	152
Say, Niger	E11	64
Sayán, Peru	D3	82
Sayan Mountains (Sajany), mts., Asia	G11	28
Sayaxché, Guat.	I14	90
Saybrook, Il., U.S.	C5	120
Saybrook Manor, Ct., U.S.	D6	114
Saybrook Point, Ct., U.S.	D6	114
Saydā (Sidon), Leb.	A4	50
Saydel, Ia., U.S.	e8	122
Sayhūt, Yemen	G7	47
Sayil, hist., Mex.	G15	90
Saylesville, R.I., U.S.	B4	146
Saylorsburg, Pa., U.S.	E11	145
Saylorville, Ia., U.S.	e8	122
Saylorville Lake, res., Ia., U.S.	C4	122
Saylūn, Khirbat (Shiloh), hist., W.B.	D4	50
Sayner, Wi., U.S.	B4	156
Sayre, Al., U.S.	B3	108
Sayre, Ok., U.S.	B2	143
Sayre, Pa., U.S.	C8	145
Sayreville, N.J., U.S.	C4	137
Sayula, Mex.	H8	90
Sayville, N.Y., U.S.	n15	139
Sayward, B.C., Can.	D5	99
Saywūn, Yemen	G6	47
Sazonovo, Russia	B18	22
Šazud, Taj.	B5	44
Sba, Alg.	F10	62
Sbeïtla, Tun.	N4	18
Sbiba, Tun.	N4	18
Scafell Pikes, mtn., Eng., U.K.	G10	8
Scalea, Italy	J10	18
Scales Mound, Il., U.S.	A3	120
Scalp Level, Pa., U.S.	F4	145
Scaly Mountain, N.C., U.S.	f9	140
Scammon, Ks., U.S.	E9	123
Scammon Bay, Ak., U.S.	C6	109
Scandia, Alta., Can.	D4	98
Scandia, Ks., U.S.	C6	123
Scanlon, Mn., U.S.	D6	130
Scanterbury, Man., Can.	D3	100
Scantic, Ct., U.S.	B5	114
Scapa Flow, b., Scot., U.K.	C10	8
Scapegoat Mountain, mtn., Mt., U.S.	C3	133
Ščapino, Russia	F23	28
Scappoose, Or., U.S.	B4	144
Scarborough, Ont., Can.	m15	103
Scarborough, Trin.	I14	94
Scarborough, Eng., U.K.	G13	8
Scarborough, Me., U.S.	E2	126
Scarbro, W.V., U.S.	n13	155
Scarsdale, N.Y., U.S.	h13	139
Scawfell Island, i., Austl.	C8	70
Ščelkovo, Russia	F21	22
Scenic, S.D., U.S.	D3	148
Sceptre, Sask., Can.	G1	105
Ščerbinka, Russia	F20	22
Schaefferstown, Pa., U.S.	F9	145
Schaerbeek (Schaarbeek), Bel.	G5	12
Schaffhausen, Switz.	C10	13
Schaffhausen, state, Switz.	C10	13
Schaller, Ia., U.S.	B2	122
Schärding, Aus.	G13	10
Schaumburg, Il., U.S.	h8	120
Schefferville, Que., Can.	h13	104
Scheibbs, Aus.	G15	10
Scheinfeld, Ger.	F10	10
Schelde (Escaut), stm., Eur.	D4	10
Schell City, Mo., U.S.	C3	132
Schell Creek Range, mts., Nv., U.S.	D7	135
Schenectady, N.Y., U.S.	C7	139
Schenectady, co., N.Y., U.S.	C6	139
Scherer, Lake, res., Ga., U.S.	C3	117
Schererville, In., U.S.	B3	121
Schertz, Tx., U.S.	h7	150
Schesslitz, Ger.	F11	10
Scheveningen, Neth.	D5	12
Schiedam, Neth.	E5	12
Schiermonnikoog, Neth.	B9	12
Schiermonnikoog, i., Neth.	B9	12
Schiller Park, Il., U.S.	k9	120
Schiltigheim, Fr.	D14	14
Schio, Italy	D6	18
Schipbeek, stm., Eur.	D9	12
Schkeuditz, Ger.	D12	10
Schladming, Aus.	H13	10
Schlater, Ms., U.S.	B3	131
Schleicher, co., Tx., U.S.	D2	150
Schleswig, Ger.	A9	10
Schleswig, Ia., U.S.	B2	122
Schleswig-Holstein, state, Ger.	A9	10
Schleusingen, Ger.	E10	10
Schley, co., Ga., U.S.	D2	117
Schlieren, Switz.	D9	13
Schlitz, Ger.	E9	10
Schlüchtern, Ger.	E9	10
Schmalkalden, Ger.	E10	10
Schmidmühlen, Ger.	F11	10
Schmölln, Ger.	E12	10
Schneider, In., U.S.	B3	121
Schneverdingen, Ger.	B9	10
Schodn'a, Russia	F20	22
Schoenchen, Ks., U.S.	D4	123
Schofield, Wi., U.S.	D4	156
Schofield Barracks, mil., Hi., U.S.	g9	118
Schoharie, N.Y., U.S.	C6	139
Schoharie, co., N.Y., U.S.	C6	139
Schoharie Creek, stm., N.Y., U.S.	C6	139
Schönebeck, Ger.	C11	10
Schongau, Ger.	H10	10
Schoodic Lake, I., Me., U.S.	C4	126
Schoolcraft, Mi., U.S.	F5	129
Schoolcraft, co., Mi., U.S.	B4	129
Schooleys Mountain, mtn., N.J., U.S.	B3	137
Schopfheim, Ger.	H7	10
Schorndorf, Ger.	G9	10
Schouten Island, i., Austl.	N8	70
Schouwen, i., Neth.	E4	12
Schramberg, Ger.	G8	10
Schram City, Il., U.S.	D4	120
Schriever, La., U.S.	E5	125
Schroeder, Mn., U.S.	C8	130
Schroffenstein, mtn., Nmb.	F4	66
Schroon Lake, N.Y., U.S.	B7	139
Schroon Lake, I., N.Y., U.S.	B7	139
Schulenburg, Tx., U.S.	E4	150
Schuler, Alta., Can.	D5	98
Schulter, Ok., U.S.	B6	143
Schultz Lake, I., N.W. Ter., Can.	D13	96
Schüpfheim, Switz.	E9	13
Schurz, Nv., U.S.	E3	135
Schuyler, Ne., U.S.	C8	134
Schuyler, Va., U.S.	C4	153
Schuyler, co., Il., U.S.	C3	120
Schuyler, co., Mo., U.S.	A5	132
Schuyler, co., N.Y., U.S.	C4	139
Schuylerville, N.Y., U.S.	B7	139
Schuylkill, co., Pa., U.S.	E9	145
Schuylkill, stm., Pa., U.S.	F10	145
Schuylkill Haven, Pa., U.S.	E9	145
Schwabach, Ger.	F11	10
Schwaben, hist. reg., Ger.	G10	10
Schwäbische Alb, mts., Ger.	G9	10
Schwäbisch Gmünd, Ger.	G9	10
Schwäbisch Hall, Ger.	F9	10
Schwabmünchen, Ger.	G10	10
Schwanden, Switz.	D11	13
Schwandorf, Ger.	F12	10
Schwaner, Pegunungan, mts., Indon.	F5	38
Schwarza, Ger.	E11	10
Schwarzach im Pongau, Aus.	H13	10
Schwarzenburg, Switz.	E7	13
Schwarzwald (Black Forest), mts., Ger.	G8	10
Schwaz, Aus.	H11	10
Schwedt, Ger.	B14	10
Schweinfurt, Ger.	E10	10
Schweizer Nationalpark, Switz.	E13	13
Schwerin, Ger.	B11	10
Schwyz, Switz.	D10	13
Schwyz, state, Switz.	D10	13
Sciacca, Italy	L8	18
Scicli, Italy	M9	18
Science Hill, Ky., U.S.	C5	124
Scilla, Italy	K10	18
Scilly, Isles of, is., Eng., U.K.	L7	8
Scio, Oh., U.S.	B4	142
Scio, Or., U.S.	C4	144
Scioto, co., Oh., U.S.	D3	142
Scioto, stm., Oh., U.S.	B2	142
Scipio, In., U.S.	F6	121
Scipio, Ut., U.S.	D3	151
Scircleville, In., U.S.	D5	121
Scituate, Ma., U.S.	B6	128
Scituate Reservoir, res., R.I., U.S.	C3	146
Scobey, Mt., U.S.	B11	133
Scofield Reservoir, res., Ut., U.S.	D4	151
Ščokino, Russia	G20	22
Scone, Austl.	I9	70
Scooba, Ms., U.S.	C5	131
Scordia, Italy	L9	18
Scotch Plains, N.J., U.S.	B4	137
Scotia, Ont., Can.	B5	103
Scotia, Ca., U.S.	B1	112
Scotia, Ne., U.S.	C7	134
Scotia, N.Y., U.S.	C7	139
Scotia Sea, S.A.	A1	73
Scotland, Ont., Can.	D4	103
Scotland, Ar., U.S.	B3	111
Scotland, Ct., U.S.	C7	114
Scotland, Ga., U.S.	D4	117
Scotland, In., U.S.	G4	121
Scotland, Pa., U.S.	G6	145
Scotland, S.D., U.S.	D8	148
Scotland, Tx., U.S.	C3	150
Scotland, co., Mo., U.S.	A5	132
Scotland, co., N.C., U.S.	C3	140
Scotland, ter., U.K.	D9	8
Scotland Neck, N.C., U.S.	A5	140
Scotlandville, La., U.S.	D4	125
Scotrun, Pa., U.S.	D11	145
Scotsburn, N.S., Can.	D7	101
Scotstown, Que., Can.	D6	104
Scott, Sask., Can.	E1	105
Scott, Ar., U.S.	C3	111
Scott, Ga., U.S.	D4	117
Scott, La., U.S.	D3	125
Scott, Ms., U.S.	B2	131
Scott, co., Ar., U.S.	C1	111
Scott, co., Il., U.S.	D3	120
Scott, co., In., U.S.	G6	121
Scott, co., Ia., U.S.	C7	122
Scott, co., Ks., U.S.	D3	123
Scott, co., Ky., U.S.	B5	124
Scott, co., Mn., U.S.	F5	130
Scott, co., Ms., U.S.	C4	131
Scott, co., Mo., U.S.	D8	132
Scott, co., Tn., U.S.	C9	149
Scott, co., Va., U.S.	f9	153
Scott, Cape, c., B.C., Can.	D3	99
Scott, Mount, mtn., Ok., U.S.	C3	143
Scott, Mount, mtn., Or., U.S.	E4	144
Scott Air Force Base, mil., Il., U.S.	E4	120
Scott Base, sci., Ant.	C8	73
Scottburgh, S. Afr.	H10	66
Scott City, Ks., U.S.	D3	123
Scott City, Mo., U.S.	D8	132
Scottdale, Ga., U.S.	h8	117
Scottdale, Pa., U.S.	F2	145
Scott Islands, is., B.C., Can.	D3	99
Scott Mountain, mtn., Id., U.S.	E3	119
Scott Peak, mtn., Id., U.S.	E6	119
Scott Reef, rf., Austl.	B4	68
Scott Reservoir, res., N.C., U.S.	A1	140
Scotts, Mi., U.S.	F5	129
Scottsbluff, Ne., U.S.	C2	134
Scotts Bluff, co., Ne., U.S.	C2	134
Scotts Bluff National Monument, Ne., U.S.	C2	134
Scottsboro, Al., U.S.	A3	108
Scottsburg, In., U.S.	G6	121
Scottsdale, Austl.	M7	70
Scottsdale, Az., U.S.	D4	110
Scotts Hill, Tn., U.S.	B3	149
Scotts Mills, Or., U.S.	B4	144
Scotts Mountain, mtn., N.J., U.S.	B2	137
Scottsville, Ky., U.S.	D3	124
Scottsville, N.Y., U.S.	B3	139
Scottsville, Va., U.S.	C4	153
Scottville, Mi., U.S.	E4	129
Scow Bay, Ak., U.S.	m23	109
Scraggly Lake, I., Me., U.S.	B4	126
Scranton, Ar., U.S.	B2	111
Scranton, Ia., U.S.	B3	122
Scranton, Ks., U.S.	D8	123
Scranton, N.D., U.S.	C2	141
Scranton, Pa., U.S.	D10	145
Scranton, S.C., U.S.	D8	147
Screven, Ga., U.S.	E4	117
Screven, co., Ga., U.S.	D5	117
Scribner, Ne., U.S.	C9	134
Ščučin, Bela.	H7	22
Ščučinsk, Kaz.	G12	26
Scugog, Lake, I., Ont., Can.	C6	103
Scuol (Schuls), Switz.	E13	13
Scurry, co., Tx., U.S.	C2	150
Scutari, Lake, I., Eur.	G3	20
Seaboard, N.C., U.S.	A5	140
Seabreeze, De., U.S.	F5	115
Sea Bright, N.J., U.S.	C5	137
Seabrook, N.H., U.S.	E5	136
Seabrook, N.J., U.S.	E2	137
Seabrook, Tx., U.S.	r14	150
Seabrook Island, i., S.C., U.S.	F7	147
Seadrift, Tx., U.S.	E4	150
Seaford, De., U.S.	F3	115
Seaford, Va., U.S.	h15	153
Seaforth, Ont., Can.	D3	103
Sea Girt, N.J., U.S.	C4	137
Seagoville, Tx., U.S.	n10	150
Seagrave, Ont., Can.	C6	103
Seagraves, Tx., U.S.	C1	150
Seahorse Point, c., N.W. Ter., Can.	D16	96
Sea Islands, is., U.S.	E10	106
Sea Isle City, N.J., U.S.	E3	137
Seal, stm., Man., Can.	f8	100
Sea Lake, Austl.	J5	70
Seal Cays, is., T./C. Is.	D9	94
Seal Cove, N.B., Can.	E3	101
Seal Cove, Newf., Can.	D3	102
Seale, Al., U.S.	C4	108
Seal Harbor, Me., U.S.	D4	126
Seal Point, c., P.E.I., Can.	C5	101
Seal Rock, Or., U.S.	C2	144
Sealy, Tx., U.S.	E4	150
Seama, N.M., U.S.	B2	138
Seaman, Oh., U.S.	D2	142
Seaman Range, mts., Nv., U.S.	F6	135
Seara, Braz.	D12	80
Searchlight, Nv., U.S.	H7	135
Searcy, Ar., U.S.	B4	111
Searcy, co., Ar., U.S.	B3	111
Searles, Al., U.S.	B2	108
Searles, Mn., U.S.	F4	130
Searles Lake, I., Ca., U.S.	E5	112
Sears Falls, wtfl, Ne., U.S.	B5	134
Searsmont, Me., U.S.	D3	126
Searsport, Me., U.S.	D4	126
Searston, Newf., Can.	E2	102
Seaside, Or., U.S.	B3	144
Seaside Heights, N.J., U.S.	D4	137
Seaside Park, N.J., U.S.	D4	137
Seaton, Il., U.S.	B3	120
Seat Pleasant, Md., U.S.	C4	127
Seattle, Wa., U.S.	B3	154
Seattle-Tacoma International Airport, Wa., U.S.	f11	154
Seaview, Wa., U.S.	C1	154
Seaville, N.J., U.S.	E3	137
Seba Beach, Alta., Can.	C3	98
Sébaco, Nic.	E8	92
Sebago Lake, Me., U.S.	E2	126
Sebakwe Recreational Area, Zimb.	B10	66
Šebalino, Russia	G15	26
Sebasco Estates, Me., U.S.	g8	126
Sebastian, Fl., U.S.	E6	116
Sebastian, co., Ar., U.S.	B1	111
Sebastian, Cape, c., Or., U.S.	E2	144
Sebastian Inlet, b., Fl., U.S.	E6	116
Sebastián Vizcaíno, Bahía, b., Mex.	C2	90
Sebasticook Lake, I., Me., U.S.	D3	126
Sebastopol, Ms., U.S.	C4	131
Sebderat, Erit.	J9	60
Sebec Lake, I., Me., U.S.	C3	126
Sebeka, Mn., U.S.	D3	130
Seberi, Braz.	D12	80
Sebeş, Rom.	D7	20
Sebes Körös (Crişul Repede), stm., Eur.	B5	20
Sebewaing, Mi., U.S.	E7	129
Sebež, Russia	E11	22
Şebinkarahisar, Tur.	A5	48
Sebiş, Rom.	C6	20
Sebnitz, Ger.	E14	10
Seboeis, stm., Me., U.S.	B4	126
Seboeis Lake, I., Me., U.S.	C4	126
Seboomook Lake, I., Me., U.S.	C3	126
Seboyeta, N.M., U.S.	B2	138
Sebree, Ky., U.S.	C2	124
Sebring, Fl., U.S.	E5	116
Sebring, Oh., U.S.	B4	142
Sebringville, Ont., Can.	D3	103
Secas, Islas, is., Pan.	J12	92
Secaucus, N.J., U.S.	h8	137
Sechelt, B.C., Can.	E6	99
Sechura, Peru	A1	82
Sechura, Bahía de, b., Peru	A1	82
Sechura, Desierto de, des., Peru	A1	82
Seclantas, Arg.	C5	80
Seco, Ky., U.S.	C7	124
Seco, stm., Arg.	B7	80
Second Lake, I., N.H., U.S.	f7	136
Second Mesa, Az., U.S.	B5	110
Secor, Il., U.S.	C4	120
Sečovce, Slvk.	G21	10
Secretary, Md., U.S.	C6	127
Secret Lake, I., R.I., U.S.	E4	146
Section, Al., U.S.	A4	108
Sécure, stm., Bol.	F9	82
Security, Co., U.S.	C6	113
Seda, China	E7	30
Seda, Lat.	D8	22
Seda, Lith.	E5	22
Sedalia, Co., U.S.	B6	113
Sedalia, Ky., U.S.	f9	124
Sedalia, Mo., U.S.	C4	132
Sedan, Fr.	C11	14
Sedan, Ks., U.S.	E7	123
Sedano, Spain	C8	16
Sedel'nikovo, Russia	F13	26
Sederot, Isr.	E3	50
Sedgewick, Alta., Can.	C5	98
Sedgewick, Mount, mtn., N.M., U.S.	B1	138
Sedgwick, Co., U.S.	A8	113
Sedgwick, Ks., U.S.	E6	123
Sedgwick, Me., U.S.	D4	126
Sedgwick, co., Co., U.S.	A8	113
Sedgwick, co., Ks., U.S.	E6	123
Sedini, Italy	I3	18
Sedlčany, Czech Rep.	F14	10
Sedley, Sask., Can.	G3	105

Name	Map Ref.	Page
Sedley, Va., U.S.	D6	153
Sedom (Sodom), hist., Isr.	F4	50
Sedona, Az., U.S.	C4	110
Sedot Yam, Isr.	D3	50
Sedova, pik, mtn., Russia	C8	26
Sedrata, Alg.	M2	18
Sedro Woolley, Wa., U.S.	A3	154
Šeduva, Lith.	F6	22
Seebe, Alta., Can.	D3	98
Seeberg, Switz.	D8	13
Seefeld in Tirol, Aus.	H11	10
Seehausen, Ger.	C11	10
Seeheim, Nmb.	F3	66
Seeis, Nmb.	D3	66
Seekonk, Ma., U.S.	C5	128
Seekonk, stm., R.I., U.S.	C4	146
Seeley, Ca., U.S.	F6	112
Seeley Lake, Mt., U.S.	C3	133
Seeleys Bay, Ont., Can.	C8	103
Seelow, Ger.	C14	10
Seelyville, In., U.S.	F3	121
Seengen, Switz.	D9	13
Sées, Fr.	D7	14
Seesen, Ger.	D10	10
Sefadu, S.L.	G4	64
Sefar, hist., Alg.	H15	62
Sefare, Bots.	D8	66
Sefīd Ābeh, Iran	F16	48
Sefrou, Mor.	D8	62
Segamat, Malay.	M7	40
Şegarcea, Rom.	E7	20
Ségbana, Benin	F11	64
Segbwema, S.L.	G4	64
Segeža, Russia	E4	26
Segni, Italy	H8	18
Segorbe, Spain	F11	16
Ségou, Mali	E6	64
Segovia, Col.	D5	84
Segovia, Spain	E7	16
Segozero, ozero, l., Russia	J23	6
Segre, stm., Eur.	D12	16
Seguam Island, i., Ak., U.S.	E5	109
Seguam Pass, strt., Ak., U.S.	E5	109
Séguédine, Niger	D9	54
Séguéla, C. Iv.	H6	64
Séguéla, Mali	D6	64
Seguí, Arg.	F8	80
Seguin, Tx., U.S.	E4	150
Segundo, Co., U.S.	D6	113
Segundo, stm., Arg.	F7	80
Segura, Port.	F5	16
Segura, stm., Spain	G11	16
Sehithwa, Bots.	C6	66
Seia, Port.	E4	16
Seibert, Co., U.S.	B8	113
Seiling, Ok., U.S.	A3	143
Seilo, Sud.	K2	60
Sein, Île de, i., Fr.	D2	14
Seinäjoki, Fin.	J18	6
Seine, stm., Fr.	C7	14
Seine, Baie de la, b., Fr.	C6	14
Seine-et-Marne, dept., Fr.	D10	14
Seine-Maritime, dept., Fr.	C8	14
Seixal, Port.	G2	16
Sejm, stm., Eur.	G4	26
Sejmčan, Russia	E22	28
Seke, Eth.	M10	60
Šeki, Azer.	I7	26
Seki, Japan	L11	36
Seki, Tur.	M13	20
Sekiu, Wa., U.S.	A1	154
Sekoma, Bots.	E6	66
Sekondi-Takoradi, Ghana	I9	64
Šekota, Eth.	K10	60
Šeksna, Russia	B21	22
Šelagskij, mys, c., Russia	C26	28
Selah, Wa., U.S.	C5	154
Selaru, Pulau, i., Indon.	G9	38
Selatan, Tanjung, c., Indon.	F5	38
Selawik, Ak., U.S.	B7	109
Selawik Lake, l., Ak., U.S.	B7	109
Selayar, Pulau, i., Indon.	G7	38
Selb, Ger.	E12	10
Selbu, Nor.	J12	6
Selby, S.D., U.S.	B5	148
Selbyville, De., U.S.	G5	115
Sel'co, Russia	H17	22
Selden, Ks., U.S.	C3	123
Seldovia, Ak., U.S.	D9	109
Selebi Phikwe, Bots.	D8	66
Selenga (Selenge), stm., Asia	G19	26
Selenge (Selenga), stm., Asia	B7	30
Selenn'ach, stm., Russia	D20	28
Sélestat, Fr.	D14	14
Selezn'ovo, Russia	A11	22
Selfridge, N.D., U.S.	C5	141
Sélibaby, Maur.	D3	64
Šelichova, zaliv, b., Russia	F23	28
Seliger, ozero, l., Russia	D16	22
Seligman, Az., U.S.	B3	110
Seligman, Mo., U.S.	E4	132
Selinsgrove, Pa., U.S.	E8	145
Selišče, Russia	E16	22
Seližarovo, Russia	E16	22
Selje, Nor.	J9	6
Seljord, Nor.	L11	6
Selkirk, Man., Can.	D3	100
Selkirk, Scot., U.K.	F11	8
Selleck, Wa., U.S.	B4	154
Sellers, Al., U.S.	C3	108
Sellers, S.C., U.S.	C9	147
Sellersburg, In., U.S.	H6	121
Sellersville, Pa., U.S.	F11	145
Sells, Az., U.S.	F4	110
Selm, Ger.	D7	10
Selma, N.S., Can.	D6	101
Selma, Al., U.S.	C2	108
Selma, Ca., U.S.	D4	112
Selma, In., U.S.	D7	121
Selma, N.C., U.S.	B4	140
Selmer, Tn., U.S.	B3	149
Seltz, Fr.	D15	14
Selva, Arg.	E7	80
Selvas, for., Braz.	E6	76
Selvin, In., U.S.	H3	121
Selway, stm., Id., U.S.	C3	119
Selwyn, Austl.	C4	70
Selwyn Mountains, mts., Can.	D6	96
Selwyn Range, mts., Austl.	C4	70
Selz, N.D., U.S.	B6	141
Seman, stm., Alb.	I3	20
Semans, Sask., Can.	F3	105
Semarang, Indon.	j15	39a
Semenivka, Ukr.	I15	22
Semeru, Gunung, mtn., Indon.	k16	39a
Semeževo, Bela.	I10	22
Semibratovo, Russia	D22	22
Seminary, Ms., U.S.	D4	131
Seminoe Mountains, mts., Wy., U.S.	D6	157
Seminoe Reservoir, res., Wy., U.S.	D6	157
Seminole, Al., U.S.	E2	108
Seminole, Ok., U.S.	B5	143
Seminole, Tx., U.S.	C1	150
Seminole, co., Fl., U.S.	D5	116
Seminole, co., Ga., U.S.	F2	117
Seminole, co., Ok., U.S.	B5	143
Seminole, Lake, res., U.S.	F2	117
Semipalatinsk, Kaz.	G8	28
Semisopochnoi Island, i., Ak., U.S.	E3	109
Semmes, Al., U.S.	E1	108
Semnān, Iran	D12	48
Semois, stm., Eur.	I7	12
Semonaicha, Kaz.	G14	26
Sem'onov, Russia	F6	26
Semporna, Malay.	E6	38
Semuliki, stm., Afr.	A5	58
Semur-en-Auxois, Fr.	E11	14
Sena, Bol.	D8	82
Sena, Moz.	E7	58
Sena, N.M., U.S.	B4	138
Senachwine Lake, l., Il., U.S.	B4	120
Senador Canedo, Braz.	D4	79
Senador Firmino, Braz.	F7	79
Senador Pompeu, Braz.	E11	76
Senahú, Guat.	B5	92
Sena Madureira, Braz.	C7	82
Senanga, Zam.	E4	58
Senath, Mo., U.S.	E7	132
Senatobia, Ms., U.S.	A4	131
Sendafa, Eth.	M10	60
Sendai, Japan	I15	36
Sêndo, China	E15	44
Seneca, Il., U.S.	B5	120
Seneca, Ks., U.S.	C7	123
Seneca, Mo., U.S.	E3	132
Seneca, Pa., U.S.	D2	145
Seneca, S.C., U.S.	B2	147
Seneca, S.D., U.S.	B6	148
Seneca, co., N.Y., U.S.	C4	139
Seneca, co., Oh., U.S.	A2	142
Seneca Falls, N.Y., U.S.	C4	139
Seneca Lake, l., N.Y., U.S.	C4	139
Senecaville Lake, res., Oh., U.S.	C4	142
Senegal (Sénégal), ctry., Afr.	F4	54
Sénégal, stm., Afr.	E4	54
Senekal, S. Afr.	G8	66
Senftenberg, Ger.	D14	10
Sengés, Braz.	H4	79
Senhor do Bonfim, Braz.	F10	76
Senica, Slvk.	G17	10
Senigallia, Italy	F8	18
Senise, Italy	I11	18
Senj, Cro.	E9	18
Senja, i., Nor.	G15	6
Senkaku-shotō, is., Japan	F11	30
Šenkursk, Russia	E6	26
Senlac, Sask., Can.	E1	105
Senlis, Fr.	C9	14
Senmonorom, Camb.	H9	40
Senneterre, Que., Can.	k11	104
Sennori, Italy	I3	18
Senoia, Ga., U.S.	C2	117
Senqu see Orange, stm., Afr.	G4	66
Sens, Fr.	D10	14
Sensuntepeque, El Sal.	D6	92
Senta, Yugo.	D4	20
Sentinel, Ok., U.S.	B2	143
Sentinel Butte, N.D., U.S.	C2	141
Sentinel Butte, mtn., N.D., U.S.	C2	141
Seo de Urgel, Spain	C13	16
Seoni, India	I8	44
Seoul see Sŏul, S. Kor.	F14	32
Sepatini, stm., Braz.	B9	82
Sepetiba, Baía de, b., Braz.	G7	79
Sepik, stm., Pap. N. Gui.	k15	68a
Sępólno Krajeńskie, Pol.	B17	10
Sepopa, Bots.	B6	66
Sepoti, stm., Braz.	B11	82
Sepotuba, stm., Braz.	F13	82
Sept-Îles (Seven Islands), Que., Can.	h13	104
Sepulga, stm., Al., U.S.	D3	108
Sequatchie, Tn., U.S.	D8	149
Sequatchie, co., Tn., U.S.	D8	149
Sequatchie, stm., Tn., U.S.	D8	149
Sequeros, Spain	E5	16
Sequim, Wa., U.S.	A2	154
Sequoia National Park, Ca., U.S.	D4	112
Sequoyah, co., Ok., U.S.	B7	143
Šerabad, Uzb.	B2	44
Serachs, Turk.	C16	48
Serafimovič, Russia	H6	26
Seraidi, Alg.	M2	18
Seraing, Bel.	G7	12
Seram (Ceram), i., Indon.	F8	38
Seram, Laut (Ceram Sea), Indon.	F8	38
Serang, Indon.	j13	39a
Serbia see Srbija, state, Yugo.	F4	20
Serdobsk, Russia	G6	26
Serebr'anyje Prudy, Russia	G21	22
Sered', Slvk.	G17	10
Seredejskij, Russia	G18	22
Seredina-Buda, Ukr.	I17	22
Seredžius, Lith.	F6	22
Seremban, Malay.	M6	40
Serengeti Plain, pl., Tan.	B6	58
Serenje, Zam.	D6	58
Šereševo, Bela.	I7	22
Seret (Siret), stm., Eur.	A9	20
Sergeant Bluff, Ia., U.S.	B1	122
Sergeja Kirova, ostrova, is., Russia	B15	26
Sergejevka, Russia	I18	28
Sergijev Posad, Russia	E21	22
Seria, Bru.	E5	38
Serian, Malay.	N11	40
Sérifos, i., Grc.	L8	20
Serkhe, Cerro, mtn., Bol.	G7	82
Šerlovaja Gora, Russia	G15	28
Sermata, Pulau, i., Indon.	G8	38
Serodino, Arg.	G8	80
Serov, Russia	F10	26
Serowe, Bots.	D8	66
Serpa, Port.	H4	16
Serpents Mouth, strt.	C12	84
Serpuchov, Russia	G20	22
Serra, Braz.	F8	79
Serra do Navio, Braz.	C8	76
Serra do Salitre, Braz.	E5	79
Sérrai, Grc.	H7	20
Serrana, Braz.	F5	79
Serrânia, Braz.	F5	79
Serranópolis, Braz.	E2	79
Serra Talhada, Braz.	E11	76
Serrezuela, Arg.	F6	80
Serrinha, Braz.	F11	76
Serro, Braz.	E7	79
Sersale, Italy	J11	18
Sertânia, Braz.	E11	76
Seruini, stm., Braz.	C8	82
Serule, Bots.	C8	66
Servia, In., U.S.	C6	121
Sêrxü, China	E6	30
Sesfontein, Nmb.	B1	66
Sesheke, Zam.	E4	58
Seskar, ostrov, i., Russia	A11	22
Sessa Aurunca, Italy	H8	18
Sesser, Il., U.S.	E4	120
Sessums, Ms., U.S.	B5	131
Sestao, Spain	B8	16
Sestri Levante, Italy	E4	18
Sestroreck, Russia	A12	22
Šešupe, stm., Eur.	G5	22
Setana, Japan	e14	36a
Sète, Fr.	I10	14
Sete Barras, Braz.	C15	80
Sete de Setembro, stm., Braz.	B2	79
Sete Lagoas, Braz.	E6	79
Sete Quedas, Parque Nacional de, Braz.	C11	80
Seth, W.V., U.S.	C3	155
Set Net, Punta, c., Nic.	E11	92
Seto, Japan	L12	36
Seto-naikai, Japan	M7	36
Seton Portage, B.C., Can.	D6	99
Settat, Mor.	D7	62
Setté Cama, Gabon	B1	58
Sette-Daban, chrebet, mts., Russia	E19	28
Setúbal, Port.	G3	16
Setúbal, Baía de, b., Port.	G3	16
Seui, Italy	J4	18
Seul, Lac, l., Ont., Can.	o16	103
Seul Choix Point, c., Mi., U.S.	C5	129
Seurre, Fr.	E12	14
Sevan, Arm.	A8	48
Sevan, ozero, l., Arm.	I7	26
Sévaré, Mali	D7	64
Sevastopol', Ukr.	I4	26
Seven Devils Lake, res., Ar., U.S.	D4	111
Seven Devils Mountains, mts., Id., U.S.	D2	119
Seven Hills, Oh., U.S.	h9	142
Seven Islands Bay, b., Newf., Can.	f9	102
Seven Mile, Oh., U.S.	C1	142
Seven Mile Beach, N.J., U.S.	E3	137
Seven Persons, Alta., Can.	E5	98
Seven Sisters Peaks, mts., B.C., Can.	B3	99
Seventy Mile House, B.C., Can.	D7	99
Severance, Co., U.S.	A6	113
Severance, N.H., U.S.	D4	136
Severn, Md., U.S.	B4	127
Severn, stm., Ont., Can.	n17	103
Severn, stm., U.K.	J11	8
Severnaja Dvina, stm., Russia	E6	26
Severnaja Osetija, state, Russia	I6	26
Severnaja Sos'va, stm., Russia	E4	28
Severnaja Zemľa, is., Russia	B17	26
Severna Park, Md., U.S.	B4	127
Severn River, b., Md., U.S.	B4	127
Severnyje uvaly, hills, Russia	B27	22
Severodvinsk, Russia	E5	26
Severo-Dvinskij kanal, Russia	B21	22
Severomorsk, Russia	D4	26
Severo-Sibirskaja nizmennost', pl., Russia	C18	26
Severoural'sk, Russia	E9	26
Severo-Zadonsk, Russia	G21	22
Severy, Ks., U.S.	E7	123
Sevier, co., Ar., U.S.	D1	111
Sevier, co., Tn., U.S.	D10	149
Sevier, co., Ut., U.S.	E4	151
Sevier, stm., Ut., U.S.	D3	151
Sevier, East Fork, stm., Ut., U.S.	F3	151
Sevier Bridge Reservoir, res., Ut., U.S.	D4	151
Sevier Desert, des., Ut., U.S.	D3	151
Sevier Lake, l., Ut., U.S.	E2	151
Sevierville, Tn., U.S.	D10	149
Sevilla, Col.	E5	84
Sevilla (Seville), Spain	H6	16
Sevilla, Isla, i., Pan.	I12	92
Seville see Sevilla, Spain	H6	16
Seville, Fl., U.S.	C5	116
Seville, Ga., U.S.	E3	117
Seville, Oh., U.S.	A4	142
Şevketiye, Tur.	I11	20
Sevsk, Russia	I17	22
Sewanee, Tn., U.S.	D8	149
Seward, Ak., U.S.	C10	109
Seward, Ne., U.S.	D8	134
Seward, co., Ks., U.S.	E3	123
Seward, co., Ne., U.S.	D8	134
Seward Peninsula, pen., Ak., U.S.	B7	109
Sewaren, N.J., U.S.	k7	137
Sewell, Chile	H3	80
Sewell, N.J., U.S.	D2	137
Sewickley, Pa., U.S.	E1	145
Sexsmith, Alta., Can.	B1	98
Sextín, stm., Mex.	E7	90
Sextonville, Wi., U.S.	E3	156
Seybaplaya, Mex.	H14	90
Seychelles, ctry., Afr.	B11	58
Seyðisfjörður, Ice.	B6	6a
Seylac, Som.	F9	56
Seymour, Austl.	K6	70
Seymour, S. Afr.	I8	66
Seymour, Ct., U.S.	D3	114
Seymour, Il., U.S.	C5	120
Seymour, In., U.S.	G6	121
Seymour, Ia., U.S.	D4	122
Seymour, Mo., U.S.	D5	132
Seymour, Tn., U.S.	D10	149
Seymour, Tx., U.S.	C3	150
Seymour, Wi., U.S.	D5	156
Seymour Inlet, b., B.C., Can.	D4	99
Seymour Johnson Air Force Base, mil., N.C., U.S.	B5	140
Seymour Lake, l., Vt., U.S.	B4	152
Seymourville, La., U.S.	h9	125
Seyssel, Fr.	G12	14
Sezela, S. Afr.	H10	66
Sfântu Gheorghe, Rom.	D9	20
Sfax, Tun.	C16	62
Sfizef, Alg.	C10	62
's-Gravenbrakel see Braine-le-Comte, Bel.	G5	12
's-Gravenhage (The Hague), Neth.	D5	12
Shaanxi (Shensi), prov., China	D8	30
Shabbona, Il., U.S.	B5	120
Shabeelle (Shebele), stm., Afr.	H9	56
Shabwah, Yemen	G5	47
Shache (Yarkand), China	A7	44
Shackelford, co., Tx., U.S.	C3	150
Shackleton Ice Shelf, Ant.	B6	73
Shādegān, Iran	F10	48
Shadehill Dam, S.D., U.S.	B3	148
Shadehill Reservoir, res., S.D., U.S.	B3	148
Shades Creek, stm., Al., U.S.	g7	108
Shades Mountain, mtn., Al., U.S.	g7	108
Shadow Mountain National Recreation Area, Co., U.S.	A4	113
Shady Cove, Or., U.S.	E4	144
Shady Dale, Ga., U.S.	C3	117
Shady Point, Ok., U.S.	B7	143
Shady Side, Md., U.S.	C4	127
Shadyside, Oh., U.S.	C5	142
Shady Spring, W.V., U.S.	D3	155
Shafer, Lake, l., In., U.S.	C4	121
Shafer Butte, mtn., Id., U.S.	F2	119
Shafter, Ca., U.S.	E4	112
Shaftsbury, Vt., U.S.	E2	152
Shagamu, Nig.	H11	64
Shageluk, Ak., U.S.	C8	109
Shag Harbour, N.S., Can.	F4	101
Shag Rocks, S. Geor.	G8	78
Shāhābād, India	E7	44
Shāhābād, India	D4	46
Shah Alam, Malay.	M6	40
Shahdād, Namakzār-e, pl., Iran	F15	48
Shahdol, India	I9	44
Shahe, China	I6	32
Shāhjahānpur, India	G8	44
Shāh Jūy, Afg.	D2	44
Shāhpur, Pak.	F3	44
Shāhpura, India	H6	44
Shahrak, Afg.	C1	44
Shahr-e Bābak, Iran	F13	48
Shahr-e Kord, Iran	E11	48
Shā'ib al-Banāt, Jabal, mtn., Egypt	H2	48
Shaikou, China	H6	34
Shakawe, Bots.	B5	66
Shaker Heights, Oh., U.S.	A4	142
Shaki, Nig.	G11	64
Shākir, Jazīrat, i., Egypt	H2	48
Shakopee, Mn., U.S.	F5	130
Shaktoolik, Ak., U.S.	C7	109
Shala, Lake, l., Eth.	N10	60
Shalatayn, Bi'r, well, Egypt	J3	48
Shaleshanto, Bots.	B6	66
Shallotte, N.C., U.S.	D4	140
Shallotte Inlet, b., N.C., U.S.	D4	140
Shallowater, Tx., U.S.	C2	150
Shallow Lake, Ont., Can.	C3	103
Shām, Bādiyat ash- (Syrian Desert), des., Asia	E6	48
Shām, Jabal ash-, mtn., Oman	C10	47
Shambe, Sud.	N6	60
Shambu, Eth.	M9	60
Shamil, Iran	H14	48
Shāmli, India	F7	44
Shamokin, Pa., U.S.	E8	145
Shamokin Dam, Pa., U.S.	E8	145
Shamrock, Sask., Can.	G2	105
Shamrock, Tx., U.S.	B2	150
Shamva, Zimb.	E6	58
Shanany, ozero, l., Ukr.	D13	20
Shanbiao, China	H1	32
Shandī, Sud.	I7	60
Shandon, Ca., U.S.	E3	112
Shandong (Shantung), prov., China	D10	30
Shandong Bandao (Shantung Peninsula), pen., China	F8	32
Shangani, Zimb.	B9	66
Shangani, stm., Zimb.	B9	66
Shangcheng, China	D4	34
Shangfu, China	G3	34
Shanggu, China	C6	32
Shanghai, China	D10	34
Shanghai Shi, China	E11	30
Shangjiaodao, China	F8	34
Shangping, China	K3	34
Shangqing, China	G6	34
Shangqiu (Zhuji), China	A4	34
Shangrao, China	G6	34
Shangshui, China	B3	34
Shangxian, China	E8	30
Shangxingzhen, China	D8	34
Shangyuan, China	B8	32
Shangzhi, China	B12	30
Shanhaiguan, China	C7	32
Shankou, China	G3	34
Shannock, R.I., U.S.	F2	146
Shannon, S. Afr.	G8	66
Shannon, Ga., U.S.	B1	117
Shannon, Il., U.S.	A4	120
Shannon, Ms., U.S.	A5	131
Shannon, co., Mo., U.S.	D6	132
Shannon, co., S.D., U.S.	D3	148
Shannon, stm., Ire.	I4	8
Shannon, Lake, l., Wa., U.S.	A4	154
Shannon Hills, Ar., U.S.	k10	111
Shannontown, S.C., U.S.	D7	147
Shanpo, China	E3	34
Shansi see Shanxi, prov., China	D9	30
Shāntipur, India	I13	44
Shantou (Swatow), China	L5	34
Shanxi (Shansi), prov., China	D9	30
Shanxian, China	I4	32
Shanxu, China	C9	40
Shanyin, China	D9	30
Shaodian, China	B3	34
Shaoguan, China	K2	34
Shaowu, China	H6	34
Shaoxing, China	E9	34
Shaoyang, China	F9	30
Shaqqā, Syria	C7	50
Shaqrā', Sau. Ar.	I8	48
Shaqrā', Yemen	H4	47
Sharafkhāneh, Iran	B8	48
Sharbatāt, Ra's ash-, c., Oman	F10	47
Sharbot Lake, Ont., Can.	C8	103
Share, Nig.	G12	64
Shark Bay, b., Austl.	E2	68
Sharkey, co., Ms., U.S.	C3	131
Shark Point, c., Fl., U.S.	H5	116
Sharm ash-Shaykh, Egypt	D8	60
Sharon, Ct., U.S.	B2	114
Sharon, Ks., U.S.	E5	123
Sharon, Ma., U.S.	B5	128
Sharon, N.D., U.S.	B8	141
Sharon, Pa., U.S.	D1	145
Sharon, Tn., U.S.	A3	149
Sharon, Vt., U.S.	D4	152
Sharon, W.V., U.S.	m13	155
Sharon, Wi., U.S.	F5	156
Sharon Hill, Pa., U.S.	p20	145
Sharon Park, Oh., U.S.	n12	142
Sharon Springs, Ks., U.S.	D2	123
Sharonville, Oh., U.S.	n13	142
Sharp, co., Ar., U.S.	A4	111
Sharpe, Lake, res., S.D., U.S.	C6	148
Sharpes, Fl., U.S.	D6	116
Sharples, W.V., U.S.	D3	155
Sharpley, De., U.S.	h7	115
Sharpsburg, Ky., U.S.	B6	124
Sharpsburg, Md., U.S.	B2	127
Sharpsburg, N.C., U.S.	B5	140
Sharpsburg, Pa., U.S.	k14	145
Sharpsville, In., U.S.	D5	121
Sharpsville, Pa., U.S.	D1	145
Sharp Top Mountain, mtn., Ar., U.S.	C2	111
Sharptown, Md., U.S.	C6	127
Sharqī, Al-Jabal ash- (Anti-Lebanon), mts., Asia	A6	50
Sharqīyah, Aṣ-Ṣaḥrā' ash- (Arabian Desert), des., Egypt	D7	60
Shasha, Eth.	N8	60
Shashe, stm., Afr.	C9	66
Shashemene, Eth.	N10	60
Shashi, China	E9	30
Shasta, co., Ca., U.S.	B3	112
Shasta, Mount, vol., Ca., U.S.	B2	112
Shasta Lake, res., Ca., U.S.	B2	112
Shatawī, Sud.	J7	60
Shatney Mountain, mtn., N.H., U.S.	f7	136
Shattuck, Ok., U.S.	A2	143
Shatuji, China	H3	32
Shaunavon, Sask., Can.	H1	105
Shaw, Ms., U.S.	B3	131
Shaw Air Force Base, mil., S.C., U.S.	D7	147
Shawangunk Mountains, mts., N.Y., U.S.	D6	139
Shawano, Wi., U.S.	D5	156
Shawano, co., Wi., U.S.	D5	156
Shawano Lake, l., Wi., U.S.	D5	156
Shawboro, N.C., U.S.	A6	140
Shawhan, Ky., U.S.	B5	124
Shawinigan, Que., Can.	C5	104
Shawinigan Lake, B.C., Can.	g12	99
Shawinigan-Sud, Que., Can.	C5	104
Shawnee, Co., U.S.	B5	113
Shawnee, Ga., U.S.	D5	117
Shawnee, Ks., U.S.	k16	123
Shawnee, Oh., U.S.	C3	142
Shawnee, Ok., U.S.	B5	143
Shawnee, co., Ks., U.S.	D8	123
Shawneetown, Il., U.S.	F5	120
Shawo, China	G3	34
Shawsheen, stm., Ma., U.S.	f11	128
Shawsville, Va., U.S.	C2	153
Shaybārā, i., Sau. Ar.	I4	48
Shay Gap, Austl.	D4	68
Shaykh, Jabal ash- (Mount Hermon), mtn., Asia	B5	50
Shaykh 'Uthmān, Yemen	H4	47
Shayuan, China	H9	34
Shebele (Shabeelle), stm., Afr.	G9	56
Shebelē Wenz, stm., Afr.	H3	42
Sheberghān, Afg.	B1	44
Sheboygan, Wi., U.S.	E6	156
Sheboygan, co., Wi., U.S.	E6	156
Sheboygan, stm., Wi., U.S.	k10	156
Sheboygan Falls, Wi., U.S.	E6	156
Shechem see Nābulus, W.B.	D4	50
Shedden, Ont., Can.	E3	103
Shediac, N.B., Can.	C5	101
Sheenjek, stm., Ak., U.S.	B11	109
Sheep Mountain, mtn., Az., U.S.	E1	110
Sheep Mountain, mtn., Wy., U.S.	B5	157
Sheep Mountain, mtn., Wy., U.S.	C2	157
Sheep Peak, mtn., Nv., U.S.	G6	135
Sheep Range, mts., Nv., U.S.	G6	135
Sheeps Heaven Mountain, mtn., Ma., U.S.	A1	128
Sheerness, Alta., Can.	D5	98
Sheet Harbour, N.S., Can.	E7	101
Shefar'am, Isr.	C4	50
Sheffield, N.Z.	E4	72
Sheffield, Eng., U.K.	H12	8
Sheffield, Al., U.S.	A2	108
Sheffield, Il., U.S.	B4	120
Sheffield, Ia., U.S.	B4	122
Sheffield, Ma., U.S.	B1	128
Sheffield, Pa., U.S.	C3	145
Sheffield, Vt., U.S.	B4	152
Sheffield Lake, Oh., U.S.	A3	142
Shegaon, India	B4	46
Sheguiandah, Ont., Can.	B3	103
Sheho, Sask., Can.	F4	105
Sheikh Hasan, Eth.	K8	60
Sheila, N.B., Can.	B5	101
Shekhūpura, Pak.	E5	44
Shelagyote Peak, mtn., B.C., Can.	B4	99
Shelbiana, Ky., U.S.	C7	124
Shelbina, Mo., U.S.	B5	132
Shelburn, In., U.S.	F3	121
Shelburne, N.S., Can.	F4	101
Shelburne, Ont., Can.	C4	103
Shelburne, Vt., U.S.	C2	152
Shelburne Falls, Ma., U.S.	A2	128
Shelburne Pond, l., Vt., U.S.	C2	152
Shelby, Al., U.S.	B3	108
Shelby, In., U.S.	B3	121
Shelby, Ia., U.S.	C2	122
Shelby, Mi., U.S.	E4	129
Shelby, Ms., U.S.	B3	131
Shelby, Mt., U.S.	B5	133
Shelby, Ne., U.S.	C8	134
Shelby, N.C., U.S.	B1	140
Shelby, Oh., U.S.	B3	142
Shelby, co., Al., U.S.	B3	108
Shelby, co., Il., U.S.	D5	120
Shelby, co., In., U.S.	E6	121
Shelby, co., Ia., U.S.	C2	122
Shelby, co., Ky., U.S.	B4	124
Shelby, co., Mo., U.S.	B5	132
Shelby, co., Oh., U.S.	B1	142
Shelby, co., Tn., U.S.	B2	149
Shelby, co., Tx., U.S.	D5	150
Shelbyville, Il., U.S.	D5	120
Shelbyville, In., U.S.	F6	121
Shelbyville, Ky., U.S.	B4	124
Shelbyville, Mo., U.S.	B5	132
Shelbyville, Tn., U.S.	B5	149
Shelbyville, Lake, res., Il., U.S.	D5	120
Sheldahl, Ia., U.S.	e8	122
Sheldon, Il., U.S.	C6	120
Sheldon, Ia., U.S.	A2	122
Sheldon, Mo., U.S.	D3	132
Sheldon, N.D., U.S.	C8	141
Sheldon, Tx., U.S.	r14	150
Sheldon, Vt., U.S.	B3	152
Sheldon Springs, Vt., U.S.	B3	152
Shelikof Strait, strt., Ak., U.S.	D9	109
Shell, Wy., U.S.	B5	157
Shell, stm., Man., Can.	D1	100
Shellbrook, Sask., Can.	D2	105
Shell Creek, Tn., U.S.	C11	149
Shell Creek, stm., U.S.	A2	113
Shell Creek, stm., Wy., U.S.	B5	157
Shelley, B.C., Can.	C6	99
Shelley, Id., U.S.	F6	119
Shellharbour, Austl.	J9	70
Shell Lake, Sask., Can.	D2	105
Shell Lake, Wi., U.S.	C2	156
Shell Lake, l., Mn., U.S.	D3	130
Shell Lake, l., Wi., U.S.	C2	156
Shellman, Ga., U.S.	E2	117
Shellman Bluff, Ga., U.S.	E5	117
Shellmouth, Man., Can.	D1	100
Shellpot Creek, stm., De., U.S.	h7	115
Shell Rock, Ia., U.S.	B5	122
Shell Rock, stm., Ia., U.S.	B5	122
Shell Rock, West Fork, stm., Ia., U.S.	B5	122
Shellsburg, Ia., U.S.	B6	122
Shelly Mountain, mtn., Id., U.S.	F5	119
Shelter Island, N.Y., U.S.	m16	139
Shelton, Ct., U.S.	D3	114
Shelton, Ne., U.S.	D7	134
Shelton, Wa., U.S.	B2	154
Shemogue, N.B., Can.	C5	101
Shemya Air Force Base, mil., Ak., U.S.	E2	109
Shenandoah, Ia., U.S.	D2	122
Shenandoah, Pa., U.S.	E9	145
Shenandoah, Va., U.S.	B4	153
Shenandoah, co., Va., U.S.	B4	153
Shenandoah, stm., U.S.	A5	153
Shenandoah, North Fork, stm., Va., U.S.	B4	153
Shenandoah, South Fork, stm., Va., U.S.	B4	153
Shenandoah Mountain, mtn., U.S.	B3	153
Shenandoah National Park, Va., U.S.	B4	153
Shenandoah Valley, val., U.S.	B4	153
Shenango River Lake, res., U.S.	D1	145
Shendam, Nig.	G14	64
Shengang, China	H5	34
Shengtian, China	H2	34
Shengze, China	E9	34
Shenipsit Lake, l., Ct., U.S.	B6	114
Shenqiu, China	B4	34
Shensi see Shaanxi, prov., China	D8	30
Shenyang (Mukden), China	B11	32
Shenzhen, China	M3	34

Name	Map Ref.	Page
Sheopur, India	H7	44
Shepard, Alta., Can.	D4	98
Shepardsville, In., U.S.	E3	121
Shepaug, stm., Ct., U.S.	C2	114
Shepaug Dam, Ct., U.S.	D2	114
Shepaug Reservoir, res., Ct., U.S.	C2	114
Shepetivka, Ukr.	G3	26
Shepherd, Mi., U.S.	E6	129
Shepherd, Mt., U.S.	E8	133
Shepherd, Tx., U.S.	D5	150
Shepherdstown, W.V., U.S.	B7	155
Shepherdsville, Ky., U.S.	C4	124
Sheppard Air Force Base, mil., Tx., U.S.	C3	150
Shepparton, Austl.	K6	70
Sheppton, Pa., U.S.	E9	145
Sheqi, China	B1	34
Sherab, Sud.	L3	60
Sherada, Eth.	N9	60
Sherard, Ms., U.S.	A3	131
Sherard, Cape, c., N.W. Ter., Can.	B16	96
Sherborn, Ma., U.S.	h10	128
Sherbro Island, i., S.L.	H3	64
Sherbrooke, N.S., Can.	D8	101
Sherbrooke, Que., Can.	D6	104
Sherburn, Mn., U.S.	G4	130
Sherburne, N.Y., U.S.	C5	139
Sherburne, co., Mn., U.S.	E5	130
Sheridan, Ar., U.S.	C3	111
Sheridan, Il., U.S.	B5	120
Sheridan, In., U.S.	D5	121
Sheridan, Me., U.S.	B4	126
Sheridan, Mi., U.S.	E5	129
Sheridan, Mo., U.S.	A3	132
Sheridan, Mt., U.S.	E4	133
Sheridan, Or., U.S.	B3	144
Sheridan, Wy., U.S.	B6	157
Sheridan, co., Ks., U.S.	C3	123
Sheridan, co., Mt., U.S.	B12	133
Sheridan, co., Ne., U.S.	B3	134
Sheridan, co., N.D., U.S.	B5	141
Sheridan, co., Wy., U.S.	B5	157
Sheridan, Mount, mtn., Wy., U.S.	B2	157
Sherman, Ms., U.S.	A5	131
Sherman, Tx., U.S.	C4	150
Sherman, co., Ks., U.S.	C2	123
Sherman, co., Ne., U.S.	C6	134
Sherman, co., Or., U.S.	B6	144
Sherman, co., Tx., U.S.	A2	150
Sherman Mills, Me., U.S.	C4	126
Sherman Mountain, mtn., Ar., U.S.	A2	111
Sherman Reservoir, res., Ne., U.S.	C7	134
Sherman Station, Me., U.S.	C4	126
Sherpur, Bngl.	H14	44
Sherrard, Il., U.S.	B3	120
Sherrelwood, Co., U.S.	*B6	113
Sherridon, Man., Can.	B1	100
Sherrill, N.Y., U.S.	B5	139
Shertallai, India	H4	46
's-Hertogenbosch, Neth.	E7	12
Sherwood, P.E.I., Can.	C6	101
Sherwood, Ar., U.S.	C3	111
Sherwood, N.D., U.S.	A4	141
Sherwood, Oh., U.S.	A1	142
Sherwood, Or., U.S.	h12	144
Sherwood, Tn., U.S.	D8	149
Sherwood, Wi., U.S.	h9	156
Sherwood Manor, Ct., U.S.	A5	114
Sherwood Park, De., U.S.	i7	115
Sheshea, stm., Peru	C5	82
Shetek, Lake, l., Mn., U.S.	G3	130
Shetland, prov., Scot., U.K.	A12	8
Shetland Islands, is., Scot., U.K.	A12	8
Shetucket, stm., Ct., U.S.	C7	114
Shevchenkove, Ukr.	D13	20
Shevlin, Mn., U.S.	C3	130
Shewa Gimira, Eth.	N8	60
Shexian, China	F7	34
Sheyenne, N.D., U.S.	B6	141
Sheyenne, stm., N.D., U.S.	C8	141
Sheyenne Lake, res., N.D., U.S.	B5	141
Sheykhābād, Afg.	C3	44
Shḥīm, Leb.	A4	50
Shiawassee, co., Mi., U.S.	F6	129
Shiba, China	C7	34
Shibām, Yemen	G6	47
Shibarni, Sud.	J3	60
Shibata, Japan	J14	36
Shibetsu, Japan	c17	36a
Shibīn al-Kawm, Egypt	B6	60
Shicheng, China	I5	34
Shickley, Ne., U.S.	D8	134
Shickshinny, Pa., U.S.	D9	145
Shidao, China	G10	32
Shideler, In., U.S.	D7	121
Shidler, Ok., U.S.	A5	143
Shifodian, China	C4	34
Shigaib, Sud.	J2	60
Shigezhuang, China	E4	32
Shiḥan, Wādī, val., Asia	E8	47
Shihe, China	D9	32
Shijiazhuang, China	E2	32
Shijing, China	K7	34
Shikārpur, Pak.	G3	44
Shikohābād, India	G8	44
Shikoku, i., Japan	N8	36
Shiliguri, India	G13	44
Shillelagh, Ire.	I7	8
Shillington, Pa., U.S.	F10	145
Shillong, India	H14	44
Shiloh, Ga., U.S.	D2	117
Shiloh, Oh., U.S.	C1	142
Shiloh, Tn., U.S.	B3	149
Shiloh see Saylūn, Khirbat, hist., W.B.	D4	50
Shiloh National Military Park, Tn., U.S.	B3	149
Shilong, China	L2	34
Shimabara, Japan	O5	36
Shimada, Japan	M13	36
Shimbiris, mtn., Som.	F10	56
Shimen, China	D6	32
Shimian, China	F7	30
Shimiaozi, China	C11	32
Shimizu, Japan	L13	36
Shimla, India	E7	44
Shimodate, Japan	K14	36
Shimoga, India	F3	46
Shimokita-hantō, pen., Japan	F16	36
Shimonoseki, Japan	N5	36
Shinall Mountain, mtn., Ar., U.S.	h10	111
Shināṣ, Oman	B10	47
Shīndand, Afg.	E17	48
Shiner, Tx., U.S.	E4	150
Shingbwiyang, Mya.	A4	40
Shinglehouse, Pa., U.S.	C5	145
Shingleton, Mi., U.S.	B4	129
Shingū, Japan	M9	36
Shingū, Japan	N10	36
Shingwidzi (Singuédeze), stm., Afr.	D10	66
Shinjō, Japan	I15	36
Shinkolobwe, Zaire	D5	58
Shinnston, W.V., U.S.	B4	155
Shinyanga, Tan.	B6	58
Shiocton, Wi., U.S.	D5	156
Shiogama, Japan	I16	36
Shiojiri, Japan	K12	36
Shiono-misaki, c., Japan	N10	36
Ship Bottom, N.J., U.S.	D4	137
Ship Harbour, N.S., Can.	E7	101
Shiping, China	C7	40
Ship Island, i., Ms., U.S.	E5	131
Ship Island Pass, strt., Ms., U.S.	g7	131
Shipman, Il., U.S.	D4	120
Shipman, Va., U.S.	C4	153
Shippegan, N.B., Can.	B5	101
Shippensburg, Pa., U.S.	F6	145
Shiprock, N.M., U.S.	A1	138
Ship Rock, mtn., N.M., U.S.	A1	138
Shipshewana, In., U.S.	A6	121
Shipu, China	F10	34
Shirakami-misaki, c., Japan	f15	36a
Shiraoi, Japan	e16	36a
Shīrāz, Iran	G12	48
Shire, stm., Afr.	E6	58
Shiretoko-misaki, c., Japan	c20	36a
Shirley, Ar., U.S.	B3	111
Shirley, In., U.S.	E6	121
Shirley, Ma., U.S.	A4	128
Shirley, W.V., U.S.	k9	155
Shirley Basin, Wy., U.S.	D6	157
Shirley Mills, Me., U.S.	C3	126
Shirley Mountains, mts., Wy., U.S.	D6	157
Shiroishi, Japan	I15	36
Shirpur, India	B3	46
Shīrvān, Iran	C14	48
Shishaldin Volcano, vol., Ak., U.S.	E7	109
Shishmaref, Ak., U.S.	B6	109
Shitan, China	L2	34
Shively, Ky., U.S.	B4	124
Shivpuri, India	H7	44
Shivwits Plateau, plat., Az., U.S.	A2	110
Shixia, China	C2	32
Shizheng, China	K4	34
Shizuoka, Japan	M13	36
Shkodër, Alb.	G3	20
Shoal, stm., Man., Can.	C1	100
Shoal Creek, stm., U.S.	B4	149
Shoal Harbour, Newf., Can.	D4	102
Shoal Lake, Man., Can.	D1	100
Shoals, In., U.S.	G4	121
Shoals, Isles of, is., Me., U.S.	E2	126
Shoalwater, Cape, c., Wa., U.S.	C1	154
Shoalwater Bay, b., Austl.	D9	70
Shobonier, Il., U.S.	E4	120
Shōdo-shima, i., Japan	M9	36
Shoe Cove, Newf., Can.	D4	102
Shoemakersville, Pa., U.S.	F10	145
Shongopovi, Az., U.S.	B5	110
Shonto, Az., U.S.	A5	110
Shop Springs, Tn., U.S.	A5	149
Shoreacres, B.C., Can.	E9	99
Shore Acres, Ma., U.S.	h13	128
Shoreham, Mi., U.S.	F4	129
Shores Acres, R.I., U.S.	E4	146
Shoreview, Mn., U.S.	m12	130
Shorewood, Il., U.S.	k8	120
Shorewood, Mn., U.S.	n11	130
Shorewood, Wi., U.S.	E6	156
Short Beach, Ct., U.S.	D4	114
Shorter, Al., U.S.	C4	108
Shorterville, Al., U.S.	D4	108
Short Mountain, mtn., Tn., U.S.	D8	149
Shortsville, N.Y., U.S.	C3	139
Shoshone, Id., U.S.	G4	119
Shoshone, co., Id., U.S.	B2	119
Shoshone, stm., Wy., U.S.	B4	157
Shoshone, North Fork, stm., Wy., U.S.	B3	157
Shoshone, South Fork, stm., Wy., U.S.	B3	157
Shoshone Falls, wtfl, Id., U.S.	G4	119
Shoshone Lake, l., Wy., U.S.	B2	157
Shoshone Mountains, mts., Nv., U.S.	E4	135
Shoshone Peak, mtn., Nv., U.S.	G5	135
Shoshone Range, mts., Nv., U.S.	C5	135
Shoshong, Bots.	D8	66
Shoshoni, Wy., U.S.	C4	157
Shostka, Ukr.	G4	26
Shouning, China	H8	34
Shouns, Tn., U.S.	C12	149
Shoup, Id., U.S.	D4	119
Shouxian, China	C5	34
Show Low, Az., U.S.	C5	110
Shreve, Oh., U.S.	B3	142
Shreveport, La., U.S.	B2	125
Shrewsbury, Eng., U.K.	I11	8
Shrewsbury, Ma., U.S.	B4	128
Shrewsbury, N.J., U.S.	C4	137
Shrewsbury, Pa., U.S.	G8	145
Shri Dūngargarh, India	F6	44
Shrīrangapattana, India	F4	46
Shropshire, co., Eng., U.K.	I11	8
Shuajingsi, China	E7	30
Shuangcheng, China	B12	30
Shuanghe, China	D5	34
Shuangjiangqiao, China	B5	40
Shuangliao, China	C11	30
Shuangmiaozi, China	A10	32
Shuangyashan, China	B13	30
Shubenacadie, N.S., Can.	D6	101
Shubert, Ne., U.S.	D10	134
Shubrā al-Khaymah, Egypt	B6	60
Shubuta, Ms., U.S.	D5	131
Shuhong, China	G9	34
Shuijing, China	A5	40
Shuikouguan, China	C9	40
Shuitouwei, China	I4	34
Shuksan, Mount, mtn., Wa., U.S.	A4	154
Shule, stm., China	C6	30
Shulerville, S.C., U.S.	E8	147
Shullsburg, Wi., U.S.	F3	156
Shumagin Islands, is., Ak., U.S.	E7	109
Shumway, Il., U.S.	D5	120
Shunchang, China	I6	34
Shunde, China	M2	34
Shungnak, Ak., U.S.	B8	109
Shuqualak, Ms., U.S.	C5	131
Shurugwi, Zimb.	B10	66
Shūsh, Iran	E10	48
Shūshtar, Iran	E10	48
Shuswap Lake, l., B.C., Can.	D8	99
Shuwak, Sud.	J8	60
Shwebo, Mya.	C3	40
Shweli (Longchuan), stm., Asia	C4	40
Shyok, stm., Asia	C7	44
Shyryayeve, Ukr.	B14	20
Siālkot, Pak.	D6	44
Siam see Thailand, ctry., Asia	B3	38
Siam, Gulf of see Thailand, Gulf of, b., Asia	I6	40
Sian see Xi'an, China	E8	30
Si'an, China	E8	34
Siapa, stm., Ven.	G10	84
Šiaškotan, ostrov, i., Russia	H22	28
Šiauliai, Lith.	F6	22
Sibāʿī, Jabal as-, mtn., Egypt	I3	48
Sibaj, Russia	E19	4
Sibasa, S. Afr.	D10	66
Sibbald, Alta., Can.	D5	98
Šibenik, Cro.	F10	18
Siberia, In., U.S.	H4	121
Siberia see Sibir', reg., Russia	D14	28
Sibert, Ky., U.S.	C6	124
Siberut, Pulau, i., Indon.	F2	38
Sibi, Pak.	F2	44
Sibir' (Siberia), reg., Russia	D14	28
Sibir'akova, ostrov, i., Russia	C13	26
Sibiti, Congo	B2	58
Sibiu, Rom.	D8	20
Sibiu, co., Rom.	D8	20
Sibley, Il., U.S.	C5	120
Sibley, Ia., U.S.	A2	122
Sibley, La., U.S.	B2	125
Sibley, Ms., U.S.	D2	131
Sibley, Mo., U.S.	h11	132
Sibley, co., Mn., U.S.	F4	130
Sibolga, Indon.	N5	40
Sibsāgar, India	G16	44
Sibuyan Island, i., Phil.	C7	38
Sibuyan Sea, Phil.	C7	38
Sicamous, B.C., Can.	D8	99
Siccus, stm., Austl.	H3	70
Sichomovi, Az., U.S.	B5	110
Sichote-Alin', mts., Russia	H19	28
Sichuan (Szechwan), prov., China	E7	30
Sichuanzhai, China	C6	40
Sicilia, prov., Italy	L9	18
Sicilia (Sicily), i., Italy	L9	18
Sicily see Sicilia, i., Italy	L9	18
Sicily, Strait of, strt.	L6	18
Sicily Island, La., U.S.	C4	125
Sicklerville, N.J., U.S.	D3	137
Sico Tinto, stm., Hond.	B9	92
Sicuani, Peru	F6	82
Šid, Yugo.	D3	20
Siddhapur, India	I5	44
Siddipet, India	C5	46
Sideling Hill, mtn., U.S.	A1	127
Sideling Hill Creek, stm., Md., U.S.	A1	127
Sidell, Il., U.S.	D6	120
Sidéradougou, Burkina	F7	64
Siderópolis, Braz.	E14	80
Sídheros, Ákra, c., Grc.	N10	20
Sidhi, India	H9	44
Sīdī ʿAbd ar-Raḥmān, Egypt	B5	60
Sidi Aïssa, Alg.	C12	62
Sidi Ali Ben Nasrallah, Tun.	N4	18
Sīdī Barrānī, Egypt	B3	60
Sidi bel Abbès, Alg.	C10	62
Sidi Bennour, Mor.	D6	62
Sidi Bou Zid, Tun.	C15	62
Sidi Daoud, Tun.	L5	18
Sīdī Ḥunaysh, Egypt	B4	60
Sidi Ifni, Mor.	F5	62
Sidi Kacem, Mor.	C8	62
Sidikalang, Indon.	M5	40
Sidi Moussa, Oued, val., Alg.	G13	62
Sidi Okba, Alg.	C13	62
Sidi Slimane, Mor.	C8	62
Sidi Smaïl, Mor.	D6	62
Sidley, Mount, mtn., Ant.	C10	73
Sidmouth, Eng., U.K.	K10	8
Sidney, B.C., Can.	E6	99
Sidney, Man., Can.	E2	100
Sidney, Ar., U.S.	A4	111
Sidney, Il., U.S.	C5	120
Sidney, In., U.S.	B6	121
Sidney, Ia., U.S.	D2	122
Sidney, Mt., U.S.	C12	133
Sidney, Ne., U.S.	C3	134
Sidney, N.Y., U.S.	C5	139
Sidney, Oh., U.S.	B1	142
Sidney Center, N.Y., U.S.	C5	139
Sidney Lanier, Lake, res., Ga., U.S.	B2	117
Sido, Mali	F6	64
Sidon see Ṣaydā, Leb.	A4	50
Sidon, Ms., U.S.	B3	131
Sidonia, Tn., U.S.	A3	149
Sidra, Gulf of see Surt, Khalīj, b., Libya	B4	56
Sidrolândia, Braz.	F1	79
Siedlce, Pol.	C22	10
Siegburg, Ger.	E7	10
Siegen, Ger.	E8	10
Siemianowice Śląskie, Pol.	E19	10
Siemiatycze, Pol.	C22	10
Siĕmréab, Camb.	H7	40
Siena, Italy	F6	18
Sieradz, Pol.	D18	10
Sierck-les-Bains, Fr.	C13	14
Sierpc, Pol.	C19	10
Sierra, co., Ca., U.S.	C3	112
Sierra, co., N.M., U.S.	D2	138
Sierra Blanca, Tx., U.S.	o12	150
Sierra Blanca Peak, mtn., N.M., U.S.	D4	138
Sierra Chica, Arg.	I8	80
Sierra City, Ca., U.S.	C3	112
Sierra Colorada, Arg.	E3	78
Sierra de Agua, Belize	I15	90
Sierra de Outes, Spain	C3	16
Sierra Estrella, mts., Az., U.S.	m8	110
Sierra Gorda, Chile	B4	80
Sierra Leone, ctry., Afr.	G4	54
Sierra Madre, Ca., U.S.	m12	112
Sierra Nevada, Parque Nacional, Ven.	C7	84
Sierras Bayas, Arg.	I8	80
Sierra Vista, Az., U.S.	F5	110
Sierre, Switz.	F8	13
Siesta Key, i., Fl., U.S.	E4	116
Siete Puntas, stm., Para.	B9	80
Sífnos, i., Grc.	M8	20
Sifton, Man., Can.	D1	100
Sig, Alg.	J11	16
Sig, Russia	I24	6
Sigean, Fr.	I9	14
Sigel, Il., U.S.	D5	120
Sighetu Marmaţiei, Rom.	B7	20
Sighişoara, Rom.	C8	20
Sigli, Indon.	L3	40
Siglufjörður, Ice.	A4	6a
Sigmaringen, Ger.	G9	10
Signal Mountain, Tn., U.S.	D8	149
Signal Mountain, mtn., Tn., U.S.	C9	149
Signal Mountain, mtn., Vt., U.S.	C4	152
Signal Mountain, mtn., Va., U.S.	g11	153
Signal Peak, mtn., Az., U.S.	D1	110
Signal Peak, mtn., Ut., U.S.	F2	151
Signy, sci., Ant.	B1	73
Signy-l'Abbaye, Fr.	C11	14
Sigourney, Ia., U.S.	C5	122
Sigre, stm., Hond.	B10	92
Sígsig, Ec.	I3	84
Siguanea, Ensenada de la, b., Cuba	D3	94
Siguatepeque, Hond.	C7	92
Sigüenza, Spain	D9	16
Siguiri, Gui.	F5	64
Sigulda, Lat.	D7	22
Sigurd, Ut., U.S.	E4	151
Sihanoukville see Kâmpóng Saôm, Camb.	I7	40
Sihu, China	I5	32
Sihuas, Peru	C3	82
Sihuas, stm., Peru	G5	82
Siirt, Tur.	C6	48
Sijiazi, China	B8	32
Sikandarābād, India	F7	44
Sīkar, India	G6	44
Sikasso, Mali	F7	64
Sikensi, C. Iv.	I7	64
Sikeston, Mo., U.S.	E8	132
Sikkim, state, India	G13	44
Şikosi, Nmb.	A6	66
Šikotan, ostrov (Shikotan-tō), i., Russia	d21	36a
Silacayoapan, Mex.	I10	90
Šilalė, Lith.	F5	22
Silandro, Italy	C5	18
Silao, Mex.	G9	90
Silas, Al., U.S.	D1	108
Sīlat az-Ẓahr, W.B.	D4	50
Silay, Phil.	C7	38
Silchar, India	H15	44
Şile, Tur.	H13	20
Siler City, N.C., U.S.	B3	140
Silesia, hist. reg., Pol.	D16	10
Silet, Alg.	I13	62
Siletz, Or., U.S.	C3	144
Silex, Mo., U.S.	B6	132
Silgaḍhī, Nepal	F9	44
Silhouette, i., Sey.	B11	58
Siliana, Tun.	M4	18
Silifke, Tur.	C2	48
Siling Co, l., China	E13	44
Silistra, Bul.	E11	20
Şilivri, Tur.	H12	20
Šilka, Russia	G15	28
Šilka, stm., Russia	G15	28
Sillamäe, Est.	B10	22
Sillery, Que., Can.	n17	104
Sillian, Aus.	I12	10
Sillustani, hist., Peru	F6	82
Siloam, Ga., U.S.	C3	117
Siloam Springs, Ar., U.S.	A1	111
Šilovo, Russia	G23	22
Silsbee, Tx., U.S.	D5	150
Silt, Co., U.S.	B3	113
Silton, Sask., Can.	G3	105
Siluko, Nig.	H12	64
Šilutė, Lith.	F4	22
Silva, Mo., U.S.	D7	132
Silvan (Miyafarkin), Tur.	B6	48
Silvânia, Braz.	D4	79
Silvaplana, Switz.	F12	13
Silver Bank Passage, strt., N.A.	D9	94
Silver Bay, Mn., U.S.	C7	130
Silver Bow, co., Mt., U.S.	E4	133
Silver City, Ia., U.S.	C2	122
Silver City, Ms., U.S.	B3	131
Silver City, Nv., U.S.	D2	135
Silver City, N.M., U.S.	E1	138
Silver Cliff, Co., U.S.	C5	113
Silver Creek, Ga., U.S.	B1	117
Silver Creek, Ms., U.S.	D3	131
Silver Creek, Ne., U.S.	C8	134
Silver Creek, N.Y., U.S.	C1	139
Silver Creek, stm., In., U.S.	H6	121
Silver Creek, stm., Ne., U.S.	g11	134
Silver Creek, stm., Or., U.S.	D7	144
Silverdale, Wa., U.S.	B3	154
Silver Grove, Ky., U.S.	h14	124
Silverhill, Al., U.S.	E2	108
Silver Hill, Md., U.S.	f9	127
Silver Island Mountains, mts., Ut., U.S.	C2	151
Silver Lake, In., U.S.	B6	121
Silver Lake, Ks., U.S.	C8	123
Silver Lake, Ma., U.S.	f11	128
Silver Lake, Mn., U.S.	F4	130
Silver Lake, N.H., U.S.	C4	136
Silver Lake, Wi., U.S.	F5	156
Silver Lake, l., De., U.S.	D3	115
Silver Lake, l., Ia., U.S.	A3	122
Silver Lake, l., Me., U.S.	C3	126
Silver Lake, l., N.H., U.S.	C4	136
Silver Lake, l., N.H., U.S.	E2	136
Silver Lake, l., Or., U.S.	D7	144
Silver Lake, l., Wa., U.S.	g13	154
Silverpeak, Nv., U.S.	F4	135
Silver Peak Range, mts., Nv., U.S.	F4	135
Silver Point, Tn., U.S.	C8	149
Silver Spring, Md., U.S.	C3	127
Silver Springs, Fl., U.S.	C4	116
Silver Springs, Nv., U.S.	D2	135
Silver Star Mountain, mtn., Wa., U.S.	A5	154
Silverthrone Mountain, mtn., B.C., Can.	D4	99
Silvertip Mountain, mtn., Mt., U.S.	C3	133
Silverton, B.C., Can.	E9	99
Silverton, Co., U.S.	D3	113
Silverton, Id., U.S.	B3	119
Silverton, N.J., U.S.	C4	137
Silverton, Oh., U.S.	o13	142
Silverton, Or., U.S.	C4	144
Silverton, Tx., U.S.	B2	150
Silvi, Italy	G9	18
Silvia, Col.	F4	84
Silvies, stm., Or., U.S.	D7	144
Silview, De., U.S.	B3	115
Silvis, Il., U.S.	B3	120
Silvretta Gruppe, mts., Eur.	E13	13
Sima, Com.	I16	67a
Sima, Russia	E22	22
Šimanovsk, Russia	G17	28
Simao, China	G7	30
Simav, Tur.	J12	20
Simcoe, Ont., Can.	E4	103
Simcoe, Lake, l., Ont., Can.	C5	103
Simeria, Rom.	D7	20
Simeulue, Pulau, i., Indon.	M4	40
Simferopol', Ukr.	I4	26
Sími, i., Grc.	M11	20
Simikoṭ, Nepal	F9	44
Simiri, Niger	D11	64
Simití, Col.	D6	84
Simi Valley, Ca., U.S.	E4	112
Simla, Co., U.S.	B6	113
Simmern, Ger.	F7	10
Simmesport, La., U.S.	D4	125
Simmie, Sask., Can.	H1	105
Simms, Mt., U.S.	C5	133
Simms Stream, stm., N.H., U.S.	g7	136
Simnas, Lith.	G6	22
Simoca, Arg.	D6	80
Simojovel, Mex.	I13	90
Simonette, stm., Alta., Can.	B1	98
Simon's Town, S. Afr.	J4	66
Šimorskoje, Russia	F25	22
Simpang-kiri, stm., Indon.	M4	40
Simplon Pass, Switz.	F9	13
Simplon Tunnel, Eur.	F9	13
Simpson, Sask., Can.	F3	105
Simpson, Ks., U.S.	C6	123
Simpson, La., U.S.	C3	125
Simpson, N.C., U.S.	B5	140
Simpson, Pa., U.S.	C11	145
Simpson, W.V., U.S.	k10	155
Simpson, co., Ky., U.S.	D3	124
Simpson, co., Ms., U.S.	D4	131
Simpson Creek, stm., W.V., U.S.	k10	155
Simpson Desert, des., Austl.	D7	68
Simpson Desert National Park, Austl.	E3	70
Simpson Strait, strt., N.W. Ter., Can.	C13	96
Simpsonville, Ky., U.S.	B4	124
Simpsonville, S.C., U.S.	B3	147
Sims, Il., U.S.	E5	120
Sims, In., U.S.	D6	121
Simsboro, La., U.S.	B3	125
Simsbury, Ct., U.S.	B4	114
Šimsk, Russia	C13	22
Simušir, ostrov, i., Russia	H22	28
Sīnā', Shibh Jazīrat (Sinai Peninsula), pen., Egypt	C7	60
Sinai, S.D., U.S.	C8	148
Sinai, Mount see Mūsā, Jabal, mtn., Egypt	C7	60
Sinaia, Rom.	D9	20
Sinai Peninsula see Sīnā', Shibh Jazīrat, pen., Egypt	C7	60
Sin'aja, stm., Russia	E16	28
Sinaloa, state, Mex.	F6	90
Sinaloa, stm., Mex.	E5	90
Sinalunga, Italy	F6	18
Sinamaica, Ven.	B7	84
Sinan, China	F8	30
Sinanju, N. Kor.	D13	32
Sin'avka, Bela.	I9	22
Sīnāwin, Libya	E16	62
Sinbo, Mya.	B4	40
Sincé, Col.	C5	84
Sincelejo, Col.	C5	84
Sinch'ang, N. Kor.	C16	32
Sinch'ŏn, N. Kor.	E13	32
Sinclair, Man., Can.	E1	100
Sinclair, Me., U.S.	A4	126
Sinclair, Wy., U.S.	E5	157
Sinclair, Lake, res., Ga., U.S.	C3	117
Sindara, Gabon	B2	58
Sindelfingen, Ger.	G9	10
Sindi, Est.	C7	22
Sındırgı, Tur.	J12	20
Sindri, India	I12	44
Sine, val., Sen.	D2	64
Sinekçi, Tur.	I11	20
Sinendé, Benin	F11	64
Sinez'orki, Russia	H17	22
Singapore, Sing.	N7	40
Singapore, ctry., Asia	E3	38
Singapore Strait, strt., Asia	N8	40
Singaraja, Indon.	G6	38
Sing Buri, Thai.	G6	40
Singen [Hohentwiel], Ger.	H8	10
Singhampton, Ont., Can.	C4	103
Singida, Tan.	B6	58
Singkaling Hkāmti, Mya.	A3	40
Singkang, Indon.	F7	38
Singkawang, Indon.	N10	40
Singkep, Pulau, i., Indon.	O8	40
Singleton, Austl.	I9	70
Singuédeze (Shingwidzi), stm., Afr.	D10	66
Sinhŭng, N. Kor.	C15	32
Sinj, Cro.	F11	18
Sinjah, Sud.	K7	60
Sinjai, Indon.	G7	38
Sinkāt, Sud.	H9	60
Sinkiang see Xinjiang Uygur Zizhiqu, prov., China	C3	30
Sinking Creek, stm., Ky., U.S.	C3	124
Sinmak, N. Kor.	E14	32
Sinnai, Italy	J4	18
Sinnamary, Fr. Gu.	B8	76
Sinnar, India	C3	46
Sinnemahoning Creek, stm., Pa., U.S.	D5	145
Sinnemahoning Creek, First Fork, stm., Pa., U.S.	D5	145
Sinnes, Nor.	L10	6
Sinnūris, Egypt	C6	60
Sinop, Tur.	G15	4
Sinp'o, N. Kor.	C16	32
Sinsheim, Ger.	C15	14
Sintaluta, Sask., Can.	G4	105
Sint-Amandsberg, Bel.	F4	12
Sintang, Indon.	E5	38
Sint Annaland, Neth.	E5	12
Sint Annaparochie, Neth.	B8	12
Sint Eustatius, i., Neth. Ant.	F13	94
Sint Maarten (Saint-Martin), i., N.A.	E13	94
Sint-Michiels, Bel.	F3	12
Sint-Niklaas (Saint-Nicolas), Bel.	F5	12
Sinton, Tx., U.S.	E4	150
Sintra, Port.	G2	16
Sint-Truiden (Saint-Trond), Bel.	G7	12
Sinú, stm., Col.	C5	84
Sinŭiju, N. Kor.	C12	32
Sió, stm., Hung.	C13	18
Siocon, Phil.	D7	38
Siófok, Hung.	I18	10
Sion (Sitten), Switz.	F7	13
Sioux, co., Ia., U.S.	A1	122
Sioux, co., Ne., U.S.	B2	134
Sioux, co., N.D., U.S.	C4	141
Sioux Center, Ia., U.S.	A1	122
Sioux City, Ia., U.S.	B1	122
Sioux Falls, S.D., U.S.	D9	148
Sioux Lookout, Ont., Can.	o17	103
Sioux Rapids, Ia., U.S.	B2	122
Sipaliwini, stm., Sur.	F14	84
Sipapo, stm., Ven.	E9	84
Siparia, Trin.	I14	94
Siping, China	C11	30
Sipiwesk Lake, l., Man., Can.	B3	100
Siple, sci., Ant.	C12	73
Siple, Mount, mtn., Ant.	C10	73
Sipsey, Al., U.S.	B2	108
Sipsey, stm., Al., U.S.	B2	108
Sipsey Fork, stm., Al., U.S.	A2	108
Sipu, China	C1	32
Šipunskij, mys, c., Russia	G24	28
Siqueira Campos, Braz.	G4	79
Siquia, stm., Nic.	E10	92
Siquirres, C.R.	G11	92
Siquisique, Ven.	B8	84
Si Racha, Thai.	H6	40
Siracuas, Para.	I11	82
Siracusa (Syracuse), Italy	L10	18
Sirājganj, Bngl.	H13	44
Sirasso, C. Iv.	G6	64
Sirba, stm., Afr.	E10	64
Sirdar, B.C., Can.	E9	99
Sir Douglas, Mount, mtn., Can.	D3	98
Sire, Eth.	M9	60
Sir Edward Pellew Group, is., Austl.	C7	68
Širega, Russia	A24	22
Siren, Wi., U.S.	C1	156
Siret (Seret), stm., Eur.	D11	20
Sirevåg, Nor.	L9	6
Sirḥān, Wādī as-, val., Sau. Ar.	F5	48
Siriya-zaki, c., Japan	F16	36
Sir James MacBrien, Mount, mtn., N.W. Ter., Can.	D7	96
Sīrjān, Iran	G13	48
Sir Joseph Banks Group, is., Austl.	J2	70
Sirohi, India	H5	44
Sironj, India	H7	44
Síros, i., Grc.	L8	20
Sirotino, Bela.	F12	22
Sir Sandford, Mount, mtn., B.C., Can.	D9	99
Sirsi, India	E3	46
Sirte, Gulf of see Surt, Khalīj, b., Libya	B4	56
Sirupa, stm., Mex.	C5	90
Sīrvān (Diyālā), stm., Asia	E8	48
Širvintos, Lith.	F7	22
Sir-Wilfrid, Mont, mtn., Que., Can.	C2	104
Sir Wilfrid Laurier, Mount, mtn., B.C., Can.	C8	99
Sís, stm., Guat.	C3	92
Sisak, Cro.	D11	18
Si Sa Ket, Thai.	G8	40
Sishen, S. Afr.	F6	66
Sishui, China	H5	32
Šišicy, Bela.	H10	22
Siskiyou, co., Ca., U.S.	B2	112
Siskiyou Mountains, mts., U.S.	F3	144

Name	Map Ref.	Page

Name | Map Ref. | Page

Name | Map Ref. | Page

Temperance, Mi., U.S. G7 129
Temperance, stm., Mn., U.S. C8 130
Temperanceville, Va., U.S. C7 153
Tempio Pausania, Italy I4 18
Tempisque, stm., C.R. G9 92
Temple, Ga., U.S. C1 117
Temple, Mi., U.S. D5 129
Temple, N.H., U.S. E3 136
Temple, Ok., U.S. C3 143
Temple, Pa., U.S. F10 145
Temple, Tx., U.S. D4 150
Temple Hill, Ky., U.S. D4 124
Temple Terrace, Fl., U.S. o11 116
Templeton, Ia., U.S. C3 122
Templeton, Ma., U.S. A3 128
Templeton, Pa., U.S. E3 145
Templeton, stm., Austl. C3 70
Templin, Ger. B13 10
Tempoal, stm., Mex. G10 90
Tempoal de Sánchez, Mex. G10 90
Tempy, Russia E20 22
Temr'uk, Russia H5 26
Temuco, Chile J2 80
Tena, Ec. H4 84
Tenabo, Mex. G14 90
Tenafly, N.J., U.S. B5 137
Tenaha, Tx., U.S. D5 150
Tenāli, India D6 46
Tenant Mountain, mtn., N.Y., U.S. B6 139
Tenants Harbor, Me., U.S. E3 126
Tenasserim, Mya. H5 40
Tendaho, Eth. F9 56
Tende, Col de, Eur. H14 14
Ten Degree Channel, strt., India J2 40
Tendoy, Id., U.S. E5 119
Tenente Marques, stm., Braz. D11 82
Tenente Portela, Braz. D12 80
Ténéré, des., Niger E9 54
Tenerife, i., Spain o24 17b
Ténès, Alg. B11 62
Teng'aopu, China B10 32
Tengchong, China B5 40
Tenggara, Nusa (Lesser Sunda Islands), is., Indon. G7 38
Tengiz, ozero, l., Kaz. G11 26
Tengtian, China H4 34
Tengtiao (Na), stm., Asia C7 40
Tengxian, China H5 32
Teniente Rodolfo Marsh, sci., Ant. B1 73
Tenino, Wa., U.S. C3 154
Tenkāsi, India H4 46
Tenke, Zaire D5 58
Tenkiller Ferry Lake, res., Ok., U.S. B6 143
Tenkodogo, Burkina F9 64
Tenmile, stm., U.S. B5 146
Tenmile Creek, stm., W.V., U.S. k10 155
Tenmile Lake, l., Mn., U.S. D4 130
Tennant Creek, Austl. C6 68
Tennessee, state, U.S. B5 149
Tennessee, stm., U.S. D9 106
Tennessee Pass, Co., U.S. B4 113
Tennessee Ridge, Tn., U.S. A4 149
Tennga, Ga., U.S. B2 117
Tennille, Ga., U.S. D4 117
Tennyson, In., U.S. H3 121
Teno, Chile H3 80
Teno (Tana), stm., Eur. F20 6
Tenosique, Mex. I14 90
Tenryū, Japan M12 36
Tensas, co., La., U.S. B4 125
Tensas, stm., La., U.S. B4 125
Tensaw, stm., Al., U.S. E2 108
Ten Sleep, Wy., U.S. B5 157
Tenstrike, Mn., U.S. C4 130
Tenterfield, Austl. G10 70
Ten Thousand Islands, is., Fl., U.S. G5 116
Teocaltiche, Mex. G8 90
Teodelina, Arg. H8 80
Teófilo Otoni, Braz. D8 79
Teotihuacán, hist., Mex. H10 90
Tepalcatepec, Mex. H8 90
Tepeaca, Mex. H11 90
Tepehuanes, Mex. E7 90
Tepehuanes, stm., Mex. E7 90
Tepeji de Ocampo, Mex. H10 90
Tepelenë, Alb. I4 20
Tepi, Eth. N8 60
Tepic, Mex. G7 90
Teplice, Czech Rep. E13 10
Teplovo, Russia F25 22
Tepoca, Bahía, b., Mex. B3 90
Tepoca, Punta, c., Mex. C3 90
Tepopa, Cabo, c., Mex. C3 90
Téra, Niger D10 64
Tera, stm., Spain D6 16
Teramo, Italy G8 18
Terang, Austl. L5 70
Terborg, Neth. E9 12
Terbuny, Russia I21 22
Terceira, i., Port. k21 62a
Tercero, stm., Arg. G7 80
Terechovka, Bela. I14 22
Tereida, Sud. L6 60
Terek, stm., Russia I7 26
Terenino, Russia G16 22
Terenos, Braz. F1 79
Teresina, Braz. E10 76
Teresópolis, Braz. G7 79
Terespol, Pol. C23 10
Teresva, Ukr. A7 20
Terhorne, Neth. B8 12
Teribe, stm., N.A. H12 92
Termas de Río Hondo, Arg. D6 80
Termez, Uzb. J11 26
Termini Imerese, Italy L8 18
Términos, Laguna de, b., Mex. H14 90
Termoli, Italy G10 18
Ternate, Indon. E8 38
Ternberg, Aus. H14 10
Ternej, Russia H19 28
Terneuzen, Neth. F4 12
Terni, Italy G7 18
Ternivka, Ukr. A13 20
Ternopil', Ukr. H3 26
Teror, Spain o25 17b
Terpenija, mys, c., Russia H20 28
Terpenija, zaliv, b., Russia H20 28
Terra Alta, W.V., U.S. B5 155
Terrace, B.C., Can. B3 99
Terracina, Italy H8 18
Terral, Ok., U.S. D4 143
Terralba, Italy J3 18
Terra Nova, Newf., Can. D4 102
Terra Nova National Park, Newf., Can. D4 102
Terra Rica, Braz. G2 79
Terra Roxa, Braz. C12 80
Terra Santa, Braz. I14 84
Terrassa, Spain D14 16
Terrebonne, Que., Can. D4 104
Terrebonne, Or., U.S. C5 144
Terrebonne, co., La., U.S. E5 125
Terrebonne Bay, b., La., U.S. E5 125
Terre Haute, In., U.S. F3 121
Terre Hill, Pa., U.S. F9 145
Terrell, N.C., U.S. B2 140
Terrell, Tx., U.S. C4 150
Terrell, co., Ga., U.S. E2 117
Terrell, co., Tx., U.S. D1 150
Terrell Hills, Tx., U.S. k7 150
Terrenceville, Newf., Can. E4 102
Terreton, Id., U.S. F6 119
Terril, Ia., U.S. A3 122
Terry, Ms., U.S. C3 131
Terry, Mt., U.S. D11 133
Terry, co., Tx., U.S. C1 150
Terry Peak, mtn., S.D., U.S. C2 148
Terrytown, Ne., U.S. C2 134
Terryville, Ct., U.S. C3 114
Terschelling, i., Neth. B7 12
Teruel, Col. F5 84
Teruel, Spain E10 16
Teša, Russia F25 22
Tesalia, Col. F5 84
Tešanj, Bos. E2 20
Tes-Chem (Tesijn), stm., Asia A5 30
Tescott, Ks., U.S. C6 123
Teseney, Erit. J9 60
Teshekpuk Lake, l., Ak., U.S. A9 109
Tesijn (Tes-Chem), stm., Asia B6 30
Teslić, Bos. E1 20
Teslin, Yukon, Can. D6 96
Teslin, stm., Can. D6 96
Teslin Lake, l., Can. D6 96
Tesouras, stm., Braz. C3 79
Tesouro, Braz. D2 79
Tessalia, Monts du, mts., Alg. J11 16
Tessalit, Mali A10 64
Tessaoua, Niger E13 64
Tessenderlo, Bel. F7 12
Tessy-sur-Vire, Fr. D5 14
Testour, Tun. M4 18
Tesuque, N.M., U.S. B4 138
Tete, Moz. E6 58
Teterow, Ger. B12 10
Teton, Id., U.S. F7 119
Teton, co., Id., U.S. F7 119
Teton, co., Mt., U.S. C4 133
Teton, co., Wy., U.S. C2 157
Teton, stm., Mt., U.S. C5 133
Tetonia, Id., U.S. F7 119
Teton Pass, Wy., U.S. C2 157
Teton Range, mts., Wy., U.S. C2 157
Teton Village, Wy., U.S. C2 157
Tétouan, Mor. C8 62
Tetovo, Mac. G4 20
Teuco, stm., Arg. C8 80
Teulada, Italy K3 18
Teulada, Capo, c., Italy K3 18
Teúl de González Ortega, Mex. G8 90
Teulon, Man., Can. D3 100
Teutopolis, Il., U.S. D5 120
Teuva, Fin. J17 6
Tevere (Tiber), stm., Italy G7 18
Teverya (Tiberias), Isr. C5 50
Tevli, Bela. I7 22
Tewkesbury, Eng., U.K. I11 8
Tewksbury, Ma., U.S. A5 128
Texada Island, i., B.C., Can. E5 99
Texarkana, Ar., U.S. D1 111
Texarkana, Tx., U.S. C5 150
Texas, Austl. G9 70
Texas, co., Mo., U.S. D5 132
Texas, co., Ok., U.S. e9 143
Texas, state, U.S. D3 150
Texas City, Tx., U.S. E5 150
Texel, i., Neth. B6 12
Texhoma, Ok., U.S. e9 143
Texico, N.M., U.S. C6 138
Texoma, Lake, res., U.S. D5 143
Teyateyaneng, Leso. G8 66
Teywarah, Afg. D1 44
Teziutlán, Mex. H11 90
Tezpur, India G15 44
Tha-anne, stm., N.W. Ter., Can. D13 96
Thabana-Ntlenyana, mtn., Leso. G9 66
Thabazimbi, S. Afr. E8 66
Thacker, W.V., U.S. D2 155
Thackerville, Ok., U.S. D4 143
Thai Binh, Viet. D9 40
Thailand (Prathet Thai), ctry., Asia B3 38
Thailand, Gulf of, b., Asia I6 40
Thai Nguyen, Viet. D8 40
Thal, Pak. D4 44
Thala, Tun. N3 18
Thalfang, Ger. F6 10
Thalwil, Switz. D10 13
Thamar, Jabal, mtn., Yemen H4 47
Thames, N.Z. B5 72
Thames, stm., Ont., Can. E3 103
Thames, stm., Eng., U.K. J12 8
Thames, stm., Ct., U.S. D7 114
Thamesville, Ont., Can. E3 103
Thāna, India C2 46
Thanbyuzayat, Mya. G4 40
Thang Binh, Viet. G10 40
Thanh Hoa, Viet. E8 40
Thanh Pho Ho Chi Minh (Saigon), Viet. I9 40
Thanjāvūr, India G5 46
Thann, Fr. E14 14
Thar Desert (Great Indian Desert), des., Asia F4 44
Thargomindah, Austl. G5 70
Thar Nhom, Sud. N6 60
Tharrawaddy, Mya. F3 40
Thásos, i., Grc. I8 20
Thatcher, Az., U.S. E6 110
Thatcher, Id., U.S. G7 119
Thaton, Mya. F4 40
Thaungdut, Mya. B3 40
Thaungyin, stm., Asia F5 40
Thawville, Il., U.S. C5 120
Thaxton, Ms., U.S. A4 131
Thaya (Dyje), stm., Eur. G15 10
Thayer, Il., U.S. D4 120
Thayer, In., U.S. B3 121
Thayer, Ks., U.S. E8 123
Thayer, Mo., U.S. E6 132
Thayer, co., Ne., U.S. D8 134
Thayetmyo, Mya. E3 40
Thayne, Wy., U.S. D1 157
Thazi, Mya. D4 40
Thealka, Ky., U.S. C7 124
Theba, Az., U.S. E3 110
The Backway, b., Newf., Can. A2 102
The Barrens, plat., Tn., U.S. B5 149
Thebes see Thívai, Grc. K7 20
Thebes, Il., U.S. F4 120
Thebes, hist., Egypt E7 60
The Colony, Tx., U.S. *C4 150
The Coteau, hills, Sask., Can. F2 105
The Dalles, Or., U.S. B5 144
The Dells, val., Wi., U.S. E4 156
Thedford, Ont., Can. D3 103
Thedford, Ne., U.S. C5 134
The Dome, mtn., Vt., U.S. F2 152
The English Companys Islands, is., Austl. B7 68
The Everglades, sw., Fl., U.S. G6 116
The Fens, reg., Eng., U.K. I14 8
The Flat Tops, mts., Co., U.S. B3 113
The Flume, wtfl, N.H., U.S. B3 136
The Graves, is., Ma., U.S. g12 128
The Hague see 's-Gravenhage, Neth. E5 12
The Heads, c., Or., U.S. E2 144
The Little Minch, strt., Scot., U.K. D7 8
Thelon, stm., N.W. Ter., Can. D12 96
The Lynd, Austl. B6 70
The Minch, strt., Scot., U.K. C8 8
The Narrows, strt., Wa., U.S. f10 154
Thenia, Alg. B12 62
Theniet el Hadd, Alg. C12 62
Theodore, Austl. E9 70
Theodore, Sask., Can. F4 105
Theodore, Al., U.S. E1 108
Theodore Roosevelt Lake, res., Az., U.S. D4 110
Theodore Roosevelt National Park (North Unit), N.D., U.S. B2 141
Theodore Roosevelt National Park (South Unit), N.D., U.S. C2 141
Theodosia, Mo., U.S. E5 132
Theólogos, Grc. I8 20
The Palisades, clf, N.J., U.S. h9 137
The Pas, Man., Can. C1 100
The Peak, mtn., N.C., U.S. A1 140
The Pinnacle, hill, Ct., U.S. B4 114
The Pinnacle, hill, Mo., U.S. B7 132
The Plains, Oh., U.S. C3 142
The Plains, Va., U.S. B5 153
The Rand see Witwatersrant, reg., S. Afr. E8 66
The Range, N.B., Can. C4 101
Theresa, N.Y., U.S. A5 139
Theresa, Wi., U.S. E5 156
Therien, Alta., Can. B5 98
Thermaïkós Kólpos, b., Grc. I6 20
Thermopílai (Thermopylae), hist., Grc. K6 20
Thermopolis, Wy., U.S. C4 157
Thermopylae see Thermopílai, hist., Grc. K6 20
The Rock, Austl. J7 70
The Rockies, mts., Wa., U.S. C3 154
The Sound, strt., Eur. N13 6
Thessalía, prov., Grc. J6 20
Thessalía, hist. reg., Grc. J6 20
Thessalon, Ont., Can. p19 103
Thessaloníki (Salonika), Grc. I6 20
Theta, Tn., U.S. B4 149
Thetford Center, Vt., U.S. D4 152
Thetford Mines, Que., Can. C6 104
The Thimbles, is., Ct., U.S. E5 114
The Valley, Anguilla E13 94
The Village, Ok., U.S. B4 143
The Wash, b., Eng., U.K. I14 8
Thibodaux, La., U.S. E5 125
Thicket Portage, Man., Can. B3 100
Thickwood Hills, hills, Sask., Can. E2 105
Thida, Ar., U.S. B4 111
Thief, stm., Mn., U.S. B2 130
Thief Lake, l., Mn., U.S. B3 130
Thief River Falls, Mn., U.S. B2 130
Thielsen, Mount, mtn., Or., U.S. D4 144
Thiene, Italy D6 18
Thiensville, Wi., U.S. E6 156
Thiers, Fr. G10 14
Thiès, Sen. D1 64
Thiesi, Italy I3 18
Thika, Kenya B7 58
Thimphu, Bhu. G13 44
Thingvellir, Ice. B3 6a
Thingvellir National Park, Ice. B3 6a
Thionville, Fr. C13 14
Thíra (Santorini), i., Grc. M9 20
Third Lake, l., N.H., U.S. f7 136
Thiruvārūr, India G5 46
Thistle Island, i., Austl. J2 70
Thívai (Thebes), Grc. K7 20
Thlewiaza, stm., N.W. Ter., Can. D13 96
Thohoyandou, S. Afr. D10 66
Thoi Binh, Viet. J8 40
Thomas, Ok., U.S. B3 143
Thomas, W.V., U.S. B5 155
Thomas, co., Ga., U.S. F3 117
Thomas, co., Ks., U.S. C2 123
Thomas, co., Ne., U.S. C5 134
Thomasboro, Il., U.S. C5 120
Thomas Creek, stm., Fl., U.S. k8 116
Thomaston, Al., U.S. C2 108
Thomaston, Ct., U.S. C3 114
Thomaston, Ga., U.S. D2 117
Thomaston, Me., U.S. D3 126
Thomaston Reservoir, res., Ct., U.S. C3 114
Thomastown, Ms., U.S. C4 131
Thomasville, Al., U.S. D2 108
Thomasville, Ga., U.S. F3 117
Thomasville, N.C., U.S. B2 140
Thompson, Man., Can. B3 100
Thompson, Ct., U.S. B8 114
Thompson, Ia., U.S. A4 122
Thompson, N.D., U.S. B8 141
Thompson, stm., U.S. A4 132
Thompson Creek, stm., Ms., U.S. D5 131
Thompson Falls, Mt., U.S. C1 133
Thompson Island, i., Ma., U.S. g11 128
Thompson Lake, l., U.S. D2 126
Thompson Peak, mtn., Ca., U.S. B2 112
Thompson Peak, mtn., N.M., U.S. h9 138
Thompson Reservoir, res., Or., U.S. E5 144
Thompsons Station, Tn., U.S. B5 149
Thompsonville, Il., U.S. F5 120
Thompsonville, Mi., U.S. D5 129
Thomson, Ga., U.S. C4 117
Thomson, Il., U.S. B3 120
Thomson, stm., Austl. E5 70
Thon Buri, Thai. H6 40
Thongwa, Mya. F4 40
Thonon-les-Bains, Fr. F13 14
Thonotosassa, Fl., U.S. D4 116
Thonze, Mya. F3 40
Thor, Ia., U.S. B3 122
Thorburn, N.S., Can. D7 101
Thoreau, N.M., U.S. B1 138
Thorhild, Alta., Can. B4 98
Thorial, Sud. M5 60
Thornburg, Ar., U.S. C3 111
Thornbury, Ont., Can. C4 103
Thorndale, Tx., U.S. D4 150
Thorndike, Ma., U.S. B3 128
Thorne Bay, Ak., U.S. n23 109
Thornhill, Man., Can. E2 100
Thornton, Ont., Can. C5 103
Thornton, Ar., U.S. D3 111
Thornton, Id., U.S. F7 119
Thornton, Ia., U.S. B4 122
Thornton, Ms., U.S. B3 131
Thornton, Tx., U.S. D4 150
Thornton, W.V., U.S. k11 155
Thornton Gap, Va., U.S. B4 153
Thorntonville, Tx., U.S. D1 150
Thorntown, In., U.S. D4 121
Thornville, Oh., U.S. C3 142
Thorny Mountain, mtn., Mo., U.S. D6 132
Thorofare, N.J., U.S. D2 137
Thorold, Ont. Can. D5 103
Thorp, Wa., U.S. B5 154
Thorp, Wi., U.S. D3 156
Thorsby, Alta., Can. C3 98
Thorsby, Al., U.S. C3 108
Thouars, Fr. F6 14
Thousand Islands, is., N.Y., U.S. A4 139
Thousand Lake Mountain, mtn., Ut., U.S. E4 151
Thousand Springs Creek, stm., U.S. B7 135
Thrace, hist. reg., Eur. H10 20
Thrakikón Pélagos, Grc. I8 20
Thrashers, Ms., U.S. A5 131
Three Fingered Jack, mtn., Or., U.S. C5 144
Three Forks, Mt., U.S. E5 133
Three Hills, Alta., Can. D4 98
Three Hummock Island, i., Austl. M6 70
Three Lakes, Wi., U.S. C4 156
Three Mile Plains, N.S., Can. E5 101
Three Oaks, Mi., U.S. G4 129
Three Pagodas Pass, Asia G5 40
Three Rivers, Ma., U.S. B3 128
Three Rivers, Mi., U.S. G5 129
Three Rivers, Ms., U.S. E5 131
Three Rivers, Tx., U.S. E3 150
Three Rock Cove, Newf., Can. D2 102
Three Sisters, S. Afr. H6 66
Three Sisters, mtn., Or., U.S. C5 144
Three Springs, Austl. E3 68
Throckmorton, Tx., U.S. C3 150
Throckmorton, co., Tx., U.S. C3 150
Throop, Pa., U.S. m18 145
Thu Dau Mot, Viet. I9 40
Thule, Grnld. B13 86
Thun, Switz. E8 13
Thunder Bay, Ont., Can. o17 103
Thunder Bay, b., Mi., U.S. D7 129
Thunder Bay, stm., Mi., U.S. D6 129
Thunder Bay, North Branch, stm., Mi., U.S. C6 129
Thunderbird, Lake, res., Ok., U.S. B4 143
Thunderbolt, Ga., U.S. D5 117
Thunder Butte, mtn., S.D., U.S. B4 148
Thunder Butte Creek, stm., S.D., U.S. B3 148
Thunersee, l., Switz. E8 13
Thung Song, Thai. J5 40
Thur, stm., Switz. C10 13
Thurgau, state, Switz. C11 13
Thüringen, state, Ger. D11 10
Thüringer Wald, mts., Ger. E10 10
Thurlow Dam, Al., U.S. C4 108
Thurman, Ia., U.S. D2 122
Thurmont, Md., U.S. A3 127
Thursday Island, Austl. B8 68
Thurso, Que., Can. D2 104
Thurso, Scot., U.K. C10 8
Thurston, Oh., U.S. C3 142
Thurston, co., Ne., U.S. B9 134
Thurston, co., Wa., U.S. C2 154
Thurston Island, i., Ant. C11 73
Thusis, Switz. E11 13
Thwaites Iceberg Tongue, Ant. C11 73
Thyolo, Mwi. E7 58
Tía Juana, Ven. B7 84
Tianchang, China C8 34
Tiandong, China C9 40
Tianfanjie, China F5 34
Tianjiazhen, China F4 34
Tianjin (Tientsin), China D5 32
Tianjin Shi, China D10 30
Tianjun, China D6 30
Tianlin, China B9 40
Tianmen, China E2 34
Tianshui, China E8 30
Tiantai, China F10 34
Tiantou, China I4 34
Tianxiyang, China I7 34
Tianzhu, China D7 30
Tianzhuang, China J2 34
Tiawah, Ok., U.S. A6 143
Tibaji, Braz. C13 80
Tibaji, stm., Braz. B13 80
Tibasti, Sarīr, des., Libya D4 56
Tibbie, Al., U.S. D1 108
Tibe, Eth. M9 60
Tiber see Tevere, stm., Italy G7 18
Tibesti, mts., Chad D4 56
Tibet see Xizang Zizhiqu, prov., China E3 30
Tibiri, Niger E13 64
Tibooburra, Austl. G5 70
Tiburón, Cabo, c. C4 84
Tiburón, Isla, i., Mex. C3 90
Tiča, Jazovir, res., Bul. F10 20
Tice, Fl., U.S. F5 116
Tichborne, Ont., Can. C8 103
Tīchīt, Maur. B5 64
Tichmenevo, Russia C21 22
Tichoreck, Russia H6 26
Tichvin, Russia B16 22
Ticino, state, Switz. F10 13
Ticino, stm., Eur. D3 18
Tickfaw, La., U.S. D5 125
Tickfaw, stm., La., U.S. C5 125
Ticonderoga, N.Y., U.S. B7 139
Ticul, Mex. G15 90
Tide Head, N.B., Can. B3 101
Tidikelt, pl., Alg. G11 62
Tidioute, Pa., U.S. C3 145
Tidjikja, Maur. B4 64
Tidore, Indon. E8 38
Tiekou, China F9 32
Tieli, China B12 30
Tieling, China A11 32
Tielt, Bel. F3 12
Tielutou, China H4 34
Tiémé, C. Iv. G6 64
T'ienchung, Tai. L9 34
Tien Shan, mts., Asia C3 30
Tientsin see Tianjin, China D5 32
Tie Plant, Ms., U.S. B4 131
Tierra Amarilla, Chile D3 80
Tierra Amarilla, N.M., U.S. A3 138
Tierra Blanca, Mex. H11 90
Tierra del Fuego, Isla Grande de, i., S.A. G3 78
Tierralta, Col. C4 84
Tieshanggang, China L2 34
Tietê, Braz. G5 79
Tietê, stm., Braz. F3 79
Tieton, Wa., U.S. C5 154
Tieton, stm., Wa., U.S. C4 154
Tieton Dam, Wa., U.S. C4 154
Tif, Alg. G11 62
Tiffany Mountain, mtn., Wa., U.S. A6 154
Tiffin, Ia., U.S. C6 122
Tiffin, Oh., U.S. A2 142
Tiffin, stm., Oh., U.S. A1 142
Tift, co., Ga., U.S. E3 117
Tifton, Ga., U.S. E3 117
Tigard, Or., U.S. h12 144
Tiger, Ga., U.S. B3 117
Tigerton, Wi., U.S. D4 156
Tighennif, Alg. C11 62
Tighina (Bender), Mol. H3 26
Tigil', Russia F23 28
Tiglid, Mor. F5 62
Tignall, Ga., U.S. C4 117
Tignish, P.E.I., Can. C5 101
Tigre, Col. F8 84
Tigre, stm., Peru J5 84
Tigre, stm., Ven. C11 84
Tigre, Cerro, mtn., C.R. I11 92
Tigrett, Tn., U.S. B2 149
Tigris (Dicle) (Dijlah), stm., Asia F9 48
Tiguabos, Cuba D7 94
Tiguentourine, Alg. G15 62
Tihāmah, pl., Asia H4 48
Tihert, Alg. C11 62
Tihuatlán, Mex. G11 90
Tijamuchi, stm., Bol. F9 82
Tijeras, N.M., U.S. B3 138
Tijesno, Cro. F10 18
Tijuana, Mex. A1 90
Tijucas, Braz. D14 80
Tijucas do Sul, Braz. C14 80
Tijuco, stm., Braz. E4 79
Tikal, hist., Guat. I15 90
Tiko, Cam. I14 64
Tikrīt, Iraq D7 48
Tikša, Russia I23 6
Tikšeozero, ozero, l., Russia H22 6
Tilarán, C.R. G10 92
Tilbalakan, Laguna, b., Hond. B10 92
Tilburg, Neth. E7 12
Tilbury, Ont., Can. E2 103
Tilcara, Arg. B6 80
Tilden, Il., U.S. E4 120
Tilden, Ne., U.S. B8 134
Tilemsès, Niger D12 64
Tilemsi, Vallée du, val., Mali B10 64
Tilghman, Md., U.S. C5 127
Tilghman Island, i., Md., U.S. C5 127
Tilhar, India G8 44
Tilimsen, Alg. C10 62
Tiline, Ky., U.S. e9 124
Tilisarao, Arg. G6 80
Tillaberi, Niger D10 64
Tillamook, Or., U.S. B3 144
Tillamook, co., Or., U.S. B3 144
Tillanchāng Dwīp, i., India J2 40
Tillar, Ar., U.S. D4 111
Tillery, Lake, res., N.C., U.S. B2 140
Tilley, Alta., Can. D5 98
Tillia, Niger C12 64
Tillman, co., Ok., U.S. C2 143
Tillmans Corner, Al., U.S. E1 108
Tillson, N.Y., U.S. D6 139
Tillsonburg, Ont., Can. E4 103
Tilpa, Austl. H6 70
Tilrhemt, Alg. D12 62
Tilston, Man., Can. E1 100
Tilting, Newf., Can. D4 102
Tilton, Ga., U.S. B2 117
Tilton, Il., U.S. C6 120
Tilton, N.H., U.S. D3 136
Tiltonsville, Oh., U.S. B5 142
Timā, Egypt D6 60
Timaná, Col. G5 84
Timane, stm., Para. I12 82
Timanskij kr'až, mtn., Russia D7 26
Timaru, N.Z. F3 72
Timbalier Island, i., La., U.S. E5 125
Timbedgha, Maur. C5 64
Timbered Knob, mtn., Mo., U.S. E5 132
Timber Lake, S.D., U.S. B4 148
Timberlake, Va., U.S. C3 153
Timberville, Va., U.S. B4 153
Timbío, Col. F4 84
Timbó, Braz. D14 80
Timbo, Lib. I5 64
Timboon, Austl. L5 70
Timbuktu see Tombouctou, Mali C8 64
Timétrine, Mali B9 64
Timgad, hist., Alg. C14 62
Timimoun, Alg. F11 62
Timinar, Sud. H6 60
Timir'azevskij, Russia F14 26
Timirist, Râs, c., Maur. B1 64
Timiș, co., Rom. D5 20
Timiș (Tamiš), stm., Eur. D5 20
Timișoara, Rom. D5 20
Timmendorfer Strand, Ger. A10 10
Timmins, Ont., Can. o19 103
Timmonsville, S.C., U.S. C8 147
Timms Hill, hill, Wi., U.S. C3 156
Timnath, Co., U.S. A5 113
Timor, i., Indon. G8 38
Timor Sea J16 158
Timotes, Ven. C7 84
Timoudi, Alg. F10 62
Timpanogos Cave National Monument, Ut., U.S. C4 151
Timpas Creek, stm., Co., U.S. D7 113
Timpson, Tx., U.S. D5 150
Tims Ford Lake, res., Tn., U.S. B5 149
Tina, Mo., U.S. B4 132
Tinaca Point, c., Phil. D8 38
Tinaco, Ven. C8 84
Tīnah, Khalīj aṭ-, b., Egypt F2 48
Tinaja, Punta, c., Peru G5 82
Ti-n-Amzi, val., Afr. B12 64
Tinaquillo, Ven. C8 84
Tindivanam, India F5 46
Tindouf, Alg. G6 62
Tindouf, Hamada de, reg., Afr. F6 62
Tindouf, Sebkha de, pl., Alg. G7 62
Tineo, Spain B5 16
Tinga, mtn., Afr. M2 60
Tingha, Austl. G9 70
Tinghert, Hamādat (Plateau du Tinghert), plat., Afr. F15 62
Tinghert, Plateau du (Hamādat Tinghert), plat., Afr. F15 62
Tingmerkpuk Mountain, mtn., Ak., U.S. B7 109
Tingo de Saposoa, Peru B3 82
Tingo María, Peru C4 82
Tingri, China F12 44
Tingsiqiao, China F3 34
Tingvoll, Nor. J11 6
Tinharé, Ilha de, i., Braz. B9 79
Tinh Bien, Viet. I8 40
Tinker Air Force Base, mil., Ok., U.S. B4 143
Tinkisso, stm., Gui. F5 64
Tinley Park, Il., U.S. k9 120
Tinnie, N.M., U.S. D4 138
Tinniswood, Mount, mtn., B.C., Can. D6 99
Tinnoset, Nor. L11 6
Tinogasta, Arg. E5 80
Tínos, Grc. L9 20
Tínos, i., Grc. L9 20
Tinquipaya, Bol. H9 82
Tinrhir, Mor. E8 62
Tinsley, Ms., U.S. C3 131
Tinsukia, India G16 44
Tinte, Cerro, mtn., S.A. J8 82
Tintina, Arg. D7 80
Tinton Falls, N.J., U.S. C4 137
Ti-n-Zaouatene, Alg. B11 64
Tio, Erit. G2 47
Tioga, La., U.S. C3 125
Tioga, N.D., U.S. A3 141
Tioga, Pa., U.S. C7 145
Tioga, W.V., U.S. C4 155
Tioga, co., N.Y., U.S. C4 139
Tioga, co., Pa., U.S. C7 145
Tioga, stm., Pa., U.S. B7 145
Tioga Terrace, N.Y., U.S. C4 139
Tiogue Lake, res., R.I., U.S. D3 146

Name — Map Ref. — Page

Tres Algarrobos, Arg. H7 80
Tres Árboles, Ur. G10 80
Tres Arroyos, Arg. J8 80
Tresckow, Pa., U.S. E10 145
Três Corações, Braz. F6 79
Três Coroas, Braz. E13 80
Três de Maio, Braz. D11 80
Tres Esquinas, Col. G5 84
Três Fronteiras, Braz. F3 79
Tres Isletas, Arg. D8 80
Três Lagoas, Braz. F3 79
Tres Lomas, Arg. I7 80
Três Marias, Braz. E6 79
Três Marias, Represa de, res., Braz. E6 79
Tres Palos, Laguna, b., Mex. I10 90
Três Passos, Braz. D12 80
Tres Picos, Cerro, mtn., Arg. J8 80
Tres Piedras, N.M., U.S. A4 138
Três Pontas, Braz. F6 79
Tres Puntas, Cabo, c., Arg. F3 78
Tres Puntas, Cabo, c., Guat. B6 92
Três Ranchos, Braz. E5 79
Três Rios, Braz. G7 79
Tres Ríos, C.R. H11 92
Tres Vírgenes, Volcán de las, vol., Mex. D3 90
Tres Zapotes, hist., Mex. H12 90
Treuchtlingen, Ger. G10 10
Treuenbrietzen, Ger. C12 10
Treutlen, co., Ga., U.S. D4 117
Treviglio, Italy D4 18
Treviso, Italy D7 18
Trevlac, In., U.S. F5 121
Trevor, Wi., U.S. n11 156
Trevorton, Pa., U.S. E8 145
Trévoux, Fr. G11 14
Treynor, Ia., U.S. C2 122
Trezevant, Tn., U.S. A3 149
Triabunna, Austl. N7 70
Triadelphia, W.V., U.S. A4 155
Triadelphia Reservoir, res., Md., U.S. B3 127
Triánda, Grc. M12 20
Triangle, Va., U.S. B5 153
Triángulos, Arrecifes, rf., Mex. G13 90
Tribbey, Ok., U.S. B4 143
Tribugá, Ensenada de, b., Col. E4 84
Tribune, Sask., Can. H4 105
Tribune, Ks., U.S. D2 123
Tricase, Italy J13 18
Trichardt, S. Afr. F9 66
Trichūr, India G4 46
Tri City, Or., U.S. E3 144
Trident Peak, mtn., Nv., U.S. B3 135
Trier, Ger. F6 10
Trieste, Italy D8 18
Trigal, Bol. H9 82
Trigg, co., Ky., U.S. D2 124
Triglav, mtn., Slvn. C8 18
Trigo Mountains, mts., Az., U.S. D1 110
Trigueros, Spain H5 16
Tríkala, Grc. J5 20
Trikhonís, Límni, l., Grc. K5 20
Trikora, Puncak, mtn., Indon. F10 38
Tri Lakes, In., U.S. B7 121
Trilby, Fl., U.S. D4 116
Trilla, Il., U.S. D5 120
Trimble, Mo., U.S. B3 132
Trimble, Tn., U.S. A2 149
Trimble, co., Ky., U.S. B4 124
Trimont, Mn., U.S. G4 130
Trin, Switz. E11 13
Trinchera Creek, stm., Co., U.S. D5 113
Trincheras, Mex. B4 90
Trincomalee, Sri L. H6 46
Trindade, Braz. D4 79
Trindade, i., Braz. G12 74
Třinec, Czech Rep. F18 10
Tring Jonction, Que., Can. C6 104
Trinidad, Bol. F9 82
Trinidad, Col. E7 84
Trinidad, Cuba D5 94
Trinidad, Hond. C6 92
Trinidad, Co., U.S. D6 113
Trinidad, Tx., U.S. C4 150
Trinidad, Ur. G10 80
Trinidad, i., Trin. I14 94
Trinidad, Isla, i., Arg. J8 80
Trinidad and Tobago, ctry., N.A. I14 94
Trinidad Head, c., Ca., U.S. B1 112
Trinity, Newf., Can. D5 102
Trinity, Newf., Can. D5 102
Trinity, Al., U.S. A2 108
Trinity, Tx., U.S. D5 150
Trinity, co., Ca., U.S. B2 112
Trinity, co., Tx., U.S. D5 150
Trinity, stm., Ca., U.S. B2 112
Trinity, stm., Tx., U.S. D5 150
Trinity, East Fork, stm., Tx., U.S. n10 150
Trinity, Elm Fork, stm., Tx., U.S. m10 150
Trinity, South Fork, stm., Ca., U.S. B2 112
Trinity, West Fork, stm., Tx., U.S. n9 150
Trinity Bay, b., Newf., Can. D5 102
Trinity Center, Ca., U.S. B2 112
Trinity Islands, is., Ak., U.S. D9 109
Trinity Mountain, mtn., Id., U.S. F3 119
Trinity Mountains, mts., Ca., U.S. B2 112
Trinity Peak, mtn., Nv., U.S. C3 135
Trinity Range, mts., Nv., U.S. C3 135
Trinkat Island, i., India J2 40
Trinkitat, Sud. H9 60
Trino, Italy D3 18
Trinway, Oh., U.S. B3 142
Trion, Ga., U.S. B1 117
Tripoli see Țarābulus, Leb. D3 48
Tripoli see Țarābulus, Libya B3 56
Tripoli, Ia., U.S. B5 122
Trípolis, Grc. L6 20
Tripolis, hist., Tur. L13 20
Tripp, S.D., U.S. D8 148
Tripp, co., S.D., U.S. D6 148
Tripura, state, India I14 44
Tristan da Cunha Group, is., St. Hel. L5 52
Tristao, Îles, is., Afr. F2 64
Triste, Golfo, b., Ven. B8 84
Triumph, La., U.S. E6 125
Trivandrum, India H4 46
Trnava, Slvk. G17 10
Trochu, Alta., Can. D4 98
Trogir, Cro. F11 18
Troia, Italy H10 18
Troick, Russia G10 26
Troicko-Pečorsk, Russia E9 26
Troina, Italy L9 18
Troisdorf, Ger. E7 10
Trois-Pistoles, Que., Can. A8 104
Trois-Rivières, Que., Can. C5 104
Trois-Rivières-Ouest, Que., Can. C5 104
Trojan, Bul. G8 20
Trojekurovo, Russia H22 22
Trollhättan, Swe. L13 6
Trombetas, stm., Braz. H14 84
Tromelin, Île, i., Afr. E10 58
Trompsburg, S. Afr. H7 66
Troms, co., Nor. G16 6
Tromsø, Nor. G16 6
Trona, Ca., U.S. E5 112
Tronador, Monte, mtn., S.A. E2 78
Troncoso, Mex. F8 90
Trondheim, Nor. J12 6
Troon, Scot., U.K. F9 8
Tropas, Rio das, stm., Braz. B13 82
Tropea, Italy K10 18
Trophy Mountain, mtn., B.C., Can. D8 99
Tropic, Ut., U.S. F3 151
Tropojë, Alb. G4 20
Troškūnai, Lith. F7 22
Trosna, Russia I18 22
Trossachs, Sask., Can. H3 105
Trostyanets', Ukr. A13 20
Trotwood, Oh., U.S. C1 142
Trou-du-Nord, Haiti E8 94
Troup, co., Ga., U.S. C1 117
Trousdale, co., Tn., U.S. A5 149
Trousers Lake, l., N.B., Can. B3 101
Trout, La., U.S. C3 125
Trout, stm., Fl., U.S. m8 116
Trout, stm., Vt., U.S. B3 152
Trout Creek, Ont., Can. B5 103
Trout Creek, Mt., U.S. C1 133
Trout Creek Pass, Co., U.S. C5 113
Trout Lake, Mi., U.S. B6 129
Trout Lake, Wa., U.S. D4 154
Trout Lake, l., B.C., Can. D9 99
Trout Lake, l., Ont., Can. o16 103
Trout Lake, l., Mn., U.S. B6 130
Trout Lake, l., Wi., U.S. B4 156
Troutman, N.C., U.S. B2 140
Trout Peak, mtn., Wy., U.S. B3 157
Trout River, Newf., Can. D2 102
Troutville, Va., U.S. C3 153
Trouville [-sur-Mer], Fr. C7 14
Trowbridge, Eng., U.K. J11 8
Troy, Al., U.S. D4 108
Troy, Id., U.S. C2 119
Troy, Il., U.S. E4 120
Troy, In., U.S. H4 121
Troy, Ks., U.S. C8 123
Troy, Mi., U.S. o15 129
Troy, Ms., U.S. A5 131
Troy, Mo., U.S. C7 132
Troy, Mt., U.S. B1 133
Troy, N.H., U.S. E2 136
Troy, N.Y., U.S. C7 139
Troy, N.C., U.S. B3 140
Troy, Oh., U.S. B1 142
Troy, Pa., U.S. C8 145
Troy, Tn., U.S. A2 149
Troy, Vt., U.S. B4 152
Troy, hist., Tur. J10 20
Troyes, Fr. D11 14
Troy Grove, Il., U.S. B4 120
Troyits'ke, Ukr. B14 20
Troy Mills, Ia., U.S. B6 122
Troy Peak, mtn., Nv., U.S. E6 135
Trstenik, Yugo. F5 20
Trubčevsk, Russia I16 22
Truchas, N.M., U.S. A4 138
Truchas Peak, mtn., N.M., U.S. B4 138
Truckee, Ca., U.S. C3 112
Truckee, stm., U.S. D2 135
Trujillo, Col. E4 84
Trujillo, Hond. B8 92
Trujillo, Peru C2 82
Trujillo, Spain F6 16
Trujillo, Ven. C7 84
Trujillo, state, Ven. C7 84
Truk Islands, is., Micron. H19 158
Truman, Mn., U.S. G4 130
Trumann, Ar., U.S. B5 111
Trumansburg, N.Y., U.S. C4 139
Trumbull, Ct., U.S. E3 114
Trumbull, Ne., U.S. D7 134
Trumbull, co., Oh., U.S. A5 142
Trumbull, Mount, mtn., Az., U.S. A2 110
Trundle, Austl. I7 70
Truro, N.S., Can. D6 101
Truro, Ia., U.S. C4 122
Truro, Ma., U.S. C7 128
Trussville, Al., U.S. B3 108
Trustom Pond, l., R.I., U.S. G3 146
Truth or Consequences (Hot Springs), N.M., U.S. D2 138
Trutnov, Czech Rep. E15 10
Truxton, Az., U.S. B2 110
Tryduby, Ukr. A14 20
Tryon, Ne., U.S. C5 134
Tryon, N.C., U.S. f10 140
Tryon, Ok., U.S. B5 143
Trzcianka, Pol. B16 10
Trzebież, Pol. B14 10
Trzebinia, Pol. E19 10
Tsala Apopka Lake, l., Fl., U.S. D4 116
Tsarabaria, Madag. n23 67b
Tsaratanana, Madag. p22 67b
Tsaratanana, Massif du, mts., Madag. o23 67b
Tsau, Bots. C6 66
Tsaukaib, Nmb. F2 66
Tsavo, Kenya B7 58
Tschetter Colony, S.D., U.S. D8 148
Tschida, Lake, res., N.D., U.S. C4 141
Tsebrykove, Ukr. B14 20
Tsekanyani, Bots. B8 66
Tsévié, Togo H10 64
Tshabong, Bots. F6 66
Tshane, Bots. E5 66
Tshangalele, Lac, l., Zaire D5 58
Tshela, Zaire B2 58
Tshesebe, Bots. C8 66
Tshidilamolomo, S. Afr. E7 66
Tshikapa, Zaire C4 58
Tshofa, Zaire C5 58
Tshukudu, Bots. D6 66
Tshwaane, Bots. D6 66
Tsiafajavona, mtn., Madag. q22 67b
Tsianaloka, Madag. q21 67b
Tsihombe, Madag. t21 67b
Tsilmamo, Eth. N8 60
Tsimilofo, Madag. t21 67b
Tsineng, S. Afr. F6 66
Tsingtao see Qingdao, China G8 32
Tsinjomitondraka, Madag. o22 67b
Tsiribihina, stm., Madag. q21 67b
Tsiroanomandidy, Madag. q22 67b
Tsitondroina, Madag. r22 67b
Tsivory, Madag. t22 67b
Tsobis, Nmb. B3 66
Tsomo, stm., S. Afr. H8 66
Tsoying, Tai. M9 34
Tsu, Japan M11 36
Tsuchiura, Japan K15 36
Tsugaru-kaikyō, strt., Japan f15 36a
Tsumeb, Nmb. B3 66
Tsumis Park, Nmb. D3 66
Tsumkwe, Nmb. B5 66
Tsuni see Zunyi, China F8 30
Tsuruga, Japan L11 36
Tsuruoka, Japan I14 36
Tsushima, is., Japan M4 36
Tsushima-kaikyō (Eastern Channel), strt., Japan N4 36
Tsuyama, Japan L9 36
Tua Chau, Viet. D7 40
Tual, Indon. G9 38
Tualatin, stm., Or., U.S. h11 144
Tuam, Ire. H5 8
Tuamotu, Îles, is., Fr. Poly. J26 158
Tuanfeng, China E3 34
Tuanlin, China D7 32
Tuanwang, China G8 32
Tuapse, Russia I5 26
Tubac, Az., U.S. F4 110
Tuba City, Az., U.S. A4 110
Tubarão, Braz. E14 80
Tübingen, Ger. G9 10
Țubruq (Tobruk), Libya A2 60
Tucacas, Ven. B8 84
Tucacas, Punta, c., Ven. B8 84
Tucannon, stm., Wa., U.S. C8 154
Tucannon Canyon, val., Wa., U.S. C8 154
Tucano, Braz. F11 76
Tucavaca, stm., Bol. H12 82
Tuchengzi, China C12 32
Tuchola, Pol. B17 10
Tuckahoe, N.J., U.S. E3 137
Tuckahoe, N.Y., U.S. h13 139
Tuckahoe, stm., N.J., U.S. E3 137
Tuckahoe Creek, stm., Md., U.S. C6 127
Tucker, Ar., U.S. C4 111
Tucker, Ga., U.S. h8 117
Tucker, co., W.V., U.S. B5 155
Tucker Island, i., N.J., U.S. E4 137
Tuckerman, Ar., U.S. B4 111
Tuckernuck Island, i., Ma., U.S. D7 128
Tuckerton, N.J., U.S. D4 137
Tučkovo, Russia F19 22
Tucson, Az., U.S. E5 110
Tucumã, mth., Braz. J9 84
Tucumán, prov., Arg. D6 80
Tucumcari, N.M., U.S. B6 138
Tucumcari Mountain, mtn., N.M., U.S. B6 138
Tucunuco, Arg. F4 80
Tucupido, Ven. C10 84
Tucupita, Ven. C11 84
Tucuruí, Braz. D9 76
Tucuruí, Represa de, res., Braz. D9 76
Tudcum, Arg. F4 80
Tudela, Spain C10 16
Tudmur (Palmyra), Syria D5 48
Tudu, Est. B9 22
Tugaloo Lake, res., U.S. B1 147
Tugaske, Sask., Can. G2 105
Tug Fork, stm., U.S. C2 155
Tuichi, stm., Bol. F8 82
Tuineje, Spain o26 17b
Tujmazy, Russia G8 26
T'ukalinsk, Russia F12 26
Tukangbesi, Kepulauan, is., Indon. G7 38
Tuktoyaktuk, N.W. Ter., Can. C6 96
Tukums, Lat. D6 22
Tukwila, Wa., U.S. f11 154
Tula, Mex. F10 90
Tula, Russia G20 22
Tulalip Indian Reservation, Wa., U.S. A3 154
Tulancingo, Mex. G10 90
Tulare, Ca., U.S. D4 112
Tulare, S.D., U.S. C7 148
Tulare, co., Ca., U.S. D4 112
Tulare Lake, l., Ca., U.S. D4 112
Tularosa, N.M., U.S. D3 138
Tularosa Mountains, mts., N.M., U.S. D1 138
Tularosa Valley, val., N.M., U.S. E3 138
Tulbagh, S. Afr. I4 66
Tulcán, Ec. G4 84
Tulcea, Rom. D12 20
Tulcea, co., Rom. D12 20
Tule, stm., Nic. F10 92
Tulelake, Ca., U.S. B3 112
Tule Lake, sw., Ca., U.S. B3 112
Tule River Indian Reservation, Ca., U.S. E4 112
Tule Valley, val., Ut., U.S. D2 151
T'ul'gan, Russia G9 26
Tuli, Zimb. C9 66
Tulia, Tx., U.S. B2 150
Tuling, China J7 34
Ţūlkarm, W.B. D4 50
Tullahoma, Tn., U.S. B5 149
Tullamore, Austl. I7 70
Tullamore, Ire. H6 8
Tulle, Fr. G8 14
Tullibigeal, Austl. I7 70
Tulln, Aus. G16 10
Tullos, La., U.S. C3 125
Tullus, Sud. L3 60
Tully, Austl. A6 70
Tuloma, stm., Russia G23 6
Tulsa, Ok., U.S. A6 143
Tulsa, co., Ok., U.S. B6 143
Tuluá, Col. E4 84
Tulum, Mex. G16 90
Tulum, hist., Mex. G16 90
Tulumayo, stm., Peru D4 82
Tulun, Russia G12 28
Tulungagung, Indon. k15 39a
Tuma, Russia F23 22
Tuma, stm., Nic. D10 92
Tumacacori, Az., U.S. F4 110
Tumacacori National Monument, Az., U.S. F4 110
Tumaco, Col. G3 84
Tumaco, Rada de, b., Col. G3 84
Tumalo, Or., U.S. C5 144
Tumatumari, Guy. E13 84
Tumba, Lac, l., Zaire B3 58
Tumbarumba, Austl. J8 70
Tumbes, Peru I2 84
Tumbes, dept., Peru F2 84
Tumbes (Puyango), stm., S.A. I2 84
Tumble Mountain, mtn., Mt., U.S. E7 133
Tumbler Ridge, B.C., Can. B7 99
Tumbling Shoals, Ar., U.S. B3 111
Tumbotino, Russia F26 22
Tumby Bay, Austl. J2 70
Tumča, stm., Eur. H21 6
Tumen, China A17 32
T'umen', Russia F11 26
Tumen (Tuman-gang), stm., Asia A18 32
Tumeremo, Ven. D12 84
Tumiritinga, Braz. E8 79
Tumkūr, India F4 46
Tummo, Libya D3 56
Tumos, stm., Nmb. D2 66
Tumpat, Malay. K7 40
Tumsar, India B5 46
Tumtum, Wa., U.S. B8 154
Tumuc-Humac Mountains, mts., S.A. C7 76
Tumut, Austl. J8 70
Tumwater, Wa., U.S. B3 154
Tunari, Cerro, mtn., Bol. G8 82
Tunas de Zaza, Cuba D5 94
Tunaydah, Egypt E5 60
Tunçbilek, Tur. J13 20
Tunduru, Tan. D7 58
Tundža, stm., Eur. G10 20
T'ung, stm., Russia E16 28
Tungabhadra Reservoir, res., India E4 46
Tungaru, Sud. L6 60
Tungkang, Tai. M9 34
Tungla, Nic. D10 92
Tungsha Tao (Pratas Island), i., Tai. G10 30
Tungshih, Tai K9 34
Tungurahua, prov., Ec. H3 84
Tuni, India D7 46
Tunica, stm., Col. G6 84
Tunica, Ms., U.S. A3 131
Tunica, co., Ms., U.S. A3 131
Tunis, Tun. M5 18
Tunis, Golfe de, b., Tun. L5 18
Tunisia (Tunisie), ctry., Afr. B8 54
Tunja, Col. E6 84
Tunkás, Mex. G15 90
Tunkhannock, Pa., U.S. C10 145
Tunk Lake, l., Me., U.S. D4 126
Tunnel Hill, Ga., U.S. B1 117
Tunnel Springs, Al., U.S. D2 108
Tunnelton, In., U.S. G5 121
Tunnelton, W.V., U.S. B5 155
Tunp Range, mts., Wy., U.S. D2 157
Tununak, Ak., U.S. C6 109
Tunungayualck Island, i., Newf., Can. g9 102
Tunuyán, Arg. G4 80
Tunuyán, stm., Arg. G5 80
Tunxi, China F7 34
Tuo, stm., China E7 30
Tuocheng, China K4 34
Tuokusidawan Ling, mtn., China B11 44
Tuolumne, Ca., U.S. D3 112
Tuolumne, co., Ca., U.S. C4 112
Tuolumne, stm., Ca., U.S. D3 112
Tupã, Braz. F3 79
Tupaciguara, Braz. E4 79
Tupana, stm., Braz. J12 84
Tupanciretã, Braz. E12 80
Tuparro, stm., Col. E8 84
Tupelo, Ar., U.S. B4 111
Tupelo, Ms., U.S. A5 131
Tupelo, Ok., U.S. C5 143
Tupinambarana, Ilha, i., Braz. I14 84
Tupi Paulista, Braz. F3 79
Tupiraçaba, Braz. C4 79
Tupiza, Bol. I9 82
Tupper, B.C., Can. B7 99
Tupper Lake, N.Y., U.S. A6 139
Tupper Lake, l., N.Y., U.S. A6 139
Tupperville, Ont., Can. E2 103
Tupungato, Arg. G4 80
Tupungato, Cerro, mtn., S.A. G4 80
Túquerres, Col. G4 84
Tura, India H14 44
Tura, stm., Russia F10 26
Turabah, Sau. Ar. D2 47
Turayf, Sau. Ar. F5 48
Turbaco, Col. B5 84
Turbacz, mtn., Pol. F20 10
Turbat, Pak. I17 48
Turbeville, S.C., U.S. D7 147
Turbo, Col. C4 84
Turbotville, Pa., U.S. D8 145
Turda, Rom. C7 20
Turdej, Russia H21 22
Turek, Pol. C18 10
Turfan see Turpan, China C4 30
Turfan Depression see Turpan Pendi, depr., China C4 30
Turgaj, Kaz. H10 26
Turgaj, stm., Kaz. H10 26
Turgajskaja ložbina, val., Kaz. G10 26
Turgajskoje plato, plat., Kaz. G10 26
Turginovo, Russia E19 22
Turgoš, Russia B18 22
Turgutlu, Tur. K11 20
Türi, Est. C8 22
Turia, stm., Spain F11 16
Turimiquire, Cerro, mtn., Ven. B11 84
Turin, Alta., Can. E4 98
Turin see Torino, Italy D2 18
Turin, Ga., U.S. C2 117
Turinsk, Russia F10 26
Turka, Ukr. F23 10
Turkestan, Kaz. I11 26
Túrkeve, Hung. H20 10
Turkey, Tx., U.S. B2 150
Turkey (Türkiye), ctry., Asia H15 4
Turkey, stm., Ia., U.S. B6 122
Turkey Creek, La., U.S. D3 125
Turkey Creek, stm., Ne., U.S. D8 134
Turkey Creek, stm., Ok., U.S. A3 143
Turkey Point, c., Md., U.S. B5 127
Turkish Republic of Northern Cyprus see Cyprus, North, ctry., Asia H14 4
Turkmenistan, ctry., Asia I9 26
Turkmeniya see Turkmenistan, ctry., Asia I9 26
Turks and Caicos Islands, dep., N.A. D9 94
Turks Island Passage, strt., T./C. Is. D9 94
Turks Islands, is., T./C. Is. D9 94
Turku (Åbo), Fin. K18 6
Turley, Ok., U.S. A6 143
Turlock, Ca., U.S. D3 112
Turmalina, Braz. D7 79
Turnbull, Mount, mtn., Az., U.S. D5 110
Turneffe Islands, is., Belize I16 90
Turner, Me., U.S. D2 126
Turner, Mt., U.S. B8 133
Turner, Or., U.S. C4 144
Turner, co., Ga., U.S. E3 117
Turner, co., S.D., U.S. D8 148
Turner Mountain, hill, Ct., U.S. C1 114
Turners Falls, Ma., U.S. A2 128
Turner Valley, Alta., Can. D3 98
Turney, Mo., U.S. B3 132
Turnhout, Bel. F6 12
Türnitz, Aus. H15 10
Turnor Lake, l., Sask., Can. m7 105
Turnu Măgurele, Rom. F8 20
Turon, Ks., U.S. E5 123
Turpan, China C4 30
Turpan Pendi, depr., China C4 30
Turpin, Ok., U.S. e10 143
Turquino, Pico, mtn., Cuba E6 94
Turrell, Ar., U.S. B5 111
Turret Peak, mtn., Az., U.S. C4 110
Turrialba, C.R. H11 92
Turrialba, Volcán, vol., C.R. G11 92
Turriff, Scot., U.K. D11 8
Turrubares, Cerro, mtn., C.R. H10 92
Turtle Creek, N.B., Can. D5 101
Turtle Creek, Pa., U.S. k14 145
Turtle Flambeau Flowage, res., Wi., U.S. B3 156
Turtleford, Sask., Can. D1 105
Turtle Lake, N.D., U.S. B5 141
Turtle Lake, Wi., U.S. C1 156
Turtle Lake, l., Sask., Can. D1 105
Turtle Mountain Indian Reservation, N.D., U.S. A6 141
Turton, S.D., U.S. B7 148
Turu, stm., Russia D12 28
Turuchan, stm., Russia D9 28
Turun-Porin lääni, prov., Fin. K18 6
Turvo, Braz. E14 80
Turvo, stm., Braz. F4 79
Turvo, stm., Braz. D3 79
Tuscaloosa, Al., U.S. B2 108
Tuscaloosa, co., Al., U.S. B2 108
Tuscany see Toscana, prov., Italy F5 18
Tuscarawas, co., Oh., U.S. B4 142
Tuscarawas, stm., Oh., U.S. B4 142
Tuscarora, Nv., U.S. B5 135
Tuscarora Indian Reservation, N.Y., U.S. B2 139
Tuscarora Mountain, mtn., Pa., U.S. F6 145
Tuscarora Mountains, mts., Nv., U.S. B5 135
Tuscola, Il., U.S. D5 120
Tuscola, Tx., U.S. C3 150
Tuscola, co., Mi., U.S. E7 129
Tusculum College, Tn., U.S. C11 149
Tuscumbia, Al., U.S. A2 108
Tushka, Ok., U.S. C5 143
Tuskegee, Al., U.S. C4 108
Tusket, N.S., Can. F4 101
Tusket, stm., N.S., Can. E4 101
Tustumena Lake, l., Ak., U.S. g16 109
Tutajev, Russia D22 22
Tutang, China F5 34
Tuticorin, India H5 46
Tutóia, Braz. D10 76
Tutrakan, Bul. E10 20
Tuttle, N.D., U.S. B6 141
Tuttle, Ok., U.S. B4 143
Tuttle Creek Dam, Ks., U.S. C7 123
Tuttle Creek Lake, res., Ks., U.S. C7 123
Tutupaca, Volcán, vol., Peru G6 82
Tututalak Mountain, mtn., Ak., U.S. B7 109
Tutwiler, Ms., U.S. A3 131
Tuva, state, Russia G16 26
Tuvalu, ctry., Oc. G24 2
Ţuwayq, Jabal, mts., Sau. Ar. D4 47
Tuxedo, N.C., U.S. f10 140
Tuxedo Park, De., U.S. i7 115
Tuxford, Sask., Can. G3 105
Tuxpan, Mex. G11 90
Tuxpan, Mex. G7 90
Tuxtepec, Mex. H11 90
Tuxtla Gutiérrez, Mex. I13 90
Tuy, stm., Ven. B9 84
Tuy An, Viet. H10 40
Tuyen Quang, Viet. D8 40
Tuy Hoa, Viet. H10 40
Tuz Gölü, l., Tur. H14 4
Tuzigoot National Monument, Az., U.S. C4 110
Ţūz Khurmātū, Iraq D8 48
Tuzla, Bos. E2 20
Tuzly, Ukr. D14 20
Tver' (Kalinin), Russia E18 22
Tweed, Ont., Can. C7 103
Tweed, stm., U.K. F11 8
Tweed Heads, Austl. G10 70
Tweedsmuir Provincial Park, B.C., Can. C4 99
Tweedy Mountain, mtn., Mt., U.S. E4 133
Twee Rivieren, S. Afr. F5 66
Twelve Mile, In., U.S. C5 121
Twelvepole Creek, stm., W.V., U.S. C2 155
Twelvepole Creek, East Fork, stm., W.V., U.S. D2 155
Twelvepole Creek, West Fork, stm., W.V., U.S. D2 155
Twentymile Creek, stm., W.V., U.S. C3 155
Twentynine Palms, Ca., U.S. E5 112
Twentynine Palms Marine Corps Base, mil., Ca., U.S. E5 112
Twiggs, co., Ga., U.S. D3 117
Twillingate, Newf., Can. D4 102
Twin Bridges, Mt., U.S. E4 133
Twin Buttes, mtn., Or., U.S. C4 144
Twin Buttes Reservoir, res., Tx., U.S. D2 150
Twin City, Ga., U.S. D4 117
Twin Creek, stm., Oh., U.S. C1 142
Twin Falls, Id., U.S. G4 119
Twin Falls, co., Id., U.S. G4 119
Twin Knolls, Az., U.S. m9 110
Twin Lakes, Ga., U.S. F3 117
Twin Lakes, In., U.S. B5 121
Twin Lakes, Wi., U.S. F5 156
Twin Lakes, l., Ct., U.S. A2 114
Twin Lakes, l., Ia., U.S. B3 122
Twin Lakes, l., Me., U.S. C4 126
Twin Lakes Mountain, mtn., N.Y., U.S. B6 139
Twin Mountain, N.H., U.S. B3 136
Twin Mountains, mtn., Wy., U.S. E7 157
Twin Peaks, mts., Id., U.S. E4 119
Twin Rivers, N.J., U.S. C4 137
Twin Rocks, Pa., U.S. F4 145
Twinsburg, Oh., U.S. A4 142
Twin Valley, Mn., U.S. C2 130
Twisp, Wa., U.S. A5 154
Two Butte Creek, stm., Co., U.S. D8 113
Twofold Bay, b., Austl. K8 70
Twoforks, stm., Sask., Can. C2 105
Two Harbors, Mn., U.S. C7 130
Two Hills, Alta., Can. C5 98
Two Mile Beach, N.J., U.S. F3 137
Two Prairie, Bayou, stm., Ar., U.S. h11 111
Two Rivers, Wi., U.S. D6 156
Two Rivers, North Branch, stm., Mn., U.S. B2 130
Two Rivers, South Branch, stm., Mn., U.S. B2 130
Tyachiv, Ukr. A7 20
Tybee Island, Ga., U.S. D6 117
Tychy, Pol. E18 10
Tygart Lake, res., W.V., U.S. B5 155
Tygart River, Falls of the, wtfl, W.V., U.S. k10 155
Tygarts Creek, stm., Ky., U.S. B7 124
Tygart Valley, stm., W.V., U.S. B4 155
Tyger, stm., S.C., U.S. B4 147
Tygh Valley, Or., U.S. B5 144
Tyler, Al., U.S. C3 108
Tyler, Mn., U.S. F2 130
Tyler, Tx., U.S. C5 150
Tyler, co., Tx., U.S. D5 150
Tyler, co., W.V., U.S. B4 155
Tyler, Lake, res., Tx., U.S. C5 150
Tyler Branch, stm., Vt., U.S. B3 152
Tyler Heights, W.V., U.S. C3 155
Tylertown, Ms., U.S. D3 131
Tym, stm., Russia E8 28
Tymochtee Creek, stm., Oh., U.S. B2 142
Tyndall, Man., Can. D3 100
Tyndall, S.D., U.S. E8 148
Tyndall Air Force Base, mil., Fl., U.S. u16 116
Tyndinskij, Russia F16 28
Tyne, stm., Eng., U.K. G11 8
Tynemouth, Eng., U.K. F12 8
Tyner, In., U.S. B5 121
Tyner, Ky., U.S. C6 124
Tyne Valley, P.E.I., Can. C6 101
Týn nad Vltavou, Czech Rep. F14 10
Tyonek, Ak., U.S. C9 109
Tyre see Şūr, Leb. B4 50
Tyrma, Russia G18 28

W

Name | Map Ref. | Page

Walhonding, stm., Oh., U.S. B3 142
Walker, Ia., U.S. B6 122
Walker, La., U.S. g10 125
Walker, Mi., U.S. E5 129
Walker, Mn., U.S. C4 130
Walker, Mo., U.S. D3 132
Walker, co., Al., U.S. B2 108
Walker, co., Ga., U.S. B1 117
Walker, co., Tx., U.S. D5 150
Walker, stm., Nv., U.S. D3 135
Walker Lake, l., Man., Can. B3 100
Walker Lake, l., Nv., U.S. E3 135
Walker Mountain, mtn., Ga., U.S. B3 117
Walker Mountain, mtn., Va., U.S. C1 153
Walker River Indian Reservation, Nv., U.S. D3 135
Walker Springs, Al., U.S. D2 108
Walkersville, Md., U.S. B3 127
Walkerton, Ont., Can. C3 103
Walkerton, In., U.S. B5 121
Walkertown, N.C., U.S. A2 140
Walkerville, Mt., U.S. D4 133
Wall, S.D., U.S. D3 148
Wallace, N.S., Can. D6 101
Wallace, Id., U.S. B3 119
Wallace, Ne., U.S. D4 134
Wallace, N.C., U.S. B4 140
Wallace, S.D., U.S. B8 148
Wallace, W.V., U.S. B4 155
Wallace, co., Ks., U.S. D2 123
Wallaceburg, Ont., Can. E2 103
Wallace Lake, res., La., U.S. B2 125
Wallacetown, Ont., Can. E3 103
Walland, Tn., U.S. D10 149
Wallangarra, Austl. G9 70
Wallaroo, Austl. I2 70
Walla Walla, Wa., U.S. C7 154
Walla Walla, co., Wa., U.S. C7 154
Walla Walla, stm., U.S. C7 154
Walled Lake, Mi., U.S. o15 129
Wallen, In., U.S. B7 121
Wallenpaupack, Lake, l., Pa., U.S. D11 145
Wallen Ridge, mtn., Tn., U.S. C10 149
Waller, Tx., U.S. q14 150
Waller, co., Tx., U.S. E4 150
Wallingford, Ct., U.S. D4 114
Wallingford, Vt., U.S. E3 152
Walling Mountain, mtn., Ma., U.S. B1 128
Wallington, N.J., U.S. h8 137
Wallis, Tx., U.S. E4 150
Wallis and Futuna, dep., Oc. G1 2
Wallisellen, Switz. D10 13
Wallis Sands, N.H., U.S. D5 136
Wallkill, N.Y., U.S. D6 139
Wallkill, stm., N.Y., U.S. D6 139
Wall Lake, Ia., U.S. B2 122
Wall Lake, l., Ia., U.S. B4 122
Walloomsac, stm., U.S. F2 152
Walloon Lake, l., Mi., U.S. C6 129
Wallowa, Or., U.S. B9 144
Wallowa, co., Or., U.S. B9 144
Wallowa Mountains, mts., Or., U.S. B9 144
Walls, Ms., U.S. A3 131
Wallsburg, Ut., U.S. C4 151
Wallula, Lake, res., U.S. C7 154
Wallum Lake, l., U.S. A1 146
Walnut, Il., U.S. B4 120
Walnut, Ia., U.S. C2 122
Walnut, Ks., U.S. E8 123
Walnut, Ms., U.S. A5 131
Walnut, N.C., U.S. f10 140
Walnut, stm., Ks., U.S. E6 123
Walnut Canyon National Monument, Az., U.S. B4 110
Walnut Cove, N.C., U.S. A2 140
Walnut Creek, Ca., U.S. h8 112
Walnut Creek, stm., Ks., U.S. D4 123
Walnut Grove, Al., U.S. A3 108
Walnut Grove, Mn., U.S. F3 130
Walnut Grove, Ms., U.S. C4 131
Walnut Grove, Mo., U.S. D4 132
Walnut Hill, Me., U.S. g7 126
Walnut Hill, hill, Ma., U.S. A2 128
Walnut Mountain, hill, Ct., U.S. B3 114
Walnutport, Pa., U.S. E10 145
Walnut Ridge, Ar., U.S. A5 111
Walpeup, Austl. J5 70
Walpole, Ma., U.S. B5 128
Walpole, N.H., U.S. D2 136
Walsenburg, Co., U.S. D6 113
Walsh, Alta., Can. E5 98
Walsh, Co., U.S. D8 113
Walsh, co., N.D., U.S. A8 141
Walsrode, Ger. C9 10
Walterboro, S.C., U.S. F6 147
Walter F. George Dam, U.S. D4 108
Walter F. George Lake, res., U.S. D4 108
Walterhill, Tn., U.S. B5 149
Walters, Ok., U.S. C3 143
Walters Falls, Ont., Can. C4 103
Waltershausen, Ger. E10 10
Waltersville, Ms., U.S. C3 131
Walterville, Or., U.S. C4 144
Walthall, Ms., U.S. B4 131
Walthall, co., Ms., U.S. D3 131
Waltham, Ma., U.S. B5 128
Waltham, Mn., U.S. G6 130
Walthill, Ne., U.S. B9 134
Walthourville, Ga., U.S. E5 117
Walton, N.S., Can. D6 101
Walton, Ont., Can. D3 103
Walton, In., U.S. C5 121
Walton, Ks., U.S. D6 123
Walton, Ky., U.S. B5 124
Walton, Ne., U.S. h11 134
Walton, N.Y., U.S. C5 139
Walton, W.V., U.S. C3 155
Walton, co., Fl., U.S. u15 116
Walton, co., Ga., U.S. C3 117
Waltonville, Il., U.S. E4 120
Walvis Bay, Nmb. D2 66
Walworth, Wi., U.S. F5 156
Walworth, co., S.D., U.S. B5 148
Walworth, co., Wi., U.S. F5 156
Wamac, Il., U.S. E4 120
Wamba, Nig. G14 64
Wamba, stm., Afr. C3 58
Wamego, Ks., U.S. C7 123
Wamesit, Ma., U.S. A5 128
Wampú, Hond. B9 92
Wampú, stm., Hond. B9 92
Wampum, Pa., U.S. E1 145
Wamsutter, Wy., U.S. E5 157
Wanaaring, Austl. G6 70
Wanaka, N.Z. F2 72
Wanamie, Pa., U.S. D9 145
Wanamingo, Mn., U.S. F6 130
Wan'an, China I3 34
Wanapum Dam, Wa., U.S. C6 154
Wanapum Lake, res., Wa., U.S. B6 154
Wanaque, N.J., U.S. A4 137
Wanaque Reservoir, res., N.J., U.S. A4 137
Wanatah, In., U.S. B4 121
Wanbi, Austl. J4 70
Wanblee, S.D., U.S. D4 148
Wanchese, N.C., U.S. B7 140
Wandering River, Alta., Can. B4 98
Wando, S. Kor. I14 32
Wando, stm., S.C., U.S. F8 147
Wandoan, Austl. F8 70
Wando Woods, S.C., U.S. k11 147
Wanette, Ok., U.S. C4 143
Wanfoxia, China C8 30
Wanganui, N.Z. C5 72
Wangaratta, Austl. K7 70
Wangary, Austl. J1 70
Wangdu Phodrang, Bhu. G13 44
Wanghu, China D1 32
Wanghuzhuang, China E5 32
Wangjiang, China E5 34
Wangpan Yang, b., China E11 30
Wangsi, China E4 32
Wangtuan, China F10 32
Wangzhong, China H4 32
Wangzhuangbu, China D1 32
Wanham, Alta., Can. B1 98
Wani, India B5 46
Wanigela, Pap. N. Gui. A9 68
Wānkāner, India I4 44
Wanli, China D9 34
Wanneroo, Austl. F3 68
Wanship, Ut., U.S. C4 151
Wanxian, China E8 30
Wanzai, China G3 34
Wanzleben, Ger. C11 10
Wapakoneta, Oh., U.S. B1 142
Wapanucka, Ok., U.S. C5 143
Wapato, Wa., U.S. C5 154
Wapawekka Lake, l., Sask., Can. C3 105
Wapella, Sask., Can. G5 105
Wapella, Il., U.S. C5 120
Wapello, Ia., U.S. C6 122
Wapello, co., Ia., U.S. C5 122
Wapiti, Wy., U.S. B3 157
Wapiti, stm., Can. B1 98
Wapiti Ridge, mtn., Wy., U.S. B3 157
Wappapello, Mo., U.S. E7 132
Wappapello, Lake, res., Mo., U.S. D7 132
Wappingers Falls, N.Y., U.S. D7 139
Wapsipinicon, stm., Ia., U.S. B6 122
Wapske, N.B., Can. C2 101
Waqqās, Jord. C5 50
War, W.V., U.S. D3 155
Waramaug, Lake, l., Ct., U.S. C2 114
Warangal, India C5 46
Waratah, Austl. M6 70
Warbreccan, Austl. E5 70
Warburg, Alta., Can. C3 98
Warburg, Ger. D9 10
Warburton, Austl. K6 70
Warburton Creek, stm., Austl. E7 68
Ward, Al., U.S. C1 108
Ward, Ar., U.S. B4 111
Ward, co., N.D., U.S. A4 141
Ward, co., Tx., U.S. D1 150
Ward, stm., Austl. E7 70
Wardell, Mo., U.S. E8 132
Warden, Que., Can. D5 104
Warden, Wa., U.S. C6 154
Wardha, India B5 46
Wardha, stm., India C5 46
Wardlow, Alta., Can. D5 98
Ward Mountain, mtn., Mt., U.S. D2 133
Wardner, B.C., Can. E10 99
Wardner, Id., U.S. B2 119
Wardsboro, Vt., U.S. E3 152
Wardsville, Ont., Can. E3 103
Ware, Ma., U.S. B3 128
Ware, co., Ga., U.S. E4 117
Ware, stm., Ma., U.S. B3 128
War Eagle Creek, stm., Ar., U.S. A2 111
War Eagle Mountain, mtn., Id., U.S. G2 119
Waregem, Bel. G3 12
Wareham, Eng., U.K. K11 8
Wareham, Ma., U.S. C6 128
Warehouse Point, Ct., U.S. B5 114
Waremme (Borgworm), Bel. G7 12
Waren, Ger. B12 10
Warendorf, Ger. D7 10
Waresboro, Ga., U.S. E4 117
Ware Shoals, S.C., U.S. C3 147
Waretown, N.J., U.S. D4 137
Warfield, B.C., Can. E9 99
Warfield, Ky., U.S. C7 124
Wargla, Alg. E13 62
Warialda, Austl. G9 70
Warin Chamrap, Thai. G8 40
Warkworth, Ont., Can. C7 103
Warman, Sask., Can. E2 105
Warmbad, Nmb. G4 66
Warmbad, S. Afr. E9 66
Warm Beach, Wa., U.S. A3 154
Warminster, Eng., U.K. J11 8
Warminster, Pa., U.S. F11 145
Warm Springs, Ga., U.S. D2 117
Warm Springs, Or., U.S. C5 144
Warm Springs, Va., U.S. B3 153
Warm Springs Indian Reservation, Or., U.S. C5 144
Warm Springs Reservoir, res., Or., U.S. D8 144
Warner, Alta., Can. E4 98
Warner, N.H., U.S. D3 136
Warner, Ok., U.S. B6 143
Warner, S.D., U.S. B7 148
Warner, stm., N.H., U.S. D3 136
Warner Mountain, mtn., Ma., U.S. B1 128
Warner Mountains, mts., Ca., U.S. B3 112
Warner Peak, mtn., Or., U.S. E7 144
Warner Robins, Ga., U.S. D3 117
Warnes, Arg. H8 80
Warnes, Bol. G10 82
Warracknabeal, Austl. K5 70
Warr Acres, Ok., U.S. B4 143
Warragul, Austl. L6 70
Warrego, stm., Austl. G6 70
Warrego Range, mts., Austl. E7 70
Warren, Austl. H7 70
Warren, Ont., Can. A4 103
Warren, Ar., U.S. D3 111
Warren, Il., U.S. A4 120
Warren, In., U.S. C7 121
Warren, Me., U.S. D3 126
Warren, Ma., U.S. B3 128
Warren, Mi., U.S. F7 129
Warren, Mn., U.S. B2 130
Warren, N.H., U.S. C3 136
Warren, Oh., U.S. A5 142
Warren, Or., U.S. B4 144
Warren, Pa., U.S. C3 145
Warren, R.I., U.S. D5 146
Warren, Tx., U.S. D5 150
Warren, Vt., U.S. C3 152
Warren, co., Ga., U.S. C4 117
Warren, co., Il., U.S. C3 120
Warren, co., In., U.S. D3 121
Warren, co., Ia., U.S. C4 122
Warren, co., Ky., U.S. C3 124
Warren, co., Ms., U.S. C3 131
Warren, co., Mo., U.S. C6 132
Warren, co., N.J., U.S. B3 137
Warren, co., N.Y., U.S. B7 139
Warren, co., N.C., U.S. A4 140
Warren, co., Oh., U.S. C1 142
Warren, co., Pa., U.S. C3 145
Warren, co., Tn., U.S. D8 149
Warren, co., Va., U.S. B4 153
Warren, stm., U.S. D5 146
Warren Park, In., U.S. k10 121
Warren Peaks, mts., Wy., U.S. B8 157
Warrens, Wi., U.S. D3 156
Warrensburg, Il., U.S. D4 120
Warrensburg, Mo., U.S. C4 132
Warrensburg, N.Y., U.S. B7 139
Warrensville Heights, Oh., U.S. h9 142
Warrenton, S. Afr. G7 66
Warrenton, Ga., U.S. C4 117
Warrenton, Mo., U.S. C6 132
Warrenton, N.C., U.S. A4 140
Warrenton, Or., U.S. A3 144
Warrenton, Va., U.S. B5 153
Warrenville, Il., U.S. k8 120
Warrenville, S.C., U.S. D4 147
Warri, Nig. I12 64
Warrick, co., In., U.S. H3 121
Warrington, Fl., U.S. u14 116
Warrior, Al., U.S. B3 108
Warrior Lake, res., Al., U.S. C2 108
Warrior Mountain, mtn., Md., U.S. k13 127
Warrnambool, Austl. L5 70
Warroad, Mn., U.S. B3 130
Warsaw, Ont., Can. C6 103
Warsaw see Warszawa, Pol. C21 10
Warsaw, Il., U.S. C2 120
Warsaw, In., U.S. B6 121
Warsaw, Ky., U.S. B5 124
Warsaw, Mo., U.S. C4 132
Warsaw, N.Y., U.S. C2 139
Warsaw, N.C., U.S. B4 140
Warsaw, N.D., U.S. A8 141
Warsaw, Oh., U.S. B3 142
Warsaw, Va., U.S. C6 153
Warspite, Alta., Can. B4 98
Warszawa (Warsaw), Pol. C21 10
Warta, stm., Pol. C15 10
Wartburg, Tn., U.S. C9 149
Wartburg, hist., Ger. E10 10
Warthen, Ga., U.S. C4 117
Wartrace, Tn., U.S. B5 149
Warud, India B5 46
Warunta, Laguna de, l., Hond. B10 92
Warwick, Austl. G10 70
Warwick, Ont., Can. D3 103
Warwick, Que., Can. D6 104
Warwick, Eng., U.K. I12 8
Warwick, Ga., U.S. E3 117
Warwick, Md., U.S. B6 127
Warwick, N.Y., U.S. D6 139
Warwick, N.D., U.S. B7 141
Warwick, R.I., U.S. D4 146
Warwick Channel, strt., Austl. B7 68
Warwick Dam, Ga., U.S. E3 117
Warwickshire, co., Eng., U.K. I12 8
Wasaga Beach, Ont., Can. C4 103
Wasagu, Nig. F12 64
Wasatch, co., Ut., U.S. C4 151
Wasatch Plateau, plat., Ut., U.S. D4 151
Wascana Creek, stm., Sask., Can. G3 105
Wasco, Ca., U.S. E4 112
Wasco, Or., U.S. B6 144
Wasco, co., Or., U.S. B5 144
Waseca, Sask., Can. D1 105
Waseca, Mn., U.S. F5 130
Waseca, co., Mn., U.S. F5 130
Washademoak Lake, l., N.B., Can. D4 101
Washago, Ont., Can. C5 103
Washakie, co., Wy., U.S. C5 157
Washakie Needles, mts., Wy., U.S. C3 157
Washburn, Il., U.S. C4 120
Washburn, Ia., U.S. B5 122
Washburn, Me., U.S. B4 126
Washburn, Mo., U.S. E4 132
Washburn, N.D., U.S. B5 141
Washburn, Tn., U.S. C10 149
Washburn, Wi., U.S. B3 156
Washburn, co., Wi., U.S. C2 156
Washburn, Mount, mtn., Wy., U.S. B2 157
Washington, Ar., U.S. D2 111
Washington, Ct., U.S. C2 114
Washington, D.C., U.S. C3 127
Washington, Ga., U.S. C4 117
Washington, Il., U.S. C4 120
Washington, In., U.S. G3 121
Washington, Ia., U.S. C6 122
Washington, Ks., U.S. C6 123
Washington, Ky., U.S. B6 124
Washington, La., U.S. D3 125
Washington, Ms., U.S. D2 131
Washington, Mo., U.S. C6 132
Washington, Ne., U.S. g12 134
Washington, N.J., U.S. B3 137
Washington, N.C., U.S. B5 140
Washington, Ok., U.S. B4 143
Washington, Pa., U.S. F1 145
Washington, Tn., U.S. D9 149
Washington, Ut., U.S. F2 151
Washington, Vt., U.S. C4 152
Washington, W.V., U.S. B3 155
Washington, co., Al., U.S. D1 108
Washington, co., Ar., U.S. A1 111
Washington, co., Co., U.S. B7 113
Washington, co., Fl., U.S. u16 116
Washington, co., Ga., U.S. C4 117
Washington, co., Id., U.S. E2 119
Washington, co., Il., U.S. E4 120
Washington, co., In., U.S. G5 121
Washington, co., Ia., U.S. C6 122
Washington, co., Ks., U.S. C6 123
Washington, co., Ky., U.S. C4 124
Washington, co., La., U.S. D5 125
Washington, co., Me., U.S. D5 126
Washington, co., Md., U.S. A2 127
Washington, co., Mn., U.S. E6 130
Washington, co., Ms., U.S. B3 131
Washington, co., Mo., U.S. D7 132
Washington, co., Ne., U.S. C9 134
Washington, co., N.Y., U.S. B7 139
Washington, co., N.C., U.S. B6 140
Washington, co., Oh., U.S. C4 142
Washington, co., Ok., U.S. A6 143
Washington, co., Or., U.S. B3 144
Washington, co., Pa., U.S. F1 145
Washington, co., R.I., U.S. E2 146
Washington, co., Tn., U.S. C11 149
Washington, co., Tx., U.S. D4 150
Washington, co., Ut., U.S. F2 151
Washington, co., Vt., U.S. C3 152
Washington, co., Va., U.S. f9 153
Washington, co., Wi., U.S. E5 156
Washington, state, U.S. B5 154
Washington, Lake, l., Fl., U.S. D6 116
Washington, Lake, l., Mn., U.S. E4 130
Washington, Lake, l., Ms., U.S. B3 131
Washington, Lake, l., Wa., U.S. e11 154
Washington, Mount, mtn., N.H., U.S. B4 136
Washington Court House, Oh., U.S. C2 142
Washington Depot, Ct., U.S. C2 114
Washington Island, i., Wi., U.S. C7 156
Washington Park, Il., U.S. E3 120
Washington Terrace, Ut., U.S. B4 151
Washita, co., Ok., U.S. B2 143
Washita, stm., Ok., U.S. C4 143
Washoe, co., Nv., U.S. C2 135
Washoe City, Nv., U.S. D2 135
Washougal, Wa., U.S. D3 154
Washow Bay, b., Man., Can. D3 100
Washta, Ia., U.S. B2 122
Washtenaw, co., Mi., U.S. F7 129
Washtucna, Wa., U.S. C7 154
Wasilków, Pol. B23 10
Wasilla, Ak., U.S. C10 109
Waskada, Man., Can. E1 100
Waskatenau, Alta., Can. B4 98
Waskesiu Lake, l., Sask., Can. D2 105
Waskom, Tx., U.S. C5 150
Waspam, Nic. C11 92
Waspuk, stm., Nic. C10 92
Wasque Point, c., Ma., U.S. D7 128
Wassaw Sound, strt., Ga., U.S. E6 117
Wassen, Switz. E10 13
Wassenaar, Neth. D5 12
Wasserafingen, Ger. G10 10
Wasserbillig, Lux. I10 12
Wasserburg am Inn, Ger. G12 10
Wasson, Il., U.S. F5 120
Wassookeag, Lake, l., Me., U.S. C3 126
Wassou, Gui. F3 64
Wassuk Range, mts., Nv., U.S. E3 135
Wassy, Fr. D11 14
Wasta, S.D., U.S. C3 148
Wataga, Il., U.S. B3 120
Watampone, Indon. F7 38
Watapi Lake, l., Sask., Can. B6 98
Watatic, Mount, mtn., Ma., U.S. A4 128
Watauga, Tn., U.S. C11 149
Watauga, co., N.C., U.S. A1 140
Watauga, stm., Tn., U.S. C12 149
Watauga Lake, res., Tn., U.S. C12 149
Watchaug Pond, l., R.I., U.S. F2 146
Watch Hill, R.I., U.S. G1 146
Watch Hill Point, c., R.I., U.S. G1 146
Watchung, N.J., U.S. B4 137
Waterberg, Nmb. C3 66
Waterberg Plateau Park, Nmb. C3 66
Waterboro, Me., U.S. E2 126
Waterbury, Ct., U.S. C3 114
Waterbury, Vt., U.S. C3 152
Waterbury Center, Vt., U.S. C3 152
Waterbury Reservoir, res., Vt., U.S. C3 152
Wateree, stm., S.C., U.S. D6 147
Wateree Lake, res., S.C., U.S. C6 147
Waterflow, N.M., U.S. A1 138
Waterford, Ire. I6 8
Waterford, Ct., U.S. D7 114
Waterford, In., U.S. A4 121
Waterford, Ms., U.S. A4 131
Waterford, N.Y., U.S. C7 139
Waterford, Oh., U.S. C4 142
Waterford, Pa., U.S. C2 145
Waterford, Va., U.S. A5 153
Waterford, Wi., U.S. F5 156
Waterford, co., Ire. I6 8
Waterford Mills, In., U.S. A6 121
Waterford Works, N.J., U.S. D3 137
Waterhen Lake, l., Man., Can. C2 100
Waterloo, Bel. G5 12
Waterloo, Ont., Can. D4 103
Waterloo, Que., Can. D5 104
Waterloo, Al., U.S. A1 108
Waterloo, Il., U.S. E3 120
Waterloo, In., U.S. B7 121
Waterloo, Ia., U.S. B5 122
Waterloo, Ne., U.S. g12 134
Waterloo, N.Y., U.S. C4 139
Waterloo, Wi., U.S. E5 156
Waterman, Il., U.S. B5 120
Waterman Reservoir, res., R.I., U.S. B3 146
Waterproof, La., U.S. C4 125
Watersmeet, Mi., U.S. n12 129
Waterton Lakes National Park, Alta., Can. E3 98
Waterton Park, Alta., Can. E4 98
Watertown, Ct., U.S. C3 114
Watertown, Fl., U.S. B4 116
Watertown, Ma., U.S. g11 128
Watertown, N.Y., U.S. B5 139
Watertown, S.D., U.S. C8 148
Watertown, Tn., U.S. A5 149
Watertown, Wi., U.S. E5 156
Water Valley, Ky., U.S. f9 124
Water Valley, Ms., U.S. A4 131
Water Village, N.H., U.S. C4 136
Waterville, N.S., Can. D5 101
Waterville, Ks., U.S. C7 123
Waterville, Me., U.S. D3 126
Waterville, Mn., U.S. F5 130
Waterville, N.Y., U.S. C5 139
Waterville, Oh., U.S. A2 142
Waterville, Wa., U.S. B5 154
Watervliet, Mi., U.S. F4 129
Watervliet, N.Y., U.S. C7 139
Watford, Ont., Can. E3 103
Watford City, N.D., U.S. B2 141
Wathena, Ks., U.S. C9 123
Watino, Alta., Can. B2 98
Watkins, Mn., U.S. E4 130
Watkins Glen, N.Y., U.S. C4 139
Watkinsville, Ga., U.S. C3 117
Watling Island see San Salvador, i., Bah. B7 94
Watonga, Ok., U.S. B3 143
Watonwan, co., Mn., U.S. F4 130
Watonwan, stm., Mn., U.S. G4 130
Watova, Ok., U.S. A6 143
Watrous, Sask., Can. F3 105
Watrous, N.M., U.S. B5 138
Watseka, Il., U.S. C6 120
Watson, Sask., Can. E3 105
Watson, Ar., U.S. D4 111
Watson, Il., U.S. D5 120
Watson, In., U.S. H6 121
Watson, Ok., U.S. C7 143
Watson Lake, Yukon, Can. D7 96
Watsontown, Pa., U.S. D8 145
Watsonville, Ca., U.S. D3 112
Wattenberg, Co., U.S. A6 113
Wattens, Aus. H11 10
Wattensaw Bayou, stm., Ar., U.S. C4 111
Wattenwil, Switz. E8 13
Watts (part of Los Angeles), Ca., U.S. n12 112
Watts, Ok., U.S. A7 143
Watts Bar Dam, Tn., U.S. D9 149
Watts Bar Lake, res., Tn., U.S. D9 149
Wattsville, Al., U.S. B3 108
Wattsville, S.C., U.S. B4 147
Wattwil, Switz. D11 13
Watubela, Kepulauan, is., Indon. F9 38
Watuppa Pond, l., Ma., U.S. C5 128
Watzmann, mtn., Ger. H12 10
Waubaushene, Ont., Can. C5 103
Waubay, S.D., U.S. B8 148
Waubay Lake, l., S.D., U.S. B8 148
Waubun, Mn., U.S. C3 130
Wauchope, Austl. H10 70
Wauchula, Fl., U.S. E5 116
Waucoma, Ia., U.S. A5 122
Wauconda, Il., U.S. h8 120
Waugh Mountain, mtn., Id., U.S. D4 119
Waukaringa, Austl. I3 70
Waukee, Ia., U.S. C4 122
Waukegan, Il., U.S. A6 120
Waukesha, Wi., U.S. F5 156
Waukesha, co., Wi., U.S. E5 156
Waukewan, Lake, l., N.H., U.S. C3 136
Waukomis, Ok., U.S. A4 143
Waukon, Ia., U.S. A6 122
Wauna, Wa., U.S. f10 154
Waunakee, Wi., U.S. E4 156
Wauneta, Ne., U.S. D4 134
Waungumbaug Lake, l., Ct., U.S. B6 114
Waupaca, Wi., U.S. D4 156
Waupaca, co., Wi., U.S. D5 156
Waupun, Wi., U.S. E5 156
Wauregan, Ct., U.S. C8 114
Waurika, Ok., U.S. C4 143
Waurika Lake, res., Ok., U.S. C3 143
Wausa, Ne., U.S. B8 134
Wausau, Wi., U.S. D4 156
Wausau, Lake, res., Wi., U.S. D4 156
Wausaukee, Wi., U.S. C6 156
Wauseon, Oh., U.S. A1 142
Waushara, co., Wi., U.S. D4 156
Wautoma, Wi., U.S. D4 156
Wauwatosa, Wi., U.S. m12 156
Wauzeka, Wi., U.S. E3 156
Wave Hill, Austl. C6 68
Waveland, In., U.S. E3 121
Waveland, Ms., U.S. E4 131
Waverley, N.S., Can. E6 101
Waverly, Al., U.S. C4 108
Waverly, Ga., U.S. E5 117
Waverly, Il., U.S. D4 120
Waverly, In., U.S. E5 121
Waverly, Ia., U.S. B5 122
Waverly, Ks., U.S. D8 123
Waverly, Ky., U.S. C2 124
Waverly, Mn., U.S. E5 130
Waverly, Mo., U.S. B4 132
Waverly, Ne., U.S. D9 134
Waverly, N.Y., U.S. C4 139
Waverly, Oh., U.S. C3 142
Waverly, Tn., U.S. A4 149
Waverly, Va., U.S. C5 153
Waverly, W.V., U.S. B3 155
Waverly Hall, Ga., U.S. D2 117
Wavre (Waver), Bel. G6 12
Wāw, Sud. N4 60
Wawa, Sud. G6 60
Wawa, stm., Nic. C11 92
Wawaka, In., U.S. B7 121
Wāw al-Kabīr, Libya C4 56
Wawanesa, Man., Can. E2 100
Wawasee, Lake, l., In., U.S. B6 121
Wawayanda Lake, l., N.J., U.S. A4 137
Wawayanda Mountain, mtn., U.S. A4 137
Wawota, Sask., Can. H4 105
Waxahachie, Tx., U.S. C4 150
Waxhaw, N.C., U.S. C2 140
Wayabula, Indon. E8 38
Wayagamac, Lac, l., Que., Can. B5 104
Waycross, Ga., U.S. E4 117
Wayland, Ia., U.S. C6 122
Wayland, Ky., U.S. C7 124
Wayland, Ma., U.S. g10 128
Wayland, Mi., U.S. F5 129
Wayland, Mo., U.S. A6 132
Wayland, N.Y., U.S. C3 139
Waylyn, S.C., U.S. k12 147
Waymart, Pa., U.S. C11 145
Wayne, Alta., Can. D4 98
Wayne, Mi., U.S. p15 129
Wayne, Ne., U.S. B8 134
Wayne, N.J., U.S. B4 137
Wayne, Oh., U.S. A2 142
Wayne, Ok., U.S. C4 143
Wayne, W.V., U.S. C2 155
Wayne, co., Ga., U.S. E5 117
Wayne, co., Il., U.S. E5 120
Wayne, co., In., U.S. E7 121
Wayne, co., Ia., U.S. D4 122
Wayne, co., Ky., U.S. D5 124
Wayne, co., Mi., U.S. F7 129
Wayne, co., Ms., U.S. D5 131
Wayne, co., Mo., U.S. D7 132
Wayne, co., Ne., U.S. B8 134
Wayne, co., N.Y., U.S. B3 139
Wayne, co., N.C., U.S. B4 140
Wayne, co., Oh., U.S. B4 142
Wayne, co., Pa., U.S. C11 145
Wayne, co., Tn., U.S. B4 149
Wayne, co., Ut., U.S. E4 151
Wayne, co., W.V., U.S. C2 155
Wayne City, Il., U.S. E5 120
Waynesboro, Ga., U.S. C4 117
Waynesboro, Ms., U.S. D5 131
Waynesboro, Pa., U.S. G6 145
Waynesboro, Tn., U.S. B4 149
Waynesboro, Va., U.S. B4 153
Waynesburg, Ky., U.S. C5 124
Waynesburg, Oh., U.S. B4 142
Waynesburg, Pa., U.S. G1 145
Waynesville, Ga., U.S. E5 117
Waynesville, Il., U.S. C4 120
Waynesville, Mo., U.S. D5 132
Waynesville, N.C., U.S. f10 140
Waynesville, Oh., U.S. C1 142
Waynetown, In., U.S. D3 121
Waynewood, Va., U.S. g12 153
Waynoka, Ok., U.S. A3 143
Wayside, Ms., U.S. B2 131
Wayzata, Mn., U.S. n11 130
Wāzah Khwāh, Afg. D3 44
Wāzin, Libya E16 62
Wazīrābād, Pak. D6 44
We, Pulau, i., Indon. L3 40
Weakley, co., Tn., U.S. A3 149
Weare, N.H., U.S. D3 136
Weatherford, Ok., U.S. B3 143
Weatherford, Tx., U.S. C4 150
Weatherly, Pa., U.S. E10 145
Weatogue, Ct., U.S. B4 114
Weaubleau, Mo., U.S. D4 132
Weaver, Al., U.S. B4 108
Weaver Mountains, mts., Az., U.S. C3 110
Weaverville, Ca., U.S. B2 112
Weaverville, N.C., U.S. f10 140
Webb, Sask., Can. G1 105
Webb, Al., U.S. D4 108
Webb, Ms., U.S. B3 131
Webb, co., Tx., U.S. F3 150
Webb City, Mo., U.S. D3 132
Webbers Falls, Ok., U.S. B6 143
Webberville, Mi., U.S. F6 129
Webb Hill, hill, Ma., U.S. B3 128
Webb Lake, l., Me., U.S. D2 126
Webbwood, Ont., Can. A3 103
Weber, co., Ut., U.S. B4 151
Weber City, Va., U.S. f9 153
Weberi Bekera, Eth. M10 60
Webster, Fl., U.S. D4 116
Webster, In., U.S. E8 121
Webster, Ma., U.S. B4 128
Webster, Mn., U.S. F5 130
Webster, N.Y., U.S. B3 139

Whit-Wino

Name — Map Ref. Page

White, stm., U.S. D5 148
White, stm., U.S. C7 151
White, stm., Az., U.S. D5 110
White, stm., In., U.S. H2 121
White, stm., Mi., U.S. E4 129
White, stm., Nv., U.S. E6 135
White, stm., Tx., U.S. C2 150
White, stm., Vt., U.S. D4 152
White, stm., Wa., U.S. B5 154
White, stm., Wa., U.S. B4 154
White, East Fork, stm., In., U.S. G5 121
White Bay, b., Newf., Can. D3 102
White Bear, stm., Newf., Can. E3 102
White Bear Lake, Mn., U.S. E5 130
White Bird, Id., U.S. D2 119
White Bluff, Tn., U.S. A4 149
White Breast Creek, stm., Ia., U.S. C4 122
White Butte, mtn., N.D., U.S. C2 141
White Cap Mountain, mtn., Me., U.S. C3 126
White Castle, La., U.S. D4 125
White Center, Wa., U.S. e11 154
White City, Fl., U.S. C1 116
White City, Ks., U.S. D7 123
White City, Or., U.S. E4 144
White Clay Creek, stm., U.S. A3 134
White Clay Creek, stm., De., U.S. B3 115
White Cliffs, Austl. H5 70
White Cloud, Ks., U.S. C8 123
White Cloud, Mi., U.S. E5 129
Whitecourt, Alta., Can. B3 98
White Creek, stm., U.S. E2 152
Whiteday, stm., W.V., U.S. h10 155
White Deer, Tx., U.S. B2 150
White Earth, Mn., U.S. C3 130
White Earth Indian Reservation, Mn., U.S. C3 130
White Earth Lake, l., Mn., U.S. C3 130
Whiteface, Tx., U.S. C1 150
Whiteface, stm., Mn., U.S. C6 130
Whiteface Mountain, mtn., N.Y., U.S. f11 139
White Face Mountain, mtn., Vt., U.S. B3 152
Whitefield, N.H., U.S. B3 136
Whitefield, Ok., U.S. B6 143
Whitefish, Mt., U.S. B2 133
Whitefish Bay, Wi., U.S. m12 156
Whitefish Bay, b., Mi., U.S. B6 129
Whitefish Falls, Ont., Can. A3 103
Whitefish Lake, l., Mn., U.S. D4 130
Whitefish Range, mts., Mt., U.S. B2 133
Whiteford, Md., U.S. A5 127
White Fox, Sask., Can. D3 105
White Hall, Al., U.S. C3 108
White Hall, Ar., U.S. C3 111
White Hall, Ga., U.S. C3 117
White Hall, Il., U.S. D3 120
Whitehall, Mi., U.S. E4 129
Whitehall, Mt., U.S. E4 133
Whitehall, N.Y., U.S. B7 139
Whitehall, Oh., U.S. m11 142
Whitehall, Wi., U.S. D2 156
Whitehall Reservoir, res., Ma., U.S. h9 128
White Haven, Pa., U.S. D10 145
White Heath, Il., U.S. C5 120
Whitehorn, Point, c., Wa., U.S. A3 154
Whitehorse, Yukon, Can. D5 96
White Horse, N.J., U.S. C3 137
Whitehorse, S.D., U.S. B5 148
White Horse Beach, Ma., U.S. C6 128
Whitehouse, Oh., U.S. A2 142
White House, Tn., U.S. A5 149
Whitehouse, Tx., U.S. C5 150
White House Station, N.J., U.S. B3 137
White Island, i., N.W. Ter., Can. C16 96
White Island Shores, Ma., U.S. C6 128
White Knob Mountains, mts., Id., U.S. F5 119
White Lake, Ont., Can. B8 103
White Lake, S.D., U.S. D7 148
White Lake, Wi., U.S. C5 156
White Lake, l., Ont., Can. B8 103
White Lake, l., La., U.S. E3 125
Whitelaw, Alta., Can. A1 98
Whitelaw, Wi., U.S. h10 156
Whiteman Air Force Base, mil., Mo., U.S. C4 132
Whitemark, Austl. M8 70
White Meadow Lake, N.J., U.S. *B3 137
White Mesa Natural Bridge, Az., U.S. A4 110
White Mountain, Ak., U.S. C7 109
White Mountain Peak, mtn., Ca., U.S. D4 112
White Mountains, mts., U.S. D4 112
White Mountains, mts., N.H., U.S. B3 136
Whitemouth, Man., Can. E4 100
Whitemouth, stm., Man., Can. E4 100
Whitemouth Lake, l., Man., Can. E4 100
White Nile (Al-Bahr al-Abyad), stm., Sud. L7 60
White Oak, Ga., U.S. E5 117
White Oak, Oh., U.S. o12 142
White Oak, Tx., U.S. C5 150
White Oak Creek, stm., Oh., U.S. D2 142
Whiteoak Creek, stm., Tn., U.S. A4 149
White Oak Lake, res., Ar., U.S. D2 111
White Oak Mountain, mtn., Ar., U.S. C2 111
White Pigeon, Mi., U.S. G5 129
White Pine, Mi., U.S. m12 129
White Pine, Tn., U.S. C10 149
White Pine, co., Nv., U.S. D6 135
White Plains, Al., U.S. B4 108
White Plains, Ga., U.S. C3 117
White Plains, Ky., U.S. C2 124
White Plains, Md., U.S. C4 127
White Plains, N.Y., U.S. D7 139
Whiteriver, Az., U.S. D6 110
White River, S.D., U.S. D5 148
White River Junction, Vt., U.S. D4 152
White River Plateau, plat., Co., U.S. B3 113
White Rock, B.C., Can. E6 99
White Rock, N.M., U.S. B3 138
White Rock, R.I., U.S. F1 146
White Rock, S.C., U.S. C5 147
White Rock Creek, stm., Ks., U.S. C5 123
Whiterocks, Ut., U.S. C6 151
White Rocks, mtn., Ky., U.S. D6 124
White Russia see Belarus, ctry., Eur. H11 26
Whitesail Lake, l., B.C., Can. C4 99
White Salmon, Wa., U.S. D4 154
White Salmon, stm., Wa., U.S. D4 154
White Sands Missile Range, mil., N.M., U.S. E3 138
White Sands National Monument, N.M., U.S. E3 138
Whitesboro, N.J., U.S. E3 137
Whitesboro, N.Y., U.S. B5 139
Whitesboro, Ok., U.S. C7 143
Whitesboro, Tx., U.S. C4 150
Whites Brook, N.B., Can. B2 101
Whitesburg, Ga., U.S. C2 117
Whitesburg, Ky., U.S. C7 124
Whites Creek, stm., Tn., U.S. g10 149
White Sea see Beloje more, Russia D5 26
Whiteside, Tn., U.S. D8 149
Whiteside, co., Il., U.S. B3 120
White Springs, Fl., U.S. B4 116
Whitestone, Ga., U.S. B2 117
White Stone, Va., U.S. C6 153
Whitestown, In., U.S. E5 121
White Sulphur Springs, Mt., U.S. D6 133
White Sulphur Springs, W.V., U.S. D4 155
Whitesville, Ky., U.S. C3 124
Whitesville, N.Y., U.S. C3 139
Whitesville, W.V., U.S. D3 155
White Swan, Wa., U.S. C5 154
Whitetail, Mt., U.S. B11 133
White Tank Mountains, mts., Az., U.S. k7 110
Whiteville, N.C., U.S. C4 140
Whiteville, Tn., U.S. B2 149
White Volta (Volta Blanche), stm., Afr. F6 54
Whitewater, Co., U.S. C2 113
Whitewater, Ks., U.S. E6 123
Whitewater, Mt., U.S. B9 133
Whitewater, Wi., U.S. F5 156
Whitewater, stm., U.S. F7 121
Whitewater, stm., Ks., U.S. E6 123
Whitewater, East Fork, stm., U.S. E8 121
Whitewater, West Branch, stm., Ks., U.S. g12 123
Whitewater Baldy, mtn., N.M., U.S. D1 138
Whitewater Bay, b., Fl., U.S. G6 116
White Woman Creek, stm., Ks., U.S. D2 123
Whitewood, Austl. C5 70
Whitewood, Sask., Can. G4 105
Whitewood, S.D., U.S. C2 148
Whitewright, Tx., U.S. C4 150
Whitfield, co., Ga., U.S. B2 117
Whitfield Estates, Fl., U.S. q10 116
Whithorn, Scot., U.K. G9 8
Whiting, In., U.S. A3 121
Whiting, Ia., U.S. B1 122
Whiting, Ks., U.S. C8 123
Whiting, N.J., U.S. D4 137
Whiting, Wi., U.S. D4 156
Whiting Field Naval Air Station, mil., Fl., U.S. u14 116
Whitingham, Vt., U.S. F3 152
Whitinsville, Ma., U.S. B4 128
Whitley, co., In., U.S. B6 121
Whitley, co., Ky., U.S. D5 124
Whitley City, Ky., U.S. D5 124
Whitman, Ma., U.S. B6 128
Whitman, Ne., U.S. B4 134
Whitman, W.V., U.S. D2 155
Whitman, co., Wa., U.S. B8 154
Whitmans Pond, l., Ma., U.S. h12 128
Whitman Square, N.J., U.S. D2 137
Whitmer, W.V., U.S. C5 155
Whitmire, S.C., U.S. B4 147
Whitmore Lake, Mi., U.S. p14 129
Whitmore Village, Hi., U.S. f9 118
Whitney, Pa., U.S. F3 145
Whitney, S.C., U.S. B4 147
Whitney, Tx., U.S. D4 150
Whitney, Lake, res., Tx., U.S. D4 150
Whitney, Mount, mtn., Ca., U.S. D4 112
Whitney Point, N.Y., U.S. C5 139
Whitney Point Lake, res., N.Y., U.S. C5 139
Whitneyville, Me., U.S. D5 126
Whitsunday Island, i., Austl. C8 70
Whittemore, Ia., U.S. A3 122
Whittemore, Mi., U.S. D7 129
Whittier, Ak., U.S. C10 109
Whittier, Ca., U.S. F4 112
Whittlesea, Austl. K6 70
Whittlesea, S. Afr. I8 66
Whittlesey, Mount, hill, Wi., U.S. B3 156
Whitwell, Tn., U.S. D8 149
Whyalla, Austl. I2 70
Whycocomagh, N.S., Can. D8 101
Wiarton, Ont., Can. C3 103
Wiawso, Ghana H8 64
Wibaux, Mt., U.S. D12 133
Wibaux, co., Mt., U.S. D12 133
Wichita, Ks., U.S. E6 123
Wichita, co., Ks., U.S. D2 123
Wichita, co., Tx., U.S. B3 150
Wichita Falls, Tx., U.S. C3 150
Wichita Mountains, mts., Ok., U.S. C3 143
Wick, Scot., U.K. C10 8
Wickenburg, Az., U.S. D3 110
Wickes, Ar., U.S. C1 111
Wickett, Tx., U.S. D1 150
Wickham, Cape, c., Austl. L5 70
Wickiup Reservoir, res., Or., U.S. E5 144
Wickliffe, Ky., U.S. f8 124
Wickliffe, Oh., U.S. A4 142
Wicklow, co., Ire. I7 8
Wicklow Mountains, mts., Ire. H7 8
Wicomico, co., Md., U.S. D6 127
Wicomico, stm., Md., U.S. D6 127
Wiconisco, Pa., U.S. E8 145
Widefield, Co., U.S. C6 113
Widen, W.V., U.S. C4 155
Widener, Ar., U.S. B5 111
Widerøe, Mount, mtn., Ant. C3 73
Wide Ruins, Az., U.S. B6 110
Wiehl, Ger. E7 10
Wiek, Ger. A13 10
Wieliczka, Pol. F20 10
Wielkopolska, reg., Pol. E17 10
Wieluń, Pol. D18 10
Wien (Vienna), Aus. G16 10
Wiener Neustadt, Aus. H16 10
Wienerwald, mts., Aus. G16 10
Wieprz, stm., Pol. D22 10
Wierden, Neth. D10 12
Wiesbaden, Ger. E8 10
Wieselburg, Aus. G15 10
Wiesloch, Ger. F8 10
Wietze, Ger. C9 10
Wigan, Eng., U.K. H11 8
Wiggins, Co., U.S. A6 113
Wiggins, Ms., U.S. E4 131
Wiggins Peak, mtn., Wy., U.S. C3 157
Wigtown, Scot., U.K. G9 8
Wijalpurā, Nepal G11 44
Wikieup, Az., U.S. C2 110
Wikwemikong, Ont., Can. B3 103
Wil, Switz. D11 13
Wilbarger, co., Tx., U.S. B3 150
Wilber, Ne., U.S. D9 134
Wilberforce, Ont., Can. B6 103
Wilberforce, Oh., U.S. C2 142
Wilbraham, Ma., U.S. B3 128
Wilbur, Or., U.S. D3 144
Wilbur, Wa., U.S. B7 154
Wilburn, Ar., U.S. B4 111
Wilburton, Ok., U.S. C6 143
Wilcannia, Austl. H5 70
Wilcox, Sask., Can. G3 105
Wilcox, Ne., U.S. D6 134
Wilcox, Pa., U.S. C4 145
Wilcox, co., Al., U.S. D2 108
Wilcox, co., Ga., U.S. E3 117
Wilcox, Mount, mtn., Ma., U.S. B1 128
Wild, stm., U.S. B4 136
Wild Ammonoosuc, stm., N.H., U.S. B3 136
Wild Branch, stm., Vt., U.S. B4 152
Wildcat Creek, stm., In., U.S. D4 121
Wildcat Creek, South Fork, stm., In., U.S. D4 121
Wildcat Top, mtn., Tn., U.S. D10 149
Wilder, Id., U.S. F2 119
Wilder, Vt., U.S. D4 152
Wilder Dam, U.S. C2 136
Wildersville, Tn., U.S. B3 149
Wilderville, Or., U.S. E3 144
Wildhaus, Switz. D11 13
Wildhay, stm., Alta., Can. C2 98
Wildhorse Creek, stm., Ok., U.S. C4 143
Wild Horse Reservoir, res., Nv., U.S. B6 135
Wildon, Aus. I15 10
Wildorado, Tx., U.S. B1 150
Wild Rice, stm., Mn., U.S. C2 130
Wild Rice, stm., N.D., U.S. C8 141
Wild Rice, South Branch, stm., Mn., U.S. C2 130
Wildrose, N.D., U.S. A2 141
Wild Rose, Wi., U.S. D4 156
Wildsville, La., U.S. C4 125
Wildwood, Alta., Can. C3 98
Wildwood, Fl., U.S. D4 116
Wildwood, Il., U.S. h9 120
Wildwood, N.J., U.S. F3 137
Wildwood Crest, N.J., U.S. F3 137
Wiley, Co., U.S. C8 113
Wiley, Wa., U.S. C5 154
Wilhelm, Mount, mtn., Pap. N. Gui. m15 68a
Wilhelmina Gebergte, mts., Sur. F14 84
Wilhelminakanaal, Neth. E7 12
Wilhelmina Peak see Trikora, Puncak, mtn., Indon. F10 38
Wilhelmshaven, Ger. B8 10
Wilhelmstal, Nmb. C3 66
Wilhoit, Az., U.S. C3 110
Wilkes, co., Ga., U.S. C4 117
Wilkes, co., N.C., U.S. A1 140
Wilkes-Barre, Pa., U.S. D10 145
Wilkesboro, N.C., U.S. A1 140
Wilkes Land, reg., Ant. C7 73
Wilkeson, Wa., U.S. B3 154
Wilkie, Sask., Can. E1 105
Wilkin, co., Mn., U.S. D2 130
Wilkinsburg, Pa., U.S. F2 145
Wilkinson, In., U.S. E6 121
Wilkinson, Ms., U.S. D2 131
Wilkinson, W.V., U.S. D3 155
Wilkinson, co., Ga., U.S. D3 117
Wilkinson, co., Ms., U.S. D2 131
Will, co., Il., U.S. B6 120
Willacoochee, Ga., U.S. E3 117
Willacy, co., Tx., U.S. F4 150
Willamette, stm., Or., U.S. C3 144
Willamette, Middle Fork, stm., Or., U.S. D4 144
Willamette Pass, Or., U.S. D4 144
Willamina, Or., U.S. B3 144
Willandra Billabong Creek, stm., Austl. I6 70
Willapa, Wa., U.S. C2 154
Willapa Bay, b., Wa., U.S. C1 154
Willard, Ks., U.S. C8 123
Willard, Ky., U.S. B7 124
Willard, Mo., U.S. D4 132
Willard, N.M., U.S. C3 138
Willard, N.Y., U.S. C4 139
Willard, Oh., U.S. A3 142
Willard, Ut., U.S. B3 151
Willard, Punta, c., Mex. C3 90
Willard Bay, b., Ut., U.S. B3 151
Willards, Md., U.S. D7 127
Willard Stream, stm., Vt., U.S. B5 152
Willcox, Az., U.S. E6 110
Willcox Playa, l., Az., U.S. E5 110
Willemstad, Neth. Ant. H10 94
William Bill Dannelly Reservoir, res., Al., U.S. C2 108
William P. Lane, Jr. Memorial Bridge, Md., U.S. B5 127
Williams, Az., U.S. B3 110
Williams, Ca., U.S. C2 112
Williams, In., U.S. G4 121
Williams, Ia., U.S. B4 122
Williams, co., N.D., U.S. A2 141
Williams, co., Oh., U.S. A1 142
Williams, stm., Austl. C4 70
Williams, stm., Vt., U.S. E3 152
Williams, stm., W.V., U.S. C4 155
Williams Air Force Base, mil., Az., U.S. D4 110
Williams Bay, Wi., U.S. F5 156
Williamsburg, Ont., Can. C9 103
Williamsburg, In., U.S. E8 121
Williamsburg, Ia., U.S. C5 122
Williamsburg, Ks., U.S. D8 123
Williamsburg, Ky., U.S. D5 124
Williamsburg, Ma., U.S. B2 128
Williamsburg, N.M., U.S. D2 138
Williamsburg, Oh., U.S. C1 142
Williamsburg, Pa., U.S. F5 145
Williamsburg, Va., U.S. C6 153
Williamsburg, W.V., U.S. D4 155
Williamsburg, co., S.C., U.S. D8 147
Williamsfield, Il., U.S. C3 120
Williams Fork, stm., Co., U.S. A3 113
Williams Harbour, Newf., Can. B4 102
Williams Lake, B.C., Can. C6 99
Williams Mountain, mtn., Ok., U.S. C7 143
Williamson, Ga., U.S. C2 117
Williamson, N.Y., U.S. B3 139
Williamson, W.V., U.S. D2 155
Williamson, co., Il., U.S. F4 120
Williamson, co., Tn., U.S. B5 149
Williamson, co., Tx., U.S. D4 150
Williamsport, In., U.S. D3 121
Williamsport, Md., U.S. A2 127
Williamsport, Oh., U.S. C2 142
Williamsport, Pa., U.S. D7 145
Williamston, Mi., U.S. F6 129
Williamston, N.C., U.S. B5 140
Williamston, S.C., U.S. B3 147
Williamstown, Ont., Can. B10 103
Williamstown, Ky., U.S. B5 124
Williamstown, Ma., U.S. A1 128
Williamstown, Mo., U.S. A6 132
Williamstown, N.J., U.S. D3 137
Williamstown, Pa., U.S. E8 145
Williamstown, Vt., U.S. C3 152
Williamstown, W.V., U.S. B3 155
Williamsville, De., U.S. G5 115
Williamsville, Il., U.S. D4 120
Williamsville, Ms., U.S. B4 131
Williamsville, Mo., U.S. E7 132
Williamsville, N.Y., U.S. C2 139
Willimantic, Ct., U.S. C7 114
Willimantic, stm., Ct., U.S. B6 114
Willimantic Reservoir, res., Ct., U.S. C7 114
Willingboro, N.J., U.S. C3 137
Willingdon, Alta., Can. C4 98
Willis, Mi., U.S. p14 129
Willis, Tx., U.S. D5 150
Willisau, Switz D9 13
Willisburg, Ky., U.S. C4 124
Willis Group, is., Austl. C10 68
Williston, S. Afr. H5 66
Williston, Fl., U.S. C4 116
Williston, N.D., U.S. A2 141
Williston, S.C., U.S. E5 147
Williston, Tn., U.S. B2 149
Williston, Vt., U.S. C2 152
Williston Basin U.S. B2 141
Williston Lake, res., B.C., Can. B6 99
Willisville, Ar., U.S. D2 111
Willisville, Il., U.S. F4 120
Willis Wharf, Va., U.S. C7 153
Willits, Ca., U.S. C2 112
Willmar, Mn., U.S. E3 130
Willoughby, Oh., U.S. A4 142
Willoughby, Cape, c., Austl. J3 70
Willoughby, Lake, l., Vt., U.S. B4 152
Willoughby Hills, Oh., U.S. A4 142
Willow, Ak., U.S. g17 109
Willow Branch, In., U.S. E6 121
Willowbrook, Sask., Can. F4 105
Willow Bunch, Sask., Can. H3 105
Willow City, N.D., U.S. A5 141
Willow Creek, Mt., U.S. E5 133
Willow Creek, stm., Nv., U.S. E5 135
Willow Creek, stm., Ut., U.S. D6 151
Willow Creek, stm., Wy., U.S. C6 157
Willow Grove, De., U.S. D3 115
Willow Grove, Pa., U.S. F11 145
Willow Grove Naval Air Station, mil., Pa., U.S. F11 145
Willow Hill, Il., U.S. E5 120
Willowick, Oh., U.S. A4 142
Willow Lake, S.D., U.S. C8 148
Willowmore, S. Afr. I6 66
Willow Reservoir, res., Wi., U.S. C3 156
Willow River, B.C., Can. B6 99
Willow River, Mn., U.S. D6 130
Willow Run, De., U.S. i7 115
Willow Run, Mi., U.S. p14 129
Willows, Ca., U.S. C2 112
Willow Springs, Il., U.S. k9 120
Willow Springs, Mo., U.S. E6 132
Wills, Lake, l., Austl. D5 68
Willsboro, N.Y., U.S. f11 139
Wills Hill, hill, Ma., U.S. f11 128
Willshire, Oh., U.S. B1 142
Willston, Va., U.S. *B5 153
Willunga, Austl. J3 70
Wilmar, Ar., U.S. D4 111
Wilmer, Al., U.S. E1 108
Wilmerding, Pa., U.S. k14 145
Wilmette, Il., U.S. A6 120
Wilmington, Austl. I3 70
Wilmington, De., U.S. B3 115
Wilmington, Il., U.S. B5 120
Wilmington, Ma., U.S. A5 128
Wilmington, N.C., U.S. C5 140
Wilmington, Oh., U.S. C2 142
Wilmington, Vt., U.S. F3 152
Wilmington Manor, De., U.S. i7 115
Wilmont, Mn., U.S. G3 130
Wilmore, Ky., U.S. C5 124
Wilmot, N.S., Can. E4 101
Wilmot, Ar., U.S. D4 111
Wilmot, S.D., U.S. B9 148
Wilmot Flat, N.H., U.S. D3 136
Wilno, Ont., Can. B7 103
Wilsall, Mt., U.S. E6 133
Wilsey, Ks., U.S. D7 123
Wilson, Austl. I3 70
Wilson, Ar., U.S. B5 111
Wilson, Ks., U.S. D5 123
Wilson, La., U.S. D4 125
Wilson, N.Y., U.S. B2 139
Wilson, N.C., U.S. B5 140
Wilson, Ok., U.S. C4 143
Wilson, Pa., U.S. E11 145
Wilson, Ut., U.S. B3 151
Wilson, Wy., U.S. C2 157
Wilson, co., Ks., U.S. E8 123
Wilson, co., N.C., U.S. B5 140
Wilson, co., Tn., U.S. A5 149
Wilson, co., Tx., U.S. E3 150
Wilson, stm., Austl. F4 70
Wilson, Cape, c., N.W. Ter., Can. C16 96
Wilson, Mount, mtn., Az., U.S. B1 110
Wilson, Mount, mtn., Ca., U.S. m12 112
Wilson, Mount, mtn., Co., U.S. D2 113
Wilson, Mount, mtn., Nv., U.S. E7 135
Wilson, Mount, mtn., Or., U.S. B5 144
Wilson Creek, stm., Wa., U.S. B5 154
Wilson Creek, stm., Wa., U.S. B6 154
Wilson Dam, Al., U.S. A2 108
Wilson Lake, res., Al., U.S. A2 108
Wilson Lake, res., Ks., U.S. D4 123
Wilsons Beach, N.B., Can. E3 101
Wilsons Mills, N.C., U.S. B4 140
Wilsons Promontory, c., Austl. L7 70
Wilsonville, Al., U.S. B3 108
Wilsonville, Ct., U.S. A8 114
Wilsonville, Il., U.S. D4 120
Wilsonville, Ne., U.S. D5 134
Wilsonville, Or., U.S. h12 144
Wilton, Al., U.S. B3 108
Wilton, Ar., U.S. D1 111
Wilton, Ct., U.S. E2 114
Wilton, Ia., U.S. C6 122
Wilton, Me., U.S. D2 126
Wilton, Mn., U.S. C3 130
Wilton, N.H., U.S. E3 136
Wilton, N.D., U.S. B5 141
Wilton, Wi., U.S. E3 156
Wilton Center, N.H., U.S. E3 136
Wiltshire, co., Eng., U.K. J12 8
Wiluna, Austl. E4 68
Wimauma, Fl., U.S. E4 116
Wimbledon, N.D., U.S. B7 141
Wimborne, Alta., Can. D4 98
Winagami Lake, l., Alta., Can. B2 98
Winamac, In., U.S. B4 121
Winburg, S. Afr. G8 66
Wincheck Pond, l., R.I., U.S. E1 146
Winchell Mountain, mtn., Ma., U.S. B2 128
Winchendon, Ma., U.S. A3 128
Winchester, Ont., Can. B9 103
Winchester, Eng., U.K. J12 8
Winchester, Ar., U.S. D4 111
Winchester, Id., U.S. C2 119
Winchester, Il., U.S. D3 120
Winchester, In., U.S. D8 121
Winchester, Ks., U.S. k15 123
Winchester, Ky., U.S. C5 124
Winchester, Ma., U.S. g11 128
Winchester, Nv., U.S. G6 135
Winchester, N.H., U.S. E2 136
Winchester, Oh., U.S. D2 142
Winchester, Tn., U.S. B5 149
Winchester, Va., U.S. A4 153
Winchester Bay, Or., U.S. D2 144
Wind, stm., Wa., U.S. D4 154
Wind, stm., Wy., U.S. C4 157
Windber, Pa., U.S. F4 145
Wind Cave National Park, S.D., U.S. D2 148
Winder, Ga., U.S. C3 117
Windermere, B.C., Can. D10 99
Windfall, In., U.S. D6 121
Windgap, Pa., U.S. E11 145
Windham, Ct., U.S. C7 114
Windham, Oh., U.S. A4 142
Windham, co., Ct., U.S. B7 114
Windham, co., Vt., U.S. F3 152
Windhoek, Nmb. D3 66
Winding Stair Mountain, mts., Ok., U.S. C6 143
Windischgarsten, Aus. H14 10
Wind Lake, Wi., U.S. F5 156
Wind Lake, l., Wi., U.S. n11 156
Windmill Point, c., Va., U.S. C6 153
Windom, Ks., U.S. D6 123
Windom, Mn., U.S. G3 130
Windom Peak, mtn., Co., U.S. D3 113
Windorah, Austl. E5 70
Window Rock, Az., U.S. B6 110
Wind Point, Wi., U.S. n12 156
Wind River Indian Reservation, Wy., U.S. C4 157
Wind River Peak, mtn., Wy., U.S. D3 157
Wind River Range, mts., Wy., U.S. C3 157
Windsor, Austl. I9 70
Windsor (part of Grand Falls-Windsor), Newf., Can. D4 102
Windsor, N.S., Can. E5 101
Windsor, Ont., Can. E1 103
Windsor, Que., Can. D5 104
Windsor, Eng., U.K. J13 8
Windsor, Co., U.S. A6 113
Windsor, Ct., U.S. B5 114
Windsor, Il., U.S. D5 120
Windsor, Mo., U.S. C4 132
Windsor, N.C., U.S. A6 140
Windsor, Pa., U.S. G8 145
Windsor, Vt., U.S. E4 152
Windsor, Va., U.S. D6 153
Windsor, co., Vt., U.S. D3 152
Windsor Heights, Ia., U.S. e8 122
Windsor Locks, Ct., U.S. B5 114
Windsorville, Ct., U.S. B5 114
Windthorst, Sask., Can. G4 105
Windward Islands, is., N.A. H14 94
Windward Passage, strt., N.A. E7 94
Windy Hill, S.C., U.S. C8 147
Windy Peak, mtn., Wa., U.S. A6 154
Winefred, stm., Alta., Can. B5 98
Winefred Lake, l., Alta., Can. B5 98
Winejok, Sud. M4 60
Winfall, N.C., U.S. A6 140
Winfield, Alta., Can. C3 98
Winfield, Al., U.S. B2 108
Winfield, Ia., U.S. C6 122
Winfield, Ks., U.S. E7 123
Winfield, Mo., U.S. C7 132
Winfield, N.J., U.S. k7 137
Winfield, Tn., U.S. C9 149
Winfield, W.V., U.S. C3 155
Wing, Al., U.S. D3 108
Wing, N.D., U.S. B5 141
Wing, stm., Mn., U.S. D3 130
Wingate, In., U.S. D3 121
Wingate, N.C., U.S. C2 140
Wingene, Bel. F3 12
Winger, Mn., U.S. C3 130
Wingham, Austl. H10 70
Wingham, Ont., Can. D3 103
Wingo, Ky., U.S. f9 124
Winifred, Mt., U.S. C7 133
Winifreda, Arg. I6 80
Winifrede, W.V., U.S. m12 155
Winigan, Mo., U.S. A5 132
Winisk, stm., Ont., Can. n18 103
Winisk Lake, l., Ont., Can. n18 103
Wink, Tx., U.S. D1 150
Winkana, Mya. G5 40
Winkelman, Az., U.S. E5 110
Winkler, Man., Can. E3 100
Winkler, co., Tx., U.S. D1 150
Winlaw, B.C., Can. E9 99
Winlock, Wa., U.S. C3 154
Winn, Me., U.S. C4 126
Winn, Mi., U.S. E6 129
Winn, co., La., U.S. C3 125
Winneba, Ghana I9 64
Winnebago, Il., U.S. A4 120
Winnebago, Mn., U.S. G4 130
Winnebago, Ne., U.S. B9 134
Winnebago, Wi., U.S. h8 156
Winnebago, co., Il., U.S. A4 120
Winnebago, co., Ia., U.S. A4 122
Winnebago, co., Wi., U.S. D5 156
Winnebago, stm., Ia., U.S. A4 122
Winnebago, Lake, l., Wi., U.S. E5 156
Winnebago Indian Reservation, Ne., U.S. B9 134
Winneconne, Wi., U.S. D5 156
Winnemucca, Nv., U.S. C4 135
Winnemucca Lake, l., Nv., U.S. C2 135
Winner, S.D., U.S. D6 148
Winneshiek, co., Ia., U.S. A6 122
Winnetka, Il., U.S. A6 120
Winnett, Mt., U.S. C8 133
Winnfield, La., U.S. C3 125
Winnibigoshish, Lake, l., Mn., U.S. C4 130
Winnipeg, Man., Can. E3 100
Winnipeg, stm., Can. D4 100
Winnipeg, Lake, l., Man., Can. C3 100
Winnipeg Beach, Man., Can. D3 100
Winnipegosis, Man., Can. D2 100
Winnipegosis, Lake, l., Man., Can. C2 100
Winnipesaukee, Lake, l., N.H., U.S. C4 136
Winnisquam, N.H., U.S. C3 136
Winnisquam Lake, l., N.H., U.S. C3 136
Winnsboro, La., U.S. B4 125
Winnsboro, S.C., U.S. C5 147
Winnsboro, Tx., U.S. C5 150
Winnsboro Mills, S.C., U.S. C5 147
Winona, Ks., U.S. C2 123
Winona, Mn., U.S. F7 130
Winona, Ms., U.S. B4 131
Winona, Mo., U.S. D6 132
Winona, W.V., U.S. C4 155
Winona, co., Mn., U.S. F7 130
Winona Lake, In., U.S. B6 121
Winona Lake, l., Vt., U.S. C2 152

World Political Information

This table lists the area, population, population density, form of government, political status, and capital for every country in the world.

The populations are estimates for January 1, 1994 made by Rand McNally on the basis of official data, United Nations estimates, and other available information. Area figures include inland water.

The political units listed in the table are categorized by political status, as follows:

A–independent countries; B–internally independent political entities which are under the protection of other countries in matters of defense and foreign affairs; C–colonies and other dependent political units; D–the major administrative subdivisions of Australia, Canada, China, the United Kingdom, and the United States. For comparison, the table also includes the continents and the world.

All footnotes to this table appear on page 260.

Country, Division or Region English (Conventional)	Area in sq. mi.	Area in sq. km.	Estimated Population 1/1/94	Pop. per sq. mi.	Pop. per sq. km.	Form of Government and Political Status	Capital
† Afghanistan	251,826	652,225	16,595,000	66	25	Islamic republic ....A	Kābol (Kabul)
Africa	11,700,000	30,300,000	683,700,000	58	23		
Alabama	52,423	135,775	4,202,000	80	31	State (U.S.) .... D	Montgomery
Alaska	656,424	1,700,139	597,000	0.9	0.4	State (U.S.) .... D	Juneau
† Albania	11,100	28,748	3,424,000	308	119	Republic ....A	Tiranë
Alberta	255,287	661,190	2,599,000	10	3.9	Province (Canada) .... D	Edmonton
† Algeria	919,595	2,381,741	26,780,000	29	11	Provisional military government ....A	El Djazaïr (Algiers)
American Samoa	77	199	53,000	688	266	Unincorporated territory (U.S.) C	Pago Pago
† Andorra	175	453	58,000	331	128	Parliamentary co-principality (Spanish and French protection) ....B	Andorra
† Angola	481,354	1,246,700	11,040,000	23	8.9	Republic ....A	Luanda
Anguilla	35	91	7,000	200	77	Dependent territory (U.K. protection) ....B	The Valley
Anhwei (Anhui)	53,668	139,000	58,850,000	1,097	423	Province (China) .... D	Hefei
Antarctica	5,400,000	14,000,000		(1)			
† Antigua and Barbuda	171	442	64,000	374	145	Parliamentary state ....A	St. John's
† Argentina	1,073,519	2,780,400	33,635,000	31	12	Republic ....A	Buenos Aires and Viedma (4)
Arizona	114,006	295,276	3,943,000	35	13	State (U.S.) .... D	Phoenix
Arkansas	53,182	137,742	2,438,000	46	18	State (U.S.) .... D	Little Rock
† Armenia	11,506	29,800	3,743,000	325	126	Republic ....A	Jerevan
Aruba	75	193	68,000	907	352	Self-governing territory (Netherlands protection) ....B	Oranjestad
Asia	17,300,000	44,900,000	3,385,900,000	196	75		
† Australia	2,966,155	7,682,300	17,950,000	6.1	2.3	Federal parliamentary state ....A	Canberra
Australian Capital Territory	927	2,400	303,000	327	126	Territory (Australia) .... D	Canberra
† Austria	32,377	83,856	7,913,000	244	94	Federal republic ....A	Wien (Vienna)
† Azerbaijan	33,436	86,600	7,481,000	224	86	Republic ....A	Bakı (Baku)
† Bahamas	5,382	13,939	270,000	50	19	Parliamentary state ....A	Nassau
† Bahrain	267	691	572,000	2,142	828	Monarchy ....A	Al-Manāmah
† Bangladesh	55,598	143,998	115,240,000	2,073	800	Republic ....A	Dhaka (Dacca)
† Barbados	166	430	260,000	1,566	605	Parliamentary state ....A	Bridgetown
† Belarus	80,155	207,600	10,380,000	129	50	Republic ....A	Minsk
† Belgium	11,783	30,518	10,050,000	853	329	Constitutional monarchy ....A	Bruxelles (Brussels)
† Belize	8,866	22,963	205,000	23	8.9	Parliamentary state ....A	Belmopan
† Benin	43,475	112,600	5,292,000	122	47	Republic ....A	Porto-Novo and Cotonou
Bermuda	21	54	76,000	3,619	1,407	Dependent territory (U.K.) C	Hamilton
† Bhutan	17,954	46,500	1,707,000	95	37	Monarchy (Indian protection) ....B	Thimphu
† Bolivia	424,165	1,098,581	7,582,000	18	6.9	Republic ....A	La Paz and Sucre
† Bosnia and Herzegovina	19,741	51,129	4,442,000	225	87	Republic ....A	Sarajevo
† Botswana	224,711	582,000	1,424,000	6.3	2.4	Republic ....A	Gaborone
† Brazil	3,286,500	8,511,996	151,310,000	46	18	Federal republic ....A	Brasília
British Columbia	365,948	947,800	3,354,000	9.2	3.5	Province (Canada) .... D	Victoria
British Indian Ocean Territory	23	60	(1)	. . .	. . .	Dependent territory (U.K.) C	
British Virgin Islands	59	153	13,000	220	85	Dependent territory (U.K.) C	Road Town
† Brunei	2,226	5,765	279,000	125	48	Monarchy ....A	Bandar Seri Begawan
† Bulgaria	42,855	110,994	8,813,000	206	79	Republic ....A	Sofija (Sofia)
† Burkina Faso	105,869	274,200	9,922,000	94	36	Republic ....A	Ouagadougou
Burma, see Myanmar							
† Burundi	10,745	27,830	6,015,000	560	216	Republic ....A	Bujumbura
California	163,707	424,002	31,905,000	195	75	State (U.S.) .... D	Sacramento
† Cambodia	69,898	181,035	10,010,000	143	55	Transitional government ....A	Phnum Pénh (Phnom Penh)
† Cameroon	183,568	475,440	12,845,000	70	27	Republic ....A	Yaoundé
† Canada	3,849,674	9,970,610	27,950,000	7.3	2.8	Federal parliamentary state ....A	Ottawa
† Cape Verde	1,557	4,033	414,000	266	103	Republic ....A	Praia
Cayman Islands	100	259	32,000	320	124	Dependent territory (U.K.) C	George Town
† Central African Republic	240,535	622,984	3,089,000	13	5.0	Republic ....A	Bangui
† Chad	495,755	1,284,000	6,149,000	12	4.8	Republic ....A	N'Djamena
Chekiang (Zhejiang)	39,305	101,800	43,455,000	1,106	427	Province (China) .... D	Hangzhou
† Chile	292,135	756,626	13,795,000	47	18	Republic ....A	Santiago
† China (excl. Taiwan)	3,689,631	9,556,100	1,184,060,000	321	124	Socialist republic ....A	Beijing (Peking)
Christmas Island	52	135	1,300	25	9.6	External territory (Australia) C	
Cocos (Keeling) Islands	5.4	14	600	111	43	Territory (Australia) C	
† Colombia	440,831	1,141,748	35,085,000	80	31	Republic ....A	Santa Fe de Bogotá
Colorado	104,100	269,620	3,528,000	34	13	State (U.S.) .... D	Denver
† Comoros (excl. Mayotte)	863	2,235	508,000	589	227	Federal Islamic republic ....A	Moroni
† Congo	132,047	342,000	2,403,000	18	7.0	Republic ....A	Brazzaville
Connecticut	5,544	14,358	3,272,000	590	228	State (U.S.) .... D	Hartford
Cook Islands	91	236	19,000	209	81	Self-governing territory (New Zealand protection) ....B	Avarua
† Costa Rica	19,730	51,100	3,285,000	166	64	Republic ....A	San José
† Cote d'Ivoire	124,518	322,500	13,930,000	112	43	Republic ....A	Abidjan and Yamoussoukro
† Croatia	21,829	56,538	4,796,000	220	85	Republic ....A	Zagreb
† Cuba	42,804	110,861	11,015,000	257	99	Socialist republic ....A	La Habana (Havana)
† Cyprus (excl. North Cyprus)	2,276	5,896	574,000	252	97	Republic ....A	Nicosia (Levkosía)
Cyprus, North (2)	1,295	3,355	193,000	149	58	Republic ....A	Nicosia (Lefkoşa)
† Czech Republic	30,450	78,864	10,400,000	342	132	Republic ....A	Praha (Prague)
Delaware	2,489	6,447	700,000	281	109	State (U.S.) .... D	Dover
† Denmark	16,639	43,094	5,181,000	311	120	Constitutional monarchy ....A	København (Copenhagen)
District of Columbia	68	177	576,000	8,471	3,254	Federal district (U.S.) .... D	Washington
† Djibouti	8,958	23,200	579,000	65	25	Republic ....A	Djibouti
† Dominica	305	790	87,000	285	110	Republic ....A	Roseau
† Dominican Republic	18,704	48,442	7,715,000	412	159	Republic ....A	Santo Domingo
† Ecuador	105,037	272,045	10,515,000	100	39	Republic ....A	Quito
† Egypt	386,662	1,001,449	56,820,000	147	57	Socialist republic ....A	Al-Qāhirah (Cairo)
† El Salvador	8,124	21,041	5,179,000	637	246	Republic ....A	San Salvador
England	50,352	130,410	48,320,000	960	371	Administrative division (U.K.) .... D	London
† Equatorial Guinea	10,831	28,051	379,000	35	14	Republic ....A	Malabo
† Eritrea	36,170	93,679	3,540,000	98	38	Republic ....A	Asmera
† Estonia	17,413	45,100	1,608,000	92	36	Republic ....A	Tallinn
† Ethiopia	446,953	1,157,603	54,170,000	121	47	Provisional military government ....A	Adis Abeba
Europe	3,800,000	9,900,000	709,300,000	187	72		
Faeroe Islands	540	1,399	48,000	89	34	Self-governing territory (Danish protection) ......B	Tórshavn
Falkland Islands (3)	4,700	12,173	2,200	0.5	0.2	Dependent territory (U.K.) C	Stanley
† Fiji	7,056	18,274	759,000	108	42	Republic ....A	Suva
† Finland	130,559	338,145	5,056,000	39	15	Republic ....A	Helsinki (Helsingfors)

257

World Political Information

Country, Division or Region English (Conventional)	Area in sq. mi.	Area in sq. km.	Estimated Population 1/1/94	Pop. per sq. mi.	Pop. per sq. km.	Form of Government and Political Status	Capital
Florida	65,758	170,313	13,855,000	211	81	State (U.S.) D	Tallahassee
† France (excl. Overseas Departments)	211,208	547,026	57,680,000	273	105	Republic A	Paris
French Guiana	35,135	91,000	134,000	3.8	1.5	Overseas department (France) C	Cayenne
French Polynesia	1,359	3,521	211,000	155	60	Overseas territory (France) C	Papeete
Fukien (Fujian)	46,332	120,000	31,375,000	677	261	Province (China) D	Fuzhou
† Gabon	103,347	267,667	1,127,000	11	4.2	Republic A	Libreville
† Gambia	4,127	10,689	919,000	223	86	Republic A	Banjul
Gaza Strip	146	378	745,000	5,103	1,971	Israeli territory with limited self-government	. . .
Georgia	59,441	153,953	6,875,000	116	45	State (U.S.) D	Atlanta
† Georgia (Sakartvelo)	26,911	69,700	5,646,000	210	81	Republic A	Tbilisi
† Germany	137,822	356,955	80,930,000	587	227	Federal republic A	Berlin and Bonn
† Ghana	92,098	238,533	16,595,000	180	70	Republic A	Accra
Gibraltar	2.3	6.0	32,000	13,913	5,333	Dependent territory (U.K.) C	Gibraltar
Golan Heights	454	1,176.0	29,000	64	25	Occupied by Israel	
† Greece	50,949	131,957	10,500,000	206	80	Republic A	Athínai (Athens)
Greenland	840,004	2,175,600	57,000	0.1	. . .	Self-governing territory (Danish protection) B	Godthåb (Nuuk)
† Grenada	133	344	91,000	684	265	Parliamentary state A	St. George's
Guadeloupe (incl. Dependencies)	687	1,780	424,000	617	238	Overseas department (France) C	Basse-Terre
Guam	209	541	147,000	703	272	Unincorporated territory (U.S.) C	Agana
† Guatemala	42,042	108,889	10,510,000	250	97	Republic A	Guatemala
Guernsey (incl. Dependencies)	30	78	63,000	2,100	808	Crown dependency (U.K. protection) B	St. Peter Port
† Guinea	94,926	245,857	6,274,000	66	26	Provisional military government A	Conakry
† Guinea-Bissau	13,948	36,125	1,078,000	77	30	Republic A	Bissau
† Guyana	83,000	214,969	732,000	8.8	3.4	Republic A	Georgetown
Hainan	13,127	34,000	6,867,000	523	202	Province (China) D	Haikou
† Haiti	10,714	27,750	6,411,000	598	231	Provisional military government A	Port-au-Prince
Hawaii	10,932	28,313	1,167,000	107	41	State (U.S.) D	Honolulu
Heilungkiang (Heilongjiang)	181,082	469,000	36,945,000	204	79	Province (China) D	Harbin
Honan (Henan)	64,479	167,000	89,520,000	1,388	536	Province (China) D	Zhengzhou
† Honduras	43,277	112,088	5,206,000	120	46	Republic A	Tegucigalpa
Hong Kong	414	1,072	5,890,000	14,227	5,494	Chinese territory under British administration C	Hong Kong (Victoria)
Hopeh (Hebei)	73,359	190,000	63,940,000	872	337	Province (China) D	Shijiazhuang
Hunan	81,081	210,000	63,580,000	784	303	Province (China) D	Changsha
† Hungary	35,919	93,030	10,295,000	287	111	Republic A	Budapest
Hupeh (Hubei)	72,356	187,400	56,480,000	781	301	Province (China) D	Wuhan
† Iceland	39,769	103,000	262,000	6.6	2.5	Republic A	Reykjavík
Idaho	83,574	216,456	1,089,000	13	5.0	State (U.S.) D	Boise
Illinois	57,918	150,007	11,750,000	203	78	State (U.S.) D	Springfield
† India (incl. part of Jammu and Kashmir)	1,237,062	3,203,975	906,770,000	733	283	Federal republic A	New Delhi
Indiana	36,420	94,328	5,733,000	157	61	State (U.S.) D	Indianapolis
† Indonesia	752,410	1,948,732	198,810,000	264	102	Republic A	Jakarta
Inner Mongolia (Nei Monggol)	456,759	1,183,000	22,495,000	49	19	Autonomous region (China) D	Hohhot
Iowa	56,276	145,754	2,827,000	50	19	State (U.S.) D	Des Moines
† Iran	632,457	1,638,057	63,940,000	101	39	Islamic republic A	Tehrān
† Iraq	169,235	438,317	19,335,000	114	44	Republic A	Baghdād
† Ireland	27,137	70,285	3,563,000	131	51	Republic A	Dublin (Baile Átha Cliath)
Isle of Man	221	572	72,000	326	126	Crown dependency (U.K. protection) B	Douglas
† Israel	8,019	20,770	4,950,000	617	238	Republic A	Yerushalayim (Jerusalem)
† Italy	116,324	301,277	56,670,000	487	188	Republic A	Roma (Rome)
Ivory Coast, see Cote d'Ivoire							
† Jamaica	4,244	10,991	2,538,000	598	231	Parliamentary state A	Kingston
† Japan	145,870	377,801	124,840,000	856	330	Constitutional monarchy A	Tōkyō
Jersey	45	116	86,000	1,911	741	Crown dependency (U.K. protection) B	St. Helier
† Jordan	35,135	91,000	3,858,000	110	42	Constitutional monarchy A	'Ammān
Kansas	82,282	213,110	2,568,000	31	12	State (U.S.) D	Topeka
Kansu (Gansu)	173,746	450,000	23,445,000	135	52	Province (China) D	Lanzhou
† Kazakhstan	1,049,156	2,717,300	17,190,000	16	6.3	Republic A	Alma-Ata (Almaty)
Kentucky	40,411	104,665	3,813,000	94	36	State (U.S.) D	Frankfort
† Kenya	224,961	582,646	28,280,000	126	49	Republic A	Nairobi
Kiangsi (Jiangxi)	64,325	166,600	39,550,000	615	237	Province (China) D	Nanchang
Kiangsu (Jiangsu)	39,614	102,600	70,210,000	1,772	684	Province (China) D	Nanjing (Nanking)
Kiribati	313	811	77,000	246	95	Republic A	Bairiki
Kirin (Jilin)	72,201	187,000	25,815,000	358	138	Province (China) D	Changchun
† Korea, North	46,540	120,538	22,735,000	489	189	Socialist republic A	P'yŏngyang
† Korea, South	38,230	99,016	44,250,000	1,157	447	Republic A	Sŏul (Seoul)
† Kuwait	6,880	17,818	1,734,000	252	97	Constitutional monarchy A	Al-Kuwayt (Kuwait)
Kwangsi Chuang (Guangxi Zhuangzu)	91,236	236,300	44,285,000	485	187	Autonomous region (China) D	Nanning
Kwangtung (Guangdong)	68,726	178,000	65,830,000	958	370	Province (China) D	Guangzhou (Canton)
Kweichow (Guizhou)	65,637	170,000	33,985,000	518	200	Province (China) D	Guiyang
† Kyrgyzstan	76,641	198,500	4,645,000	61	23	Republic A	Biškek
† Laos	91,429	236,800	4,601,000	50	19	Socialist republic A	Viangchan (Vientiane)
† Latvia	24,595	63,700	2,556,000	104	40	Republic A	Rīga
† Lebanon	4,015	10,400	3,566,000	888	343	Republic A	Bayrūt (Beirut)
† Lesotho	11,720	30,355	1,907,000	163	63	Constitutional monarchy under military rule A	Maseru
Liaoning	56,255	145,700	41,325,000	735	284	Province (China) D	Shenyang (Mukden)
† Liberia	38,250	99,067	2,901,000	76	29	Republic A	Monrovia
† Libya	679,362	1,759,540	4,917,000	7.2	2.8	Socialist republic A	Ṭarābulus (Tripoli)
† Liechtenstein	62	160	30,000	484	188	Constitutional monarchy A	Vaduz
† Lithuania	25,212	65,300	3,777,000	150	58	Republic A	Vilnius
Louisiana	51,843	134,275	4,332,000	84	32	State (U.S.) D	Baton Rouge
† Luxembourg	998	2,586	401,000	402	155	Constitutional monarchy A	Luxembourg
Macau	6.6	17	380,000	57,576	22,353	Chinese territory under Portuguese administration C	Macau
† Macedonia	9,928	25,713	2,198,000	221	85	Republic A	Skopje
† Madagascar	226,658	587,041	13,110,000	58	22	Republic A	Antananarivo
Maine	35,387	91,653	1,245,000	35	14	State (U.S.) D	Augusta
† Malawi	45,747	118,484	8,942,000	195	75	Republic A	Lilongwe
† Malaysia	127,320	329,758	19,060,000	150	58	Federal constitutional monarchy A	Kuala Lumpur
† Maldives	115	298	246,000	2,139	826	Republic A	Male'
† Mali	482,077	1,248,574	8,922,000	19	7.1	Republic A	Bamako
† Malta	122	316	365,000	2,992	1,155	Republic A	Valletta
Manitoba	250,947	649,950	1,118,000	4.5	1.7	Province (Canada) D	Winnipeg
† Marshall Islands	70	181	52,000	743	287	Republic (U.S. protection) A	Majuro (island)
Martinique	425	1,100	377,000	887	343	Overseas department (France) C	Fort-de-France
Maryland	12,407	32,135	5,006,000	403	156	State (U.S.) D	Annapolis
Massachusetts	10,555	27,337	6,106,000	578	223	State (U.S.) D	Boston
† Mauritania	395,956	1,025,520	2,142,000	5.4	2.1	Republic A	Nouakchott
† Mauritius (incl. Dependencies)	788	2,040	1,110,000	1,409	544	Republic A	Port Louis

Country, Division or Region English (Conventional)	Area in sq. mi.	Area in sq. km.	Estimated Population 1/1/94	Pop. per sq. mi.	Pop. per sq. km.	Form of Government and Political Status	Capital
Mayotte [5]	144	374	91,000	632	243	Territorial collectivity (France) C	Dzaoudzi and Mamoudzou [4]
† Mexico	759,534	1,967,183	90,870,000	120	46	Federal republic A	Ciudad de México (Mexico City)
Michigan	96,810	250,738	9,550,000	99	38	State (U.S.) D	Lansing
† Micronesia, Federated States of .	271	702	119,000	439	170	Republic (U.S. protection) A	Kolonia and Paliker [4]
Midway Islands	2.0	5.2	500	250	96	Unincorporated territory (U.S.) C	....
Minnesota	86,943	225,182	4,539,000	52	20	State (U.S.) D	St. Paul
Mississippi	48,434	125,443	2,646,000	55	21	State (U.S.) D	Jackson
Missouri	69,709	180,546	5,266,000	76	29	State (U.S.) D	Jefferson City
† Moldova	13,012	33,700	4,425,000	340	131	Republic A	Chişinău (Kishinev)
† Monaco	0.7	1.9	31,000	44,286	16,316	Constitutional monarchy A	Monaco
† Mongolia	604,829	1,566,500	2,314,000	3.8	1.5	Republic A	Ulaanbaatar (Ulan Bator)
Montana	147,046	380,850	830,000	5.6	2.2	State (U.S.) D	Helena
Montserrat	39	102	13,000	333	127	Dependent territory (U.K.) C	Plymouth
† Morocco (excl. Western Sahara) .	172,414	446,550	28,095,000	163	63	Constitutional monarchy A	Rabat
† Mozambique	308,642	799,380	16,585,000	54	21	Republic A	Maputo
† Myanmar (Burma)	261,228	676,577	43,630,000	167	64	Provisional military government A	Yangon (Rangoon)
† Namibia	318,253	824,272	1,555,000	4.9	1.9	Republic A	Windhoek
Nauru	8.1	21	10,000	1,235	476	Republic A	Yaren District
Nebraska	77,358	200,358	1,635,000	21	8.2	State (U.S.) D	Lincoln
† Nepal	56,827	147,181	20,660,000	364	140	Constitutional monarchy A	Kāthmāndū
† Netherlands	16,164	41,864	15,320,000	948	366	Constitutional monarchy A	Amsterdam and 's-Gravenhage (The Hague)
Netherlands Antilles	309	800	192,000	621	240	Self-governing territory (Netherlands protection) B	Willemstad
Nevada	110,567	286,368	1,375,000	12	4.8	State (U.S.) D	Carson City
New Brunswick	28,355	73,440	755,000	27	10	Province (Canada) D	Fredericton
New Caledonia	7,358	19,058	179,000	24	9.4	Overseas territory (France) C	Nouméa
Newfoundland	156,649	405,720	587,000	3.7	1.4	Province (Canada) D	St. John's
New Hampshire	9,351	24,219	1,167,000	125	48	State (U.S.) D	Concord
New Jersey	8,722	22,590	7,915,000	907	350	State (U.S.) D	Trenton
New Mexico	121,598	314,939	1,608,000	13	5.1	State (U.S.) D	Santa Fe
New South Wales	309,500	801,600	6,117,000	20	7.6	State (Australia) D	Sydney
New York	54,475	141,089	18,375,000	337	130	State (U.S.) D	Albany
† New Zealand	104,454	270,534	3,486,000	33	13	Parliamentary state A	Wellington
† Nicaragua	50,054	129,640	4,267,000	85	33	Republic A	Managua
† Niger	489,191	1,267,000	8,754,000	18	6.9	Provisional military government A	Niamey
† Nigeria	356,669	923,768	94,550,000	265	102	Provisional military government A	Lagos and Abuja
Ningsia Hui (Ningxia Huizu)	25,637	66,400	4,855,000	189	73	Autonomous region (China) D	Yinchuan
Niue	100	259	1,900	19	7.3	Self-governing territory (New Zealand protection) B	Alofi
Norfolk Island	14	36	2,700	193	75	External territory (Australia) C	Kingston
North America	9,500,000	24,700,000	444,600,000	47	18	....	....
North Carolina	53,821	139,397	6,955,000	129	50	State (U.S.) D	Raleigh
North Dakota	70,704	183,123	632,000	8.9	3.5	State (U.S.) D	Bismarck
Northern Ireland	5,461	14,144	1,605,000	294	113	Administrative division (U.K.) D	Belfast
Northern Mariana Islands	184	477	49,000	266	103	Commonwealth (U.S. protection) C	Saipan (island)
Northern Territory	519,771	1,346,200	172,000	0.3	0.1	Territory (Australia) D	Darwin
Northwest Territories	1,322,910	3,426,320	56,000	. . .	. . .	Territory (Canada) D	Yellowknife
† Norway (incl. Svalbard and Jan Mayen)	149,412	386,975	4,301,000	29	11	Constitutional monarchy A	Oslo
Nova Scotia	21,425	55,490	922,000	43	17	Province (Canada) D	Halifax
Oceania (incl. Australia)	3,300,000	8,500,000	28,000,000	8.5	3.3	. . .	. . .
Ohio	44,828	116,103	11,155,000	249	96	State (U.S.) D	Columbus
Oklahoma	69,903	181,049	3,242,000	46	18	State (U.S.) D	Oklahoma City
† Oman	82,030	212,457	1,659,000	20	7.8	Monarchy A	Masqaţ (Muscat)
Ontario	412,581	1,068,580	10,315,000	25	9.7	Province (Canada) D	Toronto
Oregon	98,386	254,819	3,009,000	31	12	State (U.S.) D	Salem
† Pakistan (incl. part of Jammu and Kashmir)	339,732	879,902	126,090,000	371	143	Federal Islamic republic A	Islāmābād
Palau	196	508	16,000	82	31	Under U.S. administration B	Koror and Melekeok [4]
† Panama	29,157	75,517	2,592,000	89	34	Republic A	Panamá
† Papua New Guinea	178,704	462,840	3,989,000	22	8.6	Parliamentary state A	Port Moresby
† Paraguay	157,048	406,752	4,297,000	27	11	Republic A	Asunción
Peking (Beijing)	6,487	16,800	11,365,000	1,752	676	Autonomous city (China) D	Beijing (Peking)
Pennsylvania	46,058	119,291	12,145,000	264	102	State (U.S.) D	Harrisburg
† Peru	496,225	1,285,216	23,305,000	47	18	Republic A	Lima
† Philippines	115,831	300,000	66,190,000	571	221	Republic A	Manila
Pitcairn (incl. Dependencies)	19	49	100	5.3	2.0	Dependent territory (U.K.) C	Adamstown
† Poland	121,196	313,895	38,540,000	318	123	Republic A	Warszawa (Warsaw)
† Portugal	35,516	91,985	9,961,000	280	108	Republic A	Lisboa (Lisbon)
Prince Edward Island	2,185	5,660	140,000	64	25	Province (Canada) D	Charlottetown
Puerto Rico	3,515	9,104	3,801,000	1,081	418	Commonwealth (U.S. protection) B	San Juan
† Qatar	4,412	11,427	502,000	114	44	Monarchy A	Ad-Dawḥah (Doha)
Quebec	594,860	1,540,680	7,070,000	12	4.6	Province (Canada) D	Québec
Queensland	666,876	1,727,200	3,111,000	4.7	1.8	State (Australia) D	Brisbane
Reunion	969	2,510	643,000	664	256	Overseas department (France) C	Saint-Denis
Rhode Island	1,545	4,002	1,012,000	655	253	State (U.S.) D	Providence
† Romania	91,699	237,500	22,770,000	248	96	Republic A	Bucureşti (Bucharest)
† Russia	6,592,849	17,075,400	150,500,000	23	8.8	Republic A	Moskva (Moscow)
† Rwanda	10,169	26,338	8,196,000	806	311	Provisional military government A	Kigali
St. Helena (incl. Dependencies)	121	314	7,000	58	22	Dependent territory (U.K.) C	Jamestown
† St. Kitts and Nevis	104	269	45,000	433	167	Parliamentary state A	Basseterre
† St. Lucia	238	616	151,000	634	245	Parliamentary state A	Castries
St. Pierre and Miquelon	93	242	7,000	75	29	Territorial collectivity (France) C	Saint-Pierre
† St. Vincent and the Grenadines	150	388	115,000	767	296	Parliamentary state A	Kingstown
† San Marino	24	61	24,000	1,000	393	Republic A	San Marino
† Sao Tome and Principe	372	964	125,000	336	130	Republic A	São Tomé
Saskatchewan	251,866	652,330	1,006,000	4.0	1.5	Province (Canada) D	Regina
† Saudi Arabia	830,000	2,149,690	16,585,000	20	7.7	Monarchy A	Ar-Riyāḍ (Riyadh)
Scotland	30,421	78,789	5,130,000	169	65	Administrative division (U.K.) D	Edinburgh
† Senegal	75,951	196,712	8,522,000	112	43	Republic A	Dakar
† Seychelles	175	453	72,000	411	159	Republic A	Victoria
Shanghai	2,394	6,200	13,970,000	5,835	2,253	Autonomous city (China) D	Shanghai
Shansi (Shanxi)	60,232	156,000	30,075,000	499	193	Province (China) D	Taiyuan
Shantung (Shandong)	59,074	153,000	88,450,000	1,497	578	Province (China) D	Jinan
Shensi (Shaanxi)	79,151	205,000	34,455,000	435	168	Province (China) D	Xi'an (Sian)
† Sierra Leone	27,925	72,325	4,538,000	163	63	Transitional military government A	Freetown
† Singapore	246	636	2,834,000	11,520	4,456	Republic A	Singapore
Sinkiang Uighur (Xinjiang Uygur) .	617,764	1,600,000	15,865,000	26	9.9	Autonomous region (China) D	Ürümqi
† Slovakia	18,933	49,035	5,342,000	282	109	Republic A	Bratislava

World Political Information

Country, Division or Region English (Conventional)	Area in sq. mi.	Area in sq. km.	Estimated Population 1/1/94	Pop. per sq. mi.	Pop. per sq. km.	Form of Government and Political Status		Capital
† Slovenia	7,820	20,253	1,986,000	254	98	Republic	A	Ljubljana
† Solomon Islands	10,954	28,370	376,000	34	13	Parliamentary state	A	Honiara
† Somalia	246,201	637,657	6,541,000	27	10	None	A	Muqdisho (Mogadishu)
† South Africa	471,010	1,219,909	42,320,000	90	35	Republic	A	Pretoria, Cape Town, and Bloemfontein
South America	6,900,000	17,800,000	304,500,000	44	17			...
South Australia	379,925	984,000	1,495,000	3.9	1.5	State (Australia)	D	Adelaide
South Carolina	32,007	82,898	3,657,000	114	44	State (U.S.)	D	Columbia
South Dakota	77,121	199,745	726,000	9.4	3.6	State (U.S.)	D	Pierre
South Georgia and the South Sandwich Islands	1,450	3,755	(1)	...	...	Dependent territory (U.K.)	C	...
† Spain	194,885	504,750	38,640,000	198	77	Constitutional monarchy	A	Madrid
Spanish North Africa (6)	12	32	142,000	11,833	4,438	Five possessions (Spain)	C	...
† Sri Lanka	24,962	64,652	17,970,000	720	278	Socialist republic	A	Colombo and Sri Jayawardenepura
† Sudan	967,500	2,505,813	28,900,000	30	12	Provisional military government	A	Al-Khartūm (Khartoum)
† Suriname	63,251	163,820	418,000	6.6	2.6	Republic	A	Paramaribo
† Swaziland	6,704	17,364	854,000	127	49	Monarchy	A	Mbabane and Lobamba
† Sweden	173,732	449,964	8,747,000	50	19	Constitutional monarchy	A	Stockholm
Switzerland	15,943	41,293	7,001,000	439	170	Federal republic	A	Bern (Berne)
† Syria	71,498	185,180	13,695,000	192	74	Socialist republic	A	Dimashq (Damascus)
Szechwan (Sichuan)	220,078	570,000	112,250,000	510	197	Province (China)	D	Chengdu
Taiwan	13,900	36,002	20,945,000	1,507	582	Republic	A	T'aipei
† Tajikistan	55,251	143,100	5,720,000	104	40	Republic	A	Dušanbe
† Tanzania	364,900	945,087	27,450,000	75	29	Republic	A	Dar es Salaam and Dodoma
Tasmania	26,178	67,800	483,000	18	7.1	State (Australia)	D	Hobart
Tennessee	42,146	109,158	5,058,000	120	46	State (U.S.)	D	Nashville
Texas	268,601	695,676	17,925,000	67	26	State (U.S.)	D	Austin
† Thailand	198,115	513,115	58,960,000	298	115	Constitutional monarchy	A	Krung Thep (Bangkok)
Tibet (Xizang)	471,045	1,220,000	2,250,000	4.8	1.8	Autonomous region (China)	D	Lhasa
Tientsin (Tianjin)	4,363	11,300	9,235,000	2,117	817	Autonomous city (China)	D	Tianjin (Tientsin)
† Togo	21,925	56,785	4,142,000	189	73	Provisional military government	A	Lomé
Tokelau	4.6	12	1,500	326	125	Island territory (New Zealand)	C	...
Tonga	288	747	104,000	361	139	Constitutional monarchy	A	Nuku'alofa
† Trinidad and Tobago	1,980	5,128	1,288,000	651	251	Republic	A	Port of Spain
Tsinghai (Qinghai)	277,994	720,000	4,618,000	17	6.4	Province (China)	D	Xining
† Tunisia	63,170	163,610	8,605,000	136	53	Republic	A	Tunis
† Turkey	300,948	779,452	61,540,000	204	79	Republic	A	Ankara
† Turkmenistan	188,456	488,100	3,935,000	21	8.1	Republic	A	Ašchabad (Ashgabat)
Turks and Caicos Islands	193	500	13,000	67	26	Dependent territory (U.K.)	C	Grand Turk
Tuvalu	10	26	10,000	1,000	385	Parliamentary state	A	Funafuti
† Uganda	93,104	241,139	18,425,000	198	76	Republic	A	Kampala
† Ukraine	233,090	603,700	52,240,000	224	87	Republic	A	Kyyiv (Kiev)
† United Arab Emirates	32,278	83,600	2,692,000	83	32	Federation of monarchs	A	Abū Zaby (Abu Dhabi)
† United Kingdom	94,249	244,101	57,960,000	615	237	Constitutional monarchy	A	London
† United States	3,787,425	9,809,431	259,390,000	68	26	Federal republic	A	Washington
† Uruguay	68,500	177,414	3,181,000	46	18	Republic	A	Montevideo
Utah	84,904	219,902	1,842,000	22	8.4	State (U.S.)	D	Salt Lake City
† Uzbekistan	172,742	447,400	22,240,000	129	50	Republic	A	Taškent (Toshkent)
† Vanuatu	4,707	12,190	160,000	34	13	Republic	A	Port Vila
Vatican City	0.2	0.4	900	4,500	2,250	Monarchical-sacerdotal state	A	Città del Vaticano (Vatican City)
† Venezuela	352,145	912,050	20,460,000	58	22	Federal republic	A	Caracas
Vermont	9,615	24,903	585,000	61	23	State (U.S.)	D	Montpelier
Victoria	87,877	227,600	4,566,000	52	20	State (Australia)	D	Melbourne
† Vietnam	127,428	330,036	72,080,000	566	218	Socialist republic	A	Ha Noi
Virginia	42,769	110,771	6,485,000	152	59	State (U.S.)	D	Richmond
Virgin Islands	133	344	97,000	729	282	Unincorporated territory (U.S.)	C	Charlotte Amalie
Wake Island	3.0	7.8	300	100	38	Unincorporated territory (U.S.)	C	...
Wales	8,015	20,758	2,905,000	362	140	Administrative division (U.K.)	D	Cardiff
Wallis and Futuna	98	255	14,000	143	55	Overseas territory (France)	C	Mata-Utu
Washington	71,303	184,674	5,188,000	73	28	State (U.S.)	D	Olympia
West Bank (incl. Jericho and East Jerusalem)	2,347	6,078	1,460,000	622	240	Israeli territory with limited self-government		...
Western Australia	975,101	2,525,500	1,703,000	1.7	0.7	State (Australia)	D	Perth
Western Sahara	102,703	266,000	208,000	2.0	0.8	Occupied by Morocco		El Aaiún (Laayone)
† Western Samoa	1,093	2,831	168,000	154	59	Constitutional monarchy	A	Apia
West Virginia	24,231	62,759	1,816,000	75	29	State (U.S.)	D	Charleston
Wisconsin	65,503	169,653	5,058,000	77	30	State (U.S.)	D	Madison
Wyoming	97,818	253,349	467,000	4.8	1.8	State (U.S.)	D	Cheyenne
† Yemen	203,850	527,968	10,840,000	53	21	Republic	A	San'ā'
† Yugoslavia	39,449	102,173	10,730,000	272	105	Republic	A	Beograd (Belgrade)
Yukon Territory	186,661	483,450	28,000	0.2	0.1	Territory (Canada)	D	Whitehorse
Yunnan	152,124	394,000	38,720,000	255	98	Province (China)	D	Kunming
† Zaire	905,446	2,345,095	41,675,000	46	18	Republic	A	Kinshasa
† Zambia	290,586	752,614	8,625,000	30	11	Republic	A	Lusaka
† Zimbabwe	150,873	390,759	10,605,000	70	27	Republic	A	Harare (Salisbury)
WORLD	57,900,000	150,100,000	5,556,000,000	96	37			...

† Member of the United Nations (1993).
(1) No permanent population.
(2) North Cyprus unilaterally declared its independence from Cyprus in 1983.
(3) Claimed by Argentina.
(4) Future capital.
(5) Claimed by Comoros.
(6) Comprises Ceuta, Melilla, and several small islands.

General Information

MOVEMENTS OF THE EARTH

The earth makes one complete revolution around the sun every 365 days, 5 hours, 48 minutes, and 46 seconds.

The earth makes one complete rotation on its axis in 23 hours, 56 minutes and 4 seconds.

The earth revolves in its orbit around the sun at a speed of 66,700 miles per hour (107,343 kilometers per hour).

The earth rotates on its axis at an equatorial speed of more than 1,000 miles per hour (1,600 kilometers per hour).

MEASUREMENTS OF THE EARTH

Estimated age of the earth, at least 4.6 billion years.

Equatorial diameter of the earth, 7,926.38 miles (12,756.27 kilometers).

Polar diameter of the earth, 7,899.80 miles (12,713.50 kilometers).

Mean diameter of the earth, 7,917.52 miles (12,742.01 kilometers).

Equatorial circumference of the earth, 24,901.46 miles (40,075.02 kilometers).

Polar circumference of the earth, 24,855.34 miles (40,000.79 kilometers).

Difference between equatorial and polar circumferences of the earth, 46.12 miles (74.23 kilometers).

Weight of the earth, 6,600,000,000,000,000,000,000 tons, or 6,600 billion billion tons (6,000 billion billion metric tons).

THE EARTH'S SURFACE

Total area of the earth, 197,000,000 square miles (510,000,000 square kilometers).

Total land area of the earth (including inland water and Antarctica), 57,900,000 square miles (150,100,000 square kilometers).

Highest point on the earth's surface, Mt. Everest, Asia, 29,028 feet (8,848 meters).

Lowest point on the earth's land surface, shores of the Dead Sea, Asia, 1,339 feet (408 meters) below sea level.

Greatest known depth of the ocean, the Mariana Trench, southwest of Guam, Pacific Ocean, 35,810 feet (10,915 meters).

THE EARTH'S INHABITANTS

Population of the earth is estimated to be 5,556,000,000 (January 1, 1994).

Estimated population density of the earth, 96 per square mile (37 per square kilometer).

EXTREMES OF TEMPERATURE AND RAINFALL OF THE EARTH

Highest temperature ever recorded, 136° F. (58° C.) at Al-'Azīzīyah, Libya, Africa, on September 13, 1922.

Lowest temperature ever recorded, -129° F. (-89° C.) at Vostok, Antarctica on July 21, 1983.

Highest mean annual temperature, 94° F. (34° C.) at Dalol, Ethiopia.

Lowest mean annual temperature, -70° F. (-50° C.) at Plateau Station, Antarctica.

The greatest local average annual rainfall is at Waialeale, Kauai, Hawaii, 460 inches (11,680 millimeters).

The greatest 24-hour rainfall, 74 inches (1,880 millimeters), is at Cilaos, Reunion Island, March 15-16, 1952.

The lowest local average annual rainfall is at Arica, Chile, .03 inches (8 millimeters).

The longest dry period, over 14 years, is at Arica, Chile, October 1903 to January 1918.

The Continents

CONTINENT	Area (sq. mi.) (sq. km.)	Estimated Population Jan. 1, 1994	Population per sq. mi. (sq. km.)	Mean Elevation (feet) (m.)	Highest Elevation (Feet) (m.)	Lowest Elevation (Feet) (m.)	Highest Recorded Temperature	Lowest Recorded Temperature
North America	9,500,000 (24,700,000)	444,600,000	47 (18)	2,000 (610)	Mt. McKinley, Alaska, United States 20,320 (6,194)	Death Valley, California, United States 282 (84) below sea level	Death Valley, California 134° F (57° C)	Northice, Greenland -87° F (-66° C)
South America	6,900,000 (17,800,000)	304,500,000	44 (17)	1,800 (550)	Cerro Aconcagua, Argentina 22,831 (6,959)	Salinas Chicas, Argentina 138 (42) below sea level	Rivadavia, Argentina 120° F (49° C)	Sarmiento, Argentina -27° F (-33° C)
Europe	3,800,000 (9,900,000)	709,300,000	187 (72)	980 (300)	Gora El'brus, Russia 18,510 (5,642)	Caspian Sea, Europe-Asia 92 (28) below sea level	Sevilla, Spain 122° F (50° C)	Ust' Ščugor, Russia -67° F (-55° C)
Asia	17,300,000 (44,900,000)	3,385,900,000	196 (75)	3,000 (910)	Mt. Everest, China-Nepal 29,028 (8,848)	Dead Sea, Israel-Jordan 1,339 (408) below sea level	Tirat Zevi, Israel 129° F (54° C)	Ojm'akon and Verchojansk, Russia -90° F (-68° C)
Africa	11,700,000 (30,300,000)	663,700,000	58 (23)	1,900 (580)	Kilimanjaro, Tanzania 19,340 (5,895)	Lac Assal, Djibouti 509 (155) below sea level	Al-'Azīzīyah, Libya 136° F (58° C)	Ifrane, Morocco -11° F (-24° C)
Oceania, incl. Australia	3,300,000 (8,500,000)	28,000,000	8.5 (3.3)	. . . .	Mt. Wilhelm, Papua New Guinea 14,793 (4,509)	Lake Eyre, South Australia, Australia 52 (16) below sea level	Cloncurry, Queensland, Australia 128° F (53° C)	Charlottes Pass, New South Wales, Australia -8° F (-22° C)
Australia	2,966,155 (7,682,300)	17,950,000	6.1 (2.3)	1,000 (300)	Mt. Kosciusko, New South Wales 7,310 (2,228)	Lake Eyre, South Australia 52 (16) below sea level	Cloncurry, Queensland 128° F (53° C)	Charlottes Pass, New South Wales -8° F (-22° C)
Antarctica	5,400,000 (14,000,000)	. . . .	. . . .	6,000 (1830)	Vinson Massif 16,066 (4,897)	sea level	Vanda Station 59° F (15° C)	Vostok -129° F (-89° C)
World	57,900,000 (150,100,000)	5,556,000,000	96 (37)	. . . .	Mt. Everest, China-Nepal 29,028 (8,848)	Dead Sea, Israel-Jordan 1,339 (408) below sea level	Al-'Azīzīyah, Libya 136° F (58° C)	Vostok, Antarctica -129° F (-89° C)

Historical Populations *

AREA	1650	1750	1800	1850	1900	1920	1950	1970	1980	1990
North America	5,000,000	5,000,000	13,000,000	39,000,000	106,000,000	147,000,000	219,000,000	316,600,000	365,000,000	423,600,000
South America	8,000,000	7,000,000	12,000,000	20,000,000	38,000,000	61,000,000	111,000,000	187,400,000	239,000,000	293,700,000
Europe	100,000,000	140,000,000	190,000,000	265,000,000	400,000,000	453,000,000	530,000,000	623,700,000	660,300,000	688,000,000
Asia	335,000,000	476,000,000	593,000,000	754,000,000	932,000,000	1,000,000,000	1,418,000,000	2,086,200,000	2,581,000,000	3,156,100,000
Africa	100,000,000	95,000,000	90,000,000	95,000,000	118,000,000	140,000,000	199,000,000	346,900,000	463,800,000	648,300,000
Oceania, incl. Australia	2,000,000	2,000,000	2,000,000	2,000,000	6,000,000	9,000,000	13,000,000	19,200,000	22,700,000	26,300,000
Australia	*	*	*	*	4,000,000	6,000,000	8,000,000	12,460,000	14,510,000	16,950,000
World	550,000,000	725,000,000	900,000,000	1,175,000,000	1,600,000,000	1,810,000,000	2,490,000,000	3,580,000,000	4,332,000,000	5,236,000,000

* Figures prior to 1970 are rounded to the nearest million.   *Figures in italics represent very rough estimates.*

Largest Countries : Population

		Population 1/1/94				Population 1/1/94
1	China	1,184,060,000		16	Turkey	61,540,000
2	India	906,770,000		17	Thailand	58,960,000
3	United States	259,390,000		18	United Kingdom	57,960,000
4	Indonesia	198,810,000		19	France	57,680,000
5	Brazil	151,310,000		20	Egypt	56,820,000
6	Russia	150,500,000		21	Italy	56,670,000
7	Pakistan	126,090,000		22	Ethiopia	54,170,000
8	Japan	124,840,000		23	Ukraine	52,240,000
9	Bangladesh	115,240,000		24	Korea, South	44,250,000
10	Nigeria	94,550,000		25	Myanmar (Burma)	43,630,000
11	Mexico	90,870,000		26	South Africa	42,320,000
12	Germany	80,930,000		27	Zaire	41,675,000
13	Vietnam	72,080,000		28	Spain	38,640,000
14	Philippines	66,190,000		29	Poland	38,540,000
15	Iran	63,940,000		30	Colombia	35,085,000

Largest Countries : Area

		Area (sq. mi.)	Area (sq. km.)			Area (sq. mi.)	Area (sq. km.)
1	Russia	6,592,849	17,075,400	17	Libya	679,362	1,759,540
2	Canada	3,849,674	9,970,610	18	Iran	632,457	1,638,057
3	United States	3,787,425	9,809,431	19	Mongolia	604,829	1,566,500
4	China	3,689,631	9,556,100	20	Peru	496,225	1,285,216
5	Brazil	3,286,500	8,511,996	21	Chad	495,755	1,284,000
6	Australia	2,966,155	7,682,300	22	Niger	489,191	1,267,000
7	India	1,237,062	3,203,975	23	Mali	482,077	1,248,574
8	Argentina	1,073,519	2,780,400	24	Angola	481,354	1,246,700
9	Kazakhstan	1,049,156	2,717,300	25	South Africa	471,010	1,219,909
10	Sudan	967,500	2,505,813	26	Ethiopia	446,953	1,157,603
11	Algeria	919,595	2,381,741	27	Colombia	440,831	1,141,748
12	Zaire	905,446	2,345,095	28	Bolivia	424,165	1,098,581
13	Greenland	840,004	2,175,600	29	Mauritania	395,956	1,025,520
14	Saudi Arabia	830,000	2,149,690	30	Egypt	386,662	1,001,449
15	Mexico	759,534	1,967,183				
16	Indonesia	752,410	1,948,732				

Principal Mountains

North America

	Height (feet)	Height (meters)
McKinley, Mt., Δ Alaska (Δ United States; Δ North America)	20,320	*6,194*
Logan, Mt., Δ Canada (Δ Yukon; Δ St. Elias Mts.)	19,524	*5,951*
Orizaba, Pico de, Δ Mexico	18,406	*5,610*
St. Elias, Mt., Alaska-Canada	18,008	*5,489*
Popocatépetl, Volcán, Mexico	17,930	*5,465*
Foraker, Mt., Alaska	17,400	*5,304*
Iztaccíhuatl, Mexico	17,159	*5,230*
Lucania, Mt., Canada	17,147	*5,226*
Fairweather, Mt., Alaska-Canada (Δ British Columbia)	15,300	*4,663*
Whitney, Mt., Δ California,	14,494	*4,418*
Elbert, Mt., Δ Colorado (Δ Rocky Mts.)	14,433	*4,399*
Massive, Mt., Colorado	14,421	*4,396*
Harvard, Mt., Colorado	14,420	*4,395*
Rainier, Mt., Δ Washington (Δ Cascade Range)	14,410	*4,392*
Williamson, Mt., California	14,375	*4,382*
Blanca Pk., Colorado (Δ Sangre de Cristo Mts.)	14,345	*4,372*
La Plata Pk., Colorado	14,336	*4,370*
Uncompahgre Pk., Colorado (Δ San Juan Mts.)	14,309	*4,361*
Grays Pk., Colorado (Δ Front Range)	14,270	*4,349*
Evans, Mt., Colorado	14,264	*4,348*
Longs Pk., Colorado	14,255	*4,345*
Wrangell, Mt., Alaska	14,163	*4,317*
Shasta, Mt., California	14,162	*4,317*
Pikes Pk., Colorado	14,110	*4,301*
Colima, Nevado de, Mexico	13,991	*4,240*
Tajumulco, Volcán, Δ Guatemala (Δ Central America)	13,846	*4,220*
Gannett Pk., Δ Wyoming	13,804	*4,207*
Mauna Kea, Δ Hawaii	13,796	*4,205*
Grand Teton, Wyoming	13,770	*4,197*
Mauna Loa, Hawaii	13,679	*4,169*
Kings Pk., Δ Utah	13,528	*4,123*
Cloud Pk., Wyoming (Δ Bighorn Mts.)	13,167	*4,013*
Wheeler Pk., Δ New Mexico	13,161	*4,011*
Boundary Pk., Δ Nevada	13,143	*4,006*
Waddington, Mt., Canada (Δ Coast Mts.)	13,104	*3,994*
Robson, Mt., Canada (Δ Canadian Rockies)	12,972	*3,954*
Granite Pk., Δ Montana	12,799	*3,901*
Borah Pk., Δ Idaho	12,662	*3,859*
Humphreys Pk., Δ Arizona	12,633	*3,851*
Chirripó, Cerro, Δ Costa Rica	12,533	*3,819*
Columbia, Mt., Canada (Δ Alberta)	12,294	*3,747*
Adams, Mt., Washington	12,276	*3,742*
Gunnbjørn Fjeld, Δ Greenland	12,139	*3,700*
San Gorgonio Mtn., California	11,499	*3,505*
Barú, Volcán, Δ Panama	11,411	*3,475*
Hood, Mt., Δ Oregon	11,235	*3,424*
Lassen Pk., California	10,457	*3,187*
Duarte, Pico, Δ Dominican Rep. (Δ West Indies)	10,417	*3,175*
Haleakala Crater, Hawaii (Δ Maui)	10,023	*3,055*
Paricutín, Mexico	9,186	*2,800*
El Pital, Cerro, Δ El Salvador-Honduras	8,957	*2,730*
La Selle, Morne, Δ Haiti	8,773	*2,674*
Guadalupe Pk., Δ Texas	8,749	*2,667*
Olympus, Mt., Washington (Δ Olympic Mts.)	7,965	*2,428*
Blue Mountain Pk., Δ Jamaica	7,402	*2,256*
Harney Pk., Δ South Dakota (Δ Black Hills)	7,242	*2,207*
Mitchell, Mt., Δ North Carolina (Δ Appalachian Mts.)	6,684	*2,037*
Clingmans Dome, North Carolina-Δ Tennessee (Δ Great Smoky Mts.)	6,643	*2,025*
Turquino, Pico, Δ Cuba	6,470	*1,972*
Washington, Mt., Δ New Hampshire (Δ White Mts.)	6,288	*1,917*
Rogers, Mt., Δ Virginia	5,729	*1,746*
Marcy, Mt., Δ New York (Δ Adirondack Mts.)	5,344	*1,629*
Katahdin, Mt., Δ Maine	5,268	*1,606*
Kawaikini, Hawaii (Δ Kauai)	5,243	*1,598*
Spruce Knob, Δ West Virginia	4,862	*1,482*
Pelée, Montagne, Δ Martinique	4,583	*1,397*
Mansfield, Mt., Δ Vermont (Δ Green Mts.)	4,393	*1,339*
Punta, Cerro de, Δ Puerto Rico	4,389	*1,338*
Black Mtn., Δ Kentucky-Virginia	4,145	*1,263*
Kaala, Hawaii (Δ Oahu)	4,040	*1,231*

South America

Aconcagua, Cerro, Δ Argentina; Δ Andes; (Δ South America)	22,831	*6,959*
Ojos del Salado, Nevado, Argentina-Δ Chile	22,572	*6,880*
Bonete, Cerro, Argentina	22,546	*6,872*
Huascarán, Nevado, Δ Peru	22,204	*6,768*
Llullaillaco, Volcán, Argentina-Chile	22,110	*6,739*
Yerupaja, Nevado, Peru	21,765	*6,634*
Tupungato, Cerro, Argentina-Chile	21,489	*6,550*
Sajama, Nevado, Bolivia	21,463	*6,542*
Illimani, Nevado, Δ Bolivia	21,004	*6,402*
Illampu, Nevado, Bolivia	20,873	*6,362*
Chimborazo, Δ Ecuador	20,702	*6,310*
Antofalla, Volcán, Argentina	20,013	*6,100*
Cotopaxi, Ecuador	19,347	*5,897*
Misti, Volcán, Peru	19,098	*5,821*
Huila, Nevado del, Colombia (Δ Cordillera Central)	16,896	*5,150*
Bolívar, Pico, Δ Venezuela	16,427	*5,007*
Fitzroy, Monte (Cerro Chaltel), Argentina-Chile	11,073	*3,375*
Neblina, Pico da, Δ Brazil-Venezuela	9,888	*3,014*

Europe

El'brus, gora, Δ Russia (Δ Caucasus; Δ Europe)	18,510	*5,642*
Dychtau, gora, Russia	17,073	*5,204*
Blanc, Mont (Monte Bianco), Δ France-Δ Italy (Δ Alps)	15,771	*4,807*
Dufourspitze, Italy-Δ Switzerland	15,203	*4,634*
Weisshorn, Switzerland	14,783	*4,506*
Matterhorn, Italy-Switzerland	14,692	*4,478*
Finsteraarhorn, Switzerland	14,022	*4,274*
Jungfrau, Switzerland	13,642	*4,158*
Écrins, Barre des, France	13,458	*4,102*
Viso, Monte, Italy (Δ Alpes Cottiennes)	12,602	*3,841*
Grossglockner, Δ Austria	12,457	*3,797*
Teide, Pico de, Δ Spain (Δ Canary Is.)	12,188	*3,715*
Mulhacén, Δ Spain (continental)	11,423	*3,482*
Aneto, Pico de, Spain (Δ Pyrenees)	11,168	*3,404*
Perdido, Monte, Spain	11,007	*3,355*
Etna, Monte, Italy (Δ Sicily)	10,902	*3,323*
Zugspitze, Austria-Δ Germany	9,721	*2,963*
Musala, Δ Bulgaria	9,596	*2,925*
Ólimbos, Oros (Mount Olympus), Δ Greece	9,570	*2,917*
Corno Grande, Italy (Δ Apennines)	9,554	*2,912*
Triglav, Δ Slovenia	9,396	*2,864*
Korab, Δ Albania-Macedonia	9,026	*2,751*
Cinto, Monte, France (Δ Corsica)	8,891	*2,710*
Gerlachovský Štít, Δ Slovakia (Δ Carpathian Mts.)	8,711	*2,655*
Moldoveanu, Δ Romania	8,346	*2,544*
Rysy, Czechoslovakia-Δ Poland	8,199	*2,499*
Galdhøpiggen, Δ Norway (Δ Scandinavia)	8,100	*2,469*
Parnassos, Greece	8,061	*2,457*
Ídhi, Óros, Greece (Δ Crete)	8,047	*2,453*
Pico, Ponta do, Δ Portugal (Δ Azores Is.)	7,713	*2,351*
Hvannadalshnúkur, Δ Iceland	6,952	*2,119*
Kebnekaise, Δ Sweden	6,926	*2,111*
Estrela, Δ Portugal (continental)	6,539	*1,993*
Narodnaja, gora, Russia (Δ Ural Mts.)	6,217	*1,895*
Sancy, Puy de, France (Δ Massif Central)	6,184	*1,885*
La Marmora, Punta, Italy (Δ Sardinia)	6,017	*1,834*
Hekla, Iceland	4,892	*1,491*
Nevis, Ben, Δ United Kingdom (Δ Scotland)	4,406	*1,343*
Haltiatunturi, Δ Finland-Norway	4,357	*1,328*
Vesuvio, Italy	4,190	*1,277*
Snowdon, United Kingdom (Δ Wales)	3,560	*1,085*
Carrauntoohil, Δ Ireland	3,406	*1,038*
Kékes, Δ Hungary	3,330	*1,015*
Scafell Pikes, United Kingdom (Δ England)	3,210	*978*

Asia

Everest, Mount, Δ China-Δ Nepal (Δ Tibet; Δ Himalayas; Δ Asia; Δ World)	29,028	*8,848*
K2 (Qogir Feng), China-Δ Pakistan (Δ Kashmir; Δ Karakoram Range)	28,250	*8,611*
Kānchenjunga, Δ India-Nepal	28,208	*8,598*
Makālu, China-Nepal	27,825	*8,481*
Dhawlagiri, Nepal	26,810	*8,172*
Nānga Parbat, Pakistan	26,660	*8,126*
Annapūrna, Nepal	26,504	*8,078*
Gasherbrum, China-Pakistan	26,470	*8,068*
Xixabangma Feng, China	26,286	*8,012*
Nanda Devi, India	25,645	*7,817*
Kamet, China-India	25,447	*7,756*
Namjagbarwa Feng, China	25,446	*7,756*
Muztag, China (Δ Kunlun Shan)	25,338	*7,723*
Tirich Mir, Pakistan (Δ Hindu Kush)	25,230	*7,690*
Gongga Shan, China	24,790	*7,556*
Kula Kangri, Δ Bhutan	24,784	*7,554*
Kommunizma, pik, Δ Tajikistan (Δ Pamir)	24,590	*7,495*
Nowshāk, Δ Afghanistan-Pakistan	24,557	*7,485*
Pobedy, pik, China-Russia	24,406	*7,439*
Chomo Lhari, Bhutan-China	23,997	*7,314*
Muztag, China	23,891	*7,282*
Lenina, pik, Δ Kyrgyzstan-Tajikistan	23,406	*7,134*
Api, Nepal	23,399	*7,132*
Kangrinboqê Feng, China	22,028	*6,714*
Hkakabo Razi, Δ Myanmar	19,296	*5,881*
Damāvend, Qollah-ye, Δ Iran	18,386	*5,604*
Fūlādī, Kūh-e, Afghanistan	16,854	*5,137*
Ağrı Dağı (Mount Ararat), Δ Turkey	16,804	*5,122*
Jaya, Puncak, Δ Indonesia (Δ New Guinea)	16,503	*5,030*
Kl'učevskaja Sopka, vulkan, Russia (Δ Puluostrov Kamčatka)	15,584	*4,750*
Trikora, Puncak, Indonesia	15,584	*4,750*
Belucha, gora, Kazakhstan-Russia	14,783	*4,506*
Turgen, Mount, Mongolia	14,311	*4,362*
Kinabalu, Gunong, Δ Malaysia (Δ Borneo)	13,455	*4,101*
Yü Shan, Δ Taiwan	13,114	*3,997*
Erciyes Dağı, Turkey	12,851	*3,917*
Kerinci, Gunung, Indonesia (Δ Sumatra)	12,467	*3,800*
Fuji-san, Δ Japan (Δ Honshu)	12,388	*3,776*
Nabī Shu'ayb, Jabal an-, Δ Yemen (Δ Arabian Peninsula)	12,335	*3,760*
Rinjani, Gunung, Indonesia (Δ Lombok)	12,224	*3,726*
Semeru, Gunung, Indonesia (Δ Java)	12,060	*3,676*
Rantekombola, Bulu, Indonesia (Δ Celebes)	11,335	*3,455*
Slamet, Gunung, Indonesia	11,247	*3,428*
Fan Si Pan, Δ Vietnam	10,312	*3,143*
Shām, Jabal ash-, Δ Oman	9,957	*3,035*
Apo, Mount, Δ Philippines (Δ Mindanao)	9,692	*2,954*
Pulog, Mount, Philippines (Δ Luzon)	9,626	*2,934*
Bia, Phou, Δ Laos	9,249	*2,819*
Shaykh, Jabal ash-, Lebanon-Δ Syria	9,232	*2,814*
Paektu-san, Δ North Korea-China	9,003	*2,744*
Inthanon, Doi, Δ Thailand	8,530	*2,600*
Pidurutalagala, Δ Sri Lanka	8,281	*2,524*
Mayon Volcano, Philippines	8,077	*2,462*
Asahi-dake, Japan (Δ Hokkaidō)	7,513	*2,290*
Tahan, Gunong, Malaysia (Δ Malaya)	7,174	*2,187*
Ólimbos, Δ Cyprus	6,401	*1,951*
Halla-san, Δ South Korea	6,398	*1,950*
Aôral, Phnum, Δ Cambodia	5,948	*1,813*
Kujū-san, Japan (Δ Kyūshū)	5,863	*1,787*
Ramm, Jabal, Δ Jordan	5,755	*1,754*
Meron, Hare, Δ Israel	3,963	*1,208*
Karmel, Har (Mount Carmel), Israel	1,791	*546*

Africa

Kilimanjaro, Δ Tanzania (Δ Africa)	19,340	*5,895*
Kirinyaga (Mount Kenya), Δ Kenya	17,058	*5,199*
Margherita Peak, Δ Uganda-Δ Zaire	16,763	*5,109*
Ras Dashen Terara, Δ Ethiopia	15,158	*4,620*
Meru, Mount, Tanzania	14,978	*4,565*
Karisimbi, Volcan, Δ Rwanda-Zaire	14,787	*4,507*
Elgon, Mount, Kenya-Uganda	14,178	*4,321*
Toubkal, Jebel, Δ Morocco (Δ Atlas Mts.)	13,665	*4,165*
Cameroon Mountain, Δ Cameroon	13,451	*4,100*
Ntlenyana, Thabana, Δ Lesotho	11,425	*3,482*
eNjesuthi, Δ South Africa	11,306	*3,446*
Koussi, Emi, Δ Chad (Δ Tibesti)	11,204	*3,415*
Kinyeti, Δ Sudan	10,456	*3,187*
Santa Isabel, Pico de, Δ Equatorial Guinea (Δ Bioko)	9,869	*3,008*
Tahat, Δ Algeria (Δ Ahaggar)	9,541	*2,908*
Maromokotro, Δ Madagascar	9,436	*2,876*
Kātrīnā, Jabal, Δ Egypt	8,668	*2,642*
São Tome, Pico de, Δ Sao Tome	6,640	*2,024*

Oceania

Wilhelm, Mount, Δ Papua New Guinea	14,793	*4,509*
Giluwe, Mount, Papua New Guinea	14,330	*4,368*
Bangeta, Mt., Papua New Guinea	13,520	*4,121*
Victoria, Mount, Papua New Guinea (Δ Owen Stanley Range)	13,238	*4,035*
Cook, Mount, Δ New Zealand (Δ South Island)	12,316	*3,754*
Ruapehu, New Zealand (Δ North Island)	9,177	*2,797*
Balbi, Papua New Guinea (Δ Solomon Is.)	9,000	*2,743*
Taranaki, Mount, New Zealand	8,260	*2,518*
Orohena, Mont, Δ French Polynesia (Δ Tahiti)	7,352	*2,241*
Kosciusko, Mount, Δ Australia (Δ New South Wales)	7,277	*2,218*
Silisili, Mauga, Δ Western Samoa	6,096	*1,858*
Panié, Mont, Δ New Caledonia	5,341	*1,628*
Bartle Frere, Australia (Δ Queensland)	5,322	*1,622*
Ossa, Mount, Australia (Δ Tasmania)	5,305	*1,617*
Woodroffe, Mount, Australia (Δ South Australia)	4,724	*1,440*
Sinewit, Mt., Papua New Guinea	4,462	*1,360*
Tomanivi, Δ Fiji (Δ Viti Levu)	4,341	*1,323*
Meharry, Mt., Australia (Δ Western Australia)	4,104	*1,251*
Ayers Rock, Australia	2,844	*867*

Antarctica

Vinson Massif, Δ Antarctica	16,066	*4,897*
Kirkpatrick, Mount, Antarctica	14,856	*4,528*
Markham, Mount, Antarctica	14,272	*4,350*
Jackson, Mount, Antarctica	13,747	*4,190*
Sidley, Mount, Antarctica	13,717	*4,181*
Wade, Mount, Antarctica	13,396	*4,083*

Δ Highest mountain in state, country, range, or region named.

World Oceans, Seas, Gulfs, Lakes, Rivers and Islands

Oceans, Seas and Gulfs

	Area (sq. mi.)	Area (sq. km.)		Area (sq. mi.)	Area (sq. km.)		Area (sq. mi.)	Area (sq. km.)
Pacific Ocean	63,800,000	165,200,000	South China Sea	1,331,000	3,447,000	Okhotsk, Sea of	619,000	1,603,000
Atlantic Ocean	31,800,000	82,400,000	Caribbean Sea	1,063,000	2,753,000	Norwegian Sea	597,000	1,546,000
Indian Ocean	28,900,000	74,900,000	Mediterranean Sea	967,000	2,505,000	Mexico, Gulf of	596,000	1,544,000
Arctic Ocean	5,400,000	14,000,000	Bering Sea	876,000	2,269,000	Hudson Bay	475,000	1,230,000
Arabian Sea	1,492,000	3,864,000	Bengal, Bay of	839,000	2,173,000	Greenland Sea	465,000	1,204,000

Principal Lakes

	Area (sq. mi.)	Area (sq. km.)		Area (sq. mi.)	Area (sq. km.)		Area (sq. mi.)	Area (sq. km.)
Caspian Sea, Asia—Europe. (Salt)	143,240	370,990	Ontario, Lake, Canada—U.S.	7,540	19,529	Issyk-Kul', ozero, Kyrgyzstan (Salt)	2,425	6,280
Superior, Lake, Canada—U.S.	31,700	82,100	Balchaš, ozero, Kazakhstan	Δ 7,100	18,300	Torrens, Lake, Australia (Salt)	2,300	5,900
Victoria, Lake, Kenya—Tanzania—Uganda	26,820	69,463	Ladožskoje ozero, Russia	6,833	17,700	Albert, Lake, Uganda—Zaire	2,160	5,594
Aral Sea, Kazakhstan—Uzbekistan (Salt)	24,700	64,100	Chad, Lake (Lac Tchad), Cameroon—Chad—Nigeria	6,300	16,300	Vänern, Sweden	2,156	5,584
Huron, Lake, Canada—U.S.	23,000	60,000	Onežskoje ozero, Russia	3,753	9,720	Nettilling Lake, Canada	2,140	5,542
Michigan, Lake, U.S.	22,300	57,800	Eyre, Lake, Australia (Salt)	Δ 3,700	9,500	Winnipegosis, Lake, Canada	2,075	5,374
Tanganyika, Lake, Africa	12,350	31,986	Titicaca, Lago, Bolivia—Peru	3,200	8,300	Bangweulu, Lake, Zambia	1,930	4,999
Bajkal, ozero, Russia	12,200	31,500	Nicaragua, Lago de, Nicaragua	3,150	8,158	Nipigon, Lake, Canada	1,872	4,848
Great Bear Lake, Canada	12,095	31,326	Mai-Ndombe, Lac, Zaire	Δ 3,100	8,000	Orūmīyeh, Daryācheh-ye, Iran (Salt)	Δ 1,815	4,701
Malawi, Lake (Lake Nyasa), Malawi—Mozambique—Tanzania	11,150	28,878	Athabasca, Lake, Canada	3,064	7,935	Manitoba, Lake, Canada	1,785	4,624
Great Slave Lake, Canada	11,030	28,568	Reindeer Lake, Canada	2,568	6,650	Woods, Lake of the, Canada—U.S.	1,727	4,472
Erie, Lake, Canada—U.S.	9,910	25,667	Tônlé Sab, Bœng, Cambodia	Δ 2,500	6,500	Kyoga, Lake, Uganda	1,710	4,429
Winnipeg, Lake, Canada	9,416	24,387	Rudolf, Lake, Ethiopia—Kenya (Salt)	2,473	6,405	Great Salt Lake, U.S. (Salt)	1,680	4,351

Δ Due to seasonal fluctuations in water level, areas of these lakes vary considerably.

Principal Rivers

	Length (miles)	Length (km.)		Length (miles)	Length (km.)		Length (miles)	Length (km.)
Nile, Africa	4,145	6,671	Euphrates, Asia	1,510	2,430	Canadian, North America	906	1,458
Amazon-Ucayali, South America	4,000	6,400	Ural, Asia	1,509	2,428	Brazos, North America	900	1,400
Chang (Yangtze), Asia	3,900	6,300	Arkansas, North America	1,459	2,348	Salado, South America	900	1,400
Mississippi-Missouri, North America	3,740	6,019	Colorado, North America (U.S.-Mexico)	1,450	2,334	Darling, Australia	864	1,390
Huang (Yellow), Asia	3,395	5,464	Aldan, Asia	1,412	2,273	Fraser, North America	851	1,370
Ob'-Irtyš, Asia	3,362	5,410	Syrdarja, Asia	1,370	2,205	Parnaíba, South America	850	1,368
Río de la Plata-Paraná, South America	3,030	4,876	Dnieper, Europe	1,400	2,200	Colorado, North America (Texas)	840	1,352
Congo (Zaïre), Africa	2,900	4,700	Araguaia, South America	1,400	2,200	Dniester, Europe	840	1,352
Paraná, South America	2,800	4,500	Kasai (Cassai), Africa	1,338	2,153	Rhine, Europe	820	1,320
Amur-Argun', Asia	2,761	4,444	Tarim, Asia	1,328	2,137	Narmada, Asia	800	1,300
Amur (Heilong), Asia	2,744	4,416	Kolyma, Asia	1,323	2,129	St. Lawrence, North America	800	1,300
Lena, Asia	2,700	4,400	Orange, Africa	1,300	2,100	Ottawa, North America	790	1,271
Mackenzie, North America	2,635	4,241	Negro, South America	1,300	2,100	Athabasca, North America	765	1,231
Mekong, Asia	2,600	4,200	Ayeyarwady (Irrawaddy), Asia	1,300	2,100	Pecos, North America	735	1,183
Niger, Africa	2,600	4,200	Red, North America	1,270	2,044	Severskij Donec, Europe	735	1,183
Jenisej, Asia	2,543	4,092	Jurúa, South America	1,250	2,012	Green, North America	730	1,175
Missouri-Red Rock, North America	2,533	4,076	Columbia, North America	1,200	2,000	White, North America (Ar.-Mo.)	720	1,159
Mississippi, North America	2,348	3,779	Xingu, South America	1,230	1,979	Cumberland, North America	720	1,159
Murray-Darling, Australia	2,330	3,750	Ucayali, South America	1,220	1,963	Elbe (Labe), Europe	720	1,159
Missouri, North America	2,315	3,726	Saskatchewan-Bow, North America	1,205	1,939	James, North America (N./S. Dakota)	710	1,143
Volga, Europe	2,194	3,531	Peace, North America	1,195	1,923	Gambia, Africa	680	1,094
Madeira, South America	2,013	3,240	Tigris, Asia	1,180	1,899	Yellowstone, North America	671	1,080
São Francisco, South America	1,988	3,199	Don, Europe	1,162	1,870	Tennessee, North America	652	1,049
Grande, Rio (Río Bravo), North America	1,885	3,034	Songhua, Asia	1,140	1,835	Gila, North America	630	1,014
Purús, South America	1,860	2,993	Pečora, Europe	1,124	1,809	Wisła (Vistula), Europe	630	1,014
Indus, Asia	1,800	2,900	Kama, Europe	1,122	1,805	Tagus (Tejo) (Tajo), Europe	625	1,006
Danube, Europe	1,776	2,858	Limpopo, Africa	1,100	1,800	Loire, Europe	625	1,006
Brahmaputra, Asia	1,770	2,849	Angara, Asia	1,105	1,779	Cimarron, North America	600	1,000
Yukon, North America	1,770	2,849	Snake, North America	1,038	1,670	North Platte, North America	618	995
Salween (Nu), Asia	1,750	2,816	Uruguay, South America	1,025	1,650	Albany, North America	610	982
Zambezi, Africa	1,700	2,700	Churchill, North America	1,000	1,600	Tisza (Tisa), Europe	607	977
Vil'uj, Asia	1,647	2,650	Marañón, South America	1,000	1,600	Back, North America	605	974
Tocantins, South America	1,640	2,639	Tobol, Asia	989	1,591	Ouachita, North America	605	974
Orinoco South America,	1,600	2,600	Ohio, North America	981	1,579	Sava, Europe	585	941
Paraguay, South America	1,610	2,591	Magdalena, South America	950	1,529	Nemunas (Neman), Europe	582	937
Amu Darya, Asia	1,578	2,540	Roosevelt, South America	950	1,529	Branco, South America	580	933
Murray, Australia	1,566	2,520	Oka, Europe	900	1,500	Meuse (Maas), Europe	575	925
Ganges, Asia	1,560	2,511	Xiang, Asia	930	1,497	Oder (Odra), Europe	565	909
Pilcomayo, South America	1,550	2,494	Godāvari, Asia	930	1,497	Rhône, Europe	500	800

Principal Islands

	Area (sq. mi.)	Area (sq. km.)		Area (sq. mi.)	Area (sq. km.)		Area (sq. mi.)	Area (sq. km.)
Grønland (Greenland), North America	840,000	2,175,600	Hispaniola, North America	29,400	76,200	New Caledonia, Oceania	6,252	16,192
New Guinea, Asia—Oceania	309,000	800,000	Banks Island, Canada	27,038	70,028	Timor, Indonesia	5,743	14,874
Borneo (Kalimantan), Asia	287,300	744,100	Tasmania, Australia	26,200	67,800	Flores, Indonesia	5,502	14,250
Madagascar, Africa	226,500	587,000	Sri Lanka, Asia	24,900	64,600	Samar, Philippines	5,100	13,080
Baffin Island, Canada	195,928	507,451	Devon Island, Canada	21,331	55,247	Negros, Philippines	4,907	12,710
Sumatera (Sumatra), Indonesia	182,860	473,606	Tierra del Fuego, Isla Grande de, South America	18,600	48,200	Palawan, Philippines	4,550	11,785
Honshū, Japan	89,176	230,966	Kyūshū, Japan	17,129	44,363	Panay, Philippines	4,446	11,515
Great Britain, United Kingdom	88,795	229,978	Melville Island, Canada	16,274	42,149	Jamaica, North America	4,200	11,000
Victoria Island, Canada	83,897	217,291	Southampton Island, Canada	15,913	41,214	Hawaii, United States	4,034	10,448
Ellesmere Island, Canada	75,767	196,236	Spitsbergen, Norway	15,260	39,523	Cape Breton Island, Canada	3,981	10,311
Sulawesi (Celebes), Indonesia	73,057	189,216	New Britain, Papua New Guinea	14,093	36,500	Mindoro, Philippines	3,759	9,735
South Island, New Zealand	57,708	149,463	T'aiwan, Asia	13,900	36,000	Kodiak Island, United States	3,670	9,505
Jawa (Java), Indonesia	51,038	132,187	Hainan Dao, China	13,100	34,000	Bougainville, Papua New Guinea	3,600	9,300
North Island, New Zealand	44,332	114,821	Prince of Wales Island, Canada	12,872	33,339	Cyprus, Asia	3,572	9,251
Cuba, North America	42,800	110,800	Vancouver Island, Canada	12,079	31,285	Puerto Rico, North America	3,500	9,100
Newfoundland, Canada	42,031	108,860	Sicilia (Sicily), Italy	9,926	25,709	New Ireland, Papua New Guinea	3,500	9,000
Luzon, Philippines	40,420	104,688	Somerset Island, Canada	9,570	24,786	Corse (Corsica), France	3,367	8,720
Ísland (Iceland), Europe	39,800	103,000	Sardegna (Sardinia), Italy	9,301	24,090	Kríti (Crete), Greece	3,189	8,259
Mindanao, Philippines	36,537	94,630	Shikoku, Japan	7,258	18,799	Vrangel'a, ostrov (Wrangel Island), Russia	2,800	7,300
Ireland, Europe	32,600	84,400	Seram (Ceram), Indonesia	7,191	18,625	Leyte, Philippines	2,785	7,214
Hokkaidō, Japan	32,245	83,515	Nordaustlandet (North East Land), Norway	6,350	16,446	Guadalcanal, Solomon Islands	2,060	5,336
Novaja Zeml'a (Novaya Zemlya), Russia	31,900	82,600				Long Island, United States	1,377	3,566
Sachalin, ostrov (Sakhalin), Russia	29,500	76,400						

World Populations

This table includes every urban center of 50,000 or more population in the world as well as many other important or well-known cities and towns.

The population figures are all from recent censuses (designated C) or official estimates (designated E), except for a few cities for which only unofficial estimates are available (designated U). The date of the census or estimate is specified for each country. Individual exceptions are dated in parentheses.

For many cities, a second population figure is given accompanied by a star (★). The starred population refers to the city's entire metropolitan area, including suburbs. These metropolitan areas have been defined by Rand McNally, following consistent rules to facilitate comparisons among the urban centers of various countries. Where a place is part of the metropolitan area of another city, that city's name is specified in parentheses preceded by (★). A population preceded by a triangle (▲) refers to an entire municipality, commune, or other district, which includes rural areas in addition to the urban center itself. The names of capital cities appear in CAPITALS; the largest city in each country is designated by the symbol (•).

For more recent population totals for countries, see the Rand McNally population estimates in the World Political Information table.

AFGHANISTAN / Afghānestān
1988 E ... 17,672,000
Herāt ... 177,300
Jalālābād (1982 E) ... 58,000
• KĀBOL ... 1,424,400
Kondūz (1982 E) ... 57,000
Mazār-e Sharīf ... 130,600
Qandahār ... 225,500

ALBANIA / Shqipëri
1989 C ... 3,182,400
Durrës ... 82,700
Elbasan ... 80,700
Korçë ... 63,600
Shkodër ... 79,900
• TIRANË ... 238,100
Vlorë ... 71,700

ALGERIA / Algérie / Djazaïr
1987 C ... 23,038,942
Aïn el Beïda ... 61,997
Aïn Oussera ... 44,270
Aïn Témouchent ... 47,479
Annaba (Bône) ... 305,526
Bab Ezzouar (★El Djazaïr) ... 55,211
Barika ... 56,488
Batna ... 181,601
Béchar ... 107,311
Bejaïa (Bougie) ... 114,534
Beskra ... 128,281
Bordj Bou Arreridj ... 84,264
Bordj el Kiffan (★El Djazaïr) ... 61,035
Boufarik ... 41,305
Bou Saâda ... 66,688
Ech Cheliff (Orléansville) ... 129,976
El Boulaïda ... 170,935
• EL DJAZAÏR (ALGIERS) (★ 2,547,983) ... 1,507,241
El Djelfa ... 84,207
El Eulma ... 67,933
El Wad ... 70,073
Ghardaïa ... 89,415
Ghilizane ... 80,091
Guelma ... 77,821
Jijel ... 62,793
Khemis ... 55,335
Khenchla ... 69,743
Laghouat ... 67,214
Lemdiyya ... 85,195
Maghniyya ... 52,275
Messaad ... 47,460
Mestghanem ... 114,037
Mouaskar ... 64,691
M'Sila ... 65,805
Qacentina ... 440,842
Saïda ... 80,825
Sidi bel Abbès ... 152,778
Skikda ... 128,747
Souq Ahras ... 83,015
Stif ... 170,182
Tbessa ... 107,559
Tihert ... 95,821
Tilimsen ... 126,882
Tizi-Ouzou ... 61,163
Touggourt ... 70,645
Wahran ... 628,558
Wargla ... 81,721

AMERICAN SAMOA / Amerika Samoa
1980 C ... 32,279
• PAGO PAGO ... 3,075

ANDORRA
1991 E ... 54,507
• ANDORRA ... 20,437

ANGOLA
1989 E ... 9,739,100
Benguela (1983 E) ... 155,000
Huambo (Nova Lisboa) (1983 E) ... 203,000
Lobito (1983 E) ... 150,000
• LUANDA ... 1,459,900
Lubango (1984 E) ... 95,915
Namibe (1981 E) ... 100,000

ANGUILLA
1984 C ... 6,680
South Hill ... 961
• THE VALLEY ... 1,042

ANTIGUA AND BARBUDA
1977 E ... 72,000
• SAINT JOHN'S ... 24,359

ARGENTINA
1991 C ... 32,608,560
Almirante Brown (★Buenos Aires) ... 448,762
Avellaneda (★Buenos Aires) ... 346,620
Bahía Blanca ... 255,145
Berazategui (★Buenos Aires) ... 244,881
Berisso (★Buenos Aires) ... 72,703
• BUENOS AIRES (★ 11,000,000) ... 2,960,976
Campana (★Buenos Aires) ... 67,267
Caseros (Tres de Febrero) (★Buenos Aires) ... 349,221
Comodoro Rivadavia ... 124,151
Concordia ... 116,491
Córdoba (★ 1,260,000) ... 1,148,305
Corrientes ... 257,766
Ensenada (★Buenos Aires) ... 47,192
Esteban Echeverría (★Buenos Aires) ... 274,303
Florencio Varela (★Buenos Aires) ... 249,006
Formosa ... 153,855
General San Martín (★Buenos Aires) ... 407,506
General Sarmiento (San Miguel) (★Buenos Aires) ... 646,891
Godoy Cruz (★Mendoza) ... 179,468
Gualeguaychú ... 64,620
Junín ... 70,138
Lanús (★Buenos Aires) ... 466,755
La Plata (★Buenos Aires) ... 520,449
La Rioja ... 104,494
Las Heras (★Mendoza) ... 145,823
Lomas de Zamora (★Buenos Aires) ... 572,769
Mar del Plata ... 519,707
Mendoza (★ 770,000) ... 121,739
Mercedes ... 77,137
Merlo (★Buenos Aires) ... 386,304
Moreno (★Buenos Aires) ... 285,964
Morón (★Buenos Aires) ... 641,541
Necochea ... 59,775
Neuquén ... 167,078
Olavarría ... 72,821
Paraná ... 206,848
Pergamino ... 78,200
Pilar (★Buenos Aires) ... 113,428
Presidencia Roque Sáenz Peña ... 64,476
Posadas ... 201,943
Punta Alta ... 56,165
Quilmes (★Buenos Aires) ... 509,445
Rafaela ... 67,086
Resistencia (★ 291,083) ... 228,199
Río Cuarto ... 134,677
Rosario (★ 1,190,000) ... 894,645
Salta ... 367,099
San Carlos de Bariloche ... 77,750
San Fernando (★Buenos Aires) ... 141,496
San Fernando del Valle de Catamarca (★ 133,050) ... 110,269
San Francisco (★ 58,536) ... 55,828
San Isidro (★Buenos Aires) ... 299,022
San Juan (★ 353,476) ... 119,492
San Justo (★Buenos Aires) ... 1,111,811
San Lorenzo (★Rosario) ... 38,509
San Luis ... 110,353
San Miguel de Tucumán (★ 622,348) ... 470,604
San Nicolás de los Arroyos ... 114,752
San Rafael ... 94,776
San Salvador de Jujuy ... 181,318
Santa Fe (★ 394,888) ... 342,796
Santiago del Estero (★ 255,000) ... 189,490
Tandil ... 90,427
Tigre (★Buenos Aires) ... 253,748
Trelew ... 78,089
Venado Tuerto ... 58,678
Vicente López (★Buenos Aires) ... 289,142
Villa Krause (★San Juan) ... 83,266
Villa María ... 64,763
Villa Nueva (★Mendoza) ... 200,595
Zárate ... 77,877

ARMENIA / Hayastan
1989 C ... 3,283,000
Abovjan (1987 E) ... 53,000
Ečmiadzin (★Jerevan) (1987 E) ... 53,000
• JEREVAN (★ 1,315,000) ... 1,199,000
Kirovakan (1987 E) ... 169,000
Kumajri ... 120,000
Razdan (1987 E) ... 56,000

ARUBA
1987 E ... 64,763
• ORANJESTAD ... 19,800

AUSTRALIA
1991 C ... 16,850,330
Adelaide (★ 1,023,597) ... 14,843
Albury (★ 72,871) ... 40,154
Auburn (★Sydney) ... 48,566
Ballarat (★ 78,342) ... 34,501
Bankstown (★Sydney) ... 153,904
Bayswater (★Perth) ... 44,010
Bendigo (★ 67,315) ... 30,134
Berwick (★Melbourne) ... 69,144
Blacktown (★Sydney) ... 211,710
Blue Mountains (★Sydney) ... 69,420
Box Hill (★Melbourne) ... 45,139
Brisbane (★ 1,334,017) ... 751,115
Broadmeadows (★Melbourne) ... 102,996
Brunswick (★Melbourne) ... 39,886
Camberwell (★Melbourne) ... 83,799
Campbelltown (★Sydney) ... 137,879
CANBERRA (★ 303,846) ... 276,162
Canning (★Perth) ... 65,967
Canterbury (★Sydney) ... 129,232
Caulfield (★Melbourne) ... 67,776
Coburg (★Melbourne) ... 50,625
Cockburn (★Perth) ... 50,380
Coffs Harbour ... 51,520
Dandenong (★Melbourne) ... 57,275
Darwin (★ 78,400) ... 70,072
Doncaster (★Melbourne) ... 102,898
Enfield (★Adelaide) ... 61,502
Essendon (★Melbourne) ... 52,721
Fairfield (★Sydney) ... 175,099
Footscray (★Melbourne) ... 46,844
Frankston (★Melbourne) ... 84,986
Geelong (★ 145,325) ... 13,036
Gosford ... 128,956
Gosnells (★Perth) ... 69,560
Heidelberg (★Melbourne) ... 60,468
Hobart (★ 181,832) ... 47,106
Holroyd (★Sydney) ... 79,132
Hurstville (★Sydney) ... 63,757
Ipswich (★Brisbane) ... 73,299
Keilor (★Melbourne) ... 106,076
Knox (★Melbourne) ... 121,982
Kogarah (★Sydney) ... 46,518
Lake Macquarie (★Newcastle) ... 162,026
Launceston (★ 93,581) ... 59,646
Leichhardt (★Sydney) ... 58,484
Liverpool (★Sydney) ... 98,203
Logan (★Brisbane) ... 142,595
Mackay (★ 53,934) ... 23,052
Malvern (★Melbourne) ... 41,340
Marion (★Adelaide) ... 73,942
Marrickville (★Sydney) ... 78,023
Melbourne (★ 3,022,439) ... 60,476
Melville (★Perth) ... 84,838
Mitcham (★Adelaide) ... 60,939
Moorabbin (★Melbourne) ... 94,161
Newcastle (★ 427,824) ... 131,305
Noarlunga (★Adelaide) ... 80,882
Northcote (★Melbourne) ... 46,547
North Sydney (★Sydney) ... 50,446
Nunawading (★Melbourne) ... 91,468
Oakleigh (★Melbourne) ... 55,151
Parramatta (★Sydney) ... 132,798
Penrith (★Sydney) ... 149,630
Perth (★ 1,143,249) ... 80,517
Prahran (★Melbourne) ... 42,193
Preston (★Melbourne) ... 76,996
Randwick (★Sydney) ... 115,349
Redcliffe (★Brisbane) ... 47,799
Rockdale (★Sydney) ... 84,074
Rockhampton (★ 62,797) ... 59,394
Ryde (★Sydney) ... 90,197
Saint Kilda (★Melbourne) ... 45,481
Salisbury (★Adelaide) ... 106,007
Shoalhaven ... 68,287
Southport (★ 324,429) ... 157,857
South Sydney (★Sydney) ... 77,818
Springvale (★Melbourne) ... 89,478
Stirling (★Perth) ... 172,731
Sunshine (★Melbourne) ... 94,020
• Sydney (★ 3,538,749) ... 13,501
Tea Tree Gully (★Adelaide) ... 83,969
Toowoomba ... 81,043
Townsville (★ 101,398) ... 87,288
Wagga Wagga ... 53,447
Wanneroo (★Perth) ... 167,873
Waverley (★Melbourne) ... 118,265
Waverley (★Sydney) ... 59,095
West Torrens (★Adelaide) ... 42,863
Willoughby (★Sydney) ... 51,503
Wollongong (★ 235,966) ... 173,764
Woodville (★Adelaide) ... 78,824
Woollahra (★Sydney) ... 49,904

AUSTRIA / Österreich
1991 C ... 7,795,786
Bruck an der Mur (★ 50,000) ... 14,046
Graz (★ 265,000) ... 237,810
Innsbruck (★ 200,000) ... 118,112
Klagenfurt (★ 118,000) ... 89,415
Leoben (★ 47,600) ... 28,897
Linz (★ 352,000) ... 203,044
Neunkirchen (★ 45,000) ... 10,216
Salzburg (★ 185,000) ... 143,978
Sankt Pölten (★ 69,500) ... 50,026
Steyr (★ 58,000) ... 39,337
Villach (★ 66,500) ... 54,640
Wels (★ 68,000) ... 52,594
• WIEN (VIENNA) (★ 1,900,000) ... 1,539,848

AZERBAIJAN / Azərbaycan
1991 E ... 7,136,600
Äli Bayramlı ... 61,500
• BAKI (★ 2,020,000) ... 1,080,500
Gäncä ... 282,200
Mingäçevir ... 90,900
Naxçıvan ... 61,700
Şeki ... 57,800
Šumqayıt (★Bakı) ... 236,200
Xankändi (Stepanakert) ... 55,200

BAHAMAS
1990 C ... 254,685
Freeport (▲ 171,542) ... 28,200
• NASSAU ... 141,000

BAHRAIN / Al-Bahrayn
1988 E ... 473,000
• AL-MANĀMAH (★ 273,000) (1986 E) ... 82,700
Al-Muharraq (★Al-Manāmah) ... 78,000
Jidd Ḥafṣ (★Al-Manāmah) ... 48,000

BANGLADESH
1991 C ... 104,766,143
Barisāl ... 180,014
Begamganj (1981 C) ... 69,623
Bhairab Bāzār ... 75,747
Bogra ... 93,114
Brāhmanbāria ... 114,297
Chāndpur ... 84,067
Chittagong (★ 2,342,662) ... 1,566,070
Chuādanga ... 65,222
Comilla (1981 C) ... 164,509
• DHAKA (DACCA) (★ 6,537,308) ... 3,637,892
Dinājpur ... 136,657
Farīdpur ... 72,927
Gopālpur ... 45,174
Gulshan (★Dhaka) (1981 C) ... 215,444
Jamālpur ... 108,416
Jessore ... 176,398
Jhenida ... 69,501
Khulna (★ 966,096) ... 601,051
Kishorganj ... 64,676
Kurīgrām ... 62,075
Kushtia ... 71,706
Mādārīpur ... 46,842
Mīrpur (★Dhaka) (1981 C) ... 349,031
Mymensingh ... 138,662
Naogaon ... 109,156
Nārāyanganj (★Dhaka) ... 288,008
Narsinghdi ... 100,120
Nawābganj ... 131,260
Noākhāli ... 73,766
Pābna ... 113,146
Patuākhāli ... 50,344
Rājshāhi (★ 560,013) ... 324,532
Rangpur ... 220,849
Saidpur ... 110,494
Sātkhira ... 81,199
Sherpur ... 63,030
Sirājganj ... 100,003
Sītākunda (★Chittagong) (1981 C) ... 237,520
Sylhet ... 114,284
Tangail ... 111,783
Tongi (★Dhaka) ... 165,099

BARBADOS
1980 C ... 244,228
• BRIDGETOWN (★ 115,000) ... 7,466

BELARUS / Byelarus'
1991 E ... 10,260,400
Baranoviči ... 166,700
Bobrujsk ... 223,000
Borisov ... 150,200
Brest ... 277,000
Gomel' ... 503,300
Grodno ... 284,800
Kobrin ... 48,300
Lida ... 95,000
• MINSK (★ 1,694,000) ... 1,633,600
Mogil'ov ... 363,000
Molodečno ... 93,500
Mozyr' ... 103,000
Novopolock ... 96,600
Orša ... 125,300
Pinsk ... 123,800
Polock ... 78,700
Rečica ... 69,400
Sluck ... 60,100
Soligorsk ... 96,000
Vitebsk ... 361,500
Žlobin ... 60,800
Žodino ... 56,000

BELGIUM / België / Belgique
1987 E ... 9,864,751
Aalst (Alost) (★Bruxelles) ... 77,113
Anderlecht (★Bruxelles) ... 88,849
Antwerpen (★ 1,100,000) ... 479,748
Bastogne (▲ 11,699) ... 6,900
Brugge (Bruges) (★ 223,000) ... 117,755
• BRUXELLES (★ 2,385,000) ... 136,920
Charleroi (★ 480,000) ... 209,395
Etterbeek (★Bruxelles) ... 44,240
Forest (★Bruxelles) ... 48,266
Genk (★Hasselt) ... 61,391
Gent (Gand) (★ 465,000) ... 233,856
Hasselt (★ 290,000) ... 65,563
Ixelles (★Bruxelles) ... 76,241
Kortrijk (Courtrai) (★ 202,000) ... 76,216
La Louvière (★ 147,000) ... 76,340
Leuven (Louvain) (★ 173,000) ... 84,583
Liège (Luik) (★ 750,000) ... 200,891
Mechelen (Malines) (★ 121,000) ... 75,808
Molenbeek-St.-Jean (★Bruxelles) ... 69,764
Mons (Bergen) (★ 242,000) ... 89,697
Mouscron (★Lille, France) ... 53,713
Namur (★ 147,000) ... 102,670
Oostende (Ostende) (★ 122,000) ... 68,318
Roeselare (Roulers) ... 51,963
Saint-Gilles (★Bruxelles) ... 42,482
Schaerbeek (★Bruxelles) ... 104,919
Seraing (★Liège) ... 61,731
Sint-Niklaas (Saint-Nicolas) ... 68,082
Spa ... 9,645
Tournai (Doornik) (▲ 66,998) ... 44,900
Uccle (★Bruxelles) ... 75,876
Verviers (★ 101,000) ... 53,498
Waterloo (★Bruxelles) ... 25,232
Woluwe-Saint-Lambert (Sint-Lambrechts-Woluwe) (★Bruxelles) ... 47,887

BELIZE
1990 C ... 184,340
• Belize City ... 43,621
BELMOPAN ... 5,256

BENIN / Bénin
1984 E ... 3,825,000
Abomey ... 53,000
• COTONOU (1992 C) ... 533,212
Parakou ... 92,000
PORTO-NOVO ... 164,000

BERMUDA
1985 E ... 56,000
• HAMILTON (★ 15,000) ... 1,676

BHUTAN / Druk-Yul
1982 E ... 1,333,000
• THIMPHU ... 12,000

C Census. E Official estimate. U Unofficial estimate.
• Largest city in country.
★ Population or designation of metropolitan area, including suburbs (see headnote).
▲ Population of an entire municipality, commune, or district, including rural area.

BOLIVIA

1990 E ... 7,314,000

Cochabamba ... 413,300
• LA PAZ ... 1,125,600
Montero (1988 E) ... 84,100
Oruro ... 207,700
Potosí ... 120,100
Santa Cruz de la Sierra ... 696,100
SUCRE ... 101,400
Tarija ... 74,600
Trinidad ... 51,900

BOSNIA AND HERZEGOVINA / Bosna i Hercegovina

1987 E ... 4,400,464

Banja Luka (▲ 193,890) ... 130,900
• SARAJEVO (▲ 479,688) ... 341,200
Tuzla (▲ 129,967) ... 67,300
Zenica (▲ 144,869) ... 67,500

BOTSWANA

1991 C ... 1,326,796

Francistown ... 65,244
• GABORONE ... 133,468
Selebi Phikwe ... 39,772

BRAZIL / Brasil

1991 C ... 146,917,459

Abaetetuba (▲ 100,016) ... 55,442
Abreu e Lima (▲ 76,568) ... 70,099
Alagoinhas (▲ 116,740) ... 97,819
Alegrete (▲ 78,879) ... 67,505
Almirante Tamandaré (▲ 66,090) ... 51,240
Altamira (▲ 120,441) ... 48,452
Alvorada (▲ 142,020) (★Porto Alegre) ... 132,582
Americana ... 153,592
Ananindeua (▲ 88,035) ... 73,941
Anápolis (▲ 239,047) ... 222,400
Anil (▲ 695,199) ... 81,879
Antônio Bezerra (▲ 1,765,794) (★Fortaleza) ... 193,682
Aparecida de Goiânia (▲ 178,326) ... 48,804
Apucarana (▲ 94,914) ... 80,048
Aracaju ... 401,676
Araçatuba (▲ 159,499) ... 146,977
Araguaína (▲ 103,396) ... 81,729
Araguari (▲ 91,202) ... 80,568
Arapiraca (▲ 165,379) ... 131,449
Arapongas (▲ 64,531) ... 59,996
Araraquara (▲ 166,732) ... 101,302
Araras (▲ 87,355) ... 79,002
Araucária (▲ 61,767) ... 53,522
Araxá ... 67,919
Arcoverde (▲ 55,790) ... 49,479
Assis (▲ 85,265) ... 72,004
Atibaia (▲ 86,193) ... 74,658
Avaré (▲ 61,063) ... 56,232
Bacabal (▲ 98,875) ... 64,844
Bagé (▲ 118,736) ... 89,372
Barbacena (▲ 99,895) ... 80,682
Barra Alegre (▲ 179,710) ... 58,445
Barra do Piraí (▲ 78,426) ... 59,202
Barra Mansa (▲ 171,671) (★Volta Redonda) ... 145,112
Barreiras (▲ 92,439) ... 70,701
Barreiros (▲ 139,318) (★Florianópolis) ... 58,694
Barretos (▲ 95,538) ... 88,935
Barueri (▲ 130,383) ... 66,722
Bauru ... 254,690
Bayeux (★João Pessoa) ... 77,047
Bebedouro (▲ 67,752) ... 60,792
Belém (★ 1,355,000) ... 765,476
Belford Roxo (▲ 1,293,611) (★Rio de Janeiro) ... 337,698
Belo Horizonte (★ 3,340,000) ... 1,529,566
Betim (★Belo Horizonte) ... 162,462
Birigui ... 70,547
Blumenau (▲ 211,862) ... 185,200
Boa Vista (▲ 142,902) ... 118,928
Botucatu (▲ 90,620) ... 81,528
Bragança Paulista (▲ 108,602) ... 88,336
Brás Cubas (▲ 273,255) ... 65,538
BRASÍLIA ... 1,513,470
Brusque ... 53,438
Cabo (▲ 126,756) ... 68,594
Cabo Frio (▲ 84,635) ... 70,251
Caçapava (▲ 65,889) ... 58,145
Cáceres (▲ 77,475) ... 51,891
Cachoeira do Sul (▲ 89,148) ... 69,780
Cachoeirinha (★Porto Alegre) ... 87,976
Cachoeiro de Itapemirim (▲ 143,763) ... 112,099
Camaçari (▲ 113,615) ... 88,302
Camarajibe ... 99,431
Cambé (▲ 73,803) ... 66,767
Campina Grande ... 298,331
Campinas (★ 1,290,000) ... 759,032
Campo Comprido (▲ 1,313,094) (★Curitiba) ... 105,631
Campo Grande ... 516,403
Campo Mourão (▲ 82,280) ... 69,966
Campos (▲ 388,747) ... 277,482
Campos Elísios (▲ 665,343) (★Rio de Janeiro) ... 197,833
Candeias (▲ 67,936) ... 61,432
Canoas (★Porto Alegre) ... 269,234
Capuáva (▲ 615,112) ... 92,950
Carapicuíba (▲ 283,653) (★São Paulo) ... 207,264
Carapina (▲ 221,510) (★Vit2oria) ... 141,234
Carazinho (▲ 58,770) ... 49,010
Cariacica (▲ 274,455) (★Vitória) ... 91,888
Caruaru (▲ 213,573) ... 180,654
Cascatinha (▲ 255,261) ... 56,890
Cascavel (▲ 192,884) ... 175,332
Castanhal (▲ 101,963) ... 90,364
Catanduva ... 88,024
Caucaia (▲ 165,015) (★Fortaleza) ... 66,379
Cava (▲ 1,293,611) ... 59,506
Cavaleiro (▲ 486,774) (★Recife) ... 120,065
Caxias (▲ 146,730) ... 85,332
Caxias do Sul (▲ 290,969) ... 262,983
Chapecó (▲ 122,889) ... 93,697
Codó (▲ 111,679) ... 58,163
Coelho da Rocha (▲ 424,689) (★Rio de Janeiro) ... 152,045
Colatina (▲ 106,712) ... 71,094
Colombo (▲ 117,658) (★Curitiba) ... 110,161
Conselheiro Lafaiete (▲ 88,843) ... 82,619
Contagem (▲ 448,991) (★Belo Horizonte) ... 195,705
Corumbá (▲ 88,290) ... 75,235
Cotia (▲ 106,822) ... 90,469
Coxipó da Ponte (▲ 401,303) ... 140,130
Crato (▲ 91,413) ... 56,374
Criciúma (▲ 146,162) ... 99,375
Cruz Alta (▲ 68,784) ... 61,860
Cruzeiro ... 65,935
Cubatão (★Santos) ... 90,572
Cuiabá (▲ 401,303) ... 252,784
Curitiba (★ 1,815,000) ... 841,882
Diadema (★São Paulo) ... 305,068
Divinópolis (▲ 151,382) ... 141,984
Dourados (▲ 135,786) ... 116,817
Dracena (▲ 39,576) ... 33,856
Duque de Caxias (▲ 665,343) (★Rio de Janeiro) ... 325,903
Embu (★São Paulo) ... 155,851
Erechim (▲ 72,292) ... 61,509
Esteio (★Porto Alegre) ... 70,449
Eunápolis (▲ 70,561) ... 63,553
Feira de Santana (▲ 405,848) ... 340,034
Fernandópolis (▲ 56,125) ... 51,216
Ferraz de Vasconcelos (▲ 95,973) (★São Paulo) ... 65,319
Florianópolis (★ 420,000) ... 191,664
Formosa (▲ 62,974) ... 49,135
Fortaleza (★ 2,040,000) ... 743,335
Foz do Iguaçu ... 186,362
Franca ... 227,613
Francisco Morato ... 83,361
Franco da Rocha ... 79,534
Garanhuns (▲ 103,365) ... 86,593
Goiabeiras (▲ 258,243) (★Vitória) ... 74,086
Goiânia (★ 1,130,000) ... 912,136
Governador Valadares (▲ 230,403) ... 210,396
Gravataí (▲ 181,019) (★Porto Alegre) ... 166,954
Guaíba (▲ 83,119) ... 72,739
Guarapari (▲ 61,594) ... 54,994
Guaratinguetá (▲ 102,005) ... 84,660
Guarujá (▲ 209,814) (★Santos) ... 98,918
Guarulhos (▲ 786,355) (★São Paulo) ... 546,417
Gurupi (▲ 56,741) ... 51,005
Hortolândia (▲ 226,225) ... 78,011
Ibes (▲ 265,251) (★Vitória) ... 91,071
Icoraci (▲ 1,244,688) (★Belém) ... 67,458
Igapó (▲ 606,681) ... 117,251
Igarassu (▲ 79,713) (★Recife) ... 48,598
Ijuí (▲ 75,169) ... 58,627
Ilhéus (▲ 223,482) ... 135,117
Imbariê (▲ 665,343) ... 100,687
Imperatriz (▲ 276,440) ... 209,970
Indaiatuba (▲ 100,816) ... 91,752
Inhomirim (▲ 191,249) ... 76,031
Ipatinga (▲ 179,710) ... 120,025
Ipiiba (▲ 778,831) (★Rio de Janeiro) ... 121,785
Itabira (▲ 85,284) ... 71,287
Itaboraí (▲ 161,398) ... 72,410
Itabuna (▲ 185,165) ... 170,434
Itaguaí (▲ 113,019) ... 48,274
Itaipu (▲ 435,658) ... 35,072
Itaituba (▲ 116,541) ... 62,278
Itajaí ... 114,558
Itajubá (▲ 74,618) ... 68,469
Itambi (▲ 161,398) ... 48,891
Itapecerica da Serra (▲ 92,854) (★São Paulo) ... 84,479
Itaperuna (▲ 78,017) ... 55,484
Itapetininga (▲ 105,071) ... 84,703
Itapeva (▲ 81,858) ... 55,658
Itapevi (★São Paulo) ... 107,983
Itaquaquecetuba (★São Paulo) ... 164,665
Itaquari (▲ 274,455) (★Vitória) ... 169,145
Itatiba (▲ 61,587) ... 54,044
Itaúna ... 61,891
Itú (▲ 107,176) ... 88,838
Ituiutaba (▲ 84,581) ... 78,211
Itumbiara (▲ 79,457) ... 68,673
Jaboatão (▲ 486,774) (★Recife) ... 81,178
Jaboticabal (▲ 59,130) ... 53,027
Jacareí (▲ 163,843) ... 144,141
Jandira ... 62,573
Japeri (▲ 1,293,611) ... 65,576
Jaraguá do Sul (▲ 76,994) ... 62,578
Jardim Presidente Dutra (▲ 786,355) (★São Paulo) ... 229,987
Jataí (▲ 65,921) ... 53,431
Jaú (▲ 94,138) ... 80,331
Jequié (▲ 144,572) ... 114,542
Ji-Paraná (▲ 97,719) ... 75,384
João Monlevade ... 57,413
João Pessoa (★ 670,000) ... 497,308
Joinvile ... 326,208
Juàzeiro 128,691) (★Petrolina) ... 95,676
Juazeiro do Norte ... 163,527
Juiz de Fora ... 377,538
Jundiaí (▲ 288,644) ... 265,599
Jurema (▲ 165,015) (★Fortaleza) ... 75,463
Justinópolis (▲ 143,696) (★Belo Horizonte) ... 85,452
Lages (▲ 151,100) ... 137,169
Lavras (▲ 65,857) ... 60,690
Leme ... 64,525
Limeira (▲ 207,416) ... 177,591
Linhares (▲ 119,501) ... 73,082
Lins (▲ 59,218) ... 54,868
Londrina (▲ 389,959) ... 355,062
Lorena (▲ 73,167) ... 67,766
Luziânia (▲ 207,425) ... 194,128
Macaé (▲ 100,642) ... 57,581
Macapá (▲ 179,252) ... 146,523
Maceió (▲ 628,241) ... 554,727
Manaus ... 1,005,634
Marabá (▲ 122,231) ... 102,364
Marília (▲ 160,872) ... 144,906
Maringá ... 225,516
Matão ... 59,694
Mauá (★São Paulo) ... 294,631
Mesquita (▲ 1,293,611) (★Rio de Janeiro) ... 141,326
Messejana (▲ 1,765,794) (★Fortaleza) ... 229,507
Moji das Cruzes (▲ 273,255) (★São Paulo) ... 138,995
Mojiguaçu (▲ 107,440) ... 92,440
Mojimirim (▲ 64,750) ... 57,395
Mondubim (▲ 1,765,794) (★Fortaleza) ... 331,591
Monjolo (▲ 778,831) (★Rio de Janeiro) ... 137,974
Montes Claros (▲ 249,565) ... 223,046
Mossoró (▲ 191,959) ... 177,020
Muriaé (▲ 84,507) ... 65,406
Muribeca dos Guararapes (▲ 486,774) (★Recife) ... 217,905
Natal (▲ 606,681) ... 459,827
Neves (▲ 778,831) (★Rio de Janeiro) ... 151,067
Nilópolis (▲ 157,936) (★Rio de Janeiro) ... 104,671
Niterói (▲ 435,658) (★Rio de Janeiro) ... 400,586
Nossa Senhora do Socorro ... 67,443
Nova Brasília (▲ 178,326) (★Goiânia) ... 126,701
Nova Friburgo (▲ 166,975) ... 111,020
Nova Iguaçu (▲ 1,293,611) (★Rio de Janeiro) ... 562,062
Nova Veneza (▲ 226,225) ... 82,203
Novo Hamburgo (★Porto Alegre) ... 201,334
Novo Mundo (▲ 1,313,094) (★Curitiba) ... 71,508
Olinda (★Recife) ... 341,059
Olinda (▲ 157,936) ... 53,265
Osasco (★São Paulo) ... 566,949
Ourinhos (▲ 76,912) ... 70,690
Palhoça (▲ 68,298) (★Florianópolis) ... 58,097
Paracatu (▲ 62,709) ... 49,656
Pará de Minas (▲ 61,066) ... 51,679
Paranaguá (▲ 107,601) ... 88,110
Paranavaí (▲ 71,173) ... 61,043
Parangaba (▲ 1,765,794) (★Fortaleza) ... 267,679
Parauapebas (▲ 53,312) ... 27,452
Parnaíba (▲ 127,992) ... 105,131
Parnamirim (▲ 63,253) ... 48,534
Parque Industrial (▲ 448,991) (★Belo Horizonte) ... 223,660
Passo do Sabão (▲ 169,079) (★Porto Alegre) ... 63,140
Passo Fundo (▲ 147,239) ... 135,158
Passos (▲ 84,618) ... 74,218
Patos (▲ 81,292) ... 76,378
Patos de Minas (▲ 102,766) ... 83,670
Paulista (▲ 211,017) (★Recife) ... 53,566
Paulo Afonso (▲ 86,594) ... 74,326
Pelotas (▲ 290,660) ... 260,510
Petrolina (★ 300,000) ... 123,857
Petrópolis (▲ 255,261) (★Rio de Janeiro) ... 164,849
Pindamonhangaba (▲ 101,939) ... 71,449
Pinhais (▲ 106,764) (★Curitiba) ... 71,973
Pinheirinho (▲ 1,313,094) (★Curitiba) ... 117,516
Piracicaba (▲ 283,634) ... 223,170
Poá (★São Paulo) ... 72,151
Poços de Caldas ... 105,223
Ponta Grossa ... 219,955
Porto Alegre (★ 2,850,000) ... 1,247,352
Porto Velho (▲ 286,471) ... 226,196
Porto Velho (▲ 161,611) ... 56,973
Pouso Alegre (▲ 81,776) ... 73,875
Praia da Conceição (▲ 211,017) (★Recife) ... 97,635
Praia Grande (▲ 123,494) ... 97,173
Presidente Prudente ... 157,618
Queimados (▲ 1,293,611) (★Rio de Janeiro) ... 124,121
Recife (★ 2,880,000) ... 1,296,995
Resende (▲ 91,605) ... 52,261
Ribeirão Pires ... 62,240
Ribeirão Preto ... 416,186
Rio Branco (▲ 196,871) ... 136,457
Rio Claro ... 130,364
Rio de Janeiro (★ 11,050,000) ... 5,473,909
Rio Grande (▲ 172,408) ... 157,608
Rio Verde (▲ 95,894) ... 76,818
Rondonópolis (▲ 126,082) ... 87,307
Salto ... 72,076
Salvador (★ 2,340,000) ... 2,070,296
Santa Bárbara d'Oeste ... 141,230
Santa Cruz do Sul (▲ 117,779) ... 74,295
Santa Felicidade (▲ 1,313,094) (★Curitiba) ... 53,560
Santa Inês (▲ 64,655) ... 54,006
Santa Maria (▲ 217,604) ... 193,294
Santana do Livramento (▲ 80,145) ... 72,950
Santarém (▲ 264,779) ... 168,153
Santa Rita (▲ 94,412) (★João Pessoa) ... 74,396
Santa Rosa (▲ 58,262) ... 48,211
Santo André (▲ 615,112) (★São Paulo) ... 518,272
Santo Angelo (▲ 76,461) ... 59,688
Santo Antônio de Jesus (▲ 64,198) ... 52,770
Santos (★ 1,165,000) ... 415,554
São Benedito (▲ 137,686) (★Belo Horizonte) ... 91,733
São Bernardo do Campo (★São Paulo) ... 550,030
São Borja (▲ 63,766) ... 52,493
São Caetano do Sul (★São Paulo) ... 149,203
São Carlos (▲ 158,186) ... 100,502
São Cristóvão ... 46,172
São Gabriel (▲ 59,024) ... 47,668
São Gonçalo (▲ 778,831) (★Rio de Janeiro) ... 296,021
São João da Boa Vista (▲ 69,090) ... 60,845
São João del-Rei (▲ 72,741) ... 63,680
São João de Meriti (▲ 424,689) (★Rio de Janeiro) ... 220,742
São José do Rio Preto ... 263,454
São José dos Campos (▲ 442,009) ... 385,879
São José dos Pinhais (▲ 128,170) (★Curitiba) ... 99,154
São Leopoldo (★Porto Alegre) ... 160,228
São Lourenço da Mata (▲ 85,889) (★Recife) ... 68,479
São Luís (★ 710,000) ... 164,334
São Mateus (▲ 424,689) ... 51,902
• São Paulo (★ 16,925,000) ... 9,393,753
São Vicente (★Santos) ... 268,467
Sapiranga (▲ 58,522) ... 51,387
Sapucaia do Sul (★Porto Alegre) ... 104,626
Serra (▲ 221,510) ... 62,398
Sertãozinho (▲ 78,753) ... 68,874
Sete Lagoas ... 139,910
Sete Pontes (▲ 778,831) (★Rio de Janeiro) ... 71,984
Sobral (▲ 127,459) ... 92,805
Sorocaba ... 348,952
Sumaré (▲ 226,225) ... 64,673
Susano (▲ 159,142) (★São Paulo) ... 110,414
Taboão da Serra (★São Paulo) ... 159,894
Tatuí (▲ 76,662) ... 68,808
Taubaté (▲ 206,416) ... 185,790
Teixeira de Freitas (▲ 85,227) ... 73,107
Telêmaco Borba (▲ 64,854) ... 50,774
Teófilo Otoni (▲ 140,676) ... 96,382
Teresina (★ 665,000) ... 556,073
Teresópolis (▲ 120,712) ... 96,516
Timon (▲ 107,394) (★Teresina) ... 90,577
Timóteo (▲ 58,393) ... 48,340
Toledo (▲ 94,857) ... 67,343
Três Corações (▲ 57,053) ... 49,138
Três Lagoas (▲ 68,067) ... 60,716
Três Rios (▲ 81,163) ... 60,201
Tubarão (▲ 95,058) ... 83,262
Tucuruí (▲ 81,635) ... 46,011
Tupã (▲ 61,290) ... 53,282
Ubá (▲ 66,422) ... 52,673
Uberaba (▲ 211,356) ... 198,565
Uberlândia ... 355,191
Umbará (▲ 1,313,094) (★Curitiba) ... 64,523
Umuarama (▲ 100,185) ... 66,995
Uruguaiana (▲ 117,437) ... 103,160
Valinhos (▲ 67,867) ... 59,896
Varginha (▲ 88,045) ... 82,263
Várzea Grande (▲ 161,611) ... 96,379
Várzea Paulista ... 67,911
Venda Nova (▲ 2,017,127) (★Belo Horizonte) ... 481,470
Viamão (▲ 169,079) ... 75,782
Vicente de Carvalho (▲ 209,814) (★Santos) ... 110,881
Vila Dirce (▲ 283,653) ... 59,144
Vila Velha (▲ 265,251) (★Vitória) ... 113,664
Vila Xavier (▲ 166,732) ... 50,922
Vitória (★ 810,000) ... 184,157
Vitória da Conquista (▲ 224,896) ... 179,868
Vitória de Santo Antão (▲ 106,661) ... 84,116
Volta Redonda (★ 430,000) ... 219,988
Votorantim ... 79,150
Votuporanga (▲ 66,037) ... 59,604

BRITISH VIRGIN ISLANDS

1980 C ... 12,034

• ROAD TOWN ... 2,479

BRUNEI

1981 C ... 192,832

• BANDAR SERI BEGAWAN (★ 64,000) ... 22,777
Seria ... 23,415

BULGARIA / Bâlgarija

1989 E ... 8,986,636

Asenovgrad ... 58,568
Blagoevgrad ... 74,236
Burgas ... 200,464
Dimitrovgrad ... 57,102
Dobrič ... 112,582
Gabrovo ... 80,930
Haskovo ... 93,609
Jambol ... 97,414
Kărdžali ... 58,995
Kazanlăk ... 63,776
Kjustendil ... 55,620
Loveč ... 50,872
Montana ... 55,203
Pazardžik ... 83,451
Pernik ... 97,930
Pleven ... 136,287
Plovdiv ... 364,162
Razgrad ... 56,494
Ruse ... 190,720
Silistra ... 56,907
Sliven ... 109,432
• SOFIJA (★ 1,205,000) ... 1,136,875
Stara Zagora ... 158,151
Šumen ... 107,973
Varna ... 306,300
Veliko Tărnovo ... 71,709
Vidin ... 65,892
Vraca ... 81,992

BURKINA FASO

1985 C ... 7,964,705

Bobo Dioulasso ... 228,668
Koudougou ... 51,926
• OUAGADOUGOU ... 441,514
Ouahigouya ... 38,902

BURUNDI

1990 C ... 5,356,266

• BUJUMBURA ... 226,628

CAMBODIA / Kâmpŭchéa

1990 E ... 8,567,582

Bătdâmbâng ... 94,412
Kâmpóng Saôm ... 67,452
• PHNUM PENH ... 620,000
Prey Vêng ... 41,456
Siěmréab ... 76,434
Ta Khmau ... 34,947

CAMEROON / Cameroun

1987 C ... 9,312,429

Bafoussam ... 92,381
Bamenda ... 95,455
• Douala ... 712,251
Foumban ... 46,920
Garoua ... 122,564
Kumba ... 63,911
Maroua ... 111,630
Ngaoundéré ... 62,468
Nkongsamba ... 76,887
YAOUNDE ... 560,785

CANADA

1991 C ... 27,296,859

CANADA: ALBERTA

1991 C ... 2,545,553

Calgary (★ 754,033) ... 710,677
Edmonton (★ 839,924) ... 616,741

C Census. E Official estimate. U Unofficial estimate.
• Largest city in country.

★ Population or designation of metropolitan area, including suburbs (see headnote).
▲ Population of an entire municipality, commune, or district, including rural area.

Lethbridge 60,974
Medicine Hat (★ 52,681) 43,625
Red Deer 58,134

CANADA: BRITISH COLUMBIA

1991 C 3,282,061

Burnaby (★Vancouver) 158,858
Chilliwack (★ 60,251) 49,531
Delta (★Vancouver) 95,577
Kamloops (★ 67,856) 67,057
Kelowna (★ 111,846) 75,950
Matsqui (★ 113,562) 68,064
Nanaimo (★ 73,547) 60,129
Prince George 69,653
Richmond (★Vancouver) 126,624
Saanich (★Victoria) 245,173
Surrey (★Vancouver) 84,021
Vancouver (★ 1,602,502) 471,844
Victoria (★ 287,897) 71,228

CANADA: MANITOBA

1991 C 1,091,942

Winnipeg (★ 652,354) 616,790

CANADA: NEW BRUNSWICK

1991 C 723,900

Fredericton (★ 71,869) 46,466
Moncton (★ 106,503) 57,010
Saint John (★ 124,981) 74,969

CANADA: NEWFOUNDLAND

1991 C 568,474

Saint John's (★ 171,859) 95,770

CANADA: NORTHWEST TERRITORIES

1991 C 57,649

Yellowknife 15,179

CANADA: NOVA SCOTIA

1991 C 899,942

Dartmouth (★Halifax) 67,798
Halifax (★ 320,501) 114,455
Sydney (★ 116,100) 26,063

CANADA: ONTARIO

1991 C 10,084,885

Ajax (★Toronto) 57,350
Barrie (★ 92,165) 62,728
Brampton (★Toronto) 234,445
Brantford (★ 97,106) 81,997
Burlington (★Hamilton) 129,575
Cambridge
(Galt) (★Kitchener) 92,772
Cornwall (★ 53,545) 47,137
East York (★Toronto) 102,696
Etobicoke (★Toronto) 309,993
Gloucester (★Ottawa) 101,677
Guelph (★ 97,213) 87,976
Hamilton (★ 599,760) 318,499
Kingston (★ 136,401) 56,597
Kitchener (★ 356,421) 168,282
Leamington (★ 35,792) 14,182
London (★ 381,522) 303,165
Markham (★Toronto) 153,811
Mississauga (★Toronto) 463,388
Nepean (★Ottawa) 107,627
Newcastle 49,479
Niagara Falls (★Saint
Catharines) 75,399
North Bay (★ 63,285) 55,405
North York (★Toronto) 562,564
Oakville (★Toronto) 114,670
Oshawa (★ 240,104) 129,344
OTTAWA (★ 920,857) 313,987
Peterborough (★ 98,060) 68,371
Pickering (★Toronto) 68,631
Richmond Hill (★Toronto) 80,142
Saint Catharines
(★ 364,552) 129,300
Sarnia (★ 87,870) 74,376
Sault Sainte Marie
(★ 101,800) 81,476
Scarborough (★Toronto) 524,598
Stoney
Creek (★Hamilton) 49,968
Sudbury (★ 157,613) 92,884
Thunder Bay (★ 124,427) 113,946
• Toronto (★ 3,893,046) 635,395
Vaughan (★Toronto) 111,359
Waterloo (★Kitchener) 71,181
Whitby (★Oshawa) 61,281
Windsor (★ 262,075) 191,435
York (★Toronto) 140,525

CANADA: PRINCE EDWARD ISLAND

1991 C 129,765

Charlottetown (★ 57,472) 15,396

CANADA: QUÉBEC

1991 C 6,895,963

Beauport (★Québec) 69,158
Brossard (★Montréal) 64,793
Charlesbourg (★Québec) 70,788
Chicoutimi (★ 160,928) 62,670
Drummondville
(★ 60,092) 35,462
Gatineau (★Ottawa) 92,284
Hull (★Ottawa) 60,707
Jonquière (★Chicoutimi) 57,933
La Salle (★Montréal) 73,804
Laval (★Montréal) 314,398
Lévis (★Québec) 39,452
Longueuil (★Montréal) 129,874
Montréal (★ 3,127,242) 1,017,666
Montréal-Nord
(★Montréal) 85,516
Pierrefonds (★Montréal) 48,735
Québec (★ 645,550) 167,517
Repentigny (★Montréal) 49,630
Sainte-Foy (★Québec) 71,133
Saint-Hubert (★Montréal) 74,027
Saint-Jean-sur-Richelieu
(★ 68,378) 37,607
Saint-Laurent (★Montréal) 72,402
Saint-Léonard
(★Montréal) 73,120
Shawinigan (★ 61,672) 19,931
Sherbrooke (★ 139,194) 76,429
Trois-Rivières
(★ 136,303) 49,426
Verdun (★Montréal) 61,307

CANADA: SASKATCHEWAN

1991 C 988,928

Regina (★ 191,692) 179,178
Saskatoon (★ 210,023) 186,058

CANADA: YUKON

1991 C 27,797

Whitehorse 17,925

CAPE VERDE / Cabo Verde

1990 C 341,491

Mindelo 47,109
• PRAIA 61,644

CAYMAN ISLANDS

1988 E 25,900

• GEORGE TOWN 13,700

CENTRAL AFRICAN REPUBLIC / République centrafricaine

1984 E 2,517,000

• BANGUI 473,817
Bouar (1982 E) 48,000

CHAD / Tchad

1988 E 5,428,000

Abéché 40,000
Moundou 100,000
• N'DJAMENA 500,000
Sarh 76,835

CHILE

1982 C 11,329,736

Antofagasta (1990 E) 218,800
Apoquindo (★Santiago) 175,735
Arica (1990 E) 177,300
Calama 81,684
Cerrillos (★Santiago) 67,013
Cerro Navia (★Santiago) 137,777
Chillán (1990 E) 146,000
Concepción (★ 710,000)
(1990 E) 306,500
Conchalí (★Santiago) 157,884
Copiapó 69,045
Coquimbo 62,186
Coronel (★Concepción) 65,918
Curicó 60,550
El Bosque (★Santiago) 143,717
Huechuraba (★Santiago) 56,313
Independencia (★Santiago) 86,724
Iquique (1990 E) 148,500
La Cisterna (★Santiago) 95,863
La Florida (★Santiago) 191,883
La Granja (★Santiago) 109,168
La Pintana (★Santiago) 73,932
La Reina (★Santiago) 80,452
La Serena (1990 E) 105,600
Las Rejas (★Santiago) 147,918
Linares 46,433
Lo Espejo (★Santiago) 124,462
Lo Prado (★Santiago) 103,575
Los Ángeles 70,529
Lota (★Concepción) 47,133
Macul (★Santiago) 113,100
Maipú (★Santiago) 114,117
Ñuñoa (★Santiago) 168,919
Osorno (1990 E) 117,400
Ovalle 43,023
Pedro Aguirre
Cerda (★Santiago) 145,207
Peñalolén (★Santiago) 137,298
Providencia (★Santiago) 115,449
Pudahuel (★Santiago) 97,578
Puente Alto (★Santiago)
(1990 E) 187,400
Puerto Montt (1990 E) 106,500
Punta Arenas (1990 E) 120,000
Quilpué (★Valparaíso)
(1990 E) 107,400
Quinta
Normal (★Santiago) 128,989
Rancagua (1990 E) 190,400
Recoleta (★Santiago) 164,292
Renca (★Santiago) 93,928
San Antonio 61,486
San Bernardo
(★Santiago) (1990 E) 188,200
San Joaquín (★Santiago) 123,904
San Miguel (★Santiago) 88,764
San Ramón (★Santiago) 99,410
• SANTIAGO (★ 4,100,000) 232,667
Talca (1990 E) 164,500
Talcahuano (★Concepción)
(1990 E) 246,900
Temuco (1990 E) 211,700
Valdivia (1990 E) 113,500
Vallenar 38,375
Valparaíso (★ 690,000)
(1990 E) 276,800
Villa Alemana
(★Valparaíso) 55,766
Viña del Mar
(★Valparaíso) (1990 E) 281,100
Vitacura (★Santiago) 72,038

CHINA / Zhongguo

1988 E 999,999,999

Abagnar Qi (▲ 100,700)
(1986 E) 71,700
Acheng (1985 E) 100,304
Aihui (▲ 135,000)
(1986 E) 76,700
Aksu (▲ 345,900)
(1986 E) 143,100
Altay (▲ 141,700)
(1986 E) 62,800
Anci (Langfang)
(▲ 522,800) (1986 E) 122,100
Anda (▲ 425,500)
(1986 E) 130,200
Ankang (1985 E) 89,188
Anqing (▲ 433,900)
(1986 E) 213,200
Anshan 1,330,000
Anshun (▲ 214,700)
(1986 E) 128,800
Anyang (▲ 541,900)
(1986 E) 361,200
Baicheng (▲ 282,000)
(1986 E) 198,600
Baiquan (1985 E) 50,996
Baiyin (▲ 301,900)
(1986 E) 157,100
Baoding (▲ 535,100)
(1986 E) 423,200
Baoji (▲ 359,500)
(1986 E) 286,200
Baoshan (▲ 688,400)
(1986 E) 52,300
Baotou (Paotow) 1,130,000
Baoying (1985 E) 50,479
Bei'an (▲ 440,500)
(1986 E) 199,500
Beihai (▲ 175,900)
(1986 E) 119,000
BEIJING (PEKING)
(★ 7,320,000) 6,710,000
Beipiao (▲ 603,700)
(1986 E) 180,900
Bengbu (▲ 612,600)
(1986 E) 403,900
Benxi (Penhsi) 860,000
Bijie (1985 E) 54,871
Binxian (▲ 177,900)
(1986 E) 86,700
Binxian (1982 C) 127,326
Boli (1985 E) 61,990
Bose (▲ 271,400)
(1986 E) 82,000
Boshan (1975 U) 100,000
Boxian (1985 E) 63,222
Boxing (1982 C) 57,554
Boyang (1985 E) 60,688
Butha Qi (Zalantun)
(▲ 389,500) (1986 E) 111,300
Cangshan (Bianzhuang)
(1982 C) 79,334
Cangzhou (▲ 293,600)
(1986 E) 196,700
Changchun (▲ 2,000,000) 1,822,000
Changde (▲ 220,800)
(1986 E) 178,200
Changge (1982 C) 67,002
Changji (▲ 233,400)
(1986 E) 110,500
Changqing (1982 C) 65,094
Changsha 1,230,000
Changshou (1985 E) 51,923
Changshu (▲ 998,000)
(1986 E) 281,300
Changtu (1985 E) 49,937
Changyi (1982 C) 64,513
Changzhi (▲ 463,400)
(1986 E) 273,000
Changzhou (Changchow)
(1986 E) 522,700
Chao'an (▲ 1,214,500)
(1986 E) 265,400
Chaoxian (▲ 739,500)
(1986 E) 116,800
Chaoyang, Guangdong
prov. (1985 E) 85,968
Chaoyang, Liaoning prov.
(▲ 318,900) (1986 E) 180,300
Chengde (▲ 330,400)
(1986 E) 226,600
Chengdu (Chengtu)
(▲ 2,960,000) 1,884,000
Chenghai (1985 E) 50,631
Chenxian (▲ 191,900)
(1986 E) 143,500
Chifeng (Ulanhad)
(▲ 882,900) (1986 E) 299,000
Chongqing (Chungking)
(▲ 2,890,000) 2,502,000
Chuxian (▲ 365,000)
(1986 E) 113,300
Chuxiong (▲ 379,400)
(1986 E) 67,700
Da'an (1985 E) 70,552
Dachangzhen (1975 U) 50,000
Dalian (Dairen) 2,280,000
Dandong (1986 E) 579,800
Daqing (▲ 880,000) 640,000
Dashiqiao (1985 E) 68,898
Datong (1985 E) 55,529
Datong (▲ 1,040,000) 810,000
Dawa (1985 E) 142,581
Daxian (▲ 209,400)
(1986 E) 142,000
Dehui (1985 E) 60,247
Dengfeng (1982 C) 49,746
Deqing (1982 C) 48,726
Deyang (▲ 753,400)
(1986 E) 184,800
Dezhou (▲ 276,200)
(1986 E) 161,300
Didao (1975 U) 50,000
Dinghai (1985 E) 50,161
Dongchuan (Xincun)
(▲ 275,100) (1986 E) 67,400
Dongguan (▲ 1,208,500)
(1986 E) 254,900
Dongsheng (▲ 121,300)
(1986 E) 57,500
Dongtai (1985 E) 65,788
Dongying (▲ 514,400)
(1986 E) 178,100
Dukou (▲ 551,200)
(1986 E) 380,200
Dunhua (▲ 448,000)
(1986 E) 217,100
Duyun (▲ 386,600)
(1986 E) 123,800
Echeng (▲ 938,000)
(1986 E) 217,400
Enshi (▲ 679,000)
(1986 E) 84,300
Erenhot (1986 E) 7,200
Ergun Zuoqi (1985 E) 55,970
Feixian (1982 C) 73,246
Fengcheng (1985 E) 66,745
Foshan (▲ 312,700)
(1986 E) 243,500
Fujin (1985 E) 60,948
Fuling (▲ 973,500)
(1986 E) 166,300
Fushun (Funan) 1,290,000
Fuxian (Wafangdian)
(▲ 960,700) (1986 E) 246,200
Fuxin 700,000
Fuyang (▲ 195,200)
(1986 E) 143,400
Fuyu, Heilongjiang prov.
(1985 E) 48,670
Fuyu, Jilin prov. (1985 E) 98,373
Fuzhou, Fujian prov.
(▲ 1,240,000) 910,000
Fuzhou, Jiangxi prov.
(▲ 171,800) (1986 E) 106,700
Gaixian (1985 E) 67,587
Ganhe (1985 E) 48,128
Ganzhou (▲ 346,000)
(1986 E) 191,600
Gaoqing (Tianzhen)
(1982 C) 70,411
Gaoyou (1985 E) 57,844
Gejiu (Kokiu) (▲ 341,700)
(1986 E) 193,600
Golmud (1986 E) 60,300
Gongchangling (1982 C) 49,281
Guanghua (▲ 420,000)
(1986 E) 104,400
Guangyuan (▲ 805,500)
(1986 E) 162,200
Guangzhou (Canton)
(▲ 3,420,000) 3,100,000
Guanxian, Shandong
prov. (1982 C) 49,782
Guanxian, Sichuan prov.
(1985 E) 65,039
Guilin (Kweilin)
(▲ 457,500) (1986 E) 324,200
Guixian (1985 E) 61,970
Guiyang (Kweiyang)
(▲ 1,430,000) 1,030,000
Haicheng (▲ 984,800)
(1986 E) 210,700
Haifeng (1985 E) 50,401
Haikou (▲ 289,600)
(1986 E) 209,200
Hailar (▲ 163,549)
(1986 E) 180,000
Hailin (1985 E) 58,909
Hailong (Meihekou)
(▲ 534,200) (1986 E) 117,500
Hailun (1985 E) 83,448
Haiyang (Dongcun)
(1982 C) 77,098
Hami (Kumul) (▲ 270,300)
(1986 E) 146,400
Hancheng (▲ 304,200)
(1986 E) 66,600
Handan (▲ 1,030,000) 870,000
Hangu (1975 U) 100,000
Hangzhou (Hangchow) 1,290,000
Hanzhong (▲ 415,000)
(1986 E) 151,700
Harbin 2,710,000
Hebi (▲ 321,600)
(1986 E) 158,500
Hechi (▲ 266,800)
(1986 E) 74,400
Hechuan (1985 E) 65,237
Hefei (▲ 930,000) 740,000
Hegang (1986 E) 588,300
Helong (1985 E) 62,665
Hengshui (▲ 286,500)
(1986 E) 83,100
Hengyang (▲ 601,300)
(1986 E) 419,200
Heshan (▲ 109,600)
(1986 E) 42,000
Heze (Caozhou)
(▲ 1,001,500) (1986 E) 115,400
Hohhot (▲ 830,000) 670,000
Hongjiang (▲ 67,000)
(1986 E) 54,300
Horqin Youyi Qianqi (Ulan
Hot) (▲ 192,100)
(1986 E) 129,100
Hotan (▲ 122,800)
(1986 E) 71,700
Houma (▲ 158,500)
(1986 E) 67,000
Huadian (1985 E) 75,183
Huai'an (1985 E) 65,673
Huaibei (▲ 447,200)
(1986 E) 252,100
Huaide (▲ 899,400)
(1986 E) 187,600
Huaihua (▲ 427,100)
(1986 E) 102,000
Huainan (▲ 1,110,000) 700,000
Huaiyin (Wangying)
(▲ 382,500) (1986 E) 201,700
Huanan (1985 E) 66,596
Huanggang (1982 C) 65,961
Huangshi (1986 E) 451,900
Huayun (Huarong)
(▲ 313,500) (1986 E) 81,000
Huinan (Chaoyang)
(1985 E) 52,429
Huizhou (▲ 182,100)
(1986 E) 117,000
Hulan (1985 E) 74,989
Hunjiang (Badaojiang)
(▲ 687,700) (1986 E) 442,600
Huzhou (▲ 964,400)
(1986 E) 208,500
Jiading (1985 E) 60,718
Jiamusi (Kiamusze)
(▲ 557,700) (1986 E) 429,800
Ji'an (▲ 184,300)
(1986 E) 132,200
Jiangling (1985 E) 77,887
Jiangmen (▲ 231,700)
(1986 E) 168,800
Jiangyin (1985 E) 66,476
Jiangyou (1985 E) 72,663
Jian'ou (1985 E) 55,180
Jiaohe (1985 E) 51,504
Jiaojiang (▲ 385,200)
(1986 E) 82,300
Jiaoxian (1985 E) 51,869
Jiaozuo (▲ 509,900)
(1986 E) 335,400
Jiawang (1975 U) 50,000
Jiaxing (▲ 686,500)
(1986 E) 210,200
Jiayuguan (▲ 102,100)
(1986 E) 73,800
Jiexiu (1985 E) 51,300
Jieyang (1985 E) 98,531
Jilin (Kirin) 1,200,000
Jinan (Tsinan)
(▲ 2,140,000) 1,546,000
Jinchang (Baijiazui)
(▲ 136,000) (1986 E) 90,500
Jincheng (▲ 612,700)
(1986 E) 99,900
Jingdezhen (Kingtechen)
(▲ 569,700) (1986 E) 304,000
Jingmen (▲ 946,500)
(1986 E) 227,000
Jinhua (▲ 799,900)
(1986 E) 147,800
Jining, Nei Monggol prov.
(1986 E) 163,300
Jining, Shandong prov.
(▲ 765,700) (1986 E) 222,600
Jinshi (▲ 219,700)
(1986 E) 73,700
Jinxi (▲ 634,300)
(1986 E) 223,100
Jinxian (1985 E) 95,761
Jinzhou (Chinchou)
(▲ 810,000) 710,000
Jishou (▲ 194,500)
(1986 E) 59,500
Jishu (1985 E) 75,587
Jiujiang (▲ 382,300)
(1986 E) 248,500
Jiuquan (Suzhou)
(▲ 269,900) (1986 E) 56,300
Jiutai (1985 E) 63,021
Jixi (▲ 820,000) 700,000
Jixian (1985 E) 59,725
Juancheng (1982 C) 54,110
Junan (Shizilu) (1982 C) 90,222
Junxian (▲ 423,400)
(1986 E) 97,000
Juxian (1982 C) 51,666
Kaifeng (▲ 629,100)
(1986 E) 458,800
Kaili (▲ 342,100) (1986 E) 96,600
Kaiping (1985 E) 54,145
Kaiyuan (▲ 342,100)
(1986 E) 96,600
Kaiyuan (1985 E) 85,762
Karamay (▲ 168,868)
(1986 E) 185,300
Kashi (▲ 194,500)
(1986 E) 146,300
Keshan (1985 E) 65,088
Korla (▲ 219,000)
(1986 E) 129,400
Kunming (▲ 1,550,000) 1,310,000
Kunshan (1985 E) 44,645
Kuqa (1985 E) 63,847
Kuytun (1986 E) 60,200
Laiwu (▲ 1,041,800)
(1986 E) 143,500
Langxiang (1985 E) 64,658
Lanxi (1985 E) 53,236
Lanxi (▲ 606,800)
(1986 E) 70,500
Lanzhou (Lanchow)
(▲ 1,420,000) 1,297,000
Lechang (1986 E) 56,913

C Census. E Official estimate. U Unofficial estimate.
• Largest city in country.

★ Population or designation of metropolitan area, including suburbs (see headnote).
▲ Population of an entire municipality, commune, or district, including rural area.

Langshuijiang (▲ 277,600) (1986 E)	101,700
Langshuitan (▲ 362,000) (1986 E)	60,900
Leshan (▲ 972,300) (1986 E)	307,300
Lhasa (▲ 107,700) (1986 E)	84,400
Lianyungang (Xinpu) (▲ 459,400) (1986 E)	288,000
Liaocheng (▲ 724,300) (1986 E)	119,000
Liaoyang (▲ 576,900) (1986 E)	442,600
Liaoyuan (1986 E)	370,400
Liling (▲ 856,300) (1986 E)	107,100
Linfen (▲ 530,100) (1986 E)	157,600
Lingling (▲ 515,300) (1986 E)	72,700
Lingyuan (1985 E)	66,825
Linhai (1985 E)	52,653
Linhe (▲ 365,900) (1986 E)	99,800
Linkou (1985 E)	52,936
Linqing (▲ 603,000) (1986 E)	87,000
Linqu (1982 C)	84,196
Linxia (▲ 150,200) (1986 E)	72,900
Linyi (▲ 1,365,000) (1986 E)	190,000
Liuzhou	680,000
Longjiang (1985 E)	51,156
Longyan (▲ 378,500) (1986 E)	114,500
Loudi (▲ 254,300) (1986 E)	84,200
Lu'an (▲ 163,400) (1986 E)	122,600
Lufeng (1985 E)	53,015
Luohe (▲ 159,100) (1986 E)	102,300
Luoyang (Loyang) (▲ 1,090,000)	760,000
Luzhou (▲ 360,300) (1986 E)	237,800
Ma'anshan (▲ 367,000) (1986 E)	258,900
Manzhouli (1986 E)	116,600
Maoming (▲ 434,900) (1986 E)	118,600
Meixian (▲ 740,600) (1986 E)	169,000
Mengyin (1982 C)	70,602
Mianyang, Sichuan prov. (▲ 848,500) (1986 E)	233,900
Minhang (1975 U)	60,000
Mishan (1985 E)	54,919
Mixian (1982 C)	64,776
Mudanjiang	650,000
Nahe (1985 E)	49,725
N'aizishen (1985 E)	51,982
Nancha (1975 U)	50,000
Nanchang (▲ 1,260,000)	1,090,000
Nanchong (▲ 238,100) (1986 E)	158,000
Nanjing (Nanking)	2,390,000
Nanning (▲ 1,000,000)	720,000
Nanpiao (1982 C)	67,274
Nanping (▲ 420,800) (1986 E)	157,100
Nantong (▲ 411,000) (1986 E)	308,800
Nanyang (▲ 294,800) (1986 E)	199,400
Neihuang (1982 C)	56,039
Neijiang (▲ 298,500) (1986 E)	191,100
Ning'an (1985 E)	49,334
Ningbo (▲ 1,050,000)	570,000
Ningyang (1982 C)	55,424
Nong'an (1985 E)	55,966
Nunjiang (1985 E)	59,276
Orogen Zizhiqi (1985 E)	48,042
Panshan (▲ 343,100) (1986 E)	248,100
Panshi (1985 E)	59,270
Pingdingshan (▲ 819,900) (1986 E)	363,200
Pingliang (▲ 362,500) (1986 E)	85,400
Pingxiang, Jiangxi prov. (▲ 1,286,700) (1986 E)	368,700
Pingyi (1982 C)	89,373
Pingyin (1982 C)	62,827
Potou (▲ 456,100) (1986 E)	59,000
Puqi (1985 E)	65,239
Putian (▲ 265,400) (1986 E)	64,600
Putuo (1985 E)	50,962
Puyang (▲ 1,086,100) (1986 E)	131,000
Qian Gorlos (1985 E)	79,494
Qingdao (Tsingtao)	1,300,000
Qinggang (1985 E)	43,075
Qingjiang, Jiangsu prov. (▲ 246,617) (1982 C)	150,000
Qingjiang, Jiangxi prov. (1985 E)	42,698
Qingyuan (1985 E)	51,756
Qinhuangdao (Chinwangtao) (▲ 436,000) (1986 E)	307,500
Qinzhou (▲ 923,400) (1986 E)	97,100
Qiqihar (Tsitsihar) (▲ 1,330,000)	1,180,000
Qitaihe (▲ 309,900) (1986 E)	166,400
Qixia (1982 C)	54,158
Qixian (1982 C)	53,041
Quanzhou (Chuanchou) (▲ 436,000) (1986 E)	157,000
Qujing (▲ 758,000) (1986 E)	135,000
Quxian (▲ 704,800) (1986 E)	124,000
Raoping (1985 E)	54,831
Rizhao (▲ 970,300) (1986 E)	93,300
Rongcheng (1982 C)	52,878
Rugao (1985 E)	50,643
Rui'an (1985 E)	57,993
Sanmenxia (Shanxian) (▲ 150,000) (1986 E)	79,000
Sanming (▲ 214,300) (1986 E)	144,900
• Shanghai (★ 9,300,000)	7,220,000
Shangqiu (Zhuji) (▲ 199,400) (1986 E)	135,400
Shangrao (▲ 142,500) (1986 E)	113,000
Shangshui (1982 C)	50,191
Shantou (Swatow) (▲ 790,000)	560,000
Shanwei (1985 E)	61,234
Shaoguan (1986 E)	363,100
Shaowu (▲ 266,700) (1986 E)	81,400
Shaoxing (▲ 250,900) (1986 E)	167,100
Shaoyang (▲ 465,900) (1986 E)	218,600
Shashi (1986 E)	253,700
Shenxian (1982 C)	50,208
Shenyang (Mukden) (▲ 4,370,000)	3,910,000
Shenzhen (▲ 231,900) (1986 E)	189,600
Shiguaigou (1975 U)	50,000
Shihezi (▲ 549,300) (1987 E)	304,700
Shijiazhuang	1,220,000
Shiyan (▲ 332,600) (1986 E)	227,300
Shizuishan (▲ 317,400) (1986 E)	225,500
Shouguang (1982 C)	83,400
Shuangcheng (1985 E)	91,163
Shuangliao (1985 E)	67,326
Shuangyashan (1986 E)	427,300
Shuicheng (▲ 2,216,500) (1986 E)	363,500
Shulan (1986 E)	50,582
Shunde (1985 E)	50,262
Siping (▲ 357,800) (1986 E)	280,100
Sishui (1982 C)	82,990
Songjiang (1985 E)	71,864
Songjianghe (1985 E)	53,023
Suifenhe (▲ 21,700) (1986 E)	13,900
Suihua (▲ 732,100) (1986 E)	200,400
Suileng (1985 E)	68,399
Suining (▲ 1,174,900) (1986 E)	118,500
Suixian (▲ 1,281,600) (1986 E)	187,700
Suqian (1985 E)	50,742
Suxian (▲ 218,600) (1986 E)	123,300
Suzhou (Soochow)	740,000
Tai'an (▲ 1,325,400) (1986 E)	215,900
Taiyuan (▲ 1,980,000)	1,700,000
Taizhou (▲ 210,800) (1987 E)	143,200
Tancheng (1982 C)	61,857
Tangshan (▲ 1,440,000)	1,080,000
Tao'an (1985 E)	76,269
Tengzhou (1985 E)	53,254
Tianjin (Tientsin) (▲ 5,540,000)	4,950,000
Tianshui (▲ 953,200) (1986 E)	209,500
Tiefa (▲ 146,367) (1982 C)	60,000
Tieli (1985 E)	102,527
Tieling (▲ 454,100) (1986 E)	326,100
Tongchuan (▲ 393,200) (1986 E)	268,900
Tonghua (▲ 367,400) (1986 E)	290,200
Tongliao (▲ 253,100) (1986 E)	190,100
Tongling (▲ 216,400) (1986 E)	182,900
Tongren (1985 E)	50,307
Tongxian (1985 E)	97,168
Tumen (▲ 99,700) (1986 E)	77,600
Tunxi (▲ 104,500) (1986 E)	61,800
Turpan (▲ 196,800) (1986 E)	52,300
Ürümqi	1,060,000
Wangkui (1985 E)	52,021
Wangqing (1985 E)	61,237
Wanxian (▲ 280,800) (1986 E)	138,700
Weifang (▲ 1,042,200) (1986 E)	312,500
Weihai (▲ 220,800) (1986 E)	83,000
Weinan (▲ 699,400) (1986 E)	111,300
Weishan (Xiazhen) (1982 C)	57,932
Weixian (Hanting) (1982 C)	50,180
Wenzhou (▲ 530,600) (1986 E)	372,200
Wuchang (1985 E)	64,403
Wuhai (1986 E)	266,000
Wuhan	3,570,000
Wuhu (▲ 502,200) (1986 E)	396,000
Wulian (Hongning) (1982 C)	51,718
Wusong (1982 C)	64,017
Wuwei (Liangzhou) (▲ 804,000) (1986 E)	115,500
Wuxi (Wuhsi)	880,000
Wuzhong (▲ 402,400) (1986 E)	48,600
Wuzhou (Wuchow) (▲ 261,500) (1986 E)	194,800
Xiaguan (▲ 395,800) (1986 E)	112,100
Xiamen (Amoy) (▲ 546,400) (1986 E)	343,700
Xi'an (Sian) (▲ 2,580,000)	2,210,000
Xiangfan (▲ 421,200) (1986 E)	314,900
Xiangtan (▲ 511,100) (1986 E)	389,500
Xianning (▲ 402,200) (1986 E)	122,200
Xianyang (▲ 641,800) (1986 E)	285,900
Xiaogan (▲ 1,204,400) (1986 E)	125,500
Xiaoshan (1985 E)	63,074
Xichang (▲ 161,000) (1986 E)	105,000
Xinghua (1985 E)	75,573
Xinglongzhen (1982 C)	52,961
Xingtai (▲ 350,800) (1986 E)	265,600
Xinhui (1985 E)	77,381
Xining (Sining)	620,000
Xinmin (1985 E)	47,900
Xintai (▲ 1,157,300) (1986 E)	171,400
Xinwen (Suncun) (1975 U)	50,000
Xinxian (▲ 398,600) (1986 E)	74,200
Xinxiang (▲ 540,500) (1986 E)	411,000
Xinyang (▲ 234,200) (1986 E)	169,100
Xinyu (▲ 610,600) (1986 E)	140,200
Xuancheng (1985 E)	52,387
Xuanhua (1975 U)	140,000
Xuanwei (1982 C)	70,081
Xuchang (▲ 247,200) (1986 E)	167,800
Xuguit Qi (Yakeshi) (1986 E)	390,000
Xuzhou (Süchow)	860,000
Yaan (▲ 277,600) (1986 E)	89,200
Yan'an (▲ 259,800) (1986 E)	86,700
Yancheng (▲ 1,251,400) (1986 E)	258,400
Yangcheng (1982 C)	57,255
Yangjiang (1986 E)	91,433
Yangquan (▲ 478,900) (1986 E)	295,100
Yangzhou (▲ 417,300) (1986 E)	321,500
Yanji (▲ 216,900) (1986 E)	175,000
Yanji (Longjing) (1985 E)	55,035
Yanling (1982 C)	52,679
Yantai (Chefoo) (▲ 717,300) (1986 E)	327,000
Yanzhou (1985 E)	48,972
Yaxian (Sanya) (▲ 321,700) (1986 E)	70,500
Yi'an (1986 E)	54,253
Yibin (Ipin) (▲ 636,500) (1986 E)	218,800
Yichang (Ichang) (1986 E)	410,500
Yichuan (1982 C)	58,914
Yichun, Heilongjiang prov.	840,000
Yichun, Jiangxi prov. (▲ 770,200) (1986 E)	132,600
Yidu (1985 E)	54,838
Yilan (1985 E)	50,436
Yima (▲ 84,800) (1986 E)	53,700
Yinan (Jiehu) (1982 C)	67,803
Yinchuan (▲ 396,900) (1986 E)	268,200
Yingchengzi (1985 E)	59,072
Yingkou (▲ 480,000) (1986 E)	366,900
Yingtan (▲ 116,200) (1986 E)	64,500
Yining (Kuldja) (▲ 232,000) (1986 E)	153,200
Yiyang (▲ 365,000) (1986 E)	155,300
Yiyuan (Nanma) (1982 C)	53,800
Yong'an (▲ 269,000) (1986 E)	105,100
Yongchuan (1985 E)	70,444
Yuci (▲ 420,700) (1986 E)	171,000
Yueyang (▲ 411,300) (1986 E)	239,500
Yulin, Guangxi Zhuangzu prov. (▲ 1,228,800) (1986 E)	115,600
Yulin, Shaanxi prov. (1985 E)	51,610
Yumen (Laojunmiao) (▲ 160,100) (1986 E)	84,300
Yuncheng, Shandong prov. (1982 C)	54,262
Yuncheng, Shansi prov. (▲ 434,900) (1986 E)	87,000
Yunyang (1982 C)	54,903
Yushu (1985 E)	57,222
Yuyao (▲ 772,700) (1986 E)	169,700
Zaozhuang (▲ 1,592,000) (1986 E)	292,200
Zhangjiakou (Kalgan) (▲ 640,000)	500,000
Zhangye (▲ 394,200) (1986 E)	73,000
Zhangzhou (Longxi) (▲ 310,400) (1986 E)	159,400
Zhanjiang (▲ 920,900) (1986 E)	335,500
Zhaodong (1985 E)	99,836
Zhaoqing (Gaoyao) (▲ 187,600) (1986 E)	145,700
Zhaotong (▲ 546,600) (1986 E)	77,500
Zhaoyuan (1985 E)	42,426
Zhaoyuan (1982 C)	56,389
Zhengzhou (Chengchow) (▲ 1,580,000)	1,150,000
Zhenjiang (1986 E)	412,400
Zhongshan (Shiqizhen) (▲ 1,059,700) (1986 E)	238,700
Zhoucun (1975 U)	50,000
Zhoukouzhen (▲ 220,400) (1986 E)	110,500
Zhuhai (▲ 155,000) (1986 E)	88,800
Zhumadian (▲ 149,500) (1986 E)	99,400
Zhuoxian (1985 E)	54,523
Zhuzhou (Chuchow) (▲ 499,600) (1986 E)	344,800
Zibo (Zhangdian) (▲ 2,370,000)	840,000
Zigong (Tzukung) (▲ 909,300) (1986 E)	361,700
Zixing (▲ 334,300) (1986 E)	97,100
Ziyang (1985 E)	57,349
Zouping (1982 C)	49,274
Zouxian (1985 E)	61,578
Zunyi (▲ 347,600) (1986 E)	236,600

COLOMBIA

1985 C	27,867,326
Armenia	187,130
Barrancabermeja	137,406
Barranquilla (★ 1,140,000)	899,781
Bello (★Medellín)	212,861
Bucaramanga (★ 550,000)	352,326
Buenaventura	160,342
Buga	82,992
Cali (★ 1,400,000)	1,350,565
Cartagena	531,426
Cartago	97,791
Ciénaga	56,860
Cúcuta (★ 445,000)	379,478
Dos Quebradas (★Pereira)	101,480
Duitama	56,390
Envigado (★Medellín)	91,391
Florencia	66,430
Floridablanca (★Bucaramanga)	143,824
Girardot	70,078
Ibagué	292,965
Itagüí (★Medellín)	137,623
Magangué	49,160
Maicao	46,033
Malambo (★Barranquilla)	52,584
Manizales (★ 330,000)	299,352
Medellín (★ 2,095,000)	1,468,089
Montería	157,466
Neiva	194,556
Ocaña	51,443
Palmira	175,186
Pasto	197,407
Pereira (★ 390,000)	233,271
Popayán	141,964
• SANTA FE DE BOGOTÁ (★ 4,260,000)	3,982,941
Santa Marta	177,922
Sincelejo	120,537
Soacha (★Santa Fe de Bogotá)	109,051
Sogamoso	64,437
Soledad (★Barranquilla)	165,791
Tuluá	99,721
Tunja	93,792
Valledupar	142,771
Villa Rosario (★Cúcuta)	63,615
Villavicencio	178,685
Zipaquirá	45,676

COMOROS / Al-Qumur / Comores

1990 E	452,742
• MORONI	23,432

CONGO

1989 C	2,188,367
• BRAZZAVILLE	693,712
Dolisie	57,991
Pointe-Noire	350,139

COOK ISLANDS

1986 C	18,155
• AVARUA	9,678

COSTA RICA

1988 E	2,851,000
Alajuela (▲ 147,400)	33,800
Desamparados (★San José) (1984 C)	43,352
Puerto Limón (▲ 62,600)	40,400
Puntarenas (▲ 86,400)	34,100
• SAN JOSÉ (★ 1,355,000)	278,600

CÔTE D'IVOIRE (IVORY COAST)

1988 C	10,815,694
Abengourou	59,114
• ABIDJAN	1,929,079
Agboville	46,045
Bouaké	329,850
Daloa	121,842
Divo	72,350
Gagnoa	85,563
Korhogo	109,445
Man	89,575
San Pédro	70,611
YAMOUSSOUKRO	106,786

CROATIA / Hrvatska

1987 E	4,673,517
Osijek (▲ 162,490)	106,800
Rijeka (▲ 199,282)	166,400
Split	191,074
• ZAGREB	697,925

CUBA

1991 E	10,694,465
Bayamo	139,061
Camagüey	286,404
Cárdenas (▲ 84,590)	69,800
Ciego de Ávila	101,620
Cienfuegos	136,233
Florida	51,442
Guantánamo	215,864
Holguín	236,967
• LA HABANA (HAVANA) (★ 2,210,000)	2,119,059
Las Tunas	126,678
Manzanillo	108,668
Matanzas	119,510
Morón	49,793
Palma Soriano (▲ 124,543)	66,600
Pinar del Río	136,303
Sancti Spíritus	97,522
Santa Clara	203,753
Santiago de Cuba	434,541

CYPRUS / Kıbrıs / Kípros

1982 C	512,097
Lárnax (Larnaca) (★ 48,330)	35,823
Lemesós (Limassol) (★ 107,161)	74,782
• NICOSIA (LEVKOSÍA) (★ 185,000)	48,221

CYPRUS, NORTH / Kuzey Kıbrıs

1985 E	160,287
Gazimağusa (Famagusta)	19,428
• NICOSIA (LEFKOŞA)	37,400

CZECH REPUBLIC / Česká Republika

1991 C	10,298,731
Brno (★ 450,000)	387,986
Česká Lípa	39,667
České Budějovice (★ 114,000)	97,283
Český Těšín (★Třinec)	28,737
Cheb	31,847
Chomutov (★ 80,000)	53,191
Děčín (★ 72,000)	55,112
Frýdek-Místek (★Ostrava)	65,067
Havířov (★Ostrava)	86,267
Hodonín	30,736
Hradec Králové (★ 113,000)	99,889
Jablonec nad Nisou (★Liberec)	45,918
Jihlava	52,271
Karlovy Vary (Carlsbad)	56,291
Karviná (★Ostrava)	68,368
Kladno (★ 88,500)	71,735
Kolín	31,582
Kroměříž (★ 38,500)	28,962
Liberec (★ 175,000)	101,934
Litvínov (★Most)	29,085
Mladá Boleslav	44,471
Most (★ 135,000)	70,675
Nový Jičín	29,028
Olomouc (★ 126,000)	105,690
Opava (★ 78,000)	63,601
Orlová (★Ostrava)	36,307
Ostrava (★ 760,000)	327,553
Pardubice	94,857
Písek	29,542
Plzeň (★ 210,000)	173,129
• PRAHA (★ 1,328,000)	1,212,010
Přerov	51,341
Příbram	36,869
Prostějov	50,102
Šumperk	30,446
Tábor (★ 55,500)	36,329
Teplice (★ 94,000)	53,039
Třebíč	39,348
Třinec (★ 87,500)	45,189
Trutnov	31,957
Ústí nad Labem (★ 115,000)	99,739
Valašské Meziříčí	28,153
Vsetín	31,584
Zlín (★ 124,000)	84,634
Znojmo	39,910

DENMARK / Danmark

1992 E	5,162,126
Ålborg (▲ 156,614)	115,200
Århus (▲ 267,873)	207,300
Ballerup (★København)	45,476
Esbjerg (▲ 81,843)	72,200
Fredericia (▲ 46,617)	28,700
Frederiksberg (★København)	86,372
Gentofte (★København)	66,077

C Census. E Official estimate. U Unofficial estimate.
• Largest city in country.

★ Population or designation of metropolitan area, including suburbs (see headnote).
▲ Population of an entire municipality, commune, or district, including rural area.

Gladsakse (★København) 60,604
Helsingør (Elsinore) (★København) 56,794
Horsens (▲ 55,123) 47,200
Hvidovre (★København) 48,754
• KØBENHAVN (★ 1,670,000) 464,566
Kolding (▲ 57,982) 42,700
Kongens Lyngby (★København) 49,612
Odense (▲ 179,487) 142,800
Randers 61,440
Rønne 15,236
Roskilde (▲ 50,158) (★København) 40,700
Vejle (▲ 51,845) 45,700

DJIBOUTI

1991 E 508,541

• DJIBOUTI 329,337

DOMINICA

1984 E 77,000

• ROSEAU 9,348

DOMINICAN REPUBLIC / República Dominicana

1990 E 7,169,800

Barahona 80,400
La Romana 147,800
La Vega 192,300
Mao 58,400
Puerto Plata 94,900
San Cristóbal 137,500
San Francisco de Macorís 165,300
San Juan de la Maguana 129,700
San Pedro de Macorís 144,300
Santiago de los Caballeros 489,500
• SANTO DOMINGO 2,411,900

ECUADOR

1990 C 9,648,189

Ambato 124,166
Babahoyo 50,285
Cuenca 194,981
Eloy Alfaro (★Guayaquil) 82,359
Esmeraldas 98,558
• Guayaquil 1,508,444
Ibarra 80,991
La Libertad 50,108
Loja 94,305
Machala 144,197
Manta 125,505
Milagro 93,637
Portoviejo 132,937
Quevedo 86,910
QUITO (★ 1,300,000) 1,100,847
Riobamba 94,505
Santo Domingo de los Colorados 114,422

EGYPT / Mişr

1986 C 48,205,049

Abnūb 48,302
Abū Kabīr 68,394
Abū Tīj 48,518
Akhmīm 70,494
Al-'Arīsh 67,337
Al-Fayyūm 213,070
Al-Hawāmidīyah (★Al-Qāhirah) 73,298
Al-Iskandarīyah (Alexandria) (★ 3,350,000) 2,926,859
Al-Ismā'īlīyah (★ 235,000) 158,045
Al-Jīzah (Giza) (★Al-Qāhirah) 1,883,189
Al-Maḥallah al-Kubrā 306,509
Al-Manṣūrah (★ 375,000) 317,508
Al-Manzilah 54,918
Al-Maṭarīyah 73,315
Al-Minyā 179,060
• AL-QĀHIRAH (CAIRO) (★ 9,300,000) 6,068,695
Al-Qanāṭir al-Khayrīyah 49,361
Al-Uqṣur (Luxor) 126,160
Armant 54,618
Ashmūn 54,450
As-Sinbillāwayn 60,159
As-Suways (Suez) 327,717
Aswān 190,579
Asyūṭ 272,986
Az-Zaqāzīq 244,354
Bahtīm (★Al-Qāhirah) 275,807
Banhā 115,701
Banī Mazār 47,982
Banī Suwayf 152,476
Bilbays 96,511
Bilqās Qism Awwal 73,040
Biyalā 47,702
Būlāq ad-Dakrūr (★Al-Qāhirah) 148,787
Būr Sa'īd (Port Said) 401,172
Būsh 54,655
Damanhūr 188,939
Dikirnis 48,616
Disūq 78,316
Dumyāṭ (Damietta) 89,069
Fāqūs 48,365
Hawsh 'Īsā 53,619
Idkū 70,724
Jirjā 71,564
Kafr ad-Dawwār (★Al-Iskandarīyah) 198,244
Kafr ash-Shaykh 103,301
Kafr az-Zayyāt 58,276
Kawm Umbū 52,506
Maghāghah 50,916
Mallawī 98,632
Manfalūt 52,281
Marsā Maṭrūḥ 43,157
Minūf 69,673
Mīt Ghamr (★ 100,000) 91,927
Qalyūb 84,413
Qinā 119,917
Rashīd (Rosetta) 51,789
Samālūt 62,404
Sāqiyat Makkī 51,062
Sawhāj 132,649
Shibīn al-Kawm 132,209
Shubrā al-Khaymah (★Al-Qāhirah) 714,594
Sinnūris 55,187
Ṭahṭā 58,457
Ṭalkhā (★Al-Manṣūrah) 54,923
Ṭanṭā 336,517
Ṭimā 46,824
Warrāq al-'Arab (★Al-Qāhirah) 127,108
Ziftā (★Mīt Ghamr) 69,253

EL SALVADOR

1985 E 5,337,896

Delgado (★San Salvador) 67,684
Mejicanos (★San Salvador) 91,465
Nueva San Salvador (★San Salvador) 53,688
San Miguel 88,520
• SAN SALVADOR (★ 920,000) 462,652
Santa Ana 137,879
Soyapango (★San Salvador) 60,000

EQUATORIAL GUINEA / Guinea Ecuatorial

1983 C 300,000

• MALABO 31,630

ERITREA

1991 E 2,951,000

• ASMERA (1990 E) 358,100
Mitsiwa (1986 E) 16,576

ESTONIA / Eesti

1991 E 1,581,800

Kohtla-Järve 74,700
Narva 83,000
Pärnu 54,200
• TALLINN 481,500
Tartu 115,300

ETHIOPIA / Ityopiya

1986 E 44,927,000

• ADIS ABEBA (★ 1,990,000) (1990 E) 1,912,500
Akaki Beseka (★Adis Abeba) 58,977
Awasa 39,693
Bahir Dar 59,951
Debre Zeyit 55,706
Dese 77,459
Dire Dawa (1990 E) 127,400
Gonder 88,344
Harer 67,977
Jima 67,470
Mekele 66,640
Nazret 83,091

FAEROE ISLANDS / Føroyar

1990 E 47,946

• TÓRSHAVN 14,767

FALKLAND ISLANDS

1991 C 2,050

• STANLEY 1,557

FIJI

1986 C 715,375

Lautoka (★ 39,057) 28,728
• SUVA (★ 141,273) 69,665

FINLAND / Suomi

1992 E 5,029,002

Espoo (Esbo) (★Helsinki) 175,670
• HELSINKI (HELSINGFORS) (★ 1,040,000) 497,542
Joensuu 48,182
Jyväskylä (★ 93,000) (1990 E) 67,026
Kotka 56,515
Kouvola (★ 53,821) 32,066
Kuopio 81,593
Lahti (★ 108,000) 93,414
Lappeenranta 55,358
Oulu (★ 121,000) (1990 E) 102,280
Pori 76,432
Tampere (★ 241,000) 173,797
Turku (Åbo) (★ 228,000) 159,403
Vaasa (Vasa) 53,764
Vantaa (Vanda) (★Helsinki) 157,274

FRANCE

1990 C 56,614,493

Aix-en-Provence (★Marseille) 123,842
Ajaccio 58,315
Albi (★ 54,359) 46,579
Alès (★ 76,856) 41,037
Amiens (★ 156,120) 131,872
Angers (★ 208,282) 141,404
Angoulême (★ 102,908) 42,876
Annecy (★ 126,729) 49,644
Antibes (★Cannes) 63,248
Antony (★Paris) 57,771
Argenteuil (★Paris) 93,096
Arles (★ 54,309) 39,000
Armentières (★ 57,738) 25,219
Arras (★ 79,607) 38,983
Asnières [-sur-Seine] (★Paris) 71,850
Aubervilliers (★Paris) 67,557
Aulnay-sous-Bois (★Paris) 82,314
Avignon (★ 181,136) 86,939
Bastia (★ 52,446) 37,845
Bayonne (★ 164,378) 40,051
Beauvais (★ 57,704) 54,190
Belfort (★ 77,844) 50,125
Besançon (★ 122,623) 113,828
Béthune (★ 261,535) 24,556
Béziers (★ 76,304) 70,996
Blois (★ 65,132) 49,318
Bondy (★Paris) 46,676
Bordeaux (★ 760,000) 210,336
Boulogne-Billancourt (★Paris) 101,743
Boulogne-sur-Mer (★ 91,249) 43,678
Bourg-en-Bresse (★ 55,784) 40,972
Bourges (★ 94,731) 75,609
Brest (★ 201,480) 147,956
Brive-la-Gaillarde (★ 64,379) 49,765
Bruay-en-Artois (★Béthune) 24,927
Caen (★ 191,490) 112,846
Calais (★ 101,768) 75,309
Cambrai (★ 48,133) 33,092
Cannes (★ 335,647) 68,676
Carcassonne 43,470
Castres (★ 46,482) 44,812
Châlons-sur-Marne (★ 61,452) 48,423
Chalon-sur-Saône (★ 77,764) 54,575
Chambéry (★ 103,283) 54,120
Champigny-sur-Marne (★Paris) 79,486
Charleville-Mézières (★ 67,213) 57,008
Chartres (★ 85,933) 39,595
Châteauroux (★ 67,090) 50,969
Châtellerault (★ 36,298) 34,678
Cherbourg (★ 92,045) 27,121
Cholet 55,132
Clamart (★Paris) 47,227
Clermont-Ferrand (★ 254,416) 136,181
Clichy (★Paris) 48,030
Cognac (★ 27,468) 19,528
Colmar (★ 83,816) 63,498
Colombes (★Paris) 78,513
Compiègne (★ 67,057) 41,896
Courbevoie (★Paris) 65,389
Creil (★ 97,119) 31,956
Créteil (★Paris) 82,088
Denain (★Valenciennes) 19,544
Dieppe (★ 43,348) 35,894
Dijon (★ 230,451) 146,703
Douai (★ 199,562) 42,175
Drancy (★Paris) 60,707
Dunkerque (★ 190,879) 70,331
Elbeuf (★ 53,886) 16,604
Épinal (★ 62,140) 36,732
Épinay-sur-Seine (★Paris) 48,762
Évreux (★ 57,968) 49,103
Évry (★Paris) 45,531
Fontainebleau (★ 35,706) 15,714
Fontenay-sous-Bois (★Paris) 51,868
Forbach (★ 98,758) 27,076
Fréjus (★ 73,967) 41,486
Gennevilliers (★Paris) 44,818
Grenoble (★ 404,733) 150,758
Hagondange (★ 112,061) 8,222
Hayange (★Thionville) 15,638
Issy-les-Moulineaux (★Paris) 46,127
Ivry-sur-Seine (★Paris) 53,619
La Rochelle (★ 100,264) 71,094
La Seyne-sur-Mer (★Toulon) 59,968
Laval (★ 56,855) 50,473
Le Blanc-Mesnil (★Paris) 46,956
Le Havre (★ 253,627) 195,854
Le Mans (★ 189,107) 145,502
Lens (★ 323,174) 35,017
Le Puy (★ 43,499) 21,743
Levallois-Perret (★Paris) 47,548
Lille (★ 1,050,000) 172,142
Limoges (★ 170,065) 133,464
Longwy (★ 41,300) 15,439
Lorient (★ 115,488) 59,271
Lourdes 16,300
Lyon (★ 1,335,000) 415,487
Mâcon (★ 46,714) 37,275
Maisons-Alfort (★Paris) 53,375
Mantes-la-Jolie (★Paris) 45,087
Marseille (★ 1,225,000) 800,550
Martigues (★Marseille) 31,300
Maubeuge (★ 102,772) 34,989
Meaux (★ 63,006) 48,305
Melun (★ 107,705) 35,319
Menton (★Monaco, Monaco) 29,141
Mérignac (★Bordeaux) 57,273
Metz (★ 193,117) 119,594
Meudon (★Paris) 45,339
Montargis (★ 52,804) 15,020
Montbéliard (★ 117,510) 29,005
Montceau-les-Mines (★ 47,283) 22,999
Montluçon (★ 63,018) 44,248
Montpellier (★ 248,303) 207,996
Montreuil-sous-Bois (★Paris) 94,754
Moulins (★ 41,715) 22,799
Moyeuvre-Grande (★Hagondange) 9,203
Mulhouse (Mülhausen) (★ 223,856) 108,357
Nancy (★ 329,447) 99,351
Nanterre (★Paris) 84,565
Nantes (★ 496,078) 244,995
Neuilly-sur-Seine (★Paris) 61,768
Nevers (★ 58,915) 41,968
Nice (★ 516,740) 342,439
Nîmes (★ 138,527) 128,471
Niort (★ 65,792) 57,012
Noisy-le-Grand (★Paris) 54,032
Noisy-le-Sec (★Paris) 36,309
Orléans (★ 243,153) 105,111
Orly (★Paris) 21,646
Pantin (★Paris) 47,303
• PARIS (★ 10,275,000) 2,152,423
Pau (★ 144,674) 82,157
Périgueux (★ 63,322) 30,280
Perpignan (★ 157,873) 105,983
Pessac (★Bordeaux) 51,055
Poissy (★Paris) 36,745
Poitiers (★ 107,625) 78,894
Quimper (★ 65,954) 59,437
Reims (★ 206,437) 180,620
Rennes (★ 245,065) 197,536
Roanne (★ 77,160) 41,756
Rodez (★ 39,017) 24,701
Romans-sur-Isère (★ 49,212) 32,734
Roubaix (★Lille) 97,746
Rouen (★ 380,161) 102,723
Rueil-Malmaison (★Paris) 66,401
Saint-Brieuc (★ 83,861) 44,752
Saint-Chamond (★ 81,795) 38,878
Saint-Denis (★Paris) 89,988
Saint-Dizier (★ 40,097) 33,552
Saint-Étienne (★ 313,338) 199,396
Saint-Lô (★ 2,760) 21,546
Saint-Malo 48,057
Saint-Maur-des-Fossés (★Paris) 77,206
Saint-Nazaire (★ 131,511) 64,812
Saint-Ouen (★Paris) 42,343
Saint-Quentin (★ 71,113) 60,644
Sarcelles (★Paris) 56,833
Sartrouville (★Paris) 50,329
Sevran 48,478
Soissons (★ 46,168) 29,829
Strasbourg (★ 415,000) 252,338
Suresnes (★Paris) 35,998
Tarbes (★ 77,787) 47,566
Thionville (★ 132,413) 39,712
Toulon (★ 437,553) 167,619
Toulouse (★ 650,000) 358,688
Tourcoing (★Lille) 93,765
Tours (★ 282,152) 129,509
Troyes (★ 122,763) 59,255
Valence (★ 107,965) 63,437
Valenciennes (★ 338,392) 38,441
Vénissieux (★Lyon) 60,444
Verdun-sur-Meuse (★ 26,711) 20,753
Versailles (★Paris) 87,789
Vichy (★ 61,566) 27,714
Villefranche (★ 55,249) 29,542
Villejuif (★Paris) 48,405
Villeneuve-d'Ascq (★Lille) 65,320
Villeurbanne (★Lyon) 116,872
Vitry-sur-Seine (★Paris) 82,400
Wattrelos (★Lille) 43,675

FRENCH GUIANA / Guyane française

1982 C 73,022

• CAYENNE 38,091

FRENCH POLYNESIA / Polynésie française

1988 C 188,814

• PAPEETE (★ 80,000) 23,555

GABON

1985 E 1,312,000

Franceville 58,800
Lambaréné 49,500
• LIBREVILLE 235,700
Port Gentil 124,400

GAMBIA

1983 C 687,817

• BANJUL (★ 160,000) 44,188
Brikama 19,624

GAZA STRIP

1992 E 667,000

Ghazzah (1986 E) 235,000
Khān Yūnis (1986 E) 98,370
Rafaḥ (1967 C) 49,812

GEORGIA / Sakartvelo

1991 E 5,464,200

Batumi 137,500
Gori 70,100
Kutaisi 238,200
Poti 51,100
Rustavi (★Tbilisi) 161,900
Suchumi 120,000
• TBILISI (★ 1,460,000) 1,279,000
Zugdidi 50,600

GERMANY / Deutschland

1991 E 79,753,227

Aachen (★ 540,000) 241,861
Aalen (★ 78,000) 64,781
Ahlen 54,169
Albstadt 49,021
Alsdorf (★Aachen) 46,935
Altenburg 48,926
Amberg 43,111
Arnsberg 75,864
Aschaffenburg (★ 150,000) 64,098
Augsburg (★ 420,000) 256,877
Baden-Baden 51,849
Bad Homburg (★Frankfurt am Main) 51,820
Bad Oeynhausen 46,475
Bad Salzuflen (★Herford) 53,771
Bamberg (★ 122,000) 70,521
Bautzen 48,588
Bayreuth (★ 87,000) 72,345
Bergheim (★Köln) 58,146
Bergisch Gladbach (★Köln) 104,037
Bergkamen (★Essen) 49,761
BERLIN (★ 4,150,000) 3,433,695
Bielefeld (★ 535,000) 319,037
Bitterfeld (★ 105,000) 17,988
Bocholt 68,936
Bochum (★Essen) 396,486
BONN (★ 575,000) 292,234
Bottrop (★Essen) 118,936
Brandenburg 89,889
Braunschweig (★ 320,000) 258,833
Bremen (★ 790,000) 551,219
Bremerhaven (★ 180,000) 130,446
Castrop-Rauxel (★Essen) 79,037
Celle 72,260
Chemnitz (★ 500,000) 294,244
Coburg 44,246
Cottbus 125,891
Cuxhaven 56,090
Dachau (★München) 35,387
Darmstadt (★ 315,000) 138,920
Delmenhorst (★Bremen) 75,154
Dessau (★ 138,000) 96,754
Detmold 70,074
Dinslaken (★Essen) 65,313
Dormagen (★Köln) 58,260
Dorsten (★Essen) 78,035
Dortmund (★Essen) 599,055
Dresden (★ 870,000) 490,571
Duisburg (★Essen) 535,447
Düren (★ 108,000) 86,508
Düsseldorf (★ 1,225,000) 575,794
Eberswalde 52,586
Eisenach 45,220
Eisenhüttenstadt 50,216
Emden 50,735
Erfurt 208,989
Erlangen (★Nürnberg) 102,440
Eschweiler (★Aachen) 54,675
• Essen (★ 5,050,000) 626,973
Esslingen (★Stuttgart) 91,685
Euskirchen 49,654
Flensburg (★ 98,000) 86,977
Frankenthal (★Mannheim) 46,966
Frankfurt am Main (★ 1,935,000) 644,865
Frankfurt an der Oder 86,131
Freiberg 48,609
Freiburg (★ 235,000) 191,029
Friedrichshafen 54,129
Fulda (★ 74,000) 56,289
Fürth (★Nürnberg) 103,362
Garbsen (★Hannover) 60,776
Garmisch-Partenkirchen 26,837
Gelsenkirchen (★Essen) 293,714
Gera 129,037
Giessen (★ 155,000) 74,497
Gladbeck (★Essen) 80,267
Göppingen (★ 155,000) 54,957
Görlitz 72,237
Goslar (★ 72,000) 46,251
Gotha 54,525
Göttingen 121,831
Greifswald 66,251
Grevenbroich (★Düsseldorf) 60,835
Gummersbach 50,965
Gütersloh (★Bielefeld) 86,807
Hagen (★Essen) 214,449
Halberstadt 45,364
Halle (★ 455,000) 310,234
Hamburg (★ 2,385,000) 1,652,363
Hameln (★ 65,000) 58,539

C Census. E Official estimate. U Unofficial estimate.
• Largest city in country.

★ Population or designation of metropolitan area, including suburbs (see headnote).
▲ Population of an entire municipality, commune, or district, including rural area.

Hamm 179,639
Hanau (★Frankfurt am Main) 86,913
Hannover (★ 1,000,000) 513,010
Hattingen (★Essen) 58,241
Heidelberg (★Mannheim) 136,796
Heidenheim (★ 80,000) 50,532
Heilbronn (★ 245,000) 115,843
Herford (★ 120,000) 63,893
Herne (★Essen) 178,132
Herten (★Essen) 69,245
Hilden (★Düsseldorf) 54,782
Hildesheim (★ 126,000) 105,291
Hof 52,913
Hoyerswerda 64,888
Hürth (★Köln) 50,808
Ingolstadt (★ 145,000) 105,489
Iserlohn 96,314
Jena 102,518
Kaiserslautern (★ 130,000) 99,351
Kamen (★Essen) 46,160
Karlsruhe (★ 505,000) 275,061
Kassel (★ 375,000) 194,268
Kempten (Allgäu) 61,906
Kerpen (★Köln) 57,337
Kiel (★ 325,000) 245,567
Kleve 45,963
Koblenz (★ 170,000) 108,733
Köln (★ 1,810,000) 953,551
Konstanz 75,089
Krefeld (★Essen) 244,020
Landshut 59,066
Langenfeld (★Düsseldorf) 53,455
Langenhagen (★Hannover) 47,432
Leipzig (★ 720,000) 511,079
Leverkusen (★Köln) 160,919
Lingen 49,137
Lippstadt 62,345
Lübeck (★ 250,000) 214,758
Lüdenscheid 79,401
Ludwigsburg (★Stuttgart) 82,343
Ludwigshafen (★Mannheim) 162,173
Lüneburg 61,870
Lünen (★Essen) 87,845
Magdeburg (★ 400,000) 278,807
Mainz (★Wiesbaden) 179,486
Mannheim (★ 1,525,000) 310,411
Marburg 74,146
Marl (★Essen) 91,467
Meerbusch (★Düsseldorf) 52,104
Menden 56,527
Merseburg (★Halle) 42,905
Minden (★ 121,000) 78,145
Moers (★Essen) 104,595
Mönchengladbach (★ 410,000) 259,436
Mülheim an der Ruhr (★Essen) 177,681
München (Munich) (★ 1,900,000) 1,229,026
Münster 259,438
Neubrandenburg 89,284
Neumünster 80,743
Neunkirchen/Saar (★ 125,000) 51,536
Neuss (★Düsseldorf) 147,019
Neustadt an der Weinstrasse 51,988
Neu-Ulm (★Ulm) 46,264
Neuwied (★ 157,000) 62,075
Norderstedt (★Hamburg) 68,450
Nordhausen 46,422
Nordhorn 49,359
Nürnberg (★ 1,065,000) 493,692
Oberhausen (★Essen) 223,840
Offenbach (★Frankfurt am Main) 114,992
Offenburg 52,964
Oldenburg 143,131
Osnabrück (★ 270,000) 163,168
Paderborn 120,680
Passau 50,328
Peine 46,654
Pforzheim (★ 230,000) 112,944
Pirmasens 47,680
Pirna (★Dresden) 41,798
Plauen 71,774
Potsdam (★Berlin) 139,794
Ratingen (★Düsseldorf) 91,007
Ravensburg (★ 75,000) 45,650
Recklinghausen (★Essen) 125,060
Regensburg (★ 180,000) 121,691
Remscheid (★Wuppertal) 123,155
Reutlingen (★ 170,000) 103,687
Rheine 70,452
Riesa 45,440
Rosenheim 56,340
Rostock 248,088
Rüsselsheim (★Wiesbaden) 59,430
Saarbrücken (★ 365,000) 191,694
Saarlouis (★ 115,000) 38,160
Salzgitter 114,355
Sankt Augustin (★Bonn) 51,886
Schwäbisch Gmünd 60,081
Schwedt 50,633
Schweinfurt (★ 105,000) 54,483
Schwerin 127,447
Schwerte (★Essen) 50,696
Siegburg (★ 175,000) 35,441
Siegen (★ 192,000) 109,174
Sindelfingen (★Stuttgart) 58,805
Solingen (★Wuppertal) 165,401
Speyer 46,553
Stendal 48,532
Stolberg (★Aachen) 57,231
Stralsund 72,780
Stuttgart (★ 2,005,000) 579,988
Suhl 54,731
Trier (★ 122,000) 97,835
Troisdorf (★Siegburg) 64,430
Tübingen 80,372
Ulm (★ 215,000) 110,529
Unna (★Essen) 61,552
Velbert (★Essen) 89,253
Viersen (★Mönchengladbach) 77,453
Villingen-Schwenningen 78,218
Weimar 60,326
Wesel 59,631
Wetzlar (★ 96,000) 51,737
Wiesbaden (★ 790,000) 260,301
Wilhelmshaven (★ 122,000) 90,561
Wismar 55,509
Witten (★Essen) 105,403
Wittenberg 49,682
Wolfenbüttel (★Braunschweig) 52,032
Wolfsburg 128,510
Worms (★Mannheim) 76,503
Wuppertal (★ 845,000) 383,660
Würzburg (★ 195,000) 127,777
Zweibrücken (★ 100,000) 33,918
Zwickau (★ 180,000) 114,632

GHANA

1987 E 13,577,538
• ACCRA (★ 1,390,000) 949,113
Ashiaman (★Accra) (1984 C) 49,427
Cape Coast (1984 C) 57,653
Koforidua (1984 C) 54,400
Kumasi (★ 540,000) 385,192
Obuasi (1984 C) 60,146
Sekondi (★ 175,352) (1984 C) 32,355
Tafo (★Kumasi) (1984 C) 50,432
Takoradi (★Sekondi) (1984 C) 61,527
Tamale (★ 171,661) 151,069
Tema (★ 179,076) (★Accra) 109,975
Teshie (★Accra) (1984 C) 62,954

GIBRALTAR

1988 E 30,077
• GIBRALTAR 30,077

GREECE / Ellás

1991 C 10,264,156
Aiyáleo (★Athínai) 79,560
Akharnaí 60,062
Amaroúsion (★Athínai) 63,619
Ampelókipoi (★Thessaloníki) (1981 C) 40,033
• ATHÍNAI (ATHENS) (★ 3,096,775) 748,110
Áyios Dhimítrios (★Athínai) 57,387
Ermoúpolis (★ 16,008) 12,987
Galátsion (★Athínai) 56,972
Glifádha (★Athínai) 62,310
Ilioúpolis (★Athínai) 72,623
Ioánnina 56,496
Iráklion (★ 127,600) 117,167
Kalámai (★ 45,090) 43,838
Kalamariá (★Thessaloníki) (1981 C) 51,676
Kallithéa (★Athínai) 110,738
Kardhítsa 30,451
Kateríni (★ 48,021) 46,304
Kavála 58,576
Keratsínion (★Athínai) 71,845
Khalándrion (★Athínai) 72,286
Khalkís 51,482
Khaniá (★ 65,519) 50,077
Khíos (★ 27,405) 21,261
Koridhallós (★Athínai) 63,033
Kórinthos (Corinth) 28,903
Lárisa (★ 125,623) 113,426
Návplion 11,453
Néa Ionía (★Athínai) 60,364
Néa Liósia (★Athínai) 78,029
Neápolis (★Thessaloníki) (1981 C) 31,464
Néa Smírni (★Athínai) 69,319
Níkaia (★Athínai) 87,924
Palaión Fáliron (★Athínai) 60,974
Pátrai (★ 172,763) 155,180
Peristérion (★Athínai) 145,854
Piraiévs (Piraeus) (★Athínai) 169,622
Ródhos (Rhodes) 43,619
Sérrai 50,875
Spárti (Sparta) (★ 15,496) 14,043
Thessaloníki (Salonika) (★ 739,998) 377,951
Tríkala 48,810
Trípolis 21,772
Véroia 38,871
Víron (★Athínai) 57,149
Vólos (★ 106,142) 77,907
Zográfos (★Athínai) 78,570

GREENLAND / Grønland / Kalaallit Nunaat

1990 E 55,558
Egedesminde (Aasiaat) 3,308
• GODTHÅB (NUUK) 12,217
Holsteinsborg (Sisimiut) 4,871

GRENADA

1991 C 90,691
• SAINT GEORGE'S (★ 25,000) 4,439

GUADELOUPE

1982 C 328,400
BASSE-TERRE (★ 26,600) 13,656
Les Abymes (★Pointe-à-Pitre) 56,165
• Pointe-à-Pitre (★ 83,000) 25,310

GUAM

1990 C 133,152
• AGANA (★ 50,000) 1,139

GUATEMALA

1989 E 8,935,395
Escuintla 60,673
• GUATEMALA (★ 1,400,000) 1,057,210
Quetzaltenango 88,769

GUERNSEY

1991 C 58,867
• SAINT PETER PORT (★ 36,000) 16,648

GUINEA / Guinée

1986 E 6,225,000
• CONAKRY 800,000
Kankan 100,000
Kindia 80,000
Labé 110,000
Nzérékoré (1983 C) 55,356

GUINEA-BISSAU / Guiné-Bissau

1988 E 945,000
• BISSAU 125,000

GUYANA

1983 E 918,000
• GEORGETOWN (★ 188,000) 78,500

HAITI / Haïti

1987 E 5,531,802
Cap-Haïtien 72,161
Gonaïves 37,034
• PORT-AU-PRINCE (★ 880,000) 797,000

HONDURAS

1988 C 4,443,721
Choluteca 54,481
El Progreso 60,058
La Ceiba 68,764
San Pedro Sula (★ 375,000) 287,350
• TEGUCIGALPA 576,661

HONG KONG

1986 C 5,395,997
Kowloon (Jiulong) (★Victoria) 774,781
Kwai Chung (★Victoria) 131,362
New Kowloon (Xinjiulong) (★Victoria) 1,526,910
Sha Tin (★Victoria) 355,810
Sheung Shui 87,206
Tai Po 119,679
Tsuen Wan (Quanwan) (★Victoria) 514,241
Tuen Mun (★Victoria) 262,458
• VICTORIA (★ 4,770,000) (1991 C) 1,250,993
Yuen Long 75,740

HUNGARY / Magyarország

1990 C 10,374,823
Békéscsaba 67,609
• BUDAPEST (★ 2,515,000) 2,016,774
Debrecen 212,235
Dunaújváros 59,028
Eger 61,892
Győr 129,338
Hódmezővásárhely 51,180
Kaposvár 71,788
Kecskemét 102,516
Miskolc 196,442
Nagykanizsa 54,052
Nyíregyháza 114,152
Ózd 43,592
Pécs 170,039
Salgótarján 47,822
Sopron 55,083
Szeged 175,301
Székesfehérvár 108,958
Szolnok 78,328
Szombathely 85,617
Tatabánya 74,277
Vác 34,015
Veszprém 63,867
Zalaegerszeg 62,212

ICELAND / Ísland

1991 E 259,577
Akureyri 14,436
• REYKJAVÍK (★ 149,482) 99,623

INDIA / Bharat

1991 C 846,302,688
Abohar 107,163
Achalpur 96,229
Ādilābād 84,255
Ādityapur (★Jamshedpur) 77,803
Ādoni 136,182
Agartala 157,358
Āgra (★ 948,063) 891,790
Āgra Cantonment (★Āgra) 49,755
Ahmadābād (★ 3,312,216) 2,876,710
Ahmadnagar (★ 222,088) 181,339
Aizawl 155,240
Ajmer 402,700
Akola 328,034
Akot 65,681
Alandur (★Madras) 125,244
Alīgarh 480,520
Alīpur Duār (★ 102,815) 65,241
Allahābād (★ 844,546) 792,858
Alleppey (★ 264,969) 174,666
Alwal (★Hyderābād) 66,471
Alwar (★ 210,146) 205,086
Amalner 76,442
Ambājogāi 57,159
Ambāla (★ 259,227) 119,338
Ambāla Cantonment (★Ambāla Sadar) 49,017
Ambāla Sadar 90,872
Ambāsamudram (★ 59,661) 33,893
Ambattur (★Madras) 215,424
Ambikāpur (★ 53,227) 50,277
Āmbūr 75,911
Amrāvati 421,576
Amreli (★ 69,366) 67,827
Amritsar 708,835
Amroha 137,061
Anakāpalle 84,356
Ānand (★ 174,480) 110,266
Anantapur 174,924
Anjār 51,209
Ankleshwar (★ 78,100) 51,739
Āra 157,082
Arakkonam 71,928
Arcot (★ 114,760) 45,205
Arni 54,898
Aruppukkottai 78,976
Asansol (★ 763,939) 262,188
Ashoknagar-Kalyangarh (★Hābra) 96,747
Āttūr 55,667
Auraiya 50,772
Aurangābād (★ 592,709) 573,272
Avadi (★Madras) 183,215
Āzamgarh 78,567
Badagara (★ 102,430) 72,434
Bagaha 34,327
Bāgalkot 76,903
Bahādurgarh 56,524
Baharampur (★ 126,400) 115,144
Bahraich 135,400
Baidyabāti (★Calcutta) 90,081
Bālāghāt (★ 67,151) 62,178
Balāngīr 69,920
Bāleshwar (★ 101,829) 85,442
Ballarpur (★ 92,436) 83,511
Ballia 84,063
Bālly (★Calcutta) 184,474
Bālly (★Calcutta) 73,322
Balrāmpur 59,619
Bālurghāt (★ 126,225) 119,796
Bānda 96,795
Bangalore (★ 4,130,288) 2,660,088
Bangaon 79,571
Bānkura 114,876
Bansberia (★Calcutta) 93,520
Bānswāra (★ 67,908) 66,632
Bāpatla 62,536
Bārākpur (★Calcutta) 133,265
Bārān 57,719
Baranagar (★Calcutta) 224,821
Bārāsat (★Calcutta) 102,660
Baraut 67,705
Barddhamān 245,079
Bareilly (★ 617,350) 587,211
Bargarh 51,205
Bāripada (★ 69,240) 49,619
Bārmer 68,625
Barnāla 75,430
Bārsi 88,810
Basīrhāt 101,409
Basti 87,371
Batala (★ 103,367) 86,006
Bathinda 159,114
Beāwar (★ 106,721) 105,363
Begusarai (★ 84,018) 71,424
Bela 65,945
Belampalli 66,780
Belgaum (★ 402,412) 326,399
Bellary 245,391
Bettiah 92,653
Betūl 63,534
Bhadohi 64,010
Bhadrak 76,435
Bhadrāvati (★ 149,257) 55,475
Bhadrāvati New Town (★Bhadrāvati) 74,928
Bhadreswar (★Calcutta) 72,474
Bhāgalpur (★ 260,119) 253,225
Bhandāra 71,813
Bharatpur (★ 156,880) 148,519
Bharūch (★ 139,029) 133,102
Bhātpāra (★Calcutta) 304,952
Bhavāni (★ 97,160) 35,193
Bhāvnagar (★ 405,225) 402,338
Bhawānipatna 51,062
Bhilai (★ 685,474) 386,159
Bhīlwāra 183,965
Bhīmavaram 121,314
Bhind 109,755
Bhiwandi (★ 392,214) 379,070
Bhiwāni 121,629
Bhopāl 1,062,771
Bhubaneshwar 411,542
Bhuj (★ 121,009) 102,176
Bhusāwal (★ 159,799) 145,143
Bīd 112,434
Bīdar (★ 132,408) 108,016
Bihār 201,323
Bijāpur (★ 193,131) 186,939
Bijnor (★ 73,900) 66,486
Bīkāner 416,289
Bilāspur (★ 229,615) 179,833
Bīlimora (★ 51,039) 42,052
Birlapur (★ 65,482) 20,320
Birnagar (★ 92,208) 20,015
Bishnupur 56,128
Bodhan 64,406
Bodināyakkanūr 66,500
Bokāro Steel City (★ 398,890) 333,683
Bolpur 52,760
• Bombay (★ 12,596,243) 9,925,891
Botād 64,603
Brahmapur 210,418
Brajrajnagar 69,667
Budaun 116,695
Budge Budge (★Calcutta) 72,951
Bulandshahr 127,201
Buldāna 52,767
Bulsār (★ 111,775) 57,909
Būndi 65,047
Burhānpur 172,710
Calcutta (★ 11,021,918) 4,399,819
Calicut (★ 801,190) 419,831
Cannanore (★Tellicherry) 65,238
Chāībāsa 56,729
Chākdaha 74,769
Chakradharpur (★ 47,666) 32,737
Chālisgaon 77,420
Champdāni (★Calcutta) 101,067
Chandannagar (★Calcutta) 120,378
Chandausi 82,748
Chandīgarh (★ 575,829) 504,094
Chāndpur 55,825
Chandrapur 226,105
Changanācheri 52,445
Channapatna 55,209
Chāpra 136,877
Chās 65,207
Chhatarpur (★ 75,594) 72,824
Chhindwāra (★ 96,858) 93,650
Chidambaram (★ 67,949) 58,740
Chikmagalūr 60,816
Chilakalūrupet 79,142
Chingleput 54,127
Chintāmani 50,394
Chīrāla (★ 142,778) 80,861
Chitradurga (★ 103,435) 87,069
Chittaranjan (★ 65,689) 47,186
Chittaurgarh 71,569
Chittoor 133,462
Chopda 49,234
Chūru 82,464
Cochin (★ 1,140,605) 564,589
Coimbatore (★ 1,100,746) 816,321
Contai 53,484
Coonoor (★ 100,687) 48,003
Cuddalore 144,561
Cuddapah (★ 215,866) 121,463
Cuttack (★ 440,295) 403,418
Dabgram 147,217
Dabhoi 50,641
Dāhod (★ 96,632) 66,500
Dāltenganj 56,323
Damoh (★ 105,043) 95,661
Dānāpur (★Patna) 84,616
Dandeli 52,701
Darbhanga 218,391
Darjiling 73,062
Datia 64,477
Dāvangere (★ 287,233) 266,082
Dehra Dūn (★ 368,053) 270,159
Dehri 93,694
Delhi (★ 8,419,084) 7,206,704
Delhi Cantonment (★Delhi) 94,393
Deoband 66,208
Deoghar (★ 85,902) 76,380
Deolāli (★Nāsik) 44,331
Deoria 82,168
Dewās 164,364
Dhamtari 69,357
Dhanbad (★ 815,005) 151,789
Dhār 59,246
Dhārāpuram 48,393
Dharmapuri 59,318
Dharmavaram 78,961
Dhaulpur 68,533
Dholka (★ 54,352) 49,860
Dhorāji (★ 79,479) 77,748
Dhrāngadhra 57,961
Dhuburi 66,216
Dhule 278,317
Dibrugarh (★ 125,667) 120,127
Dimāpur 57,182
Dindigul 182,477
Dīsa 62,435
Dod Ballāpur 54,609
Dum Dum (★Calcutta) 40,961
Durg (★Bhilai) 150,645
Durgāpur 425,836
Elūru 212,866
Erode (★ 361,755) 159,323
Etah 78,458
Etāwah 124,072
Faizābād (★ 176,922) 124,437
Farīdābād (★Delhi) 617,717
Farīdkot 58,244
Farrukhābād (★ 208,727) 194,657
Fatehpur 117,675
Fathpur 66,387

C Census. E Official estimate. U Unofficial estimate.
• Largest city in country.
★ Population or designation of metropolitan area, including suburbs (see headnote).
▲ Population of an entire municipality, commune, or district, including rural area.

Fāzilka 58,028
Fīrozābād (★ 270,536) 215,128
Fīrozpur 78,738
Fīrozpur Cantonment 53,094
Gadag 134,051
Gandhidham 104,585
Gāndhinagar 123,359
Ganga Ghat 50,260
Gangānagar 161,482
Gangāpur (★ 68,886) 53,689
Gangāwati (★ 85,515) 64,843
Gangtok 25,024
Gārulia (★Calcutta) 80,918
Gaya (★ 294,427) 219,675
Ghāziābād (★ 511,759) 454,156
Ghāzīpur 76,547
Girīdīh 78,097
Godhra (★ 100,662) 96,813
Gokāk 52,080
Gonda 95,553
Gondal (★ 81,611) 80,584
Gondia 109,470
Gopichettipālaiyam 48,364
Gorakhpur 505,566
Gudivāda 101,656
Gudiyāttam (★ 90,557) 83,232
Gūdūr 55,984
Gulbarga (★ 310,920) 304,099
Guna 100,490
Guntakal 107,592
Guntūr 471,051
Gurdāspur 54,733
Gurgaon (★ 135,884) 121,486
Guruvayur (★ 118,632) 20,216
Guwāhāti 584,342
Gwalior (★ 717,780) 690,765
Hābra (★ 196,970) 100,223
Hājīpur 87,687
Haldwāni 104,195
Hālisahar (★Calcutta) 114,028
Hānsi 59,653
Hanumāngarh (★ 82,733) 78,525
Hāora (★Calcutta) 950,435
Hāpur 146,262
Hardoi 88,651
Haridwār (★ 187,392) 147,305
Harihar 66,647
Hassan (★ 108,706) 90,803
Hāthras 113,285
Hazārībāg 97,824
Himatnagar 51,461
Hindaun 60,780
Hindupur 104,651
Hinganghāt 78,715
Hingoli 54,457
Hisār (★ 181,255) 172,677
Hoshangābād 70,914
Hoshiārpur 122,705
Hospet (★ 134,799) 96,322
Hubli-Dhārwār 648,298
Hugli-Chinsurah (★Calcutta) 151,806
Hyderābād (★ 4,344,437) 30,443,896
Ichalkaranji (★ 235,979) 214,950
Imphāl (★ 202,839) 198,535
Indore (★ 1,109,056) 1,091,674
Ingrāj Bāzār (★ 177,164) 139,204
Itānagar 16,545
Itārsi (★ 84,626) 77,334
Jabalpur (★ 888,916) 741,927
Jabalpur Cantonment (★Jabalpur) 56,124
Jagādhri (★Yamunānagar) 67,386
Jagdalpur (★ 84,578) 66,154
Jagtiāl 67,591
Jahānābād 52,332
Jaipur (★ 1,518,235) 1,458,483
Jalandhar 509,510
Jālgaon 242,193
Jālna 174,985
Jalpāiguri 68,732
Jamālpur 86,112
Jamkhandi 48,143
Jammu (★ 223,361) (1981 C) 206,135
Jāmnagar (★ 381,646) 341,637
Jamshedpur (★ 829,171) 460,577
Jaora (★ 56,023) 54,997
Jaunpur 136,062
Jaypur 65,246
Jetpur (★ 95,397) 73,560
Jhānsi (★ 368,154) 300,850
Jharia (★Dhanbād) 69,641
Jhārsuguda 65,054
Jhunjhunūn 72,187
Jīnd 85,315
Jodhpur 666,279
Jorhāt (★ 112,030) 58,358
Jūnāgadh (★ 167,110) 130,484
Kadaiyanallūr 68,819
Kadiri 63,378
Kagaznagar 57,535
Kairāna 56,079
Kaithal 71,142
Kākināda (★ 327,541) 279,980
Kalamassery (★Cochin) 54,342
Kālol (★ 92,550) 82,137
Kalyān (★Bombay) 1,014,557
Kāmāreddi 48,666
Kāmārhāti (★Calcutta) 266,889
Kambam 52,435
Kāmthi (★ 127,151) 78,612
Kānchipuram (★ 171,129) 144,955
Kānchrāpāra (★Calcutta) 100,194
Kānnangād (★ 118,214) 57,165
Kannauj 58,932
Kānpur (★ 2,029,889) 1,874,409
Kānpur Cantonment (★Kānpur) 95,021
Kapra (★Hyderābād) 87,747
Kapūrthala 64,567
Karād 56,819
Kāraikāl 61,804
Kāraikkudi (★ 110,926) 71,965
Kāranja 48,866
Karauli 49,008
Karīmnagar 148,583
Karnāl (★ 176,131) 173,751
Karūr (★ 113,669) 73,418
Kārwār 51,022
Kāsaragod 50,126
Kāsganj 75,634
Kāshīpur 69,870
Katihār (★ 154,367) 135,436
Kātwa 55,541
Kāvali 65,910
Kāyankulam 67,151
Keshod 50,172
Khadki Cantonment (★Pune) 78,323
Khambhāt (★ 89,834) 76,746
Khāmgaon 73,692
Khammam (★ 149,077) 127,992
Khandwa 145,133
Khanna 71,990
Kharagpur (★ 264,842) 177,989
Kharagpur Railway Settlement (★Kharagpur) 84,252
Khardaha 88,358
Khargone 66,786
Khurja 80,305
Kishanganj 64,568
Kishangarh Bās 81,948
Koch Bihār (★ 92,820) 71,215
Kodarma 53,577
Kohīma 51,418
Kolār 83,287
Kolār Gold Fields (★ 156,746) 72,485
Kolhāpur (★ 418,538) 406,370
Konnagar (★Calcutta) 62,200
Korba 124,501
Kota 537,371
Kot Kapūra 62,430
Kottagūdem (★ 102,137) 80,440
Kottayam (★ 166,552) 63,155
Kovilpatti 78,834
Krishnagiri 60,315
Krishnanagar 121,110
Kukatpalle (★Hyderābād) 186,963
Kulti (★Asansol) 108,518
Kumārapālaiyam (★Bhavāni) 57,672
Kumbakonam (★ 150,540) 139,483
Kundla (★ 65,785) 64,815
Kurasia (★ 71,708) 15,898
Kurichi (★Coimbatore) 64,796
Kurnool (★ 275,360) 236,800
Lādnūn 48,205
Lakhīmpur 79,951
Lalbahadur Nagar (★Hyderābād) 155,514
Lalitpur 79,870
Lalitpur 79,870
Lātūr 197,408
Luckeesarai 53,360
Lucknow (★ 1,669,204) 1,619,115
Lucknow Cantonment (★Lucknow) 50,089
Ludhiāna 1,042,740
Machilīpatnam (Bandar) 159,110
Madanapalle 73,820
Madgaon (Margao) (★ 72,400) 58,951
Mādhavaram (★Madras) 49,256
Madhubani 53,747
Madras (★ 5,421,985) 3,841,396
Madurai (★ 1,085,914) 940,989
Mahbūbnagar 116,833
Mahesāna (★ 109,950) 88,201
Mahoba 56,247
Mahuva (★ 64,144) 59,912
Mainpuri 76,735
Makrāna (★ 66,720) 59,714
Malappuram (★ 142,204) 49,692
Malaut 56,868
Mālegaon 342,595
Māler Kotla 88,600
Malkajgiri (★Hyderābād) 127,178
Malkāpur 51,311
Mancheriyal 52,657
Mandsaur 95,907
Mandya 120,265
Mangalagiri 59,152
Mangalore (★ 426,341) 273,304
Mango (★Jamshedpur) 108,100
Manjeri 69,334
Manmād 61,312
Mannārgudi 56,552
Mānsa 55,089
Mathura (★ 235,922) 226,691
Maunath Bhanjan 136,697
Mawāna 51,701
Māyūram 76,837
Medinīpur 125,498
Meerut (★ 849,799) 753,778
Meerut Cantonment (★Meerut) 96,021
Melappālaiyam (★Tirunelveli) 66,748
Mettuppālaiyam 63,479
Mhow (★ 83,796) 74,987
Mira Bhayandar (★Bombay) 175,605
Miraj (★Sāngli) 121,593
Miryalaguda 65,879
Mirzāpur 169,336
Modinagar (★ 123,279) 101,660
Moga (★ 110,958) 108,304
Mokāma 59,528
Morādābād (★ 443,701) 429,214
Morbi (★ 120,117) 90,357
Morena 147,124
Mormugao (★ 90,429) 83,367
Motihāri (★ 83,255) 77,432
Mubārakpur (★ 62,733) 45,376
Muktsar 66,383
Munger 150,112
Murwāra 163,431
Muzaffarnagar (★ 247,624) 240,609
Muzaffarpur 241,107
Mysore (★ 653,345) 480,692
Nābha 54,421
Nadiād (★ 170,217) 167,051
Nagaon 93,350
Nāgappattinam (★ 99,745) 86,489
Nāgaur 68,194
Nagda 79,622
Nāgercoil 190,084
Nagīna 58,513
Nāgpur (★ 1,664,006) 1,624,752
Naihāti (★Calcutta) 132,701
Najībābād 66,860
Nalasopara (★Bombay) 67,732
Nalgonda 84,910
Nānded (★ 309,316) 275,083
Nandurbār 78,378
Nandyāl 119,813
Nangi (★Calcutta) 52,956
Narasapur 56,362
Narasaraopet 88,726
Nārnaul 51,976
Nāshik (★ 725,341) 656,925
Navadwip (★ 155,905) 125,037
Navsāri (★ 190,946) 126,089
Nawābganj (★ 77,234) 64,582
Nawāda 53,174
Nawalgarh 51,190
Nedumangād 49,875
Neemuch (★ 90,474) 86,439
Nellore 316,606
New Bārākpur (★Calcutta) 63,795
New Bombay (★Bombay) 307,724
NEW DELHI (★Delhi) 301,297
Neyveli (★ 126,889) 118,080
Nipāni 51,624
Nirmal 57,761
Nizāmābād 241,034
North Bārākpur (★Calcutta) 100,606
North Dum Dum (★Calcutta) 149,965
Ongole (★ 128,648) 100,836
Orai 98,716
Osmānābād 68,019
Pālakodu 56,969
Palani (★ 76,209) 68,907
Pālanpur (★ 90,269) 80,657
Pālayankottai (★Tirunelveli) 98,399
Pālghāt (★ 180,033) 123,289
Pāli 136,842
Pallavaram (★Madras) 111,866
Palwal 59,168
Palwancha 53,102
Panaji (Panjim) (★ 85,515) 43,349
Pandharpur 79,902
Pānihāti (★Calcutta) 275,990
Pānīpat 191,212
Panruti 51,394
Panvel 58,986
Paramakkudi 72,321
Parbhani 190,255
Parli 72,670
Pātan (★ 97,025) 96,112
Pathānkot (★ 128,198) 123,930
Patiāla (★ 253,706) 238,368
Patna (★ 1,099,647) 917,243
Pattukkottai 58,062
Payyannūr 64,032
Periyakulam 46,744
Petlād 48,552
Phagwāra (★ 88,316) 83,163
Pīlībhīt 106,605
Pilkhua 51,162
Pimpri-Chinchwad (★Pune) 517,083
Pollāchi (★ 127,132) 86,897
Pondicherry (★ 401,437) 203,065
Ponmalai (★Tiruchchirāppalli) 69,639
Ponnāni 51,770
Ponnūru Nidubrolu 54,363
Porbandar (★ 160,167) 116,671
Port Blair 74,955
Proddatūr 133,914
Pudukkottai 99,058
Puliyangudi 53,287
Pune (Poona) (★ 2,493,987) 1,566,651
Pune Cantonment (★Pune) 82,139
Puri 125,199
Pūrnia (★ 136,918) 114,912
Puruliya 92,386
Pusad 55,931
Quilon (★ 362,572) 139,852
Qutubullapur (★Hyderābād) 106,591
Rabkavi Banhatti 60,609
Rāe Bareli 129,904
Rāichūr (★ 170,577) 157,551
Raiganj (★ 159,266) 151,045
Raigarh (★ 90,265) 86,767
Raipur (★ 462,694) 438,639
Rājahmundry (★ 401,397) 324,851
Rājapālaiyam 114,202
Rajendranagar (★Hyderābād) 84,520
Rajhara-Jharandalli 55,996
Rājkot (★ 654,490) 559,407
Rāj Nāndgaon 125,371
Rājpur (★ 86,451) 60,175
Rājpura 70,983
Rāmanagaram 50,437
Rāmanāthapuram 52,879
Rāmgarh (★ 82,328) 51,264
Rāmpur 243,742
Rānāghāt (★ 127,035) 62,532
Rānchi (★ 614,795) 599,306
Rānībennur 67,442
Rānīganj (★ 155,823) 61,997
Ratangarh 55,079
Ratlām (★ 195,776) 183,375
Ratnāgiri 56,529
Raurkela (★ 398,864) 215,509
Raurkela Civil Township (★ 152,690) (★Raurkela) 142,408
Rāyagāda 48,247
Rewa 128,981
Rewāri 75,342
Rishīkesh (★ 71,704) 44,487
Rishra (★Calcutta) 102,815
Robertson Pet (★Kolār Gold Fields) 68,230
Rohtak 216,096
Roorkee (★ 91,139) 80,262
Rudrapur 61,280
Sāgar (★ 257,119) 195,346
Sahāranpur 374,945
Saharsa 80,149
Sahaswān 51,080
Sāhibganj 49,257
Salem (★ 578,291) 366,712
Sāmalkot 48,760
Sambalpur (★ 193,297) 131,138
Sambhal 150,869
Sangamner 49,061
Sangareddi 50,123
Sāngli (★ 363,751) 193,197
Sangrūr 56,419
Sankarankovil 48,846
Sardārshahr 67,954
Sarni 84,379
Sāsarām 98,122
Sātāra 95,180
Satna (★ 160,500) 156,630
Sawāi Mādhopur (★ 77,690) 72,165
Secunderābād Cantonment (★Hyderābād) 171,148
Sehore 71,456
Seoni 64,532
Serampore (★Calcutta) 137,028
Serilungampalle (★Hyderābād) 72,320
Shahdol (★ 60,529) 55,508
Shāhjahānpur (★ 260,403) 237,713
Shāmli 70,853
Shāntipur 109,956
Shikohābād 62,829
Shiliguri 216,950
Shillong (★ 223,366) 131,719
Shimoga (★ 193,028) 179,258
Shivpuri 108,277
Shrirampur (★ 79,052) 71,368
Siddhapur (★ 51,794) 50,770
Siddipet 54,091
Sikandarābād 60,992
Sīkar 148,272
Silchar 115,483
Silvassa 11,725
Simla (★ 110,360) 82,054
Sindri (★Dhānbād) 72,333
Sircilla 50,048
Sirsa 112,841
Sītāmarhi (★ 67,336) 44,935
Sītāpur 121,842
Siuri 54,298
Sivakāsi (★ 102,175) 65,593
Siwān 83,125
Solāpur (★ 620,846) 604,215
Sonīpat 143,922
South Dum Dum (★Calcutta) 232,811
Srīkākulam 88,883
Srikalahasti 88,883
Srīnagar (★ 606,002) (1981 C) 594,775
Srīrangam (★Tiruchchirāppalli) 70,109
Srīvilliputtūr 68,644
Sujāngarh 70,843
Sultānpur 76,533
Sūrat (★ 1,518,950) 1,498,817
Surendranagar (★ 166,466) 106,110
Suriāpet 60,630
Tādepallegūdem 88,878
Tādpatri 71,068
Talipparamba 60,226
Tāmbaram (★Madras) 107,187
Tānda 70,605
Tanuku 62,913
Tellicherry (★ 463,962) 103,579
Tenāli 143,726
Tenkāsi 55,189
Tezpur 55,084
Thāna (★Bombay) 803,389
Thānesar 81,255
Thanjāvūr 202,013
Theni-Allinagaram 60,050
Thiruvārūr 49,195
Thrippunithura (★Cochin) 51,078
Tīkamgarh 54,173
Tindivanam 61,579
Tinsukia 73,918
Tiruchchirāppalli (★ 711,862) 387,223
Tiruchengodu 63,027
Tirunelveli (★ 366,869) 135,825
Tirupati (★ 188,904) 174,369
Tiruppattūr 55,282
Tiruppur (★ 306,237) 235,661
Tirūr 49,453
Tiruvalla 54,780
Tiruvannāmalai 109,196
Tiruvottiyūr (★Madras) 168,642
Titāgarh (★Calcutta) 114,085
Tonk 100,079
Trichūr (★ 275,053) 74,604
Trivandrum (★ 826,225) 524,006
Ttruchchendūr (★ 75,301) 27,420
Tumkūr (★ 179,877) 138,903
Tuticorin (★ 280,091) 199,854
Udagamandalam 81,763
Udaipur 308,571
Udamalpet 58,678
Udgīr 70,453
Ujjain 362,266
Ulhāsnagar (★Bombay) 369,077
Ulubāria 155,172
Unjha 51,003
Unnāo 107,425
Upleta 51,801
Uppal Kalan (★Hyderābād) 75,644
Uttarpara-Kotrung (★Calcutta) 101,268
Vadodara (★ 1,126,824) 1,031,346
Vālpārai 106,523
Vāniyambādi (★ 92,307) 72,428
Vārānasi (Benares) (★ 1,030,863) 929,270
Vasai (Bassein) (★ 83,734) 39,781
Veerappanchattiram (★Erode) 61,649
Vejalpur (★Ahmadābād) 92,116
Velore (★ 310,776) 175,061
Verāval (★ 120,178) 93,976
Vidisha 92,922
Vijayawāda (★ 845,756) 701,827
Vikramasingapuram 49,834
Viluppuram 88,788
Viramgām 50,698
Virār (★Bombay) 57,600
Virudunagar 70,971
Vishākhapatnam (★ 1,057,118) 752,037
Visnagar (★ 59,647) 57,869
Vizianagaram (★ 177,022) 160,359
Vriddhāchalam 52,819
Wadhwan (★Surendranager) 49,791
Warangal (★ 137,757) 447,657
Wardha 102,985
Wāshīm 49,140
Yamunānagar (★ 219,754) 144,346
Yavatmāl (★ 121,816) 108,578
Yemmiganur 65,089

INDONESIA

1990 C 179,378,946

Ambon (▲ 275,888) 205,193
Balikpapan 344,147
Banda Aceh (Kuturaja) (▲ 184,650) 143,360
Bandung (★ 2,220,000) 2,058,122
Banjarmasin 480,737
Bantul (▲ 696,944) 13,700
Banyuwangi (▲ 1,455,010) 92,800
Batang (▲ 591,647) 55,200
Bekasi (▲ 951,509) (★Jakarta) 146,400
Bengkulu 170,183
Binjai (▲ 181,866) 127,184
Blitar (★ 150,000) 118,933
Bogor (★ 260,000) 271,341
Bojonegoro (▲ 1,104,031) 63,700
Brebes (▲ 1,521,835) 49,500
Bukittinggi 83,753
Cianjur (▲ 1,420,228) 108,700
Cibinong (▲ 1,812,734) 264,100
Cikampek (▲ 1,152,405) 91,200
Cilacap (▲ 1,487,308) 141,900
Ciledug (▲ 1,244,151) 293,000
Cimahi (▲ 1,909,459) (★Bandung) 196,900
Ciparay (▲ 1,909,456) 135,300
Cirebon (★ 315,000) 254,477
Denpasar (▲ 663,390) 209,500
Depok (▲ 1,812,734) (★Jakarta) 382,000
Dili (▲ 123,475) 12,900
Dumai (▲ 904,375) 71,500
Garut (▲ 1,478,757) 145,900
Genteng (▲ 1,455,010) 60,900
Gorontalo (▲ 119,745) 94,058
Gresik (▲ 856,853) 102,000
Indramayu (▲ 1,226,609) 32,700
• JAKARTA (★ 10,200,000) 8,227,746
Jambi 339,786
Jayapura (Sukarnapura) (▲ 246,389) 101,200
Jember (▲ 2,062,554) 190,000
Jepara (▲ 827,657) 36,200
Jombang (▲ 1,048,805) 65,700
Karawang (▲ 1,152,405) 143,300
Kebumen (▲ 1,120,982) 48,300
Kediri 249,538
Kendari (▲ 488,471) 70,700
Kisaran (▲ 884,594) 66,600
Klangenang (▲ 1,035,575) 291,200
Klaten (▲ 1,056,135) 120,400
Kudus (▲ 631,322) 182,600
Kuningan (▲ 739,360) 33,100
Kupang (▲ 522,944) 111,300
Lumajang (▲ 924,894) 62,100
Madiun (★ 200,000) 170,050
Magelang (★ 180,000) 123,156
Majalaya (▲ 1,909,459) 176,600
Malang 695,089
Manado 320,600
Mataram (▲ 859,273) 276,300
Medan 1,730,052
Mojokerto 99,707
Muncar (▲ 1,455,010) 48,100
Padang (▲ 631,263) 477,064
Padangsidempuan (▲ 954,184) 72,100
Palangkaraya 112,511
Palembang 1,144,047
Palu (▲ 784,647) 56,500
Pangkalpinang 113,129
Pare (▲ 1,343,125) 51,400
Parepare (▲ 101,421) 84,093
Pasuruan (★ 190,000) 152,075
Pati (▲ 1,064,115) 54,900
Payakumbuh (▲ 90,838) 50,475
Pekalongan (★ 430,000) 242,714
Pekanbaru 398,621
Pemalang (▲ 1,114,228) 86,200
Pematangsiantar (★ 250,000) 219,316
Perabumulih (▲ 582,396) 59,500
Ponorogo (▲ 837,055) 59,500
Pontianak 396,658
Pringsewu (▲ 1,825,040) 58,300
Probolinggo (▲ 176,906) 131,077
Purwakarta (▲ 437,327) 62,300
Purwokerto (▲ 1,348,825) 158,300
Purworejo (▲ 700,788) 38,600
Salatiga 98,012
Samarinda (▲ 407,174) 334,851
Semarang 1,249,230
Serang (▲ 1,201,742) 84,900
Sibolga 71,559
Sidoarjo (▲ 1,167,467) 76,800
Singaraja (▲ 540,150) 59,200
Singkawang (▲ 574,156) 64,000
Situbondo (▲ 574,156) 63,800
Sorong (▲ 199,085) 77,900
Subang (▲ 1,037,394) 52,700
Sukabumi (★ 250,000) 119,938
Sumedang (▲ 718,488) 42,900
Sumenep (▲ 933,746) 53,300
Surabaya 2,473,272
Surakarta (★ 590,000) 503,827
Taman (▲ 1,167,467) 88,100
Tangerang (▲ 1,244,151) 99,100
Tanjungbalai 107,751

C Census. E Official estimate. U Unofficial estimate.
• Largest city in country.
★ Population or designation of metropolitan area, including suburbs (see headnote).
▲ Population of an entire municipality, commune, or district, including rural area.

Tanjungkarang-Telukbetung (▲ 636,418)	457,927
Tanjungpinang	105,820
Tarakan (▲ 232,494)	61,300
Tasikmalaya (▲ 1,444,242)	194,000
Tebingtinggi	116,749
Tegal (★ 510,000)	229,553
Tembilahan (▲ 4,878,066)	62,700
Tuban (▲ 977,716)	54,700
Tulungagung (▲ 890,032)	97,000
Ujungpandang (Makasar)	944,372
Yogyakarta (★ 540,000)	412,059

IRAN / Īrān

1986 C	49,445,010
Ābādān	21,879
Abhar	41,628
Āghā Jārī	64,102
Ahar	62,145
Ahvāz	579,826
Alīgūdarz	53,843
Āmol	118,242
Andīmeshk	56,288
Arāk	265,349
Ardabīl	281,973
Bābol	115,320
Bābol Sar	28,589
Bākhtarān (Kermānshāh)	560,514
Bam	50,709
Bandar-e 'Abbās	201,642
Bandar-e Anzalī (Bandar-e Pahlavī)	87,063
Bandar-e Būshehr	120,787
Bandar-e Māh Shahr	71,808
Behbahān	78,694
Behshahr	52,461
Bīrjand	81,798
Bojnūrd	93,392
Borāzjān	67,061
Borūjerd	183,879
Dezfūl	151,420
Do Gonbadān	51,107
Do Rūd	62,517
Emāmshahr (Shāhrūd)	78,950
Eṣfahān (★ 1,175,000)	986,753
Eslāmābād	73,362
Eslāmshahr (★Tehrān)	215,129
Fasā	64,771
Ganāveh	41,883
Gonbad-e Qābūs	87,100
Gorgān	139,430
Hamadān	272,499
Īlām	89,035
Jahrom	77,174
Karaj (★Tehrān)	275,100
Kāshān	138,599
Kāshmar	49,259
Kāzerūn	73,444
Kermān	257,284
Khomeynīshahr (★Eṣfahān)	104,647
Khorramābād	208,592
Khorramshahr (1976 C)	146,706
Khvoy	115,343
Mahābād	75,238
Malāyer	103,640
Marāgheh	100,679
Marand	71,394
Marv Dasht	79,132
Mashhad	1,463,508
Masjed-e Soleymān	104,787
Mīāndoāb	59,551
Mīāneh	65,959
Nahāvand	52,265
Najafābād	129,058
Naqadeh	52,275
Neyshābūr	109,258
Orūmīyeh (Reẓā'īyeh)	300,746
Qā'emshahr	109,288
Qazvīn	248,591
Qom	543,139
Qomsheh	73,367
Qūchān	66,531
Rafsanjān	66,498
Rasht	290,897
Sabzevār	129,103
Salmās	50,573
Sanandaj	204,537
Saqqez	81,351
Sārī	141,020
Sāveh	64,081
Semnān	64,891
Shahr-e Kord	75,080
Shīrāz	848,289
Shīrvān	48,688
Shūshtar	65,840
Sīrjān	90,072
Tabrīz	971,482
• TEHRĀN (★ 7,500,000)	6,042,584
Torbat-e Ḥeydarīyeh	72,068
Varāmīn	58,311
Yazd	230,483
Zābol	75,105
Zāhedān	281,923
Zanjān	215,261

IRAQ / Al 'Irāq

1985 E	15,584,987
Ad-Dīwānīyah (1970 E)	62,300
Al-'Amārah	131,785
Al-Baṣrah	616,700
Al-Ḥillah	215,249
Al-Kūt	73,022
Al-Mawṣil	570,926
An-Najaf	242,603
An-Nāṣirīyah	138,842
Ar-Ramādī	137,388
As-Samāwah	75,293
As-Sulaymānīyah	279,424
• BAGHDĀD (1987 C)	3,841,268
Ba'qūbah	114,516
Irbīl	333,903
Karbalā'	184,574
Kirkūk (1970 E)	207,900

IRELAND / Éire

1986 C	3,540,643
Cork (★ 173,694)	133,271
• DUBLIN (BAILE ÁTHA CLIATH) (★ 1,140,000)	502,749
Dún Laoghaire (★Dublin)	54,715
Galway	47,104
Limerick (★ 76,557)	56,279
Waterford (★ 41,054)	39,529

ISLE OF MAN

1991 C	69,788
• DOUGLAS (★ 30,000)	22,214

ISRAEL / Isrā'īl / Yisra'el

1991 E	4,713,800
Ashdod	83,900
Ashqelon	59,700
Bat Yam (★Tel Aviv-Yafo)	141,300
Be'ér Sheva (Beersheba)	122,000
Bene Beraq (★Tel Aviv-Yafo)	116,700
Elat	26,300
Giv'atayim (★Tel Aviv-Yafo)	46,600
Hefa (★ 450,000)	245,900
Herzliyya (★Tel Aviv-Yafo)	77,200
Holon (★Tel Aviv-Yafo)	156,700
Kefar Sava (★Tel Aviv-Yafo)	61,100
Lod (Lydda) (★Tel Aviv-Yafo)	43,300
Nazerat (Nazareth) (★ 77,000)	53,600
Netanya (★Tel Aviv-Yafo)	132,200
Petah Tiqwa (★Tel Aviv-Yafo)	144,000
Ra'ananna (★Tel Aviv-Yafo)	53,600
Ramat Gan (★Tel Aviv-Yafo)	119,500
Rehovot (★Tel Aviv-Yafo)	80,300
Rishon LeZiyyon (★Tel Aviv-Yafo)	139,500
• Tel Aviv-Yafo (★ 1,735,000)	339,400
YERUSHALAYIM (AL-QUDS) (JERUSALEM) (★ 560,000)	524,500

ITALY / Italia

1991 C	56,411,290
Afragola (★Napoli)	59,940
Alessandria (▲ 93,351)	74,000
Altamura	57,462
Ancona	103,268
Andria	82,556
Arezzo (▲ 91,623)	74,200
Asti (▲ 74,497)	62,800
Avellino	54,343
Aversa (★Napoli)	50,361
Bari (★ 475,000)	341,273
Barletta	86,215
Benevento (▲ 62,683)	51,900
Bergamo (★ 345,000)	115,655
Biella	50,993
Bitonto	49,792
Bologna (★ 525,000)	411,803
Bolzano	100,380
Brescia	196,766
Brindisi	91,778
Busto Arsizio (★Milano)	77,001
Cagliari (★ 305,000)	211,719
Caltanissetta	62,853
Campobasso (▲ 51,307)	44,400
Carpi (▲ 60,794)	49,600
Carrara (★Massa)	68,480
Caserta	68,811
Casoria (▲ 79,315) (★Napoli)	57,800
Castellammare di Stabia (★Napoli)	68,720
Catania (★ 550,000)	330,037
Catanzaro	103,802
Cava de' Tirreni (★Salerno)	52,610
Cerignola	54,971
Cesena (▲ 89,497)	72,200
Chieti	57,535
Cinisello Balsamo (★Milano)	75,606
Civitavecchia	50,856
Collegno (★Torino)	47,192
Cologno Monzese (★Milano)	50,853
Como (★ 165,000)	85,955
Cosenza (★ 150,000)	104,483
Cremona	75,160
Crotone (▲ 61,813)	54,300
Cuneo (▲ 55,838)	47,900
Empoli (▲ 42,790)	32,300
Ercolano (★Napoli)	60,869
Ferrara (▲ 140,600)	110,700
Firenze (★ 640,000)	402,316
Foggia	155,042
Foligno (▲ 53,518)	42,500
Forlì (▲ 109,755)	90,600
Gela	79,718
Genova (Genoa) (★ 805,000)	675,639
Giugliano in Campania (★Napoli)	59,091
Grosseto (▲ 71,373)	57,000
Imola (▲ 62,352)	48,800
Imperia	41,278
L'Aquila (▲ 67,818)	43,100
La Spezia (★ 185,000)	101,701
Latina (▲ 105,543)	72,700
Lecce	102,344
Lecco	45,859
Legnano (★Milano)	50,068
Livorno	171,265
Lucca	86,437
Manfredonia	58,157
Mantova (▲ 54,228)	46,800
Marsala	77,218
Massa (★ 145,000)	67,779
Matera	54,872
Messina	274,846
Mestre (▲ 317,837) (★Venezia)	181,900
• Milano (Milan) (★ 3,750,000)	1,371,008
Modena	177,501
Molfetta	66,658
Moncalieri (★Torino)	58,433
Monopoli (▲ 43,019)	33,100
Monza (★Milano)	121,151
Napoli (Naples) (★ 2,875,000)	1,024,601
Nicastro (▲ 69,660)	53,700
Nocera Inferiore	49,021
Novara	103,349
Padova (★ 270,000)	218,186
Palermo	697,162
Parma	173,991
Pavia	80,073
Perugia (▲ 150,576)	109,500
Pesaro (▲ 90,341)	78,700
Pescara	128,553
Piacenza	102,252
Pisa	101,500
Pistoia (▲ 87,275)	73,900
Pordenone	50,222
Portici (★Napoli)	67,824
Potenza (▲ 68,499)	58,800
Pozzuoli (▲ 75,706) (★Napoli)	67,100
Prato (★ 215,000)	165,364
Quartu Sant'Elena	60,852
Ragusa	69,423
Ravenna (▲ 136,724)	87,000
Reggio di Calabria	178,496
Reggio nell'Emilia (▲ 131,880)	108,800
Rho (★Milano)	51,646
Rimini (▲ 130,896)	114,800
Rivoli (★Torino)	51,884
ROMA (★ 3,175,000)	2,693,383
Salerno (★ 250,000)	153,436
San Benedetto del Tronto	45,220
San Giorgio a Cremano (★Napoli)	62,168
San Remo	59,247
San Severo	55,376
Sassari	120,011
Savona (★ 112,000)	68,997
Scandicci (★Firenze)	53,264
Sesto Fiorentino (★Firenze)	46,899
Sesto San Giovanni (★Milano)	85,175
Siena	57,745
Siracusa	125,444
Taranto	232,200
Teramo (▲ 52,490)	36,100
Terni (▲ 109,809)	93,400
Torino (★ 1,550,000)	961,916
Torre Annunziata (★Napoli)	50,346
Torre del Greco (★Napoli)	101,456
Trani	49,337
Trapani (▲ 69,273)	59,700
Trento (▲ 102,124)	83,100
Treviso	83,886
Trieste (Triest) (Trst)	231,047
Udine (★ 126,000)	98,322
Varese	85,461
Venezia (Venice) (★ 420,000)	85,100
Vercelli	50,207
Verona	258,946
Viareggio (▲ 60,559)	51,500
Vicenza	109,333
Vigevano	61,380
Viterbo (▲ 60,213)	48,700
Vittoria	56,970

JAMAICA

1990 E	2,392,000
• KINGSTON (★ 820,000)	661,600
Montego Bay (▲ 155,700)	80,500
Portmore (★Kingston) (1982 C)	73,426
Spanish Town (▲ 358,600) (★Kingston)	96,100

JAPAN / Nihon

1990 C	123,611,167
Abiko (★Tōkyō)	120,628
Ageo (★Tōkyō)	194,947
Aizu-wakamatsu	119,080
Akashi (★Ōsaka)	270,722
Akigawa (★Tōkyō)	50,387
Akishima (★Tōkyō)	105,372
Akita	302,362
Akō	51,131
Amagasaki (★Ōsaka)	498,999
Anan (▲ 59,044)	47,000
Anjō	142,251
Aomori	287,808
Arao (★Ōmuta)	59,507
Asahikawa	359,071
Asaka (★Tōkyō)	103,617
Ashikaga	167,686
Ashiya (★Ōsaka)	87,524
Atami	47,291
Atsugi (★Tōkyō)	197,282
Ayase (★Tōkyō)	77,926
Beppu	130,334
Bisai (★Nagoya)	55,880
Chiba (★Tōkyō)	829,455
Chichibu	60,915
Chigasaki (★Tōkyō)	201,675
Chikushino (★Fukuoka)	70,303
Chiryū (★Nagoya)	54,059
Chita (★Nagoya)	75,433
Chitose	78,946
Chōfu (★Tōkyō)	197,677
Chōshi	85,138
Daitō (★Ōsaka)	126,460
Dazaifu (★Fukuoka)	62,402
Ebetsu (★Sapporo)	97,201
Ebina (★Tōkyō)	105,822
Eniwa	55,615
Fuchū (★Tōkyō)	209,396
Fuchū	45,739
Fuchū	50,060
Fuji (★ 370,000)	222,490
Fujieda (★Shizuoka)	119,815
Fujiidera (★Ōsaka)	65,922
Fujimi (★Tōkyō)	94,864
Fujinomiya (★Fuji)	117,092
Fujioka (▲ 60,981)	50,100
Fujisawa (★Tōkyō)	350,330
Fuji-yoshida	54,804
Fukaya (▲ 94,017)	75,600
Fukuchiyama (▲ 66,506)	56,700
Fukui	252,743
Fukuoka (★ 1,750,000)	1,237,062
Fukushima	277,528
Fukuyama	365,612
Funabashi (★Tōkyō)	533,270
Furukawa (▲ 64,230)	51,200
Fussa (★Tōkyō)	58,062
Gamagōri	84,819
Gifu	410,324
Ginowan	75,905
Gotemba	79,557
Gushikawa	54,018
Gyōda	83,181
Habikino (★Ōsaka)	115,049
Hachinohe	241,057
Hachiōji (★Tōkyō)	466,347
Hadano (★Tōkyō)	155,620
Hagi	50,618
Hakodate	307,249
Hamada	49,135
Hamakita	81,157
Hamamatsu	534,620
Hanamaki (▲ 70,514)	55,000
Handa (★Nagoya)	99,550
Hannō (★Tōkyō)	73,214
Hashima	61,460
Hasuda (★Tōkyō)	59,706
Hatogaya (★Tōkyō)	56,440
Hatsukaichi (★Hiroshima)	63,441
Hekinan	65,899
Higashihiroshima (★Hiroshima)	94,209
Higashikurume (★Tōkyō)	113,818
Higashimatsuyama	84,394
Higashimurayama (★Tōkyō)	134,002
Higashiōsaka (★Ōsaka)	518,319
Higashiyamato (★Tōkyō)	75,132
Hikari (★Tokuyama)	47,611
Hikone	99,519
Himeji (★ 660,000)	454,360
Himi (▲ 60,766)	51,400
Hino (★Tōkyō)	165,928
Hirakata (★Ōsaka)	390,788
Hiratsuka (★Tōkyō)	245,950
Hirosaki (▲ 174,704)	133,800
Hiroshima (★ 1,575,000)	1,085,705
Hita (▲ 64,695)	57,100
Hitachi	202,141
Hōfu	117,634
Honjō	59,098
Hōya (★Tōkyō)	95,146
Hyūga	58,442
Ibaraki (★Ōsaka)	254,078
Ichihara (★Tōkyō)	257,716
Ichikawa (★Tōkyō)	436,596
Ichinomiya (★Nagoya)	262,434
Ichinoseki (▲ 61,967)	50,100
Iida (▲ 91,859)	64,700
Iizuka (▲ 110,000)	83,131
Ikeda (★Ōsaka)	104,218
Ikoma (★Ōsaka)	99,604
Imabari	123,114
Imari (▲ 60,882)	50,000
Ina (▲ 60,062)	49,500
Inagi (★Tōkyō)	58,635
Inazawa (★Nagoya)	96,274
Inuyama (★Nagoya)	69,801
Iruma (★Tōkyō)	137,585
Isahaya	90,683
Ise (Uji-yamada)	104,164
Isehara (★Tōkyō)	89,567
Isesaki	115,938
Ishinomaki	121,976
Itami (★Ōsaka)	186,134
Itō	71,223
Iwaki (Taira)	355,812
Iwakuni	109,530
Iwamizawa	80,417
Iwata	83,521
Iwatsuki (★Tōkyō)	106,462
Izumi (★Ōsaka)	146,127
Izumi (★Sendai)	124,216
Izumi-ōtsu (★Ōsaka)	67,035
Izumi-sano (★Ōsaka)	88,866
Izumo (▲ 82,679)	69,600
Joetsu	130,116
Jōyō (★Ōsaka)	84,770
Kadoma (★Ōsaka)	142,297
Kaga	69,196
Kagoshima	536,752
Kainan (★Wakayama)	48,596
Kaizuka (★Ōsaka)	79,234
Kakamigahara	129,680
Kakegawa (▲ 72,795)	59,000
Kakogawa (★Ōsaka)	239,803
Kamagaya (★Tōkyō)	95,052
Kamaishi	52,484
Kamakura (★Tōkyō)	174,307
Kameoka	85,283
Kamifukuoka (★Tōkyō)	58,761
Kanazawa	442,868
Kani (★Nagoya)	80,012
Kanoya (▲ 77,655)	61,500
Kanuma (▲ 90,043)	74,900
Karatsu (▲ 79,207)	70,500
Kariya (★Nagoya)	120,126
Kasai	51,764
Kasaoka (▲ 59,619)	52,700
Kashihara (★Ōsaka)	115,554
Kashiwa (★Tōkyō)	305,058
Kashiwara (★Ōsaka)	76,819
Kashiwazaki (▲ 88,309)	75,300
Kasuga (★Fukuoka)	88,699
Kasugai (★Nagoya)	266,599
Kasukabe (★Tōkyō)	188,823
Katano (★Ōsaka)	65,308
Katsuta	109,825
Kawachi-nagano (★Ōsaka)	108,767
Kawagoe (★Tōkyō)	304,854
Kawaguchi (★Tōkyō)	438,680
Kawanishi (★Ōsaka)	141,253
Kawasaki (★Tōkyō)	1,173,603
Kesennuma	65,578
Kimitsu (▲ 89,242)	76,100
Kiryū	126,446
Kisarazu	123,433
Kishiwada (★Ōsaka)	188,563
Kitaibaraki	51,093
Kitakyūshū (★ 1,525,000)	1,026,455
Kitami	107,247
Kitamoto (★Tōkyō)	63,929
Kiyose (★Tōkyō)	67,539
Kōbe (★Ōsaka)	1,477,410
Kōchi	317,069
Kodaira (★Tōkyō)	164,013
Kōfu	200,626
Koga (★Tōkyō)	58,231
Koganei (★Tōkyō)	105,899
Kokubunji (★Tōkyō)	100,982
Komae (★Tōkyō)	74,189
Komaki (★Nagoya)	124,441
Komatsu	106,075
Kōnan (★Nagoya)	93,837
Kōnosu (★Tōkyō)	72,435
Kōriyama	314,642
Koshigaya (★Tōkyō)	285,259
Kudamatsu (★Tokuyama)	53,030
Kuki (★Tōkyō)	66,852
Kumagaya	152,124
Kumamoto	579,306
Kunitachi (★Tōkyō)	65,833
Kurashiki	414,693
Kure (★Hiroshima)	216,723
Kuroiso (▲ 52,344)	41,900
Kurume	228,347
Kusatsu (★Ōsaka)	94,767
Kushiro	205,639
Kuwana (★Nagoya)	97,909
Kyōto (★Ōsaka)	1,461,103
Machida (★Tōkyō)	349,050
Maebashi	286,261
Maizuru	96,333
Marugame	75,606
Matsubara (★Ōsaka)	135,919
Matsudo (★Tōkyō)	456,210
Matsue	142,956
Matsumoto	200,715
Matsusaka	118,725
Matsuyama	443,322
Mihara	85,518
Miki (★Ōsaka)	76,501
Minō (★Ōsaka)	122,120
Misato (★Tōkyō)	128,376
Mishima (★Numazu)	105,418
Mitaka (★Tōkyō)	165,564
Mito	234,968
Miura (★Tōkyō)	52,440
Miyako	58,503
Miyakonojō (▲ 130,153)	106,200
Miyazaki	287,352
Mobara	83,437
Moriguchi (★Ōsaka)	157,372
Morioka	235,434
Moriyama	58,561
Mukō (★Ōsaka)	52,928
Munakata	68,265
Muroran (★ 195,000)	117,855
Musashimurayama (★Tōkyō)	65,562
Musashino (★Tōkyō)	139,077
Mutsu	48,470
Nabari	68,963
Nagahama	55,465
Nagano	347,026
Nagaoka	185,938
Nagaokakyō (★Ōsaka)	77,191
Nagareyama (★Tōkyō)	140,059
Nagasaki	444,599
Nagoya (★ 4,800,000)	2,154,793
Naha	304,836
Nakama (★Kitakyūshū)	49,216
Nakatsu	66,388
Nakatsugawa	53,722
Nanao	50,103
Nara (★Ōsaka)	349,349
Narashino (★Tōkyō)	151,471
Narita	86,708
Naruto	64,575
Naze	46,306
Neyagawa (★Ōsaka)	256,524
Niigata	486,097
Niihama	129,149
Niitsu (▲ 63,999)	55,700
Niiza (★Tōkyō)	138,919
Nishinomiya (★Ōsaka)	426,909
Nishio	95,197
Nobeoka	130,624
Noboribetsu (★Muroran)	55,571
Noda (★Tōkyō)	114,475
Nōgata	62,530
Noshiro (▲ 55,915)	47,800
Numazu (★ 495,000)	211,732
Obihiro	167,384
Ōbu (★Nagoya)	69,720
Ōdate (▲ 68,195)	58,500
Odawara	193,417
Ōgaki	148,281
Ōita	408,501
Ōkawa	45,704
Okaya	59,849
Okayama	593,730
Okazaki	306,822
Okegawa (★Tōkyō)	69,029

C Census. E Official estimate. U Unofficial estimate.
• Largest city in country.

★ Population or designation of metropolitan area, including suburbs (see headnote).
▲ Population of an entire municipality, commune, or district, including rural area.

World Populations

Okinawa... 105,845
Okinawa... 105,852
Ōme (★Tōkyō)... 125,960
Ōmi-hachiman (★Ōsaka)... 66,066
Ōmiya (★Tōkyō)... 403,776
Ōmura... 73,435
Ōmuta (★ 225,000)... 150,453
Ōnojō (★Fukuoka)... 75,214
Onomichi... 97,103
Ōsaka (★ 16,900,000)... 2,623,801
Ōta... 139,801
Otaru (★Sapporo)... 163,211
Ōtsu (★Ōsaka)... 260,018
Owariashi (★Nagoya)... 65,675
Oyama (★ 142,262)... 120,000
Sabae... 62,283
Saga... 169,963
Sagamihara (★Tōkyō)... 531,542
Saijō... 56,821
Saiki... 52,323
Sakado (★Tōkyō)... 95,740
Sakai (★Ōsaka)... 807,765
Sakaide... 63,876
Sakata... 100,811
Saku (▲ 62,003)... 50,000
Sakura (★Tōkyō)... 144,688
Sakurai... 60,262
Sanda (▲ 64,560) (★Ōsaka)... 54,500
Sanjō... 85,823
Sano... 83,484
Sapporo (★ 1,900,000)... 1,671,742
Sasebo... 244,677
Satte... 54,342
Sayama (★Tōkyō)... 157,309
Sayama (★Ōsaka)... 54,319
Seki... 68,386
Sendai, Kagoshima pref. (▲ 71,735)... 58,000
Sendai, Miyagi pref. (★ 1,175,000)... 918,398
Sennan (★Ōsaka)... 60,065
Seto (★Nagoya)... 126,340
Settsu (★Ōsaka)... 87,453
Shibata (▲ 78,170)... 63,600
Shijōnawate (★Ōsaka)... 50,035
Shiki (★Tōkyō)... 63,491
Shimada (▲ 73,810)... 64,500
Shimizu (★Shizuoka)... 241,523
Shimodate (▲ 66,028)... 54,100
Shimonoseki (★Kitakyūshū)... 262,635
Shiogama (★Sendai)... 62,025
Shizuoka (★ 975,000)... 472,196
Sōka (★Tōkyō)... 206,132
Suita (★Ōsaka)... 345,206
Suwa... 52,464
Suzuka... 174,105
Tachikawa (★Tōkyō)... 152,824
Tagajō (★Sendai)... 58,456
Tagawa... 57,700
Tajimi (★Nagoya)... 94,036
Takaishi (★Ōsaka)... 65,086
Takamatsu... 329,684
Takaoka (★ 220,000)... 175,466
Takarazuka (★Ōsaka)... 201,862
Takasago (★Ōsaka)... 93,273
Takasaki... 236,461
Takatsuki (★Ōsaka)... 359,867
Takayama... 65,243
Takefu... 70,187
Takikawa... 49,591
Tama (★Tōkyō)... 144,489
Tamano... 73,238
Tanabe (▲ 69,859)... 59,100
Tanashi (★Tōkyō)... 75,144
Tatebayashi... 76,221
Tenri... 68,815
Tochigi... 86,216
Toda (★Tōkyō)... 87,599
Tōkai (★Nagoya)... 97,358
Toki... 64,946
Tokoname (★Nagoya)... 51,784
Tokorozawa (★Tōkyō)... 303,040
Tokushima... 263,356
Tokuyama (★ 250,000)... 110,900
• TŌKYŌ (★ 30,300,000)... 8,163,573
Tomakomai... 160,118
Tondabayashi (★Ōsaka)... 110,447
Toride (★Tōkyō)... 81,665
Tosu... 55,877
Tottori... 142,467
Toyama... 321,254
Toyoake (★Nagoya)... 62,160
Toyohashi... 337,982
Toyokawa... 111,730
Toyonaka (★Ōsaka)... 409,837
Toyota... 332,336
Tsu... 157,177
Tsuchiura... 127,471
Tsuruga... 68,041
Tsuruoka... 99,889
Tsushima (★Nagoya)... 59,343
Tsuyama... 89,400
Ube (★ 230,000)... 175,053
Ueda... 119,435
Ueno (▲ 60,242)... 51,400
Uji (★Ōsaka)... 177,010
Uozu... 49,514
Urasoe... 89,994
Urawa (★Tōkyō)... 418,271
Urayasu (★Tōkyō)... 115,675
Usa (▲ 50,829)... 38,600
Ushiku... 60,693
Utsunomiya... 426,795
Uwajima... 68,034
Wakayama (★ 495,000)... 396,553
Wakkanai... 48,232
Wakō (★Tōkyō)... 56,890
Warabi (★Tōkyō)... 73,620
Yachiyo (★Tōkyō)... 148,615
Yaizu (★Shizuoka)... 112,186
Yamagata... 249,487
Yamaguchi... 129,461
Yamato (★Tōkyō)... 194,866
Yamato-kōriyama (★Ōsaka)... 92,949
Yamato-takada (★Ōsaka)... 68,237
Yao (★Ōsaka)... 277,568
Yashio (★Tōkyō)... 72,473
Yatsushiro (▲ 108,135)... 88,300
Yawata (★Ōsaka)... 75,758
Yokkaichi... 274,180

Yokohama (★Tōkyō)... 3,220,331
Yokosuka (★Tōkyō)... 433,358
Yonago... 131,453
Yonezawa... 94,760
Yono (★Tōkyō)... 79,060
Yotsukaidō (★Tōkyō)... 72,157
Yukuhashi... 65,711
Zama (★Tōkyō)... 112,102
Zushi (★Tōkyō)... 56,704

JERSEY
1991 C... 84,082
• SAINT HELIER (★ 46,500)... 28,123

JORDAN / Al-Urdun
1989 E... 3,111,000
Al-Baq'ah (★'Ammān)... 63,985
•'AMMĀN (★ 1,625,000)... 936,300
Ar-Ruṣayfah (★'Ammān)... 72,580
As-Salt... 47,585
Az-Zarqā' (★'Ammān)... 318,055
Irbid... 167,785

KAZAKHSTAN
1991 E... 16,793,100
Aktau... 169,000
Akt'ubinsk... 265,300
• ALMA-ATA (ALMATY) (★ 1,190,000)... 1,156,200
Arkalyk... 64,900
Aterau... 152,500
Balchaš... 87,600
Čelinograd... 286,000
Čimkent... 407,900
Džambul... 312,300
Džetygara... 48,900
Džezkazgan... 111,100
Ekibastuz... 138,900
Karaganda... 608,600
Kentau... 65,100
Kokčetav... 143,300
Kustanaj... 233,900
Kzyl-Orda... 158,200
Leninogorsk... 69,500
Leninsk... 73,000
Pavlodar... 342,500
Petropavlovsk... 247,400
Rudnyj... 128,800
Šachtinsk... 65,300
Saptajev... 61,400
Saran'... 62,600
Ščučinsk... 56,000
Semipalatinsk... 344,700
Taldy-Kurgan... 124,500
Temirtau... 213,100
Turkestan... 81,200
Ural'sk... 214,000
Ust'-Kamenogorsk... 332,900
Žanatas... 53,000
Zyr'anovsk... 53,800

KENYA
1990 E... 24,870,000
Eldoret (1979 C)... 50,503
Kisumu (1984 E)... 167,100
Machakos (1983 E)... 92,300
Meru (1979 C)... 72,049
Mombasa... 537,000
• NAIROBI... 1,505,000
Nakuru (1984 E)... 101,700

KIRIBATI
1990 C... 72,298
BAIRIKI... 2,226
• Bikenibeu... 5,055

KOREA, NORTH / Chosŏn-minjujuŭi-inmīn-konghwaguk
1981 E... 18,317,000
Ch'ŏngjin... 490,000
Haeju (1983 E)... 213,000
Hamhŭng (1970 E)... 150,000
Hŭngnam (1976 E)... 260,000
Kaesŏng... 259,000
Kanggye (1967 E)... 130,000
Kimch'aek (Sŏngjin) (1967 E)... 265,000
Namp'o... 241,000
• P'YŎNGYANG... 2,355,000
Sinŭiju... 305,000
Songnim (1944 C)... 53,035
Wŏnsan... 398,000

KOREA, SOUTH / Taehan-min'guk
1990 C... 43,520,199
Andong... 116,932
Ansan (★Sŏul)... 252,157
Anyang (★Sŏul)... 480,668
Bucheon (★Sŏul)... 667,777
Changsŭngp'o... 48,614
Changwŏn (★Masan)... 323,138
Chech'on... 102,037
Cheju... 232,687
Chinhae... 120,207
Chinju... 258,365

Chŏmch'on... 47,802
Ch'ŏnan... 211,382
Ch'ŏngju... 497,429
Chŏnju... 86,850
Chŏnju, Chŏlla Pukdo prov.... 517,104
Ch'unch'ŏn... 174,153
Ch'ungju... 129,994
Ch'ungmu... 92,159
Hanam (★Sŏul)... 101,278
Inch'ŏn (★Sŏul)... 1,818,293
Iri... 203,401
Kangnŭng... 152,605
Kimch'ŏn... 81,349
Kimhae... 106,166
Kimje... 55,136
Kongju... 65,195
Kumi... 206,101
Kŭmsŏng (1985 C)... 58,897
Kunp'o (★Sŏul)... 99,956
Kunsan... 218,216
Kwachŏn (★Sŏul)... 72,328
Kwangju... 1,144,695
Kwangmyŏng (★Sŏul)... 328,803
Kyŏngju... 141,895
Kyŏngsan... 60,524
Masan (★ 625,000)... 496,639
Mikŭm (★Sŏul)... 74,688
Miryang... 52,995
Mokp'o... 253,423
Naju... 55,306
Namwŏn... 63,121
Ŏnyang... 66,379
Osan... 59,492
P'ohang... 318,595
Pusan (★ 3,800,000)... 3,797,566
P'yŏngt'aek... 79,238
Samch'ŏnp'o... 62,824
Sangju... 51,875
Shihŭng (★Sŏul)... 107,190
Sŏgwipo... 88,292
Sŏkch'o... 73,796
Sŏngnam (★Sŏul)... 540,764
Songtan... 77,460
Sŏsan... 55,930
• SŎUL (★ 15,850,000)... 10,627,790
Sunch'ŏn... 167,209
Suwŏn (★Sŏul)... 644,968
T'aebaek... 89,770
Taech'ŏn... 56,922
Taegu... 2,228,834
Taejŏn... 1,062,084
Tongduch'ŏn... 71,448
Tonghae... 89,162
Tongkwang... 70,118
Ŭijŏngbu (★Sŏul)... 212,368
Ŭiwang... 96,892
Ulsan... 682,978
Wŏnju... 173,013
Yŏch'ŏn... 63,802
Yŏngch'ŏn... 48,890
Yŏngju... 84,335
Yŏsu... 173,164

KUWAIT / Al-Kuwayt
1985 C... 1,697,301
Abraq Khīṭān (★Al-Kuwayt)... 45,120
Al-Aḥmadī (★ 285,000)... 26,899
Al-Farwānīyah (★Al-Kuwayt)... 68,701
Al-Fuhayhīl (★Al-Aḥmadī)... 50,081
Al-Jahrah (★Al-Kuwayt)... 111,222
• AL-KUWAYT (★ 1,375,000)... 44,335
Aṣ-Sālimīyah (★Al-Kuwayt)... 153,359
Aṣ-Sulaybīyah (★Al-Kuwayt)... 51,314
Hawallī (★Al-Kuwayt)... 145,126
Qalīb ash-Shuyūkh (★Al-Kuwayt)... 114,771
South Khīṭān (★Al-Kuwayt)... 69,256
Subahiya (★Al-Aḥmadī)... 60,787

KYRGYZSTAN
1991 E... 4,422,200
• BIŠKEK... 631,300
Džalal-Abad... 74,200
Kara-Balta... 55,000
Karakol (Prževal'sk)... 64,300
Oš... 218,700
Tokmak... 71,200

LAOS / Lao
1985 C... 3,584,803
Savannakhét (1975 E)... 53,000
• VIANGCHAN (VIENTIANE)... 377,409

LATVIA / Latvija
1991 E... 2,680,500
Daugavpils... 129,000
Jelgava... 74,500
Jūrmala (★Rīga)... 66,500
Liepāja... 114,900
• RĪGA (★ 1,005,000)... 910,200
Ventspils... 50,400

LEBANON / Lubnān
1982 E... 2,637,000
• BAYRŪT (★ 1,675,000)... 509,000

Ṣaydā... 105,000
Ṣūr (Tyre) (1970 E)... 12,500
Ṭarābulus (Tripoli) (★ 950,000)... 198,000

LESOTHO
1986 C... 1,577,536
• MASERU... 98,017

LIBERIA
1986 E... 2,221,000
• MONROVIA... 465,000

LIBYA / Lībiyā
1988 E... 3,772,500
Al-Baydā (Beida) (1984 C)... 67,120
Banghāzī... 446,250
Darnah (1984 C)... 62,179
Misrātah... 121,669
• TARĀBULUS (TRIPOLI)... 591,062
Tubruq (Tobruk) (1984 C)... 75,282

LIECHTENSTEIN
1992 E... 29,386
• VADUZ... 4,887

LITHUANIA / Lietuva
1992 C... 3,746,400
Alytus... 77,500
Kaunas... 433,600
Klaipėda (Memel)... 208,300
Marijampole... 52,300
Panevėžys... 132,300
Šiauliai... 149,000
• VILNIUS... 596,900

LUXEMBOURG
1991 C... 384,062
Esch-sur-Alzette (★ 83,000)... 24,012
• LUXEMBOURG (★ 136,000)... 75,377

MACAU
1989 E... 452,300
• MACAU... 452,300

MACEDONIA / Makedonija
1987 E... 2,064,581
Bitola (▲ 143,090)... 76,200
• SKOPJE (▲ 547,214)... 444,900

MADAGASCAR / Madagasikara
1988 E... 11,238,000
• ANTANANARIVO... 1,250,000
Antsirabe (▲ 100,000)... 52,700
Antsiranana... 220,000
Fianarantsoa... 300,000
Mahajanga... 200,000
Toamasina... 230,000
Toliara... 150,000

MALAWI / Malaŵi
1987 C... 7,988,507
• Blantyre... 333,120
LILONGWE... 223,318
Mzuzu... 51,904

MALAYSIA
1980 C... 13,136,109
Alor Setar... 69,435
Batu Pahat... 64,727
Butterworth (★George Town)... 77,982
George Town (Pinang) (★ 495,000)... 248,241
Ipoh... 293,849
Johor Baharu (★Singapore, Singapore)... 246,395
Kelang... 192,080
Keluang... 50,315
Kota Baharu... 167,872
Kota Kinabalu (Jesselton)... 55,997
• KUALA LUMPUR (★ 1,475,000)... 919,610
Kuala Terengganu... 180,296
Kuantan... 131,547
Kuching... 72,555
Melaka... 87,494
Miri... 52,125

Muar (Bandar Maharani)... 65,151
Petaling Jaya (★Kuala Lumpur)... 207,805
Sandakan... 70,420
Seremban... 132,911
Sibu... 85,231
Taiping... 146,000
Telok Anson... 49,148

MALDIVES
1990 C... 213,215
• MALE'... 55,130

MALI
1987 C... 7,696,348
• BAMAKO... 658,275
Gao... 55,266
Kayes... 50,993
Koutiala... 48,698
Mopti... 74,771
Ségou... 88,135
Sikasso... 73,859
Tombouctou (Timbuktu)... 31,962

MALTA
1991 E... 355,910
• VALLETTA (★ 215,000)... 9,199

MARSHALL ISLANDS
1980 C... 30,873
• Jarej-Uliga-Delap... 8,583

MARTINIQUE
1982 C... 328,566
• FORT-DE-FRANCE (★ 116,017)... 99,844

MAURITANIA / Mauritanie / Mūrītāniyā
1987 E... 2,007,000
• NOUAKCHOTT... 285,000

MAURITIUS
1989 E... 1,081,669
Beau Bassin-Rose Hill (★Port Louis)... 94,236
Curepipe (★Port Louis)... 66,704
• PORT LOUIS (★ 420,000)... 141,870
Quatre Bornes (★Port Louis)... 65,759
Vacoas-Phoenix (★Port Louis)... 56,335

MAYOTTE
1985 E... 67,205
• DZAOUDZI (★ 6,979)... 5,865

MEXICO / México
1990 C... 81,249,645
Acámbaro... 52,248
Acapulco de Juárez... 515,374
Aguascalientes... 440,425
Apatzingán de la Constitución... 76,643
Apodaca... 103,364
Atlixco... 74,233
Buenavista... 114,653
Campeche... 150,518
Cancún... 167,730
Cárdenas... 61,017
Celaya... 214,856
Chalco (★Ciudad de México)... 224,190
Chetumal... 94,158
Chicoloapan de Juárz... 57,306
Chihuahua... 516,153
Chilpancingo de los Bravo... 97,165
Chimalhuacán... 235,587
Cholula de Rivadabia (★Puebla)... 53,673
Ciudad Acuña... 52,983
Ciudad del Carmen... 83,806
• CIUDAD DE MÉXICO (★ 14,100,000)... 8,235,744
Ciudad Guzmán... 72,619
Ciudad Hidalgo... 48,476
Ciudad Juárez (★El Paso, Tex., U.S.A.)... 789,522
Ciudad Lerdo (★Torreón)... 46,593
Ciudad López Mateos... 315,059
Ciudad Madero (★Tampico)... 160,331
Ciudad Mante... 76,799
Ciudad Obregón... 219,980
Ciudad Valles... 91,402
Ciudad Victoria... 194,996

C Census.　　E Official estimate.　　U Unofficial estimate.
• Largest city in country.
★ Population or designation of metropolitan area, including suburbs (see headnote).
▲ Population of an entire municipality, commune, or district, including rural area.

Coacalco 151,255
Coatzacoalcos 198,817
Colima 106,967
Comitan de Dominguez 48,299
Córdoba 130,695
Cortazar 45,579
Cuauhtémoc 6,938
Cuautitlán Izcalli (★Ciudad de México) 313,238
Cuernavaca 279,187
Culiacán 415,046
Delicias 87,412
Durango 348,036
Ecatepec (★Ciudad de México) 1,218,135
Ensenada 169,426
Fresnillo 75,118
Garza García (★Monterrey) 113,017
General Escobedo 96,962
Gómez Palacio (★Torreón) 164,092
Guadalajara (★ 2,430,000) 1,650,042
Guadalupe (★Monterrey) 535,332
Guadalupe 46,433
Guamúchil 49,635
Guanajuato 73,108
Guasave 49,338
Guaymas 87,484
Hermosillo 406,417
Heroica Zitácuaro 66,983
Hidalgo del Parral 88,197
Iguala 83,412
Irapuato 265,042
Ixtapaluca 115,711
Jiutepec 82,845
Juchitán de Zaragoza 53,666
Lagos de Moreno 63,646
La Paz 137,641
La Piedad de Cabadas 62,625
Las Choapas 43,868
León 758,279
Los Mochis 162,659
Los Reyes la Paz 134,544
Manzanillo 67,697
Matamoros (★Brownsville, Tex., U.S.A.) 266,055
Matehuala 54,713
Mazatlán 262,705
Mérida 523,422
Metepec 116,203
Mexicali (★ 460,000) 438,377
Minatitlán 142,060
Monclova 177,792
Monterrey (★ 2,015,000) 1,068,996
Morelia 428,486
Naucalpan de Juárez (★Ciudad de México) 845,960
Navojoa 82,618
Nezahualcóyotl (★Ciudad de México) 1,255,456
Nogales 105,873
Nuevo Laredo (★Laredo, Tex., U.S.A.) 218,413
Oaxaca de Juárez 212,818
Ocotlán 62,595
Orizaba (★ 215,000) 114,216
Pachuca 174,013
Papantla de Olarte 46,075
Piedras Negras 96,178
Poza Rica 151,739
Puebla (★ 1,200,000) 1,007,170
Puerto Vallarta 93,503
Querétaro 385,503
Reynosa 265,663
Río Bravo 67,092
Sahuayo de José María Morelos 50,463
Salamanca 123,190
Salina Cruz 61,656
Saltillo 420,947
San Andrés Tuxtla 49,658
San Cristóbal de las Casas 73,388
San Francisco del Rincón 52,291
San Juan del Río 61,652
San Luis Potosí (★ 600,000) 489,238
San Luis Río Colorado 95,461
San Martín Texmelucan 57,519
San Miguel de Allende 48,935
San Nicolás de los Garza (★Monterrey) 436,603
San Pablo de las Salinas 84,217
Santa Catarina (★Monterrey) 162,707
Silao 50,828
Soledad de Graciano Sanchez 123,943
Tampico (★ 440,000) 272,690
Tapachula 138,858
Tecomán 60,938
Tehuacán 139,450
Temixco 65,058
Tepatitlán de Morelos 54,036
Tepic 206,967
Texcoco de Mora (★Ciudad de México) 74,194
Tijuana (★San Diego, Calif., U.S.A.) 698,752
Tlalnepantla (★Ciudad de México) 702,270
Tlaquepaque (★Guadalajara) 328,031
Tlaxcala de Xicoténcatl 50,486
Toluca de Lerdo 327,865
Tonalá 151,190
Torreón (★ 690,000) 439,436
Tulancingo 75,477
Tuxpan 69,224
Tuxtepec 62,788
Tuxtla Gutiérrez 289,626
Uruapan del Progreso 187,623
Valle de Santiago 56,009
Veracruz (★ 540,000) 438,821
Villa Frontera 58,216
Villahermosa 261,231
Villa Nicolás Romero 148,342
Xalapa 279,451
Zacatecas 100,051
Zamora de Hidalgo 109,751
Zapopan (★Guadalajara) 668,323

MICRONESIA, FEDERATED STATES OF

1985 E 94,534
• KOLONIA 6,306

MOLDOVA

1991 E 4,366,300
Bălţi 161,800
• CHIŞINĂU (KISHINEV) 676,700
Râbniţa (Rybnica) 62,900
Tighina 133,000
Tiraspol 186,000

MONACO

1990 C 29,972
• MONACO (★ 87,000) 29,972

MONGOLIA / Mongol Ard Uls

1989 E 2,040,000
Darchan (1985 E) 69,800
• ULAANBAATAR 548,400

MONTSERRAT

1980 C 11,606
• PLYMOUTH 1,568

MOROCCO / Al-Magreb

1982 C 20,419,555
Agadir 110,479
Beni-Mellal 95,003
Berkane 60,490
• Casablanca (Dar-el-Beida) (★ 2,475,000) 2,139,204
El-Jadida (Mazagan) 81,455
Fès (★ 535,000) 448,823
Kenitra 188,194
Khemisset 58,925
Khouribga 127,181
Ksar-el-Kebir 73,541
Larache 63,893
Marrakech (★ 535,000) 439,728
Meknès (★ 375,000) 319,783
Mohammedia (Fedala) (★Casablanca) 105,120
Nador 62,040
Oued-Zem 58,744
Oujda 260,082
RABAT (★ 980,000) 518,616
Safi 197,309
Salé (★Rabat) 289,391
Settat 65,203
Sidi Kacem 55,833
Sidi Slimane 50,457
Tanger (Tangier) (★ 370,000) 266,346
Tan-Tan 41,451
Taza 77,216
Temera (★Rabat) 48,644
Tétouan 199,615

MOZAMBIQUE / Moçambique

1989 E 15,326,476
Beira 291,604
Chimoio (1986 E) 86,928
Inhambane (1986 E) 64,274
• MAPUTO 1,069,727
Nacala 101,615
Nampula 197,379
Pemba (1986 E) 50,215
Quelimane 78,520
Tete (1986 E) 56,178
Xai-Xai (1986 E) 51,620

MYANMAR (BURMA)

1983 C 34,124,908
Bago (Pegu) 150,528
Chauk 51,437
Dawei (Tavoy) 69,882
Henzada 82,005
Kale 52,628
Lashio 88,590
Magway 54,881
Mandalay 532,949
Mawlamyine (Moulmein) 219,961
Maymyo 63,782
Meiktila 96,496
Mergui (Myeik) 88,600
Mogok 49,392
Monywa 106,843
Myingyan 77,060
Myitkyinā 56,427
Nyaunglebin 55,194
Pakokku 71,860
Pathein (Bassein) 144,096
Prome (Pyè) 83,332
Pyinmana 52,962
Sagaing 46,212
Shwebo 52,185
Sittwe (Akyab) 107,621
Taunggyi 108,231
Thaton 61,790
Toungoo 65,861
• YANGON (RANGOON) (★ 2,800,000) 2,705,039
Yenangyaung 62,582

NAMIBIA

1988 E 1,760,000
Walvis Bay (★ 22,999) (1991 C) 12,383
• WINDHOEK 114,500

NEPAL / Nepāl

1981 C 15,022,839
Bhaktapur 48,472
• KĀTHMĀNDAU (★ 320,000) 235,160
Wirātnagar 93,544

NETHERLANDS / Nederland

1992 E 15,129,150
Alkmaar (★ 124,000) 91,817
Almelo 63,383
Alphen aan den Rijn 63,573
Amersfoort 104,390
Amstelveen (★Amsterdam) 71,939
• AMSTERDAM (★ 1,875,000) 713,407
Apeldoorn 148,745
Arnhem (★ 305,000) 132,928
Assen 50,880
Bergen op Zoom 47,259
Breda (★ 165,000) 126,709
Delft (★'s-Gravenhage) 90,066
Den Helder 61,225
Deventer 68,004
Dordrecht (★ 209,000) 111,791
Ede (▲ 96,044) 50,700
Eindhoven (★ 384,000) 193,966
Emmen (▲ 93,107) 37,000
Enschede (★ 252,000) 147,199
Geleen (★ 179,000) 33,922
Gouda 67,416
Groningen (★ 208,000) 169,387
Haarlem (★Amsterdam) 149,788
Haarlemmermeer (▲ 100,659) (★Amsterdam) 14,000
Heerlen (★ 267,500) 53,600
Helmond 70,574
Hengelo (★Enschede) 76,726
Hilversum (★Amsterdam) 84,674
Hoorn 59,028
IJmuiden (★Amsterdam) 61,506
Kerkrade (★Heerlen) 53,364
Leeuwarden 86,405
Leiden (★ 190,000) 112,976
Maastricht (★ 163,000) 118,152
Nieuwegein (★Utrecht) 58,882
Nijmegen (★ 242,000) 146,344
Oss 52,132
Purmerend (★Amsterdam) 62,504
Ridderkerk (★Rotterdam) 45,834
Rijswijk (★'s-Gravenhage) 47,456
Roosendaal 61,354
Rotterdam (★ 1,120,000) 589,707
Schiedam (★Rotterdam) 71,117
'S-GRAVENHAGE (THE HAGUE) (★ 773,000) 445,287
's-Hertogenbosch (★ 200,000) 93,171
Soest (★Amersfoort) 41,693
Spijkenisse (★Rotterdam) 69,655
Tilburg (★ 235,000) 160,618
Utrecht (★ 528,000) 232,705
Veenendaal 50,791
Venlo (★ 88,000) 64,890
Vlaardingen (★Rotterdam) 73,893
Vlissingen (Flushing) (▲ 43,913) 25,000
Zaanstad (★Amsterdam) 131,273
Zeist (★Utrecht) 59,211
Zoetermeer (★'s-Gravenhage) 100,623
Zwolle 97,131

NETHERLANDS ANTILLES / Nederlandse Antillen

1990 E 189,687
• WILLEMSTAD (★ 130,000) (1981 C) 31,883

NEW CALEDONIA / Nouvelle-Calédonie

1989 C 164,173
• NOUMÉA (★ 97,581) 65,110

NEW ZEALAND

1991 C 3,434,950
• Auckland (★ 855,571) 315,668
Christchurch (★ 307,179) 292,858
Dunedin 116,577
Hamilton (★ 148,625) 101,448
Invercargill 56,148
Lower Hutt (★Wellington) 94,540
Manukau (★Auckland) 226,147
Napier (★ 110,216) 51,645
Palmerston North (★ 70,951) 70,318
Rotorua (★ 53,702) 45,144
Takapuna (★Auckland) 74,360
Tauranga (★ 70,803) 46,308
Waitemata (★Auckland) 136,716
WELLINGTON (★ 375,000) 150,301
Whangarei (★ 44,183) 40,101

NICARAGUA

1985 E 3,272,100
Chinandega 75,000
Granada (1981 E) 64,642
León 101,000
• MANAGUA 682,000
Masaya 75,000
Matagalpa 68,000

NIGER

1988 C 7,220,089
Agadez 49,361
Maradi 104,386
• NIAMEY 392,165
Tahoua 49,948
Zinder 119,838

NIGERIA

1987 E 101,907,000
Aba 239,800
Abakaliki 56,800
Abeokuta 341,300
ABUJA (1993 U) 250,000
Ado-Ekiti 287,000
Afikpo 65,790
Agege 83,810
Akure 129,600
Amaigbo 53,690
Apomu 49,570
Aramoko 48,280
Asaba 47,410
Awka 88,800
Azare 50,020
Bauchi 68,840
Benin City 183,200
Bida 100,200
Calabar 139,800
Deba 110,600
Duku 52,880
Ede 245,200
Effon-Alaiye 122,300
Ejigbo 84,570
Emure-Ekiti 58,750
Enugu 252,500
Epe 80,560
Erin-Oshogbo 59,940
Eruwa 49,140
Fiditi 49,440
Gboko 49,390
Gbongan 53,990
Gombe 86,120
Gusau 126,200
Ibadan 1,144,000
Idah 60,550
Idanre 56,080
Ife 237,000
Ifon-Oshogbo 65,980
Igbasa-Odo 48,040
Igboho 85,230
Igbo-Ora 68,060
Igede-Ekiti 56,570
Ihiala 73,240
Ijebu-Igbo 78,680
Ijebu-Ode 124,900
Ijero-Ekiti 76,420
Ikare 112,500
Ikerre 195,400
Ikire 94,450
Ikirun 144,900
Ikole 71,860
Ikorodu 147,700
Ikot Ekpene 69,440
Ila 210,800
Ilawe-Ekiti 147,300
Ilesha 302,100
Ilobu 159,000
Ilorin 380,000
Inisa 95,630
Ipoti-Ekiti 53,220
Ise-Ekiti 82,580
Iseyin 173,500
Iwo 289,100
Jega (1985 E) 47,000
Jimeta 66,130
Jos 164,700
Kaduna 273,200
Kano 538,300
Katsina 165,000
Kaura Namoda 52,910
Keffi 57,790
Kishi 77,210
Kumo 118,200
Lafia 97,810
Lafiagi 57,580
• LAGOS (★ 3,800,000) 1,213,000
Lalupon 56,130
Lere 49,670
Maiduguri 255,100
Makurdi 98,350
Minna 109,300
Mubi 51,190
Mushin (★Lagos) 266,100
Nguru 78,770
Nsukka 47,760
Ode-Ekiti 48,910
Offa 157,500
Ogbomosho 582,900
Oka 114,400
Oke-Mesi 55,040
Okwe 52,550
Olupona 65,720
Ondo 135,300
Onitsha 298,200
Opobo 64,620
Oron 62,260
Oshogbo 380,800
Owerri (1985 E) 37,000
Owo 146,600
Oyan 50,930
Oyo 204,700
Pindiga 64,130
Port Harcourt 327,300
Potiskum 56,490
Sapele 111,200
Shagamu 93,610
Shaki 139,000
Shomolu (★Lagos) 120,700
Sokoto 163,700
Ugep 81,910
Umuahia 52,550
Uyo 60,500
Warri 100,700
Zaria 302,800

NIUE

1989 C 2,267
• ALOFI 706

NORTHERN MARIANA ISLANDS

1980 C 16,780
• Chalan Kanoa 2,678
Garapan 2,063

NORWAY / Norge

1987 E 4,190,000
Bærum (★Oslo) (1985 E) 83,000
Bergen (★ 239,000) 209,320
Drammen (★ 73,000) (1985 E) 50,700
Fredrikstad (★ 52,000) (1983 E) 27,618
Hammerfest (1983 E) 7,208
Kristiansand (1985 E) 62,200
Narvik (1983 E) 19,080
• OSLO (★ 720,000) 452,415
Skien (★ 77,981) (1985 E) 46,700
Stavanger (★ 132,000) (1985 E) 94,200
Tromsø (1985 E) 47,800
Trondheim 135,010

OMAN / 'Umān

1983 E 1,131,000
• MASQAṬ (MUSCAT) 30,000
Maṭraḥ (1971 E) 14,000
Ṣūr 30,000

PAKISTAN / Pākistān

1981 C 84,253,644
Abbottābād (★ 65,996) 32,188
Ahmadpur East 56,979
Attock (★ 39,986) 26,233
Bahāwalnagar 74,533
Bahāwalpur (★ 180,263) 152,009
Bannu (★ 43,210) 35,170
Bhakkar 41,934
Chārsadda 62,530
Chīchāwatni 50,241
Chiniot 105,559
Chishtiān Mandi 61,959
Daska 55,555
Dera Ghāzi Khān 102,007
Dera Ismāīl Khān (★ 68,145) 64,358
Drigh Road Cantonment (★Karāchi) 56,742
Faisalabad (Lyallpur) 1,104,209
Gojra 68,000
Gujrānwāla (★ 658,753) 600,993
Gujrānwāla Cantonment (★Gujrānwāla) 57,760
Gujrāt 155,058
Hāfizābād 83,464
Hyderābād (★ 800,000) 702,539
Hyderābād Cantonment (★Hyderābād) 48,990
ISLAMABAD (★Rāwalpindi) 204,364
Jacobābād 79,365
Jarānwāla 69,459
Jhang Sadar 195,558
Jhelum (★ 106,462) 92,646
Kamālia 61,107
Kāmoke 71,097
• Karāchi (★ 5,300,000) 4,901,627
Karāchi Cantonment (★Karāchi) 181,981
Kasūr 155,523
Khairpur 61,447
Khānewāl 89,090
Khānpur 70,589
Khāriān Cantonment (★ 51,506) 16,042
Khushāb 56,274
Kohāt (★ 77,604) 55,832
Lahore (★ 3,025,000) 2,707,215
Lahore Cantonment (★Lahore) 245,474
Lārkāna 123,890
Leiah 51,482
Malir Cantonment (★Karāchi) 47,588
Mandi Būrewāla 86,311
Mardān (★ 147,977) 141,842

C Census. E Official estimate. U Unofficial estimate.
• Largest city in country.
★ Population or designation of metropolitan area, including suburbs (see headnote).
▲ Population of an entire municipality, commune, or district, including rural area.

Miānwāli ... 59,159
Mingāora ... 88,078
Mīrpur Khās ... 124,371
Multān (★ 732,070) ... 696,316
Muzaffargarh ... 53,000
Nawābshāh ... 102,139
Nowshera (★ 74,913) ... 38,875
Okāra (★ 153,483) ... 127,455
Pākpattan ... 69,820
Peshāwar (★ 566,248) ... 506,896
Peshāwar Cantonment (★Peshāwar) ... 59,352
Quetta (★ 285,719) ... 244,842
Rahīmyār Khān (★ 132,635) ... 119,036
Rāwalpindi (★ 1,040,000) ... 457,091
Rāwalpindi Cantonment (★Rāwalpindi) ... 337,752
Sādiqābād ... 63,935
Sāhīwal ... 150,954
Sargodha (★ 291,362) ... 231,895
Sargodha Cantonment (★Sargodha) ... 59,467
Shekhūpura ... 141,168
Shikārpur ... 88,138
Shorkot (★ 50,568) ... 18,533
Siālkot (★ 302,009) ... 258,147
Sukkur ... 190,551
Tando Ādam ... 62,744
Turbat ... 52,337
Vihāri ... 53,799
Wāh Cantonment ... 122,335
Wazīrābād ... 62,725

PALAU / Belau

1986 C ... 13,873
• KOROR ... 8,629

PANAMA / Panamá

1990 C ... 2,315,047
Balboa (▲ 11,327) (★Panamá) ... 3,500
Colón (★ 96,000) ... 54,469
David ... 65,635
• PANAMÁ (★ 770,000) ... 411,549
San Miguelito (★Panamá) ... 242,529

PAPUA NEW GUINEA

1990 C ... 3,534,038
Lae ... 78,265
• PORT MORESBY ... 193,242
Rabaul ... 16,883

PARAGUAY

1992 C ... 4,123,550
• ASUNCIÓN (★ 700,000) ... 502,426
Caaguazú ... 38,200
Capiatá ... 83,189
Ciudad del Este ... 133,896
Encarnación ... 55,359
Fernando de la Mora (★Asunción) ... 95,287
Lambaré (★Asunción) ... 99,681
Pedro Juan Caballero ... 53,601
San Lorenzo (★Asunción) ... 133,311

PERU / Perú

1981 C ... 17,031,221
Arequipa (★ 446,942) ... 108,023
Ayacucho (★ 69,533) ... 57,432
Barranco (★Lima) ... 46,478
Breña (★Lima) ... 112,398
Cajamarca ... 62,259
Callao (★Lima) ... 264,133
Cerro de Pasco (★ 66,373) ... 55,597
Chiclayo (★ 279,527) ... 213,095
Chimbote ... 223,341
Chorrillos (★Lima) ... 141,881
Chosica ... 65,139
Cusco (★ 184,550) ... 89,563
Huacho ... 43,398
Huancayo (★ 164,954) ... 84,845
Huánuco ... 61,812
Ica ... 114,786
Iquitos ... 178,738
Jesús Maria (★Lima) ... 83,179
Juliaca ... 87,651
La Victoria (★Lima) ... 270,778
• LIMA (★ 4,608,010) ... 371,122
Lince (★Lima) ... 80,456
Magdalena (★Lima) ... 55,535
Miraflores (★Lima) ... 103,453
Pisco ... 55,604
Piura (★ 207,934) ... 144,609
Pucallpa ... 112,263
Pueblo Libre (★Lima) ... 83,985
Puno ... 67,397
Rímac (★Lima) ... 184,484
San Isidro (★Lima) ... 71,203
San Martin de Porras (★Lima) ... 404,856
Santiago de Surco (★Lima) ... 146,636
Sullana ... 89,037
Surquillo (★Lima) ... 134,158
Tacna ... 97,173
Talara ... 57,351
Trujillo (★ 354,301) ... 202,469
Tumbes ... 47,936
Vitarte (★Lima) ... 145,504

PHILIPPINES / Pilipinas

1990 C ... 60,477,000
Angeles ... 236,685
Antipolo (▲ 207,842) ... 83,641
Bacolod ... 364,000
Bacoor (★Manila) ... 159,685
Baguio ... 183,102
Baliuag ... 89,719
Biñan (★Manila) ... 134,553
Binangonan ... 127,561
Bislig (▲ 81,615) (1980 C) ... 49,498
Bocaue ... 67,243
Butuan (▲ 228,000) ... 99,000
Cabanatuan (▲ 173,065) ... 74,966
Cagayan de Oro (▲ 340,000) ... 255,000
Cainta (★Manila) ... 126,839
Calamba (▲ 173,453) ... 97,623
Caloocan (★Manila) ... 761,011
Carmona (★Manila) ... 28,247
Cavite (★ 195,000) ... 91,641
Cebu (★ 825,000) ... 610,000
Cotabato ... 127,000
Dagupan ... 122,247
Davao (▲ 850,000) ... 569,300
Dumaguete ... 80,000
General Santos (Dadiangas) (▲ 250,000) ... 157,600
Guagua ... 88,290
Iloilo ... 311,000
Isabela (Basilan) (▲ 49,891) (1980 C) ... 11,491
Jolo (1980 C) ... 52,429
Lapu-Lapu (Opon) ... 146,000
Las Piñas (★Manila) ... 296,851
Legaspi (▲ 121,000) ... 63,000
Lucena ... 150,624
Mabalacat (▲ 121,115) ... 64,261
Makati (★Manila) ... 452,734
Malabon (★Manila) ... 278,380
Malolos ... 125,178
Mandaluyong (★Manila) ... 244,538
Mandaue (★Cebu) ... 180,000
Mangaldan ... 65,947
• MANILA (★ 9,650,000) ... 1,598,918
Marawi ... 92,000
Marikina (★Manila) ... 310,010
Meycauayan (★Manila) ... 123,982
Muntinglupa (★Manila) ... 276,972
Naga ... 115,000
Navotas (★Manila) ... 186,799
Olongapo ... 193,327
Pagadian (▲ 107,000) ... 52,400
Parañaque (★Manila) ... 307,717
Pasay (★Manila) ... 366,623
Pasig (★Manila) ... 397,309
Puerto Princesa (▲ 92,147) ... 47,461
Quezon City (★Manila) ... 1,666,766
San Fernando ... 157,851
San Juan del Monte (★Manila) ... 126,708
San Pablo (▲ 161,630) ... 80,671
San Pedro ... 156,486
Santa Cruz ... 76,603
Santa Rosa (★Manila) ... 94,719
Tacloban ... 138,000
Tagbilaran ... 56,000
Tagig (★Manila) ... 266,080
Taytay (★Manila) ... 112,403
Valenzuela (★Manila) ... 340,050
Zamboanga (▲ 444,000) ... 107,000

PITCAIRN

1988 C ... 59
• ADAMSTOWN ... 59

POLAND / Polska

1991 E ... 38,183,200
Będzin (★Katowice) ... 76,200
Bełchatów ... 57,400
Biała Podlaska ... 53,100
Białystok ... 270,600
Bielsko-Biała ... 181,300
Bydgoszcz ... 381,500
Bytom (Beuthen) (★Katowice) ... 231,200
Chełm ... 66,400
Chorzów (★Katowice) ... 131,900
Częstochowa ... 258,000
Dąbrowa Górnicza (★Katowice) ... 136,900
Dzierżoniów (Reichenbach) (★ 89,000) ... 38,000
Elbląg (Elbing) ... 126,100
Ełk ... 52,400
Gdańsk (Danzig) (★ 909,000) ... 465,100
Gdynia (★Gdańsk) ... 251,500
Gliwice (Gleiwitz) (★Katowice) ... 214,200
Głogów ... 73,300
Gniezno ... 70,400
Gorzów Wielkopolski (Landsberg an der Warthe) ... 124,300
Grudziądz ... 102,300
Inowrocław ... 77,700
Jastrzębie-Zdrój ... 103,700
Jaworzno (★Katowice) ... 99,500
Jelenia Góra (Hirschberg) ... 93,400
Kalisz ... 106,200
• Katowice (★ 2,778,000) ... 366,800
Kędzierzyn Kozle ... 71,700
Kielce ... 214,200
Konin ... 80,300
Koszalin (Köslin) ... 108,700
Kraków (★ 828,000) ... 750,500
Krosno ... 49,700
Kutno ... 50,400
Legionowo (★Warszawa) ... 50,800
Legnica (Liegnitz) ... 105,200
Leszno ... 58,300
Łódź (★ 1,061,000) ... 848,200
Łomża ... 59,300
Lubin ... 82,300
Lublin (★ 389,000) ... 351,400
Mielec ... 61,800
Mysłowice (★Katowice) ... 93,800
Nowy Sącz ... 78,200
Olsztyn (Allenstein) ... 162,900
Opole (Oppeln) ... 128,400
Ostrołęka ... 50,700
Ostrowiec Świętokrzyski ... 78,600
Ostrów Wielkopolski ... 73,300
Pabianice (★Łódź) ... 75,200
Piekary Śląskie (★Katowice) ... 68,500
Piła (Schneidemühl) ... 72,300
Piotrków Trybunalski ... 81,000
Płock ... 123,400
Poznań (★ 672,000) ... 590,100
Pruszków (★Warszawa) ... 53,700
Przemyśl ... 68,500
Puławy ... 85,700
Racibórz (Ratibor) ... 64,400
Radom ... 228,500
Radomsko ... 50,400
Ruda Śląska (★Katowice) ... 171,000
Rybnik ... 144,000
Rzeszów ... 153,000
Siedlce ... 72,000
Siemianowice Śląskie (★Katowice) ... 81,100
Skarżysko-Kamienna ... 50,900
Słupsk (Stolp) ... 101,200
Sopot (★Gdańsk) ... 46,700
Sosnowiec (★Katowice) ... 259,400
Stalowa Wola ... 70,000
Starachowice ... 56,600
Stargard Szczeciński (Stargard in Pommern) ... 71,000
Starogard Gdański ... 49,500
Suwałki ... 61,300
Świdnica (Schweidnitz) ... 63,300
Świętochłowice (★Katowice) ... 60,500
Świnoujście (Swinemünde) ... 43,300
Szczecin (Stettin) (★ 449,000) ... 413,400
Tarnów ... 121,200
Tarnowskie Góry (★Katowice) ... 74,100
Tczew ... 59,500
Tomaszów Mazowiecki ... 69,900
Toruń ... 202,300
Tychy (★Katowice) ... 191,700
Wałbrzych (Waldenburg) (★ 207,000) ... 141,000
WARSZAWA (★ 2,323,000) ... 1,655,700
Włocławek ... 122,200
Wodzisław Śląski ... 111,800
Wrocław (Breslau) ... 643,200
Zabrze (Hindenburg) (★Katowice) ... 205,000
Zamość ... 61,800
Zawiercie ... 56,600
Zgierz (★Łódź) ... 59,000
Zielona Góra (Grünberg) ... 114,100
Żory ... 67,000

PORTUGAL

1981 C ... 9,833,014
Amadora (★Lisboa) ... 95,518
Barreiro (★Lisboa) ... 50,863
Braga ... 63,033
Coimbra ... 74,616
• LISBOA (★ 2,250,000) ... 807,167
Ponta Delgada ... 21,187
Porto (★ 1,225,000) ... 327,368
Setúbal ... 77,885
Vila Nova de Gaia (★Porto) ... 62,469

PUERTO RICO

1990 C ... 3,522,037
Arecibo (★ 160,500) ... 49,545
Bayamón (▲ 220,262) (★San Juan) ... 202,103
Caguas (▲ 133,447) (★San Juan) ... 92,429
Carolina (▲ 177,806) (★San Juan) ... 162,404
Guaynabo (▲ 92,886) (★San Juan) ... 73,385
Mayagüez (★ 200,600) ... 83,010
Ponce (★ 232,700) ... 159,151
• SAN JUAN (★ 1,877,000) ... 426,832

QATAR / Qaṭar

1986 C ... 369,079
• AD-DAWḤAH (DOHA) (★ 310,000) ... 217,294
Ar-Rayyān (★Ad-Dawḥah) ... 91,996

REUNION / Réunion

1982 C ... 515,814
• SAINT-DENIS (▲ 109,072) ... 84,400

ROMANIA / România

1992 C ... 22,760,449
Alba Iulia ... 71,254
Alexandria ... 58,582
Arad ... 190,088
Bacău ... 204,495
Baia Mare ... 148,815
Bistrița ... 87,793
Botoșani ... 126,204
Brăila ... 234,706
• BUCUREȘTI (BUCHAREST) (★ 2,300,000) ... 2,064,474
Buzău ... 148,247
Călărași ... 76,886
Cluj-Napoca ... 328,008
Constanța ... 350,476
Craiova ... 303,520
Deva ... 78,366
Drobeta-Turnu Severin ... 115,526
Focșani ... 101,296
Galați ... 325,788
Giurgiu ... 74,236
Hunedoara ... 81,198
Iași ... 342,994
Lugoj ... 50,983
Medgidia ... 46,586
Mediaș ... 64,488
Miercurea-Ciuc ... 46,029
Onești ... 59,008
Oradea ... 220,848
Petroșani (★ 76,000) ... 52,532
Piatra Neamț ... 123,175
Pitești ... 179,479
Ploiești (★ 310,000) ... 252,073
Râmnicu Vâlcea ... 113,356
Reșița ... 96,798
Roman ... 80,192
Satu Mare ... 131,859
Sfântu Gheorghe ... 68,070
Sibiu ... 169,696
Slatina ... 85,336
Slobozia ... 55,614
Suceava ... 114,355
Târgoviște ... 97,876
Târgu Jiu ... 98,267
Târgu Mureș ... 163,625
Tecuci ... 46,735
Timișoara ... 334,278
Tulcea ... 97,500
Turda ... 61,135
Vaslui ... 80,151
Zalău ... 68,322

RUSSIA

1991 E ... 148,542,700
Abakan ... 157,300
Achtubinsk ... 50,800
Ačinsk ... 122,000
Alapajevsk ... 50,300
Alatyr' ... 47,700
Aleksandrov ... 68,600
Aleksin ... 74,200
Al'metjevsk ... 132,700
Amursk ... 59,600
Anapa ... 55,900
Angarsk ... 268,500
Anžero-Sudžensk ... 107,000
Apatity ... 88,600
Archangel'sk ... 420,400
Armavir ... 162,200
Arsenjev ... 71,200
Art'om ... 70,100
Arzamas ... 111,800
Asbest ... 84,900
Astrachan' ... 511,900
Azov ... 80,700
Balakovo ... 201,300
Balašicha (★Moskva) ... 137,600
Balašov ... 97,300
Barnaul (★ 673,000) ... 606,800
Batajsk (★Rostov-na-Donu) ... 93,300
Belebej ... 54,500
Belgorod ... 311,400
Belogorsk ... 74,300
Belorečensk ... 51,900
Beloreck ... 73,100
Belovo ... 92,900
Berdsk (★Novosibirsk) ... 80,400
Berezniki ... 199,700
Ber'ozovskij ... 51,900
Bijsk ... 234,600
Birobidžan ... 86,300
Blagoveščensk ... 211,000
Bor (★Nižnij Novgorod) ... 64,500
Borisoglebsk ... 72,100
Boroviči ... 62,800
Br'ansk ... 458,900
Bratsk ... 259,400
Bud'onnovsk ... 57,500
Bugul'ma ... 91,100
Buguruslan ... 54,100
Buj ... 32,900
Bujnaksk ... 57,900
Buzuluk ... 85,100
Čajkovskij ... 88,300
Čapajevsk ... 96,000
Čebarkul' ... 50,700
Čeboksary ... 436,000
Čechov ... 60,200
Čel'abinsk (★ 1,325,000) ... 1,148,300
Čeremchovo ... 73,600
Čerepovec ... 315,900
Čerkessk ... 117,000
Černogorsk ... 79,700
Chabarovsk ... 613,300
Chasavjurt ... 72,800
Chimki (★Moskva) ... 135,500
Cholmsk ... 51,800
Čistopol' ... 66,600
Čita ... 376,300
Čusovoj ... 58,000
Derbent ... 81,500
Dimitrovgrad ... 127,000
Dmitrov ... 65,600
Dolgoprudnyj (★Moskva) ... 71,100
Domodedovo (★Moskva) ... 56,300
Doneck ... 48,900
Dubna ... 67,200
Dzeržinsk (★Nižnij Novgorod) ... 286,700
Elektrostal' ... 153,000
Elista ... 92,700
Engel's (★Saratov) ... 183,600
Fr'azino (★Moskva) ... 54,000
Furmanov ... 45,900
Gatčina (★Sankt-Peterburg) ... 80,600
Gelendžik ... 48,600
Georgijevsk ... 63,700
Georgiu-Dež ... 54,600
Glazov ... 106,000
Gorno-Altajsk ... 47,500
Gr'azi ... 47,700
Groznyj ... 401,400
Gubkin ... 76,400
Gukovo ... 67,700
Gus'-Chrustal'nyj ... 77,000
Inta ... 60,900
Irbit ... 51,300
Irkutsk ... 640,500
Išim ... 65,900
Išimbaj ... 71,000
Iskitim ... 68,700
Ivanovo ... 482,200
Ivantejevka (★Moskva) ... 53,200
Iževsk ... 646,800
Jakutsk ... 193,300
Jarcevo ... 54,000
Jaroslavl' ... 638,100
Jefremov ... 56,600
Jegorjevsk ... 74,200
Jejsk ... 79,400
Jelec ... 121,300
Jelizovo ... 48,700
Jermolajevo ... 65,600
Jessentuki ... 86,300
Joškar-Ola ... 247,800
Jurga ... 94,000
Južno-Sachalinsk ... 164,000
Kaliningrad (★Moskva) ... 161,500
Kaliningrad (Königsberg) ... 408,100
Kaluga ... 315,500
Kamensk-Šachtinskij ... 73,100
Kamensk-Ural'skij ... 208,700
Kamyšin ... 124,400
Kanaš ... 56,100
Kandalakša ... 54,300
Kansk ... 109,900
Kaspijsk ... 61,900
Kazan' (★ 1,165,000) ... 1,107,300
Kemerovo ... 520,700
Kimry ... 62,000
Kinel' ... 33,800
Kinešma ... 104,900
Kingisepp ... 50,600
Kiriši ... 53,100
Kirov ... 491,200
Kirovo-Čepeck ... 95,600
Kisel'ovsk (★Prokopjevsk) ... 126,900
Kislovodsk ... 116,800
Kizel ... 36,600
Klimovsk (★Moskva) ... 57,600
Klin ... 95,100
Klincy ... 71,200
Kogalym ... 48,200
Kol'čugino ... 45,600
Kolomna ... 163,500
Kolpino (★Sankt-Peterburg) ... 144,500
Komsomol'sk-na-Amure ... 318,800
Kopejsk (★Čel'abinsk) ... 78,300
Korkino ... 44,800
Korsakov ... 45,300
Kostroma ... 281,800
Kotlas ... 68,900
Kovrov ... 161,900
Krasnodar ... 631,200
Krasnogorsk (★Moskva) ... 91,700
Krasnojarsk ... 924,400
Krasnokamensk ... 67,000
Krasnokamsk ... 57,800
Krasnoturjinsk ... 67,200
Krasnoufimsk ... 46,100
Krasnoural'sk ... 34,800
Krasnyj Sulin ... 43,200
Kropotkin ... 76,600
Krymsk ... 51,100
Kstovo (★Nižnij Novgord) ... 65,300
Kujbyšev ... 51,600
Kungur ... 81,800
Kurgan ... 363,800
Kursk ... 433,300
Kušva ... 43,300
Kuzneck ... 100,000
Kyzyl ... 88,000
Labinsk ... 58,600
Leninogorsk ... 63,300
Leninsk-Kuzneckij ... 133,400
Lesosibirsk ... 69,300
Lipeck ... 460,100
Livny ... 52,600
Lobn'a (★Moskva) ... 61,000
L'ubercy (★Moskva) ... 164,900
Lys'va ... 77,800
Lytkarino (★Moskva) ... 51,700
Machačkala ... 333,500
Magadan ... 154,900
Magnitogorsk ... 443,900
Majkop ... 152,500
Mcensk ... 49,200
Meleuz ... 55,200
Meždurečensk ... 107,500
Miass ... 169,700
Michajlovka ... 58,700
Mičurinsk ... 109,400
Mineral'nyje Vody ... 72,500
Minusinsk ... 74,200
Mončegorsk ... 68,100
Moršansk ... 50,500
• MOSKVA (MOSCOW) (★ 13,150,000) ... 8,801,500
Murmansk ... 472,900
Murom ... 126,000
Mytišči (★Moskva) ... 153,900
Naberežnyje Čelny ... 510,100
Nachodka ... 164,500
Nadym ... 52,200

C Census. E Official estimate. U Unofficial estimate.
• Largest city in country.

★ Population or designation of metropolitan area, including suburbs (see headnote).
▲ Population of an entire municipality, commune, or district, including rural area.

Nal'čik 240,600
Naro-Fominsk 58,800
Nazarovo 65,200
Neftejugansk 65,500
Ner'ungri 77,200
Nevinnomyssk 123,300
Nikolo-Berjozovka 110,500
Nižnekamsk 196,200
Nižnevartovsk 247,400
Nižnij Novgorod (Gorky) (★ 2,025,000) 1,445,000
Nižnij Tagil 439,200
Njagan 59,800
Noginsk 122,700
Nojabr'sk 88,900
Noril'sk 169,000
Novgorod 233,800
Novoaltajsk (★Barnaul) 55,200
Novočeboksarsk 119,300
Novočerkassk 188,500
Novodvinsk 50,300
Novokujbyševsk (★Samara) 113,200
Novokuzneck 601,900
Novomoskovsk, Tula oblast' (★ 365,000) 145,800
Novorossijsk 188,600
Novošachtinsk 107,300
Novosibirsk (★ 1,600,000) 1,446,300
Novotroick 107,600
Novyj Urengoj 93,600
Obninsk 103,700
Odincovo (★Moskva) 128,400
Okt'abr'skij 106,700
Omsk (★ 1,190,000) 1,166,800
Orechovo-Zujevo (★ 205,000) 136,800
Orel 345,200
Orenburg 556,500
Orsk 272,200
Osinniki 63,200
Otradnyj 49,600
Partizansk 50,000
P'atigorsk 131,100
Pavlovo 72,200
Pavlovskij Posad 70,800
Pečora 65,500
Penza 551,100
Perm' (★ 1,180,000) 1,110,400
Pervoural'sk 143,700
Petrodvorec (★Sankt-Peterburg) 83,800
Petropavlovsk-Kamčatskij 272,900
Petrozavodsk 277,400
Podol'sk (★Moskva) 208,500
Polevskoj 71,900
Prochladnyj 58,500
Prokopjevsk (★ 410,000) 272,600
Pskov 207,500
Puškin (★Sankt-Peterburg) 95,300
Puškino (★Moskva) 75,800
Ramenskoje 88,800
Rasskazovo 49,800
R'azan' 527,200
Reutov (★Moskva) 68,900
Revda 66,000
Roslavl' 60,700
Rossoš' 58,900
Rostov-na-Donu (★ 1,165,000) 1,027,600
Rubcovsk 172,500
Ruzajevka 52,100
Rybinsk 252,600
Ržev 70,900
Šachty 227,700
Šadrinsk 87,500
Safonovo 56,300
Sajanogorsk 53,000
Salavat 151,400
Sal'sk 61,700
Samara (★ 1,505,000) 1,257,300
Sankt-Peterburg (Saint Petersburg) (★ 5,525,000) 4,466,800
Saransk 319,600
Sarapul 110,600
Saratov (★ 1,155,000) 911,100
Šatka 51,100
Ščelkovo (★Moskva) 109,600
Ščokino 68,800
Šelechov 48,600
Sergijev Posad (Zagorsk) 115,600
Serov 103,800
Serpuchov 141,200
Severodvinsk 251,500
Severomorsk 66,200
Slav'ansk-Na-Kubani 58,500
Smolensk 349,800
Soči 341,500
Sokol 46,700
Solikamsk 110,200
Solnečnogorsk (★Moskva) 56,700
Sosnovyj Bor 56,700
Spassk-Dal'nij 61,100
Staryj Oskol 181,900
Stavropol' 328,300
Sterlitamak 252,200
Stupino 74,600
Šuja 69,000
Surgut 261,100
Sverdlovsk (★ 1,620,000) 1,375,400
Svetlogorsk 71,600
Svobodnyj 80,900
Syktyvkar 224,000
Syzran' 174,900
Taganrog 293,600
Talnach 65,600
Tambov 309,600
Tichoreck 67,600
Tichvin 71,800
Tobol'sk 96,800
Toljatti 654,700
Tomsk 505,600
Toržok 50,500
Troick 89,800
Tuapse 63,800
Tujmazy 59,800
Tula (★ 640,000) 543,600
Tulun 53,700
T'umen' 494,200
Tver' 455,300
Tyndinskij 64,700
Uchta 112,100
Ufa (★ 1,118,000) 1,097,000
Uglič 40,000
Ulan-Ude 362,400
Uljanovsk 648,300
Usinsk 52,300
Usolje-Sibirskoje 106,800
Ussurijsk 160,200
Ust'-Ilimsk 112,200
Ust'-Kut 61,800
Uzlovaja (★Novomoskovsk) 64,000
V'az'ma 59,900
Velikije Luki 115,400
Verchn'aja Pyšma (★Sverdlovsk) 53,500
Verchn'aja Salda 55,100
Vičuga 49,700
Vidnoje (★Moskva) 56,900
Vladikavkaz 306,000
Vladimir 355,600
Vladivostok 648,000
Volchov 50,100
Volgodonsk 180,700
Volgograd (Stalingrad) (★ 1,360,000) 1,007,300
Vologda 289,200
Vol'sk 65,500
Volžsk 62,000
Volžskij (★Volgograd) 278,400
Vorkuta 117,400
Voronež 900,000
Voskresensk 81,400
Votkinsk 104,500
Vyborg 81,100
Vyksa 62,200
Vyšnij Voloček 64,600
Zarinsk 51,800
Zelenograd (★Moskva) 162,700
Železnodorožnyj (★Moskva) 99,300
Železnogorsk 89,200
Zel'onodol'sk 97,000
Žigulevsk 45,000
Zlatoust 208,200
Žukovskij 101,300

RWANDA

1991 C 6,762,145
• KIGALI 232,733

SAINT HELENA

1987 C 5,644
• JAMESTOWN 1,413

SAINT KITTS AND NEVIS

1980 C 44,404
• BASSETERRE 14,725
Charlestown 1,771

SAINT LUCIA

1987 E 142,342
• CASTRIES 53,933

SAINT PIERRE AND MIQUELON / Saint-Pierre-et-Miquelon

1982 C 6,041
• SAINT-PIERRE 5,371

SAINT VINCENT AND THE GRENADINES

1987 E 112,589
• KINGSTOWN (★ 28,936) 19,028

SAN MARINO

1989 E 23,000
• SAN MARINO 2,794

SAO TOME AND PRINCIPE / São Tomé e Príncipe

1991 C 117,504
• SÃO TOMÉ 5,245

SAUDI ARABIA / Al-ʿArabīyah as-Suʿūdīyah

1980 E 9,229,000
Abhā (1974 C) 30,150
Ad-Dammām 200,000
Al-Hufūf (1974 C) 101,271
Al-Khubar (1974 C) 48,817
Al-Madīnah (Medina) 290,000
Al-Mubarraz (1974 C) 54,325
AR-RIYĀḌ (RIYADH) 1,250,000
Aṭ-Ṭā'if 300,000
Buraydah (1974 C) 69,940
Hā'il (1974 C) 40,502
• Jiddah (Jeddah) 1,300,000
Khamīs Mushayṭ (1974 C) 49,581
Makkah (Mecca) 550,000
Najran (1974 C) 47,501
Tabūk (1974 C) 74,825

SENEGAL / Sénégal

1988 C 6,892,720
• DAKAR 1,490,450
Diourbel 77,548
Kaolack 152,007
Louga 52,763
Saint-Louis 160,689
Thiès 184,902
Ziguinchor 124,283

SEYCHELLES

1984 E 64,718
• VICTORIA 23,000

SIERRA LEONE

1985 C 3,515,812
Bo 59,768
• FREETOWN (★ 525,000) 469,776
Kenema 52,473
Koidu 82,474
Makeni 49,038

SINGAPORE

1990 C 2,690,100
• SINGAPORE (★ 3,025,000) 2,690,100

SLOVAKIA / Slovenská Republika

1991 C 5,268,935
Banská Bystrica 85,007
• BRATISLAVA 441,453
Komárno 37,370
Košice 234,840
Martin 58,338
Michalovce 38,866
Nitra 89,888
Nové Zámky 42,851
Poprad 52,878
Považská Bystrica 39,801
Prešov 87,788
Prievidza 53,393
Spišská Nová Ves 39,187
Trenčín 56,733
Trnava 71,641
Žilina 83,853
Zvolen 41,935

SLOVENIA / Slovenija

1987 E 1,936,606
• LJUBLJANA (▲ 316,607) 233,200
Maribor (▲ 187,651) 107,400

SOLOMON ISLANDS

1986 C 285,176
• HONIARA 30,413

SOMALIA / Somaliya

1984 E 5,423,000
Berbera 65,000
Hargeysa 70,000
Kismaayo 70,000
Marka 60,000
• MUQDISHO 600,000

SOUTH AFRICA / Suid-Afrika

1991 C 30,986,920
Alberton (★Johannesburg) 76,642
Alexandra (★Johannesburg) 124,586
Atteridgeville (★Pretoria) 92,008
Bellville (★Cape Town) 78,822
Benoni (★Johannesburg) 113,501
Bloemfontein (★ 280,000) 126,867
Boksburg (★Johannesburg) 119,890
Botshabelo (★Bloemfontein) 117,926
Brakpan (★Johannesburg) 53,522
CAPE TOWN (KAAPSTAD) (★ 1,900,000) 854,616
Carletonville (★ 175,000) 118,699
Daveyton (★Johannesburg) 151,659
Diepmeadow (★Johannesburg) 241,099
Durban (★ 1,740,000) 715,669
East London (Oos-Londen) (★ 365,000) 102,325
Edendale (★Pietermaritzburg) 72,063
Elsies River (★Cape Town) 82,045
Evaton (★Vereeniging) 201,026
Galeshewe (★Kimberley) 72,118
Ga-Rankuwa (1980 C) 48,300
Germiston (★Johannesburg) 134,005
Grassy Park (★Cape Town) 52,675
Guguletu (★Cape Town) 54,635
• Johannesburg (★ 4,000,000) 712,507
Kagiso (★Johannesburg) 61,680
Katlehong (★Johannesburg) 201,785
Kempton Park (★Johannesburg) 106,606
Kimberley (★ 160,000) 80,082
Klerksdorp (★ 275,000) 58,923
Krugersdorp (★Johannesburg) 81,584
Kwa Mashu (★Durban) 156,679
KwaNdengezi (★Durban) 50,835
KwaNobuhle (★Port Elizabeth) 92,381
Kwa-Thema (★Johannesburg) 81,345
Ladysmith (★ 37,885) 29,589
Lekoa (Shapeville) (★Vereeniging) 217,582
Madadeni (★Newcastle) 95,931
Mafikeng (★ 16,000) (1980 C) 6,500
Mamelodi (★Pretoria) 154,845
Mangaung (★Bloemfontein) 125,545
Mdantsane (★East London) (1986 E) 242,823
Ntuzuma (★Durban) 102,310
Nyanga (★Cape Town) 92,896
Osizweni (★Durban) 78,079
Paarl (★Cape Town) 73,415
Parow (★Cape Town) 68,081
Pietermaritzburg (★ 265,000) 156,473
Pinetown (★Durban) 70,001
Port Elizabeth (★ 810,000) 303,353
PRETORIA (★ 1,100,000) 525,583
Randburg (★Johannesburg) 90,557
Randfontein (★Johannesburg) 51,940
Roodepoort-Maraisburg (★Johannesburg) 162,632
Sandton (★Johannesburg) 101,197
Soshanguve (★Pretoria) 146,334
Soweto (★Johannesburg) 596,632
Springs (★Johannesburg) 72,647
Tembisa (★Johannesburg) 209,238
Thabong (★Welkom) 88,547
Uitenhage (★Port Elizabeth) 67,581
Umlazi (★Durban) 299,275
Umtata (1978 E) 30,000
Vanderbijlpark (★Vereeniging) 67,291
Vereeniging (★ 675,000) 70,255
Verwoerdburg (★Pretoria) 50,552
Vosloorus (★Johannesburg) 76,015
Welkom (★ 156,658) 68,111
Westonaria (★Johannesburg) 57,177

SPAIN / España

1988 E 39,217,804
Alacant (Alicante) 261,051
Albacete 125,997
Alcalá de Guadaira 50,935
Alcalá de Henares (★Madrid) 150,021
Alcobendas (★Madrid) 73,455
Alcoi (Alcoy) 66,074
Alcorcón (★Madrid) 139,796
Algeciras 99,528
Almería 157,644
Avilés (★ 131,000) 87,811
Badajoz (▲ 122,407) 106,400
Badalona (★Barcelona) 225,229
Baracaldo (★Bilbao) 113,502
Barcelona (★ 4,040,000) 1,714,355
Bilbao (★ 985,000) 384,733
Burgos 160,561
Cáceres 71,598
Cádiz (★ 240,000) 156,591
Cartagena (▲ 172,710) 70,000
Castelló de la Plana 131,809
Ciudad Real 56,300
Córdoba 302,301
Cornellà de Llobregat (★Barcelona) 86,866
Coslada (★Madrid) 68,765
Donostia (San Sebastián) (★ 285,000) 177,622
Dos Hermanas (▲ 68,456) 60,600
Elda 56,756
El Ferrol del Caudillo (★ 129,000) 86,503
El Prat de Llobregat (★Barcelona) 64,193
El Puerto de Santa María (▲ 62,285) 49,900
Elx (Elche) (▲ 180,256) 158,300
Fuenlabrada (★Madrid) 128,872
Gernika-Lumo (Guernica y Luno) (▲ 17,836) (1981 C) 12,214
Getafe (★Madrid) 135,367
Gijón 262,156
Granada 263,334
Granollers (★Barcelona) 49,045
Guadalajara 61,309
Huelva 137,826
Irún 54,886
Jaén 106,435
Jerez de la Frontera (▲ 183,007) 156,200
La Coruña 248,862
La Línea 60,956
Las Palmas de Gran Canaria (▲ 366,347) 319,000
Leganés (★Madrid) 168,403
León (★ 159,000) 136,558
L'Hospitalet de Llobregat (★Barcelona) 278,449
Linares 58,622
Lleida (Lérida) (▲ 109,795) 91,500
Logroño 119,038
Lugo (▲ 78,795) 68,700
• MADRID (★ 4,650,000) 3,102,846
Málaga 574,456
Manresa 65,607
Mataró 100,817
Mérida 52,363
Móstoles (★Madrid) 181,648
Murcia (▲ 314,124) 149,800
Orense 106,042
Oviedo (▲ 190,073) 168,900
Palencia 76,692
Palma (▲ 314,608) 249,000
Pamplona 180,593
Parla (★Madrid) 66,253
Portugalete (★Bilbao) 57,813
Puertollano 52,284
Reus 83,800
Rubí (★Barcelona) 48,807
Sabadell (★Barcelona) 189,489
Salamanca 159,342
San Baudilio de Llobrega (★Barcelona) 77,502
San Cristóbal de la Laguna (▲ 111,533) 25,900
San Fernando (★Cádiz) 81,975
San Sebastián de los Reyes (★Madrid) 51,653
Santa Coloma de Gramanet (★Barcelona) 136,042
Santa Cruz de Tenerife 215,228
Santander (▲ 190,795) 166,800
Santiago de Compostela (▲ 88,110) 68,800
Santurce-Antiguo (★Bilbao) 52,334
Segovia 54,402
Sevilla (★ 945,000) 663,132
Talavera de la Reina 68,158
Tarragona (▲ 109,586) 63,500
Tarrasa (★Barcelona) 161,410
Toledo 59,551
Torrejón de Ardoz (★Madrid) 83,267
Torrent (★València) 55,751
València (★ 1,270,000) 743,933
Valladolid 331,461
Vigo (▲ 271,128) 179,500
Vitoria (Gasteiz) 204,264
Zamora 62,047
Zaragoza 582,239

SPANISH NORTH AFRICA / Plazas de Soberanía en el Norte de África

1988 E 122,905
• Ceuta 67,188
Melilla 55,717

SRI LANKA

1989 E 16,806,000
Battaramulla (★Colombo) (1981 C) 56,535
Batticaloa 50,000
• COLOMBO (★ 2,050,000) 612,000
Dehiwala-Mount Lavinia (★Colombo) 193,000
Galle 83,000
Jaffna 128,000
Kandy 103,000
Moratuwa (★Colombo) 166,000
Negombo 64,000
SRI JAYAWARDENEPURA (KOTTE) (★Colombo) 108,000
Trincomalee 49,000

SUDAN / As-Sūdān

1983 C 20,594,197
Al-Fāshir 84,298
• AL-KHARṬŪM (★ 1,450,000) 473,597
Al-Kharṭūm Baḥrī (★Al-Kharṭūm) 340,857
Al-Qaḍārif 116,876
Al-Ubayyiḍ 137,582
'Aṭbarah 72,835
Būr Sūdān (Port Sudan) 206,038
Jūbā 84,377
Kassalā 141,429
Kūstī 89,135
Nyala 111,693
Umm Durmān (Omdurman) (★Al-Kharṭūm) 526,192
Wad Madanī 145,015
Wāw 90,960

SURINAME

1988 E 392,000
• PARAMARIBO (★ 296,000) 241,000
Wanica (★Paramaribo) 55,000

SWAZILAND

1986 C 712,131
LOBAMBA
Manzini (★ 30,000) 18,084
• MBABANE 38,290

SWEDEN / Sverige

1991 E 8,590,630
Borås (▲ 101,766) 59,400
Eskilstuna (▲ 89,765) 59,800
Gävle (▲ 88,568) 88,600
Göteborg (★ 710,894) 433,042

C Census. E Official estimate. U Unofficial estimate.
• Largest city in country.
★ Population or designation of metropolitan area, including suburbs (see headnote).
▲ Population of an entire municipality, commune, or district, including rural area.

Halmstad (▲ 80,061) 48,900
Helsingborg (▲ 109,267) 82,000
Huddinge (★Stockholm) 73,829
Järfälla (★Stockholm) 56,359
Jönköping (▲ 111,486) 76,300
Karlstad (▲ 76,467) 53,100
Linköping (▲ 122,268) 82,700
Luleå (▲ 68,412) 42,700
Lund (▲ 87,681) (★Malmö) 63,700
Malmö (★ 475,224) 233,887
Mölndal (★Göteborg) 52,028
Nacka (★Stockholm) 64,056
Norrköping (▲ 120,522) 82,600
Örebro (▲ 120,944) 86,000
Södertälje (▲ 81,786) (★Stockholm) 58,100
Sollentuna (★Stockholm) 51,377
Solna (★Stockholm) 51,841
• STOCKHOLM (★ 1,491,726) 674,452
Sundsvall (▲ 93,808) 50,300
Täby (★Stockholm) 56,714
Trollhättan (▲ 51,047) 41,000
Tumba (★Stockholm) 68,542
Umeå (▲ 91,258) 61,300
Uppsala (▲ 167,508) 110,000
Västerås (▲ 119,761) 98,300
Växjö (▲ 69,547) 48,000

SWITZERLAND / Schweiz / Suisse / Svizzera

1990 C 6,873,687

Aarau (★ 59,500) 16,481
Arbon (★ 41,400) 11,043
Baden (★ 73,200) 15,718
Basel (Bâle) (★ 587,000) 178,428
BERN (BERNE) (★ 300,400) 136,338
Biel (Bienne) (★ 83,100) 51,893
Fribourg (Freiburg) (★ 62,500) 36,355
Genève (Geneva) (★ 470,000) 171,042
Lausanne (★ 265,000) 128,112
Locarno (★ 42,200) 13,796
Lugano (★ 94,700) 25,344
Luzern (★ 165,000) 61,034
Neuchâtel (★ 67,500) 33,579
Sankt Gallen (★ 127,000) 75,237
Schaffhausen (★ 53,800) 34,225
Thun (★ 79,500) 38,211
Vevey (★ 65,900) 15,968
Winterthur (★ 110,500) 86,959
Zug (★ 69,000) 21,705
• Zürich (★ 870,000) 365,043

SYRIA / Sūrīyah

1988 E 11,338,000

Al-Hasakah (1981 C) 73,426
Al-Lādhiqīyah (Latakia) 249,000
Al-Qāmishlī 126,236
Ar-Raqqah 113,000
As-Suwaydā' 46,844
Dar'ā (1981 C) 49,534
Dārayyā (★Dimashq) 53,204
Dayr az-Zawr 112,000
• DIMASHQ (DAMASCUS) (★ 2,000,000) 1,326,000
Dūmā (★Dimashq) 66,130
Ḥalab (Aleppo) (★ 1,335,000) 1,261,000
Ḥamāh 222,000
Ḥimṣ 447,000
Idlib (1981 C) 51,682
Jaramānah (★Dimashq) 96,681
Kābir aṣ Ṣaghīr 47,728
Madīnat ath Thawrah 58,151
Ṭarṭūs (1981 C) 52,589

TAIWAN / T'aiwan

1991 E 20,352,966

Changhua (▲ 215,224) 165,000
Chiai (1992 E) 258,713
Chilung (1992 E) 357,000
Chungho (★T'aipei) 374,339
Chungli 269,804
Chutung (1988 E) 104,797
Fangshan (★Kaohsiung) 290,777
Fengyüan (▲ 151,642) 121,100
Hsichih (★T'aipei) (1980 C) 70,031
Hsinchu (1992 E) 330,576
Hsinchuang (★T'aipei) 299,174
Hsintien (★T'aipei) 225,517
Hualien 107,552
Ilan (▲ 81,751) (1980 C) 70,900
Kangshan (1980 C) 78,049
Kaohsiung (★ 1,900,000) (1992 E) 1,401,239
Lotung (1980 C) 57,925
Lukang (1980 C) 72,019
Miaoli (1980 C) 81,500
Nant'ou (1980 C) 84,038
P'ingchen (★T'aipei) 147,030
P'ingtung (▲ 210,801) 172,400
Sanchung (★T'aipei) 375,996
Shulin (★T'aipei) 111,993
Tach'i (1980 C) 67,209
T'aichung (1992 E) 785,182
T'ainan (1992 E) 692,116
• T'AIPEI (★ 6,200,000) (1992 E) 2,706,453
T'aipeihsien (★T'aipei) 538,954
T'aitung (▲ 108,196) 79,100
Taoyüan 241,263
T'oufen (1980 C) 66,536
T'uch'eng (▲ 136,928) (★T'aipei) 80,300
Yangmei (1980 C) 84,353
Yüanlin (▲ 121,251) 53,200
Yungho (★T'aipei) 249,736
Yungkang (▲ 136,705) 70,900

TAJIKISTAN

1991 E 5,358,300

Chudžand (Leninabad) 164,500
• DUŠANBE 582,400
Kul'ab 79,300
Kurgan-T'ube 58,400

TANZANIA

1985 E 21,733,000

Arusha (1984 E) 69,000
• DAR ES SALAAM 1,096,000
DODOMA 85,000
Iringa (1984 E) 67,000
Kigoma (1978 C) 50,044
Mbeya 194,000
Morogoro (1984 E) 72,000
Moshi (1984 E) 62,000
Mtwara (1978 C) 48,510
Mwanza 252,000
Tabora 214,000
Tanga 172,000
Ujiji (1967 C) 21,369
Zanzibar 133,000

THAILAND / Prathet Thai

1991 E 56,961,030

Chiang Mai 161,541
Chon Buri 45,763
Hat Yai 142,351
Khon Kaen 131,478
• KRUNG THEP (BANGKOK) (★ 7,060,000) 5,620,591
Nakhon Ratchasima 202,503
Nakhon Sawan 108,569
Nakhon Si Thammarat 74,219
Nonthaburi (★Krung Thep) 264,201
Pattaya 64,731
Phitsanulok 77,672
Phra Nakhon Si Ayutthaya 60,561
Phuket 42,913
Sakon Nakhon 47,869
Samut Prakan (★Krung Thep) 71,538
Samut Sakhon 55,509
Saraburi 64,915
Songkhla 82,167
Trang 48,589
Ubon Ratchathani 98,950
Udon Thani 78,489
Yala 68,834

TOGO

1987 E 3,148,000

• LOMÉ 500,000
Sokodé 55,000

TONGA

1986 C 94,535

• NUKU'ALOFA 21,265

TRINIDAD AND TOBAGO

1990 C 1,234,388

• PORT OF SPAIN (★ 370,000) 50,878
San Fernando (★ 75,000) 30,092

TUNISIA / Tunis / Tunisie

1984 C 6,975,450

Ariana (★Tunis) 98,655
Bardo (★Tunis) 65,669
Ben Arous (★Tunis) 52,105
Bizerte 94,509
Gabès 92,258
Gafsa 60,970
Hammam Lif (★Tunis) 47,009
Houmt Essouk 92,269
Kairouan 72,254
Kasserine 47,606
La Goulette (★Tunis) 61,609
Menzel Bourguiba 51,399
Sfax (★ 310,000) 231,911
Sousse (★ 160,000) 83,509
• TUNIS (★ 1,225,000) 596,654
Zarzis 49,063

TURKEY / Türkiye

1990 C 56,473,035

Adana 916,150
Adıyaman 100,045
Afyon 95,643
Ağrı 58,038
Akhisar 73,944
Aksaray 90,698
Akşehir 51,746
Alanya 52,460
Amasya 57,288
ANKARA (★ 2,650,000) 2,559,471
Antalya 378,208
Aydın 107,011
Bafra 65,600
Balıkesir 170,589
Bandırma 77,444
Batman 147,347
Bilecik 23,273
Bolu 60,789
Burdur 56,432
Bursa 834,576
Çanakkale 53,995
Ceyhan 85,308
Cizre 50,023
Çorlu 74,681
Çorum 116,810
Darıca 53,560
Denizli 204,118
Diyarbakır 381,144
Düzce 61,878
Edirne 102,345
Elazığ 204,603
Elbistan 54,741
Ereğli, Konya prov. 74,283
Ereğli, Zonguldak prov. 63,987
Erzincan 91,772
Erzurum 242,391
Esenyurt (★İstanbul) 70,280
Eskişehir 413,082
Gaziantep 603,434
Gebze (★İstanbul) 159,116
Gelibolu 18,670
Gemlik 50,237
Giresun 67,604
Gölcük 64,911
Gümüşhane 26,014
Hakkâri 30,407
Hatay (Antioch) 123,871
İçel (Mersin) 422,357
İnegöl 71,120
İskenderun 154,807
Isparta 112,117
• İstanbul (★ 7,550,000) 6,620,241
İzmir (★ 1,900,000) 1,757,414
İzmit 256,882
Kadirli 55,061
Kahramanmaraş 228,129
Karabük 105,373
Karaman 76,525
Kars 78,455
Kastamonu 51,560
Kayseri 421,362
Kilis 82,882
Kırıkkale 185,431
Kırşehir 73,538
Kızıltepe 60,134
Konya 513,346
Körfez 65,786
Kozan 54,451
Kütahya 130,994
Lüleburgaz 52,384
Malatya 281,776
Manisa 158,928
Mardin 53,005
Muş 44,019
Nazilli 80,277
Nevşehir 52,719
Niğde 55,035
Nizip 58,604
Nusaybin 49,671
Ödemiş 51,620
Ordu 102,107
Osmaniye 123,307
Polatlı 60,158
Rize 52,031
Sakarya 171,225
Salihli 70,861
Samsun 303,979
Şanlıurfa 276,528
Siirt 68,320
Silvan (Miyafarkin) 59,865
Sinop 25,537
Sivas 221,512
Siverek 63,049
Söke 50,866
Soma 49,977
Sultanbeyli (★İstanbul) 82,298
Tarsus 187,508
Tatvan 54,071
Tekirdağ 80,442
Tokat 83,058
Trabzon 143,941
Tunceli 24,513
Turgutlu 73,634
Turhal 68,384
Uşak 105,270
Van 153,111
Viranşehir 57,461
Yalova (★İstanbul) 65,823
Yozgat 50,335
Zonguldak (★ 220,000) 116,725

TURKMENISTAN

1991 E 3,714,100

• AŠCHABAD (ASHGABAT) 412,200
Čardžou 166,400
Krasnovodsk 59,500
Mary 94,900
Nebit-Dag 89,100
Tašauz 117,000

TURKS AND CAICOS ISLANDS

1990 C 11,465

• GRAND TURK 3,691

TUVALU

1979 C 7,349

• FUNAFUTI 2,191

UGANDA

1991 C 16,582,700

Jinja 60,979
• KAMPALA 773,463
Masaka 49,070
Mbale 53,634

UKRAINE / Ukrayina

1991 E 51,944,400

Alchevs'k 126,000
Antratsyt (★Krasnyy Luch) 72,800
Artemivs'k 90,800
Berdyans'k 135,200
Berdychivv 93,400
Bila Tserkva 204,400
Bilhorod-Dnistrovs'kyy 56,800
Boryspil' (★Kyyiv) 52,700
Brovary (★Kyyiv) 84,800
Bryanka (★Stakhanov) 64,500
Cherkasy 302,200
Chernihiv 305,700
Chernivtsi 258,800
Chervonohrad 74,000
Dniprodzerzhyns'k (★Dnipropetrovs'k) 284,400
Dnipropetrovs'k (★ 1,600,000) 1,189,300
Donets'k (★ 2,125,000) 1,121,300
Drohobych 79,200
Druzhkivka (★Kramators'k) 74,400
Dymytrov (★Krasnoarmiys'k) 63,800
Dzerzhyns'k (★Horlivka) 50,500
Dzhankoy 54,500
Enerhodar 51,500
Fastiv 54,400
Feodosiya 85,600
Horlivka (★ 700,000) 336,600
Illichivs'k (★Odesa) 56,000
Ivano-Frankivs'k 225,800
Izmayil 95,100
Izyum 64,800
Kalush 69,400
Kam'yanets'-Podil's'kyy 104,900
Kerch 178,300
Kharkiv (Kharkov) (★ 2,050,000) 1,622,800
Khartsyz'k (★Donets'k) 69,300
Kherson 365,400
Khmel'nyts'kyy 244,500
Kirovohrad 277,900
Kolomyya 66,200
Komsomol's'k 53,000
Konotop 97,700
Korosten' 67,500
Kostyantynivka 107,800
Kovel' 69,700
Kramators'k (★ 515,000) 201,300
Krasnoarmiys'k (★ 180,000) 73,300
Krasnodon (★ 165,000) 54,800
Krasnyy Luch (★ 320,000) 113,400
Kremenchuk 240,600
Kryvyy Rih 724,000
• KYYIV (KIEV) (★ 3,250,000) 2,635,000
Lozova 74,100
Lubny 60,300
Luhans'k (★ 650,000) 503,900
Luts'k 209,500
L'viv 802,200
Lysychans'k (★ 415,000) 126,400
Makiyivka (★Donets'k) 423,900
Marhanets' 54,700
Mariupol' (Ždanov) 521,800
Melitopol' 176,900
Mukacheve 88,000
Mykolayiv 511,600
Nikopol' 159,000
Nizhyn 82,000
Nova Kakhovka 59,000
Novohrad-Volyns'kyy 56,100
Novomoskovs'k 76,600
Novovolyns'k 56,400
Odesa (★ 1,185,000) 1,100,700
Okhtyrka 52,000
Oleksandriya 104,900
Pavlohrad 134,300
Pervomays'k (★Stakhanov) 52,000
Pervomays'k 83,800
Poltava 320,100
Pryluky 72,900
Rivne 239,300
Romny 57,300
Roven'ky 58,500
Rubizhne (★Lysychans'k) 75,100
Sevastopol' 366,200
Shakhtars'k (★Torez) 73,100
Shepetivka 51,900
Shostka 95,200
Simferopol' 352,600
Slov'yans'k (★Kramators'k) 137,100
Smila 81,100
Snizhne (★Torez) 68,900
Stakhanov (★ 700,000) 112,700
Stryy 68,200
Sumy 300,900
Sverdlovs'k (★ 145,000) 83,700
Svitlovods'k 57,900
Syeverodonets'k (★Lysychans'k) 133,300
Ternopil' 218,400
Torez (★ 320,000) 88,100
Uman' 92,700
Uzhhorod 122,600
Vinnytsya 380,900
Yalta 89,300
Yenakiyeve (★Horlivka) 120,100
Yevpatoriya 110,500
Zaporizhzhya 896,600
Zhovti Vody 63,900
Zhytomyr 297,500

UNITED ARAB EMIRATES / Al-Imārāt al-'Arabīyah al-Muttaḥidah

1980 C 980,000

ABŪ ZABY (ABU DHABI) 242,975
Al-'Ayn 101,663
Ash-Shāriqah 125,149
• Dubayy 265,702
Ra's al-Khaymah 42,000

UNITED KINGDOM

1981 C 55,678,079

UNITED KINGDOM: ENGLAND

1981 C 46,220,955

Aldershot (★London) 53,665
Ashton-under-Lyne (★Manchester) 43,605
Aylesbury 51,999
Barnsley 76,783
Barrow-in-Furness 50,174
Basildon (★London) 94,800
Basingstoke 73,027
Bath 84,283
Bebington (★Liverpool) 62,618
Bedford 75,632
Beeston and Stapleford (★Nottingham) 64,785
Benfleet (★London) 50,783
Birkenhead (★Liverpool) 99,075
Birmingham (★ 2,675,000) 1,013,995
Blackburn (★ 221,900) 109,564
Blackpool (★ 280,000) 146,297
Bognor Regis 50,323
Bolton (★Manchester) 143,960
Bootle 70,860
Bournemouth (★ 315,000) 142,829
Bracknell (★London) 52,257
Bradford (★Leeds) 293,336
Brentwood (★London) 51,212
Brighton (★ 420,000) 134,581
Bristol (★ 630,000) 413,861
Burnley (★ 160,000) 76,365
Burton upon Trent 59,040
Bury (★Manchester) 61,785
Bury Saint Edmunds 30,563
Cambridge 87,111
Cannock (★Birmingham) 54,503
Canterbury 34,546
Carlisle 72,206
Carlton (★Nottingham) 46,053
Chatham (★London) 65,835
Cheadle and Gatley (★Manchester) 59,478
Chelmsford (★London) 91,109
Cheltenham 87,188
Cheshunt (★London) 49,616
Chester 80,154
Chesterfield (★ 127,000) 73,352
Clacton-on-Sea 39,618
Colchester 87,476
Corby 48,704
Coventry (★ 645,000) 318,718
Crawley (★London) 80,113
Crewe 59,097
Crosby (★Liverpool) 54,103
Darlington 85,519
Dartford (★London) 62,032
Derby (★ 275,000) 218,026
Dewsbury (★Leeds) 49,612
Doncaster 74,727
Dover 33,461
Dudley (★Birmingham) 186,513
Dunstable (★Luton) 48,436
Durham 38,105
Eastbourne 86,715
Eastleigh (★Southampton) 58,585
Ellesmere Port (★Liverpool) 65,829
Epsom and Ewell (★London) 65,830
Esher / Molesey (★London) 46,688
Exeter 88,235
Fareham / Portchester (★Portsmouth) 55,563
Farnborough (★London) 48,063
Folkestone 42,949
Frimley and Camberley (★London) 45,108
Gateshead (★Newcastle) 91,429
Gillingham (★London) 92,531
Gloucester (★ 115,000) 106,526
Gosport (★Portsmouth) 69,664
Gravesend (★London) 53,450
Grays (★London) 45,881
Greasby / Moreton (★Liverpool) 56,410
Great Yarmouth 54,777
Grimsby (★ 145,000) 91,532
Guildford (★London) 61,509
Halesowen (★Birmingham) 57,533
Halifax 76,675
Harlow (★London) 79,150
Harrogate 63,637
Hartlepool (★Middlesbrough) 91,749
Hastings 74,979
Havant (★Portsmouth) 50,098
Hemel Hempstead (★London) 80,110
Hereford 48,277
Hertford (★London) 21,350
High Wycombe (▲ 156,800) 69,575
Hove (★Brighton) 65,587
Huddersfield (▲ 377,400) 147,825
Huyton-with-Roby (★Liverpool) 62,011
Ipswich 129,661
Keighley (★Leeds) 49,188
Kidderminster 50,385

C Census. E Official estimate. U Unofficial estimate.
• Largest city in country.
★ Population or designation of metropolitan area, including suburbs (see headnote).
▲ Population of an entire municipality, commune, or district, including rural area.

Kingston upon Hull (★ 350,000) 322,144
Kingswood (★Bristol) 54,736
Kirkby (★Liverpool) 52,825
Lancaster 43,902
Leeds (★ 1,540,000) 445,242
Leicester (★ 495,000) 324,394
Lincoln 79,980
Littlehampton 46,028
Liverpool (★ 1,525,000) 538,809
• LONDON (★ 11,100,000) 6,574,009
Loughborough 44,895
Lowestoft 59,430
Luton (★ 220,000) 163,209
Macclesfield 47,525
Maidenhead (★London) 59,809
Maidstone 86,067
Manchester (★ 2,775,000) 437,612
Mansfield (★ 198,000) 71,325
Margate 53,137
Middlesbrough (★ 580,000) 158,516
Middleton (★Manchester) 51,373
Milton Keynes 36,886
Newcastle-under-Lyme (★Stoke-on-Trent) 73,208
Newcastle upon Tyne (★ 1,300,000) 199,064
Northampton 154,172
Norwich (★ 230,000) 169,814
Nottingham (★ 655,000) 273,300
Nuneaton (★Coventry) 60,337
Oldbury / Smethwick (★Birmingham) 153,268
Oldham (★Manchester) 107,095
Oxford (★ 230,000) 113,847
Penzance 18,501
Peterborough 113,404
Plymouth (★ 290,000) 238,583
Poole (★Bournemouth) 122,815
Portsmouth (★ 485,000) 174,218
Preston (★ 250,000) 166,675
Ramsgate 36,678
Reading (★ 200,000) 194,727
Redditch (★Birmingham) 61,639
Reigate / Redhill (★London) 48,241
Rochdale (★Manchester) 97,292
Rotherham (★Sheffield) 122,374
Royal Leamington Spa (★Coventry) 56,552
Royal Tunbridge Wells 57,699
Rugby 59,039
Runcorn (★Liverpool) 63,995
Saint Albans (★London) 76,709
Saint Helens 114,397
Sale (★Manchester) 57,872
Salford (★Manchester) 96,525
Salisbury 36,890
Scarborough 36,665
Scunthorpe 79,043
Sheffield (★ 710,000) 470,685
Shrewsbury 57,731
Slough (★London) 106,341
Solihull (★Birmingham) 93,940
Southampton (★ 415,000) 211,321
Southend-on-Sea (★London) 155,720
Southport (★Liverpool) 88,596
South Shields (★Newcastle) 86,488
Stafford 60,915
Staines (★London) 51,949
Stevenage 74,757
Stockport (★Manchester) 135,489
Stockton-on-Tees (★Middlesbrough) 86,699
Stoke-on-Trent (★ 440,000) 272,446
Stourbridge (★Birmingham) 55,136
Stratford-upon-Avon 20,941
Stretford (★Manchester) 47,522
Sunderland (★Newcastle) 195,064
Sutton Coldfield (★Birmingham) 102,572
Swindon 127,348
Tamworth 63,260
Taunton 47,793
Torquay (★ 112,400) 54,430
Wakefield (★Leeds) 74,764
Wallasey (★Liverpool) 62,465
Walsall (★Birmingham) 177,923
Walton and Weybridge (★London) 50,031
Warrington 81,366
Washington (★Newcastle) 48,856
Waterlooville (★Portsmouth) 57,296
Watford (★London) 109,503
West Bromwich (★Birmingham) 153,725
Weston-super-Mare 60,821
Widnes 55,973
Wigan (★Manchester) 88,725
Woking (★London) 92,667
Wolverhampton (★Birmingham) 263,501
Worcester 75,466
Worthing (★Brighton) 90,687
York (★ 145,000) 123,126

UNITED KINGDOM: NORTHERN IRELAND

1990 E 1,589,400

Bangor (★Belfast) 72,600
Belfast (★ 685,000) 295,100
Castlereagh (★Belfast) 58,100
Londonderry (Derry) 100,500
Lurgan (★ 63,000) (1981 C) 20,991
Newtownabbey (★Belfast) 72,900

UNITED KINGDOM: SCOTLAND

1990 E 5,102,400

Aberdeen 211,080
Ayr (★ 100,000) (1981 C) 48,493
Clydebank (★Glasgow) (1981 C) 51,832
Coatbridge (1981 C) 50,831
Cumbernauld (★Glasgow) 50,700
Dundee 172,860
Dunfermline (★ 125,817) (1981 C) 52,105
East Kilbride (★Glasgow) 70,500
Edinburgh (★ 630,000) 434,520
Falkirk (★ 148,171) (1981 C) 36,372
Glasgow (★ 1,800,000) 689,210
Greenock (★ 101,000) (1981 C) 58,436
Hamilton (★Glasgow) (1981 C) 51,666
Irvine (★ 94,000) 56,000
Kilmarnock (★ 84,000) (1981 C) 51,799
Kirkcaldy (★ 148,171) (1981 C) 46,356
Motherwell (★Glasgow) (1981 C) 30,616
Paisley (★Glasgow) (1981 C) 84,330
Perth (1981 C) 41,916
Stirling (★ 61,000) (1981 C) 36,640

UNITED KINGDOM: WALES

1981 C 2,790,462

Cardiff (★ 625,000) 262,313
Cwmbran (★Newport) 44,592
Llanelli 45,336
Merthyr Tydfil 38,893
Neath (★Swansea) 48,687
Newport (★ 310,000) 115,896
Pontypool (★Newport) 36,064
Port Talbot (★ 130,000) 40,078
Rhondda (★Cardiff) 70,980
Swansea (★ 275,000) 172,433
Wrexham 39,929

UNITED STATES

1990 C 248,709,873

UNITED STATES: ALABAMA

1990 C 4,040,587

Anniston (★ 116,034) 26,623
Auburn (★ 61,100) 33,830
Birmingham (★ 907,810) 265,968
Decatur (★ 131,556) 48,761
Dothan (★ 130,964) 53,589
Florence (★ 131,327) 36,426
Gadsden (★ 99,840) 42,523
Huntsville (★ 238,912) 159,789
Mobile (★ 476,923) 196,278
Montgomery (★ 292,517) 187,106
Tuscaloosa (★ 150,522) 77,759

UNITED STATES: ALASKA

1990 C 550,043

Anchorage (★ 248,400) 226,338
Fairbanks (★ 59,500) 30,843
Juneau 26,751

UNITED STATES: ARIZONA

1990 C 3,665,228

Chandler (★Phoenix) 90,533
Glendale (★Phoenix) 148,134
Mesa (★Phoenix) 288,091
Nogales (★Nogales, Mexico) 19,489
Phoenix (★ 2,122,101) 900,013
Scottsdale (★Phoenix) 130,069
Tempe (★Phoenix) 141,865
Tucson (★ 666,880) 405,390
Yuma (★ 106,895) 54,923

UNITED STATES: ARKANSAS

1990 C 2,350,725

Fayetteville (★ 113,409) 42,099
Fort Smith (★ 175,911) 72,798
Hot Springs National Park (★ 56,500) 32,462
Jonesboro (★ 49,300) 46,535
Little Rock (★ 513,117) 175,795
North Little Rock (★Little Rock) 61,741
Pine Bluff (★ 85,487) 57,140

UNITED STATES: CALIFORNIA

1990 C 29,760,021

Alameda (★Oakland) 76,459
Alhambra (★Los Angeles) 82,106
Anaheim (★ 2,410,556) (★Los Angeles) 266,406
Antioch (★Oakland) 62,195
Arden (★Sacramento) 62,900
Bakersfield (★ 543,477) 174,820
Baldwin Park (★Los Angeles) 69,330
Bellflower (★Los Angeles) 61,815
Berkeley (★Oakland) 102,724
Buena Park (★Anaheim) 68,784
Burbank (★Los Angeles) 93,643
Calexico (★Mexicali, Mexico) 18,633
Camarillo (★Oxnard) 52,303
Carlsbad (★San Diego) 63,126
Carmichael (★Sacramento) 48,702
Carson (★Los Angeles) 83,995
Cerritos (★Los Angeles) 53,240
Chico (★ 182,120) 40,079
Chino (★Riverside) 59,682
Chula Vista (★San Diego) 135,163
Citrus Heights (★Sacramento) 112,800
Clovis (★Fresno) 50,323
Compton (★Los Angeles) 90,454
Concord (★Oakland) 111,348
Corona (★Riverside) 76,095
Costa Mesa (★Anaheim) 96,357
Cucamonga (★Riverside) 101,409
Daly City (★San Francisco) 92,311
Diamond Bar (★Los Angeles) 53,672
Downey (★Los Angeles) 91,444
East Los Angeles (★Los Angeles) 126,379
El Cajon (★San Diego) 88,693
El Monte (★Los Angeles) 106,209
El Toro (★Anaheim) 62,685
Escondido (★San Diego) 108,635
Eureka (★ 89,800) 27,025
Fairfield (★Vallejo) 77,211
Fontana (★Riverside) 87,535
Fountain Valley (★Anaheim) 53,691
Fremont (★Oakland) 173,339
Fresno (★ 667,490) 354,202
Fullerton (★Anaheim) 114,144
Gardena (★Los Angeles) 49,847
Garden Grove (★Anaheim) 143,050
Glendale (★Los Angeles) 180,038
Hacienda Heights (★Los Angeles) 58,200
Hawthorne (★Los Angeles) 71,349
Hayward (★Oakland) 111,498
Hemet (★Riverside) 36,094
Huntington Beach (★Anaheim) 181,519
Huntington Park (★Los Angeles) 56,065
Inglewood (★Los Angeles) 109,602
Irvine (★Anaheim) 110,330
La Habra (★Anaheim) 51,266
Lakewood (★Los Angeles) 73,557
La Mesa (★San Diego) 52,931
Lancaster (★ 189,300) (★Los Angeles) 97,291
Livermore (★Oakland) 56,741
Lodi (★Stockton) 51,874
Lompoc (★Santa Barbara) 37,649
Long Beach (★Los Angeles) 429,433
Los Angeles (★ 14,531,529) 3,485,398
Lynwood (★Los Angeles) 61,945
Merced (★ 178,403) 56,216
Milpitas (★San Jose) 50,686
Mission Viejo (★Anaheim) 72,820
Modesto (★ 370,522) 164,730
Montebello (★Los Angeles) 59,564
Monterey (★Salinas) 31,954
Monterey Park (★Los Angeles) 60,738
Mountain View (★San Jose) 67,460
Napa (★Vallejo) 61,842
National City (★San Diego) 54,249
Newport Beach (★Anaheim) 66,643
Norwalk (★Los Angeles) 94,279
Oakland (★ 2,082,914) (★San Francisco) 372,242
Oceanside (★San Diego) 128,398
Ontario (★Riverside) 133,179
Orange (★Anaheim) 110,658
Oxnard (★ 669,016) (★Los Angeles) 142,216
Palm Springs (★Riverside) 40,181
Palo Alto (★San Jose) 55,900
Pasadena (★Los Angeles) 131,591
Pico Rivera (★Los Angeles) 59,177
Pleasanton (★Oakland) 50,553
Pomona (★Los Angeles) 131,723
Porterville (★Visalia) 29,563
Rancho Cordova (★Sacramento) 48,731
Redding (★ 147,036) 66,462
Redlands (★Riverside) 60,394
Redondo Beach (★Los Angeles) 60,167
Redwood City (★San Francisco) 66,072
Rialto (★Riverside) 72,388
Richmond (★Oakland) 87,425
Riverside (★ 2,588,793) (★Los Angeles) 226,505
Rosemead (★Los Angeles) 51,638
Sacramento (★ 1,481,102) 369,365
Salinas (★ 355,660) 108,777
San Bernardino (★Riverside) 164,164
San Diego (★ 2,949,000) 1,110,549
San Francisco (★ 6,253,311) 723,959
San Jose (★ 1,497,577) (★San Francisco) 782,248
San Leandro (★Oakland) 68,223
San Mateo (★San Francisco) 85,486
Santa Ana (★Anaheim) 293,742
Santa Barbara (★ 369,608) 85,571
Santa Clara (★San Jose) 93,613
Santa Cruz (★ 229,734) (★San Francisco) 49,040
Santa Maria (★Santa Barbara) 61,284
Santa Monica (★Los Angeles) 86,905
Santa Rosa (★ 388,222) (★San Francisco) 113,313
Santee (★San Diego) 52,902
Simi Valley (★Oxnard) 100,217
South Gate (★Los Angeles) 86,284
South San Francisco (★San Francisco) 54,312
South Whittier (★Los Angeles) 51,100
Spring Valley (★San Diego) 54,600
Stockton (★ 480,628) 210,943
Sunnyvale (★San Jose) 117,229
Thousand Oaks (★Oxnard) 104,352
Torrance (★Los Angeles) 133,107
Tustin (★Anaheim) 50,689
Union City (★Oakland) 53,762
Upland (★Riverside) 63,374
Vacaville (★Vallejo) 71,479
Vallejo (★ 451,186) (★San Francisco) 109,199
Ventura (San Buenaventura) (★Oxnard) 92,575
Visalia (★ 311,921) 75,636
Vista (★San Diego) 71,872
Walnut Creek (★Oakland) 60,569
Watsonville (★Santa Cruz) 31,099
West Covina (★Los Angeles) 96,086
Westminster (★Anaheim) 78,118
Whittier (★Los Angeles) 77,671
Yorba Linda (★Anaheim) 52,422
Yuba City (★ 122,643) 27,437

UNITED STATES: COLORADO

1990 C 3,294,394

Arvada (★Denver) 89,235
Aurora (★Denver) 222,103
Boulder (★ 225,339) (★Denver) 83,312
Colorado Springs (★ 397,014) 281,140
Denver (★ 1,848,319) 467,610
Fort Collins (★ 186,136) 87,758
Grand Junction (★ 85,200) 29,034
Greeley (★ 131,821) 60,536
Lakewood (★Denver) 126,481
Longmont (★Boulder) 51,555
Loveland (★Fort Collins) 37,352
Pueblo (★ 123,051) 98,640
Thornton (★Denver) 55,031
Westminster (★Denver) 74,625

UNITED STATES: CONNECTICUT

1990 C 3,287,116

Bridgeport (★ 443,722) (★New York, N.Y.) 141,686
Bristol (★ 79,488) (★Hartford) 60,640
Danbury (★ 187,867) (★New York, N.Y.) 65,585
East Hartford (★Hartford) 50,452
Fairfield (★Bridgeport) 53,418
Greenwich (★Stamford) 58,441
Hamden (★New Haven) 53,100
Hartford (★ 1,085,837) 139,739
Manchester (★Hartford) 51,000
Meriden (★New Haven) 59,479
Milford (★Bridgeport) 48,168
New Britain (★ 148,188) (★Hartford) 75,491
New Haven (★ 530,180) 130,474
New London (★ 266,819) 28,540
Norwalk (★ 127,378) (★New York, N.Y.) 78,331
Stamford (★ 202,557) (★New York, N.Y.) 108,056
Stratford (★Bridgeport) 49,389
Torrington (★ 58,800) 33,687
Waterbury (★ 221,629) 108,961
West Hartford (★Hartford) 59,100
West Haven (★New Haven) 54,021

UNITED STATES: DELAWARE

1990 C 666,168

Dover (★ 78,900) 27,630
Wilmington (★Philadelphia, Pa.) 71,529

UNITED STATES: DISTRICT OF COLUMBIA

1990 C 606,900

WASHINGTON (★ 3,923,574) 606,900

UNITED STATES: FLORIDA

1990 C 12,937,926

Boca Raton (★West Palm Beach) 61,492
Brandon (★Tampa) 57,985
Cape Coral (★Fort Myers) 74,991
Carol City (★Miami) 52,800
City of Sunrise (★Fort Lauderdale) 64,407
Clearwater (★Tampa) 98,784
Daytona Beach (★ 370,712) 61,921
De Land (★Daytona Beach) 16,491
Fort Lauderdale (★ 1,255,488) (★Miami) 149,377
Fort Myers (★ 335,113) 45,206
Fort Pierce (★ 251,071) 36,830
Fort Walton Beach (★ 143,776) 21,471
Gainesville (★ 204,111) 84,770
Hialeah (★Miami) 188,004
Hollywood (★Fort Lauderdale) 121,697
Jacksonville (★ 906,727) 635,230
Kendall (★Miami) 53,100
Lakeland (★ 405,382) 70,576
Largo (★Tampa) 65,674
Melbourne (★ 398,978) 59,646
Miami (★ 3,192,582) 358,548
Miami Beach (★Miami) 92,639
Naples (★ 152,099) 19,505
Ocala (★ 194,833) 42,045
Orlando (★ 1,072,748) 164,693
Panama City (★ 126,994) 34,378
Pembroke Pines (★Fort Lauderdale) 65,452
Pensacola (★ 344,406) 58,165
Plantation (★Fort Lauderdale) 66,692
Pompano Beach (★Fort Lauderdale) 72,411
Saint Petersburg (★Tampa) 238,629
Sarasota (★ 277,776) 50,961
Tallahassee (★ 233,598) 124,773
Tampa (★ 2,067,959) 280,015
Venice (★Sarasota) 16,922
West Palm Beach (★ 863,518) 67,643
Winter Haven (★Lakeland) 24,725

UNITED STATES: GEORGIA

1990 C 6,478,216

Albany (★ 112,561) 78,122
Athens (★ 156,267) 45,734
Atlanta (★ 2,833,511) 394,017
Augusta (★ 396,809) 44,639
Columbus (★ 243,072) 178,681
Macon (★ 281,103) 106,612
Rome (★ 74,900) 30,326
Savannah (★ 242,622) 137,560
Valdosta (★ 64,000) 39,806
Warner Robins (★Macon) 43,726

UNITED STATES: HAWAII

1990 C 1,108,229

Hilo (★ 47,600) 37,808
Honolulu (★ 836,231) 365,272

UNITED STATES: IDAHO

1990 C 1,006,749

Boise (★ 205,775) 125,738
Idaho Falls (★ 72,700) 43,929
Lewiston (★ 44,300) 28,082
Nampa (★ 70,500) 28,365
Pocatello (★ 56,700) 46,080

UNITED STATES: ILLINOIS

1990 C 11,430,602

Arlington Heights (★Chicago) 75,460
Aurora (★ 356,884) (★Chicago) 99,581
Bloomington (★ 129,180) 51,972
Champaign (★ 173,025) 63,502
Chicago (★ 8,065,633) 2,783,726
Cicero (★Chicago) 67,436
Danville (★ 68,000) 33,828
Decatur (★ 117,206) 83,885
De Kalb (★ 52,200) 34,925
Des Plaines (★Chicago) 53,223
East Saint Louis (★Saint Louis, Mo.) 40,944
Elgin (★Aurora) 77,010
Evanston (★Chicago) 73,233
Galesburg (★ 40,600) 33,530
Joliet (★ 389,650) (★Chicago) 76,836
Kankakee (★ 96,255) 27,575
Mount Prospect (★Chicago) 53,170
Naperville (★Chicago) 85,351
Oak Lawn (★Chicago) 56,182

C Census. E Official estimate. U Unofficial estimate.
• Largest city in country.

★ Population or designation of metropolitan area, including suburbs (see headnote).
▲ Population of an entire municipality, commune, or district, including rural area.

Oak Park (★Chicago) 53,648
Peoria (★ 339,172) 113,504
Quincy (★ 50,600) 39,681
Rockford (★ 283,719) 139,426
Schaumburg (★Chicago) 68,586
Skokie (★Chicago) 59,432
Springfield (★ 189,550) 105,227
Waukegan (★Chicago) 69,392
Wheaton (★Chicago) 51,464

UNITED STATES: INDIANA

1990 C 5,544,159

Anderson (★ 130,669) 59,459
Bloomington (★ 108,978) 60,633
Columbus (★ 59,000) 31,802
Elkhart (★ 156,198) 43,627
Evansville (★ 278,990) 126,272
Fort Wayne (★ 363,811) 173,072
Gary (★ 604,526) (★Chicago, Il.) 116,646
Hammond (★Gary) 84,236
Indianapolis (★ 1,249,822) 731,327
Kokomo (★ 96,946) 44,962
Lafayette (★ 130,598) 43,764
Marion (★ 76,900) 32,618
Michigan City (★ 55,600) 33,822
Muncie (★ 119,659) 71,035
Richmond (★ 64,100) 38,705
South Bend (★ 247,052) 105,511
Terre Haute (★ 130,812) 57,483

UNITED STATES: IOWA

1990 C 2,776,755

Ames (★ 65,400) 47,198
Cedar Rapids (★ 168,767) 108,751
Clinton (★ 39,600) 29,201
Council Bluffs (★Omaha, Ne.) 54,315
Davenport (★ 350,861) 95,333
Des Moines (★ 392,928) 193,187
Dubuque (★ 86,403) 57,546
Iowa City (★ 96,119) 59,738
Mason City 29,040
Sioux City (★ 115,018) 80,505
Waterloo (★ 146,611) 66,467

UNITED STATES: KANSAS

1990 C 2,477,574

Hutchinson (★ 46,800) 39,308
Kansas City (★Kansas City, Mo.) 149,767
Lawrence (★ 81,798) 65,608
Manhattan (★ 47,400) 37,712
Olathe (★Kansas City, Mo.) 63,352
Overland Park (★Kansas City, Mo.) 111,790
Salina (★ 42,700) 42,303
Topeka (★ 160,976) 119,883
Wichita (★ 485,270) 304,011

UNITED STATES: KENTUCKY

1990 C 3,685,296

Bowling Green (★ 59,100) 40,641
Covington (★Cincinnati, Oh.) 43,264
Frankfort 25,968
Lexington (★ 348,428) 225,366
Louisville (★ 952,662) 269,063
Owensboro (★ 87,189) 53,549
Paducah (★ 63,000) 27,256

UNITED STATES: LOUISIANA

1990 C 4,219,973

Alexandria (★ 131,556) 49,188
Baton Rouge (★ 528,264) 219,531
Bossier City (★Shreveport) 52,721
Houma (★ 182,842) 96,982
Kenner (★New Orleans) 72,033
Lafayette (★ 208,740) 94,440
Lake Charles (★ 168,134) 70,580
Metairie (★New Orleans) 149,428
Monroe (★ 142,191) 54,909
New Iberia (★ 49,000) 31,828
New Orleans (★ 1,238,816) 496,938
Shreveport (★ 334,341) 198,525

UNITED STATES: MAINE

1990 C 1,227,928

Augusta (★ 56,700) 21,325
Bangor (★ 88,745) 33,181
Lewiston (★ 88,141) 39,757
Portland (★ 215,281) 64,358

UNITED STATES: MARYLAND

1990 C 4,781,468

Annapolis (★Baltimore) 33,187
Baltimore (★ 2,382,172) 736,014
Bethesda (★Washington, D.C.) 62,936
Columbia (★Baltimore) 75,883
Cumberland (★ 101,643) 23,706
Dundalk (★Baltimore) 65,800
Hagerstown (★ 121,393) 35,445
Salisbury (★ 72,400) 20,592
Silver Spring (★Washington, D.C.) 76,046
Towson (★Baltimore) 49,445
Wheaton (★Washington, D.C.) (1989) 58,300

UNITED STATES: MASSACHUSETTS

1990 C 6,016,425

Amherst (★ 44,700) 17,824
Boston (★ 4,171,643) 574,283
Brockton (★ 189,478) (★Boston) 92,788
Brookline (★Boston) 54,718
Cambridge (★Boston) 95,802
Chicopee (★Springfield) 56,632
Fall River (★ 157,272) (★Providence, R.I.) 92,703
Fitchburg (★ 102,797) 41,194
Framingham (★Boston) 64,989
Haverhill (★Lawrence) 51,418
Lawrence (★ 393,516) (★Boston) 70,207
Lowell (★ 273,067) (★Boston) 103,439
Lynn (★Salem) 81,245
Malden (★Boston) 53,884
Medford (★Boston) 57,407
New Bedford (★ 175,641) 99,922
Newton (★Boston) 82,585
Northampton (★Springfield) 29,289
Pittsfield (★ 79,250) 48,622
Quincy (★Boston) 84,985
Somerville (★Boston) 76,210
Springfield (★ 529,519) 156,983
Taunton (★ 59,700) 49,832
Waltham (★Boston) 57,878
Weymouth (★Boston) 54,063
Worcester (★ 436,905) 169,759

UNITED STATES: MICHIGAN

1990 C 9,295,297

Ann Arbor (★ 282,937) (★Detroit) 109,592
Battle Creek (★ 135,982) 53,540
Benton Harbor (★ 161,378) 12,818
Clinton Township (★Detroit) 77,900
Dearborn (★Detroit) 89,286
Dearborn Heights (★Detroit) 60,838
Detroit (★ 4,665,236) 1,027,974
East Lansing (★Lansing) 50,677
Farmington Hills (★Detroit) 74,652
Flint (★ 430,459) 140,761
Grand Rapids (★ 688,399) 189,126
Holland (★Grand Rapids) 30,745
Jackson (★ 149,756) 37,446
Kalamazoo (★ 223,411) 80,277
Lansing (★ 432,674) 127,321
Livonia (★Detroit) 100,850
Monroe (★ 62,600) (★Detroit) 22,902
Muskegon (★ 158,983) 40,283
Pontiac (★Detroit) 71,166
Port Huron (★Sarnia, Canada) 33,694
Redford Township (★Detroit) 54,387
Roseville (★Detroit) 51,412
Royal Oak (★Detroit) 65,410
Saginaw (★ 399,320) 69,512
Saint Clair Shores (★Detroit) 68,107
Sault Sainte Marie 14,689
Southfield (★Detroit) 75,728
Sterling Heights (★Detroit) 117,810
Taylor (★Detroit) 70,811
Troy (★Detroit) 72,884
Warren (★Detroit) 144,864
Westland (★Detroit) 84,724
Wyoming (★Grand Rapids) 63,891

UNITED STATES: MINNESOTA

1990 C 4,375,099

Bloomington (★Minneapolis) 86,335
Brooklyn Park (★Minneapolis) 56,381
Burnsville (★Minneapolis) 51,288
Coon Rapids (★Minneapolis) 52,978
Duluth (★ 239,971) 85,493
Mankato (★ 48,400) 31,477
Minneapolis (★ 2,464,124) 368,383
Plymouth (★Minneapolis) 50,889
Rochester (★ 106,470) 70,745
Saint Cloud (★ 190,921) 48,812
Saint Paul (★Minneapolis) 272,235

UNITED STATES: MISSISSIPPI

1990 C 2,573,216

Biloxi (★ 197,125) 46,319
Columbus (★ 52,100) 23,799
Greenville (★ 48,500) 45,226
Gulfport (★Biloxi) 40,775
Hattiesburg (★ 71,600) 41,882
Jackson (★ 395,396) 196,637
Laurel (★ 47,300) 18,827
Meridian (★ 60,600) 41,036
Natchez (★ 45,700) 19,460
Pascagoula (★ 115,243) 25,899
Vicksburg (★ 43,500) 20,908

UNITED STATES: MISSOURI

1990 C 5,117,073

Cape Girardeau (★ 59,100) 34,438
Columbia (★ 112,379) 69,101
Florissant (★Saint Louis) 51,206
Independence (★Kansas City) 112,301
Jefferson City (★ 60,100) 35,481
Joplin (★ 134,910) 40,961
Kansas City (★ 1,566,280) 435,146
Saint Charles (★Saint Louis) 54,555
Saint Joseph (★ 83,083) 71,852
Saint Louis (★ 2,444,099) 396,685
Springfield (★ 240,593) 140,494

UNITED STATES: MONTANA

1990 C 799,065

Billings (★ 113,419) 81,151
Butte (★ 33,900) 33,336
Great Falls (★ 77,691) 55,097
Helena 24,569
Missoula (★ 65,700) 42,918

UNITED STATES: NEBRASKA

1990 C 1,578,385

Grand Island (★ 42,200) 39,386
Lincoln (★ 213,641) 191,972
Omaha (★ 618,262) 335,795

UNITED STATES: NEVADA

1990 C 1,201,833

Carson City 40,443
Henderson (★Las Vegas) 64,942
Las Vegas (★ 741,459) 258,295
Paradise (★Las Vegas) 124,682
Reno (★ 254,667) 133,850
Sparks (★Reno) 53,367
Sunrise Manor (★Las Vegas) 95,362

UNITED STATES: NEW HAMPSHIRE

1990 C 1,109,252

Concord (★ 73,300) 36,006
Manchester (★ 147,809) 99,567
Nashua (★ 180,557) (★Boston, Ma.) 79,662
Portsmouth (★ 223,578) 25,925

UNITED STATES: NEW JERSEY

1990 C 7,730,188

Atlantic City (★ 319,416) 37,986
Bayonne (★Jersey City) 61,444
Bloomfield (★Newark) 45,061
Brick Township (★New York, N.Y.) 66,473
Camden (★Philadelphia, Pa.) 87,492
Cherry Hill (★Philadelphia, Pa.) 69,319
Clifton (★New York, N.Y.) 71,742
East Orange (★Newark) 73,552
Edison (★New York, N.Y.) 88,680
Elizabeth (★Newark) 110,002
Irvington (★Newark) 59,774
Jersey City (★ 553,099) (★New York, N.Y.) 228,537
Middletown (★New York, N.Y.) 62,298
Newark (★ 1,824,321) (★New York, N.Y.) 275,221
Passaic (★New York, N.Y.) 58,041
Paterson (★New York, N.Y.) 140,891
Trenton (★ 325,824) (★Philadelphia, Pa.) 88,675
Union (★Newark) 50,024
Union City (★Jersey City) 58,012
Vineland (★ 138,053) (★Philadelphia, Pa.) 54,780

UNITED STATES: NEW MEXICO

1990 C 1,515,069

Albuquerque (★ 480,577) 384,736
Farmington (★ 50,300) 33,997
Las Cruces (★ 135,510) 62,126
Roswell (★ 50,600) 44,654
Santa Fe (★ 117,043) 55,859

UNITED STATES: NEW YORK

1990 C 17,990,455

Albany (★ 874,304) 101,082
Auburn (★ 52,900) 31,258
Binghamton (★ 264,497) 53,008
Buffalo (★ 1,189,288) 328,123
Cheektowaga (★Buffalo) 84,387
Elmira (★ 95,195) 33,724
Glens Falls (★ 118,539) 15,023
Hempstead (★New York) 49,453
Irondequoit (★Rochester) 52,322
Ithaca (★ 82,700) 29,541
Jamestown (★ 141,895) 34,681
Kingston (★ 88,200) 23,095
Levittown (★New York) 53,286
Lockport (★ 57,500) (★Buffalo) 24,426
Mount Vernon (★New York) 67,153
Newburgh (★ 102,300) (★New York) 26,454
New Rochelle (★New York) 67,265
• New York (★ 18,087,251) 7,322,564
Niagara Falls (★ 220,756) (★Buffalo) 61,840
Poughkeepsie (★ 259,462) 28,844
Rochester (★ 1,002,410) 231,636
Schenectady (★Albany) 65,566
Syracuse (★ 659,864) 163,860
Troy (★Albany) 54,269
Utica (★ 316,633) 68,637
West Seneca (★Buffalo) 47,866
Yonkers (★New York) 188,082

UNITED STATES: NORTH CAROLINA

1990 C 6,628,637

Asheville (★ 174,821) 61,607
Burlington (★ 108,213) 39,498
Charlotte (★ 1,162,093) 395,934
Durham (★Raleigh) 136,611
Fayetteville (★ 274,566) 75,695
Gastonia (★Charlotte) 54,732
Goldsboro (★ 94,200) 40,709
Greensboro (★ 942,091) 183,521
Hickory (★ 221,700) 28,301
High Point (★Greensboro) 69,496
Jacksonville (★ 149,838) 30,013
Kannapolis (★Charlotte) 29,696
Raleigh (★ 735,480) 207,951
Rocky Mount (★ 83,400) 48,997
Salisbury (★Charlotte) 23,087
Wilmington (★ 120,284) 55,530
Winston-Salem (★Greenboro) 143,485

UNITED STATES: NORTH DAKOTA

1990 C 638,800

Bismarck (★ 83,831) 49,256
Fargo (★ 153,296) 74,111
Grand Forks (★ 70,683) 49,425
Minot (★ 39,800) 34,544

UNITED STATES: OHIO

1990 C 10,347,115

Akron (★ 657,575) (★Cleveland) 223,019
Alliance (★Canton) 23,376
Ashtabula (★ 40,900) 21,633
Brunswick (★Cleveland) 28,230
Canton (★ 394,106) 84,161
Cincinnati (★ 1,744,124) 364,040
Cleveland (★ 2,759,823) 505,616
Cleveland Heights (★Cleveland) 54,052
Columbus (★ 1,377,419) 632,910
Dayton (★ 951,270) 182,044
East Liverpool (★ 44,400) 13,654
Elyria (★Lorain) 56,746
Euclid (★Cleveland) 54,875
Hamilton (★ 291,479) (★Cincinnati) 61,368
Kettering (★Dayton) 60,569
Lakewood (★Cleveland) 59,718
Lancaster (★Columbus) 34,507
Lima (★ 154,340) 45,549
Lorain (★ 271,126) (★Cleveland) 71,245
Mansfield (★ 126,137) 50,627
Marion (★ 53,900) 34,075
Middletown (★ 107,200) (★Cincinnati) 46,022
Newark (★Columbus) 44,389
Parma (★Cleveland) 87,876
Portsmouth (★ 64,300) 22,676
Sandusky (★ 79,800) 29,764
Springfield (★Dayton) 70,487
Steubenville (★ 142,523) 22,125
Toledo (★ 614,128) 332,943
Warren (★Youngstown) 50,793
Youngstown (★ 492,619) 95,732
Zanesville (★ 67,800) 26,778

UNITED STATES: OKLAHOMA

1990 C 3,145,585

Broken Arrow (★Tulsa) 58,043
Edmond (★Oklahoma City) 52,315
Enid (★ 56,735) 45,309
Lawton (★ 111,486) 80,561
Midwest City (★Oklahoma City) 52,267
Muskogee (★ 49,500) 37,708
Norman (★Oklahoma City) 80,071
Oklahoma City (★ 958,839) 444,719
Tulsa (★ 708,954) 367,302

UNITED STATES: OREGON

1990 C 2,842,321

Beaverton (★Portland) 53,310
Corvallis (★ 98,700) 44,757
Eugene (★ 282,912) 112,669
Gresham (★Portland) 68,235
Medford (★ 146,389) 46,951
Portland (★ 1,477,895) 437,319
Salem (★ 278,024) 107,786

UNITED STATES: PENNSYLVANIA

1990 C 11,881,643

Abington (★Philadelphia) 59,300
Allentown (★ 686,688) 105,090
Altoona (★ 130,542) 51,881
Bensalem (★Philadelphia) 56,788
Bethlehem (★Allentown) 71,428
Bristol (★Philadelphia) 57,129
Butler (★ 86,500) 15,714
Coatesville (★ 93,400) (★Philadelphia) 11,038
Erie (★ 275,572) 108,718
Hanover (★York) 14,399
Harrisburg (★ 587,986) 52,376
Haverford (★Philadelphia) 49,848
Hazleton (★Scranton) 24,730
Johnstown (★ 241,247) 28,134
Lancaster (★ 422,822) 55,551
Lebanon (★Harrisburg) 24,800
Lower Merion Township (★Philadelphia) 58,003
New Castle (★ 68,400) 28,334
Oil City (★ 42,000) 11,949
Penn Hills (★Pittsburgh) 51,430
Philadelphia (★ 5,899,345) 1,585,577
Pittsburgh (★ 2,242,798) 369,879
Pottstown (★ 88,300) (★Philadelphia) 21,831
Pottsville (★ 54,200) 16,603
Reading (★ 336,523) 78,380
Scranton (★ 734,175) 81,805
Sharon (★ 121,003) 17,493
State College (★ 123,786) 38,923
Uniontown (★ 53,200) (★Pittsburgh) 12,034
Upper Darby (★Philadelphia) 84,054
Washington (★ 66,000) (★Pittsburgh) 15,864
Wilkes-Barre (★Scranton) 47,523
Williamsport (★ 118,710) 31,933
York (★ 417,848) 42,192

UNITED STATES: RHODE ISLAND

1990 C 1,003,464

Cranston (★Providence) 76,060
East Providence (★Providence) 50,380
Newport (★ 64,500) 28,227
Pawtucket (★ 329,384) (★Providence) 72,644
Providence (★ 1,141,510) 160,728
Warwick (★Providence) 85,427

UNITED STATES: SOUTH CAROLINA

1990 C 3,486,703

Anderson (★ 145,196) 26,184
Charleston (★ 506,875) 80,414
Columbia (★ 453,331) 98,052
Florence (★ 114,344) 29,813
Greenville (★ 640,861) 58,282
North Charleston (★Charleston) 70,218
Rock Hill (★Charlotte, N.C.) 41,643
Spartanburg (★Greenville) 43,467
Sumter (★ 90,300) 41,943

UNITED STATES: SOUTH DAKOTA

1990 C 696,004

Pierre 12,906
Rapid City (★ 81,343) 54,523
Sioux Falls (★ 123,809) 100,814

UNITED STATES: TENNESSEE

1990 C 4,877,185

Bristol (★Johnson City) 23,421
Chattanooga (★ 433,210) 152,466
Clarksville (★ 169,439) 75,494
Jackson (★ 77,982) 48,949
Johnson City (★ 436,047) 49,381
Kingsport (★Johnson City) 36,365
Knoxville (★ 604,816) 165,121
Memphis (★ 981,747) 610,337
Murfreesboro (★Nashville) 44,922
Nashville (★ 985,026) 487,969

UNITED STATES: TEXAS

1990 C 16,986,510

Abilene (★ 119,655) 106,654
Amarillo (★ 187,547) 157,615
Arlington (★Fort Worth) 261,721
Austin (★ 781,572) 465,622
Baytown (★Houston) 63,850
Beaumont (★ 361,226) 114,323

C Census. E Official estimate. U Unofficial estimate.
• Largest city in country.

★ Population or designation of metropolitan area, including suburbs (see headnote).
▲ Population of an entire municipality, commune, or district, including rural area.

Brownsville (★ 460,000) 98,962
Bryan (★ 121,862) 55,002
Carrollton (★Dallas) 82,169
College Station (★Bryan) 52,456
Corpus Christi
(★ 349,894) 257,453
Dallas (★ 3,885,415) 1,006,877
Denton (★Dallas) 66,270
El Paso (★ 650,000) 515,342
Fort Worth
(★ 1,332,053) (★Dallas) 447,619
Freeport
(★ 88,600) (★Houston) 11,389
Galveston
(★ 217,399) (★Houston) 59,070
Garland (★Dallas)............... 180,650
Grand Prairie (★Dallas)...........99,616
Harlingen (★Brownsville) 48,735
Houston (★ 3,711,043)....... 1,630,553
Irving (★Dallas)................. 155,037
Killeen (★ 255,301)...............63,535
Laredo (★ 354,000) 122,899
Longview (★ 162,431) 70,311
Lubbock (★ 222,636) 186,206
Lufkin (★ 56,000) 30,206
McAllen (★ 383,545)..............84,021
Mesquite (★Dallas) 101,484
Midland (★ 106,611) 89,443
Odessa (★ 118,934)...............89,699
Pasadena (★Houston).......... 119,363
Plano (★Dallas)................. 128,713
Port Arthur (★Beaumont) 58,724
Richardson (★Dallas) 74,840
San Angelo (★ 98,458)...........84,474
San Antonio
(★ 1,302,099) 935,933
Sherman (★ 95,021) 31,601
Temple (★Killeen) 46,109
Texarkana (★ 120,132) 31,656
Tyler (★ 151,309) 75,450
Victoria (★ 74,361) 55,076
Waco (★ 189,123)............. 103,590
Wichita Falls (★ 122,378) 96,259

UNITED STATES: UTAH

1990 C 1,722,850

Logan (★ 60,300) 32,762
Ogden (★Salt Lake City) 63,909
Orem (★Provo) 67,561
Provo (★ 263,590) 86,835
Salt Lake City
(★ 1,072,227) 159,936
Sandy (★Salt Lake City) 75,058
West Valley City (★Salt
Lake City) 86,976

UNITED STATES: VERMONT

1990 C 562,758

Burlington (★ 131,439) 39,127
Montpelier (★ 52,800) 8,247
Rutland (★ 53,000)...............18,230

UNITED STATES: VIRGINIA

1990 C 6,187,358

Alexandria (★Washington,
D.C.) 111,183
Annandale (★Washington,
D.C.) 50,975
Arlington (★Washington,
D.C.) 170,936
Charlottesville
(★ 131,107) 40,341
Chesapeake (★Norfolk) 151,976
Danville (★ 108,711) 53,056
Hampton (★Norfolk)............ 133,793
Lynchburg (★ 142,199) 66,049
Martinsville (★ 67,100) 16,162
Newport News (★Norfolk) 170,045
Norfolk (★ 1,396,107).......... 261,229
Portsmouth (★Norfolk) 103,907
Richmond (★ 865,640)......... 203,056
Roanoke (★ 224,477) 96,397
Suffolk (★Norfolk) 52,141
Virginia Beach (★Norfolk) 393,069

UNITED STATES: WASHINGTON

1990 C 4,866,692

Bellevue (★Seattle)...............86,874
Bellingham (★ 127,780) 52,179
Bremerton (★ 189,731) 38,142
Everett (★Seattle) 69,961
Lakes District (★Tacoma) 58,412
Longview (★ 67,100).............31,499
Olympia (★ 161,238) 33,840
Pasco (★Richland).................20,337
Seattle (★ 2,559,164) 516,259
Spokane (★ 361,364) 177,196
Tacoma
(★ 586,203) (★Seattle) 176,664
Yakima (★ 188,823)..............54,827

UNITED STATES: WEST VIRGINIA

1990 C 1,793,477

Beckley (★ 64,300)...............18,296
Charleston (★ 250,454) 57,287
Clarksburg (★ 53,800) 18,059
Fairmont (★ 53,700)..............20,210
Huntington (★ 312,529) 54,844
Morgantown (★ 71,500) 25,879
Parkersburg (★ 149,169) 33,862
Wheeling (★ 159,301) 34,882

UNITED STATES: WISCONSIN

1990 C 4,891,769

Appleton (★ 315,121) 65,695
Beloit (★Janesville) 35,573
Eau Claire (★ 137,543)...........56,856
Fond du Lac (★ 52,400) 37,757
Green Bay (★ 194,594) 96,466
Janesville (★ 139,510) 52,133
Kenosha (★ 128,181)
(★Chicago, Il.) 80,352
La Crosse (★ 97,904) 51,003
Madison (★ 367,085)........... 191,262
Manitowoc (★ 57,300) 32,520
Milwaukee (★ 1,607,183) 628,088
Oshkosh (★Appleton) 55,006
Racine
(★ 175,034) (★Milwaukee)......84,298
Sheboygan (★ 103,877) 49,676
Waukesha (★Milwaukee) 56,958
Wausau (★ 115,400) 37,060
Wauwatosa (★Milwaukee) 49,366
West Allis (★Milwaukee) 63,221

UNITED STATES: WYOMING

1990 C 453,588

Casper (★ 61,226) 46,742
Cheyenne (★ 73,142) 50,008

URUGUAY

1985 C 2,955,241

Las
Piedras (★Montevideo) 58,288
Melo..............................42,615
Mercedes.........................36,702
Minas.............................34,661
• MONTEVIDEO
(★ 1,550,000) 1,251,647
Paysandú.........................76,191
Rivera 57,316
Salto 80,823

UZBEKISTAN

1991 E 20,708,200

Almalyk......................... 116,400
Andižan 298,300
Angren 132,600
Bekabad...........................82,800
Buchara 249,600
Chodžejli 61,200
Čirčik (★Taškent)............... 158,400
Denau 49,300
Džizak 109,700
Fergana 193,700
Gulistan 54,500
Jangijul' 56,900
Kagan 49,800
Karši............................. 168,000
Kattakurgan 59,600
Kokand 175,000
Margilan 124,900
Namangan...................... 319,200
Navoi 111,600
Nukus 179,600
Šachrichan 47,600
Šachrisabz 53,200
Samarkand 370,500
• TAŠKENT (TASHKENT)
(★ 2,325,000) 2,113,300
Termez 90,400
Urgenč 130,400

VANUATU

1989 C 142,944

• PORT VILA (★ 23,000)...........19,311

VATICAN CITY / Città del Vaticano

1988 E 766

VENEZUELA

1990 C 18,105,265

Acarigua........................ 116,551
Anaco 61,386
Araure 55,299
Barcelona 221,792
Barinas 153,630
Barquisimeto 625,450
Baruta (★Caracas) 182,941
Cabimas........................ 165,755
Cagua 73,465
Calabozo 79,578
• CARACAS (★ 4,000,000) ... 1,822,465
Carora............................70,715
Carúpano.........................92,333
Catia La Mar (★Caracas) 100,104
Chacao (★Caracas) 66,897
Ciudad Bolívar.................. 225,340
Ciudad Guayana 453,047
Ciudad Ojeda (Lagunillas) 73,473
Coro............................ 124,506
Cumaná 212,432
El Limón..........................90,030
El Tigre...........................93,229
Guacara 100,766
Guanare 84,904
Guarenas (★Caracas) 134,158
La Asunción......................16,552
La Victoria........................77,326
Los Dos
Caminos (★Caracas)...........59,141
Los Teques (★Caracas) 140,617
Maiquetía (★Caracas) 62,834
Maracaibo 1,249,670
Maracay 354,196
Mariara 69,404
Maturín 206,654
Mérida.......................... 170,902
Palo Negro 50,718
Petare (★Caracas)............. 338,417
Porlamar 62,732
Pozuelos (1981 C) 80,342
Puerto Ayacucho 36,107
Puerto Cabello 128,825
Puerto la Cruz.................. 115,731
Punto Fijo 88,681
San Carlos 50,708
San Cristóbal................... 220,675
San Felipe 65,509
San Fernando 72,716
San Juan de los Morros 67,791
Trujillo 33,241
Tucupita 41,117
Turmero 174,280
Valencia 903,621
Valera 97,012
Valle de la Pascua 67,100
Villa de Cura 51,096

VIETNAM / Viet Nam

1989 C 64,411,668

Bac Giang 50,879
Bac Lieu...........................83,483
Bien Hoa 273,879
Buon Me Thuot 97,044
Ca Mau 81,901
Cam Pha 105,336
Can Tho......................... 208,078
Chau Doc 50,935
Da Lat........................... 102,583
Da Nang........................ 369,734
Hai Duong.........................53,370
Hai Phong (▲ 1,447,523) 351,919
HA NOI (★ 1,275,000) 905,939
Hoa Binh 69,323
Hon Gai 123,102
Hue............................. 211,718
Long Xuyen 128,814
Minh Hai (1979 C)................72,517
My Tho.......................... 104,724
Nam Dinh 165,629
Nha Trang 213,460
Phan Rang 71,111
Phan Thiet 114,236
Play Cu............................76,991
Qui Nhon 159,852
Rach Gia 137,784
Sa Dec 50,733
Soc Trang 87,899
Soc Trang 87,899
Tan An 50,288
Thai Binh 57,640
Thai Nguyen.................... 124,871
Thanh Hoa 84,951
• Thanh Pho Ho Chi Minh
(Saigon) (★ 3,300,000) ... 2,796,229
Tra Vinh 47,785
Tuy Hoa 54,081
Uong Bi 49,595
Viet Tri 73,347
Vinh 110,793
Vinh Long 81,620
Vung Tau........................ 123,528
Yen Bai............................58,645

VIRGIN ISLANDS OF THE UNITED STATES

1990 C 101,809

• CHARLOTTE AMALIE
(★ 32,000) 12,331

WALLIS AND FUTUNA / Wallis et Futuna

1983 E 12,408

• MATĀ'UTU 815
Ono (1976 C)......................... 624

WEST BANK

1992 E 1,653,000

Al - Quds (Jerusalem)
(★Yerushalayim, Israel) 285,000
Arīḥā (Jericho)
(Independent City)
(1967 C) 6,829
Bayt Lahm (Bethlehem)
(1971 E)........................25,000
Nābulus (1971 E).................64,000

WESTERN SAHARA

1982 E 142,000

• EL AAIÚN 93,875

WESTERN SAMOA / Samoa i Sisifo

1981 C 156,349

• APIA..............................33,170

YEMEN / Al-Yaman

1990 E 15,267,000

'Adan (★ 318,000)
(1984 E)...................... 176,100
Al-Hudaydah (1986 C).......... 155,110
Al-Mukallā (1984 E) 58,000
• ṢAN'Ā' (1986 C) 427,150
Ta'izz (1986 C)................. 178,043

YUGOSLAVIA / Jugoslavija

1991 C 10,337,920

• BEOGRAD (★ 1,554,826) ... 1,136,786
Čačak 72,392
Kragujevac 146,607
Kraljevo 56,616
Kruševac 58,114
Leskovac..........................61,963
Niš............................... 175,555
Novi Pazar 51,906
Novi Sad 178,896
Pančevo (★Beograd) 72,717
Podgorica 118,059
Priština (▲ 244,830)
(1987 E)...................... 125,400
Šabac 54,829
Smederevo 64,257
Sombor............................48,789
Subotica........................ 100,219
Užice 53,666
Valjevo 58,324
Vranje 51,695
Zrenjanin 81,382

ZAIRE / Zaïre

1984 C 30,729,443

Bandundu 63,642
Beni 44,141
Boma............................ 197,617
Bukavu 167,950
Bumba 51,197
Bunia 59,598
Butembo 73,312
Gandajika 64,878
Gbadolite 27,063
Gemena 63,052
Goma.............................77,908
Ilebo (Port-Francqui).............53,887
Isiro 78,268
Kalemie (Albertville) 73,528
Kamina 62,789
Kananga (Luluabourg).......... 298,693
Kikwit 149,296
Kindu 66,812
• KINSHASA
(LÉOPOLDVILLE)
(1986 E).................... 3,000,000
Kipushi 53,207
Kisangani (Stanleyville) 317,581
Kolwezi......................... 416,122
Likasi (Jadotville) 213,862
Lubumbashi
(Élisabethville)................ 564,830
Matadi.......................... 138,798
Mbandaka (Coquilhatville) 137,291
Mbuji-Mayi (Bakwanga) 486,235
Mwene-Ditu 94,560
Tshikapa 116,016
Uvira 74,432

ZAMBIA

1990 C 7,818,447

Chililabombwe (Bancroft)
(★ 76,848) 35,200
Chingola......................... 167,954
Kabwe (Broken Hill) 166,519
Kalulushi..........................75,197
Kitwe (★ 338,207).............. 247,100
Livingstone 82,218
Luanshya (★ 146,275) 79,500
• LUSAKA......................... 982,362
Mufulira (★ 152,944) 85,000
Ndola........................... 376,311

ZIMBABWE

1983 E 7,740,000

Bulawayo....................... 429,000
Chitungwiza (★Harare) 202,000
Gweru (1982 C) 78,940
• HARARE (★ 890,000).......... 681,000
Mutare (1982 C)..................75,358

C Census. E Official estimate. U Unofficial estimate.
• Largest city in country.

★ Population or designation of metropolitan area, including suburbs (see headnote).
▲ Population of an entire municipality, commune, or district, including rural area.

United States General Information

Geographical Facts

ELEVATION

The highest elevation in the United States is Mount McKinley, Alaska, 20,320 feet.

The lowest elevation in the United States is in Death Valley, California, 282 feet below sea level.

The average elevation of the United States is 2,500 feet.

EXTREMITIES

Direction	Location	Latitude	Longitude
North	Point Barrow, Ak.	71° 23'N.	156° 29'W.
South	Ka Lae (point) Hi.	18° 56'N.	155° 41'W.
East	West Quoddy Head, Me.	44° 49'N.	66° 57'W.
West	Cape Wrangell, Ak.	52° 55'N.	172° 27'E.

LENGTH OF BOUNDARIES

The total length of the Canadian boundary of the United States is 5,525 miles.

The total length of the Mexican boundary of the United States is 1,933 miles.

The total length of the Atlantic coastline of the United States is 2,069 miles.

The total length of the Pacific and Arctic coastline of the United States is 8,683 miles.

The total length of the Gulf of Mexico coastline of the United States is 1,631 miles.

The total length of all coastlines and land boundaries of the United States is 19,841 miles.

The total length of the tidal shoreline and land boundaries of the United States is 96,091 miles.

GEOGRAPHIC CENTERS

The geographic center of the United States (including Alaska and Hawaii) is in Butte County, South Dakota at 44° 58'N., 103° 46'W.

The geographic center of North America is in North Dakota, a few miles west of Devils Lake, at 48° 10'N., 100° 10'W.

EXTREMES OF TEMPERATURE

The highest temperature ever recorded in the United States was 134° F., at Greenland Ranch, Death Valley, California, on July 10, 1913.

The lowest temperature ever recorded in the United States was -80° F., at Prospect Creek, Alaska, on January 23, 1971.

Historical Facts

TERRITORIAL ACQUISITIONS

Accession	Date	Area (sq. mi.)	Cost in Dollars
Original territory of the Thirteen States	1790	888,685	
Purchase of Louisiana Territory, from France	1803	827,192	$11,250,000
By treaty with Spain: Florida	1819	58,560	5,000,000
Other areas	1819	13,443	
Annexation of Texas	1845	390,144	
Oregon Territory, by treaty with Great Britain	1846	285,580	
Mexican Cession	1848	529,017	$15,000,000
Gadsden Purchase, from Mexico	1853	29,640	$10,000,000
Purchase of Alaska, from Russia	1867	586,412	7,200,000
Annexation of Hawaiian Islands	1898	6,450	
Puerto Rico, by treaty with Spain	1899	3,435	
Guam, by treaty with Spain	1899	212	
American Samoa, by treaty with Great Britain and Germany	1900	76	
Virgin Islands, by purchase from Denmark	1917	133	$25,000,000

Note: The Philippines, ceded by Spain in 1898 for $20,000,000 were a territorial possession of the United States from 1898 to 1946. On July 4, 1946 they became the independent Republic of the Philippines.

Note: The Canal Zone, ceded by Panama in 1903 for $10,000,000 was a territory of the United States from 1903 to 1979. As a result of treaties signed in 1977, sovereignty over the Canal Zone reverted to Panama in 1979.

WESTWARD MOVEMENT OF CENTER OF POPULATION

Year	U.S.Population Total at Census	Approximate Location
1790	3,929,214	23 miles east of Baltimore, Md.
1800	5,308,483	18 miles west of Baltimore, Md.
1810	7,239,881	40 miles northwest of Washington, D.C.
1820	9,638,453	16 miles east of Moorefield, W. Va.
1830	12,866,020	19 miles southwest of Moorefield, W. Va.
1840	17,069,453	16 miles south of Clarksburg, W. Va.
1850	23,191,876	23 miles southeast of Parkersburg, W. Va.
1860	31,443,321	20 miles southeast of Chillicothe, Ohio
1870	39,818,449	48 miles northeast of Cincinnati, Ohio
1880	50,155,783	8 miles southwest of Cincinnati, Ohio
1890	62,947,714	20 miles east of Columbus, Ind.
1900	75,994,575	6 miles southeast of Columbus, Ind.
1910	91,972,266	Bloomington, Ind.
1920	105,710,620	8 miles southwest of Spencer, Ind.
1930	122,775,046	3 miles northeast of Linton, Ind.
1940	131,669,275	2 miles southeast of Carlisle, Ind.
1950	150,697,361	8 miles northwest of Olney, Ill.
1960	179,323,175	6 miles northwest of Centralia, Ill.
1970	204,816,296	5 miles southeast of Mascoutah, Ill.
1980	226,549,010	1/4 mile west of DeSoto, Mo.
1990	248,709,873	10 miles southeast of Steelville, Mo.

State Areas and Populations

STATE	Land Area* square miles	Water Area* square miles	Total Area* square miles	Area Rank land area	1990 Population	1990 Population per square mile	1980 Population	1970 Population	1960 Population	Population Rank 1990	Population Rank 1980	Population Rank 1970
Alabama	50,750	1,673	52,423	28	4,040,587	80	3,894,046	3,444,354	3,266,740	22	22	21
Alaska	570,374	86,051	656,424	1	550,043	1.0	401,851	302,583	226,167	49	50	50
Arizona	113,642	364	114,006	6	3,665,228	32	2,716,756	1,775,399	1,302,161	24	29	33
Arkansas	52,075	1,107	53,182	27	2,350,725	45	2,286,357	1,923,322	1,786,272	33	33	32
California	155,973	7,734	163,707	3	29,760,021	191	23,667,372	19,971,069	15,717,204	1	1	1
Colorado	103,730	371	104,100	8	3,294,394	32	2,889,735	2,209,596	1,753,947	26	28	30
Connecticut	4,845	698	5,544	48	3,287,116	678	3,107,576	3,032,217	2,535,234	27	25	24
Delaware	1,955	535	2,489	49	666,168	341	594,317	548,104	446,292	46	47	41
District of Columbia	61	7	68	.....	606,900	9,949	638,432	756,668	763,956	.....	.....	.....
Florida	53,997	11,761	65,758	26	12,937,926	240	9,747,015	6,791,418	4,951,560	4	7	9
Georgia	57,919	1,522	59,441	21	6,478,216	112	5,462,982	4,587,930	3,943,116	11	13	15
Hawaii	6,423	4,508	10,932	47	1,108,229	173	964,691	769,913	632,772	41	39	40
Idaho	82,751	823	83,574	11	1,006,749	12	944,127	713,015	667,191	42	41	43
Illinois	55,593	2,325	57,918	24	11,430,602	206	11,427,414	11,110,285	10,081,158	6	5	5
Indiana	35,870	550	36,420	38	5,544,159	155	5,490,212	5,195,392	4,662,498	14	12	11
Iowa	55,875	401	56,276	23	2,776,755	50	2,913,808	2,825,368	2,757,537	30	27	25
Kansas	81,823	459	82,282	13	2,477,574	30	2,364,236	2,249,071	2,178,611	32	32	28
Kentucky	39,732	679	40,411	36	3,685,296	93	3,660,324	3,220,711	3,038,156	23	23	23
Louisiana	43,566	8,277	51,843	33	4,219,973	97	4,206,098	3,644,637	3,257,022	21	19	20
Maine	30,865	4,523	35,387	39	1,227,928	40	1,125,043	993,722	969,265	38	38	38
Maryland	9,775	2,633	12,407	42	4,781,468	489	4,216,933	3,923,897	3,100,689	19	18	18
Massachusetts	7,838	2,717	10,555	45	6,016,425	768	5,737,093	5,689,170	5,148,578	13	11	10
Michigan	56,809	40,001	96,810	22	9,295,297	164	9,262,044	8,881,826	7,823,194	8	8	7
Minnesota	79,617	7,326	86,943	14	4,375,099	55	4,075,970	3,806,103	3,413,864	20	21	19
Mississippi	46,914	1,520	48,434	31	2,573,216	55	2,520,698	2,216,994	2,178,141	31	31	29
Missouri	68,898	811	69,709	18	5,117,073	74	4,916,759	4,677,623	4,319,813	15	15	13
Montana	145,556	1,490	147,046	4	799,065	5.5	786,690	694,409	674,767	44	44	44
Nebraska	76,878	481	77,358	15	1,578,385	21	1,569,825	1,485,333	1,411,330	36	35	35
Nevada	109,806	761	110,567	7	1,201,833	11	800,508	488,738	285,278	39	43	47
New Hampshire	8,969	382	9,351	44	1,109,252	124	920,610	737,681	606,921	40	42	42
New Jersey	7,419	1,303	8,722	46	7,730,188	1,042	7,365,011	7,171,112	6,066,782	9	9	8
New Mexico	121,365	234	121,598	5	1,515,069	12	1,303,542	1,017,055	951,023	37	37	37
New York	47,224	7,251	54,475	30	17,990,455	381	17,558,165	18,241,391	16,782,304	2	2	2
North Carolina	48,718	5,103	53,821	29	6,628,637	136	5,880,415	5,084,411	4,556,155	10	10	12
North Dakota	68,994	1,710	70,704	17	638,800	9.3	652,717	617,792	632,446	47	46	46
Ohio	40,953	3,875	44,828	35	10,847,115	265	10,797,603	10,657,423	9,706,397	7	6	6
Oklahoma	68,679	1,224	69,903	19	3,145,585	46	3,025,487	2,559,463	2,328,284	28	26	27
Oregon	96,003	2,383	98,386	10	2,842,321	30	2,633,156	2,091,533	1,768,687	29	30	31
Pennsylvania	44,820	1,239	46,058	32	11,881,643	265	11,864,751	11,800,766	11,319,366	5	4	3
Rhode Island	1,045	500	1,545	50	1,003,464	960	947,154	949,723	859,488	43	40	39
South Carolina	30,111	1,896	32,007	40	3,486,703	116	3,120,730	2,590,713	2,382,594	25	24	26
South Dakota	75,898	1,224	77,121	16	696,004	9.2	690,768	666,257	680,514	45	45	45
Tennessee	41,220	926	42,146	34	4,877,185	118	4,591,023	3,926,018	3,567,089	17	17	17
Texas	261,914	6,687	268,601	2	16,986,510	65	14,225,288	11,198,655	9,579,677	3	3	4
Utah	82,168	2,736	84,904	12	1,722,850	21	1,461,037	1,059,273	890,627	35	36	36
Vermont	9,249	366	9,615	43	562,758	61	511,456	444,732	389,881	48	48	48
Virginia	39,598	3,171	42,769	37	6,187,358	156	5,346,797	4,651,448	3,966,949	12	14	14
Washington	66,582	4,721	71,303	20	4,866,692	73	4,132,353	3,413,244	2,853,214	18	20	22
West Virginia	24,087	145	24,231	41	1,793,477	74	1,950,186	1,744,237	1,860,421	34	34	34
Wisconsin	54,314	11,190	65,503	25	4,891,769	90	4,705,642	4,417,821	3,951,777	16	16	16
Wyoming	97,105	714	97,818	9	453,588	4.7	469,557	332,416	330,066	50	49	49
United States	3,536,342	251,083	3,787,425	.....	248,709,873	70	226,542,360	203,302,031	179,323,175	.....	.....	.....

*The sum of the area figures for all states does not equal U.S. total due to rounding.

United States 1990 Populations and Zip Codes

The following alphabetical list shows populations for all counties and over 15,000 selected cities and towns in the United States. ZIP codes are shown for all of the cities listed in the table. The state abbreviation following each name is that used by the United States Postal Service.

ZIP codes are listed for cities and towns after the state abbreviations. For each city with more than one ZIP code, the range of numbers assigned to the city is shown: For example, the ZIP code range for Chicago is 60601–99, and this indicates that the numbers between 60601 and 60699 are valid Chicago ZIP codes. ZIP codes are not listed for counties.

Populations for cities and towns appear as *italics* after the ZIP codes, and populations for counties appear after the state abbreviations. These populations are either 1990 census figures or, where census data are not available, estimates created by Rand McNally. City populations are for central cities, not metropolitan areas. For New England, 1990 census populations are given for incorporated cities. Estimates are used for unincorporated places that are not treated separately by the census. 'Town' (or 'township') populations are not included unless the town is considered to be primarily urban and contains only one commonly used placename.

Counties are identified by a square symbol (□).

Abbreviations for State Names

AK	Alaska	**IA**	Iowa	**MS**	Mississippi	**PA**	Pennsylvania
AL	Alabama	**ID**	Idaho	**MT**	Montana	**RI**	Rhode Island
AR	Arkansas	**IL**	Illinois	**NC**	North Carolina	**SC**	South Carolina
AZ	Arizona	**IN**	Indiana	**ND**	North Dakota	**SD**	South Dakota
CA	California	**KS**	Kansas	**NE**	Nebraska	**TN**	Tennessee
CO	Colorado	**KY**	Kentucky	**NH**	New Hampshire	**TX**	Texas
CT	Connecticut	**LA**	Louisiana	**NJ**	New Jersey	**UT**	Utah
DC	District of Columbia	**MA**	Massachusetts	**NM**	New Mexico	**VA**	Virginia
DE	Delaware	**MD**	Maryland	**NV**	Nevada	**VT**	Vermont
FL	Florida	**ME**	Maine	**NY**	New York	**WA**	Washington
GA	Georgia	**MI**	Michigan	**OH**	Ohio	**WI**	Wisconsin
HI	Hawaii	**MN**	Minnesota	**OK**	Oklahoma	**WV**	West Virginia
		MO	Missouri	**OR**	Oregon	**WY**	Wyoming

A

Abbeville, AL 36310 • *3,173*
Abbeville, LA 70510–11 • *11,187*
Abbeville, SC 29620 • *5,778*
Abbeville □, SC • *23,862*
Abbotsford, WI 54405 • *1,916*
Abbott Run Valley, RI 02864 • *1,050*
Aberdeen, ID 83210 • *1,406*
Aberdeen, MD 21001 • *13,087*
Aberdeen, MS 39730 • *6,837*
Aberdeen, NC 28315 • *2,700*
Aberdeen, OH 45101 • *1,329*
Aberdeen, SD 57401–02 • *24,927*
Aberdeen, WA 98520 • *16,565*
Abernathy, TX 79311 • *2,720*
Abilene, KS 67410 • *6,242*
Abilene, TX 79601–08 • *106,654*
Abingdon, IL 61410 • *3,597*
Abingdon, VA 24210 • *7,003*
Abington, MA 02351 • *13,817*
Abington [Township], PA 19001 • *59,084*
Abita Springs, LA 70420 • *1,296*
Absarokee, MT 59001 • *1,067*
Absecon, NJ 08201 • *7,298*
Academia, OH 43050 • *1,447*
Acadia □, LA • *55,882*
Accomack □, VA • *31,703*
Ackerman, MS 39735 • *1,573*
Ackley, IA 50601 • *1,696*
Acton, CA 93510 • *1,471*
Acton, MA 01720 • *2,300*
Acushnet, MA 02743 • *6,030*
Acworth, GA 30101 • *4,519*
Ada, MN 56510 • *1,708*
Ada, OH 45810 • *5,413*
Ada, OK 74820–21 • *15,820*
Ada □, ID • *205,775*
Adair □, IA • *8,409*
Adair □, KY • *15,360*
Adair □, MO • *24,577*
Adair □, OK • *18,421*
Adairsville, GA 30103 • *2,131*
Adams, CO 80022 • *2,200*
Adams, MA 01220 • *6,356*
Adams, NY 13605 • *1,753*
Adams, WI 53910 • *1,715*
Adams □, CO • *265,038*
Adams □, ID • *3,254*
Adams □, IL • *66,090*
Adams □, IN • *31,095*
Adams □, IA • *4,866*
Adams □, MS • *35,356*
Adams □, NE • *29,625*
Adams □, ND • *3,174*
Adams □, OH • *25,371*
Adams □, PA • *78,274*
Adams □, WA • *13,603*
Adams □, WI • *15,682*
Adams Center, NY 13606 • *1,675*
Adamstown, PA 19501 • *1,108*
Adamsville, AL 35005 • *4,161*
Adamsville, RI 02801 • *600*
Adamsville, TN 38310 • *1,745*
Addis, LA 70710 • *1,222*
Addison, CT 06033 • *2,460*
Addison, IL 60101 • *32,058*
Addison, NY 14801 • *1,842*
Addison, TX 75001 • *8,783*
Addison □, VT • *32,953*
Addyston, OH 45001 • *1,198*
Adel, GA 31620 • *5,093*
Adel, IA 50003 • *3,304*
Adelanto, CA 92301 • *8,517*
Adelphi, MD 20783 • *13,524*
Adobe Acres, NM 87105 • *2,400*
Adrian, MI 49221 • *22,097*
Adrian, MN 56110 • *1,141*
Adrian, MO 64720 • *1,582*
Advance, MO 63730 • *1,139*
Affton, MO 63123 • *21,106*
Afton, DE 19810 • *1,200*
Afton, MN 55001 • *2,645*
Afton, WY 83110 • *1,394*
Agawam, MA 01001 • *10,190*
Agoura Hills, CA 91301 • *20,390*
Ahoskie, NC 27910 • *4,391*
Aiea, HI 96701 • *8,906*
Aiken, SC 29801–03 • *19,872*
Aiken □, SC • *120,940*
Ainsworth, NE 69210 • *1,870*
Air Park West, NE 68524 • *3,100*
Aitkin, MN 56431 • *1,698*
Aitkin □, MN • *12,425*
Ajo, AZ 85321 • *2,919*
Akiachak, AK 99551 • *400*
Akron, CO 80720 • *1,599*
Akron, IA 51001 • *1,450*
Akron, NY 14001 • *2,906*
Akron, OH 44301–98 • *223,019*
Akron, PA 17501 • *3,869*
Alabaster, AL 35007 • *14,732*
Alachua, FL 32615 • *4,529*
Alachua □, FL • *181,596*
Alakanuk, AK 99554 • *544*
Alamance □, NC • *108,213*
Alameda, CA 94501 • *76,459*
Alameda, NM 87114 • *5,900*
Alameda □, CA • *1,279,182*
Alamo, CA 94507 • *12,277*
Alamo, NV 89001 • *400*
Alamo, TN 38001 • *2,426*
Alamo, TX 78516 • *8,210*
Alamogordo, NM 88310–11 • *27,596*
Alamo Heights, TX 78208 • *6,502*
Alamosa, CO 81101–02 • *7,579*
Alamosa □, CO • *13,617*
Alamosa East, CO 81101 • *1,389*
Albany, CA 94706 • *16,327*
Albany, GA 31701–07 • *78,122*
Albany, IN 47320 • *2,357*
Albany, KY 42602 • *2,062*
Albany, MN 56307 • *1,548*
Albany, MO 64402 • *1,958*
Albany, NY 12201–60 • *101,082*
Albany, OR 97321 • *29,462*
Albany, TX 76430 • *1,962*
Albany, WI 53502 • *1,140*
Albany □, NY • *292,594*
Albany □, WY • *30,797*
Albemarle, NC 28001–02 • *14,939*
Albemarle □, VA • *68,040*
Albert Lea, MN 56007 • *18,310*
Albertson, NY 11507 • *5,166*
Albertville, AL 35950 • *14,507*
Albertville, MN 55301 • *1,251*
Albia, IA 52531 • *3,870*
Albion, IL 62806 • *2,116*
Albion, IN 46701 • *1,823*
Albion, MI 49224 • *10,066*
Albion, NE 68620 • *1,916*
Albion, NY 14411 • *5,863*
Albion, PA 16401 • *1,575*
Albion, RI 02802 • *1,600*
Albuquerque, NM 87101–99 • *384,736*
Alburtis, PA 18011 • *1,415*
Alcester, SD 57001 • *843*
Alcoa, TN 37701 • *6,400*
Alcona □, MI • *10,145*
Alcorn □, MS • *31,722*
Alden, NY 14004 • *2,457*
Alderson, WV 24910 • *1,152*
Alderwood Manor, WA 98011 • *16,524*
Aledo, IL 61231 • *3,681*
Alexander □, IL • *10,626*
Alexander □, NC • *27,544*
Alexander City, AL 35010 • *14,917*
Alexandria, IN 46001 • *5,709*
Alexandria, KY 41001 • *5,592*
Alexandria, LA 71301–15 • *49,188*
Alexandria, MN 56308 • *7,838*
Alexandria, VA 22301–20 • *111,183*
Alexandria Bay, NY 13607 • *1,194*
Alfalfa □, OK • *6,416*
Alfred, NY 14802 • *4,559*
Alger □, MI • *8,972*
Algoma, WI 54201 • *3,353*
Algona, IA 50511 • *6,015*
Algona, WA 98001 • *1,694*
Algonac, MI 48001 • *4,551*
Algonquin, IL 60102 • *11,663*
Algood, TN 38501 • *2,399*
Alhambra, CA 91801–99 • *82,106*
Alice, TX 78332–33 • *19,788*
Aliceville, AL 35442 • *3,009*
Aliquippa, PA 15001 • *13,374*
Allamakee □, IA • *13,855*
Allegan, MI 49010 • *4,547*
Allegan □, MI • *90,509*
Allegany, NY 14706 • *1,980*
Allegany □, MD • *74,946*
Allegany □, NY • *50,470*
Alleghany □, NC • *9,590*
Alleghany □, VA • *13,176*
Allegheny □, PA • *1,336,449*
Allen, TX 75002 • *18,309*
Allen, TX 75002 • *18,309*
Allen □, IN • *300,836*
Allen □, KS • *14,638*
Allen □, KY • *14,628*
Allen □, LA • *21,226*
Allen □, OH • *109,755*
Allendale, NJ 07401 • *5,900*
Allendale, SC 29810 • *4,410*
Allendale □, SC • *11,722*
Allen Park, MI 48101 • *31,092*
Allenton, RI 02852 • *600*
Allentown, NJ 08501 • *1,828*
Allentown, PA 18101–95 • *105,090*
Alliance, NE 69301 • *9,765*
Alliance, OH 44601 • *23,376*
Allison, IA 50602 • *1,000*
Allison Park, PA 15101 • *5,600*
Allouez, WI 54301 • *14,431*
Alloway, NJ 08001 • *1,371*
Allyn, WA 98524 • *1,100*
Alma, AR 72921 • *2,959*
Alma, GA 31510 • *3,663*
Alma, MI 48801 • *9,034*
Alma, NE 68920 • *1,226*
Almont, MI 48003 • *2,354*
Aloha, OR 97006 • *34,284*
Alondra Park, CA 90249 • *12,215*
Alpena, MI 49707 • *11,354*
Alpena □, MI • *30,605*
Alpha, NJ 08865 • *2,530*
Alpharetta, GA 30201–02 • *13,002*
Alpine, CA 91901 • *9,695*
Alpine, NJ 07620 • *1,716*
Alpine, TX 79830–31 • *5,637*
Alpine, UT 84003 • *3,492*
Alpine □, CA • *1,113*
Alsip, IL 60658 • *18,227*
Alta, IA 51002 • *1,820*
Altadena, CA 91001–02 • *42,658*
Altamont, IL 62411 • *2,296*
Altamont, KS 67330 • *1,048*
Altamont, NY 12009 • *1,519*
Altamont, OR 97601 • *18,591*
Altamonte Springs, FL 32701 • *34,879*
Alta Sierra, CA 95949 • *5,709*
Altavista, VA 24517 • *3,686*
Alto, TX 75925 • *1,027*
Alton, IL 62002 • *32,905*
Alton, IA 51003 • *1,063*
Alton, NH 03809 • *975*
Alton Bay, NH 03810 • *1,000*
Altoona, FL 32702 • *1,300*
Altoona, IA 50009 • *7,191*
Altoona, PA 16601–03 • *51,881*
Altoona, WI 54720 • *5,889*
Alturas, CA 96101 • *3,231*
Altus, OK 73521–23 • *21,910*
Alva, FL 33920 • *1,200*
Alva, OK 73717 • *5,495*
Alvarado, TX 76009 • *2,918*
Alvin, TX 77511–12 • *19,220*
Amador □, CA • *30,039*
Amagansett, NY 11930 • *2,188*
Amana, IA 52203 • *540*
Amarillo, TX 79101–76 • *157,615*
Ambler, PA 19002 • *6,609*
Amboy, IL 61310 • *2,377*
Ambridge, PA 15003 • *8,133*
Amelia, LA 70340 • *2,447*
Amelia, OH 45102 • *1,837*
Amelia □, VA • *8,787*
Amenia, NY 12501 • *1,057*
American Canyon, CA 94589 • *7,706*
American Falls, ID 83211 • *3,757*
American Fork, UT 84003–04 • *15,696*
Americus, GA 31709 • *16,512*
Amery, WI 54001 • *2,657*
Ames, IA 50010 • *47,198*
Amesbury, MA 01913 • *12,109*
Amherst, MA 01002–04 • *17,824*
Amherst, NH 03031 • *850*
Amherst, NY 14226 • *45,600*
Amherst, OH 44001 • *10,332*
Amherst, VA 24521 • *1,060*
Amherst □, VA • *28,578*
Amherstdale, WV 25607 • *1,200*
Amite, LA 70422 • *4,236*
Amite □, MS • *13,328*
Amity, OR 97101 • *1,175*
Amityville, NY 11701 • *9,286*
Ammon, ID 83401 • *5,002*
Amory, MS 38821 • *7,093*
Amsterdam, NY 12010 • *20,714*
Anaconda, MT 59711 • *10,278*
Anacortes, WA 98221 • *11,451*
Anadarko, OK 73005 • *6,586*
Anaheim, CA 92801–25 • *266,406*
Anahola, HI 96703 • *1,181*
Anahuac, TX 77514 • *1,993*
Anamosa, IA 52205 • *5,100*
Anandale, LA 71301 • *2,000*
Anchorage, AK 99501–40 • *226,338*
Anchorage, KY 40223 • *2,082*
Andalusia, AL 36420 • *9,269*
Anderson, AK 99744 • *628*
Anderson, CA 96007 • *8,299*
Anderson, IN 46011–18 • *59,459*
Anderson, MO 64831 • *1,432*
Anderson, SC 29621–25 • *26,184*
Anderson □, KS • *7,803*
Anderson □, KY • *14,571*
Anderson □, SC • *145,196*
Anderson □, TN • *68,250*
Anderson □, TX • *48,024*
Andover, KS 67002 • *4,047*
Andover, MA 01810 • *8,242*
Andover, MN 55304 • *15,216*
Andover, NY 14806 • *1,125*
Andover, OH 44003 • *1,216*
Andrew □, MO • *14,632*
Andrews, IN 46702 • *1,118*
Andrews, NC 28901 • *2,551*
Andrews, SC 29510 • *3,050*
Andrews, TX 79714 • *10,678*
Andrews □, TX • *14,338*
Androscoggin □, ME • *105,259*
Angelina □, TX • *69,884*
Angels Camp, CA 95222 • *2,409*
Angier, NC 27501 • *2,235*
Angle Lake, WA 98188 • *5,000*
Angleton, TX 77515–16 • *17,140*
Angola, IN 46703 • *5,824*
Angola, NY 14006 • *2,231*
Angoon, AK 99820 • *638*
Aniak, AK 99557 • *540*
Anita, IA 50020 • *1,068*
Ankeny, IA 50021 • *18,482*
Anna, IL 62906 • *4,805*
Anna, OH 45302 • *1,164*
Annalee Heights, VA 22042 • *1,750*
Anna Maria, FL 34216 • *1,744*
Annandale, MN 55302 • *2,054*
Annandale, VA 22003 • *50,975*
Annapolis, MD 21401–05 • *33,187*
Ann Arbor, MI 48103–08 • *109,592*
Anne Arundel □, MD • *427,239*
Anniston, AL 36201–06 • *26,623*
Annville, PA 17003 • *4,294*
Anoka, MN 55303–04 • *17,192*
Anoka □, MN • *243,641*
Anson, TX 79501 • *2,644*
Anson □, NC • *23,474*
Ansonia, CT 06401 • *18,403*
Ansonia, OH 45303 • *1,279*
Ansted, WV 25812 • *1,643*
Antelope □, NE • *7,965*
Anthony, FL 32617 • *1,200*
Anthony, KS 67003 • *2,516*
Anthony, NM 88021 • *5,160*
Anthony, RI 02816 • *2,980*
Anthony, TX 88021 • *3,328*
Antigo, WI 54409 • *8,276*
Antioch, CA 94509 • *62,195*
Antioch, IL 60002 • *6,105*
Antlers, OK 74523 • *2,524*
Anton, TX 79313 • *1,212*
Antrim, NH 03440 • *1,325*
Antrim □, MI • *18,185*
Antwerp, OH 45813 • *1,677*
Apache, OK 73006 • *1,591*
Apache □, AZ • *61,591*
Apache Junction, AZ 85217–20 • *18,100*
Apalachicola, FL 32320 • *2,602*
Apalachin, NY 13732 • *1,208*
Apex, NC 27502 • *4,968*
Aplington, IA 50604 • *1,034*
Apollo, PA 15613 • *1,895*
Apollo Beach, FL 33572 • *6,025*
Apopka, FL 32703–04 • *13,512*
Appalachia, VA 24216 • *1,994*
Appanoose □, IA • *13,743*
Appleton, MN 56208 • *1,552*
Appleton, WI 54911–15 • *65,695*
Appleton City, MO 64724 • *1,280*
Apple Valley, CA 92307–08 • *46,079*
Apple Valley, MN 55124 • *34,598*
Applewood, CO 80401 • *11,069*
Appleyard, WA 98801 • *1,207*
Appling □, GA • *15,744*
Appomattox, VA 24522 • *1,707*
Appomattox □, VA • *12,298*
Aptos, CA 95003 • *9,061*
Aquia Harbour, VA 22554 • *6,308*
Arab, AL 35016 • *6,321*
Arabi, LA 70032 • *8,787*
Aransas □, TX • *17,892*
Aransas Pass, TX 78336 • *7,180*
Arapahoe, NE 68922 • *1,001*
Arapahoe □, CO • *391,511*
Arbuckle, CA 95912 • *1,912*
Arcade, CA 95821 • *47,900*
Arcade, NY 14009 • *2,081*
Arcadia, CA 91006–07 • *48,290*
Arcadia, FL 33821 • *6,488*
Arcadia, IN 46030 • *1,468*
Arcadia, LA 71001 • *3,079*
Arcadia, SC 29320 • *2,088*
Arcadia, WI 54612 • *2,166*
Arcanum, OH 45304 • *1,953*
Arcata, CA 95521 • *15,197*
Archbald, PA 18403 • *6,291*
Archbold, OH 43502 • *3,440*
Archdale, NC 27263 • *6,913*
Archer, FL 32618 • *1,372*
Archer □, TX • *7,973*
Archer City, TX 76351 • *1,748*
Archuleta □, CO • *5,345*
Arco, ID 83213 • *1,016*
Arcola, IL 61910 • *2,678*
Arden, CA 95825 • *62,900*
Arden Hills, MN 55112 • *9,199*
Ardmore, AL 35739 • *1,090*
Ardmore, IN 46628 • *2,250*
Ardmore, OK 73401–03 • *23,079*
Ardsley, NY 10502 • *4,272*
Arenac □, MI • *14,931*
Argos, IN 46501 • *1,642*
Arizona Sunsites, AZ 85625 • *1,100*
Arkadelphia, AR 71923 • *10,014*
Arkansas □, AR • *21,653*
Arkansas City, KS 67005 • *12,762*
Arkoma, OK 74901 • *2,393*
Arlington, GA 31713 • *1,513*
Arlington, MA 02174 • *44,630*
Arlington, MN 55307 • *1,886*
Arlington, NE 68002 • *1,178*
Arlington, NY 12603 • *11,948*
Arlington, OH 45814 • *1,267*
Arlington, SD 57212 • *908*
Arlington, TN 38002 • *1,541*
Arlington, TX 76010–18 • *261,721*
Arlington, VT 05250 • *1,311*
Arlington, VA 22201–19 • *170,936*
Arlington, WA 98223 • *4,037*
Arlington □, VA • *170,936*
Arlington Heights, IL 60004–07 • *75,460*
Arma, KS 66712 • *1,542*
Armada, MI 48005 • *1,548*
Armijo, NM 87105 • *14,600*
Armonk, NY 10504 • *2,745*
Armour, SD 57313 • *854*
Armstrong, IA 50514 • *1,025*
Armstrong □, PA • *73,478*
Armstrong □, TX • *2,021*
Arnaudville, LA 70512 • *1,444*
Arnold, MD 21012 • *20,261*
Arnold, MN 55803 • *1,500*
Arnold, MO 63010 • *18,828*
Arnold, PA 15068 • *6,113*
Arnold Mills, RI 02864 • *600*
Aroostook □, ME • *86,936*
Arroyo Grande, CA 93420–21 • *14,378*
Artesia, CA 90701–03 • *15,464*
Artesia, NM 88210–11 • *10,610*
Arthur, IL 61911 • *2,112*
Arthur □, NE • *462*
Arundel Village, MD 21225 • *3,370*
Arvada, CO 80001–06 • *89,235*
Arvin, CA 93203 • *9,286*
Asbury Park, NJ 07712 • *16,799*
Ascension □, LA • *58,214*
Ashaway, RI 02804 • *1,584*
Ashburn, GA 31714 • *4,827*
Ashburnham, MA 01430 • *1,300*
Ashdown, AR 71822 • *5,150*
Ashe □, NC • *22,209*
Asheboro, NC 27203 • *16,362*
Asherton, TX 78827 • *1,608*
Asheville, NC 28801–16 • *61,607*
Ashford, AL 36312 • *1,926*
Ash Grove, MO 65604 • *1,128*
Ashland, AL 36251 • *2,034*
Ashland, CA 94541 • *16,590*
Ashland, IL 62612 • *1,257*
Ashland, KS 67831 • *1,032*
Ashland, KY 41101–05 • *23,622*
Ashland, MA 01721 • *9,165*
Ashland, MO 65010 • *1,252*
Ashland, NE 68003 • *2,136*
Ashland, NH 03217 • *1,915*
Ashland, OH 44805 • *20,079*
Ashland, OR 97520 • *16,234*
Ashland, PA 17921 • *3,859*
Ashland, VA 23005 • *5,864*
Ashland, WI 54806 • *8,695*
Ashland □, OH • *47,507*
Ashland □, WI • *16,307*
Ashland City, TN 37015 • *2,552*
Ashley, ND 58413 • *1,052*
Ashley, OH 43003 • *1,059*
Ashley, PA 18706 • *3,291*
Ashley □, AR • *24,319*
Ashtabula, OH 44004 • *21,633*
Ashtabula □, OH • *99,821*
Ashton, ID 83420 • *1,114*
Ashton, IL 61006 • *1,042*
Ashton, MD 20861 • *1,800*
Ashton, RI 02864 • *820*
Ashville, AL 35953 • *1,494*
Ashville, OH 43103 • *2,254*
Ashwaubenon, WI 54304 • *16,376*
Asotin □, WA • *17,605*
Aspen, CO 81611–15 • *5,049*
Aspen Hill, MD 20906 • *45,494*
Aspermont, TX 79502 • *1,214*
Aspinwall, PA 15215 • *2,880*
Assinippi, MA 02339 • *1,400*
Assonet, MA 02702 • *1,200*
Assumption, IL 62510 • *1,244*
Assumption □, LA • *22,753*
Astoria, IL 61501 • *1,205*
Astoria, OR 97103 • *10,069*
Atascadero, CA 93422–23 • *23,138*
Atascosa □, TX • *30,533*
Atchison, KS 66002 • *10,656*
Atchison □, KS • *16,932*
Atchison □, MO • *7,457*
Atco, NJ 08004 • *2,020*
Athens, AL 35611 • *16,901*
Athens, GA 30601–13 • *45,734*
Athens, IL 62613 • *1,404*
Athens, NY 12015 • *1,708*
Athens, OH 45701 • *21,265*
Athens, PA 18810 • *3,468*
Athens, TN 37303 • *12,054*
Athens, TX 75751 • *10,967*
Athens □, OH • *59,549*
Atherton, CA 94027 • *7,163*
Athol, MA 01331 • *8,732*
Atkins, AR 72823 • *2,834*
Atkins, VA 24311 • *1,130*
Atkinson, NE 68713 • *1,380*
Atkinson □, GA • *613*
Atlanta, GA 30301–83 • *394,017*
Atlanta, IL 61723 • *1,616*
Atlanta, TX 75551 • *6,118*
Atlantic, IA 50022 • *7,432*
Atlantic □, NJ • *224,327*
Atlantic Beach, FL 32233 • *11,636*
Atlantic City, NJ 08401–06 • *37,986*
Atlantic Highlands, NJ 07716 • *4,629*
Atmore, AL 36502 • *8,046*
Atoka, OK 74525 • *3,298*
Atoka □, OK • *12,778*
Attala □, MS • *18,481*
Attalla, AL 35954 • *6,859*
Attica, IN 47918 • *3,457*
Attica, NY 14011 • *2,630*
Attleboro, MA 02703 • *38,383*
Atwater, CA 95301 • *22,282*
Atwater, MN 56209 • *1,053*
Atwood, IL 61913 • *1,253*
Atwood, KS 67730 • *1,388*
Atwood, TN 38220 • *1,066*
Auberry, CA 93602 • *1,866*
Auburn, AL 36830–49 • *33,830*
Auburn, CA 95603–04 • *10,592*
Auburn, GA 30203 • *3,139*
Auburn, IL 62615 • *3,724*

United States Populations and ZIP Codes

Auburn, IN 46706 • *9,379*
Auburn, KY 42206 • *1,273*
Auburn, ME 04210–12 • *24,309*
Auburn, MA 01501 • *14,845*
Auburn, MI 48611 • *1,855*
Auburn, NE 68305 • *3,443*
Auburn, NY 13021–24 • *31,258*
Auburn, WA 98001–02 • *33,102*
Auburndale, FL 33823 • *8,858*
Auburn Heights, MI 48321 • *17,076*
Audrain □, MO • *23,599*
Audubon, IA 50025 • *2,524*
Audubon, NJ 08106 • *9,205*
Audubon, PA 19407 • *6,328*
Audubon □, IA • *7,334*
Auglaize □, OH • *44,585*
August, CA 95201 • *6,376*
Augusta, AR 72006 • *2,759*
Augusta, GA 30901–19 • *44,639*
Augusta, KS 67010 • *7,876*
Augusta, KY 41002 • *1,336*
Augusta, ME 04330–38 • *21,325*
Augusta, WI 54722 • *1,510*
Augusta □, VA • *54,677*
Aulander, NC 27805 • *1,209*
Ault, CO 80610 • *1,107*
Aumsville, OR 97325 • *1,650*
Aurora, CO 80010–19 • *222,103*
Aurora, IL 60504–07 • *99,581*
Aurora, IN 47001 • *3,825*
Aurora, MN 55705 • *1,965*
Aurora, MO 65605 • *6,459*
Aurora, NE 68818 • *3,810*
Aurora, OH 44202 • *9,192*
Aurora □, SD • *3,135*
Au Sable, MI 48750 • *1,542*
Au Sable Forks, NY 12912 • *2,100*
Austell, GA 30001 • *4,173*
Austin, IN 47102 • *4,310*
Austin, MN 55912 • *21,907*
Austin, NV 89310 • *370*
Austin, TX 78701–89 • *465,622*
Austin □, TX • *19,832*
Austintown, OH 44512 • *32,371*
Autauga □, AL • *34,222*
Ava, MO 65608 • *2,938*
Avalon, CA 90704 • *2,918*
Avalon, NJ 08202 • *1,809*
Avalon, PA 15202 • *5,784*
Avella, PA 15312 • *1,200*
Avenal, CA 93204 • *9,770*
Avenel, MD • *5,600*
Avenel, NJ 07001 • *15,504*
Aventura, FL 33180 • *14,914*
Averill Park, NY 12018 • *1,656*
Avery □, NC • *14,867*
Avilla, IN 46710 • *1,366*
Avis, PA 17721 • *1,506*
Avoca, IA 51521 • *1,497*
Avoca, NY 14809 • *1,033*
Avoca, PA 18641 • *2,897*
Avocado Heights, CA 91746 • *14,232*
Avon, CT 06001 • *13,937*
Avon, MA 02322 • *5,026*
Avon, NY 14414 • *2,995*
Avon, OH 44011 • *7,337*
Avon by the Sea, NJ 07717 • *2,165*
Avondale, AZ 85323 • *16,169*
Avondale, LA 70094 • *5,813*
Avondale, OH 45404 • *5,000*
Avondale Estates, GA 30002 • *2,209*
Avon Lake, OH 44012 • *15,066*
Avonmore, PA 15618 • *1,089*
Avon Park, FL 33825 • *8,042*
Avoyelles □, LA • *39,159*
Ayden, NC 28513 • *4,740*
Ayer, MA 01432 • *2,889*
Azalea Park, FL 32807 • *8,926*
Azle, TX 76020 • *8,868*
Aztec, NM 87410 • *5,479*
Azusa, CA 91702 • *41,333*

B

Babbitt, MN 55706 • *1,562*
Babbitt, NV • *1,800*
Babylon, NY 11702–04 • *12,249*
Baca □, CO • *4,556*
Bacliff, TX 77518 • *5,549*
Bacon □, GA • *9,566*
Bad Axe, MI 48413 • *3,484*
Baden, PA 15005 • *5,074*
Badin, NC 28009 • *1,481*
Bagdad, AZ 86321 • *1,858*
Bagdad, FL 32530 • *1,457*
Baggs, WY 82321 • *272*
Bagley, MN 56621 • *1,388*
Bailey □, TX • *7,064*
Baileys Crossroads, VA 22041 • *19,507*
Bainbridge, GA 31717 • *10,712*
Bainbridge, NY 13733 • *1,550*
Baird, TX 79504 • *1,658*
Bairdford, PA 15006 • *1,200*
Baker, LA 70714 • *13,233*
Baker, MT 59313 • *1,818*
Baker, OR 97814 • *9,140*
Baker □, FL • *18,486*
Baker □, GA • *3,615*
Baker □, OR • *15,317*
Bakersfield, CA 93301–89 • *174,820*
Balch Springs, TX 75180 • *17,406*
Bald Knob, AR 72010 • *2,653*
Baldwin, FL 32234 • *1,450*
Baldwin, GA 30511 • *1,439*
Baldwin, LA 70514 • *2,379*
Baldwin, NY 11510 • *22,719*
Baldwin, PA 15234 • *21,923*
Baldwin, WI 54002 • *2,022*
Baldwin □, AL • *98,280*
Baldwin □, GA • *39,530*
Baldwin City, KS 66006 • *2,961*
Baldwin Park, CA 91706 • *69,330*
Baldwinsville, NY 13027 • *6,591*
Baldwinville, MA 01436 • *1,795*
Baldwyn, MS 38824 • *3,204*
Balfour, NC 28706 • *1,118*
Ball, LA 71405 • *3,305*
Ballard □, KY • *7,902*
Ballardvale, MA 01810 • *1,270*
Ballinger, TX 76821 • *3,975*
Ballston Spa, NY 12020 • *4,937*
Ballwin, MO 63011 • *21,816*
Balmville, NY 12550 • *2,963*
Baltic, CT 06330 • *2,000*
Baltimore, MD 21201–99 • *736,014*
Baltimore, OH 43105 • *2,971*
Baltimore □, MD • *692,134*
Baltimore Highlands, MD 21227 • *7,300*
Bamberg, SC 29003 • *3,843*
Bamberg □, SC • *16,902*
Bandera □, TX • *10,562*
Bandon, OR 97411 • *2,215*
Bangor, ME 04401–02 • *33,181*
Bangor, MI 49013 • *1,922*
Bangor, PA 18013 • *5,383*
Bangor, WI 54614 • *1,076*
Bangor Township, MI 48706 • *17,494*
Bangs, TX 76823 • *1,555*
Banks □, GA • *10,308*
Banner □, NE • *852*
Banning, CA 92220 • *20,570*
Bannock □, ID • *66,026*
Baraboo, WI 53913 • *9,203*
Baraga, MI 49908 • *1,231*
Baraga □, MI • *7,954*
Barataria, LA 70036 • *1,160*
Barber □, KS • *5,874*
Barberton, OH 44203 • *27,623*
Barbour □, AL • *25,417*
Barbour □, WV • *15,699*
Barboursville, WV 25504 • *2,774*
Barbourville, KY 40906 • *3,658*
Bardstown, KY 40004 • *6,801*
Bargersville, IN 46106 • *1,681*
Bar Harbor, ME 04609 • *2,768*
Barker Heights, NC 28739 • *1,137*
Barling, AR 72923 • *4,078*
Barnegat, NJ 08005 • *1,160*
Barnes □, ND • *12,545*
Barnesboro, PA 15714 • *2,530*
Barnesville, GA 30204 • *4,747*
Barnesville, MN 56514 • *2,066*
Barnesville, OH 43713 • *4,326*
Barnsdall, OK 74002 • *1,316*
Barnstable, MA 02630 • *2,790*
Barnstable □, MA • *186,605*
Barnwell, SC 29812 • *5,255*
Barnwell □, SC • *20,293*
Barrackville, WV 26559 • *1,443*
Barre, MA 01005 • *1,094*
Barre, VT 05641 • *9,482*
Barren □, KY • *34,001*
Barrington, IL 60010–11 • *9,504*
Barrington, NJ 08007 • *6,774*
Barrington, RI 02806 • *15,849*
Barron, WI 54812 • *2,986*
Barron □, WI • *40,750*
Barron Lake, MI 49120 • *1,600*
Barrow, AK 99723 • *3,469*
Barrow □, GA • *29,721*
Barry, IL 62312 • *1,391*
Barry □, MI • *50,057*
Barry □, MO • *27,547*
Barstow, CA 92310–12 • *21,472*
Bartholomew □, IN • *63,657*
Bartlesville, OK 74003–06 • *34,256*
Bartlett, IL 60103 • *19,373*
Bartlett, TN 38134 • *26,989*
Bartlett, TX 76511 • *1,439*
Barton, OH 43905 • *1,039*
Barton, VT 05822 • *908*
Barton □, KS • *29,382*
Barton □, MO • *11,312*
Bartonville, IL 61607 • *5,643*
Bartow, FL 33830 • *14,716*
Bartow □, GA • *55,911*
Barview, OR 97420 • *1,402*
Basalt, CO 81621 • *1,128*
Basehor, KS 66007 • *1,591*
Basile, LA 70515 • *1,808*
Basin, WY 82410 • *1,180*
Basking Ridge, NJ 07920 • *3,060*
Bassett, VA 24055 • *1,579*
Bass Lake, IN 46534 • *1,500*
Bastrop, LA 71220–21 • *13,916*
Bastrop, TX 78602 • *4,044*
Bastrop □, TX • *38,263*
Batavia, IL 60510 • *17,076*
Batavia, NY 14020–21 • *16,310*
Batavia, OH 45103 • *1,700*
Bates □, MO • *15,025*
Batesburg, SC 29006 • *4,082*
Batesville, AR 72501–03 • *9,187*
Batesville, IN 47006 • *4,720*
Batesville, MS 38606 • *6,403*
Bath, ME 04530 • *9,799*
Bath, NY 14810 • *5,801*
Bath, PA 18014 • *2,358*
Bath, SC 29816 • *2,242*
Bath □, KY • *9,692*
Bath □, VA • *4,799*
Baton Rouge, LA 70801–98 • *219,531*
Battle Creek, MI 49015–17 • *53,540*
Battle Ground, WA 98604 • *3,758*
Battle Mountain, NV 89820 • *3,542*
Baudette, MN 56623 • *1,146*
Bawcomville, LA 71291 • *2,250*
Baxley, GA 31513 • *3,841*
Baxter, MN 56425 • *3,695*
Baxter, TN 38544 • *1,289*
Baxter □, AR • *31,186*
Baxter Springs, KS 66713 • *4,351*
Bay, AR 72411 • *1,660*
Bay □, FL • *126,994*
Bay □, MI • *111,723*
Bayard, NE 69334 • *1,196*
Bayard, NM 88023 • *2,598*
Bayberry, NY 13088 • *6,710*
Bay City, MI 48706–08 • *38,936*
Bay City, OR 97107 • *1,027*
Bay City, TX 77414 • *18,170*
Bayfield, CO 81122 • *1,090*
Bayfield □, WI • *14,008*
Bay Head, NJ 08742 • *1,226*
Baylor □, TX • *4,385*
Bay Minette, AL 36507 • *7,168*
Bayonet Point, FL 34667 • *21,860*
Bayonne, NJ 07002 • *61,444*
Bayou Cane, LA 70359 • *15,876*
Bayou George, FL 32401 • *1,500*
Bayou La Batre, AL 36509 • *2,456*
Bay Pines, FL 33504 • *4,171*
Bayport, MN 55003 • *3,200*
Bayport, NY 11705 • *7,702*
Bay Ridge, MD 21403 • *1,989*
Bay Saint Louis, MS 39520–21 • *8,063*
Bay Shore, NY 11706 • *21,279*
Bayshore Gardens, FL 34207 • *17,062*
Bayside, WI 53217 • *4,789*
Bay Springs, MS 39422 • *1,729*
Baytown, TX 77520–22 • *63,850*
Bay Village, OH 44140 • *17,000*
Bayville, NY 11709 • *7,193*
Beach, IL 60085 • *9,513*
Beach, ND 58621 • *1,205*
Beach Haven, NJ 08008 • *1,475*
Beachwood, NJ 08722 • *9,324*
Beachwood, OH 44122 • *10,677*
Beacon, NY 12508 • *13,243*
Beacon Falls, CT 06403 • *1,285*
Beacon Square, FL 34652 • *6,265*
Beadle □, SD • *18,253*
Bear, DE 19701 • *1,200*
Bearden, AR 71720 • *1,021*
Beardstown, IL 62618 • *5,270*
Bear Lake □, ID • *6,084*
Bear Town, MS 39648 • *1,277*
Beatrice, NE 68310 • *12,354*
Beatty, NV 89003 • *1,623*
Beattyville, KY 41311 • *1,131*
Beaufort, NC 28516 • *3,808*
Beaufort, SC 29901–03 • *9,576*
Beaufort □, NC • *42,283*
Beaufort □, SC • *86,425*
Beaumont, CA 92223 • *9,685*
Beaumont, MS 39423 • *1,054*
Beaumont, TX 77701–26 • *114,323*
Beauregard □, LA • *30,083*
Beaver, OK 73932 • *1,584*
Beaver, PA 15009 • *5,028*
Beaver, UT 84713 • *1,998*
Beaver, WV 25813 • *1,244*
Beaver □, OK • *6,023*
Beaver □, PA • *186,093*
Beaver □, UT • *4,765*
Beavercreek, OH 45385 • *33,626*
Beaverdale, PA 15921 • *1,000*
Beaver Dam, KY 42320 • *2,904*
Beaver Dam, WI 53916 • *14,196*
Beaver Falls, PA 15010 • *10,687*
Beaverhead □, MT • *8,424*
Beaverton, MI 48612 • *1,150*
Beaverton, OR 97005–07 • *53,310*
Beckemeyer, IL 62219 • *1,070*
Becker □, MN • *27,881*
Beckham □, OK • *18,812*
Beckley, WV 25801–02 • *18,296*
Bedford, IN 47421 • *13,817*
Bedford, IA 50833 • *1,528*
Bedford, MA 01730 • *13,067*
Bedford, NH 03102 • *1,400*
Bedford, OH 44146 • *14,822*
Bedford, PA 15522 • *3,137*
Bedford, TX 76021–22 • *43,762*
Bedford, VA 24523 • *6,073*
Bedford □, PA • *47,919*
Bedford □, TN • *30,411*
Bedford □, VA • *45,656*
Bedford Heights, OH 44146 • *12,131*
Bedford Hills, NY 10507 • *3,140*
Bee □, TX • *25,135*
Beebe, AR 72012 • *4,455*
Beecher, IL 60401 • *2,032*
Beecher, MI 48458 • *14,465*
Beech Grove, IN 46107 • *13,383*
Beech Island, SC 29842 • *1,500*
Bee Ridge, FL 34233 • *6,406*
Beeville, TX 78102–04 • *13,547*
Beggs, OK 74421 • *1,150*
Bel Air, MD 21014 • *8,860*
Bel Aire, KS 67220 • *3,695*
Belchertown, MA 01007 • *2,339*
Belcourt, ND 58316 • *2,458*
Belding, MI 48809 • *5,969*
Belen, NM 87002 • *6,547*
Belfast, ME 04915 • *6,355*
Belfast, NY 14711 • *1,100*
Belfield, ND 58622 • *887*
Belford, NJ 07718 • *6,300*
Belgrade, MT 59714 • *3,411*
Belhaven, NC 27810 • *2,269*
Belington, WV 26250 • *1,850*
Belknap □, NH • *49,216*
Bell, CA 90201 • *34,365*
Bell □, KY • *31,506*
Bell □, TX • *191,088*
Bellair, FL 32073 • *5,200*
Bellaire, MI 49615 • *1,104*
Bellaire, OH 43906 • *6,028*
Bellaire, TX 77401–02 • *13,842*
Bella Vista, AR 72712 • *9,083*
Bellbrook, OH 45305 • *6,511*
Belle, MO 65013 • *1,218*
Belle, WV 25015 • *1,421*
Belleair, FL 34616 • *3,968*
Belle Chasse, LA 70037 • *8,512*
Bellefontaine, OH 43311 • *12,142*
Bellefontaine Neighbors, MO 63137 • *10,922*
Bellefonte, DE 19809 • *1,243*
Bellefonte, PA 16823 • *6,358*
Belle Fourche, SD 57717 • *4,335*
Belle Glade, FL 33430 • *16,177*
Belle Isle, FL 32809 • *5,272*
Belle Meade, TN 37205 • *2,839*
Bellemoor, DE 19802 • *1,040*
Belle Plaine, IA 52208 • *2,834*
Belle Plaine, KS 67013 • *1,649*
Belle Plaine, MN 56011 • *3,149*
Belle Vernon, PA 15012 • *1,213*
Belleview, FL 32506 • *8,000*
Belleview, FL 32620 • *2,666*
Belle View, VA 22307 • *3,500*
Belleville, IL 62220–25 • *42,785*
Belleville, KS 66935 • *2,517*
Belleville, MI 48111–12 • *3,270*
Belleville, NJ 07109 • *34,213*
Belleville, PA 17004 • *1,589*
Belleville, WI 53508 • *1,456*
Bellevue, ID 83313 • *1,275*
Bellevue, IA 52031 • *2,239*
Bellevue, KY 41073 • *6,997*
Bellevue, MI 49021 • *1,401*
Bellevue, NE 68005 • *30,982*
Bellevue, OH 44811 • *8,146*
Bellevue, PA 15202 • *9,126*
Bellevue, WA 98004–09 • *86,874*
Bellflower, CA 90706–07 • *61,815*
Bell Gardens, CA 90201 • *42,355*
Bellingham, MA 02019 • *4,535*
Bellingham, WA 98225–27 • *52,179*
Bellmawr, NJ 08031 • *12,603*
Bellmead, TX 76705 • *8,336*
Bellmore, NY 11710 • *16,438*
Bellows Falls, VT 05101 • *3,313*
Bellport, NY 11713 • *2,572*
Bells, TN 38006 • *1,643*
Bellville, OH 44813 • *1,568*
Bellville, TX 77418 • *3,378*
Bellwood, IL 60104 • *20,241*
Bellwood, PA 16617 • *1,976*
Bellwood, VA 23234 • *6,178*
Belmar, NJ 07719 • *5,877*
Belmond, IA 50421 • *2,500*
Belmont, CA 94002 • *24,127*
Belmont, MA 02178 • *24,720*
Belmont, MS 38827 • *1,554*
Belmont, NY 14813 • *1,006*
Belmont, NC 28012 • *8,434*
Belmont □, OH • *71,074*
Bel-Nor, MO 63133 • *2,935*
Beloit, KS 67420 • *4,066*
Beloit, OH 44609 • *1,037*
Beloit, WI 53511–12 • *35,573*
Beloit North, WI 53511 • *5,457*
Belpre, OH 45714 • *6,796*
Belt, MT 59412 • *571*
Belton, MO 64012 • *18,150*
Belton, SC 29627 • *4,646*
Belton, TX 76513 • *12,476*
Beltrami □, MN • *34,384*
Beltsville, MD 20705 • *14,476*
Belvedere, GA 30032 • *6,100*
Belvedere, SC 29841 • *6,133*
Belvedere Park, GA 30032 • *18,089*
Belvidere, IL 61008 • *15,958*
Belvidere, NJ 07823 • *2,669*
Belzoni, MS 39038 • *2,536*
Bement, IL 61813 • *1,668*
Bemidji, MN 56601–19 • *11,245*
Benavides, TX 78341 • *1,788*
Benbrook, TX 76126 • *19,564*
Bend, OR 97701–09 • *20,469*
Benewah □, ID • *7,937*
Ben Hill □, GA • *16,245*
Benicia, CA 94510 • *24,437*
Benkelman, NE 69021 • *1,193*
Benld, IL 62009 • *1,604*
Ben Lomond, CA 95005 • *7,884*
Bennett, CO 80102 • *1,757*
Bennett □, SD • *3,206*
Bennettsville, SC 29512 • *9,345*
Bennington, VT 05201 • *9,532*
Bennington □, VT • *35,845*
Bennion, UT 84118 • *9,575*
Bensalem, PA 19020–21 • *52,368*
Bensenville, IL 60106 • *17,767*
Bensley, VA 23234 • *5,093*
Benson, AZ 85602 • *3,824*
Benson, MN 56215 • *3,235*
Benson, NC 27504 • *2,810*
Benson □, ND • *7,198*
Bent □, CO • *5,048*
Bentleyville, PA 15314 • *2,673*
Benton, AR 72015 • *18,177*
Benton, IL 62812 • *7,216*
Benton, KY 42025 • *3,899*
Benton, LA 71006 • *2,047*
Benton □, AR • *97,499*
Benton □, IN • *9,441*
Benton □, IA • *22,429*
Benton □, MN • *30,185*
Benton □, MS • *8,046*
Benton □, MO • *13,859*
Benton □, OR • *70,811*
Benton □, TN • *14,524*
Benton □, WA • *112,560*
Benton City, WA 99320 • *1,806*
Benton Harbor, MI 49022–23 • *12,818*
Benton Heights, MI 49022 • *5,465*
Bentonville, AR 72712–14 • *11,257*
Benwood, WV 26031 • *1,669*
Benzie □, MI • *12,200*
Beowawe, NV 89821 • *250*
Berea, KY 40403 • *9,126*
Berea, OH 44017 • *19,051*
Berea, SC 29611 • *13,535*
Beresford, SD 57004 • *1,849*
Bergen, NY 14416 • *1,103*
Bergen □, NJ • *825,380*
Bergenfield, NJ 07621 • *24,458*
Berkeley, CA 94701–10 • *102,724*
Berkeley, IL 60163 • *5,137*
Berkeley, MO 63134 • *12,450*
Berkeley, RI 02864 • *830*
Berkeley □, SC • *128,776*
Berkeley □, WV • *59,253*
Berkeley Heights, NJ 07922 • *11,980*
Berkley, MI 48072 • *16,960*
Berks □, PA • *336,523*
Berkshire □, MA • *139,352*
Berlin, CT 06037 • *1,040*
Berlin, MD 21811 • *2,616*
Berlin, NH 03570 • *11,824*
Berlin, NJ 08009 • *5,672*
Berlin, NY 12022 • *1,200*
Berlin, PA 15530 • *2,064*
Berlin, WI 54923 • *5,371*
Bernalillo, NM 87004 • *5,960*
Bernalillo □, NM • *480,577*
Bernardsville, NJ 07924 • *6,597*
Berne, IN 46711 • *3,559*
Bernice, LA 71222 • *1,543*
Bernie, MO 63822 • *1,847*
Berrien □, GA • *14,153*
Berrien □, MI • *161,378*
Berrien Springs, MI 49103 • *1,927*
Berry, AL 35546 • *1,218*
Berryville, AR 72616 • *3,212*
Berryville, VA 22611 • *3,097*
Berthoud, CO 80513 • *2,990*
Bertie □, NC • *20,388*
Bertrand, MI 49120 • *5,500*
Berwick, LA 70342 • *4,375*
Berwick, ME 03901 • *2,378*
Berwick, PA 18603 • *10,976*
Berwyn, IL 60402 • *45,426*
Berwyn, PA 19312 • *8,150*
Bessemer, AL 35020–23 • *33,497*
Bessemer, MI 49911 • *2,272*
Bessemer, PA 16112 • *1,196*
Bessemer City, NC 28016 • *4,698*
Bethalto, IL 62010 • *9,507*
Bethany, CT 06525 • *1,170*
Bethany, IL 61914 • *1,369*
Bethany, MO 64424 • *3,005*
Bethany, OK 73008 • *20,075*
Bethany, WV 26032 • *1,139*
Bethany Beach, DE 19930 • *326*
Bethel, AK 99559 • *4,674*
Bethel, CT 06801 • *8,835*
Bethel, ME 04217 • *1,225*
Bethel, NC 27812 • *1,842*
Bethel, OH 45106 • *2,407*
Bethel, VT 05032 • *1,866*
Bethel Acres, OK 74801 • *2,505*
Bethel Park, PA 15102 • *33,823*
Bethesda, MD 20813–17 • *62,936*
Bethesda, OH 43719 • *1,161*
Bethlehem, CT 06751 • *1,976*
Bethlehem, PA 18015–18 • *71,428*
Bethpage, NY 11714 • *15,761*
Bettendorf, IA 52722 • *28,132*
Beulah, ND 58523 • *3,363*
Beverly, MA 01915 • *38,195*
Beverly, NJ 08010 • *2,973*
Beverly, OH 45715 • *1,444*
Beverly Hills, CA 90209–13 • *31,971*
Beverly Hills, FL 32665 • *6,163*
Beverly Hills, MI 48009 • *10,610*
Bexar □, TX • *1,185,394*
Bexley, OH 43209 • *13,088*
Bibb □, AL • *16,576*
Bibb □, GA • *149,967*
Bicknell, IN 47512 • *3,357*
Biddeford, ME 04005 • *20,710*
Bienville □, LA • *15,979*
Big Bear City, CA 92314 • *3,500*
Big Bend, WI 53103 • *1,299*
Big Delta, AK 99737 • *400*
Big Flats, NY 14814 • *2,658*
Bigfork, MT 59911 • *1,080*
Biggs, CA 95917 • *1,581*
Big Horn □, MT • *11,337*
Big Horn □, WY • *10,525*
Big Lake, MN 55309 • *3,113*
Big Lake, TX 76932 • *3,672*
Big Pine, CA 93513 • *1,158*
Big Piney, WY 83113 • *454*
Big Rapids, MI 49307 • *12,603*
Big Sandy, MT 59520 • *740*
Big Sandy, TX 75755 • *1,185*
Big Spring, TX 79720–21 • *23,093*
Big Stone □, MN • *6,285*
Big Stone Gap, VA 24219 • *4,748*
Big Timber, MT 59011 • *1,557*
Billerica, MA 01821–22 • *6,840*
Billings, MT 59101–08 • *81,151*
Billings □, ND • *1,108*
Billings Heights, MT 59105 • *8,480*
Biloxi, MS 39530–35 • *46,319*
Biltmore Forest, NC 28803 • *1,327*
Bingham, ME 04920 • *1,071*
Bingham □, ID • *37,583*
Binghamton, NY 13901–05 • *53,008*
Birchwood City, MD 20745 • *4,870*
Birchwood Park, DE 19711 • *2,250*
Bird Island, MN 55310 • *1,326*
Birdsboro, PA 19508 • *4,222*
Birmingham, AL 35201–61 • *265,968*
Birmingham, MI 48009–12 • *19,997*
Bisbee, AZ 85603 • *6,288*
Biscayne Gardens, FL 33168 • *13,000*
Biscayne Park, FL 33161 • *3,068*
Biscoe, NC 27209 • *1,484*
Bishop, CA 93514–15 • *3,475*
Bishop, TX 78343 • *3,337*
Bishopville, SC 29010 • *3,560*
Bismarck, MO 63624 • *1,579*
Bismarck, ND 58501–07 • *49,256*
Biwabik, MN 55708 • *1,097*
Bixby, OK 74008 • *9,502*
Black Canyon City, AZ 85324 • *1,811*
Black Creek, WI 54106 • *1,152*
Black Diamond, WA 98010 • *1,422*
Black Earth, WI 53515 • *1,248*
Blackfoot, ID 83221 • *9,646*
Blackford □, IN • *14,067*
Black Forest, CO 80908 • *8,143*
Black Hawk, SD 57718 • *1,955*
Black Hawk □, IA • *123,798*
Black Jack, MO 63031 • *6,128*
Black Lick, PA 15716 • *1,100*
Blacklick Estates, OH 43227 • *10,080*
Black Mountain, NC 28711 • *5,418*
Black Point Beach Club, CT 06357 • *1,200*
Black River, NY 13612 • *1,349*
Black River Falls, WI 54615 • *3,490*
Blacksburg, SC 29702 • *1,907*
Blacksburg, VA 24060–63 • *34,590*
Blackshear, GA 31516 • *3,263*
Blackstone, MA 01504 • *4,460*
Blackstone, VA 23824 • *3,497*
Blackville, SC 29817 • *2,688*
Blackwell, OK 74631 • *7,538*
Blackwood, NJ 08012 • *5,120*
Bladen □, NC • *28,663*
Bladenboro, NC 28320 • *1,821*
Bladensburg, MD 20710 • *8,064*
Blades, DE 19973 • *834*
Blaine, MN 55433 • *38,975*
Blaine, TN 37709 • *1,326*
Blaine, WA 98230 • *2,489*
Blaine □, ID • *13,552*
Blaine □, MT • *6,728*
Blaine □, NE • *675*
Blaine □, OK • *11,470*
Blair, NE 68008 • *6,860*
Blair, WI 54616 • *1,126*
Blair □, PA • *130,542*
Blairsville, PA 15717 • *3,595*
Blakely, GA 31723 • *5,595*
Blakely, PA 18447 • *7,222*
Blanchard, LA 71009 • *1,175*
Blanchard, OK 73010 • *1,922*
Blanchester, OH 45107 • *4,206*
Blanco, TX 78606 • *1,238*
Blanco □, TX • *5,972*
Bland □, VA • *6,514*
Blanding, UT 84511 • *3,162*
Blasdell, NY 14219 • *2,900*
Blauvelt, NY 10913 • *4,470*
Blawnox, PA 15238 • *1,626*
Bleckley □, GA • *10,430*
Bledsoe □, TN • *9,669*

Blende, CO 81006 • 1,330
Blennerhassett, WV 26101 • 2,924
Blissfield, MI 49228 • 3,172
Block Island, RI 02807 • 620
Bloomer, WI 54724 • 3,085
Bloomfield, CT 06002 • 7,120
Bloomfield, IN 47424 • 2,592
Bloomfield, IA 52537 • 2,580
Bloomfield, MO 63825 • 1,800
Bloomfield, NE 68718 • 1,181
Bloomfield, NJ 07003 • 45,061
Bloomfield, NM 87413 • 5,214
Bloomfield Hills, MI 48302–04 • 4,288
Bloomfield Township, MI 48302 • 42,137
Bloomingdale, GA 31302 • 2,271
Bloomingdale, IL 60108 • 16,614
Bloomingdale, NJ 07403 • 7,530
Bloomingdale, TN 37660 • 10,953
Blooming Prairie, MN 55917 • 2,043
Bloomington, CA 92316 • 15,116
Bloomington, IL 61701–04 • 51,972
Bloomington, IN 47401–08 • 60,633
Bloomington, MN 55420 • 86,335
Bloomington, TX 77951 • 1,888
Bloomsburg, PA 17815 • 12,439
Blossburg, PA 16912 • 1,571
Blossom, TX 75416 • 1,440
Blount □, AL • 39,248
Blount □, TN • 85,969
Blountstown, FL 32424 • 2,404
Blountsville, AL 35031 • 1,527
Blountville, TN 37617 • 2,605
Blowing Rock, NC 28605 • 1,257
Blue Ash, OH 45242 • 11,860
Blue Diamond, NV 89004 • 420
Blue Earth, MN 56013 • 3,745
Blue Earth □, MN • 54,044
Bluefield, VA 24605 • 5,363
Bluefield, WV 24701 • 12,756
Blue Grass, IA 52726 • 1,214
Blue Hills, CT 06002 • 3,206
Blue Island, IL 60406 • 21,203
Blue Lake, CA 95525 • 1,235
Blue Mound, IL 62513 • 1,161
Blue Rapids, KS 66411 • 1,131
Blue Ridge, GA 30513 • 1,336
Blue Ridge, VA 24064 • 2,840
Blue Ridge Summit, PA 17214 • 1,800
Blue Springs, MO 64014–15 • 40,153
Bluewell, WV 24701 • 2,752
Bluff City, TN 37618 • 1,390
Bluffdale, UT 84065 • 2,152
Bluff Park, AL 35226 • 8,000
Bluffton, IN 46714 • 9,020
Bluffton, OH 45817 • 3,367
Blythe, CA 92225–26 • 8,428
Blytheville, AR 72315–19 • 22,906
Boalsburg, PA 16827 • 2,206
Boardman, OH 44512 • 38,596
Boardman, OR 97818 • 1,387
Boaz, AL 35957 • 6,928
Boca Grande, FL 33921 • 1,200
Boca Raton, FL 33431–34 • 61,492
Boerne, TX 78006 • 4,274
Bogalusa, LA 70427–29 • 14,280
Bogart, GA 30622 • 1,018
Bogata, TX 75417 • 1,421
Boger City, NC 28092 • 1,373
Bogota, NJ 07603 • 7,824
Bohemia, NY 11716 • 9,556
Boiling Springs, NC 28017 • 2,445
Boiling Springs, PA 17007 • 1,978
Boise, ID 83701–15 • 125,738
Boise □, ID • 3,509
Boise City, OK 73933 • 1,509
Bolingbrook, IL 60440 • 40,843
Bolivar, MO 65613 • 6,845
Bolivar, NY 14715 • 1,261
Bolivar, TN 38008 • 5,969
Bolivar □, MS • 41,875
Bollinger □, MO • 10,619
Bolton Landing, NY 12814 • 1,600
Bon Air, VA 23235 • 16,413
Bonaventure, FL 33317 • 6,000
Bond □, IL • 14,991
Bondsville, MA 01009 • 1,992
Bonduel, WI 54107 • 1,210
Bondurant, IA 50035 • 1,584
Bonham, TX 75418 • 6,686
Bon Homme □, SD • 7,089
Bonifay, FL 32425 • 2,612
Bonita, CA 91903 • 12,542
Bonita Springs, FL 33923 • 13,600
Bonneauville, PA 17325 • 1,282
Bonner □, ID • 26,622
Bonners Ferry, ID 83805 • 2,193
Bonner Springs, KS 66012 • 6,413
Bonne Terre, MO 63628 • 3,871
Bonneville □, ID • 72,207
Bonney Lake, WA 98390 • 7,494
Bonnie Doone, NC 28303 • 3,893
Bono, AR 72416 • 1,220
Booker, TX 79005 • 1,236
Boomer, WV 25031 • 1,051
Boone, IA 50036 • 12,392
Boone, NC 28607 • 12,915
Boone □, AR • 28,297
Boone □, IL • 30,806
Boone □, IN • 38,147
Boone □, IA • 25,186
Boone □, KY • 57,589
Boone □, MO • 112,379
Boone □, NE • 6,667
Boone □, WV • 25,870
Booneville, AR 72927 • 3,804
Booneville, MS 38829 • 7,955
Boonsboro, MD 21713 • 2,445
Boonton, NJ 07005 • 8,343
Boonville, CA 95415 • 1,000
Boonville, IN 47601 • 6,724
Boonville, MO 65233 • 7,095
Boonville, NY 13309 • 2,220
Boonville, NC 27011 • 1,009
Boothbay Harbor, ME 04538 • 1,267
Borden □, TX • 799
Bordentown, NJ 08505 • 4,341
Borger, TX 79007–08 • 15,675
Boron, CA 93516 • 2,101
Borrego Springs, CA 92004 • 2,244
Boscobel, WI 53805 • 2,706
Bosque □, TX • 15,125
Bossert Estates, NJ 08505 • 1,830
Bossier □, LA • 86,088
Bossier City, LA 71111–13 • 52,721
Boston, GA 31626 • 1,395
Boston, MA 02101–99 • 574,283
Boswell, PA 15531 • 1,485
Botetourt □, VA • 24,992
Bothell, WA 98011–12 • 12,345
Botkins, OH 45306 • 1,340
Bottineau, ND 58318 • 2,598
Bottineau □, ND • 8,011
Boulder, CO 80301–08 • 83,312
Boulder, MT 59632 • 1,316
Boulder □, CO • 225,339
Boulder City, NV 89005–06 • 12,567
Boulder Creek, CA 95006 • 6,725
Boulder Hill, IL 60538 • 8,894
Boulevard Heights, MD 20743 • 1,820
Boundary □, ID • 8,332
Bound Brook, NJ 08805 • 9,487
Bountiful, UT 84010–11 • 36,659
Bourbon, IN 46504 • 1,672
Bourbon, MO 65441 • 1,188
Bourbon □, KS • 14,966
Bourbon □, KY • 19,236
Bourbonnais, IL 60914 • 13,934
Bourg, LA 70343 • 2,073
Bourne, MA 02532 • 1,284
Boutte, LA 70039 • 1,200
Bovina, TX 79009 • 1,549
Bowdon, GA 30108 • 1,981
Bowie, MD 20715–21 • 37,589
Bowie, TX 76230 • 4,990
Bowie □, TX • 81,665
Bowling Green, FL 33834 • 1,836
Bowling Green, KY 42101–04 • 40,641
Bowling Green, MO 63334 • 2,976
Bowling Green, OH 43402 • 28,176
Bowman, ND 58623 • 1,741
Bowman, SC 29018 • 1,063
Bowman □, ND • 3,596
Box Butte □, NE • 13,130
Box Elder, SD 57719 • 2,680
Box Elder □, UT • 36,485
Boxford, MA 01921 • 2,072
Boyce, LA 71409 • 1,361
Boyd □, KY • 51,150
Boyd □, NE • 2,835
Boyertown, PA 19512 • 3,759
Boyes Hot Springs, CA 95416 • 5,973
Boyle □, KY • 25,641
Boyne City, MI 49712 • 3,478
Boynton Beach, FL 33435–37 • 46,194
Bozeman, MT 59715 • 22,660
Bracken □, KY • 7,766
Brackenridge, PA 15014 • 3,784
Brackettville, TX 78832 • 1,740
Braddock, PA 15104 • 4,682
Braddock Heights, MD 21714 • 4,778
Bradenton, FL 34201–10 • 43,779
Bradenville, PA 15620 • 1,100
Bradford, OH 45308 • 2,005
Bradford, PA 16701 • 9,625
Bradford, RI 02808 • 1,604
Bradford, TN 38316 • 1,154
Bradford, VT 05033 • 672
Bradford □, FL • 22,515
Bradford □, PA • 60,967
Bradfordwoods, PA 15015 • 1,329
Bradley, FL 33835 • 1,108
Bradley, IL 60915 • 10,792
Bradley, WV 25818 • 2,144
Bradley □, AR • 11,793
Bradley □, TN • 73,712
Bradley Beach, NJ 07720 • 4,475
Bradner, OH 43406 • 1,093
Brady, TX 76825 • 5,946
Braham, MN 55006 • 1,139
Braidwood, IL 60408 • 3,584
Brainerd, MN 56401 • 12,353
Braintree, MA 02184 • 33,836
Branch □, MI • 41,502
Branch Village, RI 02895 • 400
Branchville, SC 29432 • 1,107
Brandenburg, KY 40108 • 1,857
Brandon, FL 33510 • 57,985
Brandon, MS 39042–43 • 11,077
Brandon, SC 29611 • 2,170
Brandon, SD 57005 • 3,543
Brandon, VT 05733 • 1,902
Brandywine, MD 20613 • 1,406
Branford, CT 06405 • 27,603
Branford Hills, CT 06405 • 3,460
Branson, MO 65616 • 3,706
Brantley, AL 36009 • 1,015
Brantley □, GA • 11,077
Brant Rock, MA 02020 • 1,850
Bratenahl, OH 44108 • 1,356
Brattleboro, VT 05301–04 • 8,612
Brawley, CA 92227 • 18,923
Braxton □, WV • 12,998
Brazil, IN 47834 • 7,640
Brazoria, TX 77422 • 2,717
Brazoria □, TX • 191,707
Brazos □, TX • 121,862
Brea, CA 92621–22 • 32,873
Breathitt □, KY • 15,703
Breaux Bridge, LA 70517 • 6,515
Breckenridge, CO 80424 • 1,285
Breckenridge, MI 48615 • 1,301
Breckenridge, MN 56520 • 3,708
Breckenridge, TX 76024 • 5,665
Breckenridge Hills, MO 63114 • 5,404
Breckinridge □, KY • 16,312
Brecksville, OH 44141 • 11,818
Breese, IL 62230 • 3,567
Bremen, GA 30110 • 4,356
Bremen, IN 46506 • 4,725
Bremen, OH 43107 • 1,386
Bremer □, IA • 22,813
Bremerton, WA 98310–15 • 38,142
Bremond, TX 76629 • 1,110
Brenham, TX 77833–34 • 11,952
Brent, AL 35034 • 2,776
Brent, FL 32503 • 21,624
Brentwood, CA 94513 • 7,563
Brentwood, MD 20722 • 3,005
Brentwood, MO 63144 • 8,150
Brentwood, NY 11717 • 45,218
Brentwood, NY • 45,218
Brentwood, OH 45231 • 3,568
Brentwood, PA 15227 • 10,823
Brentwood, SC 29405 • 2,000
Brentwood, TN 37027 • 16,392
Brevard, NC 28712 • 5,388
Brevard □, FL • 398,978
Brewer, ME 04412 • 9,021
Brewster, MA 02631 • 1,818
Brewster, NY 10509 • 1,566
Brewster, OH 44613 • 2,307
Brewster, WA 98812 • 1,633
Brewster □, TX • 8,681
Brewton, AL 36426–27 • 5,885
Briarcliff Manor, NY 10510 • 7,070
Brick [Township], NJ 08723 • 55,473
Bridge City, LA 70094 • 8,327
Bridge City, TX 77611 • 8,034
Bridgehampton, NY 11932 • 1,997
Bridgeport, AL 35740 • 2,936
Bridgeport, CT 06601–50 • 141,686
Bridgeport, IL 62417 • 2,118
Bridgeport, MI 48722 • 8,569
Bridgeport, NE 69336 • 1,581
Bridgeport, OH 43912 • 2,318
Bridgeport, PA 19405 • 4,292
Bridgeport, TX 76026 • 3,581
Bridgeport, WA 98813 • 1,498
Bridgeport, WV 26330 • 6,739
Bridger, MT 59014 • 692
Bridgeton, MO 63044 • 17,779
Bridgeton, NJ 08302 • 18,942
Bridgetown, OH 45211 • 11,460
Bridgeview, IL 60455 • 14,402
Bridgeville, DE 19933 • 1,210
Bridgeville, PA 15017 • 5,445
Bridgewater, MA 02324 • 7,242
Bridgewater, NJ 08807 • 5,630
Bridgewater, VA 22812 • 3,918
Bridgman, MI 49106 • 2,140
Bridgton, ME 04009 • 2,195
Brielle, NJ 08730 • 4,406
Brigantine, NJ 08203 • 11,354
Brigham City, UT 84302 • 15,644
Brighton, AL 35020 • 4,518
Brighton, CO 80601 • 14,203
Brighton, IL 62012 • 2,270
Brighton, MI 48116 • 5,686
Brighton, NY 14610 • 34,455
Brilliant, OH 43913 • 1,672
Brillion, WI 54110 • 2,840
Brinkley, AR 72021 • 4,234
Briscoe □, TX • 1,971
Bristol, CT 06010–11 • 60,640
Bristol, IN 46507 • 1,133
Bristol, NH 03222 • 1,483
Bristol, RI 02809 • 21,625
Bristol, TN 37620–25 • 23,421
Bristol, VT 05443 • 1,801
Bristol, VA 24201–03 • 18,426
Bristol □, MA • 506,325
Bristol □, RI • 48,859
Bristol [Township], PA 19007 • 58,773
Bristow, OK 74010 • 4,062
Britt, IA 50423 • 2,133
Britton, SD 57430 • 1,394
Broadalbin, NY 12025 • 1,397
Broad Brook, CT 06016 • 1,280
Broadkill Beach, DE 19968 • 390
Broadus, MT 59317 • 572
Broadview, IL 60153 • 8,713
Broadview Heights, OH 44141 • 12,219
Broadview Park, FL 33314 • 6,109
Broadwater □, MT • 3,318
Broadway, VA 22815 • 1,209
Brockport, NY 14420 • 8,749
Brockton, MA 02401–05 • 92,788
Brockway, PA 15824 • 2,207
Brocton, NY 14716 • 1,387
Brodhead, KY 40409 • 1,140
Brodhead, WI 53520 • 3,165
Brodheadsville, PA 18322 • 1,500
Broken Arrow, OK 74011–14 • 58,043
Broken Bow, NE 68822 • 3,778
Broken Bow, OK 74728 • 3,961
Bronson, MI 49028 • 2,342
Bronx □, NY • 1,203,789
Bronxville, NY 10708 • 6,028
Brooke □, WV • 26,992
Brookfield, CT 06804 • 1,500
Brookfield, IL 60513 • 18,876
Brookfield, MA 01506 • 2,968
Brookfield, MO 64628 • 4,888
Brookfield, VA 22021 • 2,100
Brookfield, WI 53005 • 35,184
Brookfield Center, CT 06804 • 1,400
Brookhaven, MS 39601 • 10,243
Brookhaven, PA 19015 • 8,567
Brookhaven, WV 26505 • 3,836
Brookings, OR 97415 • 4,400
Brookings, SD 57006 • 16,270
Brookings □, SD • 25,207
Brooklawn, NJ 08030 • 1,805
Brookline, MA 02146 • 54,718
Brooklyn, CT 06234 • 1,400
Brooklyn, IN 46111 • 1,162
Brooklyn, IA 52211 • 1,439
Brooklyn, OH 44144 • 11,706
Brooklyn, SC 29720 • 1,850
Brooklyn Center, MN 55429 • 28,887
Brooklyn Park, MD 21225 • 10,987
Brooklyn Park, MN 55443 • 56,381
Brookneal, VA 24528 • 1,344
Brook Park, OH 44142 • 22,865
Brookport, IL 62910 • 1,070
Brooks, KY 40109 • 2,464
Brooks □, GA • 15,398
Brooks □, TX • 8,204
Brookshire, TX 77423 • 2,922
Brookside, AL 35036 • 1,365
Brookside, DE 19713 • 15,307
Brookston, IN 47923 • 1,804
Brooksville, FL 34601–14 • 7,440
Brooksville, MS 39739 • 1,098
Brookville, IN 47012 • 2,529
Brookville, NY 11545 • 3,716
Brookville, OH 45309 • 4,621
Brookville, PA 15825 • 4,184
Brookwood, NJ 08527 • 5,500
Broomall, PA 19008 • 10,930
Broome □, NY • 212,160
Broomfield, CO 80020–21 • 24,638
Broussard, LA 70518 • 3,213
Broward □, FL • 1,255,488
Browardale, FL 33311 • 6,257
Brown □, IL • 5,836
Brown □, IN • 14,080
Brown □, KS • 11,128
Brown □, MN • 26,984
Brown □, NE • 3,657
Brown □, OH • 34,966
Brown □, SD • 35,580
Brown □, TX • 34,371
Brown □, WI • 194,594
Brown City, MI 48416 • 1,244
Brown Deer, WI 53209 • 12,236
Brownfield, TX 79316 • 9,560
Brownfields, LA 70811 • 5,229
Browning, MT 59417 • 1,170
Brownsburg, IN 46112 • 7,628
Browns Mills, NJ 08015 • 11,429
Brownstown, IN 47220 • 2,872
Brownsville, FL 33142 • 15,607
Brownsville, OR 97327 • 1,281
Brownsville, PA 15417 • 3,164
Brownsville, TN 38012 • 10,019
Brownsville, TX 78520–26 • 98,962
Brownville, LA 71291 • 1,700
Brownville, NY 13615 • 1,138
Brownwood, TX 76803–04 • 18,387
Broxton, GA 31519 • 1,211
Broyhill Park, VA 22042 • 3,600
Bruce, MS 38915 • 2,127
Bruceton, TN 38317 • 1,586
Brule □, SD • 5,485
Brundidge, AL 36010 • 2,472
Brunswick, GA 31520–22 • 16,433
Brunswick, ME 04011 • 14,683
Brunswick, MD 21716 • 5,117
Brunswick, MO 65236 • 1,074
Brunswick, OH 44212 • 28,230
Brunswick □, NC • 50,985
Brunswick □, VA • 15,987
Brush, CO 80723 • 4,165
Brusly, LA 70719 • 1,824
Bryan, OH 43506 • 8,348
Bryan, TX 77801–06 • 55,002
Bryan □, GA • 15,438
Bryan □, OK • 32,089
Bryans Road, MD 20616 • 3,809
Bryant, AR 72022 • 5,269
Bryantville, MA 02327 • 1,800
Bryn Mawr, WA 98178 • 1,500
Bryson City, NC 28713 • 1,145
Buchanan, GA 30113 • 1,009
Buchanan, MI 49107 • 4,992
Buchanan, VA 24066 • 1,222
Buchanan □, IA • 20,844
Buchanan □, MO • 83,083
Buchanan □, VA • 31,333
Buckeye, AZ 85326 • 5,038
Buckeye Lake, OH 43008 • 2,986
Buckhannon, WV 26201 • 5,909
Buckingham □, VA • 12,873
Buckley, WA 98321 • 3,516
Bucknell Manor, VA 22307 • 2,300
Buckner, MO 64016 • 2,873
Bucks □, PA • 541,174
Bucksport, ME 04416 • 2,989
Bucksport, SC 29527 • 1,022
Bucyrus, OH 44820 • 13,496
Buda, TX 78610 • 1,795
Budd Lake 0L, NJ • 7,272
Buechel, KY 40218 • 7,081
Buena, NJ 08310 • 4,441
Buena Park, CA 90620–24 • 68,784
Buena Vista, CO 81211 • 1,752
Buena Vista, FL 34691 • 3,000
Buena Vista, GA 31803 • 1,472
Buena Vista, VA 24416 • 6,406
Buena Vista □, IA • 19,965
Buffalo, IA 52728 • 1,260
Buffalo, MN 55313 • 6,856
Buffalo, MO 65622 • 2,414
Buffalo, NY 14201–40 • 328,123
Buffalo, OK 73834 • 1,312
Buffalo, SC 29321 • 1,569
Buffalo, TX 75831 • 1,555
Buffalo, WY 82834 • 3,302
Buffalo □, NE • 37,447
Buffalo □, SD • 1,759
Buffalo □, WI • 13,584
Buffalo Center, IA 50424 • 1,081
Buffalo Grove, IL 60089 • 36,427
Buford, GA 30518 • 8,771
Buhl, ID 83316 • 3,516
Buhler, KS 67522 • 1,277
Buies Creek, NC 27506 • 2,085
Bullhead City, AZ 86430 • 21,951
Bullitt □, KY • 47,567
Bulloch □, GA • 43,125
Bullock □, AL • 11,042
Bull Shoals, AR 72619 • 1,534
Buna, TX 77612 • 1,900
Bunche Park, FL 33054 • 4,000
Buncombe □, NC • 174,821
Bunker Hill, IL 62014 • 1,722
Bunker Hill, OR 97420 • 1,242
Bunkerville, NV 89007 • 300
Bunkie, LA 71322 • 5,044
Bunnell, FL 32110 • 1,873
Buras, LA 70041 • 1,600
Burbank, CA 91501–10 • 93,643
Burbank, IL 60459 • 27,600
Burdickville, RI 02808 • 500
Bureau □, IL • 35,688
Burgaw, NC 28425 • 1,807
Burgettstown, PA 15021 • 1,634
Burgin, KY 40310 • 1,009
Burien, WA 98062 • 25,089
Burkburnett, TX 76354 • 10,145
Burke, SD 57523 • 756
Burke, VA 22015 • 57,734
Burke □, GA • 20,579
Burke □, NC • 75,744
Burke □, ND • 3,002
Burkesville, KY 42717 • 1,815
Burleigh □, ND • 60,131
Burleson, TX 76028 • 16,113
Burleson □, TX • 13,625
Burley, ID 83318 • 8,702
Burlingame, CA 94010–11 • 26,801
Burlingame, KS 66413 • 1,074
Burlington, CO 80807 • 2,941
Burlington, IA 52601 • 27,208
Burlington, KS 66839 • 2,735
Burlington, KY 41005 • 6,070
Burlington, MA 01803 • 23,302
Burlington, NJ 08016 • 9,835
Burlington, NC 27215–17 • 39,498
Burlington, ND 58722 • 995
Burlington, VT 05401–04 • 39,127
Burlington, WA 98233 • 4,349
Burlington, WI 53105 • 8,855
Burlington □, NJ • 395,066
Burnet, TX 78611 • 3,423
Burnet □, TX • 22,677
Burnett □, WI • 13,084
Burney, CA 96013 • 3,423
Burnham, PA 17009 • 2,197
Burns, OR 97720 • 2,913
Burns, TN 37029 • 1,127
Burns, WY 82053 • 254
Burns Flat, OK 73624 • 1,027
Burnsville, MN 55337 • 51,288
Burnsville, NC 28714 • 1,482
Burnt Hills, NY 12027 • 1,550
Burr Ridge, IL 60521 • 7,669
Burt □, NE • 7,868
Burton, MI 48509 • 27,617
Burton, OH 44021 • 1,349
Burton, SC 29902 • 6,917
Burtonsville, MD 20866 • 5,853
Burwell, NE 68823 • 1,278
Bushnell, FL 33513 • 1,998
Bushnell, IL 61422 • 3,288
Butler, AL 36904 • 1,872
Butler, GA 31006 • 1,673
Butler, IN 46721 • 2,601
Butler, MO 64730 • 4,099
Butler, NJ 07405 • 7,392
Butler, PA 16001–03 • 15,714
Butler, WI 53007 • 2,079
Butler □, AL • 21,892
Butler □, IA • 15,731
Butler □, KS • 50,580
Butler □, KY • 11,245
Butler □, MO • 38,765
Butler □, NE • 8,601
Butler □, OH • 291,479
Butler □, PA • 152,013
Butner, NC 27509 • 4,679
Butte, MT 59701–03 • 33,336
Butte □, CA • 182,120
Butte □, ID • 2,918
Butte □, SD • 7,914
Buttonwillow, CA 93206 • 1,301
Butts □, GA • 15,326
Buxton, NC 27920 • 1,300
Buzzards Bay, MA 02532 • 3,250
Byers, CO 80103 • 1,065
Byesville, OH 43723 • 2,435
Byfield, MA 01922 • 1,200
Bylas, AZ 85530 • 1,219
Byron, GA 31008 • 2,276
Byron, IL 61010 • 2,284
Byron, MN 55920 • 2,441
Byron, WY 82412 • 470

C

Cabarrus □, NC • 98,935
Cabell □, WV • 96,827
Cabin Creek, WV 25035 • 1,300
Cabin John, MD 20818 • 1,690
Cabool, MO 65689 • 2,006
Cabot, AR 72023 • 8,319
Cache, OK 73527 • 2,251
Cache □, UT • 70,183
Caddo □, LA • 248,253
Caddo □, OK • 29,550
Cadillac, MI 49601 • 10,104
Cadiz, KY 42211 • 2,148
Cadiz, OH 43907 • 3,439
Cadott, WI 54727 • 1,328
Cahaba Heights, AL 35243 • 4,778
Cahokia, IL 62206 • 17,550
Cairnbrook, PA 15924 • 1,081
Cairo, GA 31728 • 9,035
Cairo, IL 62914 • 4,846
Cairo, NY 12413 • 1,273
Calais, ME 04619 • 3,963
Calaveras □, CA • 31,998
Calavo Gardens, CA 91941 • 6,100
Calcasieu □, LA • 168,134
Calcutta, OH 43920 • 1,212
Caldwell, ID 83605–06 • 18,400
Caldwell, KS 67022 • 1,351
Caldwell, NJ 07006 • 7,549
Caldwell, OH 43724 • 1,786
Caldwell, TX 77836 • 3,181
Caldwell □, KY • 13,232
Caldwell □, LA • 9,810
Caldwell □, MO • 8,380
Caldwell □, NC • 70,709
Caldwell □, TX • 26,392
Caledonia, MN 55921 • 2,846
Caledonia, NY 14423 • 2,262
Caledonia □, VT • 27,846
Calera, AL 35040 • 2,136
Calera, OK 74730 • 1,536
Calexico, CA 92231–32 • 18,633
Calhoun, GA 30701 • 7,135
Calhoun □, AL • 116,034
Calhoun □, AR • 5,826
Calhoun □, FL • 11,011
Calhoun □, GA • 5,013
Calhoun □, IL • 5,322
Calhoun □, IA • 11,508
Calhoun □, MI • 135,982
Calhoun □, MS • 14,908
Calhoun □, SC • 12,753
Calhoun □, TX • 19,053
Calhoun □, WV • 7,885
Calhoun City, MS 38916 • 1,838
Calhoun Falls, SC 29628 • 2,328
Caliente, NV 89008 • 1,111
Califon, NJ 07830 • 1,073
California, MD 20619 • 7,626
California, MO 65018 • 3,465
California, PA 15419 • 5,748
Calipatria, CA 92233 • 2,690
Calistoga, CA 94515 • 4,468
Callahan □, TX • 11,859
Callaway, FL 32401 • 12,253
Callaway □, MO • 32,809
Calloway □, KY • 30,735
Calmar, IA 52132 • 1,026
Calumet □, WI • 34,291
Calumet City, IL 60409 • 37,840
Calumet Park, IL 60643 • 8,418
Calvert, TX 77837 • 1,536
Calvert □, MD • 51,372
Calvert City, KY 42029 • 2,531
Calverton, MD 20705 • 12,046

United States Populations and ZIP Codes

Calverton Park, MO 63136 • 1,404
Camanche, IA 52730 • 4,436
Camarillo, CA 93010–11 • 52,303
Camas, WA 98607 • 6,442
Camas □, ID • 727
Cambria, CA 93428 • 5,382
Cambria □, PA • 163,029
Cambrian Park, CA 95124 • 2,998
Cambridge, IL 61238 • 2,124
Cambridge, MD 21613 • 11,514
Cambridge, MA 02138 • 95,802
Cambridge, MN 55008 • 5,094
Cambridge, NE 69022 • 1,107
Cambridge, NY 12816 • 1,906
Cambridge, OH 43725 • 11,748
Cambridge City, IN 47327 • 2,091
Cambridge Springs, PA 16403 • 1,837
Camden, AL 36726 • 2,414
Camden, AR 71701 • 14,380
Camden, DE 19934 • 1,899
Camden, ME 04843 • 4,022
Camden, NJ 08101–10 • 87,492
Camden, NY 13316 • 2,552
Camden, OH 45311 • 2,210
Camden, SC 29020 • 6,696
Camden, TN 38320 • 3,643
Camden □, GA • 30,167
Camden □, MO • 27,495
Camden □, NJ • 502,824
Camden □, NC • 5,904
Camdenton, MO 65020 • 2,561
Camelot, WA 98002 • 4,900
Cameron, LA 70631 • 2,041
Cameron, MO 64429 • 4,831
Cameron, TX 76520 • 5,580
Cameron, WV 26033 • 1,177
Cameron, WI 54822 • 1,273
Cameron □, LA • 9,260
Cameron □, PA • 5,913
Cameron □, TX • 260,120
Cameron Park, CA 95682 • 11,897
Camilla, GA 31730 • 5,008
Camino, CA 95709 • 1,500
Camp □, TX • 9,904
Campbell, CA 95008–09 • 36,048
Campbell, FL 34746 • 3,884
Campbell, MO 63933 • 2,165
Campbell, OH 44405 • 10,038
Campbell □, KY • 83,866
Campbell □, SD • 1,965
Campbell □, TN • 35,079
Campbell □, VA • 47,572
Campbell □, WY • 29,370
Campbellsport, WI 53010 • 1,732
Campbellsville, KY 42718–19 • 9,577
Camp Hill, AL 36850 • 1,415
Camp Hill, PA 17011 • 7,831
Camp Point, IL 62320 • 1,230
Camp Springs, MD 20748 • 16,392
Camp Verde, AZ 86322 • 6,243
Canaan, CT 06018 • 1,194
Canadensis, PA 18325 • 1,200
Canadian, TX 79014 • 2,417
Canadian □, OK • 74,409
Canajoharie, NY 13317 • 2,278
Canal Fulton, OH 44614 • 4,157
Canal Winchester, OH 43110 • 2,617
Canandaigua, NY 14424–25 • 10,725
Canastota, NY 13032 • 4,673
Canby, MN 56220 • 1,826
Canby, OR 97013 • 8,983
Candler □, GA • 7,744
Candlewood Isle, CT 06812 • 1,100
Candlewood Shores, CT 06804 • 1,620
Cando, ND 58324 • 1,564
Caney, KS 67333 • 2,062
Canfield, OH 44406 • 5,409
Canisteo, NY 14823 • 2,421
Cannelton, IN 47520 • 1,786
Cannon □, TN • 10,467
Cannon Beach, OR 97110 • 1,221
Cannondale, CT 06897 • 1,500
Cannon Falls, MN 55009 • 3,232
Canon City, CO 81212 • 12,687
Canonsburg, PA 15317 • 9,200
Canterbury, DE 19943 • 500
Canton, CT 06019 • 1,563
Canton, GA 30114 • 4,817
Canton, IL 61520 • 13,922
Canton, MA 02021 • 18,182
Canton, MI 48187 • 57,047
Canton, MS 39046 • 10,062
Canton, MO 63435 • 2,623
Canton, NY 13617 • 6,379
Canton, NC 28716 • 3,790
Canton, OH 44701–99 • 84,161
Canton, PA 17724 • 1,966
Canton, SD 57013 • 2,787
Canton, TX 75103 • 2,949
Cantonment, FL 32533 • 3,200
Cantutillo, TX 79835 • 4,500
Canyon, TX 79015 • 11,365
Canyon □, ID • 90,076
Canyon Lake, CA 92380 • 7,938
Canyon Lake, TX 78130 • 9,975
Canyonville, OR 97417 • 1,219
Capac, MI 48014 • 1,583
Cape Canaveral, FL 32920 • 8,014
Cape Charles, VA 23310 • 1,398
Cape Coral, FL 33904 • 74,991
Cape Elizabeth, ME 04107 • 8,854
Cape Girardeau, MO 63701–02 • 34,438
Cape Girardeau □, MO • 61,633
Cape May, NJ 08204 • 4,668
Cape May □, NJ • 95,089
Cape May Court House, NJ 08210 • 4,426
Cape Saint Claire, MD 21401 • 7,878
Capitola, CA 95010 • 10,171
Capitol Heights, MD 20743 • 3,633
Capitol View, SC 29209 • 10,456
Captain Cook, HI 96704 • 2,595
Captiva, FL 33924 • 1,200
Caraway, AR 72419 • 1,178
Carbon □, MT • 8,080
Carbon □, PA • 56,846
Carbon □, UT • 20,228
Carbon □, WY • 16,659
Carbondale, CO 81623 • 3,004
Carbondale, IL 62901–03 • 27,033
Carbondale, KS 66414 • 1,526
Carbondale, PA 18407 • 10,664
Carbon Hill, AL 35549 • 2,115
Cardington, OH 43315 • 1,770
Carencro, LA 70520 • 5,429
Carey, OH 43316 • 3,684
Caribou, ME 04736 • 9,415
Caribou □, ID • 6,963
Carle Place, NY 11514 • 5,107
Carleton, MI 48117 • 2,770
Carlin, NV 89822 • 2,220
Carlinville, IL 62626 • 5,416
Carlisle, AR 72024 • 2,253
Carlisle, IA 50047 • 3,241
Carlisle, KY 40311 • 1,639
Carlisle, OH 45005 • 4,872
Carlisle, PA 17013 • 18,419
Carlisle □, KY • 5,238
Carl Junction, MO 64834 • 4,123
Carlsbad, CA 92008–09 • 63,126
Carlsbad, NM 88220–21 • 24,952
Carlstadt, NJ 07072 • 5,510
Carlton, OR 97111 • 1,289
Carlton □, MN • 29,259
Carlyle, IL 62231 • 3,474
Carmel, CA 93921–23 • 4,239
Carmel, IN 46032 • 25,380
Carmel, NY 10512 • 3,395
Carmi, IL 62821 • 5,564
Carmichael, CA 95608–09 • 48,702
Carnation, WA 98014 • 1,243
Carnegie, OK 73015 • 1,593
Carnegie, PA 15106 • 9,278
Carney, MD 21234 • 25,578
Carneys Point, NJ 08069 • 7,686
Carnot, PA 15108 • 4,750
Caro, MI 48723 • 4,054
Carol City, FL 33055 • 53,331
Caroleen, NC 28019 • 1,100
Carolina Beach, NC 28428 • 3,630
Caroline □, MD • 27,035
Caroline □, VA • 19,217
Carol Stream, IL 60188 • 31,716
Carpentersville, IL 60110 • 23,049
Carpinteria, CA 93013–14 • 13,747
Carrabelle, FL 32322 • 1,200
Carrboro, NC 27510 • 11,553
Carrier Mills, IL 62917 • 1,991
Carrington, ND 58421 • 2,267
Carrizo Springs, TX 78834 • 5,745
Carrizozo, NM 88301 • 1,075
Carroll, IA 51401 • 9,579
Carroll □, AR • 18,654
Carroll □, GA • 71,422
Carroll □, IL • 16,805
Carroll □, IN • 18,809
Carroll □, IA • 21,423
Carroll □, KY • 9,292
Carroll □, MD • 123,372
Carroll □, MS • 9,237
Carroll □, MO • 10,748
Carroll □, NH • 35,410
Carroll □, OH • 26,521
Carroll □, TN • 27,514
Carroll □, VA • 26,594
Carrollton, AL 35447 • 1,170
Carrollton, GA 30117 • 16,029
Carrollton, IL 62016 • 2,507
Carrollton, KY 41008 • 3,715
Carrollton, MI 48724 • 6,521
Carrollton, MO 64633 • 4,406
Carrollton, OH 44615 • 3,042
Carrollton, TX 75006–08 • 82,169
Carrolltown, PA 15722 • 1,286
Carrollwood, FL 33618 • 11,400
Carson, CA 90749 • 83,995
Carson □, TX • 6,576
Carson City, MI 48811 • 1,158
Carson City, NV 89701–21 • 40,443
Carter □, KY • 24,340
Carter □, MO • 5,515
Carter □, MT • 1,503
Carter □, OK • 42,919
Carter □, TN • 51,505
Carteret, NJ 07008 • 19,025
Carteret □, NC • 52,556
Carter Lake, IA 51510 • 3,200
Cartersville, GA 30120 • 12,035
Carterville, IL 62918 • 3,630
Carterville, MO 64835 • 2,013
Carthage, IL 62321 • 2,657
Carthage, MS 39051 • 3,819
Carthage, MO 64836 • 10,747
Carthage, NY 13619 • 4,344
Carthage, TN 37030 • 2,386
Carthage, TX 75633 • 6,496
Caruthersville, MO 63830 • 7,389
Carver, MA 02330 • 1,500
Carver □, MN • 47,915
Carver Ranch Estates, FL 33023 • 5,600
Carville, LA 70721 • 1,108
Cary, IL 60013 • 10,043
Cary, NC 27511 • 43,858
Caryville, TN 37714 • 1,751
Casa de Oro, CA 92077 • 9,500
Casa Grande, AZ 85222 • 19,082
Casas Adobes, AZ 85704 • 12,155
Cascade, CO 80809 • 1,000
Cascade, ID 83611 • 877
Cascade, IA 52033 • 1,812
Cascade, MT 59421 • 729
Cascade □, MT • 77,691
Cascade Vista, WA 98058 • 7,800
Casey, IL 62420 • 2,914
Casey □, KY • 14,211
Cashion, AZ 85329 • 3,014
Cashmere, WA 98815 • 2,544
Casper, WY 82601–15 • 46,742
Caspian, MI 49915 • 1,031
Cass □, IL • 13,437
Cass □, IN • 38,413
Cass □, IA • 15,128
Cass □, MI • 49,477
Cass □, MN • 21,791
Cass □, MO • 63,808
Cass □, NE • 21,318
Cass □, ND • 102,874
Cass □, TX • 29,982
Cass City, MI 48726 • 2,276
Casselberry, FL 32707–08 • 18,911
Casselton, ND 58012 • 1,601
Cassia □, ID • 19,532
Cassopolis, MI 49031 • 1,822
Cassville, MO 65625 • 2,371
Cassville, WI 53806 • 1,144
Castanea, PA 17726 • 1,123
Castile, NY 14427 • 1,078
Castle Dale, UT 84513 • 1,704
Castle Hayne, NC 28429 • 1,182
Castle Hills, DE 19720 • 1,475
Castle Park, CA 92011 • 6,300
Castle Point, MO 63136 • 7,800
Castle Rock, CO 80104 • 8,708
Castle Rock, WA 98611 • 2,067
Castle Shannon, PA 15234 • 9,135
Castleton, VT 05735 • 600
Castleton on Hudson, NY 12033 • 1,491
Castlewood, VA 24224 • 2,110
Castro □, TX • 9,070
Castro Valley, CA 94546 • 48,619
Castroville, TX 78009 • 2,159
Caswell □, NC • 20,693
Catahoula □, LA • 11,065
Catalina Foothills, AZ 85718 • 1,470
Catasauqua, PA 18032 • 6,662
Cataumet, MA 02534 • 1,500
Catawba □, NC • 118,412
Catawissa, PA 17820 • 1,683
Cathedral City, CA 92234–35 • 30,085
Catlettsburg, KY 41129 • 2,231
Catlin, IL 61817 • 2,173
Catonsville, MD 21228 • 35,233
Catoosa, OK 74015 • 2,954
Catoosa □, GA • 42,464
Catron □, NM • 2,563
Catskill, NY 12414 • 4,690
Cattaraugus, NY 14719 • 1,100
Cattaraugus □, NY • 84,234
Cavalier, ND 58220 • 1,508
Cavalier □, ND • 6,064
Cave City, AR 72521 • 1,503
Cave City, KY 42127 • 1,953
Cave Creek, AZ 85331 • 2,925
Cave Junction, OR 97523 • 1,126
Cave Spring, VA 24018 • 24,053
Cavetown, MD 21720 • 1,533
Cayce, SC 29033 • 11,163
Cayuga, IN 47928 • 1,083
Cayuga □, NY • 82,313
Cayuga Heights, NY 14850 • 3,457
Cazenovia, NY 13035 • 3,007
Cecil □, MD • 71,347
Cedar □, IA • 17,381
Cedar □, MO • 12,093
Cedar □, NE • 10,131
Cedar Bluff, AL 35959 • 1,174
Cedar Bluff Two, TN 37722 • 2,000
Cedarburg, WI 53012 • 9,895
Cedar City, UT 84720–22 • 13,443
Cedar Crest, NM 87008 • 1,200
Cedaredge, CO 81413 • 1,380
Cedar Falls, IA 50613 • 34,298
Cedar Grove, NJ 07009 • 12,053
Cedar Grove, WV 25039 • 1,213
Cedar Grove, WI 53013 • 1,521
Cedar Hill, MO 63016 • 1,966
Cedar Hill, TX 75104 • 19,976
Cedar Hills, OR 97005 • 9,294
Cedarhurst, NY 11516 • 5,716
Cedar Lake, IN 46303 • 8,885
Cedar Rapids, IA 52401–10 • 108,751
Cedar Springs, MI 49319 • 2,600
Cedartown, GA 30125 • 7,978
Cedarville, NJ 08311 • 1,100
Cedarville, OH 45314 • 3,210
Celina, OH 45822 • 9,650
Celina, TN 38551 • 1,493
Celina, TX 75009 • 1,737
Celoron, NY 14720 • 1,232
Cementon, PA 18052 • 1,050
Center, CO 81125 • 1,963
Center, ND 58530 • 826
Center, TX 75935 • 4,950
Centerburg, OH 43011 • 1,323
Centereach, NY 11720 • 26,720
Center Line, MI 48015 • 9,026
Center Moriches, NY 11934 • 5,987
Center Point, AL 35215 • 22,657
Center Point, IA 52213 • 1,693
Centerville, IN 47330 • 2,398
Centerville, IA 52544 • 5,936
Centerville, MA 02632 • 9,190
Centerville, OH 45459 • 21,082
Centerville, PA 15417 • 3,842
Centerville, SD 57014 • 887
Centerville, TN 37033 • 3,616
Centerville, UT 84014 • 11,500
Central, NM 88026 • 1,835
Central, SC 29630 • 2,438
Central City, CO 80427 • 335
Central City, IL 62801 • 1,390
Central City, IA 52214 • 1,063
Central City, KY 42330 • 4,979
Central City, NE 68826 • 2,868
Central City, PA 15926 • 1,246
Central Falls, RI 02863 • 17,637
Central Heights, AZ 85501 • 1,500
Centralia, IL 62801 • 14,274
Centralia, MO 65240 • 3,414
Centralia, WA 98531 • 12,101
Central Islip, NY 11722 • 26,028
Central Park, WA 98520 • 2,669
Central Point, OR 97502 • 7,509
Central Square, NY 13036 • 1,671
Central Valley, CA 96019 • 4,340
Central Valley, NY 10917 • 1,929
Central Village, CT 06332 • 1,600
Centre, AL 35960 • 2,893
Centre □, PA • 123,786
Centre City, NJ 08051 • 2,070
Centre Hall, PA 16828 • 1,203
Centreville, AL 35042 • 2,508
Centreville, IL 62207 • 7,489
Centreville, MD 21617 • 2,097
Centreville, MI 49032 • 1,516
Centreville, MS 39631 • 1,771
Centreville, VA 22020 • 26,585
Century, FL 32535 • 1,989
Century Village, FL 33409 • 8,363
Ceredo, WV 25507 • 1,916
Ceres, CA 95307 • 26,314
Cerritos, CA 90703 • 53,240
Cerro Gordo, IL 61818 • 1,436
Cerro Gordo □, IA • 46,733
Chadbourn, NC 28431 • 2,005
Chadds Ford, PA 19317 • 1,200
Chadron, NE 69337 • 5,588
Chadwicks, NY 13319 • 2,000
Chaffee, MO 63740 • 3,059
Chaffee □, CO • 12,684
Chaffin, MA 01520 • 3,980
Chagrin Falls, OH 44022 • 4,146
Chalfonte, DE 19810 • 1,740
Challis, ID 83226 • 1,073
Chalmette, LA 70043–44 • 31,860
Chama, NM 87520 • 1,048
Chamberlain, SD 57325 • 2,347
Chambers □, AL • 36,876
Chambers □, TX • 20,088
Chambersburg, PA 17201 • 16,647
Chamblee, GA 30341 • 7,668
Champaign, IL 61820–21 • 63,502
Champaign □, IL • 173,025
Champaign □, OH • 36,019
Champion, OH 44481 • 5,270
Champlain, NY 12919 • 1,273
Champlin, MN 55316 • 16,849
Chandler, AZ 85224–27 • 90,533
Chandler, IN 47610 • 3,099
Chandler, OK 74834 • 2,596
Chandler, TX 75758 • 1,630
Chandler Heights, AZ 85227 • 1,000
Chanhassen, MN 55317 • 11,732
Channahon, IL 60410 • 4,266
Channel Lake, IL 60002 • 1,660
Channelview, TX 77530 • 25,564
Chantilly, VA 22021–22 • 29,337
Chanute, KS 66720 • 9,488
Chapel Hill, NC 27514–16 • 38,719
Chapel Square, VA 22003 • 2,400
Chapman, KS 67431 • 1,264
Chapmanville, WV 25508 • 1,110
Chappaqua, NY 10514 • 6,380
Chardon, OH 44024 • 4,446
Chariton, IA 50049 • 4,616
Chariton □, MO • 9,202
Charleroi, PA 15022 • 5,014
Charles □, MD • 101,154
Charles City, IA 50616 • 7,878
Charles City □, VA • 6,282
Charles Mix □, SD • 9,131
Charleston, AR 72933 • 2,128
Charleston, IL 61920 • 20,398
Charleston, MS 38921 • 2,328
Charleston, MO 63834 • 5,085
Charleston, SC 29401–22 • 80,414
Charleston, WV 25301–75 • 57,287
Charleston □, SC • 295,039
Charlestown, IN 47111 • 5,889
Charlestown, NH 03603 • 1,173
Charlestown, RI 02813 • 1,500
Charles Town, WV 25414 • 3,122
Charlevoix, MI 49720 • 3,116
Charlevoix □, MI • 21,468
Charlotte, MI 48813 • 8,083
Charlotte, NC 28201–41 • 395,934
Charlotte, TX 78011 • 1,475
Charlotte □, FL • 110,975
Charlotte □, VA • 11,688
Charlotte Hall, MD 20622 • 1,992
Charlotte Harbor, FL 33980 • 3,327
Charlottesville, VA 22901–08 • 40,341
Charlton □, GA • 8,496
Charlton City, MA 01508 • 1,400
Charter Oak, CA 91724 • 8,858
Chase □, KS • 3,021
Chase □, NE • 4,381
Chase City, VA 23924 • 2,442
Chaska, MN 55318 • 11,339
Chatfield, MN 55923 • 2,226
Chatham, IL 62629 • 6,074
Chatham, MA 02633 • 1,916
Chatham, NJ 07928 • 8,007
Chatham, NY 12037 • 1,920
Chatham, VA 24531 • 1,354
Chatham □, GA • 216,935
Chatham □, NC • 38,759
Chatom, AL 36518 • 1,094
Chatsworth, GA 30705 • 2,865
Chatsworth, IL 60921 • 1,186
Chattahoochee, FL 32324 • 4,382
Chattahoochee □, GA • 16,934
Chattanooga, TN 37401–22 • 152,466
Chattaroy, WV 25667 • 1,182
Chattooga □, GA • 22,242
Chautauqua □, KS • 4,407
Chautauqua □, NY • 141,895
Chauvin, LA 70344 • 3,375
Chaves □, NM • 57,849
Chazy, NY 12921 • 1,000
Cheatham □, TN • 27,140
Cheboygan, MI 49721 • 4,999
Cheboygan □, MI • 21,398
Checotah, OK 74426 • 3,290
Cheektowaga, NY 14225 • 84,387
Chehalis, WA 98532 • 6,527
Chelan, WA 98816 • 2,969
Chelan □, WA • 52,250
Chelmsford, MA 01824 • 32,388
Chelsea, MA 02150 • 28,710
Chelsea, MI 48118 • 3,772
Chelsea, OK 74016 • 1,620
Chelsea Estates, DE 19720 • 1,320
Cheltenham Township, PA 19012 • 35,509
Chemung □, NY • 95,195
Chenango □, NY • 51,768
Chenango Bridge, NY 13745 • 2,890
Cheney, KS 67025 • 1,560
Cheney, WA 99004 • 7,723
Cheneyville, LA 71325 • 1,005
Chenoa, IL 61726 • 1,732
Chenoweth, OR 97058 • 3,246
Chepachet, RI 02814 • 900
Cheraw, SC 29520 • 5,505
Cherokee, AL 35616 • 1,479
Cherokee, IA 51012 • 6,026
Cherokee, OK 73728 • 1,787
Cherokee □, AL • 19,543
Cherokee □, GA • 90,204
Cherokee □, IA • 14,098
Cherokee □, KS • 21,374
Cherokee □, NC • 20,170
Cherokee □, OK • 34,049
Cherokee □, SC • 44,506
Cherokee □, TX • 41,049
Cherokee Village, AR 72525 • 3,200
Cherry □, NE • 6,307
Cherry Hill, NJ 08002–03 • 69,319
Cherry Hills Village, CO 80110 • 5,245
Cherryland, CA 94541 • 11,088
Cherryvale, KS 67335 • 2,464
Cherry Valley, CA 92223 • 5,945
Cherry Valley, IL 61016 • 1,615
Cherry Valley, MA 01611 • 1,120
Cherryville, NC 28021 • 4,756
Chesaning, MI 48616 • 2,567
Chesapeake, OH 45619 • 1,073
Chesapeake, VA 23320–28 • 151,976
Chesapeake, WV 25315 • 1,896
Chesapeake Beach, MD 20732 • 2,403
Cheshire, CT 06410 • 25,684
Cheshire, MA 01225 • 1,100
Cheshire □, NH • 70,121
Chesilhurst, NJ 08089 • 1,526
Chesnee, SC 29323 • 1,280
Chester, CA 96020 • 2,082
Chester, CT 06412 • 1,563
Chester, IL 62233 • 8,194
Chester, MT 59522 • 942
Chester, NJ 07930 • 1,214
Chester, NY 10918 • 3,270
Chester, PA 19013–16 • 41,856
Chester, SC 29706 • 7,158
Chester, VT 05143 • 550
Chester, VA 23831 • 14,896
Chester, WV 26034 • 2,905
Chester □, PA • 376,396
Chester □, SC • 32,170
Chester □, TN • 12,819
Chester Depot, VT 05144 • 500
Chesterfield, IN 46017 • 2,730
Chesterfield, SC 29709 • 1,373
Chesterfield □, SC • 38,577
Chesterfield □, VA • 209,274
Chesterton, IN 46304 • 9,124
Chestertown, MD 21620 • 4,005
Chester Township, PA 19013 • 5,399
Chestnut Hill Estates, DE 19713 • 1,730
Chestnut Ridge, NY 10952 • 7,517
Cheswick, PA 15024 • 1,971
Cheswold, DE 19936 • 321
Chetek, WI 54728 • 1,953
Chetopa, KS 67336 • 1,357
Chevak, AK 99563 • 598
Cheverly, MD 20785 • 6,023
Cheviot, OH 45211 • 9,616
Chevy Chase, MD 20815 • 8,559
Chewelah, WA 99109 • 1,945
Cheyenne, WY 82001–09 • 50,008
Cheyenne □, CO • 2,397
Cheyenne □, KS • 3,243
Cheyenne □, NE • 9,494
Cheyenne Wells, CO 80810 • 1,128
Chicago, IL 60601–66 • 2,783,726
Chicago Heights, IL 60411 • 33,072
Chicago Ridge, IL 60415 • 13,643
Chickamauga, GA 30707 • 2,149
Chickasaw, AL 36611 • 6,649
Chickasaw □, IA • 13,295
Chickasaw □, MS • 18,085
Chickasha, OK 73018 • 14,988
Chico, CA 95926–28 • 40,079
Chicopee, MA 01013–22 • 56,632
Chicora, PA 16025 • 1,058
Chiefland, FL 32626 • 1,917
Childersburg, AL 35044 • 4,579
Childress, TX 79201 • 5,055
Childress □, TX • 5,953
Chilhowie, VA 24319 • 1,971
Chili Center, NY 14624 • 4,360
Chillicothe, IL 61523 • 5,959
Chillicothe, MO 64601 • 8,804
Chillicothe, OH 45601 • 21,923
Chillum, MD 20783 • 31,309
Chilton, WI 53014 • 3,240
Chilton □, AL • 32,458
Chimayo, NM 87522 • 2,789
China Grove, NC 28023 • 2,732
Chincoteague, VA 23336 • 3,572
Chinle, AZ 86503 • 5,059
Chino, CA 91708–10 • 59,682
Chinook, MT 59523 • 1,512
Chino Valley, AZ 86323 • 4,837
Chipley, FL 32428 • 3,866
Chippewa □, MI • 34,604
Chippewa □, MN • 13,228
Chippewa □, WI • 52,360
Chippewa Falls, WI 54729 • 12,727
Chisago □, MN • 30,521
Chisago City, MN 55013 • 2,009
Chisholm, ME 04239 • 1,653
Chisholm, MN 55719 • 5,290
Chittenango, NY 13037 • 4,734
Chittenden □, VT • 131,761
Choctaw, OK 73020 • 8,545
Choctaw □, AL • 16,018
Choctaw □, MS • 9,071
Choctaw □, OK • 15,302
Choteau, MT 59422 • 1,741
Chouteau, OK 74337 • 1,771
Chouteau □, MT • 5,452
Chowan □, NC • 13,506
Chowchilla, CA 93610 • 5,930
Chrisman, IL 61924 • 1,136
Christian □, IL • 34,418
Christian □, KY • 68,941
Christian □, MO • 32,644
Christiana, DE 19702 • 500
Christiana, PA 17509 • 1,045
Christiansburg, VA 24073 • 15,004
Christmas, FL 32709 • 1,200
Christopher, IL 62822 • 2,774
Chubbuck, ID 83202 • 7,791
Chugwater, WY 82210 • 192
Chula Vista, CA 91909–15 • 135,163
Church Hill, TN 37642 • 4,834
Churchill, OH 44505 • 7,700
Churchill □, NV • 17,938
Church Point, LA 70525 • 4,677
Churchville, NY 14428 • 1,731
Churubusco, IN 46723 • 1,781
Cibola □, NM • 23,794
Cicero, IL 60650 • 67,436
Cicero, IN 46034 • 3,268
Cimarron, KS 67835 • 1,626
Cimarron □, OK • 3,301
Cimarron Hills, CO 80906 • 11,160
Cincinnati, OH 45201–75 • 364,040
Cinnaminson, NJ 08077 • 14,583
Circle, MT 59215 • 805
Circle Pines, MN 55014 • 4,704
Circleville, OH 43113 • 11,666
Cisco, TX 76437 • 3,813
Citra, FL 32113 • 1,500
Citronelle, AL 36522 • 3,671
Citrus, CA 91702 • 9,481

Citrus □, FL • 93,515
Citrus Heights, CA 95610–11 • 107,439
City Of Sunrise, FL 33313 • 64,407
City View, SC 29611 • 1,490
Clackamas, OR 97015 • 2,578
Clackamas □, OR • 278,850
Claiborne, LA 71291 • 8,300
Claiborne □, LA • 17,405
Claiborne □, MS • 11,370
Claiborne □, TN • 26,137
Clair-Mel City, FL 33619 • 7,000
Clairton, PA 15025 • 9,656
Clallam □, WA • 56,464
Clanton, AL 35045 • 7,669
Clara City, MN 56222 • 1,307
Clare, MI 48617 • 3,021
Clare □, MI • 24,952
Claremont, CA 91711 • 32,503
Claremont, NH 03743 • 13,902
Claremore, OK 74017–18 • 13,280
Clarence, MO 63437 • 1,026
Clarendon, AR 72029 • 2,072
Clarendon, TX 79226 • 2,067
Clarendon □, SC • 28,450
Clarendon Hills, IL 60514 • 6,994
Claridge, PA 15623 • 1,200
Clarinda, IA 51632 • 5,104
Clarion, IA 50525 • 2,703
Clarion, PA 16214 • 6,457
Clarion □, PA • 41,699
Clark, NJ 07066 • 14,629
Clark, SD 57225 • 1,292
Clark □, AR • 21,437
Clark □, ID • 762
Clark □, IL • 15,921
Clark □, IN • 87,777
Clark □, KS • 2,418
Clark □, KY • 29,496
Clark □, MO • 7,547
Clark □, NV • 741,459
Clark □, OH • 147,548
Clark □, SD • 4,403
Clark □, WA • 238,053
Clark □, WI • 31,647
Clarkdale, AZ 86324 • 2,144
Clarke □, AL • 27,240
Clarke □, GA • 87,594
Clarke □, IA • 8,287
Clarke □, MS • 17,313
Clarke □, VA • 12,101
Clarkesville, GA 30523 • 1,151
Clarksburg, WV 26301–02 • 18,059
Clarksdale, MS 38614 • 19,717
Clarks Summit, PA 18411 • 5,433
Clarkston, GA 30021 • 5,385
Clarkston, MI 48346–48 • 1,005
Clarkston, WA 99403 • 6,753
Clarksville, AR 72830 • 5,833
Clarksville, DE 19970 • 500
Clarksville, IN 47129 • 19,833
Clarksville, IA 50619 • 1,382
Clarksville, TN 37040–43 • 75,494
Clarksville, TX 75426 • 4,311
Clarksville, VA 23927 • 1,243
Clarkton, MO 63837 • 1,113
Clatskanie, OR 97016 • 1,629
Clatsop □, OR • 33,301
Claude, TX 79019 • 1,199
Clawson, MI 48017 • 13,874
Claxton, GA 30417 • 2,464
Clay, KY 42404 • 1,173
Clay □, AL • 13,252
Clay □, AR • 18,107
Clay □, FL • 105,986
Clay □, GA • 3,364
Clay □, IL • 14,460
Clay □, IN • 24,705
Clay □, IA • 17,585
Clay □, KS • 9,158
Clay □, KY • 21,746
Clay □, MN • 50,422
Clay □, MS • 21,120
Clay □, MO • 153,411
Clay □, NE • 7,123
Clay □, NC • 7,155
Clay □, SD • 13,186
Clay □, TN • 7,238
Clay □, TX • 10,024
Clay □, WV • 9,983
Clay Center, KS 67432 • 4,613
Clay City, KY 40312 • 1,258
Claymont, DE 19702 • 9,800
Claypool, AZ 85532 • 1,942
Claysburg, PA 16625 • 1,399
Clayton, AL 36016 • 1,564
Clayton, DE 19938 • 1,163
Clayton, GA 30525 • 1,613
Clayton, MO 63105 • 13,874
Clayton, NJ 08312 • 6,155
Clayton, NM 88415 • 2,484
Clayton, NY 13624 • 2,160
Clayton, NC 27520 • 4,756
Clayton □, GA • 182,052
Clayton □, IA • 19,054
Clear Creek □, CO • 7,619
Clearfield, KY 40313 • 1,250
Clearfield, PA 16830 • 6,633
Clearfield, UT 84015 • 21,435
Clearfield □, PA • 78,097
Clearlake, CA 95422 • 11,804
Clear Lake, IA 50428 • 8,183
Clear Lake, SD 57226 • 1,247
Clearlake, WA 98235 • 1,100
Clear Lake Shores, TX 77565 • 1,096
Clearwater, FL 34615–30 • 98,784
Clearwater, KS 67026 • 1,875
Clearwater, SC 29822 • 4,731
Clearwater □, ID • 8,505
Clearwater □, MN • 8,309
Cleburne, TX 76031–33 • 22,205
Cleburne □, AL • 12,730
Cleburne □, AR • 19,411
Cle Elum, WA 98922 • 1,778
Cleland Heights, DE 19805 • 1,120
Clementon, NJ 08021 • 5,601
Clemmons, NC 27012 • 6,020
Clemson, SC 29631–33 • 11,096
Clendenin, WV 25045 • 1,203
Cleona, PA 17042 • 2,322
Clermont, FL 34711–12 • 6,910
Clermont □, OH • 150,187
Cleveland, GA 30528 • 1,653
Cleveland, MS 38732–33 • 15,384
Cleveland, OH 44101–99 • 505,616
Cleveland, OK 74020 • 3,156
Cleveland, TN 37311–12 • 30,354
Cleveland, TX 77327–28 • 7,124
Cleveland, WI 53015 • 1,398
Cleveland □, AR • 7,781
Cleveland □, NC • 84,714
Cleveland □, OK • 174,253
Cleveland Heights, OH 44118 • 54,052
Cleves, OH 45002 • 2,208
Clewiston, FL 33440 • 6,085
Cliffside Park, NJ 07010 • 20,393
Clifton, AZ 85533 • 2,840
Clifton, CO 81520 • 12,671
Clifton, IL 60927 • 1,347
Clifton, NJ 07011–15 • 71,742
Clifton, TX 76634 • 3,195
Clifton Forge, VA 24422 • 4,679
Clifton Heights, PA 19018 • 7,111
Clifton Knolls, NY 12065 • 5,636
Clifton Springs, NY 14432 • 2,175
Clinch □, GA • 6,160
Clint, TX 79836 • 1,035
Clinton, AR 72031 • 2,213
Clinton, CT 06413 • 3,439
Clinton, IL 61727 • 7,437
Clinton, IN 47842 • 5,040
Clinton, IA 52732–33 • 29,201
Clinton, KY 42031 • 1,547
Clinton, LA 70722 • 1,904
Clinton, ME 04927 • 1,485
Clinton, MD 20735 • 19,987
Clinton, MA 01510 • 7,943
Clinton, MI 49236 • 2,475
Clinton, MS 39056 • 21,847
Clinton, MO 64735 • 8,703
Clinton, NJ 08809 • 2,054
Clinton, NY 13323 • 2,238
Clinton, NC 28328 • 8,204
Clinton, OK 73601 • 9,298
Clinton, SC 29325 • 7,987
Clinton, TN 37716 • 8,972
Clinton, UT 84015 • 7,945
Clinton, WA 98236 • 2,000
Clinton, WI 53525 • 1,849
Clinton □, IL • 33,944
Clinton □, IN • 30,974
Clinton □, IA • 51,040
Clinton □, KY • 9,135
Clinton □, MI • 57,883
Clinton □, MO • 16,595
Clinton □, NY • 85,969
Clinton □, OH • 35,415
Clinton □, PA • 37,182
Clinton Township, MI 48043 • 85,866
Clintonville, WI 54929 • 4,351
Clintwood, VA 24228 • 1,542
Clio, AL 36017 • 1,365
Clio, MI 48420 • 2,629
Clive, IA 50322 • 7,462
Cloquet, MN 55720 • 10,885
Closter, NJ 07624 • 8,094
Cloud □, KS • 11,023
Clover, SC 29710 • 3,422
Cloverdale, CA 95425 • 4,924
Cloverdale, IN 46120 • 1,681
Cloverleaf, TX 77015 • 18,230
Cloverport, KY 40111 • 1,207
Clovis, CA 93612–13 • 50,323
Clovis, NM 88101–03 • 30,954
Clute, TX 77531 • 8,910
Clyde, NY 14433 • 2,409
Clyde, NC 28721 • 1,041
Clyde, OH 43410 • 5,776
Clyde, TX 79510 • 3,002
Clymer, PA 15728 • 1,499
Coachella, CA 92236 • 16,896
Coahoma, TX 79511 • 1,133
Coahoma □, MS • 31,665
Coal □, OK • 5,780
Coal City, IL 60416 • 3,907
Coal Fork, WV 25306 • 2,100
Coalgate, OK 74538 • 1,895
Coal Grove, OH 45638 • 2,251
Coalinga, CA 93210 • 8,212
Coalville, UT 84017 • 1,065
Coatesville, PA 19320 • 11,038
Coats, NC 27521 • 1,493
Cobb □, GA • 447,745
Cobden, IL 62920 • 1,090
Cobleskill, NY 12043 • 5,268
Cochise □, AZ • 97,624
Cochituate, MA 01778 • 6,046
Cochran, GA 31014 • 4,390
Cochran □, TX • 4,377
Cochranton, PA 16314 • 1,174
Cocke □, TN • 29,141
Cockeysville, MD 21030 • 18,668
Cockrell Hill, TX 75211 • 3,746
Cocoa, FL 32922–27 • 17,722
Cocoa Beach, FL 32931–32 • 12,123
Coconino □, AZ • 96,591
Coconut Creek, FL 33060 • 27,485
Codington □, SD • 22,698
Cody, WY 82414 • 7,897
Coeburn, VA 24230 • 2,165
Coeur d'Alene, ID 83814 • 24,563
Coffee □, AL • 40,240
Coffee □, GA • 29,592
Coffee □, TN • 40,339
Coffey □, KS • 8,404
Coffeyville, KS 67337 • 12,917
Cohasset, MA 02025 • 6,900
Cohoes, NY 12047 • 16,825
Cokato, MN 55321 • 2,180
Coke □, TX • 3,424
Cokeville, WY 83114 • 493
Colbert, OK 74733 • 1,043
Colbert □, AL • 51,666
Colby, KS 67701 • 5,396
Colby, WI 54421 • 1,532
Colchester, CT 06415 • 3,212
Colchester, IL 62326 • 1,645
Cold Bay, AK 99571 • 148
Cold Spring, KY 41076 • 2,880
Cold Spring, MN 56320 • 2,459
Cold Spring Harbor, NY 11724 • 4,789
Coldwater, MI 49036 • 9,607
Coldwater, MS 38618 • 1,502
Coldwater, OH 45828 • 4,335
Cole □, MO • 63,579
Colebrook, NH 03576 • 2,444
Cole Camp, MO 65325 • 1,054
Coleman, MI 48618 • 1,237
Coleman, TX 76834 • 5,410
Coleman □, TX • 9,710
Coleraine, MN 55722 • 1,041
Coles □, IL • 51,644
Colfax, CA 95713 • 1,306
Colfax, IA 50054 • 2,462
Colfax, LA 71417 • 1,696
Colfax, WA 99111 • 2,713
Colfax, WI 54730 • 1,110
Colfax □, NE • 9,139
Colfax □, NM • 12,925
College, AK 99701 • 11,249
Collegedale, TN 37315 • 5,048
College Park, GA 30337 • 20,457
College Park, MD 20740–41 • 21,927
College Place, WA 99324 • 6,308
College Station, AR 72053 • 3,800
College Station, TX 77840–45 • 52,456
Collegeville, PA 19426 • 4,227
Colleton □, SC • 34,377
Colleyville, TX 76034 • 12,724
Collier □, FL • 152,099
Collierville, TN 38017 • 14,427
Collin □, TX • 264,036
Collingdale, PA 19023 • 9,175
Collingswood, NJ 08108 • 15,289
Collingsworth □, TX • 3,573
Collins, MS 39428 • 2,541
Collins Park, DE 19720 • 2,100
Collinsville, AL 35961 • 1,429
Collinsville, CT 06022 • 2,591
Collinsville, IL 62234 • 22,446
Collinsville, OK 74021 • 3,612
Collinsville, VA 24078 • 7,280
Collinwood, TN 38450 • 1,014
Colmar Manor, MD 20722 • 1,249
Coloma, MI 49038 • 1,679
Colon, MI 49040 • 1,224
Colonia, NJ 07067 • 18,238
Colonial Beach, VA 22443 • 3,132
Colonial Heights, TN 37663 • 6,716
Colonial Heights, VA 23834 • 16,064
Colonial Park, PA 17109 • 13,777
Colonie, NY 12212 • 8,019
Colorado □, TX • 18,383
Colorado City, AZ 86021 • 2,426
Colorado City, CO 81019 • 1,149
Colorado City, TX 79512 • 4,749
Colorado Springs, CO 80901–99 • 281,140
Colquitt, GA 31737 • 1,991
Colquitt □, GA • 36,645
Colstrip, MT 59323 • 3,035
Colton, CA 92324 • 40,213
Columbia, CA 95310 • 1,799
Columbia, IL 62236 • 5,524
Columbia, KY 42728 • 3,845
Columbia, MD 21044–46 • 75,883
Columbia, MS 39429 • 6,815
Columbia, MO 65201–05 • 69,101
Columbia, PA 17512 • 10,701
Columbia, SC 29201–92 • 98,052
Columbia, TN 38401–02 • 28,583
Columbia □, AR • 25,691
Columbia □, FL • 42,613
Columbia □, GA • 66,031
Columbia □, NY • 62,982
Columbia □, OR • 37,557
Columbia □, PA • 63,202
Columbia □, WA • 4,024
Columbia □, WI • 45,088
Columbia City, IN 46725 • 5,706
Columbia City, OR 97018 • 1,003
Columbia Falls, MT 59912 • 2,942
Columbia Heights, MN 55421 • 18,910
Columbiana, AL 35051 • 2,968
Columbiana, OH 44408 • 4,961
Columbiana □, OH • 108,276
Columbine, CO 80123 • 23,969
Columbus, GA 31901–09 • 178,681
Columbus, IN 47201–03 • 31,802
Columbus, KS 66725 • 3,268
Columbus, MS 39701–05 • 23,799
Columbus, MT 59019 • 1,573
Columbus, NE 68601 • 19,480
Columbus, OH 43201–91 • 632,910
Columbus, TX 78934 • 3,367
Columbus, WI 53925 • 4,093
Columbus □, NC • 49,587
Columbus Grove, OH 45830 • 2,231
Columbus Junction, IA 52738 • 1,616
Colusa, CA 95932 • 4,934
Colusa □, CA • 16,275
Colver, PA 15927 • 1,024
Colville, WA 99114 • 4,360
Colwich, KS 67030 • 1,091
Comal □, TX • 51,832
Comanche, OK 73529 • 1,695
Comanche, TX 76442 • 4,087
Comanche □, KS • 2,313
Comanche □, OK • 111,486
Comanche □, TX • 13,381
Combee Settlement, FL 33801 • 5,463
Combined Locks, WI 54113 • 2,190
Comfort, TX 78013 • 1,477
Commack, NY 11725 • 36,124
Commerce, CA 90040 • 12,135
Commerce, GA 30529 • 4,108
Commerce, OK 74339 • 2,426
Commerce, TX 75428 • 6,825
Commerce City, CO 80022 • 16,466
Common Fence Point, RI 02871 • 860
Como, MS 38619 • 1,387
Compton, CA 90220–24 • 90,454
Comstock, MI 49041 • 5,600
Comstock Park, MI 49321 • 6,530
Concho □, TX • 3,044
Concord, CA 94518–24 • 111,348
Concord, MA 01742 • 4,680
Concord, MO 63128 • 19,859
Concord, NH 03301–03 • 36,006
Concord, NC 28025–27 • 27,347
Concord, TN 37901 • 3,420
Concordia, KS 66901 • 6,167
Concordia, MO 64020 • 2,160
Concordia □, LA • 20,828
Conecuh □, AL • 14,054
Conejos □, CO • 7,453
Conemaugh, PA 15909 • 1,470
Congers, NY 10920 • 8,003
Conklin, NY 13748 • 1,800
Conley, GA 30027 • 5,528
Conneaut, OH 44030 • 13,241
Connell, WA 99326 • 2,005
Connellsville, PA 15425 • 9,229
Connersville, IN 47331 • 15,550
Conover, NC 28613 • 5,465
Conrad, MT 59425 • 2,891
Conroe, TX 77301–05 • 27,610
Conshohocken, PA 19428 • 8,064
Constantia, NY 13044 • 1,140
Constantine, MI 49042 • 2,032
Continental, OH 45831 • 1,214
Contoocook, NH 03229 • 1,334
Contra Costa □, CA • 803,732
Converse, IN 46919 • 1,144
Converse, SC 29329 • 1,173
Converse, TX 78109 • 8,887
Converse □, WY • 11,128
Convoy, OH 45832 • 1,200
Conway, AR 72032 • 26,481
Conway, FL 32809 • 13,159
Conway, NH 03818 • 1,604
Conway, PA 15027 • 2,424
Conway, SC 29526–27 • 9,819
Conway □, AR • 19,151
Conway Springs, KS 67031 • 1,384
Conyers, GA 30207–08 • 7,380
Cook □, GA • 13,456
Cook □, IL • 5,105,067
Cook □, MN • 3,868
Cooke □, TX • 30,777
Cookeville, TN 38501–02 • 21,744
Coolidge, AZ 85228 • 6,927
Coon Rapids, IA 50058 • 1,266
Coon Rapids, MN 55433 • 52,978
Cooper, TX 75432 • 2,153
Cooper □, MO • 14,835
Cooper City, FL 33328 • 20,791
Cooper Road, LA 71107 • 11,050
Coopersburg, PA 18036 • 2,599
Cooperstown, NY 13326 • 2,180
Cooperstown, ND 58425 • 1,247
Coopersville, MI 49404 • 3,421
Coos □, NH • 34,828
Coos □, OR • 60,273
Coosa □, AL • 11,063
Coos Bay, OR 97420 • 15,076
Copake, NY 12516 • 1,200
Copiague, NY 11726 • 20,769
Copiah □, MS • 27,592
Coplay, PA 18037 • 3,267
Copperas Cove, TX 76522 • 24,079
Coquille, OR 97423 • 4,121
Coral Gables, FL 33134 • 40,091
Coral Hills, MD 20743 • 11,032
Coral Springs, FL 33065 • 79,443
Coral Terrace, FL 33157 • 23,255
Coralville, IA 52241 • 10,347
Coral Way Village, FL 33155 • 9,000
Coram, NY 11727 • 30,111
Coraopolis, PA 15108 • 6,747
Corbin, KY 40701–02 • 7,419
Corcoran, CA 93212 • 13,364
Corcoran, MN 55340 • 5,199
Cordaville, MA 01772 • 1,530
Cordele, GA 31015 • 10,321
Cordell, OK 73632 • 2,903
Cordova, AL 35550 • 2,623
Cordova, AK 99574 • 2,110
Cordova, NC 28330 • 1,200
Corinth, MS 38834 • 11,820
Corinth, NY 12822 • 2,760
Cornelia, GA 30531 • 3,219
Cornelius, NC 28031 • 2,581
Cornelius, OR 97113 • 6,148
Cornell, WI 54732 • 1,541
Corning, AR 72422 • 3,323
Corning, CA 96021 • 5,870
Corning, IA 50841 • 1,806
Corning, NY 14830 • 11,938
Cornville, AZ 86325 • 1,200
Cornwall, PA 17016 • 3,231
Cornwall on Hudson, NY 12520 • 3,093
Corona, CA 91718–20 • 76,095
Coronado, CA 92118 • 26,540
Coronado, CO 80229 • 6,890
Corpus Christi, TX 78401–82 • 257,453
Corrigan, TX 75939 • 1,764
Corriganville, MD 21524 • 1,020
Corry, PA 16407 • 7,216
Corsicana, TX 75110 • 22,911
Corson □, SD • 4,195
Corte Madera, CA 94925 • 8,272
Cortez, CO 81321 • 7,284
Cortez, FL 34215 • 4,509
Cortland, NY 13045 • 19,801
Cortland, OH 44410 • 5,666
Cortland □, NY • 48,963
Corunna, MI 48817 • 3,091
Corvallis, OR 97330–33 • 44,757
Corydon, IN 47112 • 2,661
Corydon, IA 50060 • 1,675
Coryell □, TX • 64,213
Coshocton, OH 43812 • 12,193
Coshocton □, OH • 35,427
Cosmopolis, WA 98537 • 1,372
Costa Mesa, CA 92626–28 • 96,357
Costilla □, CO • 3,190
Cottage Grove, MN 55016 • 22,935
Cottage Grove, OR 97424 • 7,402
Cottle □, TX • 2,247
Cottleville, MO 63338 • 2,936
Cotton □, OK • 6,651
Cottondale, AL 35453 • 1,960
Cotton Plant, AR 72036 • 1,150
Cottonport, LA 71327 • 2,600
Cotton Valley, LA 71018 • 1,130
Cottonwood, AL 36320 • 1,385
Cottonwood, AZ 86326 • 5,918
Cottonwood, CA 96022 • 1,747
Cottonwood, ID 83522 • 822
Cottonwood, UT 84121 • 11,554
Cottonwood □, MN • 12,694
Cottonwood Heights, UT 84121 • 28,766
Cotuit, MA 02635 • 1,750
Cotulla, TX 78014 • 3,694
Coudersport, PA 16915 • 2,854
Coulee Dam, WA 99116 • 1,087
Council, ID 83612 • 831
Council Bluffs, IA 51501–03 • 54,315
Council Grove, KS 66846 • 2,228
Country Club Hills, IL 60478 • 15,431
Country Homes, WA 99218 • 5,126
Countryside, IL 60525 • 5,716
Coupeville, WA 98239 • 1,377
Coushatta, LA 71019 • 1,845
Covedale, OH 45238 • 6,669
Covelo, CA 95428 • 1,057
Coventry, CT 06238 • 10,063
Coventry, DE 19720 • 1,165
Coventry, RI 02816 • 6,980
Covina, CA 91722–24 • 43,207
Covington, GA 30209 • 10,026
Covington, IN 47932 • 2,747
Covington, KY 41011–18 • 43,264
Covington, LA 70433–34 • 7,691
Covington, OH 45318 • 2,603
Covington, TN 38019 • 7,487
Covington, VA 24426 • 6,991
Covington □, AL • 36,478
Covington □, MS • 16,527
Cowan, TN 37318 • 1,738
Cowarts, AL 36321 • 1,400
Coweta, OK 74429 • 6,159
Coweta □, GA • 53,853
Cowley, WY 82420 • 477
Cowley □, KS • 36,915
Cowlitz □, WA • 82,119
Cowpens, SC 29330 • 2,176
Coxsackie, NY 12051 • 2,789
Cozad, NE 69130 • 3,823
Crab Orchard, WV 25827 • 2,919
Crabtree, PA 15624 • 1,000
Crafton, PA 15205 • 7,188
Craig, AK 99921 • 1,260
Craig, CO 81625–26 • 8,091
Craig □, OK • 14,104
Craig □, VA • 4,372
Craighead □, AR • 68,956
Craigsville, WV 26205 • 1,955
Cramerton, NC 28032 • 2,371
Cranbury, NJ 08512 • 1,255
Crandall, TX 75114 • 1,652
Crandon, WI 54520 • 1,958
Crane, AZ 85365 • 2,650
Crane, MO 65633 • 1,218
Crane, TX 79731 • 3,533
Crane □, TX • 4,652
Cranford, NJ 07016 • 22,624
Cranston, RI 02910 • 76,060
Craven □, NC • 81,613
Crawford, NE 69339 • 1,115
Crawford □, AR • 42,493
Crawford □, GA • 8,991
Crawford □, IL • 19,464
Crawford □, IN • 9,914
Crawford □, IA • 16,775
Crawford □, KS • 35,568
Crawford □, MI • 12,260
Crawford □, MO • 19,173
Crawford □, OH • 47,870
Crawford □, PA • 86,169
Crawford □, WI • 15,940
Crawfordsville, IN 47933 • 13,584
Crawfordville, FL 32327 • 1,110
Creedmoor, NC 27522 • 1,504
Creek □, OK • 60,915
Creighton, NE 68729 • 1,223
Creighton, PA 15030 • 1,658
Crenshaw □, AL • 13,635
Creola, AL 36525 • 1,896
Cresaptown, MD 21502 • 4,645
Crescent, OK 73028 • 1,236
Crescent City, CA 95531 • 4,380
Crescent City, FL 32112 • 1,859
Crescent Springs, KY 41016 • 2,179
Cresco, IA 52136 • 3,669
Cresskill, NJ 07626 • 7,558
Cresson, PA 16630 • 1,784
Cressona, PA 17929 • 1,694
Cresthaven, FL 33064 • 2,400
Crest Hill, IL 60435 • 10,643
Crestline, CA 92325 • 8,594
Crestline, OH 44827 • 4,934
Creston, IA 50801 • 7,911
Creston, OH 44217 • 1,848
Crestview, FL 32536 • 9,886
Crestview, HI 96797 • 1,000
Crestwood, IL 60445 • 10,823
Crestwood, KY 40014 • 1,435
Crestwood, MO 63126 • 11,234
Crestwood Village, NJ 08759 • 8,030
Creswell, OR 97426 • 2,431
Crete, IL 60417 • 6,773
Crete, NE 68333 • 4,841
Creve Coeur, IL 61611 • 5,938
Creve Coeur, MO 63141 • 12,304
Crewe, VA 23930 • 2,276
Cricket, NC 28659 • 2,015
Cridersville, OH 45806 • 1,885
Crisfield, MD 21817 • 2,880
Crisp □, GA • 20,011
Crittenden □, AR • 49,939
Crittenden □, KY • 9,196
Crocker, MO 65452 • 1,077
Crockett, CA 94525 • 3,228
Crockett, TX 75835 • 7,024
Crockett □, TN • 13,378
Crockett □, TX • 4,078
Crofton, MD 21114 • 12,781
Cromwell, CT 06416 • 1,100
Crook □, OR • 14,111
Crook □, WY • 5,294
Crookston, MN 56716 • 8,119
Crooksville, OH 43731 • 2,601
Crosby, MN 56441 • 2,073
Crosby, ND 58730 • 1,312
Crosby, TX 77532 • 1,811
Crosby □, TX • 7,304
Crosbyton, TX 79322 • 2,026
Cross □, AR • 19,225
Cross City, FL 32628 • 2,041
Crossett, AR 71635 • 6,282
Crosslake, MN 56442 • 1,132
Cross Lanes, WV 25313 • 10,878
Cross Plains, TN 37049 • 1,025
Cross Plains, TX 76443 • 1,063
Cross Plains, WI 53528 • 2,098
Crossville, AL 35962 • 1,350
Crossville, TN 38555 • 6,930
Croswell, MI 48422 • 2,174
Crothersville, IN 47229 • 1,687
Croton-on-Hudson, NY 10520 • 7,018
Crow Agency, MT 59022 • 1,446
Crowell, TX 79227 • 1,230
Crowley, LA 70526–27 • 13,983
Crowley, TX 76036 • 6,974

Crowley □, CO • 3,946
Crown Point, IN 46307 • 17,728
Crownpoint, NM 87313 • 2,108
Crow Wing □, MN • 44,249
Crozet, VA 22932 • 2,256
Crystal, MN 55428 • 23,788
Crystal Bay, NV 89402 • 1,200
Crystal Beach, FL 34681 • 1,450
Crystal City, MO 63019 • 4,088
Crystal City, TX 78839 • 8,263
Crystal Falls, MI 49920 • 1,922
Crystal Lake, CT 06029 • 1,200
Crystal Lake, FL 33803 • 5,300
Crystal Lake, IL 60014 • 24,512
Crystal Lawns, IL 60435 • 1,660
Crystal River, FL 32629 • 4,044
Crystal Springs, MS 39059 • 5,643
Cuba, IL 61427 • 1,440
Cuba, MO 65453 • 2,537
Cuba, NY 14727 • 1,690
Cuba City, WI 53807 • 2,024
Cucamonga, CA 91730 • 101,409
Cudahy, CA 90201 • 22,817
Cudahy, WI 53110 • 18,659
Cuero, TX 77954 • 6,700
Culberson □, TX • 3,407
Culbertson, MT 59218 • 796
Cullen, LA 71021 • 1,642
Cullman, AL 35055–56 • 13,367
Cullman □, AL • 67,613
Culloden, WV 25510 • 2,907
Cullowhee, NC 28723 • 1,200
Culpeper, VA 22701 • 8,581
Culpeper □, VA • 27,791
Culver, IN 46511 • 1,404
Culver City, CA 90230–33 • 38,793
Cumberland, KY 40823 • 3,112
Cumberland, MD 21501–05 • 23,706
Cumberland, WI 54829 • 2,163
Cumberland □, IL • 10,670
Cumberland □, KY • 6,784
Cumberland □, ME • 243,135
Cumberland □, NJ • 138,053
Cumberland □, NC • 274,566
Cumberland □, PA • 195,257
Cumberland □, TN • 34,736
Cumberland □, VA • 7,825
Cumberland Center, ME 04021 • 1,890
Cumberland Foreside, ME 04110 • 1,000
Cumberland Hill, RI 02864 • 6,379
Cuming □, NE • 10,117
Cumming, GA 30130 • 2,828
Cupertino, CA 95014–16 • 40,263
Currituck □, NC • 13,736
Curry □, NM • 42,207
Curry □, OR • 19,327
Curtisville, PA 15032 • 1,285
Curwensville, PA 16833 • 2,924
Cushing, OK 74023 • 7,218
Cusseta, GA 31805 • 1,107
Custer, SD 57730 • 1,741
Custer □, CO • 1,926
Custer □, ID • 4,133
Custer □, MT • 11,697
Custer □, NE • 12,270
Custer □, OK • 26,897
Custer □, SD • 6,179
Cut Bank, MT 59427 • 3,329
Cutchogue, NY 11935 • 1,730
Cuthbert, GA 31740 • 3,730
Cutler, FL 33157 • 16,201
Cutler Ridge, FL 33157 • 21,268
Cutlerville, MI 49508 • 11,228
Cut Off, LA 70345 • 5,325
Cuyahoga □, OH • 1,412,140
Cuyahoga Falls, OH 44221–24 • 48,950
Cynthiana, KY 41031 • 6,497
Cypress, CA 90630 • 42,655
Cypress Lake, FL 33919 • 10,491
Cypress Quarters, FL 34972 • 1,343
Cyril, OK 73029 • 1,072

D

Dacono, CO 80514 • 2,228
Dacula, GA 30211 • 2,217
Dade □, FL • 1,937,094
Dade □, GA • 13,147
Dade □, MO • 7,449
Dade City, FL 33525–26 • 5,633
Dadeville, AL 36853 • 3,276
Daggett □, UT • 690
Dagsboro, DE 19939 • 398
Dahlonega, GA 30533 • 3,086
Daingerfield, TX 75638 • 2,572
Dakota □, MN • 275,227
Dakota □, NE • 16,742
Dakota City, IA 50529 • 1,024
Dakota City, NE 68731 • 1,470
Dale, IN 47523 • 1,553
Dale □, AL • 49,633
Dale City, VA 22193 • 47,170
Daleville, AL 36322 • 5,117
Daleville, IN 47334 • 1,681
Dalhart, TX 79022 • 6,246
Dallam □, TX • 5,461
Dallas, GA 30132 • 2,810
Dallas, NC 28034 • 3,012
Dallas, OR 97338 • 9,422
Dallas, PA 18612 • 2,567
Dallas, TX 75201–99 • 1,006,877
Dallas □, AL • 48,130
Dallas □, AR • 9,614
Dallas □, IA • 29,755
Dallas □, MO • 12,646
Dallas □, TX • 1,852,810
Dallas Center, IA 50063 • 1,454
Dallas City, IL 62330 • 1,037
Dallastown, PA 17313 • 3,974
Dalton, GA 30720–22 • 21,761
Dalton, MA 01226–27 • 6,797
Dalton, OH 44618 • 1,377
Dalton, PA 18414 • 1,369
Dalton Gardens, ID 83814 • 1,951
Daly City, CA 94014–17 • 92,311
Damascus, MD 20872 • 9,817
Dana Point, CA 92629 • 31,896
Danbury, CT 06810–13 • 65,585
Danbury, TX 77534 • 1,447
Dandridge, TN 37725 • 1,540
Dane □, WI • 367,085
Dania, FL 33004 • 13,024
Daniels □, MT • 2,266
Danielson, CT 06239 • 4,441
Dannemora, NY 12929 • 4,005
Dansville, NY 14437 • 5,002
Dante, VA 24237 • 1,083
Danvers, MA 01923 • 24,174
Danville, AR 72833 • 1,585
Danville, CA 94526 • 31,306
Danville, IL 61832–34 • 33,828
Danville, IN 46122 • 4,345
Danville, KY 40422–23 • 12,420
Danville, OH 43014 • 1,001
Danville, PA 17821 • 5,165
Danville, VA 24540–43 • 53,056
Daphne, AL 36526 • 11,290
Darby, PA 19023 • 11,140
Darby Township, PA 19036 • 10,955
Dardanelle, AR 72834 • 3,722
Dare □, NC • 22,746
Darien, CT 06820 • 18,130
Darien, GA 31305 • 1,783
Darien, IL 60559 • 18,341
Darien, WI 53114 • 1,158
Darke □, OH • 53,619
Darley Woods, DE 19810 • 1,220
Darlington, SC 29532 • 7,311
Darlington, WI 53530 • 2,235
Darlington □, SC • 61,851
Darrington, WA 98241 • 1,042
Dartmouth Woods, DE 19810 • 1,970
Dassel, MN 55325 • 1,082
Dauphin □, PA • 237,813
Davenport, FL 33837 • 1,529
Davenport, IA 52801–09 • 95,333
Davenport, WA 99122 • 1,502
David City, NE 68632 • 2,522
Davidson, NC 28036 • 4,046
Davidson □, NC • 126,677
Davidson □, TN • 510,784
Davidsville, PA 15928 • 1,167
Davie, FL 33328 • 47,217
Davie □, NC • 27,859
Daviess □, IN • 27,533
Daviess □, KY • 87,189
Daviess □, MO • 7,865
Davis, CA 95616–17 • 46,209
Davis, OK 73030 • 2,543
Davis □, IA • 8,312
Davis □, UT • 187,941
Davison, MI 48423 • 5,693
Davison □, SD • 17,503
Davisville, RI 02852 • 500
Dawes □, NE • 9,021
Dawson, GA 31742 • 5,295
Dawson, MN 56232 • 1,626
Dawson □, GA • 9,429
Dawson □, MT • 9,505
Dawson □, NE • 19,940
Dawson □, TX • 14,349
Dawson Springs, KY 42408 • 3,129
Day □, SD • 6,978
Dayton, KY 41074 • 6,576
Dayton, MN 55327 • 4,443
Dayton, NV 89403 • 2,217
Dayton, NJ 08810 • 1,200
Dayton, OH 45401–90 • 182,044
Dayton, OR 97114 • 1,526
Dayton, TN 37321 • 5,671
Dayton, TX 77535 • 5,151
Dayton, WA 99328 • 2,468
Dayton, WY 82836 • 565
Daytona Beach, FL 32114–25 • 61,921
Dayville, CT 06241 • 1,500
Deadwood, SD 57732 • 1,830
Deaf Smith □, TX • 19,153
Deal, NJ 07723 • 1,179
Deale, MD 20751 • 4,151
Dearborn, MI 48120–26 • 89,286
Dearborn □, IN • 38,835
Dearborn Heights, MI 48127 • 60,838
De Baca □, NM • 2,252
De Bary, FL 32713 • 7,176
Decatur, AL 35601–03 • 48,761
Decatur, GA 30030–37 • 17,336
Decatur, IL 62521–26 • 83,885
Decatur, IN 46733 • 8,644
Decatur, MI 49045 • 1,760
Decatur, MS 39327 • 1,248
Decatur, TN 37322 • 1,361
Decatur, TX 76234 • 4,252
Decatur □, GA • 25,511
Decatur □, IN • 23,645
Decatur □, IA • 8,338
Decatur □, KS • 4,021
Decatur □, TN • 10,472
Decherd, TN 37324 • 2,196
Deckerville, MI 48427 • 1,015
Decorah, IA 52101 • 8,063
Dedham, MA 02026 • 23,782
Deep River, CT 06417 • 2,520
Deerfield, IL 60015 • 17,327
Deerfield, WI 53531 • 1,617
Deerfield Beach, FL 33441–43 • 46,325
Deer Lodge, MT 59722 • 3,378
Deer Lodge □, MT • 10,278
Deer Park, NY 11729 • 28,840
Deer Park, OH 45236 • 6,181
Deer Park, TX 77536 • 27,652
Deer Park, WA 99006 • 2,278
Defiance, OH 43512 • 16,768
Defiance □, OH • 39,350
De Forest, WI 53532 • 4,882
De Funiak Springs, FL 32433 • 5,120
De Graff, OH 43318 • 1,331
De Kalb, IL 60115 • 34,925
De Kalb, MS 39328 • 1,073
De Kalb, TX 75559 • 1,976
De Kalb □, AL • 54,651
De Kalb □, GA • 545,837
De Kalb □, IL • 77,932
De Kalb □, IN • 35,324
De Kalb □, MO • 9,967
De Kalb □, TN • 14,360
Delafield, WI 53018 • 5,347
Del Aire, CA 90250 • 8,040
Delanco, NJ 08075 • 3,316
De Land, FL 32720–24 • 16,491
Delano, CA 93215–16 • 22,762
Delano, MN 55328 • 2,709
Delavan, IL 61734 • 1,642
Delavan, WI 53115 • 6,073
Delavan Lake, WI 53115 • 2,177
Delaware, OH 43015 • 20,030
Delaware □, IN • 119,659
Delaware □, IA • 18,035
Delaware □, NY • 47,225
Delaware □, OH • 66,929
Delaware □, OK • 28,070
Delaware □, PA • 547,651
Delaware City, DE 19706 • 1,682
Delcambre, LA 70528 • 1,978
Del City, OK 73115 • 23,928
De Leon, TX 76444 • 2,190
De Leon Springs, FL 32130 • 1,481
Delevan, NY 14042 • 1,214
Delhi, LA 71232 • 3,169
Delhi, NY 13753 • 3,064
Delhi Hills, OH 45238 • 27,647
Dell Rapids, SD 57022 • 2,484
Dellwood, MO 63136 • 5,245
Del Mar, CA 92014 • 4,860
Delmar, DE 19940 • 962
Delmar, MD 21875 • 1,430
Delmar, NY 12054 • 8,360
Del Norte, CO 81132 • 1,674
Del Norte □, CA • 23,460
Del Park Manor, DE 19808 • 1,550
Delphi, IN 46923 • 2,531
Delphos, OH 45833 • 7,093
Delran, NJ 08075 • 14,811
Delray Beach, FL 33444–47 • 47,181
Del Rio, FL 33617 • 8,248
Del Rio, TX 78840–42 • 30,705
Delta, CO 81416 • 3,789
Delta, OH 43515 • 2,849
Delta, UT 84624 • 2,998
Delta □, CO • 20,980
Delta □, MI • 37,780
Delta □, TX • 4,857
Delta Junction, AK 99737 • 652
Deltaville, VA 23043 • 1,082
Deltona, FL 32725 • 50,828
Demarest, NJ 07627 • 4,800
Deming, NM 88030–31 • 10,970
Demopolis, AL 36732 • 7,512
Demorest, GA 30535 • 1,088
Demotte, IN 46310 • 2,482
Denham Springs, LA 70726–27 • 8,381
Denison, IA 51442 • 6,604
Denison, TX 75020–21 • 21,505
Denmark, SC 29042 • 3,762
Denmark, WI 54208 • 1,612
Dennis, MA 02638 • 2,500
Dennison, OH 44621 • 3,282
Dennis Port, MA 02639 • 2,775
Denny Terrace, SC 29203 • 1,885
Dent □, MO • 13,702
Denton, MD 21629 • 2,977
Denton, NC 27239 • 1,292
Denton, TX 76201–06 • 66,270
Denton □, TX • 273,525
Dentsville, SC 29204 • 11,839
Denver, CO 80201–95 • 467,610
Denver, IA 50622 • 1,600
Denver, PA 17517 • 2,861
Denver □, CO • 467,610
Denver City, TX 79323 • 5,145
Denville, NJ 07834 • 14,380
De Pere, WI 54115 • 16,569
Depew, NY 14043 • 17,673
Deposit, NY 13754 • 1,936
Depue, IL 61322 • 1,729
De Queen, AR 71832 • 4,633
De Quincy, LA 70633 • 3,474
Derby, CT 06418 • 12,199
Derby, KS 67037 • 14,699
Derby, NY 14047 • 1,200
Derby Line, VT 05830 • 855
De Ridder, LA 70634 • 9,868
Dermott, AR 71638 • 4,715
Derry, NH 03038 • 20,446
Derry, PA 15627 • 2,950
Derwood, MD 20855 • 1,500
Des Allemands, LA 70030 • 2,504
Des Arc, AR 72040 • 2,001
Deschutes □, OR • 74,958
Desert Hot Springs, CA 92240 • 11,668
Desha □, AR • 16,798
Deshler, OH 43516 • 1,876
Desloge, MO 63601 • 4,150
De Smet, SD 57231 • 1,172
Des Moines, IA 50301–95 • 193,187
Des Moines, WA 98188 • 17,283
Des Moines □, IA • 42,614
De Soto, IL 62924 • 1,500
De Soto, IA 50069 • 1,033
De Soto, KS 66018 • 2,291
De Soto, MO 63020 • 5,993
De Soto, TX 75115 • 30,544
De Soto □, FL • 23,865
De Soto □, LA • 25,346
De Soto □, MS • 67,910
Despard, WV 26301 • 1,018
Des Peres, MO 63131 • 8,395
Des Plaines, IL 60016–19 • 53,223
Destin, FL 32540–41 • 8,080
Destrehan, LA 70047 • 8,031
Detroit, MI 48201–44 • 1,027,974
Detroit Lakes, MN 56501–02 • 6,635
Deuel □, NE • 2,237
Deuel □, SD • 4,522
Devils Lake, ND 58301 • 7,782
Devine, TX 78016 • 3,928
Devola, OH 45750 • 2,736
Devon, PA 19333 • 6,620
Devonshire, DE 19810 • 2,120
Dewey, OK 74029 • 3,326
Dewey □, OK • 5,551
Dewey □, SD • 5,523
Dewey Beach, DE 19971 • 204
Deweyville, TX 77614 • 1,218
De Witt, AR 72042 • 3,553
De Witt, IA 52742 • 4,514
De Witt, MI 48820 • 3,964
De Witt, NY 13214 • 8,244
De Witt □, IL • 16,516
De Witt □, TX • 18,840
Dexter, ME 04930 • 2,650
Dexter, MI 48130 • 1,497
Dexter, MO 63841 • 7,559
Dexter, NY 13634 • 1,030
Diamond Bar, CA 91765 • 53,672
Diamond Hill, RI 02864 • 810
Diamond Lake, IL 60060 • 1,500
Diamond Springs, CA 95619 • 2,872
Diamondville, WY 83116 • 864
Diaz, AR 72043 • 1,363
D'Iberville, MS 39532 • 6,566
Diboll, TX 75941 • 4,341
Dickens □, TX • 2,571
Dickenson □, VA • 17,620
Dickey □, ND • 6,107
Dickinson, ND 58601–02 • 16,097
Dickinson, TX 77539 • 9,497
Dickinson □, IA • 14,909
Dickinson □, KS • 18,958
Dickinson □, MI • 26,831
Dickson, TN 37055 • 8,791
Dickson □, TN • 35,061
Dickson City, PA 18519 • 6,276
Dierks, AR 71833 • 1,263
Dighton, KS 67839 • 1,361
Dighton, MA 02715 • 1,100
Dillard, OR 97432 • 1,000
Dilley, TX 78017 • 2,632
Dillingham, AK 99576 • 2,017
Dillon, MT 59725 • 3,991
Dillon, SC 29536 • 6,829
Dillon □, SC • 29,114
Dillsboro, IN 47018 • 1,200
Dillsburg, PA 17019 • 1,925
Dilworth, MN 56529 • 2,562
Dimmit □, TX • 10,433
Dimmitt, TX 79027 • 4,408
Dimondale, MI 48821 • 1,247
Dingmans Ferry, PA 18328 • 1,200
Dinuba, CA 93618 • 12,743
Dinwiddie □, VA • 20,960
Dishman, WA 99213 • 9,671
District Heights-Forestville, MD 20747 • 6,704
Divernon, IL 62530 • 1,178
Divide □, ND • 2,899
Dixfield, ME 04224 • 1,300
Dix Hills, NY 11746 • 25,849
Dixie □, FL • 10,585
Dixon, CA 95620 • 10,401
Dixon, IL 61021 • 15,144
Dixon, MO 65459 • 1,585
Dixon □, NE • 6,143
Dixonville, PA 15734 • 1,000
Dobbs Ferry, NY 10522 • 9,940
Dobson, NC 27017 • 1,195
Docena, AL 35060 • 1,000
Dock Junction, GA 31520 • 7,094
Doddridge □, WV • 6,994
Dodge □, GA • 17,607
Dodge □, MN • 15,731
Dodge □, NE • 34,500
Dodge □, WI • 76,559
Dodge Center, MN 55927 • 1,954
Dodge City, KS 67801 • 21,129
Dodge Park, MD 20785 • 4,842
Dodgeville, WI 53533 • 3,882
Dolgeville, NY 13329 • 2,452
Dolomite, AL 35061 • 2,590
Dolores □, CO • 1,504
Dolton, IL 60419 • 23,930
Dona Ana, NM 88032 • 950
Dona Ana □, NM • 135,510
Donaldsonville, LA 70346 • 7,949
Donalsonville, GA 31745 • 2,761
Doneraile, SC 29532 • 1,276
Doniphan, MO 63935 • 1,713
Doniphan □, KS • 8,134
Donley □, TX • 3,696
Donna, TX 78537 • 12,652
Donora, PA 15033 • 5,928
Dooly □, GA • 9,901
Door □, WI • 25,690
Dora, AL 35062 • 2,214
Doraville, GA 30340 • 7,626
Dorchester □, MD • 30,236
Dorchester □, SC • 83,060
Dormont, PA 15216 • 9,772
Dorothy Pond, MA 01527 • 1,670
Dorr, MI 49323 • 1,450
Dorset, VT 05251 • 550
Dorsey, MD 21227 • 1,186
Dothan, AL 36301–04 • 53,589
Double Springs, AL 35553 • 1,138
Dougherty □, GA • 96,311
Douglas, AZ 85607–08 • 12,822
Douglas, GA 31533 • 10,464
Douglas, MI 49406 • 1,040
Douglas, WY 82633 • 5,076
Douglas □, CO • 60,391
Douglas □, GA • 71,120
Douglas □, IL • 19,464
Douglas □, KS • 81,798
Douglas □, MN • 28,674
Douglas □, MO • 11,876
Douglas □, NE • 416,444
Douglas □, NV • 27,637
Douglas □, OR • 94,649
Douglas □, SD • 3,746
Douglas □, WA • 26,205
Douglas □, WI • 41,758
Douglass, KS 67039 • 1,722
Douglasville, GA 30133–35 • 11,635
Dousman, WI 53118 • 1,277
Dover, AR 72837 • 1,055
Dover, DE 19901–03 • 27,630
Dover, FL 33527 • 2,606
Dover, MA 02030 • 2,163
Dover, NH 03820 • 25,042
Dover, NJ 07801 • 15,115
Dover, OH 44622 • 11,329
Dover, PA 17315 • 1,884
Dover, TN 37058 • 1,341
Dover-Foxcroft, ME 04426 • 3,077
Dover Plains, NY 12522 • 1,847
Dowagiac, MI 49047 • 6,409
Downers Grove, IL 60515–17 • 46,858
Downey, CA 90239–42 • 91,444
Downingtown, PA 19335 • 7,749
Downs, KS 67437 • 1,119
Downsville, NY 13755 • 1,100
Doylestown, OH 44230 • 2,668
Doylestown, PA 18901 • 8,575
Dracut, MA 01826 • 25,594
Drain, OR 97435 • 1,011
Draper, UT 84020 • 7,257
Drayton, ND 58225 • 961
Drayton, SC 29333 • 1,443
Drayton Plains, MI 48330 • 18,000
Dreamland Villa, AZ 85205 • 3,400
Dresden, OH 43821 • 1,581
Dresden, TN 38225 • 2,488
Dresslerville, NV 89410 • 180
Drew, MS 38737 • 2,349
Drew □, AR • 17,369
Drexel, NC 28619 • 1,746
Drexel, OH 45427 • 5,143
Drexel Hill, PA 19026 • 29,744
Dripping Springs, TX 78620 • 1,033
Druid Hills, GA 30333 • 12,174
Drumright, OK 74030 • 2,799
Dryden, NY 13053 • 1,908
Dry Ridge, KY 41035 • 1,601
Duarte, CA 91010 • 20,688
Dublin, CA 94568 • 23,229
Dublin, GA 31021 • 16,312
Dublin, OH 43017 • 16,366
Dublin, PA 18917 • 1,985
Dublin, TX 76446 • 3,190
Dublin, VA 24084 • 2,012
Du Bois, PA 15801 • 8,286
Dubois, WY 82513 • 895
Dubois □, IN • 36,616
Duboistown, PA 17701 • 1,201
Dubuque, IA 52001–04 • 57,546
Dubuque □, IA • 86,403
Duchesne, UT 84021 • 1,308
Duchesne □, UT • 12,645
Dudley, MA 01570–71 • 3,700
Due West, SC 29639 • 1,220
Dukes □, MA • 11,639
Dulce, NM 87528 • 2,438
Duluth, GA 30136 • 9,029
Duluth, MN 55801–16 • 85,493
Dumas, AR 71639 • 5,520
Dumas, TX 79029 • 12,871
Dumfries, VA 22026 • 4,282
Dumont, NJ 07628 • 17,187
Dunaire, GA 30032 • 7,170
Dunbar, PA 15431 • 1,213
Dunbar, WV 25064 • 8,697
Duncan, OK 73533–34 • 21,732
Duncan, SC 29334 • 2,152
Duncan Falls, OH 43734 • 1,200
Duncannon, PA 17020 • 1,450
Duncansville, PA 16635 • 1,309
Duncanville, TX 75116 • 35,748
Dundalk, MD 21222 • 65,800
Dundee, FL 33838 • 2,335
Dundee, IL 60118 • 3,728
Dundee, MI 48131 • 2,664
Dundee, NY 14837 • 1,588
Dundee, OR 97115 • 1,663
Dundy □, NE • 2,582
Dunedin, FL 34697–98 • 34,012
Dunellen, NJ 08812 • 6,528
Dunkirk, IN 47336 • 2,739
Dunkirk, NY 14048 • 13,989
Dunklin □, MO • 33,112
Dunlap, IN 46514 • 5,705
Dunlap, IA 51529 • 1,251
Dunlap, TN 37327 • 3,731
Dunleith, DE 19801 • 2,600
Dunmore, PA 18512 • 15,403
Dunn, NC 28334–35 • 8,336
Dunn □, ND • 4,005
Dunn □, WI • 35,909
Dunnellon, FL 32630 • 1,624
Dunn Loring Woods, VA 22180 • 2,800
Dunseith, ND 58329 • 723
Dunsmuir, CA 96025 • 2,129
Dunwoody, GA 30338 • 26,302
Du Page □, IL • 781,666
Duplin □, NC • 39,995
Dupont, CO 80024 • 5,200
Dupont, PA 18641 • 2,984
Dupont Manor, DE 19901 • 1,059
Duquesne, PA 15110 • 8,525
Du Quoin, IL 62832 • 6,697
Durand, IL 61024 • 1,100
Durand, MI 48429 • 4,283
Durand, WI 54736 • 2,003
Durango, CO 81301–02 • 12,430
Durant, IA 52747 • 1,549
Durant, MS 39063 • 2,838
Durant, OK 74701–02 • 12,823
Durham, CA 95938 • 1,500
Durham, CT 06422 • 2,650
Durham, NH 03824 • 9,236
Durham, NC 27701–22 • 136,611
Durham □, NC • 181,835
Duryea, PA 18642 • 4,869
Duson, LA 70529 • 1,465
Dutchess □, NY • 259,462
Duval □, FL • 672,971
Duval □, TX • 12,918
Duxbury, MA 02331–32 • 1,637
Dwight, IL 60420 • 4,230
Dyer, IN 46311 • 10,923
Dyer, TN 38330 • 2,204
Dyer □, TN • 34,854
Dyersburg, TN 38024–25 • 16,317
Dyersville, IA 52040 • 3,703
Dysart, IA 52224 • 1,230

E

Eagan, MN 55121 • 47,409
Eagar, AZ 85925 • 4,025
Eagle, CO 81631 • 1,580
Eagle, ID 83616 • 3,327
Eagle, NE 68347 • 1,047
Eagle, WI 53119 • 1,182
Eagle □, CO • 21,928
Eagle Grove, IA 50533 • 3,671
Eagle Lake, MN 56024 • 1,703
Eagle Lake, TX 77434 • 3,551
Eagle Lake, WI 53139 • 1,000
Eagle Pass, TX 78852–53 • 20,651
Eagle Point, OR 97524 • 3,008
Eagle River, WI 54521 • 1,374
Eagleton Village, TN 37801 • 5,331
Earle, AR 72331 • 3,393
Earlham, IA 50072 • 1,157
Earlimart, CA 93219 • 5,881
Earlington, KY 42410 • 1,833
Earlville, IL 60518 • 1,435
Early □, GA • 11,854
Earth, TX 79031 • 1,228
Easley, SC 29640–42 • 15,195
East Alton, IL 62024 • 7,063
East Arlington, VT 05252 • 600
East Aurora, NY 14052 • 6,647
East Bangor, PA 18013 • 1,006
East Barre, VT 05649 • 700
East Baton Rouge □, LA • 380,105

East Berlin, PA 17316 • *1,175*
East Bernard, TX 77435 • *1,544*
East Bethel, MN 55005 • *8,050*
East Billerica, MA 01821 • *3,830*
East Brady, PA 16028 • *1,047*
East Brewton, AL 36426 • *2,579*
East Bridgewater, MA 02333 • *3,270*
East Brookfield, MA 01515 • *1,396*
East Brooklyn, CT 06239 • *1,481*
East Brunswick, NJ 08816 • *43,548*
East Carbon, UT 84520 • *1,270*
East Carroll □, LA • *9,709*
Eastchester, NY 10709 • *18,537*
East Chicago, IN 46312 • *33,892*
East Cleveland, OH 44112 • *33,096*
East Compton, CA 90221 • *7,967*
East Dennis, MA 02641 • *1,500*
East Detroit, MI 48021 • *35,283*
East Douglas, MA 01516 • *1,945*
East Dubuque, IL 61025 • *1,914*
East Falmouth, MA 02536 • *5,577*
East Farmingdale, NY 11735 • *4,510*
East Feliciana □, LA • *19,211*
East Flat Rock, NC 28726 • *3,218*
East Gaffney, SC 29340 • *3,278*
Eastgate, WA 98007 • *4,434*
East Glenville, NY 12302 • *6,518*
East Granby, CT 06026 • *1,200*
East Grand Forks, MN 56721 • *8,658*
East Grand Rapids, MI 49506 • *10,807*
East Greenville, PA 18041 • *3,117*
East Greenwich, RI 02818 • *11,865*
East Half Hollow Hills, NY 11746 • *7,010*
Eastham, MA 02642 • *1,150*
East Hampton, CT 06424 • *2,167*
Easthampton, MA 01027 • *15,580*
East Hampton, NY 11937 • *1,402*
East Hanover, NJ • *9,926*
East Hartford, CT 06128 • *50,452*
East Haven, CT 06512 • *26,144*
East Helena, MT 59635 • *1,538*
East Hemet, CA 92343 • *17,611*
East Hills, NY 11576 • *6,746*
East Islip, NY 11730 • *14,325*
East Jordan, MI 49727 • *2,240*
Eastlake, OH 44094 • *21,161*
East La Mirada, CA 90638 • *9,367*
Eastland, TX 76448 • *3,690*
Eastland □, TX • *18,488*
East Lansing, MI 48823–26 • *50,677*
East Las Vegas, NV 89112 • *11,087*
East Liverpool, OH 43920 • *13,654*
East Longmeadow, MA 01028 • *12,905*
East Los Angeles, CA 90022 • *126,379*
East Lyme, CT 06333 • *1,200*
Eastman, GA 31023 • *5,153*
East Marietta, GA 30062 • *11,900*
East Marion, NY 11939 • *1,500*
East Matunuck, RI 02879 • *500*
East Meadow, NY 11554 • *36,609*
East Middlebury, VT 05740 • *500*
East Midvale, UT 84047 • *3,800*
East Millinocket, ME 04430 • *2,075*
East Moline, IL 61244 • *20,147*
East Montpelier, VT 05651 • *600*
East Naples, FL 33962 • *22,951*
East Newark, NJ 07029 • *2,157*
East Newnan, GA 30263 • *1,173*
East Norriton, PA 19401 • *13,324*
East Northport, NY 11731 • *20,411*
Easton, MD 21601 • *9,372*
Easton, PA 18042–44 • *26,276*
East Orange, NJ 07017–19 • *73,552*
East Orleans, MA 02643 • *1,850*
Eastover, SC 29044 • *1,044*
East Palatka, FL 32131 • *1,989*
East Palestine, OH 44413 • *5,168*
East Palo Alto, CA 94303 • *23,451*
East Patchogue, NY 11772 • *20,195*
East Pea Ridge, WV 25705 • *4,980*
East Peoria, IL 61611 • *21,378*
East Pepperell, MA 01463 • *2,296*
East Petersburg, PA 17520 • *4,197*
East Pittsburgh, PA 15112 • *2,160*
Eastpoint, FL 32328 • *1,577*
East Point, GA 30344 • *34,402*
Eastport, ME 04631 • *1,965*
Eastport, NY 11941 • *1,500*
East Porterville, CA 93257 • *5,790*
East Port Orchard, WA 98366 • *5,409*
East Prairie, MO 63845 • *3,416*
East Providence, RI 02914 • *50,380*
East Quogue, NY 11942 • *4,372*
East Richmond, CA 94805 • *5,100*
East Ridge, TN 37412 • *21,101*
East River, CT 06443 • *3,440*
East Rochester, NY 14445 • *6,932*
East Rockaway, NY 11518 • *10,152*
East Rockingham, NC 28379 • *4,158*
East Rutherford, NJ 07073 • *7,902*
East Saint Louis, IL 62201–08 • *40,944*
Eastsound, WA 98245 • *1,100*
East Spencer, NC 28039 • *2,055*
East Stroudsburg, PA 18301 • *8,781*
East Tawas, MI 48730 • *2,887*
East Templeton, MA 01438 • *1,300*
East Troy, WI 53120 • *2,664*
East Tustin, CA 92705 • *10,000*
East Vestal, NY 13902 • *6,310*
East View, WV 26301 • *1,222*
East Walpole, MA 02032 • *3,760*
East Wareham, MA 02538 • *1,500*
East Washington, PA 15301 • *2,126*
East Wenatchee, WA 98802 • *2,701*
East Windsor, NJ 08520 • *15,000*
Eastwood, MI 49001 • *6,340*
Eastwood Hills, UT 84106 • *1,200*
Eaton, CO 80615 • *1,959*
Eaton, IN 47338 • *1,614*
Eaton, OH 45320 • *7,396*
Eaton □, MI • *92,879*
Eaton Rapids, MI 48827 • *4,695*
Eatonton, GA 31024 • *4,737*
Eatontown, NJ 07724 • *13,800*
Eatonville, WA 98328 • *1,374*
Eau Claire, WI 54701–03 • *56,856*
Eau Claire □, WI • *85,183*
Ebensburg, PA 15931 • *3,872*
Eccles, WV 25836 • *1,162*
Echo Bay, NV 89040 • *120*
Echols □, GA • *2,334*
Eckhart Mines, MD 21528 • *1,333*
Eclectic, AL 36024 • *1,087*

Economy, PA 15005 • *9,519*
Ecorse, MI 48229 • *12,180*
Ector □, TX • *118,934*
Edcouch, TX 78538 • *2,878*
Eddy □, NM • *48,605*
Eddy □, ND • *2,951*
Eddystone, PA 19013 • *2,446*
Eddyville, IA 52553 • *1,010*
Eddyville, KY 42038 • *1,889*
Eden, NY 14057 • *3,088*
Eden, NC 27288 • *15,238*
Eden, TX 76837 • *1,567*
Eden Prairie, MN 55344 • *39,311*
Edenton, NC 27932 • *5,268*
Edgar, WI 54426 • *1,318*
Edgar □, IL • *19,595*
Edgartown, MA 02539 • *3,062*
Edgecombe □, NC • *56,558*
Edgefield, SC 29824 • *2,563*
Edgefield □, SC • *18,375*
Edgeley, ND 58433 • *680*
Edgemere, MD 21221 • *9,226*
Edgemont, SD 57735 • *906*
Edgemoor, DE 19802 • *5,853*
Edgerton, KS 66021 • *1,244*
Edgerton, MN 56128 • *1,106*
Edgerton, OH 43517 • *1,896*
Edgerton, WI 53534 • *4,254*
Edgerton, WY 82635 • *247*
Edgewater, AL 35224 • *1,120*
Edgewater, CO 80214 • *4,613*
Edgewater, FL 32132 • *15,337*
Edgewater, MD 21037 • *1,600*
Edgewater, NJ 07020 • *5,001*
Edgewater Park, NJ 08010 • *8,388*
Edgewood, IN 46011 • *2,057*
Edgewood, KY 41017 • *8,143*
Edgewood, MD • *3,470*
Edgewood, MD 21040 • *23,903*
Edgewood, OH 44004 • *5,189*
Edgewood, PA 15218 • *3,581*
Edgewood, WA 98372 • *2,650*
Edgeworth, PA 15143 • *1,670*
Edina, MN 55410 • *46,070*
Edina, MO 63537 • *1,283*
Edinboro, PA 16412 • *7,736*
Edinburg, TX 78539–40 • *29,885*
Edinburgh, IN 46124 • *4,536*
Edison, GA 31746 • *1,182*
Edison, NJ 08817–20 • *88,680*
Edmond, OK 73034 • *52,315*
Edmonds, WA 98020 • *30,744*
Edmondson Heights, MD 21207 • *4,750*
Edmonson □, KY • *10,357*
Edmonton, KY 42129 • *1,477*
Edmore, MI 48829 • *1,126*
Edmunds □, SD • *4,356*
Edna, TX 77957 • *5,343*
Edwards, MS 39066 • *1,279*
Edwards □, IL • *7,440*
Edwards □, KS • *3,787*
Edwards □, TX • *2,266*
Edwardsburg, MI 49112 • *1,142*
Edwardsville, IL 62025 • *14,579*
Edwardsville, KS 66113 • *3,979*
Edwardsville, PA 18704 • *5,399*
Effingham, IL 62401 • *11,851*
Effingham □, GA • *25,687*
Effingham □, IL • *31,704*
Egg Harbor City, NJ 08215 • *4,583*
Egypt, MA 02066 • *1,100*
Egypt Lake, FL 33614 • *14,580*
Ehrenberg, AZ 85334 • *1,500*
Elba, AL 36323 • *4,011*
Elbert □, CO • *9,646*
Elbert □, GA • *18,949*
Elberta, GA 31093 • *1,559*
Elberton, GA 30635 • *5,682*
Elbow Lake, MN 56531 • *1,186*
Elburn, IL 60119 • *1,275*
El Cajon, CA 92019–22 • *88,693*
El Campo, TX 77437 • *10,511*
El Centro, CA 92243–44 • *31,384*
El Cerrito, CA 94530 • *22,869*
Eldersburg, MD 21784 • *9,720*
Eldon, IA 52554 • *1,070*
Eldon, MO 65026 • *4,419*
Eldora, IA 50627 • *3,038*
El Dorado, AR 71730–31 • *23,146*
Eldorado, IL 62930 • *4,536*
El Dorado, KS 67042 • *11,504*
Eldorado, TX 76936 • *2,019*
El Dorado □, CA • *125,995*
El Dorado Hills, CA 95630 • *6,395*
El Dorado Springs, MO 64744 • *3,830*
Eldridge, IA 52748 • *3,378*
Eleanor, WV 25070 • *1,256*
Electra, TX 76360 • *3,113*
Eleele, HI 96705 • *1,489*
El Encanto Heights, CA 93117 • *7,700*
Elfers, FL 34680 • *12,356*
Elgin, IL 60120–23 • *77,010*
Elgin, ND 58533 • *765*
Elgin, OR 97827 • *1,586*
Elgin, TX 78621 • *4,846*
Elida, OH 45807 • *1,486*
Elizabeth, NJ 07201–08 • *110,002*
Elizabeth City, NC 27906–09 • *14,292*
Elizabethton, TN 37643–44 • *11,931*
Elizabethtown, KY 42701–02 • *18,167*
Elizabethtown, NC 28337 • *3,704*
Elizabethtown, PA 17022 • *9,952*
Elizabethville, PA 17023 • *1,467*
Elk □, KS • *3,327*
Elk □, PA • *34,878*
Elkader, IA 52043 • *1,510*
Elk City, OK 73644 • *10,428*
Elk Grove, CA 95624 • *17,483*
Elk Grove Village, IL 60009 • *33,429*
Elkhart, IN 46514–17 • *43,627*
Elkhart, KS 67950 • *2,318*
Elkhart, TX 75839 • *1,076*
Elkhart □, IN • *156,198*
Elkhart Lake, WI 53020 • *1,019*
Elkhorn, NE 68022 • *1,398*
Elkhorn, WI 53121 • *5,337*
Elkin, NC 28621 • *3,790*
Elkins, WV 26241 • *7,420*
Elkland, PA 16920 • *1,849*
Elk Mountain, WY 82324 • *174*
Elko, NV 89801–02 • *14,736*
Elko □, NV • *33,530*
Elk Point, SD 57025 • *1,423*

Elk Rapids, MI 49629 • *1,626*
Elkridge, MD 21227 • *12,953*
Elk River, MN 55330 • *11,143*
Elkton, KY 42220 • *1,789*
Elkton, MD 21921–22 • *9,073*
Elkton, VA 22827 • *1,935*
Elkview, WV 25071 • *1,047*
Ellaville, GA 31806 • *1,724*
Ellendale, DE 19941 • *313*
Ellendale, ND 58436 • *1,798*
Ellensburg, WA 98926 • *12,361*
Ellenton, FL 34222 • *2,573*
Ellenville, NY 12428 • *4,243*
Ellerbe, NC 28338 • *1,132*
Ellerslie, MD 21529 • *1,500*
Ellettsville, IN 47429 • *3,275*
Ellicott City, MD 21043 • *41,396*
Ellijay, GA 30540 • *1,178*
Ellington, CT 06029 • *1,500*
Ellinwood, KS 67526 • *2,329*
Elliott □, KY • *6,455*
Ellis, KS 67637 • *1,814*
Ellis □, KS • *26,004*
Ellis □, OK • *4,497*
Ellis □, TX • *85,167*
Ellisville, MS 39437 • *3,634*
Ellisville, MO 63011 • *7,545*
Ellport, PA 16117 • *1,243*
Ellsworth, KS 67439 • *2,294*
Ellsworth, ME 04605 • *5,975*
Ellsworth, PA 15331 • *1,048*
Ellsworth, WI 54011 • *2,706*
Ellsworth □, KS • *6,586*
Ellwood City, PA 16117 • *8,894*
Elma, WA 98541 • *3,011*
Elm City, NC 27822 • *1,624*
Elmer, NJ 08318 • *1,571*
Elm Grove, WI 53122 • *6,261*
Elmhurst, IL 60126 • *42,029*
Elmira, NY 14901–05 • *33,724*
El Mirage, AZ 85335 • *5,001*
Elmira Heights, NY 14903 • *4,359*
Elmont, NY 11003 • *28,612*
El Monte, CA 91731–34 • *106,209*
Elmora, PA 15737 • *1,500*
Elmore, OH 43416 • *1,334*
Elmore □, AL • *49,210*
Elmore □, ID • *21,205*
Elmwood, IL 61529 • *1,841*
Elmwood Park, IL 60635 • *23,206*
Elmwood Park, NJ 07407 • *17,623*
Elmwood Place, OH 45216 • *2,937*
Eloise, FL 33880 • *1,408*
Elon College, NC 27244 • *4,394*
Eloy, AZ 85231 • *7,211*
El Paso, IL 61738 • *2,499*
El Paso, TX 79901–99 • *515,342*
El Paso □, CO • *397,014*
El Paso □, TX • *591,610*
El Portal, FL 33138 • *2,457*
El Reno, OK 73036 • *15,414*
Elroy, WI 53929 • *1,533*
Elsa, TX 78543 • *5,242*
Elsberry, MO 63343 • *1,898*
El Segundo, CA 90245 • *15,223*
Elsmere, DE 19805 • *5,935*
Elsmere, KY 41018 • *6,847*
Elsmere, NY 12054 • *4,180*
El Sobrante, CA 94803 • *9,852*
Elton, LA 70532 • *1,277*
El Toro, CA 92630 • *62,685*
Elvins, MO 63601 • *1,391*
Elwood, IN 46036 • *9,494*
Elwood, KS 66024 • *1,079*
Elwood, NJ 08217 • *1,400*
Elwood, NY 11731 • *10,916*
Ely, MN 55731 • *3,968*
Ely, NV 89301 • *4,756*
Elyria, OH 44035–39 • *56,746*
Elysburg, PA 17824 • *1,890*
Emanuel □, GA • *20,546*
Emerson, GA 30137 • *1,201*
Emerson, NJ 07630 • *6,930*
Emery □, UT • *10,332*
Eminence, KY 40019 • *2,055*
Emmaus, PA 18049 • *11,157*
Emmet □, IA • *11,569*
Emmet □, MI • *25,040*
Emmetsburg, IA 50536 • *3,940*
Emmett, ID 83617 • *4,601*
Emmitsburg, MD 21727 • *1,688*
Emmonak, AK 99581 • *642*
Emmons □, ND • *4,830*
Empire, NV 89405 • *300*
Emporia, KS 66801 • *25,512*
Emporia, VA 23847 • *5,306*
Emporium, PA 15834 • *2,513*
Emsworth, PA 15202 • *2,892*
Encampment, WY 82325 • *490*
Encinitas, CA 92023–24 • *55,386*
Enderlin, ND 58027 • *997*
Endicott, NY 13760 • *13,531*
Endwell, NY 13760 • *12,602*
Enfield (Thompsonville), CT 06082–83 • *8,458*
Enfield, NH 03748 • *1,560*
Enfield, NC 27823 • *3,082*
England, AR 72046 • *3,351*
Engleside, VA 22309 • *24,058*
Englewood, CO 80110–12 • *29,387*
Englewood, FL 34223–24 • *15,025*
Englewood, NJ 07631–32 • *24,850*
Englewood, OH 45322 • *11,432*
Englewood, TN 37329 • *1,611*
Englewood Cliffs, NJ 07632 • *5,634*
Englishtown, NJ 07726 • *1,268*
Enid, OK 73701–06 • *45,309*
Enka, NC 28728 • *5,567*
Ennis, MT 59729 • *773*
Ennis, TX 75119–20 • *13,883*
Enoch, UT 84720 • *1,947*
Enola, PA 17025 • *5,961*
Enon, OH 45323 • *2,605*
Enoree, SC 29335 • *1,107*
Enosburg Falls, VT 05450 • *1,350*
Ensley, FL 32504 • *16,362*
Enterprise, AL 36330–31 • *20,123*
Enterprise, OR 97828 • *1,905*
Enterprise, WV 26568 • *1,058*
Enumclaw, WA 98022 • *7,227*
Ephraim, UT 84627 • *3,363*
Ephrata, PA 17522 • *12,133*
Ephrata, WA 98823 • *5,349*

Epping, NH 03042 • *1,384*
Epworth, IA 52045 • *1,297*
Erath, LA 70533 • *2,428*
Erath □, TX • *27,991*
Erial, NJ 08081 • *2,500*
Erick, OK 73645 • *1,083*
Erie, CO 80516 • *1,258*
Erie, IL 61250 • *1,572*
Erie, KS 66733 • *1,276*
Erie, PA 16501–65 • *108,718*
Erie □, NY • *968,532*
Erie □, OH • *76,779*
Erie □, PA • *275,572*
Erin, TN 37061 • *1,586*
Erlanger, KY 41018 • *15,979*
Erma, NJ 08204 • *2,045*
Errol Heights, OR 97266 • *10,487*
Erwin, NC 28339 • *4,061*
Erwin, TN 37650 • *5,015*
Escalon, CA 95320 • *4,437*
Escambia □, AL • *35,518*
Escambia □, FL • *262,798*
Escanaba, MI 49829 • *13,659*
Escatawpa, MS 39552 • *3,902*
Escondido, CA 92025–27 • *108,635*
Esmeralda □, NV • *1,344*
Esmond, RI 02917 • *4,320*
Espanola, NM 87532 • *8,389*
Esparto, CA 95627 • *1,487*
Esperance, WA 98043 • *11,236*
Espy, PA 17815 • *1,430*
Essex, CT 06426 • *2,500*
Essex, MD 21221 • *40,872*
Essex, MA 01929 • *1,507*
Essex, VT 05451 • *800*
Essex □, MA • *670,080*
Essex □, NJ • *778,206*
Essex □, NY • *37,152*
Essex □, VT • *6,405*
Essex □, VA • *8,689*
Essex Fells, NJ 07021 • *2,363*
Essex Junction, VT 05452–53 • *8,396*
Essexville, MI 48732 • *4,088*
Estacada, OR 97023 • *2,016*
Estelle, LA 70072 • *14,091*
Estell Manor, NJ 08319 • *1,404*
Estes Park, CO 80517 • *3,184*
Estherville, IA 51334 • *6,720*
Estill, SC 29918 • *2,387*
Estill □, KY • *14,614*
Estill Springs, TN 37330 • *1,408*
Etna, PA 15223 • *4,200*
Etowah, TN 37331 • *3,815*
Etowah □, AL • *99,840*
Ettrick, VA 23803 • *5,290*
Euclid, OH 44117 • *54,875*
Eudora, AR 71640 • *3,155*
Eudora, KS 66025 • *3,006*
Eufaula, AL 36027 • *13,220*
Eufaula, OK 74432 • *2,652*
Eugene, OR 97401–05 • *112,669*
Euless, TX 76039–40 • *38,149*
Eunice, LA 70535 • *11,162*
Eunice, NM 88231 • *2,676*
Eupora, MS 39744 • *2,145*
Eureka, CA 95501–02 • *27,025*
Eureka, IL 61530 • *4,435*
Eureka, KS 67045 • *2,974*
Eureka, MO 63025 • *4,683*
Eureka, MT 59917 • *1,043*
Eureka, NV 89316 • *650*
Eureka, SC 29706 • *1,738*
Eureka, SD 57437 • *1,197*
Eureka □, NV • *1,547*
Eureka Springs, AR 72632 • *1,900*
Eustis, FL 32726–27 • *12,967*
Eutaw, AL 35462 • *2,281*
Evangeline □, LA • *33,274*
Evans, CO 80620 • *5,877*
Evans, GA 30809 • *2,000*
Evans □, GA • *8,724*
Evans City, PA 16033 • *2,054*
Evansdale, IA 50707 • *4,638*
Evanston, IL 60201–04 • *73,233*
Evanston, WY 82930–31 • *10,903*
Evansville, IN 47701–37 • *126,272*
Evansville, WI 53536 • *3,174*
Evansville, WY 82636 • *1,403*
Evart, MI 49631 • *1,744*
Evarts, KY 40828 • *1,063*
Eveleth, MN 55734 • *4,064*
Everett, MA 02149 • *35,701*
Everett, PA 15537 • *1,777*
Everett, WA 98201–08 • *69,961*
Evergreen, AL 36401 • *3,911*
Evergreen, CO 80439 • *7,582*
Evergreen Park, IL 60642 • *20,874*
Everman, TX 76140 • *5,672*
Everson, WA 98247 • *1,490*
Ewa, HI 96706 • *3,780*
Ewa Beach, HI 96706–07 • *14,315*
Ewing Township, NJ 08618 • *34,185*
Excelsior Springs, MO 64024 • *10,354*
Exeter, CA 93221 • *7,276*
Exeter, NH 03833 • *9,556*
Exeter, PA 18643 • *5,691*
Exmore, VA 23350 • *1,115*
Experiment, GA 30223 • *3,762*
Eyota, MN 55934 • *1,448*

F

Fabens, TX 79838 • *5,599*
Factoryville, PA 18419 • *1,310*
Fairbank, IA 50629 • *1,018*
Fairbanks, AK 99701 • *30,843*
Fair Bluff, NC 28439 • *1,068*
Fairborn, OH 45324 • *31,300*
Fairburn, GA 30213 • *4,013*
Fairbury, IL 61739 • *3,643*
Fairbury, NE 68352 • *4,335*
Fairchance, PA 15436 • *1,918*
Fairdale, KY 40118 • *6,563*
Fairfax, CA 94930 • *6,931*
Fairfax, DE 19803 • *2,075*
Fairfax, MN 55332 • *1,276*
Fairfax, OK 74637 • *1,749*
Fairfax, SC 29827 • *2,317*
Fairfax, VA 22030–39 • *19,622*
Fairfax □, VA • *818,584*
Fairfield, AL 35064 • *12,200*
Fairfield, CA 94533 • *77,211*
Fairfield, CT 06430–32 • *53,418*

Fairfield, IL 62837 • *5,439*
Fairfield, IA 52556 • *9,768*
Fairfield, ME 04937 • *2,794*
Fairfield, NJ 07004 • *7,615*
Fairfield, OH 45014 • *39,729*
Fairfield, TX 75840 • *3,234*
Fairfield □, CT • *827,645*
Fairfield □, OH • *103,461*
Fairfield □, SC • *22,295*
Fairfield Bay, AR 72088 • *2,332*
Fair Grove, NC 27360 • *1,500*
Fairhaven, MA 02719 • *15,759*
Fair Haven, NJ 07704 • *5,270*
Fair Haven, VT 05743 • *2,432*
Fairhope, AL 36532–33 • *8,485*
Fair Lawn, NJ 07410 • *30,548*
Fairlawn, OH 44313 • *5,779*
Fairlawn, VA 24141 • *2,399*
Fairlea, WV 24902 • *1,743*
Fairless Hills, PA 19030 • *9,026*
Fairmont, IL 60441 • *2,260*
Fairmont, MN 56031 • *11,265*
Fairmont, NC 28340 • *2,489*
Fairmont, WV 26554–55 • *20,210*
Fairmount, IN 46928 • *3,130*
Fairmount, NY 13031 • *12,266*
Fairmount Heights, MD 20743 • *1,238*
Fair Oaks, CA 95628 • *26,867*
Fair Oaks, GA 30060 • *6,996*
Fairoaks, PA 15003 • *1,854*
Fair Plain, MI 49022 • *8,051*
Fairport, NY 14450 • *5,943*
Fairport Harbor, OH 44077 • *2,978*
Fairton, NJ 08320 • *1,359*
Fairview, MT 59221 • *869*
Fairview, NJ 07022 • *10,733*
Fairview, OK 73737 • *2,936*
Fairview, OR 97024 • *2,391*
Fairview, PA 16415 • *1,988*
Fairview, TN 37062 • *4,210*
Fairview Heights, IL 62208 • *14,351*
Fairview Park, IN 47842 • *1,446*
Fairview Park, OH 44126 • *18,028*
Fairview Shores, FL 32804 • *13,192*
Fairway, KS 66205 • *4,173*
Fairwood, WA 98058 • *2,000*
Fairwood, WA 99218 • *5,807*
Falconer, NY 14733 • *2,653*
Falcon Heights, MN 55113 • *5,380*
Falfurrias, TX 78355 • *5,788*
Falkville, AL 35622 • *1,337*
Fall Branch, TN 37656 • *1,203*
Fallbrook, CA 92028 • *22,095*
Fall City, WA 98024 • *1,582*
Fall Creek, WI 54742 • *1,034*
Fallon, NV 89406 • *6,438*
Fallon □, MT • *3,103*
Fall River, MA 02720–26 • *92,703*
Fall River □, SD • *7,353*
Falls □, TX • *17,712*
Falls Church, VA 22040–46 • *9,578*
Falls City, NE 68355 • *4,769*
Falls Creek, PA 15840 • *1,087*
Fallston, MD 21047 • *5,730*
Falls Township, PA 19054 • *36,083*
Falmouth, KY 41040 • *2,378*
Falmouth, ME 04105 • *7,610*
Falmouth, MA 02540 • *4,047*
Falmouth, VA 22405 • *3,541*
Fannin □, GA • *15,992*
Fannin □, TX • *24,804*
Fanwood, NJ 07023 • *7,115*
Fargo, ND 58102–09 • *74,111*
Faribault, MN 55021 • *17,085*
Faribault □, MN • *16,937*
Farley, IA 52046 • *1,354*
Farmer City, IL 61842 • *2,114*
Farmers Branch, TX 75234 • *24,250*
Farmersburg, IN 47850 • *1,159*
Farmersville, CA 93223 • *6,235*
Farmerville, LA 71241 • *3,334*
Farmingdale, ME 04345 • *2,070*
Farmingdale, NJ 07727 • *1,462*
Farmingdale, NY 11735 • *8,022*
Farmington, AR 72730 • *1,322*
Farmington, CT 06032 • *2,500*
Farmington, IL 61531 • *2,535*
Farmington, ME 04938 • *4,197*
Farmington, MI 48335–36 • *10,132*
Farmington, MN 55024 • *5,940*
Farmington, MO 63640 • *11,598*
Farmington, NH 03835 • *3,567*
Farmington, NM 87401–02 • *33,997*
Farmington, UT 84025 • *9,028*
Farmington Hills, MI 48331–34 • *74,652*
Farmingville, NY 11738 • *14,842*
Farmland, IN 47340 • *1,412*
Farmville, NC 27828 • *4,392*
Farmville, VA 23901 • *6,046*
Farragut, TN 37922 • *12,793*
Farrell, PA 16121 • *6,841*
Farwell, TX 79325 • *1,373*
Faulk □, SD • *2,744*
Faulkland Heights, DE 19808 • *1,300*
Faulkner □, AR • *60,006*
Faulkton, SD 57438 • *809*
Fauquier □, VA • *48,741*
Fayette, AL 35555 • *4,909*
Fayette, IA 52142 • *1,317*
Fayette, MS 39069 • *1,853*
Fayette, MO 65248 • *2,888*
Fayette, OH 43521 • *1,248*
Fayette □, AL • *17,962*
Fayette □, GA • *62,415*
Fayette □, IL • *20,893*
Fayette □, IN • *26,015*
Fayette □, IA • *21,843*
Fayette □, KY • *225,366*
Fayette □, OH • *27,466*
Fayette □, PA • *145,351*
Fayette □, TN • *25,559*
Fayette □, TX • *20,095*
Fayette □, WV • *47,952*
Fayetteville, AR 72701–03 • *42,099*
Fayetteville, GA 30214 • *5,827*
Fayetteville, NC 28301–14 • *75,695*
Fayetteville, PA 17222 • *3,033*
Fayetteville, TN 37334 • *6,921*
Fayetteville, WV 25840 • *2,182*
Fayville, MA 01745 • *1,000*
Federal Heights, CO 80221 • *9,342*
Federalsburg, MD 21632 • *2,365*
Federal Way, WA 98003 • *67,554*

Feeding Hills, MA 01030 • 5,470
Fellowship, NJ 08057 • 4,250
Fellsmere, FL 32948 • 2,179
Felton, CA 95041 • 5,350
Felton, DE 19943 • 683
Fennimore, WI 53809 • 2,378
Fennville, MI 49408 • 1,023
Fenton, MI 48430 • 8,444
Fentress □, TN • 14,669
Ferdinand, IN 47532 • 2,318
Fergus □, MT • 12,083
Fergus Falls, MN 56537–38 • 12,362
Ferguson, MO 63135 • 22,286
Fernandina Beach, FL 32034 • 8,765
Fern Creek, KY 40291 • 16,406
Ferndale, CA 95536 • 1,331
Ferndale, MD 21061 • 16,355
Ferndale, MI 48220 • 25,084
Ferndale, PA 15905 • 2,020
Ferndale, WA 98248 • 5,398
Fernley, NV 89408 • 5,164
Fern Park, FL 32730 • 8,294
Fernway, PA 16063 • 9,072
Ferriday, LA 71334 • 4,111
Ferris, TX 75125 • 2,212
Ferron, UT 84523 • 1,606
Ferry □, WA • 6,295
Ferry Farms, VA 22405 • 1,600
Fessenden, ND 58438 • 655
Festus, MO 63028 • 8,105
Fieldale, VA 24089 • 1,018
Fig Garden, CA 93704 • 9,000
Filer, ID 83328 • 1,511
Fillmore, CA 93015–16 • 11,992
Fillmore, UT 84631 • 1,956
Fillmore □, MN • 20,777
Fillmore □, NE • 7,103
Findlay, OH 45839–40 • 35,703
Finley, TN 38030 • 1,014
Finney □, KS • 33,070
Fircrest, WA 98466 • 5,258
Firebaugh, CA 93622 • 4,429
Firestone, CO 80520 • 1,358
Fisher, IL 61843 • 1,526
Fisher □, TX • 4,842
Fishers, IN 46038 • 7,508
Fishkill, NY 12524 • 1,957
Fiskdale, MA 01518 • 2,189
Fitchburg, MA 01420 • 41,194
Fitzgerald, GA 31750 • 8,612
Five Points, NM 87105 • 4,200
Flagler □, FL • 28,701
Flagler Beach, FL 32136 • 3,820
Flagstaff, AZ 86001–16 • 45,857
Flanders, NJ 07836 • 3,040
Flandreau, SD 57028 • 2,311
Flathead □, MT • 59,218
Flatonia, TX 78941 • 1,295
Flat River, MO 63601 • 4,823
Flat Rock, MI 48134 • 7,290
Flat Rock, NC 28731 • 1,200
Flatwoods, KY 41139 • 7,799
Fleetwood, PA 19522 • 3,478
Fleming □, KY • 12,292
Flemingsburg, KY 41041 • 3,071
Flemington, NJ 08822 • 4,047
Flemington, PA 17745 • 1,321
Fletcher, NC 28732 • 2,787
Fletcher, OK 73541 • 1,002
Flint, MI 48501–32 • 140,761
Flint City, AL 35601 • 1,033
Flippin, AR 72634 • 1,006
Flomaton, AL 36441 • 1,811
Flora, IL 62839 • 5,054
Flora, IN 46929 • 2,179
Flora, MS 39071 • 1,482
Florala, AL 36442 • 2,075
Floral City, FL 32636 • 2,609
Floral Park, NY 11001–05 • 15,947
Florence, AL 35630–33 • 36,426
Florence, AZ 85232 • 7,510
Florence, CA 90001 • 43,900
Florence, CO 81226 • 2,990
Florence, KY 41042 • 18,624
Florence, MS 39073 • 1,831
Florence, NJ 08518 • 4,203
Florence, OR 97439 • 5,162
Florence, SC 29501–06 • 29,813
Florence □, SC • 114,344
Florence □, WI • 4,590
Floresville, TX 78114 • 5,247
Florham Park, NJ 07932 • 8,521
Florida, NY 10921 • 2,497
Florida City, FL 33034 • 5,806
Florida Ridge, FL 32960 • 12,218
Florin, CA 95828 • 24,330
Florissant, MO 63031–34 • 51,206
Flossmoor, IL 60422 • 8,651
Flower Hill, NY 11050 • 4,490
Flowery Branch, GA 30542 • 1,251
Flowood, MS 39208 • 2,860
Floyd □, GA • 81,251
Floyd □, IN • 64,404
Floyd □, IA • 17,058
Floyd □, KY • 43,586
Floyd □, TX • 8,497
Floyd □, VA • 12,005
Floydada, TX 79235 • 3,896
Flushing, MI 48433 • 8,542
Flushing, OH 43977 • 1,042
Fluvanna □, VA • 12,429
Foard □, TX • 1,794
Folcroft, PA 19032 • 7,506
Foley, AL 36535–36 • 4,937
Foley, MN 56329 • 1,854
Folkston, GA 31537 • 2,285
Follansbee, WV 26037 • 3,339
Folly Beach, SC 29439 • 1,398
Folsom, CA 95630 • 29,802
Folsom, NJ 08037 • 2,181
Fonda, NY 12068 • 1,007
Fond du Lac, WI 54935–36 • 37,757
Fond du Lac □, WI • 90,083
Fontana, CA 92334–36 • 87,535
Fontana, WI 53125 • 1,635
Foothill Farms, CA 95841 • 17,135
Ford □, IL • 14,275
Ford □, KS • 27,463
Ford City, CA 93268 • 3,781
Ford City, PA 16226 • 3,413
Ford Heights, IL 60411 • 4,259
Fords, NJ 08863 • 14,392
Fords Prairie, WA 98531 • 2,480
Fordyce, AR 71742 • 4,729
Foreman, AR 71836 • 1,267
Forest, MS 39074 • 5,060
Forest, OH 45843 • 1,594
Forest □, PA • 4,802
Forest □, WI • 8,776
Forest Acres, SC 29206 • 7,197
Forest City, IA 50436 • 4,430
Forest City, NC 28043 • 7,475
Forest City, PA 18421 • 1,846
Forestdale, AL 35214 • 10,395
Forestdale, RI 02824 • 530
Forest Dale, VT 05745 • 350
Forest Grove, OR 97116 • 13,559
Forest Hill, TX 76119 • 11,482
Forest Hills, PA 15221 • 7,335
Forest Knolls, CA 94933 • 2,000
Forest Lake, MN 55025 • 5,833
Forest Park, GA 30050–51 • 16,925
Forest Park, IL 60130 • 14,918
Forest Park, LA 71291 • 1,400
Forest Park, OH 45240 • 18,609
Forked River, NJ 08731 • 1,950
Forks, WA 98331 • 2,862
Forney, TX 75126 • 4,070
Forrest, IL 61741 • 1,124
Forrest □, MS • 68,314
Forrest City, AR 72335 • 13,364
Forreston, IL 61030 • 1,361
Forsyth, GA 31029 • 4,268
Forsyth, IL 62535 • 1,275
Forsyth, MO 65653 • 1,175
Forsyth, MT 59327 • 2,178
Forsyth □, GA • 44,083
Forsyth □, NC • 265,878
Fort Ashby, WV 26719 • 1,288
Fort Atkinson, WI 53538 • 10,227
Fort Bend □, TX • 225,421
Fort Benton, MT 59442 • 1,660
Fort Bragg, CA 95437 • 6,078
Fort Branch, IN 47648 • 2,447
Fort Collins, CO 80521–26 • 87,758
Fort Covington, NY 12937 • 1,200
Fort Davis, TX 79734 • 1,100
Fort Defiance, AZ 86504 • 4,489
Fort Deposit, AL 36032 • 1,240
Fort Dodge, IA 50501 • 25,894
Fort Edward, NY 12828 • 3,561
Fort Fairfield, ME 04742 • 1,729
Fort Gaines, GA 31751 • 1,248
Fort Gibson, OK 74434 • 3,359
Fort Hall, ID 83203 • 2,681
Fort Kent, ME 04743 • 2,123
Fort Laramie, WY 82212 • 243
Fort Lauderdale, FL 33301–51 • 149,377
Fort Lee, NJ 07024 • 31,997
Fort Loramie, OH 45845 • 1,042
Fort Loudon, PA 17224 • 1,200
Fort Lupton, CO 80621 • 5,159
Fort Madison, IA 52627 • 11,618
Fort McKinley, OH 45426 • 9,740
Fort Meade, FL 33841 • 4,976
Fort Mill, SC 29715 • 4,930
Fort Mitchell, KY 41017 • 7,438
Fort Morgan, CO 80701 • 9,068
Fort Myers, FL 33901–19 • 45,206
Fort Myers Beach, FL 33931–32 • 9,284
Fort Myers Shores, FL 33905 • 5,460
Fort Oglethorpe, GA 30742 • 5,880
Fort Payne, AL 35967 • 11,838
Fort Pierce, FL 34945–54 • 36,830
Fort Pierre, SD 57532 • 1,854
Fort Plain, NY 13339 • 2,416
Fort Recovery, OH 45846 • 1,313
Fort Scott, KS 66701 • 8,362
Fort Shawnee, OH 45806 • 4,128
Fort Smith, AR 72901–17 • 72,798
Fort Stockton, TX 79735 • 8,524
Fort Sumner, NM 88119 • 1,269
Fort Thomas, KY 41075 • 16,032
Fortuna, CA 95540 • 8,788
Fort Valley, GA 31030 • 8,198
Fortville, IN 46040 • 2,690
Fort Walton Beach, FL 32547–48 • 21,471
Fort Washington Forest, MD 20744 • 1,010
Fort Wayne, IN 46801–99 • 173,072
Fort Wingate, NM 87316 • 950
Fort Worth, TX 76101–85 • 447,619
Fort Wright, KY 41011 • 6,570
Forty Fort, PA 18704 • 5,049
Fort Yukon, AK 99740 • 580
Fosston, MN 56542 • 1,529
Foster □, ND • 3,983
Foster City, CA 94404 • 28,176
Foster Village, HI 96818 • 3,700
Fostoria, OH 44830 • 14,983
Fountain, CO 80817 • 9,984
Fountain □, IN • 17,808
Fountain Hill, PA 18015 • 4,637
Fountain Inn, SC 29644 • 4,388
Fountain Place, LA • 9,200
Fountain Valley, CA 92708 • 53,691
Four Corners, OR 97301 • 12,156
Four Oaks, NC 27524 • 1,308
Fowler, CA 93625 • 3,208
Fowler, CO 81039 • 1,154
Fowler, IN 47944 • 2,333
Fowlerville, MI 48836 • 2,648
Foxboro, MA 02035 • 5,706
Fox Chapel, PA 15238 • 5,319
Fox Lake, IL 60020 • 7,478
Fox Lake, WI 53933 • 1,269
Fox Point, WI 53217 • 7,238
Fox River Grove, IL 60021 • 3,551
Frackville, PA 17931 • 4,700
Framingham, MA 01701 • 64,994
Franconia, VA 22310 • 19,882
Frankenmuth, MI 48734 • 4,408
Frankford, DE 19945 • 591
Frankfort, IL 60423 • 7,180
Frankfort, IN 46041 • 14,754
Frankfort, KY 40601–22 • 25,968
Frankfort, MI 49635 • 1,546
Frankfort, NY 13340 • 2,693
Frankfort, OH 45628 • 1,065
Franklin, IN 46131 • 12,907
Franklin, KY 42134–35 • 7,607
Franklin, LA 70538 • 9,004
Franklin, MA 02038 • 9,965
Franklin, NE 68939 • 1,112
Franklin, NH 03235 • 8,304
Franklin, NJ 07416 • 4,977
Franklin, NC 28734 • 2,873
Franklin, OH 45005 • 11,026
Franklin, PA 16323 • 7,329
Franklin, TN 37064–65 • 20,098
Franklin, TX 77856 • 1,336
Franklin, VA 23851 • 7,864
Franklin, WI 53132 • 21,855
Franklin □, AL • 27,814
Franklin □, AR • 14,897
Franklin □, FL • 8,967
Franklin □, GA • 16,650
Franklin □, ID • 9,232
Franklin □, IL • 40,319
Franklin □, IN • 19,580
Franklin □, IA • 11,364
Franklin □, KS • 21,994
Franklin □, KY • 43,781
Franklin □, LA • 22,387
Franklin □, ME • 29,008
Franklin □, MA • 70,092
Franklin □, MS • 8,377
Franklin □, MO • 80,603
Franklin □, NE • 3,938
Franklin □, NY • 46,540
Franklin □, NC • 36,414
Franklin □, OH • 961,437
Franklin □, PA • 121,082
Franklin □, TN • 34,725
Franklin □, TX • 7,802
Franklin □, VT • 39,980
Franklin □, VA • 39,549
Franklin □, WA • 37,473
Franklin Lakes, NJ 07417 • 9,873
Franklin Park, IL 60131 • 18,485
Franklin Park, PA 15143 • 10,109
Franklin Square, NY 11010 • 28,205
Franklinton, LA 70438 • 4,007
Franklinton, NC 27525 • 1,615
Franklinville, NJ 08322 • 1,020
Franklinville, NY 14737 • 1,739
Frankston, TX 75763 • 1,127
Frankton, IN 46044 • 1,736
Fraser, MI 48026 • 13,899
Frazee, MN 56544 • 1,176
Frazeysburg, OH 43822 • 1,165
Frazier Park, CA 93225 • 2,201
Frederic, WI 54837 • 1,124
Frederica, DE 19946 • 761
Frederick, MD 21701–02 • 40,148
Frederick, OK 73542 • 5,221
Frederick □, MD • 150,208
Frederick □, VA • 45,723
Fredericksburg, IA 50630 • 1,011
Fredericksburg, TX 78624 • 6,934
Fredericksburg, VA 22401–08 • 19,027
Fredericktown, MO 63645 • 3,950
Fredericktown, OH 43019 • 2,443
Fredericktown, PA 15333 • 1,052
Fredonia, AZ 86022 • 1,207
Fredonia, KS 66736 • 2,599
Fredonia, NY 14063 • 10,436
Fredonia, WI 53021 • 1,558
Freeborn □, MN • 33,060
Freeburg, IL 62243 • 3,115
Freedom, CA 95019 • 8,361
Freedom, PA 15042 • 1,897
Freedom, WY 83120 • 450
Freehold, NJ 07728 • 10,742
Freeland, MI 48623 • 1,421
Freeland, PA 18224 • 3,909
Freeman, SD 57029 • 1,293
Freemansburg, PA 18017 • 1,946
Freeport, IL 61032 • 25,840
Freeport, ME 04032 • 1,829
Freeport, NY 11520 • 39,894
Freeport, PA 16229 • 1,983
Freeport, TX 77541 • 11,389
Freer, TX 78357 • 3,271
Freestone □, TX • 15,818
Fremont, CA 94536–39 • 173,339
Fremont, IN 46737 • 1,407
Fremont, MI 49412 • 3,875
Fremont, NE 68025 • 23,680
Fremont, NC 27830 • 1,710
Fremont, OH 43420 • 17,648
Fremont □, CO • 32,273
Fremont □, ID • 10,937
Fremont □, IA • 8,226
Fremont □, WY • 33,662
French Island, WI 54601 • 4,478
French Lick, IN 47432 • 2,087
Frenchtown, NJ 08825 • 1,528
Fresno, CA 93701–94 • 354,202
Fresno □, CA • 667,490
Frewsburg, NY 14738 • 1,817
Friars Point, MS 38631 • 1,334
Friday Harbor, WA 98250 • 1,492
Fridley, MN 55432 • 28,335
Friend, NE 68359 • 1,111
Friendship, NY 14739 • 1,423
Friendswood, TX 77546 • 22,814
Frio □, TX • 13,472
Friona, TX 79035 • 3,688
Frisco, CO 80443 • 1,601
Frisco City, AL 36445 • 1,581
Fritch, TX 79036 • 2,335
Frontenac, KS 66762 • 2,588
Frontier □, NE • 3,101
Front Royal, VA 22630 • 11,880
Frostburg, MD 21532 • 8,075
Frostproof, FL 33843 • 2,808
Fruita, CO 81521 • 4,045
Fruit Heights, UT 84037 • 3,900
Fruitland, ID 83619 • 2,400
Fruitland, MD 21826 • 3,511
Fruitland Park, FL 34731 • 2,754
Fruitport, MI 49415 • 1,090
Fruitvale, CO 81504 • 1,070
Fruitvale, WA 98902 • 4,125
Fruitville, FL 34232 • 9,808
Fryeburg, ME 04037 • 1,580
Fulda, MN 56131 • 1,212
Fullerton, CA 92631–35 • 114,144
Fullerton, NE 68638 • 1,452
Fulton, IL 61252 • 3,698
Fulton, KY 42041 • 3,078
Fulton, MS 38843 • 3,387
Fulton, MO 65251 • 10,033
Fulton, NY 13069 • 12,929
Fulton □, AR • 10,037
Fulton □, GA • 648,951
Fulton □, IL • 38,080
Fulton □, IN • 18,840
Fulton □, KY • 8,271
Fulton □, NY • 54,191
Fulton □, OH • 38,498
Fulton □, PA • 13,837
Fultondale, AL 35068 • 6,400
Funkstown, MD 21734 • 1,136
Fuquay-Varina, NC 27526 • 4,562
Furnas □, NE • 5,553
Fyffe, AL 35971 • 1,094

G

Gabbs, NV 89409 • 667
Gadsden, AL 35901–05 • 42,523
Gadsden □, FL • 41,105
Gaffney, SC 29340–42 • 13,145
Gage □, NE • 22,794
Gages Lake, IL 60030 • 8,349
Gahanna, OH 43230 • 27,791
Gaines □, TX • 14,123
Gainesboro, TN 38562 • 1,002
Gainesville, FL 32601–14 • 84,770
Gainesville, GA 30501–07 • 17,885
Gainesville, TX 76240 • 14,256
Gaithersburg, MD 20877–79 • 39,542
Galax, VA 24333 • 6,670
Galena, AK 99741 • 833
Galena, IL 61036 • 3,647
Galena, KS 66739 • 3,308
Galesburg, IL 61401–02 • 33,530
Galesburg, MI 49053 • 1,863
Gales Ferry, CT 06335 • 1,191
Galesville, WI 54630 • 1,278
Galeton, PA 16922 • 1,370
Galeville, NY 13088 • 4,695
Galion, OH 44833 • 11,859
Gallatin, MO 64640 • 1,864
Gallatin, TN 37066 • 18,794
Gallatin □, IL • 6,909
Gallatin □, KY • 5,393
Gallatin □, MT • 50,463
Gallia □, OH • 30,954
Galliano, LA 70354 • 4,294
Gallipolis, OH 45631 • 4,831
Gallitzin, PA 16641 • 2,003
Gallup, NM 87301–05 • 19,154
Galt, CA 95632 • 8,889
Galva, IL 61434 • 2,742
Galveston, IN 46932 • 1,609
Galveston, TX 77550–54 • 59,070
Galveston □, TX • 217,399
Gambell, AK 99742 • 525
Gambier, OH 43022 • 2,073
Gambrills, MD 21054 • 1,200
Ganado, AZ 86505 • 3,400
Ganado, TX 77962 • 1,701
Gang Mills, NY 14870 • 2,738
Gantt, SC 29605 • 13,891
Gap, PA 17527 • 1,200
Garberville, CA 95440 • 1,200
Garden □, NE • 2,460
Gardena, CA 90247–49 • 49,847
Garden City, GA 31408 • 7,410
Garden City, ID 83704 • 6,369
Garden City, KS 67846 • 24,097
Garden City, MI 48135–36 • 31,846
Garden City, MO 64747 • 1,225
Garden City, NY 11530 • 21,686
Garden City Park, NY 11040 • 7,437
Gardendale, AL 35071 • 9,251
Garden Grove, CA 92640–45 • 143,050
Garden Home, OR 97223 • 5,500
Gardiner, ME 04345 • 6,746
Gardner, IL 60424 • 1,237
Gardner, KS 66030 • 3,191
Gardner, MA 01440 • 20,125
Gardnerville, NV 89410 • 2,177
Gardnerville Ranchos, NV 89410 • 7,455
Garfield, NJ 07026 • 26,727
Garfield □, CO • 29,974
Garfield □, MT • 1,589
Garfield □, NE • 2,141
Garfield □, OK • 56,735
Garfield □, UT • 3,980
Garfield □, WA • 2,248
Garfield Heights, OH 44125 • 31,739
Garfield Park, DE 19720 • 1,415
Garland, TX 75040–48 • 180,650
Garland, UT 84312 • 1,637
Garland □, AR • 73,397
Garner, IA 50438 • 2,916
Garner, NC 27529 • 14,967
Garnett, KS 66032 • 3,210
Garrard □, KY • 11,579
Garretson, SD 57030 • 924
Garrett, IN 46738 • 5,349
Garrett □, MD • 28,138
Garrettsville, OH 44231 • 2,014
Garrison, MD 21055 • 5,045
Garrison, ND 58540 • 1,530
Garvin □, OK • 26,605
Garwood, NJ 07027 • 4,227
Gary, IN 46401–11 • 116,646
Gary, WV 24836 • 1,355
Garysburg, NC 27831 • 1,057
Garyville, LA 70051 • 3,181
Garza □, TX • 5,143
Gas City, IN 46933 • 6,296
Gasconade □, MO • 14,006
Gasport, NY 14067 • 1,336
Gassville, AR 72635 • 1,167
Gaston, NC 27832 • 1,003
Gaston □, NC • 175,093
Gastonia, NC 28051–56 • 54,732
Gate City, VA 24251 • 2,214
Gates, NY 14624 • 30,000
Gates □, NC • 9,305
Gatesville, TX 76528 • 11,492
Gatlinburg, TN 37738 • 3,417
Gautier, MS 39553 • 10,088
Gaylord, MI 49735 • 3,256
Gaylord, MN 55334 • 1,935
Gearhart, OR 97138 • 1,027
Geary, OK 73040 • 1,347
Geary □, KS • 30,453
Geauga □, OH • 81,129
Geistown, PA 15904 • 2,749
Gem □, ID • 11,844
Genesee, ID 83832 • 725
Genesee, MI 48437 • 1,400
Genesee □, MI • 430,459
Genesee □, NY • 60,060
Geneseo, IL 61254 • 5,990
Geneseo, NY 14454 • 7,187
Geneva, AL 36340 • 4,681
Geneva, IL 60134 • 12,617
Geneva, IN 46740 • 1,280
Geneva, NE 68361 • 2,310
Geneva, NY 14456 • 14,143
Geneva, OH 44041 • 6,597
Geneva □, AL • 23,647
Geneva-on-the-Lake, OH 44041 • 1,626
Genoa, IL 60135 • 3,083
Genoa, NE 68640 • 1,082
Genoa, NV 89411 • 190
Genoa, OH 43430 • 2,262
Genoa City, WI 53128 • 1,277
Gentry, AR 72734 • 1,726
Gentry □, MO • 6,848
George, IA 51237 • 1,066
George □, MS • 16,673
Georgetown, CA 95634 • 2,000
Georgetown, CT 06829 • 1,694
Georgetown, DE 19947 • 3,732
Georgetown, IL 61846 • 3,678
Georgetown, IN 47122 • 2,092
Georgetown, KY 40324 • 11,414
Georgetown, MA 01833 • 2,100
Georgetown, OH 45121 • 3,627
Georgetown, SC 29440–42 • 9,517
Georgetown, TX 78626–28 • 14,842
Georgetown □, SC • 46,302
George West, TX 78022 • 2,586
Georgiana, AL 36033 • 1,933
Gering, NE 69341 • 7,946
Gerlach, NV 89412 • 200
Germantown, IL 62245 • 1,167
Germantown, MD 20874 • 41,145
Germantown, OH 45327 • 4,916
Germantown, TN 38138 • 32,893
Germantown, WI 53022 • 13,658
Gettysburg, PA 17325 • 7,025
Gettysburg, SD 57442 • 1,510
Giants Neck, CT 06357 • 1,200
Gibbon, NE 68840 • 1,525
Gibbstown, NJ 08027 • 5,404
Gibsland, LA 71028 • 1,224
Gibson □, IN • 31,913
Gibson □, TN • 46,315
Gibsonburg, OH 43431 • 2,579
Gibson City, IL 60936 • 3,396
Gibsonia, FL 33805 • 5,168
Gibsonia, PA 15044 • 3,500
Gibsonton, FL 33534 • 7,706
Gibsonville, NC 27249 • 3,441
Giddings, TX 78942 • 4,093
Gideon, MO 63848 • 1,104
Gifford, FL 32960 • 6,278
Gig Harbor, WA 98335 • 3,236
Gila □, AZ • 40,216
Gila Bend, AZ 85337 • 1,747
Gilbert, AZ 85234 • 29,188
Gilbert, MN 55741 • 1,934
Gilbert, OR 97266 • 4,000
Gilbertsville, PA 19525 • 3,994
Gilbertville, MA 01031 • 1,029
Gilchrist □, FL • 9,667
Gilcrest, CO 80623 • 1,084
Giles □, TN • 25,741
Giles □, VA • 16,366
Gilford Park, NJ 08753 • 8,668
Gillespie, IL 62033 • 3,645
Gillespie □, TX • 17,204
Gillett, WI 54124 • 1,303
Gillette, WY 82716–17 • 17,635
Gilliam □, OR • 1,717
Gilman, IL 60938 • 1,816
Gilman, VT 05904 • 500
Gilmer, TX 75644 • 4,822
Gilmer □, GA • 13,368
Gilmer □, WV • 7,669
Gilpin □, CO • 3,070
Gilroy, CA 95020–21 • 31,487
Girard, IL 62640 • 2,164
Girard, KS 66743 • 2,794
Girard, OH 44420 • 11,304
Girard, PA 16417 • 2,879
Girardville, PA 17935 • 1,889
Glacier □, MT • 12,121
Glades □, FL • 7,591
Glade Spring, VA 24340 • 1,435
Gladeview, FL 33138 • 15,637
Gladewater, TX 75647 • 6,027
Gladstone, MI 49837 • 4,565
Gladstone, MO 64118 • 26,243
Gladstone, NJ 07934 • 2,111
Gladstone, OR 97027 • 10,152
Gladwin, MI 48624 • 2,682
Gladwin □, MI • 21,896
Glasco, NY 12432 • 1,538
Glascock □, GA • 2,357
Glasford, IL 61533 • 1,115
Glasgow, KY 42141–42 • 12,351
Glasgow, MO 65254 • 1,295
Glasgow, MT 59230 • 3,572
Glasgow, VA 24555 • 1,140
Glasgow Village, MO 63137 • 5,199
Glassboro, NJ 08028 • 15,614
Glasscock □, TX • 1,447
Glassport, PA 15045 • 5,582
Glastonbury, CT 06033 • 7,082
Gleason, TN 38229 • 1,402
Glen Allen, VA 23060 • 9,010
Glen Avon, CA • 12,663
Glenbrook, NV 89413 • 400
Glen Burnie, MD 21061 • 37,305
Glen Burnie Park, MD 21061 • 3,260
Glen Carbon, IL 62034 • 7,731
Glencoe, AL 35905 • 4,670
Glencoe, IL 60022 • 8,499
Glencoe, MN 55336 • 4,648
Glen Cove, NY 11542 • 24,149
Glendale, AZ 85301–12 • 148,134
Glendale, CA 91201–14 • 180,038
Glendale, CO 80222 • 2,453
Glendale, MS 39401 • 1,329
Glendale, MO 63122 • 5,945
Glendale, OH 45246 • 2,445
Glendale, RI 02826 • 700
Glendale, SC 29346 • 1,049
Glen Dale, WV 26038 • 1,612
Glendale, WI 53209 • 14,088
Glendale Heights, IL 60139 • 27,973
Glendive, MT 59330 • 4,802
Glendo, WY 82213 • 195

Glendola, NJ 07719 • *2,340*
Glendora, CA 91740 • *47,828*
Glendora, NJ 08029 • *5,201*
Glen Ellyn, IL 60137–38 • *24,944*
Glen Gardner, NJ 08826 • *1,665*
Glenham, NY 12527 • *2,832*
Glen Head, NY 11545 • *6,870*
Glen Lyon, PA 18617 • *2,082*
Glenmora, LA 71433 • *1,686*
Glenn □, CA • *24,798*
Glennallen, AK 99588 • *451*
Glenn Dale, MD 20769 • *9,689*
Glenns Ferry, ID 83623 • *1,304*
Glennville, GA 30427 • *3,676*
Glenolden, PA 19036 • *7,260*
Glenpool, OK 74033 • *6,688*
Glen Raven, NC 27215 • *2,616*
Glen Ridge, NJ 07028 • *7,076*
Glen Rock, NJ 07452 • *10,883*
Glen Rock, PA 17327 • *1,688*
Glenrock, WY 82637 • *2,153*
Glen Rose, TX 76043 • *1,949*
Glens Falls, NY 12801 • *15,023*
Glenside, PA 19038 • *8,704*
Glen Ullin, ND 58631 • *927*
Glenview, IL 60025 • *37,093*
Glenville, WV 26351 • *1,923*
Glenwood, AR 71943 • *1,354*
Glenwood, IL 60425 • *9,289*
Glenwood, IA 51534 • *4,571*
Glenwood, MN 56334 • *2,573*
Glenwood, VA 24541 • *2,276*
Glenwood City, WI 54013 • *1,026*
Glenwood Farms, VA 23223 • *3,200*
Glenwood Hills, GA 30032 • *5,240*
Glenwood Springs, CO 81601–02 • *6,561*
Glidden, IA 51443 • *1,099*
Globe, AZ 85501–02 • *6,062*
Gloster, MS 39638 • *1,323*
Gloucester, MA 01930–31 • *28,716*
Gloucester, VA 23061 • *1,200*
Gloucester □, NJ • *230,082*
Gloucester □, VA • *30,131*
Gloucester City, NJ 08030 • *12,649*
Gloucester Point, VA 23062 • *8,509*
Glouster, OH 45732 • *2,001*
Gloversville, NY 12078 • *16,656*
Gloverville, SC 29828 • *2,753*
Glynn □, GA • *62,496*
Gnadenhutten, OH 44629 • *1,226*
Goddard, KS 67052 • *1,804*
Godfrey, IL 62035 • *5,436*
Goffstown, NH 03045 • *2,700*
Gogebic □, MI • *18,052*
Golconda, NV 89414 • *200*
Gold Bar, WA 98251 • *1,078*
Gold Beach, OR 97444 • *1,546*
Golden, CO 80401–03 • *13,116*
Goldendale, WA 98620 • *3,319*
Golden Gate, FL 33999 • *14,148*
Golden Glades, FL 33055 • *25,474*
Golden Meadow, LA 70357 • *2,049*
Golden Valley, MN 55427 • *20,971*
Golden Valley □, MT • *912*
Golden Valley □, ND • *2,108*
Goldfield, NV 89013 • *600*
Goldsboro, NC 27530–34 • *40,709*
Goldthwaite, TX 76844 • *1,658*
Goleta, CA 93117 • *28,600*
Golf Manor, OH 45237 • *4,154*
Goliad, TX 77963 • *1,946*
Goliad □, TX • *5,980*
Gonzales, CA 93926 • *4,660*
Gonzales, LA 70737 • *7,003*
Gonzales, TX 78629 • *6,527*
Gonzales □, TX • *17,205*
Gonzalez, FL 32560 • *7,669*
Goochland □, VA • *14,163*
Goodhue □, MN • *40,690*
Gooding, ID 83330 • *2,820*
Gooding □, ID • *11,633*
Goodland, FL 33933 • *1,000*
Goodland, IN 47948 • *1,033*
Goodland, KS 67735 • *4,983*
Goodlettsville, TN 37072 • *11,219*
Goodman, MS 39079 • *1,256*
Goodman, MO 64843 • *1,094*
Goodsprings, NV 89019 • *150*
Goodview, MN 55987 • *2,878*
Goodwater, AL 35072 • *1,840*
Goodwell, OK 73939 • *1,065*
Goodyear, AZ 85338 • *6,258*
Goose Creek, SC 29445 • *24,692*
Gordo, AL 35466 • *1,918*
Gordon, GA 31031 • *2,468*
Gordon, NE 69343 • *1,803*
Gordon □, GA • *35,072*
Gordonsville, VA 22942 • *1,351*
Gorham, ME 04038 • *3,618*
Gorham, NH 03581 • *1,910*
Gorman, TX 76454 • *1,290*
Goshen, IN 46526 • *23,797*
Goshen, NY 10924 • *5,255*
Goshen, OH 45122 • *1,400*
Goshen □, WY • *12,373*
Gosnell, AR 72319 • *3,783*
Gosper □, NE • *1,928*
Gothenburg, NE 69138 • *3,232*
Gould, AR 71643 • *1,470*
Goulding, FL 32503 • *4,159*
Goulds, FL 33170 • *7,284*
Gouverneur, NY 13642 • *4,604*
Gove □, KS • *3,231*
Gowanda, NY 14070 • *2,901*
Gower, MO 64454 • *1,249*
Gowrie, IA 50543 • *1,028*
Grace, ID 83241 • *973*
Graceville, FL 32440 • *2,675*
Gracewood, GA 30812 • *1,000*
Grady □, GA • *20,279*
Grady □, OK • *41,747*
Grafton, MA 01519 • *1,520*
Grafton, ND 58237 • *4,840*
Grafton, OH 44044 • *3,344*
Grafton, WV 26354 • *5,524*
Grafton, WI 53024 • *9,340*
Grafton □, NH • *74,929*
Graham, CA 90002 • *10,600*
Graham, NC 27253 • *10,426*
Graham, TX 76046 • *8,986*
Graham □, AZ • *26,554*
Graham □, KS • *3,543*
Graham □, NC • *7,196*
Grainger □, TN • *17,095*
Grain Valley, MO 64029 • *1,898*
Grambling, LA 71245 • *5,484*
Gramercy, LA 70052 • *2,412*
Granbury, TX 76048–49 • *4,045*
Granby, CT 06035 • *9,369*
Granby, MA 01033 • *1,327*
Granby, MO 64844 • *1,945*
Grand □, CO • *7,966*
Grand □, UT • *6,620*
Grand Bay, AL 36541 • *3,383*
Grand Blanc, MI 48439 • *7,760*
Grand Caillou, LA 70360 • *1,400*
Grand Canyon, AZ 86023 • *1,499*
Grand Coteau, LA 70541 • *1,118*
Grandfield, OK 73546 • *1,224*
Grand Forks, ND 58201–06 • *49,425*
Grand Forks □, ND • *70,683*
Grand Haven, MI 49417 • *11,951*
Grand Island, NE 68801–03 • *39,386*
Grand Isle, LA 70358 • *1,455*
Grand Isle □, VT • *5,318*
Grand Junction, CO 81501–06 • *29,034*
Grand Ledge, MI 48837 • *7,579*
Grand Marais, MN 55604 • *1,171*
Grand Prairie, TX 75050–54 • *99,616*
Grand Rapids, MI 49501–99 • *189,126*
Grand Rapids, MN 55744 • *7,976*
Grand Saline, TX 75140 • *2,630*
Grand Terrace, CA 92324 • *10,946*
Grand Traverse □, MI • *64,273*
Grandview, MO 64030 • *24,967*
Grandview, WA 98930 • *7,169*
Grandview Heights, OH 43212 • *7,010*
Grandville, MI 49418 • *15,624*
Granger, IN 46530 • *20,241*
Granger, TX 76530 • *1,190*
Granger, WA 98932 • *2,053*
Grangeville, ID 83530 • *3,226*
Granite, OK 73547 • *1,844*
Granite □, MT • *2,548*
Granite City, IL 62040 • *32,862*
Granite Falls, MN 56241 • *3,083*
Granite Falls, NC 28630 • *3,253*
Granite Falls, WA 98252 • *1,060*
Granite Quarry, NC 28072 • *1,646*
Graniteville, MA 01886 • *1,010*
Graniteville, SC 29829 • *1,158*
Graniteville, VT 05654 • *500*
Grant, NE 69140 • *1,239*
Grant □, AR • *13,948*
Grant □, IN • *74,169*
Grant □, KS • *7,159*
Grant □, KY • *15,737*
Grant □, LA • *17,526*
Grant □, MN • *6,246*
Grant □, NE • *769*
Grant □, NM • *27,676*
Grant □, ND • *3,549*
Grant □, OK • *5,689*
Grant □, OR • *7,853*
Grant □, SD • *8,372*
Grant □, WA • *54,758*
Grant □, WV • *10,428*
Grant □, WI • *49,264*
Grant Park, IL 60940 • *1,024*
Grants, NM 87020 • *8,626*
Grantsburg, WI 54840 • *1,144*
Grants Pass, OR 97526–27 • *17,488*
Grantsville, UT 84029 • *4,500*
Grantville, GA 30220 • *1,180*
Granville, IL 61326 • *1,407*
Granville, NY 12832 • *2,646*
Granville, OH 43023 • *4,353*
Granville □, NC • *38,345*
Grapeland, TX 75844 • *1,450*
Grapevine, TX 76051 • *29,202*
Grasonville, MD 21638 • *2,439*
Grass Lake, IL 60002 • *2,191*
Grass Valley, CA 95945 • *9,048*
Gratiot □, MI • *38,982*
Graves □, KY • *33,550*
Gravette, AR 72736 • *1,412*
Gray, GA 31032 • *2,189*
Gray, LA 70359 • *1,500*
Gray □, KS • *5,396*
Gray □, TX • *23,967*
Grayling, MI 49738 • *1,944*
Graylyn Crest, DE 19810 • *4,380*
Grays Harbor □, WA • *64,175*
Grayslake, IL 60030 • *7,388*
Grayson, KY 41143 • *3,510*
Grayson □, KY • *21,050*
Grayson □, TX • *95,021*
Grayson □, VA • *16,278*
Graysville, AL 35073 • *2,241*
Graysville, TN 37338 • *1,301*
Grayville, IL 62844 • *2,043*
Great Barrington, MA 01230 • *2,810*
Great Bend, KS 67530 • *15,427*
Great Falls, MT 59401–06 • *55,097*
Great Falls, SC 29055 • *2,307*
Great Falls, VA 22066 • *6,945*
Great Neck, NY 11020–27 • *8,745*
Great Neck Estates, NY 11021 • *2,790*
Greece, NY 14626 • *15,632*
Greece, NY • *15,632*
Greeley, CO 80631–34 • *60,536*
Greeley □, KS • *1,774*
Greeley □, NE • *3,006*
Green, OR 97470 • *5,076*
Green □, KY • *10,371*
Green □, WI • *30,339*
Greenacres, CA 93308 • *7,379*
Green Acres, DE 19803 • *1,140*
Greenacres, WA 99016 • *4,250*
Greenacres City, FL 33463 • *18,683*
Green Bay, WI 54301–24 • *96,466*
Greenbelt, MD 20770 • *21,096*
Greenbriar, VA 22033 • *6,200*
Greenbrier, AR 72058 • *2,130*
Green Brier, TN 37073 • *2,873*
Greenbrier □, WV • *34,693*
Green Brook, NJ 08812 • *2,380*
Greencastle, IN 46135 • *8,984*
Greencastle, PA 17225 • *3,600*
Green Cove Springs, FL 32043 • *4,497*
Greendale, IN 47025 • *3,881*
Greendale, WI 53129 • *15,128*
Greene, IA 50636 • *1,142*
Greene, NY 13778 • *1,812*
Greene □, AL • *10,153*
Greene □, AR • *31,804*
Greene □, GA • *11,793*
Greene □, IL • *15,317*
Greene □, IN • *30,410*
Greene □, IA • *10,045*
Greene □, MS • *10,220*
Greene □, MO • *207,949*
Greene □, NY • *44,739*
Greene □, NC • *15,384*
Greene □, OH • *136,731*
Greene □, PA • *39,550*
Greene □, TN • *55,853*
Greene □, VA • *10,297*
Greeneville, TN 37743–44 • *13,532*
Greenfield, CA 93927 • *7,464*
Greenfield, IL 62044 • *1,162*
Greenfield, IN 46140 • *11,657*
Greenfield, IA 50849 • *2,074*
Greenfield, MA 01301–02 • *14,016*
Greenfield, MO 65661 • *1,416*
Greenfield, OH 45123 • *5,172*
Greenfield, TN 38230 • *2,105*
Greenfield, WI 53220 • *33,403*
Greenfield Plaza, IA 50315 • *2,200*
Green Forest, AR 72638 • *2,050*
Green Harbor, MA 02041 • *1,900*
Greenhills, OH 45218 • *4,393*
Green Island, NY 12183 • *2,490*
Green Lake, WI 54941 • *1,064*
Green Lake □, WI • *18,651*
Greenlawn, NY 11740 • *13,208*
Greenlee □, AZ • *8,008*
Greenock, PA 15047 • *2,500*
Greenport, NY 11944 • *2,070*
Green River, WY 82935 • *12,711*
Green Rock, IL 61241 • *2,615*
Greensboro, AL 36744 • *3,047*
Greensboro, GA 30642 • *2,860*
Greensboro, MD 21639 • *1,441*
Greensboro, NC 27401–95 • *183,521*
Greensburg, IN 47240 • *9,286*
Greensburg, KS 67054 • *1,792*
Greensburg, KY 42743 • *1,990*
Greensburg, PA 15601 • *16,318*
Green Springs, OH 44836 • *1,446*
Greensville □, VA • *8,853*
Greentown, IN 46936 • *2,172*
Green Tree, PA 15220 • *4,905*
Greenup, IL 62428 • *1,616*
Greenup, KY 41144 • *1,158*
Greenup □, KY • *36,742*
Green Valley, AZ 85614 • *13,231*
Green Valley, MD 21771 • *9,424*
Greenview, SC 29203 • *5,515*
Greenville, AL 36037 • *7,492*
Greenville, CA 95947 • *1,396*
Greenville, DE 19807 • *800*
Greenville, GA 30222 • *1,167*
Greenville, IL 62246 • *4,806*
Greenville, KY 42345 • *4,689*
Greenville, ME 04441 • *1,601*
Greenville, MI 48838 • *8,101*
Greenville, MS 38701–04 • *45,226*
Greenville, NH 03048 • *1,135*
Greenville, NY 10583 • *9,528*
Greenville, NC 27834–36 • *44,972*
Greenville, OH 45331 • *12,863*
Greenville, PA 16125 • *6,734*
Greenville, RI 02828 • *8,303*
Greenville, SC 29601–16 • *58,282*
Greenville, TX 75401–03 • *23,071*
Greenville □, SC • *320,167*
Greenwich, CT 06830–36 • *58,441*
Greenwich, NY 12834 • *1,961*
Greenwich, OH 44837 • *1,442*
Greenwood, AR 72936 • *3,984*
Greenwood, DE 19950 • *578*
Greenwood, IN 46142 • *26,265*
Greenwood, LA 71033 • *2,092*
Greenwood, MS 38930 • *18,906*
Greenwood, MO 64034 • *1,505*
Greenwood, PA 16601 • *1,650*
Greenwood, SC 29646–49 • *20,807*
Greenwood □, KS • *7,847*
Greenwood □, SC • *59,567*
Greenwood Lake, NY 10925 • *3,208*
Greenwood Village, CO 80111 • *7,589*
Greer, SC 29650–52 • *10,322*
Greer □, OK • *6,559*
Gregg □, TX • *104,948*
Gregory, SD 57533 • *1,384*
Gregory □, SD • *5,359*
Greilickville, MI 49684 • *1,060*
Grenada, MS 38901 • *10,864*
Grenada □, MS • *21,555*
Gresham, OR 97030 • *68,235*
Gresham Park, GA 30316 • *9,000*
Gretna, FL 32332 • *1,981*
Gretna, LA 70053–54 • *17,208*
Gretna, NE 68028 • *2,249*
Gretna, VA 24557 • *1,339*
Greybull, WY 82426 • *1,789*
Gridley, CA 95948 • *4,631*
Gridley, IL 61744 • *1,304*
Griffin, GA 30223–24 • *21,347*
Griffith, IN 46319 • *17,916*
Grifton, NC 28530 • *2,393*
Griggs □, ND • *3,303*
Griggsville, IL 62340 • *1,218*
Grimes, IA 50111 • *2,653*
Grimes □, TX • *18,828*
Grindall Creek, VA 23234 • *1,710*
Grinnell, IA 50112 • *8,902*
Griswold, IA 51535 • *1,049*
Groesbeck, OH 45239 • *6,684*
Groesbeck, TX 76642 • *3,185*
Grosse Ile, MI 48138 • *9,781*
Grosse Pointe, MI 48236 • *5,681*
Grosse Pointe Farms, MI 48236 • *10,092*
Grosse Pointe Park, MI 48230 • *12,857*
Grosse Pointe Woods, MI 48225 • *17,715*
Grossmont, CA 91941 • *2,600*
Groton, CT 06340 • *9,837*
Groton, MA 01450 • *1,044*
Groton, NY 13073 • *2,398*
Groton, SD 57445 • *1,196*
Grottoes, VA 24441 • *1,455*
Grove, OK 74344 • *4,020*
Grove City, FL 34224 • *2,374*
Grove City, OH 43123 • *19,661*
Grove City, PA 16127 • *8,240*
Grove Hill, AL 36451 • *1,551*
Groveland, FL 34736 • *2,300*
Groveland, MA 01834 • *3,780*
Groveport, OH 43125 • *2,948*
Grover City, CA 93433 • *11,656*
Groves, TX 77619 • *16,513*
Groveton, NH 03582 • *1,255*
Groveton, TX 75845 • *1,071*
Groveton, VA 22303 • *19,997*
Groveton Gardens, VA 22303 • *2,600*
Grovetown, GA 30813 • *3,596*
Groveville, NJ 08620 • *2,900*
Gruetli-Laager, TN 37339 • *1,810*
Grulla, TX 78548 • *1,335*
Grundy, VA 24614 • *1,305*
Grundy □, IL • *32,337*
Grundy □, IA • *12,029*
Grundy □, MO • *10,536*
Grundy □, TN • *13,362*
Grundy Center, IA 50638 • *2,491*
Gruver, TX 79040 • *1,172*
Guadalupe, AZ 85283 • *5,458*
Guadalupe, CA 93434 • *5,479*
Guadalupe □, NM • *4,156*
Guadalupe □, TX • *64,873*
Guernsey, WY 82214 • *1,155*
Guernsey □, OH • *39,024*
Gueydan, LA 70542 • *1,611*
Guilford, CT 06437 • *2,588*
Guilford, ME 04443 • *1,082*
Guilford □, NC • *347,420*
Guin, AL 35563 • *2,464*
Gulf □, FL • *11,504*
Gulf Breeze, FL 32561 • *5,530*
Gulf Gate Estates, FL 34231 • *11,622*
Gulfport, FL 33707 • *11,727*
Gulfport, MS 39501–07 • *40,775*
Gulf Shores, AL 36542 • *3,261*
Gumboro, DE 19945 • *200*
Gunnison, CO 81230 • *4,636*
Gunnison, UT 84634 • *1,298*
Gunnison □, CO • *10,273*
Guntersville, AL 35976 • *7,038*
Gurdon, AR 71743 • *2,199*
Gurley, AL 35748 • *1,007*
Gurnee, IL 60031 • *13,701*
Gustine, CA 95322 • *3,931*
Guthrie, KY 42234 • *1,504*
Guthrie, OK 73044 • *10,518*
Guthrie □, IA • *10,935*
Guthrie Center, IA 50115 • *1,614*
Guttenberg, IA 52052 • *2,257*
Guttenberg, NJ 07093 • *8,268*
Guymon, OK 73942 • *7,803*
Gwinhurst, DE 19809 • *1,340*
Gwinn, MI 49841 • *2,370*
Gwinner, ND 58040 • *585*
Gwinnett □, GA • *352,910*
Gypsum, CO 81637 • *1,750*

H

Haakon □, SD • *2,624*
Habersham □, GA • *27,621*
Hacienda Heights, CA 91745 • *52,354*
Hackensack, NJ 07601–08 • *37,049*
Hackettstown, NJ 07840 • *8,120*
Hackleburg, AL 35564 • *1,161*
Haddam, CT 06438 • *1,200*
Haddonfield, NJ 08033 • *11,628*
Haddon Heights, NJ 08035 • *7,860*
Hadlock, WA 98339 • *1,752*
Hagerman, NM 88232 • *961*
Hagerstown, IN 47346 • *1,835*
Hagerstown, MD 21740 • *35,445*
Hahira, GA 31632 • *1,353*
Hahnville, LA 70057 • *2,599*
Hailey, ID 83333 • *3,687*
Haines, AK 99827 • *1,238*
Haines City, FL 33844 • *11,683*
Hainesport, NJ 08036 • *1,250*
Halawa Heights, HI 96701 • *7,000*
Hale □, AL • *15,498*
Hale □, TX • *34,671*
Hale Center, TX 79041 • *2,067*
Haledon, NJ 07508 • *6,951*
Haleiwa, HI 96712 • *2,442*
Hales Corners, WI 53130 • *7,623*
Halethorpe, MD 21227 • *19,750*
Haleyville, AL 35565 • *4,452*
Half Hollow Hills, NY 11746 • *5,110*
Half Moon, NC 28540 • *6,306*
Half Moon Bay, CA 94019 • *8,886*
Halfway, MD 21740 • *8,873*
Halifax □, NC • *55,516*
Halifax □, VA • *29,033*
Haliimaile, HI 96768 • *841*
Hall □, GA • *95,428*
Hall □, NE • *48,925*
Hall □, TX • *3,905*
Hallandale, FL 33009 • *30,996*
Hallettsville, TX 77964 • *2,718*
Hallie, WI 54729 • *1,300*
Hallock, MN 56728 • *1,304*
Hallowell, ME 04347 • *2,534*
Halls, TN 37918 • *6,450*
Halls, TN 38040 • *2,431*
Halls Crossroads, TN 37918 • *1,900*
Hallstead, PA 18822 • *1,274*
Hallsville, TX 75650 • *2,288*
Halstead, KS 67056 • *2,015*
Haltom City, TX 76117 • *32,856*
Hamblen □, TN • *50,480*
Hamburg, AR 71646 • *3,098*
Hamburg, IA 51640 • *1,248*
Hamburg, NJ 07419 • *2,566*
Hamburg, NY 14075 • *10,442*
Hamburg, PA 19526 • *3,987*
Hamden, CT 06514 • *52,434*
Hamel, MN 55340 • *3,096*
Hamilton, AL 35570 • *5,787*
Hamilton, IL 62341 • *3,281*
Hamilton, MA 01936 • *1,000*
Hamilton, MI 49419 • *1,000*
Hamilton, MO 64644 • *1,737*
Hamilton, MT 59840 • *2,737*
Hamilton, NY 13346 • *3,790*
Hamilton, OH 45011–18 • *61,368*
Hamilton, TX 76531 • *2,937*
Hamilton □, FL • *10,930*
Hamilton □, IL • *8,499*
Hamilton □, IN • *108,936*
Hamilton □, IA • *16,071*
Hamilton □, KS • *2,388*
Hamilton □, NE • *8,862*
Hamilton □, NY • *5,279*
Hamilton □, OH • *866,228*
Hamilton □, TN • *285,536*
Hamilton □, TX • *7,733*
Hamilton City, CA 95951 • *1,811*
Hamilton Square, NJ 08690 • *10,970*
Ham Lake, MN 55304 • *8,924*
Hamlet, NC 28345 • *6,196*
Hamlin, TX 79520 • *2,791*
Hamlin, WV 25523 • *1,030*
Hamlin □, SD • *4,974*
Hammond, IN 46320–27 • *84,236*
Hammond, LA 70401–04 • *15,871*
Hammond, WI 54015 • *1,097*
Hammonton, NJ 08037 • *12,208*
Hampden, ME 04444 • *3,895*
Hampden □, MA • *456,310*
Hampden Highlands, ME 04444 • *1,540*
Hampshire, IL 60140 • *1,843*
Hampshire □, MA • *146,568*
Hampshire □, WV • *16,498*
Hampstead, MD 21074 • *2,608*
Hampton, AR 71744 • *1,562*
Hampton, GA 30228 • *2,694*
Hampton, IA 50441 • *4,133*
Hampton, NH 03842 • *7,989*
Hampton, NJ 08827 • *1,515*
Hampton, SC 29924 • *2,997*
Hampton, TN 37658 • *2,236*
Hampton, VA 23651–70 • *133,793*
Hampton □, SC • *18,191*
Hampton Bays, NY 11946 • *7,893*
Hamtramck, MI 48212 • *18,372*
Hana, HI 96713 • *683*
Hanahan, SC 29406 • *13,176*
Hanamaulu, HI 96715 • *3,611*
Hanapepe, HI 96716 • *1,395*
Hanceville, AL 35077 • *2,246*
Hancock, MD 21750 • *1,926*
Hancock, MI 49930 • *4,547*
Hancock, NY 13783 • *1,330*
Hancock □, GA • *8,908*
Hancock □, IL • *21,373*
Hancock □, IN • *45,527*
Hancock □, IA • *12,638*
Hancock □, KY • *7,864*
Hancock □, ME • *46,948*
Hancock □, MS • *31,760*
Hancock □, OH • *65,536*
Hancock □, TN • *6,739*
Hancock □, WV • *35,233*
Hand □, SD • *4,272*
Hanford, CA 93230–32 • *30,897*
Hankinson, ND 58041 • *1,038*
Hanna, WY 82327 • *1,076*
Hanna City, IL 61536 • *1,205*
Hannibal, MO 63401 • *18,004*
Hanover, IN 47243 • *3,610*
Hanover, MA 02339 • *2,500*
Hanover, NH 03755 • *6,538*
Hanover, PA 17331 • *14,399*
Hanover □, VA • *63,306*
Hanover Center, MA 02339 • *1,000*
Hanover Park, IL 60103 • *32,895*
Hanover Township, NJ 07981 • *11,538*
Hansen, ID 83334 • *848*
Hansford □, TX • *5,848*
Hanson, MA 02341 • *2,188*
Hanson □, SD • *2,994*
Hapeville, GA 30354 • *5,483*
Happy Valley, OR 97236 • *1,519*
Harahan, LA 70123 • *9,927*
Haralson □, GA • *21,966*
Harbeson, DE 19951 • *500*
Harbor, OR 97415 • *2,143*
Harbor Beach, MI 48441 • *2,089*
Harborcreek, PA 16421 • *1,500*
Harbor Springs, MI 49740 • *1,540*
Hardee □, FL • *19,499*
Hardeeville, SC 29927 • *1,583*
Hardeman □, TN • *23,377*
Hardeman □, TX • *5,283*
Hardin, IL 62047 • *1,071*
Hardin, MT 59034 • *2,940*
Hardin □, IL • *5,189*
Hardin □, IA • *19,094*
Hardin □, KY • *89,240*
Hardin □, OH • *31,111*
Hardin □, TN • *22,633*
Hardin □, TX • *41,320*
Harding □, NM • *987*
Harding □, SD • *1,669*
Hardinsburg, KY 40143 • *1,906*
Hardwick, GA 31034 • *8,800*
Hardwick, VT 05843 • *1,400*
Hardy □, WV • *10,977*
Harford □, MD • *182,132*
Hargill, TX 78549 • *1,030*
Harker Heights, TX 76543 • *12,841*
Harkers Island, NC 28531 • *1,759*
Harlan, IN 46743 • *1,200*
Harlan, IA 51537 • *5,148*
Harlan, KY 40831 • *2,686*
Harlan □, KY • *36,574*
Harlan □, NE • *3,810*
Harlem, FL 33440 • *2,826*
Harlem, GA 30814 • *2,199*
Harlem, MT 59526 • *882*
Harleysville, PA 19438 • *7,405*
Harlingen, TX 78550–52 • *48,735*
Harlowton, MT 59036 • *1,049*
Harmon □, OK • *3,793*
Harmony, MN 55939 • *1,081*
Harmony, PA 16037 • *1,054*
Harmony, RI 02829 • *820*
Harnett □, NC • *67,822*
Harney □, OR • *7,060*
Harper, KS 67058 • *1,735*
Harper □, KS • *7,124*
Harper □, OK • *4,063*
Harpers Ferry, WV 25425 • *308*
Harper Woods, MI 48225 • *14,903*
Harrah, OK 73045 • *4,206*
Harriman, TN 37748 • *7,119*
Harrington, DE 19952 • *2,311*
Harrington Park, NJ 07640 • *4,623*
Harris, RI 02816 • *1,050*
Harris □, GA • *17,788*
Harris □, TX • *2,818,199*
Harrisburg, AR 72432 • *1,943*
Harrisburg, IL 62946 • *9,289*
Harrisburg, OR 97446 • *1,939*
Harrisburg, PA 17101–13 • *52,376*
Harris Hill, NY 14221 • *4,577*

United States Populations and ZIP Codes

Harrison, AR 72601-02 • 9,922
Harrison, MI 48625 • 1,835
Harrison, NJ 07029 • 13,425
Harrison, NY 10528 • 23,308
Harrison, OH 45030 • 7,518
Harrison, TN 37341 • 7,191
Harrison □, IN • 29,890
Harrison □, IA • 14,730
Harrison □, KY • 16,248
Harrison □, MS • 165,365
Harrison □, MO • 8,469
Harrison □, OH • 16,085
Harrison □, TX • 57,483
Harrison □, WV • 69,371
Harrisonburg, VA 22801 • 30,707
Harrison Township, MI 48045 • 24,685
Harrisonville, MO 64701 • 7,683
Harristown, IL 62537 • 1,319
Harrisville, RI 02830 • 1,654
Harrisville, UT 84404 • 3,004
Harrisville, WV 26362 • 1,839
Harrodsburg, KY 40330 • 7,335
Hart, MI 49420 • 1,942
Hart, TX 79043 • 1,221
Hart □, GA • 19,712
Hart □, KY • 14,890
Hartford, AL 36344 • 2,448
Hartford, CT 06101-99 • 139,739
Hartford, IL 62048 • 1,676
Hartford, KY 42347 • 2,532
Hartford, MI 49057 • 2,341
Hartford, SD 57033 • 1,262
Hartford, VT 05047 • 500
Hartford, WI 53027 • 8,188
Hartford □, CT • 851,783
Hartford City, IN 47348 • 6,960
Hartington, NE 68739 • 1,583
Hartland, ME 04943 • 1,038
Hartland, WI 53029 • 6,906
Hartley, IA 51346 • 1,632
Hartley □, TX • 3,634
Hartsdale, NY 10530 • 9,587
Hartselle, AL 35640 • 10,795
Hartshorne, OK 74547 • 2,120
Hartsville, SC 29550 • 8,372
Hartsville, TN 37074 • 2,188
Hartville, OH 44632 • 2,031
Hartwell, GA 30643 • 4,555
Harvard, IL 60033 • 5,975
Harvard, MA 01451 • 1,200
Harvey, IL 60426 • 29,771
Harvey, LA 70058 • 21,222
Harvey, MI 49855 • 1,377
Harvey, ND 58341 • 2,263
Harvey □, KS • 31,028
Harwich, MA 02645 • 4,399
Harwich Port, MA 02646 • 2,300
Harwinton, CT 06791 • 5,228
Harwood Heights, IL 60656 • 7,680
Hasbrouck Heights, NJ 07604 • 11,488
Haskell, AR 72015 • 1,342
Haskell, OK 74436 • 2,143
Haskell, TX 79521 • 3,362
Haskell □, KS • 3,886
Haskell □, OK • 10,940
Haskell □, TX • 6,820
Haslett, MI 48840 • 10,230
Hastings, MI 49058 • 6,549
Hastings, MN 55033 • 15,445
Hastings, NE 68901-02 • 22,837
Hastings, PA 16646 • 1,431
Hastings-on-Hudson, NY 10706 • 8,000
Hatboro, PA 19040 • 7,382
Hatch, NM 87937 • 1,136
Hatfield, MA 01038 • 1,234
Hatfield, PA 19440 • 2,650
Hatteras, NC 27943 • 1,000
Hattiesburg, MS 39401-07 • 41,882
Hatton, ND 58240 • 800
Haubstadt, IN 47639 • 1,455
Haughton, LA 71037 • 1,664
Hauppauge, NY 11788 • 19,750
Hauula, HI 96717 • 3,479
Havana, FL 32333 • 1,654
Havana, IL 62644 • 3,610
Havelock, NC 28532 • 20,268
Haven, KS 67543 • 1,198
Haverford [Township], PA 19083 • 52,371
Haverhill, MA 01830-35 • 51,418
Haverstraw, NY 10927 • 9,438
Havre, MT 59501 • 10,201
Havre de Grace, MD 21078 • 8,952
Havre North, MT 59501 • 1,110
Hawaii □, HI • 120,317
Hawaiian Gardens, CA 90716 • 13,639
Hawarden, IA 51023 • 2,439
Hawi, HI 96719 • 924
Hawkins □, TN • 44,565
Hawkinsville, GA 31036 • 3,527
Hawley, MN 56549 • 1,655
Hawley, PA 18428 • 1,244
Haworth, NJ 07641 • 3,384
Haw River, NC 27258 • 1,855
Hawthorne, CA 90250-51 • 71,349
Hawthorne, FL 32640 • 1,305
Hawthorne, NV 89415-16 • 4,162
Hawthorne, NJ 07506 • 17,084
Hawthorne, NY 10532 • 4,764
Hayden, CO 81639 • 1,444
Hayden, ID 83835 • 3,744
Hayes □, NE • 1,222
Hayesville, OR 97303 • 14,318
Hayfield, MN 55940 • 1,283
Hayfield, VA 22310 • 2,300
Hayfork, CA 96041 • 2,605
Haynesville, LA 71038 • 2,854
Hays, KS 67601 • 17,767
Hays □, TX • 65,614
Haysville, KS 67060 • 8,364
Hayti, MO 63851 • 3,280
Hayward, CA 94540-46 • 111,498
Hayward, WI 54843 • 1,897
Hayward Addition, SD 57106 • 1,000
Haywood □, NC • 46,942
Haywood □, TN • 19,437
Hazard, KY 41701 • 5,416
Hazardville, CT 06082 • 5,179
Hazel Crest, IL 60429 • 13,334
Hazel Dell, WA 98660 • 15,386
Hazel Green, AL 35750 • 2,208
Hazel Green, WI 53811 • 1,171
Hazel Park, MI 48030 • 20,051
Hazelwood, MO 63042-45 • 15,324
Hazelwood, NC 28738 • 1,678
Hazen, AR 72064 • 1,668
Hazen, ND 58545 • 2,818
Hazlehurst, GA 31539 • 4,202
Hazlehurst, MS 39083 • 4,221
Hazlet, NJ 07730 • 23,013
Hazleton, PA 18201 • 24,730
Headland, AL 36345 • 3,266
Healdsburg, CA 95448 • 9,469
Healdton, OK 73438 • 2,872
Healy, AK 99743 • 487
Heard □, GA • 8,628
Hearne, TX 77859 • 5,132
Heath, OH 43056 • 7,231
Heavener, OK 74937 • 2,601
Hebbronville, TX 78361 • 4,465
Heber City, UT 84032 • 4,782
Heber Springs, AR 72543 • 5,628
Hebron, IN 46341 • 3,183
Hebron, KY 41048 • 1,200
Hebron, NE 68370 • 1,765
Hebron, ND 58638 • 888
Hebron, OH 43025 • 2,076
Hector, MN 55342 • 1,145
Heeia, HI 96744 • 5,010
Heflin, AL 36264 • 2,906
Hegins, PA 17938 • 1,200
Helena, AL 35080 • 3,918
Helena, AR 72342 • 7,491
Helena, GA 31037 • 1,256
Helena, MT 59601-26 • 24,569
Helena, OK 73741 • 1,043
Hellam, PA 17406 • 1,375
Hellertown, PA 18055 • 5,662
Helmetta, NJ 08828 • 1,211
Helotes, TX 78023 • 1,535
Helper, UT 84526 • 2,148
Hemet, CA 92343-44 • 36,094
Hemlock, MI 48626 • 1,601
Hemphill, TX 75948 • 1,182
Hemphill □, TX • 3,720
Hempstead, NY 11550-54 • 49,453
Hempstead, TX 77445 • 3,551
Hempstead □, AR • 21,621
Henagar, AL 35978 • 1,934
Henderson, KY 42420 • 25,945
Henderson, LA 70517 • 1,543
Henderson, NV 89015-16 • 64,942
Henderson, NC 27536 • 15,655
Henderson, TN 38340 • 4,760
Henderson, TX 75652-53 • 11,139
Henderson □, IL • 8,096
Henderson □, KY • 43,044
Henderson □, NC • 69,285
Henderson □, TN • 21,844
Henderson □, TX • 58,543
Henderson's Point, MS 39571 • 1,114
Hendersonville, NC 28739 • 7,284
Hendersonville, TN 37075 • 32,188
Hendricks □, IN • 75,717
Hendry □, FL • 25,773
Hennepin □, MN • 1,032,431
Hennessey, OK 73742 • 1,902
Henniker, NH 03242 • 1,693
Henrico □, VA • 217,881
Henrietta, NY 14467 • 1,200
Henrietta, NC 28076 • 1,412
Henrietta, TX 76365 • 2,896
Henry, IL 61537 • 2,591
Henry □, AL • 15,374
Henry □, GA • 58,741
Henry □, IL • 51,159
Henry □, IN • 48,139
Henry □, IA • 19,226
Henry □, KY • 12,823
Henry □, MO • 20,044
Henry □, OH • 29,108
Henry □, TN • 27,888
Henry □, VA • 56,942
Henryetta, OK 74437 • 5,872
Henryville, IN 47126 • 1,132
Hephzibah, GA 30815 • 2,466
Heppner, OR 97836 • 1,412
Herculaneum, MO 63048 • 2,263
Hercules, CA 94547 • 16,829
Hereford, TX 79045 • 14,745
Herington, KS 67449 • 2,685
Heritage Village, CT 06488 • 9,700
Herkimer, NY 13350 • 7,945
Herkimer □, NY • 65,797
Hermann, MO 65041 • 2,754
Hermantown, MN 55811 • 6,761
Herminie, PA 15637 • 2,000
Hermiston, OR 97838 • 10,040
Hermitage, PA 16148 • 15,300
Hermosa Beach, CA 90254 • 18,219
Hernando, FL 32642 • 2,103
Hernando, MS 38632 • 3,125
Hernando □, FL • 101,115
Herndon, VA 22070-71 • 16,139
Herrin, IL 62948 • 10,857
Herscher, IL 60941 • 1,278
Hershey, PA 17033 • 11,860
Hertford, NC 27944 • 2,105
Hertford □, NC • 22,523
Hesperia, CA 92345 • 50,418
Hesston, KS 67062 • 3,012
Hettinger, ND 58639 • 1,574
Hettinger □, ND • 3,445
Hewitt, TX 76643 • 8,983
Hewlett, NY 11557 • 6,620
Heyburn, ID 83336 • 2,714
Heyworth, IL 61745 • 1,627
Hialeah, FL 33010-16 • 188,004
Hiawatha, IA 52233 • 4,986
Hiawatha, KS 66434 • 3,603
Hibbing, MN 55746-47 • 18,046
Hickman, KY 42050 • 2,689
Hickman, NE 68372 • 1,081
Hickman □, KY • 5,566
Hickman □, TN • 16,754
Hickory, NC 28601-03 • 28,301
Hickory □, MO • 7,335
Hickory Hills, IL 60457 • 13,021
Hicksville, NY 11801-05 • 40,174
Hicksville, OH 43526 • 3,664
Hico, TX 76457 • 1,342
Hidalgo, TX 78557 • 3,292
Hidalgo □, NM • 5,958
Hidalgo □, TX • 383,545
Higganum, CT 06441 • 1,692
Higginsville, MO 64037 • 4,693
High Bridge, NJ 08829 • 3,886
Highland, CA 92346 • 34,439
Highland, IL 62249 • 7,525
Highland, IN 46322 • 23,696
Highland, MI 48356-57 • 750
Highland, NY 12528 • 4,492
Highland □, OH • 35,728
Highland □, VA • 2,635
Highland Falls, NY 10928 • 3,937
Highland Heights, OH 44124 • 6,249
Highland Lakes, NJ 07422 • 4,550
Highland Park, IL 60035 • 30,575
Highland Park, MI 48203 • 20,121
Highland Park, NJ 08904 • 13,279
Highland Park, TX 75205 • 8,739
Highlands, NJ 07732 • 4,849
Highlands, TX 77562 • 6,632
Highlands □, FL • 68,432
Highland Springs, VA 23075 • 13,823
Highmore, SD 57345 • 835
High Point, NC 27260-65 • 69,496
High Ridge, MO 63049 • 2,380
High Spire, PA 17034 • 2,668
High Springs, FL 32643 • 3,144
Hightstown, NJ 08520 • 5,126
Highview, KY 40228 • 14,814
Highwood, IL 60040 • 5,331
Hilbert, WI 54129 • 1,211
Hildale, UT 84784 • 1,325
Hill □, MT • 17,654
Hill □, TX • 27,146
Hill City, KS 67642 • 1,835
Hillcrest, NY 10977 • 6,447
Hillcrest Center, CA 93306 • 26,900
Hillcrest Heights, MD 20748 • 17,136
Hilliard, FL 32046 • 1,751
Hilliard, OH 43026 • 11,796
Hillsboro, IL 62049 • 4,400
Hillsboro, KS 67063 • 2,704
Hillsboro, MO 63050 • 1,625
Hillsboro, NH 03244 • 1,826
Hillsboro, ND 58045 • 1,488
Hillsboro, OH 45133 • 6,235
Hillsboro, OR 97123-24 • 37,520
Hillsboro, TX 76645 • 7,072
Hillsboro, WI 54634 • 1,288
Hillsborough, CA 94010 • 10,667
Hillsborough, NC 27278 • 4,263
Hillsborough □, FL • 834,054
Hillsborough □, NH • 336,073
Hillsdale, MI 49242 • 8,170
Hillsdale, NJ 07642 • 9,750
Hillsdale □, MI • 43,431
Hillside, IL 60162 • 7,672
Hillside, NJ 07205 • 21,044
Hillside Heights, DE 19711 • 1,500
Hillsville, VA 24343 • 2,008
Hillview, KY 40229 • 6,119
Hilo, HI 96720-21 • 37,808
Hilton, NY 14468 • 5,216
Hilton Head Island, SC 29928 • 23,694
Hinckley, IL 60520 • 1,682
Hinds □, MS • 254,441
Hines, OR 97738 • 1,452
Hinesville, GA 31313 • 21,603
Hingham, MA 02043 • 5,454
Hinsdale, IL 60521-22 • 16,029
Hinsdale, NH 03451 • 1,718
Hinsdale □, CO • 467
Hinton, OK 73047 • 1,233
Hinton, WV 25951 • 3,433
Hiram, GA 30141 • 1,389
Hiram, OH 44234 • 1,330
Hitchcock, TX 77563 • 5,868
Hitchcock □, NE • 3,750
Hitchcock Lake, CT 06716 • 1,640
Hobart, IN 46342 • 21,822
Hobart, OK 73651 • 4,305
Hobbs, NM 88240-41 • 29,115
Hobe Sound, FL 33455 • 11,507
Hoboken, NJ 07030 • 33,397
Hockessin, DE 19707 • 2,430
Hocking □, OH • 25,533
Hockley □, TX • 24,199
Hodgeman □, KS • 2,177
Hodgenville, KY 42748 • 2,721
Hoffman Estates, IL 60194-95 • 46,561
Hogansville, GA 30230 • 2,976
Hohenwald, TN 38462 • 3,760
Ho-Ho-Kus, NJ 07423 • 3,935
Hoisington, KS 67544 • 3,182
Hoke □, NC • 22,856
Hokes Bluff, AL 35903 • 3,739
Holbrook, AZ 86025-29 • 4,686
Holbrook, MA 02343 • 11,041
Holbrook, NY 11741 • 25,273
Holcomb, KS 67851 • 1,400
Holden, MA 01520 • 4,040
Holden, MO 64040 • 2,389
Holden, WV 25625 • 1,246
Holden Heights, FL 32805 • 4,387
Holdenville, OK 74848 • 4,792
Holdrege, NE 68949 • 5,671
Holgate, OH 43527 • 1,290
Holiday, FL 34690 • 19,360
Holiday City at Berkeley, NJ 08757 • 5,750
Holladay, UT 84117 • 22,189
Holland, MI 49422-24 • 30,745
Holland, NY 14080 • 1,288
Holland, OH 43528 • 1,210
Holland, PA 18966 • 5,250
Holland, TX 76534 • 1,118
Hollandale, MS 38748 • 3,576
Holley, NY 14470 • 1,890
Holliday, TX 76366 • 1,475
Hollidaysburg, PA 16648 • 5,624
Hollins, VA 24019 • 13,305
Hollis, OK 73550 • 2,584
Hollister, CA 95023-24 • 19,212
Hollister, MO 65672 • 2,628
Holliston, MA 01746 • 12,622
Holly, MI 48442 • 5,595
Holly Hill, FL 32117 • 11,141
Holly Hill, SC 29059 • 1,478
Holly Springs, GA 30142 • 2,406
Holly Springs, MS 38634-35 • 7,261
Hollywood, FL 33019-29 • 121,697
Hollywood, SC 29449 • 2,094
Holmen, WI 54636 • 3,220
Holmes □, FL • 15,778
Holmes □, MS • 21,604
Holmes □, OH • 32,849
Holstein, IA 51025 • 1,449
Holt, AL 35404 • 4,125
Holt, MI 48842 • 11,744
Holt □, MO • 6,034
Holt □, NE • 12,599
Holton, KS 66436 • 3,196
Holtsville, NY 11742 • 14,972
Holtville, CA 92250 • 4,820
Holualoa, HI 96725 • 3,834
Holyoke, CO 80734 • 1,931
Holyoke, MA 01040-41 • 43,704
Homedale, ID 83628 • 1,963
Home Gardens, CA 91720 • 7,780
Homeland Park, SC 29621 • 6,569
Home Place, IN 46240 • 1,300
Homer, AK 99603 • 3,660
Homer, IL 61849 • 1,264
Homer, LA 71040 • 4,152
Homer, MI 49245 • 1,758
Homer, NY 13077 • 3,476
Homer City, PA 15748 • 1,809
Homerville, GA 31634 • 2,560
Homestead, FL 33030-35 • 26,866
Homestead, PA 15120 • 4,179
Hometown, IL 60456 • 4,769
Homewood, AL 35209 • 22,922
Homewood, IL 60430 • 19,278
Homewood, OH 45015 • 2,550
Hominy, OK 74035 • 2,342
Homosassa, FL 32646 • 2,113
Hondo, TX 78861 • 6,018
Honea Path, SC 29654 • 3,841
Honeoye Falls, NY 14472 • 2,340
Honesdale, PA 18431 • 4,972
Honey Brook, PA 19344 • 1,184
Honey Grove, TX 75446 • 1,681
Honeypot Glen, CT 06410 • 1,200
Honeyville, UT 84314 • 1,112
Honokaa, HI 96727 • 2,186
Honolulu, HI 96801-50 • 365,272
Honolulu □, HI • 836,231
Honomu, HI 96728 • 532
Hood □, TX • 28,981
Hood River, OR 97031 • 4,632
Hood River □, OR • 16,903
Hoodsport, WA 98548 • 1,100
Hooker, OK 73945 • 1,551
Hooker □, NE • 793
Hooksett, NH 03106 • 2,573
Hoonah, AK 99829 • 795
Hooper Bay, AK 99604 • 845
Hoopeston, IL 60942 • 5,871
Hoosick Falls, NY 12090 • 3,490
Hoover, AL 35216 • 39,788
Hooverson Heights, WV 26037 • 3,056
Hopatcong, NJ 07843 • 15,586
Hope, AR 71801 • 9,643
Hope, IN 47246 • 2,171
Hope, RI 02831 • 270
Hopedale, MA 01747 • 3,961
Hope Mills, NC 28348 • 8,184
Hope Valley, RI 02832 • 1,446
Hopewell, NJ 08525 • 1,968
Hopewell, VA 23860 • 23,101
Hopewell Junction, NY 12533 • 1,786
Hopkins, MN 55343-47 • 16,534
Hopkins, SC 29061 • 1,600
Hopkins □, KY • 46,126
Hopkins □, TX • 28,833
Hopkinsville, KY 42240-41 • 29,809
Hopkinton, MA 01748 • 2,305
Hopkinton, RI 02833 • 550
Hopwood, PA 15445 • 2,021
Hoquiam, WA 98550 • 8,972
Horicon, WI 53032 • 3,873
Hornell, NY 14843 • 9,877
Horn Lake, MS 38637 • 9,069
Horry □, SC • 144,053
Horse Cave, KY 42749 • 2,284
Horseheads, NY 14844-45 • 6,802
Horsham, PA 19044 • 15,051
Horton, KS 66439 • 1,885
Hortonville, WI 54944 • 2,029
Hot Spring □, AR • 26,115
Hot Springs, SD 57747 • 4,325
Hot Springs □, WY • 4,809
Hot Springs National Park, AR 71901-14 • 32,462
Hot Springs Village, AR 71901 • 6,361
Houghton, MI 49931 • 7,498
Houghton, NY 14744 • 1,740
Houghton □, MI • 35,446
Houghton Lake, MI 48629 • 3,353
Houghton Lake Heights, MI 48630 • 2,449
Houlton, ME 04730 • 5,627
Houma, LA 70360-64 • 96,982
Housatonic, MA 01236 • 1,184
Houston, DE 19954 • 487
Houston, MN 55943 • 1,013
Houston, MS 38851 • 3,903
Houston, MO 65483 • 2,118
Houston, PA 15342 • 1,445
Houston, TX 77001-99 • 1,630,553
Houston □, AL • 81,331
Houston □, GA • 89,208
Houston □, MN • 18,497
Houston □, TN • 7,018
Houston □, TX • 21,375
Houtzdale, PA 16651 • 1,204
Howard, SD 57349 • 1,156
Howard, WI 54303 • 9,874
Howard □, AR • 13,569
Howard □, IN • 80,827
Howard □, IA • 9,809
Howard □, MD • 187,328
Howard □, MO • 9,631
Howard □, NE • 6,055
Howard □, TX • 32,343
Howard City, MI 49329 • 1,351
Howard Lake, MN 55349 • 1,343
Howards Grove-Millersville, WI 53083 • 2,329
Howell, MI 48843-44 • 8,184
Howell □, MO • 31,447
Howland, ME 04448 • 1,304
Howland, OH 44484 • 6,732
Hoxie, AR 72433 • 2,676
Hoxie, KS 67740 • 1,342
Hoyt Lakes, MN 55750 • 2,348
Huachuca City, AZ 85616 • 1,782
Hubbard, OH 44425 • 8,248
Hubbard, OR 97032 • 1,881
Hubbard, TX 76648 • 1,589
Hubbard □, MN • 14,939
Hubbell, MI 49934 • 1,174
Huber Heights, OH 45424 • 38,696
Huber Ridge, OH 43081 • 5,255
Huber South, OH 45439 • 4,800
Hudson, FL 34667 • 7,344
Hudson, IL 61748 • 1,006
Hudson, IA 50643 • 2,037
Hudson, MA 01749 • 14,267
Hudson, MI 49247 • 2,580
Hudson, NH 03051 • 7,626
Hudson, NY 12534 • 8,034
Hudson, NC 28638 • 2,819
Hudson, OH 44236 • 5,159
Hudson, WI 54016 • 6,378
Hudson, WY 82515 • 392
Hudson □, NJ • 553,099
Hudson Falls, NY 12839 • 7,651
Hudson Lake, IN 46552 • 1,347
Hudsonville, MI 49426 • 6,170
Hudspeth □, TX • 2,915
Huerfano □, CO • 6,009
Hueytown, AL 35023 • 15,280
Huffakers, NV 89501 • 150
Hughes, AR 72348 • 1,810
Hughes □, OK • 13,023
Hughes □, SD • 14,817
Hughesville, MD 20637 • 1,319
Hughesville, PA 17737 • 2,049
Hugo, MN 55038 • 4,417
Hugo, OK 74743 • 5,978
Hugoton, KS 67951 • 3,179
Hulett, WY 82720 • 429
Hull, IA 51239 • 1,724
Hull, MA 02045 • 10,466
Humansville, MO 65674 • 1,084
Humble, TX 77338-39 • 12,060
Humboldt, IA 50548 • 4,438
Humboldt, KS 66748 • 2,178
Humboldt, NE 68376 • 1,003
Humboldt, TN 38343 • 9,651
Humboldt □, CA • 119,118
Humboldt □, IA • 10,756
Humboldt □, NV • 12,844
Hummels Wharf, PA 17831 • 1,069
Humphreys □, MS • 12,134
Humphreys □, TN • 15,795
Hunt □, TX • 64,343
Hunterdon □, NJ • 107,776
Huntertown, IN 46748 • 1,330
Huntingburg, IN 47542 • 5,242
Huntingdon, PA 16652 • 6,843
Huntingdon, TN 38344 • 4,180
Huntingdon □, PA • 44,164
Huntington, IN 46750 • 16,389
Huntington, MA 01050 • 1,200
Huntington, NY 11743 • 18,243
Huntington, TX 75949 • 1,794
Huntington, UT 84528 • 1,875
Huntington, VA 22303 • 7,489
Huntington, WV 25701-79 • 54,844
Huntington □, IN • 35,427
Huntington Bay, NY 11743 • 1,521
Huntington Beach, CA 92646-49 • 181,519
Huntington Park, CA 90255 • 56,065
Huntington Station, NY 11746 • 28,247
Huntington Woods, MI 48070 • 6,419
Huntley, IL 60142 • 2,453
Huntsville, AL 35801-24 • 159,789
Huntsville, AR 72740 • 1,605
Huntsville, MO 65259 • 1,567
Huntsville, TX 77340-44 • 27,925
Hurley, NM 88043 • 1,534
Hurley, NY 12443 • 4,644
Hurley, WI 54534 • 1,782
Hurlock, MD 21643 • 1,706
Huron, OH 44839 • 7,030
Huron, SD 57350 • 12,448
Huron □, MI • 34,951
Huron □, OH • 56,240
Hurricane, UT 84737 • 3,915
Hurricane, WV 25526 • 4,461
Hurst, TX 76053-54 • 33,574
Hurt, VA 24563 • 1,294
Hutchins, TX 75141 • 2,719
Hutchinson, KS 67501-05 • 39,308
Hutchinson, MN 55350 • 11,523
Hutchinson □, SD • 8,262
Hutchinson □, TX • 25,689
Huxley, IA 50124 • 2,047
Hyannis, MA 02601 • 14,120
Hyannis Port, MA 02647 • 1,100
Hyattsville, MD 20780-89 • 13,864
Hybla Valley, VA 22306 • 15,491
Hydaburg, AK 99922 • 384
Hyde, PA 16843 • 1,643
Hyde □, NC • 5,411
Hyde □, SD • 1,696
Hyde Park, NY 12538 • 2,550
Hyde Park, UT 84318 • 2,190
Hydeville, VT 05750 • 450
Hyndman, PA 15545 • 1,019
Hyrum, UT 84319 • 4,829

I

Iberia □, LA • 68,297
Iberville □, LA • 31,049
Ida, MI 48140 • 1,000
Ida □, IA • 8,365
Idabel, OK 74745 • 6,957
Ida Grove, IA 51445 • 2,357
Idaho □, ID • 13,783
Idaho Falls, ID 83401-15 • 43,929
Idaho Springs, CO 80452 • 1,834
Idalou, TX 79329 • 2,074
Ilion, NY 13357 • 8,888
Illmo, MO 63780 • 1,368
Imlay, NV 89418 • 250
Imlay City, MI 48444 • 2,921
Immokalee, FL 33934 • 14,120
Imperial, CA 92251 • 4,113
Imperial, NE 69033 • 2,007
Imperial, PA 15126 • 3,200
Imperial □, CA • 109,303
Imperial Beach, CA 91932-33 • 26,512
Incline Village, NV 89450 • 4,500
Independence, CA 93526 • 1,000
Independence, IA 50644 • 5,972
Independence, KS 67301 • 9,942
Independence, KY 41051 • 10,444
Independence, LA 70443 • 1,632
Independence, MO 64050-58 • 112,301
Independence, OH 44131 • 6,500

Independence, OR 97351 • 4,425
Independence, WI 54747 • 1,041
Independence □, AR • 31,192
Indiana, PA 15701 • 15,174
Indiana □, PA • 89,994
Indianapolis, IN 46201–90 • 731,327
Indian Harbour Beach, FL 32937 • 6,933
Indian Head, MD 20640 • 3,531
Indian Heights, IN 46902 • 3,669
Indian Hills, CO 80454 • 2,000
Indian Neck, CT 06405 • 2,430
Indianola, IA 50125 • 11,340
Indianola, MS 38751 • 11,809
Indian Ridge Estates, AZ 85715 • 1,260
Indian River □, FL • 90,208
Indian Rocks Beach, FL 34635 • 3,963
Indian Springs, NV 89018 • 1,164
Indiantown, FL 34956 • 4,794
Indian Trail, NC 28079 • 1,942
Indio, CA 92201–02 • 36,793
Ingalls Park, IL 60431 • 2,730
Ingham □, MI • 281,912
Ingleside, TX 78362 • 5,696
Inglewood, CA 90301–12 • 109,602
Inglewood, TX 98011 • 6,500
Ingram, PA 15205 • 3,901
Inkom, ID 83245 • 769
Inkster, MI 48141 • 30,772
Inman, KS 67546 • 1,035
Inman, SC 29349 • 1,742
Inniswold, LA 70809 • 1,100
Inola, OK 74036 • 1,444
Institute, WV 25112 • 1,400
Interlachen, FL 32148 • 1,160
International Falls, MN 56649 • 8,325
Inver Grove Heights, MN 55076–77 • 22,477
Inverness, CA 94937 • 1,422
Inverness, FL 32650–52 • 5,797
Inverness, IL 60067 • 6,503
Inverness, MS 38753 • 1,174
Inwood, FL 33880 • 6,824
Inwood, NY 11696 • 7,767
Inwood, WV 25428 • 1,360
Inyo □, CA • 18,281
Iola, KS 66749 • 6,351
Iola, WI 54945 • 1,125
Iona, ID 83427 • 1,049
Ione, CA 95640 • 6,516
Ionia, MI 48846 • 5,935
Ionia □, MI • 57,024
Iosco □, MI • 30,209
Iota, LA 70543 • 1,256
Iowa, LA 70647 • 2,588
Iowa □, IA • 14,630
Iowa □, WI • 20,150
Iowa City, IA 52240–46 • 59,738
Iowa Falls, IA 50126 • 5,424
Iowa Park, TX 76367 • 6,072
Ipswich, MA 01938 • 4,132
Ipswich, SD 57451 • 965
Iraan, TX 79744 • 1,322
Iredell □, NC • 92,931
Irion □, TX • 1,629
Irmo, SC 29063 • 11,280
Iron □, MI • 13,175
Iron □, MO • 10,726
Iron □, UT • 20,789
Iron □, WI • 6,153
Irondale, AL 35210 • 9,454
Irondequoit, NY 14617 • 52,322
Ironia, NJ 07845 • 1,110
Iron Mountain, MI 49801 • 8,525
Iron River, MI 49935 • 2,095
Ironton, MO 63650 • 1,539
Ironton, OH 45638 • 12,751
Ironwood, MI 49938 • 6,849
Iroquois □, IL • 30,787
Irvine, CA 92713–20 • 110,330
Irvine, KY 40336 • 2,836
Irving, TX 75060–63 • 155,037
Irvington, KY 40146 • 1,180
Irvington, NJ 07111 • 59,774
Irvington, NY 10533 • 6,348
Irwin, PA 15642 • 4,604
Irwin □, GA • 8,649
Isabella □, MI • 54,624
Isanti, MN 55040 • 1,228
Isanti □, MN • 25,921
Iselin, NJ 08830 • 16,141
Ishpeming, MI 49849 • 7,200
Islamorada, FL 33036 • 1,220
Island □, WA • 60,195
Island Heights, NJ 08732 • 1,470
Island Park, NY 11558 • 4,860
Island Park, RI 02871 • 1,240
Island Pond, VT 05846 • 1,222
Isla Vista, CA 93117 • 20,395
Isle of Palms, SC 29451 • 3,680
Isle of Wight □, VA • 25,053
Isleta, NM 87022 • 1,703
Islington, MA 02090 • 4,920
Islip, NY 11751 • 18,924
Islip Terrace, NY 11752 • 5,530
Issaquah, WA 98027 • 7,786
Issaquena □, MS • 1,909
Italy, TX 76651 • 1,699
Itasca, IL 60143 • 6,947
Itasca, TX 76055 • 1,523
Itasca □, MN • 40,863
Itawamba □, MS • 20,017
Ithaca, MI 48847 • 3,009
Ithaca, NY 14850–52 • 29,541
Itta Bena, MS 38941 • 2,377
Iuka, MS 38852 • 3,122
Iva, SC 29655 • 1,174
Ives Estates, FL 33162 • 13,531
Ivins, UT 84738 • 1,630
Ivoryton, CT 06442 • 2,200
Izard □, AR • 11,364

J

Jacinto City, TX 77029 • 9,343
Jack □, TX • 6,981
Jackpot, NV 89825 • 570
Jacksboro, TN 37757 • 1,568
Jacksboro, TX 76056 • 3,350
Jackson, AL 36545 • 5,819
Jackson, CA 95642 • 3,545
Jackson, GA 30233 • 4,076
Jackson, KY 41339 • 2,466
Jackson, LA 70748 • 3,891
Jackson, MI 49201–04 • 37,446
Jackson, MN 56143 • 3,559
Jackson, MS 39201–98 • 196,637
Jackson, MO 63755 • 9,256
Jackson, OH 45640 • 6,144
Jackson, SC 29831 • 1,681
Jackson, TN 38301–08 • 48,949
Jackson, WI 53037 • 2,486
Jackson, WY 83001–02 • 4,472
Jackson □, AL • 47,796
Jackson □, AR • 18,944
Jackson □, CO • 1,605
Jackson □, FL • 41,375
Jackson □, GA • 30,005
Jackson □, IL • 61,067
Jackson □, IN • 37,730
Jackson □, IA • 19,950
Jackson □, KS • 11,525
Jackson □, KY • 11,955
Jackson □, LA • 15,705
Jackson □, MI • 149,756
Jackson □, MN • 11,677
Jackson □, MS • 115,243
Jackson □, MO • 633,232
Jackson □, NC • 26,846
Jackson □, OH • 30,230
Jackson □, OK • 28,764
Jackson □, OR • 146,389
Jackson □, SD • 2,811
Jackson □, TN • 9,297
Jackson □, TX • 13,039
Jackson □, WV • 25,938
Jackson □, WI • 16,588
Jackson Center, OH 45334 • 1,398
Jacksonville, AL 36265 • 10,283
Jacksonville, AR 72076 • 29,101
Jacksonville, FL 32201–98 • 635,230
Jacksonville, IL 62650–51 • 19,324
Jacksonville, NC 28540–46 • 30,013
Jacksonville, OR 97530 • 1,896
Jacksonville, TX 75766 • 12,765
Jacksonville Beach, FL 32250 • 17,839
Jaffrey, NH 03452 • 2,558
Jal, NM 88252 • 2,156
Jamesburg, NJ 08831 • 5,294
James City, NC 28560 • 4,279
James City □, VA • 34,859
James Island, SC 29412 • 24,124
Jamestown, CA 95327 • 2,178
Jamestown, KY 42629 • 1,641
Jamestown, NY 14701–02 • 34,681
Jamestown, NC 27282 • 2,600
Jamestown, ND 58401–02 • 15,571
Jamestown, OH 45335 • 1,794
Jamestown, RI 02835 • 2,156
Jamestown, TN 38556 • 1,862
James Town, WY 82935 • 280
Janesville, CA 96114 • 1,200
Janesville, MN 56048 • 1,969
Janesville, WI 53545–47 • 52,133
Jarrettsville, MD 21084 • 2,148
Jasmine Estates, FL 34668 • 17,136
Jasonville, IN 47438 • 2,200
Jasper, AL 35501–02 • 13,553
Jasper, FL 32052 • 2,099
Jasper, GA 30143 • 1,772
Jasper, IN 47546–47 • 10,030
Jasper, TN 37347 • 2,780
Jasper, TX 75951 • 6,959
Jasper □, GA • 8,453
Jasper □, IL • 10,609
Jasper □, IN • 24,960
Jasper □, IA • 34,795
Jasper □, MS • 17,114
Jasper □, MO • 90,465
Jasper □, SC • 15,487
Jasper □, TX • 31,102
Jay, OK 74346 • 2,220
Jay □, IN • 21,512
Jean, NV 89019 • 150
Jeanerette, LA 70544 • 6,205
Jeannette, PA 15644 • 11,221
Jeff Davis □, GA • 12,032
Jeff Davis □, TX • 1,946
Jefferson, GA 30549 • 2,763
Jefferson, IA 50129 • 4,292
Jefferson, LA 70121 • 14,521
Jefferson, NC 28640 • 1,300
Jefferson, OH 44047 • 3,331
Jefferson, OR 97352 • 1,805
Jefferson, PA 15025 • 9,533
Jefferson, TX 75657 • 2,199
Jefferson, WI 53549 • 6,078
Jefferson □, AL • 651,525
Jefferson □, AR • 85,487
Jefferson □, CO • 438,430
Jefferson □, FL • 11,296
Jefferson □, GA • 17,408
Jefferson □, ID • 16,543
Jefferson □, IL • 37,020
Jefferson □, IN • 29,797
Jefferson □, IA • 16,310
Jefferson □, KS • 15,905
Jefferson □, KY • 664,937
Jefferson □, LA • 448,306
Jefferson □, MS • 8,653
Jefferson □, MO • 171,380
Jefferson □, MT • 7,939
Jefferson □, NE • 8,759
Jefferson □, NY • 110,943
Jefferson □, OH • 80,298
Jefferson □, OK • 7,010
Jefferson □, OR • 13,676
Jefferson □, PA • 46,083
Jefferson □, TN • 33,016
Jefferson □, TX • 239,397
Jefferson □, WA • 20,146
Jefferson □, WV • 35,926
Jefferson □, WI • 67,783
Jefferson City, MO 65101–10 • 35,481
Jefferson City, TN 37760 • 5,494
Jefferson Davis □, LA • 30,722
Jefferson Davis □, MS • 14,051
Jefferson Farms, DE 19720 • 3,130
Jefferson Manor, VA 22303 • 2,300
Jeffersontown, KY 40299 • 23,221
Jefferson Valley, NY 10535 • 6,420
Jefferson Village, VA 22042 • 2,500
Jeffersonville, GA 31044 • 1,545
Jeffersonville, IN 47129–31 • 21,841
Jeffersonville, KY 40337 • 1,854
Jeffersonville, OH 43128 • 1,281
Jeffrey City, WY 82310 • 1,882
Jellico, TN 37762 • 2,447
Jemez Pueblo, NM 87024 • 1,301
Jemison, AL 35085 • 1,898
Jena, LA 71342 • 2,626
Jenison, MI 49428–29 • 17,882
Jenkins, KY 41537 • 2,751
Jenkins □, GA • 8,247
Jenkintown, PA 19046 • 4,574
Jenks, OK 74037 • 7,493
Jennings, LA 70546 • 11,305
Jennings, MO 63136 • 15,905
Jennings □, IN • 23,661
Jennings Lodge, OR 97222 • 11,480
Jensen Beach, FL 34957–58 • 9,884
Jerauld □, SD • 2,425
Jericho, NY 11753 • 13,141
Jericho, VT 05465 • 1,300
Jermyn, PA 18433 • 2,263
Jerome, ID 83338 • 6,529
Jerome, PA 15937 • 1,074
Jerome □, ID • 15,138
Jersey □, IL • 20,539
Jersey City, NJ 07301–11 • 228,537
Jersey Shore, PA 17740 • 4,353
Jerseyville, IL 62052 • 7,382
Jessamine □, KY • 30,508
Jessup, MD 20794 • 6,537
Jessup, PA 18434 • 4,605
Jesup, GA 31545 • 8,958
Jesup, IA 50648 • 2,121
Jewell, IA 50130 • 1,106
Jewell □, KS • 4,251
Jewett City, CT 06351 • 3,349
Jim Hogg □, TX • 5,109
Jim Thorpe, PA 18229 • 5,048
Jim Wells □, TX • 37,679
Joanna, SC 29351 • 1,735
Jo Daviess □, IL • 21,821
John Day, OR 97845 • 1,836
Johnson, KS 67855 • 1,348
Johnson, VT 05656 • 1,470
Johnson □, AR • 18,221
Johnson □, GA • 8,329
Johnson □, IL • 11,347
Johnson □, IN • 88,109
Johnson □, IA • 96,119
Johnson □, KS • 355,054
Johnson □, KY • 23,248
Johnson □, MO • 42,514
Johnson □, NE • 4,673
Johnson □, TN • 13,766
Johnson □, TX • 97,165
Johnson □, WY • 6,145
Johnsonburg, PA 15845 • 3,350
Johnson City, NY 13790 • 16,890
Johnson City, TN 37601–15 • 49,381
Johnson Creek, WI 53038 • 1,259
Johnsonville, SC 29555 • 1,415
Johnston, IA 50131 • 4,702
Johnston, RI 02919 • 26,542
Johnston, SC 29832 • 2,688
Johnston □, NC • 81,306
Johnston □, OK • 10,032
Johnston City, IL 62951 • 3,706
Johnstown, CO 80534 • 1,579
Johnstown, NY 12095 • 9,058
Johnstown, OH 43031 • 3,237
Johnstown, PA 15901–09 • 28,134
Joliet, IL 60431–36 • 76,836
Jones, OK 73049 • 2,424
Jones □, GA • 20,739
Jones □, IA • 19,444
Jones □, MS • 62,031
Jones □, NC • 9,414
Jones □, SD • 1,324
Jones □, TX • 16,490
Jonesboro, AR 72401–03 • 46,535
Jonesboro, GA 30236–37 • 3,635
Jonesboro, IL 62952 • 1,728
Jonesboro, IN 46938 • 2,073
Jonesboro, LA 71251 • 4,305
Jonesborough, TN 37659 • 3,091
Jones Creek, TX 77541 • 2,160
Jonesport, ME 04649 • 1,525
Jonestown, MS 38639 • 1,467
Jonesville, LA 71343 • 2,720
Jonesville, MI 49250 • 2,283
Jonesville, NC 28642 • 1,549
Jonesville, SC 29353 • 1,205
Joplin, MO 64801–04 • 40,961
Joppatowne, MD 21085 • 11,084
Jordan, MN 55352 • 2,909
Jordan, NY 13080 • 1,325
Joseph, OR 97846 • 1,073
Josephine □, OR • 62,649
Joshua, TX 76058 • 3,828
Joshua Tree, CA 92252 • 3,898
Jourdanton, TX 78026 • 3,220
Juab □, UT • 5,817
Juanita, WA 98033 • 10,500
Judith Basin □, MT • 2,282
Judsonia, AR 72081 • 1,915
Julesburg, CO 80737 • 1,295
Julian, CA 92036 • 1,284
Junction, TX 76849 • 2,654
Junction City, KS 66441 • 20,604
Junction City, KY 40440 • 1,983
Junction City, OR 97448 • 3,670
Juneau, AK 99801–03 • 26,751
Juneau, WI 53039 • 2,157
Juneau □, WI • 21,650
Juniata □, PA • 20,625
Jupiter, FL 33458 • 24,986
Justice, IL 60458 • 11,137
Justin, TX 76247 • 1,234

K

Kaaawa, HI 96730 • 1,138
Kadoka, SD 57543 • 736
Kahaluu, HI 96725 • 380
Kahaluu, HI 96744 • 3,068
Kahoka, MO 63445 • 2,195
Kahuku, HI 96731 • 2,063
Kahului, HI 96732–33 • 16,889
Kailua, HI 96734 • 36,818
Kailua Kona, HI 96739–40 • 9,126
Kake, AK 99830 • 700
Kalaheo, HI 96741 • 3,592
Kalama, WA 98625 • 1,210
Kalamazoo, MI 49001–09 • 80,277
Kalamazoo □, MI • 223,411
Kalawao □, HI • 130
Kalispell, MT 59901 • 11,917
Kalkaska, MI 49646 • 1,952
Kalkaska □, MI • 13,497
Kalona, IA 52247 • 1,942
Kamas, UT 84036 • 1,061
Kamiah, ID 83536 • 1,157
Kamuela (Waimea), HI 96743 • 5,972
Kanab, UT 84741 • 3,289
Kanabec □, MN • 12,802
Kanawha □, WV • 207,619
Kandiyohi □, MN • 38,761
Kane, PA 16735 • 4,590
Kane □, IL • 317,471
Kane □, UT • 5,169
Kaneohe, HI 96744 • 35,448
Kankakee, IL 60901 • 27,575
Kankakee □, IL • 96,255
Kannapolis, NC 28081–83 • 29,696
Kansas City, KS 66101–19 • 149,767
Kansas City, MO 64101–99 • 435,146
Kapaa, HI 96746 • 8,149
Kapaau, HI 96755 • 1,083
Kaplan, LA 70548 • 4,535
Karnes □, TX • 12,455
Karnes City, TX 78118 • 2,916
Karns, TN 37921 • 1,458
Kasson, MN 55944 • 3,514
Kathleen, FL 33849 • 2,743
Katy, TX 77449–50 • 8,005
Kauai □, HI • 51,177
Kaufman, TX 75142 • 5,238
Kaufman □, TX • 52,220
Kaukauna, WI 54130 • 11,982
Kaumakani, HI 96747 • 803
Kaunakakai, HI 96748 • 2,658
Kay □, OK • 48,056
Kaycee, WY 82639 • 256
Kayenta, AZ 86033 • 4,372
Kaysville, UT 84037 • 13,961
Keaau, HI 96749 • 1,584
Kealakekua, HI 96750 • 1,453
Kealia, HI 96751 • 700
Keansburg, NJ 07734 • 11,069
Kearney, MO 64060 • 1,790
Kearney, NE 68847–48 • 24,396
Kearney □, NE • 6,629
Kearns, UT 84118 • 28,374
Kearny, AZ 85237 • 2,262
Kearny, NJ 07031–32 • 34,874
Kearny □, KS • 4,027
Keego Harbor, MI 48320 • 2,932
Keene, NH 03431 • 22,430
Keene, TX 76059 • 3,944
Keeseville, NY 12944 • 1,854
Keewatin, MN 55753 • 1,118
Keith □, NE • 8,584
Keizer, OR 97303 • 21,884
Kekaha, HI 96752 • 3,506
Keller, TX 76248 • 13,683
Kellogg, ID 83837 • 2,591
Kelseyville, CA 95451 • 2,861
Kelso, WA 98626 • 11,820
Kemmerer, WY 83101 • 3,020
Kemp, TX 75143 • 1,184
Kemper □, MS • 10,356
Kenai, AK 99611 • 6,327
Kenbridge, VA 23944 • 1,264
Ken Caryl, CO 80123 • 24,391
Kendall, FL 33156 • 87,271
Kendall □, IL • 39,413
Kendall □, TX • 14,589
Kendall Park, NJ 08824 • 7,127
Kendallville, IN 46755 • 7,773
Kenedy, TX 78119 • 3,763
Kenedy □, TX • 460
Kenilworth, IL 60043 • 2,402
Kenilworth, NJ 07033 • 7,574
Kenly, NC 27542 • 1,549
Kenmare, ND 58746 • 1,214
Kenmore, NY 14217 • 17,180
Kenmore, WA 98028 • 8,917
Kennebec □, ME • 115,904
Kennebunk, ME 04043 • 4,206
Kennebunkport, ME 04046 • 1,100
Kennedy Heights, LA 70094 • 2,000
Kennedy Township, PA 15108 • 7,152
Kenner, LA 70062–65 • 72,033
Kennesaw, GA 30144 • 8,936
Kennett, MO 63857 • 10,941
Kennett Square, PA 19348 • 5,218
Kennewick, WA 99336–37 • 42,155
Kennydale, WA 98056 • 2,000
Kenosha, WI 53140–44 • 80,352
Kenosha □, WI • 128,181
Kenova, WV 25530 • 3,748
Ken Rock, IL 61109 • 3,300
Kensett, AR 72082 • 1,741
Kensington, CA 94707 • 4,974
Kensington, CT 06037 • 8,306
Kensington, MD 20895 • 1,713
Kent, OH 44240 • 28,835
Kent, WA 98031–32 • 37,960
Kent □, DE • 110,993
Kent □, MD • 17,842
Kent □, MI • 500,631
Kent □, RI • 161,135
Kent □, TX • 1,010
Kentfield, CA 94904 • 6,030
Kentland, IN 47951 • 1,798
Kenton, DE 19955 • 232
Kenton, OH 43326 • 8,356
Kenton, TN 38233 • 1,366
Kenton □, KY • 142,031
Kentwood, LA 70444 • 2,468
Kentwood, MI 49508 • 37,826
Kenvil, NJ 07847 • 3,050
Kenwood, OH 45236 • 7,469
Kenyon, MN 55946 • 1,552
Kenyon, RI 02836 • 400
Keokea, HI 96790 • 900
Keokuk, IA 52632 • 12,451
Keokuk □, IA • 11,624
Keosauqua, IA 52565 • 1,020
Keota, IA 52248 • 1,000
Kerens, TX 75144 • 1,702
Kerhonkson, NY 12446 • 1,629
Kermit, TX 79745 • 6,875
Kern □, CA • 543,477
Kernersville, NC 27284–85 • 10,836
Kernville, CA 93238 • 1,656
Kerr □, TX • 36,304
Kerrville, TX 78028–29 • 17,384
Kershaw, SC 29067 • 1,814
Kershaw □, SC • 43,599
Ketchikan, AK 99901 • 8,263
Ketchum, ID 83340 • 2,523
Kettering, MD 20772 • 9,901
Kettering, OH 45429 • 60,569
Kettle Falls, WA 99141 • 1,272
Kewanee, IL 61443 • 12,969
Kewaskum, WI 53040 • 2,515
Kewaunee, WI 54216 • 2,750
Kewaunee □, WI • 18,878
Keweenaw □, MI • 1,701
Keya Paha □, NE • 1,029
Key Biscayne, FL 33149 • 8,854
Key Largo, FL 33037 • 11,336
Keyport, NJ 07735 • 7,586
Keyser, WV 26726 • 5,870
Keystone Heights, FL 32656 • 1,315
Key West, FL 33040–41 • 24,832
Kiana, AK 99749 • 385
Kidder □, ND • 3,332
Kiel, WI 53042 • 2,910
Kihei, HI 96753 • 11,107
Kilauea, HI 96754 • 1,685
Kilgore, TX 75662–63 • 11,066
Killdeer, ND 58640 • 722
Killeen, TX 76540–47 • 63,535
Killen, AL 35645 • 1,047
Kilmarnock, VA 22482 • 1,109
Kimball, NE 69145 • 2,574
Kimball □, NE • 4,108
Kimberly, AL 35091 • 1,096
Kimberly, ID 83341 • 2,367
Kimberly, WI 54136 • 5,406
Kimble □, TX • 4,122
Kincaid, IL 62540 • 1,353
Kinder, LA 70648 • 2,246
Kinderhook, NY 12106 • 1,293
King, NC 27021 • 4,059
King □, TX • 354
King □, WA • 1,507,319
King and Queen □, VA • 6,289
King City, CA 93930 • 7,634
King Cove, AK 99612 • 451
Kingfisher, OK 73750 • 4,095
Kingfisher □, OK • 13,212
King George □, VA • 13,527
Kingman, AZ 86401–02 • 12,722
Kingman, KS 67068 • 3,196
Kingman □, KS • 8,292
King of Prussia, PA 19406 • 18,406
Kings, MS 39180 • 1,165
Kings □, CA • 101,469
Kings □, NY • 2,300,664
King Salmon, AK 99613 • 696
Kingsburg, CA 93631 • 7,205
Kingsbury □, SD • 5,925
Kingsford, MI 49801 • 5,480
Kingsgate, WA 98011 • 14,259
Kingsland, GA 31548 • 4,699
Kingsland, TX 78639 • 2,725
Kingsley, IA 51028 • 1,129
Kings Mountain, NC 28086 • 8,763
Kings Park, NY 11754 • 17,773
Kings Park, VA 22151 • 6,000
Kings Park West, VA 22032 • 6,000
Kings Point, FL 33484 • 12,422
Kings Point, NY 11024 • 4,843
Kingsport, TN 37660–65 • 36,365
Kingston, ID 83839 • 1,000
Kingston, MA 02364 • 4,774
Kingston, NJ 08528 • 1,200
Kingston, NY 12401 • 23,095
Kingston, OH 45644 • 1,153
Kingston, OK 73439 • 1,237
Kingston, PA 18704 • 14,507
Kingston, RI 02881 • 6,504
Kingston, TN 37763 • 4,552
Kingston Springs, TN 37082 • 1,529
Kingstown, MD 21620 • 1,660
Kingstree, SC 29556 • 3,858
Kingsville, MD 21087 • 3,550
Kingsville (North Kingsville), OH 44048 • 1,243
Kingsville, TX 78363–64 • 25,276
King William □, VA • 10,913
Kingwood, TX 77339 • 37,397
Kingwood, WV 26537 • 3,243
Kinloch, MO 63140 • 2,702
Kinnelon, NJ 07405 • 8,470
Kinney □, TX • 3,119
Kinsey, AL 36301 • 1,679
Kinsley, KS 67547 • 1,875
Kinston, NC 28501–03 • 25,295
Kiowa, KS 67070 • 1,160
Kiowa □, CO • 1,688
Kiowa □, KS • 3,660
Kiowa □, OK • 11,347
Kipnuk, AK 99614 • 470
Kirby, TX 78219 • 8,326
Kirbyville, TX 75956 • 1,871
Kirkland, IL 60146 • 1,011
Kirkland, WA 98033–34 • 40,052
Kirksville, MO 63501 • 17,152
Kirkwood, DE 19708 • 350
Kirkwood, MO 63122 • 27,291
Kirtland, NM 87417 • 3,552
Kirtland, OH 44094 • 5,881
Kissimmee, FL 34741–46 • 30,050
Kit Carson □, CO • 7,140
Kitsap □, WA • 189,731
Kittanning, PA 16201 • 5,120
Kittery, ME 03904 • 5,151
Kittery Point, ME 03905 • 1,093
Kittitas □, WA • 26,725
Kittson □, MN • 5,767
Kitty Hawk, NC 27949 • 1,937
Klamath □, OR • 57,702
Klamath Falls, OR 97601–03 • 17,737
Klawock, AK 99925 • 722
Kleberg □, TX • 30,274
Klein, TX 77379 • 12,000
Klickitat □, WA • 16,616
Knightdale, NC 27545 • 1,884
Knights Landing, CA 95645 • 1,000
Knightstown, IN 46148 • 2,048
Knob Noster, MO 65336 • 2,261
Knott □, KY • 17,906
Knox, IN 46534 • 3,705
Knox, PA 16232 • 1,182
Knox □, IL • 56,393
Knox □, IN • 39,884
Knox □, KY • 29,676
Knox □, ME • 36,310

Knox □, MO • 4,482
Knox □, NE • 9,534
Knox □, OH • 47,473
Knox □, TN • 335,749
Knox □, TX • 4,837
Knox City, TX 79529 • 1,440
Knoxville, IL 61448 • 3,243
Knoxville, IA 50138 • 8,232
Knoxville, TN 37901-50 • 165,121
Kodiak, AK 99615 • 6,365
Kohler, WI 53044 • 1,817
Kokomo, IN 46901-04 • 44,962
Koloa, HI 96756 • 1,791
Konawa, OK 74849 • 1,508
Koochiching □, MN • 16,299
Koontz Lake, IN 46574 • 1,615
Kootenai □, ID • 69,795
Koppel, PA 16136 • 1,024
Kosciusko, MS 39090 • 6,986
Kosciusko □, IN • 65,294
Kossuth □, IA • 18,591
Kotlik, AK 99620 • 461
Kotzebue, AK 99752 • 2,751
Kountze, TX 77625 • 2,056
Kouts, IN 46347 • 1,603
Krebs, OK 74554 • 1,955
Kremmling, CO 80459 • 1,166
Krotz Springs, LA 70750 • 1,285
Kula, HI 96790 • 1,300
Kulpmont, PA 17834 • 3,233
Kuna, ID 83634 • 1,955
Kurtistown, HI 96760 • 910
Kutztown, PA 19530 • 4,704
Kwethluk, AK 99621 • 558
Kwigillingok, AK 99622 • 278
Kyle, TX 78640 • 2,225

L

Labadieville, LA 70372 • 1,821
La Barge, WY 83123 • 493
La Belle, FL 33935 • 2,703
Labette □, KS • 23,693
La Canada Flintridge, CA 91011 • 19,378
Lac du Flambeau, WI 54538 • 1,180
La Center, KY 42056 • 1,040
Lacey, WA 98503 • 19,279
Lackawanna, NY 14218 • 20,585
Lackawanna □, PA • 219,039
Laclede □, MO • 27,158
Lacombe, LA 70445 • 6,523
Lacon, IL 61540 • 1,986
Laconia, NH 03246-47 • 15,743
Lacoochee, FL 33537 • 2,072
Lac qui Parle □, MN • 8,924
La Crescent, MN 55947 • 4,311
La Crescenta, CA 91214 • 12,500
La Crosse, KS 67548 • 1,427
La Crosse, WI 54601-03 • 51,003
La Crosse □, WI • 97,904
La Cygne, KS 66040 • 1,066
Ladd, IL 61329 • 1,283
Ladera Heights, CA 90045 • 6,316
Ladoga, IN 47954 • 1,124
Ladson, SC 29456 • 13,540
Ladue, MO 63124 • 8,847
Lady Lake, FL 32159 • 8,071
Ladysmith, WI 54848 • 3,938
Lafayette, AL 36862 • 3,151
Lafayette, CA 94549 • 23,501
Lafayette, CO 80026 • 14,548
Lafayette, GA 30728 • 6,313
Lafayette, IN 47901-06 • 43,764
Lafayette, LA 70501-09 • 94,440
Lafayette, NC 28304 • 3,200
Lafayette, OR 97127 • 1,292
La Fayette, RI 02852 • 640
Lafayette, TN 37083 • 3,641
Lafayette □, AR • 9,643
Lafayette □, FL • 5,578
Lafayette □, LA • 164,762
Lafayette □, MS • 31,826
Lafayette □, MO • 31,107
Lafayette □, WI • 16,076
Lafayette Southwest, LA • 5,500
La Feria, TX 78559 • 4,360
Lafitte, LA 70067 • 1,507
La Follette, TN 37766 • 7,192
Lafourche □, LA • 85,860
La Grande, OR 97850 • 11,766
La Grange, GA 30240-41 • 25,597
La Grange, IL 60525 • 15,362
Lagrange, IN 46761 • 2,382
La Grange, KY 40031 • 3,853
La Grange, MO 63448 • 1,102
La Grange, NC 28551 • 2,805
Lagrange, OH 44050 • 1,199
La Grange, TX 78945 • 3,951
Lagrange □, IN • 29,477
La Grange Highlands, IL 60525 • 3,660
La Grange Park, IL 60525 • 12,861
Laguna Beach, CA 92651-54 • 23,170
Laguna Hills, CA 92653 • 46,731
Laguna Niguel, CA 92677 • 44,400
La Habra, CA 90631-33 • 51,266
Lahaina, HI 96761 • 9,073
La Harpe, IL 61450 • 1,407
Laie, HI 96762 • 5,577
Laingsburg, MI 48848 • 1,148
La Junta, CO 81050 • 7,637
Lake □, CA • 50,631
Lake □, CO • 6,007
Lake □, FL • 152,104
Lake □, IL • 516,418
Lake □, IN • 475,594
Lake □, MI • 8,583
Lake □, MN • 10,415
Lake □, MT • 21,041
Lake □, OH • 215,499
Lake □, OR • 7,186
Lake □, SD • 10,550
Lake □, TN • 7,129
Lake Alfred, FL 33850 • 3,622
Lake Andes, SD 57356 • 846
Lake Arrowhead, CA 92317 • 6,539
Lake Arthur, LA 70549 • 3,194
Lake Barcroft, VA 22041 • 8,686
Lake Bluff, IL 60044 • 5,513
Lake Butler, FL 32054 • 2,116
Lake Carmel, NY 10512 • 8,489
Lake Charles, LA 70601-29 • 70,580
Lake City, AR 72437 • 1,833
Lake City, FL 32055-56 • 10,005
Lake City, IA 51449 • 1,841
Lake City, MN 55041 • 4,391
Lake City, PA 16423 • 2,519
Lake City, SC 29560 • 7,153
Lake City, TN 37769 • 2,166
Lake Crystal, MN 56055 • 2,084
Lake Delta, NY 13440 • 1,980
Lake Delton, WI 53940 • 1,470
Lake Elmo, MN 55042 • 5,903
Lake Elsinore, CA 92330-31 • 18,285
Lake Erie Beach, NY 14006 • 4,509
Lakefield, MN 56150 • 1,679
Lake Forest, FL 33023 • 5,400
Lake Forest, IL 60045 • 17,836
Lake Geneva, WI 53147 • 5,979
Lake Grove, NY 11755 • 9,612
Lake Hamilton, AR 71913 • 1,331
Lake Havasu City, AZ 86403-05 • 24,363
Lake Helen, FL 32744 • 2,344
Lakehurst, NJ 08733 • 3,078
Lake in the Hills, IL 60102 • 5,866
Lake Jackson, TX 77566 • 22,776
Lake Katrine, NY 12449 • 1,998
Lakeland, FL 33801-13 • 70,576
Lakeland, GA 31635 • 2,467
Lakeland Highlands, FL 33801 • 9,972
Lakeland Village, CA 92330 • 5,159
Lake Linden, MI 49945 • 1,203
Lake Lorraine, FL 32569 • 6,779
Lake Luzerne, NY 12846 • 1,160
Lake Magdalene, FL 33612 • 15,973
Lake Mary, FL 32746 • 5,929
Lake Mills, IA 50450 • 2,143
Lake Mills, WI 53551 • 4,143
Lakemore, OH 44250 • 2,684
Lake Odessa, MI 48849 • 2,256
Lake Of The Woods □, MN • 4,076
Lake Orion, MI 48360-62 • 3,057
Lake Oswego, OR 97034-35 • 30,576
Lake Park, FL 33403 • 6,704
Lake Placid, FL 33852 • 1,158
Lake Placid, NY 12946 • 2,485
Lakeport, CA 95453 • 4,390
Lake Preston, SD 57249 • 663
Lake Providence, LA 71254 • 5,380
Lake Ridge, VA 22192 • 23,862
Lake Ronkonkoma, NY 11779 • 18,997
Lake Shore, MD 21122 • 13,269
Lakeside, CA 92040 • 39,412
Lakeside, CT 06488 • 1,200
Lakeside, FL 32073 • 29,137
Lakeside, OR 97449 • 1,437
Lakeside, VA 23228 • 12,081
Lakeside Park, KY 41017 • 3,131
Lakeside-Pinetop, AZ 85935 • 2,422
Lake Station, IN 46405 • 13,899
Lake Stevens, WA 98258 • 3,380
Lake Telemark, NJ 07866 • 1,121
Lakeview, GA 30741 • 5,237
Lake View, IA 51450 • 1,303
Lakeview, MI 48850 • 1,108
Lake View, NY 14085 • 1,460
Lakeview, NY 11552 • 5,476
Lakeview, OH 43331 • 1,056
Lakeview, OR 97630 • 2,526
Lake Villa, IL 60046 • 2,857
Lake Village, AR 71653 • 2,791
Lakeville, CT 06039 • 1,800
Lakeville, MA 02346 • 1,948
Lakeville, MN 55044 • 24,854
Lakeville, NY 14480 • 1,000
Lake Wales, FL 33853 • 9,670
Lake Wissota, WI 54729 • 2,175
Lakewood, CA 90711-16 • 73,557
Lakewood, CO 80215 • 126,481
Lakewood, IL 60014 • 1,609
Lakewood, IA 50211 • 1,950
Lakewood, NJ 08701 • 26,095
Lakewood, NY 14750 • 3,564
Lakewood, OH 44107 • 59,718
Lakewood, WA 98259 • 58,412
Lakewood Center, WA 98499 • 58,412
Lakewood Park, FL 34951 • 7,211
Lake Worth, FL 33460-67 • 28,564
Lake Zurich, IL 60047 • 14,947
Lakin, KS 67860 • 2,060
Lakota, ND 58344 • 898
La Luz, NM 88337 • 1,625
Lamar, CO 81052 • 8,343
Lamar, MO 64759 • 4,168
Lamar, PA 16848 • 1,200
Lamar, SC 29069 • 1,125
Lamar □, AL • 15,715
Lamar □, GA • 13,038
Lamar □, MS • 30,424
Lamar □, TX • 43,949
La Marque, TX 77568 • 14,120
Lamb □, TX • 15,072
Lambert, MS 38643 • 1,131
Lambertville, MI 48144 • 7,860
Lambertville, NJ 08530 • 3,927
La Mesa, CA 91941-44 • 52,931
La Mesa, NM 88044 • 900
Lamesa, TX 79331 • 10,809
La Mirada, CA 90637-38 • 40,452
Lamoille, NV 89828 • 110
Lamoille □, VT • 19,735
Lamoni, IA 50140 • 2,319
Lamont, CA 93241 • 11,517
La Moure, ND 58458 • 970
La Moure □, ND • 5,383
Lampasas, TX 76550 • 6,382
Lampasas □, TX • 13,521
Lanai City, HI 96763 • 2,400
Lanark, IL 61046 • 1,382
Lancashire, DE 19810 • 1,175
Lancaster, CA 93534-39 • 97,291
Lancaster, KY 40444 • 3,421
Lancaster, NH 03584 • 1,859
Lancaster, NY 14086 • 11,940
Lancaster, OH 43130 • 34,507
Lancaster, PA 17601-05 • 55,551
Lancaster, SC 29720-21 • 8,914
Lancaster, TX 75146 • 22,117
Lancaster, WI 53813 • 4,192
Lancaster □, NE • 213,641
Lancaster □, PA • 422,822
Lancaster □, SC • 54,516
Lancaster □, VA • 10,896
Lancaster Village, DE 19805 • 1,100
Landen, OH 45040 • 9,263
Lander, WY 82520 • 7,023
Lander □, NV • 6,266
Landess, IN 46944 • 1,500
Landis, NC 28088 • 2,333
Land O' Lakes, FL 34639 • 7,892
Landover, MD 20784 • 5,052
Landrum, SC 29356 • 2,347
Lane □, KS • 2,375
Lane □, OR • 282,912
Lanesboro, MA 01237 • 1,000
Lanett, AL 36863 • 8,985
Langdon, ND 58249 • 2,241
Langeloth, PA 15054 • 1,112
Langhorne, PA 19047 • 1,361
Langlade □, WI • 19,505
Langley, SC 29834 • 1,714
Langley Park, MD 20783 • 17,474
Langston, OK 73050 • 1,471
Lanham, MD 20706 • 5,000
Lanier □, GA • 5,531
Lansdale, PA 19446 • 16,362
Lansdowne, MD 21227 • 9,430
Lansdowne, PA 19050 • 11,712
L'Anse, MI 49946 • 2,151
Lansford, PA 18232 • 4,583
Lansing, IL 60438 • 28,086
Lansing, IA 52151 • 1,007
Lansing, KS 66043 • 7,120
Lansing, MI 48901-33 • 127,321
Lantana, FL 33462 • 8,392
La Palma, CA 90623 • 15,392
La Paz □, AZ • 13,844
Lapeer, MI 48446 • 7,759
Lapeer □, MI • 74,768
Lapel, IN 46051 • 1,742
La Place, LA 70068-69 • 24,194
La Plata, MD 20646 • 5,841
La Plata, MO 63549 • 1,401
La Plata □, CO • 32,284
Laporte, CO 80535 • 1,300
La Porte, IN 46350 • 21,507
La Porte, TX 77571-72 • 27,910
La Porte □, IN • 107,066
La Porte City, IA 50651 • 2,128
La Pryor, TX 78872 • 1,343
La Puente, CA 91744-49 • 36,955
Lapwai, ID 83540 • 932
Laramie, WY 82063-71 • 26,687
Laramie □, WY • 73,142
Larchmont, NY 10538 • 6,181
Larchmont North, NY 10538 • 11,240
Laredo, TX 78040-44 • 122,899
Largo, FL 34640-49 • 65,674
Larimer □, CO • 186,136
Larimore, ND 58251 • 1,464
La Riviera, CA 95826 • 10,986
Larkspur, CA 94939 • 11,070
Larksville, PA 18704 • 4,700
Larned, KS 67550 • 4,490
Larose, LA 70373 • 5,772
Larue □, KY • 11,679
La Salle, CO 80645 • 1,783
La Salle, IL 61301 • 9,717
La Salle □, IL • 106,913
La Salle □, LA • 13,662
La Salle □, TX • 5,254
Las Animas, CO 81054 • 2,481
Las Animas □, CO • 13,765
Las Cruces, NM 88001-08 • 62,126
Lassen □, CA • 27,598
Las Vegas, NV 89101-99 • 258,295
Las Vegas, NM 87701 • 14,753
Latah □, ID • 30,617
Lathrop, MO 64465 • 1,794
Lathrop Wells, NV 89020 • 350
Latimer □, OK • 10,333
Laton, CA 93242 • 1,415
Latrobe, PA 15650 • 9,265
Latta, SC 29565 • 1,565
Lauderdale □, AL • 79,661
Lauderdale □, MS • 75,555
Lauderdale □, TN • 23,491
Lauderdale Lakes, FL 33313 • 27,341
Lauderhill, FL 33313 • 49,708
Laughlin, NV 89028-29 • 140
Laughlintown, PA 15655 • 1,000
Laurel, DE 19956 • 3,226
Laurel, FL 34272 • 8,245
Laurel, MD 20707-09 • 19,438
Laurel, MS 39440-42 • 18,827
Laurel, MT 59044 • 5,686
Laurel, VA 23060 • 13,011
Laurel □, KY • 43,438
Laurel Bay, SC 29902 • 4,972
Laureldale, PA 19605 • 3,726
Laurel Hill, NC 28351 • 2,314
Laurence Harbor, NJ 08879 • 6,361
Laurens, IA 50554 • 1,550
Laurens, SC 29360 • 9,694
Laurens □, GA • 39,988
Laurens □, SC • 58,092
Laurinburg, NC 28352-53 • 11,643
Laurium, MI 49913 • 2,268
Lavaca, AR 72941 • 1,253
Lavaca □, TX • 18,690
La Vale, MD 21502 • 5,000
Lavallette, NJ 08735 • 2,299
La Vergne, TN 37086 • 7,499
La Verkin, UT 84745 • 1,771
La Verne, CA 91750 • 30,897
Laverne, OK 73848 • 1,269
La Vista, GA 30329 • 4,900
La Vista, NE 68128 • 9,840
Lavonia, GA 30553 • 1,840
Lawai, HI 96765 • 1,787
Lawndale, CA 90260-61 • 27,331
Lawnside, NJ 08045 • 2,841
Lawrence, IN 46226 • 26,763
Lawrence, KS 66044-46 • 65,608
Lawrence, MA 01840-45 • 70,207
Lawrence, NY 11559 • 6,513
Lawrence □, AL • 31,513
Lawrence □, AR • 17,457
Lawrence □, IL • 15,972
Lawrence □, IN • 42,836
Lawrence □, KY • 13,998
Lawrence □, MS • 12,458
Lawrence □, MO • 30,236
Lawrence □, OH • 61,834
Lawrence □, PA • 96,246
Lawrence □, TN • 35,303
Lawrenceburg, IN 47025 • 4,375
Lawrenceburg, KY 40342 • 5,911
Lawrenceburg, TN 38464 • 10,412
Lawrence Park, PA 16511 • 4,310
Lawrenceville, GA 30243-46 • 16,848
Lawrenceville, IL 62439 • 4,897
Lawrenceville, NJ 08648 • 6,446
Lawrenceville, VA 23868 • 1,486
Lawson, MO 64062 • 1,876
Lawsonia, MD 21817 • 1,326
Lawtell, LA 70550 • 1,014
Lawton, MI 49065 • 1,685
Lawton, OK 73501-07 • 80,561
Layton, UT 84040-41 • 41,784
Laytonville, CA 95454 • 1,133
Lea □, NM • 55,765
Leachville, AR 72438 • 1,743
Lead, SD 57754 • 3,632
Leadville, CO 80461 • 2,629
Leadwood, MO 63653 • 1,247
League City, TX 77573-74 • 30,159
Leake □, MS • 18,436
Leakesville, MS 39451 • 1,129
Lealman, FL 33714 • 21,748
Leavenworth, KS 66048 • 38,495
Leavenworth, WA 98826 • 1,692
Leavenworth □, KS • 64,371
Leavittsburg, OH 44430 • 2,220
Leawood, KS 66206 • 19,693
Lebanon, DE 19901 • 130
Lebanon, IL 62254 • 3,688
Lebanon, IN 46052 • 12,059
Lebanon, KY 40033 • 5,695
Lebanon, MO 65536 • 9,983
Lebanon, NH 03766 • 12,183
Lebanon, NJ 08833 • 1,036
Lebanon, OH 45036 • 10,453
Lebanon, OR 97355 • 10,950
Lebanon, PA 17042 • 24,800
Lebanon, TN 37087-88 • 15,208
Lebanon, VA 24266 • 3,386
Lebanon □, PA • 113,744
Lebanon Junction, KY 40150 • 1,741
Le Center, MN 56057 • 2,006
Le Claire, IA 52753 • 2,734
Lecompte, LA 71346 • 1,592
Lee, MA 01238 • 2,020
Lee □, AL • 87,146
Lee □, AR • 13,053
Lee □, FL • 335,113
Lee □, GA • 16,250
Lee □, IL • 34,392
Lee □, IA • 38,687
Lee □, KY • 7,422
Lee □, MS • 65,581
Lee □, NC • 41,374
Lee □, SC • 18,437
Lee □, TX • 12,854
Lee □, VA • 24,496
Leechburg, PA 15656 • 2,504
Leedom Estates, DE 19720 • 1,100
Leeds, AL 35094 • 9,946
Leelanau □, MI • 16,527
Lee Park, PA 18702 • 3,800
Leesburg, FL 34748-49 • 14,903
Leesburg, GA 31763 • 1,452
Leesburg, OH 45135 • 1,063
Leesburg, VA 22075 • 16,202
Lees Summit, MO 64063-64 • 46,418
Leesville, LA 71446 • 7,638
Leesville, SC 29070 • 2,025
Leetonia, OH 44431 • 2,070
Leetsdale, PA 15056 • 1,387
Leflore □, MS • 37,341
Le Flore □, OK • 43,270
Le Grand, CA 95333 • 1,205
Lehi, UT 84043 • 8,475
Lehigh □, PA • 291,130
Lehigh Acres, FL 33936 • 13,611
Lehighton, PA 18235 • 5,914
Leicester, MA 01524 • 3,200
Leipsic, DE 19901 • 236
Leipsic, OH 45856 • 2,203
Leisure City, FL 33033 • 19,379
Leitchfield, KY 42754-55 • 4,965
Leland, MS 38756 • 6,366
Le Mars, IA 51031 • 8,454
Lemay, MO 63125 • 18,005
Lemhi □, ID • 6,899
Lemmon, SD 57638 • 1,614
Lemmon Valley, NV 89501 • 4,100
Lemon Grove, CA 91945-46 • 23,984
Lemont, IL 60439 • 7,348
Lemont, PA 16851 • 2,613
Lemoore, CA 93245 • 13,622
Lena, IL 61048 • 2,605
Lenawee □, MI • 91,476
Lenexa, KS 66215 • 34,034
Lennox, CA 90304 • 22,757
Lennox, SD 57039 • 1,767
Lenoir, NC 28645 • 14,192
Lenoir □, NC • 57,274
Lenoir City, TN 37771 • 6,147
Lenox, IA 50851 • 1,303
Lenox, MA 01240 • 1,687
Leo, IN 46765 • 1,200
Leominster, MA 01453 • 38,145
Leon, IA 50144 • 2,047
Leon □, FL • 192,493
Leon □, TX • 12,665
Leonard, TX 75452 • 1,744
Leonardo, NJ 07737 • 3,720
Leonardtown, MD 20650 • 1,475
Leonia, NJ 07605 • 8,365
Leon Valley, TX 78238 • 9,581
Leoti, KS 67861 • 1,738
Lepanto, AR 72354 • 2,033
Le Roy, IL 61752 • 2,777
Le Roy, NY 14482 • 4,974
Leslie, MI 49251 • 1,872
Leslie, SC 29730 • 1,102
Leslie □, KY • 13,642
Lester Prairie, MN 55354 • 1,180
Le Sueur, MN 56058 • 3,714
Le Sueur □, MN • 23,239
Letcher □, KY • 27,000
Levelland, TX 79336-38 • 13,986
Levittown, NY 11756 • 53,286
Levittown, PA 19058 • 55,362
Levy □, FL • 25,923
Lewes, DE 19958 • 2,295
Lewis □, ID • 3,516
Lewis □, KY • 13,029
Lewis □, MO • 10,233
Lewis □, NY • 26,796
Lewis □, TN • 9,247
Lewis □, WA • 59,358
Lewis □, WV • 17,223
Lewis and Clark □, MT • 47,495
Lewisburg, OH 45338 • 1,584
Lewisburg, PA 17837 • 5,785
Lewisburg, TN 37091 • 9,879
Lewisburg, WV 24901 • 3,598
Lewisport, KY 42351 • 1,778
Lewiston, ID 83501 • 28,082
Lewiston, ME 04240-43 • 39,757
Lewiston, MN 55952 • 1,298
Lewiston, NY 14092 • 3,048
Lewiston, UT 84320 • 1,532
Lewistown, IL 61542 • 2,572
Lewistown, MT 59457 • 6,051
Lewistown, PA 17044 • 9,341
Lewisville, AR 71845 • 1,424
Lewisville, TX 75067 • 46,521
Lexington, IL 61753 • 1,809
Lexington, KY 40501-96 • 225,366
Lexington, MA 02173 • 28,974
Lexington, MS 39095 • 2,227
Lexington, MO 64067 • 4,860
Lexington, NE 68850 • 6,601
Lexington, NC 27292-93 • 16,581
Lexington, OH 44904 • 4,124
Lexington, OK 73051 • 1,776
Lexington, SC 29071-73 • 3,289
Lexington, TN 38351 • 5,810
Lexington, VA 24450 • 6,959
Lexington □, SC • 167,611
Lexington Park, MD 20653 • 9,943
Libby, MT 59923 • 2,532
Liberal, KS 67901-05 • 16,573
Liberty, IN 47353 • 2,051
Liberty, KY 42539 • 1,937
Liberty, MO 64068 • 20,459
Liberty, NY 12754 • 4,128
Liberty, NC 27298 • 2,047
Liberty, SC 29657 • 3,228
Liberty, TX 77575 • 7,733
Liberty □, FL • 5,569
Liberty □, GA • 52,745
Liberty □, MT • 2,295
Liberty □, TX • 52,726
Liberty Acres, CA 90250 • 4,700
Liberty Center, OH 43532 • 1,084
Liberty Lake, WA 99019 • 2,015
Libertyville, IL 60048 • 19,174
Licking, MO 65542 • 1,328
Licking □, OH • 128,300
Lidgerwood, ND 58053 • 799
Lighthouse Point, FL 33064 • 10,378
Ligonier, IN 46767 • 3,443
Ligonier, PA 15658 • 1,638
Lihue, HI 96766 • 5,536
Lilbourn, MO 63862 • 1,378
Lilburn, GA 30247 • 9,301
Lillington, NC 27546 • 2,048
Lilly, PA 15938 • 1,162
Lima, NY 14485 • 2,165
Lima, OH 45801-09 • 45,549
Limestone, ME 04750-51 • 1,245
Limestone □, AL • 54,135
Limestone □, TX • 20,946
Limon, CO 80828 • 1,831
Lincoln, AL 35096 • 2,941
Lincoln, AR 72744 • 1,460
Lincoln, CA 95648 • 7,248
Lincoln, DE 19960 • 500
Lincoln, IL 62656 • 15,418
Lincoln, KS 67455 • 1,381
Lincoln, ME 04457 • 3,399
Lincoln, MA 01773 • 2,860
Lincoln, NE 68501-72 • 191,972
Lincoln □, AR • 13,690
Lincoln □, CO • 4,529
Lincoln □, GA • 7,442
Lincoln □, ID • 3,308
Lincoln □, KS • 3,653
Lincoln □, KY • 20,045
Lincoln □, LA • 41,745
Lincoln □, ME • 30,357
Lincoln □, MN • 6,890
Lincoln □, MS • 30,278
Lincoln □, MO • 28,892
Lincoln □, MT • 17,481
Lincoln □, NE • 32,508
Lincoln □, NV • 3,775
Lincoln □, NM • 12,219
Lincoln □, NC • 50,319
Lincoln □, OK • 29,216
Lincoln □, OR • 38,889
Lincoln □, SD • 15,427
Lincoln □, TN • 28,157
Lincoln □, WA • 8,864
Lincoln □, WV • 21,382
Lincoln □, WI • 26,993
Lincoln □, WY • 12,625
Lincoln Acres, CA 91947 • 1,800
Lincoln City, OR 97367 • 5,892
Lincoln Heights, OH 45215 • 4,805
Lincoln Park, CO 81212 • 3,728
Lincoln Park, GA 30286 • 1,755
Lincoln Park, MI 48146 • 41,832
Lincoln Park, NJ 07035 • 10,978
Lincolnshire, IL 60069 • 4,931
Lincolnton, GA 30817 • 1,476
Lincolnton, NC 28092 • 6,847
Lincoln Village, CA 95207 • 4,236
Lincoln Village, OH 43228 • 9,958
Lincolnwood, IL 60645 • 11,365
Lincroft, NJ 07738 • 4,740
Linda, CA 95901 • 13,033
Lindale, GA 30147 • 4,187
Lindale, TX 75771 • 2,428
Linden, AL 36748 • 2,548
Linden, MI 48451 • 2,415
Linden, NJ 07036 • 36,701
Linden, TN 37096 • 1,099
Linden, TX 75563 • 2,375
Lindenhurst, IL 60046 • 8,038
Lindenhurst, NY 11757 • 26,879
Lindenwold, NJ 08021 • 18,734
Lindgren Acres, FL 33177 • 22,290
Lindon, UT 84042 • 3,818
Lindsay, CA 93247 • 8,338
Lindsay, OK 73052 • 2,947
Lindsborg, KS 67456 • 3,076
Lindstrom, MN 55045 • 2,461
Linesville, PA 16424 • 1,166
Lineville, AL 36266 • 2,394
Lingle, WY 82223 • 473
Linglestown, PA 17112 • 3,700

Linn, MO 65051 • 1,148
Linn □, IA • 168,767
Linn □, KS • 8,254
Linn □, MO • 13,885
Linn □, OR • 91,227
Lino Lakes, MN 55014 • 8,807
Linthicum Heights, MD • 2,950
Linthicum Heights, MD 21090 • 7,547
Linton, IN 47441 • 5,814
Linton, ND 58552 • 1,410
Linwood, NJ 08221 • 6,866
Lipscomb, AL 35020 • 2,892
Lipscomb □, TX • 3,143
Lisbon, IA 52253 • 1,452
Lisbon, ME 04250 • 1,240
Lisbon, NH 03585 • 1,246
Lisbon, ND 58054 • 2,177
Lisbon, OH 44432 • 3,037
Lisbon Falls, ME 04252 • 4,674
Lisle, IL 60532 • 19,512
Litchfield, CT 06759 • 1,378
Litchfield, IL 62056 • 6,883
Litchfield, MI 49252 • 1,317
Litchfield, MN 55355 • 6,041
Litchfield □, CT • 174,092
Litchfield Park, AZ 85340 • 3,303
Lithia Springs, GA 30057 • 11,403
Lithonia, GA 30058 • 2,448
Lititz, PA 17543 • 8,280
Little Canada, MN 55110 • 8,971
Little Chute, WI 54140 • 9,207
Little Compton, RI 02837 • 500
Little Creek, DE 19961 • 167
Little Falls, MN 56345 • 7,232
Little Falls, NJ 07424 • 11,294
Little Falls, NY 13365 • 5,829
Little Ferry, NJ 07643 • 9,989
Littlefield, TX 79339 • 6,489
Little River □, AR • 13,966
Little Rock, AR 72201–31 • 175,795
Little Silver, NJ 07739 • 5,721
Littlestown, PA 17340 • 2,974
Littleton, CO 80120–27 • 33,685
Littleton, MA 01460 • 2,867
Littleton, NH 03561 • 4,633
Little Valley, NY 14755 • 1,188
Live Oak, CA 95062 • 15,212
Live Oak, CA 95953 • 4,320
Live Oak, FL 32060 • 6,332
Live Oak, TX 78233 • 10,023
Live Oak □, TX • 9,556
Live Oak Manor, LA 70094 • 2,150
Livermore, CA 94550 • 56,741
Livermore, KY 42352 • 1,534
Livermore Falls, ME 04254 • 1,935
Livingston, AL 35470 • 3,530
Livingston, CA 95334 • 7,317
Livingston, MT 59047 • 6,701
Livingston, NJ 07039 • 26,609
Livingston, TN 38570 • 3,809
Livingston, TX 77351 • 5,019
Livingston □, IL • 39,301
Livingston □, KY • 9,062
Livingston □, LA • 70,526
Livingston □, MI • 115,645
Livingston □, MO • 14,592
Livingston □, NY • 62,372
Livingston Manor, NY 12758 • 1,482
Livonia, MI 48150–54 • 100,850
Livonia, NY 14487 • 1,434
Llangollen Estates, DE 19720 • 1,070
Llano, TX 78643 • 2,962
Llano □, TX • 11,631
Lloyd Harbor, NY 11743 • 3,343
Lochearn, MD 21207 • 25,240
Loch Lomond, VA 22110 • 3,292
Lockhart, FL 32810 • 11,636
Lockhart, TX 78644 • 9,205
Lock Haven, PA 17745 • 9,230
Lockland, OH 45215 • 4,357
Lockney, TX 79241 • 2,207
Lockport, IL 60441 • 9,401
Lockport, LA 70374 • 2,503
Lockport, NY 14094 • 24,426
Lockwood, MO 65682 • 1,041
Lockwood, MT 59101 • 3,967
Locust, NC 28097 • 1,940
Locust Grove, GA 30248 • 1,681
Locust Grove, OK 74352 • 1,326
Lodi, CA 95240–42 • 51,874
Lodi, NJ 07644 • 22,355
Lodi, OH 44254 • 3,042
Lodi, WI 53555 • 2,093
Logan, IA 51546 • 1,401
Logan, OH 43138 • 6,725
Logan, UT 84321 • 32,762
Logan, WV 25601 • 2,206
Logan □, AR • 20,557
Logan □, CO • 17,567
Logan □, IL • 30,798
Logan □, KS • 3,081
Logan □, KY • 24,416
Logan □, NE • 878
Logan □, ND • 2,847
Logan □, OH • 42,310
Logan □, OK • 29,011
Logan □, WV • 43,032
Logandale, NV 89021 • 500
Logansport, IN 46947 • 16,812
Logansport, LA 71049 • 1,390
Loganville, GA 30249 • 3,180
Lolo, MT 59847 • 2,746
Loma Linda, CA 92354 • 17,400
Lombard, IL 60148 • 39,408
Lomira, WI 53048 • 1,542
Lomita, CA 90717 • 19,382
Lompoc, CA 93436 • 37,649
Lonaconing, MD 21539 • 1,122
London, KY 40741 • 5,757
London, OH 43140 • 7,807
Londonderry, NH 03053 • 10,114
Londontown, MD 21037 • 6,992
Lone Grove, OK 73443 • 4,114
Lone Pine, CA 93545 • 1,818
Long □, GA • 6,202
Long Beach, CA 90801–88 • 429,433
Long Beach, IN 46360 • 2,044
Long Beach, MS 39560 • 15,804
Long Beach, NY 11561 • 33,510
Long Beach, WA 98631 • 1,236
Longboat Key, FL 34228 • 5,937
Long Branch, NJ 07740 • 28,658
Long Lake, IL 60041 • 2,888
Longmeadow, MA 01106 • 15,467
Longmont, CO 80501–02 • 51,555
Longport, NJ 08403 • 1,224
Long Prairie, MN 56347 • 2,786
Long Valley, NJ 07853 • 1,744
Long View, NC 28601 • 3,229
Longview, TX 75601–15 • 70,311
Longview, WA 98632 • 31,499
Longwood, FL 32750 • 13,316
Lonoke, AR 72086 • 4,022
Lonoke □, AR • 39,268
Lonsdale, MN 55046 • 1,252
Lonsdale, RI 02865 • 3,850
Loogootee, IN 47553 • 2,884
Lookout Mountain, TN 37350 • 1,901
Lorain, OH 44052–55 • 71,245
Lorain □, OH • 271,126
Lordsburg, NM 88045 • 2,951
Lorenzo, TX 79343 • 1,208
Loretto, PA 15940 • 1,072
Loretto, TN 38469 • 1,515
Loris, SC 29569 • 2,067
Lorton, VA 22079 • 15,385
Los Alamitos, CA 90720–21 • 11,676
Los Alamos, NM 87544 • 11,455
Los Alamos □, NM • 18,115
Los Altos, CA 94022–24 • 26,303
Los Altos Hills, CA 94022 • 7,514
Los Angeles, CA 90001–99 • 3,485,398
Los Angeles □, CA • 8,863,164
Los Banos, CA 93635 • 14,519
Los Fresnos, TX 78566 • 2,473
Los Gatos, CA 95030–32 • 27,357
Los Lunas, NM 87031 • 6,013
Los Molinos, CA 96055 • 1,709
Los Nietos, CA 90606 • 7,100
Los Osos, CA 93402 • 8,000
Los Padillas, NM 87105 • 2,400
Los Ranchos de Albuquerque, NM 87107 • 3,955
Los Serranos, CA 91709 • 7,099
Lost Hills, CA 93249 • 1,212
Loudon, TN 37774 • 4,026
Loudon □, TN • 31,255
Loudonville, NY 12211 • 10,822
Loudonville, OH 44842 • 2,915
Loudoun □, VA • 86,129
Louisa, KY 41230 • 1,990
Louisa, VA 23093 • 1,088
Louisa □, IA • 11,592
Louisa □, VA • 20,325
Louisburg, KS 66053 • 1,964
Louisburg, NC 27549 • 3,037
Louisiana, MO 63353 • 3,967
Louisville, CO 80027 • 12,361
Louisville, GA 30434 • 2,429
Louisville, IL 62858 • 1,098
Louisville, KY 40201–99 • 269,063
Louisville, MS 39339 • 7,169
Louisville, OH 44641 • 8,087
Loup □, NE • 683
Loup City, NE 68853 • 1,104
Love □, OK • 8,157
Loveland, CO 80537–39 • 37,352
Loveland, OH 45140 • 9,990
Loveland Park, OH 45140 • 1,357
Lovell, WY 82431 • 2,131
Lovelock, NV 89419 • 2,069
Loves Park, IL 61111 • 15,462
Loving, NM 88256 • 1,243
Loving □, TX • 107
Lovington, IL 61937 • 1,143
Lovington, NM 88260 • 9,322
Lowell, AR 72745 • 1,224
Lowell, IN 46356 • 6,430
Lowell, MA 01850–54 • 103,439
Lowell, MI 49331 • 3,983
Lowell, NC 28098 • 2,704
Lowellville, OH 44436 • 1,349
Lower Burrell, PA 15068 • 12,251
Lower Merion Township, PA 19003 • 59,629
Lower Paia, HI 96779 • 1,500
Lowndes □, AL • 12,658
Lowndes □, GA • 75,981
Lowndes □, MS • 59,308
Lowville, NY 13367 • 3,632
Loxley, AL 36551 • 1,161
Loyal, WI 54446 • 1,244
Loyall, KY 40854 • 1,100
Lubbock, TX 79401–99 • 186,206
Lubbock □, TX • 222,636
Lucas □, IA • 9,070
Lucas □, OH • 462,361
Lucasville, OH 45648 • 1,575
Luce □, MI • 5,763
Lucedale, MS 39452 • 2,592
Lucerne, CA 95458 • 2,011
Lucernemines, PA 15754 • 1,074
Lucerne Valley, CA 92356 • 1,300
Luck, WI 54853 • 1,022
Ludington, MI 49431 • 8,507
Ludlow, KY 41016 • 4,736
Ludlow, MA 01056 • 18,150
Ludlow, VT 05149 • 1,123
Ludowici, GA 31316 • 1,291
Lufkin, TX 75901–03 • 30,206
Lugoff, SC 29078 • 3,211
Lula, GA 30554 • 1,018
Luling, LA 70070 • 2,803
Luling, TX 78648 • 4,661
Lumber City, GA 31549 • 1,429
Lumberport, WV 26386 • 1,014
Lumberton, MS 39455 • 2,121
Lumberton, NC 28358–59 • 18,601
Lumpkin, GA 31815 • 1,250
Lumpkin □, GA • 14,573
Luna □, NM • 18,110
Luna Pier, MI 48157 • 1,507
Lund, NV 89317 • 330
Lunenburg, MA 01462 • 1,694
Lunenburg □, VA • 11,419
Luray, VA 22835 • 4,587
Lusk, WY 82225 • 1,504
Lutcher, LA 70071 • 3,907
Luther, OK 73054 • 1,560
Lutherville-Timonium, MD 21093 • 16,442
Lutz, FL 33549 • 10,552
Luverne, AL 36049 • 2,555
Luverne, MN 56156 • 4,382
Luxemburg, WI 54217 • 1,151
Luxora, AR 72358 • 1,338
Luzerne, PA 18709 • 3,206
Luzerne □, PA • 328,149
Lycoming □, PA • 118,710
Lyford, TX 78569 • 1,674
Lykens, PA 17048 • 1,986
Lyman, SC 29365 • 2,271
Lyman, WY 82937 • 1,896
Lyman □, SD • 3,638
Lynbrook, NY 11563 • 19,208
Lynch, KY 40855 • 1,166
Lynchburg, OH 45142 • 1,212
Lynchburg, TN 37352 • 4,721
Lynchburg, VA 24501–06 • 66,049
Lyncourt, NY 13208 • 4,516
Lynden, WA 98264 • 5,709
Lyndhurst, NJ 07071 • 18,262
Lyndhurst, OH 44124 • 15,982
Lyndon, KY 40222 • 8,037
Lyndonville, VT 05851 • 1,255
Lyndora, PA 16045 • 3,000
Lynn, IN 47355 • 1,183
Lynn, MA 01901–08 • 81,245
Lynn □, TX • 6,758
Lynne Acres, MD 21207 • 5,910
Lynnfield, MA 01940 • 11,274
Lynn Garden, TN 37665 • 7,213
Lynn Garden, TN 37665 • 3,950
Lynn Haven, FL 32444 • 9,298
Lynnwood, WA 98036–37 • 28,695
Lynwood, CA 90262 • 61,945
Lyon □, IA • 11,952
Lyon □, KS • 34,732
Lyon □, KY • 6,624
Lyon □, MN • 24,789
Lyon □, NV • 20,001
Lyon Mountain, NY 12952 • 1,000
Lyons, CO 80540 • 1,227
Lyons, GA 30436 • 4,502
Lyons, IL 60534 • 9,828
Lyons, KS 67554 • 3,688
Lyons, NE 68038 • 1,144
Lyons, NY 14489 • 4,280
Lytle, TX 78052 • 2,255

M

Mabank, TX 75147 • 1,739
Mableton, GA 30059 • 25,725
Mabscott, WV 25871 • 1,543
Mabton, WA 98935 • 1,482
MacClenny, FL 32063 • 3,966
Macedon, NY 14502 • 1,400
Macedonia, OH 44056 • 7,509
Machesney Park, IL 61111 • 19,033
Machias, ME 04654 • 1,773
Mackinac □, MI • 10,674
Mackinaw, IL 61755 • 1,331
Mackinaw City, MI 49701 • 875
Macomb, IL 61455 • 19,952
Macomb □, MI • 717,400
Macon, GA 31201–95 • 106,612
Macon, IL 62544 • 1,282
Macon, MS 39341 • 2,256
Macon, MO 63552 • 5,571
Macon □, AL • 24,928
Macon □, GA • 13,114
Macon □, IL • 117,206
Macon □, MO • 15,345
Macon □, NC • 23,499
Macon □, TN • 15,906
Macoupin □, IL • 47,679
Macungie, PA 18062 • 2,597
Madawaska, ME 04756 • 3,653
Madeira, OH 45243 • 9,141
Madelia, MN 56062 • 2,237
Madera, CA 93637–39 • 29,281
Madera □, CA • 88,090
Madill, OK 73446 • 3,069
Madison, AL 35758 • 14,904
Madison, AR 72359 • 1,263
Madison, CT 06443 • 2,139
Madison, FL 32340 • 3,345
Madison, GA 30650 • 3,483
Madison, IL 62060 • 4,629
Madison, IN 47250 • 12,006
Madison, ME 04950 • 2,956
Madison, MN 56256 • 1,951
Madison, MS 39110 • 7,471
Madison, NE 68748 • 2,135
Madison, NJ 07940 • 15,850
Madison, NC 27025 • 2,371
Madison, OH 44057 • 2,477
Madison, SD 57042 • 6,257
Madison, WV 25130 • 3,051
Madison, WI 53701–19 • 191,262
Madison □, AL • 238,912
Madison □, AR • 11,618
Madison □, FL • 16,569
Madison □, GA • 21,050
Madison □, ID • 23,674
Madison □, IL • 249,238
Madison □, IN • 130,669
Madison □, IA • 12,483
Madison □, KY • 57,508
Madison □, LA • 12,463
Madison □, MS • 53,794
Madison □, MO • 11,127
Madison □, MT • 5,989
Madison □, NE • 32,655
Madison □, NY • 69,120
Madison □, NC • 16,953
Madison □, OH • 37,068
Madison □, TN • 77,982
Madison □, TX • 10,931
Madison □, VA • 11,949
Madison Heights, MI 48071 • 32,196
Madison Heights, VA 24572 • 11,700
Madisonville, KY 42431 • 16,200
Madisonville, TN 37354 • 3,033
Madisonville, TX 77864 • 3,569
Madras, OR 97741 • 3,443
Madrid, IA 50156 • 2,395
Maeser, UT 84078 • 2,598
Magalia, CA 95954 • 8,987
Magdalena, NM 87825 • 861
Magee, MS 39111 • 3,607
Magna, UT 84044 • 17,829
Magnolia, AR 71753 • 11,151
Magnolia, MS 39652 • 2,245
Magnolia, NJ 08049 • 4,861
Magoffin □, KY • 13,077
Mahanoy City, PA 17948 • 5,209
Mahaska □, IA • 21,522
Mahnomen, MN 56557 • 1,154
Mahnomen □, MN • 5,044
Mahomet, IL 61853 • 3,103
Mahoning □, OH • 264,806
Mahopac, NY 10541 • 7,755
Mahwah, NJ 07430 • 7,500
Maiden, NC 28650 • 2,574
Maili, HI 96792 • 6,059
Maine, NY 13802 • 1,110
Maitland, FL 32751 • 9,110
Maize, KS 67101 • 1,520
Major □, OK • 8,055
Makaha, HI 96792 • 7,990
Makakilo City, HI 96706 • 9,828
Makawao, HI 96768 • 5,405
Makaweli, HI 96769 • 700
Malabar, FL 32950 • 1,977
Malad City, ID 83252 • 1,946
Malaga, NJ 08328 • 2,140
Malakoff, TX 75148 • 2,038
Malden, MA 02148 • 53,884
Malden, MO 63863 • 5,123
Malheur □, OR • 26,038
Malibu, CA 90264–65 • 10,000
Malone, NY 12953 • 6,777
Malta, MT 59538 • 2,340
Malvern, AR 72104 • 9,256
Malvern, IA 51551 • 1,210
Malvern, OH 44644 • 1,112
Malvern, PA 19355 • 2,944
Malverne, NY 11565 • 9,054
Mamaroneck, NY 10543 • 17,325
Mammoth, AZ 85618 • 1,845
Mammoth Lakes, CA 93546 • 4,785
Mammoth Spring, AR 72554 • 1,097
Mamou, LA 70554 • 3,483
Manahawkin, NJ 08050 • 1,594
Manasquan, NJ 08736 • 5,369
Manassas, VA 22110–11 • 27,957
Manassas Park, VA 22111 • 6,734
Manatee □, FL • 211,707
Manawa, WI 54949 • 1,169
Mancelona, MI 49659 • 1,370
Manchaug, MA 01526 • 1,000
Manchester, CT 06040 • 51,618
Manchester, GA 31816 • 4,104
Manchester, IA 52057 • 5,137
Manchester, KY 40962 • 1,634
Manchester, MD 21102 • 2,810
Manchester, MA 01944 • 5,424
Manchester, MI 48158 • 1,753
Manchester, MO 63011 • 6,542
Manchester, NH 03101–10 • 99,567
Manchester, NY 14504 • 1,598
Manchester, OH 45144 • 2,223
Manchester, PA 17345 • 1,830
Manchester, TN 37355 • 7,709
Manchester, VT 05254 • 561
Manchester Center, VT 05255 • 1,574
Mandan, ND 58554 • 15,177
Mandeville, LA 70448 • 7,083
Mangum, OK 73554 • 3,344
Manhasset, NY 11030 • 7,718
Manhattan, KS 66502 • 37,712
Manhattan, MT 59741 • 1,034
Manhattan Beach, CA 90266 • 32,063
Manheim, PA 17545 • 5,011
Manila, AR 72442 • 2,635
Manistee, MI 49660 • 6,734
Manistee □, MI • 21,265
Manistique, MI 49854 • 3,456
Manito, IL 61546 • 1,711
Manitou Springs, CO 80829 • 4,535
Manitowoc, WI 54220–21 • 32,520
Manitowoc □, WI • 80,421
Mankato, KS 66956 • 1,037
Mankato, MN 56001–03 • 31,477
Manlius, NY 13104 • 4,764
Manly, IA 50456 • 1,349
Mannford, OK 74044 • 1,826
Manning, IA 51455 • 1,484
Manning, SC 29102 • 4,428
Mannington, WV 26582 • 2,184
Manokotak, AK 99628 • 385
Manomet, MA 02345 • 1,500
Manor, TX 78653 • 1,041
Manorhaven, NY 11050 • 5,672
Mansfield, AR 72944 • 1,018
Mansfield, LA 71052 • 5,389
Mansfield, MA 02048 • 7,170
Mansfield, MO 65704 • 1,429
Mansfield, OH 44901–07 • 50,627
Mansfield, PA 16933 • 3,538
Mansfield, TX 76063 • 15,607
Mansfield Center, CT 06250 • 1,043
Manson, IA 50563 • 1,844
Mansura, LA 71350 • 1,601
Manteca, CA 95336 • 40,773
Manteno, IL 60950 • 3,488
Manti, UT 84642 • 2,268
Manton, MI 49663 • 1,161
Mantua, NJ 08051 • 1,350
Mantua, OH 44255 • 1,178
Mantua Hills, VA 22031 • 1,600
Manvel, TX 77578 • 3,733
Manville, NJ 08835 • 10,567
Manville, RI 02838 • 3,030
Many, LA 71449 • 3,112
Many Farms, AZ 86538 • 1,294
Maple Bluff, WI 53704 • 1,352
Maple Grove, MN 55369 • 38,736
Maple Heights, OH 44137 • 27,089
Maple Lake, MN 55358 • 1,394
Maple Plain, MN 55359 • 2,005
Maple Shade, NJ 08052 • 19,211
Mapleton, IA 51034 • 1,294
Mapleton, MN 56065 • 1,526
Mapleton, UT 84663 • 3,572
Maple Valley, WA 98038 • 1,211
Mapleville, RI 02839 • 1,300
Maplewood, MN 55109 • 30,954
Maplewood, MO 63143 • 9,962
Maplewood, NJ 07040 • 21,756
Maquoketa, IA 52060 • 6,111
Marana, AZ 85653 • 2,187
Marathon, FL 33050 • 8,857
Marathon, NY 13803 • 1,107
Marathon, WI 54448 • 1,606
Marathon □, WI • 115,400
Marble Falls, TX 78654 • 4,007
Marblehead, MA 01945 • 19,971
Marble Hill, MO 63764 • 1,447
Marbleton, WY 83113 • 634
Marbury, MD 20658 • 1,244
Marceline, MO 64658 • 2,645
Marcellus, MI 49067 • 1,193
Marco, FL 33937 • 9,493
Marcus, IA 51035 • 1,171
Marcus Hook, PA 19061 • 2,546
Marengo, IL 60152 • 4,768
Marengo, IA 52301 • 2,270
Marengo □, AL • 23,084
Marfa, TX 79843 • 2,424
Margate, FL 33063 • 42,985
Margate, MD 21060 • 1,900
Margate City, NJ 08402 • 8,431
Marianna, AR 72360 • 5,910
Marianna, FL 32446 • 6,292
Maricopa, AZ 85239 • 1,600
Maricopa, CA 93252 • 1,193
Maricopa □, AZ • 2,122,101
Mariemont, OH 45227 • 3,118
Marienville, PA 16239 • 1,400
Maries □, MO • 7,976
Marietta, GA 30060–68 • 44,129
Marietta, OH 45750 • 15,026
Marietta, OK 73448 • 2,306
Marin □, CA • 230,096
Marina, CA 93933 • 26,436
Marina del Rey, CA 90292 • 7,431
Marine City, MI 48039 • 4,556
Marinette, WI 54143 • 11,843
Marinette □, WI • 40,548
Maringouin, LA 70757 • 1,149
Marion, AL 36756 • 4,211
Marion, AR 72364 • 4,391
Marion, IL 62959 • 14,545
Marion, IN 46952–53 • 32,618
Marion, IA 52302 • 20,403
Marion, KS 66861 • 1,906
Marion, KY 42064 • 3,320
Marion, MA 02738 • 1,426
Marion, MS 39342 • 1,359
Marion, NY 14505 • 1,080
Marion, NC 28752 • 4,765
Marion, OH 43301–02 • 34,075
Marion, PA 17235 • 1,000
Marion, SC 29571 • 7,658
Marion, SD 57043 • 831
Marion, VA 24354 • 6,630
Marion, WI 54950 • 1,242
Marion □, AL • 29,830
Marion □, AR • 12,001
Marion □, FL • 194,833
Marion □, GA • 5,590
Marion □, IL • 41,561
Marion □, IN • 797,159
Marion □, IA • 30,001
Marion □, KS • 12,888
Marion □, KY • 16,499
Marion □, MS • 25,544
Marion □, MO • 27,682
Marion □, OH • 64,274
Marion □, OR • 228,483
Marion □, SC • 33,899
Marion □, TN • 24,860
Marion □, TX • 9,984
Marion □, WV • 57,249
Marionville, MO 65705 • 1,920
Mariposa, CA 95338 • 1,152
Mariposa □, CA • 14,302
Marissa, IL 62257 • 2,375
Marked Tree, AR 72365 • 3,100
Markesan, WI 53946 • 1,496
Markham, IL 60426 • 13,136
Markham, TX 77456 • 1,206
Markle, IN 46770 • 1,208
Marks, MS 38646 • 1,758
Marksville, LA 71351 • 5,526
Marlboro, NY 12542 • 2,200
Marlboro □, SC • 29,361
Marlborough, CT 06447 • 5,535
Marlborough, MA 01752 • 31,813
Marlborough, NH 03455 • 1,211
Marlene Village, OR 97005 • 1,500
Marlette, MI 48453 • 1,924
Marley, MD 21060 • 7,100
Marlin, TX 76661 • 6,386
Marlinton, WV 24954 • 1,148
Marlow, OK 73055 • 4,416
Marlow Heights, MD 20748 • 5,885
Marlton, NJ 08053 • 10,228
Marmaduke, AR 72443 • 1,164
Marmet, WV 25315 • 1,879
Maroa, IL 61756 • 1,602
Marquette, MI 49855 • 21,977
Marquette □, MI • 70,887
Marquette □, WI • 12,321
Marquette Heights, IL 61554 • 3,077
Marrero, LA 70072–73 • 36,671
Mars, PA 16046 • 1,713
Marseilles, IL 61341 • 4,811
Marshall, AR 72650 • 1,318
Marshall, IL 62441 • 3,555
Marshall, MI 49068 • 6,891
Marshall, MN 56258 • 12,023
Marshall, MO 65340 • 12,711
Marshall, TX 75670–71 • 23,682
Marshall, WI 53559 • 2,329
Marshall □, AL • 70,832
Marshall □, IL • 12,846
Marshall □, IN • 42,182
Marshall □, IA • 38,276
Marshall □, KS • 11,705
Marshall □, KY • 27,205
Marshall □, MN • 10,993
Marshall □, MS • 30,361
Marshall □, OK • 10,829
Marshall □, SD • 4,844
Marshall □, TN • 21,539
Marshall □, WV • 37,356
Marshallton, DE 19808 • 1,765
Marshalltown, IA 50158 • 25,178
Marshallville, GA 31057 • 1,457
Marshfield, MA 02050 • 4,002
Marshfield, MO 65706 • 4,374
Marshfield, WI 54449 • 19,291
Marshfield Hills, MA 02051 • 2,201
Mars Hill, ME 04758 • 1,500
Mars Hill, NC 28754 • 1,611
Marshville, NC 28103 • 2,020
Marsing, ID 83639 • 798
Marstons Mills, MA 02648 • 8,017
Mart, TX 76664 • 2,004
Martha Lake, WA 98012 • 10,155
Martin, SD 57551 • 1,151
Martin, TN 38237 • 8,600

United States Populations and ZIP Codes

Martin □, FL • *100,900*
Martin □, IN • *10,369*
Martin □, KY • *12,526*
Martin □, MN • *22,914*
Martin □, NC • *25,078*
Martin □, TX • *4,956*
Martinez, CA 94553 • *31,808*
Martinez, GA 30907 • *33,731*
Martinsburg, PA 16662 • *2,119*
Martinsburg, WV 25401 • *14,073*
Martins Ferry, OH 43935 • *7,990*
Martinsville, IL 62442 • *1,161*
Martinsville, IN 46151 • *11,677*
Martinsville, VA 24112–15 • *16,162*
Marvell, AR 72366 • *1,545*
Maryland City, MD 20724 • *6,813*
Maryland Heights, MO 63043 • *25,407*
Marysville, CA 95901 • *12,324*
Marysville, KS 66508 • *3,359*
Marysville, MI 48040 • *8,515*
Marysville, OH 43040 • *9,656*
Marysville, PA 17053 • *2,425*
Marysville, WA 98270 • *10,328*
Maryville, MO 64468 • *10,663*
Maryville, TN 37801–04 • *19,208*
Mascot, TN 37806 • *2,138*
Mascoutah, IL 62258 • *5,511*
Mason, MI 48854 • *6,768*
Mason, NV 89447 • *400*
Mason, OH 45040 • *11,452*
Mason, TX 76856 • *2,041*
Mason, WV 25260 • *1,053*
Mason □, IL • *16,269*
Mason □, KY • *16,666*
Mason □, MI • *25,537*
Mason □, TX • *3,423*
Mason □, WA • *38,341*
Mason □, WV • *25,178*
Masonboro, NC 28403 • *7,010*
Mason City, IL 62664 • *2,323*
Mason City, IA 50401 • *29,040*
Masontown, PA 15461 • *3,759*
Massac □, IL • *14,752*
Massapequa, NY 11758 • *22,018*
Massapequa Park, NY 11762 • *18,044*
Massena, NY 13662 • *11,719*
Massillon, OH 44646–48 • *31,007*
Mastic, NY 11950 • *13,778*
Mastic Beach, NY 11951 • *10,293*
Masury, OH 44438 • *1,836*
Matagorda □, TX • *36,928*
Matamoras, PA 18336 • *1,934*
Matawan, NJ 07747 • *9,270*
Mather, PA 15346 • *1,300*
Mathews □, VA • *8,348*
Mathis, TX 78368 • *5,423*
Matoaca, VA 23803 • *1,967*
Mattapoisett, MA 02739 • *2,949*
Matteson, IL 60443 • *11,378*
Matthews, NC 28105–06 • *13,651*
Mattituck, NY 11952 • *3,902*
Mattoon, IL 61938 • *18,441*
Mattydale, NY 13211 • *6,418*
Matunuck, RI 02879 • *550*
Maud, OK 74854 • *1,204*
Maugansville, MD 21767 • *1,707*
Maui □, HI • *100,374*
Mauldin, SC 29662 • *11,587*
Maumee, OH 43537 • *15,561*
Maunaloa, HI 96770 • *405*
Maunawili, HI 96734 • *4,847*
Maury □, TN • *54,812*
Mauston, WI 53948 • *3,439*
Maverick □, TX • *36,378*
Maxton, NC 28364 • *2,373*
Maxwell Acres, WV 26041 • *1,000*
Mayer, AZ 86333 • *1,800*
Mayes □, OK • *33,366*
Mayfield, KY 42066 • *9,935*
Mayfield, PA 18433 • *1,890*
Mayfield Heights, OH 44124 • *19,847*
Mayflower, AR 72106 • *1,415*
Mayflower Village, CA 91016 • *4,978*
Maynard, MA 01754 • *10,325*
Maynardville, TN 37807 • *1,298*
Mayo, MD 21106 • *2,537*
Mayodan, NC 27027 • *2,471*
Mays Landing, NJ 08330 • *2,090*
Maysville, KY 41056 • *7,169*
Maysville, MO 64469 • *1,176*
Maysville, OK 73057 • *1,203*
Mayville, MI 48744 • *1,010*
Mayville, NY 14757 • *1,636*
Mayville, ND 58257 • *2,092*
Mayville, WI 53050 • *4,374*
Maywood, CA 90270 • *27,850*
Maywood, IL 60153–54 • *27,139*
Maywood, NJ 07607 • *9,473*
Mazomanie, WI 53560 • *1,377*
McAdoo, PA 18237 • *2,459*
McAlester, OK 74501–02 • *16,370*
McAllen, TX 78501–04 • *84,021*
McAlmont, AR 72117 • *1,800*
McAlpine, MD 21043 • *2,230*
McArthur, OH 45651 • *1,541*
McCall, ID 83638 • *2,005*
McCamey, TX 79752 • *2,493*
McCandless, PA 15237 • *28,781*
McCaysville, GA 30555 • *1,065*
McClain □, OK • *22,795*
McCleary, WA 98557 • *1,235*
McCloud, CA 96057 • *1,555*
McClure, PA 17841 • *1,070*
McColl, SC 29570 • *2,685*
McComb, MS 39648 • *11,591*
McComb, OH 45858 • *1,544*
McCone □, MT • *2,276*
McConnellsburg, PA 17233 • *1,106*
McConnelsville, OH 43756 • *1,804*
McCook, NE 69001 • *8,112*
McCook □, SD • *5,688*
McCormick, SC 29835 • *1,659*
McCormick □, SC • *8,868*
McCracken □, KY • *62,879*
McCreary □, KY • *15,603*
McCrory, AR 72101 • *1,971*
McCulloch □, TX • *8,778*
McCurtain □, OK • *33,433*
McDermitt, NV 89421 • *373*
McDonald □, MO • *16,938*
McDonough, GA 30253 • *2,929*
McDonough □, IL • *35,244*
McDowell □, NC • *35,681*
McDowell □, WV • *35,233*
McDuffie □, GA • *20,119*
McEwen, TN 37101 • *1,442*
McFarland, CA 93250 • *7,005*
McFarland, WI 53558 • *5,232*
McGehee, AR 71654 • *4,997*
McGill, NV 89318 • *1,258*
McGrath, AK 99627 • *528*
McGraw, NY 13101 • *1,074*
McGregor, TX 76657 • *4,683*
McHenry, IL 60050–51 • *16,177*
McHenry □, IL • *183,241*
McHenry □, ND • *6,528*
McIntosh □, GA • *8,634*
McIntosh □, ND • *4,021*
McIntosh □, OK • *16,779*
McKean □, PA • *47,131*
McKee City, NJ 08232 • *1,200*
McKeesport, PA 15130–35 • *26,016*
McKees Rocks, PA 15136 • *7,691*
McKenzie, TN 38201 • *5,168*
McKenzie □, ND • *6,383*
McKinley □, NM • *60,686*
McKinleyville, CA 95521 • *10,749*
McKinney, TX 75069–70 • *21,283*
McLaughlin, SD 57642 • *780*
McLean, VA 22101 • *38,168*
McLean □, IL • *129,180*
McLean □, KY • *9,628*
McLean □, ND • *10,457*
McLeansboro, IL 62859 • *2,677*
McLennan □, TX • *189,123*
McLeod □, MN • *32,030*
McLoud, OK 74851 • *2,493*
McMechen, WV 26040 • *2,130*
McMinn □, TN • *42,383*
McMinnville, OR 97128 • *17,894*
McMinnville, TN 37110 • *11,194*
McMullen □, TX • *817*
McNairy □, TN • *22,422*
McPherson, KS 67460 • *12,422*
McPherson □, KS • *27,268*
McPherson □, NE • *546*
McPherson □, SD • *3,228*
McQueeney, TX 78123 • *2,063*
McRae, GA 31055 • *3,007*
McRoberts, KY 41835 • *1,101*
McSherrystown, PA 17344 • *2,769*
Mead, WA 99021 • *2,150*
Meade, KS 67864 • *1,526*
Meade □, KS • *4,247*
Meade □, KY • *24,170*
Meade □, SD • *21,878*
Meadowbrook, FL 32808 • *5,200*
Meadowood, DE 19711 • *2,100*
Meadville, PA 16335 • *14,318*
Meagher □, MT • *1,819*
Mebane, NC 27302 • *4,754*
Mecca, CA 92254 • *1,966*
Mechanic Falls, ME 04256 • *2,388*
Mechanicsburg, OH 43044 • *1,803*
Mechanicsburg, PA 17055 • *9,452*
Mechanicsville, IA 52306 • *1,012*
Mechanicsville, VA 23111 • *22,027*
Mechanicville, NY 12118 • *5,249*
Mecklenburg □, NC • *511,433*
Mecklenburg □, VA • *29,241*
Mecosta □, MI • *37,308*
Medfield, MA 02052 • *5,985*
Medford, MA 02155 • *57,407*
Medford, NJ 08055 • *1,800*
Medford, NY 11763 • *21,274*
Medford, OK 73759 • *1,172*
Medford, OR 97501–04 • *46,951*
Medford, WI 54451 • *4,283*
Medford Lakes, NJ 08055 • *4,462*
Media, PA 19063–65 • *5,957*
Mediapolis, IA 52637 • *1,637*
Medical Lake, WA 99022 • *3,664*
Medicine Bow, WY 82329 • *389*
Medicine Lodge, KS 67104 • *2,453*
Medina, NY 14103 • *6,686*
Medina, OH 44256 • *19,231*
Medina, WA 98039 • *2,981*
Medina □, OH • *122,354*
Medina □, TX • *27,312*
Medway, MA 02053 • *3,890*
Meeker, CO 81641 • *2,098*
Meeker, OK 74855 • *1,003*
Meeker □, MN • *20,846*
Meeteetse, WY 82433 • *368*
Mehlville, MO 63129 • *27,557*
Meigs, GA 31765 • *1,120*
Meigs □, OH • *22,987*
Meigs □, TN • *8,033*
Meiners Oaks, CA 93023 • *3,329*
Melbourne, AR 72556 • *1,562*
Melbourne, FL 32901–10 • *59,646*
Melbourne Beach, FL 32951 • *3,021*
Melcher, IA 50163 • *1,302*
Mellette □, SD • *2,137*
Melrose, FL 32666 • *1,700*
Melrose, MA 02176 • *28,150*
Melrose, MN 56352 • *2,561*
Melrose Park, FL 33312 • *6,477*
Melrose Park, IL 60160–63 • *20,859*
Melville, LA 71353 • *1,562*
Melville, NY 11747 • *12,586*
Melvindale, MI 48122 • *11,216*
Memphis, FL 34221 • *6,760*
Memphis, MI 48041 • *1,221*
Memphis, MO 63555 • *2,094*
Memphis, TN 38101–87 • *610,337*
Memphis, TX 79245 • *2,465*
Mena, AR 71953 • *5,475*
Menahga, MN 56464 • *1,076*
Menands, NY 12204 • *4,333*
Menard, TX 76859 • *1,606*
Menard □, IL • *11,164*
Menard □, TX • *2,252*
Menasha, WI 54952 • *14,711*
Mendenhall, MS 39114 • *2,463*
Mendham, NJ 07945 • *4,890*
Mendocino, CA 95460 • *1,008*
Mendocino □, CA • *80,345*
Mendota, CA 93640 • *6,821*
Mendota, IL 61342 • *7,018*
Mendota Heights, MN 55118 • *9,431*
Menifee □, KY • *5,092*
Menlo Park, CA 94025–28 • *28,040*
Menno, SD 57045 • *768*
Menominee, MI 49858 • *9,398*
Menominee □, MI • *24,920*
Menominee □, WI • *3,890*
Menomonee Falls, WI 53051–52 • *26,840*
Menomonie, WI 54751 • *13,547*
Mentor, OH 44060–61 • *47,358*
Mentor-on-the-Lake, OH 44060 • *8,271*
Mequon, WI 53092 • *18,885*
Meraux, LA 70075 • *8,000*
Merced, CA 95339–44 • *56,216*
Merced □, CA • *178,403*
Mercedes, TX 78570 • *12,694*
Mercer, PA 16137 • *2,444*
Mercer, WI 54547 • *1,300*
Mercer □, IL • *17,290*
Mercer □, KY • *19,148*
Mercer □, MO • *3,723*
Mercer □, NJ • *325,824*
Mercer □, ND • *9,808*
Mercer □, OH • *39,443*
Mercer □, PA • *121,003*
Mercer □, WV • *64,980*
Mercer Island, WA 98040 • *20,816*
Mercersburg, PA 17236 • *1,640*
Mercerville, NJ 08619 • *15,600*
Merchantville, NJ 08109 • *4,095*
Meredith, NH 03253 • *1,654*
Meredosia, IL 62665 • *1,134*
Meriden, CT 06450 • *59,479*
Meridian, ID 83642 • *9,596*
Meridian, MS 39301–09 • *41,036*
Meridian, PA 16001 • *3,473*
Meridian, TX 76665 • *1,390*
Meridian Hills, IN 46260 • *1,728*
Meridianville, AL 35759 • *2,852*
Meriwether □, GA • *22,411*
Merkel, TX 79536 • *2,469*
Merriam, KS 66203 • *11,821*
Merrick, NY 11566 • *23,042*
Merrick □, NE • *8,042*
Merrifield, VA 22031 • *8,399*
Merrill, WI 54452 • *9,860*
Merrillville, IN 46410 • *27,257*
Merrimac, MA 01860 • *2,050*
Merrimack, NH 03054 • *1,300*
Merrimack □, NH • *120,005*
Merritt Island, FL 32952–54 • *32,886*
Merryville, LA 70653 • *1,235*
Merton, WI 53056 • *1,199*
Mesa, AZ 85201–16 • *288,091*
Mesa □, CO • *93,145*
Mescalero, NM 88340 • *1,159*
Mesilla, NM 88046 • *1,975*
Mesquite, NV 89024 • *1,871*
Mesquite, TX 75149–50 • *101,484*
Metairie, LA 70001–11 • *149,428*
Metamora, IL 61548 • *2,520*
Metcalfe, MS 38760 • *1,092*
Metcalfe □, KY • *8,963*
Methuen, MA 01844 • *39,990*
Metlakatla, AK 99926 • *1,407*
Metropolis, IL 62960 • *6,734*
Metter, GA 30439 • *3,707*
Metuchen, NJ 08840 • *12,804*
Metzger, OR 97223 • *3,149*
Mexia, TX 76667 • *6,933*
Mexico, ME 04257 • *2,302*
Mexico, MO 65265 • *11,290*
Mexico, NY 13114 • *1,555*
Meyersdale, PA 15552 • *2,518*
Miami, AZ 85539 • *2,018*
Miami, FL 33101–99 • *358,548*
Miami, OK 74354–55 • *13,142*
Miami □, IN • *36,897*
Miami □, KS • *23,466*
Miami □, OH • *93,182*
Miami Beach, FL 33139 • *92,639*
Miami Lakes, FL 33014 • *12,750*
Miamisburg, OH 45342–43 • *17,834*
Miami Shores, FL 33138 • *10,084*
Miami Springs, FL 33166 • *13,268*
Micco, FL 32958 • *8,757*
Michigan Center, MI 49254 • *4,863*
Michigan City, IN 46360 • *33,822*
Middleboro (Middleborough Center), MA 02346 • *6,837*
Middleburg, FL 32068 • *6,223*
Middleburg, PA 17842 • *1,422*
Middleburgh, NY 12122 • *1,436*
Middleburg Heights, OH 44130 • *14,702*
Middlebury, CT 06762 • *4,140*
Middlebury, IN 46540 • *2,004*
Middlebury, VT 05753 • *6,007*
Middlefield, CT 06455 • *1,200*
Middlefield, OH 44062 • *1,898*
Middle Island, NY 11953 • *7,848*
Middleport, NY 14105 • *1,876*
Middleport, OH 45760 • *2,725*
Middle River, MD 21220 • *24,616*
Middlesboro, KY 40965 • *11,328*
Middlesex, NJ 08846 • *13,055*
Middlesex □, CT • *143,196*
Middlesex □, MA • *1,398,468*
Middlesex □, NJ • *671,780*
Middlesex □, VA • *8,653*
Middleton, ID 83644 • *1,851*
Middleton, MA 01949 • *4,135*
Middleton, WI 53562 • *13,289*
Middletown, CA 95461 • *2,000*
Middletown, CT 06457 • *42,762*
Middletown, DE 19709 • *3,834*
Middletown, IN 47356 • *2,333*
Middletown, KY 40243 • *5,016*
Middletown, MD 21769 • *1,834*
Middletown, NJ 07718 • *62,298*
Middletown, NY 10940 • *24,160*
Middletown, OH 45042–44 • *46,022*
Middletown, PA 17057 • *9,254*
Middletown, RI 02840 • *3,350*
Middletown, VA 22645 • *1,061*
Middletown Township, PA 19037 • *6,866*
Middleville, MI 49333 • *1,966*
Midfield, AL 35228 • *5,559*
Midland, MI 48640–42 • *38,053*
Midland, PA 15059 • *3,321*
Midland, TX 79701–12 • *89,443*
Midland □, MI • *75,651*
Midland □, TX • *106,611*
Midland City, AL 36350 • *1,819*
Midland Park, KS 67216 • *1,200*
Midland Park, NJ 07432 • *7,047*
Midland Park, SC 29405 • *1,300*
Midlothian, IL 60445 • *14,372*
Midlothian, TX 76065 • *5,141*
Midvale, UT 84047 • *11,886*
Midway, DE 19971 • *500*
Midway, KY 40347 • *1,290*
Midway, OR 97233 • *19,000*
Midway, PA 15060 • *1,043*
Midway, UT 84049 • *1,554*
Midwest, WY 82643 • *495*
Midwest City, OK 73110 • *52,267*
Mifflin □, PA • *46,197*
Mifflinburg, PA 17844 • *3,480*
Mifflinville, PA 18631 • *1,329*
Milaca, MN 56353 • *2,182*
Milam □, TX • *22,946*
Milan, GA 31060 • *1,056*
Milan, IL 61264 • *5,831*
Milan, IN 47031 • *1,529*
Milan, MI 48160 • *4,040*
Milan, MO 63556 • *1,767*
Milan, NM 87021 • *1,911*
Milan, OH 44846 • *1,464*
Milan, TN 38358 • *7,512*
Milbank, SD 57252 • *3,879*
Milesburg, PA 16853 • *1,144*
Miles City, MT 59301 • *8,461*
Milford, CT 06460 • *48,168*
Milford, DE 19963 • *6,040*
Milford, IL 60953 • *1,512*
Milford, IN 46542 • *1,388*
Milford, IA 51351 • *2,170*
Milford, ME 04461 • *2,228*
Milford, MA 01757 • *23,339*
Milford, MI 48380–82 • *5,511*
Milford, NE 68405 • *1,886*
Milford, NH 03055 • *8,015*
Milford, NJ 08848 • *1,273*
Milford, OH 45150 • *5,660*
Milford, PA 18337 • *1,064*
Milford, UT 84751 • *1,107*
Mililani Town, HI 96789 • *29,359*
Millard □, UT • *11,333*
Millbrae, CA 94030 • *20,412*
Millbrook, AL 36054 • *6,050*
Millbrook, NY 12545 • *1,339*
Millburn, NJ 07041 • *18,630*
Millbury, MA 01527 • *4,940*
Millbury, OH 43447 • *1,081*
Mill City, OR 97360 • *1,555*
Millcreek, UT 84109 • *32,230*
Millcreek Township, PA 16505 • *46,100*
Milledgeville, GA 31061 • *17,727*
Milledgeville, IL 61051 • *1,076*
Mille Lacs □, MN • *18,670*
Millen, GA 30442 • *3,808*
Miller, SD 57362 • *1,678*
Miller □, AR • *38,467*
Miller □, GA • *6,280*
Miller □, MO • *20,700*
Miller Place, NY 11764 • *9,315*
Millersburg, OH 44654 • *3,051*
Millersburg, PA 17061 • *2,729*
Millers Falls, MA 01349 • *1,084*
Millersport, OH 43046 • *1,010*
Millersville, PA 17551 • *8,099*
Mill Hall, PA 17751 • *1,702*
Milliken, CO 80543 • *1,605*
Millington, MI 48746 • *1,114*
Millington, TN 38053 • *17,866*
Millinocket, ME 04462 • *6,922*
Millis, MA 02054 • *3,777*
Millport, AL 35576 • *1,203*
Mills, WY 82644 • *1,574*
Mills □, IA • *13,202*
Mills □, TX • *4,531*
Millsboro, DE 19966 • *1,643*
Millstadt, IL 62260 • *2,566*
Milltown, NJ 08850 • *6,968*
Millvale, PA 15209 • *4,341*
Mill Valley, CA 94941–42 • *13,038*
Millville, MA 01529 • *1,693*
Millville, NJ 08332 • *25,992*
Millville, UT 84326 • *1,202*
Millwood, WA 99212 • *1,559*
Milnor, ND 58060 • *651*
Milo, ME 04463 • *2,129*
Milpitas, CA 95035–36 • *50,686*
Milroy, PA 17063 • *1,456*
Milstead, GA 30207 • *1,500*
Milton, DE 19968 • *1,417*
Milton, FL 32570–71 • *7,216*
Milton, MA 02186 • *25,725*
Milton, NH 03851 • *1,000*
Milton, NY 12547 • *1,140*
Milton, PA 17847 • *6,746*
Milton, VT 05468 • *1,578*
Milton, WA 98354 • *4,995*
Milton, WV 25541 • *2,242*
Milton, WI 53563 • *4,434*
Milton-Freewater, OR 97862 • *5,533*
Milwaukee, WI 53201–95 • *628,088*
Milwaukee □, WI • *959,275*
Milwaukie, OR 97222 • *18,692*
Mimosa Park, LA 70070 • *4,516*
Mims, FL 32754 • *9,412*
Mina, NV 89422 • *400*
Minco, OK 73059 • *1,411*
Minden, LA 71055 • *13,661*
Minden, NE 68959 • *2,749*
Minden, NV 89423 • *1,441*
Mine Hill, NJ 07801 • *3,250*
Mineola, NY 11501 • *18,994*
Mineola, TX 75773 • *4,321*
Miner, MO 63801 • *1,218*
Miner □, SD • *3,272*
Mineral □, CO • *558*
Mineral □, MT • *3,315*
Mineral □, NV • *6,475*
Mineral □, WV • *26,697*
Mineral Point, WI 53565 • *2,428*
Mineral Springs, AR 71851 • *1,004*
Mineral Wells, TX 76067 • *14,870*
Minersville, PA 17954 • *4,877*
Minerva, OH 44657 • *4,318*
Minetto, NY 13115 • *1,252*
Mineville, NY 12956 • *1,000*
Mingo □, WV • *33,739*
Mingo Junction, OH 43938 • *4,297*
Minidoka □, ID • *19,361*
Minier, IL 61759 • *1,155*
Minneapolis, KS 67467 • *1,983*
Minneapolis, MN 55401–80 • *368,383*
Minnehaha □, SD • *123,809*
Minneota, MN 56264 • *1,417*
Minnetonka, MN 55345 • *48,370*
Minocqua, WI 54548 • *1,280*
Minonk, IL 61760 • *1,982*
Minooka, IL 60447 • *2,561*
Minot, ND 58701–02 • *34,544*
Minquadale, DE 19720 • *790*
Minster, OH 45865 • *2,650*
Mint Hill, NC 28212 • *11,567*
Minturn, CO 81645 • *1,066*
Mio, MI 48647 • *1,500*
Mira Loma, CA 91752 • *15,786*
Miramar, FL 33023 • *40,663*
Misenheimer, NC 28109 • *1,000*
Mishawaka, IN 46544–46 • *42,608*
Mishicot, WI 54228 • *1,296*
Missaukee □, MI • *12,147*
Mission, KS 66205 • *9,504*
Mission, TX 78572 • *28,653*
Mission Hills, KS 66205 • *3,446*
Mission Viejo, CA 92691 • *72,820*
Mississippi □, AR • *57,525*
Mississippi □, MO • *14,442*
Mississippi State, MS 39762 • *12,400*
Missoula, MT 59801–07 • *42,918*
Missoula □, MT • *78,687*
Missouri City, TX 77459 • *36,176*
Missouri Valley, IA 51555 • *2,888*
Mitchell, IL 62040 • *1,320*
Mitchell, IN 47446 • *4,669*
Mitchell, NE 69357 • *1,743*
Mitchell, SD 57301 • *13,798*
Mitchell □, GA • *20,275*
Mitchell □, IA • *10,928*
Mitchell □, KS • *7,203*
Mitchell □, NC • *14,433*
Mitchell □, TX • *8,016*
Mitchellville, IA 50169 • *1,670*
Mizpah, NJ 08342 • *1,000*
Moab, UT 84532 • *3,971*
Moberly, MO 65270 • *12,839*
Mobile, AL 36601–95 • *196,278*
Mobile □, AL • *378,643*
Mobridge, SD 57601 • *3,768*
Mocanaqua, PA 18655 • *1,100*
Mocksville, NC 27028 • *3,399*
Modesto, CA 95350–56 • *164,730*
Modoc □, CA • *9,678*
Moenkopi, AZ 86045 • *1,200*
Moffat □, CO • *11,357*
Mogadore, OH 44260 • *4,008*
Mohall, ND 58761 • *931*
Mohave □, AZ • *93,497*
Mohawk, NY 13407 • *2,986*
Mohnton, PA 19540 • *2,484*
Mojave, CA 93501–02 • *3,763*
Mokena, IL 60448 • *6,128*
Molalla, OR 97038 • *3,651*
Moline, IL 61265 • *43,202*
Molino, FL 32577 • *1,207*
Momence, IL 60954 • *2,968*
Monaca, PA 15061 • *6,739*
Monahans, TX 79756 • *8,101*
Monarch Mills, SC 29379 • *2,214*
Moncks Corner, SC 29461 • *5,607*
Mondovi, WI 54755 • *2,491*
Monee, IL 60449 • *1,044*
Monessen, PA 15062 • *9,901*
Monett, MO 65708 • *6,529*
Monette, AR 72447 • *1,115*
Monfort Heights, OH 45239 • *9,745*
Moniteau □, MO • *12,298*
Monmouth, IL 61462 • *9,489*
Monmouth, OR 97361 • *6,288*
Monmouth □, NJ • *553,124*
Monmouth Beach, NJ 07750 • *3,303*
Monmouth Junction, NJ 08852 • *1,570*
Mono □, CA • *9,956*
Monon, IN 47959 • *1,585*
Monona, IA 52159 • *1,520*
Monona, WI 53716 • *8,637*
Monona □, IA • *10,034*
Monongah, WV 26554 • *1,018*
Monongahela, PA 15063 • *4,928*
Monongalia □, WV • *75,509*
Monroe, GA 30655 • *9,759*
Monroe, IA 50170 • *1,739*
Monroe, LA 71201–13 • *54,909*
Monroe, MI 48161 • *22,902*
Monroe, NY 10950 • *6,672*
Monroe, NC 28110–12 • *16,127*
Monroe, OH 45050 • *4,490*
Monroe, UT 84754 • *1,472*
Monroe, WA 98272 • *4,278*
Monroe, WI 53566 • *10,241*
Monroe □, AL • *23,968*
Monroe □, AR • *11,333*
Monroe □, FL • *78,024*
Monroe □, GA • *17,113*
Monroe □, IL • *22,422*
Monroe □, IN • *108,978*
Monroe □, IA • *8,114*
Monroe □, KY • *11,401*
Monroe □, MI • *133,600*
Monroe □, MS • *36,582*
Monroe □, MO • *9,104*
Monroe □, NY • *713,968*
Monroe □, OH • *15,497*
Monroe □, PA • *95,709*
Monroe □, TN • *30,541*
Monroe □, WV • *12,406*
Monroe □, WI • *36,633*
Monroe Center, CT 06468 • *7,900*
Monroe City, MO 63456 • *2,701*
Monroe Park, DE 19807 • *1,000*
Monroeville, AL 36460–61 • *6,993*
Monroeville, IN 46773 • *1,232*
Monroeville, OH 44847 • *1,381*
Monroeville, PA 15146 • *29,169*
Monrovia, CA 91016 • *35,761*
Monsey, NY 10952 • *13,986*
Monson, MA 01057 • *2,101*
Montague, CA 96064 • *1,415*
Montague, MI 49437 • *2,276*
Montague □, TX • *17,274*
Mont Alto, PA 17237 • *1,395*
Montauk, NY 11954 • *3,001*
Mont Belvieu, TX 77580 • *1,323*
Montcalm □, MI • *53,059*
Montchanin, DE 19710 • *500*
Montclair, CA 91763 • *28,434*
Montclair, NJ 07042–44 • *37,729*
Mont Clare, PA 19453 • *1,800*
Monteagle, TN 37356 • *1,138*
Montebello, CA 90640 • *59,564*
Montecito, CA 93108 • *9,300*

Montello, NV 89830 • 200
Montello, WI 53949 • 1,329
Monterey, CA 93940 • 31,954
Monterey, TN 38574 • 2,559
Monterey □, CA • 355,660
Monterey Park, CA 91754 • 60,738
Montesano, WA 98563 • 3,064
Montevallo, AL 35115 • 4,239
Montevideo, MN 56265 • 5,499
Monte Vista, CO 81144 • 4,324
Montezuma, GA 31063 • 4,506
Montezuma, IN 47862 • 1,134
Montezuma, IA 50171 • 1,651
Montezuma □, CO • 18,672
Montgomery, AL 36101–99 • 187,106
Montgomery, IL 60538 • 4,267
Montgomery, MN 56069 • 2,399
Montgomery, NY 12549 • 2,696
Montgomery, OH 45242 • 9,753
Montgomery, PA 17752 • 1,631
Montgomery, WV 25136 • 2,449
Montgomery □, AL • 209,085
Montgomery □, AR • 7,841
Montgomery □, GA • 7,163
Montgomery □, IL • 30,728
Montgomery □, IN • 34,436
Montgomery □, IA • 12,076
Montgomery □, KS • 38,816
Montgomery □, KY • 19,561
Montgomery □, MD • 757,027
Montgomery □, MS • 12,388
Montgomery □, MO • 11,355
Montgomery □, NY • 51,981
Montgomery □, NC • 23,346
Montgomery □, OH • 573,809
Montgomery □, PA • 678,111
Montgomery □, TN • 100,498
Montgomery □, TX • 182,201
Montgomery □, VA • 73,913
Montgomery City, MO 63361 • 2,281
Montgomery Village, MD 20879 • 32,315
Monticello, AR 71655 • 8,116
Monticello, FL 32344 • 2,573
Monticello, GA 31064 • 2,289
Monticello, IL 61856 • 4,549
Monticello, IN 47960 • 5,237
Monticello, IA 52310 • 3,522
Monticello, KY 42633 • 5,357
Monticello, MN 55362 • 4,941
Monticello, MS 39654 • 1,755
Monticello, NY 12701 • 6,597
Monticello, UT 84535 • 1,806
Monticello, WI 53570 • 1,140
Montmorency □, MI • 8,936
Montour □, PA • 17,735
Montour Falls, NY 14865 • 1,845
Montoursville, PA 17754 • 4,983
Montpelier, ID 83254 • 2,656
Montpelier, IN 47359 • 1,880
Montpelier, OH 43543 • 4,299
Montpelier, VT 05601–02 • 8,247
Montrose, AL 36559 • 1,400
Montrose, CO 81401–02 • 8,854
Montrose, MI 48457 • 1,811
Montrose, PA 18801 • 1,982
Montrose, VA 23231 • 6,405
Montrose □, CO • 24,423
Montvale, NJ 07645 • 6,946
Montville, CT 06353 • 16,673
Montville, NJ 07045 • 2,600
Monument, CO 80132 • 1,020
Monument Beach, MA 02553 • 1,800
Monument Heights, VA 23226 • 2,500
Moodus, CT 06469 • 1,170
Moody, TX 76557 • 1,329
Moody □, SD • 6,507
Moonachie, NJ 07074 • 2,817
Moorcroft, WY 82721 • 768
Moore, OK 73160 • 40,318
Moore □, NC • 59,013
Moore □, TN • 4,721
Moore □, TX • 17,865
Moorefield, WV 26836 • 2,148
Moore Haven, FL 33471 • 1,432
Mooreland, OK 73852 • 1,157
Moorestown, NJ 08057 • 16,500
Mooresville, IN 46158 • 5,541
Mooresville, NC 28115 • 9,317
Moorhead, MN 56560–61 • 32,295
Moorhead, MS 38761 • 2,417
Moorpark, CA 93020–21 • 25,494
Moose Lake, MN 55767 • 1,206
Moosic, PA 18507 • 5,339
Moosup, CT 06354 • 3,289
Mora, MN 55051 • 2,905
Mora, NM 87732 • 1,200
Mora □, NM • 4,264
Moraga, CA 94556 • 15,852
Moraine, OH 45439 • 5,989
Moravia, NY 13118 • 1,559
Morehead, KY 40351 • 8,357
Morehead City, NC 28557 • 6,046
Morehouse, MO 63868 • 1,068
Morehouse □, LA • 31,938
Morenci, AZ 85540 • 1,799
Morenci, MI 49256 • 2,342
Moreno Valley, CA 92387–88 • 118,779
Morgan, UT 84050 • 2,023
Morgan □, AL • 100,043
Morgan □, CO • 21,939
Morgan □, GA • 12,883
Morgan □, IL • 36,397
Morgan □, IN • 55,920
Morgan □, KY • 11,648
Morgan □, MO • 15,574
Morgan □, OH • 14,194
Morgan □, TN • 17,300
Morgan □, UT • 5,528
Morgan □, WV • 12,128
Morgan City, LA 70380–81 • 14,531
Morganfield, KY 42437 • 3,776
Morgan Hill, CA 95037–38 • 23,928
Morganton, NC 28655 • 15,085
Morgantown, KY 42261 • 2,284
Morgantown, MS 39120 • 3,288
Morgantown, WV 26502–07 • 25,879
Moriarty, NM 87035 • 1,399
Morningdale, MA 01505 • 1,130
Morocco, IN 47963 • 1,044
Moroni, UT 84646 • 1,115
Morrill □, NE • 5,423
Morrilton, AR 72110 • 6,551
Morris, AL 35116 • 1,136
Morris, IL 60450 • 10,270
Morris, MN 56267 • 5,613
Morris, OK 74445 • 1,216
Morris □, KS • 6,198
Morris □, NJ • 421,353
Morris □, TX • 13,200
Morrison, IL 61270 • 4,363
Morrison □, MN • 29,604
Morrison City, TN 37660 • 2,032
Morrisonville, IL 62546 • 1,113
Morrisonville, NY 12962 • 1,742
Morris Plains, NJ 07950 • 5,219
Morristown, NJ 07960–63 • 16,189
Morristown, TN 37813–15 • 21,385
Morrisville, NY 13408 • 2,732
Morrisville, PA 19067 • 9,765
Morrisville, VT 05661 • 1,984
Morro Bay, CA 93442–43 • 9,664
Morrow, GA 30260 • 5,168
Morrow, OH 45152 • 1,206
Morrow □, OH • 27,749
Morrow □, OR • 7,625
Morton, IL 61550 • 13,799
Morton, MS 39117 • 3,212
Morton, TX 79346 • 2,597
Morton, WA 98356 • 1,130
Morton □, KS • 3,480
Morton □, ND • 23,700
Morton Grove, IL 60053 • 22,408
Moscow, ID 83843 • 18,519
Moscow, PA 18444 • 1,527
Moses Lake, WA 98837 • 11,235
Mosheim, TN 37818 • 1,451
Mosinee, WI 54455 • 3,820
Moss Bluff, LA 70611 • 8,039
Moss Point, MS 39563 • 17,837
Motley □, TX • 1,532
Mott, ND 58646 • 1,019
Moulton, AL 35650 • 3,248
Moultrie, GA 31768 • 14,865
Moultrie □, IL • 13,930
Mound, MN 55364 • 9,634
Mound Bayou, MS 38762 • 2,222
Mound City, MO 64470 • 1,273
Moundridge, KS 67107 • 1,531
Mounds, IL 62964 • 1,407
Mounds View, MN 55432 • 12,541
Moundsville, WV 26041 • 10,753
Moundville, AL 35474 • 1,348
Mountainair, NM 87036 • 926
Mountain Brook, AL 35223 • 19,810
Mountain City, NV 89831 • 110
Mountain City, TN 37683 • 2,169
Mountain Grove, MO 65711 • 4,182
Mountain Home, AR 72653 • 9,027
Mountain Home, ID 83647 • 7,913
Mountain Iron, MN 55768 • 3,362
Mountain Lake, MN 56159 • 1,906
Mountain Lake Park, MD 21550 • 1,938
Mountain Lakes, NJ 07046 • 3,847
Mountain Park, GA 30087 • 11,025
Mountainside, NJ 07092 • 6,657
Mountain View, AR 72560 • 2,439
Mountain View, CA 94039–43 • 67,460
Mountain View, CO 80521 • 2,100
Mountain View, MO 65548 • 2,036
Mountain View, NM 87105 • 2,300
Mountain View, OK 73062 • 1,086
Mountain View, WY 82604 • 1,200
Mountain View, WY 82939 • 1,189
Mountain Village, AK 99632 • 674
Mount Airy, MD 21771 • 3,730
Mount Airy, NC 27030 • 7,156
Mount Angel, OR 97362 • 2,778
Mount Arlington, NJ 07856 • 3,630
Mount Ayr, IA 50854 • 1,796
Mount Carmel, IL 62863 • 8,287
Mount Carmel, PA 17851 • 7,196
Mount Carroll, IL 61053 • 1,726
Mount Clemens, MI 48043–46 • 18,405
Mount Dora, FL 32757 • 7,196
Mount Ephraim, NJ 08059 • 4,517
Mount Freedom, NJ 07970 • 1,920
Mount Gay, WV 25637 • 1,200
Mount Gilead, NC 27306 • 1,336
Mount Gilead, OH 43338 • 2,846
Mount Healthy, OH 45231 • 7,580
Mount Holly, NJ 08060 • 10,639
Mount Holly, NC 28120 • 7,710
Mount Holly Springs, PA 17065 • 1,925
Mount Hope, WV 25880 • 1,573
Mount Horeb, WI 53572 • 4,182
Mount Jackson, VA 22842 • 1,583
Mount Jewett, PA 16740 • 1,029
Mount Joy, PA 17552 • 6,398
Mount Juliet, TN 37122 • 5,389
Mount Kisco, NY 10549 • 9,108
Mountlake Terrace, WA 98043 • 19,320
Mount Lebanon, PA 15228 • 33,362
Mount Morris, IL 61054 • 2,919
Mount Morris, MI 48458 • 3,292
Mount Morris, NY 14510 • 3,102
Mount Olive, AL 35117 • 2,270
Mount Olive, IL 62069 • 2,126
Mount Olive, NC 28365 • 4,582
Mount Olympus, UT 84117 • 7,413
Mount Orab, OH 45154 • 1,929
Mount Penn, PA 19606 • 2,883
Mount Pleasant, IA 52641 • 8,027
Mount Pleasant, MI 48858–59 • 23,285
Mount Pleasant, NC 28124 • 1,027
Mount Pleasant, PA 15666 • 4,787
Mount Pleasant, SC 29464–65 • 30,108
Mount Pleasant, TN 38474 • 4,278
Mount Pleasant, TX 75455 • 12,291
Mount Pleasant, UT 84647 • 2,092
Mount Pocono, PA 18344 • 1,795
Mount Prospect, IL 60056 • 53,170
Mount Pulaski, IL 62548 • 1,610
Mountrail □, ND • 7,021
Mount Rainier, MD 20712 • 7,954
Mount Savage, MD 21545 • 1,640
Mount Shasta, CA 96067 • 3,460
Mount Sinai, NY 11766 • 8,023
Mount Sterling, IL 62353 • 1,922
Mount Sterling, KY 40353 • 5,362
Mount Sterling, OH 43143 • 1,647
Mount Union, PA 17066 • 2,878
Mount Vernon, GA 30445 • 1,914
Mount Vernon, IL 62864 • 16,988
Mount Vernon, IN 47620 • 7,217
Mount Vernon, IA 52314 • 3,657
Mount Vernon, KY 40456 • 2,654
Mount Vernon, MO 65712 • 3,726
Mount Vernon, NY 10550–53 • 67,153
Mount Vernon, OH 43050 • 14,550
Mount Vernon, TX 75457 • 2,219
Mount Vernon, WA 98273 • 17,647
Mount View, RI 02852 • 610
Mount Washington, KY 40047 • 5,226
Mount Wolf, PA 17347 • 1,365
Mount Zion, IL 62549 • 4,522
Moville, IA 51039 • 1,306
Moweaqua, IL 62550 • 1,785
Mower □, MN • 37,385
Moyock, NC 27958 • 1,400
Muenster, TX 76252 • 1,387
Muhlenberg □, KY • 31,318
Mukilteo, WA 98275 • 7,007
Mukwonago, WI 53149 • 4,457
Mulberry, AR 72947 • 1,448
Mulberry, FL 33860 • 2,988
Mulberry, IN 46058 • 1,262
Mulberry, NC 28659 • 2,339
Muldraugh, KY 40155 • 1,376
Muldrow, OK 74948 • 2,889
Muleshoe, TX 79347 • 4,571
Mullan, ID 83846 • 821
Mullens, WV 25882 • 2,006
Mullica Hill, NJ 08062 • 1,117
Mullins, SC 29574 • 5,910
Multnomah □, OR • 583,887
Mulvane, KS 67110 • 4,674
Muncie, IN 47302–08 • 71,035
Muncy, PA 17756 • 2,702
Munday, TX 76371 • 1,600
Mundelein, IL 60060 • 21,215
Munford, TN 38058 • 2,326
Munfordville, KY 42765 • 1,556
Munhall, PA 15120 • 13,158
Munising, MI 49862 • 2,783
Munster, IN 46321 • 19,949
Murfreesboro, AR 71958 • 1,542
Murfreesboro, NC 27855 • 2,580
Murfreesboro, TN 37129–33 • 44,922
Murphy, MO 63026 • 9,342
Murphy, NC 28906 • 1,575
Murphys, CA 95247 • 1,517
Murphysboro, IL 62966 • 9,176
Murray, KY 42071 • 14,439
Murray, UT 84107 • 31,282
Murray □, GA • 26,147
Murray □, MN • 9,660
Murray □, OK • 12,042
Murrells Inlet, SC 29576 • 3,334
Murrysville, PA 15668 • 17,240
Muscatine, IA 52761 • 22,881
Muscatine □, IA • 39,907
Muscle Shoals, AL 35661 • 9,611
Muscoda, WI 53573 • 1,287
Muscogee □, GA • 179,278
Muscoy, CA 92405 • 7,541
Muse, PA 15350 • 1,250
Muskego, WI 53150 • 16,813
Muskegon, MI 49440–45 • 40,283
Muskegon □, MI • 158,983
Muskegon Heights, MI 49444 • 13,176
Muskingum □, OH • 82,068
Muskogee, OK 74401–03 • 37,708
Muskogee □, OK • 68,078
Musselshell □, MT • 4,106
Mustang, OK 73064 • 10,434
Myerstown, PA 17067 • 3,236
Myrtle Beach, SC 29577–78 • 24,848
Myrtle Grove, FL 32506 • 17,402
Myrtle Point, OR 97458 • 2,712
Mystic, CT 06355 • 2,618
Mystic Island, NJ 08087 • 7,400

N

Naalehu, HI 96772 • 1,027
Naamans Gardens, DE 19810 • 1,500
Nabnasset, MA 01886 • 3,600
Nacogdoches, TX 75961–63 • 30,872
Nacogdoches □, TX • 54,753
Nags Head, NC 27959 • 1,838
Nahant, MA 01908 • 3,828
Nahunta, GA 31553 • 1,049
Nampa, ID 83651–53 • 28,365
Nanakuli, HI 96792 • 9,575
Nance □, NE • 4,275
Nanticoke, PA 18634 • 12,267
Nantucket, MA 02554 • 3,069
Nantucket □, MA • 6,012
Nanty Glo, PA 15943 • 3,190
Nanuet, NY 10954 • 14,065
Napa, CA 94558–59 • 61,842
Napa □, CA • 110,765
Napanoch, NY 12458 • 1,068
Naperville, IL 60540 • 85,351
Naples, FL 33939–42 • 19,505
Naples, NY 14512 • 1,237
Naples, TX 75568 • 1,508
Naples, UT 84078 • 1,334
Naples Park, FL 33963 • 8,002
Napoleon, ND 58561 • 930
Napoleon, OH 43545 • 8,884
Nappanee, IN 46550 • 5,510
Naranja, FL 33032 • 5,790
Narberth, PA 19072 • 4,278
Narragansett, RI 02882 • 3,721
Narrows, VA 24124 • 2,082
Naselle, WA 98638 • 1,000
Nash, TX 75569 • 2,162
Nash □, NC • 76,677
Nashua, IA 50658 • 1,476
Nashua, NH 03060–63 • 79,662
Nashville, AR 71852 • 4,639
Nashville, GA 31639 • 4,782
Nashville, IL 62263 • 3,202
Nashville, MI 49073 • 1,654
Nashville, NC 27856 • 3,617
Nashville, TN 37201–35 • 487,969
Nashwauk, MN 55769 • 1,026
Nassau, NY 12123 • 1,254
Nassau □, FL • 43,941
Nassau □, NY • 1,287,348
Nassau Shores, NY 11758 • 5,110
Natalia, TX 78059 • 1,216
Natchez, MS 39120–22 • 19,460
Natchitoches, LA 71457–58 • 16,609
Natchitoches □, LA • 36,689
Natick, MA 01760 • 30,100
National City, CA 91950–51 • 54,249
National Park, NJ 08063 • 3,413
Natrona □, WY • 61,226
Natrona Heights, PA 15065 • 12,200
Naugatuck, CT 06770 • 30,625
Nautilus Park, CT 06340 • 6,500
Nauvoo, IL 62354 • 1,108
Navajo □, AZ • 77,658
Navarre, OH 44662 • 1,635
Navarro □, TX • 39,926
Navasota, TX 77868–69 • 6,296
Navesink, NJ 07752 • 1,420
Nazareth, PA 18064 • 5,713
Neah Bay, WA 98357 • 1,300
Nebraska City, NE 68410 • 6,547
Nederland, CO 80466 • 1,099
Nederland, TX 77627 • 16,192
Nedrow, NY 13120 • 2,980
Needham, MA 02192 • 27,557
Needles, CA 92363 • 5,191
Needville, TX 77461 • 2,199
Neenah, WI 54956–57 • 23,219
Neffs, OH 43940 • 1,213
Negaunee, MI 49866 • 4,741
Neillsville, WI 54456 • 2,680
Nekoosa, WI 54457 • 2,557
Neligh, NE 68756 • 1,742
Nelson □, KY • 29,710
Nelson □, ND • 4,410
Nelson □, VA • 12,778
Nelsonville, OH 45764 • 4,563
Nemacolin, PA 15351 • 1,097
Nemaha □, KS • 10,446
Nemaha □, NE • 7,980
Nenana, AK 99760 • 393
Neodesha, KS 66757 • 2,837
Neoga, IL 62447 • 1,678
Neosho, MO 64850 • 9,254
Neosho □, KS • 17,035
Nephi, UT 84648 • 3,515
Neptune, NJ 07753 • 28,366
Neptune Beach, FL 32233 • 6,816
Neptune City, NJ 07753 • 4,997
Nesconset, NY 11767 • 10,712
Nescopeck, PA 18635 • 1,651
Neshoba □, MS • 24,800
Nesquehoning, PA 18240 • 3,364
Ness □, KS • 4,033
Ness City, KS 67560 • 1,724
Netcong, NJ 07857 • 3,311
Nether Providence Township, PA 19013 • 13,229
Nettleton, MS 38858 • 2,462
Nevada, IA 50201 • 6,009
Nevada, MO 64772 • 8,597
Nevada □, AR • 10,101
Nevada □, CA • 78,510
Nevada City, CA 95959 • 2,855
New Albany, IN 47150–51 • 36,322
New Albany, MS 38652 • 6,775
New Albany, OH 43054 • 1,621
Newark, AR 72562 • 1,159
Newark, CA 94560 • 37,861
Newark, DE 19711–15 • 25,098
Newark, NJ 07101–75 • 275,221
Newark, NY 14513 • 9,849
Newark, OH 43055–58 • 44,389
Newark Valley, NY 13811 • 1,082
New Athens, IL 62264 • 2,010
Newaygo, MI 49337 • 1,336
Newaygo □, MI • 38,202
New Baden, IL 62265 • 2,602
New Baltimore, MI 48047 • 5,798
New Bedford, MA 02740–48 • 99,922
Newberg, OR 97132 • 13,086
New Berlin, NY 13411 • 1,220
New Berlin, WI 53151 • 33,592
New Bern, NC 28560–64 • 17,363
Newbern, TN 38059 • 2,515
Newberry, FL 32669 • 1,644
Newberry, MI 49868 • 1,873
Newberry, SC 29108 • 10,542
Newberry □, SC • 33,172
New Bethlehem, PA 16242 • 1,151
New Bloomfield, PA 17068 • 1,092
New Boston, MI 48164 • 1,200
New Boston, OH 45662 • 2,717
New Boston, TX 75570 • 5,057
New Braunfels, TX 78130–33 • 27,334
New Bremen, OH 45869 • 2,558
New Brighton, MN 55112 • 22,207
New Brighton, PA 15066 • 6,854
New Britain, CT 06050–53 • 75,491
New Brockton, AL 36351 • 1,184
New Brunswick, NJ 08901–06 • 41,711
New Buffalo, MI 49117 • 2,317
Newburg, KY 40218 • 21,647
Newburgh, IN 47629–30 • 2,880
Newburgh, NY 12550–53 • 26,454
Newburgh Heights, OH 44105 • 2,310
Newburyport, MA 01950–52 • 16,317
New Canaan, CT 06840 • 17,864
New Carlisle, IN 46552 • 1,446
New Carlisle, OH 45344 • 6,049
New Carrollton, MD 20784 • 12,002
New Cassel, NY 11590 • 10,257
New Castle, AL 35119 • 1,100
New Castle, DE 19720 • 4,837
New Castle, IN 47362 • 17,753
Newcastle, OK 73065 • 4,214
New Castle, PA 16101–08 • 28,334
Newcastle, WY 82701 • 3,003
New Castle □, DE • 441,946
New City, NY 10956 • 33,673
Newcomerstown, OH 43832 • 4,012
New Concord, OH 43762 • 2,086
New Cumberland, PA 17070 • 7,665
New Cumberland, WV 26047 • 1,363
New Egypt, NJ 08533 • 2,327
Newell, IA 50568 • 1,089
Newell, WV 26050 • 1,724
New Ellenton, SC 29809 • 2,515
Newellton, LA 71357 • 1,576
New England, ND 58647 • 663
New Fairfield, CT 06812 • 4,600
Newfane, NY 14108 • 3,001
Newfield, NJ 08344 • 1,592
New Franklin, MO 65274 • 1,107
New Freedom, PA 17349 • 2,920
New Glarus, WI 53574 • 1,899
New Hampton, IA 50659 • 3,660
New Hanover □, NC • 120,284
New Hartford, CT 06057 • 1,269
New Haven, CT 06501–36 • 130,474
New Haven, IN 46774 • 9,320
New Haven, MI 48048 • 2,331
New Haven, MO 63068 • 1,757
New Haven, WV 25265 • 1,632
New Haven □, CT • 804,219
New Holland, GA 30501 • 1,200
New Holland, PA 17557 • 4,484
New Holstein, WI 53061 • 3,342
New Hope, AL 35760 • 2,248
New Hope, MN 55428 • 21,853
New Hope, NC 27604 • 5,694
New Hope, PA 18938 • 1,400
New Hyde Park, NY 11040 • 9,728
New Iberia, LA 70560–62 • 31,828
Newington, CT 06131 • 29,208
Newington, VA 22122 • 17,965
New Johnsonville, TN 37134 • 1,643
New Kensington, PA 15068 • 15,894
New Kent □, VA • 10,445
Newkirk, OK 74647 • 2,168
New Lenox, IL 60451 • 9,627
New Lexington, OH 43764 • 5,117
New Lisbon, WI 53950 • 1,491
Newllano, LA 71461 • 2,660
New London, CT 06320 • 28,540
New London, IA 52645 • 1,922
New London, NH 03257 • 3,180
New London, OH 44851 • 2,642
New London, WI 54961 • 6,658
New London □, CT • 254,957
New Madrid, MO 63869 • 3,350
New Madrid □, MO • 20,928
Newman, CA 95360 • 4,151
Newmanstown, PA 17073 • 1,410
Newmarket, NH 03857 • 4,917
New Market, TN 37820 • 1,086
New Market, VA 22844 • 1,435
New Martinsville, WV 26155 • 6,705
New Matamoras, OH 45767 • 1,002
New Miami, OH 45011 • 2,555
New Milford, CT 06776 • 5,775
New Milford, NJ 07646 • 15,990
Newnan, GA 30263–65 • 12,497
New Orleans, LA 70101–95 • 496,938
New Oxford, PA 17350 • 1,617
New Paltz, NY 12561 • 5,463
New Paris, IN 46553 • 1,007
New Paris, OH 45347 • 1,801
New Philadelphia, OH 44663 • 15,698
New Philadelphia, PA 17959 • 1,283
New Plymouth, ID 83655 • 1,313
Newport, AR 72112 • 7,459
Newport, DE 19804 • 1,240
Newport, KY 41071–76 • 18,871
Newport, ME 04953 • 1,843
Newport, MI 48166 • 1,100
Newport, MN 55055 • 3,720
Newport, NH 03773 • 3,772
Newport, NC 28570 • 2,516
Newport, OR 97365 • 8,437
Newport, PA 17074 • 1,568
Newport, RI 02840 • 28,227
Newport, TN 37821 • 7,123
Newport, VT 05855 • 4,434
Newport, WA 99156 • 1,691
Newport □, RI • 87,194
Newport Beach, CA 92657–63 • 66,643
Newport East, RI 02840 • 11,080
Newport Hills, WA 98002 • 14,736
Newport News, VA 23601–09 • 170,045
New Port Richey, FL 34652–56 • 14,044
New Prague, MN 56071 • 3,569
New Preston, CT 06777 • 1,217
New Providence, NJ 07974 • 11,439
New Richland, MN 56072 • 1,237
New Richmond, OH 45157 • 2,408
New Richmond, WI 54017 • 5,106
New River Station, NC 28542 • 9,732
New Roads, LA 70760 • 5,303
New Rochelle, NY 10801–05 • 67,265
New Rockford, ND 58356 • 1,604
New Salem, ND 58563 • 909
New Sarpy, LA 70078 • 2,946
New Sharon, IA 50207 • 1,136
New Smyrna Beach, FL 32168–70 • 16,543
New Tazewell, TN 37825 • 1,864
Newton, AL 36352 • 1,580
Newton, IL 62448 • 3,154
Newton, IA 50208 • 14,789
Newton, KS 67114 • 16,700
Newton, MA 02158 • 82,585
Newton, MS 39345 • 3,701
Newton, NJ 07860 • 7,521
Newton, NC 28658 • 9,304
Newton, TX 75966 • 1,885
Newton □, AR • 7,666
Newton □, GA • 41,808
Newton □, IN • 13,551
Newton □, MS • 20,291
Newton □, MO • 44,445
Newton □, TX • 13,569
Newton Falls, OH 44444 • 4,866
Newtown, CT 06470 • 1,800
New Town, ND 58763 • 1,388
Newtown, OH 45244 • 1,589
Newtown Square, PA 19073 • 11,366
New Ulm, MN 56073 • 13,132
Newville, PA 17241 • 1,349
New Washington, OH 44854 • 1,057
New Washoe City, NV 89701 • 2,875
New Waterford, OH 44445 • 1,278
New Whiteland, IN 46184 • 4,097
New Wilmington, PA 16142 • 2,706
New Windsor, NY 12553 • 8,898
New York, NY 10001–99 • 7,322,564
New York □, NY • 1,487,536
Nez Perce □, ID • 33,754
Niagara, WI 54151 • 1,999
Niagara □, NY • 220,756
Niagara Falls, NY 14301–05 • 61,840
Niantic, CT 06357 • 3,048
Nibley, UT 84321 • 1,167
Niceville, FL 32578 • 10,507
Nicholas □, KY • 6,725
Nicholas □, WV • 26,775
Nicholasville, KY 40356 • 13,603
Nicholls, GA 31554 • 1,003
Nichols Hills, OK 73116 • 4,020
Nickerson, KS 67561 • 1,137
Nicollet □, MN • 28,076
Nicoma Park, OK 73066 • 2,353
Nikishka, AK 99635 • 1,109
Niland, CA 92257 • 1,183

Niles, IL 60648 • 28,284
Niles, MI 49120 • 12,458
Niles, OH 44446 • 21,128
Ninety Six, SC 29666 • 2,099
Ninilchik, AK 99639 • 456
Niobrara □, WY • 2,499
Nipomo, CA 93444 • 7,109
Niskayuna, NY 12309 • 4,942
Nisswa, MN 56468 • 1,391
Nitro, WV 25143 • 6,851
Niwot, CO 80544 • 2,666
Nixa, MO 65714 • 4,707
Nixon, NV 89424 • 150
Nixon, TX 78140 • 1,995
Noank, CT 06340 • 1,406
Noble, OK 73068 • 4,710
Noble □, IN • 37,877
Noble □, OH • 11,336
Noble □, OK • 11,045
Nobles □, MN • 20,098
Noblesville, IN 46060 • 17,655
Nocatee, FL 33864 • 1,300
Nocona, TX 76255 • 2,870
Nodaway □, MO • 21,709
Noel, MO 64854 • 1,169
Nogales, AZ 85621 • 19,489
Nokomis, FL 34274–75 • 3,448
Nokomis, IL 62075 • 2,534
Nolan □, TX • 16,594
Nome, AK 99762 • 3,500
Noorvik, AK 99763 • 531
Nora Springs, IA 50458 • 1,505
Norco, CA 91760 • 23,302
Norco, LA 70079 • 3,385
Norcross, GA 30071 • 5,947
Norfolk, CT 06058 • 1,500
Norfolk, NE 68701 • 21,476
Norfolk, NY 13667 • 1,412
Norfolk, VA 23501–93 • 261,229
Norfolk □, MA • 616,087
Norland, FL 33169 • 22,109
Normal, IL 61761 • 40,023
Norman, OK 73069–72 • 80,071
Norman □, MN • 7,975
Normandy, MO 63121 • 4,480
Norridge, IL 60656 • 14,459
Norridgewock, ME 04957 • 1,496
Norris, TN 37828 • 1,303
Norris City, IL 62869 • 1,341
Norristown, PA 19401–09 • 30,749
North Adams, MA 01247 • 16,797
North Albany, OR 97321 • 4,325
North Amherst, MA 01059 • 6,239
North Amityville, NY 11701 • 13,849
Northampton, MA 01060–61 • 29,289
Northampton, PA 18067 • 8,717
Northampton □, NC • 20,798
Northampton □, PA • 247,105
Northampton □, VA • 13,061
North Andover, MA 01845 • 20,129
North Andrews Gardens, FL 33308 • 9,002
North Apollo, PA 15673 • 1,391
North Arlington, NJ 07032 • 13,790
North Atlanta, GA 30319 • 27,812
North Attleboro, MA 02760–63 • 16,178
North Auburn, CA 95603 • 10,301
North Augusta, SC 29841 • 15,351
North Aurora, IL 60542 • 5,940
North Babylon, NY 11703 • 18,081
North Baltimore, OH 45872 • 3,139
North Bay Shore, NY 11706 • 12,799
North Beach, MD 20714 • 1,173
North Bellmore, NY 11710 • 19,707
North Bellport, NY 11713 • 8,182
North Belmont, NC 28012 • 10,762
North Bend, NE 68649 • 1,249
North Bend, OR 97459 • 9,614
North Bend, WA 98045 • 2,578
North Bennington, VT 05257 • 1,520
North Bergen, NJ 07047 • 48,414
North Berwick, ME 03906 • 1,568
North Billerica, MA 01862 • 5,400
Northborough, MA 01532 • 5,761
North Braddock, PA 15104 • 7,036
North Branch, MI 48461 • 1,023
North Branch, MN 55056 • 1,867
North Branch, NJ 08876 • 2,620
North Branford, CT 06471 • 6,600
Northbridge, MA 01534 • 3,570
Northbrook, IL 60062 • 32,308
Northbrook, OH 45231 • 11,471
North Brookfield, MA 01535 • 2,635
North Brunswick, NJ 08902 • 31,287
North Brunswick Township, NJ 08902 • 31,287
North Caldwell, NJ 07006 • 5,832
North Canton, OH 44720 • 14,748
North Cape May, NJ 08204 • 3,574
North Charleston, SC 29406 • 70,218
North Chicago, IL 60064 • 34,978
North City, WA 98155 • 8,200
North Cohasset, MA 02025 • 1,045
North College Hill, OH 45239 • 11,002
North Collins, NY 14111 • 1,335
North Conway, NH 03860 • 2,032
North Corbin, KY 40701 • 1,601
North Crossett, AR 71635 • 3,358
North Dartmouth, MA 02747 • 8,080
North Decatur, GA 30033 • 13,936
North Dighton, MA 02764 • 1,174
North Druid Hills, GA 30033 • 14,170
North Eagle Butte, SD 57625 • 1,423
North East, MD 21901 • 1,913
North East, PA 16428 • 4,617
North Eastham, MA 02651 • 1,570
Northeast Henrietta, NY 14534 • 10,650
North Easton, MA 02356 • 4,420
North Fair Oaks, CA 94025 • 13,912
North Falmouth, MA 02556 • 3,150
Northfield, IL 60093 • 4,635
Northfield, MA 01360 • 1,322
Northfield, MN 55057 • 14,684
Northfield, NH 03276 • 1,375
Northfield, NJ 08225 • 7,305
Northfield, OH 44067 • 3,624
Northfield, VT 05663 • 1,889
Northfield Falls, VT 05664 • 600
North Fond du Lac, WI 54935 • 4,292
Northford, CT 06472 • 3,180
North Fort Myers, FL 33903 • 30,027
Northglenn, CO 80233 • 27,195
North Grafton, MA 01536 • 3,050
North Great River, NY 11722 • 3,964
North Grosvenordale, CT 06255 • 1,705
North Gulfport, MS 39501 • 4,966
North Haledon, NJ 07508 • 7,987
North Hampton, NH 03862 • 1,000
North Haven, CT 06473 • 22,249
North Highlands, CA 95660 • 42,105
North Hill, WA 98166 • 5,706
North Houston, TX 77086 • 12,800
North Hudson, WI 54016 • 3,101
North Industry, OH 44707 • 3,250
North Judson, IN 46366 • 1,582
North Kansas City, MO 64116 • 4,130
North Kingstown, RI 02852–54 • 2,750
North Kingsville, OH 44068 • 2,672
North La Junta, CO 81050 • 1,076
Northlake, IL 60164 • 12,505
North Las Vegas, NV 89030–31 • 47,707
North Lauderdale, FL 33068 • 26,506
North Lewisburg, OH 43060 • 1,160
North Liberty, IN 46554 • 1,366
North Liberty, IA 52317 • 2,926
North Lindenhurst, NY 11757 • 10,563
North Little Rock, AR 72114–20 • 61,741
North Logan, UT 84321 • 3,768
North Madison, OH 44057 • 8,699
North Manchester, IN 46962 • 6,383
North Mankato, MN 56001 • 10,164
North Massapequa, NY 11758 • 19,365
North Merrick, NY 11566 • 12,113
North Merrydale, LA 70812 • 4,000
North Miami, FL 33161 • 49,998
North Miami Beach, FL 33162 • 35,359
North Muskegon, MI 49445 • 3,919
North Myrtle Beach, SC 29582 • 8,636
North Naples, FL 33963 • 13,422
North New Hyde Park, NY 11040 • 14,359
North Ogden, UT 84404 • 11,668
North Olmsted, OH 44070 • 34,204
North Oxford, MA 01537 • 1,250
North Palm Beach, FL 33408 • 11,343
North Park, IL 61111 • 15,806
North Patchogue, NY 11772 • 7,374
North Pembroke, MA 02358 • 2,485
North Plainfield, NJ 07060 • 18,820
North Platte, NE 69101–03 • 22,605
Northport, AL 35476 • 17,366
North Port, FL 34287 • 11,973
Northport, NY 11768 • 7,572
North Prairie, WI 53153 • 1,322
North Providence, RI 02911 • 32,090
North Reading, MA 01864 • 11,455
North Richland Hills, TX 76118 • 45,895
Northridge, OH 45502 • 5,939
Northridge, OH 45414 • 9,448
North Ridgeville, OH 44039 • 21,564
North Riverside, IL 60546 • 6,005
North Royalton, OH 44133 • 23,197
North Salt Lake, UT 84054 • 6,474
North Sarasota, FL 34234 • 6,702
North Scituate, MA 02060 • 4,891
North Sioux City, SD 57049 • 2,019
North Springfield, OR 97477 • 5,451
North Springfield, VT 05150 • 750
North Springfield, VA 22151 • 8,996
North Star, DE 19711 • 1,030
North St. Paul, MN 55109 • 12,376
North Sudbury, MA 01776 • 2,630
North Syracuse, NY 13212 • 7,363
North Tarrytown, NY 10591 • 8,152
North Terre Haute, IN 47805 • 2,000
North Tewksbury, MA 01876 • 1,030
North Tonawanda, NY 14120 • 34,989
North Troy, VT 05859 • 723
North Tunica, MS 38676 • 1,314
Northumberland, PA 17857 • 3,860
Northumberland □, PA • 96,771
Northumberland □, VA • 10,524
North Uxbridge, MA 01538 • 1,500
Northvale, NJ 07647 • 4,563
North Valley Stream, NY 11580 • 14,574
North Vernon, IN 47265 • 5,311
North Versailles, PA 15137 • 12,302
Northview, MI 49505 • 13,712
Northview, OH 45322 • 10,337
Northville, MI 48167 • 6,226
Northville, NY 12134 • 1,180
North Wales, PA 19454 • 3,802
North Wantagh, NY 11793 • 12,276
North Warren, PA 16365 • 1,232
North Wildwood, NJ 08260 • 5,017
North Wilkesboro, NC 28659 • 3,384
North Windham, ME 04062 • 4,077
Northwood, IA 50459 • 1,940
Northwood, ND 58267 • 1,166
Northwood, OH 43619 • 5,506
Northwoods, MO 63121 • 5,106
North York, PA 17404 • 1,689
Norton, KS 67654 • 3,017
Norton, MA 02766 • 1,899
Norton, OH 44203 • 11,477
Norton, VA 24273 • 4,247
Norton □, KS • 5,947
Norton Shores, MI 49441 • 21,755
Nortonville, KY 42442 • 1,209
Norwalk, CA 90650–52 • 94,279
Norwalk, CT 06850–56 • 78,331
Norwalk, IA 50211 • 5,726
Norwalk, OH 44857 • 14,731
Norway, ME 04268 • 3,023
Norway, MI 49870 • 2,910
Norwell, MA 02061 • 1,200
Norwich, CT 06360 • 37,391
Norwich, NY 13815 • 7,613
Norwich, VT 05055 • 1,000
Norwood, MA 02062 • 28,700
Norwood, MN 55368 • 1,351
Norwood, NJ 07648 • 4,858
Norwood, NY 13668 • 1,841
Norwood, NC 28128 • 1,617
Norwood, OH 45212 • 23,674
Norwood, PA 19074 • 6,162
Norwoodville, IA 50317 • 1,200
Nottoway □, VA • 14,993
Novato, CA 94947–49 • 47,585
Novi, MI 48374–77 • 32,998
Nowata, OK 74048 • 3,896
Nowata □, OK • 9,992
Noxubee □, MS • 12,604
Nuckolls □, NE • 5,786
Nueces □, TX • 291,145
Nulato, AK 99765 • 359
Nunda, NY 14517 • 1,347
Nutley, NJ 07110 • 27,099
Nutter Fort, WV 26301 • 1,819
Nutting Lake, MA 01865 • 3,180
Nyack, NY 10960 • 6,558
Nye □, NV • 17,781
Nyssa, OR 97913 • 2,629

O

Oak Bluffs, MA 02557 • 1,124
Oak Brook, IL 60521 • 9,178
Oak Creek, WI 53154 • 19,513
Oakdale, CA 95361 • 11,961
Oakdale, GA 30080 • 1,080
Oakdale, LA 71463 • 6,832
Oakdale, MN 55128 • 18,374
Oakdale, NY 11769 • 7,875
Oakdale, PA 15071 • 1,752
Oakes, ND 58474 • 1,775
Oakfield, NY 14125 • 1,818
Oakfield, WI 53065 • 1,003
Oak Forest, IL 60452 • 26,203
Oak Grove, KY 42262 • 2,863
Oak Grove, LA 71263 • 2,126
Oak Grove, OR 97267 • 12,576
Oak Grove, SC 29073 • 7,173
Oak Harbor, OH 43449 • 2,637
Oak Harbor, WA 98277 • 17,176
Oak Hill, MI 49660 • 1,000
Oak Hill, OH 45656 • 1,831
Oak Hill, WV 25901 • 6,812
Oakhurst, OK 74050 • 2,200
Oakland, CA 94601–62 • 372,242
Oakland, IA 51560 • 1,496
Oakland, ME 04963 • 3,510
Oakland, MD 21550 • 2,078
Oakland, NE 68045 • 1,279
Oakland, NJ 07436 • 11,997
Oakland, RI 02830 • 600
Oakland □, MI • 1,083,592
Oakland City, IN 47660 • 2,810
Oakland Park, FL 33334 • 26,326
Oak Lawn, IL 60453–59 • 56,182
Oaklawn, KS 67216 • 4,200
Oakley, CA 94561 • 18,374
Oakley, KS 67748 • 2,045
Oaklyn, NJ 08107 • 4,430
Oakmont, PA 15139 • 6,961
Oak Orchard, DE 19966 • 350
Oak Park, CA 91301 • 5,000
Oak Park, IL 60301–05 • 53,648
Oak Park, MI 48237 • 30,462
Oak Ridge, FL 32809 • 15,388
Oakridge, OR 97463 • 3,063
Oak Ridge, TN 37830 • 27,310
Oakton, VA 22124 • 24,610
Oak Valley, NJ 08090 • 5,400
Oakville, CT 06779 • 8,741
Oakville, MO 63129 • 31,750
Oakwood, GA 30566 • 1,464
Oakwood, IL 61858 • 1,533
Oakwood, OH 45419 • 9,392
Oberlin, KS 67749 • 2,197
Oberlin, LA 70655 • 1,808
Oberlin, OH 44074 • 8,191
Obetz, OH 43207 • 3,167
Obion, TN 38240 • 1,241
Obion □, TN • 31,717
Oblong, IL 62449 • 1,616
O'Brien □, IA • 15,444
Ocala, FL 32670–78 • 42,045
Ocean □, NJ • 433,203
Oceana, WV 24870 • 1,791
Oceana □, MI • 22,454
Ocean Bluff, MA 02065 • 2,500
Ocean City, FL 32548 • 5,422
Ocean City, MD 21842 • 5,146
Ocean City, NJ 08226 • 15,512
Ocean Gate, NJ 08740 • 2,078
Ocean Grove, MA 02777 • 4,560
Oceano, CA 93445 • 6,169
Ocean Park, WA 98640 • 1,650
Ocean Port, NJ 07757 • 6,146
Oceanside, CA 92054–56 • 128,398
Oceanside, NY 11572 • 32,423
Ocean Springs, MS 39564–65 • 14,658
Ocean [Township], NJ 07712 • 23,570
Ocean View, DE 19970 • 606
Oceanville, NJ 08231 • 1,000
Ochiltree □, TX • 9,128
Ocilla, GA 31774 • 3,182
Ocoee, FL 34761 • 12,778
Oconee □, GA • 17,618
Oconee □, SC • 57,494
Oconomowoc, WI 53066 • 10,993
Oconto, WI 54153 • 4,474
Oconto □, WI • 30,226
Oconto Falls, WI 54154 • 2,584
Odebolt, IA 51458 • 1,158
Odell, IL 60460 • 1,030
Odem, TX 78370 • 2,366
Odenton, MD 21113 • 12,833
Odessa, DE 19730 • 303
Odessa, MO 64076 • 3,695
Odessa, TX 79760–68 • 89,699
Odin, IL 62870 • 1,150
Odon, IN 47562 • 1,475
O'Donnell, TX 79351 • 1,102
Oelwein, IA 50662 • 6,493
O'Fallon, IL 62269 • 16,073
O'Fallon, MO 63366 • 18,698
Ogallala, NE 69153 • 5,095
Ogden, IA 50212 • 1,909
Ogden, KS 66517 • 1,494
Ogden, UT 84401–14 • 63,909
Ogdensburg, NJ 07439 • 2,722
Ogdensburg, NY 13669 • 13,521
Ogemaw □, MI • 18,681
Ogle □, IL • 45,957
Oglesby, IL 61348 • 3,619
Oglethorpe, GA 31068 • 1,302
Oglethorpe □, GA • 9,763
Ogunquit, ME 03907 • 1,492
Ohatchee, AL 36271 • 1,042
Ohio □, IN • 5,315
Ohio □, KY • 21,105
Ohio □, WV • 50,871
Ohioville, PA 15059 • 3,865
Oil City, LA 71061 • 1,282
Oil City, PA 16301 • 11,949
Oildale, CA 93308 • 26,553
Oilton, OK 74052 • 1,060
Ojai, CA 93023–24 • 7,613
Okaloosa □, FL • 143,776
Okanogan, WA 98840 • 2,370
Okanogan □, WA • 33,350
Okarche, OK 73762 • 1,160
Okauchee, WI 53069 • 2,300
Okauchee Lake, WI 53058 • 3,819
Okawville, IL 62271 • 1,274
Okeechobee, FL 34972–74 • 4,943
Okeechobee □, FL • 29,627
Okeene, OK 73763 • 1,343
Okemah, OK 74859 • 3,085
Okemos, MI 48864 • 20,216
Okfuskee □, OK • 11,551
Oklahoma □, OK • 599,611
Oklahoma City, OK 73101–80 • 444,719
Oklawaha, FL 32179 • 1,200
Okmulgee, OK 74447 • 13,441
Okmulgee □, OK • 36,490
Okolona, KY 40219 • 18,902
Okolona, MS 38860 • 3,267
Oktibbeha □, MS • 38,375
Ola, AR 72853 • 1,090
Olathe, CO 81425 • 1,263
Olathe, KS 66061–62 • 63,352
Olcott, NY 14126 • 1,432
Old Bethpage, NY 11804 • 5,610
Old Bridge, NJ 08857 • 22,151
Old Forge, NY 13420 • 1,061
Old Forge, PA 18518 • 8,834
Oldham □, KY • 33,263
Oldham □, TX • 2,278
Old Harbor, AK 99643 • 284
Old Orchard Beach, ME 04064 • 7,789
Old Saybrook, CT 06475 • 1,820
Oldsmar, FL 34677 • 8,361
Old Tappan, NJ 07675 • 4,254
Old Town, ME 04468 • 8,317
Olean, NY 14760 • 16,946
Olive Branch, MS 38654 • 3,567
Olive Hill, KY 41164 • 1,809
Olivehurst, CA 95961 • 9,738
Oliver, PA 15472 • 3,271
Oliver □, ND • 2,381
Oliver Springs, TN 37840 • 3,433
Olivet, MI 49076 • 1,604
Olivette, MO 63132 • 7,573
Olivia, MN 56277 • 2,623
Olla, LA 71465 • 1,410
Olmito, TX 78575 • 1,400
Olmos Park, TX 78212 • 2,161
Olmsted □, MN • 106,470
Olmsted Falls, OH 44138 • 6,741
Olney, IL 62450 • 8,664
Olney, MD 20832 • 23,019
Olney, TX 76374 • 3,519
Olton, TX 79064 • 2,116
Olympia, WA 98501–07 • 33,840
Olympia Heights, FL 33175 • 36,900
Olyphant, PA 18447 • 5,222
Omaha, NE 68101–72 • 335,795
Omak, WA 98841 • 4,117
Omro, WI 54963 • 2,836
Onalaska, WI 54650 • 11,284
Onancock, VA 23417 • 1,434
Onarga, IL 60955 • 1,281
Onawa, IA 51040 • 2,936
Onaway, MI 49765 • 1,039
Oneco, FL 34264 • 6,417
Oneida, NY 13421 • 10,850
Oneida, OH 45042 • 1,650
Oneida, TN 37841 • 3,502
Oneida □, ID • 3,492
Oneida □, NY • 250,836
Oneida □, WI • 31,679
O'Neill, NE 68763 • 3,852
Oneonta, AL 35121 • 4,844
Oneonta, NY 13820 • 13,954
Onida, SD 57564 • 761
Onondaga □, NY • 468,973
Onset, MA 02558 • 1,461
Onslow □, NC • 149,838
Ontario, CA 91761–62 • 133,179
Ontario, OH 44862 • 4,026
Ontario, OR 97914 • 9,392
Ontario □, NY • 95,101
Ontonagon, MI 49953 • 2,040
Ontonagon □, MI • 8,854
Oolitic, IN 47451 • 1,424
Ooltewah, TN 37363 • 1,200
Oostburg, WI 53070 • 1,931
Opal Cliffs, CA 95062 • 5,940
Opa-Locka, FL 33054–56 • 15,283
Opelika, AL 36801–03 • 22,122
Opelousas, LA 70570–71 • 18,151
Opp, AL 36467 • 6,985
Opportunity, WA 99206 • 22,326
Oquawka, IL 61469 • 1,442
Oracle, AZ 85623 • 3,043
Oradell, NJ 07649 • 8,024
Oran, MO 63771 • 1,164
Orange, CA 92664–69 • 110,658
Orange, CT 06477 • 12,830
Orange, MA 01364 • 3,791
Orange, NJ 07050–52 • 29,925
Orange, TX 77630–31 • 19,381
Orange, VA 22960 • 2,582
Orange □, CA • 2,410,556
Orange □, FL • 677,491
Orange □, IN • 18,409
Orange □, NY • 307,647
Orange □, NC • 93,851
Orange □, TX • 80,509
Orange □, VT • 26,149
Orange □, VA • 21,421
Orange Beach, AL 36561 • 2,253
Orangeburg, SC 29115–16 • 13,739
Orangeburg □, SC • 84,803
Orange City, FL 32763 • 5,347
Orange City, IA 51041 • 4,940
Orange Grove, MS 39503 • 15,676
Orange Grove, TX 78372 • 1,175
Orange Lake, FL 32681 • 1,000
Orange Park, FL 32073 • 9,488
Orangevale, CA 95662 • 26,266
Orangeville, UT 84537 • 1,459
Orchard City, CO 81410 • 2,218
Orchard Homes, MT 59801 • 10,317
Orchard Mesa, CO 81501 • 5,977
Orchard Park, NY 14127 • 3,280
Orchards, WA 98662 • 8,828
Orchard Valley, WY 82007 • 3,321
Orcutt, CA 93455 • 1,500
Ord, NE 68862 • 2,481
Ordway, CO 81063 • 1,025
Oregon, IL 61061 • 3,891
Oregon, OH 43616 • 18,334
Oregon, WI 53575 • 4,519
Oregon □, MO • 9,470
Oregon City, OR 97045 • 14,698
Orem, UT 84057–59 • 67,561
Orfordville, WI 53576 • 1,219
Orient, NY 11957 • 1,000
Orinda, CA 94563 • 16,642
Orion, IL 61273 • 1,821
Oriskany, NY 13424 • 1,450
Orland, CA 95963 • 5,052
Orlando, FL 32801–72 • 164,693
Orland Park, IL 60462 • 35,720
Orleans, IN 47452 • 2,083
Orleans, IN 47452 • 2,161
Orleans, MA 02653 • 1,699
Orleans, VT 05860 • 806
Orleans □, LA • 496,938
Orleans □, NY • 41,846
Orleans □, VT • 24,053
Orlovista, FL 32811 • 5,990
Ormond Beach, FL 32174–76 • 29,721
Ormond By The Sea, FL 32174 • 8,157
Orofino, ID 83544 • 2,868
Orono, ME 04473 • 9,789
Orono, MN 55323 • 7,285
Orosi, CA 93647 • 5,486
Oroville, CA 95965–66 • 11,960
Oroville, WA 98844 • 1,505
Orrville, OH 44667 • 7,712
Orting, WA 98360 • 2,106
Ortonville, MI 48462 • 1,252
Ortonville, MN 56278 • 2,205
Orwell, OH 44076 • 1,258
Orwigsburg, PA 17961 • 2,780
Osage, IA 50461 • 3,439
Osage, WY 82723 • 350
Osage □, KS • 15,248
Osage □, MO • 12,018
Osage □, OK • 41,645
Osage Beach, MO 65065 • 2,599
Osage City, KS 66523 • 2,689
Osakis, MN 56360 • 1,256
Osawatomie, KS 66064 • 4,590
Osborne, KS 67473 • 1,778
Osborne □, KS • 4,867
Osburn, ID 83849 • 1,579
Osceola, AR 72370 • 8,930
Osceola, IN 46561 • 1,999
Osceola, IA 50213 • 4,164
Osceola, WI 54020 • 2,075
Osceola □, FL • 107,728
Osceola □, IA • 7,267
Osceola □, MI • 20,146
Osceola Mills, PA 16666 • 1,310
Oscoda, MI 48750 • 1,061
Oscoda □, MI • 7,842
Osgood, IN 47037 • 1,688
Oshkosh, WI 54901–04 • 55,006
Oskaloosa, IA 52577 • 10,632
Oskaloosa, KS 66066 • 1,074
Osprey, FL 34229 • 2,597
Osseo, MN 55369 • 2,704
Osseo, WI 54758 • 1,551
Ossian, IN 46777 • 2,428
Ossining, NY 10562 • 22,582
Osterville, MA 02655 • 2,911
Oswego, IL 60543 • 3,876
Oswego, KS 67356 • 1,870
Oswego, NY 13126 • 19,195
Oswego □, NY • 121,771
Otay, CA 92010 • 6,400
Oteen, NC 28805 • 1,400
Otego, NY 13825 • 1,068
Otero □, CO • 20,185
Otero □, NM • 51,928
Othello, WA 99327 • 4,638
Otis Orchards, WA 99027 • 3,200
Otoe □, NE • 14,252
Otsego, MI 49078 • 3,937
Otsego □, MI • 17,957
Otsego □, NY • 60,517
Ottawa, IL 61350 • 17,451
Ottawa, KS 66067 • 10,667
Ottawa, OH 45875 • 3,999
Ottawa □, KS • 5,634
Ottawa □, MI • 187,768
Ottawa □, OH • 40,029
Ottawa □, OK • 30,561
Ottawa Hills, OH 43606 • 4,543
Otterbein, IN 47970 • 1,291
Otter Tail □, MN • 50,714
Ottumwa, IA 52501 • 24,488
Ouachita □, AR • 30,574
Ouachita □, LA • 142,191
Ouray, CO 81427 • 644
Ouray □, CO • 2,295
Outagamie □, WI • 140,510
Overland, MO 63114 • 17,987
Overland Park, KS 66204 • 111,790
Overlea, MD 21206 • 12,137
Overlook, OH 45431 • 6,000
Overton, NV 89040 • 1,111
Overton, TX 75684 • 2,105
Overton □, TN • 17,636
Ovid, MI 48866 • 1,442
Owasso, OK 74055 • 11,151
Owatonna, MN 55060 • 19,386
Owego, NY 13827 • 4,442
Owen □, IN • 17,281
Owen □, KY • 9,035
Owensboro, KY 42301–03 • 53,549
Owensville, IN 47665 • 1,053
Owensville, MO 65066 • 2,325
Owensville, OH 45160 • 1,019
Owenton, KY 40359 • 1,306
Owings Mills, MD 21117 • 9,474
Owingsville, KY 40360 • 1,491
Owosso, MI 48867 • 16,322
Owsley □, KY • 5,036
Owyhee, NV 89832 • 908
Owyhee □, ID • 8,392
Oxford, AL 36203 • 9,362
Oxford, CT 06483 • 1,600
Oxford, GA 30267 • 1,945
Oxford, IN 47971 • 1,273
Oxford, KS 67119 • 1,143
Oxford, MA 01540 • 5,969
Oxford, MI 48370–71 • 2,929
Oxford, MS 38655 • 9,984
Oxford, NJ 07863 • 1,767
Oxford, NY 13830 • 1,738

Oxford, NC 27565 • 7,913
Oxford, OH 45056 • 18,937
Oxford, PA 19363 • 3,769
Oxford □, ME • 52,602
Oxnard, CA 93030–35 • 142,216
Oxon Hill, MD 20745 • 36,267
Oyster Bay, NY 11771 • 6,687
Ozark, AL 36360–61 • 12,922
Ozark, AR 72949 • 3,330
Ozark, MO 65721 • 4,243
Ozark □, MO • 8,598
Ozaukee □, WI • 72,831
Ozona, FL 34660 • 1,500
Ozona, TX 76943 • 3,181

P

Paauilo, HI 96776 • 620
Pace, FL 32571 • 6,277
Pacific, MO 63069 • 4,350
Pacific, WA 98047 • 4,622
Pacific □, WA • 18,882
Pacifica, CA 94044 • 37,670
Pacific Beach, WA 98571 • 1,200
Pacific City, OR 97135 • 1,500
Pacific Grove, CA 93950 • 16,117
Pacific Palisades, HI 96782 • 10,000
Packwood, WA 98361 • 1,010
Pacolet, SC 29372 • 1,736
Paddock Lake, WI 53168 • 2,662
Paden City, WV 26159 • 2,862
Paducah, KY 42001–03 • 27,256
Paducah, TX 79248 • 1,788
Page, AZ 86040 • 6,598
Page □, IA • 16,870
Page □, VA • 21,690
Pageland, SC 29728 • 2,666
Page Manor, OH 45431 • 9,300
Pagosa Springs, CO 81147 • 1,207
Pahala, HI 96777 • 1,520
Pahoa, HI 96778 • 1,027
Pahokee, FL 33476 • 6,822
Pahrump, NV 89041 • 7,424
Paia, HI 96779 • 2,091
Paincourtville, LA 70391 • 1,550
Painesville, OH 44077 • 15,699
Painted Post, NY 14870 • 1,950
Paintsville, KY 41240 • 4,354
Pajarito, NM 87105 • 1,400
Palacios, TX 77465 • 4,418
Palatine, IL 60067 • 39,253
Palatka, FL 32177 • 10,201
Palestine, IL 62451 • 1,619
Palestine, TX 75801–02 • 18,042
Palisade, CO 81526 • 1,871
Palisades Park, NJ 07650 • 14,536
Palm Bay, FL 32905 • 62,632
Palm Beach, FL 33480 • 9,814
Palm Beach □, FL • 863,518
Palm Beach Gardens, FL 33410 • 22,965
Palm Coast, FL 32135 • 14,287
Palmdale, CA 93550–51 • 68,842
Palm Desert, CA 92260–61 • 23,252
Palmer, AK 99645 • 2,866
Palmer, MA 01069 • 4,069
Palmer, MS 39401 • 2,765
Palmer, TX 75152 • 1,659
Palmer Lake, CO 80133 • 1,480
Palmer Park, MD 20785 • 7,019
Palmerton, PA 18071 • 5,394
Palmetto, FL 34220–21 • 9,268
Palmetto, GA 30268 • 2,612
Palmetto Estates, FL 33157 • 12,293
Palm Harbor, FL 34682–85 • 50,256
Palm Springs, CA 92262–64 • 40,181
Palm Springs, FL 33460 • 9,763
Palm Springs North, FL 33015 • 5,300
Palm Valley, FL 32082 • 9,960
Palmyra, MO 63461 • 3,371
Palmyra, NJ 08065 • 7,056
Palmyra, NY 14522 • 3,566
Palmyra, PA 17078 • 6,910
Palmyra, WI 53156 • 1,539
Palo Alto, CA 94301–09 • 55,900
Palo Alto □, IA • 10,669
Palo Pinto □, TX • 25,055
Palos Heights, IL 60463 • 11,478
Palos Hills, IL 60465 • 17,803
Palos Park, IL 60464 • 4,199
Palos Verdes Estates, CA 90274 • 13,512
Pamlico □, NC • 11,372
Pampa, TX 79065–66 • 19,959
Pamplico, SC 29583 • 1,314
Pana, IL 62557 • 5,796
Panaca, NV 89042 • 700
Panama, OK 74951 • 1,528
Panama City, FL 32401–13 • 34,378
Panama City Beach, FL 32407–08 • 4,051
Pandora, OH 45877 • 1,009
Panguitch, UT 84759 • 1,444
Panhandle, TX 79068 • 2,353
Panola □, MS • 29,996
Panola □, TX • 22,035
Panora, IA 50216 • 1,100
Panthersville, GA 30032 • 9,874
Paola, KS 66071 • 4,698
Paoli, IN 47454 • 3,542
Paoli, PA 19301 • 5,603
Paonia, CO 81428 • 1,403
Papaikou, HI 96781 • 1,634
Papillion, NE 68046 • 10,372
Paradise, CA 95969 • 25,408
Paradise, NV 89109 • 124,682
Paradise Hills, NM 87114 • 5,513
Paradise Valley, AZ 85253 • 11,671
Paradise Valley, NV 89426 • 150
Paragould, AR 72450–51 • 18,540
Paramount, CA 90723 • 47,669
Paramount, MD 21740 • 1,878
Paramus, NJ 07652–53 • 25,067
Parchment, MI 49004 • 1,958
Pardeeville, WI 53954 • 1,630
Paris, AR 72855 • 3,674
Paris, IL 61944 • 8,987
Paris, KY 40361–62 • 8,730
Paris, MO 65275 • 1,486
Paris, TN 38242 • 9,332
Paris, TX 75460–61 • 24,699
Park □, CO • 7,174
Park □, MT • 14,562
Park □, WY • 23,178
Park City, KS 67219 • 5,050
Park City, UT 84060 • 4,468
Parke □, IN • 15,410
Parker, AZ 85344 • 2,897
Parker, CO 80134 • 5,450
Parker, FL 32401 • 4,598
Parker, SD 57053 • 984
Parker □, TX • 64,785
Parker City, IN 47368 • 1,323
Parkersburg, IA 50665 • 1,804
Parkersburg, WV 26101–06 • 33,862
Parkesburg, PA 19365 • 2,981
Park Falls, WI 54552 • 3,104
Park Forest, IL 60466 • 24,656
Park Hills, KY 41015 • 3,321
Parkin, AR 72373 • 1,847
Parkland, WA 98444 • 20,882
Park Layne, OH 45344 • 4,895
Park Rapids, MN 56470 • 2,863
Park Ridge, IL 60068 • 36,175
Park Ridge, NJ 07656 • 8,102
Park River, ND 58270 • 1,725
Parkrose, OR 97230 • 21,108
Parkston, SD 57366 • 1,572
Parkville, MD 21234 • 31,617
Parkville, MO 64152 • 2,402
Parkwater, WA 99211 • 4,300
Parkway, CA 95823 • 12,000
Parkwood, NC 27713 • 4,123
Parkwood, WA 98366 • 6,853
Parlier, CA 93648 • 7,938
Parma, ID 83660 • 1,597
Parma, OH 44129 • 87,876
Parma Heights, OH 44130 • 21,448
Parmer □, TX • 9,863
Parole, MD 21401 • 10,054
Parowan, UT 84761 • 1,873
Parrish, AL 35580 • 1,433
Parshall, ND 58770 • 943
Parsons, KS 67357 • 11,924
Parsons, TN 38363 • 2,033
Parsons, WV 26287 • 1,453
Pasadena, CA 91101–09 • 131,591
Pasadena, MD 21122 • 10,012
Pasadena, TX 77501–08 • 119,363
Pascagoula, MS 39567–68 • 25,899
Pasco, WA 99301–02 • 20,337
Pasco □, FL • 281,131
Pascoag, RI 02859 • 5,011
Paso Robles, CA 93446–47 • 18,583
Pasquotank □, NC • 31,298
Passaic, NJ 07055 • 58,041
Passaic □, NJ • 453,060
Pass Christian, MS 39571 • 5,557
Pataskala, OH 43062 • 3,046
Patchogue, NY 11772 • 11,060
Paterson, NJ 07501–44 • 140,891
Patrick □, VA • 17,473
Patten, ME 04765 • 1,256
Patterson, LA 70392 • 4,736
Patterson, NY 12563 • 1,200
Patton, PA 16668 • 2,206
Paul, ID 83347 • 901
Paulding, OH 45879 • 2,605
Paulding □, GA • 41,611
Paulding □, OH • 20,488
Paullina, IA 51046 • 1,134
Paulsboro, NJ 08066 • 6,577
Pauls Valley, OK 73075 • 6,150
Pawcatuck, CT 06379 • 5,289
Paw Creek, NC 28130 • 1,700
Pawhuska, OK 74056 • 3,825
Pawling, NY 12564 • 1,974
Pawnee, IL 62558 • 2,384
Pawnee, OK 74058 • 2,197
Pawnee □, KS • 7,555
Pawnee □, NE • 3,317
Pawnee □, OK • 15,575
Pawnee City, NE 68420 • 1,008
Paw Paw, MI 49079 • 3,169
Pawtucket, RI 02860–65 • 72,644
Paxton, IL 60957 • 4,289
Paxton, MA 01612 • 1,550
Payette, ID 83661 • 5,592
Payette □, ID • 16,434
Payne, OH 45880 • 1,244
Payne □, OK • 61,507
Paynesville, MN 56362 • 2,275
Payson, AZ 85541 • 8,377
Payson, IL 62360 • 1,114
Payson, UT 84651 • 9,510
Peabody, KS 66866 • 1,349
Peabody, MA 01960–61 • 47,039
Peace Dale, RI 02883 • 3,100
Peach □, GA • 21,189
Peach Orchard, GA 30906 • 13,800
Peachtree City, GA 30269 • 19,027
Pea Ridge, AR 72751 • 1,620
Pearisburg, VA 24134 • 2,064
Pearl, MS 39208 • 19,588
Pearland, TX 77581 • 18,697
Pearl City, HI 96782 • 30,993
Pearl River, LA 70452 • 1,507
Pearl River, NY 10965 • 15,314
Pearl River □, MS • 38,714
Pearsall, TX 78061 • 6,924
Pearson, GA 31642 • 1,714
Pecatonica, IL 61063 • 1,760
Pecos, NM 87552 • 1,012
Pecos, TX 79772 • 12,069
Pecos □, TX • 14,675
Peculiar, MO 64078 • 1,777
Pedricktown, NJ 08067 • 1,500
Peebles, OH 45660 • 1,782
Peekskill, NY 10566 • 19,536
Pegram, TN 37143 • 1,371
Pekin, IL 61554–55 • 32,254
Pekin, IN 47165 • 1,095
Pelahatchie, MS 39145 • 1,553
Pelham, AL 35124 • 9,765
Pelham, GA 31779 • 3,869
Pelham, NY 10803 • 6,413
Pelham Manor, NY 10803 • 5,443
Pelican Rapids, MN 56572 • 1,886
Pella, IA 50219 • 9,270
Pell City, AL 35125 • 8,118
Pell Lake, WI 53157 • 2,018
Pemberton, NJ 08068 • 1,367
Pemberville, OH 43450 • 1,279
Pembina □, ND • 9,238
Pembroke, GA 31321 • 1,503
Pembroke, MA 02359 • 2,000
Pembroke, NC 28372 • 2,241
Pembroke, VA 24136 • 1,064
Pembroke Park, FL 33009 • 4,933
Pembroke Pines, FL 33024 • 65,452
Pemiscot □, MO • 21,921
Pen Argyl, PA 18072 • 3,492
Penbrook, PA 17103 • 2,791
Pender, NE 68047 • 1,208
Pender □, NC • 28,855
Pendleton, IN 46064 • 2,309
Pendleton, OR 97801 • 15,126
Pendleton, SC 29670 • 3,314
Pendleton □, KY • 12,036
Pendleton □, WV • 8,054
Pendley Hills, GA 30032 • 5,400
Pend Oreille □, WA • 8,915
Penfield, NY 14526 • 6,260
Penn Acres, DE 19720 • 2,430
Penn Hills, PA 15235 • 51,430
Pennington, NJ 08534 • 2,537
Pennington □, MN • 13,306
Pennington □, SD • 81,343
Pennington Gap, VA 24277 • 1,922
Pennsauken, NJ 08110 • 34,733
Pennsboro, WV 26415 • 1,282
Pennsburg, PA 18073 • 2,460
Penns Grove, NJ 08069 • 5,228
Pennsville, NJ 08070 • 12,218
Penn Yan, NY 14527 • 5,248
Penobscot □, ME • 146,601
Pensacola, FL 32501–26 • 58,165
Pentwater, MI 49449 • 1,050
Peoria, AZ 85345 • 50,618
Peoria, IL 61601–56 • 113,504
Peoria □, IL • 182,827
Peoria Heights, IL 61614 • 6,930
Peotone, IL 60468 • 2,947
Pepeekeo, HI 96783 • 1,813
Pepin □, WI • 7,107
Pepperell, MA 01463 • 2,350
Pepper Pike, OH 44124 • 6,185
Pequannock, NJ 07440 • 12,844
Perdido, AL 36562 • 1,200
Perham, MN 56573 • 2,075
Perkasie, PA 18944 • 7,878
Perkins, OK 74059 • 1,925
Perkins □, NE • 3,367
Perkins □, SD • 3,932
Perquimans □, NC • 10,447
Perrine, FL 33157 • 15,576
Perris, CA 92370 • 21,460
Perry, FL 32347 • 7,151
Perry, GA 31069 • 9,452
Perry, IA 50220 • 6,652
Perry, MI 48872 • 2,163
Perry, NY 14530 • 4,219
Perry, OH 44081 • 1,012
Perry, OK 73077 • 4,978
Perry, UT 84302 • 1,211
Perry □, AL • 12,759
Perry □, AR • 7,969
Perry □, IL • 21,412
Perry □, IN • 19,107
Perry □, KY • 30,283
Perry □, MS • 10,865
Perry □, MO • 16,648
Perry □, OH • 31,557
Perry □, PA • 41,172
Perry □, TN • 6,612
Perry Hall, MD 21128 • 22,723
Perry Heights, OH 44646 • 9,055
Perryman, MD 21130 • 2,160
Perrysburg, OH 43551–52 • 12,551
Perryton, TX 79070 • 7,607
Perryville, AR 72126 • 1,141
Perryville, MD 21903 • 2,456
Perryville, MO 63775 • 6,933
Pershing □, NV • 4,336
Person □, NC • 30,180
Perth Amboy, NJ 08861–63 • 41,967
Peru, IL 61354 • 9,302
Peru, IN 46970 • 12,843
Peru, NE 68421 • 1,110
Peru, NY 12972 • 1,565
Peshtigo, WI 54157 • 3,154
Petal, MS 39465 • 7,883
Petaluma, CA 94952–55 • 43,184
Peterborough, NH 03458 • 2,685
Petersburg, AK 99833 • 3,207
Petersburg, IL 62675 • 2,261
Petersburg, IN 47567 • 2,449
Petersburg, MI 49270 • 1,201
Petersburg, TX 79250 • 1,292
Petersburg, VA 23801–05 • 38,386
Petersburg, WV 26847 • 2,360
Petersville, AL 35633 • 1,730
Petoskey, MI 49770 • 6,056
Petroleum □, MT • 519
Petros, TN 37845 • 1,286
Pettis □, MO • 35,437
Pevely, MO 63070 • 2,831
Pewaukee, WI 53072 • 4,941
Pewee Valley, KY 40056 • 1,283
Pharr, TX 78577 • 32,921
Phelps, KY 41553 • 1,120
Phelps, NY 14532 • 1,978
Phelps □, MO • 35,248
Phelps □, NE • 9,715
Phenix City, AL 36867–69 • 25,312
Philadelphia, MS 39350 • 6,758
Philadelphia, NY 13673 • 1,478
Philadelphia, PA 19101–96 • 1,585,577
Philadelphia □, PA • 1,585,577
Phil Campbell, AL 35581 • 1,317
Philip, SD 57567 • 1,077
Philippi, WV 26416 • 3,132
Philipsburg, MT 59858 • 925
Philipsburg, PA 16866 • 3,048
Phillips, TX 79007 • 1,729
Phillips, WI 54555 • 1,592
Phillips □, AR • 28,838
Phillips □, CO • 4,189
Phillips □, KS • 6,590
Phillips □, MT • 5,163
Phillipsburg, KS 67661 • 2,828
Phillipsburg, NJ 08865 • 15,757
Philmont, NY 12565 • 1,623
Philo, IL 61864 • 1,028
Philomath, OR 97370 • 2,983
Phoenix, AZ 85001–82 • 983,403
Phoenix, IL 60426 • 2,217
Phoenix, NY 13135 • 2,435
Phoenix, OR 97535 • 3,239
Phoenixville, PA 19460 • 15,066
Piatt □, IL • 15,548
Picayune, MS 39466 • 10,633
Picher, OK 74360 • 1,714
Pickaway □, OH • 48,255
Pickens, MS 39146 • 1,285
Pickens, SC 29671 • 3,042
Pickens □, AL • 20,699
Pickens □, GA • 14,432
Pickens □, SC • 93,894
Pickerington, OH 43147 • 5,668
Pickett □, TN • 4,548
Pico Rivera, CA 90660–61 • 59,177
Piedmont, AL 36272 • 5,288
Piedmont, CA 94611 • 10,602
Piedmont, MO 63957 • 2,166
Piedmont, OK 73078 • 2,522
Piedmont, SC 29673 • 4,143
Piedmont, WV 26750 • 1,094
Pierce, ID 83546 • 746
Pierce, NE 68767 • 1,615
Pierce □, GA • 13,328
Pierce □, NE • 7,827
Pierce □, ND • 5,052
Pierce □, WA • 586,203
Pierce □, WI • 32,765
Pierce City, MO 65723 • 1,382
Pierceton, IN 46562 • 1,030
Pierre, SD 57501 • 12,906
Pierre Part, LA 70339 • 3,053
Pierson, FL 32180 • 2,988
Pierz, MN 56364 • 1,014
Pigeon, MI 48755 • 1,207
Pigeon Cove, MA 01966 • 1,660
Pigeon Forge, TN 37863 • 3,027
Piggott, AR 72454 • 3,777
Pike □, AL • 27,595
Pike □, AR • 10,086
Pike □, GA • 10,224
Pike □, IL • 17,577
Pike □, IN • 12,509
Pike □, KY • 72,583
Pike □, MS • 36,882
Pike □, MO • 15,969
Pike □, OH • 24,249
Pike □, PA • 27,966
Pike Lake, MN 55811 • 1,004
Pikesville, MD 21208 • 24,815
Piketon, OH 45661 • 1,717
Pikeville, KY 41501–02 • 6,324
Pikeville, TN 37367 • 1,771
Pilot Mountain, NC 27041 • 1,181
Pilot Point, TX 76258 • 2,538
Pilot Rock, OR 97868 • 1,478
Pilot Station, AK 99650 • 463
Pima, AZ 85543 • 1,725
Pima □, AZ • 666,880
Pimmit Hills, VA 22043 • 6,019
Pinal □, AZ • 116,379
Pinardville, NH 03045 • 4,654
Pinckney, MI 48169 • 1,603
Pinckneyville, IL 62274 • 3,372
Pinconning, MI 48650 • 1,291
Pine □, MN • 21,264
Pine Bluff, AR 71601–13 • 57,140
Pine Bluffs, WY 82082 • 1,054
Pine Bridge, CT 06403 • 1,160
Pine Bush, NY 12566 • 1,445
Pine Castle, FL 32809 • 8,276
Pine City, MN 55063 • 2,613
Pinedale, WY 82941 • 1,181
Pine Grove, PA 17963 • 2,118
Pine Grove Mills, PA 16868 • 1,129
Pine Hill, NJ 08021 • 9,854
Pine Hills, FL 32808 • 35,322
Pinehurst, MA 01866 • 6,614
Pinehurst, NJ 08201 • 1,850
Pinehurst, NC 28374 • 5,103
Pine Island, MN 55963 • 2,125
Pine Island, NY 10969 • 1,200
Pine Knot, KY 42635 • 1,549
Pine Lawn, MO 63120 • 5,092
Pine Level, NC 27568 • 1,217
Pinellas □, FL • 851,659
Pinellas Park, FL 34664–66 • 43,426
Pine Plains, NY 12567 • 1,312
Pine Ridge, SD 57770 • 2,596
Pinetops, NC 27864 • 1,514
Pine Valley, CA 91962 • 1,297
Pineville, KY 40977 • 2,198
Pineville, LA 71360–61 • 12,251
Pineville, NC 28134 • 2,970
Pinewald, NJ 08721 • 1,700
Pinewood, FL 33168 • 15,518
Pinewood Park, FL 33168 • 8,300
Piney Point, MD 20674 • 1,200
Piney View, WV 25906 • 1,085
Pinole, CA 94564 • 17,460
Pinson, AL 35126 • 1,430
Pioche, NV 89043 • 830
Pioneer, OH 43554 • 1,287
Pipestone, MN 56164 • 4,554
Pipestone □, MN • 10,491
Piqua, OH 45356 • 20,612
Pirtleville, AZ 85626 • 1,364
Piscataquis □, ME • 18,653
Piscataway, NJ 08854–55 • 42,223
Pisgah, OH 45069 • 15,660
Pisgah Forest, NC 28768 • 1,899
Pismo Beach, CA 93448–49 • 7,669
Pitcairn, PA 15140 • 4,087
Pitkin □, CO • 12,661
Pitman, NJ 08071 • 9,365
Pitt □, NC • 107,924
Pittsboro, NC 27312 • 1,436
Pittsburg, CA 94565 • 47,564
Pittsburg, KS 66762 • 17,775
Pittsburg, TX 75686 • 4,007
Pittsburg □, OK • 40,581
Pittsburgh, PA 15201–90 • 369,879
Pittsfield, IL 62363 • 4,231
Pittsfield, ME 04967 • 3,222
Pittsfield, MA 01201–03 • 48,622
Pittsfield, NH 03263 • 1,717
Pittsford, VT 05763 • 650
Pittston, PA 18640–44 • 9,389
Pittsylvania □, VA • 55,655
Piute □, UT • 1,277
Pixley, CA 93256 • 2,457
Placentia, CA 92670 • 41,259
Placer □, CA • 172,796
Placerville, CA 95667 • 8,355
Plain City, OH 43064 • 2,278
Plain City, UT 84404 • 2,722
Plain Dealing, LA 71064 • 1,074
Plainedge, NY 11714 • 8,739
Plainfield, CT 06374 • 2,856
Plainfield, IL 60544 • 4,557
Plainfield, IN 46168 • 10,433
Plainfield, NJ 07059–63 • 46,567
Plainfield, VT 05667 • 600
Plainfield Heights, MI 49505 • 5,000
Plains, MT 59859 • 992
Plains, PA 18705 • 4,694
Plains, TX 79355 • 1,422
Plainsboro, NJ 08536 • 1,560
Plainview, MN 55964 • 2,768
Plainview, NE 68769 • 1,333
Plainview, NY 11803 • 26,207
Plainview, TX 79072–73 • 21,700
Plainville, CT 06062 • 17,392
Plainville, KS 67663 • 2,173
Plainville, MA 02762 • 5,857
Plainwell, MI 49080 • 4,057
Plaistow, NH 03865 • 1,850
Plano, IL 60545 • 5,104
Plano, TX 75074–75 • 128,713
Plantation, FL 33317 • 66,692
Plant City, FL 33564–67 • 22,754
Plantersville, MS 38862 • 1,046
Plantsite, AZ 85540 • 1,500
Plantsville, CT 06479 • 7,050
Plaquemine, LA 70764–65 • 7,186
Plaquemines □, LA • 25,575
Platte, SD 57369 • 1,311
Platte □, MO • 57,867
Platte □, NE • 29,820
Platte □, WY • 8,145
Platte City, MO 64079 • 2,947
Platteville, CO 80651 • 1,515
Platteville, WI 53818 • 9,708
Plattsburg, MO 64477 • 2,248
Plattsburgh, NY 12901 • 21,255
Plattsmouth, NE 68048 • 6,412
Pleasant Gap, PA 16823 • 1,699
Pleasant Garden, NC 27313 • 2,228
Pleasant Grove, AL 35127 • 8,458
Pleasant Grove, UT 84062 • 13,476
Pleasant Hill, CA 94523 • 31,585
Pleasant Hill, IL 62366 • 1,030
Pleasant Hill, IA 50301 • 3,671
Pleasant Hill, MO 64080 • 3,827
Pleasant Hill, OH 45359 • 1,066
Pleasant Hills, PA 15236 • 8,884
Pleasanton, CA 94566 • 50,553
Pleasanton, KS 66075 • 1,231
Pleasanton, TX 78064 • 7,678
Pleasant Prairie, WI 53158 • 11,961
Pleasants □, WV • 7,546
Pleasant Valley, MO 64068 • 2,731
Pleasant Valley, NY 12569 • 1,688
Pleasant View, CO 80401 • 3,460
Pleasant View, UT 84404 • 3,603
Pleasantville, IA 50225 • 1,536
Pleasantville, NJ 08232 • 16,027
Pleasantville, NY 10570–72 • 6,592
Pleasure Beach, CT 06385 • 1,356
Pleasure Ridge Park, KY 40258 • 25,131
Plentywood, MT 59254 • 2,136
Plover, WI 54467 • 8,176
Plum, PA 15239 • 25,609
Plumas □, CA • 19,739
Plumsteadville, PA 18949 • 1,200
Plymouth, CT 06782 • 1,070
Plymouth, FL 32768 • 2,700
Plymouth, IN 46563 • 8,303
Plymouth, MA 02360–61 • 7,258
Plymouth, MI 48170 • 9,560
Plymouth, MN 55441 • 50,889
Plymouth, NH 03264 • 3,967
Plymouth, NC 27962 • 4,328
Plymouth, OH 44865 • 1,942
Plymouth, PA 18651 • 7,134
Plymouth, WI 53073 • 6,769
Plymouth □, IA • 23,388
Plymouth □, MA • 435,276
Plymouth Township, PA 19401 • 17,168
Poca, WV 25159 • 1,124
Pocahontas, AR 72455 • 6,151
Pocahontas, IA 50574 • 2,085
Pocahontas □, IA • 9,525
Pocahontas □, WV • 9,008
Pocasset, MA 02559 • 2,200
Pocatalico, WV 25320 • 2,420
Pocatello, ID 83201–06 • 46,080
Pocola, OK 74902 • 3,664
Pocomoke City, MD 21851 • 3,922
Poinsett □, AR • 24,664
Point Clear, AL 36564 • 2,125
Pointe Coupee □, LA • 22,540
Point Hope, AK 99766 • 639
Point Marion, PA 15474 • 1,344
Point Pleasant, NJ 08742 • 18,177
Point Pleasant, WV 25550 • 4,996
Point Pleasant Beach, NJ 08742 • 5,112
Poipu, HI 96756 • 975
Polk, PA 16342 • 1,267
Polk □, AR • 17,347
Polk □, FL • 405,382
Polk □, GA • 33,815
Polk □, IA • 327,140
Polk □, MN • 32,498
Polk □, MO • 21,826
Polk □, NE • 5,675
Polk □, NC • 14,416
Polk □, OR • 49,541
Polk □, TN • 13,643
Polk □, TX • 30,687
Polk □, WI • 34,773
Polk City, FL 33868 • 1,439
Polk City, IA 50226 • 1,908
Polo, IL 61064 • 2,514
Polson, MT 59860 • 3,283
Pomeroy, OH 45769 • 2,259
Pomeroy, WA 99347 • 1,393
Pomona, CA 91765–69 • 131,723
Pomona, NJ 08240 • 2,624
Pompano Beach, FL 33060–69 • 72,411
Pompano Beach Highlands, FL 33060 • 17,915
Pompton Lakes, NJ 07442 • 10,539
Ponca City, OK 74601–04 • 26,359
Ponchatoula, LA 70454 • 5,425
Pondera □, MT • 6,433
Ponte Vedra Beach, FL 32082 • 1,700
Pontiac, IL 61764 • 11,428
Pontiac, MI 48340–43 • 71,166
Pontotoc, MS 38863 • 4,570
Pontotoc □, MS • 22,237

Pontotoc □, OK • 34,119
Pooler, GA 31322 • 4,453
Poolesville, MD 20837 • 3,796
Pope □, AR • 45,883
Pope □, IL • 4,373
Pope □, MN • 10,745
Poplar, MT 59255 • 881
Poplar Bluff, MO 63901 • 16,996
Poplarville, MS 39470 • 2,561
Poquonock Bridge, CT 06340 • 2,770
Poquoson, VA 23662 • 11,005
Portage, IN 46368 • 29,060
Portage, MI 49081 • 41,042
Portage, PA 15946 • 3,105
Portage, WI 53901 • 8,640
Portage □, OH • 142,585
Portage □, WI • 61,405
Portage Lakes, OH 44319 • 13,373
Portageville, MO 63873 • 3,401
Portales, NM 88130 • 10,690
Port Allegany, PA 16743 • 2,391
Port Allen, LA 70767 • 6,277
Port Angeles, WA 98362 • 17,710
Port Aransas, TX 78373 • 2,233
Port Arthur, TX 77640–43 • 58,724
Port Barre, LA 70577 • 2,144
Port Bolivar, TX 77650 • 1,600
Port Byron, IL 61275 • 1,002
Port Byron, NY 13140 • 1,359
Port Carbon, PA 17965 • 2,134
Port Charlotte, FL 33952 • 41,535
Port Chester, NY 10573 • 24,728
Port Clinton, OH 43452 • 7,106
Port Dickinson, NY 13901 • 1,785
Port Edwards, WI 54469 • 1,848
Porter, IN 46304 • 3,118
Porter, TX 77365 • 7,000
Porter □, IN • 128,932
Porterdale, GA 30270 • 1,278
Porterville, CA 93257–58 • 29,563
Port Ewen, NY 12466 • 3,444
Port Gibson, MS 39150 • 1,810
Port Henry, NY 12974 • 1,263
Port Hueneme, CA 93041–44 • 20,319
Port Huron, MI 48060–61 • 33,694
Port Isabel, TX 78578 • 4,467
Port Jefferson, NY 11777 • 7,455
Port Jefferson Station, NY 11776 • 7,232
Port Jervis, NY 12771 • 9,060
Portland, CT 06480 • 5,645
Portland, IN 47371 • 6,483
Portland, ME 04101–12 • 64,358
Portland, MI 48875 • 3,889
Portland, OR 97201–99 • 437,319
Portland, TN 37148 • 5,165
Portland, TX 78374 • 12,224
Port Lavaca, TX 77979 • 10,886
Port Monmouth, NJ 07758 • 3,800
Port Neches, TX 77651 • 12,974
Port Norris, NJ 08349 • 1,701
Port O'Connor, TX 77982 • 1,031
Portola, CA 96122 • 2,193
Port Orange, FL 32127 • 35,317
Port Orchard, WA 98366 • 4,984
Port Orford, OR 97465 • 1,025
Port Penn, DE 19731 • 300
Port Richey, FL 34667–74 • 2,523
Port Royal, SC 29935 • 2,985
Port Saint Joe, FL 32456 • 4,044
Port Saint Lucie, FL 34952 • 55,866
Port Salerno, FL 34992 • 7,786
Portsmouth, NH 03801–02 • 25,925
Portsmouth, OH 45662 • 22,676
Portsmouth, RI 02871 • 3,540
Portsmouth, VA 23701–09 • 103,907
Port St. John, FL 32922 • 8,933
Port Sulphur, LA 70083 • 3,523
Port Townsend, WA 98368 • 7,001
Portville, NY 14770 • 1,040
Port Vue, PA 15133 • 4,641
Port Washington, NY 11050 • 15,387
Port Washington, WI 53074 • 9,338
Port Wentworth, GA 31407 • 4,012
Posen, IL 60469 • 4,226
Posey □, IN • 25,968
Poseyville, IN 47633 • 1,089
Post, TX 79356 • 3,768
Post Falls, ID 83854 • 7,349
Postville, IA 52162 • 1,472
Poteau, OK 74953 • 7,210
Poteet, TX 78065 • 3,206
Poth, TX 78147 • 1,642
Potlatch, ID 83855 • 790
Potomac, MD 20851 • 45,634
Potomac Heights, MD 20640 • 1,524
Potomac Park, MD 21502 • 1,800
Potosi, MO 63664 • 2,683
Potsdam, NY 13676 • 10,251
Pottawatomie □, KS • 16,128
Pottawatomie □, OK • 58,760
Pottawattamie □, IA • 82,628
Potter □, PA • 16,717
Potter □, SD • 3,190
Potter □, TX • 97,874
Potter Valley, CA 95469 • 1,500
Pottstown, PA 19464 • 21,831
Pottsville, PA 17901 • 16,603
Poughkeepsie, NY 12601–03 • 28,844
Poulsbo, WA 98370 • 4,848
Poultney, VT 05764 • 1,731
Poway, CA 92064 • 43,516
Powder River □, MT • 2,090
Powder Springs, GA 30073 • 6,893
Powell, OH 43065 • 2,154
Powell, TN 37849 • 7,534
Powell, WY 82435 • 5,292
Powell □, KY • 11,686
Powell □, MT • 6,620
Powellhurst, OR 97236 • 28,756
Powellton, WV 25161 • 1,905
Power □, ID • 7,086
Poweshiek □, IA • 19,033
Powhatan □, VA • 15,328
Powhatan Point, OH 43942 • 1,807
Poydras, LA 70085 • 4,029
Poynette, WI 53955 • 1,662
Prague, OK 74864 • 2,308
Prairie □, AR • 9,518
Prairie □, MT • 1,383
Prairie City, IA 50228 • 1,360
Prairie City, OR 97869 • 1,117
Prairie du Chien, WI 53821 • 5,659
Prairie du Sac, WI 53578 • 2,380
Prairie Grove, AR 72753 • 1,761
Prairie View, TX 77446 • 4,004
Prairie Village, KS 66208 • 23,186
Pratt, KS 67124 • 6,687
Pratt □, KS • 9,702
Prattville, AL 36066–67 • 19,587
Preble □, OH • 40,113
Premont, TX 78375 • 2,914
Prentiss, MS 39474 • 1,487
Prentiss □, MS • 23,278
Prescott, AZ 86301–14 • 26,455
Prescott, AR 71857 • 3,673
Prescott, WI 54021 • 3,243
Presho, SD 57568 • 654
Presidio, TX 79845 • 3,072
Presidio □, TX • 6,637
Presque Isle, ME 04769 • 10,550
Presque Isle □, MI • 13,743
Preston, ID 83263 • 3,710
Preston, IA 52069 • 1,025
Preston, MN 55965 • 1,530
Preston □, WV • 29,037
Prestonsburg, KY 41653 • 3,558
Price, UT 84501 • 8,712
Price □, WI • 15,600
Prichard, AL 36610 • 34,311
Priest River, ID 83856 • 1,560
Primrose, RI 02895 • 500
Prince Edward □, VA • 17,320
Prince Frederick, MD 20678 • 1,885
Prince George □, VA • 27,394
Prince Georges □, MD • 729,268
Princes Lakes, IN 46164 • 1,055
Princess Anne, MD 21853 • 1,666
Princeton, FL 33032 • 7,073
Princeton, IL 61356 • 7,197
Princeton, IN 47670 • 8,127
Princeton, KY 42445 • 6,940
Princeton, MN 55371 • 3,719
Princeton, MO 64673 • 1,021
Princeton, NJ 08540–43 • 12,016
Princeton, NC 27569 • 1,181
Princeton, WV 24740 • 7,043
Princeton, WI 54968 • 1,458
Princeton Junction, NJ 08550 • 2,362
Princeville, IL 61559 • 1,421
Princeville, NC 27886 • 1,652
Prince William □, VA • 215,686
Prineville, OR 97754 • 5,355
Prior Lake, MN 55372 • 11,482
Proctor, MN 55810 • 2,974
Proctor, VT 05765 • 1,979
Proctorsville, VT 05153 • 480
Prophetstown, IL 61277 • 1,749
Prospect, CT 06712 • 6,807
Prospect, KY 40059 • 2,788
Prospect, OH 43342 • 1,148
Prospect, OR 97536 • 1,200
Prospect, PA 16052 • 1,122
Prospect Heights, IL 60070 • 15,239
Prospect Park, NJ 07508 • 5,053
Prospect Park, PA 19076 • 6,764
Prosperity, SC 29127 • 1,116
Prosperity, WV 25909 • 1,322
Prosser, WA 99350 • 4,476
Providence, KY 42450 • 4,123
Providence, RI 02901–40 • 160,728
Providence, UT 84332 • 3,344
Providence □, RI • 596,270
Provincetown, MA 02657 • 3,374
Provo, UT 84601–06 • 86,835
Prowers □, CO • 13,347
Prudenville, MI 48651 • 1,100
Prudhoe Bay, AK 99734 • 47
Pryor, OK 74361–62 • 8,327
Pueblo, CO 81001–19 • 98,640
Pueblo □, CO • 123,051
Puhi, HI 96766 • 1,210
Pukalani, HI 96788 • 5,879
Pulaski, NY 13142 • 2,525
Pulaski, TN 38478 • 7,895
Pulaski, VA 24301 • 9,985
Pulaski, WI 54162 • 2,200
Pulaski □, AR • 349,660
Pulaski □, GA • 8,108
Pulaski □, IL • 7,523
Pulaski □, IN • 12,643
Pulaski □, KY • 49,489
Pulaski □, MO • 41,307
Pulaski □, VA • 34,496
Pullman, WA 99163–65 • 23,478
Pumphrey, MD 21227 • 5,483
Punta Gorda, FL 33948–55 • 10,747
Punxsutawney, PA 15767 • 6,782
Purcell, OK 73080 • 4,784
Purcellville, VA 22132 • 1,744
Purvis, MS 39475 • 2,140
Pushmataha □, OK • 10,997
Putnam, CT 06260 • 6,835
Putnam □, FL • 65,070
Putnam □, GA • 14,137
Putnam □, IL • 5,730
Putnam □, IN • 30,315
Putnam □, MO • 5,079
Putnam □, NY • 83,941
Putnam □, OH • 33,819
Putnam □, TN • 51,373
Putnam □, WV • 42,835
Putney, VT 05346 • 1,100
Puyallup, WA 98371–74 • 23,875

Q

Quail Oaks, VA 23234 • 1,500
Quaker Hill, CT 06375 • 2,052
Quakertown, PA 18951 • 8,982
Quanah, TX 79252 • 3,413
Quarryville, PA 17566 • 1,642
Quartz Hill, CA 93536 • 9,626
Quartzsite, AZ 85346 • 1,876
Quay □, NM • 10,823
Quechee, VT 05059 • 550
Queen Annes □, MD • 33,953
Queen City, TX 75572 • 1,748
Queen Creek, AZ 85242 • 2,667
Queens □, NY • 1,951,598
Queensborough, WA 98021 • 4,850
Questa, NM 87556 • 1,707
Quidnessett, RI 02852 • 3,300
Quidnick, RI 02816 • 2,300
Quilcene, WA 98376 • 1,200
Quincy, CA 95971 • 2,700
Quincy, FL 32351 • 7,444
Quincy, IL 62301–06 • 39,681
Quincy, MA 02169 • 84,985
Quincy, MI 49082 • 1,680
Quincy, WA 98848 • 3,738
Quinebaug, CT 06262 • 1,031
Quinhagak, AK 99655 • 501
Quinlan, TX 75474 • 1,360
Quinton, OK 74561 • 1,133
Quitman, GA 31643 • 5,292
Quitman, MS 39355 • 2,736
Quitman, TX 75783 • 1,684
Quitman □, GA • 2,209
Quitman □, MS • 10,490
Quonochontaug, RI 02813 • 1,500

R

Rabun □, GA • 11,648
Raceland, KY 41169 • 2,256
Raceland, LA 70394 • 5,564
Racine, WI 53401–08 • 84,298
Racine □, WI • 175,034
Radcliff, KY 40159–60 • 19,772
Radford, VA 24141–43 • 15,940
Radnor Township, PA 19087 • 28,705
Raeford, NC 28376 • 3,469
Ragland, AL 35131 • 1,807
Rahway, NJ 07065–67 • 25,325
Rainbow City, AL 35901 • 7,673
Rainelle, WV 25962 • 1,681
Rainier, OR 97048 • 1,674
Rains □, TX • 6,715
Rainsville, AL 35986 • 3,875
Raleigh, MS 39153 • 1,291
Raleigh, NC 27601–61 • 207,951
Raleigh □, WV • 76,819
Raleigh Hills, OR 97225 • 6,066
Ralls, TX 79357 • 2,172
Ralls □, MO • 8,476
Ralston, NE 68127 • 6,236
Rambleton Acres, DE 19720 • 1,700
Ramblewood, NJ 08054 • 6,181
Ramona, CA 92065 • 13,040
Ramsay, MI 49959 • 1,075
Ramseur, NC 27316 • 1,186
Ramsey, MN 55303 • 12,408
Ramsey, NJ 07446 • 13,228
Ramsey □, MN • 485,765
Ramsey □, ND • 12,681
Ranchester, WY 82839 • 676
Rancho Cordova, CA 95670 • 48,731
Rancho Mirage, CA 92270 • 9,778
Rancho Palos Verdes, CA 90274 • 41,659
Rancho Rinconado, CA 95014 • 4,206
Ranchos de Taos, NM 87557 • 1,779
Rancocas Woods, NJ 08060 • 1,250
Rand, WV 25306 • 2,400
Randall □, TX • 89,673
Randallstown, MD 21133 • 26,277
Randleman, NC 27317 • 2,612
Randolph, ME 04345 • 1,949
Randolph, MA 02368 • 30,093
Randolph, NY 14772 • 1,298
Randolph, VT 05060 • 2,200
Randolph, WI 53956 • 1,729
Randolph □, AL • 19,881
Randolph □, AR • 16,558
Randolph □, GA • 8,023
Randolph □, IL • 34,583
Randolph □, IN • 27,148
Randolph □, MO • 24,370
Randolph □, NC • 106,546
Randolph □, WV • 27,803
Randolph Hills, MD 20852 • 4,180
Random Lake, WI 53075 • 1,439
Rangely, CO 81648 • 2,278
Ranger, TX 76470 • 2,803
Rankin, PA 15104 • 2,503
Rankin, TX 79778 • 1,011
Rankin □, MS • 87,161
Ransom □, ND • 5,921
Ransomville, NY 14131 • 1,542
Ranson, WV 25438 • 2,890
Rantoul, IL 61866 • 17,212
Raoul, GA 30510 • 1,400
Rapid City, SD 57701–09 • 54,523
Rapides □, LA • 131,556
Rapid Valley, SD 57701 • 5,968
Rappahannock □, VA • 6,622
Raritan, NJ 08869 • 5,798
Rathdrum, ID 83858 • 2,000
Raton, NM 87740 • 7,372
Ravalli □, MT • 25,010
Raven, VA 24639 • 2,640
Ravena, NY 12143 • 3,547
Ravenel, SC 29470 • 2,165
Ravenna, NE 68869 • 1,317
Ravenna, OH 44266 • 12,069
Ravenswood, WV 26164 • 4,189
Rawlins, WY 82301 • 9,380
Rawlins □, KS • 3,404
Ray, ND 58849 • 603
Ray □, MO • 21,971
Raymond, MS 39154 • 2,275
Raymond, NH 03077 • 2,516
Raymond, WA 98577 • 2,901
Raymondville, TX 78580 • 8,880
Raymore, MO 64083 • 5,592
Rayne, LA 70578 • 8,502
Raynham, MA 02767 • 3,709
Raynham Center, MA 02768 • 3,709
Raytown, MO 64133 • 30,601
Rayville, LA 71269 • 4,411
Reading, MA 01867 • 22,539
Reading, MI 49274 • 1,127
Reading, OH 45215 • 12,038
Reading, PA 19601–12 • 78,380
Reagan □, TX • 4,514
Real □, TX • 2,412
Reamstown, PA 17567 • 2,649
Rector, AR 72461 • 2,268
Red Bank, NJ 07701–04 • 10,636
Red Bank, SC 29073 • 6,112
Red Bank, TN 37415 • 12,322
Red Bay, AL 35582 • 3,451
Redbird, OH 44057 • 1,600
Red Bluff, CA 96080 • 12,363
Red Bud, IL 62278 • 2,918
Red Cloud, NE 68970 • 1,204
Redding, CA 96001–03 • 66,462
Redding, CT 06875 • 1,000
Redfield, AR 72132 • 1,082
Redfield, SD 57469 • 2,770
Redford, MI 48239 • 54,387
Redgranite, WI 54970 • 1,009
Red Hook, NY 12571 • 1,794
Redkey, IN 47373 • 1,383
Red Lake □, MN • 4,525
Red Lake Falls, MN 56750 • 1,481
Redlands, CA 92373–75 • 60,394
Red Lion, PA 17356 • 6,130
Red Lodge, MT 59068 • 1,958
Redmond, OR 97756 • 7,163
Redmond, WA 98052–53 • 35,800
Red Oak, GA 30272 • 2,800
Red Oak, IA 51566 • 6,264
Red Oak, TX 75154 • 3,124
Red Oaks, LA 70815 • 1,600
Red Oaks Mill, NY 12603 • 4,906
Redondo Beach, CA 90277–78 • 60,167
Red River □, LA • 9,387
Red River □, TX • 14,317
Red Springs, NC 28377 • 3,799
Red Willow □, NE • 11,705
Red Wing, MN 55066 • 15,134
Redwood, UT 84119 • 1,850
Redwood □, MN • 17,254
Redwood City, CA 94061–65 • 66,072
Redwood Falls, MN 56283 • 4,859
Redwood Valley, CA 95470 • 1,300
Reed City, MI 49677 • 2,379
Reedley, CA 93654 • 15,791
Reedsburg, WI 53959 • 5,834
Reedsport, OR 97467 • 4,796
Reedsville, PA 17084 • 1,030
Reedsville, WI 54230 • 1,182
Reedurban, OH 44710 • 6,650
Reese, MI 48757 • 1,414
Reeves □, TX • 15,852
Reform, AL 35481 • 2,105
Refugio, TX 78377 • 3,158
Refugio □, TX • 7,976
Rehoboth Beach, DE 19971 • 1,234
Reidland, KY 42001 • 4,054
Reidsville, GA 30453 • 2,469
Reidsville, NC 27320–23 • 12,183
Reinbeck, IA 50669 • 1,605
Reisterstown, MD 21136 • 19,314
Reliance, WY 82943 • 500
Remington, IN 47977 • 1,247
Remsen, IA 51050 • 1,513
Reno, NV 89501–70 • 133,850
Reno □, KS • 62,389
Renovo, PA 17764 • 1,526
Rensselaer, IN 47978 • 5,045
Rensselaer, NY 12144 • 8,255
Rensselaer □, NY • 154,429
Renton, WA 98055–59 • 41,688
Renville, MN 56284 • 1,315
Renville □, MN • 17,673
Renville □, ND • 3,160
Republic, MI 49879 • 1,100
Republic, MO 65738 • 6,292
Republic, PA 15475 • 1,400
Republic □, KS • 6,482
Reserve, LA 70084 • 8,847
Reston, VA 22090 • 48,556
Revere, MA 02151 • 42,786
Rexburg, ID 83440 • 14,302
Reynolds, GA 31076 • 1,166
Reynolds □, MO • 6,661
Reynoldsburg, OH 43068 • 25,748
Reynoldsville, PA 15851 • 2,818
Rhea □, TN • 24,344
Rhinebeck, NY 12572 • 2,725
Rhinelander, WI 54501 • 7,427
Rialto, CA 92376–77 • 72,388
Rice □, KS • 10,610
Rice □, MN • 49,183
Rice Lake, WI 54868 • 7,998
Rich □, UT • 1,725
Richardson, TX 75080–83 • 74,840
Richardson □, NE • 9,937
Richardson Park, DE 19804 • 1,100
Richardton, ND 58652 • 625
Richboro, PA 18954 • 5,332
Richfield, MN 55423 • 35,710
Richfield, UT 84701 • 5,593
Richfield Springs, NY 13439 • 1,565
Richford, VT 05476 • 1,425
Rich Hill, MO 64779 • 1,317
Richland, GA 31825 • 1,668
Richland, MO 65556 • 2,029
Richland, WA 99352 • 32,315
Richland □, IL • 16,545
Richland □, LA • 20,629
Richland □, MT • 10,716
Richland □, ND • 18,148
Richland □, OH • 126,137
Richland □, SC • 285,720
Richland □, WI • 17,521
Richland Center, WI 53581 • 5,018
Richland Hills, TX 76118 • 7,978
Richlands, VA 24641 • 4,456
Richlandtown, PA 18955 • 1,195
Richmond, CA 94801–08 • 87,425
Richmond, IL 60071 • 1,016
Richmond, IN 47374–75 • 38,705
Richmond, KY 40475–76 • 21,155
Richmond, ME 04357 • 1,775
Richmond, MI 48062 • 4,141
Richmond, MO 64085 • 5,738
Richmond, TX 77469 • 9,801
Richmond, UT 84333 • 1,955
Richmond, VT 05477 • 650
Richmond, VA 23201–94 • 203,056
Richmond □, GA • 189,719
Richmond □, NY • 378,977
Richmond □, NC • 44,518
Richmond □, VA • 7,273
Richmond Beach, WA 98160 • 5,000
Richmond Heights, FL 33156 • 8,583
Richmond Heights, MO 63117 • 10,448
Richmond Heights, OH 44143 • 9,611
Richmond Highlands, WA 98133 • 26,037
Richmond Hill, GA 31324 • 2,934
Rich Square, NC 27869 • 1,058
Richton, MS 39476 • 1,034
Richton Park, IL 60471 • 10,523
Richwood, OH 43344 • 2,186
Richwood, WV 26261 • 2,808
Riddle, OR 97469 • 1,143
Ridge, NY 11961 • 11,734
Ridgecrest, CA 93555 • 27,725
Ridgecrest, WA 98155 • 5,500
Ridgefield, CT 06877 • 6,363
Ridgefield, NJ 07657 • 9,996
Ridgefield, WA 98642 • 1,297
Ridgefield Park, NJ 07660 • 12,454
Ridgeland, MS 39157–58 • 11,714
Ridgeland, SC 29936 • 1,071
Ridgely, MD 21660 • 1,034
Ridgely, TN 38080 • 1,775
Ridgetop, TN 37152 • 1,132
Ridgeville, SC 29472 • 1,625
Ridgewood, NJ 07450–52 • 24,152
Ridgway, IL 62979 • 1,103
Ridgway, PA 15853 • 4,793
Ridley Park, PA 19078 • 7,592
Ridley Township, PA 19018 • 33,771
Rifle, CO 81650 • 4,636
Rigby, ID 83442 • 2,681
Riley □, KS • 67,139
Rimersburg, PA 16248 • 1,053
Rincon, GA 31326 • 2,697
Ringgold, GA 30736 • 1,675
Ringgold, LA 71068 • 1,856
Ringgold □, IA • 5,420
Ringling, OK 73456 • 1,250
Ringwood, NJ 07456 • 12,623
Rio, FL 34957 • 1,054
Rio Arriba □, NM • 34,365
Rio Blanco □, CO • 5,972
Rio Dell, CA 95562 • 3,012
Rio Del Mar, CA 95003 • 8,919
Rio Grande, NJ 08242 • 2,505
Rio Grande □, CO • 10,770
Rio Grande City, TX 78582 • 9,891
Rio Hondo, TX 78583 • 1,793
Rio Linda, CA 95673 • 9,481
Rio Rancho, NM 87124 • 32,505
Rio Vista, CA 94571 • 3,316
Ripley, MS 38663 • 5,371
Ripley, NY 14775 • 1,189
Ripley, OH 45167 • 1,816
Ripley, TN 38063 • 6,188
Ripley, WV 25271 • 3,023
Ripley □, IN • 24,616
Ripley □, MO • 12,303
Ripon, WI 54971 • 7,241
Rising Sun, DE 19934 • 540
Rising Sun, IN 47040 • 2,311
Rising Sun, MD 21911 • 1,263
Rison, AR 71665 • 1,258
Ritchie □, WV • 10,233
Rittman, OH 44270 • 6,147
Ritzville, WA 99169 • 1,725
Riverbank, CA 95367 • 8,547
Riverdale, CA 93656 • 1,980
Riverdale, GA 30274 • 9,359
Riverdale, IL 60627 • 13,671
Riverdale, MD 20737–38 • 5,185
Riverdale, NJ 07457 • 2,370
Riverdale, UT 84405 • 6,419
River Edge, NJ 07661 • 10,603
River Falls, WI 54022 • 10,610
River Forest, IL 60305 • 11,669
River Grove, IL 60171 • 9,961
Riverhead, NY 11901 • 8,814
River Heights, UT 84321 • 1,274
River Hills, WI 53217 • 1,612
River Oaks, TX 76114 • 6,580
River Pines, MA 01821 • 3,620
River Ridge, LA 70123 • 14,800
River Road, OR 97404 • 9,443
River Rouge, MI 48218 • 11,314
Riverside, AL 35135 • 1,004
Riverside, CA 92501–19 • 226,505
Riverside, IL 60546 • 8,774
Riverside, NJ 08075 • 7,974
Riverside, PA 17868 • 1,991
Riverside □, CA • 1,170,413
Riverton, IL 62561 • 2,638
Riverton, NJ 08077 • 2,775
Riverton, UT 84065 • 11,261
Riverton, VT 05663 • 150
Riverton, WY 82501 • 9,202
Riverton Heights, WA 98188 • 14,182
River Vale, NJ 07675 • 9,410
Riverview, FL 33569 • 6,478
Riverview, MI 48192 • 13,894
Rivesville, WV 26588 • 1,064
Riviera Beach, FL 33404 • 27,639
Riviera Beach, MD 21122 • 11,376
Roane □, TN • 47,227
Roane □, WV • 15,120
Roan Mountain, TN 37687 • 1,220
Roanoke, AL 36274 • 6,362
Roanoke, IL 61561 • 1,910
Roanoke, IN 46783 • 1,018
Roanoke, TX 76262 • 1,616
Roanoke, VA 24001–38 • 96,397
Roanoke □, VA • 79,332
Roanoke Rapids, NC 27870 • 15,722
Roaring Spring, PA 16673 • 2,615
Robbins, IL 60472 • 7,498
Robbinsdale, MN 55422 • 14,396
Robersonville, NC 27871 • 1,940
Robert Lee, TX 76945 • 1,276
Roberts, WI 54023 • 1,043
Roberts □, SD • 9,914
Roberts □, TX • 1,025
Robertsdale, AL 36567 • 2,401
Robertson □, KY • 2,124
Robertson □, TN • 41,494
Robertson □, TX • 15,511
Robertsville, NJ 07746 • 9,841
Robeson □, NC • 105,179
Robinson, IL 62454 • 6,740
Robinson, TX 76706 • 7,111
Robstown, TX 78380 • 12,849
Rochdale, MA 01542 • 1,105
Rochelle, GA 31079 • 1,510
Rochelle, IL 61068 • 8,769
Rochelle Park, NJ 07662 • 5,587
Rochester, IL 62563 • 2,676
Rochester, IN 46975 • 5,969
Rochester, MI 48306–09 • 7,130
Rochester, MN 55901–06 • 70,745
Rochester, NH 03867–68 • 26,630
Rochester, NY 14601–92 • 231,636
Rochester, PA 15074 • 4,156
Rochester, VT 05767 • 500
Rochester, WA 98579 • 1,150
Rochester Hills, MI 48309 • 61,766
Rock □, MN • 9,806
Rock □, NE • 2,019
Rock □, WI • 139,510
Rockaway, NJ 07866 • 6,243

Rockbridge □, VA • *18,350*
Rockcastle □, KY • *14,803*
Rock Creek, MN 55067 • *1,040*
Rock Creek 0M, OR • *8,282*
Rockdale, IL 60436 • *1,709*
Rockdale, MD 21207 • *5,885*
Rockdale, TX 76567 • *5,235*
Rockdale □, GA • *54,091*
Rock Falls, IL 61071 • *9,654*
Rockford, IL 61101-32 • *139,426*
Rockford, MI 49341 • *3,750*
Rockford, MN 55373 • *2,665*
Rockford, OH 45882 • *1,119*
Rock Hall, MD 21661 • *1,584*
Rock Hill, MO 63124 • *5,217*
Rock Hill, SC 29730-32 • *41,643*
Rockingham, NC 28379 • *9,399*
Rockingham □, NH • *245,845*
Rockingham □, NC • *86,064*
Rockingham □, VA • *57,482*
Rock Island, IL 61201-04 • *40,552*
Rock Island □, IL • *148,723*
Rockland, ME 04841 • *7,972*
Rockland, MA 02370 • *15,695*
Rockland □, NY • *265,475*
Rockledge, FL 32955-56 • *16,023*
Rockledge, PA 19111 • *2,679*
Rocklin, CA 95677 • *19,033*
Rockmart, GA 30153 • *3,356*
Rockport, IN 47635 • *2,315*
Rockport, ME 04856 • *1,100*
Rockport, MA 01966 • *4,690*
Rock Port, MO 64482 • *1,438*
Rockport, TX 78382 • *4,753*
Rock Rapids, IA 51246 • *2,601*
Rock River, WY 82083 • *190*
Rocksprings, TX 78880 • *1,339*
Rock Springs, WY 82901-02 • *19,050*
Rockton, IL 61072 • *2,928*
Rock Valley, IA 51247 • *2,540*
Rockville, IN 47872 • *2,706*
Rockville, MD 20847-59 • *44,835*
Rockville Centre, NY 11570-71 • *24,727*
Rockwall, TX 75087 • *10,486*
Rockwall □, TX • *25,604*
Rockwell, IA 50469 • *1,008*
Rockwell, NC 28138 • *1,598*
Rockwell City, IA 50579 • *1,981*
Rockwell Park, NC 28213 • *2,600*
Rockwood, MI 48173 • *3,141*
Rockwood, OR 97233 • *11,000*
Rockwood, PA 15557 • *1,014*
Rockwood, TN 37854 • *5,348*
Rocky Creek, FL 33615 • *7,800*
Rocky Ford, CO 81067 • *4,162*
Rocky Hill, CT 06067 • *14,559*
Rocky Mount, NC 27801-04 • *48,997*
Rocky Mount, VA 24151 • *4,098*
Rocky Point, NY 11778 • *8,596*
Rocky River, OH 44116 • *20,410*
Rodeo, CA 94572 • *7,589*
Roderfield, WV 24881 • *1,200*
Rodney Village, DE 19901 • *1,745*
Roebling, NJ 08554 • *2,415*
Roebuck, SC 29376 • *1,966*
Roeland Park, KS 66203 • *7,706*
Roessleville, NY 12205 • *10,753*
Roger Mills □, OK • *4,147*
Rogers, AR 72756-57 • *24,692*
Rogers, TX 76569 • *1,131*
Rogers □, OK • *55,170*
Rogers City, MI 49779 • *3,642*
Rogersville, AL 35652 • *1,125*
Rogersville, TN 37857 • *4,149*
Rogue River, OR 97537 • *1,759*
Rohnert Park, CA 94927-28 • *36,326*
Roland, IA 50236 • *1,035*
Roland, OK 74954 • *2,481*
Rolette □, ND • *12,772*
Rolla, MO 65401 • *14,090*
Rolla, ND 58367 • *1,286*
Rolling Fork, MS 39159 • *2,444*
Rolling Hills Estates, CA 90274 • *7,789*
Rolling Meadows, IL 60008 • *22,591*
Rollinsford, NH 03869 • *2,645*
Roma, TX 78584 • *8,059*
Rome, GA 30161-65 • *30,326*
Rome, IL 61562 • *1,902*
Rome, NY 13440 • *44,350*
Rome City, IN 46784 • *1,138*
Romeo, MI 48065 • *3,520*
Romeoville, IL 60441 • *14,074*
Romney, WV 26757 • *1,966*
Romulus, MI 48174 • *22,897*
Ronan, MT 59864 • *1,547*
Ronceverte, WV 24970 • *1,754*
Ronkonkoma, NY 11779 • *20,391*
Roodhouse, IL 62082 • *2,139*
Rooks □, KS • *6,039*
Roosevelt, NY 11575 • *15,030*
Roosevelt, UT 84066 • *3,915*
Roosevelt □, MT • *10,999*
Roosevelt □, NM • *16,702*
Roosevelt Park, MI 49441 • *3,885*
Rosamond, CA 93560 • *7,430*
Roscoe, IL 61073 • *2,079*
Roscoe, TX 79545 • *1,446*
Roscommon □, MI • *19,776*
Roseau, MN 56751 • *2,396*
Roseau □, MN • *15,026*
Roseboro, NC 28382 • *1,441*
Rosebud, TX 76570 • *1,638*
Rosebud □, MT • *10,505*
Roseburg, OR 97470 • *17,032*
Rosedale, MD 21237 • *18,703*
Rosedale, MS 38769 • *2,595*
Rose Hill, KS 67133 • *2,399*
Rose Hill, NC 28458 • *1,287*
Rose Hill, VA 22310 • *12,675*
Roseland, CA 95407 • *8,779*
Roseland, FL 32957 • *1,379*
Roseland, LA 70456 • *1,093*
Roseland, NJ 07068 • *4,847*
Roseland, OH 44906 • *3,000*
Roselle, IL 60172 • *20,819*
Roselle, NJ 07203 • *20,314*
Roselle Park, NJ 07204 • *12,805*
Rosemead, CA 91770 • *51,638*
Rosemont, CA 95826 • *22,851*
Rosemount, MN 55068 • *8,622*
Rosenberg, TX 77471 • *20,183*
Rosepine, LA 70659 • *1,135*
Roseto, PA 18013 • *1,555*
Roseville, CA 95678 • *44,685*
Roseville, IL 61473 • *1,151*
Roseville, MI 48066 • *51,412*
Roseville, MN 55113 • *33,485*
Roseville, OH 43777 • *1,847*
Rosewood Heights, IL 62024 • *4,821*
Rosiclare, IL 62982 • *1,378*
Roslyn Heights, NY 11577 • *6,405*
Ross, OH 45061 • *2,124*
Ross □, OH • *69,330*
Rossford, OH 43460 • *5,861*
Rossmoor, CA 90720 • *9,893*
Ross Township, PA 15237 • *33,482*
Rossville, GA 30741-42 • *3,601*
Rossville, IL 60963 • *1,334*
Rossville, IN 46065 • *1,175*
Rossville, KS 66533 • *1,052*
Roswell, GA 30075-77 • *47,923*
Roswell, NM 88201-02 • *44,654*
Rotan, TX 79546 • *1,913*
Rothschild, WI 54474 • *3,310*
Rothsville, PA 17543 • *2,097*
Rotterdam, NY 12303 • *21,228*
Roulette, PA 16746 • *1,500*
Round Lake, IL 60073 • *3,550*
Round Lake Beach, IL 60073 • *16,434*
Round Mountain, NV 89045 • *210*
Round Rock, TX 78664 • *30,923*
Roundup, MT 59072 • *1,808*
Rouses Point, NY 12979 • *2,377*
Routt □, CO • *14,088*
Rouzerville, PA 17250 • *1,188*
Rowan □, KY • *20,353*
Rowan □, NC • *110,605*
Rowland, NC 28383 • *1,139*
Rowland Heights, CA 91748 • *32,700*
Rowlett, TX 75088 • *23,260*
Rowley, MA 01969 • *1,144*
Roxboro, NC 27573 • *7,332*
Roy, UT 84067 • *24,603*
Royal Oak, MI 48067-73 • *65,410*
Royal Pines, NC 28704 • *1,600*
Royalton, IL 62983 • *1,191*
Royersford, PA 19468 • *4,458*
Royse City, TX 75089 • *2,206*
Royston, GA 30662 • *2,758*
Rubidoux, CA 92509 • *24,367*
Rugby, ND 58368 • *2,909*
Ruidoso, NM 88345 • *4,600*
Ruidoso Downs, NM 88346 • *920*
Ruleville, MS 38771 • *3,245*
Rumford, ME 04276 • *5,419*
Rumson, NJ 07760 • *6,701*
Runge, TX 78151 • *1,139*
Runnels □, TX • *11,294*
Runnemede, NJ 08078 • *9,042*
Rupert, ID 83350 • *5,455*
Rupert, WV 25984 • *1,104*
Rural Hall, NC 27045 • *1,652*
Rush □, IN • *18,129*
Rush □, KS • *3,842*
Rush City, MN 55069 • *1,497*
Rushford, MN 55971 • *1,485*
Rushmere, VA 23430 • *1,064*
Rush Springs, OK 73082 • *1,229*
Rushville, IL 62681 • *3,229*
Rushville, IN 46173 • *5,533*
Rushville, NE 69360 • *1,127*
Rusk, TX 75785 • *4,366*
Rusk □, TX • *43,735*
Rusk □, WI • *15,079*
Ruskin, FL 33570-73 • *6,046*
Russell, KS 67665 • *4,781*
Russell, KY 41169 • *4,014*
Russell, PA 16345 • *1,000*
Russell □, AL • *46,860*
Russell □, KS • *7,835*
Russell □, KY • *14,716*
Russell □, VA • *28,667*
Russell Springs, KY 42642 • *2,363*
Russellville, AL 35653 • *7,812*
Russellville, AR 72801 • *21,260*
Russellville, KY 42276 • *7,454*
Russellville, OR 97216 • *6,500*
Russellville, TN 37860 • *1,069*
Ruston, LA 71270-73 • *20,027*
Ruth, NV 89319 • *550*
Rutherford, NJ 07070-75 • *17,790*
Rutherford, TN 38369 • *1,303*
Rutherford □, NC • *56,918*
Rutherford □, TN • *118,570*
Rutherfordton, NC 28139 • *3,617*
Rutland, MA 01543 • *2,145*
Rutland, VT 05701-02 • *18,230*
Rutland □, VT • *62,142*
Rye, NH 03870 • *835*
Rye, NY 10580 • *14,936*
Rye Brook, NY 10573 • *7,765*

S

Sabattus, ME 04280 • *3,696*
Sabetha, KS 66534 • *2,341*
Sabina, OH 45169 • *2,652*
Sabinal, TX 78881 • *1,584*
Sabine □, LA • *22,646*
Sabine □, TX • *9,586*
Sac □, IA • *12,324*
Sacaton, AZ 85221 • *1,452*
Sac City, IA 50583 • *2,492*
Sachse, TX 75040 • *5,346*
Sackets Harbor, NY 13685 • *1,313*
Saco, ME 04072 • *15,181*
Sacramento, CA 95801-66 • *369,365*
Sacramento □, CA • *1,041,219*
Saddle Brook, NJ 07662 • *13,296*
Saddle River, NJ 07458 • *2,950*
Saegertown, PA 16433 • *1,066*
Safety Harbor, FL 34695 • *15,124*
Safford, AZ 85546 • *7,359*
Sagadahoc □, ME • *33,535*
Sagamore, MA 02561 • *2,589*
Sagamore Hills, OH 44067 • *4,700*
Sag Harbor, NY 11963 • *2,134*
Saginaw, MI 48601-08 • *69,512*
Saginaw, TX 76179 • *8,551*
Saginaw □, MI • *211,946*
Saguache □, CO • *4,619*
Saint Albans, VT 05478 • *7,339*
Saint Albans, WV 25177 • *11,194*
Saint Andrews, SC 29407 • *9,908*
Saint Andrews, SC 29210 • *25,692*
Saint Ann, MO 63074 • *14,489*
Saint Anne, IL 60964 • *1,153*
Saint Ansgar, IA 50472 • *1,063*
Saint Anthony, ID 83445 • *3,010*
Saint Anthony, MN 55418 • *7,727*
Saint Augustine, FL 32084-86 • *11,692*
Saint Bernard, OH 45217 • *5,344*
Saint Bernard □, LA • *66,631*
Saint Charles, IL 60174-75 • *22,501*
Saint Charles, MD 20601 • *28,717*
Saint Charles, MI 48655 • *2,144*
Saint Charles, MN 55972 • *2,642*
Saint Charles, MO 63301-03 • *54,555*
Saint Charles □, LA • *42,437*
Saint Charles □, MO • *212,907*
Saint Charles Mesa, CO 81006 • *7,050*
Saint Clair, MI 48079 • *5,116*
Saint Clair, MO 63077 • *3,917*
Saint Clair, PA 17970 • *3,524*
Saint Clair □, AL • *50,009*
Saint Clair □, IL • *262,852*
Saint Clair □, MI • *145,607*
Saint Clair □, MO • *8,457*
Saint Clair Shores, MI 48080-82 • *68,107*
Saint Clairsville, OH 43950 • *5,162*
Saint Cloud, FL 34769-73 • *12,453*
Saint Cloud, MN 56301-04 • *48,812*
Saint Croix □, WI • *50,251*
Saint Croix Falls, WI 54024 • *1,640*
Saint David, AZ 85630 • *1,500*
Saint Elmo, IL 62458 • *1,473*
Saint Francis, KS 67756 • *1,495*
Saint Francis, MN 55070 • *2,538*
Saint Francis, SD 57572 • *815*
Saint Francis, WI 53207 • *9,245*
Saint Francis □, AR • *28,497*
Saint Francisville, LA 70775 • *1,700*
Saint Francois □, MO • *48,904*
Sainte Genevieve, MO 63670 • *4,411*
Sainte Genevieve □, MO • *16,037*
Saint George, SC 29477 • *2,077*
Saint George, UT 84770-71 • *28,502*
Saint Georges, DE 19733 • *500*
Saint Helena, CA 94574 • *4,990*
Saint Helena □, LA • *9,874*
Saint Helens, OR 97051 • *7,535*
Saint Henry, OH 45883 • *1,907*
Saint Ignace, MI 49781 • *2,568*
Saint Ignatius, MT 59865 • *778*
Saint James, MN 56081 • *4,364*
Saint James, MO 65559 • *3,256*
Saint James, NY 11780 • *12,703*
Saint James □, LA • *20,879*
Saint James City, FL 33956 • *1,094*
Saint Jo, TX 76265 • *1,048*
Saint John, IN 46373 • *4,921*
Saint John, KS 67576 • *1,357*
Saint Johns, AZ 85936 • *3,294*
Saint Johns, MI 48879 • *7,284*
Saint Johns, MO 63114 • *7,466*
Saint Johns □, FL • *83,829*
Saint Johnsbury, VT 05819 • *6,424*
Saint Johnsville, NY 13452 • *1,825*
Saint John the Baptist □, LA • *39,996*
Saint Joseph, IL 61873 • *2,052*
Saint Joseph, LA 71366 • *1,517*
Saint Joseph, MI 49085 • *9,214*
Saint Joseph, MN 56374 • *3,294*
Saint Joseph, MO 64501-08 • *71,852*
Saint Joseph □, IN • *247,052*
Saint Joseph □, MI • *58,913*
Saint Landry □, LA • *80,331*
Saint Lawrence □, NY • *111,974*
Saint Leo, FL 33574 • *1,009*
Saint Louis, MI 48880 • *3,828*
Saint Louis, MO 63101-88 • *396,685*
Saint Louis □, MN • *198,213*
Saint Louis □, MO • *993,529*
Saint Louis Park, MN 55426 • *43,787*
Saint Lucie □, FL • *150,171*
Saint Maries, ID 83861 • *2,442*
Saint Martin □, LA • *43,978*
Saint Martinville, LA 70582 • *7,137*
Saint Mary □, LA • *58,086*
Saint Marys, AK 99658 • *441*
Saint Marys, GA 31558 • *8,187*
Saint Marys, IN 46556 • *1,800*
Saint Marys, KS 66536 • *1,791*
Saint Marys, OH 45885 • *8,441*
Saint Marys, PA 15857 • *5,511*
Saint Marys, WV 26170 • *2,148*
Saint Marys □, MD • *75,974*
Saint Marys City, MD 20686 • *3,200*
Saint Matthews, KY 40207 • *15,800*
Saint Matthews, SC 29135 • *2,345*
Saint Michael, MN 55376 • *2,506*
Saint Michaels, MD 21663 • *1,301*
Saint Paris, OH 43072 • *1,842*
Saint Paul, AK 99660 • *763*
Saint Paul, IN 47272 • *1,032*
Saint Paul, MN 55101-89 • *272,235*
Saint Paul, MO 63366 • *1,192*
Saint Paul, NE 68873 • *2,009*
Saint Paul, VA 24283 • *1,007*
Saint Paul Park, MN 55071 • *4,965*
Saint Pauls, NC 28384 • *1,992*
Saint Peter, MN 56082 • *9,421*
Saint Peters, MO 63376 • *45,779*
Saint Petersburg, FL 33701-84 • *238,629*
Saint Petersburg Beach, FL 33706 • *9,200*
Saint Rose, LA 70087 • *2,800*
Saint Simons Island, GA 31522 • *12,026*
Saint Stephen, SC 29479 • *1,697*
Saint Stephens, NC 28601 • *8,734*
Saint Tammany □, LA • *144,508*
Salamanca, NY 14779 • *6,566*
Sale Creek, TN 37373 • *1,050*
Salem, AR 72576 • *1,474*
Salem, IL 62881 • *7,470*
Salem, IN 47167 • *5,619*
Salem, MA 01970-71 • *38,091*
Salem, MO 65560 • *4,486*
Salem, NH 03079 • *12,000*
Salem, NJ 08079 • *6,883*
Salem, OH 44460 • *12,233*
Salem, OR 97301-14 • *107,786*
Salem, SD 57058 • *1,289*
Salem, UT 84653 • *2,284*
Salem, VA 24153 • *23,756*
Salem, WV 26426 • *2,063*
Salem, WI 53168 • *1,020*
Salem □, NJ • *65,294*
Salida, CO 81201 • *4,737*
Salina, KS 67401-02 • *42,303*
Salina, OK 74365 • *1,153*
Salina, UT 84654 • *1,943*
Salinas, CA 93901-15 • *108,777*
Saline, MI 48176 • *6,660*
Saline □, AR • *64,183*
Saline □, IL • *26,551*
Saline □, KS • *49,301*
Saline □, MO • *23,523*
Saline □, NE • *12,715*
Salineville, OH 43945 • *1,474*
Salisbury, CT 06068 • *1,600*
Salisbury, MD 21801-03 • *20,592*
Salisbury, MA 01952 • *3,729*
Salisbury, MO 65281 • *1,881*
Salisbury, NC 28144-46 • *23,087*
Sallisaw, OK 74955 • *7,122*
Salmon, ID 83467 • *2,941*
Salmon Creek, WA 98665 • *11,989*
Saltillo, MS 38866 • *1,782*
Salt Lake □, UT • *725,956*
Salt Lake City, UT 84101-90 • *159,936*
Salt Springs, FL 32113 • *1,500*
Saltville, VA 24370 • *2,300*
Saltwater, WA 98188 • *2,200*
Saluda, SC 29138 • *2,798*
Saluda □, SC • *16,357*
Salyersville, KY 41465 • *1,917*
Samoset, FL 34208 • *3,119*
Sampson □, NC • *47,297*
Samson, AL 36477 • *2,190*
Samtown, LA 71301 • *3,500*
San Andreas, CA 95249 • *2,115*
San Angelo, TX 76901-06 • *84,474*
San Anselmo, CA 94960 • *11,743*
San Antonio, TX 78201-99 • *935,933*
Sanatoga, PA 19464 • *5,534*
San Augustine, TX 75972 • *2,337*
San Augustine □, TX • *7,999*
San Benito, TX 78586 • *20,125*
San Benito □, CA • *36,697*
San Bernardino, CA 92401-27 • *164,164*
San Bernardino □, CA • *1,418,380*
Sanborn, IA 51248 • *1,345*
Sanborn □, SD • *2,833*
San Bruno, CA 94066 • *38,961*
San Carlos, AZ 85550 • *2,918*
San Carlos, CA 94070 • *26,167*
San Carlos Park, FL 33912 • *11,785*
San Clemente, CA 92672-74 • *41,100*
Sandalfoot Cove, FL 33433 • *14,214*
Sanders □, MT • *8,669*
Sanderson, TX 79848 • *1,128*
Sandersville, GA 31082 • *6,290*
Sand Hill, MA 02066 • *1,800*
Sandia, NM 87047 • *6,742*
San Diego, CA 92101-99 • *1,110,549*
San Diego, TX 78384 • *4,983*
San Diego □, CA • *2,498,016*
San Dimas, CA 91773 • *32,397*
Sandoval, IL 62882 • *1,535*
Sandoval □, NM • *63,319*
Sand Point, AK 99661 • *878*
Sandpoint, ID 83862-65 • *5,203*
Sand Springs, OK 74063 • *15,346*
Sandston, VA 23150 • *3,630*
Sandstone, MN 55072 • *2,057*
Sandusky, MI 48471 • *2,403*
Sandusky, OH 44870-71 • *29,764*
Sandusky □, OH • *61,963*
Sandwich, IL 60548 • *5,567*
Sandwich, MA 02563 • *2,998*
Sandy, OR 97055 • *4,152*
Sandy, UT 84070 • *75,058*
Sandy Hook, CT 06482 • *1,100*
Sandy Springs, GA 30328 • *67,842*
Sandy Springs, SC 29677 • *1,200*
San Felipe Pueblo, NM 87001 • *1,557*
San Fernando, CA 91340-46 • *22,580*
Sanford, FL 32771-73 • *32,387*
Sanford, ME 04073 • *10,296*
Sanford, NC 27330-31 • *14,475*
San Francisco, CA 94101-88 • *723,959*
San Francisco □, CA • *723,959*
Sangamon □, IL • *178,386*
Sanger, CA 93657 • *16,839*
Sanger, TX 76266 • *3,508*
Sanibel, FL 33957 • *5,468*
Sanilac □, MI • *39,928*
San Jacinto, CA 92383 • *16,210*
San Jacinto □, TX • *16,372*
San Joaquin □, CA • *480,628*
San Jose, CA 95101-96 • *782,248*
San Juan, TX 78589 • *10,815*
San Juan □, CO • *745*
San Juan □, NM • *91,605*
San Juan □, UT • *12,621*
San Juan □, WA • *10,035*
San Juan Capistrano, CA 92690-93 • *26,183*
San Leandro, CA 94577-79 • *68,223*
San Lorenzo, CA 94580 • *19,987*
San Luis, AZ 85634 • *4,212*
San Luis Obispo, CA 93401-12 • *41,958*
San Luis Obispo □, CA • *217,162*
San Manuel, AZ 85631 • *4,009*
San Marcos, CA 92069 • *38,974*
San Marcos, TX 78666-67 • *28,743*
San Marino, CA 91108 • *12,959*
San Mateo, CA 94401-04 • *85,486*
San Mateo □, CA • *649,623*
San Miguel □, CO • *3,653*
San Miguel □, NM • *25,743*
San Pablo, CA 94806 • *25,158*
San Patricio □, TX • *58,749*
Sanpete □, UT • *16,259*
San Rafael, CA 94901-15 • *48,404*
San Ramon, CA 94583 • *35,303*
San Remo, NY 11754 • *7,770*
San Saba, TX 76877 • *2,626*
San Saba □, TX • *5,401*
Sans Souci, SC 29609 • *7,612*
Santa Ana, CA 92701-08 • *293,742*
Santa Anna, TX 76878 • *1,249*
Santa Barbara, CA 93101-90 • *85,571*
Santa Barbara □, CA • *369,608*
Santa Clara, CA 95050-56 • *93,613*
Santa Clara, OR 97404 • *12,834*
Santa Clara, UT 84765 • *2,322*
Santa Clara □, CA • *1,497,577*
Santa Cruz, CA 95060-67 • *49,040*
Santa Cruz, NM 87567 • *975*
Santa Cruz □, AZ • *29,676*
Santa Cruz □, CA • *229,734*
Santa Fe, NM 87501-06 • *55,859*
Santa Fe, TX 77510 • *8,429*
Santa Fe □, NM • *98,928*
Santa Fe Springs, CA 90670-71 • *15,520*
Santa Margarita, CA 93453 • *1,200*
Santa Maria, CA 93454-56 • *61,284*
Santa Monica, CA 90401-11 • *86,905*
Santa Paula, CA 93060-61 • *25,062*
Santaquin, UT 84655 • *2,386*
Santa Rosa, CA 95401-09 • *113,313*
Santa Rosa, NM 88435 • *2,263*
Santa Rosa □, FL • *81,608*
Santa Venetia, CA 94901 • *6,000*
Santa Ynez, CA 93460 • *4,200*
Santee, CA 92071 • *52,902*
Santo Domingo Pueblo, NM 87052 • *2,866*
San Ygnacio, TX 78067 • *1,000*
Sappington, MO 63126 • *10,917*
Sapulpa, OK 74066-67 • *18,074*
Saraland, AL 36571 • *11,751*
Saranac, MI 48881 • *1,461*
Saranac Lake, NY 12983 • *5,377*
Sarasota, FL 34230-43 • *50,961*
Sarasota □, FL • *277,776*
Sarasota Springs, FL 34232 • *16,088*
Saratoga, CA 95070-71 • *28,061*
Saratoga, TX 77585 • *1,200*
Saratoga, WY 82331 • *1,969*
Saratoga □, NY • *181,276*
Saratoga Springs, NY 12866 • *25,001*
Sarcoxie, MO 64862 • *1,330*
Sardis, GA 30456 • *1,116*
Sardis, MS 38666 • *2,128*
Sargent □, ND • *4,549*
Sarpy □, NE • *102,583*
Sartell, MN 56377 • *5,393*
Satanta, KS 67870 • *1,073*
Satellite Beach, FL 32937 • *9,889*
Satsuma, AL 36572 • *5,194*
Saugerties, NY 12477 • *3,915*
Saugus, MA 01906 • *25,549*
Sauk □, WI • *46,975*
Sauk Centre, MN 56378 • *3,581*
Sauk City, WI 53583 • *3,019*
Sauk Rapids, MN 56379 • *7,825*
Sauk Village, IL 60411 • *9,926*
Saukville, WI 53080 • *3,695*
Sault Sainte Marie, MI 49783 • *14,689*
Saunders □, NE • *18,285*
Saunderstown, RI 02874 • *400*
Sausalito, CA 94965-66 • *7,152*
Savage, MD 20763 • *2,850*
Savage, MN 55378 • *9,906*
Savanna, IL 61074 • *3,819*
Savannah, GA 31401-20 • *137,560*
Savannah, MO 64485 • *4,352*
Savannah, TN 38372 • *6,547*
Savoonga, AK 99769 • *519*
Savoy, IL 61874 • *2,674*
Sawyer □, WI • *14,181*
Saxonburg, PA 16056 • *1,345*
Saxtons River, VT 05154 • *541*
Saybrook Manor, CT 06475 • *1,073*
Saydel, IA 50313 • *3,500*
Saylesville, RI 02865 • *3,510*
Saylorsburg, PA 18353 • *1,500*
Sayre, OK 73662 • *2,881*
Sayre, PA 18840 • *5,791*
Sayreville, NJ 08872 • *34,986*
Sayville, NY 11782 • *16,550*
Scalp Level, PA 15963 • *1,158*
Scappoose, OR 97056 • *3,529*
Scarborough, ME 04074 • *2,586*
Scarsdale, NY 10583 • *16,987*
Schaumburg, IL 60192-94 • *68,586*
Schenectady, NY 12301-09 • *65,566*
Schenectady □, NY • *149,285*
Schererville, IN 46375 • *19,926*
Schertz, TX 78154 • *10,555*
Schiller Park, IL 60176 • *11,189*
Schleicher □, TX • *2,990*
Schley □, GA • *3,588*
Schofield, WI 54476 • *2,415*
Schoharie, NY 12157 • *1,045*
Schoharie □, NY • *31,859*
Schoolcraft, MI 49087 • *1,517*
Schoolcraft □, MI • *8,302*
Schroon Lake, NY 12870 • *1,100*
Schulenburg, TX 78956 • *2,455*
Schurz, NV 89427 • *617*
Schuyler, NE 68661 • *4,052*
Schuyler □, IL • *7,498*
Schuyler □, MO • *4,236*
Schuyler □, NY • *18,662*
Schuylerville, NY 12871 • *1,364*
Schuylkill □, PA • *152,585*
Schuylkill Haven, PA 17972 • *5,610*
Scioto □, OH • *80,327*
Scituate, MA 02066 • *5,180*
Scobey, MT 59263 • *1,154*
Scotch Plains, NJ 07076 • *21,160*
Scotchtown, NY 10940 • *8,765*
Scotia, CA 95565 • *1,200*
Scotia, NY 12302 • *7,359*
Scotland, SD 57059 • *968*
Scotland □, MO • *4,822*
Scotland □, NC • *33,754*
Scotland Neck, NC 27874 • *2,575*
Scotlandville, LA 70807 • *15,113*
Scott, LA 70583 • *4,912*
Scott □, AR • *10,205*
Scott □, IL • *5,644*
Scott □, IN • *20,991*
Scott □, IA • *150,979*
Scott □, KS • *5,289*
Scott □, KY • *23,867*
Scott □, MN • *57,846*
Scott □, MS • *24,137*
Scott □, MO • *39,376*
Scott □, TN • *18,358*
Scott □, VA • *23,204*
Scott City, KS 67871 • *3,785*
Scott City, MO 63780 • *4,292*
Scottdale, GA 30079 • *8,636*
Scottdale, PA 15683 • *5,184*
Scott Lake, FL 33055 • *14,588*
Scottsbluff, NE 69361-63 • *13,711*
Scotts Bluff □, NE • *36,025*
Scottsboro, AL 35768 • *13,786*
Scottsburg, IN 47170 • *5,334*
Scottsdale, AZ 85250-71 • *130,069*
Scotts Valley, CA 95066-67 • *8,615*
Scottsville, KY 42164 • *4,278*

United States Populations and ZIP Codes

Scottsville, NY 14546 • 1,912
Scott Township, PA 15106 • 17,118
Scottville, MI 49454 • 1,287
Scranton, PA 18501–19 • 81,805
Screven □, GA • 13,842
Scurry □, TX • 18,634
Seabreeze, DE 19971 • 350
Sea Bright, NJ 07760 • 1,693
Seabrook, MD 20706 • 7,660
Seabrook, NJ 08302 • 1,457
Seabrook, TX 77586 • 6,685
Sea Cliff, NY 11579 • 5,054
Seadrift, TX 77983 • 1,277
Seaford, DE 19973 • 5,689
Seaford, NY 11783 • 15,597
Seaford, VA 23696 • 2,340
Seagate, NC 28403 • 5,444
Sea Girt, NJ 08750 • 2,099
Seagoville, TX 75159 • 8,969
Seagraves, TX 79359 • 2,398
Sea Isle City, NJ 08243 • 2,692
Seal Beach, CA 90740 • 25,098
Sealy, TX 77474 • 4,541
Seaman, OH 45679 • 1,013
Searchlight, NV 89029 • 430
Searcy, AR 72143 • 15,180
Searcy □, AR • 7,841
Searsport, ME 04974 • 1,151
Seaside, CA 93955 • 38,901
Seaside, OR 97138 • 5,359
Seaside Heights, NJ 08751 • 2,366
Seaside Park, NJ 08752 • 1,871
Seat Pleasant, MD 20743 • 5,359
Seattle, WA 98101–99 • 516,259
Sebastian, FL 32958 • 10,205
Sebastian □, AR • 99,590
Sebewaing, MI 48759 • 1,923
Sebree, KY 42455 • 1,510
Sebring, FL 33870–72 • 8,900
Sebring, OH 44672 • 4,848
Secaucus, NJ 07094 • 14,061
Security, CO 80911 • 6,660
Sedalia, MO 65301–02 • 19,800
Sedan, KS 67361 • 1,306
Sedgwick, KS 67135 • 1,438
Sedgwick □, CO • 2,690
Sedgwick □, KS • 403,662
Sedona, AZ 86336 • 7,720
Sedro Woolley, WA 98284 • 6,031
Seekonk, MA 02771 • 12,269
Seeley, CA 92273 • 1,228
Seelyville, IN 47878 • 1,090
Seguin, TX 78155–56 • 18,853
Seiling, OK 73663 • 1,031
Selah, WA 98942 • 5,113
Selawik, AK 99770 • 596
Selby, SD 57472 • 707
Selbyville, DE 19975 • 1,335
Selden, NY 11784 • 20,608
Seldovia, AK 99663 • 316
Selinsgrove, PA 17870 • 5,384
Sellersburg, IN 47172 • 5,745
Sellersville, PA 18960 • 4,479
Sells, AZ 85634 • 2,750
Selma, AL 36701–02 • 23,755
Selma, CA 93662 • 14,757
Selma, NC 27576 • 4,600
Selmer, TN 38375 • 3,838
Seminole, OK 74868 • 7,071
Seminole, TX 79360 • 6,342
Seminole □, FL • 287,529
Seminole □, GA • 9,010
Seminole □, OK • 25,412
Seminole Park, FL 34647 • 8,000
Semmes, AL 36575 • 2,250
Senath, MO 63876 • 1,622
Senatobia, MS 38668 • 4,772
Seneca, IL 61360 • 1,878
Seneca, KS 66538 • 2,027
Seneca, MO 64865 • 1,885
Seneca, PA 16346 • 1,300
Seneca, SC 29678–79 • 7,726
Seneca □, NY • 33,683
Seneca □, OH • 59,733
Seneca Falls, NY 13148 • 7,370
Sequatchie □, TN • 8,863
Sequim, WA 98382 • 3,616
Sequoyah □, OK • 33,828
Sergeant Bluff, IA 51054 • 2,772
Sesser, IL 62884 • 2,087
Seven Hills, OH 44131 • 12,339
Seven Oaks, SC 29210 • 15,722
Severn, MD 21144 • 24,499
Severna Park, MD 21146 • 25,879
Sevier □, AR • 13,637
Sevier □, TN • 51,043
Sevier □, UT • 15,431
Sevierville, TN 37862 • 7,178
Seville, OH 44273 • 1,810
Sewanee, TN 37375 • 2,128
Seward, AK 99664 • 2,699
Seward, NE 68434 • 5,634
Seward □, KS • 18,743
Seward □, NE • 15,450
Sewell, NJ 08080 • 1,870
Sewickley, PA 15143 • 4,134
Seymour, CT 06483 • 14,288
Seymour, IN 47274 • 15,576
Seymour, MO 65746 • 1,636
Seymour, TN 37865 • 7,026
Seymour, TX 76380 • 3,185
Seymour, WI 54165 • 2,782
Seymourville, LA 70764 • 2,891
Shackelford □, TX • 3,316
Shady Cove, OR 97539 • 1,351
Shady Side, MD 20764 • 4,107
Shadyside, OH 43947 • 3,934
Shady Spring, WV 25918 • 1,929
Shafter, CA 93263 • 8,409
Shaftsbury, VT 05262 • 700
Shaker Heights, OH 44120 • 30,831
Shakopee, MN 55379 • 11,739
Shaler Township, PA 15116 • 30,533
Shallowater, TX 79363 • 1,708
Shamokin, PA 17872 • 9,184
Shamokin Dam, PA 17876 • 1,690
Shamrock, TX 79079 • 2,286
Shannock, RI 02875 • 950
Shannon, GA 30172 • 1,703
Shannon, MS 38868 • 1,419
Shannon □, MO • 7,613
Shannon □, SD • 9,902
Shannontown, SC 29150 • 7,900
Sharkey □, MS • 7,066
Sharon, MA 02067 • 5,893
Sharon, PA 16146 • 17,493
Sharon, TN 38255 • 1,047
Sharon, WI 53585 • 1,250
Sharon Hill, PA 19079 • 5,771
Sharonville, OH 45241 • 13,153
Sharp □, AR • 14,109
Sharpes, FL 32922 • 3,348
Sharpley, DE 19803 • 1,250
Sharpsburg, MD 21782 • 659
Sharpsburg, NC 27878 • 1,536
Sharpsburg, PA 15215 • 3,781
Sharpsville, PA 16150 • 4,729
Shasta □, CA • 147,036
Shattuck, OK 73858 • 1,454
Shaw, MS 38773 • 2,349
Shawano, WI 54166 • 7,598
Shawano □, WI • 37,157
Shawnee, KS 66203 • 37,993
Shawnee, OK 74801–02 • 26,017
Shawnee □, KS • 160,976
Shawneetown, IL 62984 • 1,575
Sheboygan, WI 53081–83 • 49,676
Sheboygan □, WI • 103,877
Sheboygan Falls, WI 53085 • 5,823
Sheffield, AL 35660–62 • 10,380
Sheffield, IA 50475 • 1,174
Sheffield, MA 01257 • 1,100
Sheffield, PA 16347 • 1,294
Sheffield Lake, OH 44054 • 9,825
Shelbina, MO 63468 • 2,172
Shelburn, IN 47879 • 1,147
Shelburne Falls, MA 01370 • 1,996
Shelby, MI 49455 • 48,655
Shelby, MS 38774 • 2,806
Shelby, MT 59474 • 2,763
Shelby, NC 28150–51 • 14,669
Shelby, OH 44875 • 9,564
Shelby □, AL • 99,358
Shelby □, IL • 22,261
Shelby □, IN • 40,307
Shelby □, IA • 13,230
Shelby □, KY • 24,824
Shelby □, MO • 6,942
Shelby □, OH • 44,915
Shelby □, TN • 826,330
Shelby □, TX • 22,034
Shelbyville, IL 62565 • 4,943
Shelbyville, IN 46176 • 15,336
Shelbyville, KY 40065 • 6,238
Shelbyville, TN 37160 • 14,049
Sheldon, IL 60966 • 1,109
Sheldon, IA 51201 • 4,937
Sheldon, TX 77028 • 1,653
Shelley, ID 83274 • 3,536
Shell Lake, WI 54871 • 1,161
Shellman, GA 31786 • 1,162
Shell Rock, IA 50670 • 1,385
Shelter Island, NY 11964 • 1,193
Shelton, CT 06484 • 35,418
Shelton, WA 98584 • 7,241
Shenandoah, IA 51601 • 5,572
Shenandoah, PA 17976 • 6,221
Shenandoah, VA 22849 • 2,213
Shenandoah □, VA • 31,636
Shepherd, MI 48883 • 1,413
Shepherd, TX 77371 • 1,812
Shepherdstown, WV 25443 • 1,287
Shepherdsville, KY 40165 • 4,805
Sherborn, MA 01770 • 1,490
Sherburn, MN 56171 • 1,105
Sherburne, NY 13460 • 1,531
Sherburne □, MN • 41,945
Sheridan, AR 72150 • 3,098
Sheridan, CO 80110 • 4,976
Sheridan, IL 60551 • 1,288
Sheridan, IN 46069 • 2,046
Sheridan, OR 97378 • 3,979
Sheridan, WY 82801 • 13,900
Sheridan □, KS • 3,043
Sheridan □, MT • 4,732
Sheridan □, NE • 6,750
Sheridan □, ND • 2,148
Sheridan □, WY • 23,562
Sheridan Beach, WA 98155 • 6,518
Sherman, TX 75090–91 • 31,601
Sherman □, KS • 6,926
Sherman □, NE • 3,718
Sherman □, OR • 1,918
Sherman □, TX • 2,858
Sherrelwood, CO 80221 • 16,636
Sherrill, NY 13461 • 2,864
Sherwood, AR 72116 • 18,893
Sherwood, OR 97140 • 3,093
Sherwood Manor, CT 06082 • 6,357
Sherwood Park, DE 19808 • 2,000
Shiawassee □, MI • 69,770
Shickshinny, PA 18655 • 1,108
Shillington, PA 19607 • 5,062
Shiloh, OH 44878 • 11,607
Shiloh, PA 17404 • 8,245
Shiner, TX 77984 • 2,074
Shinglehouse, PA 16748 • 1,243
Shinnston, WV 26431 • 2,543
Ship Bottom, NJ 08008 • 1,352
Shippensburg, PA 17257 • 5,331
Shiprock, NM 87420 • 7,687
Shirley, MA 01464 • 1,559
Shirley, NY 11967 • 22,936
Shishmaref, AK 99772 • 456
Shively, KY 40216 • 15,535
Shoemakersville, PA 19555 • 1,443
Shore Acres, MA 02066 • 1,200
Shores Acres, RI 02852 • 410
Shoreview, MN 55112 • 24,587
Shorewood, IL 60435 • 6,264
Shorewood, MN 55331 • 5,917
Shorewood, WI 53211 • 14,116
Shorewood Hills, WI 53705 • 1,680
Short Beach, CT 06405 • 2,500
Shortsville, NY 14548 • 1,485
Shoshone, ID 83352 • 1,249
Shoshone □, ID • 13,931
Shoshoni, WY 82649 • 497
Show Low, AZ 85901 • 5,019
Shreve, OH 44676 • 1,584
Shreveport, LA 71101–10 • 198,525
Shrewsbury, MA 01545 • 23,400
Shrewsbury, MO 63119 • 6,416
Shrewsbury, NJ 07702 • 3,096
Shrewsbury, PA 17361 • 2,672
Shullsburg, WI 53586 • 1,236
Shungnak, AK 99773 • 223
Sibley, IA 51249 • 2,815
Sibley □, MN • 14,366
Sicklerville, NJ 08081 • 1,750
Sidney, IL 61877 • 1,027
Sidney, IA 51652 • 1,253
Sidney, MT 59270 • 5,217
Sidney, NE 69162 • 5,959
Sidney, NY 13838 • 4,720
Sidney, OH 45365 • 18,710
Siegle, LA 71291 • 1,600
Sierra □, CA • 3,318
Sierra □, NM • 9,912
Sierra Madre, CA 91024 • 10,762
Sierra Vista, AZ 85635–36 • 32,983
Siesta Key, FL 34242 • 7,772
Signal Hill, CA 90806 • 8,371
Signal Mountain, TN 37377 • 7,034
Sigourney, IA 52591 • 2,111
Sikeston, MO 63801 • 17,641
Siler City, NC 27344 • 4,808
Siloam Springs, AR 72761 • 8,151
Silsbee, TX 77656 • 6,368
Silt, CO 81652 • 1,095
Silver Bay, MN 55614 • 1,894
Silver Bow □, MT • 33,941
Silver City, NV 89428 • 100
Silver City, NM 88061–62 • 10,683
Silver Creek, NY 14136 • 2,927
Silverdale, WA 98383 • 7,660
Silver Grove, KY 41085 • 1,102
Silver Hill, MD 20746 • 1,580
Silver Lake, KS 66539 • 1,390
Silver Lake, MA 01887 • 2,900
Silver Lake, WI 53170 • 1,801
Silverpeak, NV 89047 • 190
Silver Spring, MD 20901–12 • 76,046
Silver Springs, FL 32688 • 1,082
Silver Springs, NV 89429 • 2,253
Silver Springs Shores, FL 32672 • 6,421
Silverton, NJ 08753 • 9,175
Silverton, OH 45236 • 5,859
Silverton, OR 97381 • 5,635
Silview, DE 19804 • 1,500
Silvis, IL 61282 • 6,926
Simi Valley, CA 93062–65 • 100,217
Simmesport, LA 71369 • 2,092
Simpson, PA 18407 • 1,670
Simpson □, KY • 15,145
Simpson □, MS • 23,953
Simpsonville, SC 29681 • 11,708
Simsbury, CT 06070 • 5,577
Sinclair, WY 82334 • 500
Sinton, TX 78387 • 5,549
Sioux □, IA • 29,903
Sioux □, NE • 1,549
Sioux □, ND • 3,761
Sioux Center, IA 51250 • 5,074
Sioux City, IA 51101–11 • 80,505
Sioux Falls, SD 57101–18 • 100,814
Siskiyou □, CA • 43,531
Sisseton, SD 57262 • 2,181
Sistersville, WV 26175 • 1,797
Sitka, AK 99835 • 8,588
Skagit □, WA • 79,555
Skagway, AK 99840 • 692
Skamania □, WA • 8,289
Skaneateles, NY 13152 • 2,724
Skiatook, OK 74070 • 4,910
Skokie, IL 60076–77 • 59,432
Skowhegan, ME 04976 • 6,990
Sky Lake, FL 32809 • 6,202
Skyland, NV 89448 • 660
Skyland, NC 28776 • 1,100
Skyway, WA 98178 • 8,500
Slackwoods, NJ 08638 • 8,100
Slater, IA 50244 • 1,268
Slater, MO 65349 • 2,186
Slater, SC 29683 • 1,000
Slatersville, RI 02876 • 2,330
Slatington, PA 18080 • 4,678
Slaton, TX 79364 • 6,078
Slayton, MN 56172 • 2,147
Sleepy Eye, MN 56085 • 3,694
Slickville, PA 15684 • 1,178
Slidell, LA 70458–61 • 24,124
Slinger, WI 53086 • 2,340
Slippery Rock, PA 16057 • 3,008
Sloan, NY 14225 • 3,830
Sloatsburg, NY 10974 • 3,035
Slocomb, AL 36375 • 1,906
Slope □, ND • 907
Smackover, AR 71762 • 2,232
Smethport, PA 16749 • 1,734
Smith □, KS • 5,078
Smith □, MS • 14,798
Smith □, TN • 14,143
Smith □, TX • 151,309
Smith Center, KS 66967 • 2,016
Smithers, WV 25186 • 1,162
Smithfield, NC 27577 • 7,540
Smithfield, PA 15478 • 1,000
Smithfield, UT 84335 • 5,566
Smithfield, VA 23430 • 4,686
Smith River, CA 95567 • 1,000
Smiths, AL 36877 • 1,700
Smithsburg, MD 21783 • 1,221
Smithton, IL 62285 • 1,587
Smithtown, NY 11787 • 25,638
Smithville, MO 64089 • 2,525
Smithville, OH 44677 • 1,354
Smithville, TN 37166 • 3,791
Smithville, TX 78957 • 3,196
Smyrna, DE 19977 • 5,231
Smyrna, GA 30080–82 • 30,981
Smyrna, TN 37167 • 13,647
Smyth □, VA • 32,370
Sneads, FL 32460 • 1,746
Sneedville, TN 37869 • 1,446
Snellville, GA 30278 • 12,084
Snohomish, WA 98290 • 6,499
Snohomish □, WA • 465,642
Snoqualmie, WA 98065 • 1,546
Snowflake, AZ 85937 • 3,679
Snow Hill, MD 21863 • 2,217
Snow Hill, NC 28580 • 1,378
Snyder, OK 73566 • 1,619
Snyder, TX 79549 • 12,195
Snyder □, PA • 36,680
Soap Lake, WA 98851 • 1,149
Socastee, SC 29577 • 10,426
Social Circle, GA 30279 • 2,755
Socorro, NM 87801 • 8,159
Socorro □, NM • 14,764
Soda Springs, ID 83276 • 3,111
Soddy-Daisy, TN 37379 • 8,240
Sodus, NY 14551 • 1,904
Sodus Point, NY 14555 • 1,190
Solana, FL 33950 • 1,128
Solana Beach, CA 92075 • 12,962
Solano □, CA • 340,421
Soldotna, AK 99669 • 3,482
Soledad, CA 93960 • 7,146
Solomons, MD 20688 • 1,500
Solon, IA 52333 • 1,050
Solon, OH 44139 • 18,548
Solvay, NY 13209 • 6,717
Somerdale, NJ 08083 • 5,440
Somers, CT 06071 • 9,108
Somerset, KY 42501–02 • 10,733
Somerset, MA 02725 • 17,655
Somerset, NJ 08873–75 • 22,070
Somerset, OH 43783 • 1,390
Somerset, PA 15501 • 6,454
Somerset, TX 78069 • 1,144
Somerset, WI 54025 • 1,065
Somerset □, ME • 49,767
Somerset □, MD • 23,440
Somerset □, NJ • 240,279
Somerset □, PA • 78,218
Somers Point, NJ 08244 • 11,216
Somersville, CT 06072 • 1,200
Somersworth, NH 03878 • 11,249
Somerton, AZ 85350 • 5,282
Somervell □, TX • 5,360
Somerville, MA 02143 • 76,210
Somerville, NJ 08876–77 • 11,632
Somerville, TN 38068 • 2,047
Somerville, TX 77879 • 1,542
Somonauk, IL 60552 • 1,263
Sonoma, CA 95476 • 8,121
Sonoma □, CA • 388,222
Sonora, CA 95370 • 4,153
Sonora, TX 76950 • 2,751
Soperton, GA 30457 • 2,797
Sophia, WV 25921 • 1,182
Soquel, CA 95073 • 9,188
Sorrento, LA 70778 • 1,119
Souderton, PA 18964 • 5,957
Sound Beach, NY 11789 • 9,102
South Acton, MA 01720 • 3,220
South Amboy, NJ 08879 • 7,863
South Amherst, MA 01002 • 5,053
South Amherst, OH 44001 • 1,765
Southampton, NY 11968–69 • 3,980
Southampton □, VA • 17,550
South Ashburnham, MA 01466 • 1,110
Southaven, MS 38671 • 17,949
South Barre, VT 05670 • 1,314
South Bay, FL 33493 • 3,558
South Belmar, NJ 07719 • 1,482
South Beloit, IL 61080 • 4,072
South Bend, IN 46601–80 • 105,511
South Bend, WA 98586 • 1,551
South Berwick, ME 03908 • 5,877
Southborough, MA 01772 • 1,450
South Boston, VA 24592 • 6,997
South Bound Brook, NJ 08880 • 4,185
South Bradenton, FL 34205 • 20,398
Southbridge, MA 01550 • 13,631
South Broadway, WA 98902 • 2,735
South Burlington, VT 05403 • 12,809
Southbury, CT 06488 • 3,000
South Charleston, OH 45368 • 1,626
South Charleston, WV 25303 • 13,645
South Chicago Heights, IL 60411 • 3,597
South Congaree, SC 29169 • 2,406
South Connellsville, PA 15425 • 2,204
South Dartmouth, MA 02748 • 9,850
South Daytona, FL 32121 • 12,482
South Decatur, GA 30034 • 19,350
South Deerfield, MA 01373 • 1,906
South Dennis, MA 02660 • 2,500
South Duxbury, MA 02332 • 3,017
South Easton, MA 02375 • 1,530
South Elgin, IL 60177 • 7,474
South El Monte, CA 91733 • 20,850
Southern Pines, NC 28387–88 • 9,129
South Euclid, OH 44121 • 23,866
South Fallsburg, NY 12779 • 2,115
South Farmingdale, NY 11735 • 15,377
Southfield, MI 48034 • 75,728
South Fork, PA 15956 • 1,197
South Fulton, TN 38257 • 2,688
South Gastonia, NC 28052 • 5,487
South Gate, CA 90280 • 86,284
Southgate, FL 34239 • 7,324
Southgate, KY 41071 • 3,266
South Gate, MD 21061 • 27,564
Southgate, MI 48195 • 30,771
South Glastonbury, CT 06073 • 1,570
Southglenn, CO 80122 • 43,087
South Glens Falls, NY 12801 • 3,506
South Grafton, MA 01560 • 2,610
South Hackensack, NJ 07606 • 2,229
South Hadley, MA 01075 • 5,340
South Hadley Falls, MA 01075 • 5,100
South Hamilton, MA 01982 • 2,720
South Haven, IN 46383 • 6,112
South Haven, MI 49090 • 5,563
South Hill, NY 14850 • 5,423
South Hill, VA 23970 • 4,217
South Hingham, MA 02043 • 4,080
South Holland, IL 60473 • 22,105
South Hooksett, NH 03106 • 3,638
South Hopkinton, RI 02813 • 900
South Houston, TX 77587 • 14,207
South Huntington, NY 11746 • 9,624
South Hutchinson, KS 67505 • 2,444
Southington, CT 06489 • 38,518
South International Falls, MN 56679 • 2,806
South Jacksonville, IL 62650 • 3,187
South Jordan, UT 84065 • 12,220
South Lake Tahoe, CA 95702 • 21,586
South Lancaster, MA 01561 • 1,772
South Laramie, WY 82070 • 1,500
South Laurel, MD 20708 • 18,591
South Lebanon, OH 45065 • 2,696
South Lockport, NY 14094 • 7,112
South Lyon, MI 48178 • 5,857
South Miami, FL 33143 • 10,404
South Miami Heights, FL 33157 • 30,030
South Milwaukee, WI 53172 • 20,958
South Nyack, NY 10960 • 3,352
South Ogden, UT 84403 • 12,105
Southold, NY 11971 • 5,192
South Orange, NJ 07079 • 16,390
South Paris, ME 04281 • 2,320
South Pasadena, CA 91030 • 23,936
South Patrick Shores, FL 32937 • 10,249
South Pekin, IL 61564 • 1,184
South Pittsburg, TN 37380 • 3,295
South Plainfield, NJ 07080 • 20,489
Southport, FL 32409 • 1,992
Southport, IN 46227 • 1,969
Southport, NY 14904 • 7,753
Southport, NC 28461 • 2,369
South Portland, ME 04106 • 23,163
South River, NJ 08882 • 13,692
South Royalton, VT 05068 • 700
South Saint Paul, MN 55075–77 • 20,197
South Salt Lake, UT 84115 • 10,129
South San Francisco, CA 94080–83 • 54,312
South San Gabriel, CA 91770 • 7,700
South San Jose Hills, CA 91744 • 17,814
South Sarasota, FL 34239 • 5,298
South Setauket, NY 11733 • 5,990
Southside, AL 35901 • 5,580
Southside Place, TX 77005 • 1,392
South Sioux City, NE 68776 • 9,677
South Stony Brook, NY 11790 • 6,120
South Streator, IL 61364 • 2,334
South Sumter, SC 29150 • 4,371
South Toms River, NJ 08757 • 3,869
South Torrington, WY 82240 • 300
South Tucson, AZ 85713 • 5,093
South Valley Stream, NY 11581 • 5,328
South Venice, FL 34293 • 11,951
South Walpole, MA 02071 • 1,300
South Waverly, PA 14892 • 1,049
South Wellfleet, MA 02663 • 2,300
South Westbury, NY 11590 • 9,732
Southwest Harbor, ME 04679 • 1,952
South Whitley, IN 46787 • 1,482
South Whittier, CA 90605 • 51,100
Southwick, MA 01077 • 1,170
South Williamsport, PA 17701 • 6,496
South Windham, CT 06266 • 1,644
South Windham, ME 04082 • 1,350
South Windsor, CT 06074 • 10,800
Southwood, CO 80120 • 2,050
Southwood Acres, CT 06082 • 8,963
South Woodstock, CT 06267 • 1,112
South Yarmouth, MA 02664 • 10,358
South Yuba City, CA 95991 • 8,816
South Zanesville, OH 43701 • 1,969
Spalding □, GA • 54,457
Spanaway, WA 98387 • 15,001
Spangler, PA 15775 • 2,068
Spanish Fork, UT 84660 • 11,272
Spanish Fort, AL 36527 • 3,732
Spanish Lake, MO 63138 • 20,322
Sparks, GA 31647 • 1,205
Sparks, NV 89431–36 • 53,367
Sparr, FL 32192 • 1,100
Sparta, GA 31087 • 1,710
Sparta, IL 62286 • 4,853
Sparta, MI 49345 • 3,968
Sparta (Lake Mohawk), NJ 07871 • 8,930
Sparta, NC 28675 • 1,957
Sparta, TN 38583 • 4,681
Sparta, WI 54656 • 7,788
Spartanburg, SC 29301–18 • 43,467
Spartanburg □, SC • 226,800
Spearfish, SD 57783 • 6,966
Spearman, TX 79081 • 3,197
Speedway, IN 46224 • 13,092
Spencer, IN 47460 • 2,609
Spencer, IA 51301 • 11,066
Spencer, MA 01562 • 6,306
Spencer, NC 28159 • 3,219
Spencer, TN 38585 • 1,125
Spencer, WV 25276 • 2,279
Spencer, WI 54479 • 1,757
Spencer □, IN • 19,490
Spencer □, KY • 6,801
Spencerport, NY 14559 • 3,606
Spencerville, MD 20868 • 1,780
Spencerville, OH 45887 • 2,288
Spicer, MN 56288 • 1,020
Spindale, NC 28160 • 4,040
Spink □, SD • 7,981
Spirit Lake, ID 83869 • 790
Spirit Lake, IA 51360 • 3,871
Spiro, OK 74959 • 2,146
Spokane, WA 99201–28 • 177,196
Spokane □, WA • 361,364
Spooner, WI 54801 • 2,464
Spotswood, NJ 08884 • 7,983
Spotsylvania □, VA • 57,403
Sprague, WV 25926 • 2,090
Spring, TX 77373 • 33,111
Spring Arbor, MI 49283 • 2,010
Springboro, OH 45066 • 6,590
Spring City, PA 19475 • 3,433
Spring City, TN 37381 • 2,199
Spring Creek 0M, NV • 5,866
Springdale, AR 72764–66 • 29,941
Springdale, OH 45246 • 10,621
Springdale, PA 15144 • 3,992
Springdale, SC 29169 • 3,226
Springer, NM 87747 • 1,262
Springerville, AZ 85938 • 1,802
Springfield, CO 81073 • 1,475
Springfield, FL 32401 • 8,715
Springfield, GA 31329 • 1,415
Springfield, IL 62701–94 • 105,227
Springfield, KY 40069 • 2,875
Springfield, MA 01101–05 • 156,983
Springfield, MI 49015 • 5,582
Springfield, MN 56087 • 2,173
Springfield, MO 65801–99 • 140,494
Springfield, NE 68059 • 1,426
Springfield, NJ 07081 • 13,240
Springfield, OH 45501–06 • 70,487
Springfield, OR 97477–78 • 44,683
Springfield, PA 19064 • 24,160
Springfield, SD 57062 • 834
Springfield, TN 37172 • 11,227
Springfield, VT 05156 • 4,207
Springfield, VA 22150 • 23,706
Spring Garden, PA 17403 • 11,127
Spring Green, WI 53588 • 1,283
Spring Grove, IL 60081 • 1,066
Spring Grove, MN 55974 • 1,153
Spring Grove, PA 17362 • 1,863
Spring Hill, FL 34606 • 31,117

Spring Hill, KS 66083 • *2,191*
Springhill, LA 71075 • *5,668*
Spring Hill, TN 37174 • *1,464*
Spring Hope, NC 27882 • *1,221*
Spring Lake, MI 49456 • *2,537*
Spring Lake, NJ 07762 • *3,499*
Spring Lake, NC 28390 • *7,524*
Spring Lake Heights, NJ 07762 • *5,341*
Spring Lake Park, MN 55432 • *6,532*
Springvale, ME 04083 • *3,542*
Spring Valley, IL 61362 • *5,246*
Spring Valley, MN 55975 • *2,461*
Spring Valley, NY 10977 • *21,802*
Spring Valley, WI 54767 • *1,051*
Springville, AL 35146 • *1,910*
Springville, IA 52336 • *1,068*
Springville, NY 14141 • *4,310*
Springville, UT 84663–64 • *13,950*
Spruce Pine, NC 28777 • *2,010*
Spur, TX 79370 • *1,300*
Staatsburg, NY 12580 • *1,100*
Stafford, KS 67578 • *1,344*
Stafford □, KS • *5,365*
Stafford □, VA • *61,236*
Stafford Springs, CT 06076 • *4,100*
Stambaugh, MI 49964 • *1,281*
Stamford, CT 06901–12 • *108,056*
Stamford, NY 12167 • *1,211*
Stamford, TX 79553 • *3,817*
Stamford, VT 05352 • *400*
Stamps, AR 71860 • *2,478*
Stanaford, WV 25927 • *1,706*
Stanberry, MO 64489 • *1,310*
Standish, MI 48658 • *1,377*
Stanfield, AZ 85272 • *1,700*
Stanfield, OR 97875 • *1,568*
Stanford, CA 94305 • *18,097*
Stanford, KY 40484 • *2,686*
Stanhope, NJ 07874 • *3,393*
Stanislaus □, CA • *370,522*
Stanley, NC 28164 • *2,823*
Stanley, ND 58784 • *1,371*
Stanley, VA 22851 • *1,186*
Stanley, WI 54768 • *2,011*
Stanley □, SD • *2,453*
Stanleytown, VA 24168 • *1,563*
Stanleyville, NC 27045 • *4,779*
Stanly □, NC • *51,765*
Stanton, CA 90680 • *30,491*
Stanton, KY 40380 • *2,795*
Stanton, MI 48888 • *1,504*
Stanton, NE 68779 • *1,549*
Stanton, TX 79782 • *2,576*
Stanton □, KS • *2,333*
Stanton □, NE • *6,244*
Stanwood, WA 98292 • *1,961*
Staples, MN 56479 • *2,754*
Stapleton, AL 36578 • *1,300*
Starbuck, MN 56381 • *1,143*
Star City, AR 71667 • *2,138*
Star City, WV 26505 • *1,251*
Stargo, AZ 85540 • *1,038*
Stark □, IL • *6,534*
Stark □, ND • *22,832*
Stark □, OH • *367,585*
Starke, FL 32091 • *5,226*
Starke □, IN • *22,747*
Starkville, MS 39759 • *18,458*
Starr □, TX • *40,518*
Startex, SC 29377 • *1,162*
State Center, IA 50247 • *1,248*
State College, PA 16801–05 • *38,923*
Stateline, NV 89449 • *1,379*
State Line, PA 17263 • *1,253*
Statesboro, GA 30458 • *15,854*
Statesville, NC 28677 • *17,567*
Statham, GA 30666 • *1,360*
Staunton, IL 62088 • *4,806*
Staunton, VA 24401 • *24,461*
Stayton, OR 97383 • *5,011*
Steamboat, NV 89511 • *450*
Steamboat Springs, CO 80487 • *6,695*
Stearns, KY 42647 • *1,550*
Stearns □, MN • *118,791*
Stebbins, AK 99671 • *400*
Steele, AL 35987 • *1,046*
Steele, MO 63877 • *2,395*
Steele, ND 58482 • *762*
Steele □, MN • *30,729*
Steele □, ND • *2,420*
Steeleville, IL 62288 • *2,059*
Steelton, PA 17113 • *5,152*
Steelville, MO 65565 • *1,465*
Steger, IL 60475 • *8,584*
Steilacoom, WA 98388 • *5,728*
Stephens, AR 71764 • *1,137*
Stephens □, GA • *23,257*
Stephens □, OK • *42,299*
Stephens □, TX • *9,010*
Stephens City, VA 22655 • *1,186*
Stephenson □, IL • *48,052*
Stephenville, TX 76401 • *13,502*
Sterling, AK 99672 • *3,802*
Sterling, CO 80751 • *10,362*
Sterling, IL 61081 • *15,132*
Sterling, KS 67579 • *2,115*
Sterling, MA 01564 • *1,250*
Sterling, VA 22170 • *20,512*
Sterling □, TX • *1,438*
Sterling City, TX 76951 • *1,096*
Sterling Heights, MI 48310–14 • *117,810*
Sterlington, LA 71280 • *1,140*
Steuben □, IN • *27,446*
Steuben □, NY • *99,088*
Steubenville, OH 43952 • *22,125*
Stevens □, KS • *5,048*
Stevens □, MN • *10,634*
Stevens □, WA • *30,948*
Stevenson, AL 35772 • *2,046*
Stevenson, WA 98648 • *1,147*
Stevens Point, WI 54481 • *23,006*
Stevensville, MI 49127 • *1,230*
Stevensville, MT 59870 • *1,221*
Stewart □, GA • *5,654*
Stewart □, TN • *9,479*
Stewartstown, PA 17363 • *1,308*
Stewartville, MN 55976 • *4,520*
Stickney, IL 60402 • *5,678*
Stigler, OK 74462 • *2,574*
Stillwater, MN 55082–83 • *13,882*
Stillwater, NY 12170 • *1,531*
Stillwater, OK 74074–76 • *36,676*
Stillwater □, MT • *6,536*
Stilwell, OK 74960 • *2,663*
Stinnett, TX 79083 • *2,166*
Stirling, NJ 07980 • *1,800*
Stockbridge, GA 30281 • *3,359*
Stockbridge, MA 01262 • *2,408*
Stockbridge, MI 49285 • *1,202*
Stockdale, TX 78160 • *1,268*
Stockholm, NJ 07460 • *1,200*
Stockton, CA 95201–19 • *210,943*
Stockton, IL 61085 • *1,871*
Stockton, KS 67669 • *1,507*
Stockton, MO 65785 • *1,579*
Stoddard □, MO • *28,895*
Stokes □, NC • *37,223*
Stokesdale, NC 27357 • *2,134*
Stollings, WV 25646 • *1,200*
Stone □, AR • *9,775*
Stone □, MS • *10,750*
Stone □, MO • *19,078*
Stoneboro, PA 16153 • *1,091*
Stoneham, MA 02180 • *22,203*
Stone Harbor, NJ 08247 • *1,025*
Stone Mountain, GA 30083 • *6,494*
Stoneville, NC 27048 • *1,109*
Stonewall, LA 71078 • *1,266*
Stonewall, MS 39363 • *1,148*
Stonewall □, TX • *2,013*
Stonewood, WV 26301 • *1,996*
Stonington, CT 06378 • *1,100*
Stonington, IL 62567 • *1,006*
Stony Brook, NY 11790 • *13,726*
Stony Point, NY 10980 • *10,587*
Stony Point, NC 28678 • *1,286*
Storey □, NV • *2,526*
Storm Lake, IA 50588 • *8,769*
Storrs, CT 06268 • *12,198*
Story, WY 82842 • *700*
Story □, IA • *74,252*
Story City, IA 50248 • *2,959*
Stottville, NY 12172 • *1,369*
Stoughton, MA 02072 • *26,777*
Stoughton, WI 53589 • *8,786*
Stow, MA 01775 • *1,200*
Stow, OH 44224 • *27,702*
Stowe, PA 19464 • *3,598*
Stowe, VT 05672 • *450*
Stowe Township, PA 15136 • *7,681*
Strabane, PA 15363 • *1,200*
Strafford, MO 65757 • *1,166*
Strafford □, NH • *104,233*
Strasburg, CO 80136 • *1,005*
Strasburg, OH 44680 • *1,995*
Strasburg, PA 17579 • *2,568*
Strasburg, VA 22657 • *3,762*
Stratford, CT 06497 • *49,389*
Stratford, DE 19720 • *1,950*
Stratford, NJ 08084 • *7,614*
Stratford, OK 74872 • *1,404*
Stratford, TX 79084 • *1,781*
Stratford, WI 54484 • *1,515*
Stratford Landing, VA 22308 • *2,800*
Strathmore, CA 93267 • *2,353*
Strathmore, NJ 07747 • *7,060*
Strawberry Point, IA 52076 • *1,357*
Streamwood, IL 60103 • *30,987*
Streator, IL 61364 • *14,121*
Streetsboro, OH 44241 • *9,932*
Stromsburg, NE 68666 • *1,241*
Strongsville, OH 44136 • *35,308*
Stroud, OK 74079 • *2,666*
Stroudsburg, PA 18360 • *5,312*
Struthers, OH 44471 • *12,284*
Stryker, OH 43557 • *1,468*
Stuart, FL 34994–97 • *11,936*
Stuart, IA 50250 • *1,522*
Stuarts Draft, VA 24477 • *5,087*
Sturbridge, MA 01566 • *2,093*
Sturgeon Bay, WI 54235 • *9,176*
Sturgis, KY 42459 • *2,184*
Sturgis, MI 49091 • *10,130*
Sturgis, SD 57785 • *5,330*
Sturtevant, WI 53177 • *3,803*
Stutsman □, ND • *22,241*
Stuttgart, AR 72160 • *10,420*
Sublette, KS 67877 • *1,378*
Sublette □, WY • *4,843*
Sublimity, OR 97385 • *1,491*
Succasunna, NJ 07876 • *7,750*
Sudbury, MA 01776 • *1,860*
Sudbury Center, MA 01776 • *2,590*
Sudley, VA 22110 • *7,321*
Suffern, NY 10901 • *11,055*
Suffield, CT 06078 • *1,353*
Suffolk, VA 23432–38 • *52,141*
Suffolk □, MA • *663,906*
Suffolk □, NY • *1,321,864*
Sugar City, ID 83448 • *1,275*
Sugar Creek, MO 64054 • *3,982*
Sugarcreek, PA 16323 • *5,532*
Sugar Grove, VA 24375 • *1,027*
Sugar Hill, GA 30518 • *4,557*
Sugar Land, TX 77478–79 • *24,529*
Sugarland Run, VA 22170 • *9,357*
Sugar Loaf, VA 24018 • *2,000*
Sugar Notch, PA 18706 • *1,044*
Suisun City, CA 94585 • *22,686*
Suitland, MD 20746 • *35,400*
Sulligent, AL 35586 • *1,886*
Sullivan, IL 61951 • *4,354*
Sullivan, IN 47882 • *4,663*
Sullivan, MO 63080 • *5,661*
Sullivan □, IN • *18,993*
Sullivan □, MO • *6,326*
Sullivan □, NH • *38,592*
Sullivan □, NY • *69,277*
Sullivan □, PA • *6,104*
Sullivan □, TN • *143,596*
Sullivans Island, SC 29482 • *1,623*
Sully □, SD • *1,589*
Sulphur, LA 70663–64 • *20,125*
Sulphur, OK 73086 • *4,824*
Sulphur Springs, TX 75482 • *14,062*
Sultan, WA 98294 • *2,236*
Sumiton, AL 35148 • *2,604*
Summerfield, NC 27358 • *2,051*
Summers □, WV • *14,204*
Summersville, WV 26651 • *2,906*
Summerville, GA 30747 • *5,025*
Summerville, SC 29483–85 • *22,519*
Summit, IL 60501 • *9,971*
Summit, MS 39666 • *1,566*
Summit, NJ 07901 • *19,757*
Summit, TN 37363 • *8,307*
Summit □, CO • *12,881*
Summit □, OH • *514,990*
Summit □, UT • *15,518*
Summit Hill, PA 18250 • *3,332*
Sumner, IL 62466 • *1,083*
Sumner, IA 50674 • *2,078*
Sumner, WA 98390 • *6,281*
Sumner □, KS • *25,841*
Sumner □, TN • *103,281*
Sumter, SC 29150–54 • *41,943*
Sumter □, AL • *16,174*
Sumter □, FL • *31,577*
Sumter □, GA • *30,228*
Sumter □, SC • *102,637*
Sunbury, OH 43074 • *2,046*
Sunbury, PA 17801 • *11,591*
Sun City, AZ 85351 • *38,126*
Sun City, CA 92381 • *14,930*
Sun City Center, FL 33573 • *8,326*
Suncook, NH 03275 • *5,214*
Sundance, WY 82729 • *1,139*
Sundown, TX 79372 • *1,759*
Sunflower □, MS • *32,867*
Sunland Park, NM 88063 • *8,179*
Sunny Isles, FL 33160 • *11,772*
Sunnyside, CA 93727 • *5,000*
Sunnyside, WA 98944 • *11,238*
Sunnyvale, CA 94086–89 • *117,229*
Sun Prairie, WI 53590 • *15,333*
Sunray, TX 79086 • *1,729*
Sunrise Manor, NV 89110 • *95,362*
Sunset, FL 33143 • *15,810*
Sunset, LA 70584 • *2,201*
Sunset, UT 84015 • *5,128*
Sunset Beach, HI 96712 • *800*
Sun Valley, ID 83353–54 • *938*
Sun Valley, NV 89433 • *11,391*
Superior, AZ 85273 • *3,468*
Superior, MT 59872 • *881*
Superior, NE 68978 • *2,397*
Superior, WI 54880 • *27,134*
Superior, WY 82945 • *273*
Suquamish, WA 98392 • *3,105*
Surf City, NJ 08008 • *1,375*
Surfside, FL 33154 • *4,108*
Surfside Beach, SC 29575 • *3,845*
Surgoinsville, TN 37873 • *1,499*
Surprise, AZ 85374 • *7,122*
Surrey, ND 58785 • *856*
Surry □, NC • *61,704*
Surry □, VA • *6,145*
Susanville, CA 96130 • *7,279*
Susquehanna, PA 18847 • *1,760*
Susquehanna □, PA • *40,380*
Sussex, NJ 07461 • *2,201*
Sussex, WI 53089 • *5,039*
Sussex □, DE • *113,229*
Sussex □, NJ • *130,943*
Sussex □, VA • *10,248*
Sutherland, NE 69165 • *1,032*
Sutherlin, OR 97479 • *5,020*
Sutter □, CA • *64,415*
Sutter Creek, CA 95685 • *1,835*
Sutton, NE 68979 • *1,353*
Sutton □, TX • *4,135*
Suwanee, GA 30174 • *2,412*
Suwannee □, FL • *26,780*
Swain □, NC • *11,268*
Swainsboro, GA 30401 • *7,361*
Swampscott, MA 01907 • *13,650*
Swannanoa, NC 28778 • *3,538*
Swansboro, NC 28584 • *1,165*
Swansea, IL 62221 • *8,201*
Swanton, OH 43558 • *3,557*
Swanton, VT 05488 • *2,360*
Swanwyck Estates, DE 19720 • *1,320*
Swarthmore, PA 19081 • *6,157*
Swartz Creek, MI 48473 • *4,851*
Swatara Township, PA 17111 • *19,700*
Swayzee, IN 46986 • *1,059*
Swedesboro, NJ 08085 • *2,024*
Sweeny, TX 77480 • *3,297*
Sweet Grass □, MT • *3,154*
Sweet Home, OR 97386 • *6,850*
Sweet Springs, MO 65351 • *1,595*
Sweetwater, FL 33152 • *13,909*
Sweetwater, TN 37874 • *5,066*
Sweetwater, TX 79556 • *11,967*
Sweetwater □, WY • *38,823*
Sweetwater Creek, FL 33614 • *18,000*
Swift □, MN • *10,724*
Swisher □, TX • *8,133*
Swissvale, PA 15218 • *10,637*
Switzer, WV 25647 • *1,004*
Switzerland, FL 32043 • *2,400*
Switzerland □, IN • *7,738*
Swoyerville, PA • *5,630*
Sycamore, AL 35149 • *1,250*
Sycamore, IL 60178 • *9,708*
Sykesville, MD 21784 • *2,303*
Sykesville, PA 15865 • *1,387*
Sylacauga, AL 35150 • *12,520*
Sylva, NC 28779 • *1,809*
Sylvan Beach, NY 13157 • *1,119*
Sylvania, GA 30467 • *2,871*
Sylvania, OH 43560 • *17,301*
Sylvan Lake, MI 48320 • *1,884*
Sylvester, GA 31791 • *5,702*
Syosset, NY 11791 • *18,967*
Syracuse, IN 46567 • *2,729*
Syracuse, KS 67878 • *1,606*
Syracuse, NE 68446 • *1,646*
Syracuse, NY 13201–90 • *163,860*
Syracuse, UT 84075 • *4,658*

T

Tabor City, NC 28463 • *2,330*
Tacoma, WA 98401–99 • *176,664*
Taft, CA 93268 • *5,902*
Taft, TX 78390 • *3,222*
Tahlequah, OK 74464–65 • *10,398*
Tahoe City, CA 95730 • *1,300*
Tahoka, TX 79373 • *2,868*
Takoma Park, MD 20912 • *16,700*
Talbot □, GA • *6,524*
Talbot □, MD • *30,549*
Talbotton, GA 31827 • *1,046*
Talent, OR 97540 • *3,274*
Taliaferro □, GA • *1,915*
Talihina, OK 74571 • *1,297*
Talladega, AL 35160 • *18,175*
Talladega □, AL • *74,107*
Tallahassee, FL 32301–17 • *124,773*
Tallahatchie □, MS • *15,210*
Tallapoosa, GA 30176 • *2,805*
Tallapoosa □, AL • *38,826*
Tallassee, AL 36078 • *5,112*
Talleyville, DE 19803 • *6,346*
Tallmadge, OH 44278 • *14,870*
Tallulah, LA 71282–84 • *8,526*
Tama, IA 52339 • *2,697*
Tama □, IA • *17,419*
Tamalpais Valley, CA 94941 • *5,000*
Tamaqua, PA 18252 • *7,943*
Tamarac, FL 33321 • *44,822*
Tamiami, FL 33165 • *33,845*
Tampa, FL 33601–97 • *280,015*
Tanana, AK 99777 • *345*
Taney □, MO • *25,561*
Taneytown, MD 21787 • *3,695*
Tangipahoa □, LA • *85,709*
Taos, NM 87571 • *4,065*
Taos □, NM • *23,118*
Taos Pueblo, NM 87571 • *1,030*
Tappahannock, VA 22560 • *1,550*
Tappan, NY 10983 • *6,867*
Tara Hills, CA 94564 • *6,000*
Tarboro, NC 27886 • *11,037*
Tarentum, PA 15084 • *5,674*
Tariffville, CT 06081 • *1,477*
Tarkio, MO 64491 • *2,243*
Tarpey, CA 93727 • *4,000*
Tarpon Springs, FL 34688–91 • *17,906*
Tarrant, AL 35217 • *8,046*
Tarrant □, TX • *1,170,103*
Tarrytown, NY 10591 • *10,739*
Tate, GA 30177 • *1,000*
Tate □, MS • *21,432*
Tattnall □, GA • *17,722*
Taunton, MA 02780 • *49,832*
Tavares, FL 32778 • *7,383*
Tavernier, FL 33070 • *2,433*
Tawas City, MI 48763–64 • *2,009*
Taylor, AZ 85939 • *2,418*
Taylor, MI 48180 • *70,811*
Taylor, PA 18517 • *6,941*
Taylor, TX 76574 • *11,472*
Taylor □, FL • *17,111*
Taylor □, GA • *7,642*
Taylor □, IA • *7,114*
Taylor □, KY • *21,146*
Taylor □, TX • *119,655*
Taylor □, WV • *15,144*
Taylor □, WI • *18,901*
Taylor Mill, KY 41015 • *5,530*
Taylors, SC 29687 • *19,619*
Taylorsville, IN 47280 • *1,044*
Taylorsville, MS 39168 • *1,412*
Taylorsville, NC 28681 • *1,566*
Taylorville, IL 62568 • *11,133*
Tazewell, TN 37879 • *2,150*
Tazewell, VA 24651 • *4,176*
Tazewell □, IL • *123,692*
Tazewell □, VA • *45,960*
Tchula, MS 39169 • *2,186*
Teague, TX 75860 • *3,268*
Teaneck, NJ 07666 • *37,825*
Teaticket, MA 02536 • *2,600*
Tecumseh, MI 49286 • *7,462*
Tecumseh, NE 68450 • *1,702*
Tecumseh, OK 74873 • *5,750*
Tehachapi, CA 93561 • *5,791*
Tehama □, CA • *49,625*
Tekamah, NE 68061 • *1,852*
Telfair □, GA • *11,000*
Telford, PA 18969 • *4,238*
Tell City, IN 47586 • *8,088*
Teller □, CO • *12,468*
Telluride, CO 81435 • *1,309*
Temecula, CA 92390 • *27,099*
Tempe, AZ 85280–85 • *141,865*
Temperance, MI 48182 • *6,542*
Temple, GA 30179 • *1,870*
Temple, OK 73568 • *1,223*
Temple, PA 19560 • *1,491*
Temple, TX 76501–05 • *46,109*
Temple City, CA 91780 • *31,100*
Temple Terrace, FL 33617 • *16,444*
Templeton, MA 01468 • *1,000*
Tenafly, NJ 07670 • *13,326*
Tenaha, TX 75974 • *1,072*
Tenino, WA 98589 • *1,292*
Tennessee Ridge, TN 37178 • *1,271*
Tennille, GA 31089 • *1,552*
Tensas □, LA • *7,103*
Ten Sleep, WY 82442 • *311*
Terra Alta, WV 26764 • *1,713*
Terrebonne □, LA • *96,982*
Terre Haute, IN 47801–08 • *57,483*
Terre Hill, PA 17581 • *1,282*
Terrell, TX 75160 • *12,490*
Terrell □, GA • *10,653*
Terrell □, TX • *1,410*
Terrell Hills, TX 78209 • *4,592*
Terry, MT 59349 • *659*
Terry □, TX • *13,218*
Terrytown, LA 70053 • *23,787*
Terryville, CT 06786 • *5,426*
Terryville, NY 11776 • *7,380*
Tesuque, NM 87574 • *1,490*
Teton □, ID • *3,439*
Teton □, MT • *6,271*
Teton □, WY • *11,172*
Teton Village, WY 83025 • *250*
Teutopolis, IL 62467 • *1,417*
Tewksbury, MA 01876 • *10,540*
Texarkana, AR 75502 • *22,631*
Texarkana, TX 75501–05 • *31,656*
Texas □, MO • *21,476*
Texas □, OK • *16,419*
Texas City, TX 77590–92 • *40,822*
Texico, NM 88135 • *966*
Thatcher, AZ 85552 • *3,763*
Thayer, MO 65791 • *1,996*
Thayer □, NE • *6,635*
Thayne, WY 83127 • *267*
The Colony, TX 75056 • *22,113*
The Dalles, OR 97058 • *11,060*
Theodore, AL 36582 • *6,509*
The Plains, OH 45780 • *2,644*
Thermalito, CA 95965 • *5,646*
Thermopolis, WY 82443 • *3,247*
The Village, OK 73120 • *10,353*
The Village of Indian Hill, OH 45243 • *5,383*
The Woodlands, TX 77380 • *29,205*
Thibodaux, LA 70301–02 • *14,035*
Thief River Falls, MN 56701 • *8,010*
Thiensville, WI 53092 • *3,301*
Thomas, OK 73669 • *1,246*
Thomas □, GA • *38,986*
Thomas □, KS • *8,258*
Thomas □, NE • *851*
Thomasboro, IL 61878 • *1,250*
Thomaston, CT 06787 • *3,590*
Thomaston, GA 30286 • *9,127*
Thomaston, ME 04861 • *2,445*
Thomasville, AL 36784 • *4,301*
Thomasville, GA 31792 • *17,457*
Thomasville, NC 27360–61 • *15,915*
Thompson, ND 58278 • *930*
Thompson Falls, MT 59873 • *1,319*
Thomson, GA 30824 • *6,862*
Thonotosassa, FL 33592 • *1,500*
Thoreau, NM 87323 • *1,099*
Thorndale, TX 76577 • *1,092*
Thorndike, MA 01079 • *1,100*
Thornton, CO 80229 • *55,031*
Thorntown, IN 46071 • *1,506*
Thornwood, NY 10594 • *7,025*
Thorofare, NJ 08086 • *1,800*
Thorp, WI 54771 • *1,657*
Thorsby, AL 35171 • *1,465*
Thousand Oaks, CA 91359–62 • *104,352*
Three Forks, MT 59752 • *1,203*
Three Oaks, MI 49128 • *1,786*
Three Rivers, MA 01080 • *3,006*
Three Rivers, MI 49093 • *7,413*
Three Rivers, TX 78071 • *1,889*
Throckmorton, TX 76083 • *1,036*
Throckmorton □, TX • *1,880*
Throop, PA 18512 • *4,070*
Thunderbolt, GA 31404 • *2,786*
Thurmont, MD 21788 • *3,398*
Thurston □, NE • *6,936*
Thurston □, WA • *161,238*
Tiburon, CA 94920 • *7,532*
Tice, FL 33905 • *3,971*
Ticonderoga, NY 12883 • *2,770*
Tierra Amarilla, NM 87575 • *900*
Tiffin, OH 44883 • *18,604*
Tift □, GA • *34,998*
Tifton, GA 31793–94 • *14,215*
Tigard, OR 97223 • *29,344*
Tillamook, OR 97141 • *4,001*
Tillamook □, OR • *21,570*
Tillman □, OK • *10,384*
Tillmans Corner, AL 36619 • *17,988*
Tillson, NY 12486 • *1,688*
Tilton, IL 61833 • *2,729*
Tilton, NH 03276 • *1,380*
Tiltonsville, OH 43963 • *1,517*
Timberlake, VA 24502 • *10,314*
Timberville, VA 22853 • *1,596*
Timmonsville, SC 29161 • *2,182*
Timpson, TX 75975 • *1,029*
Tinley Park, IL 60477 • *37,121*
Tinton Falls, NJ 07724 • *12,361*
Tioga, LA 71477 • *1,200*
Tioga, ND 58852 • *1,278*
Tioga □, NY • *52,337*
Tioga □, PA • *41,126*
Tippah □, MS • *19,523*
Tipp City, OH 45371 • *6,027*
Tippecanoe □, IN • *130,598*
Tipton, CA 93272 • *1,383*
Tipton, IN 46072 • *4,751*
Tipton, IA 52772 • *2,998*
Tipton, MO 65081 • *2,026*
Tipton, OK 73570 • *1,043*
Tipton □, IN • *16,119*
Tipton □, TN • *37,568*
Tiptonville, TN 38079 • *2,149*
Tishomingo, OK 73460 • *3,116*
Tishomingo □, MS • *17,683*
Titus □, TX • *24,009*
Titusville, FL 32780–83 • *39,394*
Titusville, PA 16354 • *6,434*
Tiverton, RI 02878 • *7,259*
Tivoli, NY 12583 • *1,035*
Toast, NC 27049 • *2,125*
Tobyhanna, PA 18466 • *1,200*
Toccoa, GA 30577 • *8,266*
Todd □, KY • *10,940*
Todd □, MN • *23,363*
Todd □, SD • *8,352*
Todd Estates, DE 19713 • *2,000*
Togiak, AK 99678 • *613*
Tohatchi, NM 87325 • *661*
Tok, AK 99780 • *935*
Toledo, IL 62468 • *1,199*
Toledo, IA 52342 • *2,380*
Toledo, OH 43601–99 • *332,943*
Toledo, OR 97391 • *3,174*
Tolland, CT 06084 • *1,200*
Tolland □, CT • *128,699*
Tolleson, AZ 85353 • *4,434*
Tolono, IL 61880 • *2,605*
Toluca, IL 61369 • *1,315*
Tomah, WI 54660 • *7,570*
Tomahawk, WI 54487 • *3,328*
Tomball, TX 77375 • *6,370*
Tombstone, AZ 85638 • *1,220*
Tom Green □, TX • *98,458*
Tompkins □, NY • *94,097*
Tompkinsville, KY 42167 • *2,861*
Toms River, NJ 08753–57 • *7,524*
Tonawanda, NY 14150–51 • *17,284*
Tonawanda, NY 14223 • *65,284*
Tonganoxie, KS 66086 • *2,347*
Tonkawa, OK 74653 • *3,127*
Tonopah, NV 89049 • *3,616*
Tooele, UT 84074 • *13,887*
Tooele □, UT • *26,601*
Toole □, MT • *5,046*
Toombs □, GA • *24,072*
Topeka, KS 66601–99 • *119,883*
Toppenish, WA 98948 • *7,419*
Topsfield, MA 01983 • *2,711*
Topsham, ME 04086 • *6,147*
Topton, PA 19562 • *1,987*
Toronto, OH 43964 • *6,127*
Torrance, CA 90501–10 • *133,107*
Torrance □, NM • *10,285*
Torrington, CT 06790 • *33,687*
Torrington, WY 82240 • *5,651*
Totowa, NJ 07512 • *10,177*
Touisset, MA 02777 • *1,520*

United States Populations and ZIP Codes

Toulon, IL 61483 • 1,328
Towaco, NJ 07082 • 1,020
Towanda, KS 67144 • 1,289
Towanda, PA 18848 • 3,242
Tower City, PA 17980 • 1,518
Town and Country, WA 99210 • 4,921
Town Creek, AL 35672 • 1,379
Towner, ND 58788 • 669
Towner □, ND • 3,627
Town 'n Country, FL 33615 • 60,946
Towns □, GA • 6,754
Townsend, DE 19734 • 322
Townsend, MA 01469 • 1,164
Townsend, MT 59644 • 1,635
Towson, MD 21204 • 49,445
Tracy, CA 95376–78 • 33,558
Tracy, MN 56175 • 2,059
Tracy City, TN 37387 • 1,556
Tracyton, WA 98393 • 2,621
Traer, IA 50675 • 1,552
Trafford, PA 15085 • 3,345
Trail Creek, IN 46360 • 2,463
Traill □, ND • 8,752
Transylvania □, NC • 25,520
Travelers Rest, SC 29690 • 3,069
Traverse □, MN • 4,463
Traverse City, MI 49684 • 15,155
Travis □, TX • 576,407
Treasure □, MT • 874
Treasure Island, FL 33706 • 7,266
Trego □, KS • 3,694
Tremont, IL 61568 • 2,088
Tremont, PA 17981 • 1,814
Tremonton, UT 84337 • 4,264
Trempealeau, WI 54661 • 1,039
Trempealeau □, WI • 25,263
Trenton, FL 32693 • 1,287
Trenton, GA 30752 • 1,994
Trenton, IL 62293 • 2,481
Trenton, MI 48183 • 20,586
Trenton, MO 64683 • 6,129
Trenton, NJ 08601–91 • 88,675
Trenton, OH 45067 • 6,189
Trenton, TN 38382 • 4,836
Tresckow, PA 18254 • 1,033
Treutlen □, GA • 5,994
Trevorton, PA 17881 • 2,058
Triangle, VA 22172 • 4,740
Tri City, OR 97457 • 3,585
Trigg □, KY • 10,361
Tri Lakes, IN 46725 • 3,299
Trimble □, KY • 6,090
Trinidad, CO 81082 • 8,580
Trinidad, TX 75163 • 1,056
Trinity, AL 35673 • 1,380
Trinity, NC 27370 • 5,469
Trinity, TX 75862 • 2,648
Trinity □, CA • 13,063
Trinity □, TX • 11,445
Trion, GA 30753 • 1,661
Tripoli, IA 50676 • 1,188
Tripp □, SD • 6,924
Triumph, LA 70041 • 1,200
Trona, CA 93562 • 1,400
Trooper, PA 19401 • 5,137
Trotwood, OH 45426 • 8,816
Troup □, GA • 55,536
Trousdale □, TN • 5,920
Troutdale, OR 97060 • 7,852
Troutman, NC 28166 • 1,493
Troy, AL 36081 • 13,051
Troy, ID 83871 • 699
Troy, IL 62294 • 6,046
Troy, KS 66087 • 1,073
Troy, MI 48083–84 • 72,884
Troy, MO 63379 • 3,811
Troy, MT 59935 • 953
Troy, NH 03465 • 2,097
Troy, NY 12180–83 • 54,269
Troy, NC 27371 • 3,404
Troy, OH 45373 • 19,478
Troy, PA 16947 • 1,262
Troy, TN 38260 • 1,047
Truckee, CA 95734 • 3,484
Truman, MN 56088 • 1,292
Trumann, AR 72472 • 6,304
Trumansburg, NY 14886 • 1,611
Trumbull, CT 06611 • 32,000
Trumbull □, OH • 227,813
Trussville, AL 35173 • 8,266
Truth or Consequences (Hot Springs), NM 87901 • 6,221
Tryon, NC 28782 • 1,680
Tualatin, OR 97062 • 15,013
Tuba City, AZ 86045 • 7,323
Tuckahoe, NY 10707 • 6,302
Tucker, GA 30084 • 25,781
Tucker □, WV • 7,728
Tuckerman, AR 72473 • 2,020
Tuckerton, NJ 08087 • 3,048
Tucson, AZ 85701–51 • 405,390
Tucumcari, NM 88401 • 6,831
Tukwila, WA 98188 • 11,874
Tulare, CA 93274–75 • 33,249
Tulare □, CA • 311,921
Tularosa, NM 88352 • 2,615
Tulelake, CA 96134 • 1,010
Tulia, TX 79088 • 4,699
Tullahoma, TN 37388 • 16,761
Tulsa, OK 74101–94 • 367,302
Tulsa □, OK • 503,341
Tumwater, WA 98502 • 9,976
Tunica, MS 38676 • 1,175
Tunica □, MS • 8,164
Tunkhannock, PA 18657 • 2,251
Tununak, AK 99681 • 316
Tuolumne, CA 95379 • 1,686
Tuolumne □, CA • 48,456
Tupelo, MS 38801–03 • 30,685
Tupper Lake, NY 12986 • 4,087
Turley, OK 74156 • 2,930
Turlock, CA 95380–81 • 42,198
Turner, OR 97392 • 1,281
Turner □, GA • 8,703
Turner □, SD • 8,576
Turners Falls, MA 01376 • 4,731
Turtle Creek, PA 15145 • 6,556
Turtle Lake, ND 58575 • 681
Tuscaloosa, AL 35401–06 • 77,759
Tuscaloosa □, AL • 150,522
Tuscarawas □, OH • 84,090
Tuscola, IL 61953 • 4,155
Tuscola □, MI • 55,498
Tuscumbia, AL 35674 • 8,413
Tuskegee, AL 36083 • 12,257
Tustin, CA 92680–81 • 50,689
Tuttle, OK 73089 • 2,807
Tutwiler, MS 38963 • 1,391
Tuxedo Park, DE 19804 • 1,300
Twentynine Palms, CA 92277–78 • 11,821
Twiggs □, GA • 9,806
Twin City, GA 30471 • 1,466
Twin Falls, ID 83301–03 • 27,591
Twin Falls □, ID • 53,580
Twin Knolls, AZ 85207 • 5,210
Twin Lakes, CA 95060 • 5,379
Twin Lakes, WI 53181 • 3,989
Twin Rivers, NJ 08520 • 7,715
Twinsburg, OH 44087 • 9,606
Two Harbors, MN 55616 • 3,651
Two Rivers, WI 54241 • 13,030
Tybee Island, GA 31328 • 2,842
Tyler, MN 56178 • 1,257
Tyler, TX 75701–13 • 75,450
Tyler □, TX • 16,646
Tyler □, WV • 9,796
Tyler Heights, WV 25312 • 4,070
Tylertown, MS 39667 • 1,938
Tyndall, SD 57066 • 1,201
Tyrone, NM 88065 • 950
Tyrone, PA 16686 • 5,743
Tyrrell □, NC • 3,856
Tysons Corner, VA 22102 • 13,124

U

Ucon, ID 83454 • 895
Uhrichsville, OH 44683 • 5,604
Uinta □, WY • 18,705
Uintah □, UT • 22,211
Ukiah, CA 95482 • 14,599
Uleta, FL 33162 • 10,000
Ulster □, NY • 165,304
Ulysses, KS 67880 • 5,474
Umatilla, FL 32784 • 2,350
Umatilla, OR 97882 • 3,046
Umatilla □, OR • 59,249
Unadilla, GA 31091 • 1,620
Unadilla, NY 13849 • 1,265
Unalakleet, AK 99684 • 714
Unalaska, AK 99685 • 3,089
Uncasville, CT 06382 • 1,597
Underwood, AL 35630 • 1,950
Underwood, ND 58576 • 976
Unicoi □, TN • 16,549
Union, KY 41091 • 1,001
Union, MS 39365 • 1,875
Union, MO 63084 • 5,909
Union, NJ 07083 • 50,024
Union, OH 45322 • 5,501
Union, OR 97883 • 1,847
Union, SC 29379 • 9,836
Union, UT 84047 • 13,684
Union □, AR • 46,719
Union □, FL • 10,252
Union □, GA • 11,993
Union □, IL • 17,619
Union □, IN • 6,976
Union □, IA • 12,750
Union □, KY • 16,557
Union □, LA • 20,690
Union □, MS • 22,085
Union □, NJ • 493,819
Union □, NM • 4,124
Union □, NC • 84,211
Union □, OH • 31,969
Union □, OR • 23,598
Union □, PA • 36,176
Union □, SC • 30,337
Union □, SD • 10,189
Union □, TN • 13,694
Union Beach, NJ 07735 • 6,156
Union City, CA 94587 • 53,762
Union City, GA 30291 • 8,375
Union City, IN 47390 • 3,612
Union City, MI 49094 • 1,767
Union City, NJ 07087 • 58,012
Union City, OH 45390 • 1,984
Union City, OK 73090 • 1,000
Union City, PA 16438 • 3,537
Union City, TN 38261 • 10,513
Uniondale, NY 11553 • 20,328
Union Gap, WA 98903 • 3,120
Union Grove, WI 53182 • 3,669
Union Lake, MI 48386–87 • 8,500
Union Park, FL 32817 • 6,890
Union Pier, MI 49129 • 1,039
Union Point, GA 30669 • 1,753
Union Springs, AL 36089 • 3,975
Union Springs, NY 13160 • 1,142
Uniontown, AL 36786 • 1,730
Uniontown, KY 42461 • 1,008
Uniontown, OH 44685 • 1,500
Uniontown, PA 15401 • 12,034
Union Village, RI 02895 • 2,150
Unionville, CT 06085 • 3,500
Unionville, MO 63565 • 1,989
Universal City, TX 78148 • 13,057
University City, MO 63130 • 40,087
University Gardens, NY 11020 • 4,600
University Heights, IA 52240 • 1,042
University Heights, OH 44118 • 14,790
University Park, IL 60466 • 6,204
University Park, NM 88003 • 4,520
University Park, TX 75205 • 22,259
University Place, WA 98465 • 27,701
Upland, CA 91785–86 • 63,374
Upland, IN 46989 • 3,295
Upper Arlington, OH 43221 • 34,128
Upper Darby, PA 19082–83 • 84,054
Upper Dublin Township, PA 19002 • 22,348
Upper Greenwood Lake, NJ 07421 • 2,734
Upper Merion Township, PA 19406 • 26,138
Upper Moreland Township, PA 19090 • 25,874
Upper Providence Township, PA 19063 • 9,727
Upper Saddle River, NJ 07458 • 7,198
Upper Saint Clair, PA 15241 • 19,692
Upper Sandusky, OH 43351 • 5,906
Upshur □, TX • 31,370
Upshur □, WV • 22,867
Upson □, GA • 26,300
Upton, MA 01568 • 1,500
Upton, WY 82730 • 980
Upton □, TX • 4,447
Urbana, IL 61801 • 36,344
Urbana, OH 43078 • 11,353
Urbandale, IA 50322 • 23,500
Usquepaug, RI 02892 • 400
Utah □, UT • 263,590
Utica, MI 48315–18 • 5,081
Utica, MS 39175 • 1,033
Utica, NY 13501–05 • 68,637
Utica, OH 43080 • 1,997
Uvalde, TX 78801–02 • 14,729
Uvalde □, TX • 23,340
Uxbridge, MA 01569 • 3,340

V

Vacaville, CA 95687–88 • 71,479
Vacherie, LA 70090 • 2,169
Vadnais Heights, MN 55110 • 11,041
Vail, CO 81657–58 • 3,659
Valatie, NY 12184 • 1,487
Valdese, NC 28690 • 3,914
Valdez, AK 99686 • 4,068
Valdosta, GA 31601–04 • 39,806
Vale, OR 97918 • 1,491
Valencia, AZ 85326 • 1,200
Valencia □, NM • 45,235
Valencia Heights, SC 29205 • 4,122
Valentine, NE 69201 • 2,826
Valhalla, NY 10595 • 6,200
Valinda, CA 91744 • 18,735
Vallejo, CA 94589–92 • 109,199
Valle Vista, CA 92343 • 8,751
Valley, AL 36854 • 8,173
Valley, NE 68064 • 1,775
Valley □, ID • 6,109
Valley □, MT • 8,239
Valley □, NE • 5,169
Valley Center, KS 67147 • 3,624
Valley City, ND 58072 • 7,163
Valley Cottage, NY 10989 • 9,007
Valley Falls, KS 66088 • 1,253
Valley Falls, RI 02864 • 11,175
Valley Forge, PA 19481–82 • 1,500
Valley Mills, TX 76689 • 1,085
Valley Park, MO 63088 • 4,165
Valley Ridge, WA 98188 • 6,500
Valley Springs, SD 57068 • 739
Valley Station, KY 40272 • 22,840
Valley Stream, NY 11580–82 • 33,946
Valley View, PA 17983 • 1,749
Valparaiso, FL 32580 • 4,672
Valparaiso, IN 46383–84 • 24,414
Val Verda, UT 84010 • 3,712
Val Verde □, TX • 38,721
Van, TX 75790 • 1,854
Van Alstyne, TX 75095 • 2,090
Van Buren, AR 72956 • 14,979
Van Buren, ME 04785 • 2,759
Van Buren □, AR • 14,008
Van Buren □, IA • 7,676
Van Buren □, MI • 70,060
Van Buren □, TN • 4,846
Vance □, NC • 38,892
Vanceburg, KY 41179 • 1,713
Vancleave, MS 39564 • 3,214
Vancouver, WA 98660–68 • 46,380
Vandalia, IL 62471 • 6,114
Vandalia, MO 63382 • 2,683
Vandalia, OH 45377 • 13,882
Vandenberg Village, CA 93436 • 5,871
Vander, NC 28301 • 1,179
Vanderburgh □, IN • 165,058
Vandergrift, PA 15690 • 5,904
Van Horn, TX 79855 • 2,930
Van Lear, KY 41265 • 1,050
Vansant, VA 24656 • 1,187
Van Vleck, TX 77482 • 1,534
Van Wert, OH 45891 • 10,891
Van Wert □, OH • 30,464
Van Zandt □, TX • 37,944
Varina, VA 23231 • 2,500
Varnville, SC 29944 • 1,970
Vassar, MI 48768 • 2,559
Vaughn, MT 59487 • 2,270
Veazie, ME 04401 • 1,610
Veedersburg, IN 47987 • 2,192
Velda Rose Estates, AZ 85205 • 2,330
Velva, ND 58790 • 968
Venango □, PA • 59,381
Veneta, OR 97487 • 2,519
Venice, FL 34292–93 • 16,922
Venice, IL 62090 • 3,571
Venice Gardens, FL 34293 • 7,701
Ventnor City, NJ 08406 • 11,005
Ventura (San Buenaventura), CA 93001–07 • 92,575
Ventura □, CA • 669,016
Veradale, WA 99037 • 7,836
Verda, KY 40828 • 1,133
Verdi, NV 89439 • 1,140
Vergennes, VT 05491 • 2,578
Vermilion, OH 44089 • 11,127
Vermilion □, IL • 88,257
Vermilion □, LA • 50,055
Vermillion, SD 57069 • 10,034
Vermillion □, IN • 16,773
Vernal, UT 84078–79 • 6,644
Vernon, AL 35592 • 2,247
Vernon, CT 06066 • 30,200
Vernon, TX 76384 • 12,001
Vernon □, LA • 61,961
Vernon □, MO • 19,041
Vernon □, WI • 25,617
Vernon Hills, IL 60061 • 15,319
Vernonia, OR 97064 • 1,808
Vero Beach, FL 32960–68 • 17,350
Verona, MS 38879 • 2,893
Verona, NJ 07044 • 13,597
Verona, PA 15147 • 3,260
Verona, WI 53593 • 5,374
Versailles, IN 47042 • 1,791
Versailles, KY 40383 • 7,269
Versailles, MO 65084 • 2,365
Versailles, OH 45380 • 2,351
Vestal, NY 13850–51 • 5,530
Vestavia Hills, AL 35216 • 19,749
Vevay, IN 47043 • 1,393
Vian, OK 74962 • 1,414
Vicksburg, MI 49097 • 2,216
Vicksburg, MS 39180–82 • 20,908
Victor, NY 14564 • 2,308
Victoria, KS 67671 • 1,157
Victoria, TX 77901–05 • 55,076
Victoria, VA 23974 • 1,830
Victoria □, TX • 74,361
Victorville, CA 92392–93 • 40,674
Vidalia, GA 30474 • 11,078
Vidalia, LA 71373 • 4,953
Vidor, TX 77662 • 10,935
Vienna, GA 31092 • 2,708
Vienna, IL 62995 • 1,446
Vienna, VA 22180–83 • 14,852
Vienna, WV 26105 • 10,862
View Park, CA 90043 • 5,900
Vigo □, IN • 106,107
Vilas □, WI • 17,707
Villa Grove, IL 61956 • 2,734
Villa Hills, KY 41016 • 7,739
Villa Park, CA 92667 • 6,299
Villa Park, IL 60181 • 22,253
Villa Rica, GA 30180 • 6,542
Villas, NJ 08251 • 8,136
Ville Platte, LA 70586 • 9,037
Villisca, IA 50864 • 1,332
Vilonia, AR 72173 • 1,133
Vincennes, IN 47591 • 19,859
Vincent, AL 35178 • 1,767
Vine Grove, KY 40175 • 3,586
Vineland, NJ 08360 • 54,780
Vineyard Haven, MA 02568 • 1,762
Vinita, OK 74301 • 5,804
Vinton, IA 52349 • 5,103
Vinton, LA 70668 • 3,154
Vinton, VA 24179 • 7,665
Vinton □, OH • 11,098
Viola, NY 10952 • 4,504
Violet, LA 70092 • 8,574
Virden, IL 62690 • 3,635
Virginia, IL 62691 • 1,767
Virginia, MN 55792 • 9,410
Virginia Beach, VA 23450–67 • 393,069
Virginia City, NV 89440 • 920
Viroqua, WI 54665 • 3,922
Visalia, CA 93277–79 • 75,636
Vista, CA 92083–84 • 71,872
Vivian, LA 71082 • 4,156
Volcano, HI 96785 • 1,516
Volga, SD 57071 • 1,263
Volusia □, FL • 370,712

W

Wabash, IN 46992 • 12,127
Wabash □, IL • 13,111
Wabash □, IN • 35,069
Wabasha, MN 55981 • 2,384
Wabasha □, MN • 19,744
Wabasso, FL 32970 • 1,145
Wabaunsee □, KS • 6,603
Waco, TX 76701–16 • 103,590
Waconia, MN 55387 • 3,498
Wade Hampton, SC 29607 • 20,014
Wadena, MN 56482 • 4,131
Wadena □, MN • 13,154
Wadesboro, NC 28170 • 3,645
Wading River, NY 11792 • 5,317
Wadley, GA 30477 • 2,473
Wadsworth, IL 60083 • 1,826
Wadsworth, NV 89442 • 640
Wadsworth, OH 44281 • 15,718
Wagner, SD 57380 • 1,462
Wagoner, OK 74467 • 6,894
Wagoner □, OK • 47,883
Wahiawa, HI 96786 • 17,386
Wahkiakum □, WA • 3,327
Wahoo, NE 68066 • 3,681
Wahpeton, ND 58074–75 • 8,751
Waialua, HI 96791 • 3,943
Waianae, HI 96792 • 8,758
Waikapu, HI 96793 • 729
Wailua, HI 96746 • 2,018
Wailuku, HI 96793 • 10,688
Waimanalo, HI 96795 • 3,508
Waimea, HI 96712 • 600
Waimea, HI 96796 • 5,972
Wainwright, AK 99782 • 492
Waipahu, HI 96797 • 31,435
Waipio Acres, HI 96786 • 5,304
Waite Park, MN 56387 • 5,020
Wakarusa, IN 46573 • 1,667
Wake □, NC • 423,380
Wa Keeney, KS 67672 • 2,161
Wakefield, MA 01880 • 24,825
Wakefield, MI 49968 • 2,318
Wakefield, NE 68784 • 1,082
Wakefield, RI 02879–83 • 3,450
Wakefield, VA 23888 • 1,070
Wake Forest, NC 27587–88 • 5,769
Wakulla □, FL • 14,202
Walbridge, OH 43465 • 2,736
Walcott, IA 52773 • 1,356
Walden, NY 12586 • 5,836
Waldo, AR 71770 • 1,495
Waldo, FL 32694 • 1,017
Waldo □, ME • 33,018
Waldoboro, ME 04572 • 1,420
Waldport, OR 97394 • 1,595
Waldron, AR 72958 • 3,024
Waldwick, NJ 07463 • 9,757
Walhalla, ND 58282 • 1,131
Walhalla, SC 29691 • 3,755
Walker, LA 70785 • 3,727
Walker, MI 49504 • 17,279
Walker □, AL • 67,670
Walker □, GA • 58,340
Walker □, TX • 50,917
Walkersville, MD 21793 • 4,145
Walkerton, IN 46574 • 2,061
Walkertown, NC 27051 • 1,200
Walkerville, MT 59701 • 605
Wall, SD 57790 • 834
Wallace, ID 83873 • 1,010
Wallace, NC 28466 • 2,939
Wallace □, KS • 1,821
Walla Walla, WA 99362 • 26,478
Walla Walla □, WA • 48,439
Walled Lake, MI 48390 • 6,278
Wallen, IN 46806 • 1,000
Waller, TX 77484 • 1,493
Waller □, TX • 23,390
Wallingford, CT 06492 • 17,827
Wallingford, VT 05773 • 1,148
Wallington, NJ 07057 • 10,828
Wallis, TX 77485 • 1,001
Wallkill, NY 12589 • 2,125
Wallowa □, OR • 6,911
Walnut, CA 91789 • 29,105
Walnut, IL 61376 • 1,463
Walnut Cove, NC 27052 • 1,088
Walnut Creek, CA 94593–98 • 60,569
Walnut Park, CA 90255 • 14,722
Walnutport, PA 18088 • 2,055
Walnut Ridge, AR 72476 • 4,388
Walpole, MA 02081 • 5,495
Walsenburg, CO 81089 • 3,300
Walsh □, ND • 13,840
Walterboro, SC 29488 • 5,492
Walters, OK 73572 • 2,519
Walthall □, MS • 14,352
Waltham, MA 02154 • 57,878
Walthourville, GA 31333 • 2,024
Walton, IN 46994 • 1,053
Walton, KY 41094 • 2,034
Walton, NY 13856 • 3,326
Walton □, FL • 27,760
Walton □, GA • 38,586
Walworth, WI 53184 • 1,614
Walworth □, SD • 6,087
Walworth □, WI • 75,000
Wamac, IL 62801 • 1,501
Wamego, KS 66547 • 3,706
Wamesit, MA 01876 • 2,700
Wamsutter, WY 82336 • 240
Wanaque, NJ 07465 • 9,711
Wanchese, NC 27981 • 1,380
Wando Woods, SC 29405 • 5,253
Wantagh, NY 11793 • 18,567
Wapakoneta, OH 45895 • 9,214
Wapato, WA 98951 • 3,795
Wapello, IA 52653 • 2,013
Wapello □, IA • 35,687
Wappingers Falls, NY 12590 • 4,605
War, WV 24892 • 1,081
Ward, AR 72176 • 1,269
Ward □, ND • 57,921
Ward □, TX • 13,115
Warden, WA 98857 • 1,639
Ware, MA 01082 • 6,533
Ware □, GA • 35,471
Wareham, MA 02571 • 2,607
Warehouse Point, CT 06088 • 1,880
Ware Shoals, SC 29692 • 2,497
Waretown, NJ 08758 • 1,283
Warminster, PA 18974 • 35,463
Warner, OK 74469 • 1,479
Warner Robins, GA 31088 • 43,726
Warr Acres, OK 73132 • 9,288
Warren, AR 71671 • 6,455
Warren, IL 61087 • 1,550
Warren, IN 46792 • 1,185
Warren, MA 01083 • 1,516
Warren, MI 48089–93 • 144,864
Warren, MN 56762 • 1,813
Warren, OH 44481–85 • 50,793
Warren, PA 16365 • 11,122
Warren, RI 02885 • 11,385
Warren, VT 05674 • 350
Warren □, GA • 6,078
Warren □, IL • 19,181
Warren □, IN • 8,176
Warren □, IA • 36,033
Warren □, KY • 76,673
Warren □, MS • 47,880
Warren □, MO • 19,534
Warren □, NJ • 91,607
Warren □, NY • 59,209
Warren □, NC • 17,265
Warren □, OH • 113,909
Warren □, PA • 45,050
Warren □, TN • 32,992
Warren □, VA • 26,142
Warren Park, IN 46219 • 1,763
Warrensburg, IL 62573 • 1,274
Warrensburg, MO 64093 • 15,244
Warrensburg, NY 12885 • 3,204
Warrensville Heights, OH 44122 • 15,745
Warrenton, GA 30828 • 2,056
Warrenton, MO 63383 • 3,564
Warrenton, OR 97146 • 2,681
Warrenton, VA 22186 • 4,830
Warrenville, IL 60555 • 11,333
Warrenville, SC 29851 • 1,029
Warrick □, IN • 44,920
Warrington, FL 32507 • 16,040
Warrington, PA 18976 • 6,980
Warrior, AL 35180 • 3,280
Warroad, MN 56763 • 1,679
Warsaw, IL 62379 • 1,882
Warsaw, IN 46580–81 • 10,968
Warsaw, KY 41095 • 1,202
Warsaw, MO 65355 • 1,696
Warsaw, NY 14569 • 3,830
Warsaw, NC 28398 • 2,859
Warwick, NY 10990 • 5,984
Warwick, RI 02886–89 • 85,427
Wasatch □, UT • 10,089
Wasco, CA 93280 • 12,412
Wasco □, OR • 21,683
Waseca, MN 56093 • 8,385
Waseca □, MN • 18,079
Washakie □, WY • 8,388
Washburn, IL 61570 • 1,075
Washburn, IA 50706 • 1,400
Washburn, ME 04786 • 1,880
Washburn, ND 58577 • 1,506
Washburn, WI 54891 • 2,285
Washburn □, WI • 13,772
Washington, DC 20001–99 • 606,900
Washington, GA 30673 • 4,279
Washington, IL 61571 • 10,099
Washington, IN 47501 • 10,838
Washington, IA 52353 • 7,074
Washington, KS 66968 • 1,304
Washington, LA 70589 • 1,253
Washington, MO 63090 • 10,704
Washington, NJ 07882 • 6,474
Washington, NC 27889 • 9,075
Washington, PA 15301 • 15,864
Washington, UT 84780 • 4,198
Washington □, AL • 16,694
Washington □, AR • 113,409
Washington □, CO • 4,812
Washington □, FL • 16,919
Washington □, GA • 19,112
Washington □, ID • 8,550
Washington □, IL • 14,965
Washington □, IN • 23,717

Washington □, IA • 19,612
Washington □, KS • 7,073
Washington □, KY • 10,441
Washington □, LA • 43,185
Washington □, ME • 35,308
Washington □, MD • 121,393
Washington □, MN • 145,896
Washington □, MS • 67,935
Washington □, MO • 20,380
Washington □, NE • 16,607
Washington □, NY • 59,330
Washington □, NC • 13,997
Washington □, OH • 62,254
Washington □, OK • 48,066
Washington □, OR • 311,554
Washington □, PA • 204,584
Washington □, RI • 110,006
Washington □, TN • 92,315
Washington □, TX • 26,154
Washington □, UT • 48,560
Washington □, VT • 54,928
Washington □, VA • 45,887
Washington □, WI • 95,328
Washington Court House, OH 43160 • 12,983
Washington Park, FL 33314 • 6,930
Washington Park, IL 62204 • 7,431
Washington Terrace, UT 84403 • 8,189
Washington Township, NJ 07675 • 9,245
Washita □, OK • 11,441
Washoe □, NV • 254,667
Washoe City, NV 89701 • 400
Washougal, WA 98671 • 4,764
Washtenaw □, MI • 282,937
Wasilla, AK 99687 • 4,028
Waskom, TX 75692 • 1,812
Watauga, TX 76148 • 20,009
Watauga □, NC • 36,952
Watchung, NJ 07060 • 5,110
Waterbury, CT 06701–26 • 108,961
Waterbury, VT 05676 • 1,702
Waterbury Center, VT 05677 • 500
Waterford, CT 06385 • 17,930
Waterford, MI 48327–29 • 66,692
Waterford, NY 12188 • 2,370
Waterford, PA 16441 • 1,492
Waterford, WI 53185 • 2,431
Waterford Works, NJ 08089 • 1,200
Waterloo, IL 62298 • 5,072
Waterloo, IN 46793 • 2,040
Waterloo, IA 50701–07 • 66,467
Waterloo, NY 13165 • 5,116
Waterloo, WI 53594 • 2,712
Waterman, IL 60556 • 1,074
Waterproof, LA 71375 • 1,080
Watertown, CT 06795 • 20,456
Watertown, FL 32055 • 3,340
Watertown, MA 02172 • 33,284
Watertown, NY 13601–03 • 29,429
Watertown, SD 57201 • 17,592
Watertown, TN 37184 • 1,250
Watertown, WI 53094 • 19,142
Water Valley, MS 38965 • 3,610
Waterville, ME 04901–03 • 17,173
Waterville, MN 56096 • 1,771
Waterville, NY 13480 • 1,664
Waterville, OH 43566 • 4,517
Watervliet, MI 49098 • 1,867
Watervliet, NY 12189 • 11,061
Watford City, ND 58854 • 1,784
Wathena, KS 66090 • 1,160
Watkins Glen, NY 14891 • 2,207
Watkinsville, GA 30677 • 1,600
Watonga, OK 73772 • 3,408
Watonwan □, MN • 11,682
Watseka, IL 60970 • 5,424
Watsontown, PA 17777 • 2,310
Watsonville, CA 95076–77 • 31,099
Wattsville, SC 29360 • 1,324
Wauchula, FL 33873 • 3,253
Wauconda, IL 60084 • 6,294
Waukee, IA 50263 • 2,512
Waukegan, IL 60085–87 • 69,392
Waukesha, WI 53186–88 • 56,958
Waukesha □, WI • 304,715
Waukomis, OK 73773 • 1,322
Waukon, IA 52172 • 4,019
Waunakee, WI 53597 • 5,897
Waupaca, WI 54981 • 4,957
Waupaca □, WI • 46,104
Waupun, WI 53963 • 8,207
Wauregan, CT 06387 • 1,200
Waurika, OK 73573 • 2,088
Wausau, WI 54401–02 • 37,060
Wauseon, OH 43567 • 6,322
Waushara □, WI • 19,385
Wautoma, WI 54982 • 1,784
Wauwatosa, WI 53213 • 49,366
Waveland, MS 39576 • 5,369
Waverly, IL 62692 • 1,402
Waverly, IA 50677 • 8,539
Waverly, MI 48917 • 15,614
Waverly, NE 68462 • 1,869
Waverly, NY 14892 • 4,787
Waverly, OH 45690 • 4,477
Waverly, TN 37185 • 3,925
Waverly, VA 23890 • 2,223
Waxahachie, TX 75165 • 18,168
Waxhaw, NC 28173 • 1,294
Waycross, GA 31501 • 16,410
Wayland, MA 01778 • 2,550
Wayland, MI 49348 • 2,751
Wayland, NY 14572 • 1,976
Waylyn, SC 29405 • 2,400
Waymart, PA 18472 • 1,337
Wayne, MI 48184–88 • 19,899
Wayne, NE 68787 • 5,142
Wayne, NJ 07470–74 • 47,025
Wayne, WV 25570 • 1,128
Wayne □, GA • 22,356
Wayne □, IL • 17,241
Wayne □, IN • 71,951
Wayne □, IA • 7,067
Wayne □, KY • 17,468
Wayne □, MI • 2,111,687
Wayne □, MS • 19,517
Wayne □, MO • 11,543
Wayne □, NE • 9,364
Wayne □, NY • 89,123
Wayne □, NC • 104,666
Wayne □, OH • 101,461
Wayne □, PA • 39,944
Wayne □, TN • 13,935
Wayne □, UT • 2,177
Wayne □, WV • 41,636
Wayne City, IL 62895 • 1,099
Waynesboro, GA 30830 • 5,701
Waynesboro, MS 39367 • 5,143
Waynesboro, PA 17268 • 9,578
Waynesboro, TN 38485 • 1,824
Waynesboro, VA 22980 • 18,549
Waynesburg, OH 44688 • 1,068
Waynesburg, PA 15370 • 4,270
Waynesville, MO 65583 • 3,207
Waynesville, NC 28786 • 6,758
Waynesville, OH 45068 • 1,949
Waynewood, VA 22308 • 5,000
Wayzata, MN 55391 • 3,806
Weakley □, TN • 31,972
Weatherford, OK 73096 • 10,124
Weatherford, TX 76086–87 • 14,804
Weatherly, PA 18255 • 2,640
Weatogue, CT 06089 • 2,521
Weaver, AL 36277 • 2,715
Weaverville, CA 96093 • 3,370
Weaverville, NC 28787 • 2,107
Webb, AL 36376 • 1,039
Webb □, TX • 133,239
Webb City, MO 64870 • 7,449
Webberville, MI 48892 • 1,698
Weber □, UT • 158,330
Weber City, VA 24251 • 1,377
Webster, MA 01570 • 11,849
Webster, NY 14580 • 5,464
Webster, PA 15087 • 1,000
Webster, SD 57274 • 2,017
Webster □, GA • 2,263
Webster □, IA • 40,342
Webster □, KY • 13,955
Webster □, LA • 41,989
Webster □, MS • 10,222
Webster □, MO • 23,753
Webster □, NE • 4,279
Webster □, WV • 10,729
Webster City, IA 50595 • 7,894
Webster Groves, MO 63119 • 22,987
Websterville, VT 05678 • 600
Wedgewood, MO 63031 • 6,700
Weed, CA 96094 • 3,062
Weed Heights, NV 89447 • 230
Weedsport, NY 13166 • 1,996
Weehawken, NJ 07087 • 12,385
Weeping Water, NE 68463 • 1,008
Weigelstown, PA 17315 • 8,665
Weimar, TX 78962 • 2,052
Weippe, ID 83553 • 532
Weirsdale, FL 32195 • 1,500
Weirton, WV 26062 • 22,124
Weiser, ID 83672 • 4,571
Wekiva Springs, FL 32750 • 23,026
Welch, WV 24801 • 3,028
Welcome, SC 29611 • 6,560
Weld □, CO • 131,821
Weldon, NC 27890 • 1,392
Weleetka, OK 74880 • 1,112
Wellesley, MA 02181 • 26,615
Wellfleet, MA 02667 • 1,200
Wellford, SC 29385 • 2,511
Wellington, CO 80549 • 1,340
Wellington, FL 33414 • 20,670
Wellington, KS 67152 • 8,411
Wellington, NV 89444 • 280
Wellington, OH 44090 • 4,140
Wellington, TX 79095 • 2,456
Wellington, UT 84542 • 1,632
Wellman, IA 52356 • 1,085
Wells, ME 04090 • 1,200
Wells, MI 49894 • 1,150
Wells, MN 56097 • 2,465
Wells, NV 89835 • 1,256
Wells □, IN • 25,948
Wells □, ND • 5,864
Wellsboro, PA 16901 • 3,430
Wellsburg, WV 26070 • 3,385
Wellston, OH 45692 • 6,049
Wellsville, KS 66092 • 1,563
Wellsville, MO 63384 • 1,430
Wellsville, NY 14895 • 5,241
Wellsville, OH 43968 • 4,532
Wellsville, UT 84339 • 2,206
Wellton, AZ 85356 • 1,066
Welsh, LA 70591 • 3,299
Wenatchee, WA 98801–07 • 21,756
Wendell, ID 83355 • 1,963
Wendell, NC 27591 • 2,822
Wendover, UT 84083 • 1,127
Wenham, MA 01984 • 3,897
Wenonah, NJ 08090 • 2,331
Wentzville, MO 63385 • 5,088
Weslaco, TX 78596 • 21,877
Wesleyville, PA 16510 • 3,655
Wessington Springs, SD 57382 • 1,083
Wesson, MS 39191 • 1,510
West, TX 76691 • 2,515
West Acton, MA 01720 • 5,230
West Alexandria, OH 45381 • 1,460
West Allis, WI 53214 • 63,221
West Andover, MA 01810 • 1,970
West Athens, CA 90247 • 8,859
West Babylon, NY 11704 • 42,410
West Barnstable, MA 02668 • 1,000
West Baton Rouge □, LA • 19,419
West Bay Shore, NY 11706 • 4,907
West Bend, WI 53095 • 23,916
West Berlin, NJ 08091 • 2,970
West Billerica, MA 01862 • 1,920
West Blocton, AL 35184 • 1,468
Westborough, MA 01581 • 3,917
West Bountiful, UT 84087 • 4,477
West Boylston, MA 01583 • 3,130
West Bradenton, FL 34205 • 4,528
West Branch, IA 52358 • 1,908
West Branch, MI 48661 • 1,914
West Bridgewater, MA 02379 • 2,140
Westbrook, CT 06498 • 2,060
Westbrook, ME 04092 • 16,121
West Brookfield, MA 01585 • 1,419
West Burlington, IA 52655 • 3,083
Westbury, NY 11590 • 13,060
Westby, WI 54667 • 1,866
West Caldwell, NJ 07004 • 10,422
West Cape May, NJ 08204 • 1,026
West Carroll □, LA • 12,093
West Carrollton, OH 45449 • 14,403
West Carson, CA 90502 • 20,143
West Carthage, NY 13619 • 2,166
West Chatham, MA 02669 • 1,504
Westchester, FL 33136 • 29,883
Westchester, IL 60153 • 17,301
West Chester, PA 19380–82 • 18,041
Westchester □, NY • 874,866
West Chicago, IL 60185–86 • 14,796
West Columbia, SC 29169–72 • 10,588
West Columbia, TX 77486 • 4,372
West Compton, CA 90220 • 5,451
West Concord, MA 01742 • 5,761
West Concord, NC 28027 • 5,859
West Covina, CA 91790–93 • 96,086
West Crossett, AR 71635 • 2,019
West Dennis, MA 02670 • 2,307
West Des Moines, IA 50265 • 31,702
West Elmira, NY 14905 • 5,218
Westerly, RI 02891 • 16,477
Westernport, MD 21562 • 2,454
Western Springs, IL 60558 • 11,984
Westerville, OH 43081–82 • 30,269
West Fairview, PA 17025 • 1,403
West Falmouth, MA 02574 • 1,600
West Fargo, ND 58078 • 12,287
West Feliciana □, LA • 12,915
Westfield, IN 46074 • 3,304
Westfield, MA 01085–86 • 38,372
Westfield, NJ 07090–92 • 28,870
Westfield, NY 14787 • 3,451
Westfield, PA 16950 • 1,119
Westfield, WI 53964 • 1,125
Westford, MA 01886 • 1,200
West Fork, AR 72774 • 1,607
West Frankfort, IL 62896 • 8,526
West Freehold, NJ 07728 • 11,166
Westgate, FL 33401 • 2,100
West Gate, VA 22110 • 6,565
West Gate of Lomond, VA 22110 • 5,400
West Glens Falls, NY 12801 • 5,964
West Goshen, PA 19380 • 8,948
West Grove, PA 19390 • 2,128
Westham, VA 23229 • 3,200
West Hanover, MA 02339 • 1,700
West Hartford, CT 06127 • 60,110
West Haven, CT 06516 • 54,021
West Haven, OR 97225 • 3,400
West Haverstraw, NY 10993 • 9,183
West Hazleton, PA 18201 • 4,136
West Helena, AR 72390 • 9,695
West Hempstead, NY 11552 • 17,689
West Hollywood, CA 90069 • 36,118
Westhope, ND 58793 • 578
West Hyannisport, MA 02672 • 1,200
West Islip, NY 11795 • 28,419
West Jefferson, NC 28694 • 1,002
West Jefferson, OH 43162 • 4,504
West Jordan, UT 84084 • 42,892
West Kingston, RI 02892 • 1,150
West Lafayette, IN 47906–07 • 25,907
West Lafayette, OH 43845 • 2,129
Westlake, LA 70669 • 5,007
Westlake, OH 44145 • 27,018
Westlake Village, CA 91361 • 7,455
Westland, MI 48185 • 84,724
West Lawn, PA 19609 • 1,606
West Liberty, IA 52776 • 2,935
West Liberty, KY 41472 • 1,887
West Liberty, OH 43357 • 1,613
West Liberty, WV 26074 • 1,434
West Linn, OR 97068 • 16,367
West Long Branch, NJ 07764 • 7,690
West Marion, NC 28752 • 1,291
West Medway, MA 02053 • 1,940
West Melbourne, FL 32901 • 8,399
West Memphis, AR 72301 • 28,259
Westmere, NY 12203 • 6,750
West Miami, FL 33174 • 5,727
West Mifflin, PA 15122–23 • 23,644
West Milford, NJ 07480 • 25,430
West Milton, OH 45383 • 4,348
West Milwaukee, WI 53214 • 3,973
Westminster, CA 92683–84 • 78,118
Westminster, CO 80030–31 • 74,625
Westminster, MD 21157 • 13,068
Westminster, SC 29693 • 3,120
West Modesto, CA 95351 • 6,135
West Monroe, LA 71291–94 • 14,096
Westmont, CA 90044 • 31,100
Westmont, IL 60559 • 21,228
Westmont, NJ 08108 • 5,630
Westmont, PA 15905 • 5,789
Westmoreland, TN 37186 • 1,726
Westmoreland □, PA • 370,321
Westmoreland □, VA • 15,480
Westmorland, CA 92281 • 1,380
West Mystic, CT 06388 • 3,595
West Newton, PA 15089 • 3,152
West New York, NJ 07093 • 38,125
West Norriton, PA 19401 • 15,209
West Nyack, NY 10960 • 3,437
Weston, CT 06883 • 1,370
Weston, MA 02193 • 11,169
Weston, MO 64098 • 1,528
Weston, OH 43569 • 1,716
Weston, WV 26452 • 4,994
Weston, WI 54476 • 9,714
Weston □, WY • 6,518
West Orange, NJ 07052 • 39,103
Westover, WV 26505 • 4,201
West Palm Beach, FL 33401–20 • 67,643
West Pasco, WA 99301 • 7,312
West Paterson, NJ 07424 • 10,982
West Pawlet, VT 05775 • 350
West Pensacola, FL 32505 • 22,107
West Peoria, IL 61604 • 5,314
West Pittsburg, CA 94565 • 17,453
West Pittsburg, PA 16160 • 1,133
West Pittston, PA 18643 • 5,590
West Plains, MO 65775 • 8,913
West Point, CA 95255 • 1,500
West Point, GA 31833 • 3,571
West Point, IA 52656 • 1,079
West Point, KY 40177 • 1,216
West Point, MS 39773 • 8,489
West Point, NE 68788 • 3,250
West Point, NY 10996–97 • 8,024
West Point, UT 84015 • 4,258
West Point, VA 23181 • 2,938
Westport, CT 06880–83 • 24,407
Westport, IN 47283 • 1,478
Westport, WA 98595 • 1,892
West Portsmouth, OH 45662 • 3,551
West Puente Valley, CA 91744 • 20,254
West Reading, PA 19611 • 4,142
West Rutland, VT 05777 • 2,246
West Sacramento, CA 95691 • 28,898
West Saint Paul, MN 55118 • 19,248
West Salem, IL 62476 • 1,042
West Salem, OH 44287 • 1,534
West Salem, WI 54669 • 3,611
West Sayville, NY 11796 • 4,680
West Seneca, NY 14224 • 47,866
West Simsbury, CT 06092 • 2,149
West Slope, OR 97225 • 7,959
West Springfield, MA 01089–90 • 27,537
West Springfield, VA 22152 • 28,126
West Swanzey, NH 03469 • 1,055
West Terre Haute, IN 47885 • 2,495
West Union, IA 52175 • 2,490
West Union, OH 45693 • 3,096
West Unity, OH 43570 • 1,677
West University Place, TX 77005 • 12,920
West Upton, MA 01587 • 1,300
Westvale, NY 13219 • 5,952
West Valley City, UT 84120 • 86,976
Westview, FL 33168 • 9,668
West View, PA 15229 • 7,734
Westville, IL 61883 • 3,387
Westville, IN 46391 • 5,255
Westville, NJ 08093 • 4,573
Westville, OK 74965 • 1,374
West Wareham, MA 02576 • 2,059
West Warren, MA 01092 • 1,200
West Warwick, RI 02893 • 29,268
West Webster, NY 14580 • 8,690
Westwego, LA 70094–96 • 11,218
West Whittier, CA 90606 • 13,800
West Willow, MI 48198 • 4,300
Westwood, CA 96137 • 2,017
Westwood, KS 66205 • 1,772
Westwood, KY 41101 • 5,300
Westwood, MA 02090 • 6,500
Westwood, MI 49007 • 8,957
Westwood, NJ 07675 • 10,446
Westwood Lakes, FL 33165 • 11,522
West Wyoming, PA 18644 • 3,117
West Yarmouth, MA 02673 • 5,409
West Yellowstone, MT 59758 • 913
West York, PA 17404 • 4,283
Wethersfield, CT 06129 • 25,651
Wetumka, OK 74883 • 1,427
Wetumpka, AL 36092 • 4,670
Wetzel □, WV • 19,258
Wewahitchka, FL 32465 • 1,779
Wewoka, OK 74884 • 4,050
Wexford □, MI • 26,360
Weyauwega, WI 54983 • 1,665
Weymouth, MA 02188 • 54,063
Whalom, MA 01420 • 1,340
Wharton, NJ 07885 • 5,405
Wharton, TX 77488 • 9,011
Wharton □, TX • 39,955
Whatcom □, WA • 127,780
Wheatland, CA 95692 • 1,631
Wheatland, WY 82201 • 3,271
Wheatland □, MT • 2,246
Wheaton, IL 60187–89 • 51,464
Wheaton, MD 20902 • 58,300
Wheaton, MN 56296 • 1,615
Wheat Ridge, CO 80033–34 • 29,419
Wheeler, TX 79096 • 1,393
Wheeler □, GA • 4,903
Wheeler □, NE • 948
Wheeler □, OR • 1,396
Wheeler □, TX • 5,879
Wheelersburg, OH 45694 • 5,113
Wheeling, IL 60090 • 29,911
Wheeling, WV 26003 • 34,882
Whitacres, CT 06082 • 2,410
White □, AR • 54,676
White □, GA • 13,006
White □, IL • 16,522
White □, IN • 23,265
White □, TN • 20,090
White Bear Lake, MN 55110 • 24,704
White Bluff, TN 37187 • 1,988
White Castle, LA 70788 • 2,102
White Center, WA 98126 • 15,700
White City, OR 97503 • 5,891
White City, UT 84070 • 6,506
White Cloud, MI 49349 • 1,147
White Deer, TX 79097 • 1,125
Whitefield, NH 03598 • 1,041
Whitefish, MT 59937 • 4,368
Whitefish Bay, WI 53217 • 14,272
White Hall, AR 71602 • 3,849
White Hall, IL 62092 • 2,814
Whitehall, MI 49461 • 3,027
Whitehall, MT 59759 • 1,067
Whitehall, NY 12887 • 3,071
Whitehall, OH 43213 • 20,572
Whitehall, PA 15227 • 14,451
Whitehall, WI 54773 • 1,494
White Haven, PA 18661 • 1,132
White Horse, NJ 08610 • 9,397
White Horse Beach, MA 02381 • 1,200
Whitehouse, OH 43571 • 2,528
White House, TN 37188 • 2,987
White House Station, NJ 08889 • 1,400
White Island Shores, MA 02538 • 2,000
White Meadow Lake, NJ 07866 • 8,002
White Oak, MD 20901 • 18,671
White Oak, OH 45239 • 12,430
White Oak, PA 15131 • 8,761
White Pigeon, MI 49099 • 1,458
White Pine, MI 49971 • 1,142
White Pine, TN 37890 • 1,771
White Pine □, NV • 9,264
White Plains, MD 20695 • 3,560
White Plains, NY 10601–07 • 48,718
Whiteriver, AZ 85941 • 3,775
White River Junction, VT 05001 • 2,521
White Rock, NM 87544 • 6,192
White Salmon, WA 98672 • 1,861
Whitesboro, NY 13492 • 4,195
Whitesboro, TX 76273 • 3,209
Whitesburg, KY 41858 • 1,636
White Settlement, TX 76108 • 15,472
Whiteside □, IL • 60,186
White Sulphur Springs, MT 59645 • 963
White Sulphur Springs, WV 24986 • 2,779
Whiteville, NC 28472 • 5,078
Whiteville, TN 38075 • 1,050
Whitewater, WI 53190 • 12,636
Whitewood, SD 57793 • 891
Whitewright, TX 75491 • 1,713
Whitfield □, GA • 72,462
Whitfield Estates, FL 34243 • 3,152
Whiting, IN 46394 • 5,155
Whiting, WI 54481 • 1,838
Whitinsville, MA 01588 • 5,639
Whitley □, IN • 27,651
Whitley □, KY • 33,326
Whitley City, KY 42653 • 1,133
Whitman, MA 02382 • 13,534
Whitman, WV 25652 • 1,651
Whitman □, WA • 38,775
Whitman Square, NJ 08012 • 3,490
Whitmire, SC 29178 • 1,702
Whitmore Lake, MI 48189 • 3,251
Whitmore Village, HI 96786 • 3,373
Whitney, SC 29303 • 4,052
Whitney, TX 76692 • 1,626
Whitney Point, NY 13862 • 1,054
Whittier, AK 99693 • 243
Whittier, CA 90601–12 • 77,671
Whitwell, TN 37397 • 1,622
Wibaux, MT 59353 • 628
Wibaux □, MT • 1,191
Wichita, KS 67201–78 • 304,011
Wichita □, KS • 2,758
Wichita □, TX • 122,378
Wichita Falls, TX 76301–11 • 96,259
Wickenburg, AZ 85358 • 4,515
Wickliffe, OH 44092 • 14,558
Wickliffe, OH 44515 • 7,240
Wicomico □, MD • 74,339
Wiconisco, PA 17097 • 1,321
Widefield, CO 80911 • 12,112
Wiggins, MS 39577 • 3,185
Wilbarger □, TX • 15,121
Wilber, NE 68465 • 1,527
Wilberforce, OH 45384 • 2,639
Wilbraham, MA 01095 • 3,352
Wilburton, OK 74578 • 3,092
Wilcox, PA 15870 • 1,000
Wilcox □, AL • 13,568
Wilcox □, GA • 7,008
Wilder, ID 83676 • 1,232
Wilder, VT 05088 • 1,576
Wildorado, TX 79098 • 2,000
Wildwood, FL 34785 • 3,421
Wildwood, IL 60030 • 2,034
Wildwood, NJ 08260 • 4,484
Wildwood Crest, NJ 08260 • 3,631
Wilkes □, GA • 10,597
Wilkes □, NC • 59,393
Wilkes-Barre, PA 18701–73 • 47,523
Wilkesboro, NC 28697 • 2,573
Wilkin □, MN • 7,516
Wilkinsburg, PA 15221 • 21,080
Wilkinson □, GA • 10,228
Wilkinson □, MS • 9,678
Wilkins Township, PA 15145 • 7,487
Will □, IL • 357,313
Willacoochee, GA 31650 • 1,205
Willacy □, TX • 17,705
Willamina, OR 97396 • 1,717
Willard, MO 65781 • 2,177
Willard, NY 14588 • 1,339
Willard, OH 44890 • 6,210
Willard, UT 84340 • 1,298
Willcox, AZ 85643 • 3,122
Williams, AZ 86046 • 2,532
Williams, CA 95987 • 2,297
Williams □, ND • 21,129
Williams □, OH • 36,956
Williams Bay, WI 53191 • 2,108
Williamsburg, IA 52361 • 2,174
Williamsburg, KY 40769 • 5,493
Williamsburg, MA 01096 • 1,200
Williamsburg, OH 45176 • 2,322
Williamsburg, PA 16693 • 1,456
Williamsburg, VA 23185–88 • 11,530
Williamsburg □, SC • 36,815
Williamson, NY 14589 • 1,768
Williamson, WV 25661 • 4,154
Williamson □, IL • 57,733
Williamson □, TN • 81,021
Williamson □, TX • 139,551
Williamsport, IN 47993 • 1,798
Williamsport, MD 21795 • 2,103
Williamsport, PA 17701–03 • 31,933
Williamston, MI 48895 • 2,922
Williamston, NC 27892 • 5,503
Williamston, SC 29697 • 3,876
Williamstown, KY 41097 • 3,023
Williamstown, MA 01267 • 4,791
Williamstown, NJ 08094 • 10,891
Williamstown, PA 17098 • 1,509
Williamstown, VT 05679 • 650
Williamstown, WV 26187 • 2,774
Williamsville, IL 62693 • 1,140
Williamsville, NY 14221 • 5,583
Willimantic, CT 06226 • 14,746
Willingboro, NJ 08046 • 36,291
Willis, TX 77378 • 2,764
Williston, FL 32696 • 2,179
Williston, ND 58801–02 • 13,131
Williston, SC 29853 • 3,099
Williston Park, NY 11596 • 7,516
Willits, CA 95490 • 5,027
Willmar, MN 56201 • 17,531
Willoughby, OH 44094–95 • 20,510
Willoughby Hills, OH 44092 • 8,427
Willow Brook, CA 90222 • 32,772
Willowbrook, IL 60521 • 8,598
Willow Grove, PA 19090 • 16,325
Willowick, OH 44094 • 15,269
Willow Run, DE 19805 • 1,600
Willow Run, MI 48198 • 7,200
Willows, CA 95988 • 5,988
Willow Springs, IL 60480 • 4,509
Willow Springs, MO 65793 • 2,038
Willston, VA 22044 • 2,000
Wilmerding, PA 15148 • 2,222
Wilmette, IL 60091 • 26,690
Wilmington, DE 19801–99 • 71,529
Wilmington, IL 60481 • 4,743
Wilmington, MA 01887 • 17,654
Wilmington, NC 28401–12 • 55,530
Wilmington, OH 45177 • 11,199
Wilmington, VT 05363 • 550
Wilmington Island, GA 31410 • 11,230
Wilmington Manor, DE 19720 • 8,568
Wilmington Manor Gardens, DE 19720 • 1,500
Wilmore, KY 40390 • 4,215
Wilmot, AR 71676 • 1,047
Wilson, AR 72395 • 1,068

United States Populations and ZIP Codes

Wilson, NY 14172 • 1,307
Wilson, NC 27893-95 • 36,930
Wilson, OK 73463 • 1,639
Wilson, PA 18042 • 7,830
Wilson, WY 83014 • 500
Wilson □, KS • 10,289
Wilson □, NC • 66,061
Wilson □, TN • 67,675
Wilson □, TX • 22,650
Wilsonville, AL 35186 • 1,185
Wilsonville, OR 97070 • 7,106
Wilton, CT 06897 • 7,200
Wilton, IA 52778 • 2,577
Wilton, ME 04294 • 2,453
Wilton, NH 03086 • 1,165
Wilton, ND 58579 • 728
Wilton Manors, FL 33334 • 11,804
Wimauma, FL 33598 • 2,932
Winamac, IN 46996 • 2,262
Winchendon, MA 01475 • 4,316
Winchester, IN 47394 • 5,095
Winchester, KY 40391-92 • 15,799
Winchester, MA 01890 • 20,267
Winchester, NH 03470 • 1,735
Winchester, NV 89101 • 23,365
Winchester, TN 37398 • 6,305
Winchester, VA 22601 • 21,947
Windber, PA 15963 • 4,756
Windcrest, TX 78239 • 5,331
Winder, GA 30680 • 7,373
Windgap, PA 18091 • 2,741
Windham, CT 06280 • 1,100
Windham, NH 44288 • 2,943
Windham □, CT • 102,525
Windham □, VT • 41,588
Wind Lake, WI 53185 • 3,000
Windom, MN 56101 • 4,283
Window Rock, AZ 86515 • 3,306
Wind Point, WI 53402 • 1,941
Windsor, CO 80550 • 5,062
Windsor, CT 06095 • 27,817
Windsor, IL 61957 • 1,143
Windsor, MO 65360 • 3,044
Windsor, NC 27983 • 2,056
Windsor, PA 17366 • 1,355
Windsor, VT 05089 • 3,478
Windsor, VA 23487 • 1,025
Windsor □, VT • 54,055
Windsor Heights, IA 50311 • 5,190
Windsor Hills, CA 90052 • 6,200
Windsor Locks, CT 06096 • 12,358
Windy Hill, SC 29506 • 1,622
Windy Hills, DE 19711 • 1,130
Winfield, AL 35594 • 3,689
Winfield, IA 52659 • 1,051
Winfield, KS 67156 • 11,931
Winfield, NJ 07036 • 1,785
Winfield, WV 25213 • 1,164
Wingate, NC 28174 • 2,821
Wink, TX 79789 • 1,189
Winkler □, TX • 8,626
Winlock, WA 98596 • 1,027
Winn □, LA • 16,269
Winnebago, IL 61088 • 1,840
Winnebago, MN 56098 • 1,565
Winnebago, WI 54985 • 1,433
Winnebago □, IL • 252,913
Winnebago □, IA • 12,122
Winnebago □, WI • 140,320
Winneconne, WI 54986 • 2,059
Winnemucca, NV 89445 • 6,134
Winner, SD 57580 • 3,354
Winneshiek □, IA • 20,847
Winnetka, IL 60093 • 12,174
Winnfield, LA 71483 • 6,138
Winnsboro, LA 71295 • 5,755

Winnsboro, SC 29180 • 3,475
Winnsboro, TX 75494 • 2,904
Winnsboro Mills, SC 29180 • 2,275
Winona, MN 55987 • 25,399
Winona, MS 38967 • 5,705
Winona, MO 65588 • 1,081
Winona □, MN • 47,828
Winona Lake, IN 46590 • 4,053
Winooski, VT 05404 • 6,649
Winslow, AZ 86047 • 8,190
Winslow, ME 04901 • 5,436
Winsted, CT 06098 • 8,254
Winsted, MN 55395 • 1,581
Winston, FL 33801 • 9,118
Winston, OR 97496 • 3,773
Winston □, AL • 22,053
Winston □, MS • 19,433
Winston-Salem, NC 27101-27 • 143,485
Winter Garden, FL 34787 • 9,745
Winter Haven, FL 33880-84 • 24,725
Winter Park, FL 32789-90 • 22,242
Winter Park, NC 28403 • 4,504
Winterport, ME 04496 • 1,274
Winters, CA 95694 • 4,639
Winters, TX 79567 • 2,905
Winterset, IA 50273 • 4,196
Winter Springs, FL 32708 • 22,151
Wintersville, OH 43952 • 4,102
Winterville, NC 28590 • 2,816
Winthrop, ME 04364 • 2,819
Winthrop, MA 02152 • 18,127
Winthrop, MN 55396 • 1,279
Winthrop Harbor, IL 60096 • 6,240
Winton, CA 95388 • 7,559
Wirt □, WV • 5,192
Wiscasset, ME 04578 • 1,350
Wisconsin Dells, WI 53965 • 2,393
Wisconsin Rapids, WI 54494-95 • 18,245
Wise, VA 24293 • 3,193
Wise □, TX • 34,679
Wise □, VA • 39,573
Wishek, ND 58495 • 1,171
Wisner, LA 71378 • 1,153
Wisner, NE 68791 • 1,253
Withamsville, OH 45245 • 5,000
Witherbee, NY 12998 • 1,000
Wittenberg, WI 54499 • 1,145
Wixom, MI 48393 • 8,550
Woburn, MA 01801 • 35,943
Wolcott, CT 06716 • 6,070
Wolcott, NY 14590 • 1,544
Wolfe □, KY • 6,503
Wolfeboro, NH 03894 • 2,783
Wolfe City, TX 75496 • 1,505
Wolf Lake, MI 49442 • 4,110
Wolf Point, MT 59201 • 2,880
Wolf Trap, VA 22182 • 13,133
Womelsdorf, PA 19567 • 2,270
Wonder Lake, IL 60097 • 6,664
Wood □, OH • 113,269
Wood □, TX • 29,380
Wood □, WV • 86,915
Wood □, WI • 73,605
Woodbine, GA 31569 • 1,212
Woodbine, IA 51579 • 1,500
Woodbine, NJ 08270 • 2,678
Woodbourne, NY 12788 • 1,155
Woodbourne, OH 45459 • 6,000
Woodbridge, CT 06525 • 7,924
Woodbridge, NJ 07095 • 17,434
Woodbridge, VA 22191-94 • 26,401
Woodbridge [Township], NJ 07095 • 17,434
Woodburn, IA 46797 • 1,321
Woodburn, OR 97071 • 13,404
Woodbury, CT 06798 • 1,212
Woodbury, GA 30293 • 1,429

Woodbury, MN 55125 • 20,075
Woodbury, NJ 08096 • 10,904
Woodbury, NY 11797 • 8,008
Woodbury, TN 37190 • 2,287
Woodbury □, IA • 98,276
Woodcliff Lake, NJ 07675 • 5,303
Wood Dale, IL 60191 • 12,425
Woodfield, SC 29206 • 8,862
Woodford □, IL • 32,653
Woodford □, KY • 19,955
Woodhaven, MI 48183 • 11,631
Woodlake, CA 93286 • 5,678
Woodland, CA 95695 • 39,802
Woodland, ME 04694 • 1,287
Woodland, WA 98674 • 2,500
Woodland Park, CO 80863 • 4,610
Woodlawn, KY 42001 • 1,600
Woodlawn, MD 21207 • 5,329
Woodlawn, MD 20784 • 5,329
Woodlawn, OH 45215 • 2,674
Woodlawn, VA 24381 • 1,689
Woodlynne, NJ 08107 • 2,547
Woodmere, NY 11598 • 15,578
Woodmont, CT 06460 • 1,770
Woodmoor, MD 21207 • 8,630
Woodridge, IL 60517 • 26,256
Wood-Ridge, NJ 07075 • 7,506
Wood River, IL 62095 • 11,490
Wood River, NE 68883 • 1,156
Woodruff, SC 29388 • 4,365
Woodruff, WI 54568 • 1,500
Woodruff □, AR • 9,520
Woods □, OK • 9,103
Woodsboro, TX 78393 • 1,731
Woods Cross, UT 84087 • 5,384
Woodsfield, OH 43793 • 2,832
Woods Hole, MA 02543 • 1,080
Woodside, CA 94062 • 5,035
Woodson □, KS • 4,116
Woodstock, GA 30188 • 4,361
Woodstock, IL 60098 • 14,353
Woodstock, NY 12498 • 1,870
Woodstock, VT 05091 • 1,037
Woodstock, VA 22664 • 3,182
Woodstown, NJ 08098 • 3,154
Woodsville, NH 03785 • 1,122
Woodville, FL 32362 • 2,760
Woodville, MS 39669 • 1,393
Woodville, OH 43469 • 1,953
Woodville, TX 75979 • 2,636
Woodward, IA 50276 • 1,197
Woodward, OK 73801-02 • 12,340
Woodward □, OK • 18,976
Woodway, TX 76710 • 8,695
Woonsocket, RI 02895 • 43,877
Woonsocket, SD 57385 • 766
Wooster, OH 44691 • 22,191
Worcester, MA 01601-15 • 169,759
Worcester □, MD • 35,028
Worcester □, MA • 709,705
Worland, WY 82401 • 5,742
Worth, IL 60482 • 11,208
Worth □, GA • 19,745
Worth □, IA • 7,991
Worth □, MO • 2,440
Wortham, TX 76693 • 1,020
Worthington, IN 47471 • 1,473
Worthington, KY 41183 • 1,751
Worthington, MN 56187 • 9,977
Worthington, OH 43085 • 14,869
Wrangell, AK 99929 • 2,479
Wray, CO 80758 • 1,998
Wrens, GA 30833 • 2,414
Wrentham, MA 02093 • 2,110
Wright, FL 32548 • 18,945
Wright □, IA • 14,269

Wright □, MN • 68,710
Wright □, MO • 16,758
Wright City, MO 63390 • 1,250
Wrightstown, NJ 08562 • 3,843
Wrightstown, WI 54180 • 1,262
Wrightsville, AR 72183 • 1,062
Wrightsville, GA 31096 • 2,331
Wrightsville, PA 17368 • 2,396
Wrightsville Beach, NC 28480 • 2,937
Wrightwood, CA 92397 • 3,308
Wurtsboro, NY 12790 • 1,048
Wyandanch, NY 11798 • 8,950
Wyandot □, OH • 22,254
Wyandotte, MI 48192 • 30,938
Wyandotte □, KS • 161,993
Wyanet, IL 61379 • 1,017
Wyckoff, NJ 07481 • 15,372
Wymore, NE 68466 • 1,611
Wynne, AR 72396-97 • 8,187
Wynnewood, OK 73098 • 2,451
Wyoming, DE 19934 • 977
Wyoming, IL 61491 • 1,462
Wyoming, MI 49509 • 63,891
Wyoming, MN 55092 • 2,142
Wyoming, OH 45215 • 8,128
Wyoming, PA 18644 • 3,255
Wyoming □, NY • 42,507
Wyoming □, PA • 28,076
Wyoming □, WV • 28,990
Wyomissing, PA 19610 • 7,332
Wythe □, VA • 25,466
Wytheville, VA 24382 • 8,038

X

Xenia, OH 45385 • 24,664

Y

Yadkin □, NC • 30,488
Yadkinville, NC 27055 • 2,525
Yakima, WA 98901-09 • 54,827
Yakima □, WA • 188,823
Yakutat, AK 99689 • 534
Yale, MI 48097 • 1,977
Yale, OK 74085 • 1,392
Yalobusha □, MS • 12,033
Yamhill □, OR • 65,551
Yancey □, NC • 15,419
Yanceyville, NC 27379 • 1,973
Yankton, SD 57078 • 12,703
Yankton □, SD • 19,252
Yaphank, NY 11980 • 5,000
Yardley, PA 19067 • 2,288
Yardville, NJ 08620 • 6,190
Yarmouth, ME 04096 • 3,338
Yarmouth, MA 02675 • 1,200
Yarnell, AZ 85362 • 1,500
Yates □, NY • 22,810
Yates Center, KS 66783 • 1,815
Yavapai □, AZ • 107,714
Yazoo □, MS • 25,506
Yazoo City, MS 39194 • 12,427
Yeadon, PA 19050 • 11,980
Yeagertown, PA 17099 • 1,150
Yell □, AR • 17,759
Yellow Medicine □, MN • 11,684
Yellow Springs, OH 45387 • 3,973
Yellowstone □, MT • 113,419
Yellowstone National Park, WY 82190 • 400
Yellowstone National Park □, MT • 52
Yellville, AR 72687 • 1,181
Yelm, WA 98597 • 1,337
Yerington, NV 89447 • 2,367

Yermo, CA 92398 • 1,092
Yoakum, TX 77995 • 5,611
Yoakum □, TX • 8,786
Yolo □, CA • 141,092
Yonkers, NY 10701-10 • 188,082
Yorba Linda, CA 92686 • 52,422
York, AL 36925 • 3,160
York, ME 03909 • 3,130
York, NE 68467 • 7,884
York, PA 17401-07 • 42,192
York, SC 29745 • 6,709
York □, ME • 164,587
York □, NE • 14,428
York □, PA • 339,574
York □, SC • 131,497
York □, VA • 42,422
Yorketown, NJ 07726 • 6,313
York Harbor, ME 03911 • 2,555
Yorkshire, NY 14173 • 1,340
Yorktown, IN 47396 • 4,106
Yorktown, NY 10598 • 5,270
Yorktown, TX 78164 • 2,207
Yorktown, VA 23690-93 • 270
Yorktown Heights, NY 10598 • 7,690
Yorktown Manor, RI 02852 • 2,520
Yorkville, IL 60560 • 3,925
Yorkville, NY 13495 • 2,972
Yorkville, OH 43971 • 1,246
Yosemite National Park, CA 95389 • 1,073
Young □, TX • 18,126
Youngstown, NY 14174 • 2,075
Youngstown, OH 44501-15 • 95,732
Youngsville, LA 70592 • 1,195
Youngsville, PA 16371 • 1,775
Youngtown, AZ 85363 • 2,542
Youngwood, PA 15697 • 3,372
Ypsilanti, MI 48197-98 • 24,846
Yreka, CA 96097 • 6,948
Yuba □, CA • 58,228
Yuba City, CA 95991-92 • 27,437
Yucaipa, CA 92399 • 20,000
Yucca Valley, CA 92284-86 • 13,701
Yukon, OK 73099 • 20,935
Yulee, FL 32097 • 6,915
Yuma, AZ 85364-69 • 54,923
Yuma, CO 80759 • 2,719
Yuma □, AZ • 106,895
Yuma □, CO • 8,954

Z

Zachary, LA 70791 • 9,036
Zanesville, OH 43701-02 • 26,778
Zapata, TX 78076 • 7,119
Zapata □, TX • 9,279
Zavala □, TX • 12,162
Zebulon, GA 30295 • 1,035
Zebulon, NC 27597 • 3,173
Zeeland, MI 49464 • 5,417
Zeigler, IL 62999 • 1,746
Zelienople, PA 16063 • 4,158
Zenith, WA 98188 • 1,100
Zephyr Cove, NV 89448 • 1,700
Zephyrhills, FL 33539-44 • 8,220
Ziebach □, SD • 2,220
Zillah, WA 98953 • 1,911
Zilwaukee, MI 48604 • 1,850
Zimmerman, MN 55398 • 1,350
Zion, IL 60099 • 19,775
Zionsville, IN 46077 • 5,281
Zolfo Springs, FL 33890 • 1,219
Zumbrota, MN 55992 • 2,312
Zuni (Zuni Pueblo), NM 87327 • 5,857
Zwolle, LA 71486 • 1,779